OFFICIAL BASEBALL REGISTER

1994 EDITION

Editor/Official Baseball Register
MARK SHIMABUKURO

Contributing Editors/Official Baseball Register
JOHN DUXBURY
GEORGE PURO

PUBLISHING CO.

Francis P. Pandolfi, Chairman and Chief Executive Officer; **Nicholas H. Niles**, Publisher and President; **John D. Rawlings**, Editorial Director; **Kathy Kinkeade**, Vice President/Production; **Mike Nahrstedt**, Managing Editor; **Joe Hoppel**, Senior Editor; **Craig Carter, Tom Dienhart and Dave Sloan**, Associate Editors; **Mark Shimabukuro**, Assistant Editor; **George Puro**, Production Assistant; **Craig Mulcahy**, Editorial Assistant; **Bill Perry**, Director of Graphic Presentation; **Michael Bruner**, Art Director/Yearbooks and Books; **Steve Levin**, Photo Editor; **Gary Levy**, Editor of Special Projects; **Gary Brinker**, Director of Electronic Information Development; **Corby Ann Dolan**, Database Analyst; **Vern Kasal**, Composing Room Supervisor.

A Times Mirror Company

Major league statistics compiled by STATS, Inc., Lincolnwood, Ill.
Minor league statistics compiled by Howe Sportsdata International Inc., Boston.
Additional assistance provided by MLB-IBM Baseball Information System.

ISBN: 0-89204-486-1 (perfect-bound)
0-89204-489-6 (comb-bound)

10 9 8 7 6 5 4 3 2 1

CONTENTS

EXPLANATION OF FOOTNOTES AND ABBREVIATIONS

Note for statistical comparisons: Player strikes forced the cancellation of games in the 1972 season (10 days missed) and the 1981 season (50 days missed).

Positions are listed in descending order of games played; because of limited space, designated hitter, pinch-hitter and pinch-runner are listed in the regular-season section only if a player did not play a defensive position.

- ★ Led league. For fielding statistics, the player led the league at the position shown.
- • Tied for league lead. For fielding statistics, the player tied for the league lead at the position shown.
- † Led league, but number indicated is total figure for two or more positions. Actual league-leading figure for a position is mentioned in "Statistical Notes" section.
- ‡ Tied for league lead, but number indicated is total figure for two or more positions. Actual league-tying figure for a position is mentioned in "Statistical Notes" section.
- ■ Indicates a player's movement from one major league organization to another major league organization or to an independent minor league organization.
- ... Statistic unavailable, inapplicable, unofficial or mathematically impossible to calculate.
- — Manager statistic inapplicable.

LEAGUES: A.A., Am. Assoc.: American Association. **A.L.**: American. **Ala.-Fla.**: Alabama-Florida. **App., Appal.**: Appalachian. **Ar., Ariz.**: Arizona. **Cal., Calif.**: California. **Can.-Am.**: Canadian-American. **Car., Caro.**: Carolina. **CRL**: Cocoa Rookie. **DSL**: Dominican Summer. **East.**: Eastern. **Evan.**: Evangeline. **Fla. St., Florida St., FSL**: Florida State. **GCL**: Gulf Coast. **GSL**: Gulf States. **In.-Am.**: Inter-American. **Int'l.**: International. **Jp. Cen., Jp. Cn.**: Japan Central. **Jp. Pac.**: Japan Pacific. **Mex.**: Mexican. **Mex. Cen.**: Mexican Center. **Mid., Midw.**: Midwest. **Miss.-O.V.**: Mississippi-Ohio Valley. **N.C. St.**: North Carolina State. **N.L.**: National. **North.**: Northern. **N'west**: Northwest. **N.Y.-Penn, NYP**: New York-Pennsylvania. **Pac. Coast, PCL**: Pacific Coast. **Pio.**: Pioneer. **S. Atl., SAL**: South Atlantic. **Soph.**: Sophomore. **Sou., South.**: Southern. **Taiw.**: Taiwan. **Tex.**: Texas. **W. Car., W. Caro.**: Western Carolinas.

TEAMS: Aguascal.: Aguascalientes. **Alb./Colon.**: Albany/Colonie. **Albuq.**: Albuquerque. **App.**: Appleton. **Ariz.**: Arizona. **Ark.**: Arkansas. **Atl.**: Atlanta. **Balt.**: Baltimore. **Belling.**: Bellingham. **Birm.**: Birmingham. **Bos.**: Boston. **Buff.**: Buffalo. **Bur.**: Burlington. **Calg.**: Calgary. **Calif.**: California. **Cant./Akr.**: Canton/Akron. **Caro.**: Carolina. **Ced. Rap.**: Cedar Rapids. **Cent. Ore.**: Central Oregon. **Central Vall.**: Central Valley. **Char.**: Charleston. **Charl.**: Charlotte. **Chatt.**: Chattanooga. **Chi.**: Chicago. **Cin.**: Cincinnati. **Ciu. Juarez**: Ciudad Juarez. **Clev.**: Cleveland. **Colo.**: Colorado. **Col. S., Col. Sp., Colo. Springs**: Colorado Springs. **Colu., Colum.**: Columbus. **Dall./Fort W.**: Dallas/Fort Worth. **Day. Beach.**: Daytona Beach. **Den.**: Denver. **Det.**: Detroit. **Dom.**: Dominican. **Duned.**: Dunedin. **Edm.**: Edmonton. **Elizabeth.**: Elizabethton. **Eve.**: Everett. **Fla.**: Florida. **Fort Lauder.**: Fort Lauderdale. **Fukuoka**: Fukuoka Daiei. **GC**: Gulf Coast. **GC Astros-Or.**: Gulf Coast Astros-Orange. **GC Royals-B**: Gulf Coast Royals-Blue. **GC Royals-G**: Gulf Coast Royals-Gold. **GC Whi. Sox**: Gulf Coast White Sox. **Grays Har.**: Grays Harbor. **Greens.**: Greensboro. **Greenw.**: Greenwood. **Guana.**: Guanajuato. **Hiroshima**: Hiroshima Toyo. **Hou.**: Houston. **H.P.**: High Point. **Hunt.**: Huntsville. **Hunting.**: Huntington. **Ind.**: Indianapolis. **Jacks., Jacksonv.**: Jacksonville. **Johns. City**: Johnson City. **Kane Co.**: Kane County. **K.C.**: Kansas City. **Knox.**: Knoxville. **L.A.**: Los Angeles. **Lake Charl.**: Lake Charles. **Louis.**: Louisville. **L.V.**: Las Vegas. **M.C.**: Mexico City. **M.C. Red Dev.**: Mexico City Red Devils. **Me.**: Maine. **Mem.**: Memphis. **Mil.**: Milwaukee. **Minn.**: Minnesota. **Monc.**: Monclova. **Mont.**: Montreal. **Nash.**: Nashville. **Niag. Falls**: Niagara Falls. **Nor.**: Norfolk. **N.Y.**: New York. **Oak.**: Oakland. **Okla. C., Okla. City**: Oklahoma City. **Oma.**: Omaha. **Pan. City**: Panama City. **Phil.**: Philadelphia. **Phoe.**: Phoenix. **Pitts.**: Pittsburgh. **Pomp. Beach**: Pompano Beach. **Port.**: Portland. **Pres. Lions**: President Lions. **Prin. William**: Prince William. **Pue. Rico**: Puerto Rico. **Quad C.**: Quad City. **Rancho Cuca.**: Rancho Cucamonga. **Ric., Rich.**: Richmond. **Roc., Roch.**: Rochester. **Rock.**: Rockford. **Salt.**: Saltillo. **Salt L. City**: Salt Lake City. **San. Dom., Santo Dom.**: Santo Domingo. **San Luis Pot.**: San Luis Potosi. **Santa Barb.**: Santa Barbara. **S.B., San Bern.**: San Bernardino. **Schen.**: Schenectady. **Scr/WB, Scran./W.B.**: Scranton/Wilkes-Barre. **S.D.**: San Diego. **Sea.**: Seattle. **S.F.**: San Francisco. **S.F. de Mac.**: San Francisco de Macoris. **S. Oregon**: Southern Oregon. **Spartan., Sp'rt'brg**: Spartanburg. **St. Cathar.**: St. Catharines. **St.L.**: St. Louis. **St. Luc.**: St. Lucie. **St. Peters.**: St. Petersburg. **States.**: Statesville. **Stock.**: Stockton. **Syrac.**: Syracuse. **Tac.**: Tacoma. **Tam.**: Tampa. **Thomas.**: Thomasville. **Tide.**: Tidewater. **Tol.**: Toledo. **Tor.**: Toronto. **T.-C.**: Tri-Cities. **Tucs.**: Tucson. **Vanc.**: Vancouver. **Vent. Co.**: Ventura County. **Water.**: Watertown. **Well.**: Welland. **W.H.**: Winter Haven. **Winst.-Salem**: Winston-Salem. **Wis. Rap.**: Wisconsin Rapids. **W.P.B., W.P. Beach**: West Palm Beach. **Yoko. Tai.**: Yokohama Taiyo.

STATISTICS: A: assists. **AB**: at-bats. **Avg.**: average. **BB**: bases on balls. **CG**: complete games. **E**: errors. **ER**: earned runs. **ERA**: earned-run average. **G**: games. **GS**: games started. **H**: hits. **HR**: home runs. **IP**: innings pitched. **L**: losses. **Pct.**: winning percentage. **PO**: putouts. **Pos.**: position. **R**: runs. **RBI**: runs batted in. **SB**: stolen bases. **ShO**: shutouts. **SO**: strikeouts. **Sv.**: saves. **W**: wins. **2B**: doubles. **3B**: triples.

ON THE COVER: Jack McDowell of the Chicago White Sox led the American League with 22 victories and four shutouts and won the A.L. Cy Young Award in 1993. (Photo by Tom DiPace)

PLAYERS

ABBOTT, JIM

P, YANKEES

PERSONAL: Born September 19, 1967, in Flint, Mich. . . . 6-3/210. . . . Throws left, bats left. . . . Full name: James Anthony Abbott.
HIGH SCHOOL: Flint (Mich.) Central.
COLLEGE: Michigan.
TRANSACTIONS/CAREER NOTES: Selected by Toronto Blue Jays organization in 36th round of free-agent draft (June 3, 1985).... Selected by California Angels organization in first round (eighth pick overall) of free-agent draft (June 1, 1988).... On disabled list (July 12-August 8, 1992).... Traded by Angels to New York Yankees for 1B J.T. Snow, P Jerry Nielsen and P Russ Springer (December 6, 1992).... On disabled list (June 10-25, 1993).
HONORS: Named Golden Spikes Award winner by USA Baseball (1987).... Named lefthanded pitcher on THE SPORTING NEWS college All-America team (1988).... Named lefthanded pitcher on THE SPORTING NEWS A.L. All-Star team (1991).
STATISTICAL NOTES: Tied for A.L. lead with four balks in 1991.... Pitched 4-0 no-hit victory against Cleveland (September 4, 1993).
MISCELLANEOUS: Member of 1988 U.S. Olympic baseball team.

Year	Team (League)	W	L	Pct.	ERA	G	GS	CG	ShO	Sv.	IP	H	R	ER	BB	SO
1989	—California (A.L.)	12	12	.500	3.92	29	29	4	2	0	181⅓	190	95	79	74	115
1990	—California (A.L.)	10	14	.417	4.51	33	33	4	1	0	211⅔	*246	116	106	72	105
1991	—California (A.L.)	18	11	.621	2.89	34	34	5	1	0	243	222	85	78	73	158
1992	—California (A.L.)	7	15	.318	2.77	29	29	7	0	0	211	208	73	65	68	130
1993	—New York (A.L.)■	11	14	.440	4.37	32	32	4	1	0	214	221	115	104	73	95
Major league totals (5 years)		58	66	.468	3.66	157	157	24	5	0	1061	1087	484	432	360	603

ABBOTT, KURT

SS, MARLINS

PERSONAL: Born June 2, 1969, in Zanesville, O. . . . 6-0/170. . . . Throws right, bats right. . . . Full name: Kurt Thomas Abbott.
HIGH SCHOOL: Dixie Hollins (St. Petersburg, Fla.).
COLLEGE: St. Petersburg (Fla.) Junior College.
TRANSACTIONS/CAREER NOTES: Selected by Oakland Athletics organization in 15th round of free-agent draft (June 5, 1989).... On Modesto disabled list (May 26-June 6, 1991).... Traded by A's to Florida Marlins for OF Kerwin Moore (December 20, 1993).
STATISTICAL NOTES: Led Arizona League shortstops with .922 fielding percentage in 1989.... Led Southern League shortstops with 87 double plays in 1992.

			BATTING												FIELDING			
Year	Team (League)	Pos.	G	AB	R	H	2B	3B	HR	RBI	Avg.	BB	SO	SB	PO	A	E	Avg.
1989	—Ariz. A's (Arizona)	SS-2B-3B	36	155	27	42	5	3	0	25	.271	8	40	0	59	90	10	†.937
	—S. Oregon (N'west)	SS	5	10	2	1	0	0	0	1	.100	0	3	1	6	7	1	.929
1990	—Madison (Midwest)	SS-2B-3B	104	362	38	84	18	0	0	28	.232	47	74	21	180	268	40	.918
1991	—Modesto (Calif.)	SS	58	216	36	55	8	2	3	25	.255	29	55	6	78	130	9	.959
	—Huntsville (South.)	SS	53	182	18	46	6	1	0	11	.253	17	39	6	89	164	13	.951
1992	—Huntsville (South.)	SS	124	452	64	115	14	5	9	52	.254	31	75	16	196	342	29	*.949
	—Tacoma (PCL)	SS	11	39	2	6	1	0	0	1	.154	4	9	1	21	32	4	.930
1993	—Tacoma (PCL)	SS	133	480	75	153	36	11	12	79	.319	33	123	19	*210	367	30	.951
	—Oakland (A.L.)	OF-SS-2B	20	61	11	15	1	0	3	9	.246	3	20	2	36	13	2	.961
Major league totals (1 year)			20	61	11	15	1	0	3	9	.246	3	20	2	36	13	2	.961

ABBOTT, PAUL

P, ROYALS

PERSONAL: Born September 15, 1967, in Van Nuys, Calif. . . . 6-3/194. . . . Throws right, bats right. . . . Full name: Paul David Abbott.
HIGH SCHOOL: Sunny Hills (Fullerton, Calif.).
TRANSACTIONS/CAREER NOTES: Selected by Minnesota Twins organization in third round of free-agent draft (June 3, 1985).... On Minnesota disabled list (March 28-June 5 and August 14-September 1, 1992).... Released by Twins (March 2, 1993).... Signed by Charlotte, Cleveland Indians organization (March 27, 1993).... On Charlotte disabled list (April 8-May 6, 1993).... Granted free agency (October 15, 1993).... Signed by Omaha, Kansas City Royals organization (November 21, 1993).
STATISTICAL NOTES: Pitched 3-0 no-hit victory against Palm Springs (June 26, 1988, seven innings).

Year	Team (League)	W	L	Pct.	ERA	G	GS	CG	ShO	Sv.	IP	H	R	ER	BB	SO
1985	—Elizabeth. (Appal.)	1	5	.167	6.94	10	10	1	0	0	35	33	32	27	32	34
1986	—Kenosha (Midwest)	6	10	.375	4.50	25	15	1	0	0	98	102	62	49	73	73
1987	—Kenosha (Midwest)	13	6	.684	3.65	26	25	1	0	0	145⅓	102	76	59	103	138
1988	—Visalia (California)	11	9	.550	4.18	28	•28	4	2	0	172⅓	141	95	80	*143	*205
1989	—Orlando (Southern)	9	3	.750	4.37	17	17	1	0	0	90⅔	71	48	44	48	102
1990	—Portland (PCL)	5	14	.263	4.56	23	23	4	1	0	128⅓	110	75	65	82	129
	—Minnesota (A.L.)	0	5	.000	5.97	7	7	0	0	0	34⅔	37	24	23	28	25
1991	—Portland (PCL)	2	3	.400	3.89	8	8	1	1	0	44	36	19	19	28	40
	—Minnesota (A.L.)	3	1	.750	4.75	15	3	0	0	0	47⅓	38	27	25	36	43
1992	—Portland (PCL)	4	1	.800	2.33	7	7	0	0	0	46⅓	30	13	12	31	46
	—Minnesota (A.L.)	0	0	...	3.27	6	0	0	0	0	11	12	4	4	5	13
1993	—Cant./Akr. (East.)■	4	5	.444	4.06	13	12	1	0	0	75⅓	72	34	34	28	86
	—Cleveland (A.L.)	0	1	.000	6.38	5	5	0	0	0	18⅓	19	15	13	11	7
	—Charlotte (Int'l)	0	1	.000	6.63	4	4	0	0	0	19	25	16	14	7	12
Major league totals (4 years)		3	7	.300	5.25	33	15	0	0	0	111⅓	106	70	65	80	88

ACRE, MARK

P, ATHLETICS

PERSONAL: Born September 16, 1968, in Concord, Calif. . . . 6-8/235. . . . Throws right, bats right. . . . Full name: Mark Robert Acre.
HIGH SCHOOL: Corning (Calif.) Union.
COLLEGE: New Mexico State.
TRANSACTIONS/CAREER NOTES: Signed as free agent by Oakland Athletics organization (August 5, 1991). . . . On Modesto disabled list (April 8-23, 1993).

Year	Team (League)	W	L	Pct.	ERA	G	GS	CG	ShO	Sv.	IP	H	R	ER	BB	SO
1991	—Ariz. A's (Arizona)	2	0	1.000	2.70	6	0	0	0	0	10	10	3	3	6	6
1992	—Reno (California)	4	4	.500	4.56	35	8	0	0	2	77	67	56	39	50	65
1993	—Madison (Midwest)	0	0	...	0.29	28	0	0	0	20	31⅓	9	1	1	13	41
	—Huntsville (South.)	1	1	.500	2.42	19	0	0	0	10	22⅓	22	10	6	3	21

AGOSTO, JUAN

P

PERSONAL: Born February 23, 1958, in Rio Piedras, Puerto Rico. . . . 6-2/190. . . . Throws left, bats left. . . . Full name: Juan Roberto Agosto.
TRANSACTIONS/CAREER NOTES: Signed as free agent by Boston Red Sox organization (August 29, 1974). . . . Released by Red Sox organization (September 21, 1978). . . . Signed by Puerto Rico of Inter-American League (March 10, 1979). . . . Declared free agent when Inter-American League folded (June 30, 1979). . . . Signed by Chicago White Sox organization (January 18, 1980). . . . Contract sold by White Sox organization to Minnesota Twins in exchange for Twins loaning P Pete Filson to Buffalo, White Sox organization (April 30, 1986); Filson was returned to Minnesota and traded to White Sox for P Kurt Walker (September 3, 1986). . . . Released by Twins organization (December 20, 1986). . . . Signed by Tucson, Houston Astros organization (February 13, 1987). . . . Granted free agency (November 5, 1990). . . . Signed by St. Louis Cardinals (December 14, 1990). . . . Released by Cardinals (June 13, 1992). . . . Signed by Seattle Mariners (June 19, 1992). . . . Released by Mariners (October 5, 1992). . . . Signed by San Diego Padres organization (January 11, 1993). . . . Released by Las Vegas, Padres organization (May 20, 1993). . . . Signed by Tucson, Houston Astros organization (May 24, 1993). . . . Granted free agency (October 15, 1993).
STATISTICAL NOTES: Led Carolina League with four balks in 1977 and five in 1978.

Year	Team (League)	W	L	Pct.	ERA	G	GS	CG	ShO	Sv.	IP	H	R	ER	BB	SO
1975	—Winter Haven (FSL)	0	4	.000	5.79	6	6	0	0	0	28	35	23	18	24	19
	—Elmira (N.Y.-Penn)	1	4	.200	8.61	9	5	0	0	0	23	27	37	22	34	22
1976	—Winter Haven (FSL)	5	11	.313	4.63	28	13	3	0	0	107	97	70	55	69	80
1977	—Winst.-Salem (Car.)	4	9	.308	5.97	30	23	0	0	0	119	128	106	79	*111	98
1978	—Winter Haven (FSL)	0	0	...	18.00	1	1	0	0	0	1	5	2	2	0	0
	—Winst.-Salem (Car.)	5	11	.313	3.83	23	19	9	2	0	120	114	76	51	89	74
1979	—Pue. Rico (In.-Am.)■	3	2	.600	2.61	10	...	0	0	1	31	31	13	9	17	9
1980	—Glens Falls (East.)■	1	0	1.000	6.95	8	0	0	0	1	22	26	18	17	18	8
	—Appleton (Midw.)	11	6	.647	2.69	23	16	5	1	1	144	118	60	43	52	93
1981	—Edmonton (PCL)	7	10	.412	3.90	48	4	2	0	7	120	128	61	52	49	57
	—Chicago (A.L.)	0	0	...	4.50	2	0	0	0	0	6	5	3	3	0	3
1982	—Edmonton (PCL)	3	4	.429	5.00	50	3	1	0	11	95⅓	101	63	53	49	39
	—Chicago (A.L.)	0	0	...	18.00	1	0	0	0	0	2	7	4	4	0	1
1983	—Denver (A.A.)	4	1	.800	2.08	19	0	0	0	7	26	19	8	6	10	19
	—Chicago (A.L.)	2	2	.500	4.10	39	0	0	0	7	41⅔	41	20	19	11	29
1984	—Chicago (A.L.)	2	1	.667	3.09	49	0	0	0	7	55⅓	54	20	19	34	26
1985	—Chicago (A.L.)	4	3	.571	3.58	54	0	0	0	1	60⅓	45	27	24	23	39
	—Buffalo (A.A.)	0	0	...	2.13	6	0	0	0	2	12⅔	13	3	3	2	11
1986	—Chi.-Minn. (A.L.)■	1	4	.200	8.64	26	1	0	0	1	25	49	30	24	18	12
	—Toledo (Int'l)	4	3	.571	2.31	21	0	0	0	6	35	33	11	9	14	29
1987	—Tucson (PCL)■	4	2	.667	1.98	44	0	0	0	7	50	48	16	11	19	31
	—Houston (N.L.)	1	1	.500	2.63	27	0	0	0	2	27⅓	26	12	8	10	6
1988	—Houston (N.L.)	10	2	.833	2.26	75	0	0	0	4	91⅔	74	27	23	30	33
1989	—Houston (N.L.)	4	5	.444	2.93	71	0	0	0	1	83	81	32	27	32	46
1990	—Houston (N.L.)	9	8	.529	4.29	*82	0	0	0	4	92⅓	91	46	44	39	50
1991	—St. Louis (N.L.)■	5	3	.625	4.81	72	0	0	0	2	86	92	52	46	39	34
1992	—St. Louis (N.L.)	2	4	.333	6.25	22	0	0	0	0	31⅔	39	24	22	9	13
	—Seattle (A.L.)■	0	0	...	5.89	17	1	0	0	0	18⅓	27	12	12	3	12
	—Calgary (PCL)	1	0	1.000	4.98	10	0	0	0	1	21⅔	20	12	12	13	12
1993	—L.V.-Tucson (PCL)■	7	3	.700	5.29	51	0	0	0	3	51	66	32	30	29	33
	—Houston (N.L.)	0	0	...	6.00	6	0	0	0	0	6	8	4	4	0	3
A.L. totals (7 years)		9	10	.474	4.53	188	2	0	0	16	208⅔	228	116	105	89	122
N.L. totals (7 years)		31	23	.574	3.75	355	0	0	0	13	418	411	197	174	159	185
Major league totals (13 years)		40	33	.548	4.01	543	2	0	0	29	626⅔	639	313	279	248	307

CHAMPIONSHIP SERIES RECORD

Year	Team (League)	W	L	Pct.	ERA	G	GS	CG	ShO	Sv.	IP	H	R	ER	BB	SO
1983	—Chicago (A.L.)	0	0	...	0.00	1	0	0	0	0	⅓	0	0	0	0	0

AGUILERA, RICK

P, TWINS

PERSONAL: Born December 31, 1961, in San Gabriel, Calif. . . . 6-5/203. . . . Throws right, bats right. . . . Full name: Richard Warren Aguilera. . . . Name pronounced AG-ah-LAIR-uh.
HIGH SCHOOL: Edgewood (West Covina, Calif.).
COLLEGE: Brigham Young.
TRANSACTIONS/CAREER NOTES: Selected by St. Louis Cardinals organization in 37th round of free-agent draft (June 3, 1980). . . . Selected by New York Mets organization in third round of free-agent draft (June 6, 1983). . . . On New York disabled list (September 3-15, 1985). . . . On New York disabled list (May 23-August 24, 1987); included rehabilitation assignment to Tidewater (August 10-24). . . . On New York disabled list (April 19-June 19 and July 12-September 7, 1988); included rehabilitation assignment to St. Lucie (June 7-14) and Tidewater (June 15-19). . . . Traded by Mets with P David West and three play-

ers to be named later to Minnesota Twins for P Frank Viola (July 31, 1989); Portland, Twins organization, acquired P Kevin Tapani and P Tim Drummond (August 1, 1989), and Twins acquired P Jack Savage to complete deal (October 16, 1989).

Year	Team (League)	W	L	Pct.	ERA	G	GS	CG	ShO	Sv.	IP	H	R	ER	BB	SO
1983	—Little Falls (NYP)	5	6	.455	3.72	16	15	4	•2	0	104	★109	55	43	26	84
1984	—Lynchburg (Caro.)	8	3	.727	2.34	13	13	6	•3	0	88⅓	72	29	23	28	101
	—Jackson (Texas)	4	4	.500	4.57	11	11	2	1	0	67	68	37	34	19	71
1985	—Tidewater (Int'l)	6	4	.600	2.51	11	11	2	1	0	79	64	24	22	17	55
	—New York (N.L.)	10	7	.588	3.24	21	19	2	0	0	122⅓	118	49	44	37	74
1986	—New York (N.L.)	10	7	.588	3.88	28	20	2	0	0	141⅔	145	70	61	36	104
1987	—New York (N.L.)	11	3	.786	3.60	18	17	1	0	0	115	124	53	46	33	77
	—Tidewater (Int'l)	1	1	.500	0.69	3	3	0	0	0	13	8	2	1	1	10
1988	—New York (N.L.)	0	4	.000	6.93	11	3	0	0	0	24⅔	29	20	19	10	16
	—St. Lucie (Fla. St.)	0	0	...	1.29	2	2	0	0	0	7	8	1	1	1	5
	—Tidewater (Int'l)	0	0	...	1.50	1	1	0	0	0	6	6	1	1	1	4
1989	—New York (N.L.)	6	6	.500	2.34	36	0	0	0	7	69⅓	59	19	18	21	80
	—Minnesota (A.L.)■	3	5	.375	3.21	11	11	3	0	0	75⅔	71	32	27	17	57
1990	—Minnesota (A.L.)	5	3	.625	2.76	56	0	0	0	32	65⅓	55	27	20	19	61
1991	—Minnesota (A.L.)	4	5	.444	2.35	63	0	0	0	42	69	44	20	18	30	61
1992	—Minnesota (A.L.)	2	6	.250	2.84	64	0	0	0	41	66⅔	60	28	21	17	52
1993	—Minnesota (A.L.)	4	3	.571	3.11	65	0	0	0	34	72⅓	60	25	25	14	59
	A.L. totals (5 years)	18	22	.450	2.86	259	11	3	0	149	349	290	132	111	97	290
	N.L. totals (5 years)	37	27	.578	3.58	114	59	5	0	7	473	475	211	188	137	351
	Major league totals (9 years)	55	49	.529	3.27	373	70	8	0	156	822	765	343	299	234	641

CHAMPIONSHIP SERIES RECORD

Year	Team (League)	W	L	Pct.	ERA	G	GS	CG	ShO	Sv.	IP	H	R	ER	BB	SO
1986	—New York (N.L.)	0	0	...	0.00	2	0	0	0	0	5	2	1	0	2	2
1988	—New York (N.L.)	0	0	...	1.29	3	0	0	0	0	7	3	1	1	2	4
1991	—Minnesota (A.L.)	0	0	...	0.00	3	0	0	0	3	3⅓	1	0	0	0	3
	Champ. series totals (3 years)	0	0	...	0.59	8	0	0	0	3	15⅓	6	2	1	4	9

WORLD SERIES RECORD

WORLD SERIES NOTES: Flied out in only appearance as pinch-hitter (1991).

Year	Team (League)	W	L	Pct.	ERA	G	GS	CG	ShO	Sv.	IP	H	R	ER	BB	SO
1986	—New York (N.L.)	1	0	1.000	12.00	2	0	0	0	0	3	8	4	4	1	4
1991	—Minnesota (A.L.)	1	1	.500	1.80	4	0	0	0	2	5	6	1	1	1	3
	World Series totals (2 years)	2	1	.667	5.63	6	0	0	0	2	8	14	5	5	2	7

ALL-STAR GAME RECORD

Year	League	W	L	Pct.	ERA	GS	CG	ShO	Sv.	IP	H	R	ER	BB	SO
1991	—American	0	0	...	0.00	0	0	0	0	1⅓	2	0	0	0	3
1992	—American	0	0	...	13.50	0	0	0	0	⅔	1	1	1	0	0
1993	—American	0	0	...	0.00	0	0	0	0	1	2	0	0	0	2
	All-Star totals (3 years)	0	0	...	3.00	0	0	0	0	3	5	1	1	0	5

ALDRED, SCOTT

P

PERSONAL: Born June 12, 1968, in Flint, Mich. . . . 6-4/215. . . . Throws left, bats left. . . . Full name: Scott Phillip Aldred.

HIGH SCHOOL: Hill McCloy (Montrose, Mich.).

TRANSACTIONS/CAREER NOTES: Selected by Detroit Tigers organization in 16th round of free-agent draft (June 2, 1986). . . . Selected by Colorado Rockies in first round (15th pick overall) of expansion draft (November 17, 1992). . . . Claimed on waivers by Montreal Expos (April 29, 1993). . . . On Montreal disabled list (May 15-September 11, 1993). . . . Released by Expos (September 11, 1993).

Year	Team (League)	W	L	Pct.	ERA	G	GS	CG	ShO	Sv.	IP	H	R	ER	BB	SO
1987	—Fayetteville (SAL)	4	9	.308	3.60	21	20	0	0	0	110	101	56	44	69	91
1988	—Lakeland (Fla. St.)	8	7	.533	3.56	25	25	1	1	0	131⅓	122	61	52	72	102
1989	—London (Eastern)	10	6	.625	3.84	20	20	3	1	0	122	98	55	52	59	97
1990	—Toledo (Int'l)	6	15	.286	4.90	29	★29	2	0	0	158	145	93	86	81	133
	—Detroit (A.L.)	1	2	.333	3.77	4	3	0	0	0	14⅓	13	6	6	10	7
1991	—Toledo (Int'l)	8	8	.500	3.92	22	20	2	0	1	135⅓	127	65	59	72	95
	—Detroit (A.L.)	2	4	.333	5.18	11	11	1	0	0	57⅓	58	37	33	30	35
1992	—Detroit (A.L.)	3	8	.273	6.78	16	13	0	0	0	65	80	51	49	33	34
	—Toledo (Int'l)	4	6	.400	5.13	16	13	3	0	0	86	92	57	49	47	81
1993	—Colo.-Mont. (N.L.)■	1	0	1.000	9.00	8	0	0	0	0	12	19	14	12	10	9
	A.L. totals (3 years)	6	14	.300	5.80	31	27	1	0	0	136⅔	151	94	88	73	76
	N.L. totals (1 year)	1	0	1.000	9.00	8	0	0	0	0	12	19	14	12	10	9
	Major league totals (4 years)	7	14	.333	6.05	39	27	1	0	0	148⅔	170	108	100	83	85

ALDRETE, MIKE

1B/OF, ATHLETICS

PERSONAL: Born January 29, 1961, in Carmel, Calif. . . . 5-11/185. . . . Throws left, bats left. . . . Full name: Michael Peter Aldrete. . . . Brother of Rich Aldrete, minor league first baseman (1987-92). . . . Name pronounced owl-DRET-ee.

HIGH SCHOOL: Monterey (Calif.).

COLLEGE: Stanford (bachelor of arts degree in communication).

TRANSACTIONS/CAREER NOTES: Selected by San Francisco Giants organization in seventh round of free-agent draft (June 6, 1983). . . . Traded by Giants to Montreal Expos for OF Tracy Jones (December 8, 1988). . . . On Montreal disabled list (August 16-September 1, 1989); included rehabilitation assignment to Indianapolis (August 21-September 1). . . . Released by Expos (March 30, 1991). . . . Signed by San Diego Padres (April 5, 1991). . . . Released by Padres (May 10, 1991). . . . Signed by Col-

orado Springs, Cleveland Indians organization (May 17, 1991).... Released by Indians (March 31, 1992).... Signed by Colorado Springs (April 7, 1992).... Released by Charlotte, Indians organization (March 24, 1993).... Signed by Oakland Athletics organization (March 27, 1993).... On Tacoma disabled list (April 8-15, 1993).... Granted free agency (November 1, 1993).... Re-signed by A's (November 16, 1993).
STATISTICAL NOTES: Led California League with 225 total bases in 1984.

Year	Team (League)	Pos.	G	AB	R	H	2B	3B	HR	RBI	Avg.	BB	SO	SB	PO	A	E	Avg.
			BATTING												FIELDING			
1983	—Great Falls (Pio.)	1B-OF	38	132	30	55	11	2	4	31	.417	31	22	7	257	17	4	.986
	—Fresno (California)	1B	20	68	5	14	4	0	1	12	.206	11	17	2	189	9	2	.990
1984	—Fresno (California)	1B	136	457	89	155	28	3	12	72	.339	109	77	14	1180	74	8	*.994
1985	—Shreveport (Texas)	1B-OF	127	441	80	147	32	1	15	77	.333	94	57	16	854	41	9	.990
	—Phoenix (PCL)	OF	3	8	0	1	1	0	0	1	.125	0	3	0	3	0	0	1.000
1986	—Phoenix (PCL)	OF-1B	47	159	36	59	14	0	6	35	.371	36	24	0	131	8	1	.993
	—San Francisco (N.L.)	1B-OF	84	216	27	54	18	3	2	25	.250	33	34	1	317	36	1	.997
1987	—San Francisco (N.L.)	OF-1B	126	357	50	116	18	2	9	51	.325	43	50	6	328	18	3	.991
1988	—San Francisco (N.L.)	OF-1B	139	389	44	104	15	0	3	50	.267	56	65	6	272	8	4	.986
1989	—Montreal (N.L.)■	OF-1B	76	136	12	30	8	1	1	12	.221	19	30	1	109	9	1	.992
	—Indianapolis (A.A.)	1B-OF	10	31	4	4	1	0	0	2	.129	8	10	0	41	3	0	1.000
1990	—Montreal (N.L.)	OF-1B	96	161	22	39	7	1	1	18	.242	37	31	1	160	12	1	.994
1991	—San Diego (N.L.)■	OF	12	15	2	0	0	0	0	1	.000	3	4	0	7	1	0	1.000
	—Colo. Springs (PCL)■	OF-1B	23	76	4	22	5	0	0	8	.289	8	17	0	77	8	1	.988
	—Cleveland (A.L.)	1B-OF	85	183	22	48	6	1	1	19	.262	36	37	1	334	23	2	.994
1992	—Colo. Springs (PCL)	1B-OF	128	463	69	149	42	2	8	84	.322	65	113	1	567	38	3	.995
1993	—Tacoma (PCL)■	OF-1B	37	122	20	39	11	2	7	21	.320	26	22	2	75	5	1	.988
	—Oakland (A.L.)	1B-OF	95	255	40	68	13	1	10	33	.267	34	45	1	407	28	2	.995
American League totals (2 years)			180	438	62	116	19	2	11	52	.265	70	82	2	741	51	4	.995
National League totals (6 years)			533	1274	157	343	66	7	16	157	.269	191	214	15	1193	84	10	.992
Major league totals (7 years)			713	1712	219	459	85	9	27	209	.268	261	296	17	1934	135	14	.993

CHAMPIONSHIP SERIES RECORD

Year	Team (League)	Pos.	G	AB	R	H	2B	3B	HR	RBI	Avg.	BB	SO	SB	PO	A	E	Avg.
			BATTING												FIELDING			
1987	—San Francisco (N.L.)	PH-OF	5	10	0	1	0	0	0	1	.100	0	2	0	5	0	0	1.000

ALEXANDER, MANNY

SS, ORIOLES

PERSONAL: Born March 20, 1971, in San Pedro de Macoris, Dominican Republic. ... 5-10/165.... Throws right, bats right.... Full name: Manuel DeJesus Alexander.
TRANSACTIONS/CAREER NOTES: Signed as free agent by Baltimore Orioles organization (February 4, 1988).... On disabled list (April 26-July 23, 1990).... On Rochester disabled list (May 9-19 and June June 9-17, 1993).
STATISTICAL NOTES: Led Appalachian League shortstops with 349 total chances in 1989. ... Led Carolina League shortstops with 651 total chances and 93 double plays in 1991.

Year	Team (League)	Pos.	G	AB	R	H	2B	3B	HR	RBI	Avg.	BB	SO	SB	PO	A	E	Avg.
			BATTING												FIELDING			
1988	—		Dominican Summer League statistics unavailable.															
1989	—Bluefield (Appal.)	SS	65	*274	49	*85	13	2	2	34	.310	20	49	19	*140	177	*32	.908
1990	—Wausau (Midwest)	SS	44	152	16	27	3	1	0	11	.178	12	41	8	66	99	11	.938
1991	—Hagerstown (East.)	SS	3	9	3	3	1	0	0	2	.333	1	3	0	5	4	0	1.000
	—Frederick (Caro.)	SS	134	548	•81	*143	17	3	3	42	.261	44	68	47	*226	*393	32	*.951
1992	—Hagerstown (East.)	SS	127	499	69	129	23	8	2	41	.259	25	62	43	216	253	36	.929
	—Rochester (Int'l)	SS	6	24	3	7	1	0	0	3	.292	1	3	2	12	25	1	.974
	—Baltimore (A.L.)	SS	4	5	1	1	0	0	0	0	.200	0	3	0	3	3	0	1.000
1993	—Rochester (Int'l)	SS	120	471	55	115	23	8	6	51	.244	22	60	19	184	335	18	*.966
	—Baltimore (A.L.)	PR	3	0	1	0	0	0	0	0	...	0	0	0	...	...	...	...
Major league totals (2 years)			7	5	2	1	0	0	0	0	.200	0	3	0	3	3	0	1.000

ALICEA, LUIS

2B, CARDINALS

PERSONAL: Born July 29, 1965, in Santurce, Puerto Rico. ... 5-9/177. ... Throws right, bats both.... Full name: Luis Rene Alicea.... Name pronounced AH-la-SAY-uh.
HIGH SCHOOL: Liceo Castro (Rio Piedras, Puerto Rico).
COLLEGE: Florida State.
TRANSACTIONS/CAREER NOTES: Selected by St. Louis Cardinals organization in first round (23rd pick overall) of free-agent draft (June 2, 1986).... On disabled list (April 6-June 4, 1990).... On Louisville disabled list (April 25-May 25, 1991).... On St. Louis disabled list (June 1-July 6, 1992); included rehabilitation assignment to Louisville (July 2-6).
HONORS: Named second baseman on THE SPORTING NEWS college All-America team (1986).

Year	Team (League)	Pos.	G	AB	R	H	2B	3B	HR	RBI	Avg.	BB	SO	SB	PO	A	E	Avg.
			BATTING												FIELDING			
1986	—Erie (N.Y.-Penn)	2B	47	163	40	46	6	1	3	18	.282	37	20	27	94	163	12	.955
	—Arkansas (Texas)	2B-SS	25	68	8	16	3	0	0	3	.235	5	11	0	39	63	4	.962
1987	—Arkansas (Texas)	2B	101	337	57	91	14	3	4	47	.270	49	28	13	184	251	11	*.975
	—Louisville (A.A.)	2B	29	105	18	32	10	2	2	20	.305	9	9	4	69	81	4	.974
1988	—Louisville (A.A.)	2B-SS-OF	49	191	21	53	11	6	1	21	.277	11	21	8	116	165	0	1.000
	—St. Louis (N.L.)	2B	93	297	20	63	10	4	1	24	.212	25	32	1	206	240	14	.970
1989	—Louisville (A.A.)	2B	124	412	53	102	20	3	8	48	.248	59	55	13	240	310	16	.972
1990	—St. Peters. (FSL)	2B	29	95	14	22	1	4	0	12	.232	20	14	9	20	23	0	1.000
	—Arkansas (Texas)	2B	14	49	11	14	3	1	0	4	.286	7	8	2	24	34	4	.935
	—Louisville (A.A.)	3B	25	92	10	32	6	3	0	10	.348	5	12	0	14	39	6	.898

Year	Team (League)	Pos.	G	AB	R	H	2B	3B	HR	RBI	Avg.	BB	SO	SB	PO	A	E	Avg.
				BATTING											FIELDING			
1991	—Louisville (A.A.)	2B	31	112	26	44	6	3	4	16	.393	14	8	5	68	95	5	.970
	—St. Louis (N.L.)	2B-3B-SS	56	68	5	13	3	0	0	0	.191	8	19	0	19	23	0	1.000
1992	—Louisville (A.A.)	2B-SS	20	71	11	20	8	0	0	6	.282	16	6	0	44	52	4	.960
	—St. Louis (N.L.)	2B-SS	85	265	26	65	9	11	2	32	.245	27	40	2	136	233	7	.981
1993	—St. Louis (N.L.)	2B-OF-3B	115	362	50	101	19	3	3	46	.279	47	54	11	210	281	11	.978
	Major league totals (4 years)		349	992	101	242	41	18	6	102	.244	107	145	14	571	777	32	.977

ALLANSON, ANDY

C, GIANTS

PERSONAL: Born December 22, 1961, in Richmond, Va. . . . 6-5/225. . . . Throws right, bats right. . . . Full name: Andrew Neal Allanson.
HIGH SCHOOL: Varina (Richmond, Va.).
COLLEGE: Richmond.
TRANSACTIONS/CAREER NOTES: Selected by Cleveland Indians organization in second round of free-agent draft (June 6, 1983). . . . On Cleveland disabled list (June 19-29, 1984 and July 16-August 5, 1988). . . . Released by Indians (March 27, 1990). . . . Signed by Oklahoma City, Texas Rangers organization (April 2, 1990). . . . Released by Oklahoma City (May 8, 1990). . . . Signed by Salinas, independent (July 23, 1990). . . . Released by Salinas (August 29, 1990). . . . Signed by Omaha, Kansas City Royals organization (January 18, 1991). . . . Traded by Royals to Detroit Tigers organization for C Jim Baxter (March 30, 1991). . . . Granted free agency (December 20, 1991). . . . Signed by Denver, Milwaukee Brewers organization (January 23, 1992). . . . On Milwaukee disabled list (May 18-June 30, 1992); included rehabilitation assignment to Denver (June 11-30). . . . Released by Brewers (October 15, 1992). . . . Signed by Phoenix, San Francisco Giants organization (January 14, 1993). . . . Granted free agency (October 15, 1993). . . . Re-signed by Giants organization (November 29, 1993).
STATISTICAL NOTES: Led A.L. catchers with 762 total chances and 11 double plays in 1988.

Year	Team (League)	Pos.	G	AB	R	H	2B	3B	HR	RBI	Avg.	BB	SO	SB	PO	A	E	Avg.
				BATTING											FIELDING			
1983	—Waterloo (Midw.)	C	17	50	4	10	0	0	0	0	.200	7	10	1	99	8	3	.973
	—Batavia (NY-Penn)	C	51	145	27	38	3	0	0	6	.262	25	16	3	372	27	5	.988
1984	—Buffalo (Eastern)	C	39	111	12	28	4	0	0	11	.252	15	18	0	154	15	3	.983
	—Waterloo (Midw.)	C	46	144	14	39	5	0	0	10	.271	10	16	6	68	9	1	.987
1985	—Waterbury (East.)	C	120	420	69	131	17	1	0	47	*.312	52	25	22	578	64	10	.985
1986	—Cleveland (A.L.)	C	101	293	30	66	7	3	1	29	.225	14	36	10	446	33	*20	.960
1987	—Buffalo (A.A.)	C	76	276	21	75	8	0	4	39	.272	9	36	2	428	30	•12	.974
	—Cleveland (A.L.)	C	50	154	17	41	6	0	3	16	.266	9	30	1	252	22	4	.986
1988	—Cleveland (A.L.)	C	133	434	44	114	11	0	05	50	.263	25	63	5	*691	60	•11	.986
1989	—Cleveland (A.L.)	C	111	323	30	75	9	1	3	17	.232	23	47	4	570	53	9	.986
1990	—Okla. City (A.A.)■	C	13	40	3	4	0	0	0	4	.100	6	7	0	79	12	2	.978
	—Salinas (Calif.)■	C	36	127	21	37	6	1	3	19	.291	19	22	6	223	28	2	.992
1991	—Detroit (A.L.)■	C-1B	60	151	10	35	10	0	1	16	.232	7	31	0	219	22	5	.980
1992	—Milwaukee (A.L.)■	C	9	25	6	8	1	0	0	0	.320	1	2	3	30	3	2	.943
	—Denver (A.A.)	C-1B-OF	72	266	42	79	16	3	4	31	.297	23	29	9	279	30	3	.990
1993	—Phoenix (PCL)■	C-1-0-3	50	161	31	57	15	2	6	23	.354	10	18	7	243	26	8	.971
	—San Francisco (N.L.)	C-1B	13	24	3	4	1	0	0	2	.167	1	2	0	38	0	0	1.000
	American League totals (6 years)		464	1380	137	339	44	4	13	128	.246	79	209	23	2208	193	51	.979
	National League totals (1 year)		13	24	3	4	1	0	0	2	.167	1	2	0	38	0	0	1.000
	Major league totals (7 years)		477	1404	140	343	45	4	13	130	.244	80	211	23	2246	193	51	.980

ALOMAR, ROBERTO

2B, BLUE JAYS

PERSONAL: Born February 5, 1968, in Ponce, Puerto Rico. . . . 6-0/185. . . . Throws right, bats both. . . . Full name: Roberto Velazquez Alomar. . . . Son of Sandy Alomar Sr., current minor league instructor, Chicago Cubs organization, major league infielder with six teams (1964-78) and coach, San Diego Padres (1986-90); and brother of Sandy Alomar Jr., catcher, Cleveland Indians.
TRANSACTIONS/CAREER NOTES: Signed as free agent by San Diego Padres organization (February 16, 1985). . . . Traded by Padres with OF Joe Carter to Toronto Blue Jays for 1B Fred McGriff and SS Tony Fernandez (December 5, 1990).
RECORDS: Shares A.L. single-season record for fewest errors by second baseman (150 or more games)—5 (1992).
HONORS: Won A.L. Gold Glove at second base (1991-93). . . . Named second baseman on THE SPORTING NEWS A.L. All-Star team (1992). . . . Named second baseman on THE SPORTING NEWS A.L. Silver Slugger team (1992).
STATISTICAL NOTES: Led South Atlantic League second basemen with 35 errors in 1985. . . . Led Texas League shortstops with 167 putouts and 34 errors in 1987. . . . Led N.L. with 17 sacrifice hits in 1989. . . . Led N.L. second basemen with 17 errors in 1990. . . . Switch-hit home runs in one game (May 10, 1991).

Year	Team (League)	Pos.	G	AB	R	H	2B	3B	HR	RBI	Avg.	BB	SO	SB	PO	A	E	Avg.
				BATTING											FIELDING			
1985	—Char., S.C. (S. Atl.)	2B-SS	*137	*546	89	160	14	3	0	54	.293	61	73	36	298	339	†36	.947
1986	—Reno (California)	2B	90	356	53	123	16	4	4	49	*.346	32	38	14	198	265	18	.963
1987	—Wichita (Texas)	SS-2B	130	536	88	171	41	4	12	68	.319	49	74	43	†188	309	†36	.932
1988	—Las Vegas (PCL)	2B	9	37	5	10	1	0	2	14	.270	1	4	3	22	29	1	.981
	—San Diego (N.L.)	2B	143	545	84	145	24	6	9	41	.266	47	83	24	319	459	16	.980
1989	—San Diego (N.L.)	2B	158	623	82	184	27	1	7	56	.295	53	76	42	341	472	*28	.967
1990	—San Diego (N.L.)	2B-SS	147	586	80	168	27	5	6	60	.287	48	72	24	316	404	†19	.974
1991	—Toronto (A.L.)■	2B	161	637	88	188	41	11	9	69	.295	57	86	53	333	447	15	.981
1992	—Toronto (A.L.)	2B	152	571	105	177	27	8	8	76	.310	87	52	49	287	378	5	.993
1993	—Toronto (A.L.)	2B	153	589	109	192	35	6	17	93	.326	80	67	55	254	439	14	.980
	American League totals (3 years)		466	1797	302	557	103	25	34	238	.310	224	205	157	874	1264	34	.984
	National League totals (3 years)		448	1754	246	497	78	12	22	157	.283	148	231	90	976	1335	63	.973
	Major league totals (6 years)		914	3551	548	1054	181	37	56	395	.297	372	436	247	1850	2599	97	.979

CHAMPIONSHIP SERIES RECORD

CHAMPIONSHIP SERIES NOTES: Named A.L. Championship Series Most Valuable Player (1992).

Year	Team (League)	Pos.	G	AB	R	H	2B	3B	HR	RBI	Avg.	BB	SO	SB	PO	A	E	Avg.
			BATTING												FIELDING			
1991	—Toronto (A.L.)	2B	5	19	3	9	0	0	0	4	.474	2	3	2	14	9	0	1.000
1992	—Toronto (A.L.)	2B	6	26	4	11	1	0	2	4	.423	2	1	5	16	15	0	1.000
1993	—Toronto (A.L.)	2B	6	24	3	7	1	0	0	4	.292	4	3	4	14	19	0	1.000
Championship series totals (3 years)			17	69	10	27	2	0	2	12	.391	8	7	11	44	43	0	1.000

WORLD SERIES RECORD

WORLD SERIES NOTES: Shares record for most at-bats in one inning—2 (October 20, 1993, eighth inning).

Year	Team (League)	Pos.	G	AB	R	H	2B	3B	HR	RBI	Avg.	BB	SO	SB	PO	A	E	Avg.
			BATTING												FIELDING			
1992	—Toronto (A.L.)	2B	6	24	3	5	1	0	0	0	.208	3	3	3	5	12	0	1.000
1993	—Toronto (A.L.)	2B	6	25	5	12	2	1	0	6	.480	2	3	4	9	21	2	.938
World Series totals (2 years)			12	49	8	17	3	1	0	6	.347	5	6	7	14	33	2	.959

ALL-STAR GAME RECORD

ALL-STAR GAME NOTES: Shares single-game record for most stolen bases—2 (July 14, 1992).

Year	League	Pos.	AB	R	H	2B	3B	HR	RBI	Avg.	BB	SO	SB	PO	A	E	Avg.
			BATTING											FIELDING			
1990	—National	2B	1	0	0	0	0	0	0	.000	0	0	0	1	2	0	1.000
1991	—American	2B	4	0	0	0	0	0	0	.000	0	0	0	2	5	0	1.000
1992	—American	2B	3	1	1	0	0	0	0	.333	0	0	2	0	1	0	1.000
1993	—American	2B	3	1	1	0	0	1	1	.333	0	0	0	0	0	0	...
All-Star Game totals (4 years)			11	2	2	0	0	1	1	.182	0	0	2	3	8	0	1.000

ALOMAR, SANDY

C, INDIANS

PERSONAL: Born June 18, 1966, in Salinas, Puerto Rico. . . . 6-5/215. . . . Throws right, bats right. . . . Full name: Santos Velazquez Alomar Jr. . . . Son of Sandy Alomar Sr., current minor league instructor, Chicago Cubs organization, major league infielder with six teams (1964-78) and coach, San Diego Padres (1986-90); and brother of Roberto Alomar, second baseman, Toronto Blue Jays.
HIGH SCHOOL: Luis Munoz Rivera (Salinas, Puerto Rico).
TRANSACTIONS/CAREER NOTES: Signed as free agent by San Diego Padres organization (October 21, 1983). . . . Traded by Padres with OF Chris James and 3B Carlos Baerga to Cleveland Indians for OF Joe Carter (December 6, 1989). . . . On Cleveland disabled list (May 15-June 17 and July 29, 1991-remainder of season); included rehabilitation assignment to Colorado Springs (June 8-17 and August 9-12). . . . On disabled list (May 2-18, 1992). . . . On suspended list (July 29-August 2, 1992). . . . On Cleveland disabled list (May 1-August 7, 1993); included rehabilitation assignment to Charlotte, S.C. (July 22-August 7).
HONORS: Named Minor League co-Player of the Year by THE SPORTING NEWS (1988). . . . Named Pacific Coast League Player of the Year (1988-89). . . . Named Minor League Player of the Year by THE SPORTING NEWS (1989). . . . Named A.L. Rookie Player of the Year by THE SPORTING NEWS (1990). . . . Won A.L. Gold Glove at catcher (1990). . . . Named A.L. Rookie of the Year by Baseball Writers' Association of America (1990).
STATISTICAL NOTES: Led Northwest League catchers with .985 fielding percentage and 421 putouts in 1984. . . . Led Pacific Coast League catchers with 14 errors in 1988. . . . Led Pacific Coast League catchers with 573 putouts in 1988 and 702 in 1989. . . . Led Pacific Coast League catchers with 633 total chances in 1988 and 761 in 1989.
MISCELLANEOUS: Batted as switch-hitter (1984-86).

Year	Team (League)	Pos.	G	AB	R	H	2B	3B	HR	RBI	Avg.	BB	SO	SB	PO	A	E	Avg.
			BATTING												FIELDING			
1984	—Spokane (N'west)	C-1B	59	219	13	47	5	0	0	21	.215	13	20	3	†465	51	8	†.985
1985	—Char., S.C. (S. Atl.)	C-OF	100	352	38	73	7	0	3	43	.207	31	30	3	779	75	18	.979
1986	—Beaumont (Texas)	C	100	346	36	83	15	1	4	27	.240	15	35	2	505	60	*18	.969
1987	—Wichita (Texas)	C	103	375	50	115	19	1	8	65	.307	21	37	1	*606	50	*15	.978
1988	—Las Vegas (PCL)	C-OF	93	337	59	100	9	5	16	71	.297	28	35	1	†574	46	†14	.978
	—San Diego (N.L.)	PH	1	1	0	0	0	0	0	0	.000	0	1	0	...	...	...	...
1989	—Las Vegas (PCL)	C-OF	131	*523	88	160	33	8	13	101	.306	42	58	3	†706	47	12	.984
	—San Diego (N.L.)	C	7	19	1	4	1	0	1	6	.211	3	3	0	33	1	0	1.000
1990	—Cleveland (A.L.)■	C	132	445	60	129	26	2	9	66	.290	25	46	4	686	46	*14	.981
1991	—Cleveland (A.L.)	C	51	184	10	40	9	0	0	7	.217	8	24	0	280	19	4	.987
	—Colo. Springs (PCL)	C	12	35	5	14	2	0	1	10	.400	5	0	0	5	0	1	.833
1992	—Cleveland (A.L.)	C	89	299	22	75	16	0	2	26	.251	13	32	3	477	39	2	.996
1993	—Cleveland (A.L.)	C	64	215	24	58	7	1	6	32	.270	11	28	3	342	25	6	.984
	—Charlotte (Int'l)	C	12	44	8	16	5	0	1	8	.364	5	8	0	20	1	0	1.000
American League totals (4 years)			336	1143	116	302	58	3	17	131	.264	57	130	10	1785	129	26	.987
National League totals (2 years)			8	20	1	4	1	0	1	6	.200	3	4	0	33	1	0	1.000
Major league totals (6 years)			344	1163	117	306	59	3	18	137	.263	60	134	10	1818	130	26	.987

ALL-STAR GAME RECORD

Year	League	Pos.	AB	R	H	2B	3B	HR	RBI	Avg.	BB	SO	SB	PO	A	E	Avg.
			BATTING											FIELDING			
1990	—American	C	3	1	2	0	0	0	0	.667	0	0	0	3	0	0	1.000
1991	—American	C	2	0	0	0	0	0	0	.000	0	0	0	2	0	0	1.000
1992	—American	C	3	0	1	0	0	0	0	.333	0	0	0	3	0	0	1.000
All-Star Game totals (3 years)			8	1	3	0	0	0	0	.375	0	0	0	8	0	0	1.000

ALOU, MOISES

OF, EXPOS

PERSONAL: Born July 3, 1966, in Atlanta. . . . 6-3/190. . . . Throws right, bats right. . . . Full name: Moises Rojas Alou. . . . Son of Felipe Alou, current manager, Montreal Expos, and major league outfielder/first baseman with six teams (1958-74); nephew of Jesus Alou, major league outfielder with four teams (1963-75 and 1978-79); and nephew of Matty Alou, major

league outfielder with six teams (1960-74).... Name pronounced MOY-SEZZ ah-LOO.
HIGH SCHOOL: C.E.E. (Santo Domingo, Dominican Republic).
COLLEGE: Canada College (Calif.).
TRANSACTIONS/CAREER NOTES: Selected by Pittsburgh Pirates organization in first round (second pick overall) of free-agent draft (January 14, 1986).... Traded by Pirates organization to Montreal Expos (August 16, 1990), completing deal in which Expos traded P Zane Smith to Pirates for P Scott Ruskin, SS Willie Greene and a player to be named later (August 8, 1990).... On Montreal disabled list (March 19, 1991-entire season; July 7-27, 1992 and September 18, 1993-remainder of season).
STATISTICAL NOTES: Led American Association outfielders with seven double plays in 1990.

			BATTING											FIELDING			
Year Team (League)	**Pos.**	**G**	**AB**	**R**	**H**	**2B**	**3B**	**HR**	**RBI**	**Avg.**	**BB**	**SO**	**SB**	**PO**	**A**	**E**	**Avg.**
1986 —Watertown (NYP).....	OF	69	254	30	60	9	*8	6	35	.236	22	72	14	134	6	7	.952
1987 —Macon (S. Atl.).........	OF	4	8	1	1	0	0	0	0	.125	2	4	0	6	0	0	1.000
—Watertown (NYP).....	OF	39	117	20	25	6	2	4	8	.214	16	36	6	43	1	2	.957
1988 —Augusta (S. Atl.)......	OF	105	358	58	112	23	5	7	62	.313	51	84	24	220	10	9	.962
1989 —Salem (Carolina)......	OF	86	321	50	97	29	2	14	53	.302	35	69	12	166	12	10	.947
—Harrisburg (East.)....	OF	54	205	36	60	5	2	3	19	.293	17	38	8	89	1	2	.978
1990 —Harrisburg (East.)....	OF	36	132	19	39	12	2	3	22	.295	16	21	7	93	2	1	.990
—Buffalo-Ind. (A.A.)■.	OF	90	326	44	86	5	6	5	37	.264	33	50	13	196	12	8	.963
—Pitts.-Mont. (N.L.)...	OF	16	20	4	4	0	1	0	0	.200	0	3	0	9	1	0	1.000
1991 —..................................							Did not play.										
1992 —Montreal (N.L.)........	OF	115	341	53	96	28	2	9	56	.282	25	46	16	170	6	4	.978
1993 —Montreal (N.L.)........	OF	136	482	70	138	29	6	18	85	.286	38	53	17	254	11	4	.985
Major league totals (3 years)..................		267	843	127	238	57	9	27	141	.282	63	102	33	433	18	8	.983

ALVAREZ, TAVO
P, EXPOS

PERSONAL: Born November 25, 1971, in Obregon, Mexico.... 6-3/225.... Throws right, bats right.... Full name: Cesar Octavo Alvarez.
HIGH SCHOOL: Tucson (Ariz.).
TRANSACTIONS/CAREER NOTES: Selected by Montreal Expos organization in second round of free-agent draft (June 4, 1990); pick received as part of compensation for New York Yankees signing Type A free agent Pascual Perez.... On disabled list (August 30, 1991-remainder of season; June 17-24 and August 1-16, 1993).

Year Team (League)	**W**	**L**	**Pct.**	**ERA**	**G**	**GS**	**CG**	**ShO**	**Sv.**	**IP**	**H**	**R**	**ER**	**BB**	**SO**
1990 —GC Expos (GCL).........	5	2	.714	2.60	11	10	0	0	0	52	42	17	15	16	47
1991 —Sumter (S. Atl.)..........	12	10	.545	3.24	25	25	3	1	0	152⅔	151	68	55	58	158
1992 —W.P. Beach (FSL)......	13	4	.765	*1.49	19	19	•7	*4	0	139	124	30	23	24	83
—Harrisburg (East.).....	4	1	.800	2.85	7	7	2	1	0	47⅓	48	15	15	9	42
1993 —Ottawa (Int'l).............	7	10	.412	4.22	25	25	1	0	0	140⅔	163	80	66	55	77

ALVAREZ, WILSON
P, WHITE SOX

PERSONAL: Born March 24, 1970, in Maracaibo, Venezuela.... 6-1/235.... Throws left, bats left.... Full name: Wilson Eduardo Alvarez.
TRANSACTIONS/CAREER NOTES: Signed as free agent by Texas Rangers organization (September 23, 1986).... Traded by Rangers with IF Scott Fletcher and OF Sammy Sosa to Chicago White Sox for OF Harold Baines and IF Fred Manrique (July 29, 1989).
STATISTICAL NOTES: Tied for Gulf Coast League lead with six home runs allowed in 1987.... Pitched 7-0 no-hit victory for Chicago against Baltimore (August 11, 1991).

Year Team (League)	**W**	**L**	**Pct.**	**ERA**	**G**	**GS**	**CG**	**ShO**	**Sv.**	**IP**	**H**	**R**	**ER**	**BB**	**SO**
1987 —Gastonia (S. Atl.).......	1	5	.167	6.47	8	6	0	0	0	32	39	24	23	23	19
—GC Rangers (GCL)......	2	5	.286	5.24	10	10	0	0	0	44⅔	41	29	26	21	46
1988 —Gastonia (S. Atl.).......	4	11	.267	2.98	23	23	1	0	0	127	113	63	42	49	134
—Okla. City (A.A.).........	1	1	.500	3.78	5	3	0	0	0	16⅔	17	8	7	6	9
1989 —Charlotte (Fla. St.).....	7	4	.636	2.11	13	13	3	2	0	81	68	29	19	21	51
—Tulsa (Texas)............	2	2	.500	2.06	7	7	1	1	0	48	40	14	11	16	29
—Texas (A.L.)..............	0	1	.000	...	1	1	0	0	0	0	3	3	3	2	0
—Birm. (Southern)■......	2	1	.667	3.03	6	6	0	0	0	35⅔	32	12	12	16	18
1990 —Birm. (Southern)........	5	1	.833	4.27	7	7	1	0	0	46⅓	44	24	22	25	36
—Vancouver (PCL).......	7	7	.500	6.00	17	15	1	0	0	75	91	54	50	51	35
1991 —Birm. (Southern)........	10	6	.625	1.83	23	23	3	2	0	152⅓	109	46	31	74	165
—Chicago (A.L.)............	3	2	.600	3.51	10	9	2	1	0	56⅓	47	26	22	29	32
1992 —Chicago (A.L.)............	5	3	.625	5.20	34	9	0	0	1	100⅓	103	64	58	65	66
1993 —Chicago (A.L.)............	15	8	.652	2.95	31	31	1	1	0	207⅔	168	78	68	*122	155
—Nashville (A.A.).........	0	1	.000	2.84	1	1	0	0	0	6⅓	7	7	2	2	8
Major league totals (4 years)..	23	14	.622	3.73	76	50	3	2	1	364⅓	321	171	151	218	253

CHAMPIONSHIP SERIES RECORD

Year Team (League)	**W**	**L**	**Pct.**	**ERA**	**G**	**GS**	**CG**	**ShO**	**Sv.**	**IP**	**H**	**R**	**ER**	**BB**	**SO**
1993 —Chicago (A.L.)...........	1	0	1.000	1.00	1	1	1	0	0	9	7	1	1	2	6

AMARAL, RICH
2B, MARINERS

PERSONAL: Born April 1, 1962, in Visalia, Calif.... 6-0/175.... Throws right, bats right.... Full name: Richard Louis Amaral.... Name pronounced AM-ar-all.
HIGH SCHOOL: Estancia (Costa Mesa, Calif.).
COLLEGE: Orange Coast College (Calif.) and UCLA.
TRANSACTIONS/CAREER NOTES: Selected by Chicago Cubs organization in second round of free-agent draft (June 6, 1983).... Selected by Chicago White Sox organization from Cubs organization in Rule 5 minor league draft (December 6, 1988).... Granted free agency (October 15, 1990).... Signed by Seattle Mariners organization (November 25, 1990).... On Seattle disabled list (May 29-July 17, 1991); included rehabilitation assignment to Calgary (July 11-17).... On disabled list (August 1-16, 1993).

HONORS: Named second baseman on THE SPORTING NEWS college All-America team (1983).
STATISTICAL NOTES: Tied for New York-Pennsylvania League lead in double plays by second baseman with 39 in 1984. . . . Tied for Carolina League lead in errors by second baseman with 25 in 1985. . . . Led Pacific Coast League with .433 on-base percentage in 1991.

			BATTING												FIELDING			
Year	Team (League)	Pos.	G	AB	R	H	2B	3B	HR	RBI	Avg.	BB	SO	SB	PO	A	E	Avg.
1983	—Geneva (NY-Penn)...	2B-3B-SS	67	269	63	68	17	3	1	24	.253	45	47	22	135	205	14	.960
1984	—Quad Cities (Mid.)	2B-SS	34	119	21	25	1	0	0	7	.210	24	29	12	62	73	6	.957
1985	—Winst.-Salem (Car.) ..	2B-3B	124	428	62	116	15	5	3	36	.271	59	68	26	228	318	‡27	.953
1986	—Pittsfield (Eastern) ..	2B	114	355	43	89	12	0	0	24	.251	39	65	25	228	266	14	.972
1987	—Pittsfield (Eastern) ..	2B-1B	104	315	45	80	8	5	0	28	.254	43	50	28	242	274	18	.966
1988	—Pittsfield (Eastern) ..	2-3-1-S-0	122	422	66	117	15	4	4	47	.277	56	53	54	288	262	19	.967
1989	—Birm. (Southern)■....	2B-SS-3B	122	432	*90	123	15	6	4	48	.285	88	66	57	198	256	23	.952
1990	—Vancouver (PCL)	S-3-2-0-1	130	462	87	139	*39	5	4	56	.301	88	68	20	154	260	15	.965
1991	—Calgary (PCL)■........	SS-2B	86	347	79	120	26	2	3	36	*.346	53	37	30	148	284	15	.966
	—Seattle (A.L.)	2-3-S-1	14	16	2	1	0	0	0	0	.063	1	5	0	13	16	2	.935
1992	—Calgary (PCL)..........	SS-2B-OF	106	403	79	128	21	8	0	21	.318	67	69	*53	192	329	22	.959
	—Seattle (A.L.)	S-3-0-1-2	35	100	9	24	3	0	1	7	.240	5	16	4	33	68	3	.971
1993	—Seattle (A.L.)	2-3-S-1	110	373	53	108	24	1	1	44	.290	33	54	19	180	270	10	.978
Major league totals (3 years)			159	489	64	133	27	1	2	51	.272	39	75	23	226	354	15	.975

AMARO, RUBEN

OF, INDIANS

PERSONAL: Born February 12, 1965, in Philadelphia. . . . 5-10/175. . . . Throws right, bats both. . . . Son of Ruben Amaro Sr., current scout, Detroit Tigers and major league infielder with four teams (1958 and 1960-69).
HIGH SCHOOL: William Penn Charter (Philadelphia).
COLLEGE: Stanford (bachelor of science degree in human biology, 1987).
TRANSACTIONS/CAREER NOTES: Selected by California Angels organization in 11th round of free-agent draft (June 2, 1987). . . . Traded by Angels with P Kyle Abbott to Philadelphia Phillies for OF Von Hayes (December 8, 1991). . . . On Scranton/Wilkes-Barre disabled list (April 26-May 7, 1993). . . . Traded by Phillies to Cleveland Indians for P Heathcliff Slocumb (November 2, 1993).
STATISTICAL NOTES: Led Northwest League in caught stealing with 11 in 1987. . . . Tied for Texas League lead in being hit by pitch with nine in 1990.

			BATTING												FIELDING			
Year	Team (League)	Pos.	G	AB	R	H	2B	3B	HR	RBI	Avg.	BB	SO	SB	PO	A	E	Avg.
1987	—Salem (Northwest)...	0-3-1-S-2	71	241	51	68	7	3	3	41	.282	49	28	27	243	53	17	.946
1988	—Palm Springs (Cal.)..	2-0-C-S	115	417	96	111	13	3	4	50	.266	105	61	42	258	188	18	.961
	—Midland (Texas).......	2B	13	31	5	4	1	0	0	2	.129	4	5	4	14	30	1	.978
1989	—Quad City (Midw.)....	OF-2B	59	200	50	72	9	4	3	27	.360	45	25	20	94	34	4	.970
	—Midland (Texas).......	OF	29	110	28	42	9	2	3	9	.382	10	19	7	34	2	2	.947
1990	—Midland (Texas).......	OF	57	224	50	80	15	6	4	38	.357	29	23	8	97	8	0	1.000
	—Edmonton (PCL).......	OF-1B	82	318	53	92	15	4	3	32	.289	40	43	32	161	5	2	.988
1991	—Edmonton (PCL).......	OF-2B-1B	121	472	*95	154	*42	6	3	42	.326	63	48	36	167	23	5	.974
	—California (A.L.)	OF-2B	10	23	0	5	1	0	0	2	.217	3	3	0	9	6	1	.938
1992	—Philadelphia (N.L.)■.	OF	126	374	43	82	15	6	7	34	.219	37	54	11	232	5	2	.992
	—Scran./W.B. (Int'l)...	OF	18	68	8	20	4	1	1	10	.294	9	6	2	35	1	0	1.000
1993	—Scran./W.B. (Int'l)...	OF-2B	101	412	76	120	30	5	9	37	.291	31	44	25	272	8	5	.982
	—Philadelphia (N.L.)...	OF	25	48	7	16	2	2	1	6	.333	6	5	0	25	1	1	.963
American League totals (1 year)			10	23	0	5	1	0	0	2	.217	3	3	0	9	6	1	.938
National League totals (2 years)			151	422	50	98	17	8	8	40	.232	43	59	11	257	6	3	.989
Major league totals (3 years)			161	445	50	103	18	8	8	42	.231	46	62	11	266	12	4	.986

ANDERSEN, LARRY

P, PHILLIES

PERSONAL: Born May 6, 1953, in Portland, Ore. . . . 6-3/205. . . . Throws right, bats right. . . . Full name: Larry Eugene Andersen.
HIGH SCHOOL: Interlake (Seattle).
COLLEGE: Bellevue (Wash.) Community College.
TRANSACTIONS/CAREER NOTES: Selected by Cleveland Indians organization in seventh round of free-agent draft (June 8, 1971). . . . Traded by Indians to Pittsburgh Pirates for OF Larry Littleton and P John Burden (December 21, 1979). . . . Traded by Pirates organization to Seattle Mariners (October 29, 1980), completing deal in which Mariners traded P Odell Jones to Pirates for a player to be named later (April 1, 1980). . . . On Seattle disabled list (August 11-September 1, 1982); included rehabilitation assignment to Salt Lake City (August 11-31). . . . Loaned by Mariners organization to Portland, Philadelphia Phillies organization (April 1, 1983). . . . Contract sold by Mariners to Phillies (July 29, 1983). . . . Released by Phillies (May 13, 1986). . . . Signed by Houston Astros (May 16, 1986). . . . Granted free agency (November 12, 1986). . . . Re-signed by Astros (December 21, 1986). . . . Granted free agency (November 9, 1987). . . . Re-signed by Astros (January 8, 1988). . . . On disabled list (April 26-May 11, 1988; April 25-May 10 and August 20-September 4, 1989). . . . Traded by Astros to Boston Red Sox for 3B Jeff Bagwell (August 30, 1990). . . . Granted free agency (December 7, 1990). . . . Signed by San Diego Padres (December 21, 1990). . . . On disabled list (May 8-30 and August 20-September 9, 1991). . . . On San Diego disabled list (March 28-April 12, 1992). . . . On San Diego disabled list (April 27-June 8, 1992); included rehabilitation assignment to High Desert (May 29-June 8). . . . On San Diego disabled list (August 24-September 8, 1992). . . . Granted free agency (October 26, 1992). . . . Signed by Phillies organization (December 18, 1992). . . . On disabled list (May 8-27, 1993). . . . Granted free agency (October 29, 1993). . . . Re-signed by Phillies organization (January 18, 1994).
STATISTICAL NOTES: Pitched 6-0 no-hit victory against Victoria (June 1, 1974). . . . Led American Association with four balks in 1975.
MISCELLANEOUS: Appeared as first baseman with no chances with Toledo (1977).

Year	Team (League)	W	L	Pct.	ERA	G	GS	CG	ShO	Sv.	IP	H	R	ER	BB	SO
1971	—Reno (California)	1	0	1.000	6.75	7	3	0	0	0	24	37	20	18	9	10
	—GC Indians (GCL)	0	3	.000	3.00	4	2	0	0	0	15	15	7	5	7	10

Year	Team (League)	W	L	Pct.	ERA	G	GS	CG	ShO	Sv.	IP	H	R	ER	BB	SO
1972	—Reno (California)	4	14	.222	6.53	27	19	2	0	0	124	166	102	90	57	79
1973	—Reno (California)	10	8	.556	3.95	29	29	3	0	0	164	173	91	72	67	115
1974	—San Antonio (Tex.)	10	6	.625	3.83	25	22	9	1	0	169	176	84	72	51	64
1975	—Okla. City (A.A.)	10	11	.476	4.21	25	23	11	1	0	156	179	87	73	52	64
	—Cleveland (A.L.)	0	0	...	4.50	3	0	0	0	0	6	4	3	3	2	4
1976	—Toledo (Int'l)	0	2	.000	12.91	6	5	0	0	0	23	47	33	33	6	8
	—Williamsport (East.)	9	6	.600	2.71	21	15	12	1	0	133	117	47	40	34	74
1977	—Toledo (Int'l)	5	6	.455	1.94	45	0	0	0	9	65	52	20	14	37	40
	—Cleveland (A.L.)	0	1	.000	3.21	11	0	0	0	0	14	10	7	5	9	8
1978	—Portland (PCL)	10	7	.588	3.45	57	0	0	0	*25	99	92	42	38	45	65
1979	—Tacoma (PCL)	10	6	.625	4.02	27	12	4	0	4	112	124	59	50	32	52
	—Cleveland (A.L.)	0	0	...	7.41	8	0	0	0	0	17	25	14	14	4	7
1980	—Portland (PCL)■	5	7	.417	1.74	52	0	0	0	15	93	78	24	18	16	65
1981	—Seattle (A.L.)■	3	3	.500	2.65	41	0	0	0	5	68	57	27	20	18	40
1982	—Seattle (A.L.)	0	0	...	5.99	40	1	0	0	1	79⅔	100	56	53	23	32
	—Salt Lake City (PCL)	1	0	1.000	0.00	5	0	0	0	4	6⅔	2	0	0	3	8
1983	—Portland (PCL)■	7	8	.467	2.05	52	0	0	0	*22	70⅓	63	35	16	30	64
	—Philadelphia (N.L.)	1	0	1.000	2.39	17	0	0	0	0	26⅓	19	7	7	9	14
1984	—Philadelphia (N.L.)	3	7	.300	2.38	64	0	0	0	4	90⅔	85	32	24	25	54
1985	—Philadelphia (N.L.)	3	3	.500	4.32	57	0	0	0	3	73	78	41	35	26	50
1986	—Phil.-Hou. (N.L.)■	2	1	.667	3.03	48	0	0	0	1	77⅓	83	30	26	26	42
1987	—Houston (N.L.)	9	5	.643	3.45	67	0	0	0	5	101⅔	95	46	39	41	94
1988	—Houston (N.L.)	2	4	.333	2.94	53	0	0	0	5	82⅔	82	29	27	20	66
1989	—Houston (N.L.)	4	4	.500	1.54	60	0	0	0	3	87⅔	63	19	15	24	85
1990	—Houston (N.L.)	5	2	.714	1.95	50	0	0	0	6	73⅔	61	19	16	24	68
	—Boston (A.L.)■	0	0	...	1.23	15	0	0	0	1	22	18	3	3	3	25
1991	—San Diego (N.L.)■	3	4	.429	2.30	38	0	0	0	13	47	39	13	12	13	40
1992	—San Diego (N.L.)	1	1	.500	3.34	34	0	0	0	2	35	26	14	13	8	35
	—High Desert (Calif.)	0	1	.000	2.25	5	2	0	0	0	8	7	5	2	2	10
1993	—Philadelphia (N.L.)■	3	2	.600	2.92	64	0	0	0	0	61⅔	54	22	20	21	67
	A.L. totals (6 years)	3	4	.429	4.27	118	1	0	0	7	206⅔	214	110	98	59	116
	N.L. totals (11 years)	36	33	.522	2.78	552	0	0	0	42	756⅔	685	272	234	237	615
	Major league totals (16 years)	39	37	.513	3.10	670	1	0	0	49	963⅓	899	382	332	296	731

CHAMPIONSHIP SERIES RECORD

Year	Team (League)	W	L	Pct.	ERA	G	GS	CG	ShO	Sv.	IP	H	R	ER	BB	SO
1986	—Houston (N.L.)	0	0	...	0.00	2	0	0	0	0	5	1	0	0	2	3
1990	—Boston (A.L.)	0	1	.000	6.00	3	0	0	0	0	3	3	2	2	3	3
1993	—Philadelphia (N.L.)	0	0	...	15.43	3	0	0	0	1	2⅓	4	4	4	1	3
	Champ. series totals (3 years)	0	1	.000	5.23	8	0	0	0	1	10⅓	8	6	6	6	9

WORLD SERIES RECORD

Year	Team (League)	W	L	Pct.	ERA	G	GS	CG	ShO	Sv.	IP	H	R	ER	BB	SO
1983	—Philadelphia (N.L.)	0	0	...	2.25	2	0	0	0	0	4	4	1	1	0	1
1993	—Philadelphia (N.L.)	0	0	...	12.27	4	0	0	0	0	3⅔	5	5	5	3	3
	World Series totals (2 years)	0	0	...	7.04	6	0	0	0	0	7⅔	9	6	6	3	4

ANDERSON, BRADY

OF, ORIOLES

PERSONAL: Born January 18, 1964, in Silver Spring, Md. . . . 6-1/195. . . . Throws left, bats left. . . . Full name: Brady Kevin Anderson.

HIGH SCHOOL: Carlsbad (Calif.).

COLLEGE: UC Irvine.

TRANSACTIONS/CAREER NOTES: Selected by Boston Red Sox organization in 10th round of free-agent draft (June 3, 1985). . . . Traded by Red Sox with P Curt Schilling to Baltimore Orioles for P Mike Boddicker (July 29, 1988). . . . On Baltimore disabled list (June 8-July 20, 1990); included rehabilitation assignment to Hagerstown (July 5-12) and Frederick (July 13-17). . . . On Baltimore disabled list (May 28-June 14, 1991 and June 23-July 8, 1993).

STATISTICAL NOTES: Led A.L. outfielders with six double plays in 1992.

			BATTING												FIELDING			
Year	Team (League)	Pos.	G	AB	R	H	2B	3B	HR	RBI	Avg.	BB	SO	SB	PO	A	E	Avg.
1985	—Elmira (N.Y.-Penn)	OF	71	215	36	55	7	*6	5	21	.256	*67	32	13	119	5	3	.976
1986	—Winter Haven (FSL)	OF	126	417	86	133	19	11	12	87	.319	*107	47	44	280	5	1	*.997
1987	—New Britain (East.)	OF	52	170	30	50	4	3	6	35	.294	45	24	7	127	2	2	.985
	—Pawtucket (Int'l)	OF	23	79	18	30	4	0	2	8	.380	16	8	2	48	1	0	1.000
1988	—Pawtucket (Int'l)	OF	49	167	27	48	6	1	4	19	.287	26	33	8	115	4	2	.983
	—Boston-Balt. (A.L.)■	OF	94	325	31	69	13	4	1	21	.212	23	75	10	243	4	4	.984
1989	—Baltimore (A.L.)	OF	94	266	44	55	12	2	4	16	.207	43	45	16	191	3	3	.985
	—Rochester (Int'l)	OF	21	70	14	14	1	2	1	8	.200	12	13	2	1	0	0	1.000
1990	—Baltimore (A.L.)	OF	89	234	24	54	5	2	3	24	.231	31	46	15	149	3	2	.987
	—Hagerstown (East.)	OF	9	34	8	13	0	2	1	5	.382	5	5	2	8	1	0	1.000
	—Frederick (Caro.)	OF	2	7	2	3	1	0	0	3	.429	1	1	0	1	0	0	1.000
1991	—Baltimore (A.L.)	OF	113	256	40	59	12	3	2	27	.230	38	44	12	150	3	3	.981
	—Rochester (Int'l)	OF	7	26	5	10	3	0	0	2	.385	7	4	4	19	1	0	1.000
1992	—Baltimore (A.L.)	OF	159	623	100	169	28	10	21	80	.271	98	98	53	382	10	8	.980
1993	—Baltimore (A.L.)	OF	142	560	87	147	36	8	13	66	.263	82	99	24	296	7	2	.993
	Major league totals (6 years)		691	2264	326	553	106	29	44	234	.244	315	407	130	1411	30	22	.985

ALL-STAR GAME RECORD

Year	League	Pos.	BATTING AB	R	H	2B	3B	HR	RBI	Avg.	BB	SO	SB	FIELDING PO	A	E	Avg.
1992	—American	OF	3	0	0	0	0	0	0	.000	0	0	0	1	0	0	1.000

ANDERSON, BRIAN
P, ANGELS

PERSONAL: Born April 26, 1972, in Portsmouth, Va.... 6-1/190.... Throws left, bats both.... Full name: Brian James Anderson.
HIGH SCHOOL: Geneva (O.).
COLLEGE: Wright State.
TRANSACTIONS/CAREER NOTES: Selected by California Angels organization in first round (third pick overall) of free-agent draft (June 3, 1993).

Year	Team (League)	W	L	Pct.	ERA	G	GS	CG	ShO	Sv.	IP	H	R	ER	BB	SO
1993	—Midland (Texas)	0	1	.000	3.38	2	2	0	0	0	10⅔	16	5	4	0	9
	—Vancouver (PCL)	0	1	.000	12.38	2	2	0	0	0	8	13	12	11	6	2
	—California (A.L.)	0	0	...	3.97	4	1	0	0	0	11⅓	11	5	5	2	4
Major league totals (1 year)		0	0	...	3.97	4	1	0	0	0	11⅓	11	5	5	2	4

ANDERSON, GARRET
OF, ANGELS

PERSONAL: Born June 30, 1972, in Los Angeles.... 6-3/190.... Throws left, bats left.... Full name: Garret Joseph Anderson.
HIGH SCHOOL: John F. Kennedy (Granada Hills, Calif.) and Palos Verdes Estates (Calif.).
TRANSACTIONS/CAREER NOTES: Selected by California Angels organization in fourth round of free-agent draft (June 4, 1990). ... On disabled list (June 12, 1991-remainder of season).

Year	Team (League)	Pos.	BATTING G	AB	R	H	2B	3B	HR	RBI	Avg.	BB	SO	SB	FIELDING PO	A	E	Avg.
1990	—Ariz. Angels (Ariz.)	OF	32	127	5	27	2	0	0	14	.213	2	24	3	53	2	2	.965
	—Boise (Northwest)	OF	25	83	11	21	3	1	1	8	.253	4	18	0	38	0	2	.950
1991	—Quad City (Midw.)	OF	105	392	40	102	22	2	2	42	.260	20	89	5	158	7	10	.943
1992	—Palm Springs (Cal.)	OF	81	322	46	104	15	2	1	62	.323	21	61	1	137	4	6	.959
	—Midland (Texas)	OF	39	146	16	40	5	0	2	19	.274	9	30	2	62	6	1	.986
1993	—Vancouver (PCL)	OF-1B	124	467	57	137	34	4	4	71	.293	31	95	3	198	13	2	.991

ANDERSON, MIKE
P, CUBS

PERSONAL: Born July 30, 1966, in Austin, Tex.... 6-3/205.... Throws right, bats right. ... Full name: Michael James Anderson.
HIGH SCHOOL: Georgetown (Tex.).
COLLEGE: Southwestern University (Tex.).
TRANSACTIONS/CAREER NOTES: Signed as free agent by Cincinnati Reds organization (June 10, 1988).... On Chattanooga disabled list (April 8-25, 1993).... Traded by Reds with P Larry Luebbers and C Darron Cox to Chicago Cubs for P Chuck McElroy (December 10, 1993).
STATISTICAL NOTES: Pitched six-inning, 5-0 no-hit victory against Columbia (July 27, 1989, first game).

Year	Team (League)	W	L	Pct.	ERA	G	GS	CG	ShO	Sv.	IP	H	R	ER	BB	SO
1988	—GC Reds (GCL)	0	1	.000	4.91	2	2	0	0	0	7⅓	6	7	4	5	11
	—Billings (Pioneer)	3	1	.750	3.25	17	4	0	0	2	44⅓	36	17	16	21	52
1989	—Greensboro (S. Atl.)	11	6	.647	2.86	25	25	4	2	0	154⅓	117	64	49	72	154
1990	—Ced. Rap. (Midw.)	10	5	.667	3.38	23	23	2	0	0	138⅓	134	67	52	62	101
1991	—Chatt. (South.)	10	9	.526	4.40	28	26	3	•3	0	155⅓	142	*94	76	93	115
1992	—Chatt. (South.)	•13	7	.650	2.52	28	26	4	•4	0	171⅔	155	59	48	61	149
1993	—Chatt. (South.)	1	1	.500	1.20	2	2	1	0	0	15	10	3	2	1	14
	—Indianapolis (A.A.)	10	6	.625	3.75	23	23	2	1	0	151	150	73	63	56	111
	—Cincinnati (N.L.)	0	0	...	18.56	3	0	0	0	0	5⅓	12	11	11	3	4
Major league totals (1 year)		0	0	...	18.56	3	0	0	0	0	5⅓	12	11	11	3	4

ANDREWS, SHANE
3B, EXPOS

PERSONAL: Born August 28, 1971, in Dallas.... 6-1/215.... Throws right, bats right. ... Full name: Darrell Shane Andrews.
HIGH SCHOOL: Carlsbad (N.M.) Senior.
TRANSACTIONS/CAREER NOTES: Selected by Montreal Expos organization in first round (11th pick overall) of free-agent draft (June 4, 1990).... On disabled list (August 3-11, 1993).
STATISTICAL NOTES: Led South Atlantic League third basemen with 98 putouts in 1992.

Year	Team (League)	Pos.	BATTING G	AB	R	H	2B	3B	HR	RBI	Avg.	BB	SO	SB	FIELDING PO	A	E	Avg.
1990	—GC Expos (GCL)	3B	56	190	31	46	7	1	3	24	.242	29	46	11	42	105	17	.896
1991	—Sumter (S. Atl.)	3B	105	356	46	74	16	7	11	49	.208	65	132	5	71	205	29	.905
1992	—Albany (S. Atl.)	3B-1B	136	453	76	104	18	1	*25	87	.230	*107	*174	8	†125	212	26	.928
1993	—Harrisburg (East.)	3B-SS	124	442	77	115	29	2	18	70	.260	64	118	10	74	217	23	.927

ANDUJAR, LUIS
P, WHITE SOX

PERSONAL: Born November 22, 1972, in Bani, Dominican Republic.... 6-1/160.... Throws right, bats right.... Full name: Luis Sanchez Andujar.
TRANSACTIONS/CAREER NOTES: Signed as free agent by Chicago White Sox organization (February 25, 1991).... On disabled list (July 8-18, 1992).... On Birmingham disabled list (September 2, 1993-remainder of season).

Year	Team (League)	W	L	Pct.	ERA	G	GS	CG	ShO	Sv.	IP	H	R	ER	BB	SO
1991	—GC Whi. Sox (GCL)	4	4	.500	2.45	10	10	1	•1	0	62⅓	60	27	17	10	52
1992	—South Bend (Mid.)	6	5	.545	2.92	32	15	1	1	3	120⅓	109	49	39	47	91
1993	—Sarasota (Fla. St.)	6	6	.500	1.99	18	11	2	0	1	86	67	26	19	28	76
	—Birm. (Southern)	5	0	1.000	1.82	6	6	0	0	0	39⅔	31	9	8	18	48

ANSLEY, WILLIE

OF, ASTROS

PERSONAL: Born December 15, 1969, in Dallas. . . . 6-2/200. . . . Throws right, bats right. . . . Full name: Willie Carl Ansley Jr.

HIGH SCHOOL: Plainview (Tex.).

TRANSACTIONS/CAREER NOTES: Selected by Houston Astros organization in first round (seventh pick overall) of free-agent draft (June 1, 1988). . . . On Jackson disabled list (June 9-July 11, 1991 and April 10-July 22, 1992).

			BATTING												FIELDING			
Year	Team (League)	Pos.	G	AB	R	H	2B	3B	HR	RBI	Avg.	BB	SO	SB	PO	A	E	Avg.
1989	—Asheville (S. Atl.)	OF	103	340	81	105	14	2	6	55	.309	73	90	53	179	12	5	.974
	—Columbus (South.) ...	OF	30	104	16	26	3	0	0	7	.250	26	37	37	63	1	0	1.000
1990	—Columbus (South.) ...	OF	120	415	69	106	9	7	9	37	.255	54	121	33	198	7	11	.949
1991	—Osceola (Fla. St.)......	DH	15	46	3	4	0	0	0	3	.087	13	18	3	...	...	...	...
	—Jackson (Texas)	OF	77	233	43	54	15	5	1	20	.232	43	66	9	41	2	2	.956
1992	—GC Astros (GCL)	OF	10	35	9	13	3	0	0	7	.371	7	6	5	15	0	0	1.000
	—Jackson (Texas)	OF	35	120	18	29	8	1	0	3	.242	22	33	10	52	1	2	.964
1993	—Tucson (PCL)	OF	125	382	71	100	20	7	5	61	.262	79	93	22	174	9	8	.958

ANTHONY, ERIC

OF, MARINERS

PERSONAL: Born November 8, 1967, in San Diego. . . . 6-2/195. . . . Throws left, bats left. . . . Full name: Eric Todd Anthony.

HIGH SCHOOL: Sharstown (Houston).

TRANSACTIONS/CAREER NOTES: Selected by Houston Astros organization in 34th round of free-agent draft (June 2, 1986). . . . On Houston disabled list (April 10-30, 1990); included rehabilitation assignment to Columbus (April 25-30). . . . Traded by Astros to Seattle Mariners for OF Mike Felder and P Mike Hampton (December 10, 1993).

HONORS: Named Southern League Most Valuable Player (1989).

STATISTICAL NOTES: Led Gulf Coast League with 110 total bases in 1987. . . . Led South Atlantic League with .558 slugging percentage in 1988. . . . Led Southern League with .558 slugging percentage in 1989.

			BATTING												FIELDING			
Year	Team (League)	Pos.	G	AB	R	H	2B	3B	HR	RBI	Avg.	BB	SO	SB	PO	A	E	Avg.
1986	—GC Astros (GCL)	OF	13	12	2	3	0	0	0	0	.250	5	5	1	2	1	0	1.000
1987	—GC Astros (GCL)	OF	60	216	38	57	11	6	*10	*46	.264	26	58	2	100	•11	5	.957
1988	—Asheville (S. Atl.)	OF	115	439	73	120	*36	1	*29	89	.273	40	101	10	152	8	14	.920
1989	—Columbus (South.) ...	OF	107	403	67	121	16	2	*28	79	.300	35	127	14	178	17	8	.961
	—Houston (N.L.)	OF	25	61	7	11	2	0	4	7	.180	9	16	0	34	1	0	1.000
	—Tucson (PCL)	OF	12	46	10	10	3	0	3	11	.217	6	11	0	21	0	0	1.000
1990	—Houston (N.L.)	OF	84	239	26	46	8	0	10	29	.192	29	78	5	124	5	4	.970
	—Columbus (South.) ...	OF	4	12	2	2	0	0	1	3	.167	3	4	0	3	0	0	1.000
	—Tucson (PCL)	OF	40	161	28	46	10	2	6	26	.286	17	40	8	84	7	4	.958
1991	—Tucson (PCL)	OF-1B	79	318	57	107	22	2	9	63	.336	25	58	11	154	9	4	.976
	—Houston (N.L.)	OF	39	118	11	18	6	0	1	7	.153	12	41	1	64	5	1	.986
1992	—Houston (N.L.)	OF	137	440	45	105	15	1	19	80	.239	38	98	5	173	6	5	.973
1993	—Houston (N.L.)	OF	145	486	70	121	19	4	15	66	.249	49	88	3	233	6	3	.988
Major league totals (5 years)			430	1344	159	301	50	5	49	189	.224	137	321	14	628	23	13	.980

APPIER, KEVIN

P, ROYALS

PERSONAL: Born December 6, 1967, in Lancaster, Calif. . . . 6-2/195. . . . Throws right, bats right. . . . Full name: Robert Kevin Appier. . . . Name pronounced AY-pee-er.

HIGH SCHOOL: Antelope Valley (Lancaster, Calif.).

COLLEGE: Fresno State and Antelope Valley College (Calif.).

TRANSACTIONS/CAREER NOTES: Selected by Kansas City Royals organization in first round (ninth pick overall) of free-agent draft (June 2, 1987).

HONORS: Named A.L. Rookie Pitcher of the Year by THE SPORTING NEWS (1990).

Year	Team (League)	W	L	Pct.	ERA	G	GS	CG	ShO	Sv.	IP	H	R	ER	BB	SO
1987	—Eugene (N'west)	5	2	.714	3.04	15	•15	0	0	0	77	81	43	26	29	72
1988	—Baseball City (FSL)....	10	9	.526	2.75	24	24	1	0	0	147⅓	134	58	45	39	112
	—Memphis (South.)	2	0	1.000	1.83	3	3	0	0	0	19⅔	11	5	4	7	18
1989	—Omaha (A.A.)	8	8	.500	3.95	22	22	3	2	0	139	141	70	61	42	109
	—Kansas City (A.L.)	1	4	.200	9.14	6	5	0	0	0	21⅔	34	22	22	12	10
1990	—Omaha (A.A.)	2	0	1.000	1.50	3	3	0	0	0	18	15	3	3	3	17
	—Kansas City (A.L.)	12	8	.600	2.76	32	24	3	3	0	185⅔	179	67	57	54	127
1991	—Kansas City (A.L.)	13	10	.565	3.42	34	31	6	3	0	207⅔	205	97	79	61	158
1992	—Kansas City (A.L.)	15	8	.652	2.46	30	30	3	0	0	208⅓	167	59	57	68	150
1993	—Kansas City (A.L.)	18	8	.692	*2.56	34	34	5	1	0	238⅔	183	74	68	81	186
Major league totals (5 years) ..		59	38	.608	2.95	136	124	17	7	0	862	768	319	283	276	631

AQUINO, LUIS

P, MARLINS

PERSONAL: Born May 19, 1965, in Rio Piedras, Puerto Rico. . . . 6-1/190. . . . Throws right, bats right. . . . Full name: Luis Antonio Colon Aquino. . . . Name pronounced uh-KEE-no.

HIGH SCHOOL: Gabriela Mistra (Rio Piedras, Puerto Rico).

TRANSACTIONS/CAREER NOTES: Signed as free agent by Toronto Blue Jays organization (June 15, 1981). . . . Traded by Blue Jays organization to Kansas City Royals organization for OF Juan Beniquez (July 14, 1987). . . . On disabled list (May 31-June 15, 1989 and July 21-September 24, 1990). . . . On Kansas City disabled list (April 11-July 19,

1992); included rehabilitation assignment to Omaha (July 8-19).... Contract sold by Royals to Florida Marlins (March 27, 1993).... On disabled list (July 4-August 3, 1993).... Granted free agency (December 20, 1993).... Re-signed by Marlins organization (January 17, 1994).

STATISTICAL NOTES: Pitched 2-0 no-hit victory for Omaha against Columbus (June 20, 1988).

Year	Team (League)	W	L	Pct.	ERA	G	GS	CG	ShO	Sv.	IP	H	R	ER	BB	SO
1982	—GC Blue Jays (GCL)	4	7	.364	3.31	13	11	4	0	0	73⅓	60	33	27	17	52
1983	—Florence (S. Atl.)	7	9	.438	5.25	29	21	5	1	0	133⅔	128	91	78	61	104
1984	—Kinston (Carolina)	5	6	.455	2.70	*53	0	0	0	20	70	50	21	21	37	78
	—Knoxville (South.)	0	0	...	9.00	3	0	0	0	0	4	3	4	4	3	7
1985	—Knoxville (South.)	5	7	.417	2.60	50	0	0	0	*20	83	58	29	24	32	82
1986	—Syracuse (Int'l)	3	7	.300	2.88	43	6	0	0	10	84⅓	70	30	27	34	60
	—Toronto (A.L.)	1	1	.500	6.35	7	0	0	0	0	11⅓	14	8	8	3	5
1987	—Syracuse (Int'l)	6	7	.462	4.78	26	11	0	0	0	84⅔	75	46	45	51	68
	—Omaha (A.A.)■	3	2	.600	2.31	14	4	1	0	1	50⅔	42	15	13	16	29
1988	—Omaha (A.A.)	8	3	.727	2.85	25	16	1	1	0	129⅓	106	43	41	50	93
	—Kansas City (A.L.)	1	0	1.000	2.79	7	5	1	1	0	29	33	15	9	17	11
1989	—Kansas City (A.L.)	6	8	.429	3.50	34	16	2	1	0	141⅓	148	62	55	35	68
1990	—Kansas City (A.L.)	4	1	.800	3.16	20	3	1	0	0	68⅓	59	25	24	27	28
1991	—Kansas City (A.L.)	8	4	.667	3.44	38	18	1	1	3	157	152	67	60	47	80
1992	—Kansas City (A.L.)	3	6	.333	4.52	15	13	0	0	0	67⅔	81	35	34	20	11
	—Omaha (A.A.)	0	0	...	2.61	2	2	0	0	0	10⅓	13	3	3	4	3
1993	—Florida (N.L.)■	6	8	.429	3.42	38	13	0	0	0	110⅔	115	43	42	40	67
A.L. totals (6 years)		23	20	.535	3.60	121	55	5	3	3	474⅔	487	212	190	149	203
N.L. totals (1 year)		6	8	.429	3.42	38	13	0	0	0	110⅔	115	43	42	40	67
Major league totals (7 years)		29	28	.509	3.57	159	68	5	3	3	585⅓	602	255	232	189	270

ARIAS, ALEX
IF, MARLINS

PERSONAL: Born November 20, 1967, in New York.... 6-3/185.... Throws right, bats right.... Full name: Alejandro Arias.... Name pronounced air-REE-ahs.

HIGH SCHOOL: George Washington (New York).

TRANSACTIONS/CAREER NOTES: Selected by Chicago Cubs organization in third round of free-agent draft (June 2, 1987).... Traded by Cubs with 3B Gary Scott to Florida Marlins for P Greg Hibbard (November 17, 1992).

STATISTICAL NOTES: Led Midwest League shortstops with 655 total chances and 83 double plays in 1989.... Led Southern League shortstops with 583 total chances and 81 double plays in 1991.

			BATTING												FIELDING			
Year	Team (League)	Pos.	G	AB	R	H	2B	3B	HR	RBI	Avg.	BB	SO	SB	PO	A	E	Avg.
1987	—Wytheville (Appal.)	SS-3B	61	233	41	69	7	0	0	24	.296	27	29	16	77	141	16	.932
1988	—Char., W.Va. (SAL)	SS-3B-2B	127	472	57	122	12	1	0	33	.258	54	44	41	184	396	32	.948
1989	—Peoria (Midwest)	SS	*136	506	74	140	10	*11	2	64	.277	49	67	31	*210	*408	37	.944
1990	—Charlotte (South.)	SS	119	419	55	103	16	3	4	38	.246	42	53	12	171	284	*42	.915
1991	—Charlotte (South.)	SS	134	488	69	134	26	0	4	47	.275	47	42	23	*203	*351	29	*.950
1992	—Iowa (Am. Assoc.)	SS-2B	106	409	52	114	23	3	5	40	.279	44	27	14	183	290	14	.971
	—Chicago (N.L.)	SS	32	99	14	29	6	0	0	7	.293	11	13	0	43	74	4	.967
1993	—Florida (N.L.)■	2B-3B-SS	96	249	27	67	5	1	2	20	.269	27	18	1	94	144	6	.975
Major league totals (2 years)			128	348	41	96	11	1	2	27	.276	38	31	1	137	218	10	.973

ARMAS, MARCOS
1B, ATHLETICS

PERSONAL: Born August 5, 1969, in Puerto Piritu, Venezuela.... 6-5/195.... Throws right, bats right.... Full name: Marcos Rafael Armas.... Brother of Tony Armas, major league outfielder with four teams (1976-89).

TRANSACTIONS/CAREER NOTES: Signed as free agent by Oakland Athletics organization (December 15, 1987).... On Tacoma disabled list (April 27-May 5, 1993).

STATISTICAL NOTES: Led Southern League first basemen with 1,271 total chances and 122 double plays in 1992.

			BATTING												FIELDING			
Year	Team (League)	Pos.	G	AB	R	H	2B	3B	HR	RBI	Avg.	BB	SO	SB	PO	A	E	Avg.
1988	—Ariz. A's (Arizona)	1B-3B-2B	17	58	14	17	2	1	0	10	.293	5	17	0	89	9	1	.990
1989	—S. Oregon (N'west)	OF-3B-1B	36	136	18	43	5	2	3	22	.316	6	42	1	40	18	9	.866
1990	—Madison (Midwest)	3B-OF	75	260	32	62	13	0	7	33	.238	10	80	3	52	51	14	.880
1991	—Modesto (Calif.)	1B-OF-3B	36	140	21	39	7	0	8	33	.279	10	41	0	144	13	2	.987
	—Huntsville (South.)	1B-OF	81	305	40	69	16	1	8	53	.226	18	89	2	492	35	8	.985
1992	—Huntsville (South.)	1B	132	509	83	144	30	6	17	84	.283	41	133	9	*1177	75	*19	.985
1993	—Tacoma (PCL)	1B-3B-OF	117	434	69	126	27	8	15	89	.290	35	113	4	538	42	10	.983
	—Oakland (A.L.)	1B-OF	15	31	7	6	2	0	1	1	.194	1	12	1	77	4	0	1.000
Major league totals (1 year)			15	31	7	6	2	0	1	1	.194	1	12	1	77	4	0	1.000

ARMSTRONG, JACK
P, RANGERS

PERSONAL: Born March 7, 1965, in Englewood, N.J.... 6-5/220.... Throws right, bats right.... Full name: Jack William Armstrong.

HIGH SCHOOL: Neptune (N.J.).

COLLEGE: Rider (N.J.) and Oklahoma (degree in economics, 1987).

TRANSACTIONS/CAREER NOTES: Selected by San Francisco Giants organization in third round of free-agent draft (June 2, 1986).... Selected by Cincinnati Reds organization in first round (18th pick overall) of free-agent draft (June 2, 1987).... On Cincinnati disabled list (August 25-September 9, 1990).... Traded by Reds with P Scott Scudder and P Joe Turek to Cleveland Indians for P Greg Swindell (November 15, 1991).... Selected by Florida Marlins in second round (39th pick overall) of expansion draft (November 17, 1992).... Granted free agency (December 20, 1993).... Signed by Texas Rangers (January 7, 1994).

STATISTICAL NOTES: Pitched 4-0 no-hit victory for Nashville against Indianapolis (August 7, 1988).... Tied for N.L. lead with five balks in 1990.

Year	Team (League)	W	L	Pct.	ERA	G	GS	CG	ShO	Sv.	IP	H	R	ER	BB	SO
1987	—Billings (Pioneer)	2	1	.667	2.66	5	4	0	0	0	20⅓	16	7	6	12	29
	—Vermont (Eastern)	1	2	.333	3.03	5	5	2	1	0	35⅔	24	12	12	23	39
1988	—Nashville (A.A.)	5	5	.500	3.00	17	17	4	1	0	120	84	44	40	38	116
	—Cincinnati (N.L.)	4	7	.364	5.79	14	13	0	0	0	65⅓	63	44	42	38	45
1989	—Nashville (A.A.)	•13	9	.591	2.91	25	24	*12	*6	0	182⅔	144	63	59	58	152
	—Cincinnati (N.L.)	2	3	.400	4.64	9	8	0	0	0	42⅔	40	24	22	21	23
1990	—Cincinnati (N.L.)	12	9	.571	3.42	29	27	2	1	0	166	151	72	63	59	110
1991	—Cincinnati (N.L.)	7	13	.350	5.48	27	24	1	0	0	139⅔	158	90	85	54	93
	—Nashville (A.A.)	2	0	1.000	2.65	6	6	2	0	0	37⅓	31	14	11	5	28
1992	—Cleveland (A.L.)■	6	15	.286	4.64	35	23	1	0	0	166⅔	176	100	86	67	114
1993	—Florida (N.L.)■	9	17	.346	4.49	36	33	0	0	0	196⅓	210	105	98	78	118
	A.L. totals (1 year)	6	15	.286	4.64	35	23	1	0	0	166⅔	176	100	86	67	114
	N.L. totals (5 years)	34	49	.410	4.57	115	105	3	1	0	610	622	335	310	250	389
	Major league totals (6 years)	40	64	.385	4.59	150	128	4	1	0	776⅔	798	435	396	317	503

CHAMPIONSHIP SERIES RECORD

Year	Team (League)	W	L	Pct.	ERA	G	GS	CG	ShO	Sv.	IP	H	R	ER	BB	SO
1990	—Cincinnati (N.L.)							Did not play.								

WORLD SERIES RECORD

Year	Team (League)	W	L	Pct.	ERA	G	GS	CG	ShO	Sv.	IP	H	R	ER	BB	SO
1990	—Cincinnati (N.L.)	0	0	...	0.00	1	0	0	0	0	3	1	0	0	0	3

ALL-STAR GAME RECORD

Year	League	W	L	Pct.	ERA	GS	CG	ShO	Sv.	IP	H	R	ER	BB	SO
1990	—National	0	0	...	0.00	1	0	0	0	2	1	0	0	0	2

AROCHA, RENE

P, CARDINALS

PERSONAL: Born February 24, 1966, in Havana, Cuba. . . . 6-0/180. . . . Throws right, bats right.
HIGH SCHOOL: Regla (Cuba).
TRANSACTIONS/CAREER NOTES: Signed as free agent by St. Louis Cardinals organization (November 21, 1991). . . . On disabled list (April 21-May 13, 1993).
HONORS: Named American Association Most Valuable Pitcher (1992).
MISCELLANEOUS: Member of Cuban national baseball team (1986-91).

Year	Team (League)	W	L	Pct.	ERA	G	GS	CG	ShO	Sv.	IP	H	R	ER	BB	SO
1992	—Louisville (A.A.)	•12	7	.632	2.70	25	25	3	1	0	166⅔	145	59	50	65	128
1993	—St. Louis (N.L.)	11	8	.579	3.78	32	29	1	0	0	188	197	89	79	31	96
	Major league totals (1 year)	11	8	.579	3.78	32	29	1	0	0	188	197	89	79	31	96

ARTEAGA, IVAN

P, ROCKIES

PERSONAL: Born July 20, 1972, in Cabello, Venezuela. . . . 6-2/220. . . . Throws right, bats left. . . . Full name: Ivan Jose Arteaga. . . . Name pronounced ar-tee-AH-guh.
TRANSACTIONS/CAREER NOTES: Signed as free agent by Montreal Expos organization (May 11, 1989). . . . Not on disabled list but did not play (1992). . . . Traded by Expos with P Rodney Pedraza to Colorado Rockies for IF Freddie Benavides (January 7, 1994).

Year	Team (League)	W	L	Pct.	ERA	G	GS	CG	ShO	Sv.	IP	H	R	ER	BB	SO
1991	—Dom. Expos (DSL)	6	4	.600	1.91	14	13	3	1	0	85	58	24	18	45	60
1992	—							Did not play.								
1993	—Burlington (Midw.)	6	5	.545	2.83	20	20	2	0	0	127	114	57	40	47	111
	—W.P. Beach (FSL)	0	3	.000	8.04	4	4	0	0	0	15⅔	23	15	14	9	10

RECORD AS POSITION PLAYER

			BATTING												FIELDING			
Year	Team (League)	Pos.	G	AB	R	H	2B	3B	HR	RBI	Avg.	BB	SO	SB	PO	A	E	Avg.
1989	—Dom. Expos (DSL)	IF	25	54	6	13	1	0	1	9	.241	13	16	0	...	...	...	...
1990	—Dom. Expos (DSL)	IF	66	199	26	48	10	3	3	33	.241	52	50	2	...	...	...	...

ASHBY, ANDY

P, PADRES

PERSONAL: Born July 11, 1967, in Kansas City, Mo. . . . 6-5/190. . . . Throws right, bats right. . . . Full name: Andrew Jason Ashby.
HIGH SCHOOL: Park Hill (Kansas City, Mo.).
COLLEGE: Crowder College (Mo.).
TRANSACTIONS/CAREER NOTES: Signed as free agent by Philadelphia Phillies organization (May 4, 1986). . . . On Spartanburg disabled list (April 7-July 10, 1988). . . . On disabled list (April 6-26, 1989). . . . On Philadelphia disabled list (April 27-August 11, 1992); included rehabilitation assignment to Scranton/Wilkes-Barre (July 8-August 2 and August 6-10). . . . Selected by Colorado Rockies in first round (25th pick overall) of expansion draft (November 17, 1992). . . . Traded by Rockies to San Diego Padres (July 27, 1993), completing deal in which Padres traded P Bruce Hurst and P Greg W. Harris to Rockies for C Brad Ausmus, P Doug Bochtler and a player to be named later (July 26, 1993).
RECORDS: Shares major league record by striking out side on nine pitches (June 15, 1991, fourth inning).

Year	Team (League)	W	L	Pct.	ERA	G	GS	CG	ShO	Sv.	IP	H	R	ER	BB	SO
1986	—Bend (Northwest)	1	2	.333	4.95	16	6	0	0	2	60	56	40	33	34	45
1987	—Spartanburg (SAL)	4	6	.400	5.60	13	13	1	0	0	64⅓	73	45	40	38	52
	—Utica (N.Y.-Penn)	3	7	.300	4.05	13	13	0	0	0	60	56	38	27	36	51
1988	—Spartanburg (SAL)	1	1	.500	2.70	3	3	0	0	0	16⅔	13	7	5	7	16
	—Batavia (NY-Penn)	3	1	.750	1.61	6	6	2	1	0	44⅔	25	11	8	16	32

Year	Team (League)	W	L	Pct.	ERA	G	GS	CG	ShO	Sv.	IP	H	R	ER	BB	SO
1989	—Spartanburg (SAL)......	5	9	.357	2.87	17	17	3	1	0	106⅔	95	48	34	49	100
	—Clearwater (FSL).......	1	4	.200	1.24	6	6	2	1	0	43⅔	28	9	6	21	44
1990	—Reading (Eastern)......	10	7	.588	3.42	23	23	4	1	0	139⅔	134	65	53	48	94
1991	—Scran./W.B. (Int'l).....	11	11	.500	3.46	26	26	•6	•3	0	161⅓	144	78	62	60	113
	—Philadelphia (N.L.).....	1	5	.167	6.00	8	8	0	0	0	42	41	28	28	19	26
1992	—Philadelphia (N.L.).....	1	3	.250	7.54	10	8	0	0	0	37	42	31	31	21	24
	—Scran./W.B. (Int'l).....	0	3	.000	3.00	7	7	1	0	0	33	23	13	11	14	18
1993	—Colo.-S.D. (N.L.)■......	3	10	.231	6.80	32	21	0	0	1	123	168	100	93	56	77
	—Colo. Springs (PCL).....	4	2	.667	4.10	7	6	1	0	0	41⅔	45	25	19	12	35
	Major league totals (3 years)...	5	18	.217	6.77	50	37	0	0	1	202	251	159	152	96	127

ASHLEY, BILLY

OF, DODGERS

PERSONAL: Born July 11, 1970, in Taylor, Mich.... 6-7/227.... Throws right, bats right.... Full name: Billy Manual Ashley.

HIGH SCHOOL: Belleville (Mich.).

TRANSACTIONS/CAREER NOTES: Selected by Los Angeles Dodgers organization in third round of free-agent draft (June 1, 1988).... On disabled list (April 10-May 1, May 19-31 and June 8-July 8, 1991).

STATISTICAL NOTES: Led Texas League with .534 slugging percentage in 1992.

			BATTING												FIELDING			
Year	Team (League)	Pos.	G	AB	R	H	2B	3B	HR	RBI	Avg.	BB	SO	SB	PO	A	E	Avg.
1988	—GC Dodgers (GCL)....	OF	9	26	3	4	0	0	0	0	.154	1	9	1	8	2	0	1.000
1989	—GC Dodgers (GCL)....	OF	48	160	23	38	6	2	1	19	.238	19	42	16	50	3	5	.914
1990	—Bakersfield (Calif.)...	OF	99	331	48	72	13	1	9	40	.218	25	135	17	122	3	10	.926
1991	—Vero Beach (FSL).....	OF	61	206	18	52	11	2	7	42	.252	7	69	9	39	1	0	1.000
1992	—San Antonio (Tex.)....	OF-1B	101	380	60	106	23	1	*24	66	.279	16	111	13	129	9	3	.979
	—Albuquerque (PCL)..	OF	25	95	11	20	7	0	2	10	.211	6	42	1	39	1	2	.952
	—Los Angeles (N.L.)...	OF	29	95	6	21	5	0	2	6	.221	5	34	0	34	2	6	.857
1993	—Albuquerque (PCL)..	OF	125	482	88	143	31	4	26	*100	.297	35	*143	6	211	7	*11	.952
	—Los Angeles (N.L.)...	OF	14	37	0	9	0	0	0	0	.243	2	11	0	11	3	0	1.000
	Major league totals (2 years)..................		43	132	6	30	5	0	2	6	.227	7	45	0	45	5	6	.893

ASSENMACHER, PAUL

P, YANKEES

PERSONAL: Born December 10, 1960, in Allen Park, Mich.... 6-3/210.... Throws left, bats left.... Full name: Paul Andre Assenmacher.... Name pronounced OSS-en-MOCK-er.

HIGH SCHOOL: Aquinas (Southgate, Mich.).

COLLEGE: Aquinas, Mich. (degree in business administration).

TRANSACTIONS/CAREER NOTES: Signed as free agent by Atlanta Braves organization (July 10, 1983).... On Atlanta disabled list (April 29-May 9, 1987 and August 10-25, 1988).... Traded by Braves organization to Chicago Cubs for two players to be named later (August 24, 1989); Braves acquired C Kelly Mann and P Pat Gomez to complete deal (September 1, 1989).... On disabled list (May 19-June 4, 1992).... Traded by Cubs to New York Yankees as part of a three-way deal in which Yankees sent P John Habyan to Kansas City Royals and Royals sent OF Karl Rhodes to Cubs (July 30, 1993).

RECORDS: Shares major league record for most strikeouts in one inning—4 (August 22, 1989, fifth inning).

Year	Team (League)	W	L	Pct.	ERA	G	GS	CG	ShO	Sv.	IP	H	R	ER	BB	SO
1983	—GC Braves (GCL)........	1	0	1.000	2.21	10	3	1	1	2	36⅔	35	14	9	4	44
1984	—Durham (Carolina).....	6	11	.353	4.28	26	24	3	1	0	147⅓	153	78	70	52	147
1985	—Durham (Carolina).....	3	2	.600	3.29	14	0	0	0	1	38⅓	38	16	14	13	36
	—Greenville (South.).....	6	0	1.000	2.56	29	0	0	0	4	52⅔	47	16	15	11	59
1986	—Atlanta (N.L.)............	7	3	.700	2.50	61	0	0	0	7	68⅓	61	23	19	26	56
1987	—Atlanta (N.L.)............	1	1	.500	5.10	52	0	0	0	2	54⅔	58	41	31	24	39
	—Richmond (Int'l).........	1	2	.333	3.65	4	4	0	0	0	24⅔	30	11	10	8	21
1988	—Atlanta (N.L.)............	8	7	.533	3.06	64	0	0	0	5	79⅓	72	28	27	32	71
1989	—Atl.-Chicago (N.L.)■..	3	4	.429	3.99	63	0	0	0	0	76⅔	74	37	34	28	79
1990	—Chicago (N.L.)...........	7	2	.778	2.80	74	1	0	0	10	103	90	33	32	36	95
1991	—Chicago (N.L.)...........	7	8	.467	3.24	75	0	0	0	15	102⅔	85	41	37	31	117
1992	—Chicago (N.L.)...........	4	4	.500	4.10	70	0	0	0	8	68	72	32	31	26	67
1993	—Chicago (N.L.)...........	2	1	.667	3.49	46	0	0	0	0	38⅔	44	15	15	13	34
	—New York (A.L.)■.......	2	2	.500	3.12	26	0	0	0	0	17⅓	10	6	6	9	11
	A.L. totals (1 year)...............	2	2	.500	3.12	26	0	0	0	0	17⅓	10	6	6	9	11
	N.L. totals (8 years)............	39	30	.565	3.44	505	1	0	0	47	591⅓	556	250	226	216	558
	Major league totals (8 years)..	41	32	.562	3.43	531	1	0	0	47	608⅔	566	256	232	225	569

CHAMPIONSHIP SERIES RECORD

Year	Team (League)	W	L	Pct.	ERA	G	GS	CG	ShO	Sv.	IP	H	R	ER	BB	SO
1989	—Chicago (N.L.)...........	0	0	...	13.50	2	0	0	0	0	⅔	3	1	1	0	0

ASTACIO, PEDRO

P, DODGERS

PERSONAL: Born November 28, 1969, in Hato Mayor, Dominican Republic.... 6-2/190.... Throws right, bats right.... Full name: Pedro Julio Astacio.... Name pronounced ah-STA-see-oh.

HIGH SCHOOL: Pilar Rondon (Dominican Republic).

TRANSACTIONS/CAREER NOTES: Signed as free agent by Los Angeles Dodgers organization (November 21, 1987).... On Albuquerque disabled list (April 26-May 21, 1992).

STATISTICAL NOTES: Led N.L. with nine balks in 1993.

Year	Team (League)	W	L	Pct.	ERA	G	GS	CG	ShO	Sv.	IP	H	R	ER	BB	SO
1989	—GC Dodgers (GCL)......	7	3	.700	3.17	12	12	1	•1	0	76⅔	77	30	27	12	52
1990	—Vero Beach (FSL).......	1	5	.167	6.32	8	8	0	0	0	47	54	39	33	23	41

Year	Team (League)	W	L	Pct.	ERA	G	GS	CG	ShO	Sv.	IP	H	R	ER	BB	SO
	—Yakima (N'west)	2	0	1.000	1.74	3	3	0	0	0	20⅔	9	8	4	4	22
	—Bakersfield (Calif.)	5	2	.714	2.77	10	7	1	0	0	52	46	22	16	15	34
1991	—Vero Beach (FSL)	5	3	.625	1.67	9	9	3	1	0	59⅓	44	19	11	8	45
	—San Antonio (Tex.)	4	11	.267	4.78	19	19	2	1	0	113	142	67	60	39	62
1992	—Albuquerque (PCL)	6	6	.500	5.47	24	15	1	0	0	98⅔	115	68	60	44	66
	—Los Angeles (N.L.)	5	5	.500	1.98	11	11	4	4	0	82	80	23	18	20	43
1993	—Los Angeles (N.L.)	14	9	.609	3.57	31	31	3	2	0	186⅓	165	80	74	68	122
Major league totals (2 years)		19	14	.576	3.09	42	42	7	6	0	268⅓	245	103	92	88	165

AUDE, RICH

1B, PIRATES

PERSONAL: Born July 13, 1971, in Van Nuys, Calif. . . . 6-5/209. . . . Throws right, bats right. . . . Full name: Richard Thomas Aude. . . . Name pronounced AW-day.
HIGH SCHOOL: Chatsworth (Calif.).
TRANSACTIONS/CAREER NOTES: Selected by Pittsburgh Pirates organization in second round of free-agent draft (June 5, 1989).

			BATTING												FIELDING			
Year	Team (League)	Pos.	G	AB	R	H	2B	3B	HR	RBI	Avg.	BB	SO	SB	PO	A	E	Avg.
1989	—GC Pirates (GCL)	3B	24	88	13	19	3	0	0	7	.216	5	17	2	23	32	12	.821
1990	—Augusta (S. Atl.)	1B-3B	128	475	48	111	23	1	6	61	.234	41	133	4	522	110	29	.956
1991	—Salem (Carolina)	1B-3B	103	366	45	97	12	2	3	43	.265	27	72	4	558	46	17	.973
1992	—Salem (Carolina)	1B-3B	122	447	63	128	26	4	9	60	.286	50	79	11	1120	58	10	.992
	—Carolina (South.)	1B-3B	6	20	4	4	1	0	2	3	.200	1	3	0	17	1	0	1.000
1993	—Carolina (South.)	1B	120	422	66	122	25	3	18	73	.289	50	79	8	790	49	13	.985
	—Buffalo (A.A.)	1B	21	64	17	24	9	0	4	16	.375	10	15	0	174	13	1	.995
	—Pittsburgh (N.L.)	1B-OF	13	26	1	3	1	0	0	4	.115	1	7	0	47	3	1	.980
Major league totals (1 year)			13	26	1	3	1	0	0	4	.115	1	7	0	47	3	1	.980

AUSMUS, BRAD

C, PADRES

PERSONAL: Born April 14, 1969, in New Haven, Conn. . . . 5-11/190. . . . Throws right, bats right. . . . Full name: Bradley David Ausmus.
HIGH SCHOOL: Cheshire (Conn.).
COLLEGE: Dartmouth.
TRANSACTIONS/CAREER NOTES: Selected by New York Yankees organization in 47th round of free-agent draft (June 2, 1987). . . . Selected by Colorado Rockies in third round (54th pick overall) of expansion draft (November 17, 1992). . . . Traded by Rockies with P Doug Bochtler and a player to be named later to San Diego Padres for P Bruce Hurst and P Greg W. Harris (July 26, 1993); Padres acquired P Andy Ashby to complete deal (July 27, 1993).
STATISTICAL NOTES: Led Gulf Coast League catchers with 434 total chances in 1988. . . . Led International League catchers with 666 putouts and 738 total chances in 1992.

			BATTING												FIELDING			
Year	Team (League)	Pos.	G	AB	R	H	2B	3B	HR	RBI	Avg.	BB	SO	SB	PO	A	E	Avg.
1988	—Oneonta (NYP)	C	2	4	0	1	0	0	0	0	.250	0	2	0	0	0	0	...
	—Sarasota (Fla. St.)	C	43	133	22	34	2	0	0	15	.256	11	25	5	*378	*47	9	.979
1989	—Oneonta (NYP)	C-3B	52	165	29	43	6	0	1	18	.261	22	28	6	401	43	7	.984
1990	—Prin. William (Car.)	C	107	364	46	86	12	2	0	27	.236	32	73	2	662	84	5	*.993
1991	—Prin. William (Car.)	C	63	230	28	70	14	3	2	30	.304	24	37	17	419	54	5	.990
	—Alb./Colon. (East.)	C	67	229	36	61	9	2	1	29	.266	27	36	14	470	56	4	.992
1992	—Alb./Colon. (East.)	C	5	18	0	3	0	1	0	1	.167	2	3	2	30	2	1	.970
	—Columbus (Int'l)	C-OF	111	364	48	88	14	3	2	35	.242	40	56	19	†666	63	9	.988
1993	—Colo. Springs (PCL)■	C-OF	76	241	31	65	10	4	2	33	.270	27	41	10	393	57	6	.987
	—San Diego (N.L.)■	C	49	160	18	41	8	1	5	12	.256	6	28	2	272	34	8	.975
Major league totals (1 year)			49	160	18	41	8	1	5	12	.256	6	28	2	272	34	8	.975

AUSTIN, JAMES

P, YANKEES

PERSONAL: Born December 7, 1963, in Farmville, Va. . . . 6-2/200. . . . Throws right, bats right. . . . Full name: James Parker Austin.
HIGH SCHOOL: Dinwiddie (Va.) Senior.
COLLEGE: Virginia Commonwealth.
TRANSACTIONS/CAREER NOTES: Selected by San Diego Padres organization in sixth round of free-agent draft (June 2, 1986). . . . Traded by Padres organization with P Todd Simmons to Milwaukee Brewers organization for P Dan Murphy (February 15, 1989). . . . On Denver disabled list (May 7-23 and June 13-23, 1991). . . . On Milwaukee disabled list (July 30-August 31, 1991 and April 15-30, 1993). . . . Released by Brewers (October 5, 1993). . . . Signed by New York Yankees organization (December 21, 1993).

Year	Team (League)	W	L	Pct.	ERA	G	GS	CG	ShO	Sv.	IP	H	R	ER	BB	SO
1986	—Spokane (N'west)	5	4	.556	2.26	28	0	0	0	5	59⅔	53	24	15	22	74
1987	—Char., S.C. (S. Atl.)	7	10	.412	4.20	31	21	2	1	0	152	138	89	71	56	123
1988	—Riverside (Calif.)	6	2	.750	2.70	12	12	2	1	0	80	65	31	24	35	73
	—Wichita (Texas)	5	6	.455	4.81	12	12	4	1	0	73	76	46	39	23	52
1989	—Stockton (Calif.)■	3	3	.500	2.61	7	7	0	0	0	48⅓	51	19	14	14	44
	—El Paso (Texas)	3	10	.231	5.82	22	13	2	0	1	85	121	60	55	34	69
1990	—El Paso (Texas)	11	3	.786	2.44	38	3	0	0	6	92⅓	91	36	25	26	77
1991	—Denver (A.A.)	6	3	.667	2.45	20	3	0	0	3	44	35	12	12	24	37
	—Milwaukee (A.L.)	0	0	...	8.31	5	0	0	0	0	8⅔	8	8	8	11	3
1992	—Milwaukee (A.L.)	5	2	.714	1.85	47	0	0	0	0	58⅓	38	13	12	32	30
1993	—Milwaukee (A.L.)	1	2	.333	3.82	31	0	0	0	0	33	28	15	14	13	15
	—New Orleans (A.A.)	1	2	.333	5.06	8	3	0	0	0	16	17	11	9	7	7
Major league totals (3 years)		6	4	.600	3.06	83	0	0	0	0	100	74	36	34	56	48

AVERY, STEVE

P, BRAVES

PERSONAL: Born April 14, 1970, in Trenton, Mich. . . . 6-4/190. . . . Throws left, bats left. . . . Full name: Steven Thomas Avery. . . . Son of Ken Avery, minor league pitcher (1962-63).
HIGH SCHOOL: John F. Kennedy (Taylor, Mich.).
TRANSACTIONS/CAREER NOTES: Selected by Atlanta Braves organization in first round (third pick overall) of free-agent draft (June 1, 1988).
HONORS: Named lefthanded pitcher on THE SPORTING NEWS N.L. All-Star team (1993).
MISCELLANEOUS: Received base on balls in only appearance as pinch-hitter and appeared in one game as pinch-runner (1991).

Year	Team (League)	W	L	Pct.	ERA	G	GS	CG	ShO	Sv.	IP	H	R	ER	BB	SO
1988	—Pulaski (Appal.)	7	1	.875	1.50	10	10	3	•2	0	66	38	16	11	19	80
1989	—Durham (Carolina)	6	4	.600	1.45	13	13	3	1	0	86⅔	59	22	14	20	90
	—Greenville (South.)	6	3	.667	2.77	13	13	1	0	0	84⅓	68	32	26	34	75
1990	—Richmond (Int'l)	5	5	.500	3.39	13	13	3	0	0	82⅓	85	35	31	21	69
	—Atlanta (N.L.)	3	11	.214	5.64	21	20	1	1	0	99	121	79	62	45	75
1991	—Atlanta (N.L.)	18	8	.692	3.38	35	35	3	1	0	210⅓	189	89	79	65	137
1992	—Atlanta (N.L.)	11	11	.500	3.20	35	•35	2	2	0	233⅔	216	95	83	71	129
1993	—Atlanta (N.L.)	18	6	.750	2.94	35	35	3	1	0	223⅓	216	81	73	43	125
Major league totals (4 years)		50	36	.581	3.49	126	125	9	5	0	766⅓	742	344	297	224	466

CHAMPIONSHIP SERIES RECORD

CHAMPIONSHIP SERIES NOTES: Named N.L. Championship Series Most Valuable Player (1991). . . . Holds career record for most consecutive scoreless innings—22⅓ (1991-92). . . . Holds single-series record for most consecutive scoreless innings—16⅓ (1991).

Year	Team (League)	W	L	Pct.	ERA	G	GS	CG	ShO	Sv.	IP	H	R	ER	BB	SO
1991	—Atlanta (N.L.)	2	0	1.000	0.00	2	2	0	0	0	16⅓	9	0	0	4	17
1992	—Atlanta (N.L.)	1	1	.500	9.00	3	2	0	0	0	8	13	8	8	2	3
1993	—Atlanta (N.L.)	0	0	...	2.77	2	2	0	0	0	13	9	5	4	6	10
Champ. series totals (3 years)		3	1	.750	2.89	7	6	0	0	0	37⅓	31	13	12	12	30

WORLD SERIES RECORD

Year	Team (League)	W	L	Pct.	ERA	G	GS	CG	ShO	Sv.	IP	H	R	ER	BB	SO
1991	—Atlanta (N.L.)	0	0	...	3.46	2	2	0	0	0	13	10	6	5	1	8
1992	—Atlanta (N.L.)	0	1	.000	3.75	2	2	0	0	0	12	11	5	5	3	11
World Series totals (2 years)		0	1	.000	3.60	4	4	0	0	0	25	21	11	10	4	19

ALL-STAR GAME RECORD

Year	League	W	L	Pct.	ERA	GS	CG	ShO	Sv.	IP	H	R	ER	BB	SO
1993	—National	0	0	...	0.00	0	0	0	0	1	1	3	0	1	1

AYALA, BOBBY

P, MARINERS

PERSONAL: Born July 8, 1969, in Ventura, Calif. . . . 6-3/200. . . . Throws right, bats right. . . . Full name: Robert Joesph Ayala. . . . Name pronounced eye-YAH-luh.
HIGH SCHOOL: Rio Mesa (Oxnard, Calif.).
TRANSACTIONS/CAREER NOTES: Signed as free agent by Cincinnati Reds organization (June 27, 1988). . . . Traded by Reds with C Dan Wilson to Seattle Mariners for P Erik Hanson and 2B Bret Boone (November 2, 1993).

Year	Team (League)	W	L	Pct.	ERA	G	GS	CG	ShO	Sv.	IP	H	R	ER	BB	SO
1988	—GC Reds (GCL)	0	4	.000	3.82	20	0	0	0	3	33	34	23	14	12	24
1989	—Greensboro (S. Atl.)	5	8	.385	4.10	22	19	1	0	0	105⅓	97	73	48	50	70
1990	—Ced. Rap. (Midw.)	3	2	.600	3.38	18	7	3	1	1	53⅓	40	24	20	18	59
	—Char., W.Va. (SAL)	6	1	.857	2.43	21	4	2	1	2	74	48	23	20	21	73
1991	—Chatt. (South.)	3	1	.750	4.67	39	8	1	0	4	90⅔	79	52	47	58	92
1992	—Chatt. (South.)	12	6	.667	3.54	27	27	3	3	0	162⅔	152	75	64	58	154
	—Cincinnati (N.L.)	2	1	.667	4.34	5	5	0	0	0	29	33	15	14	13	23
1993	—Indianapolis (A.A.)	0	2	.000	5.67	5	5	0	0	0	27	36	19	17	12	19
	—Cincinnati (N.L.)	7	10	.412	5.60	43	9	0	0	3	98	106	72	61	45	65
Major league totals (2 years)		9	11	.450	5.31	48	14	0	0	3	127	139	87	75	58	88

AYRAULT, BOB

P, DODGERS

PERSONAL: Born April 27, 1966, in South Lake Tahoe, Calif. . . . 6-4/235. . . . Throws right, bats right. . . . Full name: Robert Cunningham Ayrault.
HIGH SCHOOL: Carson City (Nev.).
COLLEGE: Moorpark (Calif.) Junior College and UNLV.
TRANSACTIONS/CAREER NOTES: Selected by San Diego Padres organization in ninth round of free-agent draft (January 14, 1986). . . . Selected by Pittsburgh Pirates organization in 26th round of free-agent draft (June 2, 1987). . . . Signed as free agent by Reno, independent (June 2, 1989). . . . Contract sold by Reno to Philadelphia Phillies organization (July 29, 1989). . . . Traded by Phillies to Seattle Mariners for P Kevin Foster (June 12, 1993). . . . Claimed on waivers by Los Angeles Dodgers (August 9, 1993).

Year	Team (League)	W	L	Pct.	ERA	G	GS	CG	ShO	Sv.	IP	H	R	ER	BB	SO
1989	—Reno (California)	7	4	.636	3.78	24	14	3	0	0	109⅔	104	56	46	57	91
	—Batavia (NY-Penn)■	2	1	.667	1.38	4	3	2	1	0	26	13	5	4	7	20
	—Reading (Eastern)	0	0	...	1.04	2	1	0	0	0	8⅔	3	1	1	4	8
1990	—Reading (Eastern)	4	6	.400	2.30	44	9	0	0	10	109⅓	77	33	28	34	84
1991	—Scran./W.B. (Int'l)	8	5	.615	4.83	*68	0	0	0	3	98⅔	91	58	53	47	103
1992	—Scran./W.B. (Int'l)	5	1	.833	4.97	20	0	0	0	6	25⅓	19	15	14	15	30
	—Philadelphia (N.L.)	2	2	.500	3.12	30	0	0	0	0	43⅓	32	16	15	17	27
1993	—Philadelphia (N.L.)	2	0	1.000	9.58	10	0	0	0	0	10⅓	18	11	11	10	8
	—Scran./W.B. (Int'l)	0	1	.000	1.23	5	1	0	0	0	7⅓	8	2	1	3	9

Year	Team (League)	W	L	Pct.	ERA	G	GS	CG	ShO	Sv.	IP	H	R	ER	BB	SO
	—Seattle (A.L.)■	1	1	.500	3.20	14	0	0	0	0	19⅔	18	8	7	6	7
	—Calg.-Albuq. (PCL)■	2	2	.500	7.11	14	0	0	0	1	19	29	15	15	9	16
A.L. totals (1 year)		1	1	.500	3.20	14	0	0	0	0	19⅔	18	8	7	6	7
N.L. totals (2 years)		4	2	.667	4.36	40	0	0	0	0	53⅔	50	27	26	27	35
Major league totals (2 years)		5	3	.625	4.05	54	0	0	0	0	73⅓	68	35	33	33	42

AYRAULT, JOE

C, BRAVES

PERSONAL: Born October 8, 1971, in Rochester, Mich.... 6-3/190.... Throws right, bats right. ... Full name: Joseph Allen Ayrault.

HIGH SCHOOL: Sarasota (Fla.).

TRANSACTIONS/CAREER NOTES: Selected by Atlanta Braves organization in fifth round of free-agent draft (June 4, 1990).... On disabled list (August 9-22, 1992).

STATISTICAL NOTES: Led Appalachian League catchers with 495 total chances and seven double plays and tied for lead with 12 passed balls in 1991.

			BATTING												FIELDING			
Year	Team (League)	Pos.	G	AB	R	H	2B	3B	HR	RBI	Avg.	BB	SO	SB	PO	A	E	Avg.
1990	—GC Braves (GCL)	C	30	87	8	24	2	2	0	12	.276	9	15	1	182	30	3	.986
1991	—Pulaski (Appal.)	C	55	202	22	52	12	0	3	27	.257	13	49	0	425	*64	6	.988
1992	—Macon (S. Atl.)	C	90	297	24	77	12	0	6	24	.259	24	68	1	584	101	19	.973
1993	—Durham (Carolina)	C	119	390	45	99	21	0	6	52	.254	23	103	1	*739	98	7	*.992

BACKMAN, WALLY

IF

PERSONAL: Born September 22, 1959, in Hillsboro, Ore.... 5-9/168.... Throws right, bats both.... Full name: Walter Wayne Backman.

HIGH SCHOOL: Aloha (Beaverton, Ore.).

TRANSACTIONS/CAREER NOTES: Selected by New York Mets organization in first round (16th pick overall) of free-agent draft (June 7, 1977).... On suspended list (June 18-20, 1981).... On Tidewater disabled list (July 9-September 1, 1981).... On New York disabled list (August 15-September 8, 1982; June 9-29, 1987; and August 27-September 11, 1988).... Traded by Mets with P Mike Santiago to Minnesota Twins for P Jeff Bumgarner, P Steve Gasser and P Toby Nivens (December 7, 1988).... On disabled list (May 8-25 and July 9-August 4, 1989).... Granted free agency (November 13, 1989).... Signed by Pittsburgh Pirates (January 31, 1990).... Granted free agency (November 5, 1990).... Signed by Philadelphia Phillies (January 10, 1991).... On disabled list (August 5, 1992-remainder of season).... Granted free agency (November 5, 1992).... Signed by Atlanta Braves organization (January 25, 1993).... Released by Braves organization (April 1, 1993).... Signed by Seattle Mariners (April 5, 1993).... On disabled list (April 11-27, 1993).... Released by Mariners (May 17, 1993).

STATISTICAL NOTES: Led Carolina League in caught stealing with 17 in 1978.... Tied for N.L. lead with 14 sacrifice hits in 1985. ... Led N.L second basemen with .989 fielding percentage in 1985.... Collected six hits in one game (April 27, 1990).

			BATTING												FIELDING			
Year	Team (League)	Pos.	G	AB	R	H	2B	3B	HR	RBI	Avg.	BB	SO	SB	PO	A	E	Avg.
1977	—Little Falls (NYP)	SS-3B	69	255	44	83	10	2	6	30	.325	28	53	20	96	185	19	.937
1978	—Lynchburg (Caro.)	SS	132	494	86	149	19	•9	3	38	.302	74	99	42	*202	*329	30	*.947
1979	—Jackson (Texas)	SS-2B	110	404	63	114	11	5	2	19	.282	35	50	23	184	259	31	.935
1980	—Tidewater (Int'l)	2B-SS	125	400	53	117	15	5	1	51	.293	*87	67	11	237	320	22	.962
	—New York (N.L.)	2B-SS	27	93	12	30	1	1	0	9	.323	11	14	2	62	55	1	.992
1981	—New York (N.L.)	2B-3B	26	36	5	10	2	0	0	0	.278	4	7	1	14	21	2	.946
	—Tidewater (Int'l)	SS-3B-2B	21	59	6	9	3	1	0	6	.153	10	8	2	12	38	1	.980
1982	—New York (N.L.)	2B-3B-SS	96	261	37	71	13	2	3	22	.272	49	47	8	173	209	16	.960
1983	—New York (N.L.)	2B-3B	26	42	6	7	0	1	0	3	.167	2	8	0	16	15	2	.939
	—Tidewater (Int'l)	2B-SS-3B	101	361	69	114	11	3	1	28	.316	68	47	37	175	278	13	.972
1984	—New York (N.L.)	2B-SS	128	436	68	122	19	2	1	26	.280	56	63	32	223	306	10	.981
1985	—New York (N.L.)	2B-SS	145	520	77	142	24	5	1	38	.273	36	72	30	273	370	7	†.989
1986	—New York (N.L.)	2B	124	387	67	124	18	2	1	27	.320	36	32	13	186	290	17	.966
1987	—New York (N.L.)	2B	94	300	43	75	6	1	1	23	.250	25	43	11	131	210	6	.983
1988	—New York (N.L.)	2B	99	294	44	89	12	0	0	17	.303	41	49	9	128	219	4	.989
1989	—Minnesota (A.L.)■	2B	87	299	33	69	9	2	1	26	.231	32	45	1	146	187	6	.982
1990	—Pittsburgh (N.L.)■	3B-2B	104	315	62	92	21	3	2	28	.292	42	53	6	56	136	12	.941
1991	—Philadelphia (N.L.)■	2B-3B	94	185	20	45	12	0	0	15	.243	30	30	3	54	79	4	.971
1992	—Philadelphia (N.L.)	2B-3B	42	48	6	13	1	0	0	6	.271	6	9	1	10	20	1	.968
1993	—Seattle (A.L.)■	3B-2B	10	29	2	4	0	0	0	0	.138	1	8	0	4	15	3	.864
American League totals (2 years)			97	328	35	73	9	2	1	26	.223	33	53	1	150	202	9	.975
National League totals (12 years)			1005	2917	447	820	129	17	9	214	.281	338	427	116	1326	1930	82	.975
Major league totals (14 years)			1102	3245	482	893	138	19	10	240	.275	371	480	117	1476	2132	91	.975

CHAMPIONSHIP SERIES RECORD

			BATTING												FIELDING			
Year	Team (League)	Pos.	G	AB	R	H	2B	3B	HR	RBI	Avg.	BB	SO	SB	PO	A	E	Avg.
1986	—New York (N.L.)	2B-PH	6	21	5	5	0	0	0	2	.238	2	4	1	9	17	0	1.000
1988	—New York (N.L.)	2B	7	22	2	6	1	0	0	2	.273	2	5	1	7	19	2	.929
1990	—Pittsburgh (N.L.)	3B-PH	3	7	1	1	1	0	0	0	.143	1	1	1	1	3	0	1.000
Championship series totals (3 years)			16	50	8	12	2	0	0	4	.240	5	10	3	17	39	2	.966

WORLD SERIES RECORD

			BATTING												FIELDING			
Year	Team (League)	Pos.	G	AB	R	H	2B	3B	HR	RBI	Avg.	BB	SO	SB	PO	A	E	Avg.
1986	—New York (N.L.)	2B-PR	6	18	4	6	0	0	0	1	.333	3	2	1	9	13	0	1.000

BAERGA, CARLOS

2B, INDIANS

PERSONAL: Born November 4, 1968, in San Juan, Puerto Rico. . . . 5-11/200. . . . Throws right, bats both. . . . Full name: Carlos Obed Ortiz Baerga. . . . Name pronounced by-AIR-guh.
HIGH SCHOOL: Barbara Ann Rooshart (Rio Piedra, Puerto Rico).
TRANSACTIONS/CAREER NOTES: Signed as free agent by San Diego Padres organization (November 4, 1985). . . . Traded by Padres organization with C Sandy Alomar and OF Chris James to Cleveland Indians for OF Joe Carter (December 6, 1989).
RECORDS: Holds major league record for switch-hitting home runs in one inning (April 8, 1993, seventh inning). . . . Shares major league record for most home runs in one inning—2 (April 8, 1993, seventh inning).
HONORS: Named second baseman on THE SPORTING NEWS A.L. All-Star team (1993). . . . Named second baseman on THE SPORTING NEWS A.L. Silver Slugger team (1993).
STATISTICAL NOTES: Led South Atlantic League second basemen with 29 errors in 1987. . . . Led Texas League shortstops with 61 double plays in 1988. . . . Led Pacific Coast League third basemen with 380 total chances in 1989. . . . Led A.L. second basemen with 138 double plays in 1992. . . . Led A.L. second basemen with 894 total chances in 1992 and 809 in 1993. . . . Collected six hits in one game (April 11, 1992). . . . Switch-hit home runs in one game (April 8, 1993). . . . Hit three home runs in one game (June 17, 1993).

			BATTING												FIELDING			
Year	**Team (League)**	**Pos.**	**G**	**AB**	**R**	**H**	**2B**	**3B**	**HR**	**RBI**	**Avg.**	**BB**	**SO**	**SB**	**PO**	**A**	**E**	**Avg.**
1986	—Char., S.C. (S. Atl.)	2B-SS	111	378	57	102	14	4	7	41	.270	26	60	6	202	245	27	.943
1987	—Char., S.C. (S. Atl.)	2B-SS	134	515	83	157	23	•9	7	50	.305	38	107	26	253	341	†36	.943
1988	—Wichita (Texas)	SS-2B	122	444	67	121	28	1	12	65	.273	31	83	4	221	325	33	.943
1989	—Las Vegas (PCL)	3B	132	520	63	143	28	2	10	74	.275	30	98	6	*92	256	*32	.916
1990	—Cleveland (A.L.)■	3B-SS-2B	108	312	46	81	17	2	7	47	.260	16	57	0	79	164	17	.935
	—Colo. Springs (PCL)	3B	12	50	11	19	2	1	1	11	.380	5	4	1	18	31	4	.925
1991	—Cleveland (A.L.)	3B-2B-SS	158	593	80	171	28	2	11	69	.288	48	74	3	217	421	27	.959
1992	—Cleveland (A.L.)	2B	161	657	92	205	32	1	20	105	.312	35	76	10	*400	*475	19	.979
1993	—Cleveland (A.L.)	2B	154	624	105	200	28	6	21	114	.321	34	68	15	*347	*445	17	.979
Major league totals (4 years)			581	2186	323	657	105	11	59	335	.301	133	275	28	1043	1505	80	.970

ALL-STAR GAME RECORD

			BATTING										FIELDING			
Year	**League**	**Pos.**	**AB**	**R**	**H**	**2B**	**3B**	**HR**	**RBI**	**Avg.**	**BB**	**SO**	**SB**	**PO**	**A**	**E**	**Avg.**
1992	—American	2B	1	1	1	1	0	0	1	1.000	0	0	0	1	2	0	1.000
1993	—American	2B	2	1	0	0	0	0	0	.000	0	1	0	0	1	0	1.000
All-Star Game totals (2 years)			3	2	1	1	0	0	1	.333	0	1	0	1	3	0	1.000

BAEZ, KEVIN

SS, METS

PERSONAL: Born January 10, 1967, in Brooklyn, N.Y. . . . 6-0/170. . . . Throws right, bats right. . . . Full name: Kevin Richard Baez. . . . Name pronounced BY-EZ.
HIGH SCHOOL: Lafayette (Brooklyn, N.Y.).
COLLEGE: Dominican College (N.Y.).
TRANSACTIONS/CAREER NOTES: Selected by New York Mets organization in seventh round of free-agent draft (June 1, 1988). . . . On Jackson disabled list (July 26-August 12, 1990). . . . On disabled list (June 24, 1991-remainder of season). . . . On New York disabled list (April 27-May 14, 1992).
STATISTICAL NOTES: Led New York-Pennsylvania League shortstops with 317 total chances in 1988. . . . Led Texas League shortstops with 509 total chances in 1990.

			BATTING												FIELDING			
Year	**Team (League)**	**Pos.**	**G**	**AB**	**R**	**H**	**2B**	**3B**	**HR**	**RBI**	**Avg.**	**BB**	**SO**	**SB**	**PO**	**A**	**E**	**Avg.**
1988	—Little Falls (NYP)	SS	70	218	23	58	7	1	1	19	.266	32	30	7	93	198	26	.918
1989	—Columbia (S. Atl.)	SS	123	426	59	108	20	1	5	44	.254	58	53	11	181	327	36	*.934
1990	—Jackson (Texas)	SS	106	326	29	76	11	0	2	29	.233	37	44	3	*184	301	24	.953
	—New York (N.L.)	SS	5	12	0	2	1	0	0	0	.167	0	0	0	5	7	0	1.000
1991	—Tidewater (Int'l)	SS	65	210	18	36	8	0	0	13	.171	12	32	0	128	227	15	.959
1992	—Tidewater (Int'l)	SS	109	352	30	83	16	1	2	33	.236	13	57	1	147	305	19	.960
	—New York (N.L.)	SS	6	13	0	2	0	0	0	0	.154	0	0	0	5	11	2	.889
1993	—Norfolk (Int'l)	SS	63	209	23	54	11	1	2	21	.258	20	29	0	94	193	15	.950
	—New York (N.L.)	SS	52	126	10	23	9	0	0	7	.183	13	17	0	57	117	6	.967
Major league totals (3 years)			63	151	10	27	10	0	0	7	.179	13	17	0	67	135	8	.962

BAGWELL, JEFF

1B, ASTROS

PERSONAL: Born May 27, 1968, in Boston. . . . 6-0/195. . . . Throws right, bats right. . . . Full name: Jeffrey Robert Bagwell.
HIGH SCHOOL: Xavier (Middletown, Conn.).
COLLEGE: Hartford.
TRANSACTIONS/CAREER NOTES: Selected by Boston Red Sox organization in fourth round of free-agent draft (June 5, 1989). . . . Traded by Red Sox to Houston Astros for P Larry Andersen (August 31, 1990).
HONORS: Named Eastern League Most Valuable Player (1990). . . . Named N.L. Rookie Player of the Year by THE SPORTING NEWS (1991). . . . Named N.L. Rookie of the Year by Baseball Writers' Association of America (1991).
STATISTICAL NOTES: Led Eastern League with 220 total bases and 12 intentional bases on balls received in 1990. . . . Led N.L. in being hit by pitch with 13 in 1991. . . . Led N.L. with 13 sacrifice flies in 1992.

			BATTING												FIELDING			
Year	**Team (League)**	**Pos.**	**G**	**AB**	**R**	**H**	**2B**	**3B**	**HR**	**RBI**	**Avg.**	**BB**	**SO**	**SB**	**PO**	**A**	**E**	**Avg.**
1989	—GC Red Sox (GCL)	3B-2B	5	19	3	6	1	0	0	3	.316	3	0	0	2	12	2	.875
	—Winter Haven (FSL)	3B-2B-1B	64	210	27	65	13	2	2	19	.310	22	25	1	53	109	12	.931
1990	—New Britain (East.)	3B	136	481	63	*160	•34	7	4	61	.333	73	57	5	93	267	34	.914
1991	—Houston (N.L.)■	1B	156	554	79	163	26	4	15	82	.294	75	116	7	1270	106	12	.991
1992	—Houston (N.L.)	1B	•162	586	87	160	34	6	18	96	.273	84	97	10	1334	133	7	.995
1993	—Houston (N.L.)	1B	142	535	76	171	37	4	20	88	.320	62	73	13	1200	113	9	.993
Major league totals (3 years)			460	1675	242	494	97	14	53	266	.295	221	286	30	3804	352	28	.993

BAILEY, CORY

P, RED SOX

PERSONAL: Born January 24, 1971, in Herrin, Ill. . . . 6-1/208. . . . Throws right, bats right. . . . Full name: Phillip Cory Bailey.
HIGH SCHOOL: Marion (Ill.).
COLLEGE: Southeastern Illinois College.
TRANSACTIONS/CAREER NOTES: Selected by Boston Red Sox organization in 15th round of free-agent draft (June 3, 1991).

Year	Team (League)	W	L	Pct.	ERA	G	GS	CG	ShO	Sv.	IP	H	R	ER	BB	SO
1991	—GC Red Sox (GCL)	0	0	...	0.00	1	0	0	0	1	2	2	1	0	1	1
	—Elmira (N.Y.-Penn)	2	4	.333	1.85	28	0	0	0	*15	39	19	10	8	12	54
1992	—Lynchburg (Caro.)	5	7	.417	2.44	49	0	0	0	*23	66⅓	43	20	18	30	87
1993	—Pawtucket (Int'l)	4	5	.444	2.88	52	0	0	0	20	65⅔	48	21	21	31	59
	—Boston (A.L.)	0	1	.000	3.45	11	0	0	0	0	15⅔	12	7	6	12	11
Major league totals (1 year)		0	1	.000	3.45	11	0	0	0	0	15⅔	12	7	6	12	11

BAINES, HAROLD

DH, ORIOLES

PERSONAL: Born March 15, 1959, in St. Michaels, Md. . . . 6-2/195. . . . Throws left, bats left. . . . Full name: Harold Douglas Baines.
HIGH SCHOOL: St. Michaels (Easton, Md.).
TRANSACTIONS/CAREER NOTES: Selected by Chicago White Sox organization in first round (first pick overall) of free-agent draft (June 7, 1977). . . . On disabled list (April 7-May 8, 1987). . . . Traded by White Sox with IF Fred Manrique to Texas Rangers for SS Scott Fletcher, OF Sammy Sosa and P Wilson Alvarez (July 29, 1989). . . . Traded by Rangers to Oakland Athletics for two players to be named later (August 29, 1990); Rangers acquired P Joe Bitker and P Scott Chiamparino to complete deal (September 4, 1990). . . . Granted free agency (October 27, 1992); accepted arbitration. . . . Traded by A's to Baltimore Orioles for P Bobby Chouinard and P Allen Plaster (January 14, 1993). . . . Signed by Orioles (January 14, 1993). . . . On Baltimore disabled list (May 5-27, 1993); included rehabilitation assignment to Bowie (May 25-27). . . . Granted free agency (November 1, 1993). . . . Re-signed by Orioles (December 2, 1993).
RECORDS: Shares major league single-game record for most plate appearances—12 (May 8, finished May 9, 1984, 25 innings). . . . Shares A.L. record for longest errorless game by outfielder—25 innings (May 8, finished May 9, 1984). . . . Shares A.L. single-game record for most innings by outfielder—25 (May 8, finished May 9, 1984).
HONORS: Named outfielder on THE SPORTING NEWS A.L. All-Star team (1985). . . . Named designated hitter on THE SPORTING NEWS A.L. All-Star team (1988-89). . . . Named designated hitter on THE SPORTING NEWS A.L. Silver Slugger team (1989).
STATISTICAL NOTES: Tied for American Association lead in double plays by outfielder with four in 1979. . . . Hit three home runs in one game (July 7, 1982; September 17, 1984 and May 7, 1991). . . . Led A.L. with 22 game-winning RBIs in 1983. . . . Led A.L. with .541 slugging percentage in 1984.

			BATTING												FIELDING			
Year	Team (League)	Pos.	G	AB	R	H	2B	3B	HR	RBI	Avg.	BB	SO	SB	PO	A	E	Avg.
1977	—Appleton (Midw.)	OF	69	222	37	58	11	2	5	29	.261	36	62	2	94	10	7	.937
1978	—Knoxville (South.)	OF-1B	137	502	70	138	16	6	13	72	.275	43	91	3	291	22	13	.960
1979	—Iowa (Am. Assoc.)	OF	125	466	87	139	25	8	22	87	.298	33	80	5	222	•16	11	.956
1980	—Chicago (A.L.)	OF	141	491	55	125	23	6	13	49	.255	19	65	2	229	6	9	.963
1981	—Chicago (A.L.)	OF	82	280	42	80	11	7	10	41	.286	12	41	6	120	10	2	.985
1982	—Chicago (A.L.)	OF	161	608	89	165	29	8	25	105	.271	49	95	10	326	10	7	.980
1983	—Chicago (A.L.)	OF	156	596	76	167	33	2	20	99	.280	49	85	7	312	10	9	.973
1984	—Chicago (A.L.)	OF	147	569	72	173	28	10	29	94	.304	54	75	1	307	8	6	.981
1985	—Chicago (A.L.)	OF	160	640	86	198	29	3	22	113	.309	42	89	1	318	8	2	.994
1986	—Chicago (A.L.)	OF	145	570	72	169	29	2	21	88	.296	38	89	2	295	15	5	.984
1987	—Chicago (A.L.)	OF	132	505	59	148	26	4	20	93	.293	46	82	0	13	0	0	1.000
1988	—Chicago (A.L.)	OF	158	599	55	166	39	1	13	81	.277	67	109	0	14	1	2	.882
1989	—Chi.-Texas (A.L.)■	OF	146	505	73	156	29	1	16	72	.309	73	79	0	54	0	2	.964
1990	—Texas-Oak. (A.L.)■	OF	135	415	52	118	15	1	16	65	.284	67	80	0	5	0	1	.833
1991	—Oakland (A.L.)	OF	141	488	76	144	25	1	20	90	.295	72	67	0	11	1	1	.923
1992	—Oakland (A.L.)	OF	140	478	58	121	18	0	16	76	.253	59	61	1	27	0	1	.964
1993	—Baltimore (A.L.)■	DH	118	416	64	130	22	0	20	78	.313	57	52	0	...	...	...	...
	—Bowie (Eastern)	DH	2	6	0	0	0	0	0	0	.000	1	1	0	...	...	...	...
Major league totals (14 years)			1962	7160	929	2060	356	46	261	1144	.288	704	1069	30	2031	69	47	.978

CHAMPIONSHIP SERIES RECORD

			BATTING												FIELDING			
Year	Team (League)	Pos.	G	AB	R	H	2B	3B	HR	RBI	Avg.	BB	SO	SB	PO	A	E	Avg.
1983	—Chicago (A.L.)	OF	4	16	0	2	0	0	0	0	.125	1	3	0	5	1	0	1.000
1990	—Oakland (A.L.)	DH	4	14	2	5	1	0	0	3	.357	2	1	1	...	...	...	...
1992	—Oakland (A.L.)	DH	6	25	6	11	2	0	1	4	.440	0	3	0	...	...	...	...
Championship series totals (3 years)			14	55	8	18	3	0	1	7	.327	3	7	1	5	1	0	1.000

WORLD SERIES RECORD

			BATTING												FIELDING			
Year	Team (League)	Pos.	G	AB	R	H	2B	3B	HR	RBI	Avg.	BB	SO	SB	PO	A	E	Avg.
1990	—Oakland (A.L.)	DH-PH	3	7	1	1	0	0	1	2	.143	1	2	0	...	...	...	...

ALL-STAR GAME RECORD

			BATTING											FIELDING			
Year	League	Pos.	AB	R	H	2B	3B	HR	RBI	Avg.	BB	SO	SB	PO	A	E	Avg.
1985	—American	PH	1	0	1	0	0	0	0	1.000	0	0	0	...	...	...	...
1986	—American	PH	1	0	0	0	0	0	0	.000	0	0	0	...	...	...	...
1987	—American	PH	1	0	0	0	0	0	0	.000	0	0	0	...	...	...	...
1989	—American	DH	3	1	1	0	0	0	1	.333	0	1	0	...	...	...	...
1991	—American	PH-DH	1	0	0	0	0	0	1	.000	0	0	0	...	...	...	...
All-Star Game totals (5 years)			7	1	2	0	0	0	2	.286	0	1	0	...	...	...	...

BAKER, SCOTT

P, ATHLETICS

PERSONAL: Born May 18, 1970, in San Jose, Calif.... 6-2/175.... Throws left, bats left.
HIGH SCHOOL: Basic (Henderson, Nev.).
COLLEGE: Taft (Calif.) College.
TRANSACTIONS/CAREER NOTES: Selected by St. Louis Cardinals organization in seventh round of free-agent draft (June 4, 1990).... Selected by Florida Marlins in third round (65th pick overall) of expansion draft (November 17, 1992).... Traded by Marlins to Oakland Athletics organization (November 20, 1992), completing deal in which A's traded SS Walt Weiss to Marlins for C Eric Helfand and a player to be named later (November 17, 1992).... On disabled list (August 10-17, 1993).

Year	Team (League)	W	L	Pct.	ERA	G	GS	CG	ShO	Sv.	IP	H	R	ER	BB	SO
1990	—Johns. City (App.)	4	2	.667	2.28	*32	0	0	0	0	51⅓	44	21	13	29	65
1991	—Savannah (S. Atl.)	2	3	.400	2.89	8	8	0	0	0	46⅔	42	27	15	25	41
	—St. Peters. (FSL)	3	9	.250	4.42	19	16	1	0	0	93⅔	98	47	46	42	50
1992	—St. Peters. (FSL)	10	9	.526	1.96	24	24	0	0	0	151⅔	123	48	33	54	125
1993	—Huntsville (South.)■	10	4	.714	4.14	25	25	1	1	0	130⅓	141	73	60	84	97

BALBONI, STEVE

DH, ROYALS

PERSONAL: Born January 16, 1957, in Brockton, Mass.... 6-3/250.... Throws right, bats right.... Full name: Stephen Charles Balboni.
HIGH SCHOOL: Memorial (Manchester, N.H.).
COLLEGE: Eckerd (Fla.).
TRANSACTIONS/CAREER NOTES: Selected by New York Yankees organization in fourth round of free-agent draft (June 6, 1978).... Traded by Yankees with P Roger Erickson to Kansas City Royals for P Mike Armstrong and C Duane Dewey (December 8, 1983).... Released by Royals (December 18, 1986).... Re-signed by Royals (February 25, 1987).... Released by Royals (December 21, 1987).... Re-signed by Royals (February 18, 1988).... Released by Royals (May 27, 1988).... Signed by Seattle Mariners (June 1, 1988).... Traded by Mariners to Yankees for P Dana Ridenour (March 27, 1989).... Released by Yankees (April 1, 1991).... Signed by Oklahoma City, Texas Rangers organization (June 2, 1991).... Granted free agency (October 15, 1991).... Re-signed by Oklahoma City (March 28, 1992).... On Oklahoma City disabled list (June 26-July 20, 1992).... Granted free agency (October 15, 1992).... Re-signed by Oklahoma City (February 8, 1993).... Granted free agency (October 4, 1993).... Signed by Royals organization (January 27, 1994).
HONORS: Named designated hitter on THE SPORTING NEWS college All-America team (1978).... Named Florida State League Most Valuable Player (1979).... Named Southern League Most Valuable Player (1980).
STATISTICAL NOTES: Led Florida State League first basemen with 106 double plays in 1979.... Led Southern League with 288 total bases and with 17 intentional bases on balls received in 1980.... Led Southern League first basemen with 125 double plays in 1980.... Led A.L. first basemen with 1,686 total chances in 1985.... Tied for American Association lead with six bases on balls received in 1992.

			BATTING											FIELDING			
Year	Team (League)	Pos.	G	AB	R	H	2B	3B	HR	RBI	Avg.	BB	SO	SB	PO	A	E	Avg.
1978	—West Haven (East.)	DH	2	2	0	0	0	0	0	0	.000	0	0	0	...	...	...	...
	—Fort Lauder. (FSL)	1B	60	176	19	36	5	0	1	19	.205	20	47	1	475	19	4	.992
1979	—Fort Lauder. (FSL)	1B	*140	*504	69	127	19	2	*26	*91	.252	69	*154	2	*1297	*97	11	*.992
1980	—Nashville (South.)	1B	141	521	*101	157	25	2	*34	*122	.301	82	162	4	*1218	76	13	*.990
1981	—Columbus (Int'l)	1B	125	434	68	107	21	2	*33	*98	.247	55	*146	0	631	55	*14	.980
	—New York (A.L.)	1B	4	7	2	2	1	1	0	2	.286	1	4	0	14	1	0	1.000
1982	—Columbus (Int'l)	1B	83	313	57	89	17	1	*32	86	.284	38	58	0	426	38	8	.983
	—New York (A.L.)	1B	33	107	8	20	2	1	2	4	.187	6	34	0	194	13	2	.990
1983	—Columbus (Int'l)	1B	84	317	72	87	14	0	27	81	.274	48	91	1	479	47	11	.980
	—New York (A.L.)	1B	32	86	8	20	2	0	5	17	.233	8	23	0	178	9	3	.984
1984	—Kansas City (A.L.)■	1B	126	438	58	107	23	2	28	77	.244	45	139	0	1102	79	•15	.987
1985	—Kansas City (A.L.)	1B	160	600	74	146	28	2	36	88	.243	52	*166	1	*1573	101	12	.993
1986	—Kansas City (A.L.)	1B	138	512	54	117	25	1	29	88	.229	43	146	0	1236	98	*18	.987
1987	—Kansas City (A.L.)	1B	121	386	44	80	11	1	24	60	.207	34	97	0	521	41	6	.989
1988	—K.C.-Sea. (A.L.)■	1B	118	413	46	97	17	1	23	66	.235	24	87	0	428	30	4	.991
1989	—New York (A.L.)■	1B	110	300	33	71	12	2	17	59	.237	25	67	0	150	7	1	.994
1990	—New York (A.L.)	1B	116	266	24	51	6	0	17	34	.192	35	91	0	183	7	3	.984
1991	—Okla. City (A.A.)■	1B	83	301	44	81	15	1	20	63	.269	33	74	0	62	6	2	.971
1992	—Okla. City (A.A.)	1B	117	454	75	114	26	2	*30	*104	.251	55	100	0	22	2	0	1.000
1993	—Okla. City (A.A.)	1B	126	471	67	115	22	0	*36	108	.244	51	98	0	59	10	0	1.000
	—Texas (A.L.)	DH	2	5	0	3	0	0	0	0	.600	0	2	0	...	...	...	...
Major league totals (11 years)			960	3120	351	714	127	11	181	495	.229	273	856	1	5579	386	64	.989

CHAMPIONSHIP SERIES RECORD

CHAMPIONSHIP SERIES NOTES: Shares A.L. single-series record for most strikeouts—8 (1985).

			BATTING											FIELDING			
Year	Team (League)	Pos.	G	AB	R	H	2B	3B	HR	RBI	Avg.	BB	SO	SB	PO	A	E	Avg.
1984	—Kansas City (A.L.)	1B	3	11	0	1	0	0	0	0	.091	1	4	0	20	3	1	.958
1985	—Kansas City (A.L.)	1B	7	25	1	3	0	0	0	1	.120	2	8	0	72	7	2	.975
Championship series totals (2 years)			10	36	1	4	0	0	0	1	.111	3	12	0	92	10	3	.971

WORLD SERIES RECORD

WORLD SERIES NOTES: Shares record for most at-bats in one inning—2 (October 27, 1985, fifth inning).

			BATTING											FIELDING			
Year	Team (League)	Pos.	G	AB	R	H	2B	3B	HR	RBI	Avg.	BB	SO	SB	PO	A	E	Avg.
1985	—Kansas City (A.L.)	1B	7	25	2	8	0	0	0	3	.320	5	4	0	70	3	0	1.000

BALDWIN, JAMES

P, WHITE SOX

PERSONAL: Born July 15, 1971, in Southern Pines, N.C.... 6-3/210.... Throws right, bats right.
HIGH SCHOOL: Pinecrest (Southern Pines, N.C.).
TRANSACTIONS/CAREER NOTES: Selected by Chicago White Sox organization in fourth

round of free-agent draft (June 4, 1990).

Year	Team (League)	W	L	Pct.	ERA	G	GS	CG	ShO	Sv.	IP	H	R	ER	BB	SO
1990	—GC Whi. Sox (GCL)	1	6	.143	4.10	9	7	0	0	0	37⅓	32	29	17	18	32
1991	—GC Whi. Sox (GCL)	3	1	.750	2.12	6	6	0	0	0	34	16	8	8	16	48
	—Utica (N.Y.-Penn)	1	4	.200	5.30	7	7	1	0	0	37⅓	40	26	22	27	23
1992	—South Bend (Mid.)	9	5	.643	2.42	21	21	1	1	0	137⅔	118	53	37	45	137
	—Sarasota (Fla. St.)	1	2	.333	2.87	6	6	1	0	0	37⅔	31	13	12	7	39
1993	—Birm. (Southern)	8	5	.615	*2.25	17	17	•4	0	0	120	94	48	30	43	107
	—Nashville (A.A.)	5	4	.556	2.61	10	10	1	0	0	69	43	21	20	36	61

B

BALLARD, JEFF

P, PIRATES

PERSONAL: Born August 13, 1963, in Billings, Mont. . . . 6-2/203. . . . Throws left, bats left. . . . Full name: Jeffrey Scott Ballard.
HIGH SCHOOL: Billings (Mont.) West.
COLLEGE: Stanford (degree in geophysics).
TRANSACTIONS/CAREER NOTES: Selected by Milwaukee Brewers organization in 16th round of free-agent draft (June 8, 1981). . . . Selected by Baltimore Orioles organization in 27th round of free-agent draft (June 4, 1984). . . . Selected by Orioles organization in seventh round of free-agent draft (June 3, 1985). . . . Granted free agency (October 18, 1991). . . . Signed by Louisville, St. Louis Cardinals organization (January 22, 1992). . . . Released by Louisville (December 10, 1992). . . . Signed by Tacoma, Oakland Athletics organization (January 26, 1993). . . . Released by Tacoma (March 12, 1993). . . . Signed by Buffalo, Pittsburgh Pirates organization (April 27, 1993). . . . On Buffalo disabled list (May 17-25, 1993).

Year	Team (League)	W	L	Pct.	ERA	G	GS	CG	ShO	Sv.	IP	H	R	ER	BB	SO
1985	—Newark (NY-Penn)	•10	2	.833	1.41	13	13	6	•3	0	96	78	20	15	20	91
1986	—Hagerstown (Car.)	9	5	.643	*1.85	17	17	5	2	0	112	106	39	23	32	115
	—Charlotte (South.)	5	2	.714	3.32	10	10	0	0	0	59⅔	70	29	22	20	35
	—Rochester (Int'l)	0	2	.000	7.11	2	2	0	0	0	6⅓	11	6	5	3	7
1987	—Rochester (Int'l)	13	4	.765	3.09	23	23	4	1	0	160⅓	151	60	55	35	114
	—Baltimore (A.L.)	2	8	.200	6.59	14	14	0	0	0	69⅔	100	60	51	35	27
1988	—Rochester (Int'l)	4	3	.571	2.97	9	8	3	1	0	60⅔	56	26	20	11	32
	—Baltimore (A.L.)	8	12	.400	4.40	25	25	6	1	0	153⅓	167	83	75	42	41
1989	—Baltimore (A.L.)	18	8	.692	3.43	35	35	4	1	0	215⅓	240	95	82	57	62
1990	—Baltimore (A.L.)	2	11	.154	4.93	44	17	0	0	0	133⅓	152	79	73	42	50
1991	—Baltimore (A.L.)	6	12	.333	5.60	26	22	0	0	0	123⅔	153	91	77	28	37
	—Rochester (Int'l)	3	3	.500	4.41	7	7	3	0	0	51	63	27	25	10	19
1992	—Louisville (A.A.)■	•12	8	.600	2.52	24	24	3	1	0	160⅔	164	57	45	34	76
1993	—Buffalo (A.A.)■	6	1	.857	2.29	12	12	1	0	0	74⅔	79	22	19	17	40
	—Pittsburgh (N.L.)	4	1	.800	4.86	25	5	0	0	0	53⅔	70	31	29	15	16
A.L. totals (5 years)		36	51	.414	4.63	144	113	10	2	0	695⅓	812	408	358	204	217
N.L. totals (1 year)		4	1	.800	4.86	25	5	0	0	0	53⅔	70	31	29	15	16
Major league totals (6 years)		40	52	.435	4.65	169	118	10	2	0	749	882	439	387	219	233

BANKHEAD, SCOTT

P, RED SOX

PERSONAL: Born July 31, 1963, in Raleigh, N.C. . . . 5-10/185. . . . Throws right, bats right. . . . Full name: Michael Scott Bankhead.
HIGH SCHOOL: Reidsville (N.C.).
COLLEGE: North Carolina.
TRANSACTIONS/CAREER NOTES: Selected by Pittsburgh Pirates organization in 17th round of free-agent draft (June 8, 1981). . . . Selected by Kansas City Royals organization in first round (16th pick overall) of free-agent draft (June 4, 1984). . . . Traded by Royals with P Steve Shields and OF Mike Kingery to Seattle Mariners for OF Danny Tartabull and P Rick Luecken (December 10, 1986). . . . On disabled list (June 24-July 13, 1987). . . . On Seattle disabled list (March 20-May 14, 1988); included rehabilitation assignment to San Bernardino (April 23-May 2) and Calgary (May 3-10). . . . On Seattle disabled list (April 16-May 18 and June 3, 1990-remainder of season); included rehabilitation assignment to Calgary (May 1-7). . . . On Seattle disabled list (May 11-31 and June 12-September 1, 1991); included rehabilitation assignment to San Bernardino (August 5-14), Bellingham (August 14-18) and Calgary (August 18-September 1). . . . Granted free agency (December 20, 1991). . . . Signed by Cincinnati Reds (January 22, 1992). . . . Granted free agency (October 28, 1992). . . . Signed by Boston Red Sox (December 8, 1992).
MISCELLANEOUS: Member of 1984 U.S. Olympic baseball team.

Year	Team (League)	W	L	Pct.	ERA	G	GS	CG	ShO	Sv.	IP	H	R	ER	BB	SO
1985	—Memphis (South.)	8	6	.571	3.59	24	24	2	1	0	140⅓	117	63	56	56	•128
1986	—Omaha (A.A.)	2	2	.500	1.49	7	7	2	0	0	48⅓	31	11	8	14	34
	—Kansas City (A.L.)	8	9	.471	4.61	24	17	0	0	0	121	121	66	62	37	94
1987	—Seattle (A.L.)■	9	8	.529	5.42	27	25	2	0	0	149⅓	168	96	90	37	95
1988	—San Bern. (Calif.)	0	0	...	1.64	2	2	0	0	0	11	6	3	2	4	6
	—Calgary (PCL)	1	1	.500	7.36	2	2	0	0	0	11	15	9	9	5	5
	—Seattle (A.L.)	7	9	.438	3.07	21	21	2	1	0	135	115	53	46	38	102
1989	—Seattle (A.L.)	14	6	.700	3.34	33	33	3	2	0	210⅓	187	84	78	63	140
1990	—Seattle (A.L.)	0	2	.000	11.08	4	4	0	0	0	13	18	16	16	7	10
	—Calgary (PCL)	0	1	.000	6.43	2	2	0	0	0	7	9	6	5	3	7
1991	—Seattle (A.L.)	3	6	.333	4.90	17	9	0	0	0	60⅔	73	35	33	21	28
	—San Bern. (Calif.)	0	1	.000	5.06	2	2	0	0	0	5⅓	4	4	3	2	4
	—Belling. (N'west)	1	0	1.000	0.00	1	0	0	0	0	4	1	0	0	1	8
	—Calgary (PCL)	0	0	...	1.04	5	0	0	0	1	8⅔	7	1	1	1	10
1992	—Cincinnati (N.L.)■	10	4	.714	2.93	54	0	0	0	1	70⅔	57	26	23	29	53
1993	—Boston (A.L.)■	2	1	.667	3.50	40	0	0	0	0	64⅓	59	28	25	29	47
A.L. totals (7 years)		43	41	.512	4.18	166	109	7	3	0	753⅔	741	378	350	232	516
N.L. totals (1 year)		10	4	.714	2.93	54	0	0	0	1	70⅔	57	26	23	29	53
Major league totals (8 years)		53	45	.541	4.07	220	109	7	3	1	824⅓	798	404	373	261	569

BANKS, WILLIE

P, CUBS

PERSONAL: Born February 27, 1969, in Jersey City, N.J. . . . 6-1/202. . . . Throws right, bats right. . . . Full name: Willie Anthony Banks.
HIGH SCHOOL: St. Anthony (Jersey City, N.J.).
TRANSACTIONS/CAREER NOTES: Selected by Minnesota Twins organization in first round (third pick overall) of free-agent draft (June 2, 1987). . . . Traded by Twins to Chicago Cubs for P Dave Stevens and C Matt Walbeck (November 24, 1993).
STATISTICAL NOTES: Led Appalachian League with 28 wild pitches and tied for lead with three balks in 1987. . . . Pitched 1-0 no-hit victory for Visalia against Palm Springs (May 24, 1989). . . . Led California League with 22 wild pitches in 1989. . . . Tied for Pacific Coast League lead with 14 wild pitches in 1991. . . . Tied for A.L. lead with five balks in 1993.

Year	Team (League)	W	L	Pct.	ERA	G	GS	CG	ShO	Sv.	IP	H	R	ER	BB	SO
1987	—Elizabeth. (Appal.)	1	8	.111	6.99	13	13	0	0	0	65⅔	73	*71	*51	*62	71
1988	—Kenosha (Midwest)	10	10	.500	3.72	24	24	0	0	0	125⅔	109	73	52	*107	113
1989	—Visalia (California)	12	9	.571	2.59	27	27	7	•4	0	174	122	70	50	85	*173
	—Orlando (Southern)	1	0	1.000	5.14	1	1	0	0	0	7	10	4	4	0	9
1990	—Orlando (Southern)	7	9	.438	3.93	28	28	1	0	0	162⅔	161	93	71	98	114
1991	—Portland (PCL)	9	8	.529	4.55	25	24	1	1	0	146⅓	156	81	74	76	63
	—Minnesota (A.L.)	1	1	.500	5.71	5	3	0	0	0	17⅓	21	15	11	12	16
1992	—Portland (PCL)	6	1	.857	1.92	11	11	2	1	0	75	62	20	16	34	41
	—Minnesota (A.L.)	4	4	.500	5.70	16	12	0	0	0	71	80	46	45	37	37
1993	—Minnesota (A.L.)	11	12	.478	4.04	31	30	0	0	0	171⅓	186	91	77	78	138
	Major league totals (3 years)	16	17	.485	4.61	52	45	0	0	0	259⅔	287	152	133	127	191

BARBERIE, BRET

2B, MARLINS

PERSONAL: Born August 16, 1967, in Long Beach, Calif. . . . 5-11/180. . . . Throws right, bats both. . . . Full name: Bret Edward Barberie. . . . Son of Edward Barberie, minor league catcher/shortstop (1961-66). . . . Name pronounced BAR-ber-ee.
HIGH SCHOOL: Gahr (Cerritos, Calif.).
COLLEGE: Cerritos College (Calif.) and Southern California (received degree, 1988).
TRANSACTIONS/CAREER NOTES: Selected by St. Louis Cardinals organization in second round of free-agent draft (January 14, 1986). . . . Selected by Oakland Athletics organization in secondary phase of free-agent draft (June 2, 1986). . . . Selected by Kansas City Royals organization in 65th round of free-agent draft (June 2, 1987). . . . Selected by Montreal Expos organization in seventh round of free-agent draft (June 1, 1988). . . . On Montreal disabled list (August 20-September 5, 1992). . . . Selected by Florida Marlins in first round (sixth pick overall) of expansion draft (November 17, 1992). . . . On Florida disabled list (April 17-May 28, 1993); included rehabilitation assignment to Edmonton (May 22-28). . . . On Florida disabled list (June 28-July 25, 1993); included rehabilitation assignment to Gulf Coast Marlins (July 23-25).
STATISTICAL NOTES: Switch-hit home runs in one game for Montreal (August 2, 1991).
MISCELLANEOUS: Member of 1988 U.S. Olympic baseball team.

			BATTING											FIELDING			
Year	Team (League)	Pos.	G	AB	R	H	2B	3B	HR	RBI	Avg.	BB	SO	SB	PO	A	E	Avg.
1989	—W.P. Beach (FSL)	2B	124	457	63	122	16	4	4	34	.267	64	39	10	247	343	16	.974
1990	—Jacksonv. (South.)	2B	133	431	71	112	18	3	7	56	.260	86	64	20	263	322	14	*.977
1991	—Indianapolis (A.A.)	3-2-S-1	71	218	45	68	10	4	10	48	.312	59	47	10	83	162	13	.950
	—Montreal (N.L.)	S-2-3-1	57	136	16	48	12	2	2	18	.353	20	22	0	53	90	5	.966
1992	—Montreal (N.L.)	3B-2B-SS	111	285	26	66	11	0	1	24	.232	47	62	9	66	188	13	.951
	—Indianapolis (A.A.)	2B-3B-SS	10	43	4	17	3	0	3	8	.395	1	9	0	25	20	3	.938
1993	—Florida (N.L.)■	2B	99	375	45	104	16	2	5	33	.277	33	58	2	201	303	9	.982
	—Edmonton (PCL)	2B	4	19	3	8	2	0	1	8	.421	0	2	0	8	12	1	.952
	—GC Marlins (GCL)	2B	2	8	0	2	0	0	0	1	.250	1	1	0	3	4	0	1.000
	Major league totals (3 years)		267	796	87	218	39	4	8	75	.274	100	142	11	320	581	27	.971

BARFIELD, JESSE

OF, ASTROS

PERSONAL: Born October 29, 1959, in Joliet, Ill. . . . 6-1/201. . . . Throws right, bats right. . . . Full name: Jesse Lee Barfield.
HIGH SCHOOL: Joliet (Ill.) Central.
TRANSACTIONS/CAREER NOTES: Selected by Toronto Blue Jays organization in ninth round of free-agent draft (June 7, 1977). . . . On disabled list (August 15-29, 1980 and May 16-31, 1988). . . . Traded by Blue Jays to New York Yankees for P Al Leiter (April 30, 1989). . . . On disabled list (July 29, 1991-remainder of season). . . . On New York disabled list (May 24-June 17, 1992); included rehabilitation assignment to Albany/Colonie (June 15-17). . . . On New York disabled list (June 18, 1992-remainder of season). . . . Granted free agency (November 4, 1992). . . . Signed by Yomiuri Giants of Japan Central League (December 2, 1992). . . . Signed as free agent by Yakult Swallows of Japan Central League (December 14, 1993). . . . Signed as free agent by Houston Astros organization (December 28, 1993).
HONORS: Won A.L. Gold Glove as outfielder (1986-87). . . . Named outfielder on THE SPORTING NEWS A.L. Silver Slugger team (1986).
STATISTICAL NOTES: Led A.L. outfielders with eight double plays in 1985 and 1986.

			BATTING											FIELDING			
Year	Team (League)	Pos.	G	AB	R	H	2B	3B	HR	RBI	Avg.	BB	SO	SB	PO	A	E	Avg.
1977	—Utica (N.Y.-Penn)	OF	70	234	37	53	9	3	5	35	.226	38	78	4	122	6	•13	.908
1978	—Dunedin (Fla. St.)	OF	133	441	40	91	12	3	2	34	.206	30	*125	1	229	*22	*15	.944
1979	—Kinston (Carolina)	OF	136	477	66	126	24	5	8	71	.264	49	126	6	284	19	17	.947
1980	—Knoxville (South.)	OF	124	433	63	104	12	8	14	65	.240	57	113	11	309	14	12	.964
1981	—Knoxville (South.)	OF	141	524	83	137	24	13	16	70	.261	59	111	25	270	*23	6	.980
	—Toronto (A.L.)	OF	25	95	7	22	3	2	2	9	.232	4	19	4	71	2	0	1.000
1982	—Toronto (A.L.)	OF	139	394	54	97	13	2	18	58	.246	42	79	1	217	15	9	.963
1983	—Toronto (A.L.)	OF	128	388	58	98	13	3	27	68	.253	22	110	2	213	16	8	.966
1984	—Toronto (A.L.)	OF	110	320	51	91	14	1	14	49	.284	35	81	8	190	9	10	.952
1985	—Toronto (A.L.)	OF	155	539	94	156	34	9	27	84	.289	66	143	22	349	*22	4	.989
1986	—Toronto (A.L.)	OF	158	589	107	170	35	2	*40	108	.289	69	146	8	368	*20	3	.992
1987	—Toronto (A.L.)	OF	159	590	89	155	25	3	28	84	.263	58	141	3	341	•17	3	.992

Year	Team (League)	Pos.	G	AB	R	H	2B	3B	HR	RBI	Avg.	BB	SO	SB	PO	A	E	Avg.
			BATTING												FIELDING			
1988	—Toronto (A.L.)	OF	137	468	62	114	21	5	18	56	.244	41	108	7	325	12	4	.988
1989	—Tor.-N.Y. (A.L.)■	OF	150	521	79	122	23	1	23	67	.234	87	150	5	340	*20	•10	.973
1990	—New York (A.L.)	OF	153	476	69	117	21	2	25	78	.246	82	150	4	305	*16	9	.973
1991	—New York (A.L.)	OF	84	284	37	64	12	0	17	48	.225	36	80	1	178	10	0	1.000
1992	—New York (A.L.)	OF	30	95	8	13	2	0	2	7	.137	9	27	1	54	3	2	.966
	—Alb./Colon. (East.)	OF	2	8	2	3	0	0	1	2	.375	1	1	0	4	1	0	1.000
1993	—Yomiuri (Jp. Cen.)■	...	104	344	52	74	8	2	26	53	.215	70	*127	1	...	...	...	...
Major league totals (12 years)			1428	4759	715	1219	216	30	241	716	.256	551	1234	66	2951	162	62	.980

CHAMPIONSHIP SERIES RECORD

Year	Team (League)	Pos.	G	AB	R	H	2B	3B	HR	RBI	Avg.	BB	SO	SB	PO	A	E	Avg.
			BATTING												FIELDING			
1985	—Toronto (A.L.)	OF	7	25	3	7	1	0	1	4	.280	3	7	1	21	0	1	.955

ALL-STAR GAME RECORD

Year	League	Pos.	AB	R	H	2B	3B	HR	RBI	Avg.	BB	SO	SB	PO	A	E	Avg.
			BATTING											FIELDING			
1986	—American	PH-OF	3	0	0	0	0	0	0	.000	0	0	0	2	0	0	1.000

BARK, BRIAN

P, BRAVES

PERSONAL: Born August 26, 1968, in Baltimore. . . . 5-9/160. . . . Throws left, bats left. . . . Full name: Brian Stuart Bark. . . . Son of Jerry Bark, minor league pitcher (1965-68).
HIGH SCHOOL: Randallstown (Md.).
COLLEGE: North Carolina State.
TRANSACTIONS/CAREER NOTES: Selected by Baltimore Orioles organization in 28th round of free-agent draft (June 5, 1989). . . . Selected by Atlanta Braves organization in 12th round of free-agent draft (June 4, 1990). . . . On Greenville disabled list (July 26-September 12, 1991).

Year	Team (League)	W	L	Pct.	ERA	G	GS	CG	ShO	Sv.	IP	H	R	ER	BB	SO
1990	—Pulaski (Appal.)	2	2	.500	2.66	5	5	0	0	0	23⅔	17	19	7	13	33
1991	—Durham (Carolina)	4	3	.571	2.51	13	13	0	0	0	82⅓	66	23	23	24	76
	—Greenville (South.)	2	1	.667	3.57	9	3	1	0	1	17⅔	19	10	7	8	15
1992	—Greenville (South.)	5	0	1.000	1.15	11	11	2	1	0	55	36	11	7	13	49
	—Richmond (Int'l)	1	2	.333	6.00	22	4	0	0	2	42	63	32	28	15	50
1993	—Richmond (Int'l)	12	9	.571	3.67	29	28	1	1	0	162	153	81	66	*72	110

BARNES, BRIAN

P, INDIANS

PERSONAL: Born March 25, 1967, in Roanoke Rapids, N.C. . . . 5-9/170. . . . Throws left, bats left. . . . Full name: Brian Keith Barnes.
HIGH SCHOOL: Roanoke Rapids (N.C.).
COLLEGE: Clemson.
TRANSACTIONS/CAREER NOTES: Selected by Baltimore Orioles organization in 25th round of free-agent draft (June 1, 1988). . . . Selected by Montreal Expos organization in fourth round of free-agent draft (June 5, 1989). . . . On Expos disabled list (March 28-May 5, 1991); included rehabilitation assignment to West Palm Beach (April 15-21) and Indianapolis (April 21-May 5). . . . Traded by Expos to Cleveland Indians (December 17, 1993), completing deal in which Indians traded 1B Randy Milligan to Expos for a player to be named later (December 13, 1993).
HONORS: Named Southern League Most Outstanding Pitcher (1990).
MISCELLANEOUS: Struck out in one game as pinch-hitter (1993).

Year	Team (League)	W	L	Pct.	ERA	G	GS	CG	ShO	Sv.	IP	H	R	ER	BB	SO
1989	—Jamestown (NYP)	1	0	1.000	1.00	2	2	0	0	0	9	4	1	1	3	15
	—W.P. Beach (FSL)	4	3	.571	0.72	7	7	4	3	0	50	25	9	4	16	67
	—Indianapolis (A.A.)	1	0	1.000	1.50	1	1	0	0	0	6	5	1	1	2	5
1990	—Jacksonv. (South.)	13	7	.650	2.77	29	28	3	1	0	*201⅓	144	78	62	87	*213
	—Montreal (N.L.)	1	1	.500	2.89	4	4	1	0	0	28	25	10	9	7	23
1991	—Montreal (N.L.)	5	8	.385	4.22	28	27	1	0	0	160	135	82	75	84	117
	—W.P. Beach (FSL)	0	0	...	0.00	2	2	0	0	0	7	3	0	0	4	6
	—Indianapolis (A.A.)	2	0	1.000	1.64	2	2	0	0	0	11	6	2	2	8	10
1992	—Indianapolis (A.A.)	4	4	.500	3.69	13	13	2	1	0	83	69	35	34	30	77
	—Montreal (N.L.)	6	6	.500	2.97	21	17	0	0	0	100	77	34	33	46	65
1993	—Montreal (N.L.)	2	6	.250	4.41	52	8	0	0	3	100	105	53	49	48	60
Major league totals (4 years)		14	21	.400	3.85	105	56	2	0	3	388	342	179	166	185	265

BARNES, SKEETER

IF/OF, TIGERS

PERSONAL: Born March 7, 1957, in Cincinnati. . . . 5-10/180. . . . Throws right, bats right. . . . Full name: William Henry Barnes III.
HIGH SCHOOL: Woodward (Cincinnati).
COLLEGE: Cincinnati.
TRANSACTIONS/CAREER NOTES: Selected by Cincinnati Reds organization in 16th round of free-agent draft (June 6, 1978). . . . Traded by Reds organization to Montreal Expos organization for OF Max Venable (April 26, 1985). . . . Traded by Expos organization with P Dan Schatzeder to Philadelphia Phillies for IF Tom Foley and P Larry Sorensen (July 24, 1986). . . . Granted free agency (October 15, 1986). . . . Signed by Louisville, St. Louis Cardinals organization (January 26, 1987). . . . Contract sold by Cardinals to Denver, Milwaukee Brewers organization (July 16, 1987). . . . Granted free agency (October 15, 1987). . . . Signed by Buffalo, Pittsburgh Pirates organization (November 20, 1987). . . . Released by Pirates organization (May 7, 1988). . . . Signed by Nashville, Reds organization (May 14, 1988). . . . Granted free agency (October 15, 1988). . . . Re-signed by Reds (November 5, 1988). . . . Granted free agency (October 22, 1989). . . . Re-signed by Reds (January 29, 1990). . . . Granted free agency (October 15, 1990). . . . Signed by Toledo, Detroit Tigers organization (January 21, 1991). . . . On suspended list (September 22-23, 1992).
STATISTICAL NOTES: Tied for Pioneer League lead with six sacrifice flies in 1978. . . . Led Eastern League third basemen with 104

putouts in 1981 and .947 fielding percentage in 1982. . . . Tied for American Association lead with eight sacrifice flies in 1989. . . . Led American Association outfielders with 24 assists in 1990.

			BATTING												FIELDING			
Year	Team (League)	Pos.	G	AB	R	H	2B	3B	HR	RBI	Avg.	BB	SO	SB	PO	A	E	Avg.
1978	—Billings (Pioneer)	0-3-S-2-1	68	277	66	102	*22	5	3	*76	.368	29	27	21	56	50	16	.869
1979	—Nashville (South.)	3B	•145	500	54	133	19	4	12	77	.266	27	64	5	123	*291	*35	.922
1980	—Waterbury (East.)	OF	*138	533	62	156	27	6	4	64	.293	24	54	18	264	15	13	.955
1981	—Indianapolis (A.A.)	1B-OF-3B	36	118	10	31	6	1	1	11	.263	9	10	1	254	23	3	.989
	—Waterbury (East.)	3-0-1-2	96	363	45	93	17	0	6	49	.256	33	29	15	†115	185	15	.952
1982	—Waterbury (East.)	3B-1B-SS	112	418	67	128	24	6	12	72	.306	44	32	31	252	192	19	†.959
	—Indianapolis (A.A.)	3B-1B	18	59	8	18	5	1	1	3	.305	1	6	1	25	25	2	.962
1983	—Indianapolis (A.A.)	3-1-0-2	109	377	67	127	19	6	7	56	.337	26	42	10	203	140	16	.955
	—Cincinnati (N.L.)	1B-3B	15	34	5	7	0	0	1	4	.206	7	3	2	45	11	1	.982
1984	—Wichita (A.A.)	3-1-0-2	92	360	59	118	23	4	14	67	.328	26	30	24	143	122	13	.953
	—Cincinnati (N.L.)	3B-OF	32	42	5	5	0	0	1	3	.119	4	6	0	7	15	0	1.000
1985	—Denver-Ind. (A.A.)■	3-1-0-2	95	340	51	95	16	0	8	63	.279	38	45	20	308	154	10	.979
	—Montreal (N.L.)	3B-OF-1B	19	26	0	4	1	0	0	0	.154	0	2	0	13	6	0	1.000
1986	—Indianapolis (A.A.)	3B-OF-1B	85	300	40	80	18	5	5	40	.267	26	28	16	95	137	18	.928
	—Portland (PCL)■	3-0-S-1	38	141	21	52	8	4	1	29	.369	7	9	3	44	60	6	.945
1987	—Louis.-Den. (A.A.)■	3B-1B-OF	110	431	79	131	33	5	16	76	.304	41	38	17	315	127	17	.963
	—St. Louis (N.L.)	3B	4	4	1	1	0	0	1	3	.250	0	0	0	0	0	0	...
1988	—Buff.-Nash. (A.A.)■	1-0-3-P	122	379	47	96	16	0	6	39	.253	17	47	15	461	38	3	.994
1989	—Nashville (A.A.)	OF-1B-3B	124	472	57	143	*39	3	6	55	.303	32	59	15	305	24	7	.979
	—Cincinnati (N.L.)	PR-PH	5	3	1	0	0	0	0	0	.000	0	0	0	...	...	...	...
1990	—Nashville (A.A.)■	OF-1B-3B	*144	*548	83	*156	21	2	7	66	.285	47	57	34	281	†30	5	.984
1991	—Toledo (Int'l)■	OF-3B-1B	62	233	48	77	14	0	9	40	.330	23	26	27	209	69	7	.975
	—Detroit (A.L.)	0-3-1-2	75	159	28	46	13	2	5	17	.289	9	24	10	92	38	2	.985
1992	—Detroit (A.L.)	3-1-0-2	95	165	27	45	8	1	3	25	.273	10	18	3	127	78	11	.949
1993	—Detroit (A.L.)	1-0-3-2-S	84	160	24	45	8	1	2	27	.281	11	19	5	158	37	4	.980
American League totals (3 years)			254	484	79	136	29	4	10	69	.281	30	61	18	377	153	17	.969
National League totals (5 years)			75	109	12	17	1	0	3	10	.156	11	11	2	65	32	1	.990
Major league totals (8 years)			329	593	91	153	30	4	13	79	.258	41	72	20	442	185	18	.972

RECORD AS PITCHER

Year	Team (League)	W	L	Pct.	ERA	G	GS	CG	ShO	Sv.	IP	H	R	ER	BB	SO
1988	—Nashville (A.A.)	0	0	...	...	1	0	0	0	0	0	4	6	6	3	0

BASS, KEVIN

OF, ASTROS

PERSONAL: Born May 12, 1959, in Redwood City, Calif. . . . 6-0/190. . . . Throws right, bats both. . . . Full name: Kevin Charles Bass. . . . Brother of Richard Bass, minor league outfielder (1976-77); and cousin of James Lofton, Philadelphia Eagles, National Football League.
HIGH SCHOOL: Menlo Park (Calif.).

TRANSACTIONS/CAREER NOTES: Selected by Milwaukee Brewers organization in second round of free-agent draft (June 7, 1977). . . . On disabled list (July 29-September 1, 1981). . . . Traded by Brewers organization with P Mike Madden and P Frank DiPino to Houston Astros (September 3, 1982), completing deal in which Houston traded P Don Sutton to Brewers for three players to be named later (August 30, 1982). . . . On disabled list (March 29-April 13, 1984). . . . On Houston disabled list (May 28-August 11, 1989); included rehabilitation assignment to Tucson (August 4-22). . . . Granted free agency (November 13, 1989). . . . Signed by San Francisco Giants (November 16, 1989). . . . On San Francisco disabled list (May 27-September 3, 1990); included rehabilitation assignment to San Jose (August 20-26) and Phoenix (August 27-September 3). . . . On San Francisco disabled list (June 19-July 23, 1991); included rehabilitation assignment to San Jose (July 4-10) and Phoenix (July 10-23). . . . On disabled list (March 29-April 19, 1992). . . . Traded by Giants to New York Mets for a player to be named later (August 8, 1992); Giants acquired OF Rob Katzaroff to complete deal (October 1, 1992). . . . Granted free agency (November 3, 1992). . . . Signed by Astros (January 5, 1993). . . . Granted free agency (November 1, 1993). . . . Re-signed by Astros (December 7, 1993).

RECORDS: Shares major league single-season record for most games with switch-hit home runs—2 (1987). . . . Holds N.L. career record for most games with switch-hit home runs—4.

STATISTICAL NOTES: Led Midwest League in being hit by pitch with 10 in 1978. . . . Led Eastern League outfielders with seven double plays in 1980. . . . Switch-hit home runs in one game (August 3 and September 2, 1987; August 20, 1989, and August 2, 1992, second game).

			BATTING												FIELDING			
Year	Team (League)	Pos.	G	AB	R	H	2B	3B	HR	RBI	Avg.	BB	SO	SB	PO	A	E	Avg.
1977	—Newark (NY-Penn)	OF	48	189	30	56	11	•7	1	33	.296	19	17	11	56	2	3	.951
1978	—Burlington (Midw.)	OF	129	499	81	132	27	5	18	69	.265	40	63	36	*281	14	11	.964
1979	—Holyoke (Eastern)	OF	135	490	69	129	15	4	8	54	.263	37	77	17	280	•16	*17	.946
1980	—Holyoke (Eastern)	OF	136	490	79	147	*31	7	4	51	.300	41	59	35	305	14	*18	.947
1981	—Vancouver (PCL)	OF	97	339	40	87	10	5	2	30	.257	43	36	29	175	14	7	.964
1982	—Milwaukee (A.L.)	OF	18	9	4	0	0	0	0	0	.000	1	1	0	7	0	0	1.000
	—Vancouver (PCL)	OF	102	413	70	130	23	7	17	65	.315	44	44	23	199	15	10	.955
	—Houston (N.L.)■	OF	12	24	2	1	0	0	0	1	.042	0	8	0	11	0	1	.917
1983	—Houston (N.L.)	OF	88	195	25	46	7	3	2	18	.236	6	27	2	68	1	4	.945
1984	—Houston (N.L.)	OF	121	331	33	86	17	5	2	29	.260	6	57	5	149	4	4	.975
1985	—Houston (N.L.)	OF	150	539	72	145	27	5	16	68	.269	31	63	19	328	10	1	*.997
1986	—Houston (N.L.)	OF	157	591	83	184	33	5	20	79	.311	38	72	22	303	12	5	.984
1987	—Houston (N.L.)	OF	157	592	83	168	31	5	19	85	.284	53	77	21	287	11	4	.987
1988	—Houston (N.L.)	OF	157	541	57	138	27	2	14	72	.255	42	65	31	267	7	6	.979
1989	—Houston (N.L.)	OF	87	313	42	94	19	4	5	44	.300	29	44	11	186	6	3	.985
	—Tucson (PCL)	OF	6	17	1	5	1	0	0	2	.294	1	2	0	8	0	0	1.000
1990	—San Francisco (N.L.)■	OF	61	214	25	54	9	1	7	32	.252	14	26	2	88	2	3	.968
	—San Jose (Calif.)	OF	6	22	2	8	1	0	0	4	.364	0	1	1	3	0	0	1.000

Year	Team (League)	Pos.	G	AB	R	H	2B	3B	HR	RBI	Avg.	BB	SO	SB	PO	A	E	Avg.
			BATTING												FIELDING			
	—Phoenix (PCL)	OF	8	33	2	8	2	0	0	4	.242	0	4	1	5	2	0	1.000
1991	—San Francisco (N.L.)	OF	124	361	43	84	10	4	10	40	.233	36	56	7	159	9	4	.977
	—San Jose (Calif.)	OF	5	19	1	2	2	0	0	1	.105	2	3	2	7	1	1	.889
	—Phoenix (PCL)	OF	10	41	8	13	3	1	2	7	.317	2	4	1	20	0	0	1.000
1992	—S.F.-N.Y. (N.L.)■	OF	135	402	40	108	23	5	9	39	.269	23	70	14	191	2	3	.985
1993	—Houston (N.L.)■	OF	111	229	31	65	18	0	3	37	.284	26	31	7	83	3	1	.989
American League totals (1 year)			18	9	4	0	0	0	0	0	.000	1	1	0	7	0	0	1.000
National League totals (12 years)			1360	4332	536	1173	221	39	107	544	.271	304	596	141	2120	67	39	.982
Major league totals (12 years)			1378	4341	540	1173	221	39	107	544	.270	305	597	141	2127	67	39	.983

CHAMPIONSHIP SERIES RECORD

CHAMPIONSHIP SERIES NOTES: Shares single-game record for most times caught stealing—2 (October 15, 1986, 16 innings).... Shares N.L. single-series record for most times caught stealing—3 (1986).

Year	Team (League)	Pos.	G	AB	R	H	2B	3B	HR	RBI	Avg.	BB	SO	SB	PO	A	E	Avg.
			BATTING												FIELDING			
1986	—Houston (N.L.)	OF	6	24	0	7	2	0	0	0	.292	4	4	2	16	0	1	.941

ALL-STAR GAME RECORD

Year	League	Pos.	AB	R	H	2B	3B	HR	RBI	Avg.	BB	SO	SB	PO	A	E	Avg.
			BATTING											FIELDING			
1986	—National	PH	1	0	0	0	0	0	0	.000	0	0	0	...	...	...	...

BATCHELOR, RICHARD

P, CARDINALS

PERSONAL: Born April 8, 1967, in Florence, S.C.... 6-1/195.... Throws right, bats right.... Full name: Richard Anthony Batchelor.
HIGH SCHOOL: Hartsville (S.C.).
COLLEGE: South Carolina-Aiken.
TRANSACTIONS/CAREER NOTES: Selected by Chicago White Sox organization in seventh round of free-agent draft (June 1, 1988).... Selected by New York Yankees organization in 38th round of free-agent draft (June 5, 1989).... Signed as free agent by Yankees organization (April 17, 1990).... Traded by Yankees organization to St. Louis Cardinals for P Lee Smith (August 31, 1993).

Year	Team (League)	W	L	Pct.	ERA	G	GS	CG	ShO	Sv.	IP	H	R	ER	BB	SO
1990	—Greensboro (S. Atl.)	2	2	.500	1.58	27	0	0	0	8	51⅓	39	15	9	14	38
1991	—Fort Lauder. (FSL)	4	7	.364	2.76	50	0	0	0	•25	62	55	28	19	22	58
	—Alb./Colon. (East.)	0	0	...	45.00	1	0	0	0	0	1	5	5	5	1	0
1992	—Alb./Colon. (East.)	4	5	.444	4.20	58	0	0	0	7	70⅔	79	40	33	34	45
1993	—Alb./Colon. (East.)	1	3	.250	0.89	36	0	0	0	19	40⅓	27	9	4	12	40
	—Columbus (Int'l)	1	1	.500	2.76	15	0	0	0	6	16⅓	14	5	5	8	17
	—St. Louis (N.L.)■	0	0	...	8.10	9	0	0	0	0	10	14	12	9	3	4
Major league totals (1 year)		0	0	...	8.10	9	0	0	0	0	10	14	12	9	3	4

BATISTA, MIGUEL

P, EXPOS

PERSONAL: Born February 19, 1971, in Santo Domingo, Dominican Republic.... 6-1/170.... Throws right, bats right.... Full name: Miguel Jerez Decartes Batista.
HIGH SCHOOL: Nuevo Horizondes (Dominican Republic).
TRANSACTIONS/CAREER NOTES: Signed as free agent by Montreal Expos organization (February 29, 1988).... Selected by Pittsburgh Pirates organization from Expos organization in Rule 5 major league draft (December 9, 1991).... Returned to Expos (April 23, 1992).

Year	Team (League)	W	L	Pct.	ERA	G	GS	CG	ShO	Sv.	IP	H	R	ER	BB	SO
1988	—	Dominican Summer League statistics unavailable.														
1989	—Dom. Expos (DSL)	1	7	.125	4.24	13	11	0	0	0	68	56	46	32	50	60
1990	—GC Expos (GCL)	4	3	.571	2.06	9	6	0	0	0	39⅓	33	16	9	17	21
	—Rockford (Midw.)	0	1	.000	8.76	3	2	0	0	0	12⅓	16	13	12	5	7
1991	—Rockford (Midw.)	11	5	.688	4.04	23	23	2	1	0	133⅔	126	74	60	57	90
1992	—Pittsburgh (N.L.)■	0	0	...	9.00	1	0	0	0	0	2	4	2	2	3	1
	—W.P. Beach (FSL)■	7	7	.500	3.79	24	24	1	0	0	135⅓	130	69	57	54	92
1993	—Harrisburg (East.)	13	5	.722	4.34	26	26	0	0	0	141	139	79	68	86	91
Major league totals (1 year)		0	0	...	9.00	1	0	0	0	0	2	4	2	2	3	1

BATISTE, KIM

3B/SS, PHILLIES

PERSONAL: Born March 15, 1968, in New Orleans.... 6-0/200.... Throws right, bats right.... Full name: Kimothy Emil Batiste.... Name pronounced buh-TEEST.
HIGH SCHOOL: St. Amant (La.).
TRANSACTIONS/CAREER NOTES: Selected by Philadelphia Phillies organization in third round of free-agent draft (June 2, 1987).
STATISTICAL NOTES: Led Eastern League shortstops with 550 total chances in 1990.

Year	Team (League)	Pos.	G	AB	R	H	2B	3B	HR	RBI	Avg.	BB	SO	SB	PO	A	E	Avg.
			BATTING												FIELDING			
1987	—Utica (N.Y.-Penn)	SS-3B	46	150	15	26	8	1	2	10	.173	7	65	4	64	90	16	.906
1988	—Spartanburg (SAL)	SS	122	430	51	107	19	6	6	52	.249	14	100	16	202	363	60	.904
1989	—Clearwater (FSL)	SS-3B	114	385	36	90	12	4	3	33	.234	17	67	13	168	309	35	.932
1990	—Reading (Eastern)	SS	125	486	57	134	14	4	6	33	.276	13	73	28	*182	*333	*35	.936
1991	—Scran./W.B. (Int'l)	SS	122	462	54	135	25	6	1	41	.292	11	72	18	181	344	*37	.934
	—Philadelphia (N.L.)	SS	10	27	2	6	0	0	0	1	.222	1	8	0	10	22	1	.970
1992	—Philadelphia (N.L.)	SS	44	136	9	28	4	0	1	10	.206	4	18	0	69	85	13	.922
	—Scran./W.B. (Int'l)	SS	71	269	30	70	12	6	2	29	.260	7	42	6	105	160	16	.943

Year	Team (League)	Pos.	G	AB	R	H	2B	3B	HR	RBI	Avg.	BB	SO	SB	PO	A	E	Avg.
			BATTING												FIELDING			
1993	—Philadelphia (N.L.)...	3B-SS	79	156	14	44	7	1	5	29	.282	3	29	0	72	108	10	.947
Major league totals (3 years)			133	319	25	78	11	1	6	40	.245	8	55	0	151	215	24	.938

CHAMPIONSHIP SERIES RECORD

Year	Team (League)	Pos.	G	AB	R	H	2B	3B	HR	RBI	Avg.	BB	SO	SB	PO	A	E	Avg.
			BATTING												FIELDING			
1993	—Philadelphia (N.L.)...	3B	4	1	0	1	0	0	0	1	1.000	0	0	0	2	0	2	.500

WORLD SERIES RECORD

Year	Team (League)	Pos.	G	AB	R	H	2B	3B	HR	RBI	Avg.	BB	SO	SB	PO	A	E	Avg.
			BATTING												FIELDING			
1993	—Philadelphia (N.L.)...	3B	2	0	0	0	0	0	0	0	...	0	0	0	0	1	0	1.000

BATTLE, ALLEN

OF, WHITE SOX

PERSONAL: Born November 29, 1968, in Grantham, N.C. . . . 6-0/170. . . . Throws right, bats right.

HIGH SCHOOL: Southern Wayne (Dudley, N.C.).

COLLEGE: South Alabama.

TRANSACTIONS/CAREER NOTES: Selected by Chicago White Sox organization in 45th round of free-agent draft (June 4, 1990). . . . Selected by St. Louis Cardinals organization in 10th round of free-agent draft (June 3, 1991). . . . On disabled list (April 24-May 6, 1993). . . . Selected by White Sox from Cardinals organization in Rule 5 major league draft (December 13, 1993).

Year	Team (League)	Pos.	G	AB	R	H	2B	3B	HR	RBI	Avg.	BB	SO	SB	PO	A	E	Avg.
			BATTING												FIELDING			
1991	—Johns. City (App.)....	OF	17	62	26	24	6	1	0	7	.387	14	6	7	29	0	0	1.000
	—Savannah (S. Atl.)...	OF	48	169	28	41	7	1	0	20	.243	27	34	12	83	2	1	.988
1992	—Springfield (Midw.)..	OF	67	235	49	71	10	4	4	24	.302	41	34	22	136	3	4	.972
	—St. Peters. (FSL).......	OF	60	222	34	71	9	2	1	15	.320	35	38	21	165	3	2	.988
1993	—Arkansas (Texas)....	OF	108	390	71	107	24	*12	3	40	.274	45	75	20	241	5	5	.980

BATTLE, HOWARD

3B, BLUE JAYS

PERSONAL: Born March 25, 1972, in Biloxi, Miss. . . . 6-0/208. . . . Throws right, bats right. . . . Full name: Howard Dion Battle.

HIGH SCHOOL: Mercy Cross (Biloxi, Miss.).

TRANSACTIONS/CAREER NOTES: Selected by Toronto Blue Jays organization in fourth round of free-agent draft (June 4, 1990).

STATISTICAL NOTES: Led Southern League third basemen with 436 total chances in 1993.

Year	Team (League)	Pos.	G	AB	R	H	2B	3B	HR	RBI	Avg.	BB	SO	SB	PO	A	E	Avg.
			BATTING												FIELDING			
1990	—Medicine Hat (Pio.)..	3B	61	233	25	62	17	1	5	32	.266	15	38	5	25	92	*34	.775
1991	—Myrtle Beach (SAL)..	3B	138	520	82	145	33	4	20	87	.279	48	87	15	86	184	29	.903
1992	—Dunedin (Fla. St.).....	3B	*136	520	76	132	27	3	17	85	.254	49	89	6	58	292	33	.914
1993	—Knoxville (South.)....	3B	141	521	66	145	21	5	7	70	.278	45	94	12	88	*319	*29	.933

BAUTISTA, DANNY

OF, TIGERS

PERSONAL: Born May 24, 1972, in Santo Domingo, Dominican Republic. . . . 5-11/170. . . . Throws right, bats right.

TRANSACTIONS/CAREER NOTES: Signed as free agent by Detroit Tigers organization (June 24, 1989). . . . On disabled list (May 24-July 10, 1991).

Year	Team (League)	Pos.	G	AB	R	H	2B	3B	HR	RBI	Avg.	BB	SO	SB	PO	A	E	Avg.
			BATTING												FIELDING			
1989	—..................................		Dominican Summer League statistics unavailable.															
1990	—Bristol (Appal.).........	OF	27	95	9	26	3	0	2	12	.274	8	21	2	43	2	0	1.000
1991	—Fayetteville (SAL).....	OF	69	234	21	45	6	4	1	30	.192	21	65	7	137	6	4	.973
1992	—Fayetteville (SAL)....	OF	121	453	59	122	22	0	5	52	.269	29	76	18	210	17	6	.974
1993	—London (Eastern).....	OF	117	424	55	121	21	1	6	48	.285	32	69	28	256	13	3	.989
	—Detroit (A.L.)............	OF	17	61	6	19	3	0	1	9	.311	1	10	3	38	2	0	1.000
Major league totals (1 year)			17	61	6	19	3	0	1	9	.311	1	10	3	38	2	0	1.000

BAUTISTA, JOSE

P, CUBS

PERSONAL: Born July 25, 1964, in Bani, Dominican Republic. . . . 6-2/205. . . . Throws right, bats right. . . . Full name: Jose Joaquin Bautista. . . . Name pronounced bough-TEES-tuh.

HIGH SCHOOL: Bani (Dominican Republic) School.

TRANSACTIONS/CAREER NOTES: Signed as free agent by New York Mets organization (April 25, 1981). . . . Selected by Baltimore Orioles from Mets organization in Rule 5 major league draft (December 7, 1987). . . . On Baltimore disabled list (May 20-June 11, 1989); included rehabilitation assignment to Rochester (May 29-June 11). . . . Sent by Orioles outright to Miami, independent (April 24, 1991); returned to Orioles organization (June 1, 1991). . . . Loaned by Orioles organization to Oklahoma City (June 1-July 11, 1991). . . . Granted free agency (September 23, 1991). . . . Signed by Omaha, Kansas City Royals organization (December 20, 1991). . . . Granted free agency (October 15, 1992). . . . Signed by Chicago Cubs organization (December 17, 1992). . . . On suspended list (September 10-13, 1993).

STATISTICAL NOTES: Pitched 6-0 no-hit victory against Prince William (May 26, 1985, first game).

MISCELLANEOUS: Appeared in two games as pinch-runner (1993).

Year	Team (League)	W	L	Pct.	ERA	G	GS	CG	ShO	Sv.	IP	H	R	ER	BB	SO
1981	—Kingsport (Appal.).....	3	6	.333	4.64	13	11	3	2	0	66	84	54	34	17	34
1982	—Kingsport (Appal.).....	0	4	.000	8.92	14	4	0	0	5	38⅓	61	44	38	19	13
1983	—GC Mets (GCL)...........	4	3	.571	2.31	13	13	2	0	0	81⅔	66	31	21	32	44

Year	Team (League)	W	L	Pct.	ERA	G	GS	CG	ShO	Sv.	IP	H	R	ER	BB	SO
1984	—Columbia (S. Atl.)	13	4	.765	3.13	19	18	5	3	0	135	121	52	47	35	96
1985	—Lynchburg (Caro.)	15	8	.652	2.34	27	25	7	3	1	169	145	49	44	33	109
1986	—Jackson (Texas)	0	1	.000	8.31	7	4	0	0	0	21⅔	36	22	20	8	13
	—Lynchburg (Caro.)	8	8	.500	3.94	18	18	5	1	0	118⅔	120	58	52	24	62
1987	—Jackson (Texas)	10	5	.667	3.24	28	25	2	0	0	169⅓	174	76	61	43	95
1988	—Baltimore (A.L.)■	6	15	.286	4.30	33	25	3	0	0	171⅔	171	86	82	45	76
1989	—Baltimore (A.L.)	3	4	.429	5.31	15	10	0	0	0	78	84	46	46	15	30
	—Rochester (Int'l)	4	4	.500	2.83	15	13	3	1	0	98⅔	84	41	31	26	47
1990	—Baltimore (A.L.)	1	0	1.000	4.05	22	0	0	0	0	26⅔	28	15	12	7	15
	—Rochester (Int'l)	7	8	.467	4.06	27	13	3	0	2	108⅔	115	51	49	15	50
1991	—Baltimore (A.L.)	0	1	.000	16.88	5	0	0	0	0	5⅓	13	10	10	5	3
	—Miami (Florida St.)■	8	2	*.800	2.71	11	11	4	•3	0	76⅓	63	23	23	11	69
	—Okla. City (A.A.)■	0	3	.000	5.29	11	3	0	0	0	32⅓	38	19	19	6	22
	—Rochester (Int'l)■	1	0	1.000	0.59	6	0	0	0	1	15⅓	8	1	1	3	7
1992	—Omaha (A.A.)■	2	10	.167	4.90	40	7	1	0	2	108⅓	125	66	59	28	60
	—Memphis (South.)	1	0	1.000	4.50	1	1	0	0	0	6	6	3	3	2	7
1993	—Chicago (N.L.)■	10	3	.769	2.82	58	7	1	0	2	111⅔	105	38	35	27	63
A.L. totals (4 years)		10	20	.333	4.79	75	35	3	0	0	281⅔	296	157	150	72	124
N.L. totals (1 year)		10	3	.769	2.82	58	7	1	0	2	111⅔	105	38	35	27	63
Major league totals (5 years)		20	23	.465	4.23	133	42	4	0	2	393⅓	401	195	185	99	187

BEAN, BILLY

OF, PADRES

PERSONAL: Born May 11, 1964, in Santa Ana, Calif. . . . 6-0/190. . . . Throws left, bats left. . . . Full name: William Daro Bean.
HIGH SCHOOL: Santa Ana (Calif.).
COLLEGE: Loyola Marymount (bachelor of arts degree in business administration).
TRANSACTIONS/CAREER NOTES: Selected by New York Yankees organization in 24th round of free-agent draft (June 3, 1985). . . . Selected by Detroit Tigers organization in fourth round of free-agent draft (June 2, 1986). . . . Traded by Tigers organization to Los Angeles Dodgers organization for OF Steve Green and 1B/OF Domingo Michel (July 17, 1989). . . . Selected by Edmonton, Angels organization, from San Antonio, Dodgers organization, in Rule 5 minor league draft (December 9, 1991). . . . Released by Edmonton (January 21, 1992). . . . Signed by Kintetsu Buffaloes of Japan Pacific League (1992). . . . Released by Kintetsu (July 1992). . . . Signed by Edmonton, Angels organization (July 14, 1992). . . . Granted free agency (October 15, 1992). . . . Signed by Wichita, San Diego Padres organization (December 15, 1992).
RECORDS: Shares modern major league record for most hits in first game in majors (nine innings)—4 (April 25, 1987).

			BATTING												FIELDING			
Year	Team (League)	Pos.	G	AB	R	H	2B	3B	HR	RBI	Avg.	BB	SO	SB	PO	A	E	Avg.
1986	—Glens Falls (East.)	OF	80	279	43	77	10	3	8	49	.276	36	27	3	189	4	3	.985
1987	—Toledo (Int'l)	OF	104	357	51	98	18	2	8	43	.275	38	52	14	228	1	7	.970
	—Detroit (A.L.)	OF	26	66	6	17	2	0	0	4	.258	5	11	1	54	1	0	1.000
1988	—Toledo (Int'l)	OF-1B	•138	484	59	124	19	1	6	40	.256	41	45	12	664	43	12	.983
	—Detroit (A.L.)	OF-1B	10	11	2	2	0	1	0	0	.182	0	2	0	8	1	0	1.000
1989	—Detroit (A.L.)	OF-1B	9	11	0	0	0	0	0	0	.000	2	3	0	12	0	2	.857
	—Toledo (Int'l)	OF-1B	76	267	43	84	14	2	4	29	.315	27	35	7	231	14	4	.984
	—Albuquerque (PCL)■	OF	3	9	1	2	0	1	0	3	.222	2	0	0	7	0	0	1.000
	—Los Angeles (N.L.)	OF	51	71	7	14	4	0	0	3	.197	4	10	0	49	0	0	1.000
1990	—Albuquerque (PCL)	OF-1B-3B	129	427	85	126	26	5	7	67	.295	69	63	16	209	14	8	.965
1991	—Albuquerque (PCL)	OF	103	259	35	77	22	6	2	35	.297	23	32	7	112	5	1	.992
1992	—Kintetsu (Jp. Pac.)■	OF	7	24	2	5	2	0	0	2	.208	1	5	0	...	...	...	...
	—Edmonton (PCL)■	OF	39	138	17	34	8	2	1	24	.246	7	13	5	35	3	0	1.000
1993	—Las Vegas (PCL)■	OF-1B	53	167	31	59	11	2	7	40	.353	32	14	3	149	20	1	.994
	—San Diego (N.L.)	OF-1B	88	177	19	46	9	0	5	32	.260	6	29	2	122	9	1	.992
American League totals (3 years)			45	88	8	19	2	1	0	4	.216	7	16	1	74	2	2	.974
National League totals (2 years)			139	248	26	60	13	0	5	35	.242	10	39	2	171	9	1	.994
Major league totals (4 years)			184	336	34	79	15	1	5	39	.235	17	55	3	245	11	3	.988

BECK, ROD

P, GIANTS

PERSONAL: Born August 3, 1968, in Burbank, Calif. . . . 6-1/236. . . . Throws right, bats right. . . . Full name: Rodney Roy Beck.
HIGH SCHOOL: Grant (Sherman Oaks, Calif.).
TRANSACTIONS/CAREER NOTES: Selected by Oakland Athletics organization in 13th round of free-agent draft (June 2, 1986). . . . Traded by A's organization to San Francisco Giants organization for P Charlie Corbell (March 23, 1988).

Year	Team (League)	W	L	Pct.	ERA	G	GS	CG	ShO	Sv.	IP	H	R	ER	BB	SO
1986	—Medford (N'west)	1	3	.250	5.23	13	6	0	0	1	32⅔	47	25	19	11	21
1987	—Medford (N'west)	5	8	.385	5.18	17	12	2	0	0	92	106	74	53	26	69
1988	—Clinton (Midwest)■	12	7	.632	3.00	28	23	5	1	0	177	177	68	59	27	123
1989	—San Jose (Calif.)	11	2	*.846	2.40	13	13	4	0	0	97⅓	91	29	26	26	88
	—Shreveport (Texas)	7	3	.700	3.55	16	14	4	1	0	99	108	45	39	16	74
1990	—Shreveport (Texas)	10	3	.769	2.23	14	14	2	1	0	93	85	26	23	17	71
	—Phoenix (PCL)	4	7	.364	4.93	12	12	2	0	0	76⅔	100	51	42	18	43
1991	—Phoenix (PCL)	4	3	.571	2.02	23	5	3	0	6	71⅓	56	18	16	13	35
	—San Francisco (N.L.)	1	1	.500	3.78	31	0	0	0	1	52⅓	53	22	22	13	38
1992	—San Francisco (N.L.)	3	3	.500	1.76	65	0	0	0	17	92	62	20	18	15	87
1993	—San Francisco (N.L.)	3	1	.750	2.16	76	0	0	0	48	79⅓	57	20	19	13	86
Major league totals (3 years)		7	5	.583	2.37	172	0	0	0	66	223⅔	172	62	59	41	211

ALL-STAR GAME RECORD

Year	League	W	L	Pct.	ERA	GS	CG	ShO	Sv.	IP	H	R	ER	BB	SO
1993	—National	0	0	...	9.00	0	0	0	0	1	2	1	1	0	1

BECKER, RICH

OF, TWINS

PERSONAL: Born February 1, 1972, in Aurora, Ill. . . . 5-10/180. . . . Throws left, bats both. . . . Full name: Richard Goodhard Becker.
HIGH SCHOOL: Aurora (Ill.) West.
TRANSACTIONS/CAREER NOTES: Selected by Minnesota Twins organization in third round of free-agent draft (June 4, 1990). . . . On Minnesota disabled list (September 13, 1993-remainder of season).
STATISTICAL NOTES: Led Appalachian League with .448 on-base percentage in 1990. . . . Led Midwest League with 215 total bases in 1991. . . . Led California League outfielders with 355 total chances in 1992.

		BATTING												FIELDING			
Year Team (League)	Pos.	G	AB	R	H	2B	3B	HR	RBI	Avg.	BB	SO	SB	PO	A	E	Avg.
1990 —Elizabeth. (Appal.)	OF	56	194	54	56	5	1	6	24	.289	*53	54	18	87	2	9	.908
1991 —Kenosha (Midwest)	OF	130	494	100	132	*38	3	13	53	.267	72	108	19	270	19	11	.963
1992 —Visalia (California)	OF	*136	506	*118	160	37	2	15	82	.316	*114	122	29	*332	17	6	.983
1993 —Nashville (South.)	OF	138	516	•93	148	25	7	15	66	.287	94	117	29	303	5	6	.981
—Minnesota (A.L.)	OF	3	7	3	2	2	0	0	0	.286	5	4	1	7	0	1	.875
Major league totals (1 year)		3	7	3	2	2	0	0	0	.286	5	4	1	7	0	1	.875

B

BECKETT, ROBBIE

P, PADRES

PERSONAL: Born July 16, 1972, in Austin, Tex. . . . 6-5/235. . . . Throws left, bats right. . . . Full name: Robert Joseph Beckett.
HIGH SCHOOL: McCallum (Austin, Tex.).
TRANSACTIONS/CAREER NOTES: Selected by San Diego Padres organization in first round (25th pick overall) of free-agent draft (June 4, 1990); pick received as part of compensation for Kansas City Royals signing Type A free agent Mark Davis.
STATISTICAL NOTES: Led California League with 25 wild pitches in 1993.

Year Team (League)	W	L	Pct.	ERA	G	GS	CG	ShO	Sv.	IP	H	R	ER	BB	SO
1990 —Ariz. Padres (Ariz.)	2	5	.286	4.38	10	10	0	0	0	49⅓	40	28	24	*45	54
—Riverside (Calif.)	2	1	.667	7.02	3	3	0	0	0	16⅔	18	13	13	11	11
1991 —Char., S.C. (S. Atl.)	2	*14	.125	8.23	28	26	1	0	0	109⅓	115	•111	*100	*117	96
1992 —Waterloo (Midw.)	4	10	.286	4.77	24	24	1	1	0	120⅔	77	88	64	*140	147
1993 —Rancho Cuca. (Cal.)	2	4	.333	6.02	37	10	0	0	4	83⅔	75	62	56	93	88

BEDROSIAN, STEVE

P, BRAVES

PERSONAL: Born December 6, 1957, in Methuen, Mass. . . . 6-3/205. . . . Throws right, bats right. . . . Full name: Stephen Wayne Bedrosian. . . . Name pronounced bed-ROHZ-ee-un.
HIGH SCHOOL: Methuen (Mass.).
COLLEGE: North Essex Community College (Mass.) and New Haven (Conn.).
TRANSACTIONS/CAREER NOTES: Selected by Atlanta Braves organization in third round of free-agent draft (June 6, 1978). . . . On disabled list (June 24-September 18, 1979 and August 20-September 4, 1984). . . . Traded by Braves with OF Milt Thompson to Philadelphia Phillies for C Ozzie Virgil and P Pete Smith (December 10, 1985). . . . On Philadelphia disabled list (March 21-May 20, 1988); included rehabilitation assignment to Maine (May 9-19). . . . Traded by Phillies with a player to be named later to San Francisco Giants for P Dennis Cook, P Terry Mulholland and 3B Charlie Hayes (June 18, 1989); Giants organization acquired IF Rick Parker to complete deal (August 7, 1989). . . . Traded by Giants to Minnesota Twins for P Johnny Ard and a player to be named later (December 5, 1990); Giants acquired P Jimmy Williams to complete deal (December 18, 1990). . . . Granted free agency (November 7, 1991). . . . Signed by Braves organization (December 17, 1992).
HONORS: Named N.L. Rookie Pitcher of the Year by THE SPORTING NEWS (1982). . . . Named N.L. Fireman of the Year by THE SPORTING NEWS (1987). . . . Named N.L. Cy Young Award winner by Baseball Writers' Association of America (1987).

Year Team (League)	W	L	Pct.	ERA	G	GS	CG	ShO	Sv.	IP	H	R	ER	BB	SO
1978 —Kingsport (Appal.)	2	2	.500	3.08	6	6	1	0	0	38	38	18	13	25	29
—Greenw. (W. Car.)	5	1	.833	2.13	8	8	1	0	0	55	45	17	13	34	58
1979 —Savannah (South.)	5	5	.500	3.03	13	13	4	2	0	89	71	36	30	58	73
1980 —Savannah (South.)	14	10	.583	3.19	29	•29	9	2	0	*203	167	91	72	96	*161
1981 —Richmond (Int'l)	10	10	.500	2.69	26	25	8	1	0	184	143	76	55	99	144
—Atlanta (N.L.)	1	2	.333	4.50	15	1	0	0	0	24	15	14	12	15	9
1982 —Atlanta (N.L.)	8	6	.571	2.42	64	3	0	0	11	137⅔	102	39	37	57	123
1983 —Atlanta (N.L.)	9	10	.474	3.60	70	1	0	0	19	120	100	50	48	51	114
1984 —Atlanta (N.L.)	9	6	.600	2.37	40	4	0	0	11	83⅔	65	23	22	33	81
1985 —Atlanta (N.L.)	7	15	.318	3.83	37	37	0	0	0	206⅔	198	101	88	111	134
1986 —Philadelphia (N.L.)■	8	6	.571	3.39	68	0	0	0	29	90⅓	79	39	34	34	82
1987 —Philadelphia (N.L.)	5	3	.625	2.83	65	0	0	0	40	89	79	31	28	28	74
1988 —Maine (Int'l)	0	0	...	0.00	5	0	0	0	0	6⅔	6	0	0	2	5
—Philadelphia (N.L.)	6	6	.500	3.75	57	0	0	0	28	74⅓	75	34	31	27	61
1989 —Phil.-S.F. (N.L.)■	3	7	.300	2.87	68	0	0	0	23	84⅔	56	31	27	39	58
1990 —San Francisco (N.L.)	9	9	.500	4.20	68	0	0	0	17	79⅓	72	40	37	44	43
1991 —Minnesota (A.L.)■	5	3	.625	4.42	56	0	0	0	6	77⅓	70	42	38	35	44
1992 —	Out of organized baseball.														
1993 —Atlanta (N.L.)■	5	2	.714	1.63	49	0	0	0	0	49⅔	34	11	9	14	33
A.L. totals (1 year)	5	3	.625	4.42	56	0	0	0	6	77⅓	70	42	38	35	44
N.L. totals (11 years)	70	72	.493	3.23	601	46	0	0	178	1039⅓	875	413	373	453	812
Major league totals (12 years)	75	75	.500	3.31	657	46	0	0	184	1116⅔	945	455	411	488	856

CHAMPIONSHIP SERIES RECORD

CHAMPIONSHIP SERIES NOTES: Shares N.L. single-series record for most saves—3 (1989).

Year Team (League)	W	L	Pct.	ERA	G	GS	CG	ShO	Sv.	IP	H	R	ER	BB	SO
1982 —Atlanta (N.L.)	0	0	...	18.00	2	0	0	0	0	1	3	2	2	1	2
1989 —San Francisco (N.L.)	0	0	...	2.70	4	0	0	0	3	3⅓	4	1	1	2	2
1991 —Minnesota (A.L.)	0	0	...	0.00	2	0	0	0	0	1⅓	3	2	0	2	2
1993 —Atlanta (N.L.)	Did not play.														
Champ. series totals (3 years)	0	0	...	4.76	8	0	0	0	3	5⅔	10	5	3	5	6

WORLD SERIES RECORD

Year	Team (League)	W	L	Pct.	ERA	G	GS	CG	ShO	Sv.	IP	H	R	ER	BB	SO
1989	—San Francisco (N.L.).....	0	0	...	0.00	2	0	0	0	0	2⅔	0	0	0	2	2
1991	—Minnesota (A.L.).........	0	0	...	5.40	3	0	0	0	0	3⅓	3	2	2	0	2
World Series totals (2 years)...		0	0	...	3.00	5	0	0	0	0	6	3	2	2	2	4

ALL-STAR GAME RECORD

Year	League	W	L	Pct.	ERA	GS	CG	ShO	Sv.	IP	H	R	ER	BB	SO
1987	—National........................	0	0	...	0.00	0	0	0	0	1	0	0	0	2	0

BELCHER, TIM

P, TIGERS

PERSONAL: Born October 19, 1961, in Sparta, O.... 6-3/220.... Throws right, bats right.... Full name: Timothy Wayne Belcher.
HIGH SCHOOL: Highland (Sparta, O.).
COLLEGE: Mt. Vernon Nazarene (O.).

TRANSACTIONS/CAREER NOTES: Selected by Minnesota Twins organization in first round (first pick overall) of free-agent draft (June 6, 1983).... Selected by New York Yankees organization in secondary phase of free-agent draft (January 17, 1984).... Selected by Oakland Athletics organization in player compensation pool draft (February 8, 1984); A's received compensation for Baltimore Orioles signing Type A free-agent P Tom Underwood (February 7, 1984).... On disabled list (April 10-May 4 and May 5-July 23, 1986).... Traded by A's organization to Los Angeles Dodgers (September 3, 1987), completing deal in which Dodgers traded P Rick Honeycutt to A's for a player to be named later (August 29, 1987).... On disabled list (August 17, 1990-remainder of season).... Traded by Dodgers with P John Wetteland to Cincinnati Reds for OF Eric Davis and P Kip Gross (November 27, 1991).... Traded by Reds to Chicago White Sox for P Johnny Ruffin and P Jeff Pierce (July 31, 1993).... Granted free agency (October 26, 1993).... Signed by Detroit Tigers (February 7, 1994).
HONORS: Named righthanded pitcher on THE SPORTING NEWS college All-America team (1983).... Named N.L. Rookie Pitcher of the Year by THE SPORTING NEWS (1988).

Year	Team (League)	W	L	Pct.	ERA	G	GS	CG	ShO	Sv.	IP	H	R	ER	BB	SO
1984	—Madison (Midwest)....	9	4	.692	3.57	16	16	3	1	0	98⅓	80	45	39	48	111
	—Alb./Colon. (East.)....	3	4	.429	3.33	10	10	2	0	0	54	37	30	20	41	40
1985	—Huntsville (South.).....	11	10	.524	4.69	29	26	3	1	0	149⅔	145	99	78	99	90
1986	—Huntsville (South.).....	2	5	.286	6.57	9	9	0	0	0	37	50	28	27	22	25
1987	—Tacoma (PCL)...........	9	11	.450	4.42	29	28	2	1	0	163	143	89	80	*133	136
	—Los Angeles (N.L.)■...	4	2	.667	2.38	6	5	0	0	0	34	30	11	9	7	23
1988	—Los Angeles (N.L.).....	12	6	.667	2.91	36	27	4	1	4	179⅔	143	65	58	51	152
1989	—Los Angeles (N.L.).....	15	12	.556	2.82	39	30	•10	*8	1	230	182	81	72	80	200
1990	—Los Angeles (N.L.).....	9	9	.500	4.00	24	24	5	2	0	153	136	76	68	48	102
1991	—Los Angeles (N.L.).....	10	9	.526	2.62	33	33	2	1	0	209⅓	189	76	61	75	156
1992	—Cincinnati (N.L.)■......	15	14	.517	3.91	35	34	2	1	0	227⅔	201	*104	*99	80	149
1993	—Cincinnati (N.L.)........	9	6	.600	4.47	22	22	4	2	0	137	134	72	68	47	101
	—Chicago (A.L.)■.........	3	5	.375	4.40	12	11	1	1	0	71⅔	64	36	35	27	34
A.L. totals (1 year)		3	5	.375	4.40	12	11	1	1	0	71⅔	64	36	35	27	34
N.L. totals (7 years)		74	58	.561	3.34	195	175	27	15	5	1170⅔	1015	485	435	388	883
Major league totals (7 years)..		77	63	.550	3.40	207	186	28	16	5	1242⅓	1079	521	470	415	917

CHAMPIONSHIP SERIES RECORD

Year	Team (League)	W	L	Pct.	ERA	G	GS	CG	ShO	Sv.	IP	H	R	ER	BB	SO
1988	—Los Angeles (N.L.).....	2	0	1.000	4.11	2	2	0	0	0	15⅓	12	7	7	4	16
1993	—Chicago (A.L.)...........	1	0	1.000	2.45	1	0	0	0	0	3⅔	3	1	1	3	1
Champ. series totals (2 years)		3	0	1.000	3.79	3	2	0	0	0	19	15	8	8	7	17

WORLD SERIES RECORD

Year	Team (League)	W	L	Pct.	ERA	G	GS	CG	ShO	Sv.	IP	H	R	ER	BB	SO
1988	—Los Angeles (N.L.).....	1	0	1.000	6.23	2	2	0	0	0	8⅔	10	7	6	6	10

BELINDA, STAN

P, ROYALS

PERSONAL: Born August 6, 1966, in Huntingdon, Pa.... 6-3/215.... Throws right, bats right.... Full name: Stanley Peter Belinda.
HIGH SCHOOL: State College (Pa.) Area.
COLLEGE: Allegany Community College (Md.).

TRANSACTIONS/CAREER NOTES: Selected by Pittsburgh Pirates organization in 10th round of free-agent draft (June 2, 1986).... On Gulf Coast Pirates disabled list (June 21-30, 1986).... Traded by Pirates to Kansas City Royals for P Jon Lieber and P Dan Miceli (July 31, 1993).

Year	Team (League)	W	L	Pct.	ERA	G	GS	CG	ShO	Sv.	IP	H	R	ER	BB	SO
1986	—Watertown (NYP)......	0	0	...	3.38	5	0	0	0	2	8	5	3	3	2	5
	—GC Pirates (GCL)........	3	2	.600	2.66	17	0	0	0	7	20⅓	23	12	6	2	17
1987	—Macon (S. Atl.)...........	6	4	.600	2.09	50	0	0	0	16	82	59	26	19	27	75
1988	—Salem (Carolina).........	6	4	.600	2.76	53	0	0	0	14	71⅔	54	33	22	32	63
1989	—Harrisburg (East.).....	1	4	.200	2.33	32	0	0	0	13	38⅔	32	13	10	25	33
	—Buffalo (A.A.).............	2	2	.500	0.95	19	0	0	0	9	28⅓	13	5	3	13	28
	—Pittsburgh (N.L.)........	0	1	.000	6.10	8	0	0	0	0	10⅓	13	8	7	2	10
1990	—Buffalo (A.A.).............	3	1	.750	1.90	15	0	0	0	5	23⅔	20	8	5	8	25
	—Pittsburgh (N.L.)........	3	4	.429	3.55	55	0	0	0	8	58⅓	48	23	23	29	55
1991	—Pittsburgh (N.L.)........	7	5	.583	3.45	60	0	0	0	16	78⅓	50	30	30	35	71
1992	—Pittsburgh (N.L.)........	6	4	.600	3.15	59	0	0	0	18	71⅓	58	26	25	29	57
1993	—Pittsburgh (N.L.)........	3	1	.750	3.61	40	0	0	0	19	42⅓	35	18	17	11	30
	—Kansas City (A.L.)■...	1	1	.500	4.28	23	0	0	0	0	27⅓	30	13	13	6	25
A.L. totals (1 year)		1	1	.500	4.28	23	0	0	0	0	27⅓	30	13	13	6	25
N.L. totals (5 years)		19	15	.559	3.52	222	0	0	0	61	260⅔	204	105	102	106	223
Major league totals (5 years)..		20	16	.556	3.59	245	0	0	0	61	288	234	118	115	112	248

CHAMPIONSHIP SERIES RECORD

Year	Team (League)	W	L	Pct.	ERA	G	GS	CG	ShO	Sv.	IP	H	R	ER	BB	SO
1990	—Pittsburgh (N.L.)........	0	0	...	2.45	3	0	0	0	0	3⅔	3	1	1	0	4
1991	—Pittsburgh (N.L.)........	1	0	1.000	0.00	3	0	0	0	0	5	0	0	0	3	4
1992	—Pittsburgh (N.L.)........	0	0	...	0.00	2	0	0	0	0	1⅔	2	0	0	1	2
Champ. series totals (3 years)		1	0	1.000	0.87	8	0	0	0	0	10⅓	5	1	1	4	10

BELL, DAVID

3B, INDIANS

PERSONAL: Born September 14, 1972, in Cincinnati. . . . 5-10/170. . . . Throws right, bats right. . . . Full name: David Michael Bell. . . . Son of Buddy Bell, current coach, Cleveland Indians, and major league infielder with four teams (1972-89) and grandson of Gus Bell, major league outfielder with four teams (1950-64).

HIGH SCHOOL: Moeller (Cincinnati).

TRANSACTIONS/CAREER NOTES: Selected by Cleveland Indians organization in seventh round of free-agent draft (June 4, 1990).

STATISTICAL NOTES: Led South Atlantic League in grounding into double plays with 22 in 1991. . . . Led South Atlantic League third basemen with 389 total chances in 1991. . . . Led Eastern League third basemen with 32 double plays in 1993.

			BATTING												FIELDING			
Year	**Team (League)**	**Pos.**	**G**	**AB**	**R**	**H**	**2B**	**3B**	**HR**	**RBI**	**Avg.**	**BB**	**SO**	**SB**	**PO**	**A**	**E**	**Avg.**
1990	—GC Indians (GCL)	3B	30	111	18	29	5	1	0	13	.261	10	8	1	29	50	7	.919
	—Burlington (Appal.) ..	3B	12	42	4	7	1	1	0	2	.167	2	5	2	8	27	3	.921
1991	—Columbus (S. Atl.)	3B	136	491	47	113	24	1	5	63	.230	37	50	3	90	*268	31	.920
1992	—Kinston (Carolina) ...	3B	123	464	52	117	17	2	6	47	.252	54	66	2	83	264	20	.946
1993	—Cant./Akr. (East.)....	3B-2B-SS	129	483	69	141	20	2	9	60	.292	43	54	3	117	283	21	.950

BELL, DEREK

OF, PADRES

PERSONAL: Born December 11, 1968, in Tampa, Fla. . . . 6-2/215. . . . Throws right, bats right. . . . Full name: Derek Nathaniel Bell.

HIGH SCHOOL: King (Tampa, Fla.).

TRANSACTIONS/CAREER NOTES: Selected by Toronto Blue Jays organization in second round of free-agent draft (June 2, 1987). . . . On Knoxville disabled list (July 30, 1988-remainder of season; June 13-21 and July 2-12, 1990). . . . On Toronto disabled list (April 9-May 8, 1992); included rehabilitation assignment to Dunedin (April 27-May 4). . . . Traded by Blue Jays with OF Stoney Briggs to San Diego Padres for OF Darrin Jackson (March 30, 1993). . . . On suspended list (July 9-12, 1993).

HONORS: Named International League Most Valuable Player (1991).

STATISTICAL NOTES: Led International League with 243 total bases in 1991. . . . Led International League outfielders with seven double plays in 1991.

			BATTING												FIELDING			
Year	**Team (League)**	**Pos.**	**G**	**AB**	**R**	**H**	**2B**	**3B**	**HR**	**RBI**	**Avg.**	**BB**	**SO**	**SB**	**PO**	**A**	**E**	**Avg.**
1987	—St. Cathar. (NYP)	OF	74	273	46	72	11	3	10	42	.264	18	60	12	126	6	2	.985
1988	—Knoxville (South.)	OF	14	52	5	13	3	1	0	4	.250	1	14	2	18	2	2	.909
1989	—Knoxville (South.)	OF	136	513	72	124	22	6	16	75	.242	26	92	15	216	12	9	.962
1990	—Syracuse (Int'l)	OF	109	402	57	105	13	5	7	56	.261	23	75	21	220	9	5	.979
1991	—Syracuse (Int'l)	OF	119	457	*89	*158	22	•12	13	*93	*.346	57	69	27	278	*15	*16	.948
	—Toronto (A.L.)...........	OF	18	28	5	4	0	0	0	1	.143	6	5	3	16	0	2	.889
1992	—Toronto (A.L.)...........	OF	61	161	23	39	6	3	2	15	.242	15	34	7	105	4	0	1.000
	—Dunedin (Fla. St.).....	OF	7	25	7	6	2	0	0	4	.240	4	4	3	13	0	2	.867
1993	—San Diego (N.L.)■.....	OF-3B	150	542	73	142	19	1	21	72	.262	23	122	26	334	37	17	.956
American League totals (2 years)			79	189	28	43	6	3	2	16	.228	21	39	10	121	4	2	.984
National League totals (1 year)			150	542	73	142	19	1	21	72	.262	23	122	26	334	37	17	.956
Major league totals (3 years)			229	731	101	185	25	4	23	88	.253	44	161	36	455	41	19	.963

CHAMPIONSHIP SERIES RECORD

			BATTING												FIELDING			
Year	**Team (League)**	**Pos.**	**G**	**AB**	**R**	**H**	**2B**	**3B**	**HR**	**RBI**	**Avg.**	**BB**	**SO**	**SB**	**PO**	**A**	**E**	**Avg.**
1992	—Toronto (A.L.)..........	PR-OF	2	0	1	0	0	0	0	0	...	1	0	0	1	0	0	1.000

WORLD SERIES RECORD

			BATTING												FIELDING			
Year	**Team (League)**	**Pos.**	**G**	**AB**	**R**	**H**	**2B**	**3B**	**HR**	**RBI**	**Avg.**	**BB**	**SO**	**SB**	**PO**	**A**	**E**	**Avg.**
1992	—Toronto (A.L.)..........	PH	2	1	1	0	0	0	0	0	.000	1	0	0	...	...	...	...

BELL, ERIC

P

PERSONAL: Born October 27, 1963, in Modesto, Calif. . . . 6-0/165. . . . Throws left, bats left. . . . Full name: Eric Alvin Bell.

HIGH SCHOOL: Beyer (Modesto, Calif.).

TRANSACTIONS/CAREER NOTES: Selected by Baltimore Orioles organization in ninth round of free-agent draft (June 7, 1982). . . . On Hagerstown disabled list (May 3-June 18, 1984). . . . On Rochester disabled list (May 9, 1988-remainder of season; and April 5-June 10, 1989). . . . Granted free agency (October 4, 1990). . . . Signed by Cleveland Indians (October 14, 1990). . . . On Canton/Akron disabled list (June 3-28, 1991). . . . Granted free agency (October 16, 1992). . . . Signed by Tucson, Houston Astros organization (January 12, 1993). . . . Granted free agency (October 15, 1993).

Year	Team (League)	W	L	Pct.	ERA	G	GS	CG	ShO	Sv.	IP	H	R	ER	BB	SO
1982	—Bluefield (Appal.)	4	1	.800	2.10	11	9	0	0	0	51⅓	42	19	12	36	30
1983	—Newark (NY-Penn)....	3	2	.600	4.95	18	5	2	0	6	60	71	44	33	30	56
1984	—Hagerstown (Car.).....	0	0	...	9.82	3	1	0	0	0	3⅔	6	4	4	5	6
	—Newark (NY-Penn)....	8	3	.727	2.46	15	15	4	1	0	102⅓	82	40	28	26	114
1985	—Hagerstown (Car.).....	11	6	.647	3.13	26	•26	5	2	0	158⅓	141	73	55	63	*162
	—Baltimore (A.L.)	0	0	...	4.76	4	0	0	0	0	5⅔	4	3	3	4	4

Year	Team (League)	W	L	Pct.	ERA	G	GS	CG	ShO	Sv.	IP	H	R	ER	BB	SO
1986	—Charlotte (South.)	9	6	.600	*3.05	18	18	6	1	0	129⅔	109	49	44	66	104
	—Rochester (Int'l)	7	3	*.700	3.05	11	11	4	0	0	76⅔	68	26	26	35	59
	—Baltimore (A.L.)	1	2	.333	5.01	4	4	0	0	0	23⅓	23	14	13	14	18
1987	—Baltimore (A.L.)	10	13	.435	5.45	33	29	2	0	0	165	174	113	100	78	111
1988	—Rochester (Int'l)	3	1	.750	1.98	7	7	0	0	0	36⅓	28	10	8	13	33
1989	—Rochester (Int'l)	1	2	.333	4.99	7	7	0	0	0	39⅔	40	24	22	15	27
	—Hagerstown (East.)	4	2	.667	1.88	9	7	0	0	1	43	32	11	9	11	35
1990	—Rochester (Int'l)	9	6	.600	4.86	27	27	3	0	0	148	168	90	80	65	90
1991	—Cant./Akr. (East.)■	9	5	.643	2.89	18	16	1	0	0	93⅓	82	47	30	37	84
	—Colo. Springs (PCL)	2	1	.667	2.13	4	4	1	1	0	25⅓	23	6	6	11	16
	—Cleveland (A.L.)	4	0	1.000	0.50	10	0	0	0	0	18	5	2	1	5	7
1992	—Cleveland (A.L.)	0	2	.000	7.63	7	1	0	0	0	15⅓	22	13	13	9	10
	—Colo. Springs (PCL)	10	7	.588	3.73	26	18	5	0	1	137⅔	161	64	57	30	56
1993	—Houston (N.L.)■	0	1	.000	6.14	10	0	0	0	0	7⅓	10	5	5	2	2
	—Tucson (PCL)	4	6	.400	4.05	22	16	3	1	0	106⅔	131	59	48	39	53
A.L. totals (5 years)		15	17	.469	5.15	58	34	2	0	0	227⅓	228	145	130	110	150
N.L. totals (1 year)		0	1	.000	6.14	10	0	0	0	0	7⅓	10	5	5	2	2
Major league totals (6 years)		15	18	.455	5.18	68	34	2	0	0	234⅔	238	150	135	112	152

BELL, GEORGE

DH

PERSONAL: Born October 21, 1959, in San Pedro de Macoris, Dominican Republic. . . . 6-1/210. . . . Throws right, bats right. . . . Full name: George Antonio Mathey Bell. . . . Brother of Juan Bell, infielder, Milwaukee Brewers; and brother of Rolando Bell, minor league infielder (1985-87).

TRANSACTIONS/CAREER NOTES: Signed as free agent by Philadelphia Phillies organization (June 23, 1978). . . . On disabled list (June 22, 1980-remainder of season). . . . Selected by Toronto Blue Jays from Phillies organization in Rule 5 major league draft (December 8, 1980). . . . On disabled list (April 20-May 1, June 14-30 and July 8, 1982-remainder of season). . . . On suspended list (July 31-August 2, 1989). . . . Granted free agency (November 5, 1990). . . . Signed by Chicago Cubs (December 6, 1990). . . . Traded by Cubs to Chicago White Sox for OF Sammy Sosa and P Ken Patterson (March 30, 1992). . . . On Chicago disabled list (July 22-September 1, 1993); included rehabilitation assignment to South Bend (August 26-September 1). . . . Released by White Sox (October 13, 1993).

RECORDS: Shares major league single-game record for most sacrifice flies—3 (August 14, 1990).

HONORS: Named outfielder on THE SPORTING NEWS A.L. All-Star team (1986-87). . . . Named outfielder on THE SPORTING NEWS A.L. Silver Slugger team (1985-87). . . . Named Major League Player of the Year by THE SPORTING NEWS (1987). . . . Named A.L. Player of the Year by THE SPORTING NEWS (1987). . . . Named A.L. Most Valuable Player by Baseball Writers' Association of America (1987).

STATISTICAL NOTES: Led Western Carolinas League with 270 total bases in 1979. . . . Tied for International League lead in double plays by outfielder with four in 1983. . . . Tied for A.L. lead in errors by outfielder with 11 in 1985. . . . Tied for A.L. lead with 15 game-winning RBIs in 1986. . . . Led A.L. with 369 total bases in 1987. . . . Hit three home runs in one game (April 4, 1988). . . . Led A.L. with 14 sacrifice flies in 1989. . . . Led A.L. in grounding into double plays with 29 in 1992.

			BATTING												FIELDING			
Year	Team (League)	Pos.	G	AB	R	H	2B	3B	HR	RBI	Avg.	BB	SO	SB	PO	A	E	Avg.
1978	—Helena (Pioneer)	OF	33	106	20	33	6	1	0	14	.311	9	18	3	39	4	4	.915
1979	—Sp'rt'brg (W. Caro.)	OF	130	491	78	150	24	*15	22	*102	.305	26	98	10	206	14	8	.965
1980	—Reading (Eastern)	OF	22	55	11	17	5	2	0	11	.309	3	8	3	24	0	1	.960
1981	—Toronto (A.L.)	OF	60	163	19	38	2	1	5	12	.233	5	27	3	92	3	3	.969
1982	—Syracuse (Int'l)	OF	37	125	11	25	5	4	3	19	.200	1	42	2	72	3	1	.987
1983	—Syracuse (Int'l)	OF	85	317	37	86	11	4	15	59	.271	23	54	5	135	12	6	.961
	—Toronto (A.L.)	OF	39	112	5	30	5	4	2	17	.268	4	17	1	61	1	3	.954
1984	—Toronto (A.L.)	OF-3B	159	606	85	177	39	4	26	87	.292	24	86	11	289	13	9	.971
1985	—Toronto (A.L.)	OF-1B	157	607	87	167	28	6	28	95	.275	43	90	21	320	14	‡11	.968
1986	—Toronto (A.L.)	OF-3B	159	641	101	198	38	6	31	108	.309	41	62	7	270	17	10	.966
1987	—Toronto (A.L.)	OF-2B-3B	156	610	111	188	32	4	47	*134	.308	39	75	5	249	14	11	.960
1988	—Toronto (A.L.)	OF	156	614	78	165	27	5	24	97	.269	34	66	4	253	8	15	.946
1989	—Toronto (A.L.)	OF	153	613	88	182	41	2	18	104	.297	33	60	4	258	4	•10	.963
1990	—Toronto (A.L.)	OF	142	562	67	149	25	0	21	86	.265	32	80	3	226	4	5	.979
1991	—Chicago (N.L.)■	OF	149	558	63	159	27	0	25	86	.285	32	62	2	249	6	*10	.962
1992	—Chicago (A.L.)■	OF	155	627	74	160	27	0	25	112	.255	31	97	5	27	0	1	.964
1993	—Chicago (A.L.)	DH	102	410	36	89	17	2	13	64	.217	13	49	1	...	...	...	...
	—South Bend (Mid.)	DH	2	8	1	1	0	0	0	0	.125	1	0	0	...	...	...	...
American League totals (11 years)			1438	5565	751	1543	281	34	240	916	.277	299	709	65	2045	78	78	.965
National League totals (1 year)			149	558	63	159	27	0	25	86	.285	32	62	2	249	6	10	.962
Major league totals (12 years)			1587	6123	814	1702	308	34	265	1002	.278	331	771	67	2294	84	88	.964

CHAMPIONSHIP SERIES RECORD

			BATTING												FIELDING			
Year	Team (League)	Pos.	G	AB	R	H	2B	3B	HR	RBI	Avg.	BB	SO	SB	PO	A	E	Avg.
1985	—Toronto (A.L.)	OF	7	28	4	9	3	0	0	1	.321	0	4	0	13	0	0	1.000
1989	—Toronto (A.L.)	DH-OF	5	20	2	4	0	0	1	2	.200	0	3	0	3	1	0	1.000
1993	—Chicago (A.L.)								Did not play.									
Championship series totals (2 years)			12	48	6	13	3	0	1	3	.271	0	7	0	16	1	0	1.000

ALL-STAR GAME RECORD

			BATTING										FIELDING			
Year	League	Pos.	AB	R	H	2B	3B	HR	RBI	Avg.	BB	SO	SB	PO	A	E	Avg.
1987	—American	OF	3	0	0	0	0	0	0	.000	0	0	0	1	0	0	1.000
1990	—American	PH-OF	2	0	0	0	0	0	0	.000	0	1	0	2	0	0	1.000
1991	—National	PH	1	0	0	0	0	0	0	.000	0	1	0	...	...	...	...
All-Star Game totals (3 years)			6	0	0	0	0	0	0	.000	0	2	0	3	0	0	1.000

BELL, JAY

SS, PIRATES

PERSONAL: Born December 11, 1965, at Eglin AFB, Fla. . . . 6-0/185. . . . Throws right, bats right. . . . Full name: Jay Stuart Bell.

HIGH SCHOOL: Tate (Gonzalez, Fla.).

TRANSACTIONS/CAREER NOTES: Selected by Minnesota Twins organization in first round (eighth pick overall) of free-agent draft (June 4, 1984). . . . Traded by Twins with P Curt Wardle, OF Jim Weaver and a player to be named later to Cleveland Indians for P Bert Blyleven (August 1, 1985); Indians organization acquired P Rich Yett to complete deal (September 17, 1985). . . . Traded by Indians to Pittsburgh Pirates for SS Felix Fermin (March 25, 1989).

HONORS: Named shortstop on THE SPORTING NEWS N.L. All-Star team (1993). . . . Won N.L. Gold Glove at shortstop (1993). . . . Named shortstop on THE SPORTING NEWS N.L. Silver Slugger team (1993).

STATISTICAL NOTES: Led Appalachian League shortstops with 352 total chances and 43 double plays in 1984. . . . Led California League shortstops with 84 double plays in 1985. . . . Hit home run in first major league at-bat on first pitch (September 29, 1986). . . . Led Eastern League shortstops with 613 total chances in 1986. . . . Led American Association shortstops with 198 putouts, 322 assists, 30 errors and 550 total chances in 1987. . . . Led N.L. with 39 sacrifice hits in 1990 and 30 in 1991. . . . Led N.L. shortstops with 741 total chances in 1990, 754 in 1991, 816 in 1992 and 794 in 1993. . . . Led N.L. shortstops with 94 double plays in 1992.

			BATTING												FIELDING			
Year	Team (League)	Pos.	G	AB	R	H	2B	3B	HR	RBI	Avg.	BB	SO	SB	PO	A	E	Avg.
1984	—Elizabeth. (Appal.)	SS	66	245	43	54	12	1	6	30	.220	42	50	4	*109	*218	25	.929
1985	—Visalia (California)	SS	106	376	56	106	16	6	9	59	.282	41	73	10	176	330	53	.905
	—Waterbury (East.)■	SS	29	114	13	34	11	2	1	14	.298	9	16	3	41	79	6	.952
1986	—Waterbury (East.)	SS	138	494	86	137	28	4	7	74	.277	87	65	10	197	*371	*45	.927
	—Cleveland (A.L.)	2B	5	14	3	5	2	0	1	4	.357	2	3	0	1	6	2	.778
1987	—Buffalo (A.A.)	SS-2B	110	362	71	94	15	4	17	60	.260	70	84	6	†201	†325	†30	.946
	—Cleveland (A.L.)	SS	38	125	14	27	9	1	2	13	.216	8	31	2	67	93	9	.947
1988	—Cleveland (A.L.)	SS	73	211	23	46	5	1	2	21	.218	21	53	4	103	170	10	.965
	—Colo. Springs (PCL)	SS	49	181	35	50	12	2	7	24	.276	26	27	3	87	171	18	.935
1989	—Pittsburgh (N.L.)■	SS	78	271	33	70	13	3	2	27	.258	19	47	5	109	197	10	.968
	—Buffalo (A.A.)	SS-3B	86	298	49	85	15	3	10	54	.285	38	55	12	110	223	16	.954
1990	—Pittsburgh (N.L.)	SS	159	583	93	148	28	7	7	52	.254	65	109	10	*260	459	22	.970
1991	—Pittsburgh (N.L.)	SS	157	608	96	164	32	8	16	67	.270	52	99	10	239	*491	*24	.968
1992	—Pittsburgh (N.L.)	SS	159	632	87	167	36	6	9	55	.264	55	103	7	*268	*526	22	.973
1993	—Pittsburgh (N.L.)	SS	154	604	102	187	32	9	9	51	.310	77	122	16	*256	*527	11	*.986
American League totals (3 years)			116	350	40	78	16	2	5	38	.223	31	87	6	171	269	21	.954
National League totals (5 years)			707	2698	411	736	141	33	43	252	.273	268	480	48	1132	2200	89	.974
Major league totals (8 years)			823	3048	451	814	157	35	48	290	.267	299	567	54	1303	2469	110	.972

CHAMPIONSHIP SERIES RECORD

CHAMPIONSHIP SERIES NOTES: Holds N.L. single-series record for most singles—9 (1991).

			BATTING												FIELDING			
Year	Team (League)	Pos.	G	AB	R	H	2B	3B	HR	RBI	Avg.	BB	SO	SB	PO	A	E	Avg.
1990	—Pittsburgh (N.L.)	SS	6	20	3	5	1	0	1	1	.250	4	3	0	4	22	1	.963
1991	—Pittsburgh (N.L.)	SS	7	29	2	12	2	0	1	1	.414	0	10	0	13	19	1	.970
1992	—Pittsburgh (N.L.)	SS	7	29	3	5	2	0	1	4	.172	3	4	0	6	8	1	.933
Championship series totals (3 years)			20	78	8	22	5	0	3	6	.282	7	17	0	23	49	3	.960

ALL-STAR GAME RECORD

			BATTING											FIELDING			
Year	League	Pos.	AB	R	H	2B	3B	HR	RBI	Avg.	BB	SO	SB	PO	A	E	Avg.
1993	—National	2B	1	0	0	0	0	0	0	.000	0	0	0	1	1	0	1.000

BELL, JUAN

2B/SS, BREWERS

PERSONAL: Born March 29, 1968, in San Pedro de Macoris, Dominican Republic. . . . 5-11/175. . . . Throws right, bats both. . . . Full name: Juan Mathey Bell. . . . Brother of George Bell, major league designated hitter/outfielder, Toronto Blue Jays, Chicago Cubs and Chicago White Sox (1981-93); and brother of Rolando Bell, minor league infielder (1985-87).

HIGH SCHOOL: Gastone F. Deligne (San Pedro de Macoris, Dominican Republic).

TRANSACTIONS/CAREER NOTES: Signed as free agent by Los Angeles Dodgers organization (September 1, 1984). . . . Traded by Dodgers organization with P Brian Holton and P Ken Howell to Baltimore Orioles for 1B Eddie Murray (December 4, 1988). . . . On Rochester disabled list (July 6-August 27, 1990). . . . Loaned by Rochester, Orioles organization, to Oklahoma City, Texas Rangers organization (June 2-August 11, 1992). . . . On Oklahoma City disabled list (June 8-July 24, 1992). . . . Traded by Orioles to Philadelphia Phillies for IF Steve Scarsone (August 11, 1992). . . . Claimed on waivers by Milwaukee Brewers (June 1, 1993).

STATISTICAL NOTES: Led Gulf Coast League shortstops with 293 total chances in 1986. . . . Led California League shortstops with 719 total chances in 1987.

MISCELLANEOUS: Batted righthanded only with Gulf Coast Dodgers (1986) and San Antonio (1988).

			BATTING												FIELDING			
Year	Team (League)	Pos.	G	AB	R	H	2B	3B	HR	RBI	Avg.	BB	SO	SB	PO	A	E	Avg.
1985	—GC Dodgers (GCL)	SS-2B	42	106	11	17	0	0	0	8	.160	12	20	2	56	73	20	.866
1986	—GC Dodgers (GCL)	SS	59	217	38	52	6	2	0	26	.240	29	28	12	78	*193	22	.925
1987	—Bakersfield (Calif.)	SS	134	473	54	116	15	3	4	58	.245	73	91	21	235	*431	*53	.926
1988	—San Antonio (Tex.)	SS	61	215	37	60	4	2	5	21	.279	16	37	11	106	182	20	.935
	—Albuquerque (PCL)	SS	73	257	42	77	9	3	8	45	.300	16	70	7	114	249	23	.940
1989	—Rochester (Int'l)■	SS	116	408	50	107	15	6	2	32	.262	39	92	17	190	297	36	.931
	—Baltimore (A.L.)	2B-SS	8	4	2	0	0	0	0	0	.000	0	1	1	2	6	0	1.000
1990	—Rochester (Int'l)	SS	82	326	59	93	12	5	6	35	.285	36	59	16	131	240	22	.944
	—Baltimore (A.L.)	SS	5	2	1	0	0	0	0	0	.000	0	1	0	1	1	0	1.000
1991	—Baltimore (A.L.)	2B-SS-OF	100	209	26	36	9	2	1	15	.172	8	51	0	107	199	9	.971
1992	—Rochester (Int'l)	SS-2B	39	138	21	27	6	3	2	14	.196	14	40	2	60	86	5	.967

Year	Team (League)	Pos.	G	AB	R	H	2B	3B	HR	RBI	Avg.	BB	SO	SB	PO	A	E	Avg.
			BATTING												FIELDING			
	—Okla. City (A.A.)■	SS	24	82	12	21	4	1	1	9	.256	4	19	2	35	62	5	.951
	—Philadelphia (N.L.)■	SS	46	147	12	30	3	1	1	8	.204	18	29	5	82	129	6	.972
1993	—Philadelphia (N.L.)	SS	24	65	5	13	6	1	0	7	.200	5	12	0	33	57	9	.909
	—Milwaukee (A.L.)■	2B-SS-OF	91	286	42	67	6	2	5	29	.234	36	64	6	185	224	12	.971
American League totals (4 years)			204	501	71	103	15	4	6	44	.206	44	117	7	295	430	21	.972
National League totals (2 years)			70	212	17	43	9	2	1	15	.203	23	41	5	115	186	15	.953
Major league totals (5 years)			274	713	88	146	24	6	7	59	.205	67	158	12	410	616	36	.966

BELLE, ALBERT

OF, INDIANS

PERSONAL: Born August 25, 1966, in Shreveport, La. ... 6-2/210. ... Throws right, bats right. ... Full name: Albert Jojuan Belle. ... Formerly known as Joey Belle.
HIGH SCHOOL: Huntington (Shreveport, La.).
COLLEGE: Louisiana State.
TRANSACTIONS/CAREER NOTES: Selected by Cleveland Indians organization in second round of free-agent draft (June 2, 1987). ... On suspended list (July 12-18, 1991; August 4-8, 1992 and June 4-7, 1993).
RECORDS: Shares A.L. single-season record for fewest errors by outfielder who led league in errors—9 (1991).
HONORS: Named outfielder on THE SPORTING NEWS A.L. All-Star team (1993). ... Named outfielder on THE SPORTING NEWS A.L. Silver Slugger team (1993).
STATISTICAL NOTES: Hit three home runs in one game (September 4, 1992). ... Led A.L. with 14 sacrifice flies in 1993. ... Led A.L. outfielders with seven double plays in 1993.

Year	Team (League)	Pos.	G	AB	R	H	2B	3B	HR	RBI	Avg.	BB	SO	SB	PO	A	E	Avg.
			BATTING												FIELDING			
1987	—Kinston (Carolina)	OF	10	37	5	12	2	0	3	9	.324	8	16	0	5	0	0	1.000
1988	—Kinston (Carolina)	OF	41	153	21	46	16	0	8	39	.301	18	45	2	43	5	5	.906
	—Waterloo (Midw.)	OF	9	28	2	7	1	0	1	2	.250	1	9	0	11	1	0	1.000
1989	—Cant./Akr. (East.)	OF	89	312	48	88	20	0	20	69	.282	32	82	8	136	4	3	.979
	—Cleveland (A.L.)	OF	62	218	22	49	8	4	7	37	.225	12	55	2	92	3	2	.979
1990	—Cleveland (A.L.)	OF	9	23	1	4	0	0	1	3	.174	1	6	0	0	0	0	...
	—Colo. Springs (PCL)	OF	24	96	16	33	3	1	5	19	.344	5	16	4	31	0	2	.939
	—Cant./Akr. (East.)	DH	9	32	4	8	1	0	0	3	.250	3	7	0	...	...	...	...
1991	—Cleveland (A.L.)	OF	123	461	60	130	31	2	28	95	.282	25	99	3	170	8	•9	.952
	—Colo. Springs (PCL)	OF	16	61	9	20	3	2	2	16	.328	2	8	1	19	1	1	.952
1992	—Cleveland (A.L.)	OF	153	585	81	152	23	1	34	112	.260	52	128	8	94	1	3	.969
1993	—Cleveland (A.L.)	OF	159	594	93	172	36	3	38	*129	.290	76	96	23	338	16	5	.986
Major league totals (5 years)			506	1881	257	507	98	10	108	376	.270	166	384	36	694	28	19	.974

ALL-STAR GAME RECORD

Year	League	Pos.	AB	R	H	2B	3B	HR	RBI	Avg.	BB	SO	SB	PO	A	E	Avg.
			BATTING											FIELDING			
1993	—American	PH-DH	1	2	1	0	0	0	1	1.000	1	0	0	...	...	...	...

BELLIARD, RAFAEL

SS, BRAVES

PERSONAL: Born October 24, 1961, in Pueblo Nuevo, Mao, Dominican Republic. ... 5-6/160. ... Throws right, bats right. ... Full name: Rafael Leonidas Matias Belliard. ... Name pronounced BELL-ee-ard.
TRANSACTIONS/CAREER NOTES: Signed as free agent by Pittsburgh Pirates organization (July 10, 1980). ... On Buffalo disabled list (April 19-July 24, 1982). ... On Pittsburgh disabled list (June 28-August 28, 1984; July 28-August 12, 1986; August 27, 1987-remainder of season; and May 19-June 3, 1988). ... Granted free agency (November 5, 1990). ... Signed by Atlanta Braves (December 18, 1990).
STATISTICAL NOTES: Led Carolina League with 12 sacrifice hits and tied for lead in caught stealing with 15 in 1981. ... Tied for Eastern League lead in double plays by shortstop with 69 in 1983. ... Led N.L. shortstops with .977 fielding percentage in 1988.

Year	Team (League)	Pos.	G	AB	R	H	2B	3B	HR	RBI	Avg.	BB	SO	SB	PO	A	E	Avg.
			BATTING												FIELDING			
1980	—GC Pirates (GCL)	SS-2B-3B	12	42	6	9	1	0	0	2	.214	0	3	1	24	39	1	.984
	—Shelby (S. Atl.)	SS	8	24	1	3	0	0	0	2	.125	1	3	0	10	27	5	.881
1981	—Alexandria (Caro.)	SS	127	472	58	102	6	5	0	33	.216	26	92	42	•205	330	29	.949
1982	—Buffalo (Eastern)	SS	40	124	14	34	1	1	0	19	.274	8	16	6	56	87	5	.966
	—Pittsburgh (N.L.)	SS	9	2	3	1	0	0	0	0	.500	0	0	1	2	2	0	1.000
1983	—Lynn (Eastern)	SS-2B	127	431	63	113	13	2	2	37	.262	30	54	12	203	307	26	.951
	—Pittsburgh (N.L.)	SS	4	1	1	0	0	0	0	0	.000	0	1	0	1	3	0	1.000
1984	—Pittsburgh (N.L.)	SS-2B	20	22	3	5	0	0	0	0	.227	0	1	0	12	13	3	.893
1985	—Pittsburgh (N.L.)	SS	17	20	1	4	0	0	0	1	.200	0	5	0	13	23	2	.947
	—Hawaii (PCL)	SS-2B	100	341	35	84	12	4	1	18	.246	4	49	9	172	289	5	.989
1986	—Pittsburgh (N.L.)	SS-2B	117	309	33	72	5	2	0	31	.233	26	54	12	147	317	12	.975
1987	—Pittsburgh (N.L.)	SS-2B	81	203	26	42	4	3	1	15	.207	20	25	5	113	191	6	.981
	—Harrisburg (East.)	SS	37	145	24	49	5	2	0	9	.338	6	16	7	59	115	7	.961
1988	—Pittsburgh (N.L.)	SS-2B	122	286	28	61	0	4	0	11	.213	26	47	7	134	261	9	†.978
1989	—Pittsburgh (N.L.)	SS-2B-3B	67	154	10	33	4	0	0	8	.214	8	22	5	71	138	3	.986
1990	—Pittsburgh (N.L.)	2B-SS-3B	47	54	10	11	3	0	0	6	.204	5	13	1	37	36	2	.973
1991	—Atlanta (N.L.)■	SS	149	353	36	88	9	2	0	27	.249	22	63	3	168	361	18	.967
1992	—Atlanta (N.L.)	SS-2B	144	285	20	60	6	1	0	14	.211	14	43	0	152	291	14	.969
1993	—Atlanta (N.L.)	SS-2B	91	79	6	18	5	0	0	6	.228	4	13	0	53	99	1	.993
Major league totals (12 years)			868	1768	177	395	36	12	1	119	.223	125	287	34	903	1735	70	.974

CHAMPIONSHIP SERIES RECORD

Year	Team (League)	Pos.	BATTING G	AB	R	H	2B	3B	HR	RBI	Avg.	BB	SO	SB	FIELDING PO	A	E	Avg.
1990	—Pittsburgh (N.L.)		Did not play.															
1991	—Atlanta (N.L.)	SS	7	19	0	4	0	0	0	1	.211	3	3	0	9	15	1	.960
1992	—Atlanta (N.L.)	SS-2B-PR	4	2	1	0	0	0	0	0	.000	1	0	0	2	3	0	1.000
1993	—Atlanta (N.L.)	PH-2-PR-S	2	1	1	0	0	0	0	0	.000	0	1	0	0	0	0	...
Championship series totals (3 years)			13	22	2	4	0	0	0	1	.182	4	4	0	11	18	1	.967

WORLD SERIES RECORD

Year	Team (League)	Pos.	BATTING G	AB	R	H	2B	3B	HR	RBI	Avg.	BB	SO	SB	FIELDING PO	A	E	Avg.
1991	—Atlanta (N.L.)	SS	7	16	0	6	1	0	0	4	.375	1	2	0	8	21	0	1.000
1992	—Atlanta (N.L.)	SS-2B	4	4	0	0	0	0	0	0	.000	0	0	0	3	2	0	1.000
World Series totals (2 years)			11	20	0	6	1	0	0	4	.300	1	2	0	11	23	0	1.000

BELTRE, ESTEBAN

SS, WHITE SOX

PERSONAL: Born December 26, 1967, in Ingenio Quisfuella, Dominican Republic. . . . 5-10/172. . . . Throws right, bats right. . . . Full name: Esteban Valera Beltre. . . . Name pronounced BELL-tray.

HIGH SCHOOL: Eugenio Mariade Hostos (Dominican Republic).

TRANSACTIONS/CAREER NOTES: Signed as a free agent by the Montreal Expos (May 9, 1989). . . . Loaned by Expos organization to Utica, independent (June 16-September 16, 1985). . . . Granted free agency (January 1, 1991). . . . Signed by Vancouver, Milwaukee Brewers organization (March 16, 1991). . . . Traded by Brewers organization to Chicago White Sox organization for OF John Cangelosi (May 23, 1991).

STATISTICAL NOTES: Led American Association shortstops with 580 total chances in 1990 and 624 in 1993.

Year	Team (League)	Pos.	BATTING G	AB	R	H	2B	3B	HR	RBI	Avg.	BB	SO	SB	FIELDING PO	A	E	Avg.
1984	—Calgary (Pioneer)	SS	18	20	1	4	0	0	0	2	.200	2	8	1	13	13	10	.722
1985	—Utica (N.Y.-Penn)■	SS	72	241	19	48	6	2	0	22	.199	18	58	8	106	206	26	.923
1986	—W.P. Beach (FSL)■	SS	97	285	24	69	11	1	1	20	.242	16	59	4	116	273	23	.944
1987	—Jacksonv. (South.)	SS	142	491	55	104	15	4	4	34	.212	40	98	9	*198	*358	*35	.941
1988	—Jacksonv. (South.)	SS	35	113	5	17	2	0	0	6	.150	3	28	1	39	87	11	.920
	—W.P. Beach (FSL)	SS	69	226	23	63	5	6	0	15	.279	11	38	4	99	204	19	.941
1989	—Rockford (Midw.)	SS	104	375	42	80	15	3	2	33	.213	33	83	9	183	336	30	*.945
1990	—Indianapolis (A.A.)	SS	133	407	33	92	11	2	1	37	.226	32	77	8	215	*335	*30	.948
1991	—Denver (A.A.)■	SS	27	78	11	14	1	3	0	9	.179	9	16	3	52	64	13	.899
	—Vancouver (PCL)■	SS-2B	88	347	48	94	11	3	0	30	.271	23	61	8	129	243	26	.935
	—Chicago (A.L.)	SS	8	6	0	1	0	0	0	0	.167	1	1	1	1	5	0	1.000
1992	—Vancouver (PCL)	SS	40	161	17	43	5	2	0	16	.267	8	27	4	70	109	10	.947
	—Chicago (A.L.)	SS	49	110	21	21	2	0	1	10	.191	3	18	1	53	92	12	.924
1993	—Nashville (A.A.)	SS	134	489	67	143	24	4	8	52	.292	33	102	18	190	*404	*30	.952
Major league totals (2 years)			57	116	21	22	2	0	1	10	.190	4	19	2	54	97	12	.926

BENAVIDES, FREDDIE

SS/2B, EXPOS

PERSONAL: Born April 7, 1966, in Laredo, Tex. . . . 6-2/185. . . . Throws right, bats right. . . . Full name: Alfredo Benavides III. . . . Name pronounced BEN-uh-VEE-diss.

HIGH SCHOOL: Nixon (Laredo, Tex.).

COLLEGE: Texas Christian.

TRANSACTIONS/CAREER NOTES: Selected by Cincinnati Reds organization in second round of free-agent draft (June 2, 1987). . . . Selected by Colorado Rockies in second round (28th pick overall) of expansion draft (November 17, 1992). . . . On Colorado disabled list (May 6-21, 1993). . . . On Colorado disabled list (May 29-June 24, 1993); included rehabilitation assignment to Colorado Springs (June 18-24). . . . Traded by Rockies to Montreal Expos for P Ivan Arteaga and P Rodney Pedraza (January 7, 1994).

Year	Team (League)	Pos.	BATTING G	AB	R	H	2B	3B	HR	RBI	Avg.	BB	SO	SB	FIELDING PO	A	E	Avg.
1987	—Ced. Rap. (Midw.)	SS	5	15	2	2	1	0	0	0	.133	0	7	0	7	7	4	.778
1988	—Ced. Rap. (Midw.)	SS	88	314	38	70	9	2	1	32	.223	35	75	18	118	210	24	.932
1989	—Chatt. (South.)	SS	88	284	25	71	14	3	0	27	.250	22	46	1	129	230	20	.947
	—Nashville (A.A.)	SS	31	94	9	16	4	0	1	12	.170	6	24	0	40	73	7	.942
1990	—Chatt. (South.)	SS	55	197	20	51	10	1	1	28	.259	11	25	4	76	157	7	.971
	—Nashville (A.A.)	SS	77	266	30	56	7	3	2	20	.211	12	50	3	134	200	16	.954
1991	—Nashville (A.A.)	SS-2B	94	331	24	80	8	0	0	21	.242	16	55	7	148	269	11	.974
	—Cincinnati (N.L.)	SS-2B	24	63	11	18	1	0	0	3	.286	1	15	1	33	53	2	.977
1992	—Cincinnati (N.L.)	2B-SS-3B	74	173	14	40	10	1	1	17	.231	10	34	0	80	129	6	.972
1993	—Colorado (N.L.)■	S-2-3-1	74	213	20	61	10	3	3	26	.286	6	27	3	98	158	13	.952
	—Colo. Springs (PCL)	SS	5	16	3	7	1	0	0	2	.438	1	0	0	4	12	0	1.000
Major league totals (3 years)			172	449	45	119	21	4	4	46	.265	17	76	4	211	340	21	.963

BENES, ANDY

P, PADRES

PERSONAL: Born August 20, 1967, in Evansville, Ind. . . . 6-6/240. . . . Throws right, bats right. . . . Full name: Andrew Charles Benes. . . . Brother of Alan Benes, pitcher, St. Louis Cardinals organization. . . . Name pronounced BEN-ess.

HIGH SCHOOL: Central (Evansville, Ind.).

COLLEGE: Evansville.

TRANSACTIONS/CAREER NOTES: Selected by San Diego Padres organization in first round (first pick overall) of free-agent draft (June 1, 1988). . . . On suspended list (September 28, 1993-remainder of season).

RECORDS: Holds major league single-season record for fewest hits allowed for leader in most hits allowed—230 (1992).
HONORS: Named N.L. Rookie Pitcher of the Year by THE SPORTING NEWS (1989).... Named Texas League Pitcher of the Year (1989).
STATISTICAL NOTES: Tied for N.L. lead with five balks in 1990.
MISCELLANEOUS: Member of 1988 U.S. Olympic baseball team.

Year	Team (League)	W	L	Pct.	ERA	G	GS	CG	ShO	Sv.	IP	H	R	ER	BB	SO
1989	—Wichita (Texas)	8	4	.667	2.16	16	16	5	*3	0	108⅓	79	32	26	39	115
	—Las Vegas (PCL)	2	1	.667	8.10	5	5	0	0	0	26⅔	41	29	24	12	29
	—San Diego (N.L.)	6	3	.667	3.51	10	10	0	0	0	66⅔	51	28	26	31	66
1990	—San Diego (N.L.)	10	11	.476	3.60	32	31	2	0	0	192⅓	177	87	77	69	140
1991	—San Diego (N.L.)	15	11	.577	3.03	33	33	4	1	0	223	194	76	75	59	167
1992	—San Diego (N.L.)	13	14	.481	3.35	34	34	2	2	0	231⅓	*230	90	86	61	169
1993	—San Diego (N.L.)	15	15	.500	3.78	34	34	4	2	0	230⅔	200	111	97	86	179
Major league totals (5 years)		59	54	.522	3.44	143	142	12	5	0	944	852	392	361	306	721

ALL-STAR GAME RECORD

Year	League	W	L	Pct.	ERA	GS	CG	ShO	Sv.	IP	H	R	ER	BB	SO
1993	—National	0	0	...	4.50	0	0	0	0	2	2	1	1	0	2

BENITEZ, ARMANDO

P, ORIOLES

PERSONAL: Born November 3, 1972, in Ramon Santana, Dominican Republic.... 6-4/180.... Throws right, bats right.
TRANSACTIONS/CAREER NOTES: Signed as free agent by Baltimore Orioles organization (April 1, 1990).

Year	Team (League)	W	L	Pct.	ERA	G	GS	CG	ShO	Sv.	IP	H	R	ER	BB	SO
1990	—	Dominican Summer League statistics unavailable.														
1991	—GC Orioles (GCL)	3	2	.600	2.72	14	3	0	0	0	36⅓	35	16	11	11	33
1992	—Bluefield (Appal.)	1	2	.333	4.31	25	0	0	0	5	31⅓	35	31	15	23	37
1993	—Albany (S. Atl.)	5	1	.833	1.52	40	0	0	0	14	53⅓	31	10	9	19	83
	—Frederick (Caro.)	3	0	1.000	0.66	12	0	0	0	4	13⅔	7	1	1	4	29

BENITEZ, YAMIL

OF, EXPOS

PERSONAL: Born October 5, 1972, in San Juan, Puerto Rico.... 6-2/190.... Throws right, bats right.... Full name: Yamil Antonio Benitez.
TRANSACTIONS/CAREER NOTES: Signed as free agent by Montreal Expos organization (October 26, 1989).

			BATTING											FIELDING			
Year	Team (League)	Pos.	G	AB	R	H	2B	3B	HR	RBI	Avg.	BB	SO	SB	PO	A	E	Avg.
1990	—GC Expos (GCL)	OF	22	83	6	19	1	0	1	5	.229	8	18	0	38	2	1	.976
1991	—GC Expos (GCL)	OF	54	197	20	47	9	5	5	38	.239	12	55	10	85	2	3	.967
1992	—Albany (S. Atl.)	OF	23	79	6	13	3	2	1	6	.165	5	49	0	30	0	1	.968
	—Jamestown (NYP)	OF	44	162	24	44	6	6	3	23	.272	14	52	19	61	2	1	.984
1993	—Burlington (Midw.)	OF	111	411	70	112	21	5	15	61	.273	29	99	18	167	4	10	.945

BENJAMIN, MIKE

IF, GIANTS

PERSONAL: Born November 22, 1965, in Euclid, O.... 6-0/169.... Throws right, bats right.... Full name: Michael Paul Benjamin.
HIGH SCHOOL: Bellflower (Calif.).
COLLEGE: Cerritos College (Calif.) and Arizona State.
TRANSACTIONS/CAREER NOTES: Selected by Minnesota Twins organization in seventh round of free-agent draft (January 9, 1985).... Selected by San Francisco Giants organization in third round of free-agent draft (June 2, 1987).... On San Francisco disabled list (March 31-June 5, 1992); included rehabilitation assignment to Phoenix (April 20-May 10).... On San Francisco disabled list (July 8-August 6, 1993); included rehabilitation assignment to San Jose (August 4-6).
STATISTICAL NOTES: Led Pacific Coast League shortstops with 626 total chances in 1990.

			BATTING											FIELDING			
Year	Team (League)	Pos.	G	AB	R	H	2B	3B	HR	RBI	Avg.	BB	SO	SB	PO	A	E	Avg.
1987	—Fresno (California)	SS	64	212	25	51	6	4	6	24	.241	24	71	6	89	188	21	.930
1988	—Shreveport (Texas)	SS	89	309	48	73	19	5	6	37	.236	22	63	14	134	248	11	.972
	—Phoenix (PCL)	SS	37	106	13	18	4	1	0	6	.170	13	32	2	41	74	4	.966
1989	—Phoenix (PCL)	SS-2B	113	363	44	94	17	6	3	36	.259	18	82	10	149	332	15	.970
	—San Francisco (N.L.)	SS	14	6	6	1	0	0	0	0	.167	0	1	0	4	4	0	1.000
1990	—Phoenix (PCL)	SS	118	419	61	105	21	7	5	39	.251	25	89	13	*216	*386	24	.962
	—San Francisco (N.L.)	SS	22	56	7	12	3	1	2	3	.214	3	10	1	29	53	1	.988
1991	—San Francisco (N.L.)	SS-3B	54	106	12	13	3	0	2	8	.123	7	26	3	64	123	3	.984
	—Phoenix (PCL)	SS	64	226	34	46	13	2	6	31	.204	20	67	3	109	252	9	.976
1992	—San Francisco (N.L.)	SS-3B	40	75	4	13	2	1	1	3	.173	4	15	1	34	71	1	.991
	—Phoenix (PCL)	SS-2B	31	108	15	33	10	2	0	17	.306	3	18	4	51	92	2	.986
1993	—San Francisco (N.L.)	SS-2B-3B	63	146	22	29	7	0	4	16	.199	9	23	0	74	133	5	.976
	—San Jose (Calif.)	SS-2B	2	8	1	0	0	0	0	0	.000	1	0	0	1	5	0	1.000
Major league totals (5 years)			193	389	51	68	15	2	9	30	.175	23	75	5	205	384	10	.983

BENZINGER, TODD

1B/OF, GIANTS

PERSONAL: Born February 11, 1963, in Dayton, Ky.... 6-1/195.... Throws right, bats both.... Full name: Todd Eric Benzinger.... Nephew of Don Gross, pitcher, Cincinnati Reds and Pittsburgh Pirates (1955-60).... Name pronounced BEN-zing-er.
HIGH SCHOOL: New Richmond (Richmond, O.).
TRANSACTIONS/CAREER NOTES: Selected by Boston Red Sox organization in fourth round of free-agent draft (June 8, 1981).... On disabled list (August 10, 1984-remainder of season; April 10-June 11, 1985; April 11-21 and June 26-July 17, 1986; and

June 3-22, 1988).... Traded by Red Sox with P Jeff Sellers and a player to be named later to Cincinnati Reds for 1B Nick Esasky and P Rob Murphy (December 13, 1988); Reds acquired P Luis Vasquez to complete deal (January 12, 1989).... Traded by Reds to Kansas City Royals for 1B/OF Carmelo Martinez (July 11, 1991).... Traded by Royals to Los Angeles Dodgers for OF Chris Gwynn and 2B Domingo Mota (December 11, 1991).... Granted free agency (December 19, 1992).... Signed by San Francisco Giants (January 13, 1993).
STATISTICAL NOTES: Switch-hit home runs in one game (August 30, 1993).

			BATTING											FIELDING			
Year	Team (League)	Pos.	G	AB	R	H	2B	3B	HR	RBI	Avg.	BB	SO	SB	PO	A	E	Avg.
1981	—Elmira (N.Y.-Penn)..	OF-1B	41	141	21	34	10	1	2	8	.241	20	32	4	131	9	2	.986
1982	—Winst.-Salem (Car.)..	OF-1B	121	443	54	97	19	1	5	46	.219	41	71	4	438	28	8	.983
1983	—Winter Haven (FSL)..	OF-1B-3B	125	480	56	134	34	5	7	68	.279	43	75	4	206	10	8	.964
1984	—New Britain (East.)..	OF-1B	110	391	49	101	25	5	10	60	.258	33	89	0	465	29	14	.972
1985	—Pawtucket (Int'l)	OF	70	256	31	64	13	1	11	47	.250	12	49	0	106	3	3	.973
1986	—Pawtucket (Int'l)	OF-1B	90	314	41	79	13	2	11	32	.252	23	76	7	156	4	2	.988
1987	—Pawtucket (Int'l)	OF-1B	65	257	47	83	17	3	13	49	.323	16	41	7	256	16	2	.993
	—Boston (A.L.)	OF-1B	73	223	36	62	11	1	8	43	.278	22	41	5	155	7	2	.988
1988	—Boston (A.L.)	1B-OF	120	405	47	103	28	1	13	70	.254	22	80	2	602	38	6	.991
1989	—Cincinnati (N.L.)■	1B	161	*628	79	154	28	3	17	76	.245	44	120	3	1417	73	7	.995
1990	—Cincinnati (N.L.).......	1B-OF	118	376	35	95	14	2	5	46	.253	19	69	3	733	52	6	.992
1991	—Cincinnati (N.L.).......	1B-OF	51	123	7	23	3	2	1	11	.187	10	20	2	146	13	2	.988
	—Kansas City (A.L.)■.	1B	78	293	29	86	15	3	2	40	.294	17	46	2	651	38	3	.996
1992	—Los Angeles (N.L.)■.	OF-1B	121	293	24	70	16	2	4	31	.239	15	54	2	263	18	1	.996
1993	—San Francisco (N.L.)■	1B-OF-3B	86	177	25	51	7	2	6	26	.288	13	35	0	299	15	0	1.000
American League totals (3 years)			271	921	112	251	54	5	23	153	.273	61	167	9	1408	83	11	.993
National League totals (5 years)			537	1597	170	393	68	11	33	190	.246	101	298	10	2858	171	16	.995
Major league totals (7 years)			808	2518	282	644	122	16	56	343	.256	162	465	19	4266	254	27	.994

CHAMPIONSHIP SERIES RECORD

			BATTING											FIELDING			
Year	Team (League)	Pos.	G	AB	R	H	2B	3B	HR	RBI	Avg.	BB	SO	SB	PO	A	E	Avg.
1988	—Boston (A.L.)	1B-PH	4	11	0	1	0	0	0	0	.091	1	3	0	21	1	0	1.000
1990	—Cincinnati (N.L.).......	PH-1B	5	9	0	3	0	0	0	0	.333	2	0	0	17	0	0	1.000
Championship series totals (2 years)			9	20	0	4	0	0	0	0	.200	3	3	0	38	1	0	1.000

WORLD SERIES RECORD

			BATTING											FIELDING			
Year	Team (League)	Pos.	G	AB	R	H	2B	3B	HR	RBI	Avg.	BB	SO	SB	PO	A	E	Avg.
1990	—Cincinnati (N.L.).......	1B-PH	4	11	1	2	0	0	0	0	.182	0	0	0	24	0	0	1.000

BERE, JASON
P, WHITE SOX

PERSONAL: Born May 26, 1971, in Cambridge, Mass.... 6-3/185.... Throws right, bats right.... Full name: Jason Phillip Bere.... Name pronounced burr-AY.
HIGH SCHOOL: Wilmington (Mass.).
COLLEGE: Middlesex Community College (Mass.).
TRANSACTIONS/CAREER NOTES: Selected by Chicago White Sox organization in 36th round of free-agent draft (June 4, 1990).

Year	Team (League)	W	L	Pct.	ERA	G	GS	CG	ShO	Sv.	IP	H	R	ER	BB	SO
1990	—GC Whi. Sox (GCL)	0	4	.000	2.37	16	2	0	0	1	38	26	19	10	19	41
1991	—South Bend (Mid.)	9	12	.429	2.87	27	27	2	1	0	163	116	66	52	*100	158
1992	—Sarasota (Fla. St.)	7	2	.778	2.41	18	18	1	1	0	116	84	35	31	34	106
	—Birm. (Southern)	4	4	.500	3.00	8	8	4	2	0	54	44	22	18	20	45
	—Vancouver (PCL)	0	0	...	0.00	1	0	0	0	0	1	2	0	0	0	2
1993	—Nashville (A.A.)	5	1	.833	2.37	8	8	0	0	0	49⅓	36	19	13	25	52
	—Chicago (A.L.)............	12	5	.706	3.47	24	24	1	0	0	142⅔	109	60	55	81	129
Major league totals (1 year) ...		12	5	.706	3.47	24	24	1	0	0	142⅔	109	60	55	81	129

CHAMPIONSHIP SERIES RECORD

Year	Team (League)	W	L	Pct.	ERA	G	GS	CG	ShO	Sv.	IP	H	R	ER	BB	SO
1993	—Chicago (A.L.)............	0	0	...	11.57	1	1	0	0	0	2⅓	5	3	3	2	3

BERGMAN, SEAN
P, TIGERS

PERSONAL: Born April 11, 1970, in Joliet, Ill.... 6-4/205.... Throws right, bats right.... Full name: Sean Frederick Bergman.
HIGH SCHOOL: Joliet (Ill.) Catholic Academy.
COLLEGE: Southern Illinois.
TRANSACTIONS/CAREER NOTES: Selected by Detroit Tigers organization in fourth round of free-agent draft (June 3, 1991).

Year	Team (League)	W	L	Pct.	ERA	G	GS	CG	ShO	Sv.	IP	H	R	ER	BB	SO
1991	—Niag. Falls (NYP)	5	7	.417	4.46	15	15	0	0	0	84⅔	87	57	42	42	77
1992	—Lakeland (Fla. St.)	5	2	.714	2.49	13	13	0	0	0	83	61	28	23	14	67
	—London (Eastern)........	4	7	.364	4.28	14	14	1	0	0	88⅓	85	52	42	45	59
1993	—Toledo (Int'l)	8	9	.471	4.38	19	19	3	0	0	117	124	62	57	53	91
	—Detroit (A.L.)	1	4	.200	5.67	9	6	1	0	0	39⅔	47	29	25	23	19
Major league totals (1 year) ...		1	4	.200	5.67	9	6	1	0	0	39⅔	47	29	25	23	19

BERROA, GERONIMO
OF

PERSONAL: Born March 18, 1965, in Santo Domingo, Dominican Republic.... 6-0/195.... Throws right, bats right.... Full name: Geronimo Emiliano Berroa.... Name pronounced her-ON-i-mo bur-OH-uh.
TRANSACTIONS/CAREER NOTES: Signed as free agent by Toronto Blue Jays organi-

zation (September 4, 1983).... Selected by Atlanta Braves from Blue Jays organization in Rule 5 major league draft (December 5, 1988).... Released by Braves (February 1, 1991).... Signed by Calgary, Seattle Mariners organization (February 27, 1991).... Contract sold by Mariners organization to Colorado Springs, Cleveland Indians organization (March 28, 1991).... Granted free agency (October 15, 1991).... Signed by Nashville, Cincinnati Reds organization (October 31, 1991).... Released by Reds (November 20, 1992).... Signed by Florida Marlins (December 9, 1992).... Granted free agency (October 15, 1993).

STATISTICAL NOTES: Led Southern League with 297 total bases in 1987.... Led International League in being hit by pitch with 10 and tied for lead with eight sacrifice flies in 1988.... Led International League in grounding into double plays with 17 in 1990.

			BATTING												FIELDING			
Year	Team (League)	Pos.	G	AB	R	H	2B	3B	HR	RBI	Avg.	BB	SO	SB	PO	A	E	Avg.
1984	—GC Blue Jays (GCL)..	OF-1B	62	235	31	59	16	1	3	34	.251	12	34	2	104	2	5	.955
1985	—Kinston (Carolina)...	OF	19	43	4	8	0	0	1	4	.186	4	10	0	13	1	1	.933
	—Medicine Hat (Pio.)..	OF	54	201	39	69	*22	2	6	45	.343	18	40	7	58	3	3	.953
	—Florence (S. Atl.)......	OF	19	66	7	21	2	0	3	20	.318	6	13	0	24	0	2	.923
1986	—Ventura (Calif.)........	OF	128	459	76	137	22	5	21	73	.298	38	92	12	194	9	14	.935
	—Knoxville (South.)....	OF	1	4	0	0	0	0	0	0	.000	0	1	0	2	0	0	1.000
1987	—Knoxville (South.)....	OF	134	523	87	150	33	3	36	108	.287	46	104	2	236	6	•15	.942
1988	—Syracuse (Int'l)........	OF	131	470	55	122	•29	1	8	64	.260	38	88	7	243	12	5	.981
1989	—Atlanta (N.L.)■.........	OF	81	136	7	36	4	0	2	9	.265	7	32	0	67	1	2	.971
1990	—Richmond (Int'l).......	OF	135	499	56	134	17	2	12	80	.269	34	89	4	200	10	7	.968
	—Atlanta (N.L.)...........	OF	7	4	0	0	0	0	0	0	.000	1	1	0	1	0	0	1.000
1991	—Colo. Springs (PCL)■	OF	125	478	81	154	31	7	18	91	.322	35	88	2	151	14	5	.971
1992	—Nashville (A.A.)■......	OF	112	461	73	151	33	2	22	88	.328	32	69	8	194	16	5	.977
	—Cincinnati (N.L.).......	OF	13	15	2	4	1	0	0	0	.267	2	1	0	2	1	0	1.000
1993	—Edmonton (PCL)■.....	OF-1B	90	327	64	107	33	4	16	68	.327	36	71	1	210	10	7	.969
	—Florida (N.L.)...........	OF	14	34	3	4	1	0	0	0	.118	2	7	0	9	1	2	.833
Major league totals (4 years)..................			115	189	12	44	6	0	2	9	.233	12	41	0	79	3	4	.953

BERRY, SEAN

3B, EXPOS

PERSONAL: Born March 22, 1966, in Santa Monica, Calif.... 5-11/200.... Throws right, bats right.... Full name: Sean Robert Berry.

HIGH SCHOOL: West Torrance (Torrance, Calif.).

COLLEGE: UCLA.

TRANSACTIONS/CAREER NOTES: Selected by Boston Red Sox organization in fourth round of free-agent draft (June 4, 1984).... Selected by Kansas City Royals organization in secondary phase of free-agent draft (January 14, 1986).... On disabled list (April 16-May 3, 1987).... Traded by Royals with P Archie Corbin to Montreal Expos for P Bill Sampen and P Chris Haney (August 29, 1992).

STATISTICAL NOTES: Led Northwest League third basemen with 11 double plays in 1986.

			BATTING												FIELDING			
Year	Team (League)	Pos.	G	AB	R	H	2B	3B	HR	RBI	Avg.	BB	SO	SB	PO	A	E	Avg.
1986	—Eugene (N'west).......	3B	65	238	53	76	20	2	5	44	.319	44	72	10	*63	96	21	.883
1987	—Fort Myers (FSL)......	3B	66	205	26	52	7	2	2	30	.254	46	65	5	39	101	23	.859
1988	—Baseball City (FSL)..	3B-SS-OF	94	304	34	71	6	4	4	30	.234	31	62	24	84	161	28	.897
1989	—Baseball City (FSL)..	3-0-2-S	116	399	67	106	19	7	4	44	.266	44	68	37	100	199	24	.926
1990	—Memphis (South.)....	3B	135	487	73	142	25	4	14	77	.292	44	89	18	79	238	27	.922
	—Kansas City (A.L.)....	3B	8	23	2	5	1	1	0	4	.217	2	5	0	7	10	1	.944
1991	—Omaha (A.A.)...........	3B-SS-2B	103	368	62	97	21	9	11	54	.264	48	70	8	75	206	20	.934
	—Kansas City (A.L.)....	3B	31	60	5	8	3	0	0	1	.133	5	23	0	13	52	2	.970
1992	—Omaha (A.A.)...........	3B	122	439	61	126	22	2	21	77	.287	39	87	6	86	239	21	*.939
	—Montreal (N.L.)■.......	3B	24	57	5	19	1	0	1	4	.333	1	11	2	10	19	4	.879
1993	—Montreal (N.L.).........	3B	122	299	50	78	15	2	14	49	.261	41	70	12	66	153	15	.936
American League totals (2 years)............			39	83	7	13	4	1	0	5	.157	7	28	0	20	62	3	.965
National League totals (2 years).............			146	356	55	97	16	2	15	53	.272	42	81	14	76	172	19	.929
Major league totals (4 years)..................			185	439	62	110	20	3	15	58	.251	49	109	14	96	234	22	.938

BERRYHILL, DAMON

C, RED SOX

PERSONAL: Born December 3, 1963, in South Laguna, Calif.... 6-0/205.... Throws right, bats both.... Full name: Damon Scott Berryhill.

HIGH SCHOOL: Laguna Beach (Calif.).

COLLEGE: Orange Coast College (Calif.).

TRANSACTIONS/CAREER NOTES: Selected by Chicago White Sox organization in 13th round of free-agent draft (January 11, 1983).... Selected by Chicago Cubs organization in first round (fourth pick overall) of free-agent draft (January 17, 1984).... On Chicago disabled list (June 30-July 15, 1988).... On Chicago disabled list (March 9-May 1, 1989); included rehabilitation assignment to Iowa (April 24-May 1).... On Chicago disabled list (August 19-September 29, 1989).... On Chicago disabled list (April 8-August 15, 1990); included rehabilitation assignment to Peoria (July 16-23) and Iowa (July 24-August 4).... Traded by Cubs with P Mike Bielecki to Atlanta Braves for P Turk Wendell and P Yorkis Perez (September 29, 1991).... Granted free agency (December 20, 1993).... Signed by Boston Red Sox organization (February 1, 1994).

STATISTICAL NOTES: Led Carolina League with 18 passed balls in 1985.... Led American Association catchers with .990 fielding percentage, 603 putouts, 66 assists, 676 total chances, 11 double plays and 15 passed balls in 1987.

MISCELLANEOUS: Batted righthanded only (1984).

			BATTING												FIELDING			
Year	Team (League)	Pos.	G	AB	R	H	2B	3B	HR	RBI	Avg.	BB	SO	SB	PO	A	E	Avg.
1984	—Quad Cities (Mid.)....	C-1B	62	217	30	60	14	0	0	31	.276	16	44	4	314	31	8	.977
1985	—Winst.-Salem (Car.)..	C-1B	117	386	31	90	25	1	9	50	.233	32	90	4	625	71	11	.984
1986	—Pittsfield (Eastern)..	C-OF	112	345	33	71	13	1	6	35	.206	37	54	2	449	61	12	.977
1987	—Iowa (Am. Assoc.)....	C-1B	121	429	54	123	22	1	18	67	.287	32	58	5	†607	†67	7	†.990
	—Chicago (N.L.)..........	C	12	28	2	5	1	0	0	1	.179	3	5	0	37	3	4	.909

Year	Team (League)	Pos.	G	AB	R	H	2B	3B	HR	RBI	Avg.	BB	SO	SB	PO	A	E	Avg.
			BATTING												FIELDING			
1988	—Iowa (Am. Assoc.)	C	21	73	11	16	5	1	2	11	.219	7	21	0	117	15	0	1.000
	—Chicago (N.L.)	C	95	309	19	80	19	1	7	38	.259	17	56	1	448	54	9	.982
1989	—Iowa (Am. Assoc.)	C	7	30	4	6	1	0	2	4	.200	1	8	0	40	5	2	.957
	—Chicago (N.L.)	C	91	334	37	86	13	0	5	41	.257	16	54	1	473	41	4	.992
1990	—Peoria (Midwest)	C	7	26	10	10	2	0	3	8	.385	3	6	0	75	4	1	.988
	—Iowa (Am. Assoc.)	C	22	79	8	17	1	0	3	6	.215	4	18	0	115	13	2	.985
	—Chicago (N.L.)	C	17	53	6	10	4	0	1	9	.189	5	14	0	87	3	2	.978
1991	—Chicago-Atl. (N.L.)■	C	63	160	13	30	7	0	5	14	.188	11	42	1	214	24	8	.967
	—Iowa (Am. Assoc.)	C	26	97	20	32	4	1	8	24	.330	12	25	0	90	14	2	.981
1992	—Atlanta (N.L.)	C	101	307	21	70	16	1	10	43	.228	17	67	0	426	31	1	.998
1993	—Atlanta (N.L.)	C	115	335	24	82	18	2	8	43	.245	21	64	0	570	52	6	.990
Major league totals (7 years)			494	1526	122	363	78	4	36	189	.238	90	302	3	2255	208	34	.986

CHAMPIONSHIP SERIES RECORD

Year	Team (League)	Pos.	G	AB	R	H	2B	3B	HR	RBI	Avg.	BB	SO	SB	PO	A	E	Avg.
			BATTING												FIELDING			
1992	—Atlanta (N.L.)	C	7	24	1	4	1	0	0	1	.167	3	2	0	43	5	0	1.000
1993	—Atlanta (N.L.)	C	6	19	2	4	0	0	1	3	.211	1	5	0	42	0	0	1.000
Championship series totals (2 years)			13	43	3	8	1	0	1	4	.186	4	7	0	85	5	0	1.000

WORLD SERIES RECORD

Year	Team (League)	Pos.	G	AB	R	H	2B	3B	HR	RBI	Avg.	BB	SO	SB	PO	A	E	Avg.
			BATTING												FIELDING			
1992	—Atlanta (N.L.)	C	6	22	1	2	0	0	1	3	.091	1	11	0	32	3	0	1.000

BERUMEN, ANDRES

P, PADRES

PERSONAL: Born April 5, 1971, in Tijuana, Mexico. . . . 6-1/205. . . . Throws right, bats right.
HIGH SCHOOL: Banning (Calif.).
TRANSACTIONS/CAREER NOTES: Selected by Kansas City Royals organization in 27th round of free-agent draft (June 5, 1989). . . . On Appleton disabled list (July 11-28, 1991). . . . Selected by Florida Marlins in second round (45th pick overall) of expansion draft (November 17, 1992). . . . Traded by Marlins with P Trevor Hoffman and P Jose Martinez to San Diego Padres for 3B Gary Sheffield and P Rich Rodriguez (June 24, 1993). . . . On Wichita disabled list (August 11, 1993-remainder of season).

Year	Team (League)	W	L	Pct.	ERA	G	GS	CG	ShO	Sv.	IP	H	R	ER	BB	SO
1989	—GC Royals (GCL)	2	4	.333	4.78	12	10	0	0	0	49	57	29	26	17	24
1990	—GC Royals (GCL)	0	2	.000	2.38	5	4	0	0	1	22⅔	24	9	6	8	18
	—Baseball City (FSL)	3	5	.375	4.30	9	9	1	1	0	44	30	27	21	28	35
1991	—Appleton (Midw.)	2	6	.250	3.51	13	13	0	0	0	56⅓	55	33	22	26	49
	—Baseball City (FSL)	0	5	.000	4.14	7	7	0	0	0	37	34	18	17	18	24
1992	—Appleton (Midw.)	5	2	.714	2.65	46	0	0	0	13	57⅔	50	25	17	23	52
1993	—High Desert (Calif.)■	9	2	*.818	3.62	14	13	1	0	0	92	85	45	37	36	74
	—Wichita (Texas)■	3	1	.750	5.74	7	7	0	0	0	26⅔	35	17	17	11	17

BICHETTE, DANTE

OF, ROCKIES

PERSONAL: Born November 18, 1963, in West Palm Beach, Fla. . . . 6-3/225. . . . Throws right, bats right. . . . Full name: Alphonse Dante Bichette. . . . Name pronounced bih-SHETT.
HIGH SCHOOL: Jupiter (Fla.).
COLLEGE: Palm Beach Junior College (Fla.).
TRANSACTIONS/CAREER NOTES: Selected by California Angels organization in 16th round of free-agent draft (June 4, 1984). . . . Traded by Angels to Milwaukee Brewers for DH Dave Parker (March 14, 1991). . . . Traded by Brewers to Colorado Rockies for OF Kevin Reimer (November 17, 1992).
STATISTICAL NOTES: Led A.L. outfielders with seven double plays in 1991.

Year	Team (League)	Pos.	G	AB	R	H	2B	3B	HR	RBI	Avg.	BB	SO	SB	PO	A	E	Avg.
			BATTING												FIELDING			
1984	—Salem (Northwest)	OF-1B-3B	64	250	27	58	9	2	4	30	.232	6	53	6	224	24	11	.958
1985	—Quad Cities (Mid.)	1B-OF-C	137	547	58	145	28	4	11	78	.265	25	89	25	300	21	15	.955
1986	—Palm Springs (Cal.)	OF-3B	68	290	39	79	15	0	10	73	.272	21	53	2	78	68	11	.930
	—Midland (Texas)	OF-3B	62	243	43	69	16	2	12	36	.284	18	50	3	131	30	11	.936
1987	—Edmonton (PCL)	OF-3B	92	360	54	108	20	3	13	50	.300	26	68	3	169	21	9	.955
1988	—Edmonton (PCL)	OF	132	509	64	136	29	•10	14	81	.267	25	78	7	218	*22	*15	.941
	—California (A.L.)	OF	21	46	1	12	2	0	0	8	.261	0	7	0	44	2	1	.979
1989	—California (A.L.)	OF	48	138	13	29	7	0	3	15	.210	6	24	3	95	6	1	.990
	—Edmonton (PCL)	OF	61	226	39	55	11	2	11	40	.243	24	39	4	92	9	1	.990
1990	—California (A.L.)	OF	109	349	40	89	15	1	15	53	.255	16	79	5	183	12	7	.965
1991	—Milwaukee (A.L.)■	OF-3B	134	445	53	106	18	3	15	59	.238	22	107	14	270	14	7	.976
1992	—Milwaukee (A.L.)	OF	112	387	37	111	27	2	5	41	.287	16	74	18	188	6	2	.990
1993	—Colorado (N.L.)■	OF	141	538	93	167	43	5	21	89	.310	28	99	14	308	14	9	.973
American League totals (5 years)			424	1365	144	347	69	6	38	176	.254	60	291	40	780	40	18	.979
National League totals (1 year)			141	538	93	167	43	5	21	89	.310	28	99	14	308	14	9	.973
Major league totals (6 years)			565	1903	237	514	112	11	59	265	.270	88	390	54	1088	54	27	.977

BIELECKI, MIKE

P

PERSONAL: Born July 31, 1959, in Baltimore. . . . 6-3/195. . . . Throws right, bats right. . . . Full name: Michael Joseph Bielecki. . . . Name pronounced bill-LECK-ee.
HIGH SCHOOL: Dundalk (Baltimore).
COLLEGE: Loyola College (Md.) and Valencia Community College (Fla.).

TRANSACTIONS/CAREER NOTES: Selected by Kansas City Royals organization in sixth round of free-agent draft (January 9, 1979).... Selected by Pittsburgh Pirates organization in secondary phase of free-agent draft (June 5, 1979).... Traded by Pirates to Chicago Cubs for P Mike Curtis (March 31, 1988).... Traded by Cubs with C Damon Berryhill to Atlanta Braves for P Turk Wendell and P Yorkis Perez (September 29, 1991).... On disabled list (July 29, 1992-remainder of season).... Granted free agency (October 30, 1992).... Signed by Cleveland Indians (December 14, 1992).... Released by Indians (June 19, 1993).... Signed by Rochester, Baltimore Orioles organization (June 29, 1993).... Released by Rochester (August 15, 1993).
STATISTICAL NOTES: Tied for Eastern League lead with 24 home runs allowed in 1982.

Year	Team (League)	W	L	Pct.	ERA	G	GS	CG	ShO	Sv.	IP	H	R	ER	BB	SO
1979	—GC Pirates (GCL)	1	4	.200	2.29	9	9	1	0	0	51	48	21	13	21	35
1980	—Shelby (S. Atl.)	3	5	.375	4.55	29	6	1	0	3	99	106	60	50	58	78
1981	—Greenwood (S. Atl.)	12	11	.522	3.42	28	•28	10	2	0	192	172	95	73	82	163
1982	—Buffalo (Eastern)	7	12	.368	4.86	25	25	4	0	0	157⅓	165	96	•85	75	135
1983	—Lynn (Eastern)	•15	7	.682	3.19	25	25	7	1	0	163⅔	126	73	58	69	*143
1984	—Hawaii (PCL)	*19	3	.864	2.97	28	28	9	2	0	187⅔	162	70	62	88	*162
	—Pittsburgh (N.L.)	0	0	...	0.00	4	0	0	0	0	4⅓	4	0	0	0	1
1985	—Pittsburgh (N.L.)	2	3	.400	4.53	12	7	0	0	0	45⅔	45	26	23	31	22
	—Hawaii (PCL)	8	6	.571	3.83	20	20	2	0	0	129⅓	117	58	55	56	111
1986	—Pittsburgh (N.L.)	6	11	.353	4.66	31	27	0	0	0	148⅔	149	87	77	83	83
1987	—Vancouver (PCL)	12	10	.545	3.78	26	26	3	3	0	181	194	89	76	78	140
	—Pittsburgh (N.L.)	2	3	.400	4.73	8	8	2	0	0	45⅔	43	25	24	12	25
1988	—Chicago (N.L.)■	2	2	.500	3.35	19	5	0	0	0	48⅓	55	22	18	16	33
	—Iowa (Am. Assoc.)	3	2	.600	2.63	23	3	1	1	5	54⅔	34	19	16	20	50
1989	—Chicago (N.L.)	18	7	.720	3.14	33	33	4	3	0	212⅓	187	82	74	81	147
1990	—Chicago (N.L.)	8	11	.421	4.93	36	29	0	0	1	168	188	101	92	70	103
1991	—Chicago-Atl. (N.L.)■	13	11	.542	4.46	41	25	0	0	0	173⅔	171	91	86	56	75
1992	—Atlanta (N.L.)	2	4	.333	2.57	19	14	1	1	0	80⅔	77	27	23	27	62
1993	—Cleveland (A.L.)■	4	5	.444	5.90	13	13	0	0	0	68⅔	90	47	45	23	38
	—Rochester (Int'l)■	5	3	.625	5.03	9	9	0	0	0	48⅓	56	33	27	16	31
A.L. totals (1 year)		4	5	.444	5.90	13	13	0	0	0	68⅔	90	47	45	23	38
N.L. totals (9 years)		53	52	.505	4.05	203	148	7	4	1	927⅓	919	461	417	376	551
Major league totals (10 years)		57	57	.500	4.17	216	161	7	4	1	996	1009	508	462	399	589

CHAMPIONSHIP SERIES RECORD

Year	Team (League)	W	L	Pct.	ERA	G	GS	CG	ShO	Sv.	IP	H	R	ER	BB	SO
1989	—Chicago (N.L.)	0	1	.000	3.65	2	2	0	0	0	12⅓	7	5	5	6	11

BIGGIO, CRAIG

2B, ASTROS

PERSONAL: Born December 14, 1965, in Smithtown, N.Y.... 5-11/180.... Throws right, bats right.... Full name: Craig Alan Biggio.... Name pronounced BEE-jee-oh.
HIGH SCHOOL: Kings Park (N.Y.).
COLLEGE: Seton Hall.
TRANSACTIONS/CAREER NOTES: Selected by Houston Astros organization in first round (22nd pick overall) of free-agent draft (June 2, 1987).
HONORS: Named catcher on THE SPORTING NEWS college All-America team (1987).... Named catcher on THE SPORTING NEWS N.L. Silver Slugger team (1989).
STATISTICAL NOTES: Led N.L. catchers with 889 putouts, 963 total chances and 13 passed balls in 1991.

				BATTING											FIELDING			
Year	Team (League)	Pos.	G	AB	R	H	2B	3B	HR	RBI	Avg.	BB	SO	SB	PO	A	E	Avg.
1987	—Asheville (S. Atl.)	C-OF	64	216	59	81	17	2	9	49	.375	39	33	31	378	46	2	.995
1988	—Tucson (PCL)	C-OF	77	281	60	90	21	4	3	41	.320	40	39	19	318	33	6	.983
	—Houston (N.L.)	C	50	123	14	26	6	1	3	5	.211	7	29	6	292	28	3	.991
1989	—Houston (N.L.)	C-OF	134	443	64	114	21	2	13	60	.257	49	64	21	742	56	9	.989
1990	—Houston (N.L.)	C-OF	150	555	53	153	24	2	4	42	.276	53	79	25	657	60	13	.982
1991	—Houston (N.L.)	C-2B-OF	149	546	79	161	23	4	4	46	.295	53	71	19	†894	73	11	.989
1992	—Houston (N.L.)	2B	•162	613	96	170	32	3	6	39	.277	94	95	38	*344	413	12	.984
1993	—Houston (N.L.)	2B	155	610	98	175	41	5	21	64	.287	77	93	15	306	*447	14	.982
Major league totals (6 years)			800	2890	404	799	147	17	51	256	.276	333	431	124	3235	1077	62	.986

ALL-STAR GAME RECORD

			BATTING										FIELDING			
Year	League	Pos.	AB	R	H	2B	3B	HR	RBI	Avg.	BB	SO	SB	PO	A	E	Avg.
1991	—National	C	1	0	0	0	0	0	0	.000	0	0	0	2	0	1	.667
1992	—National	2B	2	0	0	0	0	0	0	.000	0	0	0	0	2	0	1.000
All-Star Game totals (2 years)			3	0	0	0	0	0	0	.000	0	0	0	2	2	1	.800

BIRKBECK, MIKE

P, BRAVES

PERSONAL: Born March 10, 1961, in Orrville, O.... 6-2/190.... Throws right, bats right.... Full name: Michael Lawrence Birkbeck.
HIGH SCHOOL: Orrville (O.).
COLLEGE: Akron.
TRANSACTIONS/CAREER NOTES: Selected by Chicago Cubs organization in 11th round of free-agent draft (June 7, 1982).... Selected by Milwaukee Brewers organization in fourth round of free-agent draft (June 8, 1983).... On Milwaukee disabled list (June 2-September 5, 1987); included rehabilitation assignment to Beloit (June 19-23) and Denver (June 24-July 1).... On Milwaukee disabled list (May 31-August 29, 1989); included rehabilitation assignment to Denver (August 6-25).... Released by Brewers organization (October 16, 1990).... Signed by Cleveland Indians organization (April 8, 1991).... On Canton/Akron disabled list (April 10-May 8, 1991).... Released by Colorado Springs, Indians organization (September 25, 1991).... Signed by Tidewater, New York Mets organization (January 2, 1992).... On Tidewater disabled list (April 25-May 6 and July 11-26, 1992).... Granted free agency (October 16, 1992).... Signed by Richmond, Atlanta Braves organization (December 22, 1992).

Year	Team (League)	W	L	Pct.	ERA	G	GS	CG	ShO	Sv.	IP	H	R	ER	BB	SO
1983	—Paintsville (Appal.)	3	1	.750	1.88	7	5	0	0	0	28⅔	17	12	6	17	38
	—Beloit (Midwest)	2	4	.333	3.43	7	7	0	0	0	42	35	22	16	17	38
1984	—Beloit (Midwest)	14	3	.824	2.18	26	25	6	2	0	177⅔	134	57	43	64	164
1985	—El Paso (Texas)	9	9	.500	3.43	24	24	4	0	0	155	154	67	59	64	103
1986	—Vancouver (PCL)	12	6	.667	4.62	23	23	2	0	0	134⅓	160	82	69	39	81
	—Milwaukee (A.L.)	1	1	.500	4.50	7	4	0	0	0	22	24	12	11	12	13
1987	—Milwaukee (A.L.)	1	4	.200	6.20	10	10	1	0	0	45	63	33	31	19	25
	—Beloit (Midwest)	0	0	...	2.08	1	1	0	0	0	4⅓	4	4	1	1	7
	—Denver (A.A.)	0	1	.000	9.64	1	1	0	0	0	4⅔	9	11	5	3	1
1988	—Milwaukee (A.L.)	10	8	.556	4.72	23	23	0	0	0	124	141	69	65	37	64
	—Denver (A.A.)	4	1	.800	2.01	5	5	4	0	0	44⅔	30	10	10	10	30
1989	—Milwaukee (A.L.)	0	4	.000	5.44	9	9	1	0	0	44⅔	57	32	27	22	31
	—Denver (A.A.)	2	2	.500	3.04	5	5	0	0	0	23⅔	26	9	8	10	9
1990	—Denver (A.A.)	3	8	.273	5.33	21	20	0	0	0	96⅓	102	73	57	36	69
1991	—Cant./Akr. (East.)■	2	3	.400	3.89	21	2	0	0	5	39⅓	39	17	17	18	40
	—Colo. Springs (PCL)	0	0	...	0.00	3	1	0	0	0	7	4	0	0	3	3
1992	—Tidewater (Int'l)■	4	10	.286	4.08	21	19	3	0	0	117	108	61	53	31	101
	—New York (N.L.)	0	1	.000	9.00	1	1	0	0	0	7	12	7	7	1	2
1993	—Richmond (Int'l)■	*13	8	.619	3.11	27	26	1	0	0	159⅓	143	67	55	41	*136
	A.L. totals (4 years)	12	17	.414	5.12	49	46	2	0	0	235⅔	285	146	134	90	133
	N.L. totals (1 year)	0	1	.000	9.00	1	1	0	0	0	7	12	7	7	1	2
	Major league totals (5 years)	12	18	.400	5.23	50	47	2	0	0	242⅔	297	153	141	91	135

BLACK, BUD

P, GIANTS

PERSONAL: Born June 30, 1957, in San Mateo, Calif. . . . 6-2/188. . . . Throws left, bats left. . . . Full name: Harry Ralston Black.
HIGH SCHOOL: Mark Morris (Longview, Wash.).
COLLEGE: Lower Columbia College (Wash.) and San Diego State (bachelor of arts degree in finance, 1979).
TRANSACTIONS/CAREER NOTES: Selected by San Francisco Giants organization in third round of free-agent draft (January 11, 1977). . . . Selected by New York Mets organization in secondary phase of free-agent draft (June 7, 1977). . . . Selected by Seattle Mariners organization in 17th round of free-agent draft (June 5, 1979). . . . Traded by Mariners to Kansas City Royals (March 2, 1982), completing deal in which Royals traded IF Manny Castillo to Mariners for a player to be named later (October 23, 1981). . . . On disabled list (June 8-July 4, 1987). . . . Traded by Royals to Cleveland Indians for 1B Pat Tabler (June 3, 1988). . . . On Cleveland disabled list (July 19-August 21, 1988); included rehabilitation assignment to Williamsport (August 16-21). . . . Granted free agency (November 4, 1988). . . . Re-signed by Indians (December 5, 1988). . . . Traded by Indians to Toronto Blue Jays for P Mauro Gozzo and two players to be named later (September 16, 1990); Indians acquired P Steve Cummings (September 21, 1990) and P Alex Sanchez (September 24, 1990) to complete deal. . . . Granted free agency (November 5, 1990). . . . Signed by San Francisco Giants (November 9, 1990). . . . On San Francisco disabled list (March 27-May 7, 1992); included rehabilitation assignment to Phoenix (April 23-May 7). . . . On San Francisco disabled list (April 9-29 and July 10-28, 1993). . . . On San Francisco disabled list (August 4, 1993-remainder of season); included rehabilitation assignment to San Jose (August 23-24).
RECORDS: Shares major league single-season record for fewest double plays by pitcher who led league in double plays—4 (1992). . . . Shares major league record for most hit batsmen in one inning—3 (July 8, 1988, fourth inning).
STATISTICAL NOTES: Led A.L. with seven balks in 1982. . . . Led N.L. with six balks in 1991 and tied for lead with seven in 1992. . . . Led N.L. with 23 home runs allowed in 1992.
MISCELLANEOUS: Made an out in only appearance as pinch-hitter (1991).

Year	Team (League)	W	L	Pct.	ERA	G	GS	CG	ShO	Sv.	IP	H	R	ER	BB	SO
1979	—Belling. (N'west)	0	0	...	0.00	2	0	0	0	0	5	3	0	0	5	8
	—San Jose (Calif.)	0	1	.000	3.00	17	2	0	0	1	27	17	11	9	16	24
1980	—San Jose (Calif.)	5	3	.625	3.45	32	5	4	0	2	86	67	34	33	49	73
1981	—Lynn (Eastern)	2	6	.250	3.00	22	11	2	1	2	87	78	38	29	23	86
	—Spokane (PCL)	1	0	1.000	4.50	4	0	0	0	0	8	12	4	4	2	4
	—Seattle (A.L.)	0	0	...	0.00	2	0	0	0	0	1	2	0	0	3	0
1982	—Kansas City (A.L.)■	4	6	.400	4.58	22	14	0	0	0	88⅓	92	48	45	34	40
	—Omaha (A.A.)	3	1	.750	2.48	4	4	3	1	0	29	23	9	8	10	20
1983	—Omaha (A.A.)	3	1	.750	3.34	5	5	3	0	0	35	31	13	13	13	32
	—Kansas City (A.L.)	10	7	.588	3.79	24	24	3	0	0	161⅓	159	75	68	43	58
1984	—Kansas City (A.L.)	17	12	.586	3.12	35	35	8	1	0	257	226	99	89	64	140
1985	—Kansas City (A.L.)	10	15	.400	4.33	33	33	5	2	0	205⅔	216	111	99	59	122
1986	—Kansas City (A.L.)	5	10	.333	3.20	56	4	0	0	9	121	100	49	43	43	68
1987	—Kansas City (A.L.)	8	6	.571	3.60	29	18	0	0	1	122⅓	126	63	49	35	61
1988	—K.C.-Clev. (A.L.)■	4	4	.500	5.00	33	7	0	0	1	81	82	47	45	34	63
	—Williamsport (East.)	1	0	1.000	0.00	1	1	0	0	0	5	0	0	0	0	5
1989	—Cleveland (A.L.)	12	11	.522	3.36	33	32	6	3	0	222⅓	213	95	83	52	88
1990	—Clev.-Tor. (A.L.)■	13	11	.542	3.57	32	31	5	2	0	206⅔	181	86	82	61	106
1991	—San Francisco (N.L.)■	12	*16	.429	3.99	34	34	3	3	0	214⅓	201	104	95	71	104
1992	—Phoenix (PCL)	2	0	1.000	0.86	3	3	1	1	0	21	21	3	2	5	7
	—San Francisco (N.L.)	10	12	.455	3.97	28	28	2	1	0	177	178	88	78	59	82
1993	—San Francisco (N.L.)	8	2	.800	3.56	16	16	0	0	0	93⅔	89	44	37	33	45
	—San Jose (Calif.)	0	0	...	9.00	1	1	0	0	0	1	2	1	1	0	2
	A.L. totals (10 years)	83	82	.503	3.70	299	198	27	8	11	1466⅔	1397	673	603	428	746
	N.L. totals (3 years)	30	30	.500	3.90	78	78	5	4	0	485	468	236	210	163	231
	Major league totals (13 years)	113	112	.502	3.75	377	276	32	12	11	1951⅔	1865	909	813	591	977

CHAMPIONSHIP SERIES RECORD

Year	Team (League)	W	L	Pct.	ERA	G	GS	CG	ShO	Sv.	IP	H	R	ER	BB	SO
1984	—Kansas City (A.L.)	0	1	.000	7.20	1	1	0	0	0	5	7	4	4	1	3

Year	Team (League)	W	L	Pct.	ERA	G	GS	CG	ShO	Sv.	IP	H	R	ER	BB	SO
1985	—Kansas City (A.L.)	0	0	...	1.69	3	1	0	0	0	10⅔	11	3	2	4	8
	Champ. series totals (2 years)	0	1	.000	3.45	4	2	0	0	0	15⅔	18	7	6	5	11

WORLD SERIES RECORD

Year	Team (League)	W	L	Pct.	ERA	G	GS	CG	ShO	Sv.	IP	H	R	ER	BB	SO
1985	—Kansas City (A.L.)	0	1	.000	5.06	2	1	0	0	0	5⅓	4	3	3	5	4

BLAIR, WILLIE

P, ROCKIES

PERSONAL: Born December 18, 1965, in Paintsville, Ky. . . . 6-1/185. . . . Throws right, bats right. . . . Full name: William Allen Blair.
HIGH SCHOOL: Johnson Central (Paintsville, Ky.).
COLLEGE: Morehead State.
TRANSACTIONS/CAREER NOTES: Selected by Toronto Blue Jays organization in 11th round of free-agent draft (June 2, 1986). . . . Traded by Blue Jays to Cleveland Indians for P Alex Sanchez (November 6, 1990). . . . Traded by Indians with C Eddie Taubensee to Houston Astros for OF Kenny Lofton and IF Dave Rohde (December 10, 1991). . . . Selected by Colorado Rockies in first round (21st pick overall) of expansion draft (November 17, 1992).
STATISTICAL NOTES: Combined with starter Pat Hentgen and Enrique Burgos in 2-1 no-hit victory for Dunedin against Osceola (May 10, 1988).

Year	Team (League)	W	L	Pct.	ERA	G	GS	CG	ShO	Sv.	IP	H	R	ER	BB	SO
1986	—St. Cathar. (NYP)	5	0	1.000	1.68	21	0	0	0	*12	53⅔	32	10	10	20	55
1987	—Dunedin (Fla. St.)	2	9	.182	4.43	50	0	0	0	13	85⅓	99	51	42	29	72
1988	—Dunedin (Fla. St.)	2	0	1.000	2.70	4	0	0	0	0	6⅔	5	2	2	4	5
	—Knoxville (South.)	5	5	.500	3.62	34	9	0	0	3	102	94	49	41	35	76
1989	—Syracuse (Int'l)	5	6	.455	3.97	19	17	3	1	0	106⅔	94	55	47	38	76
1990	—Toronto (A.L.)	3	5	.375	4.06	27	6	0	0	0	68⅔	66	33	31	28	43
	—Syracuse (Int'l)	0	2	.000	4.74	3	3	1	0	0	19	20	13	10	8	6
1991	—Colo. Springs (PCL)■...	9	6	.600	4.99	26	15	0	0	4	113⅔	130	74	63	30	57
	—Cleveland (A.L.)	2	3	.400	6.75	11	5	0	0	0	36	58	27	27	10	13
1992	—Tucson (PCL)■...........	4	4	.500	2.39	21	2	1	0	2	52⅔	50	20	14	12	35
	—Houston (N.L.)	5	7	.417	4.00	29	8	0	0	0	78⅔	74	47	35	25	48
1993	—Colorado (N.L.)■..........	6	10	.375	4.75	46	18	1	0	0	146	184	90	77	42	84
	A.L. totals (2 years)	5	8	.385	4.99	38	11	0	0	0	104⅔	124	60	58	38	56
	N.L. totals (2 years)	11	17	.393	4.49	75	26	1	0	0	224⅔	258	137	112	67	132
	Major league totals (4 years) ...	16	25	.390	4.65	113	37	1	0	0	329⅓	382	197	170	105	188

BLANCO, HENRY

3B, DODGERS

PERSONAL: Born August 29, 1971, in Caracas, Venezuela. . . . 5-11/168. . . . Throws right, bats right. . . . Full name: Henry Ramon Blanco.
HIGH SCHOOL: Antonio Jose de Sucre (Venezuela).
TRANSACTIONS/CAREER NOTES: Signed as free agent by Los Angeles Dodgers organization (November 12, 1989). . . . On disabled list (June 16-25, 1993).
STATISTICAL NOTES: Led Pioneer League third basemen with .947 fielding percentage and 10 double plays in 1991. . . . Led California League third basemen with 345 total chances and 34 double plays in 1992. . . . Led Texas League third basemen with .944 fielding percentage, 92 putouts and 270 total chances in 1993.

				BATTING											FIELDING			
Year	Team (League)	Pos.	G	AB	R	H	2B	3B	HR	RBI	Avg.	BB	SO	SB	PO	A	E	Avg.
1990	—GC Dodgers (GCL)	3B	60	178	23	39	8	0	1	19	.219	26	41	7	*48	129	11	.941
1991	—Vero Beach (FSL)	3B-SS	5	7	0	1	0	0	0	0	.143	2	0	0	6	4	0	1.000
	—Great Falls (Pio.)	3B-1B	62	216	35	55	7	1	5	28	.255	27	39	3	93	99	8	†.960
1992	—Bakersfield (Calif.) ...	3B	124	401	42	94	21	2	5	52	.234	51	91	10	*95	*236	14	*.959
1993	—San Antonio (Tex.) ...	3B-1B-SS	117	374	33	73	19	1	10	42	.195	29	80	3	†150	169	16	†.952

BLANKENSHIP, LANCE

OF/2B, ATHLETICS

PERSONAL: Born December 6, 1963, in Portland, Ore. . . . 6-0/185. . . . Throws right, bats right. . . . Full name: Lance Robert Blankenship.
HIGH SCHOOL: Ygnacio Valley (Concord, Calif.).
COLLEGE: California.
TRANSACTIONS/CAREER NOTES: Selected by Oakland Athletics organization in 10th round of free-agent draft (June 2, 1986). . . . On Oakland disabled list (July 8-August 10, 1992); included rehabilitation assignment to Tacoma (August 4-10). . . . On disabled list (August 16, 1993-remainder of season).
HONORS: Named third baseman on THE SPORTING NEWS college All-America team (1985).
STATISTICAL NOTES: Led Pacific Coast League second basemen with 390 assists and 682 total chances in 1988.

				BATTING											FIELDING			
Year	Team (League)	Pos.	G	AB	R	H	2B	3B	HR	RBI	Avg.	BB	SO	SB	PO	A	E	Avg.
1986	—Medford (N'west)	OF	14	52	22	21	3	0	2	17	.404	17	9	10	22	1	1	.958
	—Modesto (Calif.)	OF-3B	55	171	47	50	5	3	6	25	.292	41	39	15	88	27	7	.943
1987	—Modesto (Calif.)	3-O-S-2	22	84	14	23	9	2	0	17	.274	12	29	12	26	30	8	.875
	—Huntsville (South.) ...	OF-2B-3B	107	390	64	99	21	3	4	39	.254	67	61	34	185	99	8	.973
1988	—Tacoma (PCL)	2B-OF	131	437	84	116	21	8	9	52	.265	*96	75	40	272	†390	21	.969
	—Oakland (A.L.)	2B	10	3	1	0	0	0	0	0	.000	0	1	0	1	1	0	1.000
1989	—Tacoma (PCL)	2B	25	98	25	29	8	2	2	9	.296	19	15	5	39	81	2	.984
	—Oakland (A.L.)	OF-2B	58	125	22	29	5	1	1	4	.232	8	31	5	69	49	1	.992
1990	—Oakland (A.L.)	3-O-2-1	86	136	18	26	3	0	0	10	.191	20	23	3	66	69	5	.964
	—Tacoma (PCL)	2B-OF-3B	24	93	18	24	7	1	1	9	.258	14	16	7	39	57	2	.980
1991	—Oakland (A.L.)	2B-OF-3B	90	185	33	46	8	0	3	21	.249	23	42	12	123	122	3	.988
	—Tacoma (PCL)	S-2-3-O	30	109	19	32	7	0	1	11	.294	22	27	9	51	90	8	.946
1992	—Tacoma (PCL)	2B-OF	5	19	3	3	0	0	1	5	.158	2	7	0	11	9	0	1.000

Year	Team (League)	Pos.	G	AB	R	H	2B	3B	HR	RBI	Avg.	BB	SO	SB	PO	A	E	Avg.
			BATTING												FIELDING			
	—Oakland (A.L.)	2B-OF-1B	123	349	59	84	24	1	3	34	.241	82	57	21	286	226	6	.988
1993	—Oakland (A.L.)	0-2-1-S	94	252	43	48	8	1	2	23	.190	67	64	13	207	65	5	.982
Major league totals (6 years)			461	1050	176	233	48	3	9	92	.222	200	218	54	752	532	20	.985

CHAMPIONSHIP SERIES RECORD

Year	Team (League)	Pos.	G	AB	R	H	2B	3B	HR	RBI	Avg.	BB	SO	SB	PO	A	E	Avg.
			BATTING												FIELDING			
1989	—Oakland (A.L.)	2B	1	0	0	0	0	0	0	0	...	0	0	0	0	1	0	1.000
1990	—Oakland (A.L.)	PR	3	0	1	0	0	0	0	0	...	0	0	1	...	...	...	...
1992	—Oakland (A.L.)	2B-PR	5	13	2	3	0	0	0	0	.231	3	4	1	11	13	2	.923
Championship series totals (3 years)			9	13	3	3	0	0	0	0	.231	3	4	2	11	14	2	.926

WORLD SERIES RECORD

Year	Team (League)	Pos.	G	AB	R	H	2B	3B	HR	RBI	Avg.	BB	SO	SB	PO	A	E	Avg.
			BATTING												FIELDING			
1989	—Oakland (A.L.)	PH-2B	1	2	1	1	0	0	0	0	.500	0	0	0	1	0	0	1.000
1990	—Oakland (A.L.)	PH	1	1	0	0	0	0	0	0	.000	0	1	0	...	...	...	...
World Series totals (2 years)			2	3	1	1	0	0	0	0	.333	0	1	0	1	0	0	1.000

BLAUSER, JEFF

SS, BRAVES

PERSONAL: Born November 8, 1965, in Los Gatos, Calif. . . . 6-0/170. . . . Throws right, bats right. . . . Full name: Jeffrey Michael Blauser. . . . Name pronounced BLAU-zer.

HIGH SCHOOL: Placer (Sacramento, Calif.).

COLLEGE: Sacramento (Calif.) City College.

TRANSACTIONS/CAREER NOTES: Selected by St. Louis Cardinals organization in first round (eighth pick overall) of free-agent draft (January 17, 1984). . . . Selected by Atlanta Braves organization in secondary phase of free-agent draft (June 4, 1984). . . . On disabled list (May 14-30, 1990).

STATISTICAL NOTES: Led Carolina League shortstops with 506 total chances in 1986. . . . Hit three home runs in one game (July 12, 1992). . . . Led N.L. in being hit by pitch with 16 in 1993.

Year	Team (League)	Pos.	G	AB	R	H	2B	3B	HR	RBI	Avg.	BB	SO	SB	PO	A	E	Avg.
			BATTING												FIELDING			
1984	—Pulaski (Appal.)	SS	62	217	41	54	6	1	3	24	.249	38	47	14	61	162	24	.903
1985	—Sumter (S. Atl.)	SS	125	422	74	99	19	0	5	49	.235	82	94	36	150	306	35	.929
1986	—Durham (Carolina)	SS	123	447	94	128	27	3	13	52	.286	81	92	36	167	*314	25	*.951
1987	—Richmond (Int'l)	SS-2B	33	113	11	20	1	0	1	12	.177	11	24	3	56	106	9	.947
	—Atlanta (N.L.)	SS	51	165	11	40	6	3	2	15	.242	18	34	7	65	166	9	.963
	—Greenville (South.)	SS	72	265	35	66	13	3	4	32	.249	34	49	5	101	225	8	.976
1988	—Richmond (Int'l)	SS	69	271	40	77	19	1	5	23	.284	19	53	6	93	156	15	.943
	—Atlanta (N.L.)	2B-SS	18	67	7	16	3	1	2	7	.239	2	11	0	35	59	4	.959
1989	—Atlanta (N.L.)	3-2-S-0	142	456	63	123	24	2	12	46	.270	38	101	5	137	254	21	.949
1990	—Atlanta (N.L.)	S-2-3-0	115	386	46	104	24	3	8	39	.269	35	70	3	169	288	16	.966
1991	—Atlanta (N.L.)	SS-2B-3B	129	352	49	91	14	3	11	54	.259	54	59	5	136	219	17	.954
1992	—Atlanta (N.L.)	SS-2B-3B	123	343	61	90	19	3	14	46	.262	46	82	5	119	225	14	.961
1993	—Atlanta (N.L.)	SS	161	597	110	182	29	2	15	73	.305	85	109	16	189	426	19	.970
Major league totals (7 years)			739	2366	347	646	119	17	64	280	.273	278	466	41	850	1637	100	.961

CHAMPIONSHIP SERIES RECORD

Year	Team (League)	Pos.	G	AB	R	H	2B	3B	HR	RBI	Avg.	BB	SO	SB	PO	A	E	Avg.
			BATTING												FIELDING			
1991	—Atlanta (N.L.)	SS-PH	2	2	0	0	0	0	0	0	.000	0	0	0	0	1	1	.500
1992	—Atlanta (N.L.)	SS	7	24	3	5	0	1	1	4	.208	3	2	0	7	15	2	.917
1993	—Atlanta (N.L.)	SS	6	25	5	7	1	0	2	4	.280	4	7	0	6	14	0	1.000
Championship series totals (3 years)			15	51	8	12	1	1	3	8	.235	7	9	0	13	30	3	.935

WORLD SERIES RECORD

Year	Team (League)	Pos.	G	AB	R	H	2B	3B	HR	RBI	Avg.	BB	SO	SB	PO	A	E	Avg.
			BATTING												FIELDING			
1991	—Atlanta (N.L.)	SS-PH	5	6	0	1	0	0	0	0	.167	1	1	0	3	3	0	1.000
1992	—Atlanta (N.L.)	SS	6	24	2	6	0	0	0	0	.250	1	9	2	7	22	0	1.000
World Series totals (2 years)			11	30	2	7	0	0	0	0	.233	2	10	2	10	25	0	1.000

ALL-STAR GAME RECORD

Year	League	Pos.	AB	R	H	2B	3B	HR	RBI	Avg.	BB	SO	SB	PO	A	E	Avg.
			BATTING											FIELDING			
1993	—National	SS	1	0	0	0	0	0	0	.000	0	1	0	1	2	1	.750

BLOMDAHL, BEN

P, TIGERS

PERSONAL: Born December 30, 1970, in Long Beach, Calif. . . . 6-2/185. . . . Throws right, bats right. . . . Full name: Benjamin Earl Blomdahl. . . . Name pronounced BLOOM-doll.

HIGH SCHOOL: Riverside (Calif.) Polytech.

COLLEGE: Riverside (Calif.) Community College.

TRANSACTIONS/CAREER NOTES: Selected by Detroit Tigers organization in 14th round of free-agent draft (June 4, 1990).

STATISTICAL NOTES: Pitched 1-0 perfect game for Fayetteville against Spartanburg (June 4, 1992, second game).

Year	Team (League)	W	L	Pct.	ERA	G	GS	CG	ShO	Sv.	IP	H	R	ER	BB	SO
1991	—Niag. Falls (NYP)	6	6	.500	4.46	16	13	0	0	0	78⅔	72	43	39	50	30
1992	—Fayetteville (SAL)	10	4	.714	2.70	17	17	2	2	0	103⅓	94	46	31	26	65

Year	Team (League)	W	L	Pct.	ERA	G	GS	CG	ShO	Sv.	IP	H	R	ER	BB	SO
	—Lakeland (Fla. St.).....	5	3	.625	4.65	10	10	2	0	0	62	77	35	32	5	41
1993	—London (Eastern).......	6	6	.500	3.71	17	17	3	0	0	119	108	58	49	42	72
	—Toledo (Int'l)	3	4	.429	4.88	11	10	0	0	0	62⅔	67	34	34	19	27

BLOSSER, GREG

OF, RED SOX

PERSONAL: Born June 26, 1971, in Bradenton, Fla. . . . 6-3/200. . . . Throws left, bats left. . . . Full name: Gregory Brent Blosser.

HIGH SCHOOL: Sarasota (Fla.).

TRANSACTIONS/CAREER NOTES: Selected by Boston Red Sox organization in first round (16th pick overall) of free-agent draft (June 5, 1989); pick received as part of compensation for San Diego Padres signing Type A free agent Bruce Hurst. . . . On Pawtucket disabled list (September 4, 1992-remainder of season).

STATISTICAL NOTES: Led Eastern League with nine intentional bases on balls received in 1992.

B

				BATTING											FIELDING			
Year	Team (League)	Pos.	G	AB	R	H	2B	3B	HR	RBI	Avg.	BB	SO	SB	PO	A	E	Avg.
1989	—GC Red Sox (GCL)	OF	40	146	17	42	7	3	2	20	.288	25	19	3	54	2	4	.933
	—Winter Haven (FSL)..	OF	28	94	6	24	1	1	2	14	.255	8	14	1	52	4	4	.933
1990	—Lynchburg (Caro.) ...	OF	119	447	63	126	23	1	*18	62	.282	55	99	5	171	8	14	.927
1991	—New Britain (East.) ..	OF	134	452	47	98	21	3	8	46	.217	63	114	9	178	15	•11	.946
1992	—New Britain (East.) ..	OF	129	434	59	105	23	4	22	71	.242	64	122	0	189	9	7	.966
	—Pawtucket (Int'l)......	PH	1	0	1	0	0	0	0	0	...	1	0	0	...	...	...	...
1993	—Pawtucket (Int'l)......	OF	130	478	66	109	22	2	23	66	.228	58	139	3	199	•13	7	.968
	—Boston (A.L.)...........	OF	17	28	1	2	1	0	0	1	.071	2	7	1	11	1	0	1.000
Major league totals (1 year).....................			17	28	1	2	1	0	0	1	.071	2	7	1	11	1	0	1.000

BLOWERS, MIKE

3B, MARINERS

PERSONAL: Born April 24, 1965, in Wurzburg, West Germany. . . . 6-2/210. . . . Throws right, bats right. . . . Full name: Michael Roy Blowers.

HIGH SCHOOL: Bethel (Wash.).

COLLEGE: Tacoma (Wash.) Community College and Washington.

TRANSACTIONS/CAREER NOTES: Selected by Seattle Mariners organization in eighth round of free-agent draft (January 17, 1984). . . . Selected by San Francisco Giants organization in secondary phase of free-agent draft (June 4, 1984). . . . Selected by Baltimore Orioles organization in secondary phase of free-agent draft (January 9, 1985). . . . Selected by Montreal Expos organization in 10th round of free-agent draft (June 2, 1986). . . . Traded by Expos to New York Yankees (August 31, 1989), completing deal in which Yankees traded P John Candelaria to Expos for a player to be named later (August 29, 1989). . . . Traded by Yankees to Mariners for a player to be named later and cash (May 17, 1991); Yankees acquired P Jim Blueberg to complete deal (June 22, 1991).

RECORDS: Shares A.L. single-game record for most errors by third baseman—4 (May 3, 1990).

STATISTICAL NOTES: Led Florida State League third basemen with .944 fielding percentage and 27 double plays in 1987. . . . Led Southern League third basemen with 125 putouts and 27 double plays in 1988. . . . Led American Association third basemen with .930 fielding percentage in 1989.

				BATTING											FIELDING			
Year	Team (League)	Pos.	G	AB	R	H	2B	3B	HR	RBI	Avg.	BB	SO	SB	PO	A	E	Avg.
1986	—Jamestown (NYP)	SS-3B	32	95	13	24	9	2	1	6	.253	17	18	3	48	73	16	.883
	—GC Expos (GCL)........	SS	31	115	14	25	3	1	2	17	.217	15	25	2	50	84	15	.899
1987	—W.P. Beach (FSL).....	3B-SS-1B	136	491	68	124	30	3	16	71	.253	48	118	4	75	239	18	†.946
1988	—Jacksonv. (South.) ..	3B-SS-2B	137	460	58	115	20	6	15	60	.250	68	114	6	†125	241	34	.915
1989	—Indianapolis (A.A.)...	3B-SS	131	461	49	123	29	6	14	56	.267	41	109	3	91	214	23	†.930
	—New York (A.L.)■......	3B	13	38	2	10	0	0	0	3	.263	3	13	0	9	14	4	.852
1990	—New York (A.L.)........	3B	48	144	16	27	4	0	5	21	.188	12	50	1	26	63	10	.899
	—Columbus (Int'l)	3B-1B-2B	62	230	30	78	20	6	6	50	.339	29	40	3	64	89	8	.950
1991	—New York (A.L.)........	3B	15	35	3	7	0	0	1	1	.200	4	3	0	4	16	3	.870
	—Calgary (PCL)■........	3B-SS-1B	90	329	56	95	20	2	9	59	.289	40	74	3	56	163	19	.920
1992	—Calgary (PCL)..........	3B-1B-OF	83	300	56	95	28	2	9	67	.317	50	64	2	99	87	5	.974
	—Seattle (A.L.)	3B-1B	31	73	7	14	3	0	1	2	.192	6	20	0	28	44	1	.986
1993	—Seattle (A.L.)	3-O-1-C	127	379	55	106	23	3	15	57	.280	44	98	1	70	225	15	.952
Major league totals (5 years)..................			234	669	83	164	30	3	22	84	.245	69	184	2	137	362	33	.938

BOCHTLER, DOUG

P, PADRES

PERSONAL: Born July 5, 1970, in West Palm Beach, Fla. . . . 6-3/185. . . . Throws right, bats right. . . . Full name: Douglas Eugene Bochtler. . . . Name pronounced BOCK-ler.

HIGH SCHOOL: John I. Leonard (Lake Worth, Fla.).

COLLEGE: Indian River Community College (Fla.).

TRANSACTIONS/CAREER NOTES: Selected by Montreal Expos organization in ninth round of free-agent draft (June 5, 1989). . . . On disabled list (June 18-September 6, 1992). . . . Selected by Colorado Rockies in second round (32nd pick overall) of expansion draft (November 17, 1992). . . . On Colorado Springs disabled list (April 18-26, 1993). . . . Traded by Rockies with C Brad Ausmus and a player to be named later to San Diego Padres for P Bruce Hurst and P Greg W. Harris (July 26, 1993); Padres acquired P Andy Ashby to complete deal (July 27, 1993).

Year	Team (League)	W	L	Pct.	ERA	G	GS	CG	ShO	Sv.	IP	H	R	ER	BB	SO
1989	—GC Expos (GCL)	2	2	.500	3.21	9	9	1	0	0	47⅔	46	22	17	20	45
1990	—Rockford (Midw.)	9	12	.429	3.50	25	25	1	1	0	139	142	82	54	54	109
1991	—W.P. Beach (FSL)	•12	9	.571	2.92	26	24	7	2	0	160⅓	148	63	52	55	109
1992	—Harrisburg (East.)	6	5	.545	2.32	13	13	2	1	0	77⅔	50	25	20	36	89
1993	—Colo. Sp.-L.V. (PCL)■	1	9	.100	6.18	19	18	1	0	0	90⅓	123	67	62	37	68
	—Central Vall. (Cal.)	3	1	.750	3.40	8	8	0	0	0	47⅔	40	23	18	28	43

BODDICKER, MIKE

P

PERSONAL: Born August 23, 1957, in Cedar Rapids, Ia. . . . 5-11/185. . . . Throws right, bats right. . . . Full name: Michael James Boddicker. . . . Name pronounced BOD-dick-er.
HIGH SCHOOL: Norway (Ia.).
COLLEGE: Iowa.
TRANSACTIONS/CAREER NOTES: Selected by Montreal Expos organization in eighth round of free-agent draft (June 4, 1975). . . . Selected by Baltimore Orioles organization in sixth round of free-agent draft (June 6, 1978). . . . On disabled list (April 20-May 10, 1986). . . . Traded by Orioles to Boston Red Sox for OF Brady Anderson and P Curt Schilling (July 29, 1988). . . . Granted free agency (November 5, 1990). . . . Signed by Kansas City Royals (November 21, 1990). . . . On disabled list (May 13-29, 1991 and July 26-August 21 and September 4, 1992-remainder of season). . . . On disabled list (March 27-April 26, 1993); included rehabilitation assignment to Omaha (April 13-26). . . . Traded by Royals to Milwaukee Brewers for a player to be named later (April 26, 1993); deal settled in cash. . . . On Milwaukee disabled list (June 14-July 23, 1993); included rehabilitation assignment to Beloit (June 30-July 2). . . . Placed on voluntarily retired list (July 26, 1993).
RECORDS: Shares modern major league single-season record for most putouts by pitcher—49 (1984).
HONORS: Named A.L. Rookie Pitcher of the Year by THE SPORTING NEWS (1983). . . . Named righthanded pitcher on THE SPORTING NEWS A.L. All-Star team (1984). . . . Won A.L. Gold Glove at pitcher (1990).
STATISTICAL NOTES: Tied for A.L. lead with 13 hit batsmen in 1991.
MISCELLANEOUS: Appeared in one game as pinch-runner (1984). . . . Appeared in two games as pinch-runner (1985).

Year	Team (League)	W	L	Pct.	ERA	G	GS	CG	ShO	Sv.	IP	H	R	ER	BB	SO
1978	—Bluefield (Appal.)	2	1	.667	0.47	8	1	0	0	2	19	9	2	1	10	28
	—Charlotte (South.)	4	3	.571	1.94	10	8	5	2	0	65	42	15	14	17	48
	—Rochester (Int'l)	1	0	1.000	1.80	1	1	0	0	0	5	4	1	1	2	3
1979	—Charlotte (South.)	9	3	.750	3.00	14	14	8	2	0	102	82	40	34	36	89
	—Rochester (Int'l)	4	6	.400	6.00	15	12	2	1	0	72	88	48	48	27	48
1980	—Rochester (Int'l)	12	9	.571	2.18	25	25	13	4	0	190	149	57	46	35	109
	—Baltimore (A.L.)	0	1	.000	6.43	1	1	0	0	0	7	6	6	5	5	4
1981	—Rochester (Int'l)	10	10	.500	4.20	30	29	8	3	0	182	182	91	85	66	109
	—Baltimore (A.L.)	0	0	...	4.50	2	0	0	0	0	6	6	4	3	2	2
1982	—Rochester (Int'l)	10	5	.667	3.58	20	19	5	1	0	133⅓	121	59	53	36	82
	—Baltimore (A.L.)	1	0	1.000	3.51	7	0	0	0	0	25⅔	25	10	10	12	20
1983	—Rochester (Int'l)	3	1	.750	1.90	4	4	1	1	0	23⅔	17	6	5	13	18
	—Baltimore (A.L.)	16	8	.667	2.77	27	26	10	*5	0	179	141	65	55	52	120
1984	—Baltimore (A.L.)	*20	11	.645	*2.79	34	34	16	4	0	261⅓	218	95	81	81	128
1985	—Baltimore (A.L.)	12	17	.414	4.07	32	32	9	2	0	203⅓	227	104	92	89	135
1986	—Baltimore (A.L.)	14	12	.538	4.70	33	33	7	0	0	218⅓	214	125	114	74	175
1987	—Baltimore (A.L.)	10	12	.455	4.18	33	33	7	2	0	226	212	114	105	78	152
1988	—Balt.-Boston (A.L.)■	13	15	.464	3.39	36	35	5	1	0	236	234	102	89	77	156
1989	—Boston (A.L.)	15	11	.577	4.00	34	34	3	2	0	211⅔	217	101	94	71	145
1990	—Boston (A.L.)	17	8	.680	3.36	34	34	4	0	0	228	225	92	85	69	143
1991	—Kansas City (A.L.)■	12	12	.500	4.08	30	29	1	0	0	180⅔	188	89	82	59	79
1992	—Kansas City (A.L.)	1	4	.200	4.98	29	8	0	0	3	86⅔	92	50	48	37	47
1993	—Omaha (A.A.)	0	2	.000	4.60	3	3	0	0	0	15⅔	18	9	8	4	12
	—Milwaukee (A.L.)■	3	5	.375	5.67	10	10	1	0	0	54	77	35	34	15	24
	—Beloit (Midwest)	0	0	...	2.25	1	1	0	0	0	4	3	1	1	1	4
Major league totals (14 years)		134	116	.536	3.80	342	309	63	16	3	2123⅔	2082	992	897	721	1330

CHAMPIONSHIP SERIES RECORD

CHAMPIONSHIP SERIES NOTES: Named A.L. Championship Series Most Valuable Player (1983). . . . Shares single-game record for most strikeouts—14 (October 6, 1983).

Year	Team (League)	W	L	Pct.	ERA	G	GS	CG	ShO	Sv.	IP	H	R	ER	BB	SO
1983	—Baltimore (A.L.)	1	0	1.000	0.00	1	1	1	1	0	9	5	0	0	3	14
1988	—Boston (A.L.)	0	1	.000	20.25	1	1	0	0	0	2⅔	8	6	6	1	2
1990	—Boston (A.L.)	0	1	.000	2.25	1	1	1	0	0	8	6	4	2	3	7
Champ. series totals (3 years)		1	2	.333	3.66	3	3	2	1	0	19⅔	19	10	8	7	23

WORLD SERIES RECORD

Year	Team (League)	W	L	Pct.	ERA	G	GS	CG	ShO	Sv.	IP	H	R	ER	BB	SO
1983	—Baltimore (A.L.)	1	0	1.000	0.00	1	1	1	0	0	9	3	1	0	0	6

ALL-STAR GAME RECORD

Year	League	W	L	Pct.	ERA	GS	CG	ShO	Sv.	IP	H	R	ER	BB	SO
1984	—American	Did not play.													

BOEHRINGER, BRIAN

P, WHITE SOX

PERSONAL: Born January 8, 1969, in St. Louis. . . . 6-2/180. . . . Throws right, bats both. . . . Full name: Brian Edward Boehringer. . . . Name pronounced BO-ring-er.
HIGH SCHOOL: Northwest (House Springs, Mo.).
COLLEGE: St. Louis Community College at Meramec (Mo.) and UNLV.
TRANSACTIONS/CAREER NOTES: Selected by Houston Astros organization in 10th round of free-agent draft (June 4, 1990). . . . Selected by Chicago White Sox organization in fourth round of free-agent draft (June 3, 1991). . . . On Utica disabled list (June 29-August 25, 1991). . . . On disabled list (June 24-August 25, 1992).

Year	Team (League)	W	L	Pct.	ERA	G	GS	CG	ShO	Sv.	IP	H	R	ER	BB	SO
1991	—GC Whi. Sox (GCL)	1	1	.500	6.57	5	1	0	0	0	12⅓	14	9	9	5	10
	—Utica (N.Y.-Penn)	1	1	.500	2.37	4	4	0	0	0	19	14	8	5	8	19
1992	—South Bend (Mid.)	6	7	.462	4.38	15	15	2	0	0	86⅓	87	52	42	40	59
1993	—Sarasota (Fla. St.)	10	4	.714	2.80	18	17	3	0	0	119	103	47	37	51	92
	—Birm. (Southern)	2	1	.667	3.54	7	7	1	0	0	40⅔	41	20	16	14	29

BOEVER, JOE

P, TIGERS

PERSONAL: Born October 4, 1960, in St. Louis. . . . 6-1/200. . . . Throws right, bats right. . . . Full name: Joseph Martin Boever. . . . Name pronounced BAY-vur.
HIGH SCHOOL: Lindbergh (St. Louis).
COLLEGE: Crowder College (Mo.), St. Louis Community College at Meramec (Mo.) and UNLV.
TRANSACTIONS/CAREER NOTES: Signed as free agent by St. Louis Cardinals organization (June 25, 1982). . . . Traded by Cardinals to Atlanta Braves for P Randy O'Neal (July 25, 1987). . . . Traded by Braves to Philadelphia Phillies for P Marvin Freeman (July 23, 1990). . . . Granted free agency (December 20, 1991). . . . Signed by Houston Astros organization (January 27, 1992). . . . Granted free agency (December 19, 1992). . . . Signed by Oakland Athletics organization (January 21, 1993). . . . Released by A's (August 15, 1993). . . . Signed by Detroit Tigers (August 21, 1993). . . . Granted free agency (November 7, 1993). . . . Re-signed by Tigers (November 7, 1993).

Year	Team (League)	W	L	Pct.	ERA	G	GS	CG	ShO	Sv.	IP	H	R	ER	BB	SO
1982	—Erie (N.Y.-Penn)	2	3	.400	1.93	19	0	0	0	9	32⅔	20	8	7	12	63
	—Springfield (Midw.)	0	0	...	2.25	3	0	0	0	0	4	3	1	1	2	7
1983	—St. Peters. (FSL)	5	6	.455	3.02	53	0	0	0	*26	80⅓	61	29	27	37	57
1984	—Arkansas (Texas)	0	1	.000	8.18	8	0	0	0	3	11	10	11	10	12	12
	—St. Peters. (FSL)	6	4	.600	3.01	48	0	0	0	*14	77⅔	52	31	26	45	81
1985	—Arkansas (Texas)	3	1	.750	1.19	27	0	0	0	9	37⅔	21	5	5	23	45
	—Louisville (A.A.)	3	2	.600	2.04	21	0	0	0	1	35⅓	28	11	8	22	37
	—St. Louis (N.L.)	0	0	...	4.41	13	0	0	0	0	16⅓	17	8	8	4	20
1986	—St. Louis (N.L.)	0	1	.000	1.66	11	0	0	0	0	21⅔	19	5	4	11	8
	—Louisville (A.A.)	4	5	.444	2.25	51	0	0	0	5	88	71	25	22	48	75
1987	—Louisville (A.A.)	3	2	.600	3.36	43	0	0	0	*21	59	52	22	22	27	79
	—Atlanta (N.L.)■	1	0	1.000	7.36	14	0	0	0	0	18⅓	29	15	15	12	18
	—Richmond (Int'l)	1	0	1.000	1.00	6	0	0	0	1	9	8	1	1	4	8
1988	—Richmond (Int'l)	6	3	.667	2.14	48	0	0	0	*22	71⅓	47	17	17	22	71
	—Atlanta (N.L.)	0	2	.000	1.77	16	0	0	0	1	20⅓	12	4	4	1	7
1989	—Atlanta (N.L.)	4	11	.267	3.94	66	0	0	0	21	82⅓	78	37	36	34	68
1990	—Atl.-Phil. (N.L.)■	3	6	.333	3.36	67	0	0	0	14	88⅓	77	35	33	51	75
1991	—Philadelphia (N.L.)	3	5	.375	3.84	68	0	0	0	0	98⅓	90	45	42	54	89
1992	—Houston (N.L.)■	3	6	.333	2.51	*81	0	0	0	2	111⅓	103	38	31	45	67
1993	—Oakland-Det. (A.L.)■	6	3	.667	3.61	61	0	0	0	3	102⅓	101	50	41	44	63
A.L. totals (1 year)		6	3	.667	3.61	61	0	0	0	3	102⅓	101	50	41	44	63
N.L. totals (8 years)		14	31	.311	3.41	336	0	0	0	38	457	425	187	173	212	352
Major league totals (9 years)		20	34	.370	3.44	397	0	0	0	41	559⅓	526	237	214	256	415

BOGAR, TIM

IF, METS

PERSONAL: Born October 28, 1966, in Indianapolis. . . . 6-2/198. . . . Throws right, bats right. . . . Full name: Timothy Paul Bogar.
HIGH SCHOOL: Buffalo Grove (Ill.).
COLLEGE: Eastern Illinois.
TRANSACTIONS/CAREER NOTES: Selected by New York Mets organization in eighth round of free-agent draft (June 2, 1987). . . . On disabled list (June 14, 1990-remainder of season). . . . On New York disabled list (August 16-September 1, 1993).
STATISTICAL NOTES: Order of frequency of positions played at Tidewater (1991): SS-2B-3B-C-1B-OF-P.
MISCELLANEOUS: Played all nine positions in one game for Tidewater (September 4, 1991).

			BATTING												FIELDING			
Year	Team (League)	Pos.	G	AB	R	H	2B	3B	HR	RBI	Avg.	BB	SO	SB	PO	A	E	Avg.
1987	—Little Falls (NYP)	SS-2B	58	205	31	48	9	0	0	23	.234	18	39	2	79	194	24	.919
1988	—Columbia (S. Atl.)	2B-SS	45	142	19	40	4	2	3	21	.282	22	29	5	89	120	8	.963
	—St. Lucie (Fla. St.)	2B-SS-3B	76	236	34	65	7	1	2	30	.275	34	57	9	141	214	19	.949
1989	—Jackson (Texas)	SS	112	406	44	108	13	5	4	45	.266	41	57	8	185	351	29	.949
1990	—Tidewater (Int'l)	SS	33	117	10	19	2	0	0	4	.162	8	22	1	57	89	10	.936
1991	—Williamsport (East.)	3-2-1-S	63	243	33	61	12	2	2	25	.251	20	44	13	100	137	8	.967
	—Tidewater (Int'l)	I-C-O-P	65	218	23	56	11	0	1	23	.257	20	35	1	111	183	11	.964
1992	—Tidewater (Int'l)	2-S-3-P-1	129	481	54	134	32	1	5	38	.279	14	65	7	211	327	15	.973
1993	—New York (N.L.)	SS-3B-2B	78	205	19	50	13	0	3	25	.244	14	29	0	105	217	9	.973
Major league totals (1 year)			78	205	19	50	13	0	3	25	.244	14	29	0	105	217	9	.973

RECORD AS PITCHER

Year	Team (League)	W	L	Pct.	ERA	G	GS	CG	ShO	Sv.	IP	H	R	ER	BB	SO
1991	—Tidewater (Int'l)	0	0	...	27.00	1	0	0	0	0	⅓	0	1	1	0	1
1992	—Tidewater (Int'l)	0	0	...	12.00	3	0	0	0	0	3	4	4	4	3	1

BOGGS, WADE

3B, YANKEES

PERSONAL: Born June 15, 1958, in Omaha, Neb. . . . 6-2/197. . . . Throws right, bats left. . . . Full name: Wade Anthony Boggs.
HIGH SCHOOL: H.B. Plant (Tampa, Fla.).
COLLEGE: Hillsborough Community College (Fla.).
TRANSACTIONS/CAREER NOTES: Selected by Boston Red Sox organization in seventh round of free-agent draft (June 8, 1976). . . . On disabled list (April 20-May 2, 1979). . . . Granted free agency (October 26, 1992). . . . Signed by New York Yankees (December 15, 1992).
RECORDS: Holds major league records for most seasons and most consecutive seasons leading league in intentional bases on balls received—6 (1987-92). . . . Holds A.L. record for most consecutive years with 200 or more hits—7 (1983-89). . . . Holds A.L. rookie-season record for highest batting average (100 or more games)—.349 (1982). . . . Shares major league single-season record for most games with one or more hits—135 (1985). . . . Holds A.L. single-season record for most singles—187 (1985). . . . Shares A.L. single-season record for fewest double plays by third baseman (150 or more games)—17 (1988). . . . Shares major league single-season record for fewest chances accepted by third baseman (150 or more games)—349 (1990).
HONORS: Named third baseman on THE SPORTING NEWS A.L. All-Star team (1983, 1985-88 and 1991). . . . Named third base-

man on THE SPORTING NEWS A.L. Silver Slugger team (1983, 1986-89, 1991 and 1993).
STATISTICAL NOTES: Led Eastern League third basemen with .953 fielding percentage in 1979. . . . Led A.L with .449 on-base percentage in 1983, .450 in 1985, .453 in 1986, .461 in 1987, .476 in 1988 and .430 in 1989. . . . Led A.L. third basemen with 30 double plays in 1984, 37 in 1987, 29 in 1989 and 29 in 1993. . . . Led A.L. third basemen with 486 total chances in 1985. . . . Led A.L. with 19 intentional bases on balls received in 1987, 1989, 1990 and 1992, with 25 in 1991 and tied for lead with 18 in 1988. . . . Led A.L. in grounding into double plays with 23 in 1988.

			BATTING											FIELDING			
Year	Team (League)	Pos.	G	AB	R	H	2B	3B	HR	RBI	Avg.	BB	SO	SB	PO	A	E	Avg.
1976	—Elmira (N.Y.-Penn)	3B	57	179	29	47	6	0	0	15	*.263	29	15	2	36	75	16	.874
1977	—Winst.-Salem (Car.)	3B-2B-SS	117	422	67	140	13	1	2	55	.332	65	22	8	145	223	27	.932
1978	—Bristol (Eastern)	3-S-2-0	109	354	63	110	14	2	1	32	.311	53	25	1	62	107	7	.960
1979	—Bristol (Eastern)	3B-SS-2B	113	406	56	132	17	2	0	41	.325	66	21	11	94	213	15	†.953
1980	—Pawtucket (Int'l)	3B-1B	129	418	51	128	21	0	1	45	.306	64	25	3	108	156	12	.957
1981	—Pawtucket (Int'l)	3B-1B	137	498	67	*167	*41	3	5	60	*.335	89	41	4	359	238	26	.958
1982	—Boston (A.L.)	1B-3B-OF	104	338	51	118	14	1	5	44	.349	35	21	1	489	168	8	.988
1983	—Boston (A.L.)	3B	153	582	100	210	44	7	5	74	*.361	92	36	3	118	368	*27	.947
1984	—Boston (A.L.)	3B	158	625	109	203	31	4	6	55	.325	89	44	3	141	330	•20	.959
1985	—Boston (A.L.)	3B	161	653	107	*240	42	3	8	78	*.368	96	61	2	134	335	17	.965
1986	—Boston (A.L.)	3B	149	580	107	207	47	2	8	71	*.357	*105	44	0	*121	267	19	.953
1987	—Boston (A.L.)	3B-1B	147	551	108	200	40	6	24	89	*.363	105	48	1	112	277	14	.965
1988	—Boston (A.L.)	3B	155	584	*128	214	*45	6	5	58	*.366	*125	34	2	*122	250	11	.971
1989	—Boston (A.L.)	3B	156	621	•113	205	*51	7	3	54	.330	107	51	2	*123	264	17	.958
1990	—Boston (A.L.)	3B	155	619	89	187	44	5	6	63	.302	87	68	0	108	241	20	.946
1991	—Boston (A.L.)	3B	144	546	93	181	42	2	8	51	.332	89	32	1	89	276	12	.968
1992	—Boston (A.L.)	3B	143	514	62	133	22	4	7	50	.259	74	31	1	70	229	15	.952
1993	—New York (A.L.)■	3B	143	560	83	169	26	1	2	59	.302	74	49	0	75	*311	12	*.970
Major league totals (12 years)			1768	6773	1150	2267	448	48	87	746	.335	1078	519	16	1702	3316	192	.963

CHAMPIONSHIP SERIES RECORD

CHAMPIONSHIP SERIES NOTES: Shares single-series record for most sacrifice flies—2 (1988).

			BATTING											FIELDING			
Year	Team (League)	Pos.	G	AB	R	H	2B	3B	HR	RBI	Avg.	BB	SO	SB	PO	A	E	Avg.
1986	—Boston (A.L.)	3B	7	30	3	7	1	1	0	2	.233	4	1	0	7	13	2	.909
1988	—Boston (A.L.)	3B	4	13	2	5	0	0	0	3	.385	3	4	0	6	6	0	1.000
1990	—Boston (A.L.)	3B	4	16	1	7	1	0	1	1	.438	0	3	0	6	10	0	1.000
Championship series totals (3 years)			15	59	6	19	2	1	1	6	.322	7	8	0	19	29	2	.960

WORLD SERIES RECORD

			BATTING											FIELDING			
Year	Team (League)	Pos.	G	AB	R	H	2B	3B	HR	RBI	Avg.	BB	SO	SB	PO	A	E	Avg.
1986	—Boston (A.L.)	3B	7	31	3	9	3	0	0	3	.290	4	2	0	4	15	0	1.000

ALL-STAR GAME RECORD

			BATTING										FIELDING			
Year	League	Pos.	AB	R	H	2B	3B	HR	RBI	Avg.	BB	SO	SB	PO	A	E	Avg.
1985	—American	3B	0	0	0	0	0	0	0	...	1	0	0	0	0	0	...
1986	—American	3B	3	0	1	0	0	0	0	.333	1	0	0	0	1	0	1.000
1987	—American	3B	3	0	0	0	0	0	0	.000	0	0	0	0	3	0	1.000
1988	—American	3B	3	0	1	0	0	0	0	.333	0	0	0	0	1	0	1.000
1989	—American	3B	3	1	1	0	0	1	1	.333	0	0	0	1	1	0	1.000
1990	—American	3B	2	0	2	0	0	0	0	1.000	1	0	0	0	4	0	1.000
1991	—American	3B	2	1	1	0	0	0	0	.500	1	0	0	1	2	0	1.000
1992	—American	3B	3	1	1	0	0	0	0	.333	0	1	0	1	0	0	1.000
1993	—American	3B	1	0	0	0	0	0	0	.000	1	0	0	1	0	0	1.000
All-Star Game totals (9 years)			20	3	7	0	0	1	1	.350	5	1	0	4	12	0	1.000

BOHANON, BRIAN

P, RANGERS

PERSONAL: Born August 1, 1968, in Denton, Tex. . . . 6-2/220. . . . Throws left, bats left. . . . Full name: Brian Edward Bohanon.
HIGH SCHOOL: North Shore (Houston).
TRANSACTIONS/CAREER NOTES: Selected by Texas Rangers organization in first round (19th pick overall) of free-agent draft (June 2, 1987). . . . On disabled list (April 17, 1988-remainder of season). . . . On Charlotte disabled list (April 7-May 2, 1989). . . . On Texas disabled list (April 7-July 1, 1991); included rehabilitation assignment to Charlotte (June 1-10), Tulsa (June 10-23) and Oklahoma City (June 23-30). . . . On Texas disabled list (April 28-May 13, 1992). . . . On Texas disabled list (June 9-30, 1993); included rehabilitation assignment to Oklahoma City (June 21-30).

Year	Team (League)	W	L	Pct.	ERA	G	GS	CG	ShO	Sv.	IP	H	R	ER	BB	SO
1987	—GC Rangers (GCL)	0	2	.000	4.71	5	4	0	0	0	21	15	13	11	5	21
1988	—Charlotte (Fla. St.)	0	1	.000	5.40	2	2	0	0	0	6⅔	6	4	4	5	9
1989	—Charlotte (Fla. St.)	0	3	.000	1.81	11	7	0	0	1	54⅔	40	16	11	20	33
	—Tulsa (Texas)	5	0	1.000	2.20	11	11	1	1	0	73⅔	59	20	18	27	44
1990	—Texas (A.L.)	0	3	.000	6.62	11	6	0	0	0	34	40	30	25	18	15
	—Okla. City (A.A.)	1	2	.333	3.66	14	4	0	0	1	32	35	16	13	8	22
1991	—Charlotte (Fla. St.)	1	0	1.000	3.86	2	2	0	0	0	11⅔	6	5	5	4	7
	—Tulsa (Texas)	0	1	.000	2.31	2	2	0	0	0	11⅔	9	8	3	11	6
	—Okla. City (A.A.)	0	4	.000	2.91	7	7	0	0	0	46⅓	49	19	15	15	37
	—Texas (A.L.)	4	3	.571	4.84	11	11	1	0	0	61⅓	66	35	33	23	34
1992	—Okla. City (A.A.)	4	2	.667	2.73	9	9	3	0	0	56	53	21	17	15	24
	—Texas (A.L.)	1	1	.500	6.31	18	7	0	0	0	45⅔	57	38	32	25	29
	—Tulsa (Texas)	2	1	.667	1.27	6	6	1	0	0	28⅓	25	7	4	9	25

Year	Team (League)	W	L	Pct.	ERA	G	GS	CG	ShO	Sv.	IP	H	R	ER	BB	SO
1993	—Texas (A.L.)	4	4	.500	4.76	36	8	0	0	0	92⅔	107	54	49	46	45
	—Okla. City (A.A.)	0	1	.000	6.43	2	2	0	0	0	7	7	6	5	3	7
Major league totals (4 years)		9	11	.450	5.35	76	32	1	0	0	233⅔	270	157	139	112	123

BOLICK, FRANK

3B/1B, PIRATES

PERSONAL: Born June 28, 1966, in Ashland, Pa. . . . 5-10/175. . . . Throws right, bats both. . . . Full name: Frank Charles Bolick. . . . Son of Frank Bolick, minor league pitcher (1966-77).

HIGH SCHOOL: Mt. Carmel (Pa.).

COLLEGE: Georgia Tech.

TRANSACTIONS/CAREER NOTES: Selected by Montreal Expos organization in 23rd round of free-agent draft (June 3, 1985). . . . Selected by Milwaukee Brewers organization in ninth round of free-agent draft (June 2, 1987). . . . Traded by Brewers organization to Seattle Mariners organization for OF Mickey Brantley (June 6, 1990). . . . Traded by Mariners with a player to be named later to Montreal Expos for P Dave Wainhouse and P Kevin Foster (November 20, 1992); Expos organization acquired C Miah Bradbury to complete deal (December 8, 1992). . . . Granted free agency (October 15, 1993). . . . Signed by Buffalo, Pittsburgh Pirates organization (November 27, 1993).

HONORS: Named California League Most Valuable Player (1990).

STATISTICAL NOTES: Tied for California League lead with 13 sacrifice flies in 1990.

			BATTING												FIELDING			
Year	Team (League)	Pos.	G	AB	R	H	2B	3B	HR	RBI	Avg.	BB	SO	SB	PO	A	E	Avg.
1987	—Helena (Pioneer)	3B	52	156	41	39	8	1	10	28	.250	41	44	4	5	13	1	.947
1988	—Beloit (Midwest)	3B	55	180	28	41	14	1	2	16	.228	43	49	3	38	81	14	.895
	—Ariz. Brewers (Ar.)	3B	23	80	20	30	9	3	1	20	.375	22	8	1	23	55	4	.951
	—Helena (Pioneer)	3B	40	131	35	39	10	1	10	38	.298	32	31	5	28	65	10	.903
1989	—Beloit (Midwest)	3B-1B-OF	88	299	44	90	23	0	9	41	.301	47	52	9	47	108	15	.912
1990	—Stock.-S.B. (Calif.)■	3B-1B	128	441	100	143	33	5	18	*102	.324	91	86	8	114	209	20	.942
1991	—Jacksonv. (South.)	3B-SS	136	468	69	119	19	0	16	73	.254	*84	115	5	88	256	17	.953
1992	—Jacksonv. (South.)	3B-1B	63	224	32	60	9	0	13	42	.268	42	38	1	51	126	5	.973
	—Calgary (PCL)	3B	78	274	35	79	18	6	14	54	.288	39	52	4	36	121	14	.918
1993	—Montreal (N.L.)■	1B-3B	95	213	25	45	13	0	4	24	.211	23	37	1	338	63	8	.980
	—Ottawa (Int'l)	3B	2	8	0	1	0	0	0	0	.125	0	0	0	0	4	0	1.000
Major league totals (1 year)			95	213	25	45	13	0	4	24	.211	23	37	1	338	63	8	.980

BOLTON, RODNEY

P, WHITE SOX

PERSONAL: Born September 23, 1968, in Chattanooga, Tenn. . . . 6-2/190. . . . Throws right, bats right. . . . Full name: Rodney Earl Bolton.

HIGH SCHOOL: Ooltewah (Tenn.).

COLLEGE: Chattanooga (Tenn.) State Community Technical College, then Kentucky (bachelor's degree in marketing).

TRANSACTIONS/CAREER NOTES: Selected by Chicago White Sox in 13th round of free-agent draft (June 4, 1990). . . . On Vancouver disabled list (September 15-October 9, 1992).

Year	Team (League)	W	L	Pct.	ERA	G	GS	CG	ShO	Sv.	IP	H	R	ER	BB	SO
1990	—Utica (N.Y.-Penn)	5	1	.833	0.41	6	6	1	1	0	44	27	4	2	11	45
	—South Bend (Mid.)	5	1	.833	1.94	7	7	3	1	0	51	34	14	11	12	50
1991	—Sarasota (Fla. St.)	7	6	.538	1.91	15	15	5	2	0	103⅔	81	29	22	23	77
	—Birm. (Southern)	8	4	.667	1.62	12	12	3	2	0	89	73	26	16	21	57
1992	—Vancouver (PCL)	11	9	.550	2.93	27	27	3	2	0	*187⅓	174	72	61	59	111
1993	—Chicago (A.L.)	2	6	.250	7.44	9	8	0	0	0	42⅓	55	40	35	16	17
	—Nashville (A.A.)	10	1	*.909	*2.88	18	16	1	0	1	115⅔	108	40	37	37	75
Major league totals (1 year)		2	6	.250	7.44	9	8	0	0	0	42⅓	55	40	35	16	17

BOLTON, TOM

P, TIGERS

PERSONAL: Born May 6, 1962, in Nashville, Tenn. . . . 6-3/185. . . . Throws left, bats left. . . . Full name: Thomas Edward Bolton.

HIGH SCHOOL: Antioch (Tenn.).

TRANSACTIONS/CAREER NOTES: Selected by Boston Red Sox organization in 20th round of free-agent draft (June 3, 1980). . . . On New Britain disabled list (June 27-July 9, 1983). . . . On disabled list (April 11-May 26, 1986 and July 22-August 13, 1991). . . . Traded by Red Sox to Cincinnati Reds for OF Billy Hatcher (July 9, 1992). . . . Released by Reds (November 30, 1992). . . . Signed by Detroit Tigers (December 10, 1992).

Year	Team (League)	W	L	Pct.	ERA	G	GS	CG	ShO	Sv.	IP	H	R	ER	BB	SO
1980	—Elmira (N.Y.-Penn)	6	2	.750	2.41	23	1	1	1	5	56	43	26	15	22	43
1981	—Winter Haven (FSL)	2	9	.182	4.50	24	16	0	0	0	92	125	62	46	41	47
1982	—Winter Haven (FSL)	9	8	.529	2.99	28	25	4	0	0	162⅔	161	67	54	63	77
1983	—New Britain (East.)	7	3	.700	2.89	16	16	2	1	0	99⅔	93	36	32	41	62
	—Pawtucket (Int'l)	0	5	.000	6.52	6	6	0	0	0	29	33	26	21	25	20
1984	—New Britain (East.)	4	5	.444	4.14	33	9	0	0	1	87	87	54	40	34	66
1985	—New Britain (East.)	5	6	.455	4.28	34	10	1	0	1	101	106	53	48	40	74
1986	—Pawtucket (Int'l)	3	4	.429	2.72	29	7	1	0	2	86	80	30	26	25	58
1987	—Pawtucket (Int'l)	2	1	.667	5.40	5	4	0	0	0	21⅔	25	14	13	12	8
	—Boston (A.L.)	1	0	1.000	4.38	29	0	0	0	0	61⅔	83	33	30	27	49
1988	—Pawtucket (Int'l)	3	0	1.000	2.79	18	1	0	0	0	19⅓	17	7	6	10	15
	—Boston (A.L.)	1	3	.250	4.75	28	0	0	0	1	30⅓	35	17	16	14	21
1989	—Pawtucket (Int'l)	12	5	.706	2.89	25	22	5	2	1	143⅓	140	57	46	47	99
	—Boston (A.L.)	0	4	.000	8.31	4	4	0	0	0	17⅓	21	18	16	10	9
1990	—Pawtucket (Int'l)	1	0	1.000	3.86	4	2	0	0	0	11⅔	9	6	5	7	8
	—Boston (A.L.)	10	5	.667	3.38	21	16	3	0	0	119⅔	111	46	45	47	65
1991	—Boston (A.L.)	8	9	.471	5.24	25	19	0	0	0	110	136	72	64	51	64

Year	Team (League)	W	L	Pct.	ERA	G	GS	CG	ShO	Sv.	IP	H	R	ER	BB	SO
1992	—Boston (A.L.)	1	2	.333	3.41	21	1	0	0	0	29	34	11	11	14	23
	—Cincinnati (N.L.)■	3	3	.500	5.24	16	8	0	0	0	46⅓	52	28	27	23	27
1993	—Detroit (A.L.)■	6	6	.500	4.47	43	8	0	0	0	102⅔	113	57	51	45	66
	A.L. totals (7 years)	27	29	.482	4.46	171	48	3	0	1	470⅔	533	254	233	208	297
	N.L. totals (1 year)	3	3	.500	5.24	16	8	0	0	0	46⅓	52	28	27	23	27
	Major league totals (7 years)	30	32	.484	4.53	187	56	3	0	1	517	585	282	260	231	324

CHAMPIONSHIP SERIES RECORD

Year	Team (League)	W	L	Pct.	ERA	G	GS	CG	ShO	Sv.	IP	H	R	ER	BB	SO
1988	—Boston (A.L.)							Did not play.								
1990	—Boston (A.L.)	0	0	...	0.00	2	0	0	0	0	3	2	0	0	2	3
	Champ. series totals (1 year)	0	0	...	0.00	2	0	0	0	0	3	2	0	0	2	3

B

BONDS, BARRY

OF, GIANTS

PERSONAL: Born July 24, 1964, in Riverside, Calif. . . . 6-1/185. . . . Throws left, bats left. . . . Full name: Barry Lamar Bonds. . . . Son of Bobby Bonds, current coach, San Francisco Giants; major league outfielder with eight teams (1968-81) and coach, Cleveland Indians (1984-87).

HIGH SCHOOL: Serra (San Mateo, Calif.).

COLLEGE: Arizona State.

TRANSACTIONS/CAREER NOTES: Selected by San Francisco Giants organization in second round of free-agent draft (June 7, 1982). . . . Selected by Pittsburgh Pirates organization in first round (sixth pick overall) of free-agent draft (June 3, 1985). . . . On disabled list (June 15-July 4, 1992). . . . Granted free agency (October 26, 1992). . . . Signed by Giants (December 8, 1992).

RECORDS: Shares major league single-season record for fewest assists by outfielder who led league in assists—14 (1990).

HONORS: Named outfielder on THE SPORTING NEWS college All-America team (1985). . . . Named Major League Player of the Year by THE SPORTING NEWS (1990). . . . Named N.L. Player of the Year by THE SPORTING NEWS (1990-91). . . . Named outfielder on THE SPORTING NEWS N.L. All-Star team (1990-93). . . . Won N.L. Gold Glove as outfielder (1990-93). . . . Named outfielder on THE SPORTING NEWS N.L. Silver Slugger team (1990-93). . . . Named N.L. Most Valuable Player by Baseball Writers' Association of America (1990 and 1992-93).

STATISTICAL NOTES: Led N.L. with .565 slugging percentage in 1990, .624 in 1992 and .677 in 1993. . . . Led N.L. with 32 intentional bases on balls received in 1992 and 43 in 1993. . . . Led N.L. with .456 on-base percentage in 1992 and .458 in 1993. . . . Led N.L. with 365 total bases in 1993.

			BATTING												FIELDING			
Year	Team (League)	Pos.	G	AB	R	H	2B	3B	HR	RBI	Avg.	BB	SO	SB	PO	A	E	Avg.
1985	—Prin. William (Car.)	OF	71	254	49	76	16	4	13	37	.299	37	52	15	202	4	5	.976
1986	—Hawaii (PCL)	OF	44	148	30	46	7	2	7	37	.311	33	31	16	109	4	2	.983
	—Pittsburgh (N.L.)	OF	113	413	72	92	26	3	16	48	.223	65	102	36	280	9	5	.983
1987	—Pittsburgh (N.L.)	OF	150	551	99	144	34	9	25	59	.261	54	88	32	330	15	5	.986
1988	—Pittsburgh (N.L.)	OF	144	538	97	152	30	5	24	58	.283	72	82	17	292	5	6	.980
1989	—Pittsburgh (N.L.)	OF	159	580	96	144	34	6	19	58	.248	93	93	32	365	14	6	.984
1990	—Pittsburgh (N.L.)	OF	151	519	104	156	32	3	33	114	.301	93	83	52	338	•14	6	.983
1991	—Pittsburgh (N.L.)	OF	153	510	95	149	28	5	25	116	.292	107	73	43	321	13	3	.991
1992	—Pittsburgh (N.L.)	OF	140	473	*109	147	36	5	34	103	.311	*127	69	39	310	4	3	.991
1993	—San Francisco (N.L.)■	OF	159	539	129	181	38	4	*46	*123	.336	126	79	29	310	7	5	.984
	Major league totals (8 years)		1169	4123	801	1165	258	40	222	679	.283	737	669	280	2546	81	39	.985

CHAMPIONSHIP SERIES RECORD

CHAMPIONSHIP SERIES NOTES: Shares record for most hits in one inning—2 (October 13, 1992, second inning).

			BATTING												FIELDING			
Year	Team (League)	Pos.	G	AB	R	H	2B	3B	HR	RBI	Avg.	BB	SO	SB	PO	A	E	Avg.
1990	—Pittsburgh (N.L.)	OF	6	18	4	3	0	0	0	1	.167	6	5	2	13	0	0	1.000
1991	—Pittsburgh (N.L.)	OF	7	27	1	4	1	0	0	0	.148	2	4	3	14	1	1	.938
1992	—Pittsburgh (N.L.)	OF	7	23	5	6	1	0	1	2	.261	6	4	1	17	0	0	1.000
	Championship series totals (3 years)		20	68	10	13	2	0	1	3	.191	14	13	6	44	1	1	.978

ALL-STAR GAME RECORD

			BATTING											FIELDING			
Year	League	Pos.	AB	R	H	2B	3B	HR	RBI	Avg.	BB	SO	SB	PO	A	E	Avg.
1990	—National	OF	1	0	0	0	0	0	0	.000	1	0	0	2	0	0	1.000
1992	—National	OF	3	1	1	1	0	0	0	.333	0	0	0	2	0	0	1.000
1993	—National	OF	3	2	2	2	0	0	0	.667	0	0	0	1	0	0	1.000
	All-Star Game totals (3 years)		7	3	3	3	0	0	0	.429	1	0	0	5	0	0	1.000

BONES, RICKY

P, BREWERS

PERSONAL: Born April 7, 1969, in Salinas, Puerto Rico. . . . 6-0/190. . . . Throws right, bats right. . . . Name pronounced BO-nuss.

TRANSACTIONS/CAREER NOTES: Signed as free agent by San Diego Padres organization (May 13, 1986). . . . Traded by Padres with IF Jose Valentin and OF Matt Mieske to Milwaukee Brewers for 3B Gary Sheffield and P Geoff Kellogg (March 27, 1992).

STATISTICAL NOTES: Led Texas League with 22 home runs allowed in 1989.

MISCELLANEOUS: Appeared in one game as outfielder with no chances (1993).

Year	Team (League)	W	L	Pct.	ERA	G	GS	CG	ShO	Sv.	IP	H	R	ER	BB	SO
1986	—Spokane (N'west)	1	3	.250	5.59	18	9	0	0	0	58	63	44	36	29	46
1987	—Char., S.C. (S. Atl.)	12	5	.706	3.65	26	26	4	1	0	170⅓	*183	81	69	45	130
1988	—Riverside (Calif.)	15	6	.714	3.64	25	25	5	2	0	175⅓	162	80	71	64	129
1989	—Wichita (Texas)	10	9	.526	5.74	24	24	2	0	0	136⅓	162	103	87	47	88

Year	Team (League)	W	L	Pct.	ERA	G	GS	CG	ShO	Sv.	IP	H	R	ER	BB	SO
1990	—Wichita (Texas)	6	4	.600	3.48	21	21	2	1	0	137	138	66	53	45	96
	—Las Vegas (PCL)	2	1	.667	3.47	5	5	0	0	0	36⅓	45	17	14	10	25
1991	—Las Vegas (PCL)	8	6	.571	4.22	23	23	1	0	0	136⅓	155	90	64	43	95
	—San Diego (N.L.)	4	6	.400	4.83	11	11	0	0	0	54	57	33	29	18	31
1992	—Milwaukee (A.L.)■	9	10	.474	4.57	31	28	0	0	0	163⅓	169	90	83	48	65
1993	—Milwaukee (A.L.)	11	11	.500	4.86	32	31	3	0	0	203⅔	222	122	110	63	63
A.L. totals (2 years)		20	21	.488	4.73	63	59	3	0	0	367	391	212	193	111	128
N.L. totals (1 year)		4	6	.400	4.83	11	11	0	0	0	54	57	33	29	18	31
Major league totals (3 years)		24	27	.471	4.75	74	70	3	0	0	421	448	245	222	129	159

BONILLA, BOBBY

OF, METS

PERSONAL: Born February 23, 1963, in New York. . . . 6-3/240. . . . Throws right, bats both. . . . Full name: Roberto Martin Antonio Bonilla. . . . Name pronounced bo-NEE-yah.
HIGH SCHOOL: Lehman (Bronx, N.Y.).
COLLEGE: New York Technical College.
TRANSACTIONS/CAREER NOTES: Signed as free agent by Pittsburgh Pirates organization (July 11, 1981). . . . On Pittsburgh disabled list (March 25-July 19, 1985). . . . Selected by Chicago White Sox from Pirates organization in Rule 5 major league draft (December 10, 1985). . . . Traded by White Sox to Pittsburgh Pirates for P Jose DeLeon (July 23, 1986). . . . Granted free agency (October 28, 1991). . . . Signed by New York Mets (December 2, 1991). . . . On suspended list (July 27-28, 1992). . . . On disabled list (August 3-19, 1992).
RECORDS: Shares major league single-season record for most games with switch-hit home runs—2 (1993).
HONORS: Named third baseman on THE SPORTING NEWS N.L. All-Star team (1988). . . . Named third baseman on THE SPORTING NEWS N.L. Silver Slugger team (1988). . . . Named outfielder on THE SPORTING NEWS N.L. All-Star team (1990-91). . . . Named outfielder on THE SPORTING NEWS N.L. Silver Slugger team (1990-91).
STATISTICAL NOTES: Led Eastern League outfielders with 15 errors in 1984. . . . Switch-hit home runs in one game (July 3, 1987; April 6, 1988; April 6, 1992 and April 23 and June 10, 1993). . . . Led N.L. third basemen with 489 total chances in 1988. . . . Led N.L. third basemen with 35 errors in 1989. . . . Led N.L. third basemen with 31 double plays in 1989. . . . Led N.L. with 15 sacrifice flies in 1990.

			BATTING												FIELDING			
Year	Team (League)	Pos.	G	AB	R	H	2B	3B	HR	RBI	Avg.	BB	SO	SB	PO	A	E	Avg.
1981	—GC Pirates (GCL)	1B-C-3B	22	69	6	15	5	0	0	7	.217	7	17	2	124	23	5	.967
1982	—GC Pirates (GCL)	1B	47	167	20	38	3	0	5	26	.228	11	20	2	318	36	*14	.962
1983	—Alexandria (Caro.)	OF-1B	•136	504	88	129	19	7	11	59	.256	78	105	28	259	12	15	.948
1984	—Nashua (Eastern)	OF-1B	136	484	74	128	19	5	11	71	.264	49	89	15	312	8	†15	.955
1985	—Prin. William (Car.)	1B-3B	39	130	15	34	4	1	3	11	.262	16	29	1	180	9	2	.990
1986	—Chicago (A.L.)■	OF-1B	75	234	27	63	10	2	2	26	.269	33	49	4	361	22	2	.995
	—Pittsburgh (N.L.)■	OF-1B-3B	63	192	28	46	6	2	1	17	.240	29	39	4	90	16	3	.972
1987	—Pittsburgh (N.L.)	3B-OF-1B	141	466	58	140	33	3	15	77	.300	39	64	3	142	139	16	.946
1988	—Pittsburgh (N.L.)	3B	159	584	87	160	32	7	24	100	.274	85	82	3	121	*336	*32	.935
1989	—Pittsburgh (N.L.)	3B-1B-OF	•163	616	96	173	37	10	24	86	.281	76	93	8	190	334	†35	.937
1990	—Pittsburgh (N.L.)	OF-3B-1B	160	625	112	175	39	7	32	120	.280	45	103	4	315	35	15	.959
1991	—Pittsburgh (N.L.)	OF-3B-1B	157	577	102	174	*44	6	18	100	.302	90	67	2	247	144	15	.963
1992	—New York (N.L.)■	OF-1B	128	438	62	109	23	0	19	70	.249	66	73	4	277	9	4	.986
1993	—New York (N.L.)	OF-3B-1B	139	502	81	133	21	3	34	87	.265	72	96	3	238	112	17	.954
American League totals (1 year)			75	234	27	63	10	2	2	26	.269	33	49	4	361	22	2	.995
National League totals (8 years)			1110	4000	626	1110	235	38	167	657	.278	502	617	31	1620	1125	137	.952
Major league totals (8 years)			1185	4234	653	1173	245	40	169	683	.277	535	666	35	1981	1147	139	.957

CHAMPIONSHIP SERIES RECORD

			BATTING												FIELDING			
Year	Team (League)	Pos.	G	AB	R	H	2B	3B	HR	RBI	Avg.	BB	SO	SB	PO	A	E	Avg.
1990	—Pittsburgh (N.L.)	OF-3B	6	21	0	4	1	0	0	1	.190	3	1	0	4	5	1	.900
1991	—Pittsburgh (N.L.)	OF	7	23	2	7	2	0	0	1	.304	6	2	0	12	1	0	1.000
Championship series totals (2 years)			13	44	2	11	3	0	0	2	.250	9	3	0	16	6	1	.957

ALL-STAR GAME RECORD

			BATTING											FIELDING			
Year	League	Pos.	AB	R	H	2B	3B	HR	RBI	Avg.	BB	SO	SB	PO	A	E	Avg.
1988	—National	3B	4	0	0	0	0	0	0	.000	0	0	0	0	2	0	1.000
1989	—National	PH-DH	2	0	2	0	0	0	0	1.000	0	0	0	...	...	...	...
1990	—National	1B	1	0	0	0	0	0	0	.000	0	0	0	1	0	0	1.000
1991	—National	DH	4	0	2	0	0	0	1	.500	0	1	0	...	...	...	...
1993	—National	OF	1	0	1	0	0	0	0	1.000	0	0	0	2	0	0	1.000
All-Star Game totals (5 years)			12	0	5	0	0	0	1	.417	0	1	0	3	2	0	1.000

BOONE, BRET

2B, REDS

PERSONAL: Born April 6, 1969, in El Cajon, Calif. . . . 5-10/180. . . . Throws right, bats right. . . . Full name: Bret Robert Boone. . . . Grandson of Ray Boone, major league infielder with six teams (1948-60); son of Bob Boone, current coach, Cincinnati Reds, and catcher, Philadelphia Phillies, California Angels and Kansas City Royals (1972-90); and nephew of Rodney Boone, minor league catcher/outfielder (1972-75).
HIGH SCHOOL: El Dorado (Yorba Linda, Calif.).
COLLEGE: Southern California.
TRANSACTIONS/CAREER NOTES: Selected by Minnesota Twins organization in 28th round of free-agent draft (June 2, 1987). . . . Selected by Seattle Mariners organization in fifth round of free-agent draft (June 4, 1990). . . . Traded by Mariners with P Erik Hanson to Cincinnati Reds for P Bobby Ayala and C Dan Wilson (November 2, 1993).
STATISTICAL NOTES: Tied for Southern League lead in grounding into double plays with 21 in 1991. . . . Led Southern League second basemen with 288 putouts in 1991. . . . Led Pacific Coast League second basemen with 90 double plays in 1992.

Year	Team (League)	Pos.	G	AB	R	H	2B	3B	HR	RBI	Avg.	BB	SO	SB	PO	A	E	Avg.
			BATTING												FIELDING			
1990	—Peninsula (Caro.)	2B	74	255	42	68	13	2	8	38	.267	47	57	5	154	216	19	.951
1991	—Jacksonv. (South.)	2B-3B	•139	475	64	121	18	1	19	75	.255	72	123	9	†300	369	21	.970
1992	—Calgary (PCL)	2B-SS	118	439	73	138	26	5	13	73	.314	60	88	17	268	366	10	.984
	—Seattle (A.L.)	2B-3B	33	129	15	25	4	0	4	15	.194	4	34	1	72	96	6	.966
1993	—Calgary (PCL)	2B	71	274	48	91	18	3	8	56	.332	28	58	3	146	180	8	.976
	—Seattle (A.L.)	2B	76	271	31	68	12	2	12	38	.251	17	52	2	140	177	3	.991
Major league totals (2 years)			109	400	46	93	16	2	16	53	.233	21	86	3	212	273	9	.982

BORBON, PEDRO

P, BRAVES

PERSONAL: Born November 15, 1967, in Mao, Dominican Republic. . . . 6-1/205. . . . Throws left, bats left. . . . Full name: Pedro Felix Borbon Jr. . . . Son of Pedro Borbon, major league pitcher with four teams (1969-80). . . . Name pronounced bor-BONE.

HIGH SCHOOL: DeWitt Clinton (Bronx, N.Y.).

COLLEGE: Ranger (Tex.) Junior College.

TRANSACTIONS/CAREER NOTES: Selected by Milwaukee Brewers organization in 35th round of free-agent draft (June 3, 1985). . . . Selected by Los Angeles Dodgers organization in secondary phase of free-agent draft (January 14, 1986). . . . Signed as free agent by Chicago White Sox organization (June 4, 1988). . . . Released by White Sox organization (April 1, 1989). . . . Signed by Atlanta Braves organization (August 25, 1989).

STATISTICAL NOTES: Led Gulf Coast League with 14 balks in 1988.

Year	Team (League)	W	L	Pct.	ERA	G	GS	CG	ShO	Sv.	IP	H	R	ER	BB	SO
1988	—GC Whi. Sox (GCL)	5	3	.625	2.41	16	11	1	1	1	74⅔	52	28	20	17	67
1989	—							Did not play.								
1990	—Burlington (Midw.)■	11	3	.786	1.47	14	14	6	2	0	97⅔	73	25	16	23	76
	—Durham (Carolina)	4	5	.444	5.43	11	11	0	0	0	61⅓	73	40	37	16	37
1991	—Durham (Carolina)	4	3	.571	2.27	37	6	1	0	5	91	85	40	23	35	79
	—Greenville (South.)	0	1	.000	2.79	4	4	0	0	0	29	23	12	9	10	22
1992	—Greenville (South.)	8	2	.800	3.06	39	10	0	0	3	94	73	36	32	42	79
	—Atlanta (N.L.)	0	1	.000	6.75	2	0	0	0	0	1⅓	2	1	1	1	1
1993	—Richmond (Int'l)	5	5	.500	4.23	52	0	0	0	1	76⅔	71	40	36	42	95
	—Atlanta (N.L.)	0	0	...	21.60	3	0	0	0	0	1⅔	3	4	4	3	2
Major league totals (2 years)		0	1	.000	15.00	5	0	0	0	0	3	5	5	5	4	3

BORDERS, PAT

C, BLUE JAYS

PERSONAL: Born May 14, 1963, in Columbus, O. . . . 6-2/200. . . . Throws right, bats right. . . . Full name: Patrick Lance Borders. . . . Brother of Todd Borders, minor league catcher (1988).

HIGH SCHOOL: Lake Wales (Fla.).

TRANSACTIONS/CAREER NOTES: Selected by Toronto Blue Jays organization in sixth round of free-agent draft (June 7, 1982). . . . On Toronto disabled list (July 5-August 19, 1988); included rehabilitation assignment to Syracuse (July 30-August 19).

STATISTICAL NOTES: Tied for Southern League lead with 16 passed balls in 1987. . . . Led A.L. catchers with 880 total chances in 1992 and 962 in 1993.

Year	Team (League)	Pos.	G	AB	R	H	2B	3B	HR	RBI	Avg.	BB	SO	SB	PO	A	E	Avg.
			BATTING												FIELDING			
1982	—Medicine Hat (Pio.)	3B	61	217	30	66	12	2	5	33	.304	24	52	1	23	96	*25	.826
1983	—Florence (S. Atl.)	3B	131	457	62	125	31	4	5	54	.274	46	116	4	70	233	*41	.881
1984	—Florence (S. Atl.)	1B-3B-OF	131	467	69	129	32	5	12	85	.276	56	109	3	650	77	25	.967
1985	—Kinston (Carolina)	1B	127	460	43	120	16	1	10	60	.261	45	116	6	854	42	*20	.978
1986	—Florence (S. Atl.)	C-OF	16	40	8	15	7	0	3	9	.375	2	9	0	22	1	0	1.000
	—Knoxville (South.)	C-1B	12	34	3	12	1	0	2	5	.353	1	6	0	45	5	3	.943
	—Kinston (Carolina)	C-1B-OF	49	174	24	57	10	0	6	26	.328	10	42	0	211	26	7	.971
1987	—Dunedin (Fla. St.)	1B	3	11	0	4	0	0	0	1	.364	0	3	0	21	1	0	1.000
	—Knoxville (South.)	C-3B	94	349	44	102	14	1	11	51	.292	20	56	2	432	49	12	.976
1988	—Toronto (A.L.)	C-2B-3B	56	154	15	42	6	3	5	21	.273	3	24	0	205	19	7	.970
	—Syracuse (Int'l)	C	35	120	11	29	8	0	3	14	.242	16	22	0	202	17	2	.991
1989	—Toronto (A.L.)	C	94	241	22	62	11	1	3	29	.257	11	45	2	261	27	6	.980
1990	—Toronto (A.L.)	C	125	346	36	99	24	2	15	49	.286	18	57	0	515	46	4	.993
1991	—Toronto (A.L.)	C	105	291	22	71	17	0	5	36	.244	11	45	0	505	48	4	.993
1992	—Toronto (A.L.)	C	138	480	47	116	26	2	13	53	.242	33	75	1	784	*88	8	.991
1993	—Toronto (A.L.)	C	138	488	38	124	30	0	9	55	.254	20	66	2	869	*80	*13	.986
Major league totals (6 years)			656	2000	180	514	114	8	50	243	.257	96	312	5	3139	308	42	.988

CHAMPIONSHIP SERIES RECORD

Year	Team (League)	Pos.	G	AB	R	H	2B	3B	HR	RBI	Avg.	BB	SO	SB	PO	A	E	Avg.
			BATTING												FIELDING			
1989	—Toronto (A.L.)	PH-C	1	1	0	1	0	0	0	1	1.000	0	0	0	1	0	0	1.000
1991	—Toronto (A.L.)	C	5	19	0	5	1	0	0	2	.263	0	0	0	38	4	2	.955
1992	—Toronto (A.L.)	C	6	22	3	7	0	0	1	3	.318	1	1	0	38	3	1	.976
1993	—Toronto (A.L.)	C	6	24	1	6	1	0	0	3	.250	0	6	1	41	4	0	1.000
Championship series totals (4 years)			18	66	4	19	2	0	1	9	.288	1	7	1	118	11	3	.977

WORLD SERIES RECORD

WORLD SERIES NOTES: Named Most Valuable Player (1992).

Year	Team (League)	Pos.	G	AB	R	H	2B	3B	HR	RBI	Avg.	BB	SO	SB	PO	A	E	Avg.
			BATTING												FIELDING			
1992	—Toronto (A.L.)	C	6	20	2	9	3	0	1	3	.450	2	1	0	48	5	1	.981
1993	—Toronto (A.L.)	C	6	23	2	7	0	0	0	1	.304	2	1	0	50	2	1	.981
World Series totals (2 years)			12	43	4	16	3	0	1	4	.372	4	2	0	98	7	2	.981

BORDICK, MIKE
SS, ATHLETICS

PERSONAL: Born July 21, 1965, in Marquette, Mich. . . . 5-11/175. . . . Throws right, bats right. . . . Full name: Michael Todd Bordick.
HIGH SCHOOL: Hampden (Me.) Academy.
COLLEGE: Maine.
TRANSACTIONS/CAREER NOTES: Signed as free agent by Oakland Athletics organization (July 10, 1986). . . . On Tacoma disabled list (April 14-May 13, 1991).
STATISTICAL NOTES: Led Pacific Coast League shortstops with .972 fielding percentage and 82 double plays in 1990. . . . Led A.L. shortstops with 280 putouts and tied for lead with 108 double plays in 1993.

			BATTING												FIELDING			
Year	**Team (League)**	**Pos.**	**G**	**AB**	**R**	**H**	**2B**	**3B**	**HR**	**RBI**	**Avg.**	**BB**	**SO**	**SB**	**PO**	**A**	**E**	**Avg.**
1986	—Medford (N'west)	SS	46	187	30	48	3	1	0	19	.257	40	21	6	68	143	18	.921
1987	—Modesto (Calif.)	SS	133	497	73	133	17	0	3	75	.268	87	92	8	216	305	17	*.968
1988	—Huntsville (South.) ...	2B-SS-3B	132	481	48	130	13	2	0	28	.270	87	50	7	260	406	24	.965
1989	—Tacoma (PCL)	2B-SS-3B	136	487	55	117	17	1	1	43	.240	58	51	4	261	431	33	.954
1990	—Oakland (A.L.)	3B-SS-2B	25	14	0	1	0	0	0	0	.071	1	4	0	9	8	0	1.000
	—Tacoma (PCL)	SS-2B	111	348	49	79	16	1	2	30	.227	46	40	3	210	366	16	†.973
1991	—Tacoma (PCL)	SS	26	81	15	22	4	1	2	14	.272	17	10	0	35	79	3	.974
	—Oakland (A.L.)	SS-2B-3B	90	235	21	56	5	1	0	21	.238	14	37	3	146	213	11	.970
1992	—Oakland (A.L.)	2B-SS	154	504	62	151	19	4	3	48	.300	40	59	12	311	449	16	.979
1993	—Oakland (A.L.)	SS-2B	159	546	60	136	21	2	3	48	.249	60	58	10	†285	420	13	.982
Major league totals (4 years)	....		428	1299	143	344	45	7	6	117	.265	115	158	25	751	1090	40	.979

CHAMPIONSHIP SERIES RECORD

			BATTING												FIELDING			
Year	**Team (League)**	**Pos.**	**G**	**AB**	**R**	**H**	**2B**	**3B**	**HR**	**RBI**	**Avg.**	**BB**	**SO**	**SB**	**PO**	**A**	**E**	**Avg.**
1992	—Oakland (A.L.)	SS-2B	6	19	1	1	0	0	0	0	.053	1	2	1	15	14	0	1.000

WORLD SERIES RECORD

			BATTING												FIELDING			
Year	**Team (League)**	**Pos.**	**G**	**AB**	**R**	**H**	**2B**	**3B**	**HR**	**RBI**	**Avg.**	**BB**	**SO**	**SB**	**PO**	**A**	**E**	**Avg.**
1990	—Oakland (A.L.)	SS-PR	3	0	0	0	0	0	0	0	...	0	0	0	0	2	0	1.000

BORLAND, TOBY
P, PHILLIES

PERSONAL: Born May 29, 1969, in Quitman, La. . . . 6-6/186. . . . Throws right, bats right. . . . Full name: Toby Shawn Borland.
HIGH SCHOOL: Quitman (La.).
TRANSACTIONS/CAREER NOTES: Selected by Philadelphia Phillies organization in 27th round of free-agent draft (June 2, 1987).
STATISTICAL NOTES: Tied for Eastern League lead with three balks in 1991. . . . Pitched one inning, combining with starter Craig Holman (two innings), Gregory Brown (two innings) and Ricky Bottalico (two innings) in 2-0 no-hit victory for Reading against New Britain (September 4, 1993, first game).

Year	**Team (League)**	**W**	**L**	**Pct.**	**ERA**	**G**	**GS**	**CG**	**ShO**	**Sv.**	**IP**	**H**	**R**	**ER**	**BB**	**SO**
1988	—Martinsville (App.)	2	3	.400	4.04	34	0	0	0	*12	49	42	26	22	29	43
1989	—Spartanburg (SAL)	4	5	.444	2.97	47	0	0	0	9	66⅔	62	29	22	35	48
1990	—Clearwater (FSL)	1	2	.333	2.26	44	0	0	0	5	59⅔	44	21	15	35	44
	—Reading (Eastern)	4	1	.800	1.44	14	0	0	0	0	25	16	6	4	11	26
1991	—Reading (Eastern)	8	3	.727	2.70	*59	0	0	0	•24	76⅔	68	31	23	56	72
1992	—Scran./W.B. (Int'l)	0	1	.000	7.24	27	0	0	0	1	27⅓	25	23	22	26	25
	—Reading (Eastern)	2	4	.333	3.43	32	0	0	0	5	42	39	23	16	32	45
1993	—Reading (Eastern)	2	2	.500	2.52	44	0	0	0	13	53⅔	38	17	15	20	74
	—Scran./W.B. (Int'l)	2	4	.333	5.76	26	0	0	0	1	29⅔	31	20	19	20	26

BOSIO, CHRIS
P, MARINERS

PERSONAL: Born April 3, 1963, in Carmichael, Calif. . . . 6-3/225. . . . Throws right, bats right. . . . Full name: Christopher Louis Bosio. . . . Name pronounced BAHZ-ee-o.
HIGH SCHOOL: Cordova (Calif.).
COLLEGE: Sacramento (Calif.) City College.
TRANSACTIONS/CAREER NOTES: Selected by Pittsburgh Pirates organization in 29th round of free-agent draft (June 8, 1981). . . . Selected by Milwaukee Brewers organization in secondary phase of free-agent draft (January 12, 1982). . . . On Milwaukee disabled list (June 29-July 15, 1990); included rehabilitation assignment to Beloit (July 9-15). . . . On Milwaukee disabled list (August 2, 1990-remainder of season). . . . On disabled list (July 1-16, 1991). . . . Granted free agency (October 26, 1992). . . . Signed by Seattle Mariners (December 3, 1992). . . . On disabled list (April 28-May 28 and June 7-25, 1993). . . . On suspended list (June 28-July 3, 1993).
STATISTICAL NOTES: Pitched 7-0 no-hit victory against Boston (April 22, 1993).
MISCELLANEOUS: Appeared in one game as designated hitter but made no plate appearance (1993).

Year	**Team (League)**	**W**	**L**	**Pct.**	**ERA**	**G**	**GS**	**CG**	**ShO**	**Sv.**	**IP**	**H**	**R**	**ER**	**BB**	**SO**
1982	—Pikeville (Appal.)	3	2	.600	4.91	13	3	2	1	1	51⅓	60	31	28	17	53
1983	—Beloit (Midwest)	3	10	.231	5.60	17	17	3	0	0	107⅔	125	82	67	41	71
	—Paintsville (Appal.)	2	2	.500	2.84	7	7	2	2	0	44⅓	30	18	14	18	43
1984	—Beloit (Midwest)	*17	6	.739	2.73	26	26	11	2	0	181	159	83	55	56	156
1985	—El Paso (Texas)	11	6	.647	3.82	28	25	6	1	2	181⅓	186	108	77	49	*155
1986	—Vancouver (PCL)	7	3	.700	2.28	44	0	0	0	•16	67	47	18	17	13	60
	—Milwaukee (A.L.)	0	4	.000	7.01	10	4	0	0	0	34⅔	41	27	27	13	29
1987	—Milwaukee (A.L.)	11	8	.579	5.24	46	19	2	1	2	170	187	102	99	50	150
1988	—Milwaukee (A.L.)	7	15	.318	3.36	38	22	9	1	6	182	190	80	68	38	84
	—Denver (A.A.)	1	0	1.000	3.86	2	2	1	0	0	14	13	6	6	4	12
1989	—Milwaukee (A.L.)	15	10	.600	2.95	33	33	8	2	0	234⅔	225	90	77	48	173
1990	—Milwaukee (A.L.)	4	9	.308	4.00	20	20	4	1	0	132⅔	131	67	59	38	76
	—Beloit (Midwest)	0	0	...	3.00	1	1	0	0	0	3	4	2	1	1	2

Year	Team (League)	W	L	Pct.	ERA	G	GS	CG	ShO	Sv.	IP	H	R	ER	BB	SO
1991	—Milwaukee (A.L.)	14	10	.583	3.25	32	32	5	1	0	204⅔	187	80	74	58	117
1992	—Milwaukee (A.L.)	16	6	.727	3.62	33	33	4	2	0	231⅓	223	100	93	44	120
1993	—Seattle (A.L.)■...........	9	9	.500	3.45	29	24	3	1	1	164⅓	138	75	63	59	119
Major league totals (8 years)..		76	71	.517	3.72	241	187	35	9	9	1354⅓	1322	621	560	348	868

BOSKIE, SHAWN

P, CUBS

PERSONAL: Born March 28, 1967, in Hawthorne, Nev. . . . 6-3/200. . . . Throws right, bats right. . . . Full name: Shawn Kealoha Boskie. . . . Name pronounced BAH-skee.

HIGH SCHOOL: Reno (Nev.).

COLLEGE: Modesto (Calif.) Junior College.

TRANSACTIONS/CAREER NOTES: Selected by Chicago Cubs organization in first round (10th pick overall) of free-agent draft (January 14, 1986). . . . On Chicago disabled list (August 5-September 26, 1990). . . . On Chicago disabled list (July 27-September 1, 1992); included rehabilitation assignment to Iowa (August 24-September 1). . . . On suspended list (August 31-September 3, 1993). . . . Granted free agency (December 20, 1993). . . . Re-signed by Cubs (December 22, 1993).

STATISTICAL NOTES: Led Appalachian League with 15 wild pitches in 1986. . . . Led Carolina League with 17 hit batsmen in 1988. . . . Led Southern League with 19 hit batsmen in 1989.

MISCELLANEOUS: Appeared in one game as pinch-runner and made an out in only appearance as pinch-hitter with Chicago (1991).

Year	Team (League)	W	L	Pct.	ERA	G	GS	CG	ShO	Sv.	IP	H	R	ER	BB	SO
1986	—Wytheville (Appal.)....	4	4	.500	5.33	14	12	1	0	0	54	42	41	32	57	40
1987	—Peoria (Midwest)	9	11	.450	4.35	26	25	1	0	0	149	149	91	72	56	100
1988	—Winst.-Salem (Car.).....	12	7	.632	3.39	27	27	4	2	0	186	176	83	70	89	164
1989	—Charlotte (South.).......	11	8	.579	4.38	28	28	5	0	0	181	*196	105	88	84	*164
1990	—Iowa (Am. Assoc.).......	4	2	.667	3.18	8	8	1	0	0	51	46	22	18	21	51
	—Chicago (N.L.)............	5	6	.455	3.69	15	15	1	0	0	97⅔	99	42	40	31	49
1991	—Chicago (N.L.)............	4	9	.308	5.23	28	20	0	0	0	129	150	78	75	52	62
	—Iowa (Am. Assoc.).......	2	2	.500	3.57	7	6	2	0	0	45⅓	43	19	18	11	29
1992	—Chicago (N.L.)............	5	11	.313	5.01	23	18	0	0	0	91⅔	96	55	51	36	39
	—Iowa (Am. Assoc.).......	0	0	...	3.68	2	2	0	0	0	7⅓	8	4	3	3	3
1993	—Chicago (N.L.)............	5	3	.625	3.43	39	2	0	0	0	65⅔	63	30	25	21	39
	—Iowa (Am. Assoc.).......	6	1	.857	4.27	11	11	1	0	0	71⅔	70	35	34	21	35
Major league totals (4 years)...		19	29	.396	4.48	105	55	1	0	0	384	408	205	191	140	189

BOSTON, DARYL

OF, YANKEES

PERSONAL: Born January 4, 1963, in Cincinnati. . . . 6-3/195. . . . Throws left, bats left. . . . Full name: Daryl Lamont Boston.

HIGH SCHOOL: Woodward (Cincinnati).

TRANSACTIONS/CAREER NOTES: Selected by Chicago White Sox organization in first round (seventh pick overall) of free-agent draft (June 8, 1981). . . . Claimed on waivers by New York Mets (April 30, 1990). . . . Granted free agency (October 31, 1991). . . . Re-signed by Mets (February 25, 1992). . . . Granted free agency (October 30, 1992). . . . Signed by Colorado Rockies (December 21, 1992). . . . Granted free agency (November 1, 1993). . . . Signed by New York Yankees organization (January 13, 1994).

STATISTICAL NOTES: Led Midwest League outfielders with 312 total chances in 1982. . . . Tied for American Association lead with 11 sacrifice flies in 1984. . . . Tied for American Association lead in double plays by outfielder with four in 1984.

			BATTING												FIELDING			
Year	Team (League)	Pos.	G	AB	R	H	2B	3B	HR	RBI	Avg.	BB	SO	SB	PO	A	E	Avg.
1981	—GC Whi. Sox (GCL)...	OF	56	189	30	55	6	3	1	30	.291	16	45	12	84	9	3	.969
1982	—Appleton (Midw.).....	OF	*139	512	86	143	19	9	15	77	.279	44	147	28	*293	9	10	.968
1983	—Glens Falls (East.)...	OF	113	435	65	104	15	1	18	50	.239	51	*133	21	271	8	13	.955
	—Denver (A.A.)...........	OF	14	51	11	13	4	1	2	7	.255	7	14	0	26	1	5	.844
1984	—Denver (A.A.)...........	OF	127	471	94	147	21	*19	15	82	.312	65	82	40	311	11	•10	.970
	—Chicago (A.L.)..........	OF	35	83	8	14	3	1	0	3	.169	4	20	6	59	2	6	.910
1985	—Chicago (A.L.)..........	OF	95	232	20	53	13	1	3	15	.228	14	44	8	179	7	2	.989
	—Buffalo (A.A.)...........	OF	63	241	45	66	12	1	10	36	.274	33	48	16	151	3	3	.981
1986	—Buffalo (A.A.)...........	OF	96	360	57	109	16	3	5	41	.303	42	45	37	210	1	5	.977
	—Chicago (A.L.)..........	OF	56	199	29	53	11	3	5	22	.266	21	33	9	152	3	5	.969
1987	—Chicago (A.L.)..........	OF	103	337	51	87	21	2	10	29	.258	25	68	12	207	3	2	.991
	—Hawaii (PCL)............	OF	21	77	14	23	3	0	5	13	.299	10	10	10	43	3	0	1.000
1988	—Chicago (A.L.)..........	OF	105	281	37	61	12	2	15	31	.217	21	44	9	190	4	10	.951
1989	—Chicago (A.L.)..........	OF	101	218	34	55	3	4	5	23	.252	24	31	7	134	2	4	.971
1990	—Chicago (A.L.)..........	OF	5	1	0	0	0	0	0	0	.000	0	0	1	0	0	0	...
	—New York (N.L.)■......	OF	115	366	65	100	21	2	12	45	.273	28	50	18	203	3	3	.986
1991	—New York (N.L.)........	OF	137	255	40	70	16	4	4	21	.275	30	42	15	156	2	3	.981
1992	—New York (N.L.)........	OF	130	289	37	72	14	2	11	35	.249	38	60	12	133	5	1	.993
1993	—Colorado (N.L.)■.......	OF	124	291	46	76	15	1	14	40	.261	26	57	1	124	5	2	.985
American League totals (7 years)............			500	1351	179	323	63	13	38	123	.239	109	240	52	921	21	29	.970
National League totals (4 years)............			506	1201	188	318	66	9	41	141	.265	122	209	46	616	15	9	.986
Major league totals (10 years)................			1006	2552	367	641	129	22	79	264	.251	231	449	98	1537	36	38	.976

BOTTALICO, RICKY

P, PHILLIES

PERSONAL: Born August 26, 1969, in New Britain, Conn. . . . 6-1/200. . . . Throws right, bats left. . . . Full name: Richard Paul Bottalico.

HIGH SCHOOL: South Catholic (Hartford, Conn.).

COLLEGE: Florida Southern and Central Connecticut State.

TRANSACTIONS/CAREER NOTES: Signed as free agent by Philadelphia Phillies organization (July 21, 1991).

STATISTICAL NOTES: Pitched two innings, combining with starter Craig Holman (two innings), Gregory Brown (two innings) and Toby Borland (one inning) in 2-0 no-hit victory for Reading against New Britain (September 4, 1993, first game).

Year	Team (League)	W	L	Pct.	ERA	G	GS	CG	ShO	Sv.	IP	H	R	ER	BB	SO
1991	—Martinsville (App.)	3	2	.600	4.09	7	6	2	•1	0	33	32	20	15	13	38
	—Spartanburg (SAL)	2	0	1.000	0.00	2	2	0	0	0	15	4	0	0	2	11
1992	—Spartanburg (SAL)	5	10	.333	2.41	42	11	1	0	13	119⅔	94	41	32	56	118
1993	—Clearwater (FSL)	1	0	1.000	2.75	13	0	0	0	4	19⅔	19	6	6	5	19
	—Reading (Eastern)	3	3	.500	2.25	49	0	0	0	20	72	63	22	18	26	65

BOTTENFIELD, KENT

P, ROCKIES

PERSONAL: Born November 14, 1968, in Portland, Ore. . . . 6-3/225. . . . Throws right, bats both. . . . Full name: Kent Dennis Bottenfield. . . . Twin brother of Keven Bottenfield, minor league catcher/infielder (1986-87).

HIGH SCHOOL: James Madison (Portland, Ore.).

TRANSACTIONS/CAREER NOTES: Selected by Montreal Expos organization in fourth round of free-agent draft (June 2, 1986). . . . Traded by Expos to Colorado Rockies for P Butch Henry (July 16, 1993).

Year	Team (League)	W	L	Pct.	ERA	G	GS	CG	ShO	Sv.	IP	H	R	ER	BB	SO
1986	—GC Expos (GCL)	5	6	.455	3.27	13	13	2	0	0	74⅓	73	•42	27	30	41
1987	—Burlington (Midw.)	9	13	.409	4.53	27	27	6	3	0	161	175	98	81	42	103
1988	—W.P. Beach (FSL)	10	8	.556	3.33	27	27	9	4	0	181	165	80	67	47	120
1989	—Jacksonv. (South.)	3	*17	.150	5.26	25	25	1	0	0	138⅔	137	101	81	73	91
1990	—Jacksonv. (South.)	12	10	.545	3.41	29	28	2	1	0	169	158	72	64	67	121
1991	—Indianapolis (A.A.)	8	15	.348	4.06	29	27	•5	2	0	166⅓	155	97	75	61	108
1992	—Indianapolis (A.A.)	•12	8	.600	3.43	25	23	3	1	0	152⅓	139	64	58	58	111
	—Montreal (N.L.)	1	2	.333	2.23	10	4	0	0	1	32⅓	26	9	8	11	14
1993	—Mont.-Colo. (N.L.)■	5	10	.333	5.07	37	25	1	0	0	159⅔	179	102	90	71	63
Major league totals (2 years)		6	12	.333	4.59	47	29	1	0	1	192	205	111	98	82	77

BOUCHER, DENIS

P, EXPOS

PERSONAL: Born March 7, 1968, in Montreal, Que. . . . 6-1/195. . . . Throws left, bats right. . . . Name pronounced DEN-ee boo-SHAY.

TRANSACTIONS/CAREER NOTES: Signed as a free agent by the Toronto Blue Jays organization (August 18, 1987). . . . Traded by Blue Jays with OF Glenallen Hill, OF Mark Whiten and a player to be named later to Cleveland Indians for P Tom Candiotti and OF Turner Ward (June 27, 1991); Indians acquired cash instead of player to complete deal (October 15, 1991). . . . Selected by Colorado Rockies in third round (72nd pick overall) of expansion draft (November 17, 1992). . . . Traded by Rockies to San Diego Padres for 1B Jay Gainer (March 21, 1993). . . . Traded by Padres to Montreal Expos for IF Austin Manahan and future considerations (July 10, 1993); deal settled in cash.

STATISTICAL NOTES: Led South Atlantic League with 21 balks in 1988. . . . Tied for A.L. lead with four balks in 1991.

Year	Team (League)	W	L	Pct.	ERA	G	GS	CG	ShO	Sv.	IP	H	R	ER	BB	SO
1988	—Myrtle Beach (SAL)	13	12	.520	2.84	33	•32	1	0	0	196⅔	161	81	62	63	169
1989	—Dunedin (Fla. St.)	10	10	.500	3.06	33	28	1	1	0	164⅔	142	80	56	58	117
1990	—Dunedin (Fla. St.)	7	0	1.000	0.75	9	9	2	2	0	60	45	8	5	8	62
	—Syracuse (Int'l)	8	5	.615	3.85	17	17	2	1	0	107⅔	100	52	46	37	80
1991	—Tor.-Clev. (A.L.)■	1	7	.125	6.05	12	12	0	0	0	58	74	41	39	24	29
	—Syracuse (Int'l)	2	1	.667	3.18	8	8	1	0	0	56⅔	57	24	20	19	28
	—Colo. Springs (PCL)	1	0	1.000	5.02	3	3	0	0	0	14⅓	14	8	8	2	9
1992	—Colo. Springs (PCL)	11	4	.733	3.48	20	18	*6	0	0	124	119	50	48	30	40
	—Cleveland (A.L.)	2	2	.500	6.37	8	7	0	0	0	41	48	29	29	20	17
1993	—Las Vegas (PCL)■	4	7	.364	6.43	24	7	1	0	1	70	101	59	50	27	46
	—Ottawa (Int'l)■	6	0	1.000	2.72	11	6	0	0	0	43	36	13	13	11	22
	—Montreal (N.L.)	3	1	.750	1.91	5	5	0	0	0	28⅓	24	7	6	3	14
A.L. totals (2 years)		3	9	.250	6.18	20	19	0	0	0	99	122	70	68	44	46
N.L. totals (1 year)		3	1	.750	1.91	5	5	0	0	0	28⅓	24	7	6	3	14
Major league totals (3 years)		6	10	.375	5.23	25	24	0	0	0	127⅓	146	77	74	47	60

BOURNIGAL, RAFAEL

SS, DODGERS

PERSONAL: Born May 12, 1966, in Azua, Dominican Republic. . . . 5-11/165. . . . Throws right, bats right. . . . Full name: Rafael Antonio Bournigal.

HIGH SCHOOL: Domax (Dominican Republic).

COLLEGE: Canada College (Calif.) and Florida State.

TRANSACTIONS/CAREER NOTES: Selected by Texas Rangers organization in 11th round of free-agent draft (January 9, 1985). . . . Selected by Baltimore Orioles organization in 10th round of free-agent draft (January 14, 1986). . . . Selected by Los Angeles Dodgers organization in 19th round of free-agent draft (June 2, 1987).

STATISTICAL NOTES: Led Northwest League shortstops with .953 fielding percentage in 1988. . . . Led Pacific Coast League shortstops with 636 total chances and 97 double plays in 1993.

MISCELLANEOUS: Served as player/coach with Vero Beach (1991).

			BATTING												FIELDING			
Year	Team (League)	Pos.	G	AB	R	H	2B	3B	HR	RBI	Avg.	BB	SO	SB	PO	A	E	Avg.
1987	—Great Falls (Pio.)	2B-SS	30	82	5	12	4	0	0	4	.146	3	7	0	49	47	4	.960
1988	—Salem (Northwest)	SS-2B-3B	70	275	54	86	10	1	0	25	.313	38	32	11	76	179	12	†.955
1989	—Vero Beach (FSL)	2B-SS	132	484	74	128	11	1	1	37	.264	33	21	18	219	378	15	.975
1990	—San Antonio (Tex.)	SS-2B-3B	69	194	20	41	4	2	0	14	.211	8	25	2	99	136	6	.975
1991	—Vero Beach (FSL)	SS-3B	20	66	6	16	2	0	0	3	.242	1	3	2	29	56	1	.988
	—San Antonio (Tex.)	3B-SS-2B	16	65	6	21	2	0	0	9	.323	2	7	2	28	43	0	1.000
	—Albuquerque (PCL)	SS-2B-3B	66	215	34	63	5	5	0	29	.293	14	13	4	100	188	9	.970
1992	—Albuquerque (PCL)	SS	122	395	47	128	18	1	0	34	.324	22	7	5	*201	369	9	*.984
	—Los Angeles (N.L.)	SS	10	20	1	3	1	0	0	0	.150	1	2	0	12	17	1	.967
1993	—Albuquerque (PCL)	SS	134	465	75	129	25	0	4	55	.277	29	18	3	196	*427	13	*.980
	—Los Angeles (N.L.)	SS-2B	8	18	0	9	1	0	0	3	.500	0	2	0	5	14	0	1.000
Major league totals (2 years)			18	38	1	12	2	0	0	3	.316	1	4	0	17	31	1	.980

BOWEN, RYAN

P, MARLINS

PERSONAL: Born February 10, 1968, in Hanford, Calif. . . . 6-0/185. . . . Throws right, bats right. . . . Full name: Ryan Eugene Bowen.

HIGH SCHOOL: Hanford (Calif.).

TRANSACTIONS/CAREER NOTES: Selected by Houston Astros organization in first round (13th pick overall) of free-agent draft (June 2, 1986). . . . Selected by Florida Marlins in third round (63rd pick overall) of expansion draft (November 17, 1992).

MISCELLANEOUS: Appeared in three games as pinch-runner with Houston (1991). . . . Appeared in four games as pinch-runner with Houston (1992).

Year	Team (League)	W	L	Pct.	ERA	G	GS	CG	ShO	Sv.	IP	H	R	ER	BB	SO
1987	—Asheville (S. Atl.)	12	5	.706	4.04	26	26	6	2	0	160⅓	143	86	72	78	126
1988	—Osceola (Fla. St.)	1	0	1.000	3.95	4	4	0	0	0	13⅔	12	8	6	10	12
1989	—Columbus (South.)	8	6	.571	4.25	27	27	1	1	0	139⅔	123	83	66	116	136
1990	—Columbus (South.)	8	4	.667	3.74	18	18	2	2	0	113	103	59	47	49	109
	—Tucson (PCL)	1	3	.250	9.35	10	7	0	0	0	34⅔	41	36	36	38	29
1991	—Tucson (PCL)	5	5	.500	4.38	18	18	2	2	0	98⅔	114	56	48	56	78
	—Houston (N.L.)	6	4	.600	5.15	14	13	0	0	0	71⅔	73	43	41	36	49
1992	—Houston (N.L.)	0	7	.000	10.96	11	9	0	0	0	33⅔	48	43	41	30	22
	—Tucson (PCL)	7	6	.538	4.12	21	20	1	1	0	122⅓	128	68	56	64	94
1993	—Florida (N.L.)■	8	12	.400	4.42	27	27	2	1	0	156⅔	156	83	77	87	98
Major league totals (3 years)		14	23	.378	5.46	52	49	2	1	0	262	277	169	159	153	169

BOWERS, BRENT

OF, BLUE JAYS

PERSONAL: Born May 2, 1971, in Oak Lawn, Ill. . . . 6-3/190. . . . Throws right, bats left. . . . Full name: Brent Raymond Bowers.

HIGH SCHOOL: St. Laurence (Burbank, Ill.).

TRANSACTIONS/CAREER NOTES: Selected by Toronto Blue Jays organization in supplemental round ("sandwich pick" between second and third round) of free-agent draft (June 5, 1989); pick received as compensation for Texas Rangers signing Type C free agent Rick Leach.

			BATTING												FIELDING			
Year	Team (League)	Pos.	G	AB	R	H	2B	3B	HR	RBI	Avg.	BB	SO	SB	PO	A	E	Avg.
1989	—Medicine Hat (Pio.)	OF	54	207	16	46	2	2	0	13	.222	19	55	6	80	4	1	.988
1990	—Medicine Hat (Pio.)	OF	60	212	30	58	7	3	3	27	.274	30	35	19	117	7	1	*.992
1991	—Myrtle Beach (SAL)	OF	120	402	53	103	8	4	2	44	.256	31	77	35	199	1	7	.966
1992	—Dunedin (Fla. St.)	OF	128	•524	74	133	10	3	3	46	.254	34	99	31	247	7	3	.988
1993	—Knoxville (South.)	OF	141	*577	63	143	23	4	5	43	.248	21	121	36	285	8	5	.983

BOZE, MARSHALL

P, BREWERS

PERSONAL: Born May 23, 1971, in San Manuel, Ariz. . . . 6-1/212. . . . Throws right, bats right. . . . Full name: Marshall Wayne Boze.

HIGH SCHOOL: Soldotna (Alaska).

COLLEGE: Southwestern College (Calif.).

TRANSACTIONS/CAREER NOTES: Selected by Milwaukee Brewers organization in 12th round of free-agent draft (June 4, 1990).

Year	Team (League)	W	L	Pct.	ERA	G	GS	CG	ShO	Sv.	IP	H	R	ER	BB	SO
1990	—Ariz. Brewers (Ar.)	1	0	1.000	7.84	15	0	0	0	3	20⅔	27	22	18	13	17
1991	—Helena (Pioneer)	3	3	.500	7.07	16	8	0	0	0	56	59	49	44	47	64
	—Beloit (Midwest)	0	1	.000	5.68	3	1	0	0	0	6⅓	8	4	4	7	4
1992	—Beloit (Midwest)	13	7	.650	2.83	26	22	4	1	0	146⅓	117	59	46	82	126
1993	—Stockton (Calif.)	7	2	.778	2.65	14	14	0	0	0	88⅓	82	36	26	41	54
	—El Paso (Texas)	10	3	.769	2.71	13	13	1	0	0	86⅓	78	36	26	32	48

BRADSHAW, TERRY

OF, CARDINALS

PERSONAL: Born February 3, 1969, in Franklin, Va. . . . 6-0/180. . . . Throws right, bats left. . . . Full name: Terry Leon Bradshaw.

HIGH SCHOOL: Windsor (Va.).

COLLEGE: Norfolk (Va.) State.

TRANSACTIONS/CAREER NOTES: Selected by New York Yankees organization in 17th round of free-agent draft (June 2, 1987). . . . Selected by St. Louis Cardinals organization in ninth round of free-agent draft (June 4, 1990). . . . On Arkansas disabled list (April 10, 1992-entire season).

STATISTICAL NOTES: Led South Atlantic League outfielders with 309 total chances in 1991.

			BATTING												FIELDING			
Year	Team (League)	Pos.	G	AB	R	H	2B	3B	HR	RBI	Avg.	BB	SO	SB	PO	A	E	Avg.
1990	—Hamilton (NYP)	OF	68	235	37	55	5	1	3	13	.234	24	60	15	106	1	2	.982
1991	—Savannah (S. Atl.)	OF	132	443	91	105	17	1	7	42	.237	99	118	*65	*297	4	8	.974
1992	—	Did not play.																
1993	—St. Peters. (FSL)	OF	125	461	84	134	25	6	5	51	.291	82	60	43	*293	10	1	*.997

BRANSON, JEFF

IF, REDS

PERSONAL: Born January 26, 1967, in Waynesboro, Miss. . . . 6-0/175. . . . Throws right, bats left. . . . Full name: Jeffery Glenn Branson.

HIGH SCHOOL: Southern Choctaw (Silas, Ala.).

COLLEGE: Livingston (Ala.) University.

TRANSACTIONS/CAREER NOTES: Selected by Cincinnati Reds organization in second round of free-agent draft (June 1, 1988).

MISCELLANEOUS: Member of 1988 U.S. Olympic baseball team.

			BATTING												FIELDING			
Year	Team (League)	Pos.	G	AB	R	H	2B	3B	HR	RBI	Avg.	BB	SO	SB	PO	A	E	Avg.
1989	—Ced. Rap. (Midw.)	SS	127	469	70	132	28	1	10	68	.281	41	90	5	172	394	33	.945
1990	—Ced. Rap. (Midw.)	SS	62	239	37	60	13	4	6	24	.251	24	44	11	96	152	7	.973
	—Chatt. (South.)	2B-SS	63	233	19	49	9	1	2	29	.210	13	48	3	122	151	13	.955
1991	—Chatt. (South.)	SS-2B	88	304	35	80	13	3	2	28	.263	31	51	3	126	212	12	.966

Year	Team (League)	Pos.	G	AB	R	H	2B	3B	HR	RBI	Avg.	BB	SO	SB	PO	A	E	Avg.
			BATTING												FIELDING			
	—Nashville (A.A.)	SS-2B-OF	43	145	10	35	4	1	0	11	.241	8	31	5	61	93	8	.951
1992	—Nashville (A.A.)	S-3-2-O	36	123	18	40	6	3	4	12	.325	9	19	0	59	76	5	.964
	—Cincinnati (N.L.)	2B-3B-SS	72	115	12	34	7	1	0	15	.296	5	16	0	46	63	7	.940
1993	—Cincinnati (N.L.)	S-2-3-1	125	381	40	92	15	1	3	22	.241	19	73	4	185	260	11	.976
	Major league totals (2 years)		197	496	52	126	22	2	3	37	.254	24	89	4	231	323	18	.969

BRANTLEY, JEFF

P, REDS

PERSONAL: Born September 5, 1963, in Florence, Ala. . . . 5-10/189. . . . Throws right, bats right. . . . Full name: Jeffrey Hoke Brantley.
HIGH SCHOOL: W.A. Berry (Florence, Ala.).
COLLEGE: Mississippi State.

TRANSACTIONS/CAREER NOTES: Selected by Montreal Expos organization in 13th round of free-agent draft (June 4, 1984). . . . Selected by San Francisco Giants organization in sixth round of free-agent draft (June 3, 1985). . . . Granted free agency (December 20, 1993). . . . Signed by Cincinnati Reds (January 6, 1994).
STATISTICAL NOTES: Tied for Pacific Coast League lead with 11 hit batsmen in 1987.

Year	Team (League)	W	L	Pct.	ERA	G	GS	CG	ShO	Sv.	IP	H	R	ER	BB	SO
1985	—Fresno (California)	8	2	.800	3.33	14	13	3	0	0	94⅔	83	39	35	37	85
1986	—Shreveport (Texas)	8	10	.444	3.48	26	26	•8	3	0	165⅔	139	78	64	68	125
1987	—Shreveport (Texas)	0	1	.000	3.09	2	2	0	0	0	11⅔	12	7	4	4	7
	—Phoenix (PCL)	6	11	.353	4.65	29	28	2	0	0	170⅓	187	110	88	82	111
1988	—Phoenix (PCL)	9	5	.643	4.33	27	19	1	0	0	122⅔	130	65	59	39	83
	—San Francisco (N.L.)	0	1	.000	5.66	9	1	0	0	1	20⅔	22	13	13	6	11
1989	—San Francisco (N.L.)	7	1	.875	4.07	59	1	0	0	0	97⅓	101	50	44	37	69
	—Phoenix (PCL)	1	1	.500	1.26	7	0	0	0	3	14⅓	6	2	2	6	20
1990	—San Francisco (N.L.)	5	3	.625	1.56	55	0	0	0	19	86⅔	77	18	15	33	61
1991	—San Francisco (N.L.)	5	2	.714	2.45	67	0	0	0	15	95⅓	78	27	26	52	81
1992	—San Francisco (N.L.)	7	7	.500	2.95	56	4	0	0	7	91⅔	67	32	30	45	86
1993	—San Francisco (N.L.)	5	6	.455	4.28	53	12	0	0	0	113⅔	112	60	54	46	76
	Major league totals (6 years)	29	20	.592	3.24	299	18	0	0	42	505⅓	457	200	182	219	384

CHAMPIONSHIP SERIES RECORD

Year	Team (League)	W	L	Pct.	ERA	G	GS	CG	ShO	Sv.	IP	H	R	ER	BB	SO
1989	—San Francisco (N.L.)	0	0	...	0.00	3	0	0	0	0	5	1	0	0	2	3

WORLD SERIES RECORD

Year	Team (League)	W	L	Pct.	ERA	G	GS	CG	ShO	Sv.	IP	H	R	ER	BB	SO
1989	—San Francisco (N.L.)	0	0	...	4.15	3	0	0	0	0	4⅓	5	2	2	3	1

ALL-STAR GAME RECORD

Year	League	W	L	Pct.	ERA	GS	CG	ShO	Sv.	IP	H	R	ER	BB	SO
1990	—National	0	1	.000	54.00	0	0	0	0	⅓	2	2	2	0	0

BREAM, SID

1B, ASTROS

PERSONAL: Born August 3, 1960, in Carlisle, Pa. . . . 6-4/220. . . . Throws left, bats left. . . . Full name: Sidney Eugene Bream.
HIGH SCHOOL: Carlisle (Pa.).
COLLEGE: Liberty (Va.).

TRANSACTIONS/CAREER NOTES: Selected by Los Angeles Dodgers organization in second round of free-agent draft (June 8, 1981). . . . Traded by Dodgers with OF Cecil Espy to Pittsburgh Pirates (September 9, 1985), completing deal in which Pirates traded 3B Bill Madlock to Dodgers for three players to be named later (August 31, 1985); Pirates acquired OF R.J. Reynolds as partial completion of deal (September 3, 1985). . . . On disabled list (April 16-May 9 and May 29, 1989-remainder of season). . . . Granted free agency (November 5, 1990). . . . Signed by Atlanta Braves (December 5, 1990). . . . On disabled list (June 26-August 2 and August 5-29, 1991). . . . Granted free agency (October 27, 1993). . . . Signed by Houston Astros (January 26, 1994).
STATISTICAL NOTES: Led Pacific Coast League first basemen with 1,411 total chances in 1983 and 1,200 in 1984. . . . Led Pacific Coast League first basemen with 106 double plays in 1984. . . . Led N.L. first basemen with 166 assists, 17 errors and 1,503 total chances in 1986.

Year	Team (League)	Pos.	G	AB	R	H	2B	3B	HR	RBI	Avg.	BB	SO	SB	PO	A	E	Avg.
			BATTING												FIELDING			
1981	—Vero Beach (FSL)	1B	70	260	35	85	12	5	1	47	.327	31	31	0	613	45	10	.985
1982	—Vero Beach (FSL)	1B	63	226	41	70	13	5	4	43	.310	32	25	1	523	40	5	.991
	—San Antonio (Tex.)	1B	70	259	43	83	18	0	8	50	.320	34	41	0	621	40	12	.982
	—Albuquerque (PCL)	1B	3	8	3	3	1	0	1	2	.375	0	2	6	11	0	0	1.000
1983	—Albuquerque (PCL)	1B	138	485	115	149	23	4	•32	*118	.307	93	80	0	1264	*123	24	.983
	—Los Angeles (N.L.)	1B	15	11	0	2	0	0	0	2	.182	2	2	0	8	0	0	1.000
1984	—Albuquerque (PCL)	1B	114	429	82	147	25	4	20	90	.343	67	62	1	1071	*112	17	.986
	—Los Angeles (N.L.)	1B	27	49	2	9	3	0	0	6	.184	6	9	5	95	11	0	1.000
1985	—Albuquerque (PCL)	1B-OF	85	297	51	110	25	3	17	57	.370	34	38	2	381	51	2	.995
	—L.A.-Pitts. (N.L.)■	1B	50	148	18	34	7	0	6	21	.230	11	24	1	367	35	3	.993
1986	—Pittsburgh (N.L.)	1B-OF	154	522	73	140	37	5	16	77	.268	60	73	0	1320	†166	†17	.989
1987	—Pittsburgh (N.L.)	1B	149	516	64	142	25	3	13	65	.275	49	69	13	1236	127	*17	.988
1988	—Pittsburgh (N.L.)	1B	148	462	50	122	37	0	10	65	.264	47	64	9	1118	*140	6	.995
1989	—Pittsburgh (N.L.)	1B	19	36	3	8	3	0	0	4	.222	12	10	9	111	7	1	.992
1990	—Pittsburgh (N.L.)	1B	147	389	39	105	23	2	15	67	.270	48	65	0	971	104	8	.993
1991	—Atlanta (N.L.)■	1B	91	265	32	67	12	0	11	45	.253	25	31	0	668	50	3	.996
1992	—Atlanta (N.L.)	1B	125	372	30	97	25	1	10	61	.261	46	51	6	856	73	10	.989
1993	—Atlanta (N.L.)	1B	117	277	33	72	14	1	9	35	.260	31	43	4	627	62	3	.996
	Major league totals (11 years)		1042	3047	344	798	186	12	90	448	.262	337	441	47	7377	775	68	.992

CHAMPIONSHIP SERIES RECORD

Year	Team (League)	Pos.	G	AB	R	H	2B	3B	HR	RBI	Avg.	BB	SO	SB	PO	A	E	Avg.
			BATTING												FIELDING			
1990	—Pittsburgh (N.L.)......	1B-PH	4	8	1	4	1	0	1	3	.500	2	3	0	26	3	0	1.000
1991	—Atlanta (N.L.)...........	1B-PH	4	10	1	3	0	0	1	3	.300	0	1	0	19	4	0	1.000
1992	—Atlanta (N.L.)...........	1B	7	22	5	6	3	0	1	2	.273	3	0	0	53	4	0	1.000
1993	—Atlanta (N.L.)...........	1B	1	1	1	1	0	0	0	0	1.000	0	0	0	1	0	0	1.000
Championship series totals (4 years)			16	41	8	14	4	0	3	8	.341	5	4	0	99	11	0	1.000

WORLD SERIES RECORD

Year	Team (League)	Pos.	G	AB	R	H	2B	3B	HR	RBI	Avg.	BB	SO	SB	PO	A	E	Avg.
			BATTING												FIELDING			
1991	—Atlanta (N.L.)...........	1B	7	24	0	3	2	0	0	0	.125	3	4	0	69	7	0	1.000
1992	—Atlanta (N.L.)...........	1B	5	15	1	3	0	0	0	0	.200	4	0	0	42	1	1	.977
World Series totals (2 years)			12	39	1	6	2	0	0	0	.154	7	4	0	111	8	1	.992

B

BRENNAN, BILL

P, CUBS

PERSONAL: Born January 15, 1963, in Tampa, Fla.... 6-3/185.... Throws right, bats right. ... Full name: William Raymond Brennan Jr.
HIGH SCHOOL: Hillwood (Nashville, Tenn.).
COLLEGE: Mercer.
TRANSACTIONS/CAREER NOTES: Signed as free agent by Los Angeles Dodgers organization (September 1, 1984).... On disabled list (August 14-28, 1986).... Selected by Houston Astros from Albuquerque, Dodgers organization, in Rule 5 major league draft (December 4, 1989).... Granted free agency (October 12, 1990).... Signed by Atlanta Braves organization (January 13, 1991).... Released by Richmond, Braves organization (April 5, 1991).... Signed by Harrisburg, Montreal Expos organization (June 21, 1991).... Granted free agency (October 15, 1991).... Signed by Detroit Tigers organization (December 11, 1991).... Released by Toledo, Tigers organization (June 8, 1992).... Signed by Iowa, Chicago Cubs organization (July 21, 1992).... Granted free agency (October 15, 1992).... Re-signed by Iowa, Cubs organization (October 30, 1992).... Released by Cubs (December 10, 1993).... Signed by Cubs organization (January 11, 1994).
STATISTICAL NOTES: Led American Association with 15 hit batsmen and 23 wild pitches in 1993.

Year	Team (League)	W	L	Pct.	ERA	G	GS	CG	ShO	Sv.	IP	H	R	ER	BB	SO
1985	—Vero Beach (FSL).......	10	9	.526	2.85	22	21	5	1	0	142	121	64	45	59	74
1986	—San Antonio (Tex.).....	7	9	.438	3.87	26	21	3	0	0	146⅔	149	75	63	61	83
1987	—Albuquerque (PCL)....	10	9	.526	4.31	28	28	4	1	0	171⅓	188	95	82	67	95
1988	—Albuquerque (PCL)....	14	8	.636	3.82	29	28	5	2	0	167⅓	177	85	71	51	83
	—Los Angeles (N.L.).....	0	1	.000	6.75	4	2	0	0	0	9⅓	13	7	7	6	7
1989	—Albuquerque (PCL)....	6	9	.400	5.23	34	17	2	0	0	129	149	87	75	57	104
1990	—Tucson (PCL)■...........	8	7	.533	4.73	41	8	2	0	0	110⅓	104	68	58	89	88
1991	—Harrisburg (East.)■...	3	2	.600	3.12	21	0	0	0	1	34⅔	35	21	12	30	33
1992	—Toledo (Int'l)■...........	0	4	.000	8.10	12	3	0	0	1	26⅔	29	29	24	23	28
	—Iowa (Am. Assoc.)■...	1	4	.200	6.37	19	1	0	0	0	29⅔	43	27	21	12	34
1993	—Iowa (Am. Assoc.).....	10	7	.588	4.42	•28	28	2	1	0	179	*180	96	88	64	*143
	—Chicago (N.L.)...........	2	1	.667	4.20	8	1	0	0	0	15	16	8	7	8	11
Major league totals (2 years) ..		2	2	.500	5.18	12	3	0	0	0	24⅓	29	15	14	14	18

BRETT, GEORGE

DH/1B

PERSONAL: Born May 15, 1953, in Glen Dale, W.Va.... 6-0/205.... Throws right, bats left. ... Full name: George Howard Brett.... Brother of Ken Brett, major league pitcher with 10 teams (1967 and 1969-81); brother of John Brett, minor league infielder (1968); and brother of Bob Brett, minor league outfielder (1972).
HIGH SCHOOL: El Segundo (Calif.).
COLLEGE: Longview Community College (Mo.) and El Camino College (Calif.).
TRANSACTIONS/CAREER NOTES: Selected by Kansas City Royals organization in second round of free-agent draft (June 8, 1971). ... On disabled list (April 29-May 11, 1972; May 4-19 and July 27-August 14, 1978; June 11-July 10, 1980; June 8-29, 1983; April 1-May 18, 1984; April 20-May 13 and May 16-June 12, 1987; April 30-June 10, 1989; and April 26-May 24, 1991).... Placed on voluntarily retired list (October 4, 1993).
RECORDS: Holds major league single-season record for most consecutive games with three or more hits—6 (May 8-13, 1976). ... Shares major league record for most home runs in month of October—4 (1985).... Holds A.L. career record for most intentional bases on balls received—220.... Holds A.L. record for most seasons with 10 or more intentional bases on balls received—11.... Holds A.L. single-season record for fewest putouts by third baseman who led league in putouts—140 (1976).
HONORS: Named third baseman on THE SPORTING NEWS A.L. All-Star team (1976, 1979 and 1980).... Named Man of the Year by THE SPORTING NEWS (1980).... Named Major League Player of the Year by THE SPORTING NEWS (1980).... Named A.L. Player of the Year by THE SPORTING NEWS (1980).... Named third baseman on THE SPORTING NEWS A.L. Silver Slugger team (1980 and 1985).... Named A.L. Most Valuable Player by Baseball Writers' Association of America (1980).... Won A.L. Gold Glove at third base (1985).... Named first baseman on THE SPORTING NEWS A.L. All-Star team (1988).... Named first baseman on THE SPORTING NEWS A.L. Silver Slugger team (1988).
STATISTICAL NOTES: Led California League with eight sacrifice hits in 1972.... Led California League third basemen with 172 assists and 30 errors in 1972.... Tied for A.L. lead in errors by third baseman with 26 in 1975.... Led A.L. with 298 total bases in 1976.... Led A.L. third basemen with 140 putouts in 1976.... Led A.L. third basemen with 373 assists, 30 errors and 532 total chances in 1979.... Hit three home runs in one game (July 22, 1979 and April 20, 1983).... Led A.L. with .461 on-base percentage in 1980.... Led A.L. with .664 slugging percentage in 1980, .563 in 1983 and .585 in 1985.... Led A.L. third basemen with 33 double plays in 1985.... Led A.L. with 31 intentional bases on balls received in 1985 and 18 in 1986.... Hit for the cycle (May 28, 1979 and July 25, 1990).

Year	Team (League)	Pos.	G	AB	R	H	2B	3B	HR	RBI	Avg.	BB	SO	SB	PO	A	E	Avg.
			BATTING												FIELDING			
1971	—Billings (Pioneer).....	SS-3B	68	258	44	75	8	5	5	44	.291	32	38	3	87	140	28	.890
1972	—San Jose (Calif.).......	3B-SS-2B	117	431	66	118	13	5	10	68	.274	53	53	2	101	†213	†30	.913

Year	Team (League)	Pos.	BATTING G	AB	R	H	2B	3B	HR	RBI	Avg.	BB	SO	SB	FIELDING PO	A	E	Avg.
1973	—Omaha (A.A.)............	3B-OF	117	405	66	115	16	4	8	64	.284	48	45	3	92	219	26	.923
	—Kansas City (A.L.)....	3B	13	40	2	5	2	0	0	0	.125	0	5	0	9	28	1	.974
1974	—Omaha (A.A.)............	3B	16	64	9	17	2	0	2	14	.266	6	1	1	8	31	4	.907
	—Kansas City (A.L.)....	3B-SS	133	457	49	129	21	5	2	47	.282	21	38	8	102	279	21	.948
1975	—Kansas City (A.L.)....	3B-SS	159	★634	84	★195	35	•13	11	89	.308	46	49	13	132	356	‡26	.949
1976	—Kansas City (A.L.)....	3B-SS	159	★645	94	★215	34	★14	7	67	★.333	49	36	21	†146	350	26	.950
1977	—Kansas City (A.L.)....	3B-SS	139	564	105	176	32	13	22	88	.312	55	24	14	115	325	21	.954
1978	—Kansas City (A.L.)....	3B-SS	128	510	79	150	★45	8	9	62	.294	39	35	23	104	289	16	.961
1979	—Kansas City (A.L.)....	3B-1B	154	645	119	★212	42	★20	23	107	.329	51	36	17	176	†378	†31	.947
1980	—Kansas City (A.L.)....	3B-1B	117	449	87	175	33	9	24	118	★.390	58	22	15	107	256	17	.955
1981	—Kansas City (A.L.)....	3B	89	347	42	109	27	7	6	43	.314	27	23	14	74	170	14	.946
1982	—Kansas City (A.L.)....	3B-OF	144	552	101	166	32	9	21	82	.301	71	51	6	130	295	17	.962
1983	—Kansas City (A.L.)....	3B-1B-OF	123	464	90	144	38	2	25	93	.310	57	39	0	210	192	25	.941
1984	—Kansas City (A.L.)....	3B	104	377	42	107	21	3	13	69	.284	38	37	0	59	201	14	.949
1985	—Kansas City (A.L.)....	3B	155	550	108	184	38	5	30	112	.335	103	49	9	107	★339	15	.967
1986	—Kansas City (A.L.)....	3B-SS	124	441	70	128	28	4	16	73	.290	80	45	1	97	218	16	.952
1987	—Kansas City (A.L.)....	1B-3B	115	427	71	124	18	2	22	78	.290	72	47	6	805	69	9	.990
1988	—Kansas City (A.L.)....	1B-SS	157	589	90	180	42	3	24	103	.306	82	51	14	1126	70	10	.992
1989	—Kansas City (A.L.)....	1B-OF	124	457	67	129	26	3	12	80	.282	59	47	14	898	80	2	.998
1990	—Kansas City (A.L.)....	1B-OF-3B	142	544	82	179	•45	7	14	87	★.329	56	63	9	880	67	7	.993
1991	—Kansas City (A.L.)....	1B	131	505	77	129	40	2	10	61	.255	58	75	2	87	5	1	.989
1992	—Kansas City (A.L.)....	1B-3B	152	592	55	169	35	5	7	61	.285	35	69	8	139	17	3	.981
1993	—Kansas City (A.L.)....	DH	145	560	69	149	31	3	19	75	.266	39	67	7	...	...	...	...
Major league totals (21 years)			2707	10349	1583	3154	665	137	317	1595	.305	1096	908	201	5503	3984	292	.970

DIVISION SERIES RECORD

Year	Team (League)	Pos.	BATTING G	AB	R	H	2B	3B	HR	RBI	Avg.	BB	SO	SB	FIELDING PO	A	E	Avg.
1981	—Kansas City (A.L.)....	3B	3	12	0	2	0	0	0	0	.167	0	0	0	1	6	1	.875

CHAMPIONSHIP SERIES RECORD

CHAMPIONSHIP SERIES NOTES: Named A.L. Championship Series Most Valuable Player (1985).... Holds career records for highest slugging average (50 or more at-bats)—.728; most runs—22; most triples—4; most home runs—9; most total bases—75; and most long hits—18.... Holds single-game record for most total bases—12 (October 6, 1978).... Shares career record for most game-winning RBIs—3.... Shares single-series record for most triples—2 (1977); and game-winning RBIs—2 (1985).... Shares single-game record for most runs—4 (October 11, 1985); home runs—3 (October 6, 1978).... Holds A.L. single-series record for highest slugging average—1.056 (1978).... Shares A.L. single-series record for most home runs—3 (1978 and 1985).... Shares A.L. single-game record for most long hits—3 (October 6, 1978 and October 11, 1985).

Year	Team (League)	Pos.	BATTING G	AB	R	H	2B	3B	HR	RBI	Avg.	BB	SO	SB	FIELDING PO	A	E	Avg.
1976	—Kansas City (A.L.)....	3B	5	18	4	8	1	1	1	5	.444	2	1	0	3	7	3	.769
1977	—Kansas City (A.L.)....	3B	5	20	2	6	0	2	0	2	.300	1	0	0	5	12	2	.895
1978	—Kansas City (A.L.)....	3B	4	18	7	7	1	1	3	3	.389	0	1	0	3	8	1	.917
1980	—Kansas City (A.L.)....	3B	3	11	3	3	1	0	2	4	.273	1	0	0	2	7	0	1.000
1984	—Kansas City (A.L.)....	3B	3	13	0	3	0	0	0	0	.231	0	2	0	2	7	0	1.000
1985	—Kansas City (A.L.)....	3B	7	23	6	8	2	0	3	5	.348	7	5	0	7	8	2	.882
Championship series totals (6 years)			27	103	22	35	5	4	9	19	.340	11	9	0	22	49	8	.899

WORLD SERIES RECORD

Year	Team (League)	Pos.	BATTING G	AB	R	H	2B	3B	HR	RBI	Avg.	BB	SO	SB	FIELDING PO	A	E	Avg.
1980	—Kansas City (A.L.)....	3B	6	24	3	9	2	1	1	3	.375	2	4	1	4	17	1	.955
1985	—Kansas City (A.L.)....	3B	7	27	5	10	1	0	0	1	.370	4	7	0	10	19	1	.967
World Series totals (2 years)			13	51	8	19	3	1	1	4	.373	6	11	1	14	36	2	.962

ALL-STAR GAME RECORD

ALL-STAR GAME NOTES: Holds career record for most sacrifice flies—3.... Named to A.L. All-Star team for 1986 game; replaced by Brook Jacoby due to injury.... Named to A.L. All-Star team for 1987 game; replaced by Kevin Seitzer due to injury.

Year	League	Pos.	BATTING AB	R	H	2B	3B	HR	RBI	Avg.	BB	SO	SB	FIELDING PO	A	E	Avg.
1976	—American..................	3B	2	0	0	0	0	0	0	.000	1	0	0	0	1	0	1.000
1977	—American..................	3B	2	0	0	0	0	0	0	.000	1	0	0	2	1	0	1.000
1978	—American..................	3B	3	1	2	1	0	0	2	.667	0	0	1	0	2	0	1.000
1979	—American..................	3B	3	1	0	0	0	0	0	.000	0	0	0	1	2	0	1.000
1980	—American..................	Selected, did not play—injured.															
1981	—American..................	3B	3	0	0	0	0	0	0	.000	0	2	0	0	1	0	1.000
1982	—American..................	3B	2	0	2	0	0	0	0	1.000	0	0	0	0	0	0	...
1983	—American..................	3B	4	2	2	1	1	0	1	.500	0	0	0	1	5	0	1.000
1984	—American..................	3B	3	1	1	0	0	1	1	.333	0	1	0	3	0	0	1.000
1985	—American..................	3B	1	0	0	0	0	0	1	.000	1	0	0	2	1	0	1.000
1986	—American..................	Selected, did not play—injured.															
1987	—American..................	Selected, did not play—injured.															
1988	—American..................	PH	1	0	0	0	0	0	0	.000	0	0	0	...	...	...	...
All-Star Game totals (10 years)			24	5	7	2	1	1	5	.292	3	3	1	9	13	0	1.000

BREWER, BILLY

P, ROYALS

PERSONAL: Born April 15, 1968, in Fort Worth, Tex. . . . 6-1/175. . . . Throws left, bats left. . . . Full name: William Robert Brewer.
HIGH SCHOOL: Spring Hill (Longview, Tex.).
COLLEGE: Dallas Baptist.

TRANSACTIONS/CAREER NOTES: Selected by Cleveland Indians organization in 26th round of free-agent draft (June 5, 1989). . . . Selected by Montreal Expos organization in 28th round of free-agent draft (June 4, 1990). . . . On disabled list (April 12-June 11, 1991). . . . Selected by Kansas City Royals from Expos organization in Rule 5 major league draft (December 7, 1992).

Year	Team (League)	W	L	Pct.	ERA	G	GS	CG	ShO	Sv.	IP	H	R	ER	BB	SO
1990	—Jamestown (NYP)	2	2	.500	2.93	11	2	0	0	1	27⅔	23	10	9	13	37
1991	—Rockford (Midw.)	3	3	.500	1.98	29	0	0	0	5	41	32	12	9	25	43
1992	—W.P. Beach (FSL)	2	2	.500	1.73	28	0	0	0	8	36⅓	27	10	7	14	37
	—Harrisburg (East.)	2	0	1.000	5.01	20	0	0	0	0	23⅓	25	15	13	18	18
1993	—Kansas City (A.L.)■	2	2	.500	3.46	46	0	0	0	0	39	31	16	15	20	28
Major league totals (1 year)		2	2	.500	3.46	46	0	0	0	0	39	31	16	15	20	28

BREWER, ROD

1B/OF, CARDINALS

PERSONAL: Born February 24, 1966, in Eustis, Fla. . . . 6-3/218. . . . Throws left, bats left. . . . Full name: Rodney Lee Brewer.
HIGH SCHOOL: Apopka (Fla.).
COLLEGE: Florida.

TRANSACTIONS/CAREER NOTES: Selected by Toronto Blue Jays organization in 25th round of free-agent draft (June 4, 1984). . . . Selected by St. Louis Cardinals organization in fifth round of free-agent draft (June 2, 1987). . . . On Louisville disabled list (June 9-July 1, 1991).

HONORS: Named first baseman on THE SPORTING NEWS college All-America team (1987).

STATISTICAL NOTES: Led Appalachian League first basemen with .990 fielding percentage, 554 putouts, 45 assists and 605 total chances in 1987. . . . Led Appalachian League with five intentional bases on balls received in 1987. . . . Led Midwest League first basemen with 106 double plays in 1988. . . . Led American Association first basemen with 1,153 putouts, 126 assists, 1,292 total chances and 118 double plays in 1990. . . . Tied for American Association lead with six intentional bases on balls received in 1992.

			BATTING												FIELDING			
Year	Team (League)	Pos.	G	AB	R	H	2B	3B	HR	RBI	Avg.	BB	SO	SB	PO	A	E	Avg.
1987	—Johns. City (App.)	1B-OF	67	238	33	60	11	2	10	42	.252	36	40	2	†557	†45	6	†.990
1988	—Springfield (Midw.)	1B	133	457	57	136	25	2	8	64	.298	63	52	6	*1249	78	10	*.993
1989	—Arkansas (Texas)	1B	128	470	71	130	25	2	10	93	.277	46	46	2	1084	97	•12	.990
1990	—Louisville (A.A.)	1B-P	•144	514	60	129	15	5	12	83	.251	54	62	0	†1153	†126	13	.990
	—St. Louis (N.L.)	1B	14	25	4	6	1	0	0	2	.240	0	4	0	46	6	1	.981
1991	—Louisville (A.A.)	1B-OF	104	382	39	86	21	1	8	52	.225	35	57	4	588	42	3	.995
	—St. Louis (N.L.)	1B-OF	19	13	0	1	0	0	0	1	.077	0	5	0	30	3	1	.971
1992	—Louisville (A.A.)	OF-1B	120	423	57	122	20	2	18	86	.288	49	60	0	399	27	5	.988
	—St. Louis (N.L.)	1B-OF	29	103	11	31	6	0	0	10	.301	8	12	0	220	19	0	1.000
1993	—St. Louis (N.L.)	OF-1B-P	110	147	15	42	8	0	2	20	.286	17	26	1	148	6	3	.981
Major league totals (4 years)			172	288	30	80	15	0	2	33	.278	25	47	1	444	34	5	.990

RECORD AS PITCHER

Year	Team (League)	W	L	Pct.	ERA	G	GS	CG	ShO	Sv.	IP	H	R	ER	BB	SO
1990	—Louisville (A.A.)	0	0	...	0.00	1	0	0	0	0	1	0	0	0	0	0
1993	—St. Louis (N.L.)	0	0	...	45.00	1	0	0	0	0	1	3	5	5	2	1
Major league totals (1 year)		0	0	...	45.00	1	0	0	0	0	1	3	5	5	2	1

BRILEY, GREG

OF

PERSONAL: Born May 24, 1965, in Greenville, N.C. . . . 5-8/180. . . . Throws right, bats left.
HIGH SCHOOL: North Pitt (Bethel, N.C.).
COLLEGE: Louisburg (N.C.) College and North Carolina State.

TRANSACTIONS/CAREER NOTES: Selected by Los Angeles Dodgers organization in third round of free-agent draft (January 9, 1985). . . . Selected by Cleveland Indians organization in secondary phase of free-agent draft (June 3, 1985). . . . Selected by Seattle Mariners organization in secondary phase of free-agent draft (June 2, 1986). . . . On disabled list (July 7-31 and August 9-September 1, 1992). . . . Released by Mariners (March 25, 1993). . . . Signed by Florida Marlins (March 31, 1993). . . . Released by Marlins (September 27, 1993).

			BATTING												FIELDING			
Year	Team (League)	Pos.	G	AB	R	H	2B	3B	HR	RBI	Avg.	BB	SO	SB	PO	A	E	Avg.
1986	—Belling. (N'west)	2B	63	218	52	65	12	•4	7	46	.298	50	29	26	132	146	24	.921
1987	—Chatt. (South.)	2B	137	539	81	148	21	5	7	61	.275	41	59	34	221	346	*29	.951
1988	—Calgary (PCL)	OF-2B	112	445	74	139	29	9	11	66	.312	40	51	27	237	132	15	.961
	—Seattle (A.L.)	OF	13	36	6	9	2	0	1	4	.250	5	6	0	13	0	1	.929
1989	—Seattle (A.L.)	OF-2B	115	394	52	105	22	4	13	52	.266	39	82	11	197	38	9	.963
	—Calgary (PCL)	3B-2B-OF	25	94	27	32	8	1	4	20	.340	13	10	14	22	44	5	.930
1990	—Seattle (A.L.)	OF	125	337	40	83	18	2	5	29	.246	37	48	16	177	4	2	.989
1991	—Seattle (A.L.)	OF-2B-3B	139	381	39	99	17	3	2	26	.260	27	51	23	187	5	4	.980
1992	—Seattle (A.L.)	OF-3B-2B	86	200	18	55	10	0	5	12	.275	4	31	9	65	13	4	.951
1993	—Florida (N.L.)■	OF	120	170	17	33	6	0	3	12	.194	12	42	6	71	2	1	.986
American League totals (5 years)			478	1348	155	351	69	9	26	123	.260	112	218	59	639	60	20	.972
National League totals (1 year)			120	170	17	33	6	0	3	12	.194	12	42	6	71	2	1	.986
Major league totals (6 years)			598	1518	172	384	75	9	29	135	.253	124	260	65	710	62	21	.974

BRINK, BRAD

P, PHILLIES

PERSONAL: Born January 20, 1965, in Roseville, Calif. . . . 6-2/208. . . . Throws right, bats right. . . . Full name: Bradford Albert Brink.
HIGH SCHOOL: Downey (Modesto, Calif.).
COLLEGE: Southern California.

TRANSACTIONS/CAREER NOTES: Selected by New York Yankees organization in 17th round of free-agent draft (June 6, 1983).... Selected by Philadelphia Phillies organization in first round (seventh pick overall) of free-agent draft (June 2, 1986).... On disabled list (July 29, 1986-remainder of season; July 15, 1988-remainder of season; April 6-26 and May 11, 1989-remainder of season, and April 6, 1990-entire season).... On Scranton/Wilkes-Barre disabled list (April 10-July 3, 1991 and April 30-July 2, 1993).

Year	Team (League)	W	L	Pct.	ERA	G	GS	CG	ShO	Sv.	IP	H	R	ER	BB	SO
1986	—Reading (Eastern)	0	4	.000	3.80	5	4	0	0	0	23⅔	22	12	10	20	8
1987	—Clearwater (FSL)	4	7	.364	3.82	17	17	2	1	0	94⅓	99	50	40	39	64
	—Reading (Eastern)	3	2	.600	5.00	12	11	1	1	0	72	76	42	40	23	50
1988	—Maine (Int'l)	5	5	.500	4.29	17	17	13	1	0	86	100	43	41	21	58
1989	—Scran./W.B. (Int'l)	0	1	.000	4.09	3	3	0	0	0	11	11	7	5	6	3
1990	—							Did not play.								
1991	—Spartanburg (SAL)	2	1	.667	1.65	3	3	1	0	0	16⅓	15	3	3	5	16
	—Clearwater (FSL)	2	0	1.000	0.69	2	2	0	0	0	13	6	1	1	3	10
	—Reading (Eastern)	2	2	.500	3.71	5	5	0	0	0	34	32	14	14	6	27
1992	—Reading (Eastern)	1	1	.500	3.29	3	3	0	0	0	13⅔	14	6	5	3	12
	—Scran./W.B. (Int'l)	8	2	.800	3.48	17	17	5	2	0	111⅓	100	47	43	34	92
	—Philadelphia (N.L.)	0	4	.000	4.14	8	7	0	0	0	41⅓	53	27	19	13	16
1993	—Scran./W.B. (Int'l)	7	7	.500	4.22	18	18	2	2	0	106⅔	104	53	50	27	89
	—Philadelphia (N.L.)	0	0	...	3.00	2	0	0	0	0	6	3	2	2	3	8
Major league totals (2 years)		0	4	.000	3.99	10	7	0	0	0	47⅓	56	29	21	16	24

BRISCOE, JOHN

P, ATHLETICS

PERSONAL: Born September 22, 1967, in LaGrange, Ill.... 6-3/185.... Throws right, bats right.... Full name: John Eric Briscoe.
HIGH SCHOOL: Berkner (Tex.).
COLLEGE: Texarkana (Tex.) College and Texas Christian.
TRANSACTIONS/CAREER NOTES: Selected by Milwaukee Brewers organization in third round of free-agent draft (January 14, 1986).... Selected by Toronto Blue Jays organization in secondary phase of free-agent draft (June 2, 1986).... Selected by Oakland Athletics organization in third round of free-agent draft (June 1, 1988).... On Tacoma disabled list (June 22-July 31, 1992).

Year	Team (League)	W	L	Pct.	ERA	G	GS	CG	ShO	Sv.	IP	H	R	ER	BB	SO
1988	—Ariz. A's (Arizona)	1	1	.500	3.51	7	6	0	0	0	25⅔	26	14	10	6	23
1989	—Madison (Midwest)	7	5	.583	4.21	21	20	1	0	0	117⅔	121	66	55	57	69
1990	—Modesto (Calif.)	3	6	.333	4.59	29	12	1	0	4	86⅓	72	50	44	52	66
	—Huntsville (South.)	0	0	...	13.50	3	0	0	0	0	4⅔	9	7	7	7	7
1991	—Huntsville (South.)	2	0	1.000	0.00	2	0	0	0	0	4⅓	1	2	0	2	6
	—Oakland (A.L.)	0	0	...	7.07	11	0	0	0	0	14	12	11	11	10	9
	—Tacoma (PCL)	3	5	.375	3.66	22	9	0	0	1	76⅓	73	35	31	44	66
1992	—Oakland (A.L.)	0	1	.000	6.43	2	2	0	0	0	7	12	6	5	9	4
	—Tacoma (PCL)	2	5	.286	5.88	33	6	0	0	0	78	78	62	51	68	66
1993	—Huntsville (South.)	4	0	1.000	3.03	30	0	0	0	16	38⅔	28	14	13	16	62
	—Oakland (A.L.)	1	0	1.000	8.03	17	0	0	0	0	24⅔	26	25	22	26	24
	—Tacoma (PCL)	1	1	.500	2.92	9	0	0	0	6	12⅓	13	5	4	9	16
Major league totals (3 years)		1	1	.500	7.49	30	2	0	0	0	45⅔	50	42	38	45	37

BRITO, BERNARDO

OF, TWINS

PERSONAL: Born December 4, 1963, in San Cristobal, Domincan Republic.... 6-1/190.... Throws right, bats right.
HIGH SCHOOL: Sabana Palenque (San Cristobal, Dominican Republic).
TRANSACTIONS/CAREER NOTES: Signed as free agent by Cleveland Indians organization (October 8, 1980).... Released by Indians (March 25, 1988).... Signed by Minnesota Twins organization (March 31, 1988).... Granted free agency (December 19, 1992).... Signed by Portland, Twins organization (January 15, 1993).... Granted free agency (October 15, 1993).... Re-signed by Portland (October 24, 1993).
STATISTICAL NOTES: Led New-York Pennsylvania League with 171 total bases in 1984.... Led Midwest League with 244 total bases in 1985.

			BATTING												FIELDING			
Year	Team (League)	Pos.	G	AB	R	H	2B	3B	HR	RBI	Avg.	BB	SO	SB	PO	A	E	Avg.
1981	—Batavia (NY-Penn)	OF	12	29	1	6	0	0	0	2	.207	2	9	0	2	0	0	1.000
1982	—Batavia (NY-Penn)	OF	41	123	10	29	2	0	4	15	.236	8	34	1	40	0	6	.870
1983	—Waterloo (Midw.)	OF	35	119	13	24	4	0	4	17	.202	10	40	3	41	2	3	.935
	—Batavia (NY-Penn)	OF	60	206	18	50	10	3	7	34	.243	15	65	5	54	7	8	.884
1984	—Batavia (NY-Penn)	OF	•76	*297	41	89	•19	3	*19	57	.300	14	67	3	100	8	8	.931
1985	—Waterloo (Midw.)	OF	135	498	66	128	27	1	*29	78	.257	24	133	1	160	15	9	.951
1986	—Waterbury (East.)	OF-SS	129	479	61	118	17	1	*18	75	.246	22	*127	0	67	1	1	.986
1987	—Williamsport (East.)	OF-1B	124	452	64	125	20	4	*24	79	.277	24	121	2	48	1	6	.891
1988	—Orlando (Southern)■	OF	135	508	55	122	20	4	24	76	.240	20	138	2	119	3	6	.953
1989	—Portland (PCL)	OF	111	355	51	90	12	7	22	74	.254	31	111	1	83	2	2	.977
1990	—Portland (PCL)	OF	113	376	48	106	26	3	*25	79	.282	27	102	1	40	0	2	.952
1991	—Portland (PCL)	OF	115	428	65	111	17	2	•27	83	.259	28	110	1	1	0	0	1.000
1992	—Portland (PCL)	OF	•140	*564	80	152	27	7	26	96	.270	32	*124	0	87	6	5	.949
	—Minnesota (A.L.)	OF	8	14	1	2	1	0	0	2	.143	0	4	0	3	0	1	.750
1993	—Portland (PCL)	OF	85	319	64	108	18	3	20	72	.339	26	65	0	37	2	2	.951
	—Minnesota (A.L.)	OF	27	54	8	13	2	0	4	9	.241	1	20	0	12	1	0	1.000
Major league totals (2 years)			35	68	9	15	3	0	4	11	.221	1	24	0	15	1	1	.941

BRITO, TILSON

SS, BLUE JAYS

PERSONAL: Born May 28, 1972, in Santo Domingo, Dominican Republic. . . . 6-0/170. . . . Throws right, bats right. . . . Full name: Tilson Manuel Brito.

TRANSACTIONS/CAREER NOTES: Signed as free agent by Toronto Blue Jays organization (January 10, 1990).

STATISTICAL NOTES: Tied for Florida State League lead in errors by shortstop with 37 in 1993.

			BATTING												FIELDING			
Year	**Team (League)**	**Pos.**	**G**	**AB**	**R**	**H**	**2B**	**3B**	**HR**	**RBI**	**Avg.**	**BB**	**SO**	**SB**	**PO**	**A**	**E**	**Avg.**
1990	—Santo Dom. (DSL)	IF	39	130	31	33	8	2	0	14	.254	13	9	4	...	...	...	...
1991	—Santo Dom. (DSL)	IF	70	253	56	85	16	2	4	55	.336	44	19	11	...	...	...	...
1992	—GC Blue Jays (GCL)..	3B-2B-SS	54	189	36	58	10	4	3	36	.307	22	22	16	56	127	17	.915
	—Knoxville (South.)	SS	7	24	2	5	1	2	0	2	.208	0	9	0	6	19	5	.833
1993	—Dunedin (Fla. St.)	SS-3B-2B	126	465	80	125	21	3	6	44	.269	59	60	27	200	387	‡38	.939

BROCAIL, DOUG

P, PADRES

PERSONAL: Born May 16, 1967, in Clearfield, Pa. . . . 6-5/235. . . . Throws right, bats left. . . . Full name: Douglas Keith Brocail.

HIGH SCHOOL: Lamar (Colo.).

COLLEGE: Lamar (Colo.) Community College.

TRANSACTIONS/CAREER NOTES: Selected by San Diego Padres organization in first round (12th pick overall) of free-agent draft (January 14, 1986). . . . On Las Vegas disabled list (May 5-12, 1993).

MISCELLANEOUS: Appeared in six games as pinch-runner for San Diego (1993).

Year	**Team (League)**	**W**	**L**	**Pct.**	**ERA**	**G**	**GS**	**CG**	**ShO**	**Sv.**	**IP**	**H**	**R**	**ER**	**BB**	**SO**
1986	—Spokane (N'west)	5	4	.556	3.81	16	•15	0	0	0	85	85	52	36	53	77
1987	—Char., S.C. (S. Atl.)	2	6	.250	4.09	19	18	0	0	0	92⅓	94	51	42	28	68
1988	—Char., S.C. (S. Atl.)	8	6	.571	2.69	22	13	5	0	2	107	107	40	32	25	107
1989	—Wichita (Texas)	5	9	.357	5.21	23	22	1	1	0	134⅔	158	88	78	50	95
1990	—Wichita (Texas)	2	2	.500	4.33	12	9	0	0	0	52	53	30	25	24	27
1991	—Wichita (Texas)	10	7	.588	3.87	34	16	3	•3	6	146⅓	147	77	63	43	108
1992	—Las Vegas (PCL)	10	10	.500	3.97	29	25	4	0	0	172⅓	187	82	76	63	103
	—San Diego (N.L.)	0	0	...	6.43	3	3	0	0	0	14	17	10	10	5	15
1993	—Las Vegas (PCL)	4	2	.667	3.68	10	8	0	0	1	51⅓	51	26	21	14	32
	—San Diego (N.L.)	4	13	.235	4.56	24	24	0	0	0	128⅓	143	75	65	42	70
Major league totals (2 years) ..		4	13	.235	4.74	27	27	0	0	0	142⅓	160	85	75	47	85

BROGNA, RICO

1B, TIGERS

PERSONAL: Born April 18, 1970, in Turner Falls, Mass. . . . 6-2/200. . . . Throws left, bats left. . . . Full name: Rico Joseph Brogna. . . . Name pronounced BRONE-yah.

HIGH SCHOOL: Watertown (Conn.).

TRANSACTIONS/CAREER NOTES: Selected by Detroit Tigers organization in first round (26th pick overall) of free-agent draft (June 1, 1988). . . . On Toledo disabled list (May 25-June 2, 1991).

STATISTICAL NOTES: Led Eastern League first basemen with 1,261 total chances and 117 double plays in 1990.

			BATTING												FIELDING			
Year	**Team (League)**	**Pos.**	**G**	**AB**	**R**	**H**	**2B**	**3B**	**HR**	**RBI**	**Avg.**	**BB**	**SO**	**SB**	**PO**	**A**	**E**	**Avg.**
1988	—Bristol (Appal.)	1B-OF	60	209	37	53	11	2	7	33	.254	25	42	3	319	26	6	.983
1989	—Lakeland (Fla. St.) ...	1B	128	459	47	108	20	7	5	51	.235	38	82	2	1098	83	13	.989
1990	—London (Eastern)	1B	137	488	70	128	21	3	*21	•77	.262	50	100	1	*1155	*93	13	.990
1991	—Toledo (Int'l)	1B	41	132	13	29	6	1	2	13	.220	4	26	2	311	37	5	.986
	—London (Eastern)	1B-OF	77	293	40	80	13	1	13	51	.273	25	59	0	368	46	6	.986
1992	—Toledo (Int'l)	1B	121	387	45	101	19	4	10	58	.261	31	85	1	896	76	9	.991
	—Detroit (A.L.)	1B	9	26	3	5	1	0	1	3	.192	3	5	0	48	6	1	.982
1993	—Toledo (Int'l)	1B	129	483	55	132	30	3	11	59	.273	31	94	7	937	97	8	.992
Major league totals (1 year)			9	26	3	5	1	0	1	3	.192	3	5	0	48	6	1	.982

BRONKEY, JEFF

P, BREWERS

PERSONAL: Born September 18, 1965, in Kabul, Afghanistan. . . . 6-3/210. . . . Throws right, bats right. . . . Full name: Jacob Jeffery Bronkey.

HIGH SCHOOL: Klamath Union (Klamath Falls, Ore.).

COLLEGE: Oklahoma State.

TRANSACTIONS/CAREER NOTES: Selected by Philadelphia Phillies organization in eighth round of free-agent draft (June 6, 1983). . . . Selected by Minnesota Twins organization in second round of free-agent draft (June 2, 1986). . . . Released by Twins organization (January 3, 1990). . . . Signed by Texas Rangers organization (May 25, 1990). . . . On Tulsa disabled list (May 21, 1991-remainder of season). . . . Traded by Rangers to Milwaukee Brewers for P David Pike (January 13, 1994).

STATISTICAL NOTES: Tied for Texas League lead with four balks in 1992.

Year	**Team (League)**	**W**	**L**	**Pct.**	**ERA**	**G**	**GS**	**CG**	**ShO**	**Sv.**	**IP**	**H**	**R**	**ER**	**BB**	**SO**
1986	—Kenosha (Midwest)	4	6	.400	3.83	14	6	1	0	0	49⅓	41	24	21	30	25
1987	—Orlando (Southern)	1	6	.143	6.29	24	4	1	0	7	48⅔	70	40	34	28	23
	—Visalia (California)	2	5	.286	3.82	27	0	0	0	5	35⅓	26	21	15	32	31
1988	—Visalia (California)	4	6	.400	3.38	44	6	1	1	9	85⅓	66	44	32	67	58
1989	—Orlando (Southern)	1	2	.333	5.40	16	13	0	0	0	61⅔	74	53	37	35	47
1990	—Okla. City (A.A.)■	2	0	1.000	4.35	28	0	0	0	0	51⅔	58	28	25	28	18
1991	—Okla. City (A.A.)	1	0	1.000	10.80	7	0	0	0	0	10	16	13	12	4	7
	—Tulsa (Texas)	0	0	...	9.39	4	0	0	0	0	7⅔	11	9	8	5	5
1992	—Tulsa (Texas)	2	7	.222	2.55	45	0	0	0	13	70⅔	51	27	20	25	58
	—Okla. City (A.A.)	0	1	.000	7.47	13	0	0	0	3	15⅔	26	13	13	7	10
1993	—Okla. City (A.A.)	2	2	.500	2.65	29	0	0	0	14	37⅓	29	11	11	7	19
	—Texas (A.L.)	1	1	.500	4.00	21	0	0	0	1	36	39	20	16	11	18
Major league totals (1 year) ...		1	1	.500	4.00	21	0	0	0	1	36	39	20	16	11	18

BROOKS, HUBIE

DH/OF, ROYALS

PERSONAL: Born September 24, 1956, in Los Angeles. . . . 6-0/205. . . . Throws right, bats right. . . . Full name: Hubert Brooks Jr. . . . Cousin of Donnie Moore, major league pitcher with five teams (1975 and 1977-88).
HIGH SCHOOL: Dominguez (Compton, Calif.).
COLLEGE: Mesa (Ariz.) Community College and Arizona State (bachelor of science degree in health science).
TRANSACTIONS/CAREER NOTES: Selected by Montreal Expos organization in 19th round of free-agent draft (June 5, 1974). . . . Selected by Kansas City Royals organization in secondary phase of free-agent draft (January 7, 1976). . . . Selected by Chicago White Sox organization in secondary phase of free-agent draft (June 8, 1976). . . . Selected by Oakland Athletics organization in secondary phase of free-agent draft (January 11, 1977). . . . Selected by White Sox organization in secondary phase of free-agent draft (June 7, 1977). . . . Selected by New York Mets organization in first round (third pick overall) of free-agent draft (June 6, 1978). . . . On disabled list (June 28-July 22, 1982). . . . Traded by Mets with C Mike Fitzgerald, OF Herm Winningham and P Floyd Youmans to Montreal Expos for C Gary Carter (December 10, 1984). . . . On disabled list (August 2, 1986-remainder of season and April 11-May 25, 1987). . . . Granted free agency (November 13, 1989). . . . Signed by Los Angeles Dodgers (December 21, 1989). . . . Traded by Dodgers to Mets for P Bob Ojeda and P Greg Hansell (December 15, 1990). . . . On disabled list (August 19, 1991-remainder of season). . . . Traded by Mets to California Angels for OF Dave Gallagher (December 10, 1991). . . . On California disabled list (June 20-September 4, 1992); included rehabilitation assignment to Edmonton (August 25-September 4). . . . Granted free agency (October 30, 1992). . . . Signed by Royals organization (January 27, 1993). . . . Granted free agency (October 29, 1993). . . . Re-signed by Royals organization (January 7, 1994).
HONORS: Named outfielder on THE SPORTING NEWS college All-America team (1977). . . . Named shortstop on THE SPORTING NEWS college All-America team (1978). . . . Named shortstop on THE SPORTING NEWS N.L. Silver Slugger team (1985-86).
STATISTICAL NOTES: Led N.L. third basemen with 21 errors in 1981.

			BATTING												FIELDING			
Year	Team (League)	Pos.	G	AB	R	H	2B	3B	HR	RBI	Avg.	BB	SO	SB	PO	A	E	Avg.
1978	—Jackson (Texas)	SS-OF-3B	45	153	19	33	8	1	3	16	.216	13	34	3	49	84	14	.905
1979	—Jackson (Texas)	3B-SS	112	406	68	124	21	2	3	28	.305	51	59	14	92	218	29	.914
	—Tidewater (Int'l)	SS-3B-OF	5	15	1	6	1	0	1	3	.400	1	2	0	4	8	1	.923
1980	—Tidewater (Int'l)	OF-3B-SS	113	417	50	124	18	5	3	50	.297	36	56	14	152	90	18	.931
	—New York (N.L.)	3B	24	81	8	25	2	1	1	10	.309	5	9	1	16	40	2	.966
1981	—New York (N.L.)	3B-OF-SS	98	358	34	110	21	2	4	38	.307	23	65	9	67	193	†21	.925
1982	—New York (N.L.)	3B	126	457	40	114	21	2	2	40	.249	28	76	6	89	237	24	.931
1983	—New York (N.L.)	3B-2B	150	586	53	147	18	4	5	58	.251	24	96	6	116	303	21	.952
1984	—New York (N.L.)	3B-SS	153	561	61	159	23	2	16	73	.283	48	79	6	112	284	29	.932
1985	—Montreal (N.L.)■	SS	156	605	67	163	34	7	13	100	.269	34	79	6	203	441	28	.958
1986	—Montreal (N.L.)	SS	80	306	50	104	18	5	14	58	.340	25	60	4	116	222	15	.958
1987	—Montreal (N.L.)	SS	112	430	57	113	22	3	14	72	.263	24	72	4	131	271	20	.953
1988	—Montreal (N.L.)	OF	151	588	61	164	35	2	20	90	.279	35	108	7	261	8	9	.968
1989	—Montreal (N.L.)	OF	148	542	56	145	30	1	14	70	.268	39	108	6	234	6	9	.964
1990	—Los Angeles (N.L.)■	OF	153	568	74	151	28	1	20	91	.266	33	108	2	255	9	10	.964
1991	—New York (N.L.)■	OF	103	357	48	85	11	1	16	50	.238	44	62	3	166	6	5	.972
1992	—California (A.L.)■	1B	82	306	28	66	13	0	8	36	.216	12	46	3	64	4	1	.986
	—Edmonton (PCL)	1B	8	24	2	7	2	1	1	11	.292	1	2	0	16	0	0	1.000
1993	—Kansas City (A.L.)■	OF-1B	75	168	14	48	12	0	1	24	.286	11	27	0	72	6	2	.975
American League totals (2 years)			157	474	42	114	25	0	9	60	.241	23	73	3	136	10	3	.980
National League totals (12 years)			1454	5439	609	1480	263	31	139	750	.272	362	922	60	1766	2020	193	.951
Major league totals (14 years)			1611	5913	651	1594	288	31	148	810	.270	385	995	63	1902	2030	196	.953

ALL-STAR GAME RECORD

			BATTING										FIELDING			
Year	League	Pos.	AB	R	H	2B	3B	HR	RBI	Avg.	BB	SO	SB	PO	A	E	Avg.
1986	—National	PH-SS	2	1	0	0	0	0	0	.000	0	1	0	1	0	0	1.000
1987	—National	SS	3	1	1	0	0	0	0	.333	0	0	0	1	2	0	1.000
All-Star Game totals (2 years)			5	2	1	0	0	0	0	.200	0	1	0	2	2	0	1.000

BROOKS, JERRY

C/OF, DODGERS

PERSONAL: Born March 23, 1967, in Syracuse, N.Y. . . . 6-0/195. . . . Throws right, bats right. . . . Full name: Jerome Edward Brooks.
HIGH SCHOOL: George W. Fowler (Syracuse, N.Y.).
COLLEGE: Clemson.
TRANSACTIONS/CAREER NOTES: Selected by Los Angeles Dodgers organization in 12th round of free-agent draft (June 1, 1988). . . . On disabled list (June 2-9, 1992).
STATISTICAL NOTES: Led Texas League outfielders with five double plays in 1990.

			BATTING												FIELDING			
Year	Team (League)	Pos.	G	AB	R	H	2B	3B	HR	RBI	Avg.	BB	SO	SB	PO	A	E	Avg.
1988	—Great Falls (Pio.)	OF-3B	68	*285	63	*99	•21	3	8	60	.347	24	25	7	60	20	3	.964
1989	—Bakersfield (Calif.)	OF-3B	141	*565	70	164	39	1	16	87	.290	25	79	9	247	16	11	.960
1990	—San Antonio (Tex.)	OF	106	391	52	118	20	0	9	58	.302	26	39	5	153	8	3	.982
1991	—Albuquerque (PCL)	OF-C	125	429	64	126	20	7	13	82	.294	29	49	4	190	7	2	.990
1992	—Albuquerque (PCL)	OF	129	467	77	124	36	1	14	78	.266	39	68	3	196	9	7	.967
1993	—Albuquerque (PCL)	C-OF	116	421	67	145	28	4	11	71	.344	21	44	3	433	44	11	.977
	—Los Angeles (N.L.)	OF	9	9	2	2	1	0	1	1	.222	0	2	0	0	0	0	...
Major league totals (1 year)			9	9	2	2	1	0	1	1	.222	0	2	0	0	0	0	...

BROSIUS, SCOTT

OF/3B, ATHLETICS

PERSONAL: Born August 15, 1966, in Hillsboro, Ore. . . . 6-1/185. . . . Throws right, bats right. . . . Full name: Scott David Brosius. . . . Name pronounced BRO-shus.
HIGH SCHOOL: Rex Putnam (Milwaukie, Ore.).
COLLEGE: Linfield College (Ore.).
TRANSACTIONS/CAREER NOTES: Selected by Oakland Athletics organization in 20th round of free-agent draft (June 2, 1987). . . .

On Tacoma disabled list (April 17-May 29, 1991).... On Oakland disabled list (April 18-May 12, 1992); included rehabilitation assignment to Tacoma (May 6-12).... On Oakland disabled list (July 13-August 3, 1992); included rehabilitation assignment to Tacoma (July 27-August 3).... On Tacoma disabled list (July 28-August 5, 1993).
STATISTICAL NOTES: Led Northwest League with seven sacrifice flies in 1987.... Led Southern League with 274 total bases in 1990.... Tied for Pacific Coast League lead in double plays by third baseman with 24 in 1992.

			BATTING												FIELDING			
Year	Team (League)	Pos.	G	AB	R	H	2B	3B	HR	RBI	Avg.	BB	SO	SB	PO	A	E	Avg.
1987	—Medford (N'west)	3-S-2-1-P	65	255	34	73	18	1	3	49	.286	26	36	5	123	148	38	.877
1988	—Madison (Midwest)	S-3-0-1	132	504	82	153	28	2	9	58	.304	56	67	13	151	305	61	.882
1989	—Huntsville (South.)	2-3-S-1	128	461	68	125	22	2	7	60	.271	58	62	4	225	316	34	.941
1990	—Huntsville (South.)	SS-2B-3B	•142	547	94	*162	*39	2	23	88	.296	81	81	12	253	419	41	.942
	—Tacoma (PCL)	2B	3	7	2	1	0	1	0	0	.143	1	3	0	3	5	0	1.000
1991	—Tacoma (PCL)	3B-SS-2B	65	245	28	70	16	3	8	31	.286	18	29	4	49	168	14	.939
	—Oakland (A.L.)	2B-OF-3B	36	68	9	16	5	0	2	4	.235	3	11	3	31	16	0	1.000
1992	—Oakland (A.L.)	0-3-1-S	38	87	13	19	2	0	4	13	.218	3	13	3	68	15	1	.988
	—Tacoma (PCL)	3B-OF	63	236	29	56	13	0	9	31	.237	23	44	8	50	167	10	.956
1993	—Oakland (A.L.)	0-1-3-S	70	213	26	53	10	1	6	25	.249	14	37	6	173	29	2	.990
	—Tacoma (PCL)	3-0-2-1-S	56	209	38	62	13	2	8	41	.297	21	50	8	101	109	13	.942
Major league totals (3 years)			144	368	48	88	17	1	12	42	.239	20	61	12	272	60	3	.991

RECORD AS PITCHER

Year	Team (League)	W	L	Pct.	ERA	G	GS	CG	ShO	Sv.	IP	H	R	ER	BB	SO
1987	—Medford (N'west)	0	0	...	0.00	1	0	0	0	0	2	0	0	0	0	1

BROSS, TERRY

P, CUBS

PERSONAL: Born March 30, 1966, in El Paso, Tex.... 6-9/230.... Throws right, bats right.... Full name: Terrence Paul Bross.... Name pronounced BRAHSS.
HIGH SCHOOL: Immaculata (Somerville, N.J.).
COLLEGE: St. John's.
TRANSACTIONS/CAREER NOTES: Selected by New York Mets organization in 13th round of free-agent draft (June 2, 1987).... On disabled list (May 31-June 29, 1989).... On Tidewater disabled list (April 10-17, 1991).... Traded by Mets to San Diego Padres for 3B Craig Bullock (March 30, 1992).... On disabled list (April 18-25, 1992).... Traded by Padres to Texas Rangers for P Pat Gomez (December 16, 1992).... Released by Rangers (March 20, 1993).... Signed by Phoenix, San Francisco Giants organization (March 26, 1993).... Granted free agency (December 20, 1993).... Signed by Chicago Cubs organization (January 11, 1994).

Year	Team (League)	W	L	Pct.	ERA	G	GS	CG	ShO	Sv.	IP	H	R	ER	BB	SO
1987	—Little Falls (NYP)	2	0	1.000	3.86	10	3	0	0	0	28	22	23	12	20	21
1988	—Little Falls (NYP)	2	1	.667	3.09	20	6	0	0	1	55⅓	43	25	19	38	59
1989	—St. Lucie (Fla. St.)	8	2	•.800	2.79	35	0	0	0	11	58	39	21	18	26	47
1990	—Jackson (Texas)	3	4	.429	2.64	58	0	0	0	*28	71⅔	46	21	21	40	51
1991	—Tidewater (Int'l)	2	0	1.000	4.36	27	0	0	0	2	33	31	21	16	32	23
	—Williamsport (East.)	2	0	1.000	2.49	20	0	0	0	5	25⅓	13	12	7	11	27
	—New York (N.L.)	0	0	...	1.80	8	0	0	0	0	10	7	2	2	3	5
1992	—Las Vegas (PCL)■	7	3	.700	3.26	49	0	0	0	0	85⅔	83	36	31	30	42
1993	—Phoenix (PCL)■	4	4	.500	3.97	54	0	0	0	5	79⅓	76	37	35	37	69
	—San Francisco (N.L.)	0	0	...	9.00	2	0	0	0	0	2	3	2	2	1	1
Major league totals (2 years)		0	0	...	3.00	10	0	0	0	0	12	10	4	4	4	6

BROW, SCOTT

P, BLUE JAYS

PERSONAL: Born March 17, 1969, in Butte, Mont.... 6-3/200.... Throws right, bats right.... Full name: Scott John Brow.... Name pronounced BRAUH.
HIGH SCHOOL: Hillsboro (Ore.).
COLLEGE: Washington.
TRANSACTIONS/CAREER NOTES: Selected by Toronto Blue Jays organization in seventh round of free-agent draft (June 4, 1990).

Year	Team (League)	W	L	Pct.	ERA	G	GS	CG	ShO	Sv.	IP	H	R	ER	BB	SO
1990	—St. Cathar. (NYP)	3	1	.750	2.27	9	7	0	0	0	39⅔	34	18	10	11	39
1991	—Dunedin (Fla. St.)	3	7	.300	4.78	15	12	0	0	0	69⅔	73	50	37	28	31
1992	—Dunedin (Fla. St.)	14	2	.875	2.43	25	25	3	1	0	*170⅔	143	53	46	44	107
1993	—Knoxville (South.)	1	2	.333	3.32	3	3	1	0	0	19	13	8	7	9	12
	—Toronto (A.L.)	1	1	.500	6.00	6	3	0	0	0	18	19	15	12	10	7
	—Syracuse (Int'l)	6	8	.429	4.38	20	19	2	0	0	121⅓	119	63	59	37	64
Major league totals (1 year)		1	1	.500	6.00	6	3	0	0	0	18	19	15	12	10	7

BROWN, JARVIS

OF, BRAVES

PERSONAL: Born March 26, 1967, in Waukegan, Ill.... 5-7/170.... Throws right, bats right.... Full name: Jarvis Ardel Brown.
HIGH SCHOOL: St. Joseph (Kenosha, Wis.).
COLLEGE: Triton College (Ill.).
TRANSACTIONS/CAREER NOTES: Selected by Minnesota Twins organization in first round (ninth pick overall) of free-agent draft (January 14, 1986).... On Portland disabled list (July 25-August 1, 1992).... Granted free agency (October 16, 1992).... Signed by San Diego Padres organization (November 20, 1992).... Claimed on waivers by Atlanta Braves (November 18, 1993).
STATISTICAL NOTES: Led Midwest League outfielders with 334 total chances in 1988.... Led California League outfielders with seven double plays in 1989.... Tied for Southern League lead in double plays by outfielder with four in 1990.

			BATTING												FIELDING			
Year	Team (League)	Pos.	G	AB	R	H	2B	3B	HR	RBI	Avg.	BB	SO	SB	PO	A	E	Avg.
1986	—Elizabeth. (Appal.)	2B-OF-SS	49	180	28	41	4	0	3	23	.228	18	41	15	90	107	17	.921
1987	—Kenosha (Midwest)	2B-OF	43	117	22	37	4	1	3	16	.316	19	24	6	74	82	15	.912

Year	Team (League)	Pos.	G	AB	R	H	2B	3B	HR	RBI	Avg.	BB	SO	SB	PO	A	E	Avg.
			BATTING												FIELDING			
	—Elizabeth. (Appal.)	OF	67	258	52	63	9	1	1	15	.244	48	50	30	106	6	*16	.875
1988	—Kenosha (Midwest)	OF	138	531	*108	*156	25	7	7	45	.294	71	89	72	311	15	8	.976
1989	—Visalia (California)	OF	141	545	*95	131	21	6	4	46	.240	73	112	49	291	16	6	.981
1990	—Orlando (Southern)	OF	135	527	*104	137	22	7	14	57	.260	80	79	33	316	12	10	.970
1991	—Portland (PCL)	OF	108	436	62	126	5	8	3	37	.289	36	66	27	243	11	4	.984
	—Minnesota (A.L.)	OF	38	37	10	8	0	0	0	0	.216	2	8	7	21	0	1	.955
1992	—Minnesota (A.L.)	OF	35	15	8	1	0	0	0	0	.067	2	4	2	20	0	1	.952
	—Portland (PCL)	OF	62	224	25	56	8	2	2	16	.250	20	37	17	135	4	4	.972
1993	—Las Vegas (PCL)■	OF	100	402	74	124	27	9	3	47	.308	41	55	22	217	*16	9	.963
	—San Diego (N.L.)	OF	47	133	21	31	9	2	0	8	.233	15	26	3	109	2	2	.982
American League totals (2 years)			73	52	18	9	0	0	0	0	.173	4	12	9	41	0	2	.953
National League totals (1 year)			47	133	21	31	9	2	0	8	.233	15	26	3	109	2	2	.982
Major league totals (3 years)			120	185	39	40	9	2	0	8	.216	19	38	12	150	2	4	.974

CHAMPIONSHIP SERIES RECORD

Year	Team (League)	Pos.	G	AB	R	H	2B	3B	HR	RBI	Avg.	BB	SO	SB	PO	A	E	Avg.
			BATTING												FIELDING			
1991	—Minnesota (A.L.)	PR-DH	1	0	1	0	0	0	0	0	...	0	0	0	...	...	...	...

WORLD SERIES RECORD

Year	Team (League)	Pos.	G	AB	R	H	2B	3B	HR	RBI	Avg.	BB	SO	SB	PO	A	E	Avg.
			BATTING												FIELDING			
1991	—Minnesota (A.L.)	OF-PH-PR	3	2	0	0	0	0	0	0	.000	0	0	0	0	0	0	...

BROWN, KEVIN

P, RANGERS

PERSONAL: Born March 14, 1965, in McIntyre, Ga. . . . 6-4/195. . . . Throws right, bats right. . . . Full name: James Kevin Brown.
HIGH SCHOOL: Wilkinson County (Irwinton, Ga.).
COLLEGE: Georgia Tech.
TRANSACTIONS/CAREER NOTES: Selected by Texas Rangers organization in first round (fourth pick overall) of free-agent draft (June 2, 1986). . . . On disabled list (August 14-29, 1990 and March 27-April 11, 1993).
HONORS: Named righthanded pitcher on THE SPORTING NEWS college All-America team (1986).
STATISTICAL NOTES: Tied for A.L. lead with 13 hit batsmen in 1991.
MISCELLANEOUS: Made an out in only appearance as pinch-hitter (1990). . . . Appeared in one game as pinch-runner (1993).

Year	Team (League)	W	L	Pct.	ERA	G	GS	CG	ShO	Sv.	IP	H	R	ER	BB	SO
1986	—GC Rangers (GCL)	0	0	...	6.00	3	0	0	0	0	6	7	4	4	2	1
	—Tulsa (Texas)	0	0	...	4.50	3	2	0	0	0	10	9	7	5	5	10
	—Texas (A.L.)	1	0	1.000	3.60	1	1	0	0	0	5	6	2	2	0	4
1987	—Tulsa (Texas)	1	4	.200	7.29	8	8	0	0	0	42	53	36	34	18	26
	—Okla. City (A.A.)	0	5	.000	10.73	5	5	0	0	0	24⅓	32	32	29	17	9
	—Charlotte (Fla. St.)	0	2	.000	2.72	6	6	1	0	0	36⅓	33	14	11	17	21
1988	—Tulsa (Texas)	12	10	.545	3.51	26	26	5	0	0	174⅓	174	94	68	61	118
	—Texas (A.L.)	1	1	.500	4.24	4	4	1	0	0	23⅓	33	15	11	8	12
1989	—Texas (A.L.)	12	9	.571	3.35	28	28	7	0	0	191	167	81	71	70	104
1990	—Texas (A.L.)	12	10	.545	3.60	26	26	6	2	0	180	175	84	72	60	88
1991	—Texas (A.L.)	9	12	.429	4.40	33	33	0	0	0	210⅔	233	116	103	90	96
1992	—Texas (A.L.)	•21	11	.656	3.32	35	35	11	1	0	*265⅔	*262	117	98	76	173
1993	—Texas (A.L.)	15	12	.556	3.59	34	34	12	3	0	233	228	105	93	74	142
Major league totals (7 years)		71	55	.563	3.65	161	161	37	6	0	1108⅔	1104	520	450	378	619

ALL-STAR GAME RECORD

Year	League	W	L	Pct.	ERA	GS	CG	ShO	Sv.	IP	H	R	ER	BB	SO
1992	—American	1	0	1.000	0.00	1	0	0	0	1	0	0	0	0	1

BROWN, MICHAEL

1B, PIRATES

PERSONAL: Born November 4, 1971, in Martinez, Calif. . . . 6-7/235. . . . Throws left, bats left.
HIGH SCHOOL: Vacaville (Calif.).
TRANSACTIONS/CAREER NOTES: Selected by Pittsburgh Pirates organization in fifth round of free-agent draft (June 5, 1989). . . . On disabled list (July 22-August 3, 1991 and April 9-20, 1992).
STATISTICAL NOTES: Tied for Carolina League lead with four intentional bases on balls received in 1993.

Year	Team (League)	Pos.	G	AB	R	H	2B	3B	HR	RBI	Avg.	BB	SO	SB	PO	A	E	Avg.
			BATTING												FIELDING			
1989	—GC Pirates (GCL)	1B	39	140	18	31	5	2	0	11	.221	19	28	2	263	29	15	.951
1990	—Welland (NYP)	1B	65	192	23	56	7	0	2	31	.292	22	35	5	427	16	12	.974
1991	—Augusta (S. Atl.)	1B	94	314	24	73	13	4	3	34	.232	47	79	12	559	34	15	.975
1992	—Augusta (S. Atl.)	1B	102	322	34	82	11	9	2	33	.255	37	69	11	626	38	13	.981
1993	—Salem (Carolina)	1B	126	436	71	118	25	3	21	70	.271	61	109	6	1082	73	13	*.989

BROWNE, BYRON

P, BREWERS

PERSONAL: Born August 8, 1970, in Camden, N.J. . . . 6-7/190. . . . Throws right, bats right. . . . Full name: Byron Ellis Browne Jr.
HIGH SCHOOL: St. Joseph (Mo.) Central.
COLLEGE: Grand Canyon (Ariz.).
TRANSACTIONS/CAREER NOTES: Selected by Milwaukee Brewers organization in 13th round of free-agent draft (June 3, 1991).
STATISTICAL NOTES: Led Midwest League with 24 wild pitches in 1992.

Year	Team (League)	W	L	Pct.	ERA	G	GS	CG	ShO	Sv.	IP	H	R	ER	BB	SO
1991	—Ariz. Brewers (Ar.).....	1	6	.143	8.07	13	11	0	0	0	58	69	*65	*52	67	68
1992	—Beloit (Midwest).........	9	8	.529	5.08	25	25	2	0	0	134⅔	109	84	76	114	111
1993	—Stockton (Calif.)	10	5	.667	4.07	27	•27	0	0	0	143⅔	117	73	65	117	110

BROWNE, JERRY

IF/OF, MARLINS

PERSONAL: Born February 3, 1966, in St. Croix, Virgin Islands. . . . 5-10/170. . . . Throws right, bats both. . . . Full name: Jerome Austin Browne.
HIGH SCHOOL: Central (Killshill, Va.).
TRANSACTIONS/CAREER NOTES: Signed as free agent by Texas Rangers organization (March 3, 1983). . . . On disabled list (August 24-September 8, 1987). . . . Traded by Rangers with 1B Pete O'Brien and OF Oddibe McDowell to Cleveland Indians for 2B Julio Franco (December 6, 1988). . . . Released by Indians (March 31, 1992). . . . Signed by Tacoma, Oakland Athletics organization (April 11, 1992). . . . On Oakland disabled list (April 19-July 18, 1993); included rehabilitation assignment to Tacoma (July 6-11). . . . Granted free agency (October 26, 1993). . . . Signed by Florida Marlins organization (January 5, 1994).
STATISTICAL NOTES: Led Carolina League second basemen with 675 total chances in 1985. . . . Led Texas League second basemen with .984 fielding percentage in 1986. . . . Led A.L. with 16 sacrifice hits in 1992.

			BATTING												FIELDING			
Year	Team (League)	Pos.	G	AB	R	H	2B	3B	HR	RBI	Avg.	BB	SO	SB	PO	A	E	Avg.
1983	—GC Rangers (GCL)....	2B	48	181	34	51	2	2	0	20	.282	31	16	8	92	123	14	.939
1984	—Burlington (Midw.)...	SS-2B	127	420	70	99	10	1	0	18	.236	71	76	31	231	311	43	.926
1985	—Salem (Carolina)......	2B	122	460	69	123	18	4	3	58	.267	82	62	24	*265	*390	20	.970
1986	—Tulsa (Texas)...........	2B-SS	128	491	82	149	15	7	2	57	.303	62	61	39	282	307	19	†.969
	—Texas (A.L.)..............	2B	12	24	6	10	2	0	0	3	.417	1	4	0	9	15	2	.923
1987	—Texas (A.L.)..............	2B	132	454	63	123	16	6	1	38	.271	61	50	27	258	338	12	.980
1988	—Okla. City (A.A.).......	2B	76	286	45	72	15	2	5	34	.252	37	29	14	190	231	10	.977
	—Texas (A.L.)..............	2B	73	214	26	49	9	2	1	17	.229	25	33	7	112	139	11	.958
1989	—Cleveland (A.L.)■.....	2B	153	598	83	179	31	4	5	45	.299	68	64	14	305	380	15	.979
1990	—Cleveland (A.L.).......	2B	140	513	92	137	26	5	6	50	.267	72	46	12	286	382	10	.985
1991	—Cleveland (A.L.).......	2B-OF-3B	107	290	28	66	5	2	1	29	.228	27	29	2	113	141	14	.948
1992	—Tacoma (PCL)■........	2B	4	17	1	7	1	1	0	3	.412	3	1	0	9	16	0	1.000
	—Oakland (A.L.)..........	3-O-2-S	111	324	43	93	12	2	3	40	.287	40	40	3	149	88	5	.979
1993	—Oakland (A.L.)..........	O-3-2-1	76	260	27	65	13	0	2	19	.250	22	17	4	149	28	6	.967
	—Tacoma (PCL)..........	3B-2B-OF	6	25	3	6	0	0	0	2	.240	0	4	1	7	12	2	.905
Major league totals (8 years).....................			804	2677	368	722	114	21	19	241	.270	316	283	69	1381	1511	75	.975

CHAMPIONSHIP SERIES RECORD

CHAMPIONSHIP SERIES NOTES: Shares single-game record for most singles—4 (October 12, 1992).

			BATTING												FIELDING			
Year	Team (League)	Pos.	G	AB	R	H	2B	3B	HR	RBI	Avg.	BB	SO	SB	PO	A	E	Avg.
1992	—Oakland (A.L.)..........	3B-OF-PH	4	10	3	4	0	0	0	2	.400	2	0	0	6	0	0	1.000

BROWNING, TOM

P, REDS

PERSONAL: Born April 28, 1960, in Casper, Wyo. . . . 6-1/190. . . . Throws left, bats left. . . . Full name: Thomas Leo Browning.
HIGH SCHOOL: Franklin Academy (Malone, N.Y.).
COLLEGE: Tennessee Wesleyan College and Le Moyne College (N.Y.).
TRANSACTIONS/CAREER NOTES: Selected by Cincinnati Reds organization in ninth round of free-agent draft (June 7, 1982). . . . Granted free agency (November 5, 1990). . . . Re-signed by Reds (November 21, 1990). . . . On disabled list (July 2, 1992-remainder of season and August 7, 1993-remainder of season).
HONORS: Named N.L. Rookie Pitcher of the Year by THE SPORTING NEWS (1985).
STATISTICAL NOTES: Pitched seven-inning, 2-0 no-hit victory for Wichita against Iowa (July 31, 1984). . . . Tied for American Association lead with 24 home runs allowed in 1984. . . . Pitched 1-0 perfect game against Los Angeles (September 16, 1988). . . . Led N.L. with 36 home runs allowed in 1988, 31 in 1989 and 32 in 1991.

Year	Team (League)	W	L	Pct.	ERA	G	GS	CG	ShO	Sv.	IP	H	R	ER	BB	SO
1982	—Billings (Pioneer).......	4	•8	.333	3.89	14	14	3	0	0	88	96	53	38	41	*87
1983	—Tampa (Fla. St.).........	8	1	.889	1.49	11	11	4	1	0	78⅔	53	19	13	36	101
	—Waterbury (East.)......	4	10	.286	3.53	18	18	3	1	0	117⅓	100	62	46	63	101
1984	—Wichita (A.A.)............	12	10	.545	3.95	30	28	8	1	0	189⅓	169	88	83	73	*160
	—Cincinnati (N.L.)........	1	0	1.000	1.54	3	3	0	0	0	23⅓	27	4	4	5	14
1985	—Cincinnati (N.L.)........	20	9	.690	3.55	38	38	6	4	0	261⅓	242	111	103	73	155
1986	—Cincinnati (N.L.)........	14	13	.519	3.81	39	•39	4	2	0	243⅓	225	123	103	70	147
1987	—Cincinnati (N.L.)........	10	13	.435	5.02	32	31	2	0	0	183	201	107	102	61	117
	—Nashville (A.A.)..........	2	3	.400	6.07	5	5	1	1	0	29⅔	37	22	20	12	28
1988	—Cincinnati (N.L.)........	18	5	.783	3.41	36	•36	5	2	0	250⅔	205	98	95	64	124
1989	—Cincinnati (N.L.)........	15	12	.556	3.39	37	*37	9	2	0	249⅔	241	109	94	64	118
1990	—Cincinnati (N.L.)........	15	9	.625	3.80	35	•35	2	1	0	227⅔	235	98	96	52	99
1991	—Cincinnati (N.L.)........	14	14	.500	4.18	36	36	1	0	0	230⅓	241	*124	*107	56	115
1992	—Cincinnati (N.L.)........	6	5	.545	5.07	16	16	0	0	0	87	108	49	49	28	33
1993	—Cincinnati (N.L.)........	7	7	.500	4.74	21	20	0	0	0	114	159	61	60	20	53
Major league totals (10 years)		120	87	.580	3.91	293	291	29	11	0	1870⅓	1884	884	813	493	975

CHAMPIONSHIP SERIES RECORD

Year	Team (League)	W	L	Pct.	ERA	G	GS	CG	ShO	Sv.	IP	H	R	ER	BB	SO
1990	—Cincinnati (N.L.)........	1	1	.500	3.27	2	2	0	0	0	11	9	4	4	6	5

WORLD SERIES RECORD

Year	Team (League)	W	L	Pct.	ERA	G	GS	CG	ShO	Sv.	IP	H	R	ER	BB	SO
1990	—Cincinnati (N.L.)	1	0	1.000	4.50	1	1	0	0	0	6	6	3	3	2	2

ALL-STAR GAME RECORD

Year	League	W	L	Pct.	ERA	GS	CG	ShO	Sv.	IP	H	R	ER	BB	SO
1991	—National	Did not play.													

BRUETT, J.T.

OF, TWINS

PERSONAL: Born October 8, 1967, in Milwaukee. . . . 5-11/180. . . . Throws left, bats left. . . . Full name: Joseph Timothy Bruett. . . . Name pronounced BREW-et.
HIGH SCHOOL: Oconomowoc (Wis.).
COLLEGE: Minnesota.
TRANSACTIONS/CAREER NOTES: Selected by Minnesota Twins organization in 11th round of free-agent draft (June 1, 1988).
STATISTICAL NOTES: Led Midwest League in caught stealing with 27 in 1989. . . . Tied for Midwest League lead in double plays by outfielder with five in 1989. . . . Led California League with .439 on-base percentage in 1990.

				BATTING											FIELDING			
Year	Team (League)	Pos.	G	AB	R	H	2B	3B	HR	RBI	Avg.	BB	SO	SB	PO	A	E	Avg.
1988	—Elizabeth. (Appal.) ...	OF	28	91	23	27	3	0	0	3	.297	19	15	17	53	2	2	.965
	—Kenosha (Midwest) ..	OF	3	10	2	2	0	0	0	0	.200	3	0	1	6	1	0	1.000
1989	—Kenosha (Midwest) ..	OF	120	445	82	119	9	1	3	29	.267	89	64	*61	234	10	3	*.988
1990	—Visalia (California) ...	OF	123	437	86	134	15	3	1	33	.307	101	60	50	268	13	4	.986
	—Portland (PCL)	OF	10	34	8	8	2	0	0	3	.235	11	4	2	20	0	0	1.000
1991	—Portland (PCL)	OF	99	345	51	98	6	3	0	35	.284	40	41	21	211	10	2	.991
1992	—Portland (PCL)	OF	77	280	41	70	10	3	0	17	.250	60	27	29	204	11	0	1.000
	—Minnesota (A.L.)	OF	56	76	7	19	4	0	0	2	.250	6	12	6	46	1	1	.979
1993	—Minnesota (A.L.)	OF	17	20	2	5	2	0	0	1	.250	1	4	0	12	0	2	.857
	—Portland (PCL)	OF	90	320	70	103	17	6	2	40	.322	55	38	12	213	11	2	.991
Major league totals (2 years)			73	96	9	24	6	0	0	3	.250	7	16	6	58	1	3	.952

BRUMFIELD, JACOB

OF, REDS

PERSONAL: Born May 27, 1965, in Bogalusa, La. . . . 6-0/185. . . . Throws right, bats right. . . . Full name: Jacob Donnell Brumfield.
HIGH SCHOOL: Hammond (La.).
TRANSACTIONS/CAREER NOTES: Selected by Chicago Cubs organization in seventh round of free-agent draft (June 6, 1983). . . . On disabled list (June 21, 1984-remainder of season). . . . Released by Cubs organization (April 9, 1985). . . . Signed by Kansas City Royals organization (August 16, 1986). . . . Granted free agency (October 15, 1991). . . . Signed by Cincinnati Reds organization (November 12, 1991). . . . On Nashville disabled list (June 12-July 25, 1992).
STATISTICAL NOTES: Led Florida State League with .429 on-base percentage in 1990. . . . Led American Association in caught stealing with 16 in 1991.

				BATTING											FIELDING			
Year	Team (League)	Pos.	G	AB	R	H	2B	3B	HR	RBI	Avg.	BB	SO	SB	PO	A	E	Avg.
1983	—Pikeville (Appal.)	OF	42	113	17	29	0	1	3	15	.257	25	34	8	34	3	5	.881
1984	—	Did not play.																
1985	—	Did not play.																
1986	—Fort Myers (FSL)■....	SS	12	41	3	13	3	1	1	5	.317	2	11	0	18	16	8	.810
1987	—Fort Myers (FSL)	OF-3B	114	379	56	93	14	*10	6	34	.245	45	78	43	235	53	19	.938
	—Memphis (South.)	OF	9	39	7	13	3	2	1	6	.333	3	8	2	35	0	2	.946
1988	—Memphis (South.)	OF	128	433	70	98	15	5	6	28	.226	52	104	47	239	2	6	.976
1989	—Memphis (South.)	OF	104	346	43	79	14	2	1	25	.228	53	74	28	217	2	8	.965
1990	—Baseball City (FSL) ..	OF	109	372	66	125	24	3	0	40	*.336	60	44	47	186	*17	8	.962
	—Omaha (A.A.)	OF	24	77	10	25	6	1	2	11	.325	7	14	10	45	3	0	1.000
1991	—Omaha (A.A.)	OF	111	397	62	106	14	7	3	43	.267	33	64	*36	227	10	2	.992
1992	—Cincinnati (N.L.)■....	OF	24	30	6	4	0	0	0	2	.133	2	4	6	20	1	0	1.000
	—Nashville (A.A.)	OF	56	208	32	59	10	3	5	19	.284	26	35	22	137	4	6	.959
1993	—Indianapolis (A.A.) ...	OF	33	126	23	41	14	1	4	19	.325	6	14	11	74	4	4	.951
	—Cincinnati (N.L.)	OF-2B	103	272	40	73	17	3	6	23	.268	21	47	20	178	16	7	.965
Major league totals (2 years)			127	302	46	77	17	3	6	25	.255	23	51	26	198	17	7	.968

BRUMLEY, DUFF

P, RANGERS

PERSONAL: Born August 25, 1970, in Cleveland, Tenn. . . . 6-4/195. . . . Throws right, bats right. . . . Full name: Duff Lechaun Brumley.
HIGH SCHOOL: Cleveland (Tenn.).
COLLEGE: Cleveland (Tenn.) State Community College.
TRANSACTIONS/CAREER NOTES: Selected by St. Louis Cardinals organization in 24th round of free-agent draft (June 4, 1990). . . . Traded by Cardinals organization to Texas Rangers organization (July 30, 1993), completing deal in which Rangers traded P Todd Burns to Cardinals for a player to be named later (July 22, 1993).

Year	Team (League)	W	L	Pct.	ERA	G	GS	CG	ShO	Sv.	IP	H	R	ER	BB	SO
1990	—Johns. City (App.)	2	6	.250	6.14	12	11	0	0	0	55⅔	62	48	38	29	43
1991	—Hamilton (NYP)	2	6	.250	3.64	15	15	0	0	0	89	90	49	36	24	80
1992	—Hamilton (NYP)	6	0	1.000	2.72	9	9	2	0	0	59⅔	38	19	18	21	83
	—Savannah (S. Atl.)	2	1	.667	1.74	5	5	0	0	0	31	17	9	6	14	46
1993	—St. Peters. (FSL)	5	1	.833	0.64	8	8	0	0	0	56	26	5	4	13	67
	—Ark.-Tulsa (Tex.)■....	7	7	.500	2.93	18	18	2	1	0	110⅔	87	43	36	35	121

BRUMLEY, MIKE

IF/OF, ANGELS

PERSONAL: Born April 9, 1963, in Oklahoma City. . . . 5-10/155. . . . Throws right, bats both. . . . Full name: Anthony Michael Brumley. . . . Son of Mike Brumley, catcher, Washington Senators (1964-66).
HIGH SCHOOL: Union (Broken Arrow, Okla.).
COLLEGE: Texas.
TRANSACTIONS/CAREER NOTES: Selected by Philadelphia Phillies organization in 16th round of free-agent draft (June 3, 1980). . . . Selected by Boston Red Sox organization in second round of free-agent draft (June 6, 1983); pick received as compensation for Oakland Athletics signing Type A free agent Tom Burgmeier. . . . Traded by Red Sox organization with P Dennis Eckersley to Chicago Cubs for 1B/OF Bill Buckner (May 25, 1984). . . . Traded by Cubs with IF Keith Moreland to San Diego Padres for P Rich Gossage and P Ray Hayward (February 12, 1988). . . . Traded by Padres organization to Detroit Tigers for IF Luis Salazar (March 23, 1989). . . . Traded by Tigers organization to Baltimore Orioles for DH Larry Sheets (January 10, 1990). . . . Released by Orioles (April 3, 1990). . . . Signed by Seattle Mariners (April 6, 1990). . . . On Seattle disabled list (June 6-July 11, 1990); included rehabilitation assignment to Calgary (July 4-11). . . . Released by Mariners (September 27, 1990). . . . Signed by Pawtucket, Red Sox organization (January 23, 1991). . . . On Pawtucket disabled list (June 3-14 and 19-26, 1992). . . . Granted free agency (October 16, 1992). . . . Signed by Tucson, Houston Astros organization (February 22, 1993). . . . On Tucson disabled list (May 17-June 13, 1993). . . . Claimed on waivers by California Angels (October 4, 1993).
STATISTICAL NOTES: Led American Association shortstops with 597 total chances in 1986.

			BATTING											FIELDING			
Year	**Team (League)**	**Pos.**	**G**	**AB**	**R**	**H**	**2B**	**3B**	**HR**	**RBI**	**Avg.**	**BB**	**SO**	**SB**	**PO**	**A**	**E**	**Avg.**
1983	—Winter Haven (FSL)	SS-OF	44	153	25	48	6	4	1	18	.314	16	31	4	51	92	20	.877
1984	—New Britain (East.)	OF-SS	34	121	14	28	6	2	0	9	.231	18	33	3	71	6	6	.928
	—Midland (Texas)■	OF	73	255	37	55	11	3	6	21	.216	48	49	5	128	4	5	.964
1985	—Pittsfield (Eastern)	SS-OF	131	460	66	127	23	*14	3	58	.276	74	95	29	182	333	33	.940
1986	—Iowa (Am. Assoc.)	SS	139	458	74	103	21	5	10	44	.225	63	102	35	177	*400	20	.966
1987	—Iowa (Am. Assoc.)	SS-2B-OF	92	319	44	81	20	5	6	42	.254	35	61	27	147	240	24	.942
	—Chicago (N.L.)	SS-2B	39	104	8	21	2	2	1	9	.202	10	30	7	43	93	5	.965
1988	—Las Vegas (PCL)■	S-0-3-2	113	425	77	134	16	7	3	41	.315	56	84	41	139	322	28	.943
1989	—Detroit (A.L.)■	S-2-3-0	92	212	33	42	5	2	1	11	.198	14	45	8	80	160	12	.952
	—Toledo (Int'l)	SS	8	26	4	6	2	2	0	1	.231	3	11	1	9	14	2	.920
1990	—Seattle (A.L.)■	S-2-3-0	62	147	19	33	5	4	0	7	.224	10	22	2	63	123	5	.974
	—Calgary (PCL)	SS	8	28	4	9	1	0	0	1	.321	1	3	3	13	23	2	.947
1991	—Pawtucket (Int'l)■	SS-2B-OF	32	108	25	29	2	2	4	16	.269	24	21	8	49	77	7	.947
	—Boston (A.L.)	S-3-2-0	63	118	16	25	5	0	0	5	.212	10	22	2	46	116	7	.959
1992	—Pawtucket (Int'l)	0-2-S-3	101	365	50	96	16	5	4	41	.263	37	76	14	133	83	13	.943
	—Boston (A.L.)	PH-PR	2	1	0	0	0	0	0	0	.000	0	0	0	...	...	...	...
1993	—Tucson (PCL)■	0-S-1-3	93	346	65	122	25	8	0	47	.353	44	71	24	161	76	14	.944
	—Houston (N.L.)	OF-SS-3B	8	10	1	3	0	0	0	2	.300	1	3	0	1	1	0	1.000
American League totals (4 years)			219	478	68	100	15	6	1	23	.209	34	89	12	189	399	24	.961
National League totals (2 years)			47	114	9	24	2	2	1	11	.211	11	33	7	44	94	5	.965
Major league totals (6 years)			266	592	77	124	17	8	2	34	.209	45	122	19	233	493	29	.962

BRUMMETT, GREG

P, TWINS

PERSONAL: Born April 20, 1967, in Wichita, Kan. . . . 6-0/186. . . . Throws right, bats right. . . . Full name: Gregory Scott Brummett. . . . Name pronounced BRUM-et.
HIGH SCHOOL: Northwest (Wichita, Kan.).
COLLEGE: Wichita State (received undergraduate degree, 1990).
TRANSACTIONS/CAREER NOTES: Selected by San Francisco Giants organization in 11th round of free-agent draft (June 5, 1989). . . . On disabled list (June 8, 1990-remainder of season). . . . On Shreveport disabled list (April 12-June 8, 1991). . . . On San Jose disabled list (May 11-July 8, 1992). . . . Traded by Giants to Minnesota Twins (September 1, 1993), completing deal in which Twins traded P Jim Deshaies to Giants for P Aaron Fultz, SS Andres Duncan and a player to be named later (August 28, 1993).

Year	**Team (League)**	**W**	**L**	**Pct.**	**ERA**	**G**	**GS**	**CG**	**ShO**	**Sv.**	**IP**	**H**	**R**	**ER**	**BB**	**SO**
1989	—Everett (N'west)	4	2	.667	2.88	14	10	1	0	0	72	63	34	23	24	76
	—San Jose (Calif.)	0	1	.000	5.59	2	2	0	0	0	9⅔	15	7	6	8	3
1990	—Clinton (Midwest)	2	2	.500	3.51	6	4	0	0	0	25⅔	18	14	10	9	22
1991	—Clinton (Midwest)	10	5	.667	2.72	16	16	5	2	0	112⅓	91	39	34	32	74
1992	—San Jose (Calif.)	10	4	.714	2.61	19	13	2	•2	0	100	74	32	29	21	68
	—Phoenix (PCL)	0	1	.000	7.71	3	1	0	0	0	4⅔	8	4	4	1	2
1993	—Phoenix (PCL)	7	7	.500	3.62	18	18	1	0	0	107	114	56	43	27	84
	—San Francisco (N.L.)	2	3	.400	4.70	8	8	0	0	0	46	53	25	24	13	20
	—Minnesota (A.L.)■	2	1	.667	5.74	5	5	0	0	0	26⅔	29	17	17	15	10
A.L. totals (1 year)		2	1	.667	5.74	5	5	0	0	0	26⅔	29	17	17	15	10
N.L. totals (1 year)		2	3	.400	4.70	8	8	0	0	0	46	53	25	24	13	20
Major league totals (1 year)		4	4	.500	5.08	13	13	0	0	0	72⅔	82	42	41	28	30

BRUNANSKY, TOM

OF, BREWERS

PERSONAL: Born August 20, 1960, in Covina, Calif. . . . 6-4/220. . . . Throws right, bats right. . . . Full name: Thomas Andrew Brunansky.
HIGH SCHOOL: West Covina (Calif.).
COLLEGE: Cal Poly Pomona.
TRANSACTIONS/CAREER NOTES: Selected by California Angels organization in first round (14th pick overall) of free-agent draft (June 6, 1978). . . . On Salt Lake City disabled list (August 8-31, 1981). . . . Traded by Angels organization with P Mike Walters and cash to Minnesota Twins for P Doug Corbett and 2B Rob Wilfong (May 12, 1982). . . . Traded by Twins to St. Louis Cardinals for 2B Tom Herr (April 22, 1988). . . . Traded by Cardinals to Boston Red Sox for P Lee Smith (May 4, 1990). . . . Granted free agency (November 5, 1990). . . . Re-signed by Red Sox (December 19, 1990). . . . Granted free agency (October 28, 1992). . . . Signed by Milwaukee Brewers (January 28, 1993). . . . On disabled list (August 5, 1993-remainder of season).
STATISTICAL NOTES: Tied for Texas League lead in double plays by outfielder with four in 1980. . . . Led A.L. outfielders with eight double plays in 1983 and six in 1984. . . . Hit three home runs in one game (September 29, 1990).

Year	Team (League)	Pos.	G	AB	R	H	2B	3B	HR	RBI	Avg.	BB	SO	SB	PO	A	E	Avg.
			BATTING												FIELDING			
1978	—Idaho Falls (Pio.)	OF	48	190	55	63	14	4	6	45	.332	45	34	17	85	1	8	.915
1979	—Salinas (Calif.)	OF	*140	485	85	131	23	1	23	76	.270	100	116	20	279	11	6	.980
1980	—El Paso (Texas)	OF	128	495	103	160	24	8	24	97	.323	75	96	23	306	17	*14	.958
	—Salt Lake City (PCL)	OF	9	32	7	11	2	2	1	8	.344	5	3	0	28	1	0	1.000
1981	—Salt Lake City (PCL)	OF	96	343	61	114	17	10	22	81	.332	57	74	6	250	14	5	.981
	—California (A.L.)	OF	11	33	7	5	0	0	3	6	.152	8	10	1	27	3	2	.938
1982	—Spokane (PCL)	OF	25	88	12	18	6	1	1	6	.205	15	19	4	44	7	1	.981
	—Minnesota (A.L.)■	OF	127	463	77	126	30	1	20	46	.272	71	101	1	343	8	5	.986
1983	—Minnesota (A.L.)	OF	151	542	70	123	24	5	28	82	.227	61	95	2	375	16	6	.985
1984	—Minnesota (A.L.)	OF	155	567	75	144	21	0	32	85	.254	57	94	4	304	13	5	.984
1985	—Minnesota (A.L.)	OF	157	567	71	137	28	4	27	90	.242	71	86	5	300	14	5	.984
1986	—Minnesota (A.L.)	OF	157	593	69	152	28	1	23	75	.256	53	98	12	315	10	6	.982
1987	—Minnesota (A.L.)	OF	155	532	83	138	22	2	32	85	.259	74	104	11	273	10	3	.990
1988	—Minnesota (A.L.)	OF	14	49	5	9	1	0	1	6	.184	7	10	1	19	0	3	.864
	—St. Louis (N.L.)■	OF	143	523	69	128	22	4	22	79	.245	79	82	16	267	10	1	*.996
1989	—St. Louis (N.L.)	OF-1B	158	556	67	133	29	3	20	85	.239	59	107	5	291	9	7	.977
1990	—St. Louis (N.L.)	OF	19	57	5	9	3	0	1	2	.158	12	10	0	37	1	2	.950
	—Boston (A.L.)■	OF	129	461	61	123	24	5	15	71	.267	54	105	5	267	7	5	.982
1991	—Boston (A.L.)	OF	142	459	54	105	24	1	16	70	.229	49	72	1	265	5	3	.989
1992	—Boston (A.L.)	OF-1B	138	458	47	122	31	3	15	74	.266	66	96	2	373	16	6	.985
1993	—Milwaukee (A.L.)■	OF	80	224	20	41	7	3	6	29	.183	25	59	3	146	4	2	.987
American League totals (12 years)			1416	4948	639	1225	240	25	218	719	.248	596	930	48	3007	106	51	.984
National League totals (3 years)			320	1136	141	270	54	7	43	166	.238	150	199	21	595	20	10	.984
Major league totals (13 years)			1736	6084	780	1495	294	32	261	885	.246	746	1129	69	3602	126	61	.984

CHAMPIONSHIP SERIES RECORD

Year	Team (League)	Pos.	G	AB	R	H	2B	3B	HR	RBI	Avg.	BB	SO	SB	PO	A	E	Avg.
			BATTING												FIELDING			
1987	—Minnesota (A.L.)	OF	5	17	5	7	4	0	2	9	.412	4	3	0	10	0	0	1.000
1990	—Boston (A.L.)	OF	4	12	0	1	0	0	0	1	.083	1	3	0	13	0	0	1.000
Championship series totals (2 years)			9	29	5	8	4	0	2	10	.276	5	6	0	23	0	0	1.000

WORLD SERIES RECORD

Year	Team (League)	Pos.	G	AB	R	H	2B	3B	HR	RBI	Avg.	BB	SO	SB	PO	A	E	Avg.
			BATTING												FIELDING			
1987	—Minnesota (A.L.)	OF	7	25	5	5	0	0	0	2	.200	4	4	1	14	0	0	1.000

ALL-STAR GAME RECORD

Year	League	Pos.	AB	R	H	2B	3B	HR	RBI	Avg.	BB	SO	SB	PO	A	E	Avg.
			BATTING											FIELDING			
1985	—American	OF	1	0	0	0	0	0	0	.000	0	0	0	0	0	0	...

BRUNO, JULIO

3B, PADRES

PERSONAL: Born October 15, 1972, in Puerto Plata, Dominican Republic. . . . 5-10/170. . . . Throws right, bats right. . . . Full name: Julio Cesar Marte Bruno.

HIGH SCHOOL: Referara (Puerto Plata, Dominican Republic).

TRANSACTIONS/CAREER NOTES: Signed as free agent by San Diego Padres organization (November 7, 1989).

Year	Team (League)	Pos.	G	AB	R	H	2B	3B	HR	RBI	Avg.	BB	SO	SB	PO	A	E	Avg.
			BATTING												FIELDING			
1990	—Char., S.C. (S. Atl.)	3B	19	75	11	17	1	1	0	5	.227	1	21	0	9	22	11	.738
	—Spokane (N'west)	3B	68	251	36	63	7	2	2	22	.251	25	78	7	38	122	*22	.879
1991	—Waterloo (Midw.)	3B	86	277	34	64	10	3	1	25	.231	29	78	11	48	172	16	.932
1992	—High Desert (Calif.)	3B	118	418	57	116	22	5	3	62	.278	33	92	2	70	224	23	.927
1993	—Rancho Cuca. (Cal.)	3B	54	201	37	62	11	2	3	16	.308	19	56	15	39	107	21	.874
	—Wichita (Texas)	3B	70	246	34	70	17	1	3	24	.285	11	46	3	51	115	15	.917

BRYANT, SHAWN

P, INDIANS

PERSONAL: Born June 10, 1969, in Oklahoma City. . . . 6-3/205. . . . Throws left, bats right. . . . Full name: Shawn Wayne Bryant.

HIGH SCHOOL: Putnam City (Oklahoma City).

COLLEGE: Oklahoma City University.

TRANSACTIONS/CAREER NOTES: Selected by Cleveland Indians organization in eighth round of free-agent draft (June 4, 1990). . . . On disabled list (May 2-11, 1993).

Year	Team (League)	W	L	Pct.	ERA	G	GS	CG	ShO	Sv.	IP	H	R	ER	BB	SO
1990	—Kinston (Carolina)	1	1	.500	5.19	2	2	0	0	0	8⅔	10	6	5	7	13
	—Burlington (Appal.)	1	0	1.000	0.84	2	2	0	0	0	10⅔	5	2	1	6	17
	—Watertown (NYP)	6	3	.667	2.77	10	10	2	0	0	61⅔	49	24	19	23	56
1991	—Kinston (Carolina)	11	9	.550	4.02	29	28	2	1	0	154⅔	154	91	69	*106	112
1992	—Kinston (Carolina)	10	8	.556	3.81	27	27	3	1	0	167⅔	152	85	71	69	121
1993	—Cant./Akr. (East.)	10	5	.667	3.72	27	27	0	0	0	172	179	80	71	61	111

BUCKLEY, TRAVIS

P, MARINERS

PERSONAL: Born June 15, 1970, in Ottawa, Kan. . . . 6-4/210. . . . Throws right, bats right. . . . Full name: Travis Royce Buckley.

HIGH SCHOOL: Shawnee Mission South (Overland Park, Kan.).

COLLEGE: Johnson County Community College (Kan.).

TRANSACTIONS/CAREER NOTES: Selected by Texas Rangers organization in 23rd round of free-agent draft (June 5, 1989).... Traded by Rangers organization to Expos organization (September 1, 1991), completing deal in which Expos traded P Oil Can Boyd to Rangers for P Jonathan Hurst, P Joey Eischen and a player to be named later (July 21, 1991).... Traded by Expos organization to Colorado Rockies organization for a player to be named later (November 9, 1992); Expos organization acquired P Matt Connolly to complete deal (December 8, 1992).... Claimed on waivers by Cincinnati Reds (April 29, 1993).... Traded by Reds to Seattle Mariners for 1B Charles "Bubba" Smith (May 24, 1993).... On Jacksonville disabled list (July 18, 1993-remainder of season).
STATISTICAL NOTES: Tied for Eastern League lead with 12 hit batsmen in 1992.

Year	Team (League)	W	L	Pct.	ERA	G	GS	CG	ShO	Sv.	IP	H	R	ER	BB	SO
1989	—GC Rangers (GCL)	3	3	.500	3.40	16	4	0	0	0	50⅓	41	28	19	24	34
1990	—Gastonia (S. Atl.)	12	6	.667	2.84	27	26	3	0	0	161⅔	149	66	51	61	149
1991	—Charlotte (Fla. St.)	8	9	.471	3.23	28	21	3	•3	1	128	115	58	46	67	131
1992	—Harrisburg (East.)■	7	7	.500	2.87	26	26	0	0	0	160	146	58	51	64	123
1993	—Colo. Springs (PCL)■	1	2	.333	6.00	6	1	0	0	0	9	12	13	6	7	5
	—Chatt.-Jacks. (Sou.)■	2	4	.333	5.75	12	11	0	0	0	56⅓	64	41	36	22	44

BUECHELE, STEVE

3B, CUBS

PERSONAL: Born September 26, 1961, in Lancaster, Calif.... 6-2/200.... Throws right, bats right.... Full name: Steven Bernard Buechele.... Name pronounced BOO-SHELL.
HIGH SCHOOL: Servite (Anaheim, Calif.).
COLLEGE: Stanford.
TRANSACTIONS/CAREER NOTES: Selected by Chicago White Sox organization in first round (ninth pick overall) of free-agent draft (June 5, 1979).... Selected by Texas Rangers organization in fifth round of free-agent draft (June 7, 1982).... On Texas disabled list (April 22-May 25, 1990).... On Texas disabled list (June 18-July 20, 1990); included rehabilitation assignment to Oklahoma City (July 16-20).... On suspended list (August 24-27, 1990).... Traded by Rangers to Pittsburgh Pirates for P Kurt Miller and a player to be named later (August 30, 1991); Rangers acquired P Hector Fajardo to complete deal (September 6, 1991).... Granted free agency (October 28, 1991).... Re-signed by Pirates (December 12, 1991).... Traded by Pirates to Chicago Cubs for P Danny Jackson (July 11, 1992).... On disabled list (June 13-28, 1993).
HONORS: Named American Association Most Valuable Player (1985).
STATISTICAL NOTES: Led A.L. third basemen with .991 fielding percentage in 1991.... Led N.L. third basemen with .975 fielding percentage in 1993.

			BATTING												FIELDING			
Year	Team (League)	Pos.	G	AB	R	H	2B	3B	HR	RBI	Avg.	BB	SO	SB	PO	A	E	Avg.
1982	—Tulsa (Texas)	2B-3B	62	213	21	63	12	2	5	33	.296	18	42	2	111	174	8	.973
1983	—Tulsa (Texas)	2B-3B	117	437	62	121	12	4	14	62	.277	54	69	5	182	259	18	.961
	—Okla. City (A.A.)	2B-3B	9	34	6	9	5	0	1	4	.265	4	6	0	17	22	1	.975
1984	—Okla. City (A.A.)	2B-3B	131	447	48	118	25	3	7	59	.264	36	72	7	236	329	17	.971
1985	—Okla. City (A.A.)	3B-2B	89	350	56	104	20	7	9	64	.297	33	62	6	84	170	7	.973
	—Texas (A.L.)	3B-2B	69	219	22	48	6	3	6	21	.219	14	38	3	52	138	6	.969
1986	—Texas (A.L.)	3B-2B-OF	153	461	54	112	19	2	18	54	.243	35	98	5	174	292	12	.975
1987	—Texas (A.L.)	3B-2B-OF	136	363	45	86	20	0	13	50	.237	28	66	2	89	211	9	.971
1988	—Texas (A.L.)	3B-2B	155	503	68	126	21	4	16	58	.250	65	79	2	114	300	16	.963
1989	—Texas (A.L.)	3B-2B-SS	155	486	60	114	22	2	16	59	.235	36	107	1	128	288	12	.972
1990	—Texas (A.L.)	3B-2B	91	251	30	54	10	0	7	30	.215	27	63	1	72	160	8	.967
	—Okla. City (A.A.)	3B	6	21	1	3	0	0	1	1	.143	2	4	0	4	15	0	1.000
1991	—Texas (A.L.)	3B-2B-SS	121	416	58	111	17	2	18	66	.267	39	69	0	99	275	3	†.992
	—Pittsburgh (N.L.)■	3B	31	114	16	28	5	1	4	19	.246	10	28	0	22	64	4	.956
1992	—Pitts.-Chi. (N.L.)■	3B-2B	145	524	52	137	23	4	9	64	.261	52	105	1	103	289	17	.958
1993	—Chicago (N.L.)	3B-1B	133	460	53	125	27	2	15	65	.272	48	87	1	97	232	8	†.976
American League totals (7 years)			880	2699	337	651	115	13	94	338	.241	244	520	14	728	1664	66	.973
National League totals (3 years)			309	1098	121	290	55	7	28	148	.264	110	220	2	222	585	29	.965
Major league totals (9 years)			1189	3797	458	941	170	20	122	486	.248	354	740	16	950	2249	95	.971

CHAMPIONSHIP SERIES RECORD

CHAMPIONSHIP SERIES NOTES: Shares N.L. single-series record for most consecutive hits—5 (1991).

			BATTING												FIELDING			
Year	Team (League)	Pos.	G	AB	R	H	2B	3B	HR	RBI	Avg.	BB	SO	SB	PO	A	E	Avg.
1991	—Pittsburgh (N.L.)	3B	7	23	2	7	2	0	0	0	.304	4	6	0	8	14	0	1.000

BUFORD, DAMON

OF, ORIOLES

PERSONAL: Born June 12, 1970, in Baltimore.... 5-10/170.... Throws right, bats right.... Full name: Damon Jackson Buford.... Son of Don Buford, current coach, Baltimore Orioles, and major league outfielder, Chicago White Sox and Orioles (1963-72); and brother of Don Buford Jr., minor league infielder (1987-89).
HIGH SCHOOL: Birmingham (Calif.).
COLLEGE: Southern California.
TRANSACTIONS/CAREER NOTES: Selected by Baltimore Orioles organization in 10th round of free-agent draft (June 4, 1990).
STATISTICAL NOTES: Led Eastern League outfielders with 279 total chances in 1992.

			BATTING												FIELDING			
Year	Team (League)	Pos.	G	AB	R	H	2B	3B	HR	RBI	Avg.	BB	SO	SB	PO	A	E	Avg.
1990	—Wausau (Midwest)	OF	41	160	31	48	7	2	1	14	.300	21	32	15	89	2	2	.978
1991	—Frederick (Caro.)	OF	133	505	71	138	25	6	8	54	.273	51	92	50	293	7	5	.984
1992	—Hagerstown (East.)	OF	101	373	53	89	17	3	1	30	.239	42	62	41	*264	13	2	.993
	—Rochester (Int'l)	OF	45	155	29	44	10	2	1	12	.284	14	23	23	100	1	3	.971
1993	—Rochester (Int'l)	OF	27	116	24	33	6	1	1	4	.284	7	16	10	73	3	3	.962
	—Baltimore (A.L.)	OF	53	79	18	18	5	0	2	9	.228	9	19	2	61	2	1	.984
Major league totals (1 year)			53	79	18	18	5	0	2	9	.228	9	19	2	61	2	1	.984

BUHNER, JAY

OF, MARINERS

PERSONAL: Born August 13, 1964, in Louisville, Ky. . . . 6-3/210. . . . Throws right, bats right. . . . Full name: Jay Campbell Buhner. . . . Name pronounced BYOO-ner.
HIGH SCHOOL: Clear Creek (League City, Tex.).
COLLEGE: McLennan Community College (Tex.).
TRANSACTIONS/CAREER NOTES: Selected by Atlanta Braves organization in ninth round of free-agent draft (June 6, 1983). . . . Selected by Pittsburgh Pirates organization in secondary phase of free-agent draft (January 17, 1984). . . . Traded by Pirates organization with IF Dale Berra and P Alfonso Pulido to New York Yankees for OF Steve Kemp, IF Tim Foli and cash (December 20, 1984). . . . On disabled list (April 11-July 28, 1986). . . . Traded by Yankees with P Rich Balabon and a player to be named later to Seattle Mariners for DH Ken Phelps (July 21, 1988); Mariners acquired P Troy Evers to complete deal (October 12, 1988). . . . On Seattle disabled list (June 29-August 19, 1989); included rehabilitation assignment to Calgary (August 16-19). . . . On Seattle disabled list (March 31-June 1, 1990); included rehabilitation assignment to Calgary (May 18-June 1). . . . On Seattle disabled list (June 17-August 23, 1990).
RECORDS: Shares major league records for most strikeouts in two consecutive nine-inning games—8 (August 23-24, 1990); most strikeouts in three consecutive games—10 (August 23-25, 1990).
STATISTICAL NOTES: Tied for International League lead in double plays by outfielder with six in 1987. . . . Hit for the cycle (June 23, 1993).

			BATTING												FIELDING			
Year	**Team (League)**	**Pos.**	**G**	**AB**	**R**	**H**	**2B**	**3B**	**HR**	**RBI**	**Avg.**	**BB**	**SO**	**SB**	**PO**	**A**	**E**	**Avg.**
1984	—Watertown (NYP)	OF	65	229	43	74	16	3	9	•58	.323	42	58	3	106	8	1	.991
1985	—Fort Lauder. (FSL)■	OF	117	409	65	121	18	10	11	76	.296	65	76	6	235	12	7	.972
1986	—Fort Lauder. (FSL)	OF	36	139	24	42	9	1	7	31	.302	15	30	1	84	7	3	.968
1987	—Columbus (Int'l)	OF	134	502	83	140	23	1	*31	85	.279	55	124	4	275	*20	6	.980
	—New York (A.L.)	OF	7	22	0	5	2	0	0	1	.227	1	6	0	11	1	0	1.000
1988	—Columbus (Int'l)	OF	38	129	26	33	5	0	8	18	.256	19	33	1	83	3	1	.989
	—N.Y.-Seattle (A.L.)■	OF	85	261	36	56	13	1	13	38	.215	28	93	1	186	9	3	.985
1989	—Calgary (PCL)	OF	56	196	43	61	12	1	11	45	.311	44	56	4	97	8	2	.981
	—Seattle (A.L.)	OF	58	204	27	56	15	1	9	33	.275	19	55	1	106	6	4	.966
1990	—Calgary (PCL)	OF	13	34	6	7	1	0	2	5	.206	7	11	0	14	1	0	1.000
	—Seattle (A.L.)	OF	51	163	16	45	12	0	7	33	.276	17	50	2	55	1	2	.966
1991	—Seattle (A.L.)	OF	137	406	64	99	14	4	27	77	.244	53	117	0	244	15	5	.981
1992	—Seattle (A.L.)	OF	152	543	69	132	16	3	25	79	.243	71	146	0	314	14	2	.994
1993	—Seattle (A.L.)	OF	158	563	91	153	28	3	27	98	.272	100	144	2	263	8	6	.978
	Major league totals (7 years)		648	2162	303	546	100	12	108	359	.253	289	611	6	1179	54	22	.982

BULLETT, SCOTT

OF, PIRATES

PERSONAL: Born December 25, 1968, in Martinsburg, W.Va. . . . 6-2/190. . . . Throws left, bats left. . . . Full name: Scott Douglas Bullett.
HIGH SCHOOL: Martinsburg (W.Va.).
TRANSACTIONS/CAREER NOTES: Signed as free agent by Pittsburgh Pirates organization (June 20, 1988).
STATISTICAL NOTES: Led American Association in caught stealing with 17 in 1993.

			BATTING												FIELDING			
Year	**Team (League)**	**Pos.**	**G**	**AB**	**R**	**H**	**2B**	**3B**	**HR**	**RBI**	**Avg.**	**BB**	**SO**	**SB**	**PO**	**A**	**E**	**Avg.**
1988	—GC Pirates (GCL)	OF	21	61	6	11	1	0	0	8	.180	7	9	2	28	2	1	.968
1989	—GC Pirates (GCL)	OF-1B	46	165	24	42	7	3	1	16	.255	12	31	15	141	4	7	.954
1990	—Welland (NYP)	OF	74	255	46	77	11	4	3	33	.302	13	50	30	110	5	5	.958
1991	—Augusta (S. Atl.)	OF	95	384	61	109	22	6	1	36	.284	27	79	48	195	8	5	.976
	—Salem (Carolina)	OF	39	156	22	52	7	5	2	15	.333	8	29	15	87	3	4	.957
	—Pittsburgh (N.L.)	OF	11	4	2	0	0	0	0	0	.000	0	3	1	2	0	0	1.000
1992	—Carolina (South.)	OF	132	518	59	140	20	5	8	45	.270	28	98	29	260	7	6	.978
	—Buffalo (A.A.)	OF	3	10	1	4	0	2	0	0	.400	0	2	0	7	0	0	1.000
1993	—Buffalo (A.A.)	OF	110	408	62	117	13	6	1	30	.287	39	67	28	222	6	7	.970
	—Pittsburgh (N.L.)	OF	23	55	2	11	0	2	0	4	.200	3	15	3	35	1	0	1.000
	Major league totals (2 years)		34	59	4	11	0	2	0	4	.186	3	18	4	37	1	0	1.000

BULLINGER, JIM

P, CUBS

PERSONAL: Born August 21, 1965, in New Orleans. . . . 6-2/185. . . . Throws right, bats right. . . . Full name: James Eric Bullinger. . . . Name pronounced BULL-in-jer.
HIGH SCHOOL: Archbishop Rummel (Metairie, La.).
COLLEGE: New Orleans.
TRANSACTIONS/CAREER NOTES: Selected by Chicago Cubs organization in ninth round of free-agent draft (June 2, 1986). . . . On Iowa disabled list (August 5-21, 1993).
STATISTICAL NOTES: Led Carolina League shortstops with 92 double plays in 1987. . . . Hit home run in first major league at-bat (June 8, 1992, first game).

Year	**Team (League)**	**W**	**L**	**Pct.**	**ERA**	**G**	**GS**	**CG**	**ShO**	**Sv.**	**IP**	**H**	**R**	**ER**	**BB**	**SO**
1989	—Charlotte (South.)	0	0	...	0.00	2	0	0	0	0	3	3	0	0	3	5
1990	—Winst.-Salem (Car.)	7	6	.538	3.70	14	13	3	0	0	90	81	43	37	46	85
	—Charlotte (South.)	3	4	.429	5.11	9	9	0	0	0	44	42	30	25	18	33
1991	—Iowa (Am. Assoc.)	3	4	.429	5.40	8	8	0	0	0	46⅔	47	32	28	23	30
	—Charlotte (South.)	9	9	.500	3.53	20	20	•8	0	0	142⅔	132	62	56	61	128
1992	—Iowa (Am. Assoc.)	1	2	.333	2.45	20	0	0	0	14	22	17	6	6	12	15
	—Chicago (N.L.)	2	8	.200	4.66	39	9	1	0	7	85	72	49	44	54	36
1993	—Iowa (Am. Assoc.)	4	6	.400	3.42	49	3	0	0	20	73⅔	64	29	28	43	74
	—Chicago (N.L.)	1	0	1.000	4.32	15	0	0	0	1	16⅔	18	9	8	9	10
	Major league totals (2 years)	3	8	.273	4.60	54	9	1	0	8	101⅔	90	58	52	63	46

RECORD AS POSITION PLAYER

Year	Team (League)	Pos.	G	AB	R	H	2B	3B	HR	RBI	Avg.	BB	SO	SB	PO	A	E	Avg.
				BATTING											FIELDING			
1986	—Geneva (NY-Penn)...	SS	*78	248	35	61	•16	1	3	33	.246	*48	50	7	104	207	26	.923
1987	—Winst.-Salem (Car.)..	SS	129	437	58	112	12	3	9	48	.256	50	79	3	210	383	28	.955
1988	—Pittsfield (Eastern)..	SS	88	242	21	41	6	1	3	33	.169	25	53	1	129	256	21	.948
	—Winst.-Salem (Car.)..	SS	32	104	13	20	4	2	1	11	.192	13	26	4	49	80	11	.921
1989	—Charlotte (South.)....	SS-3B-P	124	320	34	69	13	1	3	28	.216	39	56	3	188	281	26	.947

BURBA, DAVE

P, GIANTS

PERSONAL: Born July 7, 1966, in Dayton, O. ... 6-4/240. ... Throws right, bats right. ... Full name: David Allen Burba. ... Nephew of Ray Hathaway, pitcher, Brooklyn Dodgers (1945).
HIGH SCHOOL: Kenton Ridge (Springfield, O.).
COLLEGE: Ohio State.
TRANSACTIONS/CAREER NOTES: Selected by Seattle Mariners organization in second round of free-agent draft (June 2, 1987). ... Traded by Mariners with P Bill Swift and P Mike Jackson to San Francisco Giants for OF Kevin Mitchell and P Mike Remlinger (December 11, 1991).

Year	Team (League)	W	L	Pct.	ERA	G	GS	CG	ShO	Sv.	IP	H	R	ER	BB	SO
1987	—Belling. (N'west)........	3	1	.750	1.93	5	5	0	0	0	23⅓	20	10	5	3	24
	—Salinas (Calif.)..........	1	6	.143	4.61	9	9	0	0	0	54⅔	53	31	28	29	46
1988	—San Bern. (Calif.).......	5	7	.417	2.68	20	20	0	0	0	114	106	41	34	54	102
1989	—Williamsport (East.).....	11	7	.611	3.16	25	25	5	1	0	156⅔	138	69	55	55	89
1990	—Calgary (PCL).............	10	6	.625	4.67	31	18	1	0	2	113⅔	124	64	59	45	47
	—Seattle (A.L.)..............	0	0	...	4.50	6	0	0	0	0	8	8	6	4	2	4
1991	—Calgary (PCL).............	6	4	.600	3.53	23	9	0	0	4	71⅓	82	35	28	27	42
	—Seattle (A.L.)..............	2	2	.500	3.68	22	2	0	0	1	36⅔	34	16	15	14	16
1992	—San Francisco (N.L.)■...	2	7	.222	4.97	23	11	0	0	0	70⅔	80	43	39	31	47
	—Phoenix (PCL)............	5	5	.500	4.72	13	13	0	0	0	74⅓	86	40	39	24	44
1993	—San Francisco (N.L.).....	10	3	.769	4.25	54	5	0	0	0	95⅓	95	49	45	37	88
	A.L. totals (2 years)...............	2	2	.500	3.83	28	2	0	0	1	44⅔	42	22	19	16	20
	N.L. totals (2 years)...............	12	10	.545	4.55	77	16	0	0	0	166	175	92	84	68	135
	Major league totals (4 years)...	14	12	.538	4.40	105	18	0	0	1	210⅔	217	114	103	84	155

BURGOS, ENRIQUE

P, ROYALS

PERSONAL: Born October 7, 1965, in Chorrera, Panama. ... 6-4/230. ... Throws left, bats left.
TRANSACTIONS/CAREER NOTES: Signed as free agent by Toronto Blue Jays organization (January 31, 1983). ... Loaned by Blue Jays organization to Miami, independent (May 17-July 3, 1989). ... Granted free agency (October 22, 1989). ... Played in Taiwan (1990-92). ... Signed as free agent by Kansas City Royals organization (December 31, 1992).
STATISTICAL NOTES: Combined with starter Pat Hentgen and Willie Blair in 2-1 no-hit victory for Dunedin against Osceola (May 10, 1988).

Year	Team (League)	W	L	Pct.	ERA	G	GS	CG	ShO	Sv.	IP	H	R	ER	BB	SO
1983	—GC Blue Jays (GCL)...	0	•9	.000	4.78	13	8	1	0	0	49	52	37	26	32	19
1984	—Florence (S. Atl.)........	0	0	...	18.00	2	0	0	0	0	1	2	2	2	1	1
	—GC Blue Jays (GCL)...	4	5	.444	2.39	12	10	1	0	0	71⅔	74	37	19	22	38
1985	—Florence (S. Atl.)........	3	1	.750	6.61	26	0	0	0	1	47⅔	55	39	35	44	32
	—Kinston (Carolina).....	0	2	.000	11.88	7	1	0	0	0	8⅓	12	11	11	10	5
1986	—Florence (S. Atl.)........	3	8	.273	6.46	28	10	0	0	2	85	92	76	61	70	71
	—Vent. Co. (Calif.)........	1	3	.250	3.94	9	9	0	0	0	45⅔	46	27	20	31	37
1987	—Knoxville (South.)......	2	3	.400	4.37	17	5	0	0	1	45⅓	33	27	22	55	45
	—Myrtle Beach (SAL).....	5	2	.714	2.11	23	0	0	0	7	38⅓	22	15	9	24	46
1988	—Syracuse (Int'l)..........	0	0	...	7.71	2	0	0	0	0	2⅓	4	2	2	2	2
	—Dunedin (Fla. St.).......	1	5	.167	4.71	33	4	0	0	1	49⅔	61	28	26	37	55
1989	—Duned.-Miami (FSL)■....	3	1	.750	3.24	23	1	0	0	0	33⅓	28	21	12	20	33
	—Myrtle Beach (SAL).....	0	2	.000	2.70	16	1	0	0	1	16⅔	16	11	5	20	15
1990	—Pres. Lions (Taiw.)■...	9	8	.529	2.60	33	21	7	0	2	173	153	87	50	86	177
1991	—Pres. Lions (Taiw.).....	7	9	.438	2.68	31	22	8	2	2	174⅓	135	79	52	78	138
1992	—Pres. Lions (Taiw.).....	7	9	.438	4.37	22	20	6	0	0	136	128	85	66	102	131
1993	—Omaha (A.A.)■............	2	4	.333	3.16	48	0	0	0	9	62⅔	36	26	22	37	91
	—Kansas City (A.L.).......	0	1	.000	9.00	5	0	0	0	0	5	5	5	5	6	6
	Major league totals (1 year).....	0	1	.000	9.00	5	0	0	0	0	5	5	5	5	6	6

BURKETT, JOHN

P, GIANTS

PERSONAL: Born November 28, 1964, in New Brighton, Pa. ... 6-2/211. ... Throws right, bats right. ... Full name: John David Burkett. ... Name pronounced bur-KETT.
HIGH SCHOOL: Beaver (Pa.).
TRANSACTIONS/CAREER NOTES: Selected by San Francisco Giants organization in sixth round of free-agent draft (June 6, 1983).
STATISTICAL NOTES: Led N.L. with 10 hit batsmen in 1991.

Year	Team (League)	W	L	Pct.	ERA	G	GS	CG	ShO	Sv.	IP	H	R	ER	BB	SO
1983	—Great Falls (Pio.)........	2	6	.250	6.26	13	9	0	0	0	50⅓	73	44	35	30	38
1984	—Clinton (Midwest)......	7	6	.538	4.33	20	20	2	0	0	126⅔	128	81	61	38	83
1985	—Fresno (California)....	7	4	.636	2.87	20	20	1	1	0	109⅔	98	43	35	46	72
1986	—Fresno (California)....	0	3	.000	5.47	4	4	0	0	0	24⅔	34	19	15	8	14
	—Shreveport (Texas)....	10	6	.625	2.66	22	21	4	2	0	128⅔	99	46	38	42	73
1987	—Shreveport (Texas)....	•14	8	.636	3.34	27	27	6	1	0	*177⅔	181	75	66	53	126
	—San Francisco (N.L.).....	0	0	...	4.50	3	0	0	0	0	6	7	4	3	3	5

B

Year	Team (League)	W	L	Pct.	ERA	G	GS	CG	ShO	Sv.	IP	H	R	ER	BB	SO
1988	—Phoenix (PCL)	5	11	.313	5.21	21	21	0	0	0	114	141	79	66	49	74
	—Shreveport (Texas)	5	1	.833	2.13	7	7	2	1	0	50⅔	33	15	12	18	34
1989	—Phoenix (PCL)	10	11	.476	5.05	28	•28	2	1	0	167⅔	197	111	94	59	105
1990	—Phoenix (PCL)	2	1	.667	2.74	3	3	2	1	0	23	18	8	7	3	9
	—San Francisco (N.L.)	14	7	.667	3.79	33	32	2	0	1	204	201	92	86	61	118
1991	—San Francisco (N.L.)	12	11	.522	4.18	36	34	3	1	0	206⅔	223	103	96	60	131
1992	—San Francisco (N.L.)	13	9	.591	3.84	32	32	3	1	0	189⅔	194	96	81	45	107
1993	—San Francisco (N.L.)	•22	7	.759	3.65	34	34	2	1	0	231⅔	224	100	94	40	145
Major league totals (5 years)		61	34	.642	3.87	138	132	10	3	1	838	849	395	360	209	506

ALL-STAR GAME RECORD

Year	League	W	L	Pct.	ERA	GS	CG	ShO	Sv.	IP	H	R	ER	BB	SO
1993	—National	0	1	.000	40.50	0	0	0	0	⅔	4	3	3	0	1

B

BURKS, ELLIS

OF, ROCKIES

PERSONAL: Born September 11, 1964, in Vicksburg, Miss. . . . 6-2/205. . . . Throws right, bats right. . . . Full name: Ellis Rena Burks.
HIGH SCHOOL: Everman (Tex.).
COLLEGE: Ranger (Tex.) Junior College.

TRANSACTIONS/CAREER NOTES: Selected by Boston Red Sox organization in first round (20th pick overall) of free-agent draft (January 11, 1983). . . . On disabled list (March 26-April 12, 1988). . . . On Boston disabled list (June 15-August 1, 1989); included rehabilitation assignment to Pawtucket (July 26-August 1). . . . On disabled list (June 25, 1992-remainder of season). . . . Granted free agency (December 19, 1992). . . . Signed by Chicago White Sox (January 4, 1993). . . . Granted free agency (October 27, 1993). . . . Signed by Colorado Rockies (November 30, 1993).
RECORDS: Shares major league record for most home runs in one inning—2 (August 27, 1990, fourth inning).
HONORS: Named outfielder on THE SPORTING NEWS A.L. All-Star team (1990). . . . Named outfielder on THE SPORTING NEWS A.L. Silver Slugger team (1990). . . . Won A.L. Gold Glove as outfielder (1990).
STATISTICAL NOTES: Tied for Florida State League lead in double plays by outfielder with six in 1984.

			BATTING												FIELDING			
Year	Team (League)	Pos.	G	AB	R	H	2B	3B	HR	RBI	Avg.	BB	SO	SB	PO	A	E	Avg.
1983	—Elmira (N.Y.-Penn)	OF	53	174	30	42	9	0	2	23	.241	17	43	9	89	5	2	.979
1984	—Winter Haven (FSL)	OF	112	375	52	96	15	4	6	43	.256	42	68	29	196	12	5	.977
1985	—New Britain (East.)	OF	133	476	66	121	25	7	10	61	.254	42	85	17	306	9	8	.975
1986	—New Britain (East.)	OF	124	462	70	126	20	3	14	55	.273	44	75	31	318	5	5	.985
1987	—Pawtucket (Int'l)	OF	11	40	11	9	3	1	3	6	.225	7	7	1	25	0	0	1.000
	—Boston (A.L.)	OF	133	558	94	152	30	2	20	59	.272	41	98	27	320	15	4	.988
1988	—Boston (A.L.)	OF	144	540	93	159	37	5	18	92	.294	62	89	25	370	9	9	.977
1989	—Boston (A.L.)	OF	97	399	73	121	19	6	12	61	.303	36	52	21	245	7	6	.977
	—Pawtucket (Int'l)	OF	5	21	4	3	1	0	0	0	.143	2	3	0	16	0	0	1.000
1990	—Boston (A.L.)	OF	152	588	89	174	33	8	21	89	.296	48	82	9	324	7	2	.994
1991	—Boston (A.L.)	OF	130	474	56	119	33	3	14	56	.251	39	81	6	283	2	2	.993
1992	—Boston (A.L.)	OF	66	235	35	60	8	3	8	30	.255	25	48	5	120	3	2	.984
1993	—Chicago (A.L.)■	OF	146	499	75	137	24	4	17	74	.275	60	97	6	313	6	6	.982
Major league totals (7 years)			868	3293	515	922	184	31	110	461	.280	311	547	99	1975	49	31	.985

CHAMPIONSHIP SERIES RECORD

			BATTING												FIELDING			
Year	Team (League)	Pos.	G	AB	R	H	2B	3B	HR	RBI	Avg.	BB	SO	SB	PO	A	E	Avg.
1988	—Boston (A.L.)	OF	4	17	2	4	1	0	0	1	.235	0	3	0	10	0	0	1.000
1990	—Boston (A.L.)	OF	4	15	1	4	2	0	0	0	.267	1	1	1	9	1	0	1.000
1993	—Chicago (A.L.)	OF	6	23	4	7	1	0	1	3	.304	3	5	0	15	0	0	1.000
Championship series totals (3 years)			14	55	7	15	4	0	1	4	.273	4	9	1	34	1	0	1.000

ALL-STAR GAME RECORD

ALL-STAR GAME NOTES: Named to A.L. All-Star team for 1990 game; replaced by Brook Jacoby due to injury.

			BATTING											FIELDING			
Year	League	Pos.	AB	R	H	2B	3B	HR	RBI	Avg.	BB	SO	SB	PO	A	E	Avg.
1990	—American		Selected, did not play—injured.														

BURNITZ, JEROMY

OF, METS

PERSONAL: Born April 15, 1969, in Westminster, Calif. . . . 6-0/190. . . . Throws right, bats left. . . . Full name: Jeromy Neal Burnitz.
HIGH SCHOOL: Conroe (Tex.).
COLLEGE: Oklahoma State.

TRANSACTIONS/CAREER NOTES: Selected by Milwaukee Brewers organization in 24th round of free-agent draft (June 2, 1987). . . . Selected by New York Mets organization in first round (17th pick overall) of free-agent draft (June 4, 1990). . . . On disabled list (August 23-September 18, 1992).
STATISTICAL NOTES: Led New York-Pennsylvania League with .444 on-base percentage and tied for lead with six intentional bases on balls received in 1990.

			BATTING												FIELDING			
Year	Team (League)	Pos.	G	AB	R	H	2B	3B	HR	RBI	Avg.	BB	SO	SB	PO	A	E	Avg.
1990	—Pittsfield (NYP)	OF	51	173	37	52	6	5	6	22	.301	45	39	12	79	2	0	1.000
	—St. Lucie (Fla. St.)	OF	11	32	6	5	1	0	0	3	.156	7	12	1	18	1	0	1.000
1991	—Williamsport (East.)	OF	135	457	80	103	16	•10	*31	•85	.225	*104	127	31	237	13	•11	.958
1992	—Tidewater (Int'l)	OF	121	445	56	108	21	3	8	40	.243	33	84	30	222	11	8	.967
1993	—Norfolk (Int'l)	OF	65	255	33	58	15	3	8	44	.227	25	53	10	133	9	1	.993
	—New York (N.L.)	OF	86	263	49	64	10	6	13	38	.243	38	66	3	165	6	4	.977
Major league totals (1 year)			86	263	49	64	10	6	13	38	.243	38	66	3	165	6	4	.977

BURNS, TODD

P, MARINERS

PERSONAL: Born July 6, 1963, in Maywood, Calif. . . . 6-2/195. . . . Throws right, bats right. . . . Full name: Todd Edward Burns.
HIGH SCHOOL: Santa Fe (Calif.).
COLLEGE: Oral Roberts.
TRANSACTIONS/CAREER NOTES: Selected by Oakland Athletics organization in seventh round of free-agent draft (June 4, 1984). . . . On A's disabled list (April 13-June 13, 1991); included rehabilitation assignment to Modesto (June 6-13). . . . Granted free agency (October 18, 1991). . . . Signed by Texas Rangers organization (December 20, 1991). . . . Traded by Rangers to St. Louis Cardinals for a player to be named later (July 22, 1993); Rangers acquired P Duff Brumley to complete deal (July 30, 1993). . . . Released by Cardinals (September 20, 1993). . . . Signed by Seattle Mariners organization (February 1, 1994).

Year	Team (League)	W	L	Pct.	ERA	G	GS	CG	ShO	Sv.	IP	H	R	ER	BB	SO
1984	—Medford (N'west)	3	0	1.000	0.50	22	0	0	0	8	36⅓	21	4	2	12	63
	—Madison (Midwest)	3	2	.600	2.57	10	0	0	0	1	14	11	4	4	3	20
1985	—Madison (Midwest)	8	8	.500	3.66	20	19	5	3	0	123	109	55	50	40	94
	—Huntsville (South.)	3	1	.750	1.19	4	4	1	1	0	22⅔	16	6	3	13	8
1986	—Huntsville (South.)	7	7	.500	3.75	20	18	5	•3	0	124⅔	122	59	52	39	77
	—Tacoma (PCL)	0	1	.000	2.16	11	0	0	0	2	16⅔	11	4	4	12	14
1987	—Huntsville (South.)	3	4	.429	2.97	34	0	0	0	7	63⅔	49	24	21	17	54
	—Tacoma (PCL)	2	2	.500	4.88	21	0	0	0	0	27⅔	27	16	15	16	30
1988	—Tacoma (PCL)	4	3	.571	3.68	21	5	1	0	1	73⅓	74	39	30	26	59
	—Oakland (A.L.)	8	2	.800	3.16	17	14	2	0	1	102⅔	93	38	36	34	57
1989	—Oakland (A.L.)	6	5	.545	2.24	50	2	0	0	8	96⅓	66	27	24	28	49
1990	—Oakland (A.L.)	3	3	.500	2.97	43	2	0	0	3	78⅔	78	28	26	32	43
1991	—Oakland (A.L.)	1	0	1.000	3.38	9	0	0	0	0	13⅓	10	5	5	8	3
	—Modesto (Calif.)	1	0	1.000	10.50	2	1	0	0	0	6	9	7	7	3	8
	—Tacoma (PCL)	0	2	.000	5.33	13	0	0	0	2	25⅓	30	16	15	7	24
1992	—Okla. City (A.A.)■	3	2	.600	2.55	8	7	0	0	0	42⅓	32	15	12	13	16
	—Texas (A.L.)	3	5	.375	3.84	35	10	0	0	1	103	97	54	44	32	55
1993	—Texas (A.L.)	0	4	.000	4.57	25	5	0	0	0	65	63	36	33	32	35
	—St. Louis (N.L.)■	0	4	.000	6.16	24	0	0	0	0	30⅔	32	21	21	9	10
	A.L. totals (6 years)	21	19	.525	3.29	179	33	2	0	13	459	407	188	168	166	242
	N.L. totals (1 year)	0	4	.000	6.16	24	0	0	0	0	30⅔	32	21	21	9	10
	Major league totals (6 years)	21	23	.477	3.47	203	33	2	0	13	489⅔	439	209	189	175	252

CHAMPIONSHIP SERIES RECORD

Year	Team (League)	W	L	Pct.	ERA	G	GS	CG	ShO	Sv.	IP	H	R	ER	BB	SO
1988	—Oakland (A.L.)							Did not play.								
1989	—Oakland (A.L.)							Did not play.								
1990	—Oakland (A.L.)							Did not play.								

WORLD SERIES RECORD

Year	Team (League)	W	L	Pct.	ERA	G	GS	CG	ShO	Sv.	IP	H	R	ER	BB	SO
1988	—Oakland (A.L.)	0	0	...	0.00	1	0	0	0	0	⅓	0	0	0	0	0
1989	—Oakland (A.L.)	0	0	...	0.00	2	0	0	0	0	1⅔	1	0	0	1	0
1990	—Oakland (A.L.)	0	0	...	16.20	2	0	0	0	0	1⅔	5	3	3	2	0
	World Series totals (3 years)	0	0	...	7.36	5	0	0	0	0	3⅔	6	3	3	3	0

BURROWS, TERRY

P, RANGERS

PERSONAL: Born November 28, 1968, in Lake Charles, La. . . . 6-1/185. . . . Throws left, bats left. . . . Full name: Terry Dale Burrows.
HIGH SCHOOL: Catholic-Point Coupee (New Roads, La.).
COLLEGE: McNeese State.
TRANSACTIONS/CAREER NOTES: Selected by Texas Rangers organization in seventh round of free-agent draft (June 4, 1990). . . . On disabled list (April 25-May 2, 1993).
STATISTICAL NOTES: Tied for American Association lead with five balks in 1993.

Year	Team (League)	W	L	Pct.	ERA	G	GS	CG	ShO	Sv.	IP	H	R	ER	BB	SO
1990	—Butte (Pioneer)	3	6	.333	4.02	14	11	1	0	0	62⅔	56	35	28	35	64
1991	—Gastonia (S. Atl.)	12	8	.600	4.45	27	26	0	0	0	147⅔	107	79	73	78	151
1992	—Charlotte (Fla. St.)	4	2	.667	2.03	14	14	0	0	0	80	71	22	18	25	66
	—Tulsa (Texas)	6	3	.667	2.13	14	13	1	0	0	76	66	22	18	35	59
	—Okla. City (A.A.)	1	0	1.000	1.13	1	1	0	0	0	8	3	1	1	5	0
1993	—Okla. City (A.A.)	7	*15	.318	6.39	27	25	1	0	0	138	171	*107	*98	76	74

BURTON, DARREN

OF, ROYALS

PERSONAL: Born September 16, 1972, in Somerset, Ky. . . . 6-1/185. . . . Throws right, bats both. . . . Full name: Darren Scott Burton.
HIGH SCHOOL: Pulaski County (Somerset, Ky.).
TRANSACTIONS/CAREER NOTES: Selected by Kansas City Royals organization in fifth round of free-agent draft (June 4, 1990).
STATISTICAL NOTES: Led Midwest League outfielders with 313 total chances in 1991. . . . Led Florida State League outfielders with six double plays in 1992. . . . Tied for Carolina League lead with 13 sacrifice hits in 1993.
MISCELLANEOUS: Batted righthanded only (1990-91).

			BATTING											FIELDING			
Year	Team (League)	Pos.	G	AB	R	H	2B	3B	HR	RBI	Avg.	BB	SO	SB	PO	A	E	Avg.
1990	—GC Royals (GCL)	OF	15	58	10	12	0	1	0	2	.207	4	17	6	31	1	1	.970
1991	—Appleton (Midw.)	OF	*134	*531	78	143	32	6	2	51	.269	45	122	38	*288	16	9	.971
1992	—Baseball City (FSL)	OF	123	431	54	106	15	6	4	36	.246	49	93	16	282	16	5	.983
1993	—Wilmington (Caro.)	OF	134	549	82	152	23	5	10	45	.277	48	111	30	303	14	9	.972

BUSCH, MIKE

3B/1B, DODGERS

PERSONAL: Born July 7, 1968, in Davenport, Ia. . . . 6-5/241. . . . Throws right, bats right. . . . Full name: Michael Anthony Busch.
HIGH SCHOOL: North Scott (Eldridge, Ia.).
COLLEGE: Iowa State.
TRANSACTIONS/CAREER NOTES: Selected by Los Angeles Dodgers organization in fourth round of free-agent draft (June 4, 1990). . . . On disabled list (May 17-28 and June 6-September 10, 1991 and May 19-June 2, 1992).
STATISTICAL NOTES: Led Pioneer League with 134 total bases and .605 slugging percentage in 1990. . . . Led Pioneer League first basemen with 56 double plays in 1990. . . . Led Pacific Coast League third basemen with 312 total chances, 218 assists and 37 errors in 1993.

			BATTING												FIELDING			
Year	Team (League)	Pos.	G	AB	R	H	2B	3B	HR	RBI	Avg.	BB	SO	SB	PO	A	E	Avg.
1990	—Great Falls (Pio.)	1B	61	220	48	72	19	2	*13	47	.327	38	49	3	481	*47	4	*.992
1991	—Bakersfield (Calif.)	1B	21	72	13	20	3	1	4	16	.278	12	21	0	161	17	7	.962
1992	—San Antonio (Tex.)	3B-OF-1B	115	416	58	99	14	2	18	51	.238	36	111	3	180	161	31	.917
1993	—Albuquerque (PCL)	3B-1B	122	431	87	122	32	4	22	70	.283	53	89	1	169	†231	†40	.909

BUSH, RANDY

OF/1B

PERSONAL: Born October 5, 1958, in Dover, Del. . . . 6-1/190. . . . Throws left, bats left. . . . Full name: Robert Randall Bush.
HIGH SCHOOL: Carol City (Fla.).
COLLEGE: Miami-Dade (North) Community College and New Orleans.
TRANSACTIONS/CAREER NOTES: Selected by Minnesota Twins organization in second round of free-agent draft (June 5, 1979). . . . On Toledo disabled list (May 25-June 27, 1980). . . . Granted free agency (November 4, 1988). . . . Re-signed by Twins (December 12, 1988). . . . On Minnesota disabled list (May 19-July 19, 1990); included rehabilitation assignment to Portland (June 27-30). . . . On Minnesota disabled list (August 23-September 7, 1990). . . . Granted free agency (November 5, 1990). . . . Re-signed by Twins (December 18, 1990). . . . Granted free agency (October 28, 1992). . . . Signed by Twins organization (January 8, 1993). . . . Released by Twins (June 27, 1993).
RECORDS: Shares A.L. record for most home runs by pinch-hitter in consecutive at-bats—2 (June 20 and 23, 1986).
STATISTICAL NOTES: Led Southern League in being hit by pitch with eight in 1979 and 12 in 1981.

			BATTING												FIELDING			
Year	Team (League)	Pos.	G	AB	R	H	2B	3B	HR	RBI	Avg.	BB	SO	SB	PO	A	E	Avg.
1979	—Orlando (Southern)	1B	76	243	33	62	12	2	6	34	.255	50	50	1	653	38	13	.982
1980	—Toledo (Int'l)	OF-1B	40	108	11	21	1	0	1	7	.194	25	33	2	112	6	1	.992
	—Orlando (Southern)	1B	51	175	32	41	2	1	7	26	.234	30	46	1	458	28	4	.992
1981	—Orlando (Southern)	OF-1B	136	482	98	140	26	3	22	94	.290	85	93	14	174	7	5	.973
1982	—Toledo (Int'l)	OF	49	160	21	52	14	0	8	27	.325	26	20	2	68	0	1	.986
	—Minnesota (A.L.)	OF	55	119	13	29	6	1	4	13	.244	8	28	0	7	0	0	1.000
1983	—Minnesota (A.L.)	1B	124	373	43	93	24	3	11	56	.249	34	51	0	21	3	0	1.000
1984	—Minnesota (A.L.)	1B	113	311	46	69	17	1	11	43	.222	31	60	1	5	0	0	1.000
1985	—Minnesota (A.L.)	OF-1B	97	234	26	56	13	3	10	35	.239	24	30	3	79	0	2	.975
1986	—Minnesota (A.L.)	OF-1B	130	357	50	96	19	7	7	45	.269	39	63	5	182	2	4	.979
1987	—Minnesota (A.L.)	OF-1B	122	293	46	74	10	2	11	46	.253	43	49	10	164	5	4	.977
1988	—Minnesota (A.L.)	OF-1B	136	394	51	103	20	3	14	51	.261	58	49	8	206	5	4	.981
1989	—Minnesota (A.L.)	OF-1B	141	391	60	103	17	4	14	54	.263	48	73	5	339	14	3	.992
1990	—Minnesota (A.L.)	OF-1B	73	181	17	44	8	0	6	18	.243	21	27	0	64	3	0	1.000
	—Portland (PCL)	OF	3	9	2	2	2	0	0	1	.222	3	1	0	0	0	0	...
1991	—Minnesota (A.L.)	OF-1B	93	165	21	50	10	1	6	23	.303	24	25	0	85	5	2	.978
1992	—Minnesota (A.L.)	OF-1B	100	182	14	39	8	1	2	22	.214	11	37	1	51	1	0	1.000
1993	—Minnesota (A.L.)	1B-OF	35	45	1	7	2	0	0	3	.156	7	13	0	13	0	0	1.000
Major league totals (12 years)			1219	3045	388	763	154	26	96	409	.251	348	505	33	1216	38	19	.985

CHAMPIONSHIP SERIES RECORD

CHAMPIONSHIP SERIES NOTES: Shares record for most stolen bases in one inning—2 (October 8, 1987, fourth inning).

			BATTING												FIELDING			
Year	Team (League)	Pos.	G	AB	R	H	2B	3B	HR	RBI	Avg.	BB	SO	SB	PO	A	E	Avg.
1987	—Minnesota (A.L.)	DH	4	12	4	3	0	1	0	2	.250	3	2	3	...	...	...	...
1991	—Minnesota (A.L.)							Did not play.										
Championship series totals (1 year)			4	12	4	3	0	1	0	2	.250	3	2	3	...	...	...	...

WORLD SERIES RECORD

			BATTING												FIELDING			
Year	Team (League)	Pos.	G	AB	R	H	2B	3B	HR	RBI	Avg.	BB	SO	SB	PO	A	E	Avg.
1987	—Minnesota (A.L.)	PH-DH	4	6	1	1	1	0	0	2	.167	0	1	0	...	...	...	...
1991	—Minnesota (A.L.)	PH-3B	3	4	0	1	0	0	0	0	.250	0	1	0	0	0	0	...
World Series totals (2 years)			7	10	1	2	1	0	0	2	.200	0	2	0	0	0	0	...

BUSHING, CHRIS

P, WHITE SOX

PERSONAL: Born November 4, 1967, in Rockville Center, N.Y. . . . 6-0/190. . . . Throws right, bats right. . . . Full name: Christopher Shaun Bushing.
HIGH SCHOOL: South Broward (Hollywood, Fla.).
COLLEGE: Broward County (Fla.).
TRANSACTIONS/CAREER NOTES: Signed as free agent by Baltimore Orioles organization (July 14, 1986). . . . Released by Orioles organization (March 28, 1988). . . . Signed by New York Yankees organization (April 4, 1989). . . . Loaned by Yankees organization to Peninsula, independent (April 4, 1989-entire season). . . . Released by Yankees organization (January 9, 1990). . . . Signed by Montreal Expos organization (March 2, 1990). . . . Selected by Scranton/Wilkes-Barre, Philadelphia Phillies organization, from Harrisburg, Expos organization, in the Rule 5 minor league draft (December 9, 1991). . . . On Reading disabled list (July 22-August 11, 1992). . . . Traded by Phillies organization to Cincinnati Reds organization for OF Nick Capra (August 20, 1992). . . . Granted free agency (October 15, 1992). . . . Signed by Nashville, Reds organization (November 18, 1992). . . . Released by Reds (November 19, 1993). . . . Signed by Chicago White Sox organization (January 5, 1994).

Year	Team (League)	W	L	Pct.	ERA	G	GS	CG	ShO	Sv.	IP	H	R	ER	BB	SO
1986	—Bluefield (Appal.)	2	0	1.000	1.37	13	1	0	0	2	26⅓	14	5	4	12	30
1987	—Bluefield (Appal.)	2	0	1.000	3.65	20	0	0	0	6	37	27	20	15	18	51
1988	—							Did not play.								
1989	—Peninsula (Caro.)■	2	7	.222	4.33	35	14	1	1	3	99⅔	96	64	48	79	99
1990	—Rockford (Midw.)■	3	6	.333	3.28	46	0	0	0	12	79⅔	62	38	29	38	99
1991	—W.P. Beach (FSL)	2	1	.667	1.94	46	0	0	0	9	65	41	15	14	40	68
	—Harrisburg (East.)	1	0	1.000	1.04	3	1	0	0	0	8⅔	3	2	1	8	8
1992	—Reading (Eastern)■	3	6	.333	4.35	22	8	0	0	1	70⅓	68	38	34	30	72
	—Nashville (A.A.)■	1	0	1.000	3.48	5	0	0	0	0	10⅓	8	4	4	6	6
1993	—Chatt. (South.)	6	1	.857	2.31	•61	0	0	0	*29	70	50	20	18	23	84
	—Cincinnati (N.L.)	0	0	...	12.46	6	0	0	0	0	4⅓	9	7	6	4	3
	Major league totals (1 year)	0	0	...	12.46	6	0	0	0	0	4⅓	9	7	6	4	3

B

BUTCHER, MIKE

P, ANGELS

PERSONAL: Born May 10, 1965, in Davenport, Ia. . . . 6-1/200. . . . Throws right, bats right. . . . Full name: Michael Dana Butcher.
HIGH SCHOOL: United Township (East Moline, Ill.).
COLLEGE: Northeastern Oklahoma A&M.
TRANSACTIONS/CAREER NOTES: Selected by Cincinnati Reds organization in fourth round of free-agent draft (January 14, 1986). . . . Selected by Kansas City Royals organization in secondary phase of free-agent draft (June 2, 1986). . . . Released by Royals organization (July 3, 1988). . . . Signed by California Angels organization (July 8, 1988). . . . On California disabled list (April 2-June 15, 1993); included rehabilitation assignment to Vancouver (May 17-June 15).

Year	Team (League)	W	L	Pct.	ERA	G	GS	CG	ShO	Sv.	IP	H	R	ER	BB	SO
1986	—Eugene (N'west)	5	4	.556	3.86	14	14	1	0	0	72⅓	51	39	31	49	68
1987	—Appleton (Midw.)	10	4	.714	2.67	20	19	3	1	0	121⅓	101	50	36	56	89
	—Fort Myers (FSL)	2	2	.500	5.46	5	5	1	0	0	31⅓	33	20	19	8	17
1988	—Baseball City (FSL)	1	4	.200	3.86	6	6	0	0	0	32⅔	32	19	14	10	20
	—App.-Quad C. (Mid.)■	0	1	.000	3.38	7	4	0	0	0	24	23	10	9	9	14
	—Palm Springs (Cal.)	3	2	.600	5.70	7	7	0	0	0	42⅔	57	33	27	19	37
1989	—Midland (Texas)	2	6	.250	6.55	15	15	0	0	0	68⅔	92	54	50	41	49
1990	—Midland (Texas)	3	7	.300	6.21	35	8	0	0	0	87	109	68	60	55	84
1991	—Midland (Texas)	9	6	.600	5.22	41	6	0	0	3	88	93	54	51	46	70
1992	—Edmonton (PCL)	5	2	.714	3.07	26	0	0	0	4	29⅓	24	12	10	18	32
	—California (A.L.)	2	2	.500	3.25	19	0	0	0	0	27⅔	29	11	10	13	24
1993	—Vancouver (PCL)	2	3	.400	4.44	14	1	0	0	3	24⅓	21	16	12	12	12
	—California (A.L.)	1	0	1.000	2.86	23	0	0	0	8	28⅓	21	12	9	15	24
	Major league totals (2 years)	3	2	.600	3.05	42	0	0	0	8	56	50	23	19	28	48

BUTLER, BRETT

OF, DODGERS

PERSONAL: Born June 15, 1957, in Los Angeles. . . . 5-10/161. . . . Throws left, bats left. . . . Full name: Brett Morgan Butler.
HIGH SCHOOL: Libertyville (Ill.).
TRANSACTIONS/CAREER NOTES: Selected by Atlanta Braves organization in 23rd round of free-agent draft (June 5, 1979). . . . Traded by Braves with IF Brook Jacoby to Cleveland Indians (October 21, 1983), completing deal in which Indians traded P Len Barker to Braves for three players to be named later (August 28, 1983); Indians acquired P Rick Behenna as partial completion of deal (September 2, 1983). . . . On disabled list (April 11-30, 1987). . . . Granted free agency (November 9, 1987). . . . Signed by San Francisco Giants (December 1, 1987). . . . Granted free agency (December 7, 1990). . . . Signed by Los Angeles Dodgers (December 14, 1990).
RECORDS: Shares major league single-season records for fewest double plays by outfielder who led league in double plays—3 (1991); fewest double plays by outfielder (150 or more games)—0 (1990); highest fielding percentage by outfielder (150 or more games)—1.000 (1991 and 1993); and fewest errors by outfielder (150 games or more)—0 (1991 and 1993). . . . Holds N.L. record for most consecutive years leading league in singles—4 (1990-93). . . . Shares N.L. record for most years leading league in singles—4 (1990-93). . . . Shares modern N.L. single-game record for most bases on balls received—5 (April 12, 1990).
HONORS: Named International League Most Valuable Player (1981).
STATISTICAL NOTES: Tied for N.L. lead in double plays by outfielder with four in 1983 and three in 1991. . . . Led A.L. in caught stealing with 22 in 1984 and 20 in 1985. . . . Led N.L. in caught stealing with 28 in 1991. . . . Tied for N.L. lead in total chances by outfielder with 380 in 1991. . . . Led N.L. with 24 sacrifice hits in 1992.

			BATTING												FIELDING			
Year	Team (League)	Pos.	G	AB	R	H	2B	3B	HR	RBI	Avg.	BB	SO	SB	PO	A	E	Avg.
1979	—Greenw. (W. Car.)	OF	35	117	26	37	2	4	1	11	.316	24	27	20	45	2	0	1.000
	—GC Braves (GCL)	OF	30	111	36	41	7	5	3	20	.369	19	15	5	66	5	0	1.000
1980	—Anderson (S. Atl.)	OF	70	255	73	76	12	6	1	26	.298	67	29	44	190	5	1	.995
	—Durham (Carolina)	OF	66	224	47	82	15	6	2	39	.366	67	30	36	156	4	3	.982
1981	—Richmond (Int'l)	OF	125	466	*93	156	19	4	3	36	.335	*103	63	44	286	15	3	.990
	—Atlanta (N.L.)	OF	40	126	17	32	2	3	0	4	.254	19	17	9	76	2	1	.987
1982	—Atlanta (N.L.)	OF	89	240	35	52	2	0	0	7	.217	25	35	21	129	2	0	1.000
	—Richmond (Int'l)	OF	41	157	22	57	8	3	1	22	.363	22	19	12	101	2	1	.990
1983	—Atlanta (N.L.)	OF	151	549	84	154	21	*13	5	37	.281	54	56	39	284	13	4	.987
1984	—Cleveland (A.L.)■	OF	159	602	108	162	25	9	3	49	.269	86	62	52	448	13	4	.991
1985	—Cleveland (A.L.)	OF	152	591	106	184	28	14	5	50	.311	63	42	47	437	19	1	*.998
1986	—Cleveland (A.L.)	OF	161	587	92	163	17	*14	4	51	.278	70	65	32	434	9	3	.993
1987	—Cleveland (A.L.)	OF	137	522	91	154	25	8	9	41	.295	91	55	33	393	4	4	.990
1988	—San Francisco (N.L.)■	OF	157	568	*109	163	27	9	6	43	.287	97	64	43	395	3	5	.988
1989	—San Francisco (N.L.)	OF	154	594	100	168	22	4	4	36	.283	59	69	31	407	11	6	.986
1990	—San Francisco (N.L.)	OF	160	622	108	•192	20	9	3	44	.309	90	62	51	420	4	6	.986
1991	—Los Angeles (N.L.)■	OF	*161	615	*112	182	13	5	2	38	.296	*108	79	38	*372	8	0	*1.000

Year	Team (League)	Pos.	G	AB	R	H	2B	3B	HR	RBI	Avg.	BB	SO	SB	PO	A	E	Avg.
			BATTING												FIELDING			
1992	—Los Angeles (N.L.) ...	OF	157	553	86	171	14	11	3	39	.309	95	67	41	353	9	2	.995
1993	—Los Angeles (N.L.) ...	OF	156	607	80	181	21	10	1	42	.298	86	69	39	369	6	0	•1.000
American League totals (4 years)			609	2302	397	663	95	45	21	191	.288	310	224	164	1712	45	12	.993
National League totals (9 years)			1225	4474	731	1295	142	64	24	290	.289	633	518	312	2805	58	24	.992
Major league totals (13 years)			1834	6776	1128	1958	237	109	45	481	.289	943	742	476	4517	103	36	.992

CHAMPIONSHIP SERIES RECORD

Year	Team (League)	Pos.	G	AB	R	H	2B	3B	HR	RBI	Avg.	BB	SO	SB	PO	A	E	Avg.
			BATTING												FIELDING			
1982	—Atlanta (N.L.)	OF-PH	2	1	0	0	0	0	0	0	.000	0	0	0	0	0	0	...
1989	—San Francisco (N.L.) ..	OF	5	19	6	4	0	0	0	0	.211	3	3	0	9	0	0	1.000
Championship series totals (2 years)			7	20	6	4	0	0	0	0	.200	3	3	0	9	0	0	1.000

WORLD SERIES RECORD

Year	Team (League)	Pos.	G	AB	R	H	2B	3B	HR	RBI	Avg.	BB	SO	SB	PO	A	E	Avg.
			BATTING												FIELDING			
1989	—San Francisco (N.L.) ..	OF	4	14	1	4	1	0	0	1	.286	2	1	2	9	0	0	1.000

ALL-STAR GAME RECORD

Year	League	Pos.	AB	R	H	2B	3B	HR	RBI	Avg.	BB	SO	SB	PO	A	E	Avg.
			BATTING											FIELDING			
1991	—National	PR-OF	1	0	0	0	0	0	0	.000	0	0	0	0	0	0	...

BUTLER, ROB

OF, BLUE JAYS

PERSONAL: Born April 10, 1970, in East York, Ont. . . . 5-11/185. . . . Throws left, bats left. . . . Full name: Robert Frank John Butler.

HIGH SCHOOL: East York (Ont.) Collegiate.

TRANSACTIONS/CAREER NOTES: Signed as free agent by Toronto Blue Jays organization (September 24, 1990). . . . On disabled list (August 7, 1992-remainder of season). . . . On Syracuse disabled list (May 12-28, 1993). . . . On Toronto disabled list (June 23-September 1, 1993); included rehabilitation assignment to Syracuse (August 13-September 1).

HONORS: Named New York-Pennsylvania League Player of the Year (1991).

STATISTICAL NOTES: Led New York-Pennsylvania League with 152 total bases and five intentional bases on balls received in 1991.

Year	Team (League)	Pos.	G	AB	R	H	2B	3B	HR	RBI	Avg.	BB	SO	SB	PO	A	E	Avg.
			BATTING												FIELDING			
1991	—St. Cathar. (NYP)	OF	76	*311	71	*105	16	5	7	45	.338	20	21	33	147	8	3	.981
1992	—Dunedin (Fla. St.)	OF	92	391	67	140	13	7	4	41	*.358	22	36	19	186	8	5	.975
1993	—Syracuse (Int'l)	OF	55	208	30	59	11	2	1	14	.284	15	29	7	93	1	1	.989
	—Toronto (A.L.)	OF	17	48	8	13	4	0	0	2	.271	7	12	2	32	0	1	.970
Major league totals (1 year)			17	48	8	13	4	0	0	2	.271	7	12	2	32	0	1	.970

CHAMPIONSHIP SERIES RECORD

Year	Team (League)	Pos.	G	AB	R	H	2B	3B	HR	RBI	Avg.	BB	SO	SB	PO	A	E	Avg.
			BATTING												FIELDING			
1993	—Toronto (A.L.)								Did not play.									

WORLD SERIES RECORD

Year	Team (League)	Pos.	G	AB	R	H	2B	3B	HR	RBI	Avg.	BB	SO	SB	PO	A	E	Avg.
			BATTING												FIELDING			
1993	—Toronto (A.L.)	PH	2	2	1	1	0	0	0	0	.500	0	0	0	...	...	...	...

BYRD, JIM

SS, RED SOX

PERSONAL: Born October 3, 1968, in WeWahitchka, Fla. . . . 6-1/185. . . . Throws right, bats right. . . . Full name: James Edward Byrd.

HIGH SCHOOL: Lawton (Okla.).

COLLEGE: Seminole (Okla.) Junior College.

TRANSACTIONS/CAREER NOTES: Selected by Cincinnati Reds organization in 31st round of free-agent draft (June 2, 1986). . . . Selected by Boston Red Sox organization in eighth round of free-agent draft (June 2, 1987).

MISCELLANEOUS: Batted as switch-hitter (1988-89).

Year	Team (League)	Pos.	G	AB	R	H	2B	3B	HR	RBI	Avg.	BB	SO	SB	PO	A	E	Avg.
			BATTING												FIELDING			
1988	—Ariz. Co-op (Ariz.)	S-2-3-0-P	33	121	18	36	7	2	2	13	.298	6	19	7	48	81	14	.902
1989	—Winter Haven (FSL) ..	SS-2B	126	447	42	88	17	2	3	25	.197	25	104	22	256	377	43	.936
1990	—Lynchburg (Caro.) ...	SS	131	511	59	115	20	1	8	45	.225	38	139	24	*223	348	*44	.928
	—New Britain (East.) ..	2B	2	5	1	1	1	0	0	0	.200	0	1	0	5	4	0	1.000
1991	—New Britain (East.) ..	SS	79	292	28	70	9	1	0	15	.240	28	53	14	167	235	18	.957
	—Lynchburg (Caro.) ...	SS	52	206	29	49	10	0	1	18	.238	13	50	10	62	131	18	.915
1992	—Winter Haven (FSL) ..	SS-2B	18	71	12	19	2	1	0	1	.268	5	7	4	34	40	5	.937
	—New Britain (East.) ..	SS-3B	20	63	5	14	1	2	0	6	.222	3	13	2	23	39	4	.939
	—Pawtucket (Int'l)	2B-SS-3B	72	246	27	55	5	1	2	18	.224	7	48	2	156	181	15	.957
1993	—Pawtucket (Int'l)	SS	117	378	33	67	12	4	3	26	.177	18	111	10	*202	314	33	.940
	—Boston (A.L.)	PR	2	0	0	0	0	0	0	0	...	0	0	0	...	...	...	...
Major league totals (1 year)			2	0	0	0	0	0	0	0	...	0	0	0	...	...	...	...

RECORD AS PITCHER

Year	Team (League)	W	L	Pct.	ERA	G	GS	CG	ShO	Sv.	IP	H	R	ER	BB	SO
1988	—Ariz. Co-op (Ariz.)	0	0	...	18.00	1	0	0	0	0	1	1	2	2	1	2

CABRERA, FRANCISCO

1B/C

PERSONAL: Born October 10, 1966, in Santo Domingo, Dominican Republic. . . . 6-4/193. . . . Throws right, bats right. . . . Full name: Francisco Paulino Cabrera. . . . Name pronounced kuh-BREH-ah.
HIGH SCHOOL: Santa Cruz (Santo Domingo, Dominican Republic).
TRANSACTIONS/CAREER NOTES: Signed as free agent by Toronto Blue Jays organization (February 28, 1986). . . . Traded by Blue Jays to Atlanta Braves organization (August 24, 1989), completing deal in which Braves traded P Jim Acker to Blue Jays for P Tony Castillo and a player to be named later (August 24, 1989). . . . Released by Braves (November 24, 1993). . . . Signed by Orix Blue Wave of Japan Pacific League (November 24, 1993).
STATISTICAL NOTES: Led South Atlantic League catchers with 959 total chances in 1987. . . . Led Southern League catchers with 874 total chances and tied for lead with six double plays in 1988. . . . Led International League with eight sacrifice flies in 1989. . . . Led International League catchers with 12 errors and 13 passed balls in 1989. . . . Led International League catchers with 12 errors in 1992.

			BATTING												FIELDING			
Year	**Team (League)**	**Pos.**	**G**	**AB**	**R**	**H**	**2B**	**3B**	**HR**	**RBI**	**Avg.**	**BB**	**SO**	**SB**	**PO**	**A**	**E**	**Avg.**
1986	—Vent. Co. (Calif.)	C	6	12	2	2	1	0	0	3	.167	0	4	1	26	3	1	.967
	—St. Cathar. (NYP)	C	68	246	31	73	13	2	6	35	.297	16	48	7	449	50	6	.988
1987	—Myrtle Beach (SAL)	C	129	449	61	124	27	1	14	72	.276	40	82	4	*849	89	•21	.978
1988	—Dunedin (Fla. St.)	C	9	35	2	14	4	0	1	9	.400	1	2	0	74	9	3	.965
	—Knoxville (South.)	C	119	429	59	122	19	1	20	54	.284	26	75	4	*783	*68	*23	.974
1989	—Syrac.-Rich. (Int'l)	C-1B	116	434	59	130	31	5	9	72	.300	20	72	4	554	35	†12	.980
	—Toronto (A.L.)	DH	3	12	1	2	1	0	0	0	.167	1	3	0	...	...	...	...
	—Atlanta (N.L.)■	C-1B	4	14	0	3	2	0	0	0	.214	0	3	0	27	1	1	.966
1990	—Richmond (Int'l)	1B-C-OF	35	132	12	30	3	1	7	20	.227	7	23	2	269	25	4	.987
	—Atlanta (N.L.)	1B-C	63	137	14	38	5	1	7	25	.277	5	21	1	269	19	3	.990
1991	—Atlanta (N.L.)	C-1B	44	95	7	23	6	0	4	23	.242	6	20	1	137	13	3	.980
	—Richmond (Int'l)	1B-C-OF	32	119	22	31	7	1	7	24	.261	10	21	0	145	13	2	.988
1992	—Atlanta (N.L.)	C	12	10	2	3	0	0	2	3	.300	1	1	0	0	0	0	...
	—Richmond (Int'l)	C-1B	81	301	30	82	11	0	9	35	.272	17	49	0	541	50	†12	.980
1993	—Atlanta (N.L.)	1B-C	70	83	8	20	3	0	4	11	.241	8	21	0	65	10	0	1.000
American League totals (1 year)			3	12	1	2	1	0	0	0	.167	1	3	0	0	0	0	...
National League totals (5 years)			193	339	31	87	16	1	17	62	.257	20	66	2	498	43	7	.987
Major league totals (5 years)			196	351	32	89	17	1	17	62	.254	21	69	2	498	43	7	.987

CHAMPIONSHIP SERIES RECORD

			BATTING												FIELDING			
Year	**Team (League)**	**Pos.**	**G**	**AB**	**R**	**H**	**2B**	**3B**	**HR**	**RBI**	**Avg.**	**BB**	**SO**	**SB**	**PO**	**A**	**E**	**Avg.**
1991	—Atlanta (N.L.)							Did not play.										
1992	—Atlanta (N.L.)	PH	2	2	0	1	0	0	0	2	.500	0	0	0	...	...	...	...
1993	—Atlanta (N.L.)	PH-C	3	3	0	2	0	0	0	1	.667	0	1	0	1	0	0	1.000
Championship series totals (2 years)			5	5	0	3	0	0	0	3	.600	0	1	0	1	0	0	1.000

WORLD SERIES RECORD

			BATTING												FIELDING			
Year	**Team (League)**	**Pos.**	**G**	**AB**	**R**	**H**	**2B**	**3B**	**HR**	**RBI**	**Avg.**	**BB**	**SO**	**SB**	**PO**	**A**	**E**	**Avg.**
1991	—Atlanta (N.L.)	PH-C	3	1	0	0	0	0	0	0	.000	0	0	0	0	0	0	...
1992	—Atlanta (N.L.)	PH	1	1	0	0	0	0	0	0	.000	0	0	0	...	...	...	...
World Series totals (2 years)			4	2	0	0	0	0	0	0	.000	0	0	0	0	0	0	...

CADARET, GREG

P, BLUE JAYS

PERSONAL: Born February 27, 1962, in Detroit. . . . 6-3/215. . . . Throws left, bats left. . . . Full name: Gregory James Cadaret. . . . Name pronounced CAD-uh-ray.
HIGH SCHOOL: Central Montacalm (Stanton, Mich.).
COLLEGE: Grand Valley State (Mich.).
TRANSACTIONS/CAREER NOTES: Selected by Oakland Athletics organization in 11th round of free-agent draft (June 6, 1983). . . . Traded by A's organization with P Eric Plunk and OF Luis Polonia to New York Yankees for OF Rickey Henderson (June 21, 1989). . . . Contract sold by Yankees to Cincinnati Reds (November 6, 1992). . . . Released by Reds (July 26, 1993). . . . Signed by Kansas City Royals (July 30, 1993). . . . Granted free agency (October 25, 1993). . . . Signed by Toronto Blue Jays organization (December 21, 1993).

Year	**Team (League)**	**W**	**L**	**Pct.**	**ERA**	**G**	**GS**	**CG**	**ShO**	**Sv.**	**IP**	**H**	**R**	**ER**	**BB**	**SO**
1983	—Medford (N'west)	7	3	.700	4.36	12	11	1	1	0	64	73	36	31	36	51
1984	—Modesto (Calif.)	13	8	.619	3.05	26	26	6	2	0	171⅓	162	79	58	82	138
1985	—Huntsville (South.)	3	7	.300	6.12	17	17	0	0	0	82⅓	96	61	56	57	60
	—Modesto (Calif.)	3	9	.250	5.87	12	12	1	1	0	61⅓	59	50	40	54	43
1986	—Huntsville (South.)	12	5	.706	5.41	28	28	1	0	0	141⅓	166	106	85	98	113
1987	—Huntsville (South.)	5	2	.714	2.90	24	0	0	0	9	40⅓	31	16	13	20	48
	—Tacoma (PCL)	1	2	.333	3.46	7	0	0	0	1	13	5	6	5	13	12
	—Oakland (A.L.)	6	2	.750	4.54	29	0	0	0	0	39⅔	37	22	20	24	30
1988	—Oakland (A.L.)	5	2	.714	2.89	58	0	0	0	3	71⅔	60	26	23	36	64
1989	—Oak.-N.Y. (A.L.)■	5	5	.500	4.05	46	13	3	1	0	120	130	62	54	57	80
1990	—New York (A.L.)	5	4	.556	4.15	54	6	0	0	3	121⅓	120	62	56	64	80
1991	—New York (A.L.)	8	6	.571	3.62	68	5	0	0	3	121⅔	110	52	49	59	105
1992	—New York (A.L.)	4	8	.333	4.25	46	11	1	1	1	103⅔	104	53	49	74	73
1993	—Cincinnati (N.L.)■	2	1	.667	4.96	34	0	0	0	1	32⅔	40	19	18	23	23
	—Kansas City (A.L.)■	1	1	.500	2.93	13	0	0	0	0	15⅓	14	5	5	7	2
A.L. totals (7 years)		34	28	.548	3.88	314	35	4	2	10	593⅓	575	282	256	321	434
N.L. totals (1 year)		2	1	.667	4.96	34	0	0	0	1	32⅔	40	19	18	23	23
Major league totals (7 years)		36	29	.554	3.94	348	35	4	2	11	626	615	301	274	344	457

CHAMPIONSHIP SERIES RECORD

Year	Team (League)	W	L	Pct.	ERA	G	GS	CG	ShO	Sv.	IP	H	R	ER	BB	SO
1988	—Oakland (A.L.)	0	0	...	27.00	1	0	0	0	0	⅓	1	1	1	0	0

WORLD SERIES RECORD

Year	Team (League)	W	L	Pct.	ERA	G	GS	CG	ShO	Sv.	IP	H	R	ER	BB	SO
1988	—Oakland (A.L.)	0	0	...	0.00	3	0	0	0	0	2	2	0	0	0	3

CALDERON, IVAN

OF/DH

PERSONAL: Born March 19, 1962, in Fajardo, Puerto Rico. . . . 6-1/221. . . . Throws right, bats right. . . . Full name: Ivan Perez Calderon. . . . Name pronounced CALL-dur-OWN.
HIGH SCHOOL: Madiania Alta Intermediate (Luiza, Puerto Rico).
TRANSACTIONS/CAREER NOTES: Signed as free agent by Seattle Mariners organization (July 30, 1979). . . . On Salt Lake City disabled list (May 25-July 2, 1984). . . . On Seattle disabled list (August 26-September 12, 1984). . . . Traded by Mariners to Chicago White Sox organization (July 1, 1986), completing deal in which White Sox traded C Scott Bradley to Mariners for a player to be named later (June 26, 1986). . . . On disabled list (May 16-31, 1987; June 27-July 12 and July 31, 1988-remainder of season). . . . Traded by White Sox with P Barry Jones to Montreal Expos for OF Tim Raines, P Jeff Carter and a player to be named later (December 23, 1990); White Sox acquired P Mario Brito to complete deal (February 15, 1991). . . . On Montreal disabled list (April 30-May 19 and May 24-June 11, 1992). . . . On Montreal disabled list (June 13-September 3, 1992); included rehabilitation assignment to West Palm Beach (August 26-September 3). . . . Traded by Expos to Boston Red Sox for P Mike Gardiner and P Terry Powers (December 8, 1992). . . . On disabled list (July 11-30, 1993). . . . Released by Red Sox (August 17, 1993). . . . Signed by White Sox (August 31, 1993). . . . Granted free agency (November 1, 1993).
STATISTICAL NOTES: Tied for Southern League lead with 267 total bases in 1983. . . . Led A.L. in grounding into double plays with 26 in 1990.

C

				BATTING											FIELDING			
Year	Team (League)	Pos.	G	AB	R	H	2B	3B	HR	RBI	Avg.	BB	SO	SB	PO	A	E	Avg.
1980	—Belling. (N'west)	OF	57	195	44	62	7	*9	4	32	.318	15	41	7	56	4	7	.896
1981	—Wausau (Midwest) ..	OF-SS	117	402	79	123	19	1	20	62	.306	39	96	26	130	17	6	.961
1982	—Wausau (Midwest) ..	S-0-3-1	126	461	91	132	22	5	24	89	.286	45	90	26	215	202	45	.903
1983	—Chatt. (South.)	OF	139	546	92	•170	34	*15	11	80	*.311	34	70	25	251	10	13	.953
1984	—Salt Lake City (PCL)	OF	66	255	61	93	7	9	4	45	.365	21	32	18	132	9	8	.946
	—Seattle (A.L.)	OF	11	24	2	5	1	0	1	1	.208	2	5	1	22	0	0	1.000
1985	—Seattle (A.L.)	OF-1B	67	210	37	60	16	4	8	28	.286	19	45	4	108	5	2	.983
1986	—Calgary (PCL)...........	OF	24	81	17	27	3	0	3	18	.333	15	8	5	34	2	1	.973
	—Seattle-Chi. (A.L.)■.	OF	50	164	16	41	7	1	2	15	.250	9	39	3	64	4	5	.932
	—Buffalo (A.A.)	OF	27	105	11	23	9	0	5	22	.219	9	28	0	30	1	5	.861
1987	—Chicago (A.L.)	OF	144	542	93	159	38	2	28	83	.293	60	109	10	295	8	5	.984
1988	—Chicago (A.L.)	OF	73	264	40	56	14	0	14	35	.212	34	66	4	141	5	7	.954
1989	—Chicago (A.L.)	OF-1B	157	622	83	178	34	9	14	87	.286	43	94	7	384	17	9	.978
1990	—Chicago (A.L.)	OF	158	607	85	166	44	2	14	74	.273	51	79	32	269	7	7	.975
1991	—Montreal (N.L.)■.......	OF-1B	134	470	69	141	22	3	19	75	.300	53	64	31	284	5	7	.976
1992	—Montreal (N.L.).........	OF	48	170	19	45	14	2	3	24	.265	14	22	1	79	2	1	.988
	—W.P. Beach (FSL).....	OF	9	26	2	3	0	0	0	2	.115	4	6	0	9	0	0	1.000
1993	—Boston-Chi. (A.L.)■.	OF	82	239	26	50	10	2	1	22	.209	21	33	4	94	2	0	1.000
American League totals (8 years)............			742	2672	382	715	164	20	82	345	.268	239	470	65	1377	48	35	.976
National League totals (2 years)			182	640	88	186	36	5	22	99	.291	67	86	32	363	7	8	.979
Major league totals (10 years)................			924	3312	470	901	200	25	104	444	.272	306	556	97	1740	55	43	.977

ALL-STAR GAME RECORD

			BATTING										FIELDING			
Year	League	Pos.	AB	R	H	2B	3B	HR	RBI	Avg.	BB	SO	SB	PO	A	E	Avg.
1991	—National....................	OF	2	0	1	0	0	0	0	.500	0	0	1	1	0	0	1.000

CAMERON, STANTON

OF, PIRATES

PERSONAL: Born July 5, 1969, in Knoxville, Tenn. . . . 6-5/195. . . . Throws right, bats right. . . . Full name: Stanton McGhee Cameron.
HIGH SCHOOL: Powell (Tenn.).
COLLEGE: Tennessee.
TRANSACTIONS/CAREER NOTES: Selected by New York Mets organization in 24th round of free-agent draft (June 2, 1987). . . . Selected by Hagerstown, Baltimore Orioles organization, from St. Lucie, Mets organization, in Rule 5 minor league draft (December 9, 1991). . . . On disabled list (September 6, 1993-remainder of season). . . . Traded by Orioles organization with P Terry Farrar to Pittsburgh Pirates organization (September 14, 1993), completing deal in which Pirates traded OF Lonnie Smith to Orioles for two players to be named later (September 8, 1993).
STATISTICAL NOTES: Led Gulf Coast League outfielders with four double plays in 1988.

				BATTING											FIELDING			
Year	Team (League)	Pos.	G	AB	R	H	2B	3B	HR	RBI	Avg.	BB	SO	SB	PO	A	E	Avg.
1987	—Kingsport (Appal.) ...	OF	26	53	6	7	1	0	1	5	.132	10	24	1	23	2	3	.893
1988	—GC Mets (GCL)..........	OF-1B	51	171	24	40	10	1	1	15	.234	25	33	10	103	7	7	.940
1989	—Pittsfield (NYP)	OF-1B	71	253	35	65	13	1	10	50	.257	41	71	7	290	18	9	.972
1990	—Columbia (S. Atl.).....	OF-1B	87	302	57	90	19	1	15	57	.298	52	68	3	94	5	3	.971
1991	—St. Lucie (Fla. St.)....	OF	83	232	25	43	7	0	2	26	.185	46	82	2	88	4	3	.968
1992	—Frederick (Caro.)■....	OF	127	409	76	101	16	1	29	92	.247	90	121	2	219	15	7	.971
1993	—Bowie (Eastern)	OF-1B	118	384	65	106	27	1	21	64	.276	84	103	6	208	13	6	.974

CAMINITI, KEN

3B, ASTROS

PERSONAL: Born April 21, 1963, in Hanford, Calif. . . . 6-0/200. . . . Throws right, bats both. . . . Full name: Kenneth Gene Caminiti. . . . Name pronounced CAM-uh-NET-ee.
HIGH SCHOOL: Leigh (San Jose, Calif.).
COLLEGE: San Jose State.

TRANSACTIONS/CAREER NOTES: Selected by Houston Astros organization in third round of free-agent draft (June 4, 1984).... On disabled list (April 19-May 11, 1992).
HONORS: Named third baseman on THE SPORTING NEWS college All-America team (1984).
STATISTICAL NOTES: Led Southern League third basemen with 34 double plays in 1986.... Led Pacific Coast League third basemen with 382 total chances and 25 double plays in 1988.

			BATTING												FIELDING			
Year	**Team (League)**	**Pos.**	**G**	**AB**	**R**	**H**	**2B**	**3B**	**HR**	**RBI**	**Avg.**	**BB**	**SO**	**SB**	**PO**	**A**	**E**	**Avg.**
1985	—Osceola (Fla. St.)	3B	126	468	83	133	26	9	4	73	.284	51	54	14	53	193	20	.925
1986	—Columbus (South.)	3B	137	513	82	154	29	3	12	81	.300	56	79	5	105	*299	33	.924
1987	—Columbus (South.)	3B	95	375	66	122	25	2	15	69	.325	25	58	11	55	205	21	.925
	—Houston (N.L.)	3B	63	203	10	50	7	1	3	23	.246	12	44	0	50	98	8	.949
1988	—Tucson (PCL)	3B	109	416	54	113	24	7	5	66	.272	29	54	13	*105	*250	27	.929
	—Houston (N.L.)	3B	30	83	5	15	2	0	1	7	.181	5	18	0	12	43	3	.948
1989	—Houston (N.L.)	3B	161	585	71	149	31	3	10	72	.255	51	93	4	126	335	22	.954
1990	—Houston (N.L.)	3B	153	541	52	131	20	2	4	51	.242	48	97	9	118	243	21	.945
1991	—Houston (N.L.)	3B	152	574	65	145	30	3	13	80	.253	46	85	4	129	293	23	.948
1992	—Houston (N.L.)	3B	135	506	68	149	31	2	13	62	.294	44	68	10	102	210	11	.966
1993	—Houston (N.L.)	3B	143	543	75	142	31	0	13	75	.262	49	88	8	123	264	24	.942
Major league totals (7 years)			837	3035	346	781	152	11	57	370	.257	255	493	35	660	1486	112	.950

CAMPBELL, KEVIN

P, TWINS

PERSONAL: Born December 6, 1964, in Marianna, Ark.... 6-2/225.... Throws right, bats right.... Full name: Kevin Wade Campbell.
HIGH SCHOOL: Des Arc (Ark.).
COLLEGE: Arkansas.
TRANSACTIONS/CAREER NOTES: Selected by Philadelphia Phillies organization in 13th round of free-agent draft (June 6, 1983). ... Selected by Los Angeles Dodgers organization in fifth round of free-agent draft (June 2, 1986).... Traded by Dodgers organization to Oakland Athletics organization for P David Veres (January 15, 1991).... Granted free agency (December 19, 1992).... Re-signed by A's organization (January 21, 1993).... Granted free agency (October 15, 1993).... Signed by Portland, Minnesota Twins organization (December 6, 1993).

Year	**Team (League)**	**W**	**L**	**Pct.**	**ERA**	**G**	**GS**	**CG**	**ShO**	**Sv.**	**IP**	**H**	**R**	**ER**	**BB**	**SO**
1986	—Great Falls (Pio.)	5	6	.455	4.66	15	15	3	0	0	85	99	62	44	32	66
1987	—Vero Beach (FSL)	7	14	.333	3.91	28	28	5	1	0	184	200	100	80	64	112
1988	—Vero Beach (FSL)	8	12	.400	2.75	26	26	5	1	0	163⅔	166	67	50	49	115
1989	—San Antonio (Tex.)	1	5	.167	6.67	17	0	0	0	2	27	29	22	20	16	28
	—Bakersfield (Calif.)	5	3	.625	2.54	31	0	0	0	6	60⅓	43	23	17	28	63
1990	—San Antonio (Tex.)	2	6	.250	2.33	49	0	0	0	8	81	67	29	21	25	84
1991	—Tacoma (PCL)■	9	2	*.818	1.80	35	0	0	0	2	75	53	18	15	35	56
	—Oakland (A.L.)	1	0	1.000	2.74	14	0	0	0	0	23	13	7	7	14	16
1992	—Tacoma (PCL)	2	2	.500	4.05	10	0	0	0	0	13⅓	16	6	6	8	14
	—Oakland (A.L.)	2	3	.400	5.12	32	5	0	0	1	65	66	39	37	45	38
1993	—Tacoma (PCL)	3	5	.375	2.75	40	0	0	0	12	55⅔	42	19	17	19	46
	—Oakland (A.L.)	0	0	...	7.31	11	0	0	0	0	16	20	13	13	11	9
Major league totals (3 years)		3	3	.500	4.93	57	5	0	0	1	104	99	59	57	70	63

CANATE, WILLIE

OF, BLUE JAYS

PERSONAL: Born December 11, 1971, in Maracaibo, Venezuela.... 6-0/170.... Throws right, bats right.... Full name: Emisael William Canate.... Name pronounced kuh-NOT-ay.
TRANSACTIONS/CAREER NOTES: Signed as free agent by Cleveland Indians organization (June 22, 1989).... Selected by Cincinnati Reds from Indians organization in Rule 5 major league draft (December 7, 1992). ... On Cincinnati disabled list (March 26-April 13, 1993); included rehabilitation assignment to Indianapolis (April 8-13).... Contract sold by Reds to Toronto Blue Jays (April 13, 1993).... On Toronto disabled list (June 3-July 5, 1993); included rehabilitation assignment to Knoxville (June 20-29) and Syracuse (June 29-July 5).
STATISTICAL NOTES: Tied for South Atlantic League lead in double plays by outfielder with three in 1991.

			BATTING												FIELDING			
Year	**Team (League)**	**Pos.**	**G**	**AB**	**R**	**H**	**2B**	**3B**	**HR**	**RBI**	**Avg.**	**BB**	**SO**	**SB**	**PO**	**A**	**E**	**Avg.**
1989	—GC Indians (GCL)	OF	11	24	4	5	2	0	0	0	.208	0	8	0	6	0	1	.857
1990	—Watertown (NYP)	OF	57	199	28	52	5	2	2	15	.261	10	43	9	120	3	5	.961
1991	—Kinston (Carolina)	OF	51	189	28	41	3	1	1	12	.217	14	29	4	99	4	1	.990
	—Columbus (S. Atl.)	OF	62	204	32	49	13	2	4	20	.240	25	32	14	125	9	4	.971
1992	—Columbus (S. Atl.)	OF	133	528	*110	*167	*37	8	5	63	.316	56	66	25	185	15	5	.976
1993	—Indianapolis (A.A.)■	OF	3	5	0	0	0	0	0	0	.000	0	1	0	0	0	0	...
	—Toronto (A.L.)■	OF	38	47	12	10	0	0	1	3	.213	6	15	1	38	2	0	1.000
	—Knoxville (South.)	OF	9	37	8	10	2	0	1	4	.270	5	2	2	17	1	0	1.000
	—Syracuse (Int'l)	OF	7	24	3	6	0	0	2	5	.250	5	3	0	9	2	0	1.000
Major league totals (1 year)			38	47	12	10	0	0	1	3	.213	6	15	1	38	2	0	1.000

CHAMPIONSHIP SERIES RECORD

			BATTING												FIELDING			
Year	**Team (League)**	**Pos.**	**G**	**AB**	**R**	**H**	**2B**	**3B**	**HR**	**RBI**	**Avg.**	**BB**	**SO**	**SB**	**PO**	**A**	**E**	**Avg.**
1993	—Toronto (A.L.)								Did not play.									

WORLD SERIES RECORD

			BATTING												FIELDING			
Year	**Team (League)**	**Pos.**	**G**	**AB**	**R**	**H**	**2B**	**3B**	**HR**	**RBI**	**Avg.**	**BB**	**SO**	**SB**	**PO**	**A**	**E**	**Avg.**
1993	—Toronto (A.L.)	PR	1	0	0	0	0	0	0	0	...	0	0	0	...	...	...	...

CANDAELE, CASEY

IF/OF, REDS

PERSONAL: Born January 12, 1961, in Lompoc, Calif. . . . 5-9/165. . . . Throws right, bats both. . . . Full name: Casey Todd Candaele. . . . Son of Helen St. Aubin, former women's professional baseball player. . . . Name pronounced kan-DELL.
HIGH SCHOOL: Lompoc (Calif.).
COLLEGE: Arizona.
TRANSACTIONS/CAREER NOTES: Signed as free agent by Montreal Expos organization (August 15, 1982). . . . Traded by Expos to Houston Astros for C Mark Bailey (July 23, 1988). . . . On disabled list (June 9-July 22, 1989). . . . On Houston disabled list (July 17-August 9, 1993); included rehabilitation assignment to Tucson (August 2-9). . . . Granted free agency (October 4, 1993). . . . Signed by Cincinnati Reds organization (November 24, 1993).
STATISTICAL NOTES: Led Florida State League second basemen with 391 assists, 30 errors and 87 double plays in 1983. . . . Led American Association with 11 sacrifice hits in 1986. . . . Tied for American Association lead in double plays by second baseman with 68 in 1986.

			BATTING												FIELDING			
Year	Team (League)	Pos.	G	AB	R	H	2B	3B	HR	RBI	Avg.	BB	SO	SB	PO	A	E	Avg.
1983	—W.P. Beach (FSL)	2-0-3-S	127	*511	77	156	26	9	0	45	.305	51	44	22	271	†403	†32	.955
	—Memphis (South.)	3B	5	19	4	4	1	0	0	1	.211	1	3	1	2	11	0	1.000
1984	—Jacksonv. (South.)	S-0-2-3	132	532	68	145	23	2	2	53	.273	30	35	26	224	352	18	.970
1985	—Indianapolis (A.A.)	0-2-S-3	127	390	55	101	13	5	0	35	.259	44	33	13	266	160	6	.986
1986	—Indianapolis (A.A.)	2B-OF	119	480	77	145	32	6	2	42	.302	46	29	16	240	319	13	.977
	—Montreal (N.L.)	2B-3B	30	104	9	24	4	1	0	6	.231	5	15	3	45	74	2	.983
1987	—Montreal (N.L.)	2-0-S-1	138	449	62	122	23	4	1	23	.272	38	28	7	237	176	8	.981
1988	—Indianapolis (A.A.)	SS-2B-OF	60	239	23	63	11	6	2	36	.264	12	20	5	105	161	3	.989
	—Mont.-Hou. (N.L.)■	2B-OF-3B	57	147	11	25	8	1	0	5	.170	11	17	1	79	126	2	.990
	—Tucson (PCL)	0-2-S-3	17	66	8	17	3	0	0	5	.258	4	6	4	35	29	3	.955
1989	—Tucson (PCL)	0-3-2-S-1	68	206	22	45	6	1	0	17	.218	20	37	6	94	59	5	.968
1990	—Tucson (PCL)	2B	7	28	2	6	1	0	0	2	.214	3	2	1	14	24	1	.974
	—Houston (N.L.)	0-2-S-3	130	262	30	75	8	6	3	22	.286	31	42	7	147	120	3	.989
1991	—Houston (N.L.)	2B-OF-3B	151	461	44	121	20	7	4	50	.262	40	49	9	244	318	10	.983
1992	—Houston (N.L.)	S-3-0-2	135	320	19	68	12	1	1	18	.213	24	36	7	130	196	11	.967
1993	—Houston (N.L.)	2-0-S-3	75	121	18	29	8	0	1	7	.240	10	14	2	46	40	3	.966
	—Tucson (PCL)	OF-SS-2B	6	27	4	8	1	0	0	4	.296	3	2	1	12	10	3	.880
Major league totals (7 years)			716	1864	193	464	83	20	10	131	.249	159	201	36	928	1050	39	.981

CANDELARIA, JOHN

P

PERSONAL: Born November 6, 1953, in Brooklyn, N.Y. . . . 6-6/225. . . . Throws left, bats right. . . . Full name: John Robert Candelaria.
HIGH SCHOOL: LaSalle Academy (New York).
TRANSACTIONS/CAREER NOTES: Selected by Pittsburgh Pirates organization in second round of free-agent draft (June 6, 1972). . . . On disabled list (May 11, 1981-remainder of season). . . . Traded by Pirates with P Al Holland and OF George Hendrick to California Angels for P Pat Clements, OF Mike Brown and a player to be named later (August 2, 1985); Pirates organization acquired P Bob Kipper to complete deal (August 16, 1985). . . . On California disabled list (April 15-July 8, 1986); included rehabilitation assignment to Palm Springs (June 26-July 2). . . . On disabled list (May 14-29 and June 19-August 5, 1987). . . . Traded by Angels to New York Mets for P Shane Young and P Jeff Richardson (September 15, 1987). . . . Granted free agency (November 9, 1987). . . . Signed by New York Yankees (January 15, 1988). . . . On New York disabled list (May 6-August 19, 1989); included rehabilitation assignment to Gulf Coast Yankees (August 11-19). . . . Traded by Yankees to Montreal Expos for a player to be named later (August 29, 1989); Yankees acquired 3B Mike Blowers to complete deal (August 31, 1989). . . . Released by Expos (January 24, 1990). . . . Signed by Minnesota Twins (February 28, 1990). . . . Traded by Twins to Toronto Blue Jays for 2B Nelson Liriano and OF Pedro Munoz (July 27, 1990). . . . Granted free agency (November 5, 1990). . . . Signed by Los Angeles Dodgers (March 25, 1991). . . . Granted free agency (November 3, 1992). . . . Signed by Pirates (December 16, 1992). . . . On disabled list (April 25-May 12, 1993). . . . Released by Pirates (July 9, 1993).
HONORS: Named A.L. Comeback Player of the Year by THE SPORTING NEWS (1986).
STATISTICAL NOTES: Led Carolina League with 17 home runs allowed in 1974. . . . Pitched 2-0 no-hit victory against Los Angeles (August 9, 1976). . . . Tied for N.L. lead with 29 home runs allowed in 1977.

Year	Team (League)	W	L	Pct.	ERA	G	GS	CG	ShO	Sv.	IP	H	R	ER	BB	SO
1973	—Char., S.C. (W. Car.)	10	2	*.833	3.79	18	17	2	1	0	95	84	45	40	38	60
1974	—Salem (Carolina)	11	8	.579	3.68	25	24	9	2	1	154	146	80	63	63	147
	—Char., W.Va. (Int'l)	0	0	...	1.64	1	1	0	0	0	11	7	2	2	1	10
1975	—Pittsburgh (N.L.)	8	6	.571	2.75	18	18	4	1	0	121	95	47	37	36	95
	—Char., W.Va. (Int'l)	7	1	.875	1.77	10	9	4	3	1	61	53	15	12	17	48
1976	—Pittsburgh (N.L.)	16	7	.696	3.15	32	31	11	4	1	220	173	87	77	60	138
1977	—Pittsburgh (N.L.)	20	5	*.800	*2.34	33	33	6	1	0	231	197	64	60	50	133
1978	—Pittsburgh (N.L.)	12	11	.522	3.24	30	29	3	1	1	189	191	73	68	49	94
1979	—Pittsburgh (N.L.)	14	9	.609	3.22	33	30	8	0	0	207	201	83	74	41	101
1980	—Pittsburgh (N.L.)	11	14	.440	4.02	35	34	7	0	1	233	246	114	104	50	97
1981	—Pittsburgh (N.L.)	2	2	.500	3.51	6	6	0	0	0	41	42	17	16	11	14
1982	—Pittsburgh (N.L.)	12	7	.632	2.94	31	30	1	1	1	174⅔	166	62	57	37	133
1983	—Pittsburgh (N.L.)	15	8	.652	3.23	33	32	2	0	0	197⅔	191	73	71	45	157
1984	—Pittsburgh (N.L.)	12	11	.522	2.72	33	28	3	1	2	185⅓	179	69	56	34	133
1985	—Pittsburgh (N.L.)	2	4	.333	3.64	37	0	0	0	9	54⅓	57	23	22	14	47
	—California (A.L.)■	7	3	.700	3.80	13	13	1	1	0	71	70	33	30	24	53
1986	—California (A.L.)	10	2	.833	2.55	16	16	1	1	0	91⅔	68	30	26	26	81
	—Palm Springs (Cal.)	0	0	...	2.57	2	2	0	0	0	7	4	2	2	2	8
1987	—California (A.L.)	8	6	.571	4.71	20	20	0	0	0	116⅔	127	70	61	20	74
	—New York (N.L.)■	2	0	1.000	5.84	3	3	0	0	0	12⅓	17	8	8	3	10
1988	—New York (A.L.)	13	7	.650	3.38	25	24	6	2	1	157	150	69	59	23	121
1989	—New York (A.L.)	3	3	.500	5.14	10	6	1	0	0	49	49	28	28	12	37
	—GC Yankees (GCL)	1	0	1.000	0.00	2	2	0	0	0	8	6	0	0	1	12
	—Montreal (N.L.)■	0	2	.000	3.31	12	0	0	0	0	16⅓	17	8	6	4	14

Year	Team (League)	W	L	Pct.	ERA	G	GS	CG	ShO	Sv.	IP	H	R	ER	BB	SO
1990	—Minn.-Tor. (A.L.)■	7	6	.538	3.95	47	3	0	0	5	79⅔	87	36	35	20	63
1991	—Los Angeles (N.L.)■	1	1	.500	3.74	59	0	0	0	2	33⅔	31	16	14	11	38
1992	—Los Angeles (N.L.)	2	5	.286	2.84	50	0	0	0	5	25⅓	20	9	8	13	23
1993	—Pittsburgh (N.L.)■	0	3	.000	8.24	24	0	0	0	1	19⅔	25	19	18	9	17
	A.L. totals (6 years)	48	27	.640	3.81	131	82	9	4	6	565	551	266	239	125	429
	N.L. totals (16 years)	129	95	.576	3.19	469	274	45	9	23	1961⅓	1848	772	696	467	1244
	Major league totals (19 years)	177	122	.592	3.33	600	356	54	13	29	2526⅓	2399	1038	935	592	1673

CHAMPIONSHIP SERIES RECORD

CHAMPIONSHIP SERIES NOTES: Shares single-game records for most strikeouts—14; most consecutive strikeouts—4 (October 7, 1975).

Year	Team (League)	W	L	Pct.	ERA	G	GS	CG	ShO	Sv.	IP	H	R	ER	BB	SO
1975	—Pittsburgh (N.L.)	0	0	...	3.52	1	1	0	0	0	7⅔	3	3	3	2	14
1979	—Pittsburgh (N.L.)	0	0	...	2.57	1	1	0	0	0	7	5	2	2	1	4
1986	—California (A.L.)	1	1	.500	0.84	2	2	0	0	0	10⅔	11	8	1	6	7
	Champ. series totals (3 years)	1	1	.500	2.13	4	4	0	0	0	25⅓	19	13	6	9	25

WORLD SERIES RECORD

Year	Team (League)	W	L	Pct.	ERA	G	GS	CG	ShO	Sv.	IP	H	R	ER	BB	SO
1979	—Pittsburgh (N.L.)	1	1	.500	5.00	2	2	0	0	0	9	14	6	5	2	4

ALL-STAR GAME RECORD

Year	League	W	L	Pct.	ERA	GS	CG	ShO	Sv.	IP	H	R	ER	BB	SO
1977	—National						Did not play.								

C

CANDIOTTI, TOM

P, DODGERS

PERSONAL: Born August 31, 1957, in Walnut Creek, Calif. . . . 6-2/215. . . . Throws right, bats right. . . . Full name: Thomas Caesar Candiotti. . . . Name pronounced KAN-dee-AH-tee.

HIGH SCHOOL: St. Mary's (Calif.).

COLLEGE: St. Mary's, Calif. (bachelor of science degree in business administration, 1979).

TRANSACTIONS/CAREER NOTES: Signed as free agent by Victoria, independent (July 17, 1979). . . . Released by Victoria (January 4, 1980). . . . Signed by Ft. Myers, Kansas City Royals organization (January 5, 1980). . . . On Jacksonville disabled list (June 7-26, 1980). . . . Selected by Vancouver, Milwaukee Brewers organization, from Royals organization in Rule 5 minor league draft (December 9, 1980). . . . On disabled list (April 10-May 12, 1981 and April 13, 1982-remainder of season). . . . On Vancouver disabled list (May 30-June 15, 1984). . . . On Milwaukee disabled list (August 2-September 1, 1984); included rehabilitation assignment to Beloit (August 24-31). . . . Granted free agency (October 15, 1985). . . . Signed by Cleveland Indians (December 12, 1985). . . . On disabled list (August 4-19, 1988; July 2-17, 1989; and May 7-22, 1990). . . . Traded by Indians with OF Turner Ward to Toronto Blue Jays for P Denis Boucher, OF Glenallen Hill, OF Mark Whiten and a player to be named later (June 27, 1991); Indians acquired cash instead of player to complete deal (October 15, 1991). . . . Granted free agency (November 7, 1991). . . . Signed by Los Angeles Dodgers (December 3, 1991). . . . On disabled list (August 9-24, 1992).

Year	Team (League)	W	L	Pct.	ERA	G	GS	CG	ShO	Sv.	IP	H	R	ER	BB	SO
1979	—Victoria (N'west)	5	1	.833	2.44	12	9	3	0	1	70	63	23	19	16	66
1980	—Fort Myers (FSL)■	3	2	.600	2.25	7	5	3	0	0	44	32	16	11	9	31
	—Jacksonv. (South.)	7	8	.467	2.77	17	17	8	2	0	117	98	45	36	40	93
1981	—El Paso (Texas)■	7	6	.538	2.80	21	14	6	1	0	119	137	51	37	27	68
1982	—							Did not play.								
1983	—El Paso (Texas)	1	0	1.000	2.92	7	0	0	0	2	24⅔	23	10	8	7	18
	—Vancouver (PCL)	6	4	.600	2.81	15	14	5	2	0	99⅓	87	35	31	16	61
	—Milwaukee (A.L.)	4	4	.500	3.23	10	8	2	1	0	55⅔	62	21	20	16	21
1984	—Vancouver (PCL)	8	4	.667	2.89	15	15	4	0	0	96⅔	96	36	31	22	53
	—Milwaukee (A.L.)	2	2	.500	5.29	8	6	0	0	0	32⅓	38	21	19	10	23
	—Beloit (Midwest)	0	1	.000	2.70	2	2	0	0	0	10	12	5	3	5	12
1985	—El Paso (Texas)	1	0	1.000	2.76	4	4	2	1	0	29⅓	29	11	9	7	16
	—Vancouver (PCL)	9	13	.409	3.94	24	24	0	0	0	150⅔	178	83	66	36	97
1986	—Cleveland (A.L.)■	16	12	.571	3.57	36	34	*17	3	0	252⅓	234	112	100	106	167
1987	—Cleveland (A.L.)	7	18	.280	4.78	32	32	7	2	0	201⅔	193	132	107	93	111
1988	—Cleveland (A.L.)	14	8	.636	3.28	31	31	11	1	0	216⅔	225	86	79	53	137
1989	—Cleveland (A.L.)	13	10	.565	3.10	31	31	4	0	0	206	188	80	71	55	124
1990	—Cleveland (A.L.)	15	11	.577	3.65	31	29	3	1	0	202	207	92	82	55	128
1991	—Clev.-Tor. (A.L.)■	13	13	.500	2.65	34	34	6	0	0	238	202	82	70	73	167
1992	—Los Angeles (N.L.)■	11	•15	.423	3.00	32	30	6	2	0	203⅔	177	78	68	63	152
1993	—Los Angeles (N.L.)	8	10	.444	3.12	33	32	2	0	0	213⅔	192	86	74	71	155
	A.L. totals (8 years)	84	78	.519	3.51	213	205	50	8	0	1404⅔	1349	626	548	461	878
	N.L. totals (2 years)	19	25	.432	3.06	65	62	8	2	0	417⅓	369	164	142	134	307
	Major league totals (10 years)	103	103	.500	3.41	278	267	58	10	0	1822	1718	790	690	595	1185

CHAMPIONSHIP SERIES RECORD

Year	Team (League)	W	L	Pct.	ERA	G	GS	CG	ShO	Sv.	IP	H	R	ER	BB	SO
1991	—Toronto (A.L.)	0	1	.000	8.22	2	2	0	0	0	7⅔	17	9	7	2	5

CANSECO, JOSE

OF, RANGERS

PERSONAL: Born July 2, 1964, in Havana, Cuba. . . . 6-4/240. . . . Throws right, bats right. . . . Identical twin of Ozzie Canseco, outfielder, Milwaukee Brewers organization. . . . Name pronounced can-SAY-co.

HIGH SCHOOL: Miami Coral Park Senior.

TRANSACTIONS/CAREER NOTES: Selected by Oakland Athletics organization in 15th round of free-agent draft (June 7, 1982). . . . On Huntsville disabled list (May 14-June 3, 1985). . . . On Oakland disabled list (March 23-July 13, 1989); included rehabilitation assign-

ment to Huntsville (May 6 and June 28-July 13).... On disabled list (June 8-23, 1990 and July 1-16, 1992).... Traded by A's to Texas Rangers for OF Ruben Sierra, P Jeff Russell, P Bobby Witt and cash (August 31, 1992).... On disabled list (June 24, 1993-remainder of season).
RECORDS: Shares major league single-season record for most consecutive bases on balls received—7 (August 4-5, 1992).... Shares A.L. single-season record for fewest errors by outfielder who led league in errors—9 (1991).
HONORS: Named Minor League Player of the Year by THE SPORTING NEWS (1985).... Named Southern League Most Valuable Player (1985).... Named A.L. Rookie Player of the Year by THE SPORTING NEWS (1986).... Named A.L. Rookie of the Year by Baseball Writers' Association of America (1986).... Named A.L. Player of the Year by THE SPORTING NEWS (1988).... Named outfielder on THE SPORTING NEWS A.L. All-Star team (1988 and 1990-91).... Named outfielder on THE SPORTING NEWS A.L. Silver Slugger team (1988 and 1990-91).... Named A.L. Most Valuable Player by Baseball Writers' Association of America (1988).
STATISTICAL NOTES: Led California League outfielders with eight double plays in 1984.... Hit three home runs in one game (July 3, 1988).... Led A.L. with .569 slugging percentage in 1988.

			BATTING											FIELDING			
Year	Team (League)	Pos.	G	AB	R	H	2B	3B	HR	RBI	Avg.	BB	SO	SB	PO	A	E	Avg.
1982	—Miami (Florida St.)	3B	6	9	0	1	0	0	0	0	.111	1	3	0	3	1	1	.800
	—Idaho Falls (Pio.)	3B-OF	28	57	13	15	3	0	2	7	.263	9	13	3	6	17	3	.885
1983	—Madison (Midwest)	OF	34	88	8	14	4	0	3	10	.159	10	36	2	23	2	1	.962
	—Medford (N'west)	OF	59	197	34	53	15	2	11	40	.269	30	*78	6	46	5	5	.911
1984	—Modesto (Calif.)	OF	116	410	61	113	21	2	15	73	.276	74	127	10	216	17	9	.963
1985	—Huntsville (South.)	OF	58	211	47	67	10	2	25	80	.318	30	55	6	117	9	7	.947
	—Tacoma (PCL)	OF	60	233	41	81	16	1	11	47	.348	40	66	5	81	7	2	.978
	—Oakland (A.L.)	OF	29	96	16	29	3	0	5	13	.302	4	31	1	56	2	3	.951
1986	—Oakland (A.L.)	OF	157	600	85	144	29	1	33	117	.240	65	175	15	319	4	•14	.958
1987	—Oakland (A.L.)	OF	159	630	81	162	35	3	31	113	.257	50	157	15	263	12	7	.975
1988	—Oakland (A.L.)	OF	158	610	120	187	34	0	*42	*124	.307	78	128	40	304	11	7	.978
1989	—Huntsville (South.)	OF	9	29	2	6	0	0	0	3	.207	5	11	1	9	0	0	1.000
	—Oakland (A.L.)	OF	65	227	40	61	9	1	17	57	.269	23	69	6	119	5	3	.976
1990	—Oakland (A.L.)	OF	131	481	83	132	14	2	37	101	.274	72	158	19	182	7	1	.995
1991	—Oakland (A.L.)	OF	154	572	115	152	32	1	•44	122	.266	78	152	26	245	5	•9	.965
1992	—Oak.-Texas (A.L.)■	OF	119	439	74	107	15	0	26	87	.244	63	128	6	195	5	3	.985
1993	—Texas (A.L.)	OF-P	60	231	30	59	14	1	10	46	.255	16	62	6	94	4	3	.970
Major league totals (9 years)			1032	3886	644	1033	185	9	245	780	.266	449	1060	134	1777	55	50	.973

CHAMPIONSHIP SERIES RECORD

CHAMPIONSHIP SERIES NOTES: Shares A.L. single-series record for most home runs—3 (1988).

			BATTING											FIELDING			
Year	Team (League)	Pos.	G	AB	R	H	2B	3B	HR	RBI	Avg.	BB	SO	SB	PO	A	E	Avg.
1988	—Oakland (A.L.)	OF	4	16	4	5	1	0	3	4	.313	1	2	1	6	0	0	1.000
1989	—Oakland (A.L.)	OF-PH	5	17	1	5	0	0	1	3	.294	3	7	0	6	1	1	.875
1990	—Oakland (A.L.)	OF	4	11	3	2	0	0	0	1	.182	5	5	2	14	0	0	1.000
Championship series totals (3 years)			13	44	8	12	1	0	4	8	.273	9	14	3	26	1	1	.964

WORLD SERIES RECORD

WORLD SERIES NOTES: Hit home run in first at-bat (October 15, 1988).... Shares single-game record for most grand slams—1 (October 15, 1988).... Shares record for most runs batted in in one inning—4 (October 15, 1988, second inning).

			BATTING											FIELDING			
Year	Team (League)	Pos.	G	AB	R	H	2B	3B	HR	RBI	Avg.	BB	SO	SB	PO	A	E	Avg.
1988	—Oakland (A.L.)	OF	5	19	1	1	0	0	1	5	.053	2	4	1	8	0	0	1.000
1989	—Oakland (A.L.)	OF	4	14	5	5	0	0	1	3	.357	4	3	1	6	0	0	1.000
1990	—Oakland (A.L.)	OF-PH-DH	4	12	1	1	0	0	1	2	.083	2	3	0	4	0	0	1.000
World Series totals (3 years)			13	45	7	7	0	0	3	10	.156	8	10	2	18	0	0	1.000

ALL-STAR GAME RECORD

			BATTING										FIELDING			
Year	League	Pos.	AB	R	H	2B	3B	HR	RBI	Avg.	BB	SO	SB	PO	A	E	Avg.
1986	—American								Did not play.								
1988	—American	OF	4	0	0	0	0	0	0	.000	0	1	0	3	0	0	1.000
1989	—American						Selected, did not play—injured.										
1990	—American	OF	4	0	0	0	0	0	0	.000	1	1	1	1	0	0	1.000
1992	—American						Selected, did not play—injured.										
All-Star Game totals (2 years)			8	0	0	0	0	0	0	.000	1	2	1	4	0	0	1.000

RECORD AS PITCHER

Year	Team (League)	W	L	Pct.	ERA	G	GS	CG	ShO	Sv.	IP	H	R	ER	BB	SO
1993	—Texas (A.L.)	0	0	...	27.00	1	0	0	0	0	1	2	3	3	3	0

CANSECO, OZZIE

OF, BREWERS

PERSONAL: Born July 2, 1964, in Havana, Cuba. ... 6-3/220. ... Throws right, bats right. ... Full name: Osvaldo Capas Canseco.... Identical twin of Jose Canseco, outfielder, Texas Rangers.... Name pronounced can-SAY-co.
HIGH SCHOOL: Miami Coral Park Senior.
COLLEGE: Miami-Dade (South) Community College.
TRANSACTIONS/CAREER NOTES: Selected by New York Yankees organization in second round of free-agent draft (January 11, 1983).... On Greensboro temporary inactive list (April 18-May 14 and June 2-6, 1984).... Released by Yankees organization (July 4, 1986).... Signed by Oakland Athletics organization (July 10, 1986).... On Oakland disabled list (March 19-April 27, 1989).... Released by A's (December 20, 1990).... Signed by Kintetsu Buffaloes of Japan Pacific League (February 1991); played with Kintetsu, western league farm team of Kintetsu Buffaloes.... Left Kintetsu club (July 9, 1991).... Signed by Louisville, St. Louis Cardinals organization (January 15, 1992).... On Louisville disabled list (May 12-30, 1992).... On Louisville disqualified list (June 12-December 14, 1993)....

Traded by Cardinals organization to Milwaukee Brewers organization for OF Tony Diggs (December 14, 1993).
MISCELLANEOUS: Played only with junior team of Kintetsu Buffaloes (1991).

			BATTING												FIELDING			
Year	Team (League)	Pos.	G	AB	R	H	2B	3B	HR	RBI	Avg.	BB	SO	SB	PO	A	E	Avg.
1984	—Greensboro (S. Atl.)	P-OF	8	1	1	0	0	0	0	0	.000	0	0	0	3	1	2	.667
1985	—GC Yankees (GCL)	P-OF	20	39	2	7	0	1	1	5	.179	2	18	0	4	15	4	.826
1986	—GC Yankees (GCL)	OF	7	15	3	2	1	0	1	3	.133	5	9	0	4	0	1	.800
	—Madison (Midwest)■	OF-P-1B	42	128	17	20	1	1	3	17	.156	22	47	1	72	1	2	.973
1987	—Madison (Midwest)	OF	92	309	64	82	12	4	11	54	.265	67	104	6	131	6	13	.913
1988	—Madison (Midwest)	OF	99	359	63	98	17	7	12	68	.273	49	84	15	187	9	5	.975
	—Huntsville (South.)	OF	27	99	6	22	7	0	3	12	.222	6	31	3	29	0	1	.967
1989	—Huntsville (South.)	OF-P	91	317	52	74	17	2	12	52	.233	51	88	1	148	8	4	.975
1990	—Huntsville (South.)	OF	97	325	50	73	21	0	20	67	.225	47	103	2	157	5	8	.953
	—Oakland (A.L.)	OF	9	19	1	2	1	0	0	1	.105	1	10	0	3	0	0	1.000
1991	—Kintetsu (Japan)■	...	38	112	...	31	...	...	8	27	.277	...	...	...	...	...	...	...
1992	—Louisville (A.A.)■	OF-1B	98	308	53	82	19	1	22	57	.266	43	96	1	116	13	5	.963
	—St. Louis (N.L.)	OF	9	29	7	8	5	0	0	3	.276	7	4	0	8	0	1	.889
1993	—Louisville (A.A.)	OF-1B	44	154	20	37	6	1	13	33	.240	15	59	1	113	9	3	.976
	—St. Louis (N.L.)	OF	6	17	0	3	0	0	0	0	.176	1	3	0	1	0	1	.500
American League totals (1 year)			9	19	1	2	1	0	0	1	.105	1	10	0	3	0	0	1.000
National League totals (2 years)			15	46	7	11	5	0	0	3	.239	8	7	0	9	0	2	.818
Major league totals (3 years)			24	65	8	13	6	0	0	4	.200	9	17	0	12	0	2	.857

RECORD AS PITCHER

Year	Team (League)	W	L	Pct.	ERA	G	GS	CG	ShO	Sv.	IP	H	R	ER	BB	SO
1983	—Greensboro (S. Atl.)	3	6	.333	5.05	27	13	1	1	0	87⅓	98	62	49	49	59
1984	—Greensboro (S. Atl.)	1	1	.500	4.86	6	2	0	0	0	16⅔	19	13	9	22	9
	—Oneonta (NYP)	1	6	.143	3.53	14	4	1	1	0	43⅓	44	29	17	21	40
1985	—Fort Lauder. (FSL)	5	4	.556	3.61	11	11	1	0	0	57⅓	42	33	23	42	37
	—GC Yankees (GCL)	3	2	.600	1.57	9	7	1	0	0	51⅔	43	19	9	11	39
1986	—Madison (Midwest)	1	0	1.000	0.00	2	0	0	0	0	4	2	0	0	2	3
1989	—Huntsville (South.)	0	0	...	7.20	3	0	0	0	0	5	5	4	4	1	1

CARABALLO, GARY

3B, ROYALS

PERSONAL: Born July 11, 1971, in Brooklyn, N.Y.... 5-11/205.... Throws right, bats right.
HIGH SCHOOL: Luis Monoz Marin (Yauco, Puerto Rico).
TRANSACTIONS/CAREER NOTES: Selected by Kansas City Royals organization in 12th round of free-agent draft (June 5, 1989).... On disabled list (May 25-June 7 and June 10-August 27, 1993).

			BATTING												FIELDING			
Year	Team (League)	Pos.	G	AB	R	H	2B	3B	HR	RBI	Avg.	BB	SO	SB	PO	A	E	Avg.
1989	—GC Royals (GCL)	3B	46	160	18	38	6	0	1	25	.238	16	18	4	31	80	11	.910
	—Baseball City (FSL)	3B	3	9	0	3	0	0	0	0	.333	0	2	0	1	2	0	1.000
1990	—Appleton (Midw.)	3B	123	406	37	87	14	3	6	50	.214	39	62	6	80	230	36	.896
1991	—Appleton (Midw.)	3B	79	275	39	69	16	1	2	44	.251	34	33	13	63	187	14	.947
	—Baseball City (FSL)	3B	50	179	28	40	9	3	3	24	.223	22	32	4	43	105	13	.919
1992	—Baseball City (FSL)	3B-SS	67	239	30	69	9	4	4	40	.289	24	43	6	53	153	20	.912
	—Memphis (South.)	3B-SS	58	195	17	41	6	2	3	17	.210	7	37	1	48	106	5	.969
1993	—Wilmington (Caro.)	3B	39	145	20	44	8	3	2	26	.303	20	25	3	36	61	13	.882

CARABALLO, RAMON

2B, BRAVES

PERSONAL: Born May 23, 1969, in Rio San Juan, Dominican Republic.... 5-7/150.... Throws right, bats both.... Name pronounced CAR-uh-BY-oh.
HIGH SCHOOL: Liceo Antorcha del Futero (Dominican Republic).
TRANSACTIONS/CAREER NOTES: Signed as free agent by Atlanta Braves organization (April 10, 1988).
STATISTICAL NOTES: Led Carolina League in caught stealing with 23 in 1991.... Led International League in caught stealing with 16 in 1992.

			BATTING												FIELDING			
Year	Team (League)	Pos.	G	AB	R	H	2B	3B	HR	RBI	Avg.	BB	SO	SB	PO	A	E	Avg.
1989	—GC Braves (GCL)	SS-OF-2B	20	77	9	19	3	1	1	10	.247	10	14	5	39	47	6	.935
	—Sumter (S. Atl.)	SS	45	171	22	45	10	5	1	32	.263	16	38	9	57	151	18	.920
1990	—Burlington (Midw.)	SS	102	390	83	113	18	★14	7	55	.290	49	68	41	139	280	35	.923
1991	—Durham (Carolina)	2B	120	444	73	111	13	8	6	52	.250	38	91	★53	217	341	★28	.952
1992	—Greenville (South.)	2B	24	93	15	29	4	4	1	8	.312	14	13	10	32	74	6	.946
	—Richmond (Int'l)	2B	101	405	42	114	20	3	2	40	.281	22	60	19	217	284	14	★.973
1993	—Richmond (Int'l)	2B-OF	126	470	73	128	25	9	3	41	.272	30	81	20	211	345	23	.960
	—Atlanta (N.L.)	2B	6	0	0	0	0	0	0	0	...	0	0	0	4	3	0	1.000
Major league totals (1 year)			6	0	0	0	0	0	0	0	...	0	0	0	4	3	0	1.000

CAREY, PAUL

1B, ORIOLES

PERSONAL: Born January 8, 1968, in Boston.... 6-4/215.... Throws right, bats left.... Full name: Paul Stephen Carey.... Brother of Jim Carey, goaltender, Washington Capitals organization of National Hockey League.
HIGH SCHOOL: Boston College.
COLLEGE: Stanford.
TRANSACTIONS/CAREER NOTES: Selected by Seattle Mariners organization in 27th round of free-agent draft (June 2, 1986).... Selected by Detroit Tigers organization in fourth round of free-agent draft (June 5, 1989).... Selected by Miami (independent, Florida State League) in fourth round of free-agent draft (June 4, 1990).... Contract sold by Miami to Baltimore Orioles orga-

nization (March 18, 1991).
STATISTICAL NOTES: Tied for Eastern League lead with eight intentional bases on balls received in 1991. . . . Led Eastern League outfielders with four double plays in 1991. . . . Led International League with 11 intentional bases on balls received in 1993.

			BATTING												FIELDING			
Year	**Team (League)**	**Pos.**	**G**	**AB**	**R**	**H**	**2B**	**3B**	**HR**	**RBI**	**Avg.**	**BB**	**SO**	**SB**	**PO**	**A**	**E**	**Avg.**
1990	—Miami (Florida St.)	OF-1B	49	153	23	50	5	3	4	20	.327	43	39	4	70	7	3	.963
1991	—Hagerstown (East.)■	OF	114	373	63	94	29	1	12	65	.252	68	109	5	163	10	7	.961
1992	—Frederick (Caro.)	DH	41	136	24	41	6	0	9	26	.301	28	22	0	...	...	...	...
	—Rochester (Int'l)	1B	30	87	9	20	4	1	1	7	.230	6	16	0	72	4	1	.987
	—Hagerstown (East.)	1B	48	163	17	44	8	0	4	18	.270	15	37	3	250	23	6	.978
1993	—Rochester (Int'l)	1B	96	325	63	101	20	4	12	50	.311	65	92	0	752	53	6	.993
	—Baltimore (A.L.)	1B	18	47	1	10	1	0	0	3	.213	5	14	0	64	1	2	.970
	Major league totals (1 year)		18	47	1	10	1	0	0	3	.213	5	14	0	64	1	2	.970

CARIDAD, RON
P, TWINS

PERSONAL: Born March 22, 1972, in Caracas, Venezuela. . . . 5-10/181. . . . Throws right, bats right. . . . Full name: Ronald Jose Caridad. . . . Name pronounced CARE-uh-DAD.
HIGH SCHOOL: Westminister Christian (Miami).
TRANSACTIONS/CAREER NOTES: Selected by Minnesota Twins organization in second round of free-agent draft (June 4, 1990); pick received as part of compensation for Boston Red Sox signing Type A free agent Jeff Reardon.

Year	**Team (League)**	**W**	**L**	**Pct.**	**ERA**	**G**	**GS**	**CG**	**ShO**	**Sv.**	**IP**	**H**	**R**	**ER**	**BB**	**SO**
1990	—GC Twins (GCL)	0	0	...	7.71	5	1	0	0	0	7	5	6	6	8	2
1991	—Elizabeth. (Appal.)	0	4	.000	4.87	6	6	0	0	0	20⅓	24	19	11	13	17
1992	—Elizabeth. (Appal.)	5	3	.625	4.08	12	11	0	0	0	64	56	35	29	35	53
1993	—Fort Wayne (Mid.)	6	8	.429	3.51	27	27	0	0	0	143⅔	138	68	56	91	124

CARLSON, DAN
P, GIANTS

PERSONAL: Born January 26, 1970, in Portland, Ore. . . . 6-1/185. . . . Throws right, bats right. . . . Full name: Dan Scott Carlson.
HIGH SCHOOL: Reynolds (Troutdale, Ore.).
COLLEGE: Mt. Hood Community College (Ore.).
TRANSACTIONS/CAREER NOTES: Selected by San Francisco Giants organization in 33rd round of free-agent draft (June 5, 1989).
STATISTICAL NOTES: Tied for Texas League lead with 15 home runs allowed in 1992.

Year	**Team (League)**	**W**	**L**	**Pct.**	**ERA**	**G**	**GS**	**CG**	**ShO**	**Sv.**	**IP**	**H**	**R**	**ER**	**BB**	**SO**
1990	—Everett (N'west)	2	6	.250	5.34	17	11	0	0	0	62⅓	60	42	37	33	77
1991	—Clinton (Midwest)	•16	7	.696	3.08	27	27	5	3	0	181⅓	149	69	62	76	164
1992	—Shreveport (Texas)	*15	9	.625	3.19	27	•27	4	1	0	*186	166	85	66	60	*157
1993	—Phoenix (PCL)	5	6	.455	6.56	13	12	0	0	0	70	79	54	51	32	48
	—Shreveport (Texas)	7	4	.636	2.24	15	15	2	1	0	100⅓	86	30	25	26	81

CARPENTER, CRIS
P, RANGERS

PERSONAL: Born April 5, 1965, in St. Augustine, Fla. . . . 6-1/185. . . . Throws right, bats right. . . . Full name: Cris Howell Carpenter.
HIGH SCHOOL: Gainesville (Fla.).
COLLEGE: Georgia.
TRANSACTIONS/CAREER NOTES: Selected by Toronto Blue Jays organization in seventh round of free-agent draft (June 2, 1986). . . . Selected by St. Louis Cardinals organization in first round (14th pick overall) of free-agent draft (June 2, 1987). . . . Selected by Florida Marlins in second round (37th pick overall) of expansion draft (November 17, 1992). . . . Traded by Marlins to Texas Rangers for P Robb Nen and P Kurt Miller (July 17, 1993).

Year	**Team (League)**	**W**	**L**	**Pct.**	**ERA**	**G**	**GS**	**CG**	**ShO**	**Sv.**	**IP**	**H**	**R**	**ER**	**BB**	**SO**
1988	—Louisville (A.A.)	6	2	.750	2.87	13	13	1	1	0	87⅔	81	28	28	26	45
	—St. Louis (N.L.)	2	3	.400	4.72	8	8	1	0	0	47⅔	56	27	25	9	24
1989	—St. Louis (N.L.)	4	4	.500	3.18	36	5	0	0	0	68	70	30	24	26	35
	—Louisville (A.A.)	5	3	.625	3.19	27	0	0	0	11	36⅔	39	17	13	9	29
1990	—St. Louis (N.L.)	0	0	...	4.50	4	0	0	0	0	8	5	4	4	2	6
	—Louisville (A.A.)	10	8	.556	3.70	22	22	2	1	0	143⅓	146	61	59	21	100
1991	—St. Louis (N.L.)	10	4	.714	4.23	59	0	0	0	0	66	53	31	31	20	47
1992	—St. Louis (N.L.)	5	4	.556	2.97	73	0	0	0	1	88	69	29	29	27	46
1993	—Florida (N.L.)■	0	1	.000	2.89	29	0	0	0	0	37⅓	29	15	12	13	26
	—Texas (A.L.)■	4	1	.800	4.22	27	0	0	0	1	32	35	15	15	12	27
	A.L. totals (1 year)	4	1	.800	4.22	27	0	0	0	1	32	35	15	15	12	27
	N.L. totals (6 years)	21	16	.568	3.57	209	13	1	0	1	315	282	136	125	97	184
	Major league totals (6 years)	25	17	.595	3.63	236	13	1	0	2	347	317	151	140	109	211

CARR, CHUCK
OF, MARLINS

PERSONAL: Born August 10, 1968, in San Bernardino, Calif. . . . 5-10/165. . . . Throws right, bats both. . . . Full name: Charles Lee Glenn Carr Jr.
HIGH SCHOOL: Fontana (Calif.).
TRANSACTIONS/CAREER NOTES: Selected by Cincinnati Reds organization in ninth round of free-agent draft (June 2, 1986). . . . Released by Reds organization (March 1987). . . . Signed by Bellingham, Seattle Mariners organization (June 15, 1987). . . . Traded by Mariners organization to New York Mets organization for P Reggie Dobie (November 18, 1988). . . . On Tidewater disabled list (April 10-17 and July 15-August 9, 1991). . . . On New York disabled list (August 29-September 13, 1991). . . . Traded by Mets to St. Louis Cardinals for P Clyde Keller (December 13, 1991). . . . On Louisville disabled list (July 31-August 7, 1992). . . . Selected by Florida Marlins in first round (14th pick overall) of expansion draft (November 17, 1992). . . . On Florida disabled list (July 1-18, 1993); included rehabilitation assignment to Gulf Coast Marlins (July 11-14).
STATISTICAL NOTES: Led N.L. in caught stealing with 22 in 1993.

Year	Team (League)	Pos.	BATTING G	AB	R	H	2B	3B	HR	RBI	Avg.	BB	SO	SB	FIELDING PO	A	E	Avg.
1986	—GC Reds (GCL)	2B	44	123	13	21	5	0	0	10	.171	10	27	9	75	100	11	.941
1987	—Belling. (N'west)■	S-0-2-3	44	165	31	40	1	1	1	11	.242	12	38	20	50	58	14	.885
1988	—Wausau (Midwest)	OF-SS	82	304	58	91	14	2	6	30	.299	14	49	41	170	17	12	.940
	—Vermont (Eastern)	OF	41	159	26	39	4	2	1	13	.245	8	33	21	105	6	6	.949
1989	—Jackson (Texas)■	OF	116	444	45	107	13	1	0	22	.241	27	66	47	280	11	8	.973
1990	—Jackson (Texas)	OF	93	361	60	93	19	9	3	24	.258	43	77	48	226	12	8	.967
	—Tidewater (Int'l)	OF	20	81	13	21	5	1	0	8	.259	4	12	6	40	3	0	1.000
	—New York (N.L.)	OF	4	2	0	0	0	0	0	0	.000	0	2	1	0	0	0	...
1991	—Tidewater (Int'l)	OF	64	246	34	48	6	1	1	11	.195	18	37	27	141	8	6	.961
	—New York (N.L.)	OF	12	11	1	2	0	0	0	1	.182	0	2	1	9	0	0	1.000
1992	—Arkansas (Texas)■	OF	28	111	17	29	5	1	1	6	.261	8	23	8	70	3	1	.986
	—Louisville (A.A.)	OF	96	377	68	116	11	9	3	28	.308	31	60	*53	244	9	5	.981
	—St. Louis (N.L.)	OF	22	64	8	14	3	0	0	3	.219	9	6	10	39	1	0	1.000
1993	—Florida (N.L.)■	OF	142	551	75	147	19	2	4	41	.267	49	74	*58	393	7	6	.985
	—GC Marlins (GCL)	OF	3	12	4	5	1	0	1	3	.417	0	2	3	9	0	1	.900
Major league totals (4 years)			180	628	84	163	22	2	4	45	.260	58	84	70	441	8	6	.987

CARRASCO, HECTOR

P, REDS

PERSONAL: Born October 22, 1969, in San Pedro de Macoris, Dominican Republic. . . . 6-2/175. . . . Throws right, bats right. . . . Full name: Hector Pacheco Pipo Carrasco.

HIGH SCHOOL: Liceo Mattias Mella (San Pedro de Macoris, Dominican Republic).

TRANSACTIONS/CAREER NOTES: Signed as free agent by New York Mets organization (March 20, 1988). . . . Released by Mets organization (January 6, 1992). . . . Signed by Houston Astros organization (January 21, 1992). . . . Traded by Astros organization with P Brian Griffiths to Florida Marlins organization for P Tom Edens (November 17, 1992). . . . Traded by Marlins to Cincinnati Reds (September 10, 1993), completing deal in which Reds traded P Chris Hammond to Marlins for 3B Gary Scott and a player to be named later (March 27, 1993).

Year	Team (League)	W	L	Pct.	ERA	G	GS	CG	ShO	Sv.	IP	H	R	ER	BB	SO
1988	—GC Mets (GCL)	0	2	.000	4.17	14	2	0	0	0	36⅔	37	29	17	13	21
1989	—Kingsport (Appal.)	1	6	.143	5.74	12	10	0	0	0	53⅓	69	49	34	34	55
1990	—Kingsport (Appal.)	0	0	...	4.05	3	1	0	0	0	6⅔	8	3	3	1	5
1991	—Pittsfield (NYP)	0	1	.000	5.40	12	1	0	0	1	23⅓	25	17	14	21	20
1992	—Asheville (S. Atl.)■	5	5	.500	2.99	49	0	0	0	8	78⅓	66	30	26	47	67
1993	—Kane Co. (Midw.)■	6	12	.333	4.11	28	*28	0	0	0	149	153	90	68	76	127

CARREON, MARK

OF, GIANTS

PERSONAL: Born July 9, 1963, in Chicago. . . . 6-0/195. . . . Throws left, bats right. . . . Full name: Mark Steven Carreon. . . . Son of Camilo Carreon, catcher, Chicago White Sox, Cleveland Indians and Baltimore Orioles (1959-66). . . . Name pronounced CARE-ee-on.

HIGH SCHOOL: Salpointe (Tucson, Ariz.).

TRANSACTIONS/CAREER NOTES: Selected by New York Mets organization in eighth round of free-agent draft (June 8, 1981). . . . On New York disabled list (March 28-April 24, 1989); included rehabilitation assignment to Tidewater (April 5-24). . . . On disabled list (August 21, 1990-remainder of season). . . . Traded by Mets with P Tony Castillo to Detroit Tigers for P Paul Gibson and P Randy Marshall (January 22, 1992). . . . On Detroit disabled list (June 10-28, 1992). . . . Granted free agency (December 19, 1992). . . . Signed by San Francisco Giants organization (January 13, 1993).

STATISTICAL NOTES: Led Carolina League with 11 sacrifice flies in 1983.

Year	Team (League)	Pos.	BATTING G	AB	R	H	2B	3B	HR	RBI	Avg.	BB	SO	SB	FIELDING PO	A	E	Avg.
1981	—Kingsport (Appal.)	OF-C	64	232	30	67	8	0	1	36	.289	24	13	12	101	7	4	.964
1982	—Shelby (S. Atl.)	OF	133	486	*120	160	29	6	2	79	.329	78	37	33	183	8	5	.974
1983	—Lynchburg (Caro.)	OF	128	491	94	164	13	8	1	67	.334	76	39	36	173	8	14	.928
1984	—Jackson (Texas)	OF	119	435	64	122	14	3	1	43	.280	38	24	12	146	1	4	.974
1985	—Tidewater (Int'l)	OF	7	15	1	2	1	0	1	2	.133	2	5	0	2	0	0	1.000
	—Jackson (Texas)	OF	123	447	96	140	23	5	6	51	.313	87	32	23	201	8	1	.995
1986	—Tidewater (Int'l)	OF	115	426	62	123	23	2	10	64	.289	50	42	11	192	6	6	.971
1987	—Tidewater (Int'l)	OF	133	525	83	164	*41	5	10	89	.312	34	46	31	237	8	5	.980
	—New York (N.L.)	OF	9	12	0	3	0	0	0	1	.250	1	1	0	4	0	1	.800
1988	—Tidewater (Int'l)	OF	102	365	48	96	13	3	14	55	.263	40	53	11	111	6	2	.983
	—New York (N.L.)	OF	7	9	5	5	2	0	1	1	.556	2	1	0	1	0	0	1.000
1989	—Tidewater (Int'l)	OF-1B	32	122	22	34	4	0	1	21	.279	13	20	8	26	0	0	1.000
	—New York (N.L.)	OF	68	133	20	41	6	0	6	16	.308	12	17	2	57	0	1	.983
1990	—New York (N.L.)	OF	82	188	30	47	12	0	10	26	.250	15	29	1	87	1	0	1.000
1991	—New York (N.L.)	OF	106	254	18	66	6	0	4	21	.260	12	26	2	96	4	3	.971
1992	—Detroit (A.L.)■	OF	101	336	34	78	11	1	10	41	.232	22	57	3	178	5	4	.979
1993	—San Francisco (N.L.)■	OF-1B	78	150	22	49	9	1	7	33	.327	13	16	1	54	4	3	.951
American League totals (1 year)			101	336	34	78	11	1	10	41	.232	22	57	3	178	5	4	.979
National League totals (6 years)			350	746	95	211	35	1	28	98	.283	55	90	6	299	9	8	.975
Major league totals (7 years)			451	1082	129	289	46	2	38	139	.267	77	147	9	477	14	12	.976

CARRILLO, MATIAS

OF, MARLINS

PERSONAL: Born February 24, 1963, in Los Mochis Sinaloa, Mexico. . . . 5-11/190. . . . Throws left, bats left. . . . Full name: Matias Garcia Carrillo. . . . Name pronounced muh-TEE-us kuh-REE-yo.

HIGH SCHOOL: Los Mochis Sinaloa (Mexico).

TRANSACTIONS/CAREER NOTES: Signed by Poza Rica of Mexican League (1982). . . . Contract sold to Hawaii, Pittsburgh Pirates organization (December 15, 1985). . . . Loaned by Pittsburgh organization to Mexico City Tigers of Mexican League (May 8-September, 1986). . . . Selected by Milwaukee Brewers organization from Pirates organization in Rule 5 minor league draft (De-

cember 8, 1987).... On suspended list (May 15-29, 1988).... On Denver disabled list (May 9, 1990-remainder of season).... Loaned by Denver to Mexico City Tigers of Mexican League (March 27-September 17, 1992).... Granted free agency (October 15, 1992).... Played with Mexico City Tigers (1993).... Contract sold by Mexico City to Florida Marlins (September 1, 1993).
STATISTICAL NOTES: Tied for Mexican League lead with 16 intentional bases on balls received in 1984.... Tied for Mexican League lead in double plays by outfielder with four in 1985.

			BATTING												FIELDING			
Year	Team (League)	Pos.	G	AB	R	H	2B	3B	HR	RBI	Avg.	BB	SO	SB	PO	A	E	Avg.
1982	—Poza Rica (Mex.)	OF-1B	99	301	59	93	9	5	0	29	.309	39	54	17	150	13	6	.964
1983	—Poza Rica (Mex.)	OF	91	360	54	112	13	11	6	39	.311	34	56	25	128	12	1	.993
1984	—M.C. Tigers (Mex.)	OF	113	442	100	154	32	6	14	76	.348	74	82	*30	281	13	12	.961
1985	—M.C. Tigers (Mex.)	OF	126	465	114	164	21	8	20	102	.353	73	86	46	320	13	10	.971
1986	—Nashua (Eastern)■	OF	15	52	3	8	1	0	0	0	.154	4	13	2	28	0	0	1.000
	—M.C. Tigers (Mex.)■	OF	60	216	39	70	15	5	11	64	.324	24	47	8	123	6	1	.992
1987	—Salem (Carolina)■	OF	90	284	42	77	11	3	8	37	.271	19	41	15	55	3	3	.951
1988	—El Paso (Texas)■	OF	106	396	76	118	17	2	12	55	.298	26	81	11	232	*18	2	*.992
1989	—Denver (A.A.)	OF-1B	125	400	46	104	14	4	10	43	.260	24	90	21	236	15	7	.973
1990	—Denver (A.A.)	OF	21	75	15	20	6	2	2	10	.267	2	16	0	47	1	1	.980
1991	—Denver (A.A.)	OF-1B	120	421	56	116	18	5	8	56	.276	32	85	10	279	7	5	.983
	—Milwaukee (A.L.)	OF	3	0	0	0	0	0	0	0	...	0	0	0	0	0	0	...
1992	—M.C. Tigers (Mex.)■	OF-1B	114	437	96	158	26	8	26	110	.362	51	53	27	595	20	4	.994
1993	—M.C. Tigers (Mex.)	OF-1B	115	414	*113	143	36	0	*38	*125	.345	59	61	28	418	23	4	.991
	—Florida (N.L.)■	OF	24	55	4	14	6	0	0	3	.255	1	7	0	21	0	0	1.000
American League totals (1 year)			3	0	0	0	0	0	0	0	...	0	0	0	0	0	0	...
National League totals (1 year)			24	55	4	14	6	0	0	3	.255	1	7	0	21	0	0	1.000
Major league totals (2 years)			27	55	4	14	6	0	0	3	.255	1	7	0	21	0	0	1.000

CARTER, JOE

OF, BLUE JAYS

PERSONAL: Born March 7, 1960, in Oklahoma City.... 6-3/225.... Throws right, bats right.... Full name: Joseph Chris Carter.... Brother of Fred Carter, minor league outfielder (1985-88).
HIGH SCHOOL: Millwood (Oklahoma City).
COLLEGE: Wichita State.
TRANSACTIONS/CAREER NOTES: Selected by Chicago Cubs organization in first round (second pick overall) of free-agent draft (June 8, 1981).... On disabled list (April 9-19, 1982).... Traded by Cubs organization with OF Mel Hall, P Don Schulze and P Darryl Banks to Cleveland Indians for C Ron Hassey, P Rick Sutcliffe and P George Frazier (June 13, 1984).... On Cleveland disabled list (July 2-17, 1984).... Traded by Indians to San Diego Padres for C Sandy Alomar, OF Chris James and 3B Carlos Baerga (December 6, 1989).... Traded by Padres with 2B Roberto Alomar to Toronto Blue Jays for 1B Fred McGriff and SS Tony Fernandez (December 5, 1990).... Granted free agency (October 30, 1992).... Re-signed by Blue Jays (December 7, 1992).
RECORDS: Shares major league records for most home runs in two consecutive games—5 (July 18 [2] and 19 [3], 1989).... Shares major league single-season record for most games with three or more home runs—2 (1989).... Shares major league record for most home runs in one inning—2 (October 3, 1993, second inning).... Holds A.L. career record for most games with three or more home runs—5.
HONORS: Named outfielder on THE SPORTING NEWS college All-America team (1980-81).... Named College Player of the Year by THE SPORTING NEWS (1981).... Named outfielder on THE SPORTING NEWS A.L. All-Star team (1991-92).... Named outfielder on THE SPORTING NEWS A.L. Silver Slugger team (1991-92).
STATISTICAL NOTES: Led American Association with 265 total bases in 1983.... Hit three home runs in one game (August 29, 1986; May 28, 1987; June 24 and July 19, 1989; and August 23, 1993).... Led A.L. first basemen with 12 errors in 1987.... Led A.L. in being hit by pitch with 10 in 1991.... Led A.L. with 13 sacrifice flies in 1992.

			BATTING												FIELDING			
Year	Team (League)	Pos.	G	AB	R	H	2B	3B	HR	RBI	Avg.	BB	SO	SB	PO	A	E	Avg.
1981	—Midland (Texas)	OF	67	249	42	67	15	3	5	35	.269	8	30	12	100	10	4	.965
1982	—Midland (Texas)	OF	110	427	84	136	22	8	25	98	.319	26	51	15	182	6	5	.974
1983	—Iowa (Am. Assoc.)	OF	124	*522	82	160	27	6	22	83	.307	17	•103	40	204	9	12	.947
	—Chicago (N.L.)	OF	23	51	6	9	1	1	0	1	.176	0	21	1	26	0	0	1.000
1984	—Iowa (Am. Assoc.)	OF	61	248	45	77	12	7	14	67	.310	20	31	11	142	6	2	.987
	—Cleveland (A.L.)■	OF-1B	66	244	32	67	6	1	13	41	.275	11	48	2	169	11	6	.968
1985	—Cleveland (A.L.)	O-1-2-3	143	489	64	128	27	0	15	59	.262	25	74	24	311	17	6	.982
1986	—Cleveland (A.L.)	OF-1B	162	663	108	200	36	9	29	*121	.302	32	95	29	800	55	10	.988
1987	—Cleveland (A.L.)	1B-OF	149	588	83	155	27	2	32	106	.264	27	105	31	782	46	†17	.980
1988	—Cleveland (A.L.)	OF	157	621	85	168	36	6	27	98	.271	27	98	27	444	8	7	.985
1989	—Cleveland (A.L.)	OF-1B	•162	•651	84	158	32	4	35	105	.243	39	112	13	443	20	9	.981
1990	—San Diego (N.L.)■	OF-1B	*162	*634	79	147	27	1	24	115	.232	48	93	22	492	16	11	.979
1991	—Toronto (A.L.)■	OF	•162	638	89	174	42	3	33	108	.273	49	112	20	283	13	8	.974
1992	—Toronto (A.L.)	OF-1B	158	622	97	164	30	7	34	119	.264	36	109	12	284	13	9	.971
1993	—Toronto (A.L.)	OF	155	603	92	153	33	5	33	121	.254	47	113	8	289	7	8	.974
American League totals (9 years)			1314	5119	734	1367	269	37	251	878	.267	293	866	166	3805	190	80	.980
National League totals (2 years)			185	685	85	156	28	2	24	116	.228	48	114	23	518	16	11	.980
Major league totals (11 years)			1499	5804	819	1523	297	39	275	994	.262	341	980	189	4323	206	91	.980

CHAMPIONSHIP SERIES RECORD

CHAMPIONSHIP SERIES NOTES: Shares A.L. single-game record for most at-bats—6 (October 11, 1992, 11 innings).

			BATTING												FIELDING			
Year	Team (League)	Pos.	G	AB	R	H	2B	3B	HR	RBI	Avg.	BB	SO	SB	PO	A	E	Avg.
1991	—Toronto (A.L.)	OF-DH	5	19	3	5	2	0	1	4	.263	1	5	0	4	1	0	1.000
1992	—Toronto (A.L.)	OF-1B	6	26	2	5	0	0	1	3	.192	2	4	2	16	1	1	.944
1993	—Toronto (A.L.)	OF	6	27	2	7	0	0	0	2	.259	1	5	0	12	1	0	1.000
Championship series totals (3 years)			17	72	7	17	2	0	2	9	.236	4	14	2	32	3	1	.972

WORLD SERIES RECORD

WORLD SERIES NOTES: Holds career record for most sacrifice flies—4. . . . Holds single-series record for most sacrifice flies—3 (1993).

			BATTING											FIELDING			
Year	**Team (League)**	**Pos.**	**G**	**AB**	**R**	**H**	**2B**	**3B**	**HR**	**RBI**	**Avg.**	**BB**	**SO**	**SB**	**PO**	**A**	**E**	**Avg.**
1992	—Toronto (A.L.)	OF-1B	6	22	2	6	2	0	2	3	.273	3	2	0	27	1	0	1.000
1993	—Toronto (A.L.)	OF	6	25	6	7	1	0	2	8	.280	0	4	0	13	0	2	.867
World Series totals (2 years)			12	47	8	13	3	0	4	11	.277	3	6	0	40	1	2	.953

ALL-STAR GAME RECORD

			BATTING										FIELDING			
Year	**League**	**Pos.**	**AB**	**R**	**H**	**2B**	**3B**	**HR**	**RBI**	**Avg.**	**BB**	**SO**	**SB**	**PO**	**A**	**E**	**Avg.**
1991	—American	OF	1	1	1	0	0	0	0	1.000	1	0	0	1	0	0	1.000
1992	—American	OF	3	1	2	0	0	0	1	.667	0	0	0	1	0	0	1.000
1993	—American	OF	3	0	1	0	0	0	0	.333	0	1	0	1	0	0	1.000
All-Star Game totals (3 years)			7	2	4	0	0	0	1	.571	1	1	0	3	0	0	1.000

CARTER, JOHN

P, INDIANS

PERSONAL: Born February 16, 1972, in Chicago. . . . 6-1/195. . . . Throws right, bats right. . . . Full name: John Christopher Carter.
HIGH SCHOOL: Neal F. Simeon (Chicago).
COLLEGE: Kishwaukee College (Ill.).

TRANSACTIONS/CAREER NOTES: Selected by Pittsburgh Pirates organization in 37th round of free-agent draft (June 4, 1990). . . . Traded by Pirates organization with OF Tony Mitchell to Cleveland Indians organization for OF Alex Cole (July 4, 1992).

Year	Team (League)	W	L	Pct.	ERA	G	GS	CG	ShO	Sv.	IP	H	R	ER	BB	SO
1991	—GC Pirates (GCL)	5	4	.556	3.29	10	9	0	0	0	41	42	20	15	13	28
1992	—Well.-Water. (NYP)■	4	7	.364	4.00	16	14	3	0	0	78⅔	67	47	35	39	54
	—Augusta (S. Atl.)	0	0	...	0.00	1	1	0	0	0	5	3	0	0	1	4
1993	—Columbus (S. Atl.)	*17	7	.708	2.79	29	•29	1	0	0	180⅓	147	72	56	48	134

CARUSO, JOE

P, RED SOX

PERSONAL: Born September 16, 1970, in Brooklyn, N.Y. . . . 6-3/195. . . . Throws right, bats right. . . . Full name: Joseph James Caruso.
HIGH SCHOOL: Casa Grande (Petaluma, Calif.).
COLLEGE: Loyola Marymount.

TRANSACTIONS/CAREER NOTES: Selected by Texas Rangers organization in 59th round of free-agent draft (June 1, 1988). . . . Selected by Boston Red Sox organization in third round of free-agent draft (June 3, 1991).
STATISTICAL NOTES: Combined with starter Francisco Rodriguez in 3-0 no-hit victory against Winston-Salem (April 30, 1992).

Year	Team (League)	W	L	Pct.	ERA	G	GS	CG	ShO	Sv.	IP	H	R	ER	BB	SO
1991	—GC Red Sox (GCL)	2	0	1.000	4.50	2	0	0	0	0	6	6	3	3	4	4
	—Elmira (N.Y.-Penn)	2	1	.667	2.84	21	4	0	0	2	66⅔	56	23	21	29	68
1992	—Lynchburg (Caro.)	6	4	.600	*1.98	49	0	0	0	15	118	68	36	26	40	133
1993	—Pawtucket (Int'l)	5	10	.333	5.44	36	17	2	0	0	122⅓	138	82	74	68	65

CARY, CHUCK

P

PERSONAL: Born March 3, 1960, in Whittier, Calif. . . . 6-4/216. . . . Throws left, bats left. . . . Full name: Charles Douglas Cary.
HIGH SCHOOL: California (San Ramon, Calif.).
COLLEGE: California.

TRANSACTIONS/CAREER NOTES: Selected by Detroit Tigers organization in seventh round of free-agent draft (June 8, 1981). . . . On Birmingham disabled list (April 18-May 12, 1983; June 24-July 11 and August 4-17, 1984). . . . Traded by Tigers organization with P Randy O'Neal to Atlanta Braves for OF Terry Harper and OF Freddy Tiburcio (January 27, 1987). . . . On Atlanta disabled list (April 10-August 17, 1988); included rehabilitation assignment to Bradenton (July 29-August 10) and Richmond (August 11-17). . . . Released by Braves organization (December 4, 1988). . . . Signed by Columbus, New York Yankees organization (January 26, 1989). . . . On New York disabled list (June 15-July 11, 1989); included rehabilitation assignment to Columbus (July 4-11). . . . On New York disabled list (April 9-May 15, 1990); included rehabilitation assignment to Tampa but did not play (May 1-14). . . . On Columbus disabled list (August 18-September 17, 1991). . . . Released by Yankees (October 28, 1991). . . . Signed by Yomiuri Giants of Japan Central League for 1992. . . . Signed as free agent by Chicago White Sox organization (January 8, 1993). . . . On Chicago disabled list (April 20-August 10, 1993); included rehabilitation assignment to Nashville (July 12-15) and South Bend (July 15-August 10). . . . On Chicago disabled list (September 14-29, 1993). . . . Granted free agency (October 19, 1993).
STATISTICAL NOTES: Tied for Southern League lead with three balks in 1982.

Year	Team (League)	W	L	Pct.	ERA	G	GS	CG	ShO	Sv.	IP	H	R	ER	BB	SO
1981	—Macon (S. Atl.)	5	5	.500	2.59	13	13	4	0	0	87	77	32	25	19	55
1982	—Birm. (Southern)	8	14	.364	4.17	28	28	5	1	0	166	162	93	77	64	125
1983	—Birm. (Southern)	6	8	.429	3.61	17	17	5	1	0	104⅔	103	50	42	42	69
	—Evansville (A.A.)	1	1	.500	4.41	15	1	0	0	1	16⅓	21	10	8	8	8
1984	—Birm. (Southern)	6	4	.600	4.82	22	20	1	0	0	108⅓	118	61	58	46	62
1985	—Nashville (A.A.)	2	1	.667	3.00	48	0	0	0	8	66	55	27	22	27	54
	—Detroit (A.L.)	0	1	.000	3.42	16	0	0	0	2	23⅔	16	9	9	8	22
1986	—Detroit (A.L.)	1	2	.333	3.41	22	0	0	0	0	31⅔	33	18	12	15	21
	—Nashville (A.A.)	1	4	.200	5.47	22	0	0	0	0	26⅓	29	21	16	15	19
1987	—Richmond (Int'l)■	4	6	.400	4.68	40	9	1	0	3	105⅔	104	64	55	43	128
	—Atlanta (N.L.)	1	1	.500	3.78	13	0	0	0	1	16⅔	17	7	7	4	15
1988	—Atlanta (N.L.)	0	0	...	6.48	7	0	0	0	0	8⅓	8	6	6	4	7
	—GC Braves (GCL)	0	2	.000	3.75	4	4	0	0	0	12	11	10	5	2	18
	—Richmond (Int'l)	0	0	...	1.42	5	0	0	0	1	6⅓	4	1	1	2	3

Year	Team (League)	W	L	Pct.	ERA	G	GS	CG	ShO	Sv.	IP	H	R	ER	BB	SO
1989	—Columbus (Int'l)■	1	1	.500	3.09	11	2	0	0	0	23⅓	17	9	8	13	27
	—New York (A.L.)	4	4	.500	3.26	22	11	2	0	0	99⅓	78	42	36	29	79
1990	—New York (A.L.)	6	12	.333	4.19	28	27	2	0	0	156⅔	155	77	73	55	134
1991	—New York (A.L.)	1	6	.143	5.91	10	9	0	0	0	53⅓	61	35	35	32	34
	—Columbus (Int'l)	5	3	.625	5.72	8	8	0	0	0	45⅔	44	31	29	26	27
1992	—Yomiuri (Jp. Cen.)■	3	5	.375	3.61	19	4	0	0	1	57⅓	46	...	23	29	35
1993	—Chicago (A.L.)■	1	0	1.000	5.23	16	0	0	0	0	20⅔	22	12	12	11	10
	—Nashville (A.A.)	0	1	.000	9.00	1	0	0	0	0	2	4	2	2	2	1
	—South Bend (Mid.)	1	1	.500	2.00	8	3	0	0	1	18	13	4	4	1	28
A.L. totals (6 years)		13	25	.342	4.13	114	47	4	0	2	385⅓	365	193	177	150	300
N.L. totals (2 years)		1	1	.500	4.68	20	0	0	0	1	25	25	13	13	8	22
Major league totals (8 years)		14	26	.350	4.17	134	47	4	0	3	410⅓	390	206	190	158	322

CASIAN, LARRY

P, TWINS

PERSONAL: Born October 28, 1965, in Lynwood, Calif. . . . 6-0/173. . . . Throws left, bats right. . . . Full name: Lawrence Paul Casian. . . . Name pronounced CASS-ee-un.
HIGH SCHOOL: Lakewood (Calif.).
COLLEGE: Cal State Fullerton.
TRANSACTIONS/CAREER NOTES: Selected by Minnesota Twins organization in sixth round of free-agent draft (June 2, 1987). . . . On Minnesota disabled list (April 14-May 28, 1993); included rehabilitation assignment to Portland (May 14-27).
STATISTICAL NOTES: Pitched two innings, combining with starter David West (six innings) and Greg Johnson (one inning) in 5-0 no-hit victory for Portland against Vancouver (June 7, 1992).

Year	Team (League)	W	L	Pct.	ERA	G	GS	CG	ShO	Sv.	IP	H	R	ER	BB	SO
1987	—Visalia (California)	10	3	.769	2.51	18	15	2	1	2	97	89	35	27	49	96
1988	—Orlando (Southern)	9	9	.500	2.95	27	26	4	1	0	174	165	72	57	62	104
	—Portland (PCL)	0	1	.000	0.00	1	0	0	0	0	2⅔	5	3	0	0	2
1989	—Portland (PCL)	7	12	.368	4.52	28	27	0	0	0	169⅓	201	97	85	63	65
1990	—Portland (PCL)	9	9	.500	4.48	37	23	1	0	0	156⅔	171	90	78	59	89
	—Minnesota (A.L.)	2	1	.667	3.22	5	3	0	0	0	22⅓	26	9	8	4	11
1991	—Minnesota (A.L.)	0	0	...	7.36	15	0	0	0	0	18⅓	28	16	15	7	6
	—Portland (PCL)	3	2	.600	3.46	34	6	0	0	1	52	51	25	20	16	24
1992	—Portland (PCL)	4	0	1.000	2.32	58	0	0	0	11	62	54	16	16	13	43
	—Minnesota (A.L.)	1	0	1.000	2.70	6	0	0	0	0	6⅔	7	2	2	1	2
1993	—Minnesota (A.L.)	5	3	.625	3.02	54	0	0	0	1	56⅔	59	23	19	14	31
	—Portland (PCL)	1	0	1.000	0.00	7	0	0	0	2	7⅔	9	0	0	2	2
Major league totals (4 years)		8	4	.667	3.81	80	3	0	0	1	104	120	50	44	26	50

CASTELLANO, PEDRO

3B/1B, ROCKIES

PERSONAL: Born March 11, 1970, in Lara, Venezuela. . . . 6-1/180. . . . Throws right, bats right. . . . Full name: Pedro Orlando Castellano. . . . Name pronounced KASS-ta-YAH-no.
HIGH SCHOOL: Jose Dominguez (Lara, Venezuela).
TRANSACTIONS/CAREER NOTES: Signed as free agent by Chicago Cubs organization (April 14, 1988). . . . Selected by Colorado Rockies in third round (64th pick overall) of expansion draft (November 17, 1992).
HONORS: Named Carolina League Most Valuable Player (1991).

			BATTING												FIELDING			
Year	Team (League)	Pos.	G	AB	R	H	2B	3B	HR	RBI	Avg.	BB	SO	SB	PO	A	E	Avg.
1989	—Wytheville (Appal.)	SS-3B-1B	66	244	•55	76	17	4	9	42	.311	46	44	5	91	138	19	.923
1990	—Peoria (Midwest)	3B-SS	117	417	61	115	27	4	2	44	.276	63	73	7	93	213	17	.947
	—Winst.-Salem (Car.)	3B	19	66	6	13	0	0	1	8	.197	10	11	1	14	37	2	.962
1991	—Charlotte (South.)	3B	7	19	2	8	0	0	0	2	.421	1	6	0	2	11	0	1.000
	—Winst.-Salem (Car.)	3B-SS	129	459	59	139	25	3	10	*87	.303	72	97	11	132	318	26	.945
1992	—Iowa (Am. Assoc.)	3B-SS	74	238	25	59	14	4	2	20	.248	32	42	2	43	133	10	.946
	—Charlotte (South.)	3B-SS	45	147	16	33	3	0	1	15	.224	19	21	0	36	104	10	.933
1993	—Colo. Springs (PCL)■	3B-1B	90	304	61	95	21	2	12	60	.313	36	63	3	312	145	13	.972
	—Colorado (N.L.)	3-1-S-2	34	71	12	13	2	0	3	7	.183	8	16	1	55	33	4	.957
Major league totals (1 year)			34	71	12	13	2	0	3	7	.183	8	16	1	55	33	4	.957

CASTILLA, VINNY

SS, ROCKIES

PERSONAL: Born July 4, 1967, in Oaxaca, Mexico. . . . 6-1/180. . . . Throws right, bats right. . . . Full name: Vinicio Soria Castilla.
HIGH SCHOOL: Instituto Carlos Graciga (Oaxaca, Mexico).
TRANSACTIONS/CAREER NOTES: Signed as free agent by Saltillo of Mexican League. . . . Contract sold by Saltillo to Atlanta Braves organization (March 19, 1990). . . . Selected by Colorado Rockies in second round (40th pick overall) of expansion draft (November 17, 1992). . . . On disabled list (May 20-June 4, 1993).
STATISTICAL NOTES: Led International League shortstops with 550 total chances and 72 double plays in 1992.

			BATTING												FIELDING			
Year	Team (League)	Pos.	G	AB	R	H	2B	3B	HR	RBI	Avg.	BB	SO	SB	PO	A	E	Avg.
1987	—Saltillo (Mexican)	3B	13	27	0	5	2	0	0	1	.185	0	5	0	10	31	1	.976
1988	—Salt.-Monc. (Mex.)■	SS	50	124	22	30	2	2	5	18	.242	8	29	1	53	105	13	.924
1989	—Saltillo (Mexican)■	SS-3B	128	462	70	142	25	13	10	58	.307	33	70	11	224	427	34	.950
1990	—Sumter (S. Atl.)■	SS	93	339	47	91	15	2	9	53	.268	28	54	2	139	320	23	.952
	—Greenville (South.)	SS	46	170	20	40	5	1	4	16	.235	13	23	4	71	167	7	.971
1991	—Greenville (South.)	SS	66	259	34	70	17	3	7	44	.270	9	35	0	86	221	11	.965
	—Richmond (Int'l)	SS	67	240	25	54	7	4	7	36	.225	14	32	1	93	208	12	.962
	—Atlanta (N.L.)	SS	12	5	1	1	0	0	0	0	.200	0	2	0	6	6	0	1.000

Year	Team (League)	Pos.	G	AB	R	H	2B	3B	HR	RBI	Avg.	BB	SO	SB	PO	A	E	Avg.
			BATTING												FIELDING			
1992	—Richmond (Int'l)	SS	127	449	49	113	29	1	7	44	.252	21	68	1	162	357	*31	.944
	—Atlanta (N.L.)	SS-3B	9	16	1	4	1	0	0	1	.250	1	4	0	2	12	1	.933
1993	—Colorado (N.L.)■	SS	105	337	36	86	9	7	9	30	.255	13	45	2	141	282	11	.975
Major league totals (3 years)			126	358	38	91	10	7	9	31	.254	14	51	2	149	300	12	.974

CASTILLO, BRAULIO

OF, ASTROS

PERSONAL: Born May 13, 1968, in Elias Pina, Dominican Republic. . . . 6-0/160. . . . Throws right, bats right. . . . Full name: Braulio Robinson Medrano Castillo.

HIGH SCHOOL: Licey Miguel Angel Garrido (Dominican Republic).

TRANSACTIONS/CAREER NOTES: Signed as free agent by Los Angeles Dodgers organization (October 10, 1985). . . . On disabled list (August 9, 1990-remainder of season). . . . Traded by Dodgers with P Mike Hartley to Philadelphia Phillies for P Roger McDowell (July 31, 1991). . . . Selected by Colorado Rockies in third round (70th pick overall) of expansion draft (November 17, 1992). . . . Traded by Rockies to Houston Astros for P Mark Grant (May 20, 1993). . . . On Tucson disabled list (May 29-August 26, 1993).

Year	Team (League)	Pos.	G	AB	R	H	2B	3B	HR	RBI	Avg.	BB	SO	SB	PO	A	E	Avg.
			BATTING												FIELDING			
1987	—GC Dodgers (GCL)	OF	49	140	21	28	4	2	1	19	.200	16	41	7	40	2	2	.955
1988	—Salem (Northwest)	OF	73	306	51	86	20	•5	8	40	.281	22	72	16	•180	40	6	.973
1989	—Bakersfield (Calif.)	OF	126	494	83	147	28	•8	18	82	.298	42	132	31	232	9	*11	.956
1990	—San Antonio (Tex.)	OF	75	241	34	55	11	3	3	24	.228	14	72	11	125	7	8	.943
1991	—San Antonio (Tex.)	OF	87	297	49	89	19	3	8	48	.300	32	73	22	187	4	5	.974
	—Scran./W.B. (Int'l)■	OF	16	60	14	21	9	1	0	15	.350	6	7	2	29	1	0	1.000
	—Philadelphia (N.L.)	OF	28	52	3	9	3	0	0	2	.173	1	15	1	40	2	1	.977
1992	—Scran./W.B. (Int'l)	OF	105	386	59	95	21	5	13	47	.246	40	96	8	216	7	6	.974
	—Philadelphia (N.L.)	OF	28	76	12	15	3	1	2	7	.197	4	15	1	43	0	2	.956
1993	—Col.S.-Tucs. (PCL)■	OF	56	212	40	77	20	4	2	37	.363	22	54	9	91	5	3	.970
Major league totals (2 years)			56	128	15	24	6	1	2	9	.188	5	30	2	83	2	3	.966

CASTILLO, FRANK

P, CUBS

PERSONAL: Born April 1, 1969, in El Paso, Tex. . . . 6-1/190. . . . Throws right, bats right. . . . Full name: Frank Anthony Castillo.

HIGH SCHOOL: Eastwood (El Paso, Tex.).

TRANSACTIONS/CAREER NOTES: Selected by Chicago Cubs organization in sixth round of free-agent draft (June 2, 1987). . . . On disabled list (April 1-July 23, 1988). . . . On Iowa disabled list (April 12-June 6, 1991). . . . On Chicago disabled list (August 11-27, 1991). . . . On suspended list (September 20-24, 1993).

HONORS: Named Appalachian League Player of the Year (1987).

STATISTICAL NOTES: Pitched 4-0 no-hit victory against Huntsville (July 13, 1990, first game).

Year	Team (League)	W	L	Pct.	ERA	G	GS	CG	ShO	Sv.	IP	H	R	ER	BB	SO
1987	—Wytheville (Appal.)	*10	1	*.909	2.29	12	12	•5	0	0	90⅓	86	31	23	21	83
	—Geneva (NY-Penn)	1	0	1.000	0.00	1	1	0	0	0	6	3	1	0	1	6
1988	—Peoria (Midwest)	6	1	.857	0.71	9	8	2	2	0	51	25	5	4	10	58
1989	—Winst.-Salem (Car.)	9	6	.600	2.51	18	18	8	1	0	129⅓	118	42	36	24	114
	—Charlotte (South.)	3	4	.429	3.84	10	10	4	0	0	68	73	35	29	12	43
1990	—Charlotte (South.)	6	6	.500	3.88	18	18	4	1	0	111⅓	113	54	48	27	112
1991	—Iowa (Am. Assoc.)	3	1	.750	2.52	4	4	1	1	0	25	20	7	7	7	20
	—Chicago (N.L.)	6	7	.462	4.35	18	18	4	0	0	111⅔	107	56	54	33	73
1992	—Chicago (N.L.)	10	11	.476	3.46	33	33	0	0	0	205⅓	179	91	79	63	135
1993	—Chicago (N.L.)	5	8	.385	4.84	29	25	2	0	0	141⅓	162	83	76	39	84
Major league totals (3 years)		21	26	.447	4.10	80	76	6	0	0	458⅓	448	230	209	135	292

CASTILLO, JUAN

P, METS

PERSONAL: Born June 23, 1970, in Caracas, Venezuela. . . . 6-5/205. . . . Throws right, bats right. . . . Full name: Juan Francisco Castillo.

TRANSACTIONS/CAREER NOTES: Signed as free agent by New York Mets organization (May 2, 1988). . . . On disabled list (June 12-23, 1993).

STATISTICAL NOTES: Led Eastern League with 27 home runs allowed in 1993.

Year	Team (League)	W	L	Pct.	ERA	G	GS	CG	ShO	Sv.	IP	H	R	ER	BB	SO
1988	—GC Mets (GCL)	0	2	.000	6.41	9	3	0	0	0	19⅔	28	19	14	9	16
1989	—GC Mets (GCL)	4	7	.364	2.88	14	•13	2	•1	0	*84⅓	84	41	27	29	59
1990	—Pittsfield (NYP)	5	•8	.385	4.73	16	14	0	0	0	70⅓	64	52	37	58	65
1991	—Columbia (S. Atl.)	12	9	.571	3.82	28	•27	3	1	0	157⅔	148	82	67	89	144
1992	—St. Lucie (Fla. St.)	11	8	.579	2.58	24	24	•7	3	0	153⅔	135	53	44	27	80
1993	—Binghamton (East.)	7	11	.389	4.56	26	26	2	0	0	165⅔	167	93	84	55	118

CASTILLO, TONY

P, BLUE JAYS

PERSONAL: Born March 1, 1963, in Lara, Venezuela. . . . 5-10/188. . . . Throws left, bats left. . . . Full name: Antonio Jose Castillo. . . . Name pronounced cass-TEE-yo.

TRANSACTIONS/CAREER NOTES: Signed as free agent by Toronto Blue Jays organization (February 16, 1983). . . . On disabled list (April 10, 1986-entire season). . . . Traded by Blue Jays organization with a player to be named later to Atlanta Braves for P Jim Acker (August 24, 1989); Braves organization acquired C Francisco Cabrera to complete deal (August 24, 1989). . . . Traded by Braves with a player to be named later to New York Mets for P Alejandro Pena (August 28, 1991); Mets acquired P Joe Roa to complete deal (August 29, 1991). . . . Traded by Mets with OF Mark Carreon to Detroit Tigers for P Paul Gibson and P Randy Marshall (January 22, 1992). . . . On disabled list (June 8-August 29, 1992). . . . Granted free agency (October 15, 1992). . . . Signed by Blue Jays organization (January 11, 1993).

Year	Team (League)	W	L	Pct.	ERA	G	GS	CG	ShO	Sv.	IP	H	R	ER	BB	SO
1983	—GC Blue Jays (GCL) ...	0	0	...	3.00	1	0	0	0	1	3	3	1	1	0	4
1984	—Florence (S. Atl.)	11	8	.579	3.41	25	24	4	1	0	137⅓	123	71	52	50	96
1985	—Kinston (Carolina)	11	7	.611	1.90	36	12	0	0	3	127⅔	111	44	27	48	136
1986	—..................................							Did not play.								
1987	—Dunedin (Fla. St.)	6	2	.750	3.36	39	0	0	0	6	69⅔	62	30	26	19	62
1988	—Dunedin (Fla. St.)	4	3	.571	1.48	30	0	0	0	12	42⅔	31	9	7	10	46
	—Knoxville (South.)	1	0	1.000	0.00	5	0	0	0	2	8	2	0	0	1	11
	—Toronto (A.L.)	1	0	1.000	3.00	14	0	0	0	0	15	10	5	5	2	14
1989	—Toronto (A.L.)	1	1	.500	6.11	17	0	0	0	1	17⅔	23	14	12	10	10
	—Syracuse (Int'l)	1	3	.250	2.81	27	0	0	0	5	41⅔	33	15	13	15	37
	—Atlanta (N.L.)■..........	0	1	.000	4.82	12	0	0	0	0	9⅓	8	5	5	4	5
1990	—Atlanta (N.L.)	5	1	.833	4.23	52	3	0	0	1	76⅔	93	41	36	20	64
	—Richmond (Int'l)	3	1	.750	2.52	5	4	1	1	0	25	14	7	7	6	27
1991	—Richmond (Int'l)	5	6	.455	2.90	23	17	0	0	0	118	89	47	38	32	78
	—Atl.-N.Y. (N.L.)■	2	1	.667	3.34	17	3	0	0	0	32⅓	40	16	12	11	18
1992	—Toledo (Int'l)■	2	3	.400	3.63	12	9	0	0	2	44⅔	48	23	18	14	24
1993	—Syracuse (Int'l)■	0	0	...	0.00	1	1	0	0	0	6	4	2	0	0	2
	—Toronto (A.L.)	3	2	.600	3.38	51	0	0	0	0	50⅔	44	19	19	22	28
A.L. totals (3 years)		5	3	.625	3.89	82	0	0	0	1	83⅓	77	38	36	34	52
N.L. totals (3 years)		7	3	.700	4.03	81	6	0	0	1	118⅓	141	62	53	35	87
Major league totals (5 years) ..		12	6	.667	3.97	163	6	0	0	2	201⅔	218	100	89	69	139

CHAMPIONSHIP SERIES RECORD

Year	Team (League)	W	L	Pct.	ERA	G	GS	CG	ShO	Sv.	IP	H	R	ER	BB	SO
1993	—Toronto (A.L.)	0	0	...	0.00	2	0	0	0	0	2	0	0	0	1	1

WORLD SERIES RECORD

Year	Team (League)	W	L	Pct.	ERA	G	GS	CG	ShO	Sv.	IP	H	R	ER	BB	SO
1993	—Toronto (A.L.)	1	0	1.000	8.10	2	0	0	0	0	3⅓	6	3	3	3	1

CASTRO, NELSON

P, DODGERS

PERSONAL: Born December 10, 1971, in San Pedro de Macoris, Dominican Republic. . . . 6-1/165. . . . Throws right, bats right. . . . Full name: Nelson Jimenez Castro.
HIGH SCHOOL: El Soco (San Pedro de Macoris, Dominican Republic).
TRANSACTIONS/CAREER NOTES: Signed as free agent by Los Angeles Dodgers organization (August 2, 1989). . . . On Bakersfield disabled list (April 9, 1992-entire season).

Year	Team (League)	W	L	Pct.	ERA	G	GS	CG	ShO	Sv.	IP	H	R	ER	BB	SO
1990	—GC Dodgers (GCL)	3	1	.750	4.25	10	10	0	0	0	55	65	30	26	7	35
1991	—Great Falls (Pio.)	7	4	.636	5.26	14	14	1	1	0	75⅓	81	51	44	13	63
1992	—..................................							Did not play.								
1993	—Bakersfield (Calif.)	4	7	.364	4.27	20	20	0	0	0	86⅓	100	47	41	37	54
	—San Antonio (Tex.)	2	1	.667	4.94	5	5	0	0	0	27⅓	35	16	15	4	15

CEDENO, ANDUJAR

SS, ASTROS

PERSONAL: Born August 21, 1969, in La Romana, Dominican Republic. . . . 6-1/168. . . . Throws right, bats right. . . . Name pronounced seh-DAIN-yo.
TRANSACTIONS/CAREER NOTES: Signed as free agent by Houston Astros organization (October 1, 1986).
STATISTICAL NOTES: Led Southern League shortstops with 572 total chances in 1990. . . . Led Southern League with 12 sacrifice hits in 1991. . . . Hit for the cycle (August 25, 1992).

			BATTING												FIELDING			
Year	Team (League)	Pos.	G	AB	R	H	2B	3B	HR	RBI	Avg.	BB	SO	SB	PO	A	E	Avg.
1988	—GC Rangers (GCL)	SS	46	165	25	47	5	2	1	20	.285	11	34	10	58	145	25	.890
1989	—Asheville (S. Atl.)	SS-3B	126	487	76	*146	23	6	14	93	.300	29	124	23	182	346	62	.895
1990	—Columbus (South.) ...	SS	132	495	57	119	21	*11	19	64	.240	33	135	6	167	354	*51	.911
	—Houston (N.L.)	SS	7	8	0	0	0	0	0	0	.000	0	5	0	3	2	1	.833
1991	—Tucson (PCL)	SS	93	347	49	105	19	6	7	55	.303	19	68	5	131	262	31	.927
	—Houston (N.L.)	SS	67	251	27	61	13	2	9	36	.243	9	74	4	88	151	18	.930
1992	—Houston (N.L.)	SS	71	220	15	38	13	2	2	13	.173	14	71	2	82	175	11	.959
	—Tucson (PCL)	SS	74	280	27	82	18	4	6	56	.293	18	49	6	112	211	22	.936
1993	—Houston (N.L.)	SS-3B	149	505	69	143	24	4	11	56	.283	48	97	9	155	376	25	.955
Major league totals (4 years)			294	984	111	242	50	8	22	105	.246	71	247	15	328	704	55	.949

CEDENO, DOMINGO

SS/2B, BLUE JAYS

PERSONAL: Born November 4, 1968, in La Romana, Dominican Republic. . . . 6-1/165. . . . Throws right, bats both.
TRANSACTIONS/CAREER NOTES: Signed as free agent by Toronto Blue Jays organization (August 4, 1987). . . . Played in Dominican Summer League (1988). . . . On disabled list (April 22-May 28, 1991).
STATISTICAL NOTES: Led Florida State League shortstops with 633 total chances and 74 double plays in 1990. . . . Led Southern League with 12 sacrifice hits in 1991.

			BATTING												FIELDING			
Year	Team (League)	Pos.	G	AB	R	H	2B	3B	HR	RBI	Avg.	BB	SO	SB	PO	A	E	Avg.
1988	—..................................						Dominican Summer League statistics unavailable.											
1989	—Myrtle Beach (SAL) ..	SS	9	35	4	7	0	0	0	2	.200	3	12	1	12	20	7	.821
	—Dunedin (Fla. St.)	SS	9	28	3	6	0	1	0	1	.214	3	10	0	9	21	1	.968
	—Medicine Hat (Pio.) ..	SS	53	194	28	45	6	4	1	20	.232	23	65	6	100	141	•25	.906

Year	Team (League)	Pos.	G	AB	R	H	2B	3B	HR	RBI	Avg.	BB	SO	SB	PO	A	E	Avg.
			BATTING												FIELDING			
1990	—Dunedin (Fla. St.).....	SS	124	493	64	109	12	10	7	61	.221	48	127	10	*215	*382	36	.943
1991	—Knoxville (South.)....	SS	100	336	39	75	7	6	1	26	.223	29	81	11	140	272	24	.945
1992	—Knoxville (South.)....	2B-SS	106	337	31	76	7	7	2	21	.226	18	88	8	189	254	28	.941
	—Syracuse (Int'l)........	2B-SS	18	57	4	11	4	0	0	5	.193	3	14	0	36	43	0	1.000
1993	—Syracuse (Int'l)........	SS-2B	103	382	58	104	16	10	2	28	.272	33	67	15	150	242	21	.949
	—Toronto (A.L.)...........	SS-2B	15	46	5	8	0	0	0	7	.174	1	10	1	10	39	1	.980
Major league totals (1 year)			15	46	5	8	0	0	0	7	.174	1	10	1	10	39	1	.980

CHAMBERLAIN, WES

OF, PHILLIES

PERSONAL: Born April 13, 1966, in Chicago. . . . 6-2/216. . . . Throws right, bats right. . . . Full name: Wesley Polk Chamberlain.
HIGH SCHOOL: Neal F. Simeon (Chicago).
COLLEGE: Jackson State.

TRANSACTIONS/CAREER NOTES: Selected by Pittsburgh Pirates organization in fifth round of free-agent draft (June 4, 1984). . . . Selected by Pirates organization in fourth round of free-agent draft (June 2, 1987). . . . Traded by Pirates organization with OF Julio Peguero and a player to be named later to Philadelphia Phillies for OF/1B Carmelo Martinez (August 30, 1990); Phillies acquired OF Tony Longmire to complete deal (September 28, 1990). . . . On Philadelphia disabled list (August 19, 1992-remainder of season). . . . On disabled list (June 16-July 4, 1993).
HONORS: Named Eastern League Most Valuable Player (1989).
STATISTICAL NOTES: Tied for New York-Pennsylvania League lead in double plays by outfielder with three in 1987. . . . Led Eastern League with 239 total bases in 1989.

Year	Team (League)	Pos.	G	AB	R	H	2B	3B	HR	RBI	Avg.	BB	SO	SB	PO	A	E	Avg.
			BATTING												FIELDING			
1987	—Watertown (NYP).....	OF	66	258	50	67	13	4	5	35	.260	25	48	22	121	9	7	.949
1988	—Augusta (S. Atl.)......	OF	27	107	22	36	7	2	1	17	.336	11	11	1	49	4	1	.981
	—Salem (Carolina)......	OF	92	365	66	100	15	1	11	50	.274	38	59	14	161	11	9	.950
1989	—Harrisburg (East.)....	OF	129	471	65	*144	26	3	21	*87	.306	32	82	11	205	*14	*15	.936
1990	—Buffalo (A.A.)...........	OF	123	416	43	104	24	2	6	52	.250	34	58	14	203	16	9	.961
	—Philadelphia (N.L.)■.	OF	18	46	9	13	3	0	2	4	.283	1	9	4	23	0	1	.958
1991	—Philadelphia (N.L.)...	OF	101	383	51	92	16	3	13	50	.240	31	73	9	199	4	3	.985
	—Scran./W.B. (Int'l)...	OF	39	144	12	37	7	2	2	20	.257	8	13	7	63	2	3	.956
1992	—Philadelphia (N.L.)...	OF	76	275	26	71	18	0	9	41	.258	10	55	4	132	3	4	.971
	—Scran./W.B. (Int'l)...	OF	34	127	16	42	6	2	4	26	.331	11	13	6	51	4	0	1.000
1993	—Philadelphia (N.L.)...	OF	96	284	34	80	20	2	12	45	.282	17	51	2	131	10	1	.993
Major league totals (4 years)			291	988	120	256	57	5	36	140	.259	59	188	19	485	17	9	.982

CHAMPIONSHIP SERIES RECORD

Year	Team (League)	Pos.	G	AB	R	H	2B	3B	HR	RBI	Avg.	BB	SO	SB	PO	A	E	Avg.
			BATTING												FIELDING			
1993	—Philadelphia (N.L.)...	OF-PH	4	11	1	4	3	0	0	1	.364	1	3	0	2	2	0	1.000

WORLD SERIES RECORD

Year	Team (League)	Pos.	G	AB	R	H	2B	3B	HR	RBI	Avg.	BB	SO	SB	PO	A	E	Avg.
			BATTING												FIELDING			
1993	—Philadelphia (N.L.)...	PH	2	2	0	0	0	0	0	0	.000	0	1	0	...	...	...	...

CHARLTON, NORM

P, PHILLIES

PERSONAL: Born January 6, 1963, in Fort Polk, La. . . . 6-3/205. . . . Throws left, bats both. . . . Full name: Norman Wood Charlton III.
HIGH SCHOOL: James Madison (San Antonio).
COLLEGE: Rice (degree in political science, religion, and physical education, 1986).

TRANSACTIONS/CAREER NOTES: Selected by Montreal Expos organization in supplemental round ("sandwich pick" between first and second round, 28th pick overall) of free-agent draft (June 4, 1984); pick received as compensation for San Francisco Giants signing Type B free agent Manny Trillo. . . . Traded by Expos organization with a player to be named later to Cincinnati Reds for IF Wayne Krenchicki (March 31, 1986); Reds acquired 2B Tim Barker to complete deal (April 2, 1986). . . . On Cincinnati disabled list (April 6-June 26, 1987); included rehabilitation assignment to Nashville (June 9-26). . . . On disabled list (May 26-June 11, 1991 and June 17-July 19, 1991). . . . On suspended list (September 29 and October 4-6, 1991). . . . Traded by Reds to Seattle Mariners for OF Kevin Mitchell (November 17, 1992). . . . On suspended list (July 9-16, 1993). . . . On disabled list (July 21-August 5 and August 8, 1993-remainder of season). . . . Granted free agency (November 18, 1993). . . . Signed by Philadelphia Phillies organization (February 3, 1994).
STATISTICAL NOTES: Led American Association with 13 wild pitches in 1988.
MISCELLANEOUS: Appeared in two games as pinch-runner (1991).

Year	Team (League)	W	L	Pct.	ERA	G	GS	CG	ShO	Sv.	IP	H	R	ER	BB	SO
1984	—W.P. Beach (FSL)......	1	4	.200	4.58	8	8	0	0	0	39⅓	51	27	20	22	27
1985	—W.P. Beach (FSL)......	7	10	.412	4.57	24	23	5	2	0	128	135	79	65	79	71
1986	—Vermont (Eastern)■...	10	6	.625	2.83	22	22	6	1	0	136⅔	109	55	43	74	96
1987	—Nashville (A.A.).........	2	8	.200	4.30	18	17	3	1	0	98⅓	97	57	47	44	74
1988	—Nashville (A.A.).........	11	10	.524	3.02	27	27	8	1	0	182	149	69	61	56	*161
	—Cincinnati (N.L.)........	4	5	.444	3.96	10	10	0	0	0	61⅓	60	27	27	20	39
1989	—Cincinnati (N.L.)........	8	3	.727	2.93	69	0	0	0	0	95⅓	67	38	31	40	98
1990	—Cincinnati (N.L.)........	12	9	.571	2.74	56	16	1	1	2	154⅓	131	53	47	70	117
1991	—Cincinnati (N.L.)........	3	5	.375	2.91	39	11	0	0	1	108⅓	92	37	35	34	77
1992	—Cincinnati (N.L.)........	4	2	.667	2.99	64	0	0	0	26	81⅓	79	39	27	26	90
1993	—Seattle (A.L.)■...........	1	3	.250	2.34	34	0	0	0	18	34⅔	22	12	9	17	48
A.L. totals (1 year)		1	3	.250	2.34	34	0	0	0	18	34⅔	22	12	9	17	48
N.L. totals (5 years)		31	24	.564	3.00	238	37	1	1	29	500⅔	429	194	167	190	421
Major league totals (6 years)		32	27	.542	2.96	272	37	1	1	47	535⅓	451	206	176	207	469

CHAMPIONSHIP SERIES RECORD

Year	Team (League)	W	L	Pct.	ERA	G	GS	CG	ShO	Sv.	IP	H	R	ER	BB	SO
1990	—Cincinnati (N.L.)	1	1	.500	1.80	4	0	0	0	0	5	4	2	1	3	3

WORLD SERIES RECORD

Year	Team (League)	W	L	Pct.	ERA	G	GS	CG	ShO	Sv.	IP	H	R	ER	BB	SO
1990	—Cincinnati (N.L.)	0	0	...	0.00	1	0	0	0	0	1	1	0	0	0	0

ALL-STAR GAME RECORD

Year	League	W	L	Pct.	ERA	GS	CG	ShO	Sv.	IP	H	R	ER	BB	SO
1992	—National	0	0	...	0.00	0	0	0	0	1	0	0	0	0	1

CHIAMPARINO, SCOTT

P

PERSONAL: Born August 22, 1966, in San Mateo, Calif. ... 6-2/205. ... Throws right, bats left. ... Full name: Scott Michael Chiamparino. ... Name pronounced CHAMP-uh-REE-no.
HIGH SCHOOL: Serra (San Mateo, Calif.).
COLLEGE: Santa Clara.
TRANSACTIONS/CAREER NOTES: Selected by Oakland Athletics organization in fourth round of free-agent draft (June 2, 1987). ... Traded by A's with P Joe Bitker to Texas Rangers (September 4, 1990), completing deal in which Rangers traded OF/DH Harold Baines to A's for two players to be named later (August 29, 1990). ... On disabled list (May 26, 1991-remainder of season). ... On Texas disabled list (April 5-July 27, 1992); included rehabilitation assignment to Gulf Coast Rangers (July 11-16), Charlotte (July 16-26) and Tulsa (July 26-27). ... Selected by Florida Marlins in second round (41st pick overall) of expansion draft (November 17, 1992). ... On Florida disabled list (March 27, 1993-entire season). ... Released by Marlins (October 4, 1994).

Year	Team (League)	W	L	Pct.	ERA	G	GS	CG	ShO	Sv.	IP	H	R	ER	BB	SO
1987	—Medford (N'west)	5	4	.556	2.53	13	11	3	0	0	67⅔	64	29	19	20	65
1988	—Modesto (Calif.)	5	7	.417	2.70	16	16	5	0	0	106⅔	89	40	32	56	117
	—Huntsville (South.)	4	5	.444	3.21	13	13	4	0	0	84	88	36	30	26	49
1989	—Huntsville (South.)	8	6	.571	4.60	17	17	2	1	0	101⅔	109	60	52	29	87
1990	—Tacoma (PCL)	13	9	.591	3.28	26	26	4	•2	0	173	174	79	63	72	110
	—Texas (A.L.)■	1	2	.333	2.63	6	6	0	0	0	37⅔	36	14	11	12	19
1991	—Texas (A.L.)	1	0	1.000	4.03	5	5	0	0	0	22⅓	26	11	10	12	8
1992	—GC Rangers (GCL)	0	1	.000	0.00	1	1	0	0	0	7	8	2	0	0	5
	—Charlotte (Fla. St.)	1	1	.500	2.31	2	2	0	0	0	11⅔	6	3	3	3	8
	—Tulsa (Texas)	0	0	...	1.93	3	3	0	0	0	18⅔	17	5	4	5	18
	—Okla. City (A.A.)	2	1	.667	2.87	5	5	0	0	0	31⅓	29	11	10	13	9
	—Texas (A.L.)	0	4	.000	3.55	4	4	0	0	0	25⅓	25	11	10	5	13
1993	—■							Did not play.								
Major league totals (3 years)		2	6	.250	3.27	15	15	0	0	0	85⅓	87	36	31	29	40

CHITREN, STEVE

P, ORIOLES

PERSONAL: Born June 8, 1967, in Tokyo, Japan. ... 6-0/180. ... Throws right, bats right. ... Full name: Stephen Vincent Chitren.
HIGH SCHOOL: Valley (Las Vegas).
COLLEGE: Stanford.
TRANSACTIONS/CAREER NOTES: Selected by Seattle Mariners organization in ninth round of free-agent draft (June 1, 1988). ... Selected by Oakland Athletics organization in sixth round of free-agent draft (June 5, 1989). ... On disabled list (April 26-May 6 and May 9-June 6, 1992). ... Selected by Rochester, Baltimore Orioles organization, from Huntsville, A's organization, in Rule 5 minor league draft (December 13, 1993).
STATISTICAL NOTES: Tied for Pacific Coast League lead with 10 hit batsmen in 1992.

Year	Team (League)	W	L	Pct.	ERA	G	GS	CG	ShO	Sv.	IP	H	R	ER	BB	SO
1989	—Madison (Midwest)	2	1	.667	1.19	20	0	0	0	7	22⅔	13	3	3	4	17
	—S. Oregon (N'west)	0	0	...	1.80	2	0	0	0	0	5	3	2	1	2	3
1990	—Huntsville (South.)	2	4	.333	1.68	48	0	0	0	*27	53⅔	32	18	10	22	61
	—Tacoma (PCL)	0	0	...	0.00	1	0	0	0	0	⅔	1	0	0	0	2
	—Oakland (A.L.)	1	0	1.000	1.02	8	0	0	0	0	17⅔	7	2	2	4	19
1991	—Oakland (A.L.)	1	4	.200	4.33	56	0	0	0	4	60⅓	59	31	29	32	47
1992	—Tacoma (PCL)	4	7	.364	6.82	29	7	0	0	0	62	64	53	47	46	37
1993	—Huntsville (South.)	2	1	.667	5.17	32	0	0	0	1	55⅔	53	38	32	35	39
	—Tacoma (PCL)	1	0	1.000	3.00	14	0	0	0	1	24	21	9	8	14	27
Major league totals (2 years)		2	4	.333	3.58	64	0	0	0	4	78	66	33	31	36	66

CHOLOWSKY, DAN

3B/2B, CARDINALS

PERSONAL: Born October 30, 1970, in Yonkers, N.Y. ... 6-0/195. ... Throws right, bats right. ... Full name: Daniel John Cholowsky.
HIGH SCHOOL: Bellarmine College Prep School (San Jose, Calif.).
COLLEGE: California.
TRANSACTIONS/CAREER NOTES: Selected by Cincinnati Reds organization in 39th round of free-agent draft (June 1, 1988). ... Selected by St. Louis Cardinals organization in supplemental round ("sandwich pick" between first and second round, 39th pick overall) of free-agent draft (June 3, 1991); pick received as part of compensation for Toronto Blue Jays signing Type A free agent Ken Dayley.

			BATTING											FIELDING			
Year	Team (League)	Pos.	G	AB	R	H	2B	3B	HR	RBI	Avg.	BB	SO	SB	PO	A	E	Avg.
1991	—Hamilton (NYP)	2B-3B	20	69	9	16	1	1	1	6	.232	9	17	6	46	47	8	.921
1992	—Savannah (S. Atl.)	2B-3B	69	232	44	76	6	4	8	34	.328	51	48	34	103	178	17	.943
	—St. Peters. (FSL)	2B	59	201	19	57	8	0	1	17	.284	33	31	14	88	120	8	.963
1993	—St. Peters. (FSL)	2B-3B	54	208	30	60	12	0	2	22	.288	20	54	6	75	140	10	.956
	—Arkansas (Texas)	3B-SS	68	212	31	46	10	2	3	16	.217	38	54	10	41	117	21	.883

CHRISTOPHER, MIKE

P, TIGERS

PERSONAL: Born November 3, 1963, in Petersburg, Va. . . . 6-5/205. . . . Throws right, bats right. . . . Full name: Michael Wayne Christopher.
HIGH SCHOOL: Dinwiddie (Va.) County.
COLLEGE: East Carolina.
TRANSACTIONS/CAREER NOTES: Selected by New York Yankees organization in seventh round of free-agent draft (June 3, 1985). . . . On Albany/Colonie disabled list (May 2-20, 1989). . . . Selected by Los Angeles Dodgers organization from Yankees organization in Rule 5 minor league draft (December 5, 1989). . . . Traded by Dodgers with P Dennis Cook to Cleveland Indians for P Rudy Seanez (December 10, 1991). . . . Released by Indians (November 29, 1993). . . . Signed by Detroit Tigers organization (January 21, 1994).

Year	Team (League)	W	L	Pct.	ERA	G	GS	CG	ShO	Sv.	IP	H	R	ER	BB	SO
1985	—Oneonta (NYP)	8	1	.889	1.46	15	9	2	2	0	80⅓	58	21	13	22	84
1986	—Fort Lauder. (FSL)	7	3	.700	2.63	15	14	3	1	0	102⅔	92	37	30	36	56
	—Alb./Colon. (East.)	3	5	.375	5.04	11	11	2	0	0	60⅔	75	48	34	12	34
1987	—Fort Lauder. (FSL)	13	8	.619	2.44	24	24	9	4	0	169⅓	183	63	46	28	81
1988	—Alb./Colon. (East.)	13	7	.650	3.83	24	24	5	1	0	152⅔	166	75	65	44	67
1989	—Alb./Colon. (East.)	6	1	.857	2.52	8	8	3	0	0	53⅔	48	17	15	7	33
	—Columbus (Int'l)	5	6	.455	4.81	13	11	1	0	0	73	95	45	39	21	42
1990	—Albuquerque (PCL)■	6	1	.857	1.97	54	0	0	0	8	68⅔	62	20	15	23	47
1991	—Albuquerque (PCL)	7	2	.778	2.44	63	0	0	0	16	77⅓	73	25	21	30	67
	—Los Angeles (N.L.)	0	0	...	0.00	3	0	0	0	0	4	2	0	0	3	2
1992	—Colo. Springs (PCL)■	4	4	.500	2.91	49	0	0	0	26	58⅔	59	21	19	13	39
	—Cleveland (A.L.)	0	0	...	3.00	10	0	0	0	0	18	17	8	6	10	13
1993	—Cleveland (A.L.)	0	0	...	3.86	9	0	0	0	0	11⅔	14	6	5	2	8
	—Charlotte (Int'l)	3	6	.333	3.22	50	0	0	0	22	50⅓	51	21	18	6	36
A.L. totals (2 years)		0	0	...	3.34	19	0	0	0	0	29⅔	31	14	11	12	21
N.L. totals (1 year)		0	0	...	0.00	3	0	0	0	0	4	2	0	0	3	2
Major league totals (3 years)		0	0	...	2.94	22	0	0	0	0	33⅔	33	14	11	15	23

CHRISTOPHERSON, ERIC

C, MARINERS

PERSONAL: Born April 25, 1969, in Long Beach, Calif. . . . 6-0/195. . . . Throws right, bats right. . . . Full name: Eric Spencer Christopherson.
HIGH SCHOOL: Ocean View (Huntington Beach, Calif.).
COLLEGE: San Diego State.
TRANSACTIONS/CAREER NOTES: Selected by San Francisco Giants organization in first round (19th pick overall) of free-agent draft (June 4, 1990); pick received as part of compensation for San Diego Padres signing Type A free agent Craig Lefferts. . . . On suspended list (July 27-August 31, 1990). . . . On Shreveport disabled list (July 29-August 14 and September 1-8, 1992 and April 9-August 3 and September 2-7, 1993). . . . Selected by Seattle Mariners from Giants organization in Rule 5 major league draft (December 13, 1993).
STATISTICAL NOTES: Led Midwest League catchers with 840 total chances and tied for lead in double plays by catcher with eight in 1991.

			BATTING											FIELDING			
Year	Team (League)	Pos.	G	AB	R	H	2B	3B	HR	RBI	Avg.	BB	SO	SB	PO	A	E	Avg.
1990	—Everett (N'west)	C	48	162	20	43	8	1	1	22	.265	31	29	7	299	34	3	★.991
	—San Jose (Calif.)	C	7	23	4	4	0	0	0	1	.174	3	6	0	42	1	1	.977
1991	—Clinton (Midwest)	C	110	345	45	93	18	0	5	58	.270	68	53	10	★758	73	9	.989
1992	—Shreveport (Texas)	C	80	270	36	68	10	1	6	34	.252	37	44	1	604	66	4	.994
1993	—Ariz. Giants (Ariz.)	C	8	22	7	9	1	1	0	4	.409	9	1	0	40	4	0	1.000
	—Shreveport (Texas)	C	15	46	5	7	2	0	0	2	.152	9	10	1	98	8	2	.981

CIANFROCCO, ARCHI

3B/1B, PADRES

PERSONAL: Born October 6, 1966, in Rome, N.Y. . . . 6-5/215. . . . Throws right, bats right. . . . Full name: Angelo Dominic Cianfrocco. . . . Name pronounced AR-kee SEE-un-FROCK-oh.
HIGH SCHOOL: Rome (N.Y.) Free Academy.
COLLEGE: Onondaga Community College (N.Y.) and Purdue.
TRANSACTIONS/CAREER NOTES: Selected by Pittsburgh Pirates organization in 11th round of free-agent draft (January 14, 1986). . . . Selected by Pirates organization in secondary phase of free-agent draft (June 2, 1986). . . . Selected by Montreal Expos organization in fifth round of free-agent draft (June 2, 1987). . . . On disabled list (June 27, 1990-remainder of season). . . . On Ottawa disabled list (June 3-10, 1993). . . . Traded by Expos to San Diego Padres for P Tim Scott (June 23, 1993).
STATISTICAL NOTES: Led Southern League third basemen with 37 errors in 1989. . . . Led Eastern League in being hit by pitch with nine in 1991. . . . Led Eastern League first basemen with 95 assists and 110 double plays in 1991.

			BATTING											FIELDING			
Year	Team (League)	Pos.	G	AB	R	H	2B	3B	HR	RBI	Avg.	BB	SO	SB	PO	A	E	Avg.
1987	—Jamestown (NYP)	2B-SS-1B	70	251	28	62	8	4	2	27	.247	9	59	2	125	179	22	.933
1988	—Rockford (Midw.)	3B	126	455	54	115	34	0	15	65	.253	26	99	6	94	240	29	★.920
1989	—Jacksonv. (South.)	3B-2B-1B	132	429	46	105	22	7	7	50	.245	37	126	3	99	221	†38	.894
1990	—Jacksonv. (South.)	1B-3B-OF	62	196	18	43	10	0	5	29	.219	12	45	0	244	54	7	.977
1991	—Harrisburg (East.)	1B-OF	124	456	71	144	21	•10	9	77	.316	38	112	11	1023	†95	11	.990
1992	—Montreal (N.L.)	1B-3B-OF	86	232	25	56	5	2	6	30	.241	11	66	3	387	66	8	.983
	—Indianapolis (A.A.)	1B-3B-SS	15	59	12	18	3	0	4	16	.305	5	15	1	62	14	5	.938
1993	—Mont.-S.D. (N.L.)■	3B-1B	96	296	30	72	11	2	12	48	.243	17	69	2	243	97	10	.971
	—Ottawa (Int'l)	OF-1B-3B	50	188	21	56	14	2	4	27	.298	7	33	4	188	26	3	.986
Major league totals (2 years)			182	528	55	128	16	4	18	78	.242	28	135	5	630	163	18	.978

CICCARELLA, JOE

P, RED SOX

PERSONAL: Born December 29, 1969, in Cincinnati. . . . 6-3/200. . . . Throws left, bats left. . . . Full name: Joseph Michael Ciccarella. . . . Name pronounced CHICK-uh-RELL-uh.
HIGH SCHOOL: Mater Dei (Santa Ana, Calif.).

COLLEGE: Loyola Marymount.
TRANSACTIONS/CAREER NOTES: Selected by Philadelphia Phillies organization in fourth round of free-agent draft (June 1, 1988). ... Selected by Boston Red Sox organization in fourth round of free-agent draft (June 3, 1991).

Year	Team (League)	W	L	Pct.	ERA	G	GS	CG	ShO	Sv.	IP	H	R	ER	BB	SO
1992	—Winter Haven (FSL)	2	1	.667	2.66	38	0	0	0	12	40⅔	35	13	12	26	45
1993	—Pawtucket (Int'l)	0	1	.000	5.60	12	0	0	0	0	17⅔	27	13	11	12	8
	—New Britain (East.)	0	4	.000	4.22	30	0	0	0	15	32	31	19	15	23	34

RECORD AS POSITION PLAYER

				BATTING											FIELDING			
Year	Team (League)	Pos.	G	AB	R	H	2B	3B	HR	RBI	Avg.	BB	SO	SB	PO	A	E	Avg.
1991	—GC Red Sox (GCL)	1B	8	23	5	7	2	0	1	6	.304	6	3	0	77	3	0	1.000
	—Winter Haven (FSL)..	1B	32	99	12	23	3	0	0	11	.232	18	29	1	234	10	1	.996

CIMORELLI, FRANK

P, CARDINALS

PERSONAL: Born August 2, 1968, in Poughkeepsie, N.Y. ... 6-0/175. ... Throws right, bats right. ... Full name: Frank Thomas Cimorelli. ... Name pronounced SIM-er-RELL-ee.
HIGH SCHOOL: F.D. Roosevelt (Hyde Park, N.Y.).
COLLEGE: Dutchess Community College (N.Y.) and Dominican (N.Y.).
TRANSACTIONS/CAREER NOTES: Selected by St. Louis Cardinals organization in 37th round of free-agent draft (June 5, 1989).

Year	Team (League)	W	L	Pct.	ERA	G	GS	CG	ShO	Sv.	IP	H	R	ER	BB	SO
1989	—Johns. City (App.)......	2	4	.333	4.57	12	12	1	0	0	65	78	40	33	17	36
1990	—Springfield (Midw.)	4	8	.333	4.56	41	15	1	0	0	120⅓	125	80	61	41	86
1991	—Springfield (Midw.)	8	•14	.364	3.38	29	*29	3	0	0	191⅔	202	94	72	51	98
1992	—Springfield (Midw.)	4	2	.667	1.73	*65	0	0	0	9	72⅔	48	22	14	22	66
1993	—Arkansas (Texas)	1	1	.500	2.54	37	0	0	0	1	56⅔	44	20	16	23	36
	—Louisville (A.A.)	2	1	.667	2.72	27	0	0	0	2	43	34	15	13	25	24

CIRILLO, JEFF

3B/2B, BREWERS

PERSONAL: Born September 23, 1969, in Pasadena, Calif. ... 6-2/190. ... Throws right, bats right. ... Full name: Jeffrey Howard Cirillo.
HIGH SCHOOL: Providence (Burbank, Calif.).
COLLEGE: Southern California.
TRANSACTIONS/CAREER NOTES: Selected by Chicago Cubs organization in 37th round of free-agent draft (June 2, 1987). ... Selected by Milwaukee Brewers organization in 11th round of free-agent draft (June 3, 1991). ... On New Orleans disabled list (July 22-August 6, 1993).
STATISTICAL NOTES: Led Pioneer League in grounding into double plays with 11 in 1991. ... Led Pioneer League third basemen with 60 putouts, 104 assists and 179 total chances in 1991. ... Tied for Midwest League lead with six intentional bases on balls received in 1992.

				BATTING											FIELDING			
Year	Team (League)	Pos.	G	AB	R	H	2B	3B	HR	RBI	Avg.	BB	SO	SB	PO	A	E	Avg.
1991	—Helena (Pioneer)	3B-OF	•70	286	60	100	16	2	10	51	.350	31	28	3	†71	†104	15	.921
1992	—Stockton (Calif.)	3B	7	27	2	6	1	0	0	5	.222	2	0	0	7	10	0	1.000
	—Beloit (Midwest)	3B-2B	126	444	65	135	27	3	9	71	.304	84	85	21	115	309	26	.942
1993	—El Paso (Texas)	2B-3B	67	249	53	85	16	2	9	41	.341	26	37	2	83	142	9	.962
	—New Orleans (A.A.) ..	3B-2B-SS	58	215	31	63	13	2	3	32	.293	29	33	2	46	145	5	.974

CLARK, DAVE

OF, PIRATES

PERSONAL: Born September 3, 1962, in Tupelo, Miss. ... 6-2/209. ... Throws right, bats left. ... Full name: David Earl Clark. ... Brother of Louis Clark, wide receiver, Seattle Seahawks, National Football League (1987-92).
HIGH SCHOOL: Shannon (Miss.).
COLLEGE: Jackson State.
TRANSACTIONS/CAREER NOTES: Selected by Cleveland Indians organization in first round (11th pick overall) of free-agent draft (June 6, 1983). ... Traded by Indians to Chicago Cubs for OF Mitch Webster (November 20, 1989). ... Released by Cubs (April 1, 1991). ... Signed by Omaha, Kansas City Royals organization (April 29, 1991). ... Released by Royals (December 20, 1991). ... Signed by Pittsburgh Pirates organization (January 29, 1992). ... On Buffalo disabled list (May 11-18, 1992).
HONORS: Named outfielder on THE SPORTING NEWS college All-America team (1983).

				BATTING											FIELDING			
Year	Team (League)	Pos.	G	AB	R	H	2B	3B	HR	RBI	Avg.	BB	SO	SB	PO	A	E	Avg.
1983	—Waterloo (Midw.)	OF	58	159	20	44	8	1	4	20	.277	19	32	2	37	4	1	.976
1984	—Waterloo (Midw.)	OF	110	363	74	112	16	3	15	63	.309	57	68	20	128	10	4	.972
	—Buffalo (Eastern)	OF	17	56	12	10	1	0	3	10	.179	9	13	1	23	2	1	.962
1985	—Waterbury (East.)....	OF	132	463	75	140	24	7	12	64	.302	86	79	27	204	11	11	.951
1986	—Maine (Int'l)	OF	106	355	56	99	17	2	19	58	.279	52	70	6	150	4	6	.963
	—Cleveland (A.L.)	OF	18	58	10	16	1	0	3	9	.276	7	11	1	26	0	0	1.000
1987	—Buffalo (A.A.)	OF	108	420	83	143	22	3	30	80	.340	52	62	14	181	*22	6	.971
	—Cleveland (A.L.)	OF	29	87	11	18	5	0	3	12	.207	2	24	1	24	1	0	1.000
1988	—Cleveland (A.L.)	OF	63	156	11	41	4	1	3	18	.263	17	28	0	36	0	2	.947
	—Colo. Springs (PCL) ..	OF	47	165	27	49	10	2	4	31	.297	27	37	4	85	6	3	.968
1989	—Cleveland (A.L.)	OF	102	253	21	60	12	0	8	29	.237	30	63	0	27	0	1	.964
1990	—Chicago (N.L.)■........	OF	84	171	22	47	4	2	5	20	.275	8	40	7	60	2	0	1.000
1991	—Omaha (A.A.)■..........	OF-1B	104	359	45	108	24	3	13	64	.301	30	53	6	264	11	4	.986
	—Kansas City (A.L.)....	OF	11	10	1	2	0	0	0	1	.200	1	1	0	0	0	0	...

Year	Team (League)	Pos.	BATTING G	AB	R	H	2B	3B	HR	RBI	Avg.	BB	SO	SB	FIELDING PO	A	E	Avg.
1992	—Buffalo (A.A.)■	OF-1B	78	253	43	77	17	6	11	55	.304	34	51	6	171	6	6	.967
	—Pittsburgh (N.L.)	OF	23	33	3	7	0	0	2	7	.212	6	8	0	10	0	0	1.000
1993	—Pittsburgh (N.L.)	OF	110	277	43	75	11	2	11	46	.271	38	58	1	132	3	6	.957
American League totals (5 years)			223	564	54	137	22	1	17	69	.243	57	127	2	113	1	3	.974
National League totals (3 years)			217	481	68	129	15	4	18	73	.268	52	106	8	202	5	6	.972
Major league totals (8 years)			440	1045	122	266	37	5	35	142	.255	109	233	10	315	6	9	.973

CLARK, JERALD

OF/1B

PERSONAL: Born August 10, 1963, in Crockett, Tex. . . . 6-4/205. . . . Throws right, bats right. . . . Full name: Jerald Dwayne Clark. . . . Brother of Phil Clark, outfielder/first baseman, San Diego Padres; and brother of Isaiah Clark, minor league infielder (1984-90).
HIGH SCHOOL: Crockett (Tex.).
COLLEGE: Lamar.
TRANSACTIONS/CAREER NOTES: Selected by Los Angeles Dodgers organization in 23rd round of free-agent draft (June 4, 1984). . . . Selected by San Diego Padres organization in 12th round of free-agent draft (June 3, 1985). . . . On disabled list (May 1-20, 1991). . . . Selected by Colorado Rockies in first round (seventh pick overall) of expansion draft (November 17, 1992). . . . Granted free agency (December 20, 1993). . . . Signed by Yakult Swallows of Japan Central League (January 25, 1994).
HONORS: Named Northwest League Most Valuable Player (1985).

Year	Team (League)	Pos.	BATTING G	AB	R	H	2B	3B	HR	RBI	Avg.	BB	SO	SB	FIELDING PO	A	E	Avg.
1985	—Spokane (N'west)	OF	73	283	45	92	•24	3	2	50	.325	34	38	9	145	7	6	.962
1986	—Reno (California)	OF	95	389	76	118	34	3	7	58	.303	29	46	5	135	6	5	.966
	—Beaumont (Texas)	OF	16	56	9	18	4	1	0	6	.321	5	9	1	39	1	2	.952
1987	—Wichita (Texas)	OF	132	531	86	165	36	8	18	95	.311	40	82	6	262	10	3	.989
1988	—Las Vegas (PCL)	OF-3B-1B	107	408	65	123	27	7	9	67	.301	17	66	6	194	11	7	.967
	—San Diego (N.L.)	OF	6	15	0	3	1	0	0	3	.200	0	4	0	10	1	0	1.000
1989	—Las Vegas (PCL)	OF-1B	107	419	84	131	27	4	22	83	.313	38	81	5	213	8	8	.965
	—San Diego (N.L.)	OF	17	41	5	8	2	0	1	7	.195	3	9	0	16	2	1	.947
1990	—San Diego (N.L.)	1B-OF	53	101	12	27	4	1	5	11	.267	5	24	0	102	6	1	.991
	—Las Vegas (PCL)	1B-OF	40	161	30	49	7	4	12	32	.304	5	35	2	236	10	2	.992
1991	—San Diego (N.L.)	OF-1B	118	369	26	84	16	0	10	47	.228	31	90	2	245	10	2	.992
1992	—San Diego (N.L.)	OF-1B	146	496	45	120	22	6	12	58	.242	22	97	3	344	10	3	.992
1993	—Colorado (N.L.)■	OF-1B	140	478	65	135	26	6	13	67	.282	20	60	9	476	23	12	.977
Major league totals (6 years)			480	1500	153	377	71	13	41	193	.251	81	284	14	1193	52	19	.985

CLARK, MARK

P, INDIANS

PERSONAL: Born May 12, 1968, in Bath, Ill. . . . 6-5/225. . . . Throws right, bats right. . . . Full name: Mark William Clark.
HIGH SCHOOL: Balyki (Bath, Ill.).
COLLEGE: Lincoln Land Community College (Ill.).
TRANSACTIONS/CAREER NOTES: Selected by St. Louis Cardinals organization in ninth round of free-agent draft (June 1, 1988). . . . On Arkansas disabled list (April 12-May 8, 1991). . . . Traded by Cardinals with SS Juan Andujar to Cleveland Indians for OF Mark Whiten (March 31, 1993). . . . On Cleveland disabled list (July 17-September 9, 1993).

Year	Team (League)	W	L	Pct.	ERA	G	GS	CG	ShO	Sv.	IP	H	R	ER	BB	SO
1988	—Hamilton (NYP)	6	7	.462	3.05	15	15	2	0	0	94⅓	88	39	32	32	60
1989	—Savannah (S. Atl.)	•14	9	.609	2.44	27	27	4	2	0	173⅔	143	61	47	52	132
1990	—St. Peters. (FSL)	3	2	.600	3.05	10	10	1	1	0	62	63	33	21	14	58
	—Arkansas (Texas)	5	11	.313	3.82	19	19	*5	0	0	115⅓	111	56	49	37	87
1991	—Arkansas (Texas)	5	5	.500	4.00	15	15	4	1	0	92⅓	99	50	41	30	76
	—Louisville (A.A.)	3	2	.600	2.98	7	6	1	1	0	45⅓	43	17	15	15	29
	—St. Louis (N.L.)	1	1	.500	4.03	7	2	0	0	0	22⅓	17	10	10	11	13
1992	—Louisville (A.A.)	4	4	.500	2.80	9	9	4	*3	0	61	56	20	19	15	38
	—St. Louis (N.L.)	3	10	.231	4.45	20	20	1	1	0	113⅓	117	59	56	36	44
1993	—Cleveland (A.L.)■	7	5	.583	4.28	26	15	1	0	0	109⅓	119	55	52	25	57
	—Charlotte (Int'l)	1	0	1.000	2.08	2	2	0	0	0	13	9	5	3	2	12
A.L. totals (1 year)		7	5	.583	4.28	26	15	1	0	0	109⅓	119	55	52	25	57
N.L. totals (2 years)		4	11	.267	4.38	27	22	1	1	0	135⅔	134	69	66	47	57
Major league totals (3 years)		11	16	.407	4.33	53	37	2	1	0	245	253	124	118	72	114

CLARK, PHIL

OF/1B, PADRES

PERSONAL: Born May 6, 1968, in Crockett, Tex. . . . 6-0/200. . . . Throws right, bats right. . . . Full name: Phillip Benjamin Clark. . . . Brother of Jerald Clark, outfielder/first baseman, Yakult Swallows of Japan Central League; and brother of Isaiah Clark, minor league infielder (1984-90).
HIGH SCHOOL: Crockett (Tex.).
TRANSACTIONS/CAREER NOTES: Selected by Detroit Tigers organization in first round (18th pick overall) of free-agent draft (June 2, 1986). . . . Claimed on waivers by San Diego Padres (April 2, 1993).
STATISTICAL NOTES: Led Appalachian League catchers with 11 errors in 1986. . . . Led South Atlantic League catchers with 23 passed balls and tied for lead in errors by catcher with 21 in 1987. . . . Tied for Eastern League lead in double plays by catcher with eight in 1989.

Year	Team (League)	Pos.	BATTING G	AB	R	H	2B	3B	HR	RBI	Avg.	BB	SO	SB	FIELDING PO	A	E	Avg.
1986	—Bristol (Appal.)	C-OF	66	247	40	*82	4	2	4	36	*.332	19	42	12	354	25	†11	.972
1987	—Fayetteville (SAL)	C-OF-3B	135	*542	83	160	26	•9	8	79	.295	25	43	25	480	82	‡28	.953
1988	—Lakeland (Fla. St.)	C-OF	109	403	60	120	17	4	9	66	.298	15	43	16	413	35	8	.982
1989	—London (Eastern)	C-OF-3B	104	373	43	108	15	4	8	42	.290	31	49	2	505	56	7	.988
1990	—Toledo (Int'l)	C-OF	75	207	15	47	14	1	2	22	.227	14	35	1	156	13	2	.988

Year	Team (League)	Pos.	G	AB	R	H	2B	3B	HR	RBI	Avg.	BB	SO	SB	PO	A	E	Avg.
			BATTING												FIELDING			
1991	—Toledo (Int'l)	OF-C	110	362	47	92	14	4	4	45	.254	21	49	6	196	12	13	.941
1992	—Toledo (Int'l)	OF-C	79	271	29	76	20	0	10	39	.280	16	35	4	145	13	7	.958
	—Detroit (A.L.)	OF	23	54	3	22	4	0	1	5	.407	6	9	1	27	0	2	.931
1993	—San Diego (N.L.)■	0-1-C-3	102	240	33	75	17	0	9	33	.313	8	31	2	243	35	8	.972
American League totals (1 year)			23	54	3	22	4	0	1	5	.407	6	9	1	27	0	2	.931
National League totals (1 year)			102	240	33	75	17	0	9	33	.313	8	31	2	243	35	8	.972
Major league totals (2 years)			125	294	36	97	21	0	10	38	.330	14	40	3	270	35	10	.968

CLARK, TIM

OF, MARLINS

PERSONAL: Born February 10, 1969, in Philadelphia. . . . 6-3/210. . . . Throws right, bats left. . . . Full name: Timothy Patrick Clark.
HIGH SCHOOL: Roman Catholic (Philadelphia).
COLLEGE: Seminole (Okla.) Junior College and Louisiana State.
TRANSACTIONS/CAREER NOTES: Selected by Milwaukee Brewers organization in eighth round of free-agent draft (June 4, 1990). . . . Released by Stockton, Brewers organization (April 2, 1992). . . . Signed by Salt Lake, independent (May 22, 1992). . . . Contract sold by Salt Lake to Florida Marlins organization (August 1, 1992). . . . Loaned by Marlins organization to Salt Lake (August 1, 1992-remainder of season).
HONORS: Named California League Most Valuable Player (1993).
STATISTICAL NOTES: Led Pioneer League with 159 total bases and .585 slugging percentage in 1992. . . . Led California League with 298 total bases and 13 sacrifice flies in 1993.

Year	Team (League)	Pos.	G	AB	R	H	2B	3B	HR	RBI	Avg.	BB	SO	SB	PO	A	E	Avg.
			BATTING												FIELDING			
1990	—Beloit (Midwest)	OF	67	219	27	57	13	1	4	44	.260	31	45	3	103	9	4	.966
1991	—Stockton (Calif.)	OF-P	125	424	51	116	19	4	9	56	.274	57	60	9	164	12	7	.962
1992	—Salt Lake (Pioneer)■	OF	69	272	57	*97	*25	2	11	53	*.357	28	36	1	106	6	2	.982
1993	—High Desert (Calif.)	OF-1B	128	510	109	*185	42	*10	17	*126	*.363	56	65	2	278	23	8	.974

RECORD AS PITCHER

Year	Team (League)	W	L	Pct.	ERA	G	GS	CG	ShO	Sv.	IP	H	R	ER	BB	SO
1991	—Stockton (Calif.)	0	0	...	0.00	1	0	0	0	0	1	1	0	0	0	1

CLARK, TONY

OF, TIGERS

PERSONAL: Born June 15, 1972, in Newton, Kan. . . . 6-8/205. . . . Throws right, bats both. . . . Full name: Anthony Christopher Clark.
HIGH SCHOOL: Valhalla (El Cajon, Calif.) and Christian (El Cajon, Calif.).
COLLEGE: Arizona and San Diego State.
TRANSACTIONS/CAREER NOTES: Selected by Detroit Tigers organization in first round (second pick overall) of free-agent draft (June 4, 1990). . . . On Niagara Falls temporary inactive list (June 17, 1991-remainder of season and August 17, 1992-remainder of season). . . . On disabled list (August 24, 1993-remainder of season).

Year	Team (League)	Pos.	G	AB	R	H	2B	3B	HR	RBI	Avg.	BB	SO	SB	PO	A	E	Avg.
			BATTING												FIELDING			
1990	—Bristol (Appal.)	OF	25	73	2	12	2	0	1	8	.164	6	28	0	23	3	0	1.000
1991	—								Did not play.									
1992	—Niag. Falls (NYP)	OF	27	85	12	26	9	0	5	17	.306	9	34	1	18	1	0	1.000
1993	—Lakeland (Fla. St.)	OF	36	117	14	31	4	1	1	22	.265	18	32	0	34	0	2	.944

CLARK, WILL

1B, RANGERS

PERSONAL: Born March 13, 1964, in New Orleans. . . . 6-0/196. . . . Throws left, bats left. . . . Full name: William Nuschler Clark Jr.
HIGH SCHOOL: Jesuit (New Orleans).
COLLEGE: Mississippi State.
TRANSACTIONS/CAREER NOTES: Selected by Kansas City Royals organization in fourth round of free-agent draft (June 7, 1982). . . . Selected by San Francisco Giants organization in first round (second pick overall) of free-agent draft (June 3, 1985). . . . On San Francisco disabled list (June 4-July 24, 1986); included rehabilitation assignment to Phoenix (July 7-24). . . . On disabled list (August 26-September 10, 1993). . . . Granted free agency (October 25, 1993). . . . Signed by Texas Rangers (November 22, 1993).
HONORS: Named designated hitter on THE SPORTING NEWS college All-America team (1984). . . . Named Golden Spikes Award winner by USA Baseball (1985). . . . Named first baseman on THE SPORTING NEWS college All-America team (1985). . . . Named first baseman on THE SPORTING NEWS N.L. All-Star team (1988-89 and 1991). . . . Named first baseman on THE SPORTING NEWS N.L. Silver Slugger team (1989 and 1991). . . . Won N.L. Gold Glove at first base (1991).
STATISTICAL NOTES: Led N.L. first basemen with 130 double plays in 1987, 126 in 1988, 118 in 1990, 115 in 1991 and 130 in 1992. . . . Led N.L. with 27 intentional bases on balls received in 1988. . . . Led N.L. first basemen with 1,608 total chances in 1988, 1,566 in 1989 and 1,587 in 1990. . . . Led N.L. with .536 slugging percentage and tied for lead with 303 total bases in 1991.
MISCELLANEOUS: Member of 1984 U.S. Olympic baseball team. . . . Hit home run in first minor league at-bat (June 21, 1985) and first major league at-bat (April 8, 1986); both were on the first swing.

Year	Team (League)	Pos.	G	AB	R	H	2B	3B	HR	RBI	Avg.	BB	SO	SB	PO	A	E	Avg.
			BATTING												FIELDING			
1985	—Fresno (California)	1B-OF	65	217	41	67	14	0	10	48	.309	62	46	11	523	51	6	.990
1986	—San Francisco (N.L.)	1B	111	408	66	117	27	2	11	41	.287	34	76	4	942	72	11	.989
	—Phoenix (PCL)	DH	6	20	3	5	0	0	0	1	.250	4	2	1	...	...	...	...
1987	—San Francisco (N.L.)	1B	150	529	89	163	29	5	35	91	.308	49	98	5	1253	103	13	.991
1988	—San Francisco (N.L.)	1B	*162	575	102	162	31	6	29	*109	.282	*100	129	9	*1492	104	12	.993
1989	—San Francisco (N.L.)	1B	159	588	•104	196	38	9	23	111	.333	74	103	8	*1445	111	10	.994
1990	—San Francisco (N.L.)	1B	154	600	91	177	25	5	19	95	.295	62	97	8	*1456	119	12	.992
1991	—San Francisco (N.L.)	1B	148	565	84	170	32	7	29	116	.301	51	91	4	1273	110	4	*.997

			BATTING												FIELDING			
Year	Team (League)	Pos.	G	AB	R	H	2B	3B	HR	RBI	Avg.	BB	SO	SB	PO	A	E	Avg.
1992	—San Francisco (N.L.)..	1B	144	513	69	154	40	1	16	73	.300	73	82	12	1275	105	10	.993
1993	—San Francisco (N.L.)..	1B	132	491	82	139	27	2	14	73	.283	63	68	2	1078	88	14	.988
Major league totals (8 years)			1160	4269	687	1278	249	37	176	709	.299	506	744	52	10214	812	86	.992

CHAMPIONSHIP SERIES RECORD

CHAMPIONSHIP SERIES NOTES: Named N.L. Championship Series Most Valuable Player (1989).... Holds single-series records for most hits—13; and most total bases—24 (1989).... Holds single-game record for most runs batted in—6 (October 4, 1989).... Shares single-series records for most runs—8; and most long hits—6 (1989).... Shares single-game records for most runs—4; and most grand slams—1 (October 4, 1989).... Shares record for most runs batted in in one inning—4 (October 4, 1989, fourth inning).... Shares N.L. single-series record for most consecutive hits—5 (1989).... Shares N.L. single-game record for most hits—4 (October 4, 1989).

			BATTING												FIELDING			
Year	Team (League)	Pos.	G	AB	R	H	2B	3B	HR	RBI	Avg.	BB	SO	SB	PO	A	E	Avg.
1987	—San Francisco (N.L.)..	1B	7	25	3	9	2	0	1	3	.360	3	6	1	63	7	1	.986
1989	—San Francisco (N.L.)..	1B	5	20	8	13	3	1	2	8	.650	2	2	0	43	6	0	1.000
Championship series totals (2 years)			12	45	11	22	5	1	3	11	.489	5	8	1	106	13	1	.992

WORLD SERIES RECORD

			BATTING												FIELDING			
Year	Team (League)	Pos.	G	AB	R	H	2B	3B	HR	RBI	Avg.	BB	SO	SB	PO	A	E	Avg.
1989	—San Francisco (N.L.)..	1B	4	16	2	4	1	0	0	0	.250	1	3	0	40	2	0	1.000

ALL-STAR GAME RECORD

			BATTING											FIELDING			
Year	League	Pos.	AB	R	H	2B	3B	HR	RBI	Avg.	BB	SO	SB	PO	A	E	Avg.
1988	—National	1B	2	0	0	0	0	0	0	.000	0	0	0	4	1	0	1.000
1989	—National	1B	2	0	0	0	0	0	0	.000	0	1	0	5	0	0	1.000
1990	—National	1B	3	0	1	0	0	0	0	.333	0	0	0	6	0	0	1.000
1991	—National	1B	2	0	1	0	0	0	0	.500	1	0	0	2	0	0	1.000
1992	—National	PH-1B	2	1	1	0	0	1	3	.500	0	1	0	1	0	0	1.000
All-Star Game totals (5 years)			11	1	3	0	0	1	3	.273	1	2	0	18	1	0	1.000

CLAYTON, CRAIG

3B, MARINERS

PERSONAL: Born November 29, 1970, in Bellflower, Calif.... 6-0/185.... Throws right, bats right.... Full name: Craig Cory Clayton.

HIGH SCHOOL: Loara (Anaheim, Calif.).

COLLEGE: Cal State Northridge.

TRANSACTIONS/CAREER NOTES: Selected by Seattle Mariners organization in sixth round of free-agent draft (June 3, 1991).... On disabled list (May 13-July 15, 1992).

STATISTICAL NOTES: Led Northwest League with seven sacrifice flies in 1991.

			BATTING												FIELDING			
Year	Team (League)	Pos.	G	AB	R	H	2B	3B	HR	RBI	Avg.	BB	SO	SB	PO	A	E	Avg.
1991	—Belling. (N'west)	3B-P	43	159	16	42	10	0	3	22	.264	15	30	0	14	63	10	.885
	—San Bern. (Calif.)	3B	20	75	8	25	3	0	3	9	.333	8	11	3	12	28	1	.976
1992	—San Bern. (Calif.)......	3B-OF-2B	63	217	21	54	14	2	2	20	.249	19	21	1	32	71	25	.805
1993	—Riverside (Calif.)	3B	60	235	37	77	13	2	1	32	.328	30	30	4	39	127	14	.922
	—Jacksonv. (South.) ..	3-O-P-2	59	215	23	64	8	2	1	23	.298	17	29	10	34	79	10	.919

RECORD AS PITCHER

Year	Team (League)	W	L	Pct.	ERA	G	GS	CG	ShO	Sv.	IP	H	R	ER	BB	SO
1991	—Belling. (N'west)	0	0	...	0.00	1	0	0	0	0	⅔	1	0	0	0	0
1993	—Jacksonv. (South.)	0	0	...	0.00	3	0	0	0	0	4	3	0	0	1	1

CLAYTON, ROYCE

SS, GIANTS

PERSONAL: Born January 2, 1970, in Burbank, Calif.... 6-0/183.... Throws right, bats right.... Full name: Royce Spencer Clayton.

HIGH SCHOOL: St. Bernard (Inglewood, Calif.).

TRANSACTIONS/CAREER NOTES: Selected by San Francisco Giants organization in first round (15th pick overall) of free-agent draft (June 1, 1988); pick received as compensation for Cincinnati Reds signing Type B free agent Eddie Milner.

STATISTICAL NOTES: Led Texas League shortstops with 80 double plays in 1991.... Led N.L. shortstops with 103 double plays 1993.

			BATTING												FIELDING			
Year	Team (League)	Pos.	G	AB	R	H	2B	3B	HR	RBI	Avg.	BB	SO	SB	PO	A	E	Avg.
1988	—Everett (N'west).......	SS	60	212	35	55	4	0	3	29	.259	27	54	10	75	166	35	.873
1989	—Clinton (Midwest)	SS	104	385	39	91	13	3	0	24	.236	39	101	28	182	332	31	.943
	—San Jose (Calif.).......	SS	28	92	5	11	2	0	0	4	.120	13	27	10	53	71	8	.939
1990	—San Jose (Calif.).......	SS	123	460	80	123	15	10	7	71	.267	68	98	33	*202	358	37	.938
1991	—Shreveport (Texas)..	SS	126	485	84	136	22	8	5	68	.280	61	104	36	174	379	29	.950
	—San Francisco (N.L.)..	SS	9	26	0	3	1	0	0	2	.115	1	6	0	16	6	3	.880
1992	—San Francisco (N.L.)..	SS-3B	98	321	31	72	7	4	4	24	.224	26	63	8	142	257	11	.973
	—Phoenix (PCL)	SS	48	192	30	46	6	2	3	18	.240	17	25	15	81	150	7	.971
1993	—San Francisco (N.L.)..	SS	153	549	54	155	21	5	6	70	.282	38	91	11	251	449	27	.963
Major league totals (3 years)			260	896	85	230	29	9	10	96	.257	65	160	19	409	712	41	.965

CLEMENS, ROGER

P, RED SOX

PERSONAL: Born August 4, 1962, in Dayton, O. . . . 6-4/220. . . . Throws right, bats right. . . . Full name: William Roger Clemens.
HIGH SCHOOL: Spring Woods (Houston).
COLLEGE: San Jacinto (North) College (Tex.) and Texas.

TRANSACTIONS/CAREER NOTES: Selected by New York Mets organization in 12th round of free-agent draft (June 8, 1981). . . . Selected by Boston Red Sox organization in first round (19th pick overall) of free-agent draft (June 6, 1983). . . . On disabled list (July 8-August 3 and August 21, 1985-remainder of season). . . . On suspended list (April 26-May 3, 1991). . . . On Boston disabled list (June 19-July 16, 1993); included rehabilitation assignment to Pawtucket (July 11-16).
RECORDS: Holds major league single-game record for most strikeouts (nine-inning game)—20 (April 29, 1986). . . . Shares major league record for most putouts by pitcher in one inning—3 (June 27, 1992, sixth inning). . . . Shares A.L. record for most consecutive years with 200 or more strikeouts—7 (1986-92). . . . Shares A.L. single-game record for most consecutive strikeouts—8 (April 29, 1986).
HONORS: Named Major League Player of the Year by THE SPORTING NEWS (1986). . . . Named A.L. Pitcher of the Year by THE SPORTING NEWS (1986 and 1991). . . . Named righthanded pitcher on THE SPORTING NEWS A.L. All-Star team (1986-87 and 1991). . . . Named A.L. Most Valuable Player by Baseball Writers' Association of America (1986). . . . Named A.L. Cy Young Award winner by Baseball Writers' Association of America (1986-87 and 1991).

Year	Team (League)	W	L	Pct.	ERA	G	GS	CG	ShO	Sv.	IP	H	R	ER	BB	SO
1983	—Winter Haven (FSL)	3	1	.750	1.24	4	4	3	1	0	29	22	4	4	0	36
	—New Britain (East.)	4	1	.800	1.38	7	7	1	1	0	52	31	8	8	12	59
1984	—Pawtucket (Int'l)	2	3	.400	1.93	7	6	3	1	0	46⅔	39	12	10	14	50
	—Boston (A.L.)	9	4	.692	4.32	21	20	5	1	0	133⅓	146	67	64	29	126
1985	—Boston (A.L.)	7	5	.583	3.29	15	15	3	1	0	98⅓	83	38	36	37	74
1986	—Boston (A.L.)	*24	4	*.857	*2.48	33	33	10	1	0	254	179	77	70	67	238
1987	—Boston (A.L.)	•20	9	.690	2.97	36	36	*18	*7	0	281⅔	248	100	93	83	256
1988	—Boston (A.L.)	18	12	.600	2.93	35	35	•14	*8	0	264	217	93	86	62	*291
1989	—Boston (A.L.)	17	11	.607	3.13	35	35	8	3	0	253⅓	215	101	88	93	230
1990	—Boston (A.L.)	21	6	.778	*1.93	31	31	7	•4	0	228⅓	193	59	49	54	209
1991	—Boston (A.L.)	18	10	.643	*2.62	35	•35	13	*4	0	*271⅓	219	93	79	65	*241
1992	—Boston (A.L.)	18	11	.621	*2.41	32	32	11	*5	0	246⅔	203	80	66	62	208
1993	—Boston (A.L.)	11	14	.440	4.46	29	29	2	1	0	191⅔	175	99	95	67	160
	—Pawtucket (Int'l)	0	0	...	0.00	1	1	0	0	0	3⅔	1	0	0	4	8
Major league totals (10 years)		163	86	.655	2.94	302	301	91	35	0	2222⅔	1878	807	726	619	2033

CHAMPIONSHIP SERIES RECORD

CHAMPIONSHIP SERIES NOTES: Holds single-series record for most hits allowed—22 (1986). . . . Shares single-series record for most earned runs allowed—11 (1986). . . . Shares single-game records for most earned runs allowed—7 (October 7, 1986); and most consecutive strikeouts—4 (October 6, 1988). . . . Holds A.L. single-series record for most innings pitched—22⅔ (1986). . . . Shares A.L. single-game record for most runs allowed—8 (October 7, 1986).

Year	Team (League)	W	L	Pct.	ERA	G	GS	CG	ShO	Sv.	IP	H	R	ER	BB	SO
1986	—Boston (A.L.)	1	1	.500	4.37	3	3	0	0	0	22⅔	22	12	11	7	17
1988	—Boston (A.L.)	0	0	...	3.86	1	1	0	0	0	7	6	3	3	0	8
1990	—Boston (A.L.)	0	1	.000	3.52	2	2	0	0	0	7⅔	7	3	3	5	4
Champ. series totals (3 years)		1	2	.333	4.10	6	6	0	0	0	37⅓	35	18	17	12	29

WORLD SERIES RECORD

Year	Team (League)	W	L	Pct.	ERA	G	GS	CG	ShO	Sv.	IP	H	R	ER	BB	SO
1986	—Boston (A.L.)	0	0	...	3.18	2	2	0	0	0	11⅓	9	5	4	6	11

ALL-STAR GAME RECORD

ALL-STAR GAME NOTES: Named Most Valuable Player (1986).

Year	League	W	L	Pct.	ERA	GS	CG	ShO	Sv.	IP	H	R	ER	BB	SO
1986	—American	1	0	1.000	0.00	1	0	0	0	3	0	0	0	0	2
1988	—American	0	0	...	0.00	0	0	0	0	1	0	0	0	0	1
1990	—American						Did not play.								
1991	—American	0	0	...	9.00	0	0	0	0	1	1	1	1	0	0
1992	—American	0	0	...	0.00	0	0	0	0	1	2	0	0	0	0
All-Star totals (4 years)		1	0	1.000	1.50	1	0	0	0	6	3	1	1	0	3

COLBERT, CRAIG

C, INDIANS

PERSONAL: Born February 13, 1965, in Iowa City, Ia. . . . 6-0/214. . . . Throws right, bats right. . . . Full name: Craig Charles Colbert.
HIGH SCHOOL: Manhattan (Kan.).
COLLEGE: Oral Roberts.

TRANSACTIONS/CAREER NOTES: Selected by San Francisco Giants organization in 20th round of free-agent draft (June 2, 1986). . . . On disabled list (May 3-June 5 and June 22-August 11, 1991). . . . On San Francisco disabled list (August 6-21, 1992). . . . On San Francisco disabled list (June 4-August 22, 1993); included rehabilitation assignment to Phoenix (July 23-30, August 9-11 and August 16-22). . . . Released by Giants (November 18, 1993). . . . Signed by Cleveland Indians organization (December 14, 1993).
STATISTICAL NOTES: Tied for California League lead in double plays by third baseman with 22 in 1987.

			BATTING												FIELDING			
Year	Team (League)	Pos.	G	AB	R	H	2B	3B	HR	RBI	Avg.	BB	SO	SB	PO	A	E	Avg.
1986	—Clinton (Midwest)	3B	72	263	26	60	12	0	1	17	.228	23	53	4	49	153	15	.931
1987	—Fresno (California)	3B	115	388	41	95	12	4	6	51	.245	22	89	5	86	225	34	.901
1988	—Clinton (Midwest)	3B-1B-OF	124	455	56	106	19	2	11	64	.233	41	100	8	541	158	25	.965
1989	—Shreveport (Texas)	S-3-0-1	106	363	47	94	19	3	7	34	.259	23	67	3	122	203	23	.934
1990	—Phoenix (PCL)	3-C-S-1	111	400	41	112	22	2	8	47	.280	31	80	4	281	166	18	.961
1991	—Phoenix (PCL)	C-3-0-1-S	42	142	9	35	6	2	2	13	.246	11	38	0	130	127	6	.977
1992	—San Francisco (N.L.)	C-3B-2B	49	126	10	29	5	2	1	16	.230	9	22	1	147	24	1	.994
	—Phoenix (PCL)	3-C-S-0	36	140	16	45	8	1	1	12	.321	3	16	0	61	50	5	.957

Year	Team (League)	Pos.	G	AB	R	H	2B	3B	HR	RBI	Avg.	BB	SO	SB	PO	A	E	Avg.
			BATTING												FIELDING			
1993	—San Francisco (N.L.)..	C-2B-3B	23	37	2	6	2	0	1	5	.162	3	13	0	52	5	1	.983
	—Phoenix (PCL)	C-3B-1B	13	45	5	10	2	1	1	7	.222	0	11	0	73	9	2	.976
Major league totals (2 years)			72	163	12	35	7	2	2	21	.215	12	35	1	199	29	2	.991

COLBRUNN, GREG

1B, MARLINS

PERSONAL: Born July 26, 1969, in Fontana, Calif. . . . 6-0/200. . . . Throws right, bats right. . . . Full name: Gregory Joseph Colbrunn.

HIGH SCHOOL: Fontana (Calif.).

TRANSACTIONS/CAREER NOTES: Selected by Montreal Expos organization in sixth round of free-agent draft (June 2, 1987). . . . On disabled list (April 10, 1991-entire season). . . . On Indianapolis disabled list (April 9-May 5, 1992). . . . On Montreal disabled list (August 2-18, 1992); included rehabilitation assignment to Indianapolis (August 13-18). . . . On Montreal disabled list (April 5-21, 1993); included rehabilitation assignment to West Palm Beach (April 9-20). . . . On Montreal disabled list (July 12, 1993-remainder of season); included rehabilitation assignment to Ottawa (July 27-August 2). . . . Claimed on waivers by Florida Marlins (October 7, 1993).

Year	Team (League)	Pos.	G	AB	R	H	2B	3B	HR	RBI	Avg.	BB	SO	SB	PO	A	E	Avg.
			BATTING												FIELDING			
1988	—Rockford (Midw.)	C	115	417	55	111	18	2	7	46	.266	22	60	5	595	81	15	.978
1989	—W.P. Beach (FSL).....	C	59	228	20	54	8	0	0	25	.237	6	29	3	376	49	5	.988
	—Jacksonv. (South.) ..	C	55	178	21	49	11	1	3	18	.275	13	33	0	304	34	4	.988
1990	—Jacksonv. (South.) ..	C	125	458	57	138	29	1	13	76	.301	38	78	1	698	58	15	.981
1991	—								Did not play.									
1992	—Indianapolis (A.A.)...	1B	57	216	32	66	19	1	11	48	.306	7	41	1	441	27	4	.992
	—Montreal (N.L.).........	1B	52	168	12	45	8	0	2	18	.268	6	34	3	363	29	3	.992
1993	—W.P. Beach (FSL).....	1B	8	31	6	12	2	1	1	5	.387	4	1	0	74	5	1	.988
	—Montreal (N.L.).........	1B	70	153	15	39	9	0	4	23	.255	6	33	4	372	27	2	.995
	—Ottawa (Int'l)............	1B	6	22	4	6	1	0	0	8	.273	1	2	1	50	1	0	1.000
Major league totals (2 years)			122	321	27	84	17	0	6	41	.262	12	67	7	735	56	5	.994

COLE, ALEX

OF

PERSONAL: Born August 17, 1965, in Fayetteville, N.C. . . . 6-0/170. . . . Throws left, bats left. . . . Full name: Alexander Cole Jr.

HIGH SCHOOL: George Wythe (Richmond, Va.).

COLLEGE: Manatee Junior College (Fla.).

TRANSACTIONS/CAREER NOTES: Selected by Pittsburgh Pirates organization in 11th round of free-agent draft (January 17, 1984). . . . Selected by St. Louis Cardinals organization in second round of free-agent draft (January 9, 1985). . . . Traded by Cardinals organization with P Steve Peters to San Diego Padres for P Omar Olivares (February 27, 1990). . . . Traded by Padres organization to Cleveland Indians for C Tom Lampkin (July 11, 1990). . . . On Cleveland disabled list (May 4-26, 1991); included rehabilitation assignment to Colorado Springs (May 17-26). . . . Traded by Indians to Pirates for OF Tony Mitchell and P John Carter (July 4, 1992). . . . Selected by Colorado Rockies in first round (17th pick overall) of expansion draft (November 17, 1992). . . . Granted free agency (October 21, 1993).

STATISTICAL NOTES: Led Appalachian League outfielders with 142 total chances in 1985. . . . Led Appalachian League in caught stealing with eight in 1985. . . . Led Florida State League in caught stealing with 22 in 1986. . . . Led Texas League in caught stealing with 29 in 1987. . . . Tied for Texas League lead in double plays by outfielder with five in 1987. . . . Led American Association outfielders with 342 total chances in 1989. . . . Tied for Pacific Coast League lead in caught stealing with 18 in 1990.

Year	Team (League)	Pos.	G	AB	R	H	2B	3B	HR	RBI	Avg.	BB	SO	SB	PO	A	E	Avg.
			BATTING												FIELDING			
1985	—Johns. City (App.)....	OF	66	232	*60	61	5	1	1	13	.263	30	27	*46	*127	*12	3	.979
1986	—St. Peters. (FSL).......	OF	74	286	76	98	9	1	0	26	.343	54	37	56	201	4	8	.962
	—Louisville (A.A.)	OF	63	200	25	50	2	4	1	16	.250	17	30	24	135	6	9	.940
1987	—Arkansas (Texas)....	OF	125	477	68	122	12	4	2	27	.256	44	55	*68	289	14	10	.968
1988	—Louisville (A.A.)	OF	120	392	44	91	7	8	0	24	.232	42	59	40	276	13	1	.997
1989	—St. Peters. (FSL).......	OF	8	32	2	6	0	0	0	1	.188	3	7	4	13	0	0	1.000
	—Louisville (A.A.)	OF	127	455	75	128	5	5	2	29	.281	71	76	*47	*320	14	8	.977
1990	—L.V.-Col. Sp. (PCL)■	OF	104	390	71	120	9	4	0	31	.308	55	69	38	181	6	9	.954
	—Cleveland (A.L.)	OF	63	227	43	68	5	4	0	13	.300	28	38	40	145	3	6	.961
1991	—Cleveland (A.L.)	OF	122	387	58	114	17	3	0	21	.295	58	47	27	256	6	8	.970
	—Colo. Springs (PCL) ..	OF	8	32	6	6	0	1	0	3	.188	4	3	1	18	2	2	.909
1992	—Cleveland (A.L.)	OF	41	97	11	20	1	0	0	5	.206	10	21	9	33	1	1	.971
	—Pittsburgh (N.L.)■....	OF	64	205	33	57	3	7	0	10	.278	18	46	7	85	5	1	.989
1993	—Colorado (N.L.)■......	OF	126	348	50	89	9	4	0	24	.256	43	58	30	219	5	4	.982
American League totals (3 years)			226	711	112	202	23	7	0	39	.284	96	106	76	434	10	15	.967
National League totals (2 years)			190	553	83	146	12	11	0	34	.264	61	104	37	304	10	5	.984
Major league totals (4 years)			416	1264	195	348	35	18	0	73	.275	157	210	113	738	20	20	.974

CHAMPIONSHIP SERIES RECORD

Year	Team (League)	Pos.	G	AB	R	H	2B	3B	HR	RBI	Avg.	BB	SO	SB	PO	A	E	Avg.
			BATTING												FIELDING			
1992	—Pittsburgh (N.L.)......	OF-PH	4	10	2	2	0	0	0	1	.200	3	2	0	7	1	0	1.000

COLEMAN, PAUL

P/OF, CARDINALS

PERSONAL: Born December 9, 1970, in Jacksonville, Tex. . . . 5-11/200. . . . Throws right, bats right. . . . Full name: Paul Marwin Coleman.

HIGH SCHOOL: Frankston (Tex.).

TRANSACTIONS/CAREER NOTES: Selected by St. Louis Cardinals organization in first round (sixth pick overall) of free-agent draft (June 5, 1989). . . . On disabled list (April 12-July 18, 1991). . . . On Arkansas disabled list (April 10-June 24, 1992). . . . On Arkansas suspended list (June 24-July 22, 1992). . . . On Arkansas disabled list (July 22-August 8, 1992).

Year	Team (League)	Pos.	G	AB	R	H	2B	3B	HR	RBI	Avg.	BB	SO	SB	PO	A	E	Avg.
			BATTING												FIELDING			
1989	—Johns. City (App.)	OF	53	172	26	40	11	0	3	24	.233	16	58	7	91	4	•9	.913
1990	—Savannah (S. Atl.) ...	OF	104	340	33	71	12	4	6	35	.209	23	66	9	213	8	6	.974
1991	—Springfield (Midw.) ..	OF	45	178	9	33	5	1	2	14	.185	1	49	0	71	6	8	.906
1992	—St. Peters. (FSL)	OF	21	70	10	19	1	0	1	7	.271	2	14	3	30	1	1	.969
1993	—Arkansas (Texas)	OF	123	401	44	98	24	3	7	30	.244	32	97	8	197	10	9	.958

COLEMAN, VINCE

OF, ROYALS

PERSONAL: Born September 22, 1961, in Jacksonville, Fla. . . . 6-1/185. . . . Throws right, bats both. . . . Full name: Vincent Maurice Coleman. . . . Cousin of Greg Coleman, National Football League player (1977-88).
HIGH SCHOOL: Raines (Jacksonville, Fla.).
COLLEGE: Florida A&M (degree in physical education).
TRANSACTIONS/CAREER NOTES: Selected by Philadelphia Phillies organization in 20th round of free-agent draft (June 8, 1981). . . . Selected by St. Louis Cardinals organization in 10th round of free-agent draft (June 7, 1982). . . . Granted free agency (November 5, 1990). . . . Signed by New York Mets (December 5, 1990). . . . On disabled list (June 15-July 25 and August 14-September 27, 1991). . . . On New York disabled list (April 10-May 1, 1992). . . . On New York disabled list (May 2-28, 1992); included rehabilitation assignment to St. Lucie (May 23-28). . . . On New York disabled list (June 27-July 27, 1992). . . . Traded by Mets with cash to Kansas City Royals for OF Kevin McReynolds (January 5, 1994).
RECORDS: Holds major league rookie-season records for most stolen bases—110; and most times caught stealing—25 (1985). . . . Holds major league career record for most consecutive stolen bases without being caught stealing—50 (September 18, 1988-July 26, 1989). . . . Shares major league single-game record for most sacrifice flies—3 (May 1, 1986). . . . Shares N.L. record for most consecutive years leading league in stolen bases—6 (1985-90).
HONORS: Named South Atlantic League Most Valuable Player (1983). . . . Named N.L. Rookie Player of the Year by THE SPORTING NEWS (1985). . . . Named N.L. Rookie of the Year by Baseball Writers' Association of America (1985).
STATISTICAL NOTES: Led South Atlantic League in caught stealing with 31 in 1983. . . . Led American Association in caught stealing with 36 in 1984. . . . Led American Association outfielders with 381 total chances in 1984. . . . Led N.L. in caught stealing with 25 in 1985, 22 in 1987 and tied for lead with 27 in 1988.

Year	Team (League)	Pos.	G	AB	R	H	2B	3B	HR	RBI	Avg.	BB	SO	SB	PO	A	E	Avg.
			BATTING												FIELDING			
1982	—Johns. City (App.)	OF	58	212	40	53	2	1	0	16	.250	29	49	•43	123	7	8	.942
1983	—Macon (S. Atl.)	OF	113	446	99	156	8	7	0	53	*.350	56	85	*145	225	18	8	.968
1984	—Louisville (A.A.)	OF	152	*608	*97	156	21	7	4	48	.257	55	112	*101	357	14	•10	.974
1985	—Louisville (A.A.)	OF	5	21	1	3	0	0	0	0	.143	0	2	0	8	0	0	1.000
	—St. Louis (N.L.)	OF	151	636	107	170	20	10	1	40	.267	50	115	*110	305	16	7	.979
1986	—St. Louis (N.L.)	OF	154	600	94	139	13	8	0	29	.232	60	98	*107	300	12	•9	.972
1987	—St. Louis (N.L.)	OF	151	623	121	180	14	10	3	43	.289	70	126	*109	274	16	9	.970
1988	—St. Louis (N.L.)	OF	153	616	77	160	20	10	3	38	.260	49	111	*81	290	14	9	.971
1989	—St. Louis (N.L.)	OF	145	563	94	143	21	9	2	28	.254	50	90	*65	247	5	•10	.962
1990	—St. Louis (N.L.)	OF	124	497	73	145	18	9	6	39	.292	35	88	*77	244	12	5	.981
1991	—New York (N.L.)■......	OF	72	278	45	71	7	5	1	17	.255	39	47	37	132	5	3	.979
1992	—New York (N.L.)	OF	71	229	37	63	11	1	2	21	.275	27	41	24	112	2	1	.991
	—St. Lucie (Fla. St.)	OF	6	22	4	8	0	0	0	2	.364	2	6	3	9	0	0	1.000
1993	—New York (N.L.)	OF	92	373	64	104	14	8	2	25	.279	21	58	38	162	5	3	.982
Major league totals (9 years)			1113	4415	712	1175	138	70	20	280	.266	401	774	648	2066	87	56	.975

CHAMPIONSHIP SERIES RECORD

CHAMPIONSHIP SERIES NOTES: Shares N.L. career record for most times caught stealing—4.

Year	Team (League)	Pos.	G	AB	R	H	2B	3B	HR	RBI	Avg.	BB	SO	SB	PO	A	E	Avg.
			BATTING												FIELDING			
1985	—St. Louis (N.L.)	OF	3	14	2	4	0	0	0	1	.286	0	2	1	8	0	0	1.000
1987	—St. Louis (N.L.)	OF	7	26	3	7	1	0	0	4	.269	4	6	1	9	1	0	1.000
Championship series totals (2 years)			10	40	5	11	1	0	0	5	.275	4	8	2	17	1	0	1.000

WORLD SERIES RECORD

Year	Team (League)	Pos.	G	AB	R	H	2B	3B	HR	RBI	Avg.	BB	SO	SB	PO	A	E	Avg.
			BATTING												FIELDING			
1985	—St. Louis (N.L.)							Did not play.										
1987	—St. Louis (N.L.)	OF	7	28	5	4	2	0	0	2	.143	2	10	6	10	2	0	1.000
World Series totals (1 year)			7	28	5	4	2	0	0	2	.143	2	10	6	10	2	0	1.000

ALL-STAR GAME RECORD

Year	League	Pos.	AB	R	H	2B	3B	HR	RBI	Avg.	BB	SO	SB	PO	A	E	Avg.
			BATTING											FIELDING			
1988	—National.....................	OF	2	1	1	0	0	0	0	.500	0	0	1	3	0	0	1.000
1989	—National.....................	PR-OF	0	0	0	0	0	0	0	...	0	0	0	0	0	0	...
All-Star Game totals (2 years)			2	1	1	0	0	0	0	.500	0	0	1	3	0	0	1.000

COLES, DARNELL

OF/3B, BLUE JAYS

PERSONAL: Born June 2, 1962, in San Bernardino, Calif. . . . 6-1/185. . . . Throws right, bats right. . . . Name pronounced dar-NELL.
HIGH SCHOOL: Eisenhower (Rialto, Calif.).
COLLEGE: Orange Coast College (Calif.).
TRANSACTIONS/CAREER NOTES: Selected by Seattle Mariners organization in first round (sixth pick overall) of free-agent draft (June 3, 1980). . . . On Seattle disabled list (March 29-April 24, 1984); included rehabilitation assignment to Salt Lake City (April 12-24). . . . On Calgary disabled list (August 8-September 9, 1985). . . . Traded by Mariners to Detroit Tigers for P Rich Monteleone (December 12, 1985). . . . On disabled list (June 16-July 1, 1986). . . . On Detroit disabled list (May 25-June 27,

1987); included rehabilitation assignment to Toledo (June 16-27).... Traded by Tigers organization with a player to be named later to Pittsburgh Pirates for 3B Jim Morrison (August 7, 1987); Pirates organization acquired P Morris Madden to complete deal (August 12, 1987).... Traded by Pirates to Mariners for OF Glenn Wilson (July 22, 1988).... Traded by Mariners to Tigers for OF Tracy Jones (June 18, 1990).... Granted free agency (November 5, 1990).... Signed by Phoenix, San Francisco Giants organization (March 30, 1991).... Granted free agency (October 16, 1991).... Signed by Cincinnati Reds organization (November 12, 1991).... On Cincinnati disabled list (August 26, 1992-remainder of season).... Granted free agency (October 28, 1992).... Signed by Toronto Blue Jays (November 27, 1992).
STATISTICAL NOTES: Led Midwest League shortstops with 66 double plays in 1981.... Hit three home runs in one game (September 30, 1987, second game).

			BATTING												FIELDING			
Year	**Team (League)**	**Pos.**	**G**	**AB**	**R**	**H**	**2B**	**3B**	**HR**	**RBI**	**Avg.**	**BB**	**SO**	**SB**	**PO**	**A**	**E**	**Avg.**
1980	—Belling. (N'west)	SS	35	117	23	25	3	1	2	12	.214	22	24	1	37	80	*28	.807
1981	—Wausau (Midwest)	SS	111	354	53	97	20	3	9	48	.274	42	67	9	154	335	52	.904
1982	—Bakersfield (Calif.)	SS	136	482	91	146	24	4	11	55	.303	68	61	27	200	419	*73	.895
1983	—Chatt. (South.)	SS	72	261	49	75	10	4	5	24	.287	41	39	12	131	232	30	.924
	—Salt Lake City (PCL)	SS	61	234	43	74	12	5	10	41	.316	20	19	11	100	178	25	.917
	—Seattle (A.L.)	3B	27	92	9	26	7	0	1	6	.283	7	12	0	17	47	4	.941
1984	—Salt Lake City (PCL)	3B	69	242	57	77	22	3	14	68	.318	48	41	7	45	164	16	.929
	—Seattle (A.L.)	3B-OF	48	143	15	23	3	1	0	6	.161	17	26	2	31	63	8	.922
1985	—Calgary (PCL)	3B-SS-OF	31	97	16	31	8	0	4	24	.320	17	15	2	16	49	5	.929
	—Seattle (A.L.)	SS-3B-OF	27	59	8	14	4	0	1	5	.237	9	17	0	25	44	6	.920
1986	—Detroit (A.L.)■	3B-OF-SS	142	521	67	142	30	2	20	86	.273	45	84	6	111	242	23	.939
1987	—Detroit (A.L.)	3-1-0-S	53	149	14	27	5	1	4	15	.181	15	23	0	84	67	17	.899
	—Toledo (Int'l)	3B-OF-SS	10	37	7	12	5	0	1	8	.324	4	2	0	7	8	1	.938
	—Pittsburgh (N.L.)■	OF-3B-1B	40	119	20	27	8	0	6	24	.227	19	20	1	39	20	3	.952
1988	—Pittsburgh (N.L.)	OF-1B-3B	68	211	20	49	13	1	5	36	.232	20	41	1	100	0	2	.980
	—Seattle (A.L.)■	OF-1B	55	195	32	57	10	1	10	34	.292	17	26	3	66	3	1	.986
1989	—Seattle (A.L.)	OF-3B-1B	146	535	54	135	21	3	10	59	.252	27	61	5	317	76	12	.970
1990	—Sea.-Detroit (A.L.)■	OF-3B-1B	89	215	22	45	7	1	3	20	.209	16	38	0	69	42	9	.925
1991	—Phoenix (PCL)■	3B-OF-1B	83	328	43	95	23	2	6	65	.290	27	43	0	102	118	17	.928
	—San Francisco (N.L.)	OF-1B	11	14	1	3	0	0	0	0	.214	0	2	0	4	0	0	1.000
1992	—Nashville (A.A.)■	3B-1B	22	81	19	24	5	0	6	16	.296	8	13	1	69	35	5	.954
	—Cincinnati (N.L.)	3B-1B-OF	55	141	16	44	11	2	3	18	.312	3	15	1	161	42	0	1.000
1993	—Toronto (A.L.)■	OF-3B-1B	64	194	26	49	9	1	4	26	.253	16	29	1	77	20	7	.933
American League totals (9 years)			651	2103	247	518	96	10	53	257	.246	169	316	17	797	604	87	.942
National League totals (4 years)			174	485	57	123	32	3	14	78	.254	42	78	3	304	62	5	.987
Major league totals (11 years)			825	2588	304	641	128	13	67	335	.248	211	394	20	1101	666	92	.951

CHAMPIONSHIP SERIES RECORD

			BATTING												FIELDING			
Year	**Team (League)**	**Pos.**	**G**	**AB**	**R**	**H**	**2B**	**3B**	**HR**	**RBI**	**Avg.**	**BB**	**SO**	**SB**	**PO**	**A**	**E**	**Avg.**
1993	—Toronto (A.L.)								Did not play.									

WORLD SERIES RECORD

			BATTING												FIELDING			
Year	**Team (League)**	**Pos.**	**G**	**AB**	**R**	**H**	**2B**	**3B**	**HR**	**RBI**	**Avg.**	**BB**	**SO**	**SB**	**PO**	**A**	**E**	**Avg.**
1993	—Toronto (A.L.)								Did not play.									

CONE, DAVID

P, ROYALS

PERSONAL: Born January 2, 1963, in Kansas City, Mo.... 6-1/190.... Throws right, bats left.... Full name: David Brian Cone.
HIGH SCHOOL: Rockhurst (Kansas City, Mo.).
TRANSACTIONS/CAREER NOTES: Selected by Kansas City Royals organization in third round of free-agent draft (June 8, 1981).... On disabled list (April 8, 1983-entire season).... Traded by Royals with C Chris Jelic to New York Mets for C Ed Hearn, P Rick Anderson and P Mauro Gozzo (March 27, 1987).... On New York disabled list (May 28-August 14, 1987); included rehabilitation assignment to Tidewater (July 30-August 14).... Traded by Mets to Toronto Blue Jays for IF Jeff Kent and a player to be named later (August 27, 1992); Mets acquired OF Ryan Thompson to complete deal (September 1, 1992).... Granted free agency (October 30, 1992).... Signed by Royals (December 8, 1992).
RECORDS: Shares major league record for striking out side on nine pitches (August 30, 1991, seventh inning).... Shares N.L. single-game record for most strikeouts—19 (October 6, 1991).
STATISTICAL NOTES: Led Southern League with 27 wild pitches in 1984.... Tied for N.L. lead with 10 balks in 1988.

Year	**Team (League)**	**W**	**L**	**Pct.**	**ERA**	**G**	**GS**	**CG**	**ShO**	**Sv.**	**IP**	**H**	**R**	**ER**	**BB**	**SO**
1981	—GC Royals-B (GCL)	6	4	.600	2.55	14	12	0	0	0	67	52	24	19	33	45
1982	—Char., S.C. (S. Atl.)	9	2	.818	2.06	16	16	1	1	0	104⅔	84	38	24	47	87
	—Fort Myers (FSL)	7	1	.875	2.12	10	9	6	1	0	72⅓	56	21	17	25	57
1983	—								Did not play.							
1984	—Memphis (South.)	8	12	.400	4.28	29	29	9	1	0	178⅔	162	103	85	114	110
1985	—Omaha (A.A.)	9	15	.375	4.65	28	27	5	1	0	158⅔	157	90	82	*93	115
1986	—Omaha (A.A.)	8	4	.667	2.79	39	2	2	0	14	71	60	23	22	25	63
	—Kansas City (A.L.)	0	0	...	5.56	11	0	0	0	0	22⅔	29	14	14	13	21
1987	—New York (N.L.)■	5	6	.455	3.71	21	13	1	0	1	99⅓	87	46	41	44	68
	—Tidewater (Int'l)	0	1	.000	5.73	3	3	0	0	0	11	10	8	7	6	7
1988	—New York (N.L.)	20	3	*.870	2.22	35	28	8	4	0	231⅓	178	67	57	80	213
1989	—New York (N.L.)	14	8	.636	3.52	34	33	7	2	0	219⅔	183	92	86	74	190
1990	—New York (N.L.)	14	10	.583	3.23	31	30	6	2	0	211⅔	177	84	76	65	*233
1991	—New York (N.L.)	14	14	.500	3.29	34	34	5	2	0	232⅔	204	95	85	73	*241
1992	—New York (N.L.)	13	7	.650	2.88	27	27	7	•5	0	196⅔	162	75	63	*82	214
	—Toronto (A.L.)■	4	3	.571	2.55	8	7	0	0	0	53	39	16	15	29	47

Year	Team (League)	W	L	Pct.	ERA	G	GS	CG	ShO	Sv.	IP	H	R	ER	BB	SO
1993	—Kansas City (A.L.)■	11	14	.440	3.33	34	34	6	1	0	254	205	102	94	114	191
A.L. totals (3 years)		15	17	.469	3.36	53	41	6	1	0	329⅔	273	132	123	156	259
N.L. totals (6 years)		80	48	.625	3.08	182	165	34	15	1	1191⅓	991	459	408	418	1159
Major league totals (8 years)		95	65	.594	3.14	235	206	40	16	1	1521	1264	591	531	574	1418

CHAMPIONSHIP SERIES RECORD

Year	Team (League)	W	L	Pct.	ERA	G	GS	CG	ShO	Sv.	IP	H	R	ER	BB	SO
1988	—New York (N.L.)	1	1	.500	4.50	3	2	1	0	0	12	10	6	6	5	9
1992	—Toronto (A.L.)	1	1	.500	3.00	2	2	0	0	0	12	11	7	4	5	9
Champ. series totals (2 years)		2	2	.500	3.75	5	4	1	0	0	24	21	13	10	10	18

WORLD SERIES RECORD

Year	Team (League)	W	L	Pct.	ERA	G	GS	CG	ShO	Sv.	IP	H	R	ER	BB	SO
1992	—Toronto (A.L.)	0	0	...	3.48	2	2	0	0	0	10⅓	9	5	4	8	8

ALL-STAR GAME RECORD

Year	League	W	L	Pct.	ERA	GS	CG	ShO	Sv.	IP	H	R	ER	BB	SO
1988	—National	0	0	...	0.00	0	0	0	0	1	0	0	0	0	1
1992	—National	0	0	...	0.00	0	0	0	0	1	0	0	0	0	1
All-Star totals (2 years)		0	0	...	0.00	0	0	0	0	2	0	0	0	0	2

CONINE, JEFF

OF, MARLINS

PERSONAL: Born June 27, 1966, in Tacoma, Wash. . . . 6-1/220. . . . Throws right, bats right. . . . Full name: Jeffrey Guy Conine.

HIGH SCHOOL: Eisenhower (Yakima, Wash.).

COLLEGE: UCLA.

TRANSACTIONS/CAREER NOTES: Selected by Kansas City Royals organization in 58th round of free-agent draft (June 2, 1987). . . . On disabled list (June 28, 1991-remainder of season). . . . Selected by Florida Marlins in first round (22nd pick overall) of expansion draft (November 17, 1992).

RECORDS: Shares major league rookie-season record for most games—162 (1993).

HONORS: Named Southern League Most Valuable Player (1990).

STATISTICAL NOTES: Led Southern League first basemen with 1,164 putouts, 95 assists, 22 errors, 1,281 total chances and 108 double plays in 1990.

				BATTING											FIELDING			
Year	Team (League)	Pos.	G	AB	R	H	2B	3B	HR	RBI	Avg.	BB	SO	SB	PO	A	E	Avg.
1988	—Baseball City (FSL)	1B-3B	118	415	63	113	23	9	10	59	.272	46	77	26	661	51	22	.970
1989	—Baseball City (FSL)	1B	113	425	68	116	12	7	14	60	.273	40	91	32	830	65	18	.980
1990	—Memphis (South.)	1B-3B	137	487	89	156	37	8	15	95	.320	94	88	21	†1164	†95	†22	.983
	—Kansas City (A.L.)	1B	9	20	3	5	2	0	0	2	.250	2	5	0	39	4	1	.977
1991	—Omaha (A.A.)	1B-OF	51	171	23	44	9	1	3	15	.257	26	39	0	392	41	7	.984
1992	—Omaha (A.A.)	1B-OF	110	397	69	120	24	5	20	72	.302	54	67	4	845	60	6	.993
	—Kansas City (A.L.)	OF-1B	28	91	10	23	5	2	0	9	.253	8	23	0	75	3	0	1.000
1993	—Florida (N.L.)■	OF-1B	*162	595	75	174	24	3	12	79	.292	52	135	2	403	25	2	.995
American League totals (2 years)			37	111	13	28	7	2	0	11	.252	10	28	0	114	7	1	.992
National League totals (1 year)			162	595	75	174	24	3	12	79	.292	52	135	2	403	25	2	.995
Major league totals (3 years)			199	706	88	202	31	5	12	90	.286	62	163	2	517	32	3	.995

CONROY, BRIAN

P, RED SOX

PERSONAL: Born August 29, 1968, in Needham, Mass. . . . 6-2/185. . . . Throws right, bats both. . . . Full name: Brian Christopher Conroy.

HIGH SCHOOL: Catholic Memorial (Boston).

COLLEGE: Northeastern, then Massachusetts.

TRANSACTIONS/CAREER NOTES: Selected by Boston Red Sox organization in 22nd round of free-agent draft (June 5, 1989). . . . On disabled list (July 29, 1993-remainder of season).

STATISTICAL NOTES: Pitched 2-0 no-hit victory for New Britain against Reading (May 22, 1991).

Year	Team (League)	W	L	Pct.	ERA	G	GS	CG	ShO	Sv.	IP	H	R	ER	BB	SO
1989	—GC Red Sox (GCL)	4	2	.667	2.25	7	7	2	0	0	44	33	15	11	9	31
	—Winter Haven (FSL)	3	3	.500	2.95	8	6	2	2	0	39⅔	38	19	13	11	30
1990	—Lynchburg (Caro.)	10	12	.455	3.53	26	26	*8	*4	0	186⅓	160	84	73	51	147
	—New Britain (East.)	0	1	.000	6.00	1	1	0	0	0	6	7	4	4	1	3
1991	—New Britain (East.)	1	5	.167	3.02	10	10	1	1	0	65⅔	51	27	22	26	34
	—Pawtucket (Int'l)	6	4	.600	4.58	17	16	1	0	0	98⅓	95	60	50	51	66
1992	—Pawtucket (Int'l)	7	5	.583	4.62	15	13	1	1	0	85⅔	91	49	44	31	57
	—New Britain (East.)	4	6	.400	3.82	11	11	3	1	0	75⅓	70	33	32	17	40
1993	—Pawtucket (Int'l)	5	7	.417	5.86	19	19	0	0	0	106	126	74	69	40	64

CONVERSE, JIM

P, MARINERS

PERSONAL: Born August 17, 1971, in San Francisco. . . . 5-9/180. . . . Throws right, bats left. . . . Full name: James Daniel Converse.

HIGH SCHOOL: Orangevale (Calif.)-Casa Roble.

TRANSACTIONS/CAREER NOTES: Selected by Seattle Mariners organization in 16th round of free-agent draft (June 4, 1990).

HONORS: Named Southern League co-Pitcher of the Year (1992).

STATISTICAL NOTES: Led Northwest League with 10 balks in 1990.

Year	Team (League)	W	L	Pct.	ERA	G	GS	CG	ShO	Sv.	IP	H	R	ER	BB	SO
1990	—Belling. (N'west)	2	4	.333	3.92	12	12	0	0	0	66⅔	50	31	29	32	75
1991	—Peninsula (Caro.)	6	15	.286	4.97	26	26	1	0	0	137⅔	143	90	76	97	137

Year	Team (League)	W	L	Pct.	ERA	G	GS	CG	ShO	Sv.	IP	H	R	ER	BB	SO
1992	—Jacksonv. (South.)	12	7	.632	2.66	27	26	2	0	0	159	134	61	47	*82	*157
1993	—Calgary (PCL)	7	8	.467	5.40	23	22	•4	0	0	121⅔	144	86	73	64	78
	—Seattle (A.L.)	1	3	.250	5.31	4	4	0	0	0	20⅓	23	12	12	14	10
Major league totals (1 year)		1	3	.250	5.31	4	4	0	0	0	20⅓	23	12	12	14	10

COOK, ANDY

P

PERSONAL: Born August 30, 1967, in Memphis, Tenn.... 6-5/205.... Throws right, bats right.... Full name: Andrew Bernard Cook.
HIGH SCHOOL: Christian Brothers (Memphis, Tenn.).
COLLEGE: Memphis State.
TRANSACTIONS/CAREER NOTES: Selected by New York Yankees organization in 11th round of free-agent draft (June 1, 1988).... On Columbus disabled list (April 9-30, 1992 and July 3-19 and August 26-31, 1993).... Released by Yankees (August 31, 1993).

Year	Team (League)	W	L	Pct.	ERA	G	GS	CG	ShO	Sv.	IP	H	R	ER	BB	SO
1988	—Oneonta (NYP)	8	4	.667	3.62	16	•16	2	0	0	102	*116	50	41	21	65
1989	—Prin. William (Car.)	8	12	.400	3.29	25	24	5	1	0	153	123	68	56	49	83
1990	—Alb./Colon. (East.)	12	8	.600	3.45	24	24	5	0	0	156⅔	146	69	60	52	53
1991	—Alb./Colon. (East.)	6	3	.667	3.95	14	14	1	0	0	82	94	46	36	27	46
	—Columbus (Int'l)	5	5	.500	3.52	13	13	2	0	0	79⅓	63	34	31	38	40
1992	—Columbus (Int'l)	7	5	.583	3.16	32	9	0	0	2	99⅔	85	41	35	36	58
1993	—Columbus (Int'l)	6	7	.462	6.54	21	20	0	0	0	118⅓	149	91	86	49	47
	—New York (A.L.)	0	1	.000	5.06	4	0	0	0	0	5⅓	4	3	3	7	4
Major league totals (1 year)		0	1	.000	5.06	4	0	0	0	0	5⅓	4	3	3	7	4

C

COOK, DENNIS

P, WHITE SOX

PERSONAL: Born October 4, 1962, in Lamarque, Tex.... 6-3/185.... Throws left, bats left.... Full name: Dennis Bryan Cook.
HIGH SCHOOL: Dickinson (Tex.).
COLLEGE: Angelina College (Tex.) and Texas.
TRANSACTIONS/CAREER NOTES: Selected by San Diego Padres organization in sixth round of free-agent draft (January 11, 1983).... Selected by San Francisco Giants organization in 18th round of free-agent draft (June 3, 1985).... Traded by Giants with P Terry Mulholland and 3B Charlie Hayes to Philadelphia Phillies for P Steve Bedrosian and a player to be named later (June, 18, 1989); Giants organization acquired IF Rick Parker to complete deal (August 7, 1989).... Traded by Phillies to Los Angeles Dodgers for C Darrin Fletcher (September 13, 1990).... Traded by Dodgers with P Mike Christopher to Cleveland Indians for P Rudy Seanez (December 10, 1991).... Granted free agency (October 15, 1993).... Signed by Chicago White Sox organization (January 5, 1994).
HONORS: Named Texas League Pitcher of the Year (1987).
STATISTICAL NOTES: Led A.L. with five balks in 1992.

Year	Team (League)	W	L	Pct.	ERA	G	GS	CG	ShO	Sv.	IP	H	R	ER	BB	SO
1985	—Clinton (Midwest)	5	4	.556	3.36	13	13	1	0	0	83	73	35	31	27	40
1986	—Fresno (California)	12	7	.632	3.97	27	25	2	1	1	170	141	92	75	100	*173
1987	—Shreveport (Texas)	9	2	.818	2.13	16	16	1	1	0	105⅔	94	32	25	20	98
	—Phoenix (PCL)	2	5	.286	5.23	12	11	1	0	0	62	72	45	36	26	24
1988	—Phoenix (PCL)	11	9	.550	3.88	26	25	5	1	0	141⅓	138	73	61	51	110
	—San Francisco (N.L.)	2	1	.667	2.86	4	4	1	1	0	22	9	8	7	11	13
1989	—Phoenix (PCL)	7	4	.636	3.12	12	12	3	1	0	78	73	29	27	19	85
	—S.F.-Phil. (N.L.)■	7	8	.467	3.72	23	18	2	1	0	121	110	59	50	38	67
1990	—Phil.-L.A. (N.L.)■	9	4	.692	3.92	47	16	2	1	1	156	155	74	68	56	64
1991	—Albuquerque (PCL)	7	3	.700	3.63	14	14	1	0	0	91⅔	73	46	37	32	84
	—Los Angeles (N.L.)	1	0	1.000	0.51	20	1	0	0	0	17⅔	12	3	1	7	8
	—San Antonio (Tex.)	1	3	.250	2.49	7	7	1	0	0	50⅔	43	20	14	10	45
1992	—Cleveland (A.L.)■	5	7	.417	3.82	32	25	1	0	0	158	156	79	67	50	96
1993	—Cleveland (A.L.)	5	5	.500	5.67	25	6	0	0	0	54	62	36	34	16	34
	—Charlotte (Int'l)	3	2	.600	5.06	12	6	0	0	0	42⅔	46	26	24	6	40
A.L. totals (2 years)		10	12	.455	4.29	57	31	1	0	0	212	218	115	101	66	130
N.L. totals (4 years)		19	13	.594	3.58	94	39	5	3	1	316⅔	286	144	126	112	152
Major league totals (6 years)		29	25	.537	3.86	151	70	6	3	1	528⅔	504	259	227	178	282

COOK, MIKE

P, ORIOLES

PERSONAL: Born August 14, 1963, in Charleston, S.C.... 6-3/225.... Throws right, bats left.... Full name: Michael Horace Cook.
HIGH SCHOOL: St. Andrews Parish (Charleston, S.C.).
COLLEGE: South Carolina.
TRANSACTIONS/CAREER NOTES: Selected by Philadelphia Phillies organization in sixth round of free-agent draft (June 7, 1982).... Selected by California Angels organization in first round (19th pick overall) of free-agent draft (June 3, 1985); pick received as compensation for Baltimore Orioles signing Type A free agent Fred Lynn.... On temporary inactive list (July 9, 1985-remainder of season).... Traded by Angels organization with P Rob Wassenaar and 1B Paul Sorrento to Minnesota Twins organization for P Bert Blyleven and P Kevin Trudeau (November 3, 1988).... Released by Twins organization (April 5, 1991).... Signed by Seattle Mariners organization (April 19, 1991).... On disabled list (April 19-26, May 21-June 7 and June 19-26, 1991).... Released by Mariners organization (July 4, 1991).... Signed by Louisville, St. Louis Cardinals organization (December 18, 1991).... Granted free agency (October 15, 1992).... Signed by Rochester, Baltimore Orioles organization (January 23, 1993).

Year	Team (League)	W	L	Pct.	ERA	G	GS	CG	ShO	Sv.	IP	H	R	ER	BB	SO
1985	—Quad Cities (Mid.)	0	0	...	1.80	2	2	0	0	0	10	6	3	2	7	10
1986	—Midland (Texas)	4	6	.400	3.50	15	15	2	0	0	105⅓	101	54	41	52	82
	—California (A.L.)	0	2	.000	9.00	5	1	0	0	0	9	13	12	9	7	6
	—Edmonton (PCL)	4	1	.800	5.37	9	9	0	0	0	55⅓	49	42	33	24	35

Year	Team (League)	W	L	Pct.	ERA	G	GS	CG	ShO	Sv.	IP	H	R	ER	BB	SO
1987	—California (A.L.)	1	2	.333	5.50	16	1	0	0	0	34⅓	34	21	21	18	27
	—Edmonton (PCL)	4	7	.364	6.48	15	15	4	2	0	83⅓	81	64	60	54	54
1988	—Edmonton (PCL)	5	9	.357	4.85	51	5	0	0	10	91	93	56	49	41	84
	—California (A.L.)	0	1	.000	4.91	3	3	0	0	0	3⅔	4	2	2	1	2
1989	—Minnesota (A.L.)■	0	1	.000	5.06	15	0	0	0	0	21⅓	22	12	12	17	15
	—Portland (PCL)	5	3	.625	3.66	42	0	0	0	12	64	53	29	26	35	55
1990	—Portland (PCL)	6	8	.429	*3.20	19	19	2	1	0	115⅓	105	54	41	59	63
1991	—Calgary (PCL)■	2	4	.333	9.68	10	6	0	0	0	30⅔	45	35	33	24	18
1992	—Louisville (A.A.)■	3	2	.600	4.60	43	0	0	0	0	58⅔	58	31	30	31	56
1993	—Rochester (Int'l)■	6	7	.462	3.10	57	0	0	0	13	81⅓	77	39	28	48	74
	—Baltimore (A.L.)	0	0	...	0.00	2	0	0	0	0	3	1	0	0	2	3
Major league totals (5 years)		1	6	.143	5.55	41	5	0	0	0	71⅓	74	47	44	45	53

COOKE, STEVE

P, PIRATES

PERSONAL: Born January 14, 1970, in Kauai, Hawaii. ... 6-6/229. ... Throws left, bats right. ... Full name: Stephen Montague Cooke.
HIGH SCHOOL: Tigard (Ore.).
COLLEGE: Southern Idaho.
TRANSACTIONS/CAREER NOTES: Selected by Philadelphia Phillies organization in 53rd round of free-agent draft (June 1, 1988). ... Selected by Pittsburgh Pirates organization in 35th round of free-agent draft (June 5, 1989). ... On Buffalo disabled list (May 18-28, 1992).

Year	Team (League)	W	L	Pct.	ERA	G	GS	CG	ShO	Sv.	IP	H	R	ER	BB	SO
1990	—Welland (NYP)	2	3	.400	2.35	11	11	0	0	0	46	36	21	12	17	43
1991	—Augusta (S. Atl.)	5	4	.556	2.82	11	11	1	0	0	60⅔	50	28	19	35	52
	—Salem (Carolina)	1	0	1.000	4.85	2	2	0	0	0	13	14	8	7	2	5
	—Carolina (South.)	0	0	...	2.84	3	9	1	1	0	12⅔	9	4	4	7	18
1992	—Carolina (South.)	2	2	.500	3.00	6	6	0	0	0	36	31	13	12	12	38
	—Buffalo (A.A.)	6	3	.667	3.75	13	13	0	0	0	74⅓	71	35	31	36	52
	—Pittsburgh (N.L.)	2	0	1.000	3.52	11	0	0	0	1	23	22	9	9	4	10
1993	—Pittsburgh (N.L.)	10	10	.500	3.89	32	32	3	1	0	210⅔	207	101	91	59	132
Major league totals (2 years)		12	10	.545	3.85	43	32	3	1	1	233⅔	229	110	100	63	142

COOMER, RON

3B, DODGERS

PERSONAL: Born November 18, 1966, in Crest Hill, Ill. ... 5-11/195. ... Throws right, bats right. ... Full name: Ronald Bryan Coomer.
HIGH SCHOOL: Lockport (Ill.) Township.
COLLEGE: Taft (Calif.) College.
TRANSACTIONS/CAREER NOTES: Selected by Oakland Athletics organization in 14th round of free-agent draft (June 2, 1987). ... Released by A's organization (August 1, 1990). ... Signed as free agent by Chicago White Sox organization (March 18, 1991). ... On disabled list (June 5-19, 1992). ... On Birmingham disabled list (June 12-21, 1993). ... Traded by White Sox to Los Angeles Dodgers for P Isidro Martinez (December 27, 1993).
STATISTICAL NOTES: Led Southern League with eight sacrifice flies and tied for lead in grounding into double plays with 21 in 1991. ... Led Southern League third basemen with 94 putouts, 396 total chances, 24 double plays and tied for lead with 26 errors in 1991.

				BATTING											FIELDING			
Year	Team (League)	Pos.	G	AB	R	H	2B	3B	HR	RBI	Avg.	BB	SO	SB	PO	A	E	Avg.
1987	—Medford (N'west)	3B-1B	45	168	23	58	10	2	1	26	.345	19	22	1	54	78	11	.923
1988	—Modesto (Calif.)	3B-1B	131	495	67	138	23	2	17	85	.279	60	88	2	78	105	16	.920
1989	—Madison (Midwest)	3B-1B	61	216	28	69	15	0	4	28	.319	30	34	0	67	64	6	.956
1990	—Huntsville (South.)	2B-1B-3B	66	194	22	43	7	0	3	27	.222	21	40	3	200	100	11	.965
1991	—Birm. (Southern)■	3B-1B	137	505	*81	129	27	5	13	76	.255	59	78	0	†113	278	‡26	.938
1992	—Vancouver (PCL)	3B	86	262	29	62	10	0	9	40	.237	16	36	3	49	115	13	.927
1993	—Birm. (Southern)	3B-1B	69	262	44	85	18	0	13	50	.324	15	43	1	43	106	11	.931
	—Nashville (A.A.)	3B	59	211	34	66	19	0	13	51	.313	10	29	1	30	107	16	.895

COOPER, SCOTT

3B, RED SOX

PERSONAL: Born October 13, 1967, in St. Louis. ... 6-3/205. ... Throws right, bats left. ... Full name: Scott Kendrick Cooper.
HIGH SCHOOL: Pattonville (Maryland Heights, Mo.).
TRANSACTIONS/CAREER NOTES: Selected by Boston Red Sox organization in third round of free-agent draft (June 2, 1986).
STATISTICAL NOTES: Led Carolina League with 234 total bases in 1988. ... Led International League third basemen with 94 putouts and tied for lead with 240 assists in 1990. ... Led International League with 11 intentional bases on balls received in 1991. ... Led International League third basemen with 106 putouts, 232 assists, 26 errors and 364 total chances in 1991.

				BATTING											FIELDING			
Year	Team (League)	Pos.	G	AB	R	H	2B	3B	HR	RBI	Avg.	BB	SO	SB	PO	A	E	Avg.
1986	—Elmira (N.Y.-Penn)	3B	51	191	23	55	9	0	9	43	.288	19	32	1	22	62	9	.903
1987	—Greensboro (S. Atl.)	3B-1B-P	119	370	52	93	21	2	15	63	.251	58	69	1	150	153	21	.935
1988	—Lynchburg (Caro.)	3B-1B-OF	130	497	90	•148	*45	7	9	73	.298	58	74	0	116	198	27	.921
1989	—New Britain (East.)	3B	124	421	50	104	24	2	7	39	.247	55	84	1	91	212	22	.932
1990	—Pawtucket (Int'l)	3B-SS	124	433	56	115	17	1	12	44	.266	39	75	2	†96	‡244	22	.939
	—Boston (A.L.)	PH-PR	2	1	0	0	0	0	0	0	.000	0	1	0	...	...	...	...
1991	—Pawtucket (Int'l)	3B-SS	137	483	55	134	21	2	15	72	.277	50	58	3	†115	†241	†26	.932
	—Boston (A.L.)	3B	14	35	6	16	4	2	0	7	.457	2	2	0	6	22	2	.933
1992	—Boston (A.L.)	1-3-S-2	123	337	34	93	21	0	5	33	.276	37	33	1	472	136	9	.985
1993	—Boston (A.L.)	3B-1B-SS	156	526	67	147	29	3	9	63	.279	58	81	5	112	244	24	.937
Major league totals (4 years)			295	899	107	256	54	5	14	103	.285	97	117	6	590	402	35	.966

ALL-STAR GAME RECORD

Year	League	Pos.	AB	R	H	2B	3B	HR	RBI	Avg.	BB	SO	SB	PO	A	E	Avg.
			BATTING											FIELDING			
1993	—American	3B	2	0	0	0	0	0	0	.000	0	1	0	1	0	0	1.000

RECORD AS PITCHER

Year	Team (League)	W	L	Pct.	ERA	G	GS	CG	ShO	Sv.	IP	H	R	ER	BB	SO
1987	—Greensboro (S. Atl.)	0	0	...	0.00	2	0	0	0	0	2	2	1	0	2	3

CORA, JOEY

2B, WHITE SOX

PERSONAL: Born May 14, 1965, in Caguas, Puerto Rico. . . . 5-8/155. . . . Throws right, bats both. . . . Full name: Jose Manuel Cora.

COLLEGE: Vanderbilt.

TRANSACTIONS/CAREER NOTES: Selected by San Diego Padres organization in first round (23rd pick overall) of free-agent draft (June 3, 1985); pick received as compensation for New York Yankees signing free agent Ed Whitson. . . . On disabled list (June 22-August 15, 1986). . . . Traded by Padres with IF Kevin Garner and OF Warren Newson to Chicago White Sox for P Adam Peterson and P Steve Rosenberg (March 31, 1991). . . . On Chicago disabled list (June 22-July 11, 1991); included rehabilitation assignment to South Bend (July 9-11).

STATISTICAL NOTES: Led Pacific Coast League second basemen with 24 errors in both 1988 and 1989. . . . Led A.L. with 19 sacrifice hits in 1993. . . . Led A.L. second basemen with 19 errors in 1993.

Year	Team (League)	Pos.	G	AB	R	H	2B	3B	HR	RBI	Avg.	BB	SO	SB	PO	A	E	Avg.
			BATTING												FIELDING			
1985	—Spokane (N'west)	2B	43	170	48	55	11	2	3	26	.324	27	24	13	92	123	9	.960
1986	—Beaumont (Texas)	2B-SS	81	315	54	96	5	5	3	41	.305	47	29	24	217	267	19	.962
1987	—San Diego (N.L.)	2B-SS	77	241	23	57	7	2	0	13	.237	28	26	15	123	200	10	.970
	—Las Vegas (PCL)	2B-SS	81	293	50	81	9	1	1	24	.276	62	39	12	186	249	9	.980
1988	—Las Vegas (PCL)	2B-3B-OF	127	460	73	136	15	3	3	55	.296	44	19	31	285	346	†26	.960
1989	—Las Vegas (PCL)	2B-SS	119	507	79	157	25	4	0	37	.310	42	31	★40	245	349	†27	.957
	—San Diego (N.L.)	SS-3B-2B	12	19	5	6	1	0	0	1	.316	1	0	1	11	15	2	.929
1990	—San Diego (N.L.)	SS-2B-C	51	100	12	27	3	0	0	2	.270	6	9	8	59	49	11	.908
	—Las Vegas (PCL)	SS-2B	51	211	41	74	13	9	0	24	.351	29	16	15	125	148	14	.951
1991	—Chicago (A.L.)■	2B-SS	100	228	37	55	2	3	0	18	.241	20	21	11	107	192	10	.968
	—South Bend (Mid.)	2B	1	5	1	1	0	0	0	0	.200	0	1	1	2	4	0	1.000
1992	—Chicago (A.L.)	2B-SS-3B	68	122	27	30	7	1	0	9	.246	22	13	10	60	84	3	.980
1993	—Chicago (A.L.)	2B-3B	153	579	95	155	15	13	2	51	.268	67	63	20	296	413	†19	.974
American League totals (3 years)			321	929	159	240	24	17	2	78	.258	109	97	41	463	689	32	.973
National League totals (3 years)			140	360	40	90	11	2	0	16	.250	35	35	24	193	264	23	.952
Major league totals (6 years)			461	1289	199	330	35	19	2	94	.256	144	132	65	656	953	55	.967

CHAMPIONSHIP SERIES RECORD

Year	Team (League)	Pos.	G	AB	R	H	2B	3B	HR	RBI	Avg.	BB	SO	SB	PO	A	E	Avg.
			BATTING												FIELDING			
1993	—Chicago (A.L.)	2B	6	22	1	3	0	0	0	1	.136	3	6	0	18	20	3	.927

CORDERO, WILFREDO

SS, EXPOS

PERSONAL: Born October 3, 1971, in Mayaguez, Puerto Rico. . . . 6-2/190. . . . Throws right, bats right. . . . Full name: Wilfredo Nieva Cordero. . . . Name pronounced cor-DARE-oh.

HIGH SCHOOL: Centro de Servicios Education de Mayaguez (Puerto Rico).

TRANSACTIONS/CAREER NOTES: Signed as free agent by Montreal Expos organization (May 24, 1988). . . . On Indianapolis disabled list (August 1, 1991-remainder of season; and May 12-June 11 and July 7-20, 1992).

Year	Team (League)	Pos.	G	AB	R	H	2B	3B	HR	RBI	Avg.	BB	SO	SB	PO	A	E	Avg.
			BATTING												FIELDING			
1988	—Jamestown (NYP)	SS	52	190	18	49	3	0	2	22	.258	15	44	3	82	159	31	.886
1989	—W.P. Beach (FSL)	SS	78	289	37	80	12	2	6	29	.277	33	58	2	121	224	29	.922
	—Jacksonv. (South.)	SS	39	121	9	26	6	1	3	17	.215	12	33	1	62	93	7	.957
1990	—Jacksonv. (South.)	SS	131	444	63	104	18	4	7	40	.234	56	122	9	179	349	41	.928
1991	—Indianapolis (A.A.)	SS	98	360	48	94	16	4	11	52	.261	26	89	9	157	287	27	.943
1992	—Indianapolis (A.A.)	SS	52	204	32	64	11	1	6	27	.314	24	54	6	75	146	12	.948
	—Montreal (N.L.)	SS-2B	45	126	17	38	4	1	2	8	.302	9	31	0	51	92	8	.947
1993	—Montreal (N.L.)	SS-3B	138	475	56	118	32	2	10	58	.248	34	60	12	163	373	36	.937
Major league totals (2 years)			183	601	73	156	36	3	12	66	.260	43	91	12	214	465	44	.939

CORDOVA, MARTY

OF, TWINS

PERSONAL: Born July 10, 1969, in Las Vegas. . . . 6-0/200. . . . Throws right, bats right. . . . Full name: Martin Keevin Cordova.

HIGH SCHOOL: Bishop Gorman (Las Vegas).

COLLEGE: Orange Coast College (Calif.) and UNLV.

TRANSACTIONS/CAREER NOTES: Selected by San Diego Padres organization in eighth round of free-agent draft (June 2, 1987). . . . Selected by Minnesota Twins organization in 10th round of free-agent draft (June 5, 1989). . . . On Kenosha disabled list (April 12-May 20, 1991).

HONORS: Named California League Most Valuable Player (1992).

STATISTICAL NOTES: Led California League with 302 total bases and .589 slugging percentage and tied for lead in grounding into double plays with 20 in 1992.

Year	Team (League)	Pos.	G	AB	R	H	2B	3B	HR	RBI	Avg.	BB	SO	SB	PO	A	E	Avg.
			BATTING												FIELDING			
1989	—Elizabeth. (Appal.)	OF-3B	38	148	32	42	2	3	8	29	.284	14	29	2	6	9	4	.789
1990	—Kenosha (Midwest)	OF	81	269	35	58	7	5	7	25	.216	28	73	6	87	5	5	.948

Year	Team (League)	Pos.	G	AB	R	H	2B	3B	HR	RBI	Avg.	BB	SO	SB	PO	A	E	Avg.
			BATTING												FIELDING			
1991	—Visalia (California)...	OF	71	189	31	40	6	1	7	19	.212	17	46	2	58	2	5	.923
1992	—Visalia (California)...	OF	134	513	103	175	31	6	*28	*131	.341	76	99	13	173	10	3	.984
1993	—Nashville (South.)....	OF	138	508	83	127	30	5	19	77	.250	64	*153	10	209	7	2	*.991

CORMIER, RHEAL

P, CARDINALS

PERSONAL: Born April 23, 1967, in Moncton, New Brunswick, Canada. . . . 5-10/185. . . . Throws left, bats left. . . . Full name: Rheal Paul Cormier. . . . Name pronounced ree-AL COR-mee-AY.
COLLEGE: Community College of Rhode Island.
TRANSACTIONS/CAREER NOTES: Selected by St. Louis Cardinals organization in sixth round of free-agent draft (June 6, 1988). . . . On Louisville disabled list (April 10-29, 1991). . . . On disabled list (August 12-September 7, 1993).
MISCELLANEOUS: Member of 1988 Canadian Olympic baseball team.

Year	Team (League)	W	L	Pct.	ERA	G	GS	CG	ShO	Sv.	IP	H	R	ER	BB	SO
1989	—St. Peters. (FSL)	12	7	.632	2.23	26	26	4	1	0	169⅔	141	63	42	33	122
1990	—Arkansas (Texas)......	5	•12	.294	5.04	22	21	3	1	0	121⅓	133	81	68	30	102
	—Louisville (A.A.).........	1	1	.500	2.25	4	4	0	0	0	24	18	8	6	3	9
1991	—Louisville (A.A.).........	7	9	.438	4.23	21	21	3	*3	0	127⅔	140	64	60	31	74
	—St. Louis (N.L.)...........	4	5	.444	4.12	11	10	2	0	0	67⅔	74	35	31	8	38
1992	—Louisville (A.A.).........	0	1	.000	6.75	1	1	0	0	0	4	8	4	3	0	1
	—St. Louis (N.L.)...........	10	10	.500	3.68	31	30	3	0	0	186	194	83	76	33	117
1993	—St. Louis (N.L.)...........	7	6	.538	4.33	38	21	1	0	0	145⅓	163	80	70	27	75
Major league totals (3 years)		21	21	.500	3.99	80	61	6	0	0	399	431	198	177	68	230

CORNELIUS, REID

P, EXPOS

PERSONAL: Born June 2, 1970, in Thomasville, Ala. . . . 6-0/185. . . . Throws right, bats right. . . . Full name: Jonathan Reid Cornelius.
HIGH SCHOOL: Thomasville (Alabaster, Ala.).
TRANSACTIONS/CAREER NOTES: Selected by Montreal Expos organization in 11th round of free-agent draft (June 1, 1988). . . . On West Palm Beach disabled list (May 27-August 2, 1990 and May 20-June 3, 1991). . . . On Harrisburg disabled list (August 6, 1991-remainder of season and April 27-September 6, 1992).

Year	Team (League)	W	L	Pct.	ERA	G	GS	CG	ShO	Sv.	IP	H	R	ER	BB	SO
1989	—Rockford (Midw.)	5	6	.455	4.27	17	17	0	0	0	84⅓	71	58	40	63	66
1990	—W.P. Beach (FSL)	2	3	.400	3.38	11	11	0	0	0	56	54	25	21	25	47
1991	—W.P. Beach (FSL)	8	3	.727	2.39	17	17	0	0	0	109⅓	79	31	29	43	81
	—Harrisburg (East.)	2	1	.667	2.89	3	3	1	1	0	18⅔	15	6	6	7	12
1992	—Harrisburg (East.)	1	0	1.000	3.13	4	4	0	0	0	23	11	8	8	8	17
1993	—Harrisburg (East.)	10	7	.588	4.17	27	27	1	0	0	157⅔	146	95	73	82	119

CORREA, JOSE

P, TWINS

PERSONAL: Born June 21, 1972, in Guarenas, Venezuela. . . . 6-2/194. . . . Throws right, bats right. . . . Full name: Jose Nunez Correa.
HIGH SCHOOL: Menca de Leoni (Guarenas, Venezuela).
TRANSACTIONS/CAREER NOTES: Signed as free agent by Minnesota Twins organization (October 24, 1989).

Year	Team (League)	W	L	Pct.	ERA	G	GS	CG	ShO	Sv.	IP	H	R	ER	BB	SO
1990	—GC Twins (GCL)	4	5	.444	4.55	14	8	1	0	0	59⅓	55	37	30	13	47
1991	—GC Twins (GCL)	2	2	.500	2.59	*27	0	0	0	6	48⅔	39	20	14	15	53
1992	—Elizabeth. (Appal.).....	7	2	.778	2.25	22	0	0	0	3	44	27	13	11	18	50
1993	—Fort Wayne (Mid.)......	4	5	.444	2.63	41	0	0	0	9	96	81	33	28	36	107

CORREIA, ROD

SS/2B, ANGELS

PERSONAL: Born September 13, 1967, in Providence, R.I. . . . 5-11/180. . . . Throws right, bats right. . . . Full name: Ronald Douglas Correia. . . . Name pronounced KOR-ee-ah.
HIGH SCHOOL: Dighton-Rehoboth Regional (Rehoboth, Mass.).
COLLEGE: Southeastern Massachusetts University.
TRANSACTIONS/CAREER NOTES: Selected by Oakland Athletics organization in 15th round of free-agent draft (June 1, 1988). . . . On Tacoma disabled list (May 7-14, 1991). . . . Traded by A's organization to California Angels organization for OF Dan Grunhard (January 17, 1992).
STATISTICAL NOTES: Led Texas League shortstops with 621 total chances in 1992.

Year	Team (League)	Pos.	G	AB	R	H	2B	3B	HR	RBI	Avg.	BB	SO	SB	PO	A	E	Avg.
			BATTING												FIELDING			
1988	—S. Oregon (N'west)...	2B-SS	56	207	23	52	7	3	1	19	.251	18	42	6	97	137	15	.940
1989	—Modesto (Calif.)........	2-S-0-3	107	339	31	71	9	3	0	26	.209	34	64	7	183	197	20	.950
1990	—Modesto (Calif.)........	2-3-0-S	87	246	27	60	6	3	0	16	.244	22	41	4	125	167	18	.942
1991	—Modesto (Calif.)........	3B-2B	5	19	8	5	0	0	0	3	.263	2	1	1	7	6	1	.929
	—Tacoma (PCL)	3B-2B	17	56	9	14	0	0	1	7	.250	4	6	0	23	41	3	.955
	—Huntsville (South.)...	2-S-0-3	87	290	25	64	10	1	1	22	.221	31	50	2	142	162	17	.947
1992	—Midland (Texas)■.....	SS	123	482	73	140	23	1	6	56	.290	28	72	20	*204	*385	32	.948
1993	—Vancouver (PCL)	SS-2B	60	207	43	56	10	4	4	28	.271	15	25	11	105	159	14	.950
	—California (A.L.)	SS-2B-3B	64	128	12	34	5	0	0	9	.266	6	20	2	87	121	3	.986
Major league totals (1 year)			64	128	12	34	5	0	0	9	.266	6	20	2	87	121	3	.986

CORSI, JIM

P, MARLINS

PERSONAL: Born September 9, 1961, in Newton, Mass. . . . 6-1/220. . . . Throws right, bats right. . . . Full name: James Bernard Corsi.
HIGH SCHOOL: Newton (Mass.) North.
COLLEGE: St. Leo (Fla.) College (bachelor of arts degree in management).

TRANSACTIONS/CAREER NOTES: Selected by New York Yankees organization in 25th round of free-agent draft (June 7, 1982).... On Fort Lauderdale disabled list (April 8-May 11, 1983).... Released by Yankees organization (April 3, 1984).... Signed by Greensboro, Boston Red Sox organization (April 1, 1985).... Released by Red Sox organization (January 31, 1986).... Re-signed by Red Sox organization (April 5, 1986).... Released by Red Sox organization (April 2, 1987).... Signed by Modesto, Oakland Athletics organization (April 12, 1987).... On Oakland disabled list (March 29, 1990-entire season); included rehabilitation assignment to Tacoma (June 29-July 25).... Granted free agency (December 20, 1990).... Signed by Tucson, Houston Astros organization (March 19, 1991).... Released by Astros (November 18, 1991).... Signed by Tacoma, A's organization (March 16, 1992).... Selected by Florida Marlins in second round (49th pick overall) of expansion draft (November 17, 1992).... On Florida disabled list (March 27-April 30, 1993); included rehabilitation assignment to High Desert (April 20-30).... On Florida disabled list (July 6, 1993-remainder of season).... Granted free agency (October 15, 1993).... Re-signed by Marlins organization (January 24, 1994).

Year	Team (League)	W	L	Pct.	ERA	G	GS	CG	ShO	Sv.	IP	H	R	ER	BB	SO
1982	—Oneonta (NYP)	0	0	...	10.80	1	0	0	0	0	3⅓	5	4	4	2	6
	—Paintsville (Appal.)	0	2	.000	2.90	8	4	0	0	0	31	32	11	10	13	20
1983	—Greensboro (S. Atl.)	2	2	.500	4.09	12	7	1	0	1	50⅔	59	37	23	33	37
	—Oneonta (NYP)	3	6	.333	4.25	11	10	2	0	0	59⅓	76	38	28	21	47
1984	—	Out of organized baseball.														
1985	—Greensboro (S. Atl.)■	5	8	.385	4.23	41	2	1	0	9	78⅔	94	49	37	23	84
1986	—New Britain (East.)	2	3	.400	2.28	29	0	0	0	3	51⅓	52	13	13	20	38
1987	—Modesto (Calif.)■	3	1	.750	3.60	19	0	0	0	6	30	23	16	12	10	45
	—Huntsville (South.)	8	1	.889	2.81	28	0	0	0	4	48	30	17	15	15	33
1988	—Tacoma (PCL)	2	5	.286	2.75	50	0	0	0	16	59	60	25	18	23	48
	—Oakland (A.L.)	0	1	.000	3.80	11	1	0	0	0	21⅓	20	10	9	6	10
1989	—Tacoma (PCL)	2	3	.400	4.13	23	0	0	0	8	28⅓	40	17	13	9	23
	—Oakland (A.L.)	1	2	.333	1.88	22	0	0	0	0	38⅓	26	8	8	10	21
1990	—Tacoma (PCL)	0	0	...	1.50	5	0	0	0	0	6	9	2	1	1	3
1991	—Tucson (PCL)■	0	0	...	0.00	2	0	0	0	0	3	2	0	0	0	4
	—Houston (N.L.)	0	5	.000	3.71	47	0	0	0	0	77⅔	76	37	32	23	53
1992	—Tacoma (PCL)■	0	0	...	1.23	26	0	0	0	12	29⅓	22	8	4	10	21
	—Oakland (A.L.)	4	2	.667	1.43	32	0	0	0	0	44	44	12	7	18	19
1993	—High Desert (Calif.)■	0	1	.000	3.00	3	3	0	0	0	9	11	3	3	2	6
	—Florida (N.L.)	0	2	.000	6.64	15	0	0	0	0	20⅓	28	15	15	10	7
A.L. totals (3 years)		5	5	.500	2.08	65	1	0	0	0	103⅔	90	30	24	34	50
N.L. totals (2 years)		0	7	.000	4.32	62	0	0	0	0	98	104	52	47	33	60
Major league totals (5 years)		5	12	.294	3.17	127	1	0	0	0	201⅔	194	82	71	67	110

CHAMPIONSHIP SERIES RECORD

Year	Team (League)	W	L	Pct.	ERA	G	GS	CG	ShO	Sv.	IP	H	R	ER	BB	SO
1992	—Oakland (A.L.)	0	0	...	0.00	3	0	0	0	0	2	2	0	0	3	0

COSTO, TIM

1B/OF, REDS

PERSONAL: Born February 16, 1969, in Melrose Park, Ill.... 6-5/230.... Throws right, bats right.... Full name: Timothy Roger Costo.

HIGH SCHOOL: Glenbard (Glen Ellyn, Ill.).

COLLEGE: Iowa.

TRANSACTIONS/CAREER NOTES: Selected by Cincinnati Reds organization in 41st round of free-agent draft (June 2, 1987).... Selected by Cleveland Indians organization in first round (eighth pick overall) of free-agent draft (June 4, 1990).... Traded by Indians organization to Reds organization for 1B Reggie Jefferson (June 14, 1991).... On Chattanooga disabled list (May 5-14, 1992).

HONORS: Named shortstop on THE SPORTING NEWS college All-America team (1990).

STATISTICAL NOTES: Tied for Carolina League lead with eight sacrifice flies in 1990.

			BATTING												FIELDING			
Year	Team (League)	Pos.	G	AB	R	H	2B	3B	HR	RBI	Avg.	BB	SO	SB	PO	A	E	Avg.
1990	—Kinston (Carolina)	1B-SS	56	206	34	65	13	1	4	42	.316	23	47	4	298	75	15	.961
1991	—Cant./Akr. (East.)	1B-SS	52	192	28	52	10	3	1	24	.271	15	44	2	464	29	7	.986
	—Chatt. (South.)■	1B-SS	85	293	31	82	19	3	5	29	.280	20	65	11	505	62	7	.988
1992	—Chatt. (South.)	1B	121	424	63	102	18	2	*28	71	.241	48	128	4	973	62	7	.993
	—Cincinnati (N.L.)	1B	12	36	3	8	2	0	0	2	.222	5	6	0	84	8	0	1.000
1993	—Cincinnati (N.L.)	OF-3B-1B	31	98	13	22	5	0	3	12	.224	4	17	0	51	3	1	.982
	—Indianapolis (A.A.)	1-0-3-S	106	362	49	118	30	2	11	57	.326	22	60	3	516	61	9	.985
Major league totals (2 years)			43	134	16	30	7	0	3	14	.224	9	23	0	135	11	1	.993

COTTO, HENRY

OF, ORIOLES

PERSONAL: Born January 5, 1961, in New York.... 6-2/180.... Throws right, bats right.... Full name: Henry Suarez Cotto.... Name pronounced KOTT-oh.

HIGH SCHOOL: Colonel Bautista (Caguas, Puerto Rico).

TRANSACTIONS/CAREER NOTES: Signed as free agent by Chicago Cubs organization (June 7, 1980).... On disabled list (May 10-30, 1983).... Traded by Cubs organization with C Ron Hassey, P Rich Bordi and P Porfi Altamirano to New York Yankees for P Ray Fontenot and OF Brian Dayett (December 4, 1984).... On New York disabled list (May 25-July 5, 1985); included rehabilitation assignment to Columbus (June 19-July 5).... Traded by Yankees with P Steve Trout to Seattle Mariners for P Lee Guetterman, P Clay Parker and P Wade Taylor (December 22, 1987).... On disabled list (August 3, 1991-remainder of season).... Granted free agency (October 27, 1992).... Re-signed by Mariners (February 2, 1993).... Traded by Mariners with P Jeff Darwin to Florida Marlins for 3B Dave Magadan (June 27, 1993).... Granted free agency (October 25, 1993).... Signed by Baltimore Orioles organization (February 3, 1994).

STATISTICAL NOTES: Led Texas League outfielders with 333 total chances in 1982.... Tied for American Association lead in caught stealing with 17 in 1983.... Tied for International League lead in double plays by outfielder with three in 1986.

Year	Team (League)	Pos.	G	AB	R	H	2B	3B	HR	RBI	Avg.	BB	SO	SB	PO	A	E	Avg.
			BATTING												FIELDING			
1980	—GC Cubs (GCL)	OF	43	166	24	47	7	5	0	30	.283	12	15	12	93	6	3	.971
	—Quad Cities (Mid.)	OF	19	78	9	22	1	1	0	5	.282	4	10	8	27	2	4	.879
1981	—Quad Cities (Mid.)	OF	128	493	80	144	15	6	1	46	.292	59	62	52	249	*23	13	.954
1982	—Midland (Texas)	OF	130	524	103	161	12	5	1	36	.307	59	79	*52	*310	16	7	.979
1983	—Iowa (Am. Assoc.)	OF	104	426	52	111	7	10	0	35	.261	35	67	32	253	8	7	.974
1984	—Chicago (N.L.)	OF	105	146	24	40	5	0	0	8	.274	10	23	9	117	3	2	.984
	—Iowa (Am. Assoc.)	OF	8	30	3	6	2	0	0	0	.200	2	3	1	12	3	0	1.000
1985	—New York (A.L.)■	OF	34	56	4	17	1	0	1	6	.304	3	12	1	41	2	1	.977
	—Columbus (Int'l)	OF	75	272	38	70	16	2	7	36	.257	19	53	16	158	5	2	.988
1986	—New York (A.L.)	OF	35	80	11	17	3	0	1	6	.213	2	17	3	59	1	0	1.000
	—Columbus (Int'l)	OF	97	359	45	89	17	6	7	48	.248	19	53	16	215	5	8	.965
1987	—Columbus (Int'l)	OF	34	129	26	39	13	2	3	20	.302	10	16	14	73	3	2	.974
	—New York (A.L.)	OF	68	149	21	35	10	0	5	20	.235	6	35	4	89	2	1	.989
1988	—Seattle (A.L.)■	OF	133	386	50	100	18	1	8	33	.259	23	53	27	253	6	2	.992
1989	—Seattle (A.L.)	OF	100	295	44	78	11	2	9	33	.264	12	44	10	153	9	2	.988
1990	—Seattle (A.L.)	OF	127	355	40	92	14	3	4	33	.259	22	52	21	194	4	2	.990
1991	—Seattle (A.L.)	OF	66	177	35	54	6	2	6	23	.305	10	27	16	104	2	2	.981
1992	—Seattle (A.L.)	OF	108	294	42	76	11	1	5	27	.259	14	49	23	170	2	0	1.000
1993	—Seattle (A.L.)	OF	54	105	10	20	1	0	2	7	.190	2	22	5	59	0	1	.983
	—Florida (N.L.)■	OF	54	135	15	40	7	0	3	14	.296	3	18	11	85	1	2	.977
American League totals (9 years)			725	1897	257	489	75	9	41	188	.258	94	311	110	1122	28	11	.991
National League totals (2 years)			159	281	39	80	12	0	3	22	.285	13	41	20	202	4	4	.981
Major league totals (10 years)			884	2178	296	569	87	9	44	210	.261	107	352	130	1324	32	15	.989

CHAMPIONSHIP SERIES RECORD

Year	Team (League)	Pos.	G	AB	R	H	2B	3B	HR	RBI	Avg.	BB	SO	SB	PO	A	E	Avg.
			BATTING												FIELDING			
1984	—Chicago (N.L.)	OF-PR	3	1	1	1	0	0	0	0	1.000	0	0	0	2	0	0	1.000

COURTRIGHT, JOHN

P, REDS

PERSONAL: Born May 30, 1970, in Marion, O.... 6-2/185.... Throws left, bats left.... Full name: John Charles Courtright.

HIGH SCHOOL: Harding (Marion, O.).

COLLEGE: Duke.

TRANSACTIONS/CAREER NOTES: Selected by Cincinnati Reds organization in eighth round of free-agent draft (June 3, 1991).

Year	Team (League)	W	L	Pct.	ERA	G	GS	CG	ShO	Sv.	IP	H	R	ER	BB	SO
1991	—Billings (Pioneer)	1	0	1.000	0.00	1	1	0	0	0	6	2	0	0	1	4
1992	—Char., W.Va. (SAL)	10	5	.667	2.50	27	26	1	1	0	173	147	64	48	55	147
1993	—Chatt. (South.)	5	11	.313	3.50	27	27	1	0	0	175	179	81	68	70	96

COX, DANNY

P, BLUE JAYS

PERSONAL: Born September 21, 1959, in Northampton, England.... 6-4/250.... Throws right, bats right.... Full name: Danny Bradford Cox.

HIGH SCHOOL: Warner Robins (Ga.).

COLLEGE: Chattahoochee Valley Community College (Ala.) and Troy State.

TRANSACTIONS/CAREER NOTES: Selected by St. Louis Cardinals organization in 13th round of free-agent draft (June 8, 1981).... On Arkansas disabled list (April 8-21, 1983).... On St. Louis disabled list (March 30-April 24, 1986); included rehabilitation assignment to Louisville (April 17-24).... On disabled list (July 10-August 8, 1987).... On St. Louis disabled list (April 30-June 27, 1988); included rehabilitation assignment to Louisville (June 16-27).... On St. Louis disabled list (August 7, 1988-remainder of season).... On disabled list (March 27, 1989-entire season).... Granted free agency (November 13, 1989).... Re-signed by Cardinals (November 30, 1989).... On St. Louis disabled list (March 31, 1990-entire season); included rehabilitation assignment to Louisville (May 17-31 and June 13-18), Springfield (June 6-7) and Arkansas (June 8-12).... Granted free agency (October 19, 1990).... Signed by Scranton/Wilkes-Barre, Philadelphia Phillies organization (December 17, 1990).... On Philadelphia disabled list (May 19-June 17, 1991); included rehabilitation assignment to Scranton/Wilkes-Barre (June 14-15).... Granted free agency (October 31, 1991).... Re-signed by Phillies organization (December 9, 1991).... Released by Phillies (June 7, 1992).... Signed by Buffalo, Pittsburgh Pirates organization (June 19, 1992).... On Buffalo disabled list (July 11-24, 1992).... Granted free agency (November 3, 1992).... Signed by Toronto Blue Jays organization (December 8, 1992).... Granted free agency (October 29, 1993).... Re-signed by Blue Jays organization (November 8, 1993).

HONORS: Named Appalachian League Player of the Year (1981).

STATISTICAL NOTES: Pitched 11-0 no-hit victory against Bristol (August 9, 1981).... Tied for N.L. lead with seven hit batsmen in 1984.... Pitched seven innings, combining with Bob Gaddy (two innings) in nine inning no-hit victory for Clearwater against Baseball City (April 21, 1991).

Year	Team (League)	W	L	Pct.	ERA	G	GS	CG	ShO	Sv.	IP	H	R	ER	BB	SO
1981	—Johns. City (App.)	9	4	.692	*2.06	13	13	*10	*4	0	*109	80	27	25	36	*87
1982	—Springfield (Midw.)	5	3	.625	2.56	15	13	2	0	0	84⅓	82	46	24	29	68
1983	—St. Peters. (FSL)	2	2	.500	2.53	5	5	2	0	0	32	26	10	9	14	22
	—Arkansas (Texas)	8	3	.727	2.29	11	11	7	1	0	86⅓	60	31	22	24	73
	—Louisville (A.A.)	0	0	...	2.45	2	2	0	0	0	11	10	3	3	0	8
	—St. Louis (N.L.)	3	6	.333	3.25	12	12	0	0	0	83	92	38	30	23	36
1984	—St. Louis (N.L.)	9	11	.450	4.03	29	27	1	1	0	156⅓	171	81	70	54	70
	—Louisville (A.A.)	4	1	.800	2.13	6	6	4	0	0	42⅓	34	16	10	7	34
1985	—St. Louis (N.L.)	18	9	.667	2.88	35	35	10	4	0	241	226	91	77	64	131
1986	—St. Louis (N.L.)	12	13	.480	2.90	32	32	8	0	0	220	189	85	71	60	108
1987	—St. Louis (N.L.)	11	9	.550	3.88	31	31	2	0	0	199⅓	224	99	86	71	101
1988	—St. Louis (N.L.)	3	8	.273	3.98	13	13	0	0	0	86	89	40	38	25	47
	—Louisville (A.A.)	0	0	...	3.09	3	3	0	0	0	11⅔	11	7	4	6	7

Year	Team (League)	W	L	Pct.	ERA	G	GS	CG	ShO	Sv.	IP	H	R	ER	BB	SO
1989 —	....							Did not play.								
1990 —	Louisville (A.A.)	0	3	.000	15.55	4	3	0	0	0	11	22	20	19	10	6
	— Springfield (Midw.)	0	0	...	0.00	1	1	0	0	0	5	1	0	0	0	3
	— Arkansas (Texas)	1	0	1.000	1.29	1	1	0	0	0	7	3	1	1	1	3
1991 —	Clearwater (FSL)■	3	0	1.000	0.00	3	3	0	0	0	18	4	0	0	4	15
	— Philadelphia (N.L.)	4	6	.400	4.57	23	17	0	0	0	102⅓	98	57	52	39	46
	— Scran./W.B. (Int'l)	1	0	1.000	3.00	1	1	0	0	0	6	5	2	2	2	3
1992 —	Phil.-Pitts. (N.L.)■	5	3	.625	4.60	25	7	0	0	3	62⅔	66	37	32	27	48
	— Buffalo (A.A.)■	1	1	.500	1.70	8	8	0	0	0	42⅓	28	11	8	18	30
1993 —	Toronto (A.L.)■	7	6	.538	3.12	44	0	0	0	2	83⅔	73	31	29	29	84
A.L. totals (1 year)		7	6	.538	3.12	44	0	0	0	2	83⅔	73	31	29	29	84
N.L. totals (8 years)		65	65	.500	3.57	200	174	21	5	3	1150⅔	1155	528	456	363	587
Major league totals (9 years) ..		72	71	.504	3.54	244	174	21	5	5	1234⅓	1228	559	485	392	671

CHAMPIONSHIP SERIES RECORD

CHAMPIONSHIP SERIES NOTES: Shares single-series record for most complete games pitched—2 (1987).... Shares N.L. career record for most complete games pitched—2.

Year	Team (League)	W	L	Pct.	ERA	G	GS	CG	ShO	Sv.	IP	H	R	ER	BB	SO
1985 —	St. Louis (N.L.)	1	0	1.000	3.00	1	1	0	0	0	6	4	2	2	5	4
1987 —	St. Louis (N.L.)	1	1	.500	2.12	2	2	2	1	0	17	17	4	4	3	11
1992 —	Pittsburgh (N.L.)	0	0	...	0.00	2	0	0	0	0	1⅓	1	0	0	1	1
1993 —	Toronto (A.L.)	0	0	...	0.00	2	0	0	0	0	5	3	0	0	2	5
Champ. series totals (4 years)		2	1	.667	1.84	7	3	2	1	0	29⅓	25	6	6	11	21

WORLD SERIES RECORD

WORLD SERIES NOTES: Shares single-game record for most earned runs allowed—7 (October 18, 1987).... Shares record for most earned runs allowed in one inning—6 (October 18, 1987, fourth inning).

Year	Team (League)	W	L	Pct.	ERA	G	GS	CG	ShO	Sv.	IP	H	R	ER	BB	SO
1985 —	St. Louis (N.L.)	0	0	...	1.29	2	2	0	0	0	14	14	2	2	4	13
1987 —	St. Louis (N.L.)	1	2	.333	7.71	3	2	0	0	0	11⅔	13	10	10	8	9
1993 —	Toronto (A.L.)	0	0	...	8.10	3	0	0	0	0	3⅓	6	3	3	5	6
World Series totals (3 years) .		1	2	.333	4.66	8	4	0	0	0	29	33	15	15	17	28

COX, DARRON

C, CUBS

PERSONAL: Born November 21, 1967, in Oklahoma City.... 6-1/205.... Throws right, bats right.... Full name: James Darron Cox.

HIGH SCHOOL: Mustang (Okla.).

COLLEGE: Oklahoma.

TRANSACTIONS/CAREER NOTES: Selected by Cincinnati Reds organization in fifth round of free-agent draft (June 5, 1989).... On disabled list (June 24-July 22, 1993).... Traded by Reds with P Larry Luebbers and P Mike Anderson to Chicago Cubs for P Chuck McElroy (December 10, 1993).

			BATTING												FIELDING			
Year	Team (League)	Pos.	G	AB	R	H	2B	3B	HR	RBI	Avg.	BB	SO	SB	PO	A	E	Avg.
1989 —	Billings (Pioneer)	C	49	157	20	43	6	0	0	18	.274	21	34	11	192	24	4	.982
1990 —	Char., W.Va. (SAL) ...	C	103	367	53	93	11	3	1	44	.253	40	75	14	486	★89	10	.983
1991 —	Ced. Rap. (Midw.)	C	21	60	12	16	4	0	0	4	.267	8	11	7	93	12	8	.929
	— Char., W.Va. (SAL) ..	C	79	294	37	71	14	1	2	28	.241	24	39	8	500	73	2	.997
	— Chatt. (South.)	C	13	38	2	7	1	0	0	3	.184	2	9	0	74	6	1	.988
1992 —	Chatt. (South.)	C	98	331	29	84	19	1	1	38	.254	15	63	8	654	★91	6	★.992
1993 —	Chatt. (South.)	C	89	300	35	65	9	5	3	26	.217	38	63	7	519	87	8	.987

CRAWFORD, CARLOS

P, INDIANS

PERSONAL: Born October 4, 1971, in Charlotte, N.C.... 6-1/185.... Throws right, bats right.... Full name: Carlos Lamonte Crawford.

HIGH SCHOOL: South Mecklenburg (Charlotte, N.C.).

COLLEGE: Montreat (N.C.)-Anderson College.

TRANSACTIONS/CAREER NOTES: Selected by Cleveland Indians organization in 51st round of free-agent draft (June 4, 1990).

Year	Team (League)	W	L	Pct.	ERA	G	GS	CG	ShO	Sv.	IP	H	R	ER	BB	SO
1990 —	GC Indians (GCL)	2	3	.400	4.36	10	9	0	0	0	53⅔	68	43	26	25	39
1991 —	Burlington (Appal.)	6	3	.667	2.46	13	13	2	•1	0	80⅓	62	28	22	14	80
1992 —	Columbus (S. Atl.)	10	11	.476	2.92	28	•28	•6	•3	0	•188⅓	167	78	61	85	127
1993 —	Kinston (Carolina)	7	9	.438	3.65	28	28	4	1	0	165	158	87	67	46	124

CREEK, DOUG

P, CARDINALS

PERSONAL: Born March 1, 1969, in Winchester, Va.... 5-10/205.... Throws left, bats left.... Full name: Paul Douglas Creek.

HIGH SCHOOL: Martinsburg (W.Va.).

COLLEGE: Georgia Tech.

TRANSACTIONS/CAREER NOTES: Selected by California Angels organization in fifth round of free-agent draft (June 4, 1990).... Selected by St. Louis Cardinals organization in seventh round of free-agent draft (June 3, 1991).... On Arkansas disabled list (April 10-May 21, 1992 and July 25-August 1, 1993).

Year	Team (League)	W	L	Pct.	ERA	G	GS	CG	ShO	Sv.	IP	H	R	ER	BB	SO
1991 —	Hamilton (NYP)	3	2	.600	5.12	9	5	0	0	1	38⅔	39	22	22	18	45
	— Savannah (S. Atl.)	2	1	.667	4.45	5	5	0	0	0	28⅓	24	14	14	17	32
1992 —	Springfield (Midw.)	4	1	.800	2.58	6	6	0	0	0	38⅓	32	11	11	13	43
	— St. Peters. (FSL)	5	4	.556	2.82	13	13	0	0	0	73⅓	57	31	23	37	63
1993 —	Louisville (A.A.)	0	0	...	3.21	2	2	0	0	0	14	10	5	5	9	9
	— Arkansas (Texas)	11	10	.524	4.02	25	25	1	1	0	147⅔	142	75	66	48	128

CRIM, CHUCK

P, CUBS

PERSONAL: Born July 23, 1961, in Van Nuys, Calif. . . . 6-0/185. . . . Throws right, bats right. . . . Full name: Charles Robert Crim.
HIGH SCHOOL: Thousands Oaks (Calif.).
COLLEGE: Hawaii.
TRANSACTIONS/CAREER NOTES: Selected by Chicago Cubs organization in third round of free-agent draft (June 5, 1979). . . . Selected by Milwaukee Brewers organization in 17th round of free-agent draft (June 7, 1982). . . . On Milwaukee disabled list (July 22-August 10, 1990); included rehabilitation assignment to Beloit (August 7). . . . Traded by Brewers to California Angels for P Mike Fetters and P Glenn Carter (December 10, 1991). . . . Released by Angels (May 31, 1993). . . . Signed by Cubs organization (January 11, 1994).
MISCELLANEOUS: Appeared in one game as first baseman with no chances (1989).

Year	Team (League)	W	L	Pct.	ERA	G	GS	CG	ShO	Sv.	IP	H	R	ER	BB	SO
1982	—Pikeville (Appal.)	4	6	.400	2.56	11	11	*8	1	0	77⅓	62	32	22	18	76
1983	—Beloit (Midwest)	11	10	.524	3.47	25	23	•11	2	0	163⅓	150	83	63	50	154
1984	—El Paso (Texas)	7	4	.636	1.50	55	0	0	0	17	90	77	20	15	25	69
1985	—Vancouver (PCL)	3	6	.333	4.56	48	5	0	0	6	106⅔	110	58	54	38	68
1986	—Vancouver (PCL)	0	3	.000	4.96	26	0	0	0	1	45⅓	64	32	25	15	26
	—El Paso (Texas)	2	4	.333	2.77	16	0	0	0	6	39	35	16	12	2	32
1987	—Milwaukee (A.L.)	6	8	.429	3.67	53	5	0	0	12	130	133	60	53	39	56
1988	—Milwaukee (A.L.)	7	6	.538	2.91	*70	0	0	0	9	105	95	38	34	28	58
1989	—Milwaukee (A.L.)	9	7	.563	2.83	*76	0	0	0	7	117⅔	114	42	37	36	59
1990	—Milwaukee (A.L.)	3	5	.375	3.47	67	0	0	0	11	85⅔	88	39	33	23	39
	—Beloit (Midwest)	0	0	...	4.50	1	1	0	0	0	2	3	2	1	0	0
1991	—Milwaukee (A.L.)	8	5	.615	4.63	66	0	0	0	3	91⅓	115	52	47	25	39
1992	—California (A.L.)■	7	6	.538	5.17	57	0	0	0	1	87	100	56	50	29	30
1993	—California (A.L.)	2	2	.500	5.87	11	0	0	0	0	15⅓	17	11	10	5	10
Major league totals (7 years)		42	39	.519	3.76	400	5	0	0	43	632	662	298	264	185	291

CROMER, TRIPP

SS, CARDINALS

PERSONAL: Born November 21, 1967, in Lake City, S.C. . . . 6-2/165. . . . Throws right, bats right. . . . Full name: Roy Bunyan Cromer III. . . . Son of Roy Cromer, current scout, St. Louis Cardinals and minor league pitcher/second baseman (1960-63); brother of Brandon Cromer, shortstop, Toronto Blue Jays organization; brother of D.T. Cromer, outfielder, Oakland Athletics organization; and brother of Burke Cromer, pitcher, Atlanta Braves organization.
HIGH SCHOOL: Lake City (S.C.).
COLLEGE: South Carolina.
TRANSACTIONS/CAREER NOTES: Selected by St. Louis Cardinals organization in third round of free-agent draft (June 5, 1989). . . . On Arkansas disabled list (May 14-26, 1992). . . . On Louisville disabled list (April 30-May 28 and July 5-August 3, 1993).

			BATTING											FIELDING			
Year	Team (League)	Pos.	G	AB	R	H	2B	3B	HR	RBI	Avg.	BB	SO	SB	PO	A	E	Avg.
1989	—Hamilton (NYP)	SS	35	137	18	36	6	3	0	6	.263	17	30	4	66	85	11	.932
1990	—St. Peters. (FSL)	SS	121	408	53	88	12	5	5	38	.216	46	78	7	202	334	32	.944
1991	—St. Peters. (FSL)	SS	43	137	11	28	3	1	0	10	.204	9	17	0	79	134	3	.986
	—Arkansas (Texas)	SS	73	227	28	52	12	1	1	18	.229	15	37	0	117	198	10	.969
1992	—Arkansas (Texas)	SS	110	339	30	81	16	6	7	29	.239	22	82	4	135	315	18	*.962
	—Louisville (A.A.)	SS	6	25	5	5	1	1	1	7	.200	1	6	0	13	20	0	1.000
1993	—Louisville (A.A.)	SS	85	309	39	85	8	4	11	33	.275	15	60	1	123	253	12	.969
	—St. Louis (N.L.)	SS	10	23	1	2	0	0	0	0	.087	1	6	0	13	18	3	.912
Major league totals (1 year)			10	23	1	2	0	0	0	0	.087	1	6	0	13	18	3	.912

CRUZ, FAUSTO

SS/3B, ATHLETICS

PERSONAL: Born May 1, 1972, in Monte Cristy, Dominican Republic. . . . 5-10/165. . . . Throws right, bats right. . . . Full name: Fausto Santiago Cruz.
TRANSACTIONS/CAREER NOTES: Signed as free agent by Oakland Athletics organization (January 15, 1990).
STATISTICAL NOTES: Led Arizona League in grounding into double plays with 10 in 1991. . . . Tied for Arizona League lead with seven sacrifice flies in 1991. . . . Led Arizona League shortstops with 254 total chances and 27 double plays in 1991.

			BATTING											FIELDING			
Year	Team (League)	Pos.	G	AB	R	H	2B	3B	HR	RBI	Avg.	BB	SO	SB	PO	A	E	Avg.
1990	—		Dominican Summer League statistics unavailable.															
1991	—Ariz. A's (Arizona)	SS	52	180	38	50	2	1	2	36	.278	32	23	3	*92	147	15	*.941
	—Modesto (Calif.)	SS-2B	18	58	9	12	1	0	0	0	.207	8	13	1	22	44	7	.904
1992	—Reno (California)	SS	127	489	86	156	22	11	9	90	.319	70	66	8	*278	382	*54	.924
1993	—Modesto (Calif.)	SS	43	165	21	39	3	0	1	20	.236	25	34	6	90	117	12	.945
	—Huntsville (South.)	SS-3B	63	251	45	84	15	2	3	31	.335	20	42	2	100	143	12	.953
	—Tacoma (PCL)	3-S-2-O	21	74	13	18	2	1	0	6	.243	5	16	3	34	43	3	.963

CUMMINGS, JOHN

P, MARINERS

PERSONAL: Born May 10, 1969, in Torrance, Calif. . . . 6-3/200. . . . Throws left, bats left. . . . Full name: John Russell Cummings.
HIGH SCHOOL: Canyon (Anaheim, Calif.).
COLLEGE: Southern California.
TRANSACTIONS/CAREER NOTES: Selected by New York Yankees organization in 32nd round of free-agent draft (June 1, 1988). . . . Selected by Seattle Mariners organization in eighth round of free-agent draft (June 4, 1990). . . . On Calgary disabled list (August 1-8, 1993).
HONORS: Named Carolina League Pitcher of the Year (1992).

Year	Team (League)	W	L	Pct.	ERA	G	GS	CG	ShO	Sv.	IP	H	R	ER	BB	SO
1990	—Belling. (N'west)	1	1	.500	2.12	6	6	0	0	0	34	25	11	8	9	39
	—San Bern. (Calif.)	2	4	.333	4.20	7	7	1	0	0	40⅔	47	27	19	20	30

Year	Team (League)	W	L	Pct.	ERA	G	GS	CG	ShO	Sv.	IP	H	R	ER	BB	SO
1991	—San Bern. (Calif.)	4	10	.286	4.06	29	20	0	0	1	124	129	79	56	61	120
1992	—Peninsula (Caro.)	*16	6	.727	2.57	27	27	4	1	0	168⅓	149	71	48	63	*144
1993	—Seattle (A.L.)	0	6	.000	6.02	10	8	1	0	0	46⅓	59	34	31	16	19
	—Jacksonv. (South.)	2	2	.500	3.15	7	7	1	0	0	45⅔	50	24	16	9	35
	—Calgary (PCL)	3	4	.429	4.13	11	10	0	0	0	65⅓	69	40	30	21	42
	Major league totals (1 year)	0	6	.000	6.02	10	8	1	0	0	46⅓	59	34	31	16	19

CUMMINGS, MIDRE

OF, PIRATES

PERSONAL: Born October 14, 1971, in St. Croix, Virgin Islands. . . . 6-0/196. . . . Throws right, bats left. . . . Full name: Midre Almeric Cummings.
HIGH SCHOOL: Miami Edison Senior.
TRANSACTIONS/CAREER NOTES: Selected by Minnesota Twins organization in supplemental round ("sandwich pick" between first and second round, 29th pick overall) of free-agent draft (June 4, 1990); pick received as part of compensation for Boston Red Sox signing Type A free agent Jeff Reardon. . . . Traded by Twins organization with P Denny Neagle to Pittsburgh Pirates organization for P John Smiley (March 17, 1992).
MISCELLANEOUS: Batted as switch-hitter (1990-92).

			BATTING												FIELDING			
Year	Team (League)	Pos.	G	AB	R	H	2B	3B	HR	RBI	Avg.	BB	SO	SB	PO	A	E	Avg.
1990	—GC Twins (GCL)	OF	47	177	28	56	3	4	5	28	.316	13	32	14	73	2	6	.926
1991	—Kenosha (Midwest)	OF	106	382	59	123	20	4	4	54	*.322	22	66	28	166	6	•13	.930
1992	—Salem (Carolina)■	OF	113	420	55	128	20	5	14	75	.305	35	67	23	151	10	6	.964
1993	—Carolina (South.)	OF	63	237	33	70	17	2	6	26	.295	14	23	5	99	7	4	.964
	—Buffalo (A.A.)	OF	60	232	36	64	12	1	9	21	.276	22	45	5	90	1	2	.978
	—Pittsburgh (N.L.)	OF	13	36	5	4	1	0	0	3	.111	4	9	0	21	0	0	1.000
	Major league totals (1 year)		13	36	5	4	1	0	0	3	.111	4	9	0	21	0	0	1.000

C

CURTIS, CHAD

OF, ANGELS

PERSONAL: Born November 6, 1968, in Marion, Ind. . . . 5-10/175. . . . Throws right, bats right. . . . Full name: Chad David Curtis.
HIGH SCHOOL: Benson (Ariz.) Union.
COLLEGE: Yavapai College (Ariz.), Cochise County Community College (Ariz.) and Grand Canyon (Ariz.).
TRANSACTIONS/CAREER NOTES: Selected by California Angels organization in 45th round of free-agent draft (June 5, 1989). . . . On Edmonton disabled list (June 5-20, 1991). . . . On suspended list (June 8-12, 1993).
RECORDS: Shares A.L. single-season record for fewest errors by outfielder who led league in errors—9 (1993).
STATISTICAL NOTES: Led Midwest League with 223 total bases in 1990. . . . Tied for A.L. lead in caught stealing with 24 in 1993. . . . Led A.L. outfielders with 448 total chances and tied for lead with nine errors in 1993.

			BATTING												FIELDING			
Year	Team (League)	Pos.	G	AB	R	H	2B	3B	HR	RBI	Avg.	BB	SO	SB	PO	A	E	Avg.
1989	—Ariz. Angels (Ariz.)	2B-OF	32	122	30	37	4	4	3	20	.303	14	20	17	62	58	6	.952
	—Quad City (Midw.)	OF	23	78	7	19	3	0	2	11	.244	6	17	7	34	1	1	.972
1990	—Quad City (Midw.)	2B-OF	135	*492	87	*151	28	1	14	65	.307	57	76	64	216	221	26	.944
1991	—Edmonton (PCL)	3B-2B-OF	115	431	81	136	28	7	9	61	.316	51	56	46	124	220	25	.932
1992	—California (A.L.)	OF	139	441	59	114	16	2	10	46	.259	51	71	43	250	*16	6	.978
1993	—California (A.L.)	OF-2B	152	583	94	166	25	3	6	59	.285	70	89	48	426	13	‡9	.980
	Major league totals (2 years)		291	1024	153	280	41	5	16	105	.273	121	160	91	676	29	15	.979

CURTIS, RANDY

OF, PADRES

PERSONAL: Born January 16, 1971, in Orange, Calif. . . . 5-11/185. . . . Throws left, bats left. . . . Full name: Randall Lee Curtis.
HIGH SCHOOL: Norco (Calif.).
COLLEGE: Riverside (Calif.) Community College.
TRANSACTIONS/CAREER NOTES: Selected by Detroit Tigers organization in seventh round of free-agent draft (June 4, 1990). . . . Selected by New York Mets organization in eighth round of free-agent draft (June 3, 1991). . . . On disabled list (June 10-26, 1992). . . . Traded by Mets with a player to be named later to San Diego Padres for P Frank Seminara, OF Tracy Sanders and a player to be named later (December 10, 1993); Padres acquired P Marc Kroon and Mets acquired SS Pablo Martinez to complete deal (December 13, 1993).
HONORS: Named Florida State League Most Valuable Player (1993).
STATISTICAL NOTES: Led New York-Pennsylvania League outfielders with 224 total chances in 1991.

			BATTING												FIELDING			
Year	Team (League)	Pos.	G	AB	R	H	2B	3B	HR	RBI	Avg.	BB	SO	SB	PO	A	E	Avg.
1991	—Pittsfield (NYP)	OF	75	298	*72	86	12	1	2	33	.289	*60	63	26	*213	4	7	.969
1992	—Columbia (S. Atl.)	OF	102	353	53	104	11	5	1	56	.295	62	80	33	180	12	8	.960
1993	—St. Lucie (Fla. St.)	OF	126	467	*91	149	30	12	2	38	.319	*93	72	*52	259	16	3	.989

CUYLER, MILT

OF, TIGERS

PERSONAL: Born October 7, 1968, in Macon, Ga. . . . 5-10/185. . . . Throws right, bats both. . . . Full name: Milton Cuyler Jr. . . . Name pronounced KY-ler.
HIGH SCHOOL: Southwest Macon (Macon, Ga.).
TRANSACTIONS/CAREER NOTES: Selected by Detroit Tigers organization in second round of free-agent draft (June 2, 1986). . . . On Detroit disabled list (July 26, 1992-remainder of season and August 9, 1993-remainder of season).
STATISTICAL NOTES: Led South Atlantic League with 17 sacrifice hits in 1987. . . . Led Florida State League in caught stealing with 25 in 1988. . . . Led Eastern League outfielders with 293 total chances in 1989. . . . Led International League in caught stealing with 14 in 1990.

Year	Team (League)	Pos.	G	AB	R	H	2B	3B	HR	RBI	Avg.	BB	SO	SB	PO	A	E	Avg.
			BATTING												FIELDING			
1986	—Bristol (Appal.)	OF	45	174	24	40	3	5	1	11	.230	15	35	12	97	0	4	.960
1987	—Fayetteville (SAL)	OF	94	366	65	107	8	4	2	34	.292	34	78	27	237	13	7	.973
1988	—Lakeland (Fla. St.)	OF	132	483	*100	143	11	3	2	32	.296	71	83	50	257	8	4	.985
1989	—Toledo (Int'l)	OF	24	83	4	14	3	2	0	6	.169	8	27	4	48	3	2	.962
	—London (Eastern)	OF	98	366	69	96	8	7	7	34	.262	47	74	32	*272	13	8	.973
1990	—Toledo (Int'l)	OF	124	461	77	119	11	8	2	42	.258	60	77	*52	290	4	7	.977
	—Detroit (A.L.)	OF	19	51	8	13	3	1	0	8	.255	5	10	1	38	2	1	.976
1991	—Detroit (A.L.)	OF	154	475	77	122	15	7	3	33	.257	52	92	41	411	7	6	.986
1992	—Detroit (A.L.)	OF	89	291	39	70	11	1	3	28	.241	10	62	8	232	4	4	.983
1993	—Detroit (A.L.)	OF	82	249	46	53	11	7	0	19	.213	19	53	13	211	2	7	.968
Major league totals (4 years)			344	1066	170	258	40	16	6	88	.242	86	217	63	892	15	18	.981

DAAL, OMAR

P, DODGERS

PERSONAL: Born March 1, 1972, in Maracaibo, Venezuela. . . . 6-3/175. . . . Throws left, bats left. . . . Full name: Omar Jose Cordaro Daal.

HIGH SCHOOL: Valencia (Venezuela) Superior.

TRANSACTIONS/CAREER NOTES: Signed as free agent by Los Angeles Dodgers organization (August 24, 1990).

Year	Team (League)	W	L	Pct.	ERA	G	GS	CG	ShO	Sv.	IP	H	R	ER	BB	SO
1990	—Santo Dom. (DSL)	3	6	.333	1.18	17	13	6	0	2	91⅔	61	29	12	29	91
1991	—Santo Dom. (DSL)	7	2	.778	1.16	13	13	0	0	0	93	30	17	12	32	81
1992	—Albuquerque (PCL)	0	2	.000	7.84	12	0	0	0	0	10⅓	14	9	9	11	9
	—San Antonio (Tex.)	2	6	.250	5.02	35	5	0	0	5	57⅓	60	39	32	33	52
1993	—Albuquerque (PCL)	1	1	.500	3.38	6	0	0	0	2	5⅓	5	2	2	3	2
	—Los Angeles (N.L.)	2	3	.400	5.09	47	0	0	0	0	35⅓	36	20	20	21	19
Major league totals (1 year)		2	3	.400	5.09	47	0	0	0	0	35⅓	36	20	20	21	19

DALESANDRO, MARK

3B/C, ANGELS

PERSONAL: Born May 14, 1968, in Chicago. . . . 6-0/185. . . . Throws right, bats right. . . . Full name: Mark Anthony Dalesandro. . . . Name pronounced DELL-uh-SAN-droh.

HIGH SCHOOL: St. Ignatius College Prep School (Chicago).

COLLEGE: Illinois.

TRANSACTIONS/CAREER NOTES: Selected by California Angels organization in 18th round of free-agent draft (June 4, 1990).

STATISTICAL NOTES: Tied for California League lead in grounding into double plays with 20 in 1992.

Year	Team (League)	Pos.	G	AB	R	H	2B	3B	HR	RBI	Avg.	BB	SO	SB	PO	A	E	Avg.
			BATTING												FIELDING			
1990	—Boise (Northwest)	OF-3B-1B	55	224	35	75	10	2	6	44	.335	18	42	6	37	23	6	.909
1991	—Quad City (Midw.)	3B-1B	125	487	63	133	17	8	5	69	.273	34	58	1	198	186	25	.939
1992	—Palm Springs (Cal.)	1B-3B	126	492	72	146	30	3	7	92	.297	33	50	6	594	114	15	.979
1993	—Palm Springs (Cal.)	C-1B	46	176	22	43	5	3	1	25	.244	15	20	3	271	42	7	.978
	—Midland (Texas)	3B-C-1B	57	235	33	69	9	0	2	36	.294	8	30	1	137	60	12	.943
	—Vancouver (PCL)	3B	26	107	16	32	8	1	2	15	.299	6	13	1	19	59	7	.918

DANIELS, LEE

P, BLUE JAYS

PERSONAL: Born March 31, 1971, in Rochelle, Ga. . . . 6-4/180. . . . Throws right, bats right. . . . Full name: Lee Andrew Daniels.

HIGH SCHOOL: Wilcox County (Rochelle, Ga.).

COLLEGE: Itawamba Junior College (Mo.).

TRANSACTIONS/CAREER NOTES: Selected by Toronto Blue Jays organization in 68th round of free-agent draft (June 5, 1989).

STATISTICAL NOTES: Led Pioneer League outfielders with 127 total chances and tied for lead in putouts by outfielder with 117 in 1991.

Year	Team (League)	W	L	Pct.	ERA	G	GS	CG	ShO	Sv.	IP	H	R	ER	BB	SO
1991	—Medicine Hat (Pio.)	0	0	...	0.00	1	0	0	0	0	1⅓	1	0	0	0	2
1992	—St. Cathar. (NYP)	3	6	.333	4.34	17	4	0	0	0	58	61	34	28	20	37
1993	—Dunedin (Fla. St.)	0	1	.000	6.23	2	1	0	0	0	4⅓	6	4	3	2	5
	—Hagerstown (SAL)	2	4	.333	3.43	33	0	0	0	12	39⅓	31	20	15	26	38

RECORD AS POSITION PLAYER

Year	Team (League)	Pos.	G	AB	R	H	2B	3B	HR	RBI	Avg.	BB	SO	SB	PO	A	E	Avg.
			BATTING												FIELDING			
1990	—Medicine Hat (Pio.)	OF	31	95	3	16	3	0	0	9	.168	7	39	4	37	2	6	.867
1991	—Medicine Hat (Pio.)	OF-P	61	219	43	54	4	1	2	22	.247	34	65	18	‡117	5	5	.961

DARLING, RON

P, ATHLETICS

PERSONAL: Born August 19, 1960, in Honolulu. . . . 6-3/195. . . . Throws right, bats right. . . . Full name: Ronald Maurice Darling Jr. . . . Brother of Eddie Darling, minor league first baseman (1981-82).

HIGH SCHOOL: St. John's (Worcester, Mass.).

COLLEGE: Yale.

TRANSACTIONS/CAREER NOTES: Selected by Texas Rangers organization in first round (ninth pick overall) of free-agent draft (June 8, 1981). . . . Traded by Rangers organization with P Walt Terrell to New York Mets organization for OF Lee Mazzilli (April 1, 1982). . . . On disabled list (September 12, 1987-remainder of season). . . . Traded by Mets with P Mike Thomas to Montreal Expos for P Tim Burke (July 15, 1991). . . . Traded by Expos to Oakland Athletics for P Matt Grott and P Russell Cormier (July 31, 1991). . . . Granted free agency (October 31, 1991). . . . Re-signed by A's (January 17, 1992). . . . Granted free agency (October 28, 1992). . . . Re-signed by A's (December 17, 1992).

RECORDS: Shares N.L. single-season record for fewest assists by pitcher who led league in assists—47 (both in 1985 and 1986).
HONORS: Won N.L. Gold Glove at pitcher (1989).
MISCELLANEOUS: Appeared in one game as pinch-runner (1992).... Appeared in one game as pinch-runner (1993).

Year	Team (League)	W	L	Pct.	ERA	G	GS	CG	ShO	Sv.	IP	H	R	ER	BB	SO
1981	—Tulsa (Texas)	4	2	.667	4.44	13	13	2	2	0	71	72	43	35	33	53
1982	—Tidewater (Int'l)	7	9	.438	3.73	26	26	6	2	0	152	143	76	63	95	114
1983	—Tidewater (Int'l)	10	9	.526	4.02	27	27	5	1	0	159	137	83	71	102	107
	—New York (N.L.)	1	3	.250	2.80	5	5	1	0	0	35⅓	31	11	11	17	23
1984	—New York (N.L.)	12	9	.571	3.81	33	33	2	2	0	205⅔	179	97	87	104	136
1985	—New York (N.L.)	16	6	.727	2.90	36	35	4	2	0	248	214	93	80	*114	167
1986	—New York (N.L.)	15	6	.714	2.81	34	34	4	2	0	237	203	84	74	81	184
1987	—New York (N.L.)	12	8	.600	4.29	32	32	2	0	0	207⅔	183	111	99	96	167
1988	—New York (N.L.)	17	9	.654	3.25	34	34	7	4	0	240⅔	218	97	87	60	161
1989	—New York (N.L.)	14	14	.500	3.52	33	33	4	0	0	217⅓	214	100	85	70	153
1990	—New York (N.L.)	7	9	.438	4.50	33	18	1	0	0	126	135	73	63	44	99
1991	—N.Y.-Mont. (N.L.)■	5	8	.385	4.37	20	20	0	0	0	119⅓	121	66	58	33	69
	—Oakland (A.L.)■	3	7	.300	4.08	12	12	0	0	0	75	64	34	34	38	60
1992	—Oakland (A.L.)	15	10	.600	3.66	33	33	4	3	0	206⅓	198	98	84	72	99
1993	—Oakland (A.L.)	5	9	.357	5.16	31	29	3	0	0	178	198	107	102	72	95
	A.L. totals (3 years)	23	26	.469	4.31	76	74	7	3	0	459⅓	460	239	220	182	254
	N.L. totals (9 years)	99	72	.579	3.54	260	244	25	10	0	1637	1498	732	644	619	1159
	Major league totals (11 years)	122	98	.555	3.71	336	318	32	13	0	2096⅓	1958	971	864	801	1413

CHAMPIONSHIP SERIES RECORD

CHAMPIONSHIP SERIES NOTES: Appeared in one game as pinch-runner (1988).

Year	Team (League)	W	L	Pct.	ERA	G	GS	CG	ShO	Sv.	IP	H	R	ER	BB	SO
1986	—New York (N.L.)	0	0	...	7.20	1	1	0	0	0	5	6	4	4	2	5
1988	—New York (N.L.)	0	1	.000	7.71	2	2	0	0	0	7	11	9	6	4	7
1992	—Oakland (A.L.)	0	1	.000	3.00	1	1	0	0	0	6	4	3	2	2	3
	Champ. series totals (3 years)	0	2	.000	6.00	4	4	0	0	0	18	21	16	12	8	15

WORLD SERIES RECORD

WORLD SERIES NOTES: Shares single-game record for most wild pitches—2 (October 18, 1986).

Year	Team (League)	W	L	Pct.	ERA	G	GS	CG	ShO	Sv.	IP	H	R	ER	BB	SO
1986	—New York (N.L.)	1	1	.500	1.53	3	3	0	0	0	17⅔	13	4	3	10	12

ALL-STAR GAME RECORD

Year	League	W	L	Pct.	ERA	GS	CG	ShO	Sv.	IP	H	R	ER	BB	SO
1985	—National							Did not play.							

D

DARWIN, DANNY

P, RED SOX

PERSONAL: Born October 25, 1955, in Bonham, Tex.... 6-3/195.... Throws right, bats right.... Full name: Daniel Wayne Darwin.... Brother of Jeff Darwin, pitcher, Seattle Mariners organization.
HIGH SCHOOL: Bonham (Tex.).
COLLEGE: Grayson County College (Tex.).
TRANSACTIONS/CAREER NOTES: Signed as free agent by Texas Rangers organization (May 10, 1976).... On disabled list (April 25-May 4 and May 22-June 11, 1977; June 5-26, 1980; March 25-April 10 and August 9-September 1, 1983).... Traded by Rangers with a player to be named later to Milwaukee Brewers as part of a six-player, four-team deal in which Kansas City Royals acquired C Jim Sundberg from Brewers, Rangers acquired C Don Slaught from Royals, New York Mets organization acquired P Frank Wills from Royals and Brewers organization acquired P Tim Leary from Mets (January 18, 1985); Brewers organization acquired C Bill Hance from Rangers to complete deal (January 30, 1985).... Granted free agency (November 12, 1985).... Re-signed by Brewers (December 22, 1985).... Traded by Brewers organization to Houston Astros for P Don August and a player to be named later (August 15, 1986); Brewers organization acquired P Mark Knudson to complete deal (August 21, 1986).... Granted free agency (November 9, 1987).... Re-signed by Astros (January 8, 1988).... Granted free agency (December 7, 1990).... Signed by Boston Red Sox (December 19, 1990).... On disabled list (April 23-May 22, 1991 and July 5, 1991-remainder of season).
STATISTICAL NOTES: Tied for Western Carolinas League lead with five balks in 1976.... Tied for Texas League lead with eight hit batsmen in 1977.... Tied for A.L. lead with 34 home runs allowed in 1985.

Year	Team (League)	W	L	Pct.	ERA	G	GS	CG	ShO	Sv.	IP	H	R	ER	BB	SO
1976	—Asheville (W. Car.)	6	3	.667	3.62	16	16	6	1	0	102	96	54	41	48	76
1977	—Tulsa (Texas)	13	4	.765	2.51	23	23	6	•4	0	154	130	53	43	72	129
1978	—Tucson (PCL)	8	9	.471	6.26	23	23	4	0	0	125	147	100	87	83	126
	—Texas (A.L.)	1	0	1.000	4.00	3	1	0	0	0	9	11	4	4	1	8
1979	—Tucson (PCL)	6	6	.500	3.60	13	13	4	1	0	95	89	43	38	42	65
	—Texas (A.L.)	4	4	.500	4.04	20	6	1	0	0	78	50	36	35	30	58
1980	—Texas (A.L.)	13	4	.765	2.62	53	2	0	0	8	110	98	37	32	50	104
1981	—Texas (A.L.)	9	9	.500	3.64	22	22	6	2	0	146	115	67	59	57	98
1982	—Texas (A.L.)	10	8	.556	3.44	56	1	0	0	7	89	95	38	34	37	61
1983	—Texas (A.L.)	8	13	.381	3.49	28	26	9	2	0	183	175	86	71	62	92
1984	—Texas (A.L.)	8	12	.400	3.94	35	32	5	2	0	223⅔	249	110	98	54	123
1985	—Milwaukee (A.L.)■	8	18	.308	3.80	39	29	11	1	2	217⅔	212	112	92	65	125
1986	—Milwaukee (A.L.)	6	8	.429	3.52	27	14	5	1	0	130⅓	120	62	51	35	80
	—Houston (N.L.)■	5	2	.714	2.32	12	8	1	0	0	54⅓	50	19	14	9	40
1987	—Houston (N.L.)	9	10	.474	3.59	33	30	3	1	0	195⅔	184	87	78	69	134
1988	—Houston (N.L.)	8	13	.381	3.84	44	20	3	0	3	192	189	86	82	48	129
1989	—Houston (N.L.)	11	4	.733	2.36	68	0	0	0	7	122	92	34	32	33	104

Year	Team (League)	W	L	Pct.	ERA	G	GS	CG	ShO	Sv.	IP	H	R	ER	BB	SO
1990	—Houston (N.L.)	11	4	.733	*2.21	48	17	3	0	2	162⅔	136	42	40	31	109
1991	—Boston (A.L.)■	3	6	.333	5.16	12	12	0	0	0	68	71	39	39	15	42
1992	—Boston (A.L.)	9	9	.500	3.96	51	15	2	0	3	161⅓	159	76	71	53	124
1993	—Boston (A.L.)	15	11	.577	3.26	34	34	2	1	0	229⅓	196	93	83	49	130
A.L. totals (12 years)		94	102	.480	3.66	380	194	41	9	20	1645⅓	1551	760	669	508	1045
N.L. totals (5 years)		44	33	.571	3.05	205	75	10	1	12	726⅔	651	268	246	190	516
Major league totals (16 years)		138	135	.505	3.47	585	269	51	10	32	2372	2202	1028	915	698	1561

DARWIN, JEFF

P, MARINERS

PERSONAL: Born July 6, 1969, in Sherman, Tex. . . . 6-3/180. . . . Throws right, bats right. . . . Full name: Jeffrey Scott Darwin. . . . Brother of Danny Darwin, pitcher, Boston Red Sox.

HIGH SCHOOL: Bonham (Tex.).

COLLEGE: Alvin (Tex.) Community College.

TRANSACTIONS/CAREER NOTES: Selected by Seattle Mariners organization in 46th round of free-agent draft (June 2, 1987). . . . Selected by Mariners organization in 13th round of free-agent draft (June 1, 1988). . . . On disabled list (June 3-August 2, 1991). . . . Traded by Mariners with OF Henry Cotto to Florida Marlins for 3B Dave Magadan (June 27, 1993). . . . Traded by Marlins with cash to Mariners for 3B Dave Magadan (November 9, 1993).

STATISTICAL NOTES: Led Carolina League with nine balks in 1990.

Year	Team (League)	W	L	Pct.	ERA	G	GS	CG	ShO	Sv.	IP	H	R	ER	BB	SO
1989	—Belling. (N'west)	1	7	.125	4.92	12	12	0	0	0	64	73	42	35	24	47
1990	—Peninsula (Caro.)	8	•14	.364	4.01	25	25	1	0	0	150⅓	153	86	67	57	89
1991	—San Bern. (Calif.)	3	9	.250	6.20	16	14	0	0	0	74	80	53	51	31	58
1992	—Peninsula (Caro.)	5	11	.313	3.35	32	20	4	•2	3	139⅔	132	58	52	40	122
1993	—Jacksonv. (South.)	3	5	.375	2.97	27	0	0	0	7	36⅓	29	17	12	17	39
	—Edmonton (PCL)■	2	2	.500	8.51	25	0	0	0	2	30⅔	50	34	29	10	22

DASCENZO, DOUG

OF, METS

PERSONAL: Born June 30, 1964, in Cleveland. . . . 5-8/160. . . . Throws left, bats both. . . . Full name: Douglas Craig Dascenzo. . . . Name pronounced duh-SEN-zo.

HIGH SCHOOL: Brownsville (Pa.).

COLLEGE: Florida College and Oklahoma State.

TRANSACTIONS/CAREER NOTES: Selected by Chicago Cubs organization in 12th round of free-agent draft (June 3, 1985). . . . Granted free agency (December 19, 1992). . . . Signed by Texas Rangers (December 19, 1992). . . . Granted free agency (October 12, 1993). . . . Signed by New York Mets organization (November 17, 1993).

STATISTICAL NOTES: Led Carolina League with 12 sacrifice hits in 1986. . . . Led Eastern League outfielders with 308 total chances in 1987. . . . Led American Association in caught stealing with 21 in 1989.

			BATTING												FIELDING			
Year	Team (League)	Pos.	G	AB	R	H	2B	3B	HR	RBI	Avg.	BB	SO	SB	PO	A	E	Avg.
1985	—Geneva (NY-Penn)	OF-1B	70	252	*59	84	15	1	3	23	.333	61	20	33	133	7	4	.972
1986	—Winst.-Salem (Car.)	OF	138	545	107	*178	29	11	6	83	.327	63	44	57	299	15	8	.975
1987	—Pittsfield (Eastern)	OF	134	496	84	152	32	6	3	56	.306	73	38	36	*299	5	4	*.987
1988	—Iowa (Am. Assoc.)	OF	132	505	73	149	22	5	6	49	.295	37	41	30	261	6	4	.985
	—Chicago (N.L.)	OF	26	75	9	16	3	0	0	4	.213	9	4	6	55	1	0	1.000
1989	—Iowa (Am. Assoc.)	OF	111	431	59	121	18	4	4	33	.281	51	41	34	273	15	6	.980
	—Chicago (N.L.)	OF	47	139	20	23	1	0	1	12	.165	13	13	6	96	0	0	1.000
1990	—Chicago (N.L.)	OF-P	113	241	27	61	9	5	1	26	.253	21	18	15	174	2	0	1.000
1991	—Chicago (N.L.)	OF-P	118	239	40	61	11	0	1	18	.255	24	26	14	134	0	2	.985
1992	—Chicago (N.L.)	OF	139	376	37	96	13	4	0	20	.255	27	32	6	221	2	5	.978
1993	—Texas (A.L.)■	OF	76	146	20	29	5	1	2	10	.199	8	22	2	91	5	1	.990
	—Okla. City (A.A.)	OF	38	157	21	39	8	2	1	13	.248	16	16	6	118	4	2	.984
American League totals (1 year)			76	146	20	29	5	1	2	10	.199	8	22	2	91	5	1	.990
National League totals (5 years)			443	1070	133	257	37	9	3	80	.240	94	93	47	680	5	7	.990
Major league totals (6 years)			519	1216	153	286	42	10	5	90	.235	102	115	49	771	10	8	.990

RECORD AS PITCHER

Year	Team (League)	W	L	Pct.	ERA	G	GS	CG	ShO	Sv.	IP	H	R	ER	BB	SO
1990	—Chicago (N.L.)	0	0	. . .	0.00	1	0	0	0	0	1	1	0	0	0	0
1991	—Chicago (N.L.)	0	0	. . .	0.00	3	0	0	0	0	4	2	0	0	2	2
Major league totals (2 years)		0	0	. . .	0.00	4	0	0	0	0	5	3	0	0	2	2

DAUGHERTY, JACK

OF, ROCKIES

PERSONAL: Born July 3, 1960, in Hialeah, Fla. . . . 6-0/190. . . . Throws left, bats both. . . . Full name: John Michael Daugherty. . . . Name pronounced DAW-er-tee.

HIGH SCHOOL: Kearny (San Diego).

COLLEGE: San Diego (Calif.) Mesa College and Arizona.

TRANSACTIONS/CAREER NOTES: Signed as free agent by Oakland Athletics organization (October 9, 1982). . . . Released by A's organization (January 16, 1984). . . . Signed by Helena, independent (June 13, 1984). . . . Contract sold by Helena to West Palm Beach, Montreal Expos organization (December 4, 1984). . . . Traded by Expos organization to Texas Rangers organization (September 13, 1988), completing deal in which Rangers traded IF Tom O'Malley to Expos for a player to be named later (September 1, 1988). . . . On Texas disabled list (June 6-22, 1991); included rehabilitation assignment to Oklahoma City (June 19-22). . . . On Texas disabled list (June 23-September 1, 1991); included rehabilitation assignment to Oklahoma City (August 9-28). . . . On Texas disabled list (June 1-August 31, 1992); included rehabilitation assignment to Oklahoma City (August 4-23). . . . Granted free agency (October 8, 1992). . . . Signed by Houston Astros organization (January 5, 1993). . . . On Tucson suspended list (June 30-July 12, 1993). . . . Traded by Astros to Cincinnati Reds for OF Steve Carter (July 12, 1993). . . . Granted free agency (October 5, 1993). . . . Signed by Colorado Rockies organization (January 7, 1994).

HONORS: Named Florida State League Most Valuable Player (1985).

STATISTICAL NOTES: Led Pioneer League with 179 total bases and 10 intentional bases on balls received in 1984.... Led Pioneer League first basemen with 624 total chances in 1984.... Led Florida State League with 213 total bases in 1985.

			BATTING												FIELDING			
Year	Team (League)	Pos.	G	AB	R	H	2B	3B	HR	RBI	Avg.	BB	SO	SB	PO	A	E	Avg.
1983	—San Jose (Calif.)	1B	116	364	46	95	17	2	2	45	.261	55	71	2	670	25	7	.990
1984	—Helena (Pioneer)■	1B	66	259	*77	*104	*26	2	15	*82	*.402	•52	48	16	*583	33	8	.987
1985	—W.P. Beach (FSL)■	1B	133	481	76	152	25	3	10	*87	.316	75	58	33	1041	50	14	.987
1986	—Jacksonv. (South.)	1B	138	502	87	159	37	4	4	63	.317	79	58	15	1007	64	*19	.983
1987	—Indianapolis (A.A.)	1B-OF	117	420	65	131	35	3	7	50	.312	42	54	11	754	76	7	.992
	—Montreal (N.L.)	1B	11	10	1	1	1	0	0	1	.100	0	3	0	1	1	0	1.000
1988	—Indianapolis (A.A.)	1B-OF	137	481	82	137	33	2	6	67	.285	56	50	18	896	62	8	.992
1989	—Okla. City (A.A.)■	1B-OF	82	311	28	78	15	3	3	32	.251	39	35	2	728	54	6	.992
	—Texas (A.L.)	1B-OF	52	106	15	32	4	2	1	10	.302	11	21	2	132	14	0	1.000
1990	—Texas (A.L.)	OF-1B	125	310	36	93	20	2	6	47	.300	22	49	0	225	22	3	.988
1991	—Texas (A.L.)	OF-1B	58	144	8	28	3	2	1	11	.194	16	23	1	120	4	1	.992
	—Okla. City (A.A.)	OF	22	77	4	11	2	0	0	4	.143	8	14	1	27	2	1	.967
1992	—Texas (A.L.)	OF-1B	59	127	13	26	9	0	0	9	.205	16	21	2	70	7	2	.975
	—Okla. City (A.A.)	OF-1B	9	18	3	5	2	0	0	2	.278	3	3	0	16	1	0	1.000
1993	—Tucson (PCL)■	1B-OF	42	141	23	55	9	2	2	29	.390	26	12	1	313	19	4	.988
	—Hou.-Cin. (N.L.)■	OF-1B	50	62	7	14	2	0	2	9	.226	11	15	0	32	2	1	.971
American League totals (4 years)			294	687	72	179	36	6	8	77	.261	65	114	5	547	47	6	.990
National League totals (2 years)			61	72	8	15	3	0	2	10	.208	11	18	0	33	3	1	.973
Major league totals (6 years)			355	759	80	194	39	6	10	87	.256	76	132	5	580	50	7	.989

DAULTON, DARREN

C, PHILLIES

PERSONAL: Born January 3, 1962, in Arkansas City, Kan.... 6-2/202.... Throws right, bats left.... Full name: Darren Arthur Daulton.
HIGH SCHOOL: Arkansas City (Kan.).
COLLEGE: Crowley County Community College (Kan.).
TRANSACTIONS/CAREER NOTES: Selected by Philadelphia Phillies organization in 25th round of free-agent draft (June 3, 1980).... On disabled list (July 20-August 28, 1984).... On Philadelphia disabled list (May 17-August 9, 1985); included rehabilitation assignment to Portland (July 20-August 7).... On Philadelphia disabled list (June 22, 1986-remainder of season; April 1-16, 1987; August 28, 1988-remainder of season; and May 6-21, 1991).... On Philadelphia disabled list (May 28-June 18, 1991); included rehabilitation assignment to Scranton/Wilkes-Barre (June 15-17) and Reading (June 17-18).... On disabled list (September 7, 1991-remainder of season).
HONORS: Named catcher on THE SPORTING NEWS N.L. All-Star team (1992).... Named catcher on THE SPORTING NEWS N.L. Silver Slugger team (1992).
STATISTICAL NOTES: Tied for Eastern League lead with 10 sacrifice flies in 1983.... Tied for N.L. lead in double plays by catcher with 10 in 1990.... Led N.L. catchers with 1,057 total chances and 19 double plays in 1993.

			BATTING												FIELDING			
Year	Team (League)	Pos.	G	AB	R	H	2B	3B	HR	RBI	Avg.	BB	SO	SB	PO	A	E	Avg.
1980	—Helena (Pioneer)	C	37	100	13	20	2	1	1	10	.200	23	29	5	224	17	4	.984
1981	—Spartanburg (SAL)	C-OF-3B	98	270	44	62	11	1	3	29	.230	56	35	14	378	34	4	.990
1982	—Peninsula (Caro.)	C-1B	110	324	65	78	21	2	11	44	.241	89	51	17	654	63	9	.988
1983	—Reading (Eastern)	C-1B-OF	113	362	77	95	16	4	19	83	.262	106	87	28	557	57	14	.978
	—Philadelphia (N.L.)	C	2	3	1	1	0	0	0	0	.333	1	1	0	8	0	0	1.000
1984	—Portland (PCL)	C	80	252	45	75	19	4	7	38	.298	57	49	3	322	26	6	.983
1985	—Portland (PCL)	C	23	64	13	19	5	3	2	10	.297	16	13	6	110	9	0	1.000
	—Philadelphia (N.L.)	C	36	103	14	21	3	1	4	11	.204	16	37	3	160	15	1	.994
1986	—Philadelphia (N.L.)	C	49	138	18	31	4	0	8	21	.225	38	41	2	244	21	4	.985
1987	—Clearwater (FSL)	C-1B	9	22	1	5	3	0	1	5	.227	4	3	0	27	5	3	.914
	—Maine (Int'l)	C-1B	20	70	9	15	1	1	3	10	.214	16	15	5	138	12	0	1.000
	—Philadelphia (N.L.)	C-1B	53	129	10	25	6	0	3	13	.194	16	37	0	210	13	2	.991
1988	—Philadelphia (N.L.)	C-1B	58	144	13	30	6	0	1	12	.208	17	26	2	205	15	6	.973
1989	—Philadelphia (N.L.)	C	131	368	29	74	12	2	8	44	.201	52	58	2	627	56	11	.984
1990	—Philadelphia (N.L.)	C	143	459	62	123	30	1	12	57	.268	72	72	7	683	*70	8	.989
1991	—Philadelphia (N.L.)	C	89	285	36	56	12	0	12	42	.196	41	66	5	493	33	8	.985
	—Scran./W.B. (Int'l)	C	2	9	1	2	0	0	1	1	.222	0	0	0	14	1	0	1.000
	—Reading (Eastern)	C	1	4	0	1	0	0	0	0	.250	1	0	0	6	2	0	1.000
1992	—Philadelphia (N.L.)	C	145	485	80	131	32	5	27	*109	.270	88	103	11	760	69	11	.987
1993	—Philadelphia (N.L.)	C	147	510	90	131	35	4	24	105	.257	117	111	5	*981	67	9	.991
Major league totals (10 years)			853	2624	353	623	140	13	99	414	.237	458	552	37	4371	359	60	.987

CHAMPIONSHIP SERIES RECORD

CHAMPIONSHIP SERIES NOTES: Shares single-game record for most bases on balls received—4 (October 10, 1993).

			BATTING												FIELDING			
Year	Team (League)	Pos.	G	AB	R	H	2B	3B	HR	RBI	Avg.	BB	SO	SB	PO	A	E	Avg.
1993	—Philadelphia (N.L.)	C	6	19	2	5	1	0	1	3	.263	6	3	0	54	3	0	1.000

WORLD SERIES RECORD

			BATTING												FIELDING			
Year	Team (League)	Pos.	G	AB	R	H	2B	3B	HR	RBI	Avg.	BB	SO	SB	PO	A	E	Avg.
1993	—Philadelphia (N.L.)	C	6	23	4	5	2	0	1	4	.217	4	5	0	31	4	0	1.000

ALL-STAR GAME RECORD

			BATTING											FIELDING			
Year	League	Pos.	AB	R	H	2B	3B	HR	RBI	Avg.	BB	SO	SB	PO	A	E	Avg.
1992	—National	C	3	1	0	0	0	0	0	.000	0	0	0	5	0	0	1.000
1993	—National	C	3	0	0	0	0	0	0	.000	0	1	0	4	0	0	1.000
All-Star Game totals (2 years)			6	1	0	0	0	0	0	.000	0	1	0	9	0	0	1.000

DAVIS, BUTCH

OF, RANGERS

PERSONAL: Born June 19, 1958, in Williamston, N.C.... 6-0/196.... Throws right, bats right. ... Full name: Wallace McArthur Davis.

HIGH SCHOOL: Williamston (N.C.).

COLLEGE: St. Augustine's College (N.C.) and East Carolina (bachelor of science degree, 1980).

TRANSACTIONS/CAREER NOTES: Selected by Kansas City Royals organization in 12th round of free-agent draft (June 3, 1980). ... On disabled list (April 11, 1986-entire season).... Granted free agency (October 15, 1986).... Signed by Pittsburgh Pirates (December 4, 1986).... Granted free agency (October 15, 1987).... Signed by Charlotte, Baltimore Orioles organization (May 3, 1988).... Granted free agency (October 15, 1988).... Re-signed by Orioles organization (November 21, 1988).... Released by Orioles (December 20, 1989).... Signed by Los Angeles Dodgers organization (January 9, 1990).... Granted free agency (October 16, 1991).... Signed by Toronto Blue Jays organization (December 11, 1991).... Loaned by Syracuse, Blue Jays organization, to Las Vegas, San Diego Padres organization (September 7-14, 1992).... Granted free agency (October 15, 1992).... Signed by Oklahoma City, Texas Rangers organization (December 15, 1992).... On Texas disabled list (August 23-September 7, 1993).... Granted free agency (October 12, 1993).... Re-signed by Rangers organization (November 19, 1993).

STATISTICAL NOTES: Led Gulf Coast League with 105 total bases in 1980.... Led International League outfielders with 272 total chances in 1989.... Led Pacific Coast League with 243 total bases and 11 sacrifice flies and tied for lead in grounding into double plays with 18 in 1990.... Tied for International League lead in grounding into double plays with 20 in 1992.

			BATTING												FIELDING			
Year	**Team (League)**	**Pos.**	**G**	**AB**	**R**	**H**	**2B**	**3B**	**HR**	**RBI**	**Avg.**	**BB**	**SO**	**SB**	**PO**	**A**	**E**	**Avg.**
1980	—GC Royals (GCL)	OF	61	235	46	*74	*17	4	2	35	.315	29	36	31	117	5	3	.976
1981	—Fort Myers (FSL)	OF	126	464	*89	139	17	10	13	70	.300	54	99	44	239	5	12	.953
1982	—Jacksonv. (South.)	OF	122	450	64	115	18	4	10	57	.256	46	101	17	231	7	2	.992
1983	—Jacksonv. (South.)	OF-1B	90	331	51	105	15	7	14	63	.317	36	78	29	117	4	4	.968
	—Omaha (A.A.)	OF	46	171	27	54	10	3	5	21	.316	18	36	13	10	0	1	.909
	—Kansas City (A.L.)	OF	33	122	13	42	2	6	2	18	.344	4	19	4	83	1	2	.977
1984	—Kansas City (A.L.)	OF	41	116	11	17	3	0	2	12	.147	10	19	4	69	2	3	.959
	—Omaha (A.A.)	OF-1B	83	314	45	102	15	5	7	43	.325	24	56	9	153	13	6	.965
1985	—Omaha (A.A.)	OF-1B	109	403	58	106	26	10	6	34	.263	26	89	15	209	3	9	.959
1986	—							Did not play.										
1987	—Vancouver (PCL)■	OF	111	424	58	115	17	7	7	57	.271	22	73	22	232	8	4	.984
	—Pittsburgh (N.L.)	OF	7	7	3	1	1	0	0	0	.143	1	3	0	3	0	0	1.000
1988	—Charlotte (South.)■	OF	101	412	62	124	23	7	13	82	*.301	24	40	17	116	3	3	.975
	—Rochester (Int'l)	OF	8	28	4	4	0	2	0	0	.143	0	2	0	10	0	0	1.000
	—Baltimore (A.L.)	OF	13	25	2	6	1	0	0	0	.240	0	8	1	16	1	0	1.000
1989	—Rochester (Int'l)	OF	127	479	81	145	29	9	10	64	.303	28	57	19	*258	8	6	.978
	—Baltimore (A.L.)	OF	5	6	1	1	1	0	0	0	.167	0	3	0	3	0	0	1.000
1990	—Albuquerque (PCL)■	OF	124	480	87	164	31	9	10	85	.342	24	53	25	131	4	2	.985
1991	—Albuquerque (PCL)	OF	91	284	55	89	19	10	7	44	.313	18	51	12	56	2	0	1.000
	—Los Angeles (N.L.)	PH	1	1	0	0	0	0	0	0	.000	0	0	0	...	...	...	...
1992	—Syracuse (Int'l)■	OF	134	*550	67	154	31	•9	9	74	.280	33	77	19	201	10	2	.991
	—Las Vegas (PCL)■	PH	1	1	0	1	0	0	0	0	1.000	0	0	0	...	...	...	...
1993	—Texas (A.L.)■	OF	62	159	24	39	10	4	3	20	.245	5	28	3	94	2	4	.960
American League totals (5 years)			154	428	51	105	17	10	7	50	.245	19	77	12	265	6	9	.968
National League totals (2 years)			8	8	3	1	1	0	0	0	.125	1	3	0	3	0	0	1.000
Major league totals (7 years)			162	436	54	106	18	10	7	50	.243	20	80	12	268	6	9	.968

DAVIS, CHILI

DH, ANGELS

PERSONAL: Born January 17, 1960, in Kingston, Jamaica.... 6-3/217.... Throws right, bats both.... Full name: Charles Theodore Davis.

HIGH SCHOOL: Dorsey (Los Angeles).

TRANSACTIONS/CAREER NOTES: Selected by San Francisco Giants organization in 11th round of free-agent draft (June 7, 1977).... On Phoenix disabled list (August 19-28, 1981).... Granted free agency (November 9, 1987).... Signed by California Angels (December 1, 1987).... On disabled list (July 17-August 9, 1990).... Granted free agency (December 7, 1990).... Signed by Minnesota Twins (January 29, 1991).... Granted free agency (November 3, 1992). ... Signed by Angels (December 11, 1992).

RECORDS: Shares major league single-season record for most games with switch-hit home runs—2 (1987).

STATISTICAL NOTES: Switch-hit home runs in one game (June 5, 1983; June 27 and September 15, 1987; July 30, 1988; July 1, 1989 and October 2, 1992).... Tied for A.L. lead with 10 sacrifice flies in 1988.

MISCELLANEOUS: Original nickname was Chili Bowl, which was prompted by a friend who saw Davis after he received a haircut back in the sixth grade. The nickname was later shortened to Chili.

			BATTING												FIELDING			
Year	**Team (League)**	**Pos.**	**G**	**AB**	**R**	**H**	**2B**	**3B**	**HR**	**RBI**	**Avg.**	**BB**	**SO**	**SB**	**PO**	**A**	**E**	**Avg.**
1978	—Ced. Rap. (Midw.)	C-OF	124	424	63	119	18	5	16	73	.281	36	103	15	365	45	25	.943
1979	—Fresno (California)	OF-C	134	490	91	132	24	5	21	95	.269	80	91	30	339	43	20	.950
1980	—Shreveport (Texas)	OF-C	129	442	50	130	30	4	12	67	.294	52	94	19	184	20	12	.944
1981	—San Francisco (N.L.)	OF	8	15	1	2	0	0	0	0	.133	1	2	2	7	0	0	1.000
	—Phoenix (PCL)	OF	88	334	76	117	16	6	19	75	.350	46	54	40	175	7	6	.968
1982	—San Francisco (N.L.)	OF	154	641	86	167	27	6	19	76	.261	45	115	24	404	•16	12	.972
1983	—San Francisco (N.L.)	OF	137	486	54	113	21	2	11	59	.233	55	108	10	357	7	9	.976
	—Phoenix (PCL)	OF	10	44	12	13	2	0	2	9	.295	4	6	5	15	0	2	.882
1984	—San Francisco (N.L.)	OF	137	499	87	157	21	6	21	81	.315	42	74	12	292	9	9	.971
1985	—San Francisco (N.L.)	OF	136	481	53	130	25	2	13	56	.270	62	74	15	279	10	6	.980
1986	—San Francisco (N.L.)	OF	153	526	71	146	28	3	13	70	.278	84	96	16	303	9	•9	.972
1987	—San Francisco (N.L.)	OF	149	500	80	125	22	1	24	76	.250	72	109	16	265	6	7	.975
1988	—California (A.L.)■	OF	158	600	81	161	29	3	21	93	.268	56	118	9	299	10	*19	.942
1989	—California (A.L.)	OF	154	560	81	152	24	1	22	90	.271	61	109	3	270	5	6	.979
1990	—California (A.L.)	OF	113	412	58	109	17	1	12	58	.265	61	89	1	77	5	3	.965
1991	—Minnesota (A.L.)■	OF	153	534	84	148	34	1	29	93	.277	95	117	5	2	0	0	1.000

Year	Team (League)	Pos.	G	AB	R	H	2B	3B	HR	RBI	Avg.	BB	SO	SB	PO	A	E	Avg.
			BATTING												FIELDING			
1992	—Minnesota (A.L.)	OF-1B	138	444	63	128	27	2	12	66	.288	73	76	4	6	0	0	1.000
1993	—California (A.L.)■	DH-P	153	573	74	139	32	0	27	112	.243	71	135	4	0	0	0	...
American League totals (6 years)			869	3123	441	837	163	8	123	512	.268	417	644	26	654	20	28	.960
National League totals (7 years)			874	3148	432	840	144	20	101	418	.267	361	578	95	1907	57	52	.974
Major league totals (13 years)			1743	6271	873	1677	307	28	224	930	.267	778	1222	121	2561	77	80	.971

CHAMPIONSHIP SERIES RECORD

CHAMPIONSHIP SERIES NOTES: Shares A.L. single-series record for most strikeouts—8 (1991).

Year	Team (League)	Pos.	G	AB	R	H	2B	3B	HR	RBI	Avg.	BB	SO	SB	PO	A	E	Avg.
			BATTING												FIELDING			
1987	—San Francisco (N.L.)	OF	6	20	2	3	1	0	0	0	.150	1	4	0	11	1	1	.923
1991	—Minnesota (A.L.)	DH	5	17	3	5	2	0	0	2	.294	5	8	1	...	...	...	...
Championship series totals (2 years)			11	37	5	8	3	0	0	2	.216	6	12	1	11	1	1	.923

WORLD SERIES RECORD

Year	Team (League)	Pos.	G	AB	R	H	2B	3B	HR	RBI	Avg.	BB	SO	SB	PO	A	E	Avg.
			BATTING												FIELDING			
1991	—Minnesota (A.L.)	DH-PH-OF	6	18	4	4	0	0	2	4	.222	2	3	0	1	0	0	1.000

ALL-STAR GAME RECORD

Year	League	Pos.	AB	R	H	2B	3B	HR	RBI	Avg.	BB	SO	SB	PO	A	E	Avg.
			BATTING											FIELDING			
1984	—National	PH	1	0	0	0	0	0	0	.000	0	0	0	...	...	...	...
1986	—National	OF	1	0	0	0	0	0	0	.000	0	1	0	0	0	0	...
All-Star Game totals (2 years)			2	0	0	0	0	0	0	.000	0	1	0	0	0	0	...

RECORD AS PITCHER

Year	Team (League)	W	L	Pct.	ERA	G	GS	CG	ShO	Sv.	IP	H	R	ER	BB	SO
1993	—California (A.L.)	0	0	...	0.00	1	0	0	0	0	2	0	0	0	0	0

DAVIS, CLINT

P, CARDINALS

PERSONAL: Born September 26, 1969, in Dallas. . . . 6-3/205. . . . Throws right, bats right. . . . Full name: Clint Edward Davis.
HIGH SCHOOL: MacArthur (Irving, Tex.).
COLLEGE: Dallas Baptist.
TRANSACTIONS/CAREER NOTES: Selected by St. Louis Cardinals organization in 49th round of free-agent draft (June 3, 1991).

Year	Team (League)	W	L	Pct.	ERA	G	GS	CG	ShO	Sv.	IP	H	R	ER	BB	SO
1991	—Ariz. Cardinals (Ar.)	3	3	.500	5.74	21	0	0	0	0	26⅔	35	23	17	12	25
1992	—Savannah (S. Atl.)	4	2	.667	2.22	51	0	0	0	1	65	49	24	16	21	61
1993	—St. Peters. (FSL)	1	0	1.000	1.93	29	0	0	0	•19	28	26	8	6	10	44
	—Arkansas (Texas)	2	0	1.000	1.95	28	0	0	0	1	37	22	10	8	10	37

DAVIS, ERIC

OF, TIGERS

PERSONAL: Born May 29, 1962, in Los Angeles. . . . 6-3/185. . . . Throws right, bats right. . . . Full name: Eric Keith Davis.
HIGH SCHOOL: Fremont (Los Angeles).
TRANSACTIONS/CAREER NOTES: Selected by Cincinnati Reds organization in eighth round of free-agent draft (June 3, 1980). . . . On disabled list (August 16-September 1, 1984; May 3-18, 1989; April 25-May 19, 1990; June 12-27 and July 31-August 26, 1991). . . . Traded by Reds with P Kip Gross to Los Angeles Dodgers for P Tim Belcher and P John Wetteland (November 27, 1991). . . . On disabled list (May 23-June 19 and August 2-25, 1992). . . . Granted free agency (November 3, 1992). . . . Re-signed by Dodgers (December 1, 1992). . . . Traded by Dodgers to Detroit Tigers for a player to be named later (August 31, 1993); Dodgers acquired P John DeSilva to complete deal (September 7, 1993).
RECORDS: Holds major league career record for highest stolen-base percentage (300 or more attempts)—.870. . . . Shares major league record for most strikeouts in two consecutive games—9 (April 24 [4] and 25 [5], 1987, 21 innings). . . . Shares major league single-month record for most grand slams—3 (May 1987). . . . Holds N.L. career record for highest stolen-base percentage (300 or more attempts)—.874.
HONORS: Named outfielder on THE SPORTING NEWS N.L. All-Star team (1987 and 1989). . . . Named outfielder on THE SPORTING NEWS N.L. Silver Slugger team (1987 and 1989). . . . Won N.L. Gold Glove as outfielder (1987-89).
STATISTICAL NOTES: Hit three home runs in one game (September 10, 1986 and May 3, 1987). . . . Led N.L. outfielders with 394 total chances in 1987. . . . Led N.L. with 21 game-winning RBIs in 1988. . . . Hit for the cycle (June 2, 1989).

Year	Team (League)	Pos.	G	AB	R	H	2B	3B	HR	RBI	Avg.	BB	SO	SB	PO	A	E	Avg.
			BATTING												FIELDING			
1980	—Eugene (N'west)	SS-2B-OF	33	73	12	16	1	0	1	11	.219	14	26	10	29	36	11	.855
1981	—Eugene (N'west)	OF	62	214	*67	69	10	4	11	39	.322	57	59	*40	94	11	4	.963
1982	—Ced. Rap. (Midw.)	OF	111	434	80	120	20	5	15	56	.276	51	103	53	239	9	9	.965
1983	—Waterbury (East.)	OF	89	293	56	85	13	1	15	43	.290	65	75	39	214	8	2	.991
	—Indianapolis (A.A.)	OF	19	77	18	23	4	0	7	19	.299	8	22	9	61	1	1	.984
1984	—Wichita (A.A.)	OF	52	194	42	61	9	5	14	34	.314	25	55	27	110	5	5	.958
	—Cincinnati (N.L.)	OF	57	174	33	39	10	1	10	30	.224	24	48	10	125	4	1	.992
1985	—Cincinnati (N.L.)	OF	56	122	26	30	3	3	8	18	.246	7	39	16	75	3	1	.987
	—Denver (A.A.)	OF	64	206	48	57	10	2	15	38	.277	29	67	35	94	5	3	.971
1986	—Cincinnati (N.L.)	OF	132	415	97	115	15	3	27	71	.277	68	100	80	274	2	7	.975
1987	—Cincinnati (N.L.)	OF	129	474	120	139	23	4	37	100	.293	84	134	50	*380	10	4	.990
1988	—Cincinnati (N.L.)	OF	135	472	81	129	18	3	26	93	.273	65	124	35	300	2	6	.981
1989	—Cincinnati (N.L.)	OF	131	462	74	130	14	2	34	101	.281	68	116	21	298	2	5	.984
1990	—Cincinnati (N.L.)	OF	127	453	84	118	26	2	24	86	.260	60	100	21	257	11	2	.993

Year	Team (League)	Pos.	G	AB	R	H	2B	3B	HR	RBI	Avg.	BB	SO	SB	PO	A	E	Avg.
			BATTING												FIELDING			
1991	—Cincinnati (N.L.).......	OF	89	285	39	67	10	0	11	33	.235	48	92	14	190	5	3	.985
1992	—Los Angeles (N.L.)■.	OF	76	267	21	61	8	1	5	32	.228	36	71	19	123	0	5	.961
1993	—Los Angeles (N.L.) ...	OF	108	376	57	88	17	0	14	53	.234	41	88	33	221	7	2	.991
	—Detroit (A.L.)■.........	OF	23	75	14	19	1	1	6	15	.253	14	18	2	52	0	1	.981
American League totals (1 year)			23	75	14	19	1	1	6	15	.253	14	18	2	52	0	1	.981
National League totals (10 years)			1040	3500	632	916	144	19	196	617	.262	501	912	299	2243	46	36	.985
Major league totals (10 years)			1063	3575	646	935	145	20	202	632	.262	515	930	301	2295	46	37	.984

CHAMPIONSHIP SERIES RECORD

Year	Team (League)	Pos.	G	AB	R	H	2B	3B	HR	RBI	Avg.	BB	SO	SB	PO	A	E	Avg.
			BATTING												FIELDING			
1990	—Cincinnati (N.L.).......	OF	6	23	2	4	1	0	0	2	.174	1	9	0	12	1	0	1.000

WORLD SERIES RECORD

WORLD SERIES NOTES: Hit home run in first at-bat (October 16, 1990).

Year	Team (League)	Pos.	G	AB	R	H	2B	3B	HR	RBI	Avg.	BB	SO	SB	PO	A	E	Avg.
			BATTING												FIELDING			
1990	—Cincinnati (N.L.).......	OF	4	14	3	4	0	0	1	5	.286	0	0	0	4	0	0	1.000

ALL-STAR GAME RECORD

Year	League	Pos.	AB	R	H	2B	3B	HR	RBI	Avg.	BB	SO	SB	PO	A	E	Avg.
			BATTING											FIELDING			
1987	—National....................	OF	3	0	0	0	0	0	0	.000	0	1	0	1	0	0	1.000
1989	—National....................	OF	2	0	0	0	0	0	0	.000	1	0	1	1	0	0	1.000
All-Star Game totals (2 years)			5	0	0	0	0	0	0	.000	1	1	1	2	0	0	1.000

DAVIS, GLENN

1B, METS

PERSONAL: Born March 28, 1961, in Jacksonville, Fla.... 6-3/212.... Throws right, bats right. ... Full name: Glenn Earl Davis.

HIGH SCHOOL: University Christian (Jacksonville, Fla.).

COLLEGE: Manatee Junior College (Fla.) and Georgia.

TRANSACTIONS/CAREER NOTES: Selected by Baltimore Orioles organization in 32nd round of free-agent draft (June 5, 1979).... Selected by Houston Astros organization in secondary phase of free-agent draft (January 13, 1981).... On Houston disabled list (June 25-August 29, 1990); included rehabilitation assignment to Columbus (July 28-August 3 and August 18-28).... Traded by Astros to Baltimore Orioles for P Pete Harnisch, P Curt Schilling and OF Steve Finley (January 10, 1991).... On Baltimore disabled list (April 25-August 19, 1991); included rehabilitation assignment to Hagerstown (August 10-19).... Granted free agency (November 1, 1991).... Re-signed by Orioles (November 12, 1991).... On disabled list (April 7-May 5, 1992). ... On Baltimore disabled list (June 7-September 6, 1993); included rehabilitation assignment to Frederick (August 27-30), Rochester (August 30-September 3) and Bowie (September 3-6).... Released by Orioles (September 8, 1993).... Signed by New York Mets organization (February 9, 1994).

RECORDS: Shares major league single-game record for most times hit by pitch—3 (April 9, 1990).... Shares A.L. single-game record for most errors by first baseman—4 (April 18, 1991).... Shares N.L. single-season record for fewest double plays by first baseman (150 or more games)—89 (1987).

HONORS: Named first baseman on THE SPORTING NEWS N.L. Silver Slugger team (1986).

STATISTICAL NOTES: Led Gulf Coast League first basemen with 469 putouts, 37 assists, 14 errors and 520 total chances and tied for lead with 35 double plays in 1981.... Tied for N.L. lead with 16 game-winning RBIs in 1986.... Hit three home runs in one game (September 10, 1987 and June 1, 1990).... Led N.L. in being hit by pitch with eight in 1990.

Year	Team (League)	Pos.	G	AB	R	H	2B	3B	HR	RBI	Avg.	BB	SO	SB	PO	A	E	Avg.
			BATTING												FIELDING			
1981	—GC Astros-Or. (GCL)..	1B-OF	54	188	27	49	7	1	6	35	.261	18	31	0	†469	†37	†14	.973
1982	—Day. Beach (FSL).....	1B-3B	103	378	70	119	28	3	•19	79	.315	44	77	1	759	70	16	.981
	—Columbus (South.)...	1B	26	97	14	24	6	1	4	8	.247	5	26	7	257	11	2	.993
1983	—Columbus (South.)...	OF	118	445	68	133	19	3	•25	85	.299	40	87	1	186	17	9	.958
	—Tucson (PCL)..........	OF-1B-3B	15	57	5	12	3	0	1	8	.211	3	10	0	52	4	2	.966
1984	—Tucson (PCL)..........	1B-OF	131	471	66	140	28	7	16	94	.297	49	88	2	922	94	22	.979
	—Houston (N.L.)..........	1B	18	61	6	13	5	0	2	8	.213	4	12	0	151	15	2	.988
1985	—Tucson (PCL)..........	1B-OF	60	220	22	67	24	2	5	35	.305	13	23	1	420	29	5	.989
	—Houston (N.L.)..........	1B-OF	100	350	51	95	11	0	20	64	.271	27	68	0	766	57	12	.986
1986	—Houston (N.L.)..........	1B	158	574	91	152	32	3	31	101	.265	64	72	3	1253	111	11	.992
1987	—Houston (N.L.)..........	1B	151	578	70	145	35	2	27	93	.251	47	84	4	1283	112	12	.991
1988	—Houston (N.L.)..........	1B	152	561	78	152	26	0	30	99	.271	53	77	4	1355	103	6	*.996
1989	—Houston (N.L.)..........	1B	158	581	87	156	26	1	34	89	.269	69	123	4	1347	113	12	.992
1990	—Houston (N.L.)..........	1B	93	327	44	82	15	4	22	64	.251	46	54	8	796	55	4	.995
	—Columbus (South.)...	1B	12	37	3	11	0	0	1	8	.297	2	9	1	79	7	3	.966
1991	—Baltimore (A.L.)■.....	1B	49	176	29	40	9	1	10	28	.227	16	29	4	288	38	8	.976
	—Hagerstown (East.)..	1B	7	24	4	6	1	0	1	3	.250	1	2	0	38	1	0	1.000
1992	—Baltimore (A.L.)........	1B	106	398	46	110	15	2	13	48	.276	37	65	1	19	1	0	1.000
1993	—Baltimore (A.L.)........	1B	30	113	8	20	3	0	1	9	.177	7	29	0	190	12	2	.990
	—Frederick (Caro.)......	1B	3	11	1	3	1	0	0	2	.273	1	3	0	13	2	0	1.000
	—Rochester (Int'l).......	1B	7	24	2	6	1	1	0	3	.250	2	8	0	28	7	0	1.000
	—Bowie (Eastern).......	1B	2	6	2	2	1	0	1	1	.333	1	1	0	10	2	0	1.000
American League totals (3 years)			185	687	83	170	27	3	24	85	.247	60	123	5	497	51	10	.982
National League totals (7 years)			830	3032	427	795	150	10	166	518	.262	310	490	23	6951	566	59	.992
Major league totals (10 years)			1015	3719	510	965	177	13	190	603	.259	370	613	28	7448	617	69	.992

CHAMPIONSHIP SERIES RECORD

CHAMPIONSHIP SERIES NOTES: Hit home run in first series at-bat (October 8, 1986).... Shares single-game record for most at-bats—7 (October 15, 1986, 16 innings).

Year	Team (League)	Pos.	G	AB	R	H	2B	3B	HR	RBI	Avg.	BB	SO	SB	PO	A	E	Avg.
			BATTING												FIELDING			
1986	—Houston (N.L.)	1B	6	26	3	7	1	0	1	3	.269	1	3	0	62	3	1	.985

ALL-STAR GAME RECORD

Year	League	Pos.	AB	R	H	2B	3B	HR	RBI	Avg.	BB	SO	SB	PO	A	E	Avg.
			BATTING											FIELDING			
1986	—National	PH	1	0	0	0	0	0	0	.000	0	0	0	...	...	...	...
1989	—National	1B	1	1	1	0	0	0	0	1.000	1	0	0	7	0	0	1.000
All-Star Game totals (2 years)			2	1	1	0	0	0	0	.500	1	0	0	7	0	0	1.000

DAVIS, MARK

P, PADRES

PERSONAL: Born October 19, 1960, in Livermore, Calif.... 6-4/215.... Throws left, bats left.... Full name: Mark William Davis.

HIGH SCHOOL: Granada (Livermore, Calif.).

COLLEGE: Chabot College (Calif.).

TRANSACTIONS/CAREER NOTES: Selected by New York Mets organization in 21st round of free-agent draft (June 6, 1978).... Selected by Philadelphia Phillies organization in secondary phase of free-agent draft (January 9, 1979).... On Oklahoma City disabled list (April 14-June 11, 1981 and August 3-30, 1982).... Traded by Phillies organization with P Mike Krukow and OF Charles Penigar to San Francisco Giants for 2B Joe Morgan and P Al Holland (December 14, 1982).... Traded by Giants with 3B Chris Brown, P Keith Comstock and P Mark Grant to San Diego Padres for P Dave Dravecky, P Craig Lefferts and IF Kevin Mitchell (July 4, 1987).... Granted free agency (November 13, 1989).... Signed by Kansas City Royals (December 11, 1989).... On disabled list (August 10-September 5, 1990 and April 20-May 5, 1991).... On Kansas City disabled list (June 18-August 5, 1991); included rehabilitation assignment to Omaha (July 6-August 4).... Traded by Royals to Atlanta Braves for P Juan Berenguer (July 21, 1992).... Traded by Braves to Philadelphia Phillies for P Brad Hassinger (April 13, 1993).... Released by Phillies (July 2, 1993).... Signed by Padres (July 10, 1993).

HONORS: Named Eastern League Most Valuable Player (1980).... Named N.L. Pitcher of the Year by THE SPORTING NEWS (1989).... Named N.L. Fireman of the Year by THE SPORTING NEWS (1989).... Named lefthanded pitcher on THE SPORTING NEWS N.L. All-Star team (1989).... Named N.L. Cy Young Award winner by Baseball Writers' Association of America (1989).

STATISTICAL NOTES: Led Western Carolinas League with 18 home runs allowed and tied for lead with five balks in 1979.

Year	Team (League)	W	L	Pct.	ERA	G	GS	CG	ShO	Sv.	IP	H	R	ER	BB	SO
1979	—Spartan. (W. Caro.)	11	9	.550	3.20	26	26	9	*5	0	166	147	76	59	49	135
1980	—Reading (Eastern)	*19	6	.760	*2.47	28	•28	8	•4	0	*193	140	63	53	75	*185
	—Philadelphia (N.L.)	0	0	...	2.57	2	1	0	0	0	7	4	2	2	5	5
1981	—Okla. City (A.A.)	5	2	.714	3.88	13	13	1	0	0	65	66	34	28	47	56
	—Philadelphia (N.L.)	1	4	.200	7.74	9	9	0	0	0	43	49	37	37	24	29
1982	—Okla. City (A.A.)	5	12	.294	6.24	21	19	3	1	0	96⅔	111	75	67	50	95
1983	—Phoenix (PCL)■	6	3	.667	6.32	13	13	1	1	0	72⅔	89	57	51	33	64
	—San Francisco (N.L.)	6	4	.600	3.49	20	20	2	2	0	111	93	51	43	50	83
1984	—San Francisco (N.L.)	5	17	.227	5.36	46	27	1	0	0	174⅔	201	113	*104	54	124
1985	—San Francisco (N.L.)	5	12	.294	3.54	77	1	0	0	7	114⅓	89	49	45	41	131
1986	—San Francisco (N.L.)	5	7	.417	2.99	67	2	0	0	4	84⅓	63	33	28	34	90
1987	—S.F.-S.D. (N.L.)■	9	8	.529	3.99	63	11	1	0	2	133	123	64	59	59	98
1988	—San Diego (N.L.)	5	10	.333	2.01	62	0	0	0	28	98⅓	70	24	22	42	102
1989	—San Diego (N.L.)	4	3	.571	1.85	70	0	0	0	*44	92⅔	66	21	19	31	92
1990	—Kansas City (A.L.)■	2	7	.222	5.11	53	3	0	0	6	68⅔	71	43	39	52	73
1991	—Kansas City (A.L.)	6	3	.667	4.45	29	5	0	0	1	62⅔	55	36	31	39	47
	—Omaha (A.A.)	4	1	.800	2.02	6	6	0	0	0	35⅔	27	11	8	9	36
1992	—Kansas City (A.L.)	1	3	.250	7.18	13	6	0	0	0	36⅓	42	31	29	28	19
	—Atlanta (N.L.)■	1	0	1.000	7.02	14	0	0	0	0	16⅔	22	13	13	13	15
1993	—Phil.-S.D. (N.L.)■	1	5	.167	4.26	60	0	0	0	4	69⅔	79	37	33	44	70
A.L. totals (3 years)		9	13	.409	5.31	95	14	0	0	7	167⅔	168	110	99	119	139
N.L. totals (11 years)		42	70	.375	3.86	490	71	4	2	89	944⅔	859	444	405	397	839
Major league totals (13 years)		51	83	.381	4.08	585	85	4	2	96	1112⅓	1027	554	504	516	978

ALL-STAR GAME RECORD

Year	League	W	L	Pct.	ERA	GS	CG	ShO	Sv.	IP	H	R	ER	BB	SO
1988	—National	0	0	...	0.00	0	0	0	0	⅔	1	0	0	0	0
1989	—National	0	0	...	0.00	0	0	0	0	1	0	0	0	0	2
All-Star totals (2 years)		0	0	...	0.00	0	0	0	0	1⅔	1	0	0	0	2

DAVIS, RUSS

3B, YANKEES

PERSONAL: Born September 13, 1969, in Birmingham, Ala.... 6-0/170.... Throws right, bats right.... Full name: Russell Stuart Davis.

COLLEGE: Shelton State Junior College (Ala.).

TRANSACTIONS/CAREER NOTES: Selected by New York Yankees organization in 29th round of free-agent draft (June 1, 1988).... On disabled list (July 13-August 1, 1993).

HONORS: Named Eastern League Most Valuable Player (1992).

STATISTICAL NOTES: Tied for New York-Pennsylvania League lead in double plays by third baseman with 11 in 1989.... Led Carolina League third basemen with 336 total chances and 18 double plays in 1990.... Tied Eastern League third basemen for league lead in fielding percentage with .917, putouts with 83, assists with 205, errors with 26 and total chances with 314 in 1991.... Led Eastern League with 237 total bases and .483 slugging percentage in 1992.... Led International League third basemen with 25 errors in 1993.

Year	Team (League)	Pos.	G	AB	R	H	2B	3B	HR	RBI	Avg.	BB	SO	SB	PO	A	E	Avg.
			BATTING												FIELDING			
1988	—GC Yankees (GCL)	2B-3B	58	213	33	49	11	3	2	30	.230	16	39	6	64	105	15	.918
1989	—Fort Lauder. (FSL)	3B-2B	48	147	8	27	5	1	2	22	.184	11	38	3	32	72	17	.860

D

Year	Team (League)	Pos.	G	AB	R	H	2B	3B	HR	RBI	Avg.	BB	SO	SB	PO	A	E	Avg.
			BATTING												FIELDING			
	—Oneonta (NYP)	3B	65	236	33	68	7	5	7	42	.288	19	44	3	27	87	17	.870
1990	—Prin. William (Car.)..	3B	137	510	55	127	*37	3	16	71	.249	37	136	3	*68	*244	24	.929
1991	—Alb./Colon. (East.)...	3B-2B	135	473	57	103	23	3	8	58	.218	50	102	3	‡83	‡206	‡26	‡.917
1992	—Alb./Colon. (East.)...	3B	132	491	77	140	23	4	22	71	.285	49	93	3	78	185	23	.920
1993	—Columbus (Int'l)	3B-SS	113	424	63	108	24	1	26	83	.255	40	118	1	85	245	†26	.927

DAVIS, STORM

P, TIGERS

PERSONAL: Born December 26, 1961, in Dallas. . . . 6-4/225. . . . Throws right, bats right. . . . Full name: George Earl Davis Jr.

HIGH SCHOOL: University Christian (Jacksonville, Fla.).

TRANSACTIONS/CAREER NOTES: Selected by Baltimore Orioles organization in seventh round of free-agent draft (June 5, 1979). . . . On Baltimore disabled list (July 4-22, 1986); included rehabilitation assignment to Hagerstown (July 18-22). . . . Traded by Orioles to San Diego Padres for C Terry Kennedy and P Mark Williamson (October 30, 1986). . . . On San Diego disabled list (June 30-August 17, 1987); included rehabilitation assignment to Wichita (August 7-11) and Reno (August 12-17). . . . Traded by Padres to Oakland Athletics for two players to be named later (August 30, 1987); Padres acquired P Dave Leiper (August 31, 1987) and 1B Rob Nelson (September 8, 1987) to complete deal. . . . On disabled list (May 18-June 10, 1989). . . . Granted free agency (November 13, 1989). . . . Signed by Kansas City Royals (December 7, 1989). . . . On disabled list (May 31-June 21 and July 1-17, 1990). . . . Traded by Royals to Orioles for C Bob Melvin (December 11, 1991). . . . On disabled list (July 5-20, 1992). . . . Granted free agency (October 30, 1992). . . . Signed by A's (December 8, 1992). . . . Released by A's (July 9, 1993). . . . Signed by Detroit Tigers (July 24, 1993). . . . Granted free agency (November 5, 1993). . . . Re-signed by Tigers (November 9, 1993).

HONORS: Named A.L. Comeback Player of the Year by THE SPORTING NEWS (1988).

STATISTICAL NOTES: Tied for A.L. lead with 16 wild pitches in 1988.

MISCELLANEOUS: Nicknamed by mother after "Dr. Storm," a character in "Dates on Trial," a book she was reading while pregnant with Storm.

Year	Team (League)	W	L	Pct.	ERA	G	GS	CG	ShO	Sv.	IP	H	R	ER	BB	SO
1979	—Bluefield (Appal.)	4	4	.500	3.88	10	10	3	1	0	58	44	34	25	30	54
1980	—Miami (Florida St.)	9	12	.429	3.52	25	25	7	0	0	151	157	85	59	55	90
1981	—Charlotte (South.)	14	10	.583	3.47	28	28	6	2	0	187	*215	86	72	65	119
1982	—Rochester (Int'l)	2	1	.667	3.71	4	4	0	0	0	26⅔	25	13	11	7	27
	—Baltimore (A.L.)	8	4	.667	3.49	29	8	1	0	0	100⅔	96	40	39	28	67
1983	—Baltimore (A.L.)	13	7	.650	3.59	34	29	6	1	0	200⅓	180	90	80	64	125
1984	—Baltimore (A.L.)	14	9	.609	3.12	35	31	10	2	1	225	205	86	78	71	105
1985	—Baltimore (A.L.)	10	8	.556	4.53	31	28	8	1	0	175	172	92	88	70	93
1986	—Baltimore (A.L.)	9	12	.429	3.62	25	25	2	0	0	154	166	70	62	49	96
	—Hagerstown (Car.)	0	0	...	0.00	1	1	0	0	0	4	3	0	0	3	6
1987	—San Diego (N.L.)■.......	2	7	.222	6.18	21	10	0	0	0	62⅔	70	48	43	36	37
	—Wichita (Texas)	0	1	.000	0.00	1	1	0	0	0	4	4	3	0	0	2
	—Reno (California)	0	0	...	3.60	1	1	0	0	0	5	2	2	2	6	5
	—Oakland (A.L.)■	1	1	.500	3.26	5	5	0	0	0	30⅓	28	13	11	11	28
1988	—Oakland (A.L.)	16	7	.696	3.70	33	33	1	0	0	201⅔	211	86	83	91	127
1989	—Oakland (A.L.)	19	7	.731	4.36	31	31	1	0	0	169⅓	187	91	82	68	91
1990	—Kansas City (A.L.)■...	7	10	.412	4.74	21	20	0	0	0	112	129	66	59	35	62
1991	—Kansas City (A.L.)	3	9	.250	4.96	51	9	1	1	2	114⅓	140	69	63	46	53
1992	—Baltimore (A.L.)■.......	7	3	.700	3.43	48	2	0	0	4	89⅓	79	35	34	36	53
1993	—Oakland-Det. (A.L.)■.	2	8	.200	5.05	43	8	0	0	4	98	93	57	55	48	73
A.L. totals (12 years)............		109	85	.562	3.96	386	229	30	5	11	1670	1686	795	734	617	973
N.L. totals (1 year)...............		2	7	.222	6.18	21	10	0	0	0	62⅔	70	48	43	36	37
Major league totals (12 years)		111	92	.547	4.04	407	239	30	5	11	1732⅔	1756	843	777	653	1010

CHAMPIONSHIP SERIES RECORD

Year	Team (League)	W	L	Pct.	ERA	G	GS	CG	ShO	Sv.	IP	H	R	ER	BB	SO
1983	—Baltimore (A.L.)	0	0	...	0.00	1	1	0	0	0	6	5	0	0	2	2
1988	—Oakland (A.L.)	0	0	...	0.00	1	1	0	0	0	6⅓	2	2	0	5	4
1989	—Oakland (A.L.)	0	1	.000	7.11	1	1	0	0	0	6⅓	5	6	5	2	3
Champ. series totals (3 years)		0	1	.000	2.41	3	3	0	0	0	18⅔	12	8	5	9	9

WORLD SERIES RECORD

Year	Team (League)	W	L	Pct.	ERA	G	GS	CG	ShO	Sv.	IP	H	R	ER	BB	SO
1983	—Baltimore (A.L.)	1	0	1.000	5.40	1	1	0	0	0	5	6	3	3	1	3
1988	—Oakland (A.L.)	0	2	.000	11.25	2	2	0	0	0	8	14	10	10	1	7
1989	—Oakland (A.L.)							Did not play.								
World Series totals (2 years) .		1	2	.333	9.00	3	3	0	0	0	13	20	13	13	2	10

DAWSON, ANDRE

OF, RED SOX

PERSONAL: Born July 10, 1954, in Miami. . . . 6-3/197. . . . Throws right, bats right. . . . Full name: Andre Nolan Dawson.

HIGH SCHOOL: Southwest Miami.

COLLEGE: Florida A&M.

TRANSACTIONS/CAREER NOTES: Selected by Montreal Expos organization in 11th round of free-agent draft (June 4, 1975). . . . On disabled list (June 5-30, 1986). . . . Granted free agency (November 12, 1986). . . . Signed by Chicago Cubs (March 9, 1987). . . . On disabled list (May 7-June 12, 1989). . . . On suspended list for one game (September 17, 1991). . . . Granted free agency (November 4, 1992). . . . Signed by Boston Red Sox (December 9, 1992). . . . On disabled list (May 6-25, 1993).

RECORDS: Holds major league single-game record for most intentional bases on balls received—5 (May 22, 1990, 16 innings). . . . Shares major league records for most total bases—8; and most home runs—2, in one inning (July 30, 1978, third inning, and September 24, 1985, fifth inning); and most runs batted in in one inning—6 (September 24, 1985, fifth inning). . . . Shares

major league single-season record for fewest double plays by outfielder (150 or more games)—0 (1987).
HONORS: Named N.L. Rookie Player of the Year by THE SPORTING NEWS (1977).... Named N.L. Rookie of the Year by Baseball Writers' Association of America (1977).... Named outfielder on THE SPORTING NEWS N.L. Silver Slugger team (1980-81, 1983 and 1987).... Won N.L. Gold Glove as outfielder (1980-85 and 1987-88).... Named N.L. Player of the Year by THE SPORTING NEWS (1981 and 1987).... Named outfielder on THE SPORTING NEWS N.L. All-Star team (1981, 1983 and 1987). ... Named N.L. Most Valuable Player by Baseball Writers' Association of America (1987).
STATISTICAL NOTES: Led Pioneer League in total bases with 166, in being hit by pitch with six and tied for lead in sacrifice flies with five in 1975.... Led N.L. in being hit by pitch with 12 in 1978, seven in 1981 and tied for lead with six in 1980 and nine in 1983.... Led N.L. outfielders with 344 total chances in 1981, 435 in 1982 and 450 in 1983.... Hit for the cycle (April 29, 1987). ... Led N.L. with 341 total bases in 1983 and 353 in 1987.... Led N.L. with 18 sacrifice flies in 1983.... Hit three home runs in one game (September 24, 1985 and August 1, 1987).... Tied for N.L. lead with 16 game-winning RBIs in 1987.... Tied for N.L. lead with 21 intentional bases on balls received in 1990.

			BATTING												FIELDING			
Year	**Team (League)**	**Pos.**	**G**	**AB**	**R**	**H**	**2B**	**3B**	**HR**	**RBI**	**Avg.**	**BB**	**SO**	**SB**	**PO**	**A**	**E**	**Avg.**
1975	—Lethbridge (Pio.)	OF	•72	*300	52	*99	14	7	*13	50	.330	23	59	11	*142	7	*10	.937
1976	—Quebec City (East.)	OF	40	143	27	51	6	0	8	27	.357	12	21	9	89	3	6	.939
	—Denver (A.A.)	OF	74	240	51	84	19	4	20	46	.350	23	50	10	97	2	2	.980
	—Montreal (N.L.)	OF	24	85	9	20	4	1	0	7	.235	5	13	1	61	1	2	.969
1977	—Montreal (N.L.)	OF	139	525	64	148	26	9	19	65	.282	34	93	21	352	9	4	.989
1978	—Montreal (N.L.)	OF	157	609	84	154	24	8	25	72	.253	30	128	28	411	17	5	.988
1979	—Montreal (N.L.)	OF	155	639	90	176	24	12	25	92	.275	27	115	35	394	7	5	.988
1980	—Montreal (N.L.)	OF	151	577	96	178	41	7	17	87	.308	44	69	34	410	14	6	.986
1981	—Montreal (N.L.)	OF	103	394	71	119	21	3	24	64	.302	35	50	26	*327	10	7	.980
1982	—Montreal (N.L.)	OF	148	608	107	183	37	7	23	83	.301	34	96	39	*419	8	8	.982
1983	—Montreal (N.L.)	OF	159	633	104	•189	36	10	32	113	.299	38	81	25	*435	6	9	.980
1984	—Montreal (N.L.)	OF	138	533	73	132	23	6	17	86	.248	41	80	13	297	11	8	.975
1985	—Montreal (N.L.)	OF	139	529	65	135	27	2	23	91	.255	29	92	13	248	9	7	.973
1986	—Montreal (N.L.)	OF	130	496	65	141	32	2	20	78	.284	37	79	18	200	11	3	.986
1987	—Chicago (N.L.)■	OF	153	621	90	178	24	2	*49	*137	.287	32	103	11	271	12	4	.986
1988	—Chicago (N.L.)	OF	157	591	78	179	31	8	24	79	.303	37	73	12	267	7	3	.989
1989	—Chicago (N.L.)	OF	118	416	62	105	18	6	21	77	.252	35	62	8	227	4	3	.987
1990	—Chicago (N.L.)	OF	147	529	72	164	28	5	27	100	.310	42	65	16	250	10	5	.981
1991	—Chicago (N.L.)	OF	149	563	69	153	21	4	31	104	.272	22	80	4	243	7	3	.988
1992	—Chicago (N.L.)	OF	143	542	60	150	27	2	22	90	.277	30	70	6	223	11	2	.992
1993	—Boston (A.L.)■	OF	121	461	44	126	29	1	13	67	.273	17	49	2	42	0	0	1.000
American League totals (1 year)			121	461	44	126	29	1	13	67	.273	17	49	2	42	0	0	1.000
National League totals (17 years)			2310	8890	1259	2504	444	94	399	1425	.282	552	1349	310	5035	154	84	.984
Major league totals (18 years)			2431	9351	1303	2630	473	95	412	1492	.281	569	1398	312	5077	154	84	.984

DIVISION SERIES RECORD

			BATTING												FIELDING			
Year	**Team (League)**	**Pos.**	**G**	**AB**	**R**	**H**	**2B**	**3B**	**HR**	**RBI**	**Avg.**	**BB**	**SO**	**SB**	**PO**	**A**	**E**	**Avg.**
1981	—Montreal (N.L.)	OF	5	20	1	6	0	1	0	0	.300	1	6	2	12	1	1	.929

CHAMPIONSHIP SERIES RECORD

			BATTING												FIELDING			
Year	**Team (League)**	**Pos.**	**G**	**AB**	**R**	**H**	**2B**	**3B**	**HR**	**RBI**	**Avg.**	**BB**	**SO**	**SB**	**PO**	**A**	**E**	**Avg.**
1981	—Montreal (N.L.)	OF	5	20	2	3	0	0	0	0	.150	0	4	0	12	0	0	1.000
1989	—Chicago (N.L.)	OF	5	19	0	2	1	0	0	3	.105	2	6	0	4	0	0	1.000
Championship series totals (2 years)			10	39	2	5	1	0	0	3	.128	2	10	0	16	0	0	1.000

ALL-STAR GAME RECORD

			BATTING											FIELDING			
Year	**League**	**Pos.**	**AB**	**R**	**H**	**2B**	**3B**	**HR**	**RBI**	**Avg.**	**BB**	**SO**	**SB**	**PO**	**A**	**E**	**Avg.**
1981	—National	OF	4	0	1	0	0	0	0	.250	0	1	1	4	0	0	1.000
1982	—National	OF	4	0	1	0	0	0	0	.250	0	0	0	4	0	0	1.000
1983	—National	OF	3	0	0	0	0	0	0	.000	0	1	0	3	0	0	1.000
1987	—National	OF	3	0	1	1	0	0	0	.333	0	1	0	3	0	0	1.000
1988	—National	OF	2	0	1	0	0	0	0	.500	0	0	0	0	0	0	...
1989	—National	OF	1	0	0	0	0	0	0	.000	0	0	0	1	0	0	1.000
1990	—National	OF	2	0	0	0	0	0	0	.000	0	1	0	1	0	0	1.000
1991	—National	OF	2	1	1	0	0	1	1	.500	0	0	0	0	0	0	...
All-Star Game totals (8 years)			21	1	5	1	0	1	1	.238	0	4	1	16	0	0	1.000

DAYLEY, KEN

P

PERSONAL: Born February 25, 1959, in Jerome, Idaho.... 6-0/180.... Throws left, bats left.... Full name: Kenneth Grant Dayley II.
HIGH SCHOOL: The Dalles (Ore.).
COLLEGE: Portland.
TRANSACTIONS/CAREER NOTES: Selected by Atlanta Braves organization in first round (third pick overall) of free-agent draft (June 3, 1980).... Traded by Braves with 1B Mike Jorgensen to St. Louis Cardinals for 3B Ken Oberkfell (June 15, 1984).... On disabled list (July 13, 1986-remainder of season).... Released by Cardinals (December 20, 1986).... Re-signed by Cardinals (January 19, 1987).... On St. Louis disabled list (April 5-May 21, 1987); included rehabilitation assignment to Louisville (May 12-21).... On disabled list (April 5-May 9, 1988).... Granted free agency (November 5, 1990).... Signed by Toronto Blue Jays (November 26, 1990).... On Toronto disabled list (April 3-May 24, 1991); included rehabilitation assignment to Dunedin (May 18-24).... On Toronto disabled list (June 12, 1991-remainder of season); included rehabilitation assignment to Syracuse (June 18-July 8 and September 1-5).... On Toronto disabled list (April 3, 1992-entire season); included rehabilitation assignment to Syracuse (July 9-20).... Released by Blue Jays (April 15, 1993).... Signed by Albuquerque, Los Angeles Dodgers organization (April 20, 1993).... On Albuquerque disabled list (May 4-17, 1993).... On Albuquerque temporary

inactive list (June 1-22, 1993).... Released by Albuquerque (June 22, 1993).
HONORS: Named lefthanded pitcher on THE SPORTING NEWS college All-America team (1980).

Year	Team (League)	W	L	Pct.	ERA	G	GS	CG	ShO	Sv.	IP	H	R	ER	BB	SO
1980	—Savannah (South.)	8	3	.727	2.57	16	16	3	0	0	105	86	38	30	54	104
1981	—Richmond (Int'l)	•13	8	.619	3.33	31	*31	4	1	0	*200	180	82	74	*117	*162
1982	—Richmond (Int'l)	8	3	.727	3.11	13	13	6	0	0	98⅓	89	43	34	47	79
	—Atlanta (N.L.)	5	6	.455	4.54	20	11	0	0	0	71⅓	79	39	36	25	34
1983	—Richmond (Int'l)	9	3	.750	3.28	14	14	4	1	0	90⅔	79	39	33	49	74
	—Atlanta (N.L.)	5	8	.385	4.30	24	16	0	0	0	104⅔	100	59	50	39	70
1984	—Richmond (Int'l)	5	1	.833	4.04	9	9	2	1	0	62⅓	66	31	28	24	45
	—Atl.-St.L. (N.L.)■........	0	5	.000	7.99	7	6	0	0	0	23⅔	44	28	21	11	10
	—Louisville (A.A.)	4	6	.400	3.27	13	13	3	0	0	96⅓	86	42	35	22	79
1985	—St. Louis (N.L.)	4	4	.500	2.76	57	0	0	0	11	65⅓	65	24	20	18	62
1986	—St. Louis (N.L.)	0	3	.000	3.26	31	0	0	0	5	38⅔	42	19	14	11	33
1987	—Louisville (A.A.)	0	0	...	4.50	1	1	0	0	0	2	1	1	1	1	1
	—Springfield (Midw.)	0	0	...	0.00	2	2	0	0	0	3⅔	1	0	0	1	3
	—St. Louis (N.L.)	9	5	.643	2.66	53	3	0	0	4	61	52	21	18	33	63
1988	—St. Louis (N.L.)	2	7	.222	2.77	54	0	0	0	5	55⅓	48	20	17	19	38
1989	—St. Louis (N.L.)	4	3	.571	2.87	71	0	0	0	12	75⅓	63	26	24	30	40
1990	—St. Louis (N.L.)	4	4	.500	3.56	58	0	0	0	4	73⅓	63	32	29	30	51
1991	—Dunedin (Fla. St.)■.....	0	0	...	0.00	3	2	0	0	0	6	1	000	0	2	2
	—Toronto (A.L.)	0	0	...	6.23	8	0	0	0	0	4⅓	7	3	3	5	3
	—Syracuse (Int'l)	0	1	.000	9.64	10	0	0	0	1	14	26	16	15	11	13
1992	—Syracuse (Int'l)	0	0	...	17.18	4	0	0	0	0	3⅔	3	7	7	6	4
1993	—Toronto (A.L.)	0	0	...	0.00	2	0	0	0	0	⅔	1	2	0	4	2
	—Albuquerque (PCL)■..	0	0	...	12.19	9	1	0	0	0	10⅓	14	15	14	12	9
A.L. totals (2 years)		0	0	...	5.40	10	0	0	0	0	5	8	5	3	9	5
N.L. totals (9 years)		33	45	.423	3.62	375	36	0	0	41	568⅔	556	268	229	216	401
Major league totals (11 years)		33	45	.423	3.64	385	36	0	0	41	573⅔	564	273	232	225	406

CHAMPIONSHIP SERIES RECORD

CHAMPIONSHIP SERIES NOTES: Shares single-series record for most games pitched—5 (1985).

Year	Team (League)	W	L	Pct.	ERA	G	GS	CG	ShO	Sv.	IP	H	R	ER	BB	SO
1985	—St. Louis (N.L.)	0	0	...	0.00	5	0	0	0	2	6	2	0	0	1	3
1987	—St. Louis (N.L.)	0	0	...	0.00	3	0	0	0	2	4	1	0	0	2	4
Champ. series totals (2 years)		0	0	...	0.00	8	0	0	0	4	10	3	0	0	3	7

WORLD SERIES RECORD

Year	Team (League)	W	L	Pct.	ERA	G	GS	CG	ShO	Sv.	IP	H	R	ER	BB	SO
1985	—St. Louis (N.L.)	1	0	1.000	0.00	4	0	0	0	0	6	1	0	0	3	5
1987	—St. Louis (N.L.)	0	0	...	1.93	4	0	0	0	1	4⅔	2	1	1	0	3
World Series totals (2 years)		1	0	1.000	0.84	8	0	0	0	1	10⅔	3	1	1	3	8

DEAK, DARRELL

2B, CARDINALS

PERSONAL: Born July 5, 1969, in Cumberland, Pa.... 6-0/180.... Throws right, bats both.... Full name: Darrell Scott Deak.
HIGH SCHOOL: Chaparral (Scottsdale, Ariz.).
COLLEGE: Loyola Marymount.
TRANSACTIONS/CAREER NOTES: Selected by St. Louis Cardinals organization in 18th round of free-agent draft (June 3, 1991).... On disabled list (June 2-9, 1993).
STATISTICAL NOTES: Led Midwest League with .496 slugging percentage in 1992.

			BATTING												FIELDING			
Year	Team (League)	Pos.	G	AB	R	H	2B	3B	HR	RBI	Avg.	BB	SO	SB	PO	A	E	Avg.
1991	—Johns. City (App.)	2B-SS	66	215	43	65	*23	2	9	33	.302	42	44	1	105	154	12	.956
1992	—Springfield (Midw.) ..	2B	126	428	84	122	28	7	16	79	.285	65	71	12	199	*291	18	.965
1993	—Arkansas (Texas)	2B	121	414	63	100	22	1	19	73	.242	58	103	4	219	273	17	.967

DECKER, STEVE

C, MARLINS

PERSONAL: Born October 25, 1965, in Rock Island, Ill.... 6-3/210.... Throws right, bats right.... Full name: Steven Michael Decker.
HIGH SCHOOL: Rock Island (Ill.).
COLLEGE: Lewis-Clark State College (Idaho).
TRANSACTIONS/CAREER NOTES: Selected by San Francisco Giants organization in 21st round of free-agent draft (June 1, 1988).... Selected by Florida Marlins in second round (35th pick overall) of expansion draft (November 17, 1992).... On disabled list (May 18, 1993-remainder of season).
STATISTICAL NOTES: Led Pacific Coast League catchers with 626 putouts and 694 total chances in 1992.

			BATTING												FIELDING			
Year	Team (League)	Pos.	G	AB	R	H	2B	3B	HR	RBI	Avg.	BB	SO	SB	PO	A	E	Avg.
1988	—Everett (N'west)	C	13	42	11	22	2	0	2	13	.524	7	5	0	37	3	2	.952
	—San Jose (Calif.)	C	47	175	31	56	9	0	4	34	.320	21	21	0	199	26	5	.978
1989	—San Jose (Calif.)	C-1B	64	225	27	65	12	0	3	46	.289	44	36	8	417	51	7	.985
	—Shreveport (Texas) ..	C-1B	44	142	19	46	8	0	1	18	.324	11	24	0	229	22	5	.980
1990	—Shreveport (Texas) ..	C	116	403	52	118	22	1	15	80	.293	40	64	3	650	71	10	.986
	—San Francisco (N.L.) ..	C	15	54	5	16	2	0	3	8	.296	1	10	0	75	11	1	.989
1991	—San Francisco (N.L.) ..	C	79	233	11	48	7	1	5	24	.206	16	44	0	385	41	7	.984
	—Phoenix (PCL)	C	31	111	20	28	5	1	6	14	.252	13	29	0	156	16	1	.994
1992	—Phoenix (PCL)	C-1B	125	450	50	127	22	2	8	74	.282	47	64	2	†650	65	5	.993
	—San Francisco (N.L.) ..	C	15	43	3	7	1	0	0	1	.163	6	7	0	94	4	0	1.000

Year	Team (League)	Pos.	G	AB	R	H	2B	3B	HR	RBI	Avg.	BB	SO	SB	PO	A	E	Avg.
			BATTING												FIELDING			
1993	—Florida (N.L.)■	C	8	15	0	0	0	0	0	1	.000	3	3	0	28	2	1	.968
Major league totals (4 years)			117	345	19	71	10	1	8	34	.206	26	64	0	582	58	9	.986

DEER, ROB

OF

PERSONAL: Born September 29, 1960, in Orange, Calif. . . . 6-3/225. . . . Throws right, bats right. . . . Full name: Robert George Deer.
HIGH SCHOOL: Canyon (Anaheim, Calif.).
COLLEGE: Fresno (Calif.) City College.
TRANSACTIONS/CAREER NOTES: Selected by San Francisco Giants organization in fourth round of free-agent draft (June 6, 1978). . . . Traded by Giants to Milwaukee Brewers for P Dean Freeland and P Eric Pilkington (December 18, 1985). . . . On disabled list (July 4-27, 1988 and August 9-25, 1989). . . . Granted free agency (November 5, 1990). . . . Signed by Detroit Tigers (November 23, 1990). . . . On disabled list (June 24-July 13 and July 19-August 14, 1992 and June 2-17, 1993). . . . Traded by Tigers to Boston Red Sox for a player to be named later (August 21, 1993). . . . Granted free agency (November 1, 1993). . . . Signed by Hanshin Tigers of Japan Central League (December 16, 1993).
RECORDS: Shares major league records for most grand slams in two consecutive games—2 (August 19 and 20, 1987); most strikeouts in nine-inning game—5 (August 8, 1987, first game). . . . Holds A.L. single-season record for most strikeouts—186 (1987).
STATISTICAL NOTES: Led A.L. outfielders with seven double plays in 1990.

Year	Team (League)	Pos.	G	AB	R	H	2B	3B	HR	RBI	Avg.	BB	SO	SB	PO	A	E	Avg.
			BATTING												FIELDING			
1978	—Great Falls (Pio.)	OF	48	137	20	34	6	5	0	18	.248	30	58	2	83	3	4	.956
1979	—Ced. Rap. (Midw.)	OF	29	86	7	18	0	1	1	16	.209	7	34	3	35	1	4	.900
	—Great Falls (Pio.)	OF	63	218	49	69	18	7	7	44	.317	39	62	4	95	10	5	.955
1980	—Clinton (Midwest)	OF	127	434	60	114	31	5	13	58	.263	34	115	20	184	•17	11	.948
1981	—Fresno (California)	OF	135	479	86	137	24	4	*33	107	.286	70	*146	18	211	14	6	.974
1982	—Shreveport (Texas)	OF-1B	128	410	58	85	26	0	27	73	.207	53	*177	6	184	10	11	.946
1983	—Shreveport (Texas)	OF	132	448	89	97	15	1	*35	99	.217	85	*185	18	252	13	7	.974
1984	—Phoenix (PCL)	OF	133	449	88	102	21	1	*31	69	.227	96	*175	9	251	*19	9	.968
	—San Francisco (N.L.)	OF	13	24	5	4	0	0	3	3	.167	7	10	1	19	0	2	.905
1985	—San Francisco (N.L.)	OF-1B	78	162	22	30	5	1	8	20	.185	23	71	0	127	2	2	.985
1986	—Milwaukee (A.L.)■	OF-1B	134	466	75	108	17	3	33	86	.232	72	179	5	312	8	8	.976
1987	—Milwaukee (A.L.)	OF-1B	134	474	71	113	15	2	28	80	.238	86	*186	12	304	16	8	.976
1988	—Milwaukee (A.L.)	OF	135	492	71	124	24	0	23	85	.252	51	•153	9	284	10	3	.990
1989	—Milwaukee (A.L.)	OF	130	466	72	98	18	2	26	65	.210	60	158	4	267	10	8	.972
1990	—Milwaukee (A.L.)	OF-1B	134	440	57	92	15	1	27	69	.209	64	147	2	373	25	10	.975
1991	—Detroit (A.L.)■	OF	134	448	64	80	14	2	25	64	.179	89	*175	1	310	8	7	.978
1992	—Detroit (A.L.)	OF	110	393	66	97	20	1	32	64	.247	51	131	4	229	8	4	.983
1993	—Det.-Boston (A.L.)■	OF	128	466	66	98	17	1	21	55	.210	58	*169	5	286	7	8	.973
American League totals (8 years)			1039	3645	542	810	140	12	215	568	.222	531	1298	42	2365	92	56	.978
National League totals (2 years)			91	186	27	34	5	1	11	23	.183	30	81	1	146	2	4	.974
Major league totals (10 years)			1130	3831	569	844	145	13	226	591	.220	561	1379	43	2511	94	60	.977

DE LA HOYA, JAVIER

P, MARLINS

PERSONAL: Born February 21, 1970, in Durango, Mexico. . . . 6-0/162. . . . Throws right, bats right. . . . Full name: Javier Jaime De La Hoya.
HIGH SCHOOL: U.S. Grant (Van Nuys, Calif.).
TRANSACTIONS/CAREER NOTES: Selected by Los Angeles Dodgers organization in fourth round of free-agent draft (June 5, 1989). . . . On Vero Beach disabled list (April 9-May 8, 1992). . . . On disabled list (May 14-June 17, 1993). . . . Claimed on waivers by Florida Marlins (September 22, 1993).
STATISTICAL NOTES: Tied for Northwest League lead with seven hit batsmen in 1990.

Year	Team (League)	W	L	Pct.	ERA	G	GS	CG	ShO	Sv.	IP	H	R	ER	BB	SO
1989	—GC Dodgers (GCL)	4	3	.571	1.46	9	8	2	•1	0	55⅓	28	13	9	19	70
1990	—Bakersfield (Calif.)	4	1	.800	5.95	9	7	0	0	0	39⅓	50	30	26	24	37
	—Vero Beach (FSL)	1	2	.333	5.57	4	4	0	0	0	21	14	14	13	20	22
	—Yakima (N'west)	3	5	.375	4.46	14	14	0	0	0	70⅔	65	52	35	39	71
1991	—Bakersfield (Calif.)	6	4	.600	3.67	27	11	1	0	2	98	92	47	40	44	102
1992	—Vero Beach (FSL)	4	5	.444	2.81	14	14	2	2	0	80	68	25	25	26	92
	—San Antonio (Tex.)	2	1	.667	2.84	5	5	0	0	0	25⅓	20	11	8	17	24
1993	—San Antonio (Tex.)	8	10	.444	3.66	21	21	1	0	0	125⅓	122	61	51	42	107

DeLEON, JOSE

P, WHITE SOX

PERSONAL: Born December 20, 1960, in Rancho Viejo, LaVega, Dominican Republic. . . . 6-3/226. . . . Throws right, bats right. . . . Full name: Jose Chestaro DeLeon. . . . Name pronounced DAY-lee-own.
HIGH SCHOOL: Perth Amboy (N.J.).
TRANSACTIONS/CAREER NOTES: Selected by Pittsburgh Pirates organization in third round of free-agent draft (June 5, 1979); pick received as compensation for Montreal Expos signing free agent Duffy Dyer. . . . On disabled list (July 5-29, 1982). . . . Traded by Pirates organization to Chicago White Sox for OF Bobby Bonilla (July 23, 1986). . . . Traded by White Sox to St. Louis Cardinals for P Rick Horton, OF Lance Johnson and cash (February 9, 1988). . . . Released by Cardinals (August 31, 1992). . . . Signed by Philadelphia Phillies (September 9, 1992). . . . Traded by Phillies to Chicago White Sox for P Bobby Thigpen (August 10, 1993). . . . Granted free agency (November 1, 1993). . . . Re-signed by White Sox organization (December 7, 1993).
STATISTICAL NOTES: Led Gulf Coast League with seven home runs allowed and tied for lead with nine wild pitches in 1979. . . . Tied for South Atlantic League lead with 19 home runs allowed in 1980.
MISCELLANEOUS: Appeared in one game as outfielder with one putout (1988).

Year	Team (League)	W	L	Pct.	ERA	G	GS	CG	ShO	Sv.	IP	H	R	ER	BB	SO
1979	—GC Pirates (GCL)	2	4	.333	6.41	11	9	2	0	1	59	76	47	42	38	33
1980	—Shelby (S. Atl.)	10	15	.400	4.82	26	26	7	0	0	168	160	108	★90	69	118
1981	—Buffalo (Eastern)	12	6	.667	3.11	25	25	2	0	0	159	136	72	55	94	158
1982	—Portland (PCL)	10	7	.588	5.97	24	23	3	0	0	119	138	81	79	65	94
1983	—Hawaii (PCL)	11	6	.647	★3.04	20	20	6	1	0	127⅓	90	50	43	68	128
	—Pittsburgh (N.L.)	7	3	.700	2.83	15	15	3	2	0	108	75	36	34	47	118
1984	—Pittsburgh (N.L.)	7	13	.350	3.74	30	28	5	1	0	192⅓	147	86	80	92	153
1985	—Pittsburgh (N.L.)	2	★19	.095	4.70	31	25	1	0	3	162⅔	138	93	85	89	149
	—Hawaii (PCL)	4	0	1.000	0.88	5	5	4	2	0	41	15	4	4	10	45
1986	—Hawaii (PCL)	5	8	.385	2.46	15	14	7	1	0	106	87	32	29	44	83
	—Pittsburgh (N.L.)	1	3	.250	8.27	9	1	0	0	1	16⅓	17	16	15	17	11
	—Chicago (A.L.)■	4	5	.444	2.96	13	13	1	0	0	79	49	30	26	42	68
1987	—Chicago (A.L.)	11	12	.478	4.02	33	31	2	0	0	206	177	106	92	97	153
1988	—St. Louis (N.L.)■	13	10	.565	3.67	34	34	3	1	0	225⅓	198	95	92	86	208
1989	—St. Louis (N.L.)	16	12	.571	3.05	36	36	5	3	0	244⅔	173	96	83	80	★201
1990	—St. Louis (N.L.)	7	★19	.269	4.43	32	32	0	0	0	182⅔	168	96	90	86	164
1991	—St. Louis (N.L.)	5	9	.357	2.71	28	28	1	0	0	162⅔	144	57	49	61	118
1992	—St. L.-Phil. (N.L.)■	2	8	.200	4.37	32	18	0	0	0	117⅓	111	63	57	48	79
1993	—Philadelphia (N.L.)	3	0	1.000	3.26	24	3	0	0	0	47	39	25	17	27	34
	—Chicago (A.L.)■	0	0	...	1.74	11	0	0	0	0	10⅓	5	2	2	3	6
A.L. totals (3 years)		15	17	.469	3.66	57	44	3	0	0	295⅓	231	138	120	142	227
N.L. totals (10 years)		63	96	.396	3.71	271	220	18	7	4	1459	1210	663	602	633	1235
Major league totals (11 years)		78	113	.408	3.70	328	264	21	7	4	1754⅓	1441	801	722	775	1462

CHAMPIONSHIP SERIES RECORD

Year	Team (League)	W	L	Pct.	ERA	G	GS	CG	ShO	Sv.	IP	H	R	ER	BB	SO
1993	—Chicago (A.L.)	0	0	...	1.93	2	0	0	0	0	4⅔	7	1	1	1	6

DELGADO, CARLOS

C, BLUE JAYS

PERSONAL: Born June 25, 1972, in Aguadilla, Puerto Rico. . . . 6-3/220. . . . Throws right, bats left. . . . Full name: Carlos Juan Delgado.
HIGH SCHOOL: Jose de Diego (Aguadilla, Puerto Rico).
TRANSACTIONS/CAREER NOTES: Signed as free agent by Toronto Blue Jays organization (October 9, 1988).
HONORS: Named Florida State League Most Valuable Player (1992). . . . Named Southern League Most Valuable Player (1993).
STATISTICAL NOTES: Led New York-Pennsylvania League catchers with 540 total chances and six double plays in 1990. . . . Led South Atlantic League with 29 passed balls in 1991. . . . Led Florida State League with 281 total bases, .579 slugging percentage, .402 on-base percentage and 11 intentional bases on balls received in 1992. . . . Led Florida State League catchers with 784 total chances in 1992. . . . Led Southern League with .524 slugging percentage, .430 on-base percentage and 18 intentional bases on balls received in 1993. . . . Led Southern League catchers with 800 total chances in 1993.

			BATTING											FIELDING			
Year	Team (League)	Pos.	G	AB	R	H	2B	3B	HR	RBI	Avg.	BB	SO	SB	PO	A	E	Avg.
1989	—St. Cathar. (NYP)	C	31	89	9	16	5	0	0	11	.180	23	39	0	63	13	2	.974
1990	—St. Cathar. (NYP)	C	67	228	30	64	13	0	6	39	.281	35	65	2	★471	★62	7	.987
1991	—Myrtle Beach (SAL)	C	132	441	72	126	18	2	18	70	.286	75	97	9	679	★100	19	.976
	—Syracuse (Int'l)	C	1	3	0	0	0	0	0	0	.000	0	2	0	5	0	0	1.000
1992	—Dunedin (Fla. St.)	C	133	485	83	★157	•30	2	★30	★100	.324	59	91	2	★684	89	11	.986
1993	—Knoxville (South.)	C	140	468	91	142	28	0	★25	★102	.303	★102	98	10	★683	★103	★14	.983
	—Toronto (A.L.)	C	2	1	0	0	0	0	0	0	.000	1	0	0	2	0	0	1.000
Major league totals (1 year)			2	1	0	0	0	0	0	0	.000	1	0	0	2	0	0	1.000

DE LOS SANTOS, MARIANO

P, PIRATES

PERSONAL: Born July 13, 1970, in Santo Domingo, Dominican Republic. . . . 5-10/200. . . . Throws right, bats right.
TRANSACTIONS/CAREER NOTES: Signed as free agent by Pittsburgh Pirates organization (January 9, 1989). . . . On Carolina disabled list (August 31, 1993-remainder of season).

Year	Team (League)	W	L	Pct.	ERA	G	GS	CG	ShO	Sv.	IP	H	R	ER	BB	SO
1989	—GC Pirates (GCL)	2	2	.500	5.79	13	4	0	0	2	37⅓	41	27	24	19	24
1990	—Dom. Pirates (DSL)	5	5	.500	3.00	15	13	4	1	1	78	53	29	26	28	71
1991	—GC Pirates (GCL)	3	2	.600	1.35	9	5	0	0	1	33⅓	23	5	5	5	50
	—Welland (NYP)	1	3	.250	5.51	8	6	0	0	0	32⅔	41	24	20	21	22
1992	—Augusta (S. Atl.)	7	8	.467	2.25	52	1	0	0	12	96	75	33	24	38	103
1993	—Salem (Carolina)	9	5	.643	3.36	18	18	2	1	0	99	90	46	37	41	80
	—Carolina (South.)	1	2	.333	4.73	8	8	0	0	0	40	49	24	21	15	34

DeLUCIA, RICH

P, MARINERS

PERSONAL: Born October 7, 1964, in Reading, Pa. . . . 6-0/185. . . . Throws right, bats right. . . . Full name: Richard Anthony DeLucia. . . . Name pronounced duh-LOO-sha.
HIGH SCHOOL: Wyomissing (Pa.) Area.
COLLEGE: Tennessee.
TRANSACTIONS/CAREER NOTES: Selected by Toronto Blue Jays organization in 15th round of free-agent draft (June 3, 1985). . . . Selected by Seattle Mariners organization in sixth round of free-agent draft (June 2, 1986). . . . On disabled list (April 10, 1987-remainder of season). . . . On Williamsport disabled list (May 31-July 2 and July 7, 1989-remainder of season). . . . On Seattle disabled list (August 5-September 1, 1992); included rehabilitation assignment to Calgary (August 26-31). . . . On Seattle disabled list (June 28-July 22, 1993); included rehabilitation assignment to Calgary (July 16-22).
STATISTICAL NOTES: Pitched seven-inning, 1-0 no-hit victory against Everett (July 17, 1986). . . . Led A.L. with 31 home runs allowed in 1991.

Year	Team (League)	W	L	Pct.	ERA	G	GS	CG	ShO	Sv.	IP	H	R	ER	BB	SO
1986	—Belling. (N'west)	8	2	.800	*1.70	13	11	1	•1	0	74	44	20	14	24	69
1987	—Salinas (Calif.)	0	0	...	9.00	1	0	0	0	0	1	2	1	1	0	1
1988	—San Bern. (Calif.)	7	8	.467	3.10	22	22	0	0	0	127⅔	110	57	44	59	118
1989	—Williamsport (East.)	3	4	.429	3.79	10	10	0	0	0	54⅔	59	28	23	13	41
1990	—San Bern. (Calif.)	4	1	.800	2.05	5	5	1	0	0	30⅔	19	9	7	3	35
	—Williamsport (East.)	6	6	.500	2.11	18	18	2	1	0	115	92	30	27	30	76
	—Calgary (PCL)	2	2	.500	3.62	5	5	1	0	0	32⅓	30	17	13	12	23
	—Seattle (A.L.)	1	2	.333	2.00	5	5	1	0	0	36	30	9	8	9	20
1991	—Seattle (A.L.)	12	13	.480	5.09	32	31	0	0	0	182	176	107	103	78	98
1992	—Seattle (A.L.)	3	6	.333	5.49	30	11	0	0	1	83⅔	100	55	51	35	66
	—Calgary (PCL)	4	2	.667	2.45	8	5	2	1	1	40⅓	32	11	11	14	38
1993	—Seattle (A.L.)	3	6	.333	4.64	30	1	0	0	0	42⅔	46	24	22	23	48
	—Calgary (PCL)	1	5	.167	5.73	8	7	0	0	1	44	45	30	28	20	38
Major league totals (4 years)		19	27	.413	4.81	97	48	1	0	1	344⅓	352	195	184	145	232

DENSON, DREW

1B, WHITE SOX

PERSONAL: Born November 16, 1965, in Cincinnati. . . . 6-5/220. . . . Throws right, bats right.
HIGH SCHOOL: Purcell Marian (Cincinnati).
TRANSACTIONS/CAREER NOTES: Selected by Atlanta Braves organization in first round (19th pick overall) of free-agent draft (June 4, 1984). . . . On disabled list (April 24-May 4, 1985; May 3-24 and July 8-August 8, 1986). . . . Granted free agency (October 15, 1990). . . . Signed by Chicago White Sox organization (January 8, 1992). . . . On Birmingham disabled list (April 9-22, 1992).
STATISTICAL NOTES: Led Gulf Coast League with 133 total bases and .556 slugging percentage in 1984. . . . Led Southern League first basemen with 111 double plays in 1988. . . . Led International League first basemen with 1,111 putouts, 14 errors, 1,203 total chances and 126 double plays in 1989. . . . Led American Association in being hit by pitch with 23 and in grounding into double plays with 22 in 1993.
MISCELLANEOUS: Batted as switch-hitter with Greenville (1988) and Atlanta (1989).

			BATTING											FIELDING			
Year	Team (League)	Pos.	G	AB	R	H	2B	3B	HR	RBI	Avg.	BB	SO	SB	PO	A	E	Avg.
1984	—GC Braves (GCL)	OF	62	239	43	*77	*20	3	•10	45	*.322	17	41	5	65	6	2	.973
1985	—Sumter (S. Atl.)	OF	111	383	59	115	18	4	14	74	.300	53	76	5	119	5	3	.976
1986	—Durham (Carolina)	OF	72	231	31	54	6	3	4	23	.234	25	46	6	86	3	11	.890
1987	—Greenville (South.)	1B	128	447	54	98	23	1	14	55	.219	33	95	1	998	50	10	.991
1988	—Greenville (South.)	1B-OF	140	507	85	136	26	4	13	78	.268	44	116	11	1148	73	18	.985
1989	—Richmond (Int'l)	1B-OF	138	463	50	118	32	0	9	59	.255	42	*116	0	†1116	78	†14	.988
	—Atlanta (N.L.)	1B	12	36	1	9	1	0	0	5	.250	3	9	1	71	11	1	.988
1990	—Richmond (Int'l)	1B	90	295	25	68	4	1	7	29	.231	26	57	0	684	38	5	.993
1991	—							Out of organized baseball.										
1992	—Vancouver (PCL)■	1B	105	340	43	94	7	3	13	70	.276	36	58	1	92	7	5	.952
1993	—Nashville (A.A.)	1B	136	513	82	144	36	0	24	103	.281	46	98	0	534	48	•11	.981
	—Chicago (A.L.)	1B	4	5	0	1	0	0	0	0	.200	0	2	0	4	0	1	.800
American League totals (1 year)			4	5	0	1	0	0	0	0	.200	0	2	0	4	0	1	.800
National League totals (1 year)			12	36	1	9	1	0	0	5	.250	3	9	1	71	11	1	.988
Major league totals (2 years)			16	41	1	10	1	0	0	5	.244	3	11	1	75	11	2	.977

DESHAIES, JIM

P, TWINS

PERSONAL: Born June 23, 1960, in Massena, N.Y. . . . 6-5/222. . . . Throws left, bats left. . . . Full name: James Joseph Deshaies. . . . Name pronounced duh-SHAYS.
HIGH SCHOOL: Massena (N.Y.) Central.
COLLEGE: Le Moyne College, N.Y. (bachelor of arts degree, 1982).
TRANSACTIONS/CAREER NOTES: Selected by Montreal Expos organization in 13th round of free-agent draft (June 6, 1978). . . . Selected by New York Yankees organization in 21st round of free-agent draft (June 7, 1982). . . . On Columbus disabled list (April 10-25 and August 4-14, 1985). . . . Traded by Yankees organization with two players to be named later to Houston Astros for P Joe Niekro (September 15, 1985); Astros organization acquired IF Neder Horta (September 24, 1985) and P Dody Rather (January 11, 1986) to complete deal. . . . On disabled list (April 21-May 7, 1986 and July 26-August 16, 1987). . . . Granted free agency (October 28, 1991). . . . Signed by Oakland Athletics organization (January 27, 1992). . . . Released by A's organization (March 23, 1992). . . . Signed by San Diego Padres organization (April 28, 1992). . . . Granted free agency (October 27, 1992). . . . Signed by Minnesota Twins (December 9, 1992). . . . Traded by Twins to San Francisco Giants for P Aaron Fultz, SS Andres Duncan and a player to be named later (August 28, 1993); Twins acquired P Greg Brummett to complete deal (September 1, 1993). . . . Granted free agency (October 25, 1993). . . . Signed by Twins (January 13, 1994.
RECORDS: Holds modern major league record for most consecutive strikeouts at start of game—8 (September 23, 1986).
STATISTICAL NOTES: Pitched seven-inning, 5-1 no-hit victory for Nashville against Columbus (May 4, 1984). . . . Led International League with four balks in 1985. . . . Led N.L. with seven balks in 1986.

Year	Team (League)	W	L	Pct.	ERA	G	GS	CG	ShO	Sv.	IP	H	R	ER	BB	SO
1982	—Oneonta (NYP)	6	5	.545	3.32	15	14	6	1	0	108⅓	93	50	40	40	*137
1983	—Fort Lauder. (FSL)	11	3	.786	2.52	20	19	5	2	0	117⅔	105	44	33	58	128
1984	—Nashville (South.)	3	2	.600	2.80	7	7	1	0	0	45	33	20	14	29	42
	—Columbus (Int'l)	10	5	.667	*2.39	18	18	9	•4	0	135⅔	99	45	36	62	117
	—New York (A.L.)	0	1	.000	11.57	2	2	0	0	0	7	14	9	9	7	5
1985	—Columbus (Int'l)	8	6	.571	4.31	21	21	3	0	0	131⅔	124	67	63	59	106
	—Houston (N.L.)■	0	0	...	0.00	2	0	0	0	0	3	1	0	0	0	2
1986	—Houston (N.L.)	12	5	.706	3.25	26	26	1	1	0	144	124	58	52	59	128
1987	—Houston (N.L.)	11	6	.647	4.62	26	25	1	0	0	152	149	81	78	57	104
1988	—Houston (N.L.)	11	14	.440	3.00	31	31	3	2	0	207	164	77	69	72	127
1989	—Houston (N.L.)	15	10	.600	2.91	34	34	6	3	0	225⅔	180	80	73	79	153
1990	—Houston (N.L.)	7	12	.368	3.78	34	34	2	0	0	209⅓	186	93	88	84	119
1991	—Houston (N.L.)	5	12	.294	4.98	28	28	1	0	0	161	156	90	89	72	98

Year	Team (League)	W	L	Pct.	ERA	G	GS	CG	ShO	Sv.	IP	H	R	ER	BB	SO
1992	—Las Vegas (PCL)■	6	3	.667	4.03	18	8	0	0	1	58	60	28	26	17	46
	—San Diego (N.L.)	4	7	.364	3.28	15	15	0	0	0	96	92	40	35	33	46
1993	—Minnesota (A.L.)■	11	13	.458	4.41	27	27	1	0	0	167⅓	159	85	82	51	80
	—San Francisco (N.L.)■	2	2	.500	4.24	5	4	0	0	0	17	24	9	8	6	5
A.L. totals (2 years)		11	14	.440	4.70	29	29	1	0	0	174⅓	173	94	91	58	85
N.L. totals (9 years)		67	68	.496	3.64	201	197	14	6	0	1215	1076	528	492	462	782
Major league totals (10 years)		78	82	.488	3.78	230	226	15	6	0	1389⅓	1249	622	583	520	867

CHAMPIONSHIP SERIES RECORD

Year	Team (League)	W	L	Pct.	ERA	G	GS	CG	ShO	Sv.	IP	H	R	ER	BB	SO
1986	—Houston (N.L.)							Did not play.								

DeSHIELDS, DELINO

2B, DODGERS

PERSONAL: Born January 15, 1969, in Seaford, Del. . . . 6-1/175. . . . Throws right, bats left. . . . Full name: Delino Lamont DeShields. . . . Name pronounced duh-LINE-oh.
HIGH SCHOOL: Seaford (Del.).
COLLEGE: Villanova.
TRANSACTIONS/CAREER NOTES: Selected by Montreal Expos organization in first round (12th pick overall) of free-agent draft (June 2, 1987). . . . On disabled list (June 16-July 12, 1990 and August 12-September 11, 1993). . . . Traded by Expos to Los Angeles Dodgers for P Pedro Martinez (November 19, 1993).
RECORDS: Shares modern N.L. record for most hits in first major league game—4 (April 9, 1990).
STATISTICAL NOTES: Led Gulf Coast League shortstops with 22 errors in 1987.

			BATTING											FIELDING			
Year	Team (League)	Pos.	G	AB	R	H	2B	3B	HR	RBI	Avg.	BB	SO	SB	PO	A	E	Avg.
1987	—GC Expos (GCL)	SS-3B	31	111	17	24	5	2	1	4	.216	21	30	16	47	90	†22	.862
	—Jamestown (NYP)	SS	34	96	16	21	1	2	1	5	.219	24	28	14	25	57	21	.796
1988	—Rockford (Midw.)	SS	129	460	97	116	26	6	12	46	.252	95	110	59	173	344	42	.925
1989	—Jacksonv. (South.)	SS	93	307	55	83	10	6	3	35	.270	76	80	37	127	218	34	.910
	—Indianapolis (A.A.)	SS	47	181	29	47	8	4	2	14	.260	16	53	16	73	101	13	.930
1990	—Montreal (N.L.)	2B	129	499	69	144	28	6	4	45	.289	66	96	42	236	371	12	.981
1991	—Montreal (N.L.)	2B	151	563	83	134	15	4	10	51	.238	95	*151	56	285	405	*27	.962
1992	—Montreal (N.L.)	2B	135	530	82	155	19	8	7	56	.292	54	108	46	251	360	15	.976
1993	—Montreal (N.L.)	2B	123	481	75	142	17	7	2	29	.295	72	64	43	243	381	11	.983
Major league totals (4 years)			538	2073	309	575	79	25	23	181	.277	287	419	187	1015	1517	65	.975

DeSILVA, JOHN

P, DODGERS

PERSONAL: Born September 30, 1967, in Fort Bragg, Calif. . . . 6-0/190. . . . Throws right, bats right. . . . Full name: John Reed DeSilva.
HIGH SCHOOL: Fort Bragg (Calif.).
COLLEGE: Brigham Young.
TRANSACTIONS/CAREER NOTES: Selected by Chicago White Sox organization in 30th round of free-agent draft (June 1, 1988). . . . Selected by Detroit Tigers organization in eighth round of free-agent draft (June 5, 1989). . . . On Toledo disabled list (June 15-July 2, 1991 and April 4-21 and April 30-June 26, 1992). . . . Traded by Tigers to Los Angeles Dodgers (September 7, 1993), completing deal in which Dodgers traded OF Eric Davis to Tigers for a player to be named later (August 31, 1993).

Year	Team (League)	W	L	Pct.	ERA	G	GS	CG	ShO	Sv.	IP	H	R	ER	BB	SO
1989	—Niag. Falls (NYP)	3	0	1.000	1.88	4	4	0	0	0	24	15	5	5	8	24
	—Fayetteville (SAL)	2	2	.500	2.68	9	9	1	0	0	53⅔	40	23	16	21	54
1990	—Lakeland (Fla. St.)	8	1	.889	1.48	14	14	0	0	0	91	54	18	15	25	113
	—London (Eastern)	5	6	.455	3.84	14	14	1	1	0	89	87	47	38	27	76
1991	—London (Eastern)	5	4	.556	2.81	11	11	2	1	0	73⅔	51	24	23	24	80
	—Toledo (Int'l)	5	4	.556	4.60	11	11	1	0	0	58⅔	62	33	30	21	56
1992	—Toledo (Int'l)	0	3	.000	8.53	7	2	0	0	0	19	26	18	18	8	21
	—London (Eastern)	2	4	.333	4.13	9	9	1	1	0	52⅓	51	24	24	13	53
1993	—Toledo (Int'l)	7	10	.412	3.69	25	24	1	0	0	161	145	73	66	60	136
	—Detroit (A.L.)	0	0	...	9.00	1	0	0	0	0	1	2	1	1	0	0
	—Los Angeles (N.L.)■	0	0	...	6.75	3	0	0	0	0	5⅓	6	4	4	1	6
A.L. totals (1 year)		0	0	...	9.00	1	0	0	0	0	1	2	1	1	0	0
N.L. totals (1 year)		0	0	...	6.75	3	0	0	0	0	5⅓	6	4	4	1	6
Major league totals (1 year)		0	0	...	7.11	4	0	0	0	0	6⅓	8	5	5	1	6

DESTRADE, ORESTES

1B, MARLINS

PERSONAL: Born May 8, 1962, in Santiago, Cuba. . . . 6-4/230. . . . Throws right, bats both.
HIGH SCHOOL: Miami Coral Park Senior and Christopher Columbus (Miami).
COLLEGE: Florida College.
TRANSACTIONS/CAREER NOTES: Selected by California Angels organization in 23rd round of free-agent draft (June 3, 1980). . . . Signed as free agent by New York Yankees organization (May 17, 1981). . . . On disabled list (July 24, 1986-remainder of season). . . . Traded by Yankees to Pittsburgh Pirates for P Hipolito Pena (March 30, 1988). . . . Contract sold by Buffalo, Pirates organization, to Seibu Lions of Japan Pacific League (May 18, 1989). . . . Signed as free agent by Florida Marlins (December 15, 1992).
STATISTICAL NOTES: Tied for Appalachian League lead in double plays by first baseman with 42 in 1981. . . . Led Eastern League first basemen with 1,194 total chances and 99 double plays in 1985.

			BATTING											FIELDING			
Year	Team (League)	Pos.	G	AB	R	H	2B	3B	HR	RBI	Avg.	BB	SO	SB	PO	A	E	Avg.
1981	—Paintsville (Appal.)	1B	63	208	51	57	12	1	*14	46	.274	48	49	2	461	22	11	.978

			BATTING												FIELDING			
Year	Team (League)	Pos.	G	AB	R	H	2B	3B	HR	RBI	Avg.	BB	SO	SB	PO	A	E	Avg.
1982	—Greensboro (S. Atl.)	1B	43	122	9	22	4	1	1	14	.180	27	42	1	359	15	4	.989
	—Oneonta (NYP)	1B	64	194	44	45	12	1	4	30	.232	38	56	11	298	33	10	.971
1983	—Fort Lauder. (FSL)	OF-1B	127	425	61	124	24	5	18	74	.292	•82	86	3	425	24	9	.980
1984	—Nashville (South.)	OF-1B	35	121	15	29	6	0	6	12	.240	15	36	0	56	2	3	.951
	—Fort Lauder. (FSL)	1B	95	308	40	68	14	2	12	57	.221	64	82	3	764	41	•16	.981
1985	—Alb./Colon. (East.)	1B	136	471	82	119	24	5	23	72	.253	86	*129	9	*1103	73	18	.985
1986	—Columbus (Int'l)	1B	98	359	59	99	21	4	19	56	.276	40	88	1	697	63	11	.986
1987	—Columbus (Int'l)	1B	135	465	76	119	26	3	25	81	.256	79	118	0	509	47	6	.989
	—New York (A.L.)	1B	9	19	5	5	0	0	0	1	.263	5	5	0	20	1	0	1.000
1988	—Buffalo (A.A.)■	1B	77	273	37	74	16	1	12	42	.271	44	67	2	732	43	9	.989
	—Pittsburgh (N.L.)	1B	36	47	2	7	1	0	1	3	.149	5	17	0	61	2	0	1.000
1989	—Buffalo (A.A.)	1B-OF	33	100	8	23	6	0	1	17	.230	13	13	0	165	9	2	.989
	—Seibu (Jp. Pac.)■	DH	83	292	56	75	...	...	32	83	.257	60	72	0	...	...	...	...
1990	—Seibu (Jp. Pac.)	DH	*130	476	81	125	19	0	*42	*106	.263	70	165	10	...	...	...	...
1991	—Seibu (Jp. Pac.)	1B	•130	437	90	117	21	0	*39	*92	.268	*103	*119	15	...	...	...	...
1992	—Seibu (Jp. Pac.)	DH	128	448	87	119	...	...	*41	87	.266	*95	125	12	...	...	...	...
1993	—Florida (N.L.)■	1B	153	569	61	145	20	3	20	87	.255	58	130	0	1313	90	*19	.987
American League totals (1 year)			9	19	5	5	0	0	0	1	.263	5	5	0	20	1	0	1.000
National League totals (2 years)			189	616	63	152	21	3	21	90	.247	63	147	0	1374	92	19	.987
Major league totals (3 years)			198	635	68	157	21	3	21	91	.247	68	152	0	1394	93	19	.987

DEVEREAUX, MIKE

OF, ORIOLES

PERSONAL: Born April 10, 1963, in Casper, Wyo. . . . 6-0/195. . . . Throws right, bats right. . . . Name pronounced DEH-ver-oh.
HIGH SCHOOL: Kelly Walsh (Casper, Wyo.).
COLLEGE: Mesa (Ariz.) Community College and Arizona State (bachelor of arts degree in finance).
TRANSACTIONS/CAREER NOTES: Selected by Cleveland Indians organization in 26th round of free-agent draft (June 4, 1984). . . . Selected by Los Angeles Dodgers organization in fifth round of free-agent draft (June 3, 1985). . . . Traded by Dodgers to Baltimore Orioles for P Mike Morgan (March 12, 1989). . . . On Baltimore disabled list (May 17-June 15, 1990); included rehabilitation assignment to Frederick (June 9-10) and Hagerstown (June 11-15). . . . On Baltimore disabled list (May 3-27, 1993); included rehabilitation assignment to Bowie (May 25-27).
HONORS: Named outfielder on THE SPORTING NEWS A.L. All-Star team (1992).
STATISTICAL NOTES: Led Pioneer League with 152 total bases in 1985. . . . Led Texas League with 11 sacrifice flies in 1987. . . . Led Texas League outfielders with 349 total chances in 1987.

			BATTING												FIELDING			
Year	Team (League)	Pos.	G	AB	R	H	2B	3B	HR	RBI	Avg.	BB	SO	SB	PO	A	E	Avg.
1985	—Great Falls (Pio.)	OF	•70	*289	*73	*103	17	10	4	*67	.356	32	29	*40	100	4	5	.954
1986	—San Antonio (Tex.)	OF	115	431	69	130	22	2	10	53	.302	58	47	31	292	13	4	.987
1987	—San Antonio (Tex.)	OF	*135	*562	90	169	28	9	26	91	.301	48	65	33	*339	7	3	*.991
	—Albuquerque (PCL)	OF	3	11	2	3	1	0	1	1	.273	0	2	1	4	1	0	1.000
	—Los Angeles (N.L.)	OF	19	54	7	12	3	0	0	4	.222	3	10	3	21	1	0	1.000
1988	—Albuquerque (PCL)	OF	109	423	88	144	26	4	13	76	.340	44	46	33	211	5	7	.969
	—Los Angeles (N.L.)	OF	30	43	4	5	1	0	0	2	.116	2	10	0	29	0	0	1.000
1989	—Baltimore (A.L.)■	OF	122	391	55	104	14	3	8	46	.266	36	60	22	288	1	5	.983
1990	—Baltimore (A.L.)	OF	108	367	48	88	18	1	12	49	.240	28	48	13	281	4	5	.983
	—Frederick (Caro.)	OF	2	8	3	4	0	0	1	3	.500	1	2	1	4	2	0	1.000
	—Hagerstown (East.)	OF	4	20	4	5	3	0	0	3	.250	0	1	0	13	0	1	.929
1991	—Baltimore (A.L.)	OF	149	608	82	158	27	10	19	59	.260	47	115	16	399	10	3	.993
1992	—Baltimore (A.L.)	OF	156	653	76	180	29	11	24	107	.276	44	94	10	431	5	5	.989
1993	—Baltimore (A.L.)	OF	131	527	72	132	31	3	14	75	.250	43	99	3	311	8	4	.988
	—Bowie (Eastern)	OF	2	7	1	2	1	0	0	2	.286	0	2	0	5	0	0	1.000
American League totals (5 years)			666	2546	333	662	119	28	77	336	.260	198	416	64	1710	28	22	.988
National League totals (2 years)			49	97	11	17	4	0	0	6	.175	5	20	3	50	1	0	1.000
Major league totals (7 years)			715	2643	344	679	123	28	77	342	.257	203	436	67	1760	29	22	.988

DEWEY, MARK

P, PIRATES

PERSONAL: Born January 3, 1965, in Grand Rapids, Mich. . . . 6-0/216. . . . Throws right, bats right. . . . Full name: Mark Alan Dewey.
HIGH SCHOOL: Jenison (Mich.).
COLLEGE: Grand Valley State (Mich.).
TRANSACTIONS/CAREER NOTES: Selected by San Francisco Giants organization in 23rd round of free-agent draft (June 2, 1987). . . . Claimed on waivers by New York Mets (May 9, 1991). . . . On Norfolk disqualified list (April 8-May 10, 1993). . . . Claimed on waivers by Pittsburgh Pirates (May 11, 1993).

Year	Team (League)	W	L	Pct.	ERA	G	GS	CG	ShO	Sv.	IP	H	R	ER	BB	SO
1987	—Everett (N'west)	7	3	.700	3.30	19	10	1	0	1	84⅔	88	39	31	26	67
1988	—Clinton (Midwest)	10	4	.714	*1.43	37	7	1	0	7	119⅓	95	36	19	14	76
1989	—San Jose (Calif.)	1	6	.143	3.15	59	0	0	0	*30	68⅔	62	35	24	23	60
1990	—Shreveport (Texas)	1	5	.167	1.88	33	0	0	0	13	38⅓	37	11	8	10	23
	—Phoenix (PCL)	2	3	.400	2.67	19	0	0	0	8	30⅓	26	14	9	10	27
	—San Francisco (N.L.)	1	1	.500	2.78	14	0	0	0	0	22⅔	22	7	7	5	11
1991	—Phoenix (PCL)	1	2	.333	3.97	10	0	0	0	4	11⅓	16	7	5	7	4
	—Tidewater (Int'l)■	•12	3	•.800	3.34	48	0	0	0	9	64⅔	61	30	24	36	38
1992	—Tidewater (Int'l)	5	7	.417	4.31	43	0	0	0	9	54⅓	61	29	26	18	55
	—New York (N.L.)	1	0	1.000	4.32	20	0	0	0	0	33⅓	37	16	16	10	24
1993	—Buffalo (A.A.)■	2	0	1.000	1.23	22	0	0	0	6	29⅓	21	9	4	5	17
	—Pittsburgh (N.L.)	1	2	.333	2.36	21	0	0	0	7	26⅔	14	8	7	10	14
Major league totals (3 years)		3	3	.500	3.27	55	0	0	0	7	82⅔	73	31	30	25	49

DIAZ, ALEX

OF, BREWERS

PERSONAL: Born October 5, 1968, in Brooklyn, N.Y. . . . 5-11/180. . . . Throws right, bats both. . . . Son of Mario Caballero Diaz, minor league infielder (1959-64).
HIGH SCHOOL: Manuel Mendez Licihea (Puerto Rico).
TRANSACTIONS/CAREER NOTES: Signed as free agent by New York Mets organization (August 24, 1986). . . . Traded by Mets with OF Darren Reed to Montreal Expos for OF Terrel Hansen and P David Sommer (April 2, 1991). . . . On Indianapolis suspended list (August 30, 1991-remainder of season). . . . Traded by Expos organization to Milwaukee Brewers organization for IF George Canale (October 15, 1991). . . . On Milwaukee disabled list (May 3-August 30, 1993); included rehabilitation assignment to New Orleans (August 13-30). . . . Granted free agency (December 20, 1993). . . . Re-signed by Brewers (December 21, 1993).

			BATTING												FIELDING			
Year	**Team (League)**	**Pos.**	**G**	**AB**	**R**	**H**	**2B**	**3B**	**HR**	**RBI**	**Avg.**	**BB**	**SO**	**SB**	**PO**	**A**	**E**	**Avg.**
1987	—Kingsport (Appal.)	SS	54	212	29	56	9	1	0	13	.264	16	31	*34	67	126	18	.915
	—Little Falls (NYP)	SS	12	47	7	16	4	1	0	8	.340	2	3	2	13	22	4	.897
1988	—Columbia (S. Atl.)	SS	123	481	82	126	14	*11	0	37	.262	21	49	28	175	299	*72	.868
	—St. Lucie (Fla. St.)	SS	3	6	2	0	0	0	0	1	.000	0	4	0	3	3	3	.667
1989	—St. Lucie (Fla. St.)	SS-OF	102	416	54	106	11	10	1	33	.255	20	38	43	151	244	28	.934
	—Jackson (Texas)	2B	23	95	11	26	5	1	2	9	.274	3	11	3	25	65	3	.968
1990	—Tidewater (Int'l)	OF-2B-SS	124	437	55	112	15	2	1	36	.256	30	39	23	196	101	11	.964
1991	—Indianapolis (A.A.)■	0-S-3-2	108	370	48	90	14	4	1	21	.243	27	46	17	207	45	8	.969
1992	—Denver (A.A.)■	OF-2B-SS	106	455	67	122	17	4	1	41	.268	24	36	42	240	43	7	.976
	—Milwaukee (A.L.)	OF	22	9	5	1	0	0	0	1	.111	0	0	3	10	0	0	1.000
1993	—Milwaukee (A.L.)	OF	32	69	9	22	2	0	0	1	.319	0	12	5	46	1	1	.979
	—New Orleans (A.A.)	OF	16	55	8	16	2	0	0	5	.291	3	6	7	38	1	0	1.000
Major league totals (2 years)			54	78	14	23	2	0	0	2	.295	0	12	8	56	1	1	.983

DIAZ, MARIO

IF, MARLINS

PERSONAL: Born January 10, 1962, in Humacao, Puerto Rico. . . . 5-10/160. . . . Throws right, bats right. . . . Full name: Mario Rafael Torres Diaz.
HIGH SCHOOL: Teodor Aguilar Mora (Humacao, Puerto Rico).
TRANSACTIONS/CAREER NOTES: Signed as free agent by Seattle Mariners organization (December 21, 1978). . . . On Seattle disabled list (May 6-23, 1988); included rehabilitation assignment to Calgary (May 16-23). . . . On Seattle disabled list (March 31-May 4, 1990). . . . Traded by Mariners organization to Tidewater, New York Mets organization, for P Brian Givens (June 19, 1990). . . . Granted free agency (October 15, 1990). . . . Signed by Texas Rangers (December 14, 1990). . . . On disabled list (June 24-July 11, 1991). . . . Granted free agency (October 15, 1991). . . . Signed by Denver, Milwaukee Brewers organization (December 16, 1991). . . . Released by Denver (April 1, 1992). . . . Signed by Calgary, Mariners organization (April 4, 1992). . . . On Calgary disabled list (April 20-May 4, 1992). . . . Released by Calgary (May 29, 1992). . . . Signed by Oklahoma City, Rangers organization (June 19, 1992). . . . Granted free agency (October 15, 1992). . . . Re-signed by Oklahoma City (January 13, 1993). . . . Granted free agency (October 15, 1993). . . . Signed by Florida Marlins organization (December 15, 1993).
STATISTICAL NOTES: Led Southern League with 14 sacrifice hits in 1985.

			BATTING												FIELDING			
Year	**Team (League)**	**Pos.**	**G**	**AB**	**R**	**H**	**2B**	**3B**	**HR**	**RBI**	**Avg.**	**BB**	**SO**	**SB**	**PO**	**A**	**E**	**Avg.**
1979	—Belling. (N'west)	SS-3B-2B	32	96	12	19	2	0	1	5	.198	5	17	0	28	69	8	.924
1980	—Wausau (Midwest)	SS-2B	110	349	28	63	5	0	3	21	.181	19	37	5	172	328	41	.924
1981	—Lynn (Eastern)	SS	106	314	16	63	8	1	1	22	.201	16	42	1	163	318	18	*.964
1982	—Lynn (Eastern)	SS-1B	53	162	19	35	7	1	1	13	.216	19	24	2	384	172	18	.969
	—Salt Lake City (PCL)	SS	5	19	2	7	1	0	0	2	.368	0	2	0	4	15	1	.950
	—Wausau (Midwest)	SS	56	187	15	49	8	1	1	23	.262	7	23	3	78	148	16	.934
1983	—Bakersfield (Calif.)	SS-2B	51	171	23	41	5	1	0	10	.240	10	26	3	92	146	22	.915
	—Chatt. (South.)	SS	33	111	18	30	6	5	2	13	.270	5	15	0	48	80	10	.928
1984	—Chatt. (South.)	SS-2B	108	322	23	67	7	1	1	19	.208	21	18	6	179	313	26	.950
1985	—Chatt. (South.)	SS	115	400	38	101	6	7	0	38	.253	21	20	3	186	314	31	.942
1986	—Calgary (PCL)	SS	109	379	40	107	17	6	1	41	.282	13	29	1	194	302	16	.969
1987	—Calgary (PCL)	SS	108	376	52	106	17	3	4	52	.282	20	28	1	195	280	21	.958
	—Seattle (A.L.)	SS	11	23	4	7	0	1	0	3	.304	0	4	0	10	25	1	.972
1988	—Calgary (PCL)	SS	46	164	16	54	18	0	1	30	.329	9	10	1	65	138	12	.944
	—Seattle (A.L.)	S-2-1-3	28	72	6	22	5	0	0	9	.306	3	5	0	31	47	1	.987
1989	—Seattle (A.L.)	SS-2B-3B	52	74	9	10	0	0	1	7	.135	7	7	0	35	54	5	.947
	—Calgary (PCL)	2B-SS-1B	37	127	22	43	8	1	2	9	.339	8	7	1	64	73	9	.938
1990	—Calgary (PCL)	3B-SS-2B	32	105	10	35	5	1	1	19	.333	1	8	0	35	61	2	.980
	—Tidewater (Int'l)■	SS-3B	29	104	15	33	8	0	1	9	.317	6	6	1	38	92	6	.956
	—New York (N.L.)	SS-2B	16	22	0	3	1	0	0	1	.136	0	3	0	5	18	1	.958
1991	—Texas (A.L.)■	SS-2B-3B	96	182	24	48	7	0	1	22	.264	15	18	0	93	143	7	.971
1992	—Calgary (PCL)■	SS-OF	18	52	8	14	4	0	0	11	.269	0	6	1	23	26	4	.925
	—Okla. City (A.A.)■	SS-3B-2B	43	167	24	56	11	0	3	20	.335	2	12	1	81	109	5	.974
	—Texas (A.L.)	SS-2B-3B	19	31	2	7	1	0	0	1	.226	1	2	0	16	26	1	.977
1993	—Okla. City (A.A.)	3B-2B-SS	48	177	24	58	12	2	3	20	.328	7	15	3	53	105	3	.981
	—Texas (A.L.)	SS-3B-1B	71	205	24	56	10	1	2	24	.273	8	13	1	90	153	3	.988
American League totals (6 years)			277	587	69	150	23	2	4	66	.256	34	49	1	275	448	18	.976
National League totals (1 year)			16	22	0	3	1	0	0	1	.136	0	3	0	5	18	1	.958
Major league totals (7 years)			293	609	69	153	24	2	4	67	.251	34	52	1	280	466	19	.975

DIBBLE, ROB

P, REDS

PERSONAL: Born January 24, 1964, in Bridgeport, Conn. . . . 6-4/230. . . . Throws right, bats left. . . . Full name: Robert Keith Dibble.
HIGH SCHOOL: Southington (Conn.).
COLLEGE: Florida Southern.
TRANSACTIONS/CAREER NOTES: Selected by St. Louis Cardinals organization in 11th round of free-agent draft (June 7, 1982). . . . Selected by Cincinnati Reds organization in secondary phase of free-agent draft (June 6, 1983). . . . On suspended list (May 31-June 2 and July 25-28, 1989). . . . On disabled list (July 10-25, 1989). . . . On suspended list (July 19-23 and July

31-August 3, 1991).... On disabled list (March 28-April 16, 1992).... On suspended list (July 9-12, 1992).... On disabled list (April 22-May 28 and September 22, 1993-remainder of season).
RECORDS: Shares major league record by striking out side on nine pitches (June 4, 1989, eighth inning).... Shares N.L. single-game record for most consecutive strikeouts by relief pitcher—6 (April 23, 1991).

Year	Team (League)	W	L	Pct.	ERA	G	GS	CG	ShO	Sv.	IP	H	R	ER	BB	SO
1983	—Billings (Pioneer)	0	1	.000	7.82	5	2	0	0	0	12⅔	18	13	11	11	7
	—Eugene (N'west)	3	2	.600	5.73	7	7	1	0	0	37⅔	38	28	24	18	17
1984	—Tampa (Fla. St.)	5	2	.714	2.92	15	11	2	0	0	64⅔	59	31	21	29	39
1985	—Ced. Rap. (Midw.)	5	5	.500	3.84	45	1	0	0	12	65⅔	67	37	28	28	73
1986	—Vermont (Eastern)	3	2	.600	3.09	31	1	1	0	10	55⅓	53	29	19	28	37
	—Denver (A.A.)	1	0	1.000	5.40	5	0	0	0	0	6⅔	9	4	4	2	3
1987	—Nashville (A.A.)	2	4	.333	4.72	44	0	0	0	4	61	72	34	32	27	51
1988	—Nashville (A.A.)	2	1	.667	2.31	31	0	0	0	13	35	21	9	9	14	41
	—Cincinnati (N.L.)	1	1	.500	1.82	37	0	0	0	0	59⅓	43	12	12	21	59
1989	—Cincinnati (N.L.)	10	5	.667	2.09	74	0	0	0	2	99	62	23	23	39	141
1990	—Cincinnati (N.L.)	8	3	.727	1.74	68	0	0	0	11	98	62	22	19	34	136
1991	—Cincinnati (N.L.)	3	5	.375	3.17	67	0	0	0	31	82⅓	67	32	29	25	124
1992	—Cincinnati (N.L.)	3	5	.375	3.07	63	0	0	0	25	70⅓	48	26	24	31	110
1993	—Cincinnati (N.L.)	1	4	.200	6.48	45	0	0	0	19	41⅔	34	33	30	42	49
Major league totals (6 years)		26	23	.531	2.74	354	0	0	0	88	450⅔	316	148	137	192	619

CHAMPIONSHIP SERIES RECORD

CHAMPIONSHIP SERIES NOTES: Named N.L. Championship Series co-Most Valuable Player (1990).

Year	Team (League)	W	L	Pct.	ERA	G	GS	CG	ShO	Sv.	IP	H	R	ER	BB	SO
1990	—Cincinnati (N.L.)	0	0	...	0.00	4	0	0	0	1	5	0	0	0	1	10

WORLD SERIES RECORD

Year	Team (League)	W	L	Pct.	ERA	G	GS	CG	ShO	Sv.	IP	H	R	ER	BB	SO
1990	—Cincinnati (N.L.)	1	0	1.000	0.00	3	0	0	0	0	4⅔	3	0	0	1	4

ALL-STAR GAME RECORD

Year	League	W	L	Pct.	ERA	GS	CG	ShO	Sv.	IP	H	R	ER	BB	SO
1990	—National	0	0	...	0.00	0	0	0	0	1	1	0	0	1	0
1991	—National	0	0	...	0.00	0	0	0	0	1	0	0	0	1	1
All-Star totals (2 years)		0	0	...	0.00	0	0	0	0	2	1	0	0	2	1

D

DICKSON, LANCE

P, CUBS

PERSONAL: Born October 19, 1969, in Fullerton, Calif.... 6-1/190.... Throws left, bats right.... Full name: Lance Michael Dickson.
HIGH SCHOOL: Grossmont (La Mesa, Calif.).
COLLEGE: Arizona.
TRANSACTIONS/CAREER NOTES: Selected by Houston Astros organization in 37th round of free-agent draft (June 2, 1987).... Selected by Chicago Cubs organization in first round (23rd pick overall) of free-agent draft (June 4, 1990).... On Chicago disabled list (August 19-September 11, 1990).... On Iowa disabled list (June 13-August 25, 1991; April 9-May 6 and May 7-September 14, 1992; June 19-28, July 5-30 and August 5, 1993-remainder of season).

Year	Team (League)	W	L	Pct.	ERA	G	GS	CG	ShO	Sv.	IP	H	R	ER	BB	SO
1990	—Geneva (NY-Penn)	2	1	.667	0.53	3	3	0	0	0	17	5	1	1	4	29
	—Peoria (Midwest)	3	1	.750	1.51	5	5	1	0	0	35⅔	22	9	6	11	54
	—Charlotte (South.)	2	1	.667	0.38	3	3	1	1	0	23⅔	13	1	1	3	28
	—Chicago (N.L.)	0	3	.000	7.24	3	3	0	0	0	13⅔	20	12	11	4	4
1991	—Iowa (Am. Assoc.)	4	4	.500	3.11	18	18	1	1	0	101⅓	85	39	35	57	101
1992	—Iowa (Am. Assoc.)	0	1	.000	19.29	1	1	0	0	0	2⅓	6	5	5	2	2
1993	—Daytona (Fla. St.)	1	2	.333	3.18	3	3	0	0	0	17	17	7	6	3	18
	—Orlando (Southern)	2	3	.400	3.83	9	9	0	0	0	49⅓	37	22	21	17	46
	—Iowa (Am. Assoc.)	0	1	.000	10.38	2	2	0	0	0	4⅓	6	5	5	1	3
Major league totals (1 year)		0	3	.000	7.24	3	3	0	0	0	13⅔	20	12	11	4	4

DiPINO, FRANK

P

PERSONAL: Born October 22, 1956, in Syracuse, N.Y.... 6-0/194.... Throws left, bats left.... Full name: Frank Michael DiPino.
HIGH SCHOOL: West Genesee (Camillus, N.Y.).
COLLEGE: St. Leo (Fla.) College.
TRANSACTIONS/CAREER NOTES: Signed as free agent by Milwaukee Brewers organization (July 11, 1977).... On disabled list (May 19-June 11, 1979).... On Vancouver disabled list (May 9-June 10, 1981).... Traded by Brewers organization with OF Kevin Bass and P Mike Madden to Houston Astros (September 3, 1982), completing deal in which Astros traded P Don Sutton to Brewers for three players to be named later (August 30, 1982).... Traded by Astros to Chicago Cubs for OF Davey Lopes (July 21, 1986).... Granted free agency (November 4, 1988).... Signed by St. Louis Cardinals (December 21, 1988).... Granted free agency (November 13, 1989).... Re-signed by Cardinals (December 13, 1989).... On St. Louis disabled list (March 25, 1991-entire season); included rehabilitation assignment to Louisville (May 3-6).... On St. Louis disabled list (March 30-July 31, 1992); included rehabilitation assignment to Louisville (July 4-31).... On St. Louis disabled list (August 18-September 2, 1992).... Granted free agency (October 27, 1992).... Signed by Kansas City Royals organization (January 27, 1993).... On Kansas City disabled list (April 27-May 28, 1993); included rehabilitation assignment to Omaha (May 1-28).... Released by Royals (July 25, 1993).
STATISTICAL NOTES: Pitched seven-inning, 6-0 no-hit victory for Holyoke against Reading (June 8, 1980, second game).

Year	Team (League)	W	L	Pct.	ERA	G	GS	CG	ShO	Sv.	IP	H	R	ER	BB	SO
1977	—Newark (NY-Penn)	1	3	.250	2.48	14	0	0	0	2	29	14	12	8	22	41
1978	—Burlington (Midw.)	5	4	.556	4.70	15	14	2	0	0	88	98	58	46	36	68

Year	Team (League)	W	L	Pct.	ERA	G	GS	CG	ShO	Sv.	IP	H	R	ER	BB	SO
1979	—Stockton (Calif.)	5	3	.625	3.45	16	15	1	0	0	99	92	45	38	46	67
1980	—Holyoke (Eastern)	7	0	1.000	1.30	16	8	1	1	0	76	46	13	11	27	58
	—Vancouver (PCL)	3	1	.750	2.25	24	1	0	0	2	28	24	10	7	14	32
1981	—Vancouver (PCL)	3	5	.375	4.33	27	5	0	0	4	81	83	45	39	39	81
	—Milwaukee (A.L.)	0	0	...	0.00	2	0	0	0	0	2	0	0	0	3	3
1982	—Vancouver (PCL)	13	9	.591	4.03	26	26	11	3	0	189⅔	187	102	85	86	115
	—Houston (N.L.)■	2	2	.500	6.04	6	6	0	0	0	28⅓	32	20	19	11	25
1983	—Houston (N.L.)	3	4	.429	2.65	53	0	0	0	20	71⅓	52	21	21	20	67
1984	—Houston (N.L.)	4	9	.308	3.35	57	0	0	0	14	75⅓	74	32	28	36	65
1985	—Houston (N.L.)	3	7	.300	4.03	54	0	0	0	6	76	69	44	34	43	49
1986	—Hou.-Chi. (N.L.)■	3	7	.300	4.37	61	0	0	0	3	80⅓	74	45	39	30	70
1987	—Chicago (N.L.)	3	3	.500	3.15	69	0	0	0	4	80	75	31	28	34	61
1988	—Chicago (N.L.)	2	3	.400	4.98	63	0	0	0	6	90⅓	102	54	50	32	69
1989	—St. Louis (N.L.)■	9	0	1.000	2.45	67	0	0	0	0	88⅓	73	26	24	20	44
1990	—St. Louis (N.L.)	5	2	.714	4.56	62	0	0	0	3	81	92	45	41	31	49
1991	—Louisville (A.A.)	0	0	...	36.00	2	0	0	0	0	1	2	4	4	3	0
1992	—Louisville (A.A.)	0	3	.000	3.97	18	0	0	0	0	22⅔	28	15	10	8	10
	—St. Louis (N.L.)	0	0	...	1.64	9	0	0	0	0	11	9	2	2	3	8
1993	—Kansas City (A.L.)■	1	1	.500	6.89	11	0	0	0	0	15⅔	21	12	12	6	5
	—Omaha (A.A.)	1	2	.333	2.78	15	0	0	0	1	22⅔	21	9	7	4	9
A.L. totals (2 years)		1	1	.500	6.11	13	0	0	0	0	17⅔	21	12	12	9	8
N.L. totals (10 years)		34	37	.479	3.77	501	6	0	0	56	682	652	320	286	260	507
Major league totals (12 years)		35	38	.479	3.83	514	6	0	0	56	699⅔	673	332	298	269	515

DiPOTO, JERRY

P, INDIANS

PERSONAL: Born May 24, 1968, in Jersey City, N.J. . . . 6-2/200. . . . Throws right, bats right. . . . Full name: Gerard Peter DiPoto III.
HIGH SCHOOL: Toms River (N.J.).
COLLEGE: Virginia Commonwealth.
TRANSACTIONS/CAREER NOTES: Selected by Cleveland Indians organization in third round of free-agent draft (June 5, 1989).
STATISTICAL NOTES: Led Eastern League with 15 wild pitches and tied for lead with three balks in 1991.

Year	Team (League)	W	L	Pct.	ERA	G	GS	CG	ShO	Sv.	IP	H	R	ER	BB	SO
1989	—Watertown (NYP)	6	5	.545	3.61	14	14	1	0	0	87⅓	75	42	35	39	98
1990	—Kinston (Carolina)	11	4	.733	3.78	24	24	1	0	0	145⅓	129	75	61	77	143
	—Cant./Akr. (East.)	1	0	1.000	2.57	3	2	0	0	0	14	11	5	4	4	12
1991	—Cant./Akr. (East.)	6	11	.353	3.81	28	26	2	0	0	156	143	83	66	74	97
1992	—Colo. Springs (PCL)	9	9	.500	4.94	50	9	0	0	2	122	148	78	67	66	62
1993	—Charlotte (Int'l)	6	3	.667	1.93	34	0	0	0	12	46⅔	34	10	10	13	44
	—Cleveland (A.L.)	4	4	.500	2.40	46	0	0	0	11	56⅓	57	21	15	30	41
Major league totals (1 year)		4	4	.500	2.40	46	0	0	0	11	56⅓	57	21	15	30	41

DiSARCINA, GARY

SS, ANGELS

PERSONAL: Born November 19, 1967, in Malden, Mass. . . . 6-1/178. . . . Throws right, bats right. . . . Full name: Gary Thomas DiSarcina. . . . Brother of Glenn DiSarcina, shortstop, Chicago White Sox organization. . . . Name pronounced DEE-sar-SEE-na.
HIGH SCHOOL: Billerica (Mass.) Memorial.
COLLEGE: Massachusetts.
TRANSACTIONS/CAREER NOTES: Selected by California Angels organization in sixth round of free-agent draft (June 1, 1988). . . . On disabled list (August 27, 1993-remainder of season).
STATISTICAL NOTES: Led Pacific Coast League shortstops with .968 fielding percentage and 419 assists in 1991. . . . Led A.L. shortstops with 761 total chances in 1992.

			BATTING												FIELDING			
Year	Team (League)	Pos.	G	AB	R	H	2B	3B	HR	RBI	Avg.	BB	SO	SB	PO	A	E	Avg.
1988	—Bend (Northwest)	SS	71	295	40	90	11	•5	2	39	.305	27	34	7	104	*237	27	.927
1989	—Midland (Texas)	SS	126	441	65	126	18	7	4	54	.286	24	54	11	206	*411	30	*.954
	—California (A.L.)	SS	2	0	0	0	0	0	0	0	...	0	0	0	0	0	0	...
1990	—Edmonton (PCL)	SS	97	330	46	70	12	2	4	37	.212	25	46	5	165	289	24	.950
	—California (A.L.)	SS-2B	18	57	8	8	1	1	0	0	.140	3	10	1	17	57	4	.949
1991	—Edmonton (PCL)	SS-2B	119	390	61	121	21	4	4	58	.310	29	32	16	191	†425	20	†.969
	—California (A.L.)	SS-2B-3B	18	57	5	12	2	0	0	3	.211	3	4	0	29	45	4	.949
1992	—California (A.L.)	SS	157	518	48	128	19	0	3	42	.247	20	50	9	250	*486	•25	.967
1993	—California (A.L.)	SS	126	416	44	99	20	1	3	45	.238	15	38	5	193	362	14	.975
Major league totals (5 years)			321	1048	105	247	42	2	6	90	.236	41	102	15	489	950	47	.968

DiSARCINA, GLENN

SS, WHITE SOX

PERSONAL: Born April 29, 1970, in Malden, Mass. . . . 6-0/175. . . . Throws right, bats left. . . . Full name: Glenn David DiSarcina. . . . Brother of Gary DiSarcina, shortstop, California Angels. . . . Name pronounced DEE-sar-SEE-na.
HIGH SCHOOL: Billerica (Mass.) Memorial.
COLLEGE: Massachusetts.
TRANSACTIONS/CAREER NOTES: Selected by Chicago White Sox organization in 14th round of free-agent draft (June 3, 1991).
STATISTICAL NOTES: Led Midwest League shortstops with 524 total chances in 1992.

			BATTING												FIELDING			
Year	Team (League)	Pos.	G	AB	R	H	2B	3B	HR	RBI	Avg.	BB	SO	SB	PO	A	E	Avg.
1991	—Utica (N.Y.-Penn)	SS-1B-3B	56	202	27	51	10	1	0	27	.252	22	30	11	92	101	17	.919
1992	—South Bend (Mid.)	SS-2B	126	467	60	123	29	6	1	50	.263	44	105	12	183	314	29	.945
	—Sarasota (Fla. St.)	DH	1	4	0	0	0	0	0	0	.000	0	1	0	...	...	...	...

Year	Team (League)	Pos.	G	AB	R	H	2B	3B	HR	RBI	Avg.	BB	SO	SB	PO	A	E	Avg.
			BATTING												FIELDING			
1993	—Sarasota (Fla. St.)....	SS	120	477	73	135	29	5	4	47	.283	33	77	11	179	383	27	.954
	—Birm. (Southern)	SS	3	5	1	2	0	0	0	1	.400	2	2	1	4	4	1	.889

DISMUKE, JAMIE

1B, REDS

PERSONAL: Born October 17, 1969, in Syracuse, N.Y. . . . 6-1/210. . . . Throws right, bats left. . . . Full name: James Allen Dismuke.
HIGH SCHOOL: Corcoron (Syracuse, N.Y.).
TRANSACTIONS/CAREER NOTES: Selected by Cincinnati Reds organization in 12th round of free-agent draft (June 5, 1989).
STATISTICAL NOTES: Led Gulf Coast League with five intentional bases on balls received in 1990. . . . Led Midwest League first basemen with 1,136 total chances in 1991. . . . Led South Atlantic League first basemen with 88 double plays in 1992.

Year	Team (League)	Pos.	G	AB	R	H	2B	3B	HR	RBI	Avg.	BB	SO	SB	PO	A	E	Avg.
			BATTING												FIELDING			
1989	—GC Reds (GCL)..........	1B	34	98	6	18	1	0	1	5	.184	8	19	0	215	16	4	.983
1990	—GC Reds (GCL)..........	1B	39	124	22	44	8	4	*7	28	.355	28	8	3	278	22	4	.987
1991	—Ced. Rap. (Midw.).....	1B	133	492	56	125	35	1	8	72	.254	50	80	4	*1027	87	22	.981
1992	—Char., W.Va. (SAL) ..	1B	134	475	77	135	22	0	17	71	.284	67	71	3	1055	99	24	.980
1993	—Chatt. (South.)	1B	136	497	69	152	22	1	20	91	.306	48	60	4	1104	94	•17	.986

DIXON, STEVE

P, CARDINALS

PERSONAL: Born August 3, 1969, in Cincinnati. . . . 6-0/190. . . . Throws left, bats left. . . . Full name: Steven Ross Dixon.
HIGH SCHOOL: Moore (Louisville, Ky.).
COLLEGE: Paducah (Ky.) Community College and Kentucky.
TRANSACTIONS/CAREER NOTES: Selected by St. Louis Cardinals organization in 31st round of free-agent draft (June 5, 1989). . . . On Arkansas disabled list (June 3-20, 1992).

Year	Team (League)	W	L	Pct.	ERA	G	GS	CG	ShO	Sv.	IP	H	R	ER	BB	SO
1989	—Johns. City (App.)......	1	3	.250	6.02	18	3	0	0	0	43⅓	50	34	29	23	29
1990	—Savannah (S. Atl.)	7	3	.700	1.94	64	0	0	0	8	83⅔	59	34	18	38	93
1991	—St. Peters. (FSL)	5	4	.556	3.78	53	0	0	0	1	64⅓	54	32	27	24	54
1992	—Arkansas (Texas)......	2	1	.667	1.84	40	0	0	0	2	49	34	11	10	15	65
	—Louisville (A.A.)	1	2	.333	5.03	18	0	0	0	2	19⅔	20	12	11	19	16
1993	—Louisville (A.A.)	5	7	.417	5.05	57	0	0	0	20	67⅔	57	39	38	33	61
	—St. Louis (N.L.)..........	0	0	...	33.75	4	0	0	0	0	2⅔	7	10	10	5	2
Major league totals (1 year) ...		0	0	...	33.75	4	0	0	0	0	2⅔	7	10	10	5	2

DOHERTY, JOHN

P, TIGERS

PERSONAL: Born June 11, 1967, in Bronx, N.Y. . . . 6-4/210. . . . Throws right, bats right. . . . Full name: John Harold Doherty.
HIGH SCHOOL: Eastchester (N.Y.).
COLLEGE: Concordia College, N.Y. (received degree).
TRANSACTIONS/CAREER NOTES: Selected by Detroit Tigers organization in 19th round of free-agent draft (June 5, 1989). . . . On disabled list (June 9-28, 1992). . . . On suspended list (September 25-30, 1992). . . . On disabled list (May 20-June 4, 1993).
STATISTICAL NOTES: Tied for Eastern League lead with three balks in 1991.

Year	Team (League)	W	L	Pct.	ERA	G	GS	CG	ShO	Sv.	IP	H	R	ER	BB	SO
1989	—Niag. Falls (NYP)	1	1	.500	0.95	26	1	0	0	14	47⅓	30	7	5	6	45
1990	—Fayetteville (SAL)......	1	0	1.000	5.79	7	0	0	0	1	9⅓	17	12	6	1	6
	—Lakeland (Fla. St.)	5	1	.833	1.10	30	0	0	0	10	41	33	7	5	5	23
1991	—London (Eastern).......	3	3	.500	2.22	53	0	0	0	15	65	62	29	16	21	42
1992	—Detroit (A.L.).............	7	4	.636	3.88	47	11	0	0	3	116	131	61	50	25	37
1993	—Detroit (A.L.).............	14	11	.560	4.44	32	31	3	2	0	184⅔	205	104	91	48	63
Major league totals (2 years) ..		21	15	.583	4.22	79	42	3	2	3	300⅔	336	165	141	73	100

DONNELS, CHRIS

IF, ASTROS

PERSONAL: Born April 21, 1966, in Los Angeles. . . . 6-0/185. . . . Throws right, bats left. . . . Full name: Chris Barton Donnels. . . . Name pronounced DONN-uls.
HIGH SCHOOL: South Torrance (Torrance, Calif.).
COLLEGE: Loyola Marymount.
TRANSACTIONS/CAREER NOTES: Selected by New York Mets organization in first round (24th pick overall) of free-agent draft (June 2, 1987). . . . On Tidewater disabled list (June 20-28, 1991). . . . Selected by Florida Marlins in third round (67th pick overall) of expansion draft (November 17, 1992). . . . Claimed on waivers by Houston Astros (December 18, 1992).
HONORS: Named Florida State League Most Valuable Player (1989).
STATISTICAL NOTES: Led Florida State League with .510 slugging percentage and 15 intentional bases on balls received in 1989. . . . Led Florida State League third basemen with 93 putouts, 202 assists and 320 total chances in 1989. . . . Led Texas League third basemen with 79 putouts, 242 assists, 31 errors, 352 total chances and 24 double plays in 1990.

Year	Team (League)	Pos.	G	AB	R	H	2B	3B	HR	RBI	Avg.	BB	SO	SB	PO	A	E	Avg.
			BATTING												FIELDING			
1987	—Kingsport (Appal.) ...	3B	26	86	18	26	4	0	3	16	.302	17	17	4	16	44	6	.909
	—Columbia (S. Atl.).....	3B	41	136	20	35	7	0	2	17	.257	24	27	3	32	86	10	.922
1988	—St. Lucie (Fla. St.)	3B	65	198	25	43	14	2	3	22	.217	32	53	4	40	116	15	.912
	—Columbia (S. Atl.).....	3B	42	133	19	32	6	0	2	13	.241	30	25	5	29	84	7	.942
1989	—St. Lucie (Fla. St.)	3B-1B	117	386	70	121	23	1	17	*78	.313	83	65	18	†242	†209	28	.942
1990	—Jackson (Texas)	3B-1B-2B	130	419	66	114	24	0	12	63	.272	*111	81	11	†95	†244	†32	.914
1991	—Tidewater (Int'l)........	3B-2B	84	287	45	87	19	2	8	56	.303	62	56	1	88	189	14	.952
	—New York (N.L.)........	1B-3B	37	89	7	20	2	0	0	5	.225	14	19	1	131	34	2	.988
1992	—Tidewater (Int'l).......	3B-1B-2B	81	279	35	84	15	3	5	32	.301	58	45	12	160	156	16	.952

D

Year	Team (League)	Pos.	G	AB	R	H	2B	3B	HR	RBI	Avg.	BB	SO	SB	PO	A	E	Avg.
			BATTING												FIELDING			
	—New York (N.L.)	3B-2B	45	121	8	21	4	0	0	6	.174	17	25	1	34	77	5	.957
1993	—Houston (N.L.)■	3B-1B-2B	88	179	18	46	14	2	2	24	.257	19	33	2	169	54	8	.965
Major league totals (3 years)			170	389	33	87	20	2	2	35	.224	50	77	4	334	165	15	.971

DOPSON, JOHN

P, ANGELS

PERSONAL: Born July 14, 1963, in Baltimore. . . . 6-4/230. . . . Throws right, bats right. . . . Full name: John Robert Dopson Jr.

HIGH SCHOOL: Delone Catholic (Hanover, Pa.).

TRANSACTIONS/CAREER NOTES: Selected by Montreal Expos organization in second round of free-agent draft (June 7, 1982). . . . On suspended list (May 24-31, 1984). . . . On Indianapolis disabled list (June 24-July 15, 1985; April 10-May 12, May 29-June 23 and July 7, 1986-remainder of season). . . . Traded by Expos with SS Luis Rivera to Boston Red Sox for SS Spike Owen and P Dan Gakeler (December 8, 1988). . . . On Boston disabled list (August 2-28, 1989); included rehabilitation assignment to Pawtucket (August 18-28). . . . On Boston disabled list (April 28, 1990-remainder of season); included rehabilitation assignment to Pawtucket (May 15-June 4 and August 10-22). . . . On Boston disabled list (April 5-September 3, 1991); included rehabilitation assignment to Winter Haven (August 2-31). . . . On Boston disabled list (April 5-May 17, 1992); included rehabilitation assignment to Pawtucket (April 13-May 13). . . . Granted free agency (October 29, 1993). . . . Signed by California Angels organization (February 2, 1994).

STATISTICAL NOTES: Led A.L. with 15 balks in 1989.

Year	Team (League)	W	L	Pct.	ERA	G	GS	CG	ShO	Sv.	IP	H	R	ER	BB	SO
1982	—Jamestown (NYP)	6	•8	.429	3.97	15	15	6	1	0	106⅔	117	58	47	34	62
1983	—W.P. Beach (FSL)	13	6	.684	3.44	23	23	5	2	0	146⅔	141	82	56	38	69
1984	—Jacksonv. (South.)	10	8	.556	3.69	26	26	6	1	0	170⅔	198	83	70	41	76
1985	—Jacksonv. (South.)	3	0	1.000	1.11	5	5	1	0	0	32⅓	27	5	4	10	20
	—Indianapolis (A.A.)	4	7	.364	3.78	18	18	3	2	0	95⅓	88	44	40	44	48
	—Montreal (N.L.)	0	2	.000	11.08	4	3	0	0	0	13	25	17	16	4	4
1986	—W.P. Beach (FSL)	2	0	1.000	0.00	2	2	0	0	0	10⅔	8	0	0	4	8
	—Indianapolis (A.A.)	0	3	.000	4.50	4	4	0	0	0	16	18	12	8	11	6
1987	—Jacksonv. (South.)	7	5	.583	3.80	21	21	1	1	0	118⅓	123	58	50	30	75
1988	—Indianapolis (A.A.)	0	0	...	3.50	3	3	0	0	0	18	19	7	7	5	15
	—Montreal (N.L.)	3	11	.214	3.04	26	26	1	0	0	168⅔	150	69	57	58	101
1989	—Boston (A.L.)■	12	8	.600	3.99	29	28	2	0	0	169⅓	166	84	75	69	95
	—Pawtucket (Int'l)	0	2	.000	7.27	2	2	0	0	0	8⅔	13	9	7	1	9
1990	—Boston (A.L.)	0	0	...	2.04	4	4	0	0	0	17⅔	13	7	4	9	9
	—Pawtucket (Int'l)	2	1	.667	4.91	5	5	0	0	0	22	28	12	12	8	13
1991	—Boston (A.L.)	0	0	...	18.00	1	0	0	0	0	1	2	2	2	1	0
	—Winter Haven (FSL)	2	2	.500	3.38	6	6	0	0	0	26⅔	26	14	10	8	26
1992	—Pawtucket (Int'l)	1	2	.333	2.37	6	6	0	0	0	38	28	15	10	8	23
	—Boston (A.L.)	7	11	.389	4.08	25	25	0	0	0	141⅓	159	78	64	38	55
1993	—Boston (A.L.)	7	11	.389	4.97	34	28	1	1	0	155⅔	170	93	86	59	89
A.L. totals (5 years)		26	30	.464	4.29	93	85	3	1	0	485	510	264	231	176	248
N.L. totals (2 years)		3	13	.188	3.62	30	29	1	0	0	181⅔	175	86	73	62	105
Major league totals (7 years)		29	43	.403	4.10	123	114	4	1	0	666⅔	685	350	304	238	353

DORAN, BILL

2B

PERSONAL: Born May 28, 1958, in Cincinnati. . . . 6-0/180. . . . Throws right, bats both. . . . Full name: William Donald Doran. . . . Name pronounced DOOR-in.

HIGH SCHOOL: Mt. Healthy (Cincinnati).

COLLEGE: Miami of Ohio.

TRANSACTIONS/CAREER NOTES: Selected by Houston Astros organization in sixth round of free-agent draft (June 5, 1979). . . . On Houston disabled list (July 4-19, 1990). . . . Traded by Astros to Cincinnati Reds for three players to be named later (August 30, 1990); Astros acquired C Terry McGriff, P Keith Kaiser and P Butch Henry to complete deal (September 7, 1990). . . . Granted free agency (November 5, 1990). . . . Re-signed by Reds (December 5, 1990). . . . On disabled list (May 13-June 4, 1991). . . . Contract sold by Reds to Milwaukee Brewers (January 13, 1993). . . . On Milwaukee disabled list (March 27-April 14, 1993); included rehabilitation assignment to Stockton (April 8) and El Paso (April 9-14). . . . On Milwaukee disabled list (May 26-July 1 and July 9, 1993-remainder of season). . . . Placed on voluntarily retired list (October 15, 1993).

STATISTICAL NOTES: Led Gulf Coast League second basemen with 33 double plays in 1979. . . . Led Pacific Coast League second basemen with 123 double plays in 1982. . . . Led N.L. in caught stealing with 19 in 1986. . . . Led N.L. second basemen with .992 fielding percentage in 1987.

Year	Team (League)	Pos.	G	AB	R	H	2B	3B	HR	RBI	Avg.	BB	SO	SB	PO	A	E	Avg.
			BATTING												FIELDING			
1979	—GC Astros (GCL)	2B	44	164	21	42	6	0	1	16	.256	19	16	3	107	*144	11	.958
1980	—Day. Beach (FSL)	2B-SS	102	369	62	90	11	3	2	45	.244	50	53	20	232	259	21	.959
1981	—Columbus (South.)	2B-SS	124	427	83	120	17	7	5	56	.281	74	48	18	263	355	17	.973
1982	—Tucson (PCL)	2B	*142	559	100	169	32	7	1	65	.302	87	63	48	*361	*424	*23	.972
	—Houston (N.L.)	2B	26	97	11	27	3	0	0	6	.278	4	11	5	41	78	3	.975
1983	—Houston (N.L.)	2B	154	535	70	145	12	7	8	39	.271	86	67	12	*347	461	17	.979
1984	—Houston (N.L.)	2B-SS	147	548	92	143	18	11	4	41	.261	66	69	21	274	440	12	.983
1985	—Houston (N.L.)	2B	148	578	84	166	31	6	14	59	.287	71	69	23	345	440	16	.980
1986	—Houston (N.L.)	2B	145	550	92	152	29	3	6	37	.276	81	57	42	262	329	16	.974
1987	—Houston (N.L.)	2B-SS	*162	625	82	177	23	3	16	79	.283	82	64	31	300	432	7	†.991
1988	—Houston (N.L.)	2B	132	480	66	119	18	1	7	53	.248	65	60	17	260	371	8	*.987
1989	—Houston (N.L.)	2B	142	507	65	111	25	2	8	58	.219	59	63	22	254	345	12	.980
1990	—Hou.-Cin. (N.L.)■	2B-3B	126	403	59	121	29	2	7	37	.300	79	58	23	198	306	8	.984
1991	—Cincinnati (N.L.)	2B-OF-1B	111	361	51	101	12	2	6	35	.280	46	39	5	183	208	7	.982
1992	—Cincinnati (N.L.)	2B-1B	132	387	48	91	16	2	8	47	.235	64	40	7	306	249	5	.991
1993	—Stockton (Calif.)■	2B	1	2	0	1	0	0	0	0	.500	1	1	0	2	0	0	1.000

Year	Team (League)	Pos.	G	AB	R	H	2B	3B	HR	RBI	Avg.	BB	SO	SB	PO	A	E	Avg.
			BATTING												FIELDING			
	—El Paso (Texas)	2B	5	11	3	4	1	0	0	0	.364	3	2	0	4	12	0	1.000
	—Milwaukee (A.L.)	2B-1B	28	60	7	13	4	0	0	6	.217	6	3	1	44	28	2	.973
American League totals (1 year)			28	60	7	13	4	0	0	6	.217	6	3	1	44	28	2	.973
National League totals (11 years)			1425	5071	720	1353	216	39	84	491	.267	703	597	208	2770	3659	111	.983
Major league totals (12 years)			1453	5131	727	1366	220	39	84	497	.266	709	600	209	2814	3687	113	.983

CHAMPIONSHIP SERIES RECORD

CHAMPIONSHIP SERIES NOTES: Shares single-game record for most at-bats—7 (October 15, 1986, 16 innings).

Year	Team (League)	Pos.	G	AB	R	H	2B	3B	HR	RBI	Avg.	BB	SO	SB	PO	A	E	Avg.
			BATTING												FIELDING			
1986	—Houston (N.L.)	2B	6	27	3	6	0	0	1	3	.222	2	2	2	9	17	0	1.000

DORSETT, BRIAN

C/1B, REDS

PERSONAL: Born April 9, 1961, in Terre Haute, Ind. . . . 6-4/222. . . . Throws right, bats right. . . . Full name: Brian Richard Dorsett.
HIGH SCHOOL: North (Terre Haute, Ind.).
COLLEGE: Indiana State.

TRANSACTIONS/CAREER NOTES: Selected by Oakland Athletics organization in 10th round of free-agent draft (June 6, 1983). . . . On disabled list (June 18-July 24, 1984). . . . Traded by A's organization with P Darrel Akerfelds to Cleveland Indians for 2B Tony Bernazard (July 15, 1987). . . . On Cleveland disabled list (March 26-June 7, 1988). . . . Traded by Indians organization to California Angels for a player to be named later (June 7, 1988); Indians acquired P Colby Ward to complete deal (July 15, 1989). . . . Traded by Angels to New York Yankees for P Eric Schmidt (November 17, 1988). . . . Released by Yankees (November 19, 1990). . . . Signed by San Diego Padres (January 15, 1991). . . . Traded by Padres organization to Pittsburgh Pirates organization for P Lynn Carlson (August 2, 1991). . . . Granted free agency (October 15, 1991). . . . Re-signed by Pirates organization (January 22, 1992). . . . Granted free agency (October 15, 1992). . . . Signed by Cincinnati Reds organization (December 10, 1992).
STATISTICAL NOTES: Led International League with 13 passed balls in 1990. . . . Led American Association with 14 passed balls in 1992.

Year	Team (League)	Pos.	G	AB	R	H	2B	3B	HR	RBI	Avg.	BB	SO	SB	PO	A	E	Avg.
			BATTING												FIELDING			
1983	—Medford (N'west)	C	14	48	11	13	2	1	1	10	.271	5	5	0	85	8	2	.979
	—Madison (Midwest)	C	58	204	16	52	7	0	3	27	.255	17	35	2	337	51	6	.985
1984	—Modesto (Calif.)	C-1B	99	375	39	99	19	0	8	52	.264	23	93	0	511	76	13	.978
1985	—Madison (Midwest)	C	40	161	15	43	11	0	2	30	.267	12	23	0	194	40	5	.979
	—Huntsville (South.)	C	88	313	38	84	18	3	11	43	.268	38	60	2	437	51	10	.980
1986	—Tacoma (PCL)	C	117	426	49	111	33	1	10	51	.261	26	82	0	420	54	18	.963
1987	—Tacoma (PCL)	C	78	282	31	66	14	1	6	39	.234	33	50	0	341	51	4	.990
	—Buffalo (A.A.)■	C	26	86	9	22	5	1	4	14	.256	3	21	0	119	9	1	.992
	—Cleveland (A.L.)	C	5	11	2	3	0	0	1	3	.273	0	3	0	12	0	0	1.000
1988	—Col. S.-Edm. (PCL)■	C-1B	53	163	21	43	7	0	11	32	.264	28	30	0	283	37	5	.985
	—California (A.L.)	C	7	11	0	1	0	0	0	2	.091	1	5	0	19	3	0	1.000
1989	—Columbus (Int'l)■	C	110	388	45	97	21	1	17	62	.250	31	87	2	482	47	7	.987
	—New York (A.L.)	C	8	22	3	8	1	0	0	4	.364	1	3	0	29	3	0	1.000
1990	—Columbus (Int'l)	C	114	415	44	113	28	1	14	67	.272	49	71	1	548	37	11	.982
	—New York (A.L.)	C	14	35	2	5	2	0	0	0	.143	2	4	0	31	0	0	1.000
1991	—Las Vegas (PCL)■	C-1B-3B	62	215	36	66	13	1	13	38	.307	17	43	0	312	29	6	.983
	—San Diego (N.L.)	1B	11	12	0	1	0	0	0	1	.083	0	3	0	4	1	0	1.000
	—Buffalo (A.A.)■	1B-C	29	103	17	28	6	0	2	18	.272	8	19	0	186	20	7	.967
1992	—Buffalo (A.A.)	C-1B	131	492	69	142	35	0	21	102	.289	38	68	1	689	69	8	.990
1993	—Indianapolis (A.A.)■	C-1B	77	278	38	83	27	0	18	57	.299	28	53	2	439	50	7	.986
	—Cincinnati (N.L.)	C-1B	25	63	7	16	4	0	2	12	.254	3	14	0	119	5	0	1.000
American League totals (4 years)			34	79	7	17	3	0	1	9	.215	4	15	0	91	6	0	1.000
National League totals (2 years)			36	75	7	17	4	0	2	13	.227	3	17	0	123	6	0	1.000
Major league totals (6 years)			70	154	14	34	7	0	3	22	.221	7	32	0	214	12	0	1.000

DOUGHERTY, JIM

P, ASTROS

PERSONAL: Born March 8, 1968, in Brentwood, N.Y. . . . 6-0/210. . . . Throws right, bats right.
HIGH SCHOOL: Ross (Brentwood, N.Y.).
COLLEGE: North Carolina.

TRANSACTIONS/CAREER NOTES: Selected by Houston Astros organization in 26th round of free-agent draft (June 4, 1990).

Year	Team (League)	W	L	Pct.	ERA	G	GS	CG	ShO	Sv.	IP	H	R	ER	BB	SO
1991	—Asheville (S. Atl.)	3	1	.750	1.52	62	0	0	0	28	83	63	17	14	25	78
1992	—Osceola (Fla. St.)	5	2	.714	1.56	57	0	0	0	31	81	66	21	14	22	77
1993	—Jackson (Texas)	2	2	.500	1.87	52	0	0	0	*36	53	39	15	11	21	55

DOWNS, KELLY

P, ATHLETICS

PERSONAL: Born October 25, 1960, in Ogden, Utah. . . . 6-4/200. . . . Throws right, bats right. . . . Full name: Kelly Robert Downs. . . . Brother of Dave Downs, pitcher, Philadelphia Phillies (1972).
HIGH SCHOOL: Viewmont (Bountiful, Utah).

TRANSACTIONS/CAREER NOTES: Selected by Philadelphia Phillies organization in 26th round of free-agent draft (June 5, 1979). . . . Traded by Phillies organization with P George Riley to San Francisco Giants for 1B Al Oliver and a player to be named later (August 20, 1984); Phillies acquired P Renie Martin to complete deal (August 30, 1984). . . . On disabled list (August 31, 1988-remainder of season). . . . On San Francisco disabled list (May 2-August 13, 1989); included rehabilitation assignment to Phoenix (May 17-23 and August 7) and San Jose (August 8-12). . . . On San Francisco disabled list (April 3-August 10,

1990); included rehabilitation assignment to San Jose (July 31-August 6) and Phoenix (August 7-9). . . . On disabled list (April 2-17, 1991). . . . Released by Giants (June 22, 1992). . . . Signed by Oakland Athletics (June 30, 1992). . . . Granted free agency (October 27, 1992). . . . Re-signed by A's (December 9, 1992).

Year	Team (League)	W	L	Pct.	ERA	G	GS	CG	ShO	Sv.	IP	H	R	ER	BB	SO
1980	—Spartanburg (SAL)	5	7	.417	2.60	14	12	4	1	0	90	85	41	26	17	40
1981	—Peninsula (Caro.)	13	7	.650	2.98	25	25	9	2	0	175	176	79	58	35	124
1982	—Okla. City (A.A.)	2	*15	.118	5.34	32	25	5	0	1	156⅔	182	*116	93	72	70
1983	—Portland (PCL)	9	•13	.409	4.46	29	•29	5	1	0	159⅓	186	98	79	61	71
1984	—Portland (PCL)	7	12	.368	5.30	30	25	5	0	0	163	166	106	96	65	104
1985	—Phoenix (PCL)■	9	10	.474	4.01	37	19	2	1	1	137	138	69	61	56	109
1986	—Phoenix (PCL)	8	5	.615	3.42	18	18	4	0	0	108	116	54	41	28	68
	—San Francisco (N.L.)	4	4	.500	2.75	14	14	1	0	0	88⅓	78	29	27	30	64
1987	—San Francisco (N.L.)	12	9	.571	3.63	41	28	4	3	1	186	185	83	75	67	137
1988	—San Francisco (N.L.)	13	9	.591	3.32	27	26	6	3	0	168	140	67	62	47	118
1989	—San Francisco (N.L.)	4	8	.333	4.79	18	15	0	0	0	82⅔	82	47	44	26	49
	—Phoenix (PCL)	1	1	.500	8.68	3	3	0	0	0	9⅓	11	9	9	5	9
	—San Jose (Calif.)	0	0	...	0.00	1	1	0	0	0	5	1	0	0	4	7
1990	—San Jose (Calif.)	0	1	.000	1.80	1	1	0	0	0	5	5	2	1	0	3
	—Phoenix (PCL)	0	0	...	1.80	1	1	0	0	0	5	5	3	1	0	4
	—San Francisco (N.L.)	3	2	.600	3.43	13	9	0	0	0	63	56	26	24	20	31
1991	—San Francisco (N.L.)	10	4	.714	4.19	45	11	0	0	0	111⅔	99	59	52	53	62
1992	—San Francisco (N.L.)	1	2	.333	3.47	19	7	0	0	0	62⅓	65	27	24	24	33
	—Oakland (A.L.)■	5	5	.500	3.29	18	13	0	0	0	82	72	36	30	46	38
1993	—Oakland (A.L.)	5	10	.333	5.64	42	12	0	0	0	119⅔	135	80	75	60	66
A.L. totals (2 years)		10	15	.400	4.69	60	25	0	0	0	201⅔	207	116	105	106	104
N.L. totals (7 years)		47	38	.553	3.64	177	110	11	6	1	762	705	338	308	267	494
Major league totals (8 years)		57	53	.518	3.86	237	135	11	6	1	963⅔	912	454	413	373	598

CHAMPIONSHIP SERIES RECORD

Year	Team (League)	W	L	Pct.	ERA	G	GS	CG	ShO	Sv.	IP	H	R	ER	BB	SO
1987	—San Francisco (N.L.)	0	0	...	0.00	1	0	0	0	0	1⅓	1	0	0	0	0
1989	—San Francisco (N.L.)	1	0	1.000	3.12	2	0	0	0	0	8⅔	8	3	3	6	6
1992	—Oakland (A.L.)	0	1	.000	3.86	2	0	0	0	0	2⅓	3	3	1	1	0
Champ. series totals (3 years)		1	1	.500	2.92	5	0	0	0	0	12⅓	12	6	4	7	6

WORLD SERIES RECORD

Year	Team (League)	W	L	Pct.	ERA	G	GS	CG	ShO	Sv.	IP	H	R	ER	BB	SO
1989	—San Francisco (N.L.)	0	0	...	7.71	3	0	0	0	0	4⅔	3	4	4	2	4

DRABEK, DOUG

P, ASTROS

PERSONAL: Born July 25, 1962, in Victoria, Tex. . . . 6-1/185. . . . Throws right, bats right. . . . Full name: Douglas Dean Drabek. . . . Name pronounced DRAY-bek.
HIGH SCHOOL: St. Joseph (Victoria, Tex.).
COLLEGE: Houston.

TRANSACTIONS/CAREER NOTES: Selected by Cleveland Indians organization in fourth round of free-agent draft (June 3, 1980). . . . Selected by Chicago White Sox organization in 11th round of free-agent draft (June 6, 1983). . . . Traded by White Sox with P Kevin Hickey to New York Yankees organization (August 13, 1984), completing deal in which Yankees traded IF Roy Smalley to White Sox for two players to be named later (July 18, 1984). . . . Traded by Yankees with P Brian Fisher and P Logan Easley to Pittsburgh Pirates for P Rick Rhoden, P Cecilio Guante and P Pat Clements (November 26, 1986). . . . On disabled list (April 26-May 18, 1987). . . . Granted free agency (October 26, 1992). . . . Signed by Houston Astros (December 1, 1992).
RECORDS: Shares major league single-season record for fewest double plays by pitcher who led league in double plays—4 (1992).
HONORS: Named N.L. Pitcher of the Year by THE SPORTING NEWS (1990). . . . Named righthanded pitcher on THE SPORTING NEWS N.L. All-Star team (1990). . . . Named N.L. Cy Young Award winner by Baseball Writers' Association of America (1990).
MISCELLANEOUS: Appeared in one game as pinch-runner (1991). . . . Made an out in only appearance as pinch-hitter (1992).

Year	Team (League)	W	L	Pct.	ERA	G	GS	CG	ShO	Sv.	IP	H	R	ER	BB	SO
1983	—Niag. Falls (NYP)	6	7	.462	3.65	16	13	3	0	0	103⅔	99	52	42	48	103
1984	—Appleton (Midw.)	1	0	1.000	1.80	1	1	0	0	0	5	3	1	1	3	6
	—Glens Falls (East.)	12	5	.706	2.24	19	17	7	3	0	124⅔	90	34	31	44	75
	—Nashville (South.)■	1	2	.333	2.32	4	4	2	0	0	31	30	11	8	10	22
1985	—Alb./Colon. (East.)	13	7	.650	2.99	26	26	9	2	0	*192⅔	153	71	64	55	*153
1986	—Columbus (Int'l)	1	4	.200	7.29	8	8	0	0	0	42	50	36	34	25	23
	—New York (A.L.)	7	8	.467	4.10	27	21	0	0	0	131⅔	126	64	60	50	76
1987	—Pittsburgh (N.L.)■	11	12	.478	3.88	29	28	1	1	0	176⅓	165	86	76	46	120
1988	—Pittsburgh (N.L.)	15	7	.682	3.08	33	32	3	1	0	219⅓	194	83	75	50	127
1989	—Pittsburgh (N.L.)	14	12	.538	2.80	35	34	8	5	0	244⅓	215	83	76	69	123
1990	—Pittsburgh (N.L.)	*22	6	.786	2.76	33	33	9	3	0	231⅓	190	78	71	56	131
1991	—Pittsburgh (N.L.)	15	14	.517	3.07	35	35	5	2	0	234⅔	245	92	80	62	142
1992	—Pittsburgh (N.L.)	15	11	.577	2.77	34	34	10	4	0	256⅔	218	84	79	54	177
1993	—Houston (N.L.)■	9	*18	.333	3.79	34	34	7	2	0	237⅔	242	108	100	60	157
A.L. totals (1 year)		7	8	.467	4.10	27	21	0	0	0	131⅔	126	64	60	50	76
N.L. totals (7 years)		101	80	.558	3.13	233	230	43	18	0	1600⅓	1469	614	557	397	977
Major league totals (8 years)		108	88	.551	3.21	260	251	43	18	0	1732	1595	678	617	447	1053

CHAMPIONSHIP SERIES RECORD

CHAMPIONSHIP SERIES NOTES: Holds single-series record for most games lost—3 (1992). . . . Shares N.L. career record for most complete games pitched—2.

Year	Team (League)	W	L	Pct.	ERA	G	GS	CG	ShO	Sv.	IP	H	R	ER	BB	SO
1990	—Pittsburgh (N.L.)........	1	1	.500	1.65	2	2	1	0	0	16⅓	12	4	3	3	13
1991	—Pittsburgh (N.L.)........	1	1	.500	0.60	2	2	1	0	0	15	10	1	1	5	10
1992	—Pittsburgh (N.L.)........	0	3	.000	3.71	3	3	0	0	0	17	18	11	7	6	10
Champ. series totals (3 years)		2	5	.286	2.05	7	7	2	0	0	48⅓	40	16	11	14	33

DRAHMAN, BRIAN

P, MARLINS

PERSONAL: Born November 7, 1966, in Kenton, Ky.... 6-3/231.... Throws right, bats right.... Full name: Brian Stacy Drahman.... Name pronounced DRAY-man.

HIGH SCHOOL: Northeast (Fort Lauderdale, Fla.).

COLLEGE: Miami-Dade (South) Community College.

TRANSACTIONS/CAREER NOTES: Selected by Cleveland Indians organization in 13th round of free-agent draft (January 14, 1986).... Selected by Milwaukee Brewers organization in secondary phase of free-agent draft (June 2, 1986).... Traded by Brewers organization to Chicago White Sox organization for P Jerry Reuss (July 31, 1989).... On Nashville disabled list (May 9-25, 1993).... Contract sold by White Sox to Florida Marlins (November 10, 1993).

Year	Team (League)	W	L	Pct.	ERA	G	GS	CG	ShO	Sv.	IP	H	R	ER	BB	SO
1986	—Helena (Pioneer)........	4	6	.400	5.92	18	10	0	0	2	65⅓	79	49	43	33	40
1987	—Beloit (Midwest).........	6	5	.545	2.16	46	0	0	0	18	79	63	28	19	22	60
1988	—Stockton (Calif.)........	4	5	.444	2.02	44	0	0	0	14	62⅓	57	17	14	27	50
1989	—El Paso (Texas).........	3	4	.429	7.26	19	0	0	0	2	31	52	31	25	11	23
	—Stockton (Calif.)........	3	2	.600	3.25	12	0	0	0	4	27⅔	22	11	10	9	30
	—Sarasota (Fla. St.)■...	0	1	.000	3.24	7	2	0	0	1	16⅔	18	9	6	5	9
1990	—Birm. (Southern).........	6	4	.600	4.08	50	1	0	0	17	90⅓	90	50	41	24	72
1991	—Chicago (A.L.)...........	3	2	.600	3.23	28	0	0	0	0	30⅔	21	12	11	13	18
	—Vancouver (PCL).......	2	3	.400	4.44	22	0	0	0	12	24⅓	21	12	12	13	17
1992	—Vancouver (PCL).......	2	4	.333	2.01	48	0	0	0	*30	58⅓	44	16	13	31	34
	—Chicago (A.L.)...........	0	0	...	2.57	5	0	0	0	0	7	6	3	2	2	1
1993	—Nashville (A.A.).........	9	4	.692	2.91	54	0	0	0	20	55⅔	59	29	18	19	49
	—Chicago (A.L.)...........	0	0	...	0.00	5	0	0	0	1	5⅓	7	0	0	2	3
Major league totals (3 years)..		3	2	.600	2.72	38	0	0	0	1	43	34	15	13	17	22

DRAPER, MIKE

P

PERSONAL: Born September 14, 1966, in Hagerstown, Md.... 6-2/180.... Throws right, bats right.... Full name: Michael Anthony Draper.

HIGH SCHOOL: Williamsport (Md.).

COLLEGE: Hagerstown (Md.) Junior College, George Mason and Western Maryland College.

TRANSACTIONS/CAREER NOTES: Selected by New York Yankees organization in 26th round of free-agent draft (June 1, 1988).... Selected by New York Mets from Yankees organization in Rule 5 major league draft (December 7, 1992).... On New York disabled list (August 8-September 29, 1993).... Released by Mets (September 29, 1993).

STATISTICAL NOTES: Pitched 6-0 no-hit victory for Fort Lauderdale against St. Petersburg (July 21, 1990).

Year	Team (League)	W	L	Pct.	ERA	G	GS	CG	ShO	Sv.	IP	H	R	ER	BB	SO
1988	—Prin. William (Car.)....	2	3	.400	3.31	9	5	1	0	0	35⅓	37	22	13	4	20
	—Oneonta (NYP)..........	2	1	.667	0.84	8	0	0	0	3	10⅔	10	4	1	3	16
1989	—Prin. William (Car.)....	*14	8	.636	3.11	25	24	6	1	0	153⅓	147	66	53	42	84
1990	—Prin. William (Car.)....	0	2	.000	6.35	5	4	1	0	0	22⅔	31	20	16	9	8
	—Alb./Colon. (East.)....	2	2	.500	6.44	8	8	0	0	0	43⅓	51	34	31	19	15
	—Fort Lauder. (FSL).....	9	1	.900	2.25	14	14	1	1	0	96	80	30	24	22	52
1991	—Alb./Colon. (East.)....	10	6	.625	3.29	36	14	1	1	2	131⅓	125	58	48	47	71
	—Columbus (Int'l).........	1	3	.250	3.77	4	4	2	0	0	28⅔	36	21	12	5	13
1992	—Columbus (Int'l).........	5	6	.455	3.60	57	3	0	0	*37	80	70	36	32	28	42
1993	—New York (N.L.)■.......	1	1	.500	4.25	29	1	0	0	0	42⅓	53	22	20	14	16
Major league totals (1 year)...		1	1	.500	4.25	29	1	0	0	0	42⅓	53	22	20	14	16

DREIFORT, DARREN

P, DODGERS

PERSONAL: Born May 18, 1972, in Wichita, Kan.... 6-2/205.... Throws right, bats right.... Full name: Darren James Dreifort.... Name pronounced DRY-furt.

HIGH SCHOOL: Wichita (Kan.) Heights.

COLLEGE: Wichita State.

TRANSACTIONS/CAREER NOTES: Selected by New York Mets organization in 11th round of free-agent draft (June 4, 1990)... Selected by Los Angeles Dodgers organization in first round (second pick overall) of free-agent draft (June 3, 1993).

HONORS: Named righthanded pitcher on THE SPORTING NEWS college All-America team (1992-93).... Named Golden Spikes Award winner by USA Baseball (1993).

MISCELLANEOUS: Member of 1992 U.S. Olympic baseball team.

Year	Team (League)	W	L	Pct.	ERA	G	GS	CG	ShO	Sv.	IP	H	R	ER	BB	SO
1993	—................................							Did not play.								

DREYER, STEVE

P, RANGERS

PERSONAL: Born November 19, 1969, in Ames, Ia.... 6-3/180.... Throws right, bats right.... Full name: Steven William Dreyer.

HIGH SCHOOL: Ames (Ia.).

COLLEGE: Northern Iowa.

TRANSACTIONS/CAREER NOTES: Selected by Texas Rangers organization in eighth round of free-agent draft (June 4, 1990).

Year	Team (League)	W	L	Pct.	ERA	G	GS	CG	ShO	Sv.	IP	H	R	ER	BB	SO
1990	—Butte (Pioneer)..........	1	1	.500	4.54	8	8	0	0	0	35⅔	32	21	18	10	29
1991	—Gastonia (S. Atl.).......	7	10	.412	2.33	25	25	3	1	0	162	137	51	42	62	122
1992	—Charlotte (Fla. St.).....	11	7	.611	2.40	26	26	4	3	0	168⅔	164	54	45	37	111

Year	Team (League)	W	L	Pct.	ERA	G	GS	CG	ShO	Sv.	IP	H	R	ER	BB	SO
1993	—Tulsa (Texas)	2	2	.500	3.73	5	5	1	1	0	31⅓	26	13	13	8	27
	—Okla. City (A.A.)	4	6	.400	3.03	16	16	1	0	0	107	108	39	36	31	59
	—Texas (A.L.)	3	3	.500	5.71	10	6	0	0	0	41	48	26	26	20	23
Major league totals (1 year)		3	3	.500	5.71	10	6	0	0	0	41	48	26	26	20	23

DuBOSE, BRIAN

1B, TIGERS

PERSONAL: Born May 17, 1971, in Detroit. . . . 6-3/208. . . . Throws right, bats left. . . . Full name: Brian Allen DuBose.
HIGH SCHOOL: St. Mary of Redford (Detroit).
TRANSACTIONS/CAREER NOTES: Selected by Detroit Tigers organization in 53rd round of free-agent draft (June 5, 1989).

			BATTING												FIELDING			
Year	Team (League)	Pos.	G	AB	R	H	2B	3B	HR	RBI	Avg.	BB	SO	SB	PO	A	E	Avg.
1990	—Bristol (Appal.)	1B-OF-3B	67	223	31	56	8	0	6	21	.251	24	53	5	378	33	9	.979
1991	—Lakeland (Fla. St.)	1B	15	35	7	7	2	0	1	6	.200	10	12	0	14	2	0	1.000
	—Niag. Falls (NYP)	1B	44	164	26	42	7	1	7	31	.256	17	32	3	377	35	3	.993
1992	—Fayetteville (SAL)	1B	122	404	49	92	20	5	12	73	.228	64	100	19	871	110	14	.986
1993	—Lakeland (Fla. St.)	1B	122	448	74	140	27	11	8	68	.313	49	97	18	1166	*101	8	.994

DUCEY, ROB

OF, RANGERS

PERSONAL: Born May 24, 1965, in Toronto. . . . 6-2/180. . . . Throws right, bats left. . . . Full name: Robert Thomas Ducey.
HIGH SCHOOL: Glenview Park (Toronto).
COLLEGE: Seminole Community College (Fla.).
TRANSACTIONS/CAREER NOTES: Signed as free agent by Toronto Blue Jays organization (May 16, 1984). . . . On Toronto disabled list (June 9-September 2, 1989); included rehabilitation assignment to Syracuse (July 5-14 and August 24-September 2). . . . Traded by Blue Jays with C Greg Myers to California Angels for P Mark Eichhorn (July 30, 1992). . . . Released by Angels (November 19, 1992). . . . Signed by Texas Rangers organization (December 18, 1992). . . . On Oklahoma City disabled list (April 21-May 16, 1993).
STATISTICAL NOTES: Tied for Southern League lead in double plays by outfielder with six in 1986. . . . Tied for International League lead in double plays by outfielder with four in 1990.

			BATTING												FIELDING			
Year	Team (League)	Pos.	G	AB	R	H	2B	3B	HR	RBI	Avg.	BB	SO	SB	PO	A	E	Avg.
1984	—Medicine Hat (Pio.)	OF-1B	63	235	49	71	10	3	12	49	.302	41	61	13	185	11	6	.970
1985	—Florence (S. Atl.)	OF-1B	134	529	78	133	22	2	13	86	.251	49	103	12	228	8	9	.963
1986	—Ventura (Calif.)	OF-1B	47	178	36	60	11	3	12	38	.337	21	24	17	97	3	2	.980
	—Knoxville (South.)	OF	88	344	49	106	22	3	11	58	.308	29	59	7	186	10	6	.970
1987	—Syracuse (Int'l)	OF	100	359	62	102	14	•10	10	60	.284	61	89	8	171	13	6	.968
	—Toronto (A.L.)	OF	34	48	12	9	1	0	1	6	.188	8	10	2	31	0	0	1.000
1988	—Syracuse (Int'l)	OF	90	317	40	81	14	4	7	42	.256	43	81	7	233	6	4	.984
	—Toronto (A.L.)	OF	27	54	15	17	4	1	0	6	.315	5	7	1	35	1	0	1.000
1989	—Toronto (A.L.)	OF	41	76	5	16	4	0	0	7	.211	9	25	2	56	3	0	1.000
	—Syracuse (Int'l)	OF	10	29	0	3	0	1	0	3	.103	10	13	0	14	0	1	.933
1990	—Syracuse (Int'l)	OF	127	438	53	117	32	7	7	47	.267	60	87	13	262	13	13	.955
	—Toronto (A.L.)	OF	19	53	7	16	5	0	0	7	.302	7	15	1	37	0	0	1.000
1991	—Syracuse (Int'l)	OF	72	266	53	78	10	3	8	40	.293	51	58	5	120	1	0	1.000
	—Toronto (A.L.)	OF	39	68	8	16	2	2	1	4	.235	6	26	2	32	1	4	.892
1992	—Tor.-Calif. (A.L.)■	OF	54	80	7	15	4	0	0	2	.188	5	22	2	43	2	2	.957
1993	—Okla. City (A.A.)■	OF	105	389	68	118	17	•10	17	56	.303	46	97	17	244	8	7	.973
	—Texas (A.L.)	OF	27	85	15	24	6	3	2	9	.282	10	17	2	51	1	0	1.000
Major league totals (7 years)			241	464	69	113	26	6	4	41	.244	50	122	12	285	8	6	.980

CHAMPIONSHIP SERIES RECORD

			BATTING												FIELDING			
Year	Team (League)	Pos.	G	AB	R	H	2B	3B	HR	RBI	Avg.	BB	SO	SB	PO	A	E	Avg.
1989	—Toronto (A.L.)							Did not play.										
1991	—Toronto (A.L.)	PR-OF	1	1	0	0	0	0	0	0	.000	0	0	0	0	0	0	...
Championship series totals (1 year)			1	1	0	0	0	0	0	0	.000	0	0	0	0	0	0	...

DUNCAN, MARIANO

2B/SS, PHILLIES

PERSONAL: Born March 13, 1963, in San Pedro de Macoris, Dominican Republic. . . . 6-0/200. . . . Throws right, bats right.
TRANSACTIONS/CAREER NOTES: Signed as free agent by Los Angeles Dodgers organization (January 17, 1982). . . . On Los Angeles disabled list (August 19-September 17, 1986; June 19-July 4 and August 16, 1987-remainder of season; May 28-June 12 and July 1-16, 1989). . . . Traded by Dodgers with P Tim Leary to Cincinnati Reds for OF Kal Daniels and IF Lenny Harris (July 18, 1989). . . . On disabled list (May 14-30, 1990 and August 8-23, 1991). . . . Granted free agency (October 30, 1991). . . . Signed by Philadelphia Phillies (December 10, 1991). . . . On disabled list (July 3-18, 1993). . . . On suspended list (September 20-24, 1993).
STATISTICAL NOTES: Led Texas League second basemen with 84 double plays in 1984. . . . Led N.L. shortstops with 21 errors in 1987.
MISCELLANEOUS: Batted as switch-hitter (1982-88).

			BATTING												FIELDING			
Year	Team (League)	Pos.	G	AB	R	H	2B	3B	HR	RBI	Avg.	BB	SO	SB	PO	A	E	Avg.
1982	—Lethbridge (Pio.)	SS-2B	30	55	9	13	3	1	1	8	.236	8	21	1	23	35	15	.795
1983	—Vero Beach (FSL)	OF-SS-2B	109	384	73	102	10	*15	0	42	.266	44	87	*56	169	157	37	.898
1984	—San Antonio (Tex.)	2B-OF-SS	125	502	80	127	14	•11	2	44	.253	41	110	41	283	335	22	.966
1985	—Los Angeles (N.L.)	SS-2B	142	562	74	137	24	6	6	39	.244	38	113	38	224	430	30	.956

							BATTING								FIELDING			
Year	**Team (League)**	**Pos.**	**G**	**AB**	**R**	**H**	**2B**	**3B**	**HR**	**RBI**	**Avg.**	**BB**	**SO**	**SB**	**PO**	**A**	**E**	**Avg.**
1986	—Los Angeles (N.L.) ...	SS	109	407	47	93	7	0	8	30	.229	30	78	48	172	317	25	.951
1987	—Los Angeles (N.L.) ...	SS-2B-OF	76	261	31	56	8	1	6	18	.215	17	62	11	101	213	†21	.937
	—Albuquerque (PCL) ..	SS	6	22	6	6	0	0	0	0	.273	2	5	3	8	15	2	.920
1988	—Albuquerque (PCL) ..	SS-2B	56	227	48	65	4	8	0	25	.286	10	40	33	104	153	18	.935
1989	—L.A.-Cin. (N.L.)■......	SS-2B-OF	94	258	32	64	15	2	3	21	.248	8	51	9	101	155	14	.948
1990	—Cincinnati (N.L.)......	2B-SS-OF	125	435	67	133	22	★11	10	55	.306	24	67	13	265	303	18	.969
1991	—Cincinnati (N.L.)......	2B-SS-OF	100	333	46	86	7	4	12	40	.258	12	57	5	169	212	9	.977
1992	—Philadelphia (N.L.)■.	0-2-S-3	142	574	71	153	40	3	8	50	.267	17	108	23	256	210	16	.967
1993	—Philadelphia (N.L.)...	2B-SS	124	496	68	140	26	4	11	73	.282	12	88	6	180	304	21	.958
Major league totals (8 years)			912	3326	436	862	149	31	64	326	.259	158	624	153	1468	2144	154	.959

CHAMPIONSHIP SERIES RECORD

CHAMPIONSHIP SERIES NOTES: Holds single-game record for most triples—2 (October 9, 1993).... Shares single-series record for most triples—2 (1993).... Shares N.L. career record for most triples—3.

							BATTING								FIELDING			
Year	**Team (League)**	**Pos.**	**G**	**AB**	**R**	**H**	**2B**	**3B**	**HR**	**RBI**	**Avg.**	**BB**	**SO**	**SB**	**PO**	**A**	**E**	**Avg.**
1985	—Los Angeles (N.L.) ...	SS	5	18	2	4	2	1	0	1	.222	1	3	1	7	16	1	.958
1990	—Cincinnati (N.L.)......	2B	6	20	1	6	0	0	1	4	.300	0	8	0	6	11	1	.944
1993	—Philadelphia (N.L.)...	2B	3	15	3	4	0	2	0	0	.267	0	5	0	5	6	1	.917
Championship series totals (3 years)			14	53	6	14	2	3	1	5	.264	1	16	1	18	33	3	.944

WORLD SERIES RECORD

							BATTING								FIELDING			
Year	**Team (League)**	**Pos.**	**G**	**AB**	**R**	**H**	**2B**	**3B**	**HR**	**RBI**	**Avg.**	**BB**	**SO**	**SB**	**PO**	**A**	**E**	**Avg.**
1990	—Cincinnati (N.L.)......	2B	4	14	1	2	0	0	0	1	.143	2	2	1	9	9	0	1.000
1993	—Philadelphia (N.L.)...	2B-DH	6	29	5	10	0	1	0	2	.345	1	7	3	11	17	1	.966
World Series totals (2 years)			10	43	6	12	0	1	0	3	.279	3	9	4	20	26	1	.979

DUNN, STEVE

1B, TWINS

PERSONAL: Born April 18, 1970, in Champaign, Ill.... 6-4/225.... Throws left, bats left.... Full name: Steven Robert Dunn.

HIGH SCHOOL: Robinson Secondary (Fairfax, Va.).

TRANSACTIONS/CAREER NOTES: Selected by Minnesota Twins organization in fourth round of free-agent draft (June 1, 1988).... On disabled list (April 20-June 2, 1993).

STATISTICAL NOTES: Led Midwest League with eight intentional bases on balls received in 1990.... Led California League first basemen with 1,244 total chances and 117 double plays in 1992.

							BATTING								FIELDING			
Year	**Team (League)**	**Pos.**	**G**	**AB**	**R**	**H**	**2B**	**3B**	**HR**	**RBI**	**Avg.**	**BB**	**SO**	**SB**	**PO**	**A**	**E**	**Avg.**
1988	—Elizabeth. (Appal.) ...	1B	26	95	9	27	4	0	2	14	.284	8	22	0	187	14	5	.976
1989	—Kenosha (Midwest)..	1B	63	219	17	48	8	0	0	23	.219	18	55	2	470	54	7	.987
	—Elizabeth. (Appal.) ...	1B	57	210	34	64	12	3	6	42	.305	22	41	0	480	36	3	★.994
1990	—Kenosha (Midwest)..	1B	130	478	48	142	29	1	10	72	.297	49	105	13	1125	97	10	.992
1991	—Visalia (California)...	1B	125	458	64	105	16	1	13	59	.229	58	103	9	1122	★131	11	★.991
1992	—Visalia (California)...	1B	125	492	93	150	36	3	26	113	.305	41	103	8	★1125	106	13	.990
1993	—Nashville (South.)	1B	97	366	48	96	20	2	14	60	.262	35	88	1	700	73	10	.987

DUNSTON, SHAWON

SS, CUBS

PERSONAL: Born March 21, 1963, in Brooklyn, N.Y.... 6-1/180.... Throws right, bats right.... Full name: Shawon Donnell Dunston.

HIGH SCHOOL: Thomas Jefferson (Brooklyn, N.Y.).

TRANSACTIONS/CAREER NOTES: Selected by Chicago Cubs organization in first round (first pick overall) of free-agent draft (June 7, 1982).... On disabled list (May 31-June 10, 1983).... On Chicago disabled list (June 16-August 21, 1987); included rehabilitation assignment to Iowa (August 14-21).... On disabled list (May 5, 1992-remainder of season and March 27-September 1, 1993).

RECORDS: Shares modern major league single-game record for most triples—3 (July 28, 1990).

HONORS: Named shortstop on THE SPORTING NEWS N.L. All-Star team (1989).

STATISTICAL NOTES: Led N.L. shortstops with 817 total chances and tied for lead in double plays with 96 in 1986.

							BATTING								FIELDING			
Year	**Team (League)**	**Pos.**	**G**	**AB**	**R**	**H**	**2B**	**3B**	**HR**	**RBI**	**Avg.**	**BB**	**SO**	**SB**	**PO**	**A**	**E**	**Avg.**
1982	—GC Cubs (GCL)..........	SS-3B	53	190	27	61	11	0	2	28	.321	11	22	32	61	129	24	.888
1983	—Quad Cities (Mid.)	SS	117	455	65	141	17	8	4	62	.310	7	51	58	172	326	47	.914
1984	—Midland (Texas).......	SS	73	298	44	98	13	3	3	34	.329	11	38	11	164	203	32	.920
	—Iowa (Am. Assoc.)....	SS	61	210	25	49	11	1	7	27	.233	4	40	9	90	165	26	.907
1985	—Chicago (N.L.)	SS	74	250	40	65	12	4	4	18	.260	19	42	11	144	248	17	.958
	—Iowa (Am. Assoc.)....	SS	73	272	24	73	9	6	2	28	.268	5	48	17	138	176	12	.963
1986	—Chicago (N.L.)	SS	150	581	66	145	36	3	17	68	.250	21	114	13	★320	★465	★32	.961
1987	—Chicago (N.L.)	SS	95	346	40	85	18	3	5	22	.246	10	68	12	160	271	14	.969
	—Iowa (Am. Assoc.)....	SS	5	19	1	8	1	0	0	2	.421	0	3	1	6	12	1	.947
1988	—Chicago (N.L.)	SS	155	575	69	143	23	6	9	56	.249	16	108	30	★257	455	20	.973
1989	—Chicago (N.L.)	SS	138	471	52	131	20	6	9	60	.278	30	86	19	213	379	17	.972
1990	—Chicago (N.L.)	SS	146	545	73	143	22	8	17	66	.262	15	87	25	255	392	20	.970
1991	—Chicago (N.L.)	SS	142	492	59	128	22	7	12	50	.260	23	64	21	★261	383	21	.968
1992	—Chicago (N.L.)	SS	18	73	8	23	3	1	0	2	.315	3	13	2	28	42	1	.986
1993	—Chicago (N.L.)	SS	7	10	3	4	2	0	0	2	.400	0	1	0	5	0	0	1.000
Major league totals (9 years)			925	3343	410	867	158	38	73	344	.259	137	583	133	1643	2635	142	.968

CHAMPIONSHIP SERIES RECORD

Year	Team (League)	Pos.	BATTING G	AB	R	H	2B	3B	HR	RBI	Avg.	BB	SO	SB	FIELDING PO	A	E	Avg.
1989	—Chicago (N.L.)	SS	5	19	2	6	0	0	0	0	.316	1	1	1	10	14	1	.960

ALL-STAR GAME RECORD

Year	League	Pos.	BATTING AB	R	H	2B	3B	HR	RBI	Avg.	BB	SO	SB	FIELDING PO	A	E	Avg.
1988	—National		Did not play.														
1990	—National	SS	2	0	0	0	0	0	0	.000	0	0	0	0	0	0	...
All-Star Game totals (1 year)			2	0	0	0	0	0	0	.000	0	0	0	0	0	0	...

DURANT, MIKE

C, TWINS

PERSONAL: Born September 14, 1969, in Columbus, O. . . . 6-2/200. . . . Throws right, bats right. . . . Full name: Michael Joseph Durant.
HIGH SCHOOL: Watterson (Columbus, O.).
COLLEGE: Ohio State.
TRANSACTIONS/CAREER NOTES: Selected by Houston Astros organization in 19th round of free-agent draft (June 1, 1988). . . . Selected by Minnesota Twins organization in second round of free-agent draft (June 3, 1991).
STATISTICAL NOTES: Led Southern League catchers with .992 fielding percentage in 1993.

Year	Team (League)	Pos.	BATTING G	AB	R	H	2B	3B	HR	RBI	Avg.	BB	SO	SB	FIELDING PO	A	E	Avg.
1991	—Kenosha (Midwest)	C-3B-OF	66	217	27	44	10	0	2	20	.203	25	35	20	335	50	12	.970
1992	—Visalia (California)	C	119	418	61	119	18	2	6	57	.285	55	35	19	672	79	14	.982
1993	—Nashville (South.)	C-OF	123	437	58	106	23	1	8	57	.243	44	68	17	591	61	5	†.992

DURHAM, RAY

2B, WHITE SOX

PERSONAL: Born November 30, 1971, in Charlotte, N.C. . . . 5-8/170. . . . Throws right, bats both.
HIGH SCHOOL: Harding (Charlotte, N.C.).
TRANSACTIONS/CAREER NOTES: Selected by Chicago White Sox organization in fifth round of free-agent draft (June 4, 1990). . . . On Utica suspended list (April 1-May 22, 1992). . . . On Sarasota disabled list (June 16-July 9, 1992).
STATISTICAL NOTES: Led Southern League in caught stealing with 25 in 1993. . . . Led Southern League second basemen with 541 total chances in 1993.

Year	Team (League)	Pos.	BATTING G	AB	R	H	2B	3B	HR	RBI	Avg.	BB	SO	SB	FIELDING PO	A	E	Avg.
1990	—GC Whi. Sox (GCL)	2B-SS	35	116	18	32	3	3	0	13	.276	15	36	23	61	85	15	.907
1991	—Utica (N.Y.-Penn)	2B	39	142	29	36	2	7	0	17	.254	25	44	12	54	101	12	.928
	—GC Whi. Sox (GCL)	2B	6	23	3	7	1	0	0	4	.304	3	5	5	18	15	0	1.000
1992	—Sarasota (Fla. St.)	2B	57	202	37	55	6	3	0	7	.272	32	36	28	66	107	10	.945
	—GC Whi. Sox (GCL)	2B	5	13	3	7	2	0	0	2	.538	3	1	1	4	3	0	1.000
1993	—Birm. (Southern)	2B	137	528	83	143	22	*10	3	37	.271	42	100	39	227	284	*30	.945

DYKSTRA, LENNY

OF, PHILLIES

PERSONAL: Born February 10, 1963, in Santa Ana, Calif. . . . 5-10/195. . . . Throws left, bats left. . . . Full name: Leonard Kyle Dykstra. . . . Grandson of Pete Leswick, National Hockey League player (1936-37 and 1944-45); and nephew of Tony Leswick, NHL player (1945-46 through 1955-56 and 1957-58). . . . Name pronounced DIKE-struh.
HIGH SCHOOL: Garden Grove (Calif.).
TRANSACTIONS/CAREER NOTES: Selected by New York Mets organization in 12th round of free-agent draft (June 8, 1981). . . . Traded by Mets with P Roger McDowell and a player to be named later to Philadelphia Phillies for OF Juan Samuel (June 18, 1989); Phillies organization acquired P Tom Edens to complete deal (July 27, 1989). . . . On disabled list (May 6-July 15 and August 27, 1991-remainder of season; April 8-24, June 29-July 16 and August 16, 1992-remainder of season).
RECORDS: Holds N.L. single-season record for fewest assists by outfielder (150 or more games)—2 (1993).
HONORS: Named Carolina League Player of the Year (1983). . . . Named outfielder on THE SPORTING NEWS N.L. All-Star team (1993). . . . Named outfielder on THE SPORTING NEWS N.L. Silver Slugger team (1993).
STATISTICAL NOTES: Led Carolina League in caught stealing with 23 in 1983. . . . Led N.L. outfielders with 452 total chances in 1990 and 481 in 1993. . . . Led N.L. with .418 on-base percentage in 1990.

Year	Team (League)	Pos.	BATTING G	AB	R	H	2B	3B	HR	RBI	Avg.	BB	SO	SB	FIELDING PO	A	E	Avg.
1981	—Shelby (S. Atl.)	OF-SS	48	157	34	41	7	2	0	18	.261	37	31	15	86	3	4	.957
1982	—Shelby (S. Atl.)	OF	120	413	95	120	13	7	3	38	.291	95	40	77	239	11	14	.947
1983	—Lynchburg (Caro.)	OF	•136	*525	*132	*188	24	*14	8	81	*.358	*107	35	*105	268	9	7	.975
1984	—Jackson (Texas)	OF	131	501	*100	138	25	7	6	52	.275	73	45	53	256	5	2	*.992
1985	—Tidewater (Int'l)	OF	58	229	44	71	8	6	1	25	.310	31	20	26	184	4	5	.974
	—New York (N.L.)	OF	83	236	40	60	9	3	1	19	.254	30	24	15	165	6	1	.994
1986	—New York (N.L.)	OF	147	431	77	127	27	7	8	45	.295	58	55	31	283	8	3	.990
1987	—New York (N.L.)	OF	132	431	86	123	37	3	10	43	.285	40	67	27	239	4	3	.988
1988	—New York (N.L.)	OF	126	429	57	116	19	3	8	33	.270	30	43	30	270	3	1	.996
1989	—N.Y.-Phil. (N.L.)■	OF	146	511	66	121	32	4	7	32	.237	60	53	30	332	10	4	.988
1990	—Philadelphia (N.L.)	OF	149	590	106	•192	35	3	9	60	.325	89	48	33	*439	7	6	.987
1991	—Philadelphia (N.L.)	OF	63	246	48	73	13	5	3	12	.297	37	20	24	167	3	4	.977
1992	—Philadelphia (N.L.)	OF	85	345	53	104	18	0	6	39	.301	40	32	30	253	6	3	.989
1993	—Philadelphia (N.L.)	OF	161	*637	*143	*194	44	6	19	66	.305	*129	64	37	*469	2	10	.979
Major league totals (9 years)			1092	3856	676	1110	234	34	71	349	.288	513	406	257	2617	49	35	.987

CHAMPIONSHIP SERIES RECORD

CHAMPIONSHIP SERIES NOTES: Shares single-series record for most times hit by pitch—2 (1988).

		BATTING												FIELDING			
Year Team (League)	Pos.	G	AB	R	H	2B	3B	HR	RBI	Avg.	BB	SO	SB	PO	A	E	Avg.
1986 —New York (N.L.)........	OF-PH	6	23	3	7	1	1	1	3	.304	2	4	1	10	0	0	1.000
1988 —New York (N.L.)........	OF-PH	7	14	6	6	3	0	1	3	.429	4	0	0	9	0	0	1.000
1993 —Philadelphia (N.L.)...	OF	6	25	5	7	1	0	2	2	.280	5	8	0	13	0	0	1.000
Championship series totals (3 years)		19	62	14	20	5	1	4	8	.323	11	12	1	32	0	0	1.000

WORLD SERIES RECORD

		BATTING												FIELDING			
Year Team (League)	Pos.	G	AB	R	H	2B	3B	HR	RBI	Avg.	BB	SO	SB	PO	A	E	Avg.
1986 —New York (N.L.)........	OF-PH	7	27	4	8	0	0	2	3	.296	2	7	0	14	0	0	1.000
1993 —Philadelphia (N.L.)...	OF	6	23	9	8	1	0	4	8	.348	7	4	4	18	1	0	1.000
World Series totals (2 years)		13	50	13	16	1	0	6	11	.320	9	11	4	32	1	0	1.000

ALL-STAR GAME RECORD

		BATTING										FIELDING			
Year League	Pos.	AB	R	H	2B	3B	HR	RBI	Avg.	BB	SO	SB	PO	A	E	Avg.
1990 —National.....................	OF	4	0	1	0	0	0	0	.250	0	0	0	3	0	0	1.000

EASLEY, DAMION

2B, ANGELS

PERSONAL: Born November 11, 1969, in New York.... 5-11/185.... Throws right, bats right.... Full name: Jacinto Damion Easley.

HIGH SCHOOL: Lakewood (Calif.).

COLLEGE: Long Beach (Calif.) City College.

TRANSACTIONS/CAREER NOTES: Selected by California Angels organization in 30th round of free-agent draft (June 1, 1988).... On disabled list (June 19-July 4 and July 28, 1993-remainder of season).

		BATTING												FIELDING			
Year Team (League)	Pos.	G	AB	R	H	2B	3B	HR	RBI	Avg.	BB	SO	SB	PO	A	E	Avg.
1989 —Bend (Northwest).....	2B	36	131	34	39	5	1	4	21	.298	25	21	9	49	89	22	.863
1990 —Quad City (Midw.)....	SS	103	365	59	100	19	3	10	56	.274	41	60	25	136	206	41	.893
1991 —Midland (Texas).......	SS	127	452	73	115	24	5	6	57	.254	58	67	23	186	388	*47	.924
1992 —Edmonton (PCL).......	SS-3B	108	429	61	124	18	3	3	44	.289	31	44	26	152	342	30	.943
—California (A.L.).......	3B-SS	47	151	14	39	5	0	1	12	.258	8	26	9	30	102	5	.964
1993 —California (A.L.).......	2B-3B	73	230	33	72	13	2	2	22	.313	28	35	6	111	157	6	.978
Major league totals (2 years)		120	381	47	111	18	2	3	34	.291	36	61	15	141	259	11	.973

ECKERSLEY, DENNIS

P, ATHLETICS

PERSONAL: Born October 3, 1954, in Oakland, Calif.... 6-2/195.... Throws right, bats right.... Full name: Dennis Lee Eckersley.

HIGH SCHOOL: Washington (Fremont, Calif.).

TRANSACTIONS/CAREER NOTES: Selected by Cleveland Indians organization in third round of free-agent draft (June 6, 1972).... Traded by Indians with C Fred Kendall to Boston Red Sox for P Rick Wise, P Mike Paxton, 3B Ted Cox and C Bo Diaz (March 30, 1978).... Traded by Red Sox with OF Mike Brumley to Chicago Cubs for 1B/OF Bill Buckner (May 25, 1984).... Granted free agency (November 8, 1984).... Re-signed by Cubs (November 28, 1984).... On disabled list (August 11-September 7, 1985).... Traded by Cubs with IF Dan Rohn to Oakland Athletics for OF Dave Wilder, IF Brian Guinn and P Mark Leonette (April 3, 1987).... On disabled list (May 29-July 13, 1989).

RECORDS: Holds A.L. career records for most saves—275; and most consecutive errorless games by pitcher—421 (May 1, 1987 through September 26, 1993).

HONORS: Named A.L. Rookie Pitcher of the Year by THE SPORTING NEWS (1975).... Named A.L. Fireman of the Year by THE SPORTING NEWS (1988 and 1992).... Named A.L. co-Fireman of the Year by THE SPORTING NEWS (1991).... Named A.L. Most Valuable Player by Baseball Writers' Association of America (1992).... Named A.L. Cy Young Award winner by Baseball Writers' Association of America (1992).

STATISTICAL NOTES: Led Texas League with 10 hit batsmen in 1974.... Pitched 1-0 no-hit victory against California (May 30, 1977).... Led A.L. with 30 home runs allowed in 1978.

Year Team (League)	W	L	Pct.	ERA	G	GS	CG	ShO	Sv.	IP	H	R	ER	BB	SO
1972 —Reno (California)	5	5	.500	4.80	12	12	3	1	0	75	87	46	40	33	56
1973 —Reno (California)	12	8	.600	3.65	31	*31	11	•5	0	202	182	97	82	91	218
1974 —San Antonio (Tex.).....	•14	3	*.824	3.40	23	23	10	2	0	167	141	66	63	60	*163
1975 —Cleveland (A.L.)	13	7	.650	2.60	34	24	6	2	2	187	147	61	54	90	152
1976 —Cleveland (A.L.)	13	12	.520	3.44	36	30	9	3	1	199	155	82	76	78	200
1977 —Cleveland (A.L.)	14	13	.519	3.53	33	33	12	3	0	247	214	100	97	54	191
1978 —Boston (A.L.)■...........	20	8	.714	2.99	35	35	16	3	0	268	258	99	89	71	162
1979 —Boston (A.L.).............	17	10	.630	2.99	33	33	17	2	0	247	234	89	82	59	150
1980 —Boston (A.L.).............	12	14	.462	4.27	30	30	8	0	0	198	188	101	94	44	121
1981 —Boston (A.L.).............	9	8	.529	4.27	23	23	8	2	0	154	160	82	73	35	79
1982 —Boston (A.L.).............	13	13	.500	3.73	33	33	11	3	0	224⅓	228	101	93	43	127
1983 —Boston (A.L.).............	9	13	.409	5.61	28	28	2	0	0	176⅓	223	119	110	39	77
1984 —Boston (A.L.).............	4	4	.500	5.01	9	9	2	0	0	64⅔	71	38	36	13	33
—Chicago (N.L.)■.........	10	8	.556	3.03	24	24	2	0	0	160⅓	152	59	54	36	81
1985 —Chicago (N.L.)...........	11	7	.611	3.08	25	25	6	2	0	169⅓	145	61	58	19	117
1986 —Chicago (N.L.)...........	6	11	.353	4.57	33	32	1	0	0	201	226	109	102	43	137
1987 —Oakland (A.L.)■	6	8	.429	3.03	54	2	0	0	16	115⅔	99	41	39	17	113
1988 —Oakland (A.L.)	4	2	.667	2.35	60	0	0	0	45	72⅔	52	20	19	11	70
1989 —Oakland (A.L.)	4	0	1.000	1.56	51	0	0	0	33	57⅔	32	10	10	3	55
1990 —Oakland (A.L.)	4	2	.667	0.61	63	0	0	0	48	73⅓	41	9	5	4	73
1991 —Oakland (A.L.)	5	4	.556	2.96	67	0	0	0	43	76	60	26	25	9	87

Year	Team (League)	W	L	Pct.	ERA	G	GS	CG	ShO	Sv.	IP	H	R	ER	BB	SO
1992	—Oakland (A.L.)	7	1	.875	1.91	69	0	0	0	*51	80	62	17	17	11	93
1993	—Oakland (A.L.)	2	4	.333	4.16	64	0	0	0	36	67	67	32	31	13	80
A.L. totals (17 years)		156	123	.559	3.41	722	280	91	18	275	2507⅔	2291	1027	950	594	1863
N.L. totals (3 years)		27	26	.509	3.63	82	81	9	2	0	530⅔	523	229	214	98	335
Major league totals (19 years)		183	149	.551	3.45	804	361	100	20	275	3038⅓	2814	1256	1164	692	2198

CHAMPIONSHIP SERIES RECORD

CHAMPIONSHIP SERIES NOTES: Named A.L. Championship Series Most Valuable Player (1988).... Holds career record for most saves—10.... Holds single-series record for most saves—4 (1988).... Shares career record for most games pitched—15. ... Shares A.L. career records for most games pitched—14; and most games as relief pitcher—14.

Year	Team (League)	W	L	Pct.	ERA	G	GS	CG	ShO	Sv.	IP	H	R	ER	BB	SO
1984	—Chicago (N.L.)	0	1	.000	8.44	1	1	0	0	0	5⅓	9	5	5	0	0
1988	—Oakland (A.L.)	0	0	...	0.00	4	0	0	0	4	6	1	0	0	2	5
1989	—Oakland (A.L.)	0	0	...	1.59	4	0	0	0	3	5⅔	4	1	1	0	2
1990	—Oakland (A.L.)	0	0	...	0.00	3	0	0	0	2	3⅓	2	0	0	0	3
1992	—Oakland (A.L.)	0	0	...	6.00	3	0	0	0	1	3	8	2	2	0	2
Champ. series totals (5 years)		0	1	.000	3.09	15	1	0	0	10	23⅓	24	8	8	2	12

WORLD SERIES RECORD

Year	Team (League)	W	L	Pct.	ERA	G	GS	CG	ShO	Sv.	IP	H	R	ER	BB	SO
1988	—Oakland (A.L.)	0	1	.000	10.80	2	0	0	0	0	1⅔	2	2	2	1	2
1989	—Oakland (A.L.)	0	0	...	0.00	2	0	0	0	1	1⅔	0	0	0	0	0
1990	—Oakland (A.L.)	0	1	.000	6.75	2	0	0	0	0	1⅓	3	1	1	0	1
World Series totals (3 years)		0	2	.000	5.79	6	0	0	0	1	4⅔	5	3	3	1	3

ALL-STAR GAME RECORD

Year	League	W	L	Pct.	ERA	GS	CG	ShO	Sv.	IP	H	R	ER	BB	SO
1977	—American	0	0	...	0.00	0	0	0	0	2	0	0	0	0	1
1982	—American	0	1	.000	9.00	1	0	0	0	3	2	3	3	2	1
1988	—American	0	0	...	0.00	0	0	0	1	1	0	0	0	0	1
1990	—American	0	0	...	0.00	0	0	0	1	1	1	0	0	0	1
1991	—American	0	0	...	0.00	0	0	0	1	1	0	0	0	0	1
1992	—American	0	0	...	0.00	0	0	0	0	⅔	3	2	0	0	2
All-Star totals (6 years)		0	1	.000	3.12	1	0	0	3	8⅔	6	5	3	2	7

E

EDENS, TOM

P, ASTROS

PERSONAL: Born June 9, 1961, in Ontario, Ore.... 6-2/188.... Throws right, bats left.... Full name: Thomas Patrick Edens.
HIGH SCHOOL: Fruitland (Idaho).
COLLEGE: Lewis-Clark State College, Idaho (degree in business).
TRANSACTIONS/CAREER NOTES: Selected by Cincinnati Reds organization in 12th round of free-agent draft (June 5, 1979).... Selected by Kansas City Royals organization in 14th round of free-agent draft (June 6, 1983).... Traded by Royals organization to New York Mets organization for IF Tucker Ashford (April 1, 1984).... On Columbia disabled list (April 9-19 and May 21-June 18, 1984).... On disabled list (June 25-August 12, 1985).... Traded by Mets organization to Philadelphia Phillies organization (July 27, 1989), completing deal in which Phillies traded 2B Juan Samuel to Mets for OF Lenny Dykstra, P Roger McDowell and a player to be named later (June 18, 1989).... Granted free agency (October 15, 1989).... Signed by Denver, Milwaukee Brewers organization (December 6, 1989).... Granted free agency (December 20, 1990).... Signed by Minnesota Twins (January 14, 1991).... Selected by Florida Marlins in second round (43rd pick overall) of expansion draft (November 17, 1992).... Traded by Marlins to Houston Astros for P Brian Griffiths and P Hector Carrasco (November 17, 1992).... On Houston disabled list (March 29-May 6, 1993); included rehabilitation assignment to Osceola (April 19-24) and Tucson (April 24-May 3).
STATISTICAL NOTES: Pitched seven-inning, 6-1 no-hit victory against Helena (August 22, 1983, second game).

Year	Team (League)	W	L	Pct.	ERA	G	GS	CG	ShO	Sv.	IP	H	R	ER	BB	SO
1983	—Butte (Pioneer)	2	3	.400	4.32	13	12	1	0	0	58⅓	65	47	28	33	44
1984	—Columbia (S. Atl.)■	7	4	.636	3.12	16	15	4	1	0	95⅓	65	44	33	58	60
	—Lynchburg (Caro.)	1	1	.500	2.51	3	2	0	0	0	14⅓	11	6	4	8	15
1985	—Lynchburg (Caro.)	6	4	.600	3.84	16	16	0	0	0	82	86	40	35	34	48
1986	—Jackson (Texas)	9	4	.692	2.55	16	16	4	0	0	106	76	36	30	41	72
	—Tidewater (Int'l)	5	3	.625	4.55	11	11	2	1	0	61⅓	71	33	31	28	31
1987	—Tidewater (Int'l)	9	7	.563	3.59	25	22	0	0	1	138	140	69	55	55	61
	—New York (N.L.)	0	0	...	6.75	2	2	0	0	0	8	15	6	6	4	4
1988	—Tidewater (Int'l)	7	6	.538	3.46	24	21	3	0	0	135⅓	128	67	52	53	89
1989	—Tide.-Scr/WB (Int'l)■	2	6	.250	4.44	25	14	0	0	1	107⅓	121	59	53	39	47
1990	—Denver (A.A.)■	1	1	.500	5.40	19	0	0	0	4	36⅔	32	23	22	22	26
	—Milwaukee (A.L.)	4	5	.444	4.45	35	6	0	0	2	89	89	52	44	33	40
1991	—Portland (PCL)■	10	7	.588	3.01	25	24	3	1	0	161⅓	145	67	54	62	100
	—Minnesota (A.L.)	2	2	.500	4.09	8	6	0	0	0	33	34	15	15	10	19
1992	—Minnesota (A.L.)	6	3	.667	2.83	52	0	0	0	3	76⅓	65	26	24	36	57
1993	—Osceola (Fla. St.)■	1	0	1.000	0.00	3	1	0	0	0	4	5	0	0	1	4
	—Tucson (PCL)	1	0	1.000	6.14	5	0	0	0	0	7⅓	9	5	5	3	6
	—Houston (N.L.)	1	1	.500	3.12	38	0	0	0	0	49	47	17	17	19	21
A.L. totals (3 years)		12	10	.545	3.77	95	12	0	0	5	198⅓	188	93	83	79	116
N.L. totals (2 years)		1	1	.500	3.63	40	2	0	0	0	57	62	23	23	23	25
Major league totals (5 years)		13	11	.542	3.74	135	14	0	0	5	255⅓	250	116	106	102	141

EDMONDS, JIM

OF, ANGELS

PERSONAL: Born June 27, 1970, in Fullerton, Calif.... 6-1/190.... Throws left, bats left.... Full name: James Patrick Edmonds.... Name pronounced ED-muns.
HIGH SCHOOL: Diamond Bar (Calif.).
TRANSACTIONS/CAREER NOTES: Selected by California Angels organization in seventh round of free-agent draft (June 1, 1988).... On disabled list (June 19-September 2, 1989; April 10-May 7 and May 23, 1991-remainder of season).... On Vancouver disabled list (June 29-July 19, 1993).

			BATTING												FIELDING			
Year	Team (League)	Pos.	G	AB	R	H	2B	3B	HR	RBI	Avg.	BB	SO	SB	PO	A	E	Avg.
1988	—Bend (Northwest)	OF	35	122	23	27	4	0	0	13	.221	20	44	4	59	1	1	.984
1989	—Quad City (Midw.)	OF	31	92	11	24	4	0	1	4	.261	7	34	1	47	2	3	.942
1990	—Palm Springs (Cal.)	OF	91	314	36	92	18	6	3	56	.293	27	75	5	199	9	10	.954
1991	—Palm Springs (Cal.)	OF-1B-P	60	187	28	55	15	1	2	27	.294	40	57	2	97	6	0	1.000
1992	—Midland (Texas)	OF	70	246	42	77	15	2	8	32	.313	41	83	3	139	6	5	.967
	—Edmonton (PCL)	OF	50	194	37	58	15	2	6	36	.299	14	55	3	79	5	1	.988
1993	—Vancouver (PCL)	OF	95	356	59	112	28	4	9	74	.315	41	81	6	167	4	3	.983
	—California (A.L.)	OF	18	61	5	15	4	1	0	4	.246	2	16	0	47	4	1	.981
Major league totals (1 year)			18	61	5	15	4	1	0	4	.246	2	16	0	47	4	1	.981

RECORD AS PITCHER

Year	Team (League)	W	L	Pct.	ERA	G	GS	CG	ShO	Sv.	IP	H	R	ER	BB	SO
1991	—Palm Springs (Cal.)	0	0	...	0.00	1	0	0	0	0	2	1	0	0	3	2

EENHOORN, ROBERT

SS, YANKEES

PERSONAL: Born February 9, 1968, in Rotterdam, The Netherlands.... 6-3/170.... Throws right, bats right.
COLLEGE: Davidson.
TRANSACTIONS/CAREER NOTES: Selected by New York Yankees organization in second round of free-agent draft (June 4, 1990); pick received as compensation for Pittsburgh Pirates signing Type B free agent Walt Terrell.... On Prince William disabled list (May 30-June 28 and July 1-September 2, 1991).... On disabled list (July 28, 1993-remainder of season).
MISCELLANEOUS: Member of The Netherlands' 1988 Olympic baseball team.

			BATTING												FIELDING			
Year	Team (League)	Pos.	G	AB	R	H	2B	3B	HR	RBI	Avg.	BB	SO	SB	PO	A	E	Avg.
1990	—Oneonta (NYP)	SS	57	220	30	59	9	3	2	18	.268	18	29	11	83	135	9	*.960
1991	—GC Yankees (GCL)	SS	13	40	6	14	4	1	1	7	.350	3	8	1	12	29	4	.911
	—Prin. William (Car.)	SS	29	108	15	26	6	1	1	12	.241	13	21	0	45	69	6	.950
1992	—Fort Lauder. (FSL)	SS	57	203	23	62	5	2	4	33	.305	19	25	6	60	138	16	.925
	—Alb./Colon. (East.)	SS	60	196	24	46	11	2	1	23	.235	10	17	2	88	153	13	.949
1993	—Alb./Colon. (East.)	SS	82	314	48	88	24	3	6	46	.280	21	39	3	143	221	31	.922

EICHHORN, MARK

P, ORIOLES

PERSONAL: Born November 21, 1960, in San Jose, Calif.... 6-3/210.... Throws right, bats right.... Full name: Mark Anthony Eichhorn.... Name pronounced IKE-horn.
HIGH SCHOOL: Watsonville (Calif.).
COLLEGE: Cabrillo College (Calif.).
TRANSACTIONS/CAREER NOTES: Selected by Toronto Blue Jays organization in second round of free-agent draft (January 9, 1979).... On disabled list (June 16-July 1, 1986).... Contract sold by Blue Jays to Atlanta Braves (March 29, 1989).... Released by Braves (November 20, 1989).... Signed by Edmonton, California Angels organization (December 19, 1989).... Traded by Angels to Blue Jays for C Greg Myers and OF Rob Ducey (July 30, 1992).... Granted free agency (October 29, 1992).... Re-signed by Blue Jays (January 6, 1993).... Granted free agency (November 1, 1993).... Signed by Baltimore Orioles organization (December 14, 1993).
RECORDS: Shares A.L. single-season record for most games by relief pitcher—89 (1987).
HONORS: Named A.L. Rookie Pitcher of the Year by THE SPORTING NEWS (1986).

Year	Team (League)	W	L	Pct.	ERA	G	GS	CG	ShO	Sv.	IP	H	R	ER	BB	SO
1979	—Medicine Hat (Pio.)	7	6	.538	3.39	16	14	3	1	0	93	101	62	35	26	66
1980	—Kinston (Carolina)	14	10	.583	2.90	26	26	9	2	0	183	158	72	59	56	119
1981	—Knoxville (South.)	10	14	.417	3.98	30	•29	9	1	0	192	202	112	85	57	99
1982	—Syracuse (Int'l)	10	11	.476	4.54	27	27	6	1	0	156⅔	158	92	79	83	71
	—Toronto (A.L.)	0	3	.000	5.45	7	7	0	0	0	38	40	28	23	14	16
1983	—Syracuse (Int'l)	0	5	.000	7.92	7	5	0	0	0	30⅔	36	32	27	21	12
	—Knoxville (South.)	6	12	.333	4.33	21	20	3	0	0	120⅔	124	65	58	47	54
1984	—Syracuse (Int'l)	5	9	.357	5.97	36	18	3	1	0	117⅔	147	92	78	51	54
1985	—Knoxville (South.)	5	1	.833	3.02	26	10	2	1	0	116⅓	101	49	39	34	76
	—Syracuse (Int'l)	2	5	.286	4.82	8	7	0	0	0	37⅓	38	24	20	7	27
1986	—Toronto (A.L.)	14	6	.700	1.72	69	0	0	0	10	157	105	32	30	45	166
1987	—Toronto (A.L.)	10	6	.625	3.17	*89	0	0	0	4	127⅔	110	47	45	52	96
1988	—Toronto (A.L.)	0	3	.000	4.19	37	0	0	0	1	66⅔	79	32	31	27	28
	—Syracuse (Int'l)	4	4	.500	1.17	18	1	0	0	2	38⅓	35	9	5	15	34
1989	—Atlanta (N.L.)■	5	5	.500	4.35	45	0	0	0	0	68⅓	70	36	33	19	49
	—Richmond (Int'l)	1	0	1.000	1.32	25	0	0	0	*19	41	29	6	6	6	33
1990	—California (A.L.)■	2	5	.286	3.08	60	0	0	0	13	84⅔	98	36	29	23	69
1991	—California (A.L.)	3	3	.500	1.98	70	0	0	0	1	81⅔	63	21	18	13	49
1992	—Calif.-Tor. (A.L.)■	4	4	.500	3.08	65	0	0	0	2	87⅔	86	34	30	25	61
1993	—Toronto (A.L.)	3	1	.750	2.72	54	0	0	0	0	72⅔	76	26	22	22	47
A.L. totals (8 years)		36	31	.537	2.87	451	7	0	0	31	716	657	256	228	221	532
N.L. totals (1 year)		5	5	.500	4.35	45	0	0	0	0	68⅓	70	36	33	19	49
Major league totals (9 years)		41	36	.532	2.99	496	7	0	0	31	784⅓	727	292	261	240	581

CHAMPIONSHIP SERIES RECORD

Year	Team (League)	W	L	Pct.	ERA	G	GS	CG	ShO	Sv.	IP	H	R	ER	BB	SO
1992	—Toronto (A.L.)	0	0	...	0.00	1	0	0	0	0	1	0	0	0	0	0
1993	—Toronto (A.L.)	0	0	...	0.00	1	0	0	0	0	2	1	0	0	1	1
Champ. series totals (2 years)		0	0	...	0.00	2	0	0	0	0	3	1	0	0	1	1

WORLD SERIES RECORD

Year	Team (League)	W	L	Pct.	ERA	G	GS	CG	ShO	Sv.	IP	H	R	ER	BB	SO
1992	—Toronto (A.L.)	0	0	...	0.00	1	0	0	0	0	1	0	0	0	0	1
1993	—Toronto (A.L.)	0	0	...	0.00	1	0	0	0	0	⅓	1	0	0	1	0
World Series totals (2 years)		0	0	...	0.00	2	0	0	0	0	1⅓	1	0	0	1	1

EILAND, DAVE

P

PERSONAL: Born July 5, 1966, in Dade City, Fla. ... 6-3/212. ... Throws right, bats right. ... Full name: David William Eiland. ... Name pronounced EYE-land.

HIGH SCHOOL: Zephyrhills (Fla.).

COLLEGE: Florida, then South Florida.

TRANSACTIONS/CAREER NOTES: Selected by New York Yankees organization in seventh round of free-agent draft (June 2, 1987). ... On disabled list (May 28-July 12, 1991); included rehabilitation assignment to Columbus (June 16-July 12). ... Released by Yankees (January 19, 1992). ... Signed by San Diego Padres organization (January 27, 1992). ... On San Diego disabled list (May 4-June 26, 1992); included rehabilitation assignment to Las Vegas (May 27-June 25). ... On San Diego disabled list (July 5-August 26, 1992); included rehabilitation assignment to Las Vegas (July 28-August 26). ... Granted free agency (December 7, 1992). ... Signed by Wichita, Padres organization (February 28, 1993). ... Granted free agency (May 27, 1993). ... Signed by Charlotte, Cleveland Indians organization (May 29, 1993). ... Traded by Indians organization to Texas Rangers organization for P Gerald Alexander and P Allan Anderson (August 4, 1993). ... Granted free agency (October 15, 1993).

HONORS: Named International League Most Valuable Pitcher (1990).

STATISTICAL NOTES: Hit home run in first major league at-bat (April 10, 1992).

Year	Team (League)	W	L	Pct.	ERA	G	GS	CG	ShO	Sv.	IP	H	R	ER	BB	SO
1987	—Oneonta (NYP)	4	0	1.000	1.84	5	5	0	0	0	29⅓	20	6	6	3	16
	—Fort Lauder. (FSL)	5	3	.625	1.88	8	8	4	1	0	62⅓	57	17	13	8	28
1988	—Alb./Colon. (East.)	9	5	.643	2.56	18	18	•7	2	0	119⅓	95	39	34	22	66
	—Columbus (Int'l)	1	1	.500	2.59	4	4	0	0	0	24⅓	25	8	7	6	13
	—New York (A.L.)	0	0	...	6.39	3	3	0	0	0	12⅔	15	9	9	4	7
1989	—Columbus (Int'l)	9	4	.692	3.76	18	18	2	0	0	103	107	47	43	21	45
	—New York (A.L.)	1	3	.250	5.77	6	6	0	0	0	34⅓	44	25	22	13	11
1990	—Columbus (Int'l)	*16	5	.762	2.87	27	26	*11	•3	0	175⅓	155	63	56	32	96
	—New York (A.L.)	2	1	.667	3.56	5	5	0	0	0	30⅓	31	14	12	5	16
1991	—New York (A.L.)	2	5	.286	5.33	18	13	0	0	0	72⅔	87	51	43	23	18
	—Columbus (Int'l)	6	1	.857	2.40	9	9	2	0	0	60	54	22	16	7	18
1992	—San Diego (N.L.)■	0	2	.000	5.67	7	7	0	0	0	27	33	21	17	5	10
	—Las Vegas (PCL)	4	5	.444	5.23	14	14	0	0	0	63⅔	78	43	37	11	31
1993	—San Diego (N.L.)	0	3	.000	5.21	10	9	0	0	0	48⅓	58	33	28	17	14
	—Charlotte (Int'l)■	1	3	.250	5.30	8	8	0	0	0	35⅔	42	22	21	12	13
	—Okla. City (A.A.)■	3	1	.750	4.29	7	7	1	0	0	35⅔	39	18	17	9	15
A.L. totals (4 years)		5	9	.357	5.16	32	27	0	0	0	150	177	99	86	45	52
N.L. totals (2 years)		0	5	.000	5.38	17	16	0	0	0	75⅓	91	54	45	22	24
Major league totals (6 years)		5	14	.263	5.23	49	43	0	0	0	225⅓	268	153	131	67	76

EISCHEN, JOEY

P, EXPOS

PERSONAL: Born May 25, 1970, in West Covina, Calif. ... 6-1/190. ... Throws left, bats left. ... Full name: Joseph Raymond Eischen. ... Name pronounced EYE-shen.

HIGH SCHOOL: West Covina (Calif.).

COLLEGE: Pasadena (Calif.) City College.

TRANSACTIONS/CAREER NOTES: Selected by Chicago White Sox organization in fifth round of free-agent draft (June 1, 1988). ... Selected by Texas Rangers organization in fourth round of free-agent draft (June 5, 1989). ... Traded by Rangers organization with P Jonathan Hurst and a player to be named later to Montreal Expos organization for P Oil Can Boyd (July 21, 1991); Expos organization acquired P Travis Buckley to complete deal (September 1, 1991).

HONORS: Named Eastern League Pitcher of the Year (1993).

STATISTICAL NOTES: Led Pioneer League with 11 balks in 1989. ... Pitched 5-0 no-hit victory against Vero Beach (June 16, 1992, first game).

Year	Team (League)	W	L	Pct.	ERA	G	GS	CG	ShO	Sv.	IP	H	R	ER	BB	SO
1989	—Butte (Pioneer)	3	7	.300	5.30	12	12	0	0	0	52⅔	50	45	31	38	57
1990	—Gastonia (S. Atl.)	3	7	.300	2.70	17	14	0	0	0	73⅓	51	36	22	40	69
1991	—Charl.-W.P.B. (FSL)■	8	12	.400	3.87	26	26	2	1	0	146⅔	134	*86	63	79	106
1992	—W.P. Beach (FSL)	9	8	.529	3.08	27	26	3	2	0	169⅔	128	68	58	*83	167
1993	—Harrisburg (East.)	*14	4	*.778	3.62	20	20	0	0	0	119⅓	122	62	48	60	110
	—Ottawa (Int'l)	2	2	.500	3.54	6	6	0	0	0	40⅔	34	18	16	15	29

EISENREICH, JIM

OF, PHILLIES

PERSONAL: Born April 18, 1959, in St. Cloud, Minn. ... 5-11/200. ... Throws left, bats left. ... Full name: James Michael Eisenreich. ... Name pronounced EYES-en-rike.

HIGH SCHOOL: Technical (St. Cloud, Minn.).

COLLEGE: St. Cloud (Minn.) State.

TRANSACTIONS/CAREER NOTES: Selected by Minnesota Twins organization in 16th round of free-agent draft (June 3, 1980). ... On disabled list (May 6-28 and June 18-September 1, 1982). ... On disabled list (April 7, 1983); then transferred to voluntarily retired list (May 27, 1983-remainder of season). ... On disabled list (April 26-May 18, 1984). ... On voluntarily retired list

(June 4, 1984-September 29, 1986).... Claimed on waivers by Kansas City Royals (October 2, 1986).... On Kansas City disabled list (August 25-September 9, 1987 and July 22-August 6, 1989).... Granted free agency (October 30, 1991).... Re-signed by Royals (January 31, 1992).... On disabled list (August 12-September 7, 1992).... Granted free agency (October 30, 1992).... Signed by Philadelphia Phillies (January 20, 1993).... Granted free agency (October 29, 1993).... Re-signed by Phillies (November 24, 1993).
HONORS: Named Appalachian League co-Player of the Year (1980).

			BATTING												FIELDING			
Year	**Team (League)**	**Pos.**	**G**	**AB**	**R**	**H**	**2B**	**3B**	**HR**	**RBI**	**Avg.**	**BB**	**SO**	**SB**	**PO**	**A**	**E**	**Avg.**
1980	—Elizabeth. (Appal.)	OF	67	258	47	77	12	•4	3	41	.298	35	32	12	151	7	3	.981
	—Wis. Rap. (Midw.)	DH	5	16	4	7	0	0	0	5	.438	1	0	1	...	...	...	...
1981	—Wis. Rap. (Midw.)	OF	*134	489	101	•152	*27	0	23	99	.311	84	70	9	*295	17	9	.972
1982	—Minnesota (A.L.)	OF	34	99	10	30	6	0	2	9	.303	11	13	0	72	0	2	.973
1983	—Minnesota (A.L.)	OF	2	7	1	2	1	0	0	0	.286	1	1	0	6	1	0	1.000
1984	—Minnesota (A.L.)	OF	12	32	1	7	1	0	0	3	.219	2	4	2	5	0	0	1.000
1985	—	Out of organized baseball.																
1986	—	Out of organized baseball.																
1987	—Memphis (South.)■	DH	70	275	60	105	36	•10	11	57	.382	47	44	13	...	...	...	...
	—Kansas City (A.L.)	DH	44	105	10	25	8	2	4	21	.238	7	13	1	...	...	...	...
1988	—Kansas City (A.L.)	OF	82	202	26	44	8	1	1	19	.218	6	31	9	109	0	4	.965
	—Omaha (A.A.)	OF	36	142	28	41	8	3	4	14	.289	9	20	9	73	1	1	.987
1989	—Kansas City (A.L.)	OF	134	475	64	139	33	7	9	59	.293	37	44	27	273	4	3	.989
1990	—Kansas City (A.L.)	OF	142	496	61	139	29	7	5	51	.280	42	51	12	261	6	1	*.996
1991	—Kansas City (A.L.)	OF-1B	135	375	47	113	22	3	2	47	.301	20	35	5	243	12	5	.981
1992	—Kansas City (A.L.)	OF	113	353	31	95	13	3	2	28	.269	24	36	11	180	1	1	.995
1993	—Philadelphia (N.L.)■	OF-1B	153	362	51	115	17	4	7	54	.318	26	36	5	223	6	1	.996
American League totals (9 years)			698	2144	251	594	121	23	25	237	.277	150	228	67	1149	24	16	.987
National League totals (1 year)			153	362	51	115	17	4	7	54	.318	26	36	5	223	6	1	.996
Major league totals (10 years)			851	2506	302	709	138	27	32	291	.283	176	264	72	1372	30	17	.988

CHAMPIONSHIP SERIES RECORD

			BATTING												FIELDING			
Year	**Team (League)**	**Pos.**	**G**	**AB**	**R**	**H**	**2B**	**3B**	**HR**	**RBI**	**Avg.**	**BB**	**SO**	**SB**	**PO**	**A**	**E**	**Avg.**
1993	—Philadelphia (N.L.)	OF-PH	6	15	0	2	1	0	0	1	.133	0	2	0	6	0	0	1.000

WORLD SERIES RECORD

			BATTING												FIELDING			
Year	**Team (League)**	**Pos.**	**G**	**AB**	**R**	**H**	**2B**	**3B**	**HR**	**RBI**	**Avg.**	**BB**	**SO**	**SB**	**PO**	**A**	**E**	**Avg.**
1993	—Philadelphia (N.L.)	OF	6	26	3	6	0	0	1	7	.231	2	4	0	18	0	0	1.000

ELDRED, CAL

P, BREWERS

PERSONAL: Born November 24, 1967, in Cedar Rapids, Ia. ... 6-4/235. ... Throws right, bats right. ... Full name: Calvin John Eldred.
HIGH SCHOOL: Urbana (Ia.) Community.
COLLEGE: Iowa.
TRANSACTIONS/CAREER NOTES: Selected by Milwaukee Brewers organization in first round (17th pick overall) of free-agent draft (June 5, 1989).
HONORS: Named A.L. Rookie Pitcher of the Year by THE SPORTING NEWS (1992).
STATISTICAL NOTES: Led American Association with 12 hit batsmen in 1991.

Year	**Team (League)**	**W**	**L**	**Pct.**	**ERA**	**G**	**GS**	**CG**	**ShO**	**Sv.**	**IP**	**H**	**R**	**ER**	**BB**	**SO**
1989	—Beloit (Midwest)	2	1	.667	2.30	5	5	0	0	0	31⅓	23	10	8	11	32
1990	—Stockton (Calif.)	4	2	.667	1.62	7	7	3	1	0	50	31	12	9	19	75
	—El Paso (Texas)	5	4	.556	4.49	19	19	0	0	0	110⅓	126	61	55	47	93
1991	—Denver (A.A.)	13	9	.591	3.75	29	*29	3	1	0	*185	161	82	77	84	*168
	—Milwaukee (A.L.)	2	0	1.000	4.50	3	3	0	0	0	16	20	9	8	6	10
1992	—Denver (A.A.)	10	6	.625	3.00	19	19	4	1	0	141	122	49	47	42	99
	—Milwaukee (A.L.)	11	2	.846	1.79	14	14	2	1	0	100⅓	76	21	20	23	62
1993	—Milwaukee (A.L.)	16	16	.500	4.01	36	•36	8	1	0	*258	232	120	115	91	180
Major league totals (3 years)		29	18	.617	3.44	53	53	10	2	0	374⅓	328	150	143	120	252

ELLIOTT, DONNIE

P, PADRES

PERSONAL: Born September 20, 1968, in Pasadena, Tex. ... 6-4/190. ... Throws right, bats right. ... Full name: Donald Glenn Elliott.
HIGH SCHOOL: Deer Park (Tex.).
COLLEGE: San Jacinto College (Tex.).
TRANSACTIONS/CAREER NOTES: Selected by Philadelphia Phillies organization in seventh round of free-agent draft (June 2, 1987).... Selected by Seattle Mariners from Phillies organization in Rule 5 major league draft (December 9, 1991).... Returned to Phillies (April 1, 1992).... Traded by Phillies to Atlanta Braves for P Ben Rivera (May 28, 1992).... Traded by Braves with OF Mel Nieves and OF Vince Moore to San Diego Padres for 1B Fred McGriff (July 18, 1993).
STATISTICAL NOTES: Tied for Appalachian League lead with nine balks in 1988.

Year	**Team (League)**	**W**	**L**	**Pct.**	**ERA**	**G**	**GS**	**CG**	**ShO**	**Sv.**	**IP**	**H**	**R**	**ER**	**BB**	**SO**
1988	—Martinsville (App.)	4	2	.667	3.66	15	10	0	0	1	59	47	37	24	31	77
1989	—Batavia (NY-Penn)	4	1	.800	1.42	8	8	0	0	0	57	45	21	9	14	48
	—Spartanburg (SAL)	2	3	.400	2.47	7	7	1	1	0	43⅔	46	19	12	14	36
1990	—Spartanburg (SAL)	4	8	.333	3.50	20	20	0	0	0	105⅓	101	52	41	46	109
1991	—Spartanburg (SAL)	3	4	.429	4.24	10	10	0	0	0	51	42	37	24	36	81
	—Clearwater (FSL)	8	5	.615	2.78	18	18	1	1	0	107	78	34	33	51	103
1992	—Clearwater (FSL)	1	1	.500	3.00	3	3	0	0	0	18	12	6	6	8	12
	—Reading (Eastern)	3	3	.500	2.52	6	6	0	0	0	35⅔	37	10	10	11	23

Year	Team (League)	W	L	Pct.	ERA	G	GS	CG	ShO	Sv.	IP	H	R	ER	BB	SO
	—Greenville (South.)■ ...	7	2	.778	2.08	19	17	0	0	0	103⅔	76	28	24	35	100
1993	—Richmond (Int'l)	8	5	.615	4.72	18	18	1	0	0	103	108	65	54	39	99
	—Las Vegas (PCL)■......	2	5	.286	6.37	8	7	0	0	0	41	48	32	29	24	44

ELLIS, ROBERT

P, WHITE SOX

PERSONAL: Born December 15, 1970, in Baton Rouge, La. . . . 6-5/215. . . . Throws right, bats right. . . . Full name: Robert Randolph Ellis.
HIGH SCHOOL: Belaire (Baton Rouge, La.).
COLLEGE: Northwestern (La.) State, then Panola Junior College (Tex.).
TRANSACTIONS/CAREER NOTES: Selected by Chicago White Sox organization in third round of free-agent draft (June 4, 1990). . . . On South Bend disabled list (May 20-July 1, 1992).

Year	Team (League)	W	L	Pct.	ERA	G	GS	CG	ShO	Sv.	IP	H	R	ER	BB	SO
1991	—Utica (N.Y.-Penn)	3	•9	.250	4.62	15	15	1	1	0	87⅔	86	*66	45	61	66
1992	—South Bend (Mid.)	6	5	.545	2.34	18	18	1	1	0	123	90	46	32	35	97
	—GC Whi. Sox (GCL)	1	0	1.000	10.80	1	1	0	0	0	5	10	6	6	1	4
1993	—Sarasota (Fla. St.)	7	8	.467	2.51	15	15	*8	2	0	104	81	37	29	31	79
	—Birm. (Southern)	6	3	.667	3.10	12	12	2	1	0	81⅓	68	33	28	21	77

ELSTER, KEVIN

SS, PADRES

PERSONAL: Born August 3, 1964, in San Pedro, Calif. . . . 6-2/200. . . . Throws right, bats right. . . . Full name: Kevin Daniel Elster.
HIGH SCHOOL: Marina (Huntington Beach, Calif.).
COLLEGE: Golden West College (Calif.).
TRANSACTIONS/CAREER NOTES: Selected by New York Mets organization in second round of free-agent draft (January 17, 1984). . . . On Jackson disabled list (August 11, 1985-remainder of season). . . . On disabled list (August 4, 1990-remainder of season and May 6-21, 1991). . . . On New York disabled list (April 13, 1992-remainder of season). . . . Granted free agency (December 19, 1992). . . . Signed by Los Angeles Dodgers organization (January 12, 1993). . . . On Albuquerque disabled list (April 8-May 2, 1993). . . . Released by Dodgers (May 17, 1993). . . . Signed by Florida Marlins organization (May 22, 1993). . . . Released by Edmonton, Marlins organization (June 4, 1993). . . . Signed by San Diego Padres organization (December 17, 1993).
RECORDS: Holds major league single-season record for fewest putouts by shortstop who led league in putouts—235 (1989). . . . Holds N.L. career record for most consecutive errorless games by shortstop—88 (July 20, 1988-May 8, 1989).
STATISTICAL NOTES: Led New York-Pennsylvania League shortstops with 358 total chances and 45 double plays in 1984. . . . Led Texas League shortstops with 589 total chances and 83 double plays in 1986.

			BATTING												FIELDING			
Year	Team (League)	Pos.	G	AB	R	H	2B	3B	HR	RBI	Avg.	BB	SO	SB	PO	A	E	Avg.
1984	—Little Falls (NYP)	SS	71	257	35	66	7	3	3	35	.257	35	41	13	*128	214	16	*.955
1985	—Lynchburg (Caro.) ...	SS	59	224	41	66	9	0	7	26	.295	33	21	8	82	195	16	.945
	—Jackson (Texas)	SS	59	214	30	55	13	0	2	22	.257	19	29	2	107	220	10	.970
1986	—Jackson (Texas)	SS	127	435	69	117	19	3	2	52	.269	61	46	6	*196	*365	28	*.952
	—New York (N.L.)	SS	19	30	3	5	1	0	0	0	.167	3	8	0	16	35	2	.962
1987	—Tidewater (Int'l)	SS	134	*549	83	*170	33	7	8	74	.310	35	62	7	219	419	21	.968
	—New York (N.L.)	SS	5	10	1	4	2	0	0	1	.400	0	1	0	4	6	1	.909
1988	—New York (N.L.)	SS	149	406	41	87	11	1	9	37	.214	35	47	2	196	345	13	.977
1989	—New York (N.L.)	SS	151	458	52	106	25	2	10	55	.231	34	77	4	*235	374	15	.976
1990	—New York (N.L.)	SS	92	314	36	65	20	1	9	45	.207	30	54	2	159	251	17	.960
1991	—New York (N.L.)	SS	115	348	33	84	16	2	6	36	.241	40	53	2	149	299	14	.970
1992	—New York (N.L.)	SS	6	18	0	4	0	0	0	0	.222	0	2	0	8	10	0	1.000
1993	—San Antonio (Tex.)■.	SS	10	39	5	11	2	1	0	7	.282	4	4	0	14	31	4	.918
	Major league totals (7 years)		537	1584	166	355	75	6	34	174	.224	142	242	10	767	1320	62	.971

CHAMPIONSHIP SERIES RECORD

			BATTING												FIELDING			
Year	Team (League)	Pos.	G	AB	R	H	2B	3B	HR	RBI	Avg.	BB	SO	SB	PO	A	E	Avg.
1986	—New York (N.L.)	SS-PR	4	3	0	0	0	0	0	0	.000	0	1	0	2	3	0	1.000
1988	—New York (N.L.)	SS-PR	5	8	1	2	1	0	0	1	.250	3	0	0	7	7	2	.875
	Championship series totals (2 years)		9	11	1	2	1	0	0	1	.182	3	1	0	9	10	2	.905

WORLD SERIES RECORD

			BATTING												FIELDING			
Year	Team (League)	Pos.	G	AB	R	H	2B	3B	HR	RBI	Avg.	BB	SO	SB	PO	A	E	Avg.
1986	—New York (N.L.)	SS	1	1	0	0	0	0	0	0	.000	0	0	0	3	3	1	.857

EMBREE, ALAN

P, INDIANS

PERSONAL: Born January 23, 1970, in Vancouver, Wash. . . . 6-2/185. . . . Throws left, bats left. . . . Full name: Alan Duane Embree.
HIGH SCHOOL: Prairie (Vancouver, Wash.).
TRANSACTIONS/CAREER NOTES: Selected by Cleveland Indians organization in fifth round of free-agent draft (June 5, 1989). . . . On Cleveland disabled list (April 1-June 2 and June 2, 1993-remainder of season); included rehabilitation assignment to Canton/Akron (June 2-15).

Year	Team (League)	W	L	Pct.	ERA	G	GS	CG	ShO	Sv.	IP	H	R	ER	BB	SO
1990	—Burlington (Appal.)	4	4	.500	2.64	15	•15	0	0	0	81⅔	87	36	24	30	58
1991	—Columbus (S. Atl.)	10	8	.556	3.59	27	26	3	1	0	155⅓	126	80	62	77	137
1992	—Kinston (Carolina)	10	5	.667	3.30	15	15	1	0	0	101	89	48	37	32	115
	—Cant./Akr. (East.)	7	2	.778	2.28	12	12	0	0	0	79	61	24	20	28	56
	—Cleveland (A.L.)	0	2	.000	7.00	4	4	0	0	0	18	19	14	14	8	12
1993	—Cant./Akr. (East.)	0	0	...	3.38	1	1	0	0	0	5⅓	3	2	2	3	4
	Major league totals (1 year) ...	0	2	.000	7.00	4	4	0	0	0	18	19	14	14	8	12

ENCARNACION, ANGELO

C, PIRATES

PERSONAL: Born April 18, 1973, in Santo Domingo, Dominican Republic. . . . 5-8/180. . . . Throws right, bats right. . . . Full name: Angelo Benjamin Encarnacion.
HIGH SCHOOL: Francisco Espaillat College (Dominican Republic).
TRANSACTIONS/CAREER NOTES: Signed as free agent by Pittsburgh Pirates organization (June 1, 1990). . . . On Salem disabled list (June 28-July 16, 1993).
STATISTICAL NOTES: Led South Atlantic League catchers with 15 double plays in 1992.

			BATTING											FIELDING			
Year Team (League)	Pos.	G	AB	R	H	2B	3B	HR	RBI	Avg.	BB	SO	SB	PO	A	E	Avg.
1990 —Dom. Pirates (DSL) ..	...	30	96	18	32	2	0	0	19	.333	6	5	8	...	...	...	...
1991 —Welland (NYP)	C	50	181	21	46	3	2	0	15	.254	5	27	4	366	74	*18	.961
1992 —Augusta (S. Atl.)	C	94	314	39	80	14	3	1	29	.255	25	37	2	676	*121	*22	.973
1993 —Salem (Carolina)	C	70	238	20	61	12	1	3	24	.256	13	27	1	450	82	*21	.962
—Buffalo (A.A.)	C-OF	3	9	1	3	0	0	0	2	.333	0	0	0	14	1	0	1.000

ERICKSON, SCOTT

P, TWINS

PERSONAL: Born February 2, 1968, in Long Beach, Calif. . . . 6-4/222. . . . Throws right, bats right. . . . Full name: Scott Gavin Erickson.
HIGH SCHOOL: Homestead (Cupertino, Calif.).
COLLEGE: San Jose (Calif.) City College and Arizona.
TRANSACTIONS/CAREER NOTES: Selected by New York Mets organization in 36th round of free-agent draft (June 2, 1986). . . . Selected by Houston Astros organization in 34th round of free-agent draft (June 2, 1987). . . . Selected by Toronto Blue Jays organization in 44th round of free-agent draft (June 1, 1988). . . . Selected by Minnesota Twins organization in fourth round of free-agent draft (June 5, 1989). . . . On disabled list (June 30-July 15, 1991 and April 3-18, 1993).

Year Team (League)	W	L	Pct.	ERA	G	GS	CG	ShO	Sv.	IP	H	R	ER	BB	SO
1989 —Visalia (California)	3	4	.429	2.97	12	12	2	0	0	78⅔	79	29	26	22	59
1990 —Orlando (Southern)	8	3	.727	3.03	15	15	3	1	0	101	75	38	34	24	69
—Minnesota (A.L.)	8	4	.667	2.87	19	17	1	0	0	113	108	49	36	51	53
1991 —Minnesota (A.L.)	•20	8	.714	3.18	32	32	5	3	0	204	189	80	72	71	108
1992 —Minnesota (A.L.)	13	12	.520	3.40	32	32	5	3	0	212	197	86	80	83	101
1993 —Minnesota (A.L.)	8	*19	.296	5.19	34	34	1	0	0	218⅔	*266	*138	126	71	116
Major league totals (4 years) ..	49	43	.533	3.78	117	115	12	6	0	747⅔	760	353	314	276	378

CHAMPIONSHIP SERIES RECORD

Year Team (League)	W	L	Pct.	ERA	G	GS	CG	ShO	Sv.	IP	H	R	ER	BB	SO
1991 —Minnesota (A.L.)	0	0	...	4.50	1	1	0	0	0	4	3	2	2	5	2

WORLD SERIES RECORD

Year Team (League)	W	L	Pct.	ERA	G	GS	CG	ShO	Sv.	IP	H	R	ER	BB	SO
1991 —Minnesota (A.L.)	0	0	...	5.06	2	2	0	0	0	10⅔	10	7	6	4	5

ESPINOZA, ALVARO

3B/SS, INDIANS

PERSONAL: Born February 19, 1962, in Valencia, Carabobo, Venezuela. . . . 6-0/190. . . . Throws right, bats right. . . . Full name: Alvaro Alberto Ramirez Espinoza. . . . Name pronounced ESS-pin-OH-zuh.
HIGH SCHOOL: Valencia (Carabobo, Venezuela).
TRANSACTIONS/CAREER NOTES: Signed as free agent by Houston Astros organization (October 30, 1978). . . . Released by Astros organization (September 30, 1980). . . . Signed by Wisconsin Rapids, Minnesota Twins organization (March 18, 1982). . . . On Toledo disabled list (June 7-25, 1984 and June 6-July 2, 1985). . . . Granted free agency (October 15, 1987). . . . Signed by Columbus, New York Yankees organization (November 17, 1987). . . . Released by Yankees (March 17, 1992). . . . Signed by Colorado Springs, Cleveland Indians organization (April 3, 1992).
RECORDS: Shares major league single-season record for fewest runs batted in (150 or more games)—20 (1990).
STATISTICAL NOTES: Led Gulf Coast League shortstops with 114 putouts, 217 assists, 25 errors, 356 total chances and 33 double plays in 1980. . . . Led California League shortstops with 660 total chances in 1983. . . . Tied for International League lead with 16 sacrifice hits in 1984. . . . Led International League shortstops with 159 putouts in 1986. . . . Led Pacific Coast League shortstops with 631 total chances and 112 double plays in 1992.

			BATTING											FIELDING			
Year Team (League)	Pos.	G	AB	R	H	2B	3B	HR	RBI	Avg.	BB	SO	SB	PO	A	E	Avg.
1979 —GC Astros (GCL)	SS-2B-3B	11	32	3	7	0	0	0	5	.219	4	6	0	18	27	1	.978
1980 —GC Astros-Or. (GCL) ..	SS-3B	59	200	24	43	5	0	0	14	.215	15	18	6	†114	†219	†25	.930
1981 —								Out of organized baseball.									
1982 —Wis. Rap. (Midw.)■ ..	SS-3B-1B	112	379	41	101	9	0	5	29	.266	16	66	9	237	241	33	.935
1983 —Visalia (California) ...	SS	130	486	57	155	20	1	4	57	.319	14	50	6	*256	364	40	.939
1984 —Toledo (Int'l)	SS	104	344	22	80	12	5	0	30	.233	3	49	3	157	293	19	.959
—Minnesota (A.L.)	SS	1	0	0	0	0	0	0	0	...	0	0	0	0	0	0	...
1985 —Toledo (Int'l)	SS	82	266	24	61	11	0	1	33	.229	14	30	1	132	245	16	.959
—Minnesota (A.L.)	SS	32	57	5	15	2	0	0	9	.263	1	9	0	25	69	5	.949
1986 —Toledo (Int'l)	SS-2B	73	253	18	71	8	1	2	27	.281	6	30	1	†170	205	12	.969
—Minnesota (A.L.)	2B-SS	37	42	4	9	1	0	0	1	.214	1	10	0	23	52	4	.949
1987 —Portland (PCL)	SS-3B-1B	91	291	28	80	3	2	4	28	.275	12	37	2	158	236	20	.952
1988 —Columbus (Int'l)■	SS-2B-3B	119	435	42	107	10	5	2	30	.246	7	53	4	221	404	19	.970
—New York (A.L.)	2B-SS	3	3	0	0	0	0	0	0	.000	0	0	0	5	2	0	1.000
1989 —New York (A.L.)	SS	146	503	51	142	23	1	0	41	.282	14	60	3	237	471	22	.970
1990 —New York (A.L.)	SS	150	438	31	98	12	2	2	20	.224	16	54	1	268	447	17	.977
1991 —New York (A.L.)	SS-3B-P	148	480	51	123	23	2	5	33	.256	16	57	4	225	441	21	.969
1992 —Colo. Springs (PCL)■	SS	122	483	64	145	36	6	9	79	.300	21	55	2	191	*414	26	.959
1993 —Cleveland (A.L.)	3B-SS-2B	129	263	34	73	15	0	4	27	.278	8	36	2	66	157	12	.949
Major league totals (8 years)		646	1786	176	460	76	5	11	131	.258	56	226	10	849	1639	81	.968

RECORD AS PITCHER

Year	Team (League)	W	L	Pct.	ERA	G	GS	CG	ShO	Sv.	IP	H	R	ER	BB	SO
1991	—New York (A.L.)	0	0	...	0.00	1	0	0	0	0	⅔	0	0	0	0	0

ESPY, CECIL

OF

PERSONAL: Born January 20, 1963, in San Diego. . . . 6-3/195. . . . Throws right, bats both. . . . Full name: Cecil Edward Espy Jr.
HIGH SCHOOL: Point Loma (Calif.).
TRANSACTIONS/CAREER NOTES: Selected by Chicago White Sox organization in first round (eighth pick overall) of free-agent draft (June 3, 1980). . . . Traded by White Sox organization with P Burt Geiger to Los Angeles Dodgers organization for OF Rudy Law (March 30, 1982). . . . Traded by Dodgers organization with 1B Sid Bream to Pittsburgh Pirates (September 9, 1985), completing deal in which Dodgers acquired 3B Bill Madlock for three players to be named later; Pirates acquired OF R.J. Reynolds as partial completion of deal (September 3, 1985). . . . Selected by Texas Rangers from Pirates organization in Rule 5 major league draft (December 8, 1986). . . . On disabled list (May 3-18, 1988). . . . Granted free agency (October 15, 1990). . . . Signed by Pirates organization (February 11, 1991). . . . Claimed on waivers by Cincinnati Reds (November 25, 1992). . . . Released by Indianapolis, Reds organization (July 20, 1993).
STATISTICAL NOTES: Led Texas League outfielders with 348 putouts and 365 total chances in 1984. . . . Led Texas League shortstops with 50 errors in 1985. . . . Tied for Texas League lead in caught stealing with 17 in 1985. . . . Led A.L. in caught stealing with 20 in 1989.

			BATTING												FIELDING			
Year	Team (League)	Pos.	G	AB	R	H	2B	3B	HR	RBI	Avg.	BB	SO	SB	PO	A	E	Avg.
1980	—GC Whi. Sox (GCL) ...	OF	58	212	33	58	7	3	0	26	.274	26	38	23	138	4	7	.953
1981	—Appleton (Midw.)	OF	72	273	37	55	2	2	1	19	.201	30	54	11	143	5	5	.967
	—GC Whi. Sox (GCL) ...	OF	43	142	24	40	3	1	0	16	.282	11	13	9	54	1	4	.932
1982	—Vero Beach (FSL)■...	OF	131	*523	*100	*166	14	7	1	34	.317	58	70	*74	275	9	10	.966
1983	—San Antonio (Tex.) ...	OF	133	*564	88	151	16	11	4	38	.268	39	77	51	258	12	10	.964
	—Los Angeles (N.L.) ...	OF	20	11	4	3	1	0	0	1	.273	1	2	0	11	0	0	1.000
1984	—San Antonio (Tex.) ...	OF-2B-SS	*133	*535	99	146	19	8	8	60	.273	54	75	48	†348	16	5	.986
1985	—San Antonio (Tex.) ...	SS-OF	124	461	64	129	24	3	5	49	.280	47	59	20	183	346	†51	.912
1986	—Hawaii (PCL)■.........	OF-2B-SS	106	384	49	101	19	3	4	38	.263	24	83	41	172	8	5	.973
1987	—Okla. City (A.A.)■.....	OF-SS	118	443	76	134	18	6	1	37	.302	31	66	46	195	161	16	.957
	—Texas (A.L.)	OF	14	8	1	0	0	0	0	0	.000	1	3	2	8	1	0	1.000
1988	—Texas (A.L.)	O-S-C-1-2	123	347	46	86	17	6	2	39	.248	20	83	33	200	11	7	.968
1989	—Texas (A.L.)	OF	142	475	65	122	12	7	3	31	.257	38	99	45	281	5	3	.990
1990	—Texas (A.L.)	OF-2B	52	71	10	9	0	0	0	1	.127	10	20	11	56	1	0	1.000
	—Okla. City (A.A.)	OF-SS	34	126	15	34	4	1	2	20	.270	15	29	7	69	8	5	.939
1991	—Buffalo (A.A.)■.........	OF	102	398	69	124	27	10	2	43	.312	36	65	22	215	10	7	.970
	—Pittsburgh (N.L.)	OF	43	82	7	20	4	0	1	11	.244	5	17	4	54	3	2	.966
1992	—Pittsburgh (N.L.)	OF	112	194	21	50	7	3	1	20	.258	15	40	6	83	1	4	.955
1993	—Cincinnati (N.L.)■....	OF	40	60	6	14	2	0	0	5	.233	14	13	2	25	2	2	.931
	—Indianapolis (A.A.) ...	OF	25	83	10	19	3	0	0	7	.229	6	16	2	33	2	0	1.000
American League totals (4 years)			331	901	122	217	29	13	5	71	.241	69	205	91	545	18	10	.983
National League totals (4 years)			215	347	38	87	14	3	2	37	.251	35	72	12	173	6	8	.957
Major league totals (8 years)			546	1248	160	304	43	16	7	108	.244	104	277	103	718	24	18	.976

CHAMPIONSHIP SERIES RECORD

			BATTING												FIELDING			
Year	Team (League)	Pos.	G	AB	R	H	2B	3B	HR	RBI	Avg.	BB	SO	SB	PO	A	E	Avg.
1991	—Pittsburgh (N.L.)	PH	2	2	0	0	0	0	0	0	.000	0	2	0	...	...	...	...
1992	—Pittsburgh (N.L.)	PH-OF-PR	4	3	0	2	0	0	0	0	.667	0	1	0	0	0	0	...
Championship series totals (2 years)			6	5	0	2	0	0	0	0	.400	0	3	0	0	0	0	...

ETTLES, MARK

P, PADRES

PERSONAL: Born October 30, 1966, in Perth, Australia. . . . 6-0/185. . . . Throws right, bats right. . . . Full name: Mark Edward Ettles.
HIGH SCHOOL: Wesley College (Perth, Australia).
COLLEGE: West Florida and South Alabama.
TRANSACTIONS/CAREER NOTES: Selected by Detroit Tigers organization in 33rd round of free-agent draft (June 5, 1989). . . . Released by Lakeland, Tigers organization (May 9, 1991). . . . Signed by Charleston, S.C., San Diego Padres organization (May 14, 1991). . . . On disabled list (April 28-May 6, 1992).

Year	Team (League)	W	L	Pct.	ERA	G	GS	CG	ShO	Sv.	IP	H	R	ER	BB	SO
1989	—Niag. Falls (NYP)	3	0	1.000	1.02	5	0	0	0	1	17⅔	12	3	2	2	21
	—Fayetteville (SAL)	2	2	.500	2.28	19	0	0	0	4	27⅔	28	9	7	9	34
1990	—Lakeland (Fla. St.)	5	5	.500	3.31	45	0	0	0	3	68	63	34	25	16	62
1991	—Lakeland (Fla. St.)	2	1	.667	4.76	8	1	0	0	0	17	19	11	9	6	14
	—Char., S.C. (S. Atl.)■...	2	1	.667	2.36	29	0	0	0	12	45⅔	36	15	12	12	59
	—Waterloo (Midw.)	1	2	.333	2.25	14	0	0	0	8	16	6	5	4	6	24
1992	—Wichita (Texas)	3	8	.273	2.77	54	0	0	0	22	68⅓	54	23	21	23	86
1993	—Las Vegas (PCL)	3	6	.333	4.71	47	0	0	0	15	49⅔	58	28	26	22	29
	—San Diego (N.L.)	1	0	1.000	6.50	14	0	0	0	0	18	23	16	13	4	9
Major league totals (1 year) ...		1	0	1.000	6.50	14	0	0	0	0	18	23	16	13	4	9

EUSEBIO, TONY

C, ASTROS

PERSONAL: Born April 27, 1967, in San Jose de Los Llamos, Dominican Republic. . . . 6-2/180. . . . Throws right, bats right. . . . Full name: Raul Antonio Eusebio. . . . Name pronounced you-SAY-bee-o.
HIGH SCHOOL: San Rafael (Dominican Republic).
TRANSACTIONS/CAREER NOTES: Signed as free agent by Houston Astros organization (May 30, 1985). . . . On disabled list (Au-

gust 5, 1990-remainder of season; April 16-23, 1992 and August 24, 1993-remainder of season).
STATISTICAL NOTES: Tied for Southern League lead in double plays by catcher with eight in 1989. . . . Led Texas League catchers with .9963 fielding percentage and 12 double plays in 1992.

			BATTING											FIELDING			
Year	Team (League)	Pos.	G	AB	R	H	2B	3B	HR	RBI	Avg.	BB	SO	SB	PO	A	E	Avg.
1985	—GC Astros (GCL)	C	1	1	0	0	0	0	0	0	.000	0	0	0	4	0	0	1.000
1985	—	Dominican Summer League statistics unavailable.																
1986	—	Dominican Summer League statistics unavailable.																
1987	—GC Astros (GCL)	C-1B	42	125	26	26	1	2	1	15	.208	18	19	8	204	24	4	.983
1988	—Osceola (Fla. St.)	C-OF	118	392	45	96	6	3	0	40	.245	40	69	19	611	66	8	.988
1989	—Columbus (South.)	C	65	203	20	38	6	1	0	18	.187	38	47	7	355	46	7	.983
	—Osceola (Fla. St.)	C	52	175	22	50	6	3	0	30	.286	19	27	5	290	40	5	.985
1990	—Columbus (South.)	C	92	318	36	90	18	0	4	37	.283	21	80	6	558	69	4	*.994
1991	—Jackson (Texas)	C	66	222	27	58	8	3	2	31	.261	25	54	3	424	48	7	.985
	—Tucson (PCL)	C	5	20	5	8	1	0	0	2	.400	3	3	1	40	1	0	1.000
	—Houston (N.L.)	C	10	19	4	2	1	0	0	0	.105	6	8	0	49	4	1	.981
1992	—Jackson (Texas)	C	94	339	33	104	9	3	5	44	.307	25	58	1	493	51	2	*.996
1993	—Tucson (PCL)	C	78	281	39	91	20	1	1	43	.324	22	40	1	450	46	3	.994
Major league totals (1 year)			10	19	4	2	1	0	0	0	.105	6	8	0	49	4	1	.981

EVERETT, CARL

OF, MARLINS

PERSONAL: Born June 3, 1971, in Tampa, Fla. . . . 6-0/181. . . . Throws right, bats both. . . . Full name: Carl Edward Everett.
HIGH SCHOOL: Hillsborough (Tampa, Fla.).
TRANSACTIONS/CAREER NOTES: Selected by New York Yankees organization in first round (10th pick overall) of free-agent draft (June 4, 1990). . . . On Fort Lauderdale disabled list (July 7-August 15, 1992). . . . Selected by Florida Marlins in second round (27th pick overall) of expansion draft (November 17, 1992). . . . On High Desert disabled list (April 8-13, 1993).
STATISTICAL NOTES: Led South Atlantic League in being hit by pitch with 23 in 1991.

			BATTING											FIELDING			
Year	Team (League)	Pos.	G	AB	R	H	2B	3B	HR	RBI	Avg.	BB	SO	SB	PO	A	E	Avg.
1990	—GC Yankees (GCL)	OF	48	185	28	48	8	5	1	14	.259	15	38	15	64	5	5	.932
1991	—Greensboro (S. Atl.)	OF	123	468	96	127	18	0	4	40	.271	57	122	28	250	14	7	.974
1992	—Fort Lauder. (FSL)	OF	46	183	30	42	8	2	2	9	.230	12	40	11	111	5	3	.975
	—Prin. William (Car.)	OF	6	22	7	7	0	0	4	9	.318	5	7	1	12	1	0	1.000
1993	—High Desert (Calif.)■	OF	59	253	48	73	12	6	10	52	.289	22	73	24	124	6	2	.985
	—Florida (N.L.)	OF	11	19	0	2	0	0	0	0	.105	1	9	1	6	0	1	.857
	—Edmonton (PCL)	OF	35	136	28	42	13	4	6	16	.309	19	45	12	69	12	2	.976
Major league totals (1 year)			11	19	0	2	0	0	0	0	.105	1	9	1	6	0	1	.857

EVERSGERD, BRYAN

P, CARDINALS

PERSONAL: Born February 11, 1969, in Centralia, Ill. . . . 6-1/190. . . . Throws left, bats right. . . . Full name: Bryan David Eversgerd.
HIGH SCHOOL: Carlyle (Ill.).
COLLEGE: Kaskaskia Community College (Ill.).
TRANSACTIONS/CAREER NOTES: Signed as free agent by St. Louis Cardinals organization (June 14, 1989).

Year	Team (League)	W	L	Pct.	ERA	G	GS	CG	ShO	Sv.	IP	H	R	ER	BB	SO
1989	—Johns. City (App.)	2	3	.400	3.64	16	1	0	0	0	29⅔	30	16	12	12	19
1990	—Springfield (Midw.)	6	8	.429	4.14	20	15	2	0	0	104⅓	123	60	48	26	55
1991	—Savannah (S. Atl.)	1	5	.167	3.47	72	0	0	0	1	93⅓	71	43	36	34	97
1992	—St. Peters. (FSL)	3	2	.600	2.68	57	1	0	0	0	74	65	25	22	25	57
	—Arkansas (Texas)	0	1	.000	6.75	6	0	0	0	0	5⅓	7	4	4	2	4
1993	—Arkansas (Texas)	4	4	.500	2.18	*62	0	0	0	0	66	60	24	16	19	68

FAJARDO, HECTOR

P, RANGERS

PERSONAL: Born November 6, 1970, in Michoacan, Mexico. . . . 6-4/200. . . . Throws right, bats right. . . . Full name: Hector Navarrete Fajardo.
TRANSACTIONS/CAREER NOTES: Purchased by Pittsburgh Pirates organization from Mexico City Reds (April 2, 1989). . . . Traded by Pirates to Texas Rangers (September 6, 1991), completing deal in which Rangers traded 3B Steve Buechele to Pirates for P Kurt Miller and a player to be named later (August 30, 1991). . . . On Texas disabled list (March 28-July 27, 1992); included rehabilitation assignment to Gulf Coast Rangers (July 16-21) and Charlotte (July 21-27). . . . On Texas disabled list (March 27-August 31, 1993); included rehabilitation assignment to Gulf Coast Rangers (July 28-August 12) and Charlotte (August 18-31).

Year	Team (League)●	W	L	Pct.	ERA	G	GS	CG	ShO	Sv.	IP	H	R	ER	BB	SO
1989	—M.C. Reds (Mex.)	0	0	...	6.30	3	0	0	0	0	10	8	7	7	7	6
	—GC Pirates (GCL)■	0	5	.000	5.97	10	6	0	0	0	34⅔	38	24	23	20	19
1990	—GC Pirates (GCL)	1	1	.500	3.86	5	4	0	0	0	21	23	10	9	8	17
	—Augusta (S. Atl.)	2	2	.500	3.86	7	7	0	0	0	39⅔	41	18	17	15	28
1991	—Augusta (S. Atl.)	4	3	.571	2.69	11	11	1	1	0	60⅓	44	26	18	24	79
	—Salem (Carolina)	0	1	.000	2.35	1	1	1	0	0	7⅔	4	3	2	1	7
	—Carolina (South.)	3	4	.429	4.13	10	10	1	0	0	61	55	32	28	24	53
	—Pittsburgh (N.L.)	0	0	...	9.95	2	2	0	0	0	6⅓	10	7	7	7	8
	—Buffalo (A.A.)	1	0	1.000	0.96	8	0	0	0	1	9⅓	6	1	1	3	12
	—Texas (A.L.)■	0	2	.000	5.68	4	3	0	0	0	19	25	13	12	4	15
1992	—GC Rangers (GCL)	0	1	.000	5.68	1	1	0	0	0	6⅓	5	4	4	2	9
	—Charlotte (Fla. St.)	2	2	.500	2.78	4	4	0	0	0	22⅔	22	9	7	8	12
	—Tulsa (Texas)	2	1	.667	2.16	5	4	0	0	0	25	19	6	6	7	26
	—Okla. City (A.A.)	1	0	1.000	0.00	1	1	0	0	0	7	8	0	0	2	6

Year	Team (League)	W	L	Pct.	ERA	G	GS	CG	ShO	Sv.	IP	H	R	ER	BB	SO
1993	—GC Rangers (GCL)	3	1	.750	1.80	6	6	0	0	0	30	21	8	6	5	27
	—Charlotte (Fla. St.)	0	0	...	1.80	2	1	0	0	0	5	5	1	1	1	3
	—Texas (A.L.)	0	0	...	0.00	1	0	0	0	0	⅔	0	0	0	0	1
A.L. totals (2 years)		0	2	.000	5.49	5	3	0	0	0	19⅔	25	13	12	4	16
N.L. totals (1 year)		0	0	...	9.95	2	2	0	0	0	6⅓	10	7	7	7	8
Major league totals (2 years)		0	2	.000	6.58	7	5	0	0	0	26	35	20	19	11	24

FANEYTE, RIKKERT

OF, GIANTS

PERSONAL: Born May 31, 1969, in Amsterdam, The Netherlands. . . . 6-1/170. . . . Throws right, bats right. . . . Name pronounced fuh-NY-tuh.
COLLEGE: Miami-Dade Community College-Kendall.
TRANSACTIONS/CAREER NOTES: Selected by San Francisco Giants organization in 16th round of free-agent draft (June 4, 1990). . . . On temporary inactive list (April 12-May 8, 1991). . . . On disabled list (May 13-June 22, 1992).

				BATTING											FIELDING			
Year	Team (League)	Pos.	G	AB	R	H	2B	3B	HR	RBI	Avg.	BB	SO	SB	PO	A	E	Avg.
1991	—Clinton (Midwest)	OF	107	384	73	98	14	7	6	52	.255	61	106	18	211	9	3	*.987
1992	—San Jose (Calif.)	OF	94	342	69	90	13	2	9	43	.263	73	65	17	172	13	3	.984
1993	—Phoenix (PCL)	OF	115	426	71	133	23	2	11	71	.312	40	72	15	223	11	3	.987
	—San Francisco (N.L.)	OF	7	15	2	2	0	0	0	0	.133	2	4	0	10	0	0	1.000
Major league totals (1 year)			7	15	2	2	0	0	0	0	.133	2	4	0	10	0	0	1.000

FARIES, PAUL

IF, GIANTS

PERSONAL: Born February 20, 1965, in Berkeley, Calif. . . . 5-10/170. . . . Throws right, bats right. . . . Full name: Paul Tyrell Faries. . . . Name pronounced FAIR-ees.
HIGH SCHOOL: Campolindo (Moraga, Calif.).
COLLEGE: Pepperdine.
TRANSACTIONS/CAREER NOTES: Selected by San Diego Padres organization in 22nd round of free-agent draft (June 2, 1987). . . . On San Diego disabled list (May 23-June 17, 1991); included rehabilitation assignment to High Desert (June 8-17). . . . Traded by Padres to San Francisco Giants for P Jim Pena (December 10, 1992).
HONORS: Named California League Most Valuable Player (1988).
STATISTICAL NOTES: Led Northwest League second basemen with 377 total chances in 1987. . . . Led California League second basemen with .975 fielding percentage, 469 assists, 764 total chances and 81 double plays in 1988. . . . Led Texas League second basemen with .979 fielding percentage and 258 putouts in 1989. . . . Led Pacific Coast League second basemen with 363 assists in 1990.

				BATTING											FIELDING			
Year	Team (League)	Pos.	G	AB	R	H	2B	3B	HR	RBI	Avg.	BB	SO	SB	PO	A	E	Avg.
1987	—Spokane (N'west)	2B	74	280	*67	86	9	3	0	27	.307	37	25	*30	*169	*197	11	*.971
1988	—Riverside (Calif.)	2B-SS	141	*579	108	183	39	4	2	77	.316	72	79	65	288	†486	20	†.975
1989	—Wichita (Texas)	2B-SS	130	*513	79	136	25	8	6	52	.265	47	52	41	†284	391	18	†.974
1990	—Las Vegas (PCL)	2B-SS-3B	137	*552	*109	*172	29	3	5	64	.312	74	60	47	277	†418	25	.965
	—San Diego (N.L.)	2B-SS-3B	14	37	4	7	1	0	0	2	.189	4	7	0	21	34	2	.965
1991	—San Diego (N.L.)	2B-3B-SS	57	130	13	23	3	1	0	7	.177	14	21	3	80	117	2	.990
	—High Desert (Calif.)	SS-2B-3B	10	42	6	13	2	2	0	5	.310	2	3	1	14	22	6	.857
	—Las Vegas (PCL)	SS	20	75	16	23	2	1	1	12	.307	12	5	7	33	65	2	.980
1992	—Las Vegas (PCL)	3-S-2-0	125	457	77	134	15	6	1	40	.293	40	53	28	129	269	17	.959
	—San Diego (N.L.)	2B-3B-SS	10	11	3	5	1	0	0	1	.455	1	2	0	4	4	0	1.000
1993	—Phoenix (PCL)■	S-2-0-3	78	327	56	99	14	5	2	32	.303	22	30	18	121	244	3	.992
	—San Francisco (N.L.)	2B-SS-3B	15	36	6	8	2	1	0	4	.222	1	4	2	15	23	1	.974
Major league totals (4 years)			96	214	26	43	7	2	0	14	.201	20	34	5	120	178	5	.983

F

FARISS, MONTY

OF/1B, MARLINS

PERSONAL: Born October 13, 1967, in Cordell, Okla. . . . 6-4/205. . . . Throws right, bats right. . . . Full name: Monty Ted Fariss. . . . Name pronounced FARE-ess.
HIGH SCHOOL: Leedey (Okla.).
COLLEGE: Oklahoma State.
TRANSACTIONS/CAREER NOTES: Selected by New York Mets organization in seventh round of free-agent draft (June 3, 1985). . . . Selected by Texas Rangers organization in first round (sixth pick overall) of free-agent draft (June 1, 1988). . . . On Texas disabled list (April 15-May 4, 1992); included rehabilitation assignment to Oklahoma City (April 30-May 4). . . . Selected by Florida Marlins in third round (69th pick overall) of expansion draft (November 17, 1992).
HONORS: Named shortstop on THE SPORTING NEWS college All-America team (1988).
STATISTICAL NOTES: Led Texas League shortstops with 712 total chances and 94 double plays in 1988. . . . Led American Association second basemen with 276 putouts, 26 errors and 668 total chances in 1991.

				BATTING											FIELDING			
Year	Team (League)	Pos.	G	AB	R	H	2B	3B	HR	RBI	Avg.	BB	SO	SB	PO	A	E	Avg.
1988	—Butte (Pioneer)	SS	17	53	16	21	1	0	4	22	.396	20	7	2	36	52	4	.957
	—Tulsa (Texas)	SS	49	165	21	37	6	6	3	31	.224	22	39	2	77	147	18	.926
1989	—Tulsa (Texas)	SS	132	497	72	135	27	2	5	52	.272	64	112	12	*260	401	*51	.928
1990	—Tulsa (Texas)	SS	71	244	45	73	15	6	7	34	.299	33	60	8	141	190	24	.932
	—Okla. City (A.A.)	S-2-1-3	62	225	30	68	12	3	4	31	.302	34	48	1	138	151	22	.929
1991	—Okla. City (A.A.)	2B-OF	137	494	84	134	31	9	13	73	.271	91	*143	5	†288	368	†28	.959
	—Texas (A.L.)	OF-2B	19	31	6	8	1	0	1	6	.258	7	11	0	25	9	0	1.000
1992	—Texas (A.L.)	OF-2B-1B	67	166	13	36	7	1	3	21	.217	17	51	0	73	13	0	1.000
	—Okla. City (A.A.)	OF-SS	49	187	28	56	13	3	9	38	.299	31	42	5	114	5	0	1.000

Year	Team (League)	Pos.	G	AB	R	H	2B	3B	HR	RBI	Avg.	BB	SO	SB	PO	A	E	Avg.
			BATTING												FIELDING			
1993	—Florida (N.L.)■	OF	18	29	3	5	2	1	0	2	.172	5	13	0	13	0	0	1.000
	—Edmonton (PCL)	OF-1B	74	254	32	65	11	4	6	37	.256	43	74	1	285	20	3	.990
American League totals (2 years)			86	197	19	44	8	1	4	27	.223	24	62	0	98	22	0	1.000
National League totals (1 year)			18	29	3	5	2	1	0	2	.172	5	13	0	13	0	0	1.000
Major league totals (3 years)			104	226	22	49	10	2	4	29	.217	29	75	0	111	22	0	1.000

FARR, STEVE

P

PERSONAL: Born December 12, 1956, in Cheverly, Md. . . . 5-11/204. . . . Throws right, bats right. . . . Full name: Steven Michael Farr.
HIGH SCHOOL: DeMatha Catholic (Hyattsville, Md.).
COLLEGE: American and Charles County Community College (Md.).
TRANSACTIONS/CAREER NOTES: Signed as free agent by Pittsburgh Pirates organization (December 13, 1976). . . . On disabled list (June 6-22, 1979). . . . On Lynn suspended list (April 16, 1983); then transferred to restricted list (April 27-June 8, 1983). . . . Traded by Pirates organization to Buffalo, Cleveland Indians organization, for C John Malkin (June 8, 1983). . . . On Cleveland disabled list (June 20-July 5, 1984). . . . Released by Indians (March 31, 1985). . . . Signed by Kansas City Royals organization (May 9, 1985). . . . On disabled list (August 21-September 13, 1989). . . . Granted free agency (November 5, 1990). . . . Signed by New York Yankees (November 26, 1990). . . . On New York disabled list (June 30-July 18, 1992 and August 24-September 10, 1993). . . . Granted free agency (October 29, 1993).

Year	Team (League)	W	L	Pct.	ERA	G	GS	CG	ShO	Sv.	IP	H	R	ER	BB	SO
1977	—Niag. Falls (NYP)	1	5	.167	3.98	10	5	3	0	0	52	53	30	23	30	43
1978	—Char., S.C. (W. Car.)	5	3	.625	4.21	21	9	1	0	2	77	72	45	36	63	54
	—Salem (Carolina)	2	0	1.000	0.56	2	2	2	0	0	16	13	2	1	1	12
1979	—Salem (Carolina)	3	10	.231	4.99	26	15	5	0	1	119	138	81	66	47	105
1980	—Buffalo (Eastern)	11	6	.647	3.97	23	22	10	1	0	161	158	84	71	64	71
	—Portland (PCL)	0	1	.000	10.29	2	0	0	0	0	7	11	9	8	2	0
1981	—Buffalo (Eastern)	8	3	.727	3.74	29	12	0	0	3	106	102	50	44	48	82
	—Portland (PCL)	0	3	.000	7.83	4	4	0	0	0	23	39	28	20	12	19
1982	—Buffalo (Eastern)	5	8	.385	4.01	25	7	2	0	5	76⅓	72	40	34	38	84
1983	—Buffalo (Eastern)	13	1	.929	*1.61	18	15	5	2	1	112	88	28	20	50	108
1984	—Maine (Int'l)■	4	0	1.000	2.60	6	6	2	1	0	45	37	14	13	8	40
	—Cleveland (A.L.)	3	11	.214	4.58	31	16	0	0	1	116	106	61	59	46	83
1985	—Omaha (A.A.)■	10	4	.714	*2.02	17	16	7	3	0	133⅔	105	36	30	41	98
	—Kansas City (A.L.)	2	1	.667	3.11	16	3	0	0	1	37⅔	34	15	13	20	36
1986	—Kansas City (A.L.)	8	4	.667	3.13	56	0	0	0	8	109⅓	90	39	38	39	83
1987	—Kansas City (A.L.)	4	3	.571	4.15	47	0	0	0	1	91	97	47	42	44	88
	—Omaha (A.A.)	0	0	...	1.42	8	0	0	0	4	12⅔	6	3	2	6	15
1988	—Kansas City (A.L.)	5	4	.556	2.50	62	1	0	0	20	82⅔	74	25	23	30	72
1989	—Kansas City (A.L.)	2	5	.286	4.12	51	2	0	0	18	63⅓	75	35	29	22	56
1990	—Kansas City (A.L.)	13	7	.650	1.98	57	6	1	1	1	127	99	32	28	48	94
1991	—New York (A.L.)■	5	5	.500	2.19	60	0	0	0	23	70	57	19	17	20	60
1992	—New York (A.L.)	2	2	.500	1.56	50	0	0	0	30	52	34	10	9	19	37
1993	—New York (A.L.)	2	2	.500	4.21	49	0	0	0	25	47	44	22	22	28	39
Major league totals (10 years)		46	44	.511	3.17	479	28	1	1	128	796	710	305	280	316	648

CHAMPIONSHIP SERIES RECORD

Year	Team (League)	W	L	Pct.	ERA	G	GS	CG	ShO	Sv.	IP	H	R	ER	BB	SO
1985	—Kansas City (A.L.)	1	0	1.000	1.42	2	0	0	0	0	6⅓	4	1	1	1	3

WORLD SERIES RECORD

Year	Team (League)	W	L	Pct.	ERA	G	GS	CG	ShO	Sv.	IP	H	R	ER	BB	SO
1985	—Kansas City (A.L.)							Did not play.								

FARRELL, JOHN

P, ANGELS

PERSONAL: Born August 4, 1962, in Neptune, N.J. . . . 6-4/210. . . . Throws right, bats right. . . . Full name: John Edward Farrell.
HIGH SCHOOL: Shore Regional (West Long Branch, N.J.).
COLLEGE: Oklahoma State.
TRANSACTIONS/CAREER NOTES: Selected by Oakland Athletics organization in ninth round of free-agent draft (June 3, 1980). . . . Selected by Cleveland Indians organization in 16th round of free-agent draft (June 6, 1983). . . . Selected by Indians organization in second round of free-agent draft (June 4, 1984). . . . On disabled list (August 28-September 20, 1988 and March 19-April 16, 1989). . . . On Cleveland disabled list (June 25-September 21, 1990); included rehabilitation assignment to Canton/Akron (July 16-30). . . . On disabled list (April 5, 1991-entire season). . . . Granted free agency (November 22, 1991). . . . Signed by Edmonton, California Angels organization (February 12, 1992). . . . On California disabled list (April 5, 1992-entire season).
STATISTICAL NOTES: Tied for Eastern League lead with 10 hit batsmen in 1986. . . . Led American Association with 26 home runs allowed in 1987.

Year	Team (League)	W	L	Pct.	ERA	G	GS	CG	ShO	Sv.	IP	H	R	ER	BB	SO
1984	—Waterloo (Midw.)	0	5	.000	6.44	9	9	2	0	0	43⅓	59	34	31	33	29
	—Maine (Int'l)	2	1	.667	3.76	5	5	0	0	0	26⅓	20	11	11	20	12
1985	—Waterbury (East.)	7	13	.350	5.19	25	25	5	1	0	149	161	*106	86	76	75
1986	—Waterbury (East.)	9	10	.474	3.06	26	26	9	•3	0	173⅓	158	82	59	54	104
1987	—Buffalo (A.A.)	6	12	.333	5.83	25	24	2	0	0	156	155	109	101	64	91
	—Cleveland (A.L.)	5	1	.833	3.39	10	9	1	0	0	69	68	29	26	22	28
1988	—Cleveland (A.L.)	14	10	.583	4.24	31	30	4	0	0	210⅓	216	106	99	67	92
1989	—Cleveland (A.L.)	9	14	.391	3.63	31	31	7	2	0	208	196	97	84	71	132
1990	—Cleveland (A.L.)	4	5	.444	4.28	17	17	1	0	0	96⅔	108	49	46	33	44

Year	Team (League)	W	L	Pct.	ERA	G	GS	CG	ShO	Sv.	IP	H	R	ER	BB	SO
	—Cant./Akr. (East.)	1	1	.500	7.20	2	2	0	0	0	10	13	8	8	2	5
1991	—							Did not play.								
1992	—■							Did not play.								
1993	—California (A.L.)	3	12	.200	7.35	21	17	0	0	0	90⅔	110	74	74	44	45
	—Vancouver (PCL)	4	5	.444	3.99	12	12	2	0	0	85⅔	83	44	38	28	71
Major league totals (5 years)		35	42	.455	4.39	110	104	13	2	0	674⅔	698	355	329	237	341

FASSERO, JEFF

P, EXPOS

PERSONAL: Born January 5, 1963, in Springfield, Ill. . . . 6-1/195. . . . Throws left, bats left. . . . Full name: Jeffrey Joseph Fassero. . . . Name pronounced fuh-SAIR-oh.

HIGH SCHOOL: Griffin (Springfield, Ill.).

COLLEGE: Lincoln Land Community College (Ill.) and Mississippi.

TRANSACTIONS/CAREER NOTES: Selected by St. Louis Cardinals organization in 22nd round of free-agent draft (June 4, 1984). . . . Selected by Chicago White Sox organization from Cardinals organization in Rule 5 minor league draft (December 5, 1989). . . . Released by White Sox organization (April 3, 1990). . . . Signed by Cleveland Indians organization (April 9, 1990). . . . Granted free agency (October 15, 1990). . . . Signed by Indianapolis, Montreal Expos organization (January 3, 1991).

STATISTICAL NOTES: Pitched 5-0 no-hit victory for Arkansas against Jackson (June 12, 1989).

Year	Team (League)	W	L	Pct.	ERA	G	GS	CG	ShO	Sv.	IP	H	R	ER	BB	SO
1984	—Johns. City (App.)	4	7	.364	4.59	13	11	2	0	1	66⅔	65	42	34	39	59
1985	—Springfield (Midw.)	4	8	.333	4.01	29	15	1	0	1	119	125	78	53	45	65
1986	—St. Peters. (FSL)	13	7	.650	2.45	26	•26	6	1	0	*176	156	63	48	56	112
1987	—Arkansas (Texas)	10	7	.588	4.10	28	27	2	1	0	151⅓	168	90	69	67	118
1988	—Arkansas (Texas)	5	5	.500	3.58	70	1	0	0	17	78	97	48	31	41	72
1989	—Louisville (A.A.)	3	10	.231	5.22	22	19	0	0	0	112	136	79	65	47	73
	—Arkansas (Texas)	4	1	.800	1.64	6	6	2	1	0	44	32	11	8	12	38
1990	—Cant./Akr. (East.)■	5	4	.556	2.80	*61	0	0	0	6	64⅓	66	24	20	24	61
1991	—Indianapolis (A.A.)■	3	0	1.000	1.47	18	0	0	0	4	18⅓	11	3	3	7	12
	—Montreal (N.L.)	2	5	.286	2.44	51	0	0	0	8	55⅓	39	17	15	17	42
1992	—Montreal (N.L.)	8	7	.533	2.84	70	0	0	0	1	85⅔	81	35	27	34	63
1993	—Montreal (N.L.)	12	5	.706	2.29	56	15	1	0	1	149⅔	119	50	38	54	140
Major league totals (3 years)		22	17	.564	2.48	177	15	1	0	10	290⅔	239	102	80	105	245

FELDER, MIKE

OF, ASTROS

PERSONAL: Born November 18, 1962, in Vallejo, Calif. . . . 5-9/175. . . . Throws right, bats both. . . . Full name: Michael Otis Felder.

HIGH SCHOOL: John F. Kennedy (Richmond, Calif.).

COLLEGE: Contra Costa College (Calif.).

TRANSACTIONS/CAREER NOTES: Selected by Milwaukee Brewers organization in third round of free-agent draft (January 13, 1981). . . . On disabled list (April 15-26, 1984). . . . On Milwaukee disabled list (May 3-June 5, 1986); included rehabilitation assignment to El Paso (May 23-June 5). . . . On Milwaukee disabled list (May 31-August 2, 1988); included rehabilitation assignment to Denver (June 24-July 1 and July 15-28). . . . On suspended list (August 27-30, 1990). . . . Released by Brewers (April 2, 1991). . . . Signed by San Francisco Giants (April 5, 1991). . . . On disabled list (August 19-September 3, 1991). . . . Granted free agency (October 28, 1992). . . . Signed by Seattle Mariners (November 29, 1992). . . . On disabled list (August 12-September 1, 1993). . . . Traded by Mariners with P Mike Hampton to Houston Astros for OF Eric Anthony (December 10, 1993).

STATISTICAL NOTES: Led Texas League outfielders with 332 putouts and 363 total chances and tied for lead with 18 assists and 13 errors in 1983. . . . Led Texas League with nine sacrifice flies in 1984.

				BATTING											FIELDING			
Year	Team (League)	Pos.	G	AB	R	H	2B	3B	HR	RBI	Avg.	BB	SO	SB	PO	A	E	Avg.
1981	—Stockton (Calif.)	2B-OF	91	338	66	91	8	1	3	30	.269	38	42	41	172	162	13	.963
1982	—Stockton (Calif.)	OF	137	524	102	138	18	11	7	47	.263	62	79	*92	314	9	10	.970
1983	—El Paso (Texas)	OF-2B	133	554	108	156	23	10	9	78	.282	79	71	*71	†334	‡24	‡13	.965
1984	—El Paso (Texas)	OF	122	496	98	144	19	2	9	72	.290	63	57	*58	321	13	6	.982
1985	—Vancouver (PCL)	OF-2B	137	563	91	177	16	11	2	43	.314	55	70	*61	294	15	4	.987
	—Milwaukee (A.L.)	OF	15	56	8	11	1	0	0	0	.196	5	6	4	32	1	0	1.000
1986	—Milwaukee (A.L.)	OF	44	155	24	37	2	4	1	13	.239	13	13	16	98	0	0	1.000
	—El Paso (Texas)	OF	8	31	10	14	3	0	0	2	.452	5	3	7	14	0	0	1.000
	—Vancouver (PCL)	OF	39	153	21	40	3	4	1	15	.261	17	15	4	83	4	4	.956
1987	—Milwaukee (A.L.)	OF-2B	108	289	48	77	5	7	2	31	.266	28	23	34	190	10	5	.976
	—Denver (A.A.)	OF-2B	27	113	26	41	6	2	2	20	.363	14	6	17	75	3	1	.987
1988	—Milwaukee (A.L.)	OF-2B	50	81	14	14	1	0	0	5	.173	0	11	8	40	1	1	.976
	—Denver (A.A.)	OF	20	78	10	21	4	1	0	5	.269	5	10	8	55	1	1	.982
1989	—Milwaukee (A.L.)	OF-2B	117	315	50	76	11	3	3	23	.241	23	38	26	203	24	4	.983
1990	—Milwaukee (A.L.)	OF-2B-3B	121	237	38	65	7	2	3	27	.274	22	17	20	167	9	5	.972
1991	—San Francisco (N.L.)■	OF-3B	132	348	51	92	10	6	0	18	.264	30	31	21	193	8	4	.980
1992	—San Francisco (N.L.)	OF-2B	145	322	44	92	13	3	4	23	.286	21	29	14	159	3	1	.994
1993	—Seattle (A.L.)■	OF-3B	109	342	31	72	7	5	1	20	.211	22	34	15	143	12	2	.987
American League totals (7 years)			564	1475	213	352	34	21	10	119	.239	113	142	123	873	57	17	.982
National League totals (2 years)			277	670	95	184	23	9	4	41	.275	51	60	35	352	11	5	.986
Major league totals (9 years)			841	2145	308	536	57	30	14	160	.250	164	202	158	1225	68	22	.983

FELIX, JUNIOR

OF

PERSONAL: Born October 3, 1967, in Laguna Sabada, Dominican Republic. . . . 5-11/165. . . . Throws right, bats both. . . . Full name: Junior Francisco Sanchez Felix.

TRANSACTIONS/CAREER NOTES: Signed as free agent by Toronto Blue Jays organization (September 15, 1985). . . . On suspended list (July 15, 1988-remainder of season). . . . On disabled list (July 13-August 9, 1990). . . . Traded by Blue Jays with IF Luis Sojo and a player to be named later to California Angels for OF Devon White, P Willie Fraser and a player to be named later (December 2, 1990); Blue Jays acquired P Marcus Moore and

Angels acquired C Ken Rivers to complete deal (December 4, 1990).... On California disabled list (June 2-17, 1991).... On California disabled list (June 20-August 25, 1991); included rehabilitation assignment to Palm Springs (August 5-24).... On California disabled list (May 27-June 11, 1992).... Selected by Florida Marlins in third round (59th pick overall) of expansion draft (November 17, 1992).... Released by Edmonton, Marlins organization (July 6, 1993).
STATISTICAL NOTES: Led Pioneer League outfielders with 165 total chances in 1986.... Led Pioneer League in caught stealing with nine and tied for lead in being hit by pitch with six in 1986.... Led South Atlantic League in caught stealing with 28 in 1987.... Hit home run in first major league at-bat on first pitch (May 4, 1989).

			BATTING												FIELDING			
Year	**Team (League)**	**Pos.**	**G**	**AB**	**R**	**H**	**2B**	**3B**	**HR**	**RBI**	**Avg.**	**BB**	**SO**	**SB**	**PO**	**A**	**E**	**Avg.**
1986	—Medicine Hat (Pio.)	OF	67	263	57	75	9	3	4	28	.285	35	*84	*37	*152	8	5	.970
1987	—Myrtle Beach (SAL)	OF	124	466	70	135	15	•9	12	51	.290	43	124	64	188	8	9	.956
1988	—Knoxville (South.)	OF	93	360	52	91	16	5	3	25	.253	20	82	40	190	13	11	.949
1989	—Syracuse (Int'l)	OF	21	87	17	24	4	2	1	10	.276	9	18	13	42	0	1	.977
	—Toronto (A.L.)	OF	110	415	62	107	14	8	9	46	.258	33	101	18	243	9	9	.966
1990	—Toronto (A.L.)	OF	127	463	73	122	23	7	15	65	.263	45	99	13	244	11	9	.966
1991	—California (A.L.)■	OF	66	230	32	65	10	2	2	26	.283	11	55	7	126	1	3	.977
	—Palm Springs (Cal.)	OF	18	64	12	23	3	0	2	10	.359	16	11	8	30	0	1	.968
1992	—California (A.L.)	OF	139	509	63	125	22	5	9	72	.246	33	128	8	340	9	6	.983
1993	—Florida (N.L.)■	OF	57	214	25	51	11	1	7	22	.238	10	50	2	91	3	6	.940
	—Edmonton (PCL)	OF	7	31	7	11	2	0	0	5	.355	4	8	0	18	1	0	1.000
American League totals (4 years)			442	1617	230	419	69	22	35	209	.259	122	383	46	953	30	27	.973
National League totals (1 year)			57	214	25	51	11	1	7	22	.238	10	50	2	91	3	6	.940
Major league totals (5 years)			499	1831	255	470	80	23	42	231	.257	132	433	48	1044	33	33	.970

CHAMPIONSHIP SERIES RECORD

			BATTING												FIELDING			
Year	**Team (League)**	**Pos.**	**G**	**AB**	**R**	**H**	**2B**	**3B**	**HR**	**RBI**	**Avg.**	**BB**	**SO**	**SB**	**PO**	**A**	**E**	**Avg.**
1989	—Toronto (A.L.)	OF	3	11	0	3	1	0	0	3	.273	0	2	0	8	0	0	1.000

FERMIN, FELIX

SS, MARINERS

PERSONAL: Born October 9, 1963, in Mao, Valverde, Dominican Republic.... 5-11/170.... Throws right, bats right.... Full name: Felix Jose Fermin.... Name pronounced fair-MEEN.
COLLEGE: U.C.E. College (San Pedro de Macoris, Dominican Republic).
TRANSACTIONS/CAREER NOTES: Signed as free agent by Pittsburgh Pirates organization (June 11, 1983).... On Pittsburgh disabled list (July 19-August 24, 1987); included rehabilitation assignment to Harrisburg (August 12-24).... Traded by Pirates to Cleveland Indians for SS Jay Bell (March 25, 1989).... On Cleveland disabled list (April 23-May 12, 1991); included rehabilitation assignment to Colorado Springs (May 5-12).... Traded by Indians with 1B Reggie Jefferson and cash to Seattle Mariners for SS Omar Vizquel (December 20, 1993).
RECORDS: Shares major league single-game record for most sacrifice hits—4 (August 22, 1989, 10 innings).... Holds A.L. single-season records for fewest long hits (150 or more games)—10 (1989); and fewest errors by shortstop who led league in errors—23 (1993).
STATISTICAL NOTES: Tied for New York-Pennsylvania League lead in double plays by shortstop with 38 in 1983.... Led Eastern League shortstops with .964 fielding percentage, 251 putouts and 661 total chances in 1985.... Led Eastern League shortstops with .968 fielding percentage in 1987.... Led A.L. with 32 sacrifice hits in 1989.... Led A.L. shortstops with 26 errors in 1989.

			BATTING												FIELDING			
Year	**Team (League)**	**Pos.**	**G**	**AB**	**R**	**H**	**2B**	**3B**	**HR**	**RBI**	**Avg.**	**BB**	**SO**	**SB**	**PO**	**A**	**E**	**Avg.**
1983	—Watertown (NYP)	SS	67	234	27	46	6	1	0	14	.197	16	30	5	94	223	30	.914
	—GC Pirates (GCL)	SS	1	4	1	1	0	0	0	1	.250	0	0	0	1	4	0	1.000
1984	—Prin. William (Car.)	SS	119	382	34	94	13	1	0	41	.246	29	32	32	181	376	23	*.960
1985	—Nashua (Eastern)	SS-2B	137	443	32	100	10	2	0	27	.226	37	30	29	†251	387	24	†.964
1986	—Hawaii (PCL)	SS-2B	39	125	13	32	5	0	0	9	.256	7	13	1	60	99	7	.958
	—Prin. William (Car.)	SS	84	322	58	90	10	1	0	26	.280	25	19	40	158	205	19	.950
1987	—Harrisburg (East.)	SS-2B	100	399	62	107	9	5	0	35	.268	27	22	22	177	288	15	†.969
	—Pittsburgh (N.L.)	SS	23	68	6	17	0	0	0	4	.250	4	9	0	36	62	2	.980
1988	—Buffalo (A.A.)	SS	87	352	38	92	11	1	0	31	.261	17	18	8	131	268	10	.976
	—Pittsburgh (N.L.)	SS	43	87	9	24	0	2	0	2	.276	8	10	3	51	76	6	.955
1989	—Cleveland (A.L.)■	SS-2B	156	484	50	115	9	1	0	21	.238	41	27	6	253	517	†26	.967
1990	—Cleveland (A.L.)	SS-2B	148	414	47	106	13	2	1	40	.256	26	22	3	214	423	16	.975
1991	—Cleveland (A.L.)	SS	129	424	30	111	13	2	0	31	.262	26	27	5	214	372	12	.980
	—Colo. Springs (PCL)	SS	2	8	1	2	0	0	0	1	.250	0	0	0	2	5	0	1.000
1992	—Cleveland (A.L.)	S-3-2-1	79	215	27	58	7	2	0	13	.270	18	10	0	79	168	8	.969
1993	—Cleveland (A.L.)	SS	140	480	48	126	16	2	2	45	.263	24	14	4	211	346	*23	.960
American League totals (5 years)			652	2017	202	516	58	9	3	150	.256	135	100	18	971	1826	85	.971
National League totals (2 years)			66	155	15	41	0	2	0	6	.265	12	19	3	87	138	8	.966
Major league totals (7 years)			718	2172	217	557	58	11	3	156	.256	147	119	21	1058	1964	93	.970

FERNANDEZ, ALEX

P, WHITE SOX

PERSONAL: Born August 13, 1969, in Miami Beach, Fla.... 6-1/215.... Throws right, bats right.... Full name: Alexander Fernandez.
HIGH SCHOOL: Pace (Miami).
COLLEGE: Miami (Fla.) and Miami-Dade (South) Community College.
TRANSACTIONS/CAREER NOTES: Selected by Milwaukee Brewers organization in first round (24th pick overall) of free-agent draft (June 1, 1988).... Selected by Chicago White Sox organization in first round (fourth pick overall) of free-agent draft (June 4, 1990).
HONORS: Named Golden Spikes Award winner by USA Baseball (1990).

Year	Team (League)	W	L	Pct.	ERA	G	GS	CG	ShO	Sv.	IP	H	R	ER	BB	SO
1990	—GC Whi. Sox (GCL)	1	0	1.000	3.60	2	2	0	0	0	10	11	4	4	1	16
	—Sarasota (Fla. St.)	1	1	.500	1.84	2	2	0	0	0	14⅔	8	4	3	3	23
	—Birm. (Southern)	3	0	1.000	1.08	4	4	0	0	0	25	20	7	3	6	27
	—Chicago (A.L.)	5	5	.500	3.80	13	13	3	0	0	87⅔	89	40	37	34	61
1991	—Chicago (A.L.)	9	13	.409	4.51	34	32	2	0	0	191⅔	186	100	96	88	145
1992	—Chicago (A.L.)	8	11	.421	4.27	29	29	4	2	0	187⅔	199	100	89	50	95
	—Vancouver (PCL)	2	1	.667	0.94	4	3	2	1	0	28⅔	15	8	3	6	27
1993	—Chicago (A.L.)	18	9	.667	3.13	34	34	3	1	0	247⅓	221	95	86	67	169
Major league totals (4 years)		40	38	.513	3.88	110	108	12	3	0	714⅓	695	335	308	239	470

CHAMPIONSHIP SERIES RECORD

Year	Team (League)	W	L	Pct.	ERA	G	GS	CG	ShO	Sv.	IP	H	R	ER	BB	SO
1993	—Chicago (A.L.)	0	2	.000	1.80	2	2	0	0	0	15	15	6	3	6	10

FERNANDEZ, SID

P, ORIOLES

PERSONAL: Born October 12, 1962, in Honolulu. . . . 6-1/225. . . . Throws left, bats left. . . . Full name: Charles Sidney Fernandez.

HIGH SCHOOL: Kaiser (Honolulu).

TRANSACTIONS/CAREER NOTES: Selected by Los Angeles Dodgers organization in third round of free-agent draft (June 8, 1981). . . . Traded by Dodgers with IF Ross Jones to New York Mets for P Carlos Diaz and a player to be named later (December 8, 1983); Dodgers acquired IF Bob Bailor to complete deal (December 12, 1983). . . . On disabled list (August 4-22, 1987). . . . On New York disabled list (March 12-July 18, 1991); included rehabilitation assignment to St. Lucie (June 22-27), Tidewater (June 27-July 7 and July 14-16) and Williamsport (July 7-14). . . . On New York disabled list (May 1-July 29, 1993); included rehabilitation assignment to St. Lucie (July 11-17) and Binghamton (July). . . . Granted free agency (October 25, 1993). . . . Signed by Baltimore Orioles (November 22, 1993).

HONORS: Named Texas League Pitcher of the Year (1983).

STATISTICAL NOTES: Pitched 5-0 no-hit victory for Vero Beach against Winter Haven (April 24, 1982). . . . Pitched 1-0 no-hit victory for Vero Beach against Fort Lauderdale (June 8, 1982).

Year	Team (League)	W	L	Pct.	ERA	G	GS	CG	ShO	Sv.	IP	H	R	ER	BB	SO
1981	—Lethbridge (Pio.)	5	1	.833	★1.54	11	11	2	1	0	76	43	21	13	31	★128
1982	—Vero Beach (FSL)	8	1	.889	1.91	12	12	5	4	0	84⅔	38	19	18	38	★137
	—Albuquerque (PCL)	6	5	.545	5.42	13	13	5	0	0	88	76	54	53	52	86
1983	—San Antonio (Tex.)	•13	4	.765	★2.82	24	24	4	1	0	153	111	61	48	96	★209
	—Los Angeles (N.L.)	0	1	.000	6.00	2	1	0	0	0	6	7	4	4	7	9
1984	—Tidewater (Int'l)■	6	5	.545	2.56	17	17	3	0	0	105⅔	69	39	30	63	123
	—New York (N.L.)	6	6	.500	3.50	15	15	0	0	0	90	74	40	35	34	62
1985	—Tidewater (Int'l)	4	1	.800	2.04	5	5	1	0	0	35⅓	17	8	8	21	42
	—New York (N.L.)	9	9	.500	2.80	26	26	3	0	0	170⅓	108	56	53	80	180
1986	—New York (N.L.)	16	6	.727	3.52	32	31	2	1	1	204⅓	161	82	80	91	200
1987	—New York (N.L.)	12	8	.600	3.81	28	27	3	1	0	156	130	75	66	67	134
1988	—New York (N.L.)	12	10	.545	3.03	31	31	1	1	0	187	127	69	63	70	189
1989	—New York (N.L.)	14	5	.737	2.83	35	32	6	2	0	219⅓	157	73	69	75	198
1990	—New York (N.L.)	9	14	.391	3.46	30	30	2	1	0	179⅓	130	79	69	67	181
1991	—St. Lucie (Fla. St.)	0	0	...	0.00	1	1	0	0	0	3	1	0	0	1	4
	—Tidewater (Int'l)	1	0	1.000	1.15	3	3	0	0	0	15⅔	9	2	2	6	22
	—Williamsport (East.)	0	0	...	0.00	1	1	0	0	0	6	3	0	0	1	5
	—New York (N.L.)	1	3	.250	2.86	8	8	0	0	0	44	36	18	14	9	31
1992	—New York (N.L.)	14	11	.560	2.73	32	32	5	2	0	214⅔	162	67	65	67	193
1993	—New York (N.L.)	5	6	.455	2.93	18	18	1	1	0	119⅔	82	42	39	36	81
	—St. Lucie (Fla. St.)	0	0	...	4.50	1	1	0	0	0	4	3	2	2	1	7
	—Binghamton (East.)	0	1	.000	1.80	2	2	0	0	0	10	6	2	2	3	11
Major league totals (11 years)		98	79	.554	3.15	257	251	23	9	1	1590⅔	1174	605	557	603	1458

CHAMPIONSHIP SERIES RECORD

Year	Team (League)	W	L	Pct.	ERA	G	GS	CG	ShO	Sv.	IP	H	R	ER	BB	SO
1986	—New York (N.L.)	0	1	.000	4.50	1	1	0	0	0	6	3	3	3	1	5
1988	—New York (N.L.)	0	1	.000	13.50	1	1	0	0	0	4	7	6	6	1	5
Champ. series totals (2 years)		0	2	.000	8.10	2	2	0	0	0	10	10	9	9	2	10

WORLD SERIES RECORD

Year	Team (League)	W	L	Pct.	ERA	G	GS	CG	ShO	Sv.	IP	H	R	ER	BB	SO
1986	—New York (N.L.)	0	0	...	1.35	3	0	0	0	0	6⅔	6	1	1	1	10

ALL-STAR GAME RECORD

Year	League	W	L	Pct.	ERA	GS	CG	ShO	Sv.	IP	H	R	ER	BB	SO
1986	—National	0	0	...	0.00	0	0	0	0	1	0	0	0	2	3
1987	—National	0	0	...	0.00	0	0	0	1	1	0	0	0	1	1
All-Star totals (2 years)		0	0	...	0.00	0	0	0	1	2	0	0	0	3	4

FERNANDEZ, TONY

SS

PERSONAL: Born June 30, 1962, in San Pedro de Macoris, Dominican Republic. . . . 6-2/175. . . . Throws right, bats both. . . . Full name: Octavio Antonio Castro Fernandez.

HIGH SCHOOL: Gasto Fernando (San Pedro de Macoris, Dominican Republic).

TRANSACTIONS/CAREER NOTES: Signed as free agent by Toronto Blue Jays organization (April 24, 1979). . . . On Syracuse disabled list (August 10-27, 1981). . . . On disabled list (April 8-May 2, 1989). . . . Traded by Blue Jays with 1B Fred McGriff to San Diego Padres for OF Joe Carter and 2B Roberto Alomar (December 5, 1990). . . . Traded by Padres to New York Mets for P

Wally Whitehurst, OF D.J. Dozier and a player to be named later (October 26, 1992); Padres acquired C Raul Casanova from Mets to complete deal (December 7, 1992).... Traded by Mets to Blue Jays for OF Darrin Jackson (June 11, 1993).... Granted free agency (November 3, 1993).
RECORDS: Shares major league career record for highest fielding percentage by shortstop (1,000 or more games)—.980.... Shares major league record for most times caught stealing in one inning—2 (June 26, 1992, fifth inning).... Holds A.L. career record for highest fielding percentage by shortstop (1000 or more games)—.982.... Holds A.L. single-season record for most games by shortstop—163 (1986).... Shares A.L. single-season record for most games by switch-hitter—163 (1986).
HONORS: Named shortstop on THE SPORTING NEWS A.L. All-Star team (1986).... Won A.L. Gold Glove at shortstop (1986-89).
STATISTICAL NOTES: Led International League shortstops with 87 double plays in 1983.... Led A.L. shortstops with 791 total chances in 1985 and 786 in 1990.

			BATTING												FIELDING			
Year	**Team (League)**	**Pos.**	**G**	**AB**	**R**	**H**	**2B**	**3B**	**HR**	**RBI**	**Avg.**	**BB**	**SO**	**SB**	**PO**	**A**	**E**	**Avg.**
1980	—Kinston (Carolina) ...	SS	62	187	28	52	6	2	0	12	.278	28	17	7	93	205	28	.914
1981	—Kinston (Carolina) ...	SS	75	280	57	89	10	6	1	13	.318	49	20	15	121	227	19	.948
	—Syracuse (Int'l)	SS	31	115	13	32	6	2	1	9	.278	7	15	9	69	80	3	.980
1982	—Syracuse (Int'l)	SS	134	523	78	158	21	6	4	56	.302	42	31	22	*246	364	23	*.964
1983	—Syracuse (Int'l)	SS	117	437	65	131	18	6	5	38	.300	57	27	35	*211	361	26	.957
	—Toronto (A.L.)...........	SS	15	34	5	9	1	1	0	2	.265	2	2	0	16	17	0	1.000
1984	—Syracuse (Int'l)	SS	26	94	12	24	1	0	0	6	.255	13	9	1	46	72	5	.959
	—Toronto (A.L.)...........	SS-3B	88	233	29	63	5	3	3	19	.270	17	15	5	119	195	9	.972
1985	—Toronto (A.L.)...........	SS	161	564	71	163	31	10	2	51	.289	43	41	13	283	*478	30	.962
1986	—Toronto (A.L.)...........	SS	*163	*687	91	213	33	9	10	65	.310	27	52	25	*294	445	13	*.983
1987	—Toronto (A.L.)...........	SS	146	578	90	186	29	8	5	67	.322	51	48	32	*270	396	14	.979
1988	—Toronto (A.L.)...........	SS	154	648	76	186	41	4	5	70	.287	45	65	15	247	470	14	.981
1989	—Toronto (A.L.)...........	SS	140	573	64	147	25	9	11	64	.257	29	51	22	260	475	6	*.992
1990	—Toronto (A.L.)...........	SS	161	635	84	175	27	*17	4	66	.276	71	70	26	*297	*480	9	.989
1991	—San Diego (N.L.)■.....	SS	145	558	81	152	27	5	4	38	.272	55	74	23	247	440	20	.972
1992	—San Diego (N.L.)	SS	155	622	84	171	32	4	4	37	.275	56	62	20	240	405	11	.983
1993	—New York (N.L.)	SS	48	173	20	39	5	2	1	14	.225	25	19	6	83	150	6	.975
	—Toronto (A.L.)■	SS	94	353	45	108	18	9	4	50	.306	31	26	15	196	260	7	.985
American League totals (9 years)			1122	4305	555	1250	210	70	44	454	.290	316	370	153	1982	3216	102	.981
National League totals (3 years)			348	1353	185	362	64	11	9	89	.268	136	155	49	570	995	37	.977
Major league totals (11 years)			1470	5658	740	1612	274	81	53	543	.285	452	525	202	2552	4211	139	.980

CHAMPIONSHIP SERIES RECORD

			BATTING												FIELDING			
Year	**Team (League)**	**Pos.**	**G**	**AB**	**R**	**H**	**2B**	**3B**	**HR**	**RBI**	**Avg.**	**BB**	**SO**	**SB**	**PO**	**A**	**E**	**Avg.**
1985	—Toronto (A.L.)...........	SS	7	24	2	8	2	0	0	2	.333	1	2	0	11	15	2	.929
1989	—Toronto (A.L.)...........	SS	5	20	6	7	3	0	0	1	.350	1	2	5	9	15	0	1.000
1993	—Toronto (A.L.)...........	SS	6	22	1	7	0	0	0	1	.318	2	4	0	12	8	0	1.000
Championship series totals (3 years)			18	66	9	22	5	0	0	4	.333	4	8	5	32	38	2	.972

WORLD SERIES RECORD

			BATTING												FIELDING			
Year	**Team (League)**	**Pos.**	**G**	**AB**	**R**	**H**	**2B**	**3B**	**HR**	**RBI**	**Avg.**	**BB**	**SO**	**SB**	**PO**	**A**	**E**	**Avg.**
1993	—Toronto (A.L.)...........	SS	6	21	2	7	1	0	0	9	.333	3	3	0	11	8	0	1.000

ALL-STAR GAME RECORD

			BATTING											FIELDING			
Year	**League**	**Pos.**	**AB**	**R**	**H**	**2B**	**3B**	**HR**	**RBI**	**Avg.**	**BB**	**SO**	**SB**	**PO**	**A**	**E**	**Avg.**
1986	—American..................	SS	0	0	0	0	0	0	0	...	0	0	0	0	0	0	...
1987	—American..................	SS	2	0	0	0	0	0	0	.000	0	0	0	1	3	0	1.000
1989	—American..................	PR-SS	1	0	0	0	0	0	0	.000	0	0	0	2	2	0	1.000
1992	—National....................	SS	2	1	1	0	0	0	0	.500	0	0	0	3	0	0	1.000
All-Star Game totals (4 years)			5	1	1	0	0	0	0	.200	0	0	0	6	5	0	1.000

FERRY, MIKE

P, REDS

PERSONAL: Born July 26, 1969, in Appleton, Wis.... 6-3/200.... Throws right, bats right.... Full name: Michael Edward Ferry.
HIGH SCHOOL: Central High of Tuscaloosa (Tuscaloosa, Ala.).
COLLEGE: Auburn.
TRANSACTIONS/CAREER NOTES: Selected by Cincinnati Reds organization in fourth round of free-agent draft (June 4, 1990).... On disabled list (May 4-14, 1992).

Year	**Team (League)**	**W**	**L**	**Pct.**	**ERA**	**G**	**GS**	**CG**	**ShO**	**Sv.**	**IP**	**H**	**R**	**ER**	**BB**	**SO**
1990	—Billings (Pioneer)	2	5	.286	2.84	27	0	0	0	*11	31⅔	29	13	10	12	29
1991	—Ced. Rap. (Midw.)	2	2	.500	6.66	16	0	0	0	3	25⅔	25	19	19	21	27
	—Char., W.Va. (SAL)	1	3	.250	4.47	22	1	0	0	2	44⅓	41	23	22	21	51
1992	—Ced. Rap. (Midw.)	13	4	.765	2.71	25	25	6	0	0	162⅔	134	57	49	40	143
1993	—Chatt. (South.)	•13	8	.619	3.42	28	•28	•4	1	0	*186⅔	176	85	71	30	111

FETTERS, MIKE

P, BREWERS

PERSONAL: Born December 19, 1964, in Van Nuys, Calif.... 6-4/215.... Throws right, bats right.... Full name: Michael Lee Fetters.
HIGH SCHOOL: Iolani (Hawaii).
COLLEGE: Pepperdine.
TRANSACTIONS/CAREER NOTES: Selected by Los Angeles Dodgers organization in 22nd round of free-agent draft (June 6, 1983).... Selected by California Angels organization in supplemental round ("sandwich pick" between first and second round, 27th

pick overall) of free-agent draft (June 2, 1986); pick received as compensation for Baltimore Orioles signing Type A free agent Juan Beniquez. . . . Traded by Angels with P Glenn Carter to Milwaukee Brewers for P Chuck Crim (December 10, 1991). . . . On disabled list (May 3-19, 1992).

Year	Team (League)	W	L	Pct.	ERA	G	GS	CG	ShO	Sv.	IP	H	R	ER	BB	SO
1986	—Salem (Northwest).....	4	2	.667	3.38	12	12	1	0	0	72	60	39	27	51	72
1987	—Palm Springs (Cal.)....	9	7	.563	3.57	19	19	2	0	0	116	106	62	46	73	105
1988	—Midland (Texas)	8	8	.500	5.92	20	20	2	0	0	114	116	78	75	67	101
	—Edmonton (PCL)	2	0	1.000	1.93	2	2	1	0	0	14	8	3	3	10	11
1989	—Edmonton (PCL)	12	8	.600	3.80	26	26	•6	2	0	168	160	80	71	72	*144
	—California (A.L.)	0	0	...	8.10	1	0	0	0	0	3⅓	5	4	3	1	4
1990	—Edmonton (PCL)	1	1	.500	0.99	5	5	1	1	0	27⅓	22	9	3	13	26
	—California (A.L.)	1	1	.500	4.12	26	2	0	0	1	67⅔	77	33	31	20	35
1991	—Edmonton (PCL)	2	7	.222	4.87	11	11	1	0	0	61	65	39	33	26	43
	—California (A.L.)	2	5	.286	4.84	19	4	0	0	0	44⅔	53	29	24	28	24
1992	—Milwaukee (A.L.)■.....	5	1	.833	1.87	50	0	0	0	2	62⅔	38	15	13	24	43
1993	—Milwaukee (A.L.)	3	3	.500	3.34	45	0	0	0	0	59⅓	59	29	22	22	23
	Major league totals (5 years).	11	10	.524	3.52	141	6	0	0	3	237⅔	232	110	93	95	129

FIELDER, CECIL

1B, TIGERS

PERSONAL: Born September 21, 1963, in Los Angeles. . . . 6-3/250. . . . Throws right, bats right. . . . Full name: Cecil Grant Fielder.
HIGH SCHOOL: Nogales (La Puente, Calif.).
COLLEGE: UNLV.

TRANSACTIONS/CAREER NOTES: Selected by Baltimore Orioles organization in 31st round of free-agent draft (June 8, 1981). . . . Selected by Kansas City Royals organization in secondary phase of free-agent draft (June 7, 1982). . . . Traded by Royals organization to Toronto Blue Jays organization for OF Leon Roberts (February 4, 1983). . . . Contract sold by Blue Jays to Hanshin Tigers of Japan Central League (December 22, 1988). . . . Signed as free agent by Detroit Tigers (January 15, 1990).
RECORDS: Shares major league records for most consecutive years leading league in runs batted in—3 (1990-92); most years without a stolen base (150 games or more per year)—4. . . . Shares major league single-season record for most games with three home runs—2 (1990).
HONORS: Named A.L. Player of the Year by THE SPORTING NEWS (1990). . . . Named first baseman on THE SPORTING NEWS A.L. All-Star team (1990-91). . . . Named first baseman on THE SPORTING NEWS A.L. Silver Slugger team (1990-91).
STATISTICAL NOTES: Led Pioneer League in total bases with 176 and in being hit by pitch with eight in 1982. . . . Led A.L. with 339 total bases and .592 slugging percentage in 1990. . . . Led A.L. first basemen with 137 double plays in 1990. . . . Hit three home runs in one game (May 6 and June 6, 1990).

			BATTING												FIELDING			
Year	Team (League)	Pos.	G	AB	R	H	2B	3B	HR	RBI	Avg.	BB	SO	SB	PO	A	E	Avg.
1982	—Butte (Pioneer).........	1B	69	273	73	88	*28	0	*20	68	.322	37	62	3	247	18	4	.985
1983	—Florence (S. Atl.)■....	1B	140	500	81	156	28	2	16	94	.312	58	90	2	957	64	16	.985
1984	—Kinston (Carolina) ...	1B	61	222	42	63	12	1	19	49	.284	28	44	2	533	24	9	.984
	—Knoxville (South.)	1B	64	236	33	60	12	2	9	44	.254	22	48	0	173	10	4	.979
1985	—Knoxville (South.)	1B	96	361	52	106	26	2	18	81	.294	45	83	0	444	26	6	.987
	—Toronto (A.L.)...........	1B	30	74	6	23	4	0	4	16	.311	6	16	0	171	17	4	.979
1986	—Toronto (A.L.)..........	1B-3B-OF	34	83	7	13	2	0	4	13	.157	6	27	0	37	4	1	.976
	—Syracuse (Int'l)	OF-1B	88	325	47	91	13	3	18	68	.280	32	91	0	117	5	1	.992
1987	—Toronto (A.L.)...........	1B-3B	82	175	30	47	7	1	14	32	.269	20	48	0	98	6	0	1.000
1988	—Toronto (A.L.)..........	1B-3B-2B	74	174	24	40	6	1	9	23	.230	14	53	0	101	12	1	.991
1989	—Hanshin (Jp. Cn.)■...	...	106	384	60	116	11	0	38	81	.302	67	107	0	...	...	...	...
1990	—Detroit (A.L.)■..........	1B	159	573	104	159	25	1	*51	*132	.277	90	*182	0	1190	111	14	.989
1991	—Detroit (A.L.)	1B	•162	624	102	163	25	0	•44	*133	.261	78	151	0	1055	83	8	.993
1992	—Detroit (A.L.)	1B	155	594	80	145	22	0	35	*124	.244	73	151	0	957	92	10	.991
1993	—Detroit (A.L.)	1B	154	573	80	153	23	0	30	117	.267	90	125	0	971	78	10	.991
	Major league totals (8 years)		850	2870	433	743	114	3	191	590	.259	377	753	0	4580	403	48	.990

CHAMPIONSHIP SERIES RECORD

			BATTING												FIELDING			
Year	Team (League)	Pos.	G	AB	R	H	2B	3B	HR	RBI	Avg.	BB	SO	SB	PO	A	E	Avg.
1985	—Toronto (A.L.)...........	PH	3	3	0	1	1	0	0	0	.333	0	0	0	...	...	...	...

ALL-STAR GAME RECORD

			BATTING											FIELDING			
Year	League	Pos.	AB	R	H	2B	3B	HR	RBI	Avg.	BB	SO	SB	PO	A	E	Avg.
1990	—American..................	PH-1B	1	0	0	0	0	0	0	.000	0	0	0	3	1	0	1.000
1991	—American..................	1B	3	0	0	0	0	0	0	.000	0	1	0	6	2	0	1.000
1993	—American..................	1B	1	0	0	0	0	0	0	.000	0	0	0	4	0	0	1.000
	All-Star Game totals (3 years)		5	0	0	0	0	0	0	.000	0	1	0	13	3	0	1.000

FINLEY, CHUCK

P, ANGELS

PERSONAL: Born November 26, 1962, in Monroe, La. . . . 6-6/214. . . . Throws left, bats left. . . . Full name: Charles Edward Finley.
HIGH SCHOOL: West Monroe (La.).
COLLEGE: Northeast Louisiana.

TRANSACTIONS/CAREER NOTES: Selected by California Angels organization in 15th round of free-agent draft (June 4, 1984). . . . Selected by Angels organization in secondary phase of free-agent draft (January 9, 1985). . . . On disabled list (August 22-September 15, 1989 and April 6-22, 1992).
HONORS: Named lefthanded pitcher on THE SPORTING NEWS A.L. All-Star team (1989-90).

Year	Team (League)	W	L	Pct.	ERA	G	GS	CG	ShO	Sv.	IP	H	R	ER	BB	SO
1985	—Salem (Northwest)	3	1	.750	4.66	18	0	0	0	5	29	34	21	15	10	32
1986	—Quad Cities (Mid.)	1	0	1.000	0.00	10	0	0	0	6	12	4	0	0	3	16
	—California (A.L.)	3	1	.750	3.30	25	0	0	0	0	46⅓	40	17	17	23	37
1987	—California (A.L.)	2	7	.222	4.67	35	3	0	0	0	90⅔	102	54	47	43	63
1988	—California (A.L.)	9	15	.375	4.17	31	31	2	0	0	194⅓	191	95	90	82	111
1989	—California (A.L.)	16	9	.640	2.57	29	29	9	1	0	199⅔	171	64	57	82	156
1990	—California (A.L.)	18	9	.667	2.40	32	32	7	2	0	236	210	77	63	81	177
1991	—California (A.L.)	18	9	.667	3.80	34	34	4	2	0	227⅓	205	102	96	101	171
1992	—California (A.L.)	7	12	.368	3.96	31	31	4	1	0	204⅓	212	99	90	98	124
1993	—California (A.L.)	16	14	.533	3.15	35	35	*13	2	0	251⅓	243	108	88	82	187
Major league totals (8 years)		89	76	.539	3.40	252	195	39	8	0	1450	1374	616	548	592	1026

CHAMPIONSHIP SERIES RECORD

Year	Team (League)	W	L	Pct.	ERA	G	GS	CG	ShO	Sv.	IP	H	R	ER	BB	SO
1986	—California (A.L.)	0	0	...	0.00	3	0	0	0	0	2	1	0	0	0	1

ALL-STAR GAME RECORD

Year	League	W	L	Pct.	ERA	GS	CG	ShO	Sv.	IP	H	R	ER	BB	SO
1989	—American	Did not play.													
1990	—American	0	0	...	0.00	0	0	0	0	1	0	0	0	1	1
All-Star totals (1 year)		0	0	...	0.00	0	0	0	0	1	0	0	0	1	1

FINLEY, STEVE

OF, ASTROS

PERSONAL: Born March 12, 1965, in Union City, Tenn.... 6-2/180.... Throws left, bats left.... Full name: Steven Allen Finley.
HIGH SCHOOL: Paducah (Ky.) Tilghman.
COLLEGE: Southern Illinois (degree in physiology).
TRANSACTIONS/CAREER NOTES: Selected by Atlanta Braves organization in 11th round of free-agent draft (June 2, 1986).... Selected by Baltimore Orioles organization in 13th round of free-agent draft (June 2, 1987).... On Baltimore disabled list (April 4-22, 1989).... On Baltimore disabled list (July 29-September 1, 1989); included rehabilitation assignment to Hagerstown (August 21-23).... Traded by Orioles with P Pete Harnisch and P Curt Schilling to Houston Astros for 1B Glenn Davis (January 10, 1991).... On disabled list (April 25-May 14, 1993).
STATISTICAL NOTES: Led International League outfielders with 315 total chances in 1988.

			BATTING												FIELDING			
Year	Team (League)	Pos.	G	AB	R	H	2B	3B	HR	RBI	Avg.	BB	SO	SB	PO	A	E	Avg.
1987	—Newark (NY-Penn)	OF	54	222	40	65	13	2	3	33	.293	22	24	26	122	7	4	.970
	—Hagerstown (Car.)	OF	15	65	9	22	3	2	1	5	.338	1	6	7	32	3	0	1.000
1988	—Hagerstown (Car.)	OF	8	28	2	6	2	0	0	3	.214	4	3	4	17	0	0	1.000
	—Charlotte (South.)	OF	10	40	7	12	4	2	1	6	.300	4	3	2	14	0	0	1.000
	—Rochester (Int'l)	OF	120	456	61	*143	19	7	5	54	*.314	28	55	20	*289	14	*12	.962
1989	—Baltimore (A.L.)	OF	81	217	35	54	5	2	2	25	.249	15	30	17	144	1	2	.986
	—Rochester (Int'l)	OF	7	25	2	4	0	0	0	2	.160	1	5	3	17	2	0	1.000
	—Hagerstown (East.)	OF	11	48	11	20	3	1	0	7	.417	4	3	4	35	2	3	.925
1990	—Baltimore (A.L.)	OF	142	464	46	119	16	4	3	37	.256	32	53	22	298	4	7	.977
1991	—Houston (N.L.)■	OF	159	596	84	170	28	10	8	54	.285	42	65	34	323	13	5	.985
1992	—Houston (N.L.)	OF	•162	607	84	177	29	13	5	55	.292	58	63	44	417	8	3	.993
1993	—Houston (N.L.)	OF	142	545	69	145	15	*13	8	44	.266	28	65	19	329	12	4	.988
American League totals (2 years)			223	681	81	173	21	6	5	62	.254	47	83	39	442	5	9	.980
National League totals (3 years)			463	1748	237	492	72	36	21	153	.281	128	193	97	1069	33	12	.989
Major league totals (5 years)			686	2429	318	665	93	42	26	215	.274	175	276	136	1511	38	21	.987

FINNVOLD, GAR

P, RED SOX

PERSONAL: Born March 11, 1968, in Boynton Beach, Fla.... 6-5/195.... Throws right, bats right.... Full name: Anders Gar Finnvold.
HIGH SCHOOL: Pope John Paul II (Boca Raton, Fla.).
COLLEGE: Palm Beach Junior College (Fla.) and Florida State.
TRANSACTIONS/CAREER NOTES: Selected by Seattle Mariners organization in 42nd round of free-agent draft (June 2, 1987).... Selected by Boston Red Sox organization in sixth round of free-agent draft (June 4, 1990).

Year	Team (League)	W	L	Pct.	ERA	G	GS	CG	ShO	Sv.	IP	H	R	ER	BB	SO
1990	—Elmira (N.Y.-Penn)	5	5	.500	3.13	15	15	*5	1	0	95	91	43	33	22	89
1991	—Lynchburg (Caro.)	2	3	.400	3.32	6	6	0	0	0	38	30	16	14	7	29
	—New Britain (East.)	5	8	.385	3.82	16	16	0	0	0	101⅓	97	46	43	36	80
	—Pawtucket (Int'l)	1	2	.333	6.60	3	3	0	0	0	15	19	13	11	7	12
1992	—New Britain (East.)	7	13	.350	3.49	25	25	3	0	0	165	156	69	64	52	135
1993	—Pawtucket (Int'l)	5	9	.357	3.77	24	24	0	0	0	136	128	68	57	51	123

FISK, CARLTON

C

PERSONAL: Born December 26, 1947, in Bellows Falls, Vt.... 6-2/225.... Throws right, bats right.... Full name: Carlton Ernest Fisk.
HIGH SCHOOL: Charlestown (N.H.).
COLLEGE: New Hampshire.
TRANSACTIONS/CAREER NOTES: Selected by Baltimore Orioles organization in 36th round of free-agent draft (June 8, 1965).... Selected by Boston Red Sox organization in first round (fourth pick overall) of free-agent draft (January 1967).... On temporary inactive list (April 17, 1967); transferred to military list (May 18, 1967-April 19, 1968).... On temporary inactive list (August 5-20, 1968).... On disabled list (March 21-April 26 and June 28, 1974-remainder of season; March 24-June 23, 1975; and April 14-May 21, 1979).... Granted free agency by arbitrator's ruling (February 12, 1981).... Signed by Chicago White Sox (March 18, 1981).... On disabled list (June 13-July 5, 1984).... Granted free agency (November 12, 1985)....

F

Re-signed by White Sox (January 8, 1986).... Granted free agency (January 22, 1988).... Re-signed by White Sox (February 9, 1988).... On disabled list (May 11-July 28, 1988 and April 11-June 1, 1989).... Granted free agency (November 4, 1991).... Re-signed by White Sox (December 11, 1991).... On Chicago disabled list (March 28-June 4, 1992); included rehabilitation assignment to South Bend (May 26-27) and Sarasota (May 27-June 4).... Granted free agency (December 19, 1992).... Re-signed by White Sox (February 5, 1993).... Released by White Sox (June 28, 1993).

RECORDS: Holds major league career records for most games by catcher—2,226; and most home runs by catcher—351.... Holds major league records for longest game with no passed balls—25 innings; most innings played by catcher in game—25 (May 8, finished May 9, 1984, 25 innings).... Shares major league single-game records for most at-bats—11; and plate appearances—12 (May 8, finished May 9, 1984, 25 innings).... Shares modern major league record for most long hits in one inning—2 (May 15, 1975, eighth inning, and June 30, 1977, eighth inning).... Holds A.L. career catching records for most years—24; putouts—11,369; chances accepted—12,417.... Holds A.L. single-season record for most home runs by catcher—33 (1985; also hit four home runs as designated hitter).... Holds A.L. single-season record for fewest assists by catcher (150 or more games)—69 (1977).... Shares A.L. single-season record for fewest passed balls (150 or more games)—4 (1977).

HONORS: Named A.L. Rookie Player of the Year by THE SPORTING NEWS (1972).... Named catcher on THE SPORTING NEWS A.L. All-Star team (1972, 1977, 1983, 1985 and 1990).... Won A.L. Gold Glove at catcher (1972).... Named A.L. Rookie of the Year by Baseball Writers' Association of America (1972).... Named catcher on THE SPORTING NEWS A.L. Silver Slugger team (1981, 1985 and 1988).

STATISTICAL NOTES: Led International League catchers with 12 double plays in 1971.... Led A.L. catchers with 933 total chances in 1972, 803 in 1973, 519 in 1981 and 871 in 1985.... Led A.L. catchers with 17 errors in 1978 and 10 in 1980.... Led A.L. in being hit by pitch with 13 in 1980.... Led A.L. catchers with 470 putouts in 1981.... Led A.L. catchers with 10 double plays in 1981 and 15 in 1987.... Led A.L. with 11 passed balls in 1983.... Hit for the cycle (May 16, 1984).

			BATTING												FIELDING			
Year	Team (League)	Pos.	G	AB	R	H	2B	3B	HR	RBI	Avg.	BB	SO	SB	PO	A	E	Avg.
1967 —								In military service.										
1968 —	Waterloo (Midw.)	C	62	195	31	66	11	2	12	34	.338	21	49	2	385	42	8	.982
1969 —	Pittsfield (Eastern)	C	97	309	38	75	18	3	10	41	.243	33	60	2	551	65	*22	.966
—	Boston (A.L.)	C	2	5	0	0	0	0	0	0	.000	0	2	0	2	0	0	1.000
1970 —	Pawtucket (East.)	C-OF-1B	93	284	43	65	18	1	12	44	.229	42	66	6	482	50	7	.987
1971 —	Louisville (Int'l)	C-OF-3B	94	308	45	81	10	4	10	43	.263	35	61	4	588	51	13	.980
—	Boston (A.L.)	C	14	48	7	15	2	1	2	6	.313	1	10	0	72	6	2	.975
1972 —	Boston (A.L.)	C	131	457	74	134	28	•9	22	61	.293	52	83	5	*846	*72	•15	.984
1973 —	Boston (A.L.)	C	135	508	65	125	21	0	26	71	.246	37	99	7	*739	50	*14	.983
1974 —	Boston (A.L.)	C	52	187	36	56	12	1	11	26	.299	24	23	5	267	26	6	.980
1975 —	Boston (A.L.)	C	79	263	47	87	14	4	10	52	.331	27	32	4	347	30	8	.979
1976 —	Boston (A.L.)	C	134	487	76	124	17	5	17	58	.255	56	71	12	649	73	12	.984
1977 —	Boston (A.L.)	C	152	536	106	169	26	3	26	102	.315	75	85	7	779	69	11	.987
1978 —	Boston (A.L.)	C-OF	157	571	94	162	39	5	20	88	.284	71	83	7	734	90	†17	.980
1979 —	Boston (A.L.)	C	91	320	49	87	23	2	10	42	.272	10	38	3	155	8	3	.982
1980 —	Boston (A.L.)	C-1-0-3	131	478	73	138	25	3	18	62	.289	36	62	11	543	56	†11	.982
1981 —	Chicago (A.L.)■	C-1-3-0	96	338	44	89	12	0	7	45	.263	38	37	3	†479	46	6	.989
1982 —	Chicago (A.L.)	C	135	476	66	127	17	3	14	65	.267	46	60	17	648	63	5	.993
1983 —	Chicago (A.L.)	C	138	488	85	141	26	4	26	86	.289	46	88	9	*709	46	7	.991
1984 —	Chicago (A.L.)	C	102	359	54	83	20	1	21	43	.231	26	60	6	421	38	6	.987
1985 —	Chicago (A.L.)	C	153	543	85	129	23	1	37	107	.238	52	81	17	*801	60	10	.989
1986 —	Chicago (A.L.)	C	125	457	42	101	11	0	14	63	.221	22	92	2	455	44	8	.984
1987 —	Chicago (A.L.)	C	135	454	68	116	22	1	23	71	.256	39	72	1	597	66	7	.990
1988 —	Chicago (A.L.)	C	76	253	37	70	8	1	19	50	.277	37	40	0	338	36	2	.995
1989 —	Chicago (A.L.)	C	103	375	47	110	25	2	13	68	.293	36	60	1	419	37	3	*.993
1990 —	Chicago (A.L.)	C	137	452	65	129	21	0	18	65	.285	61	73	7	660	63	4	.994
1991 —	Chicago (A.L.)	C-1B	134	460	42	111	25	0	18	74	.241	32	86	1	625	65	6	.991
1992 —	South Bend (Mid.)	C	1	2	1	1	0	0	1	3	.500	1	0	0	4	0	1	.800
—	Sarasota (Fla. St.)	C	7	25	3	3	1	0	1	2	.120	3	6	1	31	3	0	1.000
—	Chicago (A.L.)	C	62	188	12	43	4	1	3	21	.229	23	38	3	252	26	2	.993
1993 —	Chicago (A.L.)	C	25	53	2	10	0	0	1	4	.189	2	11	0	75	5	0	1.000
Major league totals (24 years)			2499	8756	1276	2356	421	47	376	1330	.269	849	1386	128	11612	1075	165	.987

CHAMPIONSHIP SERIES RECORD

			BATTING												FIELDING			
Year	Team (League)	Pos.	G	AB	R	H	2B	3B	HR	RBI	Avg.	BB	SO	SB	PO	A	E	Avg.
1975 —	Boston (A.L.)	C	3	12	4	5	1	0	0	2	.417	0	2	1	15	0	0	1.000
1983 —	Chicago (A.L.)	C	4	17	0	3	1	0	0	0	.176	1	3	0	27	3	0	1.000
Championship series totals (2 years)			7	29	4	8	2	0	0	2	.276	1	5	1	42	3	0	1.000

WORLD SERIES RECORD

WORLD SERIES NOTES: Shares single-inning record for most at-bats—2 (October 15, 1975, fourth inning).

			BATTING												FIELDING			
Year	Team (League)	Pos.	G	AB	R	H	2B	3B	HR	RBI	Avg.	BB	SO	SB	PO	A	E	Avg.
1975 —	Boston (A.L.)	C	7	25	5	6	0	0	2	4	.240	7	7	0	37	3	2	.952

ALL-STAR GAME RECORD

			BATTING											FIELDING			
Year	League	Pos.	AB	R	H	2B	3B	HR	RBI	Avg.	BB	SO	SB	PO	A	E	Avg.
1972 —	American	C	2	1	1	0	0	0	0	.500	0	1	0	2	0	0	1.000
1973 —	American	C	2	0	0	0	0	0	0	.000	0	0	0	3	0	0	1.000
1974 —	American						Selected, did not play—injured.										
1976 —	American	C	1	0	0	0	0	0	0	.000	0	0	0	1	0	0	1.000
1977 —	American	C	2	0	0	0	0	0	0	.000	0	1	0	6	1	0	1.000
1978 —	American	C	2	0	0	0	0	0	1	.000	0	0	0	4	0	0	1.000

Year	League	Pos.	AB	R	H	2B	3B	HR	RBI	Avg.	BB	SO	SB	PO	A	E	Avg.
			BATTING											FIELDING			
1980	—American	C	2	0	0	0	0	0	0	.000	0	2	0	5	0	0	1.000
1981	—American	C	3	1	1	0	0	0	0	.333	0	1	0	4	0	0	1.000
1982	—American	C	2	0	0	0	0	0	0	.000	0	1	0	2	0	0	1.000
1985	—American	C	2	0	0	0	0	0	0	.000	0	0	0	2	0	0	1.000
1991	—American	C	2	0	1	0	0	0	0	.500	0	1	0	5	0	0	1.000
All-Star Game totals (10 years)			20	2	3	0	0	0	1	.150	0	7	0	34	1	0	1.000

FLAHERTY, JOHN

C, RED SOX

PERSONAL: Born October 21, 1967, in New York. . . . 6-1/195. . . . Throws right, bats right. . . . Full name: John Timothy Flaherty.
HIGH SCHOOL: St. Joseph's Regional (Montvale, N.J.).
COLLEGE: George Washington.
TRANSACTIONS/CAREER NOTES: Selected by Boston Red Sox organization in 25th round of free-agent draft (June 1, 1988).
STATISTICAL NOTES: Tied for Florida State League lead with 19 passed balls in 1989.

Year	Team (League)	Pos.	G	AB	R	H	2B	3B	HR	RBI	Avg.	BB	SO	SB	PO	A	E	Avg.
				BATTING											FIELDING			
1988	—Elmira (N.Y.-Penn)	C	46	162	17	38	3	0	3	16	.235	12	23	2	235	39	7	.975
1989	—Winter Haven (FSL)	C-1B	95	334	31	87	14	2	4	28	.260	20	44	1	369	60	9	.979
1990	—Pawtucket (Int'l)	C-3B	99	317	35	72	18	0	4	32	.227	24	43	1	509	59	10	.983
	—Lynchburg (Caro.)	C	1	4	0	0	0	0	0	1	.000	0	1	0	3	2	0	1.000
1991	—New Britain (East.)	C	67	225	27	65	9	0	3	18	.289	31	22	0	337	46	9	.977
	—Pawtucket (Int'l)	C	45	156	18	29	7	0	3	13	.186	15	14	0	270	18	•9	.970
1992	—Boston (A.L.)	C	35	66	3	13	2	0	0	2	.197	3	7	0	102	7	2	.982
	—Pawtucket (Int'l)	C	31	104	11	26	3	0	0	7	.250	5	8	0	158	17	4	.978
1993	—Pawtucket (Int'l)	C	105	365	29	99	22	0	6	35	.271	26	41	0	626	78	10	.986
	—Boston (A.L.)	C	13	25	3	3	2	0	0	2	.120	2	6	0	35	9	0	1.000
Major league totals (2 years)			48	91	6	16	4	0	0	4	.176	5	13	0	137	16	2	.987

FLEMING, DAVE

P, MARINERS

PERSONAL: Born November 7, 1969, in Queens, N.Y. . . . 6-3/200. . . . Throws left, bats left. . . . Full name: David Anthony Fleming.
HIGH SCHOOL: Mahopac (N.Y.).
COLLEGE: Georgia.
TRANSACTIONS/CAREER NOTES: Selected by Seattle Mariners organization in third round of free-agent draft (June 4, 1990). . . . On Seattle disabled list (March 26-May 23, 1993); included rehabilitation assignment to Jacksonville (May 3-21).
HONORS: Named lefthanded pitcher on THE SPORTING NEWS A.L. All-Star team (1992).

Year	Team (League)	W	L	Pct.	ERA	G	GS	CG	ShO	Sv.	IP	H	R	ER	BB	SO
1990	—San Bern. (Calif.)	7	3	.700	2.60	12	12	4	0	0	79⅔	64	29	23	30	77
1991	—Jacksonv. (South.)	10	6	.625	2.64	21	20	6	1	0	140	129	50	41	25	109
	—Seattle (A.L.)	1	0	1.000	6.62	9	3	0	0	0	17⅔	19	13	13	3	11
	—Calgary (PCL)	2	0	1.000	1.13	3	2	1	0	0	16	11	2	2	3	16
1992	—Seattle (A.L.)	17	10	.630	3.39	33	33	7	4	0	228⅓	225	95	86	60	112
1993	—Jacksonv. (South.)	0	2	.000	4.41	4	4	0	0	0	16⅓	16	9	8	7	10
	—Seattle (A.L.)	12	5	.706	4.36	26	26	1	1	0	167⅓	189	84	81	67	75
Major league totals (3 years)		30	15	.667	3.92	68	62	8	5	0	413⅓	433	192	180	130	198

FLENER, HUCK

P, BLUE JAYS

PERSONAL: Born February 25, 1969, in Austin, Tex. . . . 5-11/185. . . . Throws left, bats both. . . . Full name: Gregory Alan Flener. . . . Name pronounced FLENN-er.
HIGH SCHOOL: Armijo (Fairfield, Calif.).
COLLEGE: Cal State Fullerton.
TRANSACTIONS/CAREER NOTES: Selected by Toronto Blue Jays organization in 10th round of free-agent draft (June 4, 1990).
STATISTICAL NOTES: Led Southern League with eight balks in 1993.

Year	Team (League)	W	L	Pct.	ERA	G	GS	CG	ShO	Sv.	IP	H	R	ER	BB	SO
1990	—St. Cathar. (NYP)	4	3	.571	3.36	14	7	0	0	1	61⅔	45	29	23	33	46
1991	—Myrtle Beach (SAL)	6	4	.600	1.82	55	0	0	0	13	79	58	28	16	41	107
1992	—Dunedin (Fla. St.)	7	3	.700	2.24	41	8	0	0	8	112⅓	70	35	28	50	93
1993	—Knoxville (South.)	•13	6	.684	3.30	38	16	2	2	4	136⅓	130	56	50	39	114
	—Toronto (A.L.)	0	0	...	4.05	6	0	0	0	0	6⅔	7	3	3	4	2
Major league totals (1 year)		0	0	...	4.05	6	0	0	0	0	6⅔	7	3	3	4	2

FLETCHER, DARRIN

C, EXPOS

PERSONAL: Born October 3, 1966, in Elmhurst, Ill. . . . 6-1/198. . . . Throws right, bats left. . . . Full name: Darrin Glen Fletcher. . . . Son of Tom Fletcher, pitcher, Detroit Tigers (1962).
HIGH SCHOOL: Oakwood (Ill.).
COLLEGE: Illinois.
TRANSACTIONS/CAREER NOTES: Selected by Los Angeles Dodgers organization in sixth round of free-agent draft (June 2, 1987). . . . Traded by Dodgers to Philadelphia Phillies for P Dennis Cook (September 13, 1990). . . . Traded by Phillies with cash to Montreal Expos for P Barry Jones (December 9, 1991). . . . On Montreal disabled list (May 12-June 15, 1992); included rehabilitation assignment to Indianapolis (May 31-June 14).
STATISTICAL NOTES: Tied for Texas League lead in double plays by catcher with nine in 1988. . . . Led Pacific Coast League catchers with 787 total chances in 1990.

Year	Team (League)	Pos.	G	AB	R	H	2B	3B	HR	RBI	Avg.	BB	SO	SB	PO	A	E	Avg.
				BATTING											FIELDING			
1987	—Vero Beach (FSL)	C	43	124	13	33	7	0	0	15	.266	22	12	0	212	35	3	.988

F

Year	Team (League)	Pos.	G	AB	R	H	2B	3B	HR	RBI	Avg.	BB	SO	SB	PO	A	E	Avg.
							BATTING								FIELDING			
1988	—San Antonio (Tex.)...	C	89	279	19	58	8	0	1	20	.208	17	42	2	529	64	5	*.992
1989	—Albuquerque (PCL)..	C	100	315	34	86	16	1	5	44	.273	30	38	1	632	63	9	.987
	—Los Angeles (N.L.)...	C	5	8	1	4	0	0	1	2	.500	1	0	0	16	1	0	1.000
1990	—Albuquerque (PCL)..	C	105	350	58	102	23	1	13	65	.291	40	37	1	*715	64	8	.990
	—L.A.-Phil. (N.L.)■.....	C	11	23	3	3	1	0	0	1	.130	1	6	0	30	3	0	1.000
1991	—Scran./W.B. (Int'l)...	C-1B	90	306	39	87	13	1	8	50	.284	23	29	1	491	44	5	.991
	—Philadelphia (N.L.)...	C	46	136	5	31	8	0	1	12	.228	5	15	0	242	22	2	.992
1992	—Montreal (N.L.)■.......	C	83	222	13	54	10	2	2	26	.243	14	28	0	360	33	2	.995
	—Indianapolis (A.A.)...	C	13	51	2	13	2	0	1	9	.255	2	10	0	65	7	1	.986
1993	—Montreal (N.L.).........	C	133	396	33	101	20	1	9	60	.255	34	40	0	620	41	8	.988
Major league totals (5 years)			278	785	55	193	39	3	13	101	.246	55	89	0	1268	100	12	.991

FLETCHER, PAUL

P, PHILLIES

PERSONAL: Born January 14, 1967, in Gallipolis, O. . . . 6-1/185. . . . Throws right, bats right. . . . Full name: Edward Paul Fletcher.
HIGH SCHOOL: Ravenswood (W.Va.).
COLLEGE: South Carolina-Aiken and West Virginia State College.
TRANSACTIONS/CAREER NOTES: Selected by Philadelphia Phillies organization in 40th round of free-agent draft (June 1, 1988). . . . On Reading disabled list (May 5-23, 1992).
STATISTICAL NOTES: Led New York-Pennsylvania League with 13 home runs allowed in 1989. . . . Led International League with 21 wild pitches in 1993.

Year	Team (League)	W	L	Pct.	ERA	G	GS	CG	ShO	Sv.	IP	H	R	ER	BB	SO
1988	—Martinsville (App.).....	1	3	.250	4.67	15	14	1	0	1	69⅓	81	44	36	33	61
1989	—Batavia (NY-Penn)....	7	5	.583	3.28	14	14	3	0	0	82⅓	77	41	30	28	58
1990	—Spartanburg (SAL)....	2	4	.333	3.28	9	9	1	0	0	49⅓	46	24	18	18	53
	—Clearwater (FSL).......	5	8	.385	3.38	20	18	2	0	1	117⅓	104	56	44	49	104
1991	—Clearwater (FSL).......	0	1	.000	1.23	14	4	0	0	1	29⅓	22	6	4	8	27
	—Reading (Eastern).....	7	9	.438	3.51	21	19	3	1	0	120⅔	111	56	47	56	90
1992	—Reading (Eastern).....	9	4	.692	2.83	22	20	2	1	0	127	103	45	40	47	103
	—Scran./W.B. (Int'l).....	3	0	1.000	2.78	4	4	0	0	0	22⅔	17	8	7	2	26
1993	—Scran./W.B. (Int'l).....	4	12	.250	5.66	34	19	2	1	0	140	146	99	*88	60	116
	—Philadelphia (N.L.).....	0	0	...	0.00	1	0	0	0	0	⅓	0	0	0	0	0
Major league totals (1 year)...		0	0	...	0.00	1	0	0	0	0	⅓	0	0	0	0	0

FLETCHER, SCOTT

2B, RED SOX

PERSONAL: Born July 30, 1958, in Fort Walton Beach, Fla. . . . 5-11/173. . . . Throws right, bats right. . . . Full name: Scott Brian Fletcher. . . . Son of Richard Fletcher, minor league pitcher (1952-59).
HIGH SCHOOL: Wadsworth (O.).
COLLEGE: Toledo, Valencia Community College (Fla.) and Georgia Southern.
TRANSACTIONS/CAREER NOTES: Selected by Los Angeles Dodgers organization in 33rd round of free-agent draft (June 8, 1976). . . . Selected by Oakland Athletics organization in secondary phase of free-agent draft (January 10, 1978). . . . Selected by Houston Astros organization in secondary phase of free-agent draft (June 6, 1978). . . . Selected by Chicago Cubs organization in secondary phase of free-agent draft (June 5, 1979). . . . Traded by Cubs with P Dick Tidrow, P Randy Martz and IF Pat Tabler to Chicago White Sox for P Steve Trout and P Warren Brusstar (January 25, 1983). . . . Traded by White Sox with P Ed Correa and a player to be named later to Texas Rangers for IF Wayne Tolleson and P Dave Schmidt (November 25, 1985); Rangers acquired IF Jose Mota to complete deal (December 12, 1985). . . . Granted free agency (November 4, 1988). . . . Re-signed by Rangers (November 30, 1988). . . . On Texas disabled list (July 5-20, 1989). . . . Traded by Rangers with OF Sammy Sosa and P Wilson Alvarez to Chicago White Sox for OF Harold Baines and IF Fred Manrique (July 29, 1989). . . . Granted free agency (November 4, 1991). . . . Signed by Milwaukee Brewers organization (February 23, 1992). . . . Granted free agency (October 30, 1992). . . . Signed by Boston Red Sox (December 1, 1992). . . . On disabled list (June 10-25, 1993).
STATISTICAL NOTES: Led Texas League second basemen with 354 putouts, 390 assists, 29 errors, 773 total chances and 112 double plays in 1980. . . . Led American Association in being hit by pitch with nine and grounding into double plays with 20 in 1981. . . . Led American Association shortstops with 607 total chances in 1982. . . . Led A.L. second basemen with 115 double plays in 1990.

F

Year	Team (League)	Pos.	G	AB	R	H	2B	3B	HR	RBI	Avg.	BB	SO	SB	PO	A	E	Avg.
							BATTING								FIELDING			
1979	—Geneva (NY-Penn)...	SS	67	261	59	81	12	3	4	43	.310	56	29	10	99	195	18	*.942
1980	—Midland (Texas).......	2B-SS	130	501	*111	164	16	*11	6	65	.327	82	65	20	†354	†390	†29	.962
1981	—Iowa (Am. Assoc.)....	SS	119	458	66	117	26	4	4	33	.255	51	72	24	*222	337	28	.952
	—Chicago (N.L.)..........	2B-SS-3B	19	46	6	10	4	0	0	1	.217	2	4	0	34	44	3	.963
1982	—Iowa (Am. Assoc.)....	SS	129	502	90	157	26	3	4	60	.313	46	62	20	224	•357	26	.957
	—Chicago (N.L.)..........	SS	11	24	4	4	0	0	0	1	.167	4	5	1	11	23	0	1.000
1983	—Chicago (A.L.)■........	SS-2B-3B	114	262	42	62	16	5	3	31	.237	29	22	5	126	308	16	.964
1984	—Chicago (A.L.)..........	SS-2B-3B	149	456	46	114	13	3	3	35	.250	46	46	10	234	439	19	.973
1985	—Chicago (A.L.)..........	3B-SS-2B	119	301	38	77	8	1	2	31	.256	35	47	5	123	208	8	.976
1986	—Texas (A.L.)■...........	SS-3B-2B	147	530	82	159	34	5	3	50	.300	47	59	12	216	388	16	.974
1987	—Texas (A.L.).............	SS	156	588	82	169	28	4	5	63	.287	61	66	13	249	413	23	.966
1988	—Texas (A.L.).............	SS	140	515	59	142	19	4	0	47	.276	62	34	8	215	414	11	.983
1989	—Texas-Chi. (A.L.)■...	SS-2B	142	546	77	138	25	2	1	43	.253	64	60	2	241	362	15	.976
1990	—Chicago (A.L.)..........	2B	151	509	54	123	18	3	4	56	.242	45	63	1	305	436	9	.988
1991	—Chicago (A.L.)..........	2B-3B	90	248	14	51	10	1	1	28	.206	17	26	0	178	192	3	.992
1992	—Milwaukee (A.L.)■....	2B-SS-3B	123	386	53	106	18	3	3	51	.275	30	33	17	236	382	9	.986
1993	—Boston (A.L.)■..........	2B-SS-3B	121	480	81	137	31	5	5	45	.285	37	35	16	217	371	11	.982
American League totals (11 years)...........			1452	4821	628	1278	220	36	30	480	.265	473	491	89	2340	3913	140	.978
National League totals (2 years).............			30	70	10	14	4	0	0	2	.200	6	9	1	45	67	3	.974
Major league totals (13 years)................			1482	4891	638	1292	224	36	30	482	.264	479	500	90	2385	3980	143	.978

CHAMPIONSHIP SERIES RECORD

			BATTING											FIELDING			
Year	Team (League)	Pos.	G	AB	R	H	2B	3B	HR	RBI	Avg.	BB	SO	SB	PO	A	E	Avg.
1983	—Chicago (A.L.)..........	SS	3	7	0	0	0	0	0	0	.000	1	0	0	3	8	0	1.000

FLORA, KEVIN

2B, ANGELS

PERSONAL: Born June 10, 1969, in Fontana, Calif.... 6-0/185.... Throws right, bats right.... Full name: Kevin Scot Flora.

HIGH SCHOOL: Bonita (Calif.).

TRANSACTIONS/CAREER NOTES: Selected by California Angels organization in second round of free-agent draft (June 2, 1987).... On disabled list (June 21, 1988-remainder of season and June 14-September 8, 1992).... On temporary inactive list (April 24-July 16 and September 3, 1993-remainder of season).

STATISTICAL NOTES: Led Midwest League shortstops with 46 errors in 1989.

			BATTING											FIELDING				
Year	Team (League)	Pos.	G	AB	R	H	2B	3B	HR	RBI	Avg.	BB	SO	SB	PO	A	E	Avg.
1987	—Salem (Northwest)...	SS	35	88	17	24	5	1	0	12	.273	21	14	8	35	81	22	.841
1988	—Quad City (Midw.)....	SS	48	152	19	33	3	4	0	15	.217	18	33	5	64	121	23	.889
1989	—Quad City (Midw.)....	SS-2B	120	372	46	81	8	4	1	21	.218	57	107	30	156	281	†46	.905
1990	—Midland (Texas).......	SS-2B	71	232	35	53	17	5	5	32	.228	23	53	11	98	213	26	.923
1991	—Midland (Texas).......	2B	124	484	97	138	14	*15	12	67	.285	37	92	40	272	*348	24	.963
	—California (A.L.).......	2B	3	8	1	1	0	0	0	0	.125	1	5	1	8	3	2	.846
1992	—Edmonton (PCL).......	2B	52	170	35	55	8	4	3	19	.324	29	25	9	111	118	11	.954
1993	—Vancouver (PCL).....	2B-OF	30	94	17	31	2	0	1	12	.330	10	20	6	21	22	2	.956
Major league totals (1 year).....................			3	8	1	1	0	0	0	0	.125	1	5	1	8	3	2	.846

FLORIE, BRYCE

P, PADRES

PERSONAL: Born May 21, 1970, in Charleston, S.C.... 6-0/185.... Throws right, bats right.... Full name: Bryce Bettencourt Florie.

HIGH SCHOOL: Hanahan (Charleston, S.C.).

COLLEGE: Trident Technical College (S.C.).

TRANSACTIONS/CAREER NOTES: Selected by San Diego Padres organization in fifth round of free-agent draft (June 1, 1988).

STATISTICAL NOTES: Led Texas League with 25 wild pitches in 1993.

Year	Team (League)	W	L	Pct.	ERA	G	GS	CG	ShO	Sv.	IP	H	R	ER	BB	SO
1988	—Ariz. Padres (Ariz.)....	4	5	.444	7.98	11	6	0	0	0	38⅓	52	44	34	22	29
1989	—Spokane (N'west)......	4	5	.444	7.08	14	14	0	0	0	61	79	•66	48	40	50
	—Char., S.C. (S. Atl.).....	1	7	.125	6.95	12	12	0	0	0	44	54	47	34	42	22
1990	—Waterloo (Midw.).......	4	5	.444	4.39	14	14	1	0	0	65⅔	60	37	32	37	38
1991	—Waterloo (Midw.).......	7	6	.538	3.92	23	23	2	0	0	133	119	66	58	79	90
1992	—High Desert (Calif.)....	9	7	.563	4.12	26	24	0	0	0	137⅔	99	79	63	*114	106
	—Char., S.C. (S. Atl.).....	0	1	.000	1.80	1	1	0	0	0	5	5	3	1	0	5
1993	—Wichita (Texas).........	11	8	.579	3.96	27	•27	0	0	0	154⅔	128	80	68	*100	133

FLOYD, CLIFF

1B, EXPOS

PERSONAL: Born December 5, 1972, in Chicago.... 6-4/220.... Throws right, bats left.... Full name: Cornelius Clifford Floyd.

HIGH SCHOOL: Thornwood (South Holland, Ill.).

TRANSACTIONS/CAREER NOTES: Selected by Montreal Expos organization in first round (14th pick overall) of free-agent draft (June 3, 1991).

HONORS: Named Minor League Player of the Year by THE SPORTING NEWS (1993).... Named Eastern League Most Valuable Player (1993).

STATISTICAL NOTES: Led South Atlantic League with 261 total bases and nine intentional bases on balls received in 1992.... Led Eastern League with .600 slugging percentage and 12 intentional bases on balls received in 1993.

			BATTING											FIELDING				
Year	Team (League)	Pos.	G	AB	R	H	2B	3B	HR	RBI	Avg.	BB	SO	SB	PO	A	E	Avg.
1991	—GC Expos (GCL)........	1B	56	214	35	56	9	3	6	30	.262	19	37	13	451	27	*15	.970
1992	—Albany (S. Atl.).........	OF-1B	134	516	83	157	24	*16	16	*97	.304	45	75	32	423	29	17	.964
	—W.P. Beach (FSL).....	OF	1	4	0	0	0	0	0	1	.000	0	1	0	2	0	0	1.000
1993	—Harrisburg (East.)....	1B-OF	101	380	82	125	17	4	•26	*101	.329	54	71	31	564	27	19	.969
	—Ottawa (Int'l)............	1B	32	125	12	30	2	2	2	18	.240	16	34	2	272	23	5	.983
	—Montreal (N.L.).........	1B	10	31	3	7	0	0	1	2	.226	0	9	0	79	4	0	1.000
Major league totals (1 year).....................			10	31	3	7	0	0	1	2	.226	0	9	0	79	4	0	1.000

FOLEY, TOM

IF, PIRATES

PERSONAL: Born September 9, 1959, in Columbus, Ga.... 6-1/185.... Throws right, bats left.... Full name: Thomas Michael Foley.

HIGH SCHOOL: Palmetto (Miami).

COLLEGE: Miami-Dade (South) Community College.

TRANSACTIONS/CAREER NOTES: Selected by Cincinnati Reds organization in seventh round of free-agent draft (June 7, 1977).... Traded by Reds with C Alan Knicely, a player to be named later and cash to Philadelphia Phillies for C Bo Diaz and P Greg Simpson (August 8, 1985); Phillies acquired P Freddie Toliver to complete deal (August 27, 1985).... On Philadelphia disabled list (March 23-April 29, 1986); included rehabilitation assignment to Reading (April 25-29).... Traded by Phillies with P Larry Sorensen to Montreal Expos for P Dan Schatzeder and IF Skeeter Barnes (July 24, 1986).... On disabled list (May 17-June 2, 1987 and July 26-August 12, 1989).... Released by Expos (October 6, 1992).... Signed by Pittsburgh Pirates (December 14, 1992).... On disabled list (July 19-August 4, 1993).

STATISTICAL NOTES: Led Pioneer League in caught stealing with 10 in 1977.... Led Western Carolinas League shortstops with 98 double plays in 1978.... Led Florida State League shortstops with 71 double plays in 1979.

Year	Team (League)	Pos.	G	AB	R	H	2B	3B	HR	RBI	Avg.	BB	SO	SB	PO	A	E	Avg.
			BATTING												FIELDING			
1977	—Billings (Pioneer)	3B-SS	59	209	37	53	7	1	2	21	.254	37	43	7	53	109	24	.871
1978	—Shelby (W. Caro.)	SS	124	424	55	98	19	1	2	41	.231	50	43	8	*217	•352	30	*.950
1979	—Tampa (Fla. St.)	SS	125	414	38	95	12	6	0	37	.229	37	39	5	223	*394	35	.946
1980	—Waterbury (East.)	2B	131	477	49	119	16	4	4	41	.249	47	50	3	*222	329	31	.947
1981	—Indianapolis (A.A.)	SS	103	347	47	81	12	2	6	27	.233	27	27	6	175	267	27	.942
1982	—Indianapolis (A.A.)	SS	129	427	65	115	20	9	8	63	.269	42	48	1	*227	343	27	.955
1983	—Cincinnati (N.L.)	SS-2B	68	98	7	20	4	1	0	9	.204	13	17	1	54	76	2	.985
1984	—Cincinnati (N.L.)	SS-2B-3B	106	277	26	70	8	3	5	27	.253	24	36	3	119	228	11	.969
1985	—Cin.-Phil. (N.L.)■	SS-2B-3B	89	250	24	60	13	1	3	23	.240	19	34	2	127	202	7	.979
1986	—Reading (Eastern)	SS-2B	3	11	2	2	2	0	0	0	.182	1	0	0	2	11	0	1.000
	—Phil.-Mont. (N.L.)■	SS-2B-3B	103	263	26	70	15	3	1	23	.266	30	37	10	117	190	6	.981
1987	—Montreal (N.L.)	SS-2B-3B	106	280	35	82	18	3	5	28	.293	11	40	6	134	190	9	.973
1988	—Montreal (N.L.)	2B-SS-3B	127	377	33	100	21	3	5	43	.265	30	49	2	204	324	15	.972
1989	—Montreal (N.L.)	2-3-S-P	122	375	34	86	19	2	7	39	.229	45	53	2	203	317	8	.985
1990	—Montreal (N.L.)	S-2-3-1	73	164	11	35	2	1	0	12	.213	12	22	0	80	123	5	.976
1991	—Montreal (N.L.)	SS-3B-2B	86	168	12	35	11	1	0	15	.208	14	30	2	52	84	5	.965
1992	—Montreal (N.L.)	S-2-1-3-0	72	115	7	20	3	1	0	5	.174	8	21	3	74	97	5	.972
1993	—Pittsburgh (N.L.)■	2-1-3-S	86	194	18	49	11	1	3	22	.253	11	26	0	116	105	5	.978
Major league totals (11 years)			1038	2561	233	627	125	20	29	246	.245	217	365	31	1280	1936	78	.976

RECORD AS PITCHER

Year	Team (League)	W	L	Pct.	ERA	G	GS	CG	ShO	Sv.	IP	H	R	ER	BB	SO
1989	—Montreal (N.L.)	0	0	...	27.00	1	0	0	0	0	⅓	1	1	1	0	0

FORDYCE, BROOK

C, METS

PERSONAL: Born May 7, 1970, in New London, Conn. . . . 6-1/185. . . . Throws right, bats right. . . . Full name: Brook Alexander Fordyce. . . . Name pronounced FOR-DICE.
HIGH SCHOOL: St. Bernard's (Uncasville, Conn.).
TRANSACTIONS/CAREER NOTES: Selected by New York Mets organization in third round of free-agent draft (June 5, 1989).
STATISTICAL NOTES: Led Appalachian League catchers with .991 fielding percentage in 1989. . . . Led South Atlantic League in slugging percentage with .478 and tied for lead in grounding into double plays with 18 in 1990. . . . Led South Atlantic League with 30 passed balls in 1990. . . . Led Eastern League catchers with 795 total chances in 1992. . . . Led International League catchers with 810 total chances and tied for lead in double plays by catcher with 11 in 1993.

Year	Team (League)	Pos.	G	AB	R	H	2B	3B	HR	RBI	Avg.	BB	SO	SB	PO	A	E	Avg.
			BATTING												FIELDING			
1989	—Kingsport (Appal.)	C-OF-3B	69	226	45	74	15	0	9	38	.327	30	26	10	311	28	4	†.988
1990	—Columbia (S. Atl.)	C	104	372	45	117	29	1	10	54	.315	39	42	4	574	63	15	.977
1991	—St. Lucie (Fla. St.)	C	115	406	42	97	19	3	7	55	.239	37	50	4	630	87	13	.982
1992	—Binghamton (East.)	C	118	425	59	118	30	0	11	61	.278	37	78	1	*713	*79	3	*.996
1993	—Norfolk (Int'l)	C	116	409	33	106	21	2	2	41	.259	26	62	2	*735	67	8	.990

FORNEY, RICK

P, ORIOLES

PERSONAL: Born October 24, 1971, in Annapolis, Md. . . . 6-4/210. . . . Throws right, bats right. . . . Full name: David Ritchard Forney Jr.
HIGH SCHOOL: Annapolis (Md.).
COLLEGE: Anne Arundel Community College (Md.).
TRANSACTIONS/CAREER NOTES: Selected by Baltimore Orioles organization in 26th round of free-agent draft (June 3, 1991). . . . On disabled list (July 22-August 10 and August 27, 1992-remainder of season).

Year	Team (League)	W	L	Pct.	ERA	G	GS	CG	ShO	Sv.	IP	H	R	ER	BB	SO
1991	—GC Orioles (GCL)	•7	0	•1.000	2.19	12	10	2	•1	0	65⅔	48	21	16	10	51
1992	—Kane Co. (Midw.)	3	6	.333	2.48	20	18	2	1	0	123⅓	114	40	34	26	104
1993	—Frederick (Caro.)	*14	8	.636	2.78	27	27	2	0	0	165	156	64	51	64	175
	—Bowie (Eastern)	0	0	...	1.29	1	1	0	0	0	7	1	1	1	1	4

FOSSAS, TONY

P, RED SOX

PERSONAL: Born September 23, 1957, in Havana, Cuba. . . . 6-0/190. . . . Throws left, bats left. . . . Full name: Emilo Anthony Fossas.
HIGH SCHOOL: St. Mary's (Brookline, Mass.).
COLLEGE: South Florida.
TRANSACTIONS/CAREER NOTES: Selected by Minnesota Twins organization in ninth round of free-agent draft (June 6, 1978). . . . Selected by Texas Rangers organization in 12th round of free-agent draft (June 5, 1979). . . . Released by Rangers organization (February 18, 1982). . . . Signed by Midland, Chicago Cubs organization (March 11, 1982). . . . Loaned by Cubs organization to Tabasco of Mexican League (March 15-April 7, 1982). . . . Released by Cubs organization (April 7, 1982). . . . Signed by Burlington, Rangers organization (May 3, 1982). . . . Granted free agency (October 15, 1985). . . . Signed by Edmonton, California Angels organization (December 13, 1985). . . . On disabled list (June 2, 1986-remainder of season). . . . Granted free agency (October 15, 1987). . . . Signed by Oklahoma City, Rangers organization (December 1, 1987). . . . Granted free agency (October 15, 1988). . . . Signed by Denver, Milwaukee Brewers organization (January 21, 1989). . . . Released by Brewers organization (December 6, 1990). . . . Signed by Boston Red Sox organization (January 23, 1991). . . . Released by Red Sox (December 11, 1992). . . . Re-signed by Red Sox organization (January 18, 1993). . . . Granted free agency (December 20, 1993). . . . Re-signed by Red Sox organization (January 20, 1994).

Year	Team (League)	W	L	Pct.	ERA	G	GS	CG	ShO	Sv.	IP	H	R	ER	BB	SO
1979	—GC Rangers (GCL)	6	3	.667	3.00	10	9	1	0	0	60	54	28	20	26	49
	—Tulsa (Texas)	1	1	.500	6.55	2	2	0	0	0	11	14	10	8	4	3
1980	—Asheville (S. Atl.)	8	2	.800	3.15	30	•27	8	2	2	*197	*187	84	69	69	140
1981	—Tulsa (Texas)	5	6	.455	4.16	38	12	1	1	2	106	113	65	49	44	57

Year	Team (League)	W	L	Pct.	ERA	G	GS	CG	ShO	Sv.	IP	H	R	ER	BB	SO
1982	—Tabasco (Mexican)■	0	3	.000	5.56	3	3	0	0	0	11⅓	15	14	7	10	6
	—Burlington (Midw.)■	8	9	.471	3.08	25	18	10	1	0	146⅓	121	63	50	33	115
1983	—Tulsa (Texas)	8	7	.533	4.20	24	16	6	1	0	133	123	77	62	46	103
	—Okla. City (A.A.)	1	2	.333	7.90	10	5	0	0	0	35⅓	55	33	31	12	23
1984	—Tulsa (Texas)	0	1	.000	4.50	4	0	0	0	2	10	12	5	5	3	7
	—Okla. City (A.A.)	5	9	.357	4.31	29	15	3	0	0	121	143	65	58	34	74
1985	—Okla. City (A.A.)	7	6	.538	4.75	30	13	2	0	2	110	121	65	58	36	49
1986	—Edmonton (PCL)■	3	3	.500	4.57	7	7	2	1	0	43⅓	53	23	22	12	15
1987	—Edmonton (PCL)	6	8	.429	4.99	40	15	1	0	0	117⅓	152	76	65	29	54
1988	—Okla. City (A.A.)■	3	0	1.000	2.84	52	0	0	0	4	66⅔	64	21	21	16	42
	—Texas (A.L.)	0	0	...	4.76	5	0	0	0	0	5⅔	11	3	3	2	0
1989	—Denver (A.A.)■	5	1	.833	2.04	24	1	0	0	0	35⅓	27	9	8	11	35
	—Milwaukee (A.L.)	2	2	.500	3.54	51	0	0	0	1	61	57	27	24	22	42
1990	—Milwaukee (A.L.)	2	3	.400	6.44	32	0	0	0	0	29⅓	44	23	21	10	24
	—Denver (A.A.)	5	2	.714	1.51	25	0	0	0	4	35⅔	29	8	6	10	45
1991	—Boston (A.L.)■	3	2	.600	3.47	64	0	0	0	1	57	49	27	22	28	29
1992	—Boston (A.L.)	1	2	.333	2.43	60	0	0	0	2	29⅔	31	9	8	14	19
1993	—Boston (A.L.)	1	1	.500	5.18	71	0	0	0	0	40	38	28	23	15	39
	Major league totals (6 years)	9	10	.474	4.08	283	0	0	0	4	222⅔	230	117	101	91	153

FOSTER, KEVIN
P, PHILLIES

PERSONAL: Born January 13, 1969, in Evanston, Ill. . . . 6-1/160. . . . Throws right, bats right. . . . Full name: Kevin Christopher Foster.
HIGH SCHOOL: Evanston (Ill.) Township.
COLLEGE: Kishwaukee College (Ill.).
TRANSACTIONS/CAREER NOTES: Selected by Montreal Expos organization in 29th round of free-agent draft (June 2, 1987). . . . On Albany (Ga.) suspended list (April 9-May 6, 1992). . . . Traded by Expos organization with P Dave Wainhouse to Seattle Mariners for IF Frank Bolick and a player to be named later (November 20, 1992); Expos organization acquired C Miah Bradbury to complete deal (December 8, 1992). . . . Traded by Mariners to Philadelphia Phillies for P Bob Ayrault (June 12, 1993).

Year	Team (League)	W	L	Pct.	ERA	G	GS	CG	ShO	Sv.	IP	H	R	ER	BB	SO
1990	—GC Expos (GCL)	2	0	1.000	5.06	4	0	0	0	0	10⅔	9	6	6	6	11
	—Gate City (Pioneer)	1	7	.125	4.58	10	10	0	0	0	55	43	42	28	34	52
1991	—Sumter (S. Atl.)	10	4	.714	2.74	34	11	1	1	1	102	62	36	31	68	111
1992	—W.P. Beach (FSL)	7	2	.778	1.95	16	11	0	0	0	69⅓	45	19	15	31	66
1993	—Jacksonv. (South.)■	4	4	.500	3.97	12	12	1	1	0	65⅔	53	32	29	29	72
	—Scran./W.B. (Int'l)■	1	1	.500	3.93	17	9	1	0	0	71	63	32	31	29	59
	—Philadelphia (N.L.)	0	1	.000	14.85	2	1	0	0	0	6⅔	13	11	11	7	6
	Major league totals (1 year)	0	1	.000	14.85	2	1	0	0	0	6⅔	13	11	11	7	6

RECORD AS POSITION PLAYER

			BATTING											FIELDING			
Year	Team (League)	Pos.	G	AB	R	H	2B	3B	HR	RBI	Avg.	BB	SO	SB	PO	A	E	Avg.
1988	—GC Expos (GCL)	3B-2B-SS	49	164	21	42	10	1	2	21	.256	21	33	16	38	92	18	.878
1989	—Rockford (Midw.)	3B-2B	44	117	9	19	3	2	1	15	.162	18	44	1	29	70	12	.892
1990	—W.P. Beach (FSL)	3B	3	6	0	1	0	1	0	2	.167	1	1	0	2	1	0	1.000

FOSTER, STEVE
P, REDS

PERSONAL: Born August 16, 1966, in Dallas. . . . 6-0/180. . . . Throws right, bats right. . . . Full name: Stephen Eugene Foster Jr.
HIGH SCHOOL: DeSoto (Tex.).
COLLEGE: Blinn College (Tex.) and Texas-Arlington.
TRANSACTIONS/CAREER NOTES: Selected by Cincinnati Reds organization in 12th round of free-agent draft (June 1, 1988). . . . On Nashville disabled list (June 1-9, 1992). . . . On disabled list (May 20-June 26 and June 29, 1993-remainder of season).

Year	Team (League)	W	L	Pct.	ERA	G	GS	CG	ShO	Sv.	IP	H	R	ER	BB	SO
1988	—Billings (Pioneer)	2	3	.400	1.19	18	0	0	0	7	30⅓	15	5	4	7	27
1989	—Ced. Rap. (Midw.)	0	3	.000	2.14	51	0	0	0	23	59	46	16	14	19	55
1990	—Chatt. (South.)	5	10	.333	5.34	50	0	0	0	20	59	69	38	35	33	52
1991	—Chatt. (South.)	0	2	.000	1.15	17	0	0	0	10	15⅔	10	4	2	4	18
	—Nashville (A.A.)	2	3	.400	2.14	41	0	0	0	12	54⅔	46	17	13	29	52
	—Cincinnati (N.L.)	0	0	...	1.93	11	0	0	0	0	14	7	5	3	4	11
1992	—Cincinnati (N.L.)	1	1	.500	2.88	31	1	0	0	2	50	52	16	16	13	34
	—Nashville (A.A.)	5	3	.625	2.68	17	7	0	0	1	50⅓	53	20	15	22	28
1993	—Cincinnati (N.L.)	2	2	.500	1.75	17	0	0	0	0	25⅔	23	8	5	5	16
	Major league totals (3 years)	3	3	.500	2.41	59	1	0	0	2	89⅔	82	29	24	22	61

FOX, ANDY
3B, YANKEES

PERSONAL: Born January 12, 1971, in Sacramento, Calif. . . . 6-4/185. . . . Throws right, bats left. . . . Full name: Andrew Junipero Fox.
HIGH SCHOOL: Christian Brothers (Sacramento, Calif.).
TRANSACTIONS/CAREER NOTES: Selected by New York Yankees organization in second round of free-agent draft (June 5, 1989). . . . On disabled list (June 11-21, 1991; April 9-22, 1992 and June 10-August 1, 1993).
STATISTICAL NOTES: Led Carolina League third basemen with 96 putouts in 1992.

			BATTING											FIELDING			
Year	Team (League)	Pos.	G	AB	R	H	2B	3B	HR	RBI	Avg.	BB	SO	SB	PO	A	E	Avg.
1989	—GC Yankees (GCL)	3B	40	141	26	35	9	2	3	25	.248	31	29	6	37	78	10	.920
1990	—Greensboro (S. Atl.)	3B	134	455	68	99	19	4	9	55	.218	92	132	26	93	238	*45	.880
1991	—Prin. William (Car.)	3B	126	417	60	96	22	2	10	46	.230	81	104	15	85	247	*29	.920
1992	—Prin. William (Car.)	3B-SS	125	473	75	113	18	3	7	42	.239	54	81	28	†97	304	27	.937
1993	—Alb./Colon. (East.)	3B	65	236	44	65	16	1	3	24	.275	32	54	12	59	150	19	.917

FOX, ERIC

OF

PERSONAL: Born August 15, 1963, in LeMoore, Calif. . . . 5-10/180. . . . Throws left, bats both. . . . Full name: Eric Hollis Fox.

HIGH SCHOOL: Capistrano Valley (San Juan Capistrano, Calif.).

COLLEGE: Fresno State (degree in physical education).

TRANSACTIONS/CAREER NOTES: Selected by Toronto Blue Jays organization in 22nd round of free-agent draft (June 4, 1984).... Selected by Philadelphia Phillies organization in 13th round of free-agent draft (June 3, 1985).... Selected by Seattle Mariners organization in secondary phase of free-agent draft (January 14, 1986).... Released by Mariners organization (March 29, 1989).... Signed by Huntsville, Oakland Athletics organization (March 29, 1989).... On disabled list (June 21, 1990-remainder of season).... Granted free agency (December 19, 1992).... Re-signed by A's organization (February 2, 1993). ... Granted free agency (October 15, 1993).

STATISTICAL NOTES: Led California League in caught stealing with 27 in 1986.... Led California League outfielders with 337 total chances and seven double plays in 1986.... Tied for Southern League lead in double plays by outfielder with five in 1987. ... Led Southern League outfielders with 321 total chances in 1989.

			BATTING												FIELDING			
Year	**Team (League)**	**Pos.**	**G**	**AB**	**R**	**H**	**2B**	**3B**	**HR**	**RBI**	**Avg.**	**BB**	**SO**	**SB**	**PO**	**A**	**E**	**Avg.**
1986	—Salinas (Calif.)	OF	133	526	80	137	17	3	5	42	.260	69	78	41	*314	18	5	.985
1987	—Chatt. (South.)	OF	134	523	76	139	28	•10	8	54	.266	40	93	22	378	11	8	.980
1988	—Vermont (Eastern)	OF	129	478	55	120	20	6	3	39	.251	39	69	33	308	8	4	.988
1989	—Huntsville (South.)◼	OF	139	498	84	125	10	5	15	51	.251	72	85	49	*306	10	5	.984
1990	—Tacoma (PCL)	OF	62	221	37	61	9	2	4	34	.276	20	34	8	130	3	5	.964
1991	—Tacoma (PCL)	OF	127	522	85	141	24	8	4	52	.270	57	82	17	306	14	6	.982
1992	—Tacoma (PCL)	OF	37	121	16	24	3	1	1	7	.198	16	25	5	78	4	0	1.000
	—Huntsville (South.)	OF	59	240	42	65	16	2	5	14	.271	27	43	16	125	4	0	1.000
	—Oakland (A.L.)	OF	51	143	24	34	5	2	3	13	.238	13	29	3	92	3	1	.990
1993	—Oakland (A.L.)	OF	29	56	5	8	1	0	1	5	.143	2	7	0	47	0	0	1.000
	—Tacoma (PCL)	OF	92	317	49	99	14	5	11	52	.312	41	48	18	198	6	4	.981
Major league totals (2 years)			80	199	29	42	6	2	4	18	.211	15	36	3	139	3	1	.993

CHAMPIONSHIP SERIES RECORD

			BATTING												FIELDING			
Year	**Team (League)**	**Pos.**	**G**	**AB**	**R**	**H**	**2B**	**3B**	**HR**	**RBI**	**Avg.**	**BB**	**SO**	**SB**	**PO**	**A**	**E**	**Avg.**
1992	—Oakland (A.L.)	PR-DH-OF	4	1	0	0	0	0	0	0	.000	1	0	2	1	0	0	1.000

FRANCO, JOHN

P, METS

PERSONAL: Born September 17, 1960, in Brooklyn, N.Y. . . . 5-10/185. . . . Throws left, bats left. . . . Full name: John Anthony Franco.

HIGH SCHOOL: Lafayette (Brooklyn, N.Y.).

COLLEGE: St. John's.

TRANSACTIONS/CAREER NOTES: Selected by Los Angeles Dodgers organization in fifth round of free-agent draft (June 8, 1981). ... Traded by Dodgers organization with P Brett Wise to Cincinnati Reds organization for IF Rafael Landestoy (May 9, 1983). ... Traded by Reds with OF Don Brown to New York Mets for P Randy Myers and P Kip Gross (December 6, 1989).... On disabled list (June 30-August 1 and August 26, 1992-remainder of season; April 17-May 7 and August 3-26, 1993).

HONORS: Named N.L. Fireman of the Year by THE SPORTING NEWS (1988 and 1990).

Year	**Team (League)**	**W**	**L**	**Pct.**	**ERA**	**G**	**GS**	**CG**	**ShO**	**Sv.**	**IP**	**H**	**R**	**ER**	**BB**	**SO**
1981	—Vero Beach (FSL)	7	4	.636	3.53	13	11	3	0	0	79	78	41	31	41	60
1982	—Albuquerque (PCL)	1	2	.333	7.24	5	5	0	0	0	27⅓	41	22	22	15	24
	—San Antonio (Tex.)	10	5	.667	4.96	17	17	3	0	0	105⅓	137	70	58	46	76
1983	—Albuquerque (PCL)	0	0	...	5.40	11	0	0	0	0	15	10	11	9	11	8
	—Indianapolis (A.A.)◼	6	10	.375	4.85	23	18	2	0	2	115	148	69	62	42	54
1984	—Wichita (A.A.)	1	0	1.000	5.79	6	0	0	0	0	9⅓	8	6	6	4	11
	—Cincinnati (N.L.)	6	2	.750	2.61	54	0	0	0	4	79⅓	74	28	23	36	55
1985	—Cincinnati (N.L.)	12	3	.800	2.18	67	0	0	0	12	99	83	27	24	40	61
1986	—Cincinnati (N.L.)	6	6	.500	2.94	74	0	0	0	29	101	90	40	33	44	84
1987	—Cincinnati (N.L.)	8	5	.615	2.52	68	0	0	0	32	82	76	26	23	27	61
1988	—Cincinnati (N.L.)	6	6	.500	1.57	70	0	0	0	*39	86	60	18	15	27	46
1989	—Cincinnati (N.L.)	4	8	.333	3.12	60	0	0	0	32	80⅔	77	35	28	36	60
1990	—New York (N.L.)◼	5	3	.625	2.53	55	0	0	0	*33	67⅔	66	22	19	21	56
1991	—New York (N.L.)	5	9	.357	2.93	52	0	0	0	30	55⅓	61	27	18	18	45
1992	—New York (N.L.)	6	2	.750	1.64	31	0	0	0	15	33	24	6	6	11	20
1993	—New York (N.L.)	4	3	.571	5.20	35	0	0	0	10	36⅓	46	24	21	19	29
Major league totals (10 years)		62	47	.569	2.62	566	0	0	0	236	720⅓	657	253	210	279	517

ALL-STAR GAME RECORD

Year	**League**	**W**	**L**	**Pct.**	**ERA**	**GS**	**CG**	**ShO**	**Sv.**	**IP**	**H**	**R**	**ER**	**BB**	**SO**
1986	—National							Did not play.							
1987	—National	0	0	...	0.00	0	0	0	0	⅔	0	0	0	0	0
1989	—National							Did not play.							
1990	—National	0	0	...	0.00	0	0	0	0	1	0	0	0	0	0
1991	—National							Did not play.							
All-Star totals (2 years)		0	0	...	0.00	0	0	0	0	1⅔	0	0	0	0	0

FRANCO, JULIO

DH, WHITE SOX

PERSONAL: Born August 23, 1961, in San Pedro de Macoris, Dominican Republic. . . . 6-1/190. . . . Throws right, bats right. . . . Full name: Julio Cesar Franco.

HIGH SCHOOL: Divine Providence (San Pedro de Macoris, Dominican Republic).

TRANSACTIONS/CAREER NOTES: Signed as free agent by Philadelphia Phillies organization (June 23, 1978).... Traded by Phillies with 2B Manny Trillo, OF George Vukovich, P Jay Baller and C Jerry Willard to Cleveland Indians for OF Von Hayes (December 9, 1982).... On disabled list (July 13-August 8, 1987).... Traded by Indians to Texas

Rangers for 1B Pete O'Brien, OF Oddibe McDowell and 2B Jerry Browne (December 6, 1988).... On disabled list (March 28-April 19, May 4-June 1 and July 9, 1992-remainder of season).... Granted free agency (October 27, 1993).... Signed by Chicago White Sox (December 15, 1993).
HONORS: Named Carolina League Most Valuable Player (1980).... Named second baseman on THE SPORTING NEWS A.L. Silver Slugger team (1988-1991).... Named second baseman on THE SPORTING NEWS A.L. All-Star team (1989-1991).
STATISTICAL NOTES: Led Northwest League with 153 total bases in 1979.... Led Northwest League shortstops with 45 double plays in 1979.... Led Carolina League shortstops with 73 double plays in 1980.... Led American Association shortstops with 42 errors in 1982.... Led A.L. shortstops with 35 errors in 1985.... Led A.L. in grounding into double plays with 28 in 1986 and 27 in 1989.

				BATTING										FIELDING			
Year	Team (League)	Pos.	G	AB	R	H	2B	3B	HR	RBI	Avg.	BB	SO	SB	PO	A	E	Avg.
1978	—Butte (Pioneer)	SS	47	141	34	43	5	2	3	28	.305	17	30	4	37	52	25	.781
1979	—Cent. Ore. (N'west)	SS	•71	299	57	*98	15	5	•10	45	.328	24	59	22	103	*256	31	.921
1980	—Peninsula (Caro.)	SS	•140	*555	105	178	25	6	11	*99	.321	33	66	44	179	*412	42	.934
1981	—Reading (Eastern)	SS	*139	*532	70	160	17	3	8	74	.301	52	60	27	246	437	30	.958
1982	—Okla. City (A.A.)	SS-3B	120	463	80	139	19	5	21	66	.300	39	56	33	211	350	†42	.930
	—Philadelphia (N.L.)	SS-3B	16	29	3	8	1	0	0	3	.276	2	4	0	8	25	0	1.000
1983	—Cleveland (A.L.)■	SS	149	560	68	153	24	8	8	80	.273	27	50	32	247	438	28	.961
1984	—Cleveland (A.L.)	SS	160	*658	82	188	22	5	3	79	.286	43	68	19	280	481	*36	.955
1985	—Cleveland (A.L.)	SS-2B	160	636	97	183	33	4	6	90	.288	54	74	13	252	437	†36	.950
1986	—Cleveland (A.L.)	SS-2B	149	599	80	183	30	5	10	74	.306	32	66	10	248	413	19	.972
1987	—Cleveland (A.L.)	SS-2B	128	495	86	158	24	3	8	52	.319	57	56	32	175	313	18	.964
1988	—Cleveland (A.L.)	2B	152	613	88	186	23	6	10	54	.303	56	72	25	310	434	14	.982
1989	—Texas (A.L.)■	2B	150	548	80	173	31	5	13	92	.316	66	69	21	256	386	13	.980
1990	—Texas (A.L.)	2B	157	582	96	172	27	1	11	69	.296	82	83	31	310	444	•19	.975
1991	—Texas (A.L.)	2B	146	589	108	201	27	3	15	78	*.341	65	78	36	294	372	14	.979
1992	—Texas (A.L.)	2B-OF	35	107	19	25	7	0	2	8	.234	15	17	1	21	17	3	.927
1993	—Texas (A.L.)	DH	144	532	85	154	31	3	14	84	.289	62	95	9	...	...	...	...
American League totals (11 years)			1530	5919	889	1776	279	43	100	760	.300	559	728	229	2393	3735	200	.968
National League totals (1 year)			16	29	3	8	1	0	0	3	.276	2	4	0	8	25	0	1.000
Major league totals (12 years)			1546	5948	892	1784	280	43	100	763	.300	561	732	229	2401	3760	200	.969

ALL-STAR GAME RECORD

ALL-STAR GAME NOTES: Named Most Valuable Player (1990).

			BATTING										FIELDING			
Year	League	Pos.	AB	R	H	2B	3B	HR	RBI	Avg.	BB	SO	SB	PO	A	E	Avg.
1989	—American	2B	3	0	1	0	0	0	0	.333	0	0	0	1	1	0	1.000
1990	—American	PH-2B	3	0	1	1	0	0	2	.333	0	0	0	1	0	0	1.000
1991	—American								Did not play.								
All-Star Game totals (2 years)			6	0	2	1	0	0	2	.333	0	0	0	2	1	0	1.000

FRANCO, MATT

1B, CUBS

PERSONAL: Born August 19, 1969, in Santa Monica, Calif.... 6-2/200.... Throws right, bats left.... Full name: Matthew Neil Franco.
HIGH SCHOOL: Westlake (Calif.) Village.
TRANSACTIONS/CAREER NOTES: Selected by Chicago Cubs organization in seventh round of free-agent draft (June 2, 1987).
STATISTICAL NOTES: Led Midwest League in grounding into double plays with 19 in 1990.

				BATTING										FIELDING			
Year	Team (League)	Pos.	G	AB	R	H	2B	3B	HR	RBI	Avg.	BB	SO	SB	PO	A	E	Avg.
1987	—Wytheville (Appal.)	3B-1B-2B	62	202	25	50	10	1	1	21	.248	26	41	4	95	88	23	.888
1988	—Wytheville (Appal.)	3B-1B	20	79	14	31	9	1	0	16	.392	7	5	0	31	24	6	.902
	—Geneva (NY-Penn)	3B-1B	44	164	19	42	2	0	3	21	.256	19	13	2	190	43	14	.943
1989	—Char., W.Va. (SAL)	3-1-0-S	109	377	42	102	16	1	5	48	.271	57	40	2	113	189	22	.932
	—Peoria (Midwest)	3B	16	58	4	13	4	0	0	9	.224	5	5	0	11	32	6	.878
1990	—Peoria (Midwest)	1B-3B	123	443	52	125	*33	2	6	65	.282	43	39	4	810	75	18	.980
1991	—Winst.-Salem (Car.)	1B-3B-SS	104	307	47	66	12	1	4	41	.215	46	42	4	711	53	11	.986
1992	—Charlotte (South.)	3B-1B-OF	108	343	35	97	18	3	2	31	.283	26	46	3	248	69	13	.961
1993	—Orlando (Southern)	1B-3B	68	237	31	75	20	1	7	37	.316	29	30	3	444	40	4	.992
	—Iowa (Am. Assoc.)	1-0-2-P	62	199	24	58	17	4	5	29	.291	16	30	4	450	39	2	.996

RECORD AS PITCHER

Year	Team (League)	W	L	Pct.	ERA	G	GS	CG	ShO	Sv.	IP	H	R	ER	BB	SO
1993	—Iowa (Am. Assoc.)	0	0	...	36.00	1	0	0	0	0	1	5	4	4	1	1

FRAZIER, LOU

OF, EXPOS

PERSONAL: Born January 26, 1965, in St. Louis.... 6-2/175.... Throws right, bats both.... Full name: Arthur Louis Frazier.
HIGH SCHOOL: Jennings (Mo.).
COLLEGE: Scottsdale (Ariz.) Community College.
TRANSACTIONS/CAREER NOTES: Selected by Detroit Tigers organization in 10th round of free-agent draft (June 3, 1985).... Selected by Cleveland Indians organization in secondary phase of free-agent draft (January 14, 1986).... Selected by Houston Astros organization in secondary phase of free-agent draft (June 2, 1986).... Traded by Astros organization to Detroit Tigers organization for IF Doug Strange (March 30, 1990).... Granted free agency (October 15, 1992).... Signed by Montreal Expos organization (December 8, 1992).
STATISTICAL NOTES: Led Eastern League in caught stealing with 23 in 1993.

Year	Team (League)	Pos.	BATTING												FIELDING			
			G	AB	R	H	2B	3B	HR	RBI	Avg.	BB	SO	SB	PO	A	E	Avg.
1986	—GC Astros (GCL)	SS	51	178	39	51	7	2	1	23	.287	32	25	17	81	131	31	.872
1987	—Asheville (S. Atl.)	SS	108	399	83	103	9	2	1	33	.258	68	89	75	172	297	48	.907
1988	—Osceola (Fla. St.)	2-S-0-1	130	468	79	110	11	3	0	34	.235	90	104	★87	220	282	28	.947
1989	—Columbus (South.)	2B-OF	135	460	65	106	10	1	4	31	.230	76	101	43	228	254	15	.970
1990	—London (Eastern)■	0-2-S-3	81	242	29	53	4	1	0	15	.219	27	52	20	123	68	15	.927
1991	—London (Eastern)	OF-2B	122	439	69	105	9	4	3	40	.239	77	87	42	210	36	12	.953
1992	—London (Eastern)	OF-2B	129	477	85	120	16	3	0	34	.252	★95	107	★58	255	12	10	.964
1993	—Montreal (N.L.)■	OF-1B-2B	112	189	27	54	7	1	1	16	.286	16	24	17	98	9	2	.982
Major league totals (1 year)			112	189	27	54	7	1	1	16	.286	16	24	17	98	9	2	.982

FREDRICKSON, SCOTT

P, ROCKIES

PERSONAL: Born August 19, 1967, in Manchester, N.H. ... 6-3/215. ... Throws right, bats right. ... Full name: Scott Eric Fredrickson.
HIGH SCHOOL: Judson (Converse, Tex.).
COLLEGE: Texas.
TRANSACTIONS/CAREER NOTES: Selected by San Diego Padres organization in 14th round of free-agent draft (June 4, 1990).... On disabled list (June 21-30, 1992).... Selected by Colorado Rockies in third round (68th pick overall) of expansion draft (November 17, 1992).

Year	Team (League)	W	L	Pct.	ERA	G	GS	CG	ShO	Sv.	IP	H	R	ER	BB	SO
1990	—Spokane (N'west)	3	3	.500	3.28	26	1	0	0	8	46⅔	35	22	17	18	61
1991	—Waterloo (Midw.)	3	5	.375	1.17	26	0	0	0	6	38⅓	24	9	5	15	40
	—High Desert (Calif.)	4	1	.800	2.31	23	0	0	0	7	35	31	15	9	18	26
1992	—Wichita (Texas)	4	7	.364	3.19	56	0	0	0	5	73⅓	50	29	26	38	66
1993	—Colo. Springs (PCL)■	1	3	.250	5.47	23	0	0	0	7	26⅓	25	16	16	19	20
	—Colorado (N.L.)	0	1	.000	6.21	25	0	0	0	0	29	33	25	20	17	20
Major league totals (1 year)		0	1	.000	6.21	25	0	0	0	0	29	33	25	20	17	20

FREEMAN, MARVIN

P, ROCKIES

PERSONAL: Born April 10, 1963, in Chicago.... 6-7/222.... Throws right, bats right.
HIGH SCHOOL: Chicago Vocational.
COLLEGE: Jackson State.
TRANSACTIONS/CAREER NOTES: Selected by Montreal Expos organization in ninth round of free-agent draft (June 8, 1981).... Selected by Philadelphia Phillies organization in second round of free-agent draft (June 4, 1984).... On Philadelphia disabled list (April 25, 1989-remainder of season); included rehabilitation assignment to Scranton/Wilkes-Barre (August 24-September 1).... Traded by Phillies organization to Richmond, Atlanta Braves organization, for P Joe Boever (July 23, 1990).... On disabled list (August 18, 1991-remainder of season and May 26-June 10, 1992). ... On Atlanta disabled list (June 4-August 7, 1993); included rehabilitation assignment to Richmond (July 31-August 7).... Released by Braves (October 25, 1993).... Signed by Colorado Rockies (October 29, 1993).
STATISTICAL NOTES: Pitched 6-0 no-hit victory for Maine against Richmond (July 28, 1988, second game).

Year	Team (League)	W	L	Pct.	ERA	G	GS	CG	ShO	Sv.	IP	H	R	ER	BB	SO
1984	—Bend (Northwest)	8	5	.615	2.61	15	•15	2	1	0	89⅔	64	41	26	52	79
1985	—Clearwater (FSL)	6	5	.545	3.06	14	13	3	3	0	88⅓	72	32	30	36	55
	—Reading (Eastern)	1	7	.125	5.37	11	11	2	0	0	65⅓	51	41	39	52	35
1986	—Reading (Eastern)	13	6	.684	4.03	27	•27	4	2	0	163	130	89	73	★111	113
	—Philadelphia (N.L.)	2	0	1.000	2.25	3	3	0	0	0	16	6	4	4	10	8
1987	—Maine (Int'l)	0	7	.000	6.26	10	10	2	0	0	46	56	38	32	30	29
	—Reading (Eastern)	3	3	.500	5.07	9	9	0	0	0	49⅔	45	30	28	32	40
1988	—Maine (Int'l)	5	5	.500	4.62	18	14	2	1	0	74	62	43	38	46	37
	—Philadelphia (N.L.)	2	3	.400	6.10	11	11	0	0	0	51⅔	55	36	35	43	37
1989	—Scran./W.B. (Int'l)	1	1	.500	4.50	5	5	0	0	0	14	11	8	7	5	8
	—Philadelphia (N.L.)	0	0	...	6.00	1	1	0	0	0	3	2	2	2	5	0
1990	—Scr/WB-Ric. (Int'l)■	4	7	.364	4.84	14	14	1	1	0	74⅓	72	43	40	41	56
	—Phil.-Atl. (N.L.)	1	2	.333	4.31	25	3	0	0	1	48	41	24	23	17	38
1991	—Atlanta (N.L.)	1	0	1.000	3.00	34	0	0	0	1	48	37	19	16	13	34
1992	—Atlanta (N.L.)	7	5	.583	3.22	58	0	0	0	3	64⅓	61	26	23	29	41
1993	—Atlanta (N.L.)	2	0	1.000	6.08	21	0	0	0	0	23⅔	24	16	16	10	25
	—Richmond (Int'l)	0	0	...	2.25	2	2	0	0	0	4	4	1	1	1	5
Major league totals (7 years)		15	10	.600	4.21	153	18	0	0	5	254⅔	226	127	119	127	183

CHAMPIONSHIP SERIES RECORD

Year	Team (League)	W	L	Pct.	ERA	G	GS	CG	ShO	Sv.	IP	H	R	ER	BB	SO
1992	—Atlanta (N.L.)	0	0	...	14.73	3	0	0	0	0	3⅔	8	6	6	2	1

WORLD SERIES RECORD

Year	Team (League)	W	L	Pct.	ERA	G	GS	CG	ShO	Sv.	IP	H	R	ER	BB	SO
1992	—Atlanta (N.L.)							Did not play.								

FREY, STEVE

P, GIANTS

PERSONAL: Born July 29, 1963, in Meadowbrook, Pa.... 5-9/170.... Throws left, bats right.... Full name: Steven Francis Frey.... Name pronounced FRY.
HIGH SCHOOL: William Tennent (Warminster, Pa.).
COLLEGE: Bucks County Community College (Pa.).
TRANSACTIONS/CAREER NOTES: Selected by New York Yankees organization in 15th round of free-agent draft (June 6, 1983).... Traded by Yankees organization with OF Darren Reed and C Phil Lombardi to New York Mets for SS Rafael Santana and P Victor Garcia (December 11, 1987).... Traded by Mets organization to Indianapolis, Montreal Expos organization, for C Mark Bailey and 3B Tom O'Malley (March 28, 1989).... On Montreal disabled list (May 25-June 15, 1990); included rehabilitation assign-

ment to Indianapolis (June 11-15).... Contract sold by Expos organization to California Angels organization (March 29, 1992).... On disabled list (August 19-September 4, 1992).... Granted free agency (December 20, 1993).... Signed by San Francisco Giants (January 5, 1994).

Year	Team (League)	W	L	Pct.	ERA	G	GS	CG	ShO	Sv.	IP	H	R	ER	BB	SO
1983	—Oneonta (NYP)	4	6	.400	2.74	28	0	0	0	9	72⅓	47	27	22	35	86
1984	—Fort Lauder. (FSL)	4	2	.667	2.09	47	0	0	0	4	64⅔	46	26	15	34	66
1985	—Fort Lauder. (FSL)	1	1	.500	1.21	19	0	0	0	7	22⅓	11	4	3	12	15
	—Alb./Colon. (East.)	4	7	.364	3.82	40	0	0	0	3	61⅓	53	30	26	25	54
1986	—Alb./Colon. (East.)	3	4	.429	2.10	40	0	0	0	4	73	50	25	17	18	62
	—Columbus (Int'l)	0	2	.000	8.05	11	0	0	0	0	19	29	17	17	10	11
1987	—Alb./Colon. (East.)	0	2	.000	1.93	14	0	0	0	1	28	20	6	6	7	19
	—Columbus (Int'l)	2	1	.667	3.04	23	0	0	0	6	47⅓	45	19	16	10	35
1988	—Tidewater (Int'l)■	6	3	.667	3.13	58	1	0	0	6	54⅔	38	23	19	25	58
1989	—Indianapolis (A.A.)■	2	1	.667	1.78	21	0	0	0	3	25⅓	18	7	5	6	23
	—Montreal (N.L.)	3	2	.600	5.48	20	0	0	0	0	21⅓	29	15	13	11	15
1990	—Montreal (N.L.)	8	2	.800	2.10	51	0	0	0	9	55⅔	44	15	13	29	29
	—Indianapolis (A.A.)	0	0	...	0.00	2	0	0	0	1	3	0	0	0	1	3
1991	—Montreal (N.L.)	0	1	.000	4.99	31	0	0	0	1	39⅔	43	31	22	23	21
	—Indianapolis (A.A.)	3	1	.750	1.51	30	0	0	0	3	35⅔	25	6	6	15	45
1992	—California (A.L.)■	4	2	.667	3.57	51	0	0	0	4	45⅓	39	18	18	22	24
1993	—California (A.L.)	2	3	.400	2.98	55	0	0	0	13	48⅓	41	20	16	26	22
	A.L. totals (2 years)	6	5	.545	3.27	106	0	0	0	17	93⅔	80	38	34	48	46
	N.L. totals (3 years)	11	5	.688	3.70	102	0	0	0	10	116⅔	116	61	48	63	65
	Major league totals (5 years)	17	10	.630	3.51	208	0	0	0	27	210⅓	196	99	82	111	111

FROHWIRTH, TODD
P, ORIOLES

PERSONAL: Born September 28, 1962, in Milwaukee.... 6-4/211.... Throws right, bats right.... Full name: Todd Gerald Frohwirth.... Name pronounced FRO-worth.
HIGH SCHOOL: Messmer (Milwaukee).
COLLEGE: Northwest Missouri State.

TRANSACTIONS/CAREER NOTES: Selected by Philadelphia Phillies organization in 13th round of free-agent draft (June 4, 1984). ... Granted free agency (October 15, 1990).... Signed by Baltimore Orioles (December 12, 1990).... Granted free agency (December 20, 1993).... Re-signed by Orioles organization (January 20, 1994).

Year	Team (League)	W	L	Pct.	ERA	G	GS	CG	ShO	Sv.	IP	H	R	ER	BB	SO
1984	—Bend (Northwest)	4	4	.500	1.63	29	0	0	0	•11	49⅔	26	17	9	31	60
1985	—Peninsula (Caro.)	7	5	.583	2.20	*54	0	0	0	*18	82	70	33	20	48	74
1986	—Clearwater (FSL)	3	3	.500	3.98	32	0	0	0	10	52	54	29	23	18	39
	—Reading (Eastern)	0	4	.000	3.21	29	0	0	0	12	42	39	20	15	10	23
1987	—Reading (Eastern)	2	4	.333	1.86	36	0	0	0	*19	58	36	14	12	13	44
	—Maine (Int'l)	1	4	.200	2.51	27	0	0	0	10	32⅓	30	12	9	15	21
	—Philadelphia (N.L.)	1	0	1.000	0.00	10	0	0	0	0	11	12	0	0	2	9
1988	—Philadelphia (N.L.)	1	2	.333	8.25	12	0	0	0	0	12	16	11	11	11	11
	—Maine (Int'l)	7	3	.700	2.44	49	0	0	0	13	62⅔	52	21	17	19	39
1989	—Scran./W.B. (Int'l)	3	2	.600	2.23	21	0	0	0	7	32⅓	29	11	8	11	29
	—Philadelphia (N.L.)	1	0	1.000	3.59	45	0	0	0	0	62⅔	56	26	25	18	39
1990	—Philadelphia (N.L.)	0	1	.000	18.00	5	0	0	0	0	1	3	2	2	6	1
	—Scran./W.B. (Int'l)	9	7	.563	3.04	*67	0	0	0	*21	83	76	34	28	32	56
1991	—Rochester (Int'l)■	1	3	.250	3.65	20	0	0	0	8	24⅔	17	12	10	5	15
	—Baltimore (A.L.)	7	3	.700	1.87	51	0	0	0	3	96⅓	64	24	20	29	77
1992	—Baltimore (A.L.)	4	3	.571	2.46	65	0	0	0	4	106	97	33	29	41	58
1993	—Baltimore (A.L.)	6	7	.462	3.83	70	0	0	0	3	96⅓	91	47	41	44	50
	A.L. totals (3 years)	17	13	.567	2.71	186	0	0	0	10	298⅔	252	104	90	114	185
	N.L. totals (4 years)	3	3	.500	3.95	72	0	0	0	0	86⅔	87	39	38	37	60
	Major league totals (7 years)	20	16	.556	2.99	258	0	0	0	10	385⅓	339	143	128	151	245

FRYE, JEFF
2B, RANGERS

PERSONAL: Born August 31, 1966, in Oakland, Calif.... 5-9/165.... Throws right, bats right.... Full name: Jeffrey Dustin Frye.... Name pronounced FRY.
HIGH SCHOOL: Panama (Okla.).
COLLEGE: Southeastern Oklahoma.

TRANSACTIONS/CAREER NOTES: Selected by Texas Rangers organization in 30th round of free-agent draft (June 1, 1988).... On Texas disabled list (March 27, 1993-entire season).

STATISTICAL NOTES: Led Pioneer League second basemen with 44 double plays in 1988.... Tied for American Association lead in being hit by pitch with 11 in 1992.

			BATTING												FIELDING			
Year	Team (League)	Pos.	G	AB	R	H	2B	3B	HR	RBI	Avg.	BB	SO	SB	PO	A	E	Avg.
1988	—Butte (Pioneer)	2B	54	185	47	53	7	1	0	14	.286	35	25	16	96	149	7	.972
1989	—Gastonia (S. Atl.)	2B	125	464	85	145	26	3	1	40	*.313	72	53	33	242	340	14	*.977
1990	—Charlotte (Fla. St.)	2B	131	503	77	137	16	7	0	50	.272	80	66	29	252	350	13	*.979
1991	—Tulsa (Texas)	2B	131	503	92	152	32	11	4	41	.302	71	60	15	262	322	*26	.957
1992	—Okla. City (A.A.)	2B	87	337	64	101	26	2	2	28	.300	51	39	11	212	248	7	.985
	—Texas (A.L.)	2B	67	199	24	51	9	1	1	12	.256	16	27	1	120	196	7	.978
1993	—								Did not play.									
	Major league totals (1 year)		67	199	24	51	9	1	1	12	.256	16	27	1	120	196	7	.978

FRYMAN, TRAVIS
SS, TIGERS

PERSONAL: Born March 25, 1969, in Lexington, Ky.... 6-1/194.... Throws right, bats right.... Full name: David Travis Fryman.
HIGH SCHOOL: Tates Creek (Lexington, Ky.).
TRANSACTIONS/CAREER NOTES: Selected by Detroit Tigers organization in supplemental

round ("sandwich pick" between first and second round, 30th pick overall) of free-agent draft (June 2, 1987); pick received as compensation for Philadelphia Phillies signing Type A free agent Lance Parrish.
HONORS: Named shortstop on THE SPORTING NEWS A.L. All-Star team (1992).... Named shortstop on THE SPORTING NEWS A.L. Silver Slugger team (1992).... Named third baseman on THE SPORTING NEWS A.L. All-Star team (1993).
STATISTICAL NOTES: Led Appalachian League shortstops with 313 total chances in 1987.... Hit for the cycle (July 28, 1993).

									BATTING							FIELDING		
Year	**Team (League)**	**Pos.**	**G**	**AB**	**R**	**H**	**2B**	**3B**	**HR**	**RBI**	**Avg.**	**BB**	**SO**	**SB**	**PO**	**A**	**E**	**Avg.**
1987	—Bristol (Appal.)	SS	67	248	25	58	9	0	2	20	.234	22	39	6	*103	187	•23	.927
1988	—Fayetteville (SAL)	SS-2B	123	411	44	96	17	4	0	47	.234	24	83	16	174	390	32	.946
1989	—London (Eastern)	SS	118	426	52	113	*30	1	9	56	.265	19	78	5	192	346	*27	.952
1990	—Toledo (Int'l)	SS	87	327	38	84	22	2	10	53	.257	17	59	4	128	277	26	.940
	—Detroit (A.L.)	3B-SS	66	232	32	69	11	1	9	27	.297	17	51	3	47	145	14	.932
1991	—Detroit (A.L.)	3B-SS	149	557	65	144	36	3	21	91	.259	40	149	12	153	354	23	.957
1992	—Detroit (A.L.)	SS-3B	161	*659	87	175	31	4	20	96	.266	45	144	8	220	489	22	.970
1993	—Detroit (A.L.)	SS-3B	151	607	98	182	37	5	22	97	.300	77	128	9	169	382	23	.960
	Major league totals (4 years)		527	2055	282	570	115	13	72	311	.277	179	472	32	589	1370	82	.960

ALL-STAR GAME RECORD

							BATTING							FIELDING		
Year	**League**	**Pos.**	**AB**	**R**	**H**	**2B**	**3B**	**HR**	**RBI**	**Avg.**	**BB**	**SO**	**SB**	**PO**	**A**	**E**	**Avg.**
1992	—American	SS	1	1	1	0	0	0	1	1.000	1	0	0	0	3	0	1.000
1993	—American	SS	1	0	0	0	0	0	0	.000	0	0	0	1	1	0	1.000
	All-Star Game totals (2 years)		2	1	1	0	0	0	1	.500	1	0	0	1	4	0	1.000

GAETTI, GARY

3B/1B, ROYALS

PERSONAL: Born August 19, 1958, in Centralia, Ill.... 6-0/200.... Throws right, bats right.... Full name: Gary Joseph Gaetti.... Name pronounced guy-ETT-ee.
HIGH SCHOOL: Centralia (Ill.).
COLLEGE: Lake Land College (Ill.) and Northwest Missouri State.
TRANSACTIONS/CAREER NOTES: Selected by St. Louis Cardinals organization in fourth round of free-agent draft (January 10, 1978).... Selected by Chicago White Sox organization in secondary phase of free-agent draft (June 6, 1978).... Selected by Minnesota Twins organization in secondary phase of free-agent draft (June 5, 1979).... Granted free agency (November 9, 1987).... Re-signed by Twins (January 7, 1988).... On disabled list (August 21-September 5, 1988 and August 26-September 13, 1989).... Granted free agency (December 7, 1990).... Signed by California Angels (January 23, 1991).... Released by Angels (June 3, 1993).... Signed by Kansas City Royals (June 19, 1993).... Granted free agency (October 25, 1993).... Re-signed by Royals organization (December 16, 1993).
RECORDS: Shares major league rookie-season record for most sacrifice flies—13 (1982).
HONORS: Won A.L. Gold Glove at third base (1986-89).
STATISTICAL NOTES: Tied for Appalachian League lead in errors by third baseman with 18 in 1979.... Led Midwest League third basemen with 492 total chances and 35 double plays in 1980.... Hit home run in first major league at-bat (September 20, 1981).... Led Southern League third basemen with 122 putouts, 281 assists, 32 errors and 435 total chances in 1981.... Led A.L. with 13 sacrifice flies in 1982.... Led A.L. third basemen with 131 putouts in 1983, 142 in 1984 and 146 in 1985.... Led A.L. third basemen with 46 double plays in 1983, 36 in both 1986 and 1990 and 39 in 1991.... Led A.L. third basemen with 496 total chances in 1984, 473 in 1986, 438 in 1990 and 481 in 1991.... Led A.L. third basemen with 334 assists in both 1984 and 1986 and 318 in 1990.... Tied for A.L. lead in errors by third baseman with 20 in 1984.... Led A.L. in grounding into double plays with 25 in 1987.

									BATTING							FIELDING		
Year	**Team (League)**	**Pos.**	**G**	**AB**	**R**	**H**	**2B**	**3B**	**HR**	**RBI**	**Avg.**	**BB**	**SO**	**SB**	**PO**	**A**	**E**	**Avg.**
1979	—Elizabeth. (Appal.)	3B-SS	66	230	50	59	15	2	14	42	.257	43	40	6	70	134	‡21	.907
1980	—Wis. Rap. (Midw.)	3B	138	503	77	134	27	3	*22	82	.266	67	120	24	*94	*363	•35	.929
1981	—Orlando (Southern)	3B-1B	137	495	92	137	19	2	30	93	.277	58	105	15	†143	†283	†32	.930
	—Minnesota (A.L.)	3B	9	26	4	5	0	0	2	3	.192	0	6	0	5	17	0	1.000
1982	—Minnesota (A.L.)	3B-SS	145	508	59	117	25	4	25	84	.230	37	107	0	106	291	17	.959
1983	—Minnesota (A.L.)	3B-SS	157	584	81	143	30	3	21	78	.245	54	121	7	†131	361	17	.967
1984	—Minnesota (A.L.)	3B-OF-SS	•162	588	55	154	29	4	5	65	.262	44	81	11	†163	†335	‡21	.960
1985	—Minnesota (A.L.)	3B-OF-1B	160	560	71	138	31	0	20	63	.246	37	89	13	†162	316	18	.964
1986	—Minnesota (A.L.)	3-S-O-2	157	596	91	171	34	1	34	108	.287	52	108	14	120	†335	21	.956
1987	—Minnesota (A.L.)	3B	154	584	95	150	36	2	31	109	.257	37	92	10	•134	261	11	.973
1988	—Minnesota (A.L.)	3B-SS	133	468	66	141	29	2	28	88	.301	36	85	7	105	191	7	.977
1989	—Minnesota (A.L.)	3B-1B	130	498	63	125	11	4	19	75	.251	25	87	6	115	253	10	.974
1990	—Minnesota (A.L.)	3B-SS	154	577	61	132	27	5	16	85	.229	36	101	6	125	†319	18	.961
1991	—California (A.L.)■	3B	152	586	58	144	22	1	18	66	.246	33	104	5	111	*353	17	.965
1992	—California (A.L.)	3B-1B	130	456	41	103	13	2	12	48	.226	21	79	3	423	196	22	.966
1993	—Calif.-K.C. (A.L.)■	3B-1B	102	331	40	81	20	1	14	50	.245	21	87	1	185	153	7	.980
	Major league totals (13 years)		1745	6362	785	1604	307	29	245	922	.252	433	1147	83	1885	3381	186	.966

CHAMPIONSHIP SERIES RECORD

CHAMPIONSHIP SERIES NOTES: Named A.L. Championship Series Most Valuable Player (1987).... Hit home run in first at-bat (October 7, 1987).

									BATTING							FIELDING		
Year	**Team (League)**	**Pos.**	**G**	**AB**	**R**	**H**	**2B**	**3B**	**HR**	**RBI**	**Avg.**	**BB**	**SO**	**SB**	**PO**	**A**	**E**	**Avg.**
1987	—Minnesota (A.L.)	3B	5	20	5	6	1	0	2	5	.300	1	3	0	8	7	0	1.000

WORLD SERIES RECORD

WORLD SERIES NOTES: Shares records for most at-bats—2; and most hits—2, in one inning (October 17, 1987, fourth inning).

									BATTING							FIELDING		
Year	**Team (League)**	**Pos.**	**G**	**AB**	**R**	**H**	**2B**	**3B**	**HR**	**RBI**	**Avg.**	**BB**	**SO**	**SB**	**PO**	**A**	**E**	**Avg.**
1987	—Minnesota (A.L.)	3B	7	27	4	7	2	1	1	4	.259	2	5	2	6	15	0	1.000

ALL-STAR GAME RECORD

Year	League	Pos.	AB	R	H	2B	3B	HR	RBI	Avg.	BB	SO	SB	PO	A	E	Avg.
			BATTING											FIELDING			
1988	—American	PH	1	0	0	0	0	0	0	.000	0	0	0	...	...	...	...
1989	—American	3B	1	0	0	0	0	0	0	.000	0	1	0	1	0	0	1.000
All-Star Game totals (2 years)			2	0	0	0	0	0	0	.000	0	1	0	1	0	0	1.000

GAGNE, GREG

SS, ROYALS

PERSONAL: Born November 12, 1961, in Fall River, Mass. . . . 5-11/180. . . . Throws right, bats right. . . . Full name: Gregory Carpenter Gagne. . . . Name pronounced GAG-nee.
HIGH SCHOOL: Somerset (Mass.).
TRANSACTIONS/CAREER NOTES: Selected by New York Yankees organization in fifth round of free-agent draft (June 5, 1979). . . . On disabled list (September 4-22, 1980). . . . Traded by Yankees organization with P Ron Davis, P Paul Boris and cash to Minnesota Twins for SS Roy Smalley (April 10, 1982). . . . On Toledo disabled list (June 13-July 18, 1984). . . . On disabled list (August 10-September 1, 1985). . . . Granted free agency (October 27, 1992). . . . Signed by Kansas City Royals (December 8, 1992).
RECORDS: Shares major league single-game record for most inside-the-park home runs—2 (October 4, 1986).
STATISTICAL NOTES: Led International League shortstops with 599 total chances in 1983. . . . Led A.L. shortstops with 26 errors in 1986.

Year	Team (League)	Pos.	G	AB	R	H	2B	3B	HR	RBI	Avg.	BB	SO	SB	PO	A	E	Avg.
			BATTING												FIELDING			
1979	—Paintsville (Appal.)	SS	41	106	10	19	2	3	0	7	.179	13	25	2	28	62	14	.865
1980	—Greensboro (S. Atl.)	SS-3B-2B	98	337	39	91	20	5	3	32	.270	22	46	8	133	233	35	.913
1981	—Greensboro (S. Atl.)	2B-SS-3B	104	364	71	108	21	3	9	48	.297	49	72	14	172	280	25	.948
1982	—Fort Lauder. (FSL)	SS	1	3	0	1	0	0	0	0	.333	1	1	0	3	5	0	1.000
	—Orlando (Southern)■	SS-2B	136	504	73	117	23	5	11	57	.232	57	100	8	185	403	39	.938
1983	—Toledo (Int'l)	SS	119	392	61	100	22	4	17	66	.255	36	70	6	201	*364	*34	.943
	—Minnesota (A.L.)	SS	10	27	2	3	1	0	0	3	.111	0	6	0	10	14	2	.923
1984	—Toledo (Int'l)	3B-SS-2B	70	236	31	66	7	2	9	27	.280	34	52	2	58	168	20	.919
	—Minnesota (A.L.)	PR-PH	2	1	0	0	0	0	0	0	.000	0	0	0	...	...	...	...
1985	—Minnesota (A.L.)	SS	114	293	37	66	15	3	2	23	.225	20	57	10	149	269	14	.968
1986	—Minnesota (A.L.)	SS-2B	156	472	63	118	22	6	12	54	.250	30	108	12	228	381	†26	.959
1987	—Minnesota (A.L.)	SS-OF-2B	137	437	68	116	28	7	10	40	.265	25	84	6	196	391	18	.970
1988	—Minnesota (A.L.)	S-O-2-3	149	461	70	109	20	6	14	48	.236	27	110	15	202	373	18	.970
1989	—Minnesota (A.L.)	SS-OF	149	460	69	125	29	7	9	48	.272	17	80	11	218	389	18	.971
1990	—Minnesota (A.L.)	SS-OF	138	388	38	91	22	3	7	38	.235	24	76	8	184	377	14	.976
1991	—Minnesota (A.L.)	SS-3B	139	408	52	108	23	3	8	42	.265	26	72	11	181	377	9	.984
1992	—Minnesota (A.L.)	SS	146	439	53	108	23	0	7	39	.246	19	83	6	208	438	18	.973
1993	—Kansas City (A.L.)■	SS	159	540	66	151	32	3	10	57	.280	33	93	10	266	451	10	*.986
Major league totals (11 years)			1299	3926	518	995	215	38	79	392	.253	221	769	89	1842	3460	147	.973

CHAMPIONSHIP SERIES RECORD

Year	Team (League)	Pos.	G	AB	R	H	2B	3B	HR	RBI	Avg.	BB	SO	SB	PO	A	E	Avg.
			BATTING												FIELDING			
1987	—Minnesota (A.L.)	SS	5	18	5	5	3	0	2	3	.278	3	4	0	9	13	2	.917
1991	—Minnesota (A.L.)	SS	5	17	1	4	0	0	0	1	.235	1	5	0	9	9	2	.900
Championship series totals (2 years)			10	35	6	9	3	0	2	4	.257	4	9	0	18	22	4	.909

WORLD SERIES RECORD

WORLD SERIES NOTES: Shares record for most at-bats in one inning—2 (October 18, 1987, fourth inning).

Year	Team (League)	Pos.	G	AB	R	H	2B	3B	HR	RBI	Avg.	BB	SO	SB	PO	A	E	Avg.
			BATTING												FIELDING			
1987	—Minnesota (A.L.)	SS	7	30	5	6	1	0	1	3	.200	1	6	0	6	20	2	.929
1991	—Minnesota (A.L.)	SS	7	24	1	4	1	0	1	3	.167	0	7	0	13	24	0	1.000
World Series totals (2 years)			14	54	6	10	2	0	2	6	.185	1	13	0	19	44	2	.969

GAINER, JAY

1B, ROCKIES

PERSONAL: Born October 8, 1966, in Panama City, Fla. . . . 6-0/190. . . . Throws left, bats left. . . . Full name: Jonathan Keith Gainer.
HIGH SCHOOL: Rutherford (Springfield, Fla.).
COLLEGE: South Alabama.
TRANSACTIONS/CAREER NOTES: Selected by San Diego Padres organization in 24th round of free-agent draft (June 4, 1990). . . . On disabled list (April 27-May 22, 1992). . . . Traded by Padres to Colorado Rockies for P Denis Boucher (March 21, 1993). . . . On Colorado Springs disabled list (July 8-August 3, 1993).
STATISTICAL NOTES: Led Northwest League with .537 slugging percentage in 1990. . . . Led California League with 16 sacrifice flies in 1991. . . . Hit home run in first major league at-bat (May 14, 1993).

Year	Team (League)	Pos.	G	AB	R	H	2B	3B	HR	RBI	Avg.	BB	SO	SB	PO	A	E	Avg.
			BATTING												FIELDING			
1990	—Spokane (N'west)	1B	74	281	41	*100	•21	0	10	54	*.356	31	49	4	610	40	7	.989
1991	—High Desert (Calif.)	1B	127	499	83	131	17	0	*32	*120	.263	52	105	4	813	77	*22	.976
1992	—Wichita (Texas)	1B	105	376	57	98	12	1	23	67	.261	46	101	4	709	67	11	.986
1993	—Colo. Springs (PCL)■	1B	86	293	51	86	11	3	10	74	.294	22	70	4	504	49	6	.989
	—Colorado (N.L.)	1B	23	41	4	7	0	0	3	6	.171	4	12	1	52	2	1	.982
Major league totals (1 year)			23	41	4	7	0	0	3	6	.171	4	12	1	52	2	1	.982

G

GALARRAGA, ANDRES

1B, ROCKIES

PERSONAL: Born June 18, 1961, in Caracas, Venezuela. . . . 6-3/235. . . . Throws right, bats right. . . . Full name: Andres Jose Galarraga. . . . Name pronounced GAHL-ah-RAH-guh.

HIGH SCHOOL: Enrique Felmi (Caracas, Venezuela).

TRANSACTIONS/CAREER NOTES: Signed as free agent by Montreal Expos organization (January 19, 1979). . . . On disabled list (July 10-August 19 and August 20-September 4, 1986; and May 26-July 4, 1991). . . . Traded by Expos to St. Louis Cardinals for P Ken Hill (November 25, 1991). . . . On St. Louis disabled list (April 8-May 22, 1992); included rehabilitation assignment to Louisville (May 13-22). . . . Granted free agency (October 27, 1992). . . . Signed by Colorado Rockies (November 16, 1992). . . . On disabled list (May 10-27 and July 25-August 21, 1993). . . . Granted free agency (October 25, 1993). . . . Re-signed by Rockies (December 6, 1993).

HONORS: Named Southern League Most Valuable Player (1984). . . . Named first baseman on THE SPORTING NEWS N.L. Silver Slugger team (1988). . . . Won N.L. Gold Glove at first base (1989-90). . . . Named N.L. Comeback Player of the Year by THE SPORTING NEWS (1993).

STATISTICAL NOTES: Led Southern League with 271 total bases, .508 slugging percentage and 10 intentional bases on balls received and tied for lead in being hit by pitch with nine in 1984. . . . Led Southern League first basemen with 1,428 total chances and 130 double plays in 1984. . . . Led N.L. in being hit by pitch with 10 in 1987 and tied for lead with 13 in 1989. . . . Led N.L. with 329 total bases in 1988.

			BATTING												FIELDING			
Year	Team (League)	Pos.	G	AB	R	H	2B	3B	HR	RBI	Avg.	BB	SO	SB	PO	A	E	Avg.
1979	—W.P. Beach (FSL)	1B	7	23	3	3	0	0	0	1	.130	2	11	0	2	1	0	1.000
	—Calgary (Pioneer)	1B-3B-C	42	112	14	24	3	1	4	16	.214	9	42	1	187	21	5	.977
1980	—Calgary (Pioneer)	1-3-C-O	59	190	27	50	11	4	4	22	.263	7	55	3	287	52	21	.942
1981	—Jamestown (NYP)	C-1-0-3	47	154	24	40	5	4	6	26	.260	15	44	0	154	15	0	1.000
1982	—W.P. Beach (FSL)	1B-OF	105	338	39	95	20	2	14	51	.281	34	77	2	462	36	9	.982
1983	—W.P. Beach (FSL)	1B-OF-3B	104	401	55	116	18	3	10	66	.289	33	68	7	861	77	13	.986
1984	—Jacksonv. (South.)	1B	143	533	81	154	28	4	27	87	.289	59	122	2	*1302	*110	16	.989
1985	—Indianapolis (A.A.)	1B-OF	121	439	*75	118	15	8	25	87	.269	45	103	3	930	63	14	.986
	—Montreal (N.L.)	1B	24	75	9	14	1	0	2	4	.187	3	18	1	173	22	1	.995
1986	—Montreal (N.L.)	1B	105	321	39	87	13	0	10	42	.271	30	79	6	805	40	4	.995
1987	—Montreal (N.L.)	1B	147	551	72	168	40	3	13	90	.305	41	127	7	*1300	103	10	.993
1988	—Montreal (N.L.)	1B	157	609	99	*184	*42	8	29	92	.302	39	*153	13	1464	103	15	.991
1989	—Montreal (N.L.)	1B	152	572	76	147	30	1	23	85	.257	48	*158	12	1335	91	11	.992
1990	—Montreal (N.L.)	1B	155	579	65	148	29	0	20	87	.256	40	*169	10	1300	94	10	.993
1991	—Montreal (N.L.)	1B	107	375	34	82	13	2	9	33	.219	23	86	5	887	80	9	.991
1992	—St. Louis (N.L.)■	1B	95	325	38	79	14	2	10	39	.243	11	69	5	777	62	8	.991
	—Louisville (A.A.)	1B	11	34	3	6	0	1	2	3	.176	0	8	1	61	7	2	.971
1993	—Colorado (N.L.)■	1B	120	470	71	174	35	4	22	98	*.370	24	73	2	1018	103	11	.990
Major league totals (9 years)			1062	3877	503	1083	217	20	138	570	.279	259	932	61	9059	698	79	.992

ALL-STAR GAME RECORD

		BATTING											FIELDING			
Year	League	Pos.	AB	R	H	2B	3B	HR	RBI	Avg.	BB	SO	SB	PO	A	E	Avg.
1988	—National	1B	2	0	0	0	0	0	0	.000	0	1	0	6	0	0	1.000
1993	—National	1B	1	0	0	0	0	0	0	.000	0	0	0	0	0	0	...
All-Star Game totals (2 years)			3	0	0	0	0	0	0	.000	0	1	0	6	0	0	1.000

GALLAGHER, DAVE

OF, BRAVES

PERSONAL: Born September 20, 1960, in Trenton, N.J. . . . 6-0/185. . . . Throws right, bats right. . . . Full name: David Thomas Gallagher.

HIGH SCHOOL: Steinert (Trenton, N.J.).

COLLEGE: Mercer County Community College (N.J.).

TRANSACTIONS/CAREER NOTES: Selected by Oakland Athletics organization in first round (third pick overall) of free-agent draft (January 8, 1980). . . . Selected by Cleveland Indians organization in secondary phase of free-agent draft (June 3, 1980). . . . On disabled list (May 2-June 6, 1983). . . . Traded by Indians organization to Seattle Mariners organization for P Mark Huismann (May 12, 1987). . . . Released by Mariners organization (September 30, 1987). . . . Signed by Vancouver, Chicago White Sox organization (December 7, 1987). . . . On Chicago disabled list (April 29-May 28, 1990). . . . Claimed on waivers by Baltimore Orioles (August 1, 1990). . . . Traded by Orioles to California Angels for P David Martinez and P Mike Hook (December 4, 1990). . . . Traded by Angels to New York Mets for OF Hubie Brooks (December 10, 1991). . . . On New York disabled list (April 25-June 8, 1992); included rehabilitation assignment to Tidewater (June 5-8). . . . Granted free agency (December 19, 1992). . . . Re-signed by Mets (January 21, 1993). . . . Traded by Mets to Atlanta Braves for P Pete Smith (November 24, 1993).

STATISTICAL NOTES: Led Midwest League with 21 sacrifice hits in 1982. . . . Tied for Eastern League lead in double plays by outfielder with four in 1983. . . . Led International League outfielders with 369 total chances in 1985. . . . Led International League with 12 sacrifice hits in 1986.

			BATTING												FIELDING			
Year	Team (League)	Pos.	G	AB	R	H	2B	3B	HR	RBI	Avg.	BB	SO	SB	PO	A	E	Avg.
1980	—Batavia (NY-Penn)	OF	69	241	33	66	6	3	5	36	.274	29	16	11	114	4	2	.983
1981	—Waterloo (Midw.)	OF-3B	127	435	55	102	22	1	3	34	.234	38	67	12	224	22	7	.972
1982	—Chatt. (South.)	OF	15	54	10	12	2	1	0	4	.222	5	8	2	32	1	0	1.000
	—Waterloo (Midw.)	OF	110	409	61	118	25	7	6	47	.289	41	57	19	232	15	4	*.984
1983	—Buffalo (Eastern)	OF-3B	107	376	64	127	21	3	2	47	*.338	83	21	12	223	13	5	.979
1984	—Maine (Int'l)	OF	116	380	49	94	19	5	6	49	.247	49	42	4	208	7	3	.986
1985	—Maine (Int'l)	OF	132	488	71	118	22	3	9	55	.242	65	38	16	*357	9	3	*.992
1986	—Maine (Int'l)	OF	132	497	59	145	23	5	8	44	.292	41	41	19	341	*14	1	*.997
1987	—Cleveland (A.L.)	OF	15	36	2	4	1	1	0	1	.111	2	5	2	34	1	1	.972
	—Buffalo (A.A.)	OF	12	46	10	12	4	0	0	6	.261	11	3	1	34	1	0	1.000
	—Calgary (PCL)■	OF	75	268	45	82	27	2	3	46	.306	37	36	12	143	5	4	.974
1988	—Vancouver (PCL)■	OF	34	131	23	44	8	1	4	27	.336	12	21	5	79	2	0	1.000
	—Chicago (A.L.)	OF	101	347	59	105	15	3	5	31	.303	29	40	5	228	5	0	1.000

Year	Team (League)	Pos.	G	AB	R	H	2B	3B	HR	RBI	Avg.	BB	SO	SB	PO	A	E	Avg.
			BATTING												FIELDING			
1989	—Chicago (A.L.)	OF	161	601	74	160	22	2	1	46	.266	46	79	5	390	8	3	.993
1990	—Chi.-Balt. (A.L.)■	OF	68	126	12	32	4	1	0	7	.254	7	12	1	96	3	2	.980
1991	—California (A.L.)■	OF	90	270	32	79	17	0	1	30	.293	24	43	2	180	8	0	1.000
1992	—New York (N.L.)■	OF	98	175	20	42	11	1	1	21	.240	19	16	4	105	4	2	.982
	—Tidewater (Int'l)	OF	3	12	1	3	0	0	0	0	.250	3	2	0	13	1	0	1.000
1993	—New York (N.L.)	OF-1B	99	201	34	55	12	2	6	28	.274	20	18	1	139	7	0	1.000
American League totals (5 years)			435	1380	179	380	59	7	7	115	.275	108	179	15	928	25	6	.994
National League totals (2 years)			197	376	54	97	23	3	7	49	.258	39	34	5	244	11	2	.992
Major league totals (7 years)			632	1756	233	477	82	10	14	164	.272	147	213	20	1172	36	8	.993

GALLAHER, KEVIN

P, ASTROS

PERSONAL: Born August 1, 1968, in Fairfax, Va. . . . 6-3/190. . . . Throws right, bats right. . . . Full name: Kevin John Gallaher.

HIGH SCHOOL: Bishop Denis J. O'Connell (Arlington, Va.).

COLLEGE: St. Bonaventure.

TRANSACTIONS/CAREER NOTES: Signed as free agent by Houston Astros organization (May 8, 1991).

Year	Team (League)	W	L	Pct.	ERA	G	GS	CG	ShO	Sv.	IP	H	R	ER	BB	SO
1991	—Auburn (NY-Penn)	2	5	.286	6.94	16	8	0	0	0	48	59	48	37	37	25
1992	—Osceola (Fla. St.)	0	1	.000	2.84	1	1	0	0	0	6⅓	2	2	2	3	5
	—Burlington (Midw.)	6	10	.375	3.85	20	20	1	0	0	117	108	70	50	80	89
1993	—Osceola (Fla. St.)	7	7	.500	3.80	21	21	1	1	0	135	132	68	57	57	93
	—Jackson (Texas)	0	2	.000	2.63	4	4	0	0	0	24	14	7	7	10	30

GALLEGO, MIKE

IF, YANKEES

PERSONAL: Born October 31, 1960, in Whittier, Calif. . . . 5-8/175. . . . Throws right, bats right. . . . Full name: Michael Anthony Gallego. . . . Name pronounced guy-YAY-go.

HIGH SCHOOL: St. Paul (Sante Fe Springs, Calif.).

COLLEGE: UCLA.

TRANSACTIONS/CAREER NOTES: Selected by Oakland Athletics organization in second round of free-agent draft (June 8, 1981); pick received as compensation for Chicago White Sox signing free agent Jim Essian. . . . On Tacoma temporary inactive list (April 10-May 20, 1983). . . . On Oakland disabled list (June 13-July 29, 1987). . . . Granted free agency (October 28, 1991). . . . Signed by New York Yankees (January 9, 1992). . . . On New York disabled list (March 28-May 17, 1992); included rehabilitation assignment to Fort Lauderdale (May 14-17). . . . On New York disabled list (July 8-September 18, 1992 and June 11-26, 1993).

STATISTICAL NOTES: Led Pacific Coast League in being hit by pitch with eight in 1986. . . . Tied for A.L. lead with 17 sacrifice hits in 1990.

Year	Team (League)	Pos.	G	AB	R	H	2B	3B	HR	RBI	Avg.	BB	SO	SB	PO	A	E	Avg.
			BATTING												FIELDING			
1981	—Modesto (Calif.)	2B	60	202	38	55	9	3	0	23	.272	31	31	9	127	161	13	.957
1982	—West Haven (East.)	2B-SS	54	139	17	25	1	0	0	5	.180	13	25	3	85	111	4	.980
	—Tacoma (PCL)	2B-3B-SS	44	136	12	30	3	1	0	11	.221	7	12	4	73	111	8	.958
1983	—Tacoma (PCL)	2B	2	2	0	0	0	0	0	0	.000	0	1	0	0	1	0	1.000
	—Alb./Colon. (East.)	2B-SS-3B	90	274	31	61	6	0	0	18	.223	43	25	3	184	260	4	.991
1984	—Tacoma (PCL)	2B-SS-3B	101	288	29	70	8	1	0	18	.243	27	39	7	167	231	13	.968
1985	—Oakland (A.L.)	2B-SS-3B	76	77	13	16	5	1	1	9	.208	12	14	1	57	94	1	.993
	—Modesto (Calif.)	2B-SS-3B	6	25	1	5	1	0	0	2	.200	2	8	1	12	11	1	.958
1986	—Tacoma (PCL)	SS-3B-2B	132	443	58	122	16	5	4	46	.275	39	58	3	197	417	23	.964
	—Oakland (A.L.)	2B-3B-SS	20	37	2	10	2	0	0	4	.270	1	6	0	24	51	1	.987
1987	—Tacoma (PCL)	2B	10	41	6	11	0	2	0	6	.268	10	7	1	15	25	1	.976
	—Oakland (A.L.)	2B-3B-SS	72	124	18	31	6	0	2	14	.250	12	21	0	75	122	8	.961
1988	—Oakland (A.L.)	2B-SS-3B	129	277	38	58	8	0	2	20	.209	34	53	2	155	254	8	.981
1989	—Oakland (A.L.)	SS-2B-3B	133	357	45	90	14	2	3	30	.252	35	43	7	211	363	19	.968
1990	—Oakland (A.L.)	2-S-3-0	140	389	36	80	13	2	3	34	.206	35	50	5	207	379	13	.978
1991	—Oakland (A.L.)	2B-SS	159	482	67	119	15	4	12	49	.247	67	84	6	283	446	12	.984
1992	—Fort Lauder. (FSL)■	SS	3	10	0	2	1	0	0	2	.200	1	4	1	3	5	0	1.000
	—New York (A.L.)	2B-SS	53	173	24	44	7	1	3	14	.254	20	22	0	112	153	6	.978
1993	—New York (A.L.)	SS-2B-3B	119	403	63	114	20	1	10	54	.283	50	65	3	169	368	13	.976
Major league totals (9 years)			901	2319	306	562	90	11	36	228	.242	266	358	24	1293	2230	81	.978

CHAMPIONSHIP SERIES RECORD

CHAMPIONSHIP SERIES NOTES: Shares A.L. single-series record for most sacrifice hits—2 (1989).

Year	Team (League)	Pos.	G	AB	R	H	2B	3B	HR	RBI	Avg.	BB	SO	SB	PO	A	E	Avg.
			BATTING												FIELDING			
1988	—Oakland (A.L.)	2B	4	12	1	1	0	0	0	0	.083	0	3	0	7	6	0	1.000
1989	—Oakland (A.L.)	SS-2B	4	11	3	3	1	0	0	1	.273	0	2	0	6	14	0	1.000
1990	—Oakland (A.L.)	SS-2B	4	10	1	4	1	0	0	2	.400	1	1	0	8	9	0	1.000
Championship series totals (3 years)			12	33	5	8	2	0	0	3	.242	1	6	0	21	29	0	1.000

WORLD SERIES RECORD

Year	Team (League)	Pos.	G	AB	R	H	2B	3B	HR	RBI	Avg.	BB	SO	SB	PO	A	E	Avg.
			BATTING												FIELDING			
1988	—Oakland (A.L.)	PR-2B	1	0	0	0	0	0	0	0	...	0	0	0	0	0	0	...
1989	—Oakland (A.L.)	2B-PH-3B	2	1	0	0	0	0	0	0	.000	0	0	0	0	0	0	...
1990	—Oakland (A.L.)	SS	4	11	0	1	0	0	0	1	.091	1	3	1	7	10	1	.944
World Series totals (3 years)			7	12	0	1	0	0	0	1	.083	1	3	1	7	10	1	.944

GAMEZ, BOB

P, ANGELS

PERSONAL: Born November 18, 1968, in Los Angeles. . . . 6-5/185. . . . Throws left, bats left. . . . Full name: Robert Ernest Gamez.
HIGH SCHOOL: Neward (Calif.) Memorial.
COLLEGE: Chabot College (Calif.).
TRANSACTIONS/CAREER NOTES: Selected by Texas Rangers organization in 29th round of free-agent draft (June 1, 1988). . . . Released by Rangers organization (April 1, 1990). . . . Signed as free agent by California Angels organization (June 16, 1990).

Year	Team (League)	W	L	Pct.	ERA	G	GS	CG	ShO	Sv.	IP	H	R	ER	BB	SO
1988	—GC Rangers (GCL)	0	0	...	0.00	2	0	0	0	0	2⅔	0	0	0	4	1
1989	—GC Rangers (GCL)	2	1	.667	3.76	23	1	0	0	2	40⅔	35	17	17	18	44
1990	—Boise (Northwest)■	3	0	1.000	2.91	14	7	0	0	0	46⅓	42	19	15	15	38
1991	—Quad City (Midw.)	4	3	.571	3.64	41	5	0	0	1	76⅔	75	38	31	38	83
1992	—Palm Springs (Cal.)	8	8	.500	4.94	38	13	0	0	3	98⅓	106	63	54	44	70
1993	—Midland (Texas)	5	2	.714	3.26	44	0	0	0	0	60⅔	68	27	22	18	50
	—Vancouver (PCL)	1	0	1.000	4.73	9	0	0	0	0	13⅓	11	9	7	9	15

RECORD AS POSITION PLAYER

			BATTING												FIELDING			
Year	Team (League)	Pos.	G	AB	R	H	2B	3B	HR	RBI	Avg.	BB	SO	SB	PO	A	E	Avg.
1988	—GC Rangers (GCL)	OF-P	31	88	13	15	1	1	0	4	.170	9	16	0	30	1	0	1.000

GAMEZ, FRANCISCO

P, BREWERS

PERSONAL: Born April 2, 1970, in Hermosillo, Sonora, Mexico. . . . 6-2/185. . . . Throws right, bats right. . . . Full name: Francisco Depaula Jose Gamez.
TRANSACTIONS/CAREER NOTES: Signed by Monterrey of Mexican League (1989). . . . Contract sold by Monterrey to Milwaukee Brewers organization (October 26, 1989). . . . On disabled list (June 5-July 27, 1993).
STATISTICAL NOTES: Tied for Arizona League lead with five home runs allowed in 1990.

Year	Team (League)	W	L	Pct.	ERA	G	GS	CG	ShO	Sv.	IP	H	R	ER	BB	SO
1990	—Ariz. Brewers (Ar.)	2	3	.400	2.66	11	7	1	0	0	50⅔	42	21	15	20	31
1991	—Beloit (Midwest)	9	12	.429	3.63	25	24	1	0	0	146⅓	140	76	59	57	92
1992	—Stockton (Calif.)	9	5	.643	3.63	23	23	2	0	0	134	134	64	54	69	95
1993	—El Paso (Texas)	2	8	.200	5.40	15	14	1	0	0	68⅓	92	45	41	25	26

GANT, RON

OF, BRAVES

PERSONAL: Born March 2, 1965, in Victoria, Tex. . . . 6-0/200. . . . Throws right, bats right. . . . Full name: Ronald Edwin Gant.
HIGH SCHOOL: Victoria (Tex.).
TRANSACTIONS/CAREER NOTES: Selected by Atlanta Braves organization in fourth round of free-agent draft (June 6, 1983). . . . On suspended list for one game (July 31, 1991).
HONORS: Named outfielder on THE SPORTING NEWS N.L. All-Star team (1991). . . . Named outfielder on THE SPORTING NEWS N.L. Silver Slugger team (1991).
STATISTICAL NOTES: Led South Atlantic League second basemen with 75 double plays in 1984. . . . Led Carolina League with 271 total bases in 1986. . . . Led Southern League second basemen with 783 total chances and 108 double plays in 1987. . . . Led N.L. second basemen with 26 errors in 1988.

			BATTING												FIELDING			
Year	Team (League)	Pos.	G	AB	R	H	2B	3B	HR	RBI	Avg.	BB	SO	SB	PO	A	E	Avg.
1983	—GC Braves (GCL)	SS	56	193	32	45	2	2	1	14	.233	41	34	4	68	134	22	.902
1984	—Anderson (S. Atl.)	2B	105	359	44	85	14	6	3	38	.237	29	65	13	248	263	31	.943
1985	—Sumter (S. Atl.)	2B-SS-OF	102	305	46	78	14	4	7	37	.256	33	59	19	160	200	10	.973
1986	—Durham (Carolina)	2B	137	512	108	142	31	10	*26	102	.277	78	85	35	240	384	26	.960
1987	—Greenville (South.)	2B	140	527	78	130	27	3	14	82	.247	59	91	24	*328	*434	21	*.973
	—Atlanta (N.L.)	2B	21	83	9	22	4	0	2	9	.265	1	11	4	45	59	3	.972
1988	—Richmond (Int'l)	2B	12	45	3	14	2	2	0	4	.311	2	10	1	22	23	5	.900
	—Atlanta (N.L.)	2B-3B	146	563	85	146	28	8	19	60	.259	46	118	19	316	417	†31	.959
1989	—Atlanta (N.L.)	3B-OF	75	260	26	46	8	3	9	25	.177	20	63	9	70	103	17	.911
	—Sumter (S. Atl.)	OF	12	39	13	15	4	1	1	5	.385	11	3	4	19	1	2	.909
	—Richmond (Int'l)	OF-3B	63	225	42	59	13	2	11	27	.262	29	42	6	111	14	5	.962
1990	—Atlanta (N.L.)	OF	152	575	107	174	34	3	32	84	.303	50	86	33	357	7	8	.978
1991	—Atlanta (N.L.)	OF	154	561	101	141	35	3	32	105	.251	71	104	34	338	7	6	.983
1992	—Atlanta (N.L.)	OF	153	544	74	141	22	6	17	80	.259	45	101	32	277	5	4	.986
1993	—Atlanta (N.L.)	OF	157	606	113	166	27	4	36	117	.274	67	117	26	271	5	*11	.962
Major league totals (7 years)			858	3192	515	836	158	27	147	480	.262	300	600	157	1674	603	80	.966

CHAMPIONSHIP SERIES RECORD

CHAMPIONSHIP SERIES NOTES: Shares single-game record for most grand slams—1 (October 7, 1992). . . . Shares records for most runs batted in in one inning—4 (October 7, 1992, fifth inning); and most stolen bases in one inning—2 (October 10, 1991, third inning). . . . Holds N.L. single-series record for most stolen bases—7 (1991). . . . Shares N.L. single-game record for most stolen bases—3 (October 10, 1991).

			BATTING												FIELDING			
Year	Team (League)	Pos.	G	AB	R	H	2B	3B	HR	RBI	Avg.	BB	SO	SB	PO	A	E	Avg.
1991	—Atlanta (N.L.)	OF	7	27	4	7	1	0	1	3	.259	2	4	7	15	2	0	1.000
1992	—Atlanta (N.L.)	OF	7	22	5	4	0	0	2	6	.182	4	4	1	16	0	0	1.000
1993	—Atlanta (N.L.)	OF	6	27	4	5	3	0	0	3	.185	2	9	0	10	1	1	.917
Championship series totals (3 years)			20	76	13	16	4	0	3	12	.211	8	17	8	41	3	1	.978

WORLD SERIES RECORD

			BATTING												FIELDING			
Year	Team (League)	Pos.	G	AB	R	H	2B	3B	HR	RBI	Avg.	BB	SO	SB	PO	A	E	Avg.
1991	—Atlanta (N.L.)	OF	7	30	3	8	0	1	0	4	.267	2	3	1	19	0	0	1.000

Year	Team (League)	Pos.	G	AB	R	H	2B	3B	HR	RBI	Avg.	BB	SO	SB	PO	A	E	Avg.
			BATTING												FIELDING			
1992	—Atlanta (N.L.)	OF-PR-PH	4	8	2	1	1	0	0	0	.125	1	2	2	3	1	0	1.000
	World Series totals (2 years)		11	38	5	9	1	1	0	4	.237	3	5	3	22	1	0	1.000

ALL-STAR GAME RECORD

Year	League	Pos.	AB	R	H	2B	3B	HR	RBI	Avg.	BB	SO	SB	PO	A	E	Avg.
			BATTING											FIELDING			
1992	—National	PH-OF	2	0	0	0	0	0	0	.000	0	0	0	1	0	0	1.000

GARAGOZZO, KEITH

P, TWINS

PERSONAL: Born October 25, 1969, in Camden, N.J. ... 6-0/170. ... Throws left, bats left. ... Full name: Keith John Garagozzo. ... Name pronounced GARE-uh-GAH-zoh.
HIGH SCHOOL: Holy Cross (Delran, N.J.).
COLLEGE: Delaware.
TRANSACTIONS/CAREER NOTES: Selected by New York Yankees organization in ninth round of free-agent draft (June 3, 1991). ... Selected by Minnesota Twins from Yankees organization in Rule 5 major league draft (December 13, 1993).
STATISTICAL NOTES: Tied for South Atlantic League lead with 15 home runs allowed in 1992.

Year	Team (League)	W	L	Pct.	ERA	G	GS	CG	ShO	Sv.	IP	H	R	ER	BB	SO
1991	—Oneonta (NYP)	4	2	.667	4.40	15	15	0	0	0	75⅔	66	50	37	62	55
1992	—Greensboro (S. Atl.)	•14	8	.636	2.84	28	•28	2	0	0	174	153	77	55	70	137
1993	—Prin. William (Car.)	5	4	.556	2.59	11	11	1	0	0	66	44	23	19	21	52
	—Alb./Colon. (East.)	4	6	.400	4.48	17	14	1	0	0	86⅓	88	49	43	24	71

GARCES, RICH

P, TWINS

PERSONAL: Born May 18, 1971, in Maracay, Venezuela. ... 6-0/215. ... Throws right, bats right. ... Full name: Richard Aron Garces Jr. ... Name pronounced gar-SESS.
HIGH SCHOOL: Jose Felix Rivas (Maracay, Venezuela).
COLLEGE: Venezuela Universidad (Venezuela).
TRANSACTIONS/CAREER NOTES: Signed as free agent by Minnesota Twins organization (December 29, 1987). ... On Portland suspended list (May 17-September 16, 1991). ... On Portland disabled list (July 28, 1991-remainder of season).

Year	Team (League)	W	L	Pct.	ERA	G	GS	CG	ShO	Sv.	IP	H	R	ER	BB	SO
1988	—Elizabeth. (Appal.)	5	4	.556	2.29	17	3	1	0	5	59	51	22	15	27	69
1989	—Kenosha (Midwest)	9	10	.474	3.41	24	24	4	1	0	142⅔	117	70	54	62	84
1990	—Visalia (California)	2	2	.500	1.81	47	0	0	0	*28	54⅔	33	14	11	16	75
	—Orlando (Southern)	2	1	.667	2.08	15	0	0	0	8	17⅓	17	4	4	14	22
	—Minnesota (A.L.)	0	0	...	1.59	5	0	0	0	2	5⅔	4	2	1	4	1
1991	—Portland (PCL)	0	1	.000	4.85	10	0	0	0	3	13	10	7	7	8	13
	—Orlando (Southern)	2	1	.667	3.31	10	0	0	0	0	16⅓	12	6	6	14	17
1992	—Orlando (Southern)	3	3	.500	4.54	58	0	0	0	13	73⅓	76	46	37	39	72
1993	—Portland (PCL)	1	3	.250	8.33	35	7	0	0	0	54	70	55	50	64	48
	—Minnesota (A.L.)	0	0	...	0.00	3	0	0	0	0	4	4	2	0	2	3
	Major league totals (2 years)	0	0	...	0.93	8	0	0	0	2	9⅔	8	4	1	6	4

GARCIA, CARLOS

2B, PIRATES

PERSONAL: Born October 15, 1967, in Tachira, Venezuela. ... 6-1/193. ... Throws right, bats right. ... Full name: Carlos Jesus Garcia.
HIGH SCHOOL: Bolivar (Venezuela).
TRANSACTIONS/CAREER NOTES: Signed as free agent by Pittsburgh Pirates organization (January 9, 1987).

Year	Team (League)	Pos.	G	AB	R	H	2B	3B	HR	RBI	Avg.	BB	SO	SB	PO	A	E	Avg.
			BATTING												FIELDING			
1987	—Macon (S. Atl.)	SS	110	373	44	95	14	3	3	38	.255	23	80	20	161	262	42	.910
1988	—Augusta (S. Atl.)	SS	73	269	32	78	13	2	1	45	.290	22	46	11	138	207	29	.922
	—Salem (Carolina)	SS	62	236	21	65	9	3	1	28	.275	10	32	8	131	151	24	.922
1989	—Salem (Carolina)	SS	81	304	45	86	12	4	7	49	.283	18	51	19	137	262	32	.926
	—Harrisburg (East.)	SS	54	188	28	53	5	5	3	25	.282	8	36	6	84	131	7	.968
1990	—Harrisburg (East.)	SS	65	242	36	67	11	2	5	25	.277	16	36	12	101	209	14	.957
	—Buffalo (A.A.)	SS	63	197	23	52	10	0	5	18	.264	16	41	7	106	170	19	.936
	—Pittsburgh (N.L.)	SS	4	4	1	2	0	0	0	0	.500	0	2	0	0	4	0	1.000
1991	—Buffalo (A.A.)	SS	127	463	62	123	21	6	7	60	.266	33	78	30	*212	332	*31	.946
	—Pittsburgh (N.L.)	SS-3B-2B	12	24	2	6	0	2	0	1	.250	1	8	0	11	18	1	.967
1992	—Buffalo (A.A.)	SS-2B	113	426	73	129	28	9	13	70	.303	24	64	21	192	314	28	.948
	—Pittsburgh (N.L.)	2B-SS	22	39	4	8	1	0	0	4	.205	0	9	0	25	35	2	.968
1993	—Pittsburgh (N.L.)	2B-SS	141	546	77	147	25	5	12	47	.269	31	67	18	299	347	11	.983
	Major league totals (4 years)		179	613	84	163	26	7	12	52	.266	32	86	18	335	404	14	.981

CHAMPIONSHIP SERIES RECORD

Year	Team (League)	Pos.	G	AB	R	H	2B	3B	HR	RBI	Avg.	BB	SO	SB	PO	A	E	Avg.
			BATTING												FIELDING			
1992	—Pittsburgh (N.L.)	2B	1	1	0	0	0	0	0	0	.000	0	0	0	0	0	0	...

GARDINER, MIKE

P, TIGERS

PERSONAL: Born October 19, 1965, in Sarnia, Ont. ... 6-0/200. ... Throws right, bats both. ... Full name: Michael James Gardiner.
HIGH SCHOOL: Sarnia (Ont.) Collegiate.
COLLEGE: Indiana State (bachelor's degree in business, 1987).

TRANSACTIONS/CAREER NOTES: Selected by Seattle Mariners organization in 18th round of free-agent draft (June 2, 1987).... On disabled list (May 9-June 10, 1988).... Traded by Mariners to Boston Red Sox for P Rob Murphy (April 1, 1991).... On Boston disabled list (June 27-July 15, 1991).... Traded by Red Sox with P Terry Powers to Montreal Expos for OF Ivan Calderon (December 8, 1992).... Released by Expos (August 22, 1993).... Signed by Toledo, Detroit Tigers organization (August 28, 1993).
HONORS: Named Eastern League Pitcher of the Year (1990).
MISCELLANEOUS: Member of 1984 Canadian Olympic baseball team.

Year	Team (League)	W	L	Pct.	ERA	G	GS	CG	ShO	Sv.	IP	H	R	ER	BB	SO
1987	—Belling. (N'west)	2	0	1.000	0.00	2	1	0	0	0	10	6	0	0	1	11
	—Wausau (Midwest)	3	5	.375	5.22	13	13	2	0	0	81	91	54	47	33	80
1988	—Wausau (Midwest)	2	1	.667	3.16	11	6	0	0	1	31⅓	31	16	11	13	24
1989	—Wausau (Midwest)	4	0	1.000	0.59	15	1	0	0	7	30⅓	21	5	2	11	48
	—Williamsport (East.)	4	6	.400	2.84	30	3	1	0	2	63⅓	54	25	20	32	60
1990	—Williamsport (East.)	12	8	.600	*1.90	26	26	5	1	0	*179⅔	136	47	38	29	*149
	—Seattle (A.L.)	0	2	.000	10.66	5	3	0	0	0	12⅔	22	17	15	5	6
1991	—Pawtucket (Int'l)■	7	1	.875	2.34	8	8	2	1	0	57⅔	39	16	15	11	42
	—Boston (A.L.)	9	10	.474	4.85	22	22	0	0	0	130	140	79	70	47	91
1992	—Boston (A.L.)	4	10	.286	4.75	28	18	0	0	0	130⅔	126	78	69	58	79
	—Pawtucket (Int'l)	1	3	.250	3.31	5	5	2	0	0	32⅔	32	14	12	9	37
1993	—Montreal (N.L.)■	2	3	.400	5.21	24	2	0	0	0	38	40	28	22	19	21
	—Ottawa-Tol. (Int.)■	1	2	.333	2.70	9	5	0	0	1	30	23	11	9	11	35
	—Detroit (A.L.)	0	0	...	3.97	10	0	0	0	0	11⅓	12	5	5	7	4
A.L. totals (4 years)		13	22	.371	5.03	65	43	0	0	0	284⅔	300	179	159	117	180
N.L. totals (1 year)		2	3	.400	5.21	24	2	0	0	0	38	40	28	22	19	21
Major league totals (4 years)		15	25	.375	5.05	89	45	0	0	0	322⅔	340	207	181	136	201

GARDNER, JEFF

2B

PERSONAL: Born February 4, 1964, in Newport Beach, Calif.... 5-11/175.... Throws right, bats left.... Full name: Jeffrey Scott Gardner.
HIGH SCHOOL: Estancia (Costa Mesa, Calif.).
COLLEGE: Orange Coast College (Calif.).
TRANSACTIONS/CAREER NOTES: Selected by Houston Astros organization in 14th round of free-agent draft (January 17, 1984).... Signed as free agent by New York Mets organization (August 28, 1984).... Traded by Mets to San Diego Padres for P Steve Rosenberg (December 11, 1991).... Released by Padres (January 20, 1994).
STATISTICAL NOTES: Led South Atlantic League second basemen with 86 double plays in 1985.... Led Texas League with 14 sacrifice hits in 1988.... Led Texas League second basemen with .983 fielding percentage, 297 putouts, 398 assists, 707 total chances and 97 double plays in 1988.... Led International League second basemen with .988 fielding percentage in 1990 and .995 in 1991.

				BATTING										FIELDING			
Year	Team (League)	Pos.	G	AB	R	H	2B	3B	HR	RBI	Avg.	BB	SO	SB	PO	A	E	Avg.
1985	—Columbia (S. Atl.)	2B	123	401	80	118	9	1	0	50	.294	*142	40	31	284	*349	19	*.971
1986	—Lynchburg (Caro.)	2B	111	334	59	91	11	2	1	39	.272	81	33	6	212	321	9	*.983
1987	—Jackson (Texas)	2B-SS	119	399	55	109	10	3	0	30	.273	58	55	1	244	343	20	.967
1988	—Jackson (Texas)	2B-SS	134	432	46	109	15	2	0	33	.252	69	52	13	†300	†404	12	†.983
	—Tidewater (Int'l)	2B	2	8	3	3	1	1	0	2	.375	1	1	0	3	4	0	1.000
1989	—Tidewater (Int'l)	2B	101	269	28	75	11	0	0	24	.279	25	27	0	145	234	8	.979
1990	—Tidewater (Int'l)	2B-SS-3B	138	463	55	125	11	1	0	33	.270	84	33	3	271	385	13	†.981
1991	—Tidewater (Int'l)	2B-SS-3B	136	504	73	147	23	4	1	56	.292	*84	48	6	286	446	9	†.988
	—New York (N.L.)	SS-2B	13	37	3	6	0	0	0	1	.162	4	6	0	11	29	6	.870
1992	—Las Vegas (PCL)■	2B	120	439	82	147	30	5	1	51	.335	67	48	7	233	391	13	.980
	—San Diego (N.L.)	2B	15	19	0	2	0	0	0	0	.105	1	8	0	11	20	0	1.000
1993	—San Diego (N.L.)	2B-SS-3B	140	404	53	106	21	7	1	24	.262	45	69	2	214	294	10	.981
Major league totals (3 years)			168	460	56	114	21	7	1	25	.248	50	83	2	236	343	16	.973

GARDNER, MARK

P, MARLINS

PERSONAL: Born March 1, 1962, in Los Angeles.... 6-1/200.... Throws right, bats right.... Full name: Mark Allan Gardner.
HIGH SCHOOL: Clovis (Calif.).
COLLEGE: Fresno (Calif.) City College and Fresno State.
TRANSACTIONS/CAREER NOTES: Selected by California Angels organization in sixth round of free-agent draft (January 11, 1983).... Selected by Cleveland Indians organization in 17th round of free-agent draft (June 4, 1984).... Selected by Montreal Expos organization in eighth round of free-agent draft (June 3, 1985).... On disabled list (September 20, 1990-remainder of season).... On Montreal disabled list (April 2-May 14, 1991); included rehabilitation assignment to Indianapolis (April 11-May 8).... Traded by Expos with P Doug Piatt to Kansas City Royals for C Tim Spehr and P Jeff Shaw (December 9, 1992).... On Kansas City disabled list (July 7-August 27, 1993); included rehabilitation assignment to Omaha (July 28-August 26).... Released by Royals (December 8, 1993).... Signed by Florida Marlins organization (January 3, 1994).
RECORDS: Shares major league record for most hit batsmen in one inning—3 (August 15, 1992, first inning).
HONORS: Named American Association Pitcher of the Year (1989).
STATISTICAL NOTES: Led N.L. with nine hit batsmen in 1990.... Pitched nine hitless innings against Los Angeles Dodgers, but gave up two hits in 10th inning and lost, 1-0, when reliever Jeff Fassero gave up game-winning hit in 10th (July 26, 1991).

Year	Team (League)	W	L	Pct.	ERA	G	GS	CG	ShO	Sv.	IP	H	R	ER	BB	SO
1985	—Jamestown (NYP)	0	0	...	2.77	3	3	0	0	0	13	9	4	4	4	16
	—W.P. Beach (FSL)	5	4	.556	2.37	10	9	4	0	0	60⅔	54	24	16	18	44
1986	—Jacksonv. (South.)	10	11	.476	3.84	29	28	3	1	0	168⅔	144	88	72	90	140
1987	—Indianapolis (A.A.)	3	3	.500	5.67	9	9	0	0	0	46	48	32	29	28	41
	—Jacksonv. (South.)	4	6	.400	4.19	17	17	1	0	0	101	101	50	47	42	78
1988	—Jacksonv. (South.)	6	3	.667	1.60	15	15	4	2	0	112⅓	72	24	20	36	130
	—Indianapolis (A.A.)	4	2	.667	2.77	13	13	3	1	0	84⅓	65	30	26	32	71

G

Year	Team (League)	W	L	Pct.	ERA	G	GS	CG	ShO	Sv.	IP	H	R	ER	BB	SO
1989	—Indianapolis (A.A.)	12	4	*.750	2.37	24	23	4	2	0	163⅓	122	51	43	59	*175
	—Montreal (N.L.)	0	3	.000	5.13	7	4	0	0	0	26⅓	26	16	15	11	21
1990	—Montreal (N.L.)	7	9	.438	3.42	27	26	3	3	0	152⅔	129	62	58	61	135
1991	—Indianapolis (A.A.)	2	0	1.000	3.48	6	6	0	0	0	31	26	13	12	16	38
	—Montreal (N.L.)	9	11	.450	3.85	27	27	0	0	0	168⅓	139	78	72	75	107
1992	—Montreal (N.L.)	12	10	.545	4.36	33	30	0	0	0	179⅔	179	91	87	60	132
1993	—Kansas City (A.L.)■	4	6	.400	6.19	17	16	0	0	0	91⅔	92	65	63	36	54
	—Omaha (A.A.)	4	2	.667	2.79	8	8	1	0	0	48⅓	34	17	15	19	41
A.L. totals (1 year)		4	6	.400	6.19	17	16	0	0	0	91⅔	92	65	63	36	54
N.L. totals (4 years)		28	33	.459	3.96	94	87	3	3	0	527	473	247	232	207	395
Major league totals (5 years)		32	39	.451	4.29	111	103	3	3	0	618⅔	565	312	295	243	449

GATES, BRENT

2B, ATHLETICS

PERSONAL: Born March 14, 1970, in Grand Rapids, Mich. . . . 6-1/180. . . . Throws right, bats both. . . . Full name: Brent Robert Gates.
HIGH SCHOOL: Grandville (Mich.).
COLLEGE: Minnesota.
TRANSACTIONS/CAREER NOTES: Selected by Oakland Athletics organization in first round (26th pick overall) of free-agent draft (June 3, 1991).
STATISTICAL NOTES: Led California League second basemen with 735 total chances and 105 double plays in 1992.

				BATTING										FIELDING			
Year	Team (League)	Pos.	G	AB	R	H	2B	3B	HR	RBI	Avg.	BB	SO	SB	PO	A	E	Avg.
1991	—S. Oregon (N'west)	SS-2B-3B	58	219	41	63	11	0	3	26	.288	30	33	8	77	177	15	.944
	—Madison (Midwest)	SS-3B	4	12	4	4	2	0	0	1	.333	3	2	1	6	10	0	1.000
1992	—Modesto (Calif.)	2B	133	505	94	162	39	2	10	88	.321	85	60	9	*293	*420	•22	.970
1993	—Huntsville (South.)	2B	12	45	7	15	4	0	1	11	.333	7	9	0	32	28	0	1.000
	—Tacoma (PCL)	2B	12	44	7	15	7	0	1	4	.341	4	6	2	27	36	1	.984
	—Oakland (A.L.)	2B	139	535	64	155	29	2	7	69	.290	56	75	7	281	431	14	.981
Major league totals (1 year)			139	535	64	155	29	2	7	69	.290	56	75	7	281	431	14	.981

GEDMAN, RICH

C, ORIOLES

PERSONAL: Born September 26, 1959, in Worcester, Mass. . . . 6-0/211. . . . Throws right, bats left. . . . Full name: Richard Leo Gedman Jr.
HIGH SCHOOL: St Peter's (Worcester, Mass.).
TRANSACTIONS/CAREER NOTES: Signed as free agent by Boston Red Sox organization (August 5, 1977). . . . Granted free agency (November 12, 1986). . . . Re-signed by Red Sox (May 2, 1987). . . . On disabled list (July 7-22 and July 30, 1987-remainder of season). . . . On Boston disabled list (April 26-May 20, 1988); included rehabilitation assignment to Pawtucket (May 14-20). . . . Traded by Red Sox to Houston Astros for a player to be named later (June 8, 1990); deal settled with cash. . . . Granted free agency (November 5, 1990). . . . Signed by Louisville, St. Louis Cardinals organization (February 15, 1991). . . . Granted free agency (October 27, 1992). . . . Signed by Oakland Athletics organization (January 29, 1993). . . . Released by A's organization (March 29, 1993). . . . Signed by New York Yankees organization (May 6, 1993). . . . Granted free agency (October 15, 1993). . . . Signed by Baltimore Orioles organization (December 14, 1993).
RECORDS: Holds major league records for most putouts—36; and chances accepted—37, by catcher in two consecutive nine-inning games (April 29-30, 1986). . . . Shares major league single-game record for most putouts by catcher (nine-inning game)—20 (April 29, 1986). . . . Shares A.L. single-game record for most chances accepted by catcher (nine-inning game)—20 (April 29, 1986).
HONORS: Named A.L. Rookie Player of the Year by THE SPORTING NEWS (1981). . . . Named catcher on THE SPORTING NEWS A.L. All-Star team (1986).
STATISTICAL NOTES: Led International League catchers with 13 double plays in 1980. . . . Hit for the cycle (September 18, 1985). . . . Led A.L. catchers with 937 total chances and 14 passed balls in 1986.

				BATTING										FIELDING			
Year	Team (League)	Pos.	G	AB	R	H	2B	3B	HR	RBI	Avg.	BB	SO	SB	PO	A	E	Avg.
1978	—Winter Haven (FSL)	C	98	297	35	89	17	3	3	32	.300	43	29	0	377	39	2	*.995
1979	—Bristol (Eastern)	C	130	470	48	129	25	1	12	63	.274	49	95	0	497	58	11	*.981
1980	—Pawtucket (Int'l)	C	111	347	43	82	18	2	11	29	.236	30	64	0	367	*65	7	.984
	—Boston (A.L.)	C	9	24	2	5	0	0	0	1	.208	0	5	0	13	0	2	.867
1981	—Pawtucket (Int'l)	C	25	81	8	24	3	0	2	11	.296	9	11	0	176	20	6	.970
	—Boston (A.L.)	C	62	205	22	59	15	0	5	26	.288	9	31	0	275	30	3	.990
1982	—Boston (A.L.)	C	92	289	30	72	17	2	4	26	.249	10	37	0	397	29	10	.977
1983	—Boston (A.L.)	C	81	204	21	60	16	1	2	18	.294	15	37	0	274	26	6	.980
1984	—Boston (A.L.)	C	133	449	54	121	26	4	24	72	.269	29	72	0	693	58	*18	.977
1985	—Boston (A.L.)	C	144	498	66	147	30	5	18	80	.295	50	79	2	768	*78	*15	.983
1986	—Boston (A.L.)	C	135	462	49	119	29	0	16	65	.258	37	61	1	*866	65	6	.994
1987	—Boston (A.L.)	C	52	151	11	31	8	0	1	13	.205	10	24	0	306	14	8	.976
1988	—Boston (A.L.)	C	95	299	33	69	14	0	9	39	.231	18	49	0	570	40	5	.992
	—Pawtucket (Int'l)	C	4	15	2	7	1	0	1	1	.467	1	4	0	13	1	1	.933
1989	—Boston (A.L.)	C	93	260	24	55	9	0	4	16	.212	23	47	0	486	36	10	.981
1990	—Boston (A.L.)	C	10	15	3	3	0	0	0	0	.200	5	6	0	27	5	1	.970
	—Houston (N.L.)■	C	40	104	4	21	7	0	1	10	.202	15	24	0	180	25	0	1.000
1991	—St. Louis (N.L.)■	C	46	94	7	10	1	0	3	8	.106	4	15	0	192	13	5	.976
1992	—St. Louis (N.L.)	C	41	105	5	23	4	0	1	8	.219	11	22	0	227	12	3	.988
1993	—Columbus (Int'l)■	C-1B	89	275	30	72	15	0	12	35	.262	35	63	0	498	47	6	.989
American League totals (11 years)			906	2856	315	741	164	12	83	356	.259	206	448	3	4675	381	84	.984
National League totals (3 years)			127	303	16	54	12	0	5	26	.178	30	61	0	599	50	8	.988
Major league totals (13 years)			1033	3159	331	795	176	12	88	382	.252	236	509	3	5274	431	92	.984

CHAMPIONSHIP SERIES RECORD

			BATTING												FIELDING			
Year	Team (League)	Pos.	G	AB	R	H	2B	3B	HR	RBI	Avg.	BB	SO	SB	PO	A	E	Avg.
1986	—Boston (A.L.)	C	7	28	4	10	1	0	1	6	.357	0	4	0	45	4	0	1.000
1988	—Boston (A.L.)	C	4	14	1	5	0	0	1	1	.357	2	1	0	34	5	0	1.000
Championship series totals (2 years)			11	42	5	15	1	0	2	7	.357	2	5	0	79	9	0	1.000

WORLD SERIES RECORD

			BATTING												FIELDING			
Year	Team (League)	Pos.	G	AB	R	H	2B	3B	HR	RBI	Avg.	BB	SO	SB	PO	A	E	Avg.
1986	—Boston (A.L.)	C	7	30	1	6	1	0	1	1	.200	0	10	0	46	3	2	.961

ALL-STAR GAME RECORD

			BATTING										FIELDING			
Year	League	Pos.	AB	R	H	2B	3B	HR	RBI	Avg.	BB	SO	SB	PO	A	E	Avg.
1985	—American	C	1	0	0	0	0	0	0	.000	0	1	0	4	0	0	1.000
1986	—American	C	0	0	0	0	0	0	0	...	0	0	0	1	1	0	1.000
All-Star Game totals (2 years)			1	0	0	0	0	0	0	.000	0	1	0	5	1	0	1.000

GEREN, BOB

C

PERSONAL: Born September 22, 1961, in San Diego.... 6-3/228.... Throws right, bats right.... Full name: Robert Peter Geren III.... Name pronounced GAIR-in.

HIGH SCHOOL: Clairemont (Calif.).

TRANSACTIONS/CAREER NOTES: Selected by San Diego Padres organization in first round (24th pick overall) of free-agent draft (June 5, 1979); pick received as compensation for Los Angeles Dodgers signing free agent Derrel Thomas.... Traded by Padres organization to St. Louis Cardinals organization (December 10, 1980), completing deal in which Padres traded P Rollie Fingers, P Bob Shirley, C/1B Gene Tenace and a player to be named later to Cardinals for C Terry Kennedy, C Steve Swisher, P John Littlefield, P Al Olmsted, P Kim Seaman, P John Urrea and IF Mike Phillips (December 8, 1980).... Granted free agency (October 15, 1985).... Signed by Columbus, New York Yankees organization (November 7, 1985).... Claimed on waivers by Cincinnati Reds (December 2, 1991).... Released by Reds (March 17, 1992).... Signed by Winter Haven, Boston Red Sox organization (April 16, 1992).... Granted free agency (October 15, 1992).... Signed by Padres organization (December 2, 1992).... Granted free agency (October 15, 1993).... Named minor league catching instructor by Red Sox (November 30, 1993).

STATISTICAL NOTES: Led Florida State League catchers with 72 assists in 1982.... Led Midwest League catchers with 826 putouts, 102 assists and 939 total chances in 1983.... Led Texas League catchers with .996 fielding percentage in 1985.... Led Eastern League catchers with .994 fielding percentage in 1987.

			BATTING												FIELDING			
Year	Team (League)	Pos.	G	AB	R	H	2B	3B	HR	RBI	Avg.	BB	SO	SB	PO	A	E	Avg.
1979	—Walla Walla (N'west)	C	54	151	19	26	5	0	0	16	.172	32	39	0	183	23	9	.958
1980	—Reno (California)	C	48	157	24	45	7	1	4	23	.287	24	41	1	89	17	4	.964
	—Walla Walla (N'west)	C	51	177	19	45	8	1	2	28	.254	24	33	1	306	40	10	.972
1981	—St. Peters. (FSL)■	C	64	167	15	37	9	1	0	13	.222	13	32	0	204	24	3	.987
1982	—St. Peters. (FSL)	C-OF-1B	110	352	38	86	24	1	1	45	.244	29	68	3	500	†72	10	.983
1983	—Springfield (Midw.)	C-1B	124	434	67	115	21	3	24	73	.265	40	127	0	†829	†104	11	.988
1984	—Arkansas (Texas)	C-1B-3B	86	292	39	72	12	0	15	40	.247	34	69	1	545	56	8	.987
	—Louisville (A.A.)	C	15	40	3	7	1	0	0	3	.175	5	8	0	80	6	1	.989
1985	—Arkansas (Texas)	C-1B-OF	103	315	38	71	18	1	5	40	.225	31	74	3	562	60	4	†.994
	—Louisville (A.A.)	C	5	14	2	5	2	0	1	3	.357	0	1	0	27	1	0	1.000
1986	—Alb./Colon. (East.)■	C-1B	11	27	3	4	1	0	0	0	.148	6	12	0	51	7	0	1.000
	—Columbus (Int'l)	C-1B	68	205	24	52	15	3	7	25	.254	21	60	1	270	36	5	.984
1987	—Alb./Colon. (East.)	C-1B-3B	78	213	33	47	7	2	11	31	.221	21	42	1	319	45	3	†.992
	—Columbus (Int'l)	C	5	20	1	3	0	0	1	3	.150	0	9	0	20	3	1	.958
1988	—Columbus (Int'l)	C	95	321	37	87	13	2	8	35	.271	33	69	0	478	72	8	.986
	—New York (A.L.)	C	10	10	0	1	0	0	0	0	.100	2	3	0	18	3	0	1.000
1989	—Columbus (Int'l)	C	27	95	11	24	4	1	2	13	.253	5	25	1	137	18	2	.987
	—New York (A.L.)	C	65	205	26	59	5	1	9	27	.288	12	44	0	308	24	3	.991
1990	—New York (A.L.)	C	110	277	21	59	7	0	8	31	.213	13	73	0	487	55	4	.993
1991	—New York (A.L.)	C	64	128	7	28	3	0	2	12	.219	9	31	0	255	18	3	.989
1992	—Winter Haven (FSL)■	C	7	23	3	7	0	0	1	2	.304	1	5	0	19	4	1	.958
	—Pawtucket (Int'l)	C	66	213	28	44	7	0	9	25	.207	17	53	0	257	23	1	.996
1993	—San Diego (N.L.)■	C-3B-1B	58	145	8	31	6	0	3	6	.214	13	28	0	252	29	2	.993
American League totals (4 years)			249	620	54	147	15	1	19	70	.237	36	151	0	1068	100	10	.992
National League totals (1 year)			58	145	8	31	6	0	3	6	.214	13	28	0	252	29	2	.993
Major league totals (5 years)			307	765	62	178	21	1	22	76	.233	49	179	0	1320	129	12	.992

GIBRALTER, STEVE

OF, REDS

PERSONAL: Born October 9, 1972, in Dallas.... 6-0/185.... Throws right, bats right.... Full name: Stephan Benson Gibralter.... Brother of David Gibralter, infielder, Boston Red Sox organization.

HIGH SCHOOL: Duncanville (Tex.).

TRANSACTIONS/CAREER NOTES: Selected by Cincinnati Reds organization in sixth round of free-agent draft (June 4, 1990).

HONORS: Named Midwest League Most Valuable Player (1992).

STATISTICAL NOTES: Led Gulf Coast League outfielders with 115 total chances in 1990.... Tied for South Atlantic League lead in double plays by outfielder with three in 1991.... Led Midwest League with 257 total bases in 1992.... Led Southern League outfielders with 334 total bases in 1993.

			BATTING												FIELDING			
Year	Team (League)	Pos.	G	AB	R	H	2B	3B	HR	RBI	Avg.	BB	SO	SB	PO	A	E	Avg.
1990	—GC Reds (GCL)	OF	52	174	26	45	11	3	4	27	.259	23	30	9	100	•9	6	.948

Year	Team (League)	Pos.	G	AB	R	H	2B	3B	HR	RBI	Avg.	BB	SO	SB	PO	A	E	Avg.
			BATTING												FIELDING			
1991	—Char., W.Va. (SAL) ..	OF	*140	*544	72	145	*36	7	6	71	.267	31	117	11	234	15	10	.961
1992	—Ced. Rap. (Midw.).....	OF	•137	529	*92	*162	32	3	*19	*99	.306	51	99	12	*311	7	7	.978
1993	—Chatt. (South.)	OF	132	477	65	113	25	3	11	47	.237	20	108	7	*319	7	8	.976

GIBSON, KIRK

DH/OF, TIGERS

PERSONAL: Born May 28, 1957, in Pontiac, Mich. . . . 6-3/225. . . . Throws left, bats left. . . . Full name: Kirk Harold Gibson.
HIGH SCHOOL: Kettering (Detroit).
COLLEGE: Michigan State.
TRANSACTIONS/CAREER NOTES: Selected by Detroit Tigers organization in first round (12th pick overall) of free-agent draft (June 6, 1978). . . . On restricted list (August 15, 1978-March 1, 1979). . . . On disabled list (April 13-May 21, 1979; June 18-October 6, 1980; and July 11, 1982-remainder of season). . . . Granted free agency (November 12, 1985). . . . Re-signed by Tigers (January 8, 1986). . . . On disabled list (April 23-June 2, 1986). . . . On Detroit disabled list (March 30-May 5, 1987); included rehabilitation assignment to Toledo (April 28-May 5). . . . Granted free agency (January 22, 1988). . . . Signed by Los Angeles Dodgers (January 29, 1988). . . . On disabled list (April 26-May 23 and July 23, 1989-remainder of season). . . . On Los Angeles disabled list (March 31-June 2, 1990); included rehabilitation assignment to Albuquerque (May 24-June 2). . . . Granted free agency (November 5, 1990). . . . Signed by Kansas City Royals (December 1, 1990). . . . Traded by Royals to Pittsburgh Pirates for P Neal Heaton (March 10, 1992). . . . Released by Pirates (May 5, 1992). . . . Signed by Tigers (February 10, 1993). . . . Granted free agency (November 5, 1993). . . . Re-signed by Tigers (February 4, 1994).
HONORS: Named outfielder on THE SPORTING NEWS college All-America team (1978). . . . Named outfielder on THE SPORTING NEWS N.L. Silver Slugger team (1988). . . . Named N.L. Most Valuable Player by Baseball Writers' Association of America (1988).
MISCELLANEOUS: Named as wide receiver on THE SPORTING NEWS college football All-America team (1978). . . . Selected by St. Louis Cardinals in seventh round (173rd pick overall) of 1979 NFL draft.

Year	Team (League)	Pos.	G	AB	R	H	2B	3B	HR	RBI	Avg.	BB	SO	SB	PO	A	E	Avg.
			BATTING												FIELDING			
1978	—Lakeland (Fla. St.) ...	OF	54	175	27	42	5	4	8	40	.240	22	54	13	115	2	6	.951
1979	—Evansville (A.A.)	OF	89	327	50	80	13	5	9	42	.245	34	110	20	100	5	9	.921
	—Detroit (A.L.)	OF	12	38	3	9	3	0	1	4	.237	1	3	3	15	0	0	1.000
1980	—Detroit (A.L.)	OF	51	175	23	46	2	1	9	16	.263	10	45	4	122	1	1	.992
1981	—Detroit (A.L.)	OF	83	290	41	95	11	3	9	40	.328	18	64	17	142	1	4	.973
1982	—Detroit (A.L.)	OF	69	266	34	74	16	2	8	35	.278	25	41	9	167	4	1	.994
1983	—Detroit (A.L.)	OF	128	401	60	91	12	9	15	51	.227	53	96	14	116	2	3	.975
1984	—Detroit (A.L.)	OF	149	531	92	150	23	10	27	91	.282	63	103	29	245	4	•12	.954
1985	—Detroit (A.L.)	OF	154	581	96	167	37	5	29	97	.287	71	137	30	286	1	•11	.963
1986	—Detroit (A.L.)	OF	119	441	84	118	11	2	28	86	.268	68	107	34	190	2	2	.990
1987	—Toledo (Int'l)............	DH	6	17	2	4	0	0	0	3	.235	2	3	2	...	...	...	...
	—Detroit (A.L.)	OF	128	487	95	135	25	3	24	79	.277	71	117	26	253	6	7	.974
1988	—Los Angeles (N.L.)■.	OF	150	542	106	157	28	1	25	76	.290	73	120	31	311	6	*12	.964
1989	—Los Angeles (N.L.) ...	OF	71	253	35	54	8	2	9	28	.213	35	55	12	146	3	3	.980
1990	—Albuquerque (PCL) ..	OF	5	14	6	6	2	0	1	4	.429	4	3	1	2	0	1	.667
	—Los Angeles (N.L.) ...	OF	89	315	59	82	20	0	8	38	.260	39	65	26	191	4	1	.995
1991	—Kansas City (A.L.)■.	OF	132	462	81	109	17	6	16	55	.236	69	103	18	162	3	4	.976
1992	—Pittsburgh (N.L.)■....	OF	16	56	6	11	0	0	2	5	.196	3	12	3	25	1	0	1.000
1993	—Detroit (A.L.)■.........	OF	116	403	62	105	18	6	13	62	.261	44	87	15	76	0	1	.987
American League totals (11 years)..........			1141	4075	671	1099	175	47	179	616	.270	493	903	199	1774	24	46	.975
National League totals (4 years)			326	1166	206	304	56	3	44	147	.261	150	252	72	673	14	16	.977
Major league totals (15 years).................			1467	5241	877	1403	231	50	223	763	.268	643	1155	271	2447	38	62	.976

CHAMPIONSHIP SERIES RECORD

CHAMPIONSHIP SERIES NOTES: Named A.L. Championship Series Most Valuable Player (1984). . . . Shares single-series record for most game-winning RBIs—2 (1988). . . . Shares A.L. single-series record for most strikeouts—8 (1987).

Year	Team (League)	Pos.	G	AB	R	H	2B	3B	HR	RBI	Avg.	BB	SO	SB	PO	A	E	Avg.
			BATTING												FIELDING			
1984	—Detroit (A.L.)	OF	3	12	2	5	1	0	1	2	.417	2	1	1	7	0	0	1.000
1987	—Detroit (A.L.)	OF	5	21	4	6	1	0	1	4	.286	3	8	3	10	1	0	1.000
1988	—Los Angeles (N.L.) ...	OF	7	26	2	4	0	0	2	6	.154	3	6	2	17	1	1	.947
Championship series totals (3 years)			15	59	8	15	2	0	4	12	.254	8	15	6	34	2	1	.973

WORLD SERIES RECORD

Year	Team (League)	Pos.	G	AB	R	H	2B	3B	HR	RBI	Avg.	BB	SO	SB	PO	A	E	Avg.
			BATTING												FIELDING			
1984	—Detroit (A.L.)	OF	5	18	4	6	0	0	2	7	.333	4	4	3	5	1	2	.750
1988	—Los Angeles (N.L.) ...	PH	1	1	1	1	0	0	1	2	1.000	0	0	0	...	...	...	...
World Series totals (2 years)..................			6	19	5	7	0	0	3	9	.368	4	4	3	5	1	2	.750

G

GIBSON, PAUL

P, YANKEES

PERSONAL: Born January 4, 1960, in Center Moriches, N.Y. . . . 6-1/185. . . . Throws left, bats right. . . . Full name: Paul Marshall Gibson.
HIGH SCHOOL: Center Moriches (N.Y.).
COLLEGE: Suffolk County Community College (N.Y.).
TRANSACTIONS/CAREER NOTES: Selected by Cincinnati Reds organization in third round of free-agent draft (January 10, 1978). . . . Released by Reds organization (April 8, 1981). . . . Signed by Lakeland, Detroit Tigers organization (May 23, 1981). . . . Selected by Minnesota Twins from Tigers organization in Rule 5 major league draft (December 6, 1982). . . . On disabled list (August 4-14, 1983). . . . Granted free agency (October 15, 1984). . . . Signed by Birmingham, Tigers organization (November 9, 1984). . . . Traded by Tigers with P Randy Marshall to New York Mets for OF Mark Carreon and P Tony Castillo (January 22,

1992).... On New York disabled list (July 28-August 30, 1992); included rehabilitation assignment to Tidewater (August 24-30).... Granted free agency (December 19, 1992).... Re-signed by Mets organization (January 22, 1993).... Released by Mets organization (April 4, 1993).... Signed by Norfolk, Mets organization (April 14, 1993).... Released by Mets (June 11, 1993).... Signed by Columbus, New York Yankees organization (June 18, 1993).

Year	Team (League)	W	L	Pct.	ERA	G	GS	CG	ShO	Sv.	IP	H	R	ER	BB	SO
1978	—Shelby (W. Caro.)	9	6	.600	3.02	24	22	4	2	0	140	106	57	47	71	71
1979	—Tampa (Fla. St.)	3	8	.273	3.07	24	22	2	0	0	129	121	56	44	46	58
1980	—Ced. Rap. (Midw.)	6	*15	.286	4.93	28	26	2	2	1	146	171	97	80	53	74
1981	—Lakeland (Fla. St.)■	4	3	.571	2.95	20	3	2	0	0	64	64	25	21	21	38
1982	—Birm. (Southern)	3	3	.500	2.68	44	0	0	0	12	77⅓	60	25	23	39	71
1983	—Orlando (Southern)■	1	7	.125	6.10	40	5	0	0	3	76⅔	91	59	52	56	45
1984	—Orlando (Southern)	7	7	.500	3.87	27	12	3	1	1	121	125	71	52	54	64
1985	—Birm. (Southern)■	8	8	.500	4.12	36	14	2	2	1	144⅓	135	73	66	63	79
1986	—Glens Falls (East.)	3	1	.750	1.37	9	1	0	0	1	19⅔	16	3	3	7	21
	—Nashville (A.A.)	5	6	.455	3.97	30	14	2	0	2	113⅓	121	58	50	40	91
1987	—Toledo (Int'l)	*14	7	.667	3.47	27	27	7	•2	0	179	173	83	69	57	118
1988	—Detroit (A.L.)	4	2	.667	2.93	40	1	0	0	0	92	83	33	30	34	50
1989	—Detroit (A.L.)	4	8	.333	4.64	45	13	0	0	0	132	129	71	68	57	77
1990	—Detroit (A.L.)	5	4	.556	3.05	61	0	0	0	3	97⅓	99	36	33	44	56
1991	—Detroit (A.L.)	5	7	.417	4.59	68	0	0	0	8	96	112	51	49	48	52
1992	—New York (N.L.)■	0	1	.000	5.23	43	1	0	0	0	62	70	37	36	25	49
	—Tidewater (Int'l)	0	0	...	3.00	2	0	0	0	0	3	3	1	1	2	1
1993	—Nor.-Colum. (Int.)■	2	1	.667	0.64	17	1	0	0	8	28	14	2	2	6	36
	—New York (N.L.)	1	1	.500	5.19	8	0	0	0	0	8⅔	14	6	5	2	12
	—New York (A.L.)	2	0	1.000	3.06	20	0	0	0	0	35⅓	31	15	12	9	25
A.L. totals (5 years)		20	21	.488	3.82	234	14	0	0	11	452⅔	454	206	192	192	260
N.L. totals (2 years)		1	2	.333	5.22	51	1	0	0	0	70⅔	84	43	41	27	61
Major league totals (6 years)		21	23	.477	4.01	285	15	0	0	11	523⅓	538	249	233	219	321

GIL, BENJI

SS, RANGERS

PERSONAL: Born October 6, 1972, in Tijuana, Mexico.... 6-2/182.... Throws right, bats right.... Full name: Romar Benjamin Gil.

HIGH SCHOOL: Castle Park (Chula Vista, Calif.).

TRANSACTIONS/CAREER NOTES: Selected by Texas Rangers organization in first round (19th pick overall) of free-agent draft (June 3, 1991).

			BATTING											FIELDING			
Year	Team (League)	Pos.	G	AB	R	H	2B	3B	HR	RBI	Avg.	BB	SO	SB	PO	A	E	Avg.
1991	—Butte (Pioneer)	SS	32	129	25	37	4	3	2	15	.287	14	36	9	61	88	14	.914
1992	—Gastonia (S. Atl.)	SS	132	482	75	132	21	1	9	55	.274	50	106	26	226	384	45	.931
1993	—Texas (A.L.)	SS	22	57	3	7	0	0	0	2	.123	5	22	1	27	76	5	.954
	—Tulsa (Texas)	SS	101	342	45	94	9	1	17	59	.275	35	89	20	159	285	19	.959
Major league totals (1 year)			22	57	3	7	0	0	0	2	.123	5	22	1	27	76	5	.954

GILKEY, BERNARD

OF, CARDINALS

PERSONAL: Born September 24, 1966, in St. Louis.... 6-0/190.... Throws right, bats right.... Full name: Otis Bernard Gilkey.

HIGH SCHOOL: University City (Mo.).

TRANSACTIONS/CAREER NOTES: Signed as free agent by St. Louis Cardinals organization (August 22, 1984).... On disabled list (April 10-25, 1986 and May 29, 1987-remainder of season).... On St. Louis disabled list (June 14-July 11, 1991 and April 29-May 14, 1993).

STATISTICAL NOTES: Led New York-Pennsylvania League outfielders with 185 total chances in 1985.... Led Texas League in caught stealing with 22 in 1989.... Led American Association in caught stealing with 33 in 1990.... Led N.L. outfielders with 19 assists in 1993.

			BATTING											FIELDING			
Year	Team (League)	Pos.	G	AB	R	H	2B	3B	HR	RBI	Avg.	BB	SO	SB	PO	A	E	Avg.
1985	—Erie (N.Y.-Penn)	OF	•77	*294	57	60	9	1	7	27	.204	55	57	34	*164	*13	*8	.957
1986	—Savannah (S. Atl.)	OF	105	374	64	88	15	4	6	36	.235	84	57	32	220	7	5	.978
1987	—Springfield (Midw.)	OF	46	162	30	37	5	0	0	9	.228	39	28	18	79	5	4	.955
1988	—Springfield (Midw.)	OF	125	491	84	120	18	7	6	36	.244	65	54	54	165	10	6	.967
1989	—Arkansas (Texas)	OF	131	500	*104	139	25	3	6	57	.278	70	54	*53	236	*22	9	.966
1990	—Louisville (A.A.)	OF	132	499	83	147	26	8	3	46	.295	*75	49	45	236	18	•11	.958
	—St. Louis (N.L.)	OF	18	64	11	19	5	2	1	3	.297	8	5	6	47	2	2	.961
1991	—St. Louis (N.L.)	OF	81	268	28	58	7	2	5	20	.216	39	33	14	164	6	1	.994
	—Louisville (A.A.)	OF	11	41	5	6	2	0	0	2	.146	6	10	1	33	1	0	1.000
1992	—St. Louis (N.L.)	OF	131	384	56	116	19	4	7	43	.302	39	52	18	217	9	5	.978
1993	—St. Louis (N.L.)	OF-1B	137	557	99	170	40	5	16	70	.305	56	66	15	251	†20	8	.971
Major league totals (4 years)			367	1273	194	363	71	13	29	136	.285	142	156	53	679	37	16	.978

GIRARDI, JOE

C, ROCKIES

PERSONAL: Born October 14, 1964, in Peoria, Ill.... 5-11/195.... Throws right, bats right.... Full name: Joseph Elliott Girardi.... Name pronounced jeh-RAR-dee.

HIGH SCHOOL: Spalding Institute (Peoria, Ill.).

COLLEGE: Northwestern (degree in industrial engineering, 1986).

TRANSACTIONS/CAREER NOTES: Selected by Chicago Cubs organization in fifth round of free-agent draft (June 2, 1986).... On disabled list (August 27, 1986-remainder of season and August 7, 1988-remainder of season).... On Chicago disabled list (April 17-August 6, 1991); included rehabilitation assignment to Iowa (July 23-August 6).... Selected by Colorado Rockies in first round (19th pick overall) of expansion draft (November 17, 1992).... On Colorado disabled list (June 5-August 11, 1993); included rehabilitation assignment to Colorado Springs (August 1-11).

STATISTICAL NOTES: Led Carolina League catchers with 661 total chances and tied for lead with 17 passed balls in 1987. . . . Led Eastern League catchers with .992 fielding percentage, 448 putouts, 76 assists and 528 total chances and tied for lead with five double plays in 1988. . . . Tied for N.L. lead with 16 passed balls in 1990.

			BATTING												FIELDING			
Year	Team (League)	Pos.	G	AB	R	H	2B	3B	HR	RBI	Avg.	BB	SO	SB	PO	A	E	Avg.
1986	—Peoria (Midwest)......	C	68	230	36	71	13	1	3	28	.309	17	36	6	405	34	5	.989
1987	—Winst.-Salem (Car.)..	C	99	364	51	102	9	8	8	46	.280	33	64	9	★569	★74	18	.973
1988	—Pittsfield (Eastern) ..	C-OF	104	357	44	97	14	1	7	41	.272	29	51	7	†460	†76	6	†.989
1989	—Chicago (N.L.)	C	59	157	15	39	10	0	1	14	.248	11	26	2	332	28	7	.981
	—Iowa (Am. Assoc.)....	C	32	110	12	27	4	2	2	11	.245	5	19	3	172	21	1	.995
1990	—Chicago (N.L.)	C	133	419	36	113	24	2	1	38	.270	17	50	8	653	61	11	.985
1991	—Chicago (N.L.)	C	21	47	3	9	2	0	0	6	.191	6	6	0	95	11	3	.972
	—Iowa (Am. Assoc.)....	C	12	36	3	8	1	0	0	4	.222	4	8	2	62	5	3	.957
1992	—Chicago (N.L.)	C	91	270	19	73	3	1	1	12	.270	19	38	0	369	51	4	.991
1993	—Colorado (N.L.)■.......	C	86	310	35	90	14	5	3	31	.290	24	41	6	478	46	6	.989
	—Colo. Springs (PCL) ..	C	8	31	6	15	1	1	1	6	.484	0	3	1	40	3	1	.977
Major league totals (5 years)			390	1203	108	324	53	8	6	101	.269	77	161	16	1927	197	31	.986

CHAMPIONSHIP SERIES RECORD

			BATTING												FIELDING			
Year	Team (League)	Pos.	G	AB	R	H	2B	3B	HR	RBI	Avg.	BB	SO	SB	PO	A	E	Avg.
1989	—Chicago (N.L.)	C	4	10	1	1	0	0	0	0	.100	1	2	0	20	0	0	1.000

GLADDEN, DAN

OF

PERSONAL: Born July 7, 1957, in San Jose, Calif. . . . 5-11/184. . . . Throws right, bats right. . . . Full name: Clinton Daniel Gladden III. . . . Brother of Jeff Gladden, minor league pitcher (1980-84).
HIGH SCHOOL: Monte Vista (Cupertino, Calif.).
COLLEGE: De Anza College (Calif.) and Fresno State.
TRANSACTIONS/CAREER NOTES: Signed as free agent by San Francisco Giants organization (June 17, 1979). . . . On Phoenix disabled list (April 19-May 1, 1984). . . . On San Francisco disabled list (June 4-July 23, 1986); included rehabilitation assignment to Phoenix (July 14-23). . . . Traded by Giants with P David Blakley to Minnesota Twins for P Jose Dominguez, P Ray Velasquez and a player to be named later (March 31, 1987); Giants organization acquired P Bryan Hickerson to complete deal (June 15, 1987). . . . On disabled list (June 25-July 10 and July 17-August 7, 1989; and June 29-July 24, 1991). . . . Granted free agency (November 5, 1991). . . . Signed by Detroit Tigers (December 20, 1991). . . . On disabled list (May 13-June 13, 1992). . . . On Detroit disabled list (April 12-June 1, 1993); included rehabilitation assignment to Toledo (May 24-June 1). . . . Granted free agency (October 25, 1993). . . . Signed by Yomiuri Giants of Japan Central League (December 16, 1993).
STATISTICAL NOTES: Led Texas League in caught stealing with 26 in 1981. . . . Tied for A.L. lead in double plays by outfielder with five in 1988.
MISCELLANEOUS: Batted as switch-hitter with Phoenix (1986).

			BATTING												FIELDING			
Year	Team (League)	Pos.	G	AB	R	H	2B	3B	HR	RBI	Avg.	BB	SO	SB	PO	A	E	Avg.
1979	—Fresno (California) ..	OF-2B-SS	60	228	41	70	9	1	3	31	.307	17	30	17	56	16	3	.960
1980	—Fresno (California) ..	OF	62	237	46	72	10	2	9	41	.304	11	36	15	68	3	1	.986
	—Shreveport (Texas)..	OF-SS	74	292	51	86	11	2	9	35	.295	22	46	22	169	14	5	.973
1981	—Shreveport (Texas)..	OF-SS-2B	124	472	81	148	23	9	8	44	.314	50	58	★52	211	12	3	.987
1982	—Phoenix (PCL)	OF	130	503	93	155	40	5	10	74	.308	44	69	41	264	16	7	.976
1983	—Phoenix (PCL)	OF	127	505	113	153	30	9	12	80	.303	54	68	50	319	6	7	.979
	—San Francisco (N.L.)..	OF	18	63	6	14	2	0	1	9	.222	5	11	4	53	0	0	1.000
1984	—Phoenix (PCL)	OF	59	234	70	93	11	7	3	27	.397	45	23	32	130	4	2	.985
	—San Francisco (N.L.)..	OF	86	342	71	120	17	2	4	31	.351	33	37	31	232	8	3	.988
1985	—San Francisco (N.L.)..	OF	142	502	64	122	15	8	7	41	.243	40	78	32	273	3	7	.975
1986	—San Francisco (N.L.)..	OF	102	351	55	97	16	1	4	29	.276	39	59	27	226	7	3	.987
	—Phoenix (PCL)	OF	7	27	5	9	4	0	0	0	.333	2	2	0	11	0	0	1.000
1987	—Minnesota (A.L.)■....	OF	121	438	69	109	21	2	8	38	.249	38	72	25	223	9	3	.987
1988	—Minnesota (A.L.)	0-2-3-P	141	576	91	155	32	6	11	62	.269	46	74	28	319	12	3	.991
1989	—Minnesota (A.L.)	OF-P	121	461	69	136	23	3	8	46	.295	23	53	23	245	8	9	.966
1990	—Minnesota (A.L.)	OF	136	534	64	147	27	6	5	40	.275	26	67	25	286	12	6	.980
1991	—Minnesota (A.L.)	OF	126	461	65	114	14	9	6	52	.247	36	60	15	240	4	3	.988
1992	—Detroit (A.L.)■.........	OF	113	417	57	106	20	1	7	42	.254	30	64	4	227	9	3	.987
1993	—Detroit (A.L.)	OF	91	356	52	95	16	2	13	56	.267	21	50	8	196	9	3	.986
	—Toledo (Int'l)	OF	7	28	6	11	1	0	1	7	.393	0	6	1	11	0	2	.846
American League totals (7 years)			849	3243	467	862	153	29	58	336	.266	220	440	128	1736	63	30	.984
National League totals (4 years)			348	1258	196	353	50	11	16	110	.281	117	185	94	784	18	13	.984
Major league totals (11 years)			1197	4501	663	1215	203	40	74	446	.270	337	625	222	2520	81	43	.984

CHAMPIONSHIP SERIES RECORD

			BATTING												FIELDING			
Year	Team (League)	Pos.	G	AB	R	H	2B	3B	HR	RBI	Avg.	BB	SO	SB	PO	A	E	Avg.
1987	—Minnesota (A.L.)	OF	5	20	5	7	2	0	0	5	.350	2	1	0	12	0	0	1.000
1991	—Minnesota (A.L.)	OF	5	23	4	6	0	0	0	3	.261	1	3	3	20	0	0	1.000
Championship series totals (2 years)			10	43	9	13	2	0	0	8	.302	3	4	3	32	0	0	1.000

WORLD SERIES RECORD

WORLD SERIES NOTES: Shares single-game record for most grand slams—1 (October 17, 1987). . . . Shares record for most runs batted in in one inning—4 (October 17, 1987, fourth inning).

Year	Team (League)	Pos.	G	AB	R	H	2B	3B	HR	RBI	Avg.	BB	SO	SB	PO	A	E	Avg.
			BATTING												FIELDING			
1987	—Minnesota (A.L.)	OF	7	31	3	9	2	1	1	7	.290	3	4	2	12	0	0	1.000
1991	—Minnesota (A.L.)	OF	7	30	5	7	2	2	0	0	.233	3	4	2	25	1	1	.963
World Series totals (2 years)			14	61	8	16	4	3	1	7	.262	6	8	4	37	1	1	.974

RECORD AS PITCHER

Year	Team (League)	W	L	Pct.	ERA	G	GS	CG	ShO	Sv.	IP	H	R	ER	BB	SO
1988	—Minnesota (A.L.)	0	0	...	0.00	1	0	0	0	0	1	0	0	0	0	0
1989	—Minnesota (A.L.)	0	0	...	9.00	1	0	0	0	0	1	2	1	1	1	0
Major league totals (2 years)		0	0	...	4.50	2	0	0	0	0	2	2	1	1	1	0

GLANVILLE, DOUG

OF, CUBS

PERSONAL: Born August 25, 1970, in Hackensack, N.J. . . . 6-2/170. . . . Throws right, bats right. . . . Full name: Douglas Metunwa Glanville.
HIGH SCHOOL: Teaneck (N.J.).
COLLEGE: Pennsylvania.
TRANSACTIONS/CAREER NOTES: Selected by Chicago Cubs organization in first round (12th pick overall) of free-agent draft (June 3, 1991).
STATISTICAL NOTES: Led Carolina League outfielders with 312 total chances in 1992.

Year	Team (League)	Pos.	G	AB	R	H	2B	3B	HR	RBI	Avg.	BB	SO	SB	PO	A	E	Avg.
			BATTING												FIELDING			
1991	—Geneva (NY-Penn)...	OF	36	152	29	46	8	0	2	12	.303	11	25	17	77	4	0	1.000
1992	—Winst.-Salem (Car.)..	OF	120	485	72	125	18	4	4	36	.258	40	78	32	*293	12	7	.978
1993	—Daytona (Fla. St.).....	OF	61	239	47	70	10	1	2	21	.293	28	24	18	123	11	7	.950
	—Orlando (Southern)..	OF	73	296	42	78	14	4	9	40	.264	12	41	15	168	8	5	.972

GLAVINE, TOM

P, BRAVES

PERSONAL: Born March 25, 1966, in Concord, Mass. . . . 6-1/190. . . . Throws left, bats left. . . . Full name: Thomas Michael Glavine. . . . Name pronounced GLAV-in.
HIGH SCHOOL: Billerica (Mass.).
TRANSACTIONS/CAREER NOTES: Selected by Atlanta Braves organization in second round of free-agent draft (June 4, 1984).
HONORS: Named N.L. Pitcher of the Year by THE SPORTING NEWS (1991). . . . Named lefthanded pitcher on THE SPORTING NEWS N.L. All-Star team (1991-92). . . . Named pitcher on THE SPORTING NEWS N.L. Silver Slugger team (1991). . . . Named N.L. Cy Young Award winner by Baseball Writers' Association of America (1991).
STATISTICAL NOTES: Led Gulf Coast League with 12 wild pitches in 1984.
MISCELLANEOUS: Selected by Los Angeles Kings in fourth round (fourth Kings pick, 69th overall) of NHL entry draft (June 9, 1984). . . . Scored once and received a base on balls in one game as pinch-runner and one as pinch-hitter (1991). . . . Singled and struck out in two games as pinch-hitter (1992).

Year	Team (League)	W	L	Pct.	ERA	G	GS	CG	ShO	Sv.	IP	H	R	ER	BB	SO
1984	—GC Braves (GCL)	2	3	.400	3.34	8	7	0	0	0	32⅓	29	17	12	13	34
1985	—Sumter (S. Atl.)	9	6	.600	*2.35	26	26	2	1	0	168⅔	114	58	44	73	174
1986	—Greenville (South.).....	11	6	.647	3.41	22	22	2	1	0	145⅓	129	62	55	70	114
	—Richmond (Int'l)	1	5	.167	5.63	7	7	1	1	0	40	40	29	25	27	12
1987	—Richmond (Int'l)	6	12	.333	3.35	22	22	4	1	0	150⅓	142	70	56	56	91
	—Atlanta (N.L.)	2	4	.333	5.54	9	9	0	0	0	50⅓	55	34	31	33	20
1988	—Atlanta (N.L.)	7	*17	.292	4.56	34	34	1	0	0	195⅓	201	111	99	63	84
1989	—Atlanta (N.L.)	14	8	.636	3.68	29	29	6	4	0	186	172	88	76	40	90
1990	—Atlanta (N.L.)	10	12	.455	4.28	33	33	1	0	0	214⅓	232	111	102	78	129
1991	—Atlanta (N.L.)	•20	11	.645	2.55	34	34	•9	1	0	246⅔	201	83	70	69	192
1992	—Atlanta (N.L.)	•20	8	.714	2.76	33	33	7	•5	0	225	197	81	69	70	129
1993	—Atlanta (N.L.)	•22	6	.786	3.20	36	•36	4	2	0	239⅓	236	91	85	90	120
Major league totals (7 years)		95	66	.590	3.53	208	208	28	12	0	1357	1294	599	532	443	764

CHAMPIONSHIP SERIES RECORD

CHAMPIONSHIP SERIES NOTES: Holds records for most runs allowed in one inning—8 (October 13, 1992, second inning); and most earned runs allowed in one inning—7 (October 13, 1992, second inning). . . . Shares single-game record for most earned runs allowed—7 (October 13, 1992). . . . Shares record for most hits allowed in one inning—6 (October 13, 1992, second inning). . . . Shares N.L. career record for most hit batsmen—2. . . . Shares N.L. single-series record for most hit batsmen—2 (1992).

Year	Team (League)	W	L	Pct.	ERA	G	GS	CG	ShO	Sv.	IP	H	R	ER	BB	SO
1991	—Atlanta (N.L.)	0	2	.000	3.21	2	2	0	0	0	14	12	5	5	6	11
1992	—Atlanta (N.L.)	0	2	.000	12.27	2	2	0	0	0	7⅓	13	11	10	3	2
1993	—Atlanta (N.L.)	1	0	1.000	2.57	1	1	0	0	0	7	6	2	2	0	5
Champ. series totals (3 years)		1	4	.200	5.40	5	5	0	0	0	28⅓	31	18	17	9	18

WORLD SERIES RECORD

WORLD SERIES NOTES: Shares records for most bases on balls allowed in one inning—4 (October 24, 1991, sixth inning); and most consecutive bases on balls allowed in one inning—3 (October 24, 1991, sixth inning).

Year	Team (League)	W	L	Pct.	ERA	G	GS	CG	ShO	Sv.	IP	H	R	ER	BB	SO
1991	—Atlanta (N.L.)	1	1	.500	2.70	2	2	1	0	0	13⅓	8	6	4	7	8
1992	—Atlanta (N.L.)	1	1	.500	1.59	2	2	2	0	0	17	10	3	3	4	8
World Series totals (2 years)		2	2	.500	2.08	4	4	3	0	0	30⅓	18	9	7	11	16

ALL-STAR GAME RECORD

ALL-STAR GAME NOTES: Holds single-game record for most hits allowed—9 (July 14, 1992). . . . Holds record for most hits allowed in one inning—7 (July 14, 1992, first inning).

G

Year	League	W	L	Pct.	ERA	GS	CG	ShO	Sv.	IP	H	R	ER	BB	SO
1991	—National	0	0	...	0.00	1	0	0	0	2	1	0	0	1	3
1992	—National	0	1	.000	27.00	1	0	0	0	1⅔	9	5	5	0	2
1993	—National						Did not play.								
All-Star totals (2 years)		0	1	.000	12.27	2	0	0	0	3⅔	10	5	5	1	5

GOFF, JERRY

C, PIRATES

PERSONAL: Born April 12, 1964, in San Rafael, Calif. . . . 6-3/207. . . . Throws right, bats left. . . . Full name: Jerry Leroy Goff.

HIGH SCHOOL: San Rafael (Calif.).

COLLEGE: Marin Community College (Calif.) and California.

TRANSACTIONS/CAREER NOTES: Selected by Oakland Athletics organization in seventh round of free-agent draft (January 11, 1983). . . . Selected by New York Yankees organization in 12th round of free-agent draft (January 17, 1984). . . . Selected by Seattle Mariners organization in third round of free-agent draft (June 2, 1986). . . . Traded by Mariners organization to Montreal Expos for P Pat Pacillo (February 27, 1990). . . . On disabled list (June 14-July 11 and July 21-September 6, 1991). . . . Granted free agency (October 16, 1992). . . . Signed by Buffalo, Pittsburgh Pirates organization (January 20, 1993).

STATISTICAL NOTES: Led Northwest League catchers with seven double plays in 1986. . . . Led Midwest League with 32 passed balls in 1987. . . . Led Eastern League catchers with 17 errors in 1988. . . . Led Pacific Coast League with 14 passed balls in 1989. . . . Led American Association catchers with 499 putouts in 1993.

			BATTING												FIELDING			
Year	Team (League)	Pos.	G	AB	R	H	2B	3B	HR	RBI	Avg.	BB	SO	SB	PO	A	E	Avg.
1986	—Belling. (N'west)	C	54	168	26	32	7	2	7	25	.190	42	54	4	286	35	12	.964
1987	—Wausau (Midwest)	C-1B-3B	109	336	51	78	17	2	13	47	.232	65	87	4	589	90	16	.977
1988	—San Bern. (Calif.)	C	65	215	38	62	11	0	13	43	.288	52	59	2	383	64	6	.987
	—Vermont (Eastern)	C-OF	63	195	27	41	7	1	7	23	.210	23	58	2	283	40	†17	.950
1989	—Williamsport (East.)	C-OF	33	119	9	22	5	0	3	8	.185	14	42	1	180	21	6	.971
	—Calgary (PCL)	C-1-3-0	76	253	40	59	16	0	11	50	.233	23	62	1	346	63	12	.971
1990	—Indianapolis (A.A.)■	C-3-1-2	39	143	23	41	10	2	5	26	.287	24	33	3	162	24	6	.969
	—Montreal (N.L.)	C-1B-3B	52	119	14	27	1	0	3	7	.227	21	36	0	216	17	9	.963
1991	—Indianapolis (A.A.)	C-3B-1B	57	191	32	48	10	2	9	37	.251	22	51	2	204	44	13	.950
1992	—Indianapolis (A.A.)	3B-C-1B	94	314	37	75	17	1	14	39	.239	32	97	0	136	145	24	.921
	—Montreal (N.L.)	PH	3	3	0	0	0	0	0	0	.000	0	3	0	...	...	...	...
1993	—Buffalo (A.A.)■	C-3B	104	362	52	91	27	3	14	69	.251	55	82	1	†500	53	7	.988
	—Pittsburgh (N.L.)	C	14	37	5	11	2	0	2	6	.297	8	9	0	54	7	1	.984
Major league totals (3 years)			69	159	19	38	3	0	5	13	.239	29	48	0	270	24	10	.967

GOHR, GREG

P, TIGERS

PERSONAL: Born October 29, 1967, in Santa Clara, Calif. . . . 6-3/205. . . . Throws right, bats right. . . . Full name: Gregory James Gohr.

HIGH SCHOOL: Bellarmine Prep (San Jose, Calif.).

COLLEGE: Santa Clara.

TRANSACTIONS/CAREER NOTES: Selected by Detroit Tigers organization in first round (21st pick overall) of free-agent draft (June 5, 1989). . . . On disabled list (July 27-August 18 and August 25-September 8, 1992).

STATISTICAL NOTES: Led International League with 14 wild pitches in 1991.

Year	Team (League)	W	L	Pct.	ERA	G	GS	CG	ShO	Sv.	IP	H	R	ER	BB	SO
1989	—Fayetteville (SAL)	0	2	.000	7.15	4	4	0	0	0	11⅓	11	9	9	6	10
1990	—Lakeland (Fla. St.)	13	5	.722	2.62	25	25	0	0	0	137⅔	125	52	40	50	90
1991	—London (Eastern)	0	0	...	0.00	2	2	0	0	0	11	9	0	0	2	10
	—Toledo (Int'l)	10	8	.556	4.61	26	26	2	1	0	148⅓	125	86	76	66	96
1992	—Toledo (Int'l)	8	10	.444	3.99	22	20	2	0	0	130⅔	124	65	58	46	94
1993	—Detroit (A.L.)	0	0	...	5.96	16	0	0	0	0	22⅔	26	15	15	14	23
	—Toledo (Int'l)	3	10	.231	5.80	18	17	2	0	0	107	127	74	69	38	77
Major league totals (1 year)		0	0	...	5.96	16	0	0	0	0	22⅔	26	15	15	14	23

GOMEZ, CHRIS

SS, TIGERS

PERSONAL: Born June 16, 1971, in Los Angeles. . . . 6-1/183. . . . Throws right, bats right. . . . Full name: Christopher Cory Gomez.

HIGH SCHOOL: Lakewood (Calif.).

COLLEGE: Long Beach State.

TRANSACTIONS/CAREER NOTES: Selected by California Angels organization in 37th round of free-agent draft (June 5, 1989). . . . Selected by Detroit Tigers organization in third round of free-agent draft (June 1, 1992).

			BATTING												FIELDING			
Year	Team (League)	Pos.	G	AB	R	H	2B	3B	HR	RBI	Avg.	BB	SO	SB	PO	A	E	Avg.
1992	—London (Eastern)	SS	64	220	20	59	13	2	1	19	.268	20	34	1	100	174	14	.951
1993	—Toledo (Int'l)	SS	87	277	29	68	12	2	0	20	.245	23	37	6	133	261	16	.961
	—Detroit (A.L.)	SS-2B	46	128	11	32	7	1	0	11	.250	9	17	2	69	118	5	.974
Major league totals (1 year)			46	128	11	32	7	1	0	11	.250	9	17	2	69	118	5	.974

G

GOMEZ, LEO

3B, ORIOLES

PERSONAL: Born March 2, 1967, in Canovanas, Puerto Rico. . . . 6-0/208. . . . Throws right, bats right.

HIGH SCHOOL: Luis Hernaes Nevones (Carnovanas, Puerto Rico).

TRANSACTIONS/CAREER NOTES: Signed as free agent by Baltimore Orioles organization (December 13, 1985). . . . On disabled list (July 3-31, 1986 and May 3, 1988-remainder of season). . . . On Baltimore disabled list (July 8-September 1, 1993); included rehabilitation assignment to Rochester (August 26-September 1).

STATISTICAL NOTES: Led Eastern League third basemen with 256 assists in 1989. . . . Led International League third basemen with 26 double plays in 1990.

Year	Team (League)	Pos.	G	AB	R	H	2B	3B	HR	RBI	Avg.	BB	SO	SB	PO	A	E	Avg.
						BATTING									FIELDING			
1986	—Bluefield (Appal.).....	3B-2B-SS	27	88	23	31	7	1	7	28	.352	25	27	1	15	38	7	.883
1987	—Hagerstown (Car.)...	3B-SS	131	466	94	152	*38	2	19	110	*.326	95	85	6	75	233	33	.903
1988	—Charlotte (South.)...	3B-1B	24	89	6	26	5	0	1	10	.292	10	17	1	19	50	8	.896
1989	—Hagerstown (East.)..	3B-SS	134	448	71	126	23	3	18	78	.281	*89	102	2	79	†257	25	.931
1990	—Rochester (Int'l).......	3B-1B	131	430	*97	119	26	4	26	*97	.277	89	89	2	92	204	20	.937
	—Baltimore (A.L.)........	3B	12	39	3	9	0	0	0	1	.231	8	7	0	11	20	4	.886
1991	—Baltimore (A.L.)........	3B-1B	118	391	40	91	17	2	16	45	.233	40	82	1	78	184	7	.974
	—Rochester (Int'l).......	3B-1B	28	101	13	26	6	0	6	19	.257	16	18	0	24	46	4	.946
1992	—Baltimore (A.L.)........	3B	137	468	62	124	24	0	17	64	.265	63	78	2	106	246	18	.951
1993	—Baltimore (A.L.)........	3B	71	244	30	48	7	0	10	25	.197	32	60	0	48	145	10	.951
	—Rochester (Int'l).......	3B	4	15	3	3	1	0	0	1	.200	3	4	0	1	5	0	1.000
Major league totals (4 years)			338	1142	135	272	48	2	43	135	.238	143	227	3	243	595	39	.956

GOMEZ, PAT

P

PERSONAL: Born March 17, 1968, in Roseville, Calif. . . . 5-11/185. . . . Throws left, bats left. . . . Full name: Patrick Alexander Gomez.

HIGH SCHOOL: San Juan (Citrus Heights, Calif.).

TRANSACTIONS/CAREER NOTES: Selected by Chicago Cubs organization in fourth round of free-agent draft (June 2, 1986). . . . Traded by Cubs organization with C Kelly Mann to Atlanta Braves (September 1, 1989), completing deal in which Braves traded P Paul Assenmacher to Cubs for two players to be named later (August 24, 1989). . . . Traded by Braves organization to Texas Rangers organization for 3B Jose Oliva (December 9, 1992). . . . Traded by Rangers organization to San Diego Padres for P Terry Bross (December 16, 1992). . . . On San Diego disabled list (June 26, 1993-remainder of season); included rehabilitation assignment to Las Vegas but did not play (July 18-23). . . . Granted free agency (October 5, 1993).

MISCELLANEOUS: Struck out in one game as pinch-hitter (1993).

Year	Team (League)	W	L	Pct.	ERA	G	GS	CG	ShO	Sv.	IP	H	R	ER	BB	SO
1986	—Wytheville (Appal.)....	3	6	.333	5.17	11	11	0	0	0	54	57	51	31	46	55
1987	—Peoria (Midwest).......	3	6	.333	4.31	20	17	1	0	0	94	88	55	45	71	95
1988	—Char., W.Va. (SAL)....	2	7	.222	5.38	36	9	0	0	5	78⅔	75	53	47	52	97
1989	—Winst.-Salem (Car.).....	11	6	.647	2.75	23	21	3	1	0	137⅔	115	59	42	60	127
	—Charlotte (South.)■.....	1	0	1.000	2.51	2	2	0	0	0	14⅓	14	5	4	3	11
1990	—Richmond (Int'l)..........	1	1	.500	8.80	4	4	0	0	0	15⅓	19	16	15	10	8
	—Greenville (South.)......	6	8	.429	4.49	23	21	0	0	0	124⅓	126	75	62	71	94
1991	—Greenville (South.)......	5	2	.714	1.81	13	13	0	0	0	79⅔	58	20	16	31	71
	—Richmond (Int'l)..........	2	9	.182	4.39	16	14	0	0	0	82	99	55	40	41	41
1992	—Richmond (Int'l)..........	3	5	.375	5.45	23	11	0	0	0	71	79	47	43	42	48
	—Greenville (South.)......	7	0	1.000	1.13	8	8	1	1	0	47⅔	25	8	6	19	38
1993	—San Diego (N.L.)■........	1	2	.333	5.12	27	1	0	0	0	31⅔	35	19	18	19	26
Major league totals (1 year)....		1	2	.333	5.12	27	1	0	0	0	31⅔	35	19	18	19	26

GONZALES, LARRY

C

PERSONAL: Born March 28, 1967, in Covina, Calif. . . . 6-3/200. . . . Throws right, bats right. . . . Full name: Lawrence Christopher Gonzales.

HIGH SCHOOL: Edgewood (West Covina, Calif.).

COLLEGE: Hawaii.

TRANSACTIONS/CAREER NOTES: Selected by California Angels organization in 22nd round of free-agent draft (June 1, 1988). . . . Released by Vancouver, Angels organization (October 1, 1993).

Year	Team (League)	Pos.	G	AB	R	H	2B	3B	HR	RBI	Avg.	BB	SO	SB	PO	A	E	Avg.
						BATTING									FIELDING			
1988	—Palm Springs (Cal.)..	C-1B	35	100	11	20	0	0	0	11	.200	22	25	0	192	16	3	.986
1989	—Quad City (Midw.)....	C-1B	69	195	24	38	3	1	6	20	.195	39	34	2	500	40	7	.987
1990	—Quad City (Midw.)....	C-1B	99	309	44	95	16	1	8	75	.307	36	56	2	434	46	4	.992
1991	—Midland (Texas).......	C-1B	78	257	27	82	13	0	4	56	.319	22	33	2	350	38	7	.982
	—Edmonton (PCL).......	C	2	3	0	0	0	0	0	0	.000	1	1	0	7	1	1	.889
1992	—Edmonton (PCL).......	C-3-1-P	80	241	37	79	10	0	3	47	.328	38	24	2	288	63	6	.983
1993	—Vancouver (PCL).....	C-1-3-P	81	264	30	69	9	0	2	27	.261	26	28	5	359	51	2	.995
	—California (A.L.).......	C	2	2	0	1	0	0	0	1	.500	1	0	0	4	0	0	1.000
Major league totals (1 year)			2	2	0	1	0	0	0	1	.500	1	0	0	4	0	0	1.000

RECORD AS PITCHER

Year	Team (League)	W	L	Pct.	ERA	G	GS	CG	ShO	Sv.	IP	H	R	ER	BB	SO
1992	—Edmonton (PCL)........	0	0	...	13.50	2	0	0	0	0	1⅓	1	2	2	1	0
1993	—Vancouver (PCL).......	0	0	...	0.00	1	0	0	0	0	1	1	0	0	1	1

GONZALES, RENE

IF, ORIOLES

PERSONAL: Born September 3, 1961, in Austin, Tex. . . . 6-3/201. . . . Throws right, bats right. . . . Full name: Rene Adrian Gonzales.

HIGH SCHOOL: Rosemead (Calif.).

COLLEGE: Glendale College (Calif.) and Cal State Los Angeles.

TRANSACTIONS/CAREER NOTES: Selected by Montreal Expos organization in fifth round of free-agent draft (June 7, 1982). . . . Traded by Expos to Baltimore Orioles (December 16, 1986), completing deals in which Orioles traded P Dennis Martinez (June 16, 1986) and C John Stefero (December 8, 1986) to Expos for a player to be named later. . . . Traded by Orioles to Toronto Blue Jays for P Rob Blumberg (January 15, 1991). . . . Granted free agency (November 18, 1991). . . . Signed by California Angels organization (January 10, 1992). . . . On disabled list (August 12, 1992-remainder of season). . . . Granted free agency (October 26, 1992). . . . Re-signed by Angels (December 18, 1992). . . . Granted free agency (October 29, 1993). . . . Signed by Orioles organization (February 3, 1994).

STATISTICAL NOTES: Led Southern League shortstops with 102 double plays in 1983. . . . Led American Association shortstops with 79 double plays in 1985.

Year	Team (League)	Pos.	G	AB	R	H	2B	3B	HR	RBI	Avg.	BB	SO	SB	PO	A	E	Avg.
			BATTING												FIELDING			
1982	—Memphis (South.)	SS	56	183	10	39	3	1	1	11	.213	9	44	2	77	183	14	.949
1983	—Memphis (South.)	SS	144	476	67	128	12	2	2	44	.269	40	53	5	*258	449	20	*.972
1984	—Indianapolis (A.A.) ...	SS-3B-2B	114	359	41	84	12	2	2	32	.234	20	33	10	161	349	13	.975
	—Montreal (N.L.)	SS	29	30	5	7	1	0	0	2	.233	2	5	0	17	28	2	.957
1985	—Indianapolis (A.A.) ...	SS	130	340	21	77	11	1	0	25	.226	22	49	3	203	*345	23	.960
1986	—Indianapolis (A.A.) ...	3B-SS-2B	116	395	57	108	14	2	3	43	.273	41	47	8	208	297	23	.956
	—Montreal (N.L.)	SS-3B	11	26	1	3	0	0	0	0	.115	2	7	0	7	19	0	1.000
1987	—Baltimore (A.L.)■	3B-2B-SS	37	60	14	16	2	1	1	7	.267	3	11	1	22	43	2	.970
	—Rochester (Int'l)	3-S-2-1-0	42	170	20	51	9	3	0	24	.300	13	17	4	72	108	3	.984
1988	—Baltimore (A.L.)	3-2-S-1-0	92	237	13	51	6	0	2	15	.215	13	32	2	66	185	8	.969
1989	—Baltimore (A.L.)	2B-3B-SS	71	166	16	36	4	0	1	11	.217	12	30	5	103	146	7	.973
1990	—Baltimore (A.L.)	2-3-S-0	67	103	13	22	3	1	1	12	.214	12	14	1	68	114	2	.989
1991	—Toronto (A.L.)■	S-3-2-1	71	118	16	23	3	0	1	6	.195	12	22	0	61	118	7	.962
1992	—California (A.L.)■	3-2-1-S	104	329	47	91	17	1	7	38	.277	41	46	7	191	229	9	.979
1993	—California (A.L.)	3-1-S-2-P	118	335	34	84	17	0	2	31	.251	49	45	5	234	170	12	.971
American League totals (7 years)			560	1348	153	323	52	3	15	120	.240	142	200	21	745	1005	47	.974
National League totals (2 years)			40	56	6	10	1	0	0	2	.179	4	12	0	24	47	2	.973
Major league totals (9 years)			600	1404	159	333	53	3	15	122	.237	146	212	21	769	1052	49	.974

CHAMPIONSHIP SERIES RECORD

Year	Team (League)	Pos.	G	AB	R	H	2B	3B	HR	RBI	Avg.	BB	SO	SB	PO	A	E	Avg.
			BATTING												FIELDING			
1991	—Toronto (A.L.)	PR-1B-SS	2	0	0	0	0	0	0	0	...	0	0	0	2	0	0	1.000

RECORD AS PITCHER

Year	Team (League)	W	L	Pct.	ERA	G	GS	CG	ShO	Sv.	IP	H	R	ER	BB	SO
1993	—California (A.L.)	0	0	...	0.00	1	0	0	0	0	1	0	0	0	0	0

GONZALEZ, ALEX

SS, BLUE JAYS

PERSONAL: Born April 8, 1973, in Miami. . . . 6-0/182. . . . Throws right, bats right. . . . Full name: Alexander Scott Gonzalez.

HIGH SCHOOL: Miami (Fla.) Killian.

TRANSACTIONS/CAREER NOTES: Selected by Toronto Blue Jays organization in 14th round of free-agent draft (June 3, 1991).

STATISTICAL NOTES: Led Gulf Coast League shortstops with 247 total chances in 1991. . . . Led Southern League with 253 total bases in 1993. . . . Led Southern League shortstops with 682 total chances and 92 double plays in 1993.

Year	Team (League)	Pos.	G	AB	R	H	2B	3B	HR	RBI	Avg.	BB	SO	SB	PO	A	E	Avg.
			BATTING												FIELDING			
1991	—GC Blue Jays (GCL) ..	SS	53	191	29	40	5	4	0	10	.209	12	41	7	66	*160	21	.915
1992	—Myrtle Beach (SAL) ..	SS	134	535	83	145	22	9	10	62	.271	38	119	26	*248	*406	48	.932
1993	—Knoxville (S. Atl.)	SS	*142	561	*93	162	29	7	16	69	.289	39	110	38	*224	*428	30	*.956

GONZALEZ, JUAN

OF, RANGERS

PERSONAL: Born October 16, 1969, in Vega Baja, Puerto Rico. . . . 6-3/215. . . . Throws right, bats right. . . . Full name: Juan Alberto Vazquez Gonzalez.

HIGH SCHOOL: Vega Baja (Puerto Rico).

TRANSACTIONS/CAREER NOTES: Signed as free agent by Texas Rangers organization (May 30, 1986). . . . On disabled list (April 27-June 17, 1988 and March 30-April 26, 1991).

HONORS: Named American Association Most Valuable Player (1990). . . . Named outfielder on THE SPORTING NEWS A.L. Silver Slugger team (1992-93). . . . Named outfielder on THE SPORTING NEWS A.L. All-Star team (1993).

STATISTICAL NOTES: Led Texas League with 254 total bases in 1989. . . . Led American Association with 252 total bases in 1990. . . . Hit three home runs in one game (June 7, 1992 and August 28, 1993). . . . Led A.L. with .632 slugging percentage in 1993.

Year	Team (League)	Pos.	G	AB	R	H	2B	3B	HR	RBI	Avg.	BB	SO	SB	PO	A	E	Avg.
			BATTING												FIELDING			
1986	—GC Rangers (GCL)	OF	60	*233	24	56	4	1	0	36	.240	21	57	7	89	6	*6	.941
1987	—Gastonia (S. Atl.)	OF	127	509	69	135	21	2	14	74	.265	30	92	9	234	10	12	.953
1988	—Charlotte (Fla. St.) ...	OF	77	277	25	71	14	3	8	43	.256	25	64	5	139	5	4	.973
1989	—Tulsa (Texas)	OF	133	502	73	147	30	7	21	85	.293	31	98	1	292	15	9	.972
	—Texas (A.L.)	OF	24	60	6	9	3	0	1	7	.150	6	17	0	53	0	2	.964
1990	—Okla. City (A.A.)	OF	128	496	78	128	29	4	*29	*101	.258	32	109	2	220	7	8	.966
	—Texas (A.L.)	OF	25	90	11	26	7	1	4	12	.289	2	18	0	33	0	0	1.000
1991	—Texas (A.L.)	OF	142	545	78	144	34	1	27	102	.264	42	118	4	310	6	6	.981
1992	—Texas (A.L.)	OF	155	584	77	152	24	2	*43	109	.260	35	143	0	379	9	10	.975
1993	—Texas (A.L.)	OF	140	536	105	166	33	1	*46	118	.310	37	99	4	265	5	4	.985
Major league totals (5 years)			486	1815	277	497	101	5	121	348	.274	122	395	8	1040	20	22	.980

ALL-STAR GAME RECORD

Year	League	Pos.	AB	R	H	2B	3B	HR	RBI	Avg.	BB	SO	SB	PO	A	E	Avg.
			BATTING											FIELDING			
1993	—American	OF	1	0	0	0	0	0	0	.000	1	1	0	1	0	0	1.000

GONZALEZ, LUIS

OF, ASTROS

PERSONAL: Born September 3, 1967, in Tampa, Fla. . . . 6-2/180. . . . Throws right, bats left. . . . Full name: Luis Emilio Gonzalez.

HIGH SCHOOL: Jefferson (Tampa, Fla.).

COLLEGE: South Alabama.

TRANSACTIONS/CAREER NOTES: Selected by Houston Astros organization in fourth round of free-agent draft (June 1, 1988). . . .

G

On disabled list (May 26-July 5, 1989; August 29-September 13, 1991 and July 21-August 5, 1992).
STATISTICAL NOTES: Tied for Southern League lead with 12 sacrifice flies and nine intentional bases on balls received in 1990. . . . Led N.L. with 10 sacrifice flies in 1993.

			BATTING												FIELDING			
Year	**Team (League)**	**Pos.**	**G**	**AB**	**R**	**H**	**2B**	**3B**	**HR**	**RBI**	**Avg.**	**BB**	**SO**	**SB**	**PO**	**A**	**E**	**Avg.**
1988	—Asheville (S. Atl.)	3B	31	115	13	29	7	1	2	14	.252	12	17	2	19	62	6	.931
	—Auburn (NY-Penn)	3B-SS-1B	39	157	32	49	10	3	5	27	.312	12	19	2	37	83	13	.902
1989	—Osceola (Fla. St.)	DH	86	287	46	82	16	7	6	38	.286	37	49	2	...	...	...	...
1990	—Columbus (South.)	1B-3B	138	495	86	131	30	6	•24	89	.265	54	100	27	1039	88	23	.980
	—Houston (N.L.)	3B-1B	12	21	1	4	2	0	0	0	.190	2	5	0	22	10	0	1.000
1991	—Houston (N.L.)	OF	137	473	51	120	28	9	13	69	.254	40	101	10	294	6	5	.984
1992	—Houston (N.L.)	OF	122	387	40	94	19	3	10	55	.243	24	52	7	261	5	2	.993
	—Tucson (PCL)	OF	13	44	11	19	4	2	1	9	.432	5	7	4	26	0	1	.963
1993	—Houston (N.L.)	OF	154	540	82	162	34	3	15	72	.300	47	83	20	347	10	8	.978
Major league totals (4 years)			425	1421	174	380	83	15	38	196	.267	113	241	37	924	31	15	.985

GOODEN, DWIGHT

P, METS

PERSONAL: Born November 16, 1964, in Tampa, Fla. . . . 6-3/210. . . . Throws right, bats right. . . . Full name: Dwight Eugene Gooden. . . . Uncle of Gary Sheffield, outfielder/third baseman, San Diego Padres.
HIGH SCHOOL: Hillsborough (Tampa, Fla.).
TRANSACTIONS/CAREER NOTES: Selected by New York Mets organization in first round (fifth pick overall) of free-agent draft (June 7, 1982). . . . On New York disabled list (April 1-June 5, 1987); included rehabilitation assignment to Tidewater (May 12-17 and May 21-June 1). . . . On disabled list (July 2-September 2, 1989; August 24, 1991-remainder of season and July 18-August 8, 1992). . . . On suspended list (September 2-7, 1993).
RECORDS: Holds major league rookie-season record for most strikeouts—276 (1984). . . . Shares modern major league record for most strikeouts in two consecutive games—32 (September 12 [16] and 17 [16], 1984). . . . Holds N.L. record for most strikeouts in three consecutive games—43 (September 7 [11], 12 [16] and 17 [16], 1984).
HONORS: Named Carolina League Pitcher of the Year (1983). . . . Named N.L. Rookie Pitcher of the Year by THE SPORTING NEWS (1984). . . . Named N.L. Rookie of the Year by Baseball Writers' Association of America (1984). . . . Named N.L. Pitcher of the Year by THE SPORTING NEWS (1985). . . . Named righthanded pitcher on THE SPORTING NEWS N.L. All-Star team (1985). . . . Named N.L. Cy Young Award winner by Baseball Writers' Association of America (1985). . . . Named pitcher on THE SPORTING NEWS N.L. Silver Slugger team (1992).
STATISTICAL NOTES: Tied for N.L. lead with seven balks in 1984.
MISCELLANEOUS: Singled and made an out in two games as pinch-hitter (1992). . . . Tripled with an RBI in one game as pinch-hitter (1993).

Year	**Team (League)**	**W**	**L**	**Pct.**	**ERA**	**G**	**GS**	**CG**	**ShO**	**Sv.**	**IP**	**H**	**R**	**ER**	**BB**	**SO**
1982	—Kingsport (Appal.)	5	4	.556	2.47	9	9	4	2	0	65⅔	53	34	18	25	66
	—Little Falls (NYP)	0	1	.000	4.15	2	2	0	0	0	13	11	6	6	3	18
1983	—Lynchburg (Caro.)	*19	4	.826	*2.50	27	27	10	*6	0	191	121	58	53	*112	*300
1984	—New York (N.L.)	17	9	.654	2.60	31	31	7	3	0	218	161	72	63	73	*276
1985	—New York (N.L.)	*24	4	.857	*1.53	35	35	*16	8	0	*276⅔	198	51	47	69	*268
1986	—New York (N.L.)	17	6	.739	2.84	33	33	12	2	0	250	197	92	79	80	200
1987	—Tidewater (Int'l)	3	0	1.000	2.05	4	4	1	0	0	22	20	7	5	9	24
	—Lynchburg (Caro.)	0	0	...	0.00	1	1	0	0	0	4	2	0	0	2	3
	—New York (N.L.)	15	7	.682	3.21	25	25	7	3	0	179⅔	162	68	64	53	148
1988	—New York (N.L.)	18	9	.667	3.19	34	34	10	3	0	248⅓	242	98	88	57	175
1989	—New York (N.L.)	9	4	.692	2.89	19	17	0	0	1	118⅓	93	42	38	47	101
1990	—New York (N.L.)	19	7	.731	3.83	34	34	2	1	0	232⅔	229	106	99	70	223
1991	—New York (N.L.)	13	7	.650	3.60	27	27	3	1	0	190	185	80	76	56	150
1992	—New York (N.L.)	10	13	.435	3.67	31	31	3	0	0	206	197	93	84	70	145
1993	—New York (N.L.)	12	15	.444	3.45	29	29	7	2	0	208⅔	188	89	80	61	149
Major league totals (10 years)		154	81	.655	3.04	298	296	67	23	1	2128⅓	1852	791	718	636	1835

CHAMPIONSHIP SERIES RECORD

CHAMPIONSHIP SERIES NOTES: Holds single-series record for most strikeouts—20 (1988). . . . Shares N.L. single-game record for most innings pitched—10 (October 14, 1986).

Year	**Team (League)**	**W**	**L**	**Pct.**	**ERA**	**G**	**GS**	**CG**	**ShO**	**Sv.**	**IP**	**H**	**R**	**ER**	**BB**	**SO**
1986	—New York (N.L.)	0	1	.000	1.06	2	2	0	0	0	17	16	2	2	5	9
1988	—New York (N.L.)	0	0	...	2.95	3	2	0	0	0	18⅓	10	6	6	8	20
Champ. series totals (2 years)		0	1	.000	2.04	5	4	0	0	0	35⅓	26	8	8	13	29

WORLD SERIES RECORD

Year	**Team (League)**	**W**	**L**	**Pct.**	**ERA**	**G**	**GS**	**CG**	**ShO**	**Sv.**	**IP**	**H**	**R**	**ER**	**BB**	**SO**
1986	—New York (N.L.)	0	2	.000	8.00	2	2	0	0	0	9	17	10	8	4	9

ALL-STAR GAME RECORD

ALL-STAR GAME NOTES: Holds career record for most balks—2. . . . Shares career record for most games lost—2.

Year	**League**	**W**	**L**	**Pct.**	**ERA**	**GS**	**CG**	**ShO**	**Sv.**	**IP**	**H**	**R**	**ER**	**BB**	**SO**
1984	—National	0	0	...	0.00	0	0	0	0	2	1	0	0	0	3
1985	—National	Did not play.													
1986	—National	0	1	.000	6.00	1	0	0	0	3	3	2	2	0	2
1988	—National	0	1	.000	3.00	1	0	0	0	3	3	1	1	1	1
All-Star totals (3 years)		0	2	.000	3.38	2	0	0	0	8	7	3	3	1	6

GOODWIN, TOM

OF, ROYALS

PERSONAL: Born July 27, 1968, in Fresno, Calif. . . . 6-1/170. . . . Throws right, bats left. . . . Full name: Thomas Jones Goodwin.
HIGH SCHOOL: Central (Fresno, Calif.).
COLLEGE: Fresno State.

TRANSACTIONS/CAREER NOTES: Selected by Pittsburgh Pirates organization in sixth round of free-agent draft (June 2, 1986). . . . Selected by Los Angeles Dodgers organization in first round (22nd pick overall) of free-agent draft (June 5, 1989). . . . Claimed on waivers by Kansas City Royals (January 6, 1994).
HONORS: Named outfielder on THE SPORTING NEWS college All-America team (1989).
STATISTICAL NOTES: Tied for Pacific Coast League lead in caught stealing with 23 in 1991.
MISCELLANEOUS: Member of 1988 U.S. Olympic baseball team.

			BATTING												FIELDING			
Year	**Team (League)**	**Pos.**	**G**	**AB**	**R**	**H**	**2B**	**3B**	**HR**	**RBI**	**Avg.**	**BB**	**SO**	**SB**	**PO**	**A**	**E**	**Avg.**
1989	—Great Falls (Pio.)	OF	63	240	*55	74	12	3	2	33	.308	28	30	*60	67	3	1	.986
1990	—San Antonio (Tex.)	OF	102	428	76	119	15	4	0	28	.278	38	72	*60	264	7	3	*.989
	—Bakersfield (Calif.)	OF	32	134	24	39	6	2	0	13	.291	11	22	22	55	2	0	1.000
1991	—Albuquerque (PCL)	OF	132	509	84	139	19	4	1	45	.273	59	83	48	284	6	3	.990
	—Los Angeles (N.L.)	OF	16	7	3	1	0	0	0	0	.143	0	0	1	8	0	0	1.000
1992	—Albuquerque (PCL)	OF	82	319	48	96	10	4	2	28	.301	37	47	27	184	5	1	.995
	—Los Angeles (N.L.)	OF	57	73	15	17	1	1	0	3	.233	6	10	7	43	0	0	1.000
1993	—Los Angeles (N.L.)	OF	30	17	6	5	1	0	0	1	.294	1	4	1	8	0	0	1.000
	—Albuquerque (PCL)	OF	85	289	48	75	5	5	1	28	.260	30	51	21	145	1	2	.986
Major league totals (3 years)			103	97	24	23	2	1	0	4	.237	7	14	9	59	0	0	1.000

GORDON, KEITH

OF, REDS

PERSONAL: Born January 22, 1969, in Bethesda, Md. . . . 6-1/205. . . . Throws right, bats right. . . . Full name: Keith Bradley Gordon.
HIGH SCHOOL: Walter Johnson (Bethesda, Md.).
COLLEGE: Wright State.
TRANSACTIONS/CAREER NOTES: Selected by Cincinnati Reds organization in second round of free-agent draft (June 4, 1990).
STATISTICAL NOTES: Tied for South Atlantic League lead in double plays by outfielder with three in 1991.

			BATTING												FIELDING			
Year	**Team (League)**	**Pos.**	**G**	**AB**	**R**	**H**	**2B**	**3B**	**HR**	**RBI**	**Avg.**	**BB**	**SO**	**SB**	**PO**	**A**	**E**	**Avg.**
1990	—Billings (Pioneer)	SS	49	154	21	36	5	1	1	14	.234	24	51	6	79	134	22	.906
1991	—Char., W.Va. (SAL)	OF	123	388	63	104	14	10	8	46	.268	50	135	25	208	11	8	.965
1992	—Ced. Rap. (Midw.)	OF-3B	114	375	59	94	19	3	12	63	.251	43	135	21	147	10	7	.957
1993	—Chatt. (South.)	OF	116	419	69	122	26	3	14	59	.291	19	132	13	196	13	4	.981
	—Cincinnati (N.L.)	OF	3	6	0	1	0	0	0	0	.167	0	2	0	2	0	0	1.000
Major league totals (1 year)			3	6	0	1	0	0	0	0	.167	0	2	0	2	0	0	1.000

GORDON, TOM

P, ROYALS

PERSONAL: Born November 18, 1967, in Sebring, Fla. . . . 5-9/180. . . . Throws right, bats right. . . . Full name: Thomas Gordon. . . . Brother of Tony Gordon, pitcher, Chicago White Sox organization.
HIGH SCHOOL: Avon Park (Fla.).
TRANSACTIONS/CAREER NOTES: Selected by Kansas City Royals organization in sixth round of free-agent draft (June 2, 1986). . . . On disabled list (August 12-September 1, 1992).
HONORS: Named A.L. Rookie Pitcher of the Year by THE SPORTING NEWS (1989).
STATISTICAL NOTES: Tied for Northwest League lead with four balks in 1987.
MISCELLANEOUS: Appeared in one game as pinch-runner (1991).

Year	**Team (League)**	**W**	**L**	**Pct.**	**ERA**	**G**	**GS**	**CG**	**ShO**	**Sv.**	**IP**	**H**	**R**	**ER**	**BB**	**SO**
1986	—GC Royals (GCL)	3	1	.750	1.02	9	7	2	1	0	44	31	12	5	23	47
	—Omaha (A.A.)	0	0	. . .	47.25	1	0	0	0	0	1⅓	6	7	7	2	3
1987	—Eugene (N'west)	•9	0	•1.000	2.86	15	13	0	0	1	72⅓	48	33	23	47	91
	—Fort Myers (FSL)	1	0	1.000	2.63	3	3	0	0	0	13⅔	5	4	4	17	11
1988	—Appleton (Midw.)	7	5	.583	2.06	17	17	5	1	0	118	69	30	27	43	*172
	—Memphis (South.)	6	0	1.000	0.38	6	6	2	2	0	47⅓	16	3	2	17	62
	—Omaha (A.A.)	3	0	1.000	1.33	3	3	0	0	0	20⅓	11	3	3	15	29
	—Kansas City (A.L.)	0	2	.000	5.17	5	2	0	0	0	15⅔	16	9	9	7	18
1989	—Kansas City (A.L.)	17	9	.654	3.64	49	16	1	1	1	163	122	67	66	86	153
1990	—Kansas City (A.L.)	12	11	.522	3.73	32	32	6	1	0	195⅓	192	99	81	99	175
1991	—Kansas City (A.L.)	9	14	.391	3.87	45	14	1	0	1	158	129	76	68	87	167
1992	—Kansas City (A.L.)	6	10	.375	4.59	40	11	0	0	0	117⅔	116	67	60	55	98
1993	—Kansas City (A.L.)	12	6	.667	3.58	48	14	2	0	1	155⅔	125	65	62	77	143
Major league totals (6 years)		56	52	.519	3.87	219	89	10	2	3	805⅓	700	383	346	411	754

GOSSAGE, GOOSE

P

PERSONAL: Born July 5, 1951, in Colorado Springs, Colo. . . . 6-0/226. . . . Throws right, bats right. . . . Full name: Richard Michael Gossage.
HIGH SCHOOL: Wasson (Colorado Springs, Colo.).
COLLEGE: Southern Colorado.
TRANSACTIONS/CAREER NOTES: Selected by Chicago White Sox organization in ninth round of free-agent draft (June 4, 1970). . . . Traded by White Sox with P Terry Forster to Pittsburgh Pirates for OF Richie Zisk and P Silvio Martinez (December 10, 1976). . . . Granted free agency (October 28, 1977). . . . Signed by New York Yankees (November 23, 1977). . . . On disabled list (April 21-July 9, 1979). . . . Granted free agency (November 7, 1983). . . . Signed by San Diego Padres (January 6, 1984). . . . On disabled list (August 8-September 1, 1985). . . . On suspended list (August 29-September 1, 1986). . . . On disabled list (April 14-May 4, 1987). . . . Traded by Padres with P Ray Hayward to Chicago Cubs for IF Keith Moreland and IF Mike Brumley (February 12, 1988). . . . On disabled list (June 16-July 1, 1988). . . . Released by Cubs (March 28, 1989). . . . Signed by San Francisco Giants (April 14, 1989). . . . Claimed on waivers by New York Yankees (August 10, 1989). . . . Granted free agency (November 13, 1989). . . . Signed by Fukuoka Daiei Hawks of Japan Pacific League (July 4, 1990). . . . Signed as free agent by Texas Rangers organization (January 25, 1991). . . . On disabled list (June 17-July 11, 1991). . . . On Texas disabled list (August 5-September 1, 1991); included rehabilitation assignment to Oklahoma City (August 28-September 1). . . . Granted free

agency (October 30, 1991).... Signed by Oakland Athletics organization (January 27, 1992).... On disabled list (July 19, 1992-remainder of season).... Granted free agency (November 6, 1992).... Re-signed by A's (December 7, 1992).... On disabled list (August 30-September 25, 1993).... Granted free agency (October 29, 1993).
RECORDS: Holds N.L. single-season record for most strikeouts by relief pitcher—151 (1977).
HONORS: Named Midwest League Player of the Year (1971).... Named A.L. Fireman of the Year by THE SPORTING NEWS (1975 and 1978).

Year	Team (League)	W	L	Pct.	ERA	G	GS	CG	ShO	Sv.	IP	H	R	ER	BB	SO
1970	—GC Whi. Sox (GCL)	0	0	...	2.81	3	3	0	0	0	16	11	6	5	4	21
	—Appleton (Midw.)	0	3	.000	5.91	10	5	0	0	0	35	41	27	23	19	21
1971	—Appleton (Midw.)	*18	2	*.900	*1.83	25	24	*15	*7	0	187	141	48	38	50	149
1972	—Chicago (A.L.)	7	1	.875	4.28	36	1	0	0	2	80	72	44	38	44	57
1973	—Iowa (Am. Assoc.)	5	4	.556	3.68	12	9	5	1	1	71	59	32	29	28	66
	—Chicago (A.L.)	0	4	.000	7.38	20	4	1	0	0	50	57	44	41	37	33
1974	—Appleton (Midw.)	0	2	.000	3.38	2	2	0	0	0	8	8	6	3	4	5
	—Chicago (A.L.)	4	6	.400	4.15	39	3	0	0	1	89	92	45	41	47	64
1975	—Chicago (A.L.)	9	8	.529	1.84	62	0	0	0	*26	142	99	32	29	70	130
1976	—Chicago (A.L.)	9	17	.346	3.94	31	29	15	0	1	224	214	104	98	90	135
1977	—Pittsburgh (N.L.)■	11	9	.550	1.62	72	0	0	0	26	133	78	27	24	49	151
1978	—New York (A.L.)■	10	11	.476	2.01	63	0	0	0	*27	134	87	41	30	59	122
1979	—New York (A.L.)	5	3	.625	2.64	36	0	0	0	18	58	48	18	17	19	41
1980	—New York (A.L.)	6	2	.750	2.27	64	0	0	0	*33	99	74	29	25	37	103
1981	—New York (A.L.)	3	2	.600	0.77	32	0	0	0	20	47	22	6	4	14	48
1982	—New York (A.L.)	4	5	.444	2.23	56	0	0	0	30	93	63	23	23	28	102
1983	—New York (A.L.)	13	5	.722	2.27	57	0	0	0	22	87⅓	82	27	22	25	90
1984	—San Diego (N.L.)■	10	6	.625	2.90	62	0	0	0	25	102⅓	75	34	33	36	84
1985	—San Diego (N.L.)	5	3	.625	1.82	50	0	0	0	26	79	64	21	16	17	52
1986	—San Diego (N.L.)	5	7	.417	4.45	45	0	0	0	21	64⅔	69	36	32	20	63
1987	—San Diego (N.L.)	5	4	.556	3.12	40	0	0	0	11	52	47	18	18	19	44
1988	—Chicago (N.L.)■	4	4	.500	4.33	46	0	0	0	13	43⅔	50	23	21	15	30
1989	—San Francisco (N.L.)■	2	1	.667	2.68	31	0	0	0	4	43⅔	32	16	13	27	24
	—New York (A.L.)■	1	0	1.000	3.77	11	0	0	0	1	14⅓	14	6	6	3	6
1990	—Fukuoka (Jp. Pac.)■	2	3	.400	4.40	23	0	0	0	8	47	...	...	23	15	40
1991	—Texas (A.L.)■	4	2	.667	3.57	44	0	0	0	1	40⅓	33	16	16	16	28
	—Okla. City (A.A.)	0	0	...	18.00	2	0	0	0	0	2	2	4	4	1	3
1992	—Oakland (A.L.)■	0	2	.000	2.84	30	0	0	0	0	38	32	13	12	19	26
1993	—Oakland (A.L.)	4	5	.444	4.53	39	0	0	0	1	47⅔	49	24	24	26	40
A.L. totals (15 years)		79	73	.520	3.08	620	37	16	0	183	1243⅔	1038	472	426	534	1025
N.L. totals (7 years)		42	34	.553	2.73	346	0	0	0	126	518⅓	415	175	157	183	448
Major league totals (21 years)		121	107	.531	2.98	966	37	16	0	309	1762	1453	647	583	717	1473

DIVISION SERIES RECORD

Year	Team (League)	W	L	Pct.	ERA	G	GS	CG	ShO	Sv.	IP	H	R	ER	BB	SO
1981	—New York (A.L.)	0	0	...	0.00	3	0	0	0	2	6⅔	3	0	0	2	8

CHAMPIONSHIP SERIES RECORD

Year	Team (League)	W	L	Pct.	ERA	G	GS	CG	ShO	Sv.	IP	H	R	ER	BB	SO
1978	—New York (A.L.)	1	0	1.000	4.50	2	0	0	0	1	4	3	2	2	0	3
1980	—New York (A.L.)	0	1	.000	54.00	1	0	0	0	0	⅓	3	2	2	0	0
1981	—New York (A.L.)	0	0	...	0.00	2	0	0	0	2	2⅔	1	0	0	0	2
1984	—San Diego (N.L.)	0	0	...	4.50	3	0	0	0	1	4	5	2	2	1	5
Champ. series totals (4 years)		1	1	.500	4.91	8	0	0	0	4	11	12	6	6	1	10

WORLD SERIES RECORD

Year	Team (League)	W	L	Pct.	ERA	G	GS	CG	ShO	Sv.	IP	H	R	ER	BB	SO
1978	—New York (A.L.)	1	0	1.000	0.00	3	0	0	0	0	6	1	0	0	1	4
1981	—New York (A.L.)	0	0	...	0.00	3	0	0	0	2	5	2	0	0	2	5
1984	—San Diego (N.L.)	0	0	...	13.50	2	0	0	0	0	2⅔	3	4	4	1	2
World Series totals (3 years)		1	0	1.000	2.63	8	0	0	0	2	13⅔	6	4	4	4	11

ALL-STAR GAME RECORD

Year	League	W	L	Pct.	ERA	GS	CG	ShO	Sv.	IP	H	R	ER	BB	SO
1975	—American	0	0	...	9.00	0	0	0	0	1	1	1	1	0	0
1976	—American							Did not play.							
1977	—National	0	0	...	18.00	0	0	0	0	1	1	2	2	1	2
1978	—American	0	1	.000	36.00	0	0	0	0	1	4	4	4	1	1
1980	—American	0	0	...	0.00	0	0	0	0	1	1	0	0	0	0
1981	—American							Selected, did not play—injured.							
1982	—American							Did not play.							
1984	—National	0	0	...	0.00	0	0	0	1	1	1	0	0	0	2
1985	—National	0	0	...	0.00	0	0	0	0	1	0	0	0	1	2
All-Star totals (6 years)		0	1	.000	10.50	0	0	0	1	6	8	7	7	3	7

GOTT, JIM

P, DODGERS

PERSONAL: Born August 3, 1959, in Hollywood, Calif.... 6-4/229.... Throws right, bats right.... Full name: James William Gott.
HIGH SCHOOL: San Marino (Calif.).
COLLEGE: Brigham Young.
TRANSACTIONS/CAREER NOTES: Selected by St. Louis Cardinals organization in fourth round of free-agent draft (June 7, 1977).... On Arkansas disabled list (August 16-September 1, 1979).... Selected by Toronto Blue Jays from Cardinals organization

in Rule 5 major league draft (December 7, 1981).... Traded by Blue Jays with P Jack McKnight and IF Augie Schmidt to San Francisco Giants for P Gary Lavelle (January 26, 1985).... On San Francisco disabled list (May 9, 1986-remainder of season); included rehabilitation assignment to Phoenix (June 9-24).... Released by Giants organization (December 19, 1986). ... Re-signed by Giants (April 7, 1987).... Claimed on waivers by Pittsburgh Pirates (August 3, 1987).... On disabled list (April 7, 1989-remainder of season).... Granted free agency (November 13, 1989).... Signed by Los Angeles Dodgers (December 7, 1989).... On Los Angeles disabled list (April 7-May 25, 1990); included rehabilitation assignment to Bakersfield (May 4-25).

STATISTICAL NOTES: Led Western Carolinas League with 21 wild pitches in 1979.

Year Team (League)	W	L	Pct.	ERA	G	GS	CG	ShO	Sv.	IP	H	R	ER	BB	SO
1977 —Calgary (Pioneer)	3	4	.429	9.55	14	•14	0	0	0	65	71	*82	*69	*83	60
1978 —Gastonia (W. Car.)	9	6	.600	3.97	22	22	4	0	0	145	100	67	64	•113	130
—St. Peters. (FSL)	1	3	.250	1.29	5	5	2	0	0	28	23	9	4	12	15
1979 —St. Peters. (FSL)	0	3	.000	6.50	4	4	0	0	0	18	18	13	13	13	9
—Gastonia (W. Car.)	5	5	.500	5.61	19	11	1	0	0	77	63	57	48	88	102
—Arkansas (Texas)	0	1	.000	5.40	2	1	0	0	0	5	3	6	3	13	7
1980 —St. Peters. (FSL)	5	11	.313	4.60	25	21	4	1	0	137	138	96	70	113	103
1981 —Arkansas (Texas)	5	9	.357	3.44	28	19	4	0	0	131	133	68	50	65	93
1982 —Toronto (A.L.)■	5	10	.333	4.43	30	23	1	1	0	136	134	76	67	66	82
1983 —Toronto (A.L.)	9	14	.391	4.74	34	30	6	1	0	176⅔	195	103	93	68	121
1984 —Toronto (A.L.)	7	6	.538	4.02	35	12	1	1	2	109⅔	93	54	49	49	73
1985 —San Francisco (N.L.)■	7	10	.412	3.88	26	26	2	0	0	148⅓	144	73	64	51	78
1986 —San Francisco (N.L.)	0	0	...	7.62	9	2	0	0	1	13	16	12	11	13	9
—Phoenix (PCL)	0	0	...	6.75	2	2	0	0	0	2⅔	2	2	2	3	2
1987 —S.F.-Pitts. (N.L.)■	1	2	.333	3.41	55	3	0	0	13	87	81	43	33	40	90
1988 —Pittsburgh (N.L.)	6	6	.500	3.49	67	0	0	0	34	77⅓	68	30	30	22	76
1989 —Pittsburgh (N.L.)	0	0	...	0.00	1	0	0	0	0	⅔	1	0	0	1	1
1990 —Bakersfield (Calif.)■	0	0	...	2.77	7	3	0	0	0	13	13	5	4	4	16
—Los Angeles (N.L.)	3	5	.375	2.90	50	0	0	0	3	62	59	27	20	34	44
1991 —Los Angeles (N.L.)	4	3	.571	2.96	55	0	0	0	2	76	63	28	25	32	73
1992 —Los Angeles (N.L.)	3	3	.500	2.45	68	0	0	0	6	88	72	27	24	41	75
1993 —Los Angeles (N.L.)	4	8	.333	2.32	62	0	0	0	25	77⅔	71	23	20	17	67
A.L. totals (3 years)	21	30	.412	4.45	99	65	8	3	2	422⅓	422	233	209	183	276
N.L. totals (9 years)	28	37	.431	3.24	393	31	2	0	84	630	575	263	227	251	513
Major league totals (12 years)	49	67	.422	3.73	492	96	10	3	86	1052⅓	997	496	436	434	789

GOZZO, MAURO

P, METS

PERSONAL: Born March 7, 1966, in New Britain, Conn.... 6-3/212.... Throws right, bats right.... Full name: Mauro Paul Gozzo.

HIGH SCHOOL: Berlin (Conn.).

TRANSACTIONS/CAREER NOTES: Selected by New York Mets organization in 13th round of free-agent draft (June 4, 1984).... Traded by Mets organization with C Ed Hearn and P Rich Anderson to Kansas City Royals for C Chris Jelic and P David Cone (March 27, 1987).... Selected by Toronto Blue Jays organization from Royals organization in Rule 5 minor league draft (December 6, 1988).... Traded by Blue Jays with two players to be named later to Cleveland Indians for P Bud Black (September 16, 1990); Indians acquired P Steve Cummings (September 21, 1990) and P Alex Sanchez (September 24, 1990) to complete deal.... Granted free agency (October 15, 1991).... Signed by Portland, Minnesota Twins organization (January 7, 1992).... Granted free agency (October 15, 1992).... Signed by Mets organization (December 22, 1992).

Year Team (League)	W	L	Pct.	ERA	G	GS	CG	ShO	Sv.	IP	H	R	ER	BB	SO
1984 —Little Falls (NYP)	4	3	.571	5.63	24	0	0	0	2	38⅓	40	27	24	28	30
1985 —Columbia (S. Atl.)	11	4	.733	2.54	49	0	0	0	14	78	62	22	22	39	66
1986 —Lynchburg (Caro.)	9	4	.692	3.10	60	0	0	0	9	78⅓	80	30	27	35	50
1987 —Memphis (South.)■	6	5	.545	4.53	19	14	1	0	0	91⅓	95	58	46	36	56
1988 —Memphis (South.)	4	9	.308	5.73	33	12	0	0	3	92⅔	127	64	59	36	48
1989 —Knoxville (South.)■	7	0	1.000	2.98	18	6	2	1	0	60⅓	59	27	20	12	37
—Syracuse (Int'l)	5	1	.833	2.76	12	7	2	1	2	62	56	22	19	19	34
—Toronto (A.L.)	4	1	.800	4.83	9	3	0	0	0	31⅔	35	19	17	9	10
1990 —Syracuse (Int'l)	3	8	.273	3.58	34	10	0	0	7	98	87	46	39	44	62
—Cleveland (A.L.)■	0	0	...	0.00	2	0	0	0	0	3	2	0	0	2	2
1991 —Colo. Springs (PCL)	10	6	.625	5.25	25	20	3	0	1	130⅓	143	86	76	68	81
—Cleveland (A.L.)	0	0	...	19.29	2	2	0	0	0	4⅔	9	10	10	7	3
1992 —Portland (PCL)■	10	9	.526	3.35	37	19	3	2	1	155⅔	155	61	58	50	108
—Minnesota (A.L.)	0	0	...	27.00	2	0	0	0	0	1⅔	7	5	5	0	1
1993 —Norfolk (Int'l)■	8	11	.421	3.45	28	28	2	0	0	190⅓	*208	88	73	49	97
—New York (N.L.)	0	1	.000	2.57	10	0	0	0	1	14	11	5	4	5	6
A.L. totals (4 years)	4	1	.800	7.02	15	5	0	0	0	41	53	34	32	18	16
N.L. totals (1 year)	0	1	.000	2.57	10	0	0	0	1	14	11	5	4	5	6
Major league totals (5 years)	4	2	.667	5.89	25	5	0	0	1	55	64	39	36	23	22

G

GRACE, MARK

1B, CUBS

PERSONAL: Born June 28, 1964, in Winston-Salem, N.C.... 6-2/190.... Throws left, bats left. ... Full name: Mark Eugene Grace.

HIGH SCHOOL: Tustin (Calif.).

COLLEGE: Saddleback Community College (Calif.) and San Diego State.

TRANSACTIONS/CAREER NOTES: Selected by Minnesota Twins organization in 15th round of free-agent draft (January 17, 1984). ... Selected by Chicago Cubs organization in 24th round of free-agent draft (June 3, 1985).... On disabled list (June 5-23, 1989).

RECORDS: Shares major league record for most assists by first baseman in one inning—3 (May 23, 1990, fourth inning).... Holds N.L. single-season record for most assists by first baseman—180 (1990).

HONORS: Named Eastern League Most Valuable Player (1987).... Named N.L. Rookie Player of the Year by THE SPORTING NEWS (1988).... Won N.L. Gold Glove at first base (1992-93).
STATISTICAL NOTES: Led Midwest League first basemen with 103 double plays in 1986.... Led Eastern League with .545 slugging percentage in 1987.... Led N.L. first basemen with 1,695 total chances in 1991, 1,725 in 1992 and 1,573 in 1993.... Tied for N.L. lead in grounding into double plays with 25 in 1993.... Led N.L. first basemen with 134 double plays in 1993.... Hit for the cycle (May 9, 1993).

			BATTING												FIELDING			
Year	**Team (League)**	**Pos.**	**G**	**AB**	**R**	**H**	**2B**	**3B**	**HR**	**RBI**	**Avg.**	**BB**	**SO**	**SB**	**PO**	**A**	**E**	**Avg.**
1986	—Peoria (Midwest)	1B-OF	126	465	81	159	30	4	15	95	*.342	60	28	6	1050	69	13	.989
1987	—Pittsfield (Eastern)	1B	123	453	81	151	29	8	17	*101	.333	48	24	5	1054	*96	6	*.995
1988	—Iowa (Am. Assoc.)	1B	21	67	11	17	4	0	0	14	.254	13	4	1	189	20	1	.995
	—Chicago (N.L.)	1B	134	486	65	144	23	4	7	57	.296	60	43	3	1182	87	•17	.987
1989	—Chicago (N.L.)	1B	142	510	74	160	28	3	13	79	.314	80	42	14	1230	126	6	.996
1990	—Chicago (N.L.)	1B	157	589	72	182	32	1	9	82	.309	59	54	15	1324	*180	12	.992
1991	—Chicago (N.L.)	1B	160	*619	87	169	28	5	8	58	.273	70	53	3	*1520	*167	8	.995
1992	—Chicago (N.L.)	1B	158	603	72	185	37	5	9	79	.307	72	36	6	*1580	*141	4	.998
1993	—Chicago (N.L.)	1B	155	594	86	193	39	4	14	98	.325	71	32	8	*1456	112	5	.997
Major league totals (6 years)			906	3401	456	1033	187	22	60	453	.304	412	260	49	8292	813	52	.994

CHAMPIONSHIP SERIES RECORD

CHAMPIONSHIP SERIES NOTES: Hit home run in first series at-bat (October 4, 1989).

			BATTING												FIELDING			
Year	**Team (League)**	**Pos.**	**G**	**AB**	**R**	**H**	**2B**	**3B**	**HR**	**RBI**	**Avg.**	**BB**	**SO**	**SB**	**PO**	**A**	**E**	**Avg.**
1989	—Chicago (N.L.)	1B	5	17	3	11	3	1	1	8	.647	4	1	1	44	3	0	1.000

ALL-STAR GAME RECORD

			BATTING											FIELDING			
Year	**League**	**Pos.**	**AB**	**R**	**H**	**2B**	**3B**	**HR**	**RBI**	**Avg.**	**BB**	**SO**	**SB**	**PO**	**A**	**E**	**Avg.**
1993	—National	DH	3	0	0	0	0	0	0	.000	0	0	0	...	...	...	...

GRAFFANINO, TONY

2B, BRAVES

PERSONAL: Born June 6, 1972, in Amityville, N.Y.... 6-1/175.... Throws right, bats right.... Full name: Anthony Joseph Graffanino.
HIGH SCHOOL: East Islip (Islip Terrace, N.Y.).
TRANSACTIONS/CAREER NOTES: Selected by Atlanta Braves organization in 10th round of free-agent draft (June 4, 1990).
STATISTICAL NOTES: Led Pioneer League shortstops with 41 double plays in 1991.... Led Carolina League second basemen with .968 fielding percentage in 1993.

			BATTING												FIELDING			
Year	**Team (League)**	**Pos.**	**G**	**AB**	**R**	**H**	**2B**	**3B**	**HR**	**RBI**	**Avg.**	**BB**	**SO**	**SB**	**PO**	**A**	**E**	**Avg.**
1990	—Pulaski (Appal.)	SS	42	131	23	27	5	1	0	11	.206	26	17	6	60	105	24	.873
1991	—Idaho Falls (Pio.)	SS	66	274	53	95	16	4	4	56	.347	27	37	19	112	187	*29	.912
1992	—Macon (S. Atl.)	2B	112	400	50	96	15	5	10	31	.240	50	84	9	178	239	17	.961
1993	—Durham (Carolina)	2B-SS	123	459	78	126	30	5	15	69	.275	45	78	24	186	263	15	†.968

GRAHE, JOE

P, ANGELS

PERSONAL: Born August 14, 1967, in West Palm Beach, Fla.... 6-0/200.... Throws right, bats right.... Full name: Joseph Milton Grahe.... Name pronounced GRAY.
HIGH SCHOOL: Palm Beach Gardens (West Palm Beach, Fla.).
COLLEGE: Palm Beach Junior College (Fla.) and Miami (Fla.).
TRANSACTIONS/CAREER NOTES: Selected by Milwaukee Brewers organization in 28th round of free-agent draft (June 2, 1986).... Selected by Oakland Athletics organization in fifth round of free-agent draft (June 1, 1988).... Selected by California Angels organization in second round of free-agent draft (June 5, 1989).... On California disabled list (June 5-July 15, 1993); included rehabilitation assignment to Vancouver (July 2-15).

Year	**Team (League)**	**W**	**L**	**Pct.**	**ERA**	**G**	**GS**	**CG**	**ShO**	**Sv.**	**IP**	**H**	**R**	**ER**	**BB**	**SO**
1990	—Midland (Texas)	7	5	.583	5.29	18	18	1	0	0	119	145	75	70	34	58
	—Edmonton (PCL)	3	0	1.000	1.35	5	5	2	0	0	40	35	10	6	11	21
	—California (A.L.)	3	4	.429	4.98	8	8	0	0	0	43⅓	51	30	24	23	25
1991	—Edmonton (PCL)	9	3	.750	4.01	14	14	3	1	0	94⅓	121	55	42	30	55
	—California (A.L.)	3	7	.300	4.81	18	10	1	0	0	73	84	43	39	33	40
1992	—California (A.L.)	5	6	.455	3.52	46	7	0	0	21	94⅔	85	37	37	39	39
	—Edmonton (PCL)	1	0	1.000	3.20	3	3	0	0	0	19⅔	18	7	7	5	12
1993	—California (A.L.)	4	1	.800	2.86	45	0	0	0	11	56⅔	54	22	18	25	31
	—Vancouver (PCL)	1	1	.500	4.50	4	2	0	0	0	6	4	3	3	2	5
Major league totals (4 years)		15	18	.455	3.97	117	25	1	0	32	267⅔	274	132	118	120	135

GRANGER, JEFF

P, ROYALS

PERSONAL: Born December 16, 1971, in San Pedro, Calif.... 6-4/200.... Throws left, bats right.... Full name: Jeffrey Adam Granger.
HIGH SCHOOL: Orangefield (Tex.).
COLLEGE: Texas A&M.
TRANSACTIONS/CAREER NOTES: Selected by Minnesota Twins organization in 14th round of free agent draft (June 4, 1990).... Selected by Kansas City Royals organization in first round (fifth pick overall) of free-agent draft (June 3, 1993).
HONORS: Named lefthanded pitcher on THE SPORTING NEWS college All-America team (1993).

Year	**Team (League)**	**W**	**L**	**Pct.**	**ERA**	**G**	**GS**	**CG**	**ShO**	**Sv.**	**IP**	**H**	**R**	**ER**	**BB**	**SO**
1993	—Eugene (N'west)	3	3	.500	3.00	8	7	0	0	0	36	28	17	12	10	56
	—Kansas City (A.L.)	0	0	...	27.00	1	0	0	0	0	1	3	3	3	2	1
Major league totals (1 year)		0	0	...	27.00	1	0	0	0	0	1	3	3	3	2	1

GRANT, MARK

P

PERSONAL: Born October 24, 1963, in Aurora, Ill. . . . 6-2/215. . . . Throws right, bats right. . . . Full name: Mark Andrew Grant.

HIGH SCHOOL: Joliet (Ill.) Catholic.

TRANSACTIONS/CAREER NOTES: Selected by San Francisco Giants organization in first round (10th pick overall) of free-agent draft (June 8, 1981). . . . On San Francisco disabled list (May 4-23, 1984). . . . Traded by Giants with 3B Chris Brown, P Keith Comstock and P Mark Davis to San Diego Padres for P Dave Dravecky, P Craig Lefferts and IF Kevin Mitchell (July 4, 1987). . . . Traded by Padres to Atlanta Braves for P Derek Lilliquist (July 12, 1990). . . . On Atlanta disabled list (March 28, 1991-entire season); included rehabilitation assignment to Richmond (April 23-29). . . . Granted free agency (December 20, 1991). . . . Signed by Calgary, Seattle Mariners organization (January 27, 1992). . . . On Calgary disabled list (May 21-June 4, 1992). . . . Granted free agency (October 29, 1992). . . . Signed by Houston Astros organization (January 19, 1993). . . . Traded by Astros to Colorado Rockies for OF Braulio Castillo (May 20, 1993). . . . On Colorado disabled list (May 26-June 13 and June 25-July 11, 1993). . . . Released by Rockies (July 28, 1993). . . . Signed by Vancouver, California Angels organization (August 20, 1993). . . . On Vancouver disabled list (August 31, 1993-remainder of season). . . . Granted free agency (October 15, 1993).

STATISTICAL NOTES: Pitched 9-0 no-hit victory against Danville (August 12, 1982). . . . Led Pacific Coast League pitchers with 18 wild pitches in 1985.

Year	Team (League)	W	L	Pct.	ERA	G	GS	CG	ShO	Sv.	IP	H	R	ER	BB	SO
1981	—Great Falls (Pio.)	2	6	.250	4.36	10	10	4	0	0	64	63	36	31	35	50
1982	—Clinton (Midwest)	*16	5	*.762	2.36	27	27	12	•4	0	*198⅔	139	63	52	60	*243
1983	—Shreveport (Texas)	10	8	.556	3.66	26	26	7	2	0	*186⅔	182	83	76	71	159
1984	—Phoenix (PCL)	5	7	.417	3.96	17	17	4	1	0	111⅓	102	64	49	61	78
	—San Francisco (N.L.)	1	4	.200	6.37	11	10	0	0	1	53⅔	56	40	38	19	32
1985	—Phoenix (PCL)	8	•15	.348	4.52	29	•29	4	•3	0	183	182	101	92	90	133
1986	—Phoenix (PCL)	*14	7	.667	4.90	28	•27	*10	•3	0	181⅔	204	105	99	46	93
	—San Francisco (N.L.)	0	1	.000	3.60	4	1	0	0	0	10	6	4	4	5	5
1987	—Phoenix (PCL)	2	1	.667	3.13	3	3	2	0	0	23	20	8	8	5	12
	—S.F.-S.D. (N.L.)■	7	9	.438	4.24	33	25	2	1	1	163⅓	170	88	77	73	90
1988	—San Diego (N.L.)	2	8	.200	3.69	33	11	0	0	0	97⅔	97	41	40	36	61
1989	—San Diego (N.L.)	8	2	.800	3.33	50	0	0	0	2	116⅓	105	45	43	32	69
1990	—S.D.-Atlanta (N.L.)■	2	3	.400	4.73	59	1	0	0	3	91⅓	108	53	48	37	69
1991	—Richmond (Int'l)	0	0	...	0.00	1	1	0	0	0	3	2	0	0	1	3
1992	—Jacksonv. (South.)■	1	2	.333	1.93	5	5	0	0	0	32⅔	25	10	7	4	21
	—Calgary (PCL)	1	3	.250	4.15	4	3	1	0	0	26	32	15	12	4	11
	—Seattle (A.L.)	2	4	.333	3.89	23	10	0	0	0	81	100	39	35	22	42
1993	—Tucson-Van. (PCL)■	1	0	1.000	0.87	5	0	0	0	0	10⅓	5	1	1	6	11
	—Hou.-Colo. (N.L.)■	0	1	.000	7.46	20	0	0	0	1	25⅓	34	24	21	11	14
A.L. totals (1 year)		2	4	.333	3.89	23	10	0	0	0	81	100	39	35	22	42
N.L. totals (7 years)		20	28	.417	4.37	210	48	2	1	8	557⅔	576	295	271	213	340
Major league totals (8 years)		22	32	.407	4.31	233	58	2	1	8	638⅔	676	334	306	235	382

GRATER, MARK

P

PERSONAL: Born January 19, 1964, in Rochester, Pa. . . . 5-10/205. . . . Throws right, bats right.

HIGH SCHOOL: Monaca (Pa.).

COLLEGE: Community College of Beaver County (Pa.) and Florida International.

TRANSACTIONS/CAREER NOTES: Selected by St. Louis Cardinals organization in 23rd round of free-agent draft (June 2, 1986). . . . Granted free agency (October 15, 1992). . . . Signed by Toledo, Detroit Tigers organization (December 16, 1992). . . . Released by Toledo (July 19, 1993). . . . Signed by Calgary, Seattle Mariners organization (July 24, 1993). . . . On Calgary disabled list (August 27, 1993-remainder of season). . . . Granted free agency (October 15, 1993).

Year	Team (League)	W	L	Pct.	ERA	G	GS	CG	ShO	Sv.	IP	H	R	ER	BB	SO
1986	—Johns. City (App.)	5	2	.714	2.40	24	0	0	0	8	41⅓	25	14	11	14	46
1987	—Savannah (S. Atl.)	6	10	.375	3.04	50	0	0	0	6	74	54	35	25	48	59
1988	—Springfield (Midw.)	7	2	.778	1.78	53	0	0	0	11	81	60	23	16	27	66
1989	—St. Peters. (FSL)	3	8	.273	1.87	56	0	0	0	*32	67⅓	44	23	14	24	59
1990	—Arkansas (Texas)	2	0	1.000	2.86	29	0	0	0	17	44	31	18	14	18	43
	—Louisville (A.A.)	0	2	.000	3.18	24	0	0	0	3	28⅓	24	13	10	15	18
1991	—Louisville (A.A.)	3	5	.375	2.02	58	0	0	0	12	80⅓	68	20	18	33	54
	—St. Louis (N.L.)	0	0	...	0.00	3	0	0	0	0	3	5	0	0	2	0
1992	—Louisville (A.A.)	7	8	.467	2.13	54	0	0	0	*24	76	74	26	18	15	46
1993	—Toledo (Int'l)■	1	2	.333	8.13	28	0	0	0	4	31	42	31	28	12	31
	—Detroit (A.L.)	0	0	...	5.40	6	0	0	0	0	5	6	3	3	4	4
	—Calgary (PCL)■	0	1	.000	7.71	9	0	0	0	0	11⅔	19	10	10	6	4
A.L. totals (1 year)		0	0	...	5.40	6	0	0	0	0	5	6	3	3	4	4
N.L. totals (1 year)		0	0	...	0.00	3	0	0	0	0	3	5	0	0	2	0
Major league totals (2 years)		0	0	...	3.38	9	0	0	0	0	8	11	3	3	6	4

GRAY, DENNIS

P, BLUE JAYS

PERSONAL: Born December 24, 1969, in Riverside, Calif. . . . 6-6/210. . . . Throws left, bats left. . . . Full name: Dennis Cragg Gray.

HIGH SCHOOL: Banning (Calif.).

COLLEGE: Long Beach State.

TRANSACTIONS/CAREER NOTES: Selected by Chicago Cubs organization in ninth round of free-agent draft (June 1, 1988). . . . Selected by Toronto Blue Jays organization in second round of free-agent draft (June 3, 1991).

Year	Team (League)	W	L	Pct.	ERA	G	GS	CG	ShO	Sv.	IP	H	R	ER	BB	SO
1991	—St. Cathar. (NYP)	4	4	.500	3.74	15	14	0	0	0	77	63	42	32	54	78
1992	—Myrtle Beach (SAL)	11	12	.478	3.82	28	•28	0	0	0	155⅓	122	82	66	*93	141
1993	—Dunedin (Fla. St.)	8	10	.444	3.57	26	26	0	0	0	141⅓	115	71	56	*97	108

GREBECK, CRAIG

IF, WHITE SOX

PERSONAL: Born December 29, 1964, in Johnstown, Pa. . . . 5-7/148. . . . Throws right, bats right. . . . Full name: Craig Allen Grebeck. . . . Name pronounced GRAY-bek.
HIGH SCHOOL: Lakewood (Calif.).
COLLEGE: Cal State Dominguez Hills.
TRANSACTIONS/CAREER NOTES: Signed as free agent by Chicago White Sox organization (August 13, 1986). . . . On disabled list (August 9, 1992-remainder of season).
STATISTICAL NOTES: Led Southern League in grounding into double plays with 15 in 1989.

			BATTING												FIELDING			
Year	**Team (League)**	**Pos.**	**G**	**AB**	**R**	**H**	**2B**	**3B**	**HR**	**RBI**	**Avg.**	**BB**	**SO**	**SB**	**PO**	**A**	**E**	**Avg.**
1987	—Peninsula (Caro.)	SS-3B	104	378	63	106	22	3	15	67	.280	37	62	3	137	278	16	.963
1988	—Birm. (Southern)	2B	133	450	57	126	21	1	9	53	.280	65	72	5	238	368	19	.970
1989	—Birm. (Southern)	SS-3B-2B	•143	•533	85	*153	25	4	5	80	.287	63	77	14	234	364	28	.955
1990	—Chicago (A.L.)	3B-SS-2B	59	119	7	20	3	1	1	9	.168	8	24	0	36	98	3	.978
	—Vancouver (PCL)	SS-3B-2B	12	41	8	8	0	0	1	3	.195	6	7	1	28	26	1	.982
1991	—Chicago (A.L.)	3B-2B-SS	107	224	37	63	16	3	6	31	.281	38	40	1	104	183	10	.966
1992	—Chicago (A.L.)	SS-3B-OF	88	287	24	77	21	2	3	35	.268	30	34	0	112	283	8	.980
1993	—Chicago (A.L.)	SS-2B-3B	72	190	25	43	5	0	1	12	.226	26	26	1	91	185	5	.982
Major league totals (4 years)			326	820	93	203	45	6	11	87	.248	102	124	2	343	749	26	.977

CHAMPIONSHIP SERIES RECORD

			BATTING												FIELDING			
Year	**Team (League)**	**Pos.**	**G**	**AB**	**R**	**H**	**2B**	**3B**	**HR**	**RBI**	**Avg.**	**BB**	**SO**	**SB**	**PO**	**A**	**E**	**Avg.**
1993	—Chicago (A.L.)	PH-3B	1	1	0	1	0	0	0	0	1.000	0	0	0	0	0	0	...

GREEN, SHAWN

OF, BLUE JAYS

PERSONAL: Born November 10, 1972, in Des Plaines, Ill. . . . 6-4/190. . . . Throws left, bats left. . . . Full name: Shawn David Green.
HIGH SCHOOL: Tustin (Calif.).
TRANSACTIONS/CAREER NOTES: Selected by Toronto Blue Jays organization in first round (16th pick overall) of free-agent draft (June 3, 1991); pick received as compensation for San Francisco Giants signing Type A free agent Bud Black. . . . On disabled list (June 30-July 23, 1992). . . . On Knoxville disabled list (June 11-July 24, 1993).
STATISTICAL NOTES: Tied for Florida State League lead with eight sacrifice flies in 1992.

			BATTING												FIELDING			
Year	**Team (League)**	**Pos.**	**G**	**AB**	**R**	**H**	**2B**	**3B**	**HR**	**RBI**	**Avg.**	**BB**	**SO**	**SB**	**PO**	**A**	**E**	**Avg.**
1992	—Dunedin (Fla. St.)	OF	114	417	44	114	21	3	1	49	.273	28	66	22	182	3	5	.974
1993	—Knoxville (South.)	OF	99	360	40	102	14	2	4	34	.283	26	72	4	172	3	8	.956
	—Toronto (A.L.)	OF	3	6	0	0	0	0	0	0	.000	0	1	0	1	0	0	1.000
Major league totals (1 year)			3	6	0	0	0	0	0	0	.000	0	1	0	1	0	0	1.000

GREEN, TYLER

P, PHILLIES

PERSONAL: Born February 18, 1970, in Springfield, O. . . . 6-5/192. . . . Throws right, bats right. . . . Full name: Tyler Scott Green.
HIGH SCHOOL: Thomas Jefferson (Denver).
COLLEGE: Wichita State.
TRANSACTIONS/CAREER NOTES: Selected by Cincinnati Reds organization in third round of free-agent draft (June 1, 1988). . . . Selected by Philadelphia Phillies organization in first round (10th pick overall) of free-agent draft (June 3, 1991). . . . On Clearwater disabled list (August 7, 1991-remainder of season). . . . On Scranton/Wilkes-Barre disabled list (July 10, 1992-remainder of season and May 3-22, 1993).
STATISTICAL NOTES: Pitched 3-1 no-hit victory for Scranton/Wilkes-Barre against Ottawa (July 4, 1993, first game).

Year	**Team (League)**	**W**	**L**	**Pct.**	**ERA**	**G**	**GS**	**CG**	**ShO**	**Sv.**	**IP**	**H**	**R**	**ER**	**BB**	**SO**
1991	—Batavia (NY-Penn)	1	0	1.000	1.20	3	3	0	0	0	15	7	2	2	6	19
	—Clearwater (FSL)	2	0	1.000	1.38	2	2	0	0	0	13	3	2	2	8	20
1992	—Reading (Eastern)	6	3	.667	1.88	12	12	0	0	0	62 1/3	46	16	13	20	67
	—Scran./W.B. (Int'l)	0	1	.000	6.10	2	2	0	0	0	10 1/3	7	7	7	12	15
1993	—Philadelphia (N.L.)	0	0	...	7.36	3	2	0	0	0	7 1/3	16	9	6	5	7
	—Scran./W.B. (Int'l)	6	10	.375	3.95	28	14	4	0	0	118 1/3	102	62	52	43	87
Major league totals (1 year)		0	0	...	7.36	3	2	0	0	0	7 1/3	16	9	6	5	7

GREENE, TOMMY

P, PHILLIES

PERSONAL: Born April 6, 1967, in Lumberton, N.C. . . . 6-5/222. . . . Throws right, bats right. . . . Full name: Ira Thomas Greene.
HIGH SCHOOL: Whiteville (N.C.).
TRANSACTIONS/CAREER NOTES: Selected by Atlanta Braves organization in first round (14th pick overall) of free-agent draft (June 3, 1985). . . . Traded by Braves to Scranton/Wilkes-Barre, Philadelphia Phillies organization (August 9, 1990), as partial completion of deal in which Braves traded OF Dale Murphy and a player to be named later to Phillies for P Jeff Parrett and two players to be named later (August 3, 1990); Braves acquired OF Jim Vatcher (August 9, 1990) and SS Victor Rosario (September 4, 1990) to complete deal. . . . On Philadelphia disabled list (May 13-September 1, 1992); included rehabilitation assignment to Scranton/Wilkes-Barre (May 29-June 4, August 12-20 and August 21-September 1) and Reading (August 20-21). . . . On disabled list (July 28-August 12, 1993).
STATISTICAL NOTES: Pitched 2-0 no-hit victory against Montreal (May 23, 1991). . . . Led N.L. with 15 wild pitches in 1993.
MISCELLANEOUS: Appeared in two games as pinch-hitter (1991). . . . Appeared in one game as pinch-runner (1993).

Year	**Team (League)**	**W**	**L**	**Pct.**	**ERA**	**G**	**GS**	**CG**	**ShO**	**Sv.**	**IP**	**H**	**R**	**ER**	**BB**	**SO**
1985	—Pulaski (Appal.)	2	5	.286	7.64	12	12	1	1	0	50 2/3	49	45	43	27	32
1986	—Sumter (S. Atl.)	11	7	.611	4.69	28	*28	5	•3	0	174 2/3	162	95	91	82	169
1987	—Greenville (South.)	11	8	.579	3.29	23	23	4	2	0	142 1/3	103	60	52	66	101
1988	—Richmond (Int'l)	7	17	.292	4.77	29	29	4	•3	0	177 1/3	169	98	94	70	130
1989	—Richmond (Int'l)	9	12	.429	3.61	26	26	2	1	0	152	136	74	61	50	125

Year	Team (League)	W	L	Pct.	ERA	G	GS	CG	ShO	Sv.	IP	H	R	ER	BB	SO
	—Atlanta (N.L.)	1	2	.333	4.10	4	4	1	1	0	26⅓	22	12	12	6	17
1990	—Atl.-Phil. (N.L.)■	3	3	.500	5.08	15	9	0	0	0	51⅓	50	31	29	26	21
	—Ric.-Scr/WB (Int'l)	5	8	.385	3.49	20	18	2	0	0	116	93	49	45	67	69
1991	—Philadelphia (N.L.)	13	7	.650	3.38	36	27	3	2	0	207⅔	177	85	78	66	154
1992	—Philadelphia (N.L.)	3	3	.500	5.32	13	12	0	0	0	64⅓	75	39	38	34	39
	—Reading (Eastern)	0	0	...	9.00	1	1	0	0	0	2	3	2	2	2	2
	—Scran./W.B. (Int'l)	2	1	.667	2.49	5	5	1	1	0	21⅔	15	7	6	4	21
1993	—Philadelphia (N.L.)	16	4	.800	3.42	31	30	7	2	0	200	175	84	76	62	167
Major league totals (5 years)		36	19	.655	3.82	99	82	11	5	0	549⅔	499	251	233	194	398

CHAMPIONSHIP SERIES RECORD

CHAMPIONSHIP SERIES NOTES: Shares single-game record for most earned runs allowed—7 (October 7, 1993).

Year	Team (League)	W	L	Pct.	ERA	G	GS	CG	ShO	Sv.	IP	H	R	ER	BB	SO
1993	—Philadelphia (N.L.)	1	1	.500	9.64	2	2	0	0	0	9⅓	12	10	10	7	7

WORLD SERIES RECORD

Year	Team (League)	W	L	Pct.	ERA	G	GS	CG	ShO	Sv.	IP	H	R	ER	BB	SO
1993	—Philadelphia (N.L.)	0	0	...	27.00	1	1	0	0	0	2⅓	7	7	7	4	1

GREENE, WILLIE

3B, REDS

PERSONAL: Born September 23, 1971, in Milledgeville, Ga. . . . 5-11/184. . . . Throws right, bats left. . . . Full name: Willie Louis Greene.

HIGH SCHOOL: Jones County (Gray, Ga.).

TRANSACTIONS/CAREER NOTES: Selected by Pittsburgh Pirates organization in first round (18th pick overall) of free-agent draft (June 5, 1989). . . . Traded by Pirates organization with P Scott Ruskin and a player to be named later to Montreal Expos organization for P Zane Smith (August 8, 1990); Expos acquired OF Moises Alou to complete deal (August 16, 1990). . . . Traded by Expos organization with OF Dave Martinez and P Scott Ruskin to Cincinnati Reds organization for P John Wetteland and P Bill Risley (December 11, 1991). . . . On Cincinnati disabled list (August 21, 1993-remainder of season).

STATISTICAL NOTES: Led Florida State League third basemen with 31 errors in 1991. . . . Led Southern League third basemen with 24 double plays in 1992. . . . Led American Association third basemen with 23 errors in 1993.

			BATTING												FIELDING			
Year	Team (League)	Pos.	G	AB	R	H	2B	3B	HR	RBI	Avg.	BB	SO	SB	PO	A	E	Avg.
1989	—Princeton (Appal.)	SS	39	136	22	44	6	4	2	24	.324	9	29	4	33	69	19	.843
	—GC Pirates (GCL)	SS	23	86	17	24	3	3	5	11	.279	9	6	4	25	49	3	.961
1990	—Augusta (S. Atl.)	SS-2B	86	291	59	75	12	4	11	47	.258	61	58	7	117	209	34	.906
	—Salem (Carolina)	SS	17	60	9	11	1	1	3	9	.183	7	18	0	22	43	2	.970
	—Rockford (Midw.)■	SS	11	35	4	14	3	0	0	2	.400	6	7	2	14	37	4	.927
1991	—W.P. Beach (FSL)	3B-SS	99	322	46	70	9	3	12	43	.217	50	93	10	72	184	†32	.889
1992	—Ced. Rap. (Midw.)■	3B	34	120	26	34	8	2	12	40	.283	18	27	3	13	60	8	.901
	—Chatt. (South.)	3B	96	349	47	97	19	2	15	66	.278	46	90	9	*77	174	14	*.947
	—Cincinnati (N.L.)	3B	29	93	10	25	5	2	2	13	.269	10	23	0	15	40	3	.948
1993	—Indianapolis (A.A.)	3B-SS	98	341	62	91	19	0	22	58	.267	51	83	2	77	171	†23	.915
	—Cincinnati (N.L.)	SS-3B	15	50	7	8	1	1	2	5	.160	2	19	0	19	37	1	.982
Major league totals (2 years)			44	143	17	33	6	3	4	18	.231	12	42	0	34	77	4	.965

GREENWELL, MIKE

OF, RED SOX

PERSONAL: Born July 18, 1963, in Louisville, Ky. . . . 6-0/205. . . . Throws right, bats left. . . . Full name: Michael Lewis Greenwell.

HIGH SCHOOL: North Fort Myers (Fla.).

TRANSACTIONS/CAREER NOTES: Selected by Boston Red Sox organization in third round of free-agent draft (June 7, 1982). . . . On disabled list (April 21-May 2 and May 13-July 25, 1983; July 30-August 14, 1989; May 2-17 and June 22, 1992-remainder of season and May 18-June 2, 1993).

RECORDS: Holds A.L. single-season record for most game-winning runs batted in—23 (1988).

HONORS: Named outfielder on THE SPORTING NEWS A.L. All-Star team (1988). . . . Named outfielder on THE SPORTING NEWS A.L. Silver Slugger team (1988).

STATISTICAL NOTES: Led Carolina League in being hit by pitch with 15 in 1984. . . . Hit for the cycle (September 14, 1988). . . . Led A.L. with 23 game-winning RBIs and tied for lead with 18 intentional bases on balls received in 1988.

			BATTING												FIELDING			
Year	Team (League)	Pos.	G	AB	R	H	2B	3B	HR	RBI	Avg.	BB	SO	SB	PO	A	E	Avg.
1982	—Elmira (N.Y.-Penn)	3B-2B	72	268	57	72	10	1	6	36	.269	37	37	5	96	151	31	.888
1983	—Winst.-Salem (Car.)	OF	48	158	23	44	8	0	3	21	.278	19	23	4	28	1	1	.967
1984	—Winst.-Salem (Car.)	3B-OF	130	454	70	139	23	6	16	84	.306	56	40	9	126	132	30	.896
1985	—Pawtucket (Int'l)	OF	117	418	47	107	21	1	13	52	.256	38	45	3	178	8	7	.964
	—Boston (A.L.)	OF	17	31	7	10	1	0	4	8	.323	3	4	1	14	0	0	1.000
1986	—Pawtucket (Int'l)	OF-3B	89	320	62	96	21	1	18	59	.300	43	20	6	130	20	8	.949
	—Boston (A.L.)	OF	31	35	4	11	2	0	0	4	.314	5	7	0	18	1	0	1.000
1987	—Boston (A.L.)	OF-C	125	412	71	135	31	6	19	89	.328	35	40	5	165	8	6	.966
1988	—Boston (A.L.)	OF	158	590	86	192	39	8	22	119	.325	87	38	16	302	6	6	.981
1989	—Boston (A.L.)	OF	145	578	87	178	36	0	14	95	.308	56	44	13	220	11	8	.967
1990	—Boston (A.L.)	OF	159	610	71	181	30	6	14	73	.297	65	43	8	287	13	7	.977
1991	—Boston (A.L.)	OF	147	544	76	163	26	6	9	83	.300	43	35	15	263	9	3	.989
1992	—Boston (A.L.)	OF	49	180	16	42	2	0	2	18	.233	18	19	2	85	1	0	1.000
1993	—Boston (A.L.)	OF	146	540	77	170	38	6	13	72	.315	54	46	5	261	6	2	.993
Major league totals (9 years)			977	3520	495	1082	205	32	97	561	.307	366	276	65	1615	55	32	.981

CHAMPIONSHIP SERIES RECORD

Year	Team (League)	Pos.	G	AB	R	H	2B	3B	HR	RBI	Avg.	BB	SO	SB	PO	A	E	Avg.
			BATTING												FIELDING			
1986	—Boston (A.L.)	PH	2	2	0	1	0	0	0	0	.500	0	0	0	...	...	...	...
1988	—Boston (A.L.)	OF	4	14	2	3	1	0	1	3	.214	3	0	0	4	0	0	1.000
1990	—Boston (A.L.)	OF	4	14	1	0	0	0	0	0	.000	2	2	0	3	0	1	.750
Championship series totals (3 years)			10	30	3	4	1	0	1	3	.133	5	2	0	7	0	1	.875

WORLD SERIES RECORD

Year	Team (League)	Pos.	G	AB	R	H	2B	3B	HR	RBI	Avg.	BB	SO	SB	PO	A	E	Avg.
			BATTING												FIELDING			
1986	—Boston (A.L.)	PH	4	3	0	0	0	0	0	0	.000	1	2	0	...	...	...	...

ALL-STAR GAME RECORD

Year	League	Pos.	AB	R	H	2B	3B	HR	RBI	Avg.	BB	SO	SB	PO	A	E	Avg.
			BATTING											FIELDING			
1988	—American	OF	1	0	0	0	0	0	0	.000	0	0	0	1	0	0	1.000
1989	—American	OF	0	0	0	0	0	0	0	...	0	0	0	1	0	0	1.000
All-Star Game totals (2 years)			1	0	0	0	0	0	0	.000	0	0	0	2	0	0	1.000

GREER, KENNY

P, METS

PERSONAL: Born May 12, 1967, in Boston. . . . 6-2/215. . . . Throws right, bats right. . . . Full name: Kenneth William Greer.
HIGH SCHOOL: Portsmouth (N.H.).
COLLEGE: Massachusetts.
TRANSACTIONS/CAREER NOTES: Selected by New York Yankees organization in 10th round of free-agent draft (June 1, 1988). . . . On Columbus disabled list (June 19-July 15, 1993). . . . Traded by Yankees to New York Mets for P Frank Tanana (September 17, 1993).

Year	Team (League)	W	L	Pct.	ERA	G	GS	CG	ShO	Sv.	IP	H	R	ER	BB	SO
1988	—Oneonta (NYP)	5	5	.500	2.40	15	15	4	0	0	112 1/3	109	46	30	18	60
1989	—Prin. William (Car.)	7	3	.700	4.19	29	13	3	1	2	111 2/3	101	56	52	22	44
1990	—Fort Lauder. (FSL)	4	9	.308	5.44	38	5	0	0	1	89 1/3	115	64	54	33	55
	—Prin. William (Car.)	1	0	1.000	2.35	1	1	0	0	0	7 2/3	7	2	2	2	7
1991	—Fort Lauder. (FSL)	4	3	.571	4.24	31	1	0	0	0	57 1/3	49	31	27	22	46
1992	—Prin. William (Car.)	1	2	.333	3.67	13	0	0	0	1	27	25	11	11	9	30
	—Alb./Colon. (East.)	4	1	.800	1.83	40	1	0	0	4	68 2/3	48	19	14	30	53
	—Columbus (Int'l)	0	0	...	9.00	1	0	0	0	0	1	3	2	1	1	1
1993	—Columbus (Int'l)	9	4	.692	4.42	46	0	0	0	6	79 1/3	78	41	39	36	50
	—New York (N.L.)■	1	0	1.000	0.00	1	0	0	0	0	1	0	0	0	0	2
Major league totals (1 year)		1	0	1.000	0.00	1	0	0	0	0	1	0	0	0	0	2

GREER, RUSTY

1B, RANGERS

PERSONAL: Born January 21, 1969, in Fort Rucker, Ala. . . . 6-0/190. . . . Throws left, bats left. . . . Full name: Thurman Clyde Greer III.
HIGH SCHOOL: Albertville (Ala.).
COLLEGE: Montevallo (Ala.).
TRANSACTIONS/CAREER NOTES: Selected by Texas Rangers organization in 10th round of free-agent draft (June 4, 1990). . . . On disabled list (July 31-August 22, 1992).
STATISTICAL NOTES: Led Florida State League with .395 on-base percentage in 1991.

Year	Team (League)	Pos.	G	AB	R	H	2B	3B	HR	RBI	Avg.	BB	SO	SB	PO	A	E	Avg.
			BATTING												FIELDING			
1990	—Butte (Pioneer)	OF	62	226	48	78	12	6	10	50	.345	41	23	9	84	5	*8	.918
1991	—Charlotte (Fla. St.)	OF-1B	111	388	52	114	25	1	5	48	.294	66	48	12	213	15	7	.970
	—Tulsa (Texas)	OF	20	64	12	19	3	2	3	12	.297	17	6	2	34	0	0	1.000
1992	—Tulsa (Texas)	1B-OF	106	359	47	96	22	4	5	37	.267	60	63	2	814	50	11	.987
1993	—Tulsa (Texas)	1B	129	474	76	138	25	6	15	59	.291	53	79	10	1055	93	8	.993
	—Okla. City (A.A.)	OF	8	27	6	6	2	0	1	4	.222	6	7	0	16	0	0	1.000

G

GREGG, TOMMY

1B/OF

PERSONAL: Born July 29, 1963, in Boone, N.C. . . . 6-1/190. . . . Throws left, bats left. . . . Full name: William Thomas Gregg Jr.
HIGH SCHOOL: R.J. Reynolds (Winston-Salem, N.C.).
COLLEGE: Wake Forest.
TRANSACTIONS/CAREER NOTES: Selected by Cleveland Indians organization in ninth round of free-agent draft (June 8, 1981). . . . Selected by Indians organization in 32nd round of free-agent draft (June 4, 1984). . . . Selected by Pittsburgh Pirates organization in seventh round of free-agent draft (June 3, 1985). . . . Traded by Pirates to Atlanta Braves (September 1, 1988), completing deal in which Braves traded IF Ken Oberkfell and cash to Pirates for a player to be named later (August 28, 1988). . . . On disabled list (April 20-June 2, 1989). . . . On Atlanta disabled list (April 28-June 9, 1991); included rehabilitation assignment to Richmond (June 5-9). . . . On Atlanta disabled list (March 24-July 21, 1992); included rehabilitation assignment to Richmond (May 30-June 7, July 8-13 and July 16-20). . . . Claimed on waivers by Cincinnati Reds (December 1, 1992). . . . Released by Indianapolis, Reds organization (March 26, 1993). . . . Re-signed by Indianapolis (March 27, 1993). . . . On Indianapolis disabled list (May 15-22 and June 7-17, 1993). . . . Granted free agency (August 30, 1993).
STATISTICAL NOTES: Led Eastern League with 14 intentional bases on balls received in 1987.

Year	Team (League)	Pos.	G	AB	R	H	2B	3B	HR	RBI	Avg.	BB	SO	SB	PO	A	E	Avg.
			BATTING												FIELDING			
1985	—Macon (S. Atl.)	OF	72	259	43	81	14	2	1	18	.313	49	38	16	117	4	1	.992
1986	—Nashua (Eastern)	OF-1B	126	421	55	113	13	4	1	29	.268	66	48	11	216	7	4	.982

Year	Team (League)	Pos.	G	BATTING AB	R	H	2B	3B	HR	RBI	Avg.	BB	SO	SB	FIELDING PO	A	E	Avg.
1987	—Harrisburg (East.)	OF	133	461	99	171	22	9	10	82	*.371	84	47	35	242	12	7	.973
	—Pittsburgh (N.L.)	OF	10	8	3	2	1	0	0	0	.250	0	2	0	1	0	0	1.000
1988	—Buffalo (A.A.)	OF	72	252	34	74	12	0	6	27	.294	25	26	7	134	3	2	.986
	—Pitts.-Atl. (N.L.)■	OF	25	44	5	13	4	0	1	7	.295	3	6	0	26	1	0	1.000
1989	—Atlanta (N.L.)	OF-1B	102	276	24	67	8	0	6	23	.243	18	45	3	321	17	2	.994
1990	—Atlanta (N.L.)	1B-OF	124	239	18	63	13	1	5	32	.264	24	39	4	356	34	6	.985
1991	—Atlanta (N.L.)	OF-1B	72	107	13	20	8	1	1	4	.187	12	24	2	121	9	0	1.000
	—Richmond (Int'l)	OF	3	13	3	6	0	0	1	4	.462	1	2	1	5	0	0	1.000
1992	—Richmond (Int'l)	OF	39	125	17	36	9	2	0	12	.288	19	27	3	53	0	2	.964
	—Atlanta (N.L.)	OF	18	19	1	5	0	0	1	1	.263	1	7	1	15	0	0	1.000
1993	—Indianapolis (A.A.)■	1B-OF	71	198	34	63	12	5	7	30	.318	26	28	3	330	29	7	.981
	—Cincinnati (N.L.)	OF	10	12	1	2	0	0	0	1	.167	0	0	0	2	0	0	1.000
Major league totals (7 years)			361	705	65	172	34	2	14	68	.244	58	123	10	842	61	8	.991

CHAMPIONSHIP SERIES RECORD

Year	Team (League)	Pos.	G	BATTING AB	R	H	2B	3B	HR	RBI	Avg.	BB	SO	SB	FIELDING PO	A	E	Avg.
1991	—Atlanta (N.L.)	PH	4	4	0	1	0	0	0	0	.250	0	2	0	...	...	...	...

WORLD SERIES RECORD

Year	Team (League)	Pos.	G	BATTING AB	R	H	2B	3B	HR	RBI	Avg.	BB	SO	SB	FIELDING PO	A	E	Avg.
1991	—Atlanta (N.L.)	PH	4	3	0	0	0	0	0	0	.000	0	2	0	...	...	...	...

GRIFFEY JR., KEN

OF, MARINERS

PERSONAL: Born November 21, 1969, in Donora, Pa. . . . 6-3/205. . . . Throws left, bats left. . . . Full name: George Kenneth Griffey Jr. . . . Son of Ken Griffey Sr., current coach, Seattle Mariners organization, and major league outfielder with four teams (1973-91).
HIGH SCHOOL: Moeller (Cincinnati).

TRANSACTIONS/CAREER NOTES: Selected by Seattle Mariners organization in first round (first pick overall) of free-agent draft (June 2, 1987). . . . On San Bernardino disabled list (June 9-August 15, 1988). . . . On disabled list (July 24-August 20, 1989 and June 9-25, 1992).

RECORDS: Shares major league record for most consecutive games with one or more home runs—8 (July 20 through July 28, 1993).

HONORS: Won A.L. Gold Glove as outfielder (1990-93). . . . Named outfielder on THE SPORTING NEWS A.L. All-Star team (1991 and 1993). . . . Named outfielder on THE SPORTING NEWS A.L. Silver Slugger team (1991 and 1993).

STATISTICAL NOTES: Led A.L. outfielders with six double plays in 1989. . . . Led A.L. with 359 total bases in 1993.

Year	Team (League)	Pos.	G	BATTING AB	R	H	2B	3B	HR	RBI	Avg.	BB	SO	SB	FIELDING PO	A	E	Avg.
1987	—Belling. (N'west)	OF	54	182	43	57	9	1	14	40	.313	44	42	13	117	4	1	*.992
1988	—San Bern. (Calif.)	OF	58	219	50	74	13	3	11	42	.338	34	39	32	145	3	2	.987
	—Vermont (Eastern)	OF	17	61	10	17	5	1	2	10	.279	5	12	4	40	2	1	.977
1989	—Seattle (A.L.)	OF	127	455	61	120	23	0	16	61	.264	44	83	16	302	12	•10	.969
1990	—Seattle (A.L.)	OF	155	597	91	179	28	7	22	80	.300	63	81	16	330	8	7	.980
1991	—Seattle (A.L.)	OF	154	548	76	179	42	1	22	100	.327	71	82	18	360	15	4	.989
1992	—Seattle (A.L.)	OF	142	565	83	174	39	4	27	103	.308	44	67	10	359	8	1	.997
1993	—Seattle (A.L.)	OF-1B	156	582	113	180	38	3	45	109	.309	96	91	17	317	8	3	.991
Major league totals (5 years)			734	2747	424	832	170	15	132	453	.303	318	404	77	1668	51	25	.986

ALL-STAR GAME RECORD

ALL-STAR GAME NOTES: Named Most Valuable Player (1992).

Year	League	Pos.	BATTING AB	R	H	2B	3B	HR	RBI	Avg.	BB	SO	SB	FIELDING PO	A	E	Avg.
1990	—American	OF	2	0	0	0	0	0	0	.000	1	0	0	2	0	0	1.000
1991	—American	OF	3	0	2	0	0	0	0	.667	0	0	0	2	0	0	1.000
1992	—American	OF	3	2	3	1	0	1	2	1.000	0	0	0	1	0	0	1.000
1993	—American	OF	3	1	1	0	0	0	1	.333	0	1	0	2	0	0	1.000
All-Star Game totals (4 years)			11	3	6	1	0	1	3	.545	1	1	0	7	0	0	1.000

GRIFFIN, ALFREDO

IF

PERSONAL: Born March 6, 1957, in Santo Domingo, Dominican Republic. . . . 5-11/165. . . . Throws right, bats both. . . . Full name: Alfredo Claudino Griffin.
HIGH SCHOOL: San Esteban (Santo Domingo, Dominican Republic).

TRANSACTIONS/CAREER NOTES: Signed as free agent by Cleveland Indians organization (August 22, 1973). . . . Traded by Indians with 3B Phil Lansford to Toronto Blue Jays for P Victor Cruz (December 6, 1978). . . . Traded by Blue Jays with OF Dave Collins and cash to Oakland Athletics for P Bill Caudill (December 8, 1984). . . . Traded as part of an eight-player, three-team deal in which New York Mets traded P Jesse Orosco to A's (December 11, 1987). A's then traded Orosco with Griffin and P Jay Howell to Los Angeles Dodgers for P Bob Welch, P Matt Young and P Jack Savage. A's then traded Savage with P Wally Whitehurst and P Kevin Tapani to Mets. . . . On disabled list (May 22-July 25, 1988). . . . Granted free agency (November 4, 1988). . . . Re-signed by Dodgers (November 7, 1988). . . . On disabled list (May 8-28, 1989; May 10-15 and August 6-31, 1991). . . . Granted free agency (October 31, 1991). . . . Signed by Syracuse, Blue Jays organization (March 19, 1992). . . . Granted free agency (October 29, 1992). . . . Re-signed by Blue Jays organization (January 8, 1993). . . . On disabled list (May 29-June 23, 1993). . . . Granted free agency (October 27, 1993).

HONORS: Named A.L. co-Rookie of the Year by Baseball Writers' Association of America (1979). . . . Won A.L. Gold Glove at shortstop (1985).

STATISTICAL NOTES: Led Pacific Coast League shortstops with 40 errors in 1978. . . . Led A.L. shortstops with 31 errors in 1981. . . . Led A.L. shortstops with 824 total chances in 1982. . . . Led A.L. shortstops with 280 putouts in 1983.

Year	Team (League)	Pos.	G	AB	R	H	2B	3B	HR	RBI	Avg.	BB	SO	SB	PO	A	E	Avg.
			BATTING												FIELDING			
1974	—Reno (California)	SS	11	35	4	9	0	0	0	1	.257	1	11	3	10	22	9	.780
	—GC Indians (GCL)	SS	49	158	17	41	1	0	0	11	.259	10	24	7	67	133	*25	.889
1975	—San Jose (Calif.)	SS	124	358	42	82	4	3	0	25	.229	20	82	11	189	281	47	.909
1976	—San Jose (Calif.)	SS	64	224	40	58	3	1	0	17	.259	26	46	9	91	145	24	.908
	—Williamsport (East.)	SS	58	200	22	55	3	0	0	17	.275	14	29	13	86	172	17	.938
	—Toledo (Int'l)	SS	22	88	5	19	7	1	0	6	.216	4	13	0	44	71	7	.943
	—Cleveland (A.L.)	SS	12	4	0	1	0	0	0	0	.250	0	2	0	1	2	1	.750
1977	—Toledo (Int'l)	SS	125	457	60	114	14	5	1	32	.249	35	79	26	*223	398	*49	.927
	—Cleveland (A.L.)	SS	14	41	5	6	1	0	0	3	.146	3	5	2	17	30	3	.940
1978	—Portland (PCL)	SS-OF	133	474	82	138	22	10	5	48	.291	43	71	35	201	395	†40	.937
	—Cleveland (A.L.)	SS	5	4	1	2	1	0	0	0	.500	2	1	0	4	7	1	.917
1979	—Toronto (A.L.)■	SS	153	624	81	179	22	10	2	31	.287	40	58	21	272	501	*36	.956
1980	—Toronto (A.L.)	SS	155	653	63	166	26	•15	2	41	.254	24	58	18	295	489	*37	.955
1981	—Toronto (A.L.)	SS-3B-2B	101	388	30	81	19	6	0	21	.209	17	38	8	191	279	†31	.938
1982	—Toronto (A.L.)	SS	•162	539	57	130	20	8	1	48	.241	22	49	10	*319	479	•26	.968
1983	—Toronto (A.L.)	SS-2B	•162	528	62	132	22	9	4	47	.250	27	44	8	†287	422	25	.966
1984	—Toronto (A.L.)	SS-2B	140	419	53	101	8	2	4	30	.241	4	33	11	230	320	21	.963
1985	—Oakland (A.L.)■	SS	162	614	75	166	18	7	2	64	.270	20	50	24	278	440	30	.960
1986	—Oakland (A.L.)	SS	162	594	74	169	23	6	4	51	.285	35	52	33	282	421	25	.966
1987	—Oakland (A.L.)	SS-2B	144	494	69	130	23	5	3	60	.263	28	41	26	250	389	24	.964
1988	—Los Angeles (N.L.)■	SS	95	316	39	63	8	3	1	27	.199	24	30	7	145	264	15	.965
1989	—Los Angeles (N.L.)	SS	136	506	49	125	27	2	0	29	.247	29	57	10	208	333	14	.975
1990	—Los Angeles (N.L.)	SS	141	461	38	97	11	3	1	35	.210	29	65	6	221	382	•26	.959
1991	—Los Angeles (N.L.)	SS	109	350	27	85	6	2	0	27	.243	22	49	5	186	349	22	.961
1992	—Toronto (A.L.)■	SS-2B	63	150	21	35	7	0	0	10	.233	9	19	3	61	136	7	.966
1993	—Toronto (A.L.)	SS-2B-3B	46	95	15	20	3	0	0	3	.211	3	13	0	59	66	4	.969
American League totals (14 years)			1481	5147	606	1318	193	68	22	409	.256	234	463	164	2546	3981	271	.960
National League totals (4 years)			481	1633	153	370	52	10	2	118	.227	104	201	28	760	1328	77	.964
Major league totals (18 years)			1962	6780	759	1688	245	78	24	527	.249	338	664	192	3306	5309	348	.961

CHAMPIONSHIP SERIES RECORD

Year	Team (League)	Pos.	G	AB	R	H	2B	3B	HR	RBI	Avg.	BB	SO	SB	PO	A	E	Avg.
			BATTING												FIELDING			
1988	—Los Angeles (N.L.)	SS	7	25	1	4	1	0	0	3	.160	0	5	0	17	13	0	1.000
1992	—Toronto (A.L.)	PR-SS	2	2	0	0	0	0	0	0	.000	0	0	0	0	3	0	1.000
1993	—Toronto (A.L.)								Did not play.									
Championship series totals (2 years)			9	27	1	4	1	0	0	3	.148	0	5	0	17	16	0	1.000

WORLD SERIES RECORD

Year	Team (League)	Pos.	G	AB	R	H	2B	3B	HR	RBI	Avg.	BB	SO	SB	PO	A	E	Avg.
			BATTING												FIELDING			
1988	—Los Angeles (N.L.)	SS	5	16	2	3	0	0	0	0	.188	2	4	0	7	13	1	.952
1992	—Toronto (A.L.)	SS	2	0	0	0	0	0	0	0	...	0	0	0	0	1	1	.500
1993	—Toronto (A.L.)	PR-3B	3	0	0	0	0	0	0	0	...	0	0	0	0	0	0	...
World Series totals (3 years)			10	16	2	3	0	0	0	0	.188	2	4	0	7	14	2	.913

ALL-STAR GAME RECORD

Year	League	Pos.	AB	R	H	2B	3B	HR	RBI	Avg.	BB	SO	SB	PO	A	E	Avg.
			BATTING											FIELDING			
1984	—American	SS	0	0	0	0	0	0	0	...	0	0	0	0	1	0	1.000

GRIMSLEY, JASON

P, INDIANS

PERSONAL: Born August 7, 1967, in Cleveland, Tex. . . . 6-3/180. . . . Throws right, bats right. . . . Full name: Jason Alan Grimsley.

HIGH SCHOOL: Tarkington (Cleveland, Tex.).

TRANSACTIONS/CAREER NOTES: Selected by Philadelphia Phillies organization in 10th round of free-agent draft (June 3, 1985). . . . On disabled list (April 8-May 10, 1988). . . . On Philadelphia disabled list (June 6-August 22, 1991); included rehabilitation assignment to Scranton/Wilkes-Barre (June 15-30 and August 7-21). . . . Traded by Phillies to Houston Astros for P Curt Schilling (April 2, 1992). . . . On disabled list (May 14-June 14, 1992). . . . Released by Astros (March 30, 1993). . . . Signed by Cleveland Indians organization (April 7, 1993). . . . On Charlotte disabled list (April 15-26, 1993).

STATISTICAL NOTES: Led New York-Pennsylvania League with 11 hit batsmen and 18 wild pitches in 1986. . . . Pitched 3-0 no-hit victory for Reading against Harrisburg (May 3, 1989, first game). . . . Led International League with 18 wild pitches in 1990.

Year	Team (League)	W	L	Pct.	ERA	G	GS	CG	ShO	Sv.	IP	H	R	ER	BB	SO
1985	—Bend (Northwest)	0	1	.000	13.50	6	1	0	0	0	11⅓	12	21	17	25	10
1986	—Utica (N.Y.-Penn)	1	•10	.091	6.40	14	14	3	0	0	64⅔	63	61	46	*77	46
1987	—Spartanburg (SAL)	7	4	.636	3.16	23	9	3	0	0	88⅓	59	48	31	54	98
1988	—Clearwater (FSL)	4	7	.364	3.73	16	15	2	0	0	101⅓	80	48	42	37	90
	—Reading (Eastern)	1	3	.250	7.17	5	4	0	0	0	21⅓	20	19	17	13	14
1989	—Reading (Eastern)	11	8	.579	2.98	26	26	8	2	0	172	121	65	57	*109	134
	—Philadelphia (N.L.)	1	3	.250	5.89	4	4	0	0	0	18⅓	19	13	12	19	7
1990	—Scran./W.B. (Int'l)	8	5	.615	3.93	22	22	0	0	0	128⅓	111	68	56	78	99
	—Philadelphia (N.L.)	3	2	.600	3.30	11	11	0	0	0	57⅓	47	21	21	43	41
1991	—Philadelphia (N.L.)	1	7	.125	4.87	12	12	0	0	0	61	54	34	33	41	42
	—Scran./W.B. (Int'l)	2	3	.400	4.35	9	9	0	0	0	51⅔	48	28	25	37	43
1992	—Tucson (PCL)■	8	7	.533	5.05	26	20	0	0	0	124⅔	152	79	70	55	90

Year	Team (League)	W	L	Pct.	ERA	G	GS	CG	ShO	Sv.	IP	H	R	ER	BB	SO
1993	—Charlotte (Int'l)■	6	6	.500	3.39	28	19	3	1	0	135⅓	138	64	51	49	102
	—Cleveland (A.L.)	3	4	.429	5.31	10	6	0	0	0	42⅓	52	26	25	20	27
	A.L. totals (1 year)	3	4	.429	5.31	10	6	0	0	0	42⅓	52	26	25	20	27
	N.L. totals (3 years)	5	12	.294	4.35	27	27	0	0	0	136⅔	120	68	66	103	90
	Major league totals (4 years)	8	16	.333	4.58	37	33	0	0	0	179	172	94	91	123	117

GRISSOM, MARQUIS

OF, EXPOS

PERSONAL: Born April 17, 1967, in Atlanta. . . . 5-11/190. . . . Throws right, bats right. . . . Full name: Marquis Dean Grissom. . . . Name pronounced mar-KEESE.
HIGH SCHOOL: Lakeshore (College Park, Ga.).
COLLEGE: Florida A&M.

TRANSACTIONS/CAREER NOTES: Selected by Montreal Expos organization in third round of free-agent draft (June 1, 1988). . . . On Montreal disabled list (May 29-June 30, 1990); included rehabilitation assignment to Indianapolis (June 25-30).
HONORS: Won N.L. Gold Glove as outfielder (1993).
STATISTICAL NOTES: Led New York-Pennsylvania League with 146 total bases in 1988.

			BATTING												FIELDING			
Year	Team (League)	Pos.	G	AB	R	H	2B	3B	HR	RBI	Avg.	BB	SO	SB	PO	A	E	Avg.
1988	—Jamestown (NYP)	OF	74	*291	*69	94	14	7	8	39	.323	35	39	23	123	•11	3	.978
1989	—Jacksonv. (South.)	OF	78	278	43	83	15	4	3	31	.299	24	31	24	141	7	3	.980
	—Indianapolis (A.A.)	OF	49	187	28	52	10	4	2	21	.278	14	23	16	106	5	0	1.000
	—Montreal (N.L.)	OF	26	74	16	19	2	0	1	2	.257	12	21	1	32	1	2	.943
1990	—Montreal (N.L.)	OF	98	288	42	74	14	2	3	29	.257	27	40	22	165	5	2	.988
	—Indianapolis (A.A.)	OF	5	22	3	4	0	0	2	3	.182	0	5	1	16	0	0	1.000
1991	—Montreal (N.L.)	OF	148	558	73	149	23	9	6	39	.267	34	89	*76	350	•15	6	.984
1992	—Montreal (N.L.)	OF	159	*653	99	180	39	6	14	66	.276	42	81	*78	401	7	7	.983
1993	—Montreal (N.L.)	OF	157	630	104	188	27	2	19	95	.298	52	76	53	416	8	7	.984
	Major league totals (5 years)		588	2203	334	610	105	19	43	231	.277	167	307	230	1364	36	24	.983

ALL-STAR GAME RECORD

			BATTING											FIELDING			
Year	League	Pos.	AB	R	H	2B	3B	HR	RBI	Avg.	BB	SO	SB	PO	A	E	Avg.
1993	—National	OF	3	0	0	0	0	0	0	.000	0	1	0	1	0	0	1.000

GROOM, BUDDY

P, TIGERS

PERSONAL: Born July 10, 1965, in Dallas. . . . 6-2/200. . . . Throws left, bats left. . . . Full name: Wedsel Gary Groom.
HIGH SCHOOL: Red Oak (Tex.).
COLLEGE: University of Mary Hardin-Baylor (Tex.).

TRANSACTIONS/CAREER NOTES: Selected by Chicago White Sox organization in 12th round of free-agent draft (June 2, 1987). . . . Selected by Detroit Tigers organization from White Sox organization in Rule 5 minor league draft (December 3, 1990).

Year	Team (League)	W	L	Pct.	ERA	G	GS	CG	ShO	Sv.	IP	H	R	ER	BB	SO
1987	—GC Whi. Sox (GCL)	1	0	1.000	0.75	4	1	0	0	1	12	12	1	1	2	8
	—Day. Beach (FSL)	7	2	.778	3.59	11	10	2	0	0	67⅔	60	30	27	33	29
1988	—Tampa (Fla. St.)	13	10	.565	2.54	27	27	8	0	0	*195	181	69	55	51	118
1989	—Birm. (Southern)	13	8	.619	4.52	26	26	3	1	0	167⅓	172	101	84	78	94
1990	—Birm. (Southern)	6	8	.429	5.07	20	20	0	0	0	115⅓	135	81	65	48	66
1991	—Toledo (Int'l)■	2	5	.286	4.32	24	6	0	0	1	75	75	39	36	25	49
	—London (Eastern)	7	1	.875	3.48	11	7	0	0	0	51⅔	51	20	20	12	39
1992	—Toledo (Int'l)	7	7	.500	2.80	16	16	1	0	0	109⅓	102	41	34	23	71
	—Detroit (A.L.)	0	5	.000	5.82	12	7	0	0	1	38⅔	48	28	25	22	15
1993	—Toledo (Int'l)	9	3	.750	2.74	16	15	0	0	0	102	98	34	31	30	78
	—Detroit (A.L.)	0	2	.000	6.14	19	3	0	0	0	36⅔	48	25	25	13	15
	Major league totals (2 years)	0	7	.000	5.97	31	10	0	0	1	75⅓	96	53	50	35	30

GROSS, KEVIN

P, DODGERS

PERSONAL: Born June 8, 1961, in Downey, Calif. . . . 6-5/227. . . . Throws right, bats right. . . . Full name: Kevin Frank Gross.
HIGH SCHOOL: Fillmore (Calif.).
COLLEGE: Oxnard (Calif.) College and California Lutheran College.

TRANSACTIONS/CAREER NOTES: Selected by Baltimore Orioles organization in 32nd round of free-agent draft (June 5, 1979). . . . Selected by Philadelphia Phillies organization in secondary phase of free-agent draft (January 13, 1981). . . . Traded by Phillies to Montreal Expos for P Floyd Youmans and P Jeff Parrett (December 6, 1988). . . . On disabled list (June 28-July 20, 1990). . . . Granted free agency (November 5, 1990). . . . Signed by Los Angeles Dodgers (December 3, 1990).
STATISTICAL NOTES: Led N.L. with 28 home runs allowed in 1986. . . . Led N.L. with 11 hit batsmen in 1988 and tied for lead with eight in 1986 and 10 in 1987. . . . Pitched 2-0 no-hit victory against San Francisco (August 17, 1992).
MISCELLANEOUS: Singled and scored and struck out in two games as pinch-hitter (1991).

Year	Team (League)	W	L	Pct.	ERA	G	GS	CG	ShO	Sv.	IP	H	R	ER	BB	SO
1981	—Spartanburg (SAL)	13	12	.520	3.56	28	•28	8	2	0	192	173	94	76	62	123
1982	—Reading (Eastern)	10	15	.400	4.23	26	24	8	2	0	151	138	81	71	89	136
1983	—Portland (PCL)	3	5	.375	6.75	15	15	0	0	0	80	82	60	60	45	61
	—Philadelphia (N.L.)	4	6	.400	3.56	17	17	1	1	0	96	100	46	38	35	66
1984	—Philadelphia (N.L.)	8	5	.615	4.12	44	14	1	0	1	129	140	66	59	44	84
1985	—Philadelphia (N.L.)	15	13	.536	3.41	38	31	6	2	0	205⅔	194	86	78	81	151
1986	—Philadelphia (N.L.)	12	12	.500	4.02	37	36	7	2	0	241⅔	240	115	108	94	154
1987	—Philadelphia (N.L.)	9	16	.360	4.35	34	33	3	1	0	200⅔	205	107	97	87	110
1988	—Philadelphia (N.L.)	12	14	.462	3.69	33	33	5	1	0	231⅔	209	101	95	*89	162
1989	—Montreal (N.L.)■	11	12	.478	4.38	31	31	4	3	0	201⅓	188	105	*98	88	158

Year	Team (League)	W	L	Pct.	ERA	G	GS	CG	ShO	Sv.	IP	H	R	ER	BB	SO
1990	—Montreal (N.L.)	9	12	.429	4.57	31	26	2	1	0	163⅓	171	86	83	65	111
1991	—Los Angeles (N.L.)■	10	11	.476	3.58	46	10	0	0	3	115⅔	123	55	46	50	95
1992	—Los Angeles (N.L.)	8	13	.381	3.17	34	30	4	3	0	204⅔	182	82	72	77	158
1993	—Los Angeles (N.L.)	13	13	.500	4.14	33	32	3	0	0	202⅓	224	110	93	74	150
Major league totals (11 years)		111	127	.466	3.92	378	293	36	14	4	1992	1976	959	867	784	1399

WORLD SERIES RECORD

Year	Team (League)	W	L	Pct.	ERA	G	GS	CG	ShO	Sv.	IP	H	R	ER	BB	SO
1983	—Philadelphia (N.L.)	Did not play.														

ALL-STAR GAME RECORD

Year	League	W	L	Pct.	ERA	GS	CG	ShO	Sv.	IP	H	R	ER	BB	SO
1988	—National	0	0	...	0.00	0	0	0	0	1	0	0	0	0	1

GROSS, KIP

P, DODGERS

PERSONAL: Born August 24, 1964, in Scottsbluff, Neb. . . . 6-2/194. . . . Throws right, bats right. . . . Full name: Kip Lee Gross.
HIGH SCHOOL: Gering (Neb.).
COLLEGE: Murray State and Nebraska.
TRANSACTIONS/CAREER NOTES: Selected by St. Louis Cardinals organization in third round of free-agent draft (January 9, 1985). . . . Selected by New York Mets organization in fourth round of free-agent draft (June 2, 1986). . . . Traded by Mets organization with P Randy Myers to Cincinnati Reds for P John Franco and OF Don Brown (December 6, 1989). . . . Traded by Reds with OF Eric Davis to Los Angeles Dodgers for P Tim Belcher and P John Wetteland (November 27, 1991). . . . On Albuquerque disabled list (August 5-12, 1993).

Year	Team (League)	W	L	Pct.	ERA	G	GS	CG	ShO	Sv.	IP	H	R	ER	BB	SO
1987	—Lynchburg (Caro.)	7	4	.636	2.72	16	15	2	0	0	89⅓	92	37	27	22	39
1988	—St. Lucie (Fla. St.)	13	9	.591	2.62	28	27	7	3	0	178⅓	153	72	52	53	124
1989	—Jackson (Texas)	6	5	.545	2.49	16	16	4	0	0	112	96	47	31	13	60
	—Tidewater (Int'l)	4	4	.500	3.97	12	12	0	0	0	70⅓	72	33	31	17	39
1990	—Nashville (A.A.)■	12	7	.632	3.33	40	11	2	1	3	127	113	54	47	47	62
	—Cincinnati (N.L.)	0	0	...	4.26	5	0	0	0	0	6⅓	6	3	3	2	3
1991	—Nashville (A.A.)	5	3	.625	2.08	14	6	1	1	0	47⅔	39	13	11	16	28
	—Cincinnati (N.L.)	6	4	.600	3.47	29	9	1	0	0	85⅔	93	43	33	40	40
1992	—Albuquerque (PCL)■	6	5	.545	3.51	31	14	2	0	8	107⅔	96	48	42	36	58
	—Los Angeles (N.L.)	1	1	.500	4.18	16	1	0	0	0	23⅔	32	14	11	10	14
1993	—Albuquerque (PCL)	13	7	.650	4.05	59	7	0	0	13	124⅓	115	58	56	41	96
	—Los Angeles (N.L.)	0	0	...	0.60	10	0	0	0	0	15	13	1	1	4	12
Major league totals (4 years)		7	5	.583	3.31	60	10	1	0	0	130⅔	144	61	48	56	69

GRUBER, KELLY

3B

PERSONAL: Born February 26, 1962, in Bellaire, Tex. . . . 6-0/185. . . . Throws right, bats right. . . . Full name: Kelly Wayne Gruber.
HIGH SCHOOL: Westlake (Tex.).
COLLEGE: Texas.
TRANSACTIONS/CAREER NOTES: Selected by Cleveland Indians organization in first round (10th pick overall) of free-agent draft (June 3, 1980). . . . Selected by Toronto Blue Jays from Indians organization in Rule 5 major league draft (December 5, 1983). . . . On disabled list (August 10-25, 1989; May 2-June 12, 1991 and June 28-July 23, 1992). . . . Traded by Blue Jays with cash to California Angels for IF Luis Sojo (December 8, 1992). . . . On California disabled list (March 12-June 4, 1993); included rehabilitation assignment to Palm Springs (May 17-24) and Vancouver (May 24-June 4). . . . On California disabled list (July 4-September 7, 1993). . . . Released by Angels (September 7, 1993).
HONORS: Named third baseman on THE SPORTING NEWS A.L. All-Star team (1990). . . . Named third baseman on THE SPORTING NEWS A.L. Silver Slugger team (1990). . . . Won A.L. Gold Glove at third base (1990).
STATISTICAL NOTES: Led Southern League shortstops with 43 errors in 1982. . . . Led International League with .500 slugging percentage in 1984. . . . Led International League third basemen with 309 total chances in 1985. . . . Led A.L. third basemen with 349 assists and 477 total chances in 1988. . . . Led A.L. third basemen with 22 errors in 1989. . . . Hit for the cycle (April 16, 1989). . . . Led A.L. third basemen with 123 putouts in 1990.

			BATTING												FIELDING			
Year	Team (League)	Pos.	G	AB	R	H	2B	3B	HR	RBI	Avg.	BB	SO	SB	PO	A	E	Avg.
1980	—Batavia (NY-Penn)	SS	61	212	27	46	3	2	2	19	.217	15	46	6	87	155	21	.920
1981	—Waterloo (Midw.)	SS	127	458	64	133	25	4	14	59	.290	24	85	15	*180	*389	*56	.910
1982	—Chatt. (South.)	SS-3B	128	441	53	107	18	4	13	54	.243	21	89	11	161	333	†44	.918
1983	—Buffalo (Eastern)	3B-SS-OF	111	403	60	106	20	4	15	54	.263	23	44	15	98	170	27	.908
1984	—Toronto (A.L.)■	3B-OF-SS	15	16	1	1	0	0	1	2	.063	0	5	0	6	12	2	.900
	—Syracuse (Int'l)	3B-OF	97	342	53	92	12	2	21	55	.269	23	67	12	76	156	18	.928
1985	—Syracuse (Int'l)	3B	121	473	71	118	16	5	21	69	.249	28	92	20	78	*217	14	.955
	—Toronto (A.L.)	3B-2B	5	13	0	3	0	0	0	1	.231	0	3	0	2	6	0	1.000
1986	—Toronto (A.L.)	3-2-0-S	87	143	20	28	4	1	5	15	.196	5	27	2	43	77	7	.945
1987	—Toronto (A.L.)	3-S-2-0	138	341	50	80	14	3	12	36	.235	17	70	12	76	200	13	.955
1988	—Toronto (A.L.)	3-2-0-S	158	569	75	158	33	5	16	81	.278	38	92	23	121	†365	16	.968
1989	—Toronto (A.L.)	3B-OF-SS	135	545	83	158	24	4	18	73	.290	30	60	10	121	295	†22	.950
1990	—Toronto (A.L.)	3B-OF	150	592	92	162	36	6	31	118	.274	48	94	14	†129	280	19	.956
1991	—Toronto (A.L.)	3B	113	429	58	108	18	2	20	65	.252	31	70	12	97	231	13	.962
1992	—Toronto (A.L.)	3B	120	446	42	102	16	3	11	43	.229	26	72	7	104	215	17	.949
1993	—Palm Springs (Cal.)■	3B	5	9	0	2	0	0	0	1	.222	1	2	0	0	1	1	.500
	—Vancouver (PCL)	3B	8	24	4	11	1	0	1	5	.458	1	2	0	0	4	0	1.000
	—California (A.L.)	3B-OF	18	65	10	18	3	0	3	9	.277	2	11	0	20	42	4	.939
Major league totals (10 years)			939	3159	431	818	148	24	117	443	.259	197	504	80	719	1723	113	.956

CHAMPIONSHIP SERIES RECORD

CHAMPIONSHIP SERIES NOTES: Shares single-game record for most singles—4 (October 7, 1989).

		BATTING												FIELDING			
Year Team (League)	**Pos.**	**G**	**AB**	**R**	**H**	**2B**	**3B**	**HR**	**RBI**	**Avg.**	**BB**	**SO**	**SB**	**PO**	**A**	**E**	**Avg.**
1989—Toronto (A.L.)	3B	5	17	2	5	1	0	0	1	.294	3	2	1	4	8	0	1.000
1991—Toronto (A.L.)	3B	5	21	1	6	1	0	0	4	.286	0	4	1	3	6	3	.750
1992—Toronto (A.L.)	3B	6	22	3	2	1	0	1	2	.091	2	3	0	5	16	1	.955
Championship series totals (3 years)		16	60	6	13	3	0	1	7	.217	5	9	2	12	30	4	.913

WORLD SERIES RECORD

		BATTING												FIELDING			
Year Team (League)	**Pos.**	**G**	**AB**	**R**	**H**	**2B**	**3B**	**HR**	**RBI**	**Avg.**	**BB**	**SO**	**SB**	**PO**	**A**	**E**	**Avg.**
1992—Toronto (A.L.)	3B	6	19	2	2	0	0	1	1	.105	2	5	1	5	5	1	.909

ALL-STAR GAME RECORD

ALL-STAR GAME NOTES: Shares single-game record for most stolen bases—2 (July 10, 1990).

		BATTING											FIELDING			
Year League	**Pos.**	**AB**	**R**	**H**	**2B**	**3B**	**HR**	**RBI**	**Avg.**	**BB**	**SO**	**SB**	**PO**	**A**	**E**	**Avg.**
1989—American								Did not play.								
1990—American	PR-3B	1	0	0	0	0	0	0	.000	1	0	2	0	1	0	1.000
All-Star Game totals (1 year)		1	0	0	0	0	0	0	.000	1	0	2	0	1	0	1.000

GUARDADO, EDDIE

P, TWINS

PERSONAL: Born October 2, 1970, in Stockton, Calif.... 6-0/193.... Throws left, bats right.... Full name: Edward Adrian Guardado.... Name pronounced gwar-DAH-doh.

HIGH SCHOOL: Franklin (Stockton, Calif.).

COLLEGE: San Joaquin Delta College (Calif.).

TRANSACTIONS/CAREER NOTES: Selected by Minnesota Twins organization in 21st round of free-agent draft (June 4, 1990).

STATISTICAL NOTES: Pitched 5-0 no-hit victory against Pulaski (August 26, 1991).

Year Team (League)	W	L	Pct.	ERA	G	GS	CG	ShO	Sv.	IP	H	R	ER	BB	SO
1991—Elizabeth. (Appal.)	8	4	.667	1.86	14	13	3	•1	0	92	67	30	19	31	*106
1992—Kenosha (Midwest)	5	10	.333	4.37	18	18	2	1	0	101	106	57	49	30	103
—Visalia (California)	7	0	1.000	1.64	7	7	1	1	0	49⅓	47	13	9	10	39
1993—Nashville (South.)	4	0	1.000	1.24	10	10	2	2	0	65⅓	53	10	9	10	57
—Minnesota (A.L.)	3	8	.273	6.18	19	16	0	0	0	94⅔	123	68	65	36	46
Major league totals (1 year)	3	8	.273	6.18	19	16	0	0	0	94⅔	123	68	65	36	46

GUBICZA, MARK

P, ROYALS

PERSONAL: Born August 14, 1962, in Philadelphia.... 6-5/225.... Throws right, bats right.... Full name: Mark Steven Gubicza.... Son of Anthony Gubicza, minor league pitcher (1950-51).... Name pronounced GOO-ba-zah.

HIGH SCHOOL: William Penn Charter (Philadelphia).

TRANSACTIONS/CAREER NOTES: Selected by Kansas City Royals organization in second round of free-agent draft (June 8, 1981); pick received as compensation for St. Louis Cardinals signing free agent Darrell Porter.... On disabled list (June 29, 1982-remainder of season; June 6-21, 1986; and July 1, 1990-remainder of season).... On Kansas City disabled list (March 30-May 14, 1991); included rehabilitation assignment to Omaha (April 20-May 13).... On Kansas City disabled list (July 11, 1992-remainder of season).... Granted free agency (October 30, 1992).... Re-signed by Royals (November 25, 1992).... Granted free agency (November 3, 1993).... Re-signed by Royals (December 7, 1993).

Year Team (League)	W	L	Pct.	ERA	G	GS	CG	ShO	Sv.	IP	H	R	ER	BB	SO
1981—GC Royals-G (GCL)	•8	1	.889	2.25	11	11	0	0	0	56	39	18	14	23	40
1982—Fort Myers (FSL)	2	5	.286	4.13	11	11	0	0	0	48	49	33	22	25	36
1983—Jacksonv. (South.)	14	12	.538	3.08	28	28	5	0	0	196	146	81	67	93	*146
1984—Kansas City (A.L.)	10	14	.417	4.05	29	29	4	2	0	189	172	90	85	75	111
1985—Kansas City (A.L.)	14	10	.583	4.06	29	28	0	0	0	177⅓	160	88	80	77	99
1986—Kansas City (A.L.)	12	6	.667	3.64	35	24	3	2	0	180⅔	155	77	73	84	118
1987—Kansas City (A.L.)	13	18	.419	3.98	35	35	10	2	0	241⅔	231	114	107	120	166
1988—Kansas City (A.L.)	20	8	.714	2.70	35	35	8	4	0	269⅔	237	94	81	83	183
1989—Kansas City (A.L.)	15	11	.577	3.04	36	•36	8	2	0	255	252	100	86	63	173
1990—Kansas City (A.L.)	4	7	.364	4.50	16	16	2	0	0	94	101	48	47	38	71
1991—Omaha (A.A.)	2	1	.667	3.31	3	3	0	0	0	16⅓	20	7	6	4	12
—Kansas City (A.L.)	9	12	.429	5.68	26	26	0	0	0	133	168	90	84	42	89
1992—Kansas City (A.L.)	7	6	.538	3.72	18	18	2	1	0	111⅓	110	47	46	36	81
1993—Kansas City (A.L.)	5	8	.385	4.66	49	6	0	0	2	104⅓	128	61	54	43	80
Major league totals (10 years)	109	100	.522	3.81	308	253	37	13	2	1756	1714	809	743	661	1171

CHAMPIONSHIP SERIES RECORD

Year Team (League)	W	L	Pct.	ERA	G	GS	CG	ShO	Sv.	IP	H	R	ER	BB	SO
1985—Kansas City (A.L.)	1	0	1.000	3.24	2	1	0	0	0	8⅓	4	3	3	4	4

WORLD SERIES RECORD

Year Team (League)	W	L	Pct.	ERA	G	GS	CG	ShO	Sv.	IP	H	R	ER	BB	SO
1985—Kansas City (A.L.)							Did not play.								

ALL-STAR GAME RECORD

Year League	W	L	Pct.	ERA	GS	CG	ShO	Sv.	IP	H	R	ER	BB	SO
1988—American	0	0	...	4.50	0	0	0	0	2	3	1	1	0	2
1989—American	0	0	...	0.00	0	0	0	0	1	0	0	0	0	1
All-Star totals (2 years)	0	0	...	3.00	0	0	0	0	3	3	1	1	0	3

GUETTERMAN, LEE

P

PERSONAL: Born November 22, 1958, in Chattanooga, Tenn. . . . 6-8/230. . . . Throws left, bats left. . . . Full name: Arthur Lee Guetterman.
HIGH SCHOOL: Oceanside (Calif.).
COLLEGE: Liberty, Va. (bachelor of science degree in physical education, 1981).
TRANSACTIONS/CAREER NOTES: Selected by Seattle Mariners organization in fourth round of free-agent draft (June 8, 1981); pick received as compensation for California Angels signing free agent Juan Beniquez. . . . On Chattanooga disabled list (August 1-15, 1984). . . . On disabled list (April 11-May 31, 1985). . . . Traded by Mariners with P Clay Parker and P Wade Taylor to New York Yankees for P Steve Trout and OF Henry Cotto (December 22, 1987). . . . On disabled list (July 19-August 3, 1990). . . . Traded by Yankees to New York Mets for P Tim Burke (June 9, 1992). . . . Granted free agency (October 30, 1992). . . . Signed by Los Angeles Dodgers organization (January 13, 1993). . . . Released by Dodgers organization (March 30, 1993). . . . Signed by Louisville, St. Louis Cardinals organization (May 1, 1993). . . . Granted free agency (October 25, 1993).

Year	Team (League)	W	L	Pct.	ERA	G	GS	CG	ShO	Sv.	IP	H	R	ER	BB	SO
1981	—Belling. (N'west)	6	4	.600	2.68	13	13	3	0	0	84	85	36	25	42	55
1982	—Bakersfield (Calif.)	7	11	.389	4.44	26	26	4	1	0	154	172	100	76	69	82
1983	—Bakersfield (Calif.)	12	6	.667	3.22	25	25	6	1	0	156⅓	164	72	56	45	93
1984	—Chatt. (South.)	11	7	.611	3.38	24	24	4	2	0	157	174	68	59	38	47
	—Seattle (A.L.)	0	0	...	4.15	3	0	0	0	0	4⅓	9	2	2	2	2
1985	—Calgary (PCL)	5	8	.385	5.79	20	18	2	0	0	110⅓	138	86	71	44	48
1986	—Seattle (A.L.)	0	4	.000	7.34	41	4	1	0	0	76	108	67	62	30	38
	—Calgary (PCL)	1	0	1.000	5.59	4	4	0	0	0	19⅓	24	12	12	7	8
1987	—Calgary (PCL)	5	1	.833	2.86	16	2	1	0	1	44	41	14	14	17	29
	—Seattle (A.L.)	11	4	*.733	3.81	25	17	2	1	0	113⅓	117	60	48	35	42
1988	—New York (A.L.)■	1	2	.333	4.65	20	2	0	0	0	40⅔	49	21	21	14	15
	—Columbus (Int'l)	9	6	.600	2.76	18	18	6	0	0	120⅔	109	46	37	26	49
1989	—New York (A.L.)	5	5	.500	2.45	70	0	0	0	13	103	98	31	28	26	51
1990	—New York (A.L.)	11	7	.611	3.39	64	0	0	0	2	93	80	37	35	26	48
1991	—New York (A.L.)	3	4	.429	3.68	64	0	0	0	6	88	91	42	36	25	35
1992	—New York (A.L.)	1	1	.500	9.53	15	0	0	0	0	22⅔	35	24	24	13	5
	—New York (N.L.)■	3	4	.429	5.82	43	0	0	0	2	43⅓	57	28	28	14	15
1993	—Louisville (A.A.)■	2	1	.667	2.94	25	0	0	0	2	33⅔	35	11	11	12	20
	—St. Louis (N.L.)	3	3	.500	2.93	40	0	0	0	1	46	41	18	15	16	19
A.L. totals (8 years)		32	27	.542	4.26	302	23	3	1	21	541	587	284	256	171	236
N.L. totals (2 years)		6	7	.462	4.33	83	0	0	0	3	89⅓	98	46	43	30	34
Major league totals (9 years)		38	34	.528	4.27	385	23	3	1	24	630⅓	685	330	299	201	270

GUILLEN, OZZIE

SS, WHITE SOX

PERSONAL: Born January 20, 1964, in Oculare del Tuy, Miranda, Venezuela. . . . 5-11/164. . . . Throws right, bats left. . . . Full name: Oswaldo Jose Barrios Guillen. . . . Name pronounced GHEE-un.
TRANSACTIONS/CAREER NOTES: Signed as free agent by San Diego Padres organization (December 17, 1980). . . . Traded by Padres organization with P Tim Lollar, P Bill Long and 3B Luis Salazar to Chicago White Sox for P LaMarr Hoyt, P Kevin Kristan and P Todd Simmons (December 6, 1984). . . . On Chicago disabled list (April 22, 1992-remainder of season).
RECORDS: Shares major league single-season record for fewest bases on balls received (150 or more games)—11 (1991). . . . Holds A.L. single-season record for fewest putouts by shortstop (150 or more games)—220 (1985).
HONORS: Named A.L. Rookie Player of the Year by THE SPORTING NEWS (1985). . . . Named A.L. Rookie of the Year by Baseball Writers' Association of America (1985). . . . Won A.L. Gold Glove at shortstop (1990).
STATISTICAL NOTES: Tied for California League lead with 14 sacrifice hits in 1982. . . . Led Pacific Coast League shortstops with 362 assists and 549 total chances in 1984. . . . Led A.L. shortstops with 760 total chances in 1987 and 863 in 1988. . . . Led A.L. shortstops with 105 double plays in 1987.
MISCELLANEOUS: Batted as switch-hitter (1981-84).

			BATTING												FIELDING			
Year	Team (League)	Pos.	G	AB	R	H	2B	3B	HR	RBI	Avg.	BB	SO	SB	PO	A	E	Avg.
1981	—GC Padres (GCL)	SS-2B	55	189	26	49	4	1	0	16	.259	13	24	8	105	135	15	.941
1982	—Reno (California)	SS	130	528	*103	*183	33	1	2	54	.347	16	53	25	*240	399	41	.940
1983	—Beaumont (Texas)	SS	114	427	62	126	20	4	2	48	.295	15	29	7	185	327	*38	.931
1984	—Las Vegas (PCL)	SS-2B	122	463	81	137	26	6	5	53	.296	13	40	9	172	†364	17	.969
1985	—Chicago (A.L.)■	SS	150	491	71	134	21	9	1	33	.273	12	36	7	220	382	12	*.980
1986	—Chicago (A.L.)	SS	159	547	58	137	19	4	2	47	.250	12	52	8	261	459	22	.970
1987	—Chicago (A.L.)	SS	149	560	64	156	22	7	2	51	.279	22	52	25	266	475	19	.975
1988	—Chicago (A.L.)	SS	156	566	58	148	16	7	0	39	.261	25	40	25	273	*570	20	.977
1989	—Chicago (A.L.)	SS	155	597	63	151	20	8	1	54	.253	15	48	36	272	512	22	.973
1990	—Chicago (A.L.)	SS	160	516	61	144	21	4	1	58	.279	26	37	13	252	474	17	.977
1991	—Chicago (A.L.)	SS	154	524	52	143	20	3	3	49	.273	11	38	21	249	439	21	.970
1992	—Chicago (A.L.)	SS	12	40	5	8	4	0	0	7	.200	1	5	1	20	39	0	1.000
1993	—Chicago (A.L.)	SS	134	457	44	128	23	4	4	50	.280	10	41	5	189	361	16	.972
Major league totals (9 years)			1229	4298	476	1149	166	46	14	388	.267	134	349	141	2002	3711	149	.975

CHAMPIONSHIP SERIES RECORD

			BATTING												FIELDING			
Year	Team (League)	Pos.	G	AB	R	H	2B	3B	HR	RBI	Avg.	BB	SO	SB	PO	A	E	Avg.
1993	—Chicago (A.L.)	SS	6	22	4	6	1	0	0	2	.273	0	2	1	12	14	0	1.000

ALL-STAR GAME RECORD

ALL-STAR GAME NOTES: Named to A.L. All-Star team for 1988 game; replaced by Kurt Stillwell due to injury.

			BATTING										FIELDING			
Year	League	Pos.	AB	R	H	2B	3B	HR	RBI	Avg.	BB	SO	SB	PO	A	E	Avg.
1988	—American		Selected, did not play—injured.														
1990	—American	SS	2	0	0	0	0	0	0	.000	0	0	0	0	2	0	1.000

Year	League	Pos.	AB	R	H	2B	3B	HR	RBI	Avg.	BB	SO	SB	PO	A	E	Avg.
			BATTING											FIELDING			
1991 —American		SS	0	0	0	0	0	0	0	...	0	0	0	1	0	0	1.000
All-Star Game totals (2 years)			2	0	0	0	0	0	0	.000	0	0	0	1	2	0	1.000

GULLICKSON, BILL

P, TIGERS

PERSONAL: Born February 20, 1959, in Marshall, Minn. . . . 6-3/225. . . . Throws right, bats right. . . . Full name: William Lee Gullickson.

HIGH SCHOOL: Joliet (Ill.) Catholic.

TRANSACTIONS/CAREER NOTES: Selected by Montreal Expos organization in first round (second pick overall) of free-agent draft (June 7, 1977). . . . On disabled list (April 20-May 8, 1984 and June 17-July 8, 1985). . . . Traded by Expos with C Sal Butera to Cincinnati Reds for P Jay Tibbs, P Andy McGaffigan, P John Stuper and C Dann Bilardello (December 19, 1985). . . . Traded by Reds to New York Yankees for P Dennis Rasmussen (August 26, 1987). . . . Granted free agency (November 9, 1987). . . . Signed by Yomiuri Giants of Japan Central League (January 13, 1988). . . . Signed as free agent by Houston Astros (December 6, 1989). . . . Released by Astros (October 4, 1990). . . . Signed by Detroit Tigers (December 3, 1990). . . . Granted free agency (November 6, 1992). . . . Re-signed by Tigers (December 7, 1992). . . . On Detroit disabled list (March 31-May 10, 1993); included rehabilitation assignment to Lakeland (April 10-May 6) and Toledo (May 6-9).

RECORDS: Shares modern major league single-game record for most wild pitches—6 (April 10, 1982).

HONORS: Named N.L. Rookie Pitcher of the Year by THE SPORTING NEWS (1980).

STATISTICAL NOTES: Led N.L. with 27 home runs allowed in 1984. . . . Led A.L. with 35 home runs allowed in 1992.

MISCELLANEOUS: Had sacrifice hit in only appearance as pinch-hitter (1991).

Year	Team (League)	W	L	Pct.	ERA	G	GS	CG	ShO	Sv.	IP	H	R	ER	BB	SO
1977	—W.P. Beach (FSL)	3	3	.500	4.02	10	10	2	0	0	56	67	30	25	17	35
1978	—W.P. Beach (FSL)	9	9	.500	1.82	20	20	12	4	0	148	121	45	30	52	127
	—Memphis (South.)	1	4	.200	3.06	8	7	1	0	1	50	44	19	17	19	43
1979	—Denver (A.A.)	3	3	.500	6.67	11	11	1	0	0	54	65	44	40	26	31
	—Memphis (South.)	10	3	.769	3.65	16	16	8	1	0	116	110	52	47	42	115
	—Montreal (N.L.)	0	0	...	0.00	1	0	0	0	0	1	2	0	0	0	0
1980	—Denver (A.A.)	6	2	.750	1.91	9	9	5	2	0	66	47	14	14	29	64
	—Montreal (N.L.)	10	5	.667	3.00	24	19	5	2	0	141	127	53	47	50	120
1981	—Montreal (N.L.)	7	9	.438	2.81	22	22	3	2	0	157	142	54	49	34	115
1982	—Montreal (N.L.)	12	14	.462	3.57	34	34	6	0	0	236⅔	231	101	94	61	155
1983	—Montreal (N.L.)	17	12	.586	3.75	34	34	10	1	0	242⅓	230	108	101	59	120
1984	—Montreal (N.L.)	12	9	.571	3.61	32	32	3	0	0	226⅔	230	100	91	37	100
1985	—Montreal (N.L.)	14	12	.538	3.52	29	29	4	1	0	181⅓	187	78	71	47	68
1986	—Cincinnati (N.L.)■	15	12	.556	3.38	37	37	6	2	0	244⅔	245	103	92	60	121
1987	—Cincinnati (N.L.)	10	11	.476	4.85	27	27	3	1	0	165	172	99	89	39	89
	—New York (A.L.)■	4	2	.667	4.88	8	8	1	0	0	48	46	29	26	11	28
1988	—Yomiuri (Jp. Cen.)■	14	9	.609	3.10	26	26	14	3	0	203⅓	173	77	70	51	134
1989	—Yomiuri (Jp. Cen.)	7	5	.583	3.65	15	15	6	0	0	111	97	47	45	34	97
1990	—Houston (N.L.)■	10	14	.417	3.82	32	32	2	1	0	193⅓	221	100	82	61	73
1991	—Detroit (A.L.)■	•20	9	.690	3.90	35	•35	4	0	0	226⅓	256	109	98	44	91
1992	—Detroit (A.L.)	14	13	.519	4.34	34	34	4	1	0	221⅔	228	109	107	50	64
1993	—Lakeland (Fla. St.)	1	0	1.000	6.87	5	5	0	0	0	18⅓	24	14	14	4	9
	—Toledo (Int'l)	1	0	1.000	9.00	1	1	0	0	0	6	8	6	6	0	4
	—Detroit (A.L.)	13	9	.591	5.37	28	28	2	0	0	159⅓	186	106	95	44	70
A.L. totals (4 years)		51	33	.607	4.48	105	105	11	1	0	655⅓	716	353	326	149	253
N.L. totals (10 years)		107	98	.522	3.60	272	266	42	10	0	1789	1787	796	716	448	961
Major league totals (13 years)		158	131	.547	3.84	377	371	53	11	0	2444⅓	2503	1149	1042	597	1214

DIVISION SERIES RECORD

Year	Team (League)	W	L	Pct.	ERA	G	GS	CG	ShO	Sv.	IP	H	R	ER	BB	SO
1981	—Montreal (N.L.)	1	0	1.000	1.17	1	1	0	0	0	7⅔	6	1	1	1	3

CHAMPIONSHIP SERIES RECORD

Year	Team (League)	W	L	Pct.	ERA	G	GS	CG	ShO	Sv.	IP	H	R	ER	BB	SO
1981	—Montreal (N.L.)	0	2	.000	2.51	2	2	0	0	0	14⅓	12	5	4	6	12

GUTHRIE, MARK

P, TWINS

PERSONAL: Born September 22, 1965, in Buffalo, N.Y. . . . 6-4/206. . . . Throws left, bats right. . . . Full name: Mark Andrew Guthrie.

HIGH SCHOOL: Venice (Fla.).

COLLEGE: Louisiana State.

TRANSACTIONS/CAREER NOTES: Selected by St. Louis Cardinals organization in fourth round of free-agent draft (June 2, 1986). . . . Selected by Minnesota Twins organization in seventh round of free-agent draft (June 2, 1987). . . . On disabled list (May 29, 1993-remainder of season).

MISCELLANEOUS: Appeared in one game as pinch-runner (1991).

Year	Team (League)	W	L	Pct.	ERA	G	GS	CG	ShO	Sv.	IP	H	R	ER	BB	SO
1987	—Visalia (California)	2	1	.667	4.50	4	1	0	0	0	12	10	7	6	5	9
1988	—Visalia (California)	12	9	.571	3.31	25	25	4	1	0	171⅓	169	81	63	86	182
1989	—Orlando (Southern)	8	3	.727	1.97	14	14	0	0	0	96	75	32	21	38	103
	—Portland (PCL)	3	4	.429	3.65	7	7	1	0	0	44⅓	45	21	18	16	35
	—Minnesota (A.L.)	2	4	.333	4.55	13	8	0	0	0	57⅓	66	32	29	21	38
1990	—Minnesota (A.L.)	7	9	.438	3.79	24	21	3	1	0	144⅔	154	65	61	39	101
	—Portland (PCL)	1	3	.250	2.98	9	8	1	0	0	42⅓	47	19	14	12	39
1991	—Minnesota (A.L.)	7	5	.583	4.32	41	12	0	0	2	98	116	52	47	41	72
1992	—Minnesota (A.L.)	2	3	.400	2.88	54	0	0	0	5	75	59	27	24	23	76
1993	—Minnesota (A.L.)	2	1	.667	4.71	22	0	0	0	0	21	20	11	11	16	15
Major league totals (5 years)		20	22	.476	3.91	154	41	3	1	7	396	415	187	172	140	302

CHAMPIONSHIP SERIES RECORD

Year	Team (League)	W	L	Pct.	ERA	G	GS	CG	ShO	Sv.	IP	H	R	ER	BB	SO
1991	—Minnesota (A.L.)........	1	0	1.000	0.00	2	0	0	0	0	2⅔	0	0	0	0	0

WORLD SERIES RECORD

Year	Team (League)	W	L	Pct.	ERA	G	GS	CG	ShO	Sv.	IP	H	R	ER	BB	SO
1991	—Minnesota (A.L.)........	0	1	.000	2.25	4	0	0	0	0	4	3	1	1	4	3

GUTIERREZ, RICKY

SS, PADRES

PERSONAL: Born May 23, 1970, in Miami. . . . 6-1/175. . . . Throws right, bats right.
HIGH SCHOOL: American (Hialeah, Fla.).
TRANSACTIONS/CAREER NOTES: Selected by Baltimore Orioles organization in supplemental round ("sandwich pick" between first and second round, 28th pick overall) of free-agent draft (June 1, 1988); pick received as compensation for Orioles failing to sign 1987 No. 1 choice Brad DuVall. . . . Traded by Orioles to San Diego Padres (September 4, 1992), completing deal in which Padres traded P Craig Lefferts to Orioles for P Erik Schullstrom and a player to be named later (August 31, 1992).
STATISTICAL NOTES: Led Appalachian League shortstops with 309 total chances in 1988.

			BATTING												FIELDING			
Year	Team (League)	Pos.	G	AB	R	H	2B	3B	HR	RBI	Avg.	BB	SO	SB	PO	A	E	Avg.
1988	—Bluefield (Appal.).....	SS	62	208	35	51	8	2	2	19	.245	44	40	5	*100	175	34	.890
1989	—Frederick (Caro.)......	SS	127	456	48	106	16	2	3	41	.232	39	89	15	190	372	34	*.943
1990	—Frederick (Caro.)......	SS	112	425	54	117	16	4	1	46	.275	38	59	12	192	286	26	.948
	—Hagerstown (East.)..	SS	20	64	4	15	0	1	0	6	.234	3	8	2	31	36	4	.944
1991	—Hagerstown (East.)..	SS	84	292	47	69	6	4	0	30	.236	57	52	11	158	196	22	.941
	—Rochester (Int'l).......	SS-3B	49	157	23	48	5	3	0	15	.306	24	27	4	61	129	8	.960
1992	—Rochester (Int'l).......	2B-SS	125	431	54	109	9	3	0	41	.253	53	77	14	251	283	15	.973
	—Las Vegas (PCL)■....	SS	3	6	0	1	0	0	0	1	.167	1	3	0	1	8	0	1.000
1993	—Las Vegas (PCL)......	2B-SS	5	24	4	10	4	0	0	4	.417	0	4	4	11	14	2	.926
	—San Diego (N.L.).......	S-2-0-3	133	438	76	110	10	5	5	26	.251	50	97	4	194	305	14	.973
Major league totals (1 year).....................			133	438	76	110	10	5	5	26	.251	50	97	4	194	305	14	.973

GUZMAN, JOSE

P, CUBS

PERSONAL: Born April 9, 1963, in Santa Isabel, Puerto Rico. . . . 6-3/195. . . . Throws right, bats right. . . . Full name: Jose Alberto Mirabel Guzman.
HIGH SCHOOL: John F. Kennedy (Santa Isabel, Puerto Rico).
TRANSACTIONS/CAREER NOTES: Signed as free agent by Texas Rangers organization (February 10, 1981). . . . On disabled list (March 26-September 1, 1989). . . . On Texas disabled list (March 31-August 9, 1990); included rehabilitation assignments to Charlotte (June 6-19), Oklahoma City (July 17-19 and July 29-30) and Tulsa (July 20-25). . . . Released by Rangers (April 2, 1991). . . . Re-signed by Rangers organization (April 8, 1991). . . . Granted free agency (October 26, 1992). . . . Signed by Chicago Cubs (December 1, 1992).
HONORS: Named A.L. Comeback Player of the Year by THE SPORTING NEWS (1991).

Year	Team (League)	W	L	Pct.	ERA	G	GS	CG	ShO	Sv.	IP	H	R	ER	BB	SO
1981	—GC Rangers (GCL)......	3	3	.500	5.31	14	4	0	0	0	39	44	30	23	14	13
1982	—GC Rangers (GCL)......	5	4	.556	2.18	12	9	1	0	0	66	51	21	16	13	42
1983	—Burlington (Midw.)....	12	8	.600	2.97	25	24	2	1	0	154⅔	135	68	51	52	146
1984	—Tulsa (Texas)...........	7	9	.438	4.17	25	25	7	1	0	140⅓	137	75	65	55	82
1985	—Okla. City (A.A.)........	10	5	.667	3.13	25	23	4	1	1	149⅔	131	60	52	40	76
	—Texas (A.L.)..............	3	2	.600	2.76	5	5	0	0	0	32⅔	27	13	10	14	24
1986	—Texas (A.L.)..............	9	15	.375	4.54	29	29	2	0	0	172⅓	199	101	87	60	87
1987	—Texas (A.L.)..............	14	14	.500	4.67	37	30	6	0	0	208⅓	196	115	108	82	143
1988	—Texas (A.L.)..............	11	13	.458	3.70	30	30	6	2	0	206⅔	180	99	85	82	157
1989	—....................................							Did not play.								
1990	—Charlotte (Fla. St.).....	0	1	.000	2.16	2	2	0	0	0	8⅓	10	3	2	4	7
	—Okla. City (A.A.).........	0	3	.000	5.65	7	7	0	0	0	28⅔	35	20	18	9	26
	—Tulsa (Texas)............	0	0	...	6.00	1	1	0	0	0	3	3	2	2	0	2
1991	—Okla. City (A.A.).........	1	1	.500	3.92	3	3	0	0	0	20⅔	18	9	9	4	18
	—Texas (A.L.)..............	13	7	.650	3.08	25	25	5	1	0	169⅔	152	67	58	84	125
1992	—Texas (A.L.)..............	16	11	.593	3.66	33	33	5	0	0	224	229	103	91	73	179
1993	—Chicago (N.L.)■.........	12	10	.545	4.34	30	30	2	1	0	191	188	98	92	74	163
A.L. totals (6 years)..............		66	62	.516	3.90	159	152	24	3	0	1013⅔	983	498	439	395	715
N.L. totals (1 year)...............		12	10	.545	4.34	30	30	2	1	0	191	188	98	92	74	163
Major league totals (7 years)..		78	72	.520	3.97	189	182	26	4	0	1204⅔	1171	596	531	469	878

GUZMAN, JUAN

P, BLUE JAYS

PERSONAL: Born October 28, 1966, in Santo Domingo, Dominican Republic. . . . 5-11/195. . . . Throws right, bats right. . . . Full name: Juan Andres Correa Guzman.
HIGH SCHOOL: Liceo Las Americas (Dominican Republic).
TRANSACTIONS/CAREER NOTES: Signed as free agent by Los Angeles Dodgers organization (March 16, 1985). . . . Traded by Dodgers to Toronto Blue Jays organization for IF Mike Sharperson (September 22, 1987). . . . On Toronto disabled list (August 4-29, 1992); included rehabilitation assignment to Syracuse (August 24-25).
RECORDS: Holds A.L. single-season record for most wild pitches—26 (1993).
HONORS: Named A.L. Rookie Pitcher of the Year by THE SPORTING NEWS (1991).
STATISTICAL NOTES: Led Gulf Coast League with 15 wild pitches in 1985. . . . Led Florida State League with 16 wild pitches in 1986. . . . Led Southern League with 21 wild pitches in 1990. . . . Led A.L. with 26 wild pitches in 1993.

Year	Team (League)	W	L	Pct.	ERA	G	GS	CG	ShO	Sv.	IP	H	R	ER	BB	SO
1985	—GC Dodgers (GCL)......	5	1	.833	3.86	21	3	0	0	4	42	39	26	18	25	43
1986	—Vero Beach (FSL)......	10	9	.526	3.49	20	24	3	0	0	131⅓	114	69	51	90	96

Year	Team (League)	W	L	Pct.	ERA	G	GS	CG	ShO	Sv.	IP	H	R	ER	BB	SO
1987	—Bakersfield (Calif.)	5	6	.455	4.75	22	21	0	0	0	110	106	71	58	84	113
1988	—Knoxville (South.)■	4	5	.444	2.36	46	2	0	0	6	84	52	29	22	61	90
1989	—Syracuse (Int'l)	1	1	.500	3.98	14	0	0	0	0	20⅓	13	9	9	30	28
	—Knoxville (South.)	1	4	.200	6.23	22	8	0	0	0	47⅔	34	36	33	60	50
1990	—Knoxville (South.)	11	9	.550	4.24	37	21	2	0	1	157	145	84	74	80	138
1991	—Syracuse (Int'l)	4	5	.444	4.03	12	11	0	0	0	67	46	39	30	42	67
	—Toronto (A.L.)	10	3	.769	2.99	23	23	1	0	0	138⅔	98	53	46	66	123
1992	—Toronto (A.L.)	16	5	.762	2.64	28	28	1	0	0	180⅔	135	56	53	72	165
	—Syracuse (Int'l)	0	0	...	6.00	1	1	0	0	0	3	6	2	2	1	3
1993	—Toronto (A.L.)	14	3	*.824	3.99	33	33	2	1	0	221	211	107	98	110	194
Major league totals (3 years)		40	11	.784	3.28	84	84	4	1	0	540⅓	444	216	197	248	482

CHAMPIONSHIP SERIES RECORD

Year	Team (League)	W	L	Pct.	ERA	G	GS	CG	ShO	Sv.	IP	H	R	ER	BB	SO
1991	—Toronto (A.L.)	1	0	1.000	3.18	1	1	0	0	0	5⅔	4	2	2	4	2
1992	—Toronto (A.L.)	2	0	1.000	2.08	2	2	0	0	0	13	12	3	3	5	11
1993	—Toronto (A.L.)	2	0	1.000	2.08	2	2	0	0	0	13	8	4	3	9	9
Chp. series totals (3 years)		5	0	1.000	2.27	5	5	0	0	0	31⅔	24	9	8	18	22

WORLD SERIES RECORD

Year	Team (League)	W	L	Pct.	ERA	G	GS	CG	ShO	Sv.	IP	H	R	ER	BB	SO
1992	—Toronto (A.L.)	0	0	...	1.13	1	1	0	0	0	8	8	2	1	1	7
1993	—Toronto (A.L.)	0	1	.000	3.75	2	2	0	0	0	12	10	6	5	8	12
World Series totals (2 years)		0	1	.000	2.70	3	3	0	0	0	20	18	8	6	9	19

ALL-STAR GAME RECORD

Year	League	W	L	Pct.	ERA	GS	CG	ShO	Sv.	IP	H	R	ER	BB	SO
1992	—American	0	0	...	0.00	0	0	0	0	1	2	0	0	1	2

GWYNN, CHRIS

OF, ROYALS

PERSONAL: Born October 13, 1964, in Los Angeles.... 6-0/220.... Throws left, bats left.... Full name: Christopher Karlton Gwynn.... Brother of Tony Gwynn, outfielder, San Diego Padres.
HIGH SCHOOL: Long Beach (Calif.) Polytechnic.
COLLEGE: San Diego State.
TRANSACTIONS/CAREER NOTES: Selected by California Angels organization in fifth round of free-agent draft (June 7, 1982).... Selected by Los Angeles Dodgers organization in first round (10th pick overall) of free-agent draft (June 3, 1985).... On Los Angeles disabled list (June 12-July 6, 1989).... On Los Angeles disabled list (July 16, 1989-remainder of season); included rehabilitation assignment to Albuquerque (August 3-11).... Traded by Dodgers with 2B Domingo Mota to Kansas City Royals for 1B/OF Todd Benzinger (December 11, 1991).... On disabled list (May 29-July 16 and July 27, 1992-remainder of season).
HONORS: Named outfielder on THE SPORTING NEWS college All-America team (1985).
MISCELLANEOUS: Member of 1984 U.S. Olympic baseball team.

			BATTING												FIELDING			
Year	Team (League)	Pos.	G	AB	R	H	2B	3B	HR	RBI	Avg.	BB	SO	SB	PO	A	E	Avg.
1985	—Vero Beach (FSL)	OF	52	179	19	46	8	6	0	17	.257	16	34	2	43	2	0	1.000
1986	—San Antonio (Tex.)	OF	111	401	46	115	22	1	6	67	.287	16	44	2	186	11	2	.990
1987	—Albuquerque (PCL)	OF	110	362	54	101	12	3	5	41	.279	36	38	5	141	5	1	.993
	—Los Angeles (N.L.)	OF	17	32	2	7	1	0	0	2	.219	1	7	0	12	0	0	1.000
1988	—Albuquerque (PCL)	OF	112	411	57	123	22	•10	5	61	.299	39	39	1	134	3	4	.972
	—Los Angeles (N.L.)	OF	12	11	1	2	0	0	0	0	.182	1	2	0	0	0	0	...
1989	—Albuquerque (PCL)	OF	26	89	14	29	9	1	0	12	.326	7	7	3	27	0	0	1.000
	—Los Angeles (N.L.)	OF	32	68	8	16	4	1	0	7	.235	2	9	1	26	1	0	1.000
1990	—Los Angeles (N.L.)	OF	101	141	19	40	2	1	5	22	.284	7	28	0	39	1	0	1.000
1991	—Los Angeles (N.L.)	OF	94	139	18	35	5	1	5	22	.252	10	23	1	37	2	0	1.000
1992	—Kansas City (A.L.)■	OF	34	84	10	24	3	2	1	7	.286	3	10	0	33	0	0	1.000
1993	—Kansas City (A.L.)	OF-1B	103	287	36	86	14	4	1	25	.300	24	34	0	161	7	1	.994
American League totals (2 years)			137	371	46	110	17	6	2	32	.296	27	44	0	194	7	1	.995
National League totals (5 years)			256	391	48	100	12	3	10	53	.256	21	69	2	114	4	0	1.000
Major league totals (7 years)			393	762	94	210	29	9	12	85	.276	48	113	2	308	11	1	.997

GWYNN, TONY

OF, PADRES

PERSONAL: Born May 9, 1960, in Los Angeles.... 5-11/215.... Throws left, bats left.... Full name: Anthony Keith Gwynn.... Brother of Chris Gwynn, outfielder, Kansas City Royals.
HIGH SCHOOL: Long Beach (Calif.) Polytechnic.
COLLEGE: San Diego State.
TRANSACTIONS/CAREER NOTES: Selected by San Diego Padres organization in third round of free-agent draft (June 8, 1981).... On disabled list (August 26-September 10, 1982).... On San Diego disabled list (March 26-June 21, 1983); included rehabilitation to Las Vegas (May 31-June 20).... On disabled list (May 8-29, 1988).
RECORDS: Holds N.L. single-season record for lowest batting average by leader—.313 (1988).... Shares N.L. record for most years leading league in singles—4 (1984, 1986-87 and 1989).... Shares N.L. single-season record for most times collecting five or more hits in one game—4 (1993).
HONORS: Named Northwest League Most Valuable Player (1981).... Named outfielder on THE SPORTING NEWS N.L. All-Star team (1984, 1986-87 and 1989).... Named outfielder on THE SPORTING NEWS N.L. Silver Slugger team (1984, 1986-87 and 1989).... Won N.L. Gold Glove as outfielder (1986-87 and 1989-91).
STATISTICAL NOTES: Led N.L. with .410 on-base percentage in 1984.... Led N.L. outfielders with 360 total chances in 1986.... Collected six hits in one game (August 4, 1993, 12 innings).
MISCELLANEOUS: Selected by San Diego Clippers in 10th round (210th pick overall) of 1981 NBA draft (June 9, 1981).

Year	Team (League)	Pos.	G	AB	R	H	2B	3B	HR	RBI	Avg.	BB	SO	SB	PO	A	E	Avg.
							BATTING									FIELDING		
1981	—Walla Walla (N'west)	OF	42	178	46	59	12	1	12	37	*.331	23	21	17	76	2	3	.963
	—Amarillo (Texas)	OF	23	91	22	42	8	2	4	19	.462	5	7	5	41	1	0	1.000
1982	—Hawaii (PCL)	OF	93	366	65	120	23	2	5	46	.328	18	18	14	208	11	4	.982
	—San Diego (N.L.)	OF	54	190	33	55	12	2	1	17	.289	14	16	8	110	1	1	.991
1983	—Las Vegas (PCL)	OF	17	73	15	25	6	0	0	7	.342	6	5	3	23	2	3	.893
	—San Diego (N.L.)	OF	86	304	34	94	12	2	1	37	.309	23	21	7	163	9	1	.994
1984	—San Diego (N.L.)	OF	158	606	88	*213	21	10	5	71	*.351	59	23	33	345	11	4	.989
1985	—San Diego (N.L.)	OF	154	622	90	197	29	5	6	46	.317	45	33	14	337	14	4	.989
1986	—San Diego (N.L.)	OF	160	*642	•107	*211	33	7	14	59	.329	52	35	37	*337	19	4	.989
1987	—San Diego (N.L.)	OF	157	589	119	*218	36	13	7	54	*.370	82	35	56	298	13	6	.981
1988	—San Diego (N.L.)	OF	133	521	64	163	22	5	7	70	*.313	51	40	26	264	8	5	.982
1989	—San Diego (N.L.)	OF	158	604	82	*203	27	7	4	62	*.336	56	30	40	353	13	6	.984
1990	—San Diego (N.L.)	OF	141	573	79	177	29	10	4	72	.309	44	23	17	327	11	5	.985
1991	—San Diego (N.L.)	OF	134	530	69	168	27	11	4	62	.317	34	19	8	291	8	3	.990
1992	—San Diego (N.L.)	OF	128	520	77	165	27	3	6	41	.317	46	16	3	270	9	5	.982
1993	—San Diego (N.L.)	OF	122	489	70	175	41	3	7	59	.358	36	19	14	244	8	5	.981
Major league totals (12 years)			1585	6190	912	2039	316	78	66	650	.329	542	310	263	3339	124	49	.986

CHAMPIONSHIP SERIES RECORD

Year	Team (League)	Pos.	G	AB	R	H	2B	3B	HR	RBI	Avg.	BB	SO	SB	PO	A	E	Avg.
							BATTING									FIELDING		
1984	—San Diego (N.L.)	OF	5	19	6	7	3	0	0	3	.368	1	2	0	9	0	0	1.000

WORLD SERIES RECORD

Year	Team (League)	Pos.	G	AB	R	H	2B	3B	HR	RBI	Avg.	BB	SO	SB	PO	A	E	Avg.
							BATTING									FIELDING		
1984	—San Diego (N.L.)	OF	5	19	1	5	0	0	0	0	.263	3	2	1	12	1	1	.929

ALL-STAR GAME RECORD

Year	League	Pos.	AB	R	H	2B	3B	HR	RBI	Avg.	BB	SO	SB	PO	A	E	Avg.
						BATTING								FIELDING			
1984	—National	OF	3	0	1	0	0	0	0	.333	0	0	0	0	0	0	...
1985	—National	OF	1	0	0	0	0	0	0	.000	0	0	0	1	0	0	1.000
1986	—National	OF	3	0	0	0	0	0	0	.000	0	0	0	1	0	0	1.000
1987	—National	PH	1	0	0	0	0	0	0	.000	0	0	0	...	...	...	...
1989	—National	OF	2	1	1	0	0	0	0	.500	1	1	1	2	0	0	1.000
1990	—National	PH	0	0	0	0	0	0	0	...	1	0	0	...	...	...	...
1991	—National	OF	4	1	2	0	0	0	0	.500	0	0	0	6	0	0	1.000
1992	—National	OF	2	0	0	0	0	0	0	.000	1	0	0	0	2	0	1.000
1993	—National	OF	1	0	0	0	0	0	0	.000	0	0	0	0	0	0	...
All-Star Game totals (9 years)			17	2	4	0	0	0	0	.235	3	1	1	10	2	0	1.000

HAAS, DAVE

P, TIGERS

PERSONAL: Born October 19, 1965, in Independence, Mo. . . . 6-1/200. . . . Throws right, bats right. . . . Full name: Robert David Haas.

HIGH SCHOOL: Truman (Independence, Mo.).

COLLEGE: Wichita State.

TRANSACTIONS/CAREER NOTES: Selected by Baltimore Orioles organization in 28th round of free-agent draft (June 4, 1984). . . . Selected by Toronto Blue Jays organization in 18th round of free-agent draft (June 2, 1987). . . . Selected by Detroit Tigers organization in 15th round of free-agent draft (June 1, 1988). . . . On Detroit disabled list (June 14, 1993-remainder of season); included rehabilitation assignment to Toledo (July 16-August 6).

STATISTICAL NOTES: Pitched 5-0 no-hit victory for Lakeland against Clearwater (April 14, 1989).

Year	Team (League)	W	L	Pct.	ERA	G	GS	CG	ShO	Sv.	IP	H	R	ER	BB	SO
1988	—Fayetteville (SAL)	4	3	.571	1.81	11	11	0	0	0	54⅔	59	20	11	19	46
1989	—Lakeland (Fla. St.)	4	1	.800	2.03	10	10	1	1	0	62	50	16	14	16	46
	—London (Eastern)	3	11	.214	5.64	18	18	2	1	0	103⅔	107	69	65	51	75
1990	—London (Eastern)	13	8	.619	2.99	27	*27	3	1	0	177⅔	151	64	59	74	116
1991	—Toledo (Int'l)	8	10	.444	5.26	28	•28	1	0	0	157⅓	187	103	92	77	133
	—Detroit (A.L.)	1	0	1.000	6.75	11	0	0	0	0	10⅔	8	8	8	12	6
1992	—Toledo (Int'l)	9	8	.529	4.18	22	22	2	0	0	148⅔	149	72	69	53	112
	—Detroit (A.L.)	5	3	.625	3.94	12	11	1	1	0	61⅔	68	30	27	16	29
1993	—Detroit (A.L.)	1	2	.333	6.11	20	0	0	0	0	28	45	20	19	8	17
	—Toledo (Int'l)	0	0	...	18.69	2	2	0	0	0	4⅓	8	9	9	6	2
Major league totals (3 years)		7	5	.583	4.84	43	11	1	1	0	100⅓	121	58	54	36	52

HABYAN, JOHN

P, CARDINALS

PERSONAL: Born January 29, 1964, in Bayshore, N.Y. . . . 6-2/195. . . . Throws right, bats right. . . . Full name: John Gabriel Habyan. . . . Name pronounced HAY-bee-un.

HIGH SCHOOL: St. John the Baptist (Brentwood, N.Y.).

TRANSACTIONS/CAREER NOTES: Selected by Baltimore Orioles organization in third round of free-agent draft (June 7, 1982). . . . On Baltimore disabled list (March 30-June 9, 1989). . . . Traded by Orioles to New York Yankees organization for OF Stanley Jefferson (July 20, 1989). . . . Traded by Yankees to Kansas City Royals as part of a three-way deal in which Royals sent OF Karl Rhodes to Cubs and Cubs sent P Paul Assenmacher to Yankees (July 30, 1993). . . . Granted free agency (December 20, 1993). . . . Signed by St. Louis Cardinals organization (January 5, 1994).

STATISTICAL NOTES: Pitched 6-0 no-hit victory for Charlotte against Columbus (May 13, 1985).

Year	Team (League)	W	L	Pct.	ERA	G	GS	CG	ShO	Sv.	IP	H	R	ER	BB	SO
1982	—Bluefield (Appal.)	*9	2	.818	3.54	12	12	2	1	0	81⅓	68	35	32	24	55
	—Hagerstown (Car.)	0	0	...	67.50	1	1	0	0	0	⅔	5	5	5	2	1
1983	—Hagerstown (Car.)	2	3	.400	5.81	11	11	1	0	0	48	54	41	31	29	42
	—Newark (NY-Penn)	5	3	.625	3.39	11	11	1	1	0	71⅔	68	34	27	29	64
1984	—Hagerstown (Car.)	9	4	.692	3.54	13	13	4	0	0	81⅓	64	41	32	33	81
	—Charlotte (South.)	4	7	.364	4.44	13	13	1	0	0	77	84	46	38	34	55
1985	—Charlotte (South.)	13	5	.722	3.27	28	28	8	2	0	189⅔	157	73	69	90	123
	—Baltimore (A.L.)	1	0	1.000	0.00	2	0	0	0	0	2⅔	3	1	0	0	2
1986	—Rochester (Int'l)	12	7	.632	4.29	26	25	5	1	0	157⅓	168	82	75	69	93
	—Baltimore (A.L.)	1	3	.250	4.44	6	5	0	0	0	26⅓	24	17	13	18	14
1987	—Rochester (Int'l)	3	2	.600	3.86	7	7	2	1	0	49	47	23	21	20	39
	—Baltimore (A.L.)	6	7	.462	4.80	27	13	0	0	1	116⅓	110	67	62	40	64
1988	—Rochester (Int'l)	9	9	.500	4.46	23	23	8	1	0	147⅓	161	78	73	46	91
	—Baltimore (A.L.)	1	0	1.000	4.30	7	0	0	0	0	14⅔	22	10	7	4	4
1989	—Roch.-Colu. (Int'l)■	3	5	.375	3.98	15	13	2	0	0	83⅔	103	44	37	14	52
1990	—Columbus (Int'l)	7	7	.500	3.21	36	11	1	0	6	112	99	52	40	30	77
	—New York (A.L.)	0	0	...	2.08	6	0	0	0	0	8⅔	10	2	2	2	4
1991	—New York (A.L.)	4	2	.667	2.30	66	0	0	0	2	90	73	28	23	20	70
1992	—New York (A.L.)	5	6	.455	3.84	56	0	0	0	7	72⅔	84	32	31	21	44
1993	—N.Y.-K.C. (A.L.)■	2	1	.667	4.15	48	0	0	0	1	56⅓	59	27	26	20	39
Major league totals (8 years)		20	19	.513	3.81	218	18	0	0	11	387⅔	385	184	164	125	241

HALE, CHIP

IF, TWINS

PERSONAL: Born December 2, 1964, in Santa Clara, Calif. . . . 5-11/191. . . . Throws right, bats left. . . . Full name: Walter William Hale III.
HIGH SCHOOL: Campolindo (Moraga, Calif.).
COLLEGE: Arizona (received degree).
TRANSACTIONS/CAREER NOTES: Selected by Minnesota Twins organization in 17th round of free-agent draft (June 2, 1987).
STATISTICAL NOTES: Led Pacific Coast League second basemen with 332 assists in 1989. . . . Led Pacific Coast League second basemen with .982 fielding percentage, 311 putouts, 679 total chances and 101 double plays in 1990. . . . Led Pacific Coast League second basemen with 552 total chances and 85 double plays in 1991. . . . Led Pacific Coast League second basemen with .986 fielding percentage and 273 putouts in 1992.

			BATTING												FIELDING			
Year	Team (League)	Pos.	G	AB	R	H	2B	3B	HR	RBI	Avg.	BB	SO	SB	PO	A	E	Avg.
1987	—Kenosha (Midwest)	2B	87	339	65	117	12	7	7	65	*.345	33	26	3	164	233	10	.975
1988	—Orlando (Southern)	2B	133	482	62	126	20	1	11	65	.261	64	31	8	254	322	*23	.962
1989	—Portland (PCL)	2B-3B	108	411	49	112	16	9	2	34	.273	35	55	3	217	†333	10	.982
	—Minnesota (A.L.)	2B-3B	28	67	6	14	3	0	0	4	.209	1	6	0	15	40	1	.982
1990	—Portland (PCL)	2B-SS-3B	130	479	71	134	24	2	3	40	.280	68	57	6	†312	362	13	†.981
	—Minnesota (A.L.)	2B	1	2	0	0	0	0	0	2	.000	0	1	0	2	6	0	1.000
1991	—Portland (PCL)	2B	110	352	45	85	16	3	1	37	.241	47	22	3	*236	306	10	*.982
1992	—Portland (PCL)	2B-OF-P	132	474	77	135	25	8	1	53	.285	73	45	3	†278	361	9	†.986
1993	—Portland (PCL)	2B-3B-SS	55	211	37	59	15	3	1	24	.280	21	13	2	79	134	11	.951
	—Minnesota (A.L.)	2-3-S-1	69	186	25	62	6	1	3	27	.333	18	17	2	39	63	4	.962
Major league totals (3 years)			98	255	31	76	9	1	3	33	.298	19	24	2	56	109	5	.971

RECORD AS PITCHER

Year	Team (League)	W	L	Pct.	ERA	G	GS	CG	ShO	Sv.	IP	H	R	ER	BB	SO
1992	—Portland (PCL)	0	0	...	18.00	1	0	0	0	0	1	5	4	2	0	0

HALL, BILLY

2B, RED SOX

PERSONAL: Born June 17, 1969, in Wichita, Kan. . . . 5-9/180. . . . Throws right, bats both. . . . Full name: William Earl Hall Jr.
HIGH SCHOOL: Northwest (Wichita, Kan.).
COLLEGE: Butler County Community College (Kan.) and Wichita State.
TRANSACTIONS/CAREER NOTES: Selected by San Diego Padres organization in 17th round of free-agent draft (June 3, 1991). . . . Selected by Boston Red Sox from Padres organization in Rule 5 major league draft (December 13, 1993).
STATISTICAL NOTES: Led California League in caught stealing with 27 in 1992.

			BATTING												FIELDING			
Year	Team (League)	Pos.	G	AB	R	H	2B	3B	HR	RBI	Avg.	BB	SO	SB	PO	A	E	Avg.
1991	—Char., S.C. (S. Atl.)	2B	72	279	41	84	6	5	2	28	.301	34	54	25	114	140	16	.941
1992	—High Desert (Calif.)	2B	119	495	92	176	22	5	2	39	*.356	54	77	*49	239	348	*22	.964
1993	—Wichita (Texas)	2B	124	486	80	131	27	7	4	46	.270	36	88	29	209	*373	22	.964

HALTER, SHANE

SS, ROYALS

PERSONAL: Born November 8, 1969, in La Plata, Md. . . . 5-10/160. . . . Throws right, bats right. . . . Full name: Shane David Halter.
HIGH SCHOOL: Hooks (Tex.).
COLLEGE: Seminole (Okla.) Junior College and Texas.
TRANSACTIONS/CAREER NOTES: Selected by Cincinnati Reds organization in 16th round of free-agent draft (June 4, 1990). . . . Selected by Kansas City Royals organization in fifth round of free-agent draft (June 3, 1991).
STATISTICAL NOTES: Led Midwest League shortstops with 64 double plays in 1992.

			BATTING												FIELDING			
Year	Team (League)	Pos.	G	AB	R	H	2B	3B	HR	RBI	Avg.	BB	SO	SB	PO	A	E	Avg.
1991	—Eugene (N'west)	SS	64	236	41	55	9	1	1	18	.233	49	60	12	*118	154	21	.928
1992	—Appleton (Midw.)	SS	80	313	50	83	22	3	3	33	.265	41	54	21	150	227	16	.959
	—Baseball City (FSL)	SS	44	117	11	28	1	0	1	14	.239	24	31	5	70	115	6	.969

Year	Team (League)	Pos.	G	AB	R	H	2B	3B	HR	RBI	Avg.	BB	SO	SB	PO	A	E	Avg.
			BATTING												FIELDING			
1993	—Wilmington (Caro.) ..	SS	54	211	44	63	8	5	5	32	.299	27	55	5	84	146	15	.939
	—Memphis (South.)	SS	81	306	50	79	7	0	4	20	.258	30	74	4	142	229	16	.959

HAMELIN, BOB

1B, ROYALS

PERSONAL: Born November 29, 1967, in Elizabeth, N.J. . . . 6-0/235. . . . Throws left, bats left. . . . Full name: Robert James Hamelin III.
HIGH SCHOOL: Irvine (Calif.).
COLLEGE: UCLA and Rancho Santiago College (Calif.).
TRANSACTIONS/CAREER NOTES: Selected by Kansas City Royals organization in second round of free-agent draft (June 1, 1988). . . . On disabled list (June 25-July 2 and August 3, 1989-remainder of season; August 8, 1990-remainder of season; and May 27, 1991-remainder of season). . . . On Omaha disabled list (April 9-June 10, 1992).
STATISTICAL NOTES: Led Northwest League first basemen with 682 total chances in 1988. . . . Led American Association first basemen with 1,205 total chances and 116 double plays in 1993.

Year	Team (League)	Pos.	G	AB	R	H	2B	3B	HR	RBI	Avg.	BB	SO	SB	PO	A	E	Avg.
			BATTING												FIELDING			
1988	—Eugene (N'west).......	1B	70	235	42	70	19	1	*17	61	.298	56	67	9	*642	25	*15	.978
1989	—Memphis (South.)	1B	68	211	45	62	12	5	16	47	.294	52	52	3	487	27	8	.985
1990	—Omaha (A.A.)............	1B	90	271	31	63	11	2	8	30	.232	62	78	2	396	32	4	.991
1991	—Omaha (A.A.)............	1B	37	127	13	24	3	1	4	19	.189	16	32	0	55	4	0	1.000
1992	—Baseball City (FSL) ..	1B	11	44	7	12	0	1	1	6	.273	2	11	0	18	1	3	.864
	—Memphis (South.)	1B	35	120	23	40	8	0	6	22	.333	26	17	0	173	9	2	.989
	—Omaha (A.A.)............	1B	27	95	9	19	3	1	5	15	.200	14	15	0	230	13	3	.988
1993	—Omaha (A.A.)............	1B	•137	479	77	124	19	3	29	84	.259	*82	94	8	*1104	*90	•11	.991
	—Kansas City (A.L.)....	1B	16	49	2	11	3	0	2	5	.224	6	15	0	129	9	2	.986
Major league totals (1 year)			16	49	2	11	3	0	2	5	.224	6	15	0	129	9	2	.986

HAMILTON, DARRYL

OF, BREWERS

PERSONAL: Born December 3, 1964, in Baton Rouge, La. . . . 6-1/180. . . . Throws right, bats left. . . . Full name: Darryl Quinn Hamilton.
HIGH SCHOOL: University (Baton Rouge, La.).
COLLEGE: Nicholls State (La.).
TRANSACTIONS/CAREER NOTES: Selected by Milwaukee Brewers organization in 11th round of free-agent draft (June 2, 1986). . . . On disabled list (May 22-June 15, 1991; May 6-24, 1992 and May 2-17, 1993).
STATISTICAL NOTES: Led California League with nine intentional bases on balls received in 1987.

Year	Team (League)	Pos.	G	AB	R	H	2B	3B	HR	RBI	Avg.	BB	SO	SB	PO	A	E	Avg.
			BATTING												FIELDING			
1986	—Helena (Pioneer)	OF	65	248	*72	•97	12	•6	0	35	*.391	51	18	34	132	9	0	*1.000
1987	—Stockton (Calif.).......	OF	125	494	102	162	17	6	8	61	.328	74	59	42	221	8	1	*.996
1988	—Denver (A.A.)............	OF	72	277	55	90	11	4	0	32	.325	39	28	28	160	2	2	.988
	—Milwaukee (A.L.)......	OF	44	103	14	19	4	0	1	11	.184	12	9	7	75	1	0	1.000
1989	—Denver (A.A.)............	OF	129	497	72	142	24	4	2	40	.286	42	58	20	263	11	0	*1.000
1990	—Milwaukee (A.L.)......	OF	89	156	27	46	5	0	1	18	.295	9	12	10	120	1	1	.992
1991	—Milwaukee (A.L.)......	OF	122	405	64	126	15	6	1	57	.311	33	38	16	234	3	1	.996
1992	—Milwaukee (A.L.)......	OF	128	470	67	140	19	7	5	62	.298	45	42	41	279	10	0	*1.000
1993	—Milwaukee (A.L.)......	OF	135	520	74	161	21	1	9	48	.310	45	62	21	340	10	3	.992
Major league totals (5 years)			518	1654	246	492	64	14	17	196	.297	144	163	95	1048	25	5	.995

HAMMOND, CHRIS

P, MARLINS

PERSONAL: Born January 21, 1966, in Atlanta. . . . 6-1/195. . . . Throws left, bats left. . . . Full name: Christopher Andrew Hammond. . . . Brother of Steve Hammond, outfielder, Kansas City Royals (1982).
HIGH SCHOOL: Vestavia Hills (Birmingham, Ala.).
COLLEGE: Gulf Coast Community College (Fla.) and Alabama-Birmingham.
TRANSACTIONS/CAREER NOTES: Selected by Cincinnati Reds organization in sixth round of free-agent draft (January 14, 1986). . . . On disabled list (July 27-September 1, 1991). . . . Traded by Reds to Florida Marlins for 3B Gary Scott and a player to be named later (March 27, 1993); Reds acquired P Hector Carrasco to complete deal (September 10, 1993).
HONORS: Named American Association Pitcher of the Year (1990).
MISCELLANEOUS: Appeared in two games as pinch-runner (1992). . . . Struck out in one game as pinch-hitter (1993).

Year	Team (League)	W	L	Pct.	ERA	G	GS	CG	ShO	Sv.	IP	H	R	ER	BB	SO
1986	—GC Reds (GCL)	3	2	.600	2.81	7	7	1	0	0	41⅔	27	21	13	17	53
	—Tampa (Fla. St.).........	0	2	.000	3.32	5	5	0	0	0	21⅔	25	8	8	13	5
1987	—Tampa (Fla. St.).........	11	11	.500	3.55	25	24	6	0	0	170	174	81	67	60	126
1988	—Chatt. (South.)	*16	5	.762	*1.72	26	26	4	2	0	182⅔	127	48	35	77	127
1989	—Nashville (A.A.)	11	7	.611	3.38	24	24	3	1	0	157⅓	144	69	59	96	142
1990	—Nashville (A.A.)	*15	1	*.938	*2.17	24	24	5	*3	0	149	118	43	36	63	*149
	—Cincinnati (N.L.)	0	2	.000	6.35	3	3	0	0	0	11⅓	13	9	8	12	4
1991	—Cincinnati (N.L.)	7	7	.500	4.06	20	18	0	0	0	99⅔	92	51	45	48	50
1992	—Cincinnati (N.L.)	7	10	.412	4.21	28	26	0	0	0	147⅓	149	75	69	55	79
1993	—Florida (N.L.)■..........	11	12	.478	4.66	32	32	1	0	0	191	207	106	99	66	108
Major league totals (4 years)..		25	31	.446	4.43	83	79	1	0	0	449⅓	461	241	221	181	241

HAMMONDS, JEFFREY

OF, ORIOLES

PERSONAL: Born March 5, 1971, in Plainfield, N.J. . . . 6-0/195. . . . Throws right, bats right. . . . Full name: Jeffrey Bryan Hammonds. . . . Brother of Reggie Hammonds, outfielder, Pittsburgh Pirates organization (1984-86).
HIGH SCHOOL: Scotch Plains (N.J.)-Fanwood.

COLLEGE: Stanford.
TRANSACTIONS/CAREER NOTES: Selected by Toronto Blue Jays organization in ninth round of free-agent draft (June 5, 1989). ... Selected by Baltimore Orioles organization in first round (fourth pick overall) of free-agent draft (June 1, 1992).... On Hagerstown temporary inactive list (August 6-September 14, 1992).... On Rochester disabled list (May 17-28, 1993).... On Baltimore disabled list (August 8-September 1, 1993); included rehabilitation assignment to Bowie (August 28-September 1). ... On Baltimore disabled list (September 28, 1993-remainder of season).
HONORS: Named outfielder on THE SPORTING NEWS college All-America team (1990 and 1992).
MISCELLANEOUS: Member of 1992 U.S. Olympic baseball team.

			BATTING												FIELDING			
Year	Team (League)	Pos.	G	AB	R	H	2B	3B	HR	RBI	Avg.	BB	SO	SB	PO	A	E	Avg.
1992 —	....								Did not play.									
1993 —	Bowie (Eastern)	OF	24	92	13	26	3	0	3	10	.283	9	18	4	48	2	0	1.000
	—Rochester (Int'l)	OF	36	151	25	47	9	1	5	23	.311	5	27	6	72	1	0	1.000
	—Baltimore (A.L.)........	OF	33	105	10	32	8	0	3	19	.305	2	16	4	47	2	2	.961
Major league totals (1 year)	....		33	105	10	32	8	0	3	19	.305	2	16	4	47	2	2	.961

HAMPTON, MIKE
P, ASTROS

PERSONAL: Born September 9, 1972, in Brooksville, Fla.... 5-10/190.... Throws left, bats right.... Full name: Michael William Hampton.
HIGH SCHOOL: Crystal River (Fla.).
TRANSACTIONS/CAREER NOTES: Selected by Seattle Mariners organization in sixth round of free-agent draft (June 4, 1990).... Traded by Mariners with OF Mike Felder to Houston Astros for OF Eric Anthony (December 10, 1993).
STATISTICAL NOTES: Led Arizona League with 10 wild pitches in 1990.... Pitched 6-0 no-hit victory for San Bernardino against Visalia (May 31, 1991).

Year	Team (League)	W	L	Pct.	ERA	G	GS	CG	ShO	Sv.	IP	H	R	ER	BB	SO
1990 —	Ariz. Mariners (Ar.) ...	•7	2	.778	2.66	14	•13	0	0	0	64⅓	52	32	19	40	59
1991 —	San Bern. (Calif.)	1	7	.125	5.25	18	15	1	1	0	73⅔	71	58	43	47	57
	—Belling. (N'west)	5	2	.714	1.58	9	9	0	0	0	57	32	15	10	26	65
1992 —	San Bern. (Calif.)	13	8	.619	3.12	25	25	6	•2	0	170	163	75	59	66	132
	—Jacksonv. (South.)	0	1	.000	4.35	2	2	1	0	0	10⅓	13	5	5	1	6
1993 —	Seattle (A.L.).............	1	3	.250	9.53	13	3	0	0	1	17	28	20	18	17	8
	—Jacksonv. (South.)	6	4	.600	3.71	15	14	1	0	0	87⅓	71	43	36	33	84
Major league totals (1 year)	...	1	3	.250	9.53	13	3	0	0	1	17	28	20	18	17	8

HANCOCK, CHRIS
P, GIANTS

PERSONAL: Born September 12, 1969, in Lynwood, Calif. ... 6-3/175.... Throws left, bats left.... Full name: Christopher Martin Hancock.
HIGH SCHOOL: Fontana (Calif.).
TRANSACTIONS/CAREER NOTES: Selected by San Francisco Giants organization in second round of free-agent draft (June 1, 1988).... On disabled list (July 23, 1990-remainder of season; April 10-July 4, 1991 and May 28-June 15, 1993).

Year	Team (League)	W	L	Pct.	ERA	G	GS	CG	ShO	Sv.	IP	H	R	ER	BB	SO
1988 —	Pocatello (Pioneer)	2	5	.286	8.86	12	11	0	0	0	42⅔	60	54	42	43	31
1989 —	Everett (N'west)	2	5	.286	5.64	11	11	0	0	0	52⅔	47	52	33	53	50
	—Clinton (Midwest)	4	7	.364	5.88	18	17	0	0	0	72	63	53	47	77	62
1990 —	Clinton (Midwest)	11	3	.786	2.28	18	17	2	1	0	110⅔	78	33	28	43	123
	—San Jose (Calif.)	0	0	...	1.17	1	1	0	0	0	7⅔	7	1	1	4	7
1991 —	San Jose (Calif.)	4	3	.571	2.03	9	9	0	0	0	53⅓	42	16	12	33	59
1992 —	San Jose (Calif.)	7	4	.636	4.04	18	17	0	0	0	111⅓	104	60	50	55	80
	—Shreveport (Texas)....	2	4	.333	3.10	8	8	2	0	0	49⅓	37	22	17	18	30
1993 —	Shreveport (Texas)....	8	8	.500	4.06	23	23	0	0	0	124	126	71	56	52	93

HANEY, CHRIS
P, ROYALS

PERSONAL: Born November 16, 1968, in Baltimore.... 6-3/195.... Throws left, bats left.... Full name: Christopher Deane Haney.... Son of Larry Haney, major league catcher with five teams (1966-70 and 1972-78) and coach, Milwaukee Brewers (1978-91).
HIGH SCHOOL: Orange County (Va.).
COLLEGE: UNC Charlotte.
TRANSACTIONS/CAREER NOTES: Selected by Milwaukee Brewers organization in 25th round of free-agent draft (June 2, 1987). ... Selected by Montreal Expos organization in second round of free-agent draft (June 4, 1990).... On Indianapolis disabled list (June 17-25, 1992).... Traded by Expos with P Bill Sampen to Kansas City Royals for 3B Sean Berry and P Archie Corbin (August 29, 1992).
MISCELLANEOUS: Appeared in one game as pinch-runner with Montreal (1992).

Year	Team (League)	W	L	Pct.	ERA	G	GS	CG	ShO	Sv.	IP	H	R	ER	BB	SO
1990 —	Jamestown (NYP)......	3	0	1.000	0.96	6	5	0	0	1	28	17	3	3	10	26
	—Rockford (Midw.)	2	4	.333	2.21	8	8	3	0	0	53	40	15	13	6	45
	—Jacksonv. (South.)	1	0	1.000	0.00	1	1	0	0	0	6	6	0	0	3	6
1991 —	Harrisburg (East.)	5	3	.625	2.16	12	12	3	0	0	83⅓	65	21	20	31	68
	—Montreal (N.L.)	3	7	.300	4.04	16	16	0	0	0	84⅔	94	49	38	43	51
	—Indianapolis (A.A.).....	1	1	.500	4.35	2	2	0	0	0	10⅓	14	10	5	6	8
1992 —	Montreal (N.L.)	2	3	.400	5.45	9	6	1	1	0	38	40	25	23	10	27
	—Indianapolis (A.A.).....	5	2	.714	5.14	15	15	0	0	0	84	88	50	48	42	61
	—Kansas City (A.L.)■...	2	3	.400	3.86	7	7	1	1	0	42	35	18	18	16	27
1993 —	Omaha (A.A.)	6	1	.857	2.27	8	7	2	0	0	47⅔	43	13	12	14	32
	—Kansas City (A.L.)	9	9	.500	6.02	23	23	1	1	0	124	141	87	83	53	65
A.L. totals (2 years)	....	11	12	.478	5.48	30	30	2	2	0	166	176	105	101	69	92
N.L. totals (2 years)	....	5	10	.333	4.48	25	22	1	1	0	122⅔	134	74	61	53	78
Major league totals (3 years)	..	16	22	.421	5.05	55	52	3	3	0	288⅔	310	179	162	122	170

HANSELL, GREG

P, DODGERS

PERSONAL: Born March 12, 1971, in Bellflower, Calif. . . . 6-5/213. . . . Throws right, bats right. . . . Full name: Gregory Michael Hansell.
HIGH SCHOOL: John F. Kennedy (La Palma, Calif.).
TRANSACTIONS/CAREER NOTES: Selected by Boston Red Sox organization in 10th round of free-agent draft (June 5, 1989). . . . Traded by Red Sox organization with OF Ed Perozo and a player to be named later to New York Mets organization for 1B Mike Marshall (July 27, 1990); Mets acquired C Paul Williams to complete deal (November 19, 1990). . . . Traded by Mets organization with P Bob Ojeda to Los Angeles Dodgers organization for OF Hubie Brooks (December 15, 1990). . . . On disabled list (June 19-July 8, 1993).

Year	Team (League)	W	L	Pct.	ERA	G	GS	CG	ShO	Sv.	IP	H	R	ER	BB	SO
1989	—GC Red Sox (GCL)	3	2	.600	2.53	10	8	0	0	2	57	51	23	16	23	44
1990	—W.H.-St. Luc. (FSL)■	9	•14	.391	3.40	27	•27	2	1	0	153⅓	129	85	58	79	95
1991	—Bakersfield (Calif.)■	14	5	.737	2.87	25	25	0	0	0	150⅔	142	56	48	42	132
1992	—San Antonio (Tex.)	6	4	.600	2.83	14	14	0	0	0	92⅓	80	40	29	33	64
	—Albuquerque (PCL)	1	5	.167	5.24	13	13	0	0	0	68⅔	84	46	40	35	38
1993	—Albuquerque (PCL)	5	10	.333	6.93	26	20	0	0	0	101⅓	131	86	78	60	60

HANSEN, DAVE

3B, DODGERS

PERSONAL: Born November 24, 1968, in Long Beach, Calif. . . . 6-0/195. . . . Throws right, bats left. . . . Full name: David Andrew Hansen.
HIGH SCHOOL: Rowland (Long Beach, Calif.).
TRANSACTIONS/CAREER NOTES: Selected by Los Angeles Dodgers organization in second round of free-agent draft (June 2, 1986).
STATISTICAL NOTES: Led California League third basemen with 45 errors in 1987. . . . Led Florida State League with 210 total bases and tied for lead with nine sacrifice flies in 1988. . . . Led Florida State League third basemen with 383 total chances and 24 double plays in 1988. . . . Led Pacific Coast League third basemen with .926 fielding percentage, 254 assists, 349 total chances and 25 double plays in 1990.

			BATTING												FIELDING			
Year	Team (League)	Pos.	G	AB	R	H	2B	3B	HR	RBI	Avg.	BB	SO	SB	PO	A	E	Avg.
1986	—Great Falls (Pio.)	0-3-C-2	61	204	39	61	7	3	1	36	.299	27	28	9	54	10	7	.901
1987	—Bakersfield (Calif.)	3B-OF	132	432	68	113	22	1	3	38	.262	65	61	4	79	198	†45	.860
1988	—Vero Beach (FSL)	3B	135	512	68	*149	•28	6	7	*81	.291	56	46	2	*102	*263	18	*.953
1989	—San Antonio (Tex.)	3B	121	464	72	138	21	4	6	52	.297	50	44	3	*92	208	16	*.949
	—Albuquerque (PCL)	3B	6	30	6	8	1	0	2	10	.267	2	3	0	3	8	3	.786
1990	—Albuquerque (PCL)	3B-OF-SS	135	487	90	154	20	3	11	92	.316	*90	54	9	71	†255	26	†.926
	—Los Angeles (N.L.)	3B	5	7	0	1	0	0	0	1	.143	0	0	0	0	1	1	.500
1991	—Albuquerque (PCL)	3B-SS	68	254	42	77	11	1	5	40	.303	49	33	4	43	125	6	.966
	—Los Angeles (N.L.)	3B-SS	53	56	3	15	4	0	1	5	.268	2	12	1	5	19	0	1.000
1992	—Los Angeles (N.L.)	3B	132	341	30	73	11	0	6	22	.214	34	49	0	61	183	8	*.968
1993	—Los Angeles (N.L.)	3B	84	105	13	38	3	0	4	30	.362	21	13	0	11	27	3	.927
Major league totals (4 years)			274	509	46	127	18	0	11	58	.250	57	74	1	77	230	12	.962

HANSON, ERIK

P, REDS

PERSONAL: Born May 18, 1965, in Kinnelon, N.J. . . . 6-6/215. . . . Throws right, bats right. . . . Full name: Erik Brian Hanson.
HIGH SCHOOL: Peddie Prep (Highstown, N.J.).
COLLEGE: Wake Forest.
TRANSACTIONS/CAREER NOTES: Selected by Montreal Expos organization in seventh round of free-agent draft (June 6, 1983). . . . Selected by Seattle Mariners organization in second round of free-agent draft (June 2, 1986). . . . On inactive list (June 12-August 18, 1986). . . . On Seattle disabled list (May 25-August 4, 1989); included rehabilitation assignment to Calgary (June 14-22 and July 24-August 4). . . . On Seattle disabled list (May 12-28 and May 29-June 22, 1991); included rehabilitation assignment to Calgary (June 16-20). . . . On disabled list (August 23-September 12, 1992). . . . Traded by Mariners with 2B Bret Boone to Cincinnati Reds for P Bobby Ayala and C Dan Wilson (November 2, 1993).
STATISTICAL NOTES: Pitched 5-0 no-hit victory for Calgary against Las Vegas (August 21, 1988, second game).
MISCELLANEOUS: Scored once in two games as pinch-runner; after pinch-running in one game, became designated hitter but made no plate appearance (1993).

Year	Team (League)	W	L	Pct.	ERA	G	GS	CG	ShO	Sv.	IP	H	R	ER	BB	SO
1986	—Chatt. (South.)	0	0	...	3.86	3	2	0	0	0	9⅓	10	4	4	4	11
1987	—Chatt. (South.)	8	10	.444	2.60	21	21	1	0	0	131⅓	102	56	38	43	131
	—Calgary (PCL)	1	3	.250	3.61	8	7	0	0	0	47⅓	38	23	19	21	43
1988	—Calgary (PCL)	12	7	.632	4.23	27	26	2	1	0	161⅔	167	92	76	57	*154
	—Seattle (A.L.)	2	3	.400	3.24	6	6	0	0	0	41⅔	35	17	15	12	36
1989	—Seattle (A.L.)	9	5	.643	3.18	17	17	1	0	0	113⅓	103	44	40	32	75
	—Calgary (PCL)	4	2	.667	6.87	8	8	1	0	0	38	51	30	29	11	37
1990	—Seattle (A.L.)	18	9	.667	3.24	33	33	5	1	0	236	205	88	85	68	211
1991	—Seattle (A.L.)	8	8	.500	3.81	27	27	2	1	0	174⅔	182	82	74	56	143
	—Calgary (PCL)	0	0	...	1.50	1	1	0	0	0	6	1	1	1	2	5
1992	—Seattle (A.L.)	8	*17	.320	4.82	31	30	6	1	0	186⅔	209	110	100	57	112
1993	—Seattle (A.L.)	11	12	.478	3.47	31	30	7	0	0	215	215	91	83	60	163
Major league totals (6 years)		56	54	.509	3.69	145	143	21	3	0	967⅓	949	432	397	285	740

HARDGE, MIKE

2B, EXPOS

PERSONAL: Born January 27, 1972, in Fort Hood, Tex. . . . 5-11/190. . . . Throws right, bats right. . . . Full name: Michael Dwayne Hardge.
HIGH SCHOOL: C.E. Ellison (Killeen, Tex.).
TRANSACTIONS/CAREER NOTES: Selected by Montreal Expos organization in second round of free-agent draft (June 4, 1990); pick received as part of compensation for Los Angeles Dodgers signing Type A free agent Hubie Brooks.
STATISTICAL NOTES: Led Gulf Coast League second basemen with 126 putouts, 171 assists, 305 total chances and 28 double plays in 1991. . . . Led Midwest League second basemen with 254 putouts and 536 total chances in 1992.

			BATTING												FIELDING			
Year	Team (League)	Pos.	G	AB	R	H	2B	3B	HR	RBI	Avg.	BB	SO	SB	PO	A	E	Avg.
1990	—GC Expos (GCL)........	SS-2B	53	176	33	39	5	0	1	13	.222	15	43	6	100	147	22	.918
1991	—GC Expos (GCL)........	2B-OF	*60	*237	*45	60	*18	3	3	30	.253	23	41	20	†128	†171	8	.974
1992	—Rockford (Midw.).....	2B-OF	127	448	63	97	21	2	12	49	.217	47	141	44	†255	261	21	.961
	—W.P. Beach (FSL).....	2B	4	15	3	5	1	0	0	0	.333	2	5	2	2	13	0	1.000
1993	—W.P. Beach (FSL).....	2B	27	92	14	21	2	1	1	12	.228	14	16	5	48	66	2	.983
	—Harrisburg (East.)....	2B	99	386	70	94	15	10	6	35	.244	37	97	27	194	221	12	.972

HARE, SHAWN

OF, TIGERS

PERSONAL: Born March 26, 1967, in St. Louis. . . . 6-1/200. . . . Throws left, bats left. . . . Full name: Shawn Robert Hare.
HIGH SCHOOL: Rochester Adams (Mich.).
COLLEGE: Central Michigan.
TRANSACTIONS/CAREER NOTES: Signed as a free agent by Detroit Tigers organization (August 28, 1988). . . . On Toledo disabled list (April 26-May 11, 1991). . . . On Detroit disabled list (August 3, 1992-remainder of season).
STATISTICAL NOTES: Led International League with nine intentional bases on balls received in 1990.

			BATTING												FIELDING			
Year	Team (League)	Pos.	G	AB	R	H	2B	3B	HR	RBI	Avg.	BB	SO	SB	PO	A	E	Avg.
1989	—Lakeland (Fla. St.)...	OF-1B	93	290	32	94	16	4	2	36	.324	41	32	11	142	4	2	.986
1990	—Toledo (Int'l)............	OF-1B	127	429	53	109	25	4	9	55	.254	49	77	9	198	6	7	.967
1991	—Toledo (Int'l)............	OF-1B	80	252	44	78	18	2	9	42	.310	30	53	1	231	19	5	.980
	—London (Eastern).....	OF	31	125	20	34	12	0	4	28	.272	12	23	2	55	5	3	.952
	—Detroit (A.L.)...........	OF	9	19	0	1	1	0	0	0	.053	2	1	0	9	1	0	1.000
1992	—Toledo (Int'l)............	OF-1B	57	203	31	67	12	2	5	34	.330	31	28	6	173	7	3	.984
	—Detroit (A.L.)...........	OF-1B	15	26	0	3	1	0	0	5	.115	2	4	0	33	2	0	1.000
1993	—Toledo (Int'l)............	OF-1B-P	130	470	81	124	29	3	20	76	.264	34	90	8	190	5	5	.975
	Major league totals (2 years)..................		24	45	0	4	2	0	0	5	.089	4	5	0	42	3	0	1.000

RECORD AS PITCHER

Year	Team (League)	W	L	Pct.	ERA	G	GS	CG	ShO	Sv.	IP	H	R	ER	BB	SO
1993	—Toledo (Int'l).............	0	0	...	0.00	1	0	0	0	0	1	2	0	0	0	1

HARKEY, MIKE

P, ROCKIES

PERSONAL: Born October 25, 1966, in San Diego. . . . 6-5/235. . . . Throws right, bats right. . . . Full name: Michael Anthony Harkey.
HIGH SCHOOL: Ganesha (Pomona, Calif.).
COLLEGE: Cal State Fullerton.
TRANSACTIONS/CAREER NOTES: Selected by San Diego Padres organization in 18th round of free-agent draft (June 4, 1984). . . . Selected by Chicago Cubs organization in first round (fourth pick overall) of free-agent draft (June 2, 1987). . . . On disabled list (April 5-28 and July 4, 1989-remainder of season; May 29-June 13, 1990; and April 27, 1991-remainder of season). . . . On Chicago disabled list (March 28-July 20, 1992); included rehabilitation assignment to Peoria (June 9-13 and June 19-20), Iowa (June 20-July 9) and Charlotte (July 15-16). . . . On Chicago disabled list (March 27-April 14, 1993); included rehabilitaton assignment to Orlando (April 9-10). . . . On Chicago disabled list (June 13-July 5, 1993). . . . Granted free agency (December 20, 1993). . . . Signed by Colorado Rockies (January 4, 1994).
RECORDS: Shares major league record for most putouts by pitcher in one inning—3 (May 23, 1990, fourth inning).
HONORS: Named N.L. Rookie Pitcher of the Year by THE SPORTING NEWS (1990).

Year	Team (League)	W	L	Pct.	ERA	G	GS	CG	ShO	Sv.	IP	H	R	ER	BB	SO
1987	—Peoria (Midwest).......	2	3	.400	3.55	12	12	3	0	0	76	81	45	30	28	48
	—Pittsfield (Eastern)....	0	0	...	0.00	1	0	0	0	0	2	1	0	0	0	2
1988	—Pittsfield (Eastern)....	9	2	*.818	1.37	13	13	3	1	0	85⅔	66	29	13	35	73
	—Iowa (Am. Assoc.).....	7	2	.778	3.55	12	12	3	1	0	78⅔	55	36	31	33	62
	—Chicago (N.L.)...........	0	3	.000	2.60	5	5	0	0	0	34⅔	33	14	10	15	18
1989	—Iowa (Am. Assoc.).....	2	7	.222	4.43	12	12	0	0	0	63	67	37	31	35	37
1990	—Chicago (N.L.)...........	12	6	.667	3.26	27	27	2	1	0	173⅔	153	71	63	59	94
1991	—Chicago (N.L.)...........	0	2	.000	5.30	4	4	0	0	0	18⅔	21	11	11	6	15
1992	—Peoria (Midwest).......	1	0	1.000	3.00	2	2	0	0	0	12	15	6	4	3	17
	—Iowa (Am. Assoc.).....	0	1	.000	5.56	4	4	0	0	0	22⅔	21	15	14	13	16
	—Charlotte (South.)......	0	1	.000	5.63	1	1	0	0	0	8	9	5	5	0	5
	—Chicago (N.L.)...........	4	0	1.000	1.89	7	7	0	0	0	38	34	13	8	15	21
1993	—Orlando (Southern)....	0	0	...	1.69	1	1	0	0	0	5⅓	4	1	1	2	5
	—Chicago (N.L.)...........	10	10	.500	5.26	28	28	1	0	0	157⅓	187	100	92	43	67
	Major league totals (5 years)..	26	21	.553	3.92	71	71	3	1	0	422⅓	428	209	184	138	215

HARNISCH, PETE

P, ASTROS

PERSONAL: Born September 23, 1966, in Commack, N.Y. . . . 6-0/207. . . . Throws right, bats right. . . . Full name: Peter Thomas Harnisch.
HIGH SCHOOL: Commack (N.Y.).
COLLEGE: Fordham.
TRANSACTIONS/CAREER NOTES: Selected by Baltimore Orioles organization in supplemental round ("sandwich pick" between first and second round, 27th pick overall) of free-agent draft (June 2, 1987); pick received as compensation for Cleveland Indians signing Type A free agent Rick Dempsey. . . . Traded by Orioles with P Curt Schilling and OF Steve Finley to Houston Astros for 1B Glenn Davis (January 10, 1991). . . . On suspended list (July 7-9, 1992).
RECORDS: Shares major league record for striking out side on nine pitches (September 6, 1991, seventh inning).

Year	Team (League)	W	L	Pct.	ERA	G	GS	CG	ShO	Sv.	IP	H	R	ER	BB	SO
1987	—Bluefield (Appal.).......	3	1	.750	2.56	9	9	0	0	0	52⅔	38	19	15	26	64
	—Hagerstown (Car.).....	1	2	.333	2.25	4	4	0	0	0	20	17	7	5	14	18
1988	—Charlotte (South.)......	7	6	.538	2.58	20	20	4	2	0	132⅓	113	55	38	52	141

Year	Team (League)	W	L	Pct.	ERA	G	GS	CG	ShO	Sv.	IP	H	R	ER	BB	SO
	—Rochester (Int'l)	4	1	.800	2.16	7	7	3	2	0	58⅓	44	16	14	14	43
	—Baltimore (A.L.)	0	2	.000	5.54	2	2	0	0	0	13	13	8	8	9	10
1989	—Baltimore (A.L.)	5	9	.357	4.62	18	17	2	0	0	103⅓	97	55	53	64	70
	—Rochester (Int'l)	5	5	.500	2.58	12	12	3	1	0	87⅓	60	27	25	35	59
1990	—Baltimore (A.L.)	11	11	.500	4.34	31	31	3	0	0	188⅔	189	96	91	86	122
1991	—Houston (N.L.)■	12	9	.571	2.70	33	33	4	2	0	216⅔	169	71	65	83	172
1992	—Houston (N.L.)	9	10	.474	3.70	34	34	0	0	0	206⅔	182	92	85	64	164
1993	—Houston (N.L.)	16	9	.640	2.98	33	33	5	*4	0	217⅔	171	84	72	79	185
A.L. totals (3 years)		16	22	.421	4.49	51	50	5	0	0	305	299	159	152	159	202
N.L. totals (3 years)		37	28	.569	3.12	100	100	9	6	0	641	522	247	222	226	521
Major league totals (6 years)		53	50	.515	3.56	151	150	14	6	0	946	821	406	374	385	723

ALL-STAR GAME RECORD

Year	League	W	L	Pct.	ERA	GS	CG	ShO	Sv.	IP	H	R	ER	BB	SO
1991	—National	0	0	...	0.00	0	0	0	0	1	2	0	0	0	1

HARPER, BRIAN

C

PERSONAL: Born October 16, 1959, in Los Angeles. . . . 6-2/206. . . . Throws right, bats right. . . . Full name: Brian David Harper.

HIGH SCHOOL: San Pedro (Calif.).

TRANSACTIONS/CAREER NOTES: Selected by California Angels organization in fourth round of free-agent draft (June 7, 1977). . . . On disabled list (July 1-17, 1980). . . . Traded by Angels to Pittsburgh Pirates for SS Tim Foli (December 11, 1981). . . . On disabled list (April 12-May 10 and May 16-June 4, 1984). . . . Traded by Pirates with P John Tudor to St. Louis Cardinals for OF/1B George Hendrick and C Steve Barnard (December 12, 1984). . . . Released by Cardinals (April 1, 1986). . . . Signed by Detroit Tigers (April 25, 1986). . . . Released by Tigers (March 23, 1987). . . . Signed by San Jose, independent (May 3, 1987). . . . Contract sold by San Jose to Oakland Athletics organization (May 12, 1987). . . . Released by A's organization (October 12, 1987). . . . Signed by Portland, Minnesota Twins organization (January 4, 1988). . . . Granted free agency (November 4, 1991). . . . Re-signed by Twins (December 19, 1991). . . . Granted free agency (November 2, 1993).

STATISTICAL NOTES: Led Texas League with 19 passed balls in 1979. . . . Led Pacific Coast League with 339 total bases in 1981. . . . Led Pacific Coast League catchers with 19 errors in 1981. . . . Tied for American Association lead in errors by catcher with 13 in 1986. . . . Led Pacific Coast League with 12 sacrifice flies in 1987. . . . Led A.L. catchers with 11 errors in 1989. . . . Led A.L. with 12 passed balls in 1992 and 18 in 1993.

			BATTING												FIELDING			
Year	Team (League)	Pos.	G	AB	R	H	2B	3B	HR	RBI	Avg.	BB	SO	SB	PO	A	E	Avg.
1977	—Idaho Falls (Pio.)	C	52	186	28	60	9	3	1	33	.323	13	31	4	352	36	13	.968
1978	—Quad Cities (Mid.)	C	129	508	80	149	31	2	24	*101	.293	37	66	1	430	46	16	.967
1979	—El Paso (Texas)	C	132	531	85	167	*37	3	14	90	.315	50	47	10	443	66	*29	.946
	—California (A.L.)	DH	1	2	0	0	0	0	0	0	.000	0	1	0	...	...	...	...
1980	—El Paso (Texas)	C	105	400	61	114	23	3	12	66	.285	38	46	3	214	30	7	.972
1981	—Salt Lake City (PCL)	C-OF-1B	134	549	99	*192	45	9	28	122	.350	39	33	0	421	30	†24	.949
	—California (A.L.)	OF	4	11	1	3	0	0	0	1	.273	0	0	1	5	0	1	.833
1982	—Pittsburgh (N.L.)■	OF	20	29	4	8	1	0	2	4	.276	1	4	0	10	0	0	1.000
	—Portland (PCL)	OF-3B-C	101	395	71	112	29	8	17	73	.284	25	29	3	164	36	8	.962
1983	—Pittsburgh (N.L.)	OF-1B	61	131	16	29	4	1	7	20	.221	2	15	0	40	0	0	1.000
1984	—Pittsburgh (N.L.)	OF-C	46	112	4	29	4	0	2	11	.259	5	11	0	57	3	1	.984
1985	—St. Louis (N.L.)■	0-3-C-1	43	52	5	13	4	0	0	8	.250	2	3	0	15	5	0	1.000
1986	—Nashville (A.A.)■	C-OF-1B	95	317	41	83	11	1	11	45	.262	26	27	3	377	55	‡15	.966
	—Detroit (A.L.)	OF-1B-C	19	36	2	5	1	0	0	3	.139	3	3	0	25	2	1	.964
1987	—San Jose (Calif.)■	3B-OF-C	8	29	5	9	0	0	3	8	.310	2	0	0	21	12	5	.868
	—Tacoma (PCL)■	OF-C-P	94	323	41	100	17	0	9	62	.310	28	23	1	163	10	5	.972
	—Oakland (A.L.)	OF	11	17	1	4	1	0	0	3	.235	0	4	0	0	0	0	...
1988	—Portland (PCL)■	C-3-0-P	46	170	34	60	10	1	13	42	.353	14	7	2	181	25	5	.976
	—Minnesota (A.L.)	C-3B	60	166	15	49	11	1	3	20	.295	10	12	0	208	15	2	.991
1989	—Minnesota (A.L.)	C-0-1-3	126	385	43	125	24	0	8	57	.325	13	16	2	462	36	†11	.978
1990	—Minnesota (A.L.)	C-3B-1B	134	479	61	141	42	3	6	54	.294	19	27	3	686	58	11	.985
1991	—Minnesota (A.L.)	C-1B	123	441	54	137	28	1	10	69	.311	14	22	1	643	33	8	.988
1992	—Minnesota (A.L.)	C	140	502	58	154	25	0	9	73	.307	26	22	0	744	58	13	.984
1993	—Minnesota (A.L.)	C	147	530	52	161	26	1	12	73	.304	29	29	1	736	64	10	.988
American League totals (10 years)			765	2569	287	779	158	6	48	353	.303	114	136	8	3509	266	57	.985
National League totals (4 years)			170	324	29	79	13	1	11	43	.244	10	33	0	122	8	1	.992
Major league totals (14 years)			935	2893	316	858	171	7	59	396	.297	124	169	8	3631	274	58	.985

CHAMPIONSHIP SERIES RECORD

			BATTING												FIELDING			
Year	Team (League)	Pos.	G	AB	R	H	2B	3B	HR	RBI	Avg.	BB	SO	SB	PO	A	E	Avg.
1985	—St. Louis (N.L.)	PH	1	1	0	0	0	0	0	0	.000	0	0	0	...	...	...	...
1991	—Minnesota (A.L.)	C	5	18	1	5	2	0	0	1	.278	0	2	0	23	1	1	.960
Championship series totals (2 years)			6	19	1	5	2	0	0	1	.263	0	2	0	23	1	1	.960

WORLD SERIES RECORD

			BATTING												FIELDING			
Year	Team (League)	Pos.	G	AB	R	H	2B	3B	HR	RBI	Avg.	BB	SO	SB	PO	A	E	Avg.
1985	—St. Louis (N.L.)	PH	4	4	0	1	0	0	0	1	.250	0	1	0	...	...	...	...
1991	—Minnesota (A.L.)	C-PH	7	21	2	8	2	0	0	1	.381	2	2	0	33	5	2	.950
World Series totals (2 years)			11	25	2	9	2	0	0	2	.360	2	3	0	33	5	2	.950

RECORD AS PITCHER

Year	Team (League)	W	L	Pct.	ERA	G	GS	CG	ShO	Sv.	IP	H	R	ER	BB	SO
1987	—Tacoma (PCL)	0	0	...	3.00	1	0	0	0	0	3	3	1	1	0	1
1988	—Portland (PCL)	0	0	...	9.00	1	0	0	0	0	1	2	1	1	2	0

HARRIS, DONALD
OF, RANGERS

PERSONAL: Born November 12, 1967, in Waco, Tex. . . . 6-1/185. . . . Throws right, bats right.
HIGH SCHOOL: Jefferson-Moore (Waco, Tex.).
COLLEGE: McLennan Community College (Tex.).
TRANSACTIONS/CAREER NOTES: Selected by Texas Rangers organization in first round (fifth pick overall) of free-agent draft (June 5, 1989).
STATISTICAL NOTES: Led Pioneer League outfielders with 124 total chances and three double plays in 1989.

			BATTING												FIELDING			
Year	Team (League)	Pos.	G	AB	R	H	2B	3B	HR	RBI	Avg.	BB	SO	SB	PO	A	E	Avg.
1989	—Butte (Pioneer)	OF	65	*264	50	75	7	*8	6	37	.284	12	54	14	*115	7	2	.984
1990	—Tulsa (Texas)	OF	64	213	16	34	5	1	1	15	.160	7	69	7	123	6	8	.942
	—Gastonia (S. Atl.)	OF	58	221	27	46	10	0	3	13	.208	14	63	15	104	6	5	.957
1991	—Tulsa (Texas)	OF	130	450	47	102	17	8	11	53	.227	26	118	9	283	11	9	.970
	—Texas (A.L.)	OF	18	8	4	3	0	0	1	2	.375	1	3	1	7	0	0	1.000
1992	—Tulsa (Texas)	OF	83	303	39	77	15	2	11	39	.254	9	85	4	196	7	4	.981
	—Texas (A.L.)	OF	24	33	3	6	1	0	0	1	.182	0	15	1	36	1	1	.974
1993	—Okla. City (A.A.)	OF	96	367	48	93	13	9	6	40	.253	23	89	4	241	5	6	.976
	—Texas (A.L.)	OF	40	76	10	15	2	0	1	8	.197	5	18	0	47	3	3	.943
Major league totals (3 years)			82	117	17	24	3	0	2	11	.205	6	36	2	90	4	4	.959

HARRIS, DOUG
P, ROYALS

PERSONAL: Born September 27, 1969, in Carlisle, Pa. . . . 6-4/205. . . . Throws right, bats right. . . . Full name: Douglas William Harris.
HIGH SCHOOL: Carlisle (Pa.).
COLLEGE: James Madison.
TRANSACTIONS/CAREER NOTES: Selected by Kansas City Royals organization in fourth round of free-agent draft (June 4, 1990). . . . On Baseball City disabled list (July 1-8, 1991; April 10-May 7, May 18-June 16 and July 1-September 18, 1992). . . . On disabled list (May 29-June 7 and June 29-July 25, 1993).

Year	Team (League)	W	L	Pct.	ERA	G	GS	CG	ShO	Sv.	IP	H	R	ER	BB	SO
1990	—Eugene (N'west)	4	5	.444	4.41	15	15	0	0	0	69⅓	74	46	34	28	46
1991	—Appleton (Midw.)	2	2	.500	2.20	7	7	1	1	0	45	41	14	11	10	39
	—Baseball City (FSL)	10	6	.625	2.47	19	18	3	1	0	116⅔	92	38	32	27	84
1992	—Baseball City (FSL)	0	2	.000	2.15	7	7	0	0	0	29⅓	25	11	7	6	22
1993	—Memphis (South.)	3	6	.333	4.67	22	12	1	0	0	86⅔	99	52	45	13	38

HARRIS, GENE
P, PADRES

PERSONAL: Born December 5, 1964, in Sebring, Fla. . . . 5-11/195. . . . Throws right, bats right. . . . Full name: Tyrone Eugene Harris.
HIGH SCHOOL: Okeechobee (Fla.).
COLLEGE: Tulane.
TRANSACTIONS/CAREER NOTES: Selected by Montreal Expos organization in fifth round of free-agent draft (June 2, 1986). . . . Traded by Expos organization with P Randy Johnson and P Brian Holman to Seattle Mariners for P Mark Langston and a player to be named later (May 25, 1989); Indianapolis, Expos organization, acquired P Mike Campbell to complete deal (July 31, 1989). . . . On Seattle disabled list (July 29, 1989-remainder of season). . . . On disqualified list (April 25-June 26, 1991 and May 3-29, 1992). . . . Traded by Mariners to San Diego Padres for OF Will Taylor (May 11, 1992). . . . On Las Vegas suspended list (July 2-16, 1992).
MISCELLANEOUS: Appeared in one game as pinch-runner (Seattle 1989 and San Diego 1992).

Year	Team (League)	W	L	Pct.	ERA	G	GS	CG	ShO	Sv.	IP	H	R	ER	BB	SO
1986	—Jamestown (NYP)	0	2	.000	2.21	4	4	0	0	0	20⅓	15	8	5	11	16
	—Burlington (Midw.)	4	2	.667	1.35	7	6	4	3	0	53⅓	37	12	8	15	32
	—W.P. Beach (FSL)	0	0	...	4.09	2	2	0	0	0	11	14	7	5	7	5
1987	—W.P. Beach (FSL)	9	7	.563	4.37	26	26	7	1	0	179	178	101	87	77	121
1988	—Jacksonv. (South.)	9	5	.643	2.63	18	18	*7	0	0	126⅔	95	43	37	45	103
1989	—Montreal (N.L.)	1	1	.500	4.95	11	0	0	0	0	20	16	11	11	10	11
	—Indianapolis (A.A.)	2	0	1.000	0.00	6	0	0	0	2	11	4	0	0	10	9
	—Calgary (PCL)■	0	0	...	0.00	5	0	0	0	2	6	4	0	0	1	4
	—Seattle (A.L.)	1	4	.200	6.48	10	6	0	0	1	33⅓	47	27	24	15	14
1990	—Calgary (PCL)	3	0	1.000	2.35	6	0	0	0	2	7⅔	7	2	2	4	9
	—Seattle (A.L.)	1	2	.333	4.74	25	0	0	0	0	38	31	25	20	30	43
1991	—Seattle (A.L.)	0	0	...	4.05	8	0	0	0	1	13⅓	15	8	6	10	6
	—Calgary (PCL)	4	0	1.000	3.34	25	0	0	0	4	35	37	16	13	11	23
1992	—Seattle (A.L.)	0	0	...	7.00	8	0	0	0	0	9	8	7	7	6	6
	—San Diego (N.L.)■	0	2	.000	2.95	14	1	0	0	0	21⅓	15	8	7	9	19
	—Las Vegas (PCL)	0	2	.000	3.67	18	0	0	0	4	34⅓	36	15	14	16	35
1993	—San Diego (N.L.)	6	6	.500	3.03	59	0	0	0	23	59⅓	57	27	20	37	39
A.L. totals (4 years)		2	6	.250	5.48	51	6	0	0	2	93⅔	101	67	57	61	69
N.L. totals (3 years)		7	9	.438	3.40	84	1	0	0	23	100⅔	88	46	38	56	69
Major league totals (5 years)		9	15	.375	4.40	135	7	0	0	25	194⅓	189	113	95	117	138

HARRIS, GREG A.
P, RED SOX

PERSONAL: Born November 2, 1955, in Lynwood, Calif. . . . 6-0/175. . . . Throws right, bats both. . . . Full name: Greg Allen Harris.
HIGH SCHOOL: Los Alamitos (Calif.).
COLLEGE: Long Beach (Calif.) City College.

TRANSACTIONS/CAREER NOTES: Selected by California Angels organization in 10th round of free-agent draft (June 5, 1974).... Selected by New York Mets organization in secondary phase of free-agent draft (January 9, 1975).... Selected by Mets organization in seventh round of free-agent draft (January 7, 1976).... Signed as free agent by Mets organization (September 17, 1976).... Traded by Mets with C Alex Trevino and P Jim Kern to Cincinnati Reds for OF George Foster (February 10, 1982).... Claimed on waivers by Montreal Expos (September 27, 1983).... Traded by Expos to San Diego Padres for IF Al Newman (July 20, 1984).... Contract sold by Padres to Texas Rangers (February 13, 1985).... Released by Rangers (December 21, 1987).... Signed by Cleveland Indians (January 19, 1988).... Released by Indians (March 24, 1988).... Signed by Maine, Philadelphia Phillies organization (April 1, 1988).... Granted free agency (November 4, 1988).... Re-signed by Phillies (December 7, 1988).... Claimed on waivers by Boston Red Sox (August 7, 1989).... Granted free agency (November 13, 1989).... Re-signed by Red Sox (February 15, 1990).

Year	Team (League)	W	L	Pct.	ERA	G	GS	CG	ShO	Sv.	IP	H	R	ER	BB	SO
1977	—Jackson (Texas)	3	6	.333	5.42	30	8	0	0	0	83	96	63	50	36	56
1978	—Lynchburg (Caro.)	8	9	.471	2.16	21	21	10	2	0	154	114	52	37	74	102
	—Jackson (Texas)	2	3	.400	3.00	6	5	1	1	0	33	24	13	11	10	18
1979	—Jackson (Texas)	9	11	.450	*2.26	25	25	11	2	0	163	125	58	41	81	89
1980	—Tidewater (Int'l)	2	9	.182	2.70	39	11	1	0	2	110	99	45	33	40	92
1981	—Tidewater (Int'l)	4	0	1.000	2.06	7	7	2	0	0	48	37	14	11	16	26
	—New York (N.L.)	3	5	.375	4.43	16	14	0	0	1	69	65	36	34	28	54
1982	—Indianapolis (A.A.)■	4	1	.800	3.00	8	8	3	1	0	48	27	18	16	24	44
	—Cincinnati (N.L.)	2	6	.250	4.83	34	10	1	0	1	91⅓	96	56	49	37	67
1983	—Indianapolis (A.A.)	9	12	.429	4.14	28	0	0	0	0	152⅓	155	83	70	66	*146
	—Cincinnati (N.L.)	0	0	...	27.00	1	21	5	0	0	1	2	3	3	3	1
1984	—Mont.-S.D. (N.L.)■	2	2	.500	2.48	34	1	0	0	3	54⅓	38	18	15	25	45
	—Indianapolis (A.A.)	4	4	.500	4.43	14	6	0	0	1	44⅔	44	27	22	29	45
1985	—Texas (A.L.)■	5	4	.556	2.47	58	0	0	0	11	113	74	35	31	43	111
1986	—Texas (A.L.)	10	8	.556	2.83	73	0	0	0	20	111⅓	103	40	35	42	95
1987	—Texas (A.L.)	5	10	.333	4.86	42	19	0	0	0	140⅔	157	92	76	56	106
1988	—Maine (Int'l)■	0	1	.000	1.93	3	0	0	0	1	4⅔	5	3	1	1	5
	—Philadelphia (N.L.)	4	6	.400	2.36	66	1	0	0	1	107	80	34	28	52	71
1989	—Philadelphia (N.L.)	2	2	.500	3.58	44	0	0	0	1	75⅓	64	34	30	43	51
	—Boston (A.L.)■	2	2	.500	2.57	15	0	0	0	0	28	21	12	8	15	25
1990	—Boston (A.L.)	13	9	.591	4.00	34	30	1	0	0	184⅓	186	90	82	77	117
1991	—Boston (A.L.)	11	12	.478	3.85	53	21	1	0	2	173	157	79	74	69	127
1992	—Boston (A.L.)	4	9	.308	2.51	70	2	1	0	4	107⅔	82	38	30	60	73
1993	—Boston (A.L.)	6	7	.462	3.77	*80	0	0	0	8	112⅓	95	55	47	60	103
A.L. totals (8 years)		56	61	.479	3.55	425	72	3	0	45	970⅓	875	441	383	422	757
N.L. totals (6 years)		13	21	.382	3.60	195	47	6	0	7	398	345	181	159	188	289
Major league totals (13 years)		69	82	.457	3.56	620	119	9	0	52	1368⅓	1220	622	542	610	1046

CHAMPIONSHIP SERIES RECORD

CHAMPIONSHIP SERIES NOTES: Shares single-game record for most earned runs allowed—7 (October 2, 1984).... Shares record for most hits allowed in one inning—6 (October 2, 1984, fifth inning).

Year	Team (League)	W	L	Pct.	ERA	G	GS	CG	ShO	Sv.	IP	H	R	ER	BB	SO
1984	—San Diego (N.L.)	0	0	...	31.50	1	0	0	0	0	2	9	8	7	3	2
1990	—Boston (A.L.)	0	1	.000	27.00	1	0	0	0	0	⅓	3	1	1	0	0
Champ. series totals (2 years)		0	1	.000	30.86	2	0	0	0	0	2⅓	12	9	8	3	2

WORLD SERIES RECORD

Year	Team (League)	W	L	Pct.	ERA	G	GS	CG	ShO	Sv.	IP	H	R	ER	BB	SO
1984	—San Diego (N.L.)	0	0	...	0.00	1	0	0	0	0	5⅓	3	0	0	3	5

HARRIS, GREG W.

P, ROCKIES

PERSONAL: Born December 1, 1963, in Greensboro, N.C.... 6-2/195.... Throws right, bats right.... Full name: Gregory Wade Harris.
HIGH SCHOOL: Jordan Matthews (Siler City, N.C.).
COLLEGE: Elon College (N.C.).
TRANSACTIONS/CAREER NOTES: Selected by San Diego Padres organization in 10th round of free-agent draft (June 3, 1985).... On San Diego disabled list (April 23-July 4, 1991); included rehabilitation assignment to Las Vegas (June 12-30).... On San Diego disabled list (June 1-21, 1992).... On San Diego disabled list (June 22-August 22, 1992); included rehabilitation assignment to High Desert (August 7-12) and Las Vegas (August 12-22).... Traded by Padres with P Bruce Hurst to Colorado Rockies for C Brad Ausmus, P Doug Bochtler and a player to be named later (July 26, 1993); Padres acquired P Andy Ashby to complete deal (July 27, 1993).
STATISTICAL NOTES: Pitched 7-0 no-hit victory against Midland (August 26, 1987).... Led Texas League with 32 home runs allowed and six balks in 1987.... Led N.L. with 32 home runs allowed in 1993.

Year	Team (League)	W	L	Pct.	ERA	G	GS	CG	ShO	Sv.	IP	H	R	ER	BB	SO
1985	—Spokane (N'west)	5	4	.556	3.40	13	13	1	0	0	87⅓	80	36	33	36	90
1986	—Char., S.C. (S. Atl.)	13	7	.650	2.63	27	27	8	2	0	*191⅓	176	69	56	54	176
1987	—Wichita (Texas)	12	11	.522	4.28	27	27	*7	•2	0	174⅓	205	103	83	49	170
1988	—Las Vegas (PCL)	9	5	.643	4.11	26	25	5	2	0	159⅔	160	84	73	65	147
	—San Diego (N.L.)	2	0	1.000	1.50	3	1	1	0	0	18	13	3	3	3	15
1989	—San Diego (N.L.)	8	9	.471	2.60	56	8	0	0	6	135	106	43	39	52	106
1990	—San Diego (N.L.)	8	8	.500	2.30	73	0	0	0	9	117⅓	92	35	30	49	97
1991	—San Diego (N.L.)	9	5	.643	2.23	20	20	3	2	0	133	116	42	33	27	95
	—Las Vegas (PCL)	1	2	.333	7.40	4	4	0	0	0	20⅔	24	20	17	8	16
1992	—San Diego (N.L.)	4	8	.333	4.12	20	20	1	0	0	118	113	62	54	35	66
	—High Desert (Calif.)	0	0	...	0.00	1	1	0	0	0	5⅓	2	0	0	1	5
	—Las Vegas (PCL)	2	0	1.000	0.56	2	2	0	0	0	16	8	1	1	1	15
1993	—S.D.-Colo. (N.L.)■	11	17	.393	4.59	35	35	4	0	0	225⅓	239	*127	115	69	123
Major league totals (6 years)		42	47	.472	3.30	207	84	9	2	15	746⅔	679	312	274	235	502

H

HARRIS, LENNY

IF, REDS

PERSONAL: Born October 28, 1964, in Miami. . . . 5-10/220. . . . Throws right, bats left. . . . Full name: Leonard Anthony Harris.
HIGH SCHOOL: Jackson (Miami).
COLLEGE: Miami-Dade (North) Community College.
TRANSACTIONS/CAREER NOTES: Selected by Cincinnati Reds organization in fifth round of free-agent draft (June 6, 1983). . . . Loaned by Reds organization to Glens Falls, Detroit Tigers organization (May 6-28, 1988). . . . Traded by Reds with OF Kal Daniels to Los Angeles Dodgers for P Tim Leary and SS Mariano Duncan (July 18, 1989). . . . Granted free agency (October 8, 1993). . . . Signed by Reds (December 1, 1993).
STATISTICAL NOTES: Led Florida State League third basemen with 34 double plays in 1985. . . . Led Eastern League third basemen with 116 putouts, 28 errors and 360 total chances in 1986. . . . Led American Association in caught stealing with 22 in 1988. . . . Led American Association second basemen with 23 errors in 1988.

			BATTING												FIELDING			
Year	**Team (League)**	**Pos.**	**G**	**AB**	**R**	**H**	**2B**	**3B**	**HR**	**RBI**	**Avg.**	**BB**	**SO**	**SB**	**PO**	**A**	**E**	**Avg.**
1983	—Billings (Pioneer)	3B	56	224	37	63	8	1	1	26	.281	13	35	7	34	95	22	.854
1984	—Ced. Rap. (Midw.)	3B	132	468	52	115	15	3	6	53	.246	42	59	31	111	204	*34	.903
1985	—Tampa (Fla. St.)	3B	132	499	66	129	11	8	3	51	.259	37	57	15	89	*277	*35	.913
1986	—Vermont (Eastern)	3B-SS	119	450	68	114	17	2	10	52	.253	29	38	36	†119	220	†28	.924
1987	—Nashville (A.A.)	SS-3B	120	403	45	100	12	3	2	31	.248	27	43	30	124	210	34	.908
1988	—Nashville (A.A.)	2B-SS-3B	107	422	46	117	20	2	0	35	.277	22	36	*45	203	247	†25	.947
	—Glens Falls (East.)■	2B	17	65	9	22	5	1	1	7	.338	9	6	6	40	49	5	.947
	—Cincinnati (N.L.)■	3B-2B	16	43	7	16	1	0	0	8	.372	5	4	4	14	33	1	.979
1989	—Nashville (A.A.)	2B	8	34	6	9	2	0	3	6	.265	0	5	0	23	20	0	1.000
	—Cin.-L.A. (N.L.)■	2-3-0-S	115	335	36	79	10	1	3	26	.236	20	33	14	147	168	15	.955
1990	—Los Angeles (N.L.)	3-2-0-S	137	431	61	131	16	4	2	29	.304	29	31	15	140	205	11	.969
1991	—Los Angeles (N.L.)	3-2-S-0	145	429	59	123	16	1	3	38	.287	37	32	12	125	250	20	.949
1992	—Los Angeles (N.L.)	2-3-0-S	135	347	28	94	11	0	0	30	.271	24	24	19	199	248	27	.943
1993	—Los Angeles (N.L.)	2-3-S-0	107	160	20	38	6	1	2	11	.238	15	15	3	61	99	3	.982
Major league totals (6 years)			655	1745	211	481	60	7	10	142	.276	130	139	67	686	1003	77	.956

HARRIS, REGGIE

P, MARINERS

PERSONAL: Born August 12, 1968, in Waynesboro, Va. . . . 6-1/190. . . . Throws right, bats right. . . . Full name: Reginald Allen Harris.
HIGH SCHOOL: Waynesboro (Va.).
TRANSACTIONS/CAREER NOTES: Selected by Boston Red Sox organization in first round (26th pick overall) of free-agent draft (June 2, 1987). . . . Selected by Oakland Athletics from Red Sox organization in Rule 5 major league draft (December 4, 1989). . . . On Oakland disabled list (March 29-July 3, 1990); included rehabilitation assignment to Huntsville (May 26-June 24). . . . On Tacoma disabled list (June 17-August 4, 1991). . . . Selected by Seattle Mariners from A's organization in Rule 5 major league draft (December 7, 1992). . . . On Jacksonville disabled list (May 19-28, 1993). . . . On Calgary temporary inactive list (July 21-August 1, 1993). . . . Granted free agency (October 15, 1993). . . . Re-signed by Mariners (November 11, 1993).
STATISTICAL NOTES: Led Pacific Coast League with 20 wild pitches in 1992.

Year	**Team (League)**	**W**	**L**	**Pct.**	**ERA**	**G**	**GS**	**CG**	**ShO**	**Sv.**	**IP**	**H**	**R**	**ER**	**BB**	**SO**
1987	—Elmira (N.Y.-Penn)	2	3	.400	5.01	9	8	1	1	0	46⅔	50	29	26	22	25
1988	—Lynchburg (Caro.)	1	8	.111	7.45	17	11	0	0	0	64	86	60	53	34	48
	—Elmira (N.Y.-Penn)	3	6	.333	5.30	10	10	0	0	0	54⅓	56	37	32	28	46
1989	—Winter Haven (FSL)	10	13	.435	3.99	29	26	1	0	0	153⅓	144	81	68	77	85
1990	—Huntsville (South.)■	0	2	.000	3.03	5	5	0	0	0	29⅔	26	12	10	16	34
	—Oakland (A.L.)	1	0	1.000	3.48	16	1	0	0	0	41⅓	25	16	16	21	31
1991	—Tacoma (PCL)	5	4	.556	4.99	16	15	0	0	0	83	83	55	46	58	72
	—Oakland (A.L.)	0	0	...	12.00	2	0	0	0	0	3	5	4	4	3	2
1992	—Tacoma (PCL)	6	*16	.273	5.71	29	•28	1	0	0	149⅔	141	*108	*95	*117	111
1993	—Jacksonv. (South.)■	1	4	.200	4.78	9	8	0	0	0	37⅔	33	24	20	22	30
	—Calgary (PCL)	8	6	.571	5.20	17	15	1	0	0	88⅓	74	55	51	61	75
Major league totals (2 years)		1	0	1.000	4.06	18	1	0	0	0	44⅓	30	20	20	24	33

HARTLEY, MIKE

P

PERSONAL: Born August 31, 1961, in Hawthorne, Calif. . . . 6-1/195. . . . Throws right, bats right. . . . Full name: Michael Edward Hartley.
HIGH SCHOOL: El Cajon Valley (Calif.).
COLLEGE: Grossmont College (Calif.).
TRANSACTIONS/CAREER NOTES: Signed as free agent by St. Louis Cardinals organization (November 27, 1981). . . . Selected by Los Angeles Dodgers organization from Cardinals organization in Rule 5 minor league draft (December 9, 1986). . . . Traded by Dodgers with OF Braulio Castillo to Philadelphia Phillies for P Roger McDowell (July 31, 1991). . . . On Philadelphia disabled list (March 31-May 13, 1992); included rehabilitation assignment to Scranton/Wilkes-Barre (April 12-25). . . . Traded by Phillies to Minnesota Twins for P David West (December 5, 1992). . . . Granted free agency (October 12, 1993). . . . Signed by Midland, California Angels organization (November 22, 1993). . . . Contract sold by Angels organization to Chiba Lotte Marines of Japan Pacific League (November 1993). . . . Selected by Calgary, Seattle Mariners organization, from Midland, Angels organization, in Rule 5 minor league draft (December 13, 1993); Angels compensated Mariners with cash for selling contract to Chiba Lotte.

Year	**Team (League)**	**W**	**L**	**Pct.**	**ERA**	**G**	**GS**	**CG**	**ShO**	**Sv.**	**IP**	**H**	**R**	**ER**	**BB**	**SO**
1982	—Johns. City (App.)	3	1	.750	2.79	8	5	0	0	0	29	32	12	9	8	13
1983	—St. Peters. (FSL)	1	3	.250	3.34	9	4	1	0	0	29⅔	25	14	11	24	18
	—Macon (S. Atl.)	2	3	.400	10.24	7	7	1	0	0	29	36	36	33	30	12
	—Erie (N.Y.-Penn)	1	3	.250	6.75	7	7	0	0	0	32	36	27	24	31	25
1984	—St. Peters. (FSL)	8	14	.364	4.20	31	31	4	1	0	139⅓	142	81	65	84	88
1985	—Springfield (Midw.)	2	7	.222	5.12	33	33	0	0	0	114⅓	119	77	65	62	100
1986	—Springfield (Midw.)	0	0	...	9.60	8	0	0	0	1	15	22	17	16	14	10
	—Savannah (S. Atl.)	5	7	.417	2.89	39	0	0	0	8	56	38	31	18	37	55
1987	—Bakersfield (Calif.)■	5	4	.556	2.57	33	0	0	0	15	56	44	19	16	24	72
	—San Antonio (Tex.)	3	4	.429	1.32	25	0	0	0	3	41	21	8	6	18	37

Year	Team (League)	W	L	Pct.	ERA	G	GS	CG	ShO	Sv.	IP	H	R	ER	BB	SO
	—Albuquerque (PCL)	0	1	.000	6.75	2	0	0	0	0	2⅔	5	3	2	3	3
1988	—San Antonio (Tex.)	5	1	.833	0.80	30	0	0	0	9	45	25	5	4	18	57
	—Albuquerque (PCL)	2	2	.500	4.35	18	0	0	0	3	20⅔	22	11	10	12	16
1989	—Albuquerque (PCL)	7	4	.636	2.79	58	0	0	0	18	77⅓	53	31	24	34	76
	—Los Angeles (N.L.)	0	1	.000	1.50	5	0	0	0	0	6	2	1	1	0	4
1990	—Los Angeles (N.L.)	6	3	.667	2.95	32	6	1	1	1	79⅓	58	32	26	30	76
	—Albuquerque (PCL)	0	0	...	0.00	3	0	0	0	2	3	3	0	0	2	3
1991	—L.A.-Phil. (N.L.)■	4	1	.800	4.21	58	0	0	0	2	83⅓	74	40	39	47	63
1992	—Scran./W.B. (Int'l)	1	2	.333	4.09	3	3	0	0	0	11	9	6	5	7	10
	—Philadelphia (N.L.)	7	6	.538	3.44	46	0	0	0	0	55	54	23	21	23	53
1993	—Minnesota (A.L.)■	1	2	.333	4.00	53	0	0	0	1	81	86	38	36	36	57
	A.L. totals (1 year)	1	2	.333	4.00	53	0	0	0	1	81	86	38	36	36	57
	N.L. totals (4 years)	17	11	.607	3.50	141	6	1	1	3	223⅔	188	96	87	100	196
	Major league totals (5 years)	18	13	.581	3.63	194	6	1	1	4	304⅔	274	134	123	136	253

HARVEY, BRYAN

P, MARLINS

PERSONAL: Born June 2, 1963, in Chattanooga, Tenn.... 6-2/212.... Throws right, bats right.... Full name: Bryan Stanley Harvey.
HIGH SCHOOL: Bandys (Catawba, N.C.).
COLLEGE: UNC Charlotte.

TRANSACTIONS/CAREER NOTES: Signed as free agent by California Angels organization (August 20, 1984).... On disabled list (April 12-22, 1985 and June 7-22 and July 1, 1992-remainder of season).... Selected by Florida Marlins in first round (20th pick overall) of expansion draft (November 17, 1992).

HONORS: Named A.L. Rookie Pitcher of the Year by THE SPORTING NEWS (1988).... Named A.L. co-Fireman of the Year by THE SPORTING NEWS (1991).

Year	Team (League)	W	L	Pct.	ERA	G	GS	CG	ShO	Sv.	IP	H	R	ER	BB	SO
1985	—Quad City (Midw.)	5	6	.455	3.53	30	7	0	0	4	81⅔	66	37	32	37	111
1986	—Palm Springs (Cal.)	3	4	.429	2.68	43	0	0	0	15	57	38	24	17	38	68
1987	—Midland (Texas)	2	2	.500	2.04	43	0	0	0	20	53	40	14	12	28	78
	—California (A.L.)	0	0	...	0.00	3	0	0	0	0	5	6	0	0	2	3
1988	—Edmonton (PCL)	0	0	...	3.18	5	0	0	0	2	5⅔	7	2	2	4	10
	—California (A.L.)	7	5	.583	2.13	50	0	0	0	17	76	59	22	18	20	67
1989	—California (A.L.)	3	3	.500	3.44	51	0	0	0	25	55	36	21	21	41	78
1990	—California (A.L.)	4	4	.500	3.22	54	0	0	0	25	64⅓	45	24	23	35	82
1991	—California (A.L.)	2	4	.333	1.60	67	0	0	0	*46	78⅔	51	20	14	17	101
1992	—California (A.L.)	0	4	.000	2.83	25	0	0	0	13	28⅔	22	12	9	11	34
1993	—Florida (N.L.)■	1	5	.167	1.70	59	0	0	0	45	69	45	14	13	13	73
	A.L. totals (6 years)	16	20	.444	2.49	250	0	0	0	126	307⅔	219	99	85	126	365
	N.L. totals (1 year)	1	5	.167	1.70	59	0	0	0	45	69	45	14	13	13	73
	Major league totals (7 years)	17	25	.405	2.34	309	0	0	0	171	376⅔	264	113	98	139	438

ALL-STAR GAME RECORD

Year	League	W	L	Pct.	ERA	GS	CG	ShO	Sv.	IP	H	R	ER	BB	SO
1991	—American						Did not play.								
1993	—National	0	0	...	0.00	0	0	0	0	1	1	0	0	0	2
	All-Star totals (1 year)	0	0	...	0.00	0	0	0	0	1	1	0	0	0	2

HASELMAN, BILL

C, MARINERS

PERSONAL: Born May 25, 1966, in Long Branch, N.J.... 6-3/220.... Throws right, bats right.... Full name: William Joseph Haselman.
HIGH SCHOOL: Saratoga (Calif.).
COLLEGE: UCLA.

TRANSACTIONS/CAREER NOTES: Selected by Texas Rangers organization in first round (23rd pick overall) of free-agent draft (June 2, 1987); pick received as compensation for New York Yankees signing Type A free agent Gary Ward.... On disabled list (March 28-May 4, 1992).... Claimed on waivers by Seattle Mariners (May 29, 1992).... On suspended list (July 22-25, 1993).

STATISTICAL NOTES: Led Texas League with 12 passed balls in 1989.... Led Texas League catchers with 676 putouts, 90 assists, 20 errors, 786 total chances and 20 passed balls in 1990.... Led American Association catchers with 673 putouts and 751 total chances in 1991.

			BATTING												FIELDING			
Year	Team (League)	Pos.	G	AB	R	H	2B	3B	HR	RBI	Avg.	BB	SO	SB	PO	A	E	Avg.
1987	—Gastonia (S. Atl.)	C	61	235	35	72	13	1	8	33	.306	19	46	1	26	2	2	.933
1988	—Charlotte (Fla. St.)	C	122	453	56	111	17	2	10	54	.245	45	99	8	249	30	6	.979
1989	—Tulsa (Texas)	C	107	352	38	95	17	2	7	36	.270	40	88	5	508	63	9	.984
1990	—Tulsa (Texas)	C-1-0-3	120	430	68	137	39	2	18	80	.319	43	96	3	†722	†93	†20	.976
	—Texas (A.L.)	C	7	13	0	2	0	0	0	3	.154	1	5	0	8	0	0	1.000
1991	—Okla. City (A.A.)	C-0-1-3	126	442	57	113	22	2	9	60	.256	61	89	10	†706	71	11	.986
1992	—Okla. City (A.A.)	OF-C	17	58	8	14	5	0	1	9	.241	13	12	1	45	7	3	.945
	—Calgary (PCL)■	C-OF	88	302	49	77	14	2	19	53	.255	41	89	3	227	23	6	.977
	—Seattle (A.L.)	C-OF	8	19	1	5	0	0	0	0	.263	0	7	0	19	2	0	1.000
1993	—Seattle (A.L.)	C-OF	58	137	21	35	8	0	5	16	.255	12	19	2	236	17	2	.992
	Major league totals (3 years)		73	169	22	42	8	0	5	19	.249	13	31	2	263	19	2	.993

H

HATCHER, BILLY

OF, RED SOX

PERSONAL: Born October 4, 1960, in Williams, Ariz.... 5-10/190.... Throws right, bats right.... Full name: William Augustus Hatcher.
HIGH SCHOOL: Williams (Ariz.).
COLLEGE: Yavapai College (Ariz.).

TRANSACTIONS/CAREER NOTES: Selected by Chicago Cubs organization in sixth round of free-agent draft (January 13, 1981). . . . On Chicago disabled list (August 19-September 3, 1985). . . . Traded by Cubs with a player to be named later to Houston Astros for OF Jerry Mumphrey (December 16, 1985); Astros organization acquired P Steve Engel to complete deal (July 24, 1986). . . . On disabled list (June 28-July 13, 1986 and July 7-22, 1987). . . . Traded by Astros to Pittsburgh Pirates for OF Glenn Wilson (August 18, 1989). . . . Traded by Pirates to Cincinnati Reds for P Mike Roesler and IF Jeff Richardson (April 3, 1990). . . . On disabled list (May 5-22, 1992). . . . Traded by Reds to Boston Red Sox for P Tom Bolton (July 9, 1992). . . . Granted free agency (November 2, 1992). . . . Re-signed by Red Sox (November 27, 1992).
RECORDS: Shares major league single-game record for most doubles—4 (August 21, 1990).
STATISTICAL NOTES: Led New York-Pennsylvania League in being hit by pitch with eight in 1981. . . . Led American Association in being hit by pitch with nine in 1984. . . . Tied for N.L. lead in double plays by outfielder with six in 1987.

			BATTING												FIELDING			
Year	**Team (League)**	**Pos.**	**G**	**AB**	**R**	**H**	**2B**	**3B**	**HR**	**RBI**	**Avg.**	**BB**	**SO**	**SB**	**PO**	**A**	**E**	**Avg.**
1981	—Geneva (NY-Penn)...	OF	•75	289	57	81	15	3	4	40	.280	36	41	13	138	7	11	.929
1982	—Salinas (Calif.)	OF	138	549	92	171	18	8	8	59	.311	40	47	84	235	10	12	.953
1983	—Midland (Texas).......	OF	135	545	*132	163	33	11	10	80	.299	65	61	56	286	17	•13	.959
1984	—Iowa (Am. Assoc.)....	OF	150	595	96	164	27	18	9	59	.276	51	54	56	303	15	7	.978
	—Chicago (N.L.)	OF	8	9	1	1	0	0	0	0	.111	1	0	2	2	1	0	1.000
1985	—Iowa (Am. Assoc.)....	OF	67	279	39	78	14	5	5	19	.280	24	40	17	157	4	4	.976
	—Chicago (N.L.)	OF	53	163	24	40	12	1	2	10	.245	8	12	2	77	2	1	.988
1986	—Houston (N.L.)■........	OF	127	419	55	108	15	4	6	36	.258	22	52	38	226	7	4	.983
1987	—Houston (N.L.).........	OF	141	564	96	167	28	3	11	63	.296	42	70	53	276	16	4	.986
1988	—Houston (N.L.).........	OF	145	530	79	142	25	4	7	52	.268	37	56	32	280	7	5	.983
1989	—Hou.-Pitts. (N.L.)■...	OF	135	481	59	111	19	3	4	51	.231	30	62	24	250	1	2	.992
1990	—Cincinnati (N.L.)■....	OF	139	504	68	139	28	5	5	25	.276	33	42	30	308	10	1	*.997
1991	—Cincinnati (N.L.).......	OF	138	442	45	116	25	3	4	41	.262	26	55	11	248	4	5	.981
1992	—Cincinnati (N.L.).......	OF	43	94	10	27	3	0	2	10	.287	5	11	0	29	0	1	.967
	—Boston (A.L.)■..........	OF	75	315	37	75	16	2	1	23	.238	17	41	4	145	5	5	.968
1993	—Boston (A.L.)	OF-2B	136	508	71	146	24	3	9	57	.287	28	46	14	284	6	2	.993
American League totals (2 years)			211	823	108	221	40	5	10	80	.269	45	87	18	429	11	7	.984
National League totals (9 years)			929	3206	437	851	155	23	41	288	.265	204	360	192	1696	48	23	.987
Major league totals (10 years)			1140	4029	545	1072	195	28	51	368	.266	249	447	210	2125	59	30	.986

CHAMPIONSHIP SERIES RECORD

CHAMPIONSHIP SERIES NOTES: Shares single-game record for most at-bats—7 (October 15, 1986, 16 innings).

			BATTING												FIELDING			
Year	**Team (League)**	**Pos.**	**G**	**AB**	**R**	**H**	**2B**	**3B**	**HR**	**RBI**	**Avg.**	**BB**	**SO**	**SB**	**PO**	**A**	**E**	**Avg.**
1986	—Houston (N.L.)..........	OF	6	25	4	7	0	0	1	2	.280	3	2	3	11	0	1	.917
1990	—Cincinnati (N.L.).......	OF	4	15	2	5	1	0	1	2	.333	0	2	0	5	1	0	1.000
Championship series totals (2 years)			10	40	6	12	1	0	2	4	.300	3	4	3	16	1	1	.944

WORLD SERIES RECORD

WORLD SERIES NOTES: Holds single-series records for highest batting average—.750 (1990); and most consecutive hits—7 (October 16 [3] and 17 [4], 1990). . . . Shares record for most at-bats in one inning—2 (October 19, 1990, third inning).

			BATTING												FIELDING			
Year	**Team (League)**	**Pos.**	**G**	**AB**	**R**	**H**	**2B**	**3B**	**HR**	**RBI**	**Avg.**	**BB**	**SO**	**SB**	**PO**	**A**	**E**	**Avg.**
1990	—Cincinnati (N.L.).......	OF	4	12	6	9	4	1	0	2	.750	2	0	0	11	0	0	1.000

HATCHER, CHRIS

OF, ASTROS

PERSONAL: Born January 7, 1969, in Anaheim, Calif. . . . 6-3/220. . . . Throws right, bats right. . . . Full name: Christopher Kenneth Hatcher.
HIGH SCHOOL: Thomas Jefferson (Council Bluffs, Ia.).
COLLEGE: Iowa.
TRANSACTIONS/CAREER NOTES: Selected by Houston Astros organization in third round of free-agent draft (June 4, 1990). . . . On disabled list (June 8-July 15, 1992 and June 3-July 1, 1993).

			BATTING												FIELDING			
Year	**Team (League)**	**Pos.**	**G**	**AB**	**R**	**H**	**2B**	**3B**	**HR**	**RBI**	**Avg.**	**BB**	**SO**	**SB**	**PO**	**A**	**E**	**Avg.**
1990	—Auburn (NY-Penn) ..	OF	72	259	37	64	10	0	9	45	.247	27	86	8	62	5	5	.931
1991	—Burlington (Midw.)...	OF	129	497	69	116	23	5	13	65	.233	46	*180	10	235	10	10	.961
1992	—Osceola (Fla. St.)......	OF	97	367	49	103	19	6	17	68	.281	20	97	11	139	8	5	.967
1993	—Jackson (Texas)	OF	101	367	45	95	15	3	15	64	.259	11	104	5	78	2	5	.941

HATHAWAY, HILLY

P, ANGELS

PERSONAL: Born September 12, 1969, in Jacksonville, Fla. . . . 6-4/195. . . . Throws left, bats left. . . . Full name: Hillary Houston Hathaway.
HIGH SCHOOL: Sandalwood (Jacksonville, Fla.).
COLLEGE: Manatee Junior College (Fla.).
TRANSACTIONS/CAREER NOTES: Selected by Boston Red Sox in 18th round of free-agent draft (June 1, 1988). . . . Selected by California Angels organization in 35th round of free-agent draft (June 5, 1989). . . . On Quad City disabled list (April 9-June 3, 1992). . . . On California disabled list (August 17-September 10, 1993).

Year	**Team (League)**	**W**	**L**	**Pct.**	**ERA**	**G**	**GS**	**CG**	**ShO**	**Sv.**	**IP**	**H**	**R**	**ER**	**BB**	**SO**
1990	—Boise (Northwest)......	8	2	.800	1.47	15	15	0	0	0	86	56	18	14	25	*113
1991	—Quad City (Midw.)......	9	6	.600	3.35	20	20	1	0	0	129	126	58	48	41	110
1992	—Palm Springs (Cal.)....	2	1	.667	1.50	3	3	2	1	0	24	25	5	4	3	17
	—Midland (Texas)	7	2	.778	3.21	14	14	1	0	0	95⅓	90	39	34	10	69
	—California (A.L.)	0	0	...	7.94	2	1	0	0	0	5⅔	8	5	5	3	1
1993	—Vancouver (PCL)	7	0	1.000	4.09	12	12	0	0	0	70⅓	60	38	32	27	44
	—California (A.L.)	4	3	.571	5.02	11	11	0	0	0	57⅓	71	35	32	26	11
Major league totals (2 years)		4	3	.571	5.29	13	12	0	0	0	63	79	40	37	29	12

HATTEBERG, SCOTT

C, RED SOX

PERSONAL: Born December 14, 1969, in Salem, Ore. . . . 6-1/185. . . . Throws right, bats left. . . . Full name: Scott Allen Hatteberg. . . . Name pronounced HAT-ee-berg.
HIGH SCHOOL: Eisenhower (Yakima, Wash.).
COLLEGE: Washington State.
TRANSACTIONS/CAREER NOTES: Selected by Philadelphia Phillies organization in 12th round of free-agent draft (June 1, 1988). . . . Selected by Boston Red Sox organization in supplemental round ("sandwich pick" between first and second round, 43rd pick overall) of free-agent draft (June 3, 1991); pick received as part of compensation for Kansas City signing Type A free agent Mike Boddicker. . . . On disabled list (July 27-August 3, 1992).

			BATTING												FIELDING			
Year	**Team (League)**	**Pos.**	**G**	**AB**	**R**	**H**	**2B**	**3B**	**HR**	**RBI**	**Avg.**	**BB**	**SO**	**SB**	**PO**	**A**	**E**	**Avg.**
1991	—Winter Haven (FSL)..	C	56	191	21	53	7	3	1	25	.277	22	22	1	261	35	5	.983
	—Lynchburg (Caro.)...	C	8	25	4	5	1	0	0	2	.200	7	6	0	35	2	0	1.000
1992	—New Britain (East.)..	C	103	297	28	69	13	2	1	30	.232	41	49	1	473	44	11	.979
1993	—New Britain (East.)..	C	68	227	35	63	10	2	7	28	.278	42	38	1	410	45	10	.978
	—Pawtucket (Int'l)......	C	18	53	6	10	0	0	1	2	.189	6	12	0	131	4	5	.964

HAWBLITZEL, RYAN

P, ROCKIES

PERSONAL: Born April 30, 1971, in West Palm Beach, Fla. . . . 6-2/170. . . . Throws right, bats right. . . . Full name: Ryan Wade Hawblitzel.
HIGH SCHOOL: John I. Leonard (Lake Worth, Fla.).
TRANSACTIONS/CAREER NOTES: Selected by Chicago Cubs organization in second round of free-agent draft (June 4, 1990). . . . Selected by Colorado Rockies in second round (38th pick overall) of expansion draft (November 17, 1992).

Year	**Team (League)**	**W**	**L**	**Pct.**	**ERA**	**G**	**GS**	**CG**	**ShO**	**Sv.**	**IP**	**H**	**R**	**ER**	**BB**	**SO**
1990	—Hunting. (Appal.).......	6	5	.545	3.93	14	14	2	1	0	75⅔	72	38	33	25	71
1991	—Winst.-Salem (Car.).....	•15	2	*.882	2.42	20	20	5	•2	0	134	110	40	36	47	103
	—Charlotte (South.).......	1	2	.333	3.21	5	5	1	1	0	33⅔	31	14	12	12	25
1992	—Charlotte (South.).......	12	8	.600	3.76	28	28	3	1	0	174⅔	180	84	73	38	119
1993	—Colo. Springs (PCL)■...	8	13	.381	6.15	29	*28	2	0	0	165⅓	*221	*129	*113	49	90

HAYES, CHARLIE

3B, ROCKIES

PERSONAL: Born May 29, 1965, in Hattiesburg, Miss. . . . 6-0/215. . . . Throws right, bats right. . . . Full name: Charles Dewayne Hayes.
HIGH SCHOOL: Forrest County Agricultural (Brooklyn, Miss.).
TRANSACTIONS/CAREER NOTES: Selected by San Francisco Giants organization in fourth round of free-agent draft (June 6, 1983). . . . On disabled list (July 20, 1983-remainder of season). . . . Traded by Giants with P Dennis Cook and P Terry Mulholland to Philadelphia Phillies for P Steve Bedrosian and a player to be named later (June 18, 1989); Giants organization acquired IF Rick Parker to complete deal (August 7, 1989). . . . Traded by Phillies to New York Yankees (February 19, 1992), completing deal in which Yankees traded P Darrin Chapin to Phillies for a player to be named later (January 8, 1992). . . . Selected by Colorado Rockies in first round (third pick overall) of expansion draft (November 17, 1992). . . . On suspended list (August 10-13, 1993).
STATISTICAL NOTES: Led Texas League third basemen with 27 double plays in 1986. . . . Led Texas League third basemen with 334 total chances in 1987. . . . Led Pacific Coast League in grounding into double plays with 19 in 1988. . . . Led N.L. third basemen with 324 assists and tied for lead with 465 total chances in 1990. . . . Tied for A.L. lead in double plays by third baseman with 29 in 1992. . . . Tied for N.L. lead in grounding into double plays with 25 in 1993.

			BATTING												FIELDING			
Year	**Team (League)**	**Pos.**	**G**	**AB**	**R**	**H**	**2B**	**3B**	**HR**	**RBI**	**Avg.**	**BB**	**SO**	**SB**	**PO**	**A**	**E**	**Avg.**
1983	—Great Falls (Pio.)......	3B-OF	34	111	9	29	4	2	0	9	.261	7	26	1	13	32	9	.833
1984	—Clinton (Midwest)....	3B	116	392	41	96	17	2	2	51	.245	34	110	4	68	216	28	.910
1985	—Fresno (California)..	3B	131	467	73	132	17	2	4	68	.283	56	95	7	*100	233	18	*.949
1986	—Shreveport (Texas)..	3B	121	434	52	107	23	2	5	45	.247	28	83	1	89	*259	25	.933
1987	—Shreveport (Texas)..	3B	128	487	66	148	33	3	14	75	.304	26	76	5	*100	*212	22	*.934
1988	—Phoenix (PCL)..........	OF-3B	131	492	71	151	26	4	7	71	.307	34	91	4	206	100	23	.930
	—San Francisco (N.L.)..	OF-3B	7	11	0	1	0	0	0	0	.091	0	3	0	5	0	0	1.000
1989	—Phoenix (PCL)..........	3-0-1-S-2	61	229	25	65	15	1	7	27	.284	15	48	5	76	76	8	.950
	—S.F.-Phil. (N.L.)■......	3B	87	304	26	78	15	1	8	43	.257	11	50	3	51	174	22	.911
	—Scran./W.B. (Int'l)...	3B	7	27	4	11	3	1	1	3	.407	0	3	0	8	8	0	1.000
1990	—Philadelphia (N.L.)...	3B-1B-2B	152	561	56	145	20	0	10	57	.258	28	91	4	151	†329	20	.960
1991	—Philadelphia (N.L.)...	3B-SS	142	460	34	106	23	1	12	53	.230	16	75	3	88	240	15	.956
1992	—New York (A.L.)■......	3B-1B	142	509	52	131	19	2	18	66	.257	28	100	3	125	249	13	.966
1993	—Colorado (N.L.)■.......	3B-SS	157	573	89	175	*45	2	25	98	.305	43	82	11	123	292	20	.954
American League totals (1 year)			142	509	52	131	19	2	18	66	.257	28	100	3	125	249	13	.966
National League totals (5 years)			545	1909	205	505	103	4	55	251	.265	98	301	21	418	1035	77	.950
Major league totals (6 years)			687	2418	257	636	122	6	73	317	.263	126	401	24	543	1284	90	.953

HEATON, NEAL

P

PERSONAL: Born March 3, 1960, in Jamaica, N.Y. . . . 6-1/205. . . . Throws left, bats left.
HIGH SCHOOL: Sachem (Lake Ronkonkoma, N.Y.).
COLLEGE: Miami (Fla.).
TRANSACTIONS/CAREER NOTES: Selected by New York Mets organization in first round (first pick overall) of free-agent draft (January 9, 1979). . . . Selected by Cleveland Indians organization in second round of free-agent draft (June 8, 1981). . . . Traded by Indians to Minnesota Twins for P John Butcher (June 20, 1986). . . . Traded by Twins with P Al Cardwood, P Yorkis Perez and C Jeff Reed to Montreal Expos for P Jeff Reardon and C Tom Nieto (February 3, 1987). . . . On disabled list (April 8-29, 1988). . . . Traded by Expos to Pittsburgh Pirates for a player to be named later (March 28, 1989); Expos acquired P Brett Gideon to complete deal (March 30, 1989). . . . Granted free agency (November 13, 1989). . . . Re-signed by Pirates (December 6, 1989). . . . Traded by Pirates to Kansas City Royals for OF Kirk Gibson (March 10, 1992). . . . On suspended list (July 2-6, 1992). . . . Released by Royals (July 30, 1992). . . . Signed by Denver, Milwaukee Brewers or-

ganization (August 12, 1992).... Released by Brewers (October 15, 1992).... Signed by New York Yankees organization (February 2, 1993).... Released by Yankees (June 27, 1993).
HONORS: Named lefthanded pitcher on THE SPORTING NEWS college All-America team (1981).
MISCELLANEOUS: Appeared in one game as pinch-runner and received base on balls in only appearance as pinch-hitter (1991).

Year	Team (League)	W	L	Pct.	ERA	G	GS	CG	ShO	Sv.	IP	H	R	ER	BB	SO
1981	—Chatt. (South.)	4	4	.500	3.97	11	11	4	0	0	77	61	42	34	27	50
1982	—Char., W.Va. (Int'l)	10	5	.667	4.01	29	29	5	2	0	172⅔	194	97	77	66	105
	—Cleveland (A.L.)	0	2	.000	5.23	8	4	0	0	0	31	32	21	18	16	14
1983	—Cleveland (A.L.)	11	7	.611	4.16	39	16	4	3	7	149⅓	157	79	69	44	75
1984	—Cleveland (A.L.)	12	15	.444	5.21	38	34	4	1	0	198⅔	231	128	115	75	75
1985	—Cleveland (A.L.)	9	17	.346	4.90	36	33	5	1	0	207⅔	244	119	113	80	82
1986	—Clev.-Minn. (A.L.)■	7	15	.318	4.08	33	29	5	0	1	198⅔	201	102	90	81	90
1987	—Montreal (N.L.)■	13	10	.565	4.52	32	32	3	1	0	193⅓	207	103	97	37	105
1988	—Montreal (N.L.)	3	10	.231	4.99	32	11	0	0	2	97⅓	98	54	54	43	43
1989	—Pittsburgh (N.L.)■	6	7	.462	3.05	42	18	1	0	0	147⅓	127	55	50	55	67
1990	—Pittsburgh (N.L.)	12	9	.571	3.45	30	24	0	0	0	146	143	66	56	38	68
1991	—Pittsburgh (N.L.)	3	3	.500	4.33	42	1	0	0	0	68⅔	72	37	33	21	34
1992	—K.C.-Mil. (A.L.)■	3	1	.750	4.07	32	0	0	0	0	42	43	21	19	23	31
	—Denver (A.A.)	2	1	.667	3.52	6	4	0	0	0	23	23	10	9	8	9
1993	—New York (A.L.)■	1	0	1.000	6.00	18	0	0	0	0	27	34	19	18	11	15
A.L. totals (7 years)		43	57	.430	4.66	204	116	18	5	8	854⅓	942	489	442	330	382
N.L. totals (5 years)		37	39	.487	4.00	178	86	4	1	2	652⅔	647	315	290	194	317
Major league totals (12 years)		80	96	.455	4.37	382	202	22	6	10	1507	1589	804	732	524	699

ALL-STAR GAME RECORD

Year	League	W	L	Pct.	ERA	GS	CG	ShO	Sv.	IP	H	R	ER	BB	SO
1990	—National						Did not play.								

HELFAND, ERIC

C, ATHLETICS

PERSONAL: Born March 25, 1969, in Erie, Pa.... 6-0/195.... Throws right, bats left.... Full name: Eric James Helfand.... Name pronounced HELL-fand.
HIGH SCHOOL: Patrick Henry (San Diego).
COLLEGE: Nebraska, then Arizona State.
TRANSACTIONS/CAREER NOTES: Selected by Seattle Mariners organization in eighth round of free-agent draft (June 2, 1987).... Selected by Oakland Athletics in second round of free-agent draft (June 4, 1990); pick received as part of compensation for Kansas City Royals signing Type A free agent Storm Davis.... On Modesto disabled list (June 9-July 30, 1991).... Selected by Florida Marlins in first round (18th pick overall) of expansion draft (November 17, 1992).... Traded by Marlins with a player to be named later to A's for SS Walt Weiss (November 17, 1992); A's acquired P Scott Baker to complete deal (November 20, 1992).
STATISTICAL NOTES: Tied for Northwest League lead with 13 passed balls in 1990.... Led Southern League catchers with 12 double plays in 1993.

			BATTING												FIELDING			
Year	Team (League)	Pos.	G	AB	R	H	2B	3B	HR	RBI	Avg.	BB	SO	SB	PO	A	E	Avg.
1990	—S. Oregon (N'west)	C	57	207	29	59	12	0	2	39	.285	20	49	4	383	33	5	.988
1991	—Modesto (Calif.)	C	67	242	35	62	15	1	7	38	.256	37	56	0	314	48	8	.978
1992	—Modesto (Calif.)	C	72	249	40	72	15	0	10	44	.289	47	46	0	422	47	13	.973
	—Huntsville (South.)	C	37	114	13	26	7	0	2	9	.228	5	32	0	180	21	2	.990
1993	—Huntsville (South.)	C-OF	100	302	38	69	15	2	10	48	.228	43	78	1	603	63	10	.985
	—Oakland (A.L.)	C	8	13	1	3	0	0	0	1	.231	0	1	0	25	5	0	1.000
Major league totals (1 year)			8	13	1	3	0	0	0	1	.231	0	1	0	25	5	0	1.000

HELLING, RICK

P, RANGERS

PERSONAL: Born December 15, 1970, in Devils Lake, N.D.... 6-3/215.... Throws right, bats right.... Full name: Ricky Allen Helling.
HIGH SCHOOL: Shanley (Fargo, N.D.) and Lakota (N.D.).
COLLEGE: North Dakota, Kishwaukee College (Ill.) and Stanford.
TRANSACTIONS/CAREER NOTES: Selected by New York Mets organization in 50th round of free-agent draft (June 4, 1990).... Selected by Texas Rangers organization in first round (22nd pick overall) of free-agent draft (June 1, 1992).
MISCELLANEOUS: Member of 1992 U.S. Olympic baseball team.

Year	Team (League)	W	L	Pct.	ERA	G	GS	CG	ShO	Sv.	IP	H	R	ER	BB	SO
1992	—Charlotte (Fla. St.)	1	1	.500	2.29	3	3	0	0	0	19⅔	13	5	5	4	20
1993	—Tulsa (Texas)	12	8	.600	3.60	26	26	2	•2	0	177⅓	150	76	71	46	*188
	—Okla. City (A.A.)	1	1	.500	1.64	2	2	1	0	0	11	5	3	2	3	17

HEMOND, SCOTT

C, ATHLETICS

PERSONAL: Born November 18, 1965, in Taunton, Mass.... 6-0/215.... Throws right, bats right.... Full name: Scott Matthew Hemond.... Name pronounced HEE-mond.
HIGH SCHOOL: Dunedin (Fla.).
COLLEGE: South Florida.
TRANSACTIONS/CAREER NOTES: Selected by Kansas City Royals organization in fifth round of free-agent draft (June 6, 1983).... Selected by Oakland Athletics organization in first round (12th pick overall) of free-agent draft (June 2, 1986).... On Tacoma disabled list (May 18-July 6, 1990).... On Oakland disabled list (May 10-August 6, 1992); included rehabilitation assignment to Huntsville (June 5-15) and Tacoma (July 17-August 6).... Claimed on waivers by Chicago White Sox (August 6, 1992).... Claimed on waivers by A's (March 29, 1993).
HONORS: Named catcher on THE SPORTING NEWS college All-America team (1986).
STATISTICAL NOTES: Led Southern League third basemen with 299 assists and 427 total chances in 1988.

			BATTING												FIELDING			
Year	**Team (League)**	**Pos.**	**G**	**AB**	**R**	**H**	**2B**	**3B**	**HR**	**RBI**	**Avg.**	**BB**	**SO**	**SB**	**PO**	**A**	**E**	**Avg.**
1986	—Madison (Midwest) ..	C	22	85	9	26	2	0	2	13	.306	5	19	2	121	11	2	.985
1987	—Madison (Midwest) ..	C-OF	90	343	60	99	21	4	8	52	.289	40	79	27	408	53	16	.966
	—Huntsville (South.) ...	C-3B	33	110	10	20	3	1	1	8	.182	4	30	5	161	32	6	.970
1988	—Huntsville (South.) ...	3B-C	133	482	51	106	22	4	9	53	.220	48	114	29	93	†302	38	.912
1989	—Huntsville (South.) ...	3B-C	132	490	89	130	26	6	5	62	.265	62	77	45	272	198	31	.938
	—Oakland (A.L.)	PR	4	0	2	0	0	0	0	0	...	0	0	0	...	...	...	...
1990	—Tacoma (PCL)	2-C-3-S	72	218	32	53	11	0	8	35	.243	24	52	11	138	177	12	.963
	—Oakland (A.L.)	3B-2B	7	13	0	2	0	0	0	1	.154	0	5	0	2	5	0	1.000
1991	—Tacoma (PCL)	2-C-3-S	92	327	50	89	19	5	3	31	.272	39	69	11	280	177	12	.974
	—Oakland (A.L.)	C-2-3-S	23	23	4	5	0	0	0	0	.217	1	7	1	27	14	1	.976
1992	—Oak.-Chi. (A.L.)■	C-0-3-S-2	25	40	8	9	2	0	0	2	.225	4	13	1	34	6	1	.976
	—Huntsville (South.) ...	C-2B	9	27	3	9	0	0	0	2	.333	4	8	2	22	5	0	1.000
	—Tacoma (PCL)	2B-C	8	33	6	8	3	0	0	3	.242	5	6	1	35	16	2	.962
1993	—Oakland (A.L.)■	C-0-2-1	91	215	31	55	16	0	6	26	.256	32	55	14	404	39	4	.991
Major league totals (5 years)			150	291	45	71	18	0	6	29	.244	37	80	16	467	64	6	.989

HENDERSON, DAVE

OF, ROYALS

PERSONAL: Born July 21, 1958, in Dos Palos, Calif. ... 6-2/220. ... Throws right, bats right. ... Full name: David Lee Henderson. ... Nephew of Joe Henderson, pitcher, Chicago White Sox and Cincinnati Reds (1974, 1976-77).
HIGH SCHOOL: Dos Palos (Calif.).

TRANSACTIONS/CAREER NOTES: Selected by Seattle Mariners organization in first round (26th pick overall) of free-agent draft (June 7, 1977). ... On disabled list (June 26-July 22, 1980; May 3-18, 1982; and August 10-29, 1984). ... Traded by Mariners with IF Spike Owen to Boston Red Sox for IF Rey Quinones, a player to be named later and cash (August 19, 1986); as part of deal, Mariners claimed P Mike Brown and P Mike Trujillo on waivers from Red Sox (August 22, 1986). Mariners acquired OF John Christensen to complete deal (September 25, 1986). ... Traded by Red Sox to San Francisco Giants for a player to be named later (September 1, 1987); Red Sox acquired OF Randy Kutcher to complete deal (December 9, 1987). ... Granted free agency (November 9, 1987). ... Signed by Oakland Athletics (December 21, 1987). ... Granted free agency (November 4, 1988). ... Re-signed by A's (December 1, 1988). ... On disabled list (August 21-September 21, 1990). ... Granted free agency (December 7, 1990). ... Re-signed by A's (December 11, 1990). ... On Oakland disabled list (March 31-April 30, 1992). ... On Oakland disabled list (May 6-September 1, 1992); included rehabilitation assignment to Modesto (July 7-10 and July 13-14) and Tacoma (July 10-13). ... On Oakland disabled list (June 5-29, 1993); included rehabilitation assignment to Tacoma (June 26-29). ... Granted free agency (October 29, 1993). ... Signed by Kansas City Royals (January 27, 1994).
STATISTICAL NOTES: Hit three home runs in one game (August 3, 1991).

			BATTING												FIELDING			
Year	**Team (League)**	**Pos.**	**G**	**AB**	**R**	**H**	**2B**	**3B**	**HR**	**RBI**	**Avg.**	**BB**	**SO**	**SB**	**PO**	**A**	**E**	**Avg.**
1977	—Belling. (N'west)	OF	65	251	47	79	14	2	•16	63	.315	33	78	5	136	5	*11	.928
1978	—Stockton (Calif.)	OF	117	409	48	95	16	4	7	63	.232	62	100	11	204	12	14	.939
1979	—San Jose (Calif.)	OF	136	507	103	152	23	3	27	99	.300	56	115	19	264	18	4	.986
1980	—Spokane (PCL)	OF	109	341	48	95	26	1	7	50	.279	49	62	16	258	9	7	.974
1981	—Seattle (A.L.)	OF	59	126	17	21	3	0	6	13	.167	16	24	2	105	4	0	1.000
	—Spokane (PCL)	OF	80	272	47	76	23	1	12	50	.279	47	56	3	146	7	3	.981
1982	—Seattle (A.L.)	OF	104	324	47	82	17	1	14	48	.253	36	67	2	249	11	4	.985
1983	—Seattle (A.L.)	OF	137	484	50	130	24	5	17	55	.269	28	93	9	304	17	6	.982
1984	—Seattle (A.L.)	OF	112	350	42	98	23	0	14	43	.280	19	56	5	242	11	3	.988
1985	—Seattle (A.L.)	OF	139	502	70	121	28	2	14	68	.241	48	104	6	335	8	5	.986
1986	—Sea.-Boston (A.L.)■.	OF	139	388	59	103	22	4	15	47	.265	39	110	2	231	11	5	.980
1987	—Boston (A.L.)	OF	75	184	30	43	10	0	8	25	.234	22	48	1	114	0	5	.958
	—San Francisco (N.L.)■	OF	15	21	2	5	2	0	0	1	.238	8	5	2	10	1	0	1.000
1988	—Oakland (A.L.)■	OF	146	507	100	154	38	1	24	94	.304	47	92	2	382	5	7	.982
1989	—Oakland (A.L.)	OF	152	579	77	145	24	3	15	80	.250	54	131	8	385	5	9	.977
1990	—Oakland (A.L.)	OF	127	450	65	122	28	0	20	63	.271	40	105	3	319	5	4	.988
1991	—Oakland (A.L.)	OF-2B	150	572	86	158	33	0	25	85	.276	58	113	6	362	10	1	.997
1992	—Oakland (A.L.)	OF	20	63	1	9	1	0	0	2	.143	2	16	0	19	0	1	.950
	—Modesto (Calif.)	OF	3	13	3	4	1	0	1	2	.308	0	3	0	4	0	0	1.000
	—Tacoma (PCL)	OF	3	11	0	2	0	0	0	1	.182	0	3	0	2	0	0	1.000
1993	—Oakland (A.L.)	OF	107	382	37	84	19	0	20	53	.220	32	113	0	205	7	2	.991
	—Tacoma (PCL)	OF	3	11	1	2	1	0	0	2	.182	0	2	0	7	0	0	1.000
American League totals (13 years)			1467	4911	681	1270	270	16	192	676	.259	441	1072	46	3252	94	52	.985
National League totals (1 year)			15	21	2	5	2	0	0	1	.238	8	5	2	10	1	0	1.000
Major league totals (13 years)			1482	4932	683	1275	272	16	192	677	.259	449	1077	48	3262	95	52	.985

CHAMPIONSHIP SERIES RECORD

			BATTING												FIELDING			
Year	**Team (League)**	**Pos.**	**G**	**AB**	**R**	**H**	**2B**	**3B**	**HR**	**RBI**	**Avg.**	**BB**	**SO**	**SB**	**PO**	**A**	**E**	**Avg.**
1986	—Boston (A.L.)	OF	5	9	3	1	0	0	1	4	.111	2	2	0	11	0	0	1.000
1988	—Oakland (A.L.)	OF	4	16	2	6	1	0	1	4	.375	1	7	0	11	0	2	.846
1989	—Oakland (A.L.)	OF	5	19	4	5	3	0	1	1	.263	2	5	0	22	0	0	1.000
1990	—Oakland (A.L.)	OF	2	6	0	1	0	0	0	1	.167	0	2	1	7	0	0	1.000
Championship series totals (4 years)			16	50	9	13	4	0	3	10	.260	5	16	1	51	0	2	.962

WORLD SERIES RECORD

WORLD SERIES NOTES: Shares record for most home runs in two consecutive innings—2 (October 27, 1989, fourth and fifth innings).

			BATTING												FIELDING			
Year	**Team (League)**	**Pos.**	**G**	**AB**	**R**	**H**	**2B**	**3B**	**HR**	**RBI**	**Avg.**	**BB**	**SO**	**SB**	**PO**	**A**	**E**	**Avg.**
1986	—Boston (A.L.)	OF	7	25	6	10	1	1	2	5	.400	2	6	0	22	0	0	1.000
1988	—Oakland (A.L.)	OF	5	20	1	6	2	0	0	1	.300	2	7	0	12	0	0	1.000

Year	Team (League)	Pos.	G	AB	R	H	2B	3B	HR	RBI	Avg.	BB	SO	SB	PO	A	E	Avg.
			BATTING												FIELDING			
1989	—Oakland (A.L.)	OF	4	13	6	4	2	0	2	4	.308	4	3	0	13	0	0	1.000
1990	—Oakland (A.L.)	OF-PH	4	13	2	3	1	0	0	0	.231	1	3	0	7	0	0	1.000
World Series totals (4 years)			20	71	15	23	6	1	4	10	.324	9	19	0	54	0	0	1.000

ALL-STAR GAME RECORD

Year	League	Pos.	AB	R	H	2B	3B	HR	RBI	Avg.	BB	SO	SB	PO	A	E	Avg.
			BATTING											FIELDING			
1991	—American	OF	2	0	0	0	0	0	0	.000	0	1	0	2	0	0	1.000

HENDERSON, RICKEY

OF, ATHLETICS

PERSONAL: Born December 25, 1958, in Chicago. . . . 5-10/190. . . . Throws left, bats right. . . . Full name: Rickey Henley Henderson.

HIGH SCHOOL: Technical (Oakland, Calif.).

TRANSACTIONS/CAREER NOTES: Selected by Oakland Athletics organization in fourth round of free-agent draft (June 8, 1976). . . . Traded by A's with P Bert Bradley and cash to New York Yankees for OF Stan Javier, P Jay Howell, P Jose Rijo, P Eric Plunk and P Tim Birtsas (December 5, 1984). . . . On New York disabled list (March 30-April 22, 1985); included rehabilitation assignment to Fort Lauderdale (April 19-22). . . . On disabled list (June 5-29 and July 26-September 1, 1987). . . . Traded by Yankees to A's for P Greg Cadaret, P Eric Plunk and OF Luis Polonia (June 21, 1989). . . . Granted free agency (November 13, 1989). . . . Re-signed by A's (November 28, 1989). . . . On disabled list (April 12-27, 1991 and May 28-June 17 and June 30-July 16, 1992). . . . Traded by A's to Toronto Blue Jays for P Steve Karsay and a player to be named later (July 31, 1993); A's acquired OF Jose Herrera to complete deal (August 6, 1993). . . . Granted free agency (October 29, 1993). . . . Signed by A's (December 17, 1993).

RECORDS: Holds major league career records for most home runs as leadoff batter—63; stolen bases—1,095. . . . Holds major league single-season records for most stolen bases—130 (1982); and most times caught stealing—42 (1982). . . . Holds major league record for most years leading league in stolen bases—11. . . . Holds A.L. career record for most times caught stealing—248. . . . Holds A.L. single-season record for most home runs as leadoff batter—9 (1986). . . . Holds A.L. records for most years with 50 or more stolen bases—11; and most consecutive years with 50 or more stolen bases—7 (1980-86). . . . Shares A.L. single-season record for fewest times caught stealing (50 or more stolen bases)—8 (1993). . . . Shares A.L. record for most stolen bases in two consecutive games—7 (July 3 [4], 15 innings, and 4 [3], 1983).

HONORS: Named outfielder on THE SPORTING NEWS A.L. All-Star team (1981, 1985 and 1990). . . . Named outfielder on THE SPORTING NEWS A.L. Silver Slugger team (1981, 1985 and 1990). . . . Won A.L. Gold Glove as outfielder (1981). . . . Won THE SPORTING NEWS Silver Shoe Award (1982). . . . Won THE SPORTING NEWS Golden Shoe Award (1983). . . . Named A.L. Most Valuable Player by Baseball Writers' Association of America (1990).

STATISTICAL NOTES: Led California League in caught stealing with 22 in 1977. . . . Led Eastern League in caught stealing with 28 in 1978. . . . Led Eastern League outfielders with four double plays in 1978. . . . Led A.L. in caught stealing with 26 in 1980, 22 in 1981, 42 in 1982, 19 in 1983 and tied for lead with 18 in 1986. . . . Led A.L. outfielders with 341 total chances in 1981. . . . Tied for A.L. lead in double plays by outfielder with five in 1988. . . . Led A.L. with .439 on-base percentage in 1990.

Year	Team (League)	Pos.	G	AB	R	H	2B	3B	HR	RBI	Avg.	BB	SO	SB	PO	A	E	Avg.
			BATTING												FIELDING			
1976	—Boise (Northwest)	OF	46	140	34	47	13	2	3	23	.336	33	32	29	99	3	*12	.895
1977	—Modesto (Calif.)	OF	134	481	120	166	18	4	11	69	.345	104	67	*95	278	15	*20	.936
1978	—Jersey City (East.)	OF	133	455	81	141	14	4	0	34	.310	83	67	*81	305	•15	7	.979
1979	—Ogden (Pac. Coast)	OF	71	259	66	80	11	8	3	26	.309	53	41	44	149	6	6	.963
	—Oakland (A.L.)	OF	89	351	49	96	13	3	1	26	.274	34	39	33	215	5	6	.973
1980	—Oakland (A.L.)	OF	158	591	111	179	22	4	9	53	.303	117	54	*100	407	15	7	.984
1981	—Oakland (A.L.)	OF	108	423	*89	*135	18	7	6	35	.319	64	68	*56	*327	7	7	.979
1982	—Oakland (A.L.)	OF	149	536	119	143	24	4	10	51	.267	*116	94	*130	379	2	9	.977
1983	—Oakland (A.L.)	OF	145	513	105	150	25	7	9	48	.292	*103	80	*108	349	9	3	.992
1984	—Oakland (A.L.)	OF	142	502	113	147	27	4	16	58	.293	86	81	*66	341	7	11	.969
1985	—Fort Lauder. (FSL)■	OF	3	6	5	1	0	1	0	3	.167	5	2	1	6	0	0	1.000
	—New York (A.L.)	OF	143	547	*146	172	28	5	24	72	.314	99	65	*80	439	7	9	.980
1986	—New York (A.L.)	OF	153	608	*130	160	31	5	28	74	.263	89	81	*87	426	4	6	.986
1987	—New York (A.L.)	OF	95	358	78	104	17	3	17	37	.291	80	52	41	189	3	4	.980
1988	—New York (A.L.)	OF	140	554	118	169	30	2	6	50	.305	82	54	*93	320	7	12	.965
1989	—N.Y.-Oak. (A.L.)■	OF	150	541	•113	148	26	3	12	57	.274	*126	68	*77	335	6	4	.988
1990	—Oakland (A.L.)	OF	136	489	*119	159	33	3	28	61	.325	97	60	*65	289	5	5	.983
1991	—Oakland (A.L.)	OF	134	470	105	126	17	1	18	57	.268	98	73	*58	249	10	8	.970
1992	—Oakland (A.L.)	OF	117	396	77	112	18	3	15	46	.283	95	56	48	231	9	4	.984
1993	—Oak.-Tor. (A.L.)■	OF	134	481	114	139	22	2	21	59	.289	120	65	53	258	6	7	.974
Major league totals (15 years)			1993	7360	1586	2139	351	56	220	784	.291	1406	990	1095	4754	102	102	.979

DIVISION SERIES RECORD

Year	Team (League)	Pos.	G	AB	R	H	2B	3B	HR	RBI	Avg.	BB	SO	SB	PO	A	E	Avg.
			BATTING												FIELDING			
1981	—Oakland (A.L.)	OF	3	11	3	2	0	0	0	0	.182	2	0	2	8	0	0	1.000

CHAMPIONSHIP SERIES RECORD

CHAMPIONSHIP SERIES NOTES: Named A.L. Championship Series Most Valuable Player (1989). . . . Holds career record for most stolen bases—16. . . . Holds single-series record for most stolen bases—8 (1989). . . . Holds single-game record for most stolen bases—4 (October 4, 1989). . . . Shares records for most at-bats in one inning—2; most hits in one inning—2; most singles in one inning—2 (October 6, 1990, ninth inning); and most stolen bases in one inning—2 (October 4, 1989, fourth and seventh innings). . . . Shares single-series record for most runs—8 (1989). . . . Shares A.L. career record for most bases on balls received—17. . . . Shares A.L. single-game record for most at-bats—6 (October 5, 1993).

Year	Team (League)	Pos.	G	AB	R	H	2B	3B	HR	RBI	Avg.	BB	SO	SB	PO	A	E	Avg.
			BATTING												FIELDING			
1981	—Oakland (A.L.)	OF	3	11	0	4	2	1	0	1	.364	1	2	2	6	0	1	.857
1989	—Oakland (A.L.)	OF	5	15	8	6	1	1	2	5	.400	7	0	8	13	0	1	.929

Year	Team (League)	Pos.	G	AB	R	H	2B	3B	HR	RBI	Avg.	BB	SO	SB	PO	A	E	Avg.
			BATTING												FIELDING			
1990	—Oakland (A.L.)	OF	4	17	1	5	0	0	0	3	.294	1	2	2	10	0	0	1.000
1992	—Oakland (A.L.)	OF	6	23	5	6	0	0	0	1	.261	4	4	2	15	0	3	.833
1993	—Toronto (A.L.)	OF	6	25	4	3	2	0	0	0	.120	4	5	2	9	0	1	.900
	Championship series totals (5 years)		24	91	18	24	5	2	2	10	.264	17	13	16	53	0	6	.898

WORLD SERIES RECORD

WORLD SERIES NOTES: Shares single-game record for most at-bats—6 (October 28, 1989).

Year	Team (League)	Pos.	G	AB	R	H	2B	3B	HR	RBI	Avg.	BB	SO	SB	PO	A	E	Avg.
			BATTING												FIELDING			
1989	—Oakland (A.L.)	OF	4	19	4	9	1	2	1	3	.474	2	2	3	9	0	0	1.000
1990	—Oakland (A.L.)	OF	4	15	2	5	2	0	1	1	.333	3	4	3	12	1	0	1.000
1993	—Toronto (A.L.)	OF	6	22	6	5	2	0	0	2	.227	5	2	1	8	0	0	1.000
	World Series totals (3 years)		14	56	12	19	5	2	2	6	.339	10	8	7	29	1	0	1.000

ALL-STAR GAME RECORD

ALL-STAR GAME NOTES: Shares single-game record for most singles—3 (July 13, 1982).

Year	League	Pos.	AB	R	H	2B	3B	HR	RBI	Avg.	BB	SO	SB	PO	A	E	Avg.
			BATTING											FIELDING			
1980	—American	OF	1	0	0	0	0	0	0	.000	0	1	0	0	0	0	...
1982	—American	OF	4	1	3	0	0	0	0	.750	0	0	1	3	0	1	.750
1983	—American	OF	1	0	0	0	0	0	1	.000	0	0	0	0	0	0	...
1984	—American	OF	2	0	0	0	0	0	0	.000	0	0	0	0	0	0	...
1985	—American	OF	3	1	1	0	0	0	0	.333	0	1	1	1	0	0	1.000
1986	—American	OF	3	0	0	0	0	0	0	.000	0	1	0	2	0	0	1.000
1987	—American	OF	3	0	1	0	0	0	0	.333	0	0	0	0	0	0	...
1988	—American	OF	2	0	1	0	0	0	0	.500	1	0	0	1	0	0	1.000
1990	—American	OF	3	0	0	0	0	0	0	.000	0	1	0	2	0	0	1.000
1991	—American	OF	2	1	1	0	0	0	0	.500	0	0	0	0	0	0	...
	All-Star Game totals (10 years)		24	3	7	0	0	0	1	.292	1	4	2	9	0	1	.900

HENKE, TOM

P, RANGERS

PERSONAL: Born December 21, 1957, in Kansas City, Mo. . . . 6-5/225. . . . Throws right, bats right. . . . Full name: Thomas Anthony Henke. . . . Name pronounced HEN-kee.
HIGH SCHOOL: Blair Oaks (Jefferson City, Mo.).
COLLEGE: East Central College (Mo.).

TRANSACTIONS/CAREER NOTES: Selected by Seattle Mariners organization in 20th round of free-agent draft (June 5, 1979). . . . Selected by Chicago Cubs organization in secondary phase of free-agent draft (January 8, 1980). . . . Selected by Texas Rangers organization in secondary phase of free-agent draft (June 3, 1980). . . . Selected by Toronto Blue Jays organization in player compensation pool draft (January 24, 1985); pick received as compensation for Rangers signing Type A free agent DH Cliff Johnson (December 5, 1984). . . . On Toronto disabled list (April 12-May 17, 1991); included rehabilitation assignment to Dunedin but did not pitch (May 13-17). . . . Granted free agency (October 27, 1992). . . . Signed by Rangers (December 15, 1992).

HONORS: Named International League Pitcher of the Year (1985).

Year	Team (League)	W	L	Pct.	ERA	G	GS	CG	ShO	Sv.	IP	H	R	ER	BB	SO
1980	—GC Rangers (GCL)	3	3	.500	0.95	8	4	1	1	0	38	33	11	4	12	34
	—Asheville (S. Atl.)	0	2	.000	7.83	5	5	0	0	0	23	25	21	20	20	19
1981	—Asheville (S. Atl.)	8	6	.571	2.93	28	8	0	0	3	92	77	36	30	35	67
	—Tulsa (Texas)	4	3	.571	3.94	15	0	0	0	1	32	31	16	14	14	37
1982	—Tulsa (Texas)	3	6	.333	2.67	*52	1	0	0	14	87⅔	69	35	26	40	100
	—Texas (A.L.)	1	0	1.000	1.15	8	0	0	0	0	15⅔	14	2	2	8	9
1983	—Okla. City (A.A.)	9	6	.600	3.01	47	0	0	0	2	77⅔	71	33	26	33	90
	—Texas (A.L.)	1	0	1.000	3.38	8	0	0	0	1	16	16	6	6	4	17
1984	—Texas (A.L.)	1	1	.500	6.35	25	0	0	0	2	28⅓	36	21	20	20	25
	—Okla. City (A.A.)	6	2	.750	2.64	39	0	0	0	7	64⅔	59	21	19	25	65
1985	—Syracuse (Int'l)■	2	1	.667	0.88	39	0	0	0	•18	51⅓	13	5	5	18	60
	—Toronto (A.L.)	3	3	.500	2.03	28	0	0	0	13	40	29	12	9	8	42
1986	—Toronto (A.L.)	9	5	.643	3.35	63	0	0	0	27	91⅓	63	39	34	32	118
1987	—Toronto (A.L.)	0	6	.000	2.49	72	0	0	0	*34	94	62	27	26	25	128
1988	—Toronto (A.L.)	4	4	.500	2.91	52	0	0	0	25	68	60	23	22	24	66
1989	—Toronto (A.L.)	8	3	.727	1.92	64	0	0	0	20	89	66	20	19	25	116
1990	—Toronto (A.L.)	2	4	.333	2.17	61	0	0	0	32	74⅔	58	18	18	19	75
1991	—Toronto (A.L.)	0	2	.000	2.32	49	0	0	0	32	50⅓	33	13	13	11	53
1992	—Toronto (A.L.)	3	2	.600	2.26	57	0	0	0	34	55⅔	40	19	14	22	46
1993	—Texas (A.L.)■	5	5	.500	2.91	66	0	0	0	40	74⅓	55	25	24	27	79
	Major league totals (12 years)	37	35	.514	2.67	553	0	0	0	260	697⅓	532	225	207	225	774

CHAMPIONSHIP SERIES RECORD

Year	Team (League)	W	L	Pct.	ERA	G	GS	CG	ShO	Sv.	IP	H	R	ER	BB	SO
1985	—Toronto (A.L.)	2	0	1.000	4.26	3	0	0	0	0	6⅓	5	3	3	4	4
1989	—Toronto (A.L.)	0	0	...	0.00	3	0	0	0	0	2⅔	0	0	0	0	3
1991	—Toronto (A.L.)	0	0	...	0.00	2	0	0	0	0	2⅔	0	0	0	1	5
1992	—Toronto (A.L.)	0	0	...	0.00	4	0	0	0	3	4⅔	4	0	0	2	2
	Champ. series totals (4 years)	2	0	1.000	1.65	12	0	0	0	3	16⅓	9	3	3	7	14

WORLD SERIES RECORD

Year	Team (League)	W	L	Pct.	ERA	G	GS	CG	ShO	Sv.	IP	H	R	ER	BB	SO
1992	—Toronto (A.L.)	0	0	...	2.70	3	0	0	0	2	3⅓	2	1	1	2	1

ALL-STAR GAME RECORD

Year League	W	L	Pct.	ERA	GS	CG	ShO	Sv.	IP	H	R	ER	BB	SO
1987—American	0	0	...	0.00	0	0	0	0	2⅔	2	0	0	0	1

HENKEL, ROB

P, RED SOX

PERSONAL: Born November 23, 1970, in Dallas. . . . 6-3/190. . . . Throws right, bats right. . . . Full name: Robert Henry Henkel.
HIGH SCHOOL: Irving (Tex.).
COLLEGE: San Jacinto (Central) College (Tex.).
TRANSACTIONS/CAREER NOTES: Selected by Houston Astros organization in 38th round of free-agent draft (June 5, 1989). . . . Selected by Boston Red Sox organization in 18th round of free-agent draft (June 4, 1990). . . . On Elmira disabled list (July 2-9, 1991). . . . On disabled list (August 3, 1993-remainder of season).

Year Team (League)	W	L	Pct.	ERA	G	GS	CG	ShO	Sv.	IP	H	R	ER	BB	SO
1991—GC Red Sox (GCL)	1	0	1.000	1.80	1	1	0	0	0	5	4	1	1	1	7
—Elmira (N.Y.-Penn)	6	3	.667	2.34	18	11	0	0	2	77	58	34	20	33	87
1992—Winter Haven (FSL)	5	7	.417	3.32	19	19	3	2	0	116⅔	110	48	43	37	102
1993—Lynchburg (Caro.)	8	7	.533	4.29	18	18	*7	2	0	113⅓	120	60	54	27	96

HENNEMAN, MIKE

P, TIGERS

PERSONAL: Born December 11, 1961, in St. Charles, Mo. . . . 6-4/205. . . . Throws right, bats right. . . . Full name: Michael Alan Henneman. . . . Name pronounced HENN-uh-min.
HIGH SCHOOL: St. Pius X (Festus, Mo.).
COLLEGE: Oklahoma State.
TRANSACTIONS/CAREER NOTES: Selected by Toronto Blue Jays organization in 27th round of free-agent draft (June 7, 1982). . . . Selected by Philadelphia Phillies organization in secondary phase of free-agent draft (June 6, 1983). . . . Selected by Detroit Tigers organization in fourth round of free-agent draft (June 4, 1984). . . . On disabled list (May 22-June 6, 1988 and April 24-May 15, 1989).
HONORS: Named A.L. Rookie Pitcher of the Year by THE SPORTING NEWS (1987).
MISCELLANEOUS: Struck out in only at-bat with Detroit (1987).

Year Team (League)	W	L	Pct.	ERA	G	GS	CG	ShO	Sv.	IP	H	R	ER	BB	SO
1984—Birm. (Southern)	4	2	.667	2.43	29	1	0	0	6	59⅓	48	22	16	33	39
1985—Birm. (Southern)	3	5	.375	5.76	46	0	0	0	9	70⅓	88	50	45	28	40
1986—Nashville (A.A.)	2	5	.286	2.95	31	0	0	0	1	58	57	27	19	23	39
1987—Toledo (Int'l)	1	1	.500	1.47	11	0	0	0	4	18⅓	5	3	3	3	19
—Detroit (A.L.)	11	3	.786	2.98	55	0	0	0	7	96⅔	86	36	32	30	75
1988—Detroit (A.L.)	9	6	.600	1.87	65	0	0	0	22	91⅓	72	23	19	24	58
1989—Detroit (A.L.)	11	4	.733	3.70	60	0	0	0	8	90	84	46	37	51	69
1990—Detroit (A.L.)	8	6	.571	3.05	69	0	0	0	22	94⅓	90	36	32	33	50
1991—Detroit (A.L.)	10	2	.833	2.88	60	0	0	0	21	84⅓	81	29	27	34	61
1992—Detroit (A.L.)	2	6	.250	3.96	60	0	0	0	24	77⅓	75	36	34	20	58
1993—Detroit (A.L.)	5	3	.625	2.64	63	0	0	0	24	71⅔	69	28	21	32	58
Major league totals (7 years)	56	30	.651	3.00	432	0	0	0	128	605⅔	557	234	202	224	429

CHAMPIONSHIP SERIES RECORD

Year Team (League)	W	L	Pct.	ERA	G	GS	CG	ShO	Sv.	IP	H	R	ER	BB	SO
1987—Detroit (A.L.)	1	0	1.000	10.80	3	0	0	0	0	5	6	6	6	6	3

ALL-STAR GAME RECORD

Year League	W	L	Pct.	ERA	GS	CG	ShO	Sv.	IP	H	R	ER	BB	SO
1989—American	Did not play.													

HENRY, BUTCH

P, EXPOS

PERSONAL: Born October 7, 1968, in El Paso, Tex. . . . 6-1/195. . . . Throws left, bats left. . . . Full name: Floyd Bluford Henry III.
HIGH SCHOOL: Eastwood (El Paso, Tex.).
TRANSACTIONS/CAREER NOTES: Selected by Cincinnati Reds organization in 15th round of free-agent draft (June 2, 1987). . . . On disabled list (April 28, 1989-remainder of season). . . . Traded by Reds with C Terry McGriff and P Keith Kaiser to Houston Astros (September 7, 1990), completing deal in which Astros traded 2B Bill Doran to Reds for three players to be named later (August 30, 1990). . . . Selected by Colorado Rockies in second round (36th pick overall) of expansion draft (November 17, 1992). . . . Traded by Rockies to Montreal Expos for P Kent Bottenfield (July 16, 1993).

Year Team (League)	W	L	Pct.	ERA	G	GS	CG	ShO	Sv.	IP	H	R	ER	BB	SO
1987—Billings (Pioneer)	4	0	1.000	4.63	9	5	0	0	1	35	37	21	18	12	38
1988—Ced. Rap. (Midw.)	16	2	*.889	2.26	27	27	1	1	0	187	144	59	47	56	163
1989—Chatt. (South.)	1	3	.250	3.42	7	7	0	0	0	26⅓	22	12	10	12	19
1990—Chatt. (South.)	8	8	.500	4.21	24	22	2	0	0	143⅓	151	74	67	58	95
1991—Tucson (PCL)■	10	11	.476	4.80	27	27	2	0	0	153⅔	192	92	82	42	97
1992—Houston (N.L.)	6	9	.400	4.02	28	28	2	1	0	165⅔	185	81	74	41	96
1993—Colo.-Mont. (N.L.)■	3	9	.250	6.12	30	16	1	0	0	103	135	76	70	28	47
—Ottawa (Int'l)	3	1	.750	3.73	5	5	1	0	0	31⅓	34	15	13	1	25
Major league totals (2 years)	9	18	.333	4.82	58	44	3	1	0	268⅔	320	157	144	69	143

HENRY, DOUG

P, BREWERS

PERSONAL: Born December 10, 1963, in Sacramento, Calif. . . . 6-4/205. . . . Throws right, bats right. . . . Full name: Richard Douglas Henry.
HIGH SCHOOL: Tennyson (Hayward, Calif.).
COLLEGE: Arizona State.

TRANSACTIONS/CAREER NOTES: Selected by New York Mets organization in 16th round of free-agent draft (June 7, 1982).... Selected by Milwaukee Brewers organization in eighth round of free-agent draft (June 3, 1985).... On El Paso disabled list (April 5-June 5 and June 18-August 9, 1989).
STATISTICAL NOTES: Combined with Michael Ignasiak in 6-3 no-hit victory for Stockton against San Jose (April 15, 1990, first game).

Year	Team (League)	W	L	Pct.	ERA	G	GS	CG	ShO	Sv.	IP	H	R	ER	BB	SO
1986	—Beloit (Midwest)	7	8	.467	4.65	27	24	4	1	1	143⅓	153	95	74	56	115
1987	—Beloit (Midwest)	8	9	.471	4.88	31	15	1	0	2	132⅔	145	83	72	51	106
1988	—Stockton (Calif.)	7	1	.875	1.78	23	1	1	0	7	70⅔	46	19	14	31	71
	—El Paso (Texas)	4	0	1.000	3.15	14	3	3	1	0	45⅔	33	16	16	19	50
1989	—Stockton (Calif.)	0	1	.000	0.00	4	3	0	0	0	11	9	4	0	3	9
	—El Paso (Texas)	0	0	...	13.50	1	1	0	0	0	2	3	3	3	3	2
1990	—Stockton (Calif.)	1	0	1.000	1.13	4	0	0	0	1	8	4	1	1	3	13
	—El Paso (Texas)	1	0	1.000	2.93	15	0	0	0	9	30⅔	31	13	10	11	25
	—Denver (A.A.)	2	3	.400	4.44	27	0	0	0	8	50⅔	46	26	25	27	54
1991	—Denver (A.A.)	3	2	.600	2.18	32	0	0	0	14	57⅔	47	16	14	20	47
	—Milwaukee (A.L.)	2	1	.667	1.00	32	0	0	0	15	36	16	4	4	14	28
1992	—Milwaukee (A.L.)	1	4	.200	4.02	68	0	0	0	29	65	64	34	29	24	52
1993	—Milwaukee (A.L.)	4	4	.500	5.56	54	0	0	0	17	55	67	37	34	25	38
Major league totals (3 years)		7	9	.438	3.87	154	0	0	0	61	156	147	75	67	63	118

HENRY, DWAYNE

P

PERSONAL: Born February 16, 1962, in Elkton, Md.... 6-3/230.... Throws right, bats right.... Full name: Dwayne Allen Henry.
HIGH SCHOOL: Middletown (Del.).
TRANSACTIONS/CAREER NOTES: Selected by Texas Rangers organization in second round of free-agent draft (June 3, 1980).... On disabled list (May 4, 1982-remainder of season).... On Tulsa disabled list (April 8-July 9, 1983).... On Texas disabled list (May 31-July 8, 1986); included rehabilitation assignment to Oklahoma City (June 18-July 8).... Traded by Rangers to Atlanta Braves for P David Miller and cash (March 30, 1989).... Released by Braves organization (November 13, 1990).... Signed by Tucson, Houston Astros organization (March 29, 1991).... Claimed on waivers by Cincinnati Reds (November 26, 1991).... Contract sold by Reds to Seattle Mariners (April 13, 1993).... On disabled list (July 3-August 2, 1993).... Released by Mariners (October 4, 1993).... Signed by Chunichi Dragons of Japan Central League (December 6, 1993).

Year	Team (League)	W	L	Pct.	ERA	G	GS	CG	ShO	Sv.	IP	H	R	ER	BB	SO
1980	—GC Rangers (GCL)	5	1	.833	2.67	11	11	1	1	0	54	36	23	16	28	47
1981	—Asheville (S. Atl.)	8	7	.533	4.43	25	25	1	0	0	134	120	81	66	58	86
1982	—Burlington (Midw.)	2	0	1.000	0.00	4	4	0	0	0	18⅔	6	0	0	6	25
1983	—Tulsa (Texas)	0	0	...	5.79	9	2	0	0	1	14	16	14	9	19	14
	—GC Rangers (GCL)	0	0	...	4.00	3	2	0	0	0	9	10	6	4	1	11
1984	—Tulsa (Texas)	5	8	.385	3.39	33	12	1	1	8	85	65	42	32	60	79
	—Texas (A.L.)	0	1	.000	8.31	3	0	0	0	0	4⅓	5	4	4	7	2
1985	—Tulsa (Texas)	7	6	.538	2.66	34	11	0	0	9	81⅓	51	32	24	44	97
	—Texas (A.L.)	2	2	.500	2.57	16	0	0	0	3	21	16	7	6	7	20
1986	—Texas (A.L.)	1	0	1.000	4.66	19	0	0	0	0	19⅓	14	11	10	2	17
	—Okla. City (A.A.)	2	1	.667	5.89	28	1	0	0	3	44⅓	51	30	29	27	41
1987	—Okla. City (A.A.)	4	4	.500	4.96	30	8	0	0	3	69	66	39	38	50	55
	—Texas (A.L.)	0	0	...	9.00	5	0	0	0	0	10	12	10	10	9	7
1988	—Okla. City (A.A.)	5	5	.500	5.59	46	3	0	0	7	75⅔	57	51	47	54	98
	—Texas (A.L.)	0	1	.000	8.71	11	0	0	0	1	10⅓	15	10	10	9	10
1989	—Richmond (Int'l)■	11	5	.688	2.44	41	6	0	0	1	84⅔	43	28	23	61	101
	—Atlanta (N.L.)	0	2	.000	4.26	12	0	0	0	1	12⅔	12	6	6	5	16
1990	—Atlanta (N.L.)	2	2	.500	5.63	34	0	0	0	0	38⅓	41	26	24	25	34
	—Richmond (Int'l)	1	1	.500	2.33	13	0	0	0	2	27	12	7	7	16	36
1991	—Houston (N.L.)■	3	2	.600	3.19	52	0	0	0	2	67⅔	51	25	24	39	51
1992	—Cincinnati (N.L.)■	3	3	.500	3.33	60	0	0	0	0	83⅔	59	31	31	44	72
1993	—Cincinnati (N.L.)	0	1	.000	3.86	3	0	0	0	0	4⅔	6	8	2	4	2
	—Seattle (A.L.)■	2	1	.667	6.67	31	1	0	0	2	54	56	40	40	35	35
A.L. totals (6 years)		5	5	.500	6.05	85	1	0	0	6	119	118	82	80	69	91
N.L. totals (5 years)		8	10	.444	3.78	161	0	0	0	3	207	169	96	87	117	175
Major league totals (10 years)		13	15	.464	4.61	246	1	0	0	9	326	287	178	167	186	266

HENTGEN, PAT

P, BLUE JAYS

PERSONAL: Born November 13, 1968, in Detroit.... 6-2/200.... Throws right, bats right.... Full name: Patrick George Hentgen.... Name pronounced HENT-ghen.
HIGH SCHOOL: Fraser (Mich.).
TRANSACTIONS/CAREER NOTES: Selected by Toronto Blue Jays organization in fifth round of free-agent draft (June 2, 1986).... On Toronto disabled list (August 13-September 29, 1992); included rehabilitation assignment to Syracuse (September 1-8).
STATISTICAL NOTES: Combined with relievers Willie Blair and Enrique Burgos in 2-1 no-hit victory against Osceola (May 10, 1988).

Year	Team (League)	W	L	Pct.	ERA	G	GS	CG	ShO	Sv.	IP	H	R	ER	BB	SO
1986	—St. Cathar. (NYP)	0	4	.000	4.50	13	11	0	0	1	40	38	27	20	30	30
1987	—Myrtle Beach (SAL)	11	5	.688	2.35	32	*31	2	2	0	*188	145	62	49	60	131
1988	—Dunedin (Fla. St.)	3	12	.200	3.45	31	*30	0	0	0	151⅓	139	80	58	65	125
1989	—Dunedin (Fla. St.)	9	8	.529	2.68	29	28	0	0	0	151⅓	123	53	45	71	148
1990	—Knoxville (South.)	9	5	.643	3.05	28	26	0	0	0	153⅓	121	57	52	68	142
1991	—Syracuse (Int'l)	8	9	.471	4.47	31	•28	1	0	0	171	146	91	85	*90	*155
	—Toronto (A.L.)	0	0	...	2.45	3	1	0	0	0	7⅓	5	2	2	3	3

Year	Team (League)	W	L	Pct.	ERA	G	GS	CG	ShO	Sv.	IP	H	R	ER	BB	SO
1992	—Toronto (A.L.)	5	2	.714	5.36	28	2	0	0	0	50⅓	49	30	30	32	39
	—Syracuse (Int'l)	1	2	.333	2.66	4	4	0	0	0	20⅓	15	6	6	8	17
1993	—Toronto (A.L.)	19	9	.679	3.87	34	32	3	0	0	216⅓	215	103	93	74	122
Major league totals (3 years)		24	11	.686	4.11	65	35	3	0	0	274	269	135	125	109	164

CHAMPIONSHIP SERIES RECORD

Year	Team (League)	W	L	Pct.	ERA	G	GS	CG	ShO	Sv.	IP	H	R	ER	BB	SO
1993	—Toronto (A.L.)	0	1	.000	18.00	1	1	0	0	0	3	9	6	6	2	3

WORLD SERIES RECORD

Year	Team (League)	W	L	Pct.	ERA	G	GS	CG	ShO	Sv.	IP	H	R	ER	BB	SO
1993	—Toronto (A.L.)	1	0	1.000	1.50	1	1	0	0	0	6	5	1	1	3	6

ALL-STAR GAME RECORD

Year	League	W	L	Pct.	ERA	GS	CG	ShO	Sv.	IP	H	R	ER	BB	SO
1993	—American							Did not play.							

HEREDIA, GIL

P, EXPOS

PERSONAL: Born October 26, 1965, in Nogales, Ariz. . . . 6-1/205. . . . Throws right, bats right. . . . Name pronounced err-AY-dee-uh.

HIGH SCHOOL: Nogales (Ariz.).

COLLEGE: Pima Community College (Ariz.) and Arizona.

TRANSACTIONS/CAREER NOTES: Selected by Pittsburgh Pirates organization in first round (16th pick overall) of free-agent draft (January 17, 1984). . . . Selected by Baltimore Orioles organization in sixth round of free-agent draft (January 9, 1985). . . . Selected by San Francisco Giants organization in ninth round of free-agent draft (June 2, 1987). . . . Loaned by Giants organization to San Luis Potosi of Mexican League (1989). . . . Claimed on waivers by Montreal Expos (August 18, 1992).

Year	Team (League)	W	L	Pct.	ERA	G	GS	CG	ShO	Sv.	IP	H	R	ER	BB	SO
1987	—Everett (N'west)	2	0	1.000	3.60	3	3	1	0	0	20	24	8	8	1	14
	—Fresno (California)	5	3	.625	2.90	11	11	5	2	0	80⅔	62	28	26	23	60
1988	—San Jose (Calif.)	13	12	.520	3.49	27	27	9	0	0	*206⅓	•216	107	80	46	121
1989	—Shreveport (Texas)	1	0	1.000	2.55	7	2	1	0	0	24⅔	28	10	7	4	8
	—San Luis Pot. (Mex.)■	14	9	.609	2.99	24	24	15	3	0	180⅔	183	73	60	35	125
1990	—Phoenix (PCL)■	9	7	.563	4.10	29	19	0	0	1	147	159	81	67	37	75
1991	—Phoenix (PCL)	9	11	.450	*2.82	33	15	•5	1	1	140⅓	155	60	44	28	75
	—San Francisco (N.L.)	0	2	.000	3.82	7	4	0	0	0	33	27	14	14	7	13
1992	—Phoenix (PCL)	5	5	.500	2.01	22	7	1	1	1	80⅔	83	30	18	13	37
	—S.F.-Mont. (N.L.)■	2	3	.400	4.23	20	5	0	0	0	44⅔	44	23	21	20	22
	—Indianapolis (A.A.)	2	0	1.000	1.02	3	3	0	0	0	17⅔	18	2	2	3	10
1993	—Ottawa (Int'l)	8	4	.667	2.98	16	16	1	0	0	102⅔	97	46	34	26	66
	—Montreal (N.L.)	4	2	.667	3.92	20	9	1	0	2	57⅓	66	28	25	14	40
Major league totals (3 years)		6	7	.462	4.00	47	18	1	0	2	135	137	65	60	41	75

HERNANDEZ, CARLOS

C, DODGERS

PERSONAL: Born May 24, 1967, in San Felix, Bolivar, Venezuela. . . . 5-11/218. . . . Throws right, bats right. . . . Full name: Carlos Alberto Hernandez.

HIGH SCHOOL: Escuela Tecnica Industrial (San Felix, Bolivar, Venezuela).

TRANSACTIONS/CAREER NOTES: Signed as free agent by Los Angeles Dodgers organization (October 10, 1984). . . . On Albuquerque disabled list (May 27-June 20, 1990).

STATISTICAL NOTES: Tied for Gulf Coast League lead in double plays by catcher with three in 1986. . . . Led Texas League catchers with 737 total chances in 1989. . . . Led Pacific Coast League catchers with 684 total chances in 1991.

			BATTING											FIELDING			
Year	Team (League)	Pos.	G	AB	R	H	2B	3B	HR	RBI	Avg.	BB	SO	SB	PO	A	E	Avg.
1985	—GC Dodgers (GCL)	3B-1B	22	49	3	12	1	0	0	0	.245	3	8	0	48	16	2	.970
1986	—GC Dodgers (GCL)	C-3B	57	205	19	64	7	0	1	31	.312	5	18	1	217	36	10	.962
1987	—Bakersfield (Calif.)	C	48	162	22	37	6	1	3	22	.228	14	23	8	181	26	8	.963
1988	—Bakersfield (Calif.)	C	92	333	37	103	15	2	5	52	.309	16	39	3	480	88	14	.976
	—Albuquerque (PCL)	C	3	8	0	1	0	0	0	1	.125	0	0	0	11	0	1	.917
1989	—San Antonio (Tex.)	C	99	370	37	111	16	3	8	41	.300	12	46	2	*629	*90	*18	.976
	—Albuquerque (PCL)	C	4	14	1	3	0	0	0	1	.214	2	1	0	23	3	3	.897
1990	—Albuquerque (PCL)	C	52	143	11	45	8	1	0	16	.315	8	25	2	207	31	8	.967
	—Los Angeles (N.L.)	C	10	20	2	4	1	0	0	1	.200	0	2	0	37	2	0	1.000
1991	—Albuquerque (PCL)	C	95	345	60	119	24	2	8	44	.345	24	36	5	*592	*77	*15	.978
	—Los Angeles (N.L.)	C-3B	15	14	1	3	1	0	0	1	.214	0	5	1	24	4	1	.966
1992	—Los Angeles (N.L.)	C	69	173	11	45	4	0	3	17	.260	11	21	0	295	37	7	.979
1993	—Los Angeles (N.L.)	C	50	99	6	25	5	0	2	7	.253	2	11	0	181	15	7	.966
Major league totals (4 years)			144	306	20	77	11	0	5	26	.252	13	39	1	537	58	15	.975

HERNANDEZ, CESAR

OF

PERSONAL: Born September 28, 1966, in Yamasa, Dominican Republic. . . . 6-0/160. . . . Throws right, bats right. . . . Full name: Cesar Dario Perez Hernandez.

HIGH SCHOOL: Juan Pablo Duarte (Santo Domingo, Dominican Republic).

COLLEGE: University of Autonoma (Santo Domingo, Dominican Republic).

TRANSACTIONS/CAREER NOTES: Selected by Montreal Expos (first overall) in Dominican Draft (March 2, 1985). . . . On disabled list (June 3, 1986-remainder of season). . . . Claimed on waivers by Cincinnati Reds (December 2, 1991). . . . Released by Indianapolis, Reds organization (September 20, 1993).

STATISTICAL NOTES: Led Southern League outfielders with five double plays in 1992.

H

Year	Team (League)	Pos.	G	AB	R	H	2B	3B	HR	RBI	Avg.	BB	SO	SB	PO	A	E	Avg.
				BATTING											FIELDING			
1985	—S.F. de Mac. (DSL)	OF	64	252	58	87	9	2	2	51	.345	22	31	22	...	...	...	...
1986	—Burlington (Midw.)	OF	38	104	12	26	11	0	1	12	.250	7	24	7	62	1	3	.955
1987	—W.P. Beach (FSL)	OF	32	106	14	25	3	1	2	6	.236	4	29	6	60	4	3	.955
1988	—Rockford (Midw.)	OF	117	411	71	101	20	4	19	60	.246	25	109	28	188	9	16	.925
1989	—W.P. Beach (FSL)	OF	42	158	16	45	8	3	1	15	.285	8	32	16	53	6	0	1.000
	—Jacksonv. (South.)	OF	81	222	25	47	9	1	3	13	.212	22	60	11	109	7	11	.913
1990	—Jacksonv. (South.)	OF	118	393	58	94	21	7	10	50	.239	18	75	17	203	14	3	.986
1991	—Harrisburg (East.)	OF	128	418	58	106	15	2	13	52	.254	25	106	34	222	*21	5	.980
1992	—Chatt. (South.)■	OF	93	328	50	91	24	4	3	27	.277	19	65	12	242	14	10	.962
	—Nashville (A.A.)	OF	1	2	0	2	0	0	0	0	1.000	0	0	0	1	0	1	.500
	—Cincinnati (N.L.)	OF	34	51	6	14	4	0	0	4	.275	0	10	3	18	2	1	.952
1993	—Cincinnati (N.L.)	OF	27	24	3	2	0	0	0	1	.083	1	8	1	30	2	1	.970
	—Indianapolis (A.A.)	OF	84	272	30	70	12	4	5	22	.257	9	63	5	183	9	3	.985
Major league totals (2 years)			61	75	9	16	4	0	0	5	.213	1	18	4	48	4	2	.963

HERNANDEZ, JEREMY

P, INDIANS

PERSONAL: Born July 6, 1966, in Burbank, Calif. . . . 6-6/195. . . . Throws right, bats right. . . . Full name: Jeremy Stuart Hernandez.
HIGH SCHOOL: Francis Poly (Sun Valley, Calif.).
COLLEGE: Cal State Northridge.

TRANSACTIONS/CAREER NOTES: Selected by St. Louis Cardinals organization in second round of free-agent draft (June 2, 1987). . . . Traded by Cardinals organization to Charleston, S.C., San Diego Padres organization, for OF Randell Byers (April 24, 1989). . . . Traded by Padres to Cleveland Indians for OF Tracy Sanders and P Fernando Hernandez (June 1, 1993).
STATISTICAL NOTES: Led Texas League with 18 home runs allowed in 1990.

Year	Team (League)	W	L	Pct.	ERA	G	GS	CG	ShO	Sv.	IP	H	R	ER	BB	SO
1987	—Erie (N.Y.-Penn)	5	4	.556	2.81	16	16	1	0	0	99⅓	87	36	31	41	62
1988	—Springfield (Midw.)	12	6	.667	3.54	24	24	3	1	0	147⅓	133	73	58	34	97
1989	—St. Peters. (FSL)	0	2	.000	7.71	3	3	0	0	0	14	17	14	12	5	5
	—Char., S.C. (S. Atl.)■	3	5	.375	3.53	10	10	2	1	0	58⅔	65	37	23	16	39
	—Riverside (Calif.)	5	2	.714	1.75	9	9	4	1	0	67	55	17	13	11	65
	—Wichita (Texas)	2	1	.667	8.53	4	3	0	0	0	19	30	18	18	8	9
1990	—Wichita (Texas)	7	6	.538	4.53	26	26	1	0	0	155	163	92	78	50	101
1991	—Las Vegas (PCL)	4	8	.333	4.74	56	0	0	0	13	68⅓	76	36	36	25	67
	—San Diego (N.L.)	0	0	...	0.00	9	0	0	0	2	14⅓	8	1	0	5	9
1992	—San Diego (N.L.)	1	4	.200	4.17	26	0	0	0	1	36⅔	39	17	17	11	25
	—Las Vegas (PCL)	2	4	.333	2.91	42	0	0	0	11	55⅔	53	19	18	20	38
1993	—San Diego (N.L.)	0	2	.000	4.72	21	0	0	0	0	34⅓	41	19	18	7	26
	—Cleveland (A.L.)■	6	5	.545	3.14	49	0	0	0	8	77⅓	75	33	27	27	44
A.L. totals (1 year)		6	5	.545	3.14	49	0	0	0	8	77⅓	75	33	27	27	44
N.L. totals (3 years)		1	6	.143	3.69	56	0	0	0	3	85⅓	88	37	35	23	60
Major league totals (3 years)		7	11	.389	3.43	105	0	0	0	11	162⅔	163	70	62	50	104

HERNANDEZ, JOSE

SS, CUBS

PERSONAL: Born July 14, 1969, in Vega Alta, Puerto Rico. . . . 6-1/180. . . . Throws right, bats right. . . . Full name: Jose Antonio Hernandez.
HIGH SCHOOL: Maestro Ladi (Vega Alta, Puerto Rico).
COLLEGE: American University (Puerto Rico).

TRANSACTIONS/CAREER NOTES: Signed as free agent by Texas Rangers organization (January 13, 1987). . . . Claimed on waivers by Cleveland Indians (April 3, 1992). . . . Traded by Indians to Chicago Cubs for P Heathcliff Slocumb (June 1, 1993).
STATISTICAL NOTES: Led Gulf Coast League third basemen with .950 fielding percentage, 47 putouts and 11 double plays in 1988. . . . Led Florida State League shortstops with .959 fielding percentage in 1990.

Year	Team (League)	Pos.	G	AB	R	H	2B	3B	HR	RBI	Avg.	BB	SO	SB	PO	A	E	Avg.
				BATTING											FIELDING			
1987	—GC Rangers (GCL)	SS	24	52	5	9	1	1	0	2	.173	9	25	2	30	38	5	.932
1988	—GC Rangers (GCL)	3-2-S-1-0	55	162	19	26	7	1	1	13	.160	12	36	4	†68	115	8	†.958
1989	—Gastonia (S. Atl.)	3-S-2-0	91	215	35	47	7	6	1	16	.219	33	67	9	101	169	17	.941
1990	—Charlotte (Fla. St.)	SS-OF	121	388	43	99	14	7	1	44	.255	50	122	11	192	372	25	†.958
1991	—Tulsa (Texas)	SS	91	301	36	72	17	4	1	20	.239	26	75	4	151	300	15	*.968
	—Okla. City (A.A.)	SS	14	46	6	14	1	1	1	3	.304	4	10	0	32	43	3	.962
	—Texas (A.L.)	SS-3B	45	98	8	18	2	1	0	4	.184	3	31	0	49	111	4	.976
1992	—Cant./Akr. (East.)■	SS	130	404	56	103	16	4	3	46	.255	37	108	7	*226	320	*40	.932
	—Cleveland (A.L.)	SS	3	4	0	0	0	0	0	0	.000	0	2	0	3	3	1	.857
1993	—Cant./Akr. (East.)	SS-3B	45	150	19	30	6	0	2	17	.200	10	39	9	75	135	7	.968
	—Orlando (Southern)■	SS	71	263	42	80	8	3	8	33	.304	20	60	8	136	205	14	.961
	—Iowa (Am. Assoc.)	SS	6	24	3	6	1	0	0	3	.250	0	2	0	14	26	1	.976
Major league totals (2 years)			48	102	8	18	2	1	0	4	.176	3	33	0	52	114	5	.971

HERNANDEZ, ROBERTO

P, WHITE SOX

PERSONAL: Born November 11, 1964, in Santurce, Puerto Rico. . . . 6-4/235. . . . Throws right, bats right. . . . Full name: Roberto Manuel Hernandez.
HIGH SCHOOL: New Hampton (N.H.) Prep.
COLLEGE: South Carolina-Aiken.

TRANSACTIONS/CAREER NOTES: Selected by California Angels organization in first round (16th pick overall) of free-agent draft (June 2, 1986); pick received as compensation for Baltimore Orioles signing Type A free agent Juan Beniquez. . . . On disabled list (May 6-21 and June 4-August 14, 1987). . . . Traded by Angels with OF Mark Doran to Chicago White Sox organization for OF Mark Davis (August 2, 1989). . . . On Vancouver disabled list (May 17-August 10, 1991).

Year	Team (League)	W	L	Pct.	ERA	G	GS	CG	ShO	Sv.	IP	H	R	ER	BB	SO
1986	—Salem (Northwest)	2	2	.500	4.58	10	10	0	0	0	55	57	37	28	42	38
1987	—Quad City (Midw.)	2	3	.400	6.86	7	6	0	0	1	21	24	21	16	12	21
1988	—Quad City (Midw.)	9	10	.474	3.17	24	24	6	1	0	164⅔	157	70	58	48	114
	—Midland (Texas)	0	2	.000	6.57	3	3	0	0	0	12⅓	16	13	9	8	7
1989	—Midland (Texas)	2	7	.222	6.89	12	12	0	0	0	64	94	57	49	30	42
	—Palm Springs (Cal.)	1	4	.200	4.64	7	7	0	0	0	42⅔	49	27	22	16	33
	—South Bend (Mid.)■	1	1	.500	3.33	4	4	0	0	0	24⅓	19	9	9	7	17
1990	—Birm. (Southern)	8	5	.615	3.67	17	17	1	0	0	108	103	57	44	43	62
	—Vancouver (PCL)	3	5	.375	2.84	11	11	3	1	0	79⅓	73	33	25	26	49
1991	—Birm. (Southern)	2	1	.667	1.99	4	4	0	0	0	22⅔	11	5	5	6	25
	—Vancouver (PCL)	4	1	.800	3.22	7	7	0	0	0	44⅔	41	17	16	23	40
	—GC Whi. Sox (GCL)	0	0	...	0.00	1	1	0	0	0	6	2	0	0	0	7
	—Chicago (A.L.)	1	0	1.000	7.80	9	3	0	0	0	15	18	15	13	7	6
1992	—Chicago (A.L.)	7	3	.700	1.65	43	0	0	0	12	71	45	15	13	20	68
	—Vancouver (PCL)	3	3	.500	2.61	9	0	0	0	2	20⅔	13	9	6	11	23
1993	—Chicago (A.L.)	3	4	.429	2.29	70	0	0	0	38	78⅔	66	21	20	20	71
Major league totals (3 years)		11	7	.611	2.51	122	3	0	0	50	164⅔	129	51	46	47	145

CHAMPIONSHIP SERIES RECORD

Year	Team (League)	W	L	Pct.	ERA	G	GS	CG	ShO	Sv.	IP	H	R	ER	BB	SO
1993	—Chicago (A.L.)	0	0	...	0.00	4	0	0	0	1	4	4	0	0	0	1

HERNANDEZ, XAVIER

P, YANKEES

PERSONAL: Born August 16, 1965, in Port Arthur, Tex. . . . 6-2/185. . . . Throws right, bats left. . . . Full name: Francis Xavier Hernandez.
HIGH SCHOOL: Thomas Jefferson (Port Arthur, Tex.).
COLLEGE: Southwestern Louisiana.
TRANSACTIONS/CAREER NOTES: Selected by Toronto Blue Jays organization in fourth round of free-agent draft (June 2, 1986). . . . On disabled list (June 7-27, 1987). . . . Selected by Houston Astros from Blue Jays organization in Rule 5 major league draft (December 4, 1989). . . . On Houston disabled list (June 3-26, 1991); included rehabilitation assignment to Tucson (June 14-26). . . . Traded by Astros to New York Yankees for P Domingo Jean and IF Andy Stankiewicz (November 27, 1993).

Year	Team (League)	W	L	Pct.	ERA	G	GS	CG	ShO	Sv.	IP	H	R	ER	BB	SO
1986	—St. Cathar. (NYP)	5	5	.500	2.67	13	10	1	1	0	70⅔	55	27	21	16	69
1987	—St. Cathar. (NYP)	3	3	.500	5.07	13	11	0	0	0	55	57	39	31	16	49
1988	—Myrtle Beach (SAL)	13	6	.684	2.55	23	22	2	2	0	148	116	52	42	28	111
	—Knoxville (South.)	2	4	.333	2.90	11	11	2	0	0	68⅓	73	32	22	15	33
1989	—Knoxville (South.)	1	1	.500	4.13	4	4	1	0	0	24	25	11	11	11	17
	—Syracuse (Int'l)	5	6	.455	3.53	15	15	2	1	0	99⅓	95	42	39	22	47
	—Toronto (A.L.)	1	0	1.000	4.76	7	0	0	0	0	22⅔	25	15	12	8	7
1990	—Houston (N.L.)■	2	1	.667	4.62	34	1	0	0	0	62⅓	60	34	32	24	24
1991	—Houston (N.L.)	2	7	.222	4.71	32	6	0	0	3	63	66	34	33	32	55
	—Tucson (PCL)	2	1	.667	2.75	16	3	0	0	4	36	35	16	11	9	34
1992	—Houston (N.L.)	9	1	.900	2.11	77	0	0	0	7	111	81	31	26	42	96
1993	—Houston (N.L.)	4	5	.444	2.61	72	0	0	0	9	96⅔	75	37	28	28	101
A.L. totals (1 year)		1	0	1.000	4.76	7	0	0	0	0	22⅔	25	15	12	8	7
N.L. totals (4 years)		17	14	.548	3.22	215	7	0	0	19	333	282	136	119	126	276
Major league totals (5 years)		18	14	.563	3.31	222	7	0	0	19	355⅔	307	151	131	134	283

HERRERA, JOSE

OF, ATHLETICS

PERSONAL: Born August 30, 1972, in Santo Domingo, Dominican Republic. . . . 6-0/165. . . . Throws left, bats left. . . . Full name: Jose Ramon Catalino Herrera.
TRANSACTIONS/CAREER NOTES: Signed as free agent by Toronto Blue Jays organization (January 10, 1990). . . . Traded by Blue Jays organization to Oakland Athletics organization (August 6, 1993), completing deal in which A's traded OF Rickey Henderson to Blue Jays for P Steve Karsay and a player to be named later (July 31, 1993).

							BATTING								FIELDING			
Year	Team (League)	Pos.	G	AB	R	H	2B	3B	HR	RBI	Avg.	BB	SO	SB	PO	A	E	Avg.
1990	—Santo Dom. (DSL)	OF	50	164	18	42	7	0	2	18	.256	14	16	2	...	...	...	...
1991	—Medicine Hat (Pio.)	OF	40	143	21	35	5	1	1	11	.245	6	38	6	50	5	3	.948
	—St. Cathar. (NYP)	OF	3	9	3	3	1	0	0	2	.333	1	2	0	8	1	0	1.000
1992	—Medicine Hat (Pio.)	OF	72	265	45	72	9	2	0	21	.272	32	62	32	132	3	*10	.931
1993	—Hagerstown (SAL)	OF	95	388	60	123	22	5	5	42	.317	26	63	36	150	6	9	.945
	—Madison (Midwest)■	OF	4	14	1	3	0	0	0	0	.214	0	6	1	6	1	0	1.000

HERSHISER, OREL

P, DODGERS

PERSONAL: Born September 16, 1958, in Buffalo, N.Y. . . . 6-3/198. . . . Throws right, bats right. . . . Full name: Orel Leonard Hershiser IV. . . . Brother of Gordie Hershiser, minor league pitcher (1987-88). . . . Name pronounced her-SHY-zer.
HIGH SCHOOL: Cherry Hill (N.J.) East.
COLLEGE: Bowling Green State.
TRANSACTIONS/CAREER NOTES: Selected by Los Angeles Dodgers organization in 17th round of free-agent draft (June 5, 1979). . . . On disabled list (April 27, 1990-remainder of season). . . . On Los Angeles disabled list (March 31-May 29, 1991); included rehabilitation assignment to Bakersfield (May 8-13 and May 18-24), Albuquerque (May 13-18) and San Antonio (May 24-29). . . . Granted free agency (November 1, 1991). . . . Re-signed by Dodgers (December 3, 1991).
RECORDS: Holds major league single-season record for most consecutive scoreless innings—59 (August 30, sixth inning through September 28, 10th inning, 1988). . . . Shares N.L. single-season record for fewest games lost by pitcher who led league in games lost—15 (1989 and 1992). . . . Shares N.L. single-month record for most shutouts—5 (September 1988).
HONORS: Named Major League Player of the Year by THE SPORTING NEWS (1988). . . . Named N.L. Pitcher of the Year by THE

SPORTING NEWS (1988).... Named righthanded pitcher on THE SPORTING NEWS N.L. All-Star team (1988).... Won N.L. Gold Glove at pitcher (1988).... Named N.L. Cy Young Award winner by Baseball Writers' Association of America (1988).... Named pitcher on THE SPORTING NEWS N.L. Silver Slugger team (1993).

STATISTICAL NOTES: Tied for N.L. lead with 19 sacrifice hits in 1988.

MISCELLANEOUS: Singled once in two games as pinch-hitter (1992).... Started one game at third base but replaced before first plate appearance and never played in field (1993).

Year	Team (League)	W	L	Pct.	ERA	G	GS	CG	ShO	Sv.	IP	H	R	ER	BB	SO
1979	—Clinton (Midwest)	4	0	1.000	2.09	15	4	1	0	2	43	33	15	10	17	33
1980	—San Antonio (Tex.)	5	9	.357	3.55	49	3	1	0	14	109	120	59	43	59	75
1981	—San Antonio (Tex.)	7	6	.538	4.68	42	4	3	0	*15	102	94	54	53	50	95
1982	—Albuquerque (PCL)	9	6	.600	3.71	47	7	2	0	4	123⅔	121	73	51	63	93
1983	—Albuquerque (PCL)	10	8	.556	4.09	49	10	6	0	16	134⅓	132	73	61	57	95
	—Los Angeles (N.L.)	0	0	...	3.38	8	0	0	0	1	8	7	6	3	6	5
1984	—Los Angeles (N.L.)	11	8	.579	2.66	45	20	8	•4	2	189⅔	160	65	56	50	150
1985	—Los Angeles (N.L.)	19	3	*.864	2.03	36	34	9	5	0	239⅔	179	72	54	68	157
1986	—Los Angeles (N.L.)	14	14	.500	3.85	35	35	8	1	0	231⅓	213	112	99	86	153
1987	—Los Angeles (N.L.)	16	16	.500	3.06	37	35	10	1	1	*264⅔	247	105	90	74	190
1988	—Los Angeles (N.L.)	•23	8	.742	2.26	35	34	•15	*8	1	*267	208	73	67	73	178
1989	—Los Angeles (N.L.)	15	•15	.500	2.31	35	33	8	4	0	*256⅔	226	75	66	77	178
1990	—Los Angeles (N.L.)	1	1	.500	4.26	4	4	0	0	0	25⅓	26	12	12	4	16
1991	—Bakersfield (Calif.)	2	0	1.000	0.82	2	2	0	0	0	11	5	2	1	1	6
	—Albuquerque (PCL)	0	0	...	0.00	1	1	0	0	0	5	5	0	0	0	5
	—San Antonio (Tex.)	0	1	.000	2.57	1	1	0	0	0	7	11	3	2	1	5
	—Los Angeles (N.L.)	7	2	.778	3.46	21	21	0	0	0	112	112	43	43	32	73
1992	—Los Angeles (N.L.)	10	•15	.400	3.67	33	33	1	0	0	210⅔	209	101	86	69	130
1993	—Los Angeles (N.L.)	12	14	.462	3.59	33	33	5	1	0	215⅔	201	106	86	72	141
Major league totals (11 years)		128	96	.571	2.95	322	282	64	24	5	2020⅔	1788	770	662	611	1371

CHAMPIONSHIP SERIES RECORD

CHAMPIONSHIP SERIES NOTES: Named N.L. Championship Series Most Valuable Player (1988).... Holds single-series record for most innings pitched—24⅔ (1988).... Holds N.L. single-game record for most hit batsmen—2 (October 12, 1988).... Shares N.L. career records for most complete games—2; and most hit batsmen—2.... Shares N.L. single-series record for most hit batsmen—2 (1988).

Year	Team (League)	W	L	Pct.	ERA	G	GS	CG	ShO	Sv.	IP	H	R	ER	BB	SO
1983	—Los Angeles (N.L.)							Did not play.								
1985	—Los Angeles (N.L.)	1	0	1.000	3.52	2	2	1	0	0	15⅓	17	6	6	6	5
1988	—Los Angeles (N.L.)	1	0	1.000	1.09	4	3	1	1	1	24⅔	18	5	3	7	15
Champ. series totals (2 years)		2	0	1.000	2.03	6	5	2	1	1	40	35	11	9	13	20

WORLD SERIES RECORD

WORLD SERIES NOTES: Named Most Valuable Player (1988).

Year	Team (League)	W	L	Pct.	ERA	G	GS	CG	ShO	Sv.	IP	H	R	ER	BB	SO
1988	—Los Angeles (N.L.)	2	0	1.000	1.00	2	2	2	1	0	18	7	2	2	6	17

ALL-STAR GAME RECORD

Year	League	W	L	Pct.	ERA	GS	CG	ShO	Sv.	IP	H	R	ER	BB	SO
1987	—National	0	0	...	0.00	0	0	0	0	2	1	0	0	1	0
1988	—National	0	0	...	0.00	0	0	0	0	1	0	0	0	0	0
1989	—National							Did not play.							
All-Star totals (2 years)		0	0	...	0.00	0	0	0	0	3	1	0	0	1	0

HESKETH, JOE

P, RED SOX

PERSONAL: Born February 15, 1959, in Lackawanna, N.Y.... 6-2/173.... Throws left, bats left.... Full name: Joseph Thomas Hesketh.

HIGH SCHOOL: Central (Hamburg, N.Y.).

COLLEGE: New York-Buffalo.

TRANSACTIONS/CAREER NOTES: Selected by Montreal Expos organization in second round of free-agent draft (June 3, 1980).... On Memphis disabled list (April 9, 1981-remainder of season and April 8-July 8, 1982).... On Montreal disabled list (August 24, 1985-remainder of season; July 4, 1986-remainder of season; and August 18-September 8, 1989).... Claimed on waivers by Atlanta Braves (April 30, 1990).... Released by Braves (July 24, 1990).... Signed by Boston Red Sox (July 31, 1990).... Granted free agency (October 28, 1991).... Re-signed by Red Sox (December 19, 1991).... On disabled list (August 20, 1993-remainder of season).

HONORS: Named American Association Pitcher of the Year (1984).

Year	Team (League)	W	L	Pct.	ERA	G	GS	CG	ShO	Sv.	IP	H	R	ER	BB	SO
1980	—W.P. Beach (FSL)	8	2	.800	1.92	11	11	1	1	0	75	71	30	16	32	43
	—Memphis (South.)	1	0	1.000	4.05	3	3	0	0	0	20	20	13	9	7	20
1981	—							Did not play.								
1982	—W.P. Beach (FSL)	3	2	.600	2.76	8	8	2	1	0	45⅔	41	16	14	16	24
1983	—Memphis (South.)	6	4	.600	3.04	11	11	4	0	0	74	82	38	25	25	22
	—Wichita (A.A.)	5	5	.500	5.09	15	15	2	•2	0	88⅓	98	53	50	46	41
1984	—Indianapolis (A.A.)	12	3	.800	3.05	22	22	5	1	0	147⅔	120	60	50	54	135
	—Montreal (N.L.)	2	2	.500	1.80	11	5	1	1	1	45	38	12	9	15	32
1985	—Montreal (N.L.)	10	5	.667	2.49	25	25	2	1	0	155⅓	125	52	43	45	113
1986	—Montreal (N.L.)	6	5	.545	5.01	15	15	0	0	0	82⅔	92	46	46	31	67
1987	—GC Expos (GCL)	0	0	...	8.31	2	1	0	0	0	4⅓	7	4	4	0	8
	—Jacksonv. (South.)	1	0	1.000	2.29	6	3	0	0	1	19⅔	18	6	5	4	22
	—Montreal (N.L.)	0	0	...	3.14	18	0	0	0	1	28⅔	23	12	10	15	31
1988	—Indianapolis (A.A.)	0	0	...	3.27	8	0	0	0	2	11	10	5	4	5	16
	—Montreal (N.L.)	4	3	.571	2.85	60	0	0	0	9	72⅔	63	30	23	35	64

Year	Team (League)	W	L	Pct.	ERA	G	GS	CG	ShO	Sv.	IP	H	R	ER	BB	SO
1989	—Montreal (N.L.)	6	4	.600	5.77	43	0	0	0	3	48⅓	54	34	31	26	44
	—Indianapolis (A.A.)	0	0	...	3.86	5	1	0	0	1	9⅓	11	4	4	5	9
1990	—Mont.-Atl. (N.L.)■	1	2	.333	5.29	33	0	0	0	5	34	32	23	20	14	24
	—Boston (A.L.)■	0	4	.000	3.51	12	2	0	0	0	25⅔	37	12	10	11	26
1991	—Boston (A.L.)	12	4	*.750	3.29	39	17	0	0	0	153⅓	142	59	56	53	104
1992	—Boston (A.L.)	8	9	.471	4.36	30	25	1	0	1	148⅔	162	84	72	58	104
1993	—Boston (A.L.)	3	4	.429	5.06	28	5	0	0	1	53⅓	62	35	30	29	34
A.L. totals (4 years)		23	21	.523	3.97	109	49	1	0	2	381	403	190	168	151	268
N.L. totals (7 years)		29	21	.580	3.51	205	45	3	2	19	466⅔	427	209	182	181	375
Major league totals (10 years)		52	42	.553	3.72	314	94	4	2	21	847⅔	830	399	350	332	643

HIATT, PHIL

3B, ROYALS

PERSONAL: Born May 1, 1969, in Pensacola, Fla. . . . 6-3/200. . . . Throws right, bats right. . . . Full name: Philip Farrell Hiatt.
HIGH SCHOOL: Catholic (Pensacola, Fla.).
COLLEGE: Louisiana Tech.
TRANSACTIONS/CAREER NOTES: Selected by Kansas City Royals organization in eighth round of free-agent draft (June 4, 1990).
STATISTICAL NOTES: Led Northwest League third basemen with 145 assists, 200 total chances and 18 double plays in 1990.

				BATTING											FIELDING			
Year	Team (League)	Pos.	G	AB	R	H	2B	3B	HR	RBI	Avg.	BB	SO	SB	PO	A	E	Avg.
1990	—Eugene (N'west)	3B-SS	73	289	33	85	18	5	2	44	.294	17	70	15	41	†151	16	.923
1991	—Baseball City (FSL)	3B	81	315	41	94	21	6	5	33	.298	22	70	28	65	146	12	.946
	—Memphis (South.)	3B	56	206	29	47	7	1	6	33	.228	9	63	6	36	112	13	.919
1992	—Memphis (South.)	3B-OF-1B	129	487	71	119	20	5	27	83	.244	25	157	5	139	150	20	.935
	—Omaha (A.A.)	3B	5	14	3	3	0	0	2	4	.214	2	3	1	2	13	1	.938
1993	—Kansas City (A.L.)	3B	81	238	30	52	12	1	7	36	.218	16	82	6	45	114	16	.909
	—Omaha (A.A.)	3B	12	51	8	12	2	0	3	10	.235	4	20	0	11	24	2	.946
Major league totals (1 year)			81	238	30	52	12	1	7	36	.218	16	82	6	45	114	16	.909

HIBBARD, GREG

P, MARINERS

PERSONAL: Born September 13, 1964, in New Orleans. . . . 6-0/185. . . . Throws left, bats left. . . . Full name: James Gregory Hibbard.
HIGH SCHOOL: Harrison Central (Gulfport, Miss.).
COLLEGE: Mississippi Gulf Coast Junior College and Alabama.
TRANSACTIONS/CAREER NOTES: Selected by Houston Astros organization in eighth round of free-agent draft (January 17, 1984). . . . Selected by Kansas City Royals organization in 16th round of free-agent draft (June 2, 1986). . . . Traded by Royals with P Melido Perez, P John Davis and P Chuck Mount to Chicago White Sox for P Floyd Bannister and 3B Dave Cochrane (December 10, 1987). . . . Selected by Florida Marlins in first round (12th pick overall) of expansion draft (November 17, 1992). . . . Traded by Marlins to Chicago Cubs for 3B Gary Scott and SS Alex Arias (November 17, 1992). . . . On disabled list (June 12-July 2, 1993). . . . Granted free agency (December 20, 1993). . . . Signed by Seattle Mariners (January 14, 1994).
MISCELLANEOUS: Appeared in one game as pinch-runner (1993).

Year	Team (League)	W	L	Pct.	ERA	G	GS	CG	ShO	Sv.	IP	H	R	ER	BB	SO
1986	—Eugene (N'west)	5	2	.714	3.46	26	1	0	0	5	39	30	23	15	19	44
1987	—Appleton (Midw.)	7	2	.778	1.11	9	9	2	1	0	64⅔	53	17	8	18	61
	—Fort Myers (FSL)	2	1	.667	1.88	3	3	3	1	0	24	20	5	5	3	20
	—Memphis (South.)	7	6	.538	3.23	16	16	3	1	0	106	102	48	38	21	56
1988	—Vancouver (PCL)■	11	11	.500	4.12	25	24	4	1	0	144⅓	155	74	66	44	65
1989	—Vancouver (PCL)	2	3	.400	2.64	9	9	2	1	0	58	47	24	17	11	45
	—Chicago (A.L.)	6	7	.462	3.21	23	23	2	0	0	137⅓	142	58	49	41	55
1990	—Chicago (A.L.)	14	9	.609	3.16	33	33	3	1	0	211	202	80	74	55	92
1991	—Chicago (A.L.)	11	11	.500	4.31	32	29	5	0	0	194	196	107	93	57	71
	—Vancouver (PCL)	0	0	...	3.38	1	1	0	0	0	5⅓	4	3	2	3	3
1992	—Chicago (A.L.)	10	7	.588	4.40	31	28	0	0	1	176	187	92	86	57	69
1993	—Chicago (N.L.)■	15	11	.577	3.96	31	31	1	0	0	191	209	96	84	47	82
A.L. totals (4 years)		41	34	.547	3.78	119	113	10	1	1	718⅓	727	337	302	210	287
N.L. totals (1 year)		15	11	.577	3.96	31	31	1	0	0	191	209	96	84	47	82
Major league totals (5 years)		56	45	.554	3.82	150	144	11	1	1	909⅓	936	433	386	257	369

HICKERSON, BRYAN

P, GIANTS

PERSONAL: Born October 13, 1963, in Bemidji, Minn. . . . 6-2/203. . . . Throws left, bats left. . . . Full name: Bryan David Hickerson.
HIGH SCHOOL: Bemidji (Minn.).
COLLEGE: Minnesota (degree in sports and exercise science, 1987).
TRANSACTIONS/CAREER NOTES: Selected by St. Louis Cardinals organization in ninth round of free-agent draft (June 3, 1985). . . . Selected by Minnesota Twins organization in seventh round of free-agent draft (June 2, 1986). . . . Loaned by Twins to San Francisco Giants organization (April 1-June 14, 1987). . . . Traded by Twins organization to Giants organization (June 15, 1987), completing trade in which Twins traded P Jose Dominguez and P Ray Velasquez to Giants for P David Blakely and OF Dan Gladden (March 31, 1987). . . . On disabled list (July 14-August 17, 1987 and April 8, 1988-entire season).

Year	Team (League)	W	L	Pct.	ERA	G	GS	CG	ShO	Sv.	IP	H	R	ER	BB	SO
1986	—Visalia (California)	4	3	.571	4.23	11	11	3	0	0	72⅓	72	37	34	25	69
1987	—Clinton (Midwest)■	11	0	*1.000	1.24	17	10	2	1	1	94	60	17	13	37	103
	—Shreveport (Texas)■	1	2	.333	3.94	4	3	0	0	0	16	20	7	7	4	23
1988	—							Did not play.								
1989	—San Jose (Calif.)	11	6	.647	2.55	21	21	1	1	0	134	111	52	38	57	110
1990	—Shreveport (Texas)	3	6	.333	4.23	27	6	0	0	1	66	71	37	31	26	63
	—Phoenix (PCL)	0	4	.000	5.50	12	4	0	0	0	34⅓	48	25	21	16	26
1991	—Shreveport (Texas)	3	4	.429	3.00	23	0	0	0	2	39	36	15	13	14	41

Year	Team (League)	W	L	Pct.	ERA	G	GS	CG	ShO	Sv.	IP	H	R	ER	BB	SO
	—Phoenix (PCL)	1	1	.500	3.80	12	0	0	0	2	21⅓	29	10	9	5	21
	—San Francisco (N.L.)	2	2	.500	3.60	17	6	0	0	0	50	53	20	20	17	43
1992	—San Francisco (N.L.)	5	3	.625	3.09	61	1	0	0	0	87⅓	74	31	30	21	68
1993	—San Francisco (N.L.)	7	5	.583	4.26	47	15	0	0	0	120⅓	137	58	57	39	69
Major league totals (3 years)		14	10	.583	3.74	125	22	0	0	0	257⅔	264	109	107	77	180

HIGGINS, KEVIN

C/3B, PADRES

PERSONAL: Born January 22, 1967, in San Gabriel, Calif. . . . 5-11/185. . . . Throws right, bats left. . . . Full name: Kevin Wayne Higgins.

HIGH SCHOOL: Torrance (Calif.) Unified District.

COLLEGE: Los Angeles Harbor College and Arizona State.

TRANSACTIONS/CAREER NOTES: Selected by Detroit Tigers organization in fifth round of free-agent draft (January 14, 1986). . . . Selected by San Diego Padres organization in 12th round of free-agent draft (June 5, 1989).

STATISTICAL NOTES: Led Northwest League with nine sacrifice flies in 1989.

			BATTING												FIELDING			
Year	Team (League)	Pos.	G	AB	R	H	2B	3B	HR	RBI	Avg.	BB	SO	SB	PO	A	E	Avg.
1989	—Spokane (N'west)	2B	71	295	54	*98	9	3	2	52	.332	30	13	2	140	200	*21	.942
1990	—Riverside (Calif.)	C-1B	49	176	27	53	5	1	2	18	.301	27	15	0	299	42	2	.994
	—Wichita (Texas)	C	52	187	24	67	7	1	1	23	.358	16	8	5	236	21	6	.977
	—Las Vegas (PCL)	C	9	26	4	7	1	1	0	3	.269	4	3	0	53	4	2	.966
1991	—Las Vegas (PCL)	1-3-0-2-C	130	403	53	116	12	4	3	45	.288	47	38	2	389	121	17	.968
1992	—Las Vegas (PCL)	0-3-1-2-C-P	124	355	49	90	12	3	0	40	.254	41	31	6	173	103	10	.965
1993	—Las Vegas (PCL)	3-C-2-0-1	40	142	22	51	8	0	1	22	.359	18	8	1	74	58	4	.971
	—San Diego (N.L.)	C-3-0-1-2	71	181	17	40	4	1	0	13	.221	16	17	0	314	32	6	.983
Major league totals (1 year)			71	181	17	40	4	1	0	13	.221	16	17	0	314	32	6	.983

RECORD AS PITCHER

Year	Team (League)	W	L	Pct.	ERA	G	GS	CG	ShO	Sv.	IP	H	R	ER	BB	SO
1992	—Las Vegas (PCL)	0	1	.000	6.75	3	0	0	0	0	2⅔	4	2	2	2	0

HIGUERA, TED

P, BREWERS

PERSONAL: Born November 9, 1958, in Los Mochis, Mexico. . . . 5-10/180. . . . Throws left, bats both. . . . Full name: Teodoro Valenzuela Higuera. . . . Name pronounced he-GARE-uh.

HIGH SCHOOL: Los Mochis (Los Mochis, Sinaloa, Mexico).

TRANSACTIONS/CAREER NOTES: Contract sold to Vancouver, Milwaukee Brewers organization (September 13, 1983). . . . On Milwaukee disabled list (March 25-May 1, 1989); included rehabilitation assignment to El Paso (April 9-28). . . . On disabled list (June 14-29, 1990). . . . Granted free agency (November 5, 1990). . . . Re-signed by Brewers (December 5, 1990). . . . On Milwaukee disabled list (March 29-May 28, 1991); included rehabilitation assignment to Denver (May 19-28). . . . On disabled list (July 5, 1991-remainder of season). . . . On Milwaukee disabled list (April 5, 1992-entire season); included rehabilitation assignment to Beloit (July 5-15), El Paso (July 15-16) and Denver (July 25-August 5). . . . On Milwaukee disabled list (March 31-August 14, 1993); included rehabilitation assignment to New Orleans (May 4-10 and June 2-4).

HONORS: Named A.L. Rookie Pitcher of the Year by THE SPORTING NEWS (1985). . . . Named lefthanded pitcher on THE SPORTING NEWS A.L. All-Star team (1986).

STATISTICAL NOTES: Played a 20-team season and a 6-team short season with Ciudad Juarez of Mexican League (1980).

Year	Team (League)	W	L	Pct.	ERA	G	GS	CG	ShO	Sv.	IP	H	R	ER	BB	SO
1979	—Ciu. Juarez (Mex.)	0	1	.000	45.00	2	1	0	0	0	1	4	5	5	4	1
1980	—Ciu. Juarez (Mex.)	8	3	.727	1.85	19	17	4	0	0	117	111	30	24	59	76
	—Ciu. Juarez (Mex.)	2	5	.286	3.67	8	8	4	1	0	49	44	22	20	17	29
1981	—Ciu. Juarez (Mex.)	16	9	.640	3.10	28	28	14	5	0	203	207	81	70	69	157
1982	—Ciu. Juarez (Mex.)	9	12	.429	4.05	24	24	8	0	0	142⅓	163	77	64	53	74
1983	—Ciu. Juarez (Mex.)	•17	8	.680	2.03	27	•27	•18	3	0	*222	177	61	50	68	*165
1984	—El Paso (Texas)■	8	7	.533	*2.60	19	19	4	0	0	121	116	57	35	43	99
	—Vancouver (PCL)	1	4	.200	4.73	8	6	0	0	0	40	49	26	21	14	29
1985	—Milwaukee (A.L.)	15	8	.652	3.90	32	30	7	2	0	212⅓	186	105	92	63	127
1986	—Milwaukee (A.L.)	20	11	.645	2.79	34	34	15	4	0	248⅓	226	84	77	74	207
1987	—Milwaukee (A.L.)	18	10	.643	3.85	35	35	14	3	0	261⅔	236	120	112	87	240
1988	—Milwaukee (A.L.)	16	9	.640	2.45	31	31	8	1	0	227⅓	168	66	62	59	192
1989	—El Paso (Texas)	0	1	.000	1.80	1	1	0	0	0	5	5	2	1	1	4
	—Milwaukee (A.L.)	9	6	.600	3.46	22	22	2	1	0	135⅓	125	56	52	48	91
1990	—Milwaukee (A.L.)	11	10	.524	3.76	27	27	4	1	0	170	167	80	71	50	129
1991	—Denver (A.A.)	1	0	1.000	2.08	2	2	0	0	0	8⅔	6	3	2	6	6
	—Milwaukee (A.L.)	3	2	.600	4.46	7	6	0	0	0	36⅓	37	18	18	10	33
1992	—Beloit (Midwest)	1	0	1.000	3.27	2	2	0	0	0	11	13	4	4	1	11
	—El Paso (Texas)	0	1	.000	3.60	1	1	0	0	0	5	4	2	2	2	3
	—Denver (A.A.)	1	0	1.000	4.15	2	2	0	0	0	8⅔	7	5	4	8	4
1993	—New Orleans (A.A.)	0	1	.000	9.00	3	3	0	0	0	8	11	11	8	7	7
	—Milwaukee (A.L.)	1	3	.250	7.20	8	8	0	0	0	30	43	24	24	16	27
Major league totals (8 years)		93	59	.612	3.46	196	193	50	12	0	1321⅓	1188	553	508	407	1046

ALL-STAR GAME RECORD

Year	League	W	L	Pct.	ERA	GS	CG	ShO	Sv.	IP	H	R	ER	BB	SO
1986	—American	0	0	. . .	0.00	0	0	0	0	3	1	0	0	1	2

HILL, GLENALLEN

OF, CUBS

PERSONAL: Born March 22, 1965, in Santa Cruz, Calif. . . . 6-2/220. . . . Throws right, bats right.

HIGH SCHOOL: Santa Cruz (Calif.).

TRANSACTIONS/CAREER NOTES: Selected by Toronto Blue Jays organization in ninth

round of free-agent draft (June 6, 1983).... On disabled list (July 6-21, 1990).... Traded by Blue Jays with P Denis Boucher, OF Mark Whiten and a player to be named later to Cleveland Indians for P Tom Candiotti and OF Turner Ward (June 27, 1991); Indians acquired cash instead of player to complete deal (October 15, 1991).... On Cleveland disabled list (September 8, 1991-remainder of season).... On Cleveland disabled list (April 23-May 22, 1992); included rehabilitation assignment to Canton/Akron (May 18-22).... Traded by Indians to Chicago Cubs for OF Candy Maldonado (August 19, 1993).... Granted free agency (October 27, 1993).... Re-signed by Cubs (November 24, 1993).
STATISTICAL NOTES: Led Southern League with 287 total bases and tied for lead with 13 sacrifice flies in 1986.... Led International League with 279 total bases and .578 slugging percentage in 1989.

				BATTING											FIELDING			
Year	**Team (League)**	**Pos.**	**G**	**AB**	**R**	**H**	**2B**	**3B**	**HR**	**RBI**	**Avg.**	**BB**	**SO**	**SB**	**PO**	**A**	**E**	**Avg.**
1983	—Medicine Hat (Pio.)	OF	46	133	34	63	3	4	6	27	.474	17	49	4	63	3	6	.917
1984	—Florence (S. Atl.)	OF	129	440	75	105	19	5	16	64	.239	63	*150	30	281	9	16	.948
1985	—Kinston (Carolina)	OF	131	466	57	98	13	0	20	56	.210	57	*211	42	234	12	13	.950
1986	—Knoxville (South.)	OF	141	*570	87	159	23	6	*31	96	.279	39	*153	18	230	9	*21	.919
1987	—Syracuse (Int'l)	OF	*137	536	65	126	25	6	16	77	.235	25	*152	22	176	10	10	.949
1988	—Syracuse (Int'l)	OF	51	172	21	40	7	0	4	19	.233	15	59	7	101	2	1	.990
	—Knoxville (South.)	OF	79	269	37	71	13	2	12	38	.264	28	75	10	130	6	5	.965
1989	—Syracuse (Int'l)	OF	125	483	*86	*155	31	*15	*21	72	.321	34	107	21	242	3	*7	.972
	—Toronto (A.L.)	OF	19	52	4	15	0	0	1	7	.288	3	12	2	27	0	1	.964
1990	—Toronto (A.L.)	OF	84	260	47	60	11	3	12	32	.231	18	62	8	115	4	2	.983
1991	—Tor.-Clev. (A.L.)■	OF	72	221	29	57	8	2	8	25	.258	23	54	6	118	0	3	.975
1992	—Cleveland (A.L.)	OF	102	369	38	89	16	1	18	49	.241	20	73	9	126	5	6	.956
	—Cant./Akr. (East.)	OF	3	9	1	1	1	0	0	1	.111	3	4	0	4	0	1	.800
1993	—Cleveland (A.L.)	OF	66	174	19	39	7	2	5	25	.224	11	50	7	62	1	4	.940
	—Chicago (N.L.)■	OF	31	87	14	30	7	0	10	22	.345	6	21	1	42	2	2	.957
American League totals (5 years)			343	1076	137	260	42	8	44	138	.242	75	251	32	448	10	16	.966
National League totals (1 year)			31	87	14	30	7	0	10	22	.345	6	21	1	42	2	2	.957
Major league totals (5 years)			374	1163	151	290	49	8	54	160	.249	81	272	33	490	12	18	.965

HILL, KEN

P, EXPOS

PERSONAL: Born December 14, 1965, in Lynn, Mass.... 6-2/200.... Throws right, bats right.... Full name: Kenneth Wade Hill.
HIGH SCHOOL: Classical (Lynn, Mass.).
COLLEGE: North Adams (Mass.) State.
TRANSACTIONS/CAREER NOTES: Signed as free agent by Detroit Tigers organization (February 14, 1985).... Traded by Tigers with a player to be named later to St. Louis Cardinals for C Mike Heath (August 10, 1986); Cardinals acquired 1B Mike Laga to complete deal (September 2, 1986).... On St. Louis disabled list (March 26-May 9, 1988).... On St. Louis disabled list (August 11-September 1, 1991); included rehabilitation assignment to Louisville (August 29-30).... Traded by Cardinals to Montreal Expos for 1B Andres Galarraga (November 25, 1991).... On Montreal disabled list (June 26-July 17, 1993); included rehabilitation assignment to Ottawa (July 12-15).
RECORDS: Shares N.L. single-season record for fewest games lost by pitcher who led league in games lost—15 (1989).
MISCELLANEOUS: Made an out in one game as pinch-hitter with Montreal (1993).

Year	**Team (League)**	**W**	**L**	**Pct.**	**ERA**	**G**	**GS**	**CG**	**ShO**	**Sv.**	**IP**	**H**	**R**	**ER**	**BB**	**SO**
1985	—Gastonia (S. Atl.)	3	6	.333	4.96	15	12	0	0	0	69	60	51	38	57	48
1986	—Gastonia (S. Atl.)	9	5	.643	2.79	22	16	1	0	0	122⅔	95	51	38	80	86
	—Glens Falls (East.)	0	1	.000	5.14	1	1	0	0	0	7	4	4	4	6	4
	—Arkansas (Texas)■	1	2	.333	4.50	3	3	1	0	0	18	18	10	9	7	9
1987	—Arkansas (Texas)	3	5	.375	5.20	18	8	0	0	2	53⅔	60	33	31	30	48
	—St. Peters. (FSL)	1	3	.250	4.17	18	4	0	0	2	41	38	19	19	17	32
1988	—St. Louis (N.L.)	0	1	.000	5.14	4	1	0	0	0	14	16	9	8	6	6
	—Arkansas (Texas)	9	9	.500	4.92	22	22	3	1	0	115⅓	129	76	63	50	107
1989	—Louisville (A.A.)	0	2	.000	3.50	3	3	0	0	0	18	13	8	7	10	18
	—St. Louis (N.L.)	7	•15	.318	3.80	33	33	2	1	0	196⅔	186	92	83	*99	112
1990	—St. Louis (N.L.)	5	6	.455	5.49	17	14	1	0	0	78⅔	79	49	48	33	58
	—Louisville (A.A.)	6	1	.857	1.79	12	12	2	1	0	85⅓	47	20	17	27	104
1991	—St. Louis (N.L.)	11	10	.524	3.57	30	30	0	0	0	181⅓	147	76	72	67	121
	—Louisville (A.A.)	0	0	...	0.00	1	1	0	0	0	1	0	0	0	0	2
1992	—Montreal (N.L.)■	16	9	.640	2.68	33	33	3	3	0	218	187	76	65	75	150
1993	—Montreal (N.L.)	9	7	.563	3.23	28	28	2	0	0	183⅔	163	84	66	74	90
	—Ottawa (Int'l)	0	0	...	0.00	1	1	0	0	0	4	1	0	0	1	0
Major league totals (6 years)		48	48	.500	3.53	145	139	8	4	0	872⅓	778	386	342	354	537

HILL, MILT

P, BRAVES

PERSONAL: Born August 22, 1965, in Atlanta.... 6-0/180.... Throws right, bats right.... Full name: Milton Giles Hill.
HIGH SCHOOL: Redan (Stone Mountain, Ga.).
COLLEGE: DeKalb College (Ga.) and Georgia College.
TRANSACTIONS/CAREER NOTES: Selected by Atlanta Braves organization in 23rd round of free-agent draft (June 3, 1985).... Selected by Cincinnati Reds organization in 28th round of free-agent draft (June 2, 1987).... On Nashville disabled list (June 11-20, 1991).... On Indianapolis disabled list (August 17, 1993-remainder of season).... Claimed on waivers by Braves (October 5, 1993).

Year	**Team (League)**	**W**	**L**	**Pct.**	**ERA**	**G**	**GS**	**CG**	**ShO**	**Sv.**	**IP**	**H**	**R**	**ER**	**BB**	**SO**
1987	—Billings (Pioneer)	3	1	.750	1.65	21	0	0	0	7	32⅔	25	10	6	4	40
1988	—Ced. Rap. (Midw.)	9	4	.692	2.07	44	0	0	0	13	78⅓	52	21	18	17	69
1989	—Chatt. (South.)	6	5	.545	2.06	51	0	0	0	13	70	49	19	16	28	63
1990	—Nashville (A.A.)	4	4	.500	2.27	48	0	0	0	3	71⅓	51	20	18	18	58
1991	—Nashville (A.A.)	3	3	.500	2.94	37	0	0	0	3	67⅓	59	26	22	15	62
	—Cincinnati (N.L.)	1	1	.500	3.78	22	0	0	0	0	33⅓	36	14	14	8	20
1992	—Cincinnati (N.L.)	0	0	...	3.15	14	0	0	0	1	20	15	9	7	5	10

Year	Team (League)	W	L	Pct.	ERA	G	GS	CG	ShO	Sv.	IP	H	R	ER	BB	SO
	—Nashville (A.A.)	0	5	.000	2.66	53	0	0	0	18	74⅓	56	30	22	17	70
1993	—Indianapolis (A.A.).....	3	5	.375	4.08	20	5	0	0	2	53	53	27	24	17	45
	—Cincinnati (N.L.)	3	0	1.000	5.65	19	0	0	0	0	28⅔	34	18	18	9	23
Major league totals (3 years)..		4	1	.800	4.28	55	0	0	0	1	82	85	41	39	22	53

HILL, TYRONE

P, BREWERS

PERSONAL: Born March 7, 1972, in Yucaipa, Calif.... 6-6/195.... Throws left, bats left.... Full name: Tyrone Allen Hill.

HIGH SCHOOL: Yucaipa (Calif.).

TRANSACTIONS/CAREER NOTES: Selected by Milwaukee Brewers organization in first round (15th pick overall) of free-agent draft (June 3, 1991); pick received as compensation for Detroit Tigers signing Type A free agent Rob Deer.... On disabled list (August 11, 1992-remainder of season).... On temporary inactive list (May 28-July 7, 1993).

Year	Team (League)	W	L	Pct.	ERA	G	GS	CG	ShO	Sv.	IP	H	R	ER	BB	SO
1991	—Helena (Pioneer)	4	2	.667	3.15	11	11	0	0	0	60	43	27	21	35	76
1992	—Beloit (Midwest).........	9	5	.643	3.25	20	19	1	0	0	113⅔	76	51	41	74	133
1993	—Stockton (Calif.)	1	3	.250	4.50	19	17	0	0	1	66	43	45	33	60	65

HILLEGAS, SHAWN

P, ANGELS

PERSONAL: Born August 21, 1964, in Dos Palos, Calif.... 6-2/223.... Throws right, bats right.... Full name: Shawn Patrick Hillegas.... Name pronounced HILL-uh-gus.

HIGH SCHOOL: Forest Hills (Sidman, Pa.).

COLLEGE: Middle Georgia College.

TRANSACTIONS/CAREER NOTES: Selected by California Angels organization in 26th round of free-agent draft (June 6, 1983).... Selected by Los Angeles Dodgers organization in secondary phase of free-agent draft (January 17, 1984).... Traded by Dodgers to Chicago White Sox (September 2, 1988), completing deal in which White Sox traded P Ricky Horton to Dodgers for a player to be named later (August 30, 1988).... Traded by White Sox with P Eric King to Cleveland Indians for OF Cory Snyder and IF Lindsay Foster (December 4, 1990).... Released by Indians (March 31, 1992).... Claimed on waivers by Toronto Blue Jays (April 3, 1992).... Granted free agency (April 4, 1992).... Signed by Fort Lauderdale, New York Yankees organization (April 9, 1992).... On Fort Lauderdale disabled list (April 10-19, 1992).... Released by Yankees (August 22, 1992).... Signed by Oakland Athletics organization (August 31, 1992).... Granted free agency (October 15, 1993).... Signed by Angels organization (January 28, 1994).

Year	Team (League)	W	L	Pct.	ERA	G	GS	CG	ShO	Sv.	IP	H	R	ER	BB	SO
1984	—Vero Beach (FSL).......	5	3	.625	1.83	13	13	4	2	0	93⅓	71	25	19	33	64
1985	—San Antonio (Tex.).....	4	10	.286	3.17	23	23	3	0	0	139⅓	134	72	49	67	56
1986	—San Antonio (Tex.).....	9	5	.643	3.06	17	17	7	1	0	132⅓	107	60	45	58	97
	—Albuquerque (PCL)....	1	5	.167	6.17	9	9	1	0	0	46⅔	48	35	32	31	43
1987	—Albuquerque (PCL)....	13	5	.722	3.37	24	24	4	1	0	165⅔	172	79	62	64	105
	—Los Angeles (N.L.).....	4	3	.571	3.57	12	10	0	0	0	58	52	27	23	31	51
1988	—Albuquerque (PCL)....	6	4	.600	3.49	16	15	2	2	0	100⅔	93	44	39	22	66
	—Los Angeles (N.L.).....	3	4	.429	4.13	11	10	0	0	0	56⅔	54	26	26	17	30
	—Chicago (A.L.)■.........	3	2	.600	3.15	6	6	0	0	0	40	30	16	14	18	26
1989	—Chicago (A.L.)...........	7	11	.389	4.74	50	13	0	0	3	119⅔	132	67	63	51	76
1990	—Vancouver (PCL).......	5	3	.625	1.74	36	0	0	0	9	67⅓	49	22	13	15	52
	—Chicago (A.L.)...........	0	0	...	0.79	7	0	0	0	0	11⅓	4	1	1	5	5
1991	—Cleveland (A.L.)■.......	3	4	.429	4.34	51	3	0	0	7	83	67	42	40	46	66
1992	—Fort Lauder. (FSL)■...	1	0	1.000	0.00	1	1	0	0	0	6	3	0	0	1	2
	—Columbus (Int'l).........	2	0	1.000	3.29	4	4	0	0	0	27⅓	24	10	10	10	20
	—N.Y.-Oak. (A.L.)■.......	1	8	.111	5.23	26	9	1	1	0	86	104	57	50	37	49
1993	—Oakland (A.L.)...........	3	6	.333	6.97	18	11	0	0	0	60⅔	78	48	47	33	29
	—Tacoma (PCL)............	2	3	.400	5.48	9	9	0	0	0	47⅔	62	31	29	13	29
A.L. totals (6 years)..............		17	31	.354	4.83	158	42	1	1	10	400⅔	415	231	215	190	251
N.L. totals (2 years)..............		7	7	.500	3.85	23	20	0	0	0	114⅔	106	53	49	48	81
Major league totals (7 years)..		24	38	.387	4.61	181	62	1	1	10	515⅓	521	284	264	238	332

HILLMAN, ERIC

P, METS

PERSONAL: Born April 27, 1966, in Gary, Ind.... 6-10/225.... Throws left, bats left.... Full name: John Eric Hillman.

HIGH SCHOOL: Homewood Flossmoor (Flossmoor, Ill.).

COLLEGE: Eastern Illinois.

TRANSACTIONS/CAREER NOTES: Selected by New York Mets organization in 16th round of free-agent draft (June 2, 1987).

STATISTICAL NOTES: Tied for International League lead with 10 hit batsmen in 1991.

Year	Team (League)	W	L	Pct.	ERA	G	GS	CG	ShO	Sv.	IP	H	R	ER	BB	SO
1987	—Little Falls (NYP).......	6	4	.600	4.22	13	13	2	1	0	79	84	44	37	30	80
1988	—Columbia (S. Atl.).......	1	6	.143	5.55	17	13	0	0	1	73	73	54	45	43	60
1989	—Columbia (S. Atl.).......	2	1	.667	1.87	9	7	0	0	1	33⅔	28	17	7	21	33
	—St. Lucie (Fla. St.)......	6	6	.500	5.50	19	14	1	0	0	88⅓	96	59	54	53	67
1990	—St. Lucie (Fla. St.)......	2	0	1.000	0.67	4	3	0	0	0	27	15	2	2	8	23
	—Jackson (Texas)........	6	5	.545	3.93	15	15	0	0	0	89⅓	92	42	39	30	61
1991	—Tidewater (Int'l).........	5	12	.294	4.01	27	27	2	0	0	161⅔	184	89	72	58	91
1992	—Tidewater (Int'l).........	9	2	.818	3.65	34	9	0	0	0	91⅓	93	39	37	27	49
	—New York (N.L.)..........	2	2	.500	5.33	11	8	0	0	0	52⅓	67	31	31	10	16
1993	—Norfolk (Int'l)............	6	2	.750	2.21	10	9	3	1	0	61	52	18	15	12	27
	—New York (N.L.).........	2	9	.182	3.97	27	22	3	1	0	145	173	83	64	24	60
Major league totals (2 years)..		4	11	.267	4.33	38	30	3	1	0	197⅓	240	114	95	34	76

HITCHCOCK, STERLING

P, YANKEES

PERSONAL: Born April 29, 1971, in Fayetteville, N.C.... 6-1/192.... Throws left, bats left.... Full name: Sterling Alex Hitchcock.
HIGH SCHOOL: Armwood (Seffner, Fla.).
TRANSACTIONS/CAREER NOTES: Selected by New York Yankees organization in ninth round of free-agent draft (June 5, 1989).... On disabled list (June 26-August 14, 1991).... On Columbus disabled list (May 23-July 21, 1993).
STATISTICAL NOTES: Pitched 1-0 no-hit victory against Sumter (July 16, 1990).

Year	Team (League)	W	L	Pct.	ERA	G	GS	CG	ShO	Sv.	IP	H	R	ER	BB	SO
1989	—GC Yankees (GCL)	*9	1	.900	1.64	13	•13	0	0	0	76⅔	48	16	14	27	*98
1990	—Greensboro (S. Atl.)	12	12	.500	2.91	27	27	6	*5	0	173⅓	122	68	56	60	*171
1991	—Prin. William (Car.)	7	7	.500	2.64	19	19	2	0	0	119⅓	111	49	35	26	101
1992	—Alb./Colon. (East.)	6	9	.400	2.58	24	24	2	0	0	146⅔	116	51	42	42	*155
	—New York (A.L.)	0	2	.000	8.31	3	3	0	0	0	13	23	12	12	6	6
1993	—Columbus (Int'l)	3	5	.375	4.81	16	16	0	0	0	76⅔	80	43	41	28	85
	—New York (A.L.)	1	2	.333	4.65	6	6	0	0	0	31	32	18	16	14	26
	Major league totals (2 years)	1	4	.200	5.73	9	9	0	0	0	44	55	30	28	20	32

HOCKING, DENNY

SS, TWINS

PERSONAL: Born April 2, 1970, in Torrance, Calif.... 5-10/176.... Throws right, bats both.... Full name: Dennis Lee Hocking.
HIGH SCHOOL: West Torrance (Torrance, Calif.).
COLLEGE: El Camino College (Calif.).
TRANSACTIONS/CAREER NOTES: Selected by Minnesota Twins organization in 52nd round of free-agent draft (June 5, 1989).... On Nashville disabled list (April 8-29, 1993).
STATISTICAL NOTES: Led California League shortstops with 721 total chances in 1992.

			BATTING												FIELDING			
Year	Team (League)	Pos.	G	AB	R	H	2B	3B	HR	RBI	Avg.	BB	SO	SB	PO	A	E	Avg.
1990	—Elizabeth. (Appal.)	SS-2B-3B	54	201	45	59	6	2	6	30	.294	40	26	14	77	179	20	.928
1991	—Kenosha (Midwest)	SS	125	432	72	110	17	8	2	36	.255	77	69	22	193	308	42	.923
1992	—Visalia (California)	SS	135	*550	117	*182	34	9	7	81	.331	72	77	38	214	*469	38	.947
1993	—Nashville (South.)	SS-2B	107	409	54	109	9	4	8	50	.267	34	66	15	144	300	30	.937
	—Minnesota (A.L.)	SS-2B	15	36	7	5	1	0	0	0	.139	6	8	1	19	23	1	.977
	Major league totals (1 year)		15	36	7	5	1	0	0	0	.139	6	8	1	19	23	1	.977

HOFFMAN, TREVOR

P, PADRES

PERSONAL: Born October 13, 1967, in Bellflower, Calif.... 6-0/205.... Throws right, bats right.... Full name: Trevor William Hoffman.... Brother of Glenn Hoffman, current minor league field coordinator, Los Angeles Dodgers, and major league infielder with Boston Red Sox, Dodgers and California Angels (1980-89).
HIGH SCHOOL: Savanna (Anaheim, Calif.).
COLLEGE: Cypress (Calif.) College and Arizona.
TRANSACTIONS/CAREER NOTES: Selected by Cincinnati Reds organization in 11th round of free-agent draft (June 5, 1989).... Selected by Florida Marlins in first round (eighth pick overall) of expansion draft (November 17, 1992).... Traded by Marlins with P Jose Martinez and P Andres Berumen to San Diego Padres for 3B Gary Sheffield and P Rich Rodriguez (June 24, 1993).

Year	Team (League)	W	L	Pct.	ERA	G	GS	CG	ShO	Sv.	IP	H	R	ER	BB	SO
1991	—Ced. Rap. (Midw.)	1	1	.500	1.87	27	0	0	0	12	33⅔	22	8	7	13	52
	—Chatt. (South.)	1	0	1.000	1.93	14	0	0	0	8	14	10	4	3	7	23
1992	—Chatt. (South.)	3	0	1.000	1.52	6	6	0	0	0	29⅔	22	6	5	11	31
	—Nashville (A.A.)	4	6	.400	4.27	42	5	0	0	6	65⅓	57	32	31	32	63
1993	—Fla.-S.D. (N.L.)■	4	6	.400	3.90	67	0	0	0	5	90	80	43	39	39	79
	Major league totals (1 year)	4	6	.400	3.90	67	0	0	0	5	90	80	43	39	39	79

RECORD AS POSITION PLAYER

			BATTING												FIELDING			
Year	Team (League)	Pos.	G	AB	R	H	2B	3B	HR	RBI	Avg.	BB	SO	SB	PO	A	E	Avg.
1989	—Billings (Pioneer)	SS	61	201	22	50	5	0	1	20	.249	19	40	1	*116	140	•25	.911
1990	—Char., W.Va. (SAL)	SS-3B	103	278	41	59	10	1	2	23	.212	38	53	3	114	209	30	.915

HOILES, CHRIS

C, ORIOLES

PERSONAL: Born March 20, 1965, in Bowling Green, O.... 6-0/213.... Throws right, bats right.... Full name: Christopher Allen Hoiles.
HIGH SCHOOL: Elmwood (Wayne, O.).
COLLEGE: Eastern Michigan.
TRANSACTIONS/CAREER NOTES: Selected by Detroit Tigers organization in 19th round of free-agent draft (June 2, 1986).... Traded by Tigers organization with P Cesar Mejia and P Robinson Garces to Baltimore Orioles (September 9, 1988), completing deal in which Orioles traded OF Fred Lynn to Tigers for three players to be named later (August 31, 1988).... On Rochester disabled list (June 18-July 7, 1989).... On Baltimore disabled list (June 22-August 18, 1992); included rehabilitation assignment to Hagerstown (August 11-18).... On disabled list (August 3-24, 1993).
STATISTICAL NOTES: Led Appalachian League first basemen with .996 fielding percentage, 515 putouts and 551 total chances in 1986.... Led Appalachian League with 143 total bases in 1986.... Led Eastern League with .500 slugging percentage in 1988.... Tied for Eastern League lead in double plays by catcher with five in 1988.... Led A.L. catchers with .998 fielding percentage in 1991.

			BATTING												FIELDING			
Year	Team (League)	Pos.	G	AB	R	H	2B	3B	HR	RBI	Avg.	BB	SO	SB	PO	A	E	Avg.
1986	—Bristol (Appal.)	1B-C	•68	253	42	81	*19	2	13	*57	.320	30	20	10	†563	38	4	†.993
1987	—Glens Falls (East.)	C-1B-3B	108	380	47	105	12	0	13	53	.276	35	37	1	406	88	11	.978
1988	—Glens Falls (East.)	C-1B	103	360	67	102	21	3	•17	73	.283	50	56	4	438	57	7	.986

Year	Team (League)	Pos.	G	AB	R	H	2B	3B	HR	RBI	Avg.	BB	SO	SB	PO	A	E	Avg.
			BATTING												FIELDING			
	—Toledo (Int'l)	C	22	69	4	11	1	0	2	6	.159	2	12	1	71	2	1	.986
1989	—Rochester (Int'l)■	C-1B	96	322	41	79	19	1	10	51	.245	31	58	1	431	33	7	.985
	—Baltimore (A.L.)	C	6	9	0	1	1	0	0	1	.111	1	3	0	11	0	0	1.000
1990	—Rochester (Int'l)	C-1B	74	247	52	86	20	1	18	56	.348	44	48	4	268	13	5	.983
	—Baltimore (A.L.)	C-1B	23	63	7	12	3	0	1	6	.190	5	12	0	62	6	0	1.000
1991	—Baltimore (A.L.)	C-1B	107	341	36	83	15	0	11	31	.243	29	61	0	443	44	1	†.998
1992	—Baltimore (A.L.)	C	96	310	49	85	10	1	20	40	.274	55	60	0	500	31	3	.994
	—Hagerstown (East.)	C	7	24	7	11	1	0	1	5	.458	2	5	0	16	5	0	1.000
1993	—Baltimore (A.L.)	C	126	419	80	130	28	0	29	82	.310	69	94	1	696	64	5	.993
Major league totals (5 years)			358	1142	172	311	57	1	61	160	.272	159	230	1	1712	145	9	.995

HOLBERT, AARON

SS, CARDINALS

PERSONAL: Born January 9, 1973, in Torrance, Calif. . . . 6-0/160. . . . Throws right, bats right. . . . Full name: Aaron Keith Holbert. . . . Brother of Ray Holbert, shortstop, San Diego Padres organization.

HIGH SCHOOL: David Starr Jordan (Long Beach, Calif.).

TRANSACTIONS/CAREER NOTES: Selected by St. Louis Cardinals organization in first round (18th pick overall) of free-agent draft (June 4, 1990); pick received as part of compensation for Boston Red Sox signing Type A free agent Tony Pena. . . . On disabled list (June 5-July 17, 1991).

STATISTICAL NOTES: Led Florida State League in caught stealing with 22 in 1993.

Year	Team (League)	Pos.	G	AB	R	H	2B	3B	HR	RBI	Avg.	BB	SO	SB	PO	A	E	Avg.
			BATTING												FIELDING			
1990	—Johns. City (App.)	SS	54	174	27	30	4	1	1	18	.172	24	31	4	87	136	*30	.881
1991	—Springfield (Midw.)	SS	59	215	22	48	5	1	1	24	.223	15	28	5	112	181	15	.951
1992	—Savannah (S. Atl.)	SS	119	438	53	117	17	4	1	34	.267	40	57	62	190	314	47	.915
1993	—St. Peters. (FSL)	SS-2B	121	457	60	121	18	3	2	31	.265	28	61	45	220	351	32	.947

HOLBERT, RAY

SS, PADRES

PERSONAL: Born September 25, 1970, in Torrance, Calif. . . . 6-0/170. . . . Throws right, bats right. . . . Full name: Ray Arthur Holbert III. . . . Brother of Aaron Holbert, shortstop, St. Louis Cardinals organization.

HIGH SCHOOL: David Starr Jordan (Long Beach, Calif.).

TRANSACTIONS/CAREER NOTES: Selected by San Diego Padres organization in third round of free-agent draft (June 1, 1988). . . . On disabled list (July 7-28, 1992).

STATISTICAL NOTES: Led Arizona League shortstops with .927 fielding percentage and 132 assists in 1988. . . . Led Midwest League shortstops with 642 total chances and 75 double plays in 1990. . . . Led Texas League with nine sacrifice flies in 1993.

Year	Team (League)	Pos.	G	AB	R	H	2B	3B	HR	RBI	Avg.	BB	SO	SB	PO	A	E	Avg.
			BATTING												FIELDING			
1988	—Ariz. Padres (Ariz.)	SS-3B	49	170	38	44	1	0	3	19	.259	38	32	20	59	†137	15	†.929
1989	—Waterloo (Midw.)	SS-3B	117	354	37	55	7	1	0	20	.155	41	99	13	205	303	32	.941
1990	—Waterloo (Midw.)	SS	133	411	51	84	10	1	3	39	.204	51	117	16	*233	*378	31	.952
1991	—High Desert (Calif.)	SS	122	386	76	102	14	2	4	51	.264	56	83	19	196	331	*37	.934
1992	—Wichita (Texas)	SS	95	304	46	86	7	3	2	23	.283	42	68	26	150	217	17	.956
1993	—Wichita (Texas)	SS	112	388	56	101	13	5	5	48	.260	54	87	30	155	267	30	.934

HOLIFIELD, RICK

OF, BLUE JAYS

PERSONAL: Born March 25, 1970, in Bronx, N.Y. . . . 6-2/180. . . . Throws left, bats left. . . . Full name: Marshall Rickey Holifield.

HIGH SCHOOL: Ganesha (Pomona, Calif.).

TRANSACTIONS/CAREER NOTES: Selected by Toronto Blue Jays organization in 21st round of free-agent draft (June 1, 1988).

STATISTICAL NOTES: Led Florida State League in being hit by pitch with 16 and tied for lead with 214 total bases and .526 slugging percentage in 1993.

Year	Team (League)	Pos.	G	AB	R	H	2B	3B	HR	RBI	Avg.	BB	SO	SB	PO	A	E	Avg.
			BATTING												FIELDING			
1988	—Medicine Hat (Pio.)	OF	31	96	16	26	4	1	1	6	.271	9	27	6	36	5	*14	.745
1989	—St. Cathar. (NYP)	OF	60	209	22	46	7	1	4	21	.220	15	74	4	115	4	2	.983
1990	—Myrtle Beach (SAL)	OF	99	279	37	56	9	2	3	18	.201	28	88	13	171	2	10	.945
1991	—Myrtle Beach (SAL)	OF	114	324	37	71	15	5	1	25	.219	34	94	16	152	8	5	.970
1992	—Myrtle Beach (SAL)	OF	93	281	32	56	15	2	8	27	.199	23	81	6	157	4	11	.936
1993	—Dunedin (Fla. St.)	OF	127	407	84	112	18	12	*20	68	.275	56	*129	30	255	9	•12	.957

HOLLINS, DAVE

3B, PHILLIES

PERSONAL: Born May 25, 1966, in Buffalo, N.Y. . . . 6-1/215. . . . Throws right, bats both. . . . Full name: David Michael Hollins.

HIGH SCHOOL: Orchard Park (N.Y.).

COLLEGE: South Carolina.

TRANSACTIONS/CAREER NOTES: Selected by San Diego Padres organization in sixth round of free-agent draft (June 2, 1987). . . . Selected by Philadelphia Phillies from Padres organization in Rule 5 major league draft (December 4, 1989). . . . On Philadelphia disabled list (August 16-September 6, 1991); included rehabilitation assignment to Scranton/Wilkes-Barre (September 2-5). . . . On suspended list (September 29-October 3, 1992). . . . On disabled list (June 11-28, 1993).

STATISTICAL NOTES: Led Northwest League with seven intentional bases on balls received in 1987. . . . Led Northwest League third basemen with 241 total chances in 1987. . . . Led Texas League with 10 sacrifice flies in 1989. . . . Led N.L. in being hit by pitch with 19 in 1992.

H

Year	Team (League)	Pos.	G	AB	R	H	2B	3B	HR	RBI	Avg.	BB	SO	SB	PO	A	E	Avg.
			BATTING												FIELDING			
1987	—Spokane (N'west).....	3B	75	278	52	86	14	4	2	44	.309	53	36	20	*59	*167	15	*.938
1988	—Riverside (Calif.)......	3B-1B-SS	139	516	90	157	32	1	9	92	.304	82	67	13	102	248	29	.923
1989	—Wichita (Texas).......	3B	131	459	69	126	29	4	9	79	.275	63	88	8	77	209	25	.920
1990	—Philadelphia (N.L.)■.	3B-1B	72	114	14	21	0	0	5	15	.184	10	28	0	27	37	4	.941
1991	—Philadelphia (N.L.)...	3B-1B	56	151	18	45	10	2	6	21	.298	17	26	1	67	62	8	.942
	—Scran./W.B. (Int'l)...	3B-1B	72	229	37	61	11	6	8	35	.266	43	43	4	67	105	10	.945
1992	—Philadelphia (N.L.)...	3B-1B	156	586	104	158	28	4	27	93	.270	76	110	9	120	253	18	.954
1993	—Philadelphia (N.L.)...	3B	143	543	104	148	30	4	18	93	.273	85	109	2	73	215	27	.914
Major league totals (4 years)			427	1394	240	372	68	10	56	222	.267	188	273	12	287	567	57	.937

CHAMPIONSHIP SERIES RECORD

Year	Team (League)	Pos.	G	AB	R	H	2B	3B	HR	RBI	Avg.	BB	SO	SB	PO	A	E	Avg.
			BATTING												FIELDING			
1993	—Philadelphia (N.L.)...	3B	6	20	2	4	1	0	2	4	.200	5	4	1	5	4	0	1.000

WORLD SERIES RECORD

Year	Team (League)	Pos.	G	AB	R	H	2B	3B	HR	RBI	Avg.	BB	SO	SB	PO	A	E	Avg.
			BATTING												FIELDING			
1993	—Philadelphia (N.L.)...	3B	6	23	5	6	1	0	0	2	.261	6	5	0	9	9	0	1.000

ALL-STAR GAME RECORD

Year	League	Pos.	AB	R	H	2B	3B	HR	RBI	Avg.	BB	SO	SB	PO	A	E	Avg.
			BATTING											FIELDING			
1993	—National....................	3B	1	0	1	1	0	0	0	1.000	0	0	0	1	0	0	1.000

HOLLINS, JESSIE

P, CUBS

PERSONAL: Born January 27, 1970, in Conroe, Tex.... 6-3/235.... Throws right, bats right.... Full name: Jessie Edward Hollins.
HIGH SCHOOL: Willis (Tex.).
COLLEGE: San Jacinto College (Tex.).
TRANSACTIONS/CAREER NOTES: Selected by Chicago Cubs organization in 40th round of free-agent draft (June 1, 1988).... On Chicago disabled list (March 28, 1993-entire season).
STATISTICAL NOTES: Led New York-Pennsylvania League with 21 wild pitches in 1990.

Year	Team (League)	W	L	Pct.	ERA	G	GS	CG	ShO	Sv.	IP	H	R	ER	BB	SO
1989	—Wytheville (Appal.)....	3	1	.750	4.84	22	3	0	0	0	48⅓	59	44	26	23	31
1990	—Peoria (Midwest).......	0	0	...	5.59	5	0	0	0	0	9⅔	12	9	6	5	8
	—Geneva (NY-Penn)....	•10	3	.769	2.77	17	*16	1	0	0	97⅓	87	49	30	49	115
1991	—Winst.-Salem (Car.).....	4	8	.333	5.67	41	13	0	0	5	98⅓	107	78	62	83	74
1992	—Charlotte (South.).......	3	4	.429	3.20	63	0	0	0	25	70⅓	60	28	25	32	73
	—Chicago (N.L.)............	0	0	...	13.50	4	0	0	0	0	4⅔	8	7	7	5	0
1993	—..................................							Did not play.								
Major league totals (1 year).....		0	0	...	13.50	4	0	0	0	0	4⅔	8	7	7	5	0

HOLMAN, BRAD

P, MARINERS

PERSONAL: Born February 9, 1968, in Kansas City, Mo.... 6-5/200.... Throws right, bats right.... Full name: Bradley Thomas Holman.... Brother of Brian Holman, pitcher, Cincinnati Reds.
HIGH SCHOOL: North (Wichita, Kan.).
COLLEGE: Auburn-Montgomery.
TRANSACTIONS/CAREER NOTES: Selected by Kansas City Royals organization in 35th round of free-agent draft (June 4, 1990).... Released by Eugene, Royals organization (March 29, 1991).... Signed by Peninsula, Seattle Mariners organization (April 7, 1991).... On Seattle disabled list (August 9-28, 1993).

Year	Team (League)	W	L	Pct.	ERA	G	GS	CG	ShO	Sv.	IP	H	R	ER	BB	SO
1990	—Eugene (N'west)........	0	3	.000	4.78	17	17	4	0	0	43⅓	43	28	23	17	31
1991	—Peninsula (Caro.)■.....	6	6	.500	3.22	47	0	0	0	10	78⅓	70	34	28	33	71
1992	—Peninsula (Caro.)........	1	1	.500	3.06	13	0	0	0	5	17⅔	15	8	6	4	19
	—Jacksonv. (South.)....	3	3	.500	2.57	35	0	0	0	4	73⅔	67	24	21	21	76
1993	—Calgary (PCL)...........	8	4	.667	4.74	21	13	1	0	0	98⅔	109	59	52	42	54
	—Seattle (A.L.)............	1	3	.250	3.72	19	0	0	0	3	36⅓	27	17	15	16	17
Major league totals (1 year)...		1	3	.250	3.72	19	0	0	0	3	36⅓	27	17	15	16	17

HOLMAN, BRIAN

P, REDS

PERSONAL: Born January 25, 1965, in Denver.... 6-4/190.... Throws right, bats right.... Full name: Brian Scott Holman.... Brother of Brad Holman, pitcher, Seattle Mariners.
HIGH SCHOOL: North (Wichita, Kan.).
TRANSACTIONS/CAREER NOTES: Selected by Montreal Expos organization in first round (16th pick overall) of free-agent draft (June 6, 1983); pick received as compensation for San Francisco Giants signing Type A free agent Joel Youngblood.... On disabled list (August 3, 1983-remainder of season).... Traded by Expos with P Randy Johnson and P Gene Harris to Seattle Mariners for P Mark Langston and a player to be named later (May 25, 1989); Indianapolis, Expos organization, acquired P Mike Campbell to complete deal (July 31, 1989).... On Seattle disabled list (March 31, 1992-entire season and March 26, 1993-entire season).... Claimed on waivers by Cincinnati Reds (October 14, 1993).
HONORS: Named Southern League Pitcher of the Year (1987).
MISCELLANEOUS: Batted once in order (reached on error) after designated hitter moved to first base (1990).

Year	Team (League)	W	L	Pct.	ERA	G	GS	CG	ShO	Sv.	IP	H	R	ER	BB	SO
1983	—Jamestown (NYP)......	0	0	...	11.81	2	2	0	0	0	5⅓	7	7	7	4	5
1984	—W.P. Beach (FSL)......	0	3	.000	18.00	4	4	0	0	0	8	14	19	16	21	14

H

Year	Team (League)	W	L	Pct.	ERA	G	GS	CG	ShO	Sv.	IP	H	R	ER	BB	SO
	—Gastonia (S. Atl.)	5	8	.385	4.76	20	20	1	0	0	90⅔	76	58	48	98	94
1985	—W.P. Beach (FSL)	9	9	.500	3.96	25	24	6	2	0	143⅓	124	79	63	90	103
1986	—Jacksonv. (South.)	11	9	.550	5.14	27	27	3	0	0	157⅔	146	111	90	*122	118
1987	—Jacksonv. (South.)	14	5	.737	*2.50	22	22	*6	1	0	151⅓	114	52	42	56	115
	—Indianapolis (A.A.)	0	4	.000	6.23	6	6	0	0	0	34⅔	41	28	24	33	27
1988	—Indianapolis (A.A.)	8	1	.889	2.36	14	13	2	1	0	91⅓	78	26	24	30	70
	—Montreal (N.L.)	4	8	.333	3.23	18	16	1	1	0	100⅓	101	39	36	34	58
1989	—Montreal (N.L.)	1	2	.333	4.83	10	3	0	0	0	31⅔	34	18	17	15	23
	—Seattle (A.L.)■	8	10	.444	3.44	23	22	6	2	0	159⅔	160	68	61	62	82
1990	—Seattle (A.L.)	11	11	.500	4.03	28	28	3	0	0	189⅔	188	92	85	66	121
1991	—Seattle (A.L.)	13	14	.481	3.69	30	30	5	3	0	195⅓	199	86	80	77	108
1992	—							Did not play.								
1993	—							Did not play.								
A.L. totals (3 years)		32	35	.478	3.73	81	80	14	5	0	544⅔	547	246	226	205	311
N.L. totals (2 years)		5	10	.333	3.61	28	19	1	1	0	132	135	57	53	49	81
Major league totals (4 years)		37	45	.451	3.71	109	99	15	6	0	676⅔	682	303	279	254	392

HOLMES, DARREN

P, ROCKIES

PERSONAL: Born April 25, 1966, in Asheville, N.C. . . . 6-0/200. . . . Throws right, bats right. . . . Full name: Darren Lee Holmes.

HIGH SCHOOL: T.C. Roberson (Asheville, N.C.).

TRANSACTIONS/CAREER NOTES: Selected by Los Angeles Dodgers organization in 16th round of free-agent draft (June 4, 1984). . . . On disabled list (June 5, 1986-remainder of season). . . . Loaned by Dodgers organization to San Luis Potosi (1988). . . . Traded by Dodgers to Milwaukee Brewers for C Bert Heffernan (December 20, 1990). . . . On Milwaukee disabled list (July 3-18, 1991); included rehabilitation assignment to Beloit (July 13-18). . . . Selected by Colorado Rockies in first round (fifth pick overall) of expansion draft (November 17, 1992).

Year	Team (League)	W	L	Pct.	ERA	G	GS	CG	ShO	Sv.	IP	H	R	ER	BB	SO
1984	—Great Falls (Pio.)	2	5	.286	6.65	18	6	1	0	0	44⅔	53	41	33	30	29
1985	—Vero Beach (FSL)	4	3	.571	3.11	33	0	0	0	2	63⅔	57	31	22	35	46
1986	—Vero Beach (FSL)	3	6	.333	2.92	11	10	0	0	0	64⅔	55	30	21	39	59
1987	—Vero Beach (FSL)	6	4	.600	4.52	19	19	1	0	0	99⅔	111	60	50	53	46
1988	—San Luis Pot. (Mex.)■	9	9	.500	4.64	23	23	7	1	0	139⅔	151	88	72	92	110
	—Albuquerque (PCL)■	0	1	.000	5.06	2	1	0	0	0	5⅓	6	3	3	1	1
1989	—San Antonio (Tex.)	5	8	.385	3.83	17	16	3	2	1	110⅓	102	59	47	44	81
	—Albuquerque (PCL)	1	4	.200	7.45	9	8	0	0	0	38⅔	50	32	32	18	31
1990	—Albuquerque (PCL)	12	2	*.857	3.11	56	0	0	0	13	92⅔	78	34	32	39	99
	—Los Angeles (N.L.)	0	1	.000	5.19	14	0	0	0	0	17⅓	15	10	10	11	19
1991	—Denver (A.A.)■	0	0	...	9.00	1	0	0	0	0	1	1	1	1	2	2
	—Milwaukee (A.L.)	1	4	.200	4.72	40	0	0	0	3	76⅓	90	43	40	27	59
	—Beloit (Midwest)	0	0	...	0.00	2	0	0	0	2	2	0	0	0	0	3
1992	—Denver (A.A.)	0	0	...	1.38	12	0	0	0	7	13	7	2	2	1	12
	—Milwaukee (A.L.)	4	4	.500	2.55	41	0	0	0	6	42⅓	35	12	12	11	31
1993	—Colorado (N.L.)■	3	3	.500	4.05	62	0	0	0	25	66⅔	56	31	30	20	60
	—Colo. Springs (PCL)	1	0	1.000	0.00	3	2	0	0	0	8⅔	1	1	0	1	9
A.L. totals (2 years)		5	8	.385	3.94	81	0	0	0	9	118⅔	125	55	52	38	90
N.L. totals (2 years)		3	4	.429	4.29	76	0	0	0	25	84	71	41	40	31	79
Major league totals (4 years)		8	12	.400	4.09	157	0	0	0	34	202⅔	196	96	92	69	169

HOLZEMER, MARK

P, ANGELS

PERSONAL: Born August 20, 1969, in Littleton, Colo. . . . 6-0/165. . . . Throws left, bats left. . . . Full name: Mark Harold Holzemer. . . . Name pronounced HOLE-zeh-mer.

HIGH SCHOOL: J.K. Mullen (Denver).

COLLEGE: Seminole (Okla.) Junior College.

TRANSACTIONS/CAREER NOTES: Selected by California Angels organization in fourth round of free-agent draft (June 2, 1987). . . . On Midland disabled list (July 2-September 18, 1990; April 12-May 25 and June 7-26, 1991).

Year	Team (League)	W	L	Pct.	ERA	G	GS	CG	ShO	Sv.	IP	H	R	ER	BB	SO
1988	—Bend (Northwest)	4	6	.400	5.24	13	13	1	1	0	68⅔	59	51	40	47	72
1989	—Quad City (Midw.)	12	7	.632	3.36	25	25	3	1	0	139⅓	122	68	52	64	131
1990	—Midland (Texas)	1	7	.125	5.26	15	15	1	0	0	77	92	55	45	41	54
1991	—Midland (Texas)	0	0	...	1.42	2	2	0	0	0	6⅓	3	2	1	5	7
	—Palm Springs (Cal.)	0	4	.000	2.86	6	6	0	0	0	22	15	14	7	16	19
1992	—Palm Springs (Cal.)	3	2	.600	3.00	5	5	2	0	0	30	23	10	10	13	32
	—Midland (Texas)	2	5	.286	3.83	7	7	2	0	0	44⅔	45	22	19	13	36
	—Edmonton (PCL)	5	7	.417	6.67	17	16	4	0	0	89	114	69	66	55	49
1993	—Vancouver (PCL)	9	6	.600	4.82	24	23	2	0	0	145⅔	158	94	78	70	80
	—California (A.L.)	0	3	.000	8.87	5	4	0	0	0	23⅓	34	24	23	13	10
Major league totals (1 year)		0	3	.000	8.87	5	4	0	0	0	23⅓	34	24	23	13	10

HONEYCUTT, RICK

P, RANGERS

PERSONAL: Born June 29, 1954, in Chattanooga, Tenn. . . . 6-1/191. . . . Throws left, bats left. . . . Full name: Frederick Wayne Honeycutt.

HIGH SCHOOL: Lakeview (Fort Oglethorpe, Ga.).

COLLEGE: Tennessee (bachelor of science degree in health education).

TRANSACTIONS/CAREER NOTES: Selected by Baltimore Orioles organization in 14th round of free-agent draft (June 6, 1972). . . . Selected by Pittsburgh Pirates organization in 17th round of free-agent draft (June 8, 1976). . . . Traded by Pirates organization to Seattle Mariners (August 22, 1977), completing deal in which Mariners traded P Dave Pagan to Pirates for a player to be named later (July 27, 1977). . . . On disabled list (May 20-June 26, 1978). . . . Traded by Mariners with C Larry Cox, OF Willie Horton, OF Leon Roberts and SS Mario Mendoza to Texas Rangers for P Brian Allard, P Ken Clay, P Steve Finch, P

Jerry Don Gleaton, SS Rick Auerbach and OF Richie Zisk (December 12, 1980).... Traded by Rangers to Los Angeles Dodgers for P Dave Stewart and a player to be named later (August 19, 1983); Rangers acquired P Ricky Wright to complete deal (September 16, 1983).... Traded by Dodgers to Oakland Athletics for a player to be named later (August 29, 1987); Dodgers acquired P Tim Belcher to complete deal (September 3, 1987).... Granted free agency (November 4, 1988).... Re-signed by A's (December 21, 1988).... On Oakland disabled list (April 1-June 16, 1991); included rehabilitation assignment to Modesto (June 6-14) and Madison (June 14-16).... Granted free agency (October 30, 1992).... Re-signed by A's (December 7, 1992).... On disabled list (June 15-July 24, 1993).... Granted free agency (November 1, 1993).... Signed by Rangers (November 24, 1993).

MISCELLANEOUS: Played two games as first baseman and one game as shortstop (1976).... Appeared as shortstop with no chances with Shreveport (1977).... Made an out in both appearances as a pinch-hitter and appeared in one game as a pinch-runner (1990).

Year	Team (League)	W	L	Pct.	ERA	G	GS	CG	ShO	Sv.	IP	H	R	ER	BB	SO
1976	—Niag. Falls (NYP)	5	3	.625	2.60	13	12	•7	0	0	*97	91	36	28	20	*98
1977	—Shreveport (Texas)	10	6	.625	*2.47	21	21	6	0	0	135	144	53	37	42	82
	—Seattle (A.L.)■	0	1	.000	4.34	10	3	0	0	0	29	26	16	14	11	17
1978	—Seattle (A.L.)	5	11	.313	4.90	26	24	4	1	0	134	150	81	73	49	50
1979	—Seattle (A.L.)	11	12	.478	4.04	33	28	8	0	0	194	201	103	87	67	83
1980	—Seattle (A.L.)	10	17	.370	3.95	30	30	9	2	0	203	221	99	89	60	79
1981	—Texas (A.L.)■	11	6	.647	3.30	20	20	8	2	0	128	120	49	47	17	40
1982	—Texas (A.L.)	5	17	.227	5.27	30	26	4	1	0	164	201	103	96	54	64
1983	—Texas (A.L.)	14	8	.636	*2.42	25	25	5	2	0	174⅔	168	59	47	37	56
	—Los Angeles (N.L.)■	2	3	.400	5.77	9	7	1	0	0	39	46	26	25	13	18
1984	—Los Angeles (N.L.)	10	9	.526	2.84	29	28	6	2	0	183⅔	180	72	58	51	75
1985	—Los Angeles (N.L.)	8	12	.400	3.42	31	25	1	0	1	142	141	71	54	49	67
1986	—Los Angeles (N.L.)	11	9	.550	3.32	32	28	0	0	0	171	164	71	63	45	100
1987	—Los Angeles (N.L.)	2	12	.143	4.59	27	20	1	1	0	115⅔	133	74	59	45	92
	—Oakland (A.L.)■	1	4	.200	5.32	7	4	0	0	0	23⅔	25	17	14	9	10
1988	—Oakland (A.L.)	3	2	.600	3.50	55	0	0	0	7	79⅔	74	36	31	25	47
1989	—Oakland (A.L.)	2	2	.500	2.35	64	0	0	0	12	76⅔	56	26	20	26	52
1990	—Oakland (A.L.)	2	2	.500	2.70	63	0	0	0	7	63⅓	46	23	19	22	38
1991	—Oakland (A.L.)	2	4	.333	3.58	43	0	0	0	0	37⅔	37	16	15	20	26
	—Modesto (Calif.)	0	0	...	0.00	3	3	0	0	0	5	4	1	0	1	5
	—Madison (Midwest)	0	1	.000	18.00	1	1	0	0	0	1	4	2	2	0	2
1992	—Oakland (A.L.)	1	4	.200	3.69	54	0	0	0	3	39	41	19	16	10	32
1993	—Oakland (A.L.)	1	4	.200	2.81	52	0	0	0	1	41⅔	30	18	13	20	21
A.L. totals (14 years)		68	94	.420	3.77	512	160	38	8	30	1388⅓	1396	665	581	427	615
N.L. totals (5 years)		33	45	.423	3.58	128	108	9	3	1	651⅓	664	314	259	203	352
Major league totals (17 years)		101	139	.421	3.71	640	268	47	11	31	2039⅔	2060	979	840	630	967

CHAMPIONSHIP SERIES RECORD

CHAMPIONSHIP SERIES NOTES: Shares career record for most games as relief pitcher—15.

Year	Team (League)	W	L	Pct.	ERA	G	GS	CG	ShO	Sv.	IP	H	R	ER	BB	SO
1983	—Los Angeles (N.L.)	0	0	...	21.60	2	0	0	0	0	1⅔	4	4	4	0	2
1985	—Los Angeles (N.L.)	0	0	...	13.50	2	0	0	0	0	1⅓	4	2	2	2	1
1988	—Oakland (A.L.)	1	0	1.000	0.00	3	0	0	0	0	2	0	0	0	2	0
1989	—Oakland (A.L.)	0	0	...	32.40	3	0	0	0	0	1⅔	6	6	6	5	1
1990	—Oakland (A.L.)	0	0	...	0.00	3	0	0	0	1	1⅔	0	0	0	0	0
1992	—Oakland (A.L.)	0	0	...	0.00	2	0	0	0	0	2	0	0	0	0	1
Champ. series totals (6 years)		1	0	1.000	10.45	15	0	0	0	1	10⅓	14	12	12	9	5

WORLD SERIES RECORD

Year	Team (League)	W	L	Pct.	ERA	G	GS	CG	ShO	Sv.	IP	H	R	ER	BB	SO
1988	—Oakland (A.L.)	1	0	1.000	0.00	3	0	0	0	0	3⅓	0	0	0	0	5
1989	—Oakland (A.L.)	0	0	...	6.75	3	0	0	0	0	2⅔	4	2	2	0	2
1990	—Oakland (A.L.)	0	0	...	0.00	1	0	0	0	0	1⅔	2	0	0	1	0
World Series totals (3 years)		1	0	1.000	2.35	7	0	0	0	0	7⅔	6	2	2	1	7

ALL-STAR GAME RECORD

Year	League	W	L	Pct.	ERA	GS	CG	ShO	Sv.	IP	H	R	ER	BB	SO
1980	—American						Did not play.								
1983	—American	0	0	...	9.00	0	0	0	0	2	5	2	2	0	0
All-Star totals (1 year)		0	0	...	9.00	0	0	0	0	2	5	2	2	0	0

HOPE, JOHN

P, PIRATES

PERSONAL: Born December 21, 1970, in Fort Lauderdale, Fla.... 6-3/206.... Throws right, bats right.... Full name: John Alan Hope.

HIGH SCHOOL: Stranahan (Fort Lauderdale, Fla.).

TRANSACTIONS/CAREER NOTES: Selected by Pittsburgh Pirates organization in supplemental round ("sandwich pick" between second and third round) of free-agent draft (June 5, 1989); pick received as compensation for New York Yankees signing Type C free agent Dave LaPoint.

Year	Team (League)	W	L	Pct.	ERA	G	GS	CG	ShO	Sv.	IP	H	R	ER	BB	SO
1989	—GC Pirates (GCL)	0	1	.000	4.80	4	3	0	0	0	15	15	12	8	6	14
1990	—							Did not play.								
1991	—Welland (NYP)	2	0	1.000	0.53	3	3	0	0	0	17	12	1	1	3	15
	—Augusta (S. Atl.)	4	2	.667	3.50	7	7	0	0	0	46⅓	29	20	18	19	37
	—Salem (Carolina)	2	2	.500	6.18	6	5	0	0	0	27⅔	38	20	19	4	18
1992	—Salem (Carolina)	11	8	.579	3.47	27	27	4	0	0	176⅓	169	75	68	46	106
1993	—Carolina (South.)	9	4	.692	4.37	21	20	0	0	0	111⅓	123	69	54	29	66

Year	Team (League)	W	L	Pct.	ERA	G	GS	CG	ShO	Sv.	IP	H	R	ER	BB	SO
	—Buffalo (A.A.)	2	1	.667	6.33	4	4	0	0	0	21⅓	30	16	15	2	6
	—Pittsburgh (N.L.)	0	2	.000	4.03	7	7	0	0	0	38	47	19	17	8	8
Major league totals (1 year)		0	2	.000	4.03	7	7	0	0	0	38	47	19	17	8	8

HORN, SAM

DH/1B, YANKEES

PERSONAL: Born November 2, 1963, in Dallas. . . . 6-5/235. . . . Throws left, bats left. . . . Full name: Samuel Lee Horn.

HIGH SCHOOL: Morse (San Diego).

TRANSACTIONS/CAREER NOTES: Selected by Boston Red Sox organization in first round (16th pick overall) of free-agent draft (June 7, 1982); pick received as compensation for Texas Rangers signing Type A free agent Frank Tanana. . . . On disabled list (April 28-June 23, 1983). . . . On Boston disabled list (June 8-July 28, 1989); included rehabilitation assignment to Pawtucket (July 13-28). . . . Released by Red Sox organization (December 20, 1989). . . . Signed by Rochester, Baltimore Orioles organization (February 20, 1990). . . . On Baltimore disabled list (May 8-29, 1990); included rehabilitation assignment to Rochester (May 21-29). . . . Granted free agency (December 19, 1992). . . . Signed by Canton/Akron, Cleveland Indians organization (March 4, 1993). . . . Released by Indians (December 13, 1993). . . . Signed by New York Yankees organization (December 22, 1993).

RECORDS: Shares major league single-game record for most strikeouts—6 (July 17, 1991, 15 innings). . . . Shares A.L. record for most home runs in first two major league games—2 (July 25-26, 1987).

STATISTICAL NOTES: Led Carolina League with .538 slugging percentage in 1984. . . . Led International League with .649 slugging percentage in 1987 and .600 in 1993. . . . Tied for International League lead with 10 intentional bases on balls received in 1988.

			BATTING												FIELDING			
Year	Team (League)	Pos.	G	AB	R	H	2B	3B	HR	RBI	Avg.	BB	SO	SB	PO	A	E	Avg.
1982	—Elmira (N.Y.-Penn)	1B	61	213	47	64	13	1	11	48	.300	40	59	2	368	29	11	.973
1983	—Winst.-Salem (Car.)	1B	68	217	33	52	9	0	9	29	.240	50	78	0	363	24	10	.975
1984	—Winst.-Salem (Car.)	1B	127	403	67	126	22	3	21	89	.313	76	107	5	978	*70	*29	.973
1985	—New Britain (East.)	1B	134	457	64	129	*32	0	11	82	.282	64	107	4	751	63	*23	.973
1986	—New Britain (East.)	1B	100	345	41	85	13	0	8	46	.246	49	80	1	356	28	9	.977
	—Pawtucket (Int'l)	1B	20	77	8	15	2	0	3	14	.195	5	23	0	61	4	0	1.000
1987	—Pawtucket (Int'l)	1B	94	333	57	107	19	0	30	84	.321	33	88	0	28	2	2	.938
	—Boston (A.L.)	DH	46	158	31	44	7	0	14	34	.278	17	55	0	...	...	...	...
1988	—Boston (A.L.)	DH	24	61	4	9	0	0	2	8	.148	11	20	0	...	...	...	...
	—Pawtucket (Int'l)	1B	83	279	33	65	10	0	10	31	.233	44	82	0	6	1	1	.875
1989	—Boston (A.L.)	1B	33	54	1	8	2	0	0	4	.148	8	16	0	5	0	0	1.000
	—Pawtucket (Int'l)	DH	51	164	15	38	9	1	8	27	.232	20	46	0	...	...	...	...
1990	—Baltimore (A.L.)■	1B	79	246	30	61	13	0	14	45	.248	32	62	0	58	6	2	.970
	—Rochester (Int'l)	1B	17	58	16	24	3	0	9	26	.414	9	13	0	27	1	2	.933
	—Hagerstown (East.)	DH	7	23	2	6	2	0	1	3	.261	6	5	0	...	...	...	...
1991	—Baltimore (A.L.)	DH	121	317	45	74	16	0	23	61	.233	41	99	0	...	...	...	...
1992	—Baltimore (A.L.)	DH	63	162	13	38	10	1	5	19	.235	21	60	0	...	...	...	...
1993	—Charlotte (Int'l)■	1B	122	402	62	108	17	1	*38	96	.269	60	131	1	58	0	1	.983
	—Cleveland (A.L.)	DH	12	33	8	15	1	0	4	8	.455	1	5	0	...	...	...	...
Major league totals (7 years)			378	1031	132	249	49	1	62	179	.242	131	317	0	63	6	2	.972

HORSMAN, VINCE

P, ATHLETICS

PERSONAL: Born March 9, 1967, in Halifax, Nova Scotia. . . . 6-2/180. . . . Throws left, bats right. . . . Full name: Vincent Stanley Joseph Horsman.

HIGH SCHOOL: Prince Andrew (Dartmouth, Nova Scotia).

TRANSACTIONS/CAREER NOTES: Signed as free agent by Toronto Blue Jays organization (September 26, 1984). . . . On Knoxville disabled list (April 11-24, 1991). . . . Claimed on waivers by Oakland Athletics (March 20, 1992).

STATISTICAL NOTES: Led South Atlantic League with 20 home runs allowed in 1987.

Year	Team (League)	W	L	Pct.	ERA	G	GS	CG	ShO	Sv.	IP	H	R	ER	BB	SO
1985	—Medicine Hat (Pio.)	0	3	.000	6.25	18	1	0	0	1	40⅓	56	31	28	23	30
1986	—Florence (S. Atl.)	4	3	.571	4.07	29	9	1	1	1	90⅔	93	56	41	49	64
1987	—Myrtle Beach (SAL)	7	7	.500	3.32	30	28	0	0	0	149	144	74	55	37	109
1988	—Dunedin (Fla. St.)	3	1	.750	1.36	14	2	0	0	1	39⅔	28	7	6	12	34
	—Knoxville (South.)	3	2	.600	4.63	20	6	1	0	0	58⅓	57	34	30	28	40
1989	—Dunedin (Fla. St.)	5	6	.455	2.51	35	1	0	0	8	79	72	24	22	27	60
	—Knoxville (South.)	0	0	...	1.80	4	0	0	0	1	5	3	1	1	2	3
1990	—Dunedin (Fla. St.)	4	7	.364	3.24	28	0	0	0	1	50	53	21	18	15	41
	—Knoxville (South.)	2	1	.667	4.63	8	0	0	0	0	11⅔	11	7	6	5	10
1991	—Knoxville (South.)	4	1	.800	2.34	42	2	0	0	3	80⅔	79	23	21	19	80
	—Toronto (A.L.)	0	0	...	0.00	4	0	0	0	0	4	2	0	0	3	2
1992	—Oakland (A.L.)■	2	1	.667	2.49	58	0	0	0	1	43⅓	39	13	12	21	18
1993	—Tacoma (PCL)	1	2	.333	4.28	26	0	0	0	3	33⅔	37	25	16	9	23
	—Oakland (A.L.)	2	0	1.000	5.40	40	0	0	0	0	25	25	15	15	15	17
Major league totals (3 years)		4	1	.800	3.36	102	0	0	0	1	72⅓	66	28	27	39	37

H

HOSEY, STEVE

OF, GIANTS

PERSONAL: Born April 2, 1969, in Oakland, Calif. . . . 6-3/225. . . . Throws right, bats right. . . . Full name: Steven Bernard Hosey.

HIGH SCHOOL: Fremont (Oakland, Calif.).

COLLEGE: Fresno State.

TRANSACTIONS/CAREER NOTES: Selected by Cleveland Indians organization in 19th round of free-agent draft (June 2, 1986). . . . Selected by San Francisco Giants organization in first round (14th pick overall) of free-agent draft (June 5, 1989).

Year	Team (League)	Pos.	BATTING G	AB	R	H	2B	3B	HR	RBI	Avg.	BB	SO	SB	FIELDING PO	A	E	Avg.
1989	—Everett (N'west)	OF	73	288	44	83	14	3	13	59	.288	27	*84	15	143	8	4	.974
1990	—San Jose (Calif.)	OF	•139	479	85	111	13	6	16	78	.232	71	*139	16	239	11	8	.969
1991	—Shreveport (Texas)	OF	126	409	79	120	21	5	17	74	.293	56	88	26	243	5	7	.973
1992	—Phoenix (PCL)	OF	125	462	64	132	28	7	10	65	.286	39	98	15	268	6	*12	.958
	—San Francisco (N.L.)	OF	21	56	6	14	1	0	1	6	.250	0	15	1	24	0	1	.960
1993	—Phoenix (PCL)	OF-1B	129	455	70	133	40	4	16	85	.292	66	129	16	228	9	7	.971
	—San Francisco (N.L.)	OF	3	2	0	1	1	0	0	1	.500	1	1	0	0	0	0	...
Major league totals (2 years)			24	58	6	15	2	0	1	7	.259	1	16	1	24	0	1	.960

HOUGH, CHARLIE

P, MARLINS

PERSONAL: Born January 5, 1948, in Honolulu. . . . 6-2/190. . . . Throws right, bats right. . . . Full name: Charles Oliver Hough. . . . Son of Dick Hough, minor league third baseman (1933). . . . Name pronounced HUFF.

HIGH SCHOOL: Hialeah (Fla.).

TRANSACTIONS/CAREER NOTES: Selected by Los Angeles Dodgers organization in eighth round of free-agent draft (June 9, 1966). . . . On temporary inactive list (June 19-July 1, 1968). . . . On Spokane temporary inactive list (July 10-24, 1971). . . . On Albuquerque temporary inactive list (June 12-15, July 22-24 and August 7-12, 1972). . . . Contract sold by Dodgers to Texas Rangers (July 11, 1980). . . . On Texas disabled list (March 25-May 6, 1986); included rehabilitation assignment to Oklahoma City (May 2-6). . . . On disabled list (July 20-August 4, 1989). . . . Granted free agency (November 5, 1990). . . . Signed by Chicago White Sox (December 20, 1990). . . . On disabled list (March 29-April 13, 1991). . . . Granted free agency (October 30, 1992). . . . Signed by Florida Marlins organization (December 8, 1992). . . . Granted free agency (October 29, 1993). . . . Re-signed by Marlins (December 20, 1993).

RECORDS: Shares major league record for most strikeouts in one inning—4 (July 4, 1988, first inning). . . . Holds A.L. single-season record for most balks—9 (1987).

HONORS: Named Pacific Coast League Pitcher of the Year (1972).

STATISTICAL NOTES: Led Texas League with 17 home runs allowed in 1969. . . . Led A.L. with nine balks in 1987. . . . Led A.L. with 19 hit batsmen in 1987 and 11 in 1990. . . . Tied for A.L. lead with 28 home runs allowed in 1989.

Year	Team (League)	W	L	Pct.	ERA	G	GS	CG	ShO	Sv.	IP	H	R	ER	BB	SO
1966	—Ogden (Pioneer)	5	•7	.417	4.76	21	7	2	1	0	68	82	56	36	29	68
1967	—Santa Barb. (Calif.)	14	4	*.778	2.24	20	20	14	3	0	165	129	50	41	43	138
	—Albuquerque (Tex.)	2	1	.667	7.00	7	6	1	0	0	36	57	31	28	10	25
1968	—Albuquerque (Tex.)	6	10	.375	3.94	27	19	3	2	0	121	145	72	53	26	74
1969	—Albuquerque (Tex.)	10	9	.526	4.09	27	26	7	0	0	163	190	87	74	42	113
1970	—Spokane (PCL)	12	8	.600	1.95	49	3	2	0	*18	134	98	43	29	44	90
	—Los Angeles (N.L.)	0	0	...	5.29	8	0	0	0	2	17	18	11	10	11	8
1971	—Spokane (PCL)	10	8	.556	3.92	47	3	1	0	12	117	95	56	51	52	104
	—Los Angeles (N.L.)	0	0	...	4.50	4	0	0	0	0	4	3	3	2	3	4
1972	—Albuquerque (PCL)	14	5	.737	2.38	58	2	0	0	14	125	109	47	33	60	95
	—Los Angeles (N.L.)	0	0	...	3.00	2	0	0	0	0	3	2	1	1	2	4
1973	—Los Angeles (N.L.)	4	2	.667	2.75	37	0	0	0	5	72	52	24	22	45	70
1974	—Los Angeles (N.L.)	9	4	.692	3.75	49	0	0	0	1	96	65	45	40	40	63
1975	—Los Angeles (N.L.)	3	7	.300	2.95	38	0	0	0	4	61	43	25	20	34	34
1976	—Los Angeles (N.L.)	12	8	.600	2.20	77	0	0	0	18	143	102	43	35	77	81
1977	—Los Angeles (N.L.)	6	12	.333	3.33	70	1	0	0	22	127	98	53	47	70	105
1978	—Los Angeles (N.L.)	5	5	.500	3.29	55	0	0	0	7	93	69	38	34	48	66
1979	—Los Angeles (N.L.)	7	5	.583	4.77	42	14	0	0	0	151	152	88	80	66	76
1980	—Los Angeles (N.L.)	1	3	.250	5.63	19	1	0	0	1	32	37	21	20	21	25
	—Texas (A.L.)■	2	2	.500	3.98	16	2	2	1	0	61	54	30	27	37	47
1981	—Texas (A.L.)	4	1	.800	2.96	21	5	2	0	1	82	61	30	27	31	69
1982	—Texas (A.L.)	16	13	.552	3.95	34	34	12	2	0	228	217	111	100	72	128
1983	—Texas (A.L.)	15	13	.536	3.18	34	33	11	3	0	252	219	96	89	95	152
1984	—Texas (A.L.)	16	14	.533	3.76	36	•36	*17	1	0	266	*260	127	111	94	164
1985	—Texas (A.L.)	14	16	.467	3.31	34	34	14	1	0	250⅓	198	102	92	83	141
1986	—Okla. City (A.A.)	0	1	.000	9.00	1	1	0	0	0	5	7	5	5	1	3
	—Texas (A.L.)	17	10	.630	3.79	33	33	7	2	0	230⅓	188	115	97	89	146
1987	—Texas (A.L.)	18	13	.581	3.79	40	*40	13	0	0	*285⅓	238	*159	120	124	223
1988	—Texas (A.L.)	15	16	.484	3.32	34	34	10	0	0	252	202	111	93	*126	174
1989	—Texas (A.L.)	10	13	.435	4.35	30	30	5	1	0	182	168	97	88	95	94
1990	—Texas (A.L.)	12	12	.500	4.07	32	32	5	0	0	218⅔	190	108	99	119	114
1991	—Chicago (A.L.)■	9	10	.474	4.02	31	29	4	1	0	199⅓	167	98	89	94	107
1992	—Chicago (A.L.)	7	12	.368	3.93	27	27	4	0	0	176⅓	160	88	77	66	76
1993	—Florida (N.L.)■	9	16	.360	4.27	34	34	0	0	0	204⅓	202	109	97	71	126
A.L. totals (13 years)		155	145	.517	3.72	402	369	106	12	1	2683⅓	2322	1272	1109	1125	1635
N.L. totals (12 years)		56	62	.475	3.66	435	50	0	0	60	1003⅓	843	461	408	488	662
Major league totals (24 years)		211	207	.505	3.70	837	419	106	12	61	3686⅔	3165	1733	1517	1613	2297

CHAMPIONSHIP SERIES RECORD

Year	Team (League)	W	L	Pct.	ERA	G	GS	CG	ShO	Sv.	IP	H	R	ER	BB	SO
1974	—Los Angeles (N.L.)	0	0	...	7.71	1	0	0	0	0	2⅓	4	2	2	0	2
1977	—Los Angeles (N.L.)	0	0	...	4.50	1	0	0	0	0	2	2	1	1	0	3
1978	—Los Angeles (N.L.)	0	0	...	4.50	1	0	0	0	0	2	1	1	1	0	1
Champ. series totals (3 years)		0	0	...	5.68	3	0	0	0	0	6⅓	7	4	4	0	6

WORLD SERIES RECORD

Year	Team (League)	W	L	Pct.	ERA	G	GS	CG	ShO	Sv.	IP	H	R	ER	BB	SO
1974	—Los Angeles (N.L.)	0	0	...	0.00	1	0	0	0	0	2	0	0	0	1	4
1977	—Los Angeles (N.L.)	0	0	...	1.80	2	0	0	0	0	5	3	1	1	0	5

Year	Team (League)	W	L	Pct.	ERA	G	GS	CG	ShO	Sv.	IP	H	R	ER	BB	SO
1978	—Los Angeles (N.L.)	0	0	...	8.44	2	0	0	0	0	5⅓	10	5	5	2	5
World Series totals (3 years)		0	0	...	4.38	5	0	0	0	0	12⅓	13	6	6	3	14

ALL-STAR GAME RECORD

Year	League	W	L	Pct.	ERA	GS	CG	ShO	Sv.	IP	H	R	ER	BB	SO
1986	—American	0	0	...	5.40	0	0	0	0	1⅔	2	2	1	0	3

RECORD AS POSITION PLAYER

			BATTING												FIELDING			
Year	Team (League)	Pos.	G	AB	R	H	2B	3B	HR	RBI	Avg.	BB	SO	SB	PO	A	E	Avg.
1967	—Santa Barb. (Calif.)	P-1B	28	72	8	14	2	0	0	4	.194	11	13	0	15	25	2	.952
1968	—Albuquerque (Tex.)	P-1B-3B	56	83	10	21	4	0	0	6	.253	4	12	0	43	25	4	.944
1969	—Albuquerque (Tex.)	P-3B	31	57	10	12	0	0	1	9	.211	8	9	1	10	19	2	.935
1970	—Spokane (PCL)	P-OF-1B	49	33	1	6	0	0	1	3	.182	8	5	0	7	28	3	.921
1971	—Spokane (PCL)	P-OF	48	36	2	10	0	0	0	3	.278	2	4	0	6	20	1	.963
1972	—Albuquerque (PCL)	P-OF	58	34	4	9	1	0	0	5	.265	2	6	0	3	27	0	1.000

HOUSIE, WAYNE

OF

PERSONAL: Born May 20, 1965, in Hampton, Va. . . . 5-9/165. . . . Throws right, bats both. . . . Full name: Wayne Tyrone Housie.
HIGH SCHOOL: Notre Vista (Riverside, Calif.).
COLLEGE: Riverside (Calif.) Community College.

TRANSACTIONS/CAREER NOTES: Selected by Detroit Tigers organization in eighth round of free-agent draft (January 14, 1986). . . . Released by Tigers organization (April 2, 1990). . . . Signed by Salinas, Independent (April 25, 1990). . . . Contract sold by Salinas to Boston Red Sox organization (August 2, 1990). . . . Granted free agency (October 15, 1992). . . . Signed by New York Mets organization (December 22, 1992). . . . Traded by Mets to Milwaukee Brewers for P Josias Manzanillo (June 12, 1993). . . . Granted free agency (October 11, 1993).

			BATTING												FIELDING			
Year	Team (League)	Pos.	G	AB	R	H	2B	3B	HR	RBI	Avg.	BB	SO	SB	PO	A	E	Avg.
1986	—Gastonia (S. Atl.)	OF	90	336	55	87	10	6	2	29	.259	43	85	38	214	13	8	.966
1987	—Lakeland (Fla. St.)	OF	125	458	58	118	12	7	1	45	.258	39	74	26	248	13	6	.978
1988	—Glens Falls (East.)	OF	63	202	26	38	4	2	1	16	.188	28	35	9	128	5	1	.993
	—Lakeland (Fla. St.)	OF	55	212	31	57	11	3	0	23	.269	13	40	24	113	6	4	.967
1989	—London (Eastern)	OF	127	434	56	103	17	2	5	28	.237	52	90	23	238	13	5	.980
1990	—Salinas (Calif.)■	OF-2B	92	367	51	99	20	6	5	49	.270	22	72	27	249	12	5	.981
	—New Britain (East.)■	OF	30	113	13	31	8	3	1	12	.274	6	33	7	83	4	1	.989
1991	—New Britain (East.)	OF	113	444	58	123	24	2	6	26	.277	55	86	43	261	10	4	.985
	—Pawtucket (Int'l)	OF	21	79	14	26	9	0	2	8	.329	6	20	2	49	1	0	1.000
	—Boston (A.L.)	OF	11	8	2	2	1	0	0	0	.250	1	3	1	3	0	0	1.000
1992	—Pawtucket (Int'l)	OF	134	456	53	100	22	5	2	28	.219	32	102	20	313	11	*11	.967
1993	—New York (N.L.)■	OF	18	16	2	3	1	0	0	1	.188	1	1	0	0	0	0	...
	—Norfolk (Int'l)	OF	16	67	5	14	0	0	1	5	.209	3	13	7	40	2	1	.977
	—New Orleans (A.A.)■	OF	64	113	22	31	6	1	0	7	.274	18	21	6	86	3	0	1.000
American League totals (1 year)			11	8	2	2	1	0	0	0	.250	1	3	1	3	0	0	1.000
National League totals (1 year)			18	16	2	3	1	0	0	1	.188	1	1	0	0	0	0	...
Major league totals (2 years)			29	24	4	5	2	0	0	1	.208	2	4	1	3	0	0	1.000

HOUSTON, TYLER

C, BRAVES

PERSONAL: Born January 17, 1971, in Las Vegas. . . . 6-2/210. . . . Throws right, bats left. . . . Full name: Tyler Sam Houston.
HIGH SCHOOL: Valley (Las Vegas).
TRANSACTIONS/CAREER NOTES: Selected by Atlanta Braves organization in first round (second pick overall) of free-agent draft (June 5, 1989). . . . On Greenville disabled list (June 25-July 5, 1993).
STATISTICAL NOTES: Led Pioneer League with 14 passed balls in 1989.

			BATTING												FIELDING			
Year	Team (League)	Pos.	G	AB	R	H	2B	3B	HR	RBI	Avg.	BB	SO	SB	PO	A	E	Avg.
1989	—Idaho Falls (Pio.)	C	50	176	30	43	11	0	4	24	.244	25	41	4	148	15	5	.970
1990	—Sumter (S. Atl.)	C	117	442	58	93	14	3	13	56	.210	49	101	6	498	55	*18	.968
1991	—Macon (S. Atl.)	C	107	351	41	81	16	3	8	47	.231	39	70	10	591	75	10	.985
1992	—Durham (Carolina)	C-3B-1B	117	402	39	91	17	1	7	38	.226	20	89	5	493	65	15	.974
1993	—Greenville (South.)	C-OF	84	262	27	73	14	1	5	33	.279	13	50	5	410	34	9	.980
	—Richmond (Int'l)	C	13	36	4	5	1	1	1	3	.139	1	8	0	69	2	3	.959

HOWARD, CHRIS

P, RED SOX

PERSONAL: Born November 18, 1965, in Lynn, Mass. . . . 6-0/185. . . . Throws left, bats right.
HIGH SCHOOL: St. Mary's (Lynn, Mass.).
COLLEGE: Miami-Dade (South) Community College.

TRANSACTIONS/CAREER NOTES: Selected by Milwaukee Brewers organization in eighth round of free-agent draft (January 9, 1985). . . . Signed as a free agent by New York Yankees organization (June 16, 1986). . . . Released by Yankees organization (May 1, 1990). . . . Signed by Cleveland Indians organization (May 10, 1990). . . . Released by Indians organization (June 6, 1990). . . . Signed by Chicago White Sox organization (January 27, 1991). . . . On Vancouver disabled list (May 30-July 4 and July 9-August 18, 1992). . . . Granted free agency (December 20, 1993). . . . Signed by Boston Red Sox organization (January 20, 1994).
STATISTICAL NOTES: Pitched in relief, combining with Jose Ventura and John Hudek in 4-1 no-hit victory against Charlotte (April 18, 1991).

H

Year	Team (League)	W	L	Pct.	ERA	G	GS	CG	ShO	Sv.	IP	H	R	ER	BB	SO
1987	—Prin. William (Car.)	0	0	...	10.29	4	0	0	0	0	7	9	8	8	8	1
1988	—Prin. William (Car.)	2	2	.500	2.34	31	0	0	0	3	50	44	18	13	23	48
	—Alb./Colon. (East.)	0	0	...	13.50	2	0	0	0	0	1⅓	3	2	2	1	1
1989	—Fort Lauder. (FSL)	2	0	1.000	1.78	13	0	0	0	0	25⅓	19	6	5	13	25
	—Alb./Colon. (East.)	0	1	.000	3.44	24	0	0	0	2	34	29	14	13	17	33
1990	—Alb./Colon. (East.)	0	0	...	14.40	2	0	0	0	0	5	9	8	8	7	2
	—Kinston (Carolina)■	1	1	.500	2.45	8	0	0	0	0	14⅔	21	5	4	6	16
1991	—Birm. (Southern)■	6	1	.857	2.04	38	0	0	0	9	53	43	14	12	16	52
1992	—Vancouver (PCL)	3	1	.750	2.92	20	0	0	0	0	24⅔	18	9	8	22	23
	—GC Whi. Sox (GCL)	0	0	...	4.50	1	0	0	0	0	2	3	1	1	0	3
1993	—Nashville (A.A.)	4	3	.571	3.38	43	0	0	0	3	66⅔	55	32	25	16	53
	—Chicago (A.L.)	1	0	1.000	0.00	3	0	0	0	0	2⅓	2	0	0	3	1
Major league totals (1 year)		1	0	1.000	0.00	3	0	0	0	0	2⅓	2	0	0	3	1

RECORD AS POSITION PLAYER

			BATTING											FIELDING			
Year	Team (League)	Pos.	G	AB	R	H	2B	3B	HR	RBI	Avg.	BB	SO	SB	PO	A	E	Avg.
1986	—Oneonta (NYP)	OF	9	23	2	2	0	0	0	4	.087	5	4	1	4	1	1	.833
	—GC Yankees (GCL)	OF-1B	43	131	15	39	5	1	0	16	.298	13	25	2	101	4	3	.972
1987	—Prin. William (Car.)	OF-P	86	258	35	62	11	1	5	27	.240	10	43	2	135	15	7	.955
1988	—Prin. William (Car.)	P-1B-OF	40	11	2	1	0	0	0	0	.091	0	2	0	10	9	0	1.000

HOWARD, CHRIS H.

C, MARINERS

PERSONAL: Born February 27, 1966, in San Diego. . . . 6-2/220. . . . Throws right, bats right. . . . Full name: Christopher Hugh Howard.
HIGH SCHOOL: Bishop Miege (Roeland Park, Kan.).
COLLEGE: Oklahoma and Southwestern Louisiana.
TRANSACTIONS/CAREER NOTES: Selected by Seattle Mariners organization in 41st round of free-agent draft (June 1, 1988). . . . On Calgary disabled list (July 11-27, 1991).
STATISTICAL NOTES: Led Eastern League catchers with 783 total chances in 1990. . . . Led Pacific Coast League catchers with 18 passed balls and tied for lead in double plays with eight in 1991. . . . Led Pacific Coast League catchers with 19 passed balls in 1992. . . . Led Pacific Coast League catchers with 506 putouts, 65 assists and 578 total chances in 1993.

			BATTING											FIELDING			
Year	Team (League)	Pos.	G	AB	R	H	2B	3B	HR	RBI	Avg.	BB	SO	SB	PO	A	E	Avg.
1988	—Belling. (N'west)	C	2	9	3	3	0	0	1	3	.333	1	2	0	10	0	1	.909
	—Wausau (Midwest)	C-OF-1B	61	187	20	45	10	1	7	20	.241	18	60	1	248	33	9	.969
1989	—Wausau (Midwest)	C	36	125	13	30	8	0	4	32	.240	13	35	0	253	20	3	.989
1990	—Williamsport (East.)	C	118	401	48	95	19	1	5	49	.237	37	91	3	*680	*84	*19	.976
1991	—Calgary (PCL)	C	82	293	32	72	12	1	8	36	.246	16	56	1	381	57	10	.978
	—Seattle (A.L.)	C	9	6	1	1	1	0	0	0	.167	1	2	0	13	2	0	1.000
1992	—Calgary (PCL)	C	97	319	29	76	16	0	8	45	.238	14	73	3	383	53	11	.975
1993	—Calgary (PCL)	C-OF-P	94	331	40	106	23	0	6	55	.320	23	62	1	†506	†65	7	.988
	—Seattle (A.L.)	C	4	1	0	0	0	0	0	0	.000	0	0	0	5	0	0	1.000
Major league totals (2 years)			13	7	1	1	1	0	0	0	.143	1	2	0	18	2	0	1.000

RECORD AS PITCHER

Year	Team (League)	W	L	Pct.	ERA	G	GS	CG	ShO	Sv.	IP	H	R	ER	BB	SO
1993	—Calgary (PCL)	0	0	...	0.00	1	0	0	0	0	1	3	0	0	0	2

HOWARD, DAVID

SS, ROYALS

PERSONAL: Born February 26, 1967, in Sarasota, Fla. . . . 6-0/175. . . . Throws right, bats both. . . . Full name: David Wayne Howard. . . . Son of Bruce Howard, pitcher, Chicago White Sox, Baltimore Orioles and Washington Senators (1963-68).
HIGH SCHOOL: Riverview (Sarasota, Fla.).
COLLEGE: Manatee Junior College (Fla.).
TRANSACTIONS/CAREER NOTES: Selected by Kansas City Royals organization in 32nd round of free-agent draft (June 2, 1986). . . . On disabled list (May 12-31 and July 23-August 9, 1989). . . . On Kansas City disabled list (April 22-July 6, 1992); included rehabilitation assignment to Baseball City (June 16-20) and Omaha (June 20-July 5). . . . On Kansas City disabled list (April 19-May 17, 1993); included rehabilitation assignment to Omaha (May 10-17). . . . On Kansas City disabled list (June 7-August 10, 1993); included rehabilitation assignment to Omaha (July 15-23 and July 31-August 10).

			BATTING											FIELDING			
Year	Team (League)	Pos.	G	AB	R	H	2B	3B	HR	RBI	Avg.	BB	SO	SB	PO	A	E	Avg.
1987	—Fort Myers (FSL)	SS	89	289	26	56	9	4	1	19	.194	30	68	11	123	273	28	.934
1988	—Appleton (Midw.)	SS	110	368	48	82	9	4	1	22	.223	25	80	10	151	275	43	.908
1989	—Baseball City (FSL)	S-0-3-2	83	267	36	63	7	3	3	30	.236	23	44	12	141	225	18	.953
1990	—Memphis (South.)	SS-2B	116	384	41	96	10	4	5	44	.250	39	73	15	194	321	32	.941
1991	—Omaha (A.A.)	SS-2B	14	41	2	5	0	0	0	2	.122	7	11	1	30	43	3	.961
	—Kansas City (A.L.)	S-2-3-0	94	236	20	51	7	0	1	17	.216	16	45	3	129	248	12	.969
1992	—Kansas City (A.L.)	SS-OF	74	219	19	49	6	2	1	18	.224	15	43	3	124	204	8	.976
	—Baseball City (FSL)	SS	3	9	3	4	1	0	0	0	.444	2	0	0	3	7	1	.909
	—Omaha (A.A.)	SS	19	68	5	8	1	0	0	5	.118	3	8	1	25	52	8	.906
1993	—Kansas City (A.L.)	2-S-3-0	15	24	5	8	0	1	0	2	.333	2	5	1	17	28	3	.938
	—Omaha (A.A.)	SS	47	157	15	40	8	2	0	18	.255	7	20	3	76	137	8	.964
Major league totals (3 years)			183	479	44	108	13	3	2	37	.225	33	93	7	270	480	23	.970

HOWARD, THOMAS

OF, REDS

PERSONAL: Born December 11, 1964, in Middletown, O. . . . 6-2/208. . . . Throws right, bats both. . . . Full name: Thomas Sylvester Howard.
HIGH SCHOOL: Valley View (Germantown, O.).
COLLEGE: Ball State.

H

TRANSACTIONS/CAREER NOTES: Selected by San Diego Padres organization in first round (11th pick overall) of free-agent draft (June 2, 1986).... On disabled list (June 5-July 17, 1989).... Traded by Padres to Cleveland Indians for SS Jason Hardtke and a player to be named later (April 14, 1992); Padres acquired C Christopher Maffett to complete deal (July 10, 1992).... Traded by Indians to Cincinnati Reds (August 20, 1993), completing deal in which Reds traded 1B Randy Milligan to Indians for a player to be named later (August 17, 1993).
HONORS: Named outfielder on THE SPORTING NEWS college All-America team (1986).

			BATTING											FIELDING			
Year	Team (League)	Pos.	G	AB	R	H	2B	3B	HR	RBI	Avg.	BB	SO	SB	PO	A	E	Avg.
1986	—Spokane (N'west)	OF	13	55	16	23	3	3	2	17	.418	3	9	2	24	3	0	1.000
	—Reno (California)	OF	61	223	35	57	7	3	10	39	.256	34	49	10	104	5	6	.948
1987	—Wichita (Texas)	OF	113	401	72	133	27	4	14	60	.332	36	72	26	226	6	6	.975
1988	—Wichita (Texas)	OF	29	103	15	31	9	2	0	16	.301	13	14	6	51	2	2	.964
	—Las Vegas (PCL)	OF	44	167	29	42	9	1	0	15	.251	12	31	3	74	3	2	.975
1989	—Las Vegas (PCL)	OF	80	303	45	91	18	3	3	31	.300	30	56	22	178	7	2	.989
1990	—Las Vegas (PCL)	OF	89	341	58	112	26	8	5	51	.328	44	63	27	159	6	2	.988
	—San Diego (N.L.)	OF	20	44	4	12	2	0	0	0	.273	0	11	0	19	0	1	.950
1991	—San Diego (N.L.)	OF	106	281	30	70	12	3	4	22	.249	24	57	10	182	4	1	.995
	—Las Vegas (PCL)	OF	25	94	22	29	3	1	2	16	.309	10	16	11	54	2	2	.966
1992	—San Diego (N.L.)	PH	5	3	1	1	0	0	0	0	.333	0	0	0	...	...	...	...
	—Cleveland (A.L.)■	OF	117	358	36	99	15	2	2	32	.277	17	60	15	185	5	2	.990
1993	—Cleveland (A.L.)	OF	74	178	26	42	7	0	3	23	.236	12	42	5	81	3	2	.977
	—Cincinnati (N.L.)■	OF	38	141	22	39	8	3	4	13	.277	12	21	5	73	4	1	.987
American League totals (2 years)			191	536	62	141	22	2	5	55	.263	29	102	20	266	8	4	.986
National League totals (4 years)			169	469	57	122	22	6	8	35	.260	36	89	15	274	8	3	.989
Major league totals (4 years)			360	1005	119	263	44	8	13	90	.262	65	191	35	540	16	7	.988

HOWE, STEVE

P, YANKEES

PERSONAL: Born March 10, 1958, in Pontiac, Mich.... 5-11/198.... Throws left, bats left.... Full name: Steven Roy Howe.
HIGH SCHOOL: Clarkston (Mich.).
COLLEGE: Michigan.
TRANSACTIONS/CAREER NOTES: Selected by Los Angeles Dodgers organization in first round (16th pick overall) of free-agent draft (June 5, 1979); pick received as compensation for Pittsburgh Pirates signing free agent Lee Lacy.... On disabled list (May 28-June 29, 1983).... On suspended list (July 16-17 and September 23, 1983-remainder of season; and December 15, 1983-entire 1984 season).... On restricted list (July 1-3, 1985).... Released by Dodgers (July 3, 1985).... Signed by Minnesota Twins (August 12, 1985).... Released by Twins (September 17, 1985).... Signed by San Jose, independent (March 20, 1986).... On suspended list (May 15-June 24 and July 15, 1986-remainder of season).... Released by San Jose (December 31, 1986).... Signed by Tabasco of Mexican League (1987).... Signed as free agent by Texas Rangers organization (July 12, 1987).... Released by Rangers (January 19, 1988).... Signed by Salinas, independent (April 7, 1990).... Released by Salinas (October 24, 1990).... Signed by New York Yankees organization (February 21, 1991).... On New York disabled list (August 11-September 2, 1991).... On disqualified list (June 8-November 12, 1992).... Granted free agency (November 8, 1992).... Re-signed by Yankees (December 8, 1992).... On New York disabled list (May 7-June 5, 1993); included rehabilitation assignment to Columbus (May 31-June 5).
HONORS: Named lefthanded pitcher on THE SPORTING NEWS college All-America team (1979).... Named N.L. Rookie of the Year by Baseball Writers' Association of America (1980).

Year	Team (League)	W	L	Pct.	ERA	G	GS	CG	ShO	Sv.	IP	H	R	ER	BB	SO
1979	—San Antonio (Tex.)	6	2	.750	3.13	13	13	5	1	0	95	78	36	33	22	57
1980	—Los Angeles (N.L.)	7	9	.438	2.65	59	0	0	0	17	85	83	33	25	22	39
1981	—Los Angeles (N.L.)	5	3	.625	2.50	41	0	0	0	8	54	51	17	15	18	32
1982	—Los Angeles (N.L.)	7	5	.583	2.08	66	0	0	0	13	99⅓	87	27	23	17	49
1983	—Los Angeles (N.L.)	4	7	.364	1.44	46	0	0	0	18	68⅔	55	15	11	12	52
1984	—							Did not play.								
1985	—Los Angeles (N.L.)	1	1	.500	4.91	19	0	0	0	3	22	30	17	12	5	11
	—Minnesota (A.L.)■	2	3	.400	6.16	13	0	0	0	0	19	28	16	13	7	10
1986	—San Jose (Calif.)■	3	2	.600	1.47	14	8	0	0	2	49	40	14	8	5	37
1987	—Tabasco (Mexican)■	1	0	1.000	0.00	10	0	0	0	4	12⅓	7	0	0	7	5
	—Okla. City (A.A.)■	2	2	.500	3.48	7	3	0	0	0	20⅔	26	8	8	5	14
	—Texas (A.L.)	3	3	.500	4.31	24	0	0	0	1	31⅓	33	15	15	8	19
1988	—						Out of organized baseball.									
1989	—						Out of organized baseball.									
1990	—Salinas (Calif.)■	0	1	.000	2.12	10	6	0	0	0	17	19	8	4	5	14
1991	—Columbus (Int'l)■	2	1	.667	0.00	12	0	0	0	5	18	11	1	0	8	13
	—New York (A.L.)	3	1	.750	1.68	37	0	0	0	3	48⅓	39	12	9	7	34
1992	—New York (A.L.)	3	0	1.000	2.45	20	0	0	0	6	22	9	7	6	3	12
1993	—New York (A.L.)	3	5	.375	4.97	51	0	0	0	4	50⅔	58	31	28	10	19
	—Columbus (Int'l)	0	1	.000	10.13	2	2	0	0	0	2⅔	6	3	3	1	1
A.L. totals (5 years)		14	12	.538	3.73	145	0	0	0	14	171⅓	167	81	71	35	94
N.L. totals (5 years)		24	25	.490	2.35	231	0	0	0	59	329	306	109	86	74	183
Major league totals (9 years)		38	37	.507	2.82	376	0	0	0	73	500⅓	473	190	157	109	277

DIVISION SERIES RECORD

Year	Team (League)	W	L	Pct.	ERA	G	GS	CG	ShO	Sv.	IP	H	R	ER	BB	SO
1981	—Los Angeles (N.L.)	0	0	...	0.00	2	0	0	0	0	2	1	0	0	0	2

CHAMPIONSHIP SERIES RECORD

Year	Team (League)	W	L	Pct.	ERA	G	GS	CG	ShO	Sv.	IP	H	R	ER	BB	SO
1981	—Los Angeles (N.L.)	0	0	...	0.00	2	0	0	0	0	2	1	0	0	0	2

WORLD SERIES RECORD

Year	Team (League)	W	L	Pct.	ERA	G	GS	CG	ShO	Sv.	IP	H	R	ER	BB	SO
1981	—Los Angeles (N.L.)	1	0	1.000	3.86	3	0	0	0	1	7	7	3	3	1	4

ALL-STAR GAME RECORD

Year	League	W	L	Pct.	ERA	GS	CG	ShO	Sv.	IP	H	R	ER	BB	SO
1982	—National	0	0	...	0.00	0	0	0	0	⅓	0	0	0	0	0

HOWELL, JAY

P, RANGERS

PERSONAL: Born November 26, 1955, in Miami. . . . 6-3/203. . . . Throws right, bats right. . . . Full name: Jay Canfield Howell.
HIGH SCHOOL: Fairview (Boulder, Colo.).
COLLEGE: Colorado.

TRANSACTIONS/CAREER NOTES: Selected by Cincinnati Reds organization in 12th round of free-agent draft (June 5, 1973). . . . Selected by Reds organization in 31st round of free-agent draft (June 8, 1976). . . . Traded by Reds to Chicago Cubs for C Mike O'Berry (October 17, 1980). . . . Traded by Cubs organization to New York Yankees organization (August 2, 1982), completing deal in which Cubs acquired 2B Pat Tabler from Yankees on waivers for two players to be named later (August 19, 1981); Yankees acquired P Bill Caudill as partial completion of deal (April 1, 1982). . . . On disabled list (August 3, 1983-remainder of season). . . . Traded by Yankees with OF Stan Javier, P Jose Rijo, P Eric Plunk and P Tim Birtsas to Oakland Athletics for OF Rickey Henderson, P Bert Bradley and cash (December 5, 1984). . . . On Oakland disabled list (April 30-May 18, 1986). . . . On Oakland disabled list (May 27-July 20, 1986); included rehabilitation assignment to Modesto (July 11-16). . . . On disabled list (August 25, 1987-remainder of season). . . . Traded as part of an eight-player, three-team deal in which New York Mets traded P Jesse Orosco to A's (December 11, 1987). A's then traded Orosco with Howell and SS Alfredo Griffin to Los Angeles Dodgers for P Bob Welch, P Matt Young and P Jack Savage; A's then traded Savage with P Wally Whitehurst and P Kevin Tapani to Mets. . . . On disabled list (June 21-July 7, 1988; April 23-May 17, 1990; and June 20-July 23, 1991). . . . Granted free agency (November 1, 1991). . . . Re-signed by Dodgers (January 23, 1992). . . . On Los Angeles disabled list (April 4-May 18, 1992); included rehabilitation assignment to Vero Beach (April 13-29) and Bakersfield (April 29-May 13). . . . Granted free agency (November 4, 1992). . . . Signed by Atlanta Braves organization (January 22, 1993). . . . Granted free agency (October 29, 1993). . . . Signed by Texas Rangers (January 6, 1994).
HONORS: Named American Association Pitcher of the Year (1982).
STATISTICAL NOTES: Tied for American Association lead with six balks in 1981.

Year	Team (League)	W	L	Pct.	ERA	G	GS	CG	ShO	Sv.	IP	H	R	ER	BB	SO
1976	—Eugene (N'west)	5	4	.556	2.96	13	12	5	2	1	73	65	30	24	34	79
1977	—Tampa (Fla. St.)	7	13	.350	2.96	23	22	10	1	0	158	141	60	52	52	99
1978	—Nashville (South.)	9	14	.391	3.09	28	25	6	1	0	166	134	70	57	55	*173
1979	—Indianapolis (A.A.)	10	10	.500	5.13	24	23	2	2	0	128	121	82	73	84	79
1980	—Indianapolis (A.A.)	5	11	.313	5.05	25	17	1	0	0	98	95	70	55	71	73
	—Cincinnati (N.L.)	0	0	...	15.00	5	0	0	0	0	3	8	5	5	0	1
1981	—Iowa (Am. Assoc.)■ ...	5	10	.333	3.75	23	22	2	0	0	144	141	74	60	62	90
	—Chicago (N.L.)	2	0	1.000	4.91	10	2	0	0	0	22	23	13	12	10	10
1982	—Iowa (Am. Assoc.)	13	4	*.765	*2.36	20	20	5	•2	0	141⅓	102	45	37	48	139
	—Columbus (Int'l)■	2	1	.667	2.41	5	5	1	1	0	37⅓	18	13	10	19	33
	—New York (A.L.)	2	3	.400	7.71	6	6	0	0	0	28	42	25	24	13	21
1983	—New York (A.L.)	1	5	.167	5.38	19	12	2	0	0	82	89	53	49	35	61
1984	—New York (A.L.)	9	4	.692	2.69	61	1	0	0	7	103⅔	86	33	31	34	109
1985	—Oakland (A.L.)■	9	8	.529	2.85	63	0	0	0	29	98	98	32	31	31	68
1986	—Oakland (A.L.)	3	6	.333	3.38	38	0	0	0	16	53⅓	53	23	20	23	42
	—Modesto (Calif.)	0	0	...	13.50	2	0	0	0	0	2	5	3	3	1	1
1987	—Oakland (A.L.)	3	4	.429	5.89	36	0	0	0	16	44⅓	48	30	29	21	35
1988	—Los Angeles (N.L.)■ ...	5	3	.625	2.08	50	0	0	0	21	65	44	16	15	21	70
1989	—Los Angeles (N.L.)	5	3	.625	1.58	56	0	0	0	28	79⅔	60	15	14	22	55
1990	—Los Angeles (N.L.)	5	5	.500	2.18	45	0	0	0	16	66	59	17	16	20	59
1991	—Los Angeles (N.L.)	6	5	.545	3.18	44	0	0	0	16	51	39	19	18	11	40
1992	—Vero Beach (FSL)	0	0	...	8.10	5	0	0	0	0	6⅔	9	6	6	3	4
	—Bakersfield (Calif.)	0	1	.000	6.00	4	4	0	0	0	6	8	4	4	1	8
	—Los Angeles (N.L.)	1	3	.250	1.54	41	0	0	0	4	46⅔	41	9	8	18	36
1993	—Atlanta (N.L.)■	3	3	.500	2.31	54	0	0	0	0	58⅓	48	16	15	16	37
A.L. totals (6 years)		27	30	.474	4.05	223	19	2	0	68	409⅓	416	196	184	157	336
N.L. totals (8 years)		27	22	.551	2.37	305	2	0	0	85	391⅔	322	110	103	118	308
Major league totals (14 years)		54	52	.509	3.22	528	21	2	0	153	801	738	306	287	275	644

CHAMPIONSHIP SERIES RECORD

Year	Team (League)	W	L	Pct.	ERA	G	GS	CG	ShO	Sv.	IP	H	R	ER	BB	SO
1988	—Los Angeles (N.L.)	0	1	.000	27.00	2	0	0	0	0	⅔	1	2	2	2	1
1993	—Atlanta (N.L.)	Did not play.														
Champ. series totals (1 year) ..		0	1	.000	27.00	2	0	0	0	0	⅔	1	2	2	2	1

WORLD SERIES RECORD

Year	Team (League)	W	L	Pct.	ERA	G	GS	CG	ShO	Sv.	IP	H	R	ER	BB	SO
1988	—Los Angeles (N.L.)	0	1	.000	3.38	2	0	0	0	1	2⅔	3	1	1	1	2

ALL-STAR GAME RECORD

Year	League	W	L	Pct.	ERA	GS	CG	ShO	Sv.	IP	H	R	ER	BB	SO
1985	—American	Did not play.													
1987	—American	0	1	.000	9.00	0	0	0	0	2	3	2	2	0	3
1989	—National	0	0	...	0.00	0	0	0	0	1	1	0	0	0	1
All-Star totals (2 years)		0	1	.000	6.00	0	0	0	0	3	4	2	2	0	4

HOWITT, DANN

OF, WHITE SOX

PERSONAL: Born February 13, 1964, in Battle Creek, Mich. . . . 6-5/205. . . . Throws right, bats left. . . . Full name: Dann Paul John Howitt. . . . Brother of Shaun Howitt, minor league outfielder (1972).

HIGH SCHOOL: Hastings (Mich.).

COLLEGE: Michigan State and Cal State Fullerton.

TRANSACTIONS/CAREER NOTES: Selected by Oakland Athletics organization in 18th round of free-agent draft (June 2, 1986). . . . Granted free agency (July 8, 1992). . . . Signed by Calgary, Seattle Mariners organization (July 10, 1992). . . . Released by Mariners (October 4, 1993). . . . Signed by Nashville, Chicago White Sox organization (December 1, 1993).

STATISTICAL NOTES: Tied for Northwest League lead in double plays by outfielder with two in 1986. . . . Led California League outfielders with six double plays in 1987. . . . Led Southern League with 253 total bases in 1989. . . . Led Southern League first basemen with .992 fielding percentage in 1989.

			BATTING												FIELDING			
Year	**Team (League)**	**Pos.**	**G**	**AB**	**R**	**H**	**2B**	**3B**	**HR**	**RBI**	**Avg.**	**BB**	**SO**	**SB**	**PO**	**A**	**E**	**Avg.**
1986	—Medford (N'west)	OF	66	208	36	66	9	2	6	37	.317	49	37	5	83	5	4	.957
1987	—Modesto (Calif.)	OF-1B-P	109	336	44	70	11	2	8	42	.208	59	110	7	263	23	6	.979
1988	—Modesto (Calif.)	OF-1B-P	132	480	75	121	20	2	18	86	.252	81	106	11	475	42	12	.977
	—Tacoma (PCL)	OF-1B	4	15	1	2	1	0	0	0	.133	0	4	0	14	0	0	1.000
1989	—Huntsville (South.)	1B-OF-P	138	509	78	143	28	2	26	111	.281	68	107	2	965	74	9	†.991
	—Oakland (A.L.)	1B-OF	3	3	0	0	0	0	0	0	.000	0	2	0	2	0	0	1.000
1990	—Tacoma (PCL)	1B-OF-3B	118	437	58	116	30	1	11	69	.265	38	95	4	608	74	11	.984
	—Oakland (A.L.)	OF-1B-3B	14	22	3	3	0	1	0	1	.136	3	12	0	34	1	0	1.000
1991	—Tacoma (PCL)	OF-1B	122	449	58	120	28	6	14	73	.267	49	92	6	429	33	4	.991
	—Oakland (A.L.)	OF-1B	21	42	5	7	1	0	1	3	.167	1	12	0	36	0	0	1.000
1992	—Tac.-Calg. (PCL)■	OF-1B	93	318	54	95	22	6	7	60	.299	35	58	9	221	12	5	.979
	—Oak.-Sea. (A.L.)	OF-1B	35	85	7	16	4	1	2	10	.188	8	9	1	63	5	2	.971
1993	—Calgary (PCL)	OF	95	333	57	93	20	1	21	77	.279	39	67	7	174	5	3	.984
	—Seattle (A.L.)	OF	32	76	6	16	3	1	2	8	.211	4	18	0	42	1	0	1.000
Major league totals (5 years)			105	228	21	42	8	3	5	22	.184	16	53	1	177	7	2	.989

RECORD AS PITCHER

Year	Team (League)	W	L	Pct.	ERA	G	GS	CG	ShO	Sv.	IP	H	R	ER	BB	SO
1987	—Modesto (Calif.)	0	0	...	1.80	2	0	0	0	0	5	7	1	1	3	3
1988	—Modesto (Calif.)	0	0	...	6.43	4	0	0	0	0	7	13	8	5	3	3
1989	—Huntsville (South.)	0	0	...	0.00	2	0	0	0	0	2	2	1	0	0	2

HRBEK, KENT

1B, TWINS

PERSONAL: Born May 21, 1960, in Minneapolis. . . . 6-4/260. . . . Throws right, bats left. . . . Full name: Kent Alan Hrbek. . . . Name pronounced HER-beck.

HIGH SCHOOL: Kennedy (Bloomington, Minn.).

TRANSACTIONS/CAREER NOTES: Selected by Minnesota Twins organization in 17th round of free-agent draft (June 6, 1978). . . . On Wisconsin Rapids disabled list (April 13-June 21, 1979). . . . On Elizabethton disabled list (July 22-September 6, 1979). . . . On disabled list (May 27-June 6, 1980 and May 16-June 26, 1989). . . . Granted free agency (November 13, 1989). . . . Re-signed by Twins (December 6, 1989). . . . On disabled list (March 29-April 23 and September 7, 1992-remainder of season and June 8-23, 1993).

HONORS: Named California League Most Valuable Player (1981).

STATISTICAL NOTES: Led California League with .630 slugging percentage and tied for lead with nine sacrifice flies in 1981. . . . Led A.L. first basemen with .997 fielding percentage in 1990.

			BATTING												FIELDING			
Year	**Team (League)**	**Pos.**	**G**	**AB**	**R**	**H**	**2B**	**3B**	**HR**	**RBI**	**Avg.**	**BB**	**SO**	**SB**	**PO**	**A**	**E**	**Avg.**
1979	—Elizabeth. (Appal.)	1B	17	59	5	12	2	0	1	11	.203	7	15	2	126	11	2	.986
1980	—Wis. Rap. (Midw.)	1B	115	419	74	112	16	0	19	76	.267	61	54	1	1005	81	*20	.982
1981	—Visalia (California)	1B	121	462	119	175	25	5	27	111	*.379	59	59	12	1034	53	11	*.990
	—Minnesota (A.L.)	1B	24	67	5	16	5	0	1	7	.239	5	9	0	124	4	0	1.000
1982	—Minnesota (A.L.)	1B	140	532	82	160	21	4	23	92	.301	54	80	3	1174	88	9	.993
1983	—Minnesota (A.L.)	1B	141	515	75	153	41	5	16	84	.297	57	71	4	1151	89	13	.990
1984	—Minnesota (A.L.)	1B	149	559	80	174	31	3	27	107	.311	65	87	1	1320	99	14	.990
1985	—Minnesota (A.L.)	1B	158	593	78	165	31	2	21	93	.278	67	87	1	1339	114	8	.995
1986	—Minnesota (A.L.)	1B	149	550	85	147	27	1	29	91	.267	71	81	2	1218	104	10	.992
1987	—Minnesota (A.L.)	1B	143	477	85	136	20	1	34	90	.285	84	60	5	1179	68	5	.996
1988	—Minnesota (A.L.)	1B	143	510	75	159	31	0	25	76	.312	67	54	0	842	57	3	.997
1989	—Minnesota (A.L.)	1B	109	375	59	102	17	0	25	84	.272	53	35	3	723	60	4	.995
1990	—Minnesota (A.L.)	1B-3B	143	492	61	141	26	0	22	79	.287	69	45	5	1057	83	3	†.997
1991	—Minnesota (A.L.)	1B	132	462	72	131	20	1	20	89	.284	67	48	4	1138	95	8	.994
1992	—Minnesota (A.L.)	1B	112	394	52	96	20	0	15	58	.244	71	56	5	954	68	3	.997
1993	—Minnesota (A.L.)	1B	123	392	60	95	11	1	25	83	.242	71	57	4	940	81	5	.995
Major league totals (13 years)			1666	5918	869	1675	301	18	283	1033	.283	801	770	37	13159	1010	85	.994

CHAMPIONSHIP SERIES RECORD

			BATTING												FIELDING			
Year	**Team (League)**	**Pos.**	**G**	**AB**	**R**	**H**	**2B**	**3B**	**HR**	**RBI**	**Avg.**	**BB**	**SO**	**SB**	**PO**	**A**	**E**	**Avg.**
1987	—Minnesota (A.L.)	1B	5	20	4	3	0	0	1	1	.150	3	0	0	40	3	0	1.000
1991	—Minnesota (A.L.)	1B	5	21	0	3	0	0	0	3	.143	1	3	0	40	8	0	1.000
Championship series totals (2 years)			10	41	4	6	0	0	1	4	.146	4	3	0	80	11	0	1.000

WORLD SERIES RECORD

WORLD SERIES NOTES: Shares single-game record for most grand slams—1 (October 24, 1987). . . . Shares record for most runs batted in in one inning—4 (October 24, 1987, sixth inning).

Year	Team (League)	Pos.	G	AB	R	H	2B	3B	HR	RBI	Avg.	BB	SO	SB	PO	A	E	Avg.
			BATTING												FIELDING			
1987	—Minnesota (A.L.)......	1B	7	24	4	5	0	0	1	6	.208	5	3	0	68	2	0	1.000
1991	—Minnesota (A.L.)......	1B	7	26	2	3	1	0	1	2	.115	2	6	0	66	8	0	1.000
World Series totals (2 years)			14	50	6	8	1	0	2	8	.160	7	9	0	134	10	0	1.000

ALL-STAR GAME RECORD

Year	League	Pos.	AB	R	H	2B	3B	HR	RBI	Avg.	BB	SO	SB	PO	A	E	Avg.
			BATTING											FIELDING			
1982	—American..................	PH	1	0	0	0	0	0	0	.000	0	0	0	...	...	...	...

HUDEK, JOHN

P, ASTROS

PERSONAL: Born August 8, 1966, in Tampa, Fla. . . . 6-1/200. . . . Throws right, bats both. . . . Full name: John Raymond Hudek. . . . Name pronounced HOO-dek.

HIGH SCHOOL: H.B. Plant (Tampa, Fla.).

COLLEGE: Florida Southern.

TRANSACTIONS/CAREER NOTES: Selected by Texas Rangers organization in 30th round of free-agent draft (June 3, 1985). . . . Selected by Chicago White Sox organization in 10th round of free-agent draft (June 1, 1988). . . . Selected by Detroit Tigers from White Sox organization in Rule 5 major league draft (December 7, 1992). . . . On Toledo disabled list (April 8-28 and June 17-July 1, 1993). . . . Claimed on waivers by Houston Astros (July 29, 1993).

STATISTICAL NOTES: Combined with starter Jose Ventura and Chris Howard in 4-1 no-hit victory against Charlotte (April 18, 1991).

Year	Team (League)	W	L	Pct.	ERA	G	GS	CG	ShO	Sv.	IP	H	R	ER	BB	SO
1988	—South Bend (Mid.)......	7	2	.778	1.98	26	0	0	0	8	54⅔	45	19	12	21	35
1989	—Sarasota (Fla. St.).....	1	3	.250	1.67	27	0	0	0	15	43	22	10	8	13	39
	—Birm. (Southern)........	1	1	.500	4.24	18	0	0	0	11	17	14	8	8	9	10
1990	—Birm. (Southern)........	6	6	.500	4.58	42	10	0	0	4	92⅓	84	59	47	52	67
1991	—Birm. (Southern)........	5	10	.333	3.84	51	0	0	0	13	65⅔	58	39	28	28	49
1992	—Birm. (Southern)........	0	1	.000	2.31	5	0	0	0	1	11⅔	9	4	3	11	9
	—Vancouver (PCL).......	8	1	.889	3.16	39	3	1	1	2	85⅓	69	36	30	45	61
1993	—Toledo (Int'l)■...........	1	3	.250	5.82	16	5	0	0	0	38⅔	44	26	25	22	32
	—Tucson (PCL)■...........	3	1	.750	3.79	13	1	0	0	0	19	17	11	8	11	18

HUDLER, REX

IF/OF, GIANTS

PERSONAL: Born September 2, 1960, in Tempe, Ariz. . . . 6-0/195. . . . Throws right, bats right. . . . Full name: Rex Allen Hudler.

HIGH SCHOOL: Bullard (Fresno, Calif.).

TRANSACTIONS/CAREER NOTES: Selected by New York Yankees organization in first round (18th pick overall) of free-agent draft (June 6, 1978); pick received as compensation for Chicago White Sox signing free agent Ron Blomberg. . . . On Fort Lauderdale disabled list (May 18-31, 1979; May 10-June 15, 1980; and May 11-June 11, 1981). . . . Traded by Yankees with P Rich Bordi to Baltimore Orioles for OF Gary Roenicke and a player to be named later (December 12, 1985); Yankees acquired OF Leo Hernandez to complete deal (December 16, 1985). . . . On Baltimore disabled list (March 23-June 16, 1987); included rehabilitation assignment to Rochester (May 28-June 16). . . . Granted free agency (October 15, 1987). . . . Signed by Indianapolis, Montreal Expos organization (December 18, 1987). . . . Traded by Expos to St. Louis Cardinals for P John Costello (April 23, 1990). . . . On disabled list (May 7-June 29, 1992). . . . Released by Cardinals (December 7, 1992). . . . Played in Japan (1993). . . . Signed as free agent by San Francisco Giants organization (December 20, 1993).

STATISTICAL NOTES: Led International League second basemen with 95 double plays in 1984.

Year	Team (League)	Pos.	G	AB	R	H	2B	3B	HR	RBI	Avg.	BB	SO	SB	PO	A	E	Avg.
			BATTING												FIELDING			
1978	—Oneonta (NYP).........	SS	58	221	33	62	5	5	0	24	.281	21	29	16	123	21	22	.867
1979	—Fort Lauder. (FSL)...	S-3-2-0	116	414	37	104	14	1	1	25	.251	15	73	23	164	314	45	.914
1980	—Fort Lauder. (FSL)...	3-2-0-1	37	125	14	26	4	0	0	6	.208	2	25	2	55	71	5	.962
	—Greensboro (S. Atl.)..	2B	20	75	7	17	3	1	2	9	.227	4	14	1	51	52	5	.954
1981	—Fort Lauder. (FSL)...	2-S-3-0	79	259	35	77	11	1	2	26	.297	13	31	6	104	238	19	.947
1982	—Nashville (South.)....	2B-SS-OF	89	299	27	71	14	1	0	24	.237	9	51	9	136	219	20	.947
	—Fort Lauder. (FSL)...	2B	9	32	2	8	1	0	1	6	.250	4	5	0	23	25	2	.960
1983	—Fort Lauder. (FSL)...	2B-SS	91	345	55	93	15	2	2	50	.270	26	44	30	195	245	15	.967
	—Columbus (Int'l).......	2B-3B-SS	40	118	17	36	5	0	1	11	.305	6	25	1	55	95	4	.974
1984	—Columbus (Int'l).......	2B	114	394	49	115	26	1	1	35	.292	16	61	11	266	348	16	.975
	—New York (A.L.)........	2B	9	7	2	1	1	0	0	0	.143	1	5	0	4	7	0	1.000
1985	—Columbus (Int'l).......	2-S-0-3-1	106	380	62	95	13	4	3	18	.250	17	51	29	192	234	17	.962
	—New York (A.L.)........	2B-1B-SS	20	51	4	8	0	1	0	1	.157	1	9	0	42	51	2	.979
1986	—Rochester (Int'l)■......	2-3-0-S	77	219	29	57	12	3	2	13	.260	16	32	12	135	191	15	.956
	—Baltimore (A.L.)........	2B-3B	14	1	1	0	0	0	0	0	.000	0	0	1	2	3	1	.833
1987	—Rochester (Int'l).......	OF-2B-SS	31	106	22	27	5	1	5	10	.255	2	15	9	51	15	2	.971
1988	—Indianapolis (A.A.)■.	0-2-S-3	67	234	36	71	11	3	7	25	.303	10	35	14	102	96	4	.980
	—Montreal (N.L.).........	2B-SS-OF	77	216	38	59	14	2	4	14	.273	10	34	29	116	168	10	.966
1989	—Montreal (N.L.).........	2B-OF-SS	92	155	21	38	7	0	6	13	.245	6	23	15	59	59	7	.944
1990	—Mont.-St.L. (N.L.)■..	0-2-1-3-S	93	220	31	62	11	2	7	22	.282	12	32	18	158	42	5	.976
1991	—St. Louis (N.L.).........	OF-1B-2B	101	207	21	47	10	2	1	15	.227	10	29	12	130	6	2	.986
1992	—St. Louis (N.L.).........	2B-OF-1B	61	98	17	24	4	0	3	5	.245	2	23	2	44	39	3	.965
1993	—Yakult (Jp. Cen.)■....	...	120	410	48	123	26	3	14	64	.300	32	77	1	...	...	...	...
American League totals (3 years)			43	59	7	9	1	1	0	1	.153	2	14	1	48	61	3	.973
National League totals (5 years)			424	896	128	230	46	6	21	69	.257	40	141	76	507	314	27	.968
Major league totals (8 years)			467	955	135	239	47	7	21	70	.250	42	155	77	555	375	30	.969

HUFF, MIKE

OF, WHITE SOX

PERSONAL: Born August 11, 1963, in Honolulu. . . . 6-1/190. . . . Throws right, bats right. . . . Full name: Michael Kale Huff.

HIGH SCHOOL: New Trier (Winnetka, Ill.).

COLLEGE: Northwestern (bachelor of science degree in industrial engineering, 1985).

TRANSACTIONS/CAREER NOTES: Selected by Los Angeles Dodgers organization in 16th round of free-agent draft (June 3, 1985). . . . On disabled list (May 11, 1987-remainder of season). . . . Selected by Cleveland Indians from Dodgers organization in Rule 5 major league draft (December 3, 1990). . . . Claimed on waivers by Chicago White Sox (July 12, 1991). . . . On disabled list (August 25-September 9, 1991). . . . On Chicago disabled list (June 17-September 1, 1992); included rehabilitation assignment to Vancouver (July 31) and South Bend (August 21-September 1).
STATISTICAL NOTES: Tied for Texas League lead in double plays by outfielder with four in 1988. . . . Led American Association with .411 on-base percentage in 1993. . . . Tied for American Association lead in double plays by outfielder with five in 1993.

			BATTING											FIELDING			
Year	Team (League)	Pos.	G	AB	R	H	2B	3B	HR	RBI	Avg.	BB	SO	SB	PO	A	E	Avg.
1985	—Great Falls (Pio.)	OF	•70	247	70	78	6	6	0	35	.316	56	44	28	120	5	5	.962
1986	—Vero Beach (FSL)	OF	113	362	73	106	6	8	2	32	.293	67	67	28	257	10	1	.996
1987	—San Antonio (Tex.)	OF	31	135	23	42	5	1	3	18	.311	9	21	2	52	2	2	.964
1988	—San Antonio (Tex.)	OF	102	395	68	120	18	10	2	40	.304	37	55	33	222	12	2	.992
	—Albuquerque (PCL)	OF	2	4	0	1	1	0	0	0	.250	0	0	0	2	0	0	1.000
1989	—Albuquerque (PCL)	OF-2B	115	471	75	150	29	7	10	78	.318	38	75	32	209	13	2	.991
	—Los Angeles (N.L.)	OF	12	25	4	5	1	0	1	2	.200	3	6	0	18	0	0	1.000
1990	—Albuquerque (PCL)	OF-2B	*138	474	99	154	28	11	7	84	.325	82	68	27	285	29	5	.984
1991	—Clev.-Chi. (A.L.)■	OF-2B	102	243	42	61	10	2	3	25	.251	37	48	14	168	7	2	.989
1992	—Chicago (A.L.)	OF	60	115	13	24	5	0	0	8	.209	10	24	1	68	2	0	1.000
	—Vancouver (PCL)	OF	1	4	1	1	0	0	0	0	.250	1	0	0	4	0	0	1.000
	—South Bend (Mid.)	OF-3B	12	40	7	15	2	1	1	5	.375	11	7	2	15	2	1	.944
1993	—Nashville (A.A.)	OF-2B	92	344	65	101	12	6	8	32	.294	64	43	18	207	11	3	.986
	—Chicago (A.L.)	OF	43	44	4	8	2	0	1	6	.182	9	15	1	40	0	0	1.000
American League totals (3 years)			205	402	59	93	17	2	4	39	.231	56	87	16	276	9	2	.993
National League totals (1 year)			12	25	4	5	1	0	1	2	.200	3	6	0	18	0	0	1.000
Major league totals (4 years)			217	427	63	98	18	2	5	41	.230	59	93	16	294	9	2	.993

HUGHES, KEITH

OF

PERSONAL: Born September 12, 1963, in Bryn Mawr, Pa. . . . 6-3/210. . . . Throws left, bats left. . . . Full name: Keith Wills Hughes.
HIGH SCHOOL: Conestoga (Berwyn, Pa.).
TRANSACTIONS/CAREER NOTES: Signed as free agent by Philadelphia Phillies organization (August 24, 1981). . . . Traded by Phillies organization with P Marty Bystrom to New York Yankees for P Shane Rawley (June 30, 1984). . . . On Albany/Colonie disabled list (July 22-August 26, 1986). . . . Traded by Yankees with IF Shane Turner to Phillies organization for OF Mike Easler (June 10, 1987). . . . Traded by Phillies with IF Rick Schu and OF Jeff Stone to Baltimore Orioles for OF Mike Young and a player to be named later (March 21, 1988); Phillies acquired OF Frank Bellino to complete deal (June 14, 1988). . . . On disabled list (July 5, 1989-remainder of season). . . . Traded by Orioles organization with P Cesar Mejia to New York Mets for P John Mitchell and OF Joaquin Contreras (December 5, 1989). . . . Released by Mets (November 13, 1990). . . . Signed by Columbus, New York Yankees organization (January 7, 1991). . . . Granted free agency (October 15, 1991). . . . Signed by Portland, Minnesota Twins organization (January 24, 1992). . . . Granted free agency (October 15, 1992). . . . Signed by Cincinnati Reds organization (November 16, 1992). . . . On Indianapolis disabled list (June 2-July 15, 1993). . . . Granted free agency (October 15, 1993).
STATISTICAL NOTES: Tied for South Atlantic League lead with five intentional bases on balls received in 1983.

			BATTING											FIELDING			
Year	Team (League)	Pos.	G	AB	R	H	2B	3B	HR	RBI	Avg.	BB	SO	SB	PO	A	E	Avg.
1982	—Bend (Northwest)	OF	55	179	29	46	10	2	3	26	.257	30	42	2	90	6	5	.950
1983	—Spartanburg (SAL)	OF-1B	131	484	80	159	31	4	15	90	.329	67	83	16	171	5	7	.962
1984	—Reading (Eastern)	OF-1B	70	230	35	60	7	5	2	20	.261	31	43	1	117	7	9	.932
	—Nashville (South.)■	OF	21	50	6	9	0	0	0	5	.180	10	14	0	19	0	0	1.000
1985	—Alb./Colon. (East.)	OF-2B	104	361	53	97	22	5	10	54	.269	51	73	4	218	18	3	.987
	—Columbus (Int'l)	OF	18	54	7	16	4	0	3	8	.296	2	11	11	25	0	2	.926
1986	—Alb./Colon. (East.)	OF-1B	94	323	44	99	21	3	7	37	.307	32	53	6	247	17	7	.974
	—Columbus (Int'l)	OF	2	8	0	1	0	0	0	0	.125	0	2	0	6	0	1	.857
1987	—Colum.-Me. (Int'l)	OF-1B	90	316	48	93	15	4	17	57	.294	37	58	3	149	2	7	.956
	—New York (A.L.)	PH	4	4	0	0	0	0	0	0	.000	0	2	0	...	...	...	...
	—Philadelphia (N.L.)■	OF	37	76	8	20	2	0	0	10	.263	7	11	0	26	0	1	.963
1988	—Rochester (Int'l)■	OF	77	274	44	74	13	2	7	49	.270	43	57	11	159	2	3	.982
	—Baltimore (A.L.)	OF	41	108	10	21	4	2	2	14	.194	16	27	1	59	4	2	.969
1989	—Rochester (Int'l)	OF-1B	83	285	44	78	20	4	2	43	.274	44	47	4	180	7	5	.974
1990	—Tidewater (Int'l)■	OF-1B	117	379	77	117	24	5	10	53	.309	57	58	7	262	18	6	.979
	—New York (N.L.)	OF	8	9	0	0	0	0	0	0	.000	0	4	0	5	0	0	1.000
1991	—Columbus (Int'l)■	SS-1B	130	424	64	115	18	8	8	66	.271	60	74	6	467	22	9	.982
1992	—Portland (PCL)■	OF-P	89	221	37	60	11	3	5	26	.271	25	39	6	102	10	5	.957
1993	—Indianapolis (A.A.)■	OF-1B	82	283	55	81	28	4	13	42	.286	41	61	5	160	5	5	.971
	—Cincinnati (N.L.)	OF	3	4	0	0	0	0	0	0	.000	0	0	0	0	0	0	...
American League totals (2 years)			45	112	10	21	4	2	2	14	.188	16	29	1	59	4	2	.969
National League totals (3 years)			48	89	8	20	2	0	0	10	.225	7	15	0	31	0	1	.969
Major league totals (4 years)			93	201	18	41	6	2	2	24	.204	23	44	1	90	4	3	.969

RECORD AS PITCHER

Year	Team (League)	W	L	Pct.	ERA	G	GS	CG	ShO	Sv.	IP	H	R	ER	BB	SO
1992	—Portland (PCL)	0	0	...	4.50	2	0	0	0	0	2	2	1	1	2	0

H

HUGHES, TROY

OF, BRAVES

PERSONAL: Born January 3, 1971, in Mt. Vernon, Ill. . . . 6-4/195. . . . Throws right, bats right. . . . Full name: Troy Darnell Hughes.
HIGH SCHOOL: Mt. Vernon (Ill.) Township.
TRANSACTIONS/CAREER NOTES: Selected by Atlanta Braves organization in eighth round of free-agent draft (June 5, 1989).

Year	Team (League)	Pos.	G	AB	R	H	2B	3B	HR	RBI	Avg.	BB	SO	SB	PO	A	E	Avg.
			BATTING												FIELDING			
1989	—GC Braves (GCL)	OF	36	110	17	24	5	0	0	10	.218	11	29	8	52	5	2	.966
1990	—Pulaski (Appal.)	OF-1B	46	145	22	39	7	1	1	17	.269	16	39	5	70	8	3	.963
1991	—Macon (S. Atl.)	OF	112	404	69	121	32	2	9	80	.300	36	75	23	163	5	5	.971
1992	—Durham (Carolina)	OF	128	449	64	110	21	4	16	53	.245	49	97	12	197	7	11	.949
1993	—Greenville (South.)	OF	109	383	49	102	20	4	14	59	.266	44	67	7	172	14	6	.969

HULETT, TIM

3B, ORIOLES

PERSONAL: Born January 12, 1960, in Springfield, Ill. . . . 6-0/199. . . . Throws right, bats right. . . . Full name: Timothy Craig Hulett. . . . Name pronounced HYOO-lit.
HIGH SCHOOL: Lanphier (Springfield, Ill.).
COLLEGE: Miami-Dade (North) Community College and South Florida.

TRANSACTIONS/CAREER NOTES: Selected by Texas Rangers organization in 39th round of free-agent draft (June 6, 1978). . . . Selected by Chicago White Sox organization in secondary phase of free-agent draft (January 8, 1980). . . . Traded by White Sox organization to Montreal Expos for a player to be named later (April 13, 1988); White Sox acquired 2B Edgar Caceres to complete deal (June 15, 1988). . . . Granted free agency (October 15, 1988). . . . Signed by Rochester, Baltimore Orioles organization (November 21, 1988). . . . On Baltimore disabled list (April 4-June 12, 1990); included rehabilitation assignment to Rochester (May 29-June 21). . . . On disabled list (July 21-August 6, 1992). . . . Granted free agency (November 7, 1993). . . . Re-signed by Orioles (December 2, 1993).

STATISTICAL NOTES: Led Eastern League second basemen with 332 putouts, 415 assists, 763 total chances and 112 double plays in 1981. . . . Led Eastern League second basemen with .975 fielding percentage, 343 putouts, 386 assists, 748 total chances and 95 double plays in 1982. . . . Led American Association second basemen with 730 total chances in 1983. . . . Led American Association with nine sacrifice flies in both 1983 and 1988. . . . Tied for A.L. lead in errors by third baseman with 23 in 1985. . . . Led International League third basemen with 23 double plays in 1989.

Year	Team (League)	Pos.	G	AB	R	H	2B	3B	HR	RBI	Avg.	BB	SO	SB	PO	A	E	Avg.
			BATTING												FIELDING			
1980	—Glens Falls (East.)	SS	6	23	2	4	0	0	0	0	.174	3	5	0	14	13	2	.931
	—Iowa (Am. Assoc.)	3B	3	8	1	2	0	0	0	0	.250	0	0	1	0	6	3	.667
	—Appleton (Midw.)	2B-3B-SS	79	278	49	72	11	1	13	47	.259	34	56	5	162	258	17	.961
1981	—Glens Falls (East.)	2B-3B	134	437	59	99	27	1	10	55	.227	64	86	0	†333	†422	16	.979
1982	—Glens Falls (East.)	2B-SS	•140	*536	*113	145	28	5	22	87	.271	95	135	1	†352	†398	21	†.973
1983	—Denver (A.A.)	2B	133	477	77	130	19	4	21	88	.273	61	64	5	*286	*424	*20	.973
	—Chicago (A.L.)	2B	6	5	0	1	0	0	0	0	.200	0	0	1	8	6	2	.875
1984	—Chicago (A.L.)	3B-2B	8	7	1	0	0	0	0	0	.000	1	4	1	4	15	0	1.000
	—Denver (A.A.)	2B-3B-SS	139	475	72	125	32	6	16	80	.263	67	88	3	269	371	28	.958
1985	—Chicago (A.L.)	3B-2B-OF	141	395	52	106	19	4	5	37	.268	30	81	6	117	256	‡24	.940
1986	—Chicago (A.L.)	3B-2B	150	520	53	120	16	5	17	44	.231	21	91	4	179	331	15	.971
1987	—Chicago (A.L.)	3B-2B	68	240	20	52	10	0	7	28	.217	10	41	0	55	142	9	.956
	—Hawaii (PCL)	3B-2B	42	157	13	37	5	2	1	24	.236	9	28	4	47	81	11	.921
1988	—Indianapolis (A.A.)■	3B-2B	126	427	36	100	29	2	7	59	.234	34	106	2	118	211	25	.929
1989	—Rochester (Int'l)■	3-S-2-P	122	461	61	129	32	12	3	50	.280	38	81	2	149	289	20	.956
	—Baltimore (A.L.)	2B-3B	33	97	12	27	5	0	3	18	.278	10	17	0	70	71	4	.972
1990	—Rochester (Int'l)	2B-SS-3B	14	43	10	16	2	1	2	4	.372	11	7	0	22	35	1	.983
	—Baltimore (A.L.)	3B-2B	53	153	16	39	7	1	3	16	.255	15	41	1	44	101	4	.973
1991	—Baltimore (A.L.)	3B-2B-SS	79	206	29	42	9	0	7	18	.204	13	49	0	47	96	4	.973
1992	—Baltimore (A.L.)	3B-2B-SS	57	142	11	41	7	2	2	21	.289	10	31	0	25	92	7	.944
1993	—Baltimore (A.L.)	3B-SS-2B	85	260	40	78	15	0	2	23	.300	23	56	1	58	176	8	.967
Major league totals (10 years)			680	2025	234	506	88	12	46	205	.250	133	411	14	607	1286	77	.961

RECORD AS PITCHER

Year	Team (League)	W	L	Pct.	ERA	G	GS	CG	ShO	Sv.	IP	H	R	ER	BB	SO
1989	—Rochester (Int'l)	0	0	...	0.00	1	0	0	0	0	⅔	0	0	0	0	0

HULSE, DAVID

OF, RANGERS

PERSONAL: Born February 25, 1968, in San Angelo, Tex. . . . 5-11/170. . . . Throws left, bats left. . . . Full name: David Lindsey Hulse. . . . Name pronounced HULTZ.
HIGH SCHOOL: San Angelo (Tex.) Central.
COLLEGE: Schreiner College (Tex.).

TRANSACTIONS/CAREER NOTES: Selected by Texas Rangers organization in 13th round of free-agent draft (June 4, 1990). . . . On Charlotte disabled list (July 26-August 15, 1991). . . . On disabled list (July 25-August 12, 1993).

Year	Team (League)	Pos.	G	AB	R	H	2B	3B	HR	RBI	Avg.	BB	SO	SB	PO	A	E	Avg.
			BATTING												FIELDING			
1990	—Butte (Pioneer)	OF	64	257	54	*92	12	2	2	36	*.358	25	30	24	102	5	6	.947
1991	—Charlotte (Fla. St.)	OF	88	310	41	86	4	5	0	17	.277	36	74	44	129	6	3	.978
1992	—Tulsa (Texas)	OF	88	354	40	101	14	3	3	20	.285	20	86	17	84	2	4	.956
	—Okla. City (A.A.)	OF	8	30	7	7	1	1	0	3	.233	1	4	2	13	0	1	.929
	—Texas (A.L.)	OF	32	92	14	28	4	0	0	2	.304	3	18	3	61	0	1	.984
1993	—Texas (A.L.)	OF	114	407	71	118	9	10	1	29	.290	26	57	29	244	3	3	.988
Major league totals (2 years)			146	499	85	146	13	10	1	31	.293	29	75	32	305	3	4	.987

HUMPHREYS, MIKE

OF, YANKEES

PERSONAL: Born April 10, 1967, in Dallas. . . . 6-0/195. . . . Throws right, bats right. . . . Full name: Michael Butler Humphreys.
COLLEGE: Texas Tech.

TRANSACTIONS/CAREER NOTES: Selected by San Diego Padres organization in 15th round of free-agent draft (June 1, 1988). . . . Traded by Padres to New York Yankees (February 7, 1991), completing deal in which Yankees traded OF Oscar Azocar to Padres for a player to be named later (December 3, 1990).

STATISTICAL NOTES: Led Northwest League outfielders with .974 fielding percentage and tied for lead with 180 putouts in 1988.

. . . Led International League outfielders with .996 fielding percentage in 1992.

								BATTING								FIELDING		
Year	Team (League)	Pos.	G	AB	R	H	2B	3B	HR	RBI	Avg.	BB	SO	SB	PO	A	E	Avg.
1988	—Spokane (N'west)	OF-1B	76	303	*67	93	16	•5	6	59	.307	46	57	21	‡181	6	5	†.974
1989	—Riverside (Calif.)	OF-3B-1B	117	420	77	121	26	1	13	66	.288	72	79	23	251	10	7	.974
1990	—Wichita (Texas)	OF	116	421	*92	116	21	4	17	79	.276	67	79	38	277	8	5	.983
	—Las Vegas (PCL)	OF	12	42	7	10	1	0	2	6	.238	4	11	1	19	5	0	1.000
1991	—Columbus (Int'l)■	OF-3B	117	413	71	117	23	5	9	53	.283	63	62	34	188	51	8	.968
	—New York (A.L.)	OF-3B	25	40	9	8	0	0	0	3	.200	9	7	2	10	8	1	.947
1992	—Columbus (Int'l)	OF-3B	114	408	83	115	18	6	6	46	.282	59	70	*37	217	6	1	†.996
	—New York (A.L.)	OF	4	10	0	1	0	0	0	0	.100	0	1	0	7	1	0	1.000
1993	—New York (A.L.)	OF	25	35	6	6	2	1	1	6	.171	4	11	2	14	0	0	1.000
	—Columbus (Int'l)	OF-3B	92	330	59	95	16	2	6	42	.288	52	57	18	172	16	6	.969
Major league totals (3 years)			54	85	15	15	2	1	1	9	.176	13	19	4	31	9	1	.976

HUNDLEY, TODD

C, METS

PERSONAL: Born May 27, 1969, in Martinsville, Va. . . . 5-11/185. . . . Throws right, bats both. . . . Full name: Todd Randolph Hundley. . . . Son of Randy Hundley, major league catcher with four teams (1964-77).

HIGH SCHOOL: William Fremd (Palatine, Ill.).

COLLEGE: William Rainey Harper College (Ill.).

TRANSACTIONS/CAREER NOTES: Selected by New York Mets organization in second round of free-agent draft (June 2, 1987); pick received as compensation for Baltimore Orioles signing Type B free agent Ray Knight. . . . On Tidewater disabled list (June 29-July 6, 1991).

STATISTICAL NOTES: Led South Atlantic League in intentional bases on balls received with 10 and in grounding into double plays with 20 in 1989. . . . Led South Atlantic League catchers with 826 putouts and 930 total chances in 1989. . . . Tied for International League lead in errors by catcher with nine and double plays with 12 in 1991.

								BATTING								FIELDING		
Year	Team (League)	Pos.	G	AB	R	H	2B	3B	HR	RBI	Avg.	BB	SO	SB	PO	A	E	Avg.
1987	—Little Falls (NYP)	C	34	103	12	15	4	0	1	10	.146	12	27	0	181	25	7	.967
1988	—Little Falls (NYP)	C	52	176	23	33	8	0	2	18	.188	16	31	1	345	54	8	.980
	—St. Lucie (Fla. St.)	C	1	1	0	0	0	0	0	0	.000	2	1	0	4	0	1	.800
1989	—Columbia (S. Atl.)	C-OF	125	439	67	118	23	4	11	66	.269	54	67	6	†829	91	13	.986
1990	—Jackson (Texas)	C-3B	81	279	27	74	12	2	1	35	.265	34	44	5	474	63	9	.984
	—New York (N.L.)	C	36	67	8	14	6	0	0	2	.209	6	18	0	162	8	2	.988
1991	—Tidewater (Int'l)	C-1B	125	454	62	124	24	4	14	66	.273	51	95	1	585	63	‡9	.986
	—New York (N.L.)	C	21	60	5	8	0	1	1	7	.133	6	14	0	85	11	0	1.000
1992	—New York (N.L.)	C	123	358	32	75	17	0	7	32	.209	19	76	3	700	48	3	.996
1993	—New York (N.L.)	C	130	417	40	95	17	2	11	53	.228	23	62	1	592	63	8	.988
Major league totals (4 years)			310	902	85	192	40	3	19	94	.213	54	170	4	1539	130	13	.992

HUNTER, BRIAN L.

OF, ASTROS

PERSONAL: Born March 5, 1971, in Portland, Ore. . . . 6-4/180. . . . Throws right, bats right. . . . Full name: Brian Lee Hunter.

HIGH SCHOOL: Fort Vancouver (Vancouver, Wash.).

TRANSACTIONS/CAREER NOTES: Selected by Houston Astros organization in second round of free-agent draft (June 5, 1989); pick received as part of compensation for Texas Rangers signing Type A free agent Nolan Ryan.

								BATTING								FIELDING		
Year	Team (League)	Pos.	G	AB	R	H	2B	3B	HR	RBI	Avg.	BB	SO	SB	PO	A	E	Avg.
1989	—GC Astros (GCL)	OF	51	206	15	35	2	0	0	13	.170	7	42	12	95	4	2	.980
1990	—Asheville (S. Atl.)	OF	127	444	84	111	14	6	0	16	.250	60	72	45	219	13	11	.955
1991	—Osceola (Fla. St.)	OF	118	392	51	94	15	3	1	30	.240	45	75	32	250	7	9	.966
1992	—Osceola (Fla. St.)	OF	131	489	62	146	18	9	1	62	.299	31	76	39	295	10	9	.971
1993	—Jackson (Texas)	OF	133	523	84	154	22	5	10	52	.294	34	85	*35	276	9	*14	.953

HUNTER, BRIAN R.

1B, PIRATES

PERSONAL: Born March 4, 1968, in El Toro, Calif. . . . 6-0/195. . . . Throws left, bats right. . . . Full name: Brian Ronald Hunter.

HIGH SCHOOL: Paramount (Calif.).

COLLEGE: Cerritos College (Calif.).

TRANSACTIONS/CAREER NOTES: Selected by Atlanta Braves organization in eighth round of free-agent draft (June 2, 1987). . . . On Atlanta disabled list (April 18-May 18, 1993). . . . Traded by Braves to Pittsburgh Pirates for a player to be named later (November 17, 1993).

STATISTICAL NOTES: Led Appalachian League first basemen with 43 double plays in 1987. . . . Led Midwest League first basemen with 21 errors in 1988. . . . Tied for Southern League lead with nine sacrifice flies in 1989.

								BATTING								FIELDING		
Year	Team (League)	Pos.	G	AB	R	H	2B	3B	HR	RBI	Avg.	BB	SO	SB	PO	A	E	Avg.
1987	—Pulaski (Appal.)	1B-OF	65	251	38	58	10	2	8	30	.231	18	47	3	498	29	11	.980
1988	—Burlington (Midw.)	1B-OF	117	417	58	108	17	0	•22	71	.259	45	90	7	987	69	†22	.980
	—Durham (Carolina)	OF-1B	13	49	13	17	3	0	3	9	.347	7	8	2	52	6	0	1.000
1989	—Greenville (South.)	OF-1B	124	451	57	114	19	2	19	82	.253	33	62	5	248	15	4	.985
1990	—Richmond (Int'l)	OF-1B	43	137	13	27	4	0	5	16	.197	18	37	2	126	5	3	.978
	—Greenville (South.)	OF-1B	88	320	45	77	13	1	14	55	.241	43	62	6	189	19	8	.963
1991	—Richmond (Int'l)	OF	48	181	28	47	7	0	10	30	.260	11	24	3	121	4	4	.969
	—Atlanta (N.L.)	1B-OF	97	271	32	68	16	1	12	50	.251	17	48	0	624	46	8	.988
1992	—Atlanta (N.L.)	1B-OF	102	238	34	57	13	2	14	41	.239	21	50	1	542	50	4	.993

Year	Team (League)	Pos.	G	AB	R	H	2B	3B	HR	RBI	Avg.	BB	SO	SB	PO	A	E	Avg.
			BATTING												FIELDING			
1993	—Atlanta (N.L.)	1B-OF	37	80	4	11	3	1	0	8	.138	2	15	0	168	13	1	.995
	—Richmond (Int'l)	1B-OF	30	99	16	24	7	0	6	26	.242	10	21	4	174	15	0	1.000
Major league totals (3 years)			236	589	70	136	32	4	26	99	.231	40	113	1	1334	109	13	.991

CHAMPIONSHIP SERIES RECORD

Year	Team (League)	Pos.	G	AB	R	H	2B	3B	HR	RBI	Avg.	BB	SO	SB	PO	A	E	Avg.
			BATTING												FIELDING			
1991	—Atlanta (N.L.)	1B	5	18	2	6	2	0	1	4	.333	0	2	0	30	4	0	1.000
1992	—Atlanta (N.L.)	1B-PH	3	5	1	1	0	0	0	0	.200	0	1	0	7	0	0	1.000
Championship series totals (2 years)			8	23	3	7	2	0	1	4	.304	0	3	0	37	4	0	1.000

WORLD SERIES RECORD

Year	Team (League)	Pos.	G	AB	R	H	2B	3B	HR	RBI	Avg.	BB	SO	SB	PO	A	E	Avg.
			BATTING												FIELDING			
1991	—Atlanta (N.L.)	OF-1B-PH	7	21	2	4	1	0	1	3	.190	0	2	0	6	1	0	1.000
1992	—Atlanta (N.L.)	1B-PH-PR	4	5	0	1	0	0	0	2	.200	0	1	0	14	1	0	1.000
World Series totals (2 years)			11	26	2	5	1	0	1	5	.192	0	3	0	20	2	0	1.000

HURST, BRUCE

P, RANGERS

PERSONAL: Born March 24, 1958, in St. George, Utah . . . 6-3/220. . . . Throws left, bats left. . . . Full name: Bruce Vee Hurst.

HIGH SCHOOL: Dixie (St. George, Utah).

COLLEGE: Dixie College (Utah).

TRANSACTIONS/CAREER NOTES: Selected by Boston Red Sox organization in first round (22nd pick overall) of free-agent draft (June 8, 1976). . . . On disabled list (August 8-September 14, 1977; May 23-September 21, 1978; June 3-July 18, 1986; and July 8-24, 1988). . . . Granted free agency (November 4, 1988). . . . Signed by San Diego Padres (December 8, 1988). . . . On San Diego disabled list (March 29-May 25, 1993); included rehabilitation assignment to Las Vegas (May 14-19) and Rancho Cucamonga (May 19-25). . . . On San Diego disabled list (June 5-July 26, 1993). . . . Traded by Padres with P Greg W. Harris to Colorado Rockies for C Brad Ausmus, P Doug Bochtler and a player to be named later (July 26, 1993); Padres acquired P Andy Ashby to complete deal (July 27, 1993). . . . On Colorado disabled list (July 27-August 21, 1993); included rehabilitation assignment to Colorado Springs (August 5-21). . . . On Colorado disabled list (August 21-September 8, 1993). . . . Granted free agency (October 26, 1993). . . . Signed by Texas Rangers organization (December 20, 1993).

STATISTICAL NOTES: Led A.L. with four balks in 1985.

MISCELLANEOUS: Struck out in only appearance as pinch-hitter (1992).

Year	Team (League)	W	L	Pct.	ERA	G	GS	CG	ShO	Sv.	IP	H	R	ER	BB	SO
1976	—Elmira (N.Y.-Penn)	3	2	.600	3.00	9	9	0	0	0	42	25	18	14	38	40
1977	—Winter Haven (FSL)	5	4	.556	2.08	13	13	7	2	0	91	77	28	21	25	69
1978	—Bristol (Eastern)	1	3	.250	2.73	6	6	0	0	0	33	32	15	10	17	35
1979	—Winter Haven (FSL)	8	2	.800	1.93	12	12	4	2	0	84	57	22	18	20	64
	—Bristol (Eastern)	9	4	.692	3.58	16	15	8	1	0	113	108	56	45	49	91
1980	—Pawtucket (Int'l)	8	6	.571	3.94	17	17	4	1	0	105	101	52	46	50	54
	—Boston (A.L.)	2	2	.500	9.00	12	7	0	0	0	31	39	33	31	16	16
1981	—Pawtucket (Int'l)	12	7	.632	2.87	32	23	7	3	0	157	143	68	50	71	99
	—Boston (A.L.)	2	0	1.000	4.30	5	5	0	0	0	23	23	11	11	12	11
1982	—Boston (A.L.)	3	7	.300	5.77	28	19	0	0	0	117	161	87	75	40	53
1983	—Boston (A.L.)	12	12	.500	4.09	33	32	6	2	0	211⅓	241	102	96	62	115
1984	—Boston (A.L.)	12	12	.500	3.92	33	33	9	2	0	218	232	106	95	88	136
1985	—Boston (A.L.)	11	13	.458	4.51	35	31	6	1	0	229⅓	243	123	115	70	189
1986	—Boston (A.L.)	13	8	.619	2.99	25	25	11	4	0	174⅓	169	63	58	50	167
1987	—Boston (A.L.)	15	13	.536	4.41	33	33	15	3	0	238⅔	239	124	117	76	190
1988	—Boston (A.L.)	18	6	.750	3.66	33	32	7	1	0	216⅔	222	98	88	65	166
1989	—San Diego (N.L.)■	15	11	.577	2.69	33	33	•10	2	0	244⅔	214	84	73	66	179
1990	—San Diego (N.L.)	11	9	.550	3.14	33	33	9	•4	0	223⅔	188	85	78	63	162
1991	—San Diego (N.L.)	15	8	.652	3.29	31	31	4	0	0	221⅔	201	89	81	59	141
1992	—San Diego (N.L.)	14	9	.609	3.85	32	32	6	4	0	217⅓	223	96	93	51	131
1993	—L.V.-Colo. Sp. (PCL)■.	1	2	.333	7.78	4	4	0	0	0	19⅔	30	19	17	4	15
	—Rancho Cuca. (Cal.)	0	0	...	8.31	1	1	0	0	0	4⅓	4	5	4	1	6
	—S.D.-Colo. (N.L.)■	0	2	.000	7.62	5	5	0	0	0	13	15	12	11	6	9
A.L. totals (9 years)		88	73	.547	4.23	237	217	54	13	0	1459⅓	1569	747	686	479	1043
N.L. totals (5 years)		55	39	.585	3.29	134	134	29	10	0	920⅓	841	366	336	245	622
Major league totals (14 years)		143	112	.561	3.87	371	351	83	23	0	2379⅔	2410	1113	1022	724	1665

CHAMPIONSHIP SERIES RECORD

Year	Team (League)	W	L	Pct.	ERA	G	GS	CG	ShO	Sv.	IP	H	R	ER	BB	SO
1986	—Boston (A.L.)	1	0	1.000	2.40	2	2	1	0	0	15	18	5	4	1	8
1988	—Boston (A.L.)	0	2	.000	2.77	2	2	1	0	0	13	10	4	4	5	12
Champ. series totals (2 years)		1	2	.333	2.57	4	4	2	0	0	28	28	9	8	6	20

WORLD SERIES RECORD

Year	Team (League)	W	L	Pct.	ERA	G	GS	CG	ShO	Sv.	IP	H	R	ER	BB	SO
1986	—Boston (A.L.)	2	0	1.000	1.96	3	3	1	0	0	23	18	5	5	6	17

ALL-STAR GAME RECORD

Year	League	W	L	Pct.	ERA	GS	CG	ShO	Sv.	IP	H	R	ER	BB	SO
1987	—American	Did not play.													

H

HURST, JAMES

P, RANGERS

PERSONAL: Born June 1, 1967, in Plantation, Fla. . . . 6-0/160. . . . Throws left, bats left. . . . Full name: James Lavon Hurst.
HIGH SCHOOL: Sebring (Fla.).
COLLEGE: South Florida Community College and Florida Southern.
TRANSACTIONS/CAREER NOTES: Selected by Seattle Mariners organization in 52nd round of free-agent draft (June 2, 1987). . . . Selected by Cleveland Indians organization in 32nd round of free-agent draft (June 5, 1989). . . . Loaned by Indians organization to Reno, independent (April 23, 1990-remainder of season). . . . Released by Indians organization (March 26, 1991). . . . Signed by Gastonia, Texas Rangers organization (July 4, 1991). . . . On Tulsa disabled list (April 9-25, 1993).
STATISTICAL NOTES: Led California League with 19 home runs allowed in 1990.

Year	Team (League)	W	L	Pct.	ERA	G	GS	CG	ShO	Sv.	IP	H	R	ER	BB	SO
1990	—Reno (California)■	4	11	.267	5.47	25	21	1	0	1	131⅔	165	102	80	68	90
1991	—Gastonia (S. Atl.)■	3	3	.500	2.26	11	8	0	0	0	51⅔	41	18	13	14	44
1992	—Charlotte (Fla. St.)	3	2	.600	3.81	32	1	0	0	1	54⅓	60	29	23	12	49
	—Tulsa (Texas)	1	0	1.000	0.57	8	0	0	0	0	15⅔	10	2	1	3	12
1993	—Tulsa (Texas)	2	3	.400	3.26	11	7	0	0	1	49⅔	41	21	18	12	44
	—Okla. City (A.A.)	4	6	.400	4.53	16	14	2	0	0	91⅓	106	50	46	29	60

HUSKEY, BUTCH

3B, METS

PERSONAL: Born November 10, 1971, in Anadarko, Okla. . . . 6-3/244. . . . Throws right, bats right. . . . Full name: Robert Leon Huskey.
HIGH SCHOOL: Eisenhower (Lawton, Okla.).
TRANSACTIONS/CAREER NOTES: Selected by New York Mets in seventh round of free-agent draft (June 5, 1989).
STATISTICAL NOTES: Led Gulf Coast League third basemen with 50 putouts and 23 errors in 1989. . . . Led Appalachian League third basemen with 217 total chances and tied for lead with two double plays in 1990. . . . Led South Atlantic League with 256 total bases in 1991. . . . Led South Atlantic League third basemen with 21 double plays in 1991. . . . Led Florida State League third basemen with 456 total chances and 28 double plays in 1992. . . . Led Eastern League third basemen 101 putouts, 297 assists, 34 errors and 432 total chances in 1993.

			BATTING												FIELDING			
Year	Team (League)	Pos.	G	AB	R	H	2B	3B	HR	RBI	Avg.	BB	SO	SB	PO	A	E	Avg.
1989	—GC Mets (GCL)	3B-1B	54	190	27	50	14	2	6	34	.263	14	36	4	†73	106	†23	.886
1990	—Kingsport (Appal.)	3B	*72	*279	39	75	13	0	14	53	.269	24	74	7	45	*150	•22	.899
1991	—Columbia (S. Atl.)	3B	134	492	88	141	27	5	*26	*99	.287	54	89	22	*102	218	31	.912
1992	—St. Lucie (Fla. St.)	3B	134	493	65	125	17	1	18	75	.254	33	74	7	*108	*310	*38	.917
1993	—Binghamton (East.)	3B-SS	*139	*526	72	132	23	1	25	98	.251	48	102	11	†101	†297	†34	.921
	—New York (N.L.)	3B	13	41	2	6	1	0	0	3	.146	1	13	0	9	27	3	.923
	Major league totals (1 year)		13	41	2	6	1	0	0	3	.146	1	13	0	9	27	3	.923

HUSON, JEFF

IF, RANGERS

PERSONAL: Born August 15, 1964, in Scottsdale, Ariz. . . . 6-3/180. . . . Throws right, bats left. . . . Full name: Jeffrey Kent Huson. . . . Name pronounced HYOO-son.
HIGH SCHOOL: Mingus Union (Cottonwood, Ariz.).
COLLEGE: Glendale (Ariz.) Community College and Wyoming.
TRANSACTIONS/CAREER NOTES: Signed as free agent by Montreal Expos organization (August 18, 1985). . . . Traded by Expos to Oklahoma City, Texas Rangers organization, for P Drew Hall (April 2, 1990). . . . On Texas disabled list (August 8-31, 1991); included rehabilitation assignment to Oklahoma City (August 29-31). . . . On Texas disabled list (March 27-May 27, 1993); included rehabilitation assignment to Oklahoma City (May 24-27). . . . On Texas disabled list (June 5-July 15, 1993); included rehabilitation assignment to Oklahoma City (July 10-15). . . . On Texas disabled list (July 24-August 23, 1993); included rehabilitation assignment to Oklahoma City (July 31-August 19).

			BATTING												FIELDING			
Year	Team (League)	Pos.	G	AB	R	H	2B	3B	HR	RBI	Avg.	BB	SO	SB	PO	A	E	Avg.
1986	—Burlington (Midw.)	SS-3B-2B	133	457	85	132	19	1	16	72	.289	76	68	32	183	324	37	.932
	—Jacksonv. (South.)	3B	1	4	0	0	0	0	0	0	.000	0	0	0	0	1	0	1.000
1987	—W.P. Beach (FSL)	SS-OF-2B	131	455	54	130	15	4	1	53	.286	50	30	33	234	347	34	.945
1988	—Jacksonv. (South.)	S-2-O-3	128	471	72	117	18	1	0	34	.248	59	45	*56	217	285	26	.951
	—Montreal (N.L.)	S-2-3-O	20	42	7	13	2	0	0	3	.310	4	3	2	18	41	4	.937
1989	—Indianapolis (A.A.)	SS-OF-2B	102	378	70	115	17	4	3	35	.304	50	26	30	172	214	17	.958
	—Montreal (N.L.)	SS-2B-3B	32	74	1	12	5	0	0	2	.162	6	6	3	40	65	8	.929
1990	—Texas (A.L.)■	SS-3B-2B	145	396	57	95	12	2	0	28	.240	46	54	12	183	304	19	.962
1991	—Texas (A.L.)	SS-2B-3B	119	268	36	57	8	3	2	26	.213	39	32	8	143	269	15	.965
	—Okla. City (A.A.)	SS	2	6	0	3	1	0	0	2	.500	0	1	0	5	3	0	1.000
1992	—Texas (A.L.)	S-2-O-3	123	318	49	83	14	3	4	24	.261	41	43	18	178	250	9	.979
1993	—Okla. City (A.A.)	3-S-2-O	24	76	11	22	5	0	1	10	.289	13	10	1	39	52	3	.968
	—Texas (A.L.)	SS-2B-3B	23	45	3	6	1	1	0	2	.133	0	10	0	25	42	6	.918
	American League totals (4 years)		410	1027	145	241	35	9	6	80	.235	126	139	38	529	865	49	.966
	National League totals (2 years)		52	116	8	25	7	0	0	5	.216	10	9	5	58	106	12	.932
	Major league totals (6 years)		462	1143	153	266	42	9	6	85	.233	136	148	43	587	971	61	.962

HUTTON, MARK

P, YANKEES

PERSONAL: Born February 6, 1970, in South Adelaide, Australia. . . . 6-6/225. . . . Throws right, bats right. . . . Full name: Mark Steven Hutton.
TRANSACTIONS/CAREER NOTES: Signed as free agent by New York Yankees organization (December 15, 1988). . . . On Columbus disabled list (April 23-May 15, 1993).

Year	Team (League)	W	L	Pct.	ERA	G	GS	CG	ShO	Sv.	IP	H	R	ER	BB	SO
1989	—Oneonta (NYP)	6	2	.750	4.07	12	12	0	0	0	66⅓	70	39	30	24	62
1990	—Greensboro (S. Atl.)	1	10	.091	6.31	21	19	0	0	0	81⅓	77	78	57	62	72
1991	—Fort Lauder. (FSL)	5	8	.385	2.45	24	24	3	0	0	147	98	54	40	65	117

Year	Team (League)	W	L	Pct.	ERA	G	GS	CG	ShO	Sv.	IP	H	R	ER	BB	SO
	—Columbus (Int'l)	1	0	1.000	1.50	1	1	0	0	0	6	3	2	1	5	5
1992	—Alb./Colon. (East.)	13	7	.650	3.59	25	25	1	0	0	165⅓	146	75	66	66	128
	—Columbus (Int'l)	0	1	.000	5.40	1	0	0	0	0	5	7	4	3	2	4
1993	—Columbus (Int'l)	10	4	.714	3.18	21	21	0	0	0	133	98	52	47	53	112
	—New York (A.L.)	1	1	.500	5.73	7	4	0	0	0	22	24	17	14	17	12
Major league totals (1 year)		1	1	.500	5.73	7	4	0	0	0	22	24	17	14	17	12

HI

HYERS, TIM

1B, PADRES

PERSONAL: Born October 3, 1971, in Atlanta. . . . 6-1/185. . . . Throws left, bats left. . . . Full name: Timothy James Hyers.
HIGH SCHOOL: Newton County (Covington, Ga.).
TRANSACTIONS/CAREER NOTES: Selected by Toronto Blue Jays organization in supplemental round ("sandwich pick" between second and third round) of free-agent draft (June 4, 1990); pick received as compensation for Detroit Tigers signing Type C free agent Lloyd Moseby. . . . Selected by San Diego Padres from Blue Jays organization in Rule 5 major league draft (December 13, 1993).
STATISTICAL NOTES: Led Pioneer League first basemen with 565 total chances in 1990. . . . Led Florida State League first basemen with 1,260 total chances in 1992. . . . Led Southern League first basemen with 1,330 total chances and 105 double plays in 1993.

				BATTING											FIELDING			
Year	Team (League)	Pos.	G	AB	R	H	2B	3B	HR	RBI	Avg.	BB	SO	SB	PO	A	E	Avg.
1990	—Medicine Hat (Pio.)	1B	61	224	29	49	7	2	2	19	.219	29	22	4	*516	38	*11	.981
1991	—Myrtle Beach (SAL)	1B	132	398	31	81	8	0	3	37	.204	27	52	6	915	84	14	.986
1992	—Dunedin (Fla. St.)	1B	124	464	54	114	24	3	8	59	.246	41	54	2	*1149	102	9	.993
1993	—Knoxville (South.)	1B	140	487	72	149	26	3	3	61	.306	53	51	12	*1209	*116	5	*.996

HYZDU, ADAM

OF, REDS

PERSONAL: Born December 6, 1971, in San Jose, Calif. . . . 6-2/210. . . . Throws right, bats right. . . . Full name: Adam Davis Hyzdu. . . . Name pronounced HIZE-doo.
HIGH SCHOOL: Moeller (Cincinnati).
TRANSACTIONS/CAREER NOTES: Selected by San Francisco Giants organization in first round (15th pick overall) of free-agent draft (June 4, 1990); pick received as compensation for Houston Astros signing Type B free agent Ken Oberkfell. . . . Selected by Cincinnati Reds from Giants organization in Rule 5 major league draft (December 13, 1993).

				BATTING											FIELDING			
Year	Team (League)	Pos.	G	AB	R	H	2B	3B	HR	RBI	Avg.	BB	SO	SB	PO	A	E	Avg.
1990	—Everett (N'west)	OF	69	253	31	62	16	1	6	34	.245	28	78	2	128	2	5	.963
1991	—Clinton (Midwest)	OF	124	410	47	96	13	5	5	50	.234	64	131	4	185	8	9	.955
1992	—San Jose (Calif.)	OF	128	457	60	127	25	5	9	60	.278	55	134	10	193	8	5	.976
1993	—San Jose (Calif.)	OF	44	165	35	48	11	3	13	38	.291	29	53	1	72	5	3	.963
	—Shreveport (Texas)	OF	86	302	30	61	17	0	6	25	.202	20	82	0	136	8	4	.973

IGNASIAK, MICHAEL

P, BREWERS

PERSONAL: Born March 12, 1966, in Anchorville, Mich. . . . 5-11/190. . . . Throws right, bats both. . . . Full name: Michael James Ignasiak. . . . Name pronounced ig-NAH-shik.
HIGH SCHOOL: St. Mary's (Orchard Lake, Mich.).
COLLEGE: Michigan.
TRANSACTIONS/CAREER NOTES: Selected by St. Louis Cardinals organization in fourth round of free-agent draft (June 2, 1987). . . . Selected by Milwaukee Brewers organization in eighth round of free-agent draft (June 1, 1988). . . . On Milwaukee disabled list (August 31-September 28, 1991).
STATISTICAL NOTES: Combined with reliever Doug Henry in 6-3 no-hit victory for Stockton against San Jose (April 15, 1990, first game).

Year	Team (League)	W	L	Pct.	ERA	G	GS	CG	ShO	Sv.	IP	H	R	ER	BB	SO
1988	—Beloit (Midwest)	2	4	.333	2.72	9	9	1	0	0	56⅓	52	21	17	12	66
	—Helena (Pioneer)	2	0	1.000	3.09	7	0	0	0	1	11⅔	10	5	4	7	18
1989	—Stockton (Calif.)	11	6	.647	2.72	28	•28	4	•4	0	179	140	67	54	97	142
1990	—Stockton (Calif.)	3	1	.750	3.94	6	6	1	1	0	32	18	14	14	17	23
	—El Paso (Texas)	6	3	.667	4.35	15	15	1	0	0	82⅔	96	45	40	34	39
1991	—Denver (A.A.)	9	5	.643	4.25	24	22	1	0	1	137⅔	119	68	65	57	103
	—Milwaukee (A.L.)	2	1	.667	5.68	4	1	0	0	0	12⅔	7	8	8	8	10
1992	—Denver (A.A.)	7	4	.636	2.93	*62	0	0	0	10	92	83	37	30	33	64
1993	—New Orleans (A.A.)	6	0	1.000	1.09	35	0	0	0	9	57⅔	26	10	7	20	61
	—Milwaukee (A.L.)	1	1	.500	3.65	27	0	0	0	0	37	32	17	15	21	28
Major league totals (2 years)		3	2	.600	4.17	31	1	0	0	0	49⅔	39	25	23	29	38

ILSLEY, BLAISE

P, CUBS

PERSONAL: Born April 9, 1964, in Alpena, Mich. . . . 6-1/195. . . . Throws left, bats left. . . . Full name: Blaise Francis Ilsley.
HIGH SCHOOL: Alpena (Mich.).
COLLEGE: Indiana State.
TRANSACTIONS/CAREER NOTES: Selected by Houston Astros organization in fourth round of free-agent draft (June 3, 1985). . . . On disabled list (April 8-22 and June 13, 1988-remainder of season). . . . Granted free agency (October 15, 1991). . . . Signed by St. Louis Cardinals organization (December 20, 1991). . . . Granted free agency (October 15, 1992). . . . Signed by Chicago Cubs organization (November 17, 1992).
HONORS: Named South Atlantic League Most Outstanding Pitcher (1986).

Year	Team (League)	W	L	Pct.	ERA	G	GS	CG	ShO	Sv.	IP	H	R	ER	BB	SO
1985	—Auburn (NY-Penn)	9	1	.900	1.40	13	12	2	0	0	90	55	18	14	32	•116
1986	—Asheville (S. Atl.)	12	2	.857	*1.95	15	15	*9	•3	0	120	74	27	26	23	146
	—Osceola (Fla. St.)	8	4	.667	1.77	14	13	6	2	0	86⅔	67	24	17	19	74
1987	—Columbus (South.)	10	11	.476	3.86	26	26	3	0	0	167⅔	162	84	72	63	130
1988	—Columbus (South.)	3	1	.750	5.95	8	8	0	0	0	39⅓	49	28	26	21	38
1989	—Osceola (Fla. St.)	0	0	...	6.43	2	2	0	0	0	7	8	5	5	0	6
	—Columbus (South.)	1	1	.500	1.31	4	4	0	0	0	20⅔	19	10	3	5	11
	—Tucson (PCL)	4	9	.308	5.85	20	17	1	0	0	103	120	68	67	23	49
1990	—Tucson (PCL)	2	1	.667	6.46	20	6	1	0	2	62⅔	87	50	45	24	39
	—Columbus (South.)	6	4	.600	1.94	12	12	3	•3	0	83⅔	70	26	18	13	70
1991	—Tucson (PCL)	8	6	.571	4.27	46	4	0	0	0	86⅓	105	51	41	27	52
1992	—Louisville (A.A.)■	5	4	.556	4.30	33	10	1	0	1	98⅓	114	56	47	23	56
1993	—Iowa (Am. Assoc.)■ ...	12	7	.632	3.94	48	16	0	0	4	134⅔	147	61	59	32	78

INCAVIGLIA, PETE

OF, PHILLIES

PERSONAL: Born April 2, 1964, in Pebble Beach, Calif.... 6-1/235.... Throws right, bats right.... Full name: Peter Joseph Incaviglia.... Son of Tom Incaviglia, minor league infielder (1948-55); and brother of Tony Incaviglia, minor league third baseman (1979-83).

HIGH SCHOOL: Monterey (Pebble Beach, Calif.).

COLLEGE: Oklahoma State.

TRANSACTIONS/CAREER NOTES: Selected by San Francisco Giants organization in 10th round of free-agent draft (June 7, 1982).... Selected by Montreal Expos organization in first round (eighth pick overall) of free-agent draft (June 3, 1985).... Traded by Expos to Texas Rangers organization for P Bob Sebra and IF Jim Anderson (November 2, 1985).... On disabled list (June 15-30, 1989).... Released by Rangers (March 29, 1991).... Signed by Detroit Tigers (April 7, 1991).... On disabled list (June 13-July 5 and July 25-August 11, 1991).... Granted free agency (October 31, 1991).... Signed by Tucson, Houston Astros organization (January 27, 1992).... Granted free agency (November 3, 1992).... Signed by Philadelphia Phillies (December 8, 1992).

RECORDS: Shares major league record for most doubles in one inning—2 (May 11, 1986, second game, fourth inning).

HONORS: Named designated hitter on THE SPORTING NEWS college All-America team (1985).

			BATTING												FIELDING			
Year	Team (League)	Pos.	G	AB	R	H	2B	3B	HR	RBI	Avg.	BB	SO	SB	PO	A	E	Avg.
1986	—Texas (A.L.)	OF	153	540	82	135	21	2	30	88	.250	55	*185	3	157	6	•14	.921
1987	—Texas (A.L.)	OF	139	509	85	138	26	4	27	80	.271	48	168	9	216	8	•13	.945
1988	—Texas (A.L.)	OF	116	418	59	104	19	3	22	54	.249	39	•153	6	172	12	2	.989
1989	—Texas (A.L.)	OF	133	453	48	107	27	4	21	81	.236	32	136	5	213	7	6	.973
1990	—Texas (A.L.)	OF	153	529	59	123	27	0	24	85	.233	45	146	3	290	12	8	.974
1991	—Detroit (A.L.)■	OF	97	337	38	72	12	1	11	38	.214	36	92	1	106	4	3	.973
1992	—Houston (N.L.)■	OF	113	349	31	93	22	1	11	44	.266	25	99	2	188	8	6	.970
1993	—Philadelphia (N.L.)■.	OF	116	368	60	101	16	3	24	89	.274	21	82	1	164	4	5	.971
	American League totals (6 years)		791	2786	371	679	132	14	135	426	.244	255	880	27	1154	49	46	.963
	National League totals (2 years)		229	717	91	194	38	4	35	133	.271	46	181	3	352	12	11	.971
	Major league totals (8 years)		1020	3503	462	873	170	18	170	559	.249	301	1061	30	1506	61	57	.965

CHAMPIONSHIP SERIES RECORD

			BATTING												FIELDING			
Year	Team (League)	Pos.	G	AB	R	H	2B	3B	HR	RBI	Avg.	BB	SO	SB	PO	A	E	Avg.
1993	—Philadelphia (N.L.) ...	OF	3	12	2	2	0	0	1	1	.167	0	3	0	8	0	0	1.000

WORLD SERIES RECORD

			BATTING												FIELDING			
Year	Team (League)	Pos.	G	AB	R	H	2B	3B	HR	RBI	Avg.	BB	SO	SB	PO	A	E	Avg.
1993	—Philadelphia (N.L.) ...	OF-PH	4	8	0	1	0	0	0	1	.125	0	4	0	7	0	0	1.000

INGRAM, GAREY

2B, DODGERS

PERSONAL: Born July 25, 1970, in Columbus, Ga.... 5-11/180.... Throws right, bats right.... Full name: Garey Lamar Ingram.

HIGH SCHOOL: Columbus (Ga.).

COLLEGE: Middle Georgia College.

TRANSACTIONS/CAREER NOTES: Selected by Los Angeles Dodgers organization in 43rd round of free-agent draft (June 1, 1988).... Selected by Dodgers organization in 44th round of free-agent draft (June 5, 1989).... On Bakersfield disabled list (June 28-July 6, 1991).... On San Antonio disabled list (April 14-June 16, 1992; April 26-May 3, May 14-June 10 and July 29-August 8, 1993).

STATISTICAL NOTES: Tied for California League lead in being hit by pitch with 14 in 1991.... Led Texas League in being hit by pitch with 12 in 1992.... Tied for Texas League lead in errors by second baseman with 27 in 1993.

			BATTING												FIELDING			
Year	Team (League)	Pos.	G	AB	R	H	2B	3B	HR	RBI	Avg.	BB	SO	SB	PO	A	E	Avg.
1990	—Great Falls (Pio.)	DH	56	198	43	68	12	*8	2	21	.343	22	37	10	...	...	...	...
1991	—Bakersfield (Calif.) ...	OF	118	445	75	132	16	4	9	61	.297	52	70	30	174	5	9	.952
	—San Antonio (Tex.) ...	OF	1	1	0	0	0	0	0	1	.000	0	1	0	2	0	0	1.000
1992	—San Antonio (Tex.) ...	OF	65	198	34	57	9	5	2	17	.288	28	43	11	112	4	4	.967
1993	—San Antonio (Tex.) ...	2B-OF	84	305	43	82	14	5	6	33	.269	31	50	19	101	184	‡27	.913

INNIS, JEFF

P, TWINS

PERSONAL: Born July 5, 1962, in Decatur, Ill.... 6-1/168.... Throws right, bats right.... Full name: Jeffrey David Innis.... Name pronounced ENN-is.

HIGH SCHOOL: Eisenhower (Decatur, Ill.).

COLLEGE: Illinois.

TRANSACTIONS/CAREER NOTES: Selected by New York Mets organization in 13th round of free-agent draft (June 6, 1983).... Granted free agency (December 20, 1993).... Signed by Minnesota Twins organization (February 3, 1994).

Year	Team (League)	W	L	Pct.	ERA	G	GS	CG	ShO	Sv.	IP	H	R	ER	BB	SO
1983	—Little Falls (NYP)	8	0	1.000	1.37	28	0	0	0	8	46	29	8	7	28	68
1984	—Jackson (Texas)	6	5	.545	4.25	42	0	0	0	8	59⅓	65	34	28	40	63
1985	—Lynchburg (Caro.)	6	3	.667	2.34	53	0	0	0	14	77	46	26	20	40	91
1986	—Jackson (Texas)	4	5	.444	2.45	56	0	0	0	*25	92	69	30	25	24	75
1987	—Tidewater (Int'l)	6	1	.857	2.03	29	0	0	0	5	44⅓	26	10	10	16	28
	—New York (N.L.)	0	1	.000	3.16	17	1	0	0	0	25⅔	29	9	9	4	28
1988	—Tidewater (Int'l)	0	5	.000	3.54	34	0	0	0	4	48⅓	43	22	19	25	43
	—New York (N.L.)	1	1	.500	1.89	12	0	0	0	0	19	19	6	4	2	14
1989	—Tidewater (Int'l)	3	1	.750	2.12	25	0	0	0	10	29⅔	28	9	7	8	14
	—New York (N.L.)	0	1	.000	3.18	29	0	0	0	0	39⅔	38	16	14	8	16
1990	—New York (N.L.)	1	3	.250	2.39	18	0	0	0	1	26⅓	19	9	7	10	12
	—Tidewater (Int'l)	5	2	.714	1.71	40	0	0	0	19	52⅔	34	11	10	17	42
1991	—New York (N.L.)	0	2	.000	2.66	69	0	0	0	0	84⅔	66	30	25	23	47
1992	—New York (N.L.)	6	9	.400	2.86	76	0	0	0	1	88	85	32	28	36	39
1993	—New York (N.L.)	2	3	.400	4.11	67	0	0	0	3	76⅔	81	39	35	38	36
Major league totals (7 years)		10	20	.333	3.05	288	1	0	0	5	360	337	141	122	121	192

JACKSON, BO

DH/OF, ANGELS

PERSONAL: Born November 30, 1962, in Bessemer, Ala.... 6-1/228.... Throws right, bats right. ... Full name: Vincent Edward Jackson.
HIGH SCHOOL: McAdory (McCalla, Ala.)
COLLEGE: Auburn.

TRANSACTIONS/CAREER NOTES: Selected by New York Yankees organization in second round of free-agent draft (June 7, 1982). ... Selected by California Angels organization in 20th round of free-agent draft (June 3, 1985).... Selected by Kansas City Royals organization in fourth round of free-agent draft (June 2, 1986).... On Memphis temporary inactive list (June 20-30, 1986).... On disabled list (June 1-July 2, 1988; July 25-August 9, 1989; and July 18-August 26, 1990).... Released by Royals (March 18, 1991).... Signed by Chicago White Sox (April 3, 1991).... On Chicago disabled list (April 3-September 2, 1991); included rehabilitation assignments to Sarasota (August 25) and Birmingham (August 26-September 2).... Granted free agency (March 10, 1992).... Re-signed by White Sox (March 10, 1992).... On Chicago disabled list (April 5, 1992-entire season).... Granted free agency (November 5, 1993).... Signed by Angels (January 31, 1994).
RECORDS: Shares major league record for most consecutive home runs—4 (July 17 [3] and August 26 [1], 1990).... Shares major league single-game record (nine innings) for most strikeouts—5 (April 18, 1987).... Shares major league record for most strikeouts in one inning—2 (April 8, 1987, fourth inning).
HONORS: Named A.L. Comeback Player of the Year by THE SPORTING NEWS (1993).
STATISTICAL NOTES: Hit three home runs in one game (July 17, 1990).

				BATTING										FIELDING			
Year	Team (League)	Pos.	G	AB	R	H	2B	3B	HR	RBI	Avg.	BB	SO	SB	PO	A	E	Avg.
1986	—Memphis (South.)	OF	53	184	30	51	9	3	7	25	.277	22	81	3	116	8	7	.947
	—Kansas City (A.L.)	OF	25	82	9	17	2	1	2	9	.207	7	34	3	29	2	4	.886
1987	—Kansas City (A.L.)	OF	116	396	46	93	17	2	22	53	.235	30	158	10	180	9	9	.955
1988	—Kansas City (A.L.)	OF	124	439	63	108	16	4	25	68	.246	25	146	27	246	11	7	.973
1989	—Kansas City (A.L.)	OF	135	515	86	132	15	6	32	105	.256	39	*172	26	224	11	8	.967
1990	—Kansas City (A.L.)	OF	111	405	74	110	16	1	28	78	.272	44	128	15	230	8	12	.952
1991	—Sarasota (Fla. St.)■	DH	2	6	1	2	0	0	0	2	.333	0	0	0	...	...	...	...
	—Birm. (Southern)	DH	4	13	2	4	0	0	0	0	.308	4	2	1	...	...	...	...
	—Chicago (A.L.)	DH	23	71	8	16	4	0	3	14	.225	12	25	0	...	...	...	...
1992	—		Did not play.															
1993	—Chicago (A.L.)	OF	85	284	32	66	9	0	16	45	.232	23	106	0	89	5	1	.989
Major league totals (7 years)			619	2192	318	542	79	14	128	372	.247	180	769	81	998	46	41	.962

CHAMPIONSHIP SERIES RECORD

				BATTING										FIELDING			
Year	Team (League)	Pos.	G	AB	R	H	2B	3B	HR	RBI	Avg.	BB	SO	SB	PO	A	E	Avg.
1993	—Chicago (A.L.)	DH	3	10	1	0	0	0	0	0	.000	3	6	0	...	...	...	...

ALL-STAR GAME RECORD

ALL-STAR GAME NOTES: Named Most Valuable Player (1989).... Hit home run in first at-bat (July 11, 1989).

			BATTING									FIELDING			
Year	League	Pos.	AB	R	H	2B	3B	HR	RBI	Avg.	BB	SO	SB	PO	A	E	Avg.
1989	—American	OF	4	1	2	0	0	1	2	.500	0	1	1	2	0	0	1.000

RECORD AS FOOTBALL PLAYER

TRANSACTIONS/CAREER NOTES: Played running back.... Selected by Tampa Bay Buccaneers in first round (first pick overall) of 1986 NFL draft.... Selected by Birmingham Stallions in 1986 USFL territorial draft.... On reserve/did not sign list (entire 1986 season-April 27, 1987).... Selected by Los Angeles Raiders in seventh round (183rd pick overall) of 1987 NFL draft.... Signed by Raiders (July 17, 1987).... On reserve/did not report list (August 27-October 24, 1987).... On reserve/did not report list (August 22-October 12, 1988).... Activated from reserve/did not report list (October 15, 1988).... On reserve/did not report list (July 21-October 11, 1989).... On reserve/did not report list (July-October 21, 1990).... On reserve/did not report list (July-October 1991).... Placed on reserve/retired list (October 1991).
CHAMPIONSHIP GAME EXPERIENCE: Member of Los Angeles Raiders for AFC championship game (1990 season); inactive.
RECORDS/HONORS: Heisman Trophy winner (1985).... Named College Football Player of the Year by THE SPORTING NEWS (1985).... Named as running back on THE SPORTING NEWS college All-America team (1985).... Named to play in Pro Bowl (1990 season); replaced by John L. Williams due to injury.
PRO STATISTICS: 1987—Recovered one fumble. 1988—Recovered two fumbles.

Year	Team	G	RUSHING Att.	Yds.	Avg.	TD	RECEIVING No.	Yds.	Avg.	TD	TOTAL TD	Pts.	Fum.
1987	L.A. Raiders NFL	7	81	554	6.8	4	16	136	8.5	2	6	36	2
1988	L.A. Raiders NFL	10	136	580	4.3	3	9	79	8.8	0	3	18	5
1989	L.A. Raiders NFL	11	173	950	5.5	4	9	69	7.7	0	4	24	1
1990	L.A. Raiders NFL	10	125	698	5.6	5	6	68	11.3	0	5	30	3
	Pro totals (4 years)	38	515	2782	5.4	16	40	352	8.8	2	18	108	11

JACKSON, DANNY

P, PHILLIES

PERSONAL: Born January 5, 1962, in San Antonio. . . . 6-0/220. . . . Throws left, bats right. . . . Full name: Danny Lynn Jackson.

HIGH SCHOOL: Central (Aurora, Colo.).

COLLEGE: Oklahoma and Trinidad State Junior College (Colo.).

TRANSACTIONS/CAREER NOTES: Selected by Oakland A's organization in 24th round of free-agent draft (June 3, 1980). . . . Selected by Kansas City Royals organization in secondary phase of free-agent draft (January 17, 1982). . . . On Jacksonville disabled list (September 8, 1982-remainder of season). . . . On disabled list (April 4-21, 1986). . . . Traded by Royals with SS Angel Salazar to Cincinnati Reds for P Ted Power and SS Kurt Stillwell (November 6, 1987). . . . On disabled list (June 18-July 6 and July 25-September 1, 1989). . . . On Cincinnati disabled list (April 30-May 17, 1990); included rehabilitation assignment to Nashville (May 13-17). . . . On Cincinnati disabled list (July 18-August 8, 1990); included rehabilitation assignment to Charleston, W.Va. (August 5-8). . . . On Cincinnati disabled list (August 14-30, 1990); included rehabilitation assignment to Nashville (August 30). . . . Granted free agency (November 5, 1990). . . . Signed by Chicago Cubs (November 21, 1990). . . . On Chicago disabled list (April 20-June 9, 1991). . . . On Chicago disabled list (June 20-August 3, 1991); included rehabilitation assignment to Iowa (July 29-30). . . . Traded by Cubs to Pittsburgh Pirates for 3B Steve Buechele (July 11, 1992). . . . Selected by Florida Marlins in third round (53rd pick overall) of expansion draft (November 17, 1992). . . . Traded by Marlins to Philadelphia Phillies for P Joel Adamson and P Matt Whisenant (November 17, 1992).

HONORS: Named lefthanded pitcher on THE SPORTING NEWS N.L. All-Star team (1988).

Year	Team (League)	W	L	Pct.	ERA	G	GS	CG	ShO	Sv.	IP	H	R	ER	BB	SO
1982	Char., S.C. (S. Atl.)	10	1	.909	2.62	13	13	3	0	0	96⅓	80	37	28	39	62
	Jacksonv. (South.)	7	2	.778	2.39	14	14	3	1	0	98	78	30	26	42	74
1983	Omaha (A.A.)	7	8	.467	3.97	23	22	5	•2	0	136	126	74	60	73	93
	Kansas City (A.L.)	1	1	.500	5.21	4	3	0	0	0	19	26	12	11	6	9
1984	Kansas City (A.L.)	2	6	.250	4.26	15	11	1	0	0	76	84	41	36	35	40
	Omaha (A.A.)	5	8	.385	3.67	16	16	•10	•3	0	110⅓	91	50	45	45	82
1985	Kansas City (A.L.)	14	12	.538	3.42	32	32	4	3	0	208	209	94	79	76	114
1986	Kansas City (A.L.)	11	12	.478	3.20	32	27	4	1	1	185⅔	177	83	66	79	115
1987	Kansas City (A.L.)	9	18	.333	4.02	36	34	11	2	0	224	219	115	100	109	152
1988	Cincinnati (N.L.)■	•23	8	.742	2.73	35	35	•15	6	0	260⅔	206	86	79	71	161
1989	Cincinnati (N.L.)	6	11	.353	5.60	20	20	1	0	0	115⅔	122	78	72	57	70
1990	Cincinnati (N.L.)	6	6	.500	3.61	22	21	0	0	0	117⅓	119	54	47	40	76
	Nashville (A.A.)	1	0	1.000	0.00	2	2	0	0	0	11	9	0	0	4	3
	Char., W.Va. (SAL)	0	0	...	6.00	1	1	0	0	0	3	2	2	2	1	2
1991	Chicago (N.L.)■	1	5	.167	6.75	17	14	0	0	0	70⅔	89	59	53	48	31
	Iowa (Am. Assoc.)	0	0	...	1.80	1	1	0	0	0	5	2	1	1	2	4
1992	Chi.-Pitts. (N.L.)■	8	13	.381	3.84	34	34	0	0	0	201⅓	211	99	86	77	97
1993	Philadelphia (N.L.)■	12	11	.522	3.77	32	32	2	1	0	210⅓	214	105	88	80	120
	A.L. totals (5 years)	37	49	.430	3.69	119	107	20	6	1	712⅔	715	345	292	305	430
	N.L. totals (6 years)	56	54	.509	3.92	160	156	18	7	0	976	961	481	425	373	555
	Major league totals (11 years)	93	103	.474	3.82	279	263	38	13	1	1688⅔	1676	826	717	678	985

CHAMPIONSHIP SERIES RECORD

Year	Team (League)	W	L	Pct.	ERA	G	GS	CG	ShO	Sv.	IP	H	R	ER	BB	SO
1985	Kansas City (A.L.)	1	0	1.000	0.00	2	1	1	1	0	10	10	0	0	1	7
1990	Cincinnati (N.L.)	1	0	1.000	2.38	2	2	0	0	0	11⅓	8	3	3	7	8
1992	Pittsburgh (N.L.)	0	1	.000	21.60	1	1	0	0	0	1⅔	4	4	4	2	0
1993	Philadelphia (N.L.)	1	0	1.000	1.17	1	1	0	0	0	7⅔	9	1	1	2	6
	Champ. series totals (4 years)	3	1	.750	2.35	6	5	1	1	0	30⅔	31	8	8	12	21

WORLD SERIES RECORD

Year	Team (League)	W	L	Pct.	ERA	G	GS	CG	ShO	Sv.	IP	H	R	ER	BB	SO
1985	Kansas City (A.L.)	1	1	.500	1.69	2	2	1	0	0	16	9	3	3	5	12
1990	Cincinnati (N.L.)	0	0	...	10.13	1	1	0	0	0	2⅔	6	4	3	2	0
1993	Philadelphia (N.L.)	0	1	.000	7.20	1	1	0	0	0	5	6	4	4	1	1
	World Series totals (3 years)	1	2	.333	3.80	4	4	1	0	0	23⅔	21	11	10	8	13

ALL-STAR GAME RECORD

Year	League	W	L	Pct.	ERA	GS	CG	ShO	Sv.	IP	H	R	ER	BB	SO
1988	National	Did not play.													

JACKSON, DARRIN

OF, WHITE SOX

PERSONAL: Born August 22, 1963, in Los Angeles. . . . 6-0/185. . . . Throws right, bats right. . . . Full name: Darrin Jay Jackson.

HIGH SCHOOL: Culver City (Calif.).

TRANSACTIONS/CAREER NOTES: Selected by Chicago Cubs organization in second round of free-agent draft (June 8, 1981). . . . Traded by Cubs with P Calvin Schiraldi and a player to be named later to San Diego Padres for OF Marvell Wynne and IF Luis Salazar (August 30, 1989); Padres acquired 1B Phil Stephenson to complete deal (September 5, 1989). . . . Traded by Padres to Toronto Blue Jays for OF Derek Bell and OF Stoney Briggs (March 30, 1993). . . . Traded by Blue Jays to New York Mets for SS Tony Fernandez (June 11, 1993). . . . On New York disabled list (July

19-September 1, 1993).... Granted free agency (December 20, 1993).... Signed by Chicago White Sox organization (December 28, 1993).
STATISTICAL NOTES: Led Gulf Coast League outfielders with 127 total chances in 1981.... Tied for Texas League lead in double plays by outfielder with six in 1984.... Tied for American Association lead in double plays by outfielder with six in 1987.... Led N.L. in grounding into double plays with 21 in 1992.... Led N.L. outfielders with 455 total chances and nine double plays in 1992.

			BATTING											FIELDING			
Year	**Team (League)**	**Pos.**	**G**	**AB**	**R**	**H**	**2B**	**3B**	**HR**	**RBI**	**Avg.**	**BB**	**SO**	**SB**	**PO**	**A**	**E**	**Avg.**
1981	—GC Cubs (GCL)	OF	62	210	29	39	5	0	1	15	.186	28	53	18	*121	5	1	.992
1982	—Quad Cities (Mid.)	OF	132	529	86	146	23	5	5	48	.276	47	106	58	266	9	8	.972
1983	—Salinas (Calif.)	OF	129	509	70	126	18	5	6	54	.248	38	111	36	237	15	13	.951
1984	—Midland (Texas)	OF	132	496	63	134	18	2	15	54	.270	49	102	13	286	*19	8	.974
1985	—Iowa (Am. Assoc.)	OF	10	40	0	7	2	1	0	1	.175	3	10	1	19	0	0	1.000
	—Pittsfield (Eastern)	OF	91	325	38	82	10	1	3	30	.252	34	64	8	221	5	0	1.000
	—Chicago (N.L.)	OF	5	11	0	1	0	0	0	0	.091	0	3	0	7	0	0	1.000
1986	—Pittsfield (Eastern)	OF	137	•520	82	139	28	2	15	64	.267	43	115	42	320	*16	7	.980
1987	—Iowa (Am. Assoc.)	OF	132	474	81	130	32	5	23	81	.274	26	110	13	290	15	6	.981
	—Chicago (N.L.)	OF	7	5	2	4	1	0	0	0	.800	0	0	0	1	0	0	1.000
1988	—Chicago (N.L.)	OF	100	188	29	50	11	3	6	20	.266	5	28	4	116	1	2	.983
1989	—Chi.-S.D. (N.L.)■	OF	70	170	17	37	7	0	4	20	.218	13	34	1	121	5	5	.962
	—Iowa (Am. Assoc.)	OF	30	120	18	31	4	1	7	17	.258	7	22	4	66	12	0	1.000
1990	—San Diego (N.L.)	OF	58	113	10	29	3	0	3	9	.257	5	24	3	63	1	1	.985
	—Las Vegas (PCL)	OF	29	98	14	27	4	0	5	15	.276	9	21	3	61	4	0	1.000
1991	—San Diego (N.L.)	OF-P	122	359	51	94	12	1	21	49	.262	27	66	5	243	2	2	.992
1992	—San Diego (N.L.)	OF	155	587	72	146	23	5	17	70	.249	26	106	14	436	*18	2	.996
1993	—Toronto (A.L.)■	OF	46	176	15	38	8	0	5	19	.216	8	53	0	86	2	1	.989
	—New York (N.L.)■	OF	31	87	4	17	1	0	1	7	.195	2	22	0	51	4	0	1.000
American League totals (1 year)			46	176	15	38	8	0	5	19	.216	8	53	0	86	2	1	.989
National League totals (8 years)			548	1520	185	378	58	9	52	175	.249	78	283	27	1038	31	12	.989
Major league totals (8 years)			594	1696	200	416	66	9	57	194	.245	86	336	27	1124	33	13	.989

RECORD AS PITCHER

Year	**Team (League)**	**W**	**L**	**Pct.**	**ERA**	**G**	**GS**	**CG**	**ShO**	**Sv.**	**IP**	**H**	**R**	**ER**	**BB**	**SO**
1991	—San Diego (N.L.)	0	0	...	9.00	1	0	0	0	0	2	3	2	2	2	0

JACKSON, JEFF

OF, PHILLIES

PERSONAL: Born January 2, 1972, in Chicago.... 6-2/212.... Throws right, bats right.
HIGH SCHOOL: Neal F. Simeon (Chicago).
TRANSACTIONS/CAREER NOTES: Selected by Philadelphia Phillies organization in first round (fourth pick overall) of free-agent draft (June 5, 1989).... On disabled list (May 24-June 6, 1993).

			BATTING											FIELDING			
Year	**Team (League)**	**Pos.**	**G**	**AB**	**R**	**H**	**2B**	**3B**	**HR**	**RBI**	**Avg.**	**BB**	**SO**	**SB**	**PO**	**A**	**E**	**Avg.**
1989	—Martinsville (App.)	OF	48	163	16	37	5	1	2	21	.227	14	66	11	75	4	2	.975
1990	—Batavia (NY-Penn)	OF	63	227	30	45	11	3	3	22	.198	52	123	12	126	6	8	.943
1991	—Spartanburg (SAL)	OF	121	440	73	99	18	1	5	33	.225	52	123	29	235	8	6	.976
1992	—Clearwater (FSL)	OF	79	297	35	72	11	2	6	36	.242	23	78	6	141	6	1	.993
	—Reading (Eastern)	OF	36	108	12	20	1	2	0	6	.185	12	34	9	60	1	3	.953
1993	—Reading (Eastern)	OF	113	374	45	89	14	3	9	51	.238	30	117	20	163	4	•11	.938

JACKSON, MIKE

P, GIANTS

PERSONAL: Born December 22, 1964, in Houston.... 6-2/223.... Throws right, bats right.... Full name: Michael Ray Jackson.
HIGH SCHOOL: Forest Brook (Houston).
COLLEGE: Hill Junior College (Tex.).
TRANSACTIONS/CAREER NOTES: Selected by Philadelphia Phillies organization in 29th round of free-agent draft (June 6, 1983).... Selected by Philadelphia Phillies organization in secondary phase of free-agent draft (January 17, 1984).... On Philadelphia disabled list (August 6-21, 1987).... Traded by Phillies organization with OF Glenn Wilson and OF Dave Brundage to Seattle Mariners for OF Phil Bradley and P Tim Fortugno (December 9, 1987).... Traded by Mariners with P Bill Swift and P Dave Burba to San Francisco Giants for OF Kevin Mitchell and P Mike Remlinger (December 11, 1991).... On disabled list (July 24-August 9, 1993).
STATISTICAL NOTES: Led Carolina League with seven balks in 1985.... Tied for N.L. lead with eight balks in 1987.

Year	**Team (League)**	**W**	**L**	**Pct.**	**ERA**	**G**	**GS**	**CG**	**ShO**	**Sv.**	**IP**	**H**	**R**	**ER**	**BB**	**SO**
1984	—Spartanburg (SAL)	7	2	.778	2.68	14	0	0	0	0	80⅔	53	35	24	50	77
1985	—Peninsula (Caro.)	7	9	.438	4.60	31	18	0	0	1	125⅓	127	71	64	53	96
1986	—Reading (Eastern)	2	3	.400	1.66	30	0	0	0	6	43⅓	25	9	8	22	42
	—Portland (PCL)	3	1	.750	3.18	17	0	0	0	3	22⅔	18	8	8	13	23
	—Philadelphia (N.L.)	0	0	...	3.38	9	0	0	0	0	13⅓	12	5	5	4	3
1987	—Philadelphia (N.L.)	3	10	.231	4.20	55	7	0	0	1	109⅓	88	55	51	56	93
	—Maine (Int'l)	1	0	1.000	0.82	2	2	0	0	0	11	9	2	1	5	13
1988	—Seattle (A.L.)■	6	5	.545	2.63	62	0	0	0	4	99⅓	74	37	29	43	76
1989	—Seattle (A.L.)	4	6	.400	3.17	65	0	0	0	7	99⅓	81	43	35	54	94
1990	—Seattle (A.L.)	5	7	.417	4.54	63	0	0	0	3	77⅓	64	42	39	44	69
1991	—Seattle (A.L.)	7	7	.500	3.25	72	0	0	0	14	88⅔	64	35	32	34	74
1992	—San Francisco (N.L.)■	6	6	.500	3.73	67	0	0	0	2	82	76	35	34	33	80
1993	—San Francisco (N.L.)	6	6	.500	3.03	*81	0	0	0	1	77⅓	58	28	26	24	70
A.L. totals (4 years)		22	25	.468	3.33	262	0	0	0	28	364⅔	283	157	135	175	313
N.L. totals (4 years)		15	22	.405	3.70	212	7	0	0	4	282	234	123	116	117	246
Major league totals (8 years)		37	47	.440	3.49	474	7	0	0	32	646⅔	517	280	251	292	559

JACOME, JASON

P, METS

PERSONAL: Born November 24, 1970, in Tulsa, Okla. . . . 6-1/155. . . . Throws left, bats left. . . . Full name: Jason James Jacome.
HIGH SCHOOL: Rincon (Tucson, Ariz.).
COLLEGE: Pima Community College (Ariz.).
TRANSACTIONS/CAREER NOTES: Selected by New York Mets organization in 12th round of free-agent draft (June 3, 1991).

Year	Team (League)	W	L	Pct.	ERA	G	GS	CG	ShO	Sv.	IP	H	R	ER	BB	SO
1991	—Kingsport (Appal.)	5	4	.556	1.63	12	7	3	•1	2	55⅓	35	18	10	13	48
1992	—Columbia (S. Atl.)	4	1	.800	1.03	8	8	1	0	0	52⅔	40	7	6	15	49
	—St. Lucie (Fla. St.)	6	7	.462	2.83	17	17	5	1	0	114⅓	98	45	36	30	66
1993	—St. Lucie (Fla. St.)	6	3	.667	3.08	14	14	2	2	0	99⅓	106	37	34	23	66
	—Binghamton (East.)	8	4	.667	3.21	14	14	0	0	0	87	85	36	31	38	56

JAHA, JOHN

1B, BREWERS

PERSONAL: Born May 27, 1966, in Portland, Ore. . . . 6-1/205. . . . Throws right, bats right. . . . Full name: John Emile Jaha. . . . Name pronounced JAH-ha.
HIGH SCHOOL: David Douglas (Portland, Ore.).
TRANSACTIONS/CAREER NOTES: Selected by Milwaukee Brewers organization in 14th round of free-agent draft (June 4, 1984). . . . On disabled list (April 6-August 1, 1990).
HONORS: Named Texas League Most Valuable Player (1991).
STATISTICAL NOTES: Led Northwest League with 144 total bases and tied for lead with four intentional bases on balls received in 1986. . . . Led Texas League with 301 total bases, .619 slugging percentage and .438 on-base percentage in 1991. . . . Led Texas League first basemen with 81 assists in 1991.

			BATTING												FIELDING			
Year	Team (League)	Pos.	G	AB	R	H	2B	3B	HR	RBI	Avg.	BB	SO	SB	PO	A	E	Avg.
1985	—Helena (Pioneer)	3B	24	68	13	18	3	0	2	14	.265	14	23	4	9	32	1	.976
1986	—Tri-Cities (N'west)	1B-3B	•73	258	65	82	13	2	*15	67	.318	*70	75	9	352	101	18	.962
1987	—Beloit (Midwest)	3B-1B-SS	122	376	68	101	22	0	7	47	.269	102	86	10	493	113	18	.971
1988	—Stockton (Calif.)	1B	99	302	58	77	14	6	8	54	.255	69	85	10	793	60	5	*.994
1989	—Stockton (Calif.)	1B-3B	140	479	83	140	26	5	25	91	.292	*112	115	8	1081	62	8	.993
1990	—Stockton (Calif.)	DH	26	84	12	22	5	0	4	19	.262	18	25	0	...	...	...	...
1991	—El Paso (Texas)	1B-3B	130	486	*121	167	38	3	*30	*134	.344	78	101	12	883	†87	10	.990
1992	—Denver (A.A.)	1B	79	274	61	88	18	2	18	69	.321	50	60	6	654	50	7	.990
	—Milwaukee (A.L.)	1B-OF	47	133	17	30	3	1	2	10	.226	12	30	10	286	22	0	1.000
1993	—Milwaukee (A.L.)	1B-3B-2B	153	515	78	136	21	0	19	70	.264	51	109	13	1187	128	10	.992
Major league totals (2 years)			200	648	95	166	24	1	21	80	.256	63	139	23	1473	150	10	.994

JAMES, CHRIS

OF, RANGERS

PERSONAL: Born October 4, 1962, in Rusk, Tex. . . . 6-1/202. . . . Throws right, bats right. . . . Full name: Donald Christopher James. . . . Brother of Craig James, United States Football League and National Football League player (1983-88).
HIGH SCHOOL: Stratford (Houston).
COLLEGE: Blinn College (Tex.).
TRANSACTIONS/CAREER NOTES: Signed as free agent by Philadelphia Phillies organization (October 30, 1981). . . . On Philadelphia disabled list (May 6-July 21, 1986); included rehabilitation assignment to Portland (July 3-21). . . . Traded by Phillies to San Diego Padres for IF Randy Ready and OF John Kruk (June 2, 1989). . . . Traded by Padres with C Sandy Alomar and 3B Carlos Baerga to Cleveland Indians for OF Joe Carter (December 6, 1989). . . . On disabled list (September 11, 1991-remainder of season). . . . Granted free agency (December 20, 1991). . . . Signed by San Francisco Giants (January 15, 1992). . . . On San Francisco disabled list (August 15-September 1, 1992). . . . Granted free agency (October 29, 1992). . . . Signed by Houston Astros organization (January 8, 1993). . . . Traded by Astros to Texas Rangers for P Dave Gandolph (September 17, 1993).
STATISTICAL NOTES: Led South Atlantic League with 257 total bases and tied for lead in being hit by pitch with 12 in 1983. . . . Led Eastern League third basemen with 39 errors in 1984. . . . Led Pacific Coast League outfielders with 351 total chances in 1985. . . . Tied for Pacific Coast League lead in being hit by pitch with seven in 1985.

			BATTING												FIELDING			
Year	Team (League)	Pos.	G	AB	R	H	2B	3B	HR	RBI	Avg.	BB	SO	SB	PO	A	E	Avg.
1982	—Bend (Northwest)	3B-OF	63	227	47	72	*19	3	12	50	.317	20	56	10	93	54	10	.936
1983	—Spartanburg (SAL)	OF-3B	129	499	94	148	23	4	26	*121	.297	41	93	11	150	88	16	.937
1984	—Reading (Eastern)	3B-OF	128	457	66	117	19	*12	8	57	.256	40	74	19	104	209	†39	.889
1985	—Portland (PCL)	OF	135	507	78	160	35	8	11	73	.316	33	72	23	*328	16	7	.980
1986	—Portland (PCL)	OF-3B	69	266	30	64	6	2	12	41	.241	17	45	3	83	44	8	.941
	—Philadelphia (N.L.)	OF	16	46	5	13	3	0	1	5	.283	1	13	0	19	0	0	1.000
1987	—Philadelphia (N.L.)	OF	115	358	48	105	20	6	17	54	.293	27	67	3	198	5	2	.990
	—Maine (Int'l)	OF-3B	13	40	5	9	2	1	0	3	.225	3	9	0	22	4	0	1.000
1988	—Philadelphia (N.L.)	OF-3B	150	566	57	137	24	1	19	66	.242	31	73	7	282	51	9	.974
1989	—Phil.-S.D. (N.L.)■	OF-3B	132	482	55	117	17	2	13	65	.243	26	68	5	215	27	7	.972
1990	—Cleveland (A.L.)■	OF	140	528	62	158	32	4	12	70	.299	31	71	4	25	1	0	1.000
1991	—Cleveland (A.L.)	OF-1B	115	437	31	104	16	2	5	41	.238	18	61	3	173	10	0	1.000
1992	—San Francisco (N.L.)■	OF	111	248	25	60	10	4	5	32	.242	14	45	2	112	2	3	.974
1993	—Houston (N.L.)■	OF	65	129	19	33	10	1	6	19	.256	15	34	2	65	4	3	.958
	—Texas (A.L.)■	OF	8	31	5	11	1	0	3	7	.355	3	6	0	14	0	0	1.000
American League totals (3 years)			263	996	98	273	49	6	20	118	.274	52	138	7	212	11	0	1.000
National League totals (6 years)			589	1829	209	465	84	14	61	241	.254	114	300	19	891	89	24	.976
Major league totals (8 years)			852	2825	307	738	133	20	81	359	.261	166	438	26	1103	100	24	.980

JAMES, DION

OF

PERSONAL: Born November 9, 1962, in Philadelphia. . . . 6-1/185. . . . Throws left, bats left.
HIGH SCHOOL: McClatchy (Sacramento, Calif.).
TRANSACTIONS/CAREER NOTES: Selected by Milwaukee Brewers organization in first round (25th pick overall) of free-agent draft (June 3, 1980). . . . On disabled list (July 1-August 1, 1982).

. . . On Milwaukee disabled list (March 31-April 28, 1985); included rehabilitation assignment to Vancouver (April 12-28). . . . On Milwaukee disabled list (May 20-September 1, 1985). . . . Traded by Brewers organization to Atlanta Braves for OF Brad Komminsk (January 20, 1987). . . . Traded by Braves to Cleveland Indians for OF Oddibe McDowell (July 2, 1989). . . . Released by Indians (October 30, 1990). . . . Signed by New York Yankees (April 3, 1992). . . . Granted free agency (October 27, 1993). . . . Signed by Chunichi Dragons of Japan Central League (December 6, 1993).

STATISTICAL NOTES: Led California League outfielders with .988 fielding percentage in 1981.

			BATTING												FIELDING			
Year	**Team (League)**	**Pos.**	**G**	**AB**	**R**	**H**	**2B**	**3B**	**HR**	**RBI**	**Avg.**	**BB**	**SO**	**SB**	**PO**	**A**	**E**	**Avg.**
1980	—Butte (Pioneer)	OF-1B	59	224	57	71	14	1	0	27	.317	42	11	15	80	4	7	.923
	—Burlington (Midw.)	OF	3	10	0	1	0	0	0	1	.100	4	1	0	8	1	0	1.000
1981	—Stockton (Calif.)	OF-1B	124	451	70	137	17	3	2	49	.304	62	43	45	250	10	3	†.989
1982	—El Paso (Texas)	OF	106	422	103	136	25	3	9	72	.322	61	46	16	237	9	7	.972
1983	—Vancouver (PCL)	OF	129	467	84	157	29	5	8	68	.336	63	33	22	289	6	2	.993
	—Milwaukee (A.L.)	OF	11	20	1	2	0	0	0	1	.100	2	2	1	12	1	0	1.000
1984	—Milwaukee (A.L.)	OF	128	387	52	114	19	5	1	30	.295	32	41	10	252	7	3	.989
1985	—Vancouver (PCL)	OF	10	37	2	4	2	0	0	5	.108	4	6	0	17	0	0	1.000
	—Milwaukee (A.L.)	OF	18	49	5	11	1	0	0	3	.224	6	6	0	20	0	0	1.000
1986	—Vancouver (PCL)	OF-1B	130	485	85	137	25	6	6	55	.282	61	66	30	348	7	5	.986
1987	—Atlanta (N.L.)■	OF	134	494	80	154	37	6	10	61	.312	110	112	21	262	4	1	*.996
1988	—Atlanta (N.L.)	OF	132	386	46	99	17	5	3	30	.256	58	59	9	222	5	3	.987
1989	—Atlanta (N.L.)	OF-1B	63	170	15	44	7	0	1	11	.259	25	23	1	126	7	0	1.000
	—Cleveland (A.L.)■	OF-1B	71	245	26	75	11	0	4	29	.306	24	26	1	85	1	3	.966
1990	—Cleveland (A.L.)	1B-OF	87	248	28	68	15	2	1	22	.274	27	23	5	282	17	4	.987
1991	—		Out of organized baseball.															
1992	—New York (A.L.)■	OF	67	145	24	38	8	0	3	17	.262	22	15	1	62	1	0	1.000
1993	—New York (A.L.)	OF-1B	115	343	62	114	21	2	7	36	.332	31	31	0	141	4	5	.967
American League totals (7 years)			497	1437	198	422	75	9	16	138	.294	144	144	18	854	31	15	.983
National League totals (3 years)			329	1050	141	297	61	11	14	102	.283	193	194	31	610	16	4	.994
Major league totals (9 years)			826	2487	339	719	136	20	30	240	.289	337	338	49	1464	47	19	.988

JANICKI, PETE

P, ANGELS

PERSONAL: Born January 26, 1971, in Parma, O. . . . 6-4/190. . . . Throws right, bats right. . . . Full name: Peter Anthony Janicki.

HIGH SCHOOL: El Dorado (Placentia, Calif.).

COLLEGE: UCLA.

TRANSACTIONS/CAREER NOTES: Selected by Boston Red Sox organization in ninth round of free-agent draft (June 5, 1989). . . . Selected by California Angels organization in first round (eighth pick overall) of free-agent draft (June 1, 1992). . . . On Palm Springs disabled list (April 12-22, 1993). . . . On California disabled list (April 22, 1993-remainder of season).

Year	**Team (League)**	**W**	**L**	**Pct.**	**ERA**	**G**	**GS**	**CG**	**ShO**	**Sv.**	**IP**	**H**	**R**	**ER**	**BB**	**SO**
1993	—Palm Springs (Cal.)	0	0	...	10.80	1	1	0	0	0	1⅔	3	2	2	2	2

JARVIS, KEVIN

P, REDS

PERSONAL: Born August 1, 1969, in Lexington, Ky. . . . 6-2/200. . . . Throws right, bats left. . . . Full name: Kevin Thomas Jarvis.

HIGH SCHOOL: Tates Creek (Lexington, Ky.).

COLLEGE: Wake Forest.

TRANSACTIONS/CAREER NOTES: Selected by Cincinnati Reds organization in 21st round of free-agent draft (June 3, 1991).

Year	**Team (League)**	**W**	**L**	**Pct.**	**ERA**	**G**	**GS**	**CG**	**ShO**	**Sv.**	**IP**	**H**	**R**	**ER**	**BB**	**SO**
1991	—Princeton (Appal.)	5	6	.455	2.42	13	13	4	•1	0	85⅔	73	34	23	29	79
1992	—Ced. Rap. (Midw.)	0	0	...	0.00	1	0	0	0	0	1	1	0	0	0	0
	—Char., W.Va. (SAL)	6	8	.429	3.11	28	18	2	1	0	133	123	59	46	37	131
1993	—Winst.-Salem (Car.)	8	7	.533	3.41	21	20	2	1	0	145	133	68	55	48	101
	—Chatt. (South.)	3	1	.750	1.69	7	3	2	0	0	37⅓	26	7	7	11	18

JAVIER, STAN

OF, ATHLETICS

PERSONAL: Born January 9, 1964, in San Francisco de Macoris, Dominican Republic. . . . 6-0/185. . . . Throws right, bats both. . . . Full name: Stanley Julian Javier. . . . Son of Julian Javier, infielder, St. Louis Cardinals and Cincinnati Reds (1960-72). . . . Name pronounced HA-vee-AIR.

HIGH SCHOOL: La Altagracia (San Francisco de Macoris, Dominican Republic).

TRANSACTIONS/CAREER NOTES: Signed as free agent by St. Louis Cardinals organization (March 26, 1981). . . . Traded by Cardinals organization with SS Bob Meacham to New York Yankees organization for OF Bob Helsom, P Marty Mason and P Steve Fincher (December 14, 1982). . . . Traded by Yankees organization with P Jay Howell, P Jose Rijo, P Eric Plunk and P Tim Birtsas to Oakland A's for OF Rickey Henderson, P Bert Bradley and cash (December 5, 1984). . . . On Oakland disabled list (August 3-September 1, 1987); included rehabilitation assignment to Tacoma (August 20-September 1). . . . On disabled list (August 18-September 2, 1988 and July 7-24, 1989). . . . Traded by A's to Los Angeles Dodgers for 2B Willie Randolph (May 13, 1990). . . . Traded by Dodgers to Philadelphia Phillies for P Steve Searcy and a player to be named later (July 2, 1992); Dodgers acquired IF Julio Peguero to complete deal (July 28, 1992). . . . Granted free agency (October 27, 1992). . . . Signed by California Angels organization (January 15, 1993). . . . Granted free agency (October 29, 1993). . . . Signed by A's (December 7, 1993).

			BATTING												FIELDING			
Year	**Team (League)**	**Pos.**	**G**	**AB**	**R**	**H**	**2B**	**3B**	**HR**	**RBI**	**Avg.**	**BB**	**SO**	**SB**	**PO**	**A**	**E**	**Avg.**
1981	—Johns. City (App.)	OF	53	144	30	36	5	4	3	19	.250	40	33	2	53	2	3	.948
1982	—Johns. City (App.)	OF	57	185	45	51	3	•4	8	36	.276	42	55	11	94	8	4	.962
1983	—Greensboro (S. Atl.)■	OF	129	489	109	152	*34	6	12	77	.311	75	95	33	250	10	15	.945
1984	—New York (A.L.)	OF	7	7	1	1	0	0	0	0	.143	0	1	0	3	0	0	1.000
	—Nashville (South.)	OF	76	262	40	76	17	4	7	38	.290	39	57	17	202	4	7	.967
	—Columbus (Int'l)	OF	32	99	12	22	3	1	0	7	.222	12	26	1	77	4	2	.976

Year	Team (League)	Pos.	G	AB	R	H	2B	3B	HR	RBI	Avg.	BB	SO	SB	PO	A	E	Avg.
			BATTING												FIELDING			
1985	—Huntsville (South.)■.	OF	140	486	105	138	22	8	9	64	.284	*112	92	61	363	8	7	.981
1986	—Tacoma (PCL)	OF-1B	69	248	50	81	16	2	4	51	.327	47	46	18	172	9	6	.968
	—Oakland (A.L.)	OF	59	114	13	23	8	0	0	8	.202	16	27	8	118	1	0	1.000
1987	—Oakland (A.L.)	OF-1B	81	151	22	28	3	1	2	9	.185	19	33	3	149	5	3	.981
	—Tacoma (PCL)	OF-1B	15	51	6	11	2	0	0	2	.216	4	12	3	26	0	2	.929
1988	—Oakland (A.L.)	OF-1B	125	397	49	102	13	3	2	35	.257	32	63	20	274	7	5	.983
1989	—Oakland (A.L.)	OF-2B-1B	112	310	42	77	12	3	1	28	.248	31	45	12	221	8	2	.991
1990	—Oakland (A.L.)	OF	19	33	4	8	0	2	0	3	.242	3	6	0	19	0	0	1.000
	—Los Angeles (N.L.)■.	OF	104	276	56	84	9	4	3	24	.304	37	44	15	204	2	0	1.000
1991	—Los Angeles (N.L.)	OF-1B	121	176	21	36	5	3	1	11	.205	16	36	7	90	4	3	.969
1992	—L.A.-Phil. (N.L.)■	OF	130	334	42	83	17	1	1	29	.249	37	54	18	229	7	3	.987
1993	—California (A.L.)■	OF-1B-2B	92	237	33	69	10	4	3	28	.291	27	33	12	167	4	4	.977
American League totals (7 years)			495	1249	164	308	46	13	8	111	.247	128	208	55	951	25	14	.986
National League totals (3 years)			355	786	119	203	31	8	5	64	.258	90	134	40	523	13	6	.989
Major league totals (9 years)			850	2035	283	511	77	21	13	175	.251	218	342	95	1474	38	20	.987

CHAMPIONSHIP SERIES RECORD

Year	Team (League)	Pos.	G	AB	R	H	2B	3B	HR	RBI	Avg.	BB	SO	SB	PO	A	E	Avg.
			BATTING												FIELDING			
1988	—Oakland (A.L.)	OF-PR	2	4	0	2	0	0	0	1	.500	1	0	0	5	0	0	1.000
1989	—Oakland (A.L.)	OF	1	2	0	0	0	0	0	0	.000	0	1	0	1	0	0	1.000
Championship series totals (2 years)			3	6	0	2	0	0	0	1	.333	1	1	0	6	0	0	1.000

WORLD SERIES RECORD

Year	Team (League)	Pos.	G	AB	R	H	2B	3B	HR	RBI	Avg.	BB	SO	SB	PO	A	E	Avg.
			BATTING												FIELDING			
1988	—Oakland (A.L.)	PR-OF	3	4	0	2	0	0	0	2	.500	0	1	0	1	0	0	1.000
1989	—Oakland (A.L.)	OF	1	0	0	0	0	0	0	0	...	0	0	0	0	0	0	...
World Series totals (2 years)			4	4	0	2	0	0	0	2	.500	0	1	0	1	0	0	1.000

JEAN, DOMINGO

P, ASTROS

PERSONAL: Born January 9, 1969, in San Pedro de Macoris, Dominican Republic. . . . 6-2/175. . . . Throws right, bats right.

TRANSACTIONS/CAREER NOTES: Signed as free agent by Chicago White Sox organization (May 8, 1989). . . . Traded by White Sox organization with P Melido Perez and P Robert Wickman to New York Yankees organization for 2B Steve Sax and cash (January 10, 1992). . . . On Albany/Colonie disabled list (April 21-May 8, 1993). . . . Traded by Yankees with IF Andy Stankiewicz to Houston Astros for P Xavier Hernandez (November 27, 1993).

Year	Team (League)	W	L	Pct.	ERA	G	GS	CG	ShO	Sv.	IP	H	R	ER	BB	SO
1990	—GC Whi. Sox (GCL)	2	5	.286	2.29	13	•13	1	0	0	78⅔	55	32	20	16	65
1991	—South Bend (Mid.)	12	8	.600	3.30	25	25	2	0	0	158	121	75	58	65	141
1992	—Fort Lauder. (FSL)■	6	11	.353	2.61	23	23	5	1	0	158⅔	118	57	46	49	172
	—Alb./Colon. (East.)	0	0	...	2.25	1	1	0	0	0	4	3	2	1	3	6
1993	—Alb./Colon. (East.)	5	3	.625	2.51	11	11	1	0	0	61	42	24	17	33	41
	—Columbus (Int'l)	2	2	.500	2.82	7	7	1	0	0	44⅔	40	15	14	13	39
	—New York (A.L.)	1	1	.500	4.46	10	6	0	0	0	40⅓	37	20	20	19	20
	—Prin. William (Car.)	0	0	...	0.00	1	0	0	0	0	1⅔	1	0	0	0	1
Major league totals (1 year)		1	1	.500	4.46	10	6	0	0	0	40⅓	37	20	20	19	20

JEFFERIES, GREGG

1B, CARDINALS

PERSONAL: Born August 1, 1967, in Burlingame, Calif. . . . 5-10/185. . . . Throws right, bats both. . . . Full name: Gregory Scott Jefferies.

HIGH SCHOOL: Serra (San Mateo, Calif.).

TRANSACTIONS/CAREER NOTES: Selected by New York Mets organization in first round (20th pick overall) of free-agent draft (June 3, 1985). . . . On disabled list (April 27-May 13, 1991). . . . Traded by Mets with OF Kevin McReynolds and 2B Keith Miller to Kansas City Royals for P Bret Saberhagen and IF Bill Pecota (December 11, 1991). . . . Traded by Royals with OF Ed Gerald to St. Louis Cardinals for OF Felix Jose and IF/OF Craig Wilson (February 12, 1993).

HONORS: Named Appalachian League Player of the Year (1985). . . . Named Carolina League Most Valuable Player (1986). . . . Named Texas League Most Valuable Player (1987).

STATISTICAL NOTES: Led Carolina League with .549 slugging percentage in 1986. . . . Led Texas League with 18 intentional bases on balls received in 1987. . . . Tied for International League lead with 10 intentional bases on balls received in 1988. . . . Led International League third basemen with 240 assists in 1988. . . . Led A.L. third basemen with 26 errors in 1992.

Year	Team (League)	Pos.	G	AB	R	H	2B	3B	HR	RBI	Avg.	BB	SO	SB	PO	A	E	Avg.
			BATTING												FIELDING			
1985	—Kingsport (Appal.)	SS-2B	47	166	27	57	18	2	3	29	.343	14	16	21	78	130	21	.908
	—Columbia (S. Atl.)	2B-SS	20	64	7	18	2	2	1	12	.281	4	4	7	28	26	2	.964
1986	—Columbia (S. Atl.)	SS	25	112	29	38	6	1	5	24	.339	9	10	13	36	83	7	.944
	—Lynchburg (Caro.)	SS	95	390	66	138	25	9	11	80	*.354	33	29	43	138	273	20	.954
	—Jackson (Texas)	SS-3B	5	19	1	8	1	1	0	7	.421	2	2	1	7	9	1	.941
1987	—Jackson (Texas)	SS-3B	134	510	81	187	*48	5	20	101	.367	49	43	26	167	388	35	.941
	—New York (N.L.)	PH	6	6	0	3	1	0	0	2	.500	0	0	0	...	...	...	...
1988	—Tidewater (Int'l)	3-S-2-0	132	504	62	142	28	4	7	61	.282	32	35	32	110	†330	27	.942
	—New York (N.L.)	3B-2B	29	109	19	35	8	2	6	17	.321	8	10	5	33	46	2	.975
1989	—New York (N.L.)	2B-3B	141	508	72	131	28	2	12	56	.258	39	46	21	242	280	14	.974
1990	—New York (N.L.)	2B-3B	153	604	96	171	*40	3	15	68	.283	46	40	11	242	341	16	.973
1991	—New York (N.L.)	2B-3B	136	486	59	132	19	2	9	62	.272	47	38	26	170	271	17	.963

Year	Team (League)	Pos.	G	AB	R	H	2B	3B	HR	RBI	Avg.	BB	SO	SB	PO	A	E	Avg.
			BATTING												FIELDING			
1992	—Kansas City (A.L.)■	3B-2B	152	604	66	172	36	3	10	75	.285	43	29	19	96	304	†26	.939
1993	—St. Louis (N.L.)■	1B-2B	142	544	89	186	24	3	16	83	.342	62	32	46	1281	77	9	.993
American League totals (1 year)			152	604	66	172	36	3	10	75	.285	43	29	19	96	304	26	.939
National League totals (6 years)			607	2257	335	658	120	12	58	288	.292	202	166	109	1968	1015	58	.981
Major league totals (7 years)			759	2861	401	830	156	15	68	363	.290	245	195	128	2064	1319	84	.976

CHAMPIONSHIP SERIES RECORD

Year	Team (League)	Pos.	G	AB	R	H	2B	3B	HR	RBI	Avg.	BB	SO	SB	PO	A	E	Avg.
			BATTING												FIELDING			
1988	—New York (N.L.)	3B	7	27	2	9	2	0	0	1	.333	4	0	0	5	8	1	.929

ALL-STAR GAME RECORD

Year	League	Pos.	AB	R	H	2B	3B	HR	RBI	Avg.	BB	SO	SB	PO	A	E	Avg.
			BATTING											FIELDING			
1993	—National	PH-DH	1	0	0	0	0	0	0	.000	0	1	0	...	...	...	...

JEFFERSON, REGGIE

1B, MARINERS

PERSONAL: Born September 25, 1968, in Tallahassee, Fla.... 6-4/215.... Throws left, bats both.... Full name: Reginald Jirod Jefferson.

HIGH SCHOOL: Lincoln (Tallahassee, Fla.).

TRANSACTIONS/CAREER NOTES: Selected by Cincinnati Reds organization in third round of free-agent draft (June 2, 1986).... On disabled list (May 25, 1990-remainder of season).... Traded by Reds to Cleveland Indians for 1B Tim Costo (June 14, 1991).... On Cleveland disabled list (June 24-July 1, 1991); included rehabilitation assignment to Canton/Akron (June 25-July 1).... On Cleveland disabled list (March 28-July 4, 1992); included rehabilitation assignment to Colorado Springs (June 15-July 4).... On Colorado Springs suspended list (September 6-9, 1992).... Traded by Indians with SS Felix Fermin and cash to Seattle Mariners for SS Omar Vizquel (December 20, 1993).

STATISTICAL NOTES: Led Gulf Coast League first basemen with 624 total chances in 1986.

MISCELLANEOUS: Batted lefthanded only with Cedar Rapids (1987-88).

Year	Team (League)	Pos.	G	AB	R	H	2B	3B	HR	RBI	Avg.	BB	SO	SB	PO	A	E	Avg.
			BATTING												FIELDING			
1986	—GC Reds (GCL)	1B	59	208	28	54	4	•5	3	33	.260	24	40	10	*581	*36	7	.989
1987	—Billings (Pioneer)	1B	8	22	10	8	1	0	1	9	.364	4	2	1	21	1	0	1.000
	—Ced. Rap. (Midw.)	1B	15	54	9	12	5	0	3	11	.222	1	12	1	120	11	1	.992
1988	—Ced. Rap. (Midw.)	1B	135	517	76	149	26	2	18	*90	.288	40	89	2	1084	91	13	.989
1989	—Chatt. (South.)	1B	135	487	66	140	19	3	17	80	.287	43	73	2	1004	79	16	.985
1990	—Nashville (A.A.)	1B	37	126	24	34	11	2	5	23	.270	14	30	1	314	20	4	.988
1991	—Nashville (A.A.)	1B	28	103	15	33	3	1	3	20	.320	10	22	3	196	13	2	.991
	—Cincinnati (N.L.)	1B	5	7	1	1	0	0	1	1	.143	1	2	0	14	1	0	1.000
	—Cleveland (A.L.)■	1B	26	101	10	20	3	0	2	12	.198	3	22	0	252	24	2	.993
	—Cant./Akr. (East.)	1B	6	25	2	7	1	0	0	4	.280	1	5	0	46	3	0	1.000
	—Colo. Springs (PCL)	1B	39	136	29	42	11	0	3	21	.309	16	28	0	289	25	3	.991
1992	—Colo. Springs (PCL)	1B	57	218	49	68	11	4	11	44	.312	29	50	1	363	34	5	.988
	—Cleveland (A.L.)	1B	24	89	8	30	6	2	1	6	.337	1	17	0	129	12	1	.993
1993	—Cleveland (A.L.)	1B	113	366	35	91	11	2	10	34	.249	28	78	1	112	10	3	.976
American League totals (3 years)			163	556	53	141	20	4	13	52	.254	32	117	1	493	46	6	.989
National League totals (1 year)			5	7	1	1	0	0	1	1	.143	1	2	0	14	1	0	1.000
Major league totals (3 years)			168	563	54	142	20	4	14	53	.252	33	119	1	507	47	6	.989

JENNINGS, DOUG

1B/OF

PERSONAL: Born September 30, 1964, in Atlanta.... 5-10/175.... Throws left, bats left.... Full name: James Douglas Jennings.

HIGH SCHOOL: Leon (Tallahassee, Fla.).

COLLEGE: Brevard Community College (Fla.).

TRANSACTIONS/CAREER NOTES: Selected by California Angels organization in second round of free-agent draft (January 17, 1984).... Selected by Oakland Athletics from Angels organization in Rule 5 major league draft (December 7, 1987).... On Oakland disabled list (June 27-July 31, 1988); included rehabilitation assignment to Tacoma (July 15-31).... Granted free agency (March 18, 1992).... Signed by Rochester, Baltimore Orioles organization (March 31, 1992).... Released by Orioles organization (March 30, 1993).... Signed by Iowa, Chicago Cubs organization (April 3, 1993).... Granted free agency (November 15, 1993).

STATISTICAL NOTES: Led Texas League in being hit by pitch with 13 in 1987.... Led Pacific Coast League in being hit by pitch with 16 in 1989.... Led Pacific Coast League first basemen with 12 errors in 1989.... Led Pacific Coast League in being hit by pitch with 11 in 1991.

Year	Team (League)	Pos.	G	AB	R	H	2B	3B	HR	RBI	Avg.	BB	SO	SB	PO	A	E	Avg.
			BATTING												FIELDING			
1984	—Salem (Northwest)	OF	52	173	29	45	7	1	1	17	.260	40	45	12	82	5	9	.906
1985	—Quad Cities (Mid.)	OF	95	319	50	81	17	7	5	54	.254	62	76	10	187	12	11	.948
1986	—Palm Springs (Cal.)	OF	129	429	95	136	31	9	17	89	.317	*117	103	7	205	10	6	.973
1987	—Midland (Texas)	OF	126	464	106	157	33	1	•30	104	.338	*94	136	7	145	6	6	.962
1988	—Oakland (A.L.)■	OF-1B	71	101	9	21	6	0	1	15	.208	21	28	0	85	5	1	.989
	—Tacoma (PCL)	OF-1B	16	49	12	16	1	0	0	9	.327	18	13	5	26	1	1	.964
1989	—Tacoma (PCL)	1B-OF-P	137	497	*99	136	35	5	11	64	.274	*93	95	10	842	34	†14	.984
	—Oakland (A.L.)	OF	4	4	0	0	0	0	0	0	.000	0	2	0	2	0	0	1.000
1990	—Tacoma (PCL)	OF-1B	60	208	32	72	19	1	6	30	.346	31	36	4	123	7	5	.963
	—Oakland (A.L.)	OF-1B	64	156	19	30	7	2	2	14	.192	17	48	0	90	1	1	.989
1991	—Tacoma (PCL)	OF	95	332	43	89	17	2	3	44	.268	47	65	5	145	11	10	.940
	—Oakland (A.L.)	OF	8	9	0	1	0	0	0	0	.111	2	2	0	8	0	0	1.000

Year	Team (League)	Pos.	BATTING												FIELDING			
			G	AB	R	H	2B	3B	HR	RBI	Avg.	BB	SO	SB	PO	A	E	Avg.
1992	—Rochester (Int'l)■	1B-OF	119	396	70	109	23	5	14	76	.275	68	80	11	438	17	9	.981
1993	—Iowa (Am. Assoc.)■	1B-OF	65	228	38	67	20	1	7	37	.294	29	64	3	442	36	2	.996
	—Chicago (N.L.)	1B	42	52	8	13	3	1	2	8	.250	3	10	0	80	2	0	1.000
American League totals (4 years)			147	270	28	52	13	2	3	29	.193	40	80	0	185	6	2	.990
National League totals (1 year)			42	52	8	13	3	1	2	8	.250	3	10	0	80	2	0	1.000
Major league totals (5 years)			189	322	36	65	16	3	5	37	.202	43	90	0	265	8	2	.993

CHAMPIONSHIP SERIES RECORD

Year	Team (League)	Pos.	BATTING												FIELDING			
			G	AB	R	H	2B	3B	HR	RBI	Avg.	BB	SO	SB	PO	A	E	Avg.
1990	—Oakland (A.L.)	OF	1	1	0	0	0	0	0	0	.000	0	0	0	0	0	0	...

WORLD SERIES RECORD

Year	Team (League)	Pos.	BATTING												FIELDING			
			G	AB	R	H	2B	3B	HR	RBI	Avg.	BB	SO	SB	PO	A	E	Avg.
1990	—Oakland (A.L.)	PH	1	1	0	1	0	0	0	0	1.000	0	0	0	...	...	...	...

RECORD AS PITCHER

Year	Team (League)	W	L	Pct.	ERA	G	GS	CG	ShO	Sv.	IP	H	R	ER	BB	SO
1989	—Tacoma (PCL)	0	0	...	3.00	2	0	0	0	0	3	4	1	1	0	0

JENNINGS, LANCE

C, ROYALS

PERSONAL: Born October 3, 1971, in Redlands, Calif. . . . 6-0/195. . . . Throws right, bats right. . . . Full name: Lance Phillip Jennings.

HIGH SCHOOL: Pico Rivera (Calif.) -El Rancho.

TRANSACTIONS/CAREER NOTES: Selected by Kansas City Royals organization in supplemental round ("sandwich pick" between second and third round) of free-agent draft (June 5, 1989); pick received as compensation for New York Yankees signing Type C free agent Jamie Quirk.

Year	Team (League)	Pos.	BATTING												FIELDING			
			G	AB	R	H	2B	3B	HR	RBI	Avg.	BB	SO	SB	PO	A	E	Avg.
1989	—GC Royals (GCL)	C	47	164	15	39	3	0	1	15	.238	9	34	0	*300	41	4	.988
1990	—Eugene (N'west)	C	31	92	8	17	3	1	4	9	.185	6	21	0	191	22	5	.977
	—GC Royals (GCL)	C	15	48	4	14	4	0	0	5	.292	4	12	0	67	10	1	.987
1991	—Appleton (Midw.)	C	82	284	25	67	22	0	5	42	.236	20	65	0	481	57	7	.987
	—Baseball City (FSL)	C	10	34	1	8	1	0	0	5	.235	3	9	0	63	7	0	1.000
1992	—Baseball City (FSL)	C	51	174	16	45	7	0	7	24	.259	15	44	0	280	45	1	.997
	—Memphis (South.)	C	52	145	5	21	5	0	1	8	.145	6	33	0	287	33	2	.994
1993	—Memphis (South.)	C	98	327	27	67	11	0	4	33	.205	21	83	0	596	68	11	.984

JENSEN, MARCUS

C, GIANTS

PERSONAL: Born December 14, 1972, in Oakland, Calif. . . . 6-4/195. . . . Throws right, bats both.

HIGH SCHOOL: Skyline (Oakland, Calif.).

TRANSACTIONS/CAREER NOTES: Selected by San Francisco Giants organization in supplemental round ("sandwich pick" between first and second round, 33rd pick overall) of free-agent draft (June 4, 1990); pick received as part of compensation for San Diego Padres signing Type A free agent Craig Lefferts. . . . On disabled list (June 1-14, 1993).

STATISTICAL NOTES: Tied for Arizona League lead with three intentional bases on balls received in 1991.

Year	Team (League)	Pos.	BATTING												FIELDING			
			G	AB	R	H	2B	3B	HR	RBI	Avg.	BB	SO	SB	PO	A	E	Avg.
1990	—Everett (N'west)	C	51	171	21	29	3	0	2	12	.170	24	60	0	191	27	3	.986
1991	—Ariz. Giants (Ariz.)	C-1B	48	155	28	44	8	3	2	30	.284	34	22	4	226	29	7	.973
1992	—Clinton (Midwest)	C-1B	86	264	35	62	14	0	4	33	.235	54	87	4	493	68	10	.982
1993	—Clinton (Midwest)	C	104	324	53	85	24	2	11	56	.262	66	98	1	641	73	7	.990

JIMENEZ, MIGUEL

P, ATHLETICS

PERSONAL: Born August 19, 1969, in New York. . . . 6-2/205. . . . Throws right, bats right. . . . Full name: Miguel Anthony Jimenez.

HIGH SCHOOL: John F. Kennedy (Bronx, N.Y.).

COLLEGE: Fordham (undergraduate degree, 1991).

TRANSACTIONS/CAREER NOTES: Selected by Oakland Athletics organization in 12th round of free-agent draft (June 3, 1991).

STATISTICAL NOTES: Led Midwest League with 14 balks in 1992.

Year	Team (League)	W	L	Pct.	ERA	G	GS	CG	ShO	Sv.	IP	H	R	ER	BB	SO
1991	—S. Oregon (N'west)	0	2	.000	3.12	10	9	0	0	0	34⅔	22	21	12	34	39
1992	—Madison (Midwest)	7	7	.500	2.92	26	19	2	1	0	120⅓	78	48	39	78	135
	—Huntsville (South.)	1	0	1.000	1.80	1	1	0	0	0	5	3	1	1	3	8
1993	—Huntsville (South.)	10	6	.625	2.94	20	19	0	0	0	107	92	49	35	64	105
	—Tacoma (PCL)	2	3	.400	4.78	8	8	0	0	0	37⅔	32	23	20	24	34
	—Oakland (A.L.)	1	0	1.000	4.00	5	4	0	0	0	27	27	12	12	16	13
Major league totals (1 year)		1	0	1.000	4.00	5	4	0	0	0	27	27	12	12	16	13

JOHNSON, BRIAN

C, PADRES

PERSONAL: Born January 8, 1968, in Oakland, Calif. . . . 6-2/210. . . . Throws right, bats right. . . . Full name: Brian David Johnson.

HIGH SCHOOL: Skyline (Oakland, Calif.).

COLLEGE: Stanford.

TRANSACTIONS/CAREER NOTES: Selected by Montreal Expos organization in 36th round of free-agent draft (June 2, 1986).... Selected by New York Yankees organization in 16th round of free-agent draft (June 5, 1989).... Selected by Las Vegas, San Diego Padres organization, from Albany/Colonie, Yankees organization, in Rule 5 minor league draft (December 9, 1991).... On disabled list (April 22-May 16, 1992).
STATISTICAL NOTES: Led South Atlantic League catchers with 752 putouts and 844 total chances in 1990.... Led Florida State League catchers with 654 putouts in 1991.

			BATTING											FIELDING			
Year	Team (League)	Pos.	G	AB	R	H	2B	3B	HR	RBI	Avg.	BB	SO	SB	PO	A	E	Avg.
1989	—GC Yankees (GCL)....	C	17	61	7	22	1	1	0	8	.361	4	5	0	84	14	1	.990
1990	—Greensboro (S. Atl.)..	C-3B-1B	137	496	58	118	15	0	7	51	.238	57	65	4	†773	91	13	.985
1991	—Alb./Colon. (East.)...	C-1B	2	8	0	0	0	0	0	0	.000	0	2	0	10	2	0	1.000
	—Fort Lauder. (FSL)...	C-1B-3B	113	394	35	94	19	0	1	44	.239	34	67	4	†738	65	13	.984
1992	—Wichita (Texas)■.....	C-3B	75	245	30	71	20	0	3	26	.290	22	32	3	472	40	3	.994
1993	—Las Vegas (PCL)......	C-3B-OF	115	416	58	141	35	6	10	71	.339	41	53	0	513	67	9	.985

JOHNSON, DAVE

P

PERSONAL: Born October 24, 1959, in Baltimore.... 5-11/179.... Throws right, bats right.... Full name: David Wayne Johnson.
HIGH SCHOOL: Overlea (Baltimore).
COLLEGE: Community College of Baltimore.
TRANSACTIONS/CAREER NOTES: Selected by Kansas City Royals organization in fifth round of free-agent draft (January 13, 1981).... Signed as free agent by Pittsburgh Pirates organization (June 10, 1982).... Granted free agency (October 15, 1988).... Signed by Houston Astros (December 22, 1988).... Traded by Astros organization with OF Victor Hithe to Baltimore Orioles for C Carl Nichols (March 31, 1989).... On disabled list (August 15-September 4, 1990).... On Baltimore disabled list (May 19-July 26, 1991); included rehabilitation assignment to Hagerstown (July 2-17) and Rochester (July 17-26).... Released by Orioles (November 20, 1991).... Signed by California Angels (January 22, 1992).... Released by Angels (March 17, 1992).... Signed by Edmonton, Angels organization (March 21, 1992).... On Edmonton disabled list (April 22-May 30, 1992).... Released by Edmonton (May 30, 1992).... Signed by Toledo, Detroit Tigers organization (June 26, 1992).... Granted free agency (October 15, 1992).... Re-signed by Toledo (February 17, 1993).... On Detroit disabled list (May 23-September 15, 1993).... Released by Tigers (October 8, 1993).
STATISTICAL NOTES: Pitched 3-0 no-hit victory for Vancouver against Portland (July 23, 1987).... Led A.L. with 30 home runs allowed in 1990.

Year	Team (League)	W	L	Pct.	ERA	G	GS	CG	ShO	Sv.	IP	H	R	ER	BB	SO
1982	—Greenwood (S. Atl.)....	4	4	.500	3.86	16	6	1	1	0	58⅓	50	32	25	41	41
1983	—Alexandria (Caro.).....	7	5	.583	3.01	46	2	1	0	8	113⅔	100	52	38	42	95
1984	—Prin. William (Car.)....	7	5	.583	1.32	13	13	3	1	0	88⅓	60	22	13	35	48
	—Nashua (Eastern)......	1	8	.111	4.84	12	12	4	0	0	83⅔	95	52	45	31	47
1985	—Nashua (Eastern)......	6	9	.400	3.12	34	18	4	1	2	153	129	66	53	45	84
1986	—Hawaii (PCL).............	8	7	.533	*3.17	22	22	6	1	0	150⅓	150	68	53	35	71
1987	—Vancouver (PCL).......	8	10	.444	3.51	23	22	•9	2	0	153⅔	133	74	60	68	76
	—Pittsburgh (N.L.)........	0	0	...	9.95	5	0	0	0	0	6⅓	13	7	7	2	4
1988	—Buffalo (A.A.)............	*15	12	.556	3.51	29	•29	*9	2	0	192⅓	*213	93	75	55	90
1989	—Rochester (Int'l)■.......	7	6	.538	3.26	18	14	2	0	1	105	104	45	38	31	60
	—Baltimore (A.L.).........	4	7	.364	4.23	14	14	4	0	0	89⅓	90	44	42	28	26
1990	—Baltimore (A.L.).........	13	9	.591	4.10	30	29	3	0	0	180	196	83	82	43	68
1991	—Baltimore (A.L.).........	4	8	.333	7.07	22	14	0	0	0	84	127	68	66	24	38
	—Hagerstown (East.)......	3	0	1.000	1.00	3	3	0	0	0	18	13	3	2	3	9
	—Rochester (Int'l)..........	0	1	.000	4.15	2	2	1	0	0	13	18	7	6	5	8
1992	—Edmonton (PCL)■........	0	0	...	22.50	1	1	0	0	0	2	8	6	5	1	1
	—Toledo (Int'l)■.............	4	4	.500	4.27	25	5	1	0	3	52⅔	60	27	25	17	29
1993	—Toledo (Int'l)...............	1	0	1.000	0.00	9	0	0	0	0	17⅓	6	0	0	5	8
	—Detroit (A.L.)...............	1	1	.500	12.96	6	0	0	0	0	8⅓	13	13	12	5	7
A.L. totals (4 years)		22	25	.468	5.03	72	57	7	0	0	361⅔	426	208	202	100	139
N.L. totals (1 year)		0	0	...	9.95	5	0	0	0	0	6⅓	13	7	7	2	4
Major league totals (5 years)		22	25	.468	5.11	77	57	7	0	0	368	439	215	209	102	143

JOHNSON, ERIK

IF, GIANTS

PERSONAL: Born October 11, 1965, in Oakland, Calif.... 5-11/175.... Throws right, bats right.... Full name: Erik Anthony Johnson.
HIGH SCHOOL: De La Salle Catholic (Concord, Calif.).
COLLEGE: UC Santa Barbara (degree in business economics, 1987).
TRANSACTIONS/CAREER NOTES: Selected by New York Yankees organization in 27th round of free-agent draft (June 2, 1986).... Selected by San Francisco Giants organization in 18th round of free-agent draft (June 2, 1987).... On Phoenix disabled list (August 2-11, 1993).... Granted free agency (October 15, 1993).... Re-signed by Phoenix (November 1, 1993).

			BATTING											FIELDING			
Year	Team (League)	Pos.	G	AB	R	H	2B	3B	HR	RBI	Avg.	BB	SO	SB	PO	A	E	Avg.
1987	—Pocatello (Pioneer)..	2B-3B-SS	43	129	19	34	7	0	4	12	.264	13	21	6	73	77	6	.962
	—Shreveport (Texas)..	2B-3B	9	21	1	2	1	0	0	3	.095	0	5	0	11	7	0	1.000
1988	—Clinton (Midwest)....	2B-3B	90	322	29	72	12	3	5	38	.224	28	39	4	150	224	13	.966
	—San Jose (Calif.).......	2B	44	160	25	40	3	1	1	16	.250	18	29	4	109	115	12	.949
1989	—Shreveport (Texas)..	SS-2B-3B	87	246	28	56	5	4	3	29	.228	23	37	3	116	196	15	.954
1990	—Phoenix (PCL)..........	2B	2	3	0	0	0	0	0	0	.000	1	1	0	3	0	0	1.000
	—Shreveport (Texas)..	SS-3B-2B	91	270	35	60	6	0	1	15	.222	22	38	6	94	206	16	.949
1991	—Shreveport (Texas)..	3B-SS-2B	58	146	27	32	7	0	2	20	.219	16	20	6	44	85	10	.928
	—Phoenix (PCL)..........	SS-2B	16	34	6	11	1	1	0	4	.324	3	5	0	25	26	7	.879
1992	—Phoenix (PCL)..........	SS-2B-3B	90	229	24	55	5	1	0	19	.240	20	38	8	93	199	14	.954
1993	—Phoenix (PCL)..........	SS-2B-3B	101	363	33	90	8	5	0	33	.248	29	51	3	163	263	14	.968
	—San Francisco (N.L.)..	2B-SS-3B	4	5	1	2	2	0	0	0	.400	0	1	0	1	1	0	1.000
Major league totals (1 year)			4	5	1	2	2	0	0	0	.400	0	1	0	1	1	0	1.000

JOHNSON, HOWARD

OF/3B, ROCKIES

PERSONAL: Born November 29, 1960, in Clearwater, Fla. . . . 5-10/195. . . . Throws right, bats both. . . . Full name: Howard Michael Johnson.
HIGH SCHOOL: Clearwater (Fla.).
COLLEGE: St. Petersburg (Fla.) Junior College.

TRANSACTIONS/CAREER NOTES: Selected by New York Yankees organization in 23rd round of free-agent draft (June 6, 1978). . . . Selected by Detroit Tigers organization in secondary phase of free-agent draft (January 9, 1979). . . . On Evansville disabled list (June 2-August 8, 1983). . . . Traded by Tigers to New York Mets for P Walt Terrell (December 7, 1984). . . . On disabled list (June 2-23, 1986; August 2, 1992-remainder of season and June 11-July 2, 1993). . . . On suspended list (July 8-10, 1993). . . . On disabled list (July 23, 1993-remainder of season). . . . Granted free agency (October 26, 1993). . . . Signed by Colorado Rockies (November 19, 1993).
RECORDS: Holds N.L. single-season record for most home runs by switch-hitter—38 (1991). . . . Shares N.L. record for most home runs by switch-hitter in two consecutive seasons—61 (1990-91).
HONORS: Named third baseman on THE SPORTING NEWS N.L. All-Star team (1989). . . . Named third baseman on THE SPORTING NEWS N.L. Silver Slugger team (1989 and 1991).
STATISTICAL NOTES: Led Florida State League with 16 sacrifice hits in 1980. . . . Led Florida State League third basemen with 21 double plays in 1980. . . . Led American Association third basemen with 19 double plays in 1982. . . . Tied for N.L. lead with 16 game-winning RBIs in 1987. . . . Switch-hit home runs in one game (August 31, 1991). . . . Led N.L. with 15 sacrifice flies in 1991.

			BATTING											FIELDING			
Year Team (League)	**Pos.**	**G**	**AB**	**R**	**H**	**2B**	**3B**	**HR**	**RBI**	**Avg.**	**BB**	**SO**	**SB**	**PO**	**A**	**E**	**Avg.**
1979 —Lakeland (Fla. St.)	3B-SS-OF	132	456	49	107	9	6	3	49	.235	69	85	18	130	240	36	.911
1980 —Lakeland (Fla. St.)	3B	130	474	83	135	*28	1	10	69	.285	73	75	31	*110	*264	13	*.966
1981 —Birm. (Southern)	3B	138	488	84	130	28	7	22	83	.266	75	93	19	103	218	26	.925
1982 —Evansville (A.A.)	3B-OF	98	366	70	116	16	4	23	67	.317	46	62	35	69	139	23	.900
—Detroit (A.L.)	3B-OF	54	155	23	49	5	0	4	14	.316	16	30	7	36	40	7	.916
1983 —Detroit (A.L.)	3B	27	66	11	14	0	0	3	5	.212	7	10	0	10	30	7	.851
—Evansville (A.A.)	3B	3	9	1	2	1	0	0	0	.222	4	2	0	1	11	2	.857
1984 —Detroit (A.L.)	3-S-1-0	116	355	43	88	14	1	12	50	.248	40	67	10	63	150	14	.938
1985 —New York (N.L.)■	3B-SS-OF	126	389	38	94	18	4	11	46	.242	34	78	6	78	190	18	.937
1986 —New York (N.L.)	3B-SS-OF	88	220	30	54	14	0	10	39	.245	31	64	8	52	136	20	.904
1987 —New York (N.L.)	3B-SS-OF	157	554	93	147	22	1	36	99	.265	83	113	32	118	305	26	.942
1988 —New York (N.L.)	3B-SS	148	495	85	114	21	1	24	68	.230	86	104	23	110	274	18	.955
1989 —New York (N.L.)	3B-SS	153	571	•104	164	41	3	36	101	.287	77	126	41	97	217	24	.929
1990 —New York (N.L.)	3B-SS	154	590	89	144	37	3	23	90	.244	69	100	34	150	335	28	.945
1991 —New York (N.L.)	3B-OF-SS	156	564	108	146	34	4	*38	*117	.259	78	120	30	161	264	31	.932
1992 —New York (N.L.)	OF	100	350	48	78	19	0	7	43	.223	55	79	22	206	3	4	.981
1993 —New York (N.L.)	3B	72	235	32	56	8	2	7	26	.238	43	43	6	52	135	11	.944
American League totals (3 years)		197	576	77	151	19	1	19	69	.262	63	107	17	109	220	28	.922
National League totals (9 years)		1154	3968	627	997	214	18	192	629	.251	556	827	202	1024	1859	180	.941
Major league totals (12 years)		1351	4544	704	1148	233	19	211	698	.253	619	934	219	1133	2079	208	.939

CHAMPIONSHIP SERIES RECORD

			BATTING											FIELDING			
Year Team (League)	**Pos.**	**G**	**AB**	**R**	**H**	**2B**	**3B**	**HR**	**RBI**	**Avg.**	**BB**	**SO**	**SB**	**PO**	**A**	**E**	**Avg.**
1984 —Detroit (A.L.)								Did not play.									
1986 —New York (N.L.)	PH	2	2	0	0	0	0	0	0	.000	0	0	0	...	...	...	...
1988 —New York (N.L.)	SS-PH-3B	6	18	3	1	0	0	0	0	.056	1	6	1	6	9	1	.938
Championship series totals (2 years)		8	20	3	1	0	0	0	0	.050	1	6	1	6	9	1	.938

WORLD SERIES RECORD

			BATTING											FIELDING			
Year Team (League)	**Pos.**	**G**	**AB**	**R**	**H**	**2B**	**3B**	**HR**	**RBI**	**Avg.**	**BB**	**SO**	**SB**	**PO**	**A**	**E**	**Avg.**
1984 —Detroit (A.L.)	PH	1	1	0	0	0	0	0	0	.000	0	0	0	...	...	...	...
1986 —New York (N.L.)	3B-PH-SS	2	5	0	0	0	0	0	0	.000	0	2	0	1	0	0	1.000
World Series totals (2 years)		3	6	0	0	0	0	0	0	.000	0	2	0	1	0	0	1.000

ALL-STAR GAME RECORD

		BATTING											FIELDING			
Year League	**Pos.**	**AB**	**R**	**H**	**2B**	**3B**	**HR**	**RBI**	**Avg.**	**BB**	**SO**	**SB**	**PO**	**A**	**E**	**Avg.**
1989 —National	3B	3	0	1	0	0	0	1	.333	0	0	1	0	0	0	...
1991 —National	3B	2	0	0	0	0	0	0	.000	0	1	0	0	0	0	...
All-Star Game totals (2 years)		5	0	1	0	0	0	1	.200	0	1	1	0	0	0	...

JOHNSON, JEFF

P, INDIANS

PERSONAL: Born August 4, 1966, in Durham, N.C. . . . 6-3/200. . . . Throws left, bats right. . . . Full name: William Jeffrey Johnson.
HIGH SCHOOL: South Granville (Creedmoor, N.C.).
COLLEGE: UNC Charlotte (degree in mathematics).

TRANSACTIONS/CAREER NOTES: Selected by New York Yankees organization in sixth round of free-agent draft (June 1, 1988). . . . On Columbus disabled list (August 7-September 6, 1993). . . . Released by Yankees (September 17, 1993). . . . Signed by Cleveland Indians organization (February 9, 1994).

Year Team (League)	**W**	**L**	**Pct.**	**ERA**	**G**	**GS**	**CG**	**ShO**	**Sv.**	**IP**	**H**	**R**	**ER**	**BB**	**SO**
1988 —Oneonta (NYP)	6	1	.857	2.98	14	14	0	0	0	87⅔	67	35	29	39	91
1989 —Prin. William (Car.)	4	10	.286	2.92	25	24	0	0	0	138⅔	125	59	45	55	99
1990 —Fort Lauder. (FSL)	6	8	.429	3.65	17	17	1	0	0	103⅔	101	55	42	25	84
—Alb./Colon. (East.)	4	3	.571	1.63	9	9	3	1	0	60⅔	44	14	11	15	41
1991 —Columbus (Int'l)	4	0	1.000	2.61	10	10	0	0	0	62	58	27	18	25	40
—New York (A.L.)	6	11	.353	5.95	23	23	0	0	0	127	156	89	84	33	62

Year	Team (League)	W	L	Pct.	ERA	G	GS	CG	ShO	Sv.	IP	H	R	ER	BB	SO
1992	—New York (A.L.)	2	3	.400	6.66	13	8	0	0	0	52⅔	71	44	39	23	14
	—Columbus (Int'l)	2	1	.667	2.17	11	11	0	0	0	58	41	15	14	18	38
1993	—Columbus (Int'l)	7	6	.538	3.45	19	17	3	1	0	114⅔	125	55	44	47	59
	—New York (A.L.)	0	2	.000	30.38	2	2	0	0	0	2⅔	12	10	9	2	0
Major league totals (3 years)		8	16	.333	6.52	38	33	0	0	0	182⅓	239	143	132	58	76

JOHNSON, LANCE

OF, WHITE SOX

PERSONAL: Born July 6, 1963, in Lincoln Heights, O. . . . 5-11/160. . . . Throws left, bats left. . . . Full name: Kenneth Lance Johnson.
HIGH SCHOOL: Princeton (Cincinnati).
COLLEGE: Triton College (Ill.) and South Alabama.

TRANSACTIONS/CAREER NOTES: Selected by Pittsburgh Pirates organization in 30th round of free-agent draft (June 8, 1981). . . . Selected by Seattle Mariners organization in 31st round of free-agent draft (June 7, 1982). . . . Selected by St. Louis Cardinals organization in sixth round of free-agent draft (June 4, 1984). . . . Traded by Cardinals with P Rick Horton and cash to Chicago White Sox for P Jose DeLeon (February 9, 1988).

RECORDS: Shares major league record for most consecutive years leading league in triples—3 (1991-93). . . . Shares A.L. single-season record for fewest errors by outfielder who led league in errors—9 (1993).

HONORS: Named American Association Most Valuable Player (1987).

STATISTICAL NOTES: Led New York-Pennsylvania League outfielders with 201 total chances in 1984. . . . Led Texas League in caught stealing with 15 in 1986. . . . Led American Association outfielders with 333 total chances in 1987. . . . Led Pacific Coast League outfielders with five double plays in 1988. . . . Led Pacific Coast League outfielders with 273 total chances in 1989. . . . Led Pacific Coast League in caught stealing with 18 in 1989. . . . Led A.L. in caught stealing with 22 in 1990.

			BATTING												FIELDING			
Year	Team (League)	Pos.	G	AB	R	H	2B	3B	HR	RBI	Avg.	BB	SO	SB	PO	A	E	Avg.
1984	—Erie (N.Y.-Penn)	OF	71	283	*63	*96	7	5	1	28	.339	45	20	29	*188	5	8	.960
1985	—St. Peters. (FSL)	OF	129	497	68	134	17	10	2	55	.270	58	39	33	338	16	5	.986
1986	—Arkansas (Texas)	OF	127	445	82	128	24	6	2	33	.288	59	57	*49	262	11	7	.975
1987	—Louisville (A.A.)	OF	116	477	89	159	21	11	5	50	.333	49	45	42	*319	6	•8	.976
	—St. Louis (N.L.)	OF	33	59	4	13	2	1	0	7	.220	4	6	6	27	0	2	.931
1988	—Chicago (A.L.)■	OF	33	124	11	23	4	1	0	6	.185	6	11	6	63	1	2	.970
	—Vancouver (PCL)	OF	100	411	71	126	12	6	2	36	.307	42	52	49	262	9	5	.982
1989	—Vancouver (PCL)	OF	106	408	69	124	11	7	0	28	.304	46	36	33	*261	7	5	.982
	—Chicago (A.L.)	OF	50	180	28	54	8	2	0	16	.300	17	24	16	113	0	2	.983
1990	—Chicago (A.L.)	OF	151	541	76	154	18	9	1	51	.285	33	45	36	353	5	10	.973
1991	—Chicago (A.L.)	OF	159	588	72	161	14	•13	0	49	.274	26	58	26	425	11	2	.995
1992	—Chicago (A.L.)	OF	157	567	67	158	15	*12	3	47	.279	34	33	41	433	11	6	.987
1993	—Chicago (A.L.)	OF	147	540	75	168	18	*14	0	47	.311	36	33	35	*427	7	•9	.980
American League totals (6 years)			697	2540	329	718	77	51	4	216	.283	152	204	160	1814	35	31	.984
National League totals (1 year)			33	59	4	13	2	1	0	7	.220	4	6	6	27	0	2	.931
Major league totals (7 years)			730	2599	333	731	79	52	4	223	.281	156	210	166	1841	35	33	.983

CHAMPIONSHIP SERIES RECORD

			BATTING												FIELDING			
Year	Team (League)	Pos.	G	AB	R	H	2B	3B	HR	RBI	Avg.	BB	SO	SB	PO	A	E	Avg.
1987	—St. Louis (N.L.)	PR	1	0	1	0	0	0	0	0	...	0	0	1	...	...	...	...
1993	—Chicago (A.L.)	OF	6	23	2	5	1	1	1	6	.217	2	1	1	15	0	0	1.000
Championship series totals (2 years)			7	23	3	5	1	1	1	6	.217	2	1	2	15	0	0	1.000

WORLD SERIES RECORD

			BATTING												FIELDING			
Year	Team (League)	Pos.	G	AB	R	H	2B	3B	HR	RBI	Avg.	BB	SO	SB	PO	A	E	Avg.
1987	—St. Louis (N.L.)	PR	1	0	0	0	0	0	0	0	...	0	0	1	...	...	...	...

JOHNSON, RANDY

P, MARINERS

PERSONAL: Born September 10, 1963, in Walnut Creek, Calif. . . . 6-10/225. . . . Throws left, bats right. . . . Full name: Randall David Johnson.
HIGH SCHOOL: Livermore (Calif.).
COLLEGE: Southern California.

TRANSACTIONS/CAREER NOTES: Selected by Atlanta Braves organization in third round of free-agent draft (June 7, 1982). . . . Selected by Montreal Expos organization in second round of free-agent draft (June 3, 1985). . . . Traded by Expos organization with P Brian Holman and P Gene Harris to Seattle Mariners for P Mark Langston and a player to be named later (May 25, 1989); Indianapolis, Expos organization, acquired P Mike Campbell to complete deal (July 31, 1989). . . . On disabled list (June 11-27, 1992).

STATISTICAL NOTES: Led American Association with 20 balks in 1988. . . . Pitched 2-0 no-hit victory against Detroit (June 2, 1990). . . . Led A.L. with 18 hit batsmen in 1992 and 16 in 1993.

MISCELLANEOUS: Appeared in one game as outfielder with no chances (1993).

Year	Team (League)	W	L	Pct.	ERA	G	GS	CG	ShO	Sv.	IP	H	R	ER	BB	SO
1985	—Jamestown (NYP)	0	3	.000	5.93	8	8	0	0	0	27⅓	29	22	18	24	21
1986	—W.P. Beach (FSL)	8	7	.533	3.16	26	•26	2	1	0	119⅔	89	49	42	*94	133
1987	—Jacksonv. (South.)	11	8	.579	3.73	25	24	0	0	0	140	100	63	58	128	*163
1988	—Indianapolis (A.A.)	8	7	.533	3.26	20	19	0	0	0	113⅓	85	52	41	72	111
	—Montreal (N.L.)	3	0	1.000	2.42	4	4	1	0	0	26	23	8	7	7	25
1989	—Montreal (N.L.)	0	4	.000	6.67	7	6	0	0	0	29⅔	29	25	22	26	26
	—Indianapolis (A.A.)	1	1	.500	2.00	3	3	0	0	0	18	13	5	4	9	17
	—Seattle (A.L.)■	7	9	.438	4.40	22	22	2	0	0	131	118	75	64	70	104
1990	—Seattle (A.L.)	14	11	.560	3.65	33	33	5	2	0	219⅔	174	103	89	*120	194
1991	—Seattle (A.L.)	13	10	.565	3.98	33	33	2	1	0	201⅓	151	96	89	*152	228
1992	—Seattle (A.L.)	12	14	.462	3.77	31	31	6	2	0	210⅓	154	104	88	*144	*241

Year Team (League)	W	L	Pct.	ERA	G	GS	CG	ShO	Sv.	IP	H	R	ER	BB	SO
1993 —Seattle (A.L.)	19	8	.704	3.24	35	34	10	3	1	255⅓	185	97	92	99	*308
A.L. totals (5 years)	65	52	.556	3.73	154	153	25	8	1	1017⅔	782	475	422	585	1075
N.L. totals (2 years)	3	4	.429	4.69	11	10	1	0	0	55⅔	52	33	29	33	51
Major league totals (6 years)	68	56	.548	3.78	165	163	26	8	1	1073⅓	834	508	451	618	1126

ALL-STAR GAME RECORD

Year League	W	L	Pct.	ERA	GS	CG	ShO	Sv.	IP	H	R	ER	BB	SO
1990 —American						Did not play.								
1993 —American	0	0	...	0.00	0	0	0	0	2	0	0	0	0	1
All-Star totals (1 year)	0	0	...	0.00	0	0	0	0	2	0	0	0	0	1

JOHNSTON, JOEL

P, PIRATES

PERSONAL: Born March 8, 1967, in West Chester, Pa. . . . 6-4/234. . . . Throws right, bats right. . . . Full name: Joel Raymond Johnston.
HIGH SCHOOL: Newtown (West Chester, Pa.).
COLLEGE: Penn State.

TRANSACTIONS/CAREER NOTES: Selected by Kansas City Royals organization in third round of free-agent draft (June 1, 1988). . . . Traded by Royals with P Dennis Moeller to Pittsburgh Pirates for 2B Jose Lind (November 19, 1992). . . . On Buffalo disabled list (April 24-May 25, 1993).

Year Team (League)	W	L	Pct.	ERA	G	GS	CG	ShO	Sv.	IP	H	R	ER	BB	SO
1988 —Eugene (N'west)	4	7	.364	5.20	14	14	0	0	0	64	64	49	37	34	64
1989 —Baseball City (FSL)	9	4	.692	4.92	26	26	0	0	0	131⅔	135	84	72	63	76
1990 —Memphis (South.)	0	0	...	6.75	4	3	0	0	0	6⅔	5	9	5	16	6
—Baseball City (FSL)	2	4	.333	4.88	31	7	1	0	7	55⅓	36	37	30	49	60
—Omaha (A.A.)	0	0	...	0.00	2	0	0	0	0	3	1	0	0	1	3
1991 —Omaha (A.A.)	4	7	.364	5.21	47	0	0	0	8	74⅓	60	43	43	42	63
—Kansas City (A.L.)	1	0	1.000	0.40	13	0	0	0	0	22⅓	9	1	1	9	21
1992 —Kansas City (A.L.)	0	0	...	13.50	5	0	0	0	0	2⅔	3	4	4	2	0
—Omaha (A.A.)	5	2	.714	6.39	42	0	0	0	2	74⅔	80	54	53	45	48
1993 —Buffalo (A.A.)■	1	3	.250	7.76	26	0	0	0	1	31⅓	30	28	27	25	26
—Pittsburgh (N.L.)	2	4	.333	3.38	33	0	0	0	2	53⅓	38	20	20	19	31
A.L. totals (2 years)	1	0	1.000	1.80	18	0	0	0	0	25	12	5	5	11	21
N.L. totals (1 year)	2	4	.333	3.38	33	0	0	0	2	53⅓	38	20	20	19	31
Major league totals (3 years)	3	4	.429	2.87	51	0	0	0	2	78⅓	50	25	25	30	52

JOHNSTONE, JOHN

P, MARLINS

PERSONAL: Born November 25, 1968, in Liverpool, N.Y. . . . 6-3/195. . . . Throws right, bats right. . . . Full name: John William Johnstone.
HIGH SCHOOL: Bishop Ludden (Syracuse, N.Y.).
COLLEGE: Onondaga Community College (N.Y.).

TRANSACTIONS/CAREER NOTES: Selected by New York Mets organization in 20th round of free-agent draft (June 2, 1987). . . . On disabled list (June 24-July 7, 1992). . . . Selected by Florida Marlins in second round (31st pick overall) of expansion draft (November 17, 1992).

Year Team (League)	W	L	Pct.	ERA	G	GS	CG	ShO	Sv.	IP	H	R	ER	BB	SO
1987 —Kingsport (Appal.)	1	1	.500	7.45	17	1	0	0	0	29	42	28	24	20	21
1988 —GC Mets (GCL)	3	4	.429	2.68	12	12	3	0	0	74	65	29	22	25	57
1989 —Pittsfield (NYP)	*11	2	.846	2.77	15	15	2	1	0	104	101	47	32	28	60
1990 —St. Lucie (Fla. St.)	*15	6	.714	2.24	25	25	*9	3	0	172⅔	145	53	43	60	120
1991 —Williamsport (East.)	7	9	.438	3.97	27	•27	2	0	0	165⅓	159	94	73	79	100
1992 —Binghamton (East.)	7	7	.500	3.74	24	24	2	0	0	149⅓	132	66	62	36	121
1993 —Edmonton (PCL)■	4	*15	.211	5.18	30	21	1	0	4	144⅓	167	95	83	59	126
—Florida (N.L.)	0	2	.000	5.91	7	0	0	0	0	10⅔	16	8	7	7	5
Major league totals (1 year)	0	2	.000	5.91	7	0	0	0	0	10⅔	16	8	7	7	5

JONES, BARRY

P

PERSONAL: Born February 15, 1963, in Centerville, Ind. . . . 6-4/225. . . . Throws right, bats right. . . . Full name: Barry Louis Jones.
HIGH SCHOOL: Centerville (Ind.).
COLLEGE: Indiana.

TRANSACTIONS/CAREER NOTES: Selected by Texas Rangers organization in sixth round of free-agent draft (June 8, 1981). . . . Selected by Pittsburgh Pirates organization in third round of free-agent draft (June 4, 1984). . . . Traded by Pirates to Chicago White Sox for P Dave LaPoint (August 13, 1988). . . . On Chicago disabled list (May 4-August 24, 1989); included rehabilitation assignment to Sarasota (June 29-July 18). . . . Traded by White Sox with OF Ivan Calderon to Montreal Expos for OF Tim Raines, P Jeff Carter and a player to be named later (December 23, 1990); White Sox acquired P Mario Brito to complete deal (February 15, 1991). . . . Traded by Expos to Philadelphia Phillies for C Darrin Fletcher and cash (December 9, 1991). . . . Released by Phillies (August 8, 1992). . . . Signed by New York Mets (August 14, 1992). . . . Granted free agency (October 30, 1992). . . . Signed by White Sox organization (January 2, 1993). . . . Released by White Sox (June 4, 1993).

Year Team (League)	W	L	Pct.	ERA	G	GS	CG	ShO	Sv.	IP	H	R	ER	BB	SO
1984 —Watertown (NYP)	6	3	.667	3.43	14	14	2	1	0	86⅔	75	41	33	49	61
1985 —Prin. William (Car.)	3	2	.600	1.21	28	0	0	0	10	37⅓	26	7	5	19	42
—Nashua (Eastern)	3	2	.600	1.55	23	0	0	0	12	29	19	6	5	10	24
—Hawaii (PCL)	0	0	...	9.00	1	0	0	0	0	3	5	5	3	1	2
1986 —Hawaii (PCL)	3	6	.333	3.56	35	0	0	0	7	48	41	20	19	20	28
—Pittsburgh (N.L.)	3	4	.429	2.89	26	0	0	0	3	37⅓	29	16	12	21	29
1987 —Pittsburgh (N.L.)	2	4	.333	5.61	32	0	0	0	1	43⅓	55	34	27	23	28
—Vancouver (PCL)	1	2	.333	3.20	20	0	0	0	11	25⅓	21	9	9	14	27

Year	Team (League)	W	L	Pct.	ERA	G	GS	CG	ShO	Sv.	IP	H	R	ER	BB	SO
1988	—Pittsburgh (N.L.)	1	1	.500	3.04	42	0	0	0	2	56⅓	57	21	19	21	31
	—Chicago (A.L.)■	2	2	.500	2.42	17	0	0	0	1	26	15	7	7	17	17
1989	—South Bend (Mid.)	0	0	...	4.91	3	0	0	0	0	3⅔	6	3	2	0	2
	—GC Whi. Sox (GCL)	0	1	.000	1.47	7	4	0	0	1	18⅓	12	7	3	5	14
	—Chicago (A.L.)	3	2	.600	2.37	22	0	0	0	1	30⅓	22	12	8	8	17
1990	—Chicago (A.L.)	11	4	.733	2.31	65	0	0	0	1	74	62	20	19	33	45
1991	—Montreal (N.L.)■	4	9	.308	3.35	*77	0	0	0	13	88⅔	76	35	33	33	46
1992	—Phil.-N.Y. (N.L.)■	7	6	.538	5.68	61	0	0	0	1	69⅔	85	46	44	35	30
1993	—Nashville (A.A.)■	0	0	...	2.60	7	0	0	0	2	17⅓	16	5	5	2	19
	—Chicago (A.L.)	0	1	.000	8.59	6	0	0	0	0	7⅓	14	8	7	3	7
A.L. totals (4 years)		16	9	.640	2.68	110	0	0	0	3	137⅔	113	47	41	61	86
N.L. totals (5 years)		17	24	.415	4.11	238	0	0	0	20	295⅓	302	152	135	133	164
Major league totals (8 years)		33	33	.500	3.66	348	0	0	0	23	433	415	199	176	194	250

JONES, BOBBY

P, METS

PERSONAL: Born February 10, 1970, in Fresno, Calif. . . . 6-4/210. . . . Throws right, bats right. . . . Full name: Robert Joseph Jones.
HIGH SCHOOL: Fresno (Calif.).
COLLEGE: Fresno State.
TRANSACTIONS/CAREER NOTES: Selected by New York Mets organization in supplemental round ("sandwich pick" between first and second round, 36th pick overall) of free-agent draft (June 3, 1991); pick received as part of compensation for Los Angeles Dodgers signing Type A free agent Darryl Strawberry.
HONORS: Named Eastern League Pitcher of the Year (1992).
STATISTICAL NOTES: Led International League with 11 hit batsmen in 1993.

Year	Team (League)	W	L	Pct.	ERA	G	GS	CG	ShO	Sv.	IP	H	R	ER	BB	SO
1991	—Columbia (S. Atl.)	3	1	.750	1.85	5	5	5	0	0	24⅓	20	5	5	3	35
1992	—Binghamton (East.)	12	4	.750	*1.88	24	24	4	*4	0	158	118	40	33	43	143
1993	—Norfolk (Int'l)	12	10	.545	3.63	24	24	6	*3	0	166	149	72	67	32	126
	—New York (N.L.)	2	4	.333	3.65	9	9	0	0	0	61⅔	61	35	25	22	35
Major league totals (1 year)		2	4	.333	3.65	9	9	0	0	0	61⅔	61	35	25	22	35

JONES, CHIPPER

SS, BRAVES

PERSONAL: Born April 24, 1972, in De Land, Fla. . . . 6-3/185. . . . Throws right, bats both. . . . Full name: Larry Wayne Jones.
HIGH SCHOOL: The Bolles School (Jacksonville, Fla.).
TRANSACTIONS/CAREER NOTES: Selected by Atlanta Braves organization in first round (first pick overall) of free-agent draft (June 4, 1990).
STATISTICAL NOTES: Led South Atlantic League with 10 sacrifice flies in 1991. . . . Led South Atlantic League shortstops with 692 total chances and 71 double plays in 1991. . . . Led International League with 268 total bases in 1993. . . . Led International League shortstops with 619 total chances in 1993.

			BATTING												FIELDING			
Year	Team (League)	Pos.	G	AB	R	H	2B	3B	HR	RBI	Avg.	BB	SO	SB	PO	A	E	Avg.
1990	—GC Braves (GCL)	SS	44	140	20	32	1	1	1	18	.229	14	25	5	64	140	18	.919
1991	—Macon (S. Atl.)	SS	136	473	*104	154	24	11	15	98	.326	69	70	40	*217	*419	56	.919
1992	—Durham (Carolina)	SS	70	264	43	73	22	1	4	31	.277	31	34	10	106	200	14	.956
	—Greenville (South.)	SS	67	266	43	92	17	11	9	42	.346	11	32	14	92	218	18	.945
1993	—Richmond (Int'l)	SS	139	536	*97	*174	31	*12	13	89	.325	57	70	23	195	381	*43	.931
	—Atlanta (N.L.)	SS	8	3	2	2	1	0	0	0	.667	1	1	0	1	1	0	1.000
Major league totals (1 year)			8	3	2	2	1	0	0	0	.667	1	1	0	1	1	0	1.000

JONES, CHRIS

OF, ROCKIES

PERSONAL: Born December 16, 1965, in Utica, N.Y. . . . 6-2/205. . . . Throws right, bats right. . . . Full name: Christopher Carlos Jones.
HIGH SCHOOL: Liverpool (N.Y.).
TRANSACTIONS/CAREER NOTES: Selected by Cincinnati Reds organization in third round of free-agent draft (June 4, 1984). . . . Released by Reds (December 13, 1991). . . . Signed by Houston Astros organization (December 19, 1991). . . . Granted free agency (October 16, 1992). . . . Signed by Colorado Rockies (October 26, 1992). . . . Granted free agency (December 20, 1993). . . . Re-signed by Rockies organization (December 22, 1993).

			BATTING												FIELDING			
Year	Team (League)	Pos.	G	AB	R	H	2B	3B	HR	RBI	Avg.	BB	SO	SB	PO	A	E	Avg.
1984	—Billings (Pioneer)	3B	21	73	8	11	2	0	2	13	.151	2	24	4	6	27	5	.868
1985	—Billings (Pioneer)	OF	63	240	43	62	12	5	4	33	.258	19	72	13	112	4	*13	.899
1986	—Ced. Rap. (Midw.)	OF	128	473	65	117	13	9	20	78	.247	20	126	23	218	15	11	.955
1987	—Vermont (Eastern)	OF	113	383	50	88	11	4	10	39	.230	23	99	13	207	12	8	.965
1988	—Chatt. (South.)	OF	116	410	50	111	20	7	4	61	.271	29	102	11	185	15	8	.962
1989	—Chatt. (South.)	OF	103	378	47	95	18	2	10	54	.251	23	68	10	197	8	7	.967
	—Nashville (A.A.)	OF	21	49	8	8	1	0	2	5	.163	0	16	2	25	0	1	.962
1990	—Nashville (A.A.)	OF	134	436	53	114	23	3	10	52	.261	23	86	12	209	17	8	.966
1991	—Nashville (A.A.)	OF	73	267	29	65	5	4	9	33	.243	19	65	10	110	5	6	.950
	—Cincinnati (N.L.)	OF	52	89	14	26	1	2	2	6	.292	2	31	2	27	1	0	1.000
1992	—Houston (N.L.)■	OF	54	63	7	12	2	1	1	4	.190	7	21	3	27	0	2	.931
	—Tucson (PCL)	OF	45	170	25	55	9	8	3	28	.324	18	34	7	86	7	2	.979
1993	—Colo. Springs (PCL)■	OF	46	168	41	47	5	5	12	40	.280	19	47	8	107	5	3	.974
	—Colorado (N.L.)	OF	86	209	29	57	11	4	6	31	.273	10	48	9	114	2	2	.983
Major league totals (3 years)			192	361	50	95	14	7	9	41	.263	19	100	14	168	3	4	.977

JONES, DAX

OF, GIANTS

PERSONAL: Born August 4, 1970, in Pittsburgh. . . . 5-9/180. . . . Throws right, bats right. . . . Full name: Dax Xenos Jones.
HIGH SCHOOL: Waukegan (Ill.) West.
COLLEGE: Creighton.
TRANSACTIONS/CAREER NOTES: Selected by Toronto Blue Jays organization in 49th round of free-agent draft (June 1, 1988). . . . Selected by San Francisco Giants organization in eighth round of free-agent draft (June 3, 1991). . . . On Clinton disabled list (May 22-June 13, 1992).
STATISTICAL NOTES: Tied for Northwest League lead in double plays by outfielder with two in 1991.

			BATTING												FIELDING			
Year	Team (League)	Pos.	G	AB	R	H	2B	3B	HR	RBI	Avg.	BB	SO	SB	PO	A	E	Avg.
1991	—Everett (N'west)	OF	53	180	42	55	5	•6	5	29	.306	27	26	15	77	•10	6	.935
1992	—Clinton (Midwest)	OF	79	295	45	88	12	4	1	42	.298	21	32	18	159	13	8	.956
	—Shreveport (Texas)	OF	19	66	10	20	0	2	1	7	.303	4	6	2	24	3	3	.900
1993	—Shreveport (Texas)	OF	118	436	59	124	19	5	4	36	.284	26	53	13	236	13	7	.973

JONES, DOUG

P, PHILLIES

PERSONAL: Born June 24, 1957, in Covina, Calif. . . . 6-2/195. . . . Throws right, bats right. . . . Full name: Douglas Reid Jones.
HIGH SCHOOL: Lebanon (Ind.).
COLLEGE: Central Arizona College and Butler.
TRANSACTIONS/CAREER NOTES: Selected by Milwaukee Brewers organization in third round of free-agent draft (January 10, 1978). . . . On disabled list (June 20-July 12, 1978). . . . On Vancouver disabled list (April 11-September 1, 1983 and April 25-May 30, 1984). . . . Granted free agency (October 15, 1984). . . . Signed by Waterbury, Cleveland Indians organization (April 3, 1985). . . . Granted free agency (December 20, 1991). . . . Signed by Houston Astros organization (January 24, 1992). . . . Traded by Astros with P Jeff Juden to Philadelphia Phillies for P Mitch Williams (December 2, 1993).
HONORS: Named N.L. co-Fireman of the Year by THE SPORTING NEWS (1992).

Year	Team (League)	W	L	Pct.	ERA	G	GS	CG	ShO	Sv.	IP	H	R	ER	BB	SO
1978	—Newark (NY-Penn)	2	4	.333	5.21	15	3	1	0	2	38	49	30	22	15	27
1979	—Burlington (Midw.)	10	10	.500	★1.75	28	20	★16	•3	0	★190	144	63	37	73	115
1980	—Stockton (Calif.)	6	2	.750	2.84	11	11	5	1	0	76	63	32	24	31	54
	—Vancouver (PCL)	3	2	.600	3.23	8	8	1	1	0	53	52	19	19	15	28
	—Holyoke (Eastern)	5	3	.625	2.90	8	8	4	2	0	62	57	23	20	26	39
1981	—El Paso (Texas)	5	7	.417	5.80	15	15	3	1	0	90	121	67	58	28	62
	—Vancouver (PCL)	5	3	.625	3.04	11	10	2	0	0	80	79	29	27	22	38
1982	—Milwaukee (A.L.)	0	0	...	10.13	4	0	0	0	0	2⅔	5	3	3	1	1
	—Vancouver (PCL)	5	8	.385	2.97	23	9	4	0	2	106	109	48	35	31	60
1983	—Vancouver (PCL)	0	1	.000	10.29	3	1	0	0	0	7	10	8	8	5	4
1984	—Vancouver (PCL)	1	0	1.000	10.13	3	0	0	0	0	8	9	9	9	3	2
	—El Paso (Texas)	6	8	.429	4.28	16	16	7	0	0	109⅓	120	61	52	35	62
1985	—Waterbury (East.)■	9	4	.692	3.65	39	1	0	0	7	116	123	59	47	36	113
1986	—Maine (Int'l)	5	6	.455	★2.09	43	3	0	0	9	116⅓	105	35	27	27	98
	—Cleveland (A.L.)	1	0	1.000	2.50	11	0	0	0	1	18	18	5	5	6	12
1987	—Cleveland (A.L.)	6	5	.545	3.15	49	0	0	0	8	91⅓	101	45	32	24	87
	—Buffalo (A.A.)	5	2	.714	2.04	23	0	0	0	7	61⅔	49	18	14	12	61
1988	—Cleveland (A.L.)	3	4	.429	2.27	51	0	0	0	37	83⅓	69	26	21	16	72
1989	—Cleveland (A.L.)	7	10	.412	2.34	59	0	0	0	32	80⅔	76	25	21	13	65
1990	—Cleveland (A.L.)	5	5	.500	2.56	66	0	0	0	43	84⅓	66	26	24	22	55
1991	—Cleveland (A.L.)	4	8	.333	5.54	36	4	0	0	7	63⅓	87	42	39	17	48
	—Colo. Springs (PCL)	2	2	.500	3.28	17	2	1	1	7	35⅔	30	14	13	5	29
1992	—Houston (N.L.)■	11	8	.579	1.85	80	0	0	0	36	111⅔	96	29	23	17	93
1993	—Houston (N.L.)	4	10	.286	4.54	71	0	0	0	26	85⅓	102	46	43	21	66
A.L. totals (7 years)		26	32	.448	3.08	276	4	0	0	128	423⅔	422	172	145	99	340
N.L. totals (2 years)		15	18	.455	3.02	151	0	0	0	62	197	198	75	66	38	159
Major league totals (9 years)		41	50	.451	3.06	427	4	0	0	190	620⅔	620	247	211	137	499

ALL-STAR GAME RECORD

Year	League	W	L	Pct.	ERA	GS	CG	ShO	Sv.	IP	H	R	ER	BB	SO
1988	—American	0	0	...	0.00	0	0	0	0	⅔	0	0	0	0	1
1989	—American	0	0	...	0.00	0	0	0	1	1⅓	1	0	0	0	0
1990	—American	Did not play.													
1992	—National	0	0	...	27.00	0	0	0	0	1	4	3	3	0	2
All-Star totals (3 years)		0	0	...	9.00	0	0	0	1	3	5	3	3	0	3

JONES, JIMMY

P

PERSONAL: Born April 20, 1964, in Dallas. . . . 6-2/190. . . . Throws right, bats right. . . . Full name: James Condia Jones.
HIGH SCHOOL: Thomas Jefferson (Dallas).
TRANSACTIONS/CAREER NOTES: Selected by San Diego Padres organization in first round (third pick overall) of free-agent draft (June 7, 1982). . . . On disabled list (July 13, 1984-remainder of season; and June 29-July 11 and July 28, 1985-remainder of season). . . . Traded by Padres with P Lance McCullers and OF Stan Jefferson to New York Yankees for 1B/OF Jack Clark and P Pat Clements (October 24, 1988). . . . Granted free agency (October 4, 1990). . . . Signed by Tucson, Houston Astros organization (March 19, 1991). . . . On disabled list (August 21, 1991-remainder of season). . . . On Houston disabled list (March 29-May 12, 1992); included rehabilitation assignment to Jackson (April 27-May 12). . . . Granted free agency (December 19, 1992). . . . Signed by Montreal Expos organization (January 25, 1993). . . . On Montreal disabled list (May 25-June 8, 1993). . . . On Montreal disabled list (June 13-July 3, 1993); included rehabilitation assignment to Ottawa (June 20-July 2). . . . Granted free agency (July 14, 1993). . . . Signed by Vancouver, California Angels organization (October 25, 1993). . . . Released by Vancouver (November 16, 1993).
RECORDS: Shares modern major league record for fewest hits allowed in first major league game (nine innings)—1 (September 21, 1986).

MISCELLANEOUS: Had one sacrifice hit in only appearance as pinch-hitter with Houston (1992).

Year	Team (League)	W	L	Pct.	ERA	G	GS	CG	ShO	Sv.	IP	H	R	ER	BB	SO
1982	—Walla Walla (N'west)	4	6	.400	3.22	14	14	2	0	0	78⅓	64	49	28	71	78
1983	—Reno (California)	7	5	.583	2.70	17	17	6	1	0	116⅔	96	50	35	49	79
1984	—Beaumont (Texas)	7	2	.778	2.10	13	13	0	0	0	85⅔	63	28	20	39	49
1985	—Beaumont (Texas)	7	5	.583	4.66	16	16	1	0	0	85	84	51	44	66	57
1986	—Las Vegas (PCL)	9	10	.474	4.40	28	•27	4	2	0	157⅔	168	84	77	72	114
	—San Diego (N.L.)	2	0	1.000	2.50	3	3	1	1	0	18	10	6	5	3	15
1987	—Las Vegas (PCL)	2	0	1.000	5.92	4	4	1	0	0	24⅓	24	16	16	8	11
	—San Diego (N.L.)	9	7	.563	4.14	30	22	2	1	0	145⅔	154	85	67	54	51
1988	—San Diego (N.L.)	9	14	.391	4.12	29	29	3	0	0	179	192	98	82	44	82
1989	—Columbus (Int'l)■........	8	6	.571	3.77	20	20	4	1	0	124	110	54	52	31	94
	—New York (A.L.)	2	1	.667	5.25	11	6	0	0	0	48	56	29	28	16	25
1990	—Columbus (Int'l)	5	2	.714	2.34	11	11	3	1	0	73	46	20	19	35	78
	—New York (A.L.)	1	2	.333	6.30	17	7	0	0	0	50	72	42	35	23	25
1991	—Houston (N.L.)■...........	6	8	.429	4.39	26	22	1	1	0	135⅓	143	73	66	51	88
1992	—Jackson (Texas)	1	2	.333	2.50	3	3	1	0	0	18	20	9	5	6	20
	—Houston (N.L.)	10	6	.625	4.07	25	23	0	0	0	139⅓	135	64	63	39	69
1993	—Montreal (N.L.)■..........	4	1	.800	6.35	12	6	0	0	0	39⅔	47	34	28	9	21
	—Ottawa (Int'l)	1	0	1.000	1.20	3	3	0	0	0	15	10	2	2	5	12
A.L. totals (2 years)		3	3	.500	5.79	28	13	0	0	0	98	128	71	63	39	50
N.L. totals (6 years)		40	36	.526	4.26	125	105	7	3	0	657	681	360	311	200	326
Major league totals (8 years) ...		43	39	.524	4.46	153	118	7	3	0	755	809	431	374	239	376

JONES, TIM

2B/SS, INDIANS

PERSONAL: Born December 1, 1962, in Sumter, S.C. . . . 5-10/175. . . . Throws right, bats left. . . . Full name: William Timothy Jones.
HIGH SCHOOL: Sumter (S.C.).
COLLEGE: The Citadel (degree in health services, 1985).
TRANSACTIONS/CAREER NOTES: Selected by St. Louis Cardinals organization in second round of free-agent draft (June 3, 1985). . . . On disabled list (May 6-June 8, 1992). . . . Granted free agency (December 20, 1993). . . . Signed by Cleveland Indians organization (December 22, 1993).
STATISTICAL NOTES: Tied for Appalachian League lead with five sacrifice flies in 1985. . . . Led Appalachian League shortstops with 105 putouts and 30 double plays in 1985.

			BATTING												FIELDING			
Year	Team (League)	Pos.	G	AB	R	H	2B	3B	HR	RBI	Avg.	BB	SO	SB	PO	A	E	Avg.
1985	—Johns. City (App.)	SS-3B	68	*235	33	75	10	1	3	48	.319	27	19	28	†109	148	23	.918
1986	—St. Peters. (FSL)	SS	39	142	19	43	3	2	0	27	.303	30	8	8	67	125	8	.960
	—Arkansas (Texas)	SS	96	284	36	76	15	1	2	27	.268	42	32	7	142	277	24	.946
1987	—Arkansas (Texas)	SS-2B	61	176	23	58	12	0	3	26	.330	29	16	15	80	151	9	.963
	—Louisville (A.A.)	SS	73	276	48	78	14	3	4	43	.283	29	27	11	112	221	13	.962
1988	—Louisville (A.A.)	SS	103	370	63	95	21	2	6	38	.257	36	56	39	145	302	15	*.968
	—St. Louis (N.L.)	SS-2B-3B	31	52	2	14	0	0	0	3	.269	4	10	4	26	40	1	.985
1989	—St. Louis (N.L.)	2-S-3-0-C	42	75	11	22	6	0	0	7	.293	7	8	1	33	48	2	.976
1990	—St. Louis (N.L.)	S-2-3-P	67	128	9	28	7	1	1	12	.219	12	20	3	43	105	7	.955
1991	—Louisville (A.A.)	S-2-0-3	86	306	34	78	9	1	5	29	.255	36	59	19	120	207	12	.965
	—St. Louis (N.L.)	SS-2B	16	24	1	4	2	0	0	2	.167	2	6	0	5	16	0	1.000
1992	—St. Louis (N.L.)	S-2-3-0	67	145	9	29	4	0	0	3	.200	11	29	5	76	114	4	.979
1993	—Louisville (A.A.)	2B-SS	101	408	72	118	22	•10	5	46	.289	44	67	13	187	289	7	.986
	—St. Louis (N.L.)	SS-2B	29	61	13	16	6	0	0	1	.262	9	8	2	34	63	2	.980
Major league totals (6 years)			252	485	45	113	25	1	1	28	.233	45	81	15	217	386	16	.974

RECORD AS PITCHER

Year	Team (League)	W	L	Pct.	ERA	G	GS	CG	ShO	Sv.	IP	H	R	ER	BB	SO
1990	—St. Louis (N.L.)	0	0	...	6.75	1	0	0	0	0	1⅓	1	2	1	2	0

JONES, TODD

P, ASTROS

PERSONAL: Born April 24, 1968, in Marietta, Ga. . . . 6-3/200. . . . Throws right, bats left. . . . Full name: Todd Barton Jones.
HIGH SCHOOL: Osborne (Ga.).
COLLEGE: Jacksonville State (Ala.).
TRANSACTIONS/CAREER NOTES: Selected by New York Mets organization in 41st round of free-agent draft (June 2, 1986). . . . Selected by Houston Astros organization in supplemental round ("sandwich pick" between first and second round, 27th pick overall) of free-agent draft (June 5, 1989); pick received as part of compensation for Texas Rangers signing Type A free agent Nolan Ryan. . . . On suspended list (September 14-16, 1993).

Year	Team (League)	W	L	Pct.	ERA	G	GS	CG	ShO	Sv.	IP	H	R	ER	BB	SO
1989	—Auburn (NY-Penn)	2	3	.400	5.44	11	9	1	0	0	49⅔	47	39	30	42	71
1990	—Osceola (Fla. St.)	12	10	.545	3.51	27	•27	1	0	0	151⅓	124	81	59	*109	106
1991	—Osceola (Fla. St.)	4	4	.500	4.35	14	14	0	0	0	72⅓	69	38	35	35	51
	—Jackson (Texas)	4	3	.571	4.88	10	10	0	0	0	55⅓	51	37	30	39	37
1992	—Jackson (Texas)	3	7	.300	3.14	*61	0	0	0	25	66	52	28	23	44	60
	—Tucson (PCL)	0	1	.000	4.50	3	0	0	0	0	4	1	2	2	10	4
1993	—Tucson (PCL)	4	2	.667	4.44	41	0	0	0	12	48⅔	49	26	24	31	45
	—Houston (N.L.)	1	2	.333	3.13	27	0	0	0	2	37⅓	28	14	13	15	25
Major league totals (1 year) ...		1	2	.333	3.13	27	0	0	0	2	37⅓	28	14	13	15	25

JORDAN, BRIAN

OF, CARDINALS

PERSONAL: Born March 29, 1967, in Baltimore. . . . 6-1/205. . . . Throws right, bats right. . . . Full name: Brian O'Neal Jordan.
HIGH SCHOOL: Milford (Baltimore).
COLLEGE: Richmond.

TRANSACTIONS/CAREER NOTES: Selected by Cleveland Indians organization in 20th round of free-agent draft (June 3, 1985). . . . Selected by St. Louis Cardinals organization in supplemental round ("sandwich pick" between first and second round, 30th pick overall) of free-agent draft (June 1, 1988); pick received as part of compensation for New York Yankees signing Type A free agent Jack Clark. . . . On disabled list (May 1-8 and June 3-10, 1991). . . . On temporary inactive list (July 3, 1991-remainder of season). . . . On St. Louis disabled list (May 23-June 22, 1992); included rehabilitation assignment to Louisville (June 10-22). . . . On Louisville disabled list (June 7-14, 1993).

			BATTING												FIELDING			
Year	Team (League)	Pos.	G	AB	R	H	2B	3B	HR	RBI	Avg.	BB	SO	SB	PO	A	E	Avg.
1988	—Hamilton (NYP)	OF	19	71	12	22	3	1	4	12	.310	6	15	3	32	1	1	.971
1989	—St. Peters. (FSL)	OF	11	43	7	15	4	1	2	11	.349	0	8	0	22	2	0	1.000
1990	—Arkansas (Texas)	OF	16	50	4	8	1	0	0	0	.160	0	11	0	28	0	2	.933
	—St. Peters. (FSL)	OF	9	30	3	5	0	1	0	1	.167	2	11	0	23	0	0	1.000
1991	—Louisville (A.A.)	OF	61	212	35	56	11	4	4	24	.264	17	41	10	144	3	2	.987
1992	—Louisville (A.A.)	OF	43	155	23	45	3	1	4	16	.290	8	21	13	89	3	1	.989
	—St. Louis (N.L.)	OF	55	193	17	40	9	4	5	22	.207	10	48	7	101	4	1	.991
1993	—St. Louis (N.L.)	OF	67	223	33	69	10	6	10	44	.309	12	35	6	140	4	4	.973
	—Louisville (A.A.)	OF	38	144	24	54	13	2	5	35	.375	16	17	9	75	2	0	1.000
Major league totals (2 years)			122	416	50	109	19	10	15	66	.262	22	83	13	241	8	5	.980

RECORD AS FOOTBALL PLAYER

TRANSACTIONS/CAREER NOTES: Played safety. . . . Selected by Buffalo Bills in seventh round (173rd pick overall) of 1989 NFL draft. . . . Signed by Bills (July 17, 1989). . . . Claimed on waivers by Atlanta Falcons (September 5, 1989). . . . On injured reserve with ankle injury (September 9-October 22, 1989). . . . Transferred to developmental squad (October 23-December 2, 1989). . . . Granted free agency (February 1, 1992).
PRO STATISTICS: 1989—Recovered two fumbles. 1990—Recovered one fumble. 1991—Credited with two safeties and recovered one fumble.

			INTERCEPTIONS				SACKS	PUNT RETURNS				KICKOFF RETURNS				TOTAL		
Year	Team	G	No.	Yds.	Avg.	TD	No.	No.	Yds.	Avg.	TD	No.	Yds.	Avg.	TD	TD	Pts.	Fum.
1989	—Atlanta NFL	4	0	0	...	0	0.0	4	34	8.5	0	3	27	9.0	0	0	0	1
1990	—Atlanta NFL	16	3	14	4.7	0	0.0	2	19	9.5	0	0	0	...	0	0	0	0
1991	—Atlanta NFL	16	2	3	1.5	0	4.0	14	116	8.3	0	5	100	20.0	0	0	4	0
Pro totals (3 years)		36	5	17	3.4	0	4.0	20	169	8.5	0	8	127	15.9	0	0	4	1

JORDAN, KEVIN

2B, PHILLIES

PERSONAL: Born October 9, 1969, in San Francisco. . . . 6-1/185. . . . Throws right, bats right. . . . Full name: Kevin Wayne Jordan.
HIGH SCHOOL: Lowell (San Francisco).
COLLEGE: Canada College (Calif.) and Nebraska.

TRANSACTIONS/CAREER NOTES: Selected by Los Angeles Dodgers organization in 10th round of free-agent draft (June 5, 1989). . . . Selected by New York Yankees organization in 20th round of free-agent draft (June 4, 1990). . . . Traded by Yankees with P Bobby Munoz and P Ryan Karp to Philadelphia Phillies for P Terry Mulholland and a player to be named later (February 9, 1994).
STATISTICAL NOTES: Led Eastern League with 234 total bases in 1993. . . . Led Eastern League second basemen with 93 double plays in 1993.

			BATTING												FIELDING			
Year	Team (League)	Pos.	G	AB	R	H	2B	3B	HR	RBI	Avg.	BB	SO	SB	PO	A	E	Avg.
1990	—Oneonta (NYP)	2B	73	276	47	92	13	•7	4	54	.333	23	31	19	131	158	8	.973
1991	—Fort Lauder. (FSL)	2B-1B	121	448	61	122	25	5	4	53	.272	37	66	14	182	306	16	.968
1992	—Prin. William (Car.)	2B-3B	112	438	67	136	29	8	8	63	.311	27	54	6	192	288	20	.960
1993	—Alb./Colon. (East.)	2B	135	513	87	145	*33	4	16	87	.283	41	53	8	261	359	21	.967

JORDAN, RICKY

1B, PHILLIES

PERSONAL: Born May 26, 1965, in Richmond, Calif. . . . 6-3/210. . . . Throws right, bats right. . . . Full name: Paul Scott Jordan.
HIGH SCHOOL: Grant (Sacramento, Calif.).
TRANSACTIONS/CAREER NOTES: Selected by Philadelphia Phillies organization in first round (22nd pick overall) of free-agent draft (June 6, 1983). . . . On Philadelphia disabled list (June 13-July 4, 1990); included rehabilitation assignment to Scranton/Wilkes-Barre (June 29-July 4). . . . On Philadelphia disabled list (March 28-May 11, 1992); included rehabilitation assignment to Scranton/Wilkes-Barre (May 6-11).
STATISTICAL NOTES: Led Eastern League first basemen with 17 errors and 100 double plays in 1986. . . . Tied for Eastern League lead with nine sacrifice flies in 1987. . . . Led Eastern League first basemen with 1,255 total chances and 110 double plays in 1987. . . . Hit home run in first major league at-bat (July 17, 1988).

			BATTING												FIELDING			
Year	Team (League)	Pos.	G	AB	R	H	2B	3B	HR	RBI	Avg.	BB	SO	SB	PO	A	E	Avg.
1983	—Helena (Pioneer)	1B	60	247	32	73	7	1	5	33	.296	12	35	3	486	35	7	.987
1984	—Spartanburg (SAL)	1B	128	490	72	143	23	4	10	76	.292	32	63	8	1129	69	14	.988
1985	—Clearwater (FSL)	1B	*139	528	60	146	22	8	7	62	.277	25	59	26	1252	86	*20	.985
1986	—Reading (Eastern)	1B-OF	133	478	44	131	19	3	2	60	.274	21	44	17	1052	87	†17	.985
1987	—Reading (Eastern)	1B	132	475	78	151	28	3	16	95	.318	28	22	15	*1193	54	8	.994
1988	—Maine (Int'l)	1B	87	338	42	104	23	1	7	36	.308	6	30	10	809	41	4	.995
	—Philadelphia (N.L.)	1B	69	273	41	84	15	1	11	43	.308	7	39	1	579	35	5	.992
1989	—Philadelphia (N.L.)	1B	144	523	63	149	22	3	12	75	.285	23	62	4	1271	61	9	.993
1990	—Philadelphia (N.L.)	1B	92	324	32	78	21	0	5	44	.241	13	39	2	743	37	4	.995
	—Scran./W.B. (Int'l)	1B	27	104	8	29	1	0	2	11	.279	5	18	0	225	8	1	.996
1991	—Philadelphia (N.L.)	1B	101	301	38	82	21	3	9	49	.272	14	49	0	626	37	9	.987
1992	—Scran./W.B. (Int'l)	1B	4	19	1	5	0	0	0	2	.263	1	2	0	47	3	0	1.000

Year	Team (League)	Pos.	G	AB	R	H	2B	3B	HR	RBI	Avg.	BB	SO	SB	PO	A	E	Avg.
			BATTING												FIELDING			
	—Philadelphia (N.L.)...	1B-OF	94	276	33	84	19	0	4	34	.304	5	44	3	427	27	2	.996
1993	—Philadelphia (N.L.)...	1B	90	159	21	46	4	1	5	18	.289	8	32	0	201	4	2	.990
Major league totals (6 years)			590	1856	228	523	102	8	46	263	.282	70	265	10	3847	201	31	.992

CHAMPIONSHIP SERIES RECORD

Year	Team (League)	Pos.	G	AB	R	H	2B	3B	HR	RBI	Avg.	BB	SO	SB	PO	A	E	Avg.
			BATTING												FIELDING			
1993	—Philadelphia (N.L.)...	PH	2	1	0	0	0	0	0	0	.000	1	0	0	...	...	...	...

WORLD SERIES RECORD

Year	Team (League)	Pos.	G	AB	R	H	2B	3B	HR	RBI	Avg.	BB	SO	SB	PO	A	E	Avg.
			BATTING												FIELDING			
1993	—Philadelphia (N.L.)...	DH-PH	3	10	0	2	0	0	0	0	.200	0	2	0	...	...	...	...

JORGENSEN, TERRY

3B

PERSONAL: Born September 2, 1966, in Kewaunee, Wis. . . . 6-4/213. . . . Throws right, bats right. . . . Full name: Terry Allen Jorgensen.
HIGH SCHOOL: Luxemburg (Wis.)-Casco.
COLLEGE: Wisconsin-Oshkosh.

TRANSACTIONS/CAREER NOTES: Selected by Minnesota Twins organization in second round of free-agent draft (June 2, 1987). . . . Granted free agency (October 13, 1993).
STATISTICAL NOTES: Led Southern League third basemen with 406 total chances and tied for lead with 21 double plays in 1989. . . . Tied for Southern League lead with nine sacrifice flies in 1989. . . . Led Pacific Coast League third basemen with 102 putouts and 34 errors in 1990. . . . Led Pacific Coast League in grounding into double plays with 22 in 1991 and tied for lead with 22 in 1992. . . . Led Pacific Coast League third basemen with 398 total chances and 32 double plays in 1991. . . . Led Pacific Coast League third basemen with .972 fielding percentage, 91 putouts, 225 assists, 325 total chances and tied for lead with 24 double plays in 1992.

Year	Team (League)	Pos.	G	AB	R	H	2B	3B	HR	RBI	Avg.	BB	SO	SB	PO	A	E	Avg.
			BATTING												FIELDING			
1987	—Kenosha (Midwest)..	OF	67	254	37	80	17	0	7	33	.315	18	43	1	54	4	5	.921
1988	—Orlando (Southern)..	3B	135	472	53	116	27	4	3	43	.246	40	62	4	101	216	*39	.890
1989	—Orlando (Southern)..	3B	135	514	84	135	27	5	13	101	.263	76	78	1	*99	*274	33	.919
	—Minnesota (A.L.)......	3B	10	23	1	4	1	0	0	2	.174	4	5	0	4	19	1	.958
1990	—Portland (PCL).........	3B-SS-2B	123	440	43	114	28	3	10	50	.259	44	83	0	†104	206	†35	.899
1991	—Portland (PCL).........	3B	126	456	74	136	29	0	11	59	.298	54	41	1	*91	*277	*30	.925
1992	—Portland (PCL).........	3B-1B	135	505	78	149	32	2	14	71	.295	54	58	2	†299	†242	10	†.982
	—Minnesota (A.L.)......	1B-3B-SS	22	58	5	18	1	0	0	5	.310	3	11	1	103	25	1	.992
1993	—Minnesota (A.L.)......	3B-1B-SS	59	152	15	34	7	0	1	12	.224	10	21	1	65	95	3	.982
	—Portland (PCL).........	3B-1B-SS	61	238	37	73	18	2	4	44	.307	19	28	1	142	99	5	.980
Major league totals (3 years)			91	233	21	56	9	0	1	19	.240	17	37	2	172	139	5	.984

JOSE, FELIX

OF, ROYALS

PERSONAL: Born May 8, 1965, in Santo Domingo, Dominican Republic. . . . 6-1/220. . . . Throws right, bats both. . . . Full name: Domingo Felix Jose.
HIGH SCHOOL: Eldo Foreda Reyez de Munoz (Santo Domingo, Dominican Republic).
TRANSACTIONS/CAREER NOTES: Signed as free agent by Oakland Athletics organization (January 3, 1984). . . . Traded by A's with 3B Stan Royer and P Daryl Green to St. Louis Cardinals for OF Willie McGee (August 29, 1990). . . . On St. Louis disabled list (March 28-April 29, 1992); included rehabilitation assignment to Louisville (April 17-22) and St. Petersburg (April 22-29). . . . Traded by Cardinals with IF/OF Craig Wilson to Kansas City Royals for 3B Gregg Jefferies and OF Ed Gerald (February 12, 1993).

Year	Team (League)	Pos.	G	AB	R	H	2B	3B	HR	RBI	Avg.	BB	SO	SB	PO	A	E	Avg.
			BATTING												FIELDING			
1984	—Idaho Falls (Pio.)......	OF	45	152	16	33	6	0	1	18	.217	18	37	5	48	6	1	.982
1985	—Madison (Midwest)..	OF	117	409	46	89	13	3	3	33	.218	32	82	6	187	9	12	.942
1986	—Modesto (Calif.)........	OF	127	516	77	147	22	8	14	77	.285	36	89	14	215	12	14	.942
1987	—Huntsville (South.)...	OF	91	296	29	67	11	1	5	42	.226	28	61	9	131	7	8	.945
1988	—Tacoma (PCL)..........	OF	134	508	72	161	29	5	12	83	.317	53	75	16	253	11	8	.971
	—Oakland (A.L.)..........	OF	8	6	2	2	1	0	0	1	.333	0	1	1	8	0	0	1.000
1989	—Tacoma (PCL)..........	OF	104	387	59	111	26	0	14	63	.287	41	82	11	186	7	*10	.951
	—Oakland (A.L.)..........	OF	20	57	3	11	2	0	0	5	.193	4	13	0	35	2	1	.974
1990	—Oakland (A.L.)..........	OF	101	341	42	90	12	0	8	39	.264	16	65	8	212	5	5	.977
	—St. Louis (N.L.)■.......	OF	25	85	12	23	4	1	3	13	.271	8	16	4	42	0	0	1.000
1991	—St. Louis (N.L.).........	OF	154	568	69	173	40	6	8	77	.305	50	113	20	268	•15	3	.990
1992	—Louisville (A.A.).......	OF	2	7	0	1	0	0	0	0	.143	1	0	0	2	0	0	1.000
	—St. Peters. (FSL).......	OF	6	18	2	8	1	1	0	2	.444	1	2	1	6	0	0	1.000
	—St. Louis (N.L.).........	OF	131	509	62	150	22	3	14	75	.295	40	100	28	273	11	6	.979
1993	—Kansas City (A.L.)■.	OF	149	499	64	126	24	3	6	43	.253	36	95	31	237	6	7	.972
American League totals (4 years)			278	903	111	229	39	3	14	88	.254	56	174	40	492	13	13	.975
National League totals (3 years)			310	1162	143	346	66	10	25	165	.298	98	229	52	583	26	9	.985
Major league totals (6 years)			588	2065	254	575	105	13	39	253	.278	154	403	92	1075	39	22	.981

ALL-STAR GAME RECORD

Year	League	Pos.	AB	R	H	2B	3B	HR	RBI	Avg.	BB	SO	SB	PO	A	E	Avg.
			BATTING											FIELDING			
1991	—National....................	OF	2	0	1	0	0	0	0	.500	0	0	0	1	0	0	1.000

JOYNER, WALLY

1B, ROYALS

PERSONAL: Born June 16, 1962, in Atlanta. . . . 6-2/200. . . . Throws left, bats left. . . . Full name: Wallace Keith Joyner.
HIGH SCHOOL: Redan (Stone Mountain, Ga.).
COLLEGE: Brigham Young.
TRANSACTIONS/CAREER NOTES: Selected by California Angels organization in third round of free-agent draft (June 6, 1983); pick received as compensation for New York Yankees signing free agent Don Baylor. . . . On disabled list (July 12, 1990-remainder of season). . . . Granted free agency (October 28, 1991). . . . Signed by Kansas City Royals (December 9, 1991).
RECORDS: Shares major league record for most home runs in month of October—4 (1987).
STATISTICAL NOTES: Tied for Eastern League lead with eight intentional bases on balls received in 1984. . . . Led Pacific Coast League first basemen with 1,229 total chances and 121 double plays in 1985. . . . Led A.L. with 12 sacrifice flies in 1986. . . . Hit three home runs in one game (October 3, 1987). . . . Led A.L. first basemen with 1,520 total chances in 1988 and 1,441 in 1991. . . . Led A.L. first basemen with 148 double plays in 1988 and 138 in 1992.

		BATTING												FIELDING			
Year Team (League)	Pos.	G	AB	R	H	2B	3B	HR	RBI	Avg.	BB	SO	SB	PO	A	E	Avg.
1983 —Peoria (Midwest)	1B	54	192	25	63	16	2	3	33	.328	19	25	1	480	45	6	.989
1984 —Waterbury (East.)	1B-OF	134	467	81	148	24	7	12	72	.317	67	60	0	906	86	9	.991
1985 —Edmonton (PCL)	1B	126	477	68	135	29	5	12	73	.283	60	64	2	*1107	*107	•15	.988
1986 —California (A.L.)	1B	154	593	82	172	27	3	22	100	.290	57	58	5	1222	139	15	.989
1987 —California (A.L.)	1B	149	564	100	161	33	1	34	117	.285	72	64	8	1276	92	10	.993
1988 —California (A.L.)	1B	158	597	81	176	31	2	13	85	.295	55	51	8	*1369	*143	8	.995
1989 —California (A.L.)	1B	159	593	78	167	30	2	16	79	.282	46	58	3	*1487	99	4	*.997
1990 —California (A.L.)	1B	83	310	35	83	15	0	8	41	.268	41	34	2	727	62	4	.995
1991 —California (A.L.)	1B	143	551	79	166	34	3	21	96	.301	52	66	2	*1335	98	8	.994
1992 —Kansas City (A.L.)■	1B	149	572	66	154	36	2	9	66	.269	55	50	11	1236	137	10	.993
1993 —Kansas City (A.L.)	1B	141	497	83	145	36	3	15	65	.292	66	67	5	1116	145	7	.994
Major league totals (8 years)		1136	4277	604	1224	242	16	138	649	.286	444	448	44	9768	915	66	.994

CHAMPIONSHIP SERIES RECORD

		BATTING												FIELDING			
Year Team (League)	Pos.	G	AB	R	H	2B	3B	HR	RBI	Avg.	BB	SO	SB	PO	A	E	Avg.
1986 —California (A.L.)	1B	3	11	3	5	2	0	1	2	.455	2	0	0	24	1	0	1.000

ALL-STAR GAME RECORD

		BATTING											FIELDING			
Year League	Pos.	AB	R	H	2B	3B	HR	RBI	Avg.	BB	SO	SB	PO	A	E	Avg.
1986 —American	1B	1	0	0	0	0	0	0	.000	0	0	0	3	1	0	1.000

JUDEN, JEFF

P, PHILLIES

PERSONAL: Born January 19, 1971, in Salem, Mass. . . . 6-7/245. . . . Throws right, bats right. . . . Full name: Jeffrey Daniel Juden. . . . Name pronounced JOO-den.
HIGH SCHOOL: Salem (Mass.).
TRANSACTIONS/CAREER NOTES: Selected by Houston Astros organization in first round (12th pick overall) of free-agent draft (June 5, 1989). . . . On disabled list (June 14-21, 1992). . . . Traded by Astros with P Doug Jones to Philadelphia Phillies for P Mitch Williams (December 2, 1993).
STATISTICAL NOTES: Led Pacific Coast League with seven balks in 1992.

Year Team (League)	W	L	Pct.	ERA	G	GS	CG	ShO	Sv.	IP	H	R	ER	BB	SO
1989 —Sarasota (Fla. St.)	1	4	.200	3.40	9	8	0	0	0	39⅔	33	21	15	17	49
1990 —Osceola (Fla. St.)	10	1	*.909	2.27	15	15	2	1	0	91	72	37	23	42	85
—Columbus (South.)	1	3	.250	5.37	11	11	0	0	0	52	55	36	31	42	40
1991 —Jackson (Texas)	6	3	.667	3.10	16	16	0	0	0	95⅔	84	43	33	44	75
—Tucson (PCL)	3	2	.600	3.18	10	10	0	0	0	56⅔	56	28	20	25	51
—Houston (N.L.)	0	2	.000	6.00	4	3	0	0	0	18	19	14	12	7	11
1992 —Tucson (PCL)	9	10	.474	4.04	26	26	0	0	0	147	149	84	66	71	120
1993 —Tucson (PCL)	11	6	.647	4.63	27	27	0	0	0	169	174	102	87	*76	156
—Houston (N.L.)	0	1	.000	5.40	2	0	0	0	0	5	4	3	3	4	7
Major league totals (2 years)	0	3	.000	5.87	6	3	0	0	0	23	23	17	15	11	18

JUSTICE, DAVID

OF, BRAVES

PERSONAL: Born April 14, 1966, in Cincinnati. . . . 6-3/200. . . . Throws left, bats left. . . . Full name: David Christopher Justice.
HIGH SCHOOL: Covington (Ky.) Latin.
COLLEGE: Thomas More College (Ky.).
TRANSACTIONS/CAREER NOTES: Selected by Atlanta Braves organization in fourth round of free-agent draft (June 3, 1985). . . . On Atlanta disabled list (June 27-August 20, 1991); included rehabilitation assignment to Macon (August 16-20). . . . On disabled list (April 12-27, 1992).
RECORDS: Holds major league single-season record for fewest errors by outfielder who led league in errors—8 (1992).
HONORS: Named N.L. Rookie Player of the Year by THE SPORTING NEWS (1990). . . . Named N.L. Rookie of the Year by Baseball Writers' Association of America (1990). . . . Named outfielder on THE SPORTING NEWS N.L. All-Star team (1993). . . . Named outfielder on THE SPORTING NEWS N.L. Silver Slugger team (1993).
STATISTICAL NOTES: Tied for Appalachian League lead with five sacrifice flies in 1985.

		BATTING												FIELDING			
Year Team (League)	Pos.	G	AB	R	H	2B	3B	HR	RBI	Avg.	BB	SO	SB	PO	A	E	Avg.
1985 —Pulaski (Appal.)	OF	66	204	39	50	8	0	•10	46	.245	40	30	0	86	2	4	.957
1986 —Sumter (S. Atl.)	OF	61	220	48	66	16	0	10	61	.300	48	28	10	124	7	4	.970
—Durham (Carolina)	OF-1B	67	229	47	64	9	1	12	44	.279	46	24	2	163	5	1	.994
1987 —Greenville (South.)	OF	93	348	38	79	12	4	6	40	.227	53	48	3	199	4	8	.962
1988 —Richmond (Int'l)	OF	70	227	27	46	9	1	8	28	.203	39	55	4	136	5	4	.972
—Greenville (South.)	OF	58	198	34	55	13	1	9	37	.278	37	41	6	100	3	5	.954

Year	Team (League)	Pos.	G	AB	R	H	2B	3B	HR	RBI	Avg.	BB	SO	SB	PO	A	E	Avg.
			BATTING												FIELDING			
1989	—Richmond (Int'l)	OF-1B	115	391	47	102	24	3	12	58	.261	59	66	12	220	15	6	.975
	—Atlanta (N.L.)	OF	16	51	7	12	3	0	1	3	.235	3	9	2	24	0	0	1.000
1990	—Richmond (Int'l)	OF-1B	12	45	7	16	5	1	2	7	.356	7	6	0	23	4	2	.931
	—Atlanta (N.L.)	1B-OF	127	439	76	124	23	2	28	78	.282	64	92	11	604	42	14	.979
1991	—Atlanta (N.L.)	OF	109	396	67	109	25	1	21	87	.275	65	81	8	204	9	7	.968
	—Macon (S. Atl.)	OF	3	10	2	2	0	0	2	5	.200	2	1	0	1	0	0	1.000
1992	—Atlanta (N.L.)	OF	144	484	78	124	19	5	21	72	.256	79	85	2	313	8	*8	.976
1993	—Atlanta (N.L.)	OF	157	585	90	158	15	4	40	120	.270	78	90	3	323	9	5	.985
Major league totals (5 years)			553	1955	318	527	85	12	111	360	.270	289	357	26	1468	68	34	.978

CHAMPIONSHIP SERIES RECORD

Year	Team (League)	Pos.	G	AB	R	H	2B	3B	HR	RBI	Avg.	BB	SO	SB	PO	A	E	Avg.
			BATTING												FIELDING			
1991	—Atlanta (N.L.)	OF	7	25	4	5	1	0	1	2	.200	3	7	0	17	0	1	.944
1992	—Atlanta (N.L.)	OF	7	25	5	7	1	0	2	6	.280	6	2	0	19	3	0	1.000
1993	—Atlanta (N.L.)	OF	6	21	2	3	1	0	0	4	.143	3	3	0	14	0	1	.933
Championship series totals (3 years)			20	71	11	15	3	0	3	12	.211	12	12	0	50	3	2	.964

WORLD SERIES RECORD

Year	Team (League)	Pos.	G	AB	R	H	2B	3B	HR	RBI	Avg.	BB	SO	SB	PO	A	E	Avg.
			BATTING												FIELDING			
1991	—Atlanta (N.L.)	OF	7	27	5	7	0	0	2	6	.259	5	5	2	21	1	1	.957
1992	—Atlanta (N.L.)	OF	6	19	4	3	0	0	1	3	.158	6	5	1	15	0	1	.938
World Series totals (2 years)			13	46	9	10	0	0	3	9	.217	11	10	3	36	1	2	.949

ALL-STAR GAME RECORD

Year	League	Pos.	AB	R	H	2B	3B	HR	RBI	Avg.	BB	SO	SB	PO	A	E	Avg.
			BATTING											FIELDING			
1993	—National	OF	3	0	1	0	0	0	0	.333	0	0	0	1	0	1	.500

JK

KAISER, JEFF

P

PERSONAL: Born July 24, 1960, in Wyandotte, Mich. . . . 6-3/195. . . . Throws left, bats right. . . . Full name: Jeffrey Patrick Kaiser.

HIGH SCHOOL: Aquinas (Southgate, Mich.).

COLLEGE: Western Michigan (bachelor of arts degree in business administration).

TRANSACTIONS/CAREER NOTES: Selected by Toronto Blue Jays organization in seventh round of free-agent draft (June 8, 1981). . . . Selected by Oakland Athletics organization in 10th round of free-agent draft (June 7, 1982). . . . On Tacoma disabled list (July 20-August 3, 1984; June 21-July 7, 1985; and May 4-14, 1986). . . . Traded by A's organization to Cleveland Indians for P Curt Wardle (February 23, 1987). . . . On Cleveland disabled list (August 9-31, 1987). . . . Granted free agency (April 5, 1990). . . . Re-signed by Indians organization (April 11, 1990). . . . On Cleveland disabled list (July 8-September 4, 1990); included rehabilitation assignment to Colorado Springs (August 8-September 4). . . . Granted free agency (October 4, 1990). . . . Signed by Milwaukee Brewers organization (January 1, 1991). . . . Released by Denver, Brewers organization (May 9, 1991). . . . Signed by Toledo, Detroit Tigers organization (June 11, 1991). . . . Granted free agency (December 20, 1991). . . . Re-signed by Toledo, Tigers organization (January 17, 1992). . . . Granted free agency (October 15, 1992). . . . Signed by Cincinnati Reds organization (December 10, 1992). . . . Claimed on waivers by New York Mets (April 23, 1993). . . . On New York disabled list (May 18-June 7, 1993). . . . On Norfolk disabled list (July 7-26, 1993). . . . Granted free agency (October 15, 1993).

Year	Team (League)	W	L	Pct.	ERA	G	GS	CG	ShO	Sv.	IP	H	R	ER	BB	SO
1982	—Medford (N'west)	8	1	.889	5.31	15	15	1	0	0	78	91	56	46	57	69
1983	—Modesto (Calif.)	12	9	.571	3.83	25	25	4	0	0	164⅔	160	84	70	80	102
1984	—Alb./Colon. (East.)	5	1	.833	1.89	7	7	1	1	0	47⅔	36	11	10	15	20
	—Tacoma (PCL)	4	7	.364	4.58	14	12	0	0	1	74⅔	81	52	38	28	38
1985	—Oakland (A.L.)	0	0	...	14.58	15	0	0	0	0	16⅔	25	32	27	20	10
	—Tacoma (PCL)	4	2	.667	1.75	27	4	0	0	5	46⅓	33	10	9	18	36
1986	—Tacoma (PCL)	4	4	.500	4.31	34	18	2	1	2	110⅔	123	70	53	52	63
1987	—Buffalo (A.A.)■	5	3	.625	5.17	22	8	0	0	1	71⅓	87	52	41	32	53
	—Cleveland (A.L.)	0	0	...	16.20	2	0	0	0	0	3⅓	4	6	6	3	2
1988	—Colo. Springs (PCL)	3	2	.600	3.74	36	0	0	0	6	53	56	23	22	19	47
	—Cleveland (A.L.)	0	0	...	0.00	3	0	0	0	0	2⅔	2	0	0	1	0
1989	—Colo. Springs (PCL)	3	6	.333	4.37	31	1	0	0	3	45⅓	64	29	22	18	46
	—Cleveland (A.L.)	0	1	.000	7.36	6	0	0	0	0	3⅔	5	5	3	5	4
1990	—Colo. Springs (PCL)	2	2	.500	2.93	25	0	0	0	3	43	36	16	14	22	46
	—Cleveland (A.L.)	0	0	...	3.55	5	0	0	0	0	12⅔	16	5	5	7	9
1991	—Denver (A.A.)■	0	1	.000	3.86	8	1	0	0	0	18⅔	16	9	8	13	12
	—Toledo (Int'l)■	3	0	1.000	2.08	16	3	0	0	1	34⅔	35	9	8	11	28
	—Detroit (A.L.)	0	1	.000	9.00	10	0	0	0	2	5	6	5	5	5	4
1992	—Toledo (Int'l)	1	0	1.000	2.35	28	0	0	0	5	30⅔	25	12	8	12	33
1993	—Indianapolis (A.A.)■	0	0	...	0.00	1	0	0	0	0	1	0	0	0	0	2
	—Cin.-N.Y. (N.L.)■	0	0	...	7.88	9	0	0	0	0	8	10	7	7	5	9
	—Norfolk (Int'l)	1	1	.500	5.64	21	0	0	0	9	22⅓	23	15	14	6	23
A.L. totals (6 years)		0	2	.000	9.41	41	0	0	0	2	44	58	53	46	41	29
N.L. totals (1 year)		0	0	...	7.88	9	0	0	0	0	8	10	7	7	5	9
Major league totals (7 years)		0	2	.000	9.17	50	0	0	0	2	52	68	60	53	46	38

KAMIENIECKI, SCOTT

P, YANKEES

PERSONAL: Born April 19, 1964, in Mt. Clemens, Mich. . . . 6-0/195. . . . Throws right, bats right. . . . Full name: Scott Andrew Kamieniecki. . . . Name pronounced KAM-ah-NIK-ee.

HIGH SCHOOL: Redford St. Mary's (Detroit).

COLLEGE: Michigan (bachelor of arts degree in physical education).
TRANSACTIONS/CAREER NOTES: Selected by Detroit Tigers organization in second round of free-agent draft (June 7, 1982).... Selected by Milwaukee Brewers organization in 23rd round of free-agent draft (June 3, 1985).... Selected by New York Yankees organization in 14th round of free-agent draft (June 2, 1986).... On New York disabled list (August 3, 1991-remainder of season).... On New York disabled list (April 2-29, 1992); included rehabilitation assignment to Fort Lauderdale (April 9-17) and Columbus (April 17-29).

Year	Team (League)	W	L	Pct.	ERA	G	GS	CG	ShO	Sv.	IP	H	R	ER	BB	SO
1987	—Alb./Colon. (East.)	1	3	.250	5.35	10	7	0	0	0	37	41	25	22	33	19
	—Prin. William (Car.)	9	5	.643	4.17	19	19	1	0	0	112⅓	91	61	52	78	84
1988	—Prin. William (Car.)	6	7	.462	4.40	15	15	•7	2	0	100⅓	115	62	49	50	72
	—Fort Lauder. (FSL)	3	6	.333	3.62	12	11	1	1	0	77	71	36	31	40	51
1989	—Alb./Colon. (East.)	10	9	.526	3.70	24	23	6	3	1	151	142	67	62	57	*140
1990	—Alb./Colon. (East.)	10	9	.526	3.20	22	21	3	1	0	132	113	55	47	61	99
1991	—Columbus (Int'l)	6	3	.667	2.36	11	11	3	1	0	76⅓	61	25	20	20	58
	—New York (A.L.)	4	4	.500	3.90	9	9	0	0	0	55⅓	54	24	24	22	34
1992	—Fort Lauder. (FSL)	1	0	1.000	1.29	1	1	1	0	0	7	8	1	1	0	3
	—Columbus (Int'l)	1	0	1.000	0.69	2	2	0	0	0	13	6	1	1	4	12
	—New York (A.L.)	6	14	.300	4.36	28	28	4	0	0	188	193	100	91	74	88
1993	—New York (A.L.)	10	7	.588	4.08	30	20	2	0	1	154⅓	163	73	70	59	72
	—Columbus (Int'l)	1	0	1.000	1.50	1	1	0	0	0	6	5	1	1	0	4
Major league totals (3 years)..		20	25	.444	4.19	67	57	6	0	1	397⅔	410	197	185	155	194

KARKOVICE, RON

C, WHITE SOX

PERSONAL: Born August 8, 1963, in Union, N.J.... 6-1/219.... Throws right, bats right.... Full name: Ronald Joseph Karkovice.... Name pronounced CAR-ko-VICE.
HIGH SCHOOL: Boone (Orlando, Fla.).
TRANSACTIONS/CAREER NOTES: Selected by Chicago White Sox organization in first round (14th pick overall) of free-agent draft (June 7, 1982).... On disabled list (May 20-July 3, 1991 and June 20-July 6, 1993).
STATISTICAL NOTES: Led Gulf Coast League catchers with 394 total chances and tied for lead with five double plays in 1982.... Led Midwest League catchers with .996 fielding percentage in 1983.... Led Eastern League catchers with 13 double plays in 1985.

				BATTING											FIELDING			
Year	Team (League)	Pos.	G	AB	R	H	2B	3B	HR	RBI	Avg.	BB	SO	SB	PO	A	E	Avg.
1982	—GC Whi. Sox (GCL) ...	C	60	214	34	56	6	0	7	32	.262	29	*73	5	*331	*51	12	.970
1983	—Appleton (Midw.)	C-OF	97	326	54	78	17	3	13	48	.239	31	90	10	682	91	4	†.995
1984	—Glens Falls (East.) ...	C	88	260	37	56	9	1	13	39	.215	25	102	3	442	*68	11	.979
	—Denver (A.A.)	C	31	86	7	19	1	0	2	10	.221	8	25	1	149	28	3	.983
1985	—Glens Falls (East.) ...	C	99	324	37	70	9	3	11	37	.216	49	104	6	573	*103	*14	.980
1986	—Birm. (Southern)	C	97	319	63	90	13	1	20	53	.282	61	109	2	463	72	10	.982
	—Chicago (A.L.)	C	37	97	13	24	7	0	4	13	.247	9	37	1	227	19	1	.996
1987	—Chicago (A.L.)	C	39	85	7	6	0	0	2	7	.071	7	40	3	147	20	3	.982
	—Hawaii (PCL)	C-OF	34	104	15	19	3	0	4	11	.183	8	37	3	108	13	3	.976
1988	—Vancouver (PCL)	C	39	116	12	29	10	0	2	13	.250	8	26	2	202	16	3	.986
	—Chicago (A.L.)	C	46	115	10	20	4	0	3	9	.174	7	30	4	190	24	1	.995
1989	—Chicago (A.L.)	C	71	182	21	48	9	2	3	24	.264	10	56	0	299	47	5	.986
1990	—Chicago (A.L.)	C	68	183	30	45	10	0	6	20	.246	16	52	2	296	31	2	.994
1991	—Chicago (A.L.)	C-OF	75	167	25	41	13	0	5	22	.246	15	42	0	309	28	4	.988
1992	—Chicago (A.L.)	C-OF	123	342	39	81	12	1	13	50	.237	30	89	10	536	53	6	.990
1993	—Chicago (A.L.)	C	128	403	60	92	17	1	20	54	.228	29	126	2	769	63	5	.994
Major league totals (8 years)			587	1574	205	357	72	4	56	199	.227	123	472	22	2773	285	27	.991

CHAMPIONSHIP SERIES RECORD

				BATTING											FIELDING			
Year	Team (League)	Pos.	G	AB	R	H	2B	3B	HR	RBI	Avg.	BB	SO	SB	PO	A	E	Avg.
1993	—Chicago (A.L.)	C-PR	6	15	0	0	0	0	0	0	.000	1	7	0	30	2	0	1.000

KARROS, ERIC

1B, DODGERS

PERSONAL: Born November 4, 1967, in Hackensack, N.J.... 6-4/216.... Throws right, bats right.... Full name: Eric Peter Karros.... Name pronounced CARE-ose.
HIGH SCHOOL: Patrick Henry (San Diego).
COLLEGE: UCLA.
TRANSACTIONS/CAREER NOTES: Selected by Los Angeles Dodgers organization in sixth round of free-agent draft (June 1, 1988).
HONORS: Named N.L. Rookie Player of the Year by THE SPORTING NEWS (1992).... Named N.L. Rookie of the Year by Baseball Writers' Association of America (1992).
STATISTICAL NOTES: Tied for Pioneer League lead in errors by first baseman with 14 in 1988.... Led California League first basemen with 1,232 putouts, 110 assists and 1,358 total chances in 1989.... Led Texas League with 282 total bases in 1990.... Led Texas League first basemen with 1,337 total chances and 129 double plays in 1990.... Led Pacific Coast League with 269 total bases in 1991.... Tied for Pacific Coast League lead with eight intentional bases on balls received in 1991.... Led Pacific Coast League first basemen with 1,095 putouts, 109 assists and 1,215 total chances in 1991.

				BATTING											FIELDING			
Year	Team (League)	Pos.	G	AB	R	H	2B	3B	HR	RBI	Avg.	BB	SO	SB	PO	A	E	Avg.
1988	—Great Falls (Pio.)	1B-3B	66	268	68	98	12	1	12	55	.366	32	35	8	516	31	‡19	.966
1989	—Bakersfield (Calif.) ...	1B-3B	*142	545	86	*165	*40	1	15	86	.303	63	99	18	†1238	†113	19	.986
1990	—San Antonio (Tex.) ...	1B	•131	509	91	*179	*45	2	18	78	*.352	57	79	8	*1223	*106	8	*.994
1991	—Albuquerque (PCL) ..	1B-3B	132	488	88	154	33	8	22	101	.316	58	80	3	†1095	†109	11	.991
	—Los Angeles (N.L.) ...	1B	14	14	0	1	1	0	0	1	.071	1	6	0	33	2	0	1.000
1992	—Los Angeles (N.L.) ...	1B	149	545	63	140	30	1	20	88	.257	37	103	2	1211	126	9	.993
1993	—Los Angeles (N.L.) ...	1B	158	619	74	153	27	2	23	80	.247	34	82	0	1335	*147	12	.992
Major league totals (3 years)			321	1178	137	294	58	3	43	169	.250	72	191	2	2579	275	21	.993

KARSAY, STEVE

P, ATHLETICS

PERSONAL: Born March 24, 1972, in College Point, N.Y. . . . 6-3/205. . . . Throws right, bats right. . . . Full name: Stefan Andrew Karsay. . . . Name pronounced KAR-say.
HIGH SCHOOL: Christ the King (Queens, N.Y.).
TRANSACTIONS/CAREER NOTES: Selected by Toronto Blue Jays organization in first round (22nd pick overall) of free-agent draft (June 4, 1990). . . . On Knoxville disabled list (July 3-16, 1993). . . . Traded by Blue Jays with a player to be named later to Oakland Athletics for OF Rickey Henderson (July 31, 1993); A's acquired OF Jose Herrera to complete deal (August 6, 1993).

Year	Team (League)	W	L	Pct.	ERA	G	GS	CG	ShO	Sv.	IP	H	R	ER	BB	SO
1990	—St. Cathar. (NYP)	1	1	.500	0.79	5	5	0	0	0	22⅔	11	4	2	12	25
1991	—Myrtle Beach (SAL)	4	9	.308	3.58	20	20	1	0	0	110⅔	96	58	44	48	100
1992	—Dunedin (Fla. St.)	6	3	.667	2.73	16	16	3	2	0	85⅔	56	32	26	29	87
1993	—Knox.-Hunt. (Sou.)■	8	4	.667	3.58	21	20	1	0	0	118	111	50	47	35	122
	—Oakland (A.L.)	3	3	.500	4.04	8	8	0	0	0	49	49	23	22	16	33
Major league totals (1 year)		3	3	.500	4.04	8	8	0	0	0	49	49	23	22	16	33

KELLY, ROBERTO

OF, REDS

PERSONAL: Born October 1, 1964, in Panama City, Panama. . . . 6-2/202. . . . Throws right, bats right. . . . Full name: Roberto Conrado Kelly.
HIGH SCHOOL: Panama City (Panama).
COLLEGE: Jose Dolores Moscote College (Panama).
TRANSACTIONS/CAREER NOTES: Signed as free agent by New York Yankees organization (February 21, 1982). . . . On disabled list (July 10-August 23, 1986). . . . On New York disabled list (June 29-September 1, 1988; May 26-June 12, 1989; and July 6-August 13, 1991). . . . Traded by Yankees to Cincinnati Reds for OF Paul O'Neill and 1B Joe DeBerry (November 3, 1992). . . . On disabled list (July 14, 1993-remainder of season).
RECORDS: Holds major league single-season record for most times reaching base on catcher's interference—8 (1992). . . . Shares major league single-season record for fewest double plays by outfielder (150 or more games)—0 (1990).
STATISTICAL NOTES: Led International League outfielders with 345 total chances in 1987. . . . Led A.L. outfielders with 430 total chances in 1990.
MISCELLANEOUS: Batted as switch-hitter (1985).

			BATTING												FIELDING			
Year	Team (League)	Pos.	G	AB	R	H	2B	3B	HR	RBI	Avg.	BB	SO	SB	PO	A	E	Avg.
1982	—GC Yankees (GCL)	SS-OF	31	86	13	17	1	1	1	18	.198	10	18	3	47	79	19	.869
1983	—Oneonta (NYP)	OF-3B	48	167	17	36	1	2	2	17	.216	12	20	12	70	3	5	.936
	—Greensboro (S. Atl.)	OF-SS	20	49	6	13	0	0	0	3	.265	3	5	3	30	2	0	1.000
1984	—Greensboro (S. Atl.)	OF-1B	111	361	68	86	13	2	1	26	.238	57	49	42	228	5	4	.983
1985	—Fort Lauder. (FSL)	OF	114	417	86	103	4	*13	3	38	.247	58	70	49	187	1	1	.995
1986	—Alb./Colon. (East.)	OF	86	299	42	87	11	4	2	43	.291	29	63	10	206	8	7	.968
1987	—Columbus (Int'l)	OF	118	471	77	131	19	8	13	62	.278	33	116	*51	*331	4	10	.971
	—New York (A.L.)	OF	23	52	12	14	3	0	1	7	.269	5	15	9	42	0	2	.955
1988	—New York (A.L.)	OF	38	77	9	19	4	1	1	7	.247	3	15	5	70	1	1	.986
	—Columbus (Int'l)	OF	30	120	25	40	8	1	3	16	.333	6	29	11	51	1	0	1.000
1989	—New York (A.L.)	OF	137	441	65	133	18	3	9	48	.302	41	89	35	353	9	6	.984
1990	—New York (A.L.)	OF	*162	641	85	183	32	4	15	61	.285	33	148	42	420	5	5	.988
1991	—New York (A.L.)	OF	126	486	68	130	22	2	20	69	.267	45	77	32	268	8	4	.986
1992	—New York (A.L.)	OF	152	580	81	158	31	2	10	66	.272	41	96	28	389	8	7	.983
1993	—Cincinnati (N.L.)■	OF	78	320	44	102	17	3	9	35	.319	17	43	21	198	3	1	.995
American League totals (6 years)			638	2277	320	637	110	12	56	258	.280	168	440	151	1542	31	25	.984
National League totals (1 year)			78	320	44	102	17	3	9	35	.319	17	43	21	198	3	1	.995
Major league totals (7 years)			716	2597	364	739	127	15	65	293	.285	185	483	172	1740	34	26	.986

ALL-STAR GAME RECORD

			BATTING										FIELDING			
Year	League	Pos.	AB	R	H	2B	3B	HR	RBI	Avg.	BB	SO	SB	PO	A	E	Avg.
1992	—American	OF	2	0	1	1	0	0	2	.500	0	1	0	1	0	0	1.000
1993	—National	OF	1	0	0	0	0	0	0	.000	0	1	0	0	1	0	1.000
All-Star Game totals (2 years)			3	0	1	1	0	0	2	.333	0	2	0	1	1	0	1.000

KELLY, MIKE

OF, BRAVES

PERSONAL: Born June 2, 1970, in Los Angeles. . . . 6-4/195. . . . Throws right, bats right. . . . Full name: Michael Raymond Kelly.
HIGH SCHOOL: Los Alamitos (Calif.).
COLLEGE: Arizona State.
TRANSACTIONS/CAREER NOTES: Selected by New York Mets organization in 24th round of free-agent draft (June 1, 1988). . . . Selected by Atlanta Braves organization in first round (second pick overall) of free-agent draft (June 3, 1991).
HONORS: Named College Player of the Year by THE SPORTING NEWS (1990). . . . Named outfielder on THE SPORTING NEWS college All-America team (1990). . . . Named Golden Spikes Award winner by USA Baseball (1991).

			BATTING												FIELDING			
Year	Team (League)	Pos.	G	AB	R	H	2B	3B	HR	RBI	Avg.	BB	SO	SB	PO	A	E	Avg.
1991	—Durham (Carolina)	OF	35	124	29	31	6	1	6	17	.250	19	47	6	4	0	0	1.000
1992	—Greenville (South.)	OF	133	471	83	108	18	4	25	71	.229	65	*162	22	244	7	3	.988
1993	—Richmond (Int'l)	OF	123	424	63	103	13	1	19	58	.243	36	109	11	270	6	2	*.993

KELLY, PAT

2B, YANKEES

PERSONAL: Born October 14, 1967, in Philadelphia. . . . 6-0/182. . . . Throws right, bats right. . . . Full name: Patrick Franklin Kelly.
HIGH SCHOOL: Catashuqua (Pa.).
COLLEGE: West Chester (Pa.).

TRANSACTIONS/CAREER NOTES: Selected by New York Yankees organization in ninth round of free-agent draft (June 1, 1988). . . . On New York disabled list (April 21-May 7, 1992); included rehabilitation assignment to Albany/Colonie (May 5-7).
STATISTICAL NOTES: Led Carolina League second basemen with 76 double plays and tied for lead with 641 total chances in 1989. . . . Led Eastern League second basemen with 667 total chances and 97 double plays in 1990.

			BATTING											FIELDING			
Year	**Team (League)**	**Pos.**	**G**	**AB**	**R**	**H**	**2B**	**3B**	**HR**	**RBI**	**Avg.**	**BB**	**SO**	**SB**	**PO**	**A**	**E**	**Avg.**
1988	—Oneonta (NYP)	2B-SS	71	280	49	92	11	6	2	34	.329	15	45	25	124	207	16	.954
1989	—Prin. William (Car.)	2B	124	436	61	116	21	*7	3	45	.266	32	79	31	244	*372	25	.961
1990	—Alb./Colon. (East.)	2B	126	418	67	113	19	6	8	44	.270	37	79	31	*266	*381	*20	.970
1991	—Columbus (Int'l)	2B	31	116	27	39	9	2	3	19	.336	9	16	8	53	97	4	.974
	—New York (A.L.)	3B-2B	96	298	35	72	12	4	3	23	.242	15	52	12	78	204	18	.940
1992	—New York (A.L.)	2B	106	318	38	72	22	2	7	27	.226	25	72	8	203	296	11	.978
	—Alb./Colon. (East.)	2B	2	6	1	0	0	0	0	0	.000	2	4	0	4	8	0	1.000
1993	—New York (A.L.)	2B	127	406	49	111	24	1	7	51	.273	24	68	14	245	369	14	.978
Major league totals (3 years)			329	1022	122	255	58	7	17	101	.250	64	192	34	526	869	43	.970

KENT, JEFF

2B, METS

PERSONAL: Born March 7, 1968, in Bellflower, Calif. . . . 6-1/185. . . . Throws right, bats right. . . . Full name: Jeffrey Franklin Kent.
HIGH SCHOOL: Edison (Huntington Beach, Calif.).
COLLEGE: California.
TRANSACTIONS/CAREER NOTES: Selected by Toronto Blue Jays organization in 20th round of free-agent draft (June 5, 1989). . . . Traded by Blue Jays with a player to be named later to New York Mets for P David Cone (August 27, 1992); Mets acquired OF Ryan Thompson to complete deal (September 1, 1992).
STATISTICAL NOTES: Led Florida State League second basemen with 680 total chances and 83 double plays in 1990. . . . Led Southern League second basemen with 673 total chances and 96 double plays in 1991. . . . Led N.L. second basemen with 18 errors in 1993.

			BATTING											FIELDING			
Year	**Team (League)**	**Pos.**	**G**	**AB**	**R**	**H**	**2B**	**3B**	**HR**	**RBI**	**Avg.**	**BB**	**SO**	**SB**	**PO**	**A**	**E**	**Avg.**
1989	—St. Cathar. (NYP)	SS-3B	73	268	34	60	14	1	*13	37	.224	33	81	5	103	178	29	.906
1990	—Dunedin (Fla. St.)	2B	132	447	72	124	32	2	16	60	.277	53	98	17	*261	*404	15	.978
1991	—Knoxville (South.)	2B	•139	445	68	114	*34	1	2	61	.256	80	104	25	249	*395	*29	.957
1992	—Toronto (A.L.)	3B-2B-1B	65	192	36	46	13	1	8	35	.240	20	47	2	62	112	11	.941
	—New York (N.L.)■	2B-SS-3B	37	113	16	27	8	1	3	15	.239	7	29	0	62	93	3	.981
1993	—New York (N.L.)	2B-3B-SS	140	496	65	134	24	0	21	80	.270	30	88	4	261	341	†22	.965
American League totals (1 year)			65	192	36	46	13	1	8	35	.240	20	47	2	62	112	11	.941
National League totals (2 years)			177	609	81	161	32	1	24	95	.264	37	117	4	323	434	25	.968
Major league totals (2 years)			242	801	117	207	45	2	32	130	.258	57	164	6	385	546	36	.963

KESSINGER, KEITH

SS, REDS

PERSONAL: Born February 19, 1967, in Forrest City, Ark. . . . 6-2/185. . . . Throws right, bats both. . . . Full name: Robert Keith Kessinger. . . . Son of Don Kessinger, infielder, Chicago Cubs, St. Louis Cardinals and Chicago White Sox (1964-79), and manager, White Sox (1979).
HIGH SCHOOL: Briarcrest Baptist (Memphis, Tenn.).
COLLEGE: Mississippi.
TRANSACTIONS/CAREER NOTES: Selected by Baltimore Orioles organization in 36th round of free-agent draft (June 5, 1989). . . . On Frederick disabled list (April 11-May 29, 1991). . . . Contract sold by Orioles organization to Cincinnati Reds organization (July 2, 1991). . . . On disabled list (July 20-27, 1992). . . . On Indianapolis disabled list (July 8-August 4, 1993).
MISCELLANEOUS: Batted righthanded only (1989-90).

			BATTING											FIELDING			
Year	**Team (League)**	**Pos.**	**G**	**AB**	**R**	**H**	**2B**	**3B**	**HR**	**RBI**	**Avg.**	**BB**	**SO**	**SB**	**PO**	**A**	**E**	**Avg.**
1989	—Bluefield (Appal.)	2B-3B-SS	28	99	17	27	4	0	2	9	.273	8	12	1	45	77	2	.984
1990	—Wausau (Midwest)	SS-2B-3B	37	134	17	29	8	0	0	9	.216	6	23	1	44	76	11	.916
	—Frederick (Caro.)	SS-2B-3B	64	145	18	22	4	0	0	8	.152	20	36	0	69	135	14	.936
1991	—Frederick (Caro.)	3-2-S-1	26	56	5	10	3	0	0	4	.179	8	12	2	32	32	10	.865
	—Ced. Rap. (Midw.)■	3B-SS-2B	59	206	15	42	5	0	1	15	.204	23	46	0	74	124	11	.947
1992	—Ced. Rap. (Midw.)	3-2-S-1	95	308	41	73	15	1	4	38	.237	36	57	2	147	202	14	.961
1993	—Chatt. (South.)	S-2-3-1	56	161	24	50	9	0	3	28	.311	24	18	0	85	122	13	.941
	—Indianapolis (A.A.)	SS-2B	35	120	17	34	9	0	2	15	.283	14	14	0	50	101	2	.987
	—Cincinnati (N.L.)	SS	11	27	4	7	1	0	1	3	.259	4	4	0	7	22	2	.935
Major league totals (1 year)			11	27	4	7	1	0	1	3	.259	4	4	0	7	22	2	.935

KEY, JIMMY

P, YANKEES

PERSONAL: Born April 22, 1961, in Huntsville, Ala. . . . 6-1/185. . . . Throws left, bats right. . . . Full name: James Edward Key.
HIGH SCHOOL: Butler (Huntsville, Ala.).
COLLEGE: Clemson.
TRANSACTIONS/CAREER NOTES: Selected by Chicago White Sox organization in 10th round of free-agent draft (June 5, 1979). . . . Selected by Toronto Blue Jays organization in third round of free-agent draft (June 7, 1982). . . . On Toronto disabled list (April 15-June 29, 1988); included rehabilitation assignment to Dunedin (June 10-27). . . . On disabled list (August 4-19, 1989). . . . On Toronto disabled list (May 23-June 22, 1990); included rehabilitation assignment to Dunedin (June 7-18). . . . Granted free agency (October 27, 1992). . . . Signed by New York Yankees (December 10, 1992).
HONORS: Named A.L. Pitcher of the Year by THE SPORTING NEWS (1987). . . . Named lefthanded pitcher on THE SPORTING NEWS A.L. All-Star team (1987 and 1993).
MISCELLANEOUS: Appeared in one game as pinch-runner (1985).

Year	Team (League)	W	L	Pct.	ERA	G	GS	CG	ShO	Sv.	IP	H	R	ER	BB	SO
1982	—Medicine Hat (Pio.)	2	1	.667	2.30	5	5	1	0	0	31⅓	27	12	8	10	25
	—Florence (S. Atl.)	5	2	.714	3.72	9	9	0	0	0	58	59	33	24	18	49
1983	—Knoxville (South.)	6	5	.545	2.85	14	14	2	0	0	101	86	35	32	40	57
	—Syracuse (Int'l)	4	8	.333	4.13	16	15	2	0	0	89⅓	87	58	41	33	71
1984	—Toronto (A.L.)	4	5	.444	4.65	63	0	0	0	10	62	70	37	32	32	44
1985	—Toronto (A.L.)	14	6	.700	3.00	35	32	3	0	0	212⅔	188	77	71	50	85
1986	—Toronto (A.L.)	14	11	.560	3.57	36	35	4	2	0	232	222	98	92	74	141
1987	—Toronto (A.L.)	17	8	.680	*2.76	36	36	8	1	0	261	210	93	80	66	161
1988	—Toronto (A.L.)	12	5	.706	3.29	21	21	2	2	0	131⅓	127	55	48	30	65
	—Dunedin (Fla. St.)	2	0	1.000	0.00	4	4	0	0	0	21⅓	15	2	0	1	11
1989	—Toronto (A.L.)	13	14	.481	3.88	33	33	5	1	0	216	226	99	93	27	118
1990	—Toronto (A.L.)	13	7	.650	4.25	27	27	0	0	0	154⅔	169	79	73	22	88
	—Dunedin (Fla. St.)	2	0	1.000	2.50	3	3	0	0	0	18	21	7	5	3	14
1991	—Toronto (A.L.)	16	12	.571	3.05	33	33	2	2	0	209⅓	207	84	71	44	125
1992	—Toronto (A.L.)	13	13	.500	3.53	33	33	4	2	0	216⅔	205	88	85	59	117
1993	—New York (A.L.)■	18	6	.750	3.00	34	34	4	2	0	236⅔	219	84	79	43	173
Major league totals (10 years)		134	87	.606	3.37	351	284	32	12	10	1932⅓	1843	794	724	447	1117

CHAMPIONSHIP SERIES RECORD

Year	Team (League)	W	L	Pct.	ERA	G	GS	CG	ShO	Sv.	IP	H	R	ER	BB	SO
1985	—Toronto (A.L.)	0	1	.000	5.19	2	2	0	0	0	8⅔	15	5	5	2	5
1989	—Toronto (A.L.)	1	0	1.000	4.50	1	1	0	0	0	6	7	3	3	2	2
1991	—Toronto (A.L.)	0	0	...	3.00	1	1	0	0	0	6	5	2	2	1	1
1992	—Toronto (A.L.)	0	0	...	0.00	1	0	0	0	0	3	2	0	0	2	1
Champ. series totals (4 years)		1	1	.500	3.80	5	4	0	0	0	23⅔	29	10	10	7	9

WORLD SERIES RECORD

Year	Team (League)	W	L	Pct.	ERA	G	GS	CG	ShO	Sv.	IP	H	R	ER	BB	SO
1992	—Toronto (A.L.)	2	0	1.000	1.00	2	1	0	0	0	9	6	2	1	0	6

ALL-STAR GAME RECORD

Year	League	W	L	Pct.	ERA	GS	CG	ShO	Sv.	IP	H	R	ER	BB	SO
1985	—American	0	0	...	0.00	0	0	0	0	⅓	0	0	0	0	0
1991	—American	1	0	1.000	0.00	0	0	0	0	1	1	0	0	0	1
1993	—American	0	0	...	9.00	0	0	0	0	1	2	1	1	0	1
All-Star totals (3 years)		1	0	1.000	3.86	0	0	0	0	2⅓	3	1	1	0	2

KIEFER, MARK

P, BREWERS

PERSONAL: Born November 13, 1968, in Orange, Calif. . . . 6-4/184. . . . Throws right, bats right. . . . Full name: Mark Andrew Kiefer.

HIGH SCHOOL: Garden Grove (Calif.).

COLLEGE: Cal State Fullerton.

TRANSACTIONS/CAREER NOTES: Selected by Milwaukee Brewers organization in 21st round of free-agent draft (June 2, 1987). . . . On New Orleans disabled list (April 8-May 25, 1993). . . . On El Paso disabled list (June 2-17, 1993).

STATISTICAL NOTES: Led American Association with 25 home runs allowed in 1992.

Year	Team (League)	W	L	Pct.	ERA	G	GS	CG	ShO	Sv.	IP	H	R	ER	BB	SO
1988	—Helena (Pioneer)	4	4	.500	2.65	15	9	2	0	0	68	76	30	20	17	51
1989	—Beloit (Midwest)	9	6	.600	2.32	30	15	7	2	1	131⅔	106	44	34	32	100
1990	—Ariz. Brewers (Ar.)	0	0	...	3.38	1	1	0	0	0	2⅔	3	1	1	1	2
	—Stockton (Calif.)	5	2	.714	3.30	11	10	0	0	0	60	65	23	22	17	37
1991	—El Paso (Texas)	7	1	.875	3.33	12	12	0	0	0	75⅔	62	33	28	43	72
	—Denver (A.A.)	9	5	.643	4.62	17	17	3	2	0	101⅓	104	55	52	41	68
1992	—Denver (A.A.)	7	*13	.350	4.59	27	26	1	0	0	162⅔	168	95	83	65	*145
1993	—El Paso (Texas)	3	4	.429	4.01	11	11	0	0	0	51⅔	48	29	23	19	44
	—New Orleans (A.A.)	3	2	.600	5.08	5	5	0	0	0	28⅓	28	20	16	17	23
	—Milwaukee (A.L.)	0	0	...	0.00	6	0	0	0	1	9⅓	3	0	0	5	7
Major league totals (1 year)		0	0	...	0.00	6	0	0	0	1	9⅓	3	0	0	5	7

KIELY, JOHN

P, TIGERS

PERSONAL: Born October 4, 1964, in Boston. . . . 6-3/215. . . . Throws right, bats right. . . . Full name: John Francis Kiely. . . . Name pronounced KYE-lee.

HIGH SCHOOL: Brockton (Mass.).

COLLEGE: Bridgewater (Mass.) State College.

TRANSACTIONS/CAREER NOTES: Signed as free agent by Detroit Tigers organization (September 7, 1987). . . . Loaned by Tigers organization to Milwaukee Brewers organization (June 20-August 4, 1988).

Year	Team (League)	W	L	Pct.	ERA	G	GS	CG	ShO	Sv.	IP	H	R	ER	BB	SO
1988	—Peoria (Midwest)	3	2	.600	4.56	9	5	1	0	1	47⅓	42	25	24	12	50
	—Bristol (Appal.)■	2	2	.500	6.17	8	0	0	0	1	11⅔	9	9	8	7	14
1989	—Lakeland (Fla. St.)■	4	3	.571	2.40	36	0	0	0	8	63⅔	52	26	17	27	56
1990	—London (Eastern)	3	0	1.000	1.76	46	0	0	0	12	76⅔	62	17	15	42	52
1991	—Toledo (Int'l)	4	2	.667	2.13	42	0	0	0	6	72	55	25	17	35	60
	—Detroit (A.L.)	0	1	.000	14.85	7	0	0	0	0	6⅔	13	11	11	9	1
1992	—Toledo (Int'l)	1	1	.500	2.84	21	0	0	0	9	31⅔	25	11	10	7	31
	—Detroit (A.L.)	4	2	.667	2.13	39	0	0	0	0	55	44	14	13	28	18
1993	—Detroit (A.L.)	0	2	.000	7.71	8	0	0	0	0	11⅔	13	11	10	13	5
	—Toledo (Int'l)	3	4	.429	3.88	37	0	0	0	4	58	65	34	25	25	48
Major league totals (3 years)		4	5	.444	4.17	54	0	0	0	0	73⅓	70	36	34	50	24

KILE, DARRYL

P, ASTROS

PERSONAL: Born December 2, 1968, in Garden Grove, Calif.... 6-5/185.... Throws right, bats right.... Full name: Darryl Andrew Kile.
COLLEGE: Chaffey College (Calif.).
TRANSACTIONS/CAREER NOTES: Selected by Houston Astros organization in 30th round of free-agent draft (June 2, 1987).... On Tucson disabled list (June 25-July 5, 1992).
STATISTICAL NOTES: Led N.L. with 15 hit batsmen in 1993.... Pitched 7-1 no-hit victory against New York (September 8, 1993).

Year Team (League)	W	L	Pct.	ERA	G	GS	CG	ShO	Sv.	IP	H	R	ER	BB	SO
1988 —GC Astros (GCL)	5	3	.625	3.17	12	12	0	0	0	59⅔	48	34	21	33	54
1989 —Columbus (South.)	11	6	.647	2.58	20	20	6	•2	0	125⅔	74	47	36	68	108
—Tucson (PCL)	2	1	.667	5.96	6	6	1	1	0	25⅔	33	20	17	13	18
1990 —Tucson (PCL)	5	10	.333	6.64	26	23	1	0	0	123⅓	147	97	91	68	77
1991 —Houston (N.L.)	7	11	.389	3.69	37	22	0	0	0	153⅔	144	81	63	84	100
1992 —Houston (N.L.)	5	10	.333	3.95	22	22	2	0	0	125⅓	124	61	55	63	90
—Tucson (PCL)	4	1	.800	3.99	9	9	0	0	0	56⅓	50	31	25	32	43
1993 —Houston (N.L.)	15	8	.652	3.51	32	26	4	2	0	171⅔	152	73	67	69	141
Major league totals (3 years)	27	29	.482	3.69	91	70	6	2	0	450⅔	420	215	185	216	331

ALL-STAR GAME RECORD

Year League	W	L	Pct.	ERA	GS	CG	ShO	Sv.	IP	H	R	ER	BB	SO
1993 —National	Did not play.													

KILGUS, PAUL

P, CARDINALS

PERSONAL: Born February 2, 1962, in Bowling Green, Ky.... 6-1/185.... Throws left, bats left.... Full name: Paul Nelson Kilgus.
HIGH SCHOOL: Bowling Green (Ky.).
COLLEGE: Kentucky (bachelor of science degree in biology, 1984).
TRANSACTIONS/CAREER NOTES: Selected by Texas Rangers organization in 43rd round of free-agent draft (June 4, 1984).... Traded by Rangers with P Mitch Williams, P Steve Wilson, IF Curtis Wilkerson, IF Luis Benitez and OF Pablo Delgado to Chicago Cubs for OF Rafael Palmeiro, P Jamie Moyer and P Drew Hall (December 5, 1988).... Traded by Cubs organization to Toronto Blue Jays for P Jose Nunez (December 7, 1989).... Traded by Blue Jays to Baltimore Orioles for P Mickey Weston (December 14, 1990).... Released by Orioles (October 16, 1991).... Signed by Louisville, St. Louis Cardinals organization (January 19, 1992).... Granted free agency (October 15, 1992).... Re-signed by Louisville (December 18, 1992).... On St. Louis disabled list (June 24-September 1, 1993).

Year Team (League)	W	L	Pct.	ERA	G	GS	CG	ShO	Sv.	IP	H	R	ER	BB	SO
1984 —Tri-Cities (N'west)	7	5	.583	2.87	14	14	0	0	0	78⅓	87	38	25	31	60
1985 —Salem (Carolina)	3	1	.750	2.03	38	0	0	0	10	84⅓	69	28	19	26	67
1986 —Tulsa (Texas)	3	7	.300	3.73	41	7	2	0	8	103⅔	102	56	43	36	59
1987 —Okla. City (A.A.)	2	0	1.000	4.01	21	0	0	0	7	24⅔	23	12	11	10	14
—Texas (A.L.)	2	7	.222	4.13	25	12	0	0	0	89⅓	95	45	41	31	42
1988 —Texas (A.L.)	12	15	.444	4.16	32	32	5	3	0	203⅓	190	105	94	71	88
1989 —Chicago (N.L.)■	6	10	.375	4.39	35	23	0	0	2	145⅔	164	90	71	49	61
—Iowa (Am. Assoc.)	1	0	1.000	3.00	1	1	1	0	0	9	9	3	3	2	5
1990 —Toronto (A.L.)■	0	0	...	6.06	11	0	0	0	0	16⅓	19	11	11	7	7
—Syracuse (Int'l)	6	8	.429	2.94	20	17	7	1	0	125⅔	116	47	41	39	75
1991 —Baltimore (A.L.)■	0	2	.000	5.08	38	0	0	0	1	62	60	38	35	24	32
—Rochester (Int'l)	2	2	.500	5.76	9	6	0	0	0	45⅓	58	32	29	10	29
1992 —Louisville (A.A.)■	9	8	.529	3.80	27	26	4	1	0	168⅓	★189	90	71	28	90
1993 —Louisville (A.A.)	7	1	.875	2.65	9	9	4	1	0	68	59	21	20	19	54
—St. Louis (N.L.)	1	0	1.000	0.63	22	1	0	0	1	28⅔	18	2	2	8	21
A.L. totals (4 years)	14	24	.368	4.39	106	44	5	3	1	371	364	199	181	133	169
N.L. totals (2 years)	7	10	.412	3.77	57	24	0	0	3	174⅓	182	92	73	57	82
Major league totals (6 years)	21	34	.382	4.19	163	68	5	3	4	545⅓	546	291	254	190	251

CHAMPIONSHIP SERIES RECORD

Year Team (League)	W	L	Pct.	ERA	G	GS	CG	ShO	Sv.	IP	H	R	ER	BB	SO
1989 —Chicago (N.L.)	0	0	...	0.00	1	0	0	0	0	3	4	0	0	1	1

KING, JEFF

3B, PIRATES

PERSONAL: Born December 26, 1964, in Marion, Ind.... 6-1/183.... Throws right, bats right.... Full name: Jeffrey Wayne King.... Son of Jack King, minor league catcher (1954-55).
HIGH SCHOOL: Rampart (Colorado Springs, Colo.).
COLLEGE: Arkansas.
TRANSACTIONS/CAREER NOTES: Selected by Chicago Cubs organization in 23rd round of free-agent draft (June 6, 1983).... Selected by Pittsburgh Pirates organization in first round (first pick overall) of free-agent draft (June 2, 1986).... On Pittsburgh disabled list (May 5-31, 1991); included rehabilitation assignment to Buffalo (May 25-31).... On Pittsburgh disabled list (June 13-October 7, 1991); included rehabilitation assignment to Buffalo (August 28-September 6).
HONORS: Named College Player of the Year by THE SPORTING NEWS (1986).... Named third baseman on THE SPORTING NEWS college All-America team (1986).
STATISTICAL NOTES: Led Carolina League with .565 slugging percentage in 1987.... Led N.L. third basemen with 353 assists and 475 total chances in 1993.

			BATTING											FIELDING			
Year Team (League)	Pos.	G	AB	R	H	2B	3B	HR	RBI	Avg.	BB	SO	SB	PO	A	E	Avg.
1986 —Prin. William (Car.)	3B	37	132	18	31	4	1	6	20	.235	19	34	1	25	50	8	.904
1987 —Salem (Carolina)	1B-3B	90	310	68	86	9	1	26	71	.277	61	88	6	572	106	13	.981
—Harrisburg (East.)	1B	26	100	12	24	7	0	2	25	.240	4	27	0	107	10	1	.992
1988 —Harrisburg (East.)	3B	117	411	49	105	21	1	14	66	.255	46	87	5	97	208	24	.927

Year	Team (League)	Pos.	G	AB	R	H	2B	3B	HR	RBI	Avg.	BB	SO	SB	PO	A	E	Avg.
			BATTING												FIELDING			
1989	—Buffalo (A.A.)	1B-3B	51	169	26	43	5	2	6	29	.254	57	60	11	213	61	8	.972
	—Pittsburgh (N.L.)	1-3-2-S	75	215	31	42	13	3	5	19	.195	20	34	4	403	59	4	.991
1990	—Pittsburgh (N.L.)	3B-1B	127	371	46	91	17	1	14	53	.245	21	50	3	61	215	18	.939
1991	—Pittsburgh (N.L.)	3B	33	109	16	26	1	1	4	18	.239	14	15	3	15	62	2	.975
	—Buffalo (A.A.)	3B	9	18	3	4	1	1	0	2	.222	6	3	1	2	8	1	.909
1992	—Pittsburgh (N.L.)	3-2-1-S-0	130	480	56	111	21	2	14	65	.231	27	56	4	368	234	12	.980
	—Buffalo (A.A.)	3B-1B-2B	7	29	6	10	2	0	2	5	.345	2	2	1	21	12	0	1.000
1993	—Pittsburgh (N.L.)	3B-SS-2B	158	611	82	180	35	3	9	98	.295	59	54	8	108	†362	18	.963
Major league totals (5 years)			523	1786	231	450	87	10	46	253	.252	141	209	22	955	932	54	.972

CHAMPIONSHIP SERIES RECORD

CHAMPIONSHIP SERIES NOTES: Shares single-series record for most doubles—4 (1992).

Year	Team (League)	Pos.	G	AB	R	H	2B	3B	HR	RBI	Avg.	BB	SO	SB	PO	A	E	Avg.
			BATTING												FIELDING			
1990	—Pittsburgh (N.L.)	3B-PH	5	10	0	1	0	0	0	0	.100	1	5	0	1	4	0	1.000
1992	—Pittsburgh (N.L.)	3B	7	29	4	7	4	0	0	2	.241	0	1	0	11	19	1	.968
Championship series totals (2 years)			12	39	4	8	4	0	0	2	.205	1	6	0	12	23	1	.972

KING, KEVIN

P, MARINERS

PERSONAL: Born February 11, 1969, in Atwater, Calif.... 6-4/200.... Throws left, bats left.... Full name: Kevin Ray King.
HIGH SCHOOL: Braggs (Okla.).
COLLEGE: Oklahoma.
TRANSACTIONS/CAREER NOTES: Selected by Toronto Blue Jays organization in ninth round of free-agent draft (June 2, 1987).... Selected by Seattle Mariners organization in seventh round of free-agent draft (June 4, 1990).... On disabled list (May 29-July 20, 1991).

Year	Team (League)	W	L	Pct.	ERA	G	GS	CG	ShO	Sv.	IP	H	R	ER	BB	SO
1990	—Belling. (N'west)	3	2	.600	4.78	6	6	0	0	0	32	37	18	17	10	27
	—Peninsula (Caro.)	4	2	.667	4.46	7	7	0	0	0	36⅓	42	23	18	13	20
1991	—Peninsula (Caro.)	6	7	.462	4.37	17	17	2	1	0	92⅔	99	55	45	38	59
1992	—San Bern. (Calif.)	7	*16	.304	5.32	27	27	0	0	0	165⅔	*226	*118	*98	55	101
1993	—Riverside (Calif.)	3	2	.600	1.57	25	0	0	0	5	46	37	10	8	20	28
	—Jacksonv. (South.)	2	0	1.000	3.14	16	0	0	0	1	28⅔	25	10	10	7	13
	—Seattle (A.L.)	0	1	.000	6.17	13	0	0	0	0	11⅔	9	8	8	4	8
Major league totals (1 year)		0	1	.000	6.17	13	0	0	0	0	11⅔	9	8	8	4	8

KIRBY, WAYNE

OF, INDIANS

PERSONAL: Born January 22, 1964, in Williamsburg, Va.... 5-10/185.... Throws right, bats left.... Full name: Wayne Edward Kirby.... Brother of Terry Kirby, running back, Miami Dolphins of National Football League.
HIGH SCHOOL: Tabb (Va.).
COLLEGE: Newport News Apprentice School (Va.).
TRANSACTIONS/CAREER NOTES: Selected by Los Angeles Dodgers organization in 13th round of free-agent draft (January 11, 1983).... Granted free agency (October 15, 1990).... Signed by Cleveland Indians organization (December 3, 1990).... Granted free agency (October 15, 1991).... Signed by Colorado Springs, Indians organization (December 12, 1991).
STATISTICAL NOTES: Led Pacific Coast League in caught stealing with 20 in 1992.

Year	Team (League)	Pos.	G	AB	R	H	2B	3B	HR	RBI	Avg.	BB	SO	SB	PO	A	E	Avg.
			BATTING												FIELDING			
1983	—GC Dodgers (GCL)	OF	60	216	43	63	7	1	0	13	.292	34	19	23	89	9	1	.990
1984	—Vero Beach (FSL)	OF	76	224	39	61	6	3	0	21	.272	21	30	11	101	3	5	.954
	—Great Falls (Pio.)	OF	20	84	19	26	2	2	1	11	.310	12	9	19	35	3	2	.950
	—Bakersfield (Calif.)	OF	23	84	14	23	3	0	0	10	.274	4	5	8	10	1	3	.786
1985	—Vero Beach (FSL)	OF	122	437	70	123	9	3	0	28	.281	41	41	31	231	10	4	.984
1986	—Vero Beach (FSL)	OF-2B	114	387	60	101	9	4	2	31	.261	37	30	28	264	18	4	.986
1987	—Bakersfield (Calif.)	OF	105	416	77	112	14	3	0	34	.269	49	42	56	213	13	12	.950
	—San Antonio (Tex.)	OF	24	80	7	19	1	2	1	9	.238	4	7	6	47	1	3	.941
1988	—Bakersfield (Calif.)	OF	12	47	12	13	0	1	0	4	.277	11	4	9	20	2	2	.917
	—San Antonio (Tex.)	OF	100	334	50	80	9	2	0	21	.240	21	43	26	181	4	2	.989
1989	—San Antonio (Tex.)	OF	44	140	14	30	3	1	0	7	.214	18	17	11	77	3	4	.952
	—Albuquerque (PCL)	OF	78	310	62	106	18	8	0	30	.342	26	27	29	149	8	2	.987
1990	—Albuquerque (PCL)	OF	119	342	56	95	14	5	0	30	.278	28	36	29	185	11	9	.956
1991	—Colo. Springs (PCL)■	OF-2B	118	385	66	113	14	4	1	39	.294	34	36	29	227	14	6	.976
	—Cleveland (A.L.)	OF	21	43	4	9	2	0	0	5	.209	2	6	1	40	1	0	1.000
1992	—Colo. Springs (PCL)	OF	123	470	•101	*162	18	*16	11	74	.345	36	28	51	274	14	7	.976
	—Cleveland (A.L.)	OF	21	18	9	3	1	0	1	1	.167	3	2	0	3	0	0	1.000
1993	—Charlotte (Int'l)	OF	17	76	10	22	6	2	3	7	.289	3	10	4	38	1	0	1.000
	—Cleveland (A.L.)	OF	131	458	71	123	19	5	6	60	.269	37	58	17	273	*19	5	.983
Major league totals (3 years)			173	519	84	135	22	5	7	66	.260	42	66	18	316	20	5	.985

KLESKO, RYAN

1B, BRAVES

PERSONAL: Born June 12, 1971, in Westminster, Calif.... 6-3/220.... Throws left, bats left.... Full name: Ryan Anthony Klesko.
HIGH SCHOOL: Westminster (Calif.).
TRANSACTIONS/CAREER NOTES: Selected by Atlanta Braves organization in fifth round of free-agent draft (June 5, 1989).
HONORS: Named Southern League Most Valuable Player (1991).

Year	Team (League)	Pos.	G	AB	R	H	2B	3B	HR	RBI	Avg.	BB	SO	SB	PO	A	E	Avg.
			BATTING												FIELDING			
1989	—GC Braves (GCL)	DH	17	57	14	23	5	4	1	16	.404	6	6	4	...	...	...	...
	—Sumter (S. Atl.)	1B	25	90	17	26	6	0	1	12	.289	11	14	1	173	11	4	.979
1990	—Sumter (S. Atl.)	1B	63	231	41	85	15	1	10	38	.368	31	30	13	575	43	14	.978
	—Durham (Carolina)	1B	77	292	40	80	16	1	7	47	.274	32	53	10	490	34	13	.976
1991	—Greenville (South.)	1B	126	419	64	122	22	3	14	67	.291	75	60	14	1043	57	*17	.985
1992	—Richmond (Int'l)	1B	123	418	63	105	22	2	17	59	.251	41	72	3	947	51	*11	.989
	—Atlanta (N.L.)	1B	13	14	0	0	0	0	0	1	.000	0	5	0	25	0	0	1.000
1993	—Richmond (Int'l)	1B-OF	98	343	59	94	14	2	22	74	.274	47	69	4	587	45	12	.981
	—Atlanta (N.L.)	1B-OF	22	17	3	6	1	0	2	5	.353	3	4	0	8	0	0	1.000
Major league totals (2 years)			35	31	3	6	1	0	2	6	.194	3	9	0	33	0	0	1.000

KLINK, JOE

P, MARLINS

PERSONAL: Born February 3, 1962, in Johnstown, Pa.... 5-11/175.... Throws left, bats left.... Full name: Joseph Charles Klink.

HIGH SCHOOL: Chaminade (Hollywood, Fla.).

COLLEGE: Biscayne College (Fla.).

TRANSACTIONS/CAREER NOTES: Selected by New York Mets organization in 36th round of free-agent draft (June 6, 1983).... Traded by Mets organization with P Bill Latham and OF Billy Beane to Minnesota Twins for 2B Tim Teufel and OF Pat Crosby (January 16, 1986).... Traded by Twins organization to Oakland Athletics for a player to be named later (March 31, 1988); Twins organization acquired P Russ Kibler to complete deal (June 25, 1988).... On Oakland disabled list (June 6-July 11, 1991); included rehabilitation assignment to Modesto (July 4-11).... On Oakland disabled list (March 28, 1992-entire season).... Granted free agency (December 19, 1992).... Signed by Florida Marlins organization (January 27, 1993).

K

Year	Team (League)	W	L	Pct.	ERA	G	GS	CG	ShO	Sv.	IP	H	R	ER	BB	SO
1983	—Columbia (S. Atl.)	2	2	.500	4.62	12	1	0	0	0	25⅓	24	16	13	14	14
1984	—Columbia (S. Atl.)	5	4	.556	3.49	31	0	0	0	11	38⅔	30	19	15	28	49
1985	—Lynchburg (Caro.)	3	3	.500	2.26	44	0	0	0	5	51⅔	41	16	13	26	59
1986	—Orlando (Southern)■	4	5	.444	2.51	45	0	0	0	11	68	59	24	19	37	63
1987	—Portland (PCL)	0	0	...	4.30	12	0	0	0	0	23	25	14	11	13	14
	—Minnesota (A.L.)	0	1	.000	6.65	12	0	0	0	0	23	37	18	17	11	17
1988	—Huntsville (South.)■	1	2	.333	0.78	21	0	0	0	3	34⅔	25	6	3	14	30
	—Tacoma (PCL)	2	1	.667	5.12	27	0	0	0	1	38⅔	47	29	22	17	32
1989	—Huntsville (South.)	4	4	.500	2.82	57	0	0	0	*26	60⅔	46	19	19	23	59
	—Tacoma (PCL)	0	0	...	0.00	6	0	0	0	0	6⅔	2	0	0	2	5
1990	—Oakland (A.L.)	0	0	...	2.04	40	0	0	0	1	39⅔	34	9	9	18	19
1991	—Oakland (A.L.)	10	3	.769	4.35	62	0	0	0	2	62	60	30	30	21	34
	—Modesto (Calif.)	0	0	...	3.60	3	3	0	0	0	5	4	2	2	1	1
1992	—	Did not play.														
1993	—Florida (N.L.)■	0	2	.000	5.02	59	0	0	0	0	37⅔	37	22	21	24	22
A.L. totals (3 years)		10	4	.714	4.04	114	0	0	0	3	124⅔	131	57	56	50	70
N.L. totals (1 year)		0	2	.000	5.02	59	0	0	0	0	37⅔	37	22	21	24	22
Major league totals (4 years)		10	6	.625	4.27	173	0	0	0	3	162⅓	168	79	77	74	92

CHAMPIONSHIP SERIES RECORD

Year	Team (League)	W	L	Pct.	ERA	G	GS	CG	ShO	Sv.	IP	H	R	ER	BB	SO
1990	—Oakland (A.L.)	Did not play.														

WORLD SERIES RECORD

Year	Team (League)	W	L	Pct.	ERA	G	GS	CG	ShO	Sv.	IP	H	R	ER	BB	SO
1990	—Oakland (A.L.)	0	0	...	...	1	0	0	0	0	0	0	0	0	1	0

KMAK, JOE

C, METS

PERSONAL: Born May 3, 1963, in Napa, Calif.... 6-0/185.... Throws right, bats right.... Full name: Joseph Robert Kmak.... Name pronounced KAY-mak.

HIGH SCHOOL: Serra (San Mateo, Calif.).

COLLEGE: UC Santa Barbara.

TRANSACTIONS/CAREER NOTES: Selected by San Francisco Giants organization in 10th round of free-agent draft (June 3, 1985).... Signed as free agent by Milwaukee Brewers organization (January 20, 1990).... On disabled list (June 7-July 26, 1992).... Claimed on waivers by New York Mets (November 18, 1993).

STATISTICAL NOTES: Led American Association catchers with 10 double plays in 1991.

Year	Team (League)	Pos.	G	AB	R	H	2B	3B	HR	RBI	Avg.	BB	SO	SB	PO	A	E	Avg.
			BATTING												FIELDING			
1985	—Everett (N'west)	C	40	129	21	40	10	1	1	14	.310	20	23	0	175	21	3	.985
1986	—Fresno (California)	C	60	163	23	44	5	0	1	9	.270	15	38	3	203	26	3	.987
1987	—Fresno (California)	C	48	154	18	34	8	0	0	12	.221	15	32	1	323	35	4	.989
	—Shreveport (Texas)	C	15	41	5	8	0	1	0	3	.195	3	4	0	87	11	2	.980
1988	—Shreveport (Texas)	C	71	178	16	40	5	2	1	14	.225	11	19	0	325	35	6	.984
1989	—Reno (California)	C	78	248	39	68	10	5	4	34	.274	40	41	8	459	60	5	.990
1990	—El Paso (Texas)■	C	35	109	8	31	3	2	2	11	.284	7	22	0	194	28	2	.991
	—Denver (A.A.)	C	28	95	12	22	3	0	1	10	.232	4	16	2	160	20	6	.968
1991	—Denver (A.A.)	C	100	295	34	70	17	2	1	33	.237	28	45	7	579	*77	5	*.992
1992	—Denver (A.A.)	C	67	225	27	70	11	4	3	31	.311	19	39	6	351	54	3	.993
1993	—Milwaukee (A.L.)	C	51	110	9	24	5	0	0	7	.218	14	13	6	172	23	0	1.000
	—New Orleans (A.A.)	C	24	76	9	23	3	2	1	13	.303	8	14	1	106	18	2	.984
Major league totals (1 year)			51	110	9	24	5	0	0	7	.218	14	13	6	172	23	0	1.000

KNOBLAUCH, CHUCK
2B, TWINS

PERSONAL: Born July 7, 1968, in Houston. . . . 5-9/181. . . . Throws right, bats right. . . . Full name: Edward Charles Knoblauch. . . . Son of Ray Knoblauch, minor league pitcher (1947-56); and nephew of Ed Knoblauch, minor league outfielder (1938-42 and 1947-55). . . . Name pronounced NOB-lock.
HIGH SCHOOL: Bellaire (Houston).
COLLEGE: Texas A&M.
TRANSACTIONS/CAREER NOTES: Selected by Philadelphia Phillies organization in 18th round of free-agent draft (June 2, 1986). . . . Selected by Minnesota Twins organization in first round (25th pick overall) of free-agent draft (June 5, 1989).
HONORS: Named A.L. Rookie Player of the Year by THE SPORTING NEWS (1991). . . . Named A.L. Rookie of the Year by Baseball Writers' Association of America (1991).

			BATTING												FIELDING			
Year	Team (League)	Pos.	G	AB	R	H	2B	3B	HR	RBI	Avg.	BB	SO	SB	PO	A	E	Avg.
1989	—Kenosha (Midwest)..	SS	51	196	29	56	13	1	2	19	.286	32	23	9	60	124	21	.898
	—Visalia (California)...	SS	18	77	20	28	10	0	0	21	.364	6	11	4	23	52	10	.882
1990	—Orlando (Southern)..	2B	118	432	74	125	23	6	2	53	.289	63	31	23	275	300	20	.966
1991	—Minnesota (A.L.)......	2B	151	565	78	159	24	6	1	50	.281	59	40	25	249	460	18	.975
1992	—Minnesota (A.L.)......	2B-SS	155	600	104	178	19	6	2	56	.297	88	60	34	306	415	6	.992
1993	—Minnesota (A.L.)......	2B-SS-OF	153	602	82	167	27	4	2	41	.277	65	44	29	302	431	9	.988
Major league totals (3 years)			459	1767	264	504	70	16	5	147	.285	212	144	88	857	1306	33	.985

CHAMPIONSHIP SERIES RECORD

			BATTING												FIELDING			
Year	Team (League)	Pos.	G	AB	R	H	2B	3B	HR	RBI	Avg.	BB	SO	SB	PO	A	E	Avg.
1991	—Minnesota (A.L.)......	2B	5	20	5	7	2	0	0	3	.350	3	3	2	8	14	0	1.000

WORLD SERIES RECORD

			BATTING												FIELDING			
Year	Team (League)	Pos.	G	AB	R	H	2B	3B	HR	RBI	Avg.	BB	SO	SB	PO	A	E	Avg.
1991	—Minnesota (A.L.)......	2B	7	26	3	8	1	0	0	2	.308	4	2	4	15	14	1	.967

ALL-STAR GAME RECORD

			BATTING											FIELDING			
Year	League	Pos.	AB	R	H	2B	3B	HR	RBI	Avg.	BB	SO	SB	PO	A	E	Avg.
1992	—American..................	PH-2B	1	0	0	0	0	0	0	.000	1	0	0	0	0	0	...

KNORR, RANDY
C, BLUE JAYS

PERSONAL: Born November 12, 1968, in San Gabriel, Calif. . . . 6-2/215. . . . Throws right, bats right. . . . Full name: Randy Duane Knorr. . . . Name pronounced NOR.
HIGH SCHOOL: Baldwin Park (Calif.).
TRANSACTIONS/CAREER NOTES: Selected by Toronto Blue Jays organization in 10th round of free-agent draft (June 2, 1986). . . . On disabled list (June 24-July 4, 1986 and May 10, 1989-remainder of season). . . . On Syracuse disabled list (May 11-23, 1992). . . . On Toronto disabled list (August 20-September 30, 1992).
STATISTICAL NOTES: Led South Atlantic League catchers with 960 total chances and 25 passed balls in 1988.

			BATTING												FIELDING			
Year	Team (League)	Pos.	G	AB	R	H	2B	3B	HR	RBI	Avg.	BB	SO	SB	PO	A	E	Avg.
1986	—Medicine Hat (Pio.)..	1B	55	215	21	58	13	0	4	52	.270	17	53	0	451	29	10	.980
1987	—Myrtle Beach (SAL)..	C-1B-2B	46	129	17	34	4	0	6	21	.264	6	46	0	95	7	1	.990
	—Medicine Hat (Pio.)..	C	26	106	21	31	7	0	10	24	.292	5	26	0	70	5	4	.949
1988	—Myrtle Beach (SAL)..	C	117	364	43	85	13	0	9	42	.234	41	91	0	*870	75	15	.984
1989	—Dunedin (Fla. St.).....	C	33	122	13	32	6	0	6	23	.262	6	21	0	186	20	2	.990
1990	—Knoxville (South.)....	C	116	392	51	108	12	1	13	64	.276	31	83	0	599	72	15	.978
1991	—Knoxville (South.)....	C-1B	24	74	7	13	4	0	0	4	.176	10	18	2	136	16	2	.987
	—Syracuse (Int'l)........	C	91	342	29	89	20	0	5	44	.260	23	58	1	477	49	7	.987
	—Toronto (A.L.)..........	C	3	1	0	0	0	0	0	0	.000	1	1	0	6	1	0	1.000
1992	—Syracuse (Int'l)........	C	61	228	27	62	13	1	11	27	.272	17	38	1	220	22	3	.988
	—Toronto (A.L.)..........	C	8	19	1	5	0	0	1	2	.263	1	5	0	33	3	0	1.000
1993	—Toronto (A.L.)..........	C	39	101	11	25	3	2	4	20	.248	9	29	0	168	20	0	1.000
Major league totals (3 years)			50	121	12	30	3	2	5	22	.248	11	35	0	207	24	0	1.000

CHAMPIONSHIP SERIES RECORD

			BATTING												FIELDING			
Year	Team (League)	Pos.	G	AB	R	H	2B	3B	HR	RBI	Avg.	BB	SO	SB	PO	A	E	Avg.
1992	—Toronto (A.L.)..........							Did not play.										
1993	—Toronto (A.L.)..........							Did not play.										

WORLD SERIES RECORD

			BATTING												FIELDING			
Year	Team (League)	Pos.	G	AB	R	H	2B	3B	HR	RBI	Avg.	BB	SO	SB	PO	A	E	Avg.
1992	—Toronto (A.L.)..........							Did not play.										
1993	—Toronto (A.L.)..........	C	1	0	0	0	0	0	0	0	...	0	0	0	3	0	0	1.000
World Series totals (1 year)			1	0	0	0	0	0	0	0	...	0	0	0	3	0	0	1.000

KNUDSEN, KURT
P, TIGERS

PERSONAL: Born February 20, 1967, in Arlington Heights, Ill. . . . 6-3/200. . . . Throws right, bats right. . . . Full name: Kurt David Knudsen. . . . Name pronounced NOOD-sin.
HIGH SCHOOL: Del Campo (Fair Oaks, Calif.).
COLLEGE: American River College (Calif.) and Miami (Fla.).
TRANSACTIONS/CAREER NOTES: Selected by Pittsburgh Pirates organization in eighth round of free-agent draft (June 2, 1987).

... Selected by Detroit Tigers organization in ninth round of free-agent draft (June 1, 1988).... On London disabled list (April 10-22, 1991).... On Detroit disabled list (August 19-September 19, 1993).

Year	Team (League)	W	L	Pct.	ERA	G	GS	CG	ShO	Sv.	IP	H	R	ER	BB	SO
1988	—Bristol (Appal.)	0	0	...	0.00	2	0	0	0	0	2⅓	4	3	0	1	0
	—Fayetteville (SAL)	3	1	.750	1.35	12	0	0	0	1	20	8	4	3	9	22
	—Lakeland (Fla. St.)	0	0	...	0.96	7	0	0	0	0	9⅓	7	2	1	7	6
1989	—Lakeland (Fla. St.)	3	2	.600	2.15	45	0	0	0	10	54⅓	43	16	13	22	68
1990	—Lakeland (Fla. St.)	5	0	1.000	2.28	14	8	0	0	3	67	42	18	17	22	70
	—London (Eastern)	2	1	.667	2.08	15	0	0	0	1	26	15	6	6	11	26
1991	—London (Eastern)	2	3	.400	3.48	34	0	0	0	6	51⅔	42	29	20	30	56
	—Toledo (Int'l)	1	2	.333	1.47	12	0	0	0	0	18⅓	13	11	3	10	28
1992	—Toledo (Int'l)	3	1	.750	2.08	12	0	0	0	1	21⅔	11	5	5	6	19
	—Detroit (A.L.)	2	3	.400	4.58	48	1	0	0	5	70⅔	70	39	36	41	51
1993	—Toledo (Int'l)	2	2	.500	3.78	23	0	0	0	6	33⅓	24	15	14	11	39
	—Detroit (A.L.)	3	2	.600	4.78	30	0	0	0	2	37⅔	41	22	20	16	29
Major league totals (2 years)		5	5	.500	4.65	78	1	0	0	7	108⅓	111	61	56	57	80

KNUDSON, MARK

P

PERSONAL: Born October 28, 1960, in Denver.... 6-5/200.... Throws right, bats right. ... Full name: Mark Richard Knudson.... Name pronounced kuh-NEWT-son.
HIGH SCHOOL: Natrona County (Casper, Wyo.).
COLLEGE: Colorado State.
TRANSACTIONS/CAREER NOTES: Selected by Houston Astros organization in third round of free-agent draft (June 7, 1982).... On Houston disabled list (July 15-August 5, 1985).... Traded by Astros organization to Milwaukee Brewers organization (August 21, 1986), completing deal in which Brewers traded P Danny Darwin to Astros for P Don August and a player to be named later (August 15, 1986).... On Milwaukee disabled list (May 2-June 7, 1991); included rehabilitation assignment to Denver (May 28-June 7).... Granted free agency (October 16, 1991).... Signed by Las Vegas, San Diego Padres organization (February 29, 1992).... Granted free agency (October 15, 1992).... Signed by Colorado Rockies (October 29, 1992).... Granted free agency (May 19, 1993).

Year	Team (League)	W	L	Pct.	ERA	G	GS	CG	ShO	Sv.	IP	H	R	ER	BB	SO
1982	—Day. Beach (FSL)	2	6	.250	4.77	12	11	2	1	0	60⅓	75	35	32	23	15
1983	—Day. Beach (FSL)	5	3	.625	2.40	12	12	2	1	0	78⅔	80	29	21	22	47
	—Columbus (South.)	4	5	.444	4.26	13	13	3	0	0	69⅔	82	40	33	21	28
1984	—Columbus (South.)	4	5	.444	2.23	14	14	3	0	0	101	100	32	25	27	54
	—Tucson (PCL)	4	6	.400	3.64	13	13	1	0	0	84	93	41	34	20	42
1985	—Tucson (PCL)	8	5	.615	4.01	24	22	4	2	0	146	171	69	65	37	68
	—Houston (N.L.)	0	2	.000	9.00	2	2	0	0	0	11	21	11	11	3	4
1986	—Tucs.-Vanc. (PCL)■	6	6	.500	4.13	17	16	4	1	0	106⅔	124	54	49	26	63
	—Houston (N.L.)	1	5	.167	4.22	9	7	0	0	0	42⅔	48	23	20	15	20
	—Milwaukee (A.L.)	0	1	.000	7.64	4	1	0	0	0	17⅔	22	15	15	5	9
1987	—Denver (A.A.)	7	2	.778	5.86	14	14	1	0	0	78⅓	89	53	51	30	37
	—Milwaukee (A.L.)	4	4	.500	5.37	15	8	1	0	0	62	88	46	37	14	26
1988	—Denver (A.A.)	11	8	.579	3.40	24	22	6	0	0	164⅓	180	67	62	33	66
	—Milwaukee (A.L.)	0	0	...	1.13	5	0	0	0	0	16	17	3	2	2	7
1989	—Milwaukee (A.L.)	8	5	.615	3.35	40	7	1	0	0	123⅔	110	50	46	29	47
1990	—Milwaukee (A.L.)	10	9	.526	4.12	30	27	4	2	0	168⅓	187	84	77	40	56
1991	—Milwaukee (A.L.)	1	3	.250	7.97	12	7	0	0	0	35	54	33	31	15	23
	—Denver (A.A.)	4	4	.500	5.40	13	10	2	0	1	51⅔	73	34	31	13	28
1992	—Las Vegas (PCL)■	11	7	.611	4.47	37	20	1	1	3	147	184	90	73	47	79
1993	—Colo. Springs (PCL)■	3	1	.750	2.25	5	5	1	1	0	28	30	12	7	8	15
	—Colorado (N.L.)	0	0	...	22.24	4	0	0	0	0	5⅔	16	14	14	5	3
A.L. totals (6 years)		23	22	.511	4.43	106	50	6	2	0	422⅔	478	231	208	105	168
N.L. totals (3 years)		1	7	.125	6.83	15	9	0	0	0	59⅓	85	48	45	23	27
Major league totals (8 years)		24	29	.453	4.72	121	59	6	2	0	482	563	279	253	128	195

KOELLING, BRIAN

2B, REDS

PERSONAL: Born June 11, 1969, in Cincinnati.... 6-1/185.... Throws right, bats right. ... Full name: Brian Wayne Koelling.... Name pronounced KELL-ing.
HIGH SCHOOL: Taylor (North Bend, O.).
COLLEGE: Bowling Green State.
TRANSACTIONS/CAREER NOTES: Selected by Cincinnati Reds organization in 14th round of free-agent draft (June 3, 1991).
STATISTICAL NOTES: Led Southern League second basemen with 289 assists in 1993.

			BATTING												FIELDING			
Year	Team (League)	Pos.	G	AB	R	H	2B	3B	HR	RBI	Avg.	BB	SO	SB	PO	A	E	Avg.
1991	—Billings (Pioneer)	SS	22	85	17	30	7	1	2	13	.353	14	23	6	35	43	4	.951
	—Ced. Rap. (Midw.)	SS	35	147	27	38	6	0	1	12	.259	14	39	22	64	92	9	.945
1992	—Ced. Rap. (Midw.)	SS	129	460	81	121	18	7	5	43	.263	49	137	47	*196	280	38	.926
1993	—Chatt. (South.)	2B-SS	110	430	64	119	17	6	4	47	.277	32	105	34	231	†298	19	.965
	—Cincinnati (N.L.)	2B-SS	7	15	2	1	0	0	0	0	.067	0	2	0	6	12	1	.947
	—Indianapolis (A.A.)	2B	2	9	1	2	0	0	0	0	.222	0	1	0	5	8	0	1.000
Major league totals (1 year)			7	15	2	1	0	0	0	0	.067	0	2	0	6	12	1	.947

KOSLOFSKI, KEVIN

OF, ROYALS

PERSONAL: Born September 24, 1966, in Decatur, Ill.... 5-8/175.... Throws right, bats left.... Full name: Kevin Craig Koslofski.
HIGH SCHOOL: Maroa (Ill.)-Forsyth.
TRANSACTIONS/CAREER NOTES: Selected by Kansas City Royals organization in 20th round of free-agent draft (June 4, 1984).... Granted free agency (October 15, 1990).... Re-signed by Royals organization

(January 13, 1991).... On Memphis disabled list (May 15-27, 1991).... On Omaha disabled list (May 12-24, 1993).

Year	Team (League)	Pos.	G	AB	R	H	2B	3B	HR	RBI	Avg.	BB	SO	SB	PO	A	E	Avg.
			BATTING												FIELDING			
1984	—Eugene (N'west)	OF	53	155	23	29	2	2	1	10	.187	25	37	10	46	1	2	.959
1985	—GC Royals (GCL)	OF	33	108	17	27	4	2	0	11	.250	12	19	7	43	3	1	.979
1986	—Fort Myers (FSL)	OF	103	331	44	84	13	5	0	29	.254	47	59	12	178	*16	7	.965
1987	—Fort Myers (FSL)	OF	109	330	46	80	12	3	0	25	.242	46	63	25	185	10	6	.970
1988	—Baseball City (FSL)	OF	108	368	52	97	7	8	3	30	.264	44	71	32	174	14	2	.989
1989	—Baseball City (FSL)	OF	116	343	65	89	10	3	4	33	.259	51	57	41	224	7	8	.967
1990	—Memphis (South.)	OF	118	367	52	78	11	5	3	32	.213	54	89	12	221	*16	6	.975
1991	—Memphis (South.)	OF	81	287	41	93	15	3	7	39	.324	33	56	10	176	12	5	.974
	—Omaha (A.A.)	OF	25	94	13	28	3	2	2	19	.298	15	19	4	61	3	1	.985
1992	—Omaha (A.A.)	OF	78	280	29	87	12	5	4	32	.311	21	47	8	210	7	3	.986
	—Kansas City (A.L.)	OF	55	133	20	33	0	2	3	13	.248	12	23	2	107	5	1	.991
1993	—Omaha (A.A.)	OF	111	395	58	109	22	5	7	45	.276	43	73	15	285	13	5	.983
	—Kansas City (A.L.)	OF	15	26	4	7	0	0	1	2	.269	4	5	0	20	2	0	1.000
Major league totals (2 years)			70	159	24	40	0	2	4	15	.252	16	28	2	127	7	1	.993

KRAMER, TOM

P, INDIANS

PERSONAL: Born January 9, 1968, in Cincinnati.... 6-0/205.... Throws right, bats both.... Full name: Thomas Joseph Kramer.
HIGH SCHOOL: Roger Bacon (Cincinnati).
COLLEGE: John A. Logan College (Ill.).
TRANSACTIONS/CAREER NOTES: Selected by Cleveland Indians organization in fifth round of free-agent draft (June 2, 1987).... On Cleveland disabled list (July 3-21, 1993).

Year	Team (League)	W	L	Pct.	ERA	G	GS	CG	ShO	Sv.	IP	H	R	ER	BB	SO
1987	—Burlington (Appal.)	7	3	.700	3.01	12	11	2	1	1	71⅔	57	31	24	26	71
1988	—Waterloo (Midw.)	14	7	.667	2.54	27	27	*10	2	0	*198⅔	173	70	56	60	152
1989	—Kinston (Carolina)	9	5	.643	2.60	18	5	1	0	0	131⅔	97	44	38	44	89
	—Cant./Akr. (East.)	1	6	.143	6.23	10	8	1	0	0	43⅓	58	34	30	20	26
1990	—Kinston (Carolina)	7	4	.636	2.85	16	16	2	1	0	98	82	34	31	29	96
	—Cant./Akr. (East.)	6	3	.667	3.00	12	10	2	0	0	72	67	25	24	14	46
1991	—Cant./Akr. (East.)	7	3	.700	2.38	35	5	0	0	6	79⅓	61	23	21	34	61
	—Colo. Springs (PCL)	1	0	1.000	0.79	10	1	0	0	4	11⅓	5	1	1	5	18
	—Cleveland (A.L.)	0	0	...	17.36	4	0	0	0	0	4⅔	10	9	9	6	4
1992	—Colo. Springs (PCL)	8	3	.727	4.88	38	3	0	0	3	75⅔	88	43	41	43	72
1993	—Cleveland (A.L.)	7	3	.700	4.02	39	16	1	0	0	121	126	60	54	59	71
Major league totals (2 years)		7	3	.700	4.51	43	16	1	0	0	125⅔	136	69	63	65	75

KREUTER, CHAD

C, TIGERS

PERSONAL: Born August 26, 1964, in Greenbrae, Calif.... 6-2/195.... Throws right, bats both.... Full name: Chad Michael Kreuter.... Name pronounced CREW-ter.
HIGH SCHOOL: Redwood (Calif.).
COLLEGE: Pepperdine.
TRANSACTIONS/CAREER NOTES: Selected by Texas Rangers organization in fifth round of free-agent draft (June 3, 1985).... Granted free agency (October 15, 1991).... Signed by Toledo, Detroit Tigers organization (January 2, 1992).
RECORDS: Shares major league record for most hits in one inning in first major league game—2 (September 14, 1988, fifth inning).
STATISTICAL NOTES: Led Carolina League catchers with 21 errors and 17 double plays and tied for lead with 113 assists in 1986. ... Tied for Texas League lead in double plays by catcher with nine in 1988.... Led A.L. with 21 passed balls in 1989.... Switch-hit home runs in one game (September 7, 1993).
MISCELLANEOUS: Batted righthanded only (1985 and 1990).

Year	Team (League)	Pos.	G	AB	R	H	2B	3B	HR	RBI	Avg.	BB	SO	SB	PO	A	E	Avg.
			BATTING												FIELDING			
1985	—Burlington (Midw.)	C	69	199	25	53	9	0	4	26	.266	38	48	3	349	34	8	.980
1986	—Salem (Carolina)	C-OF-3B	125	387	55	85	21	2	6	49	.220	67	82	5	613	‡115	†21	.972
1987	—Charlotte (Fla. St.)	C-OF-3B	85	281	36	61	18	1	9	40	.217	31	32	1	380	54	8	.982
1988	—Tulsa (Texas)	C	108	358	46	95	24	6	3	51	.265	55	66	2	603	71	•13	.981
	—Texas (A.L.)	C	16	51	3	14	2	1	1	5	.275	7	13	0	93	8	1	.990
1989	—Texas (A.L.)	C	87	158	16	24	3	0	5	9	.152	27	40	0	453	26	4	.992
	—Okla. City (A.A.)	C	26	87	10	22	3	0	0	6	.253	13	11	1	146	14	2	.988
1990	—Texas (A.L.)	C	22	22	2	1	1	0	0	2	.045	8	9	0	39	4	1	.977
	—Okla. City (A.A.)	C	92	291	41	65	17	1	7	35	.223	52	80	0	559	64	10	.984
1991	—Texas (A.L.)	C	3	4	0	0	0	0	0	0	.000	0	1	0	5	0	0	1.000
	—Okla. City (A.A.)	C	24	70	14	19	6	0	1	12	.271	18	16	2	146	23	7	.960
	—Tulsa (Texas)	C	42	128	23	30	5	1	2	10	.234	29	23	1	269	27	4	.987
1992	—Detroit (A.L.)■	C	67	190	22	48	9	0	2	16	.253	20	38	0	271	22	5	.983
1993	—Detroit (A.L.)	C-1B	119	374	59	107	23	3	15	51	.286	49	92	2	522	70	7	.988
Major league totals (6 years)			314	799	102	194	38	4	23	83	.243	111	193	2	1383	130	18	.988

KRIVDA, RICK

P, ORIOLES

PERSONAL: Born January 19, 1970, in McKeesport, Pa.... 6-1/180.... Throws left, bats right. ... Full name: Rick Michael Krivda.
HIGH SCHOOL: McKeesport (Pa.) Area.
COLLEGE: California (Pa.).
TRANSACTIONS/CAREER NOTES: Selected by Baltimore Orioles organization in 23rd round of free-agent draft (June 3, 1991).

Year	Team (League)	W	L	Pct.	ERA	G	GS	CG	ShO	Sv.	IP	H	R	ER	BB	SO
1991	—Bluefield (Appal.)	7	1	.875	1.88	15	8	0	0	1	67	48	20	14	24	79
1992	—Kane Co. (Midw.)	12	5	.706	3.03	18	18	2	0	0	121⅔	108	53	41	41	124
	—Frederick (Caro.)	5	1	.833	2.98	9	9	1	1	0	57⅓	51	23	19	15	64
1993	—Bowie (Eastern)	7	5	.583	3.08	22	22	0	0	0	125⅔	114	46	43	50	108
	—Rochester (Int'l)	3	0	1.000	1.89	5	5	0	0	0	33⅓	20	7	7	16	23

KRUEGER, BILL

P, TIGERS

PERSONAL: Born April 24, 1958, in Waukegan, Ill. . . . 6-5/205. . . . Throws left, bats left. . . . Full name: William Culp Krueger. . . . Name pronounced CREW-ger.
HIGH SCHOOL: McMinnville (Ore.).
COLLEGE: Portland (bachelor of arts degree in business administration, 1979).
TRANSACTIONS/CAREER NOTES: Signed as free agent by Oakland Athletics organization (July 12, 1980). . . . On disabled list (August 5, 1983-remainder of season). . . . On Oakland disabled list (May 6-August 8, 1986); included rehabilitation assignment to Madison (July 4-8) and Tacoma (July 10-18 and July 21-27). . . . Traded by A's organization to Los Angeles Dodgers organization for P Tim Meeks (June 23, 1987). . . . Released by Dodgers (November 12, 1987). . . . Re-signed by Dodgers organization (January 1, 1988). . . . Traded by Dodgers to Pittsburgh Pirates for P Jim Neidlinger (October 3, 1988). . . . Released by Pirates (March 28, 1989). . . . Signed by Denver, Milwaukee Brewers organization (April 7, 1989). . . . On Milwaukee disabled list (August 10-31, 1990); included rehabilitation assignment to Beloit (August 29-31). . . . Granted free agency (November 5, 1990). . . . Signed by Seattle Mariners (December 19, 1990). . . . Granted free agency (October 30, 1991). . . . Signed by Minnesota Twins organization (January 29, 1992). . . . Traded by Twins to Montreal Expos for OF Darren Reed (August 31, 1992). . . . Granted free agency (October 30, 1992). . . . Signed by Detroit Tigers (December 11, 1992). . . . On Detroit disabled list (July 4-August 22, 1993); included rehabilitation assignment to Toledo (August 9-22).
STATISTICAL NOTES: Pitched seven-inning 2-0 no-hit victory for Albuquerque against Phoenix (August 14, 1987, second game).

K

Year	Team (League)	W	L	Pct.	ERA	G	GS	CG	ShO	Sv.	IP	H	R	ER	BB	SO
1980	—Medford (N'west)	0	4	.000	5.11	9	7	1	0	1	44	54	38	25	29	48
1981	—Modesto (Calif.)	3	5	.375	3.67	16	13	5	1	0	98	87	49	40	52	76
	—West Haven (East.)	3	6	.333	3.57	11	11	1	0	0	68	74	36	27	31	36
1982	—West Haven (East.)	15	9	.625	2.83	28	•27	7	•3	0	181	160	69	57	81	163
1983	—Oakland (A.L.)	7	6	.538	3.61	17	16	2	0	0	109⅔	104	54	44	53	58
1984	—Tacoma (PCL)	2	2	.500	3.69	5	5	2	0	0	31⅔	29	17	13	21	20
	—Oakland (A.L.)	10	10	.500	4.75	26	24	1	0	0	142	156	95	75	85	61
1985	—Oakland (A.L.)	9	10	.474	4.52	32	23	2	0	0	151⅓	165	95	76	69	56
	—Tacoma (PCL)	0	1	.000	9.31	2	2	0	0	0	9⅔	12	10	10	6	10
1986	—Oakland (A.L.)	1	2	.333	6.03	11	3	0	0	1	34⅓	40	25	23	13	10
	—Madison (Midwest)	0	0	. . .	0.00	1	0	0	0	0	2	1	0	0	1	1
	—Tacoma (PCL)	3	3	.500	4.64	8	8	2	1	0	52⅓	53	32	27	27	41
1987	—Oakland (A.L.)	0	3	.000	9.53	9	0	0	0	0	5⅔	9	7	6	8	2
	—Tac.-Albuq. (PCL)■	9	7	.563	4.06	24	24	6	2	0	146⅓	158	74	66	66	97
	—Los Angeles (N.L.)	0	0	. . .	0.00	2	0	0	0	0	2⅓	3	2	0	1	2
1988	—Albuquerque (PCL)	★15	5	.750	★3.01	27	26	7	★4	0	173⅓	167	74	58	69	114
	—Los Angeles (N.L.)	0	0	. . .	11.57	1	1	0	0	0	2⅓	4	3	3	2	1
1989	—Denver (A.A.)■	1	1	.500	2.03	2	2	0	0	0	13⅓	10	4	3	6	9
	—Milwaukee (A.L.)	3	2	.600	3.84	34	5	0	0	3	93⅔	96	43	40	33	72
1990	—Milwaukee (A.L.)	6	8	.429	3.98	30	17	0	0	0	129	137	70	57	54	64
	—Beloit (Midwest)	1	0	1.000	1.50	1	1	0	0	0	6	4	1	1	0	4
1991	—Seattle (A.L.)■	11	8	.579	3.60	35	25	1	0	0	175	194	82	70	60	91
1992	—Minnesota (A.L.)■	10	6	.625	4.30	27	27	2	2	0	161⅓	166	82	77	46	86
	—Montreal (N.L.)■	0	2	.000	6.75	9	2	0	0	0	17⅓	23	13	13	7	13
1993	—Detroit (A.L.)■	6	4	.600	3.40	32	7	0	0	0	82	90	43	31	30	60
	—Toledo (Int'l)	1	0	1.000	1.59	3	3	0	0	0	11⅓	11	2	2	3	8
A.L. totals (10 years)		63	59	.516	4.14	253	147	8	2	4	1084	1157	596	499	451	560
N.L. totals (3 years)		0	2	.000	6.55	12	3	0	0	0	22	30	18	16	10	16
Major league totals (11 years)		63	61	.508	4.19	265	150	8	2	4	1106	1187	614	515	461	576

KRUK, JOHN

1B, PHILLIES

PERSONAL: Born February 9, 1961, in Charleston, W.Va. . . . 5-10/220. . . . Throws left, bats left. . . . Full name: John Martin Kruk.
HIGH SCHOOL: Keyser (W.Va.).
COLLEGE: Allegany Community College (Md.).
TRANSACTIONS/CAREER NOTES: Selected by Pittsburgh Pirates organization in third round of free-agent draft (January 13, 1981). . . . Selected by San Diego Padres organization in secondary phase of free-agent draft (June 8, 1981). . . . On disabled list (May 5-21, 1989). . . . Traded by Padres with IF Randy Ready to Philadelphia Phillies for OF Chris James (June 2, 1989). . . . On disabled list (July 3-July 28, 1989).
STATISTICAL NOTES: Led Texas League with 13 sacrifice flies in 1983. . . . Led Pacific Coast League outfielders with four double plays in 1984.

				BATTING											FIELDING			
Year	Team (League)	Pos.	G	AB	R	H	2B	3B	HR	RBI	Avg.	BB	SO	SB	PO	A	E	Avg.
1981	—Walla Walla (N'west)	OF-1B	63	157	31	38	10	0	1	13	.242	56	45	7	108	5	2	.983
1982	—Reno (California)	OF-1B	125	441	82	137	30	8	11	92	.311	72	55	17	253	11	7	.974
1983	—Beaumont (Texas)	OF-1B-P	133	498	94	170	41	9	10	88	.341	69	54	13	304	22	8	.976
1984	—Las Vegas (PCL)	OF	115	340	56	111	25	6	11	57	.326	45	37	2	183	7	2	.990
1985	—Las Vegas (PCL)	OF-1B	123	422	61	148	29	4	7	59	★.351	67	48	2	356	18	7	.982
1986	—San Diego (N.L.)	OF-1B	122	278	33	86	16	2	4	38	.309	48	58	2	139	6	3	.980
	—Las Vegas (PCL)	OF-1B	6	28	6	13	3	1	0	9	.464	4	5	0	22	1	0	1.000
1987	—San Diego (N.L.)	1B-OF	138	447	72	140	14	2	20	91	.313	73	93	18	911	78	5	.995
1988	—San Diego (N.L.)	1B-OF	120	378	54	91	17	1	9	44	.241	80	68	5	634	37	3	.996

			BATTING												FIELDING			
Year	Team (League)	Pos.	G	AB	R	H	2B	3B	HR	RBI	Avg.	BB	SO	SB	PO	A	E	Avg.
1989	—S.D.-Phil. (N.L.)■	OF-1B	112	357	53	107	13	6	8	44	.300	44	53	3	212	9	4	.982
1990	—Philadelphia (N.L.)	OF-1B	142	443	52	129	25	8	7	67	.291	69	70	10	543	45	4	.993
1991	—Philadelphia (N.L.)	1B-OF	152	538	84	158	27	6	21	92	.294	67	100	7	848	53	3	.997
1992	—Philadelphia (N.L.)	1B-OF	144	507	86	164	30	4	10	70	.323	92	88	3	1037	58	8	.993
1993	—Philadelphia (N.L.)	1B	150	535	100	169	33	5	14	85	.316	111	87	6	1149	69	8	.993
Major league totals (8 years)			1080	3483	534	1044	175	34	93	531	.300	584	617	54	5473	355	38	.994

CHAMPIONSHIP SERIES RECORD

			BATTING												FIELDING			
Year	Team (League)	Pos.	G	AB	R	H	2B	3B	HR	RBI	Avg.	BB	SO	SB	PO	A	E	Avg.
1993	—Philadelphia (N.L.)	1B	6	24	4	6	2	1	1	5	.250	4	5	0	43	2	0	1.000

WORLD SERIES RECORD

			BATTING												FIELDING			
Year	Team (League)	Pos.	G	AB	R	H	2B	3B	HR	RBI	Avg.	BB	SO	SB	PO	A	E	Avg.
1993	—Philadelphia (N.L.)	1B	6	23	4	8	1	0	0	4	.348	7	7	0	42	3	0	1.000

ALL-STAR GAME RECORD

			BATTING										FIELDING			
Year	League	Pos.	AB	R	H	2B	3B	HR	RBI	Avg.	BB	SO	SB	PO	A	E	Avg.
1991	—National								Did not play.								
1992	—National	OF	2	1	2	0	0	0	0	1.000	0	0	0	0	1	1	.500
1993	—National	1B	3	0	0	0	0	0	0	.000	0	2	0	7	0	0	1.000
All-Star Game totals (2 years)			5	1	2	0	0	0	0	.400	0	2	0	7	1	1	.889

RECORD AS PITCHER

Year	Team (League)	W	L	Pct.	ERA	G	GS	CG	ShO	Sv.	IP	H	R	ER	BB	SO
1983	—Beaumont (Texas)	0	0	...	0.00	3	0	0	0	0	5	5	0	0	2	3

LAKE, STEVE

C, REDS

PERSONAL: Born March 14, 1957, in Inglewood, Calif. . . . 6-1/195. . . . Throws right, bats right. . . . Full name: Steven Michael Lake.

HIGH SCHOOL: Lennox (Calif.).

TRANSACTIONS/CAREER NOTES: Selected by Baltimore Orioles organization in third round of free-agent draft (June 4, 1975). . . . On disabled list (April 17-May 16, 1978). . . . Contract sold by Orioles organization to Milwaukee Brewers organization (December 21, 1978). . . . On disabled list (June 20-July 6, 1979). . . . Loaned by Brewers organization to Tucson, Houston Astros organization (April 5-September 7, 1982). . . . Traded by Brewers organization to Chicago Cubs for a player to be named later (April 1, 1983); Brewers organization acquired P Rich Buonantony to complete deal (October 24, 1983). . . . On Chicago disabled list (May 14-August 3, 1984); included rehabilitation assignment to Midland (July 23-August 3). . . . Released by Cubs (July 15, 1986). . . . Signed by Louisville, St. Louis Cardinals organization (July 24, 1986). . . . Traded by Cardinals with OF Curt Ford to Philadelphia Phillies for OF Milt Thompson (December 16, 1988). . . . On disabled list (August 28, 1989-remainder of season). . . . Granted free agency (November 13, 1989). . . . Re-signed by Phillies (December 6, 1989). . . . On disabled list (July 21-September 1, 1990). . . . Granted free agency (October 28, 1991). . . . Signed by Phoenix, San Francisco Giants organization (January 30, 1992). . . . Released by Phoenix (April 2, 1992). . . . Signed by Phillies (April 5, 1992). . . . On Philadelphia disabled list (July 28-September 11, 1992). . . . Granted free agency (October 27, 1992). . . . Signed by Cubs (December 2, 1992). . . . Released by Cubs (October 12, 1993). . . . Signed by Indianapolis, Cincinnati Reds organization (November 23, 1993).

STATISTICAL NOTES: Led Appalachian League with 15 passed balls in 1975.

			BATTING												FIELDING			
Year	Team (League)	Pos.	G	AB	R	H	2B	3B	HR	RBI	Avg.	BB	SO	SB	PO	A	E	Avg.
1975	—Bluefield (Appal.)	C	49	162	17	45	12	0	3	24	.278	12	21	3	254	*39	9	.970
1976	—Miami (Florida St.)	PH	1	1	0	1	0	0	0	1	1.000	0	0	0	...	...	...	...
1977	—Miami (Florida St.)	C	79	232	25	55	10	1	2	24	.237	5	36	2	357	47	6	.985
1978	—Miami (Florida St.)	C	69	223	19	57	10	0	2	26	.256	9	30	2	300	49	6	.983
1979	—Stockton (Calif.)■	C	94	329	36	93	12	3	6	40	.283	10	41	2	504	73	8	.986
1980	—Holyoke (Eastern)	C-OF	102	325	26	84	9	2	2	44	.258	13	27	3	445	107	10	.982
1981	—Vancouver (PCL)	C	109	348	27	80	14	1	2	38	.230	5	41	2	502	102	7	.989
1982	—Tucson (PCL)■	C	112	378	42	100	15	4	3	45	.265	17	28	5	504	91	12	.980
1983	—Chicago (N.L.)■	C	38	85	9	22	4	1	1	7	.259	2	6	0	115	22	0	1.000
1984	—Chicago (N.L.)	C	25	54	4	12	4	0	2	7	.222	0	7	0	72	13	4	.955
	—Midland (Texas)	C	9	25	2	4	0	0	0	1	.160	0	5	0	46	7	0	1.000
1985	—Chicago (N.L.)	C	58	119	5	18	2	0	1	11	.151	3	21	1	182	25	1	.995
1986	—Chi.-St.L. (N.L.)■	C	36	68	8	20	2	0	2	14	.294	3	7	0	105	9	2	.983
	—Iowa-Louis. (A.A.)	C	33	98	5	24	6	0	0	13	.245	2	20	0	140	21	2	.988
1987	—St. Louis (N.L.)	C	74	179	19	45	7	2	2	19	.251	10	18	0	253	21	1	.996
1988	—St. Louis (N.L.)	C	36	54	5	15	3	0	1	4	.278	3	15	0	51	8	1	.983
1989	—Philadelphia (N.L.)■	C	58	155	9	39	5	1	2	14	.252	12	20	0	262	33	3	.990
1990	—Philadelphia (N.L.)	C	29	80	4	20	2	0	0	6	.250	3	12	0	115	19	1	.993
1991	—Philadelphia (N.L.)	C	58	158	12	36	4	1	1	11	.228	2	26	0	277	25	2	.993
1992	—Philadelphia (N.L.)	C	20	53	3	13	2	0	1	2	.245	1	8	0	71	8	2	.975
1993	—Chicago (N.L.)■	C	44	120	11	27	6	0	5	13	.225	4	19	0	168	27	3	.985
Major league totals (11 years)			476	1125	89	267	41	5	18	108	.237	43	159	1	1671	210	20	.989

CHAMPIONSHIP SERIES RECORD

			BATTING												FIELDING			
Year	Team (League)	Pos.	G	AB	R	H	2B	3B	HR	RBI	Avg.	BB	SO	SB	PO	A	E	Avg.
1984	—Chicago (N.L.)	C	1	1	0	1	1	0	0	0	1.000	0	0	0	0	0	0	...

Year	Team (League)	Pos.	G	AB	R	H	2B	3B	HR	RBI	Avg.	BB	SO	SB	PO	A	E	Avg.
			BATTING												FIELDING			
1987	—St. Louis (N.L.)		Did not play.															
Championship series totals (1 year)			1	1	0	1	1	0	0	0	1.000	0	0	0	0	0	0	...

WORLD SERIES RECORD

Year	Team (League)	Pos.	G	AB	R	H	2B	3B	HR	RBI	Avg.	BB	SO	SB	PO	A	E	Avg.
			BATTING												FIELDING			
1987	—St. Louis (N.L.)	C	3	3	0	1	0	0	0	1	.333	0	0	0	8	1	0	1.000

LAKER, TIM

C, EXPOS

PERSONAL: Born November 27, 1969, in Encino, Calif. . . . 6-2/190. . . . Throws right, bats right. . . . Full name: Timothy John Laker.
HIGH SCHOOL: Simi Valley (Calif.).
COLLEGE: Oxnard (Calif.) College.
TRANSACTIONS/CAREER NOTES: Selected by Kansas City Royals organization in 49th round of free-agent draft (June 2, 1987). . . . Selected by Montreal Expos organization in sixth round of free-agent draft (June 1, 1988). . . . On Ottawa disabled list (April 30-May 14, 1993).
STATISTICAL NOTES: Led New York-Pennsylvania League with 16 passed balls in 1989. . . . Led Midwest League catchers with 125 assists, 18 errors and 944 total chances in 1990. . . . Tied for International League lead in errors by catcher with 11 in 1993.

Year	Team (League)	Pos.	G	AB	R	H	2B	3B	HR	RBI	Avg.	BB	SO	SB	PO	A	E	Avg.
			BATTING												FIELDING			
1988	—Jamestown (NYP)	C-OF	47	152	14	34	9	0	0	17	.224	8	30	2	236	22	2	.992
1989	—Rockford (Midw.)	C	14	48	4	11	1	1	0	4	.229	3	6	1	91	6	4	.960
	—Jamestown (NYP)	C	58	216	25	48	9	1	2	24	.222	16	40	8	437	61	8	.984
1990	—Rockford (Midw.)	C-OF	120	425	46	94	18	3	7	57	.221	32	83	7	802	†125	†18	.981
	—W.P. Beach (FSL)	C	2	3	0	0	0	0	0	0	.000	0	1	0	2	0	0	1.000
1991	—Harrisburg (East.)	C	11	35	4	10	1	0	1	5	.286	2	5	0	67	4	3	.959
	—W.P. Beach (FSL)	C	100	333	35	77	15	2	5	33	.231	22	51	10	560	87	*14	.979
1992	—Harrisburg (East.)	C	117	409	55	99	19	3	15	68	.242	39	89	3	630	62	*14	.980
	—Montreal (N.L.)	C	28	46	8	10	3	0	0	4	.217	2	14	1	102	8	1	.991
1993	—Montreal (N.L.)	C	43	86	3	17	2	1	0	7	.198	2	16	2	136	18	2	.987
	—Ottawa (Int'l)	C-1B	56	204	26	47	10	0	4	23	.230	21	41	3	341	37	‡11	.972
Major league totals (2 years)			71	132	11	27	5	1	0	11	.205	4	30	3	238	26	3	.989

LAMPKIN, TOM

C, GIANTS

PERSONAL: Born March 4, 1964, in Cincinnati. . . . 5-11/190. . . . Throws right, bats left. . . . Full name: Thomas Michael Lampkin.
HIGH SCHOOL: Blanchet (Seattle).
COLLEGE: Portland.
TRANSACTIONS/CAREER NOTES: Selected by Cleveland Indians organization in 11th round of free-agent draft (June 2, 1986). . . . On disabled list (July 6, 1989-remainder of season). . . . Traded by Indians organization to San Diego Padres for OF Alex Cole (July 11, 1990). . . . Traded by Padres to Milwaukee Brewers for future considerations (March 25, 1993); deal settled in cash. . . . Granted free agency (December 20, 1993). . . . Signed by San Francisco Giants organization (January 5, 1994).
STATISTICAL NOTES: Led Pacific Coast League catchers with 11 double plays in 1992.

Year	Team (League)	Pos.	G	AB	R	H	2B	3B	HR	RBI	Avg.	BB	SO	SB	PO	A	E	Avg.
			BATTING												FIELDING			
1986	—Batavia (NY-Penn) ..	C	63	190	24	49	5	1	1	20	.258	31	14	4	323	36	8	.978
1987	—Waterloo (Midw.)	C	118	398	49	106	19	2	7	55	.266	34	41	5	689	*100	15	.981
1988	—Williamsport (East.) ..	C	80	263	38	71	10	0	3	23	.270	25	20	1	431	60	9	.982
	—Colo. Springs (PCL) ..	C	34	107	14	30	5	0	0	7	.280	9	2	0	171	28	5	.975
	—Cleveland (A.L.)	C	4	4	0	0	0	0	0	0	.000	1	0	0	3	0	0	1.000
1989	—Colo. Springs (PCL) ..	C	63	209	26	67	10	3	4	32	.321	10	18	4	305	21	8	.976
1990	—Col. Sp.-L.V. (PCL)■	C-2B	70	201	32	45	7	5	1	18	.224	19	20	7	315	36	12	.967
	—San Diego (N.L.)	C	26	63	4	14	0	1	1	4	.222	4	9	0	91	10	3	.971
1991	—San Diego (N.L.)	C	38	58	4	11	3	1	0	3	.190	3	9	0	49	5	0	1.000
	—Las Vegas (PCL)	C-1B-OF	45	164	25	52	11	1	2	29	.317	10	19	2	211	26	6	.975
1992	—Las Vegas (PCL)	C	108	340	45	104	17	4	3	48	.306	53	27	15	506	*64	12	.979
	—San Diego (N.L.)	C-OF	9	17	3	4	0	0	0	0	.235	6	1	2	30	3	0	1.000
1993	—New Orleans (A.A.)■	C-OF	25	80	18	26	5	0	2	10	.325	18	4	5	152	12	3	.982
	—Milwaukee (A.L.)	C-OF	73	162	22	32	8	0	4	25	.198	20	26	7	242	24	6	.978
American League totals (2 years)			77	166	22	32	8	0	4	25	.193	21	26	7	245	24	6	.978
National League totals (3 years)			73	138	11	29	3	2	1	7	.210	13	19	2	170	18	3	.984
Major league totals (5 years)			150	304	33	61	11	2	5	32	.201	34	45	9	415	42	9	.981

LANCASTER, LES

P

PERSONAL: Born April 21, 1962, in Dallas. . . . 6-2/200. . . . Throws right, bats right. . . . Full name: Lester Wayne Lancaster.
HIGH SCHOOL: Nimitz (Irving, Tex.).
COLLEGE: Arkansas and Dallas Baptist.
TRANSACTIONS/CAREER NOTES: Selected by New York Yankees organization in 24th round of free-agent draft (June 8, 1981). . . . Selected by Texas Rangers organization in 39th round of free-agent draft (June 6, 1983). . . . Signed as free agent by Chicago Cubs organization (June 13, 1985). . . . On disabled list (July 24-August 14 and August 20-September 4, 1988). . . . Released by Cubs (March 31, 1992). . . . Signed by Detroit Tigers (April 6, 1992). . . . Granted free agency (October 26, 1992). . . . Signed as free agent by St. Louis Cardinals (January 13, 1993). . . . On disabled list (July 7-September 3, 1993). . . . Granted free agency (October 29, 1993).

STATISTICAL NOTES: Tied for N.L. lead with eight balks in 1987.
MISCELLANEOUS: Appeared in one game as outfielder with no chances with Chicago (1990).

Year	Team (League)	W	L	Pct.	ERA	G	GS	CG	ShO	Sv.	IP	H	R	ER	BB	SO
1985	—Wytheville (Appal.)	7	4	.636	3.62	20	10	*7	1	3	*102	*98	49	41	24	*81
1986	—Winst.-Salem (Car.)	8	3	.727	2.78	13	13	3	0	0	97	88	37	30	30	52
	—Pittsfield (Eastern)	5	6	.455	4.19	14	14	2	0	0	88	105	46	41	34	49
1987	—Chicago (N.L.)	8	3	.727	4.90	27	18	0	0	0	132⅓	138	76	72	51	78
	—Iowa (Am. Assoc.)	5	3	.625	3.22	15	6	0	0	4	67	59	24	24	17	62
1988	—Chicago (N.L.)	4	6	.400	3.78	44	3	1	0	5	85⅔	89	42	36	34	36
1989	—Iowa (Am. Assoc.)	5	7	.417	2.66	17	14	3	2	0	91⅓	76	38	27	43	56
	—Chicago (N.L.)	4	2	.667	1.36	42	0	0	0	8	72⅔	60	12	11	15	56
1990	—Chicago (N.L.)	9	5	.643	4.62	55	6	1	1	6	109	121	57	56	40	65
	—Iowa (Am. Assoc.)	0	1	.000	4.08	6	0	0	0	1	17⅔	20	10	8	5	15
1991	—Chicago (N.L.)	9	7	.563	3.52	64	11	1	0	3	156	150	68	61	49	102
1992	—Detroit (A.L.)■	3	4	.429	6.33	41	1	0	0	0	86⅔	101	66	61	51	35
1993	—St. Louis (N.L.)■	4	1	.800	2.93	50	0	0	0	0	61⅓	56	24	20	21	36
	A.L. totals (1 year)	3	4	.429	6.33	41	1	0	0	0	86⅔	101	66	61	51	35
	N.L. totals (6 years)	38	24	.613	3.73	282	38	3	1	22	617	614	279	256	210	373
	Major league totals (7 years)	41	28	.594	4.05	323	39	3	1	22	703⅔	715	345	317	261	408

CHAMPIONSHIP SERIES RECORD

Year	Team (League)	W	L	Pct.	ERA	G	GS	CG	ShO	Sv.	IP	H	R	ER	BB	SO
1989	—Chicago (N.L.)	1	1	.500	6.00	3	0	0	0	0	6	6	4	4	1	3

LANDRUM, BILL

P

PERSONAL: Born August 17, 1958, in Columbia, S.C. . . . 6-2/205. . . . Throws right, bats right. . . . Full name: Thomas William Landrum. . . . Son of Joe Landrum, pitcher, Brooklyn Dodgers (1950 and 1952).
HIGH SCHOOL: Spring Valley (Calif.).
COLLEGE: Spartanburg (S.C.) Methodist and South Carolina (bachelor of science degree, 1980).
TRANSACTIONS/CAREER NOTES: Signed as free agent by Chicago Cubs organization (June 22, 1980). . . . Released by Cubs organization (October 20, 1980). . . . Signed by Billings, Cincinnati Reds organization (February 7, 1981). . . . On Indianapolis disabled list (July 19-August 4, 1983). . . . Selected by Chicago White Sox from Reds organization in Rule 5 major league draft (December 3, 1984); returned to Reds organization (March 30, 1985). . . . On Denver disabled list (April 29-June 21, 1986). . . . Traded by Reds organization to Cubs for IF Luis Quinones (April 1, 1988). . . . Granted free agency (October 15, 1988). . . . Signed by Pittsburgh Pirates (January 12, 1989). . . . Released by Pirates (March 19, 1992). . . . Signed by Montreal Expos (April 1, 1992). . . . On Montreal disabled list (May 16-July 16, 1992); included rehabilitation assignment to Indianapolis (June 13-July 12). . . . On Indianapolis disabled list (August 8-29, 1992). . . . Granted free agency (October 16, 1992). . . . Signed by Reds organization (December 16, 1992). . . . On disabled list (June 4, 1993-remainder of season). . . . Granted free agency (October 10, 1993).

Year	Team (League)	W	L	Pct.	ERA	G	GS	CG	ShO	Sv.	IP	H	R	ER	BB	SO
1980	—GC Cubs (GCL)	2	0	1.000	4.14	11	0	0	0	0	37	37	21	17	11	27
1981	—Tampa (Fla. St.)■	6	8	.429	3.80	17	16	3	1	0	83	87	44	35	22	52
1982	—Waterbury (East.)	10	6	.625	4.09	*58	2	1	0	6	112⅓	109	63	51	65	104
1983	—Waterbury (East.)	1	1	.500	1.52	17	0	0	0	3	29⅔	17	5	5	14	33
	—Indianapolis (A.A.)	1	3	.250	3.06	15	0	0	0	2	17⅔	20	6	6	6	21
1984	—Wichita (A.A.)	7	4	.636	3.45	47	9	2	0	2	130⅓	12	58	50	52	120
1985	—Denver (A.A.)■	6	6	.500	3.98	29	19	3	1	2	138	148	72	61	49	88
1986	—Denver (A.A.)	1	3	.250	3.47	24	2	0	0	8	36⅓	36	20	14	25	36
	—Cincinnati (N.L.)	0	0	...	6.75	10	0	0	0	0	13⅓	23	11	10	4	14
1987	—Cincinnati (N.L.)	3	2	.600	4.71	44	2	0	0	2	65	68	35	34	34	42
	—Nashville (A.A.)	4	0	1.000	2.09	19	2	0	0	1	38⅔	30	9	9	19	47
1988	—Iowa (Am. Assoc.)■	1	0	1.000	2.95	9	0	0	0	3	21⅓	13	7	7	6	22
	—Chicago (N.L.)	1	0	1.000	5.84	7	0	0	0	0	12⅓	19	8	8	3	6
1989	—Pittsburgh (N.L.)■	2	3	.400	1.67	56	0	0	0	26	81	60	18	15	28	51
	—Buffalo (A.A.)	3	0	1.000	0.71	5	3	1	0	0	25⅓	16	2	2	6	20
1990	—Pittsburgh (N.L.)	7	3	.700	2.13	54	0	0	0	13	71⅔	69	22	17	21	39
1991	—Pittsburgh (N.L.)	4	4	.500	3.18	61	0	0	0	17	76⅓	76	32	27	19	45
1992	—Montreal (N.L.)■	1	1	.500	7.20	18	0	0	0	0	20	27	16	16	9	7
	—Indianapolis (A.A.)	1	1	.500	3.95	14	5	0	0	0	27⅓	27	15	12	4	23
1993	—Cincinnati (N.L.)■	0	2	.000	3.74	18	0	0	0	0	21⅔	18	9	9	6	14
	Major league totals (8 years)	18	15	.545	3.39	268	2	0	0	58	361⅓	360	151	136	124	218

CHAMPIONSHIP SERIES RECORD

Year	Team (League)	W	L	Pct.	ERA	G	GS	CG	ShO	Sv.	IP	H	R	ER	BB	SO
1990	—Pittsburgh (N.L.)	0	0	...	0.00	2	0	0	0	0	2	0	0	0	0	1
1991	—Pittsburgh (N.L.)	0	0	...	9.00	1	0	0	0	0	1	2	1	1	2	2
	Champ. series totals (2 years)	0	0	...	3.00	3	0	0	0	0	3	2	1	1	2	3

LANDRUM, CED

OF

PERSONAL: Born September 3, 1963, in Butler, Ala. . . . 5-9/170. . . . Throws right, bats left. . . . Full name: Cedric Bernard Landrum.
HIGH SCHOOL: Sweet Water (Ala.).
COLLEGE: North Alabama.
TRANSACTIONS/CAREER NOTES: Signed as free agent by Chicago Cubs organization (November 9, 1985). . . . On Iowa disabled list (April 9-June 27, 1992). . . . Traded by Cubs to Milwaukee Brewers for IF Jeff Kunkel (July 7, 1992). . . . Granted free agency (October 15, 1992). . . . Signed by Portland, Minnesota Twins organization (February 24, 1993). . . . Released by Portland (April 17, 1993). . . . Signed by New York Mets organization (May 14, 1993). . . . On Norfolk disabled list (June 14-25, 1993).

. . . Released by Mets (October 4, 1993).
STATISTICAL NOTES: Led Carolina League outfielders with 316 total chances and four double plays in 1987. . . . Led American Association in caught stealing with 17 in 1988. . . . Led Eastern League outfielders with 15 assists in 1988.

			BATTING											FIELDING			
Year	Team (League)	Pos.	G	AB	R	H	2B	3B	HR	RBI	Avg.	BB	SO	SB	PO	A	E	Avg.
1986	—Geneva (NY-Penn)...	OF	64	213	51	67	6	2	3	16	.315	40	33	*49	96	5	8	.927
1987	—Winst.-Salem (Car.)..	OF	126	458	82	129	13	7	4	49	.282	78	50	*79	*286	11	19	.940
1988	—Pittsfield (Eastern)..	OF-2B	128	445	*82	109	15	8	1	39	.245	55	63	*69	227	†16	8	.968
1989	—Charlotte (South.)....	OF	123	361	72	92	11	2	6	37	.255	48	54	45	226	5	8	.967
1990	—Iowa (Am. Assoc.)....	OF	123	372	71	110	10	4	0	24	.296	43	63	*46	214	3	4	.982
1991	—Iowa (Am. Assoc.)....	OF	38	131	14	44	8	2	1	11	.336	5	21	13	43	4	3	.940
	—Chicago (N.L.)..........	OF	56	86	28	20	2	1	0	6	.233	10	18	27	61	0	2	.968
1992	—Iowa-Denver (A.A)■	OF	51	164	24	51	7	0	1	19	.311	17	17	16	68	0	2	.971
1993	—Portland (PCL)■.......	OF	4	4	0	0	0	0	0	0	.000	0	0	1	1	0	0	1.000
	—Norfolk (Int'l)■.........	OF	69	275	39	80	13	5	5	29	.291	19	30	16	134	3	4	.972
	—New York (N.L.)........	OF	22	19	2	5	1	0	0	1	.263	0	5	0	0	0	0	...
Major league totals (2 years)			78	105	30	25	3	1	0	7	.238	10	23	27	61	0	2	.968

LANGSTON, MARK

P, ANGELS

PERSONAL: Born August 20, 1960, in San Diego. . . . 6-2/184. . . . Throws left, bats right. . . . Full name: Mark Edward Langston.
HIGH SCHOOL: Buchser (Santa Clara, Calif.).
COLLEGE: San Jose State.
TRANSACTIONS/CAREER NOTES: Selected by Chicago Cubs organization in 15th round of free-agent draft (June 6, 1978). . . . Selected by Seattle Mariners organization in third round of free-agent draft (June 8, 1981); pick received as compensation for Texas Rangers signing free agent Bill Stein. . . . On disabled list (June 7-July 22, 1985). . . . Traded by Mariners with a player to be named later to Montreal Expos for P Randy Johnson, P Brian Holman and P Gene Harris (May 25, 1989); Indianapolis, Expos organization, acquired P Mike Campbell to complete deal (July 31, 1989). . . . Granted free agency (November 13, 1989). . . . Signed by California Angels (December 1, 1989).
RECORDS: Holds major league single-season record for fewest assists by pitcher who led league in assists—42 (1990).
HONORS: Named A.L. Rookie Pitcher of the Year by THE SPORTING NEWS (1984). . . . Won A.L. Gold Glove at pitcher (1987-88 and 1991-93).
STATISTICAL NOTES: Pitched seven innings, combining with Mike Witt (two innings) in 1-0 no-hit victory against Seattle (April 11, 1990).
MISCELLANEOUS: Scored in only appearance as pinch-runner and struck out twice in two appearances as designated hitter (1992).

Year	Team (League)	W	L	Pct.	ERA	G	GS	CG	ShO	Sv.	IP	H	R	ER	BB	SO
1981	—Belling. (N'west)........	7	3	.700	3.39	13	13	5	1	0	85	81	37	32	46	97
1982	—Bakersfield (Calif.).....	12	7	.632	2.54	26	26	7	3	0	177⅓	143	71	50	102	161
1983	—Chatt. (South.)..........	14	9	.609	3.59	28	28	10	0	0	198	187	104	79	102	142
1984	—Seattle (A.L.).............	17	10	.630	3.40	35	33	5	2	0	225	188	99	85	*118	*204
1985	—Seattle (A.L.).............	7	14	.333	5.47	24	24	2	0	0	126⅔	122	85	77	91	72
1986	—Seattle (A.L.).............	12	14	.462	4.85	37	36	9	0	0	239⅓	234	*142	*129	123	*245
1987	—Seattle (A.L.).............	19	13	.594	3.84	35	35	14	3	0	272	242	132	116	114	*262
1988	—Seattle (A.L.).............	15	11	.577	3.34	35	35	9	3	0	261⅓	222	108	97	110	235
1989	—Seattle (A.L.).............	4	5	.444	3.56	10	10	2	1	0	73⅓	60	30	29	19	60
	—Montreal (N.L.)■.......	12	9	.571	2.39	24	24	6	4	0	176⅔	138	57	47	93	175
1990	—California (A.L.)■......	10	17	.370	4.40	33	33	5	1	0	223	215	120	109	104	195
1991	—California (A.L.).........	19	8	.704	3.00	34	34	7	0	0	246⅓	190	89	82	96	183
1992	—California (A.L.).........	13	14	.481	3.66	32	32	9	2	0	229	206	103	93	74	174
1993	—California (A.L.).........	16	11	.593	3.20	35	35	7	0	0	256⅓	220	100	91	85	196
A.L. totals (10 years)		132	117	.530	3.80	310	307	69	12	0	2152⅓	1899	1008	908	934	1826
N.L. totals (1 year)		12	9	.571	2.39	24	24	6	4	0	176⅔	138	57	47	93	175
Major league totals (10 years)		144	126	.533	3.69	334	331	75	16	0	2329	2037	1065	955	1027	2001

ALL-STAR GAME RECORD

Year	League	W	L	Pct.	ERA	GS	CG	ShO	Sv.	IP	H	R	ER	BB	SO
1987	—American......................	0	0	...	0.00	0	0	0	0	2	0	0	0	0	3
1991	—American......................	Did not play.													
1992	—American......................	0	0	...	9.00	0	0	0	0	1	2	1	1	0	1
1993	—American......................	0	0	...	9.00	1	0	0	0	2	3	2	2	1	2
All-Star totals (3 years)		0	0	...	5.40	1	0	0	0	5	5	3	3	1	6

LANKFORD, RAY

OF, CARDINALS

PERSONAL: Born June 5, 1967, in Modesto, Calif. . . . 5-11/198. . . . Throws left, bats left. . . . Full name: Raymond Lewis Lankford.
HIGH SCHOOL: Grace Davis (Modesto, Calif.).
COLLEGE: Modesto (Calif.) Junior College.
TRANSACTIONS/CAREER NOTES: Selected by Chicago Cubs organization in third round of free-agent draft (January 14, 1986). . . . Selected by St. Louis Cardinals organization in third round of free-agent draft (June 2, 1987). . . . On disabled list (June 24-July 9, 1993).
RECORDS: Shares major league single-season record for fewest double plays by outfielder (150 or more games)—0 (1992).
HONORS: Named Texas League Most Valuable Player (1989).
STATISTICAL NOTES: Led Appalachian League outfielders with 155 total chances in 1987. . . . Led Appalachian League in caught stealing with 11 in 1987. . . . Led Midwest League with 242 total bases in 1988. . . . Led Texas League outfielders with 387 total chances in 1989. . . . Led American Association outfielders with 352 total chances in 1990. . . . Tied for American Association lead with nine intentional bases on balls received in 1990. . . . Hit for the cycle (September 15, 1991). . . . Led N.L. in caught stealing with 24 in 1992.

Year	Team (League)	Pos.	G	AB	R	H	2B	3B	HR	RBI	Avg.	BB	SO	SB	PO	A	E	Avg.
			BATTING												FIELDING			
1987	—Johns. City (App.)	OF	66	253	45	78	17	4	3	32	.308	19	43	14	*143	7	5	.968
1988	—Springfield (Midw.)	OF	135	532	90	151	26	*16	11	66	.284	60	92	33	284	5	7	.976
1989	—Arkansas (Texas)	OF	*134	498	98	*158	28	*12	11	98	.317	65	57	38	*367	9	11	.972
1990	—Louisville (A.A.)	OF	132	473	61	123	25	8	10	72	.260	72	81	30	*333	8	•11	.969
	—St. Louis (N.L.)	OF	39	126	12	36	10	1	3	12	.286	13	27	8	92	1	1	.989
1991	—St. Louis (N.L.)	OF	151	566	83	142	23	*15	9	69	.251	41	114	44	367	7	6	.984
1992	—St. Louis (N.L.)	OF	153	598	87	175	40	6	20	86	.293	72	*147	42	*438	5	2	.996
1993	—St. Louis (N.L.)	OF	127	407	64	97	17	3	7	45	.238	81	111	14	312	6	7	.978
Major league totals (4 years)			470	1697	246	450	90	25	39	212	.265	207	399	108	1209	19	16	.987

LANSING, MIKE

2B, EXPOS

PERSONAL: Born April 3, 1968, in Rawlins, Wyo.... 6-0/180.... Throws right, bats right.... Full name: Michael Thomas Lansing.
HIGH SCHOOL: Natrona County (Casper, Wyo.).
COLLEGE: Wichita State.
TRANSACTIONS/CAREER NOTES: Selected by Baltimore Orioles organization in ninth round of free-agent draft (June 5, 1989).... Selected by Miami, independent, in sixth round of free-agent draft (June 4, 1990).... On disabled list (April 29-May 9, 1991).... Contract sold by Miami to Montreal Expos organization (September 18, 1991).
STATISTICAL NOTES: Led Eastern League shortstops with 76 double plays in 1992.

Year	Team (League)	Pos.	G	AB	R	H	2B	3B	HR	RBI	Avg.	BB	SO	SB	PO	A	E	Avg.
			BATTING												FIELDING			
1990	—Miami (Florida St.)	SS	61	207	20	50	5	2	2	11	.242	29	35	15	104	166	10	.964
1991	—Miami (Florida St.)	SS-2B	104	384	54	110	20	7	6	55	.286	40	75	29	148	273	27	.940
1992	—Harrisburg (East.)■.	SS	128	483	66	135	20	6	6	54	.280	52	64	46	189	*373	20	*.966
1993	—Montreal (N.L.)	3B-SS-2B	141	491	64	141	29	1	3	45	.287	46	56	23	136	336	24	.952
Major league totals (1 year)			141	491	64	141	29	1	3	45	.287	46	56	23	136	336	24	.952

LARKIN, BARRY

SS, REDS

PERSONAL: Born April 28, 1964, in Cincinnati.... 6-0/196.... Throws right, bats right.... Full name: Barry Louis Larkin.
HIGH SCHOOL: Moeller (Cincinnati).
COLLEGE: Michigan.
TRANSACTIONS/CAREER NOTES: Selected by Cincinnati Reds organization in second round of free-agent draft (June 7, 1982).... Selected by Reds organization in first round (fourth pick overall) of free-agent draft (June 3, 1985).... On disabled list (April 13-May 2, 1987).... On disabled list (July 11-September 1, 1989); included rehabilitation assignment to Nashville (August 27-September 1).... On disabled list (May 18-June 4, 1991; April 19-May 8, 1992 and August 5, 1993-remainder of season).
RECORDS: Shares major league record for most home runs in two consecutive games—5 (June 27-28, 1991).
HONORS: Named shortstop on THE SPORTING NEWS college All-America team (1985).... Named American Association Most Valuable Player (1986).... Named shortstop on THE SPORTING NEWS N.L. All-Star team (1988-92).... Named shortstop on THE SPORTING NEWS N.L. Silver Slugger team (1988-92).
STATISTICAL NOTES: Led American Association with .525 slugging percentage in 1986.... Tied for N.L. lead in double plays by shortstop with 86 in 1990.... Hit three home runs in one game (June 28, 1991).
MISCELLANEOUS: Member of 1984 U.S. Olympic baseball team.

Year	Team (League)	Pos.	G	AB	R	H	2B	3B	HR	RBI	Avg.	BB	SO	SB	PO	A	E	Avg.
			BATTING												FIELDING			
1985	—Vermont (Eastern)	SS	72	255	42	68	13	2	1	31	.267	23	21	12	110	166	17	.942
1986	—Denver (A.A.)	SS-2B	103	413	67	136	31	10	10	51	.329	31	43	19	172	287	18	.962
	—Cincinnati (N.L.)	SS-2B	41	159	27	45	4	3	3	19	.283	9	21	8	51	125	4	.978
1987	—Cincinnati (N.L.)	SS	125	439	64	107	16	2	12	43	.244	36	52	21	168	358	19	.965
1988	—Cincinnati (N.L.)	SS	151	588	91	174	32	5	12	56	.296	41	24	40	231	470	•29	.960
1989	—Cincinnati (N.L.)	SS	97	325	47	111	14	4	4	36	.342	20	23	10	142	267	10	.976
	—Nashville (A.A.)	SS	2	5	2	5	1	0	0	0	1.000	0	0	0	1	3	0	1.000
1990	—Cincinnati (N.L.)	SS	158	614	85	185	25	6	7	67	.301	49	49	30	254	*469	17	.977
1991	—Cincinnati (N.L.)	SS	123	464	88	140	27	4	20	69	.302	55	64	24	226	372	15	.976
1992	—Cincinnati (N.L.)	SS	140	533	76	162	32	6	12	78	.304	63	58	15	233	408	11	.983
1993	—Cincinnati (N.L.)	SS	100	384	57	121	20	3	8	51	.315	51	33	14	159	281	16	.965
Major league totals (8 years)			935	3506	535	1045	170	33	78	419	.298	324	324	162	1464	2750	121	.972

CHAMPIONSHIP SERIES RECORD

Year	Team (League)	Pos.	G	AB	R	H	2B	3B	HR	RBI	Avg.	BB	SO	SB	PO	A	E	Avg.
			BATTING												FIELDING			
1990	—Cincinnati (N.L.)	SS	6	23	5	6	2	0	0	1	.261	3	1	3	21	15	1	.973

WORLD SERIES RECORD

WORLD SERIES NOTES: Shares record for most at-bats in one inning—2 (October 19, 1990, third inning).

Year	Team (League)	Pos.	G	AB	R	H	2B	3B	HR	RBI	Avg.	BB	SO	SB	PO	A	E	Avg.
			BATTING												FIELDING			
1990	—Cincinnati (N.L.)	SS	4	17	3	6	1	1	0	1	.353	2	0	0	1	14	0	1.000

ALL-STAR GAME RECORD

Year	League	Pos.	AB	R	H	2B	3B	HR	RBI	Avg.	BB	SO	SB	PO	A	E	Avg.
			BATTING											FIELDING			
1988	—National	SS	2	0	0	0	0	0	0	.000	0	1	0	0	1	0	1.000
1989	—National							Did not play.									
1990	—National	PR-SS	0	0	0	0	0	0	0	...	0	0	1	1	2	0	1.000

Year	League	Pos.	AB	R	H	2B	3B	HR	RBI	Avg.	BB	SO	SB	PO	A	E	Avg.
			BATTING											FIELDING			
1991	—National	SS	1	0	0	0	0	0	0	.000	0	0	0	0	2	0	1.000
1993	—National	SS	2	0	0	0	0	0	1	.000	0	1	0	2	1	0	1.000
All-Star Game totals (4 years)			5	0	0	0	0	0	1	.000	0	2	1	3	6	0	1.000

LARKIN, GENE

OF/1B, TWINS

PERSONAL: Born October 24, 1962, in Astoria, N.Y. . . . 6-3/205. . . . Throws right, bats both. . . . Full name: Eugene Thomas Larkin.

HIGH SCHOOL: Chaminade (Mineola, N.Y.).

COLLEGE: Columbia (received degree).

TRANSACTIONS/CAREER NOTES: Selected by Minnesota Twins organization in 20th round of free-agent draft (June 4, 1984). . . . On disabled list (July 14-30, 1990 and July 2-17, 1991). . . . Granted free agency (December 19, 1992). . . . Re-signed by Twins (December 29, 1992). . . . On disabled list (June 8-July 2, July 7-29 and August 12, 1993-remainder of season). . . . Granted free agency (October 8, 1993). . . . Re-signed by Twins organization (January 27, 1994).

STATISTICAL NOTES: Led Appalachian League first basemen with 54 double plays in 1984. . . . Led California League with 14 sacrifice flies in 1985. . . . Led California League first basemen with 140 double plays in 1985. . . . Tied for Southern League lead with 13 sacrifice flies in 1986. . . . Led A.L. in being hit by pitch with 15 in 1988.

Year	Team (League)	Pos.	G	AB	R	H	2B	3B	HR	RBI	Avg.	BB	SO	SB	PO	A	E	Avg.
			BATTING												FIELDING			
1984	—Elizabeth. (Appal.)	1B	57	193	29	63	13	1	6	37	.326	29	18	1	478	19	6	*.988
1985	—Visalia (California)	1B	•142	528	90	161	25	3	13	•106	.305	81	61	0	*1227	62	12	.991
1986	—Orlando (Southern)	1B-3B	142	529	85	•170	29	6	15	104	.321	84	50	1	923	53	13	.987
1987	—Portland (PCL)	1B-OF	35	129	17	39	9	0	1	14	.302	20	11	0	191	22	4	.982
	—Minnesota (A.L.)	1B	85	233	23	62	11	2	4	28	.266	25	31	1	165	10	2	.989
1988	—Minnesota (A.L.)	1B	149	505	56	135	30	2	8	70	.267	68	55	3	466	28	3	.994
1989	—Minnesota (A.L.)	1B-OF	136	446	61	119	25	1	6	46	.267	54	57	5	524	28	4	.993
1990	—Minnesota (A.L.)	OF-1B	119	401	46	108	26	4	5	42	.269	42	55	5	299	18	2	.994
1991	—Minnesota (A.L.)	O-1-2-3	98	255	34	73	14	1	2	19	.286	30	21	2	340	20	3	.992
1992	—Minnesota (A.L.)	1B-OF	115	337	38	83	18	1	6	42	.246	28	43	7	509	35	5	.991
1993	—Minnesota (A.L.)	OF-1B-3B	56	144	17	38	7	1	1	19	.264	21	16	0	156	7	2	.988
Major league totals (7 years)			758	2321	275	618	131	12	32	266	.266	268	278	23	2459	146	21	.992

CHAMPIONSHIP SERIES RECORD

Year	Team (League)	Pos.	G	AB	R	H	2B	3B	HR	RBI	Avg.	BB	SO	SB	PO	A	E	Avg.
			BATTING												FIELDING			
1987	—Minnesota (A.L.)	PH	1	1	0	1	1	0	0	1	1.000	0	0	0	...	...	...	...
1991	—Minnesota (A.L.)	PH	3	3	0	0	0	0	0	0	.000	0	1	0	...	...	...	...
Championship series totals (2 years)			4	4	0	1	1	0	0	1	.250	0	1	0	...	...	...	...

WORLD SERIES RECORD

Year	Team (League)	Pos.	G	AB	R	H	2B	3B	HR	RBI	Avg.	BB	SO	SB	PO	A	E	Avg.
			BATTING												FIELDING			
1987	—Minnesota (A.L.)	PH-1B	5	3	1	0	0	0	0	0	.000	1	0	0	1	0	0	1.000
1991	—Minnesota (A.L.)	PH	4	4	0	2	0	0	0	1	.500	0	0	0	...	...	...	...
World Series totals (2 years)			9	7	1	2	0	0	0	1	.286	1	0	0	1	0	0	1.000

LaVALLIERE, MIKE

C, WHITE SOX

PERSONAL: Born August 18, 1960, in Charlotte, N.C. . . . 5-9/205. . . . Throws right, bats left. . . . Full name: Michael Eugene LaValliere. . . . Son of Guy LaValliere, minor league catcher (1952 and 1955-61). . . . Name pronounced luh-VAL-yur.

HIGH SCHOOL: Trinity (Manchester, N.H.).

COLLEGE: University of Massachusetts Lowell.

TRANSACTIONS/CAREER NOTES: Signed as free agent by Philadelphia Phillies organization (July 12, 1981). . . . Traded by Phillies to St. Louis Cardinals for a player to be named later (December 3, 1984); returned to Phillies due to injured status (December 13, 1984). . . . Granted free agency (December 23, 1984). . . . Signed by Louisville, Cardinals organization (January 23, 1985). . . . On Louisville disabled list (July 18-29, 1985). . . . Traded by Cardinals with OF Andy Van Slyke and P Mike Dunne to Pittsburgh Pirates for C Tony Pena (April 1, 1987). . . . On Pittsburgh disabled list (April 17-July 4, 1989); included rehabilitation assignment to Buffalo (June 26-July 4). . . . Granted free agency (October 31, 1991). . . . Re-signed by Pirates (January 3, 1992). . . . Released by Pirates (April 11, 1993). . . . Signed by Chicago White Sox organization (April 23, 1993).

HONORS: Won N.L. Gold Glove at catcher (1987). . . . Named catcher on THE SPORTING NEWS N.L. All-Star team (1988).

Year	Team (League)	Pos.	G	AB	R	H	2B	3B	HR	RBI	Avg.	BB	SO	SB	PO	A	E	Avg.
			BATTING												FIELDING			
1981	—Spartanburg (SAL)	3B-OF	39	123	15	33	9	0	2	23	.268	31	16	3	16	32	5	.906
1982	—Peninsula (Caro.)	C-3B	66	178	20	49	4	2	2	23	.275	26	20	3	306	35	6	.983
1983	—Reading (Eastern)	C-3B-P	81	218	24	64	16	2	4	43	.294	32	26	1	243	59	4	.987
1984	—Reading (Eastern)	C-3-2-P	55	147	19	37	6	0	6	22	.252	36	15	0	113	45	2	.988
	—Portland (PCL)	C	37	122	20	38	6	3	5	21	.311	15	11	0	186	16	1	.995
	—Philadelphia (N.L.)	C	6	7	0	0	0	0	0	0	.000	2	2	0	20	2	0	1.000
1985	—St. Louis (N.L.)■	C	12	34	2	5	1	0	0	6	.147	7	3	0	48	5	0	1.000
	—Louisville (A.A.)	C	83	231	19	47	12	1	4	26	.203	48	20	0	420	53	5	.990
1986	—St. Louis (N.L.)	C	110	303	18	71	10	2	3	30	.234	36	37	0	468	47	6	.988
1987	—Pittsburgh (N.L.)■	C	121	340	33	102	19	0	1	36	.300	43	32	0	584	70	5	.992
1988	—Pittsburgh (N.L.)	C	120	352	24	92	18	0	2	47	.261	50	34	3	565	55	8	.987
1989	—Pittsburgh (N.L.)	C	68	190	15	60	10	0	2	23	.316	29	24	0	306	24	3	.991
	—Buffalo (A.A.)	C	7	18	0	2	0	0	0	1	.111	3	4	0	15	1	0	1.000
1990	—Pittsburgh (N.L.)	C	96	279	27	72	15	0	3	31	.258	44	20	0	478	36	5	.990
1991	—Pittsburgh (N.L.)	C	108	336	25	97	11	2	3	41	.289	33	27	2	565	46	1	*.998

			BATTING												FIELDING			
Year	**Team (League)**	**Pos.**	**G**	**AB**	**R**	**H**	**2B**	**3B**	**HR**	**RBI**	**Avg.**	**BB**	**SO**	**SB**	**PO**	**A**	**E**	**Avg.**
1992	—Pittsburgh (N.L.)	C-3B	95	293	22	75	13	1	2	29	.256	44	21	0	421	63	3	.994
1993	—Pittsburgh (N.L.)	C	1	5	0	1	0	0	0	0	.200	0	0	0	12	0	0	1.000
	—Sarasota (Fla. St.)■	C	32	108	6	33	2	0	0	14	.306	19	5	2	141	14	2	.987
	—Chicago (A.L.)	C	37	97	6	25	2	0	0	8	.258	4	14	0	164	28	0	1.000
American League totals (1 year)			37	97	6	25	2	0	0	8	.258	4	14	0	164	28	0	1.000
National League totals (10 years)			737	2139	166	575	97	5	16	243	.269	288	200	5	3467	348	31	.992
Major league totals (10 years)			774	2236	172	600	99	5	16	251	.268	292	214	5	3631	376	31	.992

CHAMPIONSHIP SERIES RECORD

			BATTING												FIELDING			
Year	**Team (League)**	**Pos.**	**G**	**AB**	**R**	**H**	**2B**	**3B**	**HR**	**RBI**	**Avg.**	**BB**	**SO**	**SB**	**PO**	**A**	**E**	**Avg.**
1990	—Pittsburgh (N.L.)	C	3	6	1	0	0	0	0	0	.000	3	1	0	17	2	0	1.000
1991	—Pittsburgh (N.L.)	C-PH	3	6	0	2	0	0	0	1	.333	2	0	0	14	3	0	1.000
1992	—Pittsburgh (N.L.)	C	3	10	1	2	0	0	0	0	.200	0	3	0	14	0	0	1.000
1993	—Chicago (A.L.)	C	2	3	0	1	0	0	0	0	.333	1	0	0	8	0	0	1.000
Championship series totals (4 years)			11	25	2	5	0	0	0	1	.200	6	4	0	53	5	0	1.000

RECORD AS PITCHER

Year	**Team (League)**	**W**	**L**	**Pct.**	**ERA**	**G**	**GS**	**CG**	**ShO**	**Sv.**	**IP**	**H**	**R**	**ER**	**BB**	**SO**
1983	—Reading (Eastern)	0	0	...	5.40	4	0	0	0	0	3⅓	3	3	2	2	2
1984	—Reading (Eastern)	0	0	...	18.00	1	0	0	0	0	1	3	2	2	1	1

LAYANA, TIM

P

PERSONAL: Born March 2, 1964, in Inglewood, Calif. . . . 6-2/190. . . . Throws right, bats right. . . . Full name: Timothy Joseph Layana.
HIGH SCHOOL: Loyola (Los Angeles).
COLLEGE: Loyola Marymount.
TRANSACTIONS/CAREER NOTES: Selected by Chicago White Sox organization in 28th round of free-agent draft (June 7, 1982). . . . Selected by New York Mets organization in fifth round of free-agent draft (June 3, 1985). . . . Selected by New York Yankees organization in third round of free-agent draft (June 2, 1986). . . . Selected by Cincinnati Reds from Yankees organization in Rule 5 major league draft (December 4, 1989). . . . Released by Reds (March 31, 1992). . . . Signed by Rochester, Baltimore Orioles organization (April 20, 1992). . . . Released by Rochester (September 17, 1992). . . . Signed by Shreveport, San Francisco Giants organization (February 5, 1993). . . . Granted free agency (October 15, 1993).
MISCELLANEOUS: Appeared in one game as pinch-runner (1991).

Year	**Team (League)**	**W**	**L**	**Pct.**	**ERA**	**G**	**GS**	**CG**	**ShO**	**Sv.**	**IP**	**H**	**R**	**ER**	**BB**	**SO**
1986	—Oneonta (NYP)	2	0	1.000	2.37	3	3	0	0	0	19	10	5	5	5	24
	—Fort Lauder. (FSL)	5	4	.556	2.24	11	10	3	1	1	68⅓	59	19	17	19	52
1987	—Columbus (Int'l)	4	5	.444	4.76	13	13	0	0	0	70	77	37	37	37	36
	—Alb./Colon. (East.)	2	4	.333	5.05	8	7	1	0	0	46⅓	51	28	26	18	19
	—Prin. William (Car.)	2	1	.667	6.35	7	3	0	0	0	22⅔	29	22	16	11	17
1988	—Columbus (Int'l)	1	7	.125	6.04	11	9	0	0	0	47⅔	54	34	32	25	25
	—Alb./Colon. (East.)	5	7	.417	4.34	14	14	1	0	0	87	90	52	42	30	42
1989	—Alb./Colon. (East.)	7	4	.636	1.73	40	1	0	0	*17	67⅔	53	17	13	15	48
1990	—Cincinnati (N.L.)■	5	3	.625	3.49	55	0	0	0	2	80	71	33	31	44	53
1991	—Cincinnati (N.L.)	0	2	.000	6.97	22	0	0	0	0	20⅔	23	18	16	11	14
	—Nashville (A.A.)	3	1	.750	3.23	26	2	0	0	1	47⅓	41	17	17	28	43
1992	—Rochester (Int'l)■	3	3	.500	5.35	41	3	0	0	4	72⅓	79	45	43	38	48
1993	—Phoenix (PCL)■	3	2	.600	4.81	55	0	0	0	9	67⅓	80	42	36	24	55
	—San Francisco (N.L.)	0	0	...	22.50	1	0	0	0	0	2	7	5	5	1	1
Major league totals (3 years)		5	5	.500	4.56	78	0	0	0	2	102⅔	101	56	52	56	68

LEACH, JAY

OF, YANKEES

PERSONAL: Born March 14, 1969, in San Francisco. . . . 6-2/200. . . . Throws left, bats left. . . . Full name: Jalal Donnell Leach.
HIGH SCHOOL: San Marin (Novato, Calif.).
COLLEGE: Pepperdine.
TRANSACTIONS/CAREER NOTES: Selected by New York Yankees organization in seventh round of free-agent draft (June 4, 1990).

			BATTING												FIELDING			
Year	**Team (League)**	**Pos.**	**G**	**AB**	**R**	**H**	**2B**	**3B**	**HR**	**RBI**	**Avg.**	**BB**	**SO**	**SB**	**PO**	**A**	**E**	**Avg.**
1990	—Oneonta (NYP)	OF	69	257	41	74	7	1	2	18	.288	37	52	33	107	4	3	.974
1991	—Fort Lauder. (FSL)	OF	122	468	48	119	13	9	2	42	.254	44	122	28	253	9	5	.981
1992	—Prin. William (Car.)	OF	128	462	61	122	22	7	5	65	.264	47	114	18	249	9	7	.974
1993	—Alb./Colon. (East.)	OF	125	457	64	129	19	9	14	79	.282	47	113	15	210	9	9	.961

LEACH, TERRY

P

PERSONAL: Born March 13, 1954, in Selma, Ala. . . . 6-0/194. . . . Throws right, bats right. . . . Full name: Terry Hester Leach.
HIGH SCHOOL: Selma (Ala.).
COLLEGE: Auburn (business administration degree in personnel management-industrial relations).
TRANSACTIONS/CAREER NOTES: Selected by Boston Red Sox organization in seventh round of free-agent draft (January 7, 1976). . . . Signed as free agent by Baton Rouge, independent (June 29, 1976); released when Baton Rouge withdrew from league (August 13, 1976). . . . Signed as free agent by Greenwood, Atlanta Braves organization (May 28, 1977). . . . Loaned by Braves organization to Kinston, independent (June 3-October 28, 1978). . . . On Savannah disabled list (June 12-July 23, 1980). . . . Released by Braves organization (July 23, 1980). . . . Signed by Jackson, New York Mets organization (July 27, 1980). . . . Traded by Mets organization to Chicago Cubs organization for P Jim Adamczak and P Mitch Cook (September 26,

1983).... Traded by Chicago Cubs organization to Braves organization for P Ron Meridith (April 4, 1984).... Released by Braves organization (May 25, 1984).... Signed by Mets organization (May 26, 1984).... On disabled list (July 12-27, 1987). ... Traded by Mets to Kansas City Royals for a player to be named later (June 9, 1989); Mets acquired P Aguedo Vasquez to complete deal (October 1, 1989).... Released by Royals (April 2, 1990).... Signed by Minnesota Twins (April 7, 1990).... Granted free agency (November 7, 1991).... Signed by Indianapolis, Montreal Expos organization (February 14, 1992).... Released by Indianapolis (April 2, 1992).... Signed by Chicago White Sox (April 5, 1992).... On Chicago disabled list (April 24-May 25, 1993); included rehabilitation assignment to Nashville (May 19-25).... On Chicago disabled list (June 24, 1993-remainder of season); included rehabilitation assignment to Nashville (July 31-August 9) and Birmingham (August 17-September 3).... Granted free agency (October 18, 1993).

STATISTICAL NOTES: Led Gulf States League with 12 home runs allowed in 1976.

Year Team (League)	W	L	Pct.	ERA	G	GS	CG	ShO	Sv.	IP	H	R	ER	BB	SO
1976 — Baton Rouge (GSL)	2	0	1.000	6.16	5	1	1	0	0	19	43	21	13	14	15
1977 — Greenw. (W. Car.)■	3	2	.600	2.55	20	0	0	0	3	67	47	25	19	24	67
1978 — Savannah (South.)	1	0	1.000	5.04	9	2	0	0	0	25	24	17	14	13	21
— Kinston (Carolina)■	5	4	.556	3.27	34	0	0	0	8	66	57	29	24	25	46
1979 — Savannah (South.)■	2	9	.182	1.96	40	0	0	0	2	92	77	33	20	26	68
— Richmond (Int'l)	3	1	.750	1.93	7	2	1	0	1	14	14	3	3	4	12
1980 — Savannah (South.)	5	1	.833	3.21	22	6	2	0	1	87	83	36	31	17	58
— Jackson (Texas)■	5	1	.833	1.50	8	7	3	2	0	54	50	16	9	15	30
1981 — Tidewater (Int'l)	5	2	.714	2.72	15	8	4	1	0	76	63	27	23	19	42
— Jackson (Texas)	5	1	.833	1.71	8	7	2	1	0	58	47	14	11	12	43
— New York (N.L.)	1	1	.500	2.57	21	1	0	0	0	35	26	11	10	12	16
1982 — Tidewater (Int'l)	4	1	.800	2.96	30	0	0	0	5	48⅔	48	20	16	19	34
— New York (N.L.)	2	1	.667	4.17	21	1	1	1	3	45⅓	46	22	21	18	30
1983 — Tidewater (Int'l)	5	7	.417	4.46	37	7	2	0	6	113	120	66	56	42	66
1984 — Rich.-Tide. (Int'l)■	11	4	.733	3.03	43	0	0	0	1	95	98	42	32	30	59
1985 — Tidewater (Int'l)	1	0	1.000	1.59	24	0	0	0	4	45⅓	33	12	8	8	25
— New York (N.L.)	3	4	.429	2.91	22	4	1	1	1	55⅔	48	19	18	14	30
1986 — Tidewater (Int'l)	4	4	.500	2.49	34	4	1	0	7	79⅔	69	30	22	21	55
— New York (N.L.)	0	0	...	2.70	6	0	0	0	0	6⅔	6	3	2	3	4
1987 — New York (N.L.)	11	1	.917	3.22	44	12	1	1	0	131⅓	132	54	47	29	61
1988 — New York (N.L.)	7	2	.778	2.54	52	0	0	0	3	92	95	32	26	24	51
1989 — New York (N.L.)	0	0	...	4.22	10	0	0	0	0	21⅓	19	11	10	4	2
— Kansas City (A.L.)■	5	6	.455	4.15	30	3	0	0	0	73⅔	78	46	34	36	34
1990 — Minnesota (A.L.)■	2	5	.286	3.20	55	0	0	0	2	81⅔	84	31	29	21	46
1991 — Minnesota (A.L.)	1	2	.333	3.61	50	0	0	0	0	67⅓	82	28	27	14	32
1992 — Chicago (A.L.)■	6	5	.545	1.95	51	0	0	0	0	73⅔	57	17	16	20	22
1993 — Chicago (A.L.)	0	0	...	2.81	14	0	0	0	1	16	15	5	5	2	3
— Nashville (A.A.)	0	0	...	3.18	5	0	0	0	1	5⅔	4	2	2	0	4
— Birm. (Southern)	0	0	...	4.15	4	0	0	0	1	4⅓	4	2	2	2	5
A.L. totals (5 years)	14	18	.438	3.20	200	3	0	0	3	312⅓	316	127	111	93	137
N.L. totals (7 years)	24	9	.727	3.11	176	18	3	3	7	387⅓	372	152	134	104	194
Major league totals (11 years)	38	27	.585	3.15	376	21	3	3	10	699⅔	688	279	245	197	331

CHAMPIONSHIP SERIES RECORD

Year Team (League)	W	L	Pct.	ERA	G	GS	CG	ShO	Sv.	IP	H	R	ER	BB	SO
1988 — New York (N.L.)	0	0	...	0.00	3	0	0	0	0	5	4	0	0	1	4
1991 — Minnesota (A.L.)							Did not play.								
Champ. series totals (1 year)	0	0	...	0.00	3	0	0	0	0	5	4	0	0	1	4

WORLD SERIES RECORD

Year Team (League)	W	L	Pct.	ERA	G	GS	CG	ShO	Sv.	IP	H	R	ER	BB	SO
1991 — Minnesota (A.L.)	0	0	...	3.86	2	0	0	0	0	2⅓	2	1	1	0	2

LEARY, TIM

P

PERSONAL: Born December 23, 1958, in Santa Monica, Calif. ... 6-3/220. ... Throws right, bats right.... Full name: Timothy James Leary.

HIGH SCHOOL: Santa Monica (Calif.).

COLLEGE: UCLA.

TRANSACTIONS/CAREER NOTES: Selected by New York Mets organization in first round (second pick overall) of free-agent draft (June 5, 1979).... On disabled list (July 19-October 1, 1979).... On New York disabled list (April 16-August 1, 1981).... On disabled list (April 13, 1982-remainder of season).... Traded by Mets organization to Milwaukee Brewers organization as part of a six-player, four-team deal in which Kansas City Royals acquired C Jim Sundberg from Brewers, Texas Rangers acquired C Don Slaught from Royals, Mets organization acquired P Frank Wills from Royals and Brewers acquired P Danny Darwin and a player to be named later from Rangers (January 18, 1985); Brewers organization acquired C Bill Hance from Rangers to complete deal (January 30, 1985).... Traded by Brewers with P Tim Crews to Los Angeles Dodgers for 1B Greg Brock (December 10, 1986).... Traded by Dodgers with SS Mariano Duncan to Cincinnati Reds for OF Kal Daniels and IF Lenny Harris (July 18, 1989).... Traded by Reds with OF Van Snider to New York Yankees for 1B Hal Morris and P Rodney Imes (December 12, 1989). ... Granted free agency (November 5, 1990).... Re-signed by Yankees (November 19, 1990).... Traded by Yankees with cash to Seattle Mariners for OF Sean Twitty (August 22, 1992).... Granted free agency (October 29, 1993).

HONORS: Named righthanded pitcher on THE SPORTING NEWS college All-America team (1979).... Named Texas League Most Valuable Player (1980).... Named N.L. Comeback Player of the Year by THE SPORTING NEWS (1988).... Named pitcher on THE SPORTING NEWS N.L. Silver Slugger team (1988).

STATISTICAL NOTES: Led A.L. with 23 wild pitches in 1990.

Year Team (League)	W	L	Pct.	ERA	G	GS	CG	ShO	Sv.	IP	H	R	ER	BB	SO
1979 —							Did not play.								
1980 — Jackson (Texas)	•15	8	.652	2.76	26	26	11	*6	0	173	150	67	53	62	138
1981 — New York (N.L.)	0	0	...	0.00	1	1	0	0	0	2	0	0	0	1	3

Year	Team (League)	W	L	Pct.	ERA	G	GS	CG	ShO	Sv.	IP	H	R	ER	BB	SO
	—Tidewater (Int'l)........	1	3	.250	3.71	6	6	1	0	0	34	27	16	14	27	15
1982	—..................................							Did not play.								
1983	—Tidewater (Int'l)........	8	*16	.333	4.38	27	27	8	1	0	160⅓	170	100	78	73	106
	—New York (N.L.).........	1	1	.500	3.38	2	2	1	0	0	10⅔	15	10	4	4	9
1984	—New York (N.L.).........	3	3	.500	4.02	20	7	0	0	0	53⅔	61	28	24	18	29
	—Tidewater (Int'l)........	4	4	.500	4.05	10	10	0	0	0	53⅓	47	26	24	42	27
1985	—Vancouver (PCL)■.....	10	7	.588	4.00	27	27	3	1	0	177⅔	174	85	79	57	136
	—Milwaukee (A.L.).......	1	4	.200	4.05	5	5	0	0	0	33⅓	40	18	15	8	29
1986	—Milwaukee (A.L.).......	12	12	.500	4.21	33	30	3	2	0	188⅓	216	97	88	53	110
1987	—Los Angeles (N.L.)■...	3	11	.214	4.76	39	12	0	0	1	107⅔	121	62	57	36	61
1988	—Los Angeles (N.L.).....	17	11	.607	2.91	35	34	9	6	0	228⅔	201	87	74	56	180
1989	—L.A.-Cin. (N.L.)■........	8	14	.364	3.52	33	31	2	0	0	207	205	84	81	68	123
1990	—New York (A.L.)■.......	9	*19	.321	4.11	31	31	6	1	0	208	202	105	95	78	138
1991	—New York (A.L.).........	4	10	.286	6.49	28	18	1	0	0	120⅔	150	89	87	57	83
1992	—N.Y.-Sea. (A.L.)■.......	8	10	.444	5.36	26	23	3	0	0	141	131	89	84	87	46
1993	—Seattle (A.L.).............	11	9	.550	5.05	33	27	0	0	0	169⅓	202	104	95	58	68
A.L. totals (6 years)		45	64	.413	4.85	156	134	13	3	0	860⅔	941	502	464	341	474
N.L. totals (6 years)		32	40	.444	3.54	130	87	12	6	1	609⅔	603	271	240	183	405
Major league totals (12 years)		77	104	.425	4.31	286	221	25	9	1	1470⅓	1544	773	704	524	879

CHAMPIONSHIP SERIES RECORD

Year	Team (League)	W	L	Pct.	ERA	G	GS	CG	ShO	Sv.	IP	H	R	ER	BB	SO
1988	—Los Angeles (N.L.).....	0	1	.000	6.23	2	1	0	0	0	4⅓	8	4	3	3	3

WORLD SERIES RECORD

Year	Team (League)	W	L	Pct.	ERA	G	GS	CG	ShO	Sv.	IP	H	R	ER	BB	SO
1988	—Los Angeles (N.L.).....	0	0	...	1.35	2	0	0	0	0	6⅔	6	1	1	2	4

LEDESMA, AARON

SS, METS

PERSONAL: Born June 3, 1971, in Union City, Calif.... 6-2/200.... Throws right, bats right.... Full name: Aaron David Ledesma.
HIGH SCHOOL: James Logan (Union City, Calif.).
COLLEGE: Chabot College (Calif.).
TRANSACTIONS/CAREER NOTES: Selected by New York Mets organization in second round of free-agent draft (June 4, 1990).... On disabled list (April 13-May 24, 1991 and July 19, 1993-remainder of season).
STATISTICAL NOTES: Led Florida State League shortstops with 641 total chances and 79 double plays in 1992.

			BATTING											FIELDING			
Year	Team (League)	Pos.	G	AB	R	H	2B	3B	HR	RBI	Avg.	BB	SO	SB	PO	A	E	Avg.
1990	—Kingsport (Appal.)...	SS	66	243	50	81	11	1	5	38	.333	30	28	27	78	*170	24	.912
1991	—Columbia (S. Atl.).....	SS	33	115	19	39	8	0	1	14	.339	8	16	3	44	64	10	.915
1992	—St. Lucie (Fla. St.).....	SS	134	456	51	120	17	2	2	50	.263	46	66	20	185	*411	45	.930
1993	—Binghamton (East.)..	SS	66	206	23	55	12	0	5	22	.267	14	43	2	36	65	10	.910

LEE, DEREK

OF, EXPOS

PERSONAL: Born July 28, 1966, in Chicago.... 6-1/200.... Throws right, bats left.... Full name: Derek Gerald Lee.
HIGH SCHOOL: South Lakes (Reston, Va.).
COLLEGE: Manatee (Fla.) and South Florida.
TRANSACTIONS/CAREER NOTES: Selected by Pittsburgh Pirates organization in ninth round of free-agent draft (January 9, 1985).... Selected by Chicago Cubs organization in fifth round of free-agent draft (January 14, 1986).... Selected by Philadelphia Phillies organization in secondary phase of free-agent draft (June 2, 1986).... Selected by Detroit Tigers organization in eighth round of free-agent draft (June 2, 1987).... Selected by Chicago White Sox organization in 42nd round of free-agent draft (June 1, 1988).... Claimed on waivers by Minnesota Twins (October 5, 1992).... Traded by Twins to Montreal Expos for P Joe Norris (January 24, 1994).
STATISTICAL NOTES: Tied for Pacific Coast League lead in double plays by outfielder with four in 1993.

			BATTING											FIELDING			
Year	Team (League)	Pos.	G	AB	R	H	2B	3B	HR	RBI	Avg.	BB	SO	SB	PO	A	E	Avg.
1988	—Utica (N.Y.-Penn)....	OF-3B	76	252	51	86	7	5	2	47	.341	50	48	*54	130	10	7	.952
1989	—South Bend (Mid.)....	OF	125	448	*89	128	24	7	11	48	.286	87	83	45	187	6	8	.960
1990	—Birm. (Southern)......	OF	126	411	68	105	21	3	7	75	.255	71	93	14	188	6	8	.960
1991	—Birm. (Southern)......	OF	45	154	36	50	10	2	5	16	.325	46	23	9	65	5	1	.986
	—Vancouver (PCL).....	OF-1B	87	318	54	94	28	5	6	44	.296	35	62	4	162	8	7	.960
1992	—Vancouver (PCL).....	OF	115	381	58	104	20	6	7	50	.273	56	65	17	188	6	3	.985
1993	—Portland (PCL)■.......	OF	106	381	79	120	30	7	10	80	.315	60	51	16	188	10	6	.971
	—Minnesota (A.L.)......	OF	15	33	3	5	1	0	0	4	.152	1	4	0	15	0	0	1.000
Major league totals (1 year)			15	33	3	5	1	0	0	4	.152	1	4	0	15	0	0	1.000

LEE, MANUEL

SS, RANGERS

PERSONAL: Born June 17, 1965, in San Pedro de Macoris, Dominican Republic.... 5-9/166.... Throws right, bats both.... Full name: Manuel Lora Lee.
TRANSACTIONS/CAREER NOTES: Signed as free agent by New York Mets organization (May 10, 1982).... On disabled list (April 9-22, 1984).... Traded by Mets organization with OF Gerald Young to Houston Astros (August 31, 1984) as partial completion of deal in which Mets acquired IF Ray Knight from Astros for three players to be named later (August 28, 1984); Astros acquired P Mitch Cook to complete deal (September 10, 1984).... Selected by Toronto Blue Jays from Astros organization in Rule 5 major league draft (December 3, 1984).... On disabled list (March 28-April 12 and May 12-June 1, 1988; and April 30-June 6, 1989).... Granted free agency (November 4, 1992).... Signed by Texas Rangers (December 19, 1992).... On disabled list (March 27-April 16 and May 15-July 24, 1993).
STATISTICAL NOTES: Led A.L. second basemen with .993 fielding percentage in 1990.

Year	Team (League)	Pos.	G	AB	R	H	2B	3B	HR	RBI	Avg.	BB	SO	SB	PO	A	E	Avg.
				BATTING											FIELDING			
1982	—Kingsport (Appal.) ...	2B-SS	16	54	2	12	1	0	0	3	.222	3	12	0	34	34	6	.919
1983	—GC Mets (GCL)	2B-SS	32	97	8	24	2	1	0	12	.247	13	14	2	44	79	8	.939
	—Little Falls (NYP)	2B	17	45	10	13	0	0	0	5	.289	9	11	2	34	40	3	.961
1984	—Columbia (S. Atl.)	SS-2B	102	346	84	114	12	5	2	33	*.329	60	42	24	126	277	34	.922
1985	—Toronto (A.L.)■	2B-SS-3B	64	40	9	8	0	0	0	0	.200	2	9	1	34	56	3	.968
1986	—Syracuse (Int'l)	SS-2B	76	236	34	58	6	1	1	19	.246	21	39	7	132	237	18	.953
	—Knoxville (South.)	SS-2B	41	158	21	43	1	2	0	11	.272	20	29	8	70	117	8	.959
	—Toronto (A.L.)	2B-SS-3B	35	78	8	16	0	1	1	7	.205	4	10	0	36	76	2	.982
1987	—Toronto (A.L.)	2B-SS	56	121	14	31	2	3	1	11	.256	6	13	2	77	110	5	.974
	—Syracuse (Int'l)	SS	74	251	25	71	9	5	3	26	.283	18	50	2	120	177	23	.928
1988	—Toronto (A.L.)	2B-SS-3B	116	381	38	111	16	3	2	38	.291	26	64	3	250	308	12	.979
1989	—Toronto (A.L.)	2-S-3-0	99	300	27	78	9	2	3	34	.260	20	60	4	152	201	11	.970
1990	—Toronto (A.L.)	2B-SS	117	391	45	95	12	4	6	41	.243	26	90	3	265	301	4	†.993
1991	—Toronto (A.L.)	SS	138	445	41	104	18	3	0	29	.234	24	107	7	194	360	19	.967
1992	—Toronto (A.L.)	SS	128	396	49	104	10	1	3	39	.263	50	73	6	187	331	7	.987
1993	—Texas (A.L.)■	SS	73	205	31	45	3	1	1	12	.220	22	39	2	96	205	10	.968
Major league totals (9 years)			826	2357	262	592	70	18	17	211	.251	180	465	28	1291	1948	73	.978

CHAMPIONSHIP SERIES RECORD

Year	Team (League)	Pos.	G	AB	R	H	2B	3B	HR	RBI	Avg.	BB	SO	SB	PO	A	E	Avg.
				BATTING											FIELDING			
1985	—Toronto (A.L.)	PR-2B	1	0	0	0	0	0	0	0	...	0	0	0	0	0	0	...
1989	—Toronto (A.L.)	2B	2	8	2	2	0	0	0	0	.250	0	1	0	4	1	0	1.000
1991	—Toronto (A.L.)	SS	5	16	3	2	0	0	0	0	.125	1	5	0	8	16	1	.960
1992	—Toronto (A.L.)	SS	6	18	2	5	1	1	0	3	.278	1	2	0	12	15	3	.900
Championship series totals (4 years)			14	42	7	9	1	1	0	3	.214	2	8	0	24	32	4	.933

WORLD SERIES RECORD

Year	Team (League)	Pos.	G	AB	R	H	2B	3B	HR	RBI	Avg.	BB	SO	SB	PO	A	E	Avg.
				BATTING											FIELDING			
1992	—Toronto (A.L.)	SS	6	19	1	2	0	0	0	0	.105	1	2	0	14	10	1	.960

L

LEFFERTS, CRAIG

P, ANGELS

PERSONAL: Born September 29, 1957, in Munich, West Germany. . . . 6-1/230. . . . Throws left, bats left. . . . Full name: Craig Lindsay Lefferts.

HIGH SCHOOL: Northeast (St. Petersburg, Fla.).

COLLEGE: Arizona.

TRANSACTIONS/CAREER NOTES: Selected by Kansas City Royals organization in sixth round of free-agent draft (June 5, 1979). . . . Selected by Chicago Cubs organization in ninth round of free-agent draft (June 3, 1980). . . . On disabled list (April 24-June 4, 1982). . . . Traded by Cubs with 1B Carmelo Martinez and 3B Fritz Connally to San Diego Padres for P Scott Sanderson (December 7, 1983). . . . Traded by Padres with P Dave Dravecky and IF Kevin Mitchell to San Francisco Giants for 3B Chris Brown, P Keith Comstock, P Mark Davis and P Mark Grant (July 4, 1987). . . . Granted free agency (November 13, 1989). . . . Signed by San Diego Padres (December 6, 1989). . . . Traded by Padres to Baltimore Orioles for P Erik Schullstrom and a player to be named later (August 31, 1992); Padres acquired IF Ricky Gutierrez to complete deal (September 4, 1992). . . . Granted free agency (November 2, 1992). . . . Signed by Texas Rangers (January 13, 1993). . . . On Texas disabled list (May 18-June 2, 1993); included rehabilitation assignment to Oklahoma City (May 30-June 2). . . . Granted free agency (November 1, 1993). . . . Signed by California Angels (January 13, 1994).

Year	Team (League)	W	L	Pct.	ERA	G	GS	CG	ShO	Sv.	IP	H	R	ER	BB	SO
1980	—Geneva (NY-Penn)	9	1	*.900	2.78	12	12	5	1	0	94	74	35	29	24	*99
1981	—Midland (Texas)	12	•12	.500	4.14	26	25	11	3	0	185	203	95	85	36	135
1982	—Iowa (Am. Assoc.)	8	5	.615	3.05	18	14	3	0	0	97⅓	97	50	33	25	71
1983	—Chicago (N.L.)	3	4	.429	3.13	56	5	0	0	1	89	80	35	31	29	60
1984	—San Diego (N.L.)■.......	3	4	.429	2.13	62	0	0	0	10	105⅔	88	29	25	24	56
1985	—San Diego (N.L.)	7	6	.538	3.35	60	0	0	0	2	83⅓	75	34	31	30	48
1986	—San Diego (N.L.)	9	8	.529	3.09	*83	0	0	0	4	107⅔	98	41	37	44	72
1987	—S.D.-S.F. (N.L.)■........	5	5	.500	3.83	77	0	0	0	6	98⅔	92	47	42	33	57
1988	—San Francisco (N.L.)	3	8	.273	2.92	64	0	0	0	11	92⅓	74	33	30	23	58
1989	—San Francisco (N.L.)	2	4	.333	2.69	70	0	0	0	20	107	93	38	32	22	71
1990	—San Diego (N.L.)■........	7	5	.583	2.52	56	0	0	0	23	78⅔	68	26	22	22	60
1991	—San Diego (N.L.)	1	6	.143	3.91	54	0	0	0	23	69	74	35	30	14	48
1992	—San Diego (N.L.)	13	9	.591	3.69	27	27	0	0	0	163⅓	180	76	67	35	81
	—Baltimore (A.L.)■	1	3	.250	4.09	5	5	1	0	0	33	34	19	15	6	23
1993	—Texas (A.L.)■	3	9	.250	6.05	52	8	0	0	0	83⅓	102	57	56	28	58
	—Okla. City (A.A.)	0	1	.000	7.50	1	1	0	0	0	6	9	5	5	2	1
A.L. totals (2 years)		4	12	.250	5.49	57	13	1	0	0	116⅓	136	76	71	34	81
N.L. totals (10 years)		53	59	.473	3.14	609	32	0	0	100	994⅔	922	394	347	276	611
Major league totals (11 years) .		57	71	.445	3.39	666	45	1	0	100	1111	1058	470	418	310	692

CHAMPIONSHIP SERIES RECORD

Year	Team (League)	W	L	Pct.	ERA	G	GS	CG	ShO	Sv.	IP	H	R	ER	BB	SO
1984	—San Diego (N.L.)	2	0	1.000	0.00	3	0	0	0	0	4	1	0	0	1	1
1987	—San Francisco (N.L.)	0	0	...	0.00	3	0	0	0	0	2	3	0	0	1	0
1989	—San Francisco (N.L.)	0	0	...	9.00	2	0	0	0	0	1	1	1	1	2	1
Champ. series totals (3 years) .		2	0	1.000	1.29	8	0	0	0	0	7	5	1	1	4	2

WORLD SERIES RECORD

Year	Team (League)	W	L	Pct.	ERA	G	GS	CG	ShO	Sv.	IP	H	R	ER	BB	SO
1984	—San Diego (N.L.)	0	0	...	0.00	3	0	0	0	1	6	2	0	0	1	7
1989	—San Francisco (N.L.)	0	0	...	3.38	3	0	0	0	0	2⅔	2	1	1	2	1
World Series totals (2 years)		0	0	...	1.04	6	0	0	0	1	8⅔	4	1	1	3	8

LEFTWICH, PHIL

P, ANGELS

PERSONAL: Born May 19, 1969, in Lynchburg, Va.... 6-5/205.... Throws right, bats right.... Full name: Phillip Dale Leftwich.

HIGH SCHOOL: Brookville (Lynchburg, Va.).

COLLEGE: Radford.

TRANSACTIONS/CAREER NOTES: Selected by California Angels organization in second round of free-agent draft (June 4, 1990).

Year	Team (League)	W	L	Pct.	ERA	G	GS	CG	ShO	Sv.	IP	H	R	ER	BB	SO
1990	—Boise (Northwest)	8	2	.800	1.86	15	15	0	0	0	92	88	36	19	22	81
1991	—Quad City (Midw.)	11	9	.550	3.28	26	26	5	1	0	173	158	70	63	59	163
	—Midland (Texas)	1	0	1.000	3.00	1	1	0	0	0	6	5	2	2	5	3
1992	—Midland (Texas)	6	9	.400	5.88	21	21	0	0	0	121	156	90	79	37	85
1993	—Vancouver (PCL)	7	7	.500	4.64	20	20	3	1	0	126	138	74	65	45	102
	—California (A.L.)	4	6	.400	3.79	12	12	1	0	0	80⅔	81	35	34	27	31
Major league totals (1 year)		4	6	.400	3.79	12	12	1	0	0	80⅔	81	35	34	27	31

LEIBRANDT, CHARLIE

P

PERSONAL: Born October 4, 1956, in Chicago.... 6-3/200.... Throws left, bats right.... Full name: Charles Louis Leibrandt Jr.

HIGH SCHOOL: Loyola Academy (Wilmette, Ill.).

COLLEGE: Miami of Ohio (bachelor of science degree in business management).

TRANSACTIONS/CAREER NOTES: Selected by Cincinnati Reds organization in ninth round of free-agent draft (June 6, 1978).... Traded by Reds to Kansas City Royals for P Bob Tufts (June 7, 1983).... Granted free agency (November 9, 1987).... Re-signed by Royals (January 7, 1988).... Traded by Royals with P Rick Luecken to Atlanta Braves for 1B Gerald Perry and P Jim LeMasters (December 15, 1989).... On Atlanta disabled list (March 26-June 3, 1990); included rehabilitation assignment to Greenville (May 21-June 3).... Granted free agency (December 7, 1990).... Re-signed by Braves (December 20, 1990).... Traded by Braves with P Pat Gomez to Texas Rangers for 3B Jose Oliva (December 9, 1992).... On disabled list (August 4-20 and August 21-September 10, 1993).... Granted free agency (November 4, 1993).

Year	Team (League)	W	L	Pct.	ERA	G	GS	CG	ShO	Sv.	IP	H	R	ER	BB	SO
1978	—Eugene (N'west)	2	0	1.000	4.05	3	2	1	0	0	20	24	13	9	5	18
	—Tampa (Fla. St.)	4	1	.800	0.77	6	6	5	2	0	47	26	4	4	17	40
	—Indianapolis (A.A.)	2	1	.667	2.79	4	4	1	1	0	29	20	9	9	12	12
1979	—Indianapolis (A.A.)	8	★14	.364	2.94	27	•26	5	2	0	162	146	67	53	65	100
	—Cincinnati (N.L.)	0	0	...	0.00	3	0	0	0	0	4	2	2	0	2	1
1980	—Cincinnati (N.L.)	10	9	.526	4.24	36	27	5	2	0	174	200	84	82	54	62
1981	—Indianapolis (A.A.)	9	7	.563	2.93	25	25	5	1	0	169	149	76	55	75	101
	—Cincinnati (N.L.)	1	1	.500	3.60	7	4	1	1	0	30	28	12	12	15	9
1982	—Cincinnati (N.L.)	5	7	.417	5.10	36	11	0	0	2	107⅔	130	68	61	48	34
1983	—Ind.-Omaha (A.A.)■	9	10	.474	4.27	27	27	6	1	0	185⅓	181	113	88	77	128
1984	—Omaha (A.A.)	7	1	.875	1.24	9	9	4	•3	0	72⅔	51	14	10	16	38
	—Kansas City (A.L.)	11	7	.611	3.63	23	23	0	0	0	143⅔	158	65	58	38	53
1985	—Kansas City (A.L.)	17	9	.654	2.69	33	33	8	3	0	237⅔	223	86	71	68	108
1986	—Kansas City (A.L.)	14	11	.560	4.09	35	34	8	1	0	231⅓	238	112	105	63	108
1987	—Kansas City (A.L.)	16	11	.593	3.41	35	35	8	3	0	240⅓	235	104	91	74	151
1988	—Kansas City (A.L.)	13	12	.520	3.19	35	35	7	2	0	243	244	98	86	62	125
1989	—Kansas City (A.L.)	5	11	.313	5.14	33	27	3	1	0	161	196	98	92	54	73
1990	—Greenville (South.)■	1	0	1.000	0.00	2	2	0	0	0	13	5	4	0	5	12
	—Atlanta (N.L.)	9	11	.450	3.16	24	24	5	2	0	162⅓	164	72	57	35	76
1991	—Atlanta (N.L.)	15	13	.536	3.49	36	36	1	1	0	229⅔	212	105	89	56	128
1992	—Atlanta (N.L.)	15	7	.682	3.36	32	31	5	2	0	193	191	78	72	42	104
1993	—Texas (A.L.)■	9	10	.474	4.55	26	26	1	0	0	150⅓	169	84	76	45	89
A.L. totals (7 years)		85	71	.545	3.70	220	213	35	10	0	1407⅓	1463	647	579	404	707
N.L. totals (7 years)		55	48	.534	3.73	174	133	17	8	2	900⅔	927	421	373	252	414
Major league totals (14 years)		140	119	.541	3.71	394	346	52	18	2	2308	2390	1068	952	656	1121

CHAMPIONSHIP SERIES RECORD

Year	Team (League)	W	L	Pct.	ERA	G	GS	CG	ShO	Sv.	IP	H	R	ER	BB	SO
1979	—Cincinnati (N.L.)	0	0	...	0.00	1	0	0	0	0	⅓	0	0	0	0	0
1984	—Kansas City (A.L.)	0	1	.000	1.13	1	1	1	0	0	8	3	1	1	4	6
1985	—Kansas City (A.L.)	1	2	.333	5.28	3	2	0	0	0	15⅓	17	9	9	4	6
1991	—Atlanta (N.L.)	0	0	...	1.35	1	1	0	0	0	6⅔	8	2	1	3	6
1992	—Atlanta (N.L.)	0	0	...	1.93	2	0	0	0	0	4⅔	4	1	1	3	3
Champ. series totals (5 years)		1	3	.250	3.09	8	4	1	0	0	35	32	13	12	14	21

WORLD SERIES RECORD

Year	Team (League)	W	L	Pct.	ERA	G	GS	CG	ShO	Sv.	IP	H	R	ER	BB	SO
1985	—Kansas City (A.L.)	0	1	.000	2.76	2	2	0	0	0	16⅓	10	5	5	4	10
1991	—Atlanta (N.L.)	0	2	.000	11.25	2	1	0	0	0	4	8	5	5	1	3
1992	—Atlanta (N.L.)	0	1	.000	9.00	1	0	0	0	0	2	3	2	2	0	0
World Series totals (3 years)		0	4	.000	4.84	5	3	0	0	0	22⅓	21	12	12	5	13

LEITER, AL

P, BLUE JAYS

PERSONAL: Born October 23, 1965, in Toms River, N.J. . . . 6-3/215. . . . Throws left, bats left. . . . Full name: Alois Terry Leiter. . . . Brother of Mark Leiter, pitcher, Detroit Tigers; and brother of Kurt Leiter, minor league pitcher (1982-84 and 1986). . . . Name pronounced LIE-ter.
HIGH SCHOOL: Central Regional (Bayville, N.J.).
TRANSACTIONS/CAREER NOTES: Selected by New York Yankees organization in second round of free-agent draft (June 4, 1984). . . . On New York disabled list (June 22-July 26, 1988); included rehabilitation assignment to Columbus (July 17-25). . . . Traded by Yankees to Toronto Blue Jays for OF Jesse Barfield (April 30, 1989). . . . On Toronto disabled list (May 11, 1989-remainder of season); included rehabilitation assignment to Dunedin (August 12-29). . . . On Syracuse disabled list (May 20-June 13, 1990). . . . On Toronto disabled list (April 27, 1991-remainder of season); included rehabilitation assignment to Dunedin (May 20-28 and July 19-August 7). . . . On disabled list (April 24-May 9, 1993).

Year Team (League)	W	L	Pct.	ERA	G	GS	CG	ShO	Sv.	IP	H	R	ER	BB	SO
1984—Oneonta (NYP)	3	2	.600	3.63	10	10	0	0	0	57	52	32	23	26	48
1985—Oneonta (NYP)	3	2	.600	2.37	6	6	2	0	0	38	27	14	10	25	34
—Fort Lauder. (FSL)	1	6	.143	6.48	17	17	1	0	0	82	87	70	59	57	44
1986—Fort Lauder. (FSL)	4	8	.333	4.05	22	21	1	1	0	117⅔	96	64	53	90	101
1987—Columbus (Int'l)	1	4	.200	6.17	5	5	0	0	0	23⅓	21	18	16	15	23
—Alb./Colon. (East.)	3	3	.500	3.35	15	14	2	0	0	78	64	34	29	37	71
—New York (A.L.)	2	2	.500	6.35	4	4	0	0	0	22⅔	24	16	16	15	28
1988—New York (A.L.)	4	4	.500	3.92	14	14	0	0	0	57⅓	49	27	25	33	60
—Columbus (Int'l)	0	2	.000	3.46	4	4	0	0	0	13	5	7	5	14	12
1989—N.Y.-Tor. (A.L.)■	1	2	.333	5.67	5	5	0	0	0	33⅓	32	23	21	23	26
—Dunedin (Fla. St.)	0	2	.000	5.63	3	3	0	0	0	8	11	5	5	5	4
1990—Dunedin (Fla. St.)	0	0	...	2.63	6	6	0	0	0	24	18	8	7	12	14
—Syracuse (Int'l)	3	8	.273	4.62	15	14	1	1	0	78	59	43	40	68	69
—Toronto (A.L.)	0	0	...	0.00	4	0	0	0	0	6⅓	1	0	0	2	5
1991—Toronto (A.L.)	0	0	...	27.00	3	0	0	0	0	1⅔	3	5	5	5	1
—Dunedin (Fla. St.)	0	0	...	1.86	4	3	0	0	0	9⅔	5	2	2	7	5
1992—Syracuse (Int'l)	8	9	.471	3.86	27	27	2	0	0	163⅓	159	82	70	64	108
—Toronto (A.L.)	0	0	...	9.00	1	0	0	0	0	1	1	1	1	2	0
1993—Toronto (A.L.)	9	6	.600	4.11	34	12	1	1	2	105	93	52	48	56	66
Major league totals (7 years)	16	14	.533	4.59	65	35	1	1	2	227⅓	203	124	116	136	186

CHAMPIONSHIP SERIES RECORD

Year Team (League)	W	L	Pct.	ERA	G	GS	CG	ShO	Sv.	IP	H	R	ER	BB	SO
1993—Toronto (A.L.)	0	0	...	3.38	2	0	0	0	0	2⅔	4	1	1	2	2

WORLD SERIES RECORD

Year Team (League)	W	L	Pct.	ERA	G	GS	CG	ShO	Sv.	IP	H	R	ER	BB	SO
1993—Toronto (A.L.)	1	0	1.000	7.71	3	0	0	0	0	7	12	6	6	2	5

LEITER, MARK

P, TIGERS

PERSONAL: Born April 13, 1963, in Joliet, Ill. . . . 6-3/210. . . . Throws right, bats right. . . . Full name: Mark Edward Leiter. . . . Brother of Al Leiter, pitcher, Toronto Blue Jays; and brother of Kurt Leiter, minor league pitcher (1982-84 and 1986). . . . Name pronounced LIE-ter.
HIGH SCHOOL: Central Regional (Bayville, N.J.).
COLLEGE: Connors State College (Okla.) and Ramapo College of New Jersey.
TRANSACTIONS/CAREER NOTES: Selected by Baltimore Orioles organization in fourth round of free-agent draft (January 11, 1983). . . . On disabled list (April 10, 1986-entire season; April 10, 1987-entire season and April 10-June 13, 1988). . . . Released by Orioles organization (June 13, 1988). . . . Signed by Fort Lauderdale, New York Yankees organization (September 29, 1988). . . . Traded by Yankees to Detroit Tigers for IF Torey Lovullo (March 19, 1991). . . . On Detroit disabled list (June 6-23, 1991; July 24-August 24, 1992 and August 4-September 1, 1993).

Year Team (League)	W	L	Pct.	ERA	G	GS	CG	ShO	Sv.	IP	H	R	ER	BB	SO
1983—Bluefield (Appal.)	2	1	.667	2.70	6	6	2	0	0	36⅔	33	17	11	13	35
—Hagerstown (Car.)	1	5	.167	7.25	8	8	0	0	0	36	42	31	29	28	18
1984—Hagerstown (Car.)	8	•13	.381	5.62	27	24	5	1	0	139⅓	132	96	87	*108	105
1985—Hagerstown (Car.)	2	8	.200	3.46	34	6	1	0	8	83⅓	77	44	32	29	82
—Charlotte (South.)	0	1	.000	1.42	5	0	0	0	1	6⅓	3	1	1	2	8
1986—							Did not play.								
1987—							Did not play.								
1988—							Did not play.								
1989—Fort Lauder. (FSL)■	2	2	.500	1.53	6	4	1	0	1	35⅓	27	9	6	5	22
—Columbus (Int'l)	9	6	.600	5.00	22	12	0	0	0	90	102	50	50	34	70
1990—Columbus (Int'l)	9	4	.692	3.60	30	14	2	1	1	122⅔	114	56	49	27	115
—New York (A.L.)	1	1	.500	6.84	8	3	0	0	0	26⅓	33	20	20	9	21
1991—Toledo (Int'l)■	1	0	1.000	0.00	5	0	0	0	1	6⅔	6	0	0	3	7
—Detroit (A.L.)	9	7	.563	4.21	38	15	1	0	1	134⅔	125	66	63	50	103
1992—Detroit (A.L.)	8	5	.615	4.18	35	14	1	0	0	112	116	57	52	43	75
1993—Detroit (A.L.)	6	6	.500	4.73	27	13	1	0	0	106⅔	111	61	56	44	70
Major league totals (4 years)	24	19	.558	4.53	108	45	3	0	1	379⅔	385	204	191	146	269

LEIUS, SCOTT

SS, TWINS

PERSONAL: Born September 24, 1965, in Yonkers, N.Y. . . . 6-3/208. . . . Throws right, bats right. . . . Full name: Scott Thomas Leius. . . . Name pronounced LAY-us.
HIGH SCHOOL: Mamaroneck (N.Y.).
COLLEGE: Concordia College (N.Y.).
TRANSACTIONS/CAREER NOTES: Selected by Minnesota Twins organization in 13th round of free-agent draft (June 2, 1986). . . . On disabled list (August 3, 1989-remainder of season and April 22, 1993-remainder of season).
STATISTICAL NOTES: Led Appalachian League shortstops with 174 assists and 33 double plays in 1986. . . . Led Midwest League shortstops with 74 double plays in 1987.

Year	Team (League)	Pos.	G	AB	R	H	2B	3B	HR	RBI	Avg.	BB	SO	SB	PO	A	E	Avg.
			BATTING												FIELDING			
1986	—Elizabeth. (Appal.) ...	SS-3B	61	237	37	66	14	1	4	23	.278	26	45	5	67	†176	18	.931
1987	—Kenosha (Midwest) ..	SS	126	414	65	99	16	4	8	51	.239	50	88	6	183	331	31	.943
1988	—Visalia (California)...	SS	93	308	44	73	14	4	3	46	.237	42	50	3	154	234	15	.963
1989	—Orlando (Southern) ..	SS	99	346	49	105	22	2	4	45	*.303	38	74	3	148	257	22	.948
1990	—Portland (PCL)	SS-2B	103	352	34	81	13	5	2	23	.230	35	66	5	155	323	18	.964
	—Minnesota (A.L.)	SS-3B	14	25	4	6	1	0	1	4	.240	2	2	0	20	25	0	1.000
1991	—Minnesota (A.L.)	3B-SS-OF	109	199	35	57	7	2	5	20	.286	30	35	5	56	129	7	.964
1992	—Minnesota (A.L.)	3B-SS	129	409	50	102	18	2	2	35	.249	34	61	6	63	261	15	.956
1993	—Minnesota (A.L.)	SS	10	18	4	3	0	0	0	2	.167	2	4	0	10	26	2	.947
Major league totals (4 years)			262	651	93	168	26	4	8	61	.258	68	102	11	149	441	24	.961

CHAMPIONSHIP SERIES RECORD

Year	Team (League)	Pos.	G	AB	R	H	2B	3B	HR	RBI	Avg.	BB	SO	SB	PO	A	E	Avg.
			BATTING												FIELDING			
1991	—Minnesota (A.L.)	3B-PH	3	4	0	0	0	0	0	0	.000	1	1	0	1	4	0	1.000

WORLD SERIES RECORD

Year	Team (League)	Pos.	G	AB	R	H	2B	3B	HR	RBI	Avg.	BB	SO	SB	PO	A	E	Avg.
			BATTING												FIELDING			
1991	—Minnesota (A.L.)	3B-PH-SS	7	14	2	5	0	0	1	2	.357	1	2	0	5	8	1	.929

LEMKE, MARK

2B, BRAVES

PERSONAL: Born August 13, 1965, in Utica, N.Y. . . . 5-9/167. . . . Throws right, bats both. . . . Full name: Mark Alan Lemke. . . . Name pronounced LEM-kee.

HIGH SCHOOL: Notre Dame (Utica, N.Y.).

TRANSACTIONS/CAREER NOTES: Selected by Atlanta Braves organization in 27th round of free-agent draft (June 6, 1983). . . . On Atlanta disabled list (May 29-July 17, 1990); included rehabilitation assignment to Gulf Coast Braves (July 9-17).

STATISTICAL NOTES: Led Gulf Coast League second basemen with .977 fielding percentage, 175 putouts, 207 assists, 391 total chances and 39 double plays in 1984. . . . Led Carolina League second basemen with .982 fielding percentage, 355 assists and 83 double plays in 1987. . . . Led Southern League with 239 total bases in 1988. . . . Led Southern League second basemen with 739 total chances and 105 double plays in 1988. . . . Led International League second basemen with 731 total chances and 105 double plays in 1989. . . . Led N.L. second basemen with 785 total chances and 100 double plays in 1993.

Year	Team (League)	Pos.	G	AB	R	H	2B	3B	HR	RBI	Avg.	BB	SO	SB	PO	A	E	Avg.
			BATTING												FIELDING			
1983	—GC Braves (GCL)	2B	53	209	37	55	6	0	0	19	.263	30	19	10	81	101	11	.943
1984	—Anderson (S. Atl.)	2B-3B	42	121	18	18	2	0	0	5	.149	14	14	3	67	83	4	.974
	—GC Braves (GCL)	2B-SS	•63	*243	41	67	11	0	3	32	.276	29	14	2	†175	†209	9	†.977
1985	—Sumter (S. Atl.)	2B	90	231	25	50	6	0	0	20	.216	34	22	2	119	174	11	.964
1986	—Sumter (S. Atl.)	3B-2B	126	448	99	122	24	2	18	66	.272	87	31	11	134	274	16	.962
1987	—Durham (Carolina)...	2B-3B	127	489	75	143	28	3	20	68	.292	54	45	10	248	†355	11	†.982
	—Greenville (South.) ...	3B	6	26	0	6	0	0	0	4	.231	0	4	0	4	12	1	.941
1988	—Greenville (South.) ...	2B	•143	*567	81	*153	30	4	16	80	.270	52	92	18	*281	*440	18	.976
	—Atlanta (N.L.)	2B	16	58	8	13	4	0	0	2	.224	4	5	0	47	51	3	.970
1989	—Richmond (Int'l)	2B	*146	*518	69	143	22	7	5	61	.276	66	45	4	*299	*417	*15	.979
	—Atlanta (N.L.)	2B	14	55	4	10	2	1	2	10	.182	5	7	0	25	40	0	1.000
1990	—Atlanta (N.L.)	3B-2B-SS	102	239	22	54	13	0	0	21	.226	21	22	0	90	193	4	.986
	—GC Braves (GCL)	2B-3B	4	11	2	4	0	0	1	5	.364	1	3	0	5	11	1	.941
1991	—Atlanta (N.L.)	2B-3B	136	269	36	63	11	2	2	23	.234	29	27	1	162	215	10	.974
1992	—Atlanta (N.L.)	2B-3B	155	427	38	97	7	4	6	26	.227	50	39	0	236	335	9	.984
1993	—Atlanta (N.L.)	2B	151	493	52	124	19	2	7	49	.252	65	50	1	*329	442	14	.982
Major league totals (6 years)			574	1541	160	361	56	9	17	131	.234	174	150	2	889	1276	40	.982

CHAMPIONSHIP SERIES RECORD

Year	Team (League)	Pos.	G	AB	R	H	2B	3B	HR	RBI	Avg.	BB	SO	SB	PO	A	E	Avg.
			BATTING												FIELDING			
1991	—Atlanta (N.L.)	2B	7	20	1	4	1	0	0	1	.200	4	0	0	12	10	1	.957
1992	—Atlanta (N.L.)	2B-3B	7	21	2	7	1	0	0	2	.333	5	3	0	11	17	0	1.000
1993	—Atlanta (N.L.)	2B	6	24	2	5	2	0	0	4	.208	1	6	0	6	19	2	.926
Championship series totals (3 years)			20	65	5	16	4	0	0	7	.246	10	9	0	29	46	3	.962

WORLD SERIES RECORD

WORLD SERIES NOTES: Shares single-game record for most triples—2 (October 24, 1991).

Year	Team (League)	Pos.	G	AB	R	H	2B	3B	HR	RBI	Avg.	BB	SO	SB	PO	A	E	Avg.
			BATTING												FIELDING			
1991	—Atlanta (N.L.)	2B	6	24	4	10	1	3	0	4	.417	2	4	0	14	19	1	.971
1992	—Atlanta (N.L.)	2B	6	19	0	4	0	0	0	2	.211	1	3	0	18	12	0	1.000
World Series totals (2 years)			12	43	4	14	1	3	0	6	.326	3	7	0	32	31	1	.984

LEONARD, MARK

OF

PERSONAL: Born August 14, 1964, in Mountain View, Calif. . . . 6-0/212. . . . Throws right, bats left. . . . Full name: Mark David Leonard.

HIGH SCHOOL: Fremont (Calif.).

COLLEGE: UC Santa Barbara.

TRANSACTIONS/CAREER NOTES: Selected by San Francisco Giants organization in 29th round of free-agent draft (June 2, 1986). . . . Loaned by Giants organization to Tri-Cities, co-op (June 23-September 1, 1986). . . . On Phoenix disabled list (August 6, 1989-remainder of season). . . . On San Francisco disabled list (August 8-September 5, 1990); included rehabilitation assign-

ment to Phoenix (August 27-September 5).... On San Francisco disabled list (April 19-June 15, 1992); included rehabilitation assignment to Phoenix (May 26-June 14).... Traded by Giants to Baltimore Orioles for IF Steve Scarsone (March 20, 1993).... Released by Orioles (December 12, 1993).
STATISTICAL NOTES: Led California League with 283 total bases, 11 sacrifice flies and 13 intentional bases on balls received in 1988.

			BATTING											FIELDING			
Year	Team (League)	Pos.	G	AB	R	H	2B	3B	HR	RBI	Avg.	BB	SO	SB	PO	A	E	Avg.
1986	—Eve.-T.-C. (N'west)■	OF-1B-C	38	128	21	33	6	0	4	17	.258	27	21	4	63	2	4	.942
1987	—Clinton (Midwest)■	1B	128	413	57	132	31	2	15	80	.320	71	61	5	610	47	9	.986
1988	—San Jose (Calif.)	OF-1B	*142	510	102	176	*50	6	15	*118	.345	*118	82	11	178	120	9	.971
1989	—Shreveport (Texas)	OF	63	219	29	68	15	3	10	52	.311	33	40	1	90	5	0	1.000
	—Phoenix (PCL)	OF	27	78	7	21	4	0	0	6	.269	9	15	1	29	1	3	.909
1990	—Phoenix (PCL)	OF	109	390	76	130	22	2	19	82	.333	76	81	6	120	3	1	.992
	—San Francisco (N.L.)	OF	11	17	3	3	1	0	1	2	.176	3	8	0	10	0	0	1.000
1991	—San Francisco (N.L.)	OF	64	129	14	31	7	1	2	14	.240	12	25	0	41	0	0	1.000
	—Phoenix (PCL)	OF	41	146	27	37	7	0	8	25	.253	21	29	1	45	3	3	.941
1992	—San Francisco (N.L.)	OF	55	128	13	30	7	0	4	16	.234	16	31	0	61	2	1	.984
	—Phoenix (PCL)	OF	39	139	17	47	4	1	5	25	.338	21	29	1	62	2	1	.985
1993	—Rochester (Int'l)■	OF	97	330	57	91	23	1	17	58	.276	60	81	0	127	2	2	.985
	—Baltimore (A.L.)	OF	10	15	1	1	1	0	0	3	.067	3	7	0	5	0	1	.833
American League totals (1 year)			10	15	1	1	1	0	0	3	.067	3	7	0	5	0	1	.833
National League totals (3 years)			130	274	30	64	15	1	7	32	.234	31	64	0	112	2	1	.991
Major league totals (4 years)			140	289	31	65	16	1	7	35	.225	34	71	0	117	2	2	.983

LESKANIC, CURT

P, ROCKIES

PERSONAL: Born April 2, 1968, in Homestead, Pa.... 6-0/180.... Throws right, bats right.... Full name: Curtis John Leskanic.
HIGH SCHOOL: Steel Valley (Munhall, Pa.).
COLLEGE: Louisiana State.
TRANSACTIONS/CAREER NOTES: Selected by Cleveland Indians organization in eighth round of free-agent draft (June 5, 1989).... On disabled list (April 23-June 25, 1990).... Traded by Indians organization with P Oscar Munoz to Minnesota Twins organization for 1B Paul Sorrento (March 28, 1992).... Selected by Colorado Rockies in third round (66th pick overall) of expansion draft (November 17, 1992).... Loaned by Rockies organization to Wichita, Padres organization (April 7-May 20, 1993).

Year	Team (League)	W	L	Pct.	ERA	G	GS	CG	ShO	Sv.	IP	H	R	ER	BB	SO
1990	—Kinston (Carolina)	6	5	.545	3.68	14	14	2	0	0	73⅓	61	34	30	30	71
1991	—Kinston (Carolina)	•15	8	.652	2.79	28	28	0	0	0	174⅓	143	63	54	91	*163
1992	—Orlando (Southern)■	9	11	.450	4.30	26	23	3	0	0	152⅔	158	84	73	64	126
	—Portland (PCL)	1	2	.333	9.98	5	3	0	0	0	15⅓	16	17	17	8	14
1993	—Wichita (Texas)■	3	2	.600	3.45	7	7	0	0	0	44⅓	37	20	17	17	42
	—Colo. Springs (PCL)■	4	3	.571	4.47	9	7	1	1	0	44⅓	39	24	22	26	38
	—Colorado (N.L.)	1	5	.167	5.37	18	8	0	0	0	57	59	40	34	27	30
Major league totals (1 year)		1	5	.167	5.37	18	8	0	0	0	57	59	40	34	27	30

LEVIS, JESSE

C, INDIANS

PERSONAL: Born April 14, 1968, in Philadelphia.... 5-9/180.... Throws right, bats left.
HIGH SCHOOL: Northeast (Philadelphia).
COLLEGE: North Carolina.
TRANSACTIONS/CAREER NOTES: Selected by Philadelphia Phillies organization in 36th round of free-agent draft (June 2, 1986).... Selected by Cleveland Indians organization in fourth round of free-agent draft (June 5, 1989).
STATISTICAL NOTES: Led Eastern League catchers with 733 total chances in 1991.

			BATTING											FIELDING			
Year	Team (League)	Pos.	G	AB	R	H	2B	3B	HR	RBI	Avg.	BB	SO	SB	PO	A	E	Avg.
1989	—Burlington (Appal.)	C	27	93	11	32	4	0	4	16	.344	10	7	1	189	27	2	.991
	—Kinston (Carolina)	C	27	87	11	26	6	0	2	11	.299	12	15	1	95	17	2	.982
	—Colo. Springs (PCL)	PH	1	1	0	0	0	0	0	0	.000	0	0	0	...	...	...	...
1990	—Kinston (Carolina)	C	107	382	63	113	18	3	7	64	.296	64	42	4	517	63	5	.991
1991	—Cant./Akr. (East.)	C	115	382	31	101	17	3	6	45	.264	40	36	2	*644	*77	12	.984
1992	—Colo. Springs (PCL)	C	87	253	39	92	20	1	6	44	.364	37	25	1	375	47	4	.991
	—Cleveland (A.L.)	C	28	43	2	12	4	0	1	3	.279	0	5	0	59	5	1	.985
1993	—Charlotte (Int'l)	C	47	129	10	32	6	1	2	20	.248	15	12	0	266	22	4	.986
	—Cleveland (A.L.)	C	31	63	7	11	2	0	0	4	.175	2	10	0	109	7	1	.991
Major league totals (2 years)			59	106	9	23	6	0	1	7	.217	2	15	0	168	12	2	.989

LEWIS, DARREN

OF, GIANTS

PERSONAL: Born August 28, 1967, in Berkeley, Calif.... 6-0/189.... Throws right, bats right.... Full name: Darren Joel Lewis.
HIGH SCHOOL: Moreau (Hayward, Calif.).
COLLEGE: Chabot College (Calif.) and California.
TRANSACTIONS/CAREER NOTES: Selected by Los Angeles Dodgers organization in sixth round of free-agent draft (January 14, 1986).... Selected by Toronto Blue Jays organization in 45th round of free-agent draft (June 2, 1987).... Selected by Oakland Athletics organization in 18th round of free-agent draft (June 1, 1988).... Traded by A's with a player to be named later to San Francisco Giants for IF Ernest Riles (December 4, 1990); Giants acquired P Pedro Pena to complete deal (December 17, 1990).... On disabled list (August 20-September 4, 1993).
RECORDS: Holds major league records for most consecutive errorless games by outfielder—316 (August 21, 1990 through 1993); and most consecutive chances accepted without an error by outfielder—770 (August 21, 1990 through 1993).... Holds

N.L. records for most consecutive errorless games by outfielder—293 (July 13, 1991 through 1993); and most consecutive chances accepted without an error by outfielder—737 (July 13, 1991 through 1993).
STATISTICAL NOTES: Led California League outfielders with 324 total chances in 1989.

			BATTING												FIELDING			
Year	**Team (League)**	**Pos.**	**G**	**AB**	**R**	**H**	**2B**	**3B**	**HR**	**RBI**	**Avg.**	**BB**	**SO**	**SB**	**PO**	**A**	**E**	**Avg.**
1988	—Ariz. A's (Arizona)	OF	5	15	8	5	3	0	0	4	.333	6	5	4	15	1	0	1.000
	—Madison (Midwest)	OF-2B	60	199	38	49	4	1	0	11	.246	46	37	31	195	3	4	.980
1989	—Modesto (Calif.)	OF	129	503	74	150	23	5	4	39	.298	59	84	27	*311	8	5	.985
	—Huntsville (South.)	OF	9	31	7	10	1	1	1	7	.323	2	6	0	16	0	0	1.000
1990	—Huntsville (South.)	OF	71	284	52	84	11	3	3	23	.296	36	28	21	186	6	0	1.000
	—Tacoma (PCL)	OF	60	247	32	72	5	2	2	26	.291	16	35	16	132	9	2	.986
	—Oakland (A.L.)	OF	25	35	4	8	0	0	0	1	.229	7	4	2	33	0	0	1.000
1991	—Phoenix (PCL)■	OF	81	315	63	107	12	10	2	52	.340	41	36	32	243	5	2	.992
	—San Francisco (N.L.)	OF	72	222	41	55	5	3	1	15	.248	36	30	13	159	2	0	1.000
1992	—San Francisco (N.L.)	OF	100	320	38	74	8	1	1	18	.231	29	46	28	225	3	0	1.000
	—Phoenix (PCL)	OF	42	158	22	36	5	2	0	6	.228	11	15	9	93	2	0	1.000
1993	—San Francisco (N.L.)	OF	136	522	84	132	17	7	2	48	.253	30	40	46	344	4	0	•1.000
American League totals (1 year)			25	35	4	8	0	0	0	1	.229	7	4	2	33	0	0	1.000
National League totals (3 years)			308	1064	163	261	30	11	4	81	.245	95	116	87	728	9	0	1.000
Major league totals (4 years)			333	1099	167	269	30	11	4	82	.245	102	120	89	761	9	0	1.000

LEWIS, MARK

SS, INDIANS

PERSONAL: Born November 30, 1969, in Hamilton, O.... 6-1/190.... Throws right, bats right.... Full name: Mark David Lewis.
HIGH SCHOOL: Hamilton (O.).
TRANSACTIONS/CAREER NOTES: Selected by Cleveland Indians organization in first round (second pick overall) of free-agent draft (June 1, 1988).... On Kinston disabled list (May 29-June 20, 1989).
STATISTICAL NOTES: Tied for A.L. lead in errors by shortstop with 25 in 1992.... Tied for International League lead in grounding into double plays with 19 in 1993.... Led International League shortstops with 81 double plays in 1993.

			BATTING												FIELDING			
Year	**Team (League)**	**Pos.**	**G**	**AB**	**R**	**H**	**2B**	**3B**	**HR**	**RBI**	**Avg.**	**BB**	**SO**	**SB**	**PO**	**A**	**E**	**Avg.**
1988	—Burlington (Appal.)	SS	61	227	39	60	13	1	7	43	.264	25	44	14	70	*177	23	.915
1989	—Kinston (Carolina)	SS	93	349	50	94	16	3	1	32	.269	34	50	17	130	244	32	.921
	—Cant./Akr. (East.)	SS	7	25	4	5	1	0	0	1	.200	1	3	0	15	28	2	.956
1990	—Cant./Akr. (East.)	SS	102	390	55	106	19	3	10	60	.272	23	49	8	152	286	31	.934
	—Colo. Springs (PCL)	SS	34	124	16	38	8	1	1	21	.306	9	13	2	52	84	11	.925
1991	—Colo. Springs (PCL)	SS-2B-3B	46	179	29	50	10	3	2	31	.279	18	23	3	65	135	10	.952
	—Cleveland (A.L.)	2B-SS	84	314	29	83	15	1	0	30	.264	15	45	2	129	231	9	.976
1992	—Cleveland (A.L.)	SS-3B	122	413	44	109	21	0	5	30	.264	25	69	4	184	336	‡26	.952
1993	—Charlotte (Int'l)	SS	126	507	93	144	30	4	17	67	.284	34	76	9	168	*403	23	.961
	—Cleveland (A.L.)	SS	14	52	6	13	2	0	1	5	.250	0	7	3	22	31	2	.964
Major league totals (3 years)			220	779	79	205	38	1	6	65	.263	40	121	9	335	598	37	.962

LEWIS, RICHIE

P, MARLINS

PERSONAL: Born January 25, 1966, in Muncie, Ind.... 5-10/175.... Throws right, bats right.... Full name: Richie Todd Lewis.
HIGH SCHOOL: South Side (Muncie, Ind.).
COLLEGE: Florida State (received degree, 1987).
TRANSACTIONS/CAREER NOTES: Selected by Montreal Expos organization in second round of free-agent draft (June 2, 1987).... On disabled list (June 2-August 12 and August 22, 1988-remainder of season; and July 28, 1989-remainder of season).... On Jacksonville disabled list (June 1-8 and June 11, 1990-remainder of season).... Traded by Expos to Baltimore Orioles for P Chris Myers (August 24, 1991).... Selected by Florida Marlins in second round (51st pick overall) of expansion draft (November 17, 1992).
HONORS: Named righthanded pitcher on THE SPORTING NEWS college All-America team (1987).

Year	**Team (League)**	**W**	**L**	**Pct.**	**ERA**	**G**	**GS**	**CG**	**ShO**	**Sv.**	**IP**	**H**	**R**	**ER**	**BB**	**SO**
1987	—Indianapolis (A.A.)	0	0	...	9.82	2	0	0	0	0	3⅔	6	4	4	2	3
1988	—Jacksonv. (South.)	5	3	.625	3.38	12	12	1	0	0	61⅓	37	32	23	56	60
1989	—Jacksonv. (South.)	5	4	.556	2.58	17	17	0	0	0	94⅓	80	37	27	55	105
1990	—W.P. Beach (FSL)	0	1	.000	4.80	10	0	0	0	2	15	12	12	8	11	14
	—Jacksonv. (South.)	0	0	...	1.26	11	0	0	0	5	14⅓	7	2	2	5	14
1991	—Harrisburg (East.)	6	5	.545	3.74	34	6	0	0	5	74⅔	67	33	31	40	82
	—Indianapolis (A.A.)	1	0	1.000	3.58	5	4	0	0	0	27⅔	35	12	11	20	22
	—Rochester (Int'l)■	1	0	1.000	2.81	2	2	0	0	0	16	13	5	5	7	18
1992	—Rochester (Int'l)	10	9	.526	3.28	24	23	6	1	0	159⅓	136	63	58	61	154
	—Baltimore (A.L.)	1	1	.500	10.80	2	2	0	0	0	6⅔	13	8	8	7	4
1993	—Florida (N.L.)■	6	3	.667	3.26	57	0	0	0	0	77⅓	68	37	28	43	65
A.L. totals (1 year)		1	1	.500	10.80	2	2	0	0	0	6⅔	13	8	8	7	4
N.L. totals (1 year)		6	3	.667	3.26	57	0	0	0	0	77⅓	68	37	28	43	65
Major league totals (2 years)		7	4	.636	3.86	59	2	0	0	0	84	81	45	36	50	69

LEWIS, SCOTT

P, ANGELS

PERSONAL: Born December 5, 1965, in Grants Pass, Ore.... 6-3/178.... Throws right, bats right.... Full name: Scott Allen Lewis.
HIGH SCHOOL: Medford (Ore.).
COLLEGE: UNLV.
TRANSACTIONS/CAREER NOTES: Selected by California Angels organization in 11th round of free-agent draft (June 1, 1988).... On California disabled list (April 1-24, 1993); included rehabilitation assignment to Midland (April 18-24).... On Vancouver

disabled list (August 20-September 7, 1993).
STATISTICAL NOTES: Led California League with nine balks in 1989.

Year	Team (League)	W	L	Pct.	ERA	G	GS	CG	ShO	Sv.	IP	H	R	ER	BB	SO
1988	—Bend (Northwest)	5	3	.625	3.50	9	9	2	0	0	61⅔	63	33	24	12	53
	—Quad City (Midw.)	1	2	.333	4.64	3	3	1	0	0	21⅓	19	12	11	5	20
	—Palm Springs (Cal.)	0	1	.000	5.63	2	1	0	0	0	8	12	5	5	2	7
1989	—Midland (Texas)	11	12	.478	4.93	25	25	4	1	0	162⅓	195	*121	89	55	104
1990	—Edmonton (PCL)	13	11	.542	3.90	27	27	•6	0	0	177⅔	198	90	77	35	124
	—California (A.L.)	1	1	.500	2.20	2	2	1	0	0	16⅓	10	4	4	2	9
1991	—California (A.L.)	3	5	.375	6.27	16	11	0	0	0	60⅓	81	43	42	21	37
	—Edmonton (PCL)	3	9	.250	4.50	17	17	4	0	0	110	132	71	55	26	87
1992	—California (A.L.)	4	0	1.000	3.99	21	2	0	0	0	38⅓	36	18	17	14	18
	—Edmonton (PCL)	10	6	.625	4.17	22	22	5	0	0	146⅔	159	74	68	40	88
1993	—Midland (Texas)	1	0	1.000	1.50	1	1	0	0	0	6	6	1	1	0	2
	—California (A.L.)	1	2	.333	4.22	15	4	0	0	0	32	37	16	15	12	10
	—Vancouver (PCL)	3	1	.750	1.37	24	0	0	0	9	39⅓	31	7	6	9	38
	Major league totals (4 years)	9	8	.529	4.78	54	19	1	0	0	147	164	81	78	49	74

LEYRITZ, JIM

1B/OF/C, YANKEES

PERSONAL: Born December 27, 1963, in Lakewood, O. . . . 6-0/195. . . . Throws right, bats right. . . . Full name: James Joseph Leyritz. . . . Name pronounced LAY-rits.
COLLEGE: Middle Georgia College and Kentucky.
TRANSACTIONS/CAREER NOTES: Signed as free agent by New York Yankees organization (August 24, 1985).
STATISTICAL NOTES: Led Florida State League with 25 passed balls in 1987. . . . Tied for Eastern League lead in being hit by pitch with nine in 1989.

			BATTING												FIELDING			
Year	Team (League)	Pos.	G	AB	R	H	2B	3B	HR	RBI	Avg.	BB	SO	SB	PO	A	E	Avg.
1986	—Oneonta (NYP)	C	23	91	12	33	3	1	4	15	.363	5	10	1	170	21	2	.990
	—Fort Lauder. (FSL)	C	12	34	3	10	1	1	0	1	.294	4	5	0	32	8	1	.976
1987	—Fort Lauder. (FSL)	C	102	374	48	115	22	0	6	51	.307	38	54	2	458	*76	13	.976
1988	—Alb./Colon. (East.)	C-3B-1B	112	382	40	92	18	3	5	50	.241	43	62	3	418	73	6	.988
1989	—Alb./Colon. (East.)	C-OF-3B	114	375	53	118	18	2	10	66	*.315	65	51	2	421	41	3	.994
1990	—Columbus (Int'l)	3-2-1-0-C	59	204	36	59	11	1	8	32	.289	37	33	4	75	96	13	.929
	—New York (A.L.)	3B-OF-C	92	303	28	78	13	1	5	25	.257	27	51	2	117	107	13	.945
1991	—New York (A.L.)	3B-C-1B	32	77	8	14	3	0	0	4	.182	13	15	0	38	21	3	.952
	—Columbus (Int'l)	C-3-S-2	79	270	50	72	24	1	11	48	.267	38	50	1	209	48	5	.981
1992	—New York (A.L.)	C-0-3-1-2	63	144	17	37	6	0	7	26	.257	14	22	0	96	15	1	.991
1993	—New York (A.L.)	1B-OF-C	95	259	43	80	14	0	14	53	.309	37	59	0	333	15	2	.994
	Major league totals (4 years)		282	783	96	209	36	1	26	108	.267	91	147	2	584	158	19	.975

LIEBERTHAL, MIKE

C, PHILLIES

PERSONAL: Born January 18, 1972, in Glendale, Calif. . . . 6-0/170. . . . Throws right, bats right. . . . Full name: Michael Scott Lieberthal.
HIGH SCHOOL: Westlake (Westlake Village, Calif.).
TRANSACTIONS/CAREER NOTES: Selected by Philadelphia Phillies organization in first round (third pick overall) of free-agent draft (June 4, 1990). . . . On Scranton/Wilkes-Barre disabled list (August 31, 1992-remainder of season).

			BATTING												FIELDING			
Year	Team (League)	Pos.	G	AB	R	H	2B	3B	HR	RBI	Avg.	BB	SO	SB	PO	A	E	Avg.
1990	—Martinsville (App.)	C	49	184	26	42	9	0	4	22	.228	11	40	2	421	*52	5	*.990
1991	—Spartanburg (SAL)	C	72	243	34	74	17	0	0	31	.305	23	25	1	565	68	10	.984
	—Clearwater (FSL)	C	16	52	7	15	2	0	0	7	.288	3	12	0	128	9	1	.993
1992	—Reading (Eastern)	C	86	309	30	88	16	1	2	37	.285	19	26	4	524	48	7	.988
	—Scran./W.B. (Int'l)	C	16	45	4	9	1	0	0	4	.200	2	5	0	86	6	1	.989
1993	—Scran./W.B. (Int'l)	C	112	382	35	100	17	0	7	40	.262	24	32	2	659	75	•11	.985

LILLIQUIST, DEREK

P, INDIANS

PERSONAL: Born February 20, 1966, in Winter Park, Fla. . . . 5-10/195. . . . Throws left, bats left. . . . Full name: Derek Jansen Lilliquist.
HIGH SCHOOL: Sarasota (Fla.).
COLLEGE: Georgia.
TRANSACTIONS/CAREER NOTES: Selected by Boston Red Sox organization in 15th round of free-agent draft (June 4, 1984). . . . Selected by Atlanta Braves in first round (sixth pick overall) of free-agent draft (June 2, 1987). . . . Traded by Braves to San Diego Padres for P Mark Grant (July 12, 1990). . . . Claimed on waivers by Cleveland Indians (November 20, 1991).
HONORS: Named lefthanded pitcher on THE SPORTING NEWS college All-America team (1987).

Year	Team (League)	W	L	Pct.	ERA	G	GS	CG	ShO	Sv.	IP	H	R	ER	BB	SO
1987	—GC Braves (GCL)	0	0	...	0.00	2	2	0	0	0	13	3	0	0	2	16
	—Durham (Carolina)	2	1	.667	2.88	3	3	2	0	0	25	13	9	8	6	29
1988	—Richmond (Int'l)	10	12	.455	3.38	28	28	2	0	0	170⅔	179	70	64	36	80
1989	—Atlanta (N.L.)	8	10	.444	3.97	32	30	0	0	0	165⅔	202	87	73	34	79
1990	—Atlanta-S.D. (N.L.)■	5	11	.313	5.31	28	18	1	1	0	122	136	74	72	42	63
	—Richmond (Int'l)	4	0	1.000	2.57	5	5	1	0	0	35	31	11	10	11	24
1991	—Las Vegas (PCL)	4	6	.400	5.38	33	14	0	0	2	105⅓	142	79	63	33	89
	—San Diego (N.L.)	0	2	.000	8.79	6	2	0	0	0	14⅓	25	14	14	4	7
1992	—Cleveland (A.L.)■	5	3	.625	1.75	71	0	0	0	6	61⅔	39	13	12	18	47

Year	Team (League)	W	L	Pct.	ERA	G	GS	CG	ShO	Sv.	IP	H	R	ER	BB	SO
1993	—Cleveland (A.L.)	4	4	.500	2.25	56	2	0	0	10	64	64	20	16	19	40
A.L. totals (2 years)		9	7	.563	2.01	127	2	0	0	16	125⅔	103	33	28	37	87
N.L. totals (3 years)		13	23	.361	4.74	66	50	1	1	0	302	363	175	159	80	149
Major league totals (5 years)		22	30	.423	3.94	193	52	1	1	16	427⅔	466	208	187	117	236

LIMA, JOSE

P, TIGERS

PERSONAL: Born September 30, 1972, in Santiago, Dominican Republic. . . . 6-2/170. . . . Throws right, bats right.
TRANSACTIONS/CAREER NOTES: Signed as free agent by Detroit Tigers organization (July 5, 1989).
STATISTICAL NOTES: Led Florida State League with 14 home runs allowed in 1992. . . . Led Eastern League with 13 balks in 1993.

Year	Team (League)	W	L	Pct.	ERA	G	GS	CG	ShO	Sv.	IP	H	R	ER	BB	SO
1990	—Bristol (Appal.)	3	8	.273	5.02	14	12	1	0	1	75⅓	89	49	42	22	64
1991	—Lakeland (Fla. St.)	0	1	.000	10.38	4	1	0	0	0	8⅔	16	10	10	2	5
	—Fayetteville (SAL)	1	3	.250	4.97	18	7	0	0	0	58	53	38	32	25	60
1992	—Lakeland (Fla. St.)	5	11	.313	3.16	25	25	5	2	0	151	132	57	53	21	137
1993	—London (Eastern)	8	•13	.381	4.07	27	27	2	0	0	177	160	96	80	59	138

LIND, JOSE

2B, ROYALS

PERSONAL: Born May 1, 1964, in Toabaja, Puerto Rico. . . . 5-11/180. . . . Throws right, bats right. . . . Full name: Jose Salgado Lind. . . . Brother of Orlando Lind, minor league pitcher (1983-93). . . . Name pronounced LEEND.
HIGH SCHOOL: Jose Alegria (Dorado, Puerto Rico).
TRANSACTIONS/CAREER NOTES: Signed as free agent by Pittsburgh Pirates organization (December 3, 1982). . . . Traded by Pirates to Kansas City Royals for P Joel Johnston and P Dennis Moeller (November 19, 1992).
HONORS: Won N.L. Gold Glove at second base (1992).
STATISTICAL NOTES: Led Eastern League second basemen with 705 total chances and 84 double plays in 1986. . . . Led Pacific Coast League second basemen with 764 total chances and 84 double plays in 1987. . . . Led N.L. second basemen with 786 total chances in 1990 and 796 in 1991.

			BATTING												FIELDING			
Year	Team (League)	Pos.	G	AB	R	H	2B	3B	HR	RBI	Avg.	BB	SO	SB	PO	A	E	Avg.
1983	—GC Pirates (GCL)	2B-SS	45	163	26	49	3	4	0	18	.301	13	18	12	102	125	9	.962
1984	—Macon (S. Atl.)	2B-SS	121	396	39	82	5	2	0	30	.207	29	48	17	271	306	32	.947
1985	—Prin. William (Car.)	2-S-3-0	105	377	42	104	9	4	0	28	.276	32	42	11	164	221	14	.965
1986	—Nashua (Eastern)	2B	134	•520	58	137	18	5	1	33	.263	43	28	29	*314	*378	13	*.982
1987	—Vancouver (PCL)	2B	128	*533	75	143	16	3	3	30	.268	35	52	21	*311	*432	21	.973
	—Pittsburgh (N.L.)	2B	35	143	21	46	8	4	0	11	.322	8	12	2	53	139	1	.995
1988	—Pittsburgh (N.L.)	2B	154	611	82	160	24	4	2	49	.262	42	75	15	333	473	11	.987
1989	—Pittsburgh (N.L.)	2B	153	578	52	134	21	3	2	48	.232	39	64	15	309	438	18	.976
1990	—Pittsburgh (N.L.)	2B	152	514	46	134	28	5	1	48	.261	35	52	8	*330	449	7	.991
1991	—Pittsburgh (N.L.)	2B	150	502	53	133	16	6	3	54	.265	30	56	7	*349	438	9	.989
1992	—Pittsburgh (N.L.)	2B	135	468	38	110	14	1	0	39	.235	26	29	3	311	428	6	*.992
1993	—Kansas City (A.L.)■	2B	136	431	33	107	13	2	0	37	.248	13	36	3	269	362	4	*.994
American League totals (1 year)			136	431	33	107	13	2	0	37	.248	13	36	3	269	362	4	.994
National League totals (6 years)			779	2816	292	717	111	23	8	249	.255	180	288	50	1685	2365	52	.987
Major league totals (7 years)			915	3247	325	824	124	25	8	286	.254	193	324	53	1954	2727	56	.988

CHAMPIONSHIP SERIES RECORD

			BATTING												FIELDING			
Year	Team (League)	Pos.	G	AB	R	H	2B	3B	HR	RBI	Avg.	BB	SO	SB	PO	A	E	Avg.
1990	—Pittsburgh (N.L.)	2B	6	21	1	5	1	1	1	2	.238	1	4	0	19	19	0	1.000
1991	—Pittsburgh (N.L.)	2B	7	25	0	4	0	0	0	3	.160	0	6	0	12	24	1	.973
1992	—Pittsburgh (N.L.)	2B	7	27	5	6	2	1	1	5	.222	1	4	0	16	23	2	.951
Championship series totals (3 years)			20	73	6	15	3	2	2	10	.205	2	14	0	47	66	3	.974

LINDEMAN, JIM

1B, METS

PERSONAL: Born January 10, 1962, in Evanston, Ill. . . . 6-1/200. . . . Throws right, bats right. . . . Full name: James William Lindeman.
HIGH SCHOOL: Maine West (Des Plaines, Ill.).
COLLEGE: Bradley.
TRANSACTIONS/CAREER NOTES: Selected by St. Louis Cardinals organization in first round (24th pick overall) of free-agent draft (June 6, 1983). . . . On St. Louis disabled list (May 12-29, 1987); included rehabilitation assignment to Louisville (May 26-29). . . . On St. Louis disabled list (June 4-July 4, 1987); included rehabilitation assignment to Louisville (June 17-July 4). . . . On St. Louis disabled list (April 22-July 5 1988); included rehabilitation assignment to Louisville (June 16-July 5). . . . On St. Louis disabled list (July 10-August 10, 1989); included rehabilitation assignment to Louisville (July 26-August 10). . . . Traded by Cardinals with P Matt Kinzer to Detroit Tigers for 2B Pat Austin, C Bill Henderson and P Marcus Betances (December 6, 1989). . . . Granted free agency (October 4, 1990). . . . Signed by Philadelphia Phillies organization (January 11, 1991). . . . On Philadelphia disabled list (May 10-July 24, 1992); included rehabilitation assignment to Scranton/Wilkes-Barre (July 4-24). . . . On Philadelphia disabled list (August 12-September 1, 1992). . . . Granted free agency (October 9, 1992). . . . Signed by Tucson, Houston Astros organization (February 1, 1993). . . . On Tucson disabled list (May 10-22, 1993). . . . Granted free agency (October 4, 1993). . . . Signed by New York Mets organization (December 16, 1993).
STATISTICAL NOTES: Led Pacific Coast League with .562 slugging percentage in 1993.

			BATTING												FIELDING			
Year	Team (League)	Pos.	G	AB	R	H	2B	3B	HR	RBI	Avg.	BB	SO	SB	PO	A	E	Avg.
1983	—St. Peters. (FSL)	3B	70	232	45	64	13	1	8	37	.276	27	51	9	36	98	26	.838
1984	—Springfield (Midw.)	3B-SS	94	354	69	96	15	2	18	66	.271	47	81	6	78	175	30	.894
	—Arkansas (Texas)	3B	40	137	14	26	4	3	0	13	.190	10	34	3	26	67	6	.939

Year	Team (League)	Pos.	G	AB	R	H	2B	3B	HR	RBI	Avg.	BB	SO	SB	PO	A	E	Avg.
				BATTING											FIELDING			
1985	—Arkansas (Texas)	3B	128	450	54	127	30	6	10	63	.282	41	82	11	74	238	24	.929
1986	—Louisville (A.A.)	1B-3B-OF	139	509	82	128	38	5	20	*96	.251	39	95	9	718	110	19	.978
	—St. Louis (N.L.)	1B-3B-OF	19	55	7	14	1	0	1	6	.255	2	10	1	118	10	1	.992
1987	—St. Louis (N.L.)	OF-1B	75	207	20	43	13	0	8	28	.208	11	56	3	196	14	3	.986
	—Louisville (A.A.)	OF	20	78	11	24	3	1	4	10	.308	8	15	0	14	1	1	.938
1988	—St. Louis (N.L.)	OF-1B	17	43	3	9	1	0	2	7	.209	2	9	0	36	2	1	.974
	—Louisville (A.A.)	OF-1B	73	261	32	66	18	4	2	30	.253	33	59	2	308	23	4	.988
1989	—St. Louis (N.L.)	1B-OF	73	45	8	5	1	0	0	2	.111	3	18	0	93	6	1	.990
	—Louisville (A.A.)	OF-1B	29	109	18	33	8	1	5	20	.303	14	17	3	52	5	2	.966
1990	—Toledo (Int'l)■	1B-OF-3B	109	374	48	85	17	2	12	50	.227	26	83	2	709	53	8	.990
	—Detroit (A.L.)	1B-OF	12	32	5	7	1	0	2	8	.219	2	13	0	5	0	0	1.000
1991	—Scran./W.B. (Int'l)■	OF-1B	11	40	7	11	1	1	2	7	.275	5	6	0	30	2	2	.941
	—Philadelphia (N.L.)	OF-1B	65	95	13	32	5	0	0	12	.337	13	14	0	35	1	0	1.000
1992	—Philadelphia (N.L.)	OF	29	39	6	10	1	0	1	6	.256	3	11	0	6	0	0	1.000
	—Scran./W.B. (Int'l)	OF	15	53	5	16	0	1	0	8	.302	7	11	0	9	0	0	1.000
1993	—Tucson (PCL)■	1B-OF	101	390	72	141	28	7	12	88	*.362	41	68	5	743	47	12	.985
	—Houston (N.L.)	1B	9	23	2	8	3	0	0	0	.348	0	7	0	40	5	0	1.000
American League totals (1 year)			12	32	5	7	1	0	2	8	.219	2	13	0	5	0	0	1.000
National League totals (7 years)			287	507	59	121	25	0	12	61	.239	34	125	4	524	38	6	.989
Major league totals (8 years)			299	539	64	128	26	0	14	69	.237	36	138	4	529	38	6	.990

CHAMPIONSHIP SERIES RECORD

Year	Team (League)	Pos.	G	AB	R	H	2B	3B	HR	RBI	Avg.	BB	SO	SB	PO	A	E	Avg.
				BATTING											FIELDING			
1987	—St. Louis (N.L.)	1B-PH	5	13	1	4	0	0	1	3	.308	0	3	0	33	2	0	1.000

WORLD SERIES RECORD

Year	Team (League)	Pos.	G	AB	R	H	2B	3B	HR	RBI	Avg.	BB	SO	SB	PO	A	E	Avg.
				BATTING											FIELDING			
1987	—St. Louis (N.L.)	1B-PH-OF	6	15	3	5	1	0	0	2	.333	0	3	0	28	2	3	.909

L

LINDSEY, DOUG

C, WHITE SOX

PERSONAL: Born September 22, 1967, in Austin, Tex. . . . 6-2/232. . . . Throws right, bats right. . . . Full name: Michael Douglas Lindsey.
HIGH SCHOOL: Harmony (Austin, Tex.).
COLLEGE: Seminole (Okla.) Junior College.
TRANSACTIONS/CAREER NOTES: Selected by Philadelphia Phillies organization in sixth round of free-agent draft (June 2, 1987). . . . On Reading disabled list (May 29-June 5 and July 18-31, 1991). . . . On Scranton/Wilkes-Barre disabled list (June 12-20, 1993). . . . Traded by Phillies to Chicago White Sox (September 8, 1993), completing deal in which White Sox traded P Donn Pall to Phillies for a player to be named later (September 1, 1993).
STATISTICAL NOTES: Led Eastern League catchers with 12 double plays and tied for league lead with 11 passed balls in 1991.

Year	Team (League)	Pos.	G	AB	R	H	2B	3B	HR	RBI	Avg.	BB	SO	SB	PO	A	E	Avg.
				BATTING											FIELDING			
1987	—Utica (N.Y.-Penn)	C	52	169	23	41	7	0	1	25	.243	22	34	1	337	41	8	.979
1988	—Spartanburg (SAL)	C	90	324	29	76	19	0	4	46	.235	29	68	4	461	59	9	.983
1989	—Spartanburg (SAL)	C	39	136	14	31	7	0	3	17	.228	23	31	2	240	32	6	.978
	—Clearwater (FSL)	C	36	118	8	23	3	0	0	9	.195	5	18	0	190	35	4	.983
1990	—Reading (Eastern)	C-1B	107	323	16	56	11	0	1	32	.173	26	78	2	574	70	8	.988
1991	—Reading (Eastern)	C	94	313	26	81	13	0	1	34	.259	21	49	1	571	75	3	*.995
	—Philadelphia (N.L.)	C	1	3	0	0	0	0	0	0	.000	0	3	0	8	0	0	1.000
1992	—Scran./W.B. (Int'l)	C	87	274	28	57	9	0	4	27	.208	37	66	0	574	59	5	.992
1993	—Scran./W.B. (Int'l)	C-1B	38	121	9	21	4	1	2	7	.174	5	24	0	214	31	4	.984
	—Philadelphia (N.L.)	C	2	2	0	1	0	0	0	0	.500	0	1	0	3	0	0	1.000
	—Chicago (A.L.)■	C	2	1	0	0	0	0	0	0	.000	0	0	0	3	0	0	1.000
American League totals (1 year)			2	1	0	0	0	0	0	0	.000	0	0	0	3	0	0	1.000
National League totals (2 years)			3	5	0	1	0	0	0	0	.200	0	4	0	11	0	0	1.000
Major league totals (2 years)			5	6	0	1	0	0	0	0	.167	0	4	0	14	0	0	1.000

LINTON, DOUG

P, METS

PERSONAL: Born September 2, 1965, in Santa Ana, Calif. . . . 6-1/190. . . . Throws right, bats right. . . . Full name: Douglas Warren Linton.
HIGH SCHOOL: Canyon (Anaheim, Calif.).
COLLEGE: UC Irvine.
TRANSACTIONS/CAREER NOTES: Selected by Toronto Blue Jays organization in 43rd round of free-agent draft (June 2, 1986). . . . On disabled list (April 30-May 24 and July 29-September 2, 1987). . . . On Knoxville disabled list (April 7-July 21, 1988). . . . On disabled list (April 7-July 21, 1989). . . . Claimed on waivers by California Angels (June 17, 1993). . . . Released by Angels (September 14, 1993). . . . Signed by New York Mets organization (December 17, 1993).
STATISTICAL NOTES: Led International League with 21 home runs allowed and tied for lead with 10 hit batsmen in 1991.

Year	Team (League)	W	L	Pct.	ERA	G	GS	CG	ShO	Sv.	IP	H	R	ER	BB	SO
1987	—Myrtle Beach (SAL)	14	2	.875	*1.55	20	19	2	0	1	122	94	34	21	25	155
	—Knoxville (South.)	0	0	...	9.00	1	1	0	0	0	3	5	3	3	1	1
1988	—Dunedin (Fla. St.)	2	1	.667	1.63	12	0	0	0	2	27⅔	19	5	5	9	28
1989	—Dunedin (Fla. St.)	1	2	.333	2.96	9	1	0	0	2	27⅓	27	12	9	9	35
	—Knoxville (South.)	5	4	.556	2.60	14	13	3	•2	0	90	68	28	26	23	93
1990	—Syracuse (Int'l)	10	10	.500	3.40	26	26	8	•3	0	*177⅓	174	77	67	67	113
1991	—Syracuse (Int'l)	10	12	.455	5.01	30	26	3	1	0	161⅔	181	108	90	56	93

Year	Team (League)	W	L	Pct.	ERA	G	GS	CG	ShO	Sv.	IP	H	R	ER	BB	SO
1992	—Syracuse (Int'l)	12	10	.545	3.74	25	25	7	1	0	170⅔	176	83	71	70	126
	—Toronto (A.L.)	1	3	.250	8.63	8	3	0	0	0	24	31	23	23	17	16
1993	—Syracuse (Int'l)	2	6	.250	5.32	13	7	0	0	2	47⅓	48	29	28	14	42
	—Tor.-Calif. (A.L.)■	2	1	.667	7.36	23	1	0	0	0	36⅔	46	30	30	23	23
Major league totals (2 years)		3	4	.429	7.86	31	4	0	0	0	60⅔	77	53	53	40	39

LIRA, FELIPE

P, TIGERS

PERSONAL: Born April 26, 1972, in Miranda, Venezuela. . . . 6-0/170. . . . Throws right, bats right. . . . Full name: Antonio Felipe Lira.
TRANSACTIONS/CAREER NOTES: Signed as free agent by Detroit Tigers organization (February 20, 1990). . . . On Lakeland disabled list (April 10-June 10, 1991).

Year	Team (League)	W	L	Pct.	ERA	G	GS	CG	ShO	Sv.	IP	H	R	ER	BB	SO
1990	—Bristol (Appal.)	5	5	.500	2.41	13	10	2	1	1	78⅓	70	26	21	16	71
	—Lakeland (Fla. St.)	0	0	...	5.40	1	0	0	0	0	1⅔	3	1	1	3	4
1991	—Fayetteville (SAL)	5	5	.500	4.66	15	13	0	0	1	73⅓	79	43	38	19	56
1992	—Lakeland (Fla. St.)	11	5	.688	2.39	32	8	2	1	1	109	95	36	29	16	84
1993	—London (Eastern)	10	4	.714	3.38	22	22	2	0	0	152	157	63	57	39	122
	—Toledo (Int'l)	1	2	.333	4.60	5	5	0	0	0	31⅓	32	18	16	11	23

LIRIANO, NELSON

IF, ROCKIES

PERSONAL: Born June 3, 1964, in Puerto Plata, Dominican Republic. . . . 5-10/165. . . . Throws right, bats both. . . . Full name: Nelson Arturo Liriano. . . . Name pronounced LEER-ee-ON-oh.
HIGH SCHOOL: Jose Debeaw (Puerto Plata, Dominican Republic).
TRANSACTIONS/CAREER NOTES: Signed as free agent by Toronto Blue Jays organization (November 1, 1982). . . . Traded by Blue Jays with OF Pedro Munoz to Minnesota Twins for P John Candelaria (July 27, 1990). . . . Released by Twins (April 2, 1991). . . . Signed by Omaha, Kansas City Royals organization (May 1, 1991). . . . Granted free agency (October 15, 1991). . . . Signed by Colorado Springs, Cleveland Indians organization (January 31, 1992). . . . Granted free agency (October 15, 1992). . . . Signed by Colorado Rockies (October 26, 1992). . . . On Colorado Springs disabled list (April 7-30, 1993).
STATISTICAL NOTES: Led Carolina League second basemen with 79 double plays in 1985. . . . Led International League second basemen with 611 total chances and 96 double plays in 1987.

				BATTING											FIELDING			
Year	Team (League)	Pos.	G	AB	R	H	2B	3B	HR	RBI	Avg.	BB	SO	SB	PO	A	E	Avg.
1983	—Florence (S. Atl.)	2B	129	478	87	124	24	5	6	57	.259	70	81	27	214	323	34	.940
1984	—Kinston (Carolina)	2B	132	*512	68	126	22	4	5	50	.246	46	86	10	260	*357	*21	.967
1985	—Kinston (Carolina)	2B	134	451	68	130	23	1	6	36	.288	39	55	25	*261	328	•25	.959
1986	—Knoxville (South.)	2B-3B-SS	135	557	88	159	25	*15	7	59	.285	48	63	35	239	324	22	.962
1987	—Syracuse (Int'l)	2B	130	531	72	133	19	•10	10	55	.250	44	76	36	*246	*346	*19	.969
	—Toronto (A.L.)	2B	37	158	29	38	6	2	2	10	.241	16	22	13	83	107	1	.995
1988	—Toronto (A.L.)	2B-3B	99	276	36	73	6	2	3	23	.264	11	40	12	121	177	12	.961
	—Syracuse (Int'l)	2B	8	31	2	6	1	1	0	1	.194	2	4	2	14	23	0	1.000
1989	—Toronto (A.L.)	2B	132	418	51	110	26	3	5	53	.263	43	51	16	267	330	12	.980
1990	—Tor.-Minn. (A.L.)■	2B-SS	103	355	46	83	12	9	1	28	.234	38	44	8	176	260	11	.975
1991	—Omaha (A.A.)■	2B-SS	86	292	50	80	16	9	2	36	.274	31	39	6	149	218	9	.976
	—Kansas City (A.L.)	2B	10	22	5	9	0	0	0	1	.409	0	2	0	11	23	0	1.000
1992	—Colo. Springs (PCL)■	2B-3B-SS	106	361	73	110	19	9	5	52	.305	48	50	20	144	230	9	.977
1993	—Central Vall. (Cal.)■	3B-SS-2B	6	22	3	8	0	2	0	4	.364	6	0	0	4	10	0	1.000
	—Colo. Springs (PCL)	2B-SS-3B	79	293	48	105	23	6	6	46	.358	32	34	9	143	232	15	.962
	—Colorado (N.L.)	SS-2B-3B	48	151	28	46	6	3	2	15	.305	18	22	6	65	103	6	.966
American League totals (5 years)			381	1229	167	313	50	16	11	115	.255	108	159	49	658	897	36	.977
National League totals (1 year)			48	151	28	46	6	3	2	15	.305	18	22	6	65	103	6	.966
Major league totals (6 years)			429	1380	195	359	56	19	13	130	.260	126	181	55	723	1000	42	.976

CHAMPIONSHIP SERIES RECORD

				BATTING											FIELDING			
Year	Team (League)	Pos.	G	AB	R	H	2B	3B	HR	RBI	Avg.	BB	SO	SB	PO	A	E	Avg.
1989	—Toronto (A.L.)	2B	3	7	1	3	0	0	0	1	.429	2	0	3	4	3	1	.875

LISTACH, PAT

2B, BREWERS

PERSONAL: Born September 12, 1967, in Natchitoches, La. . . . 5-9/170. . . . Throws right, bats both. . . . Full name: Patrick Alan Listach. . . . Name pronounced LISS-tatch.
HIGH SCHOOL: Natchitoches (La.) Central.
COLLEGE: McLennan Community College (Tex.) and Arizona State.
TRANSACTIONS/CAREER NOTES: Selected by Seattle Mariners organization in 23rd round of free-agent draft (June 2, 1987). . . . Selected by Milwaukee Brewers organization in fifth round of free-agent draft (June 1, 1988). . . . On Milwaukee disabled list (June 2-July 18, 1993); included rehabilitation assignment to Beloit (July 14-18, 1993).
HONORS: Named A.L. Rookie Player of the Year by THE SPORTING NEWS (1992). . . . Named A.L. Rookie of the Year by Baseball Writers' Association of America (1992).
STATISTICAL NOTES: Led California League second basemen with 276 putouts in 1990.
MISCELLANEOUS: Batted righthanded only (1988-89 and 1991).

				BATTING											FIELDING			
Year	Team (League)	Pos.	G	AB	R	H	2B	3B	HR	RBI	Avg.	BB	SO	SB	PO	A	E	Avg.
1988	—Beloit (Midwest)	SS	53	200	40	48	5	1	1	18	.240	18	20	20	66	117	24	.884
1989	—Stockton (Calif.)	2B-SS	132	480	73	110	11	4	2	34	.229	58	106	37	250	351	29	.954
1990	—Stockton (Calif.)	2B-SS-OF	•139	503	*116	137	21	6	2	39	.272	*105	122	78	†319	356	25	.964
1991	—El Paso (Texas)	SS-2B	49	186	40	47	5	2	0	13	.253	25	56	14	86	131	22	.908
	—Denver (A.A.)	2B-SS-OF	89	286	51	72	10	4	1	31	.252	45	66	23	182	237	9	.979

Year	Team (League)	Pos.	G	AB	R	H	2B	3B	HR	RBI	Avg.	BB	SO	SB	PO	A	E	Avg.
				BATTING											FIELDING			
1992	—Milwaukee (A.L.)	SS-OF-2B	149	579	93	168	19	6	1	47	.290	55	124	54	238	449	24	.966
1993	—Milwaukee (A.L.)	SS-OF	98	356	50	87	15	1	3	30	.244	37	70	18	135	267	10	.976
	—Beloit (Midwest)	SS	4	12	2	3	0	0	0	1	.250	1	2	2	3	7	0	1.000
Major league totals (2 years)			247	935	143	255	34	7	4	77	.273	92	194	72	373	716	34	.970

LITTON, GREG

IF/OF, RANGERS

PERSONAL: Born July 13, 1964, in New Orleans. . . . 6-0/175. . . . Throws right, bats right. . . . Full name: Jon Gregory Litton.
HIGH SCHOOL: Woodham (Pensacola, Fla.).
COLLEGE: Pensacola (Fla.) Junior College.
TRANSACTIONS/CAREER NOTES: Selected by San Francisco Giants organization in first round (10th pick overall) of free-agent draft (January 17, 1984). . . . On San Francisco disabled list (March 28-April 21, 1990); included rehabilitation assignment to Phoenix (April 15-21). . . . On San Francisco disabled list (August 15-September 1, 1991). . . . Granted free agency (December 19, 1992). . . . Signed by Seattle Mariners (December 29, 1992). . . . Granted free agency (December 20, 1993). . . . Signed by Texas Rangers organization (January 7, 1994).
STATISTICAL NOTES: Led California League second basemen with 453 assists and 749 total chances in 1985. . . . Led Texas League second basemen with 262 putouts, 369 assists, 655 total chances and 24 errors in 1986. . . . Order of frequency of positions played at San Francisco (1991): 1B-2B-3B-SS-OF-C-P.

Year	Team (League)	Pos.	G	AB	R	H	2B	3B	HR	RBI	Avg.	BB	SO	SB	PO	A	E	Avg.
				BATTING											FIELDING			
1984	—Everett (N'west)	2B-3B	62	243	29	57	12	2	4	26	.235	27	47	2	135	160	17	.946
1985	—Fresno (California)	2B-OF	141	*564	88	150	*33	7	12	103	.266	50	86	8	269	†453	28	.963
1986	—Shreveport (Texas)	2B-SS-OF	131	455	46	112	30	3	10	55	.246	51	77	1	†265	†373	†24	.964
1987	—Shreveport (Texas)	2B-SS	72	254	34	66	6	3	8	33	.260	22	51	2	117	199	3	.991
	—Phoenix (PCL)	2B-SS	60	203	24	44	8	2	1	22	.217	18	40	0	146	173	8	.976
1988	—Shreveport (Texas)	3B-2B-SS	116	432	58	120	35	5	11	64	.278	37	84	2	116	247	13	.965
1989	—Phoenix (PCL)	2-S-3-1-C	30	89	6	16	4	2	2	6	.180	8	24	1	48	50	4	.961
	—San Francisco (N.L.)	3-2-S-0-C	71	143	12	36	5	3	4	17	.252	7	29	0	44	66	3	.973
1990	—Phoenix (PCL)	OF-2B-3B	6	22	3	6	1	0	0	4	.273	2	7	0	6	7	2	.867
	—San Francisco (N.L.)	0-2-S-3	93	204	17	50	9	1	1	24	.245	11	45	1	90	43	1	.993
1991	—San Francisco (N.L.)	IF-OF-C-P	59	127	13	23	7	1	1	15	.181	11	25	0	121	65	2	.989
	—Phoenix (PCL)	SS-3B-2B	8	27	9	11	1	0	4	9	.407	8	5	0	6	23	4	.879
1992	—Phoenix (PCL)	3B-2B	25	85	14	26	7	0	4	19	.306	8	21	0	28	53	3	.964
	—San Francisco (N.L.)	2-3-1-S-0	68	140	9	32	5	0	4	15	.229	11	33	0	82	85	4	.977
1993	—Seattle (A.L.)■	0-2-1-3-S	72	174	25	52	17	0	3	25	.299	18	30	0	135	52	0	1.000
	—Calgary (PCL)	3-2-0-S	49	170	35	54	16	3	6	27	.318	25	36	3	65	88	2	.987
American League totals (1 year)			72	174	25	52	17	0	3	25	.299	18	30	0	135	52	0	1.000
National League totals (4 years)			291	614	51	141	26	5	10	71	.230	40	132	1	337	259	10	.983
Major league totals (5 years)			363	788	76	193	43	5	13	96	.245	58	162	1	472	311	10	.987

CHAMPIONSHIP SERIES RECORD

Year	Team (League)	Pos.	G	AB	R	H	2B	3B	HR	RBI	Avg.	BB	SO	SB	PO	A	E	Avg.
				BATTING											FIELDING			
1989	—San Francisco (N.L.)	PH-3B	1	1	0	1	0	0	0	0	1.000	0	0	0	0	0	0	...

WORLD SERIES RECORD

Year	Team (League)	Pos.	G	AB	R	H	2B	3B	HR	RBI	Avg.	BB	SO	SB	PO	A	E	Avg.
				BATTING											FIELDING			
1989	—San Francisco (N.L.)	2B-PH-3B	2	6	1	3	1	0	1	3	.500	0	0	0	2	3	0	1.000

RECORD AS PITCHER

Year	Team (League)	W	L	Pct.	ERA	G	GS	CG	ShO	Sv.	IP	H	R	ER	BB	SO
1991	—San Francisco (N.L.)	0	0	...	9.00	1	0	0	0	0	1	1	1	1	3	0

LIVINGSTONE, SCOTT

3B, TIGERS

PERSONAL: Born July 15, 1965, in Dallas. . . . 6-0/198. . . . Throws right, bats left. . . . Full name: Scott Louis Livingstone.
HIGH SCHOOL: Lake Highlands (Dallas).
COLLEGE: Texas A&M.
TRANSACTIONS/CAREER NOTES: Selected by Toronto Blue Jays organization in sixth round of free-agent draft (June 4, 1984). . . . Selected by New York Yankees organization in 26th round of free-agent draft (June 2, 1986). . . . Selected by Oakland Athletics organization in third round of free-agent draft (June 2, 1987). . . . Selected by Detroit Tigers organization in second round of free-agent draft (June 1, 1988). . . . On disabled list (July 14-23 and July 28-August 7, 1990).
HONORS: Named designated hitter on THE SPORTING NEWS college All-America team (1987-88).
STATISTICAL NOTES: Tied for Eastern League lead in total chances by third baseman with 360 in 1989.

Year	Team (League)	Pos.	G	AB	R	H	2B	3B	HR	RBI	Avg.	BB	SO	SB	PO	A	E	Avg.
				BATTING											FIELDING			
1988	—Lakeland (Fla. St.)	3B	53	180	28	51	8	1	2	25	.283	11	25	1	30	115	8	.948
1989	—London (Eastern)	3B-SS	124	452	46	98	18	1	14	71	.217	52	67	1	100	265	25	.936
1990	—Toledo (Int'l)	3B	103	345	44	94	19	0	6	36	.272	21	40	1	66	181	13	.950
1991	—Toledo (Int'l)	3B-1B	92	331	48	100	13	3	3	62	.302	40	52	2	65	137	16	.927
	—Detroit (A.L.)	3B	44	127	19	37	5	0	2	11	.291	10	25	2	32	67	2	.980
1992	—Detroit (A.L.)	3B	117	354	43	100	21	0	4	46	.282	21	36	1	67	189	10	.962
1993	—Detroit (A.L.)	3B	98	304	39	89	10	2	2	39	.293	19	32	1	33	94	6	.955
Major league totals (3 years)			259	785	101	226	36	2	8	96	.288	50	93	4	132	350	18	.964

LLOYD, GRAEME

P, BREWERS

PERSONAL: Born April 9, 1967, in Victoria, Australia. . . . 6-7/230. . . . Throws left, bats left. . . . Full name: Graeme John Lloyd.
HIGH SCHOOL: Geelong Technical School (Victoria, Australia).
TRANSACTIONS/CAREER NOTES: Signed as free agent by Toronto Blue Jays organization (January 26, 1988). . . . On Myrtle Beach disabled list (June 29-September 1, 1989). . . . Selected by Philadelphia Phillies from Blue Jays organization in Rule 5 major league draft (December 7, 1992). . . . Traded by Phillies to Milwaukee Brewers for P John Trisler (December 8, 1992). . . . On disabled list (August 20-September 4, 1993). . . . On suspended list (September 5-9, 1993).

Year	Team (League)	W	L	Pct.	ERA	G	GS	CG	ShO	Sv.	IP	H	R	ER	BB	SO
1988	—Myrtle Beach (SAL)	3	2	.600	3.62	41	0	0	0	2	59⅔	71	33	24	30	43
1989	—Dunedin (Fla. St.)	0	0	...	10.13	2	0	0	0	0	2⅔	6	3	3	1	0
	—Myrtle Beach (SAL)	0	0	...	5.40	1	1	0	0	0	5	5	4	3	0	3
1990	—Myrtle Beach (SAL)	5	2	.714	2.72	19	6	0	0	6	49⅔	51	20	15	16	42
1991	—Dunedin (Fla. St.)	2	5	.286	2.24	50	0	0	0	24	60⅓	54	17	15	25	39
	—Knoxville (South.)	0	0	...	0.00	2	0	0	0	0	1⅔	1	0	0	1	2
1992	—Knoxville (South.)	4	8	.333	1.96	49	7	1	0	14	92	79	30	20	25	65
1993	—Milwaukee (A.L.)■	3	4	.429	2.83	55	0	0	0	0	63⅔	64	24	20	13	31
Major league totals (1 year)		3	4	.429	2.83	55	0	0	0	0	63⅔	64	24	20	13	31

LOFTON, KENNY

OF, INDIANS

PERSONAL: Born May 31, 1967, in East Chicago, Ind. . . . 6-0/180. . . . Throws left, bats left. . . . Full name: Kenneth Lofton.
HIGH SCHOOL: Washington (East Chicago, Ind.).
COLLEGE: Arizona.
TRANSACTIONS/CAREER NOTES: Selected by Houston Astros organization in 17th round of free-agent draft (June 1, 1988). . . . Traded by Astros with IF Dave Rohde to Cleveland Indians for P Willie Blair and C Eddie Taubensee (December 10, 1991).
RECORDS: Holds A.L. rookie-season record for most stolen bases—66 (1992). . . . Shares A.L. single-season record for fewest errors by outfielder who led league in errors—9 (1993).
HONORS: Won A.L. Gold Glove as outfielder (1993).
STATISTICAL NOTES: Tied for Pacific Coast League lead in caught stealing with 23 in 1991. . . . Led Pacific Coast League outfielders with 344 total chances in 1991.

			BATTING												FIELDING			
Year	Team (League)	Pos.	G	AB	R	H	2B	3B	HR	RBI	Avg.	BB	SO	SB	PO	A	E	Avg.
1988	—Auburn (NY-Penn)	OF	48	187	23	40	6	1	1	14	.214	19	51	26	94	5	4	.961
1989	—Auburn (NY-Penn)	OF	34	110	21	29	3	1	0	8	.264	14	30	26	37	4	8	.837
	—Asheville (S. Atl.)	OF	22	82	14	27	2	0	1	9	.329	12	10	14	38	1	2	.951
1990	—Osceola (Fla. St.)	OF	124	481	98	*159	15	5	2	35	.331	61	77	62	246	13	7	.974
1991	—Tucson (PCL)	OF	130	*545	93	*168	19	*17	2	50	.308	52	95	40	*308	*27	9	.974
	—Houston (N.L.)	OF	20	74	9	15	1	0	0	0	.203	5	19	2	41	1	1	.977
1992	—Cleveland (A.L.)■	OF	148	576	96	164	15	8	5	42	.285	68	54	*66	420	14	8	.982
1993	—Cleveland (A.L.)	OF	148	569	116	185	28	8	1	42	.325	81	83	*70	402	11	•9	.979
American League totals (2 years)			296	1145	212	349	43	16	6	84	.305	149	137	136	822	25	17	.980
National League totals (1 year)			20	74	9	15	1	0	0	0	.203	5	19	2	41	1	1	.977
Major league totals (3 years)			316	1219	221	364	44	16	6	84	.299	154	156	138	863	26	18	.980

LOGSDON, KEVIN

P, INDIANS

PERSONAL: Born December 23, 1970, in Baker, Ore. . . . 5-11/215. . . . Throws left, bats both. . . . Full name: Kevin Howard Logsdon.
HIGH SCHOOL: Baker (Ore.).
COLLEGE: Linn-Benton Community College (Ore.).
TRANSACTIONS/CAREER NOTES: Selected by Cleveland Indians organization in fifth round of free-agent draft (June 3, 1991).

Year	Team (League)	W	L	Pct.	ERA	G	GS	CG	ShO	Sv.	IP	H	R	ER	BB	SO
1991	—Watertown (NYP)	2	5	.286	4.25	13	11	0	0	0	59⅓	58	42	28	41	38
1992	—Columbus (S. Atl.)	6	5	.545	2.94	19	18	0	0	0	113⅓	104	43	37	48	86
1993	—Kinston (Carolina)	6	7	.462	6.14	31	20	1	0	3	124⅔	146	94	*85	57	105

LONG, STEVE

P, MARLINS

PERSONAL: Born July 17, 1969, in Blue Island, Ill. . . . 6-4/210. . . . Throws right, bats right. . . . Full name: Steven Jay Long.
HIGH SCHOOL: Oak Forest (Ill.).
COLLEGE: St. Xavier University (Ill.).
TRANSACTIONS/CAREER NOTES: Selected by Montreal Expos organization in sixth round of free-agent draft (June 4, 1990). . . . Traded by Expos organization to New York Mets organization for OF Terrel Hansen (March 30, 1993). . . . Selected by Florida Marlins from Mets organization in Rule 5 major league draft (December 13, 1993).

Year	Team (League)	W	L	Pct.	ERA	G	GS	CG	ShO	Sv.	IP	H	R	ER	BB	SO
1990	—Jamestown (NYP)	4	2	.667	1.37	22	0	0	0	2	39⅓	26	15	6	24	35
1991	—Sumter (S. Atl.)	3	3	.500	3.18	63	0	0	0	17	76⅓	72	34	27	31	79
1992	—W.P. Beach (FSL)	9	7	.563	2.44	26	23	4	0	0	151⅓	121	53	41	42	67
1993	—Binghamton (East.)■	12	8	.600	3.96	38	19	•4	0	1	156⅔	165	87	69	58	70

LONGMIRE, TONY

OF, PHILLIES

PERSONAL: Born August 12, 1968, in Vallejo, Calif. . . . 6-1/199. . . . Throws right, bats left. . . . Full name: Anthony Eugene Longmire.
HIGH SCHOOL: Hogan (Vallejo, Calif.).
TRANSACTIONS/CAREER NOTES: Selected by Pittsburgh Pirates organization in eighth round of free-agent draft (June 2, 1986). . . . On Salem disabled list (August 27, 1988-remainder of season). . . . On disabled list (April 10-May 24 and June 25, 1990-remainder of season). . . . Traded by Pirates organization to Philadelphia Phillies (September 28, 1990), completing deal in which Phillies traded OF/1B Carmelo Martinez to Pirates for OF Wes Chamberlain, OF

Julio Peguero and a player to be named later (August 30, 1990).... On Philadelphia disabled list (March 28, 1992-entire season).

MISCELLANEOUS: Batted as switch-hitter (1986-87, Harrisburg 1988 and 1990).

Year	Team (League)	Pos.	G	AB	R	H	2B	3B	HR	RBI	Avg.	BB	SO	SB	PO	A	E	Avg.
			BATTING												FIELDING			
1986	—GC Pirates (GCL)	OF	15	40	6	11	2	1	0	6	.275	2	2	1	19	0	2	.905
1987	—Macon (S. Atl.)	OF	127	445	63	117	15	4	5	62	.263	41	73	18	167	5	8	.956
1988	—Salem (Carolina)	OF	64	218	46	60	12	2	11	40	.275	36	44	4	91	3	3	.969
	—Harrisburg (East.)	OF	32	94	7	14	2	2	0	4	.149	9	12	0	46	2	2	.960
1989	—GC Pirates (GCL)	OF	2	5	0	0	0	0	0	0	.000	1	1	0	0	0	0	...
	—Salem (Carolina)	OF	14	62	8	20	3	1	1	6	.323	1	13	0	14	3	0	1.000
	—Harrisburg (East.)	OF	37	127	15	37	7	0	3	22	.291	12	21	1	62	1	2	.969
1990	—Harrisburg (East.)	OF	24	91	9	27	6	0	1	13	.297	7	11	5	46	4	2	.962
1991	—Reading (Eastern)■	OF	85	323	43	93	22	1	9	56	.288	32	45	10	134	3	4	.972
	—Scran./W.B. (Int'l)	OF	36	111	11	29	3	2	0	9	.261	8	20	4	54	1	4	.932
1992	—	Did not play.																
1993	—Scran./W.B. (Int'l)	OF	120	447	63	136	*36	4	6	67	.304	41	71	12	195	5	5	.976
	—Philadelphia (N.L.)	OF	11	13	1	3	0	0	0	1	.231	0	1	0	4	0	0	1.000
Major league totals (1 year)			11	13	1	3	0	0	0	1	.231	0	1	0	4	0	0	1.000

CHAMPIONSHIP SERIES RECORD

Year	Team (League)	Pos.	G	AB	R	H	2B	3B	HR	RBI	Avg.	BB	SO	SB	PO	A	E	Avg.
			BATTING												FIELDING			
1993	—Philadelphia (N.L.)	PH	1	1	0	0	0	0	0	0	.000	0	1	0	...	...	...	...

WORLD SERIES RECORD

Year	Team (League)	Pos.	G	AB	R	H	2B	3B	HR	RBI	Avg.	BB	SO	SB	PO	A	E	Avg.
			BATTING												FIELDING			
1993	—Philadelphia (N.L.)	Did not play.																

LOONEY, BRIAN

P, EXPOS

PERSONAL: Born September 26, 1969, in New Haven, Conn.... 5-10/185.... Throws left, bats left.... Full name: Brian James Looney.

HIGH SCHOOL: The Gunnery School (Washington, Conn.).

COLLEGE: Boston College.

TRANSACTIONS/CAREER NOTES: Selected by San Diego Padres organization in 43rd round of free-agent draft (June 1, 1988).... Selected by Montreal Expos organization in 10th round of free-agent draft (June 3, 1991).

Year	Team (League)	W	L	Pct.	ERA	G	GS	CG	ShO	Sv.	IP	H	R	ER	BB	SO
1991	—Jamestown (NYP)	7	1	.875	*1.16	11	11	2	1	0	62⅓	42	12	8	28	64
1992	—Rockford (Midw.)	3	1	.750	3.16	17	0	0	0	0	31⅓	28	13	11	23	34
	—Albany (S. Atl.)	3	2	.600	2.14	11	11	1	1	0	67⅓	51	22	16	30	56
1993	—W.P. Beach (FSL)	4	6	.400	3.14	18	16	0	0	0	106	108	48	37	29	109
	—Harrisburg (East.)	3	2	.600	2.38	8	8	1	1	0	56⅔	36	15	15	17	76
	—Montreal (N.L.)	0	0	...	3.00	3	1	0	0	0	6	8	2	2	2	7
Major league totals (1 year)		0	0	...	3.00	3	1	0	0	0	6	8	2	2	2	7

LOPEZ, ALBIE

P, INDIANS

PERSONAL: Born August 18, 1971, in Mesa, Ariz.... 6-2/205.... Throws right, bats right.... Full name: Albert Anthony Lopez.

HIGH SCHOOL: Westwood (Mesa, Ariz.).

COLLEGE: Mesa (Ariz.) Community College.

TRANSACTIONS/CAREER NOTES: Selected by San Francisco Giants organization in 46th round of free-agent draft (June 5, 1989).... Selected by Seattle Mariners organization in 19th round of free-agent draft (June 4, 1990).... Selected by Cleveland Indians organization in 20th round of free-agent draft (June 3, 1991).

Year	Team (League)	W	L	Pct.	ERA	G	GS	CG	ShO	Sv.	IP	H	R	ER	BB	SO
1991	—Burlington (Appal.)	4	5	.444	3.44	13	13	0	0	0	73⅓	61	33	28	23	81
1992	—Columbus (S. Atl.)	7	2	.778	2.88	16	16	1	0	0	97	80	41	31	33	117
	—Kinston (Carolina)	5	2	.714	3.52	10	10	1	1	0	64	56	28	25	26	44
1993	—Cant./Akr. (East.)	9	4	.692	3.11	16	16	2	0	0	110	79	44	38	47	80
	—Cleveland (A.L.)	3	1	.750	5.98	9	9	0	0	0	49⅔	49	34	33	32	25
	—Charlotte (Int'l)	1	0	1.000	2.25	3	2	0	0	0	12	8	3	3	2	7
Major league totals (1 year)		3	1	.750	5.98	9	9	0	0	0	49⅔	49	34	33	32	25

LOPEZ, JAVIER

C, BRAVES

PERSONAL: Born November 5, 1970, in Ponce, Puerto Rico.... 6-3/185.... Throws right, bats right.... Full name: Javier Torres Lopez.

HIGH SCHOOL: Academia Cristo Rey (Urb la Ramble Ponce, Puerto Rico).

TRANSACTIONS/CAREER NOTES: Signed as free agent by Atlanta Braves organization (November 6, 1987).... On Greenville disabled list (July 18-August 2, 1992).

HONORS: Named Southern League Most Valuable Player (1992).

STATISTICAL NOTES: Led Midwest League catchers with 11 double plays and 31 passed balls in 1990.... Led Carolina League catchers with 701 total chances and 14 double plays in 1991.... Led Southern League catchers with 763 total chances and 19 passed balls in 1992.... Led International League catchers with 15 passed balls in 1993.

Year	Team (League)	Pos.	G	AB	R	H	2B	3B	HR	RBI	Avg.	BB	SO	SB	PO	A	E	Avg.
			BATTING												FIELDING			
1988	—GC Braves (GCL)	C	31	94	8	18	4	0	1	9	.191	3	19	1	131	30	7	.958
1989	—Pulaski (Appal.)	C	51	153	27	40	8	1	3	27	.261	5	35	3	264	26	5	.983
1990	—Burlington (Midw.)	C	116	422	48	112	17	3	11	55	.265	14	84	0	724	79	11	.986

			BATTING												FIELDING			
Year	Team (League)	Pos.	G	AB	R	H	2B	3B	HR	RBI	Avg.	BB	SO	SB	PO	A	E	Avg.
1991	—Durham (Carolina)...	C	113	384	43	94	14	2	11	51	.245	25	88	10	*610	85	6	.991
1992	—Greenville (South.)...	C	115	442	63	142	28	3	16	60	.321	24	47	7	*680	75	8	.990
	—Atlanta (N.L.).........	C	9	16	3	6	2	0	0	2	.375	0	1	0	28	2	0	1.000
1993	—Richmond (Int'l).......	C	100	380	56	116	23	2	17	74	.305	12	53	1	718	70	10	.987
	—Atlanta (N.L.)...........	C	8	16	1	6	1	1	1	2	.375	0	2	0	37	2	1	.975
Major league totals (2 years)			17	32	4	12	3	1	1	4	.375	0	3	0	65	4	1	.986

CHAMPIONSHIP SERIES RECORD

			BATTING												FIELDING			
Year	Team (League)	Pos.	G	AB	R	H	2B	3B	HR	RBI	Avg.	BB	SO	SB	PO	A	E	Avg.
1992	—Atlanta (N.L.)...........	C	1	1	0	0	0	0	0	0	.000	0	0	0	2	0	0	1.000

WORLD SERIES RECORD

			BATTING												FIELDING			
Year	Team (League)	Pos.	G	AB	R	H	2B	3B	HR	RBI	Avg.	BB	SO	SB	PO	A	E	Avg.
1992	—Atlanta (N.L.)...........								Did not play.									

LOPEZ, LUIS

2B/SS, PADRES

PERSONAL: Born September 4, 1970, in Cidra, Puerto Rico. . . . 5-11/175. . . . Throws right, bats both. . . . Full name: Luis Santos Lopez.

HIGH SCHOOL: San Jose (Caguas, Puerto Rico).

TRANSACTIONS/CAREER NOTES: Signed as free agent by San Diego Padres organization (September 9, 1987).

STATISTICAL NOTES: Led South Atlantic League shortstops with 703 total chances and 78 double plays in 1989. . . . Led Pacific Coast League shortstops with 30 errors in 1992. . . . Tied for Pacific Coast League lead with 13 sacrifice hits in 1993.

			BATTING												FIELDING			
Year	Team (League)	Pos.	G	AB	R	H	2B	3B	HR	RBI	Avg.	BB	SO	SB	PO	A	E	Avg.
1988	—Spokane (N'west).....	SS	70	312	50	95	13	1	0	35	.304	18	59	14	*118	217	*47	.877
1989	—Char., S.C. (S. Atl.)...	SS	127	460	50	102	15	1	1	29	.222	17	85	12	*256	*373	*74	.895
1990	—Riverside (Calif.)......	SS	14	46	5	17	3	1	1	4	.370	3	3	4	18	38	6	.903
1991	—Wichita (Texas).......	2B-SS	125	452	43	121	17	1	1	41	.268	18	70	6	274	339	26	.959
1992	—Las Vegas (PCL)......	SS-OF	120	395	44	92	8	8	1	31	.233	19	65	6	200	358	†30	.949
1993	—Las Vegas (PCL)......	SS-2B	131	491	52	150	36	6	6	58	.305	27	62	8	230	380	29	.955
	—San Diego (N.L.).......	2B	17	43	1	5	1	0	0	1	.116	0	8	0	23	34	1	.983
Major league totals (1 year)			17	43	1	5	1	0	0	1	.116	0	8	0	23	34	1	.983

LOVULLO, TOREY

2B, ANGELS

PERSONAL: Born July 25, 1965, in Santa Monica, Calif. . . . 6-0/185. . . . Throws right, bats both. . . . Full name: Salvatore Anthony Lovullo. . . . Name pronounced leh-VOO-lo.

HIGH SCHOOL: Montclair Prep (Van Nuys, Calif.).

COLLEGE: UCLA (degree in psychology).

TRANSACTIONS/CAREER NOTES: Selected by Kansas City Royals organization in 27th round of free-agent draft (June 2, 1986). . . . Selected by Detroit Tigers organization in fifth round of free-agent draft (June 2, 1987). . . . Traded by Tigers to New York Yankees for P Mark Leiter (March 19, 1991). . . . Granted free agency (October 16, 1992). . . . Signed by California Angels (November 19, 1992).

HONORS: Named second baseman on THE SPORTING NEWS college All-America team (1987).

STATISTICAL NOTES: Tied for International League lead with 10 intentional bases on balls received in 1989. . . . Led International League with .509 slugging percentage in 1992.

			BATTING												FIELDING			
Year	Team (League)	Pos.	G	AB	R	H	2B	3B	HR	RBI	Avg.	BB	SO	SB	PO	A	E	Avg.
1987	—Fayetteville (SAL)....	3B-2B	55	191	34	49	13	0	8	32	.257	37	30	6	41	133	22	.888
	—Lakeland (Fla. St.)...	3B	18	60	11	16	3	0	1	16	.267	10	8	0	11	30	2	.953
1988	—Glens Falls (East.)...	3B-2B	78	270	37	74	17	1	9	50	.274	36	44	2	63	173	21	.918
	—Toledo (Int'l)............	2B-3B-SS	57	177	18	41	8	1	5	20	.232	9	24	2	120	149	5	.982
	—Detroit (A.L.)...........	2B-3B	12	21	2	8	1	1	1	2	.381	1	2	0	12	19	0	1.000
1989	—Toledo (Int'l)............	1-3-2-S	112	409	48	94	23	2	10	52	.230	44	57	2	217	257	20	.960
	—Detroit (A.L.)...........	1B-3B	29	87	8	10	2	0	1	4	.115	14	20	1	134	24	1	.994
1990	—Toledo (Int'l)............	2B-3B-1B	141	486	71	131	*38	1	14	58	.270	61	74	4	280	352	18	.972
1991	—New York (A.L.)■......	3B	22	51	0	9	2	0	0	2	.176	5	7	0	14	33	3	.940
	—Columbus (Int'l).......	3-1-2-0	106	395	74	107	24	5	10	75	.271	59	54	4	277	164	16	.965
1992	—Columbus (Int'l).......	2-3-1-0	131	468	69	138	*33	5	19	89	.295	64	65	9	187	206	8	.980
1993	—California (A.L.)■.....	2-3-S-0-1	116	367	42	92	20	0	6	30	.251	36	49	7	208	249	11	.976
Major league totals (4 years)			179	526	52	119	25	1	8	38	.226	56	78	8	368	325	15	.979

LOWERY, TERRELL

OF, RANGERS

PERSONAL: Born October 25, 1970, in Oakland, Calif. . . . 6-3/175. . . . Throws right, bats right. . . . Full name: Quenton Terrell Lowery. . . . Brother of Josh Lowery, minor league shortstop (1989-90).

HIGH SCHOOL: Oakland (Calif.) Technical.

COLLEGE: Loyola Marymount.

TRANSACTIONS/CAREER NOTES: Selected by Texas Rangers organization in second round of free-agent draft (June 3, 1991). . . . On Butte disabled list (June 17-27, 1992). . . . On restricted list (June 27, 1992-February 5, 1993).

			BATTING												FIELDING			
Year	Team (League)	Pos.	G	AB	R	H	2B	3B	HR	RBI	Avg.	BB	SO	SB	PO	A	E	Avg.
1991	—Butte (Pioneer).........	OF	54	214	38	64	10	7	3	33	.299	29	44	23	92	7	6	.943
1992	—................................								Did not play.									
1993	—Charlotte (Fla. St.)...	OF	65	257	46	77	7	9	3	36	.300	46	47	14	156	5	4	.976
	—Tulsa (Texas)...........	OF	66	258	29	62	5	1	3	14	.240	28	50	10	152	6	2	.988

LUEBBERS, LARRY

P, CUBS

PERSONAL: Born October 11, 1969, in Cincinnati. . . . 6-6/200. . . . Throws right, bats right. . . . Full name: Larry Christopher Luebbers.
HIGH SCHOOL: St. Henry (Erlanger, Ky.).
COLLEGE: Kentucky.

TRANSACTIONS/CAREER NOTES: Selected by Cincinnati Reds organization in eighth round of free-agent draft (June 4, 1990). . . . Traded by Reds with P Mike Anderson and C Darron Cox to Chicago Cubs for P Chuck McElroy (December 10, 1993).

Year	Team (League)	W	L	Pct.	ERA	G	GS	CG	ShO	Sv.	IP	H	R	ER	BB	SO
1990	—Billings (Pioneer)	5	4	.556	4.48	13	13	1	•1	0	72 1/3	74	46	36	31	48
1991	—Ced. Rap. (Midw.)	8	10	.444	3.12	28	28	3	0	0	184 2/3	177	85	64	64	98
1992	—Ced. Rap. (Midw.)	7	0	1.000	2.62	14	14	1	0	0	82 1/3	71	33	24	33	56
	—Chatt. (South.)	6	5	.545	2.27	14	14	1	0	0	87 1/3	86	34	22	34	56
1993	—Indianapolis (A.A.)	4	7	.364	4.16	15	15	0	0	0	84 1/3	81	45	39	47	51
	—Cincinnati (N.L.)	2	5	.286	4.54	14	14	0	0	0	77 1/3	74	49	39	38	38
	Major league totals (1 year)	2	5	.286	4.54	14	14	0	0	0	77 1/3	74	49	39	38	38

LUGO, URBANO

P, PIRATES

PERSONAL: Born August 12, 1962, in Falcon, Venezuela. . . . 5-11/197. . . . Throws right, bats right. . . . Full name: Urbano Rafael Lugo. . . . Son of Urbano Lugo, minor league pitcher (1967-70 and 1973).

TRANSACTIONS/CAREER NOTES: Signed as free agent by California Angels organization (January 31, 1982). . . . On California disabled list (August 22-September 6, 1985). . . . On California disabled list (March 31-June 5, 1986); included rehabilitation assignment to Midland (May 15-June 4). . . . Released by Angels (March 31, 1989). . . . Signed by Indianapolis, Montreal Expos organization (April 4, 1989). . . . Granted free agency (October 15, 1989). . . . Signed by Detroit Tigers (April 8, 1990). . . . Granted free agency (October 15, 1990). . . . Signed by Toledo, Tigers organization (March 12, 1991). . . . Granted free agency (October 15, 1991). . . . Re-signed by Toledo (February 25, 1992). . . . Loaned by Toledo to Jalisco of Mexican League (February 26-June 3, 1992). . . . Contract acquired by Jalisco from Tigers organization (June 3, 1992). . . . Signed as free agent by Pittsburgh Pirates organization (December 17, 1993).

Year	Team (League)	W	L	Pct.	ERA	G	GS	CG	ShO	Sv.	IP	H	R	ER	BB	SO
1982	—Danville (Midwest)	0	2	.000	10.13	10	0	0	0	0	24	35	30	27	16	13
	—Salem (Northwest)	7	3	.700	2.88	14	13	3	0	0	90 2/3	74	45	29	61	62
1983	—Peoria (Midwest)	8	5	.615	2.52	15	15	7	0	0	107	82	39	30	28	96
	—Redwood (Calif.)	5	5	.500	3.90	11	11	5	0	0	64 2/3	59	36	28	31	58
1984	—Waterbury (East.)	13	8	.619	2.79	24	24	9	1	0	164 1/3	135	63	51	68	117
1985	—Edmonton (PCL)	2	0	1.000	4.56	4	4	1	0	0	25 2/3	20	14	13	14	19
	—California (A.L.)	3	4	.429	3.69	20	10	1	0	0	83	86	36	34	29	42
1986	—Midland (Texas)	1	1	.500	1.64	2	2	0	0	0	11	9	2	2	4	4
	—Edmonton (PCL)	8	6	.571	4.66	16	16	2	0	0	100 1/3	110	58	52	41	53
	—California (A.L.)	1	1	.500	3.80	6	3	0	0	0	21 1/3	21	9	9	6	9
1987	—California (A.L.)	0	2	.000	9.32	7	5	0	0	0	28	42	34	29	18	24
	—Edmonton (PCL)	4	3	.571	3.67	15	14	4	2	0	90 2/3	89	46	37	46	47
1988	—Edmonton (PCL)	9	6	.600	5.26	38	15	2	1	1	116 1/3	148	74	68	47	69
	—California (A.L.)	0	0	. . .	9.00	1	0	0	0	0	2	2	2	2	1	1
1989	—Indianapolis (A.A.)■	12	4	*.750	2.94	22	21	0	0	0	122 1/3	100	53	40	41	79
	—Montreal (N.L.)	0	0	. . .	6.75	3	0	0	0	0	4	4	3	3	0	3
1990	—Detroit (A.L.)■	2	0	1.000	7.03	13	1	0	0	0	24 1/3	30	19	19	13	12
	—Toledo (Int'l)	2	2	.500	3.93	29	6	1	0	1	66 1/3	56	30	29	27	43
1991	—Jalisco (Mexican)	12	7	.632	3.29	25	24	8	3	1	150 2/3	150	69	55	49	110
1992	—Jalisco (Mexican)■	12	9	.571	3.65	27	27	8	1	0	187 1/3	186	84	76	67	121
1993	—Jalisco (Mexican)	•17	5	.773	2.88	29	28	10	1	0	*206	182	74	66	75	*164
	A.L. totals (5 years)	6	7	.462	5.28	47	19	1	0	0	158 2/3	181	100	93	67	88
	N.L. totals (1 year)	0	0	. . .	6.75	3	0	0	0	0	4	4	3	3	0	3
	Major league totals (6 years)	6	7	.462	5.31	50	19	1	0	0	162 2/3	185	103	96	67	91

LYDEN, MITCH

C, MARLINS

PERSONAL: Born December 14, 1964, in Portland, Ore. . . . 6-3/225. . . . Throws right, bats right. . . . Full name: Mitchell Scott Lyden.
HIGH SCHOOL: Beaverton (Ore.).

TRANSACTIONS/CAREER NOTES: Selected by New York Yankees organization in third round of free-agent draft (June 6, 1983). . . . On Albany/Colonie disabled list (April 11-July 13, 1986). . . . Granted free agency (October 15, 1990). . . . Signed by Colorado Springs, Cleveland Indians organization (January 11, 1991). . . . Released by Colorado Springs (April 2, 1991). . . . Signed by Toledo, Detroit Tigers organization (April 10, 1991). . . . Granted free agency (October 15, 1991). . . . Signed by Tidewater, New York Mets organization (February 2, 1992). . . . Granted free agency (October 15, 1992). . . . Signed by Edmonton, Florida Marlins organization (December 2, 1992). . . . On Edmonton disabled list (June 29-August 27, 1993).

STATISTICAL NOTES: Led Florida State League catchers with 678 total chances in 1985.

			BATTING												FIELDING			
Year	Team (League)	Pos.	G	AB	R	H	2B	3B	HR	RBI	Avg.	BB	SO	SB	PO	A	E	Avg.
1983	—Oneonta (NYP)	C	47	128	14	19	1	0	0	7	.148	12	36	3	310	28	3	*.991
1984	—Greensboro (S. Atl.)	C	14	32	3	7	1	0	1	2	.219	1	9	0	28	5	1	.971
	—GC Yankees (GCL)	C	54	200	21	47	4	0	1	21	.235	13	36	3	254	49	7	.977
1985	—Fort Lauder. (FSL)	C	116	400	43	102	21	1	10	58	.255	27	93	1	*607	63	8	*.988
1986	—Alb./Colon. (East.)	C	46	159	19	48	14	1	8	29	.302	4	39	0	131	25	3	.981
	—Columbus (Int'l)	C	2	7	0	0	0	0	0	0	.000	1	1	0	1	0	0	1.000
	—GC Yankees (GCL)	C	17	50	8	17	7	0	3	16	.340	7	7	0	62	8	2	.972
1987	—Alb./Colon. (East.)	C	71	233	25	59	12	2	8	36	.253	11	47	0	317	24	5	.986
	—Columbus (Int'l)	C	29	100	7	22	3	0	0	8	.220	4	22	1	120	11	4	.970
1988	—Prin. William (Car.)	1B	67	234	42	66	12	2	17	47	.282	19	59	1	5	1	3	.667
	—Alb./Colon. (East.)	DH	20	78	16	32	7	1	8	21	.410	5	15	0	. . .	. . .	. . .	. . .

Year	Team (League)	Pos.	G	AB	R	H	2B	3B	HR	RBI	Avg.	BB	SO	SB	PO	A	E	Avg.
			BATTING												FIELDING			
1989	—Prin. William (Car.)	1B-C	30	105	17	29	2	1	7	28	.276	8	26	1	208	9	2	.991
	—Alb./Colon. (East.)	1B-C	53	181	24	43	2	0	6	21	.238	12	51	1	30	1	0	1.000
1990	—Alb./Colon. (East.)	C-1B	85	311	55	92	22	1	17	63	.296	24	67	1	407	22	4	.991
	—Columbus (Int'l)	1B	41	147	18	33	8	0	7	20	.224	7	34	0	326	18	3	.991
1991	—Toledo (Int'l)■	C-1B	101	340	34	76	11	2	18	55	.224	15	108	0	368	22	3	.992
1992	—Tidewater (Int'l)■	1B-C	91	299	34	77	13	0	14	52	.258	12	95	1	369	25	5	.987
1993	—Edmonton (PCL)■	C-1B	50	160	34	49	15	1	8	31	.306	5	34	1	181	16	2	.990
	—Florida (N.L.)	C	6	10	2	3	0	0	1	1	.300	0	3	0	4	0	0	1.000
Major league totals (1 year)			6	10	2	3	0	0	1	1	.300	0	3	0	4	0	0	1.000

LYDY, SCOTT

OF, ATHLETICS

PERSONAL: Born October 26, 1968, in Mesa, Ariz.... 6-5/195.... Throws right, bats right.... Full name: Donald Scott Lydy.... Name pronounced LY-dee.

HIGH SCHOOL: Mountain View (Mesa, Ariz.).

COLLEGE: South Mountain Community College (Ariz.).

TRANSACTIONS/CAREER NOTES: Selected by Oakland Athletics organization in second round of free-agent draft (June 5, 1989).

Year	Team (League)	Pos.	G	AB	R	H	2B	3B	HR	RBI	Avg.	BB	SO	SB	PO	A	E	Avg.
			BATTING												FIELDING			
1989	—S. Oregon (N'west)	OF	67	230	37	48	11	2	3	28	.209	31	72	8	109	3	6	.949
1990	—Ariz. A's (Arizona)	1B	18	50	8	17	6	0	2	11	.340	10	14	0	6	1	0	1.000
	—Madison (Midwest)	OF	54	174	33	33	6	2	4	19	.190	25	62	7	85	3	4	.957
1991	—Madison (Midwest)	OF	127	464	64	120	26	2	12	69	.259	66	109	24	222	14	8	.967
1992	—Reno (California)	OF	33	124	29	49	13	2	2	27	.395	26	30	9	41	6	4	.922
	—Huntsville (South.)	OF	109	387	64	118	20	3	9	65	.305	67	95	16	137	4	7	.953
1993	—Tacoma (PCL)	OF	95	341	70	100	22	6	9	41	.293	50	87	12	182	9	6	.970
	—Oakland (A.L.)	OF	41	102	11	23	5	0	2	7	.225	8	39	2	67	2	3	.958
Major league totals (1 year)			41	102	11	23	5	0	2	7	.225	8	39	2	67	2	3	.958

L

LYONS, STEVE

OF/IF

PERSONAL: Born June 3, 1960, in Tacoma, Wash.... 6-3/195.... Throws right, bats left.... Full name: Stephen John Lyons.

HIGH SCHOOL: Marist (Eugene, Ore.), then Beaverton (Ore.).

COLLEGE: Oregon State.

TRANSACTIONS/CAREER NOTES: Selected by Boston Red Sox organization in first round (19th pick overall) of free-agent draft (June 8, 1981).... Traded by Red Sox to Chicago White Sox for P Tom Seaver (June 29, 1986).... Released by White Sox (April 13, 1991).... Signed by Red Sox (April 18, 1991).... Granted free agency (November 5, 1991).... Signed by Atlanta Braves (January 8, 1991).... Released by Braves (April 30, 1992).... Signed by Montreal Expos (May 8, 1992).... Contract sold by Expos to Red Sox (June 27, 1992).... Granted free agency (November 4, 1992).... Signed by Iowa, Chicago Cubs organization (February 24, 1993).... Released by Cubs organization (March 28, 1993).... Signed by Pawtucket, Red Sox organization (May 7, 1993).... Granted free agency (November 4, 1993).

STATISTICAL NOTES: Led International League third basemen with 98 putouts, 332 total chances and 25 errors in 1984.... Led A.L. third basemen with 36 double plays in 1988.

Year	Team (League)	Pos.	G	AB	R	H	2B	3B	HR	RBI	Avg.	BB	SO	SB	PO	A	E	Avg.
			BATTING												FIELDING			
1981	—Winst.-Salem (Car.)	OF-SS	64	252	43	61	9	3	6	40	.242	44	55	19	137	23	8	.952
1982	—Bristol (Eastern)	OF-SS	135	460	86	112	23	3	13	58	.243	81	119	35	275	11	9	.969
1983	—New Britain (East.)	3-O-S-P	132	456	83	112	24	7	7	62	.246	77	65	47	145	207	17	.954
1984	—Pawtucket (Int'l)	3B-OF-SS	131	444	80	119	21	2	17	62	.268	66	71	35	†141	211	†26	.931
1985	—Boston (A.L.)	OF-3B-SS	133	371	52	98	14	3	5	30	.264	32	64	12	253	6	7	.974
1986	—Boston-Chi. (A.L.)■	OF-3B-1B	101	247	30	56	9	3	1	20	.227	19	47	4	175	11	4	.979
	—Buffalo (A.A.)	3-S-O-1	20	74	18	22	5	1	3	8	.297	16	14	5	36	41	4	.951
1987	—Chicago (A.L.)	3B-OF-2B	76	193	26	54	11	1	1	19	.280	12	37	3	69	101	4	.977
	—Hawaii (PCL)	O-2-3-S	47	167	26	48	11	0	2	16	.287	22	27	7	73	71	3	.980
1988	—Chicago (A.L.)	3-O-2-C-1	146	472	59	127	28	3	5	45	.269	32	59	1	128	243	29	.928
1989	—Chicago (A.L.)	1B-OF-C	140	443	51	117	21	3	2	50	.264	35	68	9	414	245	15	.978
1990	—Chicago (A.L.)	1B-OF-P	94	146	22	28	6	1	1	11	.192	10	41	1	244	54	5	.983
1991	—Boston (A.L.)■	O-2-3-1-S-P	87	212	15	51	10	1	4	17	.241	11	35	10	118	43	3	.982
1992	—Atl.-Mont. (N.L.)■	OF-2B-1B	27	27	2	4	0	1	0	2	.148	1	7	1	14	3	0	1.000
	—Boston (A.L.)■	1B-OF-2B	21	28	3	7	0	1	0	2	.250	2	1	0	51	6	0	1.000
	—Pawtucket (Int'l)	3B-OF-P	37	135	14	35	14	2	2	12	.259	8	18	3	44	42	5	.945
1993	—Pawtucket (Int'l)	O-1-3-2-P-C	67	197	24	42	6	0	4	18	.213	26	50	3	194	28	7	.969
	—Boston (A.L.)	O-2-3-1-C	28	23	4	3	1	0	0	0	.130	2	5	1	11	15	0	1.000
American League totals (9 years)			826	2135	262	541	100	16	19	194	.253	155	357	41	1463	724	67	.970
National League totals (1 year)			27	27	2	4	0	1	0	2	.148	1	7	1	14	3	0	1.000
Major league totals (9 years)			853	2162	264	545	100	17	19	196	.252	156	364	42	1477	727	67	.970

RECORD AS PITCHER

Year	Team (League)	W	L	Pct.	ERA	G	GS	CG	ShO	Sv.	IP	H	R	ER	BB	SO
1983	—New Britain (East.)	1	0	1.000	2.45	3	0	0	0	0	3⅔	3	1	1	1	2
1990	—Chicago (A.L.)	0	0	...	4.50	1	0	0	0	0	2	2	1	1	4	1
1991	—Boston (A.L.)	0	0	...	0.00	1	0	0	0	0	1	2	0	0	0	1
1992	—Pawtucket (Int'l)	0	0	...	0.00	1	0	0	0	0	2	3	0	0	1	2
1993	—Pawtucket (Int'l)	0	0	...	9.00	2	0	0	0	0	2	3	5	2	2	4
Major league totals (2 years)		0	0	...	3.00	2	0	0	0	0	3	4	1	1	4	2

MAAS, KEVIN
DH/1B, YANKEES

PERSONAL: Born January 20, 1965, in Castro Valley, Calif. . . . 6-3/204. . . . Throws left, bats left. . . . Full name: Kevin Christian Maas. . . . Brother of Jason Maas, minor league outfielder/infielder (1985-91).
HIGH SCHOOL: Bishop O'Dowd (Oakland, Calif.).
COLLEGE: California.
TRANSACTIONS/CAREER NOTES: Selected by New York Yankees organization in 22nd round of free-agent draft (June 2, 1986). . . . On disabled list (April 19-30 and July 27, 1989-remainder of season).

			BATTING												FIELDING			
Year	**Team (League)**	**Pos.**	**G**	**AB**	**R**	**H**	**2B**	**3B**	**HR**	**RBI**	**Avg.**	**BB**	**SO**	**SB**	**PO**	**A**	**E**	**Avg.**
1986	—Oneonta (NYP)	1B	28	101	14	36	10	0	0	18	.356	7	9	5	222	19	1	.996
1987	—Fort Lauder. (FSL)	1B	116	439	77	122	28	4	11	73	.278	53	108	14	667	51	10	.986
1988	—Prin. William (Car.)	1B	29	108	24	32	7	0	12	35	.296	17	28	3	288	25	5	.984
	—Alb./Colon. (East.)	1B	109	372	66	98	14	3	16	55	.263	64	103	5	902	73	12	.988
1989	—Columbus (Int'l)	OF	83	291	42	93	23	2	6	45	.320	40	73	2	78	3	3	.964
1990	—Columbus (Int'l)	1B	57	194	37	55	15	2	13	41	.284	34	45	2	219	19	4	.983
	—New York (A.L.)	1B	79	254	42	64	9	0	21	41	.252	43	76	1	486	35	9	.983
1991	—New York (A.L.)	1B	148	500	69	110	14	1	23	63	.220	83	128	5	317	23	6	.983
1992	—New York (A.L.)	1B	98	286	35	71	12	0	11	35	.248	25	63	3	142	4	2	.986
1993	—New York (A.L.)	1B	59	151	20	31	4	0	9	25	.205	24	32	1	115	5	2	.984
	—Columbus (Int'l)	1B	28	104	14	29	6	0	4	18	.279	19	22	0	270	20	7	.976
Major league totals (4 years)			384	1191	166	276	39	1	64	164	.232	175	299	10	1060	67	19	.983

MABRY, JOHN
OF, CARDINALS

PERSONAL: Born October 17, 1970, in Wilmington, Del. . . . 6-4/195. . . . Throws right, bats left. . . . Full name: John Steven Mabry.
HIGH SCHOOL: Bohemia Manor (Chesapeake City, Md.).
COLLEGE: West Chester (Pa.).
TRANSACTIONS/CAREER NOTES: Selected by St. Louis Cardinals organization in sixth round of free-agent draft (June 3, 1991). . . . On disabled list (April 22-30 and May 6-18, 1992).
STATISTICAL NOTES: Led Texas League in grounding into double plays with 17 in 1993. . . . Led Texas League outfielders with six double plays in 1993.

			BATTING												FIELDING			
Year	**Team (League)**	**Pos.**	**G**	**AB**	**R**	**H**	**2B**	**3B**	**HR**	**RBI**	**Avg.**	**BB**	**SO**	**SB**	**PO**	**A**	**E**	**Avg.**
1991	—Hamilton (NYP)	OF	49	187	25	58	11	0	1	31	.310	17	18	9	73	*10	5	.943
	—Savannah (S. Atl.)	OF	22	86	10	20	6	1	0	8	.233	7	12	1	36	1	1	.974
1992	—Springfield (Midw.)	OF	115	438	63	115	13	6	11	57	.263	24	39	2	171	14	6	.969
1993	—Arkansas (Texas)	OF	*136	528	68	153	32	2	16	72	.290	27	68	7	262	15	3	*.989
	—Louisville (A.A.)	OF	4	7	0	1	0	0	0	1	.143	0	1	0	3	0	0	1.000

MacDONALD, BOB
P

PERSONAL: Born April 27, 1965, in East Orange, N.J. . . . 6-2/204. . . . Throws left, bats left. . . . Full name: Robert Joseph MacDonald.
HIGH SCHOOL: Point Pleasant Beach (N.J.).
COLLEGE: Rutgers.
TRANSACTIONS/CAREER NOTES: Selected by Toronto Blue Jays organization in 19th round of free-agent draft (June 2, 1987). . . . Contract sold by Blue Jays to Detroit Tigers (March 30, 1993). . . . Granted free agency (December 20, 1993).

Year	**Team (League)**	**W**	**L**	**Pct.**	**ERA**	**G**	**GS**	**CG**	**ShO**	**Sv.**	**IP**	**H**	**R**	**ER**	**BB**	**SO**
1987	—St. Cathar. (NYP)	0	0	...	4.50	1	1	0	0	0	4	8	4	2	0	4
	—Medicine Hat (Pio.)	3	1	.750	2.92	13	0	0	0	2	24⅔	22	13	8	12	26
	—Myrtle Beach (SAL)	2	1	.667	5.66	10	0	0	0	0	20⅔	24	18	13	7	12
1988	—Myrtle Beach (SAL)	3	4	.429	1.69	52	0	0	0	15	53⅓	42	13	10	18	43
1989	—Knoxville (South.)	3	5	.375	3.29	43	0	0	0	9	63	52	27	23	23	58
	—Syracuse (Int'l)	1	0	1.000	5.63	12	0	0	0	0	16	16	10	10	6	12
1990	—Syracuse (Int'l)	0	2	.000	5.40	9	0	0	0	2	8⅓	4	5	5	9	6
	—Knoxville (South.)	1	2	.333	1.89	36	0	0	0	15	57	37	17	12	29	54
	—Toronto (A.L.)	0	0	...	0.00	4	0	0	0	0	2⅓	0	0	0	2	0
1991	—Syracuse (Int'l)	1	0	1.000	4.50	7	0	0	0	1	6	5	3	3	5	8
	—Toronto (A.L.)	3	3	.500	2.85	45	0	0	0	0	53⅔	51	19	17	25	24
1992	—Toronto (A.L.)	1	0	1.000	4.37	27	0	0	0	0	47⅓	50	24	23	16	26
	—Syracuse (Int'l)	2	3	.400	4.63	17	0	0	0	2	23⅓	25	13	12	12	14
1993	—Detroit (A.L.)■	3	3	.500	5.35	68	0	0	0	3	65⅔	67	42	39	33	39
Major league totals (4 years)		7	6	.538	4.21	144	0	0	0	3	169	168	85	79	76	89

CHAMPIONSHIP SERIES RECORD

Year	**Team (League)**	**W**	**L**	**Pct.**	**ERA**	**G**	**GS**	**CG**	**ShO**	**Sv.**	**IP**	**H**	**R**	**ER**	**BB**	**SO**
1991	—Toronto (A.L.)	0	0	...	9.00	1	0	0	0	0	1	1	1	1	1	0

MACFARLANE, MIKE
C, ROYALS

PERSONAL: Born April 12, 1964, in Stockton, Calif. . . . 6-1/205. . . . Throws right, bats right. . . . Full name: Michael Andrew Macfarlane.
HIGH SCHOOL: Lincoln (Stockton, Calif.).
COLLEGE: Santa Clara.
TRANSACTIONS/CAREER NOTES: Selected by Kansas City Royals organization in fourth round of free-agent draft (June 3, 1985). . . . On disabled list (April 9-July 9, 1986 and July 16-September 14, 1991).
STATISTICAL NOTES: Tied for A.L. lead in being hit by pitch with 15 in 1992.

			BATTING												FIELDING			
Year	**Team (League)**	**Pos.**	**G**	**AB**	**R**	**H**	**2B**	**3B**	**HR**	**RBI**	**Avg.**	**BB**	**SO**	**SB**	**PO**	**A**	**E**	**Avg.**
1985	—Memphis (South.)	C	65	223	29	60	15	4	8	39	.269	11	30	0	295	24	9	.973

Year	Team (League)	Pos.	G	AB	R	H	2B	3B	HR	RBI	Avg.	BB	SO	SB	PO	A	E	Avg.
			BATTING												FIELDING			
1986	—Memphis (South.)	OF	40	141	26	34	7	2	12	29	.241	10	26	0	0	0	0	...
1987	—Omaha (A.A.)	C	87	302	53	79	25	1	13	50	.262	22	50	0	408	37	6	.987
	—Kansas City (A.L.)....	C	8	19	0	4	1	0	0	3	.211	2	2	0	29	2	0	1.000
1988	—Kansas City (A.L.)....	C	70	211	25	56	15	0	4	26	.265	21	37	0	309	18	2	.994
	—Omaha (A.A.)	C	21	76	8	18	7	2	2	8	.237	4	15	0	85	5	1	.989
1989	—Kansas City (A.L.)....	C	69	157	13	35	6	0	2	19	.223	7	27	0	249	17	1	.996
1990	—Kansas City (A.L.)....	C	124	400	37	102	24	4	6	58	.255	25	69	1	660	23	6	.991
1991	—Kansas City (A.L.)....	C	84	267	34	74	18	2	13	41	.277	17	52	1	391	28	3	.993
1992	—Kansas City (A.L.)....	C	129	402	51	94	28	3	17	48	.234	30	89	1	527	43	4	.993
1993	—Kansas City (A.L.)....	C	117	388	55	106	27	0	20	67	.273	40	83	2	647	68	11	.985
Major league totals (7 years)			601	1844	215	471	119	9	62	262	.255	142	359	5	2812	199	27	.991

MACK, SHANE

OF, TWINS

PERSONAL: Born December 7, 1963, in Los Angeles. . . . 6-0/190. . . . Throws right, bats right. . . . Full name: Shane Lee Mack. . . . Brother of Quinn Mack, outfielder, Seattle Mariners organization.
HIGH SCHOOL: Gahr (Cerritos, Calif.).
COLLEGE: UCLA.
TRANSACTIONS/CAREER NOTES: Selected by Kansas City Royals organization in fourth round of free-agent draft (June 8, 1981). . . . Selected by San Diego Padres organization in first round (11th pick overall) of free-agent draft (June 4, 1984). . . . On San Diego disabled list (March 25-May 4, 1989). . . . Selected by Minnesota Twins from Padres organization in Rule 5 major league draft (December 4, 1989). . . . On disabled list (May 15-30, 1993).
HONORS: Named outfielder on THE SPORTING NEWS college All-America team (1984).
STATISTICAL NOTES: Tied for Texas League lead in being hit by pitch with seven in 1986. . . . Led Texas League outfielders with four double plays in 1986. . . . Tied for A.L. lead in being hit by pitch with 15 in 1992.
MISCELLANEOUS: Member of 1984 U.S. Olympic baseball team.

Year	Team (League)	Pos.	G	AB	R	H	2B	3B	HR	RBI	Avg.	BB	SO	SB	PO	A	E	Avg.
			BATTING												FIELDING			
1985	—Beaumont (Texas) ...	OF-3B	125	430	59	112	23	3	6	55	.260	38	89	12	252	12	7	.974
1986	—Beaumont (Texas) ...	OF	115	452	61	127	26	3	15	68	.281	21	79	14	255	•14	8	.971
	—Las Vegas (PCL)	OF	19	69	13	25	1	6	0	6	.362	2	13	3	43	0	2	.956
1987	—Las Vegas (PCL)	OF	39	152	38	51	11	1	5	26	.336	19	32	13	97	3	1	.990
	—San Diego (N.L.)	OF	105	238	28	57	11	3	4	25	.239	18	47	4	159	1	3	.982
1988	—Las Vegas (PCL)	OF	55	196	43	68	7	1	10	40	.347	29	44	7	116	7	3	.976
	—San Diego (N.L.)	OF	56	119	13	29	3	0	0	12	.244	14	21	5	110	4	2	.983
1989	—Las Vegas (PCL)	OF	24	80	10	18	3	1	1	8	.225	14	19	4	59	3	1	.984
1990	—Minnesota (A.L.)■....	OF	125	313	50	102	10	4	8	44	.326	29	69	13	230	8	3	.988
1991	—Minnesota (A.L.)	OF	143	442	79	137	27	8	18	74	.310	34	79	13	290	6	7	.977
1992	—Minnesota (A.L.)	OF	156	600	101	189	31	6	16	75	.315	64	106	26	322	9	4	.988
1993	—Minnesota (A.L.)	OF	128	503	66	139	30	4	10	61	.276	41	76	15	347	8	5	.986
American League totals (4 years)			552	1858	296	567	98	22	52	254	.305	168	330	67	1189	31	19	.985
National League totals (2 years)			161	357	41	86	14	3	4	37	.241	32	68	9	269	5	5	.982
Major league totals (6 years)			713	2215	337	653	112	25	56	291	.295	200	398	76	1458	36	24	.984

CHAMPIONSHIP SERIES RECORD

Year	Team (League)	Pos.	G	AB	R	H	2B	3B	HR	RBI	Avg.	BB	SO	SB	PO	A	E	Avg.
			BATTING												FIELDING			
1991	—Minnesota (A.L.)	OF	5	18	4	6	1	1	0	3	.333	2	4	2	3	0	1	.750

WORLD SERIES RECORD

Year	Team (League)	Pos.	G	AB	R	H	2B	3B	HR	RBI	Avg.	BB	SO	SB	PO	A	E	Avg.
			BATTING												FIELDING			
1991	—Minnesota (A.L.)	OF	6	23	0	3	1	0	0	1	.130	0	7	0	11	0	0	1.000

MACLIN, LONNIE

OF, PADRES

PERSONAL: Born February 17, 1967, in Clayton, Mo. . . . 5-11/185. . . . Throws left, bats left. . . . Full name: Lonnie Lee Maclin Jr.
HIGH SCHOOL: Ritenour (St. Louis).
COLLEGE: St. Louis Community College at Meramec (Mo.).
TRANSACTIONS/CAREER NOTES: Selected by Cincinnati Reds organization in 10th round of free-agent draft (January 14, 1986). . . . Selected by St. Louis Cardinals organization in secondary phase of free-agent draft (June 2, 1986). . . . On Louisville disabled list (May 2-June 24, 1991 and May 28-August 11, 1993). . . . Granted free agency (October 15, 1993). . . . Signed by Las Vegas, San Diego Padres organization (November 2, 1993).

Year	Team (League)	Pos.	G	AB	R	H	2B	3B	HR	RBI	Avg.	BB	SO	SB	PO	A	E	Avg.
			BATTING												FIELDING			
1987	—Johns. City (App.)	OF	62	229	45	69	6	1	3	22	.301	24	32	21	70	1	6	.922
1988	—St. Peters. (FSL)	OF	51	175	22	33	3	1	3	12	.189	18	41	9	79	1	0	1.000
	—Savannah (S. Atl.) ...	OF	46	119	10	28	3	0	0	9	.235	12	19	8	104	7	1	.991
1989	—Springfield (Midw.) ..	OF	103	315	33	78	10	3	3	34	.248	21	56	18	135	7	5	.966
1990	—St. Peters. (FSL)	OF	31	119	18	46	6	3	2	17	.387	11	12	6	65	3	4	.944
	—Arkansas (Texas)	OF	74	264	32	82	14	5	2	25	.311	19	35	11	111	5	5	.959
	—Louisville (A.A.)	OF	17	58	9	18	3	2	0	6	.310	7	11	1	39	0	1	.975
1991	—Louisville (A.A.)	OF	84	327	35	94	12	2	4	37	.287	16	50	19	157	1	3	.981
1992	—Louisville (A.A.)	OF	111	290	29	94	17	3	1	38	.324	22	31	4	115	1	4	.967
1993	—Louisville (A.A.)	OF	62	220	29	61	10	3	4	18	.277	16	48	4	100	2	0	1.000
	—St. Louis (N.L.)	OF	12	13	2	1	0	0	0	1	.077	0	5	1	3	0	0	1.000
Major league totals (1 year)			12	13	2	1	0	0	0	1	.077	0	5	1	3	0	0	1.000

MADDUX, GREG

P, BRAVES

PERSONAL: Born April 14, 1966, in San Angelo, Tex. . . . 6-0/175. . . . Throws right, bats right. . . . Full name: Gregory Alan Maddux. . . . Brother of Mike Maddux, pitcher, New York Mets.
HIGH SCHOOL: Valley (Las Vegas).

TRANSACTIONS/CAREER NOTES: Selected by Chicago Cubs organization in second round of free-agent draft (June 4, 1984). . . . Granted free agency (October 26, 1992). . . . Signed by Atlanta Braves (December 9, 1992).
RECORDS: Holds major league single-season record for fewest complete games by pitcher who led league in complete games—8 (1993). . . . Shares major league career record for most years leading league in putouts by pitcher—5. . . . Shares major league single-game record for most putouts by pitcher—7 (April 29, 1990). . . . Shares modern N.L. single-season record for most putouts by pitcher—39 (each in 1990-91 and 1993).
HONORS: Won N.L. Gold Glove at pitcher (1990-93). . . . Named righthanded pitcher on THE SPORTING NEWS N.L. All-Star team (1992-93). . . . Named N.L. Cy Young Award winner by Baseball Writers' Association of America (1992-93). . . . Named N.L. Pitcher of the Year by THE SPORTING NEWS (1993).
STATISTICAL NOTES: Led Appalachian League with eight hit batsmen in 1984. . . . Led American Association with 12 hit batsmen in 1986. . . . Led N.L. with 14 hit batsmen in 1992.
MISCELLANEOUS: Singled and scored and struck out in two appearances as pinch-hitter (1991).

Year	Team (League)	W	L	Pct.	ERA	G	GS	CG	ShO	Sv.	IP	H	R	ER	BB	SO
1984	—Pikeville (Appal.)	6	2	.750	2.63	14	12	2	•2	0	85⅔	63	35	25	41	62
1985	—Peoria (Midwest)	13	9	.591	3.19	27	27	6	0	0	186	176	86	66	52	125
1986	—Pittsfield (Eastern)	4	3	.571	2.73	8	8	4	2	0	62⅔	49	22	19	15	35
	—Iowa (Am. Assoc.)	10	1	*.909	3.02	18	18	5	•2	0	128⅓	127	49	43	30	65
	—Chicago (N.L.)	2	4	.333	5.52	6	5	1	0	0	31	44	20	19	11	20
1987	—Chicago (N.L.)	6	14	.300	5.61	30	27	1	1	0	155⅔	181	111	97	74	101
	—Iowa (Am. Assoc.)	3	0	1.000	0.98	4	4	2	•2	0	27⅔	17	3	3	12	22
1988	—Chicago (N.L.)	18	8	.692	3.18	34	34	9	3	0	249	230	97	88	81	140
1989	—Chicago (N.L.)	19	12	.613	2.95	35	35	7	1	0	238⅓	222	90	78	82	135
1990	—Chicago (N.L.)	15	15	.500	3.46	35	•35	8	2	0	237	*242	*116	91	71	144
1991	—Chicago (N.L.)	15	11	.577	3.35	37	*37	7	2	0	*263	232	113	98	66	198
1992	—Chicago (N.L.)	•20	11	.645	2.18	35	•35	9	4	0	*268	201	68	65	70	199
1993	—Atlanta (N.L.)■	20	10	.667	*2.36	36	•36	*8	1	0	*267	228	85	70	52	197
	Major league totals (8 years)	115	85	.575	3.19	248	244	50	14	0	1709	1580	700	606	507	1134

CHAMPIONSHIP SERIES RECORD

CHAMPIONSHIP SERIES NOTES: Shares single-series record for most earned runs allowed—11 (1989). . . . Holds N.L. single-series record for most runs allowed—12 (1989). . . . Scored once in one game as pinch-runner (1989).

Year	Team (League)	W	L	Pct.	ERA	G	GS	CG	ShO	Sv.	IP	H	R	ER	BB	SO
1989	—Chicago (N.L.)	0	1	.000	13.50	2	2	0	0	0	7⅓	13	12	11	4	5
1993	—Atlanta (N.L.)	1	1	.500	4.97	2	2	0	0	0	12⅔	11	8	7	7	11
	Champ. series totals (2 years)	1	2	.333	8.10	4	4	0	0	0	20	24	20	18	11	16

ALL-STAR GAME RECORD

Year	League	W	L	Pct.	ERA	GS	CG	ShO	Sv.	IP	H	R	ER	BB	SO
1988	—National						Did not play.								
1992	—National	0	0	...	6.75	0	0	0	0	1⅓	1	1	1	0	0
	All-Star totals (1 year)	0	0	...	6.75	0	0	0	0	1⅓	1	1	1	0	0

MADDUX, MIKE

P, METS

PERSONAL: Born August 27, 1961, in Dayton, O. . . . 6-2/188. . . . Throws right, bats left. . . . Full name: Michael Ausley Maddux. . . . Brother of Greg Maddux, pitcher, Atlanta Braves.
HIGH SCHOOL: Rancho (Las Vegas).
COLLEGE: Texas-El Paso.

TRANSACTIONS/CAREER NOTES: Selected by Cincinnati Reds organization in 36th round of free-agent draft (June 5, 1979). . . . Selected by Philadelphia Phillies organization in fifth round of free-agent draft (June 7, 1982). . . . On Philadelphia disabled list (April 21-June 1, 1988); included rehabilitation assignment to Maine (May 13-22). . . . Released by Phillies organization (November 20, 1989). . . . Signed by Los Angeles Dodgers (December 21, 1989). . . . Granted free agency (October 15, 1990). . . . Signed by San Diego Padres (March 30, 1991). . . . On disabled list (April 5-26, 1992). . . . Traded by Padres to New York Mets for P Roger Mason and P Mike Freitas (December 17, 1992).

Year	Team (League)	W	L	Pct.	ERA	G	GS	CG	ShO	Sv.	IP	H	R	ER	BB	SO
1982	—Bend (Northwest)	3	6	.333	3.99	11	10	3	0	0	65⅓	68	35	29	26	59
1983	—Spartanburg (SAL)	4	6	.400	5.44	13	13	3	0	0	84⅓	98	62	51	47	85
	—Peninsula (Caro.)	8	4	.667	3.62	14	14	6	0	0	99⅓	92	46	40	35	78
	—Reading (Eastern)	0	0	...	6.00	1	1	0	0	0	3	4	2	2	1	2
1984	—Reading (Eastern)	3	•12	.200	5.04	20	19	4	0	0	116	143	82	65	49	77
	—Portland (PCL)	2	4	.333	5.84	8	8	1	0	0	44⅔	58	32	29	17	22
1985	—Portland (PCL)	9	12	.429	5.31	27	26	6	1	0	166	195	106	98	51	96
1986	—Portland (PCL)	5	2	.714	2.36	12	12	3	0	0	84	70	26	22	22	65
	—Philadelphia (N.L.)	3	7	.300	5.42	16	16	0	0	0	78	88	56	47	34	44
1987	—Maine (Int'l)	6	6	.500	4.35	18	16	3	1	0	103⅓	116	58	50	26	71
	—Philadelphia (N.L.)	2	0	1.000	2.65	7	2	0	0	0	17	17	5	5	5	15
1988	—Philadelphia (N.L.)	4	3	.571	3.76	25	11	0	0	0	88⅔	91	41	37	34	59
	—Maine (Int'l)	0	2	.000	4.18	5	3	1	0	0	23⅔	25	18	11	10	18
1989	—Philadelphia (N.L.)	1	3	.250	5.15	16	4	2	1	1	43⅔	52	29	25	14	26
	—Scran./W.B. (Int'l)	7	7	.500	3.66	19	17	3	1	0	123	119	55	50	26	100
1990	—Albuquerque (PCL)■	8	5	.615	4.25	20	19	2	0	0	108	122	59	51	32	85
	—Los Angeles (N.L.)	0	1	.000	6.53	11	2	0	0	0	20⅔	24	15	15	4	11
1991	—San Diego (N.L.)■	7	2	.778	2.46	64	1	0	0	5	98⅔	78	30	27	27	57
1992	—San Diego (N.L.)	2	2	.500	2.37	50	1	0	0	5	79⅔	71	25	21	24	60
1993	—New York (N.L.)■	3	8	.273	3.60	58	0	0	0	5	75	67	34	30	27	57
	Major league totals (8 years)	22	26	.458	3.72	247	37	2	1	16	501⅓	488	235	207	169	329

MAGADAN, DAVE

3B/1B, MARLINS

PERSONAL: Born September 30, 1962, in Tampa, Fla.... 6-3/205.... Throws right, bats left.... Full name: David Joseph Magadan.... Cousin of Lou Piniella, manager, Seattle Mariners.... Name pronounced MAG-uh-dun.
HIGH SCHOOL: Jesuit (Tampa, Fla.).
COLLEGE: Alabama.
TRANSACTIONS/CAREER NOTES: Selected by Boston Red Sox organization in 12th round of free-agent draft (June 3, 1980).... Selected by New York Mets organization in second round of free-agent draft (June 6, 1983).... On disabled list (August 7-September 10, 1984; March 29-April 17, 1987; May 5-20, 1988 and August 9, 1992-remainder of season).... Granted free agency (October 27, 1992).... Signed by Florida Marlins organization (December 8, 1992).... Traded by Marlins to Seattle Mariners for OF Henry Cotto and P Jeff Darwin (June 27, 1993).... Traded by Mariners to Marlins for P Jeff Darwin and cash (November 9, 1993).
HONORS: Named Golden Spikes Award winner by USA Baseball (1983).... Named designated hitter on THE SPORTING NEWS college All-America team (1983).
STATISTICAL NOTES: Led Carolina League with 10 intentional bases on balls received in 1984.... Led Texas League third basemen with 87 putouts, 275 assists, 393 total chances and 31 errors in 1985.... Led International League third basemen with .934 fielding percentage, 283 assists and 31 double plays in 1986.... Led N.L. first basemen with .998 fielding percentage in 1990.

			BATTING											FIELDING			
Year	**Team (League)**	**Pos.**	**G**	**AB**	**R**	**H**	**2B**	**3B**	**HR**	**RBI**	**Avg.**	**BB**	**SO**	**SB**	**PO**	**A**	**E**	**Avg.**
1983	—Columbia (S. Atl.)	1B	64	220	41	74	13	1	3	32	.336	51	29	2	520	37	7	.988
1984	—Lynchburg (Caro.)	1B	112	371	78	130	22	4	0	62	*.350	104	43	2	896	64	16	.984
1985	—Jackson (Texas)	3B-1B	134	466	84	144	22	0	0	76	.309	*106	57	0	†106	†276	†31	.925
1986	—Tidewater (Int'l)	3B-1B	133	473	68	147	33	6	1	64	.311	84	45	2	78	†284	25	†.935
	—New York (N.L.)	1B	10	18	3	8	0	0	0	3	.444	3	1	0	48	5	0	1.000
1987	—New York (N.L.)	3B-1B	85	192	21	61	13	1	3	24	.318	22	22	0	88	92	4	.978
1988	—New York (N.L.)	1B-3B	112	314	39	87	15	0	1	35	.277	60	39	0	459	99	10	.982
1989	—New York (N.L.)	1B-3B	127	374	47	107	22	3	4	41	.286	49	37	1	587	89	7	.990
1990	—New York (N.L.)	1B-3B	144	451	74	148	28	6	6	72	.328	74	55	2	837	99	3	†.997
1991	—New York (N.L.)	1B	124	418	58	108	23	0	4	51	.258	83	50	1	1035	90	5	.996
1992	—New York (N.L.)	3B-1B	99	321	33	91	9	1	3	28	.283	56	44	1	54	136	11	.945
1993	—Florida (N.L.)■	3B-1B	66	227	22	65	12	0	4	29	.286	44	30	0	55	122	7	.962
	—Seattle (A.L.)■	1B-3B	71	228	27	59	11	0	1	21	.259	36	33	2	325	72	5	.988
	American League totals (1 year)		71	228	27	59	11	0	1	21	.259	36	33	2	325	72	5	.988
	National League totals (8 years)		767	2315	297	675	122	11	25	283	.292	391	278	5	3163	732	47	.988
	Major league totals (8 years)		838	2543	324	734	133	11	26	304	.289	427	311	7	3488	804	52	.988

CHAMPIONSHIP SERIES RECORD

			BATTING											FIELDING			
Year	**Team (League)**	**Pos.**	**G**	**AB**	**R**	**H**	**2B**	**3B**	**HR**	**RBI**	**Avg.**	**BB**	**SO**	**SB**	**PO**	**A**	**E**	**Avg.**
1988	—New York (N.L.)	PH	3	3	0	0	0	0	0	0	.000	0	2	0	...	...	...	...

MAGNANTE, MIKE

P, ROYALS

PERSONAL: Born June 17, 1965, in Glendale, Calif.... 6-1/190.... Throws left, bats left.... Full name: Michael Anthony Magnante.... Name pronounced mag-NAN-tee.
HIGH SCHOOL: John Burroughs (Burbank, Calif.).
COLLEGE: UCLA (bachelor of science in applied mathematics).
TRANSACTIONS/CAREER NOTES: Selected by Kansas City Royals organization in 11th round of free-agent draft (June 1, 1988).... On disabled list (June 17, 1990-remainder of season and July 2-20, 1992).

Year	**Team (League)**	**W**	**L**	**Pct.**	**ERA**	**G**	**GS**	**CG**	**ShO**	**Sv.**	**IP**	**H**	**R**	**ER**	**BB**	**SO**
1988	—Eugene (N'west)	1	1	.500	0.56	3	3	0	0	0	16	10	6	1	2	26
	—Appleton (Midw.)	3	2	.600	3.21	9	8	0	0	0	47⅔	48	20	17	15	40
	—Baseball City (FSL)	1	1	.500	4.13	4	4	1	0	0	24	19	12	11	8	19
1989	—Memphis (South.)	8	9	.471	3.66	26	26	4	1	0	157⅓	137	70	64	53	118
1990	—Omaha (A.A.)	2	5	.286	4.11	13	13	2	0	0	76⅔	72	39	35	25	56
1991	—Omaha (A.A.)	6	1	.857	3.02	10	10	2	0	0	65⅔	53	23	22	23	50
	—Kansas City (A.L.)	0	1	.000	2.45	38	0	0	0	0	55	55	19	15	23	42
1992	—Kansas City (A.L.)	4	9	.308	4.94	44	12	0	0	0	89⅓	115	53	49	35	31
1993	—Omaha (A.A.)	2	6	.250	3.67	33	13	0	0	2	105⅓	97	46	43	29	74
	—Kansas City (A.L.)	1	2	.333	4.08	7	6	0	0	0	35⅓	37	16	16	11	16
	Major league totals (3 years)	5	12	.294	4.01	89	18	0	0	0	179⅔	207	88	80	69	89

MAGRANE, JOE

P, ANGELS

PERSONAL: Born July 2, 1964, in Des Moines, Ia.... 6-6/230.... Throws left, bats right.... Full name: Joseph David Magrane.... Name pronounced muh-GRAIN.
HIGH SCHOOL: Rowan (Morehead, Ky.).
COLLEGE: Arizona.
TRANSACTIONS/CAREER NOTES: Selected by Pittsburgh Pirates organization in third round of free-agent draft (June 7, 1982).... Selected by St. Louis Cardinals organization in first round (18th pick overall) of free-agent draft (June 3, 1985).... On St. Louis disabled list (May 30-June 18, 1987).... On St. Louis disabled list (April 17-June 11, 1988); included rehabilitation assignment to Louisville (May 23-June 11).... On disabled list (April 15-30, 1989 and March 19, 1991-entire season).... On St. Louis disabled list (March 28-June 1, 1992); included rehabilitation assignment to St. Petersburg (April 28-May 9) and Louisville (May 13-20 and May 23-28).... On St. Louis disabled list (June 2-September 1, 1992); included rehabilitation assignment to Louisville (August 3-31).... Released by Cardinals (August 15, 1993).... Signed by California Angels (August 20, 1993).
STATISTICAL NOTES: Tied for N.L. lead with 10 hit batsmen in 1987.

Year	**Team (League)**	**W**	**L**	**Pct.**	**ERA**	**G**	**GS**	**CG**	**ShO**	**Sv.**	**IP**	**H**	**R**	**ER**	**BB**	**SO**
1985	—Johns. City (App.)	2	1	.667	0.60	6	5	2	•2	0	30	15	4	2	11	31
	—St. Peters. (FSL)	3	1	.750	1.04	5	5	1	1	0	34⅔	21	8	4	14	17

M

Year	Team (League)	W	L	Pct.	ERA	G	GS	CG	ShO	Sv.	IP	H	R	ER	BB	SO
1986	—Arkansas (Texas)	8	4	.667	2.42	13	13	5	2	0	89⅓	66	29	24	31	66
	—Louisville (A.A.)	9	6	.600	2.06	15	15	•8	•2	0	113⅓	93	34	26	33	72
1987	—Louisville (A.A.)	1	0	1.000	1.93	3	3	1	1	0	23⅓	16	7	5	3	17
	—St. Louis (N.L.)	9	7	.563	3.54	27	26	4	2	0	170⅓	157	75	67	60	101
1988	—St. Louis (N.L.)	5	9	.357	*2.18	24	24	4	3	0	165⅓	133	57	40	51	100
	—Louisville (A.A.)	2	1	.667	3.15	4	4	1	0	0	20	19	7	7	7	18
1989	—St. Louis (N.L.)	18	9	.667	2.91	34	33	9	3	0	234⅔	219	81	76	72	127
1990	—St. Louis (N.L.)	10	17	.370	3.59	31	31	3	2	0	203⅓	204	86	81	59	100
1991	—							Did not play.								
1992	—St. Peters. (FSL)	0	1	.000	1.50	3	3	0	0	0	18	14	4	3	5	15
	—Louisville (A.A.)	3	4	.429	5.40	10	10	0	0	0	53⅓	60	32	32	29	35
	—St. Louis (N.L.)	1	2	.333	4.02	5	5	0	0	0	31⅓	34	15	14	15	20
1993	—St. Louis (N.L.)	8	10	.444	4.97	22	20	0	0	0	116	127	68	64	37	38
	—California (A.L.)■	3	2	.600	3.94	8	8	0	0	0	48	48	27	21	21	24
A.L. totals (1 year)		3	2	.600	3.94	8	8	0	0	0	48	48	27	21	21	24
N.L. totals (6 years)		51	54	.486	3.34	143	139	20	10	0	921	874	382	342	294	486
Major league totals (6 years)		54	56	.491	3.37	151	147	20	10	0	969	922	409	363	315	510

CHAMPIONSHIP SERIES RECORD

Year	Team (League)	W	L	Pct.	ERA	G	GS	CG	ShO	Sv.	IP	H	R	ER	BB	SO
1987	—St. Louis (N.L.)	0	0	...	9.00	1	1	0	0	0	4	4	4	4	2	3

WORLD SERIES RECORD

Year	Team (League)	W	L	Pct.	ERA	G	GS	CG	ShO	Sv.	IP	H	R	ER	BB	SO
1987	—St. Louis (N.L.)	0	1	.000	8.59	2	2	0	0	0	7⅓	9	7	7	5	5

MAHOMES, PAT

P, TWINS

PERSONAL: Born August 9, 1970, in Bryan, Tex. . . . 6-4/210. . . . Throws right, bats right. . . . Full name: Patrick Lavon Mahomes. . . . Name pronounced muh-HOMES.
HIGH SCHOOL: Lindale (Tex.).
TRANSACTIONS/CAREER NOTES: Selected by Minnesota Twins organization in sixth round of free-agent draft (June 1, 1988).

Year	Team (League)	W	L	Pct.	ERA	G	GS	CG	ShO	Sv.	IP	H	R	ER	BB	SO
1988	—Elizabeth. (Appal.)	6	3	.667	3.69	13	13	3	0	0	78	66	45	32	51	93
1989	—Kenosha (Midwest)	13	7	.650	3.28	25	25	3	1	0	156⅓	120	66	57	•100	167
1990	—Visalia (California)	11	11	.500	3.30	28	*28	5	1	0	•185⅓	136	77	68	*118	178
1991	—Orlando (Southern)	8	5	.615	*1.78	18	17	2	0	0	116	77	30	23	57	136
	—Portland (PCL)	3	5	.375	3.44	9	9	2	0	0	55	50	26	21	36	41
1992	—Minnesota (A.L.)	3	4	.429	5.04	14	13	0	0	0	69⅔	73	41	39	37	44
	—Portland (PCL)	9	5	.643	3.41	17	16	3	*3	1	111	97	43	42	43	87
1993	—Minnesota (A.L.)	1	5	.167	7.71	12	5	0	0	0	37⅓	47	34	32	16	23
	—Portland (PCL)	11	4	•.733	*3.03	17	16	3	1	0	115⅔	89	47	39	54	94
Major league totals (2 years)		4	9	.308	5.97	26	18	0	0	0	107	120	75	71	53	67

MAKSUDIAN, MIKE

1B/C, CUBS

PERSONAL: Born May 28, 1966, in Belleville, Ill. . . . 5-11/220. . . . Throws right, bats left. . . . Full name: Michael Bryant Maksudian. . . . Name pronounced mack-SOO-dee-an.
HIGH SCHOOL: Parsippany (N.J.).
COLLEGE: South Alabama.
TRANSACTIONS/CAREER NOTES: Signed as free agent by Chicago White Sox organization (July 13, 1987). . . . Traded by White Sox organization with OF Vince Harris to New York Mets organization for P Tom McCarthy and IF Steve Springer (August 3, 1988). . . . Released by Mets organization (March 30, 1989). . . . Signed by Miami, independent (May 22, 1989). . . . Selected by Knoxville, Toronto Blue Jays organization, from Miami in Rule 5 minor league draft (December 5, 1989). . . . On Knoxville disabled list (August 29, 1991-remainder of season). . . . Claimed on waivers by Minnesota Twins (October 26, 1992). . . . On Minnesota disabled list (April 3-18, 1993). . . . On Portland disabled list (July 16-August 26, 1993). . . . Granted free agency (October 15, 1993). . . . Signed by Chicago Cubs organization (December 14, 1993).
STATISTICAL NOTES: Led Midwest League with nine intentional bases on balls received in 1988.

			BATTING											FIELDING			
Year	Team (League)	Pos.	G	AB	R	H	2B	3B	HR	RBI	Avg.	BB	SO	SB	PO	A	E	Avg.
1987	—GC Whi. Sox (GCL)	1B-OF	34	109	23	38	11	3	1	28	.349	19	13	7	224	16	3	.988
1988	—South Bend (Mid.)	1B-C	102	366	51	111	26	3	4	50	.303	60	59	5	622	33	6	.991
	—Tam.-St. Luc. (FSL)■	1B	14	45	8	11	3	1	0	3	.244	8	7	0	11	2	0	1.000
1989	—Miami (Florida St.)■	O-C-1-3	83	288	36	90	18	4	9	42	.313	28	42	6	159	21	2	.989
1990	—Knoxville (South.)■	O-C-3-1	121	422	51	121	22	5	8	55	.287	50	66	6	216	27	7	.972
1991	—Syracuse (Int'l)	C-1B	31	97	13	32	6	3	1	13	.330	10	17	0	131	10	2	.986
	—Knoxville (South.)	C-1B	71	231	32	59	12	3	5	35	.255	37	43	2	307	22	3	.991
1992	—Syracuse (Int'l)	C-1B-OF	101	339	38	95	17	1	13	58	.280	32	63	4	399	30	2	.995
	—Toronto (A.L.)	1B	3	3	0	0	0	0	0	0	.000	0	0	0	0	0	0	...
1993	—Portland (PCL)■	1B-C-3B	76	264	57	83	16	7	10	49	.314	45	51	5	397	48	7	.985
	—Minnesota (A.L.)	1B-3B	5	12	2	2	1	0	0	2	.167	4	2	0	28	6	0	1.000
Major league totals (2 years)			8	15	2	2	1	0	0	2	.133	4	2	0	28	6	0	1.000

MALAVE, JOSE

OF, RED SOX

PERSONAL: Born May 31, 1971, in Cumana, Venezuela. . . . 6-2/194. . . . Throws right, bats right. . . . Full name: Jose Francisco Malave. . . . Name pronounced muh-LAH-vee. . . . Brother of Omar Malave, current manager, Hagerstown, Toronto Blue Jays organization, and minor league infielder (1981-89).

HIGH SCHOOL: Modesto Silva (Cumana, Venezuela).
TRANSACTIONS/CAREER NOTES: Signed as free agent by Boston Red Sox organization (August 15, 1989).... On disabled list (May 29-June 26 and August 3, 1993-remainder of season).

			BATTING											FIELDING			
Year	Team (League)	Pos.	G	AB	R	H	2B	3B	HR	RBI	Avg.	BB	SO	SB	PO	A	E	Avg.
1990	—Elmira (N.Y.-Penn)..	OF	13	29	4	4	1	0	0	3	.138	2	12	1	4	0	1	.800
1991	—GC Red Sox (GCL)....	1B-OF	37	146	24	47	4	2	2	28	.322	10	23	6	277	8	7	.976
1992	—Winter Haven (FSL)..	OF	8	25	1	4	0	0	0	0	.160	0	11	0	8	0	1	.889
	—Elmira (N.Y.-Penn)..	OF-1B	65	268	44	87	9	1	12	46	.325	14	48	8	306	22	5	.985
1993	—Lynchburg (Caro.)...	OF	82	312	42	94	27	1	8	54	.301	36	54	2	129	10	10	.933

MALDONADO, CANDY

OF, INDIANS

PERSONAL: Born September 5, 1960, in Humacao, Puerto Rico.... 6-0/205.... Throws right, bats right.... Full name: Candido Guadarrama Maldonado.
HIGH SCHOOL: Trina Padilla de Sanz (Humacao, Puerto Rico).
TRANSACTIONS/CAREER NOTES: Signed as free agent by Los Angeles Dodgers organization (June 6, 1978).... On disabled list (August 16-September 16, 1980).... Traded by Dodgers to San Francisco Giants for C Alex Trevino (December 11, 1985).... On disabled list (June 28-August 7, 1987).... Granted free agency (November 13, 1989).... Signed by Cleveland Indians (November 28, 1989).... Granted free agency (November 5, 1990).... Signed by Milwaukee Brewers (April 2, 1991).... On disabled list (April 11-June 25, 1991).... Traded by Brewers to Toronto Blue Jays for P Rob Wishnevski and a player to be named later (August 9, 1991); Brewers acquired IF William Suero to complete deal (August 14, 1991).... Granted free agency (October 30, 1992).... Signed by Chicago Cubs (December 11, 1992).... Traded by Cubs to Indians for OF Glenallen Hill (August 19, 1993).
RECORDS: Shares major league single-game record for most sacrifice flies—3 (August 29, 1987).
HONORS: Named California League co-Most Valuable Player (1980).
STATISTICAL NOTES: Tied for Pioneer League lead with six sacrifice flies in 1978.... Led California League with 247 total bases in 1980.... Hit for the cycle (May 4, 1987).

			BATTING											FIELDING			
Year	Team (League)	Pos.	G	AB	R	H	2B	3B	HR	RBI	Avg.	BB	SO	SB	PO	A	E	Avg.
1978	—Lethbridge (Pio.)......	OF	57	210	45	61	15	5	12	48	.290	22	48	2	112	6	8	.937
1979	—Clinton (Midwest)....	OF	50	158	25	37	13	1	2	26	.234	17	29	5	81	5	2	.977
	—Lethbridge (Pio.)......	OF	59	234	42	70	*20	3	5	33	.299	18	56	4	81	5	4	.956
1980	—Lodi (California).......	OF	121	456	75	139	27	3	25	*102	.305	41	63	12	211	13	11	.953
1981	—Albuquerque (PCL)..	OF	126	460	96	154	40	9	21	104	.335	50	104	13	221	21	8	.968
	—Los Angeles (N.L.)...	OF	11	12	0	1	0	0	0	0	.083	0	5	0	8	0	0	1.000
1982	—Albuquerque (PCL)..	OF	138	541	91	163	28	6	24	96	.301	48	89	4	303	15	10	.970
	—Los Angeles (N.L.)...	OF	6	4	0	0	0	0	0	0	.000	1	2	0	5	0	0	1.000
1983	—Los Angeles (N.L.)...	OF	42	62	5	12	1	1	1	6	.194	5	14	0	26	0	0	1.000
	—Albuquerque (PCL)..	OF-3B	38	144	23	46	6	1	4	20	.319	14	23	3	66	11	4	.951
1984	—Los Angeles (N.L.)...	OF-3B	116	254	25	68	14	0	5	28	.268	19	29	0	124	5	8	.942
1985	—Los Angeles (N.L.)...	OF	121	213	20	48	7	1	5	19	.225	19	40	1	121	6	2	.984
1986	—San Francisco (N.L.)■	OF-3B	133	405	49	102	31	3	18	85	.252	20	77	4	161	11	3	.983
1987	—San Francisco (N.L.)..	OF	118	442	69	129	28	4	20	85	.292	34	78	8	176	7	5	.973
1988	—San Francisco (N.L.)..	OF	142	499	53	127	23	1	12	68	.255	37	89	6	251	5	10	.962
1989	—San Francisco (N.L.)..	OF	129	345	39	75	23	0	9	41	.217	37	69	4	181	6	5	.974
1990	—Cleveland (A.L.)■.....	OF	155	590	76	161	32	2	22	95	.273	49	134	3	293	9	2	.993
1991	—Mil.-Toronto (A.L.)■	OF	86	288	37	72	15	0	12	48	.250	36	76	4	139	2	2	.986
1992	—Toronto (A.L.)..........	OF	137	489	64	133	25	4	20	66	.272	59	112	2	260	12	6	.978
1993	—Chicago (N.L.)■........	OF	70	140	8	26	5	0	3	15	.186	13	40	0	50	3	5	.914
	—Cleveland (A.L.)■.....	OF	28	81	11	20	2	0	5	20	.247	11	18	0	39	1	1	.976
American League totals (4 years)............			406	1448	188	386	74	6	59	229	.267	155	340	9	731	24	11	.986
National League totals (10 years)...........			888	2376	268	588	132	10	73	347	.247	185	443	23	1103	43	38	.968
Major league totals (13 years)................			1294	3824	456	974	206	16	132	576	.255	340	783	32	1834	67	49	.975

CHAMPIONSHIP SERIES RECORD

			BATTING											FIELDING			
Year	Team (League)	Pos.	G	AB	R	H	2B	3B	HR	RBI	Avg.	BB	SO	SB	PO	A	E	Avg.
1983	—Los Angeles (N.L.)...	PH	2	2	0	0	0	0	0	0	.000	0	1	0	...	...	...	...
1985	—Los Angeles (N.L.)...	OF-PH	4	7	0	1	0	0	0	1	.143	0	3	0	4	0	1	.800
1987	—San Francisco (N.L.)..	OF	5	19	2	4	1	0	0	2	.211	0	3	0	7	0	0	1.000
1989	—San Francisco (N.L.)..	OF-PH	3	3	1	0	0	0	0	1	.000	2	0	0	2	0	0	1.000
1991	—Toronto (A.L.)..........	OF	5	20	1	2	1	0	0	1	.100	1	6	0	4	0	0	1.000
1992	—Toronto (A.L.)..........	OF	6	22	3	6	0	0	2	6	.273	3	4	0	9	1	0	1.000
Championship series totals (6 years).......			25	73	7	13	2	0	2	11	.178	6	17	0	26	1	1	.964

WORLD SERIES RECORD

			BATTING											FIELDING			
Year	Team (League)	Pos.	G	AB	R	H	2B	3B	HR	RBI	Avg.	BB	SO	SB	PO	A	E	Avg.
1989	—San Francisco (N.L.)..	OF-PH	4	11	1	1	0	1	0	0	.091	0	4	0	5	0	0	1.000
1992	—Toronto (A.L.)..........	OF-PH	6	19	1	3	0	0	1	2	.158	2	5	0	8	2	0	1.000
World Series totals (2 years)..................			10	30	2	4	0	1	1	2	.133	2	9	0	13	2	0	1.000

MALDONADO, CARLOS

P

PERSONAL: Born October 18, 1966, in Chepo, Panama. ... 6-1/215. ... Throws right, bats right.... Full name: Carlos Cesar Maldonado.
HIGH SCHOOL: Venancio Fenosa Pascual (Chepo, Panama).
TRANSACTIONS/CAREER NOTES: Signed as free agent by Kansas City Royals organization (April 28, 1986).... On Appleton disabled list (April 7-May 12, 1989).... Traded by Royals organization to Milwaukee Brewers organization for SS Mike Guerrero (December 10, 1992).... Released by Brewers (November 15, 1993).

Year	Team (League)	W	L	Pct.	ERA	G	GS	CG	ShO	Sv.	IP	H	R	ER	BB	SO
1986	—GC Royals (GCL)	0	2	.000	1.83	10	4	0	0	1	34⅓	29	10	7	10	16
1987	—GC Royals (GCL)	5	1	.833	2.48	20	0	0	0	4	58	32	18	16	19	56
	—Appleton (Midw.)	0	0	...	11.57	2	0	0	0	0	2⅓	4	3	3	3	4
1988	—Baseball City (FSL)	1	5	.167	5.30	16	7	0	0	0	52⅔	46	35	31	39	44
1989	—Baseball City (FSL)	11	3	.786	1.17	28	0	0	0	9	76⅔	47	14	10	24	66
1990	—Memphis (South.)	4	5	.444	2.91	55	0	0	0	20	77⅓	61	29	25	37	77
	—Kansas City (A.L.)	0	0	...	9.00	4	0	0	0	0	6	9	6	6	4	9
1991	—Omaha (A.A.)	1	1	.500	4.28	41	1	0	0	9	61	67	31	29	42	46
	—Kansas City (A.L.)	0	0	...	8.22	5	0	0	0	0	7⅔	11	9	7	9	1
1992	—Omaha (A.A.)	7	4	.636	3.60	47	0	0	0	16	75	61	34	30	35	60
1993	—Milwaukee (A.L.)■	2	2	.500	4.58	29	0	0	0	1	37⅓	40	20	19	17	18
	—New Orleans (A.A.)	1	0	1.000	0.47	12	0	0	0	7	19⅓	13	1	1	7	14
Major league totals (3 years)		2	2	.500	5.65	38	0	0	0	1	51	60	35	32	30	28

MALLICOAT, ROB

P

PERSONAL: Born November 16, 1964, in St. Helens, Ore. . . . 6-3/180. . . . Throws left, bats left. . . . Full name: Robbin Dale Mallicoat. . . . Name pronounced MAL-uh-coat.
HIGH SCHOOL: Hillsboro (Ore.).
COLLEGE: Taft (Calif.) College.

TRANSACTIONS/CAREER NOTES: Selected by Detroit Tigers organization in eighth round of free-agent draft (June 6, 1983). . . . Selected by Houston Astros organization in secondary phase of free-agent draft (January 17, 1984). . . . On Columbus disabled list (June 24, 1986-remainder of season). . . . On disabled list (April 8, 1988-entire season and April 7, 1989-entire season). . . . On Sarasota disabled list (April 6-July 10, 1990). . . . On Houston disabled list (March 26, 1993-entire season). . . . Released by Astros (October 8, 1993).
MISCELLANEOUS: Appeared in two games as pinch-runner and made an out in only appearance as pinch-hitter with Houston (1992).

Year	Team (League)	W	L	Pct.	ERA	G	GS	CG	ShO	Sv.	IP	H	R	ER	BB	SO
1984	—Auburn (NY-Penn)	0	0	...	5.40	1	1	0	0	0	5	8	3	3	3	6
	—Asheville (S. Atl.)	3	4	.429	3.92	11	11	2	0	0	64⅓	49	30	28	36	57
1985	—Osceola (Fla. St.)	*16	6	.727	1.36	26	25	5	2	0	178⅔	119	41	27	74	*158
1986	—Tucson (PCL)	0	2	.000	6.43	3	3	0	0	0	14	18	14	10	8	9
	—Columbus (South.)	0	6	.000	4.81	10	10	1	0	0	58	61	38	31	45	52
1987	—Columbus (South.)	10	7	.588	2.89	24	24	3	0	0	152⅓	132	68	49	78	141
	—Tucson (PCL)	0	0	...	3.72	2	2	0	0	0	9⅔	9	5	4	7	8
	—Houston (N.L.)	0	0	...	6.75	4	1	0	0	0	6⅔	8	5	5	6	4
1988	—							Did not play.								
1989	—							Did not play.								
1990	—GC Astros (GCL)	0	1	.000	4.96	7	4	0	0	0	16⅓	15	15	9	15	21
	—Osceola (Fla. St.)	0	0	...	0.00	3	3	0	0	0	12	8	2	0	9	10
1991	—Jackson (Texas)	4	1	.800	3.77	18	0	0	0	1	31	20	15	13	11	34
	—Tucson (PCL)	4	4	.500	5.48	19	6	0	0	1	47⅔	43	32	29	38	32
	—Houston (N.L.)	0	2	.000	3.86	24	0	0	0	1	23⅓	22	10	10	13	18
1992	—Tucson (PCL)	1	3	.250	2.68	37	0	0	0	3	50⅓	36	17	15	21	53
	—Houston (N.L.)	0	0	...	7.23	23	0	0	0	0	23⅔	26	19	19	19	20
1993	—							Did not play.								
Major league totals (3 years)		0	2	.000	5.70	51	1	0	0	1	53⅔	56	34	34	38	42

MANAHAN, ANTHONY

IF, MARINERS

PERSONAL: Born December 15, 1968, in Elizabeth, N.J. . . . 6-0/190. . . . Throws right, bats right. . . . Full name: Anthony Charles Manahan.
HIGH SCHOOL: Horizon (Scottsdale, Ariz.).
COLLEGE: Arizona State.

TRANSACTIONS/CAREER NOTES: Selected by Houston Astros organization in 32nd round of free-agent draft (June 2, 1987). . . . Selected by Seattle Mariners organization in supplemental round ("sandwich pick" between first and second round, 38th pick overall) of free-agent draft (June 4, 1990); pick received as compensation for Mariners failure to sign 1989 No. 1 pick Scott Burrell. . . . On disabled list (April 11-21, 1991).
STATISTICAL NOTES: Led Southern League shortstops with 634 total chances in 1992.

				BATTING											FIELDING			
Year	Team (League)	Pos.	G	AB	R	H	2B	3B	HR	RBI	Avg.	BB	SO	SB	PO	A	E	Avg.
1990	—San Bern. (Calif.)	SS	51	198	46	63	10	2	7	30	.318	24	35	8	83	147	21	.916
1991	—Jacksonv. (South.)	SS	113	410	67	104	23	2	7	45	.254	54	81	11	142	278	28	.938
1992	—Jacksonv. (South.)	SS	134	505	70	130	24	6	8	49	.257	39	76	24	*227	*370	*37	.942
1993	—Calgary (PCL)	3-2-S-0	117	451	70	136	31	4	3	62	.302	38	48	19	162	302	25	.949

MANTO, JEFF

3B/1B, METS

PERSONAL: Born August 23, 1964, in Bristol, Pa. . . . 6-3/210. . . . Throws right, bats right. . . . Full name: Jeffrey Paul Manto.
HIGH SCHOOL: Bristol (Pa.).
COLLEGE: Temple.

TRANSACTIONS/CAREER NOTES: Selected by New York Yankees organization in 35th round of free-agent draft (June 7, 1982). . . . Selected by California Angels organization in 14th round of free-agent draft (June 3, 1985). . . . On disabled list (July 16, 1986-remainder of season). . . . Traded by Angels organization with P Colin Charland to Cleveland Indians for P Scott Bailes (January 9, 1990). . . . Released by Indians (November 27, 1991). . . . Signed by Richmond, Atlanta Braves organization (January 23, 1992). . . . On disabled list (May 4-14, 1992). . . . Granted free agency (October 15, 1992). . . . Signed by Philadelphia Phillies organization (December 16, 1992). . . . Granted free agency (October 15, 1993). . . . Signed by New York Mets organization (December 16, 1993).
HONORS: Named Texas League Most Valuable Player (1988).

STATISTICAL NOTES: Led California League third basemen with 245 assists and 365 total chances in 1987. . . . Tied for Texas League lead in errors by third baseman with 32 in 1988. . . . Led Texas League in grounding into double plays with 17 in 1988. . . . Led Pacific Coast League with .446 on-base percentage in 1990. . . . Led Pacific Coast League third basemen with .943 fielding percentage, 265 assists and 22 double plays in 1989. . . . Led International League with 12 sacrifice flies in 1992.

			BATTING												FIELDING			
Year	Team (League)	Pos.	G	AB	R	H	2B	3B	HR	RBI	Avg.	BB	SO	SB	PO	A	E	Avg.
1985	—Quad Cities (Mid.)	OF-3B	74	233	34	46	5	2	11	34	.197	40	74	3	87	8	3	.969
1986	—Quad Cities (Mid.)	3B	73	239	31	59	13	0	8	49	.247	37	70	2	48	114	28	.853
1987	—Palm Springs (Cal.)	3B-1B	112	375	61	96	21	4	7	63	.256	102	85	8	93	†246	37	.902
1988	—Midland (Texas)	3B-2B-1B	120	408	88	123	23	3	24	101	.301	62	76	7	82	208	‡32	.901
1989	—Edmonton (PCL)	3B-1B	127	408	89	113	25	3	23	67	.277	91	81	4	140	†266	21	†.951
1990	—Colo. Springs (PCL)■	3B-1B	96	316	73	94	27	1	18	82	.297	78	65	10	340	131	10	.979
	—Cleveland (A.L.)	1B-3B	30	76	12	17	5	1	2	14	.224	21	18	0	185	24	2	.991
1991	—Cleveland (A.L.)	3-1-C-0	47	128	15	27	7	0	2	13	.211	14	22	2	109	63	8	.956
	—Colo. Springs (PCL)	3-1-C-S-0	43	153	36	49	16	0	6	36	.320	33	24	1	169	53	11	.953
1992	—Richmond (Int'l)■	3B-2B-1B	127	450	65	131	24	1	13	68	.291	57	63	1	89	245	23	.936
1993	—Scran./W.B. (Int'l)■	3B-1B-C	106	388	62	112	30	1	17	88	.289	55	58	4	401	134	8	.985
	—Philadelphia (N.L.)	3B-SS	8	18	0	1	0	0	0	0	.056	0	3	0	2	8	0	1.000
American League totals (2 years)			77	204	27	44	12	1	4	27	.216	35	40	2	294	87	10	.974
National League totals (1 year)			8	18	0	1	0	0	0	0	.056	0	3	0	2	8	0	1.000
Major league totals (3 years)			85	222	27	45	12	1	4	27	.203	35	43	2	296	95	10	.975

MANUEL, BARRY

P, ORIOLES

PERSONAL: Born August 12, 1965, in Mamou, La. . . . 5-11/185. . . . Throws right, bats right. . . . Full name: Barry Paul Manuel. . . . Brother of Ferral Manuel, minor league catcher (1989).
HIGH SCHOOL: Mamou (La.).
COLLEGE: Louisiana State.
TRANSACTIONS/CAREER NOTES: Selected by Texas Rangers organization in second round of free-agent draft (June 2, 1987). . . . On Texas disabled list (March 27-June 20, 1993); included rehabilitation assignment to Charlotte (June 11-20). . . . Claimed on waivers by Baltimore Orioles (August 9, 1993).
STATISTICAL NOTES: Pitched one inning, combining with Cedric Shaw (seven innings) and Everett Cunningham (one inning) in 2-0 no-hit victory for Tulsa against Arkansas (April 18, 1991).

Year	Team (League)	W	L	Pct.	ERA	G	GS	CG	ShO	Sv.	IP	H	R	ER	BB	SO
1987	—GC Rangers (GCL)	0	0	...	18.00	1	0	0	0	0	1	3	2	2	1	1
	—Charlotte (Fla. St.)	1	2	.333	6.60	13	5	0	0	0	30	33	24	22	18	19
1988	—Charlotte (Fla. St.)	4	3	.571	2.54	37	0	0	0	4	60⅓	47	24	17	32	55
1989	—Tulsa (Texas)	3	4	.429	7.48	11	11	0	0	0	49⅓	49	44	41	39	40
	—Charlotte (Fla. St.)	4	7	.364	4.72	15	14	0	0	0	76⅓	77	43	40	30	51
1990	—Charlotte (Fla. St.)	1	5	.167	2.88	57	0	0	0	*36	56⅓	39	23	18	30	60
1991	—Tulsa (Texas)	2	7	.222	3.29	56	0	0	0	*25	68⅓	63	29	25	34	45
	—Texas (A.L.)	1	0	1.000	1.13	8	0	0	0	0	16	7	2	2	6	5
1992	—Okla. City (A.A.)	1	8	.111	5.27	27	0	0	0	5	27⅓	32	24	16	26	11
	—Texas (A.L.)	1	0	1.000	4.76	3	0	0	0	0	5⅔	6	3	3	1	9
	—Tulsa (Texas)	2	0	1.000	4.00	16	1	0	0	2	27	28	12	12	16	28
1993	—Charlotte (Fla. St.)	0	0	...	0.00	3	0	0	0	0	4⅔	6	0	0	2	4
	—Okla. City (A.A.)	2	2	.500	7.99	21	0	0	0	2	23⅔	29	21	21	16	19
	—Rochester (Int'l)■	1	1	.500	3.66	9	0	0	0	0	19⅔	14	8	8	7	11
Major league totals (2 years)		2	0	1.000	2.08	11	0	0	0	0	21⅔	13	5	5	7	14

M

MANWARING, KIRT

C, GIANTS

PERSONAL: Born July 15, 1965, in Elmira, N.Y. . . . 5-11/203. . . . Throws right, bats right. . . . Full name: Kirt Dean Manwaring.
HIGH SCHOOL: Horseheads (N.Y.).
COLLEGE: Coastal Carolina (S.C.).
TRANSACTIONS/CAREER NOTES: Selected by Boston Red Sox organization in 12th round of free-agent draft (June 6, 1983). . . . Selected by San Francisco Giants organization in second round of free-agent draft (June 2, 1986). . . . On disabled list (August 31-September 15, 1989 and June 24-July 18, 1990). . . . On San Francisco disabled list (May 30-July 11, 1991); included rehabilitation assignment to Phoenix (July 1-8) and San Jose (July 8-11). . . . On San Francisco disabled list (July 22-August 6, 1992).
HONORS: Won N.L. Gold Glove at catcher (1993).
STATISTICAL NOTES: Led Texas League catchers with 688 total chances and eight double plays in 1987. . . . Led N.L. catchers with 12 double plays in 1992.

			BATTING												FIELDING			
Year	Team (League)	Pos.	G	AB	R	H	2B	3B	HR	RBI	Avg.	BB	SO	SB	PO	A	E	Avg.
1986	—Clinton (Midwest)	C	49	147	18	36	7	1	2	16	.245	14	26	1	243	31	5	.982
1987	—Shreveport (Texas)	C	98	307	27	82	13	2	2	22	.267	19	33	1	603	*81	4	.994
	—San Francisco (N.L.)	C	6	7	0	1	0	0	0	0	.143	0	1	0	9	1	1	.909
1988	—Phoenix (PCL)	C	81	273	29	77	12	2	2	35	.282	14	32	3	411	51	6	.987
	—San Francisco (N.L.)	C	40	116	12	29	7	0	1	15	.250	2	21	0	162	24	4	.979
1989	—San Francisco (N.L.)	C	85	200	14	42	4	2	0	18	.210	11	28	2	289	32	6	.982
1990	—Phoenix (PCL)	C	74	247	20	58	10	2	3	14	.235	24	34	0	352	45	4	*.990
	—San Francisco (N.L.)	C	8	13	0	2	0	1	0	1	.154	0	3	0	22	3	0	1.000
1991	—San Francisco (N.L.)	C	67	178	16	40	9	0	0	19	.225	9	22	1	315	28	4	.988
	—Phoenix (PCL)	C	24	81	8	18	0	0	4	14	.222	8	15	0	100	15	3	.975
	—San Jose (Calif.)	C	1	3	1	0	0	0	0	0	.000	1	1	0	16	0	0	1.000
1992	—San Francisco (N.L.)	C	109	349	24	85	10	5	4	26	.244	29	42	2	564	68	4	.994
1993	—San Francisco (N.L.)	C	130	432	48	119	15	1	5	49	.275	41	76	1	739	70	2	*.998
Major league totals (7 years)			445	1295	114	318	45	9	10	128	.246	92	193	6	2100	226	21	.991

CHAMPIONSHIP SERIES RECORD

Year	Team (League)	Pos.	G	AB	R	H	2B	3B	HR	RBI	Avg.	BB	SO	SB	PO	A	E	Avg.
				BATTING											FIELDING			
1989	—San Francisco (N.L.)..	C-PH	3	2	0	0	0	0	0	0	.000	0	0	0	5	0	0	1.000

WORLD SERIES RECORD

Year	Team (League)	Pos.	G	AB	R	H	2B	3B	HR	RBI	Avg.	BB	SO	SB	PO	A	E	Avg.
				BATTING											FIELDING			
1989	—San Francisco (N.L.)..	C	1	1	1	1	1	0	0	0	1.000	0	0	0	0	0	0	...

MANZANILLO, JOSIAS

P, METS

PERSONAL: Born October 16, 1967, in San Pedro de Macoris, Dominican Republic. . . . 6-0/190. . . . Throws right, bats right. . . . Brother of Ravelo Manzanillo, pitcher, Chicago White Sox (1988). . . . Name pronounced hose-EYE-ess MAN-zan-EE-oh.

TRANSACTIONS/CAREER NOTES: Signed as free agent by Boston Red Sox organization (January 10, 1983). . . . On disabled list (June 8, 1987-remainder of season and April 8, 1988-entire season). . . . Granted free agency (March 24, 1992). . . . Signed by Omaha, Kansas City Royals organization (April 3, 1992). . . . Granted free agency (October 15, 1992). . . . Signed by Milwaukee Brewers (November 20, 1992). . . . Traded by Brewers to New York Mets for OF Wayne Housie (June 12, 1993).

Year	Team (League)	W	L	Pct.	ERA	G	GS	CG	ShO	Sv.	IP	H	R	ER	BB	SO
1983	—Elmira (N.Y.-Penn)....	1	5	.167	7.98	12	4	0	0	0	38⅓	52	44	34	20	19
1984	—Elmira (N.Y.-Penn)....	2	3	.400	5.26	14	0	0	0	1	25⅔	27	24	15	26	15
1985	—Greensboro (S. Atl.).....	1	1	.500	9.75	7	0	0	0	0	12	12	13	13	18	10
	—Elmira (N.Y.-Penn).....	2	4	.333	3.86	19	4	0	0	1	39⅔	36	19	17	36	43
1986	—Winter Haven (FSL).....	13	5	.722	2.27	23	21	3	2	0	142⅔	110	51	36	81	102
1987	—New Britain (East.)	2	0	1.000	4.50	2	2	0	0	0	10	8	5	5	8	12
1988	—....................................							Did not play.								
1989	—New Britain (East.)	9	10	.474	3.66	26	•26	3	1	0	147⅔	129	78	60	85	93
1990	—New Britain (East.)	4	4	.500	3.41	12	12	2	1	0	74	66	34	28	37	51
	—Pawtucket (Int'l)	4	7	.364	5.55	15	15	5	0	0	82⅔	75	57	51	45	77
1991	—Pawtucket (Int'l)	5	5	.500	5.61	20	16	0	0	0	102⅔	109	69	64	53	65
	—New Britain (East.)	2	2	.500	2.90	7	7	0	0	0	49⅔	37	25	16	28	35
	—Boston (A.L.)	0	0	...	18.00	1	0	0	0	0	1	2	2	2	3	1
1992	—Omaha (A.A.)■............	7	10	.412	4.36	26	21	0	0	0	136⅓	138	76	66	71	114
	—Memphis (South.)	0	2	.000	7.36	2	0	0	0	0	7⅓	6	6	6	6	8
1993	—Milwaukee (A.L.)■.......	1	1	.500	9.53	10	1	0	0	1	17	22	20	18	10	10
	—New Orleans (A.A.)	0	1	.000	9.00	1	0	0	0	0	1	1	1	1	0	3
	—Norfolk (Int'l)■............	1	5	.167	3.11	14	12	2	1	0	84	82	40	29	25	79
	—New York (N.L.)..........	0	0	...	3.00	6	0	0	0	0	12	8	7	4	9	11
A.L. totals (2 years)		1	1	.500	10.00	11	1	0	0	1	18	24	22	20	13	11
N.L. totals (1 year)..................		0	0	...	3.00	6	0	0	0	0	12	8	7	4	9	11
Major league totals (2 years) ...		1	1	.500	7.20	17	1	0	0	1	30	32	29	24	22	22

M

MARRERO, ORESTE

1B, EXPOS

PERSONAL: Born October 31, 1969, in Bayamon, Puerto Rico. . . . 6-0/195. . . . Throws left, bats left. . . . Full name: Oreste Vilato Marrero.

TRANSACTIONS/CAREER NOTES: Signed as free agent by Milwaukee Brewers organization (September 29, 1986). . . . Loaned by Brewers organization to Boise, independent (July 6-September 8, 1989). . . . Traded by Brewers organization with IF Charlie Montoyo to Montreal Expos organization for OF Todd Samples and P Ron Gerstein (January 20, 1993).

Year	Team (League)	Pos.	G	AB	R	H	2B	3B	HR	RBI	Avg.	BB	SO	SB	PO	A	E	Avg.
				BATTING											FIELDING			
1987	—Helena (Pioneer)	1B	51	154	30	50	8	2	7	34	.325	18	31	2	342	23	10	.973
1988	—Helena (Pioneer)	1B	67	240	52	85	15	0	16	44	.354	42	48	3	504	37	9	.984
	—Beloit (Midwest).......	1B	19	52	5	9	2	0	1	7	.173	3	16	0	92	9	2	.981
1989	—Ariz. Brewers (Ar.)...	1B	10	44	13	18	0	1	3	16	.409	2	5	2	61	1	0	1.000
	—Beloit (Midwest).......	1B	14	40	1	5	1	0	0	3	.125	3	20	1	12	0	1	.923
	—Boise (Northwest)■..	1B	54	203	38	56	8	1	11	43	.276	30	60	1	475	18	10	.980
1990	—Beloit (Midwest)■.....	1B	119	400	59	110	25	1	16	55	.275	45	107	8	650	30	7	.990
1991	—Stockton (Calif.).......	1B	123	438	63	110	15	2	13	61	.251	57	98	4	491	39	9	.983
1992	—El Paso (Texas)........	1B-OF	18	54	8	10	2	1	1	8	.185	4	13	1	42	0	0	1.000
	—Stockton (Calif.).......	OF-1B	76	243	35	67	17	0	7	51	.276	44	49	3	58	1	1	.983
1993	—Harrisburg (East.)■.	1B	85	255	39	85	18	1	10	49	.333	22	46	3	273	25	2	.993
	—Montreal (N.L.).........	1B	32	81	10	17	5	1	1	4	.210	14	16	1	194	15	2	.991
Major league totals (1 year)....................			32	81	10	17	5	1	1	4	.210	14	16	1	194	15	2	.991

MARSH, TOM

OF, PHILLIES

PERSONAL: Born December 27, 1965, in Toledo, O. . . . 6-2/180. . . . Throws right, bats right. . . . Full name: Thomas Owen Marsh.

HIGH SCHOOL: Calvin M. Woodward (Toledo, O.).

COLLEGE: Toledo.

TRANSACTIONS/CAREER NOTES: Selected by Toronto Blue Jays organization in 70th round of free-agent draft (June 2, 1987). . . . Selected by Philadelphia Phillies organization in 16th round of free-agent draft (June 1, 1988). . . . On Reading disabled list (June 22-September 7, 1990 and May 8-June 14, 1991). . . . On Philadelphia disabled list (June 27-July 28, 1992). . . . On disabled list (May 15-July 20, 1993).

STATISTICAL NOTES: Led International League outfielders with five double plays in 1993.

Year	Team (League)	Pos.	BATTING G	AB	R	H	2B	3B	HR	RBI	Avg.	BB	SO	SB	FIELDING PO	A	E	Avg.
1988	—Batavia (NY-Penn)..	OF	62	216	35	55	14	1	8	27	.255	18	54	6	99	9	4	.964
1989	—Spartanburg (SAL)..	OF	79	288	42	73	18	1	10	42	.253	29	66	8	128	10	8	.945
	—Clearwater (FSL).....	OF	43	141	12	24	2	1	1	10	.170	7	30	5	97	1	1	.990
1990	—Spartanburg (SAL)..	C	24	75	14	21	2	1	4	15	.280	8	21	5	46	6	0	1.000
	—Reading (Eastern)....	OF	41	132	13	34	6	1	1	10	.258	8	27	5	93	3	3	.970
1991	—Reading (Eastern)....	OF	67	236	27	62	12	5	7	35	.263	11	47	8	142	3	2	.986
1992	—Scran./W.B. (Int'l)...	OF	45	158	26	38	7	2	8	25	.241	10	30	5	35	1	1	.973
	—Philadelphia (N.L.)...	OF	42	125	7	25	3	2	2	16	.200	2	23	0	66	0	2	.971
1993	—Scran./W.B. (Int'l)...	OF	78	315	45	90	16	8	12	57	.286	14	47	10	145	10	7	.957
Major league totals (1 year)			42	125	7	25	3	2	2	16	.200	2	23	0	66	0	2	.971

MARTIN, AL

OF, PIRATES

PERSONAL: Born November 24, 1967, in West Covina, Calif. . . . 6-2/210. . . . Throws left, bats left. . . . Full name: Albert Lee Martin. . . . Formerly known as Albert Scales-Martin.
HIGH SCHOOL: Rowland Heights (Calif.).
COLLEGE: Southern California.

TRANSACTIONS/CAREER NOTES: Selected by Atlanta Braves organization in eighth round of free-agent draft (June 3, 1985). . . . Granted free agency (October 15, 1991). . . . Signed by Pittsburgh Pirates organization (November 11, 1991). . . . On suspended list (September 17-20, 1993).
STATISTICAL NOTES: Led Gulf Coast League first basemen with 15 errors in 1985. . . . Led American Association with .557 slugging percentage in 1992. . . . Led American Association outfielders with six double plays in 1992.

Year	Team (League)	Pos.	BATTING G	AB	R	H	2B	3B	HR	RBI	Avg.	BB	SO	SB	FIELDING PO	A	E	Avg.
1985	—GC Braves (GCL)......	1B-OF	40	138	16	32	3	0	0	9	.232	19	36	1	246	13	†15	.945
1986	—Sumter (S. Atl.).......	1B	44	156	23	38	5	0	1	24	.244	23	36	6	299	12	8	.975
	—Idaho Falls (Pio.)......	OF-1B	63	242	39	80	17	•6	4	44	.331	20	53	11	272	15	8	.973
1987	—Sumter (S. Atl.)........	OF-1B	117	375	59	95	18	5	12	64	.253	44	69	27	137	7	9	.941
1988	—Burlington (Midw.)....	OF	123	480	69	134	21	3	7	42	.279	30	88	40	224	4	8	.966
1989	—Durham (Carolina)...	OF	128	457	*84	124	26	3	9	48	.271	34	107	27	169	7	7	.962
1990	—Greenville (South.)...	OF	133	455	64	110	17	4	11	50	.242	43	102	20	200	8	7	.967
1991	—Greenville (South.)...	OF-1B	86	301	38	73	13	3	7	38	.243	32	84	19	134	7	6	.959
	—Richmond (Int'l).......	OF	44	151	20	42	11	1	5	18	.278	7	33	11	73	4	2	.975
1992	—Buffalo (A.A.)■.........	OF	125	420	85	128	16	*15	20	59	.305	35	93	20	222	10	8	.967
	—Pittsburgh (N.L.)......	OF	12	12	1	2	0	1	0	2	.167	0	5	0	6	0	0	1.000
1993	—Pittsburgh (N.L.)......	OF	143	480	85	135	26	8	18	64	.281	42	122	16	268	6	7	.975
Major league totals (2 years)			155	492	86	137	26	9	18	66	.278	42	127	16	274	6	7	.976

MARTIN, CHRIS

IF, EXPOS

PERSONAL: Born January 25, 1968, in Los Angeles. . . . 6-1/170. . . . Throws right, bats right. . . . Full name: Christopher Scott Martin.
HIGH SCHOOL: Hamilton (Los Angeles).
COLLEGE: Pepperdine.

TRANSACTIONS/CAREER NOTES: Selected by Kansas City Royals organization in 31st round of free-agent draft (June 2, 1986). . . . Selected by New York Yankees organization in 26th round of free-agent draft (June 5, 1989). . . . Selected by Montreal Expos organization in second round of free-agent draft (June 4, 1990); pick received as compensation for St. Louis Cardinals signing Type B free agent Bryn Smith. . . . On disabled list (June 20-July 18, 1991).

Year	Team (League)	Pos.	BATTING G	AB	R	H	2B	3B	HR	RBI	Avg.	BB	SO	SB	FIELDING PO	A	E	Avg.
1990	—W.P. Beach (FSL).....	SS	59	222	31	62	17	1	3	31	.279	27	37	7	96	178	14	.951
1991	—Harrisburg (East.)....	SS-1B	87	294	30	66	10	0	6	36	.224	22	60	1	125	240	15	.961
1992	—Harrisburg (East.)....	2B-SS-3B	125	383	39	87	22	1	5	31	.227	49	67	8	208	338	23	.960
1993	—Harrisburg (East.)....	S-2-O-3	116	395	68	116	23	1	7	54	.294	40	48	16	152	250	13	.969

MARTIN, NORBERTO

2B, WHITE SOX

PERSONAL: Born December 10, 1966, in Santo Domingo, Dominican Republic. . . . 5-10/164. . . . Throws right, bats right. . . . Full name: Norberto Edonal Martin. . . . Name pronounced mar-TEEN.

TRANSACTIONS/CAREER NOTES: Signed as free agent by Chicago White Sox organization (March 27, 1984). . . . On Peninsula disabled list (April 10-May 5, 1986). . . . On Appleton disabled list (May 14, 1986-remainder of season). . . . On disabled list (April 7, 1989-entire season and May 5-June 9, 1991).
STATISTICAL NOTES: Led Gulf Coast League shortstops with 37 errors in 1984. . . . Led Pacific Coast League second basemen with 681 total chances in 1992. . . . Led American Association second basemen with 291 putouts, 438 assists, 18 errors and 747 total chances in 1993.

Year	Team (League)	Pos.	BATTING G	AB	R	H	2B	3B	HR	RBI	Avg.	BB	SO	SB	FIELDING PO	A	E	Avg.
1984	—GC Whi. Sox (GCL)...	SS-OF	56	205	36	56	8	2	1	30	.273	21	31	18	66	149	†37	.853
1985	—Appleton (Midw.).....	SS	30	196	15	19	2	0	0	5	.097	9	23	2	39	86	12	.912
	—Niag. Falls (NYP).....	SS	60	217	22	55	9	0	1	13	.253	7	41	6	85	173	35	.881
1986	—Appleton (Midw.).....	SS	9	33	4	10	2	0	0	2	.303	2	5	1	13	16	6	.829
	—GC Whi. Sox (GCL)...	PR	1	0	0	0	0	0	0	0	...	0	0	0	...	...	...	...
1987	—Char., W.Va. (SAL)..	SS-OF-2B	68	250	44	78	14	1	5	35	.312	17	40	14	84	152	25	.904
	—Peninsula (Caro.).....	2B	41	162	21	42	6	1	1	18	.259	18	19	11	94	108	15	.931
1988	—Tampa (Fla. St.).......	2B	101	360	44	93	10	4	2	33	.258	17	49	24	196	268	20	.959
1989	—..................................							Did not play.										
1990	—Vancouver (PCL).....	2B	130	508	77	135	20	4	3	45	.266	27	63	10	283	324	17	.973
1991	—Vancouver (PCL).....	2B-SS	93	338	39	94	9	0	0	20	.278	21	38	11	196	265	16	.966

Year	Team (League)	Pos.	G	AB	R	H	2B	3B	HR	RBI	Avg.	BB	SO	SB	PO	A	E	Avg.
			BATTING												FIELDING			
1992	—Vancouver (PCL)	2B	135	497	72	143	12	7	0	29	.288	29	44	29	266	*395	•20	.971
1993	—Nashville (A.A.)	2B-SS	•137	*580	87	*179	21	6	9	74	.309	26	59	31	†292	†442	†18	.976
	—Chicago (A.L.)	2B	8	14	3	5	0	0	0	2	.357	1	1	0	13	9	1	.957
Major league totals (1 year)			8	14	3	5	0	0	0	2	.357	1	1	0	13	9	1	.957

MARTINEZ, ANGEL

C, BLUE JAYS

PERSONAL: Born October 3, 1972, in Villa Mella, Dominican Republic. . . . 6-4/200. . . . Throws right, bats left.

TRANSACTIONS/CAREER NOTES: Signed as free agent by Toronto Blue Jays organization (January 10, 1990). . . . On disabled list (May 15-June 8, 1993).

STATISTICAL NOTES: Led Pioneer League with 24 passed balls in 1992.

Year	Team (League)	Pos.	G	AB	R	H	2B	3B	HR	RBI	Avg.	BB	SO	SB	PO	A	E	Avg.
			BATTING												FIELDING			
1990	—Santo Dom. (DSL)	C	44	145	21	35	2	0	0	10	.241	18	15	1	...	...	...	...
1991	—Dunedin (Fla. St.)	C	12	38	3	7	1	0	0	3	.184	7	7	0	82	9	2	.978
	—Medicine Hat (Pio.) ..	C	34	98	8	17	1	0	2	16	.173	12	29	0	141	19	3	.982
1992	—Dunedin (Fla. St.)	C	4	15	4	3	1	0	2	4	.200	0	3	0	11	2	1	.929
	—Medicine Hat (Pio.) ..	C	57	206	27	52	15	0	4	39	.252	14	62	0	275	58	5	.985
1993	—Hagerstown (SAL) ...	C	94	338	41	89	16	1	9	46	.263	19	71	1	493	68	14	.976

MARTINEZ, CARLOS

3B/1B, INDIANS

PERSONAL: Born August 11, 1965, in La Guaira, Venezuela. . . . 6-5/215. . . . Throws right, bats right. . . . Full name: Carlos Alberto Martinez.

TRANSACTIONS/CAREER NOTES: Signed as free agent by New York Yankees organization (November 17, 1983). . . . On Fort Lauderdale disabled list (April 11-May 1, 1986). . . . Traded by Yankees organization with C Ron Hassey and a player to be named later to Chicago White Sox for C Joel Skinner, IF Wayne Tolleson and OF/DH Ron Kittle (July 30, 1986); Yankees traded C Bill Lindsey to White Sox organization to complete deal (December 24, 1986). . . . On Chicago disabled list (June 22-July 13, 1989); included rehabilitation assignment to South Bend (July 8-12). . . . Granted free agency (February 23, 1991). . . . Signed by Cleveland Indians (March 2, 1991). . . . On suspended list (October 5 and 6, 1991). . . . On Cleveland disabled list (March 28-May 29, 1992); included rehabilitation assignment to Colorado Springs (May 20-29).

Year	Team (League)	Pos.	G	AB	R	H	2B	3B	HR	RBI	Avg.	BB	SO	SB	PO	A	E	Avg.
			BATTING												FIELDING			
1984	—GC Yankees (GCL)....	SS	31	91	9	14	1	1	0	4	.154	6	15	3	53	103	14	.918
1985	—Fort Lauder. (FSL) ...	SS	93	311	39	77	15	7	6	44	.248	14	65	8	123	254	25	.938
1986	—Fort Lauder. (FSL) ...	SS	5	16	1	1	0	0	0	0	.063	0	6	0	7	18	0	1.000
	—Alb./Colon. (East.)...	SS-3B	69	253	34	70	18	2	8	39	.277	6	46	2	120	161	32	.898
	—Buffalo (A.A.)■.........	SS-3B	17	54	6	16	1	0	2	6	.296	2	12	0	24	20	5	.898
1987	—Birm. (Southern)	3B	9	30	2	7	1	0	0	0	.233	1	6	2	5	17	2	.917
	—Hawaii (PCL)	OF-3B-SS	83	304	32	75	15	1	3	36	.247	14	50	3	109	91	18	.917
1988	—Birm. (Southern)	OF-3B-SS	133	498	67	138	22	3	14	73	.277	36	82	25	196	139	20	.944
	—Chicago (A.L.)	3B	17	55	5	9	1	0	0	0	.164	0	12	1	7	33	4	.909
1989	—Vancouver (PCL)	1B	18	64	12	25	3	1	2	9	.391	5	14	2	178	10	1	.995
	—Chicago (A.L.)	3B-1B-OF	109	350	44	105	22	0	5	32	.300	21	57	4	283	134	20	.954
	—South Bend (Mid.)	3B	3	11	2	6	3	0	0	3	.545	1	1	2	0	9	3	.750
1990	—Chicago (A.L.)	1B-OF	92	272	18	61	6	5	4	24	.224	10	40	0	632	38	8	.988
1991	—Cant./Akr. (East.)■..	OF-1B	80	295	48	97	22	2	11	73	.329	22	47	11	37	1	2	.950
	—Cleveland (A.L.)	1B	72	257	22	73	14	0	5	30	.284	10	43	3	229	12	8	.968
1992	—Colo. Springs (PCL) ..	1B	9	32	7	10	1	0	0	5	.313	1	5	0	57	4	4	.938
	—Cleveland (A.L.)	1B-3B	69	228	23	60	9	1	5	35	.263	7	21	1	276	57	4	.988
1993	—Cleveland (A.L.)	3B-1B	80	262	26	64	10	0	5	31	.244	20	29	1	162	51	9	.959
	—Charlotte (Int'l)	1B-3B	20	79	17	29	7	1	3	12	.367	4	15	2	85	23	2	.982
Major league totals (6 years)			439	1424	138	372	62	6	24	152	.261	68	202	10	1589	325	53	.973

MARTINEZ, CHITO

OF, TWINS

PERSONAL: Born December 19, 1965, in Belize. . . . 5-10/185. . . . Throws left, bats left. . . . Full name: Reynaldo Ignacio Martinez.

HIGH SCHOOL: Brother Martin (New Orleans).

TRANSACTIONS/CAREER NOTES: Selected by Kansas City Royals organization in sixth round of free-agent draft (June 4, 1984). . . . On disabled list (July 28-August 15, 1986). . . . Granted free agency (October 15, 1990). . . . Signed by Baltimore Orioles organization (November 16, 1990). . . . On Rochester disabled list (May 5-16 and May 18-28, 1991). . . . On Bowie disabled list (April 29-May 14 and May 17-July 2, 1993). . . . On Rochester disabled list (August 10-September 1, 1993). . . . Released by Orioles (November 22, 1993). . . . Signed by Minnesota Twins organization (December 13, 1993).

STATISTICAL NOTES: Led Southern League outfielders with six double plays in 1988. . . . Led American Association with .514 slugging percentage in 1990.

Year	Team (League)	Pos.	G	AB	R	H	2B	3B	HR	RBI	Avg.	BB	SO	SB	PO	A	E	Avg.
			BATTING												FIELDING			
1984	—Eugene (N'west).......	OF	59	176	18	53	12	3	0	26	.301	24	38	4	78	2	8	.909
1985	—Fort Myers (FSL)......	OF	76	248	35	65	9	5	0	29	.262	31	42	11	161	7	4	.977
1986	—Memphis (South.)	OF	93	283	48	86	16	5	11	44	.304	42	58	4	115	6	8	.938
1987	—Omaha (A.A.)............	OF	35	121	14	26	10	1	2	14	.215	11	43	0	43	3	1	.979
	—Memphis (South.)	OF	78	283	34	74	10	3	9	43	.261	33	94	5	173	11	3	.984
1988	—Memphis (South.)	OF	141	485	67	110	16	4	13	65	.227	66	130	20	267	*23	7	.976
1989	—Memphis (South.)	OF	127	399	55	97	20	2	23	62	.243	63	*137	3	257	*18	7	.975
1990	—Omaha (A.A.)............	OF	122	364	59	96	12	8	21	67	.264	54	*129	6	228	18	6	.976
1991	—Rochester (Int'l)■.....	OF-1B	60	211	42	68	8	1	20	50	.322	26	69	2	190	12	4	.981

Year	Team (League)	Pos.	G	AB	R	H	2B	3B	HR	RBI	Avg.	BB	SO	SB	PO	A	E	Avg.
			BATTING												FIELDING			
	—Baltimore (A.L.)	OF-1B	67	216	32	58	12	1	13	33	.269	11	51	1	112	4	2	.983
1992	—Baltimore (A.L.)	OF	83	198	26	53	10	1	5	25	.268	31	47	0	104	4	3	.973
1993	—Bowie (Eastern)	OF	5	13	5	1	0	0	0	0	.077	2	2	0	5	0	0	1.000
	—Rochester (Int'l)	OF	43	145	14	38	11	0	5	23	.262	11	34	0	36	5	4	.911
	—Baltimore (A.L.)	OF	8	15	0	0	0	0	0	0	.000	4	4	0	2	0	0	1.000
Major league totals (3 years)			158	429	58	111	22	2	18	58	.259	46	102	1	218	8	5	.978

MARTINEZ, DAVE

OF, GIANTS

PERSONAL: Born September 26, 1964, in New York. . . . 5-10/175. . . . Throws left, bats left.
HIGH SCHOOL: Lake Howell (Maitland, Fla.).
COLLEGE: Valencia Community College (Fla.).

TRANSACTIONS/CAREER NOTES: Selected by Texas Rangers organization in 40th round of free-agent draft (June 7, 1982). . . . Selected by Chicago Cubs organization in secondary phase of free-agent draft (January 11, 1983). . . . On disabled list (April 27, 1984-remainder of season). . . . Traded by Cubs to Montreal Expos for OF Mitch Webster (July 14, 1988). . . . On disqualified list (October 4, 1991); reinstated (October 5, 1991). . . . Traded by Expos with P Scott Ruskin and SS Willie Greene to Cincinnati Reds for P John Wetteland and P Bill Risley (December 11, 1991). . . . Granted free agency (October 27, 1992). . . . Signed by San Francisco Giants (December 9, 1992). . . . On San Francisco disabled list (April 30-June 4, 1993); included rehabilitation assignment to Phoenix (June 1-4).

Year	Team (League)	Pos.	G	AB	R	H	2B	3B	HR	RBI	Avg.	BB	SO	SB	PO	A	E	Avg.
			BATTING												FIELDING			
1983	—Quad Cities (Mid.)	OF	44	119	17	29	6	2	0	10	.244	26	30	10	47	8	1	.982
	—Geneva (NY-Penn)	OF	64	241	35	63	15	2	5	33	.261	40	52	16	132	6	8	.945
1984	—Quad Cities (Mid.)	OF	12	41	6	9	2	2	0	5	.220	9	13	3	13	2	1	.938
1985	—Winst.-Salem (Car.)	OF	115	386	52	132	14	4	5	54	*.342	62	35	38	206	11	7	.969
1986	—Iowa (Am. Assoc.)	OF	83	318	52	92	11	5	5	32	.289	36	34	42	214	7	2	.991
	—Chicago (N.L.)	OF	53	108	13	15	1	1	1	7	.139	6	22	4	77	2	1	.988
1987	—Chicago (N.L.)	OF	142	459	70	134	18	8	8	36	.292	57	96	16	283	10	6	.980
1988	—Chi.-Mont. (N.L.)■	OF	138	447	51	114	13	6	6	46	.255	38	94	23	281	4	6	.979
1989	—Montreal (N.L.)	OF	126	361	41	99	16	7	3	27	.274	27	57	23	199	7	7	.967
1990	—Montreal (N.L.)	OF-P	118	391	60	109	13	5	11	39	.279	24	48	13	257	6	3	.989
1991	—Montreal (N.L.)	OF	124	396	47	117	18	5	7	42	.295	20	54	16	213	10	4	.982
1992	—Cincinnati (N.L.)■	OF-1B	135	393	47	100	20	5	3	31	.254	42	54	12	382	18	6	.985
1993	—San Francisco (N.L.)■	OF	91	241	28	58	12	1	5	27	.241	27	39	6	131	6	1	.993
	—Phoenix (PCL)	OF	3	15	4	7	0	0	0	2	.467	1	1	1	5	1	0	1.000
Major league totals (8 years)			927	2796	357	746	111	38	44	255	.267	241	464	113	1823	63	34	.982

RECORD AS PITCHER

Year	Team (League)	W	L	Pct.	ERA	G	GS	CG	ShO	Sv.	IP	H	R	ER	BB	SO
1990	—Montreal (N.L.)	0	0	...	54.00	1	0	0	0	0	⅓	2	2	2	2	0

MARTINEZ, DENNIS

P, INDIANS

PERSONAL: Born May 14, 1955, in Granada, Nicaragua. . . . 6-1/180. . . . Throws right, bats right. . . . Full name: Jose Dennis Martinez.

TRANSACTIONS/CAREER NOTES: Signed as free agent by Baltimore Orioles organization (December 10, 1973). . . . On Baltimore disabled list (March 28-April 20, 1980). . . . On Baltimore disabled list (June 3-July 10, 1980); included rehabilitation assignment to Miami (July 1-10). . . . On Baltimore disabled list (April 28-June 16, 1986); included rehabilitation assignment to Rochester (May 21-June 10). . . . Traded by Orioles to Montreal Expos for a player to be named later (June 16, 1986); Orioles acquired IF Rene Gonzales to complete deal (December 16, 1986). . . . Granted free agency (November 12, 1986). . . . Signed by Miami, independent (April 14, 1987). . . . Released by Miami (May 6, 1987). . . . Signed by Expos organization (May 6, 1987). . . . Granted free agency (November 9, 1987). . . . Re-signed by Expos (December 18, 1987). . . . Granted free agency (October 25, 1993). . . . Signed by Cleveland Indians (December 2, 1993).

RECORDS: Shares major league single-season record for fewest complete games by pitcher who led league in complete games—9 (1991).

HONORS: Named International League Pitcher of the Year (1976).

STATISTICAL NOTES: Tied for N.L. lead with 10 balks in 1988. . . . Pitched 2-0 perfect game against Los Angeles Dodgers (July 28, 1991).

MISCELLANEOUS: Had sacrifice hit in one game as pinch-hitter (1991). . . . Had sacrifice fly in one game as pinch-hitter (1993).

Year	Team (League)	W	L	Pct.	ERA	G	GS	CG	ShO	Sv.	IP	H	R	ER	BB	SO
1974	—Miami (Florida St.)	15	6	.714	2.06	25	25	10	4	0	179	124	48	41	53	162
1975	—Miami (Florida St.)	12	4	.750	2.61	20	20	9	3	0	145	125	54	42	35	114
	—Asheville (South.)	4	1	.800	2.60	6	6	4	1	0	45	45	16	13	12	18
	—Rochester (Int'l)	0	0	...	5.40	2	0	0	0	0	5	7	4	3	2	4
1976	—Rochester (Int'l)	*14	8	.636	*2.50	25	23	*16	1	0	180	148	64	50	50	*140
	—Baltimore (A.L.)	1	2	.333	2.57	4	2	1	0	0	28	23	8	8	8	18
1977	—Baltimore (A.L.)	14	7	.667	4.10	42	13	5	0	4	167	157	86	76	64	107
1978	—Baltimore (A.L.)	16	11	.593	3.52	40	38	15	2	0	276	257	121	108	93	142
1979	—Baltimore (A.L.)	15	16	.484	3.67	40	*39	*18	3	0	*292	279	129	119	78	132
1980	—Baltimore (A.L.)	6	4	.600	3.96	25	12	2	0	1	100	103	44	44	44	42
	—Miami (Florida St.)	0	0	...	0.00	2	2	0	0	0	12	3	1	0	5	7
1981	—Baltimore (A.L.)	•14	5	.737	3.32	25	24	9	2	0	179	173	84	66	62	88
1982	—Baltimore (A.L.)	16	12	.571	4.21	40	39	10	2	0	252	262	123	118	87	111
1983	—Baltimore (A.L.)	7	16	.304	5.53	32	25	4	0	0	153	209	108	94	45	71
1984	—Baltimore (A.L.)	6	9	.400	5.02	34	20	2	0	0	141⅔	145	81	79	37	77
1985	—Baltimore (A.L.)	13	11	.542	5.15	33	31	3	1	0	180	203	110	103	63	68

Year Team (League)	W	L	Pct.	ERA	G	GS	CG	ShO	Sv.	IP	H	R	ER	BB	SO
1986 —Baltimore (A.L.)	0	0	...	6.75	4	0	0	0	0	6⅔	11	5	5	2	2
—Rochester (Int'l)	2	1	.667	6.05	4	4	0	0	0	19⅓	18	14	13	9	14
—Montreal (N.L.)■	3	6	.333	4.59	19	15	1	1	0	98	103	52	50	28	63
1987 —Miami (Florida St.)■	1	1	.500	6.16	3	3	0	0	0	19	21	14	13	3	11
—Indianapolis (A.A.)■	3	2	.600	4.46	7	7	1	1	0	38⅓	32	20	19	13	30
—Montreal (N.L.)	11	4	*.733	3.30	22	22	2	1	0	144⅔	133	59	53	40	84
1988 —Montreal (N.L.)	15	13	.536	2.72	34	34	9	2	0	235⅓	215	94	71	55	120
1989 —Montreal (N.L.)	16	7	.696	3.18	34	33	5	2	0	232	227	88	82	49	142
1990 —Montreal (N.L.)	10	11	.476	2.95	32	32	7	2	0	226	191	80	74	49	156
1991 —Montreal (N.L.)	14	11	.560	*2.39	31	31	•9	*5	0	222	187	70	59	62	123
1992 —Montreal (N.L.)	16	11	.593	2.47	32	32	6	0	0	226⅓	172	75	62	60	147
1993 —Montreal (N.L.)	15	9	.625	3.85	35	34	2	0	1	224⅔	211	110	96	64	138
A.L. totals (11 years)	108	93	.537	4.16	319	243	69	10	5	1775⅓	1822	899	820	583	858
N.L. totals (8 years)	100	72	.581	3.06	239	233	41	13	1	1609	1439	628	547	407	973
Major league totals (18 years)	208	165	.558	3.64	558	476	110	23	6	3384⅓	3261	1527	1367	990	1831

CHAMPIONSHIP SERIES RECORD

Year Team (League)	W	L	Pct.	ERA	G	GS	CG	ShO	Sv.	IP	H	R	ER	BB	SO
1979 —Baltimore (A.L.)	0	0	...	3.24	1	1	0	0	0	8⅓	8	3	3	0	4
1983 —Baltimore (A.L.)							Did not play.								
Champ. series totals (1 year)	0	0	...	3.24	1	1	0	0	0	8⅓	8	3	3	0	4

WORLD SERIES RECORD

Year Team (League)	W	L	Pct.	ERA	G	GS	CG	ShO	Sv.	IP	H	R	ER	BB	SO
1979 —Baltimore (A.L.)	0	0	...	18.00	2	1	0	0	0	2	6	4	4	0	0
1983 —Baltimore (A.L.)							Did not play.								
World Series totals (1 year)	0	0	...	18.00	2	1	0	0	0	2	6	4	4	0	0

ALL-STAR GAME RECORD

Year League	W	L	Pct.	ERA	GS	CG	ShO	Sv.	IP	H	R	ER	BB	SO
1990 —National	0	0	...	0.00	0	0	0	0	1	0	0	0	0	1
1991 —National	0	1	.000	13.50	0	0	0	0	2	4	3	3	0	0
1992 —National	0	0	...	0.00	0	0	0	0	1	0	0	0	1	1
All-Star totals (3 years)	0	1	.000	6.75	0	0	0	0	4	4	3	3	1	2

MARTINEZ, DOMINGO

1B, BLUE JAYS

PERSONAL: Born August 4, 1967, in Santo Domingo, Dominican Republic. . . . 6-2/215. . . . Throws right, bats right. . . . Full name: Domingo Emelio Martinez.

TRANSACTIONS/CAREER NOTES: Signed as free agent by Toronto Blue Jays organization (August 23, 1984).

STATISTICAL NOTES: Led Gulf Coast League third basemen with 102 assists, 27 errors, 166 total chances and tied for lead with 37 putouts in 1985. . . . Led Southern League first basemen with 1,141 putouts, 87 assists, 21 errors and 1,249 total chances in 1988. . . . Led Southern League in grounding into double plays with 24 in 1990. . . . Led International League first basemen with 1,222 total chances and 106 double plays in 1991. . . . Led International League first basemen with 104 assists and 16 errors in 1993.

		BATTING												FIELDING			
Year Team (League)	Pos.	G	AB	R	H	2B	3B	HR	RBI	Avg.	BB	SO	SB	PO	A	E	Avg.
1985 —GC Blue Jays (GCL)	3B-2B	58	219	36	65	10	2	4	19	.297	12	42	3	‡39	†102	†27	.839
1986 —Vent. Co. (Calif.)	1B-3B	129	455	51	113	19	6	9	57	.248	36	127	9	1004	79	16	.985
1987 —Dunedin (Fla. St.)	1B	118	435	53	112	*32	2	8	65	.257	41	88	8	1014	78	16	.986
1988 —Knoxville (South.)	1B-3B	•143	516	54	136	25	2	13	70	.264	40	88	2	†1141	†88	†22	.982
1989 —Knoxville (South.)	1B	120	415	56	102	19	2	10	53	.246	42	82	2	929	93	13	.987
1990 —Knoxville (South.)	1B	128	463	53	119	20	3	17	66	.257	51	81	2	681	61	4	.995
1991 —Syracuse (Int'l)	1B	126	467	61	146	16	2	17	83	.313	41	107	6	*1110	*103	*9	*.993
1992 —Syracuse (Int'l)	1B-3B	116	438	55	120	22	0	21	62	.274	33	95	6	919	67	11	.989
—Toronto (A.L.)	1B	7	8	2	5	0	0	1	3	.625	0	1	0	12	0	0	1.000
1993 —Toronto (A.L.)	1B-3B	8	14	2	4	0	0	1	3	.286	1	7	0	25	4	0	1.000
—Syracuse (Int'l)	1B-3B-OF	127	465	50	127	24	2	24	79	.273	31	115	4	996	†108	†18	.984
Major league totals (2 years)		15	22	4	9	0	0	2	6	.409	1	8	0	37	4	0	1.000

MARTINEZ, EDGAR

3B, MARINERS

PERSONAL: Born January 2, 1963, in New York. . . . 5-11/190. . . . Throws right, bats right. . . . Cousin of Carmelo Martinez, major league first baseman/outfielder with six teams (1983-91).

HIGH SCHOOL: Dorado (Puerto Rico).

COLLEGE: American College (Puerto Rico.).

TRANSACTIONS/CAREER NOTES: Signed as free agent by Seattle Mariners organization (December 19, 1982). . . . On Seattle disabled list (April 4-May 17, 1993). . . . On Seattle disabled list (June 15-July 21, 1993); included rehabilitation assignment to Jacksonville (July 17-21). . . . On Seattle disabled list (August 17, 1993-remainder of season).

RECORDS: Shares A.L. single-game record for most errors by third baseman—4 (May 6, 1990).

HONORS: Named third baseman on THE SPORTING NEWS A.L. All-Star team (1992). . . . Named third baseman on THE SPORTING NEWS A.L. Silver Slugger team (1992).

STATISTICAL NOTES: Led Southern League third basemen with 360 total chances and 34 double plays in 1985. . . . Led Southern League with 12 sacrifice flies in 1985. . . . Led Southern League third basemen with .960 fielding percentage in 1986. . . . Led Pacific Coast League third basemen with 389 total chances and 31 double plays in 1987.

Year	Team (League)	Pos.	BATTING G	AB	R	H	2B	3B	HR	RBI	Avg.	BB	SO	SB	FIELDING PO	A	E	Avg.
1983	—Belling. (N'west)	3B	32	104	14	18	1	1	0	5	.173	18	24	1	22	58	6	.930
1984	—Wausau (Midwest)	3B	126	433	72	131	32	2	15	66	.303	84	57	11	85	246	25	.930
1985	—Chatt. (South.)	3B	111	357	43	92	15	5	3	47	.258	71	30	1	*94	*247	19	*.947
	—Calgary (PCL)	3B-2B	20	68	8	24	7	1	0	14	.353	12	7	1	15	44	4	.937
1986	—Chatt. (South.)	3B-2B	132	451	71	119	29	5	6	74	.264	89	35	2	94	263	15	†.960
1987	—Calgary (PCL)	3B	129	438	75	144	31	1	10	66	.329	82	47	3	*91	*278	20	.949
	—Seattle (A.L.)	3B	13	43	6	16	5	2	0	5	.372	2	5	0	13	19	0	1.000
1988	—Calgary (PCL)	3B-2B	95	331	63	120	19	4	8	64	*.363	66	40	9	48	185	20	.921
	—Seattle (A.L.)	3B	14	32	0	9	4	0	0	5	.281	4	7	0	5	8	1	.929
1989	—Seattle (A.L.)	3B	65	171	20	41	5	0	2	20	.240	17	26	2	40	72	6	.949
	—Calgary (PCL)	3B-2B	32	113	30	39	11	0	3	23	.345	22	13	2	22	56	12	.867
1990	—Seattle (A.L.)	3B	144	487	71	147	27	2	11	49	.302	74	62	1	89	259	*27	.928
1991	—Seattle (A.L.)	3B	150	544	98	167	35	1	14	52	.307	84	72	0	84	299	15	.962
1992	—Seattle (A.L.)	3B-1B	135	528	100	181	•46	3	18	73	*.343	54	61	14	88	211	17	.946
1993	—Seattle (A.L.)	3B	42	135	20	32	7	0	4	13	.237	28	19	0	5	11	2	.889
	—Jacksonv. (South.)	DH	4	14	2	5	0	0	1	3	.357	2	0	0	...	...	...	...
Major league totals (7 years)			563	1940	315	593	129	8	49	217	.306	263	252	17	324	879	68	.946

ALL-STAR GAME RECORD

Year	League	Pos.	BATTING AB	R	H	2B	3B	HR	RBI	Avg.	BB	SO	SB	FIELDING PO	A	E	Avg.
1992	—American	PH	1	0	0	0	0	0	0	.000	0	0	0	...	...	...	...

MARTINEZ, JOSE

P, PADRES

PERSONAL: Born April 1, 1971, in Guayubin, Dominican Republic. . . . 6-2/155. . . . Throws right, bats right. . . . Full name: Jose Miguel Martinez. . . . Brother of Ramon D. Martinez, shortstop, Florida Marlins organization.

HIGH SCHOOL: Luis Jose Antoine (Santiago, Dominican Republic).

TRANSACTIONS/CAREER NOTES: Signed as free agent by New York Mets organization (December 11, 1988). . . . Selected by Florida Marlins in first round (fourth pick overall) of expansion draft (November 17, 1992). . . . Traded by Marlins with P Trevor Hoffman and P Andres Berumen to San Diego Padres for 3B Gary Sheffield and P Rich Rodriguez (June 24, 1993). . . . On Las Vegas disabled list (July 26-August 11, 1993).

HONORS: Named South Atlantic League Most Outstanding Pitcher (1991).

Year	Team (League)	W	L	Pct.	ERA	G	GS	CG	ShO	Sv.	IP	H	R	ER	BB	SO
1989	—GC Mets (GCL)	1	4	.200	6.55	11	4	1	0	0	34⅓	54	35	25	4	22
1990	—GC Mets (GCL)	8	3	.727	1.57	13	•13	•4	*2	0	*92	68	27	16	9	*90
1991	—Columbia (S. Atl.)	*20	4	*.833	*1.49	26	26	*9	1	0	*193⅓	162	51	32	30	158
1992	—St. Lucie (Fla. St.)	6	5	.545	2.05	17	17	4	1	0	123	107	44	28	11	114
	—Binghamton (East.)	5	2	.714	1.71	9	8	3	1	0	58	47	16	11	13	38
1993	—Edm.-L.V. (PCL)■	8	7	.533	6.01	27	18	3	0	0	115⅓	148	88	77	39	45

MARTINEZ, PABLO

SS, METS

PERSONAL: Born June 29, 1969, in San Juan Baron, Dominican Republic. . . . 5-10/155. . . . Throws right, bats both. . . . Full name: Pablo Valera Martinez.

HIGH SCHOOL: Max Henrique Ureno (San Juan Baron, Dominican Republic).

TRANSACTIONS/CAREER NOTES: Signed as free agent by San Diego Padres organization (June 2, 1988). . . . Traded by Padres organization to New York Mets organization for P Marc Kroon (December 13, 1993), completing deal in which Padres traded P Frank Seminara, OF Tracy Sanders and a player to be named later to Mets for OF Randy Curtis and a player to be named later (December 10, 1993).

STATISTICAL NOTES: Led California League shortstops with 103 double plays in 1992.

Year	Team (League)	Pos.	BATTING G	AB	R	H	2B	3B	HR	RBI	Avg.	BB	SO	SB	FIELDING PO	A	E	Avg.
1989	—Ariz. Padres (Ariz.)	SS-3B-2B	45	178	31	42	3	1	0	12	.236	22	25	*29	68	164	12	.951
	—Spokane (N'west)	SS	2	8	3	2	0	0	0	0	.250	0	0	1	6	7	0	1.000
	—Char., S.C. (S. Atl.)	3B-SS-2B	31	80	13	14	2	0	0	4	.175	11	21	0	31	61	8	.920
1990	—Char., S.C. (S. Atl.)	SS-2B-3B	136	453	51	100	12	6	0	33	.221	41	104	16	238	488	47	.939
1991	—Char., S.C. (S. Atl.)	SS-2B	121	442	63	118	17	6	3	36	.267	42	64	39	220	305	32	.943
1992	—High Desert (Calif.)	SS	126	427	60	102	8	4	0	39	.239	50	74	19	209	408	32	*.951
1993	—Wichita (Texas)	SS-2B-3B	45	130	19	36	5	1	2	14	.277	11	24	8	52	108	6	.964
	—Las Vegas (PCL)	SS-2B	76	251	24	58	4	1	2	20	.231	18	46	8	97	265	24	.938

MARTINEZ, PEDRO A.

P, PADRES

PERSONAL: Born November 29, 1968, in Villa Mella, Dominican Republic. . . . 6-2/185. . . . Throws left, bats left. . . . Full name: Pedro Aquino Martinez. . . . Formerly known as Pedro Aquino.

HIGH SCHOOL: Ramon Matia Melle (Santo Domingo, Dominican Republic).

TRANSACTIONS/CAREER NOTES: Signed as free agent by San Diego Padres organization (September 30, 1986).

Year	Team (League)	W	L	Pct.	ERA	G	GS	CG	ShO	Sv.	IP	H	R	ER	BB	SO
1987	—Spokane (N'west)	4	1	.800	3.83	18	5	1	0	0	51⅔	57	31	22	36	42
1988	—Spokane (N'west)	8	3	.727	4.24	15	15	1	0	0	99⅔	108	55	47	32	89
1989	—Char., S.C. (S. Atl.)	•14	8	.636	*1.97	27	27	5	2	0	*187	147	53	41	64	158
1990	—Wichita (Texas)	6	10	.375	4.80	24	23	2	0	0	129⅓	139	83	69	70	88
1991	—Wichita (Texas)	11	10	.524	5.23	26	26	3	2	0	156⅔	169	99	*91	57	95
1992	—Wichita (Texas)	11	7	.611	2.99	26	26	1	0	0	168⅓	153	66	56	52	142
1993	—Las Vegas (PCL)	3	5	.375	4.72	15	14	1	0	0	87⅔	94	49	46	40	65
	—San Diego (N.L.)	3	1	.750	2.43	32	0	0	0	0	37	23	11	10	13	32
Major league totals (1 year)		3	1	.750	2.43	32	0	0	0	0	37	23	11	10	13	32

MARTINEZ, PEDRO J.

P, EXPOS

PERSONAL: Born July 25, 1971, in Manoguayabo, Dominican Republic. . . . 5-11/ 170. . . . Throws right, bats right. . . . Full name: Pedro Jaime Martinez. . . . Brother of Ramon J. Martinez, pitcher, Los Angeles Dodgers; and brother of Jesus Martinez, pitcher, Dodgers organization.

COLLEGE: Ohio Dominican College (Dominican Republic).

TRANSACTIONS/CAREER NOTES: Signed as a free agent by Los Angeles Dodgers organization (June 18, 1988). . . . On Albuquerque disabled list (June 20-July 2 and July 13-August 25, 1992). . . . Traded by Dodgers to Montreal Expos for 2B Delino DeShields (November 19, 1993).

HONORS: Named Minor League Player of the Year by THE SPORTING NEWS (1991).

MISCELLANEOUS: Started one game at third base for Los Angeles, but replaced before first plate appearance and never played in field (1993).

Year Team (League)	W	L	Pct.	ERA	G	GS	CG	ShO	Sv.	IP	H	R	ER	BB	SO
1988 —Santo Dom. (DSL)	5	1	.833	3.10	8	7	1	0	0	49⅓	45	25	17	16	28
1989 —Santo Dom. (DSL)	7	2	.778	2.73	13	7	2	3	1	85⅔	59	30	26	25	63
1990 —Great Falls (Pio.).........	8	3	.727	3.62	14	•14	0	0	0	77	74	39	31	40	82
1991 —Bakersfield (Calif.).....	8	0	1.000	2.05	10	10	0	0	0	61⅓	41	17	14	19	83
—San Antonio (Tex.).....	7	5	.583	1.76	12	12	4	•3	0	76⅔	57	21	15	31	74
—Albuquerque (PCL)....	3	3	.500	3.66	6	6	0	0	0	39⅓	28	17	16	16	35
1992 —Albuquerque (PCL)....	7	6	.538	3.81	20	20	3	1	0	125⅓	104	57	53	57	124
—Los Angeles (N.L.).....	0	1	.000	2.25	2	1	0	0	0	8	6	2	2	1	8
1993 —Albuquerque (PCL)....	0	0	...	3.00	1	1	0	0	0	3	1	1	1	1	4
—Los Angeles (N.L.).....	10	5	.667	2.61	65	2	0	0	2	107	76	34	31	57	119
Major league totals (2 years)..	10	6	.625	2.58	67	3	0	0	2	115	82	36	33	58	127

MARTINEZ, RAMON D.

IF, MARLINS

PERSONAL: Born September 8, 1969, in Villa Gonzalez, Dominican Republic. . . . 6-0/165. . . . Throws right, bats both. . . . Full name: Ramon Dario Martinez. . . . Brother of Jose Martinez, pitcher, San Diego Padres organization.

TRANSACTIONS/CAREER NOTES: Signed as free agent by Pittsburgh Pirates organization (August 20, 1987). . . . On disabled list (August 31-September 6, 1991). . . . Selected by Florida Marlins in second round (33rd pick overall) of expansion draft (November 17, 1992).

STATISTICAL NOTES: Led Carolina League shortstops with 603 total chances in 1992. . . . Led California League shortstops with 367 assists, 42 errors and 85 double plays in 1993.

			BATTING											FIELDING			
Year Team (League)	Pos.	G	AB	R	H	2B	3B	HR	RBI	Avg.	BB	SO	SB	PO	A	E	Avg.
1988 —..................................	Dominican Summer League statistics unavailable.																
1989 —Dom. Pirates (DSL) ..	...	52	200	37	45	4	1	2	16	.225	22	39	13	...	...	...	...
1990 —GC Pirates (GCL)......	SS	15	58	8	21	2	1	0	5	.362	2	6	2	19	40	5	.922
—Welland (NYP)..........	SS	48	151	26	35	3	1	0	15	.232	7	38	19	69	87	22	.876
1991 —Augusta (S. Atl.)......	SS	106	345	51	88	7	2	0	13	.255	10	82	35	203	232	41	.914
1992 —Salem (Carolina)......	SS	131	*533	73	*154	17	*12	3	30	.289	29	*139	35	194	359	50	.917
1993 —High Desert (Calif.)■	SS-2B	118	412	73	109	10	6	2	46	.265	49	79	46	212	†388	†44	.932

MARTINEZ, RAMON J.

P, DODGERS

PERSONAL: Born March 22, 1968, in Santo Domingo, Dominican Republic. . . . 6-4/176. . . . Throws right, bats left. . . . Full name: Ramon Jaime Martinez. . . . Brother of Pedro J. Martinez, pitcher, Montreal Expos, and Jesus Martinez, pitcher, Los Angeles Dodgers organization.

HIGH SCHOOL: Liceo Secunderia Las Americas (Dominican Republic).

TRANSACTIONS/CAREER NOTES: Signed as free agent by Los Angeles Dodgers organization (September 1, 1984). . . . On suspended list (July 8-12, 1993).

MISCELLANEOUS: Member of 1984 Dominican Republic Olympic baseball team. . . . Appeared in one game as pinch-runner (1992).

Year Team (League)	W	L	Pct.	ERA	G	GS	CG	ShO	Sv.	IP	H	R	ER	BB	SO
1985 —GC Dodgers (GCL)......	4	1	.800	2.59	23	6	0	0	1	59	57	30	17	23	42
1986 —Bakersfield (Calif.).....	4	8	.333	4.75	20	20	2	1	0	106	119	73	56	63	78
1987 —Vero Beach (FSL).......	16	5	.762	2.17	25	25	6	1	0	170⅓	128	45	41	78	148
1988 —San Antonio (Tex.)......	8	4	.667	2.46	14	14	2	1	0	95	79	29	26	34	89
—Albuquerque (PCL)....	5	2	.714	2.76	10	10	1	1	0	58⅔	43	24	18	32	49
—Los Angeles (N.L.).....	1	3	.250	3.79	9	6	0	0	0	35⅔	27	17	15	22	23
1989 —Albuquerque (PCL)....	10	2	.833	2.79	18	18	2	1	0	113	92	40	35	50	127
—Los Angeles (N.L.).....	6	4	.600	3.19	15	15	2	2	0	98⅔	79	39	35	41	89
1990 —Los Angeles (N.L.).....	20	6	.769	2.92	33	33	*12	3	0	234⅓	191	89	76	67	223
1991 —Los Angeles (N.L.).....	17	13	.567	3.27	33	33	6	4	0	220⅓	190	89	80	69	150
1992 —Los Angeles (N.L.).....	8	11	.421	4.00	25	25	1	1	0	150⅔	141	82	67	69	101
1993 —Los Angeles (N.L.).....	10	12	.455	3.44	32	32	4	3	0	211⅔	202	88	81	*104	127
Major league totals (6 years)..	62	49	.559	3.35	147	144	25	13	0	951⅓	830	404	354	372	713

MARTINEZ, TINO

1B, MARINERS

PERSONAL: Born December 7, 1967, in Tampa, Fla. . . . 6-2/210. . . . Throws right, bats left.

HIGH SCHOOL: Jefferson (Tampa, Fla.).

COLLEGE: Tampa (Fla.).

TRANSACTIONS/CAREER NOTES: Selected by Boston Red Sox organization in third round of free-agent draft (June 3, 1985). . . . Selected by Seattle Mariners organization in first round (14th pick overall) of free-agent draft (June 1, 1988). . . . On disabled list (August 10, 1993-remainder of season).

HONORS: Named first baseman on THE SPORTING NEWS college All-America team (1988). . . . Named Pacific Coast League Most Valuable Player (1991).

STATISTICAL NOTES: Led Eastern League with 13 intentional bases on balls received in 1989. . . . Led Eastern League first basemen with 1,348 total chances and 106 double plays in 1989. . . . Tied for Pacific Coast League lead with 11 intentional bases on balls received in 1990. . . . Led Pacific Coast League first basemen with .991 fielding percentage, 1,051 putouts, 98 assists, 1,159 total chances and 117 double plays in 1990. . . . Led Pacific Coast League first basemen with .992 fielding percentage and 122 double plays in 1991.

MISCELLANEOUS: Member of 1988 U.S. Olympic baseball team.

			BATTING												FIELDING			
Year	**Team (League)**	**Pos.**	**G**	**AB**	**R**	**H**	**2B**	**3B**	**HR**	**RBI**	**Avg.**	**BB**	**SO**	**SB**	**PO**	**A**	**E**	**Avg.**
1989	—Williamsport (East.) ..	1B	*137	*509	51	131	29	2	13	64	.257	59	54	7	*1260	*81	7	*.995
1990	—Calgary (PCL)	1B-3B	128	453	83	145	28	1	17	93	.320	74	37	8	†1051	†98	10	†.991
	—Seattle (A.L.)	1B	24	68	4	15	4	0	0	5	.221	9	9	0	155	12	0	1.000
1991	—Calgary (PCL)	1B-3B	122	442	94	144	34	5	18	86	.326	82	44	3	1078	106	9	†.992
	—Seattle (A.L.)	1B	36	112	11	23	2	0	4	9	.205	11	24	0	249	22	2	.993
1992	—Seattle (A.L.)	1B	136	460	53	118	19	2	16	66	.257	42	77	2	678	58	4	.995
1993	—Seattle (A.L.)	1B	109	408	48	108	25	1	17	60	.265	45	56	0	932	60	3	.997
Major league totals (4 years)			305	1048	116	264	50	3	37	140	.252	107	166	2	2014	152	9	.996

MASON, ROGER

P, PHILLIES

PERSONAL: Born September 18, 1958, in Bellaire, Mich. . . . 6-6/226. . . . Throws right, bats right. . . . Full name: Roger LeRoy Mason.

HIGH SCHOOL: Bellaire (Mich.).

COLLEGE: Saginaw Valley State College (Mich.).

TRANSACTIONS/CAREER NOTES: Signed as free agent by Detroit Tigers organization (September 21, 1980). . . . On Evansville disabled list (May 3-19, 1984). . . . Traded by Tigers to San Francisco Giants organization for OF Alejandro Sanchez (April 5, 1985). . . . On Phoenix disabled list (May 2-23, 1985). . . . On San Francisco disabled list (May 30-July 20, 1986); included rehabilitation assignment to Phoenix (July 9-17). . . . On San Francisco disabled list (July 26, 1986-remainder of season). . . . Granted free agency (October 15, 1988). . . . Signed by Tucson, Houston Astros organization (February 16, 1989). . . . Released by Astros organization (April 3, 1990). . . . Signed by Pittsburgh Pirates organization (May 18, 1990). . . . Released by Pirates (November 19, 1992). . . . Signed by New York Mets (December 2, 1992). . . . Traded by Mets with P Mike Freitas to San Diego Padres for P Mike Maddux (December 17, 1992). . . . Traded by Padres to Philadelphia Phillies for P Tim Mauser (July 3, 1993).

RECORDS: Shares N.L. record for most consecutive home runs allowed in one inning—3 (April 13, 1987, first inning).

STATISTICAL NOTES: Pitched no-hitter for nine innings for Tucson against Las Vegas (August 20, 1989); Tucson lost game in 11 innings, 1-0.

Year	**Team (League)**	**W**	**L**	**Pct.**	**ERA**	**G**	**GS**	**CG**	**ShO**	**Sv.**	**IP**	**H**	**R**	**ER**	**BB**	**SO**
1981	—Macon (S. Atl.)	10	10	.500	3.89	26	26	4	1	0	148	153	77	64	50	105
1982	—Lakeland (Fla. St.)	7	7	.500	3.46	22	22	5	1	0	132⅔	124	60	51	52	72
1983	—Birm. (Southern)	7	4	.636	*2.06	17	17	4	1	0	126⅔	116	45	29	43	83
	—Evansville (A.A.)	5	5	.500	4.23	11	11	2	0	0	78⅔	84	39	37	21	43
1984	—Evansville (A.A.)	9	7	.563	3.80	25	25	6	2	0	151⅔	175	78	64	64	88
	—Detroit (A.L.)	1	1	.500	4.50	5	2	0	0	1	22	23	11	11	10	15
1985	—Phoenix (PCL)■	12	1	*.923	3.33	24	24	5	2	0	167⅓	145	67	62	72	120
	—San Francisco (N.L.)	1	3	.250	2.12	5	5	1	1	0	29⅔	28	13	7	11	26
1986	—San Francisco (N.L.)	3	4	.429	4.80	11	11	1	0	0	60	56	35	32	30	43
	—Phoenix (PCL)	1	0	1.000	0.00	1	1	0	0	0	6	2	0	0	1	2
1987	—San Francisco (N.L.)	1	1	.500	4.50	5	5	0	0	0	26	30	15	13	10	18
	—Phoenix (PCL)	5	1	.833	4.13	10	10	1	0	0	61	62	34	28	20	49
1988	—Phoenix (PCL)	2	9	.182	4.86	19	17	1	0	0	90⅔	90	62	49	38	62
1989	—Tucson (PCL)■	7	12	.368	3.54	25	25	5	1	0	155	125	71	61	46	105
	—Houston (N.L.)	0	0	...	20.25	2	0	0	0	0	1⅓	2	3	3	2	3
1990	—Buffalo (A.A.)■	3	5	.375	2.10	29	2	0	0	3	77	78	21	18	25	45
1991	—Buffalo (A.A.)	9	5	.643	3.08	34	15	2	1	0	122⅔	115	47	42	44	80
	—Pittsburgh (N.L.)	3	2	.600	3.03	24	0	0	0	3	29⅔	21	11	10	6	21
1992	—Pittsburgh (N.L.)	5	7	.417	4.09	65	0	0	0	8	88	80	41	40	33	56
1993	—S.D.-Phil. (N.L.)■	5	12	.294	4.06	68	0	0	0	0	99⅔	90	48	45	34	71
A.L. totals (1 year)		1	1	.500	4.50	5	2	0	0	1	22	23	11	11	10	15
N.L. totals (7 years)		18	29	.383	4.04	180	21	2	1	11	334⅓	307	166	150	126	238
Major league totals (8 years) ...		19	30	.388	4.07	185	23	2	1	12	356⅓	330	177	161	136	253

CHAMPIONSHIP SERIES RECORD

Year	**Team (League)**	**W**	**L**	**Pct.**	**ERA**	**G**	**GS**	**CG**	**ShO**	**Sv.**	**IP**	**H**	**R**	**ER**	**BB**	**SO**
1991	—Pittsburgh (N.L.)	0	0	...	0.00	3	0	0	0	1	4⅓	3	0	0	1	2
1992	—Pittsburgh (N.L.)	0	0	...	0.00	2	0	0	0	0	3⅓	0	0	0	2	1
1993	—Philadelphia (N.L.)	0	0	...	0.00	2	0	0	0	0	3	1	0	0	0	2
Champ. series totals (3 years)		0	0	...	0.00	7	0	0	0	1	10⅔	4	0	0	3	5

WORLD SERIES RECORD

Year	**Team (League)**	**W**	**L**	**Pct.**	**ERA**	**G**	**GS**	**CG**	**ShO**	**Sv.**	**IP**	**H**	**R**	**ER**	**BB**	**SO**
1993	—Philadelphia (N.L.)	0	0	...	1.17	4	0	0	0	0	7⅔	4	1	1	1	7

MASSE, BILLY

OF, YANKEES

PERSONAL: Born July 6, 1966, in Manchester, Conn. . . . 6-1/185. . . . Throws right, bats right. . . . Full name: William Arthur Masse. . . . Name pronounced MASS-ee.

HIGH SCHOOL: Eastern Catholic (Manchester, Conn.).

COLLEGE: Davidson and Wake Forest.

TRANSACTIONS/CAREER NOTES: Selected by Chicago Cubs organization in 12th round of free-agent draft (June 2, 1987). . . . Selected by New York Yankees organization in seventh round of free-agent draft (June 1, 1988). . . . On disabled list (May 26-June 3, 1993).

HONORS: Named outfielder on THE SPORTING NEWS college All-America team (1988).

STATISTICAL NOTES: Led Carolina League outfielders with 18 assists in 1989. . . . Led Eastern League with .418 on-base percentage in 1991.
MISCELLANEOUS: Member of 1988 U.S. Olympic baseball team.

		BATTING												FIELDING			
Year Team (League)	Pos.	G	AB	R	H	2B	3B	HR	RBI	Avg.	BB	SO	SB	PO	A	E	Avg.
1989 —Prin. William (Car.)	OF-3B	124	377	70	90	17	4	11	50	.239	*89	57	16	213	†18	5	.979
1990 —Fort Lauder. (FSL)	OF	68	230	42	63	15	0	6	33	.274	33	28	9	123	10	2	.985
—Alb./Colon. (East.)	OF	31	96	12	18	1	0	3	8	.188	22	20	0	27	3	1	.968
1991 —Alb./Colon. (East.)	OF	108	356	67	105	17	2	11	61	.295	74	60	10	184	7	2	*.990
1992 —Columbus (Int'l)	OF	110	357	52	95	13	2	12	60	.266	51	51	7	140	6	4	.973
1993 —Columbus (Int'l)	OF	117	402	81	127	35	3	19	91	.316	*82	68	17	154	10	4	.976

MATHENY, MIKE

C, BREWERS

PERSONAL: Born September 22, 1970, in Columbus, O. . . . 6-3/205. . . . Throws right, bats both. . . . Full name: Michael Scott Matheny.
HIGH SCHOOL: Reynoldsburg (O.).
COLLEGE: Michigan.
TRANSACTIONS/CAREER NOTES: Selected by Toronto Blue Jays organization in 31st round of free-agent draft (June 1, 1988). . . . Selected by Milwaukee Brewers organization in eighth round of free-agent draft (June 3, 1991).
STATISTICAL NOTES: Led California League catchers with 20 double plays in 1992. . . . Led Texas League catchers with 18 double plays in 1993.
MISCELLANEOUS: Batted righthanded only (1991).

		BATTING												FIELDING			
Year Team (League)	Pos.	G	AB	R	H	2B	3B	HR	RBI	Avg.	BB	SO	SB	PO	A	E	Avg.
1991 —Helena (Pioneer)	C	64	253	35	72	14	0	2	34	.285	19	52	2	456	68	5	*.991
1992 —Stockton (Calif.)	C	106	333	42	73	13	2	6	46	.219	35	81	2	582	114	8	*.989
1993 —El Paso (Texas)	C	107	339	39	86	21	2	2	28	.254	17	73	1	524	*100	9	.986

MATTINGLY, DON

1B, YANKEES

PERSONAL: Born April 20, 1961, in Evansville, Ind. . . . 6-0/200. . . . Throws left, bats left. . . . Full name: Donald Arthur Mattingly.
HIGH SCHOOL: Evansville (Ind.) Memorial.
TRANSACTIONS/CAREER NOTES: Selected by New York Yankees organization in 19th round of free-agent draft (June 5, 1979). . . . On disabled list (June 9-24, 1987; May 27-June 14, 1988; July 26-September 11, 1990 and May 14-June 10, 1993).
RECORDS: Holds major league records for most home runs in seven consecutive games—9 (July 8-17, 1987); and eight consecutive games—10 (July 8-18, 1987). . . . Holds major league single-season records for most grand slams—6 (1987); and most at-bats without a stolen base—677 (1986). . . . Shares major league single-game records for most sacrifice flies—3 (May 3, 1986); and most putouts and chances accepted by first baseman in nine-inning game—22 (July 20, 1987). . . . Shares major league records for most doubles in one inning—2 (April 11, 1987, seventh inning); and most consecutive games with one or more home runs—8 (July 8 through July 18, 1987). . . . Holds A.L. single-season records for most consecutive games with one or more long hits—10 (July 7-19, 1987); and most at-bats by lefthander—677 (1986). . . . Shares A.L. career record for highest fielding percentage for first baseman—.995.
HONORS: Named South Atlantic League Most Valuable Player (1980). . . . Named A.L. Player of the Year by THE SPORTING NEWS (1984-86). . . . Named first baseman on THE SPORTING NEWS A.L. All-Star team (1984-87). . . . Named Major League Player of the Year by THE SPORTING NEWS (1985). . . . Won A.L. Gold Glove at first base (1985-89 and 1991-93). . . . Named first baseman on THE SPORTING NEWS A.L. Silver Slugger team (1985-87). . . . Named A.L. Most Valuable Player by Baseball Writers' Association of America (1985).
STATISTICAL NOTES: Led South Atlantic League with 12 sacrifice flies in 1980. . . . Led A.L. first basemen with .996 fielding percentage in both 1984 and 1986. . . . Led A.L. with 370 total bases in 1985 and 388 in 1986. . . . Led A.L. with 21 game-winning RBIs in 1985 and tied for lead with 15 in 1986. . . . Led A.L. with 15 sacrifice flies in 1985. . . . Tied for A.L. lead in double plays by first baseman with 154 in 1985. . . . Led A.L. with .573 slugging percentage in 1986. . . . Led A.L. first basemen with 1,377 putouts and 1,483 total chances in 1986. . . . Led A.L. first basemen with 135 double plays in 1991.

		BATTING												FIELDING			
Year Team (League)	Pos.	G	AB	R	H	2B	3B	HR	RBI	Avg.	BB	SO	SB	PO	A	E	Avg.
1979 —Oneonta (NYP)	OF-1B	53	166	20	58	10	2	3	31	.349	30	6	2	29	2	2	.939
1980 —Greensboro (S. Atl.)	OF-1B	133	494	92	*177	32	5	9	105	*.358	59	33	8	205	16	8	.965
1981 —Nashville (South.)	OF-1B	141	547	74	173	*35	4	7	98	.316	64	55	4	846	69	12	.987
1982 —Columbus (Int'l)	OF-1B	130	476	67	150	24	2	10	75	.315	50	24	1	271	17	5	.983
—New York (A.L.)	OF-1B	7	12	0	2	0	0	0	1	.167	0	1	0	15	1	0	1.000
1983 —New York (A.L.)	OF-1B-2B	91	279	34	79	15	4	4	32	.283	21	31	0	350	15	3	.992
—Columbus (Int'l)	1B-OF	43	159	35	54	11	3	8	37	.340	29	14	2	325	29	1	.997
1984 —New York (A.L.)	1B-OF	153	603	91	*207	*44	2	23	110	*.343	41	33	1	1143	126	6	†.995
1985 —New York (A.L.)	1B	159	652	107	211	*48	3	35	*145	.324	56	41	2	1318	87	7	*.995
1986 —New York (A.L.)	1B-3B	162	677	117	*238	*53	2	31	113	.352	53	35	0	†1378	111	7	†.995
1987 —New York (A.L.)	1B	141	569	93	186	38	2	30	115	.327	51	38	1	1239	91	5	*.996
1988 —New York (A.L.)	1B-OF	144	599	94	186	37	0	18	88	.311	41	29	1	1250	99	9	.993
1989 —New York (A.L.)	1B-OF	158	631	79	191	37	2	23	113	.303	51	30	3	1276	87	7	.995
1990 —New York (A.L.)	1B-OF	102	394	40	101	16	0	5	42	.256	28	20	1	800	78	3	.997
1991 —New York (A.L.)	1B	152	587	64	169	35	0	9	68	.288	46	42	2	1119	77	5	.996
1992 —New York (A.L.)	1B	157	640	89	184	40	0	14	86	.288	39	43	3	1209	116	4	*.997
1993 —New York (A.L.)	1B	134	530	78	154	27	2	17	86	.291	61	42	0	1258	84	3	*.998
Major league totals (12 years)		1560	6173	886	1908	390	17	209	999	.309	488	385	14	12355	972	59	.996

ALL-STAR GAME RECORD

		BATTING											FIELDING			
Year League	Pos.	AB	R	H	2B	3B	HR	RBI	Avg.	BB	SO	SB	PO	A	E	Avg.
1984 —American	PH	1	0	0	0	0	0	0	.000	0	0	0	...	...	...	...
1985 —American	1B	1	0	0	0	0	0	0	.000	0	0	0	4	0	0	1.000

Year	League	Pos.	AB	R	H	2B	3B	HR	RBI	Avg.	BB	SO	SB	PO	A	E	Avg.
			BATTING											FIELDING			
1986	—American	PH-1B	3	0	0	0	0	0	0	.000	0	2	0	7	0	0	1.000
1987	—American	1B	0	0	0	0	0	0	0	...	2	0	0	10	0	0	1.000
1988	—American	1B	2	0	0	0	0	0	0	.000	0	0	0	2	1	1	.750
1989	—American	1B	1	0	1	1	0	0	0	1.000	0	0	0	4	0	0	1.000
All-Star Game totals (6 years)			8	0	1	1	0	0	0	.125	2	2	0	27	1	1	.966

MAURER, ROB

1B, RANGERS

PERSONAL: Born January 7, 1967, in Evansville, Ind.... 6-3/210.... Throws left, bats left.... Full name: Robert John Maurer.... Name pronounced MAHW-er.
HIGH SCHOOL: Mater Dei (Evansville, Ind.).
COLLEGE: Evansville.

TRANSACTIONS/CAREER NOTES: Selected by Texas Rangers organization in sixth round of free-agent draft (June 1, 1988).... On Texas disabled list (March 27, 1993-entire season).

STATISTICAL NOTES: Tied for Pioneer League lead with three intentional bases on balls received in 1988.... Led Pioneer League first basemen with 65 double plays in 1988.... Led Florida State League first basemen with 105 double plays in 1989.... Led Texas League with .578 slugging percentage in 1990.... Led American Association with 245 total bases, .534 slugging percentage and .420 on-base percentage in 1991.... Led American Association first basemen with 1,151 total chances and 108 double plays in 1992.

Year	Team (League)	Pos.	G	AB	R	H	2B	3B	HR	RBI	Avg.	BB	SO	SB	PO	A	E	Avg.
				BATTING											FIELDING			
1988	—Butte (Pioneer)	1B	63	233	65	91	18	3	8	60	*.391	35	34	0	519	*41	6	.989
1989	—Charlotte (Fla. St.)	1B	132	456	69	126	18	9	6	51	.276	86	109	3	1094	*105	14	.988
1990	—Tulsa (Texas)	1B	104	367	55	110	31	4	21	78	.300	54	112	4	939	72	11	.989
1991	—Okla. City (A.A.)	1B	132	459	76	138	*41	3	20	77	.301	*96	135	2	941	*84	*16	.985
	—Texas (A.L.)	1B	13	16	0	1	1	0	0	2	.063	2	6	0	7	3	0	1.000
1992	—Okla. City (A.A.)	1B	135	493	76	142	34	2	10	82	.288	75	*117	1	*1057	*87	7	*.994
	—Texas (A.L.)	1B	8	9	1	2	0	0	0	1	.222	1	2	0	9	1	0	1.000
1993	—							Did not play.										
Major league totals (2 years)			21	25	1	3	1	0	0	3	.120	3	8	0	16	4	0	1.000

MAUSER, TIM

P, PADRES

PERSONAL: Born October 4, 1966, in Fort Worth, Tex.... 6-0/195.... Throws right, bats right.... Full name: Timothy Edward Mauser.
HIGH SCHOOL: Arlington Heights (Tex.).
COLLEGE: Texas Christian.

TRANSACTIONS/CAREER NOTES: Selected by Philadelphia Phillies organization in third round of free-agent draft (June 1, 1988).... Traded by Phillies to San Diego Padres for P Roger Mason (July 3, 1993).

STATISTICAL NOTES: Pitched 9-0 no-hit victory for Reading against New Britain (August 30, 1989, second game).

Year	Team (League)	W	L	Pct.	ERA	G	GS	CG	ShO	Sv.	IP	H	R	ER	BB	SO
1988	—Spartanburg (SAL)	2	1	.667	1.96	4	3	0	0	0	23	15	6	5	5	18
	—Reading (Eastern)	2	3	.400	3.49	5	5	0	0	0	28⅓	27	14	11	6	17
1989	—Clearwater (FSL)	6	7	.462	2.69	16	16	5	0	0	107	105	40	32	40	73
	—Reading (Eastern)	7	4	.636	3.63	11	11	4	2	0	72	62	36	29	33	54
1990	—Reading (Eastern)	3	4	.429	3.30	8	8	1	0	0	46⅓	35	20	17	15	40
	—Scran./W.B. (Int'l)	5	7	.417	3.66	16	16	4	1	0	98⅓	75	48	40	34	54
1991	—Scran./W.B. (Int'l)	6	11	.353	3.72	26	18	1	0	1	128⅓	119	66	53	55	75
	—Philadelphia (N.L.)	0	0	...	7.59	3	0	0	0	0	10⅔	18	10	9	3	6
1992	—Scran./W.B. (Int'l)	8	6	.571	2.97	45	5	0	0	4	100	87	37	33	45	75
1993	—Scran./W.B. (Int'l)	2	0	1.000	0.87	19	0	0	0	10	20⅔	10	2	2	5	25
	—Phil.-S.D. (N.L.)■	0	1	.000	4.00	36	0	0	0	0	54	51	28	24	24	46
Major league totals (2 years)		0	1	.000	4.59	39	0	0	0	0	64⅔	69	38	33	27	52

MAY, DERRICK

OF, CUBS

PERSONAL: Born July 14, 1968, in Rochester, N.Y.... 6-4/225.... Throws right, bats left.... Full name: Derrick Brant May.... Son of Dave May, major league outfielder with five teams (1967-78).
HIGH SCHOOL: Newark (Del.).

TRANSACTIONS/CAREER NOTES: Selected by Chicago Cubs organization in first round (ninth pick overall) of free-agent draft (June 2, 1986).... On Iowa disabled list (April 14-May 27 and June 6-24, 1991).

STATISTICAL NOTES: Tied for Carolina League lead in double plays by outfielder with four in 1988.

Year	Team (League)	Pos.	G	AB	R	H	2B	3B	HR	RBI	Avg.	BB	SO	SB	PO	A	E	Avg.
				BATTING											FIELDING			
1986	—Wytheville (Appal.)	OF	54	178	25	57	6	1	0	23	.320	16	15	17	47	3	5	.909
1987	—Peoria (Midwest)	OF	128	439	60	131	19	8	9	52	.298	42	106	5	181	13	8	.960
1988	—Winst.-Salem (Car.)	OF	130	485	76	•148	29	*9	8	65	.305	37	82	13	209	13	10	.957
1989	—Charlotte (South.)	OF	136	491	72	145	26	5	9	70	.295	34	77	19	239	8	•13	.950
1990	—Iowa (Am. Assoc.)	OF-1B	119	459	55	136	27	1	8	69	.296	23	50	5	159	10	8	.955
	—Chicago (N.L.)	OF	17	61	8	15	3	0	1	11	.246	2	7	1	34	1	1	.972
1991	—Iowa (Am. Assoc.)	OF	82	310	47	92	18	4	3	49	.297	19	38	7	130	2	5	.964
	—Chicago (N.L.)	OF	15	22	4	5	2	0	1	3	.227	2	1	0	11	1	0	1.000
1992	—Iowa (Am. Assoc.)	OF	8	30	6	11	4	1	2	8	.367	3	3	0	11	1	0	1.000
	—Chicago (N.L.)	OF	124	351	33	96	11	0	8	45	.274	14	40	5	153	3	5	.969
1993	—Chicago (N.L.)	OF	128	465	62	137	25	2	10	77	.295	31	41	10	220	8	7	.970
Major league totals (4 years)			284	899	107	253	41	2	20	136	.281	49	89	16	418	13	13	.971

MAYNE, BRENT

C, ROYALS

PERSONAL: Born April 19, 1968, in Loma Linda, Calif. . . . 6-1/190. . . . Throws right, bats left. . . . Full name: Brent Danem Mayne.
HIGH SCHOOL: Costa Mesa (Calif.).
COLLEGE: Orange Coast College (Calif.) and Cal State Fullerton.
TRANSACTIONS/CAREER NOTES: Selected by Kansas City Royals organization in first round (13th pick overall) of free-agent draft (June 5, 1989). . . . On disabled list (July 24, 1989-remainder of season).

			BATTING												FIELDING			
Year	**Team (League)**	**Pos.**	**G**	**AB**	**R**	**H**	**2B**	**3B**	**HR**	**RBI**	**Avg.**	**BB**	**SO**	**SB**	**PO**	**A**	**E**	**Avg.**
1989	—Baseball City (FSL)	C	7	24	5	13	3	1	0	8	.542	0	3	0	31	2	0	1.000
1990	—Memphis (South.)	C	115	412	48	110	16	3	2	61	.267	52	51	5	591	61	11	.983
	—Kansas City (A.L.)	C	5	13	2	3	0	0	0	1	.231	3	3	0	29	3	1	.970
1991	—Kansas City (A.L.)	C	85	231	22	58	8	0	3	31	.251	23	42	2	425	38	6	.987
1992	—Kansas City (A.L.)	C-3B	82	213	16	48	10	0	0	18	.225	11	26	0	281	33	3	.991
1993	—Kansas City (A.L.)	C	71	205	22	52	9	1	2	22	.254	18	31	3	356	27	2	.995
Major league totals (4 years)			243	662	62	161	27	1	5	72	.243	55	102	5	1091	101	12	.990

MAYSEY, MATT

P

PERSONAL: Born January 8, 1967, in Hamilton, Ont. . . . 6-4/225. . . . Throws right, bats right. . . . Full name: Matthew Samuel Maysey.
HIGH SCHOOL: Hastings (Houston).
TRANSACTIONS/CAREER NOTES: Selected by San Diego Padres organization in seventh round of free-agent draft (June 3, 1985). . . . On Charleston disabled list (May 4-July 9, 1986). . . . Released by Padres organization (February 14, 1991). . . . Signed by Indianapolis, Montreal Expos organization (March 12, 1991). . . . On Indianapolis disabled list (April 20-May 3, 1992). . . . Granted free agency (October 15, 1992). . . . Signed by Denver, Milwaukee Brewers organization (November 24, 1992). . . . Released by Brewers (October 5, 1993).
MISCELLANEOUS: Singled in only plate appearance with Milwaukee (1993).

Year	**Team (League)**	**W**	**L**	**Pct.**	**ERA**	**G**	**GS**	**CG**	**ShO**	**Sv.**	**IP**	**H**	**R**	**ER**	**BB**	**SO**
1985	—Spokane (N'west)	0	3	.000	4.66	7	4	0	0	0	29	27	18	15	16	18
1986	—Char., S.C. (S. Atl.)	3	2	.600	5.02	18	5	0	0	1	43	43	28	24	24	39
1987	—Char., S.C. (S. Atl.)	14	11	.560	3.17	41	18	5	0	7	150⅓	112	71	53	59	143
1988	—Wichita (Texas)	9	9	.500	3.71	28	•28	4	0	0	187	180	88	77	68	120
1989	—Las Vegas (PCL)	8	12	.400	4.08	28	•28	4	1	0	176⅓	173	94	80	84	96
1990	—Las Vegas (PCL)	6	10	.375	5.62	26	25	1	0	0	137⅔	155	97	86	88	72
1991	—Harrisburg (East.)■	6	5	.545	1.89	15	15	2	2	0	104⅔	90	26	22	28	86
	—Indianapolis (A.A.)	3	6	.333	5.14	12	12	0	0	0	63	60	45	36	33	45
1992	—Indianapolis (A.A.)	5	3	.625	4.30	35	1	0	0	5	67	63	32	32	28	38
	—Montreal (N.L.)	0	0	. . .	3.86	2	0	0	0	0	2⅓	4	1	1	0	1
1993	—New Orleans (A.A.)■	0	3	.000	4.13	29	5	0	0	2	52⅓	48	25	24	14	40
	—Milwaukee (A.L.)	1	2	.333	5.73	23	0	0	0	1	22	28	14	14	13	10
A.L. totals (1 year)		1	2	.333	5.73	23	0	0	0	1	22	28	14	14	13	10
N.L. totals (1 year)		0	0	. . .	3.86	2	0	0	0	0	2⅓	4	1	1	0	1
Major league totals (2 years)		1	2	.333	5.55	25	0	0	0	1	24⅓	32	15	15	13	11

McCARTHY, GREG

P

PERSONAL: Born October 30, 1968, in Norwalk, Conn. . . . 6-2/193. . . . Throws left, bats left. . . . Full name: Gregory O'Neil McCarthy.
HIGH SCHOOL: Bridgeport (Conn.) Central.
TRANSACTIONS/CAREER NOTES: Selected by Philadelphia Phillies organization in 36th round of free-agent draft (June 2, 1987). . . . Selected by Montreal Expos from Phillies organization in Rule 5 major league draft (December 3, 1990). . . . On disabled list (March 29, 1991-entire season). . . . Selected by Colorado Springs, Cleveland Indians organization, from Harrisburg, Expos organization, in Rule 5 minor league draft (December 9, 1991). . . . On disabled list (July 5-September 9, 1992). . . . Granted free agency (December 20, 1993).

Year	**Team (League)**	**W**	**L**	**Pct.**	**ERA**	**G**	**GS**	**CG**	**ShO**	**Sv.**	**IP**	**H**	**R**	**ER**	**BB**	**SO**
1987	—Utica (N.Y.-Penn)	4	1	.800	0.91	20	0	0	0	3	29⅔	14	9	3	23	40
1988	—Spartanburg (SAL)	4	2	.667	4.04	34	1	0	0	2	64⅔	52	36	29	52	65
1989	—Spartanburg (SAL)	5	8	.385	4.18	24	15	2	1	0	112	90	58	52	80	115
1990	—Clearwater (FSL)	1	3	.250	3.47	42	1	0	0	5	59⅔	47	33	23	38	67
1991	—							Did not play.								
1992	—Kinston (Carolina)■	3	0	1.000	0.00	23	0	0	0	12	27⅓	14	0	0	9	37
1993	—Kinston (Carolina)	0	0	. . .	1.69	9	0	0	0	2	10⅔	8	4	2	13	14
	—Cant./Akr. (East.)	2	3	.400	4.72	33	0	0	0	6	34⅓	28	18	18	37	39

McCARTY, DAVID

OF/1B, TWINS

PERSONAL: Born November 23, 1969, in Houston. . . . 6-5/207. . . . Throws left, bats right. . . . Full name: David Andrew McCarty.
HIGH SCHOOL: Sharpstown (Houston).
COLLEGE: Stanford.
TRANSACTIONS/CAREER NOTES: Selected by Minnesota Twins organization in first round (third pick overall) of free-agent draft (June 3, 1991).

			BATTING												FIELDING			
Year	**Team (League)**	**Pos.**	**G**	**AB**	**R**	**H**	**2B**	**3B**	**HR**	**RBI**	**Avg.**	**BB**	**SO**	**SB**	**PO**	**A**	**E**	**Avg.**
1991	—Visalia (California)	OF	15	50	16	19	3	0	3	8	.380	13	7	3	23	1	0	1.000
	—Orlando (Southern)	OF	28	88	18	23	4	0	3	11	.261	10	20	0	38	4	1	.977
1992	—Orlando (Southern)	OF-1B	129	456	75	124	16	2	18	79	.272	55	89	6	357	32	9	.977
	—Portland (PCL)	OF-1B	7	26	7	13	2	0	1	8	.500	5	3	1	40	3	1	.977
1993	—Portland (PCL)	OF-1B	40	143	42	55	11	0	8	31	.385	27	25	5	185	21	2	.990
	—Minnesota (A.L.)	OF-1B	98	350	36	75	15	2	2	21	.214	19	80	2	412	38	8	.983
Major league totals (1 year)			98	350	36	75	15	2	2	21	.214	19	80	2	412	38	8	.983

McCASKILL, KIRK
P, WHITE SOX

PERSONAL: Born April 9, 1961, in Kapuskasing, Ont. . . . 6-1/205. . . . Throws right, bats right. . . . Full name: Kirk Edward McCaskill. . . . Son of Ted McCaskill, National Hockey League and World Hockey Association player (1967-68, 1972-73 and 1973-74).
HIGH SCHOOL: Trinity Pawling (Pawling, N.Y.).
COLLEGE: Vermont.
TRANSACTIONS/CAREER NOTES: Selected by California Angels organization in fourth round of free-agent draft (June 7, 1982). . . . On suspended list (August 30, 1983); then transferred to disqualified list (September 26, 1983-April 25, 1984). . . . On California disabled list (April 24-July 11, 1987); included rehabilitation assignment to Palm Springs (June 24-July 2) and Edmonton (July 3-8). . . . On disabled list (August 9, 1988-remainder of season). . . . Granted free agency (October 30, 1991). . . . Signed by Chicago White Sox (December 28, 1991). . . . On Chicago disabled list (June 15-10, 1993); included rehabilitation assignment to South Bend (June 25-30).

Year	Team (League)	W	L	Pct.	ERA	G	GS	CG	ShO	Sv.	IP	H	R	ER	BB	SO
1982	—Salem (Northwest)	5	5	.500	4.29	11	11	1	0	0	71⅓	63	43	34	51	87
1983	—Redwood (Calif.)	6	5	.545	2.33	16	15	4	0	0	108⅓	78	39	28	60	100
	—Nashua (Eastern)	4	8	.333	4.45	13	13	3	0	0	87	90	47	43	43	63
1984	—Edmonton (PCL)	7	11	.389	5.73	24	22	2	0	0	143	162	104	91	74	75
1985	—Edmonton (PCL)	1	1	.500	2.04	3	3	0	0	0	17⅔	17	7	4	6	18
	—California (A.L.)	12	12	.500	4.70	30	29	6	1	0	189⅔	189	105	99	64	102
1986	—California (A.L.)	17	10	.630	3.36	34	33	10	2	0	246⅓	207	98	92	92	202
1987	—California (A.L.)	4	6	.400	5.67	14	13	1	1	0	74⅔	84	52	47	34	56
	—Palm Springs (Cal.)	2	0	1.000	0.00	2	2	0	0	0	10	4	1	0	3	7
	—Edmonton (PCL)	1	0	1.000	3.00	1	1	0	0	0	6	3	2	2	4	4
1988	—California (A.L.)	8	6	.571	4.31	23	23	4	2	0	146⅓	155	78	70	61	98
1989	—California (A.L.)	15	10	.600	2.93	32	32	6	4	0	212	202	73	69	59	107
1990	—California (A.L.)	12	11	.522	3.25	29	29	2	1	0	174⅓	161	77	63	72	78
1991	—California (A.L.)	10	*19	.345	4.26	30	30	1	0	0	177⅔	193	93	84	66	71
1992	—Chicago (A.L.)■	12	13	.480	4.18	34	34	0	0	0	209	193	116	97	95	109
1993	—Chicago (A.L.)	4	8	.333	5.23	30	14	0	0	2	113⅔	144	71	66	36	65
	—South Bend (Mid.)	1	0	1.000	1.50	1	1	0	0	0	6	3	2	1	3	5
Major league totals (9 years)		94	95	.497	4.01	256	237	30	11	2	1543⅔	1528	763	687	579	888

CHAMPIONSHIP SERIES RECORD

CHAMPIONSHIP SERIES NOTES: Holds single-series record for most runs allowed—13 (1986). . . . Shares record for most hits allowed in one inning—6 (October 14, 1986, third inning).

Year	Team (League)	W	L	Pct.	ERA	G	GS	CG	ShO	Sv.	IP	H	R	ER	BB	SO
1986	—California (A.L.)	0	2	.000	7.71	2	2	0	0	0	9⅓	16	13	8	5	7
1993	—Chicago (A.L.)	0	0	...	0.00	3	0	0	0	0	3⅔	3	0	0	1	3
Champ. series totals (2 years)		0	2	.000	5.54	5	2	0	0	0	13	19	13	8	6	10

RECORD AS HOCKEY PLAYER

PERSONAL: Played center/right wing. . . . shot right.
CAREER NOTES: Selected by Winnipeg Jets in fourth round (64th pick overall) of National Hockey League entry draft (June 1981).

			REGULAR SEASON					PLAYOFFS				
Season	Team	League	Gms.	G	A	Pts.	Pen.	Gms.	G	A	Pts.	Pen.
83-84	—Sherbrooke Jets	AHL	78	10	12	22	21	—	—	—	—	—

M

McCLENDON, LLOYD
OF/1B, PIRATES

PERSONAL: Born January 11, 1959, in Gary, Ind. . . . 6-0/208. . . . Throws right, bats right. . . . Full name: Lloyd Glenn McClendon.
HIGH SCHOOL: Roosevelt (Gary, Ind.).
COLLEGE: Valparaiso.
TRANSACTIONS/CAREER NOTES: Selected by New York Mets organization in eighth round of free-agent draft (June 3, 1980). . . . On disabled list (April 4-27, 1982). . . . Traded by Mets organization with P Charlie Puleo and OF Jason Felice to Cincinnati Reds for P Tom Seaver (December 16, 1982). . . . Traded by Reds organization to Chicago Cubs for OF Rolando Roomes (December 9, 1988). . . . Traded by Cubs to Pittsburgh Pirates for a player to be named later (September 7, 1990); Cubs acquired P Mike Pomeranz to complete deal (September 28, 1990).

			BATTING											FIELDING			
Year	Team (League)	Pos.	G	AB	R	H	2B	3B	HR	RBI	Avg.	BB	SO	SB	PO	A	E	Avg.
1980	—Kingsport (Appal.)	C	14	46	7	15	2	0	1	9	.326	5	7	0	19	5	3	.889
	—Little Falls (NYP)	C	40	117	25	32	9	1	3	20	.274	32	20	2	203	20	7	.970
1981	—Lynchburg (Caro.)	C-3B	103	363	55	91	12	6	7	57	.251	60	68	3	437	74	17	.968
1982	—Lynchburg (Caro.)	C-3B	108	384	61	105	25	1	18	78	.273	55	65	4	492	87	15	.975
1983	—Waterbury (East.)■	C-3B-1B	123	434	58	114	19	2	15	57	.263	42	64	4	466	99	8	.986
1984	—Vermont (Eastern)	C-1-3-O	60	202	36	56	16	0	7	27	.277	28	28	2	174	24	3	.985
	—Wichita (A.A.)	3B-1B-C	48	152	28	45	13	1	6	28	.296	21	33	2	143	45	4	.979
1985	—Denver (A.A.)	1-3-C-O	114	379	57	105	18	5	16	79	.277	51	56	4	470	104	17	.971
1986	—Denver (A.A.)	1-O-C-3	132	433	75	112	30	1	*24	88	.259	70	75	2	656	45	11	.985
1987	—Cincinnati (N.L.)	C-1-3-O	45	72	8	15	5	0	2	13	.208	4	15	1	80	5	2	.977
	—Nashville (A.A.)	1B-C	26	84	11	24	6	0	3	14	.286	17	15	1	72	3	1	.987
1988	—Cincinnati (N.L.)	C-O-1-3	72	137	9	30	4	0	3	14	.219	15	22	4	197	13	4	.981
	—Nashville (A.A.)	OF-C	2	7	0	1	0	0	0	0	.143	1	1	0	12	2	0	1.000
1989	—Iowa (Am. Assoc.)■	1B-OF-C	34	109	18	35	10	0	4	13	.321	21	19	4	115	6	6	.953
	—Chicago (N.L.)	O-1-3-C	92	259	47	74	12	1	12	40	.286	37	31	6	310	18	6	.982
1990	—Chi.-Pitts. (N.L.)■	OF-1B-C	53	110	6	18	3	0	2	12	.164	14	22	1	120	9	1	.992
	—Iowa (Am. Assoc.)	1-3-O-C	25	91	14	26	2	0	2	10	.286	8	19	3	125	12	2	.986
1991	—Pittsburgh (N.L.)	OF-1B-C	85	163	24	47	7	0	7	24	.288	18	23	2	163	12	3	.983
1992	—Pittsburgh (N.L.)	OF-1B	84	190	26	48	8	1	3	20	.253	28	24	1	136	9	3	.980
1993	—Pittsburgh (N.L.)	OF-1B	88	181	21	40	11	1	2	19	.221	23	17	0	98	5	3	.972
Major league totals (7 years)			519	1112	141	272	50	3	31	142	.245	139	154	15	1104	71	22	.982

CHAMPIONSHIP SERIES RECORD

CHAMPIONSHIP SERIES NOTES: Shares records for most hits in one inning—2 (October 13, 1992, second inning); and most singles in one inning—2 (October 13, 1992, second inning).

			BATTING												FIELDING			
Year	Team (League)	Pos.	G	AB	R	H	2B	3B	HR	RBI	Avg.	BB	SO	SB	PO	A	E	Avg.
1989	—Chicago (N.L.)	PH-C-OF	3	3	0	2	0	0	0	0	.667	1	0	0	3	0	0	1.000
1991	—Pittsburgh (N.L.)	PH-1B	3	2	0	0	0	0	0	0	.000	1	0	0	0	0	0	...
1992	—Pittsburgh (N.L.)	OF-PH	5	11	4	8	2	0	1	4	.727	4	1	0	10	0	0	1.000
Championship series totals (3 years)			11	16	4	10	2	0	1	4	.625	6	1	0	13	0	0	1.000

McCLURE, BOB

P

PERSONAL: Born April 29, 1953, in Oakland, Calif. . . . 5-11/188. . . . Throws left, bats right. . . . Full name: Robert Craig McClure.
HIGH SCHOOL: Terra Nova (Pacifica, Calif.).
COLLEGE: College of San Mateo (Calif.).

TRANSACTIONS/CAREER NOTES: Selected by Los Angeles Dodgers organization in third round of free-agent draft (January 10, 1973). . . . Selected by Kansas City Royals organization in secondary phase of free-agent draft (June 5, 1973). . . . On Jacksonville disabled list (April 15-May 13 and June 5-July 25, 1975). . . . Traded by Royals to Milwaukee Brewers (March 15, 1977), completing deal in which Royals traded IF Jamie Quirk, OF Jim Wohlford and a player to be named later to Brewers for P Jim Colborn and C Darrell Porter (December 6, 1976). . . . On Milwaukee disabled list (March 28-September 1, 1981); included rehabilitation assignment to Burlington (August 7-24). . . . Granted free agency (November 10, 1982). . . . Re-signed by Brewers (December 6, 1982). . . . On disabled list (August 22-September 12, 1983). . . . Contract sold by Brewers to Montreal Expos (June 8, 1986). . . . Granted free agency (November 9, 1987). . . . Re-signed by Expos (December 7, 1987). . . . Released by Expos (July 2, 1988). . . . Signed by New York Mets (July 13, 1988). . . . Released by Mets (October 27, 1988). . . . Signed by California Angels (January 12, 1989). . . . On California disabled list (April 6-August 14, 1990); included rehabilitation assignment to Palm Springs (August 3-14). . . . On disabled list (March 26-April 19, 1991). . . . Released by Angels (June 16, 1991). . . . Signed by St. Louis Cardinals (June 24, 1991). . . . Granted free agency (October 27, 1992). . . . Signed by Florida Marlins organization (December 15, 1992). . . . Released by Marlins (May 18, 1993).
STATISTICAL NOTES: Led A.L. with six balks in 1983.

Year	Team (League)	W	L	Pct.	ERA	G	GS	CG	ShO	Sv.	IP	H	R	ER	BB	SO
1973	—Billings (Pioneer)	*10	2	.833	2.11	14	13	6	•3	0	94	64	41	22	67	110
1974	—Omaha (A.A.)	5	8	.385	3.84	21	20	5	0	0	136	140	71	58	65	88
1975	—Jacksonv. (South.)	3	2	.600	2.36	9	4	2	1	0	42	31	18	11	23	39
	—Kansas City (A.L.)	1	0	1.000	0.00	12	0	0	0	1	15	4	0	0	14	15
1976	—Omaha (A.A.)	9	8	.529	2.98	21	21	9	2	0	133	133	61	44	41	91
	—Kansas City (A.L.)	0	0	...	9.00	8	0	0	0	0	4	3	4	4	8	3
1977	—Milwaukee (A.L.)■	2	1	.667	2.54	68	0	0	0	6	71	64	25	20	34	57
1978	—Milwaukee (A.L.)	2	6	.250	3.74	44	0	0	0	9	65	53	30	27	30	47
1979	—Milwaukee (A.L.)	5	2	.714	3.88	36	0	0	0	5	51	53	29	22	24	37
1980	—Milwaukee (A.L.)	5	8	.385	3.07	52	5	2	1	10	91	83	34	31	37	47
1981	—Burlington (Midw.)	0	2	.000	9.64	4	4	0	0	0	14	19	15	15	11	11
	—Milwaukee (A.L.)	0	0	...	3.38	4	0	0	0	0	8	7	3	3	4	6
1982	—Milwaukee (A.L.)	12	7	.632	4.22	34	26	5	0	0	172⅔	160	90	81	74	99
1983	—Milwaukee (A.L.)	9	9	.500	4.50	24	23	4	0	0	142	152	75	71	68	68
1984	—Milwaukee (A.L.)	4	8	.333	4.38	39	18	1	0	1	139⅔	154	76	68	52	68
1985	—Milwaukee (A.L.)	4	1	.800	4.31	38	1	0	0	3	85⅔	91	43	41	30	57
1986	—Milwaukee (A.L.)	2	1	.667	3.86	13	0	0	0	0	16⅓	18	7	7	10	11
	—Montreal (N.L.)■	2	5	.286	3.02	52	0	0	0	6	62⅔	53	22	21	23	42
1987	—Montreal (N.L.)	6	1	.857	3.44	52	0	0	0	5	52⅓	47	30	20	20	33
1988	—Mont.-N.Y. (N.L.)■	2	3	.400	5.40	33	0	0	0	3	30	35	18	18	8	19
1989	—California (A.L.)■	6	1	.857	1.55	48	0	0	0	3	52⅓	39	14	9	15	36
1990	—Palm Springs (Cal.)	0	0	...	0.00	2	1	0	0	0	3	0	0	0	1	6
	—California (A.L.)	2	0	1.000	6.43	11	0	0	0	0	7	7	6	5	3	6
1991	—California (A.L.)	0	0	...	9.31	13	0	0	0	0	9⅔	13	11	10	5	5
	—St. Louis (N.L.)■	1	1	.500	3.13	32	0	0	0	0	23	24	8	8	8	15
1992	—St. Louis (N.L.)	2	2	.500	3.17	71	0	0	0	0	54	52	21	19	25	24
1993	—Florida (N.L.)■	1	1	.500	7.11	14	0	0	0	0	6⅓	13	5	5	5	6
A.L. totals (15 years)		54	44	.551	3.86	444	73	12	1	38	930⅓	901	447	399	408	562
N.L. totals (6 years)		14	13	.519	3.59	254	0	0	0	14	228⅓	224	104	91	89	139
Major league totals (19 years)		68	57	.544	3.81	698	73	12	1	52	1158⅔	1125	551	490	497	701

DIVISION SERIES RECORD

Year	Team (League)	W	L	Pct.	ERA	G	GS	CG	ShO	Sv.	IP	H	R	ER	BB	SO
1981	—Milwaukee (A.L.)	0	0	...	0.00	3	0	0	0	0	3⅓	4	0	0	0	2

CHAMPIONSHIP SERIES RECORD

Year	Team (League)	W	L	Pct.	ERA	G	GS	CG	ShO	Sv.	IP	H	R	ER	BB	SO
1982	—Milwaukee (A.L.)	1	0	1.000	0.00	1	0	0	0	0	1⅔	2	0	0	0	0

WORLD SERIES RECORD

Year	Team (League)	W	L	Pct.	ERA	G	GS	CG	ShO	Sv.	IP	H	R	ER	BB	SO
1982	—Milwaukee (A.L.)	0	2	.000	4.15	5	0	0	0	2	4⅓	5	2	2	3	5

McCURRY, JEFF

P, PIRATES

PERSONAL: Born January 21, 1970, in Tokyo, Japan. . . . 6-7/210. . . . Throws right, bats right. . . . Full name: Jeffrey Dee McCurry.
HIGH SCHOOL: St. Thomas (Houston).
COLLEGE: San Jacinto (North) College (Tex.).

M

TRANSACTIONS/CAREER NOTES: Selected by Pittsburgh Pirates organization in 20th round of free-agent draft (June 5, 1989).... Selected by Pirates organization in 14th round of free-agent draft (June 4, 1990).... On Welland disabled list (June 19-July 12, 1991).

Year	Team (League)	W	L	Pct.	ERA	G	GS	CG	ShO	Sv.	IP	H	R	ER	BB	SO
1991	—GC Pirates (GCL)	1	0	1.000	2.57	6	1	0	0	0	14	19	10	4	4	8
	—Welland (NYP)	2	1	.667	0.57	9	0	0	0	0	15⅔	11	4	1	10	18
1992	—Augusta (S. Atl.)	2	1	.667	3.30	19	0	0	0	7	30	36	14	11	15	34
	—Salem (Carolina)	6	2	.750	2.87	30	0	0	0	3	62⅔	49	22	20	24	52
1993	—Salem (Carolina)	1	4	.200	3.89	41	0	0	0	22	44	41	21	19	15	32
	—Carolina (South.)	2	1	.667	2.79	23	0	0	0	0	29	24	11	9	14	14

McDAVID, RAY

OF, PADRES

PERSONAL: Born July 20, 1971, in San Diego.... 6-3/190.... Throws right, bats left.... Full name: Ray Darnell McDavid.
HIGH SCHOOL: Clairemont (San Diego).
COLLEGE: Arizona Western College.

TRANSACTIONS/CAREER NOTES: Selected by San Diego Padres organization in ninth round of free-agent draft (June 5, 1989).

			BATTING												FIELDING			
Year	Team (League)	Pos.	G	AB	R	H	2B	3B	HR	RBI	Avg.	BB	SO	SB	PO	A	E	Avg.
1990	—Ariz. Padres (Ariz.)	OF	13	41	4	6	0	2	0	1	.146	6	5	3	30	2	1	.970
1991	—Char., S.C. (S. Atl.)	OF	127	425	93	105	16	9	10	45	.247	*106	119	60	269	9	6	.979
1992	—High Desert (Calif.)	OF	123	428	94	118	22	5	24	94	.276	94	126	43	206	4	4	.981
1993	—Wichita (Texas)	OF	126	441	65	119	18	5	11	55	.270	70	104	33	259	8	10	.964

McDONALD, BEN

P, ORIOLES

PERSONAL: Born November 24, 1967, in Baton Rouge, La.... 6-7/214.... Throws right, bats right.... Full name: Larry Benard McDonald.
HIGH SCHOOL: Denham Springs (La.).
COLLEGE: Louisiana State.

TRANSACTIONS/CAREER NOTES: Selected by Atlanta Braves organization in 27th round of free-agent draft (June 2, 1986).... Selected by Baltimore Orioles organization in first round (first pick overall) of free-agent draft (June 5, 1989).... On Baltimore disabled list (April 6-May 22, 1990); included rehabilitation assignment to Hagerstown (April 24-29 and May 14) and Rochester (April 30-May 13 and May 15-21).... On Baltimore disabled list (March 29-April 19, 1991).... On Baltimore disabled list (May 23-July 1, 1991); included rehabilitation assignment to Rochester (June 19-July 1).
HONORS: Named Golden Spikes Award winner by USA Baseball (1989).... Named College Player of the Year by THE SPORTING NEWS (1989).... Named righthanded pitcher on THE SPORTING NEWS college All-America team (1989).
MISCELLANEOUS: Member of 1988 U.S. Olympic baseball team.

Year	Team (League)	W	L	Pct.	ERA	G	GS	CG	ShO	Sv.	IP	H	R	ER	BB	SO
1989	—Frederick (Caro.)	0	0	...	2.00	2	2	0	0	0	9	10	2	2	0	9
	—Baltimore (A.L.)	1	0	1.000	8.59	6	0	0	0	0	7⅓	8	7	7	4	3
1990	—Hagerstown (East.)	0	1	.000	6.55	3	3	0	0	0	11	11	8	8	3	15
	—Rochester (Int'l)	3	3	.500	2.86	7	7	0	0	0	44	33	18	14	21	37
	—Baltimore (A.L.)	8	5	.615	2.43	21	15	3	2	0	118⅔	88	36	32	35	65
1991	—Baltimore (A.L.)	6	8	.429	4.84	21	21	1	0	0	126⅓	126	71	68	43	85
	—Rochester (Int'l)	0	1	.000	7.71	2	2	0	0	0	7	10	7	6	5	7
1992	—Baltimore (A.L.)	13	13	.500	4.24	35	35	4	2	0	227	213	113	107	74	158
1993	—Baltimore (A.L.)	13	14	.481	3.39	34	34	7	1	0	220⅓	185	92	83	86	171
Major league totals (5 years)		41	40	.506	3.82	117	105	15	5	0	699⅔	620	319	297	242	482

McDOWELL, JACK

P, WHITE SOX

PERSONAL: Born January 16, 1966, in Van Nuys, Calif.... 6-5/188.... Throws right, bats right.... Full name: Jack Burns McDowell.
HIGH SCHOOL: Notre Dame (Van Nuys, Calif.).
COLLEGE: Stanford.

TRANSACTIONS/CAREER NOTES: Selected by Boston Red Sox organization in 20th round of free-agent draft (June 4, 1984).... Selected by Chicago White Sox organization in first round (fifth pick overall) of free-agent draft (June 2, 1987).... On suspended list (August 20-24, 1991).
HONORS: Named righthanded pitcher on THE SPORTING NEWS A.L. All-Star team (1992-93).... Named A.L. Pitcher of the Year by THE SPORTING NEWS (1993).... Named A.L. Cy Young Award winner by Baseball Writers' Association of America (1993).

Year	Team (League)	W	L	Pct.	ERA	G	GS	CG	ShO	Sv.	IP	H	R	ER	BB	SO
1987	—GC Whi. Sox (GCL)	0	1	.000	2.57	2	1	0	0	0	7	4	3	2	1	12
	—Birm. (Southern)	1	2	.333	7.84	4	4	1	1	0	20⅔	19	20	18	8	17
	—Chicago (A.L.)	3	0	1.000	1.93	4	4	0	0	0	28	16	6	6	6	15
1988	—Chicago (A.L.)	5	10	.333	3.97	26	26	1	0	0	158⅔	147	85	70	68	84
1989	—Vancouver (PCL)	5	6	.455	6.13	16	16	1	0	0	86⅔	97	60	59	50	65
	—GC Whi. Sox (GCL)	2	0	1.000	0.75	4	4	0	0	0	24	19	2	2	4	25
1990	—Chicago (A.L.)	14	9	.609	3.82	33	33	4	0	0	205	189	93	87	77	165
1991	—Chicago (A.L.)	17	10	.630	3.41	35	•35	*15	3	0	253⅔	212	97	96	82	191
1992	—Chicago (A.L.)	20	10	.667	3.18	34	34	*13	1	0	260⅔	247	95	92	75	178
1993	—Chicago (A.L.)	*22	10	.688	3.37	34	34	10	*4	0	256⅔	261	104	96	69	158
Major league totals (6 years)		81	49	.623	3.46	166	166	43	8	0	1162⅔	1072	480	447	377	791

CHAMPIONSHIP SERIES RECORD

CHAMPIONSHIP SERIES NOTES: Holds single-game record for most hits allowed—13 (October 5, 1993).... Shares single-game record for most earned runs allowed—7 (October 5, 1993).

Year	Team (League)	W	L	Pct.	ERA	G	GS	CG	ShO	Sv.	IP	H	R	ER	BB	SO
1993	—Chicago (A.L.)	0	2	.000	10.00	2	2	0	0	0	9	18	10	10	5	5

ALL-STAR GAME RECORD

Year	League	W	L	Pct.	ERA	GS	CG	ShO	Sv.	IP	H	R	ER	BB	SO
1991	—American	0	0	...	0.00	0	0	0	0	2	1	0	0	2	0
1992	—American	0	0	...	0.00	0	0	0	0	1	0	0	0	0	0
1993	—American	1	0	1.000	0.00	0	0	0	0	1	0	0	0	0	0
All-Star totals (3 years)		1	0	1.000	0.00	0	0	0	0	4	1	0	0	2	0

McDOWELL, ROGER

P, DODGERS

PERSONAL: Born December 21, 1960, in Cincinnati. . . . 6-1/197. . . . Throws right, bats right. . . . Full name: Roger Alan McDowell.

HIGH SCHOOL: Colerain (Cincinnati).

COLLEGE: Bowling Green State.

TRANSACTIONS/CAREER NOTES: Selected by New York Mets organization in third round of free-agent draft (June 7, 1982). . . . On disabled list (April 10-August 14, 1984 and March 29-May 14, 1987). . . . Traded by Mets with OF Lenny Dykstra and a player to be named later to Philadelphia Phillies for OF Juan Samuel (June 18, 1989); Phillies organization acquired P Tom Edens to complete deal (July 27, 1989). . . . On disabled list (July 1-18, 1991). . . . Traded by Phillies to Los Angeles Dodgers for P Mike Hartley and OF Braulio Castillo (July 31, 1991). . . . Granted free agency (October 28, 1992). . . . Re-signed by Dodgers (December 5, 1992).

MISCELLANEOUS: Appeared in one game as outfielder with no chances (1986). . . . Appeared in two games as outfielder with no chances with Los Angeles (1991).

Year	Team (League)	W	L	Pct.	ERA	G	GS	CG	ShO	Sv.	IP	H	R	ER	BB	SO
1982	—Shelby (S. Atl.)	6	4	.600	3.28	12	11	4	0	0	71⅓	61	34	26	30	40
	—Lynchburg (Caro.)	2	0	1.000	2.15	4	4	2	1	0	29⅓	26	12	7	11	23
1983	—Jackson (Texas)	11	12	.478	4.86	27	26	9	1	0	172⅓	203	111	93	71	115
1984	—Jackson (Texas)	0	0	...	3.68	3	2	0	0	0	7⅓	9	3	3	1	8
1985	—New York (N.L.)	6	5	.545	2.83	62	2	0	0	17	127⅓	108	43	40	37	70
1986	—New York (N.L.)	14	9	.609	3.02	75	0	0	0	22	128	107	48	43	42	65
1987	—New York (N.L.)	7	5	.583	4.16	56	0	0	0	25	88⅔	95	41	41	28	32
1988	—New York (N.L.)	5	5	.500	2.63	62	0	0	0	16	89	80	31	26	31	46
1989	—N.Y.-Phil. (N.L.)■	4	8	.333	1.96	69	0	0	0	23	92	79	36	20	38	47
1990	—Philadelphia (N.L.)	6	8	.429	3.86	72	0	0	0	22	86⅓	92	41	37	35	39
1991	—Phil.-L.A. (N.L.)■	9	9	.500	2.93	71	0	0	0	10	101⅓	100	40	33	48	50
1992	—Los Angeles (N.L.)	6	10	.375	4.09	65	0	0	0	14	83⅔	103	46	38	42	50
1993	—Los Angeles (N.L.)	5	3	.625	2.25	54	0	0	0	2	68	76	32	17	30	27
Major league totals (9 years)		62	62	.500	3.07	586	2	0	0	151	864⅓	840	358	295	331	426

CHAMPIONSHIP SERIES RECORD

Year	Team (League)	W	L	Pct.	ERA	G	GS	CG	ShO	Sv.	IP	H	R	ER	BB	SO
1986	—New York (N.L.)	0	0	...	0.00	2	0	0	0	0	7	1	0	0	0	3
1988	—New York (N.L.)	0	1	.000	4.50	4	0	0	0	0	6	6	3	3	2	5
Champ. series totals (2 years)		0	1	.000	2.08	6	0	0	0	0	13	7	3	3	2	8

WORLD SERIES RECORD

Year	Team (League)	W	L	Pct.	ERA	G	GS	CG	ShO	Sv.	IP	H	R	ER	BB	SO
1986	—New York (N.L.)	1	0	1.000	4.91	5	0	0	0	0	7⅓	10	5	4	6	2

McELROY, CHUCK

P, REDS

PERSONAL: Born October 1, 1967, in Port Arthur, Tex. . . . 6-0/195. . . . Throws left, bats left. . . . Full name: Charles Dwayne McElroy. . . . Name pronounced MACK-il-roy.

HIGH SCHOOL: Lincoln (Port Arthur, Tex.).

TRANSACTIONS/CAREER NOTES: Selected by Philadelphia Phillies organization in eighth round of free-agent draft (June 2, 1986). . . . Traded by Phillies with P Bob Scanlan to Chicago Cubs for P Mitch Williams (April 7, 1991). . . . Traded by Cubs to Cincinnati Reds for P Larry Luebbers, P Mike Anderson and C Darron Cox (December 10, 1993).

Year	Team (League)	W	L	Pct.	ERA	G	GS	CG	ShO	Sv.	IP	H	R	ER	BB	SO
1986	—Utica (N.Y.-Penn)	4	6	.400	2.95	14	14	5	1	0	94⅔	85	40	31	28	91
1987	—Spartanburg (SAL)	14	4	.778	3.11	24	21	5	2	0	130⅓	117	51	45	48	115
	—Clearwater (FSL)	1	0	1.000	0.00	2	2	0	0	0	7⅓	1	1	0	4	7
1988	—Reading (Eastern)	9	12	.429	4.50	28	26	4	2	0	160	•173	89	*80	70	92
1989	—Reading (Eastern)	3	1	.750	2.68	32	0	0	0	12	47	39	14	14	14	39
	—Scran./W.B. (Int'l)	1	2	.333	2.93	14	0	0	0	3	15⅓	13	6	5	11	12
	—Philadelphia (N.L.)	0	0	...	1.74	11	0	0	0	0	10⅓	12	2	2	4	8
1990	—Scran./W.B. (Int'l)	6	8	.429	2.72	57	1	0	0	7	76	62	24	23	34	78
	—Philadelphia (N.L.)	0	1	.000	7.71	16	0	0	0	0	14	24	13	12	10	16
1991	—Chicago (N.L.)■	6	2	.750	1.95	71	0	0	0	3	101⅓	73	33	22	57	92
1992	—Chicago (N.L.)	4	7	.364	3.55	72	0	0	0	6	83⅔	73	40	33	51	83
1993	—Chicago (N.L.)	2	2	.500	4.56	49	0	0	0	0	47⅓	51	30	24	25	31
	—Iowa (Am. Assoc.)	0	1	.000	4.60	9	0	0	0	2	15⅔	19	10	8	9	13
Major league totals (5 years)		12	12	.500	3.26	219	0	0	0	9	256⅔	233	118	93	147	230

McGEE, WILLIE

OF, GIANTS

PERSONAL: Born November 2, 1958, in San Francisco. . . . 6-1/185. . . . Throws right, bats both. . . . Full name: Willie Dean McGee.

HIGH SCHOOL: Ellis (Richmond, Calif.).

COLLEGE: Diablo Valley College (Calif.).

TRANSACTIONS/CAREER NOTES: Selected by Chicago White Sox organization in seventh round of free-agent draft (June 8, 1976). . . . Selected by New York Yankees organization in secondary phase of free-agent draft (January 11, 1977). . . . On disabled list (May 22-June 7 and July 14-August 7, 1980; and April 24-June 4, 1981). . . . Traded by Yankees organization to St. Louis Cardinals organization for P Bob Sykes (October 21, 1981).... On Louisville disabled list (April 13-23, 1982).... On St. Louis disabled list (March 30-April 29, 1983); included rehabilitation assignment to Arkansas (April 18-29).... On disabled list (July 12-27, 1984 and August 3-27, 1986).... On disabled list (June 7-July 18, 1989); included rehabilitation assignment to Louisville (July 8-18).... On disabled list (July 26-August 14, 1989).... Traded by Cardinals to Oakland Athletics for OF Felix Jose, 3B Stan Royer and P Daryl Green (August 29, 1990).... Granted free agency (November 5, 1990).... Signed by San Francisco Giants (December 3, 1990).... On San Francisco disabled list (July 12-August 1, 1991); included rehabilitation assignment to Phoenix (July 28-August 1).... On disabled list (July 10-30, 1993).

RECORDS: Holds modern N.L. single-season record for highest batting average by switch-hitter (100 or more games)—.353 (1985).... Shares major league single-season record for fewest double plays by outfielder who led league in double plays—3 (1991).

HONORS: Won N.L. Gold Glove as outfielder (1983, 1985-86).... Named N.L. Player of the Year by THE SPORTING NEWS (1985).... Named outfielder on THE SPORTING NEWS N.L. All-Star team (1985).... Named outfielder on THE SPORTING NEWS N.L. Silver Slugger team (1985).... Named N.L. Most Valuable Player by Baseball Writers' Association of America (1985).

STATISTICAL NOTES: Hit for the cycle (June 23, 1984).... Led N.L. in grounding into double plays with 24 in 1987.... Tied for N.L. lead in double plays by outfielder with three in 1991.

			BATTING											FIELDING			
Year	Team (League)	Pos.	G	AB	R	H	2B	3B	HR	RBI	Avg.	BB	SO	SB	PO	A	E	Avg.
1977	—Oneonta (NYP)	OF	65	225	31	53	4	3	2	22	.236	13	65	13	103	5	10	.915
1978	—Fort Lauder. (FSL)	OF	124	423	62	106	6	6	0	37	.251	50	78	25	243	12	9	.966
1979	—West Haven (East.)	OF	49	115	21	28	3	1	1	8	.243	13	17	7	88	3	3	.968
	—Fort Lauder. (FSL)	OF	46	176	25	56	8	3	1	18	.318	17	34	16	103	3	2	.981
1980	—Nashville (South.)	OF	78	223	35	63	4	5	1	22	.283	19	39	7	127	6	6	.957
1981	—Nashville (South.)	OF	100	388	77	125	20	5	7	63	.322	24	46	24	203	10	6	.973
1982	—Louisville (A.A.)■	OF	13	55	11	16	2	2	1	3	.291	2	7	5	40	0	1	.976
	—St. Louis (N.L.)	OF	123	422	43	125	12	8	4	56	.296	12	58	24	245	3	11	.958
1983	—St. Louis (N.L.)	OF	147	601	75	172	22	8	5	75	.286	26	98	39	385	7	5	.987
	—Arkansas (Texas)	OF	7	29	5	8	1	1	0	2	.276	4	6	1	7	0	0	1.000
1984	—St. Louis (N.L.)	OF	145	571	82	166	19	11	6	50	.291	29	80	43	374	10	6	.985
1985	—St. Louis (N.L.)	OF	152	612	114	*216	26	*18	10	82	*.353	34	86	56	382	11	9	.978
1986	—St. Louis (N.L.)	OF	124	497	65	127	22	7	7	48	.256	37	82	19	325	9	3	*.991
1987	—St. Louis (N.L.)	OF-SS	153	620	76	177	37	11	11	105	.285	24	90	16	354	10	7	.981
1988	—St. Louis (N.L.)	OF	137	562	73	164	24	6	3	50	.292	32	84	41	348	9	9	.975
1989	—St. Louis (N.L.)	OF	58	199	23	47	10	2	3	17	.236	10	34	8	118	2	3	.976
	—Louisville (A.A.)	OF	8	27	5	11	4	0	0	4	.407	3	4	3	20	1	1	.955
1990	—St. Louis (N.L.)	OF	125	501	76	168	32	5	3	62	*.335	38	86	28	341	13	*16	.957
	—Oakland (A.L.)■	OF	29	113	23	31	3	2	0	15	.274	10	18	3	72	1	1	.986
1991	—San Francisco (N.L.)■	OF	131	497	67	155	30	3	4	43	.312	34	74	17	259	6	6	.978
	—Phoenix (PCL)	OF	4	10	4	5	1	0	0	1	.500	3	1	2	10	0	1	.909
1992	—San Francisco (N.L.)	OF	138	474	56	141	20	2	1	36	.297	29	88	13	231	11	6	.976
1993	—San Francisco (N.L.)	OF	130	475	53	143	28	1	4	46	.301	38	67	10	224	9	5	.979
American League totals (1 year)			29	113	23	31	3	2	0	15	.274	10	18	3	72	1	1	.986
National League totals (12 years)			1563	6031	803	1801	282	82	61	670	.299	343	927	314	3586	100	86	.977
Major league totals (12 years)			1592	6144	826	1832	285	84	61	685	.298	353	945	317	3658	101	87	.977

CHAMPIONSHIP SERIES RECORD

CHAMPIONSHIP SERIES NOTES: Shares single-series record for most triples—2 (1982).... Shares N.L. career records for most triples—3; and most times caught stealing—4.... Shares N.L. single-series record for most times caught stealing—3 (1985).

			BATTING											FIELDING			
Year	Team (League)	Pos.	G	AB	R	H	2B	3B	HR	RBI	Avg.	BB	SO	SB	PO	A	E	Avg.
1982	—St. Louis (N.L.)	OF	3	13	4	4	0	2	1	5	.308	0	5	0	12	0	1	.923
1985	—St. Louis (N.L.)	OF	6	26	6	7	1	0	0	3	.269	3	6	2	18	0	0	1.000
1987	—St. Louis (N.L.)	OF	7	26	2	8	1	1	0	2	.308	0	5	0	16	0	0	1.000
1990	—Oakland (A.L.)	OF-PR-DH	3	9	3	2	1	0	0	0	.222	1	2	2	2	0	0	1.000
Championship series totals (4 years)			19	74	15	21	3	3	1	10	.284	4	18	4	48	0	1	.980

WORLD SERIES RECORD

			BATTING											FIELDING			
Year	Team (League)	Pos.	G	AB	R	H	2B	3B	HR	RBI	Avg.	BB	SO	SB	PO	A	E	Avg.
1982	—St. Louis (N.L.)	OF	6	25	6	6	0	0	2	5	.240	1	3	2	24	0	0	1.000
1985	—St. Louis (N.L.)	OF	7	27	2	7	2	0	1	2	.259	1	3	1	15	0	0	1.000
1987	—St. Louis (N.L.)	OF	7	27	2	10	2	0	0	4	.370	0	9	0	21	1	1	.957
1990	—Oakland (A.L.)	OF-PH	4	10	1	2	1	0	0	0	.200	0	2	1	5	0	0	1.000
World Series totals (4 years)			24	89	11	25	5	0	3	11	.281	2	17	4	65	1	1	.985

ALL-STAR GAME RECORD

			BATTING										FIELDING			
Year	League	Pos.	AB	R	H	2B	3B	HR	RBI	Avg.	BB	SO	SB	PO	A	E	Avg.
1983	—National	OF	2	0	1	0	0	0	0	.500	0	0	0	2	0	0	1.000
1985	—National	OF	2	0	1	1	0	0	2	.500	0	0	0	1	0	0	1.000
1987	—National	OF	4	0	0	0	0	0	0	.000	0	0	0	2	0	0	1.000
1988	—National	PR-OF	2	0	0	0	0	0	0	.000	0	0	0	1	0	0	1.000
All-Star Game totals (4 years)			10	0	2	1	0	0	2	.200	0	0	0	6	0	0	1.000

McGEHEE, KEVIN

P, ORIOLES

PERSONAL: Born January 18, 1969, in Alexandria, La.... 6-0/190.... Throws right, bats right.... Full name: George Kevin McGehee.

HIGH SCHOOL: Tioga (La.).

COLLEGE: Louisiana Tech.

M

TRANSACTIONS/CAREER NOTES: Selected by Kansas City Royals organization in 11th round of free-agent draft (June 2, 1987). . . . Selected by San Francisco Giants organization in eighth round of free-agent draft (June 4, 1990). . . . Traded by Giants to Baltimore Orioles for OF Luis Mercedes (April 29, 1993).
STATISTICAL NOTES: Led Northwest League with 16 wild pitches in 1990.

Year	Team (League)	W	L	Pct.	ERA	G	GS	CG	ShO	Sv.	IP	H	R	ER	BB	SO
1990	—Everett (N'west)	4	*8	.333	4.76	15	14	1	0	0	73⅔	74	47	39	38	86
1991	—San Jose (Calif.)	13	6	.684	2.33	26	26	2	0	0	174	129	58	45	87	171
1992	—Shreveport (Texas)	9	7	.563	2.96	25	24	1	0	0	158⅓	146	61	52	42	140
1993	—Phoenix (PCL)	0	3	.000	4.91	4	4	0	0	0	22	28	16	12	8	16
	—Rochester (Int'l)■	7	6	.538	*2.96	20	20	2	0	0	133⅔	124	53	44	37	92
	—Baltimore (A.L.)	0	0	...	5.94	5	0	0	0	0	16⅔	18	11	11	7	7
Major league totals (1 year)		0	0	...	5.94	5	0	0	0	0	16⅔	18	11	11	7	7

McGRIFF, FRED

1B, BRAVES

PERSONAL: Born October 31, 1963, in Tampa, Fla. . . . 6-3/215. . . . Throws left, bats left. . . . Full name: Frederick Stanley McGriff. . . . Cousin of Terry McGriff, catcher, St. Louis Cardinals organization; and uncle of Charles Johnson, catcher, Florida Marlins organization.
HIGH SCHOOL: Jefferson (Tampa, Fla.).
TRANSACTIONS/CAREER NOTES: Selected by New York Yankees organization in ninth round of free-agent draft (June 8, 1981). . . . Traded by Yankees organization with OF Dave Collins, P Mike Morgan and cash to Toronto Blue Jays for OF/C Tom Dodd and P Dale Murray (December 9, 1982). . . . On disabled list (June 5-August 14, 1985). . . . Traded by Blue Jays with SS Tony Fernandez to San Diego Padres for OF Joe Carter and 2B Roberto Alomar (December 5, 1990). . . . On suspended list (June 23-26, 1992). . . . Traded by Padres to Atlanta Braves for OF Mel Nieves, P Donnie Elliott and OF Vince Moore (July 18, 1993).
RECORDS: Shares major league record for most grand slams in two consecutive games—2 (August 13 and 14, 1991). . . . Shares N.L. single-season record for fewest errors by first baseman who led league in errors—12 (1992).
HONORS: Named first baseman on THE SPORTING NEWS A.L. All-Star team (1989). . . . Named first baseman on THE SPORTING NEWS A.L. Silver Slugger team (1989). . . . Named first baseman on THE SPORTING NEWS N.L. All-Star team (1992-93). . . . Named first baseman on THE SPORTING NEWS N.L. Silver Slugger team (1992-93).
STATISTICAL NOTES: Led International League first basemen with .992 fielding percentage, 1,219 putouts, 85 assists, 1,314 total chances and 108 double plays in 1986. . . . Tied for International League lead in intentional bases on balls received with eight and in grounding into double plays with 16 in 1986. . . . Led A.L. first basemen with 1,592 total chances and 148 double plays in 1989. . . . Led N.L. with 26 intentional base on balls received in 1991.

			BATTING												FIELDING			
Year	Team (League)	Pos.	G	AB	R	H	2B	3B	HR	RBI	Avg.	BB	SO	SB	PO	A	E	Avg.
1981	—GC Yankees (GCL)	1B	29	81	6	12	2	0	0	9	.148	11	20	0	176	8	7	.963
1982	—GC Yankees (GCL)	1B	62	217	38	59	11	1	*9	•41	.272	*48	63	6	514	*56	8	.986
1983	—Florence (S. Atl.)■	1B	33	119	26	37	3	1	7	26	.311	20	35	3	250	14	6	.978
	—Kinston (Carolina)	1B	94	350	53	85	14	1	21	57	.243	55	112	3	784	57	10	.988
1984	—Knoxville (South.)	1B	56	189	29	47	13	2	9	25	.249	29	55	0	481	45	10	.981
	—Syracuse (Int'l)	1B	70	238	28	56	10	1	13	28	.235	26	89	0	644	45	3	.996
1985	—Syracuse (Int'l)	1B	51	176	19	40	8	2	5	20	.227	23	53	0	433	37	5	.989
1986	—Syracuse (Int'l)	1B-OF	133	468	69	121	23	4	19	74	.259	83	119	0	†1219	†85	10	†.992
	—Toronto (A.L.)	1B	3	5	1	1	0	0	0	0	.200	0	2	0	3	0	0	1.000
1987	—Toronto (A.L.)	1B	107	295	58	73	16	0	20	43	.247	60	104	3	108	7	2	.983
1988	—Toronto (A.L.)	1B	154	536	100	151	35	4	34	82	.282	79	149	6	1344	93	5	*.997
1989	—Toronto (A.L.)	1B	161	551	98	148	27	3	*36	92	.269	119	131	7	1460	115	*17	.989
1990	—Toronto (A.L.)	1B	153	557	91	167	21	1	35	88	.300	94	108	5	1246	126	6	.996
1991	—San Diego (N.L.)■	1B	153	528	84	147	19	1	31	106	.278	105	135	4	1370	87	14	.990
1992	—San Diego (N.L.)	1B	152	531	79	152	30	4	*35	104	.286	96	108	8	1219	108	•12	.991
1993	—S.D.-Atlanta (N.L.)■	1B	151	557	111	162	29	2	37	101	.291	76	106	5	1203	92	17	.987
American League totals (5 years)			578	1944	348	540	99	8	125	305	.278	352	494	21	4161	341	30	.993
National League totals (3 years)			456	1616	274	461	78	7	103	311	.285	277	349	17	3792	287	43	.990
Major league totals (8 years)			1034	3560	622	1001	177	15	228	616	.281	629	843	38	7953	628	73	.992

CHAMPIONSHIP SERIES RECORD

			BATTING												FIELDING			
Year	Team (League)	Pos.	G	AB	R	H	2B	3B	HR	RBI	Avg.	BB	SO	SB	PO	A	E	Avg.
1989	—Toronto (A.L.)	1B	5	21	1	3	0	0	0	3	.143	0	4	0	35	2	1	.974
1993	—Atlanta (N.L.)	1B	6	23	6	10	2	0	1	4	.435	4	7	0	49	4	0	1.000
Championship series totals (2 years)			11	44	7	13	2	0	1	7	.295	4	11	0	84	6	1	.989

ALL-STAR GAME RECORD

			BATTING										FIELDING			
Year	League	Pos.	AB	R	H	2B	3B	HR	RBI	Avg.	BB	SO	SB	PO	A	E	Avg.
1992	—National	1B	3	0	2	0	0	0	1	.667	0	0	0	7	1	0	1.000

McGRIFF, TERRY

C, CARDINALS

PERSONAL: Born September 23, 1963, in Fort Pierce, Fla. . . . 6-2/195. . . . Throws right, bats right. . . . Full name: Terence Roy McGriff. . . . Cousin of Fred McGriff, first baseman, Atlanta Braves; and uncle of Charles Johnson, catcher, Florida Marlins organization.
HIGH SCHOOL: Westwood (Fla.).
TRANSACTIONS/CAREER NOTES: Selected by Cincinnati Reds organization in eighth round of free-agent draft (June 8, 1981). . . . Traded by Reds with P Keith Kaiser and P Butch Henry to Houston Astros (September 7, 1990), completing deal in which Astros traded 2B Bill Doran to Reds for three players to be named later (August 30, 1990). . . . On disabled list (August 8-30 and September 2, 1991-remainder of season). . . . Granted free agency (October 16, 1991). . . . Signed by Edmonton, California Angels organization (January 27, 1992). . . . Released by Edmonton (April 3, 1992). . . . Signed by Syracuse, Toronto Blue Jays organization (August 1, 1992). . . . Granted free agency (October 15, 1992). . . . Signed by Florida Marlins organization (December 9, 1992). . . . Granted free agency (October 12, 1993). . . . Signed by Louisville, St. Louis Cardinals organization (October 27, 1993).

STATISTICAL NOTES: Led Eastern League catchers with 731 total chances in 1985.... Led American Association catchers with eight double plays in 1986 and tied for lead with 10 in 1989.... Led American Association with 10 passed balls in 1986.... Led Pacific Coast League with .426 on-base percentage in 1993.

		BATTING												FIELDING			
Year Team (League)	Pos.	G	AB	R	H	2B	3B	HR	RBI	Avg.	BB	SO	SB	PO	A	E	Avg.
1981 —Billings (Pioneer)	C-1B	42	96	15	26	3	0	1	15	.271	18	11	0	166	14	7	.963
1982 —Eugene (N'west)	C	53	190	23	46	10	2	4	31	.242	26	47	1	320	*43	8	.978
1983 —Tampa (Fla. St.)	C	87	260	21	66	11	3	5	45	.254	26	62	2	403	67	7	.985
1984 —Tampa (Fla. St.)	C	110	345	48	96	19	0	7	41	.278	48	62	5	576	88	16	.976
1985 —Vermont (Eastern)	C	110	363	52	92	10	4	13	60	.253	54	81	1	*636	89	6	*.992
1986 —Denver (A.A.)	C	108	340	54	99	22	1	9	54	.291	41	71	0	411	*59	11	.977
1987 —Nashville (A.A.)	C	67	228	36	62	11	3	10	33	.272	25	47	0	343	36	3	.992
—Cincinnati (N.L.)	C	34	89	6	20	3	0	2	11	.225	8	17	0	160	14	3	.983
1988 —Cincinnati (N.L.)	C	35	96	9	19	3	0	1	4	.198	12	31	1	177	14	2	.990
—Nashville (A.A.)	C	35	97	8	21	3	1	1	12	.216	10	15	0	175	10	4	.979
1989 —Cincinnati (N.L.)	C	6	11	1	3	0	0	0	2	.273	2	3	0	23	3	2	.929
—Nashville (A.A.)	C	102	335	42	94	24	1	5	28	.281	29	68	1	534	74	9	.985
1990 —Cin.-Hou. (N.L.)■	C	6	9	0	0	0	0	0	0	.000	0	1	0	13	2	1	.938
—Nashville (A.A.)	C	94	325	44	91	17	0	9	54	.280	38	46	2	564	59	9	.986
1991 —Tucson (PCL)	C	51	146	18	42	15	1	0	24	.288	16	20	0	132	20	2	.987
1992 —Syracuse (Int'l)■	C	21	56	4	14	2	0	2	7	.250	9	11	1	75	6	1	.988
1993 —Edmonton (PCL)■	C	105	339	62	117	29	2	7	55	.345	49	29	2	505	38	2	*.996
—Florida (N.L.)	C	3	7	0	0	0	0	0	0	.000	1	2	0	12	0	0	1.000
Major league totals (5 years)		84	212	16	42	6	0	3	17	.198	23	54	1	385	33	8	.981

McGWIRE, MARK

1B, ATHLETICS

PERSONAL: Born October 1, 1963, in Pomona, Calif.... 6-5/225.... Throws right, bats right.... Full name: Mark David McGwire.... Brother of Dan McGwire, quarterback, Seattle Seahawks, National Football League.
HIGH SCHOOL: Damien (Claremont, Calif.).
COLLEGE: Southern California.
TRANSACTIONS/CAREER NOTES: Selected by Montreal Expos organization in eighth round of free-agent draft (June 8, 1981).... Selected by Oakland Athletics organization in first round (10th pick overall) of free-agent draft (June 4, 1984).... On disabled list (April 11-26, 1989 and August 22-September 11, 1992).... Granted free agency (October 26, 1992).... Re-signed by A's (December 24, 1992).... On disabled list (May 14-September 3, 1993).... On suspended list (September 4-8, 1993).
RECORDS: Holds major league rookie-season records for most home runs—49; and extra bases on long hits—183 (1987).... Shares major league record for most home runs in two consecutive games—5 (June 27 [3] and 28 [2], 1987).... Shares modern major league record for most runs in two consecutive games—9 (June 27 and 28, 1987).... Holds A.L. rookie-season record for highest slugging percentage—.618 (1987).
HONORS: Named College Player of the Year by THE SPORTING NEWS (1984).... Named first baseman on THE SPORTING NEWS college All-America team (1984).... Named A.L. Rookie Player of the Year by THE SPORTING NEWS (1987).... Named A.L. Rookie of the Year by Baseball Writers' Association of America (1987).... Won A.L. Gold Glove at first base (1990).... Named first baseman on THE SPORTING NEWS A.L. All-Star team (1992).... Named first baseman on THE SPORTING NEWS A.L. Silver Slugger team (1992).
STATISTICAL NOTES: Led California League third basemen with 239 assists and 354 total chances in 1985.... Hit three home runs in one game (June 27, 1987).... Led A.L. with .618 slugging percentage in 1987 and .585 in 1992.... Led A.L. first basemen with 1,429 total chances in 1990.
MISCELLANEOUS: Member of 1984 U.S. Olympic baseball team.

		BATTING												FIELDING			
Year Team (League)	Pos.	G	AB	R	H	2B	3B	HR	RBI	Avg.	BB	SO	SB	PO	A	E	Avg.
1984 —Modesto (Calif.)	1B	16	55	7	11	3	0	1	1	.200	8	21	0	107	6	1	.991
1985 —Modesto (Calif.)	3B-1B	138	489	95	134	23	3	•24	•106	.274	96	108	1	105	†240	33	.913
1986 —Huntsville (South.)	3B	55	195	40	59	15	0	10	53	.303	46	45	3	34	124	16	.908
—Tacoma (PCL)	3B	78	280	42	89	21	5	13	59	.318	42	67	1	53	126	25	.877
—Oakland (A.L.)	3B	18	53	10	10	1	0	3	9	.189	4	18	0	10	20	6	.833
1987 —Oakland (A.L.)	1B-3B-OF	151	557	97	161	28	4	*49	118	.289	71	131	1	1176	101	13	.990
1988 —Oakland (A.L.)	1B-OF	155	550	87	143	22	1	32	99	.260	76	117	0	1228	88	9	.993
1989 —Oakland (A.L.)	1B	143	490	74	113	17	0	33	95	.231	83	94	1	1170	114	6	.995
1990 —Oakland (A.L.)	1B	156	523	87	123	16	0	39	108	.235	*110	116	2	*1329	95	5	.997
1991 —Oakland (A.L.)	1B	154	483	62	97	22	0	22	75	.201	93	116	2	1191	•101	4	.997
1992 —Oakland (A.L.)	1B	139	467	87	125	22	0	42	104	.268	90	105	0	1118	71	6	.995
1993 —Oakland (A.L.)	1B	27	84	16	28	6	0	9	24	.333	21	19	0	197	14	0	1.000
Major league totals (8 years)		943	3207	520	800	134	5	229	632	.249	548	716	6	7419	604	49	.994

CHAMPIONSHIP SERIES RECORD

		BATTING												FIELDING			
Year Team (League)	Pos.	G	AB	R	H	2B	3B	HR	RBI	Avg.	BB	SO	SB	PO	A	E	Avg.
1988 —Oakland (A.L.)	1B	4	15	4	5	0	0	1	3	.333	1	5	0	24	2	0	1.000
1989 —Oakland (A.L.)	1B	5	18	3	7	1	0	1	3	.389	1	4	0	46	1	1	.979
1990 —Oakland (A.L.)	1B	4	13	2	2	0	0	0	2	.154	3	3	0	40	0	0	1.000
1992 —Oakland (A.L.)	1B	6	20	1	3	0	0	1	3	.150	5	4	0	46	2	1	.980
Championship series totals (4 years)		19	66	10	17	1	0	3	11	.258	10	16	0	156	5	2	.988

WORLD SERIES RECORD

		BATTING												FIELDING			
Year Team (League)	Pos.	G	AB	R	H	2B	3B	HR	RBI	Avg.	BB	SO	SB	PO	A	E	Avg.
1988 —Oakland (A.L.)	1B	5	17	1	1	0	0	1	1	.059	3	4	0	40	3	0	1.000
1989 —Oakland (A.L.)	1B	4	17	0	5	1	0	0	1	.294	1	3	0	28	2	0	1.000
1990 —Oakland (A.L.)	1B	4	14	1	3	0	0	0	0	.214	2	4	0	42	1	2	.956
World Series totals (3 years)		13	48	2	9	1	0	1	2	.188	6	11	0	110	6	2	.983

ALL-STAR GAME RECORD

ALL-STAR GAME NOTES: Named to A.L. All-Star team for 1991 game; replaced by Rafael Palmeiro due to injury.

Year	League	Pos.	AB	R	H	2B	3B	HR	RBI	Avg.	BB	SO	SB	PO	A	E	Avg.
			BATTING											FIELDING			
1987	—American	1B	3	0	0	0	0	0	0	.000	0	0	0	7	0	1	.875
1988	—American	1B	2	0	1	0	0	0	0	.500	0	1	0	8	0	0	1.000
1989	—American	1B	3	0	1	0	0	0	0	.333	0	0	0	5	0	0	1.000
1990	—American	1B	2	0	0	0	0	0	0	.000	0	2	0	7	0	0	1.000
1991	—American		Selected, did not play—injured.														
1992	—American	1B	3	1	1	0	0	0	2	.333	0	0	0	4	0	0	1.000
All-Star Game totals (5 years)			13	1	3	0	0	0	2	.231	0	3	0	31	0	1	.969

McINTOSH, TIM

OF/C/1B, TWINS

PERSONAL: Born March 21, 1965, in Minneapolis. . . . 5-11/195. . . . Throws right, bats right. . . . Full name: Timothy Allen McIntosh.
HIGH SCHOOL: Hopkins (Minnetonka, Minn.).
COLLEGE: Minnesota.
TRANSACTIONS/CAREER NOTES: Selected by Milwaukee Brewers organization in third round of free-agent draft (June 2, 1986). . . . On Denver disabled list (July 22-29, 1991). . . . On Milwaukee disabled list (August 17-September 1, 1992). . . . Claimed on waivers by Montreal Expos (April 14, 1993). . . . Granted free agency (October 15, 1993). . . . Signed by Portland, Minnesota Twins organization (December 7, 1993).
STATISTICAL NOTES: Led California League catchers with 99 assists and 14 double plays in 1988. . . . Led American Association catchers with 19 errors and 13 passed balls in 1990.

Year	Team (League)	Pos.	G	AB	R	H	2B	3B	HR	RBI	Avg.	BB	SO	SB	PO	A	E	Avg.
				BATTING											FIELDING			
1986	—Beloit (Midwest)	OF	49	173	26	45	3	2	4	21	.260	18	33	0	98	4	4	.962
1987	—Beloit (Midwest)	C	130	461	83	139	30	3	20	85	.302	49	96	7	624	71	6	*.991
1988	—Stockton (Calif.)	C-OF	138	519	81	147	32	6	15	92	.283	57	96	10	779	†101	17	.981
1989	—El Paso (Texas)	C-OF	120	463	72	139	30	3	17	93	.300	29	72	5	474	59	17	.969
1990	—Denver (A.A.)	C-OF	116	416	72	120	21	3	18	74	.288	26	58	6	577	72	†20	.970
	—Milwaukee (A.L.)	C	5	5	1	1	0	0	1	1	.200	0	2	0	6	1	1	.875
1991	—Denver (A.A.)	1B-OF-C	122	462	69	135	19	9	18	*91	.292	37	60	2	698	64	8	.990
	—Milwaukee (A.L.)	OF-1B	7	11	2	4	1	0	1	1	.364	0	4	0	1	0	0	1.000
1992	—Milwaukee (A.L.)	C-OF-1B	35	77	7	14	3	0	0	6	.182	3	9	1	122	10	1	.992
1993	—Milwaukee (A.L.)	C	1	0	0	0	0	0	0	0	...	0	0	0	0	0	0	...
	—Montreal (N.L.)■	OF-C	20	21	2	2	1	0	0	2	.095	0	7	0	8	1	0	1.000
	—Ottawa (Int'l)	OF-C-1B	27	106	15	31	7	1	6	21	.292	10	22	1	103	12	2	.983
American League totals (4 years)			48	93	10	19	4	0	2	8	.204	3	15	1	129	11	2	.986
National League totals (1 year)			20	21	2	2	1	0	0	2	.095	0	7	0	8	1	0	1.000
Major league totals (4 years)			68	114	12	21	5	0	2	10	.184	3	22	1	137	12	2	.987

McKNIGHT, JEFF

IF, METS

PERSONAL: Born February 18, 1963, in Conway, Ark. . . . 6-0/180. . . . Throws right, bats both. . . . Full name: Jefferson Alan McKnight. . . . Son of Jim McKnight, infielder, Chicago Cubs (1960 and 1962).
HIGH SCHOOL: South Side (Bee Branch, Ark.).
COLLEGE: Westark Community College (Ark.).
TRANSACTIONS/CAREER NOTES: Selected by Baltimore Orioles organization in 28th round of free-agent draft (June 7, 1982). . . . Selected by New York Mets organization in secondary phase of free-agent draft (January 11, 1983). . . . Released by Mets (September 29, 1989). . . . Signed by Rochester, Baltimore Orioles organization (December 5, 1989). . . . On disabled list (June 4, 1991-remainder of season). . . . Released by Orioles (October 16, 1991). . . . Signed by Tidewater, Mets organization (December 20, 1991).

Year	Team (League)	Pos.	G	AB	R	H	2B	3B	HR	RBI	Avg.	BB	SO	SB	PO	A	E	Avg.
				BATTING											FIELDING			
1983	—Little Falls (NYP)	SS	39	115	10	25	3	1	0	9	.217	15	18	1	43	72	16	.878
1984	—Columbia (S. Atl.)	S-2-3-1-O	95	251	31	64	10	1	1	27	.255	25	17	9	115	144	21	.925
1985	—Columbia (S. Atl.)	OF-1B-P	67	159	26	42	6	1	1	24	.264	21	18	6	92	16	4	.964
	—Lynchburg (Caro.)	S-3-2-O	49	150	19	33	6	1	0	21	.220	29	19	0	47	106	12	.927
1986	—Jackson (Texas)	O-2-1-3-S-P	132	469	71	118	24	3	4	55	.252	76	58	5	400	154	19	.967
1987	—Jackson (Texas)	O-3-1-2-S	16	59	5	12	3	0	2	8	.203	4	12	1	22	27	1	.980
	—Tidewater (Int'l)	2-O-1-3-S-P	87	184	21	47	7	3	2	25	.255	24	22	0	141	119	9	.967
1988	—Tidewater (Int'l)	O-2-S-1-3	113	345	36	88	14	0	2	25	.255	36	32	0	180	155	15	.957
1989	—Tidewater (Int'l)	1-S-2-3-O-C	116	425	84	106	19	2	9	48	.249	*79	56	3	665	172	15	.982
	—New York (N.L.)	2-1-S-3	6	12	2	3	0	0	0	0	.250	2	1	0	4	5	1	.900
1990	—Rochester (Int'l)■	O-S-1-2	100	339	56	95	21	3	7	45	.280	41	58	7	211	144	14	.962
	—Baltimore (A.L.)	1-O-2-S	29	75	11	15	2	0	1	4	.200	5	17	0	106	20	0	1.000
1991	—Rochester (Int'l)	SS-2B-OF	22	81	19	31	7	2	1	18	.383	14	10	1	34	60	5	.949
	—Baltimore (A.L.)	OF-1B	16	41	2	7	1	0	0	2	.171	2	7	1	22	2	0	1.000
1992	—Tidewater (Int'l)■	OF-1B-2B	102	352	43	108	21	1	4	43	.307	51	52	3	341	67	9	.978
	—New York (N.L.)	2-1-S-3-O	31	85	10	23	3	1	2	13	.271	2	8	0	82	40	3	.976
1993	—New York (N.L.)	S-2-1-3-C	105	164	19	42	3	1	2	13	.256	13	31	0	86	88	10	.946
American League totals (2 years)			45	116	13	22	3	0	1	6	.190	7	24	1	128	22	0	1.000
National League totals (3 years)			142	261	31	68	6	2	4	26	.261	17	40	0	172	133	14	.956
Major league totals (5 years)			187	377	44	90	9	2	5	32	.239	24	64	1	300	155	14	.970

RECORD AS PITCHER

Year	Team (League)	W	L	Pct.	ERA	G	GS	CG	ShO	Sv.	IP	H	R	ER	BB	SO
1985	—Columbia (S. Atl.)	0	0	...	9.00	3	0	0	0	0	4	4	5	4	3	8

Year	Team (League)	W	L	Pct.	ERA	G	GS	CG	ShO	Sv.	IP	H	R	ER	BB	SO
1986	—Jackson (Texas)........	0	0	...	1.50	5	0	0	0	0	6	4	1	1	1	1
1987	—Tidewater (Int'l)........	0	0	...	0.00	1	0	0	0	0	2	0	0	0	0	0

McLEMORE, MARK

2B, ORIOLES

PERSONAL: Born October 4, 1964, in San Diego. . . . 5-11/207. . . . Throws right, bats both. . . . Full name: Mark Tremell McLemore.

HIGH SCHOOL: Morse (San Diego).

TRANSACTIONS/CAREER NOTES: Selected by California Angels organization in ninth round of free-agent draft (June 7, 1982). . . . On disabled list (May 15-27, 1985). . . . On California disabled list (May 24-August 2, 1988); included rehabilitation assignment to Palm Springs (July 7-21) and Edmonton (July 22-27). . . . On California disabled list (May 17-August 17, 1990); included rehabilitation assignment to Edmonton (May 24-June 6) and Palm Springs (August 9-13). . . . Traded by Angels to Colorado Springs, Cleveland Indians organization (August 17, 1990), completing deal in which Indians traded C Ron Tingley to Angels for a player to be named later (September 6, 1989). . . . Released by Indians organization (December 13, 1990). . . . Signed by Tucson, Houston Astros organization (March 6, 1991). . . . On Houston disabled list (May 9-June 25, 1991); included rehabilitation assignment to Tucson (May 24-29) and Jackson (June 14-22). . . . Released by Astros (June 25, 1991). . . . Signed by Baltimore Orioles (July 5, 1991). . . . Granted free agency (October 15, 1991). . . . Re-signed by Orioles organization (February 5, 1992). . . . Granted free agency (December 19, 1992). . . . Signed by Rochester, Orioles organization (January 6, 1993).

STATISTICAL NOTES: Led California League second basemen with 400 assists and 84 double plays in 1984. . . . Led Pacific Coast League second basemen with 597 total chances and 95 double plays in 1989.

			BATTING											FIELDING			
Year	Team (League)	Pos.	G	AB	R	H	2B	3B	HR	RBI	Avg.	BB	SO	SB	PO	A	E	Avg.
1982	—Salem (Northwest)...	2B-SS	55	165	42	49	6	2	0	25	.297	39	38	14	81	125	11	.949
1983	—Peoria (Midwest)......	2B-SS	95	329	42	79	7	3	0	18	.240	53	64	15	170	250	24	.946
1984	—Redwood (Calif.).......	2B-SS	134	482	102	142	8	3	0	45	.295	106	75	59	274	†429	25	.966
1985	—Midland (Texas).......	2B-SS	117	458	80	124	17	6	2	46	.271	66	59	31	301	339	19	.971
1986	—Midland (Texas).......	2B	63	237	54	75	9	1	1	29	.316	48	18	38	155	194	13	.964
	—Edmonton (PCL).......	2B	73	286	41	79	13	1	0	23	.276	39	30	29	173	215	7	.982
	—California (A.L.)	2B	5	4	0	0	0	0	0	0	.000	1	2	0	3	10	0	1.000
1987	—California (A.L.)	2B-SS	138	433	61	102	13	3	3	41	.236	48	72	25	293	363	17	.975
1988	—California (A.L.)	2B-3B	77	233	38	56	11	2	2	16	.240	25	25	13	108	178	6	.979
	—Palm Springs (Cal.)..	2B	11	44	9	15	3	1	0	6	.341	11	7	7	18	24	1	.977
	—Edmonton (PCL).......	2B	12	45	7	12	3	0	0	6	.267	4	4	7	35	33	1	.986
1989	—Edmonton (PCL).......	2B	114	430	60	105	13	2	2	34	.244	49	67	26	*264	323	10	*.983
	—California (A.L.)	2B	32	103	12	25	3	1	0	14	.243	7	19	6	55	88	5	.966
1990	—Calif.-Clev. (A.L.)■...	2B-SS-3B	28	60	6	9	2	0	0	2	.150	4	15	1	37	39	4	.950
	—Edm.-Col. S. (PCL)...	2B-SS-3B	23	93	15	25	4	0	1	10	.269	17	18	5	47	72	6	.952
	—Palm Springs (Cal.)..	2B	6	22	3	6	0	0	0	2	.273	3	7	0	20	22	0	1.000
1991	—Houston (N.L.)■........	2B	21	61	6	9	1	0	0	2	.148	6	13	0	25	54	2	.975
	—Tucson (PCL)	2B	4	14	2	5	1	0	0	0	.357	2	1	0	8	6	0	1.000
	—Jackson (Texas)	2B	7	22	6	5	3	0	1	4	.227	6	3	1	27	24	0	1.000
	—Rochester (Int'l)■.....	2B	57	228	32	64	11	4	1	28	.281	27	29	12	134	166	5	.984
1992	—Baltimore (A.L.)........	2B	101	228	40	56	7	2	0	27	.246	21	26	11	126	186	7	.978
1993	—Baltimore (A.L.)........	OF-2B-3B	148	581	81	165	27	5	4	72	.284	64	92	21	335	80	6	.986
American League totals (7 years)			529	1642	238	413	63	13	9	172	.252	170	251	77	957	944	45	.977
National League totals (1 year)			21	61	6	9	1	0	0	2	.148	6	13	0	25	54	2	.975
Major league totals (8 years)			550	1703	244	422	64	13	9	174	.248	176	264	77	982	998	47	.977

McMICHAEL, GREG

P, BRAVES

PERSONAL: Born December 1, 1966, in Knoxville, Tenn. . . . 6-3/215. . . . Throws right, bats right. . . . Full name: Gregory Winston McMichael.

HIGH SCHOOL: Webb School of Knoxville (Knoxville, Tenn.).

COLLEGE: Tennessee.

TRANSACTIONS/CAREER NOTES: Selected by Cleveland Indians organization in seventh round of free-agent draft (June 1, 1988). . . . Released by Colorado Springs, Indians organization (April 4, 1991). . . . Signed by Durham, Atlanta Braves organization (April 16, 1991).

Year	Team (League)	W	L	Pct.	ERA	G	GS	CG	ShO	Sv.	IP	H	R	ER	BB	SO
1988	—Burlington (Appal.)....	2	0	1.000	2.57	3	3	1	1	0	21	17	9	6	4	20
	—Kinston (Carolina)	4	2	.667	2.68	11	11	2	0	0	77⅓	57	31	23	18	35
1989	—Cant./Akr. (East.)	11	11	.500	3.49	26	•26	8	•5	0	170	164	81	66	64	101
1990	—Cant./Akr. (East.)	2	3	.400	3.35	13	4	0	0	0	40⅓	39	17	15	17	19
	—Colo. Springs (PCL).....	2	3	.400	5.80	12	12	1	1	0	59	72	45	38	30	34
1991	—Durham (Carolina)■....	5	6	.455	3.62	36	6	0	0	2	79⅔	83	34	32	29	82
1992	—Greenville (South.)......	4	2	.667	1.36	15	4	0	0	1	46⅓	37	14	7	13	53
	—Richmond (Int'l)	6	5	.545	4.38	19	13	0	0	2	90⅓	89	52	44	34	86
1993	—Atlanta (N.L.)	2	3	.400	2.06	74	0	0	0	19	91⅔	68	22	21	29	89
Major league totals (1 year).....		2	3	.400	2.06	74	0	0	0	19	91⅔	68	22	21	29	89

CHAMPIONSHIP SERIES RECORD

Year	Team (League)	W	L	Pct.	ERA	G	GS	CG	ShO	Sv.	IP	H	R	ER	BB	SO
1993	—Atlanta (N.L.)............	0	1	.000	6.75	4	0	0	0	0	4	7	3	3	2	1

McNAMARA, JIM

C, RANGERS

PERSONAL: Born June 10, 1965, in Nashua, N.H. . . . 6-4/210. . . . Throws right, bats left. . . . Full name: James Patrick McNamara.

HIGH SCHOOL: James Madison (Vienna, Va.).

COLLEGE: North Carolina State.

TRANSACTIONS/CAREER NOTES: Selected by San Francisco Giants organization in fifth round of free-agent draft (June 2, 1986).

M

... Loaned by Giants organization to Salinas, independent (April 1-June 10, 1989). ... Granted free agency (October 15, 1992). ... Signed by Florida Marlins organization (November 9, 1992). ... Selected by Giants from Marlins organization in Rule 5 major league draft (December 7, 1992). ... On Phoenix disabled list (June 16-23, 1993). ... Granted free agency (October 15, 1993). ... Signed by Texas Rangers organization (November 12, 1993).
STATISTICAL NOTES: Led Midwest League catchers with 1,007 total chances and 13 double plays in 1987.

			BATTING											FIELDING			
Year	Team (League)	Pos.	G	AB	R	H	2B	3B	HR	RBI	Avg.	BB	SO	SB	PO	A	E	Avg.
1986	—Everett (N'west)	C	46	158	23	39	1	2	8	30	.247	18	39	0	266	21	4	.986
1987	—Clinton (Midwest)	C	110	385	43	95	22	1	5	53	.247	19	52	4	*908	90	9	.991
1988	—San Jose (Calif.)	C	93	315	27	59	9	0	1	41	.187	43	76	3	665	79	7	.991
1989	—Salinas-S.J. (Cal.)■	C-1B	68	220	11	55	10	0	1	18	.250	23	37	3	424	58	8	.984
	—Phoenix (PCL)	C-1B	27	69	3	12	3	0	0	4	.174	4	13	1	105	12	2	.983
1990	—San Jose (Calif.)	C-1B	53	158	20	32	2	2	1	22	.203	18	30	0	236	32	2	.993
	—Phoenix (PCL)	C	6	20	2	9	0	0	0	1	.450	3	4	0	24	6	0	1.000
	—Shreveport (Texas)	C	28	79	2	19	7	0	0	13	.241	7	9	0	110	13	2	.984
1991	—Shreveport (Texas)	C-1B	39	109	13	30	8	2	2	20	.275	21	11	2	205	19	2	.991
	—Phoenix (PCL)	C	17	53	3	9	1	0	0	2	.170	6	12	0	84	10	1	.989
1992	—San Francisco (N.L.)	C	30	74	6	16	1	0	1	9	.216	6	25	0	131	8	1	.993
	—Phoenix (PCL)	C	23	67	5	14	3	0	0	3	.209	14	13	0	137	11	0	1.000
1993	—Phoenix (PCL)■	C	50	158	10	31	5	0	1	23	.196	12	29	1	251	30	7	.976
	—San Francisco (N.L.)	C	4	7	0	1	0	0	0	1	.143	0	1	0	12	0	0	1.000
Major league totals (2 years)			34	81	6	17	1	0	1	10	.210	6	26	0	143	8	1	.993

McNEELY, JEFF

OF, RED SOX

PERSONAL: Born October 18, 1969, in Monroe, N.C. ... 6-2/190. ... Throws right, bats right. ... Full name: Jeffrey Laverne McNeely.
HIGH SCHOOL: Monroe (N.C.).
COLLEGE: Spartanburg (S.C.) Methodist.
TRANSACTIONS/CAREER NOTES: Selected by Boston Red Sox organization in second round of free-agent draft (June 5, 1989). ... On disabled list (May 22-June 4 and June 13-July 3, 1992).
STATISTICAL NOTES: Led Carolina League with .436 on-base percentage in 1991.

			BATTING											FIELDING			
Year	Team (League)	Pos.	G	AB	R	H	2B	3B	HR	RBI	Avg.	BB	SO	SB	PO	A	E	Avg.
1989	—GC Red Sox (GCL)	OF	9	32	10	13	1	1	0	4	.406	7	3	5	13	1	0	1.000
	—Elmira (N.Y.-Penn)	OF	61	208	20	52	7	0	2	21	.250	26	54	16	96	5	7	.935
1990	—Winter Haven (FSL)	OF	16	62	4	10	0	0	0	3	.161	3	19	7	41	3	1	.978
	—Elmira (N.Y.-Penn)	OF	73	246	41	77	4	5	6	37	.313	40	60	*39	124	8	7	.950
1991	—Lynchburg (Caro.)	OF	106	382	58	123	16	5	4	38	*.322	74	74	38	237	5	8	.968
1992	—New Britain (East.)	OF	85	261	30	57	8	4	2	11	.218	26	78	10	174	2	3	.983
1993	—Pawtucket (Int'l)	OF	129	498	65	130	14	3	2	35	.261	43	102	40	*284	6	11	.963
	—Boston (A.L.)	OF	21	37	10	11	1	1	0	1	.297	7	9	6	22	0	2	.917
Major league totals (1 year)			21	37	10	11	1	1	0	1	.297	7	9	6	22	0	2	.917

McRAE, BRIAN

OF, ROYALS

PERSONAL: Born August 27, 1967, in Bradenton, Fla. ... 6-0/185. ... Throws right, bats both. ... Full name: Brian Wesley McRae. ... Son of Hal McRae, current manager, Kansas City Royals; outfielder, Cincinnati Reds and Kansas City Royals (1968 and 1970-87); coach, Royals (1987); and coach, Montreal Expos (1990-91).
HIGH SCHOOL: Blue Springs (Mo.).
TRANSACTIONS/CAREER NOTES: Selected by Kansas City Royals organization in first round (17th pick overall) of free-agent draft (June 3, 1985).
RECORDS: Shares major league single-season record for fewest double plays by outfielder (150 or more games)—0 (1991). ... Shares major league single-game record for most unassisted double plays by oufielder—1 (August 23, 1992).
STATISTICAL NOTES: Led Northwest League second basemen with 373 total chances in 1986. ... Tied for Southern League lead in double plays by outfielder with five in 1989.

			BATTING											FIELDING			
Year	Team (League)	Pos.	G	AB	R	H	2B	3B	HR	RBI	Avg.	BB	SO	SB	PO	A	E	Avg.
1985	—GC Royals (GCL)	2B-SS	60	217	40	58	6	5	0	23	.267	28	34	27	116	142	18	.935
1986	—Eugene (N'west)	2B	72	306	*66	82	10	3	1	29	.268	41	49	28	146	*214	13	*.965
1987	—Fort Myers (FSL)	2B	131	481	62	121	14	1	1	31	.252	22	70	33	*284	346	18	.972
1988	—Baseball City (FSL)	2B	30	107	18	33	2	0	1	11	.308	9	11	8	70	103	4	.977
	—Memphis (South.)	2B	91	288	33	58	13	1	4	15	.201	16	60	13	147	231	18	.955
1989	—Memphis (South.)	OF	138	*533	72	121	18	8	5	42	.227	43	65	23	249	11	5	.981
1990	—Memphis (South.)	OF	116	470	78	126	24	6	10	64	.268	44	66	21	265	8	7	.975
	—Kansas City (A.L.)	OF	46	168	21	48	8	3	2	23	.286	9	29	4	120	1	0	1.000
1991	—Kansas City (A.L.)	OF	152	629	86	164	28	9	8	64	.261	24	99	20	405	2	3	.993
1992	—Kansas City (A.L.)	OF	149	533	63	119	23	5	4	52	.223	42	88	18	419	8	3	.993
1993	—Kansas City (A.L.)	OF	153	627	78	177	28	9	12	69	.282	37	105	23	394	4	7	.983
Major league totals (4 years)			500	1957	248	508	87	26	26	208	.260	112	321	65	1338	15	13	.990

McREYNOLDS, KEVIN

OF, METS

PERSONAL: Born October 16, 1959, in Little Rock, Ark. ... 6-1/225. ... Throws right, bats right. ... Full name: Walter Kevin McReynolds.
HIGH SCHOOL: Sylvan Hills (North Little Rock, Ark.).
COLLEGE: Arkansas.
TRANSACTIONS/CAREER NOTES: Selected by Milwaukee Brewers organization in 18th round of free-agent draft (June 6, 1978). ... Selected by San Diego Padres organization in first round (sixth pick overall) of free-agent draft (June 8, 1981). ... Traded by Padres with P Gene Walter and IF Adam Ging to New York Mets for OF Shawn Abner, OF Stanley Jefferson, OF Kevin Mitchell,

P Kevin Armstrong and P Kevin Brown (December 11, 1986).... Traded by Mets with IF Gregg Jefferies and 2B Keith Miller to Kansas City Royals for P Bret Saberhagen and IF Bill Pecota (December 11, 1991).... On disabled list (August 5-September 1, 1992 and May 15-June 7, 1993).... Traded by Royals to Mets for OF Vince Coleman and cash (January 5, 1994).
RECORDS: Holds major league single-season record for most stolen bases without being caught stealing—21 (1988).... Shares major league single-season records for fewest assists by outfielder who led league in assists—14 (1990); fewest double plays by outfielder (150 or more games)—0 (1987).
HONORS: Named outfielder on THE SPORTING NEWS college All-America team (1981).... Named California League Most Valuable Player (1982).... Named Minor League Player of the Year by THE SPORTING NEWS (1983).... Named Pacific Coast League Player of the Year (1983).... Named outfielder on THE SPORTING NEWS N.L. All-Star team (1988).
STATISTICAL NOTES: Led Pacific Coast League with 328 total bases in 1983.... Led N.L. outfielders with 436 total chances in 1984 and 445 in 1985.... Led N.L. outfielders with five double plays in 1988.... Hit for the cycle (August 1, 1989).

			BATTING												FIELDING			
Year	Team (League)	Pos.	G	AB	R	H	2B	3B	HR	RBI	Avg.	BB	SO	SB	PO	A	E	Avg.
1982	—Reno (California)	OF	90	338	83	127	17	5	*28	98	*.376	36	50	0	52	7	3	.952
	—Amarillo (Texas)	OF	40	162	30	57	8	3	5	39	.352	12	32	4	76	3	2	.975
1983	—Las Vegas (PCL)	OF	113	446	98	168	*46	9	•32	116	.377	41	55	14	257	3	9	.967
	—San Diego (N.L.)	OF	39	140	15	31	3	1	4	14	.221	12	29	2	87	4	1	.989
1984	—San Diego (N.L.)	OF	147	525	68	146	26	6	20	75	.278	34	69	3	*422	10	4	.991
1985	—San Diego (N.L.)	OF	152	564	61	132	24	4	15	75	.234	43	81	4	*430	12	3	.993
1986	—San Diego (N.L.)	OF	158	560	89	161	31	6	26	96	.288	66	83	8	332	9	8	.977
1987	—New York (N.L.)■	OF	151	590	86	163	32	5	29	95	.276	39	70	14	286	8	4	.987
1988	—New York (N.L.)	OF	147	552	82	159	30	2	27	99	.288	38	56	21	252	*18	4	.985
1989	—New York (N.L.)	OF	148	545	74	148	25	3	22	85	.272	46	74	15	307	10	•10	.969
1990	—New York (N.L.)	OF	147	521	75	140	23	1	24	82	.269	71	61	9	237	•14	3	.988
1991	—New York (N.L.)	OF	143	522	65	135	32	1	16	74	.259	49	46	6	281	9	2	.993
1992	—Kansas City (A.L.)■	OF	109	373	45	92	25	0	13	49	.247	67	48	7	204	4	3	.986
1993	—Kansas City (A.L.)	OF	110	351	44	86	22	4	11	42	.245	37	56	2	191	5	2	.990
American League totals (2 years)			219	724	89	178	47	4	24	91	.246	104	104	9	395	9	5	.988
National League totals (9 years)			1232	4519	615	1215	226	29	183	695	.269	398	569	82	2634	94	39	.986
Major league totals (11 years)			1451	5243	704	1393	273	33	207	786	.266	502	673	91	3029	103	44	.986

CHAMPIONSHIP SERIES RECORD

CHAMPIONSHIP SERIES NOTES: Shares N.L. single-game record for most hits—4 (October 11, 1988).

			BATTING												FIELDING			
Year	Team (League)	Pos.	G	AB	R	H	2B	3B	HR	RBI	Avg.	BB	SO	SB	PO	A	E	Avg.
1984	—San Diego (N.L.)	OF	4	10	2	3	0	0	1	4	.300	3	1	0	10	0	0	1.000
1988	—New York (N.L.)	OF	7	28	4	7	2	0	2	4	.250	3	5	2	19	0	0	1.000
Championship series totals (2 years)			11	38	6	10	2	0	3	8	.263	6	6	2	29	0	0	1.000

MEACHAM, RUSTY

P, ROYALS

PERSONAL: Born January 27, 1968, in Stuart, Fla.... 6-2/175.... Throws right, bats right.... Full name: Russell Loren Meacham.
COLLEGE: Indian River Community College (Fla.).
TRANSACTIONS/CAREER NOTES: Selected by Detroit Tigers organization in 33rd round of free-agent draft (June 2, 1987).... Claimed on waivers by Kansas City Royals (October 23, 1991).... On Kansas City disabled list (May 1-June 4, 1993); included rehabilitation assignment to Omaha (May 18-June 4).... On Kansas City disabled list (June 15, 1993-remainder of season).

Year	Team (League)	W	L	Pct.	ERA	G	GS	CG	ShO	Sv.	IP	H	R	ER	BB	SO
1988	—Fayetteville (SAL)	0	3	.000	6.20	6	5	0	0	0	24⅔	37	19	17	6	16
	—Bristol (Appal.)	•9	1	•.900	*1.43	13	9	2	•2	0	75⅓	55	14	12	22	85
1989	—Fayetteville (SAL)	10	3	.769	2.29	16	15	2	0	0	102	103	33	26	23	74
	—Lakeland (Fla. St.)	5	4	.556	1.95	11	9	4	2	0	64⅔	59	15	14	12	39
1990	—London (Eastern)	*15	9	.625	3.13	26	26	•9	•3	0	178	161	70	62	36	123
1991	—Toledo (Int'l)	9	7	.563	3.09	26	17	3	1	2	125⅓	117	53	43	40	70
	—Detroit (A.L.)	2	1	.667	5.20	10	4	0	0	0	27⅔	35	17	16	11	14
1992	—Kansas City (A.L.)■	10	4	.714	2.74	64	0	0	0	2	101⅔	88	39	31	21	64
1993	—Kansas City (A.L.)	2	2	.500	5.57	15	0	0	0	0	21	31	15	13	5	13
	—Omaha (A.A.)	0	0	...	4.82	7	0	0	0	0	9⅓	10	5	5	1	10
Major league totals (3 years)		14	7	.667	3.59	89	4	0	0	2	150⅓	154	71	60	37	91

MEARES, PAT

SS, TWINS

PERSONAL: Born September 6, 1968, in Salina, Kan.... 6-0/184.... Throws right, bats right.... Full name: Patrick James Meares.
HIGH SCHOOL: Sacred Heart (Salina, Kan.).
COLLEGE: Wichita State.
TRANSACTIONS/CAREER NOTES: Selected by Minnesota Twins organization in 15th round of free-agent draft (June 4, 1990).

			BATTING												FIELDING			
Year	Team (League)	Pos.	G	AB	R	H	2B	3B	HR	RBI	Avg.	BB	SO	SB	PO	A	E	Avg.
1990	—Kenosha (Midwest)	3B-2B	52	197	26	47	10	2	4	22	.239	25	45	2	35	94	16	.890
1991	—Visalia (California)	2B-3B-OF	89	360	53	109	21	4	6	44	.303	24	63	15	155	224	26	.936
1992	—Orlando (Southern)	SS	81	300	42	76	19	0	3	23	.253	11	57	5	91	190	35	.889
1993	—Portland (PCL)	SS	18	54	6	16	5	0	0	3	.296	3	11	0	28	48	5	.938
	—Minnesota (A.L.)	SS	111	346	33	87	14	3	0	33	.251	7	52	4	165	304	19	.961
Major league totals (1 year)			111	346	33	87	14	3	0	33	.251	7	52	4	165	304	19	.961

MEJIA, ROBERTO

2B, ROCKIES

PERSONAL: Born April 14, 1972, in Hato Mayor, Dominican Republic. . . . 5-11/165. . . . Throws right, bats right. . . . Full name: Roberto Antonio Diaz Mejia.

HIGH SCHOOL: Colegio Adventista (Dominican Republic).

TRANSACTIONS/CAREER NOTES: Signed as free agent by Los Angeles Dodgers organization (November 21, 1988). . . . On disabled list (April 29-May 19 and August 18, 1992-remainder of season). . . . Selected by Colorado Rockies in second round (30th pick overall) of expansion draft (November 17, 1992).

			BATTING											FIELDING			
Year	Team (League)	Pos.	G	AB	R	H	2B	3B	HR	RBI	Avg.	BB	SO	SB	PO	A	E	Avg.
1989	—Santo Dom. (DSL)	...	43	136	18	30	5	3	0	20	.221	24	22	7	...	...	...	...
1990	—Santo Dom. (DSL)	...	67	246	61	74	19	1	8	74	.301	48	30	9	...	...	...	...
1991	—Great Falls (Pio.)	2B	23	84	17	22	6	2	2	14	.262	7	22	3	33	54	3	.967
1992	—Vero Beach (FSL)	2B	96	330	42	82	17	1	12	40	.248	37	60	14	148	212	15	.960
1993	—Colo. Springs (PCL)■	2B	77	291	51	87	15	2	14	48	.299	18	56	12	166	204	8	.979
	—Colorado (N.L.)	2B	65	229	31	53	14	5	5	20	.231	13	63	4	126	184	12	.963
	Major league totals (1 year)		65	229	31	53	14	5	5	20	.231	13	63	4	126	184	12	.963

MELENDEZ, JOSE

P, RED SOX

PERSONAL: Born September 2, 1965, in Naguabo, Puerto Rico. . . . 6-2/175. . . . Throws right, bats right. . . . Full name: Jose Luis Melendez.

TRANSACTIONS/CAREER NOTES: Signed as free agent by Pittsburgh Pirates organization (August 29, 1983). . . . On disabled list (May 3-25 and June 9-August 12, 1985). . . . Selected by Seattle Mariners organization from Pirates organization in Rule 5 minor league draft (December 5, 1988). . . . Claimed on waivers by San Diego Padres (March 26, 1991). . . . Traded by Padres to Boston Red Sox for OF Phil Plantier (December 9, 1992). . . . On Boston disabled list (April 4-May 29, 1993); included rehabilitation assignment to Pawtucket (April 26-May 25). . . . On Boston disabled list (June 27-September 28, 1993); included rehabilitation assignment to Pawtucket (July 22-August 20).

Year	Team (League)	W	L	Pct.	ERA	G	GS	CG	ShO	Sv.	IP	H	R	ER	BB	SO
1984	—Watertown (NYP)	5	7	.417	2.77	15	15	3	1	0	91	61	37	28	40	68
1985	—Prin. William (Car.)	3	2	.600	2.44	9	8	1	0	1	44⅓	25	17	12	26	41
1986	—Prin. William (Car.)	13	10	.565	2.61	28	27	6	1	0	186⅓	141	75	54	81	146
1987	—Harrisburg (East.)	1	3	.250	10.80	6	6	0	0	0	18⅓	28	24	22	11	13
	—Salem (Carolina)	9	6	.600	4.56	20	20	1	1	0	116⅓	96	62	59	56	86
1988	—Salem (Carolina)	4	2	.667	4.02	8	8	2	0	0	53⅔	55	26	24	19	50
	—Harrisburg (East.)	5	3	.625	2.27	22	4	2	0	1	71⅓	46	20	18	19	38
1989	—Williamsport (East.)■	3	4	.429	2.45	11	11	0	0	0	73⅓	54	23	20	22	56
	—Calgary (PCL)	1	2	.333	5.75	17	2	0	0	0	40⅔	42	27	26	19	24
1990	—Calgary (PCL)	11	4	.733	3.90	45	10	1	0	2	124⅔	119	61	54	44	95
	—Seattle (A.L.)	0	0	...	11.81	3	0	0	0	0	5⅓	8	8	7	3	7
1991	—Las Vegas (PCL)■	7	0	1.000	3.99	9	8	1	0	0	58⅔	54	27	26	11	45
	—San Diego (N.L.)	8	5	.615	3.27	31	9	0	0	3	93⅔	77	35	34	24	60
1992	—San Diego (N.L.)	6	7	.462	2.92	56	3	0	0	0	89⅓	82	32	29	20	82
1993	—Pawtucket (Int'l)■	2	3	.400	5.40	19	0	0	0	2	35	37	24	21	7	31
	—Boston (A.L.)	2	1	.667	2.25	9	0	0	0	0	16	10	4	4	5	14
	A.L. totals (2 years)	2	1	.667	4.64	12	0	0	0	0	21⅓	18	12	11	8	21
	N.L. totals (2 years)	14	12	.538	3.10	87	12	0	0	3	183	159	67	63	44	142
	Major league totals (4 years)	16	13	.552	3.26	99	12	0	0	3	204⅓	177	79	74	52	163

M

MELVIN, BOB

C, RED SOX

PERSONAL: Born October 28, 1961, in Palo Alto, Calif. . . . 6-4/205. . . . Throws right, bats right. . . . Full name: Robert Paul Melvin.

HIGH SCHOOL: Menlo-Atherton (Menlo Park, Calif.).

COLLEGE: California and Canada College (Calif.).

TRANSACTIONS/CAREER NOTES: Selected by Baltimore Orioles organization in third round of free-agent draft (June 5, 1979). . . . Selected by Detroit Tigers organization in secondary phase of free-agent draft (January 13, 1981). . . . On disabled list (May 1-25, 1982). . . . Traded by Tigers with P Juan Berenguer and a player to be named later to San Francisco Giants for P Dave LaPoint, P Eric King and C Matt Nokes (October 7, 1985); Giants acquired P Scott Medvin to complete deal (December 11, 1985). . . . On disabled list (July 11-26, 1987). . . . Traded by Giants to Baltimore Orioles for C Terry Kennedy (January 24, 1989). . . . On disabled list (April 22-May 7, 1989). . . . Traded by Orioles to Kansas City Royals for P Storm Davis (December 11, 1991). . . . Granted free agency (October 26, 1992). . . . Signed by Boston Red Sox (December 14, 1992). . . . On disabled list (July 16-31, 1993).

STATISTICAL NOTES: Led Southern League catchers with .987 fielding percentage in 1982.

			BATTING											FIELDING			
Year	Team (League)	Pos.	G	AB	R	H	2B	3B	HR	RBI	Avg.	BB	SO	SB	PO	A	E	Avg.
1981	—Macon (S. Atl.)	C	114	412	56	112	19	1	14	64	.272	35	71	5	456	67	2	*.996
1982	—Birm. (Southern)	C-1B-3B	98	364	33	86	12	1	13	52	.236	24	70	1	638	54	9	†.987
1983	—Birm. (Southern)	C-1B-2B	78	285	43	82	14	2	10	56	.288	18	54	0	404	30	2	.995
	—Evansville (A.A.)	C-1B	45	142	10	27	6	0	2	11	.190	7	41	0	213	16	1	.996
1984	—Evansville (A.A.)	C-1B	44	141	12	35	13	0	0	11	.248	3	32	0	214	21	1	.996
	—Birm. (Southern)	C-1B-3B	69	271	34	73	14	1	2	33	.269	18	47	1	341	38	4	.990
1985	—Nashville (A.A.)	C-1B-OF	53	177	27	48	7	1	9	24	.271	16	38	3	276	28	2	.993
	—Detroit (A.L.)	C	41	82	10	18	4	1	0	4	.220	3	21	0	175	13	2	.989
1986	—San Francisco (N.L.)■	C-3B	89	268	24	60	14	2	5	25	.224	15	69	3	443	60	6	.988
1987	—San Francisco (N.L.)	C-1B	84	246	31	49	8	0	11	31	.199	17	44	0	414	44	1	.998
1988	—San Francisco (N.L.)	C-1B	92	273	23	64	13	1	8	27	.234	13	46	0	406	31	7	.984
	—Phoenix (PCL)	C	21	75	11	23	5	0	2	9	.307	8	13	0	123	6	1	.992
1989	—Baltimore (A.L.)■	C	85	278	22	67	10	1	1	32	.241	15	53	1	303	20	3	.991
1990	—Baltimore (A.L.)	C-1B	93	301	30	73	14	1	5	37	.243	11	53	0	365	26	1	.997
1991	—Baltimore (A.L.)	C	79	228	11	57	10	0	1	23	.250	11	46	0	383	31	1	.998

Year	Team (League)	Pos.	G	AB	R	H	2B	3B	HR	RBI	Avg.	BB	SO	SB	PO	A	E	Avg.
			BATTING												FIELDING			
1992	—Kansas City (A.L.)■	C-1B	32	70	5	22	5	0	0	6	.314	5	13	0	99	9	1	.991
1993	—Boston (A.L.)■	C-1B	77	176	13	39	7	0	3	23	.222	7	44	0	309	19	2	.994
American League totals (6 years)			407	1135	91	276	50	3	10	125	.243	52	230	1	1634	118	10	.994
National League totals (3 years)			265	787	78	173	35	3	24	83	.220	45	159	3	1263	135	14	.990
Major league totals (9 years)			672	1922	169	449	85	6	34	208	.234	97	389	4	2897	253	24	.992

CHAMPIONSHIP SERIES RECORD

Year	Team (League)	Pos.	G	AB	R	H	2B	3B	HR	RBI	Avg.	BB	SO	SB	PO	A	E	Avg.
			BATTING												FIELDING			
1987	—San Francisco (N.L.)	C-PH	3	7	0	3	0	0	0	0	.429	1	1	0	14	1	0	1.000

MENENDEZ, TONY

P, GIANTS

PERSONAL: Born February 20, 1965, in Havana, Cuba. . . . 6-2/190. . . . Throws right, bats right. . . . Full name: Antonio Gustavo Menendez.

HIGH SCHOOL: American (Hialeah, Fla.).

TRANSACTIONS/CAREER NOTES: Selected by Chicago White Sox organization in first round (20th pick overall) of free-agent draft (June 4, 1984); pick received as compensation for Toronto Blue Jays signing Type A free agent Dennis Lamp. . . . Granted free agency (October 15, 1990). . . . Signed by Indianapolis, Montreal Expos organization (January 7, 1991). . . . Released by Indianapolis (April 5, 1991). . . . Signed by Tulsa, Texas Rangers organization (May 13, 1991). . . . Granted free agency (October 15, 1991). . . . Signed by Chattanooga, Cincinnati Reds organization (November 20, 1991). . . . Granted free agency (October 15, 1992). . . . Signed by Buffalo, Pittsburgh Pirates organization (November 30, 1992). . . . Granted free agency (October 12, 1993). . . . Signed by San Francisco Giants (December 15, 1993).

Year	Team (League)	W	L	Pct.	ERA	G	GS	CG	ShO	Sv.	IP	H	R	ER	BB	SO
1984	—GC Whi. Sox (GCL)	3	2	.600	3.16	6	6	0	0	0	37	26	19	13	13	30
1985	—Appleton (Midw.)	13	4	.765	2.74	24	24	2	0	0	148	134	67	45	55	100
	—Buffalo (A.A.)	0	1	.000	19.29	1	1	0	0	0	2⅓	9	5	5	1	2
1986	—Birm. (Southern)	7	8	.467	5.70	17	17	0	0	0	96⅓	132	71	61	50	52
	—Peninsula (Caro.)	4	4	.500	4.57	11	10	1	1	0	63	58	35	32	29	43
1987	—Birm. (Southern)	10	10	.500	4.83	27	27	4	1	0	173⅓	193	111	93	76	102
1988	—Birm. (Southern)	6	11	.353	3.94	24	24	3	0	0	153	131	79	67	64	112
1989	—Birm. (Southern)	10	4	.714	3.19	27	18	2	1	1	144	123	61	51	53	115
1990	—Vancouver (PCL)	2	5	.286	3.72	24	9	2	1	0	72⅔	63	34	30	28	48
1991	—Tulsa (Texas)■	3	0	1.000	1.29	3	2	0	0	0	14	9	2	2	4	14
	—Okla. City (A.A.)	5	5	.500	5.20	21	19	0	0	0	116	107	70	67	62	82
1992	—Nashville (A.A.)■	3	5	.375	4.05	50	2	0	0	1	106⅔	98	53	48	47	92
	—Cincinnati (N.L.)	1	0	1.000	1.93	3	0	0	0	0	4⅔	1	1	1	0	5
1993	—Buffalo (A.A.)■	4	5	.444	2.42	54	0	0	0	24	63⅓	50	20	17	21	48
	—Pittsburgh (N.L.)	2	0	1.000	3.00	14	0	0	0	0	21	20	8	7	4	13
Major league totals (2 years)		3	0	1.000	2.81	17	0	0	0	0	25⅔	21	9	8	4	18

MENHART, PAUL

P, BLUE JAYS

PERSONAL: Born March 25, 1969, in St. Louis. . . . 6-2/190. . . . Throws right, bats right. . . . Full name: Paul Gerard Menhart.

HIGH SCHOOL: Robert E. Fitch Senior (Groton, Conn.).

COLLEGE: Western Carolina.

TRANSACTIONS/CAREER NOTES: Selected by Toronto Blue Jays organization in ninth round of free-agent draft (June 4, 1990). . . . On disabled list (August 12-27, 1993).

Year	Team (League)	W	L	Pct.	ERA	G	GS	CG	ShO	Sv.	IP	H	R	ER	BB	SO
1990	—St. Cathar. (NYP)	0	5	.000	4.05	8	8	0	0	0	40	34	27	18	19	38
	—Myrtle Beach (SAL)	3	0	1.000	0.59	5	4	1	0	0	30⅔	18	5	2	5	18
1991	—Dunedin (Fla. St.)	10	6	.625	2.66	20	20	3	0	0	128⅓	114	42	38	34	114
1992	—Knoxville (South.)	10	11	.476	3.85	28	28	2	1	0	177⅔	181	85	76	38	104
1993	—Syracuse (Int'l)	9	10	.474	3.64	25	25	4	0	0	151	143	74	61	67	108

MERCED, ORLANDO

OF, PIRATES

PERSONAL: Born November 2, 1966, in San Juan, Puerto Rico. . . . 5-11/185. . . . Throws right, bats left. . . . Full name: Orlando Luis Merced. . . . Name pronounced mer-SED.

HIGH SCHOOL: University Garden (San Juan, Puerto Rico).

TRANSACTIONS/CAREER NOTES: Signed as free agent by Pittsburgh Pirates organization (February 22, 1985). . . . On Macon disabled list (April 18-28, 1987). . . . On Watertown disabled list (June 23, 1987-remainder of season).

STATISTICAL NOTES: Led N.L. outfielders with five double plays in 1993.

MISCELLANEOUS: Batted as switch-hitter (1985-92).

Year	Team (League)	Pos.	G	AB	R	H	2B	3B	HR	RBI	Avg.	BB	SO	SB	PO	A	E	Avg.
			BATTING												FIELDING			
1985	—GC Pirates (GCL)	SS-3B-1B	40	136	16	31	6	0	1	13	.228	9	9	3	46	78	28	.816
1986	—Macon (S. Atl.)	OF-3B	65	173	20	34	4	1	2	24	.197	12	38	5	53	15	13	.840
	—Watertown (NYP)	3B-1B-OF	27	89	12	16	0	1	3	9	.180	14	21	6	49	28	10	.885
1987	—Macon (S. Atl.)	OF	4	4	1	0	0	0	0	0	.000	1	3	0	1	1	0	1.000
	—Watertown (NYP)	2B	4	12	4	5	0	1	0	3	.417	1	1	1	11	7	2	.900
1988	—Augusta (S. Atl.)	2B-3B-SS	37	136	19	36	6	3	1	17	.265	7	20	2	35	39	7	.914
	—Salem (Carolina)	3-2-0-S	80	298	47	87	12	7	7	42	.292	27	64	13	77	183	31	.893
1989	—Harrisburg (East.)	1B-OF-3B	95	341	43	82	16	4	6	48	.240	32	66	13	435	32	10	.979
	—Buffalo (A.A.)	1B-OF-3B	35	129	18	44	5	3	1	16	.341	7	26	0	173	15	3	.984
1990	—Buffalo (A.A.)	1B-3B-OF	101	378	52	99	12	6	9	55	.262	46	63	14	689	83	20	.975
	—Pittsburgh (N.L.)	OF-C	25	24	3	5	1	0	0	0	.208	1	9	0	0	0	0	...

Year	Team (League)	Pos.	G	AB	R	H	2B	3B	HR	RBI	Avg.	BB	SO	SB	PO	A	E	Avg.
			BATTING												FIELDING			
1991	—Buffalo (A.A.)	1B	3	12	1	2	0	0	0	0	.167	1	4	1	29	2	0	1.000
	—Pittsburgh (N.L.)	1B-OF	120	411	83	113	17	2	10	50	.275	64	81	8	916	60	12	.988
1992	—Pittsburgh (N.L.)	1B-OF	134	405	50	100	28	5	6	60	.247	52	63	5	906	75	5	.995
1993	—Pittsburgh (N.L.)	OF-1B	137	447	68	140	26	4	8	70	.313	77	64	3	485	31	10	.981
Major league totals (4 years)			416	1287	204	358	72	11	24	180	.278	194	217	16	2307	166	27	.989

CHAMPIONSHIP SERIES RECORD

CHAMPIONSHIP SERIES NOTES: Hit home run in first series at-bat (October 12, 1991).

Year	Team (League)	Pos.	G	AB	R	H	2B	3B	HR	RBI	Avg.	BB	SO	SB	PO	A	E	Avg.
			BATTING												FIELDING			
1991	—Pittsburgh (N.L.)	1B-PH	3	9	1	2	0	0	1	1	.222	0	1	0	13	0	1	.929
1992	—Pittsburgh (N.L.)	1B-PH	4	10	0	1	1	0	0	2	.100	2	4	0	27	2	1	.967
Championship series totals (2 years)			7	19	1	3	1	0	1	3	.158	2	5	0	40	2	2	.955

MERCEDES, HENRY

C, ATHLETICS

PERSONAL: Born July 23, 1969, in Santo Domingo, Dominican Republic. . . . 5-11/185. . . . Throws right, bats right. . . . Full name: Henry Felipe Perez Mercedes.

TRANSACTIONS/CAREER NOTES: Signed as free agent by Oakland Athletics organization (June 22, 1987).

STATISTICAL NOTES: Led California League catchers with 21 errors in 1991. . . . Led Pacific Coast League catchers with 12 errors and 10 double plays in 1993.

Year	Team (League)	Pos.	G	AB	R	H	2B	3B	HR	RBI	Avg.	BB	SO	SB	PO	A	E	Avg.
			BATTING												FIELDING			
1987	—		Dominican Summer League statistics unavailable.															
1988	—Ariz. A's (Arizona)	C	2	5	1	2	0	0	0	0	.400	0	0	0	13	2	0	1.000
1989	—S. Oregon (N'west)	C-3B	22	61	6	10	0	1	0	1	.164	10	24	0	129	15	3	.980
	—Modesto (Calif.)	C	16	37	6	3	0	0	1	3	.081	7	22	0	81	9	4	.957
	—Madison (Midwest)	C	51	152	11	32	3	0	2	13	.211	22	46	0	304	40	5	.986
1990	—Madison (Midwest)	C-3-2-O	90	282	29	64	13	2	3	37	.227	30	100	6	555	110	9	.987
	—Tacoma (PCL)	C	12	31	3	6	1	0	0	2	.194	3	7	0	46	4	0	1.000
1991	—Modesto (Calif.)	C-3B-P	116	388	55	100	17	3	4	61	.258	68	110	5	551	86	†24	.964
1992	—Tacoma (PCL)	C	85	246	36	57	9	2	0	20	.232	26	60	1	476	62	9	.984
	—Oakland (A.L.)	C	9	5	1	4	0	1	0	1	.800	0	1	0	7	0	1	.875
1993	—Tacoma (PCL)	C-3B-OF	85	256	37	61	13	1	4	32	.238	31	53	1	332	74	†18	.958
	—Oakland (A.L.)	C	20	47	5	10	2	0	0	3	.213	2	15	1	66	10	1	.987
Major league totals (2 years)			29	52	6	14	2	1	0	4	.269	2	16	1	73	10	2	.976

RECORD AS PITCHER

Year	Team (League)	W	L	Pct.	ERA	G	GS	CG	ShO	Sv.	IP	H	R	ER	BB	SO
1991	—Modesto (Calif.)	0	1	.000	81.00	1	0	0	0	0	1	4	9	9	6	2

MERCEDES, JOSE

P, BREWERS

PERSONAL: Born March 5, 1971, in El Seibo, Dominican Republic. . . . 6-1/180. . . . Throws right, bats right. . . . Full name: Jose Miguel Mercedes.

TRANSACTIONS/CAREER NOTES: Signed as free agent by Baltimore Orioles organization (August 10, 1989). . . . Selected by Milwaukee Brewers from Orioles organization in Rule 5 major league draft (December 13, 1993).

Year	Team (League)	W	L	Pct.	ERA	G	GS	CG	ShO	Sv.	IP	H	R	ER	BB	SO
1990	—	Dominican Summer League statistics unavailable.														
1991	—	Dominican Summer League statistics unavailable.														
1992	—GC Orioles (GCL)	2	3	.400	1.78	8	5	2	0	0	35⅓	31	12	7	13	21
	—Kane Co. (Midw.)	3	2	.600	2.66	8	8	2	•2	0	47⅓	40	26	14	15	45
1993	—Bowie (Eastern)	6	8	.429	4.78	26	23	3	0	0	147	170	86	78	65	75

MERCEDES, LUIS

OF, GIANTS

PERSONAL: Born February 20, 1968, in San Pedro de Macoris, Dominican Republic. . . . 6-3/195. . . . Throws right, bats right. . . . Full name: Luis Roberto Mercedes.

TRANSACTIONS/CAREER NOTES: Signed as free agent by Baltimore Orioles organization (February 16, 1987). . . . On Rochester disabled list (July 19-29, 1991). . . . On Rochester suspended list (August 28-September 8, 1991). . . . Traded by Orioles to San Francisco Giants for P Kevin McGehee (April 29, 1993).

STATISTICAL NOTES: Led International League with .435 on-base percentage in 1991. . . . Tied for International League lead in double plays by outfielder with five in 1992.

Year	Team (League)	Pos.	G	AB	R	H	2B	3B	HR	RBI	Avg.	BB	SO	SB	PO	A	E	Avg.
			BATTING												FIELDING			
1988	—Bluefield (Appal.)	2B	59	215	36	59	8	4	0	20	.274	32	39	16	127	152	*26	.915
1989	—Frederick (Caro.)	2B	108	401	62	124	12	5	3	36	*.309	30	62	29	204	305	25	.953
1990	—Hagerstown (East.)	OF	108	416	71	139	12	4	3	37	*.334	34	70	38	157	5	•9	.947
1991	—Rochester (Int'l)	OF-1B	102	374	68	125	14	5	2	36	.334	65	63	23	175	10	8	.959
	—Baltimore (A.L.)	OF	19	54	10	11	2	0	0	2	.204	4	9	0	20	0	0	1.000
1992	—Rochester (Int'l)	OF	103	409	62	128	15	1	3	29	•.313	44	56	35	201	12	8	.964
	—Baltimore (A.L.)	OF	23	50	7	7	2	0	0	4	.140	8	9	0	41	2	2	.956
1993	—Baltimore (A.L.)	OF	10	24	1	7	2	0	0	0	.292	5	4	1	11	1	0	1.000
	—San Francisco (N.L.)■	OF	18	25	1	4	0	1	0	3	.160	1	3	0	5	0	0	1.000
	—Phoenix (PCL)	OF	70	244	28	71	5	3	0	15	.291	36	30	14	104	6	9	.924
American League totals (3 years)			52	128	18	25	6	0	0	6	.195	17	22	1	72	3	2	.974
National League totals (1 year)			18	25	1	4	0	1	0	3	.160	1	3	0	5	0	0	1.000
Major league totals (3 years)			70	153	19	29	6	1	0	9	.190	18	25	1	77	3	2	.976

MERCKER, KENT

P, BRAVES

PERSONAL: Born February 1, 1968, in Dublin, O. . . . 6-2/195. . . . Throws left, bats left. . . . Full name: Kent Franklin Mercker.
HIGH SCHOOL: Dublin (O.).
TRANSACTIONS/CAREER NOTES: Selected by Atlanta Braves organization in first round (fifth pick overall) of free-agent draft (June 2, 1986). . . . On disabled list (March 30-May 6, 1990 and August 9-24, 1991).
HONORS: Named Carolina League co-Pitcher of the Year (1988).
STATISTICAL NOTES: Pitched six innings, combining with Mark Wohlers (two innings) and Alejandro Pena (one inning) in 1-0 no-hit victory against San Diego (September 11, 1991).

Year	Team (League)	W	L	Pct.	ERA	G	GS	CG	ShO	Sv.	IP	H	R	ER	BB	SO
1986	—GC Braves (GCL)	4	3	.571	2.47	9	8	0	0	0	47⅓	37	21	13	16	42
1987	—Durham (Carolina)	0	1	.000	5.40	3	3	0	0	0	11⅔	11	8	7	6	14
1988	—Durham (Carolina)	11	4	.733	*2.75	19	19	5	0	0	127⅔	102	44	39	47	159
	—Greenville (South.)	3	1	.750	3.35	9	9	0	0	0	48⅓	36	20	18	26	60
1989	—Richmond (Int'l)	9	12	.429	3.20	27	•27	4	0	0	168⅔	107	66	60	*95	*144
	—Atlanta (N.L.)	0	0	...	12.46	2	1	0	0	0	4⅓	8	6	6	6	4
1990	—Richmond (Int'l)	5	4	.556	3.55	12	10	0	0	1	58⅓	60	30	23	27	69
	—Atlanta (N.L.)	4	7	.364	3.17	36	0	0	0	7	48⅓	43	22	17	24	39
1991	—Atlanta (N.L.)	5	3	.625	2.58	50	4	0	0	6	73⅓	56	23	21	35	62
1992	—Atlanta (N.L.)	3	2	.600	3.42	53	0	0	0	6	68⅓	51	27	26	35	49
1993	—Atlanta (N.L.)	3	1	.750	2.86	43	6	0	0	0	66	52	24	21	36	59
Major league totals (5 years)		15	13	.536	3.15	184	11	0	0	19	260⅓	210	102	91	136	213

CHAMPIONSHIP SERIES RECORD

CHAMPIONSHIP SERIES NOTES: Shares single-series record for most games pitched—5 (1993).

Year	Team (League)	W	L	Pct.	ERA	G	GS	CG	ShO	Sv.	IP	H	R	ER	BB	SO
1991	—Atlanta (N.L.)	0	1	.000	13.50	1	0	0	0	0	⅔	0	1	1	2	0
1992	—Atlanta (N.L.)	0	0	...	0.00	2	0	0	0	0	3	1	0	0	1	1
1993	—Atlanta (N.L.)	0	0	...	1.80	5	0	0	0	0	5	3	1	1	2	4
Champ. series totals (3 years)		0	1	.000	2.08	8	0	0	0	0	8⅔	4	2	2	5	5

WORLD SERIES RECORD

Year	Team (League)	W	L	Pct.	ERA	G	GS	CG	ShO	Sv.	IP	H	R	ER	BB	SO
1991	—Atlanta (N.L.)	0	0	...	0.00	2	0	0	0	0	1	0	0	0	0	1

MERRIMAN, BRETT

P, TWINS

PERSONAL: Born July 15, 1966, in Jacksonville, Ill. . . . 6-2/216. . . . Throws right, bats right. . . . Full name: Brett Alan Merriman.
HIGH SCHOOL: Nevada (Mo.) R-5.
COLLEGE: Mesa (Ariz.) Community College and Grand Canyon University (Ariz.).
TRANSACTIONS/CAREER NOTES: Selected by Cleveland Indians organization in ninth round of free-agent draft (June 1, 1988). . . . Loaned by Indians organization to Miami, independent (March 31-May 15, 1989). . . . Released by Indians organization (March 31, 1990). . . . Signed by California Angels organization (April 3, 1990). . . . On disabled list (June 26, 1991-remainder of season). . . . Selected by Colorado Rockies in second round (42nd pick overall) of expansion draft (November 17, 1992). . . . Traded by Rockies to Minnesota Twins for P Gary Wayne and P Rob Wassenaar (March 26, 1993).

M

Year	Team (League)	W	L	Pct.	ERA	G	GS	CG	ShO	Sv.	IP	H	R	ER	BB	SO
1988	—Burlington (Appal.)	0	4	.000	2.58	8	8	0	0	0	45⅓	39	20	13	13	45
1989	—Miami (Florida St.)■	0	4	.000	8.05	5	5	0	0	0	19	30	21	17	17	8
	—Watertown (NYP)■	7	5	.583	2.64	14	14	2	2	0	92	75	50	27	44	64
1990	—Midland (Texas)■	1	0	1.000	2.25	2	0	0	0	0	4	7	1	1	0	1
	—Palm Springs (Cal.)	3	10	.231	3.75	24	16	0	0	0	100⅔	106	60	42	55	53
1991	—Palm Springs (Cal.)	4	1	.800	1.96	34	0	0	0	2	41⅓	36	20	9	30	23
1992	—Midland (Texas)	3	4	.429	2.70	38	0	0	0	9	53⅓	49	26	16	10	32
	—Edmonton (PCL)	1	3	.250	1.42	22	0	0	0	4	31⅔	31	10	5	10	15
1993	—Minnesota (A.L.)■	1	1	.500	9.67	19	0	0	0	0	27	36	29	29	23	14
	—Portland (PCL)	5	0	1.000	3.00	39	0	0	0	15	48	46	19	16	18	29
Major league totals (1 year)		1	1	.500	9.67	19	0	0	0	0	27	36	29	29	23	14

MERULLO, MATT

C, WHITE SOX

PERSONAL: Born August 4, 1965, in Ridgefield, Conn. . . . 6-2/200. . . . Throws right, bats left. . . . Full name: Matthew Bates Merullo. . . . Grandson of Lennie Merullo Sr., infielder, Chicago Cubs (1941-47); and son of Lennie Merullo Jr., minor league infielder (1961-64).
HIGH SCHOOL: Fairfield (Conn.) College Prep.
COLLEGE: North Carolina.
TRANSACTIONS/CAREER NOTES: Selected by Chicago White Sox organization in seventh round of free-agent draft (June 2, 1986). . . . On Vancouver disabled list (July 9-17 and July 25-September 16, 1992).
STATISTICAL NOTES: Led Southern League with 21 passed balls in 1988. . . . Led Southern League catchers with 18 errors in 1990.

			BATTING											FIELDING			
Year	Team (League)	Pos.	G	AB	R	H	2B	3B	HR	RBI	Avg.	BB	SO	SB	PO	A	E	Avg.
1986	—Peninsula (Caro.)	C	64	208	21	63	12	2	3	35	.303	19	16	1	225	26	6	.977
1987	—Day. Beach (FSL)	C-1B-OF	70	250	26	65	11	6	4	47	.260	20	18	1	227	28	6	.977
	—Birm. (Southern)	C	48	167	13	46	7	0	2	17	.275	6	20	1	278	24	8	.974
1988	—Birm. (Southern)	C-1B	125	449	58	117	26	0	6	60	.261	40	59	3	640	60	14	.980
1989	—Vancouver (PCL)	C	3	9	0	2	1	0	0	2	.222	2	1	0	19	1	1	.952
	—Chicago (A.L.)	C	31	81	5	18	1	0	1	8	.222	6	14	0	100	10	3	.973
	—Birm. (Southern)	C	33	119	19	35	6	0	3	23	.294	16	15	0	149	10	1	.994
1990	—Birm. (Southern)	C-1B	102	378	57	110	26	1	8	50	.291	34	49	2	561	51	†24	.962

Year	Team (League)	Pos.	G	AB	R	H	2B	3B	HR	RBI	Avg.	BB	SO	SB	PO	A	E	Avg.
			BATTING												FIELDING			
1991	—Chicago (A.L.)	C-1B	80	140	8	32	1	0	5	21	.229	9	18	0	159	14	2	.989
	—Birm. (Southern)	C	8	28	5	6	0	0	2	3	.214	2	4	0	25	3	1	.966
1992	—Chicago (A.L.)	C	24	50	3	9	1	1	0	3	.180	1	8	0	64	3	2	.971
	—Vancouver (PCL)	C-1B	14	45	2	8	1	1	1	4	.178	1	2	0	54	4	2	.967
1993	—Nashville (A.A.)	C-1B	103	352	50	117	30	1	12	65	*.332	28	47	0	435	40	8	.983
	—Chicago (A.L.)	DH	8	20	1	1	0	0	0	0	.050	0	1	0	...	...	...	...
Major league totals (4 years)			143	291	17	60	3	1	6	32	.206	16	41	0	323	27	7	.980

MESA, JOSE

P, INDIANS

PERSONAL: Born May 22, 1966, in Azua, Dominican Republic. . . . 6-3/225. . . . Throws right, bats right. . . . Full name: Jose Ramon Mesa.

HIGH SCHOOL: Santa School (Azua, Dominican Republic).

TRANSACTIONS/CAREER NOTES: Signed as free agent by Toronto Blue Jays organization (October 31, 1981). . . . On Kinston disabled list (August 27, 1984-remainder of season). . . . Traded by Blue Jays organization to Baltimore Orioles (September 4, 1987), completing deal in which Orioles traded P Mike Flanagan to Blue Jays for P Oswald Peraza and a player to be named later (August 31, 1987). . . . On Rochester disabled list (April 18-May 16 and June 30, 1988-remainder of season; May 27, 1989-remainder of season; and August 21-September 5, 1991). . . . Traded by Orioles to Cleveland Indians for OF Kyle Washington (July 14, 1992). . . . On suspended list for three games (April 5-8, 1993).

STATISTICAL NOTES: Tied for Carolina League lead with nine hit batsmen in 1985.

MISCELLANEOUS: Appeared in one game as pinch-runner for Baltimore (1991).

Year	Team (League)	W	L	Pct.	ERA	G	GS	CG	ShO	Sv.	IP	H	R	ER	BB	SO
1982	—GC Blue Jays (GCL)	6	4	.600	2.70	13	12	6	*3	1	83⅓	58	34	25	20	40
1983	—Florence (S. Atl.)	6	12	.333	5.48	28	27	1	0	0	141⅓	153	*116	86	93	91
1984	—Florence (S. Atl.)	4	3	.571	3.76	7	7	0	0	0	38⅓	38	24	16	25	35
	—Kinston (Carolina)	5	2	.714	3.91	10	9	0	0	0	50⅔	51	23	22	28	24
1985	—Kinston (Carolina)	5	10	.333	6.16	30	20	0	0	1	106⅔	110	89	73	79	71
1986	—Vent. Co. (Calif.)	10	6	.625	3.86	24	24	2	1	0	142⅓	141	71	61	58	113
	—Knoxville (South.)	2	2	.500	4.35	9	8	2	1	0	41⅓	40	32	20	23	30
1987	—Knoxville (South.)	10	•13	.435	5.21	35	*35	4	2	0	*193⅓	*206	*131	*112	104	115
	—Baltimore (A.L.)■	1	3	.250	6.03	6	5	0	0	0	31⅓	38	23	21	15	17
1988	—Rochester (Int'l)	0	3	.000	8.62	11	2	0	0	0	15⅔	21	20	15	14	15
1989	—Rochester (Int'l)	0	2	.000	5.40	7	1	0	0	0	10	10	6	6	6	3
	—Hagerstown (East.)	0	0	...	1.38	3	3	0	0	0	13	9	2	2	4	12
1990	—Hagerstown (East.)	5	5	.500	3.42	15	15	3	1	0	79	77	35	30	30	72
	—Rochester (Int'l)	1	2	.333	2.42	4	4	0	0	0	26	21	11	7	12	23
	—Baltimore (A.L.)	3	2	.600	3.86	7	7	0	0	0	46⅔	37	20	20	27	24
1991	—Baltimore (A.L.)	6	11	.353	5.97	23	23	2	1	0	123⅔	151	86	82	62	64
	—Rochester (Int'l)	3	3	.500	3.86	8	8	1	1	0	51⅓	37	25	22	30	48
1992	—Balt.-Clev. (A.L.)■	7	12	.368	4.59	28	27	1	1	0	160⅔	169	86	82	70	62
1993	—Cleveland (A.L.)	10	12	.455	4.92	34	33	3	0	0	208⅔	232	122	114	62	118
Major league totals (5 years)		27	40	.403	5.03	98	95	6	2	0	571	627	337	319	236	285

M

MEULENS, HENSLEY

OF

PERSONAL: Born June 23, 1967, in Curacao, Netherlands Antilles. . . . 6-3/210. . . . Throws right, bats right. . . . Full name: Hensley Filemon Meulens.

TRANSACTIONS/CAREER NOTES: Signed as free agent by New York Yankees organization (October 31, 1985). . . . Released by Yankees (November 26, 1993). . . . Signed by Chiba Lotte Marines of Japan Pacific League (November 26, 1993).

HONORS: Named International League Most Valuable Player (1990).

STATISTICAL NOTES: Led Gulf Coast League third basemen with 178 total chances in 1986. . . . Tied for Eastern League lead in double plays by third baseman with 18 in 1988. . . . Tied for Eastern League lead in being hit by pitch with nine in 1989. . . . Led International League with 245 total bases in 1990 and 257 in 1992. . . . Led International League third basemen with 88 putouts, 30 errors and 373 total chances in 1992.

Year	Team (League)	Pos.	G	AB	R	H	2B	3B	HR	RBI	Avg.	BB	SO	SB	PO	A	E	Avg.
			BATTING												FIELDING			
1986	—GC Yankees (GCL)	3B	59	219	36	51	10	4	4	31	.233	28	*66	4	*40	*118	20	.888
1987	—Prin. William (Car.)	3B-OF	116	430	76	129	23	2	28	103	.300	53	124	14	96	224	*37	.896
	—Fort Lauder. (FSL)	3B	17	58	2	10	3	0	0	2	.172	7	25	0	18	37	7	.887
1988	—Alb./Colon. (East.)	3B	79	278	50	68	9	1	13	40	.245	37	96	3	57	162	23	.905
	—Columbus (Int'l)	3B	55	209	27	48	9	1	6	22	.230	14	61	0	39	111	14	.915
1989	—Alb./Colon. (East.)	3B	104	335	55	86	8	2	11	45	.257	61	108	3	67	172	*29	.892
	—Columbus (Int'l)	3B	14	45	8	13	4	0	1	3	.289	8	13	0	11	27	3	.927
	—New York (A.L.)	3B	8	28	2	5	0	0	0	1	.179	2	8	0	5	23	4	.875
1990	—Columbus (Int'l)	OF-1B-3B	136	480	81	137	20	5	26	96	.285	66	132	6	359	51	13	.969
	—New York (A.L.)	OF	23	83	12	20	7	0	3	10	.241	9	25	1	49	3	2	.963
1991	—New York (A.L.)	OF-1B	96	288	37	64	8	1	6	29	.222	18	97	3	179	5	6	.968
1992	—Columbus (Int'l)	3B-2B	141	534	*96	147	28	2	*26	*100	.275	60	*168	15	†88	255	†30	.920
	—New York (A.L.)	3B	2	5	1	3	0	0	1	1	.600	1	0	0	0	3	0	1.000
1993	—Columbus (Int'l)	OF-1B-3B	75	279	39	57	14	0	14	45	.204	32	92	6	264	20	19	.937
	—New York (A.L.)	OF-1B-3B	30	53	8	9	1	1	2	5	.170	8	19	0	32	0	0	1.000
Major league totals (5 years)			159	457	60	101	16	2	12	46	.221	38	149	4	265	34	12	.961

MICELI, DAN

P, PIRATES

PERSONAL: Born September 9, 1970, in Newark, N.J. . . . 6-0/207. . . . Throws right, bats right.

HIGH SCHOOL: Dr. Phillips (Orlando, Fla.).

TRANSACTIONS/CAREER NOTES: Signed as free agent by Kansas City Royals organization (March 7, 1990). . . . Traded by Royals with P Jon Lieber to Pittsburgh Pirates for P Stan Belinda (July 31, 1993).

Year	Team (League)	W	L	Pct.	ERA	G	GS	CG	ShO	Sv.	IP	H	R	ER	BB	SO
1990	—GC Royals (GCL)	3	4	.429	3.91	*27	0	0	0	4	53	45	27	23	29	48
1991	—Eugene (N'west)	0	1	.000	2.14	25	0	0	0	10	33⅔	18	8	8	18	43
1992	—Appleton (Midw.)	1	1	.500	1.93	23	0	0	0	9	23⅓	12	6	5	4	44
	—Memphis (South.)	3	0	1.000	1.91	32	0	0	0	4	37⅔	20	10	8	13	46
1993	—Mem.-Caro. (Sou.)■	6	6	.500	4.69	53	0	0	0	17	71	65	38	37	43	87
	—Pittsburgh (N.L.)	0	0	...	5.06	9	0	0	0	0	5⅓	6	3	3	3	4
	Major league totals (1 year)	0	0	...	5.06	9	0	0	0	0	5⅓	6	3	3	3	4

MIESKE, MATT

OF, BREWERS

PERSONAL: Born February 13, 1968, in Midland, Mich. . . . 6-0/185. . . . Throws right, bats right. . . . Full name: Matthew Todd Mieske. . . . Name pronounced MEE-SKEE.
HIGH SCHOOL: Bay City Western (Auburn, Mich.).
COLLEGE: Western Michigan.

TRANSACTIONS/CAREER NOTES: Selected by Oakland Athletics organization in 20th round of free-agent draft (June 5, 1989). . . . Selected by San Diego Padres organization in 17th round of free-agent draft (June 4, 1990). . . . Traded by Padres organization with P Ricky Bones and IF Jose Valentin to Milwaukee Brewers organization for 3B Gary Sheffield and P Geoff Kellogg (March 27, 1992). . . . On New Orleans disabled list (May 25-June 10 and June 13-July 29, 1993).
HONORS: Named Northwest League Most Valuable Player (1990). . . . Named California League Most Valuable Player (1991).
STATISTICAL NOTES: Led Northwest League with 155 total bases in 1990. . . . Led Northwest League outfielders with 148 total chances in 1990. . . . Led California League with 261 total bases and .456 on-base percentage in 1991.

			BATTING												FIELDING			
Year	Team (League)	Pos.	G	AB	R	H	2B	3B	HR	RBI	Avg.	BB	SO	SB	PO	A	E	Avg.
1990	—Spokane (N'west)	OF	*76	*291	*59	99	20	0	*12	*63	.340	45	43	26	*134	7	7	.953
1991	—High Desert (Calif.)	OF	•133	492	108	*168	*36	6	15	119	*.341	*94	82	39	258	14	*15	.948
1992	—Denver (A.A.)■	OF	134	*524	80	140	29	11	19	77	.267	39	90	13	252	*23	*13	.955
1993	—New Orleans (A.A.)	OF	60	219	36	57	14	2	8	22	.260	27	46	6	114	4	2	.983
	—Milwaukee (A.L.)	OF	23	58	9	14	0	0	3	7	.241	4	14	0	43	1	3	.936
	Major league totals (1 year)		23	58	9	14	0	0	3	7	.241	4	14	0	43	1	3	.936

MILACKI, BOB

P, ROYALS

PERSONAL: Born July 28, 1964, in Trenton, N.J. . . . 6-4/225. . . . Throws right, bats right. . . . Name pronounced muh-LACK-ee.
HIGH SCHOOL: Lake Havasu (Ariz.).
COLLEGE: Yavapai College (Ariz.).

TRANSACTIONS/CAREER NOTES: Selected by San Diego Padres organization in first round (ninth pick overall) of free-agent draft (January 11, 1983). . . . Selected by Baltimore Orioles organization in secondary phase of free-agent draft (June 6, 1983). . . . On disabled list (July 2-August 28, 1984). . . . On Daytona Beach disabled list (April 12-May 11, 1985). . . . On Hagerstown disabled list (July 5-August 24, 1985). . . . On disabled list (July 31-September 1, 1990). . . . Granted free agency (December 19, 1992). . . . Signed by Oakland Athletics organization (January 29, 1993). . . . Released by A's organization (March 29, 1993). . . . Signed by Cleveland Indians organization (April 6, 1993). . . . On Charlotte disabled list (May 10-July 9, 1993). . . . Granted free agency (October 15, 1993). . . . Signed by Omaha, Kansas City Royals organization (December 9, 1993).
STATISTICAL NOTES: Lost no-hitter in 12th inning against Chattanooga (May 28, 1987); won game in 13 innings. . . . Pitched six innings, combining with Mike Flanagan (one inning), Mark Williamson (one inning) and Gregg Olson (one inning) in 2-0 no-hit victory for Baltimore against Oakland (July 13, 1991).

Year	Team (League)	W	L	Pct.	ERA	G	GS	CG	ShO	Sv.	IP	H	R	ER	BB	SO
1984	—Hagerstown (Car.)	4	5	.444	3.36	15	13	1	0	0	77⅔	69	35	29	48	62
1985	—Day. Beach (FSL)	1	4	.200	3.99	8	6	2	0	0	38⅓	32	23	17	26	24
	—Hagerstown (Car.)	3	2	.600	2.66	7	7	1	0	0	40⅔	32	16	12	22	37
1986	—Hagerstown (Car.)	4	5	.444	4.75	13	12	1	1	0	60⅔	69	59	32	37	46
	—Miami (Florida St.)	4	4	.500	3.74	12	11	0	0	0	67⅓	70	36	28	27	41
	—Charlotte (South.)	0	1	.000	6.75	1	1	0	0	0	5⅓	7	4	4	4	6
1987	—Charlotte (South.)	11	9	.550	4.56	29	24	2	0	1	148	168	86	75	66	101
1988	—Charlotte (South.)	3	1	.750	2.39	5	5	1	0	0	37⅔	26	11	10	12	29
	—Rochester (Int'l)	12	8	.600	2.70	24	24	*11	•3	0	176⅔	174	62	53	65	103
	—Baltimore (A.L.)	2	0	1.000	0.72	3	3	1	1	0	25	9	2	2	9	18
1989	—Baltimore (A.L.)	14	12	.538	3.74	37	•36	3	2	0	243	233	105	101	88	113
1990	—Baltimore (A.L.)	5	8	.385	4.46	27	24	1	1	0	135⅓	143	73	67	61	60
1991	—Hagerstown (East.)	3	0	1.000	1.06	3	3	0	0	0	17	14	3	2	3	18
	—Baltimore (A.L.)	10	9	.526	4.01	31	26	3	1	0	184	175	86	82	53	108
1992	—Baltimore (A.L.)	6	8	.429	5.84	23	20	0	0	1	115⅔	140	78	75	44	51
	—Rochester (Int'l)	7	1	.875	4.57	9	9	3	0	0	61	57	33	31	21	35
1993	—Charlotte (Int'l)■	4	3	.571	3.39	21	7	0	0	4	71⅔	59	31	27	19	46
	—Cleveland (A.L.)	1	1	.500	3.38	5	2	0	0	0	16	19	8	6	11	7
	Major league totals (6 years)	38	38	.500	4.17	126	111	8	5	1	719	719	352	333	266	357

MILCHIN, MIKE

P, DODGERS

PERSONAL: Born February 28, 1968, in Knoxville, Tenn. . . . 6-3/190. . . . Throws left, bats left. . . . Full name: Michael Wayne Milchin.
HIGH SCHOOL: Tucker (Richmond, Tenn.).
COLLEGE: Clemson.

TRANSACTIONS/CAREER NOTES: Selected by St. Louis Cardinals organization in second round of free-agent draft (June 5, 1989). . . . On Louisville disabled list (June 26-July 3 and August 23-September 5, 1991; April 9-May 5 and May 31-July 28, 1992 and July 28-August 7, 1993). . . . Claimed on waivers by Los Angeles Dodgers (October 15, 1993).
MISCELLANEOUS: Member of 1988 U.S. Olympic baseball team.

Year	Team (League)	W	L	Pct.	ERA	G	GS	CG	ShO	Sv.	IP	H	R	ER	BB	SO
1989	—Hamilton (NYP)	1	2	.333	2.18	8	8	0	0	0	41⅓	35	11	10	9	46
	—Springfield (Midw.)	3	2	.600	2.14	6	6	1	0	0	42	30	14	10	10	44

Year	Team (League)	W	L	Pct.	ERA	G	GS	CG	ShO	Sv.	IP	H	R	ER	BB	SO
1990	—St. Peters. (FSL)	6	1	.857	2.77	11	11	1	1	0	68⅓	57	25	21	20	66
	—Arkansas (Texas)	6	8	.429	4.31	17	17	4	2	0	102⅓	103	62	49	47	75
1991	—Arkansas (Texas)	3	2	.600	3.06	6	6	1	1	0	35⅓	27	13	12	8	38
	—Louisville (A.A.)	5	9	.357	5.07	18	18	2	1	0	94	132	64	53	40	47
1992	—Louisville (A.A.)	2	6	.250	5.92	12	12	1	0	0	65⅓	69	46	43	31	37
1993	—Louisville (A.A.)	3	7	.300	3.95	32	17	1	0	0	111⅔	108	56	49	43	72

MILITELLO, SAM

P, YANKEES

PERSONAL: Born November 26, 1969, in Tampa, Fla. . . . 6-3/195. . . . Throws right, bats right. . . . Full name: Sam Salvadore Militello Jr.

HIGH SCHOOL: Thomas Jefferson (Tampa, Fla.).

COLLEGE: University of Tampa (Fla.).

TRANSACTIONS/CAREER NOTES: Selected by New York Yankees organization in sixth round of free-agent draft (June 4, 1990). . . . On Columbus disabled list (May 14-July 5 and July 17-September 6, 1993).

HONORS: Named Carolina League Pitcher of the Year (1991). . . . Named International League Most Valuable Pitcher (1992).

STATISTICAL NOTES: Led International League with 14 hit batsmen in 1992.

Year	Team (League)	W	L	Pct.	ERA	G	GS	CG	ShO	Sv.	IP	H	R	ER	BB	SO
1990	—Oneonta (NYP)	8	2	.800	1.22	13	13	3	2	0	88⅔	53	14	12	24	*119
1991	—Prin. William (Car.)	12	2	.857	1.22	16	16	1	0	0	103⅓	65	19	14	27	113
	—Alb./Colon. (East.)	2	2	.500	2.35	7	7	0	0	0	46	40	14	12	18	55
1992	—Columbus (Int'l)	12	2	.857	*2.29	22	21	3	2	0	141⅓	104	45	36	46	152
	—New York (A.L.)	3	3	.500	3.45	9	9	0	0	0	60	43	24	23	32	42
1993	—New York (A.L.)	1	1	.500	6.75	3	2	0	0	0	9⅓	10	8	7	7	5
	—Columbus (Int'l)	1	3	.250	5.73	7	7	0	0	0	33	36	22	21	20	39
Major league totals (2 years)		4	4	.500	3.89	12	11	0	0	0	69⅓	53	32	30	39	47

MILLER, KEITH

3B, ROYALS

PERSONAL: Born June 12, 1963, in Midland, Mich. . . . 5-11/185. . . . Throws right, bats right. . . . Full name: Keith Alan Miller.

HIGH SCHOOL: All Saints (Bay City, Mich.).

COLLEGE: Oral Roberts.

TRANSACTIONS/CAREER NOTES: Selected by Cleveland Indians organization in 24th round of free-agent draft (June 5, 1981). . . . Selected by New York Yankees organization in second round of free-agent draft (June 4, 1984); pick received as compensation for San Diego Padres signing free agent Goose Gossage. Contract was later voided after it was discovered he had a pre-existing knee injury. . . . Signed as free agent by New York Mets organization (September 6, 1984). . . . On disabled list (April 8-May 20, 1986). . . . On New York disabled list (June 29-September 1, 1987); included rehabilitation assignment to Tidewater (August 21-September 1). . . . On disabled list (April 25-May 17 and August 15-September 1, 1990; and May 27-June 16, 1991). . . . Traded by Mets with OF Kevin McReynolds and IF Gregg Jefferies to Kansas City Royals for P Bret Saberhagen and IF Bill Pecota (December 11, 1991). . . . On disabled list (May 18-June 2 and July 11-August 14, 1992). . . . On Kansas City disabled list (April 6-21, 1993). . . . On Kansas City disabled list (June 5-August 23, 1993); included rehabilitation assignment to Omaha (August 16-23). . . . Granted free agency (December 20, 1993). . . . Re-signed by Royals (December 22, 1993).

STATISTICAL NOTES: Tied for Texas League lead in being hit by pitch with seven in 1986.

			BATTING												FIELDING			
Year	Team (League)	Pos.	G	AB	R	H	2B	3B	HR	RBI	Avg.	BB	SO	SB	PO	A	E	Avg.
1985	—Lynchburg (Caro.)	3B-2B-OF	89	325	51	98	16	5	7	54	.302	39	52	14	103	203	25	.924
	—Jackson (Texas)	2B-SS	46	165	17	37	8	1	3	22	.224	12	38	8	108	132	8	.968
1986	—Jackson (Texas)	2B	94	353	80	116	23	4	5	36	.329	62	56	23	198	272	19	.961
1987	—Tidewater (Int'l)	2B-OF	53	202	29	50	9	1	6	22	.248	14	36	14	112	129	5	.980
	—New York (N.L.)	2B	25	51	14	19	2	2	0	1	.373	2	6	8	21	38	2	.967
1988	—Tidewater (Int'l)	2-S-3-0	42	171	23	48	11	1	1	15	.281	12	19	8	81	111	12	.941
	—New York (N.L.)	2-S-3-0	40	70	9	15	1	1	1	5	.214	6	10	0	34	24	5	.921
1989	—Tidewater (Int'l)	2-0-S-3	48	184	33	49	8	2	1	15	.266	18	24	12	89	109	8	.961
	—New York (N.L.)	2-0-S-3	57	143	15	33	7	0	1	7	.231	5	27	6	90	52	5	.966
1990	—New York (N.L.)	OF-2B-SS	88	233	42	60	8	0	1	12	.258	23	46	16	168	21	4	.979
1991	—New York (N.L.)	2-0-3-S	98	275	41	77	22	1	4	23	.280	23	44	14	165	154	10	.970
1992	—Kansas City (A.L.)■	2B-OF	106	416	57	118	24	4	4	38	.284	31	46	16	230	250	15	.970
1993	—Kansas City (A.L.)	3B-OF-2B	37	108	9	18	3	0	0	3	.167	8	19	3	18	35	6	.898
	—Omaha (A.A.)	3B	6	24	2	7	1	1	0	2	.292	0	2	1	2	8	1	.909
American League totals (2 years)			143	524	66	136	27	4	4	41	.260	39	65	19	248	285	21	.962
National League totals (5 years)			308	772	121	204	40	4	7	48	.264	59	133	44	478	289	26	.967
Major league totals (7 years)			451	1296	187	340	67	8	11	89	.262	98	198	63	726	574	47	.965

MILLER, KURT

P, MARLINS

PERSONAL: Born August 24, 1972, in Tucson, Ariz. . . . 6-5/205. . . . Throws right, bats right. . . . Full name: Kurt Everett Miller.

HIGH SCHOOL: Bowie (Tex.), Tulsa (Okla.) Union and West (Bakersfield, Calif.).

TRANSACTIONS/CAREER NOTES: Selected by Pittsburgh Pirates organization in first round (fifth pick overall) of free-agent draft (June 4, 1990). . . . On Augusta disabled list (July 10-August 3, 1991). . . . Traded by Pirates with a player to be named later to Texas Rangers for 3B Steve Buechele (August 30, 1991); Rangers acquired P Hector Fajardo to complete deal (September 6, 1991). . . . Traded by Rangers with P Robb Nen to Florida Marlins for P Cris Carpenter (July 17, 1993).

STATISTICAL NOTES: Tied for Texas League lead with four balks in 1992.

Year	Team (League)	W	L	Pct.	ERA	G	GS	CG	ShO	Sv.	IP	H	R	ER	BB	SO
1990	—Welland (NYP)	3	2	.600	3.29	14	12	0	0	0	65⅔	59	39	24	37	62
1991	—Augusta (S. Atl.)	6	7	.462	2.50	21	21	2	2	0	115⅓	89	49	32	57	103
1992	—Charlotte (Fla. St.)■	5	4	.556	2.39	12	12	0	0	0	75⅓	51	23	20	29	58
	—Tulsa (Texas)	7	5	.583	3.68	16	15	0	0	0	88	82	42	36	35	73

Year	Team (League)	W	L	Pct.	ERA	G	GS	CG	ShO	Sv.	IP	H	R	ER	BB	SO
1993	—Tulsa (Texas)	6	8	.429	5.06	18	18	0	0	0	96	102	69	54	45	68
	—Edmonton (PCL)■	3	3	.500	4.50	9	9	0	0	0	48	42	24	24	34	19

MILLER, ORLANDO

SS, ASTROS

PERSONAL: Born January 13, 1969, in Changuinola, Panama. . . . 6-1/180. . . . Throws right, bats right. . . . Full name: Orlando Salmon Miller.

TRANSACTIONS/CAREER NOTES: Signed as a free agent by New York Yankees organization (September 17, 1987). . . . Traded by Yankees organization to Houston Astros organization for IF Dave Silvestri and a player to be named later (March 13, 1990); Yankees acquired P Daven Bond to complete deal (June 11, 1990). . . . On Jackson disabled list (May 10-June 8, 1991). . . . On disabled list (April 8-15 and 16-24, 1993).

STATISTICAL NOTES: Led South Atlantic League shortstops with 93 double plays in 1990.

			BATTING											FIELDING			
Year	Team (League)	Pos.	G	AB	R	H	2B	3B	HR	RBI	Avg.	BB	SO	SB	PO	A	E	Avg.
1988	—Fort Lauder. (FSL)	SS	3	11	0	3	0	0	0	1	.273	0	1	0	4	4	0	1.000
	—GC Yankees (GCL)	2B-SS	14	44	5	8	1	0	0	5	.182	3	10	1	19	30	5	.907
1989	—Oneonta (NYP)	2-S-3-0	58	213	29	62	5	2	1	25	.291	6	37	8	96	124	9	.961
1990	—Asheville (S. Atl.)■	SS	121	438	60	137	29	6	4	62	.313	25	52	12	208	348	*47	.922
1991	—Jackson (Texas)	SS	23	70	5	13	6	0	1	5	.186	5	13	0	31	66	12	.890
	—Osceola (Fla. St.)	SS	74	272	27	81	11	2	0	36	.298	13	30	1	106	205	24	.928
1992	—Jackson (Texas)	SS	115	379	51	100	26	5	5	53	.264	16	75	7	132	254	22	.946
	—Tucson (PCL)	SS	10	37	4	9	0	0	2	8	.243	1	2	0	10	26	1	.973
1993	—Tucson (PCL)	SS	122	471	86	143	29	16	16	89	.304	20	95	2	180	389	*33	.945

MILLER, PAUL

P, PIRATES

PERSONAL: Born April 27, 1965, in Burlington, Wis. . . . 6-5/215. . . . Throws right, bats right. . . . Full name: Paul Robert Miller.

HIGH SCHOOL: Burton (Richmond, Ill.).

COLLEGE: Carthage College (Wis.).

TRANSACTIONS/CAREER NOTES: Selected by Cincinnati Reds organization in 27th round of free-agent draft (June 2, 1986). . . . Selected by Pittsburgh Pirates organization in 53rd round of free-agent draft (June 2, 1987). . . . On Carolina disabled list (May 24-June 8, 1991). . . . On Pittsburgh disabled list (April 3-May 5, 1992); included rehabilitation assignment to Buffalo (April 23-May 5). . . . On Buffalo disabled list (July 2-September 15, 1992). . . . On Pittsburgh disabled list (September 16, 1992-remainder of season). . . . On Buffalo disabled list (April 8-June 2 and July 31-August 15, 1993). . . . Granted free agency (October 15, 1993). . . . Re-signed by Pirates organization (January 5, 1994).

STATISTICAL NOTES: Pitched 2-0 no-hit victory against Sarasota (July 27, 1987, first game).

Year	Team (League)	W	L	Pct.	ERA	G	GS	CG	ShO	Sv.	IP	H	R	ER	BB	SO
1987	—GC Pirates (GCL)	3	6	.333	3.20	12	12	1	1	0	70⅓	55	34	25	26	62
1988	—Augusta (S. Atl.)	6	5	.545	2.89	15	15	2	2	0	90⅓	80	34	29	28	51
1989	—Salem (Carolina)	6	12	.333	4.17	26	20	2	1	0	133⅔	138	86	62	64	82
1990	—Salem (Carolina)	8	6	.571	2.45	22	22	5	1	0	150⅔	145	58	41	33	83
	—Harrisburg (East.)	2	1	.667	2.19	5	5	2	1	0	37	27	9	9	10	11
1991	—Carolina (South.)	7	2	.778	2.42	15	15	1	0	0	89⅓	69	29	24	35	69
	—Buffalo (A.A.)	5	2	.714	1.48	10	10	2	0	0	67	41	17	11	29	30
	—Pittsburgh (N.L.)	0	0	...	5.40	1	1	0	0	0	5	4	3	3	3	2
1992	—Buffalo (A.A.)	2	3	.400	3.90	8	7	0	0	0	32⅓	38	23	14	16	18
	—Pittsburgh (N.L.)	1	0	1.000	2.38	6	0	0	0	0	11⅓	11	3	3	1	5
1993	—Carolina (South.)	2	2	.500	2.82	6	6	0	0	0	38⅓	31	15	12	12	33
	—Buffalo (A.A.)	3	1	.750	4.47	10	10	0	0	0	52⅓	57	28	26	14	25
	—Pittsburgh (N.L.)	0	0	...	5.40	3	2	0	0	0	10	15	6	6	2	2
Major league totals (3 years)		1	0	1.000	4.10	10	3	0	0	0	26⅓	30	12	12	6	9

MILLETTE, JOE

SS/2B, PHILLIES

PERSONAL: Born August 12, 1966, in Walnut Creek, Calif. . . . 6-1/180. . . . Throws right, bats right. . . . Full name: Joseph Anthony Millette. . . . Name pronounced mil-LET.

HIGH SCHOOL: Acalanes (Lafayette, Calif.).

COLLEGE: Diablo Valley College (Calif.), then St. Mary's.

TRANSACTIONS/CAREER NOTES: Signed as free agent by Philadelphia Phillies organization (September 4, 1988).

			BATTING											FIELDING			
Year	Team (League)	Pos.	G	AB	R	H	2B	3B	HR	RBI	Avg.	BB	SO	SB	PO	A	E	Avg.
1989	—Batavia (NY-Penn)	SS	11	42	4	10	3	0	0	4	.238	4	6	3	14	39	5	.914
	—Spartanburg (SAL)	SS	60	209	27	50	4	3	0	18	.239	28	36	4	90	166	24	.914
1990	—Clearwater (FSL)	SS-2B	108	295	31	54	5	0	0	18	.183	29	53	4	175	323	31	.941
1991	—Clearwater (FSL)	SS	18	55	6	14	2	0	0	6	.255	7	6	1	27	51	3	.963
	—Reading (Eastern)	SS	115	353	52	87	9	4	3	28	.246	36	54	6	170	342	*32	.941
1992	—Scran./W.B. (Int'l)	SS-3B	78	256	24	68	11	1	1	23	.266	15	30	3	95	233	12	.965
	—Philadelphia (N.L.)	SS-3B-2B	33	78	5	16	0	0	0	2	.205	5	10	1	33	86	3	.975
1993	—Scran./W.B. (Int'l)	SS-2B-3B	107	343	27	77	15	2	1	24	.224	19	56	5	168	257	21	.953
	—Philadelphia (N.L.)	SS-3B	10	10	3	2	0	0	0	2	.200	1	2	0	3	18	0	1.000
Major league totals (2 years)			43	88	8	18	0	0	0	4	.205	6	12	1	36	104	3	.979

MILLIGAN, RANDY

1B, EXPOS

PERSONAL: Born November 27, 1961, in San Diego. . . . 6-1/225. . . . Throws right, bats right. . . . Full name: Randall Andre Milligan.

HIGH SCHOOL: San Diego (Calif.).

COLLEGE: San Diego (Calif.) Mesa College.

TRANSACTIONS/CAREER NOTES: Selected by New York Mets organization in first round (third pick overall) of free-agent draft (January 13, 1981). . . . On disabled list (July 11, 1984-remainder of season). . . . Traded by Mets with P Scott Henion to Pittsburgh Pirates for C Mackey Sasser and P Tim Drummond (March 26, 1988). . . . Traded by Pirates to Baltimore Orioles for a

player to be named later (November 9, 1988); Pirates acquired P Pete Blohm to complete deal (December 7, 1988).... On disabled list (August 10-September 28, 1990).... Granted free agency (December 19, 1992).... Signed by Cincinnati Reds organization (February 1, 1993).... Traded by Reds to Cleveland Indians for a player to be named later (August 17, 1993); Reds acquired OF Thomas Howard to complete deal (August 20, 1993).... Traded by Indians to Montreal Expos for a player to be named later (December 13, 1993); Indians acquired P Brian Barnes to complete deal (December 17, 1993).
HONORS: Named Minor League Player of the Year by THE SPORTING NEWS (1987).... Named International League Player of the Year (1987).
STATISTICAL NOTES: Led International League with 272 total bases and tied for lead with 10 intentional bases on balls received in 1987.... Hit three home runs in one game (June 9, 1990).

			BATTING												FIELDING			
Year	Team (League)	Pos.	G	AB	R	H	2B	3B	HR	RBI	Avg.	BB	SO	SB	PO	A	E	Avg.
1981	—Shelby (S. Atl.)	OF-SS	130	406	90	115	16	6	7	58	.283	98	85	49	174	5	14	.927
1982	—Lynchburg (Caro.)	OF-1B	118	420	63	113	10	6	5	55	.269	54	101	25	341	12	11	.970
1983	—Lynchburg (Caro.)	1B-OF	106	349	60	102	13	5	5	56	.292	85	81	41	558	41	13	.979
1984	—Jackson (Texas)	1B	62	193	32	53	5	0	9	34	.275	53	39	15	475	67	8	.985
1985	—Jackson (Texas)	1B	119	391	60	121	22	2	13	77	.309	53	78	11	726	49	11	.986
1986	—Tidewater (Int'l)	1B	21	60	3	5	0	0	0	3	.083	9	15	0	60	4	1	.985
	—Jackson (Texas)	1B	78	269	53	85	11	3	7	53	.316	60	42	13	684	62	6	.992
1987	—Tidewater (Int'l)	1B-OF	136	457	*99	149	28	4	29	*103	*.326	*91	77	8	858	88	10	.990
	—New York (N.L.)	PH-PR	3	1	0	0	0	0	0	0	.000	1	1	0	...	...	...	...
1988	—Pittsburgh (N.L.)■	1B-OF	40	82	10	18	5	0	3	8	.220	20	24	1	213	15	3	.987
	—Buffalo (A.A.)	1B-OF	63	221	37	61	15	3	2	30	.276	36	40	1	551	48	5	.992
1989	—Baltimore (A.L.)■	1B	124	365	56	98	23	5	12	45	.268	74	75	9	914	83	5	.995
1990	—Baltimore (A.L.)	1B	109	362	64	96	20	1	20	60	.265	88	68	6	846	87	9	.990
1991	—Baltimore (A.L.)	1B-OF	141	483	57	127	17	2	16	70	.263	84	108	0	948	81	11	.989
1992	—Baltimore (A.L.)	1B	137	462	71	111	21	1	11	53	.240	106	81	0	1009	76	7	.994
1993	—Cincinnati (N.L.)■	1B-OF	83	234	30	64	11	1	6	29	.274	46	49	0	477	57	5	.991
	—Cleveland (A.L.)■	1B	19	47	7	20	7	0	0	7	.426	14	4	0	101	7	0	1.000
American League totals (5 years)			530	1719	255	452	88	9	59	235	.263	366	336	15	3818	334	32	.992
National League totals (3 years)			126	317	40	82	16	1	9	37	.259	67	74	1	690	72	8	.990
Major league totals (7 years)			656	2036	295	534	104	10	68	272	.262	433	410	16	4508	406	40	.992

MILLS, ALAN

P, ORIOLES

PERSONAL: Born October 18, 1966, in Lakeland, Fla.... 6-1/192.... Throws right, bats both.... Full name: Alan Bernard Mills.
HIGH SCHOOL: Kathleen (Fla.).
COLLEGE: Polk Community College (Fla.).
TRANSACTIONS/CAREER NOTES: Selected by Boston Red Sox organization in first round (13th pick overall) of free-agent draft (January 14, 1986).... Selected by California Angels organization in secondary phase of free-agent draft (June 2, 1986).... Traded by Angels organization to New York Yankees organization (June 22, 1987), completing deal in which Angels traded P Ron Romanick and a player to be named later to Yankees for C Butch Wynegar (December 19, 1986).... Traded by Yankees to Baltimore Orioles for two players to be named later (February 29, 1992); Yankees acquired P Francisco de la Rosa (February 29, 1992) and P Mark Carper (June 8, 1992) to complete deal.... On suspended list (June 26-30, 1993).

Year	Team (League)	W	L	Pct.	ERA	G	GS	CG	ShO	Sv.	IP	H	R	ER	BB	SO
1986	—Salem (Northwest)	6	6	.500	4.63	14	14	1	0	0	83⅔	77	58	43	60	50
1987	—Prin. William (Car.)■	2	11	.154	6.09	35	8	0	0	1	85⅔	102	75	58	64	53
1988	—Prin. William (Car.)	3	8	.273	4.13	42	5	0	0	4	93⅔	93	56	43	43	59
1989	—Prin. William (Car.)	6	1	.857	0.91	26	0	0	0	7	39⅔	22	5	4	13	44
	—Fort Lauder. (FSL)	1	4	.200	3.77	22	0	0	0	6	31	40	15	13	9	25
1990	—New York (A.L.)	1	5	.167	4.10	36	0	0	0	0	41⅔	48	21	19	33	24
	—Columbus (Int'l)	3	3	.500	3.38	17	0	0	0	6	29⅓	22	11	11	14	30
1991	—Columbus (Int'l)	7	5	.583	4.43	38	15	0	0	8	113⅔	109	65	56	75	77
	—New York (A.L.)	1	1	.500	4.41	6	2	0	0	0	16⅓	16	9	8	8	11
1992	—Rochester (Int'l)■	0	1	.000	5.40	3	0	0	0	1	5	6	3	3	2	8
	—Baltimore (A.L.)	10	4	.714	2.61	35	3	0	0	2	103⅓	78	33	30	54	60
1993	—Baltimore (A.L.)	5	4	.556	3.23	45	0	0	0	4	100⅓	80	39	36	51	68
Major league totals (4 years)		17	14	.548	3.20	122	5	0	0	6	261⅔	222	102	93	146	163

MINCHEY, NATE

P, RED SOX

PERSONAL: Born August 31, 1969, in Austin, Tex.... 6-7/210.... Throws right, bats right.... Full name: Nathan Derek Minchey.
HIGH SCHOOL: Pflugerville (Tex.).
TRANSACTIONS/CAREER NOTES: Selected by Montreal Expos organization in second round of free-agent draft (June 2, 1987); pick received as compensation for Chicago Cubs signing Type A free agent Andre Dawson.... Traded by Expos with P Sergio Valdez and OF Kevin Dean to Atlanta Braves organization for P Zane Smith (July 2, 1989).... Loaned by Braves organization to Miami, independent (April 10-June 19, 1991).... Traded by Braves with OF Sean Ross to Boston Red Sox for P Jeff Reardon (August 30, 1992).
STATISTICAL NOTES: Led Midwest League with 22 wild pitches in 1989.

Year	Team (League)	W	L	Pct.	ERA	G	GS	CG	ShO	Sv.	IP	H	R	ER	BB	SO
1987	—GC Expos (GCL)	3	4	.429	4.94	12	11	2	0	0	54⅔	62	45	30	28	61
1988	—Rockford (Midw.)	11	12	.478	4.79	28	27	0	0	0	150⅓	148	93	80	87	63
1989	—Rock.-Bur. (Midw.)■	5	12	.294	4.67	26	26	1	0	0	156	154	88	*81	82	87
1990	—Durham (Carolina)	4	11	.267	3.79	25	24	2	2	0	133	143	75	56	46	100
1991	—Durham (Carolina)	6	6	.500	2.84	15	12	3	0	0	88⅔	72	31	28	29	77
	—Miami (Florida St.)■	5	3	.625	1.89	13	13	4	1	0	95⅓	81	31	20	31	61
1992	—Greenville (South.)■	•13	6	.684	2.30	28	25	5	•4	0	172	137	51	44	40	115
	—Pawtucket (Int'l)■	2	0	1.000	0.00	2	0	0	0	0	7	3	0	0	0	4

Year	Team (League)	W	L	Pct.	ERA	G	GS	CG	ShO	Sv.	IP	H	R	ER	BB	SO
1993	—Pawtucket (Int'l)	7	*14	.333	4.02	•29	29	*7	2	0	*194⅔	182	*103	87	50	113
	—Boston (A.L.)	1	2	.333	3.55	5	5	1	0	0	33	35	16	13	8	18
Major league totals (1 year)		1	2	.333	3.55	5	5	1	0	0	33	35	16	13	8	18

MINOR, BLAS

P, PIRATES

PERSONAL: Born March 20, 1966, in Merced, Calif.... 6-3/203.... Throws right, bats right.
HIGH SCHOOL: Atwater (Calif.).
COLLEGE: Merced (Calif.) College and Arizona State.
TRANSACTIONS/CAREER NOTES: Selected by Kansas City Royals organization in 11th round of free-agent draft (January 9, 1985).... Selected by Philadelphia Phillies organization in secondary phase of free-agent draft (June 3, 1985).... Selected by Phillies organization in secondary phase of free-agent draft (January 14, 1986).... Selected by Pittsburgh Pirates organization in sixth round of free-agent draft (June 1, 1988).... On Buffalo disabled list (June 8-24 and June 28-August 12, 1991).... On suspended list (September 3-8, 1993).

Year	Team (League)	W	L	Pct.	ERA	G	GS	CG	ShO	Sv.	IP	H	R	ER	BB	SO
1988	—Princeton (Appal.)	0	1	.000	4.41	15	0	0	0	7	16⅓	18	10	8	5	23
1989	—Salem (Carolina)	3	5	.375	3.63	39	4	0	0	0	86⅔	91	43	35	31	62
1990	—Harrisburg (East.)	6	4	.600	3.06	38	6	0	0	5	94	81	41	32	29	98
	—Buffalo (A.A.)	0	1	.000	3.38	1	0	0	0	0	2⅔	2	1	1	2	2
1991	—Buffalo (A.A.)	2	2	.500	5.75	17	3	0	0	0	36	46	27	23	15	25
	—Carolina (South.)	0	0	...	2.84	3	2	0	0	0	12⅔	9	4	4	7	18
1992	—Buffalo (A.A.)	5	4	.556	2.43	45	7	0	0	18	96⅓	72	30	26	26	60
	—Pittsburgh (N.L.)	0	0	...	4.50	1	0	0	0	0	2	3	2	1	0	0
1993	—Pittsburgh (N.L.)	8	6	.571	4.10	65	0	0	0	2	94⅓	94	43	43	26	84
Major league totals (2 years)		8	6	.571	4.11	66	0	0	0	2	96⅓	97	45	44	26	84

MINUTELLI, GINO

P

PERSONAL: Born May 23, 1964, in Wilmington, Del.... 6-0/190.... Throws left, bats left.... Full name: Gino Michael Minutelli.... Name pronounced MIN-you-TELL-ee.
HIGH SCHOOL: Sweetwater (National City, Calif.).
COLLEGE: Southwestern College (Calif.).
TRANSACTIONS/CAREER NOTES: Signed as free agent by Cincinnati Reds organization (May 19, 1985).... On disabled list (April 12-23 and April 27, 1988-remainder of season).... On Plant City disabled list (April 1-August 1, 1989).... On Nashville disabled list (June 3-23, 1991).... On Cincinnati disabled list (June 30-July 15, 1991); included rehabilitation assignment to Charleston, W.Va. (July 7-15).... Granted free agency (September 22, 1992).... Signed by Phoenix, San Francisco Giants organization (December 20, 1992).... Granted free agency (December 20, 1993).
STATISTICAL NOTES: Led Southern League with 13 balks in 1990.

Year	Team (League)	W	L	Pct.	ERA	G	GS	CG	ShO	Sv.	IP	H	R	ER	BB	SO
1985	—Tri-Cities (N'west)	4	•8	.333	8.05	20	10	0	0	0	57	61	57	51	57	79
1986	—Ced. Rap. (Midw.)	15	5	.750	3.66	27	27	3	2	0	152⅔	133	73	62	76	149
1987	—Tampa (Fla. St.)	7	6	.538	3.80	17	15	5	1	0	104⅓	98	51	44	48	70
	—Vermont (Eastern)	4	1	.800	3.18	6	6	0	0	0	39⅔	34	15	14	16	39
1988	—Chatt. (South.)	0	1	.000	1.59	2	2	0	0	0	5⅔	6	2	1	4	3
1989	—GC Reds (GCL)	0	0	...	0.00	1	1	0	0	0	1	0	0	0	1	0
	—Chatt. (South.)	1	1	.500	5.28	6	6	1	0	0	29	28	19	17	23	20
1990	—Chatt. (South.)	9	5	.643	3.99	17	17	5	0	0	108⅓	106	52	48	46	75
	—Nashville (A.A.)	5	2	.714	3.22	11	11	3	0	0	78⅓	65	34	28	31	61
	—Cincinnati (N.L.)	0	0	...	9.00	2	0	0	0	0	1	0	1	1	2	0
1991	—Nashville (A.A.)	4	7	.364	1.90	13	13	1	1	0	80⅓	57	25	17	35	64
	—Cincinnati (N.L.)	0	2	.000	6.04	16	3	0	0	0	25⅓	30	17	17	18	21
	—Char., W.Va. (SAL)	1	0	1.000	0.00	2	2	0	0	0	8	2	0	0	4	8
1992	—Nashville (A.A.)	4	12	.250	4.27	29	*29	1	0	0	158	177	96	75	76	110
1993	—Phoenix (PCL)■	2	2	.500	4.02	49	0	0	0	11	53⅔	55	28	24	26	57
	—San Francisco (N.L.)	0	1	.000	3.77	9	0	0	0	0	14⅓	7	9	6	15	10
Major league totals (3 years)		0	3	.000	5.31	27	3	0	0	0	40⅔	37	27	24	35	31

MIRANDA, ANGEL

P, BREWERS

PERSONAL: Born November 9, 1969, in Arecibo, Puerto Rico.... 6-1/195.... Throws left, bats left.... Full name: Angel Luis Miranda.
HIGH SCHOOL: Maria Cadillo (Arecibo, Puerto Rico).
TRANSACTIONS/CAREER NOTES: Signed as free agent by Milwaukee Brewers organization (March 4, 1987).... Loaned by Brewers organization to Butte, co-op (March 4, 1987).... On Milwaukee disabled list (March 27-June 1, 1993); included rehabilitation assignment to New Orleans (May 4-June 1).
STATISTICAL NOTES: Led American Association with six balks in 1992.

Year	Team (League)	W	L	Pct.	ERA	G	GS	CG	ShO	Sv.	IP	H	R	ER	BB	SO
1987	—Butte-Helena (Pio.)■	1	2	.333	3.12	25	0	0	0	3	43⅓	27	22	15	26	60
1988	—Stockton (Calif.)	0	1	.000	7.18	16	0	0	0	2	26⅓	20	30	21	37	36
	—Helena (Pioneer)	5	2	.714	3.86	14	11	0	0	0	60⅔	54	32	26	58	75
1989	—Beloit (Midwest)	6	5	.545	0.86	43	0	0	0	16	63	39	13	6	32	88
1990	—Stockton (Calif.)	9	4	.692	2.66	52	9	2	1	24	108⅓	75	37	32	49	138
1991	—El Paso (Texas)	4	2	.667	2.54	38	0	0	0	11	74⅓	55	27	21	41	86
	—Denver (A.A.)	0	1	.000	6.17	11	0	0	0	2	11⅔	10	9	8	17	14
1992	—Denver (A.A.)	6	12	.333	4.77	28	27	1	1	0	160⅓	183	100	85	*77	122
1993	—New Orleans (A.A.)	0	1	.000	3.44	9	2	0	0	0	18⅓	11	8	7	10	24
	—Milwaukee (A.L.)	4	5	.444	3.30	22	17	2	0	0	120	100	53	44	52	88
Major league totals (1 year)		4	5	.444	3.30	22	17	2	0	0	120	100	53	44	52	88

MITCHELL, KEVIN

OF, REDS

PERSONAL: Born January 13, 1962, in San Diego. . . . 5-11/248. . . . Throws right, bats right. . . . Full name: Kevin Darrell Mitchell. . . . Cousin of Keith Mitchell, outfielder, Seattle Mariners organization.
HIGH SCHOOL: Clairmont (San Diego).
TRANSACTIONS/CAREER NOTES: Signed as free agent by New York Mets organization (November 16, 1980). . . . On disabled list (July 21, 1982-remainder of season and July 12-30, 1985). . . . Traded by Mets with OF Shawn Abner, OF Stanley Jefferson, P Kevin Armstrong and P Kevin Brown to San Diego Padres for OF Kevin McReynolds, P Gene Walter and IF Adam Ging (December 11, 1986). . . . Traded by Padres with P Dave Dravecky and P Craig Lefferts to San Francisco Giants for 3B Chris Brown, P Keith Comstock, P Mark Davis and P Mark Grant (July 4, 1987). . . . On suspended list for one game (May 3, 1991). . . . On disabled list (June 3-25, 1991). . . . Traded by Giants with P Mike Remlinger to Seattle Mariners for P Bill Swift, P Mike Jackson and P Dave Burba (December 11, 1991). . . . On disabled list (August 8-23 and September 2, 1992-remainder of season). . . . Traded by Mariners to Cincinnati Reds for P Norm Charlton (November 17, 1992). . . . On disabled list (July 9-24, 1993). . . . Suspended by Reds for two games (July 24-25, 1993). . . . On disabled list (September 10, 1993-remainder of season).
RECORDS: Holds major league single-season record for most intentional bases on balls received by righthanded batter—32 (1989).
HONORS: Named Major League Player of the Year by THE SPORTING NEWS (1989). . . . Named N.L. Player of the Year by THE SPORTING NEWS (1989). . . . Named outfielder on THE SPORTING NEWS N.L. All-Star team (1989). . . . Named outfielder on THE SPORTING NEWS N.L. Silver Slugger team (1989). . . . Named N.L. Most Valuable Player by Baseball Writers' Association of America (1989).
STATISTICAL NOTES: Led Texas League third basemen with 224 assists in 1983. . . . Led International League third basemen with 215 assists in 1984. . . . Led International League third basemen with 22 errors in 1985. . . . Led N.L. with 345 total bases, 32 intentional bases on balls received and .635 slugging percentage in 1989. . . . Hit three home runs in one game (May 25, 1990).

			BATTING												FIELDING			
Year	Team (League)	Pos.	G	AB	R	H	2B	3B	HR	RBI	Avg.	BB	SO	SB	PO	A	E	Avg.
1981	—Kingsport (Appal.)	3B-OF	62	221	39	74	9	2	7	45	.335	22	31	5	44	102	18	.890
1982	—Lynchburg (Caro.)	3B	29	85	19	27	5	1	1	16	.318	13	25	0	11	33	10	.815
1983	—Jackson (Texas)	3B-OF	120	441	75	132	25	2	15	85	.299	48	84	11	81	†224	21	.936
1984	—Tidewater (Int'l)	3B-1B-OF	120	432	51	105	21	3	10	54	.243	25	89	1	114	†220	22	.938
	—New York (N.L.)	3B	7	14	0	3	0	0	0	1	.214	0	3	0	1	4	1	.833
1985	—Tidewater (Int'l)	3B-1B	95	348	44	101	24	2	9	43	.290	32	60	3	56	209	†22	.923
1986	—New York (N.L.)	O-S-3-1	108	328	51	91	22	2	12	43	.277	33	61	3	158	69	10	.958
1987	—S.D.-S.F. (N.L.)■	3B-OF-SS	131	464	68	130	20	2	22	70	.280	48	88	9	76	240	15	.955
1988	—San Francisco (N.L.)	3B-OF	148	505	60	127	25	7	19	80	.251	48	85	5	118	205	22	.936
1989	—San Francisco (N.L.)	OF-3B	154	543	100	158	34	6	*47	*125	.291	87	115	3	305	10	7	.978
1990	—San Francisco (N.L.)	OF	140	524	90	152	24	2	35	93	.290	58	87	4	295	9	9	.971
1991	—San Francisco (N.L.)	OF-1B	113	371	52	95	13	1	27	69	.256	43	57	2	188	6	6	.970
1992	—Seattle (A.L.)■	OF	99	360	48	103	24	0	9	67	.286	35	46	0	130	4	0	1.000
1993	—Cincinnati (N.L.)■	OF	93	323	56	110	21	3	19	64	.341	25	48	1	149	7	7	.957
American League totals (1 year)			99	360	48	103	24	0	9	67	.286	35	46	0	130	4	0	1.000
National League totals (8 years)			894	3072	477	866	159	23	181	545	.282	342	544	27	1290	550	77	.960
Major league totals (9 years)			993	3432	525	969	183	23	190	612	.282	377	590	27	1420	554	77	.962

CHAMPIONSHIP SERIES RECORD

CHAMPIONSHIP SERIES NOTES: Shares N.L. single-series record for most at-bats—30 (1987).

			BATTING												FIELDING			
Year	Team (League)	Pos.	G	AB	R	H	2B	3B	HR	RBI	Avg.	BB	SO	SB	PO	A	E	Avg.
1986	—New York (N.L.)	OF	2	8	1	2	0	0	0	0	.250	0	1	0	3	0	0	1.000
1987	—San Francisco (N.L.)	3B	7	30	2	8	1	0	1	2	.267	0	3	1	4	11	1	.938
1989	—San Francisco (N.L.)	OF	5	17	5	6	0	0	2	7	.353	3	0	0	15	1	1	.941
Championship series totals (3 years)			14	55	8	16	1	0	3	9	.291	3	4	1	22	12	2	.944

WORLD SERIES RECORD

			BATTING												FIELDING			
Year	Team (League)	Pos.	G	AB	R	H	2B	3B	HR	RBI	Avg.	BB	SO	SB	PO	A	E	Avg.
1986	—New York (N.L.)	PH-OF-DH	5	8	1	2	0	0	0	0	.250	0	3	0	0	2	0	1.000
1989	—San Francisco (N.L.)	OF	4	17	2	5	0	0	1	2	.294	0	3	0	10	0	1	.909
World Series totals (2 years)			9	25	3	7	0	0	1	2	.280	0	6	0	10	2	1	.923

ALL-STAR GAME RECORD

			BATTING											FIELDING			
Year	League	Pos.	AB	R	H	2B	3B	HR	RBI	Avg.	BB	SO	SB	PO	A	E	Avg.
1989	—National	OF	4	1	2	0	0	0	1	.500	0	2	0	0	0	0	...
1990	—National	OF	2	0	0	0	0	0	0	.000	0	1	0	1	0	0	1.000
All-Star Game totals (2 years)			6	1	2	0	0	0	1	.333	0	3	0	1	0	0	1.000

MLICKI, DAVE

P, INDIANS

PERSONAL: Born June 8, 1968, in Cleveland. . . . 6-4/190. . . . Throws right, bats right. . . . Full name: David John Mlicki. . . . Brother of Doug Mlicki, pitcher, Houston Astros organization. . . . Name pronounced muh-LICK-ee.
HIGH SCHOOL: Cheyenne Mountain (Colorado Springs, Colo.).
COLLEGE: Oklahoma State.
TRANSACTIONS/CAREER NOTES: Selected by Seattle Mariners organization in 23rd round of free-agent draft (June 5, 1989). . . . Selected by Cleveland Indians organization in 17th round of free-agent draft (June 4, 1990). . . . On Cleveland disabled list (April 4-August 4, 1993); included rehabilitation assignment to Canton/Akron (July 19-August 4).

Year	Team (League)	W	L	Pct.	ERA	G	GS	CG	ShO	Sv.	IP	H	R	ER	BB	SO
1990	—Burlington (Appal.)	3	1	.750	3.50	8	1	0	0	0	18	16	11	7	6	17
	—Watertown (NYP)	3	0	1.000	3.38	7	4	0	0	0	32	33	15	12	11	28

Year	Team (League)	W	L	Pct.	ERA	G	GS	CG	ShO	Sv.	IP	H	R	ER	BB	SO
1991	—Columbus (S. Atl.)	8	6	.571	4.20	22	19	2	0	0	115⅔	101	70	54	70	136
1992	—Cant./Akr. (East.)	11	9	.550	3.60	27	*27	2	0	0	172⅔	143	77	69	•80	146
	—Cleveland (A.L.)	0	2	.000	4.98	4	4	0	0	0	21⅔	23	14	12	16	16
1993	—Cant./Akr. (East.)	2	1	.667	0.39	6	6	0	0	0	23	15	2	1	8	21
	—Cleveland (A.L.)	0	0	...	3.38	3	3	0	0	0	13⅓	11	6	5	6	7
	Major league totals (2 years)	0	2	.000	4.37	7	7	0	0	0	35	34	20	17	22	23

MOELLER, DENNIS

P, ROYALS

PERSONAL: Born September 15, 1967, in Tarzana, Calif.... 6-2/195.... Throws left, bats right.... Full name: Dennis Michael Moeller.... Name pronounced MOLE-ler.

HIGH SCHOOL: Cleveland (Reseda, Calif.).

COLLEGE: Los Angeles Valley College.

TRANSACTIONS/CAREER NOTES: Selected by Kansas City Royals organization in 17th round of free-agent draft (June 2, 1986).... On Memphis disabled list (July 26, 1989-remainder of season).... Traded by Royals with P Joel Johnston to Pittsburgh Pirates for 2B Jose Lind (November 19, 1992).... On Buffalo disabled list (July 10-24, 1993).... Granted free agency (October 15, 1993).... Signed by Omaha, Royals organization (November 28, 1993).

STATISTICAL NOTES: Tied for American Association lead with five balks in 1993.

Year	Team (League)	W	L	Pct.	ERA	G	GS	CG	ShO	Sv.	IP	H	R	ER	BB	SO
1986	—Eugene (N'west)	4	0	1.000	3.06	14	11	0	0	0	61⅔	54	22	21	34	65
1987	—Appleton (Midw.)	2	5	.286	7.20	18	13	0	0	0	55	72	63	44	45	49
1988	—Appleton (Midw.)	3	5	.375	3.18	20	18	0	0	0	99	94	46	35	34	88
1989	—Baseball City (FSL)	9	0	1.000	1.77	12	11	2	0	0	71	59	17	14	20	64
	—Memphis (South.)	1	1	.500	2.84	5	5	0	0	0	25⅓	16	9	8	10	21
1990	—Omaha (A.A.)	5	2	.714	4.02	11	11	1	1	0	65	63	29	29	30	53
	—Memphis (South.)	7	6	.538	6.25	14	14	0	0	0	67⅔	79	55	47	30	42
1991	—Omaha (A.A.)	7	3	.700	3.22	14	14	0	0	0	78⅓	70	36	28	40	51
	—Memphis (South.)	4	5	.444	2.55	10	10	0	0	0	53	52	24	15	21	54
1992	—Omaha (A.A.)	8	5	.615	*2.46	23	16	3	1	2	120⅔	121	36	33	34	56
	—Kansas City (A.L.)	0	3	.000	7.00	5	4	0	0	0	18	24	17	14	11	6
1993	—Pittsburgh (N.L.)■	1	0	1.000	9.92	10	0	0	0	0	16⅓	26	20	18	7	13
	—Buffalo (A.A.)	3	4	.429	4.34	24	11	0	0	0	76⅔	85	43	37	21	38
	A.L. totals (1 year)	0	3	.000	7.00	5	4	0	0	0	18	24	17	14	11	6
	N.L. totals (1 year)	1	0	1.000	9.92	10	0	0	0	0	16⅓	26	20	18	7	13
	Major league totals (2 years)	1	3	.250	8.39	15	4	0	0	0	34⅓	50	37	32	18	19

MOHLER, MIKE

P, ATHLETICS

PERSONAL: Born July 26, 1968, in Dayton, O.... 6-2/195.... Throws left, bats right.... Full name: Michael Ross Mohler.

HIGH SCHOOL: East Ascension (Gonzales, La.).

COLLEGE: Nicholls (La.) State.

TRANSACTIONS/CAREER NOTES: Selected by Oakland Athletics organization in 42nd round of free-agent draft (June 5, 1989).

Year	Team (League)	W	L	Pct.	ERA	G	GS	CG	ShO	Sv.	IP	H	R	ER	BB	SO
1990	—Madison (Midwest)	1	1	.500	3.41	42	2	0	0	1	63⅓	56	34	24	32	72
1991	—Modesto (Calif.)	9	4	.692	2.86	21	20	1	0	0	122⅔	106	48	39	45	98
	—Huntsville (South.)	4	2	.667	3.57	8	8	0	0	0	53	55	22	21	20	27
1992	—Huntsville (South.)	3	8	.273	3.59	44	6	0	0	3	80⅓	72	41	32	39	56
1993	—Oakland (A.L.)	1	6	.143	5.60	42	9	0	0	0	64⅓	57	45	40	44	42
	Major league totals (1 year)	1	6	.143	5.60	42	9	0	0	0	64⅓	57	45	40	44	42

MOLINA, ISLAY

C, ATHLETICS

PERSONAL: Born June 3, 1971, in New York.... 6-1/200.... Throws right, bats right.

HIGH SCHOOL: Christopher Columbus (Miami).

TRANSACTIONS/CAREER NOTES: Selected by Oakland Athletics organization in 22nd round of free-agent draft (June 4, 1990).

STATISTICAL NOTES: Tied for Arizona League lead in errors by catcher with six in 1990.... Tied for Midwest League lead in double plays by catcher with eight in 1991.... Tied for California League lead in grounding into double plays with 20 in 1992.... Led California League catchers with 871 total chances and 28 passed balls in 1992.... Led California League catchers with 740 putouts, 119 assists, 15 errors, 874 total chances, 11 double plays and 20 passed balls in 1993.

			BATTING												FIELDING			
Year	Team (League)	Pos.	G	AB	R	H	2B	3B	HR	RBI	Avg.	BB	SO	SB	PO	A	E	Avg.
1990	—Ariz. A's (Arizona)	C-1B	39	127	20	43	12	2	0	18	.339	9	22	5	261	17	‡6	.979
1991	—Madison (Midwest)	C	95	316	35	89	16	1	3	45	.282	15	38	6	560	63	8	.987
1992	—Reno (California)	C	116	436	71	113	17	2	10	75	.259	39	57	8	*716	*139	16	.982
	—Tacoma (PCL)	C	10	36	3	7	0	1	0	5	.194	2	6	1	52	4	0	1.000
1993	—Modesto (Calif.)	C-OF	125	444	61	116	26	5	6	69	.261	44	85	2	†740	†119	†15	.983

MOLITOR, PAUL

DH/1B, BLUE JAYS

PERSONAL: Born August 22, 1956, in St. Paul, Minn.... 6-0/180.... Throws right, bats right.... Full name: Paul Leo Molitor.

HIGH SCHOOL: Cretin (St. Paul).

COLLEGE: Minnesota.

TRANSACTIONS/CAREER NOTES: Selected by St. Louis Cardinals organization in 28th round of free-agent draft (June 5, 1974).... Selected by Milwaukee Brewers organization in first round (third pick overall) of free-agent draft (June 7, 1977).... On disabled list (June 24-July 18, 1980; May 3-August 12, 1981; May 2, 1984-remainder of season; August 13-28, 1985; May 10-30, June 2-17 and June 19-July 8, 1986; and April 30-May 26 and June 27-July 16, 1987).... Granted free agency (November 9, 1987).... Re-signed by Brewers (January 5, 1988).... On disabled list (March 30-April 14, 1989).... On Milwaukee disabled list (April 2-27, 1990).... On Milwaukee disabled list (June 17-July 30, 1990); included rehabilitation assignment to

Beloit (July 28).... Granted free agency (October 30, 1992).... Signed by Toronto Blue Jays (December 7, 1992).
RECORDS: Shares major league record for most stolen bases in one inning—3 (July 26, 1987, first inning).
HONORS: Named shortstop on THE SPORTING NEWS college All-America team (1977).... Named Midwest League Most Valuable Player (1977).... Named A.L. Rookie Player of the Year by THE SPORTING NEWS (1978).... Named designated hitter on THE SPORTING NEWS A.L. All-Star team (1987 and 1993).... Named designated hitter on THE SPORTING NEWS A.L. Silver Slugger team (1987-88 and 1993).
STATISTICAL NOTES: Hit three home runs in one game (May 12, 1982).... Led A.L. third basemen with 29 errors and 48 double plays in 1982.... Hit for the cycle (May 15, 1991).

			BATTING												FIELDING			
Year	Team (League)	Pos.	G	AB	R	H	2B	3B	HR	RBI	Avg.	BB	SO	SB	PO	A	E	Avg.
1977	—Burlington (Midw.)...	SS	64	228	52	79	12	0	8	50	.346	47	25	14	83	207	28	.912
1978	—Milwaukee (A.L.)......	2B-SS-3B	125	521	73	142	26	4	6	45	.273	19	54	30	253	401	22	.967
1979	—Milwaukee (A.L.)......	2B-SS	140	584	88	188	27	16	9	62	.322	48	48	33	309	440	16	.979
1980	—Milwaukee (A.L.)......	2B-SS-3B	111	450	81	137	29	2	9	37	.304	48	48	34	260	336	20	.968
1981	—Milwaukee (A.L.)......	OF	64	251	45	67	11	0	2	19	.267	25	29	10	119	4	3	.976
1982	—Milwaukee (A.L.)......	3B-SS	160	*666	*136	201	26	8	19	71	.302	69	93	41	134	350	†32	.938
1983	—Milwaukee (A.L.)......	3B	152	608	95	164	28	6	15	47	.270	59	74	41	105	343	16	.966
1984	—Milwaukee (A.L.)......	3B	13	46	3	10	1	0	0	6	.217	2	8	1	7	21	2	.933
1985	—Milwaukee (A.L.)......	3B	140	576	93	171	28	3	10	48	.297	54	80	21	126	263	19	.953
1986	—Milwaukee (A.L.)......	3B-OF	105	437	62	123	24	6	9	55	.281	40	81	20	86	171	15	.945
1987	—Milwaukee (A.L.)......	3B-2B	118	465	*114	164	*41	5	16	75	.353	69	67	45	60	113	5	.972
1988	—Milwaukee (A.L.)......	3B-2B	154	609	115	190	34	6	13	60	.312	71	54	41	87	188	17	.942
1989	—Milwaukee (A.L.)......	3B-2B	155	615	84	194	35	4	11	56	.315	64	67	27	106	287	18	.956
1990	—Milwaukee (A.L.)......	2B-1B-3B	103	418	64	119	27	6	12	45	.285	37	51	18	463	222	10	.986
	—Beloit (Midwest).......	DH	1	4	1	2	0	0	1	1	.500	0	0	0	...	...	...	...
1991	—Milwaukee (A.L.)......	1B	158	*665	*133	*216	32	•13	17	75	.325	77	62	19	389	32	6	.986
1992	—Milwaukee (A.L.)......	1B	158	609	89	195	36	7	12	89	.320	73	66	31	461	26	2	.996
1993	—Toronto (A.L.)■........	1B	160	636	121	*211	37	5	22	111	.332	77	71	22	178	14	3	.985
Major league totals (16 years)................			2016	8156	1396	2492	442	91	182	901	.306	832	953	434	3143	3211	206	.969

DIVISION SERIES RECORD

			BATTING												FIELDING			
Year	Team (League)	Pos.	G	AB	R	H	2B	3B	HR	RBI	Avg.	BB	SO	SB	PO	A	E	Avg.
1981	—Milwaukee (A.L.)......	OF	5	20	2	5	0	0	1	1	.250	2	5	0	12	0	0	1.000

CHAMPIONSHIP SERIES RECORD

CHAMPIONSHIP SERIES NOTES: Holds single-series record for most consecutive hits—6 (1993).... Shares career record for most consecutive hits—6 (1993).

			BATTING												FIELDING			
Year	Team (League)	Pos.	G	AB	R	H	2B	3B	HR	RBI	Avg.	BB	SO	SB	PO	A	E	Avg.
1982	—Milwaukee (A.L.)......	3B	5	19	4	6	1	0	2	5	.316	2	3	1	4	11	2	.882
1993	—Toronto (A.L.)..........	DH	6	23	7	9	2	1	1	5	.391	3	3	0	...	...	...	...
Championship series totals (2 years).......			11	42	11	15	3	1	3	10	.357	5	6	1	4	11	2	.882

WORLD SERIES RECORD

WORLD SERIES NOTES: Named Most Valuable Player (1993).... Holds single-game records for most hits—5; and most singles—5 (October 12, 1982).... Shares single-series record for most runs—10 (1993).... Shares single-game record (nine innings) for most at-bats—6 (October 12, 1982).

			BATTING												FIELDING			
Year	Team (League)	Pos.	G	AB	R	H	2B	3B	HR	RBI	Avg.	BB	SO	SB	PO	A	E	Avg.
1982	—Milwaukee (A.L.)......	3B	7	31	5	11	0	0	0	3	.355	2	4	1	4	9	0	1.000
1993	—Toronto (A.L.)..........	DH-3B-1B	6	24	10	12	2	2	2	8	.500	3	0	1	7	3	0	1.000
World Series totals (2 years)..................			13	55	15	23	2	2	2	11	.418	5	4	2	11	12	0	1.000

ALL-STAR GAME RECORD

			BATTING											FIELDING			
Year	League	Pos.	AB	R	H	2B	3B	HR	RBI	Avg.	BB	SO	SB	PO	A	E	Avg.
1980	—American..................		Selected, did not play—injured.														
1985	—American..................	3B-OF	1	0	0	0	0	0	0	.000	0	0	0	0	0	0	...
1988	—American..................	2B	3	0	0	0	0	0	0	.000	0	1	0	1	2	0	1.000
1991	—American..................	3B	0	0	0	0	0	0	0	...	0	0	0	0	0	0	...
1992	—American..................	PH-1B	2	0	1	0	0	0	0	.500	0	1	0	5	0	1	.833
1993	—American..................	DH	1	0	0	0	0	0	0	.000	1	0	0	...	...	...	...
All-Star Game totals (5 years).....................			7	0	1	0	0	0	0	.143	1	2	0	6	2	1	.889

MONDESI, RAUL

OF, DODGERS

PERSONAL: Born March 12, 1971, in San Cristobal, Dominican Republic.... 5-11/202.... Throws right, bats right.... Name pronounced MON-de-see.
HIGH SCHOOL: Liceo Manuel Maria Valencia (Dominican Republic).
TRANSACTIONS/CAREER NOTES: Signed as free agent by Los Angeles Dodgers organization (June 6, 1988).... On Bakersfield disabled list (May 8-July 5, 1991).... On Albuquerque disabled list (May 8-16, 1992).... On San Antonio disabled list (June 2-16, June 24-August 10 and August 24, 1992-remainder of season).

			BATTING												FIELDING			
Year	Team (League)	Pos.	G	AB	R	H	2B	3B	HR	RBI	Avg.	BB	SO	SB	PO	A	E	Avg.
1990	—Great Falls (Pio.)......	OF	44	175	35	53	10	4	8	31	.303	11	30	30	65	4	1	.986
1991	—Bakersfield (Calif.)...	OF	28	106	23	30	7	2	3	13	.283	5	21	9	42	5	3	.940
	—San Antonio (Tex.)...	OF	53	213	32	58	11	5	5	26	.272	8	47	8	101	6	4	.964
	—Albuquerque (PCL)..	OF	2	9	3	3	0	1	0	0	.333	0	1	1	0	0	1	.000

Year Team (League)	Pos.	BATTING G	AB	R	H	2B	3B	HR	RBI	Avg.	BB	SO	SB	FIELDING PO	A	E	Avg.
1992 —Albuquerque (PCL) ..	OF	35	138	23	43	4	7	4	15	.312	9	35	2	89	8	7	.933
—San Antonio (Tex.)...	OF	18	68	8	18	2	2	2	14	.265	1	24	3	31	6	1	.974
1993 —Albuquerque (PCL) ..	OF	110	425	65	119	22	7	12	65	.280	18	85	13	211	10	10	.957
—Los Angeles (N.L.) ...	OF	42	86	13	25	3	1	4	10	.291	4	16	4	55	3	3	.951
Major league totals (1 year)		42	86	13	25	3	1	4	10	.291	4	16	4	55	3	3	.951

MONTELEONE, RICH

P, GIANTS

PERSONAL: Born March 22, 1963, in Tampa, Fla. . . . 6-2/214. . . . Throws right, bats right. . . . Name pronounced MON-ta-lee-YONE.

HIGH SCHOOL: Tampa (Fla.) Catholic.

TRANSACTIONS/CAREER NOTES: Selected by Detroit Tigers organization in first round (20th pick overall) of free-agent draft (June 7, 1982). . . . Traded by Tigers organization to Seattle Mariners for 3B Darnell Coles (December 12, 1985). . . . Released by Mariners organization (May 9, 1988). . . . Signed by Edmonton, California Angels organization (May 13, 1988). . . . Traded by Angels organization with OF Claudell Washington to New York Yankees for OF Luis Polonia (April 28, 1990). . . . Granted free agency (October 15, 1993). . . . Signed by San Francisco Giants organization (November 9, 1993).

STATISTICAL NOTES: Led Appalachian League pitchers with eight home runs allowed in 1982.

Year Team (League)	W	L	Pct.	ERA	G	GS	CG	ShO	Sv.	IP	H	R	ER	BB	SO
1982 —Bristol (Appal.)	4	6	.400	3.89	12	12	2	0	0	71⅔	66	41	31	23	52
1983 —Lakeland (Fla. St.)	9	8	.529	4.11	24	24	1	0	0	142⅓	146	80	65	80	124
—Birm. (Southern)	1	1	.500	7.20	3	3	0	0	0	15	25	12	12	6	9
1984 —Birm. (Southern)	7	8	.467	4.66	19	19	4	0	0	123⅔	116	69	64	67	74
—Evansville (A.A.)	5	3	.625	4.50	11	11	2	0	0	64	64	33	32	36	42
1985 —Nashville (A.A.)	6	12	.333	5.08	27	26	3	0	0	145⅓	149	89	82	87	97
1986 —Calgary (PCL)■	8	12	.400	5.28	39	21	0	0	0	158⅔	177	108	93	*89	101
1987 —Seattle (A.L.)	0	0	...	6.43	3	0	0	0	0	7	10	5	5	4	2
—Calgary (PCL)	6	*13	.316	5.51	51	0	0	0	15	65⅓	59	45	40	63	38
1988 —Calg.-Edm. (PCL)■	4	7	.364	5.08	30	16	3	1	0	122⅓	141	84	69	27	97
—California (A.L.)	0	0	...	0.00	3	0	0	0	0	4⅓	4	0	0	1	3
1989 —Edmonton (PCL)	3	6	.333	3.47	13	8	2	0	0	57	50	23	22	16	47
—California (A.L.)	2	2	.500	3.18	24	0	0	0	0	39⅔	39	15	14	13	27
1990 —Edmonton (PCL)	1	0	1.000	1.93	5	1	0	0	1	14	7	3	3	4	9
—Columbus (Int'l)■	4	4	.500	2.24	38	0	0	0	9	64⅓	51	17	16	23	60
—New York (A.L.)	0	1	.000	6.14	5	0	0	0	0	7⅓	8	5	5	2	8
1991 —Columbus (Int'l)	1	3	.250	2.12	32	0	0	0	17	46⅔	36	15	11	7	52
—New York (A.L.)	3	1	.750	3.64	26	0	0	0	0	47	42	27	19	19	34
1992 —New York (A.L.)	7	3	.700	3.30	47	0	0	0	0	92⅔	82	35	34	27	62
1993 —New York (A.L.)	7	4	.636	4.94	42	0	0	0	0	85⅔	85	52	47	35	50
Major league totals (7 years) ..	19	11	.633	3.93	150	0	0	0	0	283⅔	270	139	124	101	186

MONTGOMERY, JEFF

P, ROYALS

PERSONAL: Born January 7, 1962, in Wellston, O. . . . 5-11/180. . . . Throws right, bats right. . . . Full name: Jeffrey Thomas Montgomery.

HIGH SCHOOL: Wellston (O.).

COLLEGE: Marshall (bachelor of science degree in computer science, 1984).

TRANSACTIONS/CAREER NOTES: Selected by Cincinnati Reds organization in ninth round of free-agent draft (June 6, 1983). . . . Traded by Reds to Kansas City Royals for OF Van Snider (February 15, 1988).

RECORDS: Shares major league record for striking out side on nine pitches (April 29, 1990, eighth inning).

HONORS: Named A.L. Fireman of the Year by THE SPORTING NEWS (1993).

Year Team (League)	W	L	Pct.	ERA	G	GS	CG	ShO	Sv.	IP	H	R	ER	BB	SO
1983 —Billings (Pioneer)	6	2	.750	2.42	20	0	0	0	5	44⅔	31	13	12	13	90
1984 —Tampa (Fla. St.)	5	3	.625	2.44	31	0	0	0	•14	44⅓	29	15	12	30	56
—Vermont (Eastern)	2	0	1.000	2.13	22	0	0	0	4	25⅓	14	7	6	24	20
1985 —Vermont (Eastern)	5	3	.625	2.05	*53	1	0	0	9	101	63	25	23	48	89
1986 —Denver (A.A.)	11	7	.611	4.39	30	22	2	2	1	151⅔	162	88	74	57	78
1987 —Nashville (A.A.)	8	5	.615	4.14	24	21	1	0	0	139	132	76	64	51	121
—Cincinnati (N.L.)	2	2	.500	6.52	14	1	0	0	0	19⅓	25	15	14	9	13
1988 —Omaha (A.A.)■	1	2	.333	1.91	20	0	0	0	13	28⅓	15	6	6	11	36
—Kansas City (A.L.)	7	2	.778	3.45	45	0	0	0	1	62⅔	54	25	24	30	47
1989 —Kansas City (A.L.)	7	3	.700	1.37	63	0	0	0	18	92	66	16	14	25	94
1990 —Kansas City (A.L.)	6	5	.545	2.39	73	0	0	0	24	94⅓	81	36	25	34	94
1991 —Kansas City (A.L.)	4	4	.500	2.90	67	0	0	0	33	90	83	32	29	28	77
1992 —Kansas City (A.L.)	1	6	.143	2.18	65	0	0	0	39	82⅔	61	23	20	27	69
1993 —Kansas City (A.L.)	7	5	.583	2.27	69	0	0	0	•45	87⅓	65	22	22	23	66
A.L. totals (6 years)	32	25	.561	2.37	382	0	0	0	160	509	410	154	134	167	447
N.L. totals (1 year)	2	2	.500	6.52	14	1	0	0	0	19⅓	25	15	14	9	13
Major league totals (7 years) ..	34	27	.557	2.52	396	1	0	0	160	528⅓	435	169	148	176	460

ALL-STAR GAME RECORD

Year League	W	L	Pct.	ERA	GS	CG	ShO	Sv.	IP	H	R	ER	BB	SO
1992 —American......................	0	0	...	27.00	0	0	0	0	⅔	2	2	2	0	0
1993 —American......................	0	0	...	0.00	0	0	0	0	1	0	0	0	0	1
All-Star totals (2 years)	0	0	...	10.80	0	0	0	0	1⅔	2	2	2	0	1

MONTOYO, CHARLIE

IF, EXPOS

PERSONAL: Born October 17, 1965, in Manati, Puerto Rico. . . . 5-11/170. . . . Throws right, bats right. . . . Full name: Jose Carlos Montoyo.

COLLEGE: Louisiana Tech.

TRANSACTIONS/CAREER NOTES: Selected by Milwaukee Brewers organization in

26th round of free-agent draft (June 2, 1986).... Selected by Brewers organization in sixth round of free-agent draft (June 2, 1987).... Traded by Brewers organization with 1B Orestes Marrero to Montreal Expos organization for OF Todd Samples and P Ron Gerstein (January 20, 1993).... On Ottawa disabled list (July 22-29, 1993).
STATISTICAL NOTES: Led Texas League with .428 on-base percentage in 1990.

			BATTING											FIELDING			
Year	Team (League)	Pos.	G	AB	R	H	2B	3B	HR	RBI	Avg.	BB	SO	SB	PO	A	E	Avg.
1987	—Helena (Pioneer)	2B	13	45	12	13	1	2	0	2	.289	12	3	2	29	25	2	.964
	—Beloit (Midwest)	2B-SS	55	188	46	50	9	2	5	19	.266	52	22	8	91	155	6	.976
1988	—Stockton (Calif.)	2B-SS	132	450	103	115	14	1	3	61	.256	*156	93	16	247	342	19	.969
1989	—Stockton (Calif.)	SS-2B	129	448	69	111	22	2	0	48	.248	102	40	13	193	324	15	.972
1990	—El Paso (Texas)	SS	94	322	71	93	15	3	3	44	.289	72	43	9	131	256	15	*.963
1991	—Denver (A.A.)	SS-2B-3B	120	394	68	94	13	1	12	45	.239	69	50	15	186	316	19	.964
1992	—Denver (A.A.)	2-3-0-1	84	259	40	84	7	4	2	34	.324	47	36	3	157	132	7	.976
1993	—Ottawa (Int'l)■	3-S-2-1	99	319	43	89	18	2	1	43	.279	71	37	0	101	230	15	.957
	—Montreal (N.L.)	2B	4	5	1	2	1	0	0	3	.400	0	0	0	0	0	0	...
Major league totals (1 year)			4	5	1	2	1	0	0	3	.400	0	0	0	0	0	0	...

MOORE, KERWIN

OF, ATHLETICS

PERSONAL: Born October 29, 1970, in Detroit.... 6-1/190.... Throws right, bats both.... Full name: Kerwin Lamar Moore.
HIGH SCHOOL: Martin Luther King (Detroit).
TRANSACTIONS/CAREER NOTES: Selected by Kansas City Royals organization in 16th round of free-agent draft (June 1, 1988).... Selected by Florida Marlins in third round (61st pick overall) of expansion draft (November 17, 1992).... Traded by Marlins to Oakland Athletics for IF Kurt Abbott (December 20, 1993).
MISCELLANEOUS: Batted righthanded only (1988 and Baseball City, 1989).

			BATTING											FIELDING			
Year	Team (League)	Pos.	G	AB	R	H	2B	3B	HR	RBI	Avg.	BB	SO	SB	PO	A	E	Avg.
1988	—GC Royals (GCL)	OF	53	165	19	29	5	0	0	14	.176	19	49	20	80	2	4	.953
1989	—Eugene (N'west)	OF	65	226	44	50	9	2	2	25	.221	36	75	20	127	3	6	.956
	—Baseball City (FSL)	OF	4	11	3	4	0	0	1	2	.364	1	2	0	7	0	0	1.000
1990	—Appleton (Midw.)	OF	128	451	*93	100	17	7	2	36	.222	*111	139	57	257	11	12	.957
1991	—Baseball City (FSL)	OF	*130	485	67	102	14	2	1	23	.210	77	*141	*61	306	2	4	.987
1992	—Baseball City (FSL)	OF	66	248	39	59	2	1	1	10	.238	40	67	26	148	3	4	.974
	—Memphis (South.)	OF	58	179	27	42	4	3	4	17	.235	24	39	16	141	2	2	.986
1993	—High Desert (Calif.)	OF	132	510	*120	137	20	9	6	52	.269	*114	95	*71	251	4	7	.973

MOORE, MARCUS

P, ROCKIES

PERSONAL: Born November 2, 1970, in Oakland, Calif.... 6-5/195.... Throws right, bats both.... Full name: Marcus Braymont Moore.
HIGH SCHOOL: John F. Kennedy (Richmond, Calif.).
TRANSACTIONS/CAREER NOTES: Selected by California Angels organization in 17th round of free-agent draft (June 1, 1988).... Traded by Angels organization to Toronto Blue Jays organization for C Ken Rivers (December 4, 1990); completing deal in which Angels traded OF Devon White, P Willie Fraser and a player to be named later to Blue Jays for OF Junior Felix, IF Luis Sojo and a player to be named later (December 2, 1990).... Selected by Colorado Rockies in third round (56th pick overall) of expansion draft (November 17, 1992).

M

Year	Team (League)	W	L	Pct.	ERA	G	GS	CG	ShO	Sv.	IP	H	R	ER	BB	SO
1989	—Bend (Northwest)	2	5	.286	4.52	14	14	1	0	0	81⅔	84	55	41	51	74
1990	—Quad City (Midw.)	*16	5	.762	3.31	27	27	2	1	0	160⅓	150	83	59	106	160
1991	—Dunedin (Fla. St.)■	6	13	.316	3.70	27	25	2	0	0	160⅔	139	78	66	*99	115
1992	—Knoxville (South.)	5	10	.333	5.59	36	14	1	0	0	106⅓	110	82	66	79	85
1993	—Central Vall. (Cal.)■	1	0	1.000	0.75	8	0	0	0	2	12	7	3	1	9	15
	—Colo. Springs (PCL)	1	5	.167	4.47	30	0	0	0	4	44⅓	54	26	22	29	38
	—Colorado (N.L.)	3	1	.750	6.84	27	0	0	0	0	26⅓	30	25	20	20	13
Major league totals (1 year)		3	1	.750	6.84	27	0	0	0	0	26⅓	30	25	20	20	13

MOORE, MIKE

P, TIGERS

PERSONAL: Born November 26, 1959, in Eakly, Okla.... 6-4/205.... Throws right, bats right.... Full name: Michael Wayne Moore.
HIGH SCHOOL: Eakly (Okla.).
COLLEGE: Oral Roberts.
TRANSACTIONS/CAREER NOTES: Selected by St. Louis Cardinals organization in third round of free-agent draft (June 6, 1978). ... Selected by Seattle Mariners organization in first round (first pick overall) of free-agent draft (June 8, 1981).... Granted free agency (November 4, 1988).... Signed by Oakland Athletics (November 28, 1988).... On disabled list (July 20-August 6, 1991).... Granted free agency (October 30, 1992).... Signed by Detroit Tigers (December 9, 1992).
HONORS: Named righthanded pitcher on THE SPORTING NEWS college All-America team (1981).
STATISTICAL NOTES: Led A.L. with 22 wild pitches in 1992.... Led A.L. with 35 home runs allowed in 1993.
MISCELLANEOUS: Made an out in only appearance as pinch-hitter (1987).... Appeared in one game as pinch-runner (1991).

Year	Team (League)	W	L	Pct.	ERA	G	GS	CG	ShO	Sv.	IP	H	R	ER	BB	SO
1981	—Lynn (Eastern)	6	5	.545	3.64	13	13	6	2	0	94	83	42	38	34	81
1982	—Seattle (A.L.)	7	14	.333	5.36	28	27	1	1	0	144⅓	159	91	86	79	73
	—Salt Lake City (PCL)	0	0	...	4.50	1	1	0	0	0	8	9	4	4	5	6
1983	—Seattle (A.L.)	6	8	.429	4.71	22	21	3	2	0	128	130	75	67	60	108
	—Salt Lake City (PCL)	4	4	.500	3.61	11	11	4	1	0	82⅓	78	48	33	54	80
1984	—Seattle (A.L.)	7	17	.292	4.97	34	33	6	0	0	212	236	127	117	85	158
1985	—Seattle (A.L.)	17	10	.630	3.46	35	34	14	2	0	247	230	100	95	70	155
1986	—Seattle (A.L.)	11	13	.458	4.30	38	*37	11	1	1	266	*279	141	127	94	146
1987	—Seattle (A.L.)	9	*19	.321	4.71	33	33	12	0	0	231	*268	145	*121	84	115
1988	—Seattle (A.L.)	9	15	.375	3.78	37	32	9	3	1	228⅔	196	104	96	63	182

Year	Team (League)	W	L	Pct.	ERA	G	GS	CG	ShO	Sv.	IP	H	R	ER	BB	SO
1989	—Oakland (A.L.)■	19	11	.633	2.61	35	35	6	3	0	241⅔	193	82	70	83	172
1990	—Oakland (A.L.)	13	15	.464	4.65	33	33	3	0	0	199⅓	204	113	103	84	73
1991	—Oakland (A.L.)	17	8	.680	2.96	33	33	3	1	0	210	176	75	69	105	153
1992	—Oakland (A.L.)	17	12	.586	4.12	36	•36	2	0	0	223	229	113	102	103	117
1993	—Detroit (A.L.)■	13	9	.591	5.22	36	•36	4	3	0	213⅔	227	135	124	89	89
Major league totals (12 years)		145	151	.490	4.16	400	390	74	16	2	2544⅔	2527	1301	1177	999	1541

CHAMPIONSHIP SERIES RECORD

Year	Team (League)	W	L	Pct.	ERA	G	GS	CG	ShO	Sv.	IP	H	R	ER	BB	SO
1989	—Oakland (A.L.)	1	0	1.000	0.00	1	1	0	0	0	7	3	1	0	2	3
1990	—Oakland (A.L.)	1	0	1.000	1.50	1	1	0	0	0	6	4	1	1	1	5
1992	—Oakland (A.L.)	0	2	.000	7.45	2	2	0	0	0	9⅔	11	9	8	5	7
Champ. series totals (3 years)		2	2	.500	3.57	4	4	0	0	0	22⅔	18	11	9	8	15

WORLD SERIES RECORD

WORLD SERIES NOTES: Shares single-game record for most wild pitches—2 (October 15, 1989).

Year	Team (League)	W	L	Pct.	ERA	G	GS	CG	ShO	Sv.	IP	H	R	ER	BB	SO
1989	—Oakland (A.L.)	2	0	1.000	2.08	2	2	0	0	0	13	9	3	3	3	10
1990	—Oakland (A.L.)	0	1	.000	6.75	1	1	0	0	0	2⅔	8	6	2	0	1
World Series totals (2 years)		2	1	.667	2.87	3	3	0	0	0	15⅔	17	9	5	3	11

ALL-STAR GAME RECORD

Year	League	W	L	Pct.	ERA	GS	CG	ShO	Sv.	IP	H	R	ER	BB	SO
1989	—American	0	0	...	0.00	0	0	0	0	1	0	0	0	0	1

MOORE, VINCE

OF, PADRES

PERSONAL: Born September 22, 1971, in Houston. . . . 6-1/175. . . . Throws left, bats left. . . . Full name: Vincent Craig Moore.

HIGH SCHOOL: Elsik (Alief, Tex.).

TRANSACTIONS/CAREER NOTES: Selected by Atlanta Braves organization in fifth round of free-agent draft (June 3, 1991). . . . Traded by Braves with OF Mel Nieves and P Donnie Elliott to San Diego Padres for 1B Fred McGriff (July 18, 1993).

STATISTICAL NOTES: Led South Atlantic League outfielders with 281 total chances in 1992.

MISCELLANEOUS: Batted as switch-hitter (1991-92).

			BATTING												FIELDING			
Year	Team (League)	Pos.	G	AB	R	H	2B	3B	HR	RBI	Avg.	BB	SO	SB	PO	A	E	Avg.
1991	—GC Braves (GCL)	OF	30	110	28	44	4	6	2	22	.400	13	19	7	57	2	2	.967
1992	—Macon (S. Atl.)	OF	123	436	52	99	15	5	6	48	.227	48	118	25	*266	8	7	.975
1993	—Durham (Carolina)	OF	87	319	53	93	14	1	14	64	.292	29	93	21	207	6	7	.968
	—Rancho Cuca. (Cal.)■	OF	39	159	33	41	8	0	6	23	.258	15	52	9	95	3	7	.933

MORANDINI, MICKEY

2B, PHILLIES

PERSONAL: Born April 22, 1966, in Kittanning, Pa. . . . 5-11/180. . . . Throws right, bats left. . . . Full name: Michael Robert Morandini. . . . Name pronounced MOR-an-DEEN-ee.

HIGH SCHOOL: Leechburg (Pa.) Area.

COLLEGE: Indiana.

TRANSACTIONS/CAREER NOTES: Selected by Pittsburgh Pirates organization in seventh round of free-agent draft (June 2, 1987). . . . Selected by Philadelphia Phillies organization in fifth round of free-agent draft (June 1, 1988).

STATISTICAL NOTES: Led International League second basemen with 271 putouts, 419 assists and 701 total chances in 1990.

MISCELLANEOUS: Member of 1988 U.S. Olympic baseball team. . . . Turned unassisted triple play while playing second base (September 20, 1992, sixth inning); ninth player ever to accomplish feat and first ever by second baseman during regular season.

			BATTING												FIELDING			
Year	Team (League)	Pos.	G	AB	R	H	2B	3B	HR	RBI	Avg.	BB	SO	SB	PO	A	E	Avg.
1989	—Spartanburg (SAL)	SS	63	231	43	78	19	1	1	30	.338	35	45	18	87	198	10	.966
	—Clearwater (FSL)	SS	17	63	14	19	4	1	0	4	.302	7	8	3	20	59	2	.975
	—Reading (Eastern)	SS	48	188	39	66	12	1	5	29	.351	23	32	5	73	137	10	.955
1990	—Scran./W.B. (Int'l)	2B-SS	139	503	76	131	24	*10	1	31	.260	60	90	16	†271	†419	11	.984
	—Philadelphia (N.L.)	2B	25	79	9	19	4	0	1	3	.241	6	19	3	37	61	1	.990
1991	—Scran./W.B. (Int'l)	2B	12	46	7	12	4	0	1	9	.261	5	6	2	19	38	1	.983
	—Philadelphia (N.L.)	2B	98	325	38	81	11	4	1	20	.249	29	45	13	183	254	6	.986
1992	—Philadelphia (N.L.)	2B-SS	127	422	47	112	8	8	3	30	.265	25	64	8	239	336	6	.990
1993	—Philadelphia (N.L.)	2B	120	425	57	105	19	9	3	33	.247	34	73	13	208	288	5	.990
Major league totals (4 years)			370	1251	151	317	42	21	8	86	.253	94	201	37	667	939	18	.989

CHAMPIONSHIP SERIES RECORD

			BATTING												FIELDING			
Year	Team (League)	Pos.	G	AB	R	H	2B	3B	HR	RBI	Avg.	BB	SO	SB	PO	A	E	Avg.
1993	—Philadelphia (N.L.)	2B-PH	4	16	1	4	0	1	0	2	.250	0	3	1	8	9	1	.944

WORLD SERIES RECORD

			BATTING												FIELDING			
Year	Team (League)	Pos.	G	AB	R	H	2B	3B	HR	RBI	Avg.	BB	SO	SB	PO	A	E	Avg.
1993	—Philadelphia (N.L.)	PH-2B	3	5	1	1	0	0	0	0	.200	1	2	0	2	0	0	1.000

MORGAN, MIKE

P, CUBS

PERSONAL: Born October 8, 1959, in Tulare, Calif. . . . 6-2/220. . . . Throws right, bats right. . . . Full name: Michael Thomas Morgan.

HIGH SCHOOL: Valley (Las Vegas).

TRANSACTIONS/CAREER NOTES: Selected by Oakland Athletics organization in first round (fourth pick overall) of free-agent draft (June 6, 1978). . . . On disabled list (May 14-June 27, 1980). . . . Traded by A's organization to New York Yankees for SS Fred Stanley and a player to be named later (November 3, 1980); A's acquired 2B Brian Doyle to complete deal (November 17, 1980). . . . On disabled list (April 9-22, 1981). . . . Traded by Yankees with OF/1B Dave Collins, 1B Fred McGriff and cash to Toronto Blue Jays for P Dale Murray and OF/C Tom Dodd (December 9, 1982). . . . On Toronto disabled list (July 2-August 23, 1983); included rehabilitation assignment to Syracuse (August 1-18). . . . Selected by Seattle Mariners from Blue Jays organization in Rule 5 major league draft (December 3, 1984). . . . On Seattle disabled list (April 17, 1985-remainder of season); included rehabilitation assignment to Calgary (July 19-22). . . . Traded by Mariners to Baltimore Orioles for P Ken Dixon (December 9, 1987). . . . On Baltimore disabled list (June 9-July 19, 1988); included rehabilitation assignment to Rochester (June 30-July 17). . . . On Baltimore disabled list (August 12, 1988-remainder of season). . . . Traded by Orioles to Los Angeles Dodgers for OF Mike Devereaux (March 12, 1989). . . . Granted free agency (October 28, 1991). . . . Signed by Chicago Cubs (December 3, 1991). . . . On disabled list (June 14-29, 1993).

Year	Team (League)	W	L	Pct.	ERA	G	GS	CG	ShO	Sv.	IP	H	R	ER	BB	SO
1978	—Oakland (A.L.)	0	3	.000	7.50	3	3	1	0	0	12	19	12	10	8	0
	—Vancouver (PCL)	5	6	.455	5.58	14	14	5	1	0	92	109	67	57	54	31
1979	—Ogden (Pac. Coast)	5	5	.500	3.48	13	13	6	0	0	101	93	48	39	49	42
	—Oakland (A.L.)	2	10	.167	5.96	13	13	2	0	0	77	102	57	51	50	17
1980	—Ogden (Pac. Coast)	6	9	.400	5.40	20	20	3	0	0	115	135	79	69	77	46
1981	—Nashville (South.)■	8	7	.533	4.42	26	26	7	0	0	169	164	97	83	83	100
1982	—New York (A.L.)	7	11	.389	4.37	30	23	2	0	0	150⅓	167	77	73	67	71
1983	—Toronto (A.L.)■	0	3	.000	5.16	16	4	0	0	0	45⅓	48	26	26	21	22
	—Syracuse (Int'l)	0	3	.000	5.59	5	4	0	0	1	19⅓	20	12	12	13	17
1984	—Syracuse (Int'l)	13	11	.542	4.07	34	28	10	•4	1	*185⅔	167	•101	84	•100	105
1985	—Seattle (A.L.)■	1	1	.500	12.00	2	2	0	0	0	6	11	8	8	5	2
	—Calgary (PCL)	0	0	...	4.50	1	1	0	0	0	2	3	1	1	0	0
1986	—Seattle (A.L.)	11	•17	.393	4.53	37	33	9	1	1	216⅓	243	122	109	86	116
1987	—Seattle (A.L.)	12	17	.414	4.65	34	31	8	2	0	207	245	117	107	53	85
1988	—Baltimore (A.L.)■	1	6	.143	5.43	22	10	2	0	1	71⅓	70	45	43	23	29
	—Rochester (Int'l)	0	2	.000	4.76	3	3	0	0	0	17	19	10	9	6	7
1989	—Los Angeles (N.L.)■	8	11	.421	2.53	40	19	0	0	0	152⅔	130	51	43	33	72
1990	—Los Angeles (N.L.)	11	15	.423	3.75	33	33	6	•4	0	211	216	100	88	60	106
1991	—Los Angeles (N.L.)	14	10	.583	2.78	34	33	5	1	1	236⅓	197	85	73	61	140
1992	—Chicago (N.L.)■	16	8	.667	2.55	34	34	6	1	0	240	203	80	68	79	123
1993	—Chicago (N.L.)	10	15	.400	4.03	32	32	1	1	0	207⅔	206	100	93	74	111
A.L. totals (8 years)		34	68	.333	4.89	157	119	24	3	2	785⅓	905	464	427	313	342
N.L. totals (5 years)		59	59	.500	3.14	173	151	18	7	1	1047⅔	952	416	365	307	552
Major league totals (13 years)		93	127	.423	3.89	330	270	42	10	3	1833	1857	880	792	620	894

ALL-STAR GAME RECORD

Year	League	W	L	Pct.	ERA	GS	CG	ShO	Sv.	IP	H	R	ER	BB	SO
1991	—National	0	0	...	0.00	0	0	0	0	1	0	0	0	0	1

MORMAN, ALVIN

P, ASTROS

PERSONAL: Born January 6, 1969, in Rockingham, N.C. . . . 6-3/210. . . . Throws left, bats left.

HIGH SCHOOL: Richmond Senior (Rockingham, N.C.).

COLLEGE: Wingate (N.C.).

TRANSACTIONS/CAREER NOTES: Selected by Houston Astros organization in 39th round of free-agent draft (June 3, 1991). . . . On disabled list (August 26, 1993-remainder of season).

Year	Team (League)	W	L	Pct.	ERA	G	GS	CG	ShO	Sv.	IP	H	R	ER	BB	SO
1991	—GC Astros (GCL)	1	0	1.000	2.16	11	0	0	0	1	16⅔	15	7	4	5	24
	—Osceola (Fla. St.)	0	0	...	1.50	3	0	0	0	0	6	5	3	1	2	3
1992	—Asheville (S. Atl.)	8	0	1.000	1.55	57	0	0	0	15	75⅓	60	17	13	26	70
1993	—Jackson (Texas)	8	2	*.800	2.96	19	19	0	0	0	97⅓	77	35	32	28	101

MORRIS, HAL

1B, REDS

PERSONAL: Born April 9, 1965, in Fort Rucker, Ala. . . . 6-4/210. . . . Throws left, bats left. . . . Full name: William Harold Morris. . . . Brother of Bob Morris, infielder, Chicago Cubs organization.

HIGH SCHOOL: Munster (Ind.).

COLLEGE: Michigan.

TRANSACTIONS/CAREER NOTES: Selected by New York Yankees organization in eighth round of free-agent draft (June 2, 1986). . . . On Albany/Colonie disabled list (August 14, 1986-remainder of season). . . . Traded by Yankees with P Rodney Imes to Cincinnati Reds for P Tim Leary and OF Van Snider (December 12, 1989). . . . On Cincinnati disabled list (April 16-May 17, 1992); included rehabilitation assignment to Nashville (May 14-17). . . . On Cincinnati disabled list (August 5-21, 1992). . . . On Cincinnati disabled list (March 27-June 7, 1993); included rehabilitation assignment to Indianapolis (June 4-7). . . . On suspended list for one game (August 10, 1993).

			BATTING												FIELDING			
Year	Team (League)	Pos.	G	AB	R	H	2B	3B	HR	RBI	Avg.	BB	SO	SB	PO	A	E	Avg.
1986	—Oneonta (NYP)	1B	36	127	26	48	9	2	3	30	.378	18	15	1	317	26	3	.991
	—Alb./Colon. (East.)	1B	25	79	7	17	5	0	0	4	.215	4	10	0	203	19	2	.991
1987	—Alb./Colon. (East.)	1B-OF	135	*530	65	*173	31	4	5	73	.326	36	43	7	1086	79	17	.986
1988	—Columbus (Int'l)	OF-1B	121	452	41	134	19	4	3	38	.296	36	62	8	543	26	8	.986
	—New York (A.L.)	OF	15	20	1	2	0	0	0	0	.100	0	9	0	7	0	0	1.000
1989	—Columbus (Int'l)	1B-OF	111	417	70	136	24	1	17	66	*.326	28	47	5	636	67	9	.987
	—New York (A.L.)	OF-1B	15	18	2	5	0	0	0	4	.278	1	4	0	12	0	0	1.000

Year	Team (League)	Pos.	G	AB	R	H	2B	3B	HR	RBI	Avg.	BB	SO	SB	PO	A	E	Avg.
				BATTING											FIELDING			
1990	—Cincinnati (N.L.)■	1B-OF	107	309	50	105	22	3	7	36	.340	21	32	9	595	53	4	.994
	—Nashville (A.A.)	OF	16	64	8	22	5	0	1	10	.344	5	10	4	23	1	1	.960
1991	—Cincinnati (N.L.)	1B-OF	136	478	72	152	33	1	14	59	.318	46	61	10	979	100	9	.992
1992	—Cincinnati (N.L.)	1B	115	395	41	107	21	3	6	53	.271	45	53	6	841	86	1	*.999
	—Nashville (A.A.)	1B	2	6	1	1	1	0	0	0	.167	2	1	0	13	3	0	1.000
1993	—Indianapolis (A.A.)	1B	3	13	4	6	0	1	1	5	.462	1	2	0	26	3	0	1.000
	—Cincinnati (N.L.)	1B	101	379	48	120	18	0	7	49	.317	34	51	2	746	75	5	.994
American League totals (2 years)			30	38	3	7	0	0	0	4	.184	1	13	0	19	0	0	1.000
National League totals (4 years)			459	1561	211	484	94	7	34	197	.310	146	197	27	3161	314	19	.995
Major league totals (6 years)			489	1599	214	491	94	7	34	201	.307	147	210	27	3180	314	19	.995

CHAMPIONSHIP SERIES RECORD

Year	Team (League)	Pos.	G	AB	R	H	2B	3B	HR	RBI	Avg.	BB	SO	SB	PO	A	E	Avg.
				BATTING											FIELDING			
1990	—Cincinnati (N.L.)	1B-PH	5	12	3	5	1	0	0	1	.417	1	0	0	20	2	0	1.000

WORLD SERIES RECORD

Year	Team (League)	Pos.	G	AB	R	H	2B	3B	HR	RBI	Avg.	BB	SO	SB	PO	A	E	Avg.
				BATTING											FIELDING			
1990	—Cincinnati (N.L.)	1B-DH	4	14	0	1	0	0	0	2	.071	1	1	0	18	1	0	1.000

MORRIS, JACK

P, INDIANS

PERSONAL: Born May 16, 1955, in St. Paul, Minn. . . . 6-3/210. . . . Throws right, bats right. . . . Full name: John Scott Morris.
HIGH SCHOOL: Highland Park (St. Paul, Minn.).
COLLEGE: Brigham Young.

TRANSACTIONS/CAREER NOTES: Selected by Detroit Tigers organization in fifth round of free-agent draft (June 8, 1976). . . . Granted free agency (November 12, 1986). . . . Re-signed by Tigers (December 19, 1986). . . . Granted free agency (November 9, 1987). . . . Re-signed by Tigers (December 29, 1987). . . . On Detroit disabled list (May 25-July 24, 1989); included rehabilitation assignment to Lakeland (July 10-24). . . . Granted free agency (December 7, 1990). . . . Signed by Minnesota Twins (February 5, 1991). . . . Granted free agency (November 11, 1991). . . . Signed by Toronto Blue Jays (December 18, 1991). . . . On disabled list (May 2-21, 1993). . . . Released by Blue Jays (November 5, 1993). . . . Signed by Cleveland Indians (February 10, 1994).

RECORDS: Holds A.L. career records for most consecutive starting assignments—492 (September 30, 1978 through 1993); most putouts by pitcher—375; and most wild pitches—193. . . . Holds A.L. record for most seasons leading league in wild pitches—5 (1983-85, 1987 and 1991). . . . Shares A.L. single-season record for fewest complete games by pitcher who led league in complete games—11 (1990). . . . Shares A.L. record for most years allowing 30 or more home runs—4 (1982-83 and 1986-87). . . . Shares A.L. single-game record for most wild pitches—5 (August 3, 1987, 10 innings).

HONORS: Named A.L. Pitcher of the Year by THE SPORTING NEWS (1981). . . . Named righthanded pitcher on THE SPORTING NEWS A.L. All-Star team (1981).

STATISTICAL NOTES: Led A.L. with 18 wild pitches in 1983, 14 in 1984, 15 in 1985, 24 in 1987 and 15 in 1991. . . . Pitched 4-0 no-hit victory against Chicago (April 7, 1984).

MISCELLANEOUS: Appeared in seven games as pinch-runner (1983). . . . Appeared in one game as pinch-runner (1985). . . . Made an out in only appearance as pinch-hitter (1987).

Year	Team (League)	W	L	Pct.	ERA	G	GS	CG	ShO	Sv.	IP	H	R	ER	BB	SO
1976	—Montgomery (Sou.)	2	3	.400	6.25	12	9	0	0	0	36	37	31	25	36	18
1977	—Evansville (A.A.)	6	7	.462	3.60	20	20	4	0	0	135	141	68	54	42	95
	—Detroit (A.L.)	1	1	.500	3.72	7	6	1	0	0	46	38	20	19	23	28
1978	—Detroit (A.L.)	3	5	.375	4.33	28	7	0	0	0	106	107	57	51	49	48
1979	—Evansville (A.A.)	2	2	.500	2.38	5	5	3	0	0	34	22	13	9	18	28
	—Detroit (A.L.)	17	7	.708	3.27	27	27	9	1	0	198	179	76	72	59	113
1980	—Detroit (A.L.)	16	15	.516	4.18	36	36	11	2	0	250	252	125	116	87	112
1981	—Detroit (A.L.)	•14	7	.667	3.05	25	25	15	1	0	198	153	69	67	*78	97
1982	—Detroit (A.L.)	17	16	.515	4.06	37	37	17	3	0	266⅓	247	131	120	96	135
1983	—Detroit (A.L.)	20	13	.606	3.34	37	37	20	1	0	*293⅔	257	117	109	83	*232
1984	—Detroit (A.L.)	19	11	.633	3.60	35	35	9	1	0	240⅓	221	108	96	87	148
1985	—Detroit (A.L.)	16	11	.593	3.33	35	35	13	4	0	257	212	102	95	110	191
1986	—Detroit (A.L.)	21	8	.724	3.27	35	35	15	*6	0	267	229	105	97	82	223
1987	—Detroit (A.L.)	18	11	.621	3.38	34	34	13	0	0	266	227	111	100	93	208
1988	—Detroit (A.L.)	15	13	.536	3.94	34	34	10	2	0	235	225	115	103	83	168
1989	—Detroit (A.L.)	6	14	.300	4.86	24	24	10	0	0	170⅓	189	102	92	59	115
	—Lakeland (Fla. St.)	0	0	...	2.25	3	3	0	0	0	8	7	2	2	0	2
1990	—Detroit (A.L.)	15	18	.455	4.51	36	•36	•11	3	0	249⅔	231	*144	*125	97	162
1991	—Minnesota (A.L.)■	18	12	.600	3.43	35	•35	10	2	0	246⅔	226	107	94	92	163
1992	—Toronto (A.L.)■	•21	6	.778	4.04	34	34	6	1	0	240⅔	222	114	108	80	132
1993	—Toronto (A.L.)	7	12	.368	6.19	27	27	4	1	0	152⅔	189	116	105	65	103
Major league totals (17 years)		244	180	.575	3.83	526	504	174	28	0	3683⅓	3404	1719	1569	1323	2378

CHAMPIONSHIP SERIES RECORD

CHAMPIONSHIP SERIES NOTES: Shares A.L. single-series record for most games won—2 (1991). . . . Appeared in one game as pinch-runner (1987).

Year	Team (League)	W	L	Pct.	ERA	G	GS	CG	ShO	Sv.	IP	H	R	ER	BB	SO
1984	—Detroit (A.L.)	1	0	1.000	1.29	1	1	0	0	0	7	5	1	1	1	4
1987	—Detroit (A.L.)	0	1	.000	6.75	1	1	1	0	0	8	6	6	6	3	7
1991	—Minnesota (A.L.)	2	0	1.000	4.05	2	2	0	0	0	13⅓	17	6	6	1	7
1992	—Toronto (A.L.)	0	1	.000	6.57	2	2	1	0	0	12⅓	11	9	9	9	6
Champ. series totals (4 years)		3	2	.600	4.87	6	6	2	0	0	40⅔	39	22	22	14	24

WORLD SERIES RECORD

WORLD SERIES NOTES: Named Most Valuable Player (1991).... Shares single-game records for most earned runs allowed—7 (October 22, 1992); and most wild pitches—2 (October 13, 1984).

Year	Team (League)	W	L	Pct.	ERA	G	GS	CG	ShO	Sv.	IP	H	R	ER	BB	SO
1984	—Detroit (A.L.)	2	0	1.000	2.00	2	2	2	0	0	18	13	4	4	3	13
1991	—Minnesota (A.L.)	2	0	1.000	1.17	3	3	1	1	0	23	18	3	3	9	15
1992	—Toronto (A.L.)	0	2	.000	8.44	2	2	0	0	0	10⅔	13	10	10	6	12
World Series totals (3 years)		4	2	.667	2.96	7	7	3	1	0	51⅔	44	17	17	18	40

ALL-STAR GAME RECORD

Year	League	W	L	Pct.	ERA	GS	CG	ShO	Sv.	IP	H	R	ER	BB	SO
1981	—American	0	0	...	0.00	1	0	0	0	2	2	0	0	1	2
1984	—American	0	0	...	0.00	0	0	0	0	2	2	0	0	1	2
1985	—American	0	1	.000	6.75	1	0	0	0	2⅔	5	2	2	1	1
1987	—American	0	0	...	0.00	0	0	0	0	2	1	0	0	1	2
1991	—American	0	0	...	4.50	1	0	0	0	2	4	1	1	0	1
All-Star totals (5 years)		0	1	.000	2.53	3	0	0	0	10⅔	14	3	3	4	8

MOTA, GARY

OF, ASTROS

PERSONAL: Born October 6, 1970, in Santo Domingo, Dominican Republic.... 6-0/195.... Throws right, bats right.... Full name: Manuel Rafael Mota Jr.... Son of Manny Mota, current coach, Los Angeles Dodgers, and major league outfielder with four teams (1962-80 and 1982); brother of Jose Mota and Domingo Mota, infielders, Kansas City Royals organization; and brother of Andy Mota, infielder, Astros organization.
COLLEGE: Fullerton (Calif.) College.
TRANSACTIONS/CAREER NOTES: Selected by Houston Astros organization in second round of free-agent draft (June 4, 1990).... On Burlington disabled list (April 12-August 3, 1991).... On disabled list (April 20-July 23, 1993).
HONORS: Named South Atlantic League Most Valuable Player (1992).

			BATTING												FIELDING			
Year	Team (League)	Pos.	G	AB	R	H	2B	3B	HR	RBI	Avg.	BB	SO	SB	PO	A	E	Avg.
1990	—Auburn (NY-Penn)	OF	69	248	39	64	12	4	3	19	.258	26	74	12	110	4	3	.974
1991	—Osceola (Fla. St.)	OF	22	71	10	14	2	2	0	3	.197	8	20	4	20	2	0	1.000
1992	—Asheville (S. Atl.)	OF	137	484	92	141	21	5	23	89	.291	58	131	22	166	14	7	.963
1993	—Jackson (Texas)	OF	27	90	7	13	2	0	3	8	.144	2	25	1	27	2	0	1.000

MOUTON, JAMES

2B, ASTROS

PERSONAL: Born December 29, 1968, in Denver.... 5-9/175.... Throws right, bats right.... Full name: James Raleigh Mouton.
HIGH SCHOOL: Luther Burbank Senior (Sacramento, Calif.).
COLLEGE: St. Mary's (Calif.).
TRANSACTIONS/CAREER NOTES: Selected by New York Yankees organization in 42nd round of free-agent draft (June 2, 1987).... Selected by Minnesota Twins organization in eighth round of free-agent draft (June 4, 1990).... Selected by Houston Astros organization in seventh round of free-agent draft (June 3, 1991).
HONORS: Named Pacific Coast League Most Valuable Player (1993).
STATISTICAL NOTES: Led New York-Pennsylvania League in caught stealing with 18 in 1991.... Led New York-Pennsylvania League second basemen with 382 total chances in 1991.... Led Florida State League second basemen with 623 total chances in 1992.... Led Pacific Coast League with 286 total bases and tied for lead in caught stealing with 18 in 1993.... Led Pacific Coast League second basemen with 674 total chances and 75 double plays in 1993.

			BATTING												FIELDING			
Year	Team (League)	Pos.	G	AB	R	H	2B	3B	HR	RBI	Avg.	BB	SO	SB	PO	A	E	Avg.
1991	—Auburn (NY-Penn)	2B	76	288	71	76	15	*10	2	40	.264	55	32	*60	*170	184	*28	.927
1992	—Osceola (Fla. St.)	2B	133	507	*110	143	•30	6	11	62	.282	71	78	*51	*288	294	*41	.934
1993	—Tucson (PCL)	2B	134	*546	*126	*172	*42	12	16	92	.315	72	82	40	*277	*354	*43	.936

MOYER, JAMIE

P, ORIOLES

PERSONAL: Born November 18, 1962, in Sellersville, Pa.... 6-0/170.... Throws left, bats left.... Son-in-law of Digger Phelps, Notre Dame basketball coach (1971-72 through 1990-91).
HIGH SCHOOL: Souderton (Pa.) Area.
COLLEGE: St. Joseph's (Pa.).
TRANSACTIONS/CAREER NOTES: Selected by Chicago Cubs organization in sixth round of free-agent draft (June 4, 1984).... Traded by Cubs with OF Rafael Palmeiro and P Drew Hall to Texas Rangers for P Mitch Williams, P Paul Kilgus, P Steve Wilson, IF Curtis Wilkerson, IF Luis Benitez and OF Pablo Delgado (December 5, 1988).... On Texas disabled list (May 31-September 1, 1989); included rehabilitation assignment to Gulf Coast Rangers (August 5-14) and Tulsa (August 15-24).... Released by Rangers (November 13, 1990).... Signed by Louisville, St. Louis Cardinals organization (January 9, 1991).... Released by Cardinals (October 14, 1991).... Signed by Cubs organization (January 8, 1992).... Released by Iowa, Cubs organization (March 30, 1992).... Signed by Toledo, Detroit Tigers organization (May 24, 1992).... Granted free agency (December 8, 1992).... Signed by Baltimore Orioles organization (December 14, 1992).
STATISTICAL NOTES: Led American Association with 16 home runs allowed in 1991.

Year	Team (League)	W	L	Pct.	ERA	G	GS	CG	ShO	Sv.	IP	H	R	ER	BB	SO
1984	—Geneva (NY-Penn)	•9	3	.750	1.89	14	14	5	2	0	*104⅔	59	27	22	31	*120
1985	—Winst.-Salem (Car.)	8	2	.800	2.30	12	12	6	2	0	94	82	36	24	22	94
	—Pittsfield (Eastern)	7	6	.538	3.72	15	15	3	0	0	96⅔	99	49	40	32	51
1986	—Pittsfield (Eastern)	3	1	.750	0.88	6	6	0	0	0	41	27	10	4	16	42
	—Iowa (Am. Assoc.)	3	2	.600	2.55	6	6	2	0	0	42⅓	25	14	12	11	25
	—Chicago (N.L.)	7	4	.636	5.05	16	16	1	1	0	87⅓	107	52	49	42	45
1987	—Chicago (N.L.)	12	15	.444	5.10	35	33	1	0	0	201	210	127	*114	97	147
1988	—Chicago (N.L.)	9	15	.375	3.48	34	30	3	1	0	202	212	84	78	55	121

Year	Team (League)	W	L	Pct.	ERA	G	GS	CG	ShO	Sv.	IP	H	R	ER	BB	SO
1989	—Texas (A.L.)■	4	9	.308	4.86	15	15	1	0	0	76	84	51	41	33	44
	—GC Rangers (GCL)	1	0	1.000	1.64	3	3	0	0	0	11	8	4	2	1	18
	—Tulsa (Texas)	1	1	.500	5.11	2	2	1	1	0	12⅓	16	8	7	3	9
1990	—Texas (A.L.)	2	6	.250	4.66	33	10	1	0	0	102⅓	115	59	53	39	58
1991	—St. Louis (N.L.)■	0	5	.000	5.74	8	7	0	0	0	31⅓	38	21	20	16	20
	—Louisville (A.A.)	5	10	.333	3.80	20	20	1	0	0	125⅔	125	64	53	43	69
1992	—Toledo (Int'l)■	10	8	.556	2.86	21	20	5	0	0	138⅔	128	48	44	37	80
1993	—Rochester (Int'l)■	6	0	1.000	1.67	8	8	1	1	0	54	42	13	10	13	41
	—Baltimore (A.L.)	12	9	.571	3.43	25	25	3	1	0	152	154	63	58	38	90
A.L. totals (3 years)		18	24	.429	4.14	73	50	5	1	0	330⅓	353	173	152	110	192
N.L. totals (4 years)		28	39	.418	4.50	93	86	5	2	0	521⅔	567	284	261	210	333
Major league totals (7 years)		46	63	.422	4.36	166	136	10	3	0	852	920	457	413	320	525

MULHOLLAND, TERRY

P, YANKEES

PERSONAL: Born March 9, 1963, in Uniontown, Pa. . . . 6-3/212. . . . Throws left, bats right. . . . Full name: Terence John Mulholland.
HIGH SCHOOL: Laurel Highlands (Uniontown, Pa.).
COLLEGE: Marietta College (O.).

TRANSACTIONS/CAREER NOTES: Selected by San Francisco Giants organization in first round (24th pick overall) of free-agent draft (June 4, 1984); pick received as compensation for Detroit Tigers signing free agent Darrell Evans. . . . On San Francisco disabled list (August 1, 1988-remainder of season). . . . Traded by Giants with P Dennis Cook and 3B Charlie Hayes to Philadelphia Phillies for P Steve Bedrosian and a player to be named later (June 18, 1989); Giants organization acquired IF Rick Parker to complete deal (August 7, 1989). . . . On Philadelphia disabled list (June 12-28, 1990); included rehabilitation assignment to Scranton/Wilkes-Barre (June 23-24). . . . Traded by Phillies with a player to be named later to New York Yankees for P Bobby Munoz, 2B Kevin Jordan and P Ryan Karp (February 9, 1994).
STATISTICAL NOTES: Pitched 6-0 no-hit victory for Philadelphia against San Francisco (August 15, 1990).
MISCELLANEOUS: Appeared in one game as pinch-runner (1991).

Year	Team (League)	W	L	Pct.	ERA	G	GS	CG	ShO	Sv.	IP	H	R	ER	BB	SO
1984	—Everett (N'west)	1	0	1.000	0.00	3	3	0	0	0	19	10	2	0	4	15
	—Fresno (California)	5	2	.714	2.95	9	9	0	0	0	42⅔	32	17	14	36	39
1985	—Shreveport (Texas)	9	8	.529	2.90	26	26	8	*3	0	176⅔	166	79	57	87	122
1986	—Phoenix (PCL)	8	5	.615	4.46	17	17	3	0	0	111	112	60	55	56	77
	—San Francisco (N.L.)	1	7	.125	4.94	15	10	0	0	0	54⅔	51	33	30	35	27
1987	—Phoenix (PCL)	7	12	.368	5.07	37	*29	3	1	1	172⅓	200	*124	•97	90	94
1988	—Phoenix (PCL)	7	3	.700	3.58	19	14	3	2	0	100⅔	116	45	40	44	57
	—San Francisco (N.L.)	2	1	.667	3.72	9	6	2	1	0	46	50	20	19	7	18
1989	—Phoenix (PCL)	4	5	.444	2.99	13	10	3	0	0	78⅓	67	30	26	26	61
	—S.F.-Phil. (N.L.)■	4	7	.364	4.92	25	18	2	1	0	115⅓	137	66	63	36	66
1990	—Philadelphia (N.L.)	9	10	.474	3.34	33	26	6	1	0	180⅔	172	78	67	42	75
	—Scran./W.B. (Int'l)	0	1	.000	3.00	1	1	0	0	0	6	9	4	2	2	2
1991	—Philadelphia (N.L.)	16	13	.552	3.61	34	34	8	3	0	232	231	100	93	49	142
1992	—Philadelphia (N.L.)	13	11	.542	3.81	32	32	*12	2	0	229	227	101	97	46	125
1993	—Philadelphia (N.L.)	12	9	.571	3.25	29	28	7	2	0	191	177	80	69	40	116
Major league totals (7 years)		57	58	.496	3.76	177	154	37	10	0	1048⅔	1045	478	438	255	569

CHAMPIONSHIP SERIES RECORD

Year	Team (League)	W	L	Pct.	ERA	G	GS	CG	ShO	Sv.	IP	H	R	ER	BB	SO
1993	—Philadelphia (N.L.)	0	1	.000	7.20	1	1	0	0	0	5	9	5	4	1	2

WORLD SERIES RECORD

Year	Team (League)	W	L	Pct.	ERA	G	GS	CG	ShO	Sv.	IP	H	R	ER	BB	SO
1993	—Philadelphia (N.L.)	1	0	1.000	6.75	2	2	0	0	0	10⅔	14	8	8	3	5

ALL-STAR GAME RECORD

Year	League	W	L	Pct.	ERA	GS	CG	ShO	Sv.	IP	H	R	ER	BB	SO
1993	—National	0	0	...	4.50	1	0	0	0	2	1	1	1	2	0

MUNOZ, BOBBY

P, PHILLIES

PERSONAL: Born March 3, 1968, in Rio Piedras, Puerto Rico. . . . 6-7/237. . . . Throws right, bats right.
HIGH SCHOOL: Hialeah (Fla.) Miami Lakes.
COLLEGE: Palm Beach Junior College (Fla.) and Polk Community College (Fla.).

TRANSACTIONS/CAREER NOTES: Selected by New York Yankees organization in 15th round of free-agent draft (June 1, 1988). . . . Traded by Yankees with 2B Kevin Jordan and P Ryan Karp to Philadelphia Phillies for P Terry Mulholland and a player to be named later (February 9, 1994).

Year	Team (League)	W	L	Pct.	ERA	G	GS	CG	ShO	Sv.	IP	H	R	ER	BB	SO
1989	—GC Yankees (GCL)	1	1	.500	3.48	2	2	0	0	0	10⅓	5	4	4	4	13
	—Fort Lauder. (FSL)	1	2	.333	4.73	3	3	0	0	0	13⅓	16	8	7	7	2
1990	—Greensboro (S. Atl.)	5	12	.294	3.73	25	24	0	0	0	132⅔	133	70	55	58	100
1991	—Fort Lauder. (FSL)	5	8	.385	2.33	19	19	4	2	0	108	91	45	28	40	53
	—Columbus (Int'l)	0	1	.000	24.00	1	1	0	0	0	3	8	8	8	3	2
1992	—Alb./Colon. (East.)	7	5	.583	3.28	22	22	0	0	0	112⅓	96	55	41	70	66
1993	—Columbus (Int'l)	3	1	.750	1.44	22	1	0	0	10	31⅓	24	6	5	8	16
	—New York (A.L.)	3	3	.500	5.32	38	0	0	0	0	45⅔	48	27	27	26	33
Major league totals (1 year)		3	3	.500	5.32	38	0	0	0	0	45⅔	48	27	27	26	33

MUNOZ, MIKE

P, ROCKIES

PERSONAL: Born July 12, 1965, in Baldwin Park, Calif. . . . 6-2/200. . . . Throws left, bats left. . . . Full name: Michael Anthony Munoz.
HIGH SCHOOL: Bishop Amat (La Puente, Calif.).
COLLEGE: Cal Poly Pomona.

TRANSACTIONS/CAREER NOTES: Selected by Los Angeles Dodgers organization in third round of free-agent draft (June 2, 1986). . . . Traded by Dodgers organization to Detroit Tigers for P Mike Wilkins (September 30, 1990). . . . Granted free agency (May 12, 1993). . . . Signed by Colorado Springs, Colorado Rockies organization (May 14, 1993).

Year	Team (League)	W	L	Pct.	ERA	G	GS	CG	ShO	Sv.	IP	H	R	ER	BB	SO
1986	—Great Falls (Pio.)	4	4	.500	3.21	14	14	2	2	0	81⅓	85	44	29	38	49
1987	—Bakersfield (Calif.)	8	7	.533	3.74	52	12	2	0	9	118	125	68	49	43	80
1988	—San Antonio (Tex.)	7	2	.778	1.00	56	0	0	0	14	71⅔	63	18	8	24	71
1989	—Albuquerque (PCL)	6	4	.600	3.08	60	0	0	0	6	79	72	32	27	40	81
	—Los Angeles (N.L.)	0	0	...	16.88	3	0	0	0	0	2⅔	5	5	5	2	3
1990	—Los Angeles (N.L.)	0	1	.000	3.18	8	0	0	0	0	5⅔	6	2	2	3	2
	—Albuquerque (PCL)	4	1	.800	4.25	49	0	0	0	6	59⅓	65	33	28	19	40
1991	—Toledo (Int'l)■	2	3	.400	3.83	38	1	0	0	8	54	44	30	23	35	38
	—Detroit (A.L.)	0	0	...	9.64	6	0	0	0	0	9⅓	14	10	10	5	3
1992	—Detroit (A.L.)	1	2	.333	3.00	65	0	0	0	2	48	44	16	16	25	23
1993	—Detroit (A.L.)	0	1	.000	6.00	8	0	0	0	0	3	4	2	2	6	1
	—Colo. Springs (PCL)■	1	2	.333	1.67	40	0	0	0	3	37⅔	46	10	7	9	30
	—Colorado (N.L.)	2	1	.667	4.50	21	0	0	0	0	18	21	12	9	9	16
	A.L. totals (3 years)	1	3	.250	4.18	79	0	0	0	2	60⅓	62	28	28	36	27
	N.L. totals (3 years)	2	2	.500	5.47	32	0	0	0	0	26⅓	32	19	16	14	21
	Major league totals (5 years)	3	5	.375	4.57	111	0	0	0	2	86⅔	94	47	44	50	48

MUNOZ, OSCAR

P, TWINS

PERSONAL: Born September 25, 1969, in Hialeah, Fla. . . . 6-3/210. . . . Throws right, bats right. . . . Full name: Juan Oscar Munoz.
HIGH SCHOOL: Christopher Columbus (Miami).
COLLEGE: Miami (Fla.).
TRANSACTIONS/CAREER NOTES: Selected by Cleveland Indians organization in fifth round of free-agent draft (June 4, 1990). . . . Traded by Indians organization with P Curt Leskanic to Minnesota Twins organization for 1B Paul Sorrento (March 28, 1992). . . . On disabled list (April 9-16 and June 19-August 21, 1992).
HONORS: Named Southern League Pitcher of the Year (1993).
STATISTICAL NOTES: Pitched 1-0 no-hit victory for Kinston against Prince William (May 26, 1991).

Year	Team (League)	W	L	Pct.	ERA	G	GS	CG	ShO	Sv.	IP	H	R	ER	BB	SO
1990	—Watertown (NYP)	1	1	.500	1.69	2	2	0	0	0	10⅔	8	2	2	3	9
	—Kinston (Carolina)	7	0	1.000	2.39	9	9	2	1	0	64	43	18	17	18	55
1991	—Kinston (Carolina)	6	3	.667	1.44	14	14	2	1	0	93⅔	60	23	15	36	111
	—Cant./Akr. (East.)	3	8	.273	5.72	15	15	2	1	0	85	88	54	54	51	71
1992	—Orlando (Southern)■	3	5	.375	5.05	14	12	1	0	0	67⅔	73	44	38	32	74
1993	—Nashville (South.)■	11	4	•.733	3.08	20	20	1	0	0	131⅔	123	56	45	51	139
	—Portland (PCL)	2	2	.500	4.31	5	5	0	0	0	31⅓	29	18	15	17	29

MUNOZ, PEDRO

OF, TWINS

PERSONAL: Born September 19, 1968, in Ponce, Puerto Rico. . . . 5-10/203. . . . Throws right, bats right. . . . Full name: Pedro Javier Munoz.
HIGH SCHOOL: Dr. Pila (Ponce, Puerto Rico).
TRANSACTIONS/CAREER NOTES: Signed as free agent by Toronto Blue Jays organization (May 31, 1985). . . . On disabled list (July 30-August 28, 1987). . . . Traded by Blue Jays organization with 2B Nelson Liriano to Minnesota Twins for P John Candelaria (July 27, 1990). . . . On Minnesota disabled list (July 15-30, 1991 and July 1-26, 1993).
STATISTICAL NOTES: Tied for South Atlantic League lead with four intentional bases on balls received in 1986.

			BATTING												FIELDING			
Year	Team (League)	Pos.	G	AB	R	H	2B	3B	HR	RBI	Avg.	BB	SO	SB	PO	A	E	Avg.
1985	—GC Blue Jays (GCL)	OF	40	145	14	38	3	0	2	17	.262	9	20	4	46	2	1	.980
1986	—Florence (S. Atl.)	OF	122	445	69	131	16	5	14	82	.294	54	100	9	197	14	9	.959
1987	—Dunedin (Fla. St.)	OF	92	341	55	80	11	5	8	44	.235	34	74	13	4	1	0	1.000
1988	—Dunedin (Fla. St.)	OF	133	481	59	141	21	7	8	73	.293	52	87	15	164	8	*15	.920
1989	—Knoxville (South.)	OF	122	442	54	118	15	4	19	65	.267	20	85	10	55	3	1	.983
1990	—Syracuse (Int'l)	OF	86	317	41	101	22	3	7	56	.319	24	64	16	110	4	6	.950
	—Portland (PCL)■	OF	30	110	19	35	4	0	5	21	.318	15	18	8	51	1	3	.945
	—Minnesota (A.L.)	OF	22	85	13	23	4	1	0	5	.271	2	16	3	34	1	1	.972
1991	—Portland (PCL)	OF	56	212	33	67	19	2	5	28	.316	19	42	9	109	2	2	.982
	—Minnesota (A.L.)	OF	51	138	15	39	7	1	7	26	.283	9	31	3	89	3	1	.989
1992	—Minnesota (A.L.)	OF	127	418	44	113	16	3	12	71	.270	17	90	4	220	8	3	.987
1993	—Minnesota (A.L.)	OF	104	326	34	76	11	1	13	38	.233	25	97	1	172	5	3	.983
	Major league totals (4 years)		304	967	106	251	38	6	32	140	.260	53	234	11	515	17	8	.985

MURPHY, DALE

OF

PERSONAL: Born March 12, 1956, in Portland, Ore. . . . 6-4/221. . . . Throws right, bats right. . . . Full name: Dale Bryan Murphy.
HIGH SCHOOL: Woodrow Wilson (Portland, Ore.).
COLLEGE: Portland (Ore.) Community College and Brigham Young.
TRANSACTIONS/CAREER NOTES: Selected by Atlanta Braves organization in first round (fifth pick overall) of free-agent draft (June 5, 1974). . . . On disabled list (May 25-July 19, 1979). . . . Traded by Braves with a player to be named later to Philadelphia Phillies for P Jeff Parrett and two players to be named later (August 3, 1990); Scranton/Wilkes-Barre, Phillies organization, acquired P Tommy Greene (August 9, 1990), and Braves acquired OF Jim Vatcher (August 9, 1990) and SS Victor Rosario (September 4, 1990) to complete deal. . . . On disabled list (April 15-May 8 and May 20-September 30, 1992). . . . Granted free agency (November 8, 1992). . . . Re-signed by Phillies organization (December 6, 1992). . . . Released by Phillies organization (April 3, 1993). . . . Signed by Colorado Rockies (April 3, 1993). . . . Placed on voluntarily retired list (May 27, 1993).
RECORDS: Shares major league career record for most years leading league in games by outfielder—6. . . . Shares major league single-season record for fewest double plays by outfielder (150 or more games)—0 (1983). . . . Shares major league records

for most home runs—2; and runs batted in—6, in one inning (July 27, 1989, sixth inning). . . . Shares N.L. single-season record for most intentional bases on balls by righthanded batter—29 (1987).

HONORS: Named N.L. Player of the Year by THE SPORTING NEWS (1982-83). . . . Named outfielder on THE SPORTING NEWS N.L. All-Star team (1982-85). . . . Won N.L. Gold Glove as outfielder (1982-86). . . . Named outfielder on THE SPORTING NEWS N.L. Silver Slugger team (1982-85). . . . Named N.L. Most Valuable Player by Baseball Writers' Association of America (1982-83).

STATISTICAL NOTES: Tied for International League lead with 249 total bases in 1977. . . . Led International League catchers with 510 putouts, 14 passed balls and tied for lead with seven double plays in 1977. . . . Led N.L. first basemen with 20 errors in 1978. . . . Hit three home runs in one game (May 18, 1979). . . . Tied for N.L. lead in double plays by outfielder with four in both 1981 and 1985. . . . Led N.L. with .540 slugging percentage in 1983 and .547 in 1984. . . . Led N.L. with 332 total bases in 1984. . . . Led N.L. with 29 intentional bases on balls received in 1987. . . . Led N.L. in grounding into double plays with 24 in 1988 and 22 in 1990.

			BATTING												FIELDING			
Year	Team (League)	Pos.	G	AB	R	H	2B	3B	HR	RBI	Avg.	BB	SO	SB	PO	A	E	Avg.
1974	—Kingsport (Appal.)	C	54	181	28	46	7	0	5	31	.254	24	53	0	389	28	7	.983
1975	—Greenw. (W. Car.)	C-1B	131	443	48	101	20	1	5	48	.228	36	63	5	723	81	18	.978
1976	—Savannah (South.)	C	104	352	37	94	13	5	12	55	.267	25	61	6	444	40	10	.980
	—Richmond (Int'l)	C-OF	18	50	10	13	1	1	4	8	.260	1	12	0	60	9	4	.945
	—Atlanta (N.L.)	C	19	65	3	17	6	0	0	9	.262	7	9	0	100	13	3	.974
1977	—Richmond (Int'l)	C-1B	127	466	71	142	•33	4	22	*90	.305	33	64	4	†600	50	15	.977
	—Atlanta (N.L.)	C	18	76	5	24	8	1	2	14	.316	0	8	0	114	11	6	.954
1978	—Atlanta (N.L.)	1B-C	151	530	66	120	14	3	23	79	.226	42	*145	11	1220	105	†23	.983
1979	—Atlanta (N.L.)	1B-C	104	384	53	106	7	2	21	57	.276	38	67	6	812	57	20	.978
1980	—Atlanta (N.L.)	OF-1B	156	569	98	160	27	2	33	89	.281	59	*133	9	384	15	6	.985
1981	—Atlanta (N.L.)	OF-1B	104	369	43	91	12	1	13	50	.247	44	72	14	264	11	5	.982
1982	—Atlanta (N.L.)	OF	•162	598	113	168	23	2	36	•109	.281	93	134	23	407	6	9	.979
1983	—Atlanta (N.L.)	OF	*162	589	131	178	24	4	36	*121	.302	90	110	30	373	10	6	.985
1984	—Atlanta (N.L.)	OF	*162	607	94	176	32	8	•36	100	.290	79	134	19	369	10	5	.987
1985	—Atlanta (N.L.)	OF	•162	616	*118	185	32	2	*37	111	.300	*90	•141	10	334	8	7	.980
1986	—Atlanta (N.L.)	OF	160	614	89	163	29	7	29	83	.265	75	141	7	303	6	6	.981
1987	—Atlanta (N.L.)	OF	159	566	115	167	27	1	44	105	.295	115	136	16	325	14	8	.977
1988	—Atlanta (N.L.)	OF	156	592	77	134	35	4	24	77	.226	74	125	3	340	15	3	.992
1989	—Atlanta (N.L.)	OF	154	574	60	131	16	0	20	84	.228	65	142	3	331	5	5	.985
1990	—Atl.-Phil. (N.L.)■	OF	154	563	60	138	23	1	24	83	.245	61	130	9	321	7	5	.985
1991	—Philadelphia (N.L.)	OF	153	544	66	137	33	1	18	81	.252	48	93	1	287	6	5	.983
1992	—Philadelphia (N.L.)	OF	18	62	5	10	1	0	2	7	.161	1	13	0	19	0	1	.950
1993	—Colorado (N.L.)■	OF	26	42	1	6	1	0	0	7	.143	5	15	0	16	1	0	1.000
Major league totals (18 years)			2180	7960	1197	2111	350	39	398	1266	.265	986	1748	161	6319	300	123	.982

CHAMPIONSHIP SERIES RECORD

			BATTING												FIELDING			
Year	Team (League)	Pos.	G	AB	R	H	2B	3B	HR	RBI	Avg.	BB	SO	SB	PO	A	E	Avg.
1982	—Atlanta (N.L.)	OF	3	11	1	3	0	0	0	0	.273	0	2	1	8	0	0	1.000

ALL-STAR GAME RECORD

			BATTING											FIELDING			
Year	League	Pos.	AB	R	H	2B	3B	HR	RBI	Avg.	BB	SO	SB	PO	A	E	Avg.
1980	—National	OF	1	0	0	0	0	0	0	.000	0	0	0	0	0	0	...
1982	—National	OF	2	1	0	0	0	0	0	.000	1	0	0	2	0	0	1.000
1983	—National	OF	3	0	1	0	0	0	1	.333	0	1	0	0	0	0	...
1984	—National	OF	3	1	2	0	0	1	1	.667	1	0	0	0	0	0	...
1985	—National	OF	3	0	1	1	0	0	0	.333	0	1	0	1	0	0	1.000
1986	—National	OF	2	0	0	0	0	0	0	.000	0	0	0	2	0	0	1.000
1987	—National	OF	1	0	0	0	0	0	0	.000	0	0	0	1	0	0	1.000
All-Star Game totals (7 years)			15	2	4	1	0	1	2	.267	2	2	0	6	0	0	1.000

M

MURPHY, ROB

P, CARDINALS

PERSONAL: Born May 26, 1960, in Miami. . . . 6-2/215. . . . Throws left, bats left. . . . Full name: Robert Albert Murphy Jr.

HIGH SCHOOL: Christopher Columbus (Miami).

COLLEGE: Florida.

TRANSACTIONS/CAREER NOTES: Selected by Milwaukee Brewers organization in 29th round of free-agent draft (June 6, 1978). . . . Selected by Cincinnati Reds organization in secondary phase of free-agent draft (January 13, 1981). . . . Traded by Reds with 1B Nick Esasky to Boston Red Sox for 1B Todd Benzinger, P Jeff Sellers and a player to be named later (December 13, 1988); Reds acquired P Luis Vasquez to complete deal (January 12, 1989). . . . Traded by Red Sox to Seattle Mariners for P Mike Gardiner (April 1, 1991). . . . Granted free agency (December 20, 1991). . . . Signed by Houston Astros organization (January 27, 1992). . . . On Houston disabled list (May 3-22, 1992). . . . Granted free agency (October 29, 1992). . . . Signed by St. Louis Cardinals (January 7, 1993).

Year	Team (League)	W	L	Pct.	ERA	G	GS	CG	ShO	Sv.	IP	H	R	ER	BB	SO
1981	—Tampa (Fla. St.)	6	8	.429	4.54	25	20	2	0	0	105	109	73	53	67	58
1982	—Ced. Rap. (Midw.)	3	7	.300	4.04	31	9	0	0	0	89	92	62	40	61	96
1983	—Ced. Rap. (Midw.)	6	10	.375	3.33	36	18	2	1	2	140⅔	120	66	52	69	137
1984	—Vermont (Eastern)	2	3	.400	2.71	45	1	0	0	•15	69⅔	57	23	21	35	69
1985	—Denver (A.A.)	5	5	.500	4.61	41	0	0	0	5	84	94	55	43	57	66
	—Cincinnati (N.L.)	0	0	...	6.00	2	0	0	0	0	3	2	2	2	2	1
1986	—Denver (A.A.)	3	4	.429	1.90	27	0	0	0	7	42⅔	33	12	9	24	36
	—Cincinnati (N.L.)	6	0	1.000	0.72	34	0	0	0	1	50⅓	26	4	4	21	36
1987	—Cincinnati (N.L.)	8	5	.615	3.04	87	0	0	0	3	100⅔	91	37	34	32	99
1988	—Cincinnati (N.L.)	0	6	.000	3.08	*76	0	0	0	3	84⅔	69	31	29	38	74

Year	Team (League)	W	L	Pct.	ERA	G	GS	CG	ShO	Sv.	IP	H	R	ER	BB	SO
1989	—Boston (A.L.)■	5	7	.417	2.74	74	0	0	0	9	105	97	38	32	41	107
1990	—Boston (A.L.)	0	6	.000	6.32	68	0	0	0	7	57	85	46	40	32	54
1991	—Seattle (A.L.)■	0	1	.000	3.00	57	0	0	0	4	48	47	17	16	19	34
1992	—Houston (N.L.)■	3	1	.750	4.04	59	0	0	0	0	55⅔	56	28	25	21	42
1993	—St. Louis (N.L.)■	5	7	.417	4.87	73	0	0	0	1	64⅔	73	37	35	20	41
A.L. totals (3 years)		5	14	.263	3.77	199	0	0	0	20	210	229	101	88	92	195
N.L. totals (6 years)		22	19	.537	3.23	331	0	0	0	8	359	317	139	129	134	293
Major league totals (9 years)		27	33	.450	3.43	530	0	0	0	28	569	546	240	217	226	488

CHAMPIONSHIP SERIES RECORD

Year	Team (League)	W	L	Pct.	ERA	G	GS	CG	ShO	Sv.	IP	H	R	ER	BB	SO
1990	—Boston (A.L.)	0	0	...	13.50	1	0	0	0	0	⅔	2	1	1	1	0

MURRAY, EDDIE

1B/DH, INDIANS

PERSONAL: Born February 24, 1956, in Los Angeles. . . . 6-2/220. . . . Throws right, bats both. . . . Full name: Eddie Clarence Murray. . . . Brother of Rich Murray, first baseman, San Francisco Giants (1980, 1983); brother of Leon Murray, minor league first baseman (1970); brother of Charles Murray, minor league outfielder (1962-66 and 1969); and brother of Venice Murray, minor league first baseman (1978).
HIGH SCHOOL: Locke (Los Angeles).
COLLEGE: Cal State Los Angeles.
TRANSACTIONS/CAREER NOTES: Selected by Baltimore Orioles organization in third round of free-agent draft (June 5, 1973). . . . On disabled list (July 10-August 7, 1986). . . . Traded by Orioles to Los Angeles Dodgers for P Brian Holton, P Ken Howell and SS Juan Bell (December 4, 1988). . . . Granted free agency (October 29, 1991). . . . Signed by New York Mets (November 27, 1991). . . . Granted free agency (November 1, 1993). . . . Signed by Cleveland Indians (December 2, 1993).
RECORDS: Shares major league career records for most games with switch-hit home runs—10; most games by first baseman—2,368; and most assists by first baseman—1,828. . . . Shares major league single-season record for games with switch-hit home runs—2 (1982, 1987 and 1990). . . . Holds A.L. career record for most game-winning RBIs—117. . . . Holds A.L. single-season records for most consecutive games with one or more hits by switch-hitter—22 (1984); and most intentional bases on balls by switch-hitter—25 (1984). . . . Holds N.L. single-season record for most double plays by first baseman (150 or more games)—88 (1990). . . . Shares N.L. single-season record for fewest errors by first baseman who led league in errors—12 (1992).
HONORS: Named Appalachian League Player of the Year (1973). . . . Named A.L. Rookie of the Year by Baseball Writers' Association of America (1977). . . . Won A.L. Gold Glove at first base (1982-84). . . . Named first baseman on THE SPORTING NEWS A.L. All-Star team (1983). . . . Named first baseman on THE SPORTING NEWS A.L. Silver Slugger team (1983-84). . . . Named first baseman on THE SPORTING NEWS N.L. All-Star team (1990). . . . Named first baseman on THE SPORTING NEWS N.L. Silver Slugger team (1990).
STATISTICAL NOTES: Led Florida State League with 212 total bases in 1974. . . . Led Florida State League first basemen with 113 double plays in 1974. . . . Switch-hit home runs in one game 10 times (August 3, 1977; August 29, 1979, second game, two righthanded and one lefthanded; August 16, 1981; April 24 and August 26, 1982; August 26, 1985, two lefthanded and one righthanded; May 8 and 9, 1987; and April 18 and June 9, 1990). . . . Led A.L. first basemen with 1,615 total chances in 1978, 1,694 in 1984 and 1,526 in 1987. . . . Led A.L. first basemen with 1,504 putouts in 1978. . . . Hit three home runs in one game (August 29, 1979, second game; September 14, 1980, 13 innings; and August 26, 1985). . . . Led A.L. with .410 on-base percentage and 19 game-winning RBIs in 1984. . . . Led A.L. with 25 intentional bases on balls received in 1984 and tied for lead with 18 in 1982. . . . Led A.L. first basemen with 152 double plays in 1984, 146 in 1987 and tied for lead with 154 in 1985. . . . Led N.L. first basemen with .996 fielding percentage, 137 assists and 122 double plays in 1989. . . . Tied for N.L. lead with 21 intentional bases on balls received in 1990.

				BATTING											FIELDING			
Year	Team (League)	Pos.	G	AB	R	H	2B	3B	HR	RBI	Avg.	BB	SO	SB	PO	A	E	Avg.
1973	—Bluefield (Appal.)	1B	50	188	34	54	6	0	11	32	.287	19	46	6	421	14	13	.971
1974	—Miami (Florida St.)	1B	131	460	64	133	*29	7	12	63	.289	58	85	4	*1114	*51	*25	.979
	—Asheville (South.)	1B	2	7	1	2	2	0	0	2	.286	1	1	0	17	0	0	1.000
1975	—Asheville (South.)	1B-3B	124	436	66	115	13	5	17	68	.264	53	79	7	637	58	15	.979
1976	—Charlotte (South.)	1B	88	299	46	89	15	2	12	46	.298	43	41	11	746	45	9	.989
	—Rochester (Int'l)	1B-OF-3B	54	168	35	46	6	2	11	40	.274	34	27	3	291	13	5	.984
1977	—Baltimore (A.L.)	OF-1B	160	611	81	173	29	2	27	88	.283	48	104	0	482	20	4	.992
1978	—Baltimore (A.L.)	1B-3B	161	610	85	174	32	3	27	95	.285	70	97	6	†1507	112	6	.996
1979	—Baltimore (A.L.)	1B	159	606	90	179	30	2	25	99	.295	72	78	10	*1456	107	10	.994
1980	—Baltimore (A.L.)	1B	158	621	100	186	36	2	32	116	.300	54	71	7	1369	77	9	.994
1981	—Baltimore (A.L.)	1B	99	378	57	111	21	2	•22	*78	.294	40	43	2	899	*91	1	*.999
1982	—Baltimore (A.L.)	1B	151	550	87	174	30	1	32	110	.316	70	82	7	1269	97	4	*.997
1983	—Baltimore (A.L.)	1B	156	582	115	178	30	3	33	111	.306	86	90	5	1393	114	10	.993
1984	—Baltimore (A.L.)	1B	•162	588	97	180	26	3	29	110	.306	*107	87	10	*1538	*143	13	.992
1985	—Baltimore (A.L.)	1B	156	583	111	173	37	1	31	124	.297	84	68	5	1338	152	*19	.987
1986	—Baltimore (A.L.)	1B	137	495	61	151	25	1	17	84	.305	78	49	3	1045	88	13	.989
1987	—Baltimore (A.L.)	1B	160	618	89	171	28	3	30	91	.277	73	80	1	1371	145	10	.993
1988	—Baltimore (A.L.)	1B	161	603	75	171	27	2	28	84	.284	75	78	5	867	106	11	.989
1989	—Los Angeles (N.L.)■	1B-3B	160	594	66	147	29	1	20	88	.247	87	85	7	1316	†137	6	†.996
1990	—Los Angeles (N.L.)	1B	155	558	96	184	22	3	26	95	.330	82	64	8	1180	113	10	.992
1991	—Los Angeles (N.L.)	1B-3B	153	576	69	150	23	1	19	96	.260	55	74	10	1327	128	7	.995
1992	—New York (N.L.)■	1B	156	551	64	144	37	2	16	93	.261	66	74	4	1283	96	•12	.991
1993	—New York (N.L.)	1B	154	610	77	174	28	1	27	100	.285	40	61	2	1319	111	18	.988
American League totals (12 years)			1820	6845	1048	2021	351	25	333	1190	.295	857	927	61	14534	1252	110	.993
National League totals (5 years)			778	2889	372	799	139	8	108	472	.277	330	358	31	6425	585	53	.992
Major league totals (17 years)			2598	9734	1420	2820	490	33	441	1662	.290	1187	1285	92	20959	1837	163	.993

CHAMPIONSHIP SERIES RECORD

CHAMPIONSHIP SERIES NOTES: Shares single-game record for most runs—4 (October 7, 1983).

			BATTING											FIELDING			
Year	Team (League)	Pos.	G	AB	R	H	2B	3B	HR	RBI	Avg.	BB	SO	SB	PO	A	E	Avg.
1979	—Baltimore (A.L.)	1B	4	12	3	5	0	0	1	5	.417	5	2	0	44	3	2	.959
1983	—Baltimore (A.L.)	1B	4	15	5	4	0	0	1	3	.267	3	3	1	34	3	1	.974
Championship series totals (2 years)			8	27	8	9	0	0	2	8	.333	8	5	1	78	6	3	.966

WORLD SERIES RECORD

			BATTING											FIELDING			
Year	Team (League)	Pos.	G	AB	R	H	2B	3B	HR	RBI	Avg.	BB	SO	SB	PO	A	E	Avg.
1979	—Baltimore (A.L.)	1B	7	26	3	4	1	0	1	2	.154	4	4	1	60	7	0	1.000
1983	—Baltimore (A.L.)	1B	5	20	2	5	0	0	2	3	.250	1	4	0	46	1	1	.979
World Series totals (2 years)			12	46	5	9	1	0	3	5	.196	5	8	1	106	8	1	.991

ALL-STAR GAME RECORD

			BATTING										FIELDING			
Year	League	Pos.	AB	R	H	2B	3B	HR	RBI	Avg.	BB	SO	SB	PO	A	E	Avg.
1978	—American								Did not play.								
1981	—American	PH-1B	2	0	0	0	0	0	0	.000	0	0	0	2	1	0	1.000
1982	—American	PH-1B	1	0	0	0	0	0	0	.000	1	0	0	4	0	0	1.000
1983	—American	1B	2	0	0	0	0	0	0	.000	0	0	0	4	0	0	1.000
1984	—American	1B	2	0	1	1	0	0	0	.500	0	1	0	3	0	0	1.000
1985	—American	1B	3	0	0	0	0	0	0	.000	0	0	0	5	2	0	1.000
1986	—American								Did not play.								
1991	—National	1B	1	0	0	0	0	0	0	.000	0	1	0	3	0	0	1.000
All-Star Game totals (6 years)			11	0	1	1	0	0	0	.091	1	2	0	21	3	0	1.000

MURRAY, GLENN

OF, EXPOS

PERSONAL: Born November 23, 1970, in Manning, S.C. . . . 6-2/220. . . . Throws right, bats right. . . . Full name: Glenn Everett Murray.

HIGH SCHOOL: Manning (S.C.).

TRANSACTIONS/CAREER NOTES: Selected by Montreal Expos organization in second round of free-agent draft (June 5, 1989).

			BATTING											FIELDING			
Year	Team (League)	Pos.	G	AB	R	H	2B	3B	HR	RBI	Avg.	BB	SO	SB	PO	A	E	Avg.
1989	—GC Expos (GCL)	3B-OF	27	87	10	15	6	2	0	7	.172	6	30	8	10	26	8	.818
	—Jamestown (NYP)	3B	3	10	1	3	1	0	0	1	.300	1	1	0	0	1	1	.500
1990	—Jamestown (NYP)	OF	53	165	20	37	8	4	1	14	.224	21	43	12	48	6	5	.915
1991	—Rockford (Midw.)	OF	124	479	73	113	16	*14	5	60	.236	77	136	22	222	5	7	.970
1992	—W.P. Beach (FSL)	OF	119	414	79	96	14	5	13	41	.232	*75	*150	26	229	11	1	.996
1993	—Harrisburg (East.)	OF	127	475	82	120	21	4	26	96	.253	56	111	16	270	6	7	.975

MURRAY, MATT

P, BRAVES

PERSONAL: Born September 26, 1970, in Boston. . . . 6-6/200. . . . Throws right, bats left. . . . Full name: Matthew Michael Murray.

HIGH SCHOOL: Loomis Chaffee (Windsor, Conn.).

TRANSACTIONS/CAREER NOTES: Selected by Atlanta Braves organization in second round of free-agent draft (June 1, 1988); pick received as compensation for Philadelphia Phillies signing Type B free agent David Palmer. . . . On disabled list (May 1-July 10 and July 20, 1991-remainder of season). . . . On Greenville disabled list (April 9-September 16, 1992). . . . On Atlanta disabled list (April 3-July 11, 1993); included rehabilitation assignment to Macon (June 15-July 11).

Year	Team (League)	W	L	Pct.	ERA	G	GS	CG	ShO	Sv.	IP	H	R	ER	BB	SO
1988	—Pulaski (Appal.)	2	4	.333	4.17	13	8	0	0	1	54	48	32	25	26	76
1989	—GC Braves (GCL)	1	0	1.000	0.00	2	2	0	0	0	7	3	0	0	0	10
	—Sumter (S. Atl.)	3	5	.375	4.33	12	12	0	0	0	72⅔	62	37	35	22	69
1990	—Burlington (Midw.)	11	7	.611	3.26	26	26	6	3	0	163	139	72	59	61	134
1991	—Durham (Carolina)	1	0	1.000	1.29	2	2	0	0	0	7	5	1	1	0	7
1992	—								Did not play.							
1993	—Macon (S. Atl.)	7	3	.700	1.83	15	15	3	0	0	83⅔	70	24	17	27	77

MUSSET, JOSE

P, YANKEES

PERSONAL: Born September 18, 1968, in Monte Plata, Dominican Republic. . . . 6-3/186. . . . Throws right, bats right. . . . Full name: Jose Luis Santana Musset.

TRANSACTIONS/CAREER NOTES: Signed as free agent by California Angels organization (October 31, 1986). . . . On Arizona League Angels disabled list (1991). . . . Traded by Angels to New York Yankees for SS Spike Owen and cash (December 9, 1993).

Year	Team (League)	W	L	Pct.	ERA	G	GS	CG	ShO	Sv.	IP	H	R	ER	BB	SO
1990	—Ariz. Angels (Ariz.)	2	•7	.222	6.03	13	•13	0	0	0	62⅔	63	•54	*42	41	49
	—Boise (Northwest)	0	0	...	0.00	1	0	0	0	0	⅔	0	0	0	1	0
1991	—Ariz. Angels (Ariz.)	1	1	.500	3.21	10	0	0	0	2	14	14	7	5	5	10
1992	—Quad City (Midw.)	8	2	.800	2.39	41	0	0	0	6	71⅔	41	19	19	25	104
1993	—Midland (Texas)	2	6	.250	5.49	59	0	0	0	21	62⅓	59	38	38	32	59

RECORD AS POSITION PLAYER

			BATTING											FIELDING			
Year	Team (League)	Pos.	G	AB	R	H	2B	3B	HR	RBI	Avg.	BB	SO	SB	PO	A	E	Avg.
1987	—							Dominican Summer League statistics unavailable.										

Year	Team (League)	Pos.	G	AB	R	H	2B	3B	HR	RBI	Avg.	BB	SO	SB	PO	A	E	Avg.
				BATTING											FIELDING			
1988	—			Dominican Summer League statistics unavailable.														
1989	—Ariz. Angels (Ariz.)	OF-1B	27	86	16	23	3	2	0	9	.267	4	22	4	42	6	5	.906

MUSSINA, MIKE

P, ORIOLES

PERSONAL: Born December 8, 1968, in Williamsport, Pa. . . . 6-2/185. . . . Throws right, bats right. . . . Full name: Michael Cole Mussina. . . . Name pronounced myoo-SEEN-uh.
HIGH SCHOOL: Montoursville (Pa.).
COLLEGE: Stanford (degree in economics, 1990).
TRANSACTIONS/CAREER NOTES: Selected by Baltimore Orioles organization in 11th round of free-agent draft (June 2, 1987). . . . Selected by Orioles organization in first round (20th pick overall) of free-agent draft (June 4, 1990). . . . On Rochester disabled list (May 5-12, 1991). . . . On Baltimore disabled list (July 22-August 20, 1993); included rehabilitation assignment to Bowie (August 9-20).
HONORS: Named International League Most Valuable Pitcher (1991).

Year	Team (League)	W	L	Pct.	ERA	G	GS	CG	ShO	Sv.	IP	H	R	ER	BB	SO
1990	—Hagerstown (East.)	3	0	1.000	1.49	7	7	2	1	0	42⅓	34	10	7	7	40
	—Rochester (Int'l)	0	0	...	1.35	2	2	0	0	0	13⅓	8	2	2	4	15
1991	—Rochester (Int'l)	10	4	.714	2.87	19	19	3	1	0	122⅓	108	42	39	31	107
	—Baltimore (A.L.)	4	5	.444	2.87	12	12	2	0	0	87⅔	77	31	28	21	52
1992	—Baltimore (A.L.)	18	5	*.783	2.54	32	32	8	4	0	241	212	70	68	48	130
1993	—Baltimore (A.L.)	14	6	.700	4.46	25	25	3	2	0	167⅔	163	84	83	44	117
	—Bowie (Eastern)	1	0	1.000	2.25	2	2	0	0	0	8	5	2	2	1	10
Major league totals (3 years)		36	16	.692	3.25	69	69	13	6	0	496⅓	452	185	179	113	299

ALL-STAR GAME RECORD

Year	League	W	L	Pct.	ERA	GS	CG	ShO	Sv.	IP	H	R	ER	BB	SO
1992	—American	0	0	...	0.00	0	0	0	0	1	0	0	0	0	0
1993	—American						Did not play.								
All-Star totals (1 year)		0	0	...	0.00	0	0	0	0	1	0	0	0	0	0

MUTIS, JEFF

P, MARLINS

PERSONAL: Born December 20, 1966, in Allentown, Pa. . . . 6-2/185. . . . Throws left, bats left. . . . Full name: Jeffrey Thomas Mutis. . . . Name pronounced MYOO-tis.
HIGH SCHOOL: Allentown (Pa.) Catholic.
COLLEGE: Lafayette College (Pa.).
TRANSACTIONS/CAREER NOTES: Selected by Cleveland Indians organization in 34th round of free-agent draft (June 3, 1985). . . . Selected by Indians organization in supplemental round ("sandwich pick" between first and second round, 27th pick overall) of free-agent draft (June 1, 1988); pick received as part of compensation for San Francisco Giants signing Type A free agent Brett Butler. . . . On Kinston disabled list (July 20, 1988-remainder of season; July 6-31 and August 1, 1989-remainder of season). . . . Claimed on waivers by Florida Marlins (November 29, 1993).

Year	Team (League)	W	L	Pct.	ERA	G	GS	CG	ShO	Sv.	IP	H	R	ER	BB	SO
1988	—Burlington (Appal.)	3	0	1.000	0.41	3	3	0	0	0	22	8	1	1	6	20
	—Kinston (Carolina)	1	0	1.000	1.59	1	1	0	0	0	5⅔	6	1	1	3	2
1989	—Kinston (Carolina)	7	3	.700	2.62	16	15	5	2	0	99⅔	87	42	29	20	68
1990	—Cant./Akr. (East.)	11	10	.524	3.16	26	26	7	•3	0	165	*178	73	58	44	94
1991	—Cant./Akr. (East.)	11	5	.688	*1.80	25	24	*7	*4	0	*169⅔	138	42	34	51	89
	—Cleveland (A.L.)	0	3	.000	11.68	3	3	0	0	0	12⅓	23	16	16	7	6
1992	—Colo. Springs (PCL)	9	9	.500	5.08	25	24	4	0	0	145⅓	177	99	82	57	77
	—Cleveland (A.L.)	0	2	.000	9.53	3	2	0	0	0	11⅓	24	14	12	6	8
1993	—Cleveland (A.L.)	3	6	.333	5.78	17	13	1	1	0	81	93	56	52	33	29
	—Charlotte (Int'l)	6	0	1.000	2.62	12	11	3	0	0	75⅔	64	27	22	25	59
Major league totals (3 years)		3	11	.214	6.88	23	18	1	1	0	104⅔	140	86	80	46	43

MYERS, GREG

C, ANGELS

PERSONAL: Born April 14, 1966, in Riverside, Calif. . . . 6-2/215. . . . Throws right, bats left. . . . Full name: Gregory Richard Myers.
HIGH SCHOOL: Riverside (Calif.) Polytechnical.
TRANSACTIONS/CAREER NOTES: Selected by Toronto Blue Jays organization in third round of free-agent draft (June 4, 1984). . . . On disabled list (June 17, 1988-remainder of season). . . . On Toronto disabled list (March 26-June 5, 1989); included rehabilitation assignment to Knoxville (May 17-June 5). . . . On Toronto disabled list (May 5-25, 1990); included rehabilitation assignment to Syracuse (May 21-24). . . . Traded by Blue Jays with OF Rob Ducey to California Angels for P Mark Eichhorn (July 30, 1992). . . . On California disabled list (August 27, 1992-remainder of season).
STATISTICAL NOTES: Led California League catchers with 967 total chances in 1986. . . . Led International League catchers with 698 total chances in 1987.

Year	Team (League)	Pos.	G	AB	R	H	2B	3B	HR	RBI	Avg.	BB	SO	SB	PO	A	E	Avg.
				BATTING											FIELDING			
1984	—Medicine Hat (Pio.)	C	38	133	20	42	9	0	2	20	.316	16	6	0	216	24	4	.984
1985	—Florence (S. Atl.)	C	134	489	52	109	19	2	5	62	.223	39	54	0	551	61	7	*.989
1986	—Ventura (Calif.)	C	124	451	65	133	23	4	20	79	.295	43	46	9	*849	99	19	.980
1987	—Syracuse (Int'l)	C	107	342	35	84	19	1	10	47	.246	22	46	3	*637	50	11	.984
	—Toronto (A.L.)	C	7	9	1	1	0	0	0	0	.111	0	3	0	24	1	0	1.000
1988	—Syracuse (Int'l)	C	34	120	18	34	7	1	7	21	.283	8	24	1	63	9	1	.986
1989	—Knoxville (South.)	C	29	90	11	30	10	0	5	19	.333	3	16	1	130	12	1	.993
	—Toronto (A.L.)	C	17	44	0	5	2	0	0	1	.114	2	9	0	46	6	0	1.000
	—Syracuse (Int'l)	C	24	89	8	24	6	0	1	11	.270	4	9	0	60	7	1	.985
1990	—Toronto (A.L.)	C	87	250	33	59	7	1	5	22	.236	22	33	0	411	30	3	.993
	—Syracuse (Int'l)	C	3	11	0	2	1	0	0	2	.182	1	1	0	14	0	0	1.000

Year	Team (League)	Pos.	G	AB	R	H	2B	3B	HR	RBI	Avg.	BB	SO	SB	PO	A	E	Avg.
				BATTING											FIELDING			
1991	—Toronto (A.L.)	C	107	309	25	81	22	0	8	36	.262	21	45	0	484	37	11	.979
1992	—Tor.-Calif. (A.L.)■	C	30	78	4	18	7	0	1	13	.231	5	11	0	125	16	1	.993
1993	—California (A.L.)	C	108	290	27	74	10	0	7	40	.255	17	47	3	369	44	6	.986
Major league totals (6 years)			356	980	90	238	48	1	21	112	.243	67	148	3	1459	134	21	.987

CHAMPIONSHIP SERIES RECORD

Year	Team (League)	Pos.	G	AB	R	H	2B	3B	HR	RBI	Avg.	BB	SO	SB	PO	A	E	Avg.
				BATTING											FIELDING			
1991	—Toronto (A.L.)							Did not play.										

MYERS, MIKE

P, MARLINS

PERSONAL: Born June 26, 1969, in Cook County, Ill. . . . 6-3/197. . . . Throws left, bats left. . . . Full name: Michael Stanley Myers.
HIGH SCHOOL: Crystal Lake (Ill.) Central.
COLLEGE: Iowa State.
TRANSACTIONS/CAREER NOTES: Selected by San Francisco Giants organization in fourth round of free-agent draft (June 4, 1990). . . . On Clinton disabled list (June 3-September 16, 1991; April 9-June 2 and June 21-July 6, 1992). . . . Selected by Florida Marlins from Giants organization in Rule 5 major league draft (December 7, 1992).
STATISTICAL NOTES: Led Pacific Coast League with 10 hit batsmen in 1993.

Year	Team (League)	W	L	Pct.	ERA	G	GS	CG	ShO	Sv.	IP	H	R	ER	BB	SO
1990	—Everett (N'west)	4	5	.444	3.90	15	14	1	0	0	85⅓	91	43	37	30	73
1991	—Ariz. Giants (Ariz.)	0	1	.000	12.00	1	0	0	0	0	3	5	5	4	2	2
	—Clinton (Midwest)	5	3	.625	2.62	11	11	1	0	0	65⅓	61	23	19	18	59
1992	—Clinton (Midwest)	1	2	.333	1.19	7	7	0	0	0	37⅔	28	11	5	8	32
	—San Jose (Calif.)	5	1	.833	2.30	8	8	0	0	0	54⅔	43	20	14	17	40
1993	—Edmonton (PCL)■	7	14	.333	5.18	27	27	3	0	0	161⅔	195	109	93	52	112

MYERS, RANDY

P, CUBS

PERSONAL: Born September 19, 1962, in Vancouver, Wash. . . . 6-1/230. . . . Throws left, bats left. . . . Full name: Randall Kirk Myers.
HIGH SCHOOL: Evergreen (Vancouver, Wash.).
COLLEGE: Clark Community College (Wash.).
TRANSACTIONS/CAREER NOTES: Selected by Cincinnati Reds organization in third round of free-agent draft (January 12, 1982). . . . Selected by New York Mets organization in secondary phase of free-agent draft (June 7, 1982). . . . Traded by Mets with P Kip Gross to Cincinnati Reds for P John Franco and OF Don Brown (December 6, 1989). . . . Traded by Reds to San Diego Padres for OF/2B Bip Roberts and a player to be named later (December 8, 1991); Reds acquired OF Craig Pueschner to complete deal (December 9, 1991). . . . Granted free agency (October 26, 1992). . . . Signed by Chicago Cubs (December 9, 1992).
RECORDS: Shares N.L. single-game record for most consecutive strikeouts by relief pitcher—6 (September 8, 1990). . . . Holds N.L. single-season record for most saves—53 (1993).
HONORS: Named Carolina League Pitcher of the Year (1984). . . . Named N.L. Fireman of the Year by THE SPORTING NEWS (1993).
STATISTICAL NOTES: Tied for Appalachian League lead with three balks in 1982.
MISCELLANEOUS: Had sacrifice hit in one game as pinch-hitter (1992). . . . Grounded into a double play in one game as pinch-hitter (1993).

Year	Team (League)	W	L	Pct.	ERA	G	GS	CG	ShO	Sv.	IP	H	R	ER	BB	SO
1982	—Kingsport (Appal.)	6	3	.667	4.12	13	•13	1	0	0	74⅓	68	49	34	69	•86
1983	—Columbia (S. Atl.)	14	10	.583	3.63	28	•28	3	0	0	173⅓	146	94	70	108	164
1984	—Lynchburg (Caro.)	13	5	.722	★2.06	23	22	•7	1	0	157	123	46	36	61	171
	—Jackson (Texas)	2	1	.667	2.06	5	5	1	0	0	35	29	14	8	16	35
1985	—Jackson (Texas)	4	8	.333	3.96	19	19	2	1	0	120⅓	99	61	53	69	116
	—Tidewater (Int'l)	1	1	.500	1.84	8	7	0	0	0	44	40	13	9	20	25
	—New York (N.L.)	0	0	. . .	0.00	1	0	0	0	0	2	0	0	0	1	2
1986	—Tidewater (Int'l)	6	7	.462	2.35	45	0	0	0	12	65	44	19	17	44	79
	—New York (N.L.)	0	0	. . .	4.22	10	0	0	0	0	10⅔	11	5	5	9	13
1987	—New York (N.L.)	3	6	.333	3.96	54	0	0	0	6	75	61	36	33	30	92
	—Tidewater (Int'l)	0	0	. . .	4.91	5	0	0	0	3	7⅓	6	4	4	4	13
1988	—New York (N.L.)	7	3	.700	1.72	55	0	0	0	26	68	45	15	13	17	69
1989	—New York (N.L.)	7	4	.636	2.35	65	0	0	0	24	84⅓	62	23	22	40	88
1990	—Cincinnati (N.L.)■	4	6	.400	2.08	66	0	0	0	31	86⅔	59	24	20	38	98
1991	—Cincinnati (N.L.)	6	13	.316	3.55	58	12	1	0	6	132	116	61	52	80	108
1992	—San Diego (N.L.)■	3	6	.333	4.29	66	0	0	0	38	79⅔	84	38	38	34	66
1993	—Chicago (N.L.)■	2	4	.333	3.11	73	0	0	0	★53	75⅓	65	26	26	26	86
Major league totals (9 years)		32	42	.432	3.07	448	12	1	0	184	613⅔	503	228	209	275	622

CHAMPIONSHIP SERIES RECORD

CHAMPIONSHIP SERIES NOTES: Named N.L. Championship Series co-Most Valuable Player (1990). . . . Shares N.L. single-series record for most saves—3 (1990).

Year	Team (League)	W	L	Pct.	ERA	G	GS	CG	ShO	Sv.	IP	H	R	ER	BB	SO
1988	—New York (N.L.)	2	0	1.000	0.00	3	0	0	0	0	4⅔	1	0	0	2	0
1990	—Cincinnati (N.L.)	0	0	. . .	0.00	4	0	0	0	3	5⅔	2	0	0	3	7
Champ. series totals (2 years)		2	0	1.000	0.00	7	0	0	0	3	10⅓	3	0	0	5	7

WORLD SERIES RECORD

Year	Team (League)	W	L	Pct.	ERA	G	GS	CG	ShO	Sv.	IP	H	R	ER	BB	SO
1990	—Cincinnati (N.L.)	0	0	. . .	0.00	3	0	0	0	1	3	2	0	0	0	3

ALL-STAR GAME RECORD

Year	League	W	L	Pct.	ERA	GS	CG	ShO	Sv.	IP	H	R	ER	BB	SO
1990	—National	0	0	...	0.00	0	0	0	0	1	1	0	0	2	0

NABHOLZ, CHRIS
P, EXPOS

PERSONAL: Born January 5, 1967, in Harrisburg, Pa. ... 6-5/210. ... Throws left, bats left. ... Full name: Christopher William Nabholz. ... Name pronounced NAB-holts.
HIGH SCHOOL: Pottsville (Pa.).
COLLEGE: Towson State.
TRANSACTIONS/CAREER NOTES: Selected by Cleveland Indians organization in 30th round of free-agent draft (June 3, 1985). ... Selected by Montreal Expos organization in second round of free-agent draft (June 1, 1988). ... On Montreal disabled list (June 16-August 4, 1991); included rehabilitation assignment to Indianapolis (July 16-August 4). ... On Montreal disabled list (August 11-September 11, 1993); included rehabilitation assignment to Ottawa (August 31-September 11).
STATISTICAL NOTES: Pitched eight innings, combining with Bruce Walton (one inning) in 4-0 no-hit victory for Ottawa against Richmond (May 24, 1993).

Year	Team (League)	W	L	Pct.	ERA	G	GS	CG	ShO	Sv.	IP	H	R	ER	BB	SO
1989	—Rockford (Midw.)	13	5	.722	2.18	24	23	3	3	0	161⅓	132	54	39	41	149
1990	—Jacksonv. (South.)	7	2	.778	3.03	11	11	0	0	0	74⅓	62	28	25	27	77
	—Montreal (N.L.)	6	2	.750	2.83	11	11	1	1	0	70	43	23	22	32	53
	—Indianapolis (A.A.)	0	6	.000	4.83	10	10	0	0	0	63⅓	66	38	34	28	44
1991	—Montreal (N.L.)	8	7	.533	3.63	24	24	1	0	0	153⅔	134	66	62	57	99
	—Indianapolis (A.A.)	2	2	.500	1.86	4	4	0	0	0	19⅓	13	5	4	5	16
1992	—Montreal (N.L.)	11	12	.478	3.32	32	32	1	1	0	195	176	80	72	74	130
1993	—Montreal (N.L.)	9	8	.529	4.09	26	21	1	0	0	116⅔	100	57	53	63	74
	—Ottawa (Int'l)	1	1	.500	4.39	5	5	0	0	0	26⅔	24	15	13	7	20
Major league totals (4 years)		34	29	.540	3.51	93	88	4	2	0	535⅓	453	226	209	226	356

NAEHRING, TIM
IF, RED SOX

PERSONAL: Born February 1, 1967, in Cincinnati. ... 6-2/205. ... Throws right, bats right. ... Full name: Timothy James Naehring. ... Name pronounced NAIR-ring.
HIGH SCHOOL: LaSalle (Cincinnati).
COLLEGE: Miami of Ohio.
TRANSACTIONS/CAREER NOTES: Selected by Boston Red Sox organization in eighth round of free-agent draft (June 1, 1988). ... On Boston disabled list (August 16, 1990-remainder of season and May 18, 1991-remainder of season). ... On Boston disabled list (July 25-September 3, 1992); included rehabilitation assignment to Pawtucket (August 22-September 3). ... On Boston disabled list (April 1-July 2, 1993); included rehabilitation assignment to Pawtucket (June 13-July 2).

			BATTING												FIELDING			
Year	Team (League)	Pos.	G	AB	R	H	2B	3B	HR	RBI	Avg.	BB	SO	SB	PO	A	E	Avg.
1988	—Elmira (N.Y.-Penn)	SS	19	59	6	18	3	0	1	13	.305	8	11	0	25	51	6	.927
	—Winter Haven (FSL)	SS	42	141	17	32	7	0	0	10	.227	19	24	1	77	136	20	.914
1989	—Lynchburg (Caro.)	SS	56	209	24	63	7	1	4	37	.301	23	30	2	72	131	12	.944
	—Pawtucket (Int'l)	SS-3B	79	273	32	75	16	1	3	31	.275	27	41	2	118	192	21	.937
1990	—Pawtucket (Int'l)	SS-3B-2B	82	290	45	78	16	1	15	47	.269	37	56	0	126	240	16	.958
	—Boston (A.L.)	SS-3B-2B	24	85	10	23	6	0	2	12	.271	8	15	0	36	66	9	.919
1991	—Boston (A.L.)	SS-3B-2B	20	55	1	6	1	0	0	3	.109	6	15	0	17	53	3	.959
1992	—Boston (A.L.)	S-2-3-0	72	186	12	43	8	0	3	14	.231	18	31	0	95	170	3	.989
	—Pawtucket (Int'l)	2B	11	34	7	10	0	0	2	5	.294	8	6	1	22	39	3	.953
1993	—Pawtucket (Int'l)	3B-SS-2B	55	202	38	62	9	1	7	36	.307	35	27	0	79	133	4	.981
	—Boston (A.L.)	2B-3B-SS	39	127	14	42	10	0	1	17	.331	10	26	1	45	44	2	.978
Major league totals (4 years)			155	453	37	114	25	0	6	46	.252	42	87	1	193	333	17	.969

NAGY, CHARLES
P, INDIANS

PERSONAL: Born May 5, 1967, in Fairfield, Conn. ... 6-3/200. ... Throws right, bats left. ... Full name: Charles Harrison Nagy. ... Name pronounced NAG-ee.
HIGH SCHOOL: Roger Ludlowe (Fairfield, Conn.).
COLLEGE: Connecticut.
TRANSACTIONS/CAREER NOTES: Selected by Cleveland Indians organization in first round (17th pick overall) of free-agent draft (June 1, 1988); pick received as part of compensation for San Francisco Giants signing Type A free agent Brett Butler. ... On Cleveland disabled list (May 16-October 1, 1993); included rehabilitation assignment to Canton/Akron (June 10-24).
HONORS: Named Carolina League Pitcher of the Year (1989).
MISCELLANEOUS: Member of 1988 U.S. Olympic baseball team.

Year	Team (League)	W	L	Pct.	ERA	G	GS	CG	ShO	Sv.	IP	H	R	ER	BB	SO
1989	—Kinston (Carolina)	8	4	.667	1.51	13	13	6	*4	0	95⅓	69	22	16	24	99
	—Cant./Akr. (East.)	4	5	.444	3.35	15	14	2	0	0	94	102	44	35	32	65
1990	—Cant./Akr. (East.)	13	8	.619	2.52	23	23	•9	0	0	175	132	62	49	39	99
	—Cleveland (A.L.)	2	4	.333	5.91	9	8	0	0	0	45⅔	58	31	30	21	26
1991	—Cleveland (A.L.)	10	15	.400	4.13	33	33	6	1	0	211⅓	228	103	97	66	109
1992	—Cleveland (A.L.)	17	10	.630	2.96	33	33	10	3	0	252	245	91	83	57	169
1993	—Cleveland (A.L.)	2	6	.250	6.29	9	9	1	0	0	48⅔	66	38	34	13	30
	—Cant./Akr. (East.)	0	0	...	1.13	2	2	0	0	0	8	8	1	1	2	4
Major league totals (4 years)		31	35	.470	3.94	84	83	17	4	0	557⅔	597	263	244	157	334

ALL-STAR GAME RECORD

Year	League	W	L	Pct.	ERA	GS	CG	ShO	Sv.	IP	H	R	ER	BB	SO
1992	—American	0	0	...	0.00	0	0	0	0	1	0	0	0	0	1

NATAL, BOB
C, MARLINS

PERSONAL: Born November 13, 1965, in Long Beach, Calif. ... 5-11/190. ... Throws right, bats right. ... Full name: Robert Marcel Natal.
HIGH SCHOOL: Hilltop (Chula Vista, Calif.).
COLLEGE: UC San Diego.

TRANSACTIONS/CAREER NOTES: Selected by Montreal Expos organization in 13th round of free-agent draft (June 2, 1987).... Selected by Florida Marlins in third round (55th pick overall) of expansion draft (November 17, 1992).... On Florida disabled list (June 2-23, 1993); included rehabilitation assignment to Edmonton (June 14-23).
STATISTICAL NOTES: Led Florida State League catchers with 765 total chances in 1988.

			BATTING												FIELDING			
Year	Team (League)	Pos.	G	AB	R	H	2B	3B	HR	RBI	Avg.	BB	SO	SB	PO	A	E	Avg.
1987	—Jamestown (NYP)	C	57	180	26	58	8	4	7	32	.322	12	25	6	321	52	6	.984
1988	—W.P. Beach (FSL)	C	113	387	47	93	17	0	6	51	.240	29	50	3	*671	77	17	.978
1989	—Jacksonv. (South.)	C	46	141	12	29	8	1	0	11	.206	9	24	2	324	37	7	.981
	—W.P. Beach (FSL)	C	15	48	5	6	0	0	1	2	.125	9	9	1	68	24	3	.968
1990	—Jacksonv. (South.)	C	62	171	23	42	7	1	7	25	.246	14	42	0	344	46	10	.975
1991	—Indianapolis (A.A.)	C	16	41	2	13	4	0	0	9	.317	6	9	1	62	5	2	.971
	—Harrisburg (East.)	C	100	336	47	86	16	3	13	53	.256	49	90	1	453	45	4	.992
1992	—Indianapolis (A.A.)	C-OF	96	344	50	104	19	3	12	50	.302	28	42	3	468	54	5	.991
	—Montreal (N.L.)	C	5	6	0	0	0	0	0	0	.000	1	1	0	10	0	1	.909
1993	—Edmonton (PCL)■	C	17	66	16	21	6	1	3	16	.318	8	10	0	119	19	2	.986
	—Florida (N.L.)	C	41	117	3	25	4	1	1	6	.214	6	22	1	196	18	0	1.000
Major league totals (2 years)			46	123	3	25	4	1	1	6	.203	7	23	1	206	18	1	.996

NAVARRO, JAIME

P, BREWERS

PERSONAL: Born March 27, 1968, in Bayamon, Puerto Rico.... 6-4/225.... Throws right, bats right.... Son of Julio Navarro, pitcher, Los Angeles Angels, Detroit Tigers and Atlanta Braves (1962-66 and 1970).
HIGH SCHOOL: Luis Pales Matos (Bayamon, Puerto Rico).
COLLEGE: Miami-Dade Community College-New World Center (Fla.).
TRANSACTIONS/CAREER NOTES: Selected by Baltimore Orioles organization in second round of free-agent draft (January 14, 1986).... Selected by Orioles organization in secondary phase of free-agent draft (June 2, 1986).... Selected by Milwaukee Brewers organization in third round of free-agent draft (June 2, 1987).
RECORDS: Shares A.L. single-season record for most sacrifice flies allowed—17 (1993).
STATISTICAL NOTES: Led A.L. with five balks in 1990.

Year	Team (League)	W	L	Pct.	ERA	G	GS	CG	ShO	Sv.	IP	H	R	ER	BB	SO
1987	—Helena (Pioneer)	4	3	.571	3.57	13	13	3	0	0	85⅔	87	37	34	18	95
1988	—Stockton (Calif.)	15	5	.750	3.09	26	23	8	2	0	174⅔	148	70	60	74	151
1989	—El Paso (Texas)	5	2	.714	2.47	11	11	1	0	0	76⅔	61	29	21	35	78
	—Denver (A.A.)	1	1	.500	3.60	3	3	1	0	0	20	24	8	8	7	17
	—Milwaukee (A.L.)	7	8	.467	3.12	19	17	1	0	0	109⅔	119	47	38	32	56
1990	—Milwaukee (A.L.)	8	7	.533	4.46	32	22	3	0	1	149⅓	176	83	74	41	75
	—Denver (A.A.)	2	3	.400	4.20	6	6	1	0	0	40⅔	41	27	19	14	28
1991	—Milwaukee (A.L.)	15	12	.556	3.92	34	34	10	2	0	234	237	117	102	73	114
1992	—Milwaukee (A.L.)	17	11	.607	3.33	34	34	5	3	0	246	224	98	91	64	100
1993	—Milwaukee (A.L.)	11	12	.478	5.33	35	34	5	1	0	214⅓	254	135	*127	73	114
Major league totals (5 years)		58	50	.537	4.08	154	141	24	6	1	953⅓	1010	480	432	283	459

NAVARRO, TITO

SS, METS

PERSONAL: Born September 12, 1970, in Rio Piedras, Puerto Rico.... 5-10/165.... Throws right, bats both.... Full name: Norberto Rodriguez Navarro.
HIGH SCHOOL: Colegio del Carmen (Trujillo Alto, Puerto Rico).
TRANSACTIONS/CAREER NOTES: Signed as free agent by New York Mets organization (September 2, 1987).... On Tidewater disabled list (April 9, 1992-entire season).... On Norfolk disabled list (August 2-9, 1993).
STATISTICAL NOTES: Led South Atlantic League shortstops with 212 putouts, 440 assists and 692 total chances in 1990.... Led Eastern League shortstops with 617 total chances in 1991.
MISCELLANEOUS: Batted righthanded only (1988-91).

			BATTING												FIELDING			
Year	Team (League)	Pos.	G	AB	R	H	2B	3B	HR	RBI	Avg.	BB	SO	SB	PO	A	E	Avg.
1988	—Kingsport (Appal.)	SS	54	172	26	42	3	2	0	23	.244	30	27	3	64	133	12	*.943
1989	—Pittsfield (NYP)	SS-2B	46	157	26	44	6	2	0	14	.280	18	30	13	63	128	17	.918
1990	—Columbia (S. Atl.)	SS-1B	136	497	86	156	25	4	0	54	.314	69	55	50	†224	†440	40	.943
	—Jackson (Texas)	SS	3	11	0	2	1	0	0	1	.182	2	2	0	4	11	2	.882
1991	—Williamsport (East.)	SS	128	482	69	139	9	4	2	42	.288	73	63	42	*233	353	31	*.950
1992	—								Did not play.									
1993	—Norfolk (Int'l)	SS	96	273	35	77	11	1	0	16	.282	33	39	19	14	17	5	.861
	—GC Mets (GCL)	SS	4	14	2	4	1	1	0	5	.286	3	1	1	5	5	1	.909
	—New York (N.L.)	SS	12	17	1	1	0	0	0	1	.059	0	4	0	8	7	0	1.000
Major league totals (1 year)			12	17	1	1	0	0	0	1	.059	0	4	0	8	7	0	1.000

NEAGLE, DENNY

P, PIRATES

PERSONAL: Born September 13, 1968, in Gambrills, Md.... 6-2/217.... Throws left, bats left.... Full name: Dennis Edward Neagle Jr.... Name pronounced NAY-ghul.
HIGH SCHOOL: Arundel (Gambrills, Md.).
COLLEGE: Minnesota.
TRANSACTIONS/CAREER NOTES: Selected by Minnesota Twins organization in third round of free-agent draft (June 5, 1989).... On Portland disabled list (April 5-23, 1991).... On Minnesota disabled list (July 28-August 12, 1991).... Traded by Twins with OF Midre Cummings to Pittsburgh Pirates for P John Smiley (March 17, 1992).
MISCELLANEOUS: Appeared in one game as pinch-runner (1992).

Year	Team (League)	W	L	Pct.	ERA	G	GS	CG	ShO	Sv.	IP	H	R	ER	BB	SO
1989	—Elizabeth. (Appal.)	1	2	.333	4.50	6	3	0	0	1	22	20	11	11	8	32
	—Kenosha (Midwest)	2	1	.667	1.65	6	6	1	1	0	43⅔	25	9	8	16	40
1990	—Visalia (California)	8	0	1.000	1.43	10	10	0	0	0	63	39	13	10	16	92

N

Year	Team (League)	W	L	Pct.	ERA	G	GS	CG	ShO	Sv.	IP	H	R	ER	BB	SO
	—Orlando (Southern)	12	3	.800	2.45	17	17	4	1	0	121⅓	94	40	33	31	94
1991	—Portland (PCL)	9	4	.692	3.27	19	17	1	1	0	104⅔	101	41	38	32	94
	—Minnesota (A.L.)	0	1	.000	4.05	7	3	0	0	0	20	28	9	9	7	14
1992	—Pittsburgh (N.L.)■	4	6	.400	4.48	55	6	0	0	2	86⅓	81	46	43	43	77
1993	—Pittsburgh (N.L.)	3	5	.375	5.31	50	7	0	0	1	81⅓	82	49	48	37	73
	—Buffalo (A.A.)	0	0	...	0.00	3	0	0	0	0	3⅓	3	0	0	2	6
A.L. totals (1 year)		0	1	.000	4.05	7	3	0	0	0	20	28	9	9	7	14
N.L. totals (2 years)		7	11	.389	4.88	105	13	0	0	3	167⅔	163	95	91	80	150
Major league totals (3 years)		7	12	.368	4.80	112	16	0	0	3	187⅔	191	104	100	87	164

CHAMPIONSHIP SERIES RECORD

Year	Team (League)	W	L	Pct.	ERA	G	GS	CG	ShO	Sv.	IP	H	R	ER	BB	SO
1992	—Pittsburgh (N.L.)	0	0	...	27.00	2	0	0	0	0	1⅔	4	5	5	3	0

NEEL, TROY

1B/DH, ATHLETICS

PERSONAL: Born September 14, 1965, in Freeport, Tex. . . . 6-4/215. . . . Throws right, bats left. . . . Full name: Troy Lee Neel.
HIGH SCHOOL: Brazoswood (Clute, Tex.).
COLLEGE: Texas A&M and Howard College (Tex.).
TRANSACTIONS/CAREER NOTES: Selected by Cleveland Indians organization in ninth round of free-agent draft (January 14, 1986). . . . Traded by Indians organization to Oakland Athletics organization for IF Larry Arndt (January 16, 1991). . . . On Tacoma disabled list (April 15-22, 1991). . . . On suspended list (September 23-27, 1993).
STATISTICAL NOTES: Tied for Eastern League lead in being hit by pitch with nine in 1989. . . . Led Southern League with .525 slugging percentage, .410 on-base percentage and 18 intentional bases on balls received in 1991.

			BATTING												FIELDING			
Year	Team (League)	Pos.	G	AB	R	H	2B	3B	HR	RBI	Avg.	BB	SO	SB	PO	A	E	Avg.
1986	—Batavia (NY-Penn)	1B	4	13	0	0	0	0	0	1	.000	0	8	0	2	1	0	1.000
1987	—Burlington (Appal.)	1B	59	192	36	54	17	0	10	•59	.281	25	59	0	424	33	9	.981
1988	—Waterloo (Midw.)	1B	91	331	49	96	20	1	8	57	.290	38	76	0	790	63	12	.986
1989	—Cant./Akr. (East.)	OF-1B	124	404	58	118	21	2	21	73	.292	51	87	5	239	22	7	.974
1990	—Colo. Springs (PCL)	1B-OF-3B	98	288	39	81	15	0	6	50	.281	43	52	5	523	55	7	.988
1991	—Huntsville (South.)■	1B-OF	110	364	64	101	21	0	23	68	.277	82	75	1	354	34	7	.982
	—Tacoma (PCL)	OF	18	59	7	14	3	1	0	7	.237	7	14	0	15	0	0	1.000
1992	—Tacoma (PCL)	OF-P	112	396	61	139	36	3	17	74	*.351	60	84	2	49	4	2	.964
	—Oakland (A.L.)	OF-1B	24	53	8	14	3	0	3	9	.264	5	15	0	16	1	3	.850
1993	—Oakland (A.L.)	1B	123	427	59	124	21	0	19	63	.290	49	101	3	236	22	5	.981
	—Tacoma (PCL)	DH	13	50	11	18	4	0	1	9	.360	6	9	2	...	...	...	...
Major league totals (2 years)			147	480	67	138	24	0	22	72	.288	54	116	3	252	23	8	.972

RECORD AS PITCHER

Year	Team (League)	W	L	Pct.	ERA	G	GS	CG	ShO	Sv.	IP	H	R	ER	BB	SO
1992	—Tacoma (PCL)	0	0	...	6.75	3	0	0	0	0	4	8	3	3	4	0

NELSON, GENE

P

PERSONAL: Born December 3, 1960, in Tampa, Fla. . . . 6-0/174. . . . Throws right, bats right. . . . Full name: Wayland Eugene Nelson II.
HIGH SCHOOL: Pasco (Dade City, Fla.).
TRANSACTIONS/CAREER NOTES: Selected by Texas Rangers organization in 29th round of free-agent draft (June 6, 1978). . . . Traded by Rangers organization with P Ray Fontenot to New York Yankees organization for P Bob Polinsky, P Neal Mersch and P Mark Softy (October 8, 1979), completing deal in which Yankees traded OF Mickey Rivers and three players to be named later to Rangers for 3B Amos Lewis and two players to be named later (August 1, 1979). . . . On New York disabled list (April 10-May 4, 1981); included rehabilitation assignment to Fort Lauderdale (April 17-May 4). . . . Traded by Yankees organization with P Bill Caudill, a player to be named later and cash to Seattle Mariners for P Shane Rawley (April 1, 1982); Mariners organization acquired OF Bobby Brown to complete deal (April 6, 1982). . . . On Salt Lake City disabled list (June 25-July 31, 1983). . . . Traded by Mariners organization with P Jerry Don Gleaton to Chicago White Sox for P Salome Barojas (June 27, 1984). . . . Traded by White Sox with a player to be named later to Oakland Athletics for IF Donnie Hill (December 11, 1986); A's acquired P Bruce Tanner to complete deal (December 18, 1986). . . . On disabled list (April 8-23, 1989 and April 10-May 20, 1991). . . . Released by A's (August 11, 1992). . . . Signed by California Angels organization (February 17, 1993). . . . Released by Angels (September 3, 1993). . . . Signed by Texas Rangers (September 11, 1993). . . . Granted free agency (October 15, 1993).
MISCELLANEOUS: Made an out in only plate appearance (1985). . . . Appeared in three games as pinch-runner (1988). . . . Appeared in one game as pinch-runner (1989 and 1992).

Year	Team (League)	W	L	Pct.	ERA	G	GS	CG	ShO	Sv.	IP	H	R	ER	BB	SO
1978	—GC Rangers (GCL)	5	0	•1.000	2.25	14	5	0	0	3	52	41	18	13	20	28
1979	—Asheville (W. Car.)	13	5	*.722	3.60	33	17	7	1	0	155	149	77	62	44	96
1980	—Fort Lauder. (FSL)■	*20	3	*.870	1.97	27	25	*16	*5	0	196	146	51	43	70	130
1981	—New York (A.L.)	3	1	.750	4.85	8	7	0	0	0	39	40	24	21	23	16
	—Fort Lauder. (FSL)	0	0	...	5.40	2	2	0	0	0	10	9	6	6	5	8
	—Columbus (Int'l)	4	0	1.000	2.53	5	4	0	0	1	32	25	9	9	14	37
1982	—Seattle (A.L.)■	6	9	.400	4.62	22	19	2	1	0	122⅔	133	70	63	60	71
	—Salt Lake City (PCL)	1	3	.250	3.35	5	5	2	0	0	37⅔	36	18	14	28	22
1983	—Salt Lake City (PCL)	9	4	.692	5.18	16	16	7	2	0	99	115	65	57	28	74
	—Seattle (A.L.)	0	3	.000	7.88	10	5	1	0	0	32	38	29	28	21	11
1984	—Salt Lake City (PCL)	6	8	.429	5.63	17	17	6	1	0	112	138	75	70	54	89
	—Chicago (A.L.)■	3	5	.375	4.46	20	9	2	0	1	74⅔	72	38	37	17	36
1985	—Chicago (A.L.)	10	10	.500	4.26	46	18	1	0	2	145⅔	144	74	69	67	101
1986	—Chicago (A.L.)	6	6	.500	3.85	54	1	0	0	6	114⅔	118	52	49	41	70

Year	Team (League)	W	L	Pct.	ERA	G	GS	CG	ShO	Sv.	IP	H	R	ER	BB	SO
1987	—Oakland (A.L.)■	6	5	.545	3.93	54	6	0	0	3	123⅔	120	58	54	35	94
1988	—Oakland (A.L.)	9	6	.600	3.06	54	1	0	0	3	111⅔	93	42	38	38	67
1989	—Oakland (A.L.)	3	5	.375	3.26	50	0	0	0	3	80	60	33	29	30	70
1990	—Oakland (A.L.)	3	3	.500	1.57	51	0	0	0	5	74⅔	55	14	13	17	38
1991	—Oakland (A.L.)	1	5	.167	6.84	44	0	0	0	0	48⅔	60	38	37	23	23
1992	—Oakland (A.L.)	3	1	.750	6.45	28	2	0	0	0	51⅔	68	37	37	22	23
1993	—Calif.-Tex. (A.L.)■	0	5	.000	3.12	52	0	0	0	5	60⅔	60	28	21	24	35
Major league totals (13 years)		53	64	.453	4.13	493	68	6	1	28	1079⅔	1061	537	496	418	655

CHAMPIONSHIP SERIES RECORD

CHAMPIONSHIP SERIES NOTES: Shares A.L. single-series record for most games won—2 (1988).

Year	Team (League)	W	L	Pct.	ERA	G	GS	CG	ShO	Sv.	IP	H	R	ER	BB	SO
1988	—Oakland (A.L.)	2	0	1.000	0.00	2	0	0	0	0	4⅔	5	0	0	1	0
1989	—Oakland (A.L.)	0	0	...	0.00	1	0	0	0	0	1⅓	1	0	0	0	2
1990	—Oakland (A.L.)	0	0	...	0.00	1	0	0	0	0	1⅔	3	0	0	0	0
Champ. series totals (3 years)		2	0	1.000	0.00	4	0	0	0	0	7⅔	9	0	0	1	2

WORLD SERIES RECORD

Year	Team (League)	W	L	Pct.	ERA	G	GS	CG	ShO	Sv.	IP	H	R	ER	BB	SO
1988	—Oakland (A.L.)	0	0	...	1.42	3	0	0	0	0	6⅓	4	1	1	3	3
1989	—Oakland (A.L.)	0	0	...	54.00	2	0	0	0	0	1	4	6	6	2	1
1990	—Oakland (A.L.)	0	0	...	0.00	2	0	0	0	0	5	3	0	0	2	0
World Series totals (3 years)		0	0	...	5.11	7	0	0	0	0	12⅓	11	7	7	7	4

NELSON, JEFF

P, MARINERS

PERSONAL: Born November 17, 1966, in Baltimore. . . . 6-8/235. . . . Throws right, bats right. . . . Full name: Jeffrey Allen Nelson.

HIGH SCHOOL: Catonsville (Md.).

COLLEGE: Catonsville Community College (Md.).

TRANSACTIONS/CAREER NOTES: Selected by Los Angeles Dodgers organization in 22nd round of free-agent draft (June 4, 1984). . . . On disabled list (April 10-June 4, 1986). . . . Selected by Calgary, Seattle Mariners organization from Dodgers organization in Rule 5 minor league draft (December 9, 1986). . . . On disabled list (July 16, 1989-remainder of season).

MISCELLANEOUS: Appeared in one game as outfielder with no chances with Seattle (1993).

Year	Team (League)	W	L	Pct.	ERA	G	GS	CG	ShO	Sv.	IP	H	R	ER	BB	SO
1984	—Great Falls (Pio.)	0	0	...	54.00	1	0	0	0	0	⅔	3	4	4	3	1
	—GC Dodgers (GCL)	0	0	...	1.35	9	0	0	0	0	13⅓	6	3	2	6	7
1985	—GC Dodgers (GCL)	0	5	.000	5.51	14	7	0	0	0	47⅓	72	50	29	32	31
1986	—Great Falls (Pio.)	0	0	...	13.50	3	0	0	0	0	2	5	3	3	3	1
	—Bakersfield (Calif.)	0	7	.000	6.69	24	11	0	0	0	71⅓	79	83	53	84	37
1987	—Salinas (Calif.)■	3	7	.300	5.74	17	16	1	0	0	80	80	61	51	71	43
1988	—San Bern. (Calif.)	8	9	.471	5.54	27	27	1	1	0	149⅓	163	115	92	91	94
1989	—Williamsport (East.)	7	5	.583	3.31	15	15	2	0	0	92⅓	72	41	34	53	61
1990	—Williamsport (East.)	1	4	.200	6.44	10	10	0	0	0	43⅓	65	35	31	18	14
	—Peninsula (Caro.)	2	2	.500	3.15	18	7	1	1	6	60	47	21	21	25	49
1991	—Jacksonv. (South.)	4	0	1.000	1.27	21	0	0	0	12	28⅓	23	5	4	9	34
	—Calgary (PCL)	3	4	.429	3.90	28	0	0	0	21	32⅓	39	19	14	15	26
1992	—Calgary (PCL)	1	0	1.000	0.00	2	0	0	0	0	3⅔	0	0	0	1	0
	—Seattle (A.L.)	1	7	.125	3.44	66	0	0	0	6	81	71	34	31	44	46
1993	—Calgary (PCL)	1	0	1.000	1.17	5	0	0	0	1	7⅔	6	1	1	2	6
	—Seattle (A.L.)	5	3	.625	4.35	71	0	0	0	1	60	57	30	29	34	61
Major league totals (2 years)		6	10	.375	3.83	137	0	0	0	7	141	128	64	60	78	107

NEN, ROBB

P, MARLINS

PERSONAL: Born November 28, 1969, in San Pedro, Calif. . . . 6-4/200. . . . Throws right, bats right. . . . Full name: Robert Allen Nen. . . . Son of Dick Nen, first baseman, Los Angeles Dodgers, Washington Senators and Chicago Cubs (1963, 1965-68 and 1970).

HIGH SCHOOL: Los Alamitos (Calif.).

TRANSACTIONS/CAREER NOTES: Selected by Texas Rangers organization in 32nd round of free-agent draft (June 2, 1987). . . . On Charlotte disabled list (beginning of season-April 26 and May 6-May 24, 1990). . . . On disabled list (April 23-June 10, June 28-July 8 and July 11-September 3, 1991; and May 7-September 9, 1992). . . . On Texas disabled list (June 12-July 17, 1993); included rehabilitation assignment to Oklahoma City (June 21-July 17). . . . Traded by Rangers with P Kurt Miller to Florida Marlins for P Cris Carpenter (July 17, 1993).

Year	Team (League)	W	L	Pct.	ERA	G	GS	CG	ShO	Sv.	IP	H	R	ER	BB	SO
1987	—GC Rangers (GCL)	0	0	...	7.71	2	0	0	0	0	2⅓	4	2	2	3	4
1988	—Gastonia (S. Atl.)	0	5	.000	7.45	14	10	0	0	0	48⅓	69	57	40	45	36
	—Butte (Pioneer)	4	5	.444	8.75	14	13	0	0	0	48⅓	65	55	47	45	30
1989	—Gastonia (S. Atl.)	7	4	.636	2.41	24	24	1	1	0	138⅓	96	47	37	76	146
1990	—Charlotte (Fla. St.)	1	4	.200	3.69	11	11	1	0	0	53⅔	44	28	22	36	38
	—Tulsa (Texas)	0	5	.000	5.06	7	7	0	0	0	26⅔	23	20	15	21	21
1991	—Tulsa (Texas)	0	2	.000	5.79	6	6	0	0	0	28	24	21	18	20	23
1992	—Tulsa (Texas)	1	1	.500	2.16	4	4	1	0	0	25	21	7	6	2	20
1993	—Texas (A.L.)	1	1	.500	6.35	9	3	0	0	0	22⅔	28	17	16	26	12
	—Okla. City (A.A.)	0	2	.000	6.67	6	5	0	0	0	28⅓	45	22	21	18	12
	—Florida (N.L.)■	1	0	1.000	7.02	15	1	0	0	0	33⅓	35	28	26	20	27
A.L. totals (1 year)		1	1	.500	6.35	9	3	0	0	0	22⅔	28	17	16	26	12
N.L. totals (1 year)		1	0	1.000	7.02	15	1	0	0	0	33⅓	35	28	26	20	27
Major league totals (1 year)		2	1	.667	6.75	24	4	0	0	0	56	63	45	42	46	39

NEWFIELD, MARC

1B/OF, MARINERS

PERSONAL: Born October 19, 1972, in Sacramento, Calif.... 6-4/205.... Throws right, bats right.... Full name: Marc Alexander Newfield.
HIGH SCHOOL: Marina (Huntington Beach, Calif.).
TRANSACTIONS/CAREER NOTES: Selected by Seattle Mariners organization in first round (sixth pick overall) of free-agent draft (June 4, 1990).... On disabled list (June 3, 1992-remainder of season).
HONORS: Named Arizona League Most Valuable Player (1990).

			BATTING												FIELDING			
Year	Team (League)	Pos.	G	AB	R	H	2B	3B	HR	RBI	Avg.	BB	SO	SB	PO	A	E	Avg.
1990	—Ariz. Mariners (Ar.)..	1B-OF	51	192	34	60	•13	2	6	38	.313	25	20	4	358	13	5	.987
1991	—San Bern. (Calif.)......	OF-1B	125	440	64	132	22	3	11	68	.300	59	90	12	245	10	8	.970
	—Jacksonv. (South.) ..	OF-1B	6	26	4	6	3	0	0	2	.231	0	8	0	16	0	1	.941
1992	—Jacksonv. (South.) ..	OF	45	162	15	40	12	0	4	19	.247	12	34	1	17	1	0	1.000
1993	—Jacksonv. (South.) ..	1B-OF	91	336	48	103	18	0	19	51	.307	33	35	1	435	21	3	.993
	—Seattle (A.L.)...........	OF	22	66	5	15	3	0	1	7	.227	2	8	0	0	0	0	...
Major league totals (1 year)			22	66	5	15	3	0	1	7	.227	2	8	0	0	0	0	...

NEWSON, WARREN

OF, WHITE SOX

PERSONAL: Born July 3, 1964, in Newnan, Ga.... 5-7/202.... Throws left, bats left.... Full name: Warren Dale Newson.
HIGH SCHOOL: Newnan (Ga.).
COLLEGE: Middle Georgia College.
TRANSACTIONS/CAREER NOTES: Selected by San Diego Padres organization in fourth round of free-agent draft (January 14, 1986).... Traded by Padres with IF Joey Cora and IF Kevin Garner to Chicago White Sox organization for P Adam Peterson and P Steve Rosenberg (March 31, 1991).... On Nashville disabled list (April 29-May 22, 1993).
STATISTICAL NOTES: Led Texas League with 10 intentional bases on balls received in 1989.

			BATTING												FIELDING			
Year	Team (League)	Pos.	G	AB	R	H	2B	3B	HR	RBI	Avg.	BB	SO	SB	PO	A	E	Avg.
1986	—Spokane (N'west).....	OF	54	159	29	37	8	1	2	31	.233	47	37	3	54	3	3	.950
1987	—Char., S.C. (S. Atl.)...	OF	58	191	50	66	12	2	7	32	.346	52	35	13	81	4	2	.977
	—Reno (California)......	OF	51	165	44	51	7	2	6	28	.309	39	34	2	60	5	8	.890
1988	—Riverside (Calif.)	OF	130	438	99	130	23	•7	*22	91	.297	107	102	36	182	7	11	.945
1989	—Wichita (Texas)	OF	128	427	94	130	20	6	18	70	.304	*103	99	20	191	15	5	.976
1990	—Las Vegas (PCL)	OF	123	404	80	123	20	3	13	58	.304	83	110	13	146	4	10	.938
1991	—Vancouver (PCL)■...	OF	33	111	19	41	12	1	2	19	.369	30	26	5	53	1	0	1.000
	—Chicago (A.L.).........	OF	71	132	20	39	5	0	4	25	.295	28	34	2	48	3	2	.962
1992	—Chicago (A.L.).........	OF	63	136	19	30	3	0	1	11	.221	37	38	3	67	5	0	1.000
	—Vancouver (PCL)	OF	19	59	7	15	0	0	0	9	.254	16	21	3	42	1	1	.977
1993	—Nashville (A.A.)........	OF	61	176	40	60	8	2	4	21	.341	38	38	5	74	7	1	.988
	—Chicago (A.L.).........	OF	26	40	9	12	0	0	2	6	.300	9	12	0	5	0	0	1.000
Major league totals (3 years)			160	308	48	81	8	0	7	42	.263	74	84	5	120	8	2	.985

CHAMPIONSHIP SERIES RECORD

			BATTING												FIELDING			
Year	Team (League)	Pos.	G	AB	R	H	2B	3B	HR	RBI	Avg.	BB	SO	SB	PO	A	E	Avg.
1993	—Chicago (A.L.).........	DH-PH	2	5	1	1	0	0	1	1	.200	0	1	0	...	...	...	...

NICHOLS, ROD

P

PERSONAL: Born December 29, 1964, in Burlington, Ia.... 6-2/190.... Throws right, bats right.... Full name: Rodney Lea Nichols.
HIGH SCHOOL: Highland (Alberquerque, N.M.).
COLLEGE: New Mexico.
TRANSACTIONS/CAREER NOTES: Selected by Cleveland Indians organization in fifth round of free-agent draft (June 3, 1985).... On disabled list (July 12-August 18, 1986).... On Cleveland disabled list (March 26-May 12, 1988).... On Cleveland disabled list (March 19-June 12, 1989); included rehabilitation assignment to Colorado Springs (May 24-June 12).... Granted free agency (December 19, 1992).... Signed by Los Angeles Dodgers organization (January 15, 1993).... Granted free agency (October 15, 1993).

Year	Team (League)	W	L	Pct.	ERA	G	GS	CG	ShO	Sv.	IP	H	R	ER	BB	SO
1985	—Batavia (NY-Penn)....	5	5	.500	3.00	13	13	3	0	0	84	74	40	28	33	93
1986	—Waterloo (Midw.).......	8	5	.615	4.06	20	20	3	1	0	115⅓	128	56	52	21	83
1987	—Kinston (Carolina)	4	2	.667	4.02	9	8	1	1	0	56	53	27	25	14	61
	—Williamsport (East.).....	4	3	.571	3.69	16	16	1	0	0	100	107	53	41	33	60
1988	—Kinston (Carolina)	3	1	.750	4.50	4	4	0	0	0	24	26	13	12	15	19
	—Colo. Springs (PCL).....	2	6	.250	5.68	10	9	2	0	0	58⅔	69	41	37	17	43
	—Cleveland (A.L.)..........	1	7	.125	5.06	11	10	3	0	0	69⅓	73	41	39	23	31
1989	—Colo. Springs (PCL).....	8	1	.889	3.58	10	10	2	1	0	65⅓	57	28	26	30	41
	—Cleveland (A.L.)..........	4	6	.400	4.40	15	11	0	0	0	71⅔	81	42	35	24	42
1990	—Cleveland (A.L.)..........	0	3	.000	7.88	4	2	0	0	0	16	24	14	14	6	3
	—Colo. Springs (PCL).....	12	9	.571	5.13	22	22	4	•2	0	133⅓	160	84	76	48	74
1991	—Cleveland (A.L.)..........	2	11	.154	3.54	31	16	3	1	1	137⅓	145	63	54	30	76
1992	—Cleveland (A.L.)..........	4	3	.571	4.53	30	9	0	0	0	105⅓	114	58	53	31	56
	—Colo. Springs (PCL).....	3	3	.500	5.67	9	9	1	0	0	54	65	39	34	16	35
1993	—Albuquerque (PCL)■...	8	5	.615	4.30	21	21	3	1	0	127⅔	132	68	61	50	79
	—Los Angeles (N.L.)	0	1	.000	5.68	4	0	0	0	0	6⅓	9	5	4	2	3
A.L. totals (5 years)		11	30	.268	4.39	91	48	6	1	1	399⅔	437	218	195	114	208
N.L. totals (1 year)		0	1	.000	5.68	4	0	0	0	0	6⅓	9	5	4	2	3
Major league totals (6 years)		11	31	.262	4.41	95	48	6	1	1	406	446	223	199	116	211

NIED, DAVID
P, ROCKIES

PERSONAL: Born December 22, 1968, in Dallas. . . . 6-2/185. . . . Throws right, bats right. . . . Full name: David Glen Nied. . . . Name pronounced NEED.
HIGH SCHOOL: Duncanville (Tex.).
TRANSACTIONS/CAREER NOTES: Selected by Atlanta Braves organization in 14th round of free-agent draft (June 2, 1987). . . . Selected by Colorado Rockies in first round (first pick overall) of expansion draft (November 17, 1992). . . . On Colorado disabled list (May 28-September 4, 1993); included rehabilitation assignment to Central Valley (August 19-24) and Colorado Springs (August 24-September 4).
STATISTICAL NOTES: Tied for South Atlantic League lead with 15 home runs allowed in 1988.

Year	Team (League)	W	L	Pct.	ERA	G	GS	CG	ShO	Sv.	IP	H	R	ER	BB	SO
1988	—Sumter (S. Atl.)	12	9	.571	3.76	27	27	3	1	0	165⅓	156	78	69	53	133
1989	—Durham (Carolina)	5	2	.714	6.63	12	12	0	0	0	58⅓	74	47	43	23	38
	—Burlington (Midw.)	5	6	.455	3.83	13	12	2	1	0	80	78	38	34	23	73
1990	—Durham (Carolina)	1	1	.500	3.83	10	10	0	0	0	42⅓	38	19	18	14	27
	—Burlington (Midw.)	5	3	.625	2.25	10	9	1	1	0	64	55	21	16	10	66
1991	—Greenville (South.)	7	3	.700	2.41	15	15	1	0	0	89⅔	79	26	24	20	101
	—Durham (Carolina)	8	3	.727	1.56	13	12	2	•2	0	80⅔	46	19	14	23	77
1992	—Richmond (Int'l)	*14	9	.609	2.84	26	26	*7	2	0	168	144	73	53	44	*159
	—Atlanta (N.L.)	3	0	1.000	1.17	6	2	0	0	0	23	10	3	3	5	19
1993	—Colorado (N.L.)■	5	9	.357	5.17	16	16	1	0	0	87	99	53	50	42	46
	—Central Vall. (Cal.)	0	1	.000	3.00	1	1	0	0	0	3	3	2	1	3	3
	—Colo. Springs (PCL)	0	2	.000	9.00	3	3	0	0	0	15	24	17	15	6	11
	Major league totals (2 years)	8	9	.471	4.34	22	18	1	0	0	110	109	56	53	47	65

WORLD SERIES RECORD

Year	Team (League)	W	L	Pct.	ERA	G	GS	CG	ShO	Sv.	IP	H	R	ER	BB	SO
1992	—Atlanta (N.L.)							Did not play.								

NIELSEN, JERRY
P, ANGELS

PERSONAL: Born August 5, 1966, in Sacramento, Calif. . . . 6-3/188. . . . Throws left, bats left. . . . Full name: Gerald Arthur Nielsen.
HIGH SCHOOL: Jesuit (Carmichael, Calif.).
COLLEGE: Sacramento (Calif.) City College and Florida State.
TRANSACTIONS/CAREER NOTES: Selected by New York Mets organization in 12th round of free-agent draft (January 3, 1985). . . . Selected by Mets organization in secondary phase of free-agent draft (June 3, 1985). . . . Selected by Detroit Tigers organization in secondary phase of free-agent draft (January 14, 1986). . . . Selected by Mets organization in secondary phase of free-agent draft (June 2, 1986). . . . Selected by Oakland Athletics organization in 11th round of free-agent draft (June 2, 1987). . . . Selected by New York Yankees organization in 18th round of free-agent draft (June 1, 1988). . . . Traded by Yankees with 1B J.T. Snow and P Russ Springer to California Angels for P Jim Abbott (December 6, 1992).

Year	Team (League)	W	L	Pct.	ERA	G	GS	CG	ShO	Sv.	IP	H	R	ER	BB	SO
1988	—Oneonta (NYP)	6	2	.750	0.71	19	1	0	0	0	38	27	6	3	18	35
1989	—Prin. William (Car.)	3	2	.600	2.19	39	0	0	0	4	49⅓	26	14	12	25	45
1990	—Prin. William (Car.)	7	12	.368	3.92	26	26	1	1	0	151⅔	149	76	66	79	119
1991	—Fort Lauder. (FSL)	3	3	.500	2.78	42	0	0	0	4	64⅔	50	29	20	31	66
1992	—Alb./Colon. (East.)	3	5	.375	1.19	36	0	0	0	11	53	38	8	7	15	59
	—New York (A.L.)	1	0	1.000	4.58	20	0	0	0	0	19⅔	17	10	10	18	12
	—Columbus (Int'l)	0	0	...	1.80	4	0	0	0	1	5	2	1	1	2	5
1993	—Vancouver (PCL)■	2	5	.286	4.20	33	5	0	0	0	55⅔	70	32	26	20	45
	—California (A.L.)	0	0	...	8.03	10	0	0	0	0	12⅓	18	13	11	4	8
	Major league totals (2 years)	1	0	1.000	5.91	30	0	0	0	0	32	35	23	21	22	20

NIEVES, MELVIN
OF, PADRES

PERSONAL: Born December 28, 1971, in San Juan, Puerto Rico. . . . 6-2/210. . . . Throws right, bats both. . . . Full name: Melvin Ramos Nieves. . . . Name pronounced nee-EV-es.
HIGH SCHOOL: Ivis Pales Matos (Santa Rosa, Puerto Rico).
TRANSACTIONS/CAREER NOTES: Signed as free agent by Atlanta Braves organization (May 20, 1988). . . . On Durham disabled list (April 11-June 13, 1991). . . . On Richmond disabled list (May 18-26, 1993). . . . Traded by Braves with P Donnie Elliott and OF Vince Moore to San Diego Padres for 1B Fred McGriff (July 18, 1993).

			BATTING											FIELDING			
Year	Team (League)	Pos.	G	AB	R	H	2B	3B	HR	RBI	Avg.	BB	SO	SB	PO	A	E	Avg.
1988	—GC Braves (GCL)	OF	56	170	16	30	6	0	1	12	.176	20	53	5	100	1	2	.981
1989	—Pulaski (Appal.)	OF	64	231	43	64	16	3	9	46	.277	30	59	6	45	1	6	.885
1990	—Sumter (S. Atl.)	OF	126	459	60	130	24	7	9	59	.283	53	125	10	227	7	11	.955
1991	—Durham (Carolina)	OF	64	201	31	53	11	0	9	25	.264	40	53	3	75	8	5	.943
1992	—Durham (Carolina)	OF	31	106	18	32	9	1	8	32	.302	17	33	4	61	4	2	.970
	—Greenville (South.)	OF	100	350	61	99	23	5	18	76	.283	52	98	6	127	9	5	.965
	—Atlanta (N.L.)	OF	12	19	0	4	1	0	0	1	.211	2	7	0	8	0	3	.727
1993	—Richmond (Int'l)	OF	78	273	38	76	10	3	10	36	.278	25	84	4	124	5	7	.949
	—Las Vegas (PCL)■	OF	43	159	31	49	10	1	7	24	.308	18	42	2	79	4	1	.988
	—San Diego (N.L.)	OF	19	47	4	9	0	0	2	3	.191	3	21	0	27	0	2	.931
	Major league totals (2 years)		31	66	4	13	1	0	2	4	.197	5	28	0	35	0	5	.875

NILSSON, DAVE
C, BREWERS

PERSONAL: Born December 14, 1969, in Brisbane, Queensland, Australia. . . . 6-3/215. . . . Throws right, bats left. . . . Full name: David Wayne Nilsson.
HIGH SCHOOL: Kedron (Brisbane, Australia).
TRANSACTIONS/CAREER NOTES: Signed as free agent by Milwaukee Brewers organization (February 9, 1987). . . . On disabled list (April 30-May 26, 1990). . . . On Denver disabled list (August 13, 1991-remainder of season). . . . On Milwaukee disabled list (July 6-24, 1992); included rehabilitation assignment to Denver (July 16-24). . . . On

Milwaukee disabled list (March 27-April 14, 1993); included rehabilitation assignment to El Paso (April 5-14).... On Milwaukee disabled list (May 18-June 22, 1993); included rehabilitation assignment to New Orleans (May 26-June 13).

							BATTING								FIELDING		
Year	**Team (League)**	**Pos.**	**G**	**AB**	**R**	**H**	**2B**	**3B**	**HR**	**RBI**	**Avg.**	**BB**	**SO**	**SB**	**PO**	**A**	**E**	**Avg.**
1987	—Helena (Pioneer)	C	55	188	36	74	13	0	1	21	.394	5	7	0	329	28	7	.981
1988	—Beloit (Midwest)	C-1B	95	332	28	74	15	2	4	41	.223	25	49	2	526	64	6	.990
1989	—Stockton (Calif.)	C-2B	125	472	59	115	16	6	5	56	.244	50	76	2	703	66	13	.983
1990	—Stockton (Calif.)	C-1B-3B	107	359	70	104	22	3	7	47	.290	43	36	6	600	86	12	.983
1991	—El Paso (Texas)	C-3B	65	249	52	104	24	3	5	57	.418	27	14	4	348	46	8	.980
	—Denver (A.A.)	C-1B-3B	28	95	10	22	8	0	1	14	.232	17	16	1	146	16	2	.988
1992	—Denver (A.A.)	C-1B-3B	66	240	38	76	16	7	3	39	.317	23	19	10	350	51	6	.985
	—Milwaukee (A.L.)	C-1B	51	164	15	38	8	0	4	25	.232	17	18	2	231	16	2	.992
1993	—El Paso (Texas)	C	5	17	5	8	1	0	1	7	.471	2	4	1	31	9	0	1.000
	—Milwaukee (A.L.)	C-1B	100	296	35	76	10	2	7	40	.257	37	36	3	457	33	9	.982
	—New Orleans (A.A.)	C	17	61	9	21	6	0	1	9	.344	5	6	0	55	7	1	.984
Major league totals (2 years)			151	460	50	114	18	2	11	65	.248	54	54	5	688	49	11	.985

NIXON, OTIS

OF, RED SOX

PERSONAL: Born January 9, 1959, in Evergreen, N.C.... 6-2/180.... Throws right, bats both.... Full name: Otis Junior Nixon.... Brother of Donell Nixon, outfielder, Cleveland Indians organization.
HIGH SCHOOL: Columbus (N.C.).
COLLEGE: Louisburg (N.C.) College.
TRANSACTIONS/CAREER NOTES: Selected by Cincinnati Reds organization in 21st round of free-agent draft (June 6, 1978).... Selected by California Angels organization in secondary phase of free-agent draft (January 9, 1979).... Selected by New York Yankees organization in secondary phase of free-agent draft (June 5, 1979).... Traded by Yankees with P George Frazier and a player to be named later to Cleveland Indians for 3B Toby Harrah and a player to be named later (February 5, 1984); Yankees organization acquired P Rick Browne and Indians organization acquired P Guy Elston to complete deal (February 8, 1984).... Granted free agency (October 15, 1987).... Signed by Indianapolis, Montreal Expos organization (March 5, 1988).... Traded by Expos with 3B Boi Rodriguez to Atlanta Braves for C Jimmy Kremers and a player to be named later (April 1, 1991); Sumter, Expos organization, acquired P Keith Morrison to complete deal (June 3, 1991).... On suspended list (August 13-16, 1991).... On disqualified list (September 16, 1991-April 24, 1992).... Granted free agency (November 11, 1991).... Re-signed by Braves (December 12, 1991).... Granted free agency (October 25, 1993).... Signed by Boston Red Sox (December 7, 1993).
RECORDS: Shares modern major league single-game record for most stolen bases—6 (June 16, 1991).
STATISTICAL NOTES: Led Appalachian League third basemen with .945 fielding percentage, 52 putouts, 120 assists, 182 total chances and 12 double plays in 1979.... Led International League in caught stealing with 29 in 1983.... Led International League outfielders with .992 fielding percentage, 363 putouts and 371 total chances in 1983.

							BATTING								FIELDING		
Year	**Team (League)**	**Pos.**	**G**	**AB**	**R**	**H**	**2B**	**3B**	**HR**	**RBI**	**Avg.**	**BB**	**SO**	**SB**	**PO**	**A**	**E**	**Avg.**
1979	—Paintsville (Appal.)	3B-SS	63	203	58	58	10	3	1	25	.286	*57	40	5	†54	†122	11	†.941
1980	—Greensboro (S. Atl.)	3B-SS	136	493	*124	137	12	5	3	48	.278	*113	88	*67	164	308	36	.929
1981	—Nashville (South.)	SS	127	407	89	102	9	2	0	20	.251	*110	101	71	198	348	*56	.907
1982	—Nashville (South.)	SS-2B	72	283	47	80	3	2	0	20	.283	59	56	61	126	211	23	.936
	—Columbus (Int'l)	2B-SS	59	207	43	58	4	0	0	14	.280	49	41	46	104	169	14	.951
1983	—Columbus (Int'l)	OF-2B	138	*557	*129	*162	11	6	0	41	.291	96	83	*94	†385	24	4	†.990
	—New York (A.L.)	OF	13	14	2	2	0	0	0	0	.143	1	5	2	14	1	1	.938
1984	—Cleveland (A.L.)■	OF	49	91	16	14	0	0	0	1	.154	8	11	12	81	3	0	1.000
	—Maine (Int'l)	OF	72	253	42	70	5	1	0	22	.277	44	45	39	206	7	1	.995
1985	—Cleveland (A.L.)	OF	104	162	34	38	4	0	3	9	.235	8	27	20	129	5	4	.971
1986	—Cleveland (A.L.)	OF	105	95	33	25	4	1	0	8	.263	13	12	23	90	3	3	.969
1987	—Cleveland (A.L.)	OF	19	17	2	1	0	0	0	1	.059	3	4	2	21	0	0	1.000
	—Buffalo (A.A.)	OF	59	249	51	71	13	4	2	23	.285	34	30	36	170	3	3	.983
1988	—Indianapolis (A.A.)■	OF	67	235	52	67	6	3	0	19	.285	43	28	40	130	1	1	.992
	—Montreal (N.L.)	OF	90	271	47	66	8	2	0	15	.244	28	42	46	176	2	1	.994
1989	—Montreal (N.L.)	OF	126	258	41	56	7	2	0	21	.217	33	36	37	160	2	2	.988
1990	—Montreal (N.L.)	OF-SS	119	231	46	58	6	2	1	20	.251	28	33	50	149	6	1	.994
1991	—Atlanta (N.L.)■	OF	124	401	81	119	10	1	0	26	.297	47	40	72	218	6	3	.987
1992	—Atlanta (N.L.)	OF	120	456	79	134	14	2	2	22	.294	39	54	41	333	6	3	.991
1993	—Atlanta (N.L.)	OF	134	461	77	124	12	3	1	24	.269	61	63	47	308	4	3	.990
American League totals (5 years)			290	379	87	80	8	1	3	19	.211	33	59	59	335	12	8	.977
National League totals (6 years)			713	2078	371	557	57	12	4	128	.268	236	268	293	1344	26	13	.991
Major league totals (11 years)			1003	2457	458	637	65	13	7	147	.259	269	327	352	1679	38	21	.988

CHAMPIONSHIP SERIES RECORD

CHAMPIONSHIP SERIES NOTES: Shares N.L. single-game record for most hits—4 (October 10, 1992).

							BATTING								FIELDING		
Year	**Team (League)**	**Pos.**	**G**	**AB**	**R**	**H**	**2B**	**3B**	**HR**	**RBI**	**Avg.**	**BB**	**SO**	**SB**	**PO**	**A**	**E**	**Avg.**
1992	—Atlanta (N.L.)	OF	7	28	5	8	2	0	0	2	.286	4	4	3	16	0	0	1.000
1993	—Atlanta (N.L.)	OF	6	23	3	8	2	0	0	4	.348	5	6	0	13	0	0	1.000
Championship series totals (2 years)			13	51	8	16	4	0	0	6	.314	9	10	3	29	0	0	1.000

WORLD SERIES RECORD

							BATTING								FIELDING		
Year	**Team (League)**	**Pos.**	**G**	**AB**	**R**	**H**	**2B**	**3B**	**HR**	**RBI**	**Avg.**	**BB**	**SO**	**SB**	**PO**	**A**	**E**	**Avg.**
1992	—Atlanta (N.L.)	OF	6	27	3	8	1	0	0	1	.296	1	3	5	18	0	0	1.000

NOKES, MATT

C, YANKEES

PERSONAL: Born October 31, 1963, in San Diego.... 6-1/210.... Throws right, bats left.... Full name: Matthew Dodge Nokes.
HIGH SCHOOL: Patrick Henry (San Diego).
TRANSACTIONS/CAREER NOTES: Selected by San Francisco Giants organization in 20th round of

free-agent draft (June 8, 1981).... Traded by Giants with P Dave LaPoint and P Eric King to Detroit Tigers for P Juan Berenguer, C Bob Melvin and a player to be named later (October 7, 1985); Giants acquired P Scott Medvin to complete deal (December 11, 1985).... On disabled list (June 19-August 3, 1989).... Traded by Tigers to New York Yankees for P Lance McCullers and P Clay Parker (June 4, 1990).... On disabled list (June 21-July 7, 1993).
HONORS: Named catcher on THE SPORTING NEWS A.L. All-Star team (1987).... Named catcher on THE SPORTING NEWS A.L. Silver Slugger team (1987).
STATISTICAL NOTES: Led Pioneer League with 19 passed balls in 1981.... Led California League catchers with nine double plays in 1983.... Led Texas League catchers with six double plays in 1985.... Tied for American Association lead in errors by catcher with 13 in 1986.

		BATTING												FIELDING			
Year Team (League)	Pos.	G	AB	R	H	2B	3B	HR	RBI	Avg.	BB	SO	SB	PO	A	E	Avg.
1981 —Great Falls (Pio.)	C	44	146	14	33	6	2	0	13	.226	11	23	0	288	35	*13	.961
1982 —Clinton (Midwest)	C	82	247	19	53	12	0	3	23	.215	15	44	1	363	41	13	.969
1983 —Fresno (California)	C	125	429	62	138	26	6	14	82	.322	60	92	0	595	62	16	.976
1984 —Shreveport (Texas)	C	97	308	32	89	19	2	11	61	.289	30	34	0	400	31	8	.982
1985 —Shreveport (Texas)	C	105	344	52	101	24	1	14	56	.294	41	47	2	520	40	12	.979
—San Francisco (N.L.)	C	19	53	3	11	2	0	2	5	.208	1	9	0	84	2	2	.977
1986 —Nashville (A.A.)■	C-1B-OF	125	428	55	122	25	4	10	71	.285	30	41	2	502	50	‡18	.968
—Detroit (A.L.)	C	7	24	2	8	1	0	1	2	.333	1	1	0	43	2	0	1.000
1987 —Detroit (A.L.)	C-OF-3B	135	461	69	133	14	2	32	87	.289	35	70	2	600	32	5	.992
1988 —Detroit (A.L.)	C	122	382	53	96	18	0	16	53	.251	34	58	0	574	45	7	.989
1989 —Detroit (A.L.)	C	87	268	15	67	10	0	9	39	.250	17	37	1	235	26	6	.978
1990 —Detroit-N.Y. (A.L.)■	C-OF	136	351	33	87	9	1	11	40	.248	24	47	2	237	34	2	.993
1991 —New York (A.L.)	C	135	456	52	122	20	0	24	77	.268	25	49	3	690	48	6	.992
1992 —New York (A.L.)	C	121	384	42	86	9	1	22	59	.224	37	62	0	552	47	4	.993
1993 —New York (A.L.)	C	76	217	25	54	8	0	10	35	.249	16	31	0	245	19	2	.992
American League totals (8 years)		819	2543	291	653	89	4	125	392	.257	189	355	8	3176	253	32	.991
National League totals (1 year)		19	53	3	11	2	0	2	5	.208	1	9	0	84	2	2	.977
Major league totals (9 years)		838	2596	294	664	91	4	127	397	.256	190	364	8	3260	255	34	.990

CHAMPIONSHIP SERIES RECORD

		BATTING												FIELDING			
Year Team (League)	Pos.	G	AB	R	H	2B	3B	HR	RBI	Avg.	BB	SO	SB	PO	A	E	Avg.
1987 —Detroit (A.L.)	C-PH-DH	5	14	2	2	0	0	1	2	.143	1	4	0	11	2	0	1.000

ALL-STAR GAME RECORD

		BATTING											FIELDING			
Year League	Pos.	AB	R	H	2B	3B	HR	RBI	Avg.	BB	SO	SB	PO	A	E	Avg.
1987 —American	C	2	0	0	0	0	0	0	.000	0	0	0	8	0	0	1.000

NORMAN, LES

OF, ROYALS

PERSONAL: Born February 25, 1969, in Warren, Mich.... 6-1/185.... Throws right, bats right.... Full name: Leslie Eugene Norman.
HIGH SCHOOL: Reed-Custer (Braidwood, Ill.).
COLLEGE: College of St. Francis (Ill.).
TRANSACTIONS/CAREER NOTES: Selected by Boston Red Sox organization in 26th round of free-agent draft (June 4, 1990).... Selected by Kansas City Royals organization in 25th round of free-agent draft (June 3, 1991).
STATISTICAL NOTES: Led Southern League outfielders with 17 assists in 1993.

		BATTING												FIELDING			
Year Team (League)	Pos.	G	AB	R	H	2B	3B	HR	RBI	Avg.	BB	SO	SB	PO	A	E	Avg.
1991 —Eugene (N'west)	OF	30	102	14	25	4	1	2	18	.245	9	18	2	65	5	3	.959
1992 —Appleton (Midw.)	OF-1B-3B	59	218	38	82	17	1	4	47	.376	22	18	8	119	20	3	.979
—Memphis (South.)	OF	72	271	32	74	14	5	3	20	.273	22	37	4	124	9	4	.971
1993 —Memphis (South.)	OF-1B	133	484	78	141	32	5	17	81	.291	50	88	11	273	†17	10	.967

NOVOA, RAFAEL

P, CUBS

PERSONAL: Born October 26, 1967, in New York.... 6-1/190.... Throws left, bats left.... Full name: Rafael Angel Novoa.
HIGH SCHOOL: Fordham Prep (Bronx, N.Y.).
COLLEGE: Villanova (received degree).
TRANSACTIONS/CAREER NOTES: Selected by San Francisco Giants organization in ninth round of free-agent draft (June 5, 1989).... On Phoenix disabled list (April 11-May 17, 1991).... Released by Phoenix (March 31, 1992).... Signed by El Paso, Milwaukee Brewers organization (April 17, 1992).... On Milwaukee disabled list (August 30-September 14, 1993).... Traded by Brewers with OF Mike Carter to Chicago Cubs for P Bob Scanlan (December 19, 1993).

Year Team (League)	W	L	Pct.	ERA	G	GS	CG	ShO	Sv.	IP	H	R	ER	BB	SO
1989 —Everett (N'west)	0	1	.000	4.80	3	3	0	0	0	15	20	11	8	8	20
—Clinton (Midwest)	5	4	.556	2.54	13	10	0	0	0	63⅔	58	20	18	18	61
1990 —Clinton (Midwest)	9	2	.818	2.40	15	14	3	1	0	97⅔	73	32	26	30	113
—Shreveport (Texas)	5	4	.556	2.64	11	10	2	1	0	71⅔	60	21	21	25	65
—San Francisco (N.L.)	0	1	.000	6.75	7	2	0	0	1	18⅔	21	14	14	13	14
1991 —Phoenix (PCL)	6	6	.500	5.96	17	17	0	0	0	93⅔	135	83	62	37	46
1992 —El Paso (Texas)■	10	7	.588	3.26	22	21	*6	0	0	146⅓	143	63	53	48	124
1993 —New Orleans (A.A.)	10	5	.667	3.42	20	18	2	1	0	113	105	55	43	38	74
—Milwaukee (A.L.)	0	3	.000	4.50	15	7	2	0	0	56	58	32	28	22	17
A.L. totals (1 year)	0	3	.000	4.50	15	7	2	0	0	56	58	32	28	22	17
N.L. totals (1 year)	0	1	.000	6.75	7	2	0	0	1	18⅔	21	14	14	13	14
Major league totals (2 years)	0	4	.000	5.06	22	9	2	0	1	74⅔	79	46	42	35	31

N

NUNEZ, EDWIN

P, ATHLETICS

PERSONAL: Born May 27, 1963, in Humacao, Puerto Rico. . . . 6-5/240. . . . Throws right, bats right. . . . Full name: Edwin Martinez Nunez. . . . Name pronounced NOON-yez.

HIGH SCHOOL: Roque (Humacao, Puerto Rico).

TRANSACTIONS/CAREER NOTES: Signed as free agent by Seattle Mariners organization (March 17, 1979). . . . On Seattle disabled list (April 23-May 15, 1982). . . . On Salt Lake City disabled list (June 4-29, 1982; June 30-July 14, 1983; and May 12-June 3, 1984). . . . On Seattle disabled list (April 5-29 and May 1-16, 1986; and May 20-June 4, 1987). . . . Traded by Mariners organization to New York Mets for P Gene Walter (July 11, 1988). . . . Released by Mets (March 28, 1989). . . . Signed by Toledo, Detroit Tigers organization (April 1, 1989). . . . On disabled list (July 8-August 14, 1990). . . . Granted free agency (November 5, 1990). . . . Signed by Milwaukee Brewers (December 4, 1990). . . . On Milwaukee disabled list (May 7-August 1, 1991); included rehabilitation assignment to Beloit (July 16-August 1). . . . Traded by Brewers to Texas Rangers for a player to be named later (May 25, 1992); Brewers acquired P Mark Hampton to complete deal (September 15, 1992). . . . Granted free agency (October 30, 1992). . . . Signed by Oakland Athletics organization (February 16, 1993). . . . On suspended list (September 13-23, 1993). . . . Granted free agency (October 29, 1993). . . . Re-signed by A's (December 7, 1993).

Year	Team (League)	W	L	Pct.	ERA	G	GS	CG	ShO	Sv.	IP	H	R	ER	BB	SO
1979	—Belling. (N'west)	4	1	.800	2.08	6	2	0	0	0	39	39	14	9	5	30
1980	—Wausau (Midwest)	9	7	.563	3.72	22	19	8	2	0	138	145	71	57	58	91
1981	—Wausau (Midwest)	*16	3	.842	2.47	25	25	*13	0	0	*186	143	61	51	58	*205
1982	—Seattle (A.L.)	1	2	.333	4.58	8	5	0	0	0	35⅓	36	18	18	16	27
	—Salt Lake City (PCL)	4	3	.571	3.42	11	8	1	0	0	55⅓	40	26	21	23	42
1983	—Seattle (A.L.)	0	4	.000	4.38	14	5	0	0	0	37	40	21	18	22	35
	—Salt Lake City (PCL)	4	4	.500	7.10	14	12	3	0	0	77⅓	99	70	61	36	52
1984	—Salt Lake City (PCL)	3	2	.600	3.58	18	0	0	0	3	27⅔	24	12	11	12	26
	—Seattle (A.L.)	2	2	.500	3.19	37	0	0	0	7	67⅔	55	26	24	21	57
1985	—Seattle (A.L.)	7	3	.700	3.09	70	0	0	0	16	90⅓	79	36	31	34	58
1986	—Seattle (A.L.)	1	2	.333	5.82	14	1	0	0	0	21⅔	25	15	14	5	17
	—Calgary (PCL)	1	2	.333	7.07	6	1	1	0	0	14	19	13	11	4	17
1987	—Seattle (A.L.)	3	4	.429	3.80	48	0	0	0	12	47⅓	45	20	20	18	34
1988	—Calgary (PCL)	2	0	1.000	4.70	3	3	0	0	0	15⅓	15	9	8	4	12
	—Seattle (A.L.)	1	4	.200	7.98	14	3	0	0	0	29⅓	45	33	26	14	19
	—New York (N.L.)■	1	0	1.000	4.50	10	0	0	0	0	14	21	7	7	3	8
1989	—Toledo (Int'l)■	1	5	.167	2.58	13	8	1	0	1	59⅓	47	20	17	18	53
	—Detroit (A.L.)	3	4	.429	4.17	27	0	0	0	1	54	49	33	25	36	41
1990	—Detroit (A.L.)	3	1	.750	2.24	42	0	0	0	6	80⅓	65	26	20	37	66
1991	—Milwaukee (A.L.)■	2	1	.667	6.04	23	0	0	0	8	25⅓	28	20	17	13	24
	—Beloit (Midwest)	0	1	.000	4.00	5	1	0	0	1	9	9	5	4	0	9
1992	—Mil.-Tex. (A.L.)■	1	3	.250	4.85	49	0	0	0	3	59⅓	63	34	32	22	49
1993	—Oakland (A.L.)■	3	6	.333	3.81	56	0	0	0	1	75⅔	89	36	32	29	58
A.L. totals (12 years)		27	36	.429	4.00	402	14	0	0	54	623⅓	619	318	277	267	485
N.L. totals (1 year)		1	0	1.000	4.50	10	0	0	0	0	14	21	7	7	3	8
Major league totals (12 years)		28	36	.438	4.01	412	14	0	0	54	637⅓	640	325	284	270	493

OBANDO, SHERMAN

OF/1B, ORIOLES

PERSONAL: Born January 23, 1970, in Changuinola, Panama. . . . 6-4/215. . . . Throws right, bats right. . . . Full name: Sherman Omar Obando.

TRANSACTIONS/CAREER NOTES: Signed as free agent by New York Yankees organization (September 17, 1987). . . . On Prince William disabled list (May 3-July 25, 1991). . . . On disabled list (April 9-May 11, 1992). . . . Selected by Baltimore Orioles from Yankees organization in Rule 5 major league draft (December 7, 1992). . . . On Baltimore disabled list (May 25-June 24, 1993); included rehabilitation assignment to Bowie (June 4-23). . . . On Baltimore disabled list (June 26-July 11, 1993).

			BATTING												FIELDING			
Year	Team (League)	Pos.	G	AB	R	H	2B	3B	HR	RBI	Avg.	BB	SO	SB	PO	A	E	Avg.
1988	—GC Yankees (GCL)	OF	49	172	26	44	10	2	4	27	.256	16	32	8	55	3	3	.951
1989	—Oneonta (NYP)	OF	70	276	50	86	*23	3	6	45	.312	16	45	8	50	0	6	.893
1990	—Prin. William (Car.)	OF	121	439	67	117	24	6	10	67	.267	42	85	5	156	4	7	.958
1991	—GC Yankees (GCL)	DH	4	17	3	5	2	0	0	1	.294	1	2	0	...	...	...	...
	—Prin. William (Car.)	OF	42	140	25	37	11	1	7	31	.264	19	28	0	19	1	0	1.000
1992	—Alb./Colon. (East.)	1B	109	381	71	107	19	3	17	56	.281	32	67	3	430	32	11	.977
1993	—Baltimore (A.L.)■	OF	31	92	8	25	2	0	3	15	.272	4	26	0	13	0	1	.929
	—Bowie (Eastern)	OF-1B	19	58	8	14	2	0	3	12	.241	9	11	1	32	0	1	.970
Major league totals (1 year)			31	92	8	25	2	0	3	15	.272	4	26	0	13	0	1	.929

O'BRIEN, CHARLIE

C, BRAVES

PERSONAL: Born May 1, 1961, in Tulsa, Okla. . . . 6-2/205. . . . Throws right, bats right. . . . Full name: Charles Hugh O'Brien. . . . Brother of John O'Brien, first baseman, St. Louis Cardinals organization.

HIGH SCHOOL: Bishop Kelley (Tulsa, Okla.).

COLLEGE: McLennan Community College (Tex.) and Wichita State.

TRANSACTIONS/CAREER NOTES: Selected by Texas Rangers organization in 14th round of free-agent draft (June 6, 1978). . . . Selected by Seattle Mariners organization in 21st round of free-agent draft (June 8, 1981). . . . Selected by Oakland Athletics organization in fifth round of free-agent draft (June 7, 1982). . . . On disabled list (July 31, 1983-remainder of season). . . . On Albany/Colonie disabled list (April 13-May 15, 1984). . . . Traded by A's organization with IF Steve Kiefer, P Mike Fulmer and P Pete Kendrick to Milwaukee Brewers for P Moose Haas (March 30, 1986). . . . Traded by Brewers with a player to be named later to New York Mets for two players to be named later (August 30, 1990); Brewers acquired P Julio Machado and P Kevin Brown (September 7, 1990) and Mets acquired P Kevin Carmody (September 11, 1990) to complete deal. . . . Granted free agency (October 29, 1993). . . . Signed by Atlanta Braves (November 26, 1993).

Year	Team (League)	Pos.	G	AB	R	H	2B	3B	HR	RBI	Avg.	BB	SO	SB	PO	A	E	Avg.
			BATTING												FIELDING			
1982	—Medford (N'west)	C	17	60	11	17	3	0	3	14	.283	10	10	0	116	18	4	.971
	—Modesto (Calif.)	C	41	140	23	42	6	0	3	32	.300	20	19	7	239	44	5	.983
1983	—Alb./Colon. (East.)	C-1B	92	285	50	83	12	1	14	56	.291	52	39	3	478	82	11	.981
1984	—Modesto (Calif.)	C	9	32	8	9	2	0	1	5	.281	2	4	1	41	8	0	1.000
	—Tacoma (PCL)	C-OF	69	195	33	44	11	0	9	22	.226	28	31	0	260	39	0	1.000
1985	—Huntsville (South.)	C	33	115	20	24	5	0	7	16	.209	16	20	0	182	29	5	.977
	—Oakland (A.L.)	C	16	11	3	3	1	0	0	1	.273	3	3	0	23	0	1	.958
	—Modesto (Calif.)	C	9	27	5	8	4	1	1	2	.296	2	5	0	33	8	1	.976
	—Tacoma (PCL)	C	18	57	5	9	4	0	0	7	.158	6	17	0	110	9	3	.975
1986	—Vancouver (PCL)■	C	6	17	1	2	0	0	0	1	.118	4	4	0	22	3	2	.926
	—El Paso (Texas)	C-OF-1B	92	336	72	109	20	3	15	75	.324	50	30	0	437	43	4	.992
1987	—Denver (A.A.)	C	80	266	37	75	12	1	8	35	.282	41	33	5	415	53	6	.987
	—Milwaukee (A.L.)	C	10	35	2	7	3	1	0	0	.200	4	4	0	78	11	0	1.000
1988	—Denver (A.A.)	C	48	153	16	43	5	0	4	25	.281	19	19	1	243	44	3	.990
	—Milwaukee (A.L.)	C	40	118	12	26	6	0	2	9	.220	5	16	0	210	20	2	.991
1989	—Milwaukee (A.L.)	C	62	188	22	44	10	0	6	35	.234	21	11	0	314	36	5	.986
1990	—Milwaukee (A.L.)	C	46	145	11	27	7	2	0	11	.186	11	26	0	217	24	2	.992
	—New York (N.L.)■	C	28	68	6	11	3	0	0	9	.162	10	8	0	191	21	3	.986
1991	—New York (N.L.)	C	69	168	16	31	6	0	2	14	.185	17	25	0	396	37	4	.991
1992	—New York (N.L.)	C	68	156	15	33	12	0	2	13	.212	16	18	0	287	44	7	.979
1993	—New York (N.L.)	C	67	188	15	48	11	0	4	23	.255	14	14	1	325	39	5	.986
American League totals (5 years)			174	497	50	107	27	3	8	56	.215	44	60	0	842	91	10	.989
National League totals (4 years)			232	580	52	123	32	0	8	59	.212	57	65	1	1199	141	19	.986
Major league totals (8 years)			406	1077	102	230	59	3	16	115	.214	101	125	1	2041	232	29	.987

O'BRIEN, PETE

DH/1B

PERSONAL: Born February 9, 1958, in Santa Monica, Calif. . . . 6-2/205. . . . Throws left, bats left. . . . Full name: Peter Michael O'Brien.
HIGH SCHOOL: Carmel (Calif.).
COLLEGE: Monterey Peninsula College (Calif.) and Nebraska.
TRANSACTIONS/CAREER NOTES: Selected by Texas Rangers organization in 15th round of free-agent draft (June 5, 1979). . . . Traded by Rangers with OF Oddibe McDowell and 2B Jerry Browne to Cleveland Indians for 2B Julio Franco (December 6, 1988). . . . Granted free agency (November 13, 1989). . . . Signed by Seattle Mariners (December 7, 1989). . . . On disabled list (May 5-June 19, 1990). . . . Released by Mariners (July 21, 1993).
RECORDS: Shares major league single-game record (nine innings) for most double plays started by first baseman—3 (May 22, 1984).
STATISTICAL NOTES: Led A.L. first basemen with 120 assists in 1983 and 146 in 1987. . . . Led A.L. first basemen with .997 fielding percentage in 1991.

Year	Team (League)	Pos.	G	AB	R	H	2B	3B	HR	RBI	Avg.	BB	SO	SB	PO	A	E	Avg.
			BATTING												FIELDING			
1979	—GC Rangers (GCL)	1B	50	189	39	46	10	2	0	31	.243	36	8	1	*465	*44	7	.986
1980	—Asheville (S. Atl.)	1B	134	505	98	149	34	2	17	94	.295	68	67	6	*1227	*96	14	.990
1981	—Tulsa (Texas)	1B	110	382	57	109	19	3	17	78	.285	56	87	3	973	95	11	.990
1982	—Denver (A.A.)	OF-1B	128	477	92	148	21	1	25	102	.310	56	65	0	418	37	8	.983
	—Texas (A.L.)	OF-1B	20	67	13	16	4	1	4	13	.239	6	8	1	39	3	0	1.000
1983	—Texas (A.L.)	1B-OF	154	524	53	124	24	5	8	53	.237	58	62	5	1191	†121	11	.992
1984	—Texas (A.L.)	1B-OF	142	520	57	149	26	2	18	80	.287	53	50	3	1271	105	11	.992
1985	—Texas (A.L.)	1B	159	573	69	153	34	3	22	92	.267	69	53	5	1457	98	8	.995
1986	—Texas (A.L.)	1B	156	551	86	160	23	3	23	90	.290	87	66	4	1224	115	11	.992
1987	—Texas (A.L.)	1B-OF	159	569	84	163	26	1	23	88	.286	59	61	0	1233	†146	11	.992
1988	—Texas (A.L.)	1B	156	547	57	149	24	1	16	71	.272	72	73	1	1346	140	8	.995
1989	—Cleveland (A.L.)■	1B	155	554	75	144	24	1	12	55	.260	83	48	3	1359	114	9	.994
1990	—Seattle (A.L.)■	1B-OF	108	366	32	82	18	0	5	27	.224	44	33	0	852	76	5	.995
1991	—Seattle (A.L.)	1B-OF	152	560	58	139	29	3	17	88	.248	44	61	0	1065	87	5	†.996
1992	—Seattle (A.L.)	1B	134	396	40	88	15	1	14	52	.222	40	27	2	623	54	3	.996
1993	—Seattle (A.L.)	1B-OF	72	210	30	54	7	0	7	27	.257	26	21	0	77	8	1	.988
Major league totals (12 years)			1567	5437	654	1421	254	21	169	736	.261	641	563	24	11737	1067	83	.994

OCHOA, ALEX

OF, ORIOLES

PERSONAL: Born March 29, 1972, in Miami Lakes, Fla. . . . 6-0/175. . . . Throws right, bats right.
HIGH SCHOOL: Hialeah (Fla.) Miami Lakes.
TRANSACTIONS/CAREER NOTES: Selected by Baltimore Orioles organization in third round of free-agent draft (June 3, 1991).
STATISTICAL NOTES: Led Carolina League in grounding into double plays with 15 in 1993.

Year	Team (League)	Pos.	G	AB	R	H	2B	3B	HR	RBI	Avg.	BB	SO	SB	PO	A	E	Avg.
			BATTING												FIELDING			
1991	—GC Orioles (GCL)	OF	53	179	26	55	8	3	1	30	.307	16	14	11	45	3	2	.960
1992	—Kane Co. (Midw.)	OF	133	499	65	147	22	7	1	59	.295	58	55	31	225	•17	•12	.953
1993	—Frederick (Caro.)	OF	137	532	84	147	29	5	13	90	.276	46	67	34	169	13	11	.943

O'DONOGHUE, JOHN

P, ORIOLES

PERSONAL: Born May 26, 1969, in Wilmington, Del. . . . 6-6/198. . . . Throws left, bats left. . . . Full name: John Preston O'Donoghue. . . . Son of John O'Donoghue, current pitching coach, Baltimore Orioles organization, and major league pitcher with five teams (1963-71).
HIGH SCHOOL: Elkton (Md.).
COLLEGE: Louisiana State.

TRANSACTIONS/CAREER NOTES: Signed as free agent by Baltimore Orioles organization (June 28, 1990).... On disabled list (August 2-September 10, 1991).

Year	Team (League)	W	L	Pct.	ERA	G	GS	CG	ShO	Sv.	IP	H	R	ER	BB	SO
1990	—Bluefield (Appal.)	4	2	.667	2.01	10	6	2	•2	0	49⅓	50	13	11	10	67
	—Frederick (Caro.)	0	1	.000	4.50	1	1	0	0	0	4	5	2	2	0	3
1991	—Frederick (Caro.)	7	8	.467	2.90	22	21	2	1	0	133⅔	131	55	43	50	128
1992	—Hagerstown (East.)	7	4	.636	2.24	17	16	2	0	0	112⅓	78	37	28	40	87
	—Rochester (Int'l)	5	4	.556	3.23	13	10	3	1	0	69⅔	60	31	25	19	47
1993	—Rochester (Int'l)	7	4	.636	3.88	22	20	2	1	0	127⅔	122	60	55	41	111
	—Baltimore (A.L.)	0	1	.000	4.58	11	1	0	0	0	19⅔	22	12	10	10	16
	Major league totals (1 year)	0	1	.000	4.58	11	1	0	0	0	19⅔	22	12	10	10	16

OFFERMAN, JOSE

SS, DODGERS

PERSONAL: Born November 8, 1968, in San Pedro de Macoris, Dominican Republic.... 6-0/165.... Throws right, bats both.... Full name: Jose Antonio Dono Offerman.
HIGH SCHOOL: Colegio Biblico Cristiano (Dominican Republic).
TRANSACTIONS/CAREER NOTES: Signed as free agent by Los Angeles Dodgers organization (July 24, 1986).
HONORS: Named Minor League Player of the Year by THE SPORTING NEWS (1990).... Named Pacific Coast League Player of the Year (1990).
STATISTICAL NOTES: Tied for Pioneer League lead in caught stealing with 10 in 1988.... Tied for Pacific Coast League lead in caught stealing with 18 in 1990.... Led Pacific Coast League shortstops with 36 errors in 1990.... Hit home run in first major league at-bat (August 19, 1990).... Led N.L. with 25 sacrifice hits in 1993.

			BATTING												FIELDING			
Year	Team (League)	Pos.	G	AB	R	H	2B	3B	HR	RBI	Avg.	BB	SO	SB	PO	A	E	Avg.
1987	—		Dominican Summer League statistics unavailable.															
1988	—Great Falls (Pio.)	SS	60	251	75	83	11	5	2	28	.331	38	42	*57	82	143	18	*.926
1989	—Bakersfield (Calif.)	SS	62	245	53	75	9	4	2	22	.306	35	48	37	94	179	30	.901
	—San Antonio (Tex.)	SS	68	278	47	80	6	3	2	22	.288	40	39	32	106	168	20	.932
1990	—Albuquerque (PCL)	SS-2B	117	454	104	148	16	11	0	56	.326	71	81	*60	174	361	†36	.937
	—Los Angeles (N.L.)	SS	29	58	7	9	0	0	1	7	.155	4	14	1	30	40	4	.946
1991	—Albuquerque (PCL)	SS	79	289	58	86	8	4	0	29	.298	47	58	32	126	241	17	.956
	—Los Angeles (N.L.)	SS	52	113	10	22	2	0	0	3	.195	25	32	3	50	121	10	.945
1992	—Los Angeles (N.L.)	SS	149	534	67	139	20	8	1	30	.260	57	98	23	208	398	*42	.935
1993	—Los Angeles (N.L.)	SS	158	590	77	159	21	6	1	62	.269	71	75	30	250	454	*37	.950
	Major league totals (4 years)		388	1295	161	329	43	14	3	102	.254	157	219	57	538	1013	93	.943

O'HALLORAN, GREG

C, MARLINS

PERSONAL: Born May 21, 1968, in Mississauga, Ont.... 6-2/205.... Throws right, bats left.... Full name: Gregory Joseph O'Halloran.... Brother of Mike O'Halloran, minor league pitcher (1991-92).
HIGH SCHOOL: De La Salle College Oakland (Toronto, Ont.).
COLLEGE: Orange Coast College (Calif.).
TRANSACTIONS/CAREER NOTES: Selected by Toronto Blue Jays organization in 32nd round of free-agent draft (June 1, 1988).... Contract sold by Blue Jays to Florida Marlins (November 12, 1993).
STATISTICAL NOTES: Led Southern League catchers with 12 double plays in 1992.
MISCELLANEOUS: Member of 1988 Canadian Olympic baseball team.

			BATTING												FIELDING			
Year	Team (League)	Pos.	G	AB	R	H	2B	3B	HR	RBI	Avg.	BB	SO	SB	PO	A	E	Avg.
1989	—St. Cathar. (NYP)	C	69	265	31	75	13	2	5	27	.283	21	33	7	356	40	5	*.988
1990	—Dunedin (Fla. St.)	C	121	465	70	132	26	4	11	75	.284	37	70	2	250	28	10	.965
1991	—Dunedin (Fla. St.)	C	20	74	7	21	3	1	0	4	.284	7	8	1	21	4	0	1.000
	—Knoxville (South.)	C-1B	110	350	37	89	13	3	8	53	.254	27	46	11	490	43	5	.991
1992	—Knoxville (South.)	C-1B-OF	117	409	44	111	20	5	2	34	.271	31	64	7	548	57	11	.982
1993	—Syracuse (Int'l)	C-1B	109	322	32	86	14	3	3	35	.267	13	54	2	543	49	10	.983

OJEDA, BOB

P, YANKEES

PERSONAL: Born December 17, 1957, in Los Angeles.... 6-1/195.... Throws left, bats left.... Full name: Robert Michael Ojeda.... Name pronounced oh-HEE-duh.
HIGH SCHOOL: Redwood (Visalia, Calif.).
COLLEGE: College of the Sequoias (Calif.).
TRANSACTIONS/CAREER NOTES: Signed as free agent by Boston Red Sox organization (May 20, 1978).... On disabled list (August 20-September 10, 1982 and August 16-September 1, 1984).... Traded by Red Sox with P Tom McCarthy, P John Mitchell and P Chris Bayer to New York Mets for P Calvin Schiraldi, P Wes Gardner, OF John Christensen and OF LaSchelle Tarver (November 13, 1985).... On disabled list (May 11-September 1, 1987).... Traded by Mets with P Greg Hansell to Los Angeles Dodgers for OF Hubie Brooks (December 15, 1990).... Granted free agency (October 28, 1992).... Signed by Cleveland Indians (December 8, 1992).... On disabled list (April 1-August 7, 1993).... Granted free agency (October 29, 1993).... Signed by New York Yankees organization (January 28, 1994).
HONORS: Named International League Pitcher of the Year (1981).
STATISTICAL NOTES: Tied for International League lead with three balks in 1980.

Year	Team (League)	W	L	Pct.	ERA	G	GS	CG	ShO	Sv.	IP	H	R	ER	BB	SO
1978	—Elmira (N.Y.-Penn)	1	6	.143	4.81	18	3	0	0	2	43	45	32	23	43	35
1979	—Winter Haven (FSL)	15	7	.682	2.43	29	•29	8	2	0	200	163	66	54	84	150
1980	—Pawtucket (Int'l)	6	7	.462	3.22	19	18	4	0	0	123	107	54	44	56	78
	—Boston (A.L.)	1	1	.500	6.92	7	7	0	0	0	26	39	20	20	14	12
1981	—Pawtucket (Int'l)	12	9	.571	*2.13	25	23	8	0	0	173	136	52	41	73	113
	—Boston (A.L.)	6	2	.750	3.14	10	10	2	0	0	66	50	25	23	25	28
1982	—Boston (A.L.)	4	6	.400	5.63	22	14	0	0	0	78⅓	95	53	49	29	52
1983	—Boston (A.L.)	12	7	.632	4.04	29	28	5	0	0	173⅔	173	85	78	73	94

O

Year	Team (League)	W	L	Pct.	ERA	G	GS	CG	ShO	Sv.	IP	H	R	ER	BB	SO
1984	—Boston (A.L.)	12	12	.500	3.99	33	32	8	*5	0	216⅔	211	106	96	96	137
1985	—Boston (A.L.)	9	11	.450	4.00	39	22	5	0	1	157⅔	166	74	70	48	102
1986	—New York (N.L.)■	18	5	.783	2.57	32	30	7	2	0	217⅓	185	72	62	52	148
1987	—New York (N.L.)	3	5	.375	3.88	10	7	0	0	0	46⅓	45	23	20	10	21
1988	—New York (N.L.)	10	13	.435	2.88	29	29	5	5	0	190⅓	158	74	61	33	133
1989	—New York (N.L.)	13	11	.542	3.47	31	31	5	2	0	192	179	83	74	78	95
1990	—New York (N.L.)	7	6	.538	3.66	38	12	0	0	0	118	123	53	48	40	62
1991	—Los Angeles (N.L.)■	12	9	.571	3.18	31	31	2	1	0	189⅓	181	78	67	70	120
1992	—Los Angeles (N.L.)	6	9	.400	3.63	29	29	2	1	0	166⅓	169	80	67	81	94
1993	—Cleveland (A.L.)■	2	1	.667	4.40	9	7	0	0	0	43	48	22	21	21	27
A.L. totals (7 years)		46	40	.535	4.22	149	120	20	5	1	761⅓	782	385	357	306	452
N.L. totals (7 years)		69	58	.543	3.21	200	169	21	11	0	1119⅔	1040	463	399	364	673
Major league totals (14 years)		115	98	.540	3.62	349	289	41	16	1	1881	1822	848	756	670	1125

CHAMPIONSHIP SERIES RECORD

CHAMPIONSHIP SERIES NOTES: Shares N.L. single-game record for most hits allowed—10 (October 9, 1986).

Year	Team (League)	W	L	Pct.	ERA	G	GS	CG	ShO	Sv.	IP	H	R	ER	BB	SO
1986	—New York (N.L.)	1	0	1.000	2.57	2	2	1	0	0	14	15	4	4	4	6

WORLD SERIES RECORD

Year	Team (League)	W	L	Pct.	ERA	G	GS	CG	ShO	Sv.	IP	H	R	ER	BB	SO
1986	—New York (N.L.)	1	0	1.000	2.08	2	2	0	0	0	13	13	3	3	5	9

O'LEARY, TROY

OF, BREWERS

PERSONAL: Born August 4, 1969, in Compton, Calif. . . . 6-0/190. . . . Throws left, bats left. . . . Full name: Troy Franklin O'Leary.
HIGH SCHOOL: Cypress (Calif.).
TRANSACTIONS/CAREER NOTES: Selected by Milwaukee Brewers organization in 13th round of free-agent draft (June 2, 1987).
HONORS: Named Texas League Most Valuable Player (1992).
STATISTICAL NOTES: Led Pioneer League with 144 total bases in 1989. . . . Led Texas League with 227 total bases and .399 on-base percentage in 1992. . . . Led Texas League outfielders with 242 total chances in 1992.

			BATTING												FIELDING			
Year	Team (League)	Pos.	G	AB	R	H	2B	3B	HR	RBI	Avg.	BB	SO	SB	PO	A	E	Avg.
1987	—Helena (Pioneer)	OF	3	5	0	2	0	0	0	1	.400	0	0	0	0	0	0	...
1988	—Helena (Pioneer)	OF	67	203	40	70	11	1	0	27	.345	30	32	10	64	4	3	.958
1989	—Beloit (Midwest)	OF	42	115	7	21	4	0	0	8	.183	15	20	1	55	1	1	.982
	—Helena (Pioneer)	OF	*68	263	54	*89	16	3	11	*56	.338	28	43	9	92	6	3	.970
1990	—Beloit (Midwest)	OF	118	436	73	130	29	1	6	62	.298	41	90	12	184	14	8	.961
	—Stockton (Calif.)	OF	2	6	1	3	1	0	0	0	.500	2	1	0	3	0	1	.750
1991	—Stockton (Calif.)	OF	126	418	63	110	20	4	5	46	.263	73	96	4	163	4	3	.982
1992	—El Paso (Texas)	OF	*135	*506	*92	*169	27	8	5	79	*.334	59	87	28	*220	11	*11	.955
1993	—New Orleans (A.A.)	OF-1B	111	388	65	106	32	1	7	59	.273	43	61	6	189	8	6	.970
	—Milwaukee (A.L.)	OF	19	41	3	12	3	0	0	3	.293	5	9	0	32	1	0	1.000
Major league totals (1 year)			19	41	3	12	3	0	0	3	.293	5	9	0	32	1	0	1.000

OLERUD, JOHN

1B, BLUE JAYS

PERSONAL: Born August 5, 1968, in Seattle, Wash. . . . 6-5/218. . . . Throws left, bats left. . . . Full name: John Garrett Olerud. . . . Son of John E. Olerud, minor league catcher (1965-70). . . . Name pronounced OH-luh-rude.
HIGH SCHOOL: Interlake (Bellevue, Wash.).
COLLEGE: Washington State.
TRANSACTIONS/CAREER NOTES: Selected by New York Mets organization in 27th round of free-agent draft (June 2, 1986). . . . Selected by Toronto Blue Jays organization in third round of free-agent draft (June 5, 1989).
RECORDS: Shares A.L. single-season records for most intentional bases on balls received—33 (1993); and most intentional bases on balls received by lefthanded hitter—33 (1993).
STATISTICAL NOTES: Tied for A.L. lead with 10 sacrifice flies in 1991. . . . Led A.L. with 33 intentional bases on balls received and .473 on-base percentage in 1993.

			BATTING												FIELDING			
Year	Team (League)	Pos.	G	AB	R	H	2B	3B	HR	RBI	Avg.	BB	SO	SB	PO	A	E	Avg.
1989	—Toronto (A.L.)	1B	6	8	2	3	0	0	0	0	.375	0	1	0	19	2	0	1.000
1990	—Toronto (A.L.)	1B	111	358	43	95	15	1	14	48	.265	57	75	0	133	10	2	.986
1991	—Toronto (A.L.)	1B	139	454	64	116	30	1	17	68	.256	68	84	0	1120	78	5	.996
1992	—Toronto (A.L.)	1B	138	458	68	130	28	0	16	66	.284	70	61	1	1057	81	7	.994
1993	—Toronto (A.L.)	1B	158	551	109	200	*54	2	24	107	*.363	114	65	0	1160	97	10	.992
Major league totals (5 years)			552	1829	286	544	127	4	71	289	.297	309	286	1	3489	268	24	.994

CHAMPIONSHIP SERIES RECORD

			BATTING												FIELDING			
Year	Team (League)	Pos.	G	AB	R	H	2B	3B	HR	RBI	Avg.	BB	SO	SB	PO	A	E	Avg.
1991	—Toronto (A.L.)	1B	5	19	1	3	0	0	0	3	.158	3	1	0	40	3	0	1.000
1992	—Toronto (A.L.)	1B	6	23	4	8	2	0	1	4	.348	2	5	0	51	1	0	1.000
1993	—Toronto (A.L.)	1B	6	23	5	8	1	0	0	3	.348	4	1	0	48	9	1	.983
Championship series totals (3 years)			17	65	10	19	3	0	1	10	.292	9	7	0	139	13	1	.993

WORLD SERIES RECORD

Year	Team (League)	Pos.	BATTING G	AB	R	H	2B	3B	HR	RBI	Avg.	BB	SO	SB	FIELDING PO	A	E	Avg.
1992	—Toronto (A.L.)	1B	4	13	2	4	0	0	0	0	.308	0	4	0	25	3	0	1.000
1993	—Toronto (A.L.)	1B	5	17	5	4	1	0	1	2	.235	4	1	0	36	0	0	1.000
World Series totals (2 years)			9	30	7	8	1	0	1	2	.267	4	5	0	61	3	0	1.000

ALL-STAR GAME RECORD

Year	League	Pos.	BATTING AB	R	H	2B	3B	HR	RBI	Avg.	BB	SO	SB	FIELDING PO	A	E	Avg.
1993	—American	1B	2	0	0	0	0	0	0	.000	0	0	0	4	0	0	1.000

OLIVA, JOSE

3B, BRAVES

PERSONAL: Born March 3, 1971, in San Pedro de Macoris, Dominican Republic. . . . 6-1/150. . . . Throws right, bats right. . . . Full name: Jose Galvez Oliva.
TRANSACTIONS/CAREER NOTES: Signed as free agent by Texas Rangers organization (November 12, 1987). . . . On Charlotte disabled list (July 16-25, 1991). . . . Traded by Rangers organization to Atlanta Braves organization for P Charlie Leibrandt and P Pat Gomez (December 9, 1992).
STATISTICAL NOTES: Led Texas League third basemen with 328 total chances and tied for lead with 15 double plays in 1992.

Year	Team (League)	Pos.	BATTING G	AB	R	H	2B	3B	HR	RBI	Avg.	BB	SO	SB	FIELDING PO	A	E	Avg.
1988	—GC Rangers (GCL)	SS	27	70	5	15	3	0	1	11	.214	3	14	0	16	43	6	.908
1989	—Butte (Pioneer)	SS-3B	41	114	18	24	2	3	4	13	.211	14	41	4	38	94	15	.898
1990	—Gastonia (S. Atl.)	SS-3B-2B	120	387	43	81	25	1	10	52	.209	26	104	9	163	284	44	.910
1991	—Charlotte (Fla. St.)	3B-SS	108	383	55	92	17	4	•14	59	.240	44	108	9	79	154	16	.936
	—GC Rangers (GCL)	3B	3	11	0	1	1	0	0	1	.091	2	3	0	4	3	0	1.000
1992	—Tulsa (Texas)	3B	124	445	57	120	28	6	16	75	.270	40	135	4	*75	*225	28	.915
1993	—Richmond (Int'l)■	3B-SS	125	412	63	97	20	6	21	65	.235	35	134	1	44	206	19	.929

OLIVARES, OMAR

P, CARDINALS

PERSONAL: Born July 6, 1967, in Mayaguez, Puerto Rico. . . . 6-1/193. . . . Throws right, bats right. . . . Full name: Omar Palqu Olivares. . . . Son of Ed Olivares, outfielder, St. Louis Cardinals (1960-61).
HIGH SCHOOL: Hostos (Mayaguez, Puerto Rico).
TRANSACTIONS/CAREER NOTES: Signed as free agent by San Diego Padres organization (September 15, 1986). . . . Traded by Padres organization to St. Louis Cardinals for OF Alex Cole and P Steve Peters (February 27, 1990). . . . On St. Louis disabled list (May 27-June 13, 1992 and June 4-20, 1993).
RECORDS: Shares major league single-season record for fewest double plays by pitcher who led league in double plays—4 (1992).
STATISTICAL NOTES: Tied for Texas League lead with 10 hit batsmen in 1989.
MISCELLANEOUS: Appeared in one game as pinch-runner and singled and scored in three games as pinch-hitter (1992). . . . Appeared in one game as pinch-runner and made an out in one game as pinch-hitter (1993).

Year	Team (League)	W	L	Pct.	ERA	G	GS	CG	ShO	Sv.	IP	H	R	ER	BB	SO
1987	—Char., S.C. (S. Atl.)	4	14	.222	4.60	31	24	5	0	0	170⅓	182	107	87	57	86
1988	—Char., S.C. (S. Atl.)	13	6	.684	2.23	24	24	*10	3	0	185⅓	166	63	46	43	94
	—Riverside (Calif.)	3	0	1.000	1.16	4	3	1	0	0	23⅓	18	9	3	9	16
1989	—Wichita (Texas)	12	11	.522	3.39	26	26	6	1	0	*185⅔	175	87	70	61	79
1990	—Louisville (A.A.)	10	11	.476	2.82	23	23	5	2	0	159⅓	127	58	50	59	88
	—St. Louis (N.L.)	1	1	.500	2.92	9	6	0	0	0	49⅓	45	17	16	17	20
1991	—St. Louis (N.L.)	11	7	.611	3.71	28	24	0	0	1	167⅓	148	72	69	61	91
	—Louisville (A.A.)	1	2	.333	3.47	6	6	0	0	0	36⅓	39	15	14	16	27
1992	—St. Louis (N.L.)	9	9	.500	3.84	32	30	1	0	0	197	189	84	84	63	124
1993	—St. Louis (N.L.)	5	3	.625	4.17	58	9	0	0	1	118⅔	134	60	55	54	63
Major league totals (4 years)		26	20	.565	3.79	127	69	1	0	2	532⅓	516	233	224	195	298

OLIVER, DARREN

P, RANGERS

PERSONAL: Born October 6, 1970, in Kansas City, Mo. . . . 6-1/170. . . . Throws left, bats right. . . . Full name: Darren Christopher Oliver. . . . Son of Bob Oliver, major league first baseman/outfielder with five teams (1965, 1969-75).
HIGH SCHOOL: Rio Linda (Calif.) Senior.
TRANSACTIONS/CAREER NOTES: Selected by Texas Rangers organization in third round of free-agent draft (June 1, 1988). . . . On Gulf Coast disabled list (April 6-August 9, 1990). . . . On disabled list (May 1, 1991-remainder of season). . . . On Tulsa disabled list (July 1, 1992-remainder of season).

Year	Team (League)	W	L	Pct.	ERA	G	GS	CG	ShO	Sv.	IP	H	R	ER	BB	SO
1988	—GC Rangers (GCL)	5	1	.833	2.15	12	9	0	0	0	54⅓	39	16	13	18	59
1989	—Gastonia (S. Atl.)	8	7	.533	3.16	24	23	2	1	0	122⅓	86	54	43	82	108
1990	—GC Rangers (GCL)	0	0	...	0.00	3	3	0	0	0	6	1	1	0	1	7
	—Gastonia (S. Atl.)	0	0	...	13.50	1	1	0	0	0	2	1	3	3	4	2
1991	—Charlotte (Fla. St.)	0	1	.000	4.50	2	2	0	0	0	8	6	4	4	3	12
1992	—Charlotte (Fla. St.)	1	0	1.000	0.72	8	2	1	1	2	25	11	2	2	10	33
	—Tulsa (Texas)	0	1	.000	3.14	3	3	0	0	0	14⅓	15	9	5	4	14
1993	—Tulsa (Texas)	7	5	.583	1.96	46	0	0	0	6	73⅓	51	18	16	41	77
	—Texas (A.L.)	0	0	...	2.70	2	0	0	0	0	3⅓	2	1	1	1	4
Major league totals (1 year)		0	0	...	2.70	2	0	0	0	0	3⅓	2	1	1	1	4

OLIVER, JOE

C, REDS

PERSONAL: Born July 24, 1965, in Memphis, Tenn. . . . 6-3/220. . . . Throws right, bats right. . . . Full name: Joseph Melton Oliver.
HIGH SCHOOL: Boone (Orlando, Fla.).
TRANSACTIONS/CAREER NOTES: Selected by Cincinnati Reds organization in second round of free-agent draft (June 6, 1983); pick received as compensation for New York Yankees signing Type A free agent Bob Shirley. . . . On disabled list (April 23-May 6, 1986).
STATISTICAL NOTES: Led Pioneer League catchers with .989 fielding percentage, 425 putouts, 38 assists and 468 total chances in 1983. . . . Led Midwest League catchers with 855 total chances and 30 passed balls in 1984. . . . Led Florida State League catchers with 84 assists and 33 passed balls in 1985. . . . Led American Association catchers with 13 errors in 1989. . . . Tied for N.L. lead with 16 passed balls in 1990. . . . Led N.L. catchers with 925 putouts and 997 total chances in 1992.

			BATTING												FIELDING			
Year	**Team (League)**	**Pos.**	**G**	**AB**	**R**	**H**	**2B**	**3B**	**HR**	**RBI**	**Avg.**	**BB**	**SO**	**SB**	**PO**	**A**	**E**	**Avg.**
1983	—Billings (Pioneer)	C-1B	56	186	21	40	4	0	4	28	.215	15	47	1	†426	†39	5	†.989
1984	—Ced. Rap. (Midw.)	C	102	335	34	73	11	0	3	29	.218	17	83	2	*757	85	13	.985
1985	—Tampa (Fla. St.)	C-1B	112	386	38	104	23	2	7	62	.269	32	75	1	615	†94	16	.978
1986	—Vermont (Eastern)	C	84	282	32	78	18	1	6	41	.277	21	47	2	383	62	14	.969
1987	—Vermont (Eastern)	C-1B	66	236	31	72	13	2	10	60	.305	17	30	0	247	35	10	.966
1988	—Nashville (A.A.)	C	73	220	19	45	7	2	4	24	.205	18	39	0	413	37	7	.985
	—Chatt. (South.)	C	28	105	9	26	6	0	3	12	.248	5	19	0	176	15	0	1.000
1989	—Nashville (A.A.)	C-1B	71	233	22	68	13	0	6	31	.292	13	35	0	388	37	†13	.970
	—Cincinnati (N.L.)	C	49	151	13	41	8	0	3	23	.272	6	28	0	260	21	4	.986
1990	—Cincinnati (N.L.)	C	121	364	34	84	23	0	8	52	.231	37	75	1	686	59	6	*.992
1991	—Cincinnati (N.L.)	C	94	269	21	58	11	0	11	41	.216	18	53	0	496	40	11	.980
1992	—Cincinnati (N.L.)	C-1B	143	485	42	131	25	1	10	57	.270	35	75	2	†926	64	8	.992
1993	—Cincinnati (N.L.)	C-1B-OF	139	482	40	115	28	0	14	75	.239	27	91	0	825	70	7	.992
Major league totals (5 years)			546	1751	150	429	95	1	46	248	.245	123	322	3	3193	254	36	.990

CHAMPIONSHIP SERIES RECORD

			BATTING												FIELDING			
Year	**Team (League)**	**Pos.**	**G**	**AB**	**R**	**H**	**2B**	**3B**	**HR**	**RBI**	**Avg.**	**BB**	**SO**	**SB**	**PO**	**A**	**E**	**Avg.**
1990	—Cincinnati (N.L.)	C	5	14	1	2	0	0	0	0	.143	0	2	0	27	1	0	1.000

WORLD SERIES RECORD

			BATTING												FIELDING			
Year	**Team (League)**	**Pos.**	**G**	**AB**	**R**	**H**	**2B**	**3B**	**HR**	**RBI**	**Avg.**	**BB**	**SO**	**SB**	**PO**	**A**	**E**	**Avg.**
1990	—Cincinnati (N.L.)	C	4	18	2	6	3	0	0	2	.333	0	1	0	27	1	3	.903

OLSON, GREG

C, METS

PERSONAL: Born September 6, 1960, in Marshall, Minn. . . . 6-0/200. . . . Throws right, bats right. . . . Full name: Gregory William Olson.
HIGH SCHOOL: Edina (Minn.) East.
COLLEGE: Minnesota.
TRANSACTIONS/CAREER NOTES: Selected by New York Mets organization in seventh round of free-agent draft (June 7, 1982). . . . Granted free agency (October 15, 1988). . . . Signed by Portland, Minnesota Twins organization (November 30, 1988). . . . Granted free agency (October 15, 1989). . . . Signed by Richmond, Atlanta Braves organization (November 6, 1989). . . . On disabled list (September 19, 1992-remainder of season and August 9-September 1, 1993). . . . Released by Braves (December 6, 1993). . . . Signed by New York Mets (December 20, 1993).
STATISTICAL NOTES: Led Carolina League catchers with 973 total chances in 1983. . . . Tied for International League lead with 15 passed balls in 1988.

			BATTING												FIELDING			
Year	**Team (League)**	**Pos.**	**G**	**AB**	**R**	**H**	**2B**	**3B**	**HR**	**RBI**	**Avg.**	**BB**	**SO**	**SB**	**PO**	**A**	**E**	**Avg.**
1982	—Lynchburg (Caro.)	C-3B	32	91	10	24	1	0	0	5	.264	12	5	1	149	26	6	.967
1983	—Lynchburg (Caro.)	C	107	318	56	73	7	0	0	22	.230	54	36	0	*881	*82	10	*.990
1984	—Jackson (Texas)	C	74	234	27	55	9	0	0	22	.235	30	16	1	511	51	9	.984
1985	—Jackson (Texas)	C	69	211	21	57	7	0	1	32	.270	23	20	1	353	56	6	.986
1986	—Jackson (Texas)	C	64	196	28	39	5	1	2	16	.199	30	16	0	347	49	4	.990
	—Tidewater (Int'l)	C	19	55	11	18	1	0	0	7	.327	5	7	1	104	13	3	.975
1987	—Tidewater (Int'l)	C	47	120	15	34	8	1	2	15	.283	14	13	0	219	12	3	.987
1988	—Tidewater (Int'l)	C-OF	115	344	39	92	19	1	6	48	.267	42	42	0	600	64	7	.990
1989	—Portland (PCL)■	C-3B	79	247	38	58	8	2	6	38	.235	45	27	3	440	32	5	.990
	—Minnesota (A.L.)	C	3	2	0	1	0	0	0	0	.500	0	0	0	4	0	0	1.000
1990	—Richmond (Int'l)■	C	3	7	0	0	0	0	0	0	.000	0	0	0	17	2	0	1.000
	—Atlanta (N.L.)	C-3B	100	298	36	78	12	1	7	36	.262	30	51	1	501	43	7	.987
1991	—Atlanta (N.L.)	C	133	411	46	99	25	0	6	44	.241	44	48	1	721	48	4	.995
1992	—Atlanta (N.L.)	C	95	302	27	72	14	2	3	27	.238	34	31	2	522	43	1	.998
1993	—Atlanta (N.L.)	C	83	262	23	59	10	0	4	24	.225	29	27	1	445	35	6	.988
American League totals (1 year)			3	2	0	1	0	0	0	0	.500	0	0	0	4	0	0	1.000
National League totals (4 years)			411	1273	132	308	61	3	20	131	.242	137	157	5	2189	169	18	.992
Major league totals (5 years)			414	1275	132	309	61	3	20	131	.242	137	157	5	2193	169	18	.992

CHAMPIONSHIP SERIES RECORD

			BATTING												FIELDING			
Year	**Team (League)**	**Pos.**	**G**	**AB**	**R**	**H**	**2B**	**3B**	**HR**	**RBI**	**Avg.**	**BB**	**SO**	**SB**	**PO**	**A**	**E**	**Avg.**
1991	—Atlanta (N.L.)	C	7	24	3	8	1	0	1	4	.333	4	3	1	62	1	0	1.000
1993	—Atlanta (N.L.)	C	2	3	0	1	1	0	0	0	.333	0	1	0	10	0	0	1.000
Championship series totals (2 years)			9	27	3	9	2	0	1	4	.333	4	4	1	72	1	0	1.000

WORLD SERIES RECORD

Year	Team (League)	Pos.	G	AB	R	H	2B	3B	HR	RBI	Avg.	BB	SO	SB	PO	A	E	Avg.
			BATTING												FIELDING			
1991	—Atlanta (N.L.)	C	7	27	3	6	2	0	0	1	.222	5	4	1	47	6	0	1.000

ALL-STAR GAME RECORD

Year	League	Pos.	AB	R	H	2B	3B	HR	RBI	Avg.	BB	SO	SB	PO	A	E	Avg.
			BATTING											FIELDING			
1990	—National	PH-C	1	0	0	0	0	0	0	.000	0	1	0	0	0	0	...

OLSON, GREGG

P, BRAVES

PERSONAL: Born October 11, 1966, in Omaha, Neb.... 6-4/212.... Throws right, bats right. ... Full name: Gregg William Olson.
HIGH SCHOOL: Northwest (Omaha, Neb.).
COLLEGE: Auburn.
TRANSACTIONS/CAREER NOTES: Selected by Baltimore Orioles organization in first round (fourth pick overall) of free-agent draft (June 1, 1988).... On disabled list (August 9-September 20, 1993).... Granted free agency (December 20, 1993).... Signed by Atlanta Braves (February 8, 1994).
RECORDS: Holds A.L. rookie-season record for most saves—27 (1989).
HONORS: Named righthanded pitcher on THE SPORTING NEWS college All-America team (1988).... Named A.L. Rookie of the Year by Baseball Writers' Association of America (1989).
STATISTICAL NOTES: Pitched one inning, combining with starter Bob Milacki (six innings), Mike Flanagan (one inning) and Mark Williamson (one inning) in 2-0 no-hit victory against Oakland (July 13, 1991).
MISCELLANEOUS: Struck out in only plate appearance (1993).

Year	Team (League)	W	L	Pct.	ERA	G	GS	CG	ShO	Sv.	IP	H	R	ER	BB	SO
1988	—Hagerstown (Car.)	1	0	1.000	2.00	8	0	0	0	4	9	5	2	2	2	9
	—Charlotte (South.)	0	1	.000	5.87	8	0	0	0	1	15⅓	24	13	10	6	22
	—Baltimore (A.L.)	1	1	.500	3.27	10	0	0	0	0	11	10	4	4	10	9
1989	—Baltimore (A.L.)	5	2	.714	1.69	64	0	0	0	27	85	57	17	16	46	90
1990	—Baltimore (A.L.)	6	5	.545	2.42	64	0	0	0	37	74⅓	57	20	20	31	74
1991	—Baltimore (A.L.)	4	6	.400	3.18	72	0	0	0	31	73⅔	74	28	26	29	72
1992	—Baltimore (A.L.)	1	5	.167	2.05	60	0	0	0	36	61⅓	46	14	14	24	58
1993	—Baltimore (A.L.)	0	2	.000	1.60	50	0	0	0	29	45	37	9	8	18	44
Major league totals (6 years)		17	21	.447	2.26	320	0	0	0	160	350⅓	281	92	88	158	347

ALL-STAR GAME RECORD

Year	League	W	L	Pct.	ERA	GS	CG	ShO	Sv.	IP	H	R	ER	BB	SO
1990	—American						Did not play.								

O'NEILL, PAUL

OF, YANKEES

PERSONAL: Born February 25, 1963, in Columbus, O.... 6-4/215.... Throws left, bats left.... Full name: Paul Andrew O'Neill.... Son of Charles O'Neill, minor league pitcher (1945-48).
HIGH SCHOOL: Brookhaven (Columbus, O.).
COLLEGE: Otterbein College (O.).
TRANSACTIONS/CAREER NOTES: Selected by Cincinnati Reds organization in fourth round of free-agent draft (June 8, 1981).... On disabled list (May 10-July 16, 1986).... On Cincinnati disabled list (July 21-September 1, 1989); included rehabilitation assignment to Nashville (August 27-September 1).... Traded by Reds with 1B Joe DeBerry to New York Yankees for OF Roberto Kelly (November 3, 1992).
STATISTICAL NOTES: Led American Association outfielders with 19 assists and eight double plays in 1985.

Year	Team (League)	Pos.	G	AB	R	H	2B	3B	HR	RBI	Avg.	BB	SO	SB	PO	A	E	Avg.
			BATTING												FIELDING			
1981	—Billings (Pioneer)	OF	66	241	37	76	7	2	3	29	.315	21	35	6	87	4	5	.948
1982	—Ced. Rap. (Midw.)	OF	116	386	50	105	19	2	8	71	.272	21	79	12	137	7	8	.947
1983	—Tampa (Fla. St.)	OF-1B	121	413	62	115	23	7	8	51	.278	56	70	20	218	14	10	.959
	—Waterbury (East.)	OF	14	43	6	12	0	0	0	6	.279	6	8	2	26	0	0	1.000
1984	—Vermont (Eastern)	OF	134	475	70	126	31	5	16	76	.265	52	72	29	246	5	7	.973
1985	—Denver (A.A.)	OF-1B	★137	★509	63	★155	★32	3	7	74	.305	28	73	5	248	†20	7	.975
	—Cincinnati (N.L.)	OF	5	12	1	4	1	0	0	1	.333	0	2	0	3	1	0	1.000
1986	—Cincinnati (N.L.)	PH	3	2	0	0	0	0	0	0	.000	1	1	0	...	...	...	...
	—Denver (A.A.)	OF	55	193	20	49	9	2	5	27	.254	9	28	1	98	7	4	.963
1987	—Cincinnati (N.L.)	OF-1B-P	84	160	24	41	14	1	7	28	.256	18	29	2	90	2	4	.958
	—Nashville (A.A.)	OF	11	37	12	11	0	0	3	6	.297	5	5	1	19	1	0	1.000
1988	—Cincinnati (N.L.)	OF-1B	145	485	58	122	25	3	16	73	.252	38	65	8	410	13	6	.986
1989	—Cincinnati (N.L.)	OF	117	428	49	118	24	2	15	74	.276	46	64	20	223	7	4	.983
	—Nashville (A.A.)	OF	4	12	1	4	0	0	0	0	.333	3	1	1	7	1	0	1.000
1990	—Cincinnati (N.L.)	OF	145	503	59	136	28	0	16	78	.270	53	103	13	271	12	2	.993
1991	—Cincinnati (N.L.)	OF	152	532	71	136	36	0	28	91	.256	73	107	12	301	13	2	.994
1992	—Cincinnati (N.L.)	OF	148	496	59	122	19	1	14	66	.246	77	85	6	291	12	1	★.997
1993	—New York (A.L.)■	OF	141	498	71	155	34	1	20	75	.311	44	69	2	230	7	2	.992
American League totals (1 year)			141	498	71	155	34	1	20	75	.311	44	69	2	230	7	2	.992
National League totals (8 years)			799	2618	321	679	147	7	96	411	.259	306	456	61	1589	60	19	.989
Major league totals (9 years)			940	3116	392	834	181	8	116	486	.268	350	525	63	1819	67	21	.989

CHAMPIONSHIP SERIES RECORD

Year	Team (League)	Pos.	G	AB	R	H	2B	3B	HR	RBI	Avg.	BB	SO	SB	PO	A	E	Avg.
			BATTING												FIELDING			
1990	—Cincinnati (N.L.)	OF	5	17	1	8	3	0	1	4	.471	1	1	1	9	2	0	1.000

WORLD SERIES RECORD

Year	Team (League)	Pos.	G	AB	R	H	2B	3B	HR	RBI	Avg.	BB	SO	SB	PO	A	E	Avg.
			BATTING												FIELDING			
1990	—Cincinnati (N.L.).......	OF	4	12	2	1	0	0	0	1	.083	5	2	1	11	0	0	1.000

ALL-STAR GAME RECORD

Year	League	Pos.	AB	R	H	2B	3B	HR	RBI	Avg.	BB	SO	SB	PO	A	E	Avg.
			BATTING											FIELDING			
1991	—National.....................	OF	2	0	0	0	0	0	0	.000	0	1	0	0	0	0	...

RECORD AS PITCHER

Year	Team (League)	W	L	Pct.	ERA	G	GS	CG	ShO	Sv.	IP	H	R	ER	BB	SO
1987	—Cincinnati (N.L.)	0	0	...	13.50	1	0	0	0	0	2	2	3	3	4	2

ONTIVEROS, STEVE

P, ATHLETICS

PERSONAL: Born March 5, 1961, in Tularosa, N.M.... 6-0/190.... Throws right, bats right.... Name pronounced AHN-tih-VAIR-oss.

HIGH SCHOOL: St. Joseph (South Bend, Ind.).

COLLEGE: Michigan.

TRANSACTIONS/CAREER NOTES: Selected by Oakland Athletics organization in second round of free-agent draft (June 7, 1982).... On West Haven temporarily inactive list (July 27-August 6, 1982).... On disabled list (April 16-August 8, 1984).... On Tacoma disabled list (April 16-28, 1985).... On disabled list (July 24-September 14, 1986).... On Oakland disabled list (March 30-April 24, 1987); included rehabilitation assignment to Tacoma (April 21-24).... On disabled list (June 12-August 2 and August 3, 1988-remainder of season).... Released by A's (December 21, 1988).... Signed by Philadelphia Phillies organization (February 16, 1989).... On Philadelphia disabled list (April 20-June 6, 1989); included rehabilitation assignment to Scranton/Wilkes-Barre (May 14-22).... On Philadelphia disabled list (June 21, 1989-remainder of season); included rehabilitation assignment to Scranton/Wilkes-Barre (June 28).... On Philadelphia disabled list (March 30-September 8, 1990); included rehabilitation assignment to Clearwater (August 2-16) and Reading (August 17-19 and August 27-September 2).... On disabled list (March 29, 1991-entire season); included rehabilitation assignment to Scranton/Wilkes-Barre (April 28-May 15 and August 22-September 2).... Granted free agency (November 11, 1991).... Signed by Toledo, Detroit Tigers organization (February 28, 1992).... On Toledo disabled list (April 9-16, 1992).... Released by Toledo (April 16, 1992).... Signed by Portland, Minnesota Twins organization (April 5, 1993).... Traded by Twins organization to Seattle Mariners organization for OF Greg Shockey (August 10, 1993).... Granted free agency (October 8, 1993).... Signed by A's (January 31, 1994).

MISCELLANEOUS: Appeared in one game as a pinch-runner (1986).... Appeared in two games as a pinch-runner (1988).

Year	Team (League)	W	L	Pct.	ERA	G	GS	CG	ShO	Sv.	IP	H	R	ER	BB	SO
1982	—Medford (N'west).......	1	0	1.000	0.00	4	0	0	0	0	8	3	0	0	4	9
	—West Haven (East.)....	2	2	.500	6.33	16	2	0	0	0	27	34	26	19	12	28
1983	—Alb./Colon. (East.)	8	4	.667	3.75	32	13	5	0	5	129⅔	131	62	54	36	91
1984	—Madison (Midwest)....	3	1	.750	2.05	5	5	2	0	0	30⅔	23	10	7	6	26
	—Tacoma (PCL)...........	1	1	.500	7.94	2	2	0	0	0	11⅓	18	11	10	5	6
1985	—Tacoma (PCL)...........	3	0	1.000	2.94	15	0	0	0	2	33⅔	26	13	11	21	30
	—Oakland (A.L.)	1	3	.250	1.93	39	0	0	0	8	74⅔	45	17	16	19	36
1986	—Oakland (A.L.)	2	2	.500	4.71	46	0	0	0	10	72⅔	72	40	38	25	54
1987	—Tacoma (PCL)...........	0	0	...	3.00	1	1	0	0	0	3	1	1	1	2	1
	—Oakland (A.L.)	10	8	.556	4.00	35	22	2	1	1	150⅔	141	78	67	50	97
1988	—Oakland (A.L.)	3	4	.429	4.61	10	10	0	0	0	54⅔	57	32	28	21	30
1989	—Philadelphia (N.L.)■...	2	1	.667	3.82	6	5	0	0	0	30⅔	34	15	13	15	12
	—Scran./W.B. (Int'l).....	0	0	...	0.00	1	1	0	0	0	3⅓	3	0	0	3	0
1990	—Clearwater (FSL)	0	0	...	2.35	3	3	0	0	0	7⅔	4	2	2	3	2
	—Reading (Eastern)	0	2	.000	9.00	2	2	0	0	0	6	7	6	6	2	8
	—Philadelphia (N.L.).....	0	0	...	2.70	5	0	0	0	0	10	9	3	3	3	6
1991	—Scran./W.B. (Int'l).....	2	1	.667	2.90	7	7	0	0	0	31	29	11	10	10	21
1992	—................................							Did not play.								
1993	—Portland (PCL)■.........	7	6	.538	2.87	20	16	2	0	0	103⅓	90	40	33	20	73
	—Seattle (A.L.)■...........	0	2	.000	1.00	14	0	0	0	0	18	18	3	2	6	13
A.L. totals (5 years)...............		16	19	.457	3.67	144	32	2	1	19	370⅔	333	170	151	121	230
N.L. totals (2 years)		2	1	.667	3.54	11	5	0	0	0	40⅔	43	18	16	18	18
Major league totals (7 years)..		18	20	.474	3.65	155	37	2	1	19	411⅓	376	188	167	139	248

OQUENDO, JOSE

2B/SS, CARDINALS

PERSONAL: Born July 4, 1963, in Rio Piedras, Puerto Rico.... 5-10/171.... Throws right, bats both.... Full name: Jose Manuel Oquendo.... Name pronounced oh-KEN-doh.

HIGH SCHOOL: Villamallo (Rio Piedras, Puerto Rico).

TRANSACTIONS/CAREER NOTES: Signed as free agent by New York Mets organization (April 15, 1979).... Traded by Mets organization with P Mark Jason Davis to St. Louis Cardinals organization for SS Argenis Salazar and P John Young (April 2, 1985).... On St. Louis disabled list (April 7-June 2, 1992); included rehabilitation assignment to Arkansas (May 11-13) and Louisville (May 23-June 2).... On St. Louis disabled list (June 9-July 13); included rehabilitation assignment to Louisville (July 7-13).... On St. Louis disabled list (July 22-September 1, 1992); included rehabilitation assignment to Louisville (August 20-31).... On St. Louis disabled list (August 9, 1993-remainder of season).

RECORDS: Holds major league single-season records for highest fielding percentage by second baseman (150 or more games)—.996; and fewest errors—3 (1990).... Shares major league single-season record for fewest double plays by second baseman (150 or more games)—65 (1990).... Holds N.L. single-season record for fewest chances accepted by second baseman (150 games or more)—678 (1990).

STATISTICAL NOTES: Led Northwest League shortstops with 40 errors in 1979.... Led Carolina League with 13 sacrifice hits in 1980.... Led International League with 14 sacrifice hits in 1982.... Led American Association with 15 sacrifice hits in 1985.... Led American Association shortstops with 591 total chances in 1985.... Order of frequency of positions played in 1988: 2B-3B-SS-1B-OF-C-P.... Led N.L. second basemen with 346 putouts, 500 assists, 851 total chances and 106 double plays in 1989.... Led N.L. second basemen with .994 fielding percentage in 1989 and .996 in 1990.

Year	Team (League)	Pos.	G	AB	R	H	2B	3B	HR	RBI	Avg.	BB	SO	SB	PO	A	E	Avg.
				BATTING											FIELDING			
1979	—Grays Har. (N'west) ..	SS-2B	64	220	24	50	8	0	1	14	.227	33	45	9	90	177	†40	.870
1980	—Lynchburg (Caro.) ...	SS	109	301	38	51	10	3	0	26	.169	47	59	14	126	358	31	*.940
1981	—Lynchburg (Caro.) ...	SS	124	393	59	98	8	6	0	38	.249	71	61	38	169	390	23	*.960
1982	—Tidewater (Int'l)	SS	114	337	40	72	8	3	0	22	.214	41	50	24	186	337	25	.954
1983	—Tidewater (Int'l)	SS	13	34	3	4	0	0	0	3	.118	5	6	2	20	23	4	.915
	—New York (N.L.)	SS	120	328	29	70	7	0	1	17	.213	19	60	8	182	326	21	.960
1984	—New York (N.L.)	SS	81	189	23	42	5	0	0	10	.222	15	26	10	95	152	7	.972
	—Tidewater (Int'l)	SS	38	113	8	18	1	0	1	8	.159	5	14	8	54	111	2	.988
1985	—Louisville (A.A.)■.....	SS	133	384	38	81	8	1	1	30	.211	24	41	13	*227	341	23	.961
1986	—St. Louis (N.L.)	S-2-3-O	76	138	20	41	4	1	0	13	.297	15	20	2	52	94	8	.948
1987	—St. Louis (N.L.)	O-2-S-3-1-P	116	248	43	71	9	0	1	24	.286	54	29	4	149	133	4	.986
1988	—St. Louis (N.L.)	IF-O-C-P	148	451	36	125	10	1	7	46	.277	52	40	4	268	315	11	.981
1989	—St. Louis (N.L.)	2B-SS-1B	•163	556	59	162	28	7	1	48	.291	79	59	3	†356	†523	6	†.993
1990	—St. Louis (N.L.)	2B-SS	156	469	38	118	17	5	1	37	.252	74	46	1	294	403	4	†.994
1991	—St. Louis (N.L.)	2B-SS-P	127	366	37	88	11	4	1	26	.240	67	48	1	271	368	9	.986
1992	—St. Louis (N.L.)	2B-SS	14	35	3	9	3	1	0	3	.257	5	3	0	18	30	1	.980
	—Arkansas (Texas)	2B	2	7	3	3	0	0	0	1	.429	0	0	0	3	2	0	1.000
	—Louisville (A.A.)	SS-2B	20	64	8	17	2	0	0	6	.266	11	3	0	36	55	5	.948
1993	—St. Louis (N.L.)	SS-2B	46	73	7	15	0	0	0	4	.205	12	8	0	52	82	1	.993
Major league totals (10 years)			1047	2853	295	741	94	19	12	228	.260	392	339	33	1737	2426	72	.983

CHAMPIONSHIP SERIES RECORD

Year	Team (League)	Pos.	G	AB	R	H	2B	3B	HR	RBI	Avg.	BB	SO	SB	PO	A	E	Avg.
				BATTING											FIELDING			
1987	—St. Louis (N.L.)	OF-3B-PH	5	12	3	2	0	0	1	4	.167	3	2	0	7	0	0	1.000

WORLD SERIES RECORD

Year	Team (League)	Pos.	G	AB	R	H	2B	3B	HR	RBI	Avg.	BB	SO	SB	PO	A	E	Avg.
				BATTING											FIELDING			
1987	—St. Louis (N.L.)	3B-OF	7	24	2	6	0	0	0	2	.250	1	4	0	8	10	0	1.000

RECORD AS PITCHER

Year	Team (League)	W	L	Pct.	ERA	G	GS	CG	ShO	Sv.	IP	H	R	ER	BB	SO
1987	—St. Louis (N.L.)	0	0	...	27.00	1	0	0	0	0	1	4	3	3	1	0
1988	—St. Louis (N.L.)	0	1	.000	4.50	1	0	0	0	0	4	4	2	2	6	1
1991	—St. Louis (N.L.)	0	0	...	27.00	1	0	0	0	0	1	2	3	3	0	1
Major league totals (3 years) ..		0	1	.000	12.00	3	0	0	0	0	6	10	8	8	7	2

OQUIST, MIKE

P, ORIOLES

PERSONAL: Born May 30, 1968, in La Junta, Colo. . . . 6-2/170. . . . Throws right, bats right. . . . Full name: Michael Lee Oquist. . . . Name pronounced OH-kwist.
HIGH SCHOOL: La Junta (Colo.).
COLLEGE: Arkansas.
TRANSACTIONS/CAREER NOTES: Selected by Baltimore Orioles organization in 13th round of free-agent draft (June 5, 1989).

Year	Team (League)	W	L	Pct.	ERA	G	GS	CG	ShO	Sv.	IP	H	R	ER	BB	SO
1989	—Erie (N.Y.-Penn)	7	4	.636	3.59	15	15	1	1	0	97⅔	86	43	39	25	109
1990	—Frederick (Caro.)	9	8	.529	2.81	25	25	3	1	0	166⅓	134	64	52	48	*170
1991	—Hagerstown (East.).....	10	9	.526	4.06	27	26	1	0	0	166⅓	168	82	75	62	136
1992	—Rochester (Int'l)	10	12	.455	4.11	26	24	5	0	0	153⅓	164	80	70	45	111
1993	—Rochester (Int'l)	9	8	.529	3.50	28	21	2	1	0	149⅓	144	62	58	41	128
	—Baltimore (A.L.)...........	0	0	...	3.86	5	0	0	0	0	11⅔	12	5	5	4	8
Major league totals (1 year)		0	0	...	3.86	5	0	0	0	0	11⅔	12	5	5	4	8

OROSCO, JESSE

P, BREWERS

PERSONAL: Born April 21, 1957, in Santa Barbara, Calif. . . . 6-2/205. . . . Throws left, bats right. . . . Name pronounced oh-ROSS-koh.
HIGH SCHOOL: Santa Barbara (Calif.).
COLLEGE: Santa Barbara (Calif.) City College.
TRANSACTIONS/CAREER NOTES: Selected by St. Louis Cardinals organization in seventh round of free-agent draft (January 11, 1977). . . . Selected by Minnesota Twins organization in second round of free-agent draft (January 10, 1978). . . . Traded by Twins organization to New York Mets (February 7, 1979), completing deal in which Twins traded P Greg Field and a player to be named later to Mets for P Jerry Koosman (December 8, 1978). . . . Traded by Mets as part of an eight-player, three-team deal in which Mets sent Orosco to Oakland Athletics (December 11, 1987). A's then traded Orosco, SS Alfredo Griffin and P Jay Howell to Los Angeles Dodgers for P Bob Welch, P Matt Young and P Jack Savage. A's then traded Savage, P Wally Whitehurst and P Kevin Tapani to Mets. . . . Granted free agency (November 4, 1988). . . . Signed by Cleveland Indians (December 3, 1988). . . . Traded by Indians to Milwaukee Brewers for a player to be named later (December 6, 1991); deal settled in cash. . . . Granted free agency (November 5, 1992). . . . Re-signed by Brewers (December 4, 1992).
MISCELLANEOUS: Appeared in one game as outfielder with one putout (1986). . . . Struck out in only plate appearance (1993).

Year	Team (League)	W	L	Pct.	ERA	G	GS	CG	ShO	Sv.	IP	H	R	ER	BB	SO
1978	—Elizabeth. (Appal.)	4	4	.500	1.13	20	0	0	0	6	40	29	7	5	20	48
1979	—Tidewater (Int'l)■	4	4	.500	3.89	16	15	1	0	0	81	82	45	35	43	55
	—New York (N.L.)	1	2	.333	4.89	18	2	0	0	0	35	33	20	19	22	22
1980	—Jackson (Texas)	4	4	.500	3.68	37	1	0	0	3	71	52	36	29	62	85
1981	—Tidewater (Int'l)	9	5	.643	3.31	46	10	0	0	8	87	80	39	32	32	81
	—New York (N.L.)	0	1	.000	1.59	8	0	0	0	1	17	13	4	3	6	18
1982	—New York (N.L.)	4	10	.286	2.72	54	2	0	0	4	109⅓	92	37	33	40	89
1983	—New York (N.L.)	13	7	.650	1.47	62	0	0	0	17	110	76	27	18	38	84

Year	Team (League)	W	L	Pct.	ERA	G	GS	CG	ShO	Sv.	IP	H	R	ER	BB	SO
1984	—New York (N.L.)	10	6	.625	2.59	60	0	0	0	31	87	58	29	25	34	85
1985	—New York (N.L.)	8	6	.571	2.73	54	0	0	0	17	79	66	26	24	34	68
1986	—New York (N.L.)	8	6	.571	2.33	58	0	0	0	21	81	64	23	21	35	62
1987	—New York (N.L.)	3	9	.250	4.44	58	0	0	0	16	77	78	41	38	31	78
1988	—Los Angeles (N.L.)■...	3	2	.600	2.72	55	0	0	0	9	53	41	18	16	30	43
1989	—Cleveland (A.L.)■.......	3	4	.429	2.08	69	0	0	0	3	78	54	20	18	26	79
1990	—Cleveland (A.L.)	5	4	.556	3.90	55	0	0	0	2	64⅔	58	35	28	38	55
1991	—Cleveland (A.L.)	2	0	1.000	3.74	47	0	0	0	0	45⅔	52	20	19	15	36
1992	—Milwaukee (A.L.)■	3	1	.750	3.23	59	0	0	0	1	39	33	15	14	13	40
1993	—Milwaukee (A.L.)	3	5	.375	3.18	57	0	0	0	8	56⅔	47	25	20	17	67
A.L. totals (5 years)		16	14	.533	3.14	287	0	0	0	14	284	244	115	99	109	277
N.L. totals (9 years)		50	49	.505	2.73	427	4	0	0	116	648⅓	521	225	197	270	549
Major league totals (14 years)		66	63	.512	2.86	714	4	0	0	130	932⅓	765	340	296	379	826

CHAMPIONSHIP SERIES RECORD

CHAMPIONSHIP SERIES NOTES: Holds single-series record for most games won—3 (1986).

Year	Team (League)	W	L	Pct.	ERA	G	GS	CG	ShO	Sv.	IP	H	R	ER	BB	SO
1986	—New York (N.L.)	3	0	1.000	3.38	4	0	0	0	0	8	5	3	3	2	10
1988	—Los Angeles (N.L.)	0	0	...	7.71	4	0	0	0	0	2⅓	4	2	2	3	0
Champ. series totals (2 years)		3	0	1.000	4.35	8	0	0	0	0	10⅓	9	5	5	5	10

WORLD SERIES RECORD

Year	Team (League)	W	L	Pct.	ERA	G	GS	CG	ShO	Sv.	IP	H	R	ER	BB	SO
1986	—New York (N.L.)	0	0	...	0.00	4	0	0	0	2	5⅔	2	0	0	0	6
1988	—Los Angeles (N.L.)							Did not play.								
World Series totals (1 year) ...		0	0	...	0.00	4	0	0	0	2	5⅔	2	0	0	0	6

ALL-STAR GAME RECORD

Year	League	W	L	Pct.	ERA	GS	CG	ShO	Sv.	IP	H	R	ER	BB	SO
1983	—National.........................	0	0	...	0.00	0	0	0	0	⅓	0	0	0	0	1
1984	—National.........................						Did not play.								
All-Star totals (1 year)		0	0	...	0.00	0	0	0	0	⅓	0	0	0	0	1

ORSULAK, JOE

OF, METS

PERSONAL: Born May 31, 1962, in Glen Ridge, N.J.... 6-1/205.... Throws left, bats left.... Full name: Joseph Michael Orsulak.... Name pronounced OR-suh-lack.

HIGH SCHOOL: Parsippany (N.J.).

TRANSACTIONS/CAREER NOTES: Selected by Pittsburgh Pirates organization in sixth round of free-agent draft (June 3, 1980).... On temporarily inactive list (July 10-27, 1981).... On disabled list (May 25-June 9, 1985).... On Pittsburgh disabled list (March 31-May 22, 1987); included rehabilitation assignment to Vancouver (May 4-22).... Traded by Pirates to Baltimore Orioles for SS Terry Crowley Jr. and 3B Rico Rossy (November 6, 1987).... On disabled list (August 16-September 1, 1992).... Granted free agency (October 28, 1992).... Signed by New York Mets (December 18, 1992).

STATISTICAL NOTES: Tied for South Atlantic League lead in double plays by outfielder with four in 1981.... Led Pacific Coast League outfielders with 367 total chances and eight double plays in 1983.

				BATTING											FIELDING			
Year	Team (League)	Pos.	G	AB	R	H	2B	3B	HR	RBI	Avg.	BB	SO	SB	PO	A	E	Avg.
1981	—Greenwood (S. Atl.)..	OF	118	460	80	145	18	8	6	70	.315	29	32	18	249	16	4	*.985
1982	—Alexandria (Caro.) ...	OF-1B	129	463	92	134	18	4	14	65	.289	47	46	28	286	7	10	.967
1983	—Hawaii (PCL)	OF	139	538	87	154	12	•13	10	58	.286	48	41	38	*341	•18	8	.978
	—Pittsburgh (N.L.)	OF	7	11	0	2	0	0	0	1	.182	0	2	0	2	2	0	1.000
1984	—Hawaii (PCL)	OF	98	388	51	110	19	12	3	53	.284	29	38	14	258	6	2	.992
	—Pittsburgh (N.L.)	OF	32	67	12	17	1	2	0	3	.254	1	7	3	41	1	0	1.000
1985	—Pittsburgh (N.L.)	OF	121	397	54	119	14	6	0	21	.300	26	27	24	229	10	6	.976
1986	—Pittsburgh (N.L.)	OF	138	401	60	100	19	6	2	19	.249	28	38	24	193	11	4	.981
1987	—Vancouver (PCL)	OF	39	143	20	33	6	1	1	12	.231	17	21	2	58	2	2	.968
1988	—Baltimore (A.L.)■	OF	125	379	48	109	21	3	8	27	.288	23	30	9	228	6	5	.979
1989	—Baltimore (A.L.)........	OF	123	390	59	111	22	5	7	55	.285	41	35	5	250	10	4	.985
1990	—Baltimore (A.L.)........	OF	124	413	49	111	14	3	11	57	.269	46	48	6	267	5	3	.989
1991	—Baltimore (A.L.)........	OF	143	486	57	135	22	1	5	43	.278	28	45	6	273	*22	1	.997
1992	—Baltimore (A.L.)........	OF	117	391	45	113	18	3	4	39	.289	28	34	5	228	9	4	.983
1993	—New York (N.L.)■......	OF-1B	134	409	59	116	15	4	8	35	.284	28	25	5	231	10	5	.980
American League totals (5 years)			632	2059	258	579	97	15	35	221	.281	166	192	31	1246	52	17	.987
National League totals (5 years)			432	1285	185	354	49	18	10	79	.275	83	99	56	696	34	15	.980
Major league totals (10 years)			1064	3344	443	933	146	33	45	300	.279	249	291	87	1942	86	32	.984

ORTIZ, JUNIOR

C, INDIANS

PERSONAL: Born October 24, 1959, in Humacao, Puerto Rico.... 5-11/181.... Throws right, bats right.... Full name: Adalberto Colon Ortiz Jr.... Brother of Alexander Ortiz, minor league outfielder (1978-79).... Name pronounced or-TEEZ.

HIGH SCHOOL: Ana Roque (Humacao, Puerto Rico).

TRANSACTIONS/CAREER NOTES: Signed as free agent by Pittsburgh Pirates organization (January 18, 1977).... On Charleston temporary inactive list (June 18-22, 1977).... On disabled list (June 16-September 5, 1978).... Traded by Pirates with P Art Ray to New York Mets for OF Marvell Wynne and P Steve Senteney (June 14, 1983).... Selected by Pirates from Mets organization in Rule 5 major league draft (December 3, 1984).... On disabled list (July 28-September 5, 1988).... Traded by Pirates with P Orlando Lind to Minnesota Twins for P Mike Pomeranz (April 4, 1990).... On disabled list (June 1-16, 1991).... Granted free agency (November 11, 1991).... Signed by Cleveland Indians organization (December 16, 1991).... Granted free

agency (October 30, 1992).... Re-signed by Indians organization (December 8, 1992).... Granted free agency (October 29, 1993).... Re-signed by Indians organization (December 20, 1993).
STATISTICAL NOTES: Tied for Western Carolinas League lead with 22 passed balls in 1978.... Led Carolina League catchers with 84 assists, 17 errors and 12 double plays in 1979.... Led Pacific Coast League catchers with 744 putouts, 110 assists, 19 errors, 873 total chances and 17 double plays in 1982.... Tied for A.L. lead in double plays by catcher with 13 in 1993.

			BATTING												FIELDING			
Year	Team (League)	Pos.	G	AB	R	H	2B	3B	HR	RBI	Avg.	BB	SO	SB	PO	A	E	Avg.
1977	—Char., S.C. (W. Car.)	C	21	53	2	14	3	0	0	10	.264	6	13	0	93	13	4	.964
	—GC Pirates (GCL)	C	34	118	11	24	5	1	1	12	.203	12	22	1	76	14	4	.957
1978	—Char., S.C. (W. Car.)	C	41	122	12	26	4	0	1	16	.213	7	20	1	198	44	7	.972
1979	—Salem (Carolina)	C-1B	108	396	35	112	21	2	5	66	.283	26	55	0	632	†84	†17	.977
1980	—Buffalo (Eastern)	C	126	515	79	*178	25	1	12	78	*.346	43	57	7	497	91	16	.974
	—Portland (PCL)	C	8	27	1	3	0	1	0	3	.111	1	3	0	42	10	0	1.000
1981	—Portland (PCL)	C	105	346	49	93	14	7	2	46	.269	25	33	5	606	76	15	.978
1982	—Portland (PCL)	C-OF-1B	124	449	46	131	22	0	6	57	.292	34	61	4	†751	†110	†19	.978
	—Pittsburgh (N.L.)	C	7	15	1	3	1	0	0	0	.200	1	3	0	27	3	0	1.000
1983	—Pitts.-N.Y. (N.L.)■	C	73	193	11	48	5	0	0	12	.249	4	34	1	293	31	11	.967
1984	—New York (N.L.)	C	40	91	6	18	3	0	0	11	.198	5	15	1	136	13	3	.980
1985	—Pittsburgh (N.L.)■	C	23	72	4	21	2	0	1	5	.292	3	17	1	115	14	2	.985
1986	—Pittsburgh (N.L.)	C	49	110	11	37	6	0	0	14	.336	9	13	0	165	13	3	.983
1987	—Pittsburgh (N.L.)	C	75	192	16	52	8	1	1	22	.271	15	23	0	313	39	9	.975
1988	—Pittsburgh (N.L.)	C	49	118	8	33	6	0	2	18	.280	9	9	1	152	23	3	.983
1989	—Pittsburgh (N.L.)	C	91	230	16	50	6	1	1	22	.217	20	20	2	334	32	2	.995
1990	—Minnesota (A.L.)■	C	71	170	18	57	7	1	0	18	.335	12	16	0	247	25	0	1.000
1991	—Minnesota (A.L.)	C	61	134	9	28	5	1	0	11	.209	15	12	0	203	17	1	.995
1992	—Cleveland (A.L.)■	C	86	244	20	61	7	0	0	24	.250	12	23	1	402	38	5	.989
1993	—Cleveland (A.L.)	C	95	249	19	55	13	0	0	20	.221	11	26	1	441	58	5	.990
American League totals (4 years)			313	797	66	201	32	2	0	73	.252	50	77	2	1293	138	11	.992
National League totals (8 years)			407	1021	73	262	37	2	5	104	.257	66	134	6	1535	168	33	.981
Major league totals (12 years)			720	1818	139	463	69	4	5	177	.255	116	211	8	2828	306	44	.986

CHAMPIONSHIP SERIES RECORD

			BATTING												FIELDING			
Year	Team (League)	Pos.	G	AB	R	H	2B	3B	HR	RBI	Avg.	BB	SO	SB	PO	A	E	Avg.
1991	—Minnesota (A.L.)	C	3	3	0	0	0	0	0	0	.000	0	0	0	10	0	0	1.000

WORLD SERIES RECORD

			BATTING												FIELDING			
Year	Team (League)	Pos.	G	AB	R	H	2B	3B	HR	RBI	Avg.	BB	SO	SB	PO	A	E	Avg.
1991	—Minnesota (A.L.)	C	3	5	0	1	0	0	0	1	.200	0	1	0	9	0	0	1.000

ORTIZ, LUIS

3B, RED SOX

PERSONAL: Born May 25, 1970, in Santo Domingo, Dominican Republic.... 6-0/188.... Throws right, bats right.... Full name: Luis Alberto Ortiz.
HIGH SCHOOL: De La Salle Dominican (Santo Domingo, Dominican Republic).
COLLEGE: Union University (Tenn.).
TRANSACTIONS/CAREER NOTES: Selected by Boston Red Sox organization in eighth round of free-agent draft (June 3, 1991).... On Pawtucket disabled list (June 26-July 15, 1993).

			BATTING												FIELDING			
Year	Team (League)	Pos.	G	AB	R	H	2B	3B	HR	RBI	Avg.	BB	SO	SB	PO	A	E	Avg.
1991	—GC Red Sox (GCL)	3B	42	153	21	51	11	2	4	29	.333	8	9	2	30	67	7	.933
1992	—Lynchburg (Caro.)	3B	94	355	43	103	27	1	10	61	.290	22	55	4	37	97	20	.870
1993	—Pawtucket (Int'l)	3B-OF	102	402	45	118	28	1	18	81	.294	13	74	1	45	114	12	.930
	—Boston (A.L.)	3B	9	12	0	3	0	0	0	1	.250	0	2	0	2	2	0	1.000
Major league totals (1 year)			9	12	0	3	0	0	0	1	.250	0	2	0	2	2	0	1.000

ORTON, JOHN

C

PERSONAL: Born December 8, 1965, in Santa Cruz, Calif.... 6-1/192.... Throws right, bats right.... Full name: John Andrew Orton.
HIGH SCHOOL: Soquel (Calif.).
COLLEGE: Cal Poly San Luis Obispo.
TRANSACTIONS/CAREER NOTES: Selected by New York Mets organization in 17th round of free-agent draft (June 4, 1984).... Selected by California Angels organization in first round (25th pick overall) of free-agent draft (June 2, 1987).... On disabled list (June 14-August 5, 1988).... On California disabled list (April 1-May 13, 1992); included rehabilitation assignment to Edmonton (April 24-May 13).... On California disabled list (July 4-August 29, 1992); included rehabilitation assignment to Edmonton (August 11-29).... On California disabled list (June 3-22, 1993).... On California disabled list (July 7-September 10, 1993); included rehabilitation assignment to Palm Springs (August 22-27) and Vancouver (August 27-September 10, did not play).... Granted free agency (October 7, 1993).
STATISTICAL NOTES: Led Texas League catchers with .994 fielding percentage and 12 double plays in 1989.

			BATTING												FIELDING			
Year	Team (League)	Pos.	G	AB	R	H	2B	3B	HR	RBI	Avg.	BB	SO	SB	PO	A	E	Avg.
1987	—Salem (Northwest)	OF-C	51	176	31	46	8	1	8	36	.261	32	63	6	271	15	6	.979
	—Midland (Texas)	C	5	13	1	2	1	0	0	0	.154	2	3	0	26	5	1	.969
1988	—Palm Springs (Cal.)	C	68	230	42	46	6	1	1	28	.200	45	78	5	235	27	8	.970
1989	—Midland (Texas)	C-1B	99	344	51	80	20	6	10	53	.233	37	102	2	466	56	4	†.992
	—California (A.L.)	C	16	39	4	7	1	0	0	4	.179	2	17	0	76	7	1	.988
1990	—California (A.L.)	C	31	84	8	16	5	0	1	6	.190	5	31	0	139	15	2	.987
	—Edmonton (PCL)	C	50	174	29	42	8	0	6	26	.241	19	63	4	277	36	7	.978

Year	Team (League)	Pos.	G	AB	R	H	2B	3B	HR	RBI	Avg.	BB	SO	SB	PO	A	E	Avg.
			BATTING												FIELDING			
1991	—California (A.L.)	C	29	69	7	14	4	0	0	3	.203	10	17	0	145	23	1	.994
	—Edmonton (PCL)	C	76	245	39	55	14	1	5	32	.224	31	66	5	397	49	7	.985
1992	—Edmonton (PCL)	C	49	149	28	38	9	3	3	25	.255	28	32	3	265	31	2	.993
	—California (A.L.)	C	43	114	11	25	3	0	2	12	.219	7	32	1	238	22	5	.981
1993	—California (A.L.)	C-OF	37	95	5	18	5	0	1	4	.189	7	24	1	185	17	4	.981
	—Palm Springs (Cal.)	C	2	7	0	0	0	0	0	0	.000	1	1	0	11	1	0	1.000
Major league totals (5 years)			156	401	35	80	18	0	4	29	.200	31	121	2	783	84	13	.985

OSBORNE, DONOVAN

P, CARDINALS

PERSONAL: Born June 21, 1969, in Roseville, Calif. . . . 6-2/195. . . . Throws left, bats left. . . . Full name: Donovan Alan Osborne.
HIGH SCHOOL: Carson (Carson City, Nev.).
COLLEGE: UNLV.

TRANSACTIONS/CAREER NOTES: Selected by Montreal Expos organization in ninth round of free-agent draft (June 2, 1987). . . . Selected by St. Louis Cardinals organization in first round (13th pick overall) of free-agent draft (June 4, 1990).
HONORS: Named lefthanded pitcher on THE SPORTING NEWS college All-America team (1989).
MISCELLANEOUS: Appeared in three games as pinch-runner (1993).

Year	Team (League)	W	L	Pct.	ERA	G	GS	CG	ShO	Sv.	IP	H	R	ER	BB	SO
1990	—Hamilton (NYP)	0	2	.000	3.60	4	4	0	0	0	20	21	8	8	5	14
	—Savannah (S. Atl.)	2	2	.500	2.61	6	6	1	0	0	41⅓	40	20	12	7	28
1991	—Arkansas (Texas)	8	12	.400	3.63	26	26	3	0	0	166	178	82	67	43	130
1992	—St. Louis (N.L.)	11	9	.550	3.77	34	29	0	0	0	179	193	91	75	38	104
1993	—St. Louis (N.L.)	10	7	.588	3.76	26	26	1	0	0	155⅔	153	73	65	47	83
Major league totals (2 years)		21	16	.568	3.76	60	55	1	0	0	334⅔	346	164	140	85	187

OSIK, KEITH

C, PIRATES

PERSONAL: Born October 22, 1968, in Port Jefferson, N.Y. . . . 6-0/195. . . . Throws right, bats right. . . . Full name: Keith Richard Osik. . . . Name pronounced OH-sik.
HIGH SCHOOL: Shoreham (N.Y.)-Wading River.
COLLEGE: Louisiana State.

TRANSACTIONS/CAREER NOTES: Selected by Texas Rangers organization in 47th round of free-agent draft (June 2, 1987). . . . Selected by Pittsburgh Pirates organization in 24th round of free-agent draft (June 4, 1990).

Year	Team (League)	Pos.	G	AB	R	H	2B	3B	HR	RBI	Avg.	BB	SO	SB	PO	A	E	Avg.
			BATTING												FIELDING			
1990	—Welland (NYP)	3-C-1-2-S	29	97	13	27	4	0	1	20	.278	11	12	2	59	29	2	.978
1991	—Salem (Carolina)	C-3B-2B	87	300	31	81	12	1	6	35	.270	38	48	2	307	85	12	.970
	—Carolina (South.)	C-3B	17	43	9	13	3	1	0	5	.302	5	5	0	84	13	2	.980
1992	—Carolina (South.)	3-C-2-P	129	425	41	110	17	1	5	45	.259	52	69	2	222	195	19	.956
1993	—Carolina (South.)	C-3B	103	371	47	104	21	2	10	47	.280	30	46	0	662	69	6	.992

RECORD AS PITCHER

Year	Team (League)	W	L	Pct.	ERA	G	GS	CG	ShO	Sv.	IP	H	R	ER	BB	SO
1992	—Carolina (South.)	0	0	...	0.00	2	0	0	0	0	2⅔	2	0	0	0	3

OSUNA, AL

P, ASTROS

PERSONAL: Born August 10, 1965, in Inglewood, Calif. . . . 6-3/200. . . . Throws left, bats right. . . . Name pronounced oh-SOO-na.
HIGH SCHOOL: Gahr (Cerritos, Calif.).
COLLEGE: Cerritos College (Calif.) and Stanford.

TRANSACTIONS/CAREER NOTES: Selected by Baltimore Orioles organization in fifth round of free-agent draft (January 9, 1985). . . . Selected by San Diego Padres organization in secondary phase of free-agent draft (June 3, 1985). . . . Selected by Houston Astros organization in 16th round of free-agent draft (June 2, 1987).
HONORS: Named N.L. Rookie Pitcher of the Year by THE SPORTING NEWS (1991).

Year	Team (League)	W	L	Pct.	ERA	G	GS	CG	ShO	Sv.	IP	H	R	ER	BB	SO
1987	—Auburn (NY-Penn)	1	0	1.000	5.74	8	0	0	0	0	15⅔	16	16	10	14	20
	—Asheville (S. Atl.)	2	0	1.000	2.75	14	0	0	0	2	19⅔	20	6	6	6	20
1988	—Asheville (S. Atl.)	6	1	.857	1.98	31	0	0	0	3	50	41	19	11	25	41
	—Osceola (Fla. St.)	0	1	.000	6.94	8	0	0	0	0	11⅔	12	9	9	9	5
1989	—Osceola (Fla. St.)	3	4	.429	2.66	46	0	0	0	7	67⅔	50	27	20	27	62
1990	—Columbus (South.)	7	5	.583	3.38	•60	0	0	0	6	69⅓	57	30	26	33	82
	—Houston (N.L.)	2	0	1.000	4.76	12	0	0	0	0	11⅓	10	6	6	6	6
1991	—Houston (N.L.)	7	6	.538	3.42	71	0	0	0	12	81⅔	59	39	31	46	68
1992	—Houston (N.L.)	6	3	.667	4.23	66	0	0	0	0	61⅔	52	29	29	38	37
1993	—Tucson (PCL)	3	1	.750	4.50	13	4	0	0	1	30	26	16	15	17	38
	—Houston (N.L.)	1	1	.500	3.20	44	0	0	0	2	25⅓	17	10	9	13	21
Major league totals (4 years)		16	10	.615	3.75	193	0	0	0	14	180	138	84	75	103	132

OTTO, DAVE

P, CUBS

PERSONAL: Born November 12, 1964, in Chicago. . . . 6-7/210. . . . Throws left, bats left. . . . Full name: David Alan Otto.
HIGH SCHOOL: Elk Grove (Ill.).
COLLEGE: Missouri.

TRANSACTIONS/CAREER NOTES: Selected by Baltimore Orioles organization in second round of free-agent draft (June 7, 1982). . . . Selected by Oakland Athletics organization in second round of free-agent draft (June 3, 1985). . . . On Oakland disabled list (April 29, 1990-remainder of season); included rehabilitation assignment to Tacoma (May 14-15). . . . Granted free agency (December 20, 1990). . . . Signed by Colorado Springs, Cleveland Indians organization (January 16, 1991). . . . On Cleveland

O

disabled list (May 10-26, 1992); included rehabilitation assignment to Canton/Akron (May 22).... Selected by Buffalo, Pittsburgh Pirates organization, from Canton/Akron, Cleveland Indians organization, in Rule 5 minor league draft (December 7, 1992).... Released by Pirates (August 19, 1993).... Signed by Chicago Cubs organization (January 24, 1994).
STATISTICAL NOTES: Led Pacific Coast League with 18 wild pitches in 1989.

Year	Team (League)	W	L	Pct.	ERA	G	GS	CG	ShO	Sv.	IP	H	R	ER	BB	SO
1985	—Medford (N'west)	2	2	.500	4.04	11	11	0	0	0	42⅓	42	27	19	22	27
1986	—Madison (Midwest)	13	7	.650	2.66	26	26	6	1	0	169	154	72	50	71	125
1987	—Madison (Midwest)	0	0	...	0.00	1	1	0	0	0	3	2	0	0	0	2
	—Huntsville (South.)	4	1	.800	2.34	9	8	1	0	0	50	36	14	13	11	25
	—Oakland (A.L.)	0	0	...	9.00	3	0	0	0	0	6	7	6	6	1	3
1988	—Tacoma (PCL)	4	9	.308	3.52	21	21	2	0	0	127⅔	124	71	50	63	80
	—Oakland (A.L.)	0	0	...	1.80	3	2	0	0	0	10	9	2	2	6	7
1989	—Tacoma (PCL)	10	13	.435	3.67	29	•28	2	1	0	169	164	84	69	61	122
	—Oakland (A.L.)	0	0	...	2.70	1	1	0	0	0	6⅔	6	2	2	2	4
1990	—Oakland (A.L.)	0	0	...	7.71	2	0	0	0	0	2⅓	3	3	2	3	2
	—Tacoma (PCL)	0	0	...	4.50	2	0	0	0	0	2	3	1	1	1	2
1991	—Colo. Springs (PCL)■	5	6	.455	4.75	17	15	1	0	0	94⅔	110	56	50	43	62
	—Cleveland (A.L.)	2	8	.200	4.23	18	14	1	0	0	100	108	52	47	27	47
1992	—Cleveland (A.L.)	5	9	.357	7.06	18	16	0	0	0	80⅓	110	64	63	33	32
	—Cant./Akr. (East.)	0	0	...	0.00	1	1	0	0	0	3	1	0	0	1	1
	—Colo. Springs (PCL)	3	2	.600	2.89	6	6	1	0	0	43⅔	35	14	14	10	11
1993	—Pittsburgh (N.L.)■	3	4	.429	5.03	28	8	0	0	0	68	85	40	38	28	30
A.L. totals (6 years)		7	17	.292	5.35	45	33	1	0	0	205⅓	243	129	122	72	95
N.L. totals (1 year)		3	4	.429	5.03	28	8	0	0	0	68	85	40	38	28	30
Major league totals (7 years)		10	21	.323	5.27	73	41	1	0	0	273⅓	328	169	160	100	125

OWEN, SPIKE

SS/2B, ANGELS

PERSONAL: Born April 19, 1961, in Cleburne, Tex.... 5-10/170.... Throws right, bats both.... Full name: Spike Dee Owen.... Brother of Dave Owen, shortstop, Chicago Cubs and Kansas City Royals (1983-85 and 1988).
HIGH SCHOOL: Cleburne (Tex.).
COLLEGE: Texas.
TRANSACTIONS/CAREER NOTES: Selected by Seattle Mariners organization in first round (sixth pick overall) of free-agent draft (June 7, 1982).... On disabled list (July 15-August 1, 1985).... Traded by Mariners with OF Dave Henderson to Boston Red Sox for IF Rey Quinones, a player to be named later and cash (August 19, 1986); as part of deal, Mariners claimed P Mike Brown and P Mike Trujillo on waivers from Red Sox (August 22, 1986). Mariners acquired OF John Christensen to complete deal (September 25, 1986).... Traded by Red Sox with P Dan Gakeler to Montreal Expos for P John Dopson and SS Luis Rivera (December 8, 1988).... On disabled list (July 17-August 1, 1989 and July 20-August 4, 1992).... Granted free agency (October 26, 1992).... Signed by New York Yankees (December 4, 1992).... Traded by Yankees with cash to California Angels for P Jose Musset (December 9, 1993).
RECORDS: Shares modern major league single-game record for most runs—6 (August 21, 1986).... Holds N.L. single-season record for most consecutive errorless games by shortstop—63 (April 9-June 22, 1990).
HONORS: Named shortstop on THE SPORTING NEWS college All-America team (1982).
STATISTICAL NOTES: Led A.L. shortstops with 767 total chances and 133 double plays in 1986.

			BATTING												FIELDING			
Year	Team (League)	Pos.	G	AB	R	H	2B	3B	HR	RBI	Avg.	BB	SO	SB	PO	A	E	Avg.
1982	—Lynn (Eastern)	SS	78	241	32	64	9	2	1	27	.266	44	33	18	106	207	9	.972
1983	—Salt Lake City (PCL)	SS	72	256	58	68	8	9	1	32	.266	57	23	22	111	212	14	.958
	—Seattle (A.L.)	SS	80	306	36	60	11	3	2	21	.196	24	44	10	122	233	11	.970
1984	—Seattle (A.L.)	SS	152	530	67	130	18	8	3	43	.245	46	63	16	245	463	17	.977
1985	—Seattle (A.L.)	SS	118	352	41	91	10	6	6	37	.259	34	27	11	196	361	14	.975
1986	—Sea.-Boston (A.L.)■	SS	154	528	67	122	24	7	1	45	.231	51	51	4	279	467	21	.973
1987	—Boston (A.L.)	SS	132	437	50	113	17	7	2	48	.259	53	43	11	176	336	13	.975
1988	—Boston (A.L.)	SS	89	257	40	64	14	1	5	18	.249	27	27	0	102	192	10	.967
1989	—Montreal (N.L.)■	SS	142	437	52	102	17	4	6	41	.233	76	44	3	232	388	13	*.979
1990	—Montreal (N.L.)	SS	149	453	55	106	24	5	5	35	.234	70	60	8	216	340	6	*.989
1991	—Montreal (N.L.)	SS	139	424	39	108	22	8	3	26	.255	42	61	2	189	376	8	.986
1992	—Montreal (N.L.)	SS	122	386	52	104	16	3	7	40	.269	50	30	9	188	300	9	.982
1993	—New York (A.L.)■	SS	103	334	41	78	16	2	2	20	.234	29	30	3	116	312	14	.968
American League totals (7 years)			828	2744	342	658	110	34	21	232	.240	264	285	55	1236	2364	100	.973
National League totals (4 years)			552	1700	198	420	79	20	21	142	.247	238	195	22	825	1404	36	.984
Major league totals (11 years)			1380	4444	540	1078	189	54	42	374	.243	502	480	77	2061	3768	136	.977

CHAMPIONSHIP SERIES RECORD

			BATTING												FIELDING			
Year	Team (League)	Pos.	G	AB	R	H	2B	3B	HR	RBI	Avg.	BB	SO	SB	PO	A	E	Avg.
1986	—Boston (A.L.)	SS	7	21	5	9	0	1	0	3	.429	2	2	1	12	21	5	.868
1988	—Boston (A.L.)	PH	1	0	0	0	0	0	0	0	...	0	0	0	...	...	...	...
Championship series totals (2 years)			8	21	5	9	0	1	0	3	.429	2	2	1	12	21	5	.868

WORLD SERIES RECORD

			BATTING												FIELDING			
Year	Team (League)	Pos.	G	AB	R	H	2B	3B	HR	RBI	Avg.	BB	SO	SB	PO	A	E	Avg.
1986	—Boston (A.L.)	SS	7	20	2	6	0	0	0	2	.300	5	6	0	10	13	0	1.000

OWENS, JAYHAWK

C, ROCKIES

PERSONAL: Born February 10, 1969, in Cincinnati.... 6-1/200.... Throws right, bats right.... Full name: Claude Jayhawk Owens II.
HIGH SCHOOL: Glen Este (Cincinnati).
COLLEGE: Middle Tennessee State.

TRANSACTIONS/CAREER NOTES: Selected by Boston Red Sox organization in 25th round of free-agent draft (June 2, 1987).... Selected by Minnesota Twins organization in third round of free-agent draft (June 4, 1990).... On disabled list (April 12-June 5, 1991 and August 13-September 6, 1992).... Selected by Colorado Rockies in first round (23rd pick overall) of expansion draft (November 17, 1992).
STATISTICAL NOTES: Tied for Southern League lead in errors by catcher with 14 in 1992.

			BATTING												FIELDING			
Year	Team (League)	Pos.	G	AB	R	H	2B	3B	HR	RBI	Avg.	BB	SO	SB	PO	A	E	Avg.
1990	—Kenosha (Midwest)..	OF-C	66	216	31	51	9	2	5	30	.236	39	59	15	133	8	5	.966
1991	—Visalia (California)...	OF	65	233	33	57	17	1	6	33	.245	35	70	14	123	6	1	.992
1992	—Orlando (Southern)..	C-OF	102	330	50	88	24	0	4	30	.267	36	67	10	656	62	‡14	.981
1993	—Colo. Springs (PCL)■	C-OF-1B	55	174	24	54	11	3	6	43	.310	21	56	5	207	18	10	.957
	—Colorado (N.L.).........	C	33	86	12	18	5	0	3	6	.209	6	30	1	138	19	7	.957
Major league totals (1 year)			33	86	12	18	5	0	3	6	.209	6	30	1	138	19	7	.957

PAGLIARULO, MIKE

3B

PERSONAL: Born March 15, 1960, in Medford, Mass.... 6-2/195.... Throws right, bats left.... Full name: Michael Timothy Pagliarulo.... Son of Charles Pagliarulo, minor league infielder (1958).... Name pronounced PAL-ya-ROO-lo.
HIGH SCHOOL: Medford (Mass.).
COLLEGE: Miami (Fla.).
TRANSACTIONS/CAREER NOTES: Selected by New York Yankees organization in sixth round of free-agent draft (June 8, 1981). ... On disabled list (July 25-August 11, 1988).... Traded by Yankees with P Don Schulze to San Diego Padres for P Walt Terrell and a player to be named later (July 22, 1989); Yankees acquired P Fred Toliver to complete deal (September 27, 1989).... Granted free agency (November 5, 1990).... Signed by Minnesota Twins (January 25, 1991).... Granted free agency (November 11, 1991).... Re-signed by Twins (January 7, 1992).... On Minnesota disabled list (March 28-April 14, 1992).... On Minnesota disabled list (April 22-July 23, 1992); included rehabilitation assignment to Fort Myers (July 14-23).... Granted free agency (October 30, 1992).... Re-signed by Twins (April 3, 1993).... Traded by Twins to Baltimore Orioles for a player to be named later (August 15, 1993); Twins acquired P Erik Schullstrom to complete deal (August 16, 1993).... Granted free agency (November 2, 1993).... Signed by Seibu Lions of Japan Pacific League (December 1, 1993).
STATISTICAL NOTES: Led New York-Pennsylvania League with eight intentional bases on balls received in 1981.... Led New York-Pennsylvania League third basemen with 214 total chances in 1981.... Led Southern League third basemen with 433 total chances in 1983.

			BATTING												FIELDING			
Year	Team (League)	Pos.	G	AB	R	H	2B	3B	HR	RBI	Avg.	BB	SO	SB	PO	A	E	Avg.
1981	—Oneonta (NYP).........	3B	72	245	32	53	9	4	2	28	.216	38	47	13	40	*159	15	.930
1982	—Greensboro (S. Atl.)..	3B	123	403	79	113	22	0	22	79	.280	83	76	7	73	*278	27	.929
1983	—Nashville (South.)....	3B	135	450	82	117	19	4	19	80	.260	59	100	8	*98	*315	20	*.954
1984	—Columbus (Int'l).......	3B-SS	58	146	24	31	5	1	7	25	.212	18	30	0	27	95	13	.904
	—New York (A.L.)........	3B	67	201	24	48	15	3	7	34	.239	15	46	0	44	106	7	.955
1985	—New York (A.L.)........	3B	138	380	55	91	16	2	19	62	.239	45	86	0	67	187	13	.951
1986	—New York (A.L.)........	3B-SS	149	504	71	120	24	3	28	71	.238	54	120	4	104	283	19	.953
1987	—New York (A.L.)........	3B-1B	150	522	76	122	26	3	32	87	.234	53	111	1	97	297	17	.959
1988	—New York (A.L.)........	3B	125	444	46	96	20	1	15	67	.216	37	104	1	82	232	19	.943
1989	—New York (A.L.)........	3B	74	223	19	44	10	0	4	16	.197	19	43	1	25	122	10	.936
	—San Diego (N.L.)■.....	3B	50	148	12	29	7	0	3	14	.196	18	39	2	19	83	7	.936
1990	—San Diego (N.L.).......	3B	128	398	29	101	23	2	7	38	.254	39	66	1	79	200	13	.955
1991	—Minnesota (A.L.)■....	3B-2B	121	365	38	102	20	0	6	36	.279	21	55	1	56	248	11	.965
1992	—Minnesota (A.L.)......	3B	42	105	10	21	4	0	0	9	.200	1	17	1	11	64	3	.962
	—Fort Myers (FSL)......	3B	6	20	2	4	2	0	0	2	.200	4	2	1	3	14	2	.895
1993	—Minn.-Balt. (A.L.)■..	3B-1B	116	370	55	112	25	4	9	44	.303	26	49	6	95	186	8	.972
American League totals (9 years)			982	3114	394	756	160	16	120	426	.243	271	631	15	581	1725	107	.956
National League totals (2 years)			178	546	41	130	30	2	10	52	.238	57	105	3	98	283	20	.950
Major league totals (10 years)			1160	3660	435	886	190	18	130	478	.242	328	736	18	679	2008	127	.955

CHAMPIONSHIP SERIES RECORD

			BATTING												FIELDING			
Year	Team (League)	Pos.	G	AB	R	H	2B	3B	HR	RBI	Avg.	BB	SO	SB	PO	A	E	Avg.
1991	—Minnesota (A.L.)......	3B-PH	5	15	4	5	1	0	1	3	.333	0	2	0	4	10	0	1.000

WORLD SERIES RECORD

			BATTING												FIELDING			
Year	Team (League)	Pos.	G	AB	R	H	2B	3B	HR	RBI	Avg.	BB	SO	SB	PO	A	E	Avg.
1991	—Minnesota (A.L.)......	3B-PH	6	11	1	3	0	0	1	2	.273	1	2	0	3	3	0	1.000

PAGNOZZI, TOM

C, CARDINALS

PERSONAL: Born July 30, 1962, in Tucson, Ariz.... 6-1/190.... Throws right, bats right. ... Full name: Thomas Alan Pagnozzi.... Brother of Tim Pagnozzi, minor league shortstop (1976); and brother of Mike Pagnozzi, minor league pitcher (1975-78).... Name pronounced pag-NAHZ-ee.
HIGH SCHOOL: Rincon (Tucson, Ariz.).
COLLEGE: Central Arizona College and Arkansas.
TRANSACTIONS/CAREER NOTES: Selected by Milwaukee Brewers organization in 24th round of free-agent draft (January 12, 1982).... Selected by St. Louis Cardinals organization in eighth round of free-agent draft (June 6, 1983).... On St. Louis disabled list (May 8-June 17, 1993); included rehabilitation assignment to Louisville (June 2-17).
RECORDS: Shares N.L. single-season records for highest fielding percentage by catcher (100 or more games)—.999 (1992); and fewest errors by catcher (100 or more games)—1 (1992).
HONORS: Won N.L. Gold Glove at catcher (1991-92).

Year	Team (League)	Pos.	G	AB	R	H	2B	3B	HR	RBI	Avg.	BB	SO	SB	PO	A	E	Avg.
			BATTING												FIELDING			
1983	—Erie (N.Y.-Penn)	C	45	168	28	52	9	1	6	22	.310	14	34	3	183	20	3	.985
	—Macon (S. Atl.)	C	18	57	7	14	2	1	0	6	.246	6	13	0	125	18	8	.947
1984	—Springfield (Midw.)	C	114	396	57	112	20	4	10	68	.283	31	75	3	667	*90	12	.984
1985	—Arkansas (Texas)	C-1B	41	139	15	43	7	1	5	29	.309	13	21	0	243	27	1	.996
	—Louisville (A.A.)	C	76	268	29	72	13	2	5	40	.269	21	47	0	266	25	4	.986
1986	—Louisville (A.A.)	C	30	106	12	31	4	0	1	18	.292	6	21	0	160	19	3	.984
1987	—Louisville (A.A.)	C-3B	84	320	53	100	20	2	14	71	.313	30	50	0	427	43	6	.987
	—St. Louis (N.L.)	C-1B	27	48	8	9	1	0	2	9	.188	4	13	1	61	5	0	1.000
1988	—St. Louis (N.L.)	1B-C-3B	81	195	17	55	9	0	0	15	.282	11	32	0	340	30	4	.989
1989	—St. Louis (N.L.)	C-1B-3B	52	80	3	12	2	0	0	3	.150	6	19	0	100	9	2	.982
1990	—St. Louis (N.L.)	C-1B	69	220	20	61	15	0	2	23	.277	14	37	1	345	39	4	.990
1991	—St. Louis (N.L.)	C-1B	140	459	38	121	24	5	2	57	.264	36	63	9	682	81	7	.991
1992	—St. Louis (N.L.)	C	139	485	33	121	26	3	7	44	.249	28	64	2	688	53	1	*.999
1993	—St. Louis (N.L.)	C	92	330	31	85	15	1	7	41	.258	19	30	1	421	44	4	.991
	—Louisville (A.A.)	C	12	43	5	12	3	0	1	1	.279	2	3	0	51	6	2	.966
Major league totals (7 years)			600	1817	150	464	92	9	20	192	.255	118	258	14	2637	261	22	.992

CHAMPIONSHIP SERIES RECORD

Year	Team (League)	Pos.	G	AB	R	H	2B	3B	HR	RBI	Avg.	BB	SO	SB	PO	A	E	Avg.
			BATTING												FIELDING			
1987	—St. Louis (N.L.)	PH	1	1	0	0	0	0	0	0	.000	0	0	0	...	...	...	...

WORLD SERIES RECORD

Year	Team (League)	Pos.	G	AB	R	H	2B	3B	HR	RBI	Avg.	BB	SO	SB	PO	A	E	Avg.
			BATTING												FIELDING			
1987	—St. Louis (N.L.)	DH-PH	2	4	0	1	0	0	0	0	.250	0	0	0	...	...	...	...

ALL-STAR GAME RECORD

Year	League	Pos.	AB	R	H	2B	3B	HR	RBI	Avg.	BB	SO	SB	PO	A	E	Avg.
			BATTING											FIELDING			
1992	—National	PH	1	0	0	0	0	0	0	.000	0	0	0	...	...	...	...

PAINTER, LANCE

P, ROCKIES

PERSONAL: Born July 21, 1967, in Bedford, England. . . . 6-1/195. . . . Throws left, bats left.
HIGH SCHOOL: Nicolet (Glendale, Wis.).
COLLEGE: Wisconsin.
TRANSACTIONS/CAREER NOTES: Selected by San Diego Padres organization in 25th round of free-agent draft (June 4, 1990). . . . Selected by Colorado Rockies in second round (34th pick overall) of expansion draft (November 17, 1992).
STATISTICAL NOTES: Led Texas League with 10 hit batsmen in 1992.

Year	Team (League)	W	L	Pct.	ERA	G	GS	CG	ShO	Sv.	IP	H	R	ER	BB	SO
1990	—Spokane (N'west)	7	3	.700	1.51	23	1	0	0	3	71⅔	45	18	12	15	104
1991	—Waterloo (Midw.)	14	8	.636	2.30	28	28	7	*4	0	200	162	64	51	57	201
1992	—Wichita (Texas)	10	5	*.667	3.53	27	•27	1	1	0	163⅓	138	74	64	55	137
1993	—Colo. Springs (PCL)■	9	7	.563	4.30	23	22	•4	1	0	138	165	90	66	44	91
	—Colorado (N.L.)	2	2	.500	6.00	10	6	1	0	0	39	52	26	26	9	16
Major league totals (1 year)		2	2	.500	6.00	10	6	1	0	0	39	52	26	26	9	16

PALL, DONN

P, YANKEES

PERSONAL: Born January 11, 1962, in Chicago. . . . 6-1/179. . . . Throws right, bats right. . . . Full name: Donn Steven Pall.
HIGH SCHOOL: Evergreen Park (Ill.).
COLLEGE: Illinois (received degree, 1985).
TRANSACTIONS/CAREER NOTES: Selected by Chicago White Sox organization in 23rd round of free-agent draft (June 3, 1985). . . . On Chicago disabled list (May 19-June 2, 1989); included rehabilitation assignment to South Bend (May 30-June 2). . . . Traded by White Sox to Philadelphia Phillies for a player to be named later (September 1, 1993); White Sox acquired C Doug Lindsey to complete deal (September 8, 1993). . . . Granted free agency (December 20, 1993). . . . Signed by New York Yankees (January 18, 1994).

Year	Team (League)	W	L	Pct.	ERA	G	GS	CG	ShO	Sv.	IP	H	R	ER	BB	SO
1985	—GC Whi. Sox (GCL)	•7	5	.583	1.67	13	13	•4	•2	0	*86	68	34	16	10	63
1986	—Appleton (Midw.)	5	5	.500	2.31	11	11	3	1	0	78	71	29	20	14	51
	—Birm. (Southern)	3	4	.429	4.44	21	9	0	0	1	73	77	38	36	27	41
1987	—Birm. (Southern)	8	11	.421	4.27	30	23	3	0	0	158	173	100	75	63	139
1988	—Vancouver (PCL)	5	2	.714	2.23	44	0	0	0	10	72⅔	61	21	18	20	41
	—Chicago (A.L.)	0	2	.000	3.45	17	0	0	0	0	28⅔	39	11	11	8	16
1989	—Chicago (A.L.)	4	5	.444	3.31	53	0	0	0	6	87	90	35	32	19	58
	—South Bend (Mid.)	0	0	...	0.00	2	0	0	0	0	3⅓	1	0	0	0	4
1990	—Chicago (A.L.)	3	5	.375	3.32	56	0	0	0	2	76	63	33	28	24	39
1991	—Chicago (A.L.)	7	2	.778	2.41	51	0	0	0	0	71	59	22	19	20	40
1992	—Chicago (A.L.)	5	2	.714	4.93	39	0	0	0	1	73	79	43	40	27	27
1993	—Chicago (A.L.)	2	3	.400	3.22	39	0	0	0	1	58⅔	62	25	21	11	29
	—Philadelphia (N.L.)■	1	0	1.000	2.55	8	0	0	0	0	17⅔	15	7	5	3	11
A.L. totals (6 years)		21	19	.525	3.45	255	0	0	0	10	394⅓	392	169	151	109	209
N.L. totals (1 year)		1	0	1.000	2.55	8	0	0	0	0	17⅔	15	7	5	3	11
Major league totals (6 years)		22	19	.537	3.41	263	0	0	0	10	412	407	176	156	112	220

PALMEIRO, RAFAEL

1B, ORIOLES

PERSONAL: Born September 24, 1964, in Havana, Cuba. . . . 6-0/188. . . . Throws left, bats left. . . . Full name: Rafael Corrales Palmeiro. . . . Name pronounced pal-MAIR-oh.
HIGH SCHOOL: Jackson (Miami).
COLLEGE: Mississippi State (degree in commercial art).
TRANSACTIONS/CAREER NOTES: Selected by New York Mets organization in eighth round of free-agent draft (June 7, 1982). . . . Selected by Chicago Cubs organization in first round (22nd pick overall) of free-agent draft (June 3, 1985); pick received as compensation for San Diego Padres signing Type A free agent Tim Stoddard. . . . Traded by Cubs with P Jamie Moyer and P Drew Hall to Texas Rangers for P Mitch Williams, P Paul Kilgus, P Steve Wilson, IF Curtis Wilkerson, IF Luis Benitez and OF Pablo Delgado (December 5, 1988). . . . Granted free agency (October 25, 1993). . . . Signed by Baltimore Orioles (December 12, 1993).
HONORS: Named outfielder on THE SPORTING NEWS college All-America team (1985). . . . Named Eastern League Most Valuable Player (1986).
STATISTICAL NOTES: Led Eastern League with 225 total bases, 13 sacrifice flies and 13 intentional bases on balls received in 1986. . . . Led A.L. first basemen with 1,540 total chances and 133 double plays in 1993.

					BATTING									FIELDING			
Year Team (League)	**Pos.**	**G**	**AB**	**R**	**H**	**2B**	**3B**	**HR**	**RBI**	**Avg.**	**BB**	**SO**	**SB**	**PO**	**A**	**E**	**Avg.**
1985 —Peoria (Midwest)	OF	73	279	34	83	22	4	5	51	.297	31	34	9	113	7	1	.992
1986 —Pittsfield (Eastern)	OF	•140	509	66	*156	29	2	12	*95	.306	54	32	15	248	9	3	*.988
—Chicago (N.L.)	OF	22	73	9	18	4	0	3	12	.247	4	6	1	34	2	4	.900
1987 —Iowa (Am. Assoc.)	OF-1B	57	214	36	64	14	3	11	41	.299	22	22	4	150	13	2	.988
—Chicago (N.L.)	OF-1B	84	221	32	61	15	1	14	30	.276	20	26	2	176	9	1	.995
1988 —Chicago (N.L.)	OF-1B	152	580	75	178	41	5	8	53	.307	38	34	12	322	11	5	.985
1989 —Texas (A.L.)■	1B	156	559	76	154	23	4	8	64	.275	63	48	4	1167	*119	12	.991
1990 —Texas (A.L.)	1B	154	598	72	*191	35	6	14	89	.319	40	59	3	1215	91	7	.995
1991 —Texas (A.L.)	1B	159	631	115	203	*49	3	26	88	.322	68	72	4	1305	96	*12	.992
1992 —Texas (A.L.)	1B	159	608	84	163	27	4	22	85	.268	72	83	2	1251	*143	7	.995
1993 —Texas (A.L.)	1B	160	597	*124	176	40	2	37	105	.295	73	85	22	*1388	*147	5	.997
American League totals (5 years)		788	2993	471	887	174	19	107	431	.296	316	347	35	6326	596	43	.994
National League totals (3 years)		258	874	116	257	60	6	25	95	.294	62	66	15	532	22	10	.982
Major league totals (8 years)		1046	3867	587	1144	234	25	132	526	.296	378	413	50	6858	618	53	.993

ALL-STAR GAME RECORD

				BATTING								FIELDING			
Year League	**Pos.**	**AB**	**R**	**H**	**2B**	**3B**	**HR**	**RBI**	**Avg.**	**BB**	**SO**	**SB**	**PO**	**A**	**E**	**Avg.**
1988 —National	PH-OF	0	0	0	0	0	0	0	...	1	0	0	1	0	0	1.000
1991 —American	1B	0	0	0	0	0	0	0	...	1	0	0	2	0	0	1.000
All-Star Game totals (2 years)		0	0	0	0	0	0	0	...	2	0	0	3	0	0	1.000

PALMER, DEAN

3B, RANGERS

PERSONAL: Born December 27, 1968, in Tallahassee, Fla. . . . 6-2/195. . . . Throws right, bats right. . . . Full name: Dean William Palmer.
HIGH SCHOOL: Florida (Tallahassee, Fla.).
TRANSACTIONS/CAREER NOTES: Selected by Texas Rangers organization in third round of free-agent draft (June 2, 1986). . . . On disabled list (July 19, 1988-remainder of season).
STATISTICAL NOTES: Led Texas League third basemen with 30 errors in 1989. . . . Led A.L. third basemen with 29 errors in 1993.

					BATTING									FIELDING			
Year Team (League)	**Pos.**	**G**	**AB**	**R**	**H**	**2B**	**3B**	**HR**	**RBI**	**Avg.**	**BB**	**SO**	**SB**	**PO**	**A**	**E**	**Avg.**
1986 —GC Rangers (GCL)	3B	50	163	19	34	7	1	0	12	.209	22	34	6	25	75	13	.885
1987 —Gastonia (S. Atl.)	3B	128	484	51	104	16	0	9	54	.215	36	126	5	58	209	*59	.819
1988 —Charlotte (Fla. St.)	3B	74	305	38	81	12	1	4	35	.266	15	69	0	49	144	28	.873
1989 —Tulsa (Texas)	3B-SS	133	498	82	125	32	5	*25	90	.251	41	*152	15	85	213	†31	.906
—Texas (A.L.)	3B-SS-OF	16	19	0	2	2	0	0	1	.105	0	12	0	3	4	2	.778
1990 —Tulsa (Texas)	3B	7	24	4	7	0	1	3	9	.292	4	10	0	9	6	3	.833
—Okla. City (A.A.)	3B-1B	88	316	33	69	17	4	12	39	.218	20	106	1	206	110	21	.938
1991 —Okla. City (A.A.)	3B-OF	60	234	45	70	11	2	*22	59	.299	20	61	4	49	105	11	.933
—Texas (A.L.)	3B-OF	81	268	38	50	9	2	15	37	.187	32	98	0	69	75	9	.941
1992 —Texas (A.L.)	3B	152	541	74	124	25	0	26	72	.229	62	*154	10	124	254	22	.945
1993 —Texas (A.L.)	3B-SS	148	519	88	127	31	2	33	96	.245	53	154	11	86	258	†29	.922
Major league totals (4 years)		397	1347	200	303	67	4	74	206	.225	147	418	21	282	591	62	.934

PAPPAS, ERIK

C, CARDINALS

PERSONAL: Born April 25, 1966, in Chicago. . . . 6-0/190. . . . Throws right, bats right. . . . Full name: Erik Daniel Pappas.
HIGH SCHOOL: Mount Carmel (Chicago).
TRANSACTIONS/CAREER NOTES: Selected by California Angels organization in first round (sixth pick overall) of free-agent draft (June 4, 1984). . . . On disabled list (April 8-July 20, 1986). . . . Selected by Chicago Cubs organization from Angels organization in Rule 5 minor league draft (December 6, 1988). . . . Released by Cubs (November 5, 1991). . . . Signed by Kansas City Royals organization (December 2, 1991). . . . On Omaha suspended list (June 17-July 9, 1992). . . . Traded by Royals organization to Chicago White Sox organization for P Jose Ventura (July 9, 1992). . . . Granted free agency (October 15, 1992). . . . Signed by St. Louis Cardinals organization (January 5, 1993).
STATISTICAL NOTES: Led Northwest League catchers with 26 passed balls and tied for lead with six double plays in 1984. . . . Led California League catchers with 867 total chances and 37 passed balls in 1987.

					BATTING									FIELDING			
Year Team (League)	**Pos.**	**G**	**AB**	**R**	**H**	**2B**	**3B**	**HR**	**RBI**	**Avg.**	**BB**	**SO**	**SB**	**PO**	**A**	**E**	**Avg.**
1984 —Salem (Northwest)	C	56	177	24	43	3	3	1	15	.243	31	26	10	404	38	*20	.957
1985 —Quad City (Midw.)	C	100	317	53	76	8	4	2	29	.240	61	55	16	632	74	19	.974

Year	Team (League)	Pos.	G	AB	R	H	2B	3B	HR	RBI	Avg.	BB	SO	SB	PO	A	E	Avg.
			BATTING												FIELDING			
1986	—Palm Springs (Cal.)..	C	74	248	40	61	16	2	5	38	.246	56	58	9	445	48	5	.990
1987	—Palm Springs (Cal.)..	C	119	395	50	96	20	3	3	64	.243	66	77	16	*775	82	10	.988
1988	—Midland (Texas).......	C-1B	83	275	40	76	17	2	4	38	.276	29	53	16	467	56	12	.978
1989	—Charlotte (South.)■..	C-O-1-2-3	119	354	69	106	31	1	16	49	.299	66	50	7	398	61	9	.981
1990	—Iowa (Am. Assoc.)....	C-O-1-2	131	405	56	101	19	2	16	55	.249	65	84	6	589	69	4	.994
1991	—Chicago (N.L.)..........	C	7	17	1	3	0	0	0	2	.176	1	5	0	35	1	0	1.000
	—Iowa (Am. Assoc.)....	C-OF-1B	88	284	41	78	19	1	7	48	.275	45	47	5	420	58	6	.988
1992	—Omaha (A.A.)■.........	C-OF-1B	45	138	18	30	8	1	1	11	.217	25	23	4	142	16	3	.981
	—Vancouver (PCL)■...	C	37	98	17	27	4	0	4	17	.276	14	17	4	181	12	10	.951
1993	—Louisville (A.A.)■.....	C	21	71	19	24	6	1	4	13	.338	11	12	0	131	5	3	.978
	—St. Louis (N.L.).........	C-OF-1B	82	228	25	63	12	0	1	28	.276	35	35	1	337	32	6	.984
Major league totals (2 years)			89	245	26	66	12	0	1	30	.269	36	40	1	372	33	6	.985

PAQUETTE, CRAIG

3B, ATHLETICS

PERSONAL: Born March 28, 1969, in Long Beach, Calif.... 6-0/190.... Throws right, bats right.... Full name: Craig Howard Paquette.

HIGH SCHOOL: Ranchos Alamitos (Garden Grove, Calif.).

COLLEGE: Golden West College (Calif.).

TRANSACTIONS/CAREER NOTES: Selected by Minnesota Twins organization in 36th round of free-agent draft (June 2, 1987).... Selected by Oakland Athletics organization in eighth round of free-agent draft (June 5, 1989).... On Modesto disabled list (April 10-May 5, 1991).... On Huntsville disabled list (June 1-11, 1991).

STATISTICAL NOTES: Tied for Northwest League lead with 163 total bases in 1989.... Led Northwest League third basemen with .936 fielding percentage and 12 double plays in 1989.... Led Southern League third basemen with 349 total chances in 1992.

Year	Team (League)	Pos.	G	AB	R	H	2B	3B	HR	RBI	Avg.	BB	SO	SB	PO	A	E	Avg.
			BATTING												FIELDING			
1989	—S. Oregon (N'west)...	3B-SS-2B	71	277	53	93	*22	3	14	56	.336	30	46	9	61	155	15	†.935
1990	—Modesto (Calif.)........	3B	130	495	65	118	23	4	15	59	.238	47	123	8	*88	218	26	*.922
1991	—Huntsville (South.)...	3B-1B	102	378	50	99	18	1	8	60	.262	28	87	0	51	132	16	.920
1992	—Huntsville (South.)...	3B	115	450	59	116	25	4	17	71	.258	29	118	13	69	*248	*32	.908
	—Tacoma (PCL)..........	3B	17	66	10	18	7	0	2	11	.273	2	16	3	14	33	3	.940
1993	—Tacoma (PCL)..........	3B-SS-2B	50	183	29	49	8	0	8	29	.268	14	54	3	32	116	15	.908
	—Oakland (A.L.)..........	3B-OF	105	393	35	86	20	4	12	46	.219	14	108	4	82	165	13	.950
Major league totals (1 year)			105	393	35	86	20	4	12	46	.219	14	108	4	82	165	13	.950

PARENT, MARK

C, CUBS

PERSONAL: Born September 16, 1961, in Ashland, Ore.... 6-5/220.... Throws right, bats right.... Full name: Mark Alan Parent.

HIGH SCHOOL: Anderson (Calif.).

TRANSACTIONS/CAREER NOTES: Selected by San Diego Padres organization in fourth round of free-agent draft (June 5, 1979).... On suspended list (August 27, 1983-remainder of season).... On disabled list (September 4, 1984-remainder of season).... Traded by Padres to Texas Rangers for 3B Scott Coolbaugh (December 12, 1990).... On Texas disabled list (March 9-September 6, 1991); included rehabilitation assignment to Oklahoma City (August 31-September 5).... Granted free agency (October 8, 1991).... Signed by Baltimore Orioles organization (February 5, 1992).... On Rochester disabled list (April 10-17, 1992).... Released by Orioles (December 2, 1993).... Signed by Chicago Cubs organization (December 14, 1993).

STATISTICAL NOTES: Led Northwest League catchers with .979 fielding percentage in 1980.... Led Carolina League catchers with 16 double plays in 1981.... Led Pacific Coast League catchers with .988 fielding percentage in 1987.... Led International League catchers with eight double plays in 1992.... Tied for International League lead in double plays by catcher with 11 in 1993.

Year	Team (League)	Pos.	G	AB	R	H	2B	3B	HR	RBI	Avg.	BB	SO	SB	PO	A	E	Avg.
			BATTING												FIELDING			
1979	—Walla Walla (N'west)..	C-OF	40	126	8	24	4	0	1	11	.190	8	31	8	229	34	6	.978
1980	—Reno (California)......	C	30	99	8	20	3	0	0	12	.202	16	12	0	128	23	2	.987
	—Grays Har. (N'west)..	C-1B	66	230	29	55	11	2	7	32	.239	17	30	1	381	38	9	†.979
1981	—Salem (Carolina)......	C	123	438	44	103	16	3	6	47	.235	37	90	10	*694	87	*28	.965
1982	—Amarillo (Texas)......	C	26	89	12	17	3	1	1	13	.191	11	13	2	100	6	2	.981
	—Salem (Carolina)......	C-1B	99	360	39	81	15	2	6	41	.225	32	58	2	475	64	12	.978
1983	—Beaumont (Texas)...	C	81	282	38	71	22	1	7	33	.252	33	35	1	464	71	10	*.982
1984	—Beaumont (Texas)...	C-1B	111	380	52	109	24	3	7	60	.287	38	39	1	674	68	7	.991
1985	—Las Vegas (PCL)......	C-1B	105	361	36	87	23	3	7	45	.241	29	58	1	586	54	6	.991
1986	—Las Vegas (PCL)......	C-1B	86	267	29	77	10	4	5	40	.288	23	25	0	344	40	5	.987
	—San Diego (N.L.).......	C	8	14	1	2	0	0	0	0	.143	1	3	0	16	0	2	.889
1987	—Las Vegas (PCL)......	C-1-3-0	105	387	50	113	23	2	4	43	.292	38	53	2	556	58	8	†.987
	—San Diego (N.L.).......	C	12	25	0	2	0	0	0	2	.080	0	9	0	36	3	0	1.000
1988	—San Diego (N.L.).......	C	41	118	9	23	3	0	6	15	.195	6	23	0	203	15	3	.986
1989	—San Diego (N.L.).......	C-1B	52	141	12	27	4	0	7	21	.191	8	34	1	246	17	0	1.000
1990	—San Diego (N.L.).......	C	65	189	13	42	11	0	3	16	.222	16	29	1	324	31	3	.992
1991	—Okla. City (A.A.)■.....	C	5	8	0	2	0	0	0	1	.250	0	1	0	4	0	0	1.000
	—Texas (A.L.).............	C	3	1	0	0	0	0	0	0	.000	0	1	0	5	0	0	1.000
1992	—Rochester (Int'l)■.....	C	101	356	52	102	24	0	17	69	.287	35	64	4	588	49	4	.994
	—Baltimore (A.L.)........	C	17	34	4	8	1	0	2	4	.235	3	7	0	73	7	1	.988
1993	—Rochester (Int'l).......	C	92	332	47	82	15	0	14	56	.247	40	71	0	549	63	3	*.995
	—Baltimore (A.L.)........	C	22	54	7	14	2	0	4	12	.259	3	14	0	83	5	1	.989
American League totals (3 years)			42	89	11	22	3	0	6	16	.247	6	22	0	161	12	2	.989
National League totals (5 years)			178	487	35	96	18	0	16	54	.197	31	98	2	825	66	8	.991
Major league totals (8 years)			220	576	46	118	21	0	22	70	.205	37	120	2	986	78	10	.991

PARKER, RICK

OF, METS

PERSONAL: Born March 20, 1963, in Kansas City, Mo.... 6-0/185.... Throws right, bats right. ... Full name: Richard Allen Parker.

HIGH SCHOOL: Oak Park (Kansas City, Mo.).

COLLEGE: Southwest Missouri State and Texas.

TRANSACTIONS/CAREER NOTES: Selected by Philadelphia Phillies organization in 16th round of free-agent draft (June 3, 1985). ... Traded by Phillies organization to Phoenix, San Francisco Giants organization (August 7, 1989), completing deal in which Phillies traded P Steve Bedrosian and a player to be named later to Giants for P Dennis Cook, P Terry Mulholland and 3B Charlie Hayes (June 18, 1989).... On San Francisco disabled list (March 25-May 16, 1991); included rehabilitation assignment to Phoenix (April 27-May 16).... Released by Giants (December 9, 1991).... Signed by Tucson, Houston Astros organization (January 3, 1992).... Granted free agency (October 4, 1992).... Re-signed by Tucson (December 14, 1992).... Granted free agency (October 4, 1993).... Signed by New York Mets organization (December 16, 1993).

			BATTING												FIELDING			
Year	Team (League)	Pos.	G	AB	R	H	2B	3B	HR	RBI	Avg.	BB	SO	SB	PO	A	E	Avg.
1985	—Bend (Northwest)	SS	55	205	45	51	9	1	2	20	.249	40	42	14	79	143	25	.899
1986	—Spartanburg (SAL)	SS	62	233	39	69	7	3	5	28	.296	36	39	14	87	169	18	.934
	—Clearwater (FSL)	SS	63	218	24	51	10	2	0	15	.234	21	29	8	94	197	21	.933
1987	—Clearwater (FSL)	2B-SS-3B	101	330	56	83	13	3	3	34	.252	31	36	6	130	234	27	.931
1988	—Reading (Eastern)	3-0-1-2-S	116	362	50	93	13	3	3	47	.257	36	50	24	174	114	18	.941
1989	—Reading (Eastern)	3B-OF-SS	103	388	59	92	7	*9	3	32	.237	42	62	17	123	91	22	.907
	—Phoenix (PCL)■	3B-OF-SS	18	68	5	18	2	2	0	11	.265	2	14	1	25	32	1	.983
1990	—Phoenix (PCL)	3B-OF-2B	44	173	38	58	7	4	1	18	.335	17	17	13	57	51	2	.982
	—San Francisco (N.L.)	0-2-S-3	54	107	19	26	5	0	2	14	.243	10	15	6	45	3	2	.960
1991	—Phoenix (PCL)	OF-3B-SS	85	297	41	89	10	9	6	41	.300	26	35	16	132	58	11	.945
	—San Francisco (N.L.)	OF	13	14	0	1	0	0	0	1	.071	1	5	0	5	0	0	1.000
1992	—Tucson (PCL)■	OF-3B-SS	105	319	51	103	10	11	4	38	.323	28	36	20	61	9	5	.933
1993	—Tucson (PCL)	OF-3B-1B	29	120	28	37	9	3	2	12	.308	14	20	6	77	3	3	.964
	—Houston (N.L.)	OF-SS-2B	45	45	11	15	3	0	0	4	.333	3	8	1	18	0	0	1.000
Major league totals (3 years)			112	166	30	42	8	0	2	19	.253	14	28	7	68	3	2	.973

PARKS, DEREK

C, TWINS

PERSONAL: Born September 29, 1968, in Covina, Calif.... 6-0/217.... Throws right, bats right.... Full name: Derek Gavin Parks.

HIGH SCHOOL: Montclair (Calif.).

TRANSACTIONS/CAREER NOTES: Selected by Minnesota Twins in first round (10th pick overall) of free-agent draft (June 2, 1986).... On disabled list (June 12-August 31, 1989 and August 5-15, 1991).... On Portland disabled list (August 2-14, 1993).

STATISTICAL NOTES: Led Appalachian League with 17 passed balls in 1986.... Led Southern League in being hit by pitch with 15 in 1988.

			BATTING												FIELDING			
Year	Team (League)	Pos.	G	AB	R	H	2B	3B	HR	RBI	Avg.	BB	SO	SB	PO	A	E	Avg.
1986	—Elizabeth. (Appal.)	C	62	224	39	53	10	1	10	40	.237	23	58	1	297	36	7	.979
1987	—Kenosha (Midwest)	C	129	466	70	115	19	2	4	94	.247	77	111	1	800	85	14	.984
1988	—Orlando (Southern)	C	118	400	52	94	15	0	7	42	.235	49	81	1	616	66	7	.990
1989	—Orlando (Southern)	C	31	95	16	18	3	0	2	10	.189	19	27	1	135	12	3	.980
1990	—Portland (PCL)	C	76	231	27	41	8	1	11	27	.177	18	56	0	488	45	13	.976
1991	—Orlando (Southern)	C	92	256	30	55	14	0	6	31	.215	31	65	0	476	37	8	.985
1992	—Portland (PCL)	C	79	249	33	61	12	0	12	49	.245	25	47	0	377	53	6	.986
	—Minnesota (A.L.)	C	7	6	1	2	0	0	0	0	.333	1	1	0	18	1	0	1.000
1993	—Portland (PCL)	C	107	363	63	113	23	1	17	71	.311	48	57	0	376	49	3	.993
	—Minnesota (A.L.)	C	7	20	3	4	0	0	0	1	.200	1	2	0	28	4	1	.970
Major league totals (2 years)			14	26	4	6	0	0	0	1	.231	2	3	0	46	5	1	.981

PARRA, JOSE

P, DODGERS

PERSONAL: Born November 28, 1972, in Jacagua Santiago, Dominican Republic.... 5-11/160.... Throws right, bats right.... Full name: Jose Miguel Parra.

HIGH SCHOOL: Liceo Evangelico Jacagua (Dominican Republic).

TRANSACTIONS/CAREER NOTES: Signed as free agent by Los Angeles Dodgers organization (December 7, 1989).... On disabled list (May 15-June 17 and August 13, 1993-remainder of season).

Year	Team (League)	W	L	Pct.	ERA	G	GS	CG	ShO	Sv.	IP	H	R	ER	BB	SO
1989	—Santo Dom. (DSL)	8	1	.889	1.87	13	11	4	3	2	67⅓	60	21	14	20	51
1990	—GC Dodgers (GCL)	5	3	.625	2.67	10	10	1	0	0	57⅓	50	22	17	18	50
1991	—Great Falls (Pio.)	4	6	.400	6.16	14	14	1	1	0	64⅓	86	58	44	18	55
1992	—Bakersfield (Calif.)	7	8	.467	3.59	24	23	3	0	0	143	151	73	57	47	107
	—San Antonio (Tex.)	2	0	1.000	6.14	3	3	0	0	0	14⅔	22	12	10	7	7
1993	—San Antonio (Tex.)	1	8	.111	3.15	17	17	0	0	0	111⅓	103	46	39	12	87

PARRETT, JEFF

P

PERSONAL: Born August 26, 1961, in Indianapolis.... 6-3/195.... Throws right, bats right. ... Full name: Jeffrey Dale Parrett.

HIGH SCHOOL: Lafayette (Lexington, Ky.).

COLLEGE: Kentucky.

TRANSACTIONS/CAREER NOTES: Selected by Milwaukee Brewers organization in ninth round of free-agent draft (June 6, 1983). ... Selected by Montreal Expos from Brewers organization in Rule 5 major league draft (December 10, 1985).... On disabled list (July 16-August 14, 1988).... Traded by Expos with P Floyd Youmans to Philadelphia Phillies for P Kevin Gross (December 6, 1988).... On disabled list (April 29-May 22, 1989).... Traded by Phillies with two players to be named later to Atlanta Braves for OF Dale Murphy and a player to be named later (August 3, 1990); Scranton/Wilkes-Barre, Phillies organization, acquired P Tommy Greene (August 9, 1990) and Braves acquired OF Jim Vatcher (August 9, 1990) and SS Victor Rosario (September 4, 1990) to complete deal.... Released by Braves (December 9, 1991).... Signed by Oakland Athletics organization

(February 7, 1992).... Granted free agency (December 19, 1992).... Signed by Colorado Rockies (January 21, 1993).... On disabled list (July 29, 1993-remainder of season).... Released by Rockies (November 10, 1993).

Year	Team (League)	W	L	Pct.	ERA	G	GS	CG	ShO	Sv.	IP	H	R	ER	BB	SO
1983	—Paintsville (Appal.)	2	0	1.000	2.12	3	3	0	0	0	17	12	6	4	8	21
	—Beloit (Midwest)	2	2	.500	4.02	10	8	0	0	0	47	40	26	21	29	34
1984	—Beloit (Midwest)	4	3	.571	4.52	29	5	1	1	2	91⅔	76	50	46	71	95
1985	—Stockton (Calif.)	7	4	.636	*2.75	45	2	0	0	11	127⅔	97	50	39	75	120
1986	—Montreal (N.L.)■	0	1	.000	4.87	12	0	0	0	0	20⅓	19	11	11	13	21
	—Indianapolis (A.A.)	2	5	.286	4.96	25	8	0	0	2	69	54	44	38	35	76
1987	—Indianapolis (A.A.)	2	1	.667	2.01	20	0	0	0	9	22⅓	15	5	5	13	17
	—Montreal (N.L.)	7	6	.538	4.21	45	0	0	0	6	62	53	33	29	30	56
1988	—Montreal (N.L.)	12	4	.750	2.65	61	0	0	0	6	91⅔	66	29	27	45	62
1989	—Philadelphia (N.L.)■	12	6	.667	2.98	72	0	0	0	6	105⅔	90	43	35	44	98
1990	—Phil.-Atl. (N.L.)■	5	10	.333	4.64	67	5	0	0	2	108⅔	119	62	56	55	86
1991	—Atlanta (N.L.)	1	2	.333	6.33	18	0	0	0	1	21⅓	31	18	15	12	14
	—Richmond (Int'l)	2	7	.222	4.52	19	14	0	0	0	79⅔	72	45	40	46	88
1992	—Oakland (A.L.)■	9	1	.900	3.02	66	0	0	0	0	98⅓	81	35	33	42	78
1993	—Colorado (N.L.)■	3	3	.500	5.38	40	6	0	0	1	73⅔	78	47	44	45	66
A.L. totals (1 year)		9	1	.900	3.02	66	0	0	0	0	98⅓	81	35	33	42	78
N.L. totals (7 years)		40	32	.556	4.04	315	11	0	0	22	483⅓	456	243	217	244	403
Major league totals (8 years)		49	33	.598	3.87	381	11	0	0	22	581⅔	537	278	250	286	481

CHAMPIONSHIP SERIES RECORD

Year	Team (League)	W	L	Pct.	ERA	G	GS	CG	ShO	Sv.	IP	H	R	ER	BB	SO
1992	—Oakland (A.L.)	0	0	...	11.57	3	0	0	0	0	2⅓	6	3	3	0	1

PARRISH, LANCE

C

PERSONAL: Born June 15, 1956, in McKeesport, Pa.... 6-3/224.... Throws right, bats right.... Full name: Lance Michael Parrish.

HIGH SCHOOL: Walnut (Calif.).

TRANSACTIONS/CAREER NOTES: Selected by Detroit Tigers organization in first round (16th pick overall) of free-agent draft (June 5, 1974).... On disabled list (July 31-September 29, 1986).... Granted free agency (November 12, 1986)... Signed by Philadelphia Phillies (March 13, 1987).... On disabled list (July 13-28, 1988).... Traded by Phillies to California Angels for P David Holdridge (October 3, 1988).... On disabled list (June 10-25, 1991; May 5-28 and June 8-23, 1992).... Released by Angels (June 23, 1992).... Signed by Seattle Mariners (June 28, 1992).... Granted free agency (November 3, 1992).... Signed by Los Angeles Dodgers organization (January 8, 1993).... Released by Albuquerque, Dodgers organization (May 7, 1993).... Signed as free agent by Cleveland Indians (May 7, 1993).... Released by Indians (May 30, 1993).

HONORS: Named catcher on THE SPORTING NEWS A.L. Silver Slugger team (1980, 1982-84, 1986 and 1990).... Named catcher on THE SPORTING NEWS A.L. All-Star team (1982 and 1984).... Won A.L. Gold Glove at catcher (1983-85).

STATISTICAL NOTES: Led Florida State League catchers with eight double plays and 31 passed balls in 1975.... Led Southern League with 22 passed balls in 1976.... Led American Association catchers with 10 double plays and 21 passed balls in 1977.... Led A.L. with 21 passed balls in 1979, 19 in 1991 and tied for lead with 17 in 1980.... Led A.L. with 13 sacrifice flies in 1983.... Led A.L. catchers with 772 total chances in 1983.... Led A.L. catchers with 11 double plays in 1984 and 15 in 1990.... Led N.L. catchers with 12 passed balls and tied for lead with 11 double plays in 1988.... Led A.L. catchers with 88 assists in 1990.

			BATTING											FIELDING			
Year	Team (League)	Pos.	G	AB	R	H	2B	3B	HR	RBI	Avg.	BB	SO	SB	PO	A	E	Avg.
1974	—Bristol (Appal.)	3B-OF	68	253	45	54	11	1	11	46	.213	32	*92	2	36	83	22	.844
1975	—Lakeland (Fla. St.)	C	100	341	30	75	15	2	5	37	.220	30	85	0	460	50	7	.986
1976	—Montgomery (Sou.)	C	107	340	46	75	9	2	14	55	.221	38	95	0	*600	*79	11	*.984
1977	—Evansville (A.A.)	C	115	416	74	116	21	2	25	90	.279	56	105	2	*722	*82	11	*.987
	—Detroit (A.L.)	C	12	46	10	9	2	0	3	7	.196	5	12	0	76	6	0	1.000
1978	—Detroit (A.L.)	C	85	288	37	63	11	3	14	41	.219	11	71	0	353	39	5	.987
1979	—Detroit (A.L.)	C	143	493	65	136	26	3	19	65	.276	49	105	6	707	*79	9	.989
1980	—Detroit (A.L.)	C-1B-OF	144	553	79	158	34	6	24	82	.286	31	109	6	607	67	7	.990
1981	—Detroit (A.L.)	C	96	348	39	85	18	2	10	46	.244	34	52	2	407	40	3	.993
1982	—Detroit (A.L.)	C-OF	133	486	75	138	19	2	32	87	.284	40	99	3	627	76	8	.989
1983	—Detroit (A.L.)	C	155	605	80	163	42	3	27	114	.269	44	106	1	695	73	4	.995
1984	—Detroit (A.L.)	C	147	578	75	137	16	2	33	98	.237	41	120	2	720	67	7	.991
1985	—Detroit (A.L.)	C	140	549	64	150	27	1	28	98	.273	41	90	2	695	53	5	.993
1986	—Detroit (A.L.)	C	91	327	53	84	6	1	22	62	.257	38	83	0	483	48	6	.989
1987	—Philadelphia (N.L.)■	C	130	466	42	114	21	0	17	67	.245	47	104	0	724	66	9	.989
1988	—Philadelphia (N.L.)	C-1B	123	424	44	91	17	2	15	60	.215	47	93	0	640	73	9	.988
1989	—California (A.L.)■	C	124	433	48	103	12	1	17	50	.238	42	104	1	638	63	5	.993
1990	—California (A.L.)	C-1B	133	470	54	126	14	0	24	70	.268	46	107	2	794	†90	6	.993
1991	—California (A.L.)	C-1B	119	402	38	87	12	0	19	51	.216	35	117	0	670	57	2	.997
1992	—Calif.-Sea. (A.L.)■	C-1B	93	275	26	64	13	1	12	32	.233	24	70	1	383	23	6	.985
1993	—Albuquerque (PCL)■	C	11	33	4	9	2	0	0	1	.273	5	4	0	67	7	0	1.000
	—Cleveland (A.L.)■	C	10	20	2	4	1	0	1	2	.200	4	5	1	47	10	3	.950
American League totals (15 years)			1625	5873	745	1507	253	25	285	905	.257	485	1250	27	7902	791	76	.991
National League totals (2 years)			253	890	86	205	38	2	32	127	.230	94	197	0	1364	139	18	.988
Major league totals (17 years)			1878	6763	831	1712	291	27	317	1032	.253	579	1447	27	9266	930	94	.991

CHAMPIONSHIP SERIES RECORD

			BATTING											FIELDING			
Year	Team (League)	Pos.	G	AB	R	H	2B	3B	HR	RBI	Avg.	BB	SO	SB	PO	A	E	Avg.
1984	—Detroit (A.L.)	C	3	12	1	3	1	0	1	3	.250	0	3	0	21	2	0	1.000

WORLD SERIES RECORD

Year	Team (League)	Pos.	G	AB	R	H	2B	3B	HR	RBI	Avg.	BB	SO	SB	PO	A	E	Avg.
				BATTING											FIELDING			
1984	—Detroit (A.L.)	C	5	18	3	5	1	0	1	2	.278	3	2	1	30	3	1	.971

ALL-STAR GAME RECORD

ALL-STAR GAME NOTES: Named to A.L. All-Star team for 1985 game; replaced by Rich Gedman due to injury.

Year	League	Pos.	AB	R	H	2B	3B	HR	RBI	Avg.	BB	SO	SB	PO	A	E	Avg.
			BATTING											FIELDING			
1980	—American	C	1	0	0	0	0	0	0	.000	0	1	0	0	0	0	...
1982	—American	C	2	0	1	1	0	0	0	.500	0	0	0	2	3	0	1.000
1983	—American	C	2	0	0	0	0	0	0	.000	0	1	0	1	0	0	1.000
1984	—American	C	2	0	0	0	0	0	0	.000	0	2	0	3	1	1	.800
1985	—American		Selected, did not play—injured.														
1986	—American	C	3	0	0	0	0	0	0	.000	0	0	0	4	0	0	1.000
1988	—National	C	1	0	0	0	0	0	0	.000	0	0	0	0	0	0	...
1990	—American	PH-C	1	1	1	0	0	0	0	1.000	0	0	0	3	0	0	1.000
All-Star Game totals (7 years)			12	1	2	1	0	0	0	.167	0	4	0	13	4	1	.944

PASQUA, DAN

OF/1B, WHITE SOX

PERSONAL: Born October 17, 1961, in Yonkers, N.Y. . . . 6-0/218. . . . Throws left, bats left. . . . Full name: Daniel Anthony Pasqua. . . . Name pronounced PASS-kwuh.

HIGH SCHOOL: Old Tappan (N.J.).

COLLEGE: William Paterson College (N.J.).

TRANSACTIONS/CAREER NOTES: Selected by New York Yankees organization in third round of free-agent draft (June 7, 1982). . . . Traded by Yankees organization with C Mark Salas and P Steve Rosenberg to Chicago White Sox for P Richard Dotson and P Scott Nielsen (November 12, 1987). . . . On disabled list (April 6-May 14 and August 21, 1989-remainder of season). . . . Granted free agency (October 31, 1991). . . . Re-signed by White Sox (December 4, 1991). . . . On Chicago disabled list (June 12-July 2, 1992). . . . On Chicago disabled list (July 11-27, 1992); included rehabilitation assignment to Birmingham (July 23-26).

HONORS: Named Appalachian League Player of the Year (1982). . . . Named International League Player of the Year (1985).

STATISTICAL NOTES: Led International League with .599 slugging percentage in 1985. . . . Led A.L. outfielders with .996 fielding percentage in 1988.

Year	Team (League)	Pos.	G	AB	R	H	2B	3B	HR	RBI	Avg.	BB	SO	SB	PO	A	E	Avg.
				BATTING											FIELDING			
1982	—Paintsville (Appal.)	OF	60	239	43	72	10	2	*16	•63	.301	22	42	1	114	4	4	.967
	—Oneonta (NYP)	OF	4	17	3	5	1	0	2	4	.294	2	3	1	2	1	1	.750
1983	—Fort Lauder. (FSL)	OF	131	451	83	123	25	10	19	84	.273	80	125	12	213	8	5	.978
	—Columbus (Int'l)	OF	1	3	0	0	0	0	0	0	.000	1	2	0	5	0	0	1.000
1984	—Nashville (South.)	OF	136	460	78	112	14	3	*33	91	.243	95	*148	5	244	11	*12	.955
1985	—Columbus (Int'l)	OF	78	287	52	92	16	5	18	69	.321	48	62	5	141	9	4	.974
	—New York (A.L.)	OF	60	148	17	31	3	1	9	25	.209	16	38	0	72	2	0	1.000
1986	—Columbus (Int'l)	OF	32	110	25	32	3	3	6	20	.291	32	29	1	62	0	3	.954
	—New York (A.L.)	OF-1B	102	280	44	82	17	0	16	45	.293	47	78	2	172	4	2	.989
1987	—New York (A.L.)	OF-1B	113	318	42	74	7	1	17	42	.233	40	99	0	214	10	2	.991
	—Columbus (Int'l)	OF	23	85	16	29	6	0	6	15	.341	5	21	2	55	0	1	.982
1988	—Chicago (A.L.)■	OF-1B	129	422	48	96	16	2	20	50	.227	46	100	1	316	14	2	†.994
1989	—Chicago (A.L.)	OF	73	246	26	61	9	1	11	47	.248	25	58	1	149	3	1	.993
1990	—Chicago (A.L.)	OF	112	325	43	89	27	3	13	58	.274	37	66	1	71	5	3	.962
1991	—Chicago (A.L.)	1B-OF	134	417	71	108	22	5	18	66	.259	62	86	0	587	46	6	.991
1992	—Chicago (A.L.)	OF-1B	93	265	26	56	16	1	6	33	.211	36	57	0	185	7	6	.970
	—Birm. (Southern)	OF	3	8	1	1	0	0	0	0	.125	2	2	0	3	0	0	1.000
1993	—Chicago (A.L.)	OF-1B	78	176	22	36	10	1	5	20	.205	26	51	2	204	12	3	.986
Major league totals (9 years)			894	2597	339	633	127	15	115	386	.244	335	633	7	1970	103	25	.988

CHAMPIONSHIP SERIES RECORD

Year	Team (League)	Pos.	G	AB	R	H	2B	3B	HR	RBI	Avg.	BB	SO	SB	PO	A	E	Avg.
				BATTING											FIELDING			
1993	—Chicago (A.L.)	1B	2	6	1	0	0	0	0	0	.000	1	2	0	13	2	1	.938

PATTERSON, BOB

P, ANGELS

PERSONAL: Born May 16, 1959, in Jacksonville, Fla. . . . 6-2/192. . . . Throws left, bats right. . . . Full name: Robert Chandler Patterson.

HIGH SCHOOL: Wade Hampton (Greenville, S.C.).

COLLEGE: East Carolina (degree in industrial technology).

TRANSACTIONS/CAREER NOTES: Selected by San Diego Padres organization in 21st round of free-agent draft (June 7, 1982). . . . Traded by Padres to Pittsburgh Pirates for OF Marvell Wynne (April 3, 1986). . . . On disabled list (April 28, 1988-remainder of season). . . . Released by Pirates (November 20, 1992). . . . Signed by Texas Rangers organization (December 8, 1992). . . . Granted free agency (October 4, 1993). . . . Signed by California Angels organization (January 18, 1994).

Year	Team (League)	W	L	Pct.	ERA	G	GS	CG	ShO	Sv.	IP	H	R	ER	BB	SO
1982	—GC Padres (GCL)	4	3	.571	2.94	8	6	3	0	0	52	60	18	17	7	65
	—Reno (California)	1	0	1.000	3.55	4	4	1	1	0	25⅓	28	11	10	5	10
1983	—Beaumont (Texas)	8	4	.667	4.01	43	9	2	0	11	116⅔	107	61	52	36	97
1984	—Las Vegas (PCL)	8	9	.471	3.27	*60	7	1	0	13	143⅓	129	63	52	37	97
1985	—Las Vegas (PCL)	10	11	.476	3.14	42	20	7	1	6	186⅓	187	80	65	52	146
	—San Diego (N.L.)	0	0	...	24.75	3	0	0	0	0	4	13	11	11	3	1
1986	—Hawaii (PCL)■	9	6	.600	3.40	25	21	6	1	1	156	146	68	59	44	*137
	—Pittsburgh (N.L.)	2	3	.400	4.95	11	5	0	0	0	36⅓	49	20	20	5	20

Year	Team (League)	W	L	Pct.	ERA	G	GS	CG	ShO	Sv.	IP	H	R	ER	BB	SO
1987	—Pittsburgh (N.L.)	1	4	.200	6.70	15	7	0	0	0	43	49	34	32	22	27
	—Vancouver (PCL)	5	2	.714	2.12	14	12	5	1	0	89	62	21	21	30	92
1988	—Buffalo (A.A.)	2	0	1.000	2.32	4	4	1	0	0	31	26	12	8	4	20
1989	—Buffalo (A.A.)	12	6	.667	3.35	31	25	4	1	1	177⅓	177	69	66	35	103
	—Pittsburgh (N.L.)	4	3	.571	4.05	12	3	0	0	1	26⅔	23	13	12	8	20
1990	—Pittsburgh (N.L.)	8	5	.615	2.95	55	5	0	0	5	94⅔	88	33	31	21	70
1991	—Pittsburgh (N.L.)	4	3	.571	4.11	54	1	0	0	2	65⅔	67	32	30	15	57
1992	—Pittsburgh (N.L.)	6	3	.667	2.92	60	0	0	0	9	64⅔	59	22	21	23	43
1993	—Texas (A.L.)■	2	4	.333	4.78	52	0	0	0	1	52⅔	59	28	28	11	46
A.L. totals (1 year)		2	4	.333	4.78	52	0	0	0	1	52⅔	59	28	28	11	46
N.L. totals (7 years)		25	21	.543	4.22	210	21	0	0	17	335	348	165	157	97	238
Major league totals (8 years)		27	25	.519	4.29	262	21	0	0	18	387⅔	407	193	185	108	284

CHAMPIONSHIP SERIES RECORD

Year	Team (League)	W	L	Pct.	ERA	G	GS	CG	ShO	Sv.	IP	H	R	ER	BB	SO
1990	—Pittsburgh (N.L.)	0	0	...	0.00	2	0	0	0	1	1	1	0	0	2	0
1991	—Pittsburgh (N.L.)	0	0	...	0.00	1	0	0	0	0	2	1	0	0	0	3
1992	—Pittsburgh (N.L.)	0	0	...	5.40	2	0	0	0	0	1⅔	3	1	1	1	1
Champ. series totals (3 years)		0	0	...	1.93	5	0	0	0	1	4⅔	5	1	1	3	4

PATTERSON, JEFF

P, PHILLIES

PERSONAL: Born October 1, 1968, in Anaheim, Calif. . . . 6-2/200. . . . Throws right, bats right. . . . Full name: Jeffrey Simmon Patterson.
HIGH SCHOOL: Loara (Anaheim, Calif.).
COLLEGE: Cypress (Calif.) College.

TRANSACTIONS/CAREER NOTES: Selected by Philadelphia Phillies organization in 58th round of free-agent draft (June 1, 1988).

Year	Team (League)	W	L	Pct.	ERA	G	GS	CG	ShO	Sv.	IP	H	R	ER	BB	SO
1989	—Martinsville (App.)	2	4	.333	3.61	7	7	0	0	0	42⅓	35	23	17	12	44
	—Batavia (NY-Penn)	2	4	.333	2.87	9	7	1	1	1	53⅓	44	19	17	11	41
1990	—Clearwater (FSL)	3	6	.333	2.96	11	11	0	0	0	67	63	34	22	22	28
1991	—Spartanburg (SAL)	9	8	.529	4.42	35	10	2	1	9	114	103	60	56	41	114
1992	—Clearwater (FSL)	2	1	.667	1.98	30	0	0	0	14	36⅓	29	11	8	11	33
	—Reading (Eastern)	3	1	.750	4.60	26	0	0	0	13	31⅓	30	16	16	14	22
	—Scran./W.B. (Int'l)	2	1	.667	2.63	11	0	0	0	1	13⅔	10	4	4	8	11
1993	—Scran./W.B. (Int'l)	7	5	.583	2.69	*62	0	0	0	8	93⅔	79	32	28	42	68

PATTERSON, JOHN

2B, GIANTS

PERSONAL: Born February 11, 1967, in Key West, Fla. . . . 5-9/168. . . . Throws right, bats both. . . . Full name: John Allen Patterson.
HIGH SCHOOL: Trevor G. Browne (Phoenix).
COLLEGE: Central Arizona and Grand Canyon (Ariz.).

TRANSACTIONS/CAREER NOTES: Selected by San Diego Padres organization in third round of free-agent draft (January 14, 1986). . . . Selected by San Francisco Giants organization in 23rd round of free-agent draft (June 1, 1988). . . . On disabled list (April 1, 1989-entire season). . . . On San Francisco disabled list (May 7-23, 1992). . . . On San Francisco disabled list (March 27-September 1, 1993); included rehabilitation assignment to San Jose (August 13-September 1).

			BATTING											FIELDING			
Year	Team (League)	Pos.	G	AB	R	H	2B	3B	HR	RBI	Avg.	BB	SO	SB	PO	A	E	Avg.
1988	—Everett (N'west)	2B-SS	58	232	37	58	10	4	0	26	.250	18	27	21	89	97	9	.954
1989	—							Did not play.										
1990	—San Jose (Calif.)	2B	131	530	91	160	23	6	4	66	.302	46	74	29	247	322	26	.956
1991	—Shreveport (Texas)	2B	117	464	81	137	31	13	4	56	.295	30	63	41	242	299	15	.973
1992	—San Francisco (N.L.)	2B-OF	32	103	10	19	1	1	0	4	.184	5	24	5	66	54	4	.968
	—Phoenix (PCL)	2B-OF-3B	93	362	52	109	20	6	2	37	.301	33	45	22	185	239	9	.979
1993	—San Jose (Calif.)	2B	16	68	8	16	7	0	1	14	.235	7	12	6	2	2	0	1.000
	—San Francisco (N.L.)	PH	16	16	1	3	0	0	1	2	.188	0	5	0	...	...	...	...
Major league totals (2 years)			48	119	11	22	1	1	1	6	.185	5	29	5	66	54	4	.968

PATTERSON, KEN

P, REDS

PERSONAL: Born July 8, 1964, in Costa Mesa, Calif. . . . 6-4/230. . . . Throws left, bats left. . . . Full name: Kenneth Brian Patterson.
HIGH SCHOOL: McGregor (Tex.).
COLLEGE: McLennan Community College (Tex.) and Baylor.

TRANSACTIONS/CAREER NOTES: Selected by Philadelphia Phillies organization in 29th round of free-agent draft (June 7, 1982). . . . Selected by Baltimore Orioles organization in secondary phase of free-agent draft (January 11, 1983). . . . Selected by Phillies organization in secondary phase of free-agent draft (June 6, 1983). . . . Selected by New York Yankees organization in third round of free-agent draft (June 3, 1985). . . . Traded by Yankees organization with a player to be named later to Chicago White Sox for IF/OF Jerry Royster and IF Mike Soper (August 26, 1987); White Sox acquired P Jeff Pries to complete deal (September 19, 1987). . . . Traded by White Sox with OF Sammy Sosa to Chicago Cubs for OF George Bell (March 30, 1992). . . . On Chicago disabled list (May 31-July 12, 1992); included rehabilitation assignment to Peoria (July 2-8) and Iowa (July 8-12). . . . Granted free agency (December 19, 1992). . . . Signed by California Angels (April 4, 1993). . . . Granted free agency (November 18, 1993). . . . Signed by Cincinnati Reds (December 8, 1993).

Year	Team (League)	W	L	Pct.	ERA	G	GS	CG	ShO	Sv.	IP	H	R	ER	BB	SO
1985	—Oneonta (NYP)	2	2	.500	4.84	6	6	0	0	0	22⅓	23	14	12	14	21
1986	—Fort Lauder. (FSL)	0	2	.000	7.71	5	5	0	0	0	18⅔	30	20	16	16	13
	—Oneonta (NYP)	9	3	.750	*1.35	15	15	5	*4	0	100⅓	67	25	15	45	102
1987	—Fort Lauder. (FSL)	1	3	.250	6.33	9	9	0	0	0	42⅔	46	34	30	31	36

P

Year	Team (League)	W	L	Pct.	ERA	G	GS	CG	ShO	Sv.	IP	H	R	ER	BB	SO
	—Alb./Colon. (East.)	3	6	.333	3.96	24	8	1	0	5	63⅔	59	31	28	31	47
	—Hawaii (PCL)■	0	0	...	0.00	3	0	0	0	2	3⅓	1	0	0	3	5
1988	—Vancouver (PCL)	6	5	.545	3.23	55	4	0	0	12	86⅓	64	37	31	36	89
	—Chicago (A.L.)	0	2	.000	4.79	9	2	0	0	1	20⅔	25	11	11	7	8
1989	—Vancouver (PCL)	0	1	.000	1.00	2	2	0	0	0	9	6	2	1	1	17
	—Chicago (A.L.)	6	1	.857	4.52	50	1	0	0	0	65⅔	64	37	33	28	43
1990	—Chicago (A.L.)	2	1	.667	3.39	43	0	0	0	2	66⅓	58	27	25	34	40
1991	—Chicago (A.L.)	3	0	1.000	2.83	43	0	0	0	1	63⅔	48	22	20	35	32
1992	—Chicago (N.L.)■	2	3	.400	3.89	32	1	0	0	0	41⅔	41	25	18	27	23
	—Peoria (Midwest)	0	0	...	12.00	2	0	0	0	0	3	5	4	4	2	5
	—Iowa (Am. Assoc.)	0	1	.000	21.60	1	0	0	0	0	1⅔	4	4	4	1	1
1993	—California (A.L.)■	1	1	.500	4.58	46	0	0	0	1	59	54	30	30	35	36
A.L. totals (5 years)		12	5	.706	3.89	191	3	0	0	5	275⅓	249	127	119	139	159
N.L. totals (1 year)		2	3	.400	3.89	32	1	0	0	0	41⅔	41	25	18	27	23
Major league totals (6 years)		14	8	.636	3.89	223	4	0	0	5	317	290	152	137	166	182

PAVLIK, ROGER

P, RANGERS

PERSONAL: Born October 4, 1967, in Houston. . . . 6-2/220. . . . Throws right, bats right. . . . Full name: Roger Allen Pavlik.

HIGH SCHOOL: Aldine (Houston).

TRANSACTIONS/CAREER NOTES: Selected by Texas Rangers organization in second round of free-agent draft (June 2, 1986). . . . On disabled list (June 21, 1986-remainder of season; June 4-August 6, 1987; and April 29-May 6 and May 23-July 29, 1991).

STATISTICAL NOTES: Pitched 5⅓ innings, combining with reliever Steve Peters (2⅔ innings) for eight no-hit innings in a 1-0 loss to Indianapolis (April 17, 1991).

Year	Team (League)	W	L	Pct.	ERA	G	GS	CG	ShO	Sv.	IP	H	R	ER	BB	SO
1986	—							Did not play.								
1987	—Gastonia (S. Atl.)	2	7	.222	4.95	15	14	0	0	0	67⅓	66	46	37	42	55
1988	—Gastonia (S. Atl.)	2	12	.143	4.59	18	16	0	0	0	84⅓	94	65	43	58	89
	—Butte (Pioneer)	4	0	1.000	4.59	8	8	1	1	0	49	45	29	25	34	56
1989	—Charlotte (Fla. St.)	3	8	.273	3.41	26	22	1	1	1	118⅔	92	60	45	72	98
1990	—Charlotte (Fla. St.)	5	3	.625	2.44	11	11	1	0	0	66⅓	50	21	18	40	76
	—Tulsa (Texas)	6	5	.545	2.33	16	16	2	1	0	100⅓	66	29	26	71	91
1991	—Okla. City (A.A.)	0	5	.000	5.19	8	7	0	0	0	26	19	21	15	26	43
1992	—Okla. City (A.A.)	7	5	.583	2.98	18	18	0	0	0	117⅔	90	44	39	51	104
	—Texas (A.L.)	4	4	.500	4.21	13	12	1	0	0	62	66	32	29	34	45
1993	—Okla. City (A.A.)	3	2	.600	1.70	6	6	0	0	0	37	26	12	7	14	32
	—Texas (A.L.)	12	6	.667	3.41	26	26	2	0	0	166⅓	151	67	63	80	131
Major league totals (2 years)		16	10	.615	3.63	39	38	3	0	0	228⅓	217	99	92	114	176

PECOTA, BILL

IF, BRAVES

PERSONAL: Born February 16, 1960, in Redwood City, Calif. . . . 6-2/195. . . . Throws right, bats right. . . . Full name: William Joseph Pecota. . . . Name pronounced puh-KOTE-uh.

HIGH SCHOOL: Peterson (Sunnyvale, Calif.).

COLLEGE: De Anza College (Calif.).

TRANSACTIONS/CAREER NOTES: Selected by Kansas City Royals organization in 10th round of free-agent draft (January 13, 1981). . . . Traded by Royals with P Bret Saberhagen to New York Mets for OF Kevin McReynolds, IF Gregg Jefferies and 2B Keith Miller (December 11, 1991). . . . On disabled list (April 19-May 4, 1992). . . . Granted free agency (December 19, 1992). . . . Signed by Atlanta Braves (January 4, 1993).

STATISTICAL NOTES: Led Southern League third basemen with 434 total chances in 1984. . . . Led American Association third basemen with .962 fielding percentage, 111 putouts, 247 assists, 372 total chances and 22 double plays in 1985. . . . Led American Association third basemen with 217 assists and 337 total chances in 1986.

			BATTING												FIELDING			
Year	Team (League)	Pos.	G	AB	R	H	2B	3B	HR	RBI	Avg.	BB	SO	SB	PO	A	E	Avg.
1981	—GC Royals-B (GCL)	C-3B-2B	61	208	*61	66	11	4	3	22	.317	39	18	14	112	45	6	.963
1982	—Fort Myers (FSL)	3B	135	482	71	115	16	6	4	49	.239	79	72	39	109	243	15	.959
1983	—Fort Myers (FSL)	3B	65	234	48	63	7	2	5	33	.269	45	31	28	46	114	7	.958
	—Jacksonv. (South.)	3B-SS	72	260	38	63	9	1	5	25	.242	33	39	9	54	135	19	.909
1984	—Memphis (South.)	3B	145	543	84	131	19	2	9	50	.241	99	72	43	*142	267	25	*.942
1985	—Omaha (A.A.)	3B-SS-OF	130	409	47	98	17	3	1	34	.240	57	55	21	†111	†247	14	†.962
1986	—Omaha (A.A.)	3B-SS-OF	139	474	48	125	26	2	4	54	.264	37	46	20	125	†238	11	.971
	—Kansas City (A.L.)	3B-SS	12	29	3	6	2	0	0	2	.207	3	3	0	7	31	1	.974
1987	—Omaha (A.A.)	3B-SS-2B	35	126	31	39	8	1	2	16	.310	15	15	7	38	78	8	.935
	—Kansas City (A.L.)	SS-3B-2B	66	156	22	43	5	1	3	14	.276	15	25	5	67	135	6	.971
1988	—Kansas City (A.L.)	S-3-1-0-2-C	90	178	25	37	3	3	1	15	.208	18	34	7	98	145	6	.976
1989	—Kansas City (A.L.)	S-0-2-3-1	65	83	21	17	4	2	3	5	.205	7	9	5	50	79	2	.985
	—Omaha (A.A.)	S-3-2-0	64	248	34	63	12	1	3	40	.254	29	29	10	96	206	8	.974
1990	—Kansas City (A.L.)	2-S-3-0-1	87	240	43	58	15	2	5	20	.242	33	39	8	160	195	5	.986
	—Omaha (A.A.)	3B-2B-SS	29	116	30	35	6	0	4	13	.302	17	17	11	32	80	1	.991
1991	—Kansas City (A.L.)	3-2-S-1-0-P	125	398	53	114	23	2	6	45	.286	41	45	16	163	206	4	.989
1992	—New York (N.L.)■	3-S-2-1-P	117	269	28	61	13	0	2	26	.227	25	40	9	92	218	12	.963
1993	—Atlanta (N.L.)■	3B-2B-OF	72	62	17	20	2	1	0	5	.323	2	5	1	9	13	0	1.000
American League totals (6 years)			445	1084	167	275	52	10	18	101	.254	117	155	41	545	791	24	.982
National League totals (2 years)			189	331	45	81	15	1	2	31	.245	27	45	10	101	231	12	.965
Major league totals (8 years)			634	1415	212	356	67	11	20	132	.252	144	200	51	646	1022	36	.979

CHAMPIONSHIP SERIES RECORD

Year	Team (League)	Pos.	G	AB	R	H	2B	3B	HR	RBI	Avg.	BB	SO	SB	PO	A	E	Avg.
				BATTING											FIELDING			
1993	—Atlanta (N.L.)	PH	4	3	1	1	0	0	0	0	.333	1	1	0	...	...	...	...

RECORD AS PITCHER

Year	Team (League)	W	L	Pct.	ERA	G	GS	CG	ShO	Sv.	IP	H	R	ER	BB	SO
1991	—Kansas City (A.L.)	0	0	...	4.50	1	0	0	0	0	2	4	1	1	0	0
1992	—New York (N.L.)	0	0	...	9.00	1	0	0	0	0	1	1	1	1	0	0
Major league totals (2 years)		0	0	...	6.00	2	0	0	0	0	3	5	2	2	0	0

PEGUES, STEVE

OF, PADRES

PERSONAL: Born May 21, 1968, in Pontotoc, Miss. . . . 6-2/190. . . . Throws right, bats right. . . . Full name: Steven Antone Pegues. . . . Name pronounced peh-GEEZE.
HIGH SCHOOL: Pontotoc (Miss.).
TRANSACTIONS/CAREER NOTES: Selected by Detroit Tigers organization in first round (21st pick overall) of free-agent draft (June 2, 1987). . . . Claimed on waivers by San Diego Padres (March 20, 1992). . . . On disabled list (April 9-May 7, May 25-June 1 and July 18-August 26, 1993).
STATISTICAL NOTES: Led Pacific Coast League outfielders with 24 assists in 1992.

Year	Team (League)	Pos.	G	AB	R	H	2B	3B	HR	RBI	Avg.	BB	SO	SB	PO	A	E	Avg.
				BATTING											FIELDING			
1987	—Bristol (Appal.)	OF	59	236	36	67	6	5	2	23	.284	16	42	22	114	4	10	.922
1988	—Fayetteville (SAL)	OF	118	437	50	112	7	5	6	46	.256	21	90	21	240	13	12	.955
1989	—Fayetteville (SAL)	OF	70	269	35	83	11	6	1	38	.309	15	52	16	127	8	2	.985
	—Lakeland (Fla. St.)	OF	55	193	24	49	7	2	0	15	.254	7	19	12	115	3	2	.983
1990	—London (Eastern)	OF	126	483	48	131	22	5	8	63	.271	12	58	17	244	7	•9	.965
1991	—London (Eastern)	OF	56	216	24	65	3	2	6	26	.301	8	24	4	69	4	1	.986
	—Toledo (Int'l)	OF	68	222	21	50	13	3	4	23	.225	3	31	8	84	7	4	.958
1992	—Las Vegas (PCL)■	OF-1B	123	376	51	99	21	4	9	56	.263	7	64	12	203	†24	9	.962
1993	—Las Vegas (PCL)	OF	68	270	52	95	20	5	9	50	.352	7	43	12	103	5	2	.982

PELTIER, DAN

OF/1B, RANGERS

PERSONAL: Born June 30, 1968, in Clifton Park, N.Y. . . . 6-1/200. . . . Throws left, bats left. . . . Full name: Daniel Edward Peltier. . . . Name pronounced pell-TEER.
HIGH SCHOOL: Shenendehowa Central (Clifton Park, N.Y.).
COLLEGE: Notre Dame (degree in business administration).
TRANSACTIONS/CAREER NOTES: Selected by Texas Rangers organization in third round of free-agent draft (June 5, 1989). . . . On disabled list (July 29, 1989-remainder of season and June 24-August 2, 1991).

Year	Team (League)	Pos.	G	AB	R	H	2B	3B	HR	RBI	Avg.	BB	SO	SB	PO	A	E	Avg.
				BATTING											FIELDING			
1989	—Butte (Pioneer)	OF	33	122	35	49	7	1	7	28	.402	25	16	10	28	4	2	.941
1990	—Tulsa (Texas)	OF	117	448	66	125	20	4	11	57	.279	40	67	10	173	9	8	.958
1991	—Okla. City (A.A.)	OF	94	345	38	79	16	4	3	32	.229	43	71	6	161	7	6	.966
1992	—Okla. City (A.A.)	OF	125	450	65	133	30	7	7	53	.296	60	72	1	255	12	3	.989
	—Texas (A.L.)	OF	12	24	1	4	0	0	0	2	.167	0	3	0	6	0	1	.857
1993	—Texas (A.L.)	OF-1B	65	160	23	43	7	1	1	17	.269	20	27	0	80	4	4	.955
	—Okla. City (A.A.)	1B-OF	48	187	28	60	15	4	5	33	.321	19	27	2	346	22	5	.987
Major league totals (2 years)			77	184	24	47	7	1	1	19	.255	20	30	0	86	4	5	.947

PEMBERTON, RUDY

OF, TIGERS

PERSONAL: Born December 17, 1969, in San Pedro de Macoris, Dominican Republic. . . . 6-1/185. . . . Throws right, bats right. . . . Full name: Rudy Hector Perez Pemberton.
TRANSACTIONS/CAREER NOTES: Signed as free agent by Detroit Tigers organization (June 7, 1987).
STATISTICAL NOTES: Tied for Florida State League lead in being hit by pitch with 13 in 1992.

Year	Team (League)	Pos.	G	AB	R	H	2B	3B	HR	RBI	Avg.	BB	SO	SB	PO	A	E	Avg.
				BATTING											FIELDING			
1987	—	Dominican Summer League statistics unavailable.																
1988	—Bristol (Appal.)	OF	6	5	2	0	0	0	0	0	.000	1	3	0	0	0	0	...
1989	—Bristol (Appal.)	OF	56	214	40	58	9	2	6	39	.271	14	43	19	84	4	5	.946
1990	—Fayetteville (SAL)	OF	127	454	59	126	14	5	6	61	.278	42	91	12	192	12	10	.953
1991	—Lakeland (Fla. St.)	OF	111	375	40	86	15	2	3	36	.229	25	52	25	184	9	9	.955
1992	—Lakeland (Fla. St.)	OF	104	343	41	91	16	5	3	43	.265	21	37	25	147	17	3	.982
1993	—London (Eastern)	OF	124	471	70	130	22	4	15	67	.276	24	80	14	215	11	8	.966

PENA, ALEJANDRO

P, PIRATES

PERSONAL: Born June 25, 1959, in Cambiaso, Dominican Republic. . . . 6-1/228. . . . Throws right, bats right. . . . Full name: Alejandro Vasquez Pena.
TRANSACTIONS/CAREER NOTES: Signed as free agent by Los Angeles Dodgers organization (September 10, 1978). . . . On disabled list (April 8-September 5, 1985). . . . On Los Angeles disabled list (March 23-May 26, 1986); included rehabilitation assignment to Vero Beach (May 2-19). . . . On disabled list (July 27-August 17, 1987). . . . Granted free agency (November 4, 1988). . . . Re-signed by Dodgers (November 7, 1988). . . . On disabled list (July 8-23, 1989). . . . Traded by Dodgers with OF Mike Marshall to New York Mets for OF Juan Samuel (December 20, 1989). . . . Traded by Mets to Atlanta Braves for P Tony Castillo and a player to be named later (August 28, 1991); Mets acquired P Joe Roa to complete deal (August 29, 1991). . . . Granted free agency (November 1, 1991). . . . Re-signed by Braves (February 28, 1992). . . . On disabled list (May 31-June 18 and August 21-September 5, 1992). . . . Granted

free agency (November 3, 1992). . . . Signed by Pittsburgh Pirates (December 10, 1992). . . . On Pittsburgh disabled list (March 22, 1993-entire season).
STATISTICAL NOTES: Pitched one inning, combining with starter Kent Mercker (six innings) and Mark Wohlers (two innings) in 1-0 no-hit victory for Atlanta against San Diego (September 11, 1991).

Year	Team (League)	W	L	Pct.	ERA	G	GS	CG	ShO	Sv.	IP	H	R	ER	BB	SO
1979	—Clinton (Midwest)	3	3	.500	4.18	21	5	0	0	0	71	53	39	33	44	57
1980	—Vero Beach (FSL).......	10	3	.769	3.21	35	3	0	0	8	73	57	32	26	41	46
1981	—Albuquerque (PCL)....	2	5	.286	1.61	38	0	0	0	*22	56	36	12	10	21	40
	—Los Angeles (N.L.).....	1	1	.500	2.88	14	0	0	0	2	25	18	8	8	11	14
1982	—Los Angeles (N.L.).....	0	2	.000	4.79	29	0	0	0	0	35⅔	37	24	19	21	20
	—Albuquerque (PCL)....	1	1	.500	5.34	16	0	0	0	5	28⅔	37	18	17	10	27
1983	—Los Angeles (N.L.).....	12	9	.571	2.75	34	26	4	3	1	177	152	67	54	51	120
1984	—Los Angeles (N.L.).....	12	6	.667	*2.48	28	28	8	*4	0	199⅓	186	67	55	46	135
1985	—Los Angeles (N.L.).....	0	1	.000	8.31	2	1	0	0	0	4⅓	7	5	4	3	2
1986	—Vero Beach (FSL).......	0	2	.000	7.47	4	4	0	0	0	15⅔	22	15	13	4	11
	—Los Angeles (N.L.).....	1	2	.333	4.89	24	10	0	0	1	70	74	40	38	30	46
1987	—Los Angeles (N.L.).....	2	7	.222	3.50	37	7	0	0	11	87⅓	82	41	34	37	76
1988	—Los Angeles (N.L.).....	6	7	.462	1.91	60	0	0	0	12	94⅓	75	29	20	27	83
1989	—Los Angeles (N.L.).....	4	3	.571	2.13	53	0	0	0	5	76	62	20	18	18	75
1990	—New York (N.L.)■.......	3	3	.500	3.20	52	0	0	0	5	76	71	31	27	22	76
1991	—N.Y.-Atlanta (N.L.)■..	8	1	.889	2.40	59	0	0	0	15	82⅓	74	23	22	22	62
1992	—Atlanta (N.L.)............	1	6	.143	4.07	41	0	0	0	15	42	40	19	19	13	34
1993	—■................................							Did not play.								
Major league totals (12 years)		50	48	.510	2.95	433	72	12	7	67	969⅓	878	374	318	301	743

CHAMPIONSHIP SERIES RECORD

CHAMPIONSHIP SERIES NOTES: Shares major league single-series record for most wild pitches—4 (1991). . . . Shares N.L. single-series record for most saves—3 (1991).

Year	Team (League)	W	L	Pct.	ERA	G	GS	CG	ShO	Sv.	IP	H	R	ER	BB	SO
1981	—Los Angeles (N.L.).....	0	0	...	0.00	2	0	0	0	0	2⅓	1	0	0	0	0
1983	—Los Angeles (N.L.).....	0	0	...	6.75	1	0	0	0	0	2⅔	4	2	2	1	3
1988	—Los Angeles (N.L.).....	1	1	.500	4.15	3	0	0	0	1	4⅓	1	2	2	5	1
1991	—Atlanta (N.L.)............	0	0	...	0.00	4	0	0	0	3	4⅓	1	0	0	0	4
Champ. series totals (4 years)		1	1	.500	2.63	10	0	0	0	4	13⅔	7	4	4	6	8

WORLD SERIES RECORD

Year	Team (League)	W	L	Pct.	ERA	G	GS	CG	ShO	Sv.	IP	H	R	ER	BB	SO
1981	—Los Angeles (N.L.).....							Did not play.								
1988	—Los Angeles (N.L.).....	1	0	1.000	0.00	2	0	0	0	0	5	2	0	0	1	7
1991	—Atlanta (N.L.)............	0	1	.000	3.38	3	0	0	0	0	5⅓	6	2	2	3	7
World Series totals (2 years)		1	1	.500	1.74	5	0	0	0	0	10⅓	8	2	2	4	14

PENA, GERONIMO

2B, CARDINALS

PERSONAL: Born March 29, 1967, in Distrito Nacional, Dominican Republic. . . . 6-1/195. . . . Throws right, bats both.
HIGH SCHOOL: Distrito Nacional (Dominican Republic).
TRANSACTIONS/CAREER NOTES: Signed as free agent by St. Louis Cardinals organization (August 9, 1984). . . . On St. Louis disabled list (March 25-June 5, 1989); included rehabilitation assignment to St. Petersburg (May 29-June 5). . . . On St. Louis disabled list (March 28-May 26, 1992); included rehabilitation assignment to Louisville (May 11-18 and May 21-25). . . . On St. Louis disabled list (June 28-August 17, 1992); included rehabilitation assignment to Louisville (July 16-20 and August 4-17). . . . On St. Louis disabled list (July 6-September 3, 1993); included rehabilitation assignment to Louisville (August 23-September 3).
STATISTICAL NOTES: Led Appalachian League with four intentional bases on balls received in 1986. . . . Led South Atlantic League second basemen with 324 putouts, 342 assists, 29 errors, 695 total chances and 80 double plays in 1987. . . . Led Florida State League second basemen with 723 total chances and 103 double plays in 1988. . . . Led American Association in being hit by pitch with 18 in 1990. . . . Led American Association third basemen with 20 errors in 1990.
MISCELLANEOUS: Batted righthanded only (1986-87).

			BATTING												FIELDING			
Year	Team (League)	Pos.	G	AB	R	H	2B	3B	HR	RBI	Avg.	BB	SO	SB	PO	A	E	Avg.
1985	—S.F. de Mac. (DSL)...	...	46	120	31	31	5	0	0	15	.258	23	18	13	...	...	...	...
1986	—Johns. City (App.)....	2B	56	202	*55	60	7	4	3	20	.297	46	33	27	108	144	7	.973
1987	—Savannah (S. Atl.)...	2B-SS	134	505	95	136	28	3	9	51	.269	73	98	*80	†325	†343	†29	.958
1988	—St. Peters. (FSL).......	2B	130	484	82	125	25	10	4	35	.258	88	103	35	*301	*402	20	*.972
1989	—St. Peters. (FSL).......	2B	6	21	2	4	1	0	0	2	.190	3	6	2	9	19	1	.966
	—Arkansas (Texas)....	2B	77	267	61	79	16	8	9	44	.296	38	68	14	177	208	14	.965
1990	—Louisville (A.A.).......	2B-3B	118	390	65	97	24	6	6	35	.249	69	116	24	153	261	†27	.939
	—St. Louis (N.L.).........	2B	18	45	5	11	2	0	0	2	.244	4	14	1	24	30	1	.982
1991	—St. Louis (N.L.).........	2B-OF	104	185	38	45	8	3	5	17	.243	18	45	15	101	146	6	.976
1992	—St. Louis (N.L.).........	2B	62	203	31	62	12	1	7	31	.305	24	37	13	125	184	5	.984
	—Louisville (A.A.).......	2B	28	101	16	25	9	4	3	12	.248	13	27	4	70	68	5	.965
1993	—St. Louis (N.L.).........	2B	74	254	34	65	19	2	5	30	.256	25	71	13	140	200	12	.966
	—Louisville (A.A.).......	2B	7	23	4	4	1	0	0	0	.174	1	4	1	10	18	0	1.000
Major league totals (4 years)			258	687	108	183	41	6	17	80	.266	71	167	42	390	560	24	.975

PENA, TONY

C, INDIANS

PERSONAL: Born June 4, 1957, in Monte Cristi, Dominican Republic. . . . 6-0/185. . . . Throws right, bats right. . . . Full name: Antonio Francisco Padilla Pena. . . . Brother of Ramon Pena, pitcher, Detroit Tigers (1989).
HIGH SCHOOL: Liceo Marti (Monte Cristi, Dominican Republic).

TRANSACTIONS/CAREER NOTES: Signed as free agent by Pittsburgh Pirates organization (July 22, 1975).... Traded by Pirates to St. Louis Cardinals for OF Andy Van Slyke, C Mike LaValliere and P Mike Dunne (April 1, 1987).... On St. Louis disabled list (April 11-May 22, 1987); included rehabilitation assignment to Louisville (May 19-22).... Granted free agency (November 13, 1989).... Signed by Boston Red Sox (November 27, 1989).... Granted free agency (October 29, 1993).... Signed by Cleveland Indians organization (February 7, 1994).
HONORS: Named catcher on THE SPORTING NEWS N.L. All-Star team (1983).... Won N.L. Gold Glove at catcher (1983-85).... Won A.L. Gold Glove at catcher (1991).
STATISTICAL NOTES: Led Carolina League catchers with nine double plays and tied for lead with 16 passed balls in 1977.... Led Eastern League catchers with 14 double plays in 1979.... Led N.L. catchers with 1,075 total chances in 1983, 999 in 1984 and 1,034 in 1985.... Led N.L. catchers with 15 double plays in 1984 and 13 in 1989.... Led N.L. catchers with 100 assists in 1985.... Led N.L. catchers with 18 errors in 1986.... Tied for N.L. lead in grounding into double plays with 21 in 1986.... Led N.L. catchers with .994 fielding percentage in 1988 and .997 in 1989.... Led A.L. catchers with 864 putouts and 943 total chances in 1990.... Led A.L. catchers with 929 total chances and 15 double plays in 1991.... Led A.L. catchers with 12 double plays in 1992.

			BATTING												FIELDING			
Year	Team (League)	Pos.	G	AB	R	H	2B	3B	HR	RBI	Avg.	BB	SO	SB	PO	A	E	Avg.
1976	—GC Pirates (GCL)	O-1-C-3	33	110	10	23	2	2	1	11	.209	4	17	5	108	14	4	.968
	—Char., S.C. (W. Car.)	C	14	49	4	11	2	0	1	8	.224	4	7	0	64	7	2	.973
1977	—Char., S.C. (W. Car.)	C	29	101	10	24	4	0	3	16	.238	7	21	2	172	19	6	.970
	—Salem (Carolina)	C	84	319	36	88	15	3	7	46	.276	14	60	3	★470	★66	★17	.969
1978	—Shreveport (Texas)	C	104	348	34	80	14	0	8	42	.230	15	96	3	637	54	★25	.965
1979	—Buffalo (Eastern)	C	134	515	89	161	16	4	34	97	.313	39	83	5	★768	★120	★26	.972
1980	—Portland (PCL)	C	124	452	57	148	24	13	9	77	.327	29	75	5	★639	85	★23	.969
	—Pittsburgh (N.L.)	C	8	21	1	9	1	1	0	1	.429	0	4	0	38	2	2	.952
1981	—Pittsburgh (N.L.)	C	66	210	16	63	9	1	2	17	.300	8	23	1	286	41	5	.985
1982	—Pittsburgh (N.L.)	C	138	497	53	147	28	4	11	63	.296	17	57	2	763	89	16	.982
1983	—Pittsburgh (N.L.)	C	151	542	51	163	22	3	15	70	.301	31	73	6	★976	90	9	.992
1984	—Pittsburgh (N.L.)	C	147	546	77	156	27	2	15	78	.286	36	79	12	★895	★95	9	.991
1985	—Pittsburgh (N.L.)	C-1B	147	546	53	136	27	2	10	59	.249	29	67	12	925	†102	12	.988
1986	—Pittsburgh (N.L.)	C-1B	144	510	56	147	26	2	10	52	.288	53	69	9	824	99	†18	.981
1987	—St. Louis (N.L.)■	C-1B-OF	116	384	40	82	13	4	5	44	.214	36	54	6	624	51	8	.988
	—Louisville (A.A.)	C	2	8	0	3	0	0	0	0	.375	0	2	0	7	1	0	1.000
1988	—St. Louis (N.L.)	C-1B	149	505	55	133	23	1	10	51	.263	33	60	6	796	72	6	†.993
1989	—St. Louis (N.L.)	C-OF	141	424	36	110	17	2	4	37	.259	35	33	5	675	70	2	†.997
1990	—Boston (A.L.)■	C-1B	143	491	62	129	19	1	7	56	.263	43	71	8	†866	74	5	.995
1991	—Boston (A.L.)	C	141	464	45	107	23	2	5	48	.231	37	53	8	★864	60	5	.995
1992	—Boston (A.L.)	C	133	410	39	99	21	1	1	38	.241	24	61	3	★786	57	6	.993
1993	—Boston (A.L.)	C	126	304	20	55	11	0	4	19	.181	25	46	1	698	53	4	.995
American League totals (4 years)			543	1669	166	390	74	4	17	161	.234	129	231	20	3214	244	20	.994
National League totals (10 years)			1207	4185	438	1146	193	22	82	472	.274	278	519	59	6802	711	87	.989
Major league totals (14 years)			1750	5854	604	1536	267	26	99	633	.262	407	750	79	10016	955	107	.990

CHAMPIONSHIP SERIES RECORD

			BATTING												FIELDING			
Year	Team (League)	Pos.	G	AB	R	H	2B	3B	HR	RBI	Avg.	BB	SO	SB	PO	A	E	Avg.
1987	—St. Louis (N.L.)	C	7	21	5	8	0	1	0	0	.381	3	4	1	55	5	0	1.000
1990	—Boston (A.L.)	C	4	14	0	3	0	0	0	0	.214	0	0	0	22	4	1	.963
Championship series totals (2 years)			11	35	5	11	0	1	0	0	.314	3	4	1	77	9	1	.989

WORLD SERIES RECORD

			BATTING												FIELDING			
Year	Team (League)	Pos.	G	AB	R	H	2B	3B	HR	RBI	Avg.	BB	SO	SB	PO	A	E	Avg.
1987	—St. Louis (N.L.)	C-DH	7	22	2	9	1	0	0	4	.409	3	2	1	32	1	1	.971

ALL-STAR GAME RECORD

			BATTING											FIELDING			
Year	League	Pos.	AB	R	H	2B	3B	HR	RBI	Avg.	BB	SO	SB	PO	A	E	Avg.
1982	—National	PR-C	1	0	0	0	0	0	0	.000	0	0	1	3	0	0	1.000
1984	—National	C	0	0	0	0	0	0	0	...	0	0	0	2	0	0	1.000
1985	—National	C	0	0	0	0	0	0	0	...	0	1	0	4	1	0	1.000
1986	—National	PR	0	0	0	0	0	0	0	...	0	0	0	...	...	...	...
1989	—National	PH-C	2	0	0	0	0	0	0	.000	0	0	0	2	0	0	1.000
All-Star Game totals (5 years)			3	0	0	0	0	0	0	.000	0	1	1	11	1	0	1.000

PENDLETON, TERRY

3B, BRAVES

PERSONAL: Born July 16, 1960, in Los Angeles.... 5-9/195.... Throws right, bats both.... Full name: Terry Lee Pendleton.
HIGH SCHOOL: Channel Island (Oxnard, Calif.).
COLLEGE: Oxnard (Calif.) College and Fresno State.
TRANSACTIONS/CAREER NOTES: Selected by St. Louis Cardinals organization in seventh round of free-agent draft (June 7, 1982).... On disabled list (April 8-May 23 and July 16-September 5, 1983; June 15-30, 1985; May 28-June 24, 1988; and April 24-May 9, 1990).... Granted free agency (November 5, 1990).... Signed by Atlanta Braves (December 3, 1990).
HONORS: Won N.L. Gold Glove at third base (1987, 1989 and 1992).... Named N.L. Comeback Player of the Year by THE SPORTING NEWS (1991).... Named third baseman on THE SPORTING NEWS N.L. All-Star team (1991).... Named N.L. Most Valuable Player by Baseball Writers' Association of America (1991).
STATISTICAL NOTES: Led American Association third basemen with .964 fielding percentage and 88 putouts in 1984.... Led N.L. third basemen with 133 putouts and 371 assists in 1986.... Led N.L. third basemen with 524 total chances in 1986, 512 in 1987, 520 in 1989, 481 in 1991 and 477 in 1992.... Led N.L. third basemen with 36 double plays in 1986 and 31 in 1991.... Tied for N.L. lead with 303 total bases in 1991.

Year	Team (League)	Pos.	G	AB	R	H	2B	3B	HR	RBI	Avg.	BB	SO	SB	PO	A	E	Avg.
			BATTING												FIELDING			
1982	—Johns. City (App.)	2B	43	181	38	58	14	•4	4	27	.320	12	28	13	79	105	17	.915
	—St. Peters. (FSL)	2B	20	69	4	18	2	1	1	7	.261	2	18	1	41	51	2	.979
1983	—Arkansas (Texas)	2B	48	185	29	51	10	3	4	20	.276	9	26	7	94	135	7	.970
1984	—Louisville (A.A.)	3B-2B	91	330	52	98	23	5	4	44	.297	24	51	6	†91	157	10	†.961
	—St. Louis (N.L.)	3B	67	262	37	85	16	3	1	33	.324	16	32	20	59	155	13	.943
1985	—St. Louis (N.L.)	3B	149	559	56	134	16	3	5	69	.240	37	75	17	129	361	18	.965
1986	—St. Louis (N.L.)	3B-OF	159	578	56	138	26	5	1	59	.239	34	59	24	†133	†371	20	.962
1987	—St. Louis (N.L.)	3B	159	583	82	167	29	4	12	96	.286	70	74	19	117	*369	26	.949
1988	—St. Louis (N.L.)	3B	110	391	44	99	20	2	6	53	.253	21	51	3	75	239	12	.963
1989	—St. Louis (N.L.)	3B	162	613	83	162	28	5	13	74	.264	44	81	9	113	*392	15	*.971
1990	—St. Louis (N.L.)	3B	121	447	46	103	20	2	6	58	.230	30	58	7	91	248	19	.947
1991	—Atlanta (N.L.)■	3B	153	586	94	*187	34	8	22	86	*.319	43	70	10	108	*349	24	.950
1992	—Atlanta (N.L.)	3B	160	640	98	•199	39	1	21	105	.311	37	67	5	*133	*325	19	.960
1993	—Atlanta (N.L.)	3B	161	633	81	172	33	1	17	84	.272	36	97	5	*128	319	19	.959
Major league totals (10 years)			1401	5292	677	1446	261	34	104	717	.273	368	664	119	1086	3128	185	.958

CHAMPIONSHIP SERIES RECORD

CHAMPIONSHIP SERIES NOTES: Shares record for most at-bats in one inning—2 (October 13, 1985, second inning). . . . Holds N.L. career record for most games—32; and most at-bats—129. . . . Shares N.L. single-series record for most at-bats—30 (both in 1991-92).

Year	Team (League)	Pos.	G	AB	R	H	2B	3B	HR	RBI	Avg.	BB	SO	SB	PO	A	E	Avg.
			BATTING												FIELDING			
1985	—St. Louis (N.L.)	3B	6	24	2	5	1	0	0	4	.208	1	3	0	6	18	1	.960
1987	—St. Louis (N.L.)	3B	6	19	3	4	0	1	0	1	.211	0	6	0	3	11	0	1.000
1991	—Atlanta (N.L.)	3B	7	30	1	5	1	1	0	1	.167	1	3	0	5	11	0	1.000
1992	—Atlanta (N.L.)	3B	7	30	2	7	2	0	0	3	.233	0	2	0	4	18	0	1.000
1993	—Atlanta (N.L.)	3B	6	26	4	9	1	0	1	5	.346	0	2	0	7	5	0	1.000
Championship series totals (5 years)			32	129	12	30	5	2	1	14	.233	2	16	0	25	63	1	.989

WORLD SERIES RECORD

Year	Team (League)	Pos.	G	AB	R	H	2B	3B	HR	RBI	Avg.	BB	SO	SB	PO	A	E	Avg.
			BATTING												FIELDING			
1985	—St. Louis (N.L.)	3B	7	23	3	6	1	1	0	3	.261	3	2	0	6	14	1	.952
1987	—St. Louis (N.L.)	DH-PH	3	7	2	3	0	0	0	1	.429	1	1	2	. . .	. . .	. . .	. . .
1991	—Atlanta (N.L.)	3B	7	30	6	11	3	0	2	3	.367	3	1	0	3	20	2	.920
1992	—Atlanta (N.L.)	3B	6	25	2	6	2	0	0	2	.240	1	5	0	4	19	0	1.000
World Series totals (4 years)			23	85	13	26	6	1	2	9	.306	8	9	2	13	53	3	.957

ALL-STAR GAME RECORD

Year	League	Pos.	AB	R	H	2B	3B	HR	RBI	Avg.	BB	SO	SB	PO	A	E	Avg.
			BATTING											FIELDING			
1992	—National	3B	2	0	1	0	0	0	0	.500	0	0	0	0	2	0	1.000

PENNINGTON, BRAD

P, ORIOLES

PERSONAL: Born April 14, 1969, in Salem, Ind. . . . 6-5/205. . . . Throws left, bats left. . . . Full name: Brad Lee Pennington.
HIGH SCHOOL: Eastern (Pekin, Ind.).
COLLEGE: Bellarmine College (Ky.) and Vincennes (Ind.) University.
TRANSACTIONS/CAREER NOTES: Selected by Baltimore Orioles organization in 12th round of free-agent draft (June 5, 1989).
STATISTICAL NOTES: Tied for Appalachian League lead with 14 wild pitches in 1989.

Year	Team (League)	W	L	Pct.	ERA	G	GS	CG	ShO	Sv.	IP	H	R	ER	BB	SO
1989	—Bluefield (Appal.)	2	•7	.222	6.58	15	14	0	0	0	64⅓	50	58	47	*74	81
1990	—Wausau (Midwest)	4	9	.308	5.18	32	18	1	0	0	106	81	89	61	*121	142
1991	—Frederick (Caro.)	1	4	.200	3.92	36	0	0	0	13	43⅔	32	23	19	44	58
	—Kane Co. (Midw.)	0	2	.000	5.87	23	0	0	0	4	23	16	17	15	25	43
1992	—Frederick (Caro.)	1	0	1.000	2.00	8	0	0	0	2	9	5	3	2	4	16
	—Hagerstown (East.)	1	2	.333	2.54	19	0	0	0	7	28⅓	20	9	8	17	33
	—Rochester (Int'l)	1	3	.250	2.08	29	0	0	0	5	39	12	10	9	33	56
1993	—Rochester (Int'l)	1	2	.333	3.45	17	0	0	0	8	15⅔	12	11	6	13	19
	—Baltimore (A.L.)	3	2	.600	6.55	34	0	0	0	4	33	34	25	24	25	39
Major league totals (1 year)		3	2	.600	6.55	34	0	0	0	4	33	34	25	24	25	39

PENNYFEATHER, WILLIAM

OF, PIRATES

PERSONAL: Born May 25, 1968, in Perth Amboy, N.J. . . . 6-2/215. . . . Throws right, bats right. . . . Full name: William Nathaniel Pennyfeather.
HIGH SCHOOL: Perth Amboy (N.J.).
COLLEGE: Syracuse.
TRANSACTIONS/CAREER NOTES: Signed as free agent by Pittsburgh Pirates organization (July 1, 1988).
STATISTICAL NOTES: Led New York-Pennsylvania League outfielders with 189 total chances in 1989. . . . Led South Atlantic League outfielders with six double plays in 1990. . . . Led American Association outfielders with 318 total chances in 1993.

Year	Team (League)	Pos.	G	AB	R	H	2B	3B	HR	RBI	Avg.	BB	SO	SB	PO	A	E	Avg.
			BATTING												FIELDING			
1988	—GC Pirates (GCL)	OF	17	74	6	18	2	1	1	7	.243	2	18	3	24	0	1	.960
	—Princeton (Appal.)	OF	16	57	11	19	2	0	1	5	.333	6	15	7	19	1	2	.909
1989	—Welland (NYP)	OF	•75	289	34	55	10	1	3	26	.190	12	75	18	*170	6	*13	.931

P

Year	Team (League)	Pos.	G	AB	R	H	2B	3B	HR	RBI	Avg.	BB	SO	SB	PO	A	E	Avg.
			BATTING												FIELDING			
1990	—Augusta (S. Atl.)	OF	122	465	69	122	14	4	4	48	.262	23	85	21	275	16	12	.960
1991	—Salem (Carolina)	OF	81	319	35	85	17	3	8	46	.266	8	52	11	167	12	4	.978
	—Carolina (South.)	OF	42	149	13	41	5	0	0	9	.275	7	17	3	75	4	6	.929
1992	—Buffalo (A.A.)	OF	55	160	19	38	6	2	1	12	.238	2	24	3	92	3	2	.979
	—Carolina (South.)	OF	51	199	28	67	13	1	6	25	.337	9	34	7	79	2	1	.988
	—Pittsburgh (N.L.)	OF	15	9	2	2	0	0	0	0	.222	0	0	0	8	0	0	1.000
1993	—Buffalo (A.A.)	OF	112	457	54	114	18	3	14	41	.249	18	92	10	*293	*21	4	.987
	—Pittsburgh (N.L.)	OF	21	34	4	7	1	0	0	2	.206	0	6	0	21	0	0	1.000
Major league totals (2 years)			36	43	6	9	1	0	0	2	.209	0	6	0	29	0	0	1.000

PERCIVAL, TROY

P, ANGELS

PERSONAL: Born August 9, 1969, in Fontana, Calif.... 6-3/200.... Throws right, bats right.... Full name: Troy Eugene Percival.... Name pronounced PER-sih-vol.
HIGH SCHOOL: Moreno Valley (Calif.).
COLLEGE: UC Riverside.
TRANSACTIONS/CAREER NOTES: Selected by California Angels organization in sixth round of free-agent draft (June 5, 1990).... On Palm Springs disabled list (June 3-July 2, 1992).... On disabled list (May 28, 1993-remainder of season).

Year	Team (League)	W	L	Pct.	ERA	G	GS	CG	ShO	Sv.	IP	H	R	ER	BB	SO
1991	—Boise (Northwest)	2	0	1.000	1.41	28	0	0	0	*12	38⅓	23	7	6	18	63
1992	—Palm Springs (Cal.)	1	1	.500	5.06	11	0	0	0	2	10⅔	6	7	6	8	16
	—Midland (Texas)	3	0	1.000	2.37	20	0	0	0	5	19	18	5	5	11	21
1993	—Vancouver (PCL)	0	1	.000	6.27	18	0	0	0	4	18⅔	24	14	13	13	19

RECORD AS POSITION PLAYER

Year	Team (League)	Pos.	G	AB	R	H	2B	3B	HR	RBI	Avg.	BB	SO	SB	PO	A	E	Avg.
			BATTING												FIELDING			
1990	—Boise (Northwest)	C	29	79	12	16	0	0	0	5	.203	19	25	0	215	25	5	.980

PEREZ, EDUARDO

OF, ANGELS

PERSONAL: Born September 11, 1969, in Cincinnati.... 6-4/215.... Throws right, bats right.... Full name: Eduardo Antanacio Perez.... Son of Tony Perez, current director of international relations, Florida Marlins, major league infielder with four teams (1964-86) and manager, Cincinnati Reds (1993); and brother of Victor Perez, minor league outfielder/first baseman (1990).
HIGH SCHOOL: Robinson (Santurce, Puerto Rico).
COLLEGE: Florida State.
TRANSACTIONS/CAREER NOTES: Selected by California Angels organization in first round (17th pick overall) of free-agent draft (June 3, 1991).... On Palm Springs disabled list (May 9-19, 1992).

Year	Team (League)	Pos.	G	AB	R	H	2B	3B	HR	RBI	Avg.	BB	SO	SB	PO	A	E	Avg.
			BATTING												FIELDING			
1991	—Boise (Northwest)	OF-1B	46	160	35	46	13	0	1	22	.288	19	39	12	87	6	3	.969
1992	—Palm Springs (Cal.)	3B-SS	54	204	37	64	8	4	3	35	.314	23	33	14	30	90	16	.882
	—Midland (Texas)	3B-OF-1B	62	235	27	54	8	1	3	23	.230	22	49	19	53	97	13	.920
1993	—Vancouver (PCL)	3B-1B-OF	96	363	66	111	23	6	12	70	.306	28	83	21	98	174	23	.922
	—California (A.L.)	3B	52	180	16	45	6	2	4	30	.250	9	39	5	24	101	5	.962
Major league totals (1 year)			52	180	16	45	6	2	4	30	.250	9	39	5	24	101	5	.962

PEREZ, MELIDO

P, YANKEES

PERSONAL: Born February 15, 1966, in Costa Verde, Dominican Republic.... 6-4/210.... Throws right, bats right.... Brother of Pascual Perez, pitcher, New York Yankees; brother of Vladimir Perez, pitcher, Kansas City Royals organization; brother of Dario Perez, pitcher, Royals organization; brother of Carlos Perez, pitcher, Montreal Expos organization; and brother of Valerio Perez, minor league pitcher (1983-84).
HIGH SCHOOL: San Gregorio de Nigua (San Cristobal, Dominican Republic).
TRANSACTIONS/CAREER NOTES: Signed as free agent by Kansas City Royals organization (July 22, 1983).... Traded by Royals with P John Davis, P Chuck Mount and P Greg Hibbard to Chicago White Sox for P Floyd Bannister and IF Dave Cochrane (December 10, 1987).... Traded by White Sox with P Robert Wickman and P Domingo Jean to New York Yankees for 2B Steve Sax and cash (January 10, 1992).... On disabled list (April 1-18, 1993).
STATISTICAL NOTES: Tied for Northwest League lead with 13 home runs allowed and two balks in 1985.... Pitched six-inning, 8-0 no-hit victory against New York (July 12, 1990).

Year	Team (League)	W	L	Pct.	ERA	G	GS	CG	ShO	Sv.	IP	H	R	ER	BB	SO
1984	—Char., S.C. (S. Atl.)	5	7	.417	4.35	16	15	0	0	0	89	99	52	43	19	55
1985	—Eugene (N'west)	6	7	.462	5.44	17	•15	2	0	0	101	116	65	*61	35	88
1986	—Burlington (Midw.)	10	12	.455	3.70	28	23	*13	1	0	170⅓	148	83	70	49	153
1987	—Fort Myers (FSL)	4	3	.571	2.38	8	8	5	1	0	64⅓	51	20	17	7	51
	—Memphis (South.)	8	5	.615	3.43	20	20	5	2	0	133⅔	125	60	51	20	126
	—Kansas City (A.L.)	1	1	.500	7.84	3	3	0	0	0	10⅓	18	12	9	5	5
1988	—Chicago (A.L.)■	12	10	.545	3.79	32	32	3	1	0	197	186	105	83	72	138
1989	—Chicago (A.L.)	11	14	.440	5.01	31	31	2	0	0	183⅓	187	106	102	90	141
1990	—Chicago (A.L.)	13	14	.481	4.61	35	35	3	3	0	197	177	111	101	86	161
1991	—Chicago (A.L.)	8	7	.533	3.12	49	8	0	0	1	135⅔	111	49	47	52	128
1992	—New York (A.L.)■	13	16	.448	2.87	33	33	10	1	0	247⅔	212	94	79	93	218
1993	—New York (A.L.)	6	14	.300	5.19	25	25	0	0	0	163	173	103	94	64	148
Major league totals (7 years)		64	76	.457	4.09	208	167	18	5	1	1134	1064	580	515	462	939

P

PEREZ, MIKE

P, CARDINALS

PERSONAL: Born October 19, 1964, in Yauco, Puerto Rico. . . . 6-0/187. . . . Throws right, bats right. . . . Full name: Michael Irvin Perez.
HIGH SCHOOL: Yauco (Puerto Rico).
COLLEGE: San Jose (Calif.) City College and Troy State (Ala.).
TRANSACTIONS/CAREER NOTES: Selected by St. Louis Cardinals organization in 12th round of free-agent draft (June 2, 1986). . . . On Louisville disabled list (July 25-August 6, 1991). . . . On St. Louis disabled list (July 6-August 15, 1993); included rehabilitation assignment to Arkansas (August 7-15).

Year	Team (League)	W	L	Pct.	ERA	G	GS	CG	ShO	Sv.	IP	H	R	ER	BB	SO
1986	—Johns. City (App.)	3	5	.375	2.97	18	8	2	0	3	72⅔	69	35	24	22	72
1987	—Springfield (Midw.)	6	2	.750	0.85	58	0	0	0	*41	84⅓	47	12	8	21	119
1988	—Arkansas (Texas)	1	3	.250	11.30	11	0	0	0	0	14⅓	18	18	18	13	17
	—St. Peters. (FSL)	2	2	.500	2.08	35	0	0	0	17	43⅓	24	12	10	16	45
1989	—Arkansas (Texas)	4	6	.400	3.64	57	0	0	0	*33	76⅔	68	34	31	32	74
1990	—Louisville (A.A.)	7	7	.500	4.28	•57	0	0	0	*31	67⅓	64	34	32	33	69
	—St. Louis (N.L.)	1	0	1.000	3.95	13	0	0	0	1	13⅔	12	6	6	3	5
1991	—St. Louis (N.L.)	0	2	.000	5.82	14	0	0	0	0	17	19	11	11	7	7
	—Louisville (A.A.)	3	5	.375	6.13	37	0	0	0	4	47	54	38	32	25	39
1992	—St. Louis (N.L.)	9	3	.750	1.84	77	0	0	0	0	93	70	23	19	32	46
1993	—St. Louis (N.L.)	7	2	.778	2.48	65	0	0	0	7	72⅔	65	24	20	20	58
	—Arkansas (Texas)	0	0	...	7.36	4	0	0	0	0	3⅔	7	3	3	0	4
Major league totals (4 years)		17	7	.708	2.57	169	0	0	0	8	196⅓	166	64	56	62	116

PEREZ, ROBERT

OF, BLUE JAYS

PERSONAL: Born June 4, 1969, in Bolivar, Venezuela. . . . 6-3/205. . . . Throws right, bats right. . . . Full name: Robert Alexander Jimenez Perez.
HIGH SCHOOL: Raul Leoni Otero (Bolivar, Venezuela).
TRANSACTIONS/CAREER NOTES: Signed as free agent by Toronto Blue Jays organization (May 1, 1989).
STATISTICAL NOTES: Tied for International League lead in grounding into double plays with 19 in 1993. . . . Led International League outfielders with 303 total chances in 1993.

			BATTING												FIELDING			
Year	Team (League)	Pos.	G	AB	R	H	2B	3B	HR	RBI	Avg.	BB	SO	SB	PO	A	E	Avg.
1989	—Santo Dom. (DSL)	OF	52	219	34	*79	*20	3	5	40	.361	21	23	5	...	...	...	...
1990	—St. Cathar. (NYP)	OF	52	207	21	54	10	2	5	25	.261	8	34	7	80	5	1	.988
	—Myrtle Beach (SAL)	OF	21	72	8	21	2	0	1	10	.292	3	9	2	40	1	1	.976
1991	—Dunedin (Fla. St.)	OF	127	480	50	*145	28	6	4	50	*.302	22	72	8	160	10	5	.971
	—Syracuse (Int'l)	OF	4	20	2	4	1	0	0	1	.200	0	2	0	5	0	1	.833
1992	—Knoxville (South.)	OF	*139	•526	59	137	25	5	9	59	.260	13	87	11	241	13	7	.973
1993	—Syracuse (Int'l)	OF	138	524	72	154	26	10	12	64	.294	24	65	13	278	•13	*12	.960

PERRY, GERALD

1B, CARDINALS

PERSONAL: Born October 30, 1960, in Savannah, Ga. . . . 6-0/201. . . . Throws right, bats left. . . . Full name: Gerald June Perry. . . . Nephew of Dan Driessen, major league first baseman with five teams (1973-87).
HIGH SCHOOL: H.E. McCracken (Buffton, N.C.).
TRANSACTIONS/CAREER NOTES: Selected by Atlanta Braves organization in 11th round of free-agent draft (June 6, 1978). . . . On disabled list (June 19-July 4, 1988; June 6-21 and July 10, 1989-remainder of season). . . . Traded by Braves with P Jim LeMasters to Kansas City Royals for P Charlie Leibrandt and P Rick Luecken (December 15, 1989). . . . Granted free agency (November 5, 1990). . . . Signed by St. Louis Cardinals (December 13, 1990). . . . Granted free agency (October 25, 1993). . . . Re-signed by Cardinals (December 21, 1993).
STATISTICAL NOTES: Led Gulf Coast League first basemen with 46 double plays in 1978. . . . Led Carolina League first basemen with 109 double plays in 1980.

			BATTING												FIELDING			
Year	Team (League)	Pos.	G	AB	R	H	2B	3B	HR	RBI	Avg.	BB	SO	SB	PO	A	E	Avg.
1978	—GC Braves (GCL)	1B	*55	191	32	51	*12	3	1	26	.267	23	23	7	*479	*37	6	*.989
1979	—Greenw. (W. Car.)	1B	109	400	69	133	17	4	9	71	*.333	56	63	35	881	59	19	.980
1980	—Durham (Carolina)	1B	138	497	102	124	19	5	15	92	.249	94	77	37	*1296	93	16	.989
1981	—Savannah (South.)	1B	137	476	71	132	18	3	19	84	.277	69	95	22	1221	86	18	.986
1982	—Richmond (Int'l)	1B	133	492	94	146	22	4	15	92	.297	91	79	39	1110	94	•17	.986
1983	—Richmond (Int'l)	1B	113	423	81	133	21	8	13	71	.314	73	55	26	943	88	11	.989
	—Atlanta (N.L.)	1B-OF	27	39	5	14	2	0	1	6	.359	5	4	0	55	0	1	.982
1984	—Atlanta (N.L.)	1B-OF	122	347	52	92	12	2	7	47	.265	61	38	15	550	28	12	.980
1985	—Atlanta (N.L.)	1B-OF	110	238	22	51	5	0	3	13	.214	23	28	9	541	37	9	.985
1986	—Richmond (Int'l)	OF-1B	107	384	69	125	30	5	10	75	.326	58	41	11	394	25	7	.984
	—Atlanta (N.L.)	OF-1B	29	70	6	19	2	0	2	11	.271	8	4	0	24	1	2	.926
1987	—Atlanta (N.L.)	1B-OF	142	533	77	144	35	2	12	74	.270	48	63	42	1297	72	14	.990
1988	—Atlanta (N.L.)	1B	141	547	61	164	29	1	8	74	.300	36	49	29	1282	106	•17	.988
1989	—Atlanta (N.L.)	1B	72	266	24	67	11	0	4	21	.252	32	28	10	618	51	9	.987
1990	—Kansas City (A.L.)■	1B	133	465	57	118	22	2	8	57	.254	39	56	17	394	40	6	.986
1991	—St. Louis (N.L.)■	1B-OF	109	242	29	58	8	4	6	36	.240	22	34	15	413	29	5	.989
1992	—St. Louis (N.L.)	1B	87	143	13	34	8	0	1	18	.238	15	23	3	221	11	3	.987
1993	—St. Louis (N.L.)	1B-OF	96	98	21	33	5	0	4	16	.337	18	23	1	79	3	2	.976
American League totals (1 year)			133	465	57	118	22	2	8	57	.254	39	56	17	394	40	6	.986
National League totals (10 years)			935	2523	310	676	117	9	48	316	.268	268	294	124	5080	338	74	.987
Major league totals (11 years)			1068	2988	367	794	139	11	56	373	.266	307	350	141	5474	378	80	.987

PERRY, HERBERT

1B/3B, INDIANS

PERSONAL: Born September 15, 1969, in Mayo, Fla. . . . 6-2/210. . . . Throws right, bats right. . . . Full name: Herbert Edward Perry Jr.
HIGH SCHOOL: Lafayette (Mayo, Fla.).
COLLEGE: Florida.

P

TRANSACTIONS/CAREER NOTES: Selected by Cleveland Indians organization in second round of free-agent draft (June 3, 1991). ... On disabled list (June 18-July 13, 1991 and July 23, 1993-remainder of season).
STATISTICAL NOTES: Led Eastern League in being hit by pitch with 15 in 1993.

			BATTING											FIELDING			
Year	Team (League)	Pos.	G	AB	R	H	2B	3B	HR	RBI	Avg.	BB	SO	SB	PO	A	E	Avg.
1991	—Watertown (NYP).....	DH	14	52	3	11	2	0	0	5	.212	8	7	0	...	...	...	...
1992	—Kinston (Carolina) ...	1B-OF-3B	121	449	74	125	16	1	19	77	.278	46	89	12	297	39	5	.985
1993	—Cant./Akr. (East.)....	1B-3B-OF	89	327	52	88	21	1	9	55	.269	37	47	7	378	86	10	.979

PETAGINE, ROBERTO

1B, ASTROS

PERSONAL: Born June 7, 1971, in Nueva Esparita, Venezuela. ... 6-1/172. ... Throws left, bats left. ... Full name: Roberto Antonio Petagine. ... Name pronounced PET-uh-GHEEN.
TRANSACTIONS/CAREER NOTES: Signed as free agent by Houston Astros organization (February 13, 1990).
HONORS: Named Texas League Player of the Year (1993).
STATISTICAL NOTES: Led Gulf Coast League first basemen with .990 fielding percentage and 46 double plays in 1990. ... Led Texas League with .442 on-base percentage and 14 intentional bases on balls received in 1993.

			BATTING											FIELDING			
Year	Team (League)	Pos.	G	AB	R	H	2B	3B	HR	RBI	Avg.	BB	SO	SB	PO	A	E	Avg.
1990	—GC Astros (GCL).......	1B-OF	55	187	35	54	5	4	2	24	.289	26	23	9	474	36	5	†.990
1991	—Burlington (Midw.)...	1B	124	432	72	112	24	1	12	58	.259	71	74	7	940	60	22	.978
1992	—Osceola (Fla. St.)......	1B	86	307	52	90	22	4	7	49	.293	47	47	3	701	74	10	.987
	—Jackson (Texas)......	1B	21	70	8	21	4	0	4	12	.300	6	15	1	151	15	0	1.000
1993	—Jackson (Texas)......	1B	128	437	73	146	*36	2	15	90	*.334	*84	89	6	1033	*110	14	.988

PETKOVSEK, MARK

P

PERSONAL: Born November 18, 1965, in Beaumont, Tex. ... 6-0/185. ... Throws right, bats right. ... Full name: Mark Joseph Petkovsek. ... Name pronounced PET-kie-zeck.
HIGH SCHOOL: Kelly (Beaumont, Tex.).
COLLEGE: Texas.
TRANSACTIONS/CAREER NOTES: Selected by Texas Rangers organization in supplemental round ("sandwich pick" between first and second round, 29th pick overall) of free-agent draft (June 2, 1987); pick received as compensation for New York Yankees signing Type A free agent Gary Ward. ... Granted free agency (October 16, 1991). ... Signed by Pittsburgh Pirates organization (January 22, 1992). ... Granted free agency (October 15, 1992). ... Re-signed by Pirates organization (November 9, 1992). ... On Buffalo disabled list (July 4-23, 1993). ... Granted free agency (October 12, 1993).

Year	Team (League)	W	L	Pct.	ERA	G	GS	CG	ShO	Sv.	IP	H	R	ER	BB	SO
1987	—GC Rangers (GCL)......	0	0	...	3.18	3	1	0	0	0	5⅔	4	2	2	2	7
	—Charlotte (Fla. St.).....	3	4	.429	4.02	11	10	0	0	0	56	67	36	25	17	23
1988	—Charlotte (Fla. St.).....	10	11	.476	2.97	28	28	7	•5	0	175⅔	156	71	58	42	95
1989	—Tulsa (Texas)...........	8	5	.615	3.47	21	21	1	0	0	140	144	63	54	35	66
	—Okla. City (A.A.).........	0	4	.000	7.34	6	6	0	0	0	30⅔	39	27	25	18	8
1990	—Okla. City (A.A.).........	7	*14	.333	5.25	28	28	2	1	0	151	*187	*103	88	42	81
1991	—Okla. City (A.A.).........	9	8	.529	4.93	25	24	3	1	0	149⅔	162	89	82	38	67
	—Texas (A.L.)............	0	1	.000	14.46	4	1	0	0	0	9⅓	21	16	15	4	6
1992	—Buffalo (A.A.)■..........	8	8	.500	3.53	32	22	1	0	1	150⅓	150	76	59	44	49
1993	—Buffalo (A.A.)............	3	4	.429	4.33	14	11	1	0	0	70⅔	74	38	34	16	27
	—Pittsburgh (N.L.).......	3	0	1.000	6.96	26	0	0	0	0	32⅓	43	25	25	9	14
A.L. totals (1 year)		0	1	.000	14.46	4	1	0	0	0	9⅓	21	16	15	4	6
N.L. totals (1 year)		3	0	1.000	6.96	26	0	0	0	0	32⅓	43	25	25	9	14
Major league totals (2 years)		3	1	.750	8.64	30	1	0	0	0	41⅔	64	41	40	13	20

PETRALLI, GENO

C

PERSONAL: Born September 25, 1959, in Sacramento, Calif. ... 6-1/190. ... Throws right, bats both. ... Full name: Eugene James Petralli Jr. ... Son of Gene Petralli, minor league first baseman (1948-51 and 1953). ... Name pronounced puh-TRA-lee.
HIGH SCHOOL: John F. Kennedy (Sacramento, Calif.).
COLLEGE: Sacramento (Calif.) City College.
TRANSACTIONS/CAREER NOTES: Selected by Toronto Blue Jays organization in third round of free-agent draft (January 10, 1978). ... On Dunedin suspended list (April 13-27, 1979). ... On disabled list (May 6-June 1 and June 28-August 18, 1981). ... Contract sold by Blue Jays to Maine, Cleveland Indians organization (May 8, 1984). ... On Maine disabled list (July 11, 1984-remainder of season). ... Released by Indians organization (April 23, 1985). ... Signed by Oklahoma City, Texas Rangers organization (May 17, 1985). ... On Texas disabled list (May 27-June 11, 1989). ... On Texas disabled list (June 27-August 19, 1989); included rehabilitation assignment to Tulsa (August 14-19). ... On Texas disabled list (June 19-July 29, 1991); included rehabilitation assignment to Oklahoma City (July 25-29). ... Granted free agency (October 30, 1991). ... Re-signed by Rangers (December 7, 1991). ... On Texas disabled list (March 27-May 14, 1993); included rehabilitation assignment to Oklahoma City (May 7-14). ... Granted free agency (October 29, 1993).
RECORDS: Holds modern major league single-season record for most passed balls—35 (1987). ... Shares modern major league single-game record for most passed balls—6 (August 30, 1987). ... Shares modern major league record for most passed balls in one inning—4 (August 22, 1987, seventh inning).
STATISTICAL NOTES: Tied for Pioneer League lead with 27 passed balls in 1978. ... Led International League catchers with 633 putouts, 86 assists, 19 errors, 738 total chances and 10 double plays in 1982. ... Led A.L. with 35 passed balls in 1987 and 20 in both 1988 and 1990.
MISCELLANEOUS: Batted as switch-hitter (1978-84 and 1986-87). ... Batted as lefthanded hitter (Maine, Oklahoma City, 1985) and switch-hitter (Texas, 1985). ... Batted as lefthanded hitter (1988-91). ... Batted as both lefthanded hitter and switch-hitter (1992).

Year	Team (League)	Pos.	G	AB	R	H	2B	3B	HR	RBI	Avg.	BB	SO	SB	PO	A	E	Avg.
			BATTING												FIELDING			
1978	—Medicine Hat (Pio.) ..	C-3B	65	242	42	68	14	5	2	40	.281	38	22	4	238	68	19	.942
1979	—Dunedin (Fla. St.)	C-3B-OF	52	184	18	53	13	0	1	24	.288	12	20	1	206	42	5	.980
	—Syracuse (Int'l)	C	18	56	6	13	0	1	0	7	.232	2	11	0	67	12	1	.988
1980	—Knoxville (South.)	C-1B-OF	116	382	42	109	20	2	3	38	.285	54	30	0	569	82	18	.973
1981	—Syracuse (Int'l)	C	45	151	17	40	11	0	0	16	.265	16	11	1	188	30	6	.973
1982	—Syracuse (Int'l)	C-1B-3B	126	395	57	114	19	3	9	58	.289	73	54	2	†674	†89	†20	.974
	—Toronto (A.L.)	C-3B	16	44	3	16	2	0	0	1	.364	4	6	0	51	4	1	.982
1983	—Syracuse (Int'l)	C-1B	104	327	39	80	9	2	3	40	.245	54	37	0	541	68	7	.989
	—Toronto (A.L.)	C	6	4	0	0	0	0	0	0	.000	1	1	0	7	0	0	1.000
1984	—Toronto (A.L.)	C	3	3	0	0	0	0	0	0	.000	0	0	0	1	1	0	1.000
	—Maine (Int'l)■	C-OF-1B	23	83	9	18	3	0	0	5	.217	13	10	0	122	11	6	.957
1985	—Maine (Int'l)	C	2	7	0	1	0	0	0	1	.143	0	0	0	12	1	1	.929
	—Okla. City (A.A.)■	C	27	80	11	21	8	0	1	5	.263	10	9	0	108	14	3	.976
	—Texas (A.L.)	C	42	100	7	27	2	0	0	11	.270	8	12	1	179	16	2	.990
1986	—Texas (A.L.)	C-3B-2B	69	137	17	35	9	3	2	18	.255	5	14	3	163	14	4	.978
1987	—Texas (A.L.)	C-3-1-2-0	101	202	28	61	11	2	7	31	.302	27	29	0	370	34	5	.988
1988	—Texas (A.L.)	C-3-1-2	129	351	35	99	14	2	7	36	.282	41	52	0	421	54	10	.979
1989	—Texas (A.L.)	C	70	184	18	56	7	0	4	23	.304	17	24	0	258	15	3	.989
	—Tulsa (Texas)	C	5	13	2	3	0	0	1	1	.231	2	2	0	6	1	0	1.000
1990	—Texas (A.L.)	C-3B-2B	133	325	28	83	13	1	0	21	.255	50	49	0	602	46	6	.991
1991	—Texas (A.L.)	C-3B	87	199	21	54	8	1	2	20	.271	21	25	2	294	25	11	.967
	—Okla. City (A.A.)	C	4	15	1	4	1	0	0	2	.267	2	1	0	13	1	0	1.000
1992	—Texas (A.L.)	C-3B-2B	94	192	11	38	12	0	1	18	.198	20	34	0	264	24	4	.986
1993	—Okla. City (A.A.)	C	6	20	2	4	1	0	1	1	.200	3	3	0	5	1	1	.857
	—Texas (A.L.)	C-3B-2B	59	133	16	32	5	0	1	13	.241	22	17	2	179	11	2	.990
Major league totals (12 years)			809	1874	184	501	83	9	24	192	.267	216	263	8	2789	244	48	.984

PHILLIPS, J.R.

1B, GIANTS

PERSONAL: Born April 29, 1970, in West Covina, Calif. . . . 6-1/185. . . . Throws left, bats left. . . . Full name: Charles Gene Phillips.

HIGH SCHOOL: Bishop Amat (La Puente, Calif.).

TRANSACTIONS/CAREER NOTES: Selected by California Angels organization in fourth round of free-agent draft (June 1, 1988). . . . Claimed on waivers by San Francisco Giants (December 17, 1992).

STATISTICAL NOTES: Led Northwest League first basemen with 641 putouts, 42 assists and 691 total chances in 1990. . . . Led California League first basemen with 1,166 putouts, 1,272 total chances and 117 double plays in 1991. . . . Led Texas League first basemen with 1,222 putouts, 100 assists, 17 errors, 1,339 total chances and 106 double plays in 1992. . . . Led Pacific Coast League first basemen with 1,135 putouts, 93 assists, 28 errors and 1,256 total chances in 1993.

Year	Team (League)	Pos.	G	AB	R	H	2B	3B	HR	RBI	Avg.	BB	SO	SB	PO	A	E	Avg.
			BATTING												FIELDING			
1988	—Bend (Northwest)	OF-1B	56	210	24	40	8	0	4	23	.190	21	70	3	197	9	3	.986
1989	—Quad City (Midw.)	1B-OF	125	442	41	85	29	1	8	50	.192	49	146	3	954	46	20	.980
1990	—Palm Springs (Cal.) ..	1B	46	162	14	32	4	1	1	15	.198	10	58	3	436	26	16	.967
	—Boise (Northwest)	1B-OF	70	237	30	46	6	0	10	34	.194	19	78	1	†642	†42	8	.988
1991	—Palm Springs (Cal.) ..	1B-P	130	471	64	117	22	2	20	70	.248	57	*144	15	†1166	94	12	.991
1992	—Midland (Texas)	1B-OF	127	497	58	118	32	4	14	77	.237	32	*165	5	†1223	†100	†17	.987
1993	—Phoenix (PCL)■	1B-OF	134	506	80	133	35	2	*27	94	.263	53	127	7	†1138	†93	†29	.977
	—San Francisco (N.L.) ..	1B	11	16	1	5	1	1	1	4	.313	0	5	0	32	2	1	.971
Major league totals (1 year)			11	16	1	5	1	1	1	4	.313	0	5	0	32	2	1	.971

RECORD AS PITCHER

Year	Team (League)	W	L	Pct.	ERA	G	GS	CG	ShO	Sv.	IP	H	R	ER	BB	SO
1991	—Palm Springs (Cal.)	0	0	...	4.50	2	0	0	0	0	2	3	1	1	2	3

PHILLIPS, TONY

OF/2B, TIGERS

PERSONAL: Born April 25, 1959, in Atlanta. . . . 5-10/175. . . . Throws right, bats both. . . . Full name: Keith Anthony Phillips.

HIGH SCHOOL: Roswell (Ga.).

COLLEGE: New Mexico Military Institute.

TRANSACTIONS/CAREER NOTES: Selected by Seattle Mariners organization in 16th round of free-agent draft (June 7, 1977). . . . Selected by Montreal Expos organization in secondary phase of free-agent draft (January 10, 1978). . . . On West Palm Beach temporary inactive list (April 11-May 4, 1978). . . . Traded by Expos organization with cash to San Diego Padres for 1B Willie Montanez (August 31, 1980). . . . Traded by Padres organization with P Eric Mustad and IF Kevin Bell to Oakland Athletics organization for P Bob Lacey and P Roy Moretti (March 27, 1981). . . . On Oakland disabled list (March 26-August 22, 1985); included rehabilitation assignment to Tacoma (July 30-August 5 and August 7-20). . . . On disabled list (August 14-October 3, 1986). . . . On Oakland disabled list (July 12-August 28, 1987); included rehabilitation assignment to Tacoma (August 20-28). . . . Released by A's (December 21, 1987). . . . Re-signed by A's (March 9, 1988). . . . On Oakland disabled list (May 18-July 8, 1988); included rehabilitation assignment to Tacoma (June 16-July 4). . . . Granted free agency (November 13, 1989). . . . Signed by Detroit Tigers (December 5, 1989).

RECORDS: Shares major league single-game record (nine innings) for most assists by second baseman—12 (July 6, 1986).

STATISTICAL NOTES: Led Southern League shortstops with 42 errors in 1980. . . . Led Eastern League in being hit by pitch with 10 in 1981. . . . Hit for the cycle (May 16, 1986).

Year	Team (League)	Pos.	G	AB	R	H	2B	3B	HR	RBI	Avg.	BB	SO	SB	PO	A	E	Avg.
			BATTING												FIELDING			
1978	—W.P. Beach (FSL)	3B-SS-2B	32	54	8	9	0	0	0	3	.167	9	7	2	13	33	5	.902
	—Jamestown (NYP)	SS-2B-3B	52	152	24	29	5	2	1	17	.191	27	24	3	73	146	16	.932
1979	—W.P. Beach (FSL)	2B-SS	60	203	30	47	5	1	0	18	.232	36	26	7	120	156	21	.929
	—Memphis (South.)	SS-2B	52	156	31	44	4	2	3	11	.282	19	13	3	68	134	18	.918

			BATTING											FIELDING			
Year Team (League)	Pos.	G	AB	R	H	2B	3B	HR	RBI	Avg.	BB	SO	SB	PO	A	E	Avg.
1980 —Memphis (South.)	SS-2B	136	502	100	125	18	4	5	41	.249	*98	89	50	226	408	†42	.938
1981 —West Haven (East.)■	SS	131	461	79	114	25	3	9	64	.247	67	69	40	200	391	*33	.947
—Tacoma (PCL)	2B-SS	4	11	1	4	1	0	0	2	.364	0	0	0	8	10	0	1.000
1982 —Tacoma (PCL)	SS	86	300	76	89	18	5	4	47	.297	73	63	29	138	236	30	.926
—Oakland (A.L.)	SS	40	81	11	17	2	2	0	8	.210	12	26	2	46	95	7	.953
1983 —Oakland (A.L.)	SS-2B-3B	148	412	54	102	12	3	4	35	.248	48	69	16	218	383	30	.952
1984 —Oakland (A.L.)	SS-2B-OF	154	451	62	120	24	3	4	37	.266	42	86	10	255	391	28	.958
1985 —Tacoma (PCL)	3B-2B	20	69	9	9	1	0	0	5	.130	8	28	3	15	36	4	.927
—Oakland (A.L.)	3B-2B	42	161	23	45	12	2	4	17	.280	13	34	3	54	103	3	.981
1986 —Oakland (A.L.)	2-3-0-S	118	441	76	113	14	5	5	52	.256	76	82	15	191	326	13	.975
1987 —Oakland (A.L.)	2-3-S-0	111	379	48	91	20	0	10	46	.240	57	76	7	179	299	14	.972
—Tacoma (PCL)	2B-3B	7	26	5	9	2	1	1	6	.346	4	3	1	8	10	0	1.000
1988 —Tacoma (PCL)	S-0-2-3	16	59	10	16	0	0	2	8	.271	12	13	0	25	27	2	.963
—Oakland (A.L.)	3-0-2-S-1	79	212	32	43	8	4	2	17	.203	36	50	0	84	80	10	.943
1989 —Oakland (A.L.)	2-3-S-0-1	143	451	48	118	15	6	4	47	.262	58	66	3	184	321	15	.971
1990 —Detroit (A.L.)■	3-2-S-0	152	573	97	144	23	5	8	55	.251	99	85	19	180	368	23	.960
1991 —Detroit (A.L.)	0-3-2-S	146	564	87	160	28	4	17	72	.284	79	95	10	269	237	8	.984
1992 —Detroit (A.L.)	0-2-3-S	159	606	*114	167	32	3	10	64	.276	114	93	12	301	195	11	.978
1993 —Detroit (A.L.)	OF-2B-3B	151	566	113	177	27	0	7	57	.313	*132	102	16	321	165	13	.974
Major league totals (12 years)		1443	4897	765	1297	217	37	75	507	.265	766	864	113	2282	2963	175	.968

CHAMPIONSHIP SERIES RECORD

			BATTING											FIELDING			
Year Team (League)	Pos.	G	AB	R	H	2B	3B	HR	RBI	Avg.	BB	SO	SB	PO	A	E	Avg.
1988 —Oakland (A.L.)	OF-2B	2	7	0	2	1	0	0	0	.286	1	3	0	10	0	0	1.000
1989 —Oakland (A.L.)	2B-3B	5	18	1	3	1	0	0	1	.167	2	4	2	4	14	0	1.000
Championship series totals (2 years)		7	25	1	5	2	0	0	1	.200	3	7	2	14	14	0	1.000

WORLD SERIES RECORD

			BATTING											FIELDING			
Year Team (League)	Pos.	G	AB	R	H	2B	3B	HR	RBI	Avg.	BB	SO	SB	PO	A	E	Avg.
1988 —Oakland (A.L.)	OF-2B	2	4	1	1	0	0	0	0	.250	1	2	2	3	5	0	1.000
1989 —Oakland (A.L.)	2B-3B-OF	4	17	2	4	1	0	1	3	.235	0	3	0	8	15	0	1.000
World Series totals (2 years)		6	21	3	5	1	0	1	3	.238	1	5	2	11	20	0	1.000

PIAZZA, MIKE

C, DODGERS

PERSONAL: Born September 4, 1968, in Norristown, Pa.... 6-3/197.... Throws right, bats right.... Full name: Michael Joseph Piazza.... Name pronounced pee-AH-za.
HIGH SCHOOL: Phoenixville (Pa.) Area.
COLLEGE: Miami-Dade (North) Community College.
TRANSACTIONS/CAREER NOTES: Selected by Los Angeles Dodgers organization in 62nd round of free-agent draft (June 1, 1988).
HONORS: Named N.L. Rookie Player of the Year by THE SPORTING NEWS (1993).... Named catcher on THE SPORTING NEWS N.L. All-Star team (1993).... Named catcher on THE SPORTING NEWS N.L. Silver Slugger team (1993).... Named N.L. Rookie of the Year by Baseball Writers' Association of America (1993).
STATISTICAL NOTES: Led California League in slugging percentage with .540 and in grounding into double plays with 19 in 1991.... Led N.L. catchers with 98 assists and tied for lead with 11 errors in 1993.

			BATTING											FIELDING			
Year Team (League)	Pos.	G	AB	R	H	2B	3B	HR	RBI	Avg.	BB	SO	SB	PO	A	E	Avg.
1989 —Salem (Northwest) ...	C	57	198	22	53	11	0	8	25	.268	13	51	0	230	21	6	.977
1990 —Vero Beach (FSL)	C-1B	88	272	27	68	20	0	6	45	.250	11	68	0	428	38	16	.967
1991 —Bakersfield (Calif.) ...	C-1B	117	448	71	124	27	2	29	80	.277	47	83	0	723	69	15	.981
1992 —San Antonio (Tex.) ...	C	31	114	18	43	11	0	7	21	.377	13	18	0	189	22	4	.981
—Albuquerque (PCL) ..	C-1B	94	358	54	122	22	5	16	69	.341	37	57	1	550	50	9	.985
—Los Angeles (N.L.) ...	C	21	69	5	16	3	0	1	7	.232	4	12	0	94	7	1	.990
1993 —Los Angeles (N.L.) ...	C-1B	149	547	81	174	24	2	35	112	.318	46	86	3	901	†98	‡11	.989
Major league totals (2 years)		170	616	86	190	27	2	36	119	.308	50	98	3	995	105	12	.989

ALL-STAR GAME RECORD

		BATTING											FIELDING			
Year League	Pos.	AB	R	H	2B	3B	HR	RBI	Avg.	BB	SO	SB	PO	A	E	Avg.
1993 —National	C	1	0	0	0	0	0	0	.000	0	1	0	3	0	0	1.000

PICHARDO, HIPOLITO

P, ROYALS

PERSONAL: Born August 22, 1969, in Jicome Esperanza, Dominican Republic.... 6-1/185.... Throws right, bats right.... Full name: Hipolito Antonio Pichardo.... Name pronounced ee-POL-uh-toe puh-CHAR-doh.
HIGH SCHOOL: Liceo Enriguillo (Jicome Esperanza, Dominican Republic).
TRANSACTIONS/CAREER NOTES: Signed as a free agent by Kansas City Royals organization (December 16, 1987).... On disabled list (August 14-September 1, 1993).

Year Team (League)	W	L	Pct.	ERA	G	GS	CG	ShO	Sv.	IP	H	R	ER	BB	SO
1988 —GC Royals (GCL)	0	0	...	13.50	1	0	0	0	0	1⅓	3	2	2	1	3
1989 —Appleton (Midw.)	5	4	.556	2.97	12	12	2	0	0	75⅔	58	29	25	18	50
1990 —Baseball City (FSL)	1	6	.143	3.80	11	10	0	0	0	45	47	28	19	25	40
1991 —Memphis (South.)	3	11	.214	4.27	34	11	0	0	0	99	116	56	47	38	75
1992 —Memphis (South.)	0	0	...	0.64	2	2	0	0	0	14	13	2	1	1	10
—Kansas City (A.L.)	9	6	.600	3.95	31	24	1	1	0	143⅔	148	71	63	49	59

P

Year	Team (League)	W	L	Pct.	ERA	G	GS	CG	ShO	Sv.	IP	H	R	ER	BB	SO
1993	—Kansas City (A.L.)	7	8	.467	4.04	30	25	2	0	0	165	183	85	74	53	70
Major league totals (2 years)..		16	14	.533	3.99	61	49	3	1	0	308⅔	331	156	137	102	129

PIERCE, JEFF

P, REDS

PERSONAL: Born June 7, 1969, in Rhinebeck, N.Y.... 6-1/200.... Throws right, bats right.... Full name: Jeffrey Charles Pierce.
HIGH SCHOOL: F.D. Roosevelt (Hyde Park, N.Y.).
COLLEGE: Dutchess Community College (N.Y.) and North Carolina State.
TRANSACTIONS/CAREER NOTES: Signed as free agent by Chicago White Sox organization (June 10, 1991).... On Birmingham disabled list (June 20-July 9, 1993).... Traded by White Sox with P Johnny Ruffin to Cincinnati Reds for P Tim Belcher (July 31, 1993).

Year	Team (League)	W	L	Pct.	ERA	G	GS	CG	ShO	Sv.	IP	H	R	ER	BB	SO
1992	—South Bend (Mid.)......	3	5	.375	2.07	52	0	0	0	30	69⅔	46	22	16	18	88
	—Sarasota (Fla. St.).....	0	0	...	0.00	1	0	0	0	0	⅔	0	0	0	0	1
1993	—Birm.-Chatt. (Sou.)■....	3	4	.429	2.60	46	0	0	0	22	69⅓	51	22	20	16	67

RECORD AS POSITION PLAYER

			BATTING											FIELDING			
Year	Team (League)	Pos.	G	AB	R	H	2B	3B	HR	RBI	Avg.	BB	SO	SB	PO	A	E	Avg.
1991	—Utica (N.Y.-Penn)....	OF	50	158	22	38	10	4	0	24	.241	25	26	4	46	0	3	.939

PIRKL, GREG

1B, MARINERS

PERSONAL: Born August 7, 1970, in Long Beach, Calif.... 6-5/240.... Throws right, bats right.... Full name: Gregory Daniel Pirkl.
HIGH SCHOOL: Los Alamitos (Calif.).
TRANSACTIONS/CAREER NOTES: Selected by Seattle Mariners organization in second round of free-agent draft (June 1, 1988).... On disabled list (May 31-June 22 and July 3, 1990-remainder of season).
STATISTICAL NOTES: Led Northwest League with 22 passed balls in 1988.... Led Pacific Coast League with 10 sacrifice flies in 1993.... Led Pacific Coast League first basemen with 21 double plays in 1993.

			BATTING												FIELDING			
Year	Team (League)	Pos.	G	AB	R	H	2B	3B	HR	RBI	Avg.	BB	SO	SB	PO	A	E	Avg.
1988	—Belling. (N'west)......	C	65	246	22	59	6	0	6	35	.240	12	59	1	227	19	9	.965
1989	—Belling. (N'west)......	C	70	265	31	68	6	0	8	36	.257	23	51	4	296	23	9	.973
1990	—San Bern. (Calif.)......	C	58	207	37	61	10	0	5	28	.295	13	34	3	325	40	9	.976
1991	—San Bern. (Calif.)......	C-1B	63	239	32	75	13	1	14	53	.314	12	43	4	412	33	11	.976
	—Peninsula (Caro.).....	C-1B	64	239	20	63	16	0	6	41	.264	9	42	0	322	31	5	.986
1992	—Jacksonv. (South.)..	1B-C	59	227	25	66	11	1	10	29	.291	9	45	0	473	35	5	.990
	—Calgary (PCL)..........	1B	79	286	30	76	21	3	6	32	.266	14	64	4	625	44	7	.990
1993	—Calgary (PCL)..........	1B-3B	115	445	67	137	24	1	21	94	.308	13	50	3	920	72	14	.986
	—Seattle (A.L.)...........	1B	7	23	1	4	0	0	1	4	.174	0	4	0	42	5	0	1.000
Major league totals (1 year)...................			7	23	1	4	0	0	1	4	.174	0	4	0	42	5	0	1.000

PISCIOTTA, MARC

P, ROCKIES

PERSONAL: Born August 7, 1970, in Edison, N.J.... 6-5/240.... Throws right, bats right.... Full name: Marc George Pisciotta.... Brother of Scott Pisciotta, pitcher, Montreal Expos organization.... Name pronounced pih-SHO-tuh.
HIGH SCHOOL: George Walton Comprehensive (Marietta, Ga.).
COLLEGE: Georgia Tech.
TRANSACTIONS/CAREER NOTES: Selected by Pittsburgh Pirates organization in 19th round of free-agent draft (June 3, 1991).... On disabled list (May 22-June 19, 1992).... Selected by Colorado Rockies from Pirates organization in Rule 5 major league draft (December 13, 1993).

Year	Team (League)	W	L	Pct.	ERA	G	GS	CG	ShO	Sv.	IP	H	R	ER	BB	SO
1991	—Welland (NYP)...........	1	1	.500	0.26	24	0	0	0	8	34	16	4	1	20	47
1992	—Augusta (S. Atl.)........	4	5	.444	4.54	20	12	1	0	1	79⅓	91	51	40	43	54
1993	—Augusta (S. Atl.)........	5	2	.714	2.68	34	0	0	0	12	43⅔	31	18	13	17	49
	—Salem (Carolina)........	0	0	...	2.95	20	0	0	0	12	18⅓	23	13	6	13	13

PLANTENBERG, ERIK

P, MARINERS

PERSONAL: Born October 30, 1968, in Renton, Wash.... 6-1/180.... Throws left, bats both.... Full name: Erik John Plantenberg.
HIGH SCHOOL: Newport (Bellevue, Wash.).
COLLEGE: San Diego State.
TRANSACTIONS/CAREER NOTES: Selected by Kansas City Royals organization in 66th round of free-agent draft (June 2, 1987).... Selected by Boston Red Sox organization in 16th round of free-agent draft (June 4, 1990).... On disabled list (May 13-June 11, 1991 and July 28, 1992-remainder of season).... Selected by Jacksonville, Seattle Mariners organization, from Lynchburg, Red Sox organization, in Rule 5 minor league draft (December 7, 1992).... On Jacksonville disabled list (May 25-June 10, 1993).

Year	Team (League)	W	L	Pct.	ERA	G	GS	CG	ShO	Sv.	IP	H	R	ER	BB	SO
1990	—Elmira (N.Y.-Penn)....	2	3	.400	4.02	16	5	0	0	1	40⅓	44	26	18	19	36
1991	—Lynchburg (Caro.).....	11	5	.688	3.76	20	20	0	0	0	103	116	59	43	51	73
1992	—Lynchburg (Caro.).....	2	3	.400	5.18	21	12	0	0	0	81⅔	112	69	47	36	62
1993	—Jacksonv. (South.)■..	2	1	.667	2.01	34	0	0	0	1	44⅔	38	11	10	14	49
	—Seattle (A.L.)............	0	0	...	6.52	20	0	0	0	1	9⅔	11	7	7	12	3
Major league totals (1 year)...		0	0	...	6.52	20	0	0	0	1	9⅔	11	7	7	12	3

P

PLANTIER, PHIL

OF, PADRES

PERSONAL: Born January 27, 1969, in Manchester, N.H. . . . 5-11/195. . . . Throws right, bats left. . . . Full name: Phillip Alan Plantier. . . . Name pronounced plan-TEER.
HIGH SCHOOL: Poway (Calif.).
TRANSACTIONS/CAREER NOTES: Selected by Boston Red Sox organization in 11th round of free-agent draft (June 2, 1987). . . . On Pawtucket disabled list (August 28-September 4, 1992). . . . Traded by Red Sox to San Diego Padres for P Jose Melendez (December 9, 1992). . . . On disabled list (April 26-May 11, 1993).
HONORS: Named Carolina League Most Valuable Player (1989).
STATISTICAL NOTES: Led Carolina League with 242 total bases, .546 slugging percentage and tied for lead with seven intentional bases on balls received in 1989. . . . Led International League with .549 slugging percentage in 1990.

			BATTING												FIELDING			
Year	**Team (League)**	**Pos.**	**G**	**AB**	**R**	**H**	**2B**	**3B**	**HR**	**RBI**	**Avg.**	**BB**	**SO**	**SB**	**PO**	**A**	**E**	**Avg.**
1987	—Elmira (N.Y.-Penn)..	3B	28	80	7	14	2	0	2	9	.175	9	9	0	12	34	12	.793
1988	—Winter Haven (FSL)..	OF-3B-2B	111	337	29	81	13	1	4	32	.240	51	62	0	106	72	18	.908
1989	—Lynchburg (Caro.)...	OF	131	443	73	133	26	1	★27	★105	.300	74	122	4	140	10	8	.949
1990	—Pawtucket (Int'l)......	OF	123	430	83	109	22	3	★33	79	.253	62	★148	1	245	8	★14	.948
	—Boston (A.L.)............	OF	14	15	1	2	1	0	0	3	.133	4	6	0	0	0	0	...
1991	—Pawtucket (Int'l)......	OF-3B	84	298	69	91	19	4	16	61	.305	65	64	6	173	6	0	1.000
	—Boston (A.L.)............	OF	53	148	27	49	7	1	11	35	.331	23	38	1	80	1	2	.976
1992	—Boston (A.L.)............	OF	108	349	46	86	19	0	7	30	.246	44	83	2	148	6	4	.975
	—Pawtucket (Int'l)......	OF	12	40	7	17	0	0	5	14	.425	6	6	0	23	1	0	1.000
1993	—San Diego (N.L.)■.....	OF	138	462	67	111	20	1	34	100	.240	61	124	4	272	14	3	.990
American League totals (3 years)............			175	512	74	137	27	1	18	68	.268	71	127	3	228	7	6	.975
National League totals (1 year)..............			138	462	67	111	20	1	34	100	.240	61	124	4	272	14	3	.990
Major league totals (4 years)..................			313	974	141	248	47	2	52	168	.255	132	251	7	500	21	9	.983

PLESAC, DAN

P, CUBS

PERSONAL: Born February 4, 1962, in Gary, Ind. . . . 6-5/215. . . . Throws left, bats left. . . . Full name: Daniel Thomas Plesac. . . . Name pronounced PLEE-sack.
HIGH SCHOOL: Crown Point (Ind.).
COLLEGE: North Carolina State.
TRANSACTIONS/CAREER NOTES: Selected by St. Louis Cardinals organization in second round of free-agent draft (June 3, 1980). . . . Selected by Milwaukee Brewers organization in first round (26th pick overall) of free-agent draft (June 6, 1983). . . . Granted free agency (October 27, 1992). . . . Signed by Chicago Cubs (December 8, 1992).
STATISTICAL NOTES: Led Appalachian League pitchers with three balks in 1983.

Year	**Team (League)**	**W**	**L**	**Pct.**	**ERA**	**G**	**GS**	**CG**	**ShO**	**Sv.**	**IP**	**H**	**R**	**ER**	**BB**	**SO**
1983	—Paintsville (Appal.)....	★9	1	.900	3.50	14	•14	2	0	0	82⅓	76	44	32	57	★85
1984	—Stockton (Calif.)........	6	6	.500	3.32	16	16	2	0	0	108⅓	106	51	40	50	101
	—El Paso (Texas).........	2	2	.500	3.46	7	7	0	0	0	39	43	19	15	16	24
1985	—El Paso (Texas).........	12	5	.706	4.97	25	24	2	0	0	150⅓	171	91	83	68	128
1986	—Milwaukee (A.L.).......	10	7	.588	2.97	51	0	0	0	14	91	81	34	30	29	75
1987	—Milwaukee (A.L.).......	5	6	.455	2.61	57	0	0	0	23	79⅓	63	30	23	23	89
1988	—Milwaukee (A.L.).......	1	2	.333	2.41	50	0	0	0	30	52⅓	46	14	14	12	52
1989	—Milwaukee (A.L.).......	3	4	.429	2.35	52	0	0	0	33	61⅓	47	16	16	17	52
1990	—Milwaukee (A.L.).......	3	7	.300	4.43	66	0	0	0	24	69	67	36	34	31	65
1991	—Milwaukee (A.L.).......	2	7	.222	4.29	45	10	0	0	8	92⅓	92	49	44	39	61
1992	—Milwaukee (A.L.).......	5	4	.556	2.96	44	4	0	0	1	79	64	28	26	35	54
1993	—Chicago (N.L.)■.........	2	1	.667	4.74	57	0	0	0	0	62⅔	74	37	33	21	47
A.L. totals (7 years)...............		29	37	.439	3.21	365	14	0	0	133	524⅓	460	207	187	186	448
N.L. totals (1 year)...............		2	1	.667	4.74	57	0	0	0	0	62⅔	74	37	33	21	47
Major league totals (8 years)..		31	38	.449	3.37	422	14	0	0	133	587	534	244	220	207	495

ALL-STAR GAME RECORD

Year	**League**	**W**	**L**	**Pct.**	**ERA**	**GS**	**CG**	**ShO**	**Sv.**	**IP**	**H**	**R**	**ER**	**BB**	**SO**
1987	—American......................	0	0	...	0.00	0	0	0	0	1	0	0	0	0	1
1988	—American......................	0	0	...	0.00	0	0	0	0	⅓	0	0	0	0	1
1989	—American......................	0	0	...	...	0	0	0	0	0	1	0	0	0	0
All-Star totals (3 years).........		0	0	...	0.00	0	0	0	0	1⅓	1	0	0	0	2

PLUNK, ERIC

P, INDIANS

PERSONAL: Born September 3, 1963, in Wilmington, Calif. . . . 6-6/220. . . . Throws right, bats right. . . . Full name: Eric Vaughn Plunk.
HIGH SCHOOL: Bellflower (Calif.).
COLLEGE: Cal State Dominguez Hills.
TRANSACTIONS/CAREER NOTES: Selected by New York Yankees organization in fourth round of free-agent draft (June 8, 1981). . . . On disabled list (August 11-26, 1983). . . . Traded by Yankees with OF Stan Javier, P Jay Howell, P Jose Rijo and P Tim Birtsas to Oakland Athletics for OF Rickey Henderson, P Bert Bradley and cash (December 5, 1984). . . . On disabled list (July 2-17, 1988). . . . Traded by A's with P Greg Cadaret and OF Luis Polonia to New York Yankees for OF Rickey Henderson (June 21, 1989). . . . Released by Yankees (November 20, 1991). . . . Signed by Syracuse, Toronto Blue Jays organization (December 12, 1991). . . . Released by Syracuse (March 27, 1992). . . . Signed by Canton/Akron, Cleveland Indians organization (April 9, 1992). . . . Granted free agency (October 27, 1992). . . . Re-signed by Indians (November 12, 1992).
STATISTICAL NOTES: Tied for Florida State League lead with seven balks in 1984. . . . Led A.L. with six balks in 1986.

Year	**Team (League)**	**W**	**L**	**Pct.**	**ERA**	**G**	**GS**	**CG**	**ShO**	**Sv.**	**IP**	**H**	**R**	**ER**	**BB**	**SO**
1981	—GC Yankees (GCL).....	3	4	.429	3.83	11	11	1	0	0	54	56	29	23	20	47
1982	—Paintsville (Appal.)....	6	3	.667	4.64	12	8	4	0	0	64	63	35	33	30	59
1983	—Fort Lauder. (FSL).....	8	10	.444	2.74	20	20	5	•4	0	125	115	55	38	63	109
1984	—Fort Lauder. (FSL).....	12	12	.500	2.86	28	28	7	1	0	176⅓	153	85	56	★123	★152
1985	—Huntsville (South.)■..	8	2	.800	3.40	13	13	2	1	0	79⅓	61	36	30	56	68

Year	Team (League)	W	L	Pct.	ERA	G	GS	CG	ShO	Sv.	IP	H	R	ER	BB	SO
	—Tacoma (PCL)	0	5	.000	5.77	11	10	0	0	0	53	51	41	34	50	43
1986	—Tacoma (PCL)	2	3	.400	4.68	6	6	0	0	0	32⅔	25	18	17	33	31
	—Oakland (A.L.)	4	7	.364	5.31	26	15	0	0	0	120⅓	91	75	71	102	98
1987	—Oakland (A.L.)	4	6	.400	4.74	32	11	0	0	2	95	91	53	50	62	90
	—Tacoma (PCL)	1	1	.500	1.56	24	0	0	0	9	34⅔	21	8	6	17	56
1988	—Oakland (A.L.)	7	2	.778	3.00	49	0	0	0	5	78	62	27	26	39	79
1989	—Oak.-N.Y. (A.L.)■	8	6	.571	3.28	50	7	0	0	1	104⅓	82	43	38	64	85
1990	—New York (A.L.)	6	3	.667	2.72	47	0	0	0	0	72⅔	58	27	22	43	67
1991	—New York (A.L.)	2	5	.286	4.76	43	8	0	0	0	111⅔	128	69	59	62	103
1992	—Cant./Akr. (East.)■	1	2	.333	1.72	9	0	0	0	0	15⅔	11	4	3	5	19
	—Cleveland (A.L.)	9	6	.600	3.64	58	0	0	0	4	71⅔	61	31	29	38	50
1993	—Cleveland (A.L.)	4	5	.444	2.79	70	0	0	0	15	71	61	29	22	30	77
Major league totals (8 years)		44	40	.524	3.94	375	41	0	0	27	724⅔	634	354	317	440	649

CHAMPIONSHIP SERIES RECORD

Year	Team (League)	W	L	Pct.	ERA	G	GS	CG	ShO	Sv.	IP	H	R	ER	BB	SO
1988	—Oakland (A.L.)	0	0	...	0.00	1	0	0	0	0	⅓	1	0	0	0	1

WORLD SERIES RECORD

Year	Team (League)	W	L	Pct.	ERA	G	GS	CG	ShO	Sv.	IP	H	R	ER	BB	SO
1988	—Oakland (A.L.)	0	0	...	0.00	2	0	0	0	0	1⅔	0	0	0	0	3

POLIDOR, GUS

IF

PERSONAL: Born October 26, 1961, in Caracas, Venezuela. . . . 6-0/180. . . . Throws right, bats right. . . . Full name: Gustavo Adolfo Polidor. . . . Brother of Wilfredo Polidor, infielder, Chicago White Sox organization.

TRANSACTIONS/CAREER NOTES: Signed as free agent by California Angels organization (January 5, 1981). . . . On disabled list (June 22-July 14 and July 26, 1982-remainder of season). . . . On California disabled list (June 14-July 1, 1988). . . . Traded by Angels organization to Milwaukee Brewers for C Bill Schroeder (December 7, 1988). . . . Released by Brewers organization (December 6, 1990). . . . Signed by Nashville, Cincinnati Reds organization (January 10, 1991). . . . Released by Nashville (April 1, 1991). . . . Signed by Denver, Brewers organization (May 1, 1991). . . . Traded by Brewers organization to Oakland Athletics organization for IF Trent Weaver (June 10, 1991). . . . Granted free agency (October 15, 1991). . . . Re-signed by A's organization (December 12, 1991). . . . On disabled list (April 17-May 28, 1992). . . . Granted free agency (October 15, 1992). . . . Signed by Florida Marlins organization (December 2, 1992). . . . Granted free agency (October 15, 1993).

STATISTICAL NOTES: Led Eastern League shortstops with 37 errors in 1983. . . . Tied for Eastern League lead in double plays by shortstop with 69 in 1983. . . . Led Eastern League shortstops with .951 fielding percentage and 200 putouts in 1984. . . . Led Pacific Coast League shortstops with 669 total chances in 1985. . . . Led Pacific Coast League shortstops with 93 double plays in 1985 and tied for lead with 92 in 1986. . . . Led Pacific Coast League shortstops with .986 fielding percentage in 1986.

			BATTING											FIELDING			
Year	Team (League)	Pos.	G	AB	R	H	2B	3B	HR	RBI	Avg.	BB	SO	SB	PO	A	E	Avg.
1981	—Holyoke (Eastern)	SS	130	479	46	119	17	3	2	47	.248	31	62	5	192	375	32	.947
1982	—Holyoke (Eastern)	SS	56	208	17	47	7	0	2	23	.226	5	23	2	74	149	21	.914
1983	—Nashua (Eastern)	SS-3B	105	329	32	69	7	2	0	21	.210	17	32	4	208	283	†37	.930
1984	—Waterbury (East.)	SS-P	119	394	42	88	11	1	1	32	.223	25	32	3	†200	322	27	†.951
1985	—Edmonton (PCL)	SS	132	460	56	131	18	7	2	51	.285	37	53	5	*250	*396	23	.966
	—California (A.L.)	SS-OF	2	1	1	1	0	0	0	0	1.000	0	0	0	0	2	0	1.000
1986	—Edmonton (PCL)	S-2-1-3	119	476	72	143	27	5	5	61	.300	29	41	7	213	316	7	†.987
	—California (A.L.)	2B-SS-3B	6	19	1	5	1	0	0	1	.263	1	0	0	10	13	0	1.000
1987	—California (A.L.)	SS-3B-2B	63	137	12	36	3	0	2	15	.263	2	15	0	46	92	2	.986
1988	—California (A.L.)	SS-3B-2B	54	81	4	12	3	0	0	4	.148	3	11	0	31	54	1	.988
	—Edmonton (PCL)	SS-1B	11	33	6	12	4	0	0	7	.364	3	3	0	20	23	2	.956
1989	—Milwaukee (A.L.)■	3B-2B-SS	79	175	15	34	7	0	0	14	.194	6	18	3	78	123	12	.944
1990	—Milwaukee (A.L.)	3B-2B-SS	18	15	0	1	0	0	0	1	.067	0	1	0	2	13	0	1.000
	—Denver (A.A.)	SS-2B-3B	46	165	17	50	8	0	1	16	.303	4	19	3	83	112	6	.970
1991	—Denver (A.A.)	SS-3B	30	103	8	28	2	1	0	5	.272	4	8	0	50	60	4	.965
	—Tacoma (PCL)■	SS	53	182	22	54	8	4	0	14	.297	12	15	0	64	140	10	.953
1992	—Tacoma (PCL)	SS-3B	99	363	23	101	16	0	1	43	.278	22	24	4	138	293	19	.958
1993	—Edmonton (PCL)■	SS-2B-3B	72	249	26	71	16	2	3	40	.285	17	17	1	108	210	8	.975
	—Florida (N.L.)	3B-2B	7	6	0	1	1	0	0	0	.167	0	2	0	1	0	0	1.000
American League totals (6 years)			222	428	33	89	14	0	2	35	.208	12	45	3	167	297	15	.969
National League totals (1 year)			7	6	0	1	1	0	0	0	.167	0	2	0	1	0	0	1.000
Major league totals (7 years)			229	434	33	90	15	0	2	35	.207	12	47	3	168	297	15	.969

RECORD AS PITCHER

Year	Team (League)	W	L	Pct.	ERA	G	GS	CG	ShO	Sv.	IP	H	R	ER	BB	SO
1984	—Waterbury (East.)	0	0	...	0.00	1	0	0	0	0	1	0	0	0	1	0

POLONIA, LUIS

OF, YANKEES

PERSONAL: Born October 27, 1964, in Santiago City, Dominican Republic. . . . 5-8/150. . . . Throws left, bats left. . . . Full name: Luis Andrew Almonte Polonia. . . . Name pronounced po-LONE-yuh.

HIGH SCHOOL: San Francisco (Santiago City, Dominican Republic).

TRANSACTIONS/CAREER NOTES: Signed as free agent by Oakland Athletics organization (January 3, 1984). . . . Traded by A's with P Greg Cadaret and P Eric Plunk to New York Yankees for OF Rickey Henderson (June 21, 1989). . . . Traded by Yankees to California Angels for OF Claudell Washington and P Rich Monteleone (April 28, 1990). . . . On suspended list (September 30-October 3, 1992). . . . Granted free agency (October 27, 1993). . . . Signed by Yankees (December 20, 1993).

STATISTICAL NOTES: Led Midwest League in caught stealing with 24 in 1984. . . . Led Pacific Coast League in caught stealing with 21 in 1986. . . . Led A.L. in caught stealing with 23 in 1991 and 21 in 1992 and tied for lead with 24 in 1993.
MISCELLANEOUS: Batted as switch-hitter (1984-86 and Tacoma, 1987-88).

			BATTING												FIELDING			
Year	Team (League)	Pos.	G	AB	R	H	2B	3B	HR	RBI	Avg.	BB	SO	SB	PO	A	E	Avg.
1984	—Madison (Midwest)	OF	135	*528	103	*162	21	10	8	64	.307	57	95	55	202	9	10	.955
1985	—Huntsville (South.)	OF	130	515	82	149	15	*18	2	36	.289	58	53	39	236	13	12	.954
1986	—Tacoma (PCL)	OF	134	*549	98	*165	20	4	3	63	.301	52	65	36	*318	8	10	.970
1987	—Tacoma (PCL)	OF	14	56	18	18	1	2	0	8	.321	14	6	4	28	1	1	.967
	—Oakland (A.L.)	OF	125	435	78	125	16	10	4	49	.287	32	64	29	235	2	5	.979
1988	—Tacoma (PCL)	OF	65	254	58	85	13	5	2	27	.335	29	28	31	129	7	7	.951
	—Oakland (A.L.)	OF	84	288	51	84	11	4	2	27	.292	21	40	24	155	3	2	.988
1989	—Oak.-N.Y. (A.L.)■	OF	125	433	70	130	17	6	3	46	.300	25	44	22	231	9	4	.984
1990	—N.Y.-Calif. (A.L.)■	OF	120	403	52	135	7	9	2	35	.335	25	43	21	142	3	3	.980
1991	—California (A.L.)	OF	150	604	92	179	28	8	2	50	.296	52	74	48	246	9	5	.981
1992	—California (A.L.)	OF	149	577	83	165	17	4	0	35	.286	45	64	51	192	8	4	.980
1993	—California (A.L.)	OF	152	576	75	156	17	6	1	32	.271	48	53	55	286	12	5	.983
	Major league totals (7 years)		905	3316	501	974	113	47	14	274	.294	248	382	250	1487	46	28	.982

CHAMPIONSHIP SERIES RECORD

			BATTING												FIELDING			
Year	Team (League)	Pos.	G	AB	R	H	2B	3B	HR	RBI	Avg.	BB	SO	SB	PO	A	E	Avg.
1988	—Oakland (A.L.)	PR-OF-PH	3	5	0	2	0	0	0	0	.400	1	2	0	2	0	0	1.000

WORLD SERIES RECORD

			BATTING												FIELDING			
Year	Team (League)	Pos.	G	AB	R	H	2B	3B	HR	RBI	Avg.	BB	SO	SB	PO	A	E	Avg.
1988	—Oakland (A.L.)	PH-OF	3	9	1	1	0	0	0	0	.111	0	2	0	2	0	0	1.000

POOLE, JIM

P, ORIOLES

PERSONAL: Born April 28, 1966, in Rochester, N.Y. . . . 6-2/203. . . . Throws left, bats left. . . . Full name: James Richard Poole.
HIGH SCHOOL: South College (Philadelphia).
COLLEGE: Georgia Tech.
TRANSACTIONS/CAREER NOTES: Selected by Los Angeles Dodgers organization in 34th round of free-agent draft (June 2, 1987). . . . Selected by Dodgers organization in ninth round of free-agent draft (June 1, 1988). . . . Traded by Dodgers with cash to Texas Rangers for P Steve Allen and P David Lynch (December 30, 1990). . . . Claimed on waivers by Baltimore Orioles (May 31, 1991). . . . On Baltimore disabled list (April 3-June 23, 1992); included rehabilitation assignment to Hagerstown (May 25-June 12) and Rochester (June 12-23).

Year	Team (League)	W	L	Pct.	ERA	G	GS	CG	ShO	Sv.	IP	H	R	ER	BB	SO
1988	—Vero Beach (FSL)	1	1	.500	3.77	10	0	0	0	0	14⅓	13	7	6	9	12
1989	—Vero Beach (FSL)	11	4	.733	1.61	*60	0	0	0	19	78⅓	57	16	14	24	93
	—Bakersfield (Calif.)	0	0	...	0.00	1	0	0	0	0	1⅔	2	1	0	0	1
1990	—San Antonio (Tex.)	6	7	.462	2.40	54	0	0	0	16	63⅔	55	31	17	27	77
	—Los Angeles (N.L.)	0	0	...	4.22	16	0	0	0	0	10⅔	7	5	5	8	6
1991	—Okla. City (A.A.)	0	0	...	0.00	10	0	0	0	3	12⅓	4	0	0	1	14
	—Texas-Balt. (A.L.)■	3	2	.600	2.36	29	0	0	0	1	42	29	14	11	12	38
	—Rochester (Int'l)	3	2	.600	2.79	27	0	0	0	9	29	29	11	9	9	25
1992	—Hagerstown (East.)	0	1	.000	2.77	7	3	0	0	0	13	14	4	4	1	4
	—Rochester (Int'l)	1	6	.143	5.31	32	0	0	0	10	42⅓	40	26	25	18	30
	—Baltimore (A.L.)	0	0	...	0.00	6	0	0	0	0	3⅓	3	3	0	1	3
1993	—Baltimore (A.L.)	2	1	.667	2.15	55	0	0	0	2	50⅓	30	18	12	21	29
	A.L. totals (3 years)	5	3	.625	2.16	90	0	0	0	3	95⅔	62	35	23	34	70
	N.L. totals (1 year)	0	0	...	4.22	16	0	0	0	0	10⅔	7	5	5	8	6
	Major league totals (4 years)	5	3	.625	2.37	106	0	0	0	3	106⅓	69	40	28	42	76

PORTUGAL, MARK

P, GIANTS

PERSONAL: Born October 30, 1962, in Los Angeles. . . . 6-0/190. . . . Throws right, bats right. . . . Full name: Mark Steven Portugal.
HIGH SCHOOL: Norwalk (Calif.).
TRANSACTIONS/CAREER NOTES: Signed as free agent by Minnesota Twins organization (October 23, 1980). . . . On Toledo disabled list (July 22-August 2, 1985). . . . On Minnesota disabled list (August 7-28, 1988). . . . Traded by Twins to Houston Astros for a player to be named later (December 4, 1988); Twins organization acquired P Todd McClure to complete deal (December 7, 1988). . . . On disabled list (July 18-August 13, 1991). . . . On Houston disabled list (June 13-July 4 and July 10-September 23, 1992). . . . Granted free agency (October 25, 1993). . . . Signed by San Francisco Giants (November 21, 1993).
STATISTICAL NOTES: Led Appalachian League with 12 wild pitches, 11 home runs allowed and tied for lead with five hit batsmen in 1981.
MISCELLANEOUS: Appeared in one game as pinch-runner (1991).

Year	Team (League)	W	L	Pct.	ERA	G	GS	CG	ShO	Sv.	IP	H	R	ER	BB	SO
1981	—Elizabeth. (Appal.)	7	1	.875	3.71	14	13	2	0	1	85	65	41	35	39	65
1982	—Wis. Rap. (Midw.)	9	8	.529	4.01	36	15	4	1	2	119	110	62	53	62	95
1983	—Visalia (California)	10	5	.667	4.18	24	23	2	0	0	131⅓	142	77	61	84	132
1984	—Orlando (Southern)	14	7	.667	2.98	27	27	10	3	0	196	171	80	65	113	110
1985	—Toledo (Int'l)	8	5	.615	3.78	19	19	5	1	0	128⅔	129	60	54	60	89
	—Minnesota (A.L.)	1	3	.250	5.55	6	4	0	0	0	24⅓	24	16	15	14	12
1986	—Toledo (Int'l)	5	1	.833	2.60	6	6	3	1	0	45	34	15	13	23	30
	—Minnesota (A.L.)	6	10	.375	4.31	27	15	3	0	1	112⅔	112	56	54	50	67

P

Year	Team (League)	W	L	Pct.	ERA	G	GS	CG	ShO	Sv.	IP	H	R	ER	BB	SO
1987	—Minnesota (A.L.)	1	3	.250	7.77	13	7	0	0	0	44	58	40	38	24	28
	—Portland (PCL)	1	10	.091	6.00	17	16	2	0	0	102	108	75	68	50	69
1988	—Portland (PCL)	2	0	1.000	1.37	3	3	1	1	0	19⅔	15	3	3	8	9
	—Minnesota (A.L.)	3	3	.500	4.53	26	0	0	0	3	57⅔	60	30	29	17	31
1989	—Tucson (PCL)■	7	5	.583	3.78	17	17	5	0	0	116⅔	107	55	49	32	90
	—Houston (N.L.)	7	1	.875	2.75	20	15	2	1	0	108	91	34	33	37	86
1990	—Houston (N.L.)	11	10	.524	3.62	32	32	1	0	0	196⅔	187	90	79	67	136
1991	—Houston (N.L.)	10	12	.455	4.49	32	27	1	0	1	168⅓	163	91	84	59	120
1992	—Houston (N.L.)	6	3	.667	2.66	18	16	1	1	0	101⅓	76	32	30	41	62
1993	—Houston (N.L.)	18	4	*.818	2.77	33	33	1	1	0	208	194	75	64	77	131
A.L. totals (4 years)		11	19	.367	5.13	72	26	3	0	4	238⅔	254	142	136	105	138
N.L. totals (5 years)		52	30	.634	3.34	135	123	6	3	1	782⅓	711	322	290	281	535
Major league totals (9 years)		63	49	.563	3.76	207	149	9	3	5	1021	965	464	426	386	673

POSE, SCOTT

OF, MARLINS

PERSONAL: Born February 11, 1967, in Davenport, Ia. . . . 5-11/165. . . . Throws right, bats left. . . . Full name: Scott Vernon Pose.
HIGH SCHOOL: Dowling (West Des Moines, Ia.).
COLLEGE: Arkansas.
TRANSACTIONS/CAREER NOTES: Selected by Cincinnati Reds organization in 34th round of free-agent draft (June 5, 1989). . . . Selected by Florida Marlins from Reds organization in Rule 5 major league draft (December 7, 1992).
STATISTICAL NOTES: Tied for Pioneer League lead with three intentional bases on balls received in 1989. . . . Led South Atlantic League with eight intentional bases on balls received and .435 on-base percentage in 1990. . . . Led Southern League in caught stealing with 27 and in on-base percentage with .414 in 1992.

			BATTING												FIELDING			
Year	Team (League)	Pos.	G	AB	R	H	2B	3B	HR	RBI	Avg.	BB	SO	SB	PO	A	E	Avg.
1989	—Billings (Pioneer)	OF-2B	60	210	52	74	7	2	0	25	.352	*54	31	26	94	19	7	.942
1990	—Char., W.Va. (SAL)	OF	135	480	*106	143	13	5	0	46	.298	*114	56	49	210	*17	3	*.987
1991	—Chatt. (South.)	OF	117	402	61	110	8	5	1	31	.274	69	50	17	215	9	1	*.996
	—Nashville (A.A.)	OF	15	52	7	10	0	0	0	3	.192	2	9	3	23	0	1	.958
1992	—Chatt. (South.)	OF	136	•526	*87	*180	22	8	2	45	*.342	63	66	21	216	10	1	*.996
1993	—Florida (N.L.)■	OF	15	41	0	8	2	0	0	3	.195	2	4	0	14	0	0	1.000
	—Edmonton (PCL)	OF	109	398	61	113	8	6	0	27	.284	42	36	19	192	4	6	.970
Major league totals (1 year)			15	41	0	8	2	0	0	3	.195	2	4	0	14	0	0	1.000

POTTS, MICHAEL

P, BRAVES

PERSONAL: Born September 5, 1970, in Langdale, Ala. . . . 5-9/170. . . . Throws left, bats left. . . . Full name: Michael Larry Potts.
HIGH SCHOOL: Lithonia (Ga.).
COLLEGE: Gordon College (Ga.).
TRANSACTIONS/CAREER NOTES: Selected by Cleveland Indians organization in 16th round of free-agent draft (June 5, 1989). . . . Selected by Atlanta Braves organization in 18th round of free-agent draft (June 4, 1990). . . . On disabled list (May 24-June 5, 1993).

Year	Team (League)	W	L	Pct.	ERA	G	GS	CG	ShO	Sv.	IP	H	R	ER	BB	SO
1990	—GC Braves (GCL)	5	2	.714	3.46	23	1	0	0	4	39	30	23	15	25	39
1991	—Macon (S. Atl.)	8	5	.615	3.49	34	11	2	2	1	95⅓	64	45	37	50	75
1992	—Durham (Carolina)	6	8	.429	4.02	30	21	0	0	1	127⅔	104	75	57	71	123
1993	—Greenville (South.)	7	6	.538	3.88	25	25	1	0	0	141⅔	131	79	61	86	116

POWELL, DENNIS

P, PIRATES

PERSONAL: Born August 13, 1963, in Moultrie, Ga. . . . 6-3/227. . . . Throws left, bats right. . . . Full name: Dennis Clay Powell.
HIGH SCHOOL: Colquitt County (Ga.).
TRANSACTIONS/CAREER NOTES: Signed as free agent by Los Angeles Dodgers organization (May 17, 1983). . . . On Los Angeles disabled list (April 30-June 6, 1986). . . . Traded by Dodgers organization with IF Mike Watters to Seattle Mariners for P Matt Young (December 10, 1986). . . . Granted free agency (May 1, 1990). . . . Signed by Denver, Milwaukee Brewers organization (May 7, 1990). . . . Granted free agency (October 15, 1990). . . . Signed by Baltimore Orioles (February 19, 1991). . . . Released by Orioles (April 2, 1991). . . . Signed by Calgary, Mariners organization (April 6, 1991). . . . Granted free agency (October 15, 1991). . . . Re-signed by Calgary, Mariners organization (January 15, 1992). . . . Granted free agency (October 15, 1993). . . . Signed by Pittsburgh Pirates organization (December 17, 1993).

Year	Team (League)	W	L	Pct.	ERA	G	GS	CG	ShO	Sv.	IP	H	R	ER	BB	SO
1983	—GC Dodgers (GCL)	8	2	.800	1.46	11	11	3	*2	0	74	52	22	12	23	*103
1984	—Vero Beach (FSL)	1	1	.500	1.38	4	4	0	0	0	26	19	7	4	12	14
	—San Antonio (Tex.)	9	8	.529	3.38	24	24	5	2	0	168	153	81	63	87	82
1985	—Albuquerque (PCL)	9	0	1.000	2.74	18	17	3	0	0	111⅔	106	40	34	48	55
	—Los Angeles (N.L.)	1	1	.500	5.22	16	2	0	0	1	29⅓	30	19	17	13	19
1986	—Los Angeles (N.L.)	2	7	.222	4.27	27	6	0	0	0	65⅓	65	32	31	25	31
	—Albuquerque (PCL)	3	3	.500	4.10	7	7	0	0	0	41⅔	45	23	19	15	27
1987	—Calgary (PCL)■	4	8	.333	4.91	20	20	2	1	0	117⅓	145	80	64	48	65
	—Seattle (A.L.)	1	3	.250	3.15	16	3	0	0	0	34⅓	32	13	12	15	17
1988	—Calgary (PCL)	6	4	.600	4.17	21	18	2	1	1	108	116	57	50	49	81
	—Seattle (A.L.)	1	3	.250	8.68	12	2	0	0	0	18⅔	29	20	18	11	15
1989	—Seattle (A.L.)	2	2	.500	5.00	43	1	0	0	2	45	49	25	25	21	27
	—Calgary (PCL)	3	2	.600	2.13	18	0	0	0	6	25⅓	21	10	6	12	15
1990	—Seattle-Mil. (A.L.)■	0	4	.000	7.02	11	7	0	0	0	42⅓	64	40	33	21	23
	—Denver (A.A.)	4	4	.500	3.61	11	11	2	0	0	62⅓	63	34	25	21	46
1991	—Calgary (PCL)■	9	8	.529	4.15	27	26	•5	1	0	173⅔	•200	90	80	59	96

P

Year	Team (League)	W	L	Pct.	ERA	G	GS	CG	ShO	Sv.	IP	H	R	ER	BB	SO
1992	—Seattle (A.L.)	4	2	.667	4.58	49	0	0	0	0	57	49	30	29	29	35
1993	—Calgary (PCL)	3	2	.600	3.60	12	4	0	0	1	40	37	16	16	19	30
	—Seattle (A.L.)	0	0	...	4.15	33	2	0	0	0	47⅔	42	22	22	24	32
A.L. totals (6 years)		8	14	.364	5.11	164	15	0	0	2	245	265	150	139	121	149
N.L. totals (2 years)		3	8	.273	4.56	43	8	0	0	1	94⅔	95	51	48	38	50
Major league totals (8 years)		11	22	.333	4.95	207	23	0	0	3	339⅔	360	201	187	159	199

POWELL, ROSS

P, REDS

PERSONAL: Born January 24, 1968, in Grand Rapids, Mich. . . . 6-0/180. . . . Throws left, bats left. . . . Full name: Ross John Powell.

HIGH SCHOOL: Cedar Springs (Mich.).

COLLEGE: Michigan.

TRANSACTIONS/CAREER NOTES: Selected by Cincinnati Reds organization in third round of free-agent draft (June 5, 1989).

STATISTICAL NOTES: Led American Association with 27 home runs allowed in 1993.

Year	Team (League)	W	L	Pct.	ERA	G	GS	CG	ShO	Sv.	IP	H	R	ER	BB	SO
1989	—Ced. Rap. (Midw.)	7	4	.636	3.54	13	13	1	1	0	76⅓	68	37	30	23	58
1990	—Chatt. (South.)	8	•14	.364	1.31	29	27	•6	1	0	185	172	29	27	57	132
	—Nashville (A.A.)	0	0	...	3.38	3	0	0	0	0	2⅔	1	1	1	0	4
1991	—Nashville (A.A.)	8	8	.500	4.37	24	24	1	0	0	129⅔	125	74	63	63	82
1992	—Chatt. (South.)	4	1	.800	1.26	14	5	0	0	1	57⅓	43	9	8	17	56
	—Nashville (A.A.)	4	8	.333	3.38	25	12	0	0	0	93⅓	89	37	35	42	84
1993	—Indianapolis (A.A.)	10	10	.500	4.11	28	27	4	0	0	179⅔	159	89	82	71	133
	—Cincinnati (N.L.)	0	3	.000	4.41	9	1	0	0	0	16⅓	13	8	8	6	17
Major league totals (1 year)		0	3	.000	4.41	9	1	0	0	0	16⅓	13	8	8	6	17

POWER, TED

P, MARINERS

PERSONAL: Born January 31, 1955, in Guthrie, Okla. . . . 6-4/215. . . . Throws right, bats right. . . . Full name: Ted Henry Power.

HIGH SCHOOL: Abilene (Kan.).

COLLEGE: Kansas State.

TRANSACTIONS/CAREER NOTES: Selected by Los Angeles Dodgers organization in fifth round of free-agent draft (June 8, 1976). . . . On disabled list (July 18-29 and August 20-September 4, 1977; and July 5-21, 1978). . . . Traded by Dodgers organization to Cincinnati Reds for IF Michael James Ramsey and cash (October 15, 1982). . . . Traded by Reds with SS Kurt Stillwell to Kansas City Royals for P Danny Jackson and SS Angel Salazar (November 6, 1987). . . . On disabled list (June 18-July 4, 1988). . . . Traded by Royals to Detroit Tigers for C Rey Palacios and P Mark Lee (August 31, 1988). . . . Granted free agency (November 4, 1988). . . . Re-signed by Tigers (December 7, 1988). . . . Released by Tigers (March 25, 1989). . . . Signed by Louisville, St. Louis Cardinals organization (March 28, 1989). . . . On St. Louis disabled list (May 17-June 19, 1989); included rehabilitation assignment to Louisville (June 9-19). . . . Granted free agency (November 13, 1989). . . . Signed by Pittsburgh Pirates (November 20, 1989). . . . On disabled list (June 5-July 14 and August 5-20, 1990). . . . Granted free agency (November 5, 1990). . . . Signed by Reds (December 14, 1990). . . . Granted free agency (November 4, 1991). . . . Signed by Cleveland Indians (April 5, 1992). . . . On disabled list (May 5-20, 1992). . . . On Cleveland disabled list (May 9-25, 1993). . . . On Cleveland disabled list (June 13-July 22, 1993); included rehabilitation assignment to Canton/Akron (June 18-July 17). . . . Released by Indians (July 23, 1993). . . . Signed by Seattle Mariners (July 28, 1993). . . . Granted free agency (November 5, 1993). . . . Re-signed by Mariners (November 16, 1993).

Year	Team (League)	W	L	Pct.	ERA	G	GS	CG	ShO	Sv.	IP	H	R	ER	BB	SO
1976	—Lodi (California)	1	3	.250	4.59	13	5	2	0	1	51	46	34	26	44	58
1977	—San Antonio (Tex.)	5	3	.625	3.88	12	12	2	0	0	72	51	35	31	55	60
1978	—San Antonio (Tex.)	6	5	.545	4.01	25	13	0	0	3	101	92	57	45	75	97
1979	—San Antonio (Tex.)	5	1	.833	5.20	10	10	4	1	0	64	69	44	37	43	52
	—Albuquerque (PCL)	5	5	.500	4.63	18	17	2	0	0	101	95	59	52	82	69
1980	—Albuquerque (PCL)	13	7	.650	4.53	26	26	3	0	0	155	160	93	78	95	113
1981	—Albuquerque (PCL)	*18	3	.857	3.56	27	26	8	1	0	187	165	84	74	*103	111
	—Los Angeles (N.L.)	1	3	.250	3.21	5	2	0	0	0	14	16	6	5	7	7
1982	—Los Angeles (N.L.)	1	1	.500	6.68	12	4	0	0	0	33⅔	38	27	25	23	15
	—Albuquerque (PCL)	5	4	.556	5.18	14	14	2	2	0	73	77	51	42	49	54
1983	—Cincinnati (N.L.)■	5	6	.455	4.54	49	6	1	0	2	111	120	62	56	49	57
1984	—Cincinnati (N.L.)	9	7	.563	2.82	*78	0	0	0	11	108⅔	93	37	34	46	81
1985	—Cincinnati (N.L.)	8	6	.571	2.70	64	0	0	0	27	80	65	27	24	45	42
1986	—Cincinnati (N.L.)	10	6	.625	3.70	56	10	0	0	1	129	115	59	53	52	95
1987	—Cincinnati (N.L.)	10	13	.435	4.50	34	34	2	1	0	204	213	115	102	71	133
1988	—K.C.-Det. (A.L.)■	6	7	.462	5.91	26	14	2	2	0	99	121	67	65	38	57
1989	—Louisville (A.A.)■	4	3	.571	3.16	8	7	1	1	0	37	29	13	13	15	36
	—St. Louis (N.L.)	7	7	.500	3.71	23	15	0	0	0	97	96	47	40	21	43
1990	—Pittsburgh (N.L.)■	1	3	.250	3.66	40	0	0	0	7	51⅔	50	23	21	17	42
1991	—Cincinnati (N.L.)■	5	3	.625	3.62	68	0	0	0	3	87	87	37	35	31	51
1992	—Cleveland (A.L.)■	3	3	.500	2.54	64	0	0	0	6	99⅓	88	33	28	35	51
1993	—Clev.-Seattle (A.L.)■	2	4	.333	5.36	45	0	0	0	13	45⅓	57	28	27	17	27
	—Cant./Akr. (East.)	0	0	...	4.67	7	3	0	0	0	17⅓	22	10	9	8	16
A.L. totals (3 years)		11	14	.440	4.43	135	14	2	2	19	243⅔	266	128	120	90	135
N.L. totals (10 years)		57	55	.509	3.88	429	71	3	1	51	916	893	440	395	362	566
Major league totals (13 years)		68	69	.496	4.00	564	85	5	3	70	1159⅔	1159	568	515	452	701

CHAMPIONSHIP SERIES RECORD

Year	Team (League)	W	L	Pct.	ERA	G	GS	CG	ShO	Sv.	IP	H	R	ER	BB	SO
1990	—Pittsburgh (N.L.)	0	0	...	3.60	3	1	0	0	1	5	6	2	2	2	3

PRATT, TODD

C, PHILLIES

PERSONAL: Born February 9, 1967, in Bellevue, Neb. . . . 6-3/225. . . . Throws right, bats right. . . . Full name: Todd Alan Pratt.
HIGH SCHOOL: Hilltop (Chula Vista, Calif.).
TRANSACTIONS/CAREER NOTES: Selected by Boston Red Sox organization in sixth round of free-agent draft (June 3, 1985). . . . Selected by Cleveland Indians organization from Red Sox organization in Rule 5 minor league draft (December 7, 1987). . . . Returned to Red Sox organization (March 1988). . . . Granted free agency (October 15, 1991). . . . Signed by Baltimore Orioles organization (November 13, 1991). . . . Selected by Philadelphia Phillies from Orioles organization in Rule 5 major league draft (December 9, 1991). . . . On Philadelphia disabled list (April 28-May 27, 1993); included rehabilitation assignment to Scranton/Wilkes-Barre (May 23-27).
STATISTICAL NOTES: Led South Atlantic League catchers with 660 putouts and nine double plays and tied for lead with 13 errors in 1986. . . . Led Eastern League catchers with 11 errors in 1989.

			BATTING												FIELDING			
Year	**Team (League)**	**Pos.**	**G**	**AB**	**R**	**H**	**2B**	**3B**	**HR**	**RBI**	**Avg.**	**BB**	**SO**	**SB**	**PO**	**A**	**E**	**Avg.**
1985	—Elmira (N.Y.-Penn)..	C	39	119	7	16	1	1	0	5	.134	10	27	0	254	29	6	.979
1986	—Greensboro (S. Atl.)..	C-1B	107	348	63	84	16	0	12	56	.241	75	114	0	†826	55	‡15	.983
1987	—Winter Haven (FSL)..	C-1B-OF	118	407	57	105	22	0	12	65	.258	70	94	0	672	64	15	.980
1988	—New Britain (East.) ..	C-1B	124	395	41	89	15	2	8	49	.225	41	110	1	540	46	15	.975
1989	—New Britain (East.) ..	C-1B	109	338	30	77	17	1	2	35	.228	44	66	1	435	42	†11	.977
1990	—New Britain (East.) ..	C-1B	70	195	15	45	14	1	2	22	.231	18	56	0	166	15	4	.978
1991	—Pawtucket (Int'l)	C-1B	68	219	68	64	16	0	11	41	.292	23	42	0	236	21	4	.985
1992	—Reading (Eastern)■..	C	41	132	20	44	6	1	6	26	.333	24	28	2	90	6	3	.970
	—Scran./W.B. (Int'l) ...	C-1B	41	125	20	40	9	1	7	28	.320	30	14	1	152	16	4	.977
	—Philadelphia (N.L.) ...	C	16	46	6	13	1	0	2	10	.283	4	12	0	65	4	2	.972
1993	—Philadelphia (N.L.) ...	C	33	87	8	25	6	0	5	13	.287	5	19	0	169	7	2	.989
	—Scran./W.B. (Int'l) ...	C	3	9	1	2	1	0	0	1	.222	3	1	0	11	0	0	1.000
	Major league totals (2 years)		49	133	14	38	7	0	7	23	.286	9	31	0	234	11	4	.984

CHAMPIONSHIP SERIES RECORD

			BATTING												FIELDING			
Year	**Team (League)**	**Pos.**	**G**	**AB**	**R**	**H**	**2B**	**3B**	**HR**	**RBI**	**Avg.**	**BB**	**SO**	**SB**	**PO**	**A**	**E**	**Avg.**
1993	—Philadelphia (N.L.) ...	C	1	1	0	0	0	0	0	0	.000	0	1	0	1	0	0	1.000

WORLD SERIES RECORD

			BATTING												FIELDING			
Year	**Team (League)**	**Pos.**	**G**	**AB**	**R**	**H**	**2B**	**3B**	**HR**	**RBI**	**Avg.**	**BB**	**SO**	**SB**	**PO**	**A**	**E**	**Avg.**
1993	—Philadelphia (N.L.) ...								Did not play.									

PRIDE, CURTIS

OF, EXPOS

PERSONAL: Born December 17, 1968, in Washington, D.C. . . . 5-11/200. . . . Throws right, bats left. . . . Full name: Curtis John Pride.
HIGH SCHOOL: John F. Kennedy (Silver Spring, Md.).
COLLEGE: William & Mary (received undergraduate degree).
TRANSACTIONS/CAREER NOTES: Selected by New York Mets organization in 10th round of free-agent draft (June 2, 1986). . . . Granted free agency (October 15, 1992). . . . Signed by Ottawa, Montreal Expos organization (December 8, 1992).

			BATTING												FIELDING			
Year	**Team (League)**	**Pos.**	**G**	**AB**	**R**	**H**	**2B**	**3B**	**HR**	**RBI**	**Avg.**	**BB**	**SO**	**SB**	**PO**	**A**	**E**	**Avg.**
1986	—Kingsport (Appal.) ...	OF	27	46	5	5	0	0	1	4	.109	6	24	5	17	1	0	1.000
1987	—Kingsport (Appal.) ...	OF	31	104	22	25	4	0	1	9	.240	16	34	14	39	3	5	.894
1988	—Kingsport (Appal.) ...	OF	70	268	*59	76	13	1	8	27	.284	50	48	23	118	6	5	.961
1989	—Pittsfield (NYP)	OF	55	212	35	55	7	3	6	23	.259	25	47	9	105	3	4	.964
1990	—Columbia (S. Atl.)	OF	53	191	38	51	4	4	6	25	.267	21	45	11	72	4	11	.874
1991	—St. Lucie (Fla. St.)	OF	116	392	57	102	21	7	9	37	.260	43	94	24	199	5	4	.981
1992	—Binghamton (East.) ..	OF	118	388	54	88	15	3	10	42	.227	47	110	14	214	3	8	.964
1993	—Harrisburg (East.)■.	OF	50	180	51	64	6	3	15	39	.356	12	36	21	69	0	2	.972
	—Ottawa (Int'l)	OF	69	262	55	79	11	4	6	22	.302	34	61	29	136	3	2	.986
	—Montreal (N.L.)	OF	10	9	3	4	1	1	1	5	.444	0	3	1	2	0	0	1.000
	Major league totals (1 year)		10	9	3	4	1	1	1	5	.444	0	3	1	2	0	0	1.000

PRINCE, TOM

C, DODGERS

PERSONAL: Born August 13, 1964, in Kankakee, Ill. . . . 5-11/185. . . . Throws right, bats right. . . . Full name: Thomas Albert Prince.
HIGH SCHOOL: Bradley Bourbonnais (Kankakee, Ill.).
COLLEGE: Kankakee (Ill.) Community College.
TRANSACTIONS/CAREER NOTES: Selected by Atlanta Braves organization in eighth round of free-agent draft (January 11, 1983). . . . Selected by Braves organization in secondary phase of free-agent draft (June 6, 1983). . . . Selected by Pittsburgh Pirates organization in secondary phase of free-agent draft (January 17, 1984). . . . On Pittsburgh disabled list (August 13-September 1, 1991); included rehabilitation assignment to Buffalo (August 28-September 1). . . . Granted free agency (October 15, 1993). . . . Signed by Albuquerque, Los Angeles Dodgers organization (November 12, 1993).
STATISTICAL NOTES: Led South Atlantic League catchers with 930 total chances, 10 double plays and 27 passed balls in 1985. . . . Led Carolina League catchers with 954 total chances and 15 passed balls in 1986. . . . Led Eastern League catchers with 721 total chances and nine double plays in 1987. . . . Led American Association catchers with 12 double plays in 1992.

			BATTING												FIELDING			
Year	**Team (League)**	**Pos.**	**G**	**AB**	**R**	**H**	**2B**	**3B**	**HR**	**RBI**	**Avg.**	**BB**	**SO**	**SB**	**PO**	**A**	**E**	**Avg.**
1984	—Watertown (NYP).....	C-3B	23	69	6	14	3	0	2	13	.203	9	13	0	155	26	2	.989
	—GC Pirates (GCL)......	C-1B	18	48	4	11	0	0	1	6	.229	8	10	1	75	16	4	.958
1985	—Macon (S. Atl.)	C	124	360	60	75	20	1	10	42	.208	96	92	13	*810	*101	*19	.980
1986	—Prin. William (Car.) ..	C	121	395	59	100	34	1	10	47	.253	50	74	4	*821	•113	20	.979
1987	—Harrisburg (East.)....	C	113	365	41	112	23	2	6	54	.307	51	46	6	*622	*88	•11	.985

Year	Team (League)	Pos.	G	AB	R	H	2B	3B	HR	RBI	Avg.	BB	SO	SB	PO	A	E	Avg.
				BATTING											FIELDING			
	—Pittsburgh (N.L.)	C	4	9	1	2	1	0	1	2	.222	0	2	0	14	3	0	1.000
1988	—Buffalo (A.A.)	C	86	304	35	79	16	0	14	42	.260	23	53	3	456	51	*12	.977
	—Pittsburgh (N.L.)	C	29	74	3	13	2	0	0	6	.176	4	15	0	108	8	2	.983
1989	—Buffalo (A.A.)	C	65	183	21	37	8	1	6	33	.202	22	30	2	312	22	5	.985
	—Pittsburgh (N.L.)	C	21	52	1	7	4	0	0	5	.135	6	12	1	85	11	4	.960
1990	—Pittsburgh (N.L.)	C	4	10	1	1	0	0	0	0	.100	1	2	0	16	1	0	1.000
	—Buffalo (A.A.)	C-1B	94	284	38	64	13	0	7	37	.225	39	46	4	461	62	8	.985
1991	—Pittsburgh (N.L.)	C-1B	26	34	4	9	3	0	1	2	.265	7	3	0	53	9	1	.984
	—Buffalo (A.A.)	C	80	221	29	46	8	3	6	32	.208	37	31	3	379	61	5	.989
1992	—Pittsburgh (N.L.)	C-3B	27	44	1	4	2	0	0	5	.091	6	9	1	76	8	2	.977
	—Buffalo (A.A.)	C-OF	75	244	34	64	17	0	9	35	.262	20	35	3	307	50	8	.978
1993	—Pittsburgh (N.L.)	C	66	179	14	35	14	0	2	24	.196	13	38	1	271	31	5	.984
Major league totals (7 years)			177	402	25	71	26	0	4	44	.177	37	81	3	623	71	14	.980

PUCKETT, KIRBY

OF, TWINS

PERSONAL: Born March 14, 1961, in Chicago. . . . 5-9/215. . . . Throws right, bats right.
HIGH SCHOOL: Calumet (Chicago).
COLLEGE: Bradley and Triton College (Ill.).
TRANSACTIONS/CAREER NOTES: Selected by Minnesota Twins organization in first round (third pick overall) of free-agent draft (January 12, 1982). . . . Granted free agency (October 28, 1992). . . . Re-signed by Twins (December 4, 1992).
RECORDS: Shares major league single-season record for most at-bats with no sacrifice flies—680 (1986). . . . Shares major league record for most consecutive years leading league in hits—3 (1987-89). . . . Shares major league single-game records for most doubles—4 (May 13, 1989); and most doubles in two consecutive games—6 (May 13 [4] and 14 [2], 1989). . . . Shares modern major league record for most hits in first game in majors (nine innings)—4 (May 8, 1984). . . . Holds A.L. record for most hits in two consecutive nine-inning games—10 (August 29 [4] and 30 [6], 1987). . . . Shares A.L. career record for most seasons with 400 or more putouts by outfielder—5.
HONORS: Named California League Player of the Year (1983). . . . Named outfielder on THE SPORTING NEWS A.L. All-Star team (1986-89, 1992). . . . Named outfielder on THE SPORTING NEWS A.L. Silver Slugger team (1986-89 and 1992). . . . Won A.L. Gold Glove as outfielder (1986-89 and 1991-92).
STATISTICAL NOTES: Led Appalachian League with 135 total bases in 1982. . . . Led California League outfielders with five double plays in 1983. . . . Led A.L. outfielders with 492 total chances in 1985, 465 in 1988 and 455 in 1989. . . . Hit for the cycle (August 1, 1986). . . . Collected six hits in one game (August 30, 1987 and May 23, 1991). . . . Led A.L. with 358 total bases in 1988 and 313 in 1992. . . . Led A.L. in grounding into double plays with 27 in 1991.

Year	Team (League)	Pos.	G	AB	R	H	2B	3B	HR	RBI	Avg.	BB	SO	SB	PO	A	E	Avg.
				BATTING											FIELDING			
1982	—Elizabeth. (Appal.)	OF	65	*275	*65	*105	15	3	3	35	*.382	25	27	•43	133	*11	5	.966
1983	—Visalia (California)	OF	138	*548	105	172	29	7	9	97	.314	46	62	48	253	*22	5	.982
1984	—Toledo (Int'l)	OF	21	80	9	21	2	0	1	5	.263	4	14	8	35	1	3	.923
	—Minnesota (A.L.)	OF	128	557	63	165	12	5	0	31	.296	16	69	14	438	*16	3	.993
1985	—Minnesota (A.L.)	OF	161	*691	80	199	29	13	4	74	.288	41	87	21	*465	19	8	.984
1986	—Minnesota (A.L.)	OF	161	680	119	223	37	6	31	96	.328	34	99	20	429	8	6	.986
1987	—Minnesota (A.L.)	OF	157	624	96	•207	32	5	28	99	.332	32	91	12	341	8	5	.986
1988	—Minnesota (A.L.)	OF	158	*657	109	*234	42	5	24	121	.356	23	83	6	*450	12	3	.994
1989	—Minnesota (A.L.)	OF	159	635	75	*215	45	4	9	85	*.339	41	59	11	*438	13	4	.991
1990	—Minnesota (A.L.)	O-2-3-S	146	551	82	164	40	3	12	80	.298	57	73	5	354	9	4	.989
1991	—Minnesota (A.L.)	OF	152	611	92	195	29	6	15	89	.319	31	78	11	373	13	6	.985
1992	—Minnesota (A.L.)	O-3-2-S	160	639	104	*210	38	4	19	110	.329	44	97	17	394	9	3	.993
1993	—Minnesota (A.L.)	OF	156	622	89	184	39	3	22	89	.296	47	93	8	312	13	2	.994
Major league totals (10 years)			1538	6267	909	1996	343	54	164	874	.318	366	829	125	3994	120	44	.989

CHAMPIONSHIP SERIES RECORD

CHAMPIONSHIP SERIES NOTES: Named A.L. Championship Series Most Valuable Player (1991). . . . Shares A.L. single-game record for most at-bats—6 (October 12, 1987).

Year	Team (League)	Pos.	G	AB	R	H	2B	3B	HR	RBI	Avg.	BB	SO	SB	PO	A	E	Avg.
				BATTING											FIELDING			
1987	—Minnesota (A.L.)	OF	5	24	3	5	1	0	1	3	.208	0	5	1	7	0	0	1.000
1991	—Minnesota (A.L.)	OF	5	21	4	9	1	0	2	6	.429	1	4	0	13	1	0	1.000
Championship series totals (2 years)			10	45	7	14	2	0	3	9	.311	1	9	1	20	1	0	1.000

WORLD SERIES RECORD

WORLD SERIES NOTES: Shares record for most at-bats in one inning—2 (October 18, 1987, fourth inning). . . . Shares single-game record for most runs—4 (October 24, 1987).

Year	Team (League)	Pos.	G	AB	R	H	2B	3B	HR	RBI	Avg.	BB	SO	SB	PO	A	E	Avg.
				BATTING											FIELDING			
1987	—Minnesota (A.L.)	OF	7	28	5	10	1	1	0	3	.357	2	1	1	15	1	1	.941
1991	—Minnesota (A.L.)	OF	7	24	4	6	0	1	2	4	.250	5	7	1	16	1	0	1.000
World Series totals (2 years)			14	52	9	16	1	2	2	7	.308	7	8	2	31	2	1	.971

ALL-STAR GAME RECORD

ALL-STAR GAME NOTES: Named Most Valuable Player (1993).

Year	League	Pos.	AB	R	H	2B	3B	HR	RBI	Avg.	BB	SO	SB	PO	A	E	Avg.
			BATTING										FIELDING				
1986	—American	OF	3	0	1	0	0	0	0	.333	1	0	1	5	0	0	1.000
1987	—American	PH-OF	4	0	0	0	0	0	0	.000	0	3	0	1	0	0	1.000
1988	—American	OF	1	0	0	0	0	0	0	.000	0	0	0	1	0	0	1.000

Year	League	Pos.	AB	R	H	2B	3B	HR	RBI	Avg.	BB	SO	SB	PO	A	E	Avg.
			BATTING											FIELDING			
1989	—American	OF	3	1	1	0	0	0	0	.333	0	0	0	0	0	0	...
1990	—American	PH-OF	1	0	1	0	0	0	0	1.000	0	0	0	1	0	0	1.000
1991	—American	OF	1	0	0	0	0	0	0	.000	0	0	0	0	0	0	...
1992	—American	OF	3	1	1	0	0	0	0	.333	0	1	0	2	0	0	1.000
1993	—American	OF	3	1	2	1	0	1	2	.667	0	0	0	1	0	0	1.000
All-Star Game totals (8 years)			19	3	6	1	0	1	2	.316	1	4	1	11	0	0	1.000

PUGH, TIM

P, REDS

PERSONAL: Born January 26, 1967, in Lake Tahoe, Calif. . . . 6-6/230. . . . Throws right, bats right. . . . Full name: Timothy Dean Pugh.

HIGH SCHOOL: Bartlesville (Okla.).

COLLEGE: Oklahoma State.

TRANSACTIONS/CAREER NOTES: Selected by Toronto Blue Jays organization in eighth round of free-agent draft (June 1, 1988). . . . Selected by Cincinnati Reds organization in sixth round of free-agent draft (June 5, 1989).

Year	Team (League)	W	L	Pct.	ERA	G	GS	CG	ShO	Sv.	IP	H	R	ER	BB	SO
1989	—Billings (Pioneer)	2	6	.250	3.94	13	13	2	0	0	77⅔	81	44	34	25	72
1990	—Char., W.Va. (SAL)	★15	6	.714	1.93	27	27	★8	2	0	177⅓	142	58	38	56	153
1991	—Chatt. (South.)	3	1	.750	1.64	5	5	0	0	0	38⅓	20	7	7	11	24
	—Nashville (A.A.)	7	11	.389	3.81	23	23	3	1	0	148⅔	130	68	63	56	89
1992	—Nashville (A.A.)	•12	9	.571	3.55	27	27	3	2	0	169⅔	165	75	67	65	117
	—Cincinnati (N.L.)	4	2	.667	2.58	7	7	0	0	0	45⅓	47	15	13	13	18
1993	—Cincinnati (N.L.)	10	15	.400	5.26	31	27	3	1	0	164⅓	200	102	96	59	94
Major league totals (2 years)		14	17	.452	4.68	38	34	3	1	0	209⅔	247	117	109	72	112

PULIDO, CARLOS

P, TWINS

PERSONAL: Born August 5, 1971, in Caracas, Venezuela. . . . 6-0/194. . . . Throws left, bats left. . . . Full name: Juan Carlos Pulido.

HIGH SCHOOL: Liceo Andres Bello (Caracas, Venezuela).

TRANSACTIONS/CAREER NOTES: Signed as free agent by Minnesota Twins organization (February 28, 1989).

Year	Team (League)	W	L	Pct.	ERA	G	GS	CG	ShO	Sv.	IP	H	R	ER	BB	SO
1989	—GC Twins (GCL)	3	0	1.000	2.25	22	0	0	0	2	36	22	9	9	14	46
1990	—Kenosha (Midwest)	5	5	.500	2.34	56	0	0	0	6	61⅔	55	21	16	36	70
1991	—Visalia (California)	1	5	.167	2.01	57	0	0	0	17	80⅔	77	34	18	23	102
	—Portland (PCL)	0	0	...	16.20	2	0	0	0	0	1⅔	4	3	3	1	2
1992	—Orlando (Southern)	6	2	.750	4.40	52	5	0	0	1	100⅓	99	52	49	37	87
1993	—Portland (PCL)	10	6	.625	4.19	33	22	1	0	0	146	169	74	68	45	79

PULLIAM, HARVEY

OF

PERSONAL: Born October 20, 1967, in San Francisco. . . . 6-0/210. . . . Throws right, bats right. . . . Full name: Harvey Jerome Pulliam Jr.

HIGH SCHOOL: McAteer (San Francisco).

TRANSACTIONS/CAREER NOTES: Selected by Kansas City Royals organization in third round of free-agent draft (June 2, 1986). . . . Granted free agency (October 15, 1993).

Year	Team (League)	Pos.	G	AB	R	H	2B	3B	HR	RBI	Avg.	BB	SO	SB	PO	A	E	Avg.
			BATTING												FIELDING			
1986	—GC Royals (GCL)	OF	48	168	14	35	3	0	4	23	.208	8	33	3	62	5	4	.944
1987	—Appleton (Midw.)	OF	110	395	54	109	20	1	9	55	.276	26	79	21	195	8	6	.971
1988	—Baseball City (FSL)	OF	132	457	56	111	19	4	4	42	.243	34	87	21	289	9	6	.980
1989	—Memphis (South.)	OF	116	417	67	121	28	8	10	67	.290	44	65	5	157	8	5	.971
	—Omaha (A.A.)	OF	7	22	3	4	2	0	0	2	.182	3	6	0	12	1	0	1.000
1990	—Omaha (A.A.)	OF	123	436	72	117	18	5	16	72	.268	49	82	9	188	12	4	.980
1991	—Omaha (A.A.)	OF	104	346	35	89	18	2	6	39	.257	31	62	2	162	12	3	.983
	—Kansas City (A.L.)	OF	18	33	4	9	1	0	3	4	.273	3	9	0	21	1	2	.917
1992	—Omaha (A.A.)	OF	100	359	55	97	12	2	16	60	.270	32	53	4	168	7	1	.994
	—Kansas City (A.L.)	OF	4	5	2	1	1	0	0	0	.200	1	3	0	3	0	0	1.000
1993	—Kansas City (A.L.)	OF	27	62	7	16	5	0	1	6	.258	2	14	0	33	0	1	.971
	—Omaha (A.A.)	OF	54	208	28	55	10	0	5	26	.264	17	36	1	102	7	6	.948
Major league totals (3 years)			49	100	13	26	7	0	4	10	.260	6	26	0	57	1	3	.951

PYE, EDDIE

2B, DODGERS

PERSONAL: Born February 13, 1967, in Columbia, Tenn. . . . 5-10/175. . . . Throws right, bats right. . . . Full name: Robert Edward Pye.

HIGH SCHOOL: Columbia (Tenn.) Central.

COLLEGE: Middle Tennessee State.

TRANSACTIONS/CAREER NOTES: Selected by Los Angeles Dodgers organization in 10th round of free-agent draft (June 1, 1988). . . . On disabled list (April 21-28 and May 7, 1991-remainder of season). . . . On temporary inactive list (May 2-22, 1992).

STATISTICAL NOTES: Led Texas League second basemen with 23 errors in 1990.

Year	Team (League)	Pos.	G	AB	R	H	2B	3B	HR	RBI	Avg.	BB	SO	SB	PO	A	E	Avg.
			BATTING												FIELDING			
1988	—Great Falls (Pio.)	2B-SS	61	237	50	71	8	4	2	30	.300	29	26	19	89	163	12	.955
1989	—Bakersfield (Calif.)	2B-SS	129	488	59	126	21	2	8	47	.258	41	87	19	220	371	32	.949
1990	—San Antonio (Tex.)	2B-SS	119	455	67	113	18	7	2	44	.248	45	68	19	216	379	†23	.963
1991	—Albuquerque (PCL)	2B	12	30	4	13	1	0	1	8	.433	4	4	1	18	18	2	.947
1992	—Albuquerque (PCL)	3B-2B	72	222	30	67	11	2	1	25	.302	13	41	6	52	115	13	.928
1993	—Albuquerque (PCL)	2B-SS-3B	101	365	53	120	21	7	7	66	.329	32	43	5	182	254	12	.973

QUANTRILL, PAUL

P, RED SOX

PERSONAL: Born November 3, 1968, in London, Ont. . . . 6-1/185. . . . Throws right, bats left. . . . Full name: Paul John Quantrill.
HIGH SCHOOL: Okemos (Mich.).
COLLEGE: Wisconsin.
TRANSACTIONS/CAREER NOTES: Selected by Los Angeles Dodgers organization in 26th round of free-agent draft (June 2, 1986). . . . Selected by Boston Red Sox organization in sixth round of free-agent draft (June 5, 1989).

Year	Team (League)	W	L	Pct.	ERA	G	GS	CG	ShO	Sv.	IP	H	R	ER	BB	SO
1989	—GC Red Sox (GCL)	0	0	...	0.00	2	0	0	0	2	5	2	0	0	0	5
	—Elmira (N.Y.-Penn)	5	4	.556	3.43	20	7	•5	0	2	76	90	37	29	12	57
1990	—Winter Haven (FSL)	2	5	.286	4.14	7	7	1	0	0	45⅔	46	24	21	6	14
	—New Britain (East.)	7	11	.389	3.53	22	22	1	1	0	132⅔	148	65	52	23	53
1991	—New Britain (East.)	2	1	.667	2.06	5	5	1	0	0	35	32	14	8	8	18
	—Pawtucket (Int'l)	10	7	.588	4.45	25	23	•6	2	0	155⅔	169	81	77	30	75
1992	—Pawtucket (Int'l)	6	8	.429	4.46	19	18	4	1	0	119	143	63	59	20	56
	—Boston (A.L.)	2	3	.400	2.19	27	0	0	0	1	49⅓	55	18	12	15	24
1993	—Boston (A.L.)	6	12	.333	3.91	49	14	1	1	1	138	151	73	60	44	66
Major league totals (2 years)		8	15	.348	3.46	76	14	1	1	2	187⅓	206	91	72	59	90

QUINTANA, CARLOS

OF/1B, RED SOX

PERSONAL: Born August 26, 1965, in Estado Miranda, Venezuela. . . . 6-2/220. . . . Throws right, bats right. . . . Full name: Carlos Narcis Quintana.
HIGH SCHOOL: Mamparal Miranda (Venezuela).
TRANSACTIONS/CAREER NOTES: Signed as free agent by Boston Red Sox organization (November 26, 1984). . . . On Boston disabled list (June 22-July 7, 1989 and April 5, 1992-entire season).
RECORDS: Shares major league record for most runs batted in in one inning—6 (July 30, 1991, third inning).
STATISTICAL NOTES: Led International League outfielders with 15 assists in 1988. . . . Led A.L. first basemen with 137 assists and 17 errors in 1990. . . . Tied for A.L. lead in assists by first baseman with 101 in 1991.

			BATTING												FIELDING			
Year	Team (League)	Pos.	G	AB	R	H	2B	3B	HR	RBI	Avg.	BB	SO	SB	PO	A	E	Avg.
1985	—Elmira (N.Y.-Penn)	OF	65	220	27	61	8	0	4	35	.277	29	31	3	55	5	3	.952
1986	—Greensboro (S. Atl.)	OF-1B	126	443	97	144	19	4	11	81	.325	90	54	26	224	12	9	.963
1987	—New Britain (East.)	OF	56	206	31	64	11	3	2	31	.311	24	33	3	100	4	2	.981
1988	—Pawtucket (Int'l)	OF-1B	131	471	67	134	25	3	16	66	.285	38	72	3	525	†44	11	.981
	—Boston (A.L.)	OF	5	6	1	2	0	0	0	2	.333	2	3	0	4	0	0	1.000
1989	—Pawtucket (Int'l)	1B-OF	82	272	45	78	11	2	11	52	.287	53	39	6	398	27	2	.995
	—Boston (A.L.)	OF-1B	34	77	6	16	5	0	0	6	.208	7	12	0	31	0	2	.939
1990	—Boston (A.L.)	1B-OF	149	512	56	147	28	0	7	67	.287	52	74	1	1190	†137	†17	.987
1991	—Boston (A.L.)	1B-OF	149	478	69	141	21	1	11	71	.295	61	66	1	1041	‡102	9	.992
1992	—							Did not play.										
1993	—Boston (A.L.)	1B-OF	101	303	31	74	5	0	1	19	.244	31	52	1	412	25	3	.993
Major league totals (5 years)			438	1376	163	380	59	1	19	165	.276	153	207	3	2678	264	31	.990

CHAMPIONSHIP SERIES RECORD

			BATTING												FIELDING			
Year	Team (League)	Pos.	G	AB	R	H	2B	3B	HR	RBI	Avg.	BB	SO	SB	PO	A	E	Avg.
1990	—Boston (A.L.)	1B	4	13	0	0	0	0	0	1	.000	0	0	0	29	2	0	1.000

RADINSKY, SCOTT

P, WHITE SOX

PERSONAL: Born March 3, 1968, in Glendale, Calif. . . . 6-3/204. . . . Throws left, bats left. . . . Full name: Scott David Radinsky.
HIGH SCHOOL: Simi Valley (Calif.).
TRANSACTIONS/CAREER NOTES: Selected by Chicago White Sox organization in third round of free-agent draft (June 2, 1986).

Year	Team (League)	W	L	Pct.	ERA	G	GS	CG	ShO	Sv.	IP	H	R	ER	BB	SO
1986	—GC Whi. Sox (GCL)	1	0	1.000	3.38	7	7	0	0	0	26⅔	24	20	10	17	18
1987	—Peninsula (Caro.)	1	7	.125	5.77	12	8	0	0	0	39	43	30	25	32	37
	—GC Whi. Sox (GCL)	3	3	.500	2.31	11	10	0	0	0	58⅓	43	23	15	39	41
1988	—GC Whi. Sox (GCL)	0	0	...	5.40	5	0	0	0	0	3⅓	2	2	2	4	7
1989	—South Bend (Mid.)	7	5	.583	1.75	53	0	0	0	31	61⅔	39	21	12	19	83
1990	—Chicago (A.L.)	6	1	.857	4.82	62	0	0	0	4	52⅓	47	29	28	36	46
1991	—Chicago (A.L.)	5	5	.500	2.02	67	0	0	0	8	71⅓	53	18	16	23	49
1992	—Chicago (A.L.)	3	7	.300	2.73	68	0	0	0	15	59⅓	54	21	18	34	48
1993	—Chicago (A.L.)	8	2	.800	4.28	73	0	0	0	4	54⅔	61	33	26	19	44
Major league totals (4 years)		22	15	.595	3.33	270	0	0	0	31	237⅔	215	101	88	112	187

CHAMPIONSHIP SERIES RECORD

Year	Team (League)	W	L	Pct.	ERA	G	GS	CG	ShO	Sv.	IP	H	R	ER	BB	SO
1993	—Chicago (A.L.)	0	0	...	10.80	4	0	0	0	0	1⅔	3	4	2	1	1

RAINES, TIM

OF, WHITE SOX

PERSONAL: Born September 16, 1959, in Sanford, Fla. . . . 5-8/186. . . . Throws right, bats both. . . . Brother of Ned Raines, minor league outfielder (1978-80).
HIGH SCHOOL: Seminole (Sanford, Fla.).
TRANSACTIONS/CAREER NOTES: Selected by Montreal Expos organization in fifth round of free-agent draft (June 7, 1977). . . . On disabled list (May 23-June 5, 1978). . . . Granted free agency (November 12, 1986). . . . Re-signed by Expos (May 2, 1987). . . . On disabled list (June 24-July 9, 1988 and June 25-July 10, 1990). . . . Traded by Expos with P

Jeff Carter and a player to be named later to Chicago White Sox for OF Ivan Calderon and P Barry Jones (December 23, 1990); White Sox acquired P Mario Brito to complete deal (February 15, 1991).... On Chicago disabled list (April 10-May 22, 1993); included rehabilitation assignment to Nashville (May 19-22).... Granted free agency (November 1, 1993).... Re-signed by White Sox (December 22, 1993).
RECORDS: Holds major league single-season record for most intentional bases on balls received by switch-hitter—26 (1987).
HONORS: Named Minor League Player of the Year by THE SPORTING NEWS (1980).... Named N.L. Rookie Player of the Year by THE SPORTING NEWS (1981).... Named outfielder on THE SPORTING NEWS N.L. All-Star team (1983 and 1986).... Won THE SPORTING NEWS Gold Shoe Award (1984).... Named outfielder on THE SPORTING NEWS N.L. Silver Slugger team (1986).
STATISTICAL NOTES: Led N.L. outfielders with 21 assists in 1983.... Led N.L. with .413 on-base percentage in 1986.... Hit for the cycle (August 16, 1987).... Switch-hit home runs in one game (July 16, 1988 and August 31, 1993).

			BATTING												FIELDING			
Year	Team (League)	Pos.	G	AB	R	H	2B	3B	HR	RBI	Avg.	BB	SO	SB	PO	A	E	Avg.
1977	—GC Expos (GCL)	2B-3B-OF	49	161	28	45	6	2	0	21	.280	27	16	29	79	72	13	.921
1978	—W.P. Beach (FSL)	2B-SS	100	359	67	103	10	0	0	23	.287	64	44	57	219	273	24	.953
1979	—Memphis (South.)	2B	•145	552	*104	160	25	10	5	50	.290	90	51	59	*341	*413	*23	.970
	—Montreal (N.L.)	PR	6	0	3	0	0	0	0	0	...	0	0	2	...	...	...	...
1980	—Denver (A.A.)	2B	108	429	105	152	23	•11	6	64	*.354	61	42	*77	226	338	16	.972
	—Montreal (N.L.)	2B-OF	15	20	5	1	0	0	0	0	.050	6	3	5	15	16	0	1.000
1981	—Montreal (N.L.)	OF-2B	88	313	61	95	13	7	5	37	.304	45	31	*71	162	8	4	.977
1982	—Montreal (N.L.)	OF-2B	156	647	90	179	32	8	4	43	.277	75	83	*78	293	126	8	.981
1983	—Montreal (N.L.)	OF-2B	156	615	*133	183	32	8	11	71	.298	97	70	*90	314	†23	4	.988
1984	—Montreal (N.L.)	OF-2B	160	622	106	192	•38	9	8	60	.309	87	69	*75	420	8	6	.986
1985	—Montreal (N.L.)	OF	150	575	115	184	30	13	11	41	.320	81	60	70	284	8	2	.993
1986	—Montreal (N.L.)	OF	151	580	91	194	35	10	9	62	*.334	78	60	70	270	13	6	.979
1987	—Montreal (N.L.)	OF	139	530	*123	175	34	8	18	68	.330	90	52	50	297	9	4	.987
1988	—Montreal (N.L.)	OF	109	429	66	116	19	7	12	48	.270	53	44	33	235	5	3	.988
1989	—Montreal (N.L.)	OF	145	517	76	148	29	6	9	60	.286	93	48	41	253	7	1	.996
1990	—Montreal (N.L.)	OF	130	457	65	131	11	5	9	62	.287	70	43	49	239	3	6	.976
1991	—Chicago (A.L.)■	OF	155	609	102	163	20	6	5	50	.268	83	68	51	273	12	3	.990
1992	—Chicago (A.L.)	OF	144	551	102	162	22	9	7	54	.294	81	48	45	312	12	2	.994
1993	—Chicago (A.L.)	OF	115	415	75	127	16	4	16	54	.306	64	35	21	200	5	0	*1.000
	—Nashville (A.A.)	OF	3	11	3	5	1	0	0	2	.455	2	0	2	3	0	0	1.000
American League totals (3 years)			414	1575	279	452	58	19	28	158	.287	228	151	117	785	29	5	.994
National League totals (12 years)			1405	5305	934	1598	273	81	96	552	.301	775	563	634	2782	226	44	.986
Major league totals (15 years)			1819	6880	1213	2050	331	100	124	710	.298	1003	714	751	3567	255	49	.987

CHAMPIONSHIP SERIES RECORD

CHAMPIONSHIP SERIES NOTES: Holds single-series record for most singles—10 (1993).... Shares A.L. single-series record for most hits—12 (1993).

			BATTING												FIELDING			
Year	Team (League)	Pos.	G	AB	R	H	2B	3B	HR	RBI	Avg.	BB	SO	SB	PO	A	E	Avg.
1981	—Montreal (N.L.)	OF	5	21	1	5	2	0	0	1	.238	0	3	0	9	0	0	1.000
1993	—Chicago (A.L.)	OF	6	27	5	12	2	0	0	1	.444	2	2	1	12	2	0	1.000
Championship series totals (2 years)			11	48	6	17	4	0	0	2	.354	2	5	1	21	2	0	1.000

ALL-STAR GAME RECORD

ALL-STAR GAME NOTES: Named Most Valuable Player (1987).

			BATTING											FIELDING			
Year	League	Pos.	AB	R	H	2B	3B	HR	RBI	Avg.	BB	SO	SB	PO	A	E	Avg.
1981	—National	PR-OF	0	0	0	0	0	0	0	...	0	0	0	1	0	0	1.000
1982	—National	OF	1	0	0	0	0	0	0	.000	1	1	1	0	0	0	...
1983	—National	OF	3	0	0	0	0	0	0	.000	0	1	1	2	0	0	1.000
1984	—National	OF	1	0	0	0	0	0	0	.000	0	1	0	4	0	0	1.000
1985	—National	PH-OF	0	1	0	0	0	0	0	...	1	0	0	0	0	0	...
1986	—National	PH-OF	2	0	0	0	0	0	0	.000	0	1	0	1	0	0	1.000
1987	—National	OF	3	0	3	0	1	0	2	1.000	0	0	1	1	0	0	1.000
All-Star Game totals (7 years)			10	1	3	0	1	0	2	.300	2	4	3	9	0	0	1.000

RAMIREZ, MANNY

OF, INDIANS

PERSONAL: Born May 30, 1972, in Santo Domingo, Dominican Republic.... 6-0/190.... Throws right, bats right.... Full name: Manuel Aristides Ramirez.
HIGH SCHOOL: George Washington (New York).
TRANSACTIONS/CAREER NOTES: Selected by Cleveland Indians organization in first round (13th pick overall) of free-agent draft (June 3, 1991).... On disabled list (July 10, 1992-remainder of season).
HONORS: Named Appalachian League Most Valuable Player (1991).
STATISTICAL NOTES: Led Appalachian League with 146 total bases and .679 slugging percentage in 1991.

			BATTING												FIELDING			
Year	Team (League)	Pos.	G	AB	R	H	2B	3B	HR	RBI	Avg.	BB	SO	SB	PO	A	E	Avg.
1991	—Burlington (Appal.)	OF	59	215	44	70	11	4	*19	*63	.326	34	41	7	83	2	3	.966
1992	—Kinston (Carolina)	OF	81	291	52	81	18	4	13	63	.278	45	74	1	128	3	6	.956
1993	—Cant./Akr. (East.)	OF	89	344	67	117	32	0	17	79	*.340	45	68	2	142	4	5	.967
	—Charlotte (Int'l)	OF	40	145	38	46	12	0	14	36	.317	27	35	1	70	3	3	.961
	—Cleveland (A.L.)	OF	22	53	5	9	1	0	2	5	.170	2	8	0	3	0	0	1.000
Major league totals (1 year)			22	53	5	9	1	0	2	5	.170	2	8	0	3	0	0	1.000

RAMIREZ, OMAR

OF, INDIANS

PERSONAL: Born November 2, 1970, in Santiago, Dominican Republic.... 5-9/170.... Throws right, bats right.... Full name: Victor Omar Ramirez.
HIGH SCHOOL: Sagrado Corazon de Jesus (Santiago, Dominican Republic).
COLLEGE: Hill Junior College (Tex.).

TRANSACTIONS/CAREER NOTES: Selected by Cleveland Indians organization in 31st round of free-agent draft (June 4, 1990).
STATISTICAL NOTES: Led Eastern League outfielders with 293 total chances in 1993.

			BATTING												FIELDING			
Year	Team (League)	Pos.	G	AB	R	H	2B	3B	HR	RBI	Avg.	BB	SO	SB	PO	A	E	Avg.
1990	—Santiago (DSL)	...	45	183	47	57	10	1	4	33	.311	24	16	23	...	...	...	...
	—GC Indians (GCL)	OF	18	58	6	10	0	0	0	2	.172	11	10	2	29	2	1	.969
1991	—Watertown (NYP)	OF	56	210	30	56	17	0	2	16	.267	30	29	12	92	5	4	.960
1992	—Kinston (Carolina)	OF	110	411	73	123	20	5	13	49	.299	38	53	19	236	13	5	.980
1993	—Cant./Akr. (East.)	OF	125	516	*116	*162	24	6	7	53	.314	53	49	24	*278	9	6	.980

RAMIREZ, ROBERTO

P, PIRATES

PERSONAL: Born August 17, 1972, in Veracruz, Mexico. . . . 5-11/170. . . . Throws left, bats right. . . . Full name: Roberto Sanchez Ramirez.
HIGH SCHOOL: Prepatoria (Veracruz, Mexico).
TRANSACTIONS/CAREER NOTES: Signed as free agent by Mexico City Reds of Mexican League (1989). . . . Contract sold by Mexico City to Pittsburgh Pirates organization (January 8, 1990). . . . On Augusta disabled list (April 9-May 8, 1992). . . . Loaned by Pirates organization to Mexico City Red Devils of Mexican League (May 8, 1992-remainder of season and February 18, 1993-entire season).

Year	Team (League)	W	L	Pct.	ERA	G	GS	CG	ShO	Sv.	IP	H	R	ER	BB	SO
1989	—M.C. Reds (Mex.)	0	0	...	4.91	2	1	0	0	0	3⅔	4	2	2	2	2
1990	—GC Pirates (GCL)■	2	1	.667	0.53	11	3	0	0	0	33⅔	20	4	2	18	27
1991	—Welland (NYP)	2	6	.250	4.12	16	12	0	0	1	74⅓	66	43	34	35	71
1992	—M.C. Red Devils (Mex.)■	3	9	.250	5.98	19	13	6	0	0	81⅓	102	61	54	47	57
1993	—M.C. Red Devils (Mex.)	14	5	.737	3.40	25	24	8	4	0	156⅓	136	65	59	65	100

RAMOS, JOHN

C, PADRES

PERSONAL: Born August 6, 1965, in Tampa, Fla. . . . 6-0/190. . . . Throws right, bats right. . . . Full name: John Joseph Ramos.
HIGH SCHOOL: H.B. Plant (Tampa, Fla.).
COLLEGE: Stanford.
TRANSACTIONS/CAREER NOTES: Selected by Cleveland Indians organization in 23rd round of free-agent draft (June 6, 1986). . . . Selected by New York Yankees organization in fifth round of free-agent draft (June 2, 1986). . . . Placed on Columbus disabled list (May 8, 1992). . . . On Columbus suspended list (May 10-20, 1992). . . . On Columbus disabled list (May 20-July 7, 1992). . . . On New York disabled list (July 7, 1992-remainder of season). . . . Granted free agency (October 15, 1992). . . . Signed by Columbus, Yankees organization (February 10, 1993). . . . On disabled list (April 8-May 27 and August 2-10, 1993). . . . Granted free agency (October 15, 1993). . . . Signed by San Diego Padres organization (December 14, 1993).
STATISTICAL NOTES: Led Carolina League catchers with 25 errors in 1988. . . . Led International League with nine sacrifice flies in 1991.

			BATTING												FIELDING			
Year	Team (League)	Pos.	G	AB	R	H	2B	3B	HR	RBI	Avg.	BB	SO	SB	PO	A	E	Avg.
1986	—Fort Lauder. (FSL)	C	54	184	25	49	10	1	2	28	.266	26	23	8	197	19	9	.960
	—Oneonta (NYP)	C	3	8	3	4	2	1	0	1	.500	2	1	0	22	0	0	1.000
1987	—Prin. William (Car.)	C	76	235	26	51	6	1	2	27	.217	28	30	8	283	24	19	.942
1988	—Prin. William (Car.)	C-OF	109	391	47	119	18	2	8	57	.304	49	34	8	585	37	†26	.960
	—Alb./Colon. (East.)	3B-OF-C	21	72	11	16	1	3	1	13	.222	12	9	2	24	27	2	.962
1989	—Alb./Colon. (East.)	C-OF	105	359	55	98	21	0	9	60	.273	40	65	7	561	46	11	.982
1990	—Alb./Colon. (East.)	C-3B	84	287	38	90	20	1	4	46	.314	36	39	1	230	21	4	.984
	—Columbus (Int'l)	C	2	6	0	0	0	0	0	1	.000	0	0	0	2	1	0	1.000
1991	—Columbus (Int'l)	C	104	377	52	116	18	3	10	63	.308	56	54	1	487	41	6	.989
	—New York (A.L.)	C	10	26	4	8	1	0	0	3	.308	1	3	0	23	1	0	1.000
1992	—Columbus (Int'l)	C	18	64	5	11	4	1	1	12	.172	8	14	1	31	0	2	.939
1993	—Columbus (Int'l)	1B	49	158	17	41	7	0	1	18	.259	19	32	1	48	2	0	1.000
	Major league totals (1 year)		10	26	4	8	1	0	0	3	.308	1	3	0	23	1	0	1.000

RAMOS, KEN

OF, INDIANS

PERSONAL: Born June 8, 1967, in Sidney, Neb. . . . 6-0/185. . . . Throws left, bats left. . . . Full name: Kenneth Cecil Ramos.
HIGH SCHOOL: East (Pueblo, Colo.).
COLLEGE: Otero Junior College (Colo.) and Nebraska.
TRANSACTIONS/CAREER NOTES: Selected by Chicago Cubs organization in sixth round of free-agent draft (January 14, 1986). . . . Signed as free agent by Cleveland Indians organization (June 22, 1989). . . . On disabled list (April 10-17, 1991).
STATISTICAL NOTES: Led Carolina League with .426 on-base percentage in 1990. . . . Led Eastern League with .442 on-base percentage in 1992.

			BATTING												FIELDING			
Year	Team (League)	Pos.	G	AB	R	H	2B	3B	HR	RBI	Avg.	BB	SO	SB	PO	A	E	Avg.
1989	—GC Indians (GCL)	OF	54	193	41	60	7	2	1	14	.311	*39	18	17	86	5	2	.978
	—Kinston (Carolina)	OF	8	21	6	3	0	0	0	0	.143	5	2	2	6	0	0	1.000
1990	—Kinston (Carolina)	OF	96	339	71	117	16	6	0	31	*.345	48	34	18	163	5	3	.982
	—Cant./Akr. (East.)	OF	19	73	12	24	2	2	0	11	.329	8	10	2	53	0	1	.981
1991	—Cant./Akr. (East.)	OF	74	257	41	62	6	3	2	13	.241	28	22	8	96	8	6	.945
1992	—Cant./Akr. (East.)	OF	125	442	*93	150	23	5	5	42	*.339	82	37	14	158	6	7	.959
1993	—Charlotte (Int'l)	OF	132	480	77	140	16	11	3	41	.292	47	41	12	205	11	2	.991

RANDA, JOE

3B, ROYALS

PERSONAL: Born December 18, 1969, in Milwaukee. . . . 5-11/190. . . . Throws right, bats right. . . . Full name: Joseph Gregory Randa.
HIGH SCHOOL: Kettle Moraine Public (Wales, Wis.).
COLLEGE: Indian River Community College (Fla.) and Tennessee.

TRANSACTIONS/CAREER NOTES: Selected by California Angels organization in 30th round of free-agent draft (June 5, 1989).... Selected by Kansas City Royals organization in 11th round of free-agent draft (June 3, 1991).
HONORS: Named Northwest League Most Valuable Player (1991).
STATISTICAL NOTES: Led Northwest League with 150 total bases and .438 on-base percentage in 1991. ... Led Northwest League third basemen with 182 total chances and 12 double plays in 1991.... Led Southern League with 10 sacrifice flies in 1993.

			BATTING											FIELDING			
Year	Team (League)	Pos.	G	AB	R	H	2B	3B	HR	RBI	Avg.	BB	SO	SB	PO	A	E	Avg.
1991	—Eugene (N'west).......	3B	72	275	53	*93	20	2	11	59	.338	46	29	6	*57	*111	14	*.923
1992	—Appleton (Midw.)	3B	72	266	55	80	13	0	5	43	.301	34	37	6	53	137	12	.941
	—Baseball City (FSL)..	3B-SS	51	189	22	52	7	0	1	12	.275	12	21	4	43	105	6	.961
1993	—Memphis (South.)	3B	131	505	74	149	31	5	11	72	.295	39	64	8	*97	309	25	.942

RAPP, PAT

P, MARLINS

PERSONAL: Born July 13, 1967, in Jennings, La. ... 6-3/205. ... Throws right, bats right. ... Full name: Patrick Leland Rapp.
HIGH SCHOOL: Sulphur (La.).
COLLEGE: Hinds Community College (Miss.) and Southern Mississippi.
TRANSACTIONS/CAREER NOTES: Selected by San Francisco Giants organization in 15th round of free-agent draft (June 5, 1989). ... Selected by Florida Marlins in first round (10th pick overall) of expansion draft (November 17, 1992).

Year	Team (League)	W	L	Pct.	ERA	G	GS	CG	ShO	Sv.	IP	H	R	ER	BB	SO
1989	—Pocatello (Pioneer)	4	6	.400	5.30	16	12	1	0	0	73	90	54	43	29	40
1990	—Clinton (Midwest)	14	10	.583	2.64	27	26	4	0	0	167⅓	132	60	49	79	132
1991	—San Jose (Calif.)	7	5	.583	2.50	16	15	1	0	0	90	88	41	25	37	73
	—Shreveport (Texas)....	6	2	.750	2.69	10	10	1	1	0	60⅓	52	23	18	22	46
1992	—Phoenix (PCL)...........	7	8	.467	3.05	39	12	2	1	3	121	115	54	41	40	79
	—San Francisco (N.L.).....	0	2	.000	7.20	3	2	0	0	0	10	8	8	8	6	3
1993	—Edmonton (PCL)■.......	8	3	.727	3.43	17	17	•4	1	0	107⅔	89	45	41	34	93
	—Florida (N.L.)	4	6	.400	4.02	16	16	1	0	0	94	101	49	42	39	57
	Major league totals (2 years)...	4	8	.333	4.33	19	18	1	0	0	104	109	57	50	45	60

RASMUSSEN, DENNIS

P

PERSONAL: Born April 18, 1959, in Los Angeles.... 6-7/235.... Throws left, bats left.... Full name: Dennis Lee Rasmussen.... Grandson of Bill Brubaker, infielder, Pittsburgh Pirates and Boston Braves (1932-40 and 1943).
HIGH SCHOOL: Bear Creek (Lakewood, Colo.).
COLLEGE: Creighton.
TRANSACTIONS/CAREER NOTES: Selected by Pittsburgh Pirates organization in 18th round of free-agent draft (June 7, 1977).... Selected by California Angels organization in first round (17th pick overall) of free-agent draft (June 3, 1980); pick received as compensation for Houston Astros signing free agent Nolan Ryan.... Traded by Angels organization to New York Yankees (November 24, 1982), completing deal in which Yankees traded P Tommy John to Angels for a player to be named later (August 31, 1982).... Traded by Yankees organization with 2B Edwin Rodriguez to San Diego Padres (September 12, 1983), completing deal in which Padres traded P John Montefusco to Yankees for two players to be named later (August 26, 1983).... Traded by Padres with a player to be named later to Yankees organization for 3B Graig Nettles (March 30, 1984); Yankees organization acquired P Darin Cloninger to complete deal (April 26, 1984).... Traded by Yankees to Cincinnati Reds for P Bill Gullickson (August 26, 1987).... Traded by Reds to Padres for P Candy Sierra (June 8, 1988).... Granted free agency (November 5, 1990).... Re-signed by Padres (January 9, 1991).... On San Diego disabled list (March 31-May 25, 1991); included rehabilitation assignment to Las Vegas (April 23-May 22).... Granted free agency (October 28, 1991).... Signed by Rochester, Baltimore Orioles organization (January 31, 1992).... Released by Rochester (June 2, 1992).... Signed by Iowa, Chicago Cubs organization (June 5, 1992).... On Chicago disabled list (July 2-21, 1992).... Released by Cubs (July 24, 1992).... Signed by Omaha, Kansas City Royals organization (July 27, 1992).... On Kansas City disabled list (March 26-April 27, 1993); included rehabilitation assignment to Omaha (April 15-27).... On Kansas City disabled list (May 13-June 20, 1993); included rehabilitation assignment to Omaha (May 22-June 20).... Granted free agency (October 29, 1993).
STATISTICAL NOTES: Led Eastern League with 18 wild pitches in 1981.... Led N.L. with 28 home runs allowed in 1990.
MISCELLANEOUS: Struck out in only appearance as pinch-hitter with San Diego (1991).

Year	Team (League)	W	L	Pct.	ERA	G	GS	CG	ShO	Sv.	IP	H	R	ER	BB	SO
1980	—Salinas (Calif.)...........	4	6	.400	5.45	11	11	4	1	0	76	69	51	46	52	63
1981	—Holyoke (Eastern)......	8	12	.400	3.98	24	24	6	1	0	156	134	95	69	99	125
1982	—Spokane (PCL)...........	11	8	.579	5.03	27	27	4	2	0	171⅔	166	110	96	*113	162
1983	—Columbus (Int'l)■.......	•13	10	.565	4.57	28	•28	8	1	0	181	161	106	92	108	*187
	—San Diego (N.L.)■.......	0	0	...	1.98	4	1	0	0	0	13⅔	10	5	3	8	13
1984	—Columbus (Int'l)■.......	4	1	.800	3.09	6	6	3	1	0	43⅔	24	15	15	27	30
	—New York (A.L.)	9	6	.600	4.57	24	24	1	0	0	147⅔	127	79	75	60	110
1985	—New York (A.L.)	3	5	.375	3.98	22	16	2	0	0	101⅔	97	56	45	42	63
	—Columbus (Int'l)	0	3	.000	3.80	7	7	1	0	0	45	41	24	19	25	43
1986	—New York (A.L.)	18	6	.750	3.88	31	31	3	1	0	202	160	91	87	74	131
1987	—New York (A.L.)	9	7	.563	4.75	26	25	2	0	0	146	145	78	77	55	89
	—Columbus (Int'l)	1	0	1.000	1.29	1	1	0	0	0	7	5	1	1	0	4
	—Cincinnati (N.L.)■.......	4	1	.800	3.97	7	7	0	0	0	45⅓	39	22	20	12	39
1988	—Cin.-S.D. (N.L.)■.........	16	10	.615	3.43	31	31	7	1	0	204⅔	199	84	78	58	112
1989	—San Diego (N.L.).........	10	10	.500	4.26	33	33	1	0	0	183⅔	190	100	87	72	87
1990	—San Diego (N.L.).........	11	15	.423	4.51	32	32	3	1	0	187⅔	217	110	94	62	86
1991	—Las Vegas (PCL).........	1	3	.250	5.47	5	5	1	0	0	26⅓	23	18	16	15	12
	—San Diego (N.L.).........	6	13	.316	3.74	24	24	1	1	0	146⅔	155	74	61	49	75
1992	—Rochester (Int'l)■.......	0	7	.000	5.67	9	9	1	0	0	46	49	33	29	22	33
	—Iowa-Omaha (A.A.)■.	4	4	.500	2.03	13	8	3	2	0	62	52	21	14	20	50
	—Chicago (N.L.)............	0	0	...	10.80	3	1	0	0	0	5	7	6	6	2	0
	—Kansas City (A.L.).....	4	1	.800	1.43	5	5	1	1	0	37⅔	25	7	6	6	12

Year	Team (League)	W	L	Pct.	ERA	G	GS	CG	ShO	Sv.	IP	H	R	ER	BB	SO
1993	—Omaha (A.A.)	7	8	.467	5.03	17	17	3	1	0	105⅔	124	68	59	27	59
	—Kansas City (A.L.)	1	2	.333	7.45	9	4	0	0	0	29	40	25	24	14	12
A.L. totals (6 years)		44	27	.620	4.26	117	105	9	2	0	664	594	336	314	251	417
N.L. totals (7 years)		47	49	.490	3.99	134	129	12	3	0	786⅔	817	401	349	263	412
Major league totals (11 years)		91	76	.545	4.11	251	234	21	5	0	1450⅔	1411	737	663	514	829

READY, RANDY

IF/OF, EXPOS

PERSONAL: Born January 8, 1960, in San Mateo, Calif. . . . 5-11/184. . . . Throws right, bats right. . . . Full name: Randy Max Ready.
HIGH SCHOOL: John F. Kennedy (Fremont, Calif.).
COLLEGE: Cal State Hayward and Mesa College (Colo.).

TRANSACTIONS/CAREER NOTES: Selected by Milwaukee Brewers organization in fifth round of free-agent draft (June 3, 1980). . . . On Vancouver disabled list (August 21, 1984-remainder of season). . . . On Milwaukee disabled list (April 30-June 19, 1985); included rehabilitation assignment to Vancouver (June 1-19). . . . Traded by Brewers to San Diego Padres for a player to be named later (June 12, 1986); Brewers organization acquired IF Tim Pyznarski to complete deal (October 29, 1986). . . . On San Diego disabled list (June 19-July 7, 1986). . . . On Las Vegas disabled list (July 22, 1986-remainder of season). . . . Traded by Padres with OF John Kruk to Philadelphia Phillies for OF Chris James (June 2, 1989). . . . On disabled list (June 7-July 11, 1991). . . . Granted free agency (October 28, 1991). . . . Signed by Oakland Athletics (January 14, 1992). . . . On disabled list (April 5-21 and June 17-July 8, 1992). . . . Granted free agency (October 27, 1992). . . . Signed by Omaha, Kansas City Royals organization (March 2, 1993). . . . Released by Omaha (April 8, 1993). . . . Signed by Rochester, Baltimore Orioles organization (May 7, 1993). . . . Released by Rochester (August 9, 1993). . . . Signed by Montreal Expos (August 10, 1993). . . . Granted free agency (November 3, 1993). . . . Re-signed by Expos organization (December 14, 1993).
RECORDS: Shares A.L. single-game record for most innings played by third baseman—25 (May 8, finished May 9, 1984; fielded 24⅓ innings).
STATISTICAL NOTES: Led Midwest League third basemen with 22 double plays in 1981. . . . Led Texas League with 281 total bases in 1982. . . . Led Texas League third basemen with 456 total chances and 27 double plays in 1982.

				BATTING											FIELDING			
Year	Team (League)	Pos.	G	AB	R	H	2B	3B	HR	RBI	Avg.	BB	SO	SB	PO	A	E	Avg.
1980	—Butte (Pioneer)	SS-2B-3B	61	226	*65	85	*23	4	8	50	*.376	57	32	2	86	174	22	.922
1981	—Burlington (Midw.)	3B	110	367	74	113	17	0	17	56	.308	85	54	7	72	216	21	*.932
1982	—El Paso (Texas)	3B	132	475	*122	*178	33	5	20	99	*.375	92	48	13	*115	*312	•29	.936
1983	—Vancouver (PCL)	3B	116	407	82	134	28	1	13	59	.329	*99	59	24	136	231	24	.939
	—Milwaukee (A.L.)	3B	12	37	8	15	3	2	1	6	.405	6	3	0	5	8	0	1.000
1984	—Milwaukee (A.L.)	3B	37	123	13	23	6	1	3	13	.187	14	18	0	29	76	6	.946
	—Vancouver (PCL)	2B-3B	43	151	48	49	7	4	3	18	.325	43	21	10	74	125	6	.971
1985	—Milwaukee (A.L.)	OF-3B-2B	48	181	29	48	9	5	1	21	.265	14	23	0	93	14	1	.991
	—Vancouver (PCL)	OF-3B-2B	52	190	33	62	12	3	4	29	.326	30	14	14	60	35	7	.931
1986	—Milwaukee (A.L.)	OF-2B-3B	23	79	8	15	4	0	1	4	.190	9	9	2	35	21	3	.949
	—San Diego (N.L.)■	3B	1	3	0	0	0	0	0	0	.000	0	1	0	0	2	1	.667
	—Las Vegas (PCL)	3B-OF	10	38	5	14	4	0	1	8	.368	6	2	1	12	10	0	1.000
1987	—San Diego (N.L.)	3B-2B-OF	124	350	69	108	26	6	12	54	.309	67	44	7	124	220	15	.958
1988	—San Diego (N.L.)	3B-2B-OF	114	331	43	88	16	2	7	39	.266	39	38	6	112	153	11	.960
1989	—S.D.-Phil. (N.L.)■	OF-3B-2B	100	254	37	67	13	2	8	26	.264	42	37	4	80	72	9	.944
1990	—Philadelphia (N.L.)	OF-2B	101	217	26	53	9	1	1	26	.244	29	35	3	78	86	2	.988
1991	—Philadelphia (N.L.)	2B	76	205	32	51	10	1	1	20	.249	47	25	2	127	145	3	.989
1992	—Oakland (A.L.)■	0-3-2-1	61	125	17	25	2	0	3	17	.200	25	23	1	53	19	5	.935
1993	—Rochester (Int'l)■	3-0-1-2	84	305	48	88	17	3	9	46	.289	50	37	4	156	70	6	.974
	—Montreal (N.L.)■	2B-1B-3B	40	134	22	34	8	1	1	10	.254	23	8	2	135	92	8	.966
American League totals (5 years)			181	545	75	126	24	8	9	61	.231	68	76	3	215	138	15	.959
National League totals (7 years)			556	1494	229	401	82	13	30	175	.268	247	188	24	656	770	49	.967
Major league totals (11 years)			737	2039	304	527	106	21	39	236	.258	315	264	27	871	908	64	.965

CHAMPIONSHIP SERIES RECORD

				BATTING											FIELDING			
Year	Team (League)	Pos.	G	AB	R	H	2B	3B	HR	RBI	Avg.	BB	SO	SB	PO	A	E	Avg.
1992	—Oakland (A.L.)	PH	1	1	0	0	0	0	0	0	.000	0	1	0	...	...	...	...

REARDON, JEFF

P

PERSONAL: Born October 1, 1955, in Pittsfield, Mass. . . . 6-0/205. . . . Throws right, bats right. . . . Full name: Jeffrey James Reardon.
HIGH SCHOOL: Wahconah (Dalton, Mass.).
COLLEGE: Massachusetts.

TRANSACTIONS/CAREER NOTES: Selected by Montreal Expos organization in 23rd round of free-agent draft (June 5, 1973). . . . Signed as free agent by New York Mets organization (June 14, 1977). . . . On Tidewater disabled list (June 13-24 and June 29-July 26, 1979). . . . Traded by Mets with OF Dan Norman to Montreal Expos for OF Ellis Valentine (May 29, 1981). . . . Traded by Expos with C Tom Nieto to Minnesota Twins for P Neal Heaton, P Al Cardwood, P Yorkis Perez and C Jeff Reed (February 3, 1987). . . . Granted free agency (November 13, 1989). . . . Signed by Boston Red Sox (December 6, 1989). . . . On disabled list (July 30-September 12, 1990). . . . Traded by Red Sox to Atlanta Braves for P Nate Minchey and OF Sean Ross (August 30, 1992). . . . Granted free agency (October 30, 1992). . . . Signed by Cincinnati Reds organization (January 19, 1993). . . . Granted free agency (October 29, 1993).
HONORS: Named N.L. Fireman of the Year by THE SPORTING NEWS (1985). . . . Named A.L. co-Fireman of the Year by THE SPORTING NEWS (1987).

Year	Team (League)	W	L	Pct.	ERA	G	GS	CG	ShO	Sv.	IP	H	R	ER	BB	SO
1977	—Lynchburg (Caro.)	8	3	.727	3.30	16	12	8	*3	0	101	89	42	37	30	60
1978	—Jackson (Texas)	*17	4	*.810	2.54	28	21	9	2	0	163	128	56	46	65	115
1979	—Tidewater (Int'l)	5	2	.714	2.09	30	1	1	0	0	69	46	18	16	21	64

Year	Team (League)	W	L	Pct.	ERA	G	GS	CG	ShO	Sv.	IP	H	R	ER	BB	SO
	—New York (N.L.)	1	2	.333	1.71	18	0	0	0	2	21	12	7	4	9	10
1980	—New York (N.L.)	8	7	.533	2.62	61	0	0	0	6	110	96	36	32	47	101
1981	—N.Y.-Mont. (N.L.)■	3	0	1.000	2.19	43	0	0	0	8	70	48	17	17	21	49
1982	—Montreal (N.L.)	7	4	.636	2.06	75	0	0	0	26	109	87	28	25	36	86
1983	—Montreal (N.L.)	7	9	.438	3.03	66	0	0	0	21	92	87	34	31	44	78
1984	—Montreal (N.L.)	7	7	.500	2.90	68	0	0	0	23	87	70	31	28	37	79
1985	—Montreal (N.L.)	2	8	.200	3.18	63	0	0	0	*41	87⅔	68	31	31	26	67
1986	—Montreal (N.L.)	7	9	.438	3.94	62	0	0	0	35	89	83	42	39	26	67
1987	—Minnesota (A.L.)■	8	8	.500	4.48	63	0	0	0	31	80⅓	70	41	40	28	83
1988	—Minnesota (A.L.)	2	4	.333	2.47	63	0	0	0	42	73	68	21	20	15	56
1989	—Minnesota (A.L.)	5	4	.556	4.07	65	0	0	0	31	73	68	33	33	12	46
1990	—Boston (A.L.)■	5	3	.625	3.16	47	0	0	0	21	51⅓	39	19	18	19	33
1991	—Boston (A.L.)	1	4	.200	3.03	57	0	0	0	40	59⅓	54	21	20	16	44
1992	—Boston (A.L.)	2	2	.500	4.25	46	0	0	0	27	42⅓	53	20	20	7	32
	—Atlanta (N.L.)■	3	0	1.000	1.15	14	0	0	0	3	15⅔	14	2	2	2	7
1993	—Cincinnati (N.L.)■	4	6	.400	4.09	58	0	0	0	8	61⅔	66	34	28	10	35
A.L. totals (6 years)		23	25	.479	3.58	341	0	0	0	192	379⅓	352	155	151	97	294
N.L. totals (10 years)		49	52	.485	2.87	528	0	0	0	173	743	631	262	237	258	579
Major league totals (15 years)		72	77	.483	3.11	869	0	0	0	365	1122⅓	983	417	388	355	873

DIVISION SERIES RECORD

Year	Team (League)	W	L	Pct.	ERA	G	GS	CG	ShO	Sv.	IP	H	R	ER	BB	SO
1981	—Montreal (N.L.)	0	1	.000	2.08	3	0	0	0	2	4⅓	1	1	1	1	2

CHAMPIONSHIP SERIES RECORD

CHAMPIONSHIP SERIES NOTES: Shares A.L. single-series record for most games pitched—4 (1987).

Year	Team (League)	W	L	Pct.	ERA	G	GS	CG	ShO	Sv.	IP	H	R	ER	BB	SO
1981	—Montreal (N.L.)	0	0	...	27.00	1	0	0	0	0	1	3	3	3	0	0
1987	—Minnesota (A.L.)	1	1	.500	5.06	4	0	0	0	2	5⅓	7	3	3	3	5
1990	—Boston (A.L.)	0	0	...	9.00	1	0	0	0	0	2	3	2	2	1	0
1992	—Atlanta (N.L.)	1	0	1.000	0.00	3	0	0	0	1	3	0	0	0	2	3
Champ. series totals (4 years)		2	1	.667	6.35	9	0	0	0	3	11⅓	13	8	8	6	8

WORLD SERIES RECORD

Year	Team (League)	W	L	Pct.	ERA	G	GS	CG	ShO	Sv.	IP	H	R	ER	BB	SO
1987	—Minnesota (A.L.)	0	0	...	0.00	4	0	0	0	1	4⅔	5	0	0	0	3
1992	—Atlanta (N.L.)	0	1	.000	13.50	2	0	0	0	0	1⅓	2	2	2	1	1
World Series totals (2 years)		0	1	.000	3.00	6	0	0	0	1	6	7	2	2	1	4

ALL-STAR GAME RECORD

Year	League	W	L	Pct.	ERA	GS	CG	ShO	Sv.	IP	H	R	ER	BB	SO
1985	—National	0	0	...	0.00	0	0	0	0	1	1	0	0	0	1
1986	—National						Did not play.								
1988	—American						Did not play.								
1991	—American	0	0	...	0.00	0	0	0	0	⅔	1	0	0	0	0
All-Star totals (2 years)		0	0	...	0.00	0	0	0	0	1⅔	2	0	0	0	1

REBOULET, JEFF

IF, TWINS

PERSONAL: Born April 30, 1964, in Dayton, O. . . . 6-0/169. . . . Throws right, bats right. . . . Full name: Jeffrey Allen Reboulet. . . . Name pronounced REB-uh-lay.

HIGH SCHOOL: Alter (Kettering, O.).

COLLEGE: Louisiana State.

TRANSACTIONS/CAREER NOTES: Selected by Houston Astros organization in 26th round of free-agent draft (June 3, 1985). . . . Selected by Minnesota Twins organization in 10th round of free-agent draft (June 2, 1986).

STATISTICAL NOTES: Led Southern League shortstops with 602 total chances in 1988. . . . Led Pacific Coast League with 17 sacrifice hits in 1991. . . . Led Pacific Coast League shortstops with 649 total chances and 99 double plays in 1991.

			BATTING												FIELDING			
Year	Team (League)	Pos.	G	AB	R	H	2B	3B	HR	RBI	Avg.	BB	SO	SB	PO	A	E	Avg.
1986	—Visalia (California)	SS	72	254	54	73	13	1	0	29	.287	54	33	14	118	188	20	.939
1987	—Orlando (Southern)	SS-2B-3B	129	422	52	108	15	1	1	35	.256	58	56	9	220	370	26	.958
1988	—Orlando (Southern)	SS	125	439	57	112	24	2	4	41	.255	53	55	18	*225	347	30	.950
	—Portland (PCL)	2B-SS	4	12	0	1	0	0	0	1	.083	3	2	0	8	13	1	.955
1989	—Portland (PCL)	S-2-3-O	26	65	9	16	1	0	0	3	.246	12	11	2	38	62	7	.935
	—Orlando (Southern)	SS-2B-OF	81	291	43	63	5	1	0	26	.216	49	33	11	129	228	22	.942
1990	—Orlando (Southern)	2-3-S-O-1	97	287	43	66	12	2	2	28	.230	57	37	10	131	230	12	.968
1991	—Portland (PCL)	SS	134	391	50	97	27	3	3	46	.248	57	52	5	*202	415	*32	.951
1992	—Portland (PCL)	SS	48	161	21	46	11	1	2	21	.286	35	18	3	72	141	7	.968
	—Minnesota (A.L.)	S-3-2-O	73	137	15	26	7	1	1	16	.190	23	26	3	71	163	5	.979
1993	—Minnesota (A.L.)	S-3-2-O	109	240	33	62	8	0	1	15	.258	35	37	5	122	215	6	.983
Major league totals (2 years)			182	377	48	88	15	1	2	31	.233	58	63	8	193	378	11	.981

REDUS, GARY

OF, RANGERS

PERSONAL: Born November 1, 1956, in Tanner, Ala. . . . 6-1/195. . . . Throws right, bats right. . . . Full name: Gary Eugene Redus. . . . Name pronounced REE-dus.

HIGH SCHOOL: Tanner (Ala.).

TRANSACTIONS/CAREER NOTES: Selected by Boston Red Sox organization in 17th round of free-agent draft (June 7, 1977). . . . Selected by Cincinnati Reds organization in 15th round of free-agent draft (June 6, 1978). . . . Traded by Reds with P Tom Hume to Philadelphia Phillies for P John Denny and P Jeff Gray (December 11, 1985). . . . On Philadelphia disabled list (April 28-July 1, 1986); included rehabilitation assignment to Reading (June 23-30).... Traded by Phillies to Chicago White Sox for P Joe Cowley and cash (March 26, 1987).... Traded by White Sox to Pittsburgh Pirates for OF Mike Diaz (August 19, 1988).... Granted free agency (November 4, 1988).... Re-signed by Pirates (November 15, 1988).... On disabled list (March 27-April 11 and July 25-August 9, 1989).... Granted free agency (November 5, 1990).... Re-signed by Pirates (December 10, 1990).... On disabled list (May 21-June 8 and June 14-29, 1992).... Granted free agency (October 27, 1992).... Signed by Texas Rangers (January 13, 1993).... On disabled list (June 2-19, 1993).

HONORS: Named Pioneer League Player of the Year (1978).

STATISTICAL NOTES: Led Pioneer League with 199 total bases and tied for lead with six sacrifice flies in 1978.... Tied for Western Carolinas League lead in errors by second baseman with 20 in 1979.... Led Florida State League with 220 total bases in 1980.... Tied for American Association lead with nine sacrifice flies in 1982.... Hit for the cycle (August 25, 1989).

			BATTING											FIELDING			
Year	**Team (League)**	**Pos.**	**G**	**AB**	**R**	**H**	**2B**	**3B**	**HR**	**RBI**	**Avg.**	**BB**	**SO**	**SB**	**PO**	**A**	**E**	**Avg.**
1978	—Billings (Pioneer)	2B	68	253	*100	*117	19	6	17	62	*.462	62	31	*42	124	*185	*28	.917
1979	—Nashville (South.)	OF	36	109	7	19	2	1	0	7	.174	18	27	8	74	3	3	.963
	—Greens. (W. Car.)	2B-OF	83	309	79	86	17	1	16	52	.278	58	61	41	172	193	‡21	.946
1980	—Tampa (Fla. St.)	OF-3B-1B	128	452	78	136	18	9	16	68	.301	66	78	50	213	84	27	.917
1981	—Waterbury (East.)	OF-1B	138	477	71	119	26	4	20	75	.249	82	108	48	667	34	14	.980
1982	—Indianapolis (A.A.)	OF	122	439	112	146	29	9	24	93	.333	51	93	*54	223	10	7	.971
	—Cincinnati (N.L.)	OF	20	83	12	18	3	2	1	7	.217	5	21	11	29	3	1	.970
1983	—Cincinnati (N.L.)	OF	125	453	90	112	20	9	17	51	.247	71	111	39	235	11	7	.972
1984	—Cincinnati (N.L.)	OF	123	394	69	100	21	3	7	22	.254	52	71	48	200	6	7	.967
1985	—Cincinnati (N.L.)	OF	101	246	51	62	14	4	6	28	.252	44	52	48	140	3	2	.986
1986	—Philadelphia (N.L.)■	OF	90	340	62	84	22	4	11	33	.247	47	78	25	185	8	4	.980
	—Reading (Eastern)	OF	6	24	4	6	1	0	0	0	.250	2	6	1	11	1	1	.923
1987	—Chicago (A.L.)■	OF	130	475	78	112	26	6	12	48	.236	69	90	52	262	13	6	.979
1988	—Chicago (A.L.)	OF	77	262	42	69	10	4	6	34	.263	33	52	26	140	7	2	.987
	—Pittsburgh (N.L.)■	OF	30	71	12	14	2	0	2	4	.197	15	19	5	42	2	2	.957
1989	—Pittsburgh (N.L.)	1B-OF	98	279	42	79	18	7	6	33	.283	40	51	25	583	55	9	.986
1990	—Pittsburgh (N.L.)	1B-OF	96	227	32	56	15	3	6	23	.247	33	38	11	461	36	8	.984
1991	—Pittsburgh (N.L.)	1B-OF	98	252	45	62	12	2	7	24	.246	28	39	17	403	26	6	.986
1992	—Pittsburgh (N.L.)	1B-OF	76	176	26	45	7	3	3	12	.256	17	25	11	301	16	1	.997
1993	—Texas (A.L.)■	OF-1B-2B	77	222	28	64	12	4	6	31	.288	23	35	4	124	4	3	.977
American League totals (3 years)			284	959	148	245	48	14	24	113	.255	125	177	82	526	24	11	.980
National League totals (10 years)			857	2521	441	632	134	37	66	237	.251	352	505	240	2579	166	47	.983
Major league totals (12 years)			1141	3480	589	877	182	51	90	350	.252	477	682	322	3105	190	58	.983

CHAMPIONSHIP SERIES RECORD

CHAMPIONSHIP SERIES NOTES: Shares single-series record for most doubles—4 (1992).

			BATTING											FIELDING			
Year	**Team (League)**	**Pos.**	**G**	**AB**	**R**	**H**	**2B**	**3B**	**HR**	**RBI**	**Avg.**	**BB**	**SO**	**SB**	**PO**	**A**	**E**	**Avg.**
1990	—Pittsburgh (N.L.)	PH-1B	5	8	1	2	0	0	0	0	.250	1	3	1	16	0	0	1.000
1991	—Pittsburgh (N.L.)	1B	5	19	1	3	0	0	0	0	.158	1	4	2	51	0	2	.962
1992	—Pittsburgh (N.L.)	1B-PH	5	16	4	7	4	1	0	3	.438	2	3	0	31	4	0	1.000
Championship series totals (3 years)			15	43	6	12	4	1	0	3	.279	4	10	3	98	4	2	.981

REED, DARREN

OF, PIRATES

PERSONAL: Born October 16, 1965, in Ventura, Calif.... 6-1/205.... Throws right, bats right.... Full name: Darren Douglas Reed.

HIGH SCHOOL: Ventura (Calif.).

COLLEGE: Ventura (Calif.) College.

TRANSACTIONS/CAREER NOTES: Selected by Oakland Athletics organization in 10th round of free-agent draft (January 17, 1984).... Selected by New York Yankees organization in secondary phase of free-agent draft (June 4, 1984).... On disabled list (June 17, 1986-remainder of season).... Traded by Yankees organization with C Phil Lombardi and P Steve Frey to New York Mets for SS Rafael Santana and P Victor Garcia (December 11, 1987).... Traded by Mets with OF Alex Diaz to Montreal Expos for OF Terrel Hansen and P David Sommer (April 2, 1991).... On Montreal disabled list (April 5, 1991-entire season).... On Montreal disabled list (March 28-May 12, 1992); included rehabilitation assignment to Indianapolis (April 9-11) and West Palm Beach (April 28-May 12).... Traded by Expos to Minnesota Twins for P Bill Krueger (August 31, 1992).... Traded by Twins to New York Mets for OF Pat Howell (November 18, 1992).... On New York disabled list (March 29-September 9, 1993).... Released by Mets (September 9, 1993).... Signed by Pittsburgh Pirates organization (January 25, 1994).

STATISTICAL NOTES: Led International League in grounding into double plays with 15 in 1989.

			BATTING											FIELDING			
Year	**Team (League)**	**Pos.**	**G**	**AB**	**R**	**H**	**2B**	**3B**	**HR**	**RBI**	**Avg.**	**BB**	**SO**	**SB**	**PO**	**A**	**E**	**Avg.**
1984	—Oneonta (NYP)	OF-C	40	113	17	26	7	0	2	9	.230	10	19	2	41	2	2	.956
1985	—Fort Lauder. (FSL)	OF	100	369	63	117	21	4	10	61	.317	36	56	13	191	8	7	.966
1986	—Alb./Colon. (East.)	OF	51	196	22	45	11	1	4	27	.230	15	24	1	78	2	5	.941
1987	—Alb./Colon. (East.)	OF	107	404	68	129	23	4	20	79	.319	51	50	7	174	6	4	.978
	—Columbus (Int'l)	OF	21	79	15	26	3	3	8	16	.329	4	9	0	33	2	1	.972
1988	—Tidewater (Int'l)■	OF-C	101	345	31	83	26	0	9	47	.241	32	66	0	170	5	4	.978
1989	—Tidewater (Int'l)	OF	133	444	57	119	30	6	4	50	.268	60	70	11	232	*19	5	.980
1990	—Tidewater (Int'l)	OF	104	359	58	95	21	6	17	74	.265	51	62	16	222	11	4	.983
	—New York (N.L.)	OF	26	39	5	8	4	1	1	2	.205	3	11	1	20	1	1	.955
1991	—■		Did not play.															
1992	—Indianapolis (A.A.)	OF	1	3	0	1	1	0	0	0	.333	0	1	0	1	0	0	1.000
	—W.P. Beach (FSL)	OF	10	40	6	10	4	0	2	12	.250	1	14	0	20	1	0	1.000
	—Montreal (N.L.)	OF	42	81	10	14	2	0	5	10	.173	6	23	0	37	1	0	1.000
	—Minnesota (A.L.)■	OF	14	33	2	6	2	0	0	4	.182	2	11	0	14	1	0	1.000
1993	—■		Did not play.															
American League totals (1 year)			14	33	2	6	2	0	0	4	.182	2	11	0	14	1	0	1.000
National League totals (2 years)			68	120	15	22	6	1	6	12	.183	9	34	1	57	2	1	.983
Major league totals (2 years)			82	153	17	28	8	1	6	16	.183	11	45	1	71	3	1	.987

REED, JEFF

C, GIANTS

PERSONAL: Born November 12, 1962, in Joliet, Ill. . . . 6-2/190. . . . Throws right, bats left. . . . Full name: Jeffrey Scott Reed. . . . Brother of Curtis Reed, minor league outfielder (1977-84).
HIGH SCHOOL: West (Joliet, Ill.).
TRANSACTIONS/CAREER NOTES: Selected by Minnesota Twins organization in first round (12th pick overall) of free-agent draft (June 3, 1980). . . . Traded by Twins organization with P Neal Heaton, P Al Cardwood and P Yorkis Perez to Montreal Expos for P Jeff Reardon and C Tom Nieto (February 3, 1987). . . . On Montreal disabled list (April 20-May 25, 1987); included rehabilitation assignment to Indianapolis (May 19-25). . . . Traded by Expos with OF Herm Winningham and P Randy St. Claire to Cincinnati Reds for OF Tracy Jones and P Pat Pacillo (July 13, 1988). . . . On disabled list (July 1-19, 1991). . . . On Cincinnati disabled list (April 26-September 1, 1992); included rehabilitation assignment to Nashville (August 17-September 1). . . . Granted free agency (October 27, 1992). . . . Signed by San Francisco Giants organization (January 15, 1993). . . . On San Francisco disabled list (June 30-August 3, 1993); included rehabilitation assignment to San Jose (July 21-22 and July 30-August 3).
RECORDS: Holds modern N.L. record for most errors by catcher in one inning—3 (July 28, 1987, seventh inning).
STATISTICAL NOTES: Led California League catchers with 758 total chances and tied for lead with nine double plays in 1982. . . . Led Southern League catchers with 714 total chances and 12 double plays in 1983. . . . Led International League catchers with 720 total chances in 1985.

			BATTING											FIELDING			
Year	Team (League)	Pos.	G	AB	R	H	2B	3B	HR	RBI	Avg.	BB	SO	SB	PO	A	E	Avg.
1980	—Elizabeth. (Appal.)	C	65	225	39	64	15	1	1	20	.284	51	23	2	269	*41	9	.972
1981	—Wis. Rap. (Midw.)	C	106	312	63	73	12	1	4	34	.234	86	36	4	547	*93	7	.989
	—Orlando (Southern)	C	3	4	0	1	0	0	0	0	.250	1	0	0	4	1	0	1.000
1982	—Visalia (California)	C	125	395	69	130	19	2	5	54	.329	78	32	1	*642	•106	10	.987
1983	—Orlando (Southern)	C	118	379	52	100	16	5	6	45	.264	76	40	2	*618	*88	8	*.989
	—Toledo (Int'l)	C	14	41	5	7	1	1	0	3	.171	5	9	0	77	6	1	.988
1984	—Minnesota (A.L.)	C	18	21	3	3	3	0	0	1	.143	2	6	0	41	2	1	.977
	—Toledo (Int'l)	C	94	301	30	80	16	3	3	35	.266	37	35	1	546	43	5	*.992
1985	—Toledo (Int'l)	C	122	404	53	100	15	3	5	36	.248	59	49	1	*627	*81	12	.983
	—Minnesota (A.L.)	C	7	10	2	2	0	0	0	0	.200	0	3	0	9	3	0	1.000
1986	—Minnesota (A.L.)	C	68	165	13	39	6	1	2	9	.236	16	19	1	332	19	2	.994
	—Toledo (Int'l)	C	25	71	10	22	5	3	1	14	.310	17	9	0	108	22	2	.985
1987	—Montreal (N.L.)■	C	75	207	15	44	11	0	1	21	.213	12	20	0	357	36	12	.970
	—Indianapolis (A.A.)	C	5	17	0	3	0	0	0	0	.176	1	2	0	27	2	0	1.000
1988	—Mont.-Cin. (N.L.)■	C	92	265	20	60	9	2	1	16	.226	28	41	1	468	38	3	.994
	—Indianapolis (A.A.)	C	8	22	1	7	3	0	0	1	.318	2	2	0	30	11	0	1.000
1989	—Cincinnati (N.L.)	C	102	287	16	64	11	0	3	23	.223	34	46	0	504	50	7	.988
1990	—Cincinnati (N.L.)	C	72	175	12	44	8	1	3	16	.251	24	26	0	358	26	5	.987
1991	—Cincinnati (N.L.)	C	91	270	20	72	15	2	3	31	.267	23	38	0	527	29	5	.991
1992	—Nashville (A.A.)	C	14	25	1	6	1	0	1	2	.240	2	7	0	47	4	0	1.000
	—Cincinnati (N.L.)	C	15	25	2	4	0	0	0	2	.160	1	4	0	29	2	0	1.000
1993	—San Francisco (N.L.)■	C	66	119	10	31	3	0	6	12	.261	16	22	0	180	14	0	1.000
	—San Jose (Calif.)	C	4	10	2	5	1	0	0	2	.500	1	0	0	19	2	0	1.000
American League totals (3 years)			93	196	18	44	9	1	2	10	.224	18	28	1	382	24	3	.993
National League totals (7 years)			513	1348	95	319	57	5	17	121	.237	138	197	1	2423	195	32	.988
Major league totals (10 years)			606	1544	113	363	66	6	19	131	.235	156	225	2	2805	219	35	.989

CHAMPIONSHIP SERIES RECORD

			BATTING											FIELDING			
Year	Team (League)	Pos.	G	AB	R	H	2B	3B	HR	RBI	Avg.	BB	SO	SB	PO	A	E	Avg.
1990	—Cincinnati (N.L.)	C	4	7	0	0	0	0	0	0	.000	2	0	0	24	1	0	1.000

WORLD SERIES RECORD

			BATTING											FIELDING			
Year	Team (League)	Pos.	G	AB	R	H	2B	3B	HR	RBI	Avg.	BB	SO	SB	PO	A	E	Avg.
1990	—Cincinnati (N.L.)								Did not play.									

REED, JODY

2B, BREWERS

PERSONAL: Born July 26, 1962, in Tampa, Fla. . . . 5-9/165. . . . Throws right, bats right. . . . Full name: Jody Eric Reed.
HIGH SCHOOL: Brandon (Fla.).
COLLEGE: Manatee Junior College (Fla.) and Florida State (degree in criminology, 1985).
TRANSACTIONS/CAREER NOTES: Selected by Texas Rangers organization in third round of free-agent draft (January 12, 1982). . . . Selected by San Francisco Giants organization in secondary phase of free-agent draft (June 7, 1982). . . . Selected by Rangers organization in secondary phase of free-agent draft (June 6, 1983). . . . Selected by Boston Red Sox organization in eighth round of free-agent draft (June 4, 1984). . . . Selected by Colorado Rockies in first round (13th pick overall) of expansion draft (November 17, 1992). . . . Traded by Rockies to Los Angeles Dodgers for P Rudy Seanez (November 17, 1992). . . . On disabled list (June 16-July 15, 1993). . . . Granted free agency (October 25, 1993). . . . Signed by Milwaukee Brewers organization (February 3, 1994).
RECORDS: Shares major league record for most doubles in one inning—2 (September 8, 1991, third inning). . . . Shares modern major league record for most long hits in one inning—2 (September 8, 1991, third inning).
STATISTICAL NOTES: Led Florida State League shortstops with 101 double plays in 1985. . . . Led International League shortstops with 683 total chances and 86 double plays in 1987.

			BATTING											FIELDING			
Year	Team (League)	Pos.	G	AB	R	H	2B	3B	HR	RBI	Avg.	BB	SO	SB	PO	A	E	Avg.
1984	—Winter Haven (FSL)	SS	77	273	46	74	14	1	0	20	.271	52	19	9	128	271	26	.939
1985	—Winter Haven (FSL)	SS	134	489	*95	157	25	1	0	45	*.321	*94	26	16	*256	*478	37	*.952
1986	—New Britain (East.)	SS	60	218	33	50	12	1	0	11	.229	52	9	10	114	190	14	.956
	—Pawtucket (Int'l)	SS	69	227	27	64	11	0	1	30	.282	31	18	8	115	222	12	.966
1987	—Pawtucket (Int'l)	SS	136	510	77	151	22	2	7	51	.296	69	23	9	*236	*427	20	.971
	—Boston (A.L.)	SS-2B-3B	9	30	4	9	1	1	0	8	.300	4	0	1	11	26	0	1.000
1988	—Boston (A.L.)	SS-2B-3B	109	338	60	99	23	1	1	28	.293	45	21	1	147	282	11	.975

Year	Team (League)	Pos.	G	AB	R	H	2B	3B	HR	RBI	Avg.	BB	SO	SB	PO	A	E	Avg.
			BATTING												FIELDING			
1989	—Boston (A.L.)	S-2-3-0	146	524	76	151	42	2	3	40	.288	73	44	4	255	423	19	.973
1990	—Boston (A.L.)	2B-SS	155	598	70	173	•45	0	5	51	.289	75	65	4	278	478	16	.979
1991	—Boston (A.L.)	2B	153	618	87	175	42	2	5	60	.283	60	53	6	312	444	14	.982
1992	—Boston (A.L.)	2B	143	550	64	136	27	1	3	40	.247	62	44	7	304	472	14	.982
1993	—Los Angeles (N.L.)■	2B	132	445	48	123	21	2	2	31	.276	38	40	1	280	413	5	*.993
American League totals (6 years)			715	2658	361	743	180	7	17	227	.280	319	227	23	1307	2125	74	.979
National League totals (1 year)			132	445	48	123	21	2	2	31	.276	38	40	1	280	413	5	.993
Major league totals (7 years)			847	3103	409	866	201	9	19	258	.279	357	267	24	1587	2538	79	.981

CHAMPIONSHIP SERIES RECORD

Year	Team (League)	Pos.	G	AB	R	H	2B	3B	HR	RBI	Avg.	BB	SO	SB	PO	A	E	Avg.
			BATTING												FIELDING			
1988	—Boston (A.L.)	SS	4	11	0	3	1	0	0	0	.273	2	1	0	3	10	0	1.000
1990	—Boston (A.L.)	2B-SS	4	15	0	2	0	0	0	1	.133	0	2	0	11	11	0	1.000
Championship series totals (2 years)			8	26	0	5	1	0	0	1	.192	2	3	0	14	21	0	1.000

REED, RICK

P, RANGERS

PERSONAL: Born August 16, 1964, in Huntington, W.Va. . . . 6-0/200. . . . Throws right, bats right. . . . Full name: Richard Allen Reed.
HIGH SCHOOL: Huntington (W.Va.).
COLLEGE: Marshall.
TRANSACTIONS/CAREER NOTES: Selected by Pittsburgh Pirates organization in 26th round of free-agent draft (June 2, 1986). . . . On Buffalo disabled list (May 2-13, 1991). . . . Granted free agency (April 3, 1992). . . . Signed by Omaha, Kansas City Royals organization (April 4, 1992). . . . Granted free agency (August 5, 1993). . . . Signed by Oklahoma City, Texas Rangers organization (August 11, 1993).
HONORS: Named American Association Most Valuable Pitcher (1991).

Year	Team (League)	W	L	Pct.	ERA	G	GS	CG	ShO	Sv.	IP	H	R	ER	BB	SO
1986	—GC Pirates (GCL)	0	2	.000	3.75	8	3	0	0	0	24	20	12	10	6	15
	—Macon (S. Atl.)	0	0	...	2.84	1	1	0	0	0	6⅓	5	3	2	2	1
1987	—Macon (S. Atl.)	8	4	.667	2.50	46	0	0	0	7	93⅔	80	38	26	29	92
1988	—Salem (Carolina)	6	2	.750	2.74	15	8	4	1	0	72⅓	56	28	22	17	73
	—Harrisburg (East.)	1	0	1.000	1.13	2	2	0	0	0	16	11	2	2	2	17
	—Buffalo (A.A.)	5	2	.714	1.64	10	9	3	2	0	77	62	15	14	12	50
	—Pittsburgh (N.L.)	1	0	1.000	3.00	2	2	0	0	0	12	10	4	4	2	6
1989	—Buffalo (A.A.)	9	8	.529	3.72	20	20	3	0	0	125⅔	130	58	52	28	75
	—Pittsburgh (N.L.)	1	4	.200	5.60	15	7	0	0	0	54⅔	62	35	34	11	34
1990	—Buffalo (A.A.)	7	4	.636	3.46	15	15	2	2	0	91	82	37	35	21	63
	—Pittsburgh (N.L.)	2	3	.400	4.36	13	8	1	1	1	53⅔	62	32	26	12	27
1991	—Buffalo (A.A.)	*14	4	*.778	*2.15	25	25	•5	2	0	167⅔	151	45	40	26	102
	—Pittsburgh (N.L.)	0	0	...	10.38	1	1	0	0	0	4⅓	8	6	5	1	2
1992	—Omaha (A.A.)■	5	4	.556	4.35	11	10	3	0	1	62	67	33	30	12	35
	—Kansas City (A.L.)	3	7	.300	3.68	19	18	1	1	0	100⅓	105	47	41	20	49
1993	—Oma.-Okla. C. (A.A.)■	12	7	.632	3.32	24	24	4	*2	0	162⅔	159	68	60	16	79
	—K.C.-Texas (A.L.)■	1	0	1.000	5.87	3	0	0	0	0	7⅔	12	5	5	2	5
A.L. totals (2 years)		4	7	.364	3.83	22	18	1	1	0	108	117	52	46	22	54
N.L. totals (4 years)		4	7	.364	4.98	31	18	1	1	1	124⅔	142	77	69	26	69
Major league totals (6 years)		8	14	.364	4.45	53	36	2	2	1	232⅔	259	129	115	48	123

REED, STEVE

P, ROCKIES

PERSONAL: Born March 11, 1966, in Los Angeles. . . . 6-2/205. . . . Throws right, bats right. . . . Full name: Steven Vincent Reed.
HIGH SCHOOL: Chatsworth (Calif.).
COLLEGE: Lewis-Clark State College (Idaho).
TRANSACTIONS/CAREER NOTES: Signed as free agent by San Francisco Giants organization (June 24, 1988). . . . On disabled list (July 17-August 13, 1990). . . . Selected by Colorado Rockies in third round (60th pick overall) of expansion draft (November 17, 1992).

Year	Team (League)	W	L	Pct.	ERA	G	GS	CG	ShO	Sv.	IP	H	R	ER	BB	SO
1988	—Pocatello (Pioneer)	4	1	.800	2.54	31	0	0	0	*13	46	42	20	13	8	49
1989	—Clinton (Midwest)	5	3	.625	1.05	60	0	0	0	26	94⅔	54	16	11	38	104
	—San Jose (Calif.)	0	0	...	0.00	2	0	0	0	0	2	0	0	0	1	3
1990	—Shreveport (Texas)	3	1	.750	1.64	45	1	0	0	8	60⅓	53	20	11	20	59
1991	—Shreveport (Texas)	2	0	1.000	0.83	15	0	0	0	7	21⅔	17	2	2	3	26
	—Phoenix (PCL)	2	3	.400	4.31	41	0	0	0	6	56⅓	62	33	27	12	46
1992	—Shreveport (Texas)	1	0	1.000	0.62	27	0	0	0	23	29	18	3	2	0	33
	—Phoenix (PCL)	0	1	.000	3.48	29	0	0	0	20	31	27	13	12	10	30
	—San Francisco (N.L.)	1	0	1.000	2.30	18	0	0	0	0	15⅔	13	5	4	3	11
1993	—Colorado (N.L.)■	9	5	.643	4.48	64	0	0	0	3	84⅓	80	47	42	30	51
	—Colo. Springs (PCL)	0	0	...	0.00	11	0	0	0	7	12⅓	8	1	0	3	10
Major league totals (2 years)		10	5	.667	4.14	82	0	0	0	3	100	93	52	46	33	62

REIMER, KEVIN

DH/OF

PERSONAL: Born June 28, 1964, in Macon, Ga. . . . 6-2/230. . . . Throws right, bats left. . . . Full name: Kevin Michael Reimer. . . . Son of Gerry Reimer, minor league first baseman/outfielder (1958-68). . . . Name pronounced RY-mer.
HIGH SCHOOL: A.L. Fortune (Enderby, B.C.).
COLLEGE: Orange Coast College (Calif.) and Cal State Fullerton.

TRANSACTIONS/CAREER NOTES: Selected by Texas Rangers organization in 11th round of free-agent draft (June 3, 1985).... On suspended list (August 28-31, 1991).... Selected by Colorado Rockies in first round (ninth pick overall) of expansion draft (November 17, 1992).... Traded by Rockies to Milwaukee Brewers for OF Dante Bichette (November 17, 1992).... Granted free agency (December 20, 1993).... Signed by Fukuoka Daiei Hawks of Japan Pacific League (January 12, 1994).
STATISTICAL NOTES: Tied for Texas League lead with nine intentional bases on balls received in 1988.... Collected six hits in one game (August 24, 1993, second game).

			BATTING												FIELDING			
Year	**Team (League)**	**Pos.**	**G**	**AB**	**R**	**H**	**2B**	**3B**	**HR**	**RBI**	**Avg.**	**BB**	**SO**	**SB**	**PO**	**A**	**E**	**Avg.**
1985	—Burlington (Midw.)	1B-OF	80	292	25	67	12	0	8	33	.229	22	43	0	685	29	15	.979
1986	—Salem (Carolina)	OF-1B	133	453	57	111	21	2	16	76	.245	61	71	4	412	27	32	.932
1987	—Charlotte (Fla. St.)	OF	74	271	36	66	13	7	6	34	.244	29	48	2	31	0	2	.939
1988	—Tulsa (Texas)	OF	133	486	74	147	30	*11	21	76	.302	38	95	4	63	1	7	.901
	—Texas (A.L.)	OF	12	25	2	3	0	0	1	2	.120	0	6	0	0	0	0	...
1989	—Okla. City (A.A.)	OF	133	514	59	137	37	7	10	73	.267	33	91	4	73	2	6	.926
	—Texas (A.L.)	DH	3	5	0	0	0	0	0	0	.000	0	1	0	...	...	...	...
1990	—Okla. City (A.A.)	1B-OF	51	198	24	56	18	2	4	33	.283	18	25	2	170	11	2	.989
	—Texas (A.L.)	OF	64	100	5	26	9	1	2	15	.260	10	22	0	12	0	2	.857
1991	—Texas (A.L.)	OF	136	394	46	106	22	0	20	69	.269	33	93	0	110	0	6	.948
1992	—Texas (A.L.)	OF	148	494	56	132	32	2	16	58	.267	42	103	2	198	7	*11	.949
1993	—Milwaukee (A.L.)■	OF	125	437	53	109	22	1	13	60	.249	30	72	5	75	1	3	.962
Major league totals (6 years)			488	1455	162	376	85	4	52	204	.258	115	297	7	395	8	22	.948

RENTERIA, RICK

IF, MARLINS

PERSONAL: Born December 25, 1961, in Harbor City, Calif.... 5-9/175.... Throws right, bats right.... Full name: Richard Avina Renteria.
HIGH SCHOOL: South Gate (Calif.).
TRANSACTIONS/CAREER NOTES: Selected by Pittsburgh Pirates organization in first round (20th pick overall) of free-agent draft (June 3, 1980).... On disabled list (May 10-June 1, 1983).... Loaned by Pirates organization to Mexico City Tigers (March 11-August 21, 1985).... Traded by Pirates organization to Seattle Mariners organization for a player to be named later (December 5, 1986); Pirates organization acquired P Bob Siegel to complete deal (December 8, 1986).... On Seattle disabled list (April 2-18, 1987).... On Seattle disabled list (March 27-June 30, 1989); included rehabilitation assignment to Calgary (June 14-30).... On Calgary disabled list (April 10, 1990-entire season).... Released by Mariners organization (September 18, 1990).... Signed by Toledo, Detroit Tigers organization (March 15, 1991).... Loaned by Toledo to Jalisco of Mexican League (March 19-August 2, 1991).... Released by Toledo (August 2, 1991).... Signed by Indianapolis, Montreal Expos organization (August 14, 1991).... Released by Expos organization (September 20, 1991).... Signed by Toledo, Tigers organization (February 18, 1992).... Loaned by Tigers organization to Jalisco of Mexican League (February 26-June 3, 1992).... Contract acquired by Jalisco from Tigers organization (June 3, 1992).... Granted free agency (October 16, 1992).... Signed by Edmonton, Florida Marlins organization (February 20, 1993).
STATISTICAL NOTES: Led South Atlantic League third basemen with 39 errors in 1981.... Tied for Carolina League lead in grounding into double plays with 19 in 1982.

			BATTING												FIELDING			
Year	**Team (League)**	**Pos.**	**G**	**AB**	**R**	**H**	**2B**	**3B**	**HR**	**RBI**	**Avg.**	**BB**	**SO**	**SB**	**PO**	**A**	**E**	**Avg.**
1980	—GC Pirates (GCL)	3B-SS	46	176	19	40	6	1	2	23	.227	9	15	4	32	87	16	.881
1981	—Greenwood (S. Atl.)	3B-SS	127	510	90	146	19	5	4	48	.286	26	53	8	87	232	†39	.891
1982	—Alexandria (Caro.)	2B	127	508	80	*168	24	5	14	*100	*.331	24	54	12	196	346	28	.951
1983	—Lynn (Eastern)	3B	115	424	47	121	25	0	4	40	.285	31	45	3	83	170	19	.930
1984	—Nashua (Eastern)	2B	113	443	63	121	22	7	1	34	.273	39	43	21	208	283	12	.976
	—Hawaii (PCL)	2B	19	77	8	19	3	1	0	11	.247	6	7	1	22	45	2	.971
1985	—M.C. Tigers (Mex.)■	3B-2B	125	484	89	169	29	11	19	*125	.349	35	53	8	121	241	19	.950
	—Hawaii (PCL)■	2B	7	31	2	6	2	0	0	2	.194	0	4	0	5	15	0	1.000
1986	—Hawaii (PCL)	3B-2B	112	389	51	122	20	9	1	51	.314	22	29	10	112	196	13	.960
	—Pittsburgh (N.L.)	3B	10	12	2	3	1	0	0	1	.250	0	4	0	1	2	2	.600
1987	—Seattle (A.L.)■	2B-SS	12	10	2	1	1	0	0	0	.100	1	2	1	3	4	1	.875
	—Calgary (PCL)	2B-SS-3B	69	267	41	79	14	3	1	32	.296	9	3	3	110	187	11	.964
1988	—Seattle (A.L.)	SS-3B-2B	31	88	6	18	9	0	0	6	.205	2	8	1	33	44	3	.963
	—Calgary (PCL)	SS-2B-3B	24	87	15	23	6	1	4	10	.264	5	10	3	34	64	7	.933
1989	—Calgary (PCL)	2B-3B-SS	65	234	34	69	17	0	5	36	.295	15	11	4	106	166	9	.968
1990	—								Did not play.									
1991	—Jalisco (Mexican)■	3B	104	382	90	169	30	6	24	106	*.442	50	33	17	68	210	11	.962
	—Indianapolis (A.A.)■	3B-2B	20	72	6	17	5	0	1	5	.236	6	9	0	13	45	1	.983
1992	—Jalisco (Mexican)■	3B-2B	114	420	86	142	27	4	13	83	.338	50	44	17	138	290	16	.964
1993	—Florida (N.L.)■	2B-3B-OF	103	263	27	67	9	2	2	30	.255	21	31	0	84	151	2	.992
American League totals (2 years)			43	98	8	19	10	0	0	6	.194	3	10	2	36	48	4	.955
National League totals (2 years)			113	275	29	70	10	2	2	31	.255	21	35	0	85	153	4	.983
Major league totals (4 years)			156	373	37	89	20	2	2	37	.239	24	45	2	121	201	8	.976

REVENIG, TODD

P, ATHLETICS

PERSONAL: Born June 28, 1969, in Brainerd, Minn.... 6-1/185.... Throws right, bats right.... Full name: Todd Michael Revenig.... Name pronounced REV-nig.
HIGH SCHOOL: Brainerd (Minn.).
COLLEGE: Mankato (Minn.) State.
TRANSACTIONS/CAREER NOTES: Selected by Oakland Athletics organization in 37th round of free-agent draft (June 4, 1990).... On Oakland disabled list (March 16, 1993-entire season).
STATISTICAL NOTES: Pitched one inning, combining with starter Dana Allison (eight innings) and Roger Smithberg (one inning) in 10-inning, 1-0 no-hit victory for Huntsville against Birmingham (August 3, 1992).

Year	**Team (League)**	**W**	**L**	**Pct.**	**ERA**	**G**	**GS**	**CG**	**ShO**	**Sv.**	**IP**	**H**	**R**	**ER**	**BB**	**SO**
1990	—S. Oregon (N'west)	3	2	.600	0.81	24	0	0	0	6	44⅔	33	13	4	9	46
1991	—Madison (Midwest)	1	0	1.000	0.94	26	0	0	0	13	28⅔	13	6	3	10	27

Year	Team (League)	W	L	Pct.	ERA	G	GS	CG	ShO	Sv.	IP	H	R	ER	BB	SO
	—Huntsville (South.).....	1	2	.333	0.98	12	0	0	0	0	18⅓	11	3	2	4	10
1992	—Huntsville (South.).....	1	1	.500	1.70	53	0	0	0	33	63⅔	33	14	12	11	49
	—Oakland (A.L.)	0	0	...	0.00	2	0	0	0	0	2	2	0	0	0	1
1993	—................................							Did not play.								
Major league totals (1 year) ...		0	0	...	0.00	2	0	0	0	0	2	2	0	0	0	1

REYES, CARLOS

P, ATHLETICS

PERSONAL: Born April 4, 1969, in Miami. . . . 6-1/190. . . . Throws right, bats both. . . . Full name: Carlos Alberto Reyes Jr.

HIGH SCHOOL: Tampa (Fla.) Catholic.

COLLEGE: Brevard Community College (Fla.) and Florida Southern.

TRANSACTIONS/CAREER NOTES: Signed as free agent by Atlanta Braves organization (June 21, 1991). . . . Selected by Oakland Athletics from Braves organization in Rule 5 major league draft (December 13, 1993).

Year	Team (League)	W	L	Pct.	ERA	G	GS	CG	ShO	Sv.	IP	H	R	ER	BB	SO
1991	—GC Braves (GCL)........	3	2	.600	1.77	20	0	0	0	5	45⅔	44	15	9	9	37
1992	—Macon (S. Atl.)...........	2	3	.400	2.10	23	0	0	0	2	60	57	16	14	11	57
	—Durham (Carolina).....	2	1	.667	2.43	21	0	0	0	5	40⅔	31	11	11	10	33
1993	—Greenville (South.).....	8	1	.889	2.06	33	2	0	0	2	70	64	22	16	24	57
	—Richmond (Int'l).........	1	0	1.000	3.77	18	1	0	0	1	28⅔	30	12	12	11	30

REYNOLDS, HAROLD

2B, PADRES

PERSONAL: Born November 26, 1960, in Eugene, Ore. . . . 5-11/165. . . . Throws right, bats both. . . . Full name: Harold Craig Reynolds. . . . Brother of Don Reynolds, outfielder, San Diego Padres (1978-79); and brother of Larry Reynolds, minor league shortstop/outfielder (1979-84).

HIGH SCHOOL: Corvallis (Ore.).

COLLEGE: San Diego State, Canada College (Calif.) and Long Beach State.

TRANSACTIONS/CAREER NOTES: Selected by San Diego Padres organization in fifth round of free-agent draft (June 5, 1979). . . . Selected by Seattle Mariners organization in secondary phase of free-agent draft (June 3, 1980). . . . Granted free agency (October 26, 1992). . . . Signed by Baltimore Orioles (December 11, 1992). . . . Granted free agency (October 29, 1993). . . . Signed by Padres organization (January 28, 1994).

RECORDS: Shares major league single-game record (nine innings) for most assists by second baseman—12 (August 27, 1986). . . . Shares A.L. career record for most years leading league in errors by second baseman—4.

HONORS: Won A.L. Gold Glove at second base (1988-90).

STATISTICAL NOTES: Led Midwest League second basemen with 82 double plays in 1981. . . . Led Eastern League in caught stealing with 20 in 1982. . . . Led Pacific Coast League with 14 sacrifice hits in 1983. . . . Led Pacific Coast League second basemen with 286 putouts, 410 assists, 27 errors and 723 total chances in 1983. . . . Led Pacific Coast League second basemen with 747 total chances and 104 double plays in 1984. . . . Tied for Pacific Coast League lead in caught stealing with 17 in 1984. . . . Led A.L. second basemen with 111 double plays in 1986, 1987, 1988 (111 in all three years), 133 in 1991 and 110 in 1993. . . . Led A.L. in caught stealing with 20 in 1987 and 29 in 1988. . . . Led A.L. second basemen with 874 total chances in 1987, 792 in 1988, 834 in 1989, 848 in 1990 and 829 in 1991.

			BATTING												FIELDING			
Year	Team (League)	Pos.	G	AB	R	H	2B	3B	HR	RBI	Avg.	BB	SO	SB	PO	A	E	Avg.
1981	—Wausau (Midwest) ..	2B-OF-3B	127	493	98	146	23	3	11	59	.296	56	47	*69	259	386	27	.960
1982	—Lynn (Eastern)...........	2B	102	375	58	102	14	4	2	48	.272	36	41	39	202	232	19	.958
1983	—Salt Lake City (PCL)	2B-SS	136	534	84	165	20	9	1	72	.309	47	43	54	†287	†410	†27	.963
	—Seattle (A.L.)	2B	20	59	8	12	4	1	0	1	.203	2	9	0	30	48	2	.975
1984	—Salt Lake City (PCL)	2B	135	*558	94	165	22	6	3	54	.296	73	72	37	*326	*396	*25	*.967
	—Seattle (A.L.)	2B	10	10	3	3	0	0	0	0	.300	0	1	1	8	12	0	1.000
1985	—Seattle (A.L.)	2B	67	104	15	15	3	1	0	6	.144	17	14	3	69	123	8	.960
	—Calgary (PCL)..........	2B	52	212	36	77	11	3	5	30	.363	28	18	9	119	171	13	.957
1986	—Calgary (PCL)..........	2B	29	118	20	37	7	0	1	7	.314	20	12	10	64	83	4	.974
	—Seattle (A.L.)	2B	126	445	46	99	19	4	1	24	.222	29	42	30	278	415	16	.977
1987	—Seattle (A.L.)	2B	160	530	73	146	31	8	1	35	.275	39	34	*60	*347	*507	*20	.977
1988	—Seattle (A.L.)	2B	158	598	61	169	26	•11	4	41	.283	51	51	35	303	*471	*18	.977
1989	—Seattle (A.L.)	2B	153	613	87	184	24	9	0	43	.300	55	45	25	311	*506	*17	.980
1990	—Seattle (A.L.)	2B	160	*642	100	162	36	5	5	55	.252	81	52	31	*330	*499	•19	.978
1991	—Seattle (A.L.)	2B	161	631	95	160	34	6	3	57	.254	72	63	28	*348	*463	18	.978
1992	—Seattle (A.L.)	2B-OF	140	458	55	113	23	3	3	33	.247	45	41	15	303	362	12	.982
1993	—Baltimore (A.L.)■.....	2B	145	485	64	122	20	4	4	47	.252	66	47	12	306	396	10	.986
Major league totals (11 years)			1300	4575	607	1185	220	52	21	342	.259	457	399	240	2633	3802	140	.979

ALL-STAR GAME RECORD

			BATTING										FIELDING			
Year	League	Pos.	AB	R	H	2B	3B	HR	RBI	Avg.	BB	SO	SB	PO	A	E	Avg.
1987	—American..................	2B	3	0	0	0	0	0	0	.000	0	0	0	4	4	0	1.000
1988	—American..................	2B	1	0	0	0	0	0	0	.000	0	0	0	1	1	0	1.000
All-Star Game totals (2 years)			4	0	0	0	0	0	0	.000	0	0	0	5	5	0	1.000

REYNOLDS, R.J.

OF, REDS

PERSONAL: Born April 19, 1960, in Sacramento, Calif. . . . 6-0/180. . . . Throws right, bats both. . . . Full name: Robert James Reynolds.

HIGH SCHOOL: John F. Kennedy (Sacramento, Calif.).

COLLEGE: Cosumnes River College (Calif.) and Sacramento (Calif.) City College.

TRANSACTIONS/CAREER NOTES: Selected by Los Angeles Dodgers organization in second round of free-agent draft (January 8, 1980). . . . On Los Angeles disabled list (July 2-17, 1984; April 8-23 and July 10-August 2, 1985). . . . Traded by Dodgers to Pittsburgh Pirates (September 3, 1985) as partial completion of deal in which Dodgers acquired 3B Bill Madlock for three players to be named later (August 31, 1985); Pirates acquired OF Cecil Espy and 1B Sid Bream to complete deal (September 9,

1985).... On disabled list (August 8-23, 1990).... Granted free agency (November 5, 1990).... Signed by Yokohama Taiyo Whales of Japan Central League (November 12, 1990).... Released by Yokohama (October 15, 1992).... Signed by Kintetsu Buffaloes of Japan Pacific League for 1993.... Signed as free agent by Cincinnati Reds organization (January 11, 1994).

STATISTICAL NOTES: Led California League outfielders with six double plays in 1980.... Led Florida State League outfielders with 395 total chances and six double plays in 1981.... Led Texas League outfielders with eight double plays in 1983.

			BATTING											FIELDING			
Year	Team (League)	Pos.	G	AB	R	H	2B	3B	HR	RBI	Avg.	BB	SO	SB	PO	A	E	Avg.
1980	—Lodi (California).......	OF	86	299	33	84	6	3	4	31	.281	16	48	9	188	10	12	.943
1981	—Vero Beach (FSL).....	OF	132	502	62	139	9	11	2	49	.277	44	77	32	*368	20	7	.982
1982	—Lodi (California).......	OF	108	403	67	126	19	3	6	35	.313	36	68	25	212	12	6	.974
	—San Antonio (Tex.)...	OF	3	12	3	2	0	0	1	2	.167	1	1	2	10	1	0	1.000
1983	—San Antonio (Tex.)...	OF	133	504	103	170	25	3	18	89	.337	55	60	43	255	•18	12	.958
	—Los Angeles (N.L.)...	OF	24	55	5	13	0	0	2	11	.236	3	11	5	25	2	2	.931
1984	—Albuquerque (PCL)..	OF	47	199	38	69	10	4	3	30	.347	16	22	13	104	4	6	.947
	—Los Angeles (N.L.)...	OF	73	240	24	62	12	2	2	24	.258	14	38	7	104	4	3	.973
1985	—L.A.-Pitts. (N.L.)■....	OF	104	337	44	95	15	7	3	42	.282	22	49	18	159	6	6	.965
1986	—Pittsburgh (N.L.)......	OF	118	402	63	108	30	2	9	48	.269	40	78	16	190	2	•9	.955
1987	—Pittsburgh (N.L.)......	OF	117	335	47	87	24	1	7	51	.260	34	80	14	134	7	1	.993
1988	—Pittsburgh (N.L.)......	OF	130	323	35	80	14	2	6	51	.248	20	62	15	142	7	4	.974
1989	—Pittsburgh (N.L.)......	OF	125	363	45	98	16	2	6	48	.270	34	66	22	200	6	2	.990
1990	—Pittsburgh (N.L.)......	OF	95	215	25	62	10	1	0	19	.288	23	35	12	102	3	3	.972
1991	—Yoko. Tai. (Jp. Cn.)■	OF	18	468	71	148	...	...	15	80	.316	38	77	17	...	...	...	...
1992	—Yoko. Tai. (Jp. Cn.)..	OF	113	427	57	106	...	...	19	66	.248	39	102	12	...	...	...	...
1993	—Kintetsu (Jp. Pac.)■.	...	104	336	46	100	20	1	18	50	.298	30	74	12	...	...	...	...
Major league totals (8 years)			786	2270	288	605	121	17	35	294	.267	190	419	109	1056	37	30	.973

CHAMPIONSHIP SERIES RECORD

			BATTING											FIELDING			
Year	Team (League)	Pos.	G	AB	R	H	2B	3B	HR	RBI	Avg.	BB	SO	SB	PO	A	E	Avg.
1990	—Pittsburgh (N.L.)......	PH-OF	6	10	0	2	0	0	0	0	.200	2	2	1	2	0	1	.667

REYNOLDS, SHANE

P, ASTROS

PERSONAL: Born March 26, 1968, in Bastrop, La.... 6-3/210.... Throws right, bats right.... Full name: Richard Shane Reynolds.

HIGH SCHOOL: Ouachita Christian (Monroe, La.).

COLLEGE: Faulkner State Junior College (Ala.) and Texas.

TRANSACTIONS/CAREER NOTES: Selected by Houston Astros organization in third round of free-agent draft (June 5, 1989).

Year	Team (League)	W	L	Pct.	ERA	G	GS	CG	ShO	Sv.	IP	H	R	ER	BB	SO
1989	—Auburn (NY-Penn)....	3	2	.600	2.31	6	6	1	0	0	35	36	16	9	14	23
	—Asheville (S. Atl.).......	5	3	.625	3.68	8	8	2	1	0	51⅓	53	25	21	21	33
1990	—Columbus (South.).....	9	10	.474	4.81	29	27	2	1	0	155⅓	•181	104	83	70	92
1991	—Jackson (Texas)........	8	9	.471	4.47	27	•27	2	0	0	151	165	93	75	62	116
1992	—Tucson (PCL)............	9	8	.529	3.68	25	22	2	0	1	142	156	73	58	34	106
	—Houston (N.L.)..........	1	3	.250	7.11	8	5	0	0	0	25⅓	42	22	20	6	10
1993	—Tucson (PCL)............	10	6	.625	3.62	25	20	2	0	1	139⅓	147	74	56	21	106
	—Houston (N.L.)..........	0	0	...	0.82	5	1	0	0	0	11	11	4	1	6	10
Major league totals (2 years)..		1	3	.250	5.20	13	6	0	0	0	36⅓	53	26	21	12	20

REYNOSO, ARMANDO

P, ROCKIES

PERSONAL: Born May 1, 1966, in San Luis Potosi, Mexico.... 6-0/196.... Throws right, bats right.... Full name: Martia Armando Gutierrez Reynoso.... Name pronounced ray-NO-so.

HIGH SCHOOL: Escuela Secandaria Mita del Estado (Jalisco, Mexico).

TRANSACTIONS/CAREER NOTES: Signed as free agent by Saltillo of Mexican League.... Contract sold by Saltillo to Atlanta Braves organization (August 15, 1990).... Selected by Colorado Rockies in third round (58th pick overall) of expansion draft (November 17, 1992).

STATISTICAL NOTES: Led International League with six balks in 1991 and five in 1992.... Tied for International League lead with 10 hit batsmen in 1991.

MISCELLANEOUS: Appeared in one game as pinch-runner with Colorado (1993).

Year	Team (League)	W	L	Pct.	ERA	G	GS	CG	ShO	Sv.	IP	H	R	ER	BB	SO
1988	—Saltillo (Mexican)......	11	11	.500	4.30	32	29	10	2	2	180	176	98	86	85	92
1989	—Saltillo (Mexican)......	13	9	.591	3.48	27	25	7	2	0	160⅓	155	78	62	64	107
1990	—Saltillo (Mexican)......	*20	3	.870	2.60	27	•27	12	5	0	200⅔	174	61	58	73	*170
	—Richmond (Int'l)■.......	3	1	.750	2.25	4	3	0	0	0	24	26	7	6	7	15
1991	—Richmond (Int'l).........	10	6	.625	*2.61	22	19	3	•3	0	131	117	44	38	39	97
	—Atlanta (N.L.)............	2	1	.667	6.17	6	5	0	0	0	23⅓	26	18	16	10	10
1992	—Richmond (Int'l).........	12	9	.571	2.66	28	27	4	1	0	169⅓	156	65	50	52	108
	—Atlanta (N.L.)............	1	0	1.000	4.70	3	1	0	0	1	7⅔	11	4	4	2	2
1993	—Colo. Springs (PCL)■...	2	1	.667	3.22	4	4	0	0	0	22⅓	19	10	8	8	22
	—Colorado (N.L.)...........	12	11	.522	4.00	30	30	4	0	0	189	206	101	84	63	117
Major league totals (3 years)..		15	12	.556	4.25	39	36	4	0	1	220	243	123	104	75	129

RHODES, ARTHUR

P, ORIOLES

PERSONAL: Born October 24, 1969, in Waco, Tex.... 6-2/206.... Throws left, bats left.... Full name: Arthur Lee Rhodes Jr.... Brother of Ricky Rhodes, pitcher, New York Yankees organization.

HIGH SCHOOL: LaVega (Waco, Tex.).

TRANSACTIONS/CAREER NOTES: Selected by Baltimore Orioles organization in second round of free-agent draft (June 1, 1988).

. . . On Hagerstown disabled list (May 13-June 5, 1991). . . . On Baltimore disabled list (May 16-August 2, 1993); included rehabilitation assignment to Rochester (July 4-August 2).
HONORS: Named Eastern League Pitcher of the Year (1991).

Year	Team (League)	W	L	Pct.	ERA	G	GS	CG	ShO	Sv.	IP	H	R	ER	BB	SO
1988	—Bluefield (Appal.)	3	4	.429	3.31	11	7	0	0	0	35⅓	29	17	13	15	44
1989	—Erie (N.Y.-Penn)	2	0	1.000	1.16	5	5	1	0	0	31	13	7	4	10	45
	—Frederick (Caro.)	2	2	.500	5.18	7	6	0	0	0	24⅓	19	16	14	19	28
1990	—Frederick (Caro.)	4	6	.400	2.12	13	13	3	0	0	80⅔	62	25	19	21	103
	—Hagerstown (East.)	3	4	.429	3.73	12	12	0	0	0	72⅓	62	32	30	39	60
1991	—Hagerstown (East.)	7	4	.636	2.70	19	19	2	2	0	106⅔	73	37	32	47	115
	—Baltimore (A.L.)	0	3	.000	8.00	8	8	0	0	0	36	47	35	32	23	23
1992	—Rochester (Int'l)	6	6	.500	3.72	17	17	1	0	0	101⅔	84	48	42	46	115
	—Baltimore (A.L.)	7	5	.583	3.63	15	15	2	1	0	94⅓	87	39	38	38	77
1993	—Baltimore (A.L.)	5	6	.455	6.51	17	17	0	0	0	85⅔	91	62	62	49	49
	—Rochester (Int'l)	1	1	.500	4.05	6	6	0	0	0	26⅔	26	12	12	15	33
Major league totals (3 years)		12	14	.462	5.50	40	40	2	1	0	216	225	136	132	110	149

RHODES, KARL

OF, CUBS

PERSONAL: Born August 21, 1968, in Cincinnati. . . . 6-0/195. . . . Throws left, bats left. . . . Full name: Karl Derrick Rhodes.
HIGH SCHOOL: Western Hills (Cincinnati).
TRANSACTIONS/CAREER NOTES: Selected by Houston Astros organization in third round of free-agent draft (June 2, 1986). . . . On Tucson disabled list (May 28-July 1, 1992). . . . Granted free agency (April 23, 1993). . . . Signed by Omaha, Kansas City Royals organization (April 27, 1993). . . . Traded by Royals to Chicago Cubs as part of a three-way deal in which Cubs sent P Paul Assenmacher to New York Yankees and Yankees sent P John Habyan to Royals (July 30, 1993).
STATISTICAL NOTES: Tied for Southern League lead in double plays by outfielder with five in 1989. . . . Led American Association with 295 total bases and .602 slugging percentage in 1993.

			BATTING												FIELDING			
Year	Team (League)	Pos.	G	AB	R	H	2B	3B	HR	RBI	Avg.	BB	SO	SB	PO	A	E	Avg.
1986	—GC Astros (GCL)	OF	*62	222	36	65	10	3	0	22	.293	32	33	14	113	6	0	*1.000
1987	—Asheville (S. Atl.)	OF	129	413	62	104	16	4	3	50	.252	77	82	43	163	14	9	.952
1988	—Osceola (Fla. St.)	OF-2B	132	452	69	128	4	2	1	34	.283	81	53	64	232	14	2	.992
1989	—Columbus (South.)	OF	•143	520	81	134	25	5	4	63	.258	93	105	18	262	15	11	.962
1990	—Tucson (PCL)	OF	107	385	68	106	24	11	3	59	.275	47	75	24	214	*20	8	.967
	—Houston (N.L.)	OF	39	86	12	21	6	1	1	3	.244	13	12	4	61	2	3	.955
1991	—Houston (N.L.)	OF	44	136	7	29	3	1	1	12	.213	14	26	2	87	4	4	.958
	—Tucson (PCL)	OF	84	308	45	80	17	1	1	46	.260	38	47	5	140	11	9	.944
1992	—Tucson (PCL)	OF	94	332	62	96	16	10	2	54	.289	55	63	8	210	13	6	.974
	—Houston (N.L.)	OF	5	4	0	0	0	0	0	0	.000	0	2	0	0	0	0	...
1993	—Hou.-Chi. (N.L.)■	OF	20	54	12	15	2	1	3	7	.278	11	9	2	33	1	1	.971
	—Omaha-Iowa (A.A)■	OF	123	490	*112	156	*43	3	30	89	.318	58	82	16	192	17	8	.963
Major league totals (4 years)			108	280	31	65	11	3	5	22	.232	38	49	8	181	7	8	.959

RICHARDSON, JEFF

IF

PERSONAL: Born August 26, 1965, in Grand Island, Neb. . . . 6-2/180. . . . Throws right, bats right. . . . Full name: Jeffrey Scott Richardson.
HIGH SCHOOL: Grand Island (Neb.).
COLLEGE: Arkansas and Louisiana Tech.
TRANSACTIONS/CAREER NOTES: Selected by Cincinnati Reds organization in seventh round of free-agent draft (June 2, 1986). . . . Traded by Reds with P Mike Roesler to Pittsburgh Pirates organization for OF Billy Hatcher (April 3, 1990). . . . On Buffalo disabled list (June 14-August 1, 1991). . . . Traded by Pirates to Boston Red Sox for P Daryl Irvine (April 2, 1993). . . . On Boston disabled list (May 29-June 13, 1993). . . . On Boston disabled list (June 14, 1993-remainder of season); included rehabilitation assignment to Pawtucket (July 28-August 16). . . . Granted free agency (October 15, 1993).

			BATTING												FIELDING			
Year	Team (League)	Pos.	G	AB	R	H	2B	3B	HR	RBI	Avg.	BB	SO	SB	PO	A	E	Avg.
1986	—Billings (Pioneer)	2B-SS	47	162	42	51	14	4	0	20	.315	17	25	12	48	64	6	.949
1987	—Tampa (Fla. St.)	2B-3B-SS	100	374	44	112	9	2	0	37	.299	30	35	10	180	228	17	.960
	—Vermont (Eastern)	2B-3B	35	134	24	28	4	0	0	8	.209	5	25	5	73	76	4	.974
1988	—Chatt. (South.)	SS	88	399	50	100	17	1	1	37	.251	23	56	8	186	321	23	*.957
1989	—Nashville (A.A.)	SS	88	286	36	78	19	2	1	25	.273	17	42	3	132	218	16	.956
	—Cincinnati (N.L.)	SS-3B	53	125	10	21	4	0	2	11	.168	10	23	1	50	81	4	.970
1990	—Buffalo (A.A.)■	S-2-3-1	66	164	15	34	4	0	1	15	.207	14	21	1	103	142	12	.953
1991	—Buffalo (A.A.)	2B-SS	62	186	21	48	16	2	1	24	.258	18	29	5	121	179	5	.984
	—Pittsburgh (N.L.)	3B-SS	6	4	0	1	0	0	0	0	.250	0	3	0	0	1	0	1.000
1992	—Buffalo (A.A.)	2B-SS-3B	97	328	34	95	23	2	3	29	.290	19	46	5	195	274	11	.977
1993	—Boston (A.L.)■	2B-SS-3B	15	24	3	5	2	0	0	2	.208	1	3	0	12	30	0	1.000
	—Pawtucket (Int'l)	SS-2B-3B	9	28	2	9	1	0	0	1	.321	1	6	0	8	22	3	.909
American League totals (1 year)			15	24	3	5	2	0	0	2	.208	1	3	0	12	30	0	1.000
National League totals (2 years)			59	129	10	22	4	0	2	11	.171	10	26	1	50	82	4	.971
Major league totals (3 years)			74	153	13	27	6	0	2	13	.176	11	29	1	62	112	4	.978

RIGHETTI, DAVE

P, ATHLETICS

PERSONAL: Born November 28, 1958, in San Jose, Calif. . . . 6-4/219. . . . Throws left, bats left. . . . Full name: David Allen Righetti. . . . Son of Leo Righetti, minor league infielder (1944-49 and 1951-57); and brother of Steven Righetti, minor league third baseman (1977-79). . . . Name pronounced rih-GET-tee.
HIGH SCHOOL: Pioneer (San Jose, Calif.).

COLLEGE: San Jose (Calif.) City College.
TRANSACTIONS/CAREER NOTES: Selected by Texas Rangers organization in first round (ninth pick overall) of free-agent draft (January 11, 1977).... On disabled list (July 31-September 2, 1978).... Traded by Rangers organization with P Mike Griffin, P Paul Mirabella, OF Juan Beniquez and OF Greg Jemison to New York Yankees for P Sparky Lyle, P Larry McCall, P Dave Rajsich, C Mike Heath, SS Domingo Ramos and cash (November 10, 1978).... On West Haven disabled list (May 21-June 28, 1979).... On Columbus disabled list (June 28-July 20 and August 2-23, 1979).... On disabled list (June 17-July 2, 1984). ... Granted free agency (November 9, 1987).... Re-signed by Yankees (December 23, 1987).... Granted free agency (November 5, 1990).... Signed by San Francisco Giants (December 4, 1990).... Released by Giants (November 9, 1993).... Signed by Oakland Athletics (December 23, 1993).
HONORS: Named A.L. Rookie Pitcher of the Year by THE SPORTING NEWS (1981).... Named A.L. Rookie of the Year by Baseball Writers' Association of America (1981).... Named A.L. Fireman of the Year by THE SPORTING NEWS (1986).... Named A.L. co-Fireman of the Year by THE SPORTING NEWS (1987).
STATISTICAL NOTES: Pitched 4-0 no-hit victory against Boston (July 4, 1983).
MISCELLANEOUS: Singled in only appearance as pinch-hitter (1992).

Year	Team (League)	W	L	Pct.	ERA	G	GS	CG	ShO	Sv.	IP	H	R	ER	BB	SO
1977	—Asheville (W. Car.)	11	3	*.786	3.14	17	16	3	0	0	109	98	47	38	53	101
1978	—Tulsa (Texas)	5	5	.500	3.16	13	13	6	0	0	91	66	40	32	49	127
1979	—West Haven (East.)■	4	3	.571	1.96	11	11	3	0	0	69	45	23	15	45	78
	—Columbus (Int'l)	3	2	.600	2.93	8	6	3	2	0	40	22	13	13	19	44
	—New York (A.L.)	0	1	.000	3.71	3	3	0	0	0	17	10	7	7	10	13
1980	—Columbus (Int'l)	6	10	.375	4.63	24	23	4	1	0	142	124	79	73	*101	139
1981	—Columbus (Int'l)	5	0	1.000	1.00	7	7	2	2	0	45	30	8	5	26	50
	—New York (A.L.)	8	4	.667	2.06	15	15	2	0	0	105	75	25	24	38	89
1982	—New York (A.L.)	11	10	.524	3.79	33	27	4	0	1	183	155	88	77	*108	163
	—Columbus (Int'l)	1	0	1.000	2.81	4	4	1	0	0	25⅔	22	11	8	12	33
1983	—New York (A.L.)	14	8	.636	3.44	31	31	7	2	0	217	194	96	83	67	169
1984	—New York (A.L.)	5	6	.455	2.34	64	0	0	0	31	96⅓	79	29	25	37	90
1985	—New York (A.L.)	12	7	.632	2.78	74	0	0	0	29	107	96	36	33	45	92
1986	—New York (A.L.)	8	8	.500	2.45	74	0	0	0	*46	106⅔	88	31	29	35	83
1987	—New York (A.L.)	8	6	.571	3.51	60	0	0	0	31	95	95	45	37	44	77
1988	—New York (A.L.)	5	4	.556	3.52	60	0	0	0	25	87	86	35	34	37	70
1989	—New York (A.L.)	2	6	.250	3.00	55	0	0	0	25	69	73	32	23	26	51
1990	—New York (A.L.)	1	1	.500	3.57	53	0	0	0	36	53	48	24	21	26	43
1991	—San Francisco (N.L.)■	2	7	.222	3.39	61	0	0	0	24	71⅔	64	29	27	28	51
1992	—San Francisco (N.L.)	2	7	.222	5.06	54	4	0	0	3	78⅓	79	47	44	36	47
1993	—San Francisco (N.L.)	1	1	.500	5.70	51	0	0	0	1	47⅓	58	31	30	17	31
	A.L. totals (11 years)	74	61	.548	3.11	522	76	13	2	224	1136	999	448	393	473	940
	N.L. totals (3 years)	5	15	.250	4.61	166	4	0	0	28	197⅓	201	107	101	81	129
	Major league totals (14 years)	79	76	.510	3.33	688	80	13	2	252	1333⅓	1200	555	494	554	1069

DIVISION SERIES RECORD

Year	Team (League)	W	L	Pct.	ERA	G	GS	CG	ShO	Sv.	IP	H	R	ER	BB	SO
1981	—New York (A.L.)	2	0	1.000	1.00	2	1	0	0	0	9	8	1	1	3	10

CHAMPIONSHIP SERIES RECORD

Year	Team (League)	W	L	Pct.	ERA	G	GS	CG	ShO	Sv.	IP	H	R	ER	BB	SO
1981	—New York (A.L.)	1	0	1.000	0.00	1	1	0	0	0	6	4	0	0	2	4

WORLD SERIES RECORD

Year	Team (League)	W	L	Pct.	ERA	G	GS	CG	ShO	Sv.	IP	H	R	ER	BB	SO
1981	—New York (A.L.)	0	0	...	13.50	1	1	0	0	0	2	5	3	3	2	1

ALL-STAR GAME RECORD

Year	League	W	L	Pct.	ERA	GS	CG	ShO	Sv.	IP	H	R	ER	BB	SO
1986	—American	0	0	...	0.00	0	0	0	0	⅔	2	0	0	0	0
1987	—American	0	0	...	0.00	0	0	0	0	⅓	1	0	0	0	0
	All-Star totals (2 years)	0	0	...	0.00	0	0	0	0	1	3	0	0	0	0

RIJO, JOSE

P, REDS

PERSONAL: Born May 13, 1965, in San Cristobal, Dominican Republic.... 6-2/215.... Throws right, bats right.... Full name: Jose Antonio Abreau Rijo.... Name pronounced REE-ho.
TRANSACTIONS/CAREER NOTES: Signed as free agent by New York Yankees organization (August 1, 1980).... Traded by Yankees organization with OF Stan Javier, P Jay Howell, P Eric Plunk and P Tim Birtsas to Oakland Athletics for OF Rickey Henderson, P Bert Bradley and cash (December 5, 1984).... Traded by A's organization with P Tim Birtsas to Cincinnati Reds for OF Dave Parker (December 8, 1987).... On disabled list (August 18-September 8, 1988 and July 17-September 1, 1989).... On disabled list (June 29-July 21, 1990); included rehabilitation assignment to Nashville (July 16-20).... On disabled list (June 21-July 25, 1991 and April 18-May 3, 1992).
HONORS: Named Florida State League Most Valuable Player (1983).... Named righthanded pitcher on THE SPORTING NEWS N.L. All-Star team (1991).
STATISTICAL NOTES: Led Pacific Coast League with 11 balks in 1985.... Tied for N.L. lead with five balks in 1990.
MISCELLANEOUS: Struck out in only appearance as pinch-hitter (1991).

Year	Team (League)	W	L	Pct.	ERA	G	GS	CG	ShO	Sv.	IP	H	R	ER	BB	SO
1981	—GC Yankees (GCL)	3	3	.500	4.50	11	1	0	0	1	22	37	16	11	7	22
1982	—Paintsville (Appal.)	8	4	.667	2.50	13	12	6	•3	0	79⅓	76	33	22	22	66
1983	—Fort Lauder. (FSL)	*15	5	.750	*1.68	21	21	*15	•4	0	160⅓	129	38	30	43	152
	—Nashville (South.)	3	2	.600	2.68	5	5	3	0	0	40⅓	31	12	12	22	32
1984	—New York (A.L.)	2	8	.200	4.76	24	5	0	0	2	62⅓	74	40	33	33	47
	—Columbus (Int'l)	3	3	.500	4.41	11	11	0	0	0	65⅓	67	35	32	40	47

Year	Team (League)	W	L	Pct.	ERA	G	GS	CG	ShO	Sv.	IP	H	R	ER	BB	SO
1985	—Tacoma (PCL)■	7	10	.412	2.90	24	24	3	1	0	149	116	64	48	*108	*179
	—Oakland (A.L.)	6	4	.600	3.53	12	9	0	0	0	63⅔	57	26	25	28	65
1986	—Oakland (A.L.)	9	11	.450	4.65	39	26	4	0	1	193⅔	172	116	100	108	176
1987	—Oakland (A.L.)	2	7	.222	5.90	21	14	1	0	0	82⅓	106	67	54	41	67
	—Tacoma (PCL)	2	4	.333	3.95	9	8	0	0	0	54⅔	44	27	24	28	67
1988	—Cincinnati (N.L.)■	13	8	.619	2.39	49	19	0	0	0	162	120	47	43	63	160
1989	—Cincinnati (N.L.)	7	6	.538	2.84	19	19	1	1	0	111	101	39	35	48	86
1990	—Cincinnati (N.L.)	14	8	.636	2.70	29	29	7	1	0	197	151	65	59	78	152
	—Nashville (A.A.)	0	0	...	8.31	1	1	0	0	0	4⅓	5	4	4	2	2
1991	—Cincinnati (N.L.)	15	6	•.714	2.51	30	30	3	1	0	204⅓	165	69	57	55	172
1992	—Cincinnati (N.L.)	15	10	.600	2.56	33	33	2	0	0	211	185	67	60	44	171
1993	—Cincinnati (N.L.)	14	9	.609	2.48	36	•36	2	1	0	257⅓	218	76	71	62	*227
A.L. totals (4 years)		19	30	.388	4.75	96	54	5	0	3	402	409	249	212	210	355
N.L. totals (6 years)		78	47	.624	2.56	196	166	15	4	0	1142⅔	940	363	325	350	968
Major league totals (10 years)		97	77	.557	3.13	292	220	20	4	3	1544⅔	1349	612	537	560	1323

CHAMPIONSHIP SERIES RECORD

Year	Team (League)	W	L	Pct.	ERA	G	GS	CG	ShO	Sv.	IP	H	R	ER	BB	SO
1990	—Cincinnati (N.L.)	1	0	1.000	4.38	2	2	0	0	0	12⅓	10	6	6	7	15

WORLD SERIES RECORD

WORLD SERIES NOTES: Named Most Valuable Player (1990).

Year	Team (League)	W	L	Pct.	ERA	G	GS	CG	ShO	Sv.	IP	H	R	ER	BB	SO
1990	—Cincinnati (N.L.)	2	0	1.000	0.59	2	2	0	0	0	15⅓	9	1	1	5	14

RILES, ERNEST

IF

PERSONAL: Born October 2, 1960, in Bainbridge, Ga. . . . 6-1/175. . . . Throws right, bats left.
HIGH SCHOOL: Bainbridge (Ga.).
COLLEGE: Middle Georgia College.
TRANSACTIONS/CAREER NOTES: Selected by Seattle Mariners organization in 21st round of free-agent draft (June 3, 1980). . . . Selected by Milwaukee Brewers organization in secondary phase of free-agent draft (January 13, 1981). . . . On Milwaukee disabled list (March 26-June 3, 1987); included rehabilitation assignment to El Paso (May 13-June 2). . . . Traded by Brewers to San Francisco Giants for OF Jeffrey Leonard (June 8, 1988). . . . Traded by Giants to Oakland Athletics for OF Darren Lewis and a player to be named later (December 4, 1990); Giants acquired P Pedro Pena to complete deal (December 17, 1990). . . . Granted free agency (October 28, 1991). . . . Signed by Houston Astros organization (January 27, 1992). . . . Granted free agency (October 5, 1992). . . . Signed by Pawtucket, Boston Red Sox organization (April 3, 1993). . . . Granted free agency (October 25, 1993).
STATISTICAL NOTES: Led California League shortstops with 95 double plays and tied for lead with 692 total chances in 1982. . . . Led Texas League shortstops with 670 total chances and 77 double plays in 1983.

				BATTING											FIELDING			
Year	Team (League)	Pos.	G	AB	R	H	2B	3B	HR	RBI	Avg.	BB	SO	SB	PO	A	E	Avg.
1981	—Butte (Pioneer)	SS-3B-2B	67	256	63	89	11	2	4	43	.348	31	34	9	97	217	27	.921
1982	—Stockton (Calif.)	SS	138	447	60	128	23	6	2	56	.286	*84	53	21	204	*451	37	.947
1983	—El Paso (Texas)	SS	130	476	109	166	31	3	13	91	*.349	86	54	9	*193	*445	32	*.952
1984	—Vancouver (PCL)	SS	123	424	59	113	19	7	3	54	.267	67	67	1	*190	316	17	.967
1985	—Vancouver (PCL)	SS	30	118	19	41	7	1	2	20	.347	17	13	2	47	120	6	.965
	—Milwaukee (A.L.)	SS	116	448	54	128	12	7	5	45	.286	36	54	2	183	310	22	.957
1986	—Milwaukee (A.L.)	SS	145	524	69	132	24	2	9	47	.252	54	80	7	212	327	20	.964
1987	—El Paso (Texas)	SS	41	153	45	52	10	0	6	24	.340	28	24	1	70	127	10	.952
	—Milwaukee (A.L.)	3B-SS	83	276	38	72	11	1	4	38	.261	30	47	3	76	152	13	.946
1988	—Milwaukee (A.L.)	3B-SS	41	127	7	32	6	1	1	9	.252	7	26	2	36	64	4	.962
	—San Francisco (N.L.)■	3B-2B-SS	79	187	26	55	7	2	3	28	.294	10	33	1	46	133	3	.984
1989	—San Francisco (N.L.)	3-2-S-0	122	302	43	84	13	2	7	40	.278	28	50	0	69	144	9	.959
1990	—San Francisco (N.L.)	SS-2B-3B	92	155	22	31	2	1	8	21	.200	26	26	0	53	105	3	.981
1991	—Oakland (A.L.)■	3-S-2-1	108	281	30	60	8	4	5	32	.214	31	42	3	113	143	11	.959
1992	—Tucson (PCL)■	1B-3B-SS	60	202	37	62	17	3	1	35	.307	30	33	2	347	47	5	.987
	—Houston (N.L.)	S-3-1-2	39	61	5	16	1	0	1	4	.262	2	11	1	29	15	1	.978
1993	—Boston (A.L.)■	2B-3B-1B	94	143	15	27	8	0	5	20	.189	20	40	1	26	53	0	1.000
	—Pawtucket (Int'l)	SS-3B-2B	6	18	4	5	0	0	2	6	.278	3	0	0	5	13	1	.947
American League totals (6 years)			587	1799	213	451	69	15	29	191	.251	178	289	18	646	1049	70	.960
National League totals (4 years)			332	705	96	186	23	5	19	93	.264	66	120	2	197	397	16	.974
Major league totals (9 years)			919	2504	309	637	92	20	48	284	.254	244	409	20	843	1446	86	.964

CHAMPIONSHIP SERIES RECORD

				BATTING											FIELDING			
Year	Team (League)	Pos.	G	AB	R	H	2B	3B	HR	RBI	Avg.	BB	SO	SB	PO	A	E	Avg.
1989	—San Francisco (N.L.)	PH	1	1	0	0	0	0	0	0	.000	0	0	0	...	...	...	...

WORLD SERIES RECORD

				BATTING											FIELDING			
Year	Team (League)	Pos.	G	AB	R	H	2B	3B	HR	RBI	Avg.	BB	SO	SB	PO	A	E	Avg.
1989	—San Francisco (N.L.)	DH-PH	4	8	0	0	0	0	0	0	.000	0	1	0	...	...	...	...

RIPKEN, BILL

2B/SS, RANGERS

PERSONAL: Born December 16, 1964, in Havre de Grace, Md. . . . 6-1/187. . . . Throws right, bats right. . . . Full name: William Oliver Ripken. . . . Son of Cal Ripken Sr., minor league catcher (1957-62 and 1964), manager, Baltimore Orioles (1987-88), and coach, Orioles (1976-86 and 1989-92); and brother of Cal Ripken Jr., shortstop, Orioles.

HIGH SCHOOL: Aberdeen (Md.).
TRANSACTIONS/CAREER NOTES: Selected by Baltimore Orioles organization in 11th round of free-agent draft (June 7, 1982).... On disabled list (April 20-May 3, 1984; June 23-July 6, 1985; March 27-April 14 and August 23-September 7, 1989; and August 5-20, 1990).... On Baltimore disabled list (July 15-August 15, 1991); included rehabilitation assignment to Frederick (August 12-13) and Hagerstown (August 13-15).... Released by Orioles (December 11, 1992).... Signed by Texas Rangers organization (February 1, 1993).... On Texas disabled list (May 13-28 and June 21-September 1, 1993).... Granted free agency (October 4, 1993).... Re-signed by Rangers organization (December 18, 1993).
STATISTICAL NOTES: Led Southern League second basemen with 723 total chances and 79 double plays in 1986.... Tied for Southern League lead in grounding into double plays with 21 in 1986.... Tied for A.L. lead with 17 sacrifice hits in 1990.

			BATTING												FIELDING			
Year	Team (League)	Pos.	G	AB	R	H	2B	3B	HR	RBI	Avg.	BB	SO	SB	PO	A	E	Avg.
1982	—Bluefield (Appal.)	SS-3B-2B	27	45	8	11	1	0	0	4	.244	8	6	0	15	17	3	.914
1983	—Bluefield (Appal.)	SS-3B	48	152	24	33	6	0	0	13	.217	12	13	7	82	145	23	.908
1984	—Hagerstown (Car.)	SS-2B	115	409	48	94	15	3	2	40	.230	36	64	3	187	358	28	.951
1985	—Charlotte (South.)	SS	18	51	2	7	1	0	0	3	.137	6	4	0	18	52	4	.946
	—Day. Beach (FSL)	SS-3B-2B	67	222	23	51	11	0	0	18	.230	22	24	7	90	198	8	.973
1986	—Charlotte (South.)	2B	141	530	58	142	20	3	5	62	.268	24	47	9	*305	*395	*23	.968
1987	—Rochester (Int'l)	2B-SS	74	238	32	68	15	0	0	11	.286	21	24	7	154	200	9	.975
	—Baltimore (A.L.)	2B	58	234	27	72	9	0	2	20	.308	21	23	4	133	162	3	.990
1988	—Baltimore (A.L.)	2B-3B	150	512	52	106	18	1	2	34	.207	33	63	8	310	440	12	.984
1989	—Baltimore (A.L.)	2B	115	318	31	76	11	2	2	26	.239	22	53	1	255	335	9	.985
1990	—Baltimore (A.L.)	2B	129	406	48	118	28	1	3	38	.291	28	43	5	250	366	8	.987
1991	—Baltimore (A.L.)	2B	104	287	24	62	11	1	0	14	.216	15	31	0	201	284	7	.986
	—Frederick (Caro.)	DH	1	4	2	1	0	0	0	1	.250	0	1	0	...	...	...	...
	—Hagerstown (East.)	2B	1	5	1	3	0	0	0	0	.600	0	0	1	2	1	0	1.000
1992	—Baltimore (A.L.)	2B	111	330	35	76	15	0	4	36	.230	18	26	2	217	317	4	*.993
1993	—Texas (A.L.)■	2B-SS-3B	50	132	12	25	4	0	0	11	.189	11	19	0	80	123	2	.990
	Major league totals (7 years)		717	2219	229	535	96	5	13	179	.241	148	258	20	1446	2027	45	.987

RIPKEN, CAL

SS, ORIOLES

PERSONAL: Born August 24, 1960, in Havre de Grace, Md.... 6-4/220.... Throws right, bats right.... Full name: Calvin Edwin Ripken Jr.... Son of Cal Ripken Sr., minor league catcher (1957-62 and 1964), manager, Baltimore Orioles (1987-88), and coach, Orioles (1976-86 and 1989-92); and brother of Bill Ripken, second baseman/shortstop, Texas Rangers organization.
HIGH SCHOOL: Aberdeen (Md.).
TRANSACTIONS/CAREER NOTES: Selected by Baltimore Orioles organization in second round of free-agent draft (June 6, 1978).
RECORDS: Holds major league career records for most home runs by shortstop—289; most years leading league in games by shortstop—9; and most consecutive games by shortstop—1,870.... Holds major league single-season records for most at-bats without a triple—646 (1989); highest fielding percentage by shortstop—.996 (1990); fewest errors by shortstop (150 or more games)—3 (1990); most consecutive errorless games by shortstop—95 (April 14 through July 27, 1990); and most consecutive chances accepted by shortstop without an error—431 (April 14-July 28, 1990, first game).... Shares major league career record for most years leading league in double plays by shortstop—6.... Holds A.L. career record for most years leading league in putouts by shortstop—6.... Holds A.L. single-season record for most assists by shortstop—583 (1984).... Shares A.L. career record for most years leading league in assists by shortstop—7.
HONORS: Named A.L. Rookie Player of the Year by THE SPORTING NEWS (1982).... Named A.L. Rookie of the Year by Baseball Writers' Association of America (1982).... Named Major League Player of the Year by THE SPORTING NEWS (1983 and 1991).... Named A.L. Player of the Year by THE SPORTING NEWS (1983 and 1991).... Named shortstop on THE SPORTING NEWS A.L. All-Star team (1983-85, 1989, 1991 and 1993).... Named shortstop on THE SPORTING NEWS A.L. Silver Slugger team (1983-86, 1989, 1991 and 1993)... Named A.L. Most Valuable Player by Baseball Writers' Association of America (1983 and 1991).... Won A.L. Gold Glove at shortstop (1991-92).
STATISTICAL NOTES: Tied for Appalachian League lead in double plays by shortstop with 31 in 1978.... Led Southern League third basemen with .933 fielding percentage, 119 putouts, 268 assists, 415 total chances and 34 double plays in 1980.... Tied for Southern League lead with nine sacrifice flies in 1980.... Led A.L. shortstops with 831 total chances in 1983, 906 in 1984, 815 in 1989, 806 in 1991 and 738 in 1993.... Led A.L. shortstops with 113 double plays in 1983, 122 in 1984, 123 in 1985, 119 in 1989, 114 in 1991 and 119 in 1992.... Hit for the cycle (May 6, 1984).... Tied for A.L. lead with 15 game-winning RBIs in 1986.... Tied for A.L. lead with 10 sacrifice flies in 1988.... Led A.L. with 368 total bases in 1991.

			BATTING												FIELDING			
Year	Team (League)	Pos.	G	AB	R	H	2B	3B	HR	RBI	Avg.	BB	SO	SB	PO	A	E	Avg.
1978	—Bluefield (Appal.)	SS	63	239	27	63	7	1	0	24	.264	24	46	1	*92	204	*33	.900
1979	—Miami (Florida St.)	3B-SS-2B	105	393	51	119	*28	1	5	54	.303	31	64	4	149	260	30	.932
	—Charlotte (South.)	3B	17	61	6	11	0	1	3	8	.180	3	13	1	13	26	3	.929
1980	—Charlotte (South.)	3B-SS	•144	522	91	144	28	5	25	78	.276	77	81	4	†151	†341	35	†.934
1981	—Rochester (Int'l)	3B-SS	114	437	74	126	31	4	23	75	.288	66	85	0	128	320	21	.955
	—Baltimore (A.L.)	SS-3B	23	39	1	5	0	0	0	0	.128	1	8	0	13	30	3	.935
1982	—Baltimore (A.L.)	SS-3B	160	598	90	158	32	5	28	93	.264	46	95	3	221	440	19	.972
1983	—Baltimore (A.L.)	SS	•162	*663	*121	*211	*47	2	27	102	.318	58	97	0	272	*534	25	.970
1984	—Baltimore (A.L.)	SS	•162	641	103	195	37	7	27	86	.304	71	89	2	*297	*583	26	.971
1985	—Baltimore (A.L.)	SS	161	642	116	181	32	5	26	110	.282	67	68	2	*286	474	26	.967
1986	—Baltimore (A.L.)	SS	162	627	98	177	35	1	25	81	.282	70	60	4	240	*482	13	.982
1987	—Baltimore (A.L.)	SS	*162	624	97	157	28	3	27	98	.252	81	77	3	240	*480	20	.973
1988	—Baltimore (A.L.)	SS	161	575	87	152	25	1	23	81	.264	102	69	2	*284	480	21	.973
1989	—Baltimore (A.L.)	SS	•162	646	80	166	30	0	21	93	.257	57	72	3	*276	*531	8	.990
1990	—Baltimore (A.L.)	SS	161	600	78	150	28	4	21	84	.250	82	66	3	242	435	3	*.996
1991	—Baltimore (A.L.)	SS	•162	650	99	210	46	5	34	114	.323	53	46	6	*267	*528	11	*.986
1992	—Baltimore (A.L.)	SS	*162	637	73	160	29	1	14	72	.251	64	50	4	*287	445	12	.984
1993	—Baltimore (A.L.)	SS	*162	*641	87	165	26	3	24	90	.257	65	58	1	226	*495	17	.977
	Major league totals (13 years)		1962	7583	1130	2087	395	37	297	1104	.275	817	855	33	3151	5937	204	.978

CHAMPIONSHIP SERIES RECORD

			BATTING											FIELDING			
Year	Team (League)	Pos.	G	AB	R	H	2B	3B	HR	RBI	Avg.	BB	SO	SB	PO	A	E	Avg.
1983	—Baltimore (A.L.)........	SS	4	15	5	6	2	0	0	1	.400	2	3	0	7	11	0	1.000

WORLD SERIES RECORD

			BATTING											FIELDING			
Year	Team (League)	Pos.	G	AB	R	H	2B	3B	HR	RBI	Avg.	BB	SO	SB	PO	A	E	Avg.
1983	—Baltimore (A.L.).......	SS	5	18	2	3	0	0	0	1	.167	3	4	0	6	14	0	1.000

ALL-STAR GAME RECORD

ALL-STAR GAME NOTES: Named Most Valuable Player (1991).

			BATTING										FIELDING			
Year	League	Pos.	AB	R	H	2B	3B	HR	RBI	Avg.	BB	SO	SB	PO	A	E	Avg.
1983	—American..................	SS	0	0	0	0	0	0	0	...	1	0	0	1	0	0	1.000
1984	—American..................	SS	3	0	0	0	0	0	0	.000	0	0	0	0	0	0	...
1985	—American..................	SS	3	0	1	0	0	0	0	.333	0	0	0	2	1	0	1.000
1986	—American..................	SS	4	0	0	0	0	0	0	.000	0	0	0	0	1	0	1.000
1987	—American..................	SS	2	0	1	0	0	0	0	.500	0	0	0	0	5	0	1.000
1988	—American..................	SS	3	0	0	0	0	0	0	.000	1	0	0	1	4	0	1.000
1989	—American..................	SS	3	0	1	1	0	0	0	.333	0	0	0	0	0	0	...
1990	—American..................	SS	2	0	0	0	0	0	0	.000	0	0	0	1	1	0	1.000
1991	—American..................	SS	3	1	2	0	0	1	3	.667	0	0	0	2	1	0	1.000
1992	—American..................	SS	3	0	1	0	0	0	1	.333	0	0	0	1	1	0	1.000
1993	—American..................	SS	3	0	0	0	0	0	0	.000	0	1	0	1	2	0	1.000
All-Star Game totals (11 years)........			29	1	6	1	0	1	4	.207	2	1	0	9	16	0	1.000

RISLEY, BILL

P, EXPOS

PERSONAL: Born May 29, 1967, in Chicago. . . . 6-2/215. . . . Throws right, bats right. . . . Full name: William Charles Risley. . . . Name pronounced RIZZ-lee.

HIGH SCHOOL: Marist (Chicago).

TRANSACTIONS/CAREER NOTES: Selected by Cincinnati Reds organization in 14th round of free-agent draft (June 2, 1987). . . . Traded by Reds with P John Wetteland to Montreal Expos for OF Dave Martinez, P Scott Ruskin and SS Willie Greene (December 11, 1991). . . . On Indianapolis disabled list (April 9-20 and May 16-June 3, 1992). . . . On Ottawa disabled list (April 8-23 and June 30-July 10, 1993).

STATISTICAL NOTES: Tied for Southern League lead with five balks in 1991.

Year	Team (League)	W	L	Pct.	ERA	G	GS	CG	ShO	Sv.	IP	H	R	ER	BB	SO
1987	—GC Reds (GCL)...........	1	4	.200	1.89	11	11	0	0	0	52⅓	38	24	11	26	50
1988	—Greensboro (S. Atl.).....	8	4	.667	4.11	23	23	3	3	0	120⅓	82	60	55	84	135
1989	—Ced. Rap. (Midw.)........	9	10	.474	3.90	27	27	2	0	0	140⅔	87	72	61	81	128
1990	—Ced. Rap. (Midw.)........	8	9	.471	2.81	22	22	•7	1	0	137⅔	99	51	43	68	123
1991	—Chatt. (South.)............	5	7	.417	3.16	19	19	3	0	0	108⅓	81	48	38	60	77
	—Nashville (A.A.)...........	3	5	.375	4.91	8	8	1	0	0	44	45	27	24	26	32
1992	—Indianapolis (A.A.)■....	5	8	.385	6.40	25	15	0	0	0	95⅔	105	69	68	47	64
	—Montreal (N.L.)...........	1	0	1.000	1.80	1	1	0	0	0	5	4	1	1	1	2
1993	—Ottawa (Int'l)..............	2	4	.333	2.69	41	0	0	0	1	63⅔	51	26	19	34	74
	—Montreal (N.L.)...........	0	0	...	6.00	2	0	0	0	0	3	2	3	2	2	2
Major league totals (2 years)...		1	0	1.000	3.38	3	1	0	0	0	8	6	4	3	3	4

RITCHIE, TODD

P, TWINS

PERSONAL: Born November 7, 1971, in Portsmouth, Va. . . . 6-3/190. . . . Throws right, bats right. . . . Full name: Todd Everett Ritchie.

HIGH SCHOOL: Duncanville (Tex.).

TRANSACTIONS/CAREER NOTES: Selected by Minnesota Twins organization in first round (12th pick overall) of free-agent draft (June 4, 1990). . . . On disabled list (August 19, 1991-remainder of season and June 24-July 9, 1993).

Year	Team (League)	W	L	Pct.	ERA	G	GS	CG	ShO	Sv.	IP	H	R	ER	BB	SO
1990	—Elizabeth. (Appal.).....	5	2	.714	1.94	11	11	1	0	0	65	45	22	14	24	49
1991	—Kenosha (Midwest)....	7	6	.538	3.55	21	21	0	0	0	116⅔	113	53	46	50	101
1992	—Visalia (California)....	11	9	.550	5.06	28	•28	3	1	0	172⅔	193	113	97	65	129
1993	—Nashville (South.)......	3	2	.600	3.66	12	10	0	0	0	46⅔	46	21	19	15	41

RIVERA, BEN

P, PHILLIES

PERSONAL: Born January 11, 1968, in San Pedro de Macoris, Dominican Republic. . . . 6-6/250. . . . Throws right, bats right. . . . Full name: Bienvenido Santana Rivera.

TRANSACTIONS/CAREER NOTES: Signed as free agent by Atlanta Braves organization (November 15, 1986). . . . Traded by Braves to Philadelphia Phillies for P Donnie Elliott (May 28, 1992). . . . On Philadelphia disabled list (July 8-29, 1992); included rehabilitation assignment to Scranton/Wilkes-Barre (July 20-29).

STATISTICAL NOTES: Pitched seven-inning, 2-0 no-hit victory for Scranton/Wilkes-Barre against Pawtucket (July 25, 1992, first game).

Year	Team (League)	W	L	Pct.	ERA	G	GS	CG	ShO	Sv.	IP	H	R	ER	BB	SO
1987	—GC Braves (GCL)........	1	5	.167	3.26	16	5	0	0	0	49⅔	55	26	18	19	29
1988	—Sumter (S. Atl.)..........	9	11	.450	3.17	27	27	3	2	0	173⅓	167	77	61	52	99
1989	—Durham (Carolina).....	5	7	.417	4.49	23	22	1	0	0	102⅓	113	55	51	51	58
1990	—Greenville (South.).....	1	4	.200	6.58	13	13	0	0	0	52	68	40	38	26	32
	—Durham (Carolina).....	5	3	.625	3.60	16	13	1	1	1	75	69	41	30	33	64
1991	—Greenville (South.).....	11	8	.579	3.57	26	26	3	2	0	158⅔	155	76	63	75	116
1992	—Atlanta-Phil. (N.L.)■.	7	4	.636	3.07	28	14	4	1	0	117⅓	99	40	40	45	77
	—Scran./W.B. (Int'l).....	2	0	1.000	0.00	2	2	1	1	0	12	4	0	0	2	10

Year	Team (League)	W	L	Pct.	ERA	G	GS	CG	ShO	Sv.	IP	H	R	ER	BB	SO
1993	—Philadelphia (N.L.).....	13	9	.591	5.02	30	28	1	1	0	163	175	99	91	85	123
Major league totals (2 years)..		20	13	.606	4.21	58	42	5	2	0	280⅓	274	139	131	130	200

CHAMPIONSHIP SERIES RECORD

Year	Team (League)	W	L	Pct.	ERA	G	GS	CG	ShO	Sv.	IP	H	R	ER	BB	SO
1993	—Philadelphia (N.L.).....	0	0	...	4.50	1	0	0	0	0	2	1	1	1	1	2

WORLD SERIES RECORD

Year	Team (League)	W	L	Pct.	ERA	G	GS	CG	ShO	Sv.	IP	H	R	ER	BB	SO
1993	—Philadelphia (N.L.).....	0	0	...	27.00	1	0	0	0	0	1⅓	4	4	4	2	3

RIVERA, LUIS

SS/2B, METS

PERSONAL: Born January 3, 1964, in Cidra, Puerto Rico. . . . 5-9/175. . . . Throws right, bats right. . . . Full name: Luis Antonio Rivera.
HIGH SCHOOL: Luis Munoz Iglesias (Cidra, Puerto Rico).
TRANSACTIONS/CAREER NOTES: Signed as free agent by Montreal Expos organization (September 22, 1981). . . . Traded by Expos with P John Dopson to Boston Red Sox for SS Spike Owen and P Dan Gakeler (December 8, 1988). . . . On disabled list (June 21-July 18 and August 21-September 5, 1993). . . . Granted free agency (October 25, 1993). . . . Signed by New York Mets (January 19, 1994).
STATISTICAL NOTES: Led Florida State League shortstops with 704 total chances and 95 double plays in 1983. . . . Tied for Florida State League lead in total chances by shortstop with 626 in 1984. . . . Led Southern League shortstops with 643 total chances and 107 double plays in 1985. . . . Led American Association shortstops with 84 double plays in 1987.

			BATTING												FIELDING			
Year	Team (League)	Pos.	G	AB	R	H	2B	3B	HR	RBI	Avg.	BB	SO	SB	PO	A	E	Avg.
1982	—San Jose (Calif.).......	SS	130	476	53	123	20	3	3	49	.258	27	94	12	226	389	55	.918
1983	—W.P. Beach (FSL).....	SS	129	419	63	95	18	5	5	53	.227	58	88	6	217	*436	*51	.928
1984	—W.P. Beach (FSL).....	SS	124	439	54	100	23	0	6	43	.228	50	79	14	*198	*389	39	.938
1985	—Jacksonv. (South.) ..	SS	138	*538	74	129	20	2	16	72	.240	44	69	18	*198	*412	33	.949
1986	—Indianapolis (A.A.)...	SS	108	407	60	100	17	5	7	43	.246	29	68	18	178	330	24	.955
	—Montreal (N.L.).........	SS	55	166	20	34	11	1	0	13	.205	17	33	1	64	119	9	.953
1987	—Indianapolis (A.A.)...	SS	108	433	73	135	26	3	8	53	.312	32	73	24	190	291	18	.964
	—Montreal (N.L.).........	SS	18	32	0	5	2	0	0	1	.156	1	8	0	9	27	3	.923
1988	—Montreal (N.L.).........	SS	123	371	35	83	17	3	4	30	.224	24	69	3	160	301	18	.962
1989	—Pawtucket (Int'l)■....	SS-3B	43	175	22	44	9	0	1	13	.251	11	23	5	53	106	9	.946
	—Boston (A.L.)...........	SS-2B	93	323	35	83	17	1	5	29	.257	20	60	2	127	240	16	.958
1990	—Boston (A.L.)...........	SS-2B-3B	118	346	38	78	20	0	7	45	.225	25	58	4	187	310	18	.965
1991	—Boston (A.L.)...........	SS	129	414	64	107	22	3	8	40	.258	35	86	4	180	386	*24	.959
1992	—Boston (A.L.)...........	S-0-3-2	102	288	17	62	11	1	0	29	.215	26	56	4	120	287	14	.967
1993	—Boston (A.L.)...........	SS-2B-3B	62	130	13	27	8	1	1	7	.208	11	36	1	65	111	6	.967
American League totals (5 years)............			504	1501	167	357	78	6	21	150	.238	117	296	15	679	1334	78	.963
National League totals (3 years)............			196	569	55	122	30	4	4	44	.214	42	110	4	233	447	30	.958
Major league totals (8 years)..................			700	2070	222	479	108	10	25	194	.231	159	406	19	912	1781	108	.961

CHAMPIONSHIP SERIES RECORD

			BATTING												FIELDING			
Year	Team (League)	Pos.	G	AB	R	H	2B	3B	HR	RBI	Avg.	BB	SO	SB	PO	A	E	Avg.
1990	—Boston (A.L.)...........	SS	4	9	1	2	1	0	0	0	.222	0	2	0	6	16	1	.957

RIVERA, MARIANO

P, YANKEES

PERSONAL: Born November 29, 1969, in Panama City, Panama. . . . 6-4/168. . . . Throws right, bats right.
TRANSACTIONS/CAREER NOTES: Signed as free agent by New York Yankees organization (February 17, 1990). . . . On disabled list (April 10-May 19, July 11-28 and August 12-September 8, 1992). . . . On Albany/Colonie disabled list (April 9-June 28, 1993). . . . On Greensboro disabled list (September 6, 1993-remainder of season).
STATISTICAL NOTES: Pitched seven-inning, 3-0 no-hit victory against Gulf Coast Pirates (August 31, 1990).

Year	Team (League)	W	L	Pct.	ERA	G	GS	CG	ShO	Sv.	IP	H	R	ER	BB	SO
1990	—GC Yankees (GCL)	5	1	.833	*0.17	22	1	1	1	1	52	17	3	1	7	58
1991	—Greensboro (S. Atl.).....	4	9	.308	2.75	29	15	1	0	0	114⅔	103	48	35	36	123
1992	—Fort Lauder. (FSL)	5	3	.625	2.28	10	10	3	1	0	59⅓	40	17	15	5	42
1993	—Greensboro (S. Atl.).....	1	0	1.000	2.06	10	10	0	0	0	39⅓	31	12	9	15	32
	—GC Yankees (GCL).......	0	1	.000	2.25	2	2	0	0	0	4	2	1	1	1	6

ROBERSON, KEVIN

OF, CUBS

PERSONAL: Born January 29, 1968, in Decatur, Ill. . . . 6-4/210. . . . Throws right, bats both. . . . Full name: Kevin Lynn Roberson. . . . Name pronounced RO-ber-son.
HIGH SCHOOL: Eisenhower (Decatur, Ill).
COLLEGE: Parkland College (Ill.).
TRANSACTIONS/CAREER NOTES: Selected by Chicago Cubs organization in 16th round of free-agent draft (June 1, 1988). . . . On disabled list (June 6-September 14, 1992).
STATISTICAL NOTES: Led South Atlantic League outfielders with seven double plays in 1989.

			BATTING												FIELDING			
Year	Team (League)	Pos.	G	AB	R	H	2B	3B	HR	RBI	Avg.	BB	SO	SB	PO	A	E	Avg.
1988	—Wytheville (Appal.)..	OF	63	225	39	47	12	2	3	29	.209	40	86	3	93	4	6	.942
1989	—Char., W.Va. (SAL) ..	OF	126	429	49	109	19	1	13	57	.254	70	•149	3	210	18	7	.970
1990	—Winst.-Salem (Car.)..	OF	85	313	49	84	23	3	5	45	.268	25	70	7	136	4	6	.959
	—Charlotte (South.)....	OF	31	119	14	29	6	2	5	16	.244	8	25	2	63	1	0	1.000

Year	Team (League)	Pos.	G	AB	R	H	2B	3B	HR	RBI	Avg.	BB	SO	SB	PO	A	E	Avg.
			BATTING												FIELDING			
1991	—Charlotte (South.)	OF	136	507	77	130	24	2	19	67	.256	39	*129	17	259	7	4	.985
1992	—Iowa (Am. Assoc.)	OF	51	197	25	60	15	4	6	34	.305	5	46	0	87	1	4	.957
1993	—Iowa (Am. Assoc.)	OF	67	263	48	80	20	1	16	50	.304	19	66	3	110	4	4	.966
	—Chicago (N.L.)	OF	62	180	23	34	4	1	9	27	.189	12	48	0	77	2	3	.963
Major league totals (1 year)			62	180	23	34	4	1	9	27	.189	12	48	0	77	2	3	.963

ROBERTS, BIP

2B/OF, PADRES

PERSONAL: Born October 27, 1963, in Berkeley, Calif. . . . 5-7/165. . . . Throws right, bats both. . . . Full name: Leon Joseph Roberts III.

HIGH SCHOOL: Skyline (Oakland, Calif.).

COLLEGE: Chabot College (Calif.) and UNLV.

TRANSACTIONS/CAREER NOTES: Selected by Pittsburgh Pirates organization in fifth round of free-agent draft (June 8, 1981). . . . Selected by Pirates organization in secondary phase of free-agent draft (June 7, 1982). . . . On suspended list (June 30-July 3, 1985). . . . Selected by San Diego Padres from Pirates organization in Rule 5 major league draft (December 10, 1985). . . . On disabled list (May 21-June 5, 1986 and August 17-September 9, 1991). . . . Traded by Padres with a player to be named later to Cincinnati Reds for P Randy Myers (December 8, 1991); Reds acquired OF Craig Pueschner to complete deal (December 9, 1991). . . . On disabled list (July 2-17 and August 4, 1993-remainder of season). . . . Granted free agency (October 26, 1993). . . . Signed by Padres (January 10, 1994).

RECORDS: Shares N.L. single-season record for most consecutive hits—10 (September 19, 20, 22 [second game] and 23, 1992; one base on balls).

STATISTICAL NOTES: Led South Atlantic League second basemen with .962 fielding percentage and tied for lead with 76 double plays in 1983. . . . Led Carolina League second basemen with 654 total chances and 91 double plays in 1984.

Year	Team (League)	Pos.	G	AB	R	H	2B	3B	HR	RBI	Avg.	BB	SO	SB	PO	A	E	Avg.
			BATTING												FIELDING			
1982	—GC Pirates (GCL)	2B	6	23	4	7	1	0	0	1	.304	2	4	4	14	15	0	1.000
	—Greenwood (S. Atl.)	2B	33	107	15	23	3	1	0	6	.215	15	18	10	52	82	7	.950
1983	—Greenwood (S. Atl.)	2B-SS	122	438	78	140	20	5	6	63	.320	69	43	27	273	311	24	†.961
1984	—Prin. William (Car.)	2B	134	498	81	*150	25	5	8	77	.301	44	63	50	*282	352	20	*.969
1985	—Nashua (Eastern)	2B	105	401	64	109	19	5	1	23	.272	29	43	•40	217	249	•29	.941
1986	—San Diego (N.L.)■	2B	101	241	34	61	5	2	1	12	.253	14	29	14	166	172	10	.971
1987	—Las Vegas (PCL)	2B-OF-3B	98	359	66	110	18	10	1	38	.306	37	39	27	147	150	8	.974
1988	—Las Vegas (PCL)	3B-OF-2B	100	343	73	121	21	8	7	51	.353	32	45	29	103	130	17	.932
	—San Diego (N.L.)	2B-3B	5	9	1	3	0	0	0	0	.333	1	2	0	2	3	1	.833
1989	—San Diego (N.L.)	0-3-S-2	117	329	81	99	15	8	3	25	.301	49	45	21	134	113	9	.965
1990	—San Diego (N.L.)	0-3-S-2	149	556	104	172	36	3	9	44	.309	55	65	46	227	160	13	.968
1991	—San Diego (N.L.)	2B-OF	117	424	66	119	13	3	3	32	.281	37	71	26	239	185	10	.977
1992	—Cincinnati (N.L.)■	OF-2B-3B	147	532	92	172	34	6	4	45	.323	62	54	44	209	152	7	.981
1993	—Cincinnati (N.L.)	2-0-3-S	83	292	46	70	13	0	1	18	.240	38	46	26	152	176	6	.982
Major league totals (7 years)			719	2383	424	696	116	22	21	176	.292	256	312	177	1129	961	56	.974

ALL-STAR GAME RECORD

Year	League	Pos.	AB	R	H	2B	3B	HR	RBI	Avg.	BB	SO	SB	PO	A	E	Avg.
			BATTING											FIELDING			
1992	—National	OF	2	1	2	0	0	0	2	1.000	0	0	0	0	0	0	...

ROBERTSON, JASON

OF, YANKEES

PERSONAL: Born March 24, 1971, in Chicago. . . . 6-2/200. . . . Throws left, bats left. . . . Full name: Jason James Robertson.

HIGH SCHOOL: Hillcrest (Country Club Hills, Ill.).

TRANSACTIONS/CAREER NOTES: Selected by New York Yankees organization in third round of free-agent draft (June 5, 1989).

Year	Team (League)	Pos.	G	AB	R	H	2B	3B	HR	RBI	Avg.	BB	SO	SB	PO	A	E	Avg.
			BATTING												FIELDING			
1989	—GC Yankees (GCL)	OF	58	214	27	61	12	5	0	31	.285	28	28	4	90	3	3	.969
1990	—Greensboro (S. Atl.)	OF	133	496	71	124	22	5	6	44	.250	67	110	21	234	4	12	.952
1991	—Prin. William (Car.)	OF	131	515	67	136	21	6	3	54	.264	53	138	32	236	0	*15	.940
1992	—Prin. William (Car.)	OF	68	254	34	61	6	4	5	34	.240	31	55	14	113	1	1	.991
	—Alb./Colon. (East.)	OF	55	204	18	44	12	1	3	33	.216	10	44	9	116	3	4	.967
1993	—Alb./Colon. (East.)	OF	130	483	65	110	30	4	6	41	.228	43	*126	35	274	5	4	.986

ROBERTSON, RICH

P, PIRATES

PERSONAL: Born September 15, 1968, in Nacogdoches, Tex. . . . 6-4/175. . . . Throws left, bats left. . . . Full name: Richard Wayne Robertson.

HIGH SCHOOL: Waller (Tex.).

COLLEGE: San Jacinto College (Tex.) and Texas A&M.

TRANSACTIONS/CAREER NOTES: Selected by San Diego Padres organization in 32nd round of free-agent draft (June 5, 1989). . . . Selected by Pittsburgh Pirates organization in ninth round of free-agent draft (June 4, 1990). . . . On Buffalo disabled list (June 10-19, 1993).

Year	Team (League)	W	L	Pct.	ERA	G	GS	CG	ShO	Sv.	IP	H	R	ER	BB	SO
1990	—Welland (NYP)	3	4	.429	3.08	16	13	0	0	0	64⅓	51	34	22	55	80
1991	—Augusta (S. Atl.)	4	7	.364	4.99	13	12	1	0	0	74	73	52	41	51	62
	—Salem (Carolina)	2	4	.333	4.93	12	11	0	0	0	45⅔	34	32	25	42	32
1992	—Salem (Carolina)	3	0	1.000	3.41	6	6	0	0	0	37	29	18	14	10	27
	—Carolina (South.)	6	7	.462	3.03	20	20	1	1	0	124⅔	127	51	42	41	107
1993	—Buffalo (A.A.)	9	8	.529	4.28	23	23	2	0	0	132⅓	141	67	63	52	71
	—Pittsburgh (N.L.)	0	1	.000	6.00	9	0	0	0	0	9	15	6	6	4	5
Major league totals (1 year)		0	1	.000	6.00	9	0	0	0	0	9	15	6	6	4	5

RODRIGUEZ, ALEX
SS, MARINERS

PERSONAL: Born July 27, 1975, in New York. . . . 6-3/190. . . . Throws right, bats right. . . . Full name: Alexander Emmanuel Rodriguez.
HIGH SCHOOL: Westminister Christian (Miami).
TRANSACTIONS/CAREER NOTES: Selected by Seattle Mariners organization in first round (first pick overall) of free-agent draft (June 3, 1993).

		BATTING												FIELDING			
Year Team (League)	Pos.	G	AB	R	H	2B	3B	HR	RBI	Avg.	BB	SO	SB	PO	A	E	Avg.
1993 —		Did not play.															

RODRIGUEZ, FELIX
P, DODGERS

PERSONAL: Born December 5, 1972, in Montecristy, Dominican Republic. . . . 6-1/170. . . . Throws right, bats right. . . . Full name: Felix Antonio Rodriguez.
HIGH SCHOOL: Liceo Bijiador (Montecristy, D.R.).
TRANSACTIONS/CAREER NOTES: Signed as free agent by Los Angeles Dodgers organization (October 17, 1989). . . . On disabled list (August 11, 1992-remainder of season).
STATISTICAL NOTES: Pitched 11-0 no-hit victory against Sarasota (August 28, 1993).

Year Team (League)	W	L	Pct.	ERA	G	GS	CG	ShO	Sv.	IP	H	R	ER	BB	SO
1993 — Vero Beach (FSL).......	8	8	.500	3.75	32	20	2	1	0	132	109	71	55	71	80

RECORD AS POSITION PLAYER

		BATTING												FIELDING			
Year Team (League)	Pos.	G	AB	R	H	2B	3B	HR	RBI	Avg.	BB	SO	SB	PO	A	E	Avg.
1990 — Santo Dom. (DSL)	...	63	241	23	55	10	0	2	33	.228	15	52	4	...	...	...	...
1991 — GC Dodgers (GCL)	C	45	139	15	37	8	1	2	21	.266	6	32	1	161	18	5	.973
1992 — Great Falls (Pio.)	C-OF	32	110	20	32	8	0	2	20	.291	1	16	2	221	33	2	.992

RODRIGUEZ, HENRY
OF/1B, DODGERS

PERSONAL: Born November 8, 1967, in Santo Domingo, Dominican Republic. . . . 6-1/200. . . . Throws left, bats left. . . . Full name: Henry Anderson Lorenzo Rodriguez.
HIGH SCHOOL: Liceo Republica de Paraguay.
TRANSACTIONS/CAREER NOTES: Signed as free agent by Los Angeles Dodgers organization (July 14, 1985).
HONORS: Named Texas League Most Valuable Player (1990).
STATISTICAL NOTES: Tied for Gulf Coast League lead with seven intentional bases on balls received in 1987. . . . Led Texas League with 14 sacrifice flies in 1990. . . . Tied for Pacific Coast League lead with 10 sacrifice flies in 1992.

		BATTING												FIELDING			
Year Team (League)	Pos.	G	AB	R	H	2B	3B	HR	RBI	Avg.	BB	SO	SB	PO	A	E	Avg.
1987 — GC Dodgers (GCL)	1B-SS	49	148	23	49	7	3	0	15	*.331	16	15	3	309	23	6	.982
1988 — Santo Dom. (DSL)	...	19	21	9	8	2	0	0	10	.381	10	6	4	...	...	...	...
— Salem (Northwest)...	1B	72	291	47	84	14	4	2	39	.289	21	42	14	585	*38	7	.989
1989 — Vero Beach (FSL).....	1B-OF	126	433	53	123	*33	1	10	73	.284	48	58	7	1072	66	12	.990
— Bakersfield (Calif.)...	1B	3	9	2	2	0	0	1	2	.222	0	3	0	8	0	0	1.000
1990 — San Antonio (Tex.)...	OF	129	495	82	144	22	9	*28	*109	.291	61	66	5	223	5	10	.958
1991 — Albuquerque (PCL) ..	OF-1B	121	446	61	121	22	5	10	67	.271	25	62	4	234	12	5	.980
1992 — Albuquerque (PCL) ..	1B-OF	94	365	59	111	21	5	14	72	.304	31	57	1	484	41	10	.981
— Los Angeles (N.L.) ...	OF-1B	53	146	11	32	7	0	3	14	.219	8	30	0	68	8	3	.962
1993 — Albuquerque (PCL) ..	1B-OF	46	179	26	53	13	5	4	30	.296	14	37	1	277	18	5	.983
— Los Angeles (N.L.) ...	OF-1B	76	176	20	39	10	0	8	23	.222	11	39	1	127	9	1	.993
Major league totals (2 years)		129	322	31	71	17	0	11	37	.220	19	69	1	195	17	4	.981

RODRIGUEZ, IVAN
C, RANGERS

PERSONAL: Born November 30, 1971, in Vega Baja, Puerto Rico. . . . 5-9/205. . . . Throws right, bats right.
HIGH SCHOOL: Lina Padron Rivera (Vega Baja, Puerto Rico).
TRANSACTIONS/CAREER NOTES: Signed as free agent by Texas Rangers organization (July 27, 1988). . . . On disabled list (June 6-27, 1992).
HONORS: Won A.L. Gold Glove at catcher (1992-93).
STATISTICAL NOTES: Led South Atlantic League catchers with 34 double plays in 1989. . . . Led Florida State League catchers with 842 total chances in 1990.

		BATTING												FIELDING			
Year Team (League)	Pos.	G	AB	R	H	2B	3B	HR	RBI	Avg.	BB	SO	SB	PO	A	E	Avg.
1989 — Gastonia (S. Atl.)......	C	112	386	38	92	22	1	7	42	.238	21	58	2	691	*96	11	.986
1990 — Charlotte (Fla. St.) ...	C	109	408	48	117	17	7	2	55	.287	12	50	1	*727	101	14	.983
1991 — Tulsa (Texas)...........	C	50	175	16	48	7	2	3	28	.274	6	27	1	210	33	3	.988
— Texas (A.L.)..............	C	88	280	24	74	16	0	3	27	.264	5	42	0	517	62	10	.983
1992 — Texas (A.L.)..............	C	123	420	39	109	16	1	8	37	.260	24	73	0	763	85	*15	.983
1993 — Texas (A.L.)..............	C	137	473	56	129	28	4	10	66	.273	29	70	8	801	76	8	.991
Major league totals (3 years)		348	1173	119	312	60	5	21	130	.266	58	185	8	2081	223	33	.986

ALL-STAR GAME RECORD

		BATTING											FIELDING			
Year League	Pos.	AB	R	H	2B	3B	HR	RBI	Avg.	BB	SO	SB	PO	A	E	Avg.
1992 — American....................	C	2	0	0	0	0	0	0	.000	0	1	0	4	0	0	1.000
1993 — American....................	C	2	1	1	1	0	0	0	.500	0	0	0	3	0	0	1.000
All-Star Game totals (2 years)		4	1	1	1	0	0	0	.250	0	1	0	7	0	0	1.000

RODRIGUEZ, RICH
P, MARLINS

PERSONAL: Born March 1, 1963, in Downey, Calif. . . . 6-0/200. . . . Throws left, bats left. . . . Full name: Richard Anthony Rodriguez.
HIGH SCHOOL: Mountain View (El Monte, Calif.).
COLLEGE: Tennessee.

TRANSACTIONS/CAREER NOTES: Selected by Kansas City Royals organization in 17th round of free-agent draft (June 8, 1981). . . . Selected by New York Mets organization in ninth round of free-agent draft (June 4, 1984). . . . Traded by Mets organization to Wichita, San Diego Padres organization, for 1B Brad Pounders and 1B Bill Stevenson (January 13, 1989). . . . Traded by Padres with 3B Gary Sheffield to Florida Marlins for P Trevor Hoffman, P Jose Martinez and P Andres Berumen (June 24, 1993).
MISCELLANEOUS: Appeared in one game as pinch-runner (1991). . . . Had sacrifice hit in only appearance as pinch-hitter (1992).

Year	Team (League)	W	L	Pct.	ERA	G	GS	CG	ShO	Sv.	IP	H	R	ER	BB	SO
1984	—Little Falls (NYP)	2	1	.667	2.80	25	1	0	0	0	35⅓	28	21	11	36	27
1985	—Columbia (S. Atl.)	6	3	.667	4.03	49	3	0	0	6	80⅓	89	41	36	36	71
1986	—Lynchburg (Caro.)	2	1	.667	3.57	36	0	0	0	3	45⅓	37	20	18	19	38
	—Jackson (Texas)	3	4	.429	9.00	13	5	1	0	0	33	51	35	33	15	15
1987	—Lynchburg (Caro.)	3	1	.750	2.78	*69	0	0	0	5	68	69	23	21	26	59
1988	—Jackson (Texas)	2	7	.222	2.87	47	1	0	0	6	78⅓	66	35	25	42	68
1989	—Wichita (Texas)■	8	3	.727	3.63	54	0	0	0	8	74⅓	74	30	30	37	40
1990	—Las Vegas (PCL)	3	4	.429	3.51	27	2	0	0	8	59	50	24	23	22	46
	—San Diego (N.L.)	1	1	.500	2.83	32	0	0	0	1	47⅔	52	17	15	16	22
1991	—San Diego (N.L.)	3	1	.750	3.26	64	1	0	0	0	80	66	31	29	44	40
1992	—San Diego (N.L.)	6	3	.667	2.37	61	1	0	0	0	91	77	28	24	29	64
1993	—S.D.-Fla. (N.L.)■	2	4	.333	3.79	70	0	0	0	3	76	73	38	32	33	43
	Major league totals (4 years)	12	9	.571	3.05	227	2	0	0	4	294⅔	268	114	100	122	169

ROGERS, CHARLIE

P, BREWERS

PERSONAL: Born August 21, 1968, in Arlington Heights, Ill. . . . 6-0/180. . . . Throws right, bats right. . . . Full name: Thomas Sloan Rogers.
HIGH SCHOOL: Cold Springs (Bremen, Ala.).
COLLEGE: North Alabama.
TRANSACTIONS/CAREER NOTES: Selected by Miami, independent, in free-agent draft (June 4, 1990). . . . Contract sold by Miami to Milwaukee Brewers organization (December 10, 1991). . . . On disabled list (May 5-22, 1991).
STATISTICAL NOTES: Led Florida State League with 14 balks in 1990.

Year	Team (League)	W	L	Pct.	ERA	G	GS	CG	ShO	Sv.	IP	H	R	ER	BB	SO
1990	—Miami (Florida St.)	2	5	.286	2.63	14	10	2	0	1	72	57	26	21	49	64
1991	—Miami (Florida St.)	6	7	.462	4.02	22	20	0	0	0	107⅓	107	54	48	52	71
1992	—Stockton (Calif.)■	4	4	.500	2.81	54	0	0	0	17	80	65	28	25	26	64
1993	—El Paso (Texas)	4	3	.571	1.74	48	2	0	0	23	72⅓	50	17	14	23	55

ROGERS, KENNY

P, RANGERS

PERSONAL: Born November 10, 1964, in Savannah, Ga. . . . 6-1/205. . . . Throws left, bats left. . . . Full name: Kenneth Scott Rogers.
HIGH SCHOOL: Plant City (Fla.).
TRANSACTIONS/CAREER NOTES: Selected by Texas Rangers organization in 39th round of free-agent draft (June 7, 1982). . . . On Tulsa disabled list (April 12-30, 1986).
STATISTICAL NOTES: Tied for A.L. lead with five balks in 1993.

Year	Team (League)	W	L	Pct.	ERA	G	GS	CG	ShO	Sv.	IP	H	R	ER	BB	SO
1982	—GC Rangers (GCL)	0	0	. . .	0.00	2	0	0	0	0	3	0	0	0	0	4
1983	—GC Rangers (GCL)	4	1	.800	2.36	15	6	0	0	1	53⅓	40	21	14	20	36
1984	—Burlington (Midw.)	4	7	.364	3.98	39	4	1	0	3	92⅔	87	52	41	33	93
1985	—Day. Beach (FSL)	0	1	.000	7.20	6	0	0	0	0	10	12	9	8	11	9
	—Burlington (Midw.)	2	5	.286	2.84	33	4	2	1	4	95	67	34	30	62	96
1986	—Tulsa (Texas)	0	3	.000	9.91	10	4	0	0	0	26⅓	39	30	29	18	23
	—Salem (Carolina)	2	7	.222	6.27	12	12	0	0	0	66	75	54	46	26	46
1987	—Charlotte (Fla. St.)	0	3	.000	4.76	5	3	0	0	0	17	17	13	9	8	14
	—Tulsa (Texas)	1	5	.167	5.35	28	6	0	0	2	69	80	51	41	35	59
1988	—Tulsa (Texas)	4	6	.400	4.00	13	13	2	0	0	83⅓	73	43	37	34	76
	—Charlotte (Fla. St.)	2	0	1.000	1.27	8	6	0	0	1	35⅓	22	8	5	11	26
1989	—Texas (A.L.)	3	4	.429	2.93	73	0	0	0	2	73⅔	60	28	24	42	63
1990	—Texas (A.L.)	10	6	.625	3.13	69	3	0	0	15	97⅔	93	40	34	42	74
1991	—Texas (A.L.)	10	10	.500	5.42	63	9	0	0	5	109⅔	121	80	66	61	73
1992	—Texas (A.L.)	3	6	.333	3.09	*81	0	0	0	6	78⅔	80	32	27	26	70
1993	—Texas (A.L.)	16	10	.615	4.10	35	33	5	0	0	208⅓	210	108	95	71	140
	Major league totals (5 years)	42	36	.538	3.90	321	45	5	0	28	568	564	288	246	242	420

ROGERS, KEVIN

P, GIANTS

PERSONAL: Born August 20, 1968, in Cleveland, Miss. . . . 6-1/198. . . . Throws left, bats both. . . . Full name: Charles Kevin Rogers.
HIGH SCHOOL: Cleveland (Miss.).
COLLEGE: Mississippi Delta Junior College.
TRANSACTIONS/CAREER NOTES: Selected by San Francisco Giants organization in ninth round of free-agent draft (June 1, 1988).

Year	Team (League)	W	L	Pct.	ERA	G	GS	CG	ShO	Sv.	IP	H	R	ER	BB	SO
1988	—Pocatello (Pioneer)	2	8	.200	6.20	13	13	1	0	0	69⅔	73	51	48	35	71
1989	—Clinton (Midwest)	13	8	.619	2.55	29	•28	4	0	0	169⅓	128	74	48	78	168
1990	—San Jose (Calif.)	14	5	.737	3.61	28	26	1	1	0	172	143	86	69	68	*186
1991	—Shreveport (Texas)	4	6	.400	3.36	22	22	2	0	0	118	124	63	44	54	108
1992	—Shreveport (Texas)	8	5	.615	2.58	16	16	2	2	0	101	87	34	29	29	110
	—Phoenix (PCL)	3	3	.500	4.00	11	11	1	1	0	69⅔	63	34	31	22	62
	—San Francisco (N.L.)	0	2	.000	4.24	6	6	0	0	0	34	37	17	16	13	26
1993	—San Francisco (N.L.)	2	2	.500	2.68	64	0	0	0	0	80⅔	71	28	24	28	62
	Major league totals (2 years)	2	4	.333	3.14	70	6	0	0	0	114⅔	108	45	40	41	88

ROJAS, MEL

P, EXPOS

PERSONAL: Born December 10, 1966, in Haina, Dominican Republic. . . . 5-11/195. . . . Throws right, bats right. . . . Nephew of Felipe Alou, current manager, Montreal Expos, and major league outfielder/first baseman with six teams (1958-74); nephew of Matty Alou, major league outfielder with six teams (1960-74); nephew of Jesus Alou, major league outfielder with four teams (1963-75 and 1978-79); and brother of Francisco Rojas, minor league outfielder (1978-79). . . . Name pronounced RO-hoss.
HIGH SCHOOL: Liceo Manresa (Santo Domingo, Dominican Republic).
TRANSACTIONS/CAREER NOTES: Signed as free agent by Montreal Expos organization (November 7, 1985). . . . On Rockford disabled list (May 7-June 14, 1988). . . . On West Palm Beach disabled list (August 8, 1988-remainder of season). . . . On Indianapolis disabled list (June 26-July 5, 1991). . . . On disabled list (July 4-19, 1993).

Year	Team (League)	W	L	Pct.	ERA	G	GS	CG	ShO	Sv.	IP	H	R	ER	BB	SO
1986	—GC Expos (GCL)	4	5	.444	4.88	13	12	1	0	0	55⅓	63	39	30	37	34
1987	—Burlington (Midw.)	8	9	.471	3.80	25	25	4	1	0	158⅔	146	84	67	67	100
1988	—Rockford (Midw.)	6	4	.600	2.45	12	12	0	0	0	73⅓	52	30	20	29	72
	—W.P. Beach (FSL)	1	0	1.000	3.60	2	2	0	0	0	5	4	2	2	1	4
1989	—Jacksonv. (South.)	10	7	.588	2.49	34	12	1	1	5	112	62	39	31	57	104
1990	—Indianapolis (A.A.)	2	4	.333	3.13	17	17	0	0	0	97⅔	84	42	34	47	64
	—Montreal (N.L.)	3	1	.750	3.60	23	0	0	0	1	40	34	17	16	24	26
1991	—Montreal (N.L.)	3	3	.500	3.75	37	0	0	0	6	48	42	21	20	13	37
	—Indianapolis (A.A.)	4	2	.667	4.10	14	10	0	0	1	52⅔	50	29	24	14	55
1992	—Indianapolis (A.A.)	2	1	.667	5.40	4	0	0	0	0	8⅓	10	5	5	3	7
	—Montreal (N.L.)	7	1	.875	1.43	68	0	0	0	10	100⅔	71	17	16	34	70
1993	—Montreal (N.L.)	5	8	.385	2.95	66	0	0	0	10	88⅓	80	39	29	30	48
	Major league totals (4 years)	18	13	.581	2.63	194	0	0	0	27	277	227	94	81	101	181

RONAN, MARC

C, CARDINALS

PERSONAL: Born September 19, 1969, in Ozark, Ala. . . . 6-2/190. . . . Throws right, bats left. . . . Full name: Edward Marcus Ronan.
HIGH SCHOOL: H.B. Plant (Tampa, Fla.).
COLLEGE: Florida State.
TRANSACTIONS/CAREER NOTES: Selected by St. Louis Cardinals organization in third round of free-agent draft (June 4, 1990).
STATISTICAL NOTES: Led Midwest League catchers with 919 total chances in 1992.

			BATTING											FIELDING			
Year	Team (League)	Pos.	G	AB	R	H	2B	3B	HR	RBI	Avg.	BB	SO	SB	PO	A	E	Avg.
1990	—Hamilton (NYP)	C-1B	56	167	14	38	6	0	1	15	.228	15	37	1	357	43	9	.978
1991	—Savannah (S. Atl.)	C	108	343	39	81	10	1	0	45	.236	38	54	11	678	87	9	.988
1992	—Springfield (Midw.)	C	110	376	45	81	19	2	6	48	.215	23	58	4	*818	90	11	.988
1993	—St. Peters. (FSL)	C-OF	25	87	13	27	5	0	0	6	.310	6	10	0	155	30	2	.989
	—Arkansas (Texas)	C	96	281	33	60	16	1	7	34	.214	26	47	1	564	65	4	*.994
	—St. Louis (N.L.)	C	6	12	0	1	0	0	0	0	.083	0	5	0	29	0	0	1.000
	Major league totals (1 year)		6	12	0	1	0	0	0	0	.083	0	5	0	29	0	0	1.000

ROPER, JOHN

P, REDS

PERSONAL: Born November 21, 1971, in Southern Pines, N.C. . . . 6-0/175. . . . Throws right, bats right. . . . Full name: John Christopher Roper.
HIGH SCHOOL: Hoke County (Raeford, N.C.).
TRANSACTIONS/CAREER NOTES: Selected by Cincinnati Reds organization in 12th round of free-agent draft (June 4, 1990). . . . On disabled list (July 6-August 21, 1992). . . . On Indianapolis disabled list (May 27-June 6, 1993). . . . On Cincinnati disabled list (June 19-July 19, 1993).
STATISTICAL NOTES: Pitched 1-0 no-hit victory against Birmingham (August 28, 1992, first game).

Year	Team (League)	W	L	Pct.	ERA	G	GS	CG	ShO	Sv.	IP	H	R	ER	BB	SO
1990	—GC Reds (GCL)	7	2	.778	0.97	13	•13	0	0	0	74	41	10	8	31	76
1991	—Char., W.Va. (SAL)	14	9	.609	2.27	27	•27	5	•3	0	186⅔	135	59	47	67	*189
1992	—Chatt. (South.)	10	9	.526	4.10	20	20	1	1	0	120⅔	115	57	55	37	99
1993	—Indianapolis (A.A.)	3	5	.375	4.45	12	12	0	0	0	54⅔	56	33	27	30	42
	—Cincinnati (N.L.)	2	5	.286	5.63	16	15	0	0	0	80	92	51	50	36	54
	Major league totals (1 year)	2	5	.286	5.63	16	15	0	0	0	80	92	51	50	36	54

ROSSELLI, JOE

P, GIANTS

PERSONAL: Born May 28, 1972, in Burbank, Calif. . . . 6-1/170. . . . Throws left, bats right.
HIGH SCHOOL: Mission Hills (Calif.)-Alemany.
TRANSACTIONS/CAREER NOTES: Selected by San Francisco Giants organization in supplemental round ("sandwich pick" between second and third round) of free-agent draft (June 4, 1990); pick received as compensation for Cleveland Indians signing Type C free agent Candy Maldonado. . . . On disabled list (August 1-20, 1992 and April 29, 1993-remainder of season).
HONORS: Named California League Pitcher of the Year (1992).

Year	Team (League)	W	L	Pct.	ERA	G	GS	CG	ShO	Sv.	IP	H	R	ER	BB	SO
1990	—Everett (N'west)	4	4	.500	4.71	15	15	0	0	0	78⅓	87	47	41	29	90
1991	—Clinton (Midwest)	8	7	.533	3.10	22	22	2	0	0	153⅔	144	70	53	49	127
1992	—San Jose (Calif.)	11	4	.733	*2.41	22	22	4	0	0	149⅔	145	50	40	46	111
1993	—Shreveport (Texas)	0	1	.000	3.13	4	4	0	0	0	23	22	9	8	7	19

ROSSY, RICO

IF, ROYALS

PERSONAL: Born February 16, 1964, in San Juan, Puerto Rico. . . . 5-10/175. . . . Throws right, bats right. . . . Full name: Elam Jose Rossy.
HIGH SCHOOL: Frontier (Chalmers, Ind.).
COLLEGE: Purdue.
TRANSACTIONS/CAREER NOTES: Selected by Baltimore Orioles organization in 33rd round of free-agent draft (June 3, 1985). . . .

Traded by Orioles organization with SS Terry Crowley Jr. to Pittsburgh Pirates organization for OF Joe Orsulak (November 6, 1987).... Traded by Pirates organization to Atlanta Braves organization for OF Greg Tubbs (May 2, 1990).... Traded by Braves to Kansas City Royals for OF Bobby Moore (December 10, 1991).... On Kansas City disabled list (April 12-27, 1993); included rehabilitation assignment to Omaha (April 22-27).

STATISTICAL NOTES: Led New York-Pennsylvania League third basemen with 64 putouts, 159 assists, 252 total chances and 15 double plays in 1985.

			BATTING											FIELDING			
Year	**Team (League)**	**Pos.**	**G**	**AB**	**R**	**H**	**2B**	**3B**	**HR**	**RBI**	**Avg.**	**BB**	**SO**	**SB**	**PO**	**A**	**E**	**Avg.**
1985	—Newark (NY-Penn)..	3B-SS-2B	73	246	38	53	14	2	3	25	.215	32	22	17	†67	†159	26	.897
1986	—Miami (Florida St.)...	3B-SS	38	134	26	34	7	1	1	9	.254	24	8	10	30	95	8	.940
	—Charlotte (South.)....	S-3-2-O	77	232	40	68	16	2	3	25	.293	26	19	13	121	149	10	.964
1987	—Charlotte (South.)....	3B-2B-OF	127	471	69	135	22	3	4	50	.287	43	38	20	129	255	19	.953
1988	—Buffalo (A.A.)■.........	SS-3B-2B	68	187	12	46	4	0	1	20	.246	13	17	1	101	152	10	.962
1989	—Harrisburg (East.)....	SS-3B	78	238	20	60	16	1	2	25	.252	27	19	2	107	175	12	.959
	—Buffalo (A.A.).........	SS-C-2B	38	109	11	21	5	0	0	10	.193	18	11	4	85	98	6	.968
1990	—Buffalo (A.A.)...........	SS	8	17	3	3	0	1	0	2	.176	4	2	1	9	20	2	.935
	—Greenville (South.)■.	SS	5	21	4	4	1	0	0	0	.190	1	2	0	9	23	2	.941
	—Richmond (Int'l).......	SS	107	380	58	88	13	0	4	32	.232	69	43	11	144	290	18	*.960
1991	—Richmond (Int'l).......	2B-SS-3B	*139	482	58	124	25	1	2	48	.257	67	44	4	286	408	17	.976
	—Atlanta (N.L.)...........	SS	5	1	0	0	0	0	0	0	.000	0	1	0	0	0	0	...
1992	—Omaha (A.A.)■..........	SS	48	174	29	55	10	1	4	17	.316	34	14	3	86	141	8	.966
	—Kansas City (A.L.)....	SS-3B-2B	59	149	21	32	8	1	1	12	.215	20	20	0	73	156	10	.958
1993	—Kansas City (A.L.)....	2B-3B-SS	46	86	10	19	4	0	2	12	.221	9	11	0	42	76	1	.992
	—Omaha (A.A.)............	SS-3B	37	131	25	39	10	1	5	21	.298	20	19	3	54	124	7	.962
American League totals (2 years)............			105	235	31	51	12	1	3	24	.217	29	31	0	115	232	11	.969
National League totals (1 year)...............			5	1	0	0	0	0	0	0	.000	0	1	0	0	0	0	...
Major league totals (3 years)..................			110	236	31	51	12	1	3	24	.216	29	32	0	115	232	11	.969

ROWLAND, RICH

C, TIGERS

PERSONAL: Born February 25, 1967, in Cloverdale, Calif.... 6-1/215.... Throws right, bats right.... Full name: Richard Garnet Rowland.

HIGH SCHOOL: Cloverdale (Calif.).

COLLEGE: Mendocino Community College (Calif.).

TRANSACTIONS/CAREER NOTES: Selected by Detroit Tigers organization in 17th round of free-agent draft (June 1, 1988).... On Toledo disabled list (May 3-27, 1991).

STATISTICAL NOTES: Tied for International League lead in grounding into double plays with 20 in 1992.... Led International League catchers with 68 assists in 1992.

			BATTING											FIELDING			
Year	**Team (League)**	**Pos.**	**G**	**AB**	**R**	**H**	**2B**	**3B**	**HR**	**RBI**	**Avg.**	**BB**	**SO**	**SB**	**PO**	**A**	**E**	**Avg.**
1988	—Bristol (Appal.).........	C	56	186	29	51	10	1	4	41	.274	27	39	1	253	31	7	.976
1989	—Fayetteville (SAL)....	C	108	375	43	102	17	1	9	59	.272	54	98	4	527	66	11	.982
1990	—London (Eastern).....	C	47	161	22	46	10	0	8	30	.286	20	33	1	231	24	3	.988
	—Toledo (Int'l)............	C	62	192	28	50	12	0	7	22	.260	15	33	2	305	39	*13	.964
	—Detroit (A.L.)...........	C	7	19	3	3	1	0	0	0	.158	2	4	0	29	0	1	.967
1991	—Toledo (Int'l)............	C	109	383	56	104	26	0	13	68	.272	60	77	4	614	78	4	*.994
	—Detroit (A.L.)...........	C	4	4	0	1	0	0	0	1	.250	1	2	0	2	1	0	1.000
1992	—Toledo (Int'l)............	C-1B	136	473	75	111	19	1	25	82	.235	56	112	9	628	†68	6	.991
	—Detroit (A.L.)...........	C-3B-1B	6	14	2	3	0	0	0	0	.214	3	3	0	12	1	0	1.000
1993	—Toledo (Int'l)............	C	96	325	58	87	24	2	21	59	.268	51	72	1	569	64	8	.988
	—Detroit (A.L.)...........	C	21	46	2	10	3	0	0	4	.217	5	16	0	75	7	1	.988
Major league totals (4 years)..................			38	83	7	17	4	0	0	5	.205	11	25	0	118	9	2	.984

ROYER, STAN

3B, CARDINALS

PERSONAL: Born August 31, 1967, in Olney, Ill.... 6-3/221.... Throws right, bats right.... Full name: Stanley Dean Royer.

HIGH SCHOOL: Charleston (Ill.).

COLLEGE: Eastern Illinois.

TRANSACTIONS/CAREER NOTES: Selected by Atlanta Braves organization in 10th round of free-agent draft (June 3, 1985).... Selected by Oakland Athletics organization in first round (16th pick overall) of free-agent draft (June 1, 1988).... Traded by A's organization with OF Felix Jose and P Daryl Green to St. Louis Cardinals for OF Willie McGee (August 29, 1990).

HONORS: Named Northwest League Most Valuable Player (1988).

STATISTICAL NOTES: Led Northwest League third basemen with 231 total chances in 1988.... Led California League third basemen with 342 total chances in 1989.... Led Southern League third basemen with 269 assists, 38 errors, 387 total chances and 28 double plays in 1990.... Led American Association third basemen with 100 putouts, 299 assists, 29 errors, 428 total chances and 32 double plays in 1991.... Tied for American Association lead in errors by first baseman with eight in 1992.

			BATTING											FIELDING			
Year	**Team (League)**	**Pos.**	**G**	**AB**	**R**	**H**	**2B**	**3B**	**HR**	**RBI**	**Avg.**	**BB**	**SO**	**SB**	**PO**	**A**	**E**	**Avg.**
1988	—S. Oregon (N'west)...	3B	73	286	47	91	19	3	6	48	.318	33	71	1	*50	*158	23	*.900
1989	—Modesto (Calif.)........	3B	127	476	54	120	28	1	11	69	.252	58	132	3	*99	220	23	*.933
	—Tacoma (PCL)..........	3B	6	19	2	5	1	0	0	2	.263	2	6	0	4	9	4	.765
1990	—Huntsville (South.)...	3B-OF-SS	137	527	69	136	29	3	14	89	.258	43	113	4	88	†271	†38	.904
	—Louisville (A.A.)■.....	3B	4	15	1	4	1	1	0	4	.267	2	5	0	0	7	0	1.000
1991	—Louisville (A.A.).......	3B-C	*138	*523	48	133	30	6	14	74	.254	43	126	1	†100	†299	†29	.932
	—St. Louis (N.L.).........	3B	9	21	1	6	1	0	0	1	.286	1	2	0	5	4	0	1.000
1992	—Louisville (A.A.).......	1B-3B	124	444	55	125	31	2	11	77	.282	32	74	0	953	103	‡10	.991
	—St. Louis (N.L.).........	3B-1B	13	31	6	10	2	0	2	9	.323	1	4	0	34	11	3	.938
1993	—Louisville (A.A.).......	3B-1B	98	368	46	103	19	0	16	54	.280	33	74	2	109	202	11	.966
	—St. Louis (N.L.).........	3B-1B	24	46	4	14	2	0	1	8	.304	2	14	0	22	16	3	.927
Major league totals (3 years)..................			46	98	11	30	5	0	3	18	.306	4	20	0	61	31	6	.939

RUETER, KIRK

P, EXPOS

PERSONAL: Born December 1, 1970, in Centralia, Ill. . . . 6-3/195. . . . Throws left, bats left. . . . Full name: Kirk Wesley Rueter. . . . Name pronounced REE-ter.
HIGH SCHOOL: Nashville (Ill.) Community.
COLLEGE: Murray State.
TRANSACTIONS/CAREER NOTES: Selected by Montreal Expos organization in 19th round of free-agent draft (June 3, 1991).
HONORS: Named N.L. Rookie Pitcher of the Year by THE SPORTING NEWS (1993).

Year	Team (League)	W	L	Pct.	ERA	G	GS	CG	ShO	Sv.	IP	H	R	ER	BB	SO
1991	—GC Expos (GCL)	1	1	.500	0.95	5	4	0	0	0	19	16	5	2	4	19
	—Sumter (S. Atl.)	3	1	.750	1.33	8	5	0	0	0	40⅔	32	8	6	10	27
1992	—Rockford (Midw.)	11	9	.550	2.58	26	26	6	•2	0	174⅓	150	68	50	36	153
1993	—Harrisburg (East.)	5	0	1.000	1.36	9	8	1	1	0	59⅔	47	10	9	7	36
	—Ottawa (Int'l)	4	2	.667	2.70	7	7	1	0	0	43⅓	46	20	13	3	27
	—Montreal (N.L.)	8	0	1.000	2.73	14	14	1	0	0	85⅔	85	33	26	18	31
	Major league totals (1 year)	8	0	1.000	2.73	14	14	1	0	0	85⅔	85	33	26	18	31

RUFFCORN, SCOTT

P, WHITE SOX

PERSONAL: Born December 29, 1969, in New Braunfels, Tex. . . . 6-4/210. . . . Throws right, bats right. . . . Full name: Scott Patrick Ruffcorn.
HIGH SCHOOL: S.F. Austin (Austin, Tex.).
COLLEGE: Baylor.
TRANSACTIONS/CAREER NOTES: Selected by Atlanta Braves organization in 39th round of free-agent draft (June 1, 1988). . . . Selected by Chicago White Sox organization in first round (25th pick overall) of free-agent draft (June 3, 1991).

Year	Team (League)	W	L	Pct.	ERA	G	GS	CG	ShO	Sv.	IP	H	R	ER	BB	SO
1991	—GC Whi. Sox (GCL)	0	0	...	3.18	4	2	0	0	0	11⅓	8	7	4	5	15
	—South Bend (Mid.)	1	3	.250	3.92	9	9	0	0	0	43⅔	35	26	19	25	45
1992	—Sarasota (Fla. St.)	14	5	.737	2.19	25	24	2	0	0	160⅓	122	53	39	39	140
1993	—Birm. (Southern)	9	4	.692	2.73	20	20	3	*3	0	135	108	47	41	52	*141
	—Chicago (A.L.)	0	2	.000	8.10	3	2	0	0	0	10	9	11	9	10	2
	—Nashville (A.A.)	2	2	.500	2.80	7	6	1	0	0	45	30	16	14	8	44
	Major league totals (1 year)	0	2	.000	8.10	3	2	0	0	0	10	9	11	9	10	2

RUFFIN, BRUCE

P, ROCKIES

PERSONAL: Born October 4, 1963, in Lubbock, Tex. . . . 6-2/213. . . . Throws left, bats both. . . . Full name: Bruce Wayne Ruffin.
HIGH SCHOOL: J.M. Hanks (El Paso, Tex.).
COLLEGE: Texas.
TRANSACTIONS/CAREER NOTES: Selected by Philadelphia Phillies organization in 31st round of free-agent draft (June 7, 1982). . . . Selected by Phillies organization in second round of free-agent draft (June 3, 1985); pick received as compensation for Pittsburgh Pirates signing free agent Sixto Lezcano. . . . Traded by Phillies to Milwaukee Brewers for SS/3B Dale Sveum (December 11, 1991). . . . Granted free agency (November 5, 1992). . . . Signed by Colorado Rockies (December 7, 1992).

Year	Team (League)	W	L	Pct.	ERA	G	GS	CG	ShO	Sv.	IP	H	R	ER	BB	SO
1985	—Clearwater (FSL)	5	5	.500	2.88	14	14	3	1	0	97	87	33	31	34	74
1986	—Reading (Eastern)	8	4	.667	3.29	16	13	4	2	0	90⅓	89	41	33	26	68
	—Philadelphia (N.L.)	9	4	.692	2.46	21	21	6	0	0	146⅓	138	53	40	44	70
1987	—Philadelphia (N.L.)	11	14	.440	4.35	35	35	3	1	0	204⅔	236	118	99	73	93
1988	—Philadelphia (N.L.)	6	10	.375	4.43	55	15	3	0	3	144⅓	151	86	71	80	82
1989	—Philadelphia (N.L.)	6	10	.375	4.44	24	23	1	0	0	125⅔	152	69	62	62	70
	—Scran./W.B. (Int'l)	5	1	.833	4.68	9	9	0	0	0	50	44	28	26	39	44
1990	—Philadelphia (N.L.)	6	13	.316	5.38	32	25	2	1	0	149	178	99	89	62	79
1991	—Scran./W.B. (Int'l)	4	5	.444	4.66	13	13	1	0	0	75⅓	82	43	39	41	50
	—Philadelphia (N.L.)	4	7	.364	3.78	31	15	1	1	0	119	125	52	50	38	85
1992	—Milwaukee (A.L.)■	1	6	.143	6.67	25	6	1	0	0	58	66	43	43	41	45
	—Denver (A.A.)	3	0	1.000	0.94	4	4	1	0	0	28⅔	28	12	3	8	17
1993	—Colorado (N.L.)■	6	5	.545	3.87	59	12	0	0	2	139⅔	145	71	60	69	126
	A.L. totals (1 year)	1	6	.143	6.67	25	6	1	0	0	58	66	43	43	41	45
	N.L. totals (7 years)	48	63	.432	4.12	257	146	16	3	5	1028⅔	1125	548	471	428	605
	Major league totals (8 years)	49	69	.415	4.26	282	152	17	3	5	1086⅔	1191	591	514	469	650

RUFFIN, JOHNNY

P, REDS

PERSONAL: Born July 29, 1971, in Butler, Ala. . . . 6-3/170. . . . Throws right, bats right. . . . Full name: Johnny Renando Ruffin.
HIGH SCHOOL: Choctaw County (Butler, Ala.).
TRANSACTIONS/CAREER NOTES: Selected by Chicago White Sox organization in fourth round of free-agent draft (June 1, 1988). . . . Traded by White Sox with P Jeff Pierce to Cincinnati Reds for P Tim Belcher (July 31, 1993).
STATISTICAL NOTES: Pitched 6-1 no-hit victory against Charlotte (June 14, 1991, second game).

Year	Team (League)	W	L	Pct.	ERA	G	GS	CG	ShO	Sv.	IP	H	R	ER	BB	SO
1988	—GC Whi. Sox (GCL)	4	2	.667	2.30	13	11	1	0	0	58⅔	43	27	15	22	31
1989	—Utica (N.Y.-Penn)	4	8	.333	3.36	15	15	0	0	0	88⅓	67	43	33	46	92
1990	—South Bend (Mid.)	7	6	.538	4.17	24	24	0	0	0	123	117	86	57	82	92
1991	—Sarasota (Fla. St.)	11	4	.733	3.23	26	26	6	2	0	158⅔	126	68	57	62	117
1992	—Birm. (Southern)	0	7	.000	6.04	10	10	0	0	0	47⅔	51	48	32	34	44
	—Sarasota (Fla. St.)	3	7	.300	5.89	23	8	0	0	0	62⅔	56	46	41	41	61
1993	—Birm. (Southern)	0	4	.000	2.82	11	0	0	0	2	22⅓	16	9	7	9	23
	—Nash.-Ind. (A.A.)■	4	5	.444	3.11	32	0	0	0	2	66⅔	51	25	23	18	75
	—Cincinnati (N.L.)	2	1	.667	3.58	21	0	0	0	2	37⅔	36	16	15	11	30
	Major league totals (1 year)	2	1	.667	3.58	21	0	0	0	2	37⅔	36	16	15	11	30

RUSKIN, SCOTT

P, ROYALS

PERSONAL: Born June 8, 1963, in Jacksonville, Fla.... 6-2/195.... Throws left, bats right.... Full name: Scott Drew Ruskin.
HIGH SCHOOL: Sandalwood (Jacksonville, Fla.).
COLLEGE: Florida.

TRANSACTIONS/CAREER NOTES: Selected by Cincinnati Reds organization in 14th round of free-agent draft (June 8, 1981).... Selected by Texas Rangers organization in fourth round of free-agent draft (June 4, 1984).... Selected by Cleveland Indians organization in third round of free-agent draft (June 3, 1985).... Selected by Montreal Expos organization in secondary phase of free-agent draft (January 14, 1986).... Selected by Pittsburgh Pirates organization in secondary phase of free-agent draft (June 2, 1986).... On Macon disabled list (April 7-28, 1987).... Traded by Pirates with SS Willie Greene and a player to be named later to Expos for P Zane Smith (August 8, 1990); Expos acquired OF Moises Alou to complete deal (August 16, 1990).... Traded by Expos with OF Dave Martinez and SS Willie Greene to Reds for P John Wetteland and P Bill Risley (December 11, 1991).... Granted free agency (October 5, 1993).... Signed by Omaha, Kansas City Royals organization (December 14, 1993).

Year	Team (League)	W	L	Pct.	ERA	G	GS	CG	ShO	Sv.	IP	H	R	ER	BB	SO
1989	—Salem (Carolina)	4	5	.444	2.23	14	13	3	0	1	84⅔	71	35	21	33	92
	—Harrisburg (East.)	2	3	.400	4.86	12	10	2	0	0	63	64	38	34	32	56
1990	—Pitts.-Mont. (N.L.)■	3	2	.600	2.75	67	0	0	0	2	75⅓	75	28	23	38	57
1991	—Montreal (N.L.)	4	4	.500	4.24	64	0	0	0	6	63⅔	57	31	30	30	46
1992	—Cincinnati (N.L.)■	4	3	.571	5.03	57	0	0	0	0	53⅔	56	31	30	20	43
1993	—Indianapolis (A.A.)	1	5	.167	5.14	49	2	0	0	*28	56	60	34	32	22	41
	—Cincinnati (N.L.)	0	0	...	18.00	4	0	0	0	0	1	3	2	2	2	0
	Major league totals (4 years)	11	9	.550	3.95	192	0	0	0	8	193⅔	191	92	85	90	146

RECORD AS POSITION PLAYER

				BATTING											FIELDING			
Year	Team (League)	Pos.	G	AB	R	H	2B	3B	HR	RBI	Avg.	BB	SO	SB	PO	A	E	Avg.
1986	—GC Pirates (GCL)	DH	11	31	3	11	1	0	0	4	.355	1	9	1	...	...	...	...
1987	—Macon (S. Atl.)	OF-1B	81	239	37	71	9	2	9	42	.297	25	64	7	183	11	6	.970
	—Salem (Carolina)	1B-OF	23	83	16	25	3	1	3	11	.301	11	20	10	154	16	1	.994
1988	—Salem (Carolina)	OF-1B	26	96	16	28	8	2	4	16	.292	10	26	6	83	6	4	.957
	—Harrisburg (East.)	OF-1B	90	309	27	69	14	3	3	32	.223	23	99	11	233	12	8	.968

RUSSELL, JEFF

P, RED SOX

PERSONAL: Born September 2, 1961, in Cincinnati.... 6-3/205.... Throws right, bats right.... Full name: Jeffrey Lee Russell.
HIGH SCHOOL: Wyoming (Cincinnati).
COLLEGE: Gulf Coast Community College (Fla.).

TRANSACTIONS/CAREER NOTES: Selected by Cincinnati Reds organization in fifth round of free-agent draft (June 5, 1979).... On disabled list (May 5-June 10 and July 28, 1982-remainder of season).... On Denver disabled list (May 22-June 10, 1985).... Traded by Reds to Texas Rangers organization (July 23, 1985), completing deal in which Rangers traded 3B Buddy Bell to Reds for OF Duane Walker and a player to be named later (July 19, 1985).... On Texas disabled list (March 25-May 15, 1987); included rehabilitation assignment to Charlotte (April 26-May 4) and Oklahoma City (May 5-15).... On Texas disabled list (May 29-September 10, 1990); included rehabilitation assignment to Charlotte (July 30-August 3).... Traded by Rangers with OF Ruben Sierra, P Bobby Witt and cash to Oakland Athletics for OF Jose Canseco (August 31, 1992).... Granted free agency (October 26, 1992).... Signed by Boston Red Sox (March 1, 1993).... On disabled list (August 29-September 28, 1993).
HONORS: Named A.L. Fireman of the Year by THE SPORTING NEWS (1989).
MISCELLANEOUS: Made an out in only appearance as a pinch-hitter (1988).

Year	Team (League)	W	L	Pct.	ERA	G	GS	CG	ShO	Sv.	IP	H	R	ER	BB	SO
1980	—Eugene (N'west)	6	5	.545	3.00	13	13	3	0	0	90	80	47	30	50	75
1981	—Tampa (Fla. St.)	10	4	.714	2.01	22	21	5	2	0	143	109	51	32	48	92
1982	—Waterbury (East.)	6	4	.600	2.37	14	12	2	1	0	79⅔	67	27	21	23	88
1983	—Indianapolis (A.A.)	5	5	.500	3.55	18	17	5	0	1	119	106	51	47	44	98
	—Cincinnati (N.L.)	4	5	.444	3.03	10	10	2	0	0	68⅓	58	30	23	22	40
1984	—Cincinnati (N.L.)	6	*18	.250	4.26	33	30	4	2	0	181⅔	186	97	86	65	101
1985	—Den.-Okla. C. (A.A.)■	7	4	.636	4.06	18	18	1	1	0	115⅓	105	55	52	51	94
	—Texas (A.L.)	3	6	.333	7.55	13	13	0	0	0	62	85	55	52	27	44
1986	—Okla. City (A.A.)	4	1	.800	3.95	11	11	1	0	0	70⅔	63	32	31	38	34
	—Texas (A.L.)	5	2	.714	3.40	37	0	0	0	2	82	74	40	31	31	54
1987	—Charlotte (Fla. St.)	0	0	...	2.45	2	2	0	0	0	11	8	3	3	5	3
	—Okla. City (A.A.)	0	0	...	1.42	4	0	0	0	0	6⅓	5	1	1	1	5
	—Texas (A.L.)	5	4	.556	4.44	52	2	0	0	3	97⅓	109	56	48	52	56
1988	—Texas (A.L.)	10	9	.526	3.82	34	24	5	1	0	188⅔	183	86	80	66	88
1989	—Texas (A.L.)	6	4	.600	1.98	71	0	0	0	*38	72⅔	45	21	16	24	77
1990	—Texas (A.L.)	1	5	.167	4.26	27	0	0	0	10	25⅓	23	15	12	16	16
	—Charlotte (Fla. St.)	0	1	.000	...	1	0	0	0	0	0	1	1	1	0	0
1991	—Texas (A.L.)	6	4	.600	3.29	68	0	0	0	30	79⅓	71	36	29	26	52
1992	—Texas-Oak. (A.L.)■	4	3	.571	1.63	59	0	0	0	30	66⅓	55	14	12	25	48
1993	—Boston (A.L.)■	1	4	.200	2.70	51	0	0	0	33	46⅔	39	16	14	14	45
	A.L. totals (9 years)	41	41	.500	3.67	412	39	5	1	146	720⅓	684	339	294	281	480
	N.L. totals (2 years)	10	23	.303	3.92	43	40	6	2	0	250	244	127	109	87	141
	Major league totals (11 years)	51	64	.443	3.74	455	79	11	3	146	970⅓	928	466	403	368	621

CHAMPIONSHIP SERIES RECORD

Year	Team (League)	W	L	Pct.	ERA	G	GS	CG	ShO	Sv.	IP	H	R	ER	BB	SO
1992	—Oakland (A.L.)	1	0	1.000	9.00	3	0	0	0	0	2	2	2	2	4	0

ALL-STAR GAME RECORD

Year	League	W	L	Pct.	ERA	GS	CG	ShO	Sv.	IP	H	R	ER	BB	SO
1988	—American	0	0	...	0.00	0	0	0	0	1	1	0	0	1	0
1989	—American	0	0	...	9.00	0	0	0	0	1	1	1	1	1	0
All-Star totals (2 years)		0	0	...	4.50	0	0	0	0	2	2	1	1	2	0

RUSSELL, JOHN

C

PERSONAL: Born January 5, 1961, in Oklahoma City. . . . 6-0/195. . . . Throws right, bats right. . . . Full name: John William Russell.
HIGH SCHOOL: Norman (Okla.).
COLLEGE: Oklahoma.
TRANSACTIONS/CAREER NOTES: Selected by Montreal Expos organization in fourth round of free-agent draft (June 5, 1979). . . . Selected by Philadelphia Phillies organization in first round (13th pick overall) of free-agent draft (June 7, 1982). . . . Contract sold by Phillies to Atlanta Braves (March 25, 1989). . . . Released by Braves (April 6, 1990). . . . Signed by Oklahoma City, Texas Rangers organization (May 8, 1990). . . . Granted free agency (October 22, 1990). . . . Re-signed by Oklahoma City (February 1, 1991). . . . On disabled list (May 1-June 6 and July 29-September 1, 1991). . . . Granted free agency (October 28, 1991). . . . Signed by Tulsa, Rangers organization (April 5, 1992). . . . On Texas disabled list (June 25, 1992-remainder of season). . . . Granted free agency (October 27, 1992). . . . Re-signed by Rangers (November 19, 1992). . . . Granted free agency (May 21, 1993). . . . Re-signed by Rangers (July 30, 1993). . . . Granted free agency (August 18, 1993). . . . Signed by Rangers (September 1, 1993). . . . Granted free agency (October 4, 1993).
STATISTICAL NOTES: Tied for Pacific Coast League lead with 13 passed balls in 1983. . . . Led N.L. with 17 passed balls in 1986.

			BATTING												FIELDING			
Year	Team (League)	Pos.	G	AB	R	H	2B	3B	HR	RBI	Avg.	BB	SO	SB	PO	A	E	Avg.
1982	—Reading (Eastern)	C-OF-1B	77	263	26	53	10	5	6	30	.202	23	84	3	354	44	12	.971
1983	—Portland (PCL)	C-OF-3B	128	445	71	113	23	3	27	76	.254	42	109	3	551	58	12	.981
1984	—Portland (PCL)	OF-1B-C	93	350	75	101	22	5	19	77	.289	44	91	1	182	18	5	.976
	—Philadelphia (N.L.)	OF-C	39	99	11	28	8	1	2	11	.283	12	33	0	51	1	0	1.000
1985	—Philadelphia (N.L.)	OF-1B	81	216	22	47	12	0	9	23	.218	18	72	2	170	9	4	.978
	—Portland (PCL)	OF-C-1B	16	49	8	15	2	2	4	11	.306	13	15	0	24	1	1	.962
1986	—Philadelphia (N.L.)	C	93	315	35	76	21	2	13	60	.241	25	103	0	498	39	13	.976
1987	—Philadelphia (N.L.)	OF-C	24	62	5	9	1	0	3	8	.145	3	17	0	48	1	1	.980
	—Maine (Int'l)	OF-C-3B	44	143	15	29	6	1	7	24	.203	22	37	2	107	14	2	.984
1988	—Maine (Int'l)	C-O-3-1	110	394	50	90	18	0	13	52	.228	29	108	4	363	54	10	.977
	—Philadelphia (N.L.)	C	22	49	5	12	1	0	2	4	.245	3	15	0	77	9	5	.945
1989	—Atlanta (N.L.)■	C-O-1-3-P	74	159	14	29	2	0	2	9	.182	8	53	0	196	28	4	.982
1990	—Okla. City (A.A.)■	C	6	22	7	9	4	0	2	6	.409	2	3	0	30	1	1	.969
	—Texas (A.L.)	C-O-1-3	68	128	16	35	4	0	2	8	.273	11	41	1	148	11	3	.981
1991	—Texas (A.L.)	OF-C	22	27	3	3	0	0	0	1	.111	1	7	0	24	0	0	1.000
1992	—Tulsa (Texas)	C	46	163	26	42	11	0	10	27	.258	17	42	0	264	27	1	.997
	—Texas (A.L.)	C-OF	7	10	1	1	0	0	0	2	.100	1	4	0	14	2	1	.941
1993	—Texas (A.L.)	C-O-3-1	18	22	1	5	1	0	1	3	.227	2	10	0	30	0	0	1.000
American League totals (4 years)			115	187	21	44	5	0	3	14	.235	15	62	1	216	13	4	.983
National League totals (6 years)			333	900	92	201	45	3	31	115	.223	69	293	2	1040	87	27	.977
Major league totals (10 years)			448	1087	113	245	50	3	34	129	.225	84	355	3	1256	100	31	.978

RECORD AS PITCHER

Year	Team (League)	W	L	Pct.	ERA	G	GS	CG	ShO	Sv.	IP	H	R	ER	BB	SO
1989	—Atlanta (N.L.)	0	0	...	0.00	1	0	0	0	0	⅓	0	0	0	0	0

RUSSO, PAUL

3B/1B, TWINS

PERSONAL: Born August 26, 1969, in Tampa, Fla. . . . 6-0/210. . . . Throws right, bats right. . . . Full name: Paul Anthony Russo. . . . Brother of Pat Russo, minor league pitcher (1990-91). . . . Name pronounced ROO-so.
HIGH SCHOOL: Thomas Jefferson (Tampa, Fla.).
COLLEGE: University of Tampa (Fla.).
TRANSACTIONS/CAREER NOTES: Selected by Minnesota Twins organization in 16th round of free-agent draft (June 4, 1990). . . . On disabled list (August 31, 1991-remainder of season and July 26-August 22, 1993).
HONORS: Named Appalachian League Player of the Year (1990).
STATISTICAL NOTES: Led Appalachian League with 156 total bases, .706 slugging percentage and tied for lead with five intentional bases on balls received in 1990. . . . Led Midwest League with 10 sacrifice flies in 1991.

			BATTING												FIELDING			
Year	Team (League)	Pos.	G	AB	R	H	2B	3B	HR	RBI	Avg.	BB	SO	SB	PO	A	E	Avg.
1990	—Elizabeth. (Appal.)	1B-3B-C	62	221	*58	74	10	3	*22	*67	.335	39	56	4	290	47	9	.974
1991	—Kenosha (Midwest)	3B	125	421	60	114	20	3	*20	*100	.271	64	105	4	62	*237	27	.917
1992	—Orlando (Southern)	3B-1B-OF	126	420	63	107	13	2	22	74	.255	48	122	0	303	132	10	.978
1993	—Portland (PCL)	3B-1B	83	288	43	81	24	2	10	47	.281	29	69	0	211	132	14	.961

RYAN, KEN

P, RED SOX

PERSONAL: Born October 24, 1968, in Pawtucket, R.I. . . . 6-3/215. . . . Throws right, bats right. . . . Full name: Kenneth Frederick Ryan Jr.
HIGH SCHOOL: Seekonk (Mass.).
TRANSACTIONS/CAREER NOTES: Signed as free agent by Boston Red Sox organization (June 16, 1986).

Year	Team (League)	W	L	Pct.	ERA	G	GS	CG	ShO	Sv.	IP	H	R	ER	BB	SO
1986	—Elmira (N.Y.-Penn)	2	2	.500	5.82	13	1	0	0	0	21⅔	20	14	14	21	22
1987	—Greensboro (S. Atl.)	3	12	.200	5.49	28	19	2	0	0	121⅓	139	88	74	63	75
1988	—Lynchburg (Caro.)	2	7	.222	6.18	19	14	0	0	0	71⅓	79	51	49	45	49
1989	—Winter Haven (FSL)	8	8	.500	3.15	24	22	3	0	0	137	114	58	48	81	78

Year	Team (League)	W	L	Pct.	ERA	G	GS	CG	ShO	Sv.	IP	H	R	ER	BB	SO
1990	—Lynchburg (Caro.)	6	•14	.300	5.13	28	•28	3	1	0	161⅓	182	104	92	82	109
1991	—Winter Haven (FSL)	1	3	.250	2.05	21	1	0	0	1	52⅔	40	15	12	19	53
	—New Britain (East.)	1	2	.333	1.73	14	0	0	0	1	26	23	7	5	12	26
	—Pawtucket (Int'l)	1	0	1.000	4.91	9	0	0	0	1	18⅓	15	11	10	11	14
1992	—New Britain (East.)	1	4	.200	1.95	44	0	0	0	22	50⅔	44	17	11	24	51
	—Pawtucket (Int'l)	2	0	1.000	2.08	9	0	0	0	7	8⅔	6	2	2	4	6
	—Boston (A.L.)	0	0	...	6.43	7	0	0	0	1	7	4	5	5	5	5
1993	—Boston (A.L.)	7	2	.778	3.60	47	0	0	0	1	50	43	23	20	29	49
	—Pawtucket (Int'l)	0	2	.000	2.49	18	0	0	0	8	25⅓	18	9	7	17	22
Major league totals (2 years)		7	2	.778	3.95	54	0	0	0	2	57	47	28	25	34	54

R

RYAN, NOLAN

P

PERSONAL: Born January 31, 1947, in Refugio, Tex.... 6-2/212.... Throws right, bats right.... Full name: Lynn Nolan Ryan Jr.

HIGH SCHOOL: Alvin (Tex.).

COLLEGE: Alvin (Tex.) Junior College.

TRANSACTIONS/CAREER NOTES: Selected by New York Mets organization in eighth round of free-agent draft (June, 1965).... On military list (January 3-May 13, 1967).... On Jacksonville disabled list (July 16-August 30, 1967).... On disabled list (July 30-August 30, 1968 and May 12-June 8, 1969).... On military list (August 11-September 1, 1969).... Traded by Mets with P Don Rose, OF Leroy Stanton and C Francisco Estrada to California Angels for IF Jim Fregosi (December 10, 1971).... On disabled list (June 14-July 5, 1978).... Granted free agency (November 1, 1979).... Signed by Houston Astros (November 19, 1979).... On disabled list (March 25-April 17 and May 3-June 6, 1983; June 2-17 and June 18-July 3, 1984; June 1-24 and July 28-August 12, 1986).... Granted free agency (November 4, 1988).... Signed by Texas Rangers (December 7, 1988).... On disabled list (May 18-June 6, 1990; May 14-29 and July 29-August 19, 1991; April 7-30, 1992; April 15-May 7, May 8-July 19 and August 22-September 12, 1993).... Placed on voluntarily retired list (October 14, 1993).

RECORDS: Holds major league career records for most seasons played and most seasons pitched—27; most consecutive seasons pitched—26 (1968-93); most bases on balls allowed—2,795; most strikeouts—5,714; most grand slams allowed—10; most seasons leading league in bases on balls allowed—8; most seasons with 300 or more strikeouts—6; most seasons with 200 or more strikeouts—15; most seasons with 100 or more strikeouts—24; most consecutive seasons with 300 or more strikeouts—3 (1972-74); most consecutive seasons with 100 or more strikeouts—23 (1970-92); most games with 15 or more strikeouts—26; most games with 10 or more strikeouts—213; most no-hit games—7; most low-hit (no-hit and one-hit) games—19; and most wild pitches—277.... Holds major league single-season records for most games with 10 or more strikeouts—23 (1973); and most strikeouts—383 (1973).... Holds major league records for most strikeouts in three consecutive games—47 (August 12 [19], 16 [9] and 20 [19], 1974, 27⅓ innings); and most strikeouts by losing pitcher in an extra-inning game—19 (August 20, 1974, 11 innings).... Holds modern major league record for most consecutive starting assignments—595 (July 30, 1974 through 1993).... Shares major league single-season records for most no-hit games—2 (1973); and most clubs shut out—8 (1972).... Shares major league records for striking out side on nine pitches (April 19, 1968, third inning and July 9, 1972, second inning); and most strikeouts in three consecutive nine-inning games—41 (August 7 [13], 12 [19] and 16 [9], 1974).... Holds A.L. career records for most seasons with 200 or more strikeouts—10; most games with 10 or more strikeouts—146; most games 15 or more strikeouts—23; most no-hit games—6; and most low-hit (no-hit and one-hit) games—15.... Shares A.L. career record for most seasons leading league in errors by pitcher—4.... Shares A.L. single-season record for most low-hit (no-hit and one-hit) games—3 (1973).... Shares A.L. record for most strikeouts in two consecutive games—32 (August 7 [13] and 12 [19], 1974).... Shares A.L. single-game record for most consecutive strikeouts—8 (July 9, 1972 and July 15, 1973).

HONORS: Named Western Carolinas League Pitcher of the Year (1966).... Named A.L. Pitcher of the Year by THE SPORTING NEWS (1977).... Named righthanded pitcher on THE SPORTING NEWS A.L. All-Star team (1977).... Named Man of the Year by THE SPORTING NEWS (1990).

STATISTICAL NOTES: Tied for Appalachian League lead with eight hit batsmen in 1965.... Led A.L. with 18 wild pitches in 1972, 21 in 1977, 13 in 1978 and 19 in 1989.... Pitched 3-0 no-hit victory against Kansas City (May 15, 1973).... Pitched 6-0 no-hit victory against Detroit (July 15, 1973).... Pitched 4-0 no-hit victory against Minnesota (September 28, 1974).... Pitched 1-0 no-hit victory against Baltimore (June 1, 1975).... Pitched 5-0 no-hit victory against Los Angeles (September 26, 1981).... Led N.L. with 16 wild pitches in 1981 and 15 in 1986.... Led N.L. with eight hit batsmen in 1982.... Tied for N.L. lead with 14 sacrifice hits in 1985.... Pitched 5-0 no-hit victory against Oakland (June 11, 1990).... Pitched 3-0 no-hit victory against Toronto (May 1, 1991).

Year	Team (League)	W	L	Pct.	ERA	G	GS	CG	ShO	Sv.	IP	H	R	ER	BB	SO
1965	—Marion (Appal.)	3	6	.333	4.38	13	12	2	1	0	78	61	47	38	56	115
1966	—Greenville (W. Car.)	*17	2	.895	2.51	29	*28	9	5	0	183	109	59	51	*127	*272
	—Williamsport (East.)	0	2	.000	0.95	3	3	0	0	0	19	9	6	2	12	35
	—New York (N.L.)	0	1	.000	15.00	2	1	0	0	0	3	5	5	5	3	6
1967	—Winter Haven (FSL)	0	0	...	2.25	1	1	0	0	0	4	1	1	1	2	5
	—Jacksonville (Int'l)	1	0	1.000	0.00	3	0	0	0	0	7	3	1	0	3	18
1968	—New York (N.L.)	6	9	.400	3.09	21	18	3	0	0	134	93	50	46	75	133
1969	—New York (N.L.)	6	3	.667	3.54	25	10	2	0	1	89	60	38	35	53	92
1970	—New York (N.L.)	7	11	.389	3.41	27	19	5	2	1	132	86	59	50	97	125
1971	—New York (N.L.)	10	14	.417	3.97	30	26	3	0	0	152	125	78	67	116	137
1972	—California (A.L.)■	19	16	.543	2.28	39	39	20	*9	0	284	166	80	72	*157	*329
1973	—California (A.L.)	21	16	.568	2.87	41	39	26	4	1	326	238	113	104	*162	*383
1974	—California (A.L.)	22	16	.579	2.89	42	41	26	3	0	*333	221	127	107	*202	*367
1975	—California (A.L.)	14	12	.538	3.45	28	28	10	5	0	198	152	90	76	132	186
1976	—California (A.L.)	17	*18	.486	3.36	39	39	21	*7	0	284	193	117	106	*183	*327
1977	—California (A.L.)	19	16	.543	2.77	37	37	•22	4	0	299	198	110	92	*204	*341
1978	—California (A.L.)	10	13	.435	3.71	31	31	14	3	0	235	183	106	97	*148	*260
1979	—California (A.L.)	16	14	.533	3.59	34	34	17	•5	0	223	169	104	89	114	*223
1980	—Houston (N.L.)■	11	10	.524	3.35	35	35	4	2	0	234	205	100	87	*98	200
1981	—Houston (N.L.)	11	5	.688	*1.69	21	21	5	3	0	149	99	34	28	68	140
1982	—Houston (N.L.)	16	12	.571	3.16	35	35	10	3	0	250⅓	196	100	88	*109	245
1983	—Houston (N.L.)	14	9	.609	2.98	29	29	5	2	0	196⅓	134	74	65	101	183
1984	—Houston (N.L.)	12	11	.522	3.04	30	30	5	2	0	183⅔	143	78	62	69	197

Year	Team (League)	W	L	Pct.	ERA	G	GS	CG	ShO	Sv.	IP	H	R	ER	BB	SO
1985	—Houston (N.L.)	10	12	.455	3.80	35	35	4	0	0	232	205	108	98	95	209
1986	—Houston (N.L.)	12	8	.600	3.34	30	30	1	0	0	178	119	72	66	82	194
1987	—Houston (N.L.)	8	16	.333	*2.76	34	34	0	0	0	211⅔	154	75	65	87	*270
1988	—Houston (N.L.)	12	11	.522	3.52	33	33	4	1	0	220	186	98	86	87	*228
1989	—Texas (A.L.)■	16	10	.615	3.20	32	32	6	2	0	239⅓	162	96	85	98	*301
1990	—Texas (A.L.)	13	9	.591	3.44	30	30	5	2	0	204	137	86	78	74	*232
1991	—Texas (A.L.)	12	6	.667	2.91	27	27	2	2	0	173	102	58	56	72	203
1992	—Texas (A.L.)	5	9	.357	3.72	27	27	2	0	0	157⅓	138	75	65	69	157
1993	—Texas (A.L.)	5	5	.500	4.88	13	13	0	0	0	66⅓	54	47	36	40	46
A.L. totals (13 years)		189	160	.542	3.17	420	417	171	46	1	3022	2113	1209	1063	1655	3355
N.L. totals (14 years)		135	132	.506	3.23	387	356	51	15	2	2365	1810	969	848	1140	2359
Major league totals (27 years)		324	292	.526	3.19	807	773	222	61	3	5387	3923	2178	1911	2795	5714

DIVISION SERIES RECORD

Year	Team (League)	W	L	Pct.	ERA	G	GS	CG	ShO	Sv.	IP	H	R	ER	BB	SO
1981	—Houston (N.L.)	1	1	.500	1.80	2	2	1	0	0	15	6	4	3	3	14

CHAMPIONSHIP SERIES RECORD

CHAMPIONSHIP SERIES NOTES: Shares career record for most strikeouts—46. . . . Shares single-game record for most consecutive strikeouts—4 (October 3, 1979).

Year	Team (League)	W	L	Pct.	ERA	G	GS	CG	ShO	Sv.	IP	H	R	ER	BB	SO
1969	—New York (N.L.)	1	0	1.000	2.57	1	0	0	0	0	7	3	2	2	2	7
1979	—California (A.L.)	0	0	...	1.29	1	1	0	0	0	7	4	3	1	3	8
1980	—Houston (N.L.)	0	0	...	5.40	2	2	0	0	0	13⅓	16	8	8	3	14
1986	—Houston (N.L.)	0	1	.000	3.86	2	2	0	0	0	14	9	6	6	1	17
Champ. series totals (4 years)		1	1	.500	3.70	6	5	0	0	0	41⅓	32	19	17	9	46

WORLD SERIES RECORD

Year	Team (League)	W	L	Pct.	ERA	G	GS	CG	ShO	Sv.	IP	H	R	ER	BB	SO
1969	—New York (N.L.)	0	0	...	0.00	1	0	0	0	1	2⅓	1	0	0	2	3

ALL-STAR GAME RECORD

ALL-STAR GAME NOTES: Named to A.L. All-Star team to replace Frank Tanana for 1977 game; declined.

Year	League	W	L	Pct.	ERA	GS	CG	ShO	Sv.	IP	H	R	ER	BB	SO
1972	—American							Did not play.							
1973	—American	0	0	...	9.00	0	0	0	0	2	2	2	2	2	2
1975	—American							Did not play.							
1977	—American							Selected, did not play—declined.							
1979	—American	0	0	...	13.50	1	0	0	0	2	5	3	3	1	2
1981	—National	0	0	...	0.00	0	0	0	0	1	0	0	0	0	1
1985	—National	0	0	...	0.00	0	0	0	0	3	2	0	0	2	2
1989	—American	1	0	1.000	0.00	0	0	0	0	2	1	0	0	0	3
All-Star totals (5 years)		1	0	1.000	4.50	1	0	0	0	10	10	5	5	5	10

SABERHAGEN, BRET

P, METS

PERSONAL: Born April 11, 1964, in Chicago Heights, Ill. . . . 6-1/200. . . . Throws right, bats right. . . . Full name: Bret William Saberhagen. . . . Name pronounced SAY-ber-HAY-gun.

HIGH SCHOOL: Cleveland (Reseda, Calif.).

TRANSACTIONS/CAREER NOTES: Selected by Kansas City Royals organization in 19th round of free-agent draft (June 7, 1982). . . . On disabled list (August 10-September 1, 1986; July 16-September 10, 1990; and June 15-July 13, 1991). . . . Traded by Royals with IF Bill Pecota to New York Mets for OF Kevin McReynolds, IF Gregg Jefferies and 2B Keith Miller (December 11, 1991). . . . On disabled list (May 16-July 18 and August 2-September 7, 1992 and August 3, 1993-remainder of season).

HONORS: Named A.L. Pitcher of the Year by THE SPORTING NEWS (1985 and 1989). . . . Named righthanded pitcher on THE SPORTING NEWS A.L. All-Star team (1985 and 1989). . . . Named A.L. Cy Young Award winner by Baseball Writers' Association of America (1985 and 1989). . . . Named A.L. Comeback Player of the Year by THE SPORTING NEWS (1987). . . . Won A.L. Gold Glove at pitcher (1989).

STATISTICAL NOTES: Pitched 7-0 no-hit victory against Chicago (August 26, 1991).

MISCELLANEOUS: Appeared in one game as pinch-runner (1984). . . . Appeared in three games as pinch-runner (1989).

Year	Team (League)	W	L	Pct.	ERA	G	GS	CG	ShO	Sv.	IP	H	R	ER	BB	SO
1983	—Fort Myers (FSL)	10	5	.667	2.30	16	16	3	1	0	109⅔	98	34	28	19	82
	—Jacksonv. (South.)	6	2	.750	2.91	11	11	2	1	0	77⅓	66	31	25	29	48
1984	—Kansas City (A.L.)	10	11	.476	3.48	38	18	2	1	1	157⅔	138	71	61	36	73
1985	—Kansas City (A.L.)	20	6	.769	2.87	32	32	10	1	0	235⅓	211	79	75	38	158
1986	—Kansas City (A.L.)	7	12	.368	4.15	30	25	4	2	0	156	165	77	72	29	112
1987	—Kansas City (A.L.)	18	10	.643	3.36	33	33	15	4	0	257	246	99	96	53	163
1988	—Kansas City (A.L.)	14	16	.467	3.80	35	35	9	0	0	260⅔	*271	122	110	59	171
1989	—Kansas City (A.L.)	*23	6	.793	*2.16	36	35	*12	4	0	*262⅓	209	74	63	43	193
1990	—Kansas City (A.L.)	5	9	.357	3.27	20	20	5	0	0	135	146	52	49	28	87
1991	—Kansas City (A.L.)	13	8	.619	3.07	28	28	7	2	0	196⅓	165	76	67	45	136
1992	—New York (N.L.)■	3	5	.375	3.50	17	15	1	1	0	97⅔	84	39	38	27	81
1993	—New York (N.L.)	7	7	.500	3.29	19	19	4	1	0	139⅓	131	55	51	17	93
A.L. totals (8 years)		110	78	.585	3.21	252	226	64	14	1	1660⅓	1551	650	593	331	1093
N.L. totals (2 years)		10	12	.455	3.38	36	34	5	2	0	237	215	94	89	44	174
Major league totals (10 years)		120	90	.571	3.24	288	260	69	16	1	1897⅓	1766	744	682	375	1267

CHAMPIONSHIP SERIES RECORD

Year	Team (League)	W	L	Pct.	ERA	G	GS	CG	ShO	Sv.	IP	H	R	ER	BB	SO
1984	—Kansas City (A.L.)	0	0	...	2.25	1	1	0	0	0	8	6	3	2	1	5
1985	—Kansas City (A.L.)	0	0	...	6.14	2	2	0	0	0	7⅓	12	5	5	2	6
Champ. series totals (2 years)		0	0	...	4.11	3	3	0	0	0	15⅓	18	8	7	3	11

WORLD SERIES RECORD

WORLD SERIES NOTES: Named Most Valuable Player (1985).

Year	Team (League)	W	L	Pct.	ERA	G	GS	CG	ShO	Sv.	IP	H	R	ER	BB	SO
1985	—Kansas City (A.L.)	2	0	1.000	0.50	2	2	2	1	0	18	11	1	1	1	10

ALL-STAR GAME RECORD

Year	League	W	L	Pct.	ERA	GS	CG	ShO	Sv.	IP	H	R	ER	BB	SO
1987	—American......................	0	0	...	0.00	1	0	0	0	3	1	0	0	0	0
1990	—American......................	1	0	1.000	0.00	0	0	0	0	2	0	0	0	0	1
All-Star totals (2 years)		1	0	1.000	0.00	1	0	0	0	5	1	0	0	0	1

SABO, CHRIS

3B, ORIOLES

PERSONAL: Born January 19, 1962, in Detroit. . . . 6-0/185. . . . Throws right, bats right. . . . Full name: Christopher Andrew Sabo. . . . Name pronounced SAY-bo.
HIGH SCHOOL: Detroit Catholic Central.
COLLEGE: Michigan.
TRANSACTIONS/CAREER NOTES: Selected by Montreal Expos organization in 30th round of free-agent draft (June 3, 1980). . . . Selected by Cincinnati Reds organization in second round of free-agent draft (June 6, 1983). . . . On Cincinnati disabled list (June 27-September 1, 1989); included rehabilitation assignment to Nashville (August 7-11). . . . On Cincinnati disabled list (April 8-23, 1992); included rehabilitation assignment to Nashville (April 17-21). . . . On disabled list (May 31-June 15, 1993). . . . Granted free agency (October 25, 1993). . . . Signed by Baltimore Orioles (January 14, 1994).
RECORDS: Shares major league single-game record (nine innings) for most assists by third baseman—11 (April 7, 1988).
HONORS: Named third baseman on THE SPORTING NEWS college All-America team (1983). . . . Named N.L. Rookie of the Year by Baseball Writers' Association of America (1988).
STATISTICAL NOTES: Led Eastern League third basemen with .943 fielding percentage in 1984. . . . Led Eastern League third basemen with 236 assists in 1985. . . . Led N.L. third basemen with .966 fielding percentage and 31 double plays in 1988.

				BATTING											FIELDING			
Year	Team (League)	Pos.	G	AB	R	H	2B	3B	HR	RBI	Avg.	BB	SO	SB	PO	A	E	Avg.
1983	—Ced. Rap. (Midw.).....	3B	77	274	43	75	11	6	12	37	.274	26	39	15	43	130	9	.951
1984	—Vermont (Eastern)...	3B-2B	125	441	44	94	19	1	5	38	.213	44	62	10	80	210	21	†.932
1985	—Vermont (Eastern)...	3B-SS	124	428	66	119	19	0	11	46	.278	50	39	7	97	†236	18	.949
1986	—Denver (A.A.)...........	3B	129	432	83	118	26	2	10	60	.273	48	53	9	83	202	9	*.969
1987	—Nashville (A.A.)........	3B	91	315	56	92	19	3	7	51	.292	37	25	23	43	137	12	.938
1988	—Cincinnati (N.L.).......	3B-SS	137	538	74	146	40	2	11	44	.271	29	52	46	75	318	14	†.966
1989	—Cincinnati (N.L.).......	3B	82	304	40	79	21	1	6	29	.260	25	33	14	36	145	11	.943
	—Nashville (A.A.)........	3B	7	30	0	5	2	0	0	3	.167	0	0	0	7	5	1	.923
1990	—Cincinnati (N.L.).......	3B	148	567	95	153	38	2	25	71	.270	61	58	25	70	273	12	*.966
1991	—Cincinnati (N.L.).......	3B	153	582	91	175	35	3	26	88	.301	44	79	19	86	255	12	.966
1992	—Cincinnati (N.L.).......	3B	96	344	42	84	19	3	12	43	.244	30	54	4	60	159	9	.961
	—Nashville (A.A.)........	DH	3	11	3	4	0	0	1	1	.364	1	1	0	...	...	...	...
1993	—Cincinnati (N.L.).......	3B	148	552	86	143	33	2	21	82	.259	43	105	6	79	242	11	.967
Major league totals (6 years)			764	2887	428	780	186	13	101	357	.270	232	381	114	406	1392	69	.963

CHAMPIONSHIP SERIES RECORD

				BATTING											FIELDING			
Year	Team (League)	Pos.	G	AB	R	H	2B	3B	HR	RBI	Avg.	BB	SO	SB	PO	A	E	Avg.
1990	—Cincinnati (N.L.).......	3B	6	22	1	5	0	0	1	3	.227	1	4	0	7	7	0	1.000

WORLD SERIES RECORD

WORLD SERIES NOTES: Shares record for most home runs in two consecutive innings—2 (October 19, 1990, second and third innings).

				BATTING											FIELDING			
Year	Team (League)	Pos.	G	AB	R	H	2B	3B	HR	RBI	Avg.	BB	SO	SB	PO	A	E	Avg.
1990	—Cincinnati (N.L.).......	3B	4	16	2	9	1	0	2	5	.563	2	2	0	3	14	0	1.000

ALL-STAR GAME RECORD

					BATTING								FIELDING			
Year	League	Pos.	AB	R	H	2B	3B	HR	RBI	Avg.	BB	SO	SB	PO	A	E	Avg.
1988	—National....................	PR	0	0	0	0	0	0	0	...	0	0	1	...	...	...	...
1990	—National....................	3B	2	0	0	0	0	0	0	.000	0	0	0	0	2	0	1.000
1991	—National....................	3B	2	0	0	0	0	0	0	.000	0	0	0	1	0	0	1.000
All-Star Game totals (3 years)			4	0	0	0	0	0	0	.000	0	0	1	1	2	0	1.000

SALKELD, ROGER

P, MARINERS

PERSONAL: Born March 6, 1971, in Burbank, Calif. . . . 6-5/215. . . . Throws right, bats right. . . . Grandson of Bill Salkeld, catcher with Pittsburgh Pirates, Boston Braves and Chicago White Sox (1945-50).
HIGH SCHOOL: Saugus (Calif.).
TRANSACTIONS/CAREER NOTES: Selected by Seattle Mariners organization in first round (third pick overall) of free-agent draft (June 5, 1989). . . . On disabled list (April 6-21, 1990). . . . On Calgary disabled list (April 9, 1992-entire season and April 8-June 22, 1993).

Year	Team (League)	W	L	Pct.	ERA	G	GS	CG	ShO	Sv.	IP	H	R	ER	BB	SO
1989	—Belling. (N'west)	2	2	.500	1.29	8	6	0	0	0	42	27	17	6	10	55
1990	—San Bern. (Calif.)	11	5	.688	3.40	25	25	2	0	0	153⅓	140	77	58	83	167
1991	—Jacksonv. (South.)	8	8	.500	3.05	23	23	5	0	0	153⅔	131	56	52	55	159
	—Calgary (PCL)	2	1	.667	5.12	4	4	0	0	0	19⅓	18	16	11	13	21
1992	—							Did not play.								
1993	—Jacksonv. (South.)	4	3	.571	3.27	14	14	0	0	0	77	71	39	28	29	56
	—Seattle (A.L.)	0	0	...	2.51	3	2	0	0	0	14⅓	13	4	4	4	13
Major league totals (1 year)		0	0	...	2.51	3	2	0	0	0	14⅓	13	4	4	4	13

SALMON, TIM
OF, ANGELS

PERSONAL: Born August 24, 1968, in Long Beach, Calif. . . . 6-3/220. . . . Throws right, bats right. . . . Full name: Timothy James Salmon. . . . Name pronounced SA-mon.
HIGH SCHOOL: Greenway (Phoenix).
COLLEGE: Grand Canyon (Ariz.).
TRANSACTIONS/CAREER NOTES: Selected by Atlanta Braves organization in 18th round of free-agent draft (June 2, 1986). . . . Selected by California Angels organization in third round of free-agent draft (June 5, 1989). . . . On disabled list (May 12-23 and May 27-August 7, 1990).
HONORS: Named Minor League Player of the Year by THE SPORTING NEWS (1992). . . . Named Pacific Coast League Most Valuable Player (1992). . . . Named A.L. Rookie Player of the Year by THE SPORTING NEWS (1993). . . . Named A.L. Rookie of the Year by Baseball Writers' Association of America (1993).
STATISTICAL NOTES: Led Pacific Coast League with 275 total bases, .672 slugging percentage and .469 on-base percentage in 1992.

			BATTING												FIELDING			
Year	Team (League)	Pos.	G	AB	R	H	2B	3B	HR	RBI	Avg.	BB	SO	SB	PO	A	E	Avg.
1989	—Bend (Northwest)	OF	55	196	37	48	6	5	6	31	.245	33	60	2	84	7	4	.958
1990	—Palm Springs (Cal.)	OF	36	118	19	34	6	0	2	21	.288	21	44	11	63	3	1	.985
	—Midland (Texas)	OF	27	97	17	26	3	1	3	16	.268	18	38	1	51	6	3	.950
1991	—Midland (Texas)	OF	131	465	100	114	26	4	23	94	.245	*89	*166	12	265	16	10	.966
1992	—Edmonton (PCL)	OF	118	409	•101	142	38	4	*29	*105	.347	91	103	9	231	14	3	.988
	—California (A.L.)	OF	23	79	8	14	1	0	2	6	.177	11	23	1	40	1	2	.953
1993	—California (A.L.)	OF	142	515	93	146	35	1	31	95	.283	82	135	5	335	12	7	.980
Major league totals (2 years)			165	594	101	160	36	1	33	101	.269	93	158	6	375	13	9	.977

SAMPEN, BILL
P

PERSONAL: Born January 18, 1963, in Lincoln, Ill. . . . 6-2/195. . . . Throws right, bats right. . . . Full name: William Albert Sampen.
HIGH SCHOOL: Hartsburg (Ill.)-Emden.
COLLEGE: MacMurray College (Ill.).
TRANSACTIONS/CAREER NOTES: Selected by Pittsburgh Pirates organization in 12th round of free-agent draft (June 3, 1985). . . . On Harrisburg disabled list (April 6-May 5, 1988). . . . Selected by Montreal Expos from Pirates organization in Rule 5 major league draft (December 4, 1989). . . . Traded by Expos with P Chris Haney to Kansas City Royals for 3B Sean Berry and P Archie Corbin (August 29, 1992). . . . Granted free agency (October 15, 1993).

Year	Team (League)	W	L	Pct.	ERA	G	GS	CG	ShO	Sv.	IP	H	R	ER	BB	SO
1985	—Watertown (NYP)	0	0	...	1.80	5	0	0	0	1	10	9	3	2	7	11
1986	—Watertown (NYP)	0	3	.000	4.25	9	5	0	0	2	29⅔	27	18	14	13	29
1987	—Salem (Carolina)	9	8	.529	3.84	26	26	2	1	0	152⅓	126	77	65	72	137
1988	—Harrisburg (East.)	6	3	.667	3.70	13	12	3	0	0	82⅔	72	38	34	27	65
	—Salem (Carolina)	3	3	.500	3.33	8	8	1	0	0	51⅓	47	22	19	14	59
1989	—Harrisburg (East.)	11	9	.550	3.21	26	•26	6	0	0	165⅔	148	75	59	40	134
1990	—Montreal (N.L.)■	12	7	.632	2.99	59	4	0	0	2	90⅓	94	34	30	33	69
1991	—Montreal (N.L.)	9	5	.643	4.00	43	8	0	0	0	92⅓	96	49	41	46	52
	—Indianapolis (A.A.)	4	0	1.000	2.04	7	7	1	0	0	39⅔	33	13	9	19	41
1992	—Montreal (N.L.)	1	4	.200	3.13	44	1	0	0	0	63⅓	62	22	22	29	23
	—Indianapolis (A.A.)	1	1	.500	6.00	2	0	0	0	0	3	3	5	2	3	4
	—Kansas City (A.L.)■	0	2	.000	3.66	8	1	0	0	0	19⅔	21	10	8	3	14
1993	—Omaha (A.A.)	1	2	.333	3.41	33	0	0	0	8	37	37	16	14	13	34
	—Kansas City (A.L.)	2	2	.500	5.89	18	0	0	0	0	18⅓	25	12	12	9	9
A.L. totals (2 years)		2	4	.333	4.74	26	1	0	0	0	38	46	22	20	12	23
N.L. totals (3 years)		22	16	.579	3.40	146	13	0	0	2	246	252	105	93	108	144
Major league totals (4 years)		24	20	.545	3.58	172	14	0	0	2	284	298	127	113	120	167

SAMUEL, JUAN
2B

PERSONAL: Born December 9, 1960, in San Pedro de Macoris, Dominican Republic. . . . 5-11/170. . . . Throws right, bats right. . . . Full name: Juan Milton Samuel. . . . Name pronounced sam-WELL.
HIGH SCHOOL: Licey Puerto Rico.
TRANSACTIONS/CAREER NOTES: Signed as free agent by Philadelphia Phillies organization (April 29, 1980). . . . On disabled list (April 13-May 2, 1986 and April 1-19, 1989). . . . Traded by Phillies to New York Mets for OF Lenny Dykstra, P Roger McDowell and a player to be named later (June 18, 1989); Phillies organization acquired P Tom Edens to complete deal (July 27, 1989). . . . Traded by Mets to Los Angeles Dodgers for P Alejandro Pena and OF Mike Marshall (December 20, 1989). . . . Granted free agency (November 5, 1990). . . . Re-signed by Dodgers (December 16, 1990). . . . Granted free agency (October 28, 1991). . . . Re-signed by Dodgers (February 27, 1992). . . . On disabled list (April 28-June 11, 1992). . . . Released by Dodgers (July 30, 1992). . . . Signed by Kansas City Royals (August 6, 1992). . . . Granted free agency (October 21, 1992). . . . Signed by Cincinnati Reds organization (December 11, 1992). . . . Granted free agency (October 25, 1993).
RECORDS: Holds major league single-season records for most at-bats by righthander—701 (1984); and fewest sacrifice hits with most at-bats—0 (1984). . . . Shares major league record for most consecutive seasons leading league in strikeouts—4 (1984-1987). . . . Shares major league single-game record (nine innings) for most assists by second baseman—12 (April 20,

1985). . . . Holds N.L. single-season record for most at-bats—701 (1984).
HONORS: Named Carolina League Most Valuable Player (1982). . . . Named N.L. Rookie Player of the Year by THE SPORTING NEWS (1984). . . . Named second baseman on THE SPORTING NEWS N.L. All-Star team (1987). . . . Named second baseman on THE SPORTING NEWS N.L. Silver Slugger team (1987).
STATISTICAL NOTES: Led Northwest League in caught stealing with 10 in 1980. . . . Led South Atlantic League second basemen with 739 total chances and 82 double plays in 1981. . . . Led Carolina League second basemen with 721 total chances and 82 double plays in 1982. . . . Led Carolina League with 283 total bases and tied for lead in being hit by pitch with 15 in 1982. . . . Led N.L. second basemen with 826 total chances in 1987. . . . Led N.L. second basemen with 343 putouts and 92 double plays in 1988.

				BATTING											FIELDING			
Year	**Team (League)**	**Pos.**	**G**	**AB**	**R**	**H**	**2B**	**3B**	**HR**	**RBI**	**Avg.**	**BB**	**SO**	**SB**	**PO**	**A**	**E**	**Avg.**
1980	—Cent. Ore. (N'west)...	2B	69	*298	66	84	11	2	17	44	.282	17	*87	25	162	188	*30	.921
1981	—Spartanburg (SAL) ..	2B	135	512	88	127	22	8	11	74	.248	36	132	53	*280	*409	*50	.932
1982	—Peninsula (Caro.).....	2B	135	494	*111	158	29	6	28	94	.320	31	124	64	*244	*442	*35	.951
1983	—Reading (Eastern)....	2B	47	184	36	43	10	0	11	39	.234	8	50	19	121	127	14	.947
	—Portland (PCL).........	2B	65	261	59	86	14	8	15	52	.330	22	46	33	110	168	15	.949
	—Philadelphia (N.L.)...	2B	18	65	14	18	1	2	2	5	.277	4	16	3	44	54	9	.916
1984	—Philadelphia (N.L.)...	2B	160	*701	105	191	36	•19	15	69	.272	28	*168	72	388	438	*33	.962
1985	—Philadelphia (N.L.)...	2B	161	*663	101	175	31	13	19	74	.264	33	•141	53	*389	463	15	.983
1986	—Philadelphia (N.L.)...	2B	145	591	90	157	36	12	16	78	.266	26	*142	42	290	440	*25	.967
1987	—Philadelphia (N.L.)...	2B	160	*655	113	178	37	*15	28	100	.272	60	*162	35	*374	434	*18	.978
1988	—Philadelphia (N.L.)...	2B-OF-3B	157	629	68	153	32	9	12	67	.243	39	151	33	†351	387	16	.979
1989	—Phil.-N.Y. (N.L.)■.....	OF	137	532	69	125	16	2	11	48	.235	42	120	42	339	6	4	.989
1990	—Los Angeles (N.L.)■.	2B-OF	143	492	62	119	24	3	13	52	.242	51	126	38	273	262	16	.971
1991	—Los Angeles (N.L.)...	2B	153	594	74	161	22	6	12	58	.271	49	133	23	300	442	17	.978
1992	—Los Angeles (N.L.)...	2B-OF	47	122	7	32	3	1	0	15	.262	7	22	2	76	77	5	.968
	—Kansas City (A.L.)■.	OF-2B	29	102	15	29	5	3	0	8	.284	7	27	6	45	29	6	.925
1993	—Cincinnati (N.L.)■....	2-1-3-0	103	261	31	60	10	4	4	26	.230	23	53	9	151	172	10	.970
American League totals (1 year)............			29	102	15	29	5	3	0	8	.284	7	27	6	45	29	6	.925
National League totals (11 years)...........			1384	5305	734	1369	248	86	132	592	.258	362	1234	352	2975	3175	168	.973
Major league totals (11 years)................			1413	5407	749	1398	253	89	132	600	.259	369	1261	358	3020	3204	174	.973

CHAMPIONSHIP SERIES RECORD

				BATTING											FIELDING			
Year	**Team (League)**	**Pos.**	**G**	**AB**	**R**	**H**	**2B**	**3B**	**HR**	**RBI**	**Avg.**	**BB**	**SO**	**SB**	**PO**	**A**	**E**	**Avg.**
1983	—Philadelphia (N.L.)...	PR	1	0	0	0	0	0	0	0	...	0	0	0	...	...	...	...

WORLD SERIES RECORD

				BATTING											FIELDING			
Year	**Team (League)**	**Pos.**	**G**	**AB**	**R**	**H**	**2B**	**3B**	**HR**	**RBI**	**Avg.**	**BB**	**SO**	**SB**	**PO**	**A**	**E**	**Avg.**
1983	—Philadelphia (N.L.)...	PR-PH	3	1	0	0	0	0	0	0	.000	0	0	0	...	...	...	...

ALL-STAR GAME RECORD

ALL-STAR GAME NOTES: Holds single-game record for most putouts by second baseman—7 (July 14, 1987). . . . Shares single-game record for most chances accepted by second baseman—9 (July 14, 1987).

			BATTING											FIELDING			
Year	**League**	**Pos.**	**AB**	**R**	**H**	**2B**	**3B**	**HR**	**RBI**	**Avg.**	**BB**	**SO**	**SB**	**PO**	**A**	**E**	**Avg.**
1984	—National.....................								Did not play.								
1987	—National.....................	2B	4	0	0	0	0	0	0	.000	0	1	0	7	2	0	1.000
1991	—National.....................	2B	1	0	1	0	0	0	0	1.000	0	0	0	2	1	0	1.000
All-Star Game totals (2 years)......................			5	0	1	0	0	0	0	.200	0	1	0	9	3	0	1.000

SANCHEZ, REY

SS, CUBS

PERSONAL: Born October 5, 1967, in Rio Piedras, Puerto Rico. . . . 5-9/170. . . . Throws right, bats right. . . . Full name: Rey Francisco Guadalupe Sanchez.
HIGH SCHOOL: Live Oak (Morgan Hill, Calif.).
TRANSACTIONS/CAREER NOTES: Selected by Texas Rangers organization in 13th round of free-agent draft (June 2, 1986). . . . Traded by Rangers organization to Chicago Cubs organization for IF Bryan House (January 3, 1990). . . . On disabled list (April 6, 1990-entire season). . . . On Chicago disabled list (May 6-21, 1992); included rehabilitation assignment to Iowa (May 13-21).
STATISTICAL NOTES: Led Gulf Coast League shortstops with .932 fielding percentage in 1986. . . . Led American Association shortstops with 104 double plays in 1989. . . . Led American Association shortstops with 596 total chances and 81 double plays in 1992.

				BATTING											FIELDING			
Year	**Team (League)**	**Pos.**	**G**	**AB**	**R**	**H**	**2B**	**3B**	**HR**	**RBI**	**Avg.**	**BB**	**SO**	**SB**	**PO**	**A**	**E**	**Avg.**
1986	—GC Rangers (GCL)....	SS-2B	52	169	27	49	3	1	0	23	.290	41	18	10	69	158	15	†.938
1987	—Gastonia (S. Atl.)......	SS	50	160	19	35	1	2	1	10	.219	22	17	6	88	162	18	.933
	—Butte (Pioneer).........	SS	49	189	36	69	10	6	0	25	.365	21	12	22	84	162	12	.953
1988	—Charlotte (Fla. St.)...	SS	128	418	60	128	6	5	0	38	.306	35	24	29	226	*415	35	.948
1989	—Okla. City (A.A.).......	SS	134	464	38	104	10	4	1	39	.224	21	50	4	*237	*418	29	*.958
1990	—■....................................								Did not play.									
1991	—Iowa (Am. Assoc.)....	SS	126	417	60	121	16	5	2	46	.290	37	27	13	204	*375	17	*.971
	—Chicago (N.L.)..........	SS-2B	13	23	1	6	0	0	0	2	.261	4	3	0	11	25	0	1.000
1992	—Chicago (N.L.)..........	SS-2B	74	255	24	64	14	3	1	19	.251	10	17	2	148	202	9	.975
	—Iowa (Am. Assoc.)....	SS-2B	20	76	12	26	3	0	0	3	.342	4	1	6	31	77	5	.956
1993	—Chicago (N.L.)..........	SS	105	344	35	97	11	2	0	28	.282	15	22	1	158	316	15	.969
Major league totals (3 years).................			192	622	60	167	25	5	1	49	.268	29	42	3	317	543	24	.973

SANDBERG, RYNE

2B, CUBS

PERSONAL: Born September 18, 1959, in Spokane, Wash.... 6-2/190.... Throws right, bats right.... Full name: Ryne Dee Sandberg.

HIGH SCHOOL: North Central (Spokane, Wash.).

TRANSACTIONS/CAREER NOTES: Selected by Philadelphia Phillies organization in 20th round of free-agent draft (June 6, 1978).... Traded by Phillies with SS Larry Bowa to Chicago Cubs for SS Ivan DeJesus (January 27, 1982).... On disabled list (June 14-July 11, 1987).... On Chicago disabled list (March 27-April 30, 1993); included rehabilitation assignment to Daytona (April 25-27) and Orlando (April 27-29).

RECORDS: Holds major league career records for highest fielding percentage by second baseman—.990; and most consecutive errorless games by second baseman—123 (June 21, 1989 through May 17, 1990).... Holds major league single-season record for most consecutive errorless games by second baseman—90 (June 21 through October 1, 1989).... Shares major league career record for most years with 500 or more assists by second baseman—6.... Shares major league single-game record for most assists by second baseman—12 (June 12, 1983).

HONORS: Won N.L. Gold Glove at second base (1983-91).... Named Major League Player of the Year by THE SPORTING NEWS (1984).... Named N.L. Player of the Year by THE SPORTING NEWS (1984).... Named second baseman on THE SPORTING NEWS N.L. All-Star team (1984 and 1988-92).... Named second baseman on THE SPORTING NEWS N.L. Silver Slugger team (1984-85 and 1988-92).... Named N.L. Most Valuable Player by Baseball Writers' Association of America (1984).

STATISTICAL NOTES: Led Pioneer League shortstops with 39 double plays in 1978.... Led Western Carolinas League shortstops with 80 double plays in 1979.... Led Eastern League shortstops with .964 fielding percentage, 386 assists and 81 double plays in 1980.... Led N.L. second basemen with .986 fielding percentage, 571 assists and 126 double plays in 1983.... Led N.L. second basemen with 914 total chances in 1983, 870 in 1984, 824 in 1988 and 830 in 1992.... Led N.L. with 344 total bases in 1990.

				BATTING											FIELDING			
Year	Team (League)	Pos.	G	AB	R	H	2B	3B	HR	RBI	Avg.	BB	SO	SB	PO	A	E	Avg.
1978	—Helena (Pioneer)	SS	56	190	34	59	6	6	1	23	.311	26	42	15	92	*200	24	.924
1979	—Sp'rt'brg (W. Caro.)	SS	•138	*539	83	133	21	7	4	47	.247	64	95	21	134	*467	35	*.945
1980	—Reading (Eastern)	SS-3B	129	490	95	152	21	12	11	79	.310	73	72	32	156	†388	20	†.965
1981	—Okla. City (A.A.)	SS-2B	133	519	78	152	17	5	9	62	.293	48	94	32	229	396	21	.967
	—Philadelphia (N.L.)	SS-2B	13	6	2	1	0	0	0	0	.167	0	1	0	7	7	0	1.000
1982	—Chicago (N.L.)■	3B-2B	156	635	103	172	33	5	7	54	.271	36	90	32	136	373	12	.977
1983	—Chicago (N.L.)	2B-SS	158	633	94	165	25	4	8	48	.261	51	79	37	330	†572	13	†.986
1984	—Chicago (N.L.)	2B	156	636	*114	200	36	•19	19	84	.314	52	101	32	314	*550	6	*.993
1985	—Chicago (N.L.)	2B-SS	153	609	113	186	31	6	26	83	.305	57	97	54	353	501	12	.986
1986	—Chicago (N.L.)	2B	154	627	68	178	28	5	14	76	.284	46	79	34	309	*492	5	*.994
1987	—Chicago (N.L.)	2B	132	523	81	154	25	2	16	59	.294	59	79	21	294	375	10	.985
1988	—Chicago (N.L.)	2B	155	618	77	163	23	8	19	69	.264	54	91	25	291	*522	11	.987
1989	—Chicago (N.L.)	2B	157	606	•104	176	25	5	30	76	.290	59	85	15	294	466	6	.992
1990	—Chicago (N.L.)	2B	155	615	*116	188	30	3	*40	100	.306	50	84	25	278	*469	8	.989
1991	—Chicago (N.L.)	2B	158	585	104	170	32	2	26	100	.291	87	89	22	267	*515	4	*.995
1992	—Chicago (N.L.)	2B	158	612	100	186	32	8	26	87	.304	68	73	17	283	*539	8	.990
1993	—Daytona (Fla. St.)	2B	2	5	2	1	0	0	1	2	.200	1	0	0	3	4	0	1.000
	—Orlando (Southern)	2B	4	9	0	2	0	0	0	1	.222	3	1	0	3	8	0	1.000
	—Chicago (N.L.)	2B	117	456	67	141	20	0	9	45	.309	37	62	9	209	347	7	.988
Major league totals (13 years)			1822	7161	1143	2080	340	67	240	881	.290	656	1010	323	3365	5728	102	.989

CHAMPIONSHIP SERIES RECORD

				BATTING											FIELDING			
Year	Team (League)	Pos.	G	AB	R	H	2B	3B	HR	RBI	Avg.	BB	SO	SB	PO	A	E	Avg.
1984	—Chicago (N.L.)	2B	5	19	3	7	2	0	0	2	.368	3	2	3	13	18	1	.969
1989	—Chicago (N.L.)	2B	5	20	6	8	3	1	1	4	.400	3	4	0	7	11	0	1.000
Championship series totals (2 years)			10	39	9	15	5	1	1	6	.385	6	6	3	20	29	1	.980

ALL-STAR GAME RECORD

			BATTING										FIELDING			
Year	League	Pos.	AB	R	H	2B	3B	HR	RBI	Avg.	BB	SO	SB	PO	A	E	Avg.
1984	—National	2B	4	0	1	0	0	0	0	.250	0	0	1	0	0	0	...
1985	—National	2B	1	1	0	0	0	0	0	.000	1	0	0	0	3	0	1.000
1986	—National	2B	3	0	0	0	0	0	0	.000	0	0	0	0	2	1	.667
1987	—National	2B	2	0	0	0	0	0	0	.000	0	0	0	0	2	0	1.000
1988	—National	2B	4	0	1	0	0	0	0	.250	0	2	0	2	2	0	1.000
1989	—National	2B	3	0	0	0	0	0	0	.000	0	2	0	2	4	0	1.000
1990	—National	2B	3	0	0	0	0	0	0	.000	0	0	0	1	2	0	1.000
1991	—National	2B	3	0	1	1	0	0	0	.333	0	0	0	2	1	0	1.000
1992	—National	2B	2	0	0	0	0	0	0	.000	0	1	0	2	3	0	1.000
1993	—National	2B	1	0	0	0	0	0	0	.000	1	0	0	0	2	0	1.000
All-Star Game totals (10 years)			26	1	3	1	0	0	0	.115	2	5	1	9	21	1	.968

SANDERS, DEION

OF, BRAVES

PERSONAL: Born August 9, 1967, in Fort Myers, Fla.... 6-1/195.... Throws left, bats left.... Full name: Deion Luwynn Sanders.

HIGH SCHOOL: North Ft. Myers (Fla.).

COLLEGE: Florida State.

TRANSACTIONS/CAREER NOTES: Selected by Kansas City Royals organization in sixth round of free-agent draft (June 3, 1985).... Selected by New York Yankees organization in 30th round of free-agent draft (June 1, 1988).... On disqualified list (August 1-September 24, 1990).... Released by Yankees organization (September 24, 1990).... Signed by Atlanta Braves (January 29, 1991).... Placed on Richmond temporary inactive list (August 1, 1991).... On disqualified list (April 29-May 21, 1993).... On disabled list (August 22-September 6, 1993).

Year	Team (League)	Pos.	BATTING G	AB	R	H	2B	3B	HR	RBI	Avg.	BB	SO	SB	FIELDING PO	A	E	Avg.
1988	—GC Yankees (GCL)....	OF	17	75	7	21	4	2	0	6	.280	2	10	11	33	1	2	.944
	—Fort Lauder. (FSL)...	OF	6	21	5	9	2	0	0	2	.429	1	3	2	22	2	0	1.000
	—Columbus (Int'l)	OF	5	20	3	3	1	0	0	0	.150	1	4	1	13	0	0	1.000
1989	—Alb./Colon. (East.)...	OF	33	119	28	34	2	2	1	6	.286	11	20	17	79	3	0	1.000
	—New York (A.L.)........	OF	14	47	7	11	2	0	2	7	.234	3	8	1	30	1	1	.969
	—Columbus (Int'l)	OF	70	259	38	72	12	7	5	30	.278	22	46	16	165	0	4	.976
1990	—New York (A.L.)........	OF	57	133	24	21	2	2	3	9	.158	13	27	8	69	2	2	.973
	—Columbus (Int'l)	OF	22	84	21	27	7	1	2	10	.321	17	15	9	49	1	0	1.000
1991	—Atlanta (N.L.)■.........	OF	54	110	16	21	1	2	4	13	.191	12	23	11	57	3	3	.952
	—Richmond (Int'l)	OF	29	130	20	34	6	3	5	16	.262	10	28	12	73	1	1	.987
1992	—Atlanta (N.L.)	OF	97	303	54	92	6	*14	8	28	.304	18	52	26	174	4	3	.983
1993	—Atlanta (N.L.)	OF	95	272	42	75	18	6	6	28	.276	16	42	19	137	1	2	.986
American League totals (2 years)			71	180	31	32	4	2	5	16	.178	16	35	9	99	3	3	.971
National League totals (3 years)			246	685	112	188	25	22	18	69	.274	46	117	56	368	8	8	.979
Major league totals (5 years)			317	865	143	220	29	24	23	85	.254	62	152	65	467	11	11	.978

CHAMPIONSHIP SERIES RECORD

Year	Team (League)	Pos.	BATTING G	AB	R	H	2B	3B	HR	RBI	Avg.	BB	SO	SB	FIELDING PO	A	E	Avg.
1992	—Atlanta (N.L.)	OF-PH	4	5	0	0	0	0	0	0	.000	0	3	0	1	0	0	1.000
1993	—Atlanta (N.L.)	PH-OF-PR	5	3	0	0	0	0	0	0	.000	0	1	0	0	0	0	...
Championship series totals (2 years)			9	8	0	0	0	0	0	0	.000	0	4	0	1	0	0	1.000

WORLD SERIES RECORD

Year	Team (League)	Pos.	BATTING G	AB	R	H	2B	3B	HR	RBI	Avg.	BB	SO	SB	FIELDING PO	A	E	Avg.
1992	—Atlanta (N.L.)	OF	4	15	4	8	2	0	0	1	.533	2	1	5	5	1	0	1.000

RECORD AS FOOTBALL PLAYER

TRANSACTIONS/CAREER NOTES: Plays cornerback. . . . Selected by Atlanta Falcons in first round (fifth pick overall) of 1989 NFL draft. . . . Signed by Falcons (September 7, 1989). . . . On reserve/did not report list (July 27-August 13, 1990). . . . Granted roster exemption for one game (September 1992).

HONORS: Named defensive back on THE SPORTING NEWS college All-America team (1986-1988). . . . Jim Thorpe Award winner (1988). . . . Named cornerback on THE SPORTING NEWS NFL All-Pro team (1991-93). . . . Played in Pro Bowl (1991-1993 seasons). . . . Named kick returner on THE SPORTING NEWS NFL All-Pro team (1992).

PRO STATISTICS: 1989—Caught one pass for minus eight yards and recovered one fumble. 1990—Recovered two fumbles. 1991—Caught one pass for 17 yards and recovered one fumble. 1992—Rushed once for minus four yards, caught three passes for 45 yards (15.0-yard avg.) and a touchdown and recovered two fumbles. 1993—Caught six passes for 106 yards (17.7-yard avg.) and a touchdown.

Year	Team	G	INTERCEPTIONS No.	Yds.	Avg.	TD	SACKS No.	PUNT RETURNS No.	Yds.	Avg.	TD	KICKOFF RETURNS No.	Yds.	Avg.	TD	TOTAL TD	Pts.	Fum.
1989	— Atlanta NFL	15	5	52	10.4	0	0.0	28	307	11.0	*1	35	725	20.7	0	1	6	2
1990	— Atlanta NFL	16	3	153	51.0	2	0.0	29	250	8.6	*1	39	851	21.8	0	3	18	4
1991	— Atlanta NFL	15	6	119	19.8	1	1.0	21	170	8.1	0	26	576	22.2	*1	2	12	1
1992	— Atlanta NFL	13	3	105	35.0	0	0.0	13	41	3.2	0	40	*1067	26.7	*2	3	18	3
1993	— Atlanta NFL	11	7	91	13.0	0	0.0	2	21	10.5	0	7	169	24.1	0	1	6	0
Pro totals (5 years) ...		70	24	520	21.7	3	1.0	93	789	8.5	2	147	3388	23.0	3	10	60	10

SANDERS, REGGIE

OF, REDS

PERSONAL: Born December 1, 1967, in Florence, S.C. . . . 6-1/186. . . . Throws right, bats right. . . . Full name: Reginald Laverne Sanders.

HIGH SCHOOL: Wilson (Florence, S.C.).

COLLEGE: Spartanburg (S.C.) Methodist.

TRANSACTIONS/CAREER NOTES: Selected by Cincinnati Reds organization in seventh round of free-agent draft (June 2, 1987). . . . On disabled list (July 11-September 15, 1988 and July 15-September 5, 1989). . . . On Chattanooga disabled list (June 30-July 26, 1991). . . . On Cincinnati disabled list (August 24-September 20, 1991 and May 13-29 and July 17-August 2, 1992).

HONORS: Named Midwest League Most Valuable Player (1990).

Year	Team (League)	Pos.	BATTING G	AB	R	H	2B	3B	HR	RBI	Avg.	BB	SO	SB	FIELDING PO	A	E	Avg.
1988	—Billings (Pioneer)	SS	17	64	11	15	1	1	0	3	.234	6	4	10	18	33	3	.944
1989	—Greensboro (S. Atl.)..	SS	81	315	53	91	18	5	9	53	.289	29	63	21	125	169	42	.875
1990	—Ced. Rap. (Midw.).....	OF	127	466	89	133	21	4	17	63	.285	59	97	40	241	10	10	.962
1991	—Chatt. (South.)	OF	86	302	50	95	15	•8	8	49	.315	41	67	15	158	2	3	.982
	—Cincinnati (N.L.).......	OF	9	40	6	8	0	0	1	3	.200	0	9	1	22	0	0	1.000
1992	—Cincinnati (N.L.).......	OF	116	385	62	104	26	6	12	36	.270	48	98	16	262	11	6	.978
1993	—Cincinnati (N.L.).......	OF	138	496	90	136	16	4	20	83	.274	51	118	27	312	3	8	.975
Major league totals (3 years)			263	921	158	248	42	10	33	122	.269	99	225	44	596	14	14	.978

SANDERS, SCOTT

P, PADRES

PERSONAL: Born March 25, 1969, in Hannibal, Mo. . . . 6-4/215. . . . Throws right, bats right. . . . Full name: Scott Gerald Sanders.

HIGH SCHOOL: Thibodaux (La.).

COLLEGE: Nicholls (La.) State.

TRANSACTIONS/CAREER NOTES: Selected by San Diego Padres organization in supplemental round ("sandwich pick" between first and second round, 32nd pick overall) of free-agent draft (June 4, 1990); pick received as part of compensation for Kansas

City Royals signing Type A free agent Mark Davis.

Year	Team (League)	W	L	Pct.	ERA	G	GS	CG	ShO	Sv.	IP	H	R	ER	BB	SO
1990	—Waterloo (Midw.)	2	2	.500	4.86	7	7	0	0	0	37	43	21	20	21	29
	—Spokane (N'west)	2	1	.667	0.95	3	3	0	0	0	19	12	3	2	5	21
1991	—Waterloo (Midw.)	3	0	1.000	0.68	4	4	0	0	0	26⅓	17	2	2	6	18
	—High Desert (Calif.)	9	6	.600	3.66	21	21	4	2	0	132⅔	114	72	54	72	93
1992	—Wichita (Texas)	7	5	.583	3.49	14	14	0	0	0	87⅔	85	35	34	37	95
	—Las Vegas (PCL)	3	6	.333	5.50	14	12	1	1	0	72	97	49	44	31	51
1993	—Las Vegas (PCL)	5	10	.333	4.96	24	24	•4	0	0	152⅓	170	101	84	62	*161
	—San Diego (N.L.)	3	3	.500	4.13	9	9	0	0	0	52⅓	54	32	24	23	37
Major league totals (1 year)		3	3	.500	4.13	9	9	0	0	0	52⅓	54	32	24	23	37

SANDERS, TRACY

OF, METS

PERSONAL: Born July 26, 1969, in Gastonia, N.C. . . . 6-2/200. . . . Throws right, bats left. . . . Full name: Tracy Jerome Sanders.
HIGH SCHOOL: North Gaston (Dallas, N.C.).
COLLEGE: Limestone College (S.C.).

TRANSACTIONS/CAREER NOTES: Selected by Cleveland Indians organization in 58th round of free-agent draft (June 4, 1990). . . . Traded by Indians with P Fernando Hernandez to San Diego Padres for P Jeremy Hernandez (June 1, 1993). . . . Traded by Padres with P Frank Seminara and a player to be named later to New York Mets for OF Randy Curtis and a player to be named later (December 10, 1993); Padres acquired P Marc Kroon and Mets acquired SS Pablo Martinez to complete deal (December 13, 1993).

			BATTING											FIELDING			
Year	Team (League)	Pos.	G	AB	R	H	2B	3B	HR	RBI	Avg.	BB	SO	SB	PO	A	E	Avg.
1990	—Burlington (Appal.)	OF	51	178	38	50	12	1	10	34	.281	33	36	10	63	7	3	.959
	—Kinston (Carolina)	OF	10	32	6	14	3	3	0	9	.438	7	6	1	20	0	0	1.000
1991	—Kinston (Carolina)	OF	118	421	80	112	20	8	*18	63	.266	*83	96	8	153	8	9	.947
1992	—Cant./Akr. (East.)	OF	114	381	66	92	11	3	21	87	.241	77	113	3	183	8	5	.974
1993	—Cant./Akr. (East.)	OF	42	136	20	29	6	2	5	20	.213	31	30	4	64	3	4	.944
	—Wichita (Texas)■	OF	77	266	44	86	13	4	13	47	.323	34	67	6	82	5	7	.926

SANDERSON, SCOTT

P

PERSONAL: Born July 22, 1956, in Dearborn, Mich. . . . 6-5/192. . . . Throws right, bats right. . . . Full name: Scott Douglas Sanderson.
HIGH SCHOOL: Glenbrook North (Northbrook, Ill.).
COLLEGE: Vanderbilt.

TRANSACTIONS/CAREER NOTES: Selected by Kansas City Royals organization in 11th round of free-agent draft (June 5, 1974). . . . Selected by Montreal Expos organization in third round of free-agent draft (June 7, 1977). . . . On disabled list (July 5-September 1, 1983). . . . Traded by Expos with IF Al Newman to San Diego Padres for P Gary Lucas (December 7, 1983); traded by Padres to Chicago Cubs for 1B Carmelo Martinez, P Craig Lefferts and 3B Fritz Connally (December 7, 1983). . . . On Chicago disabled list (June 1-July 5, 1984); included rehabilitation assignment to Lodi (June 29-July 5). . . . On disabled list (August 14, 1985-remainder of season; March 29-April 24 and June 22-July 7, 1987). . . . On Chicago disabled list (April 5-August 23, 1988); included rehabilitation assignment to Peoria (June 25-29) and Iowa (June 30-July 11). . . . Granted free agency (November 4, 1988). . . . Re-signed by Cubs (December 7, 1988). . . . Granted free agency (November 13, 1989). . . . Signed by Oakland Athletics (December 13, 1989). . . . Granted free agency (November 5, 1990). . . . Re-signed by A's (December 19, 1990). . . . Contract sold by A's to New York Yankees (December 31, 1990). . . . Granted free agency (October 28, 1992). . . . Signed by California Angels (February 11, 1993). . . . Claimed on waivers by San Francisco Giants (August 3, 1993). . . . Granted free agency (November 1, 1993).
RECORDS: Shares major league record for most home runs allowed in one inning—4 (May 2, 1992, fifth inning). . . . Shares N.L. record for most consecutive home runs allowed in one inning—3 (July 11, 1982, second inning).

Year	Team (League)	W	L	Pct.	ERA	G	GS	CG	ShO	Sv.	IP	H	R	ER	BB	SO
1977	—W.P. Beach (FSL)	5	2	.714	2.68	10	10	2	1	0	57	58	22	17	23	37
1978	—Memphis (South.)	5	3	.625	4.03	9	9	1	0	0	58	55	32	26	19	44
	—Denver (A.A.)	4	2	.667	6.06	9	9	1	0	0	49	47	35	33	30	36
	—Montreal (N.L.)	4	2	.667	2.51	10	9	1	1	0	61	52	20	17	21	50
1979	—Montreal (N.L.)	9	8	.529	3.43	34	24	5	3	1	168	148	69	64	54	138
1980	—Montreal (N.L.)	16	11	.593	3.11	33	33	7	3	0	211	206	76	73	56	125
1981	—Montreal (N.L.)	9	7	.563	2.96	22	22	4	1	0	137	122	50	45	31	77
1982	—Montreal (N.L.)	12	12	.500	3.46	32	32	7	0	0	224	212	98	86	58	158
1983	—Montreal (N.L.)	6	7	.462	4.65	18	16	0	0	1	81⅓	98	50	42	20	55
1984	—Chicago (N.L.)■	8	5	.615	3.14	24	24	3	0	0	140⅔	140	54	49	24	76
	—Lodi (California)	0	1	.000	3.60	1	1	0	0	0	5	7	2	2	0	2
1985	—Chicago (N.L.)	5	6	.455	3.12	19	19	2	0	0	121	100	49	42	27	80
1986	—Chicago (N.L.)	9	11	.450	4.19	37	28	1	1	1	169⅔	165	85	79	37	124
1987	—Chicago (N.L.)	8	9	.471	4.29	32	22	0	0	2	144⅔	156	72	69	50	106
1988	—Peoria (Midwest)	0	0	. . .	0.00	1	1	0	0	0	5	4	1	0	0	3
	—Iowa (Am. Assoc.)	1	0	1.000	4.73	3	3	0	0	0	13⅓	13	7	7	2	4
	—Chicago (N.L.)	1	2	.333	5.28	11	0	0	0	0	15⅓	13	9	9	3	6
1989	—Chicago (N.L.)	11	9	.550	3.94	37	23	2	0	0	146⅓	155	69	64	31	86
1990	—Oakland (A.L.)■	17	11	.607	3.88	34	34	2	1	0	206⅓	205	99	89	66	128
1991	—New York (A.L.)■	16	10	.615	3.81	34	34	2	2	0	208	200	95	88	29	130
1992	—New York (A.L.)	12	11	.522	4.93	33	33	2	1	0	193⅓	220	116	106	64	104
1993	—California (A.L.)■	7	11	.389	4.46	21	21	4	1	0	135⅓	153	77	67	27	66
	—San Francisco (N.L.)■	4	2	.667	3.51	11	8	0	0	0	48⅔	48	20	19	7	36
A.L. totals (4 years)		52	43	.547	4.24	122	122	10	5	0	743	778	387	350	186	428
N.L. totals (13 years)		102	91	.529	3.55	320	260	32	9	5	1668⅔	1615	721	658	419	1117
Major league totals (16 years)		154	134	.535	3.76	442	382	42	14	5	2411⅔	2393	1108	1008	605	1545

DIVISION SERIES RECORD

Year	Team (League)	W	L	Pct.	ERA	G	GS	CG	ShO	Sv.	IP	H	R	ER	BB	SO
1981	—Montreal (N.L.)	0	0	...	6.75	1	1	0	0	0	2⅔	4	4	2	2	2

CHAMPIONSHIP SERIES RECORD

Year	Team (League)	W	L	Pct.	ERA	G	GS	CG	ShO	Sv.	IP	H	R	ER	BB	SO
1981	—Montreal (N.L.)							Did not play.								
1984	—Chicago (N.L.)...........	0	0	...	5.79	1	1	0	0	0	4⅔	6	3	3	1	2
1989	—Chicago (N.L.)...........	0	0	...	0.00	1	0	0	0	0	2	2	0	0	0	1
1990	—Oakland (A.L.)							Did not play.								
Champ. series totals (2 years)		0	0	...	4.05	2	1	0	0	0	6⅔	8	3	3	1	3

WORLD SERIES RECORD

Year	Team (League)	W	L	Pct.	ERA	G	GS	CG	ShO	Sv.	IP	H	R	ER	BB	SO
1990	—Oakland (A.L.)	0	0	...	10.80	2	0	0	0	0	1⅔	4	2	2	1	0

ALL-STAR GAME RECORD

Year	League	W	L	Pct.	ERA	GS	CG	ShO	Sv.	IP	H	R	ER	BB	SO
1991	—American......................						Did not play.								

SANDOVAL, JOSE

SS, PIRATES

PERSONAL: Born August 25, 1969, in Los Mochis, Mexico. . . . 5-11/170. . . . Throws right, bats right. . . . Full name: Jose Luis Rodriguez Sandoval.

HIGH SCHOOL: Secundiria Technica #18 San Miguel Ahoeme Sinaloa (Mexico).

TRANSACTIONS/CAREER NOTES: Signed by Mexico City Reds of Mexican League (March 15, 1989). . . . Contract sold by Mexico City Red Devils to Buffalo, Pittsburgh Pirates organization (October 20, 1992). . . . Loaned by Pirates organization to Mexico City Red Devils (May 7-12, 1993). . . . On Buffalo disabled list (May 16-24, 1993).

			BATTING												FIELDING			
Year	Team (League)	Pos.	G	AB	R	H	2B	3B	HR	RBI	Avg.	BB	SO	SB	PO	A	E	Avg.
1990	—M.C. Red Devils (Mex.)	S-2-0-3	122	408	55	103	19	5	5	36	.252	37	80	9	200	369	30	.950
1991	—M.C. Red Devils (Mex.)	SS-OF-2B	117	421	90	143	23	4	25	80	.340	31	66	2	213	326	25	.956
1992	—M.C. Red Devils (Mex.)	SS-3B	130	501	81	142	25	3	26	89	.283	42	75	12	210	441	23	.966
1993	—Buffalo (A.A.)■.........	SS	65	209	23	48	7	2	5	21	.230	13	37	1	86	200	10	.966
	—M.C. Red Dev. (Mex.)■	SS	33	113	19	31	4	1	3	16	.274	12	15	2	61	123	5	.974

SANFORD, MO

P, TWINS

PERSONAL: Born December 24, 1966, in Americus, Ga. . . . 6-6/225. . . . Throws right, bats right. . . . Full name: Meredith Leroy Sanford Jr.

HIGH SCHOOL: Starkville (Miss.).

COLLEGE: Alabama.

TRANSACTIONS/CAREER NOTES: Selected by New York Yankees organization in third round of free-agent draft (June 4, 1984). . . . Selected by Cincinnati Reds organization in 32nd round of free-agent draft (June 1, 1988). . . . Selected by Colorado Rockies in third round (62nd pick overall) of expansion draft (November 17, 1992). . . . Granted free agency (December 20, 1993). . . . Signed by Minnesota Twins organization (January 5, 1994).

STATISTICAL NOTES: Pitched 7-0 no-hit victory against Myrtle Beach (June 2, 1989).

Year	Team (League)	W	L	Pct.	ERA	G	GS	CG	ShO	Sv.	IP	H	R	ER	BB	SO
1988	—GC Reds (GCL)	3	4	.429	3.23	14	11	0	0	1	53	34	24	19	25	64
1989	—Greensboro (S. Atl.).....	12	6	.667	2.81	25	25	3	1	0	153⅔	112	52	48	64	160
1990	—Ced. Rap. (Midw.)........	13	4	.765	2.74	25	25	2	1	0	157⅔	112	50	48	55	180
1991	—Chatt. (South.)	7	4	.636	2.74	16	16	1	1	0	95⅓	69	37	29	55	124
	—Nashville (A.A.)...........	3	0	1.000	1.60	5	5	2	2	0	33⅔	19	7	6	22	38
	—Cincinnati (N.L.)..........	1	2	.333	3.86	5	5	0	0	0	28	19	14	12	15	31
1992	—Nashville (A.A.)..........	8	8	.500	5.68	25	25	0	0	0	122	128	81	77	65	129
	—Chatt. (South.)	4	0	1.000	1.35	4	4	1	1	0	26⅔	13	5	4	6	28
1993	—Colo. Springs (PCL)■...	3	6	.333	5.23	20	17	0	0	0	105	103	64	61	57	104
	—Colorado (N.L.)...........	1	2	.333	5.30	11	6	0	0	0	35⅔	37	25	21	27	36
Major league totals (2 years) ...		2	4	.333	4.66	16	11	0	0	0	63⅔	56	39	33	42	67

SANTANA, JULIO

P, RANGERS

PERSONAL: Born January 20, 1973, in San Pedro de Macoris, Dominican Republic. . . . 6-0/175. . . . Throws right, bats right. . . . Full name: Julio Franklin Santana. . . . Nephew of Rico Carty, major league outfielder with seven teams (1963-79).

TRANSACTIONS/CAREER NOTES: Signed as free agent by Texas Rangers organization (February 18, 1990).

Year	Team (League)	W	L	Pct.	ERA	G	GS	CG	ShO	Sv.	IP	H	R	ER	BB	SO
1992	—San Pedro (DSL)	0	1	.000	3.24	4	1	0	0	0	8⅓	8	5	3	7	5
1993	—GC Rangers (GCL)......	4	1	.800	1.38	*26	0	0	0	7	39	31	9	6	7	50

RECORD AS POSITION PLAYER

			BATTING												FIELDING			
Year	Team (League)	Pos.	G	AB	R	H	2B	3B	HR	RBI	Avg.	BB	SO	SB	PO	A	E	Avg.
1990	—San Pedro (DSL).......	...	11	34	4	7	0	0	1	3	.206	5	7	0	...	...	...	...
1991	—San Pedro (DSL).......	...	55	161	27	42	7	0	2	12	.261	27	37	5	...	...	...	...
1992	—San Pedro (DSL).......	OF-IF-P	17	48	7	11	2	0	2	2	.229	11	8	0	50	2	4	.929

SANTANA, RUBEN

2B, MARINERS

PERSONAL: Born March 7, 1970, in Santo Domingo, Dominican Republic. . . . 6-2/175. . . . Throws right, bats right. . . . Full name: Ruben Ernesto Cruz Santana.

TRANSACTIONS/CAREER NOTES: Signed as free agent by Chicago Cubs organization (August 14, 1987). . . . Released by Cubs organization (April 1, 1989). . . . Signed as free agent by Seattle Mariners organization (July 8, 1989).

Year	Team (League)	Pos.	BATTING G	AB	R	H	2B	3B	HR	RBI	Avg.	BB	SO	SB	FIELDING PO	A	E	Avg.
1988	—Char., W.Va. (SAL) ..	2B	13	28	4	1	1	0	0	2	.036	3	13	0	30	27	5	.919
1989	—■		Dominican Summer League statistics unavailable.															
1990	—Peninsula (Caro.)	SS-2B	26	80	3	17	1	0	0	5	.213	1	22	6	39	65	6	.945
	—Belling. (N'west)	2B-3B	47	155	22	39	3	2	4	13	.252	18	39	10	81	109	11	.945
1991	—San Bern. (Calif.)	2B-SS-1B	108	394	55	119	16	4	3	43	.302	26	74	34	174	202	19	.952
	—Jacksonv. (South.) ..	2B-SS	5	15	2	3	0	0	1	3	.200	1	3	0	5	7	0	1.000
1992	—Peninsula (Caro.)	2B	113	401	54	118	19	4	8	61	.294	21	54	17	204	285	18	.964
1993	—Jacksonv. (South.) ..	2-0-3-S	128	499	79	150	21	2	21	84	.301	38	101	13	178	267	16	.965

SANTIAGO, BENITO

C, MARLINS

PERSONAL: Born March 9, 1965, in Ponce, Puerto Rico. ... 6-1/185. ... Throws right, bats right. ... Full name: Benito Rivera Santiago. ... Name pronounced SAHN-tee-AH-go.

HIGH SCHOOL: John F. Kennedy (Ponce, Puerto Rico).

TRANSACTIONS/CAREER NOTES: Signed as free agent by San Diego Padres organization (September 1, 1982). ... On disabled list (June 21-July 2, 1985). ... On San Diego disabled list (June 15-August 10, 1990); included rehabilitation assignment to Las Vegas (August 2-9). ... On San Diego disabled list (May 31-July 11, 1992); included rehabilitation assignment to Las Vegas (July 7-11). ... Granted free agency (October 26, 1992). ... Signed by Florida Marlins (December 16, 1992).

RECORDS: Holds major league rookie-season record for most consecutive games batted safely—34 (August 25-October 2, 1987). ... Shares major league single-season record for fewest passed balls (100 or more games)—0 (1992).

HONORS: Named N.L. Rookie Player of the Year by THE SPORTING NEWS (1987). ... Named catcher on THE SPORTING NEWS N.L. All-Star team (1987, 1989 and 1991). ... Named catcher on THE SPORTING NEWS N.L. Silver Slugger team (1987-88 and 1990-91). ... Named N.L. Rookie of the Year by Baseball Writers' Association of America (1987). ... Won N.L. Gold Glove at catcher (1988-90).

STATISTICAL NOTES: Led Florida State League catchers with 26 passed balls and 12 double plays in 1983. ... Led Texas League catchers with 78 assists and 16 passed balls in 1985. ... Led Pacific Coast League catchers with 655 total chances in 1986. ... Led N.L. with 22 passed balls in 1987, 14 in 1989 and 23 in 1993. ... Led N.L. in grounding into double plays with 21 in 1991. ... Tied for N.L. lead in double plays by catcher with 11 in 1988 and 14 in 1991. ... Led N.L. catchers with 100 assists and 14 errors in 1991.

Year	Team (League)	Pos.	BATTING G	AB	R	H	2B	3B	HR	RBI	Avg.	BB	SO	SB	FIELDING PO	A	E	Avg.
1983	—Miami (Florida St.) ...	C	122	429	34	106	25	3	5	56	.247	11	79	3	471	*69	*21	.963
1984	—Reno (California)	C	114	416	64	116	20	6	16	83	.279	36	75	5	692	96	25	.969
1985	—Beaumont (Texas) ...	C-1B-3B	101	372	55	111	16	6	5	52	.298	16	59	12	525	†78	15	.976
1986	—Las Vegas (PCL)	C	117	437	55	125	26	3	17	71	.286	17	81	19	*563	71	*21	.968
	—San Diego (N.L.)	C	17	62	10	18	2	0	3	6	.290	2	12	0	80	7	5	.946
1987	—San Diego (N.L.)	C	146	546	64	164	33	2	18	79	.300	16	112	21	817	80	*22	.976
1988	—San Diego (N.L.)	C	139	492	49	122	22	2	10	46	.248	24	82	15	725	*75	*12	.985
1989	—San Diego (N.L.)	C	129	462	50	109	16	3	16	62	.236	26	89	11	685	81	*20	.975
1990	—San Diego (N.L.)	C	100	344	42	93	8	5	11	53	.270	27	55	5	538	51	12	.980
	—Las Vegas (PCL)	C	6	20	5	6	2	0	1	8	.300	3	1	0	25	5	0	1.000
1991	—San Diego (N.L.)	C-OF	152	580	60	155	22	3	17	87	.267	23	114	8	830	†100	†14	.985
1992	—San Diego (N.L.)	C	106	386	37	97	21	0	10	42	.251	21	52	2	584	53	*12	.982
	—Las Vegas (PCL)	C	4	13	3	4	0	0	1	2	.308	1	1	0	13	2	0	1.000
1993	—Florida (N.L.)■.........	C-OF	139	469	49	108	19	6	13	50	.230	37	88	10	740	64	11	.987
Major league totals (8 years)			928	3341	361	866	143	21	98	425	.259	176	604	72	4999	511	108	.981

ALL-STAR GAME RECORD

Year	League	Pos.	BATTING AB	R	H	2B	3B	HR	RBI	Avg.	BB	SO	SB	FIELDING PO	A	E	Avg.
1989	—National	C	1	0	0	0	0	0	0	.000	0	1	0	0	0	1	.000
1990	—National		Selected, did not play—injured.														
1991	—National	C	3	0	0	0	0	0	0	.000	0	1	0	4	0	0	1.000
1992	—National	C	1	0	0	0	0	0	0	.000	0	1	0	3	0	0	1.000
All-Star Game totals (3 years)			5	0	0	0	0	0	0	.000	0	3	0	7	0	1	.875

SANTOVENIA, NELSON

C, ROYALS

PERSONAL: Born July 27, 1961, in Pino del Rio, Cuba. ... 6-3/210. ... Throws right, bats right. ... Full name: Nelson Gil Santovenia. ... Name pronounced SAN-toe-VAYN-yuh.

HIGH SCHOOL: Miami Southridge Sr.

COLLEGE: Miami-Dade (South) Community College and Miami (Fla.).

TRANSACTIONS/CAREER NOTES: Selected by Philadelphia Phillies organization in 29th round of free-agent draft (June 5, 1979). ... Selected by Montreal Expos organization in third round of free-agent draft (June 8, 1981). ... Selected by Expos organization in secondary phase of free-agent draft (June 7, 1982). ... On suspended list (May 24-31, 1984). ... On Montreal disabled list (June 4-20, 1988; May 13-June 13, 1989; and July 13-September 1, 1990). ... On Indianapolis disqualified list (June 11, 1991); reinstated (June 11, 1991). ... Released by Expos (December 9, 1991). ... Signed by Chicago White Sox organization (February 3, 1992). ... Granted free agency (October 5, 1992). ... Signed by Kansas City Royals organization (December 10, 1992). ... Granted free agency (October 15, 1993). ... Re-signed by Royals organization (November 16, 1993).

STATISTICAL NOTES: Led Southern League with 21 passed balls in 1983. ... Tied for Southern League lead in double plays by catcher with nine in 1984. ... Led Southern League catchers with 785 putouts and 867 total chances in 1987. ... Led Pacific Coast League catchers with 13 errors in 1992. ... Led American Association with 13 passed balls in 1993.

Year	Team (League)	Pos.	BATTING G	AB	R	H	2B	3B	HR	RBI	Avg.	BB	SO	SB	FIELDING PO	A	E	Avg.
1982	—W.P. Beach (FSL)	C	40	118	8	29	4	0	1	12	.246	14	12	0	127	21	5	.967
1983	—Memphis (South.)	C	94	318	27	77	13	0	3	44	.242	33	36	1	490	69	*15	.974

Year	Team (League)	Pos.	G	AB	R	H	2B	3B	HR	RBI	Avg.	BB	SO	SB	PO	A	E	Avg.
			BATTING												FIELDING			
1984	—Jacksonv. (South.) ..	C	90	255	27	55	9	0	5	29	.216	44	30	0	464	•64	4	.992
1985	—Jacksonv. (South.) ..	C	57	184	15	40	6	0	2	15	.217	14	18	2	281	20	9	.971
	—Indianapolis (A.A.)...	C	28	75	5	16	2	0	0	4	.213	7	11	1	135	20	1	.994
1986	—Jacksonv. (South.) ..	C-OF	31	72	15	22	7	0	4	11	.306	19	7	0	97	14	1	.991
	—Indianapolis (A.A.)...	C	18	57	6	12	1	0	1	2	.211	5	13	0	80	14	1	.989
1987	—Jacksonv. (South.) ..	C-1B	117	394	56	110	17	0	19	63	.279	36	58	3	†790	71	11	.987
	—Montreal (N.L.).........	C	2	1	0	0	0	0	0	0	.000	0	0	0	1	0	0	1.000
1988	—Indianapolis (A.A.)...	C	27	91	9	28	5	0	2	13	.308	4	16	0	198	23	3	.987
	—Montreal (N.L.).........	C-1B	92	309	26	73	20	2	8	41	.236	24	77	2	465	63	9	.983
1989	—Montreal (N.L.).........	C-1B	97	304	30	76	14	1	5	31	.250	24	37	2	564	66	12	.981
1990	—Montreal (N.L.).........	C	59	163	13	31	3	1	6	28	.190	8	31	0	264	24	6	.980
	—Indianapolis (A.A.)...	C	11	44	3	14	2	0	1	10	.318	1	7	0	40	7	1	.979
1991	—Montreal (N.L.).........	C-1B	41	96	7	24	5	0	2	14	.250	2	18	0	140	16	3	.981
	—Indianapolis (A.A.)...	C-1B	61	195	23	51	7	1	6	26	.262	21	25	0	333	33	5	.987
1992	—Vancouver (PCL)■...	C-1B	91	281	24	74	16	0	6	42	.263	37	49	0	441	59	†13	.975
	—Chicago (A.L.)..........	C	2	3	1	1	0	0	1	2	.333	0	0	0	3	0	0	1.000
1993	—Omaha (A.A.)■.........	C	81	274	33	65	13	0	11	42	.237	12	50	0	446	44	5	.990
	—Kansas City (A.L.)....	C	4	8	0	1	0	0	0	0	.125	1	2	0	14	1	0	1.000
American League totals (2 years)			6	11	1	2	0	0	1	2	.182	1	2	0	17	1	0	1.000
National League totals (5 years)			291	873	76	204	42	4	21	114	.234	58	163	4	1434	169	30	.982
Major league totals (7 years)			297	884	77	206	42	4	22	116	.233	59	165	4	1451	170	30	.982

S

SASSER, MACKEY

DH/OF, MARINERS

PERSONAL: Born August 3, 1962, in Fort Gaines, Ga.... 6-1/210.... Throws right, bats left.... Full name: Mack Daniel Sasser Jr.

HIGH SCHOOL: Godby (Tallahassee, Fla.).

COLLEGE: George C. Wallace Community College (Ala.) and Troy (Ala.) State.

TRANSACTIONS/CAREER NOTES: Selected by San Francisco Giants organization in fifth round of free-agent draft (January 17, 1984).... Traded by Giants organization with cash to Pittsburgh Pirates organization for P Don Robinson (July 31, 1987).... Traded by Pirates with P Tim Drummond to New York Mets for 1B Randy Milligan and P Scott Henion (March 26, 1988).... Granted free agency (December 19, 1992).... Signed by Seattle Mariners (December 23, 1992).... On disabled list (March 26-April 21, 1993).... On suspended list (July 27-30, 1993).

STATISTICAL NOTES: Led California League with 245 total bases in 1985.... Led California League with 19 passed balls in 1985.... Led Texas League with 13 intentional bases on balls received in 1986.... Led Pacific Coast League catchers with 584 putouts, 16 errors and 663 total chances in 1987.... Led N.L. catchers with 14 errors in 1990.

Year	Team (League)	Pos.	G	AB	R	H	2B	3B	HR	RBI	Avg.	BB	SO	SB	PO	A	E	Avg.
			BATTING												FIELDING			
1984	—Clinton (Midwest)	1-3-0-C	118	428	57	125	20	5	6	65	.292	30	46	15	526	95	17	.973
	—Fresno (California) ..	OF-3B-1B	16	62	8	17	1	1	0	6	.274	3	6	1	24	15	4	.907
1985	—Fresno (California) ..	0-C-1-3	133	497	79	168	27	4	14	102	.338	36	35	3	402	42	14	.969
1986	—Shreveport (Texas)..	C-1B-OF	120	441	52	129	29	5	5	72	.293	44	36	4	577	66	10	.985
1987	—Phoe.-Vanc. (PCL)■	C-3B-1B	115	400	53	127	24	1	3	56	.318	32	19	3	†588	72	†18	.973
	—S.F.-Pitts. (N.L.)	C	14	27	2	5	0	0	0	2	.185	0	2	0	29	0	0	1.000
1988	—New York (N.L.)■......	C-3B-OF	60	123	9	35	10	1	1	17	.285	6	9	0	235	17	6	.977
1989	—New York (N.L.)........	C-3B	72	182	17	53	14	2	1	22	.291	7	15	0	335	19	3	.992
1990	—New York (N.L.)........	C-1B	100	270	31	83	14	0	6	41	.307	15	19	0	501	43	†14	.975
1991	—New York (N.L.)........	C-OF-1B	96	228	18	62	14	2	5	35	.272	9	19	0	271	21	3	.990
1992	—New York (N.L.)........	C-1B-OF	92	141	7	34	6	0	2	18	.241	3	10	0	131	5	1	.993
1993	—Seattle (A.L.)■..........	OF-C-1B	83	188	18	41	10	2	1	21	.218	15	30	1	60	4	3	.955
American League totals (1 year)			83	188	18	41	10	2	1	21	.218	15	30	1	60	4	3	.955
National League totals (6 years)			434	971	84	272	58	5	15	135	.280	40	74	0	1502	105	27	.983
Major league totals (7 years)			517	1159	102	313	68	7	16	156	.270	55	104	1	1562	109	30	.982

CHAMPIONSHIP SERIES RECORD

Year	Team (League)	Pos.	G	AB	R	H	2B	3B	HR	RBI	Avg.	BB	SO	SB	PO	A	E	Avg.
			BATTING												FIELDING			
1988	—New York (N.L.)........	PH-C	4	5	0	1	0	0	0	0	.200	0	1	0	2	0	0	1.000

SAUNDERS, DOUG

2B, METS

PERSONAL: Born December 13, 1969, in Lakewood, Calif.... 6-0/172.... Throws right, bats right.... Full name: Douglas Long Saunders.

HIGH SCHOOL: Ezperanza (Anaheim, Calif.).

TRANSACTIONS/CAREER NOTES: Selected by New York Mets organization in third round of free-agent draft (June 1, 1988).... On disabled list (July 10-August 14, 1991).

STATISTICAL NOTES: Led Florida State League second basemen with 75 double plays in 1990.... Led Eastern League second basemen with 656 total chances and 94 double plays in 1992.

Year	Team (League)	Pos.	G	AB	R	H	2B	3B	HR	RBI	Avg.	BB	SO	SB	PO	A	E	Avg.
			BATTING												FIELDING			
1988	—GC Mets (GCL)..........	SS-2B	16	64	8	16	4	1	0	10	.250	9	14	2	29	48	6	.928
	—Little Falls (NYP)......	2B	29	100	10	30	6	1	0	11	.300	6	15	1	56	65	7	.945
1989	—Columbia (S. Atl.).....	2B-SS-1B	115	377	53	99	18	4	4	38	.263	35	78	5	225	294	21	.961
1990	—St. Lucie (Fla. St.)....	2B	115	408	52	92	8	4	1	43	.225	43	96	24	233	349	15	.975
1991	—St. Lucie (Fla. St.)....	2B-3B	70	230	19	54	9	2	2	18	.235	25	43	5	124	193	10	.969
1992	—Binghamton (East.)..	2B	130	435	45	108	16	2	5	38	.248	52	68	8	*272	*365	19	.971
1993	—Norfolk (Int'l)............	2B	105	356	37	88	12	6	2	24	.247	44	63	6	209	322	15	.973
	—New York (N.L.)........	2B-3B-SS	28	67	8	14	2	0	0	0	.209	3	4	0	37	52	4	.957
Major league totals (1 year)			28	67	8	14	2	0	0	0	.209	3	4	0	37	52	4	.957

SAX, STEVE

2B, WHITE SOX

PERSONAL: Born January 29, 1960, in Sacramento, Calif. ... 5-11/189. ... Throws right, bats right. ... Full name: Stephen Louis Sax. ... Brother of Dave Sax, first baseman/catcher, Los Angeles Dodgers and Boston Red Sox (1982-83 and 1985-87).

HIGH SCHOOL: James Marshall (West Sacramento, Calif.).

TRANSACTIONS/CAREER NOTES: Selected by Los Angeles Dodgers organization in ninth round of free-agent draft (June 6, 1978). ... On disabled list (April 19-May 4, 1985). ... Granted free agency (November 4, 1988). ... Signed by New York Yankees (November 23, 1988). ... Traded by Yankees with cash to Chicago White Sox for P Melido Perez, P Robert Wickman and P Domingo Jean (January 10, 1992).

HONORS: Named Texas League Most Valuable Player (1981). ... Named N.L. Rookie of the Year by Baseball Writers' Association of America (1982). ... Named second baseman on THE SPORTING NEWS N.L. All-Star team (1986). ... Named second baseman on THE SPORTING NEWS N.L. Silver Slugger team (1986).

STATISTICAL NOTES: Led Florida State League second basemen with .976 fielding percentage, 360 putouts, 438 assists, 818 total chances and 91 double plays in 1980. ... Led N.L. in caught stealing with 30 in 1983. ... Led N.L. second basemen with 22 errors in 1985. ... Led A.L. second basemen with 117 double plays in 1989.

			BATTING												FIELDING			
Year	Team (League)	Pos.	G	AB	R	H	2B	3B	HR	RBI	Avg.	BB	SO	SB	PO	A	E	Avg.
1978	—Lethbridge (Pio.)	SS	39	131	24	43	6	3	0	21	.328	16	20	0	21	40	9	.871
1979	—Clinton (Midwest)	OF-2B-3B	115	386	64	112	15	2	2	52	.290	57	30	25	111	75	18	.912
1980	—Vero Beach (FSL)	2B-OF	•139	•530	78	150	18	8	3	61	.283	51	26	33	†360	†438	20	†.976
1981	—San Antonio (Tex.)	2B	115	485	94	168	23	3	8	52	★.346	40	32	34	255	298	17	.970
	—Los Angeles (N.L.)	2B	31	119	15	33	2	0	2	9	.277	7	14	5	64	93	4	.975
1982	—Los Angeles (N.L.)	2B	150	638	88	180	23	7	4	47	.282	49	53	49	347	452	19	.977
1983	—Los Angeles (N.L.)	2B	155	623	94	175	18	5	5	41	.281	58	73	56	331	339	★30	.957
1984	—Los Angeles (N.L.)	2B	145	569	70	138	24	4	1	35	.243	47	53	34	318	450	21	.973
1985	—Los Angeles (N.L.)	2B-3B	136	488	62	136	8	4	1	42	.279	54	43	27	330	358	†22	.969
1986	—Los Angeles (N.L.)	2B	157	633	91	210	43	4	6	56	.332	59	58	40	•367	432	16	.980
1987	—Los Angeles (N.L.)	2B-OF-3B	157	610	84	171	22	7	6	46	.280	44	61	37	343	420	14	.982
1988	—Los Angeles (N.L.)	2B	160	★632	70	175	19	4	5	57	.277	45	51	42	276	429	14	.981
1989	—New York (A.L.)■	2B	158	•651	88	205	26	3	5	63	.315	52	44	43	312	460	10	★.987
1990	—New York (A.L.)	2B	155	615	70	160	24	2	4	42	.260	49	46	43	292	457	10	.987
1991	—New York (A.L.)	2B-3B	158	652	85	198	38	2	10	56	.304	41	38	31	277	454	10	.987
1992	—Chicago (A.L.)■	2B	143	567	74	134	26	4	4	47	.236	43	42	30	305	390	★20	.972
1993	—Chicago (A.L.)	OF-2B	57	119	20	28	5	0	1	8	.235	8	6	7	39	3	0	1.000
American League totals (5 years)			671	2604	337	725	119	11	24	216	.278	193	176	154	1225	1764	50	.984
National League totals (8 years)			1091	4312	574	1218	159	35	30	333	.282	363	406	290	2376	2973	140	.974
Major league totals (13 years)			1762	6916	911	1943	278	46	54	549	.281	556	582	444	3601	4737	190	.978

DIVISION SERIES RECORD

			BATTING												FIELDING			
Year	Team (League)	Pos.	G	AB	R	H	2B	3B	HR	RBI	Avg.	BB	SO	SB	PO	A	E	Avg.
1981	—Los Angeles (N.L.)	2B	1	0	0	0	0	0	0	0	...	0	0	0	0	0	0	...

CHAMPIONSHIP SERIES RECORD

CHAMPIONSHIP SERIES NOTES: Shares record for most stolen bases in one inning—2 (October 9, 1988, third inning). ... Shares N.L. single-series record for most at-bats—30 (1988). ... Shares N.L. single-game record for most stolen bases—3 (October 9, 1988, 12 innings).

			BATTING												FIELDING			
Year	Team (League)	Pos.	G	AB	R	H	2B	3B	HR	RBI	Avg.	BB	SO	SB	PO	A	E	Avg.
1981	—Los Angeles (N.L.)	2B	1	0	0	0	0	0	0	0	...	0	0	0	0	1	0	1.000
1983	—Los Angeles (N.L.)	2B	4	16	0	4	0	0	0	0	.250	1	0	1	11	12	0	1.000
1985	—Los Angeles (N.L.)	2B	6	20	1	6	3	0	0	1	.300	1	5	0	11	21	0	1.000
1988	—Los Angeles (N.L.)	2B	7	30	7	8	0	0	0	3	.267	3	3	5	12	22	0	1.000
1993	—Chicago (A.L.)									Did not play.								
Championship series totals (4 years)			18	66	8	18	3	0	0	4	.273	5	8	6	34	56	0	1.000

WORLD SERIES RECORD

			BATTING												FIELDING			
Year	Team (League)	Pos.	G	AB	R	H	2B	3B	HR	RBI	Avg.	BB	SO	SB	PO	A	E	Avg.
1981	—Los Angeles (N.L.)	PH-PR-2B	2	1	0	0	0	0	0	0	.000	0	0	0	0	0	0	...
1988	—Los Angeles (N.L.)	2B	5	20	3	6	0	0	0	0	.300	1	1	1	11	11	0	1.000
World Series totals (2 years)			7	21	3	6	0	0	0	0	.286	1	1	1	11	11	0	1.000

ALL-STAR GAME RECORD

			BATTING											FIELDING			
Year	League	Pos.	AB	R	H	2B	3B	HR	RBI	Avg.	BB	SO	SB	PO	A	E	Avg.
1982	—National	PR-2B	1	0	1	0	0	0	0	1.000	0	0	0	2	0	1	.667
1983	—National	2B	3	1	1	0	0	0	1	.333	0	0	1	2	0	1	.667
1986	—National	2B	1	0	1	0	0	0	1	1.000	0	0	1	0	1	0	1.000
1989	—American	2B	1	0	0	0	0	0	0	.000	0	0	0	1	3	0	1.000
1990	—American	2B	1	0	0	0	0	0	0	.000	1	0	1	0	1	0	1.000
All-Star Game totals (5 years)			7	1	3	0	0	0	2	.429	1	0	3	5	5	2	.833

SCANLAN, BOB

P, BREWERS

PERSONAL: Born August 9, 1966, in Los Angeles. ... 6-8/215. ... Throws right, bats right. ... Full name: Robert Guy Scanlan Jr.

HIGH SCHOOL: Harvard (North Hollywood, Calif.).

TRANSACTIONS/CAREER NOTES: Selected by Philadelphia Phillies organization in 25th round of free-agent draft (June 4, 1984). ... Traded by Phillies with P Chuck McElroy to Chicago Cubs organization for P Mitch Wil-

liams (April 7, 1991).... On suspended list (September 30-October 4, 1992 and September 17-20, 1993).... Traded by Cubs to Milwaukee Brewers for P Rafael Novoa and OF Mike Carter (December 19, 1993).
STATISTICAL NOTES: Led International League with 17 wild pitches in 1988.

Year	Team (League)	W	L	Pct.	ERA	G	GS	CG	ShO	Sv.	IP	H	R	ER	BB	SO
1984	—GC Phillies (GCL)	0	2	.000	6.48	13	6	0	0	0	33⅓	43	31	24	30	17
1985	—Spartanburg (SAL)	8	12	.400	4.14	26	25	4	0	0	152⅓	160	95	70	53	108
1986	—Clearwater (FSL)	8	12	.400	4.15	24	22	5	0	0	125⅔	146	73	58	45	51
1987	—Reading (Eastern)	*15	5	.750	5.10	27	26	3	1	0	164	187	98	93	55	91
1988	—Maine (Int'l)	5	*18	.217	5.59	28	27	4	1	0	161	181	*110	*100	50	79
1989	—Reading (Eastern)	6	10	.375	5.78	31	17	4	1	0	118⅓	124	88	•76	58	63
1990	—Scran./W.B. (Int'l)	8	1	.889	4.85	23	23	1	0	0	130	128	79	70	59	74
1991	—Iowa (Am. Assoc.)■	2	0	1.000	2.95	4	3	0	0	0	18⅓	14	8	6	10	15
	—Chicago (N.L.)	7	8	.467	3.89	40	13	0	0	1	111	114	60	48	40	44
1992	—Chicago (N.L.)	3	6	.333	2.89	69	0	0	0	14	87⅓	76	32	28	30	42
1993	—Chicago (N.L.)	4	5	.444	4.54	70	0	0	0	0	75⅓	79	41	38	28	44
Major league totals (3 years)		14	19	.424	3.75	179	13	0	0	15	273⅔	269	133	114	98	130

SCARSONE, STEVE

IF, GIANTS

PERSONAL: Born April 11, 1966, in Anaheim, Calif.... 6-2/195.... Throws right, bats right.... Full name: Steven Wayne Scarsone.... Name pronounced scar-SONE-ee.
HIGH SCHOOL: Canyon (Anaheim, Calif.).
COLLEGE: Santa Ana (Calif.) College.
TRANSACTIONS/CAREER NOTES: Selected by Philadelphia Phillies organization in second round of free-agent draft (January 14, 1986).... Traded by Phillies to Baltimore Orioles for SS Juan Bell (August 11, 1992).... Traded by Orioles to San Francisco Giants for OF Mark Leonard (March 20, 1993).... On San Francisco disabled list (March 31-June 1, 1993).... On Phoenix disabled list (June 22-29, 1993).
STATISTICAL NOTES: Led Northwest League second basemen with 147 putouts, 29 errors and 45 double plays in 1986.... Led International League second basemen with 20 errors in 1991.... Led International League second basemen with 304 assists, 26 errors and 77 double plays in 1992.

			BATTING												FIELDING			
Year	Team (League)	Pos.	G	AB	R	H	2B	3B	HR	RBI	Avg.	BB	SO	SB	PO	A	E	Avg.
1986	—Bend (Northwest)	2B-SS	65	219	42	48	10	•4	4	21	.219	30	51	11	†149	188	†30	.918
1987	—Char., W.Va. (SAL)	SS-2B-3B	95	259	35	56	11	1	1	17	.216	31	64	8	127	212	25	.931
1988	—Clearwater (FSL)	SS-3B-2B	125	456	51	120	21	4	8	46	.263	18	93	14	179	326	33	.939
1989	—Reading (Eastern)	2B-SS	75	240	30	43	5	0	4	22	.179	15	67	2	171	200	11	.971
1990	—Clearwater (FSL)	2B	59	211	20	58	9	5	3	23	.275	19	57	3	116	147	13	.953
	—Reading (Eastern)	2B-SS	74	245	26	65	12	1	3	23	.265	14	63	0	141	206	8	.977
1991	—Reading (Eastern)	2B	15	49	6	15	0	0	3	3	.306	4	15	2	43	54	3	.970
	—Scran./W.B. (Int'l)	2B-SS	111	405	52	111	20	6	6	38	.274	19	81	10	222	343	†21	.964
1992	—Scr/WB-Roc (Int'l)■	2B-3B	112	407	56	110	26	4	12	60	.270	30	86	13	210	†310	†26	.952
	—Philadelphia (N.L.)	2B	7	13	1	2	0	0	0	0	.154	1	6	0	3	3	0	1.000
	—Baltimore (A.L.)	2B-3B-SS	11	17	2	3	0	0	0	0	.176	1	6	0	6	8	2	.875
1993	—Phoenix (PCL)■	2-3-S-1	19	70	13	18	1	2	3	9	.257	8	21	2	36	48	3	.966
	—San Francisco (N.L.)	2B-3B-1B	44	103	16	26	9	0	2	15	.252	4	32	0	53	44	1	.990
American League totals (1 year)			11	17	2	3	0	0	0	0	.176	1	6	0	6	8	2	.875
National League totals (2 years)			51	116	17	28	9	0	2	15	.241	5	38	0	56	47	1	.990
Major league totals (2 years)			62	133	19	31	9	0	2	15	.233	6	44	0	62	55	3	.975

SCHALL, GENE

1B/OF, PHILLIES

PERSONAL: Born June 5, 1970, in Abington, Pa.... 6-3/190.... Throws right, bats right.... Full name: Eugene David Schall.
HIGH SCHOOL: LaSalle (Philadelphia).
COLLEGE: Villanova.
TRANSACTIONS/CAREER NOTES: Selected by Philadelphia Phillies organization in fourth round of free-agent draft (June 3, 1991). ... On disabled list (August 5, 1991-remainder of season).

			BATTING												FIELDING			
Year	Team (League)	Pos.	G	AB	R	H	2B	3B	HR	RBI	Avg.	BB	SO	SB	PO	A	E	Avg.
1991	—Batavia (NY-Penn)	1B	13	44	5	15	1	0	2	8	.341	3	16	0	28	5	0	1.000
1992	—Spartanburg (SAL)	OF	77	276	44	74	13	1	8	41	.268	29	52	3	89	9	2	.980
	—Clearwater (FSL)	OF	40	133	16	33	4	2	4	19	.248	14	29	1	56	1	2	.966
1993	—Reading (Eastern)	1B-OF	82	285	51	93	12	4	15	60	.326	24	56	2	298	25	1	.997
	—Scran./W.B. (Int'l)	1B	40	139	16	33	6	1	4	16	.237	19	38	4	287	28	3	.991

SCHILLING, CURT

P, PHILLIES

PERSONAL: Born November 14, 1966, in Anchorage, Alaska.... 6-4/225.... Throws right, bats right.... Full name: Curtis Montague Schilling.
HIGH SCHOOL: Shadow Mountain (Phoenix).
COLLEGE: Yavapai College (Ariz.).
TRANSACTIONS/CAREER NOTES: Selected by Boston Red Sox organization in second round of free-agent draft (January 14, 1986).... Traded by Red Sox organization with OF Brady Anderson to Baltimore Orioles for P Mike Boddicker (July 29, 1988). ... Traded by Orioles with P Pete Harnisch and OF Steve Finley to Houston Astros for 1B Glenn Davis (January 10, 1991).... Traded by Astros to Philadelphia Phillies for P Jason Grimsley (April 2, 1992).
STATISTICAL NOTES: Tied for International League lead with six balks in 1989.

Year	Team (League)	W	L	Pct.	ERA	G	GS	CG	ShO	Sv.	IP	H	R	ER	BB	SO
1986	—Elmira (N.Y.-Penn)	7	3	.700	2.59	16	15	2	1	0	93⅔	92	34	27	30	75
1987	—Greensboro (S. Atl.)	8	*15	.348	3.82	29	28	7	3	0	184	179	96	78	65	*189
1988	—New Britain (East.)	8	5	.615	2.97	21	17	4	1	0	106	91	44	35	40	62

Year	Team (League)	W	L	Pct.	ERA	G	GS	CG	ShO	Sv.	IP	H	R	ER	BB	SO
	—Charlotte (South.)■	5	2	.714	3.18	7	7	2	1	0	45⅓	36	19	16	23	32
	—Baltimore (A.L.)	0	3	.000	9.82	4	4	0	0	0	14⅔	22	19	16	10	4
1989	—Rochester (Int'l)	•13	11	.542	3.21	27	•27	•9	•3	0	★185⅓	176	76	66	59	109
	—Baltimore (A.L.)	0	1	.000	6.23	5	1	0	0	0	8⅔	10	6	6	3	6
1990	—Rochester (Int'l)	4	4	.500	3.92	15	14	1	0	0	87⅓	95	46	38	25	83
	—Baltimore (A.L.)	1	2	.333	2.54	35	0	0	0	3	46	38	13	13	19	32
1991	—Houston (N.L.)■	3	5	.375	3.81	56	0	0	0	8	75⅔	79	35	32	39	71
	—Tucson (PCL)	0	1	.000	3.42	13	0	0	0	3	23⅔	16	9	9	12	21
1992	—Philadelphia (N.L.)■	14	11	.560	2.35	42	26	10	4	2	226⅓	165	67	59	59	147
1993	—Philadelphia (N.L.)	16	7	.696	4.02	34	34	7	2	0	235⅓	234	114	105	57	186
A.L. totals (3 years)		1	6	.143	4.54	44	5	0	0	3	69⅓	70	38	35	32	42
N.L. totals (3 years)		33	23	.589	3.28	132	60	17	6	10	537⅓	478	216	196	155	404
Major league totals (6 years)		34	29	.540	3.43	176	65	17	6	13	606⅔	548	254	231	187	446

CHAMPIONSHIP SERIES RECORD

CHAMPIONSHIP SERIES NOTES: Named N.L. Championship Series Most Valuable Player (1993).... Holds single-game records for most consecutive strikeouts and most consecutive strikeouts from start of the game—5 (October 6, 1993).

Year	Team (League)	W	L	Pct.	ERA	G	GS	CG	ShO	Sv.	IP	H	R	ER	BB	SO
1993	—Philadelphia (N.L.)	0	0	...	1.69	2	2	0	0	0	16	11	4	3	5	19

WORLD SERIES RECORD

Year	Team (League)	W	L	Pct.	ERA	G	GS	CG	ShO	Sv.	IP	H	R	ER	BB	SO
1993	—Philadelphia (N.L.)	1	1	.500	3.52	2	2	1	1	0	15⅓	13	7	6	5	9

S

SCHOFIELD, DICK

SS, BLUE JAYS

PERSONAL: Born November 21, 1962, in Springfield, Ill.... 5-10/179.... Throws right, bats right.... Full name: Richard Craig Schofield.... Son of John Richard (Dick) Schofield, major league infielder with seven teams (1953-71).

HIGH SCHOOL: Sacred Heart-Griffin (Springfield, Ill.).

TRANSACTIONS/CAREER NOTES: Selected by California Angels organization in first round (third pick overall) of free-agent draft (June 8, 1981).... On disabled list (July 1-24, 1984; July 13-August 11, 1987; April 12-May 6 and August 11-September 21, 1989).... On California disabled list (March 31-June 6, 1990); included rehabilitation assignment to Edmonton (May 31-June 5).... Granted free agency (November 1, 1991).... Re-signed by Angels (January 17, 1992).... Traded by Angels to New York Mets for P Julio Valera and a player to be named later (April 12, 1992); Angels acquired P Julian Vasquez from Mets to complete deal (October 6, 1992).... Granted free agency (October 28, 1992).... Signed by Toronto Blue Jays organization (January 15, 1993).... On Toronto disabled list (May 13-September 1, 1993); included rehabilitation assignment to Dunedin (August 14-September 1).

STATISTICAL NOTES: Led Pioneer League shortstops with 102 putouts in 1981.... Led A.L. shortstops with .984 fielding percentage in 1987.... Led A.L. shortstops with 125 double plays in 1988.

			BATTING												FIELDING			
Year	Team (League)	Pos.	G	AB	R	H	2B	3B	HR	RBI	Avg.	BB	SO	SB	PO	A	E	Avg.
1981	—Idaho Falls (Pio.)	SS-2B	66	226	59	63	10	1	6	31	.279	★68	60	13	†102	201	22	.932
1982	—Danville (Midwest)	SS	92	308	80	111	21	★10	12	53	★.360	70	66	17	129	249	23	.943
	—Redwood (Calif.)	SS	33	102	15	25	3	3	1	8	.245	17	20	6	35	103	3	.979
	—Spokane (PCL)	SS-3B	7	30	4	9	4	1	1	12	.300	3	6	0	7	20	0	1.000
1983	—Edmonton (PCL)	SS-3B	139	521	91	148	30	7	16	94	.284	72	105	9	220	402	30	.954
	—California (A.L.)	SS	21	54	4	11	2	0	3	4	.204	6	8	0	24	67	7	.929
1984	—California (A.L.)	SS	140	400	39	77	10	3	4	21	.193	33	79	5	218	420	12	★.982
1985	—California (A.L.)	SS	147	438	50	96	19	3	8	41	.219	35	70	11	261	397	25	.963
1986	—California (A.L.)	SS	139	458	67	114	17	6	13	57	.249	48	55	23	246	389	18	.972
1987	—California (A.L.)	SS-2B	134	479	52	120	17	3	9	46	.251	37	63	19	205	351	9	†.984
1988	—California (A.L.)	SS	155	527	61	126	11	6	6	34	.239	40	57	20	278	492	13	★.983
1989	—California (A.L.)	SS	91	302	42	69	11	2	4	26	.228	28	47	9	118	276	7	.983
1990	—Edmonton (PCL)	SS	5	18	4	7	1	0	1	4	.389	3	4	0	6	14	1	.952
	—California (A.L.)	SS	99	310	41	79	8	1	1	18	.255	52	61	3	170	318	17	.966
1991	—California (A.L.)	SS	134	427	44	96	9	3	0	31	.225	50	69	8	186	398	15	.975
1992	—California (A.L.)	SS	1	3	0	1	0	0	0	0	.333	1	0	0	3	1	0	1.000
	—New York (N.L.)■	SS	142	420	52	86	18	2	4	36	.205	60	82	11	205	391	7	★.988
1993	—Toronto (A.L.)■	SS	36	110	11	21	1	2	0	5	.191	16	25	3	61	106	4	.977
	—Dunedin (Fla. St.)	SS	11	30	4	6	2	0	0	4	.200	3	7	0	14	13	1	.964
American League totals (11 years)			1097	3508	411	810	105	29	48	283	.231	346	534	101	1770	3215	127	.975
National League totals (1 year)			142	420	52	86	18	2	4	36	.205	60	82	11	205	391	7	.988
Major league totals (11 years)			1239	3928	463	896	123	31	52	319	.228	406	616	112	1975	3606	134	.977

CHAMPIONSHIP SERIES RECORD

			BATTING												FIELDING			
Year	Team (League)	Pos.	G	AB	R	H	2B	3B	HR	RBI	Avg.	BB	SO	SB	PO	A	E	Avg.
1986	—California (A.L.)	SS	7	30	4	9	1	0	1	2	.300	1	5	1	13	23	2	.947
1993	—Toronto (A.L.)								Did not play.									
Championship series totals (1 year)			7	30	4	9	1	0	1	2	.300	1	5	1	13	23	2	.947

WORLD SERIES RECORD

			BATTING												FIELDING			
Year	Team (League)	Pos.	G	AB	R	H	2B	3B	HR	RBI	Avg.	BB	SO	SB	PO	A	E	Avg.
1993	—Toronto (A.L.)								Did not play.									

SCHOOLER, MIKE

P

PERSONAL: Born August 10, 1962, in Anaheim, Calif. . . . 6-3/210. . . . Throws right, bats right. . . . Full name: Michael Ralph Schooler.
HIGH SCHOOL: Garden Grove (Calif.).
COLLEGE: Golden West College (Calif.) and Cal State Fullerton.
TRANSACTIONS/CAREER NOTES: Selected by Seattle Mariners organization in second round of free-agent draft (June 3, 1985). . . . On disabled list (August 25, 1990-remainder of season). . . . On Seattle disabled list (March 30-July 8, 1991); included rehabilitation assignment to Jacksonville (June 9-July 3). . . . On Seattle disabled list (July 8-August 14, 1992); included rehabilitation assignment to Calgary (August 9-11) and Bellingham (August 11-14). . . . Released by Mariners (March 16, 1993). . . . Signed by Oklahoma City, Texas Rangers organization (March 22, 1993). . . . Released by Rangers (September 11, 1993).
RECORDS: Shares major league single-season record for most grand slams allowed—4 (1992).

Year	Team (League)	W	L	Pct.	ERA	G	GS	CG	ShO	Sv.	IP	H	R	ER	BB	SO
1985	—Belling. (N'west)	4	3	.571	2.93	10	10	0	0	0	55⅓	42	24	18	15	48
1986	—Wausau (Midwest)	12	10	.545	3.35	26	26	6	1	0	166⅓	166	83	62	44	171
1987	—Chatt. (South.)	13	8	.619	3.96	28	28	3	2	0	175	183	87	77	48	144
1988	—Calgary (PCL)	4	4	.500	3.21	26	0	0	0	0	33⅔	33	19	12	6	47
	—Seattle (A.L.)	5	8	.385	3.54	40	0	0	0	15	48⅓	45	21	19	24	54
1989	—Seattle (A.L.)	1	7	.125	2.81	67	0	0	0	33	77	81	27	24	19	69
1990	—Seattle (A.L.)	1	4	.200	2.25	49	0	0	0	30	56	47	18	14	16	45
1991	—Jacksonv. (South.)	1	1	.500	5.56	11	2	0	0	0	11⅓	13	9	7	3	12
	—Seattle (A.L.)	3	3	.500	3.67	34	0	0	0	7	34⅓	25	14	14	10	31
1992	—Seattle (A.L.)	2	7	.222	4.70	53	0	0	0	13	51⅔	55	29	27	24	33
	—Calgary (PCL)	0	0	...	0.00	1	1	0	0	0	2	2	0	0	0	0
	—Belling. (N'west)	0	0	...	0.00	2	1	0	0	0	3	1	2	0	0	3
1993	—Okla. City (A.A.)■	1	3	.250	5.91	28	0	0	0	5	45⅔	59	33	30	11	31
	—Texas (A.L.)	3	0	1.000	5.55	17	0	0	0	0	24⅓	30	17	15	10	16
Major league totals (6 years)		15	29	.341	3.49	260	0	0	0	98	291⅔	283	126	113	103	248

SCHOUREK, PETE

P, METS

PERSONAL: Born May 10, 1969, in Austin, Tex. . . . 6-5/205. . . . Throws left, bats left. . . . Full name: Peter Alan Schourek. . . . Name pronounced SHUR-ek.
HIGH SCHOOL: George C. Marshall (Falls Church, Va.).
TRANSACTIONS/CAREER NOTES: Selected by New York Mets organization in second round of free-agent draft (June 2, 1987). . . . On disabled list (June 17, 1988-remainder of season).
MISCELLANEOUS: Appeared in one game as pinch-runner with New York (1992).

Year	Team (League)	W	L	Pct.	ERA	G	GS	CG	ShO	Sv.	IP	H	R	ER	BB	SO
1987	—Kingsport (Appal.)	4	5	.444	3.68	12	12	2	0	0	78⅓	70	37	32	34	57
1988	—							Did not play.								
1989	—Columbia (S. Atl.)	5	9	.357	2.85	27	19	5	1	1	136	120	66	43	66	131
	—St. Lucie (Fla. St.)	0	0	...	2.25	2	1	0	0	0	4	3	1	1	2	4
1990	—St. Lucie (Fla. St.)	4	1	.800	0.97	5	5	2	2	0	37	29	4	4	8	28
	—Tidewater (Int'l)	1	0	1.000	2.57	2	2	1	1	0	14	9	4	4	5	14
	—Jackson (Texas)	11	4	.733	3.04	19	19	1	0	0	124⅓	109	53	42	39	94
1991	—Tidewater (Int'l)	1	1	.500	2.52	4	4	0	0	0	25	18	7	7	10	17
	—New York (N.L.)	5	4	.556	4.27	35	8	1	1	2	86⅓	82	49	41	43	67
1992	—Tidewater (Int'l)	2	5	.286	2.73	8	8	2	1	0	52⅔	46	20	16	23	42
	—New York (N.L.)	6	8	.429	3.64	22	21	0	0	0	136	137	60	55	44	60
1993	—New York (N.L.)	5	12	.294	5.96	41	18	0	0	0	128⅓	168	90	85	45	72
Major league totals (3 years)		16	24	.400	4.65	98	47	1	1	2	350⅔	387	199	181	132	199

SCHRENK, STEVE

P, WHITE SOX

PERSONAL: Born November 20, 1968, in Great Lakes, Ill. . . . 6-3/185. . . . Throws right, bats right. . . . Full name: Steven Wayne Schrenk.
HIGH SCHOOL: North Marion (Aurora, Ore.).
TRANSACTIONS/CAREER NOTES: Selected by Chicago White Sox organization in fourth round of free-agent draft (June 2, 1987). . . . On disabled list (April 11-September 3, 1991).

Year	Team (League)	W	L	Pct.	ERA	G	GS	CG	ShO	Sv.	IP	H	R	ER	BB	SO
1987	—GC Whi. Sox (GCL)	1	2	.333	0.95	8	6	1	1	0	28⅓	23	10	3	12	19
1988	—South Bend (Mid.)	3	7	.300	5.00	21	18	1	0	0	90	95	63	50	37	58
1989	—South Bend (Mid.)	5	2	.714	4.33	16	16	1	1	0	79	71	44	38	44	49
1990	—South Bend (Mid.)	7	6	.538	2.95	20	14	2	1	0	103⅔	79	44	34	25	92
1991	—GC Whi. Sox (GCL)	1	3	.250	2.92	11	7	0	0	0	37	30	20	12	6	39
1992	—Sarasota (Fla. St.)	15	2	.882	2.05	25	22	4	2	1	154	130	48	35	40	113
	—Birm. (Southern)	1	1	.500	3.65	2	2	0	0	0	12⅓	13	5	5	11	9
1993	—Birm. (Southern)	5	1	.833	1.17	8	8	2	1	0	61⅔	31	11	8	7	51
	—Nashville (A.A.)	6	8	.429	3.90	21	20	0	0	0	122⅓	117	61	53	47	78

SCHWARZ, JEFF

P, WHITE SOX

PERSONAL: Born May 20, 1964, in Fort Pierce, Fla. . . . 6-5/190. . . . Throws right, bats right. . . . Full name: Jeffrey William Schwarz. . . . Name pronounced SHWARTZ.
HIGH SCHOOL: Fort Pierce (Fla.) Westwood.
TRANSACTIONS/CAREER NOTES: Selected by Chicago Cubs organization in 24th round of free-agent draft (June 7, 1982). . . . On disabled list (April 10-30 and July 8, 1986-remainder of season). . . . Granted free agency (October 22, 1988). . . . Signed by Rochester, Baltimore Orioles organization (November 23, 1988). . . . Released by Orioles organization (April 27, 1990). . . . Signed by Milwaukee Brewers organization (June 15, 1990). . . . Granted free agency (October 15, 1991). . . . Signed by Vancouver, Chicago White Sox organization (February 14, 1992). . . . On Chicago disabled list (August 19-September 3, 1993); included rehabilitation assignment to Nashville (August 28-September 3).
STATISTICAL NOTES: Pitched 4-0 no-hit victory against Kenosha (July 10, 1987).

Year	Team (League)	W	L	Pct.	ERA	G	GS	CG	ShO	Sv.	IP	H	R	ER	BB	SO
1982	—GC Cubs (GCL)	2	5	.286	6.07	11	9	0	0	0	43	47	39	29	37	24
1983	—Pikeville (Appal.)	3	8	.273	5.19	13	13	1	0	0	69⅓	73	61	40	45	61
1984	—Quad City (Midw.)	4	•14	.222	5.05	27	24	2	0	0	130	106	88	73	*111	123
1985	—Peoria (Midwest)	7	9	.438	3.20	27	19	6	2	0	143⅓	99	60	51	79	140
1986	—Winst.-Salem (Car.)	0	1	.000	7.50	4	2	0	0	0	12	10	10	10	12	11
1987	—Peoria (Midwest)	5	7	.417	4.58	20	13	2	2	0	92⅓	79	59	47	59	91
1988	—Winst.-Salem (Car.)	7	•12	.368	4.52	24	24	2	2	0	151⅓	133	93	76	110	153
	—Pittsfield (Eastern)	0	1	.000	5.65	3	3	0	0	0	14⅓	19	9	9	11	5
1989	—Hagerstown (East.)■	0	6	.000	3.91	17	9	0	0	1	69	66	45	30	41	78
	—Rochester (Int'l)	0	2	.000	5.84	9	0	0	0	2	12⅓	5	9	8	16	12
1990	—Rochester (Int'l)	0	0	...	7.11	5	1	0	0	0	12⅔	10	10	10	19	4
	—Stockton (Calif.)■	3	3	.500	4.79	19	8	0	0	2	56⅓	59	36	30	36	59
1991	—El Paso (Texas)	11	8	.579	4.89	27	24	3	1	0	141⅔	139	91	77	97	134
1992	—Birm. (Southern)■	2	1	.667	1.16	21	0	0	0	6	38⅔	16	5	5	9	53
	—Vancouver (PCL)	1	3	.250	3.00	23	0	0	0	3	36	26	18	12	31	42
1993	—Nashville (A.A.)	0	0	...	2.45	7	0	0	0	0	11	1	3	3	12	8
	—Chicago (A.L.)	2	2	.500	3.71	41	0	0	0	0	51	35	21	21	38	41
Major league totals (1 year)		2	2	.500	3.71	41	0	0	0	0	51	35	21	21	38	41

CHAMPIONSHIP SERIES RECORD

Year	Team (League)	W	L	Pct.	ERA	G	GS	CG	ShO	Sv.	IP	H	R	ER	BB	SO
1993	—Chicago (A.L.)	Did not play.														

SCIOSCIA, MIKE

C, RANGERS

PERSONAL: Born November 27, 1958, in Upper Darby, Pa. . . . 6-2/220. . . . Throws right, bats left. . . . Full name: Michael Lorri Scioscia. . . . Name pronounced SO-sha.
HIGH SCHOOL: Springfield (Pa.).
COLLEGE: Penn State.

TRANSACTIONS/CAREER NOTES: Selected by Los Angeles Dodgers organization in first round (19th pick overall) of free-agent draft (June 8, 1976). . . . On disabled list (May 19-August 4, 1978; April 10-20, 1980; May 15, 1983-remainder of season; May 6-21, 1984; June 10-July 15, 1986; June 1-16, 1987; and July 5-20, 1991). . . . Granted free agency (November 4, 1992). . . . Signed by San Diego Padres (February 11, 1993). . . . On San Diego disabled list (March 29, 1993-entire season). . . . Released by Padres (October 15, 1993). . . . Signed by Texas Rangers organization (December 14, 1993).

HONORS: Named catcher on THE SPORTING NEWS N.L. All-Star team (1990).

STATISTICAL NOTES: Led Midwest League catchers with 20 errors and 12 double plays in 1977. . . . Led Pacific Coast League catchers with 19 double plays and 22 passed balls in 1979. . . . Tied for Pacific Coast League lead in being hit by pitch with seven in 1979. . . . Led N.L. with 11 passed balls in 1981 and 14 in 1992. . . . Led N.L. catchers with 1,016 total chances in 1987, 915 in 1989 and 910 in 1990.

				BATTING											FIELDING			
Year	Team (League)	Pos.	G	AB	R	H	2B	3B	HR	RBI	Avg.	BB	SO	SB	PO	A	E	Avg.
1976	—Belling. (N'west)	C	46	151	25	42	6	0	7	26	.278	36	22	2	202	35	14	.944
1977	—Clinton (Midwest)	C-1B	121	364	58	92	20	1	7	44	.253	79	25	9	764	95	†22	.975
1978	—San Antonio (Tex.)	C	58	204	29	61	16	0	2	34	.299	31	20	3	214	17	4	.983
1979	—Albuquerque (PCL)	C	143	461	80	155	34	0	3	68	.336	73	33	5	*690	*86	*15	.981
1980	—Albuquerque (PCL)	C	52	160	33	53	11	1	3	33	.331	36	13	3	207	19	5	.978
	—Los Angeles (N.L.)	C	54	134	8	34	5	1	1	8	.254	12	9	1	226	26	2	.992
1981	—Los Angeles (N.L.)	C	93	290	27	80	10	0	2	29	.276	36	18	0	493	48	7	.987
1982	—Los Angeles (N.L.)	C	129	365	31	80	11	1	5	38	.219	44	31	2	631	57	10	.986
1983	—Los Angeles (N.L.)	C	12	35	3	11	3	0	1	7	.314	5	2	0	55	4	0	1.000
1984	—Los Angeles (N.L.)	C	114	341	29	93	18	0	5	38	.273	52	26	2	701	64	12	.985
1985	—Los Angeles (N.L.)	C	141	429	47	127	26	3	7	53	.296	77	21	3	818	66	•13	.986
1986	—Los Angeles (N.L.)	C	122	374	36	94	18	1	5	26	.251	62	23	3	756	64	15	.982
1987	—Los Angeles (N.L.)	C	142	461	44	122	26	1	6	38	.265	55	23	7	*925	80	11	.989
1988	—Los Angeles (N.L.)	C	130	408	29	105	18	0	3	35	.257	38	31	0	748	63	7	.991
1989	—Los Angeles (N.L.)	C	133	408	40	102	16	0	10	44	.250	52	29	0	*822	*82	11	.988
1990	—Los Angeles (N.L.)	C	135	435	46	115	25	0	12	66	.264	55	31	4	*842	58	10	.989
1991	—Los Angeles (N.L.)	C	119	345	39	91	16	2	8	40	.264	47	32	4	677	51	7	.990
1992	—Los Angeles (N.L.)	C	117	348	19	77	6	3	3	24	.221	32	31	3	641	*74	9	.988
1993	—■		Did not play.															
Major league totals (13 years)			1441	4373	398	1131	198	12	68	446	.259	567	307	29	8335	737	114	.988

DIVISION SERIES RECORD

				BATTING											FIELDING			
Year	Team (League)	Pos.	G	AB	R	H	2B	3B	HR	RBI	Avg.	BB	SO	SB	PO	A	E	Avg.
1981	—Los Angeles (N.L.)	C	4	13	0	2	0	0	0	1	.154	1	2	0	21	3	0	1.000

CHAMPIONSHIP SERIES RECORD

				BATTING											FIELDING			
Year	Team (League)	Pos.	G	AB	R	H	2B	3B	HR	RBI	Avg.	BB	SO	SB	PO	A	E	Avg.
1981	—Los Angeles (N.L.)	C	5	15	1	2	0	0	1	1	.133	2	1	0	27	1	0	1.000
1985	—Los Angeles (N.L.)	C	6	16	2	4	0	0	0	1	.250	4	0	0	31	4	1	.972
1988	—Los Angeles (N.L.)	C	7	22	3	8	1	0	1	2	.364	1	2	0	37	4	0	1.000
Championship series totals (3 years)			18	53	6	14	1	0	2	4	.264	7	3	0	95	9	1	.990

WORLD SERIES RECORD

				BATTING											FIELDING			
Year	Team (League)	Pos.	G	AB	R	H	2B	3B	HR	RBI	Avg.	BB	SO	SB	PO	A	E	Avg.
1981	—Los Angeles (N.L.)	C-PH	3	4	1	1	0	0	0	0	.250	1	0	0	7	1	0	1.000

Year	Team (League)	Pos.	G	AB	R	H	2B	3B	HR	RBI	Avg.	BB	SO	SB	PO	A	E	Avg.
			BATTING												FIELDING			
1988	—Los Angeles (N.L.) ...	C	4	14	0	3	0	0	0	1	.214	0	2	0	28	0	1	.966
World Series totals (2 years)			7	18	1	4	0	0	0	1	.222	1	2	0	35	1	1	.973

ALL-STAR GAME RECORD

Year	League	Pos.	AB	R	H	2B	3B	HR	RBI	Avg.	BB	SO	SB	PO	A	E	Avg.
			BATTING											FIELDING			
1989	—National	C	1	0	0	0	0	0	0	.000	0	0	0	3	0	0	1.000
1990	—National	C	2	0	0	0	0	0	0	.000	0	1	0	6	0	0	1.000
All-Star Game totals (2 years)			3	0	0	0	0	0	0	.000	0	1	0	9	0	0	1.000

SCOTT, DARRYL

P

PERSONAL: Born August 6, 1968, in Fresno, Calif. . . . 6-1/185. . . . Throws right, bats right. . . . Full name: Darryl Nelson Scott.

HIGH SCHOOL: Yuba City (Calif.).

COLLEGE: Loyola Marymount.

TRANSACTIONS/CAREER NOTES: Signed as free agent by California Angels organization (June 13, 1990). . . . Released by Angels (November 16, 1993).

Year	Team (League)	W	L	Pct.	ERA	G	GS	CG	ShO	Sv.	IP	H	R	ER	BB	SO
1990	—Boise (Northwest)	2	1	.667	1.34	27	0	0	0	6	53⅔	41	11	8	20	57
1991	—Quad City (Midw.)	4	3	.571	1.55	47	0	0	0	19	75⅓	35	18	13	26	123
1992	—Midland (Texas)	1	1	.500	1.82	27	0	0	0	9	29⅔	20	9	6	14	35
	—Edmonton (PCL)	0	2	.000	5.20	31	0	0	0	6	36⅓	41	21	21	21	48
1993	—Vancouver (PCL)	7	1	.875	2.09	46	0	0	0	15	51⅔	35	12	12	19	57
	—California (A.L.)	1	2	.333	5.85	16	0	0	0	0	20	19	13	13	11	13
Major league totals (1 year)		1	2	.333	5.85	16	0	0	0	0	20	19	13	13	11	13

SCOTT, GARY

3B, TWINS

PERSONAL: Born August 22, 1968, in New Rochelle, N.Y. . . . 6-0/175. . . . Throws right, bats right. . . . Full name: Gary Thomas Scott.

HIGH SCHOOL: John Bowne (Flushing, N.Y.).

COLLEGE: Villanova.

TRANSACTIONS/CAREER NOTES: Selected by Chicago Cubs organization in second round of free-agent draft (June 5, 1989). . . . On Iowa disabled list (July 31, 1991-remainder of season). . . . Traded by Cubs with SS Alex Arias to Florida Marlins for P Greg Hibbard (November 17, 1992). . . . Traded by Marlins with a player to be named later to Cincinnati Reds for P Chris Hammond (March 27, 1993); Reds acquired P Hector Carrasco to complete deal (September 10, 1993). . . . Traded by Reds to Minnesota Twins for P Alan Newman and IF Tom Houk (June 30, 1993).

HONORS: Named Carolina League Most Valuable Player (1990).

Year	Team (League)	Pos.	G	AB	R	H	2B	3B	HR	RBI	Avg.	BB	SO	SB	PO	A	E	Avg.
			BATTING												FIELDING			
1989	—Geneva (NY-Penn)	3B	48	175	33	49	10	1	10	42	.280	22	23	4	23	69	14	.868
1990	—Winst.-Salem (Car.)	3B	102	380	63	112	22	0	12	70	.295	29	66	17	63	184	29	.895
	—Charlotte (South.)	3B	35	143	21	44	9	0	4	17	.308	7	17	3	25	102	8	.941
1991	—Chicago (N.L.)	3B	31	79	8	13	3	0	1	5	.165	13	14	0	13	50	2	.969
	—Iowa (Am. Assoc.)	3B-SS	63	231	21	48	10	2	3	34	.208	20	45	0	47	116	8	.953
1992	—Chicago (N.L.)	3B-SS	36	96	8	15	2	0	2	11	.156	5	14	0	18	43	5	.924
	—Iowa (Am. Assoc.)	3B-SS	95	354	48	93	26	0	10	48	.263	37	48	3	97	217	14	.957
1993	—Indianapolis (A.A.)■	2B	77	284	39	60	12	1	3	18	.211	21	33	2	161	187	13	.964
	—Portland (PCL)■	3B-SS-2B	54	189	26	55	8	4	1	28	.291	27	33	3	72	138	12	.946
Major league totals (2 years)			67	175	16	28	5	0	3	16	.160	18	28	0	31	93	7	.947

SCOTT, TIM

P, EXPOS

PERSONAL: Born November 16, 1966, in Hanford, Calif. . . . 6-2/205. . . . Throws right, bats right. . . . Full name: Timothy Dale Scott.

HIGH SCHOOL: Hanford (Calif.).

TRANSACTIONS/CAREER NOTES: Selected by Los Angeles Dodgers organization in second round of free-agent draft (June 4, 1984). . . . On disabled list (July 23, 1985-remainder of season and April 11-May 15, 1986). . . . Granted free agency (October 15, 1990). . . . Signed by San Diego Padres organization (November 1, 1990). . . . Traded by Padres to Montreal Expos for IF/OF Archi Cianfrocco (June 23, 1993).

Year	Team (League)	W	L	Pct.	ERA	G	GS	CG	ShO	Sv.	IP	H	R	ER	BB	SO
1984	—Great Falls (Pio.)	5	4	.556	4.38	13	13	3	•2	0	78	90	58	38	44	38
1985	—Bakersfield (Calif.)	3	4	.429	5.80	12	10	2	0	0	63⅔	84	46	41	28	31
1986	—Vero Beach (FSL)	5	4	.556	3.40	20	13	3	1	0	95⅓	113	44	36	24	37
1987	—Bakersfield (Calif.)	2	3	.400	4.45	7	5	1	0	0	32⅓	33	19	16	10	29
	—San Antonio (Tex.)	0	1	.000	16.88	2	2	0	0	0	5⅓	14	10	10	2	6
1988	—Bakersfield (Calif.)	4	7	.364	3.64	36	2	0	0	7	64⅓	52	34	26	26	59
1989	—San Antonio (Tex.)	4	2	.667	3.71	48	0	0	0	4	68	71	30	28	36	64
1990	—San Antonio (Tex.)	3	3	.500	2.85	30	0	0	0	7	47⅓	35	17	15	14	52
	—Albuquerque (PCL)	2	1	.667	4.20	17	0	0	0	3	15	14	9	7	14	15
1991	—Las Vegas (PCL)■	8	8	.500	5.19	41	11	0	0	0	111	133	78	64	39	74
	—San Diego (N.L.)	0	0	...	9.00	2	0	0	0	0	1	2	2	1	0	1
1992	—Las Vegas (PCL)	1	2	.333	2.25	24	0	0	0	15	28	20	8	7	3	28
	—San Diego (N.L.)	4	1	.800	5.26	34	0	0	0	0	37⅔	39	24	22	21	30
1993	—S.D.-Mont. (N.L.)■	7	2	.778	3.01	56	0	0	0	1	71⅔	69	28	24	34	65
Major league totals (3 years)		11	3	.786	3.83	92	0	0	0	1	110⅓	110	54	47	55	96

SCUDDER, SCOTT

P, PIRATES

PERSONAL: Born February 14, 1968, in Paris, Tex. . . . 6-2/185. . . . Throws right, bats right. . . . Full name: William Scott Scudder.
HIGH SCHOOL: Prairieland (Pattonville, Tex.).
TRANSACTIONS/CAREER NOTES: Selected by Cincinnati Reds organization in first round (17th pick overall) of free-agent draft (June 2, 1986). . . . On disabled list (May 31-June 17 and June 27-August 17, 1991). . . . Traded by Reds with P Jack Armstrong and P Joe Turek to Cleveland Indians for P Greg Swindell (November 15, 1991). . . . On Cleveland disabled list (July 30-September 17, 1992); included rehabilitation assignment to Colorado Springs (September 7-17). . . . On Cleveland disabled list (April 1-May 18, 1993); included rehabilitation assignment to Charlotte (April 27-May 18). . . . Granted free agency (October 15, 1993). . . . Signed by Pittsburgh Pirates organization (December 17, 1993).
STATISTICAL NOTES: Pitched 4-0 no-hit victory for Cedar Rapids against Wausau (May 20, 1988).

Year	Team (League)	W	L	Pct.	ERA	G	GS	CG	ShO	Sv.	IP	H	R	ER	BB	SO
1986	—Billings (Pioneer)	1	3	.250	4.78	12	8	0	0	0	52⅔	43	34	28	36	38
1987	—Ced. Rap. (Midw.)	7	12	.368	4.10	26	26	0	0	0	153⅔	129	86	70	76	128
1988	—Ced. Rap. (Midw.)	7	3	.700	2.02	16	15	1	1	0	102⅓	61	30	23	41	126
	—Chatt. (South.)	7	0	1.000	2.96	11	11	0	0	0	70	53	24	23	30	52
1989	—Nashville (A.A.)	6	2	.750	2.68	12	12	3	3	0	80⅔	54	27	24	48	64
	—Cincinnati (N.L.)	4	9	.308	4.49	23	17	0	0	0	100⅓	91	54	50	61	66
1990	—Nashville (A.A.)	7	1	.875	2.34	11	11	1	0	0	80⅔	53	27	21	32	60
	—Cincinnati (N.L.)	5	5	.500	4.90	21	10	0	0	0	71⅔	74	41	39	30	42
1991	—Cincinnati (N.L.)	6	9	.400	4.35	27	14	0	0	1	101⅓	91	52	49	56	51
1992	—Cleveland (A.L.)■	6	10	.375	5.28	23	22	0	0	0	109	134	80	64	55	66
	—Colo. Springs (PCL)	0	1	.000	6.00	1	1	0	0	0	3	4	3	2	2	1
1993	—Charlotte (Int'l)	7	7	.500	5.03	23	22	2	0	0	136	148	92	76	52	64
	—Cleveland (A.L.)	0	1	.000	9.00	2	1	0	0	0	4	5	4	4	4	1
A.L. totals (2 years)		6	11	.353	5.42	25	23	0	0	0	113	139	84	68	59	67
N.L. totals (3 years)		15	23	.395	4.54	71	41	0	0	1	273⅓	256	147	138	147	159
Major league totals (5 years)		21	34	.382	4.80	96	64	0	0	1	386⅓	395	231	206	206	226

CHAMPIONSHIP SERIES RECORD

Year	Team (League)	W	L	Pct.	ERA	G	GS	CG	ShO	Sv.	IP	H	R	ER	BB	SO
1990	—Cincinnati (N.L.)	0	0	...	0.00	1	0	0	0	0	1	1	0	0	0	1

WORLD SERIES RECORD

Year	Team (League)	W	L	Pct.	ERA	G	GS	CG	ShO	Sv.	IP	H	R	ER	BB	SO
1990	—Cincinnati (N.L.)	0	0	...	0.00	1	0	0	0	0	1⅓	0	0	0	2	2

SEANEZ, RUDY

P, DODGERS

PERSONAL: Born October 20, 1968, in Brawley, Calif. . . . 5-10/185. . . . Throws right, bats right. . . . Full name: Rudy Caballero Seanez. . . . Name pronounced see-AHN-yez.
HIGH SCHOOL: Brawley (Calif.) Union.
TRANSACTIONS/CAREER NOTES: Selected by Cleveland Indians organization in fourth round of free-agent draft (June 10, 1986). . . . On disabled list (May 4-July 11 and August 9-29, 1987). . . . On Cleveland disabled list (April 1-16, 1991). . . . On Cleveland disabled list (July 30-September 2, 1991); included rehabilitation assignment to Colorado Springs (August 14-September 2). . . . Traded by Indians to Los Angeles Dodgers for P Dennis Cook and P Mike Christopher (December 10, 1991). . . . On Los Angeles disabled list (March 29, 1992-entire season). . . . Traded by Dodgers to Colorado Rockies for 2B Jody Reed (November 17, 1992). . . . On Colorado disabled list (April 4-July 16, 1993); included rehabilitation assignment to Central Valley (June 16-July 4) and Colorado Springs (July 4-15). . . . Granted free agency (July 16, 1993). . . . Signed by Las Vegas, San Diego Padres organization (July 22, 1993). . . . Released by Padres (November 18, 1993). . . . Signed by Dodgers organization (January 12, 1994).
STATISTICAL NOTES: Pitched 4-0 no-hit victory against Pulaski (August 2, 1986).

Year	Team (League)	W	L	Pct.	ERA	G	GS	CG	ShO	Sv.	IP	H	R	ER	BB	SO
1986	—Burlington (Appal.)	5	2	.714	3.20	13	12	1	1	0	76	59	37	27	32	56
1987	—Waterloo (Midw.)	0	4	.000	6.75	10	10	0	0	0	34⅔	35	29	26	23	23
1988	—Waterloo (Midw.)	6	6	.500	4.69	22	22	1	1	0	113⅓	98	69	59	68	93
1989	—Kinston (Carolina)	8	10	.444	4.14	25	25	1	0	0	113	94	66	52	*111	149
	—Colo. Springs (PCL)	0	0	...	0.00	1	0	0	0	0	1	1	0	0	0	0
	—Cleveland (A.L.)	0	0	...	3.60	5	0	0	0	0	5	1	2	2	4	7
1990	—Cant./Akr. (East.)	1	0	1.000	2.16	15	0	0	0	5	16⅔	9	4	4	12	27
	—Cleveland (A.L.)	2	1	.667	5.60	24	0	0	0	0	27⅓	22	17	17	25	24
	—Colo. Springs (PCL)	1	4	.200	6.75	12	0	0	0	1	12	15	10	9	10	7
1991	—Colo. Springs (PCL)	0	0	...	7.27	16	0	0	0	0	17⅓	17	14	14	22	19
	—Cant./Akr. (East.)	4	2	.667	2.58	25	0	0	0	7	38⅓	17	12	11	30	73
	—Cleveland (A.L.)	0	0	...	16.20	5	0	0	0	0	5	10	12	9	7	7
1992	—■							Did not play.								
1993	—Central Vall. (Cal.)■	0	2	.000	9.72	5	1	0	0	0	8⅓	9	9	9	11	7
	—Colo. Sp.-L.V. (PCL)■	0	1	.000	6.75	17	0	0	0	0	22⅔	27	18	17	12	19
	—San Diego (N.L.)	0	0	...	13.50	3	0	0	0	0	3⅓	8	6	5	2	1
A.L. totals (3 years)		2	1	.667	6.75	34	0	0	0	0	37⅓	33	31	28	36	38
N.L. totals (1 year)		0	0	...	13.50	3	0	0	0	0	3⅓	8	6	5	2	1
Major league totals (4 years)		2	1	.667	7.30	37	0	0	0	0	40⅔	41	37	33	38	39

SEBACH, KYLE

P, ANGELS

PERSONAL: Born September 6, 1971, in San Diego. . . . 6-4/195. . . . Throws right, bats right. . . . Name pronounced SEE-bock.
HIGH SCHOOL: Santana (Santee, Calif.).
COLLEGE: Grossmont College (Calif.).
TRANSACTIONS/CAREER NOTES: Selected by California Angels organization in 13th round of free-agent draft (June 3, 1991).
STATISTICAL NOTES: Tied for Arizona League lead with four home runs allowed in 1991.

Year	Team (League)	W	L	Pct.	ERA	G	GS	CG	ShO	Sv.	IP	H	R	ER	BB	SO
1991	—Ariz. Angels (Ariz.)	3	5	.375	6.26	13	11	1	0	0	64⅔	62	49	45	39	58
1992	—Quad City (Midw.)	3	4	.429	3.96	13	13	0	0	0	61⅓	52	31	27	40	50
	—Boise (Northwest)	1	5	.167	7.52	13	8	0	0	1	40⅔	50	42	34	34	41
1993	—Ced. Rap. (Midw.)	6	9	.400	3.04	26	26	4	0	0	154	138	73	52	70	138

SEEFRIED, TATE

1B, YANKEES

PERSONAL: Born April 22, 1972, in Seattle. . . . 6-4/180. . . . Throws right, bats left. . . . Full name: Tate Carsten Seefried. . . . Name pronounced SEE-FREED.
HIGH SCHOOL: El Segundo (Calif.).
TRANSACTIONS/CAREER NOTES: Selected by New York Yankees organization in third round of free-agent draft (June 4, 1990).
STATISTICAL NOTES: Tied for New York-Pennsylvania League lead with seven sacrifice flies in 1991. . . . Led New York-Pennsylvania League first basemen with 725 total chances and 56 double plays in 1991. . . . Led South Atlantic League first basemen with 1,388 total chances in 1992. . . . Tied for Carolina League lead with four intentional bases on balls received in 1993. . . . Led Carolina League first basemen with 1,234 total chances in 1993.

							BATTING								FIELDING			
Year	Team (League)	Pos.	G	AB	R	H	2B	3B	HR	RBI	Avg.	BB	SO	SB	PO	A	E	Avg.
1990	—GC Yankees (GCL)....	1B	52	178	15	28	3	0	0	20	.157	22	53	2	418	30	6	.987
1991	—Oneonta (NYP)	1B	73	264	40	65	19	0	7	51	.246	32	65	12	*667	46	*12	.983
1992	—Greensboro (S. Atl.)..	1B	*141	532	73	129	23	5	20	90	.242	51	166	8	*1257	*118	13	*.991
1993	—Prin. William (Car.)..	1B	125	464	63	123	25	4	21	89	.265	50	*150	8	*1127	91	16	.987

SEGUI, DAVID

1B/OF, ORIOLES

PERSONAL: Born July 19, 1966, in Kansas City, Kan. . . . 6-1/202. . . . Throws left, bats both. . . . Full name: David Vincent Segui. . . . Son of Diego Segui, major league pitcher with five teams (1962-75 and 1977); and brother of Dan Segui, minor league infielder (1987-90). . . . Name pronounced seh-GHEE.
HIGH SCHOOL: Bishop Ward (Kansas City, Kan.).
COLLEGE: Kansas City Kansas Community College and Louisiana Tech.
TRANSACTIONS/CAREER NOTES: Selected by Baltimore Orioles organization in 18th round of free-agent draft (June 2, 1987). . . . On Rochester disabled list (April 19-26, 1991). . . . On suspended list (August 16-19, 1993).

							BATTING								FIELDING			
Year	Team (League)	Pos.	G	AB	R	H	2B	3B	HR	RBI	Avg.	BB	SO	SB	PO	A	E	Avg.
1988	—Hagerstown (Car.) ...	1B-OF	60	190	35	51	12	4	3	31	.268	22	23	0	342	25	9	.976
1989	—Frederick (Caro.)......	1B	83	284	43	90	19	0	10	50	.317	41	32	2	707	47	4	.995
	—Hagerstown (East.)..	1B	44	173	22	56	14	1	1	27	.324	16	16	0	381	30	1	.998
1990	—Rochester (Int'l)	1B-OF	86	307	55	103	28	0	2	51	.336	45	28	5	704	62	3	.996
	—Baltimore (A.L.)........	1B	40	123	14	30	7	0	2	15	.244	11	15	0	283	26	3	.990
1991	—Rochester (Int'l)	1B-OF	28	96	9	26	2	0	1	10	.271	15	6	1	165	15	0	1.000
	—Baltimore (A.L.)........	OF-1B	86	212	15	59	7	0	2	22	.278	12	19	1	264	23	3	.990
1992	—Baltimore (A.L.)........	1B-OF	115	189	21	44	9	0	1	17	.233	20	23	1	406	35	1	.998
1993	—Baltimore (A.L.)........	1B	146	450	54	123	27	0	10	60	.273	58	53	2	1152	98	5	.996
Major league totals (4 years)			387	974	104	256	50	0	15	114	.263	101	110	4	2105	182	12	.995

SEITZER, KEVIN

3B/1B

PERSONAL: Born March 26, 1962, in Springfield, Ill. . . . 5-11/190. . . . Throws right, bats right. . . . Full name: Kevin Lee Seitzer. . . . Name pronounced SITE-ser.
HIGH SCHOOL: Lincoln (Ill.).
COLLEGE: Eastern Illinois (bachelor of science degree in industrial electronics).
TRANSACTIONS/CAREER NOTES: Selected by Kansas City Royals organization in 11th round of free-agent draft (June 6, 1983). . . . On disabled list (April 27-May 31, 1991). . . . Released by Royals (March 26, 1992). . . . Signed by Milwaukee Brewers (April 5, 1992). . . . Granted free agency (October 27, 1992). . . . Signed by Oakland Athletics (February 1, 1993). . . . Released by A's (July 26, 1993). . . . Signed by Brewers (July 29, 1993). . . . Granted free agency (October 29, 1993).
HONORS: Named South Atlantic League Most Valuable Player (1984).
STATISTICAL NOTES: Led Pioneer League third basemen with 122 assists and 172 total chances in 1983. . . . Led South Atlantic League third basemen with 409 total chances in 1984. . . . Tied for American Association lead in being hit by pitch with nine in 1986. . . . Collected six hits in one game (August 2, 1987). . . . Tied for A.L. lead in errors by third baseman with 22 in 1987. . . . Led A.L. third basemen with 26 errors in 1988. . . . Led A.L. third basemen with .969 fielding percentage in 1992.

							BATTING								FIELDING			
Year	Team (League)	Pos.	G	AB	R	H	2B	3B	HR	RBI	Avg.	BB	SO	SB	PO	A	E	Avg.
1983	—Butte (Pioneer).........	3B-SS	68	238	60	82	14	1	2	45	.345	46	36	11	52	†124	21	.893
1984	—Char., S.C. (S. Atl.)...	3B	•141	489	*96	*145	26	5	8	79	.297	*118	70	23	80	*279	*50	.878
1985	—Fort Myers (FSL).........	1B-3B	90	290	61	91	10	5	3	46	.314	85	30	28	569	88	9	.986
	—Memphis (South.)	3B-1B-OF	52	187	26	65	6	2	1	20	.348	25	21	9	79	51	10	.929
1986	—Memphis (South.)	1B	4	11	4	3	0	0	0	1	.273	7	1	2	28	3	1	.969
	—Omaha (A.A.)...........	OF-1B-3B	129	432	86	138	20	11	13	74	.319	89	57	20	338	39	9	.977
	—Kansas City (A.L.)....	1B-OF-3B	28	96	16	31	4	1	2	11	.323	19	14	0	224	19	3	.988
1987	—Kansas City (A.L.)....	3B-1B-OF	161	641	105	•207	33	8	15	83	.323	80	85	12	290	315	‡24	.962
1988	—Kansas City (A.L.)....	3B-OF	149	559	90	170	32	5	5	60	.304	72	64	10	93	297	†26	.938
1989	—Kansas City (A.L.)....	3-S-O-1	160	597	78	168	17	2	4	48	.281	102	76	17	118	277	20	.952
1990	—Kansas City (A.L.)....	3B-2B	158	622	91	171	31	5	6	38	.275	67	66	7	118	281	19	.955
1991	—Kansas City (A.L.)....	3B	85	234	28	62	11	3	1	25	.265	29	21	4	45	127	11	.940
1992	—Milwaukee (A.L.)■....	3B-2B-1B	148	540	74	146	35	1	5	71	.270	57	44	13	102	277	12	†.969
1993	—Oak.-Mil. (A.L.)■......	3-1-0-2-S-P	120	417	45	112	16	2	11	57	.269	44	48	7	275	150	12	.973
Major league totals (8 years)			1009	3706	527	1067	179	27	49	393	.288	470	418	70	1265	1743	127	.959

ALL-STAR GAME RECORD

Year	League	Pos.	AB	R	H	2B	3B	HR	RBI	Avg.	BB	SO	SB	PO	A	E	Avg.
			BATTING											FIELDING			
1987	—American	3B	2	0	0	0	0	0	0	.000	1	0	0	0	0	0	...

RECORD AS PITCHER

Year	Team (League)	W	L	Pct.	ERA	G	GS	CG	ShO	Sv.	IP	H	R	ER	BB	SO
1993	—Oakland (A.L.)	0	0	...	0.00	1	0	0	0	0	⅓	0	0	0	0	1

SELE, AARON

P, RED SOX

PERSONAL: Born June 25, 1970, in Golden Valley, Minn. . . . 6-5/205. . . . Throws right, bats right. . . . Full name: Aaron Helmer Sele. . . . Name pronounced SEE-lee.
HIGH SCHOOL: North Kitsap (Poulsbo, Wash.).
COLLEGE: Washington State.
TRANSACTIONS/CAREER NOTES: Selected by Minnesota Twins organization in 37th round of free-agent draft (June 1, 1988).... Selected by Boston Red Sox organization in first round (23rd pick overall) of free-agent draft (June 3, 1991).
HONORS: Named A.L. Rookie Pitcher of the Year by THE SPORTING NEWS (1993).... Named International League Most Valuable Pitcher (1993).
STATISTICAL NOTES: Led Carolina League with 14 hit batsmen in 1992.

Year	Team (League)	W	L	Pct.	ERA	G	GS	CG	ShO	Sv.	IP	H	R	ER	BB	SO
1991	—Winter Haven (FSL)	3	6	.333	4.96	13	11	4	0	1	69	65	42	38	32	51
1992	—Lynchburg (Caro.)	13	5	.722	2.91	20	19	2	1	0	127	104	51	41	46	112
	—New Britain (East.)	2	1	.667	6.27	7	6	1	0	0	33	43	29	23	15	29
1993	—Pawtucket (Int'l)	8	2	.800	2.19	14	14	2	1	0	94⅓	74	30	23	23	87
	—Boston (A.L.)	7	2	.778	2.74	18	18	0	0	0	111⅔	100	42	34	48	93
Major league totals (1 year)		7	2	.778	2.74	18	18	0	0	0	111⅔	100	42	34	48	93

SEMINARA, FRANK

P, METS

PERSONAL: Born May 16, 1967, in Brooklyn, N.Y. . . . 6-2/205. . . . Throws right, bats right. . . . Full name: Frank Peter Seminara. . . . Name pronounced SEM-ah-NAIR-ah.
HIGH SCHOOL: Xaverian (Brooklyn, N.Y.).
COLLEGE: Columbia (degree in history).
TRANSACTIONS/CAREER NOTES: Selected by New York Yankees organization in 12th round of free-agent draft (June 1, 1988).... Selected by San Diego Padres from Yankees organization in Rule 5 major league draft (December 3, 1990).... On Las Vegas disabled list (June 30-July 8, 1993).... Traded by Padres with OF Tracy Sanders and a player to be named later to New York Mets for OF Randy Curtis and a player to be named later (December 10, 1993); Mets acquired SS Pablo Martinez and Padres acquired P Marc Kroon to complete deal (December 13, 1993).
HONORS: Named Carolina League Pitcher of the Year (1990).

Year	Team (League)	W	L	Pct.	ERA	G	GS	CG	ShO	Sv.	IP	H	R	ER	BB	SO
1988	—Oneonta (NYP)	4	7	.364	4.37	16	13	0	0	1	78⅓	86	49	38	32	60
1989	—Oneonta (NYP)	7	2	.778	2.06	11	10	3	1	0	70	51	25	16	18	70
	—Prin. William (Car.)	2	4	.333	3.68	21	0	0	0	2	36⅔	26	23	15	22	23
1990	—Prin. William (Car.)	*16	8	.667	*1.90	25	25	4	2	0	170⅓	136	51	36	52	132
1991	—Wichita (Texas)■	*15	10	.600	3.38	27	•27	*6	1	0	*176	173	86	66	68	107
1992	—Las Vegas (PCL)	6	4	.600	4.13	13	13	1	1	0	80⅔	92	46	37	33	48
	—San Diego (N.L.)	9	4	.692	3.68	19	18	0	0	0	100⅓	98	46	41	46	61
1993	—San Diego (N.L.)	3	3	.500	4.47	18	7	0	0	0	46⅓	53	30	23	21	22
	—Las Vegas (PCL)	8	5	.615	5.43	21	19	0	0	1	114⅓	136	79	69	52	99
Major league totals (2 years)		12	7	.632	3.93	37	25	0	0	0	146⅔	151	76	64	67	83

SERVAIS, SCOTT

C, ASTROS

PERSONAL: Born June 4, 1967, in LaCrosse, Wis. . . . 6-2/195. . . . Throws right, bats right. . . . Full name: Scott Daniel Servais. . . . Name pronounced SER-viss.
HIGH SCHOOL: Westby (Wis.).
COLLEGE: Creighton.
TRANSACTIONS/CAREER NOTES: Selected by New York Mets organization in second round of free-agent draft (June 3, 1985).... Selected by Houston Astros organization in third round of free-agent draft (June 1, 1988).... On Tucson disabled list (June 29-July 1, 1991).... On Houston disabled list (August 4-September 7, 1991).
STATISTICAL NOTES: Tied for Pacific Coast League lead in double plays by catcher with nine in 1990.
MISCELLANEOUS: Member of 1988 U.S. Olympic baseball team.

Year	Team (League)	Pos.	G	AB	R	H	2B	3B	HR	RBI	Avg.	BB	SO	SB	PO	A	E	Avg.
			BATTING												FIELDING			
1989	—Osceola (Fla. St.)	C-1B	46	153	16	41	9	0	2	23	.268	16	35	0	168	24	4	.980
	—Columbus (South.)	C	63	199	20	47	5	0	1	22	.236	19	42	0	330	45	3	.992
1990	—Tucson (PCL)	C	89	303	37	66	11	3	5	37	.218	18	61	0	453	63	9	.983
1991	—Tucson (PCL)	C	60	219	34	71	12	0	2	27	.324	13	19	0	350	33	6	.985
	—Houston (N.L.)	C	16	37	0	6	3	0	0	6	.162	4	8	0	77	4	1	.988
1992	—Houston (N.L.)	C	77	205	12	49	9	0	0	15	.239	11	25	0	386	27	2	.995
1993	—Houston (N.L.)	C	85	258	24	63	11	0	11	32	.244	22	45	0	493	40	2	.996
Major league totals (3 years)			178	500	36	118	23	0	11	53	.236	37	78	0	956	71	5	.995

SERVICE, SCOTT

P, REDS

PERSONAL: Born February 26, 1967, in Cincinnati. . . . 6-6/226. . . . Throws right, bats right. . . . Full name: David Scott Service.
HIGH SCHOOL: Aiken (Cincinnati).
TRANSACTIONS/CAREER NOTES: Signed as free agent by Philadelphia Phillies organization (August 24, 1985).... Granted free agency (October 11, 1990).... Signed by Montreal Expos organization (November 15,

1990).... Released by Expos organization (July 19, 1991).... Played with Chunichi Dragons of Japan Central League (August 1991).... Signed by Expos organization (January 10, 1992).... Granted free agency (June 8, 1992).... Signed by Nashville, Cincinnati Reds organization (June 9, 1992).... On Indianapolis disabled list (May 15-22, 1993).... Claimed on waivers by Colorado Rockies (June 28, 1993).... Claimed on waivers by Reds (July 7, 1993).
MISCELLANEOUS: Made an out in only appearance as pinch-hitter with Cincinnati (1993).

Year	Team (League)	W	L	Pct.	ERA	G	GS	CG	ShO	Sv.	IP	H	R	ER	BB	SO
1986	—Spartanburg (SAL)	1	6	.143	5.83	14	9	1	0	0	58⅔	68	44	38	34	49
	—Utica (N.Y.-Penn)	5	4	.556	2.67	10	10	2	0	0	70⅔	65	30	21	18	43
	—Clearwater (FSL)	1	2	.333	3.20	4	4	1	1	0	25⅓	20	10	9	15	19
1987	—Reading (Eastern)	0	3	.000	7.78	5	4	0	0	0	19⅔	22	19	17	16	12
	—Clearwater (FSL)	13	4	.765	2.48	21	21	5	2	0	137⅔	127	46	38	32	73
1988	—Reading (Eastern)	3	4	.429	2.86	10	9	1	1	0	56⅔	52	25	18	22	39
	—Maine (Int'l)	8	8	.500	3.67	19	18	1	0	0	110⅓	109	51	45	31	87
	—Philadelphia (N.L.).....	0	0	...	1.69	5	0	0	0	0	5⅓	7	1	1	1	6
1989	—Scran./W.B. (Int'l).....	3	1	.750	2.16	23	0	0	0	6	33⅓	27	8	8	23	23
	—Reading (Eastern)	6	6	.500	3.26	23	10	1	1	1	85⅔	71	36	31	23	82
1990	—Scran./W.B. (Int'l).....	5	4	.556	4.76	45	9	0	0	2	96⅓	96	56	51	44	94
1991	—Indianapolis (A.A.)■ ..	6	7	.462	2.97	18	17	3	1	0	121⅓	83	42	40	39	91
	—Chunichi (Jp. Cn.)■....	0	0	...	9.00	1	...	...	...	0	1	...	...	1	0	0
1992	—Ind.-Nash. (A.A.)■.....	8	2	*.800	1.89	52	2	0	0	6	95	66	25	20	44	112
	—Montreal (N.L.)	0	0	...	14.14	5	0	0	0	0	7	15	11	11	5	11
1993	—Indianapolis (A.A.).....	4	2	.667	4.45	21	1	0	0	2	30⅓	25	16	15	17	28
	—Colo.-Cin. (N.L.)■	2	2	.500	4.30	29	0	0	0	2	46	44	24	22	16	43
Major league totals (3 years)	..	2	2	.500	5.25	39	0	0	0	2	58⅓	66	36	34	22	60

SHABAZZ, BASIL

OF, CARDINALS

PERSONAL: Born January 31, 1972, in Little Rock, Ark.... 6-0/190.... Throws right, bats right.... Full name: Basil Bashir Shabazz.... Name pronounced buh-ZEEL.
HIGH SCHOOL: Pine Bluff (Ark.).
TRANSACTIONS/CAREER NOTES: Selected by St. Louis Cardinals organization in third round of free-agent draft (June 3, 1991).... On disabled list (June 11-23 and June 30, 1993-remainder of season).
STATISTICAL NOTES: Tied for Appalachian League lead in caught stealing with 11 in 1992.

				BATTING											FIELDING			
Year	Team (League)	Pos.	G	AB	R	H	2B	3B	HR	RBI	Avg.	BB	SO	SB	PO	A	E	Avg.
1991	—Johns. City (App.)....	OF	40	117	18	24	3	0	0	11	.205	15	38	4	57	5	6	.912
1992	—Johns. City (App.)....	OF	56	223	33	51	7	2	3	20	.229	28	75	*43	102	3	5	.955
1993	—Springfield (Midw.) ..	OF	64	239	44	71	12	2	4	18	.297	29	66	29	107	5	7	.941

SHARPERSON, MIKE

2B/3B

PERSONAL: Born October 4, 1961, in Orangeburg, S.C.... 6-3/208.... Throws right, bats right.... Full name: Michael Tyrone Sharperson.
HIGH SCHOOL: Wilkinson (Orangeburg, S.C.).
COLLEGE: DeKalb Community College South (Ga.).
TRANSACTIONS/CAREER NOTES: Selected by Pittsburgh Pirates organization in 41st round of free-agent draft (June 5, 1979).... Selected by Montreal Expos organization in secondary phase of free-agent draft (January 8, 1980).... Selected by Detroit Tigers organization in fourth round of free-agent draft (January 13, 1981).... Selected by Toronto Blue Jays organization in secondary phase of free-agent draft (June 8, 1981).... On disabled list (August 14, 1983-remainder of season).... Traded by Blue Jays organization to Los Angeles Dodgers for P Juan Guzman (September 22, 1987).... On disabled list (May 8-30, 1991).... Granted free agency (October 8, 1993).
STATISTICAL NOTES: Led Southern League second basemen with 775 total chances and 103 double plays in 1984.... Led International League second basemen with 286 putouts and 666 total chances in 1985.... Tied for International League lead in double plays by third baseman with 16 in 1987.

				BATTING											FIELDING			
Year	Team (League)	Pos.	G	AB	R	H	2B	3B	HR	RBI	Avg.	BB	SO	SB	PO	A	E	Avg.
1982	—Florence (S. Atl.)......	SS-3B	111	326	51	83	16	1	3	33	.255	59	59	28	136	261	33	.923
1983	—Kinston (Carolina) ...	S-3-2-C	90	361	55	96	8	1	5	41	.266	39	65	20	148	286	19	.958
1984	—Knoxville (South.)....	2B	140	542	86	165	25	7	4	48	.304	48	66	20	*331	*423	21	.973
1985	—Syracuse (Int'l)	2B-SS	134	*536	*86	*155	19	*7	1	59	.289	71	75	14	†291	372	17	.975
1986	—Syracuse (Int'l)	2B-3B	133	519	*86	*150	18	*9	4	45	.289	69	67	17	258	376	18	.972
1987	—Toronto (A.L.)...........	2B	32	96	4	20	4	1	0	9	.208	7	15	2	64	69	4	.971
	—Syracuse (Int'l)	3B-2B	88	338	67	101	21	5	5	26	.299	40	41	13	81	152	8	.967
	—Los Angeles (N.L.)■.	3B-2B	10	33	7	9	2	0	0	1	.273	4	5	0	4	28	1	.970
1988	—Albuquerque (PCL)..	2B-3B-SS	56	210	55	67	10	2	0	30	.319	31	25	19	88	173	12	.956
	—Los Angeles (N.L.) ...	2B-3B-SS	46	59	8	16	1	0	0	4	.271	1	12	0	19	31	2	.962
1989	—Albuquerque (PCL)..	2B-3B-SS	98	359	81	111	15	7	3	48	.309	66	46	17	114	250	14	.963
	—Los Angeles (N.L.) ...	2-1-3-S	27	28	2	7	3	0	0	5	.250	4	7	0	11	8	0	1.000
1990	—Los Angeles (N.L.) ...	3-S-2-1	129	357	42	106	14	2	3	36	.297	45	39	15	152	193	15	.958
1991	—Los Angeles (N.L.) ...	3-S-1-2	105	216	24	60	11	2	2	20	.278	25	24	1	89	107	4	.980
1992	—Los Angeles (N.L.) ...	2B-3B-SS	128	317	48	95	21	0	3	36	.300	47	33	2	120	220	13	.963
1993	—Los Angeles (N.L.) ...	2-3-S-0-1	73	90	13	23	4	0	2	10	.256	5	17	2	29	38	5	.931
American League totals (1 year)		....	32	96	4	20	4	1	0	9	.208	7	15	2	64	69	4	.971
National League totals (7 years)		....	518	1100	144	316	56	4	10	112	.287	131	137	20	424	625	40	.963
Major league totals (7 years)		....	550	1196	148	336	60	5	10	121	.281	138	152	22	488	694	44	.964

CHAMPIONSHIP SERIES RECORD

				BATTING											FIELDING			
Year	Team (League)	Pos.	G	AB	R	H	2B	3B	HR	RBI	Avg.	BB	SO	SB	PO	A	E	Avg.
1988	—Los Angeles (N.L.) ...	PH-SS-3B	2	1	0	0	0	0	0	1	.000	1	0	0	1	0	0	1.000

ALL-STAR GAME RECORD

Year	League	Pos.	AB	R	H	2B	3B	HR	RBI	Avg.	BB	SO	SB	PO	A	E	Avg.
			BATTING											FIELDING			
1992	—National	3B	1	0	0	0	0	0	0	.000	0	1	0	1	0	0	1.000

SHAVE, JON

2B/SS, RANGERS

PERSONAL: Born November 4, 1967, in Waycross, Ga.... 6-0/180.... Throws right, bats right.... Full name: Jonathan Taylor Shave.
HIGH SCHOOL: Fernandina Beach (Fla.).
COLLEGE: Mississippi State.
TRANSACTIONS/CAREER NOTES: Selected by California Angels organization in ninth round of free-agent draft (June 2, 1986).... Selected by Toronto Blue Jays organization in 56th round of free-agent draft (June 5, 1989).... Selected by Texas Rangers organization in fifth round of free-agent draft (June 4, 1990).
STATISTICAL NOTES: Led Texas League second basemen with 233 putouts, 19 errors, 530 total chances and 63 double plays in 1992.

Year	Team (League)	Pos.	G	AB	R	H	2B	3B	HR	RBI	Avg.	BB	SO	SB	PO	A	E	Avg.
				BATTING											FIELDING			
1990	—Butte (Pioneer)	SS	64	250	41	88	9	3	2	42	.352	25	27	21	112	159	22	.925
1991	—Gastonia (S. Atl.)	SS-2B	55	213	29	62	11	0	2	24	.291	20	26	11	103	152	23	.917
	—Charlotte (Fla. St.)	SS-2B	56	189	17	43	4	1	1	20	.228	18	31	7	93	120	15	.934
1992	—Tulsa (Texas)	2B-SS	118	453	57	130	23	5	2	36	.287	37	59	6	†251	314	†21	.964
1993	—Okla. City (A.A.)	2B-SS	100	399	58	105	17	3	4	41	.263	20	60	4	190	277	13	.973
	—Texas (A.L.)	SS-2B	17	47	3	15	2	0	0	7	.319	0	8	1	22	37	3	.952
Major league totals (1 year)			17	47	3	15	2	0	0	7	.319	0	8	1	22	37	3	.952

S

SHAW, CURTIS

P, ATHLETICS

PERSONAL: Born August 16, 1969, in Charlotte, N.C.... 6-1/190.... Throws left, bats left.... Full name: Malcolm Curtis Shaw.
HIGH SCHOOL: Bartlesville (Okla.).
COLLEGE: Kansas.
TRANSACTIONS/CAREER NOTES: Selected by Oakland Athletics organization in second round of free-agent draft (June 4, 1990); pick received as compensation for Detroit Tigers signing Type B free agent Tony Phillips.... On disabled list (August 29-September 16, 1991).
STATISTICAL NOTES: Led Southern League with 14 hit batsmen and tied for lead with 19 wild pitches in 1993.

Year	Team (League)	W	L	Pct.	ERA	G	GS	CG	ShO	Sv.	IP	H	R	ER	BB	SO
1990	—S. Oregon (N'west)	4	6	.400	3.53	17	9	0	0	0	66⅓	53	28	26	30	74
1991	—Madison (Midwest)	7	5	.583	2.60	20	20	1	0	0	100⅓	82	45	29	79	87
1992	—Modesto (Calif.)	13	4	.765	3.05	27	27	2	0	0	177⅓	146	71	60	98	*154
1993	—Huntsville (South.)	6	*16	.273	4.93	28	•28	2	1	0	151⅔	141	98	83	*89	132

SHAW, JEFF

P, EXPOS

PERSONAL: Born July 7, 1966, in Washington Court House, O.... 6-2/200.... Throws right, bats right.... Full name: Jeffrey Lee Shaw.
HIGH SCHOOL: Washington Senior (Washington Court House, O.).
COLLEGE: Cuyahoga Community College-Western Campus (O.) and Rio Grande (O.) College.
TRANSACTIONS/CAREER NOTES: Selected by Cleveland Indians organization in first round (first pick overall) of free-agent draft (January 14, 1986).... Granted free agency (October 16, 1992).... Signed by Omaha, Kansas City Royals organization (November 9, 1992).... Traded by Royals organization with C Tim Spehr to Montreal Expos organization for P Mark Gardner and P Doug Piatt (December 9, 1992).
STATISTICAL NOTES: Led Eastern League with 14 hit batsmen in 1989.... Tied for Pacific Coast League lead with 10 hit batsmen in 1992.

Year	Team (League)	W	L	Pct.	ERA	G	GS	CG	ShO	Sv.	IP	H	R	ER	BB	SO
1986	—Batavia (NY-Penn)	8	4	.667	2.44	14	12	3	1	0	88⅔	79	32	24	35	71
1987	—Waterloo (Midw.)	11	11	.500	3.52	28	*28	6	*4	0	184⅓	192	89	72	56	117
1988	—Williamsport (East.)	5	*19	.208	3.63	27	•27	6	1	0	163⅔	•173	*94	66	75	61
1989	—Cant./Akr. (East.)	7	10	.412	3.62	30	22	6	3	0	154⅓	134	84	62	67	95
1990	—Colo. Springs (PCL)	10	3	.769	4.29	17	16	4	0	0	98⅔	98	54	47	52	55
	—Cleveland (A.L.)	3	4	.429	6.66	12	9	0	0	0	48⅔	73	38	36	20	25
1991	—Colo. Springs (PCL)	6	3	.667	4.64	12	12	1	0	0	75⅔	77	47	39	25	55
	—Cleveland (A.L.)	0	5	.000	3.36	29	1	0	0	1	72⅓	72	34	27	27	31
1992	—Colo. Springs (PCL)	10	5	.667	4.76	25	24	1	0	0	155	174	88	82	45	84
	—Cleveland (A.L.)	0	1	.000	8.22	2	1	0	0	0	7⅔	7	7	7	4	3
1993	—Ottawa (Int'l)■	0	0	...	0.00	2	1	0	0	0	4	5	0	0	2	1
	—Montreal (N.L.)	2	7	.222	4.14	55	8	0	0	0	95⅔	91	47	44	32	50
A.L. totals (3 years)		3	10	.231	4.90	43	11	0	0	1	128⅔	152	79	70	51	59
N.L. totals (1 year)		2	7	.222	4.14	55	8	0	0	0	95⅔	91	47	44	32	50
Major league totals (4 years)		5	17	.227	4.57	98	19	0	0	1	224⅓	243	126	114	83	109

SHEAFFER, DANNY

C, ROCKIES

PERSONAL: Born August 2, 1961, in Jacksonville, Fla.... 6-0/190.... Throws right, bats right.... Full name: Danny Todd Sheaffer.
HIGH SCHOOL: Red Land (Lewisberry, Pa.).
COLLEGE: Clemson and Harrisburg (Pa.) Junior College.
TRANSACTIONS/CAREER NOTES: Selected by Boston Red Sox organization in first round (20th pick overall) of free-agent draft (January 13, 1981).... On disabled list (May 3-14, 1982).... Granted free agency (October 15, 1988).... Signed by Colorado Springs, Cleveland Indians organization (November 15, 1988).... Granted free agency (October 15, 1989).... Signed by Buffalo, Pittsburgh Pirates organization (November 25, 1989).... Granted free agency (October 15, 1990).... Signed by Min-

nesota Twins organization (December 20, 1990).... Granted free agency (October 15, 1992).... Signed by Colorado Rockies organization (October 29, 1992).
STATISTICAL NOTES: Led Florida State League with 14 errors in 1982.... Led Pacific Coast League catchers with .994 fielding percentage in 1992.

			BATTING												FIELDING			
Year	Team (League)	Pos.	G	AB	R	H	2B	3B	HR	RBI	Avg.	BB	SO	SB	PO	A	E	Avg.
1981	—Elmira (N.Y.-Penn)..	C	62	198	39	57	9	0	8	29	.288	23	38	2	220	35	5	.981
	—Bristol (Eastern)......	C-2B	8	12	0	0	0	0	0	1	.000	0	3	0	16	3	0	1.000
1982	—Winter Haven (FSL)..	C-3B	82	260	20	65	4	0	5	25	.250	18	37	2	316	51	†16	.958
1983	—Winst.-Salem (Car.)..	C-1B-OF	112	380	48	105	14	2	15	63	.276	36	50	1	427	44	6	.987
1984	—New Britain (East.)..	C-OF	93	303	33	73	10	0	1	27	.241	29	31	2	438	47	6	.988
1985	—Pawtucket (Int'l)......	C	77	243	24	63	9	0	8	33	.259	17	35	0	289	18	6	.981
1986	—Pawtucket (Int'l)......	C-OF	79	265	34	90	16	1	2	30	.340	10	24	9	380	39	5	.988
1987	—Boston (A.L.)...........	C	25	66	5	8	1	0	1	5	.121	0	14	0	121	5	3	.977
	—Pawtucket (Int'l)......	C-1B-OF	69	242	32	62	13	2	2	25	.256	6	29	6	346	32	5	.987
1988	—Pawtucket (Int'l)......	C-1-3-O	98	299	30	82	17	1	1	28	.274	18	32	20	509	58	6	.990
1989	—Colo. Springs (PCL)■	OF-3B	107	401	62	113	26	2	3	47	.282	24	39	6	136	11	10	.936
	—Cleveland (A.L.).......	3B-OF	7	16	1	1	0	0	0	0	.063	2	2	0	4	0	0	1.000
1990	—Buffalo (A.A.)■........	C-OF-1B	55	144	23	35	7	0	2	19	.243	11	14	4	163	10	5	.972
1991	—Portland (PCL)■.......	C-1-O-2	93	330	46	100	14	2	1	43	.303	26	35	2	448	39	11	.978
1992	—Portland (PCL).........	C-OF-3B	116	442	54	122	23	4	5	56	.276	21	36	3	605	66	4	†.994
1993	—Colorado (N.L.)■.......	C-1-O-3	82	216	26	60	9	1	4	32	.278	8	15	2	337	32	2	.995
American League totals (2 years)			32	82	6	9	1	0	1	5	.110	2	16	0	125	5	3	.977
National League totals (1 year)			82	216	26	60	9	1	4	32	.278	8	15	2	337	32	2	.995
Major league totals (3 years)			114	298	32	69	10	1	5	37	.232	10	31	2	462	37	5	.990

SHEETS, LARRY

OF/1B

PERSONAL: Born December 6, 1959, in Staunton, Va.... 6-3/236.... Throws right, bats left.... Full name: Larry Kent Sheets.
HIGH SCHOOL: Robert E. Lee (Staunton, Va.).
COLLEGE: Eastern Mennonite College, Va. (degree in health and physical education, 1986).
TRANSACTIONS/CAREER NOTES: Selected by Baltimore Orioles organization in second round of free-agent draft (June 6, 1978); pick received as compensation for New York Mets signing free agent Elliott Maddox.... On Miami suspended list (May 1-August 29, 1979).... On Bluefield restricted list (June 18-23, 1980).... On restricted list (April 14-May 28 and June 18, 1981-remainder of season).... On Rochester suspended list (April 13, 1982); then transferred to restricted list (April 23-May 13, 1982).... On Hagerstown disabled list (August 23, 1982-remainder of season).... On disabled list (June 30-July 17, 1986).... Traded by Orioles to Detroit Tigers for IF Mike Brumley (January 10, 1990).... Granted free agency (November 5, 1990).... Signed by Edmonton, California Angels organization (October 14, 1991).... Released by Edmonton (November 1, 1991).... Signed by Yokohama Taiyo Whales of Japan Central League (November 20, 1991).... Signed as free agent by Denver, Milwaukee Brewers organization (November 2, 1992).... Traded by Brewers to Seattle Mariners for a player to be named later (September 2, 1993); deal settled in cash.... Released by Mariners (October 4, 1993).
STATISTICAL NOTES: Led International League outfielders with five double plays in 1984.... Led American Association with 10 sacrifice flies in 1993.

			BATTING												FIELDING			
Year	Team (League)	Pos.	G	AB	R	H	2B	3B	HR	RBI	Avg.	BB	SO	SB	PO	A	E	Avg.
1978	—Bluefield (Appal.).....	OF-1B	67	225	32	60	9	2	11	*48	.267	32	46	4	121	8	4	.970
1979	—Bluefield (Appal.).....	OF	3	12	2	4	2	0	0	2	.333	0	0	0	1	0	0	1.000
1980	—Bluefield (Appal.).....	OF	37	124	29	47	9	1	*14	47	.379	17	14	1	40	3	2	.956
	—Charlotte (South.)....	OF	13	48	1	9	4	0	0	5	.188	4	18	0	4	1	0	1.000
1981	—..................................		Did not play.															
1982	—Hagerstown (Car.)...	OF	88	324	46	96	21	0	18	59	.296	27	66	4	123	5	6	.955
1983	—Charlotte (South.)....	OF-1B	138	503	72	145	*37	3	•25	87	.288	0	4	4	256	15	7	.975
	—Rochester (Int'l).......	OF	3	13	1	2	1	0	0	2	.154	45	102	0	5	0	1	.833
1984	—Rochester (Int'l).......	OF	134	431	76	130	26	4	13	67	.302	54	73	1	201	*19	2	.991
	—Baltimore (A.L.)........	OF	8	16	3	7	1	0	1	2	.438	1	3	0	12	1	0	1.000
1985	—Baltimore (A.L.)........	OF-1B	113	328	43	86	8	0	17	50	.262	28	52	2	12	1	1	.929
1986	—Baltimore (A.L.)........	O-1-3-C	112	338	42	92	17	1	18	60	.272	21	56	2	90	8	3	.970
1987	—Baltimore (A.L.)........	OF-1B	135	469	74	148	23	0	31	94	.316	31	67	3	243	7	7	.973
1988	—Baltimore (A.L.)........	OF-1B	136	452	38	104	19	1	10	47	.230	42	72	6	159	12	4	.977
1989	—Baltimore (A.L.)........	DH	102	304	33	74	12	1	7	33	.243	26	58	3	...	...	...	...
1990	—Detroit (A.L.)■.........	OF	131	360	40	94	17	2	10	52	.261	24	42	2	98	7	2	.981
1991	—..................................		Out of organized baseball.															
1992	—Yoko. Tai. (Jp. Cn.)■	1B	131	487	61	150	...	...	26	*100	.308	40	59	1	...	...	...	...
1993	—New Orleans (A.A.)■	OF-1B	127	457	60	128	28	1	18	98	.280	31	52	3	193	13	1	.995
	—Seattle (A.L.)■.........	OF	11	17	0	2	1	0	0	1	.118	2	1	0	1	0	0	1.000
Major league totals (8 years)			748	2284	273	607	98	5	94	339	.266	175	351	18	615	36	17	.975

SHEFFIELD, GARY

OF/3B, MARLINS

PERSONAL: Born November 18, 1968, in Tampa, Fla.... 5-11/190.... Throws right, bats right.... Full name: Gary Antonian Sheffield.... Nephew of Dwight Gooden, pitcher, New York Mets.
HIGH SCHOOL: Hillsborough (Tampa, Fla.).
TRANSACTIONS/CAREER NOTES: Selected by Milwaukee Brewers organization in first round (sixth pick overall) of free-agent draft (June 2, 1986).... On Milwaukee disabled list (July 14-September 9, 1989).... On suspended list (August 31-September 3, 1990).... On disabled list (June 15-July 3 and July 25, 1991-remainder of season).... Traded by Brewers with P Geoff Kellogg to San Diego Padres for P Ricky Bones, IF Jose Valentin and OF Matt Mieske (March 27, 1992).... Traded by Padres with P Rich Rodriguez to Florida Marlins for P Trevor Hoffman, P Jose Martinez and P Andres Berumen (June 24, 1993).... On suspended list (July 9-12, 1993).
HONORS: Named Minor League co-Player of the Year by THE SPORTING NEWS (1988).... Named Major League Player of the

Year by THE SPORTING NEWS (1992).... Named N.L. Comeback Player of the Year by THE SPORTING NEWS (1992).... Named third baseman on THE SPORTING NEWS N.L. All-Star team (1992).... Named third baseman on THE SPORTING NEWS N.L. Silver Slugger team (1992).

STATISTICAL NOTES: Led Pioneer League shortstops with 34 double plays in 1986.... Led California League shortstops with 77 double plays in 1987.... Led N.L. with 323 total bases in 1992.

			BATTING												FIELDING			
Year	**Team (League)**	**Pos.**	**G**	**AB**	**R**	**H**	**2B**	**3B**	**HR**	**RBI**	**Avg.**	**BB**	**SO**	**SB**	**PO**	**A**	**E**	**Avg.**
1986	—Helena (Pioneer)	SS	57	222	53	81	12	2	15	*71	.365	20	14	14	97	149	24	.911
1987	—Stockton (Calif.)	SS	129	469	84	130	23	3	17	*103	.277	81	49	25	235	345	39	.937
1988	—El Paso (Texas)	SS-3B-OF	77	296	70	93	19	3	19	65	.314	35	41	5	130	206	23	.936
	—Denver (A.A.)	3B-SS	57	212	42	73	9	5	9	54	.344	21	22	8	54	97	8	.950
	—Milwaukee (A.L.)	SS	24	80	12	19	1	0	4	12	.238	7	7	3	39	48	3	.967
1989	—Milwaukee (A.L.)	SS-3B	95	368	34	91	18	0	5	32	.247	27	33	10	100	238	16	.955
	—Denver (A.A.)	SS	7	29	3	4	1	1	0	0	.138	2	0	0	2	6	0	1.000
1990	—Milwaukee (A.L.)	3B	125	487	67	143	30	1	10	67	.294	44	41	25	98	254	25	.934
1991	—Milwaukee (A.L.)	3B	50	175	25	34	12	2	2	22	.194	19	15	5	29	65	8	.922
1992	—San Diego (N.L.)■	3B	146	557	87	184	34	3	33	100	*.330	48	40	5	99	299	16	.961
1993	—S.D.-Florida (N.L.)■	3B	140	494	67	145	20	5	20	73	.294	47	64	17	79	225	*34	.899
	American League totals (4 years)		294	1110	138	287	61	3	21	133	.259	97	96	43	266	605	52	.944
	National League totals (2 years)		286	1051	154	329	54	8	53	173	.313	95	104	22	178	524	50	.934
	Major league totals (6 years)		580	2161	292	616	115	11	74	306	.285	192	200	65	444	1129	102	.939

ALL-STAR GAME RECORD

			BATTING											FIELDING			
Year	**League**	**Pos.**	**AB**	**R**	**H**	**2B**	**3B**	**HR**	**RBI**	**Avg.**	**BB**	**SO**	**SB**	**PO**	**A**	**E**	**Avg.**
1992	—National	3B	2	0	0	0	0	0	0	.000	0	0	0	0	0	0	...
1993	—National	3B	3	1	2	0	0	1	2	.667	0	0	0	0	2	0	1.000
	All-Star Game totals (2 years)		5	1	2	0	0	1	2	.400	0	0	0	0	2	0	1.000

SHELTON, BEN

1B/OF, EXPOS

PERSONAL: Born September 21, 1969, in Chicago.... 6-3/210.... Throws left, bats right.... Full name: Benjamin Davis Shelton.

HIGH SCHOOL: River Forest (Oak Park, Ill.).

TRANSACTIONS/CAREER NOTES: Selected by Pittsburgh Pirates organization in second round of free-agent draft (June 2, 1987).... On suspended list (August 26-September 6, 1992).... Released by Pirates (November 15, 1993).... Signed by Montreal Expos organization (December 16, 1993).

			BATTING												FIELDING			
Year	**Team (League)**	**Pos.**	**G**	**AB**	**R**	**H**	**2B**	**3B**	**HR**	**RBI**	**Avg.**	**BB**	**SO**	**SB**	**PO**	**A**	**E**	**Avg.**
1987	—GC Pirates (GCL)	1B	38	119	22	34	8	3	4	16	.286	12	48	7	290	15	3	.990
1988	—Princeton (Appal.)	1B	63	204	34	45	7	3	4	20	.221	42	82	8	475	29	*14	.973
	—Augusta (S. Atl.)	1B	38	128	25	25	2	2	5	20	.195	30	72	3	192	12	6	.971
1989	—Augusta (S. Atl.)	1B	122	386	67	95	16	4	8	50	.246	87	132	18	976	69	*27	.975
1990	—Salem (Carolina)	1B	109	320	44	66	10	2	10	36	.206	55	116	1	923	55	*18	.982
1991	—Salem (Carolina)	1B-OF	65	203	37	53	10	2	14	56	.261	45	65	4	444	43	7	.986
	—Carolina (South.)	1B-OF	55	169	19	39	8	3	1	19	.231	29	57	2	463	27	9	.982
1992	—Carolina (South.)	1B	115	368	57	86	17	0	10	51	.234	68	117	4	698	56	8	.990
1993	—Buffalo (A.A.)	1B-OF	65	173	25	48	8	1	5	22	.277	24	44	0	195	15	5	.977
	—Pittsburgh (N.L.)	OF-1B	15	24	3	6	1	0	2	7	.250	3	3	0	17	2	1	.950
	Major league totals (1 year)		15	24	3	6	1	0	2	7	.250	3	3	0	17	2	1	.950

SHEPHERD, KEITH

P, ROCKIES

PERSONAL: Born January 21, 1968, in Wabash, Ind.... 6-2/197.... Throws right, bats right.... Full name: Keith Wayne Shepherd.

HIGH SCHOOL: Wabash (Ind.).

TRANSACTIONS/CAREER NOTES: Selected by Pittsburgh Pirates organization in 11th round of free-agent draft (June 2, 1986).... Selected by Omaha, Kansas City Royals organization, from Salem, Pirates organization, in Rule 5 minor league draft (December 6, 1988).... Released by Royals organization (July 24, 1989).... Signed by Cleveland Indians organization (July 24, 1989).... Loaned by Indians organization to Reno, independent (April 4, 1990).... On Reno suspended list (May 2-June 11, 1990).... Returned to Indians organization (June 11, 1990).... Released by Indians organization (October 22, 1990).... Signed by Chicago White Sox organization (March 12, 1991).... Traded by White Sox to Philadelphia Phillies for IF Dale Sveum (August 10, 1992).... Selected by Colorado Rockies in second round (50th pick overall) of expansion draft (November 17, 1992).... On suspended list (June 21-29, 1993).

Year	**Team (League)**	**W**	**L**	**Pct.**	**ERA**	**G**	**GS**	**CG**	**ShO**	**Sv.**	**IP**	**H**	**R**	**ER**	**BB**	**SO**
1986	—GC Pirates (GCL)	0	4	.000	6.06	8	2	0	0	0	16⅓	16	17	11	15	12
1987	—Watertown (NYP)	5	2	.714	4.20	17	13	1	1	0	70⅔	66	40	33	42	57
1988	—Augusta (S. Atl.)	7	3	.700	4.02	16	16	1	1	0	85	71	45	38	50	49
	—Salem (Carolina)	2	3	.400	5.83	8	5	0	0	0	29⅓	26	24	19	29	15
1989	—Baseball City (FSL)■	1	7	.125	4.94	11	10	0	0	0	47⅓	45	33	26	32	20
	—Kinston (Carolina)■	1	2	.333	2.86	8	2	0	0	0	28⅓	25	11	9	15	23
1990	—Reno (California)■	1	4	.200	5.40	25	5	0	0	0	25	22	25	15	18	16
	—Watertown (NYP)■	3	3	.500	2.48	24	0	0	0	3	54⅓	41	22	15	29	55
1991	—South Bend (Mid.)■	1	2	.333	0.51	31	0	0	0	10	35⅓	17	4	2	19	38
	—Sarasota (Fla. St.)	1	1	.500	2.72	18	0	0	0	2	39⅔	33	16	12	20	24
1992	—Birm. (Southern)	3	3	.500	2.14	40	0	0	0	7	71⅓	50	19	17	20	64
	—Reading (Eastern)■	0	1	.000	2.78	4	3	0	0	0	22⅔	17	7	7	4	9
	—Philadelphia (N.L.)	1	1	.500	3.27	12	0	0	0	2	22	19	10	8	6	10
1993	—Colo. Springs (PCL)■	3	6	.333	6.78	37	1	0	0	8	67⅔	90	61	51	44	57
	—Colorado (N.L.)	1	3	.250	6.98	14	1	0	0	1	19⅓	26	16	15	4	7
	Major league totals (2 years)	2	4	.333	5.01	26	1	0	0	3	41⅓	45	26	23	10	17

SHERMAN, DARRELL

OF, ROCKIES

PERSONAL: Born December 4, 1967, in Los Angeles. . . . 5-9/160. . . . Throws left, bats left. . . . Full name: Darrell Edward Sherman.
HIGH SCHOOL: Lynwood, Calif.
COLLEGE: Cerritos College (Calif.) and Long Beach State.
TRANSACTIONS/CAREER NOTES: Selected by San Diego Padres organization in sixth round of free-agent draft (June 5, 1989). . . . Selected by Baltimore Orioles from Padres organization in Rule 5 major league draft (December 9, 1991). . . . Returned to Padres (March 27, 1992). . . . Claimed on waivers by Colorado Rockies (November 18, 1993).
STATISTICAL NOTES: Led Northwest League in being hit by pitch with 13 in 1989. . . . Led California League outfielders with 328 total chances in 1990. . . . Led Texas League outfielders with 342 total chances in 1991. . . . Led Pacific Coast League outfielders with six double plays in 1992.

			BATTING												FIELDING			
Year	Team (League)	Pos.	G	AB	R	H	2B	3B	HR	RBI	Avg.	BB	SO	SB	PO	A	E	Avg.
1989	—Spokane (N'west)	OF	70	258	*70	82	13	1	0	29	.318	58	29	*58	137	•9	3	.980
1990	—Riverside (Calif.)	OF	131	483	97	140	10	4	0	35	.290	89	51	74	*303	14	11	.966
	—Las Vegas (PCL)	OF	4	12	1	0	0	0	0	1	.000	1	2	1	5	1	0	1.000
1991	—Wichita (Texas)	OF	131	502	93	148	17	3	3	48	.295	74	28	43	*323	1	8	.976
1992	—Wichita (Texas)	OF	64	220	60	73	11	2	6	25	.332	40	25	26	135	7	2	.986
	—Las Vegas (PCL)	OF	71	269	48	77	8	1	3	22	.286	42	41	26	171	14	1	.995
1993	—San Diego (N.L.)	OF	37	63	8	14	1	0	0	2	.222	6	8	2	47	0	0	1.000
	—Las Vegas (PCL)	OF	82	272	52	72	8	2	0	11	.265	38	27	20	152	6	3	.981
Major league totals (1 year)			37	63	8	14	1	0	0	2	.222	6	8	2	47	0	0	1.000

S

SHIELDS, TOMMY

SS/3B, CUBS

PERSONAL: Born August 14, 1964, in Fairfax, Va. . . . 6-0/185. . . . Throws right, bats right. . . . Full name: Thomas Charles Shields.
HIGH SCHOOL: Conestoga (Berwyn, Pa.).
COLLEGE: Notre Dame (bachelor's degree in government and economics).
TRANSACTIONS/CAREER NOTES: Selected by Pittsburgh Pirates organization in 36th round of free-agent draft (June 3, 1985). . . . Selected by Pirates organization in 15th round of free-agent draft (June 2, 1986). . . . On Salem disabled list (April 1, 1987-entire season). . . . Traded by Pirates organization to Baltimore Orioles organization for a player to be named later (March 21, 1991); Pirates organization acquired IF Tony Beasley to complete deal (September 5, 1991). . . . Granted free agency (October 15, 1992). . . . Signed by Chicago Cubs (December 18, 1992).
STATISTICAL NOTES: Tied for Eastern League lead in being hit by pitch with nine in 1989. . . . Order of frequency of positions played in 1991: 3B-SS-OF-1B-2B-C-P. . . . Tied for International League lead in double plays by third baseman with 27 in 1992.
MISCELLANEOUS: Played all nine positions in game for Rochester (September 4, 1991).

			BATTING												FIELDING			
Year	Team (League)	Pos.	G	AB	R	H	2B	3B	HR	RBI	Avg.	BB	SO	SB	PO	A	E	Avg.
1986	—Watertown (NYP)	SS	43	153	25	44	6	1	4	25	.288	17	36	15	74	148	20	.917
	—Prin. William (Car.)	SS	30	112	17	31	7	1	1	12	.277	9	16	4	50	67	4	.967
1987	—							Did not play.										
1988	—Salem (Carolina)	SS	45	156	20	49	5	0	3	25	.314	16	24	10	62	112	7	.961
	—Harrisburg (East.)	SS	57	198	30	61	4	2	2	21	.308	14	25	7	78	146	12	.949
1989	—Harrisburg (East.)	3B-SS	123	417	66	120	13	4	5	47	.288	25	62	17	103	228	22	.938
1990	—Buffalo (A.A.)	3B-SS-2B	123	380	42	94	20	3	2	30	.247	21	72	12	127	260	29	.930
1991	—Rochester (Int'l)■	IF-O-C-P	116	412	69	119	18	3	6	52	.289	32	73	16	131	210	22	.939
1992	—Rochester (Int'l)	3B	121	431	58	130	23	3	10	59	.302	30	72	13	84	265	17	*.954
	—Baltimore (A.L.)	PR	2	0	0	0	0	0	0	0	...	0	0	0	...	...	...	...
1993	—Chicago (N.L.)■	3-2-0-1	20	34	4	6	1	0	0	1	.176	2	10	0	8	22	0	1.000
	—Iowa (Am. Assoc.)	SS-3B	84	314	48	90	16	1	9	48	.287	26	46	10	131	226	17	.955
American League totals (1 year)			2	0	0	0	0	0	0	0	...	0	0	0	...	...	...	...
National League totals (1 year)			20	34	4	6	1	0	0	1	.176	2	10	0	8	22	0	1.000
Major league totals (2 years)			22	34	4	6	1	0	0	1	.176	2	10	0	8	22	0	1.000

RECORD AS PITCHER

Year	Team (League)	W	L	Pct.	ERA	G	GS	CG	ShO	Sv.	IP	H	R	ER	BB	SO
1991	—Rochester (Int'l)	0	0	...	0.00	2	1	0	0	0	2	1	0	0	2	1

SHINALL, ZAK

P

PERSONAL: Born October 14, 1968, in St. Louis. . . . 6-3/215. . . . Throws right, bats right. . . . Full name: Zakary Sebastien Shinall.
HIGH SCHOOL: El Segundo (Calif.).
COLLEGE: El Camino College (Calif.).
TRANSACTIONS/CAREER NOTES: Selected by Los Angeles Dodgers organization in 29th round of free-agent draft (June 2, 1987). . . . Traded by Dodgers organization to Cleveland Indians organization for P Alan Walden (December 9, 1992). . . . On Charlotte disabled list (April 9-17, 1993). . . . Claimed on waivers by Seattle Mariners (April 26, 1993). . . . On Calgary disabled list (August 2-23, 1993). . . . Granted free agency (October 15, 1993).

Year	Team (League)	W	L	Pct.	ERA	G	GS	CG	ShO	Sv.	IP	H	R	ER	BB	SO
1987	—GC Dodgers (GCL)	1	2	.333	5.04	8	6	0	0	0	30⅓	27	17	17	15	29
1988	—Bakersfield (Calif.)	7	8	.467	4.22	28	19	1	1	0	113	90	65	53	104	63
1989	—Vero Beach (FSL)	5	7	.417	2.51	47	4	1	0	7	86	71	32	24	29	69
1990	—San Antonio (Tex.)	6	3	.667	3.55	20	15	0	0	0	91⅓	93	44	36	41	43
1991	—San Antonio (Tex.)	2	4	.333	2.96	25	5	0	0	9	54⅔	53	31	18	21	29
	—Albuquerque (PCL)	2	0	1.000	3.07	29	0	0	0	1	41	48	15	14	10	22
1992	—Albuquerque (PCL)	•13	5	.722	3.29	*64	0	0	0	6	82	91	38	30	37	46
1993	—Charlotte (Int'l)■	0	0	...	54.00	1	0	0	0	0	⅔	3	4	4	1	0
	—Calgary (PCL)■	2	1	.667	5.01	33	0	0	0	5	46⅔	55	29	26	18	25
	—Seattle (A.L.)	0	0	...	3.38	1	0	0	0	0	2⅔	4	1	1	2	0
Major league totals (1 year)		0	0	...	3.38	1	0	0	0	0	2⅔	4	1	1	2	0

SHIPLEY, CRAIG

SS/3B, PADRES

PERSONAL: Born January 7, 1963, in Sydney, Australia. . . . 6-1/190. . . . Throws right, bats right. . . . Full name: Craig Barry Shipley.
HIGH SCHOOL: Epping (Sydney, Australia).
COLLEGE: Alabama.

TRANSACTIONS/CAREER NOTES: Signed as free agent by Los Angeles Dodgers organization (May 28, 1984). . . . On Albuquerque disabled list (May 5-June 6, 1986). . . . Traded by Dodgers to New York Mets organization for C John Gibbons (April 1, 1988). . . . On disabled list (beginning of season-August 20, 1990). . . . Selected by San Diego Padres organization from Mets organization in Rule 5 minor league draft (December 2, 1990). . . . On Las Vegas disabled list (April 11-May 2, 1991). . . . On disabled list (May 6-23, 1993).

			BATTING												FIELDING			
Year	Team (League)	Pos.	G	AB	R	H	2B	3B	HR	RBI	Avg.	BB	SO	SB	PO	A	E	Avg.
1984	—Vero Beach (FSL)	SS	85	293	56	82	11	2	0	28	.280	52	44	18	137	216	17	.954
1985	—Albuquerque (PCL)	SS	124	414	50	100	9	2	0	30	.242	22	43	24	202	367	21	.964
1986	—Albuquerque (PCL)	SS	61	203	33	59	8	2	0	16	.291	11	23	6	99	173	18	.938
	—Los Angeles (N.L.)	SS-2B-3B	12	27	3	3	1	0	0	4	.111	2	5	0	16	18	3	.919
1987	—Albuquerque (PCL)	SS	49	139	17	31	6	1	1	15	.223	13	19	6	70	101	9	.950
	—San Antonio (Tex.)	3B	33	127	14	30	5	3	2	9	.236	5	17	2	19	56	3	.962
	—Los Angeles (N.L.)	SS-3B	26	35	3	9	1	0	0	2	.257	0	6	0	15	28	3	.935
1988	—Jackson (Texas)■	SS	89	335	41	88	14	3	6	41	.263	24	40	6	141	266	16	.962
	—Tidewater (Int'l)	2B-SS-3B	40	151	12	41	5	0	1	13	.272	4	15	0	54	110	2	.988
1989	—Tidewater (Int'l)	SS-3B-2B	44	131	6	27	1	0	2	9	.206	7	22	0	48	110	6	.963
	—New York (N.L.)	SS-3B	4	7	3	1	0	0	0	0	.143	0	1	0	0	4	0	1.000
1990	—Tidewater (Int'l)	PH-PR	4	3	1	0	0	0	0	0	.000	0	1	0	...	...	...	...
1991	—Las Vegas (PCL)■	SS-2B	65	230	27	69	9	5	5	34	.300	10	32	2	83	177	6	.977
	—San Diego (N.L.)	SS-2B	37	91	6	25	3	0	1	6	.275	2	14	0	39	70	7	.940
1992	—San Diego (N.L.)	SS-2B-3B	52	105	7	26	6	0	0	7	.248	2	21	1	52	74	1	.992
1993	—San Diego (N.L.)	S-3-2-O	105	230	25	54	9	0	4	22	.235	10	31	12	84	121	7	.967
Major league totals (6 years)			236	495	47	118	20	0	5	41	.238	16	78	13	206	315	21	.961

SHOUSE, BRIAN

P, PIRATES

PERSONAL: Born September 26, 1968, in Effingham, Ill. . . . 5-11/180. . . . Throws left, bats left. . . . Full name: Brian Douglas Shouse.
HIGH SCHOOL: Effingham (Ill.).
COLLEGE: Bradley.

TRANSACTIONS/CAREER NOTES: Selected by Pittsburgh Pirates organization in 13th round of free-agent draft (June 4, 1990).

Year	Team (League)	W	L	Pct.	ERA	G	GS	CG	ShO	Sv.	IP	H	R	ER	BB	SO
1990	—Welland (NYP)	4	3	.571	5.22	17	1	0	0	2	39⅔	50	27	23	7	39
1991	—Augusta (S. Atl.)	2	3	.400	3.19	26	0	0	0	8	31	22	13	11	9	32
	—Salem (Carolina)	2	1	.667	2.94	17	0	0	0	3	33⅔	35	12	11	15	25
1992	—Carolina (South.)	5	6	.455	2.44	59	0	0	0	4	77⅓	71	31	21	28	79
1993	—Buffalo (A.A.)	1	0	1.000	3.83	48	0	0	0	2	51⅔	54	24	22	17	25
	—Pittsburgh (N.L.)	0	0	...	9.00	6	0	0	0	0	4	7	4	4	2	3
Major league totals (1 year)		0	0	...	9.00	6	0	0	0	0	4	7	4	4	2	3

SHUMPERT, TERRY

2B, ROYALS

PERSONAL: Born August 16, 1966, in Paducah, Ky. . . . 5-11/185. . . . Throws right, bats right. . . . Full name: Terrance Darnell Shumpert.
HIGH SCHOOL: Paducah (Ky.) Tilghman.
COLLEGE: Kentucky.

TRANSACTIONS/CAREER NOTES: Selected by Kansas City Royals organization in second round of free-agent draft (June 2, 1987). . . . On disabled list (July 19-August 13, 1989). . . . On Kansas City disabled list (June 3-September 10, 1990); included rehabilitation assignment to Omaha (August 7-25). . . . On Kansas City disabled list (August 7-September 7, 1992).
STATISTICAL NOTES: Led American Association with 21 sacrifice hits in 1993.

			BATTING												FIELDING			
Year	Team (League)	Pos.	G	AB	R	H	2B	3B	HR	RBI	Avg.	BB	SO	SB	PO	A	E	Avg.
1987	—Eugene (N'west)	2B	48	186	38	54	16	1	4	22	.290	27	41	16	81	107	11	.945
1988	—Appleton (Midw.)	2B-OF	114	422	64	102	*37	2	7	38	.242	56	90	36	235	266	20	.962
1989	—Omaha (A.A.)	2B	113	355	54	88	29	2	4	22	.248	25	63	23	218	295	*22	.959
1990	—Omaha (A.A.)	2B	39	153	24	39	6	4	2	12	.255	14	28	18	72	95	7	.960
	—Kansas City (A.L.)	2B	32	91	7	25	6	1	0	8	.275	2	17	3	56	74	3	.977
1991	—Kansas City (A.L.)	2B	144	369	45	80	16	4	5	34	.217	30	75	17	249	368	16	.975
1992	—Kansas City (A.L.)	2B-SS	36	94	6	14	5	1	1	11	.149	3	17	2	50	77	4	.969
	—Omaha (A.A.)	2B-SS	56	210	23	42	12	0	1	14	.200	13	33	3	113	154	9	.967
1993	—Omaha (A.A.)	2B	111	413	70	124	29	1	14	59	.300	41	62	*36	190	303	14	.972
	—Kansas City (A.L.)	2B	8	10	0	1	0	0	0	0	.100	2	2	1	11	11	0	1.000
Major league totals (4 years)			220	564	58	120	27	6	6	53	.213	37	111	23	366	530	23	.975

SIDDALL, JOE

C, EXPOS

PERSONAL: Born October 25, 1967, in Windsor, Ont. . . . 6-1/195. . . . Throws right, bats left. . . . Full name: Joseph Todd Siddall.
HIGH SCHOOL: Assumption College (Windsor, Ont.).
COLLEGE: Central Michigan.

TRANSACTIONS/CAREER NOTES: Signed as free agent by Montreal Expos organization (August 5, 1987).
STATISTICAL NOTES: Led New York-Pennsylvania League catchers with seven double plays in 1988. . . . Led Midwest League with 19 passed balls in 1989.

			BATTING												FIELDING			
Year	Team (League)	Pos.	G	AB	R	H	2B	3B	HR	RBI	Avg.	BB	SO	SB	PO	A	E	Avg.
1988	—Jamestown (NYP)	C	53	178	18	38	5	3	1	16	.213	14	29	5	298	50	4	.989

Year	Team (League)	Pos.	G	AB	R	H	2B	3B	HR	RBI	Avg.	BB	SO	SB	PO	A	E	Avg.
			BATTING												FIELDING			
1989	—Rockford (Midw.)	C	98	313	36	74	15	2	4	38	.236	26	56	8	656	91	12	.984
1990	—W.P. Beach (FSL)	C	106	349	29	78	12	1	0	32	.223	20	55	6	644	*105	7	*.991
1991	—Harrisburg (East.)	C	76	235	28	54	6	1	1	23	.230	23	53	8	401	36	7	.984
1992	—Harrisburg (East.)	C	95	288	26	68	12	0	2	27	.236	29	55	4	199	28	1	.996
1993	—Ottawa (Int'l)	C-0-1-3	48	136	14	29	6	0	1	16	.213	19	33	2	221	33	5	.981
	—Montreal (N.L.)	C-OF-1B	19	20	0	2	1	0	0	1	.100	1	5	0	33	5	0	1.000
Major league totals (1 year)			19	20	0	2	1	0	0	1	.100	1	5	0	33	5	0	1.000

SIERRA, RUBEN

OF, ATHLETICS

PERSONAL: Born October 6, 1965, in Rio Piedras, Puerto Rico. . . . 6-1/200. . . . Throws right, bats both. . . . Full name: Ruben Angel Garcia Sierra.
HIGH SCHOOL: Dr. Secario Rosario (Rio Piedras, Puerto Rico).
TRANSACTIONS/CAREER NOTES: Signed as free agent by Texas Rangers organization (November 21, 1982). . . . Traded by Rangers with P Jeff Russell, P Bobby Witt and cash to Oakland Athletics for OF Jose Canseco (August 31, 1992). . . . Granted free agency (October 26, 1992). . . . Re-signed by A's (December 21, 1992).
HONORS: Named A.L. Player of the Year by THE SPORTING NEWS (1989). . . . Named outfielder on THE SPORTING NEWS A.L. All-Star team (1989). . . . Named outfielder on THE SPORTING NEWS A.L. Silver Slugger team (1989).
STATISTICAL NOTES: Switch-hit home runs in one game (September 13, 1986; August 27, 1988 and June 8, 1989). . . . Led A.L. with 12 sacrifice flies in 1987. . . . Led A.L. outfielders with six double plays in 1987. . . . Led A.L. with 344 total bases and .543 slugging percentage in 1989.
MISCELLANEOUS: Batted righthanded only (1983).

S

Year	Team (League)	Pos.	G	AB	R	H	2B	3B	HR	RBI	Avg.	BB	SO	SB	PO	A	E	Avg.
			BATTING												FIELDING			
1983	—GC Rangers (GCL)	OF	48	182	26	44	7	3	1	26	.242	16	38	3	67	6	4	.948
1984	—Burlington (Midw.)	OF	•138	482	55	127	33	5	6	75	.263	49	97	13	239	18	*20	.928
1985	—Tulsa (Texas)	OF	*137	*545	63	138	34	*8	13	74	.253	35	111	22	234	12	*15	.943
1986	—Okla. City (A.A.)	OF	46	189	31	56	11	2	9	41	.296	15	27	8	114	4	2	.983
	—Texas (A.L.)	OF	113	382	50	101	13	10	16	55	.264	22	65	7	200	7	6	.972
1987	—Texas (A.L.)	OF	158	*643	97	169	35	4	30	109	.263	39	114	16	272	•17	11	.963
1988	—Texas (A.L.)	OF	156	615	77	156	32	2	23	91	.254	44	91	18	310	11	7	.979
1989	—Texas (A.L.)	OF	•162	634	101	194	35	*14	29	*119	.306	43	82	8	313	13	9	.973
1990	—Texas (A.L.)	OF	159	608	70	170	37	2	16	96	.280	49	86	9	283	7	10	.967
1991	—Texas (A.L.)	OF	161	661	110	203	44	5	25	116	.307	56	91	16	305	15	7	.979
1992	—Texas-Oak. (A.L.)■	OF	151	601	83	167	34	7	17	87	.278	45	68	14	283	6	7	.976
1993	—Oakland (A.L.)	OF	158	630	77	147	23	5	22	101	.233	52	97	25	291	9	7	.977
Major league totals (8 years)			1218	4774	665	1307	253	49	178	774	.274	350	694	113	2257	85	64	.973

CHAMPIONSHIP SERIES RECORD

Year	Team (League)	Pos.	G	AB	R	H	2B	3B	HR	RBI	Avg.	BB	SO	SB	PO	A	E	Avg.
			BATTING												FIELDING			
1992	—Oakland (A.L.)	OF	6	24	4	8	2	1	1	7	.333	2	1	1	12	0	0	1.000

ALL-STAR GAME RECORD

Year	League	Pos.	AB	R	H	2B	3B	HR	RBI	Avg.	BB	SO	SB	PO	A	E	Avg.
			BATTING											FIELDING			
1989	—American	OF	3	1	2	0	0	0	1	.667	0	0	0	1	0	0	1.000
1991	—American	OF	2	0	0	0	0	0	0	.000	0	2	0	0	0	0	...
1992	—American	OF	2	2	1	0	0	1	2	.500	0	0	0	1	0	0	1.000
All-Star Game totals (3 years)			7	3	3	0	0	1	3	.429	0	2	0	2	0	0	1.000

SILVESTRI, DAVE

SS, YANKEES

PERSONAL: Born September 29, 1967, in St. Louis. . . . 6-0/196. . . . Throws right, bats right. . . . Full name: David Joseph Silvestri.
HIGH SCHOOL: Parkway Central (St. Louis).
COLLEGE: Missouri.
TRANSACTIONS/CAREER NOTES: Selected by Houston Astros in second round of free-agent draft (June 1, 1988); pick received as compensation for New York Yankees signing Type B free agent Jose Cruz. . . . Traded by Astros organization with a player to be named later to Yankees organization for IF Orlando Miller (March 13, 1990); Yankees acquired P Daven Bond to complete deal (June 11, 1990).
STATISTICAL NOTES: Led Florida State League shortstops with 221 putouts, 473 assists, 726 total chances and 93 double plays in 1989. . . . Led Carolina League shortstops with 622 total chances and 96 double plays in 1990. . . . Led Eastern League shortstops with 84 double plays in 1991.
MISCELLANEOUS: Member of 1988 U.S. Olympic baseball team.

Year	Team (League)	Pos.	G	AB	R	H	2B	3B	HR	RBI	Avg.	BB	SO	SB	PO	A	E	Avg.
			BATTING												FIELDING			
1989	—Osceola (Fla. St.)	SS-1B	129	437	67	111	20	1	2	50	.254	68	72	28	†238	†475	32	.957
1990	—Prin. William (Car.)■	SS	131	465	74	120	30	7	5	56	.258	77	90	37	218	*382	22	*.965
	—Alb./Colon. (East.)	SS	2	7	0	2	0	0	0	2	.286	0	1	0	3	5	1	.889
1991	—Alb./Colon. (East.)	SS	*140	512	*97	134	31	8	19	83	.262	83	126	20	218	*362	•32	.948
1992	—Columbus (Int'l)	SS	118	420	83	117	25	5	13	73	.279	58	110	19	*195	265	11	*.977
	—New York (A.L.)	SS	7	13	3	4	0	2	0	1	.308	0	3	0	4	12	2	.889
1993	—Columbus (Int'l)	SS-3B-OF	120	428	76	115	26	4	20	65	.269	68	127	6	183	299	16	.968
	—New York (A.L.)	SS-3B	7	21	4	6	1	0	1	4	.286	5	3	0	9	20	3	.906
Major league totals (2 years)			14	34	7	10	1	2	1	5	.294	5	6	0	13	32	5	.900

SINGLETON, DUANE

OF, BREWERS

PERSONAL: Born August 6, 1972, in Staten Island, N.Y. . . . 6-1/170. . . . Throws right, bats left. . . . Full name: Duane Earl Singleton.
HIGH SCHOOL: McKee Vocational & Technical (Staten Island, N.Y.).
TRANSACTIONS/CAREER NOTES: Selected by Milwaukee Brewers organization in fifth round of free-agent draft (June 4, 1990). . . . Loaned by Brewers organization to Salinas, independent (June 7-July 3, 1992).
STATISTICAL NOTES: Led Arizona League outfielders with two double plays in 1990. . . . Led California League outfielders with five double plays in 1992.

			BATTING											FIELDING			
Year	Team (League)	Pos.	G	AB	R	H	2B	3B	HR	RBI	Avg.	BB	SO	SB	PO	A	E	Avg.
1990	—Ariz. Brewers (Ar.) ...	OF	45	126	30	30	6	1	1	12	.238	*43	37	7	67	6	3	.961
1991	—Beloit (Midwest)	OF	101	388	57	112	13	7	3	44	.289	40	57	42	155	*25	6	.968
1992	—Salinas-Stock. (Cal.)■	OF	116	461	79	134	20	12	6	59	.291	45	77	38	227	*20	9	.965
1993	—El Paso (Texas)	OF	125	456	52	105	21	6	2	61	.230	34	90	23	288	*20	8	.975

SKINNER, JOEL

C, INDIANS

PERSONAL: Born February 21, 1961, in La Jolla, Calif. . . . 6-4/204. . . . Throws right, bats right. . . . Full name: Joel Patrick Skinner. . . . Son of Bob Skinner, outfielder/first baseman, Pittsburgh Pirates, Cincinnati Reds and St. Louis Cardinals (1954 and 1956-66); manager, Philadelphia Phillies (1968-69); and major league coach with four teams (1977-88).
HIGH SCHOOL: Mission Bay (Calif.).
COLLEGE: San Diego (Calif.) Mesa College.
TRANSACTIONS/CAREER NOTES: Selected by Pittsburgh Pirates organization in 36th round of free-agent draft (June 5, 1979). . . . On disabled list (June 1-13, 1981). . . . Selected by Chicago White Sox organization in player compensation pool draft (February 2, 1982); pick received as compensation for Philadelphia Phillies signing Type A free agent P Ed Farmer (January 28, 1982). . . . On Denver disabled list (July 23, 1984-remainder of season). . . . Traded by White Sox with OF/DH Ron Kittle and IF Wayne Tolleson to New York Yankees for C Ron Hassey, SS Carlos Martinez and a player to be named later (July 30, 1986); Yankees traded C Bill Lindsey to White Sox organization to complete deal (December 24, 1986). . . . Traded by Yankees with OF Turner Ward to Cleveland Indians for OF Mel Hall (March 19, 1989). . . . On Cleveland disabled list (April 1, 1992-entire season); included rehabilitation assignment to Canton/Akron (August 15-27). . . . On Cleveland disabled list (April 4, 1993-entire season); included rehabilitation assignment to Canton/Akron (August 9-28). . . . Granted free agency (October 15, 1993). . . . Re-signed by Indians organization (January 12, 1994).
STATISTICAL NOTES: Tied for South Atlantic League lead in double plays by catcher with seven in 1980. . . . Led American Association catchers with 698 total chances and 13 double plays in 1985. . . . Tied for American Association lead in grounding into double plays with 16 in 1985.

			BATTING											FIELDING			
Year	Team (League)	Pos.	G	AB	R	H	2B	3B	HR	RBI	Avg.	BB	SO	SB	PO	A	E	Avg.
1980	—Shelby (S. Atl.)	C	100	324	36	73	15	2	7	27	.225	25	77	0	536	63	18	.971
1981	—Greenwood (S. Atl.)..	C	117	428	48	114	25	2	11	63	.266	27	99	2	766	42	*22	.973
1982	—Glens Falls (East.)■.	C	120	422	49	107	11	6	7	65	.254	38	115	1	726	80	12	.985
1983	—Denver (A.A.)............	C	108	361	55	94	15	5	12	50	.260	35	53	0	550	54	5	.992
	—Chicago (A.L.)	C	6	11	2	3	0	0	0	1	.273	0	1	0	20	4	1	.960
1984	—Denver (A.A.)............	C	42	141	27	40	6	0	10	27	.284	13	31	1	255	24	5	.982
	—Chicago (A.L.)	C	43	80	4	17	2	0	0	3	.213	7	19	1	171	11	2	.989
1985	—Buffalo (A.A.)	C	115	390	47	94	13	0	12	59	.241	41	*115	0	*623	*65	10	.986
	—Chicago (A.L.)	C	22	44	9	15	4	1	1	5	.341	5	13	0	94	8	3	.971
1986	—Chi.-N.Y. (A.L.)■......	C	114	315	23	73	9	1	5	37	.232	16	83	1	507	37	9	.984
1987	—New York (A.L.)	C	64	139	9	19	4	0	3	14	.137	8	46	0	232	18	4	.984
	—Columbus (Int'l)	C	49	178	19	43	10	2	6	27	.242	10	44	0	226	25	4	.984
1988	—New York (A.L.)	C-OF-1B	88	251	23	57	15	0	4	23	.227	14	72	0	396	16	4	.990
1989	—Cleveland (A.L.)■.....	C	79	178	10	41	10	0	1	13	.230	9	42	1	280	22	3	.990
1990	—Cleveland (A.L.)	C	49	139	16	35	4	1	2	16	.252	7	44	0	222	16	1	.996
1991	—Cleveland (A.L.)	C	99	284	23	69	14	0	1	24	.243	14	67	0	504	38	5	.991
1992	—Cant./Akr. (East.)....	C	8	20	2	6	0	0	1	5	.300	0	3	0	18	0	0	1.000
1993	—Cant./Akr. (East.)....	C	15	46	6	11	3	0	2	5	.239	6	16	0	62	4	1	.985
Major league totals (9 years)			564	1441	119	329	62	3	17	136	.228	80	387	3	2426	170	32	.988

SLAUGHT, DON

C, PIRATES

PERSONAL: Born September 11, 1958, in Long Beach, Calif. . . . 6-1/185. . . . Throws right, bats right. . . . Full name: Donald Martin Slaught.
HIGH SCHOOL: Rolling Hills (Palos Verdes, Calif.).
COLLEGE: El Camino College (Calif.) and UCLA (bachelor of science degree in economics, 1983).
TRANSACTIONS/CAREER NOTES: Selected by Milwaukee Brewers organization in 19th round of free-agent draft (June 5, 1979). . . . Selected by Kansas City Royals organization in seventh round of free-agent draft (June 3, 1980). . . . On Omaha disabled list (August 16-September 29, 1981 and April 21-May 15, 1982). . . . On disabled list (May 16-June 1, 1983). . . . Traded by Royals to Texas Rangers as part of a six-player, four-team deal in which Royals acquired C Jim Sundberg from Brewers, Mets organization acquired P Frank Wills from Royals, Brewers acquired P Danny Darwin and a player to be named later from Rangers and P Tim Leary from Mets (January 18, 1985); Brewers organization acquired C Bill Hance from Rangers to complete deal (January 30, 1985). . . . On disabled list (August 9-26, 1985). . . . On Texas disabled list (May 18-July 4, 1986); included rehabilitation assignment to Oklahoma City (July 1-4). . . . Traded by Rangers to New York Yankees for a player to be named later (November 2, 1987); Rangers acquired P Brad Arnsberg to complete deal (November 10, 1987). . . . On disabled list (May 15-June 20, 1988). . . . Traded by Yankees to Pittsburgh Pirates for P Jeff D. Robinson and P Willie Smith (December 4, 1989). . . . On disabled list (June 30-July 16, 1990). . . . Granted free agency (November 5, 1990). . . . Re-signed by Pirates (December 19, 1990). . . . On disabled list (July 22-August 13, 1991). . . . On Pittsburgh disabled list (March 28-April 23, 1992); included rehabilitation assignment to Buffalo (April 17-20).

			BATTING											FIELDING			
Year	Team (League)	Pos.	G	AB	R	H	2B	3B	HR	RBI	Avg.	BB	SO	SB	PO	A	E	Avg.
1980	—Fort Myers (FSL)......	C	50	176	13	46	9	0	2	16	.261	16	11	3	175	34	4	.981
1981	—Jacksonv. (South.) ..	C-1B	96	379	45	127	21	2	6	44	.335	32	44	13	482	61	9	.984

S

Year	Team (League)	Pos.	G	AB	R	H	2B	3B	HR	RBI	Avg.	BB	SO	SB	PO	A	E	Avg.
			BATTING												FIELDING			
	—Omaha (A.A.)	C	22	71	10	21	4	0	2	8	.296	4	7	3	91	7	3	.970
1982	—Omaha (A.A.)	C	53	206	29	55	10	1	4	16	.267	7	20	6	216	25	5	.980
	—Kansas City (A.L.)	C	43	115	14	32	6	0	3	8	.278	9	12	0	156	7	1	.994
1983	—Kansas City (A.L.)	C	83	276	21	86	13	4	0	28	.312	11	27	3	299	18	12	.964
1984	—Kansas City (A.L.)	C	124	409	48	108	27	4	4	42	.264	20	55	0	547	44	11	.982
1985	—Texas (A.L.)■	C	102	343	34	96	17	4	8	35	.280	20	41	5	550	33	6	.990
1986	—Texas (A.L.)	C	95	314	39	83	17	1	13	46	.264	16	59	3	533	40	4	.993
	—Okla. City (A.A.)	C	3	12	2	4	1	0	0	1	.333	0	3	0	6	1	0	1.000
1987	—Texas (A.L.)	C	95	237	25	53	15	2	8	16	.224	24	51	0	429	39	7	.985
1988	—New York (A.L.)■	C	97	322	33	91	25	1	9	43	.283	24	54	1	496	24	•11	.979
1989	—New York (A.L.)	C	117	350	34	88	21	3	5	38	.251	30	57	1	493	44	5	.991
1990	—Pittsburgh (N.L.)■	C	84	230	27	69	18	3	4	29	.300	27	27	0	345	36	8	.979
1991	—Pittsburgh (N.L.)	C-3B	77	220	19	65	17	1	1	29	.295	21	32	1	338	31	5	.987
1992	—Buffalo (A.A.)	C	2	6	1	2	0	0	0	1	.333	0	0	0	15	3	0	1.000
	—Pittsburgh (N.L.)	C	87	255	26	88	17	3	4	37	.345	17	23	2	365	35	5	.988
1993	—Pittsburgh (N.L.)	C	116	377	34	113	19	2	10	55	.300	29	56	2	539	51	4	.993
American League totals (8 years)			756	2366	248	637	141	19	50	256	.269	154	356	13	3503	249	57	.985
National League totals (4 years)			364	1082	106	335	71	9	19	150	.310	94	138	5	1587	153	22	.988
Major league totals (12 years)			1120	3448	354	972	212	28	69	406	.282	248	494	18	5090	402	79	.986

CHAMPIONSHIP SERIES RECORD

Year	Team (League)	Pos.	G	AB	R	H	2B	3B	HR	RBI	Avg.	BB	SO	SB	PO	A	E	Avg.
			BATTING												FIELDING			
1984	—Kansas City (A.L.)	C	3	11	0	4	0	0	0	0	.364	0	0	0	17	0	3	.850
1990	—Pittsburgh (N.L.)	C	4	11	0	1	1	0	0	1	.091	2	3	0	22	1	1	.958
1991	—Pittsburgh (N.L.)	C-PH	6	17	0	4	0	0	0	1	.235	1	4	0	30	5	0	1.000
1992	—Pittsburgh (N.L.)	C-PH	5	12	5	4	1	0	1	5	.333	6	3	0	17	1	0	1.000
Championship series totals (4 years)			18	51	5	13	2	0	1	7	.255	9	10	0	86	7	4	.959

SLOCUMB, HEATHCLIFF

P, PHILLIES

PERSONAL: Born June 7, 1966, in Jamaica, N.Y. . . . 6-3/220. . . . Throws right, bats right.
HIGH SCHOOL: John Bowne (Flushing, N.Y.).
TRANSACTIONS/CAREER NOTES: Signed as free agent by New York Mets organization (July 10, 1984). . . . Selected by Chicago Cubs organization from Mets organization in Rule 5 minor league draft (December 9, 1986). . . . Traded by Cubs to Cleveland Indians for SS Jose Hernandez (June 1, 1993). . . . Traded by Indians to Philadelphia Phillies for OF Ruben Amaro (November 2, 1993).
STATISTICAL NOTES: Led Carolina League with 19 wild pitches in 1988.

Year	Team (League)	W	L	Pct.	ERA	G	GS	CG	ShO	Sv.	IP	H	R	ER	BB	SO
1984	—Kingsport (Appal.)	0	0	...	0.00	1	0	0	0	0	⅓	0	1	0	1	0
	—Little Falls (NYP)	0	0	...	11.00	4	1	0	0	0	9	8	11	11	16	10
1985	—Kingsport (Appal.)	3	2	.600	3.78	11	9	1	0	0	52⅓	47	32	22	31	29
1986	—Little Falls (NYP)	3	1	.750	1.65	25	0	0	0	1	43⅔	24	17	8	36	41
1987	—Winst.-Salem (Car.)■	1	2	.333	6.26	9	4	0	0	0	27⅓	26	25	19	26	27
	—Peoria (Midwest)	10	4	.714	2.60	16	16	3	1	0	103⅔	97	44	30	42	81
1988	—Winst.-Salem (Car.)	6	6	.500	4.96	25	19	2	1	1	119⅔	122	75	66	90	78
1989	—Peoria (Midwest)	5	3	.625	1.78	49	0	0	0	22	55⅔	31	16	11	33	52
1990	—Charlotte (South.)	3	1	.750	2.15	43	0	0	0	12	50⅓	50	20	12	32	37
	—Iowa (Am. Assoc.)	3	2	.600	2.00	20	0	0	0	1	27	16	10	6	18	21
1991	—Chicago (N.L.)	2	1	.667	3.45	52	0	0	0	1	62⅔	53	29	24	30	34
	—Iowa (Am. Assoc.)	1	0	1.000	4.05	12	0	0	0	1	13⅓	10	8	6	6	9
1992	—Chicago (N.L.)	0	3	.000	6.50	30	0	0	0	1	36	52	27	26	21	27
	—Iowa (Am. Assoc.)	1	3	.250	2.59	36	1	0	0	7	41⅔	36	13	12	16	47
1993	—Iowa (Am. Assoc.)	1	0	1.000	1.50	10	0	0	0	7	12	7	2	2	8	10
	—Chicago (N.L.)	1	0	1.000	3.38	10	0	0	0	0	10⅔	7	5	4	4	4
	—Cleveland (A.L.)■	3	1	.750	4.28	20	0	0	0	0	27⅓	28	14	13	16	18
	—Charlotte (Int'l)	3	2	.600	3.56	23	0	0	0	1	30⅓	25	14	12	11	25
A.L. totals (1 year)		3	1	.750	4.28	20	0	0	0	0	27⅓	28	14	13	16	18
N.L. totals (3 years)		3	4	.429	4.45	92	0	0	0	2	109⅓	112	61	54	55	65
Major league totals (3 years)		6	5	.545	4.41	112	0	0	0	2	136⅔	140	75	67	71	83

SLUSARSKI, JOE

P, ATHLETICS

PERSONAL: Born December 19, 1966, in Indianapolis. . . . 6-4/195. . . . Throws right, bats right. . . . Full name: Joseph Andrew Slusarski.
HIGH SCHOOL: Griffin (Springfield, Ill.).
COLLEGE: Lincoln Land Community College (Ill.) and New Orleans.
TRANSACTIONS/CAREER NOTES: Selected by Seattle Mariners organization in sixth round of free-agent draft (June 2, 1987). . . . Selected by Oakland Athletics organization in second round of free-agent draft (June 1, 1988). . . . On Huntsville disabled list (May 18-25, 1990). . . . On Tacoma disabled list (August 2-11, 1992 and July 22-August 11, 1993).
STATISTICAL NOTES: Led California League with 15 home runs allowed in 1989.
MISCELLANEOUS: Member of 1988 U.S. Olympic baseball team.

Year	Team (League)	W	L	Pct.	ERA	G	GS	CG	ShO	Sv.	IP	H	R	ER	BB	SO
1989	—Modesto (Calif.)	•13	10	.565	3.18	27	27	4	1	0	184	155	78	65	50	160
1990	—Huntsville (South.)	6	8	.429	4.47	17	17	2	0	0	108⅔	114	65	54	35	75
	—Tacoma (PCL)	4	2	.667	3.40	9	9	0	0	0	55⅔	54	24	21	22	37
1991	—Oakland (A.L.)	5	7	.417	5.27	20	19	1	0	0	109⅓	121	69	64	52	60

Year	Team (League)	W	L	Pct.	ERA	G	GS	CG	ShO	Sv.	IP	H	R	ER	BB	SO
	—Tacoma (PCL)	4	2	.667	2.72	7	7	0	0	0	46⅓	42	20	14	10	25
1992	—Oakland (A.L.)	5	5	.500	5.45	15	14	0	0	0	76	85	52	46	27	38
	—Tacoma (PCL)	2	4	.333	3.77	11	10	0	0	0	57⅓	67	30	24	18	26
1993	—Tacoma (PCL)	7	5	.583	4.76	24	21	1	1	0	113⅓	133	67	60	40	61
	—Oakland (A.L.)	0	0	...	5.19	2	1	0	0	0	8⅔	9	5	5	11	1
Major league totals (3 years)		10	12	.455	5.34	37	34	1	0	0	194	215	126	115	90	99

SMALL, AARON

P, BLUE JAYS

PERSONAL: Born November 23, 1971, in Oxnard, Calif. . . . 6-5/200. . . . Throws right, bats right. . . . Full name: Aaron James Small.
HIGH SCHOOL: South Hills (Covina, Calif.).
TRANSACTIONS/CAREER NOTES: Selected by Toronto Blue Jays organization in 22nd round of free-agent draft (June 5, 1989).

Year	Team (League)	W	L	Pct.	ERA	G	GS	CG	ShO	Sv.	IP	H	R	ER	BB	SO
1989	—Medicine Hat (Pio.)	1	7	.125	5.86	15	14	0	0	0	70⅔	80	55	46	31	40
1990	—Myrtle Beach (SAL)	9	9	.500	2.80	27	27	1	0	0	147⅔	150	72	46	56	96
1991	—Dunedin (Fla. St.)	8	7	.533	2.73	24	23	1	0	0	148⅓	129	51	45	42	92
1992	—Knoxville (South.)	5	12	.294	5.27	27	24	2	1	0	135	152	94	79	61	79
1993	—Knoxville (South.)	4	4	.500	3.39	48	9	0	0	16	93	99	44	35	40	44

S

SMILEY, JOHN

P, REDS

PERSONAL: Born March 17, 1965, in Phoenixville, Pa. . . . 6-4/212. . . . Throws left, bats left. . . . Full name: John Patrick Smiley.
HIGH SCHOOL: Perkiomen Valley (Graterford, Pa.).
TRANSACTIONS/CAREER NOTES: Selected by Pittsburgh Pirates organization in 12th round of free-agent draft (June 6, 1983). . . . On disabled list (April 27-May 27, 1984 and May 19-July 1, 1990). . . . Traded by Pirates to Minnesota Twins for P Denny Neagle and OF Midre Cummings (March 17, 1992). . . . Granted free agency (October 26, 1992). . . . Signed by Cincinnati Reds (December 1, 1992). . . . On disabled list (July 3, 1993-remainder of season).
STATISTICAL NOTES: Tied for Gulf Coast League lead with five home runs allowed in 1983.

Year	Team (League)	W	L	Pct.	ERA	G	GS	CG	ShO	Sv.	IP	H	R	ER	BB	SO
1983	—GC Pirates (GCL)	3	4	.429	5.92	12	12	0	0	0	65⅓	69	45	*43	27	42
1984	—Macon (S. Atl.)	5	11	.313	3.95	21	19	2	0	1	130	119	73	57	41	73
1985	—Prin. William (Car.)	2	2	.500	5.14	10	10	0	0	0	56	64	36	32	27	45
	—Macon (S. Atl.)	3	8	.273	4.67	16	16	1	1	0	88⅔	84	55	46	37	70
1986	—Prin. William (Car.)	2	4	.333	3.10	48	2	0	0	14	90	64	35	31	40	93
	—Pittsburgh (N.L.)	1	0	1.000	3.86	12	0	0	0	0	11⅔	4	6	5	4	9
1987	—Pittsburgh (N.L.)	5	5	.500	5.76	63	0	0	0	4	75	69	49	48	50	58
1988	—Pittsburgh (N.L.)	13	11	.542	3.25	34	32	5	1	0	205	185	81	74	46	129
1989	—Pittsburgh (N.L.)	12	8	.600	2.81	28	28	8	1	0	205⅓	174	78	64	49	123
1990	—Pittsburgh (N.L.)	9	10	.474	4.64	26	25	2	0	0	149⅓	161	83	77	36	86
1991	—Pittsburgh (N.L.)	•20	8	•.714	3.08	33	32	2	1	0	207⅔	194	78	71	44	129
1992	—Minnesota (A.L.)■	16	9	.640	3.21	34	34	5	2	0	241	205	93	86	65	163
1993	—Cincinnati (N.L.)■	3	9	.250	5.62	18	18	2	0	0	105⅔	117	69	66	31	60
A.L. totals (1 year)		16	9	.640	3.21	34	34	5	2	0	241	205	93	86	65	163
N.L. totals (7 years)		63	51	.553	3.80	214	135	19	3	4	959⅔	904	444	405	260	594
Major league totals (8 years)		79	60	.568	3.68	248	169	24	5	4	1200⅔	1109	537	491	325	757

CHAMPIONSHIP SERIES RECORD

Year	Team (League)	W	L	Pct.	ERA	G	GS	CG	ShO	Sv.	IP	H	R	ER	BB	SO
1990	—Pittsburgh (N.L.)	0	0	...	0.00	1	0	0	0	0	2	2	0	0	0	0
1991	—Pittsburgh (N.L.)	0	2	.000	23.63	2	2	0	0	0	2⅔	8	8	7	1	3
Champ. series totals (2 years)		0	2	.000	13.50	3	2	0	0	0	4⅔	10	8	7	1	3

ALL-STAR GAME RECORD

Year	League	W	L	Pct.	ERA	GS	CG	ShO	Sv.	IP	H	R	ER	BB	SO
1991	—National	0	0	...	...	0	0	0	0	0	1	1	1	0	0

SMITH, BRYN

P

PERSONAL: Born August 11, 1955, in Marietta, Ga. . . . 6-2/205. . . . Throws right, bats right. . . . Full name: Bryn Nelson Smith. . . . Name pronounced BRIN.
HIGH SCHOOL: Santa Maria (Calif.).
COLLEGE: Allan Hancock College (Calif.).
TRANSACTIONS/CAREER NOTES: Selected by St. Louis Cardinals organization in 49th round of free-agent draft (June 5, 1973). . . . Signed as free agent by Baltimore Orioles organization (December 18, 1974). . . . Traded by Orioles organization with P Rudy May and P Randy Miller to Montreal Expos organization for P Don Stanhouse, P Joe Kerrigan and OF Gary Roenicke (December 7, 1977). . . . On Memphis disabled list (August 5-17, 1978). . . . Released by Expos (December 20, 1986). . . . Re-signed by Expos (February 27, 1987). . . . On Montreal disabled list (March 23-May 1, 1987); included rehabilitation assignment to West Palm Beach (April 10). . . . Granted free agency (November 9, 1987). . . . Re-signed by Expos (December 16, 1987). . . . Granted free agency (November 13, 1989). . . . Signed by St. Louis Cardinals (November 28, 1989). . . . On disabled list (July 28-September 6, 1990). . . . On St. Louis disabled list (April 14-September 1, 1992); included rehabilitation assignment to Louisville (July 5-12). . . . Granted free agency (October 30, 1992). . . . Signed by Colorado Rockies organization (December 7, 1992). . . . On disabled list (April 26-May 12, 1993). . . . Released by Rockies (June 2, 1993).
HONORS: Named American Association Pitcher of the Year (1981).

Year	Team (League)	W	L	Pct.	ERA	G	GS	CG	ShO	Sv.	IP	H	R	ER	BB	SO
1975	—Miami (Florida St.)	11	7	.611	2.14	26	20	5	2	1	139	117	48	33	59	93
1976	—Miami (Florida St.)	10	10	.500	2.80	23	22	14	2	0	164	140	72	51	62	119
1977	—Charlotte (South.)	*15	11	.577	2.75	27	27	•16	2	0	*206	*195	78	63	57	103

Year	Team (League)	W	L	Pct.	ERA	G	GS	CG	ShO	Sv.	IP	H	R	ER	BB	SO
1978	—Denver (A.A.)■	0	6	.000	6.83	11	10	1	0	0	54	79	48	41	14	25
	—Memphis (South.)	4	6	.400	2.48	11	10	4	1	0	69	53	28	19	31	48
1979	—Memphis (South.)	11	10	.524	3.38	27	27	10	1	0	184	175	80	69	74	115
1980	—Memphis (South.)	10	9	.526	2.78	27	25	•12	1	0	181	179	75	56	54	110
1981	—Denver (A.A.)	*15	5	.750	3.05	29	24	•9	0	1	*183	166	80	62	42	127
	—Montreal (N.L.)	1	0	1.000	2.77	7	0	0	0	0	13	14	4	4	3	9
1982	—Wichita (A.A.)	2	0	1.000	1.90	3	3	1	0	0	23⅔	21	5	5	2	15
	—Montreal (N.L.)	2	4	.333	4.20	47	1	0	0	3	79⅓	81	43	37	23	50
1983	—Montreal (N.L.)	6	11	.353	2.49	49	12	5	3	3	155⅓	142	51	43	43	101
1984	—Montreal (N.L.)	12	13	.480	3.32	28	28	4	2	0	179	178	72	66	51	101
1985	—Montreal (N.L.)	18	5	.783	2.91	32	32	4	2	0	222⅓	193	85	72	41	127
1986	—Montreal (N.L.)	10	8	.556	3.94	30	30	1	0	0	187⅓	182	101	82	63	105
1987	—W.P. Beach (FSL)	0	2	.000	4.08	4	4	0	0	0	17⅔	19	10	8	1	16
	—Montreal (N.L.)	10	9	.526	4.37	26	26	2	0	0	150⅓	164	81	73	31	94
1988	—Montreal (N.L.)	12	10	.545	3.00	32	32	1	0	0	198	179	79	66	32	122
1989	—Montreal (N.L.)	10	11	.476	2.84	33	32	3	1	0	215⅔	177	76	68	54	129
1990	—St. Louis (N.L.)■	9	8	.529	4.27	26	25	0	0	0	141⅓	160	81	67	30	78
1991	—St. Louis (N.L.)	12	9	.571	3.85	31	31	3	0	0	198⅔	188	95	85	45	94
1992	—St. Louis (N.L.)	4	2	.667	4.64	13	1	0	0	0	21⅓	20	11	11	5	9
	—Louisville (A.A.)	1	0	1.000	1.80	2	2	0	0	0	10	6	2	2	2	2
1993	—Colorado (N.L.)■	2	4	.333	8.49	11	5	0	0	0	29⅔	47	29	28	11	9
Major league totals (13 years)		108	94	.535	3.53	365	255	23	8	6	1791⅓	1725	808	702	432	1028

S

SMITH, DAN

P, RANGERS

PERSONAL: Born April 20, 1969, in St. Paul, Minn. . . . 6-5/195. . . . Throws left, bats left. . . . Full name: Daniel Scott Smith.
HIGH SCHOOL: Apple Valley (Minn.).
COLLEGE: Creighton.
TRANSACTIONS/CAREER NOTES: Selected by Minnesota Twins organization in 22nd round of free-agent draft (June 2, 1987). . . . Selected by Texas Rangers organization in first round (16th pick overall) of free-agent draft (June 4, 1990). . . . On Tulsa disabled list (August 5-20, 1992). . . . On Texas disabled list (March 27-May 18, 1993); included rehabilitation assignment to Charlotte (May 17-18). . . . On Oklahoma City disabled list (June 23-September 1, 1993). . . . On Texas disabled list (September 1, 1993-remainder of season).
HONORS: Named Texas League Pitcher of the Year (1992).

Year	Team (League)	W	L	Pct.	ERA	G	GS	CG	ShO	Sv.	IP	H	R	ER	BB	SO
1990	—Butte (Pioneer)	2	0	1.000	3.65	5	5	0	0	0	24⅔	23	10	10	6	27
	—Tulsa (Texas)	3	2	.600	3.76	7	7	0	0	0	38⅓	27	16	16	16	32
1991	—Okla. City (A.A.)	4	*17	.190	5.52	28	27	3	0	0	151⅔	*195	*114	*93	75	85
1992	—Tulsa (Texas)	11	7	.611	*2.52	24	23	4	*3	0	146⅓	110	48	41	34	122
	—Texas (A.L.)	0	3	.000	5.02	4	2	0	0	0	14⅓	18	8	8	8	5
1993	—Charlotte (Fla. St.)	1	0	1.000	0.00	1	1	0	0	0	7	3	0	0	0	5
	—Okla. City (A.A.)	1	2	.333	4.70	3	3	0	0	0	15⅓	16	11	8	5	12
Major league totals (1 year)		0	3	.000	5.02	4	2	0	0	0	14⅓	18	8	8	8	5

SMITH, DWIGHT

OF, ANGELS

PERSONAL: Born November 8, 1963, in Tallahassee, Fla. . . . 5-11/190. . . . Throws right, bats left. . . . Full name: John Dwight Smith.
HIGH SCHOOL: Wade Hampton (Varnville, S.C.).
COLLEGE: Spartanburg (S.C.) Methodist.
TRANSACTIONS/CAREER NOTES: Selected by Toronto Blue Jays organization in third round of free-agent draft (January 17, 1984). . . . Selected by Chicago Cubs organization in secondary phase of free-agent draft (June 4, 1984). . . . On Chicago disabled list (July 8-August 5, 1993); included rehabilitation assignment to Daytona (July 30-August 4). . . . Granted free agency (December 20, 1993). . . . Signed by California Angels (February 1, 1994).
STATISTICAL NOTES: Tied for Appalachian League lead in double plays by outfielder with three in 1984. . . . Led Midwest League outfielders with 296 total chances in 1986. . . . Led Eastern League with 270 total bases and tied for lead in caught stealing with 18 in 1987.

			BATTING												FIELDING			
Year	Team (League)	Pos.	G	AB	R	H	2B	3B	HR	RBI	Avg.	BB	SO	SB	PO	A	E	Avg.
1984	—Pikeville (Appal.)	OF	61	195	42	46	6	2	1	17	.236	52	47	*39	77	8	•9	.904
1985	—Geneva (NY-Penn)	OF	73	232	44	67	11	2	4	32	.289	31	33	30	81	4	7	.924
1986	—Peoria (Midwest)	OF	124	471	92	146	22	*11	11	57	.310	59	92	53	*272	11	13	.956
1987	—Pittsfield (Eastern)	OF	130	498	*111	168	28	10	18	72	.337	67	79	*60	214	8	•14	.941
1988	—Iowa (Am. Assoc.)	OF	129	505	76	148	26	3	9	48	.293	54	90	25	216	11	*15	.938
1989	—Iowa (Am. Assoc.)	OF	21	83	11	27	7	3	2	7	.325	7	11	6	39	2	4	.911
	—Chicago (N.L.)	OF	109	343	52	111	19	6	9	52	.324	31	51	9	188	7	5	.975
1990	—Chicago (N.L.)	OF	117	290	34	76	15	0	6	27	.262	28	46	11	139	4	2	.986
1991	—Chicago (N.L.)	OF	90	167	16	38	7	2	3	21	.228	11	32	2	73	3	3	.962
1992	—Chicago (N.L.)	OF	109	217	28	60	10	3	3	24	.276	13	40	9	93	2	2	.979
	—Iowa (Am. Assoc.)	OF	3	8	1	2	1	0	0	1	.250	2	2	0	2	0	0	1.000
1993	—Chicago (N.L.)	OF	111	310	51	93	17	5	11	35	.300	25	51	8	163	5	8	.955
	—Daytona (Fla. St.)	OF	5	16	3	5	4	0	0	2	.313	3	4	0	3	0	0	1.000
Major league totals (5 years)			536	1327	181	378	68	16	32	159	.285	108	220	39	656	21	20	.971

CHAMPIONSHIP SERIES RECORD

CHAMPIONSHIP SERIES NOTES: Shares record for most at-bats in one inning—2 (October 5, 1989, first inning).

			BATTING												FIELDING			
Year	Team (League)	Pos.	G	AB	R	H	2B	3B	HR	RBI	Avg.	BB	SO	SB	PO	A	E	Avg.
1989	—Chicago (N.L.)	OF	4	15	2	3	1	0	0	0	.200	2	2	1	10	0	0	1.000

SMITH, LEE

P, ORIOLES

PERSONAL: Born December 4, 1957, in Jamestown, La.... 6-6/269.... Throws right, bats right.... Full name: Lee Arthur Smith.
HIGH SCHOOL: Castor (La.).
COLLEGE: Northwestern (La.) State.
TRANSACTIONS/CAREER NOTES: Selected by Chicago Cubs organization in second round of free-agent draft (June 4, 1975).... On disabled list (April 21-May 6, 1986).... Traded by Cubs to Boston Red Sox for P Al Nipper and P Calvin Schiraldi (December 8, 1987).... Traded by Red Sox to St. Louis Cardinals for OF Tom Brunansky (May 4, 1990).... Traded by Cardinals to New York Yankees for P Richard Batchelor (August 31, 1993).... Granted free agency (October 25, 1993).... Signed by Baltimore Orioles (January 29, 1994).
RECORDS: Holds major league career records for most saves—401; and most consecutive errorless games by pitcher—546 (July 5, 1982 through September 22, 1992).... Holds N.L. career record for most saves—340.
HONORS: Named N.L. co-Fireman of the Year by THE SPORTING NEWS (1983 and 1992).... Named N.L. Fireman of the Year by THE SPORTING NEWS (1991).
STATISTICAL NOTES: Tied for American Association lead with 16 wild pitches in 1980.

Year Team (League)	W	L	Pct.	ERA	G	GS	CG	ShO	Sv.	IP	H	R	ER	BB	SO
1975—GC Cubs (GCL)	3	5	.375	2.32	10	10	2	1	0	62	35	23	16	*49	35
1976—Pomp. Beach (FSL)	4	8	.333	5.35	26	18	2	1	0	101	120	76	60	74	52
1977—Pomp. Beach (FSL)	10	4	.714	4.29	26	18	4	0	0	130	131	67	62	85	82
1978—Midland (Texas)	8	10	.444	5.98	30	25	3	0	0	155	161	122	103	*128	71
1979—Midland (Texas)	9	5	.643	4.93	35	9	0	0	1	104	122	65	57	85	46
1980—Wichita (A.A.)	4	7	.364	3.70	50	2	0	0	15	90	70	49	37	56	63
—Chicago (N.L.)	2	0	1.000	2.86	18	0	0	0	0	22	21	9	7	14	17
1981—Chicago (N.L.)	3	6	.333	3.49	40	1	0	0	1	67	57	31	26	31	50
1982—Chicago (N.L.)	2	5	.286	2.69	72	5	0	0	17	117	105	38	35	37	99
1983—Chicago (N.L.)	4	10	.286	1.65	66	0	0	0	*29	103⅓	70	23	19	41	91
1984—Chicago (N.L.)	9	7	.563	3.65	69	0	0	0	33	101	98	42	41	35	86
1985—Chicago (N.L.)	7	4	.636	3.04	65	0	0	0	33	97⅔	87	35	33	32	112
1986—Chicago (N.L.)	9	9	.500	3.09	66	0	0	0	31	90⅓	69	32	31	42	93
1987—Chicago (N.L.)	4	10	.286	3.12	62	0	0	0	36	83⅔	84	30	29	32	96
1988—Boston (A.L.)■	4	5	.444	2.80	64	0	0	0	29	83⅔	72	34	26	37	96
1989—Boston (A.L.)	6	1	.857	3.57	64	0	0	0	25	70⅔	53	30	28	33	96
1990—Boston (A.L.)	2	1	.667	1.88	11	0	0	0	4	14⅓	13	4	3	9	17
—St. Louis (N.L.)■	3	4	.429	2.10	53	0	0	0	27	68⅔	58	20	16	20	70
1991—St. Louis (N.L.)	6	3	.667	2.34	67	0	0	0	*47	73	70	19	19	13	67
1992—St. Louis (N.L.)	4	9	.308	3.12	70	0	0	0	*43	75	62	28	26	26	60
1993—St. Louis (N.L.)	2	4	.333	4.50	55	0	0	0	43	50	49	25	25	9	49
—New York (A.L.)■	0	0	...	0.00	8	0	0	0	3	8	4	0	0	5	11
A.L. totals (4 years)	12	7	.632	2.90	147	0	0	0	61	176⅔	142	68	57	84	220
N.L. totals (12 years)	55	71	.437	2.91	703	6	0	0	340	948⅔	830	332	307	332	890
Major league totals (14 years)	67	78	.462	2.91	850	6	0	0	401	1125⅓	972	400	364	416	1110

CHAMPIONSHIP SERIES RECORD

Year Team (League)	W	L	Pct.	ERA	G	GS	CG	ShO	Sv.	IP	H	R	ER	BB	SO
1984—Chicago (N.L.)	0	1	.000	9.00	2	0	0	0	1	2	3	2	2	0	3
1988—Boston (A.L.)	0	1	.000	8.10	2	0	0	0	0	3⅓	6	3	3	1	4
Champ. series totals (2 years)	0	2	.000	8.44	4	0	0	0	1	5⅓	9	5	5	1	7

ALL-STAR GAME RECORD

Year League	W	L	Pct.	ERA	GS	CG	ShO	Sv.	IP	H	R	ER	BB	SO
1983—National	0	0	...	9.00	0	0	0	0	1	2	2	1	0	1
1987—National	1	0	1.000	0.00	0	0	0	0	3	2	0	0	0	4
1991—National	Did not play.													
1992—National	Did not play.													
1993—National	Did not play.													
All-Star totals (2 years)	1	0	1.000	2.25	0	0	0	0	4	4	2	1	0	5

SMITH, LONNIE

OF, ORIOLES

PERSONAL: Born December 22, 1955, in Chicago.... 5-9/170.... Throws right, bats right.
HIGH SCHOOL: Centennial (Compton, Calif.).
TRANSACTIONS/CAREER NOTES: Selected by Philadelphia Phillies organization in first round (third pick overall) of free-agent draft (June 5, 1974).... On Oklahoma City disabled list (April 14-25, 1978).... Traded by Phillies with a player to be named later to Cleveland Indians for C Bo Diaz (November 20, 1981); traded by Indians to St. Louis Cardinals for P Lary Sorensen and P Silvio Martinez (November 20, 1981). Indians organization acquired P Scott Munninghoff to complete first deal (December 9, 1981).... On disabled list (June 11-July 8, 1983).... Traded by Cardinals to Kansas City Royals for OF John Morris (May 17, 1985).... On disabled list (April 13-May 4, 1986).... Granted free agency (November 12, 1986).... Re-signed by Royals organization (May 8, 1987).... Released by Royals (December 15, 1987).... Signed by Richmond, Atlanta Braves organization (March 12, 1988).... On disabled list (May 20-June 13, 1989 and March 30-April 28, 1991).... Granted free agency (November 5, 1992).... Signed by Pittsburgh Pirates (January 4, 1993).... Traded by Pirates to Baltimore Orioles for two players to be named later (September 8, 1993); Pirates acquired OF Stanton Cameron and P Terry Farrar to complete deal (September 14, 1993).... Granted free agency (October 29, 1993).... Re-signed by Orioles organization (February 4, 1994).
RECORDS: Shares major league single-season record for fewest double plays by outfielder who led league in double plays—4 (1983).
HONORS: Named N.L. Rookie Player of the Year by THE SPORTING NEWS (1980).... Named outfielder on THE SPORTING NEWS N.L. All-Star team (1982).... Named N.L. Comeback Player of the Year by THE SPORTING NEWS (1989).
STATISTICAL NOTES: Tied for Western Carolinas League lead in caught stealing with 14 in 1975.... Led American Association outfielders with five double plays in 1978.... Led American Association in caught stealing with 19 in 1978.... Led N.L. in being hit by pitch with nine in 1982 and 1984 and tied for lead with nine in 1983.... Tied for N.L. lead in caught stealing with 26 in 1982.... Tied for N.L. lead in double plays by outfielder with four in 1983.... Led N.L. with .415 on-base percentage in 1989.

Year	Team (League)	Pos.	G	AB	R	H	2B	3B	HR	RBI	Avg.	BB	SO	SB	PO	A	E	Avg.
			BATTING												FIELDING			
1974	—Auburn (NY-Penn) ..	OF	61	210	48	60	10	4	5	27	.286	52	29	12	143	6	•9	.943
1975	—Sp'rt'brg (W. Caro.) .	OF	131	465	★114	★150	23	4	7	40	.323	96	63	★56	★317	9	11	.967
1976	—Okla. City (A.A.)	OF	134	483	★93	149	24	9	8	54	.308	60	73	26	200	4	★14	.936
1977	—Okla. City (A.A.)	OF	125	477	91	132	14	10	4	41	.277	49	63	45	231	8	★13	.948
1978	—Okla. City (A.A.)	OF	125	480	103	151	20	5	7	43	.315	79	79	★66	274	★21	★12	.961
	—Philadelphia (N.L.) ...	OF	17	4	6	0	0	0	0	0	.000	4	3	4	5	1	0	1.000
1979	—Okla. City (A.A.)	OF	110	451	★106	149	26	9	7	44	.330	56	52	34	268	13	★12	.959
	—Philadelphia (N.L.) ...	OF	17	30	4	5	2	0	0	3	.167	1	7	2	19	1	0	1.000
1980	—Philadelphia (N.L.) ...	OF	100	298	69	101	14	4	3	20	.339	26	48	33	121	2	4	.969
1981	—Philadelphia (N.L.) ...	OF	62	176	40	57	14	3	2	11	.324	18	14	21	91	10	3	.971
1982	—St. Louis (N.L.)■.......	OF	156	592	★120	182	35	8	8	69	.307	64	74	68	303	•16	10	.970
1983	—St. Louis (N.L.)	OF	130	492	83	158	31	5	8	45	.321	41	55	43	225	14	★15	.941
1984	—St. Louis (N.L.)	OF	145	504	77	126	20	4	6	49	.250	70	90	50	184	★18	•11	.948
1985	—St. Louis (N.L.)	OF	28	96	15	25	2	2	0	7	.260	15	20	12	43	1	0	1.000
	—Kansas City (A.L.)■.	OF	120	448	77	115	23	4	6	41	.257	41	69	40	195	10	9	.958
1986	—Kansas City (A.L.)....	OF	134	508	80	146	25	7	8	44	.287	46	78	26	245	5	9	.965
1987	—Omaha (A.A.)...........	OF	40	149	36	49	9	1	7	33	.329	18	22	8	51	1	3	.945
	—Kansas City (A.L.)....	OF	48	167	26	42	7	1	3	8	.251	24	31	9	52	2	5	.915
1988	—Richmond (Int'l)■.....	OF	93	290	58	87	13	5	9	51	.300	★66	65	26	120	6	2	.984
	—Atlanta (N.L.)	OF	43	114	14	27	3	0	3	9	.237	10	25	4	59	2	2	.968
1989	—Atlanta (N.L.)	OF	134	482	89	152	34	4	21	79	.315	76	95	25	289	3	2	.993
1990	—Atlanta (N.L.)	OF	135	466	72	142	27	9	9	42	.305	58	69	10	254	6	12	.956
1991	—Atlanta (N.L.)	OF	122	353	58	97	19	1	7	44	.275	50	64	9	134	5	5	.965
1992	—Atlanta (N.L.)	OF	84	158	23	39	8	2	6	33	.247	17	37	4	60	2	3	.954
1993	—Pittsburgh (N.L.)■....	OF	94	199	35	57	5	4	6	24	.286	43	42	9	104	1	2	.981
	—Baltimore (A.L.)■.....	OF	9	24	8	5	1	0	2	3	.208	8	10	0	5	1	0	1.000
American League totals (4 years)............			311	1147	191	308	56	12	19	96	.269	119	188	75	497	18	23	.957
National League totals (14 years)...........			1267	3964	705	1168	214	46	79	435	.295	493	643	294	1891	82	69	.966
Major league totals (16 years)................			1578	5111	896	1476	270	58	98	531	.289	612	831	369	2388	100	92	.964

DIVISION SERIES RECORD

Year	Team (League)	Pos.	G	AB	R	H	2B	3B	HR	RBI	Avg.	BB	SO	SB	PO	A	E	Avg.
			BATTING												FIELDING			
1981	—Philadelphia (N.L.) ...	OF	5	19	1	5	1	0	0	0	.263	0	4	0	6	1	0	1.000

CHAMPIONSHIP SERIES RECORD

Year	Team (League)	Pos.	G	AB	R	H	2B	3B	HR	RBI	Avg.	BB	SO	SB	PO	A	E	Avg.
			BATTING												FIELDING			
1980	—Philadelphia (N.L.) ...	PR-OF	3	5	2	3	0	0	0	0	.600	0	0	1	2	1	0	1.000
1982	—St. Louis (N.L.)	OF	3	11	1	3	0	0	0	1	.273	1	0	0	2	0	0	1.000
1985	—Kansas City (A.L.)....	OF	7	28	2	7	2	0	0	1	.250	6	1	1	8	3	1	.917
1991	—Atlanta (N.L.)	OF	7	24	3	6	3	0	0	0	.250	4	5	1	10	2	0	1.000
1992	—Atlanta (N.L.)	PH	6	6	1	2	0	1	0	1	.333	0	0	0	...	...	...	...
Championship series totals (5 years)......			26	74	9	21	5	1	0	3	.284	11	6	3	22	6	1	.966

WORLD SERIES RECORD

WORLD SERIES NOTES: Holds career record for most clubs played with—4. ... Shares single-game record for most grand slams—1 (October 22, 1992). ... Shares records for most at-bats in one inning—2 (October 24, 1991, seventh inning); and most runs batted in in one inning—4 (October 22, 1992, fifth inning).

Year	Team (League)	Pos.	G	AB	R	H	2B	3B	HR	RBI	Avg.	BB	SO	SB	PO	A	E	Avg.
			BATTING												FIELDING			
1980	—Philadelphia (N.L.) ...	OF-DH-PR	6	19	2	5	1	0	0	1	.263	1	1	0	4	1	0	1.000
1982	—St. Louis (N.L.)	OF-DH	7	28	6	9	4	1	0	1	.321	5	2	2	11	0	0	1.000
1985	—Kansas City (A.L.)....	OF	7	27	4	9	3	0	0	4	.333	8	2	2	7	2	0	1.000
1991	—Atlanta (N.L.)	DH-OF	7	26	5	6	0	0	3	3	.231	3	4	1	2	0	0	1.000
1992	—Atlanta (N.L.)	DH-PH	5	12	1	2	0	0	1	5	.167	1	4	0	...	...	...	...
World Series totals (5 years)..................			32	112	18	31	8	1	4	14	.277	18	13	5	24	3	0	1.000

ALL-STAR GAME RECORD

Year	League	Pos.	AB	R	H	2B	3B	HR	RBI	Avg.	BB	SO	SB	PO	A	E	Avg.
			BATTING											FIELDING			
1982	—National.....................	OF	0	0	0	0	0	0	0	...	0	0	0	1	0	0	1.000

SMITH, MARK

OF, ORIOLES

PERSONAL: Born May 7, 1970, in Pasadena, Calif. ... 6-3/205. ... Throws right, bats right. ... Full name: Mark Edward Smith.

HIGH SCHOOL: Arcadia (Calif.).

COLLEGE: Southern California.

TRANSACTIONS/CAREER NOTES: Selected by Baltimore Orioles organization in first round (ninth pick overall) of free-agent draft (June 3, 1991).

Year	Team (League)	Pos.	G	AB	R	H	2B	3B	HR	RBI	Avg.	BB	SO	SB	PO	A	E	Avg.
			BATTING												FIELDING			
1991	—Frederick (Caro.)......	OF	38	148	20	37	5	1	4	29	.250	9	24	1	49	1	1	.980
1992	—Hagerstown (East.) ..	OF	128	472	51	136	★32	6	4	62	.288	45	55	15	226	9	4	.983
1993	—Rochester (Int'l)	OF	129	485	69	136	27	1	12	68	.280	37	90	4	261	9	7	.975

SMITH, OZZIE

SS, CARDINALS

PERSONAL: Born December 26, 1954, in Mobile, Ala. . . . 5-10/168. . . . Throws right, bats both. . . . Full name: Osborne Earl Smith.
HIGH SCHOOL: Locke (Los Angeles).
COLLEGE: Cal Poly San Luis Obispo (received degree).

TRANSACTIONS/CAREER NOTES: Selected by Detroit Tigers organization in seventh round of free-agent draft (June 8, 1976). . . . Selected by San Diego Padres organization in fourth round of free-agent draft (June 7, 1977). . . . Traded by Padres to St. Louis Cardinals for SS Garry Templeton (February 11, 1982). . . . On disabled list (July 14-August 19, 1984; March 31-April 15, 1989 and June 16-July 1, 1992). . . . Granted free agency (November 2, 1992). . . . Re-signed by Cardinals (December 6, 1992).

RECORDS: Holds major league records for most years with 500 or more assists by shortstop—8; and most years leading league in assists and chances accepted by shortstop—8. . . . Holds major league single-season records for most assists by shortstop—621 (1980); fewest chances accepted by shortstop who led league in chances accepted—692 (1989); and fewest double plays by shortstop who led league in double plays—79 (1991). . . . Shares major league record for most double plays by shortstop in extra-inning game—6 (August 25, 1979, 19 innings). . . . Holds N.L. career records for most games by shortstop—2,322; most assists by shortstop—7,793; and most double plays by shortstop—1,459. . . . Holds N.L. single-season record for fewest errors by shortstop (150 or more games)—8 (1991). . . . Holds N.L. record for most years leading league in fielding percentage by shortstop (100 or more games)—7. . . . Shares N.L. records for most consecutive years leading league in assists by shortstop—4 (1979-82); highest fielding percentage by shortstop (150 or more games)—.987 (1987 and 1991); and most years leading league in double plays by shortstop—5. . . . Shares modern N.L. record for most consecutive years leading league in fielding percentage by shortstop (100 or more games)—4 (1984-87).

HONORS: Won N.L. Gold Glove at shortstop (1980-92). . . . Named shortstop on THE SPORTING NEWS N.L. All-Star team (1982, 1984-87). . . . Named shortstop on THE SPORTING NEWS N.L. Silver Slugger team (1987).

STATISTICAL NOTES: Led Northwest League shortstops with 40 double plays in 1977. . . . Led N.L. with 28 sacrifice hits in 1978 and 23 in 1980. . . . Led N.L. shortstops with 933 total chances in 1980, 658 in 1981, 844 in 1983, 827 in 1985, 771 in 1987, 775 in 1988 and 709 in 1989. . . . Led N.L. shortstops with 113 double plays in 1980, 111 in 1987, 79 in 1991 and tied for lead with 94 in 1984 and 96 in 1986.

			BATTING												FIELDING			
Year	**Team (League)**	**Pos.**	**G**	**AB**	**R**	**H**	**2B**	**3B**	**HR**	**RBI**	**Avg.**	**BB**	**SO**	**SB**	**PO**	**A**	**E**	**Avg.**
1977	—Walla Walla (N'west)..	SS	•68	*287	*69	87	10	2	1	35	.303	40	12	*30	130	*254	23	*.943
1978	—San Diego (N.L.)	SS	159	590	69	152	17	6	1	46	.258	47	43	40	264	548	25	.970
1979	—San Diego (N.L.)	SS	156	587	77	124	18	6	0	27	.211	37	37	28	256	*555	20	.976
1980	—San Diego (N.L.)	SS	158	609	67	140	18	5	0	35	.230	71	49	57	*288	*621	24	.974
1981	—San Diego (N.L.)	SS	•110	*450	53	100	11	2	0	21	.222	41	37	22	220	*422	16	*.976
1982	—St. Louis (N.L.)■.......	SS	140	488	58	121	24	1	2	43	.248	68	32	25	279	*535	13	*.984
1983	—St. Louis (N.L.)	SS	159	552	69	134	30	6	3	50	.243	64	36	34	*304	519	21	.975
1984	—St. Louis (N.L.)	SS	124	412	53	106	20	5	1	44	.257	56	17	35	233	437	12	*.982
1985	—St. Louis (N.L.)	SS	158	537	70	148	22	3	6	54	.276	65	27	31	264	*549	14	*.983
1986	—St. Louis (N.L.)	SS	153	514	67	144	19	4	0	54	.280	79	27	31	229	453	15	*.978
1987	—St. Louis (N.L.)	SS	158	600	104	182	40	4	0	75	.303	89	36	43	245	*516	10	*.987
1988	—St. Louis (N.L.)	SS	153	575	80	155	27	1	3	51	.270	74	43	57	234	*519	22	.972
1989	—St. Louis (N.L.)	SS	155	593	82	162	30	8	2	50	.273	55	37	29	209	*483	17	.976
1990	—St. Louis (N.L.)	SS	143	512	61	130	21	1	1	50	.254	61	33	32	212	378	12	.980
1991	—St. Louis (N.L.)	SS	150	550	96	157	30	3	3	50	.285	83	36	35	244	387	8	*.987
1992	—St. Louis (N.L.)	SS	132	518	73	153	20	2	0	31	.295	59	34	43	232	420	10	.985
1993	—St. Louis (N.L.)	SS	141	545	75	157	22	6	1	53	.288	43	18	21	251	451	19	.974
Major league totals (16 years)			2349	8632	1154	2265	369	63	23	734	.262	992	542	563	3964	7793	258	.979

CHAMPIONSHIP SERIES RECORD

CHAMPIONSHIP SERIES NOTES: Named N.L. Championship Series Most Valuable Player (1985).

			BATTING												FIELDING			
Year	**Team (League)**	**Pos.**	**G**	**AB**	**R**	**H**	**2B**	**3B**	**HR**	**RBI**	**Avg.**	**BB**	**SO**	**SB**	**PO**	**A**	**E**	**Avg.**
1982	—St. Louis (N.L.)	SS	3	9	0	5	0	0	0	3	.556	3	0	1	4	11	0	1.000
1985	—St. Louis (N.L.)	SS	6	23	4	10	1	1	1	3	.435	3	1	1	6	16	0	1.000
1987	—St. Louis (N.L.)	SS	7	25	2	5	0	1	0	1	.200	3	4	0	10	19	1	.967
Championship series totals (3 years)			16	57	6	20	1	2	1	7	.351	9	5	2	20	46	1	.985

WORLD SERIES RECORD

			BATTING												FIELDING			
Year	**Team (League)**	**Pos.**	**G**	**AB**	**R**	**H**	**2B**	**3B**	**HR**	**RBI**	**Avg.**	**BB**	**SO**	**SB**	**PO**	**A**	**E**	**Avg.**
1982	—St. Louis (N.L.)	SS	7	24	3	5	0	0	0	1	.208	3	0	1	22	17	0	1.000
1985	—St. Louis (N.L.)	SS	7	23	1	2	0	0	0	0	.087	4	0	1	10	16	1	.963
1987	—St. Louis (N.L.)	SS	7	28	3	6	0	0	0	2	.214	2	3	2	7	19	0	1.000
World Series totals (3 years)			21	75	7	13	0	0	0	3	.173	9	3	4	39	52	1	.989

ALL-STAR GAME RECORD

			BATTING											FIELDING			
Year	**League**	**Pos.**	**AB**	**R**	**H**	**2B**	**3B**	**HR**	**RBI**	**Avg.**	**BB**	**SO**	**SB**	**PO**	**A**	**E**	**Avg.**
1981	—National....................	SS	0	0	0	0	0	0	0	...	2	0	0	1	0	0	1.000
1982	—National....................	PR-SS	0	0	0	0	0	0	0	...	0	0	0	0	1	0	1.000
1983	—National....................	SS	2	1	1	0	0	0	0	.500	0	0	0	0	0	0	...
1984	—National....................	SS	3	0	0	0	0	0	0	.000	0	0	1	3	0	0	1.000
1985	—National....................	SS	4	0	0	0	0	0	0	.000	0	0	0	1	3	0	1.000
1986	—National....................	SS	1	0	0	0	0	0	0	.000	0	0	0	3	2	0	1.000
1987	—National....................	SS	2	0	0	0	0	0	0	.000	0	0	0	3	2	1	.833
1988	—National....................	SS	2	0	0	0	0	0	0	.000	0	1	0	1	4	0	1.000
1989	—National....................	SS	4	0	1	0	0	0	0	.250	0	0	0	1	3	0	1.000
1990	—National....................	SS	1	0	0	0	0	0	0	.000	0	0	0	1	1	0	1.000
1991	—National....................	SS	1	0	0	0	0	0	0	.000	1	0	0	0	1	0	1.000
1992	—National....................	SS	3	0	1	1	0	0	0	.333	0	1	0	1	1	0	1.000
All-Star Game totals (12 years)			23	1	3	1	0	0	0	.130	3	2	1	15	18	1	.971

SMITH, PETE

P, METS

PERSONAL: Born February 27, 1966, in Weymouth, Mass. . . . 6-2/200. . . . Throws right, bats right. . . . Full name: Peter John Smith.
HIGH SCHOOL: Burlington (Mass.).
TRANSACTIONS/CAREER NOTES: Selected by Philadelphia Phillies organization in first round (21st pick overall) of free-agent draft (June 4, 1984). . . . Traded by Phillies organization with C Ozzie Virgil to Atlanta Braves for P Steve Bedrosian and OF Milt Thompson (December 10, 1985). . . . On Atlanta disabled list (June 25-September 3, 1990); included rehabilitation assignment to Greenville (August 26-September 2). . . . On Atlanta disabled list (April 4-May 23, 1991); included rehabilitation assignment to Macon (April 12-24) and Richmond (April 24-May 9 and May 13-14). . . . On disabled list (July 25-September 1, 1993). . . . Traded by Braves to New York Mets for OF Dave Gallagher (November 24, 1993).
STATISTICAL NOTES: Led N.L. with seven balks in 1989. . . . Pitched seven-inning, 1-0 no-hit victory for Richmond against Rochester (May 3, 1992).

Year	Team (League)	W	L	Pct.	ERA	G	GS	CG	ShO	Sv.	IP	H	R	ER	BB	SO
1984	—GC Phillies (GCL)	1	2	.333	1.46	8	8	0	0	0	37	28	11	6	16	35
1985	—Clearwater (FSL)	12	10	.545	3.29	26	25	4	1	0	153	135	68	56	80	86
1986	—Greenville (South.)■	1	8	.111	5.85	24	19	0	0	0	104⅔	117	88	68	78	64
1987	—Greenville (South.)	9	9	.500	3.35	29	25	5	1	1	177⅓	162	76	66	67	119
	—Atlanta (N.L.)	1	2	.333	4.83	6	6	0	0	0	31⅔	39	21	17	14	11
1988	—Atlanta (N.L.)	7	15	.318	3.69	32	32	5	3	0	195⅓	183	89	80	88	124
1989	—Atlanta (N.L.)	5	14	.263	4.75	28	27	1	0	0	142	144	83	75	57	115
1990	—Atlanta (N.L.)	5	6	.455	4.79	13	13	3	0	0	77	77	45	41	24	56
	—Greenville (South.)	0	0	...	0.00	2	2	0	0	0	3⅓	1	0	0	0	2
1991	—Macon (S. Atl.)	0	0	...	8.38	3	3	0	0	0	9⅔	15	11	9	2	14
	—Richmond (Int'l)	3	3	.500	7.24	10	10	1	0	0	51	66	44	41	24	41
	—Atlanta (N.L.)	1	3	.250	5.06	14	10	0	0	0	48	48	33	27	22	29
1992	—Richmond (Int'l)	7	4	.636	2.14	15	15	4	1	0	109⅓	75	27	26	24	93
	—Atlanta (N.L.)	7	0	1.000	2.05	12	11	2	1	0	79	63	19	18	28	43
1993	—Atlanta (N.L.)	4	8	.333	4.37	20	14	0	0	0	90⅔	92	45	44	36	53
Major league totals (7 years)		30	48	.385	4.10	125	113	11	4	0	663⅔	646	335	302	269	431

CHAMPIONSHIP SERIES RECORD

Year	Team (League)	W	L	Pct.	ERA	G	GS	CG	ShO	Sv.	IP	H	R	ER	BB	SO
1992	—Atlanta (N.L.)	0	0	...	2.45	2	0	0	0	0	3⅔	2	1	1	3	3

WORLD SERIES RECORD

Year	Team (League)	W	L	Pct.	ERA	G	GS	CG	ShO	Sv.	IP	H	R	ER	BB	SO
1992	—Atlanta (N.L.)	0	0	...	0.00	1	0	0	0	0	3	3	0	0	0	0

SMITH, ZANE

P, PIRATES

PERSONAL: Born December 28, 1960, in Madison, Wis. . . . 6-1/207. . . . Throws left, bats left. . . . Full name: Zane William Smith.
HIGH SCHOOL: North Platte (Neb.).
COLLEGE: Indiana State.
TRANSACTIONS/CAREER NOTES: Selected by Atlanta Braves organization in third round of free-agent draft (June 7, 1982). . . . On disabled list (August 5-September 1, 1985 and August 25, 1988-remainder of season). . . . Traded by Braves to Montreal Expos for P Sergio Valdez, P Nate Minchey and OF Kevin Dean (July 2, 1989). . . . Traded by Expos to Pittsburgh Pirates for P Scott Ruskin, SS Willie Greene and a player to be named later (August 8, 1990); Expos acquired OF Moises Alou to complete deal (August 16, 1990). . . . Granted free agency (November 5, 1990). . . . Re-signed by Pirates (December 6, 1990). . . . On disabled list (July 15-August 8 and August 15-September 22, 1992). . . . On Pittsburgh disabled list (March 26-June 16, 1993); included rehabilitation assignment to Carolina (May 11-29). . . . On Pittsburgh disabled list (September 8, 1993-remainder of season).
HONORS: Named lefthanded pitcher on THE SPORTING NEWS N.L. All-Star team (1987).
STATISTICAL NOTES: Led N.L. batters with 14 sacrifice hits in 1987.
MISCELLANEOUS: Struck out in only appearance as pinch-hitter (1991). . . . Struck out twice and received a base on balls in three appearances as pinch-hitter (1992).

Year	Team (League)	W	L	Pct.	ERA	G	GS	CG	ShO	Sv.	IP	H	R	ER	BB	SO
1982	—Anderson (S. Atl.)	5	3	.625	6.86	12	10	1	1	1	63	65	53	48	34	32
1983	—Durham (Carolina)	9	•15	.375	4.90	27	27	7	0	0	170⅔	183	109	93	83	126
1984	—Greenville (South.)	7	0	1.000	1.65	9	9	3	1	0	60	47	13	11	23	35
	—Richmond (Int'l)	7	4	.636	4.15	19	19	3	0	0	123⅔	113	62	57	65	68
	—Atlanta (N.L.)	1	0	1.000	2.25	3	3	0	0	0	20	16	7	5	13	16
1985	—Atlanta (N.L.)	9	10	.474	3.80	42	18	2	2	0	147	135	70	62	80	85
1986	—Atlanta (N.L.)	8	16	.333	4.05	38	32	3	1	1	204⅔	209	109	92	105	139
1987	—Atlanta (N.L.)	15	10	.600	4.09	36	•36	9	3	0	242	245	★130	110	91	130
1988	—Atlanta (N.L.)	5	10	.333	4.30	23	22	3	0	0	140⅓	159	72	67	44	59
1989	—Atl.-Mont. (N.L.)■	1	13	.071	3.49	48	17	0	0	2	147	141	76	57	52	93
1990	—Mont.-Pitts. (N.L.)■	12	9	.571	2.55	33	31	4	2	0	215⅓	196	77	61	50	130
1991	—Pittsburgh (N.L.)	16	10	.615	3.20	35	35	6	3	0	228	234	95	81	29	120
1992	—Pittsburgh (N.L.)	8	8	.500	3.06	23	22	4	3	0	141	138	56	48	19	56
1993	—Carolina (South.)	1	2	.333	3.05	4	4	0	0	0	20⅔	20	10	7	5	13
	—Pittsburgh (N.L.)	3	7	.300	4.55	14	14	1	0	0	83	97	43	42	22	32
Major league totals (10 years)		78	93	.456	3.59	295	230	32	14	3	1568⅓	1570	735	625	505	860

CHAMPIONSHIP SERIES RECORD

Year	Team (League)	W	L	Pct.	ERA	G	GS	CG	ShO	Sv.	IP	H	R	ER	BB	SO
1990	—Pittsburgh (N.L.)	0	2	.000	6.00	2	1	0	0	0	9	14	6	6	1	8
1991	—Pittsburgh (N.L.)	1	1	.500	0.61	2	2	0	0	0	14⅔	15	1	1	3	10
Champ. series totals (2 years)		1	3	.250	2.66	4	3	0	0	0	23⅔	29	7	7	4	18

SMITHBERG, ROGER

P, ATHLETICS

PERSONAL: Born March 21, 1966, in Elgin, Ill. . . . 6-3/210. . . . Throws right, bats right. . . . Full name: Roger Craig Smithberg.
HIGH SCHOOL: Larkin (Elgin, Ill.).
COLLEGE: Bradley (undergraduate degree, 1988).
TRANSACTIONS/CAREER NOTES: Selected by San Diego Padres organization in second round of free-agent draft (June 2, 1987). . . . On Las Vegas disabled list (July 7-15, 1991). . . . Released by Wichita, Padres organization (April 2, 1992). . . . Signed by Reno, Oakland Athletics organization (June 26, 1992).

Year	Team (League)	W	L	Pct.	ERA	G	GS	CG	ShO	Sv.	IP	H	R	ER	BB	SO
1988	—Riverside (Calif.)	9	2	.818	3.31	15	15	5	0	0	103⅓	90	52	38	32	72
1989	—Las Vegas (PCL)	7	7	.500	4.47	22	22	4	0	0	137	159	79	68	35	58
1990	—Las Vegas (PCL)	2	7	.222	6.95	13	13	0	0	0	66	91	63	51	39	30
	—Riverside (Calif.)	1	2	.333	4.15	3	3	0	0	0	13	12	7	6	2	5
1991	—High Desert (Calif.)	1	1	.500	1.50	3	3	0	0	0	18	12	6	3	6	11
	—Wichita (Texas)	2	3	.400	4.79	7	7	0	0	0	41⅓	49	28	22	16	23
	—Las Vegas (PCL)	3	7	.300	6.61	17	15	1	0	0	79	112	65	58	33	34
1992	—Reno (California)■	2	1	.667	3.24	10	0	0	0	2	16⅔	23	10	6	10	11
	—Huntsville (South.)	3	3	.500	4.00	20	0	0	0	1	36	42	17	16	12	19
1993	—Huntsville (South.)	4	2	.667	2.21	27	0	0	0	0	36⅔	34	15	9	16	36
	—Tacoma (PCL)	3	3	.500	1.78	28	0	0	0	4	50⅔	50	14	10	11	25
	—Oakland (A.L.)	1	2	.333	2.75	13	0	0	0	3	19⅔	13	7	6	7	4
Major league totals (1 year)		1	2	.333	2.75	13	0	0	0	3	19⅔	13	7	6	7	4

SMOLTZ, JOHN

P, BRAVES

PERSONAL: Born May 15, 1967, in Warren, Mich. . . . 6-3/185. . . . Throws right, bats right. . . . Full name: John Andrew Smoltz.
HIGH SCHOOL: Waverly (Lansing, Mich.).
TRANSACTIONS/CAREER NOTES: Selected by Detroit Tigers organization in 22nd round of free-agent draft (June 3, 1985). . . . Traded by Tigers organization to Atlanta Braves for P Doyle Alexander (August 12, 1987).
STATISTICAL NOTES: Tied for Florida State League lead with six balks in 1986. . . . Led N.L. with 14 wild pitches in 1990, 20 in 1991 and 17 in 1992.
MISCELLANEOUS: Appeared in two games as pinch-runner (1991). . . . Struck out in only appearance as pinch-hitter (1992).

Year	Team (League)	W	L	Pct.	ERA	G	GS	CG	ShO	Sv.	IP	H	R	ER	BB	SO
1986	—Lakeland (Fla. St.)	7	8	.467	3.56	17	14	2	1	0	96	86	44	38	31	47
1987	—Glens Falls (East.)	4	10	.286	5.68	21	21	0	0	0	130	131	89	82	81	86
	—Richmond (Int'l)■	0	1	.000	6.19	3	3	0	0	0	16	17	11	11	11	5
1988	—Richmond (Int'l)	10	5	.667	2.79	20	20	3	0	0	135⅓	118	49	42	37	115
	—Atlanta (N.L.)	2	7	.222	5.48	12	12	0	0	0	64	74	40	39	33	37
1989	—Atlanta (N.L.)	12	11	.522	2.94	29	29	5	0	0	208	160	79	68	72	168
1990	—Atlanta (N.L.)	14	11	.560	3.85	34	34	6	2	0	231⅓	206	109	99	*90	170
1991	—Atlanta (N.L.)	14	13	.519	3.80	36	36	5	0	0	229⅔	206	101	97	77	148
1992	—Atlanta (N.L.)	15	12	.556	2.85	35	•35	9	3	0	246⅔	206	90	78	80	*215
1993	—Atlanta (N.L.)	15	11	.577	3.62	35	35	3	1	0	243⅔	208	104	98	100	208
Major league totals (6 years)		72	65	.526	3.52	181	181	28	6	0	1223⅓	1060	523	479	452	946

CHAMPIONSHIP SERIES RECORD

CHAMPIONSHIP SERIES NOTES: Named N.L. Championship Series Most Valuable Player (1992). . . . Holds N.L. career record for most strikeouts—44. . . . Shares N.L. career record for most games won—4. . . . Shares N.L. single-series record for most bases on balls allowed—10 (1992).

Year	Team (League)	W	L	Pct.	ERA	G	GS	CG	ShO	Sv.	IP	H	R	ER	BB	SO
1991	—Atlanta (N.L.)	2	0	1.000	1.76	2	2	1	1	0	15⅓	14	3	3	3	15
1992	—Atlanta (N.L.)	2	0	1.000	2.66	3	3	0	0	0	20⅓	14	7	6	10	19
1993	—Atlanta (N.L.)	0	1	.000	0.00	1	1	0	0	0	6⅓	8	2	0	5	10
Champ. series totals (3 years)		4	1	.800	1.93	6	6	1	1	0	42	36	12	9	18	44

WORLD SERIES RECORD

WORLD SERIES NOTES: Appeared in one game as pinch-runner (1992).

Year	Team (League)	W	L	Pct.	ERA	G	GS	CG	ShO	Sv.	IP	H	R	ER	BB	SO
1991	—Atlanta (N.L.)	0	0	...	1.26	2	2	0	0	0	14⅓	13	2	2	1	11
1992	—Atlanta (N.L.)	1	0	1.000	2.70	2	2	0	0	0	13⅓	13	5	4	7	12
World Series totals (2 years)		1	0	1.000	1.95	4	4	0	0	0	27⅔	26	7	6	8	23

ALL-STAR GAME RECORD

ALL-STAR GAME NOTES: Shares single-game record for most wild pitches—2 (July 13, 1993). . . . Shares record for most wild pitches in one inning—2 (July 13, 1993, sixth inning).

Year	League	W	L	Pct.	ERA	GS	CG	ShO	Sv.	IP	H	R	ER	BB	SO
1989	—National	0	1	.000	9.00	0	0	0	0	1	2	1	1	0	0
1992	—National	0	0	...	0.00	0	0	0	0	⅓	1	0	0	0	0
1993	—National	0	0	...	0.00	0	0	0	0	⅓	0	0	0	1	0
All-Star totals (3 years)		0	1	.000	5.40	0	0	0	0	1⅔	3	1	1	1	0

SNOW, J.T.

1B, ANGELS

PERSONAL: Born February 26, 1968, in Long Beach, Calif. . . . 6-2/202. . . . Throws left, bats both. . . . Full name: Jack Thomas Snow Jr. . . . Son of Jack Snow, National Football League player (1965-75).
HIGH SCHOOL: Los Alamitos (Calif.).
COLLEGE: Arizona.
TRANSACTIONS/CAREER NOTES: Selected by New York Yankees organization in fifth round of free-agent draft (June 5, 1989). . . . Traded by Yankees with P Jerry Nielsen and P Russ Springer to California Angels for P Jim Abbott (December 6, 1992).

HONORS: Named International League Most Valuable Player (1992).
STATISTICAL NOTES: Led New York-Pennsylvania League first basemen with 649 total chances in 1989. . . . Led Carolina League in grounding into double plays with 20 in 1990. . . . Led Carolina League first basemen with 1,298 total chances and 120 double plays in 1990. . . . Tied for Eastern League lead with 10 sacrifice flies in 1991. . . . Led Eastern League first basemen with 1,200 total chances in 1991. . . . Led International League with 11 intentional bases on balls received in 1992. . . . Led International League first basemen with .995 fielding percentage, 1,097 putouts, 93 assists, 1,196 total chances and 107 double plays in 1992.

			BATTING												FIELDING			
Year	Team (League)	Pos.	G	AB	R	H	2B	3B	HR	RBI	Avg.	BB	SO	SB	PO	A	E	Avg.
1989	—Oneonta (NYP)	1B	73	274	41	80	18	2	8	51	.292	29	35	4	*590	53	6	*.991
1990	—Prin. William (Car.)	1B	*138	520	57	133	25	1	8	72	.256	46	65	2	*1208	*78	12	.991
1991	—Alb./Colon. (East.)	1B	132	477	78	133	33	3	13	76	.279	67	78	5	*1102	90	8	*.993
1992	—Columbus (Int'l)	1B-OF	135	492	81	154	26	4	15	78	•.313	70	65	3	†1103	†93	8	†.993
	—New York (A.L.)	1B	7	14	1	2	1	0	0	2	.143	5	5	0	43	2	0	1.000
1993	—California (A.L.)■	1B	129	419	60	101	18	2	16	57	.241	55	88	3	1010	81	6	.995
	—Vancouver (PCL)	1B	23	94	19	32	9	1	5	24	.340	10	13	0	200	13	2	.991
Major league totals (2 years)			136	433	61	103	19	2	16	59	.238	60	93	3	1053	83	6	.995

SNYDER, CORY

OF/IF, DODGERS

PERSONAL: Born November 11, 1962, in Inglewood, Calif. . . . 6-3/206. . . . Throws right, bats right. . . . Full name: James Cory Snyder. . . . Son of Jim Snyder, minor league infielder (1961-62).
HIGH SCHOOL: Canyon (Canyon Country, Calif.).
COLLEGE: Brigham Young.
TRANSACTIONS/CAREER NOTES: Selected by Cleveland Indians organization in first round (fourth pick overall) of free-agent draft (June 4, 1984). . . . On Cleveland disabled list (July 14-30, 1989); included rehabilitation assignment to Canton/Akron (July 24-30). . . . Traded by Indians with IF Lindsay Foster to Chicago White Sox for P Eric King and P Shawn Hillegas (December 4, 1990). . . . Traded by White Sox to Toronto Blue Jays for OF Shawn Jeter and a player to be named later (July 14, 1991); White Sox acquired P Steve Wapnick to complete deal (September 4, 1991). . . . Released by Blue Jays (October 28, 1991). . . . Signed by San Francisco Giants organization (January 13, 1992). . . . Granted free agency (October 26, 1992). . . . Signed by Los Angeles Dodgers (December 5, 1992).
HONORS: Named shortstop on THE SPORTING NEWS college All-America team (1984). . . . Named Eastern League Most Valuable Player (1985).
STATISTICAL NOTES: Led Eastern League with 255 total bases and 12 sacrifice flies in 1985. . . . Led Eastern League third basemen with 132 putouts, 391 total chances and 26 double plays in 1985. . . . Hit three home runs in one game (May 21, 1987). . . . Led A.L. outfielders with .997 fielding percentage in 1989.
MISCELLANEOUS: Member of 1984 U.S. Olympic baseball team.

			BATTING												FIELDING			
Year	Team (League)	Pos.	G	AB	R	H	2B	3B	HR	RBI	Avg.	BB	SO	SB	PO	A	E	Avg.
1985	—Waterbury (East.)	3B-SS	*139	512	77	144	25	1	*28	*94	.281	44	123	5	†134	231	33	.917
1986	—Maine (Int'l)	3B-SS	49	192	25	58	19	0	9	32	.302	17	39	2	46	87	8	.943
	—Cleveland (A.L.)	OF-SS-3B	103	416	58	113	21	1	24	69	.272	16	123	2	213	84	10	.967
1987	—Cleveland (A.L.)	OF-SS	157	577	74	136	24	2	33	82	.236	31	166	5	313	53	15	.961
1988	—Cleveland (A.L.)	OF	142	511	71	139	24	3	26	75	.272	42	101	5	314	*16	5	.985
1989	—Cleveland (A.L.)	OF-SS	132	489	49	105	17	0	18	59	.215	23	134	6	297	32	1	†.997
	—Cant./Akr. (East.)	OF	4	11	3	5	0	0	0	2	.455	1	1	1	5	2	0	1.000
1990	—Cleveland (A.L.)	OF-SS	123	438	46	102	27	3	14	55	.233	21	118	1	229	18	7	.972
1991	—Chi.-Tor. (A.L.)■	OF-1B-3B	71	166	14	29	4	1	3	17	.175	9	60	0	198	17	3	.986
	—Syracuse (Int'l)	OF	17	67	11	18	3	0	6	17	.269	4	16	0	25	0	0	1.000
1992	—San Francisco (N.L.)■	0-1-3-2-S	124	390	48	105	22	2	14	57	.269	23	96	4	301	53	6	.983
1993	—Los Angeles (N.L.)■	0-3-1-S	143	516	61	137	33	1	11	56	.266	47	*147	4	210	46	9	.966
American League totals (6 years)			728	2597	312	624	117	10	118	357	.240	142	702	19	1564	220	41	.978
National League totals (2 years)			267	906	109	242	55	3	25	113	.267	70	243	8	511	99	15	.976
Major league totals (8 years)			995	3503	421	866	172	13	143	470	.247	212	945	27	2075	319	56	.977

SOJO, LUIS

IF, MARINERS

PERSONAL: Born January 3, 1966, in Barquisimeto, Venezuela. . . . 5-11/174. . . . Throws right, bats right. . . . Name pronounced SO-ho.
TRANSACTIONS/CAREER NOTES: Signed as free agent by Toronto Blue Jays organization (January 3, 1986). . . . Traded by Blue Jays with OF Junior Felix and a player to be named later to California Angels for OF Devon White, P Willie Fraser and a player to be named later (December 2, 1990); Blue Jays acquired P Marcus Moore and Angels acquired C Ken Rivers to complete deal (December 4, 1990). . . . Traded by Angels to Blue Jays for 3B Kelly Gruber and cash (December 8, 1992). . . . On Toronto disabled list (May 10-30, 1993). . . . Granted free agency (October 15, 1993). . . . Signed by Seattle Mariners organization (January 10, 1994).
STATISTICAL NOTES: Led International League shortstops with .957 fielding percentage in 1989. . . . Led International League with nine sacrifice flies in 1990. . . . Led A.L. with 19 sacrifice hits in 1991.

			BATTING												FIELDING			
Year	Team (League)	Pos.	G	AB	R	H	2B	3B	HR	RBI	Avg.	BB	SO	SB	PO	A	E	Avg.
1986	—		Dominican Summer League statistics unavailable.															
1987	—Myrtle Beach (SAL)	S-2-3-0	72	223	23	47	5	4	2	15	.211	17	18	5	104	123	14	.942
1988	—Myrtle Beach (SAL)	SS	135	*536	83	*155	22	5	5	56	.289	35	35	14	191	407	28	.955
1989	—Syracuse (Int'l)	SS-2B	121	482	54	133	20	5	3	54	.276	21	42	9	170	348	23	†.957
1990	—Syracuse (Int'l)	2B-SS	75	297	39	88	12	3	6	25	.296	14	23	10	138	212	10	.972
	—Toronto (A.L.)	2-S-0-3	33	80	14	18	3	0	1	9	.225	5	5	1	34	31	5	.929
1991	—California (A.L.)■	2-S-3-0	113	364	38	94	14	1	3	20	.258	14	26	4	233	335	11	.981
1992	—Edmonton (PCL)	3B-2B-SS	37	145	22	43	9	1	1	24	.297	9	17	4	32	106	4	.972
	—California (A.L.)	2B-3B-SS	106	368	37	100	12	3	7	43	.272	14	24	7	196	293	9	.982

Year	Team (League)	Pos.	G	AB	R	H	2B	3B	HR	RBI	Avg.	BB	SO	SB	PO	A	E	Avg.
			BATTING												FIELDING			
1993	—Toronto (A.L.)■	SS-2B-3B	19	47	5	8	2	0	0	6	.170	4	2	0	24	35	2	.967
	—Syracuse (Int'l)	2-0-3-S-1	43	142	17	31	7	2	1	12	.218	8	12	2	46	60	4	.964
Major league totals (4 years)			271	859	94	220	31	4	11	78	.256	37	57	12	487	694	27	.978

SORRENTO, PAUL

1B, INDIANS

PERSONAL: Born November 17, 1965, in Somerville, Mass. . . . 6-2/220. . . . Throws right, bats left. . . . Full name: Paul Anthony Sorrento.
HIGH SCHOOL: St. John's Preparatory (Danvers, Mass.).
COLLEGE: Florida State.
TRANSACTIONS/CAREER NOTES: Selected by California Angels organization in fourth round of free-agent draft (June 2, 1986). . . . Traded by Angels organization with P Mike Cook and P Rob Wassenaar to Minnesota Twins for P Bert Blyleven and P Kevin Trudeau (November 3, 1988). . . . Traded by Twins to Cleveland Indians for P Oscar Munoz and P Curt Leskanic (March 28, 1992).
STATISTICAL NOTES: Led Southern League first basemen with 103 double plays in 1989. . . . Led Pacific Coast League first basemen with 14 errors in 1991.

Year	Team (League)	Pos.	G	AB	R	H	2B	3B	HR	RBI	Avg.	BB	SO	SB	PO	A	E	Avg.
			BATTING												FIELDING			
1986	—Quad Cities (Mid.)	OF	53	177	33	63	11	2	6	34	.356	24	40	0	83	7	1	.989
	—Palm Springs (Cal.)	OF	16	62	5	15	3	0	1	7	.242	4	15	0	16	1	1	.944
1987	—Palm Springs (Cal.)	OF	114	370	66	83	14	2	8	45	.224	78	95	1	123	10	4	.971
1988	—Palm Springs (Cal.)	1B-OF	133	465	91	133	30	6	14	99	.286	110	101	3	719	55	18	.977
1989	—Orlando (Southern)■	1B	140	509	81	130	*35	2	27	*112	.255	84	119	1	1070	41	*24	.979
	—Minnesota (A.L.)	1B	14	21	2	5	0	0	0	1	.238	5	4	0	13	0	0	1.000
1990	—Portland (PCL)	1B-OF	102	354	59	107	27	1	19	72	.302	64	95	3	695	52	13	.983
	—Minnesota (A.L.)	1B	41	121	11	25	4	1	5	13	.207	12	31	1	118	7	1	.992
1991	—Portland (PCL)	1B-OF	113	409	59	126	30	2	13	79	.308	62	65	1	933	58	†14	.986
	—Minnesota (A.L.)	1B	26	47	6	12	2	0	4	13	.255	4	11	0	70	7	0	1.000
1992	—Cleveland (A.L.)■	1B	140	458	52	123	24	1	18	60	.269	51	89	0	996	78	8	.993
1993	—Cleveland (A.L.)	1B-OF	148	463	75	119	26	1	18	65	.257	58	121	3	1015	86	6	.995
Major league totals (5 years)			369	1110	146	284	56	3	45	152	.256	130	256	4	2212	178	15	.994

CHAMPIONSHIP SERIES RECORD

Year	Team (League)	Pos.	G	AB	R	H	2B	3B	HR	RBI	Avg.	BB	SO	SB	PO	A	E	Avg.
			BATTING												FIELDING			
1991	—Minnesota (A.L.)	PH	1	1	0	0	0	0	0	0	.000	0	1	0	...	...	...	...

WORLD SERIES RECORD

Year	Team (League)	Pos.	G	AB	R	H	2B	3B	HR	RBI	Avg.	BB	SO	SB	PO	A	E	Avg.
			BATTING												FIELDING			
1991	—Minnesota (A.L.)	PH-1B	3	2	0	0	0	0	0	0	.000	1	2	0	1	1	0	1.000

SOSA, SAMMY

OF, CUBS

PERSONAL: Born November 12, 1968, in San Pedro de Macoris, Dominican Republic. . . . 6-0/185. . . . Throws right, bats right.
TRANSACTIONS/CAREER NOTES: Signed as free agent by Texas Rangers organization (July 30, 1985). . . . Traded by Rangers with SS Scott Fletcher and P Wilson Alvarez to Chicago White Sox for OF Harold Baines and IF Fred Manrique (July 29, 1989). . . . Traded by White Sox with P Ken Patterson to Chicago Cubs for OF George Bell (March 30, 1992). . . . On Chicago disabled list (June 13-July 27, 1992); included rehabilitation assignment to Iowa (July 21-27). . . . On Chicago disabled list (August 7-September 16, 1992).
STATISTICAL NOTES: Led Gulf Coast League with 96 total bases in 1986. . . . Tied for South Atlantic League lead in double plays by outfielder with four in 1987. . . . Collected six hits in one game (July 2, 1993).

Year	Team (League)	Pos.	G	AB	R	H	2B	3B	HR	RBI	Avg.	BB	SO	SB	PO	A	E	Avg.
			BATTING												FIELDING			
1986	—GC Rangers (GCL)	OF	61	229	38	63	*19	1	4	28	.275	22	51	11	92	9	*6	.944
1987	—Gastonia (S. Atl.)	OF	129	519	73	145	27	4	11	59	.279	21	123	22	183	12	17	.920
1988	—Charlotte (Fla. St.)	OF	131	507	70	116	13	*12	9	51	.229	35	106	42	227	11	7	.971
1989	—Tulsa (Texas)	OF	66	273	45	81	15	4	7	31	.297	15	52	16	110	7	4	.967
	—Texas-Chi. (A.L.)■	OF	58	183	27	47	8	0	4	13	.257	11	47	7	94	2	4	.960
	—Okla. City (A.A.)	OF	10	39	2	4	2	0	0	3	.103	2	8	4	22	0	2	.917
	—Vancouver (PCL)	OF	13	49	7	18	3	0	1	5	.367	0	20	0	43	1	0	1.000
1990	—Chicago (A.L.)	OF	153	532	72	124	26	10	15	70	.233	33	150	32	315	14	*13	.962
1991	—Chicago (A.L.)	OF	116	316	39	64	10	1	10	33	.203	14	98	13	214	6	6	.973
	—Vancouver (PCL)	OF	32	116	19	31	7	2	3	19	.267	17	32	9	95	2	3	.970
1992	—Chicago (N.L.)■	OF	67	262	41	68	7	2	8	25	.260	19	63	15	145	4	6	.961
	—Iowa (Am. Assoc.)	OF	5	19	3	6	2	0	0	1	.316	1	2	5	14	0	0	1.000
1993	—Chicago (N.L.)	OF	159	598	92	156	25	5	33	93	.261	38	135	36	344	17	9	.976
American League totals (3 years)			327	1031	138	235	44	11	29	116	.228	58	295	52	623	22	23	.966
National League totals (2 years)			226	860	133	224	32	7	41	118	.260	57	198	51	489	21	15	.971
Major league totals (5 years)			553	1891	271	459	76	18	70	234	.243	115	493	103	1112	43	38	.968

SPEHR, TIM

C, EXPOS

PERSONAL: Born July 2, 1966, in Excelsior Springs, Mo. . . . 6-2/200. . . . Throws right, bats right. . . . Full name: Timothy Joseph Spehr. . . . Name pronounced SPEAR.
HIGH SCHOOL: Richfield (Waco, Tex.).
COLLEGE: Arizona State.
TRANSACTIONS/CAREER NOTES: Selected by Kansas City Royals organization in fifth round of free-agent draft (June 1, 1988).

. . . On disabled list (June 25-July 27, 1988). . . . On Baseball City disabled list (April 7-May 21, 1989). . . . Traded by Royals organization with P Jeff Shaw to Montreal Expos organization for P Mark Gardner and P Doug Piatt (December 9, 1992).
STATISTICAL NOTES: Led American Association catchers with 730 total chances and 14 double plays in 1990. . . . Tied for American Association lead in being hit by pitch with 11 in 1992.

			BATTING												FIELDING			
Year	Team (League)	Pos.	G	AB	R	H	2B	3B	HR	RBI	Avg.	BB	SO	SB	PO	A	E	Avg.
1988	—Appleton (Midw.)	C	31	110	15	29	3	0	5	22	.264	10	28	3	146	14	7	.958
1989	—Baseball City (FSL)	C	18	64	8	16	5	0	1	7	.250	5	17	1	63	7	1	.986
	—Memphis (South.)	C	61	216	22	42	9	0	8	23	.194	16	59	1	274	36	5	.984
1990	—Omaha (A.A.)	C	102	307	42	69	10	2	6	34	.225	41	88	5	*658	67	5	*.993
1991	—Omaha (A.A.)	C	72	215	27	59	14	2	6	26	.274	25	48	3	402	53	8	.983
	—Kansas City (A.L.)	C	37	74	7	14	5	0	3	14	.189	9	18	1	190	19	3	.986
1992	—Omaha (A.A.)	C	109	336	48	85	22	0	15	42	.253	61	89	4	577	65	7	.989
1993	—Montreal (N.L.)■	C	53	87	14	20	6	0	2	10	.230	6	20	2	166	22	9	.954
	—Ottawa (Int'l)	C	46	141	15	28	6	1	4	13	.199	14	35	2	248	24	6	.978
	American League totals (1 year)		37	74	7	14	5	0	3	14	.189	9	18	1	190	19	3	.986
	National League totals (1 year)		53	87	14	20	6	0	2	10	.230	6	20	2	166	22	9	.954
	Major league totals (2 years)		90	161	21	34	11	0	5	24	.211	15	38	3	356	41	12	.971

SPIERS, BILL

2B, BREWERS

PERSONAL: Born June 5, 1966, in Orangeburg, S.C. . . . 6-2/190. . . . Throws right, bats left. . . . Full name: William James Spiers III. . . . Name pronounced SPY-ers.
HIGH SCHOOL: Wade Hampton Academy (Orangeburg, S.C.).
COLLEGE: Clemson.
TRANSACTIONS/CAREER NOTES: Selected by Milwaukee Brewers organization in first round (13th pick overall) of free-agent draft (June 2, 1987). . . . On Milwaukee disabled list (April 6-May 15, 1990); included rehabilitation assignment to Denver (April 27-May 14). . . . On Milwaukee disabled list (April 5-September 2, 1992); included rehabilitation assignment to Beloit (May 6-15 and August 20-September 2). . . . Granted free agency (December 20, 1993). . . . Re-signed by Brewers (December 21, 1993).
HONORS: Named shortstop on THE SPORTING NEWS college All-America team (1987).

			BATTING												FIELDING			
Year	Team (League)	Pos.	G	AB	R	H	2B	3B	HR	RBI	Avg.	BB	SO	SB	PO	A	E	Avg.
1987	—Helena (Pioneer)	SS	6	22	4	9	1	0	0	3	.409	3	3	2	8	6	6	.700
	—Beloit (Midwest)	SS	64	258	43	77	10	1	3	26	.298	15	38	11	111	160	20	.931
1988	—Stockton (Calif.)	SS	84	353	68	95	17	3	5	52	.269	42	41	27	140	240	19	.952
	—El Paso (Texas)	SS	47	168	22	47	5	2	3	21	.280	15	20	4	73	141	13	.943
1989	—Milwaukee (A.L.)	S-3-2-1	114	345	44	88	9	3	4	33	.255	21	63	10	164	295	21	.956
	—Denver (A.A.)	SS	14	47	9	17	2	1	2	8	.362	5	6	1	32	33	2	.970
1990	—Denver (A.A.)	SS	11	38	6	12	0	0	1	7	.316	10	8	1	22	23	2	.957
	—Milwaukee (A.L.)	SS	112	363	44	88	15	3	2	36	.242	16	46	11	159	326	12	.976
1991	—Milwaukee (A.L.)	SS-OF	133	414	71	117	13	6	8	54	.283	34	55	14	201	345	17	.970
1992	—Beloit (Midwest)	SS	16	55	9	13	3	0	0	7	.236	7	7	4	12	28	3	.930
	—Milwaukee (A.L.)	SS-2B-3B	12	16	2	5	2	0	0	2	.313	1	4	1	6	6	0	1.000
1993	—Milwaukee (A.L.)	2B-OF-SS	113	340	43	81	8	4	2	36	.238	29	51	9	213	231	13	.972
	Major league totals (5 years)		484	1478	204	379	47	16	16	161	.256	101	219	45	743	1203	63	.969

SPOLJARIC, PAUL

P, BLUE JAYS

PERSONAL: Born September 24, 1970, in Kelowna, B.C. . . . 6-3/205. . . . Throws left, bats right. . . . Full name: Paul Nikola Spoljaric. . . . Name pronounced spole-JAIR-ick.
HIGH SCHOOL: Springvalley Secondary (Kelowna, B.C.).
COLLEGE: Douglas College (B.C.).
TRANSACTIONS/CAREER NOTES: Signed as free agent by Toronto Blue Jays organization (August 26, 1989).
HONORS: Named South Atlantic League Most Outstanding Pitcher (1992).

Year	Team (League)	W	L	Pct.	ERA	G	GS	CG	ShO	Sv.	IP	H	R	ER	BB	SO
1990	—Medicine Hat (Pio.)	3	7	.300	4.34	15	13	0	0	1	66⅓	57	43	32	35	62
1991	—St. Cathar. (NYP)	0	2	.000	4.82	4	4	0	0	0	18⅔	21	14	10	9	21
1992	—Myrtle Beach (SAL)	10	8	.556	2.82	26	26	1	0	0	162⅔	111	68	51	58	161
1993	—Dunedin (Fla. St.)	3	0	1.000	1.38	4	4	0	0	0	26	16	5	4	12	29
	—Knoxville (South.)	4	1	.800	2.28	7	7	0	0	0	43⅓	30	12	11	22	51
	—Syracuse (Int'l)	8	7	.533	5.29	18	18	1	1	0	95⅓	97	63	56	52	88

SPRADLIN, JERRY

P, REDS

PERSONAL: Born June 14, 1967, in Fullerton, Calif. . . . 6-7/231. . . . Throws right, bats both. . . . Full name: Jerry Carl Spradlin.
HIGH SCHOOL: Katella (Anaheim, Calif.).
COLLEGE: Fullerton (Calif.) College.
TRANSACTIONS/CAREER NOTES: Selected by Cincinnati Reds organization in 19th round of free-agent draft (June 1, 1988).
HONORS: Named Southern League co-Most Valuable Pitcher (1992).

Year	Team (League)	W	L	Pct.	ERA	G	GS	CG	ShO	Sv.	IP	H	R	ER	BB	SO
1988	—Billings (Pioneer)	4	1	.800	3.21	17	5	0	0	0	47⅔	45	25	17	14	23
1989	—Greensboro (S. Atl.)	7	2	.778	2.76	42	1	0	0	2	94⅔	88	35	29	23	56
1990	—Ced. Rap. (Midw.)	0	1	.000	3.00	5	0	0	0	0	12	13	8	4	5	6
	—Char., W.Va. (SAL)	3	4	.429	2.54	43	1	1	0	17	74⅓	74	23	21	17	39
1991	—Chatt. (South.)	7	3	.700	3.09	48	1	0	0	4	96	95	38	33	32	73
1992	—Chatt. (South.)	3	3	.500	1.38	59	0	0	0	*34	65⅓	52	11	10	13	35
	—Ced. Rap. (Midw.)	1	0	1.000	7.71	1	0	0	0	0	2⅓	5	2	2	0	4
1993	—Indianapolis (A.A.)	3	2	.600	3.49	34	0	0	0	1	56⅔	58	24	22	12	46
	—Cincinnati (N.L.)	2	1	.667	3.49	37	0	0	0	2	49	44	20	19	9	24
	Major league totals (1 year)	2	1	.667	3.49	37	0	0	0	2	49	44	20	19	9	24

SPRAGUE, ED

3B, BLUE JAYS

PERSONAL: Born July 25, 1967, in Castro Valley, Calif. . . . 6-2/210. . . . Throws right, bats right. . . . Full name: Edward Nelson Sprague. . . . Son of Ed Sprague, major league pitcher with four teams (1968-69 and 1971-76); and husband of Kristen Babb, Olympic gold-medal synchronized swimmer (1992). . . . Name pronounced SPRAYGH.

HIGH SCHOOL: St. Mary's (Stockton, Calif.).

COLLEGE: Stanford.

TRANSACTIONS/CAREER NOTES: Selected by Boston Red Sox organization in 26th round of free-agent draft (June 3, 1985). . . . Selected by Toronto Blue Jays organization in first round (25th pick overall) of free-agent draft (June 1, 1988). . . . On suspended list (August 8-10, 1993).

STATISTICAL NOTES: Led International League third basemen with 31 errors and 364 total chances and tied for lead with 240 assists in 1990. . . . Led A.L. in grounding into double plays with 23 in 1993.

MISCELLANEOUS: Member of 1988 U.S. Olympic baseball team.

			BATTING												FIELDING			
Year	**Team (League)**	**Pos.**	**G**	**AB**	**R**	**H**	**2B**	**3B**	**HR**	**RBI**	**Avg.**	**BB**	**SO**	**SB**	**PO**	**A**	**E**	**Avg.**
1989	—Dunedin (Fla. St.)	3B	52	192	21	42	9	2	7	23	.219	16	40	1	33	86	14	.895
	—Syracuse (Int'l)	3B	86	288	23	60	14	1	5	33	.208	18	73	0	51	149	*25	.889
1990	—Syracuse (Int'l)	3B-1B-C	142	*519	60	124	23	5	20	75	.239	31	100	4	171	‡246	†35	.923
1991	—Syracuse (Int'l)	C-3B	23	88	24	32	8	0	5	25	.364	10	21	2	111	17	6	.955
	—Toronto (A.L.)	3B-1B-C	61	160	17	44	7	0	4	20	.275	19	43	0	167	72	14	.945
1992	—Syracuse (Int'l)	C-1B-3B	100	369	49	102	18	2	16	50	.276	44	73	0	438	44	12	.976
	—Toronto (A.L.)	C-1B-3B	22	47	6	11	2	0	1	7	.234	3	7	0	82	5	1	.989
1993	—Toronto (A.L.)	3B	150	546	50	142	31	1	12	73	.260	32	85	1	*127	232	17	.955
Major league totals (3 years)			233	753	73	197	40	1	17	100	.262	54	135	1	376	309	32	.955

CHAMPIONSHIP SERIES RECORD

			BATTING												FIELDING			
Year	**Team (League)**	**Pos.**	**G**	**AB**	**R**	**H**	**2B**	**3B**	**HR**	**RBI**	**Avg.**	**BB**	**SO**	**SB**	**PO**	**A**	**E**	**Avg.**
1991	—Toronto (A.L.)							Did not play.										
1992	—Toronto (A.L.)	PH	2	2	0	1	0	0	0	0	.500	0	1	0	...	...	...	...
1993	—Toronto (A.L.)	3B	6	21	0	6	0	1	0	4	.286	2	4	0	5	9	0	1.000
Championship series totals (2 years)			8	23	0	7	0	1	0	4	.304	2	5	0	5	9	0	1.000

WORLD SERIES RECORD

WORLD SERIES NOTES: Hit home run in first at-bat (October 18, 1992).

			BATTING												FIELDING			
Year	**Team (League)**	**Pos.**	**G**	**AB**	**R**	**H**	**2B**	**3B**	**HR**	**RBI**	**Avg.**	**BB**	**SO**	**SB**	**PO**	**A**	**E**	**Avg.**
1992	—Toronto (A.L.)	PH-1B	3	2	1	1	0	0	1	2	.500	1	0	0	0	0	0	...
1993	—Toronto (A.L.)	3B-PH-1B	5	15	0	1	0	0	0	2	.067	1	6	0	4	9	2	.867
World Series totals (2 years)			8	17	1	2	0	0	1	4	.118	2	6	0	4	9	2	.867

SPRINGER, RUSS

P, ANGELS

PERSONAL: Born November 7, 1968, in Alexandria, La. . . . 6-4/195. . . . Throws right, bats right. . . . Full name: Russell Paul Springer.

HIGH SCHOOL: Grant (Dry Prong, La.).

COLLEGE: Louisiana State.

TRANSACTIONS/CAREER NOTES: Selected by New York Yankees organization in seventh round of free-agent draft (June 5, 1989). . . . Traded by Yankees with 1B J.T. Snow and P Jerry Nielsen to California Angels for P Jim Abbott (December 6, 1992). . . . On California disabled list (August 2, 1993-remainder of season).

Year	**Team (League)**	**W**	**L**	**Pct.**	**ERA**	**G**	**GS**	**CG**	**ShO**	**Sv.**	**IP**	**H**	**R**	**ER**	**BB**	**SO**
1989	—GC Yankees (GCL)	3	0	1.000	1.50	6	6	0	0	0	24	14	8	4	10	34
1990	—GC Yankees (GCL)	0	2	.000	1.20	4	4	0	0	0	15	10	6	2	4	17
	—Greensboro (S. Atl.)	2	3	.400	3.67	10	10	0	0	0	56⅓	51	33	23	31	51
1991	—Fort Lauder. (FSL)	5	9	.357	3.49	25	25	2	0	0	152⅓	118	68	59	62	139
	—Alb./Colon. (East.)	1	0	1.000	1.80	2	2	0	0	0	15	9	4	3	6	16
1992	—Columbus (Int'l)	8	5	.615	2.69	20	20	1	0	0	123⅔	89	46	37	54	95
	—New York (A.L.)	0	0	...	6.19	14	0	0	0	0	16	18	11	11	10	12
1993	—Vancouver (PCL)■	5	4	.556	4.27	11	9	1	0	0	59	58	37	28	33	40
	—California (A.L.)	1	6	.143	7.20	14	9	1	0	0	60	73	48	48	32	31
Major league totals (2 years)		1	6	.143	6.99	28	9	1	0	0	76	91	59	59	42	43

STAHOVIAK, SCOTT

3B, TWINS

PERSONAL: Born March 6, 1970, in Waukegan, Ill. . . . 6-5/208. . . . Throws right, bats left. . . . Full name: Scott Edmund Stahoviak. . . . Name pronounced stuh-HO-vee-ak.

HIGH SCHOOL: Carmel (Mundelein, Ill.).

COLLEGE: Creighton.

TRANSACTIONS/CAREER NOTES: Selected by Minnesota Twins organization in 27th round of free-agent draft (June 1, 1988). . . . Selected by Twins organization in supplemental round ("sandwich pick" between first and second round, 27th pick overall) of free-agent draft (June 3, 1991); pick received as compensation for California Angels signing Type A free agent Gary Gaetti. . . . On Nashville disabled list (May 12-June 24, 1993).

			BATTING												FIELDING			
Year	**Team (League)**	**Pos.**	**G**	**AB**	**R**	**H**	**2B**	**3B**	**HR**	**RBI**	**Avg.**	**BB**	**SO**	**SB**	**PO**	**A**	**E**	**Avg.**
1991	—Visalia (California)	3B	43	158	29	44	9	1	1	25	.278	22	28	9	31	89	12	.909
1992	—Visalia (California)	3B	110	409	62	126	26	3	5	68	.308	82	66	17	92	181	*40	.872
1993	—Nashville (South.)	3-1-S-0	93	331	40	90	25	1	12	56	.272	56	95	10	89	150	24	.909
	—Minnesota (A.L.)	3B	20	57	1	11	4	0	0	1	.193	3	22	0	9	38	4	.922
Major league totals (1 year)			20	57	1	11	4	0	0	1	.193	3	22	0	9	38	4	.922

STAIRS, MATT

OF, EXPOS

PERSONAL: Born February 27, 1969, in Fredericton, New Brunswick, Canada. . . . 5-9/175. . . . Throws right, bats left. . . . Full name: Matthew Wade Stairs.
HIGH SCHOOL: Fredericton (New Brunswick).
TRANSACTIONS/CAREER NOTES: Signed as free agent by Montreal Expos organization (January 17, 1989). . . . On disabled list (May 16-23, 1991). . . . On Ottawa disabled list (May 7-18, 1993). . . . Released by Expos (June 8, 1993). . . . Signed by Chunichi Dragons of Japan Central League (June 1993). . . . Signed as free agent by Expos organization (December 15, 1993).
HONORS: Named Eastern League Most Valuable Player (1991).
STATISTICAL NOTES: Led Eastern League with .509 slugging percentage, 257 total bases and tied for lead with eight intentional bases on balls received in 1991.
MISCELLANEOUS: Member of 1988 Canadian Olympic baseball team.

			BATTING												FIELDING			
Year	**Team (League)**	**Pos.**	**G**	**AB**	**R**	**H**	**2B**	**3B**	**HR**	**RBI**	**Avg.**	**BB**	**SO**	**SB**	**PO**	**A**	**E**	**Avg.**
1989	—W.P. Beach (FSL)	3B-SS-2B	36	111	12	21	3	1	1	9	.189	9	18	0	21	66	4	.956
	—Jamestown (NYP)	2B-3B	14	43	8	11	1	0	1	5	.256	3	5	1	15	35	6	.893
	—Rockford (Midw.)	3B	44	141	20	40	9	2	2	14	.284	15	29	5	30	62	7	.929
1990	—W.P. Beach (FSL)	3B-2B	55	183	30	62	9	3	3	30	.339	41	19	15	40	112	17	.899
	—Jacksonv. (South.)	3-0-2-S	79	280	26	71	17	0	3	34	.254	22	43	5	76	107	22	.893
1991	—Harrisburg (East.)	2B-3B-OF	129	505	87	*168	30	•10	13	78	*.333	66	47	23	193	314	22	.958
1992	—Indianapolis (A.A.)	OF	110	401	57	107	23	4	11	56	.267	49	61	11	188	11	3	.985
	—Montreal (N.L.)	OF	13	30	2	5	2	0	0	5	.167	7	7	0	14	0	1	.933
1993	—Ottawa (Int'l)	OF	34	125	18	35	4	2	3	20	.280	11	15	4	49	4	0	1.000
	—Montreal (N.L.)	OF	6	8	1	3	1	0	0	2	.375	0	1	0	1	0	0	1.000
	—Chunichi (Jp. Cn.)■	...	60	132	10	33	6	0	6	23	.250	7	34	1	...	...	...	...
Major league totals (2 years)			19	38	3	8	3	0	0	7	.211	7	8	0	15	0	1	.938

S

STANKIEWICZ, ANDY

2B/3B, ASTROS

PERSONAL: Born August 10, 1964, in Inglewood, Calif. . . . 5-9/165. . . . Throws right, bats right. . . . Full name: Andrew Neal Stankiewicz.
HIGH SCHOOL: St. Paul (Sante Fe Springs, Calif.).
COLLEGE: Pepperdine.
TRANSACTIONS/CAREER NOTES: Selected by Kansas City Royals organization in 26th round of free-agent draft (June 7, 1982). . . . Selected by Detroit Tigers organization in 18th round of free-agent draft (June 3, 1985). . . . Selected by New York Yankees organization in 12th round of free-agent draft (June 2, 1986). . . . On New York disabled list (May 16-31, 1992). . . . On Columbus disabled list (August 18-26, 1993). . . . Traded by Yankees with P Domingo Jean to Houston Astros for P Xavier Hernandez (November 27, 1993).
STATISTICAL NOTES: Led Eastern League with 11 sacrifice flies in 1989. . . . Led Eastern League second basemen with 615 total chances and 85 double plays in 1989.

			BATTING												FIELDING			
Year	**Team (League)**	**Pos.**	**G**	**AB**	**R**	**H**	**2B**	**3B**	**HR**	**RBI**	**Avg.**	**BB**	**SO**	**SB**	**PO**	**A**	**E**	**Avg.**
1986	—Oneonta (NYP)	2B-SS	59	216	51	64	8	3	0	17	.296	38	41	14	107	152	12	.956
1987	—Fort Lauder. (FSL)	2B	119	456	80	140	18	7	2	47	.307	62	84	26	233	347	16	.973
1988	—Alb./Colon. (East.)	2B	109	414	63	111	20	2	1	33	.268	39	53	15	230	325	*16	.972
	—Columbus (Int'l)	2B	29	114	4	25	0	0	0	4	.219	6	25	2	56	97	3	.981
1989	—Alb./Colon. (East.)	2B	133	498	*74	133	26	2	4	49	.267	57	59	*41	*242	*369	4	*.993
1990	—Columbus (Int'l)	2B-SS-3B	135	446	68	102	14	4	1	48	.229	71	63	25	237	399	10	.985
1991	—Columbus (Int'l)	2-S-3-P	125	372	47	101	12	4	1	41	.272	29	45	29	220	324	15	.973
1992	—New York (A.L.)	SS-2B	116	400	52	107	22	2	2	25	.268	38	42	9	185	346	12	.978
1993	—Columbus (Int'l)	2B-3B-SS	90	331	45	80	12	5	0	32	.242	29	46	12	138	265	6	.985
	—New York (A.L.)	2B-3B-SS	16	9	5	0	0	0	0	0	.000	1	1	0	7	15	0	1.000
Major league totals (2 years)			132	409	57	107	22	2	2	25	.262	39	43	9	192	361	12	.979

RECORD AS PITCHER

Year	**Team (League)**	**W**	**L**	**Pct.**	**ERA**	**G**	**GS**	**CG**	**ShO**	**Sv.**	**IP**	**H**	**R**	**ER**	**BB**	**SO**
1991	—Columbus (Int'l)	0	0	...	0.00	1	0	0	0	0	⅓	1	0	0	1	0

STANLEY, MIKE

C, YANKEES

PERSONAL: Born June 25, 1963, in Fort Lauderdale, Fla. . . . 6-0/192. . . . Throws right, bats right. . . . Full name: Robert Michael Stanley.
HIGH SCHOOL: St. Thomas Aquinas (Fort Lauderdale, Fla.).
COLLEGE: Florida.
TRANSACTIONS/CAREER NOTES: Selected by Texas Rangers organization in 16th round of free-agent draft (June 3, 1985). . . . On disabled list (July 24-August 14, 1988 and August 18-September 2, 1989). . . . Granted free agency (November 15, 1990). . . . Re-signed by Rangers organization (February 4, 1991). . . . Granted free agency (October 14, 1991). . . . Signed by Columbus, New York Yankees organization (January 21, 1992).
HONORS: Named catcher on THE SPORTING NEWS A.L. All-Star team (1993). . . . Named catcher on THE SPORTING NEWS A.L. Silver Slugger team (1993).

			BATTING												FIELDING			
Year	**Team (League)**	**Pos.**	**G**	**AB**	**R**	**H**	**2B**	**3B**	**HR**	**RBI**	**Avg.**	**BB**	**SO**	**SB**	**PO**	**A**	**E**	**Avg.**
1985	—Salem (Carolina)	1B-C	4	9	2	5	0	0	0	3	.556	1	1	0	19	1	1	.952
	—Burlington (Midw.)	C-1B-OF	13	42	8	13	2	0	1	6	.310	6	5	0	45	2	0	1.000
	—Tulsa (Texas)	C-1-0-2	46	165	24	51	10	0	3	17	.309	24	18	6	289	18	6	.981
1986	—Tulsa (Texas)	C-1B-3B	67	235	41	69	16	2	6	35	.294	34	26	5	379	45	2	.995
	—Texas (A.L.)	3B-C-OF	15	30	4	10	3	0	1	1	.333	3	7	1	14	8	1	.957
	—Okla. City (A.A.)	C-3B-1B	56	202	37	74	13	3	5	49	.366	44	42	1	206	55	9	.967
1987	—Okla. City (A.A.)	C-1B	46	182	43	61	8	3	13	54	.335	29	36	2	277	32	2	.994
	—Texas (A.L.)	C-1B-OF	78	216	34	59	8	1	6	37	.273	31	48	3	389	26	7	.983
1988	—Texas (A.L.)	C-1B-3B	94	249	21	57	8	0	3	27	.229	37	62	0	342	17	4	.989

Year	Team (League)	Pos.	G	AB	R	H	2B	3B	HR	RBI	Avg.	BB	SO	SB	PO	A	E	Avg.
			BATTING												FIELDING			
1989	—Texas (A.L.)	C-1B-3B	67	122	9	30	3	1	1	11	.246	12	29	1	117	8	3	.977
1990	—Texas (A.L.)	C-3B-1B	103	189	21	47	8	1	2	19	.249	30	25	1	261	25	4	.986
1991	—Texas (A.L.)	C-1-3-0	95	181	25	45	13	1	3	25	.249	34	44	0	288	20	6	.981
1992	—New York (A.L.)■	C-1B	68	173	24	43	7	0	8	27	.249	33	45	0	287	30	6	.981
1993	—New York (A.L.)	C	130	423	70	129	17	1	26	84	.305	57	85	1	652	46	3	*.996
Major league totals (8 years)			650	1583	208	420	67	5	50	231	.265	237	345	7	2350	180	34	.987

STANTON, MIKE

P, BRAVES

PERSONAL: Born June 2, 1967, in Houston. . . . 6-1/190. . . . Throws left, bats left. . . . Full name: William Michael Stanton.

HIGH SCHOOL: Midland (Tex.).

COLLEGE: Alvin (Tex.) Community College.

TRANSACTIONS/CAREER NOTES: Selected by Atlanta Braves organization in 13th round of free-agent draft (June 2, 1987). . . . On Atlanta disabled list (April 27, 1990-remainder of season); included rehabilitation assignment to Greenville (May 31-June 5 and August 21-29).

Year	Team (League)	W	L	Pct.	ERA	G	GS	CG	ShO	Sv.	IP	H	R	ER	BB	SO
1987	—Pulaski (Appal.)	4	8	.333	3.24	15	13	3	2	0	83⅓	64	37	30	42	82
1988	—Burlington (Midw.)	11	5	.688	3.62	30	23	1	1	0	154	154	86	62	69	160
	—Durham (Carolina)	1	0	1.000	1.46	2	2	1	1	0	12⅓	14	3	2	5	14
1989	—Greenville (South.)	4	1	.800	1.58	47	0	0	0	19	51⅓	32	10	9	31	58
	—Richmond (Int'l)	2	0	1.000	0.00	13	0	0	0	8	20	6	0	0	13	20
	—Atlanta (N.L.)	0	1	.000	1.50	20	0	0	0	7	24	17	4	4	8	27
1990	—Atlanta (N.L.)	0	3	.000	18.00	7	0	0	0	2	7	16	16	14	4	7
	—Greenville (South.)	0	1	.000	1.59	4	4	0	0	0	5⅔	7	1	1	3	4
1991	—Atlanta (N.L.)	5	5	.500	2.88	74	0	0	0	7	78	62	27	25	21	54
1992	—Atlanta (N.L.)	5	4	.556	4.10	65	0	0	0	8	63⅔	59	32	29	20	44
1993	—Atlanta (N.L.)	4	6	.400	4.67	63	0	0	0	27	52	51	35	27	29	43
Major league totals (5 years)		14	19	.424	3.97	229	0	0	0	51	224⅔	205	114	99	82	175

CHAMPIONSHIP SERIES RECORD

CHAMPIONSHIP SERIES NOTES: Shares single-series record for most games pitched—5 (1992).

Year	Team (League)	W	L	Pct.	ERA	G	GS	CG	ShO	Sv.	IP	H	R	ER	BB	SO
1991	—Atlanta (N.L.)	0	0	...	2.45	3	0	0	0	0	3⅔	4	1	1	3	3
1992	—Atlanta (N.L.)	0	0	...	0.00	5	0	0	0	0	4⅓	2	1	0	2	5
1993	—Atlanta (N.L.)	0	0	...	0.00	1	0	0	0	0	1	1	0	0	1	0
Champ. series totals (3 years)		0	0	...	1.00	9	0	0	0	0	9	7	2	1	6	8

WORLD SERIES RECORD

Year	Team (League)	W	L	Pct.	ERA	G	GS	CG	ShO	Sv.	IP	H	R	ER	BB	SO
1991	—Atlanta (N.L.)	1	0	1.000	0.00	5	0	0	0	0	7⅓	5	0	0	2	7
1992	—Atlanta (N.L.)	0	0	...	0.00	4	0	0	0	1	5	3	0	0	2	1
World Series totals (2 years)		1	0	1.000	0.00	9	0	0	0	1	12⅓	8	0	0	4	8

STATON, DAVE

1B/, PADRES

PERSONAL: Born April 12, 1968, in Seattle. . . . 6-5/225. . . . Throws right, bats right. . . . Full name: David Allen Staton. . . . Name pronounced STAY-ton.

HIGH SCHOOL: Tustin (Calif.).

COLLEGE: Orange Coast College (Calif.), then California.

TRANSACTIONS/CAREER NOTES: Selected by Pittsburgh Pirates organization in 22nd round of free-agent draft (June 1, 1988). . . . Selected by San Diego Padres organization in fifth round of free-agent draft (June 5, 1989). . . . On disabled list (July 20-27, 1991 and April 11-22 and August 8, 1992-remainder of season). . . . On Rancho Cucamonga disabled list (April 8-May 20 and August 3-17, 1993).

STATISTICAL NOTES: Tied for Northwest League lead with 163 total bases in 1989.

Year	Team (League)	Pos.	G	AB	R	H	2B	3B	HR	RBI	Avg.	BB	SO	SB	PO	A	E	Avg.
			BATTING												FIELDING			
1989	—Spokane (N'west)	3B	70	260	52	94	18	0	*17	*72	*.362	39	49	1	30	116	25	.854
1990	—Riverside (Calif.)	3B-1B	92	335	56	97	16	1	20	64	.290	52	78	4	149	162	13	.960
	—Wichita (Texas)	1B-3B	45	164	26	50	11	0	6	31	.305	22	37	0	326	35	4	.989
1991	—Las Vegas (PCL)	1B-3B	107	375	61	100	19	1	22	74	.267	44	89	1	553	116	24	.965
1992	—Las Vegas (PCL)	OF-1B	96	335	47	94	20	0	19	76	.281	34	95	0	186	27	2	.991
1993	—Wichita (Texas)	DH	5	12	2	5	3	0	0	2	.417	2	3	0	...	...	...	...
	—Rancho Cuca. (Cal.)	1B	58	221	37	70	21	0	18	58	.317	30	52	0	63	6	3	.958
	—Las Vegas (PCL)	1B	11	37	8	10	0	0	7	11	.270	3	9	0	88	5	3	.969
	—San Diego (N.L.)	1B	17	42	7	11	3	0	5	9	.262	3	12	0	66	14	0	1.000
Major league totals (1 year)			17	42	7	11	3	0	5	9	.262	3	12	0	66	14	0	1.000

STEFANSKI, MIKE

C, BREWERS

PERSONAL: Born September 12, 1969, in Flint, Mich. . . . 6-2/190. . . . Throws right, bats right. . . . Full name: Michael Joseph Stefanski.

HIGH SCHOOL: Redford (Mich.) Union.

COLLEGE: Detroit Mercy.

TRANSACTIONS/CAREER NOTES: Selected by Milwaukee Brewers organization in 40th round of free-agent draft (June 3, 1991). . . . On disabled list (April 13-29, 1993).

STATISTICAL NOTES: Led Arizona League catchers with 364 putouts and .988 fielding percentage in 1991.

Year	Team (League)	Pos.	G	AB	R	H	2B	3B	HR	RBI	Avg.	BB	SO	SB	PO	A	E	Avg.
			BATTING												FIELDING			
1991	—Ariz. Brewers (Ar.)...	C-1B	56	206	43	75	5	5	0	43	*.364	22	21	3	†386	40	6	†.986
1992	—Beloit (Midwest).......	C-1B-OF	116	385	66	105	12	0	4	45	.273	55	81	9	724	95	13	.984
1993	—Stockton (Calif.).......	C-3B-1B	97	345	58	111	22	2	10	57	.322	49	45	6	471	92	14	.976

STEINBACH, TERRY

C, ATHLETICS

PERSONAL: Born March 2, 1962, in New Ulm, Minn. . . . 6-1/195. . . . Throws right, bats right. . . . Full name: Terry Lee Steinbach. . . . Brother of Tom Steinbach, minor league outfielder (1983).
HIGH SCHOOL: New Ulm (Minn.).
COLLEGE: Minnesota.
TRANSACTIONS/CAREER NOTES: Selected by Cleveland Indians organization in 16th round of free-agent draft (June 3, 1980). . . . Selected by Oakland Athletics organization in ninth round of free-agent draft (June 6, 1983). . . . On disabled list (May 6-June 1, 1988; July 3-28, 1990 and April 10-25, 1992). . . . Granted free agency (October 26, 1992). . . . Re-signed by A's (December 14, 1992). . . . On disabled list (August 16, 1993-remainder of season).
HONORS: Named Southern League Most Valuable Player (1986).
STATISTICAL NOTES: Led Northwest League third basemen with 122 assists and tied for lead with 17 errors in 1983. . . . Led Midwest League third basemen with 31 double plays in 1984. . . . Led Southern League with 22 passed balls in 1986. . . . Hit home run in first major league at-bat (September 12, 1986). . . . Led A.L. catchers with 15 errors in 1991.

Year	Team (League)	Pos.	G	AB	R	H	2B	3B	HR	RBI	Avg.	BB	SO	SB	PO	A	E	Avg.
			BATTING												FIELDING			
1983	—Medford (N'west).....	3B-OF-1B	62	219	42	69	16	0	6	38	.315	28	22	8	105	†124	‡21	.916
1984	—Madison (Midwest)..	3B-1B-P	135	474	57	140	24	6	11	79	.295	49	59	5	107	257	27	.931
1985	—Huntsville (South.)...	C-3-1-O-P	128	456	64	124	31	3	9	72	.272	45	36	4	187	43	6	.975
1986	—Huntsville (South.)...	C-1B-3B	138	505	113	164	33	2	24	*132	.325	94	74	10	620	73	14	.980
	—Oakland (A.L.)..........	C	6	15	3	5	0	0	2	4	.333	1	0	0	21	4	1	.962
1987	—Oakland (A.L.)..........	C-3B-1B	122	391	66	111	16	3	16	56	.284	32	66	1	642	44	10	.986
1988	—Oakland (A.L.)..........	C-3-1-O	104	351	42	93	19	1	9	51	.265	33	47	3	536	58	9	.985
1989	—Oakland (A.L.)..........	C-O-1-3	130	454	37	124	13	1	7	42	.273	30	66	1	612	47	11	.984
1990	—Oakland (A.L.)..........	C-1B	114	379	32	95	15	2	9	57	.251	19	66	0	401	31	5	.989
1991	—Oakland (A.L.)..........	C-1B	129	456	50	125	31	1	6	67	.274	22	70	2	639	53	†15	.979
1992	—Oakland (A.L.)..........	C-1B	128	438	48	122	20	1	12	53	.279	45	58	2	598	72	10	.985
1993	—Oakland (A.L.)..........	C-1B	104	389	47	111	19	1	10	43	.285	25	65	3	524	47	7	.988
Major league totals (8 years)			837	2873	325	786	133	10	71	373	.274	207	438	12	3973	356	68	.985

CHAMPIONSHIP SERIES RECORD

Year	Team (League)	Pos.	G	AB	R	H	2B	3B	HR	RBI	Avg.	BB	SO	SB	PO	A	E	Avg.
			BATTING												FIELDING			
1988	—Oakland (A.L.)..........	C	2	4	0	1	0	0	0	0	.250	2	0	0	12	0	0	1.000
1989	—Oakland (A.L.)..........	C-DH	4	15	0	3	0	0	0	1	.200	1	5	0	17	0	0	1.000
1990	—Oakland (A.L.)..........	C	3	11	2	5	0	0	0	1	.455	1	2	0	11	0	0	1.000
1992	—Oakland (A.L.)..........	C	6	24	1	7	0	0	1	5	.292	2	7	0	30	7	0	1.000
Championship series totals (4 years)			15	54	3	16	0	0	1	7	.296	6	14	0	70	7	0	1.000

WORLD SERIES RECORD

Year	Team (League)	Pos.	G	AB	R	H	2B	3B	HR	RBI	Avg.	BB	SO	SB	PO	A	E	Avg.
			BATTING												FIELDING			
1988	—Oakland (A.L.)..........	C-DH	3	11	0	4	1	0	0	0	.364	0	2	0	11	3	0	1.000
1989	—Oakland (A.L.)..........	C	4	16	3	4	0	1	1	7	.250	2	1	0	27	2	0	1.000
1990	—Oakland (A.L.)..........	C	3	8	0	1	0	0	0	0	.125	0	1	0	8	1	0	1.000
World Series totals (3 years)			10	35	3	9	1	1	1	7	.257	2	4	0	46	6	0	1.000

ALL-STAR GAME RECORD

ALL-STAR GAME NOTES: Named Most Valuable Player (1988). . . . Hit home run in first at-bat (July 12, 1988).

Year	League	Pos.	AB	R	H	2B	3B	HR	RBI	Avg.	BB	SO	SB	PO	A	E	Avg.
			BATTING											FIELDING			
1988	—American..................	C	1	1	1	0	0	1	2	1.000	0	0	0	3	1	1	.800
1989	—American..................	C	3	0	1	0	0	0	0	.333	0	0	0	6	1	0	1.000
1993	—American..................	C	2	0	1	1	0	0	1	.500	0	1	0	6	0	0	1.000
All-Star Game totals (3 years)			6	1	3	1	0	1	3	.500	0	1	0	15	2	1	.944

RECORD AS PITCHER

Year	Team (League)	W	L	Pct.	ERA	G	GS	CG	ShO	Sv.	IP	H	R	ER	BB	SO
1984	—Madison (Midwest)....	0	0	...	9.00	2	0	0	0	0	3	2	4	3	4	0
1985	—Huntsville (South.).....	0	0	...	0.00	1	0	0	0	0	1	0	0	0	0	0

STEVENS, DAVE

P, TWINS

PERSONAL: Born March 4, 1970, in Fullerton, Calif. . . . 6-3/210. . . . Throws right, bats right. . . . Full name: David James Stevens.
HIGH SCHOOL: La Habra (Calif.).
COLLEGE: Fullerton (Calif.) College.
TRANSACTIONS/CAREER NOTES: Selected by Chicago Cubs organization in 20th round of free-agent draft (June 5, 1989). . . . On disabled list (June 17-July 4, 1991). . . . On Iowa disabled list (April 8-May 20, 1993). . . . Traded by Cubs with C Matt Walbeck to Minnesota Twins for P Willie Banks (November 24, 1993).

Year	Team (League)	W	L	Pct.	ERA	G	GS	CG	ShO	Sv.	IP	H	R	ER	BB	SO
1990	—Hunting. (Appal.).......	2	4	.333	4.61	13	11	0	0	0	56⅔	48	44	29	47	55
1991	—Geneva (NY-Penn)....	2	3	.400	2.85	9	9	1	0	0	47⅓	49	20	15	14	44

Year	Team (League)	W	L	Pct.	ERA	G	GS	CG	ShO	Sv.	IP	H	R	ER	BB	SO
1992	—Charlotte (South.)	9	13	.409	3.91	26	26	2	0	0	149⅔	147	79	65	53	89
1993	—Iowa (Am. Assoc.)	4	0	1.000	4.19	24	0	0	0	4	34⅓	24	16	16	14	29
	—Orlando (Southern)	6	1	.857	4.22	11	11	1	1	0	70⅓	69	36	33	35	49

STEWART, DAVE

P, BLUE JAYS

PERSONAL: Born February 19, 1957, in Oakland, Calif. . . . 6-2/200. . . . Throws right, bats right. . . . Full name: David Keith Stewart.

HIGH SCHOOL: St. Elizabeth (Oakland, Calif.).

COLLEGE: Merritt College (Calif.) and Cal State Hayward.

TRANSACTIONS/CAREER NOTES: Selected by Los Angeles Dodgers organization in 16th round of free-agent draft (June 4, 1975). . . . Traded by Dodgers with a player to be named later to Texas Rangers for P Rick Honeycutt (August 19, 1983); Rangers acquired P Ricky Wright to complete deal (September 16, 1983). . . . Traded by Rangers to Philadelphia Phillies for P Rick Surhoff (September 13, 1985). . . . Released by Phillies (May 9, 1986). . . . Signed by Tacoma, Oakland Athletics organization (May 23, 1986). . . . On disabled list (May 9-26, 1991 and June 30-July 24, 1992). . . . Granted free agency (October 29, 1992). . . . Signed by Toronto Blue Jays (December 8, 1992). . . . On disabled list (April 3-May 13, 1993).

RECORDS: Shares A.L. single-season record for fewest complete games by pitcher who led league in complete games—11 (1990).

HONORS: Named righthanded pitcher on THE SPORTING NEWS A.L. All-Star team (1988).

STATISTICAL NOTES: Tied for Midwest League lead with three balks in 1977. . . . Led A.L. with 16 balks in 1988. . . . Pitched 5-0 no-hit victory against Toronto (June 29, 1990).

Year	Team (League)	W	L	Pct.	ERA	G	GS	CG	ShO	Sv.	IP	H	R	ER	BB	SO
1975	—Belling. (N'west)	0	5	.000	5.51	22	5	1	0	2	49	59	46	30	49	37
1976	—Danville (Midwest)	0	2	.000	16.20	4	3	0	0	0	10	17	20	18	16	10
	—Belling. (N'west)	1	1	.500	5.04	24	2	0	0	1	50	47	35	28	58	53
1977	—Clinton (Midwest)	*17	4	*.810	2.15	24	24	•15	•3	0	176	152	52	42	72	144
	—Albuquerque (PCL)	1	0	1.000	4.50	1	1	0	0	0	6	4	3	3	6	3
1978	—San Antonio (Tex.)	14	12	.538	3.68	28	•28	5	2	0	*193	181	99	79	97	130
	—Los Angeles (N.L.)	0	0	...	0.00	1	0	0	0	0	2	1	0	0	0	1
1979	—Albuquerque (PCL)	11	12	.478	5.24	28	26	5	1	1	170	198	112	99	81	105
1980	—Albuquerque (PCL)	•15	10	.600	3.70	31	*29	11	0	1	*202	189	94	83	89	125
1981	—Los Angeles (N.L.)	4	3	.571	2.51	32	0	0	0	6	43	40	13	12	14	29
1982	—Los Angeles (N.L.)	9	8	.529	3.81	45	14	0	0	1	146⅓	137	72	62	49	80
1983	—Los Angeles (N.L.)	5	2	.714	2.96	46	1	0	0	8	76	67	28	25	33	54
	—Texas (A.L.)■	5	2	.714	2.14	8	8	2	0	0	59	50	15	14	17	24
1984	—Texas (A.L.)	7	14	.333	4.73	32	27	3	0	0	192⅓	193	106	101	87	119
1985	—Texas (A.L.)	0	6	.000	5.42	42	5	0	0	4	81⅓	86	53	49	37	64
	—Philadelphia (N.L.)■	0	0	...	6.23	4	0	0	0	0	4⅓	5	4	3	4	2
1986	—Philadelphia (N.L.)	0	0	...	6.57	8	0	0	0	0	12⅓	15	9	9	4	9
	—Tacoma (PCL)■	0	0	...	0.00	1	0	0	0	0	3	4	1	0	1	3
	—Oakland (A.L.)	9	5	.643	3.74	29	17	4	1	0	149⅓	137	67	62	65	102
1987	—Oakland (A.L.)	•20	13	.606	3.68	37	37	8	1	0	261⅓	224	121	107	105	205
1988	—Oakland (A.L.)	21	12	.636	3.23	37	*37	•14	2	0	*275⅔	240	111	99	110	192
1989	—Oakland (A.L.)	21	9	.700	3.32	36	•36	8	0	0	257⅔	*260	105	95	69	155
1990	—Oakland (A.L.)	22	11	.667	2.56	36	•36	•11	•4	0	*267	226	84	76	83	166
1991	—Oakland (A.L.)	11	11	.500	5.18	35	•35	2	1	0	226	245	*135	*130	105	144
1992	—Oakland (A.L.)	12	10	.545	3.66	31	31	2	0	0	199⅓	175	96	81	79	130
1993	—Toronto (A.L.)■	12	8	.600	4.44	26	26	0	0	0	162	146	86	80	72	96
A.L. totals (11 years)		140	101	.581	3.78	349	295	54	9	4	2131	1982	979	894	829	1397
N.L. totals (6 years)		18	13	.581	3.52	136	15	0	0	15	284	265	126	111	104	175
Major league totals (14 years)		158	114	.581	3.75	485	310	54	9	19	2415	2247	1105	1005	933	1572

DIVISION SERIES RECORD

Year	Team (League)	W	L	Pct.	ERA	G	GS	CG	ShO	Sv.	IP	H	R	ER	BB	SO
1981	—Los Angeles (N.L.)	0	2	.000	40.50	2	0	0	0	0	⅔	4	3	3	0	1

CHAMPIONSHIP SERIES RECORD

CHAMPIONSHIP SERIES NOTES: Named A.L. Championship Series Most Valuable Player (1990 and 1993). . . . Holds career records for most games won—8; most games won by undefeated pitcher—8; most innings pitched—75⅓; and most bases on balls issued—25. . . . Shares A.L. single-series record for most games won—2 (each in 1989-90 and 1993).

Year	Team (League)	W	L	Pct.	ERA	G	GS	CG	ShO	Sv.	IP	H	R	ER	BB	SO
1988	—Oakland (A.L.)	1	0	1.000	1.35	2	2	0	0	0	13⅓	9	2	2	6	11
1989	—Oakland (A.L.)	2	0	1.000	2.81	2	2	0	0	0	16	13	5	5	3	9
1990	—Oakland (A.L.)	2	0	1.000	1.13	2	2	0	0	0	16	8	2	2	2	4
1992	—Oakland (A.L.)	1	0	1.000	2.70	2	2	1	0	0	16⅔	14	5	5	6	7
1993	—Toronto (A.L.)	2	0	1.000	2.03	2	2	0	0	0	13⅓	8	3	3	8	8
Champ. series totals (5 years)		8	0	1.000	2.03	10	10	1	0	0	75⅓	52	17	17	25	39

WORLD SERIES RECORD

WORLD SERIES NOTES: Named Most Valuable Player (1989).

Year	Team (League)	W	L	Pct.	ERA	G	GS	CG	ShO	Sv.	IP	H	R	ER	BB	SO
1981	—Los Angeles (N.L.)	0	0	...	0.00	2	0	0	0	0	1⅔	1	0	0	2	1
1988	—Oakland (A.L.)	0	1	.000	3.14	2	2	0	0	0	14⅓	12	7	5	5	5
1989	—Oakland (A.L.)	2	0	1.000	1.69	2	2	1	1	0	16	10	3	3	2	14
1990	—Oakland (A.L.)	0	2	.000	2.77	2	2	1	0	0	13	10	6	4	6	5
1993	—Toronto (A.L.)	0	1	.000	6.75	2	2	0	0	0	12	10	9	9	8	8
World Series totals (5 years)		2	4	.333	3.32	10	8	2	1	0	57	43	25	21	23	33

ALL-STAR GAME RECORD

Year	League	W	L	Pct.	ERA	GS	CG	ShO	Sv.	IP	H	R	ER	BB	SO
1989	—American	0	0	...	18.00	1	0	0	0	1	3	2	2	2	0

STIEB, DAVE

P

PERSONAL: Born July 22, 1957, in Santa Ana, Calif.... 6-1/195.... Throws right, bats right.... Full name: David Andrew Stieb.... Brother of Steve Stieb, minor league catcher (1979-81).... Name pronounced STEEB.

HIGH SCHOOL: Oak Grove (San Jose, Calif.).

COLLEGE: Santa Ana (Calif.) College and Southern Illinois.

TRANSACTIONS/CAREER NOTES: Selected by Toronto Blue Jays organization in fifth round of free-agent draft (June 6, 1978).... On disabled list (May 23, 1991-remainder of season).... On Toronto disabled list (March 27-April 22, 1992); included rehabilitation assignment to Dunedin (April 11-20).... On Toronto disabled list (August 9, 1992-remainder of season).... Granted free agency (October 28, 1992).... Signed by Chicago White Sox (December 8, 1992).... On Chicago disabled list (April 5-28, 1993); included rehabilitation assignment to Sarasota (April 11-22) and Nashville (April 22-28).... Released by White Sox (May 23, 1993).... Signed by Omaha, Kansas City Royals organization (June 14, 1993).... Released by Omaha (July 31, 1993).

RECORDS: Shares major league record for most consecutive one-hit games—2 (September 24 and 30, 1988).... Shares A.L. single-season record for most low-hit (no-hit and one-hit) games—3 (1988).

HONORS: Named outfielder on THE SPORTING NEWS college All-America team (1978).... Named A.L. Pitcher of the Year by THE SPORTING NEWS (1982).... Named righthanded pitcher on THE SPORTING NEWS A.L. All-Star team (1982).

STATISTICAL NOTES: Led A.L. with 14 hit batsmen in 1983, 11 in 1984, 15 in 1986, 13 in 1989 and tied for lead with 11 in 1981.... Pitched 3-0 no-hit victory against Cleveland (September 2, 1990).

MISCELLANEOUS: Appeared in one game as outfielder with no chances and made an out in only at-bat (1980).... Appeared in one game as pinch-runner (1986 and 1988).

Year	Team (League)	W	L	Pct.	ERA	G	GS	CG	ShO	Sv.	IP	H	R	ER	BB	SO
1978	—Dunedin (Fla. St.)	2	0	1.000	2.08	4	4	1	0	0	26	23	10	6	1	8
1979	—Dunedin (Fla. St.)	5	0	1.000	4.24	8	8	2	1	0	51	54	30	24	28	38
	—Syracuse (Int'l)	5	2	.714	2.12	7	7	4	0	0	51	39	15	12	14	20
	—Toronto (A.L.)	8	8	.500	4.33	18	18	7	1	0	129	139	70	62	48	52
1980	—Toronto (A.L.)	12	15	.444	3.70	34	32	14	4	0	243	232	108	100	83	108
1981	—Toronto (A.L.)	11	10	.524	3.18	25	25	11	2	0	184	148	70	65	61	89
1982	—Toronto (A.L.)	17	14	.548	3.25	38	38	*19	*5	0	*288⅓	*271	116	104	75	141
1983	—Toronto (A.L.)	17	12	.586	3.04	36	36	14	4	0	278	223	105	94	93	187
1984	—Toronto (A.L.)	16	8	.667	2.83	35	35	11	2	0	*267	215	87	84	88	198
1985	—Toronto (A.L.)	14	13	.519	*2.48	36	36	8	2	0	265	206	89	73	96	167
1986	—Toronto (A.L.)	7	12	.368	4.74	37	34	1	1	1	205	239	128	108	87	127
1987	—Toronto (A.L.)	13	9	.591	4.09	33	31	3	1	0	185	164	92	84	87	115
1988	—Toronto (A.L.)	16	8	.667	3.04	32	31	8	4	0	207⅓	157	76	70	79	147
1989	—Toronto (A.L.)	17	8	.680	3.35	33	33	3	2	0	206⅔	164	83	77	76	101
1990	—Toronto (A.L.)	18	6	.750	2.93	33	33	2	2	0	208⅔	179	73	68	64	125
1991	—Toronto (A.L.)	4	3	.571	3.17	9	9	1	0	0	59⅔	52	22	21	23	29
1992	—Dunedin (Fla. St.)	1	1	.500	2.13	2	2	0	0	0	12⅔	7	6	3	4	11
	—Toronto (A.L.)	4	6	.400	5.04	21	14	1	0	0	96⅓	98	58	54	43	45
1993	—Sarasota (Fla. St.)■	1	1	.500	5.84	2	2	0	0	0	12⅓	18	10	8	2	14
	—Nash.-Oma. (A.A.)■	3	4	.429	6.09	10	9	1	1	0	54⅔	72	40	37	14	21
	—Chicago (A.L.)	1	3	.250	6.04	4	4	0	0	0	22⅓	27	17	15	14	11
Major league totals (15 years)		175	135	.565	3.41	424	409	103	30	1	2845⅓	2514	1194	1079	1017	1642

CHAMPIONSHIP SERIES RECORD

CHAMPIONSHIP SERIES NOTES: Holds A.L. single-series record for most strikeouts—18 (1985).

Year	Team (League)	W	L	Pct.	ERA	G	GS	CG	ShO	Sv.	IP	H	R	ER	BB	SO
1985	—Toronto (A.L.)	1	1	.500	3.10	3	3	0	0	0	20⅓	11	7	7	10	18
1989	—Toronto (A.L.)	0	2	.000	6.35	2	2	0	0	0	11⅓	12	8	8	6	10
Champ. series totals (2 years)		1	3	.250	4.26	5	5	0	0	0	31⅔	23	15	15	16	28

ALL-STAR GAME RECORD

ALL-STAR GAME NOTES: Shares single-game record for most wild pitches—2 (July 8, 1980).... Shares record for most wild pitches in one inning—2 (July 8, 1980, seventh inning).

Year	League	W	L	Pct.	ERA	GS	CG	ShO	Sv.	IP	H	R	ER	BB	SO
1980	—American	0	0	...	0.00	0	0	0	0	1	1	1	0	2	0
1981	—American	0	0	...	0.00	0	0	0	0	1⅔	1	0	0	1	1
1983	—American	1	0	1.000	0.00	1	0	0	0	3	0	1	0	1	4
1984	—American	0	1	.000	4.50	1	0	0	0	2	3	2	1	0	2
1985	—American	0	0	...	0.00	0	0	0	0	1	0	0	0	1	2
1988	—American	0	0	...	0.00	0	0	0	0	1	1	0	0	0	0
1990	—American	0	0	...	0.00	0	0	0	0	2	0	0	0	1	1
All-Star totals (7 years)		1	1	.500	0.77	2	0	0	0	11⅔	6	4	1	6	10

RECORD AS POSITION PLAYER

			BATTING											FIELDING			
Year	Team (League)	Pos.	G	AB	R	H	2B	3B	HR	RBI	Avg.	BB	SO	SB	PO	A	E	Avg.
1978	—Dunedin (Fla. St.)	OF-P	35	99	10	19	3	0	1	9	.192	9	18	2	85	7	3	.968

STILLWELL, KURT

SS/2B, REDS

PERSONAL: Born June 4, 1965, in Glendale, Calif.... 5-11/185.... Throws right, bats both.... Full name: Kurt Andrew Stillwell.... Son of Ron Stillwell, infielder, Washington Senators (1961-62); and brother of Rod Stillwell, minor league shortstop (1989-90).

HIGH SCHOOL: Thousand Oaks (Calif.).
TRANSACTIONS/CAREER NOTES: Selected by Cincinnati Reds organization in first round (second pick overall) of free-agent draft (June 6, 1983).... On disabled list (August 9, 1985-remainder of season).... Traded by Reds with P Ted Power to Kansas City Royals for P Danny Jackson and SS Angel Salazar (November 6, 1987).... On disabled list (July 6-August 3, 1989 and August 5-21, 1991).... Granted free agency (October 29, 1991).... Signed by San Diego Padres (February 28, 1992).... On disabled list (August 27-September 11, 1992).... On San Diego disabled list (April 3-27, 1993).... Released by Padres (July 26, 1993).... Signed by California Angels (August 1, 1993).... Released by Angels (October 25, 1993).... Signed by Reds organization (November 24, 1993).
RECORDS: Shares A.L. single-season record for fewest errors by shortstop who led league in errors—24 (1990).

			BATTING												FIELDING			
Year	**Team (League)**	**Pos.**	**G**	**AB**	**R**	**H**	**2B**	**3B**	**HR**	**RBI**	**Avg.**	**BB**	**SO**	**SB**	**PO**	**A**	**E**	**Avg.**
1983	—Billings (Pioneer)	SS	65	250	47	81	10	1	2	44	.324	42	28	5	73	137	*30	.875
1984	—Ced. Rap. (Midw.)	SS	112	382	63	96	15	1	4	33	.251	70	53	24	156	245	25	.941
1985	—Denver (A.A.)	SS-3B	59	182	28	48	7	4	1	22	.264	21	23	5	103	135	25	.905
1986	—Cincinnati (N.L.)	SS	104	279	31	64	6	1	0	26	.229	30	47	6	107	205	16	.951
	—Denver (A.A.)	SS	10	30	2	7	0	0	0	2	.233	2	4	2	14	21	5	.875
1987	—Cincinnati (N.L.)	SS-2B-3B	131	395	54	102	20	7	4	33	.258	32	50	4	144	247	23	.944
1988	—Kansas City (A.L.)■	SS	128	459	63	115	28	5	10	53	.251	47	76	6	170	349	13	.976
1989	—Kansas City (A.L.)	SS	130	463	52	121	20	7	7	54	.261	42	64	9	179	334	16	.970
1990	—Kansas City (A.L.)	SS	144	506	60	126	35	4	3	51	.249	39	60	0	181	350	*24	.957
1991	—Kansas City (A.L.)	SS	122	385	44	102	17	1	6	51	.265	33	56	3	163	263	18	.959
1992	—San Diego (N.L.)■	2B	114	379	35	86	15	3	2	24	.227	26	58	4	250	266	*16	.970
1993	—San Diego (N.L.)	SS-3B	57	121	9	26	4	0	1	11	.215	11	22	4	47	63	9	.924
	—California (A.L.)■	2B-SS	22	61	2	16	2	2	0	3	.262	4	11	2	46	51	5	.951
American League totals (5 years)			546	1874	221	480	102	19	26	212	.256	165	267	20	739	1347	76	.965
National League totals (4 years)			406	1174	129	278	45	11	7	94	.237	99	177	18	548	781	64	.954
Major league totals (8 years)			952	3048	350	758	147	30	33	306	.249	264	444	38	1287	2128	140	.961

ALL-STAR GAME RECORD

			BATTING											FIELDING			
Year	**League**	**Pos.**	**AB**	**R**	**H**	**2B**	**3B**	**HR**	**RBI**	**Avg.**	**BB**	**SO**	**SB**	**PO**	**A**	**E**	**Avg.**
1988	—American	SS	0	0	0	0	0	0	0	...	0	0	0	1	0	0	1.000

STINNETT, KELLY

C, METS

PERSONAL: Born February 14, 1970, in Lawton, Okla.... 5-11/195.... Throws right, bats right.... Full name: Kelly Lee Stinnett.... Name pronounced stih-NET.
HIGH SCHOOL: Lawton (Okla.).
COLLEGE: Seminole (Okla.) Junior College.
TRANSACTIONS/CAREER NOTES: Selected by Cleveland Indians organization in 11th round of free-agent draft (June 5, 1989).... Selected by New York Mets from Indians organization in Rule 5 major league draft (December 13, 1993).
STATISTICAL NOTES: Led New York-Pennsylvania League catchers with 18 errors in 1990.... Led South Atlantic League catchers with 27 errors in 1991.

			BATTING												FIELDING			
Year	**Team (League)**	**Pos.**	**G**	**AB**	**R**	**H**	**2B**	**3B**	**HR**	**RBI**	**Avg.**	**BB**	**SO**	**SB**	**PO**	**A**	**E**	**Avg.**
1990	—Watertown (NYP)	C-1B	60	192	29	46	10	2	2	21	.240	40	43	3	348	48	†18	.957
1991	—Columbus (S. Atl.)	C-1B	102	384	49	101	15	1	14	74	.263	26	70	4	685	100	†28	.966
1992	—Cant./Akr. (East.)	C	91	296	37	84	10	0	6	32	.284	16	43	7	560	57	*13	.979
1993	—Charlotte (Int'l)	C	98	288	42	79	10	3	6	33	.274	17	52	0	495	48	8	.985

STOCKER, KEVIN

SS, PHILLIES

PERSONAL: Born February 13, 1970, in Spokane, Wash.... 6-1/175.... Throws right, bats both.... Full name: Kevin Douglas Stocker.
HIGH SCHOOL: Central Valley (Veradale, Wash.).
COLLEGE: Washington.
TRANSACTIONS/CAREER NOTES: Selected by Philadelphia Phillies organization in second round of free-agent draft (June 3, 1991).

			BATTING												FIELDING			
Year	**Team (League)**	**Pos.**	**G**	**AB**	**R**	**H**	**2B**	**3B**	**HR**	**RBI**	**Avg.**	**BB**	**SO**	**SB**	**PO**	**A**	**E**	**Avg.**
1991	—Spartanburg (SAL)	SS	70	250	26	55	11	1	0	20	.220	31	37	15	83	176	18	.935
1992	—Clearwater (FSL)	SS	63	244	43	69	13	4	1	33	.283	27	31	15	102	220	16	.953
	—Reading (Eastern)	SS	62	240	31	60	9	2	1	13	.250	22	30	17	100	172	14	.951
1993	—Scran./W.B. (Int'l)	SS	83	313	54	73	14	1	3	17	.233	29	56	17	122	248	15	.961
	—Philadelphia (N.L.)	SS	70	259	46	84	12	3	2	31	.324	30	43	5	118	202	14	.958
Major league totals (1 year)			70	259	46	84	12	3	2	31	.324	30	43	5	118	202	14	.958

CHAMPIONSHIP SERIES RECORD

			BATTING												FIELDING			
Year	**Team (League)**	**Pos.**	**G**	**AB**	**R**	**H**	**2B**	**3B**	**HR**	**RBI**	**Avg.**	**BB**	**SO**	**SB**	**PO**	**A**	**E**	**Avg.**
1993	—Philadelphia (N.L.)	SS	6	22	0	4	1	0	0	1	.182	2	5	0	10	13	1	.958

WORLD SERIES RECORD

			BATTING												FIELDING			
Year	**Team (League)**	**Pos.**	**G**	**AB**	**R**	**H**	**2B**	**3B**	**HR**	**RBI**	**Avg.**	**BB**	**SO**	**SB**	**PO**	**A**	**E**	**Avg.**
1993	—Philadelphia (N.L.)	SS	6	19	1	4	1	0	0	1	.211	5	5	0	8	13	0	1.000

STOTTLEMYRE, TODD

P, BLUE JAYS

PERSONAL: Born May 20, 1965, in Yakima, Wash.... 6-3/200.... Throws right, bats left.... Full name: Todd Vernon Stottlemyre.... Son of Mel Stottlemyre Sr., current pitching coach, Houston Astros, pitcher, New York Yankees (1964-74), and pitching coach, New York Mets (1984-93); and brother of Mel

Stottlemyre Jr., pitcher, Kansas City Royals (1990).
HIGH SCHOOL: A.C. Davis (Yakima, Wash.).
COLLEGE: Yakima (Wash.) Valley College.
TRANSACTIONS/CAREER NOTES: Selected by New York Yankees organization in fifth round of free-agent draft (June 6, 1983).... Selected by St. Louis Cardinals organization in secondary phase of free-agent draft (January 9, 1985).... Selected by Toronto Blue Jays organization in secondary phase of free-agent draft (June 3, 1985).... On Toronto disabled list (June 20-July 13, 1992).... On suspended list (September 23-28, 1992).... On disabled list (May 23-June 13, 1993).

Year	Team (League)	W	L	Pct.	ERA	G	GS	CG	ShO	Sv.	IP	H	R	ER	BB	SO
1986	—Vent. Co. (Calif.)	9	4	.692	2.43	17	17	2	0	0	103⅔	76	39	28	36	104
	—Knoxville (South.)	8	7	.533	4.18	18	18	1	0	0	99	93	56	46	49	81
1987	—Syracuse (Int'l)	11	•13	.458	4.44	34	*34	1	0	0	186⅔	189	•103	*92	*87	143
1988	—Toronto (A.L.)	4	8	.333	5.69	28	16	0	0	0	98	109	70	62	46	67
	—Syracuse (Int'l)	5	0	1.000	2.05	7	7	1	0	0	48⅓	36	12	11	8	51
1989	—Toronto (A.L.)	7	7	.500	3.88	27	18	0	0	0	127⅔	137	56	55	44	63
	—Syracuse (Int'l)	3	2	.600	3.23	10	9	2	0	0	55⅔	46	23	20	15	45
1990	—Toronto (A.L.)	13	17	.433	4.34	33	33	4	0	0	203	214	101	98	69	115
1991	—Toronto (A.L.)	15	8	.652	3.78	34	34	1	0	0	219	194	97	92	75	116
1992	—Toronto (A.L.)	12	11	.522	4.50	28	27	6	2	0	174	175	99	87	63	98
1993	—Toronto (A.L.)	11	12	.478	4.84	30	28	1	1	0	176⅔	204	107	95	69	98
Major league totals (6 years)		62	63	.496	4.41	180	156	12	3	0	998⅓	1033	530	489	366	557

CHAMPIONSHIP SERIES RECORD

Year	Team (League)	W	L	Pct.	ERA	G	GS	CG	ShO	Sv.	IP	H	R	ER	BB	SO
1989	—Toronto (A.L.)	0	1	.000	7.20	1	1	0	0	0	5	7	4	4	2	3
1991	—Toronto (A.L.)	0	1	.000	9.82	1	1	0	0	0	3⅔	7	4	4	1	3
1992	—Toronto (A.L.)	0	0	...	2.45	1	0	0	0	0	3⅔	3	1	1	0	1
1993	—Toronto (A.L.)	0	1	.000	7.50	1	1	0	0	0	6	6	5	5	4	4
Champ. series totals (4 years)		0	3	.000	6.87	4	3	0	0	0	18⅓	23	14	14	7	11

WORLD SERIES RECORD

WORLD SERIES NOTES: Shares records for most bases on balls allowed in one inning—4 (October 20, 1993, first inning); and most consecutive bases on balls allowed in one inning—3 (October 20, 1993, first inning).

Year	Team (League)	W	L	Pct.	ERA	G	GS	CG	ShO	Sv.	IP	H	R	ER	BB	SO
1992	—Toronto (A.L.)	0	0	...	0.00	4	0	0	0	0	3⅔	4	0	0	0	4
1993	—Toronto (A.L.)	0	0	...	27.00	1	1	0	0	0	2	3	6	6	4	1
World Series totals (2 years)		0	0	...	9.53	5	1	0	0	0	5⅔	7	6	6	4	5

STRANGE, DOUG

2B, RANGERS

PERSONAL: Born April 13, 1964, in Greenville, S.C.... 6-2/170.... Throws right, bats both. ... Full name: Joseph Douglas Strange.
HIGH SCHOOL: Wade Hampton (Greenville, S.C.).
COLLEGE: North Carolina State.
TRANSACTIONS/CAREER NOTES: Selected by Detroit Tigers organization in seventh round of free-agent draft (June 3, 1985).... Traded by Tigers to Houston Astros organization for IF/OF Lou Frazier (March 30, 1990).... Released by Astros organization (May 25, 1990).... Signed by Chicago Cubs organization (June 11, 1990).... Granted free agency (December 19, 1992).... Signed by Texas Rangers organization (January 11, 1993).
STATISTICAL NOTES: Led Florida State League third basemen with 116 putouts and tied for lead with 20 double plays in 1986.... Led American Association third basemen with 16 double plays in 1990.... Led American Association with 10 intentional bases on balls received in 1991.
MISCELLANEOUS: Batted righthanded only (Glens Falls, 1987).

				BATTING											FIELDING			
Year	Team (League)	Pos.	G	AB	R	H	2B	3B	HR	RBI	Avg.	BB	SO	SB	PO	A	E	Avg.
1985	—Bristol (Appal.)	OF-2B-3B	65	226	43	69	16	1	6	45	.305	22	30	6	84	59	11	.929
1986	—Lakeland (Fla. St.)	3B-1B	126	466	59	119	29	4	2	63	.255	65	59	18	†202	215	37	.919
1987	—Glens Falls (East.)	3-2-0-S	115	431	63	130	31	1	13	70	.302	31	53	5	110	214	20	.942
	—Toledo (Int'l)	3B	16	45	7	11	2	0	1	5	.244	4	7	3	14	28	3	.933
1988	—Toledo (Int'l)	3B-SS-1B	82	278	23	56	8	2	6	19	.201	8	38	9	52	126	13	.932
	—Glens Falls (East.)	3B	57	218	32	61	11	1	1	36	.280	16	28	11	45	112	12	.929
1989	—Toledo (Int'l)	3B-SS	83	304	38	75	15	2	8	42	.247	34	49	8	108	197	17	.947
	—Detroit (A.L.)	3B-2B-SS	64	196	16	42	4	1	1	14	.214	17	36	3	53	118	19	.900
1990	—Tucson (PCL)■	3B-SS	37	98	7	22	3	0	0	7	.224	8	23	0	9	47	9	.862
	—Iowa (Am. Assoc.)■	3B-2B-SS	82	269	31	82	17	1	5	35	.305	28	42	6	58	149	16	.928
1991	—Iowa (Am. Assoc.)	3-2-1-S-0	131	509	76	149	35	5	8	56	.293	49	75	10	263	273	21	.962
	—Chicago (N.L.)	3B	3	9	0	4	1	0	0	1	.444	0	1	1	1	3	1	.800
1992	—Iowa (Am. Assoc.)	2B-3B	55	212	32	65	16	1	4	26	.307	9	32	3	84	126	16	.929
	—Chicago (N.L.)	3B-2B	52	94	7	15	1	0	1	5	.160	10	15	1	24	51	6	.926
1993	—Texas (A.L.)■	2B-3B-SS	145	484	58	124	29	0	7	60	.256	43	69	6	276	374	13	.980
American League totals (2 years)			209	680	74	166	33	1	8	74	.244	60	105	9	329	492	32	.962
National League totals (2 years)			55	103	7	19	2	0	1	6	.184	10	16	2	25	54	7	.919
Major league totals (4 years)			264	783	81	185	35	1	9	80	.236	70	121	11	354	546	39	.958

STRAWBERRY, DARRYL

OF, DODGERS

PERSONAL: Born March 12, 1962, in Los Angeles.... 6-6/215.... Throws left, bats left.... Full name: Darryl Eugene Strawberry.... Brother of Michael Strawberry, minor league outfielder (1980-81).
HIGH SCHOOL: Crenshaw (Los Angeles).
TRANSACTIONS/CAREER NOTES: Selected by New York Mets organization in first round (first pick overall) of free-agent draft (June 3, 1980).... On disabled list (May 12-June 28, 1985).... Granted free agency (November 5, 1990).... Signed by Los

Angeles Dodgers (November 8, 1990).... On disabled list (June 18-July 3, 1991 and May 14-July 6 and July 21-September 1, 1992).... On Los Angeles disabled list (May 13-June 5, 1993); included rehabilitation assignment to Albuquerque (May 28-June 5).... On Los Angeles disabled list (June 17, 1993-remainder of season).
HONORS: Named Texas League Most Valuable Player (1982).... Named N.L. Rookie Player of the Year by THE SPORTING NEWS (1983).... Named N.L. Rookie of the Year by Baseball Writers' Association of America (1983).... Named outfielder on THE SPORTING NEWS N.L. All-Star team (1988 and 1990).... Named outfielder on THE SPORTING NEWS N.L. Silver Slugger team (1988 and 1990).
STATISTICAL NOTES: Led Texas League in slugging percentage with .602 and in caught stealing with 22 in 1982.... Hit three home runs in one game (August 5, 1985).... Led N.L. with .545 slugging percentage in 1988.

			BATTING											FIELDING			
Year	Team (League)	Pos.	G	AB	R	H	2B	3B	HR	RBI	Avg.	BB	SO	SB	PO	A	E	Avg.
1980	—Kingsport (Appal.) ...	OF	44	157	27	42	5	2	5	20	.268	20	39	5	55	4	3	.952
1981	—Lynchburg (Caro.) ...	OF	123	420	84	107	22	6	13	78	.255	82	105	31	173	8	13	.933
1982	—Jackson (Texas)	OF	129	435	93	123	19	9	*34	97	.283	*100	145	45	211	8	9	.961
1983	—Tidewater (Int'l)	OF	16	57	12	19	4	1	3	13	.333	14	18	7	22	0	4	.846
	—New York (N.L.)........	OF	122	420	63	108	15	7	26	74	.257	47	128	19	232	8	4	.984
1984	—New York (N.L.)........	OF	147	522	75	131	27	4	26	97	.251	75	131	27	276	11	6	.980
1985	—New York (N.L.)........	OF	111	393	78	109	15	4	29	79	.277	73	96	26	211	5	2	.991
1986	—New York (N.L.)........	OF	136	475	76	123	27	5	27	93	.259	72	141	28	226	10	6	.975
1987	—New York (N.L.)........	OF	154	532	108	151	32	5	39	104	.284	97	122	36	272	6	8	.972
1988	—New York (N.L.)........	OF	153	543	101	146	27	3	*39	101	.269	85	127	29	297	4	9	.971
1989	—New York (N.L.)........	OF	134	476	69	107	26	1	29	77	.225	61	105	11	272	4	8	.972
1990	—New York (N.L.)........	OF	152	542	92	150	18	1	37	108	.277	70	110	15	268	10	3	.989
1991	—Los Angeles (N.L.)■.	OF	139	505	86	134	22	4	28	99	.265	75	125	10	209	11	5	.978
1992	—Los Angeles (N.L.) ...	OF	43	156	20	37	8	0	5	25	.237	19	34	3	67	2	1	.986
1993	—Los Angeles (N.L.) ...	OF	32	100	12	14	2	0	5	12	.140	16	19	1	37	1	4	.905
	—Albuquerque (PCL) ..	OF	5	19	3	6	2	0	1	2	.316	2	5	1	7	0	0	1.000
Major league totals (11 years)			1323	4664	780	1210	219	34	290	869	.259	690	1138	205	2367	72	56	.978

S

CHAMPIONSHIP SERIES RECORD

CHAMPIONSHIP SERIES NOTES: Shares single-series record for most strikeouts—12 (1986).... Shares N.L. single-series record for most at-bats—30 (1988).

			BATTING											FIELDING			
Year	Team (League)	Pos.	G	AB	R	H	2B	3B	HR	RBI	Avg.	BB	SO	SB	PO	A	E	Avg.
1986	—New York (N.L.)........	OF	6	22	4	5	1	0	2	5	.227	3	12	1	9	0	0	1.000
1988	—New York (N.L.)........	OF	7	30	5	9	2	0	1	6	.300	2	5	0	11	0	0	1.000
Championship series totals (2 years)			13	52	9	14	3	0	3	11	.269	5	17	1	20	0	0	1.000

WORLD SERIES RECORD

			BATTING											FIELDING			
Year	Team (League)	Pos.	G	AB	R	H	2B	3B	HR	RBI	Avg.	BB	SO	SB	PO	A	E	Avg.
1986	—New York (N.L.)........	OF	7	24	4	5	1	0	1	1	.208	4	6	3	19	0	0	1.000

ALL-STAR GAME RECORD

			BATTING										FIELDING			
Year	League	Pos.	AB	R	H	2B	3B	HR	RBI	Avg.	BB	SO	SB	PO	A	E	Avg.
1984	—National....................	OF	2	0	1	0	0	0	0	.500	0	1	0	0	0	0	...
1985	—National....................	OF	1	2	1	0	0	0	0	1.000	1	0	1	3	0	0	1.000
1986	—National....................	OF	2	0	1	0	0	0	0	.500	0	1	0	1	0	0	1.000
1987	—National....................	OF	2	0	0	0	0	0	0	.000	0	0	0	0	0	0	...
1988	—National....................	OF	4	0	1	0	0	0	0	.250	0	1	0	4	0	0	1.000
1989	—National....................		Selected, did not play—injured.														
1990	—National....................	OF	1	0	0	0	0	0	0	.000	0	1	0	3	1	1	.800
1991	—National....................		Selected, did not play—injured.														
All-Star Game totals (6 years)			12	2	4	0	0	0	0	.333	1	4	1	11	1	1	.923

STRICKLAND, CHAD

C, ROYALS

PERSONAL: Born March 16, 1972, in Oklahoma City.... 6-1/185.... Throws right, bats right.... Full name: Daniel Chad Strickland.
HIGH SCHOOL: Carl Albert (Midwest City, Okla.).
TRANSACTIONS/CAREER NOTES: Selected by Kansas City Royals organization in 13th round of free-agent draft (June 4, 1990).
STATISTICAL NOTES: Led Gulf Coast League with 15 passed balls in 1990.... Tied for Carolina League lead with nine sacrifice flies in 1993.... Led Carolina League catchers with 126 assists, 879 total chances and 11 double plays in 1993.

			BATTING											FIELDING			
Year	Team (League)	Pos.	G	AB	R	H	2B	3B	HR	RBI	Avg.	BB	SO	SB	PO	A	E	Avg.
1990	—GC Royals (GCL)	C	50	163	14	36	7	0	0	12	.221	11	24	6	232	54	6	.979
1991	—Appleton (Midw.)	C	28	81	5	14	4	0	1	5	.173	2	12	2	150	24	4	.978
	—Eugene (N'west).......	C	34	118	13	19	7	0	1	11	.161	13	16	1	269	37	4	.987
1992	—Appleton (Midw.)	C	112	396	29	101	16	1	2	49	.255	12	37	2	702	*109	*19	.977
1993	—Wilmington (Caro.) ..	C-1B	122	409	51	102	16	6	2	46	.249	23	46	4	733	†126	20	.977

STURTZE, TANYON

P, ATHLETICS

PERSONAL: Born October 12, 1970, in Worcester, Mass. ... 6-5/190. ... Throws right, bats right.... Full name: Tanyon James Sturtze.
HIGH SCHOOL: St. Peter-Marian (Worcester, Mass.).
COLLEGE: Quinsigamond Community College (Mass.).
TRANSACTIONS/CAREER NOTES: Selected by Oakland Athletics organization in 23rd round of free-agent draft (June 4, 1990).
STATISTICAL NOTES: Pitched 5-0 no-hit victory against Chattanooga (June 13, 1993).

Year	Team (League)	W	L	Pct.	ERA	G	GS	CG	ShO	Sv.	IP	H	R	ER	BB	SO
1990	—Ariz. A's (Arizona)	2	5	.286	5.44	12	10	0	0	0	48	55	41	29	27	30
1991	—Madison (Midwest)	10	5	.667	3.09	27	27	0	0	0	163	136	77	56	58	88
1992	—Modesto (Calif.)	7	11	.389	3.75	25	25	1	0	0	151	143	72	63	78	126
1993	—Huntsville (South.).....	5	12	.294	4.78	28	•28	1	1	0	165⅔	169	102	*88	85	112

SUERO, WILLIAM
2B

PERSONAL: Born November 7, 1966, in Santo Domingo, Dominican Republic. . . . 5-9/175. . . . Throws right, bats right. . . . Full name: William Urban Suero. . . . Name pronounced SWEAR-oh.

HIGH SCHOOL: Francisco Rosario Sanchez (Santo Domingo, Dominican Republic).

TRANSACTIONS/CAREER NOTES: Signed as free agent by Toronto Blue Jays organization (May 1, 1985). . . . On disabled list (June 21, 1985-remainder of season). . . . Traded by Blue Jays to Milwaukee Brewers (August 14, 1991), completing deal in which Brewers traded OF Candy Maldonado to Blue Jays for P Rob Wishnevski and a player to be named later (August 9, 1991). . . . Granted free agency (August 8, 1993).

STATISTICAL NOTES: Led Pioneer League second basemen with 360 total chances and 34 double plays in 1986. . . . Led New York-Pennsylvania League second basemen with 362 total chances in 1987. . . . Led Southern League in caught stealing with 22 in 1990.

			BATTING												FIELDING			
Year	**Team (League)**	**Pos.**	**G**	**AB**	**R**	**H**	**2B**	**3B**	**HR**	**RBI**	**Avg.**	**BB**	**SO**	**SB**	**PO**	**A**	**E**	**Avg.**
1985	—								Did not play.									
1986	—Medicine Hat (Pio.) ..	2B	64	273	39	76	7	5	2	28	.278	15	36	13	*159	*182	*19	*.947
1987	—St. Cathar. (NYP)	2B	•77	297	43	94	12	4	4	24	.316	35	35	23	*149	197	*16	.956
1988	—Myrtle Beach (SAL) ..	2B	125	493	88	140	21	6	6	52	.284	49	72	21	254	303	26	.955
1989	—Dunedin (Fla. St.)	2B	51	206	35	60	10	5	2	17	.291	16	32	9	92	155	10	.961
	—Knoxville (South.)	2B	87	324	42	84	17	5	4	29	.259	34	50	7	146	228	15	.961
1990	—Knoxville (South.)	2B	133	483	80	127	29	7	16	60	.263	78	78	40	259	333	23	.963
1991	—Syracuse (Int'l)	2B	98	393	49	78	18	1	1	28	.198	38	51	17	178	318	*19	.963
	—Denver (A.A.)■	2B	20	70	20	27	3	2	0	15	.386	10	8	3	63	57	3	.976
1992	—Milwaukee (A.L.)	2B-SS	18	16	4	3	1	0	0	0	.188	2	1	1	11	22	1	.971
	—Denver (A.A.)	2B	75	276	42	71	10	9	1	25	.257	31	33	16	178	214	10	.975
1993	—Milwaukee (A.L.)	2B-3B	15	14	0	4	0	0	0	0	.286	1	3	0	6	13	1	.950
	—New Orleans (A.A.) ..	2B-1B-OF	46	124	14	28	4	1	1	13	.226	21	17	8	83	72	7	.957
Major league totals (2 years)			33	30	4	7	1	0	0	0	.233	3	4	1	17	35	2	.963

SURHOFF, B.J.
3B/OF, BREWERS

PERSONAL: Born August 4, 1964, in Bronx, N.Y. . . . 6-1/200. . . . Throws right, bats left. . . . Full name: William James Surhoff. . . . Son of Dick Surhoff, National Basketball Association player (1952-53 and 1953-54); and brother of Rich Surhoff, pitcher, Philadelphia Phillies and Texas Rangers (1985).

HIGH SCHOOL: Rye (N.Y.).

COLLEGE: North Carolina.

TRANSACTIONS/CAREER NOTES: Selected by New York Yankees organization in fifth round of free-agent draft (June 7, 1982). . . . Selected by Milwaukee Brewers organization in first round (first pick overall) of free-agent draft (June 3, 1985). . . . On suspended list (August 23-25, 1990).

HONORS: Named College Player of the Year by THE SPORTING NEWS (1985). . . . Named catcher on THE SPORTING NEWS college All-America team (1985).

STATISTICAL NOTES: Tied for Pacific Coast League lead in double plays by catcher with 10 in 1986. . . . Led A.L. catchers with 68 assists in 1991.

MISCELLANEOUS: Member of 1984 U.S. Olympic baseball team.

			BATTING												FIELDING			
Year	**Team (League)**	**Pos.**	**G**	**AB**	**R**	**H**	**2B**	**3B**	**HR**	**RBI**	**Avg.**	**BB**	**SO**	**SB**	**PO**	**A**	**E**	**Avg.**
1985	—Beloit (Midwest)	C	76	289	39	96	13	4	7	58	.332	22	35	10	475	44	3	.994
1986	—Vancouver (PCL)	C	116	458	71	141	19	3	5	59	.308	29	30	21	539	70	7	*.989
1987	—Milwaukee (A.L.)	C-3B-1B	115	395	50	118	22	3	7	68	.299	36	30	11	648	56	11	.985
1988	—Milwaukee (A.L.)	C-3-1-S-0	139	493	47	121	21	0	5	38	.245	31	49	21	550	94	8	.988
1989	—Milwaukee (A.L.)	C-3B	126	436	42	108	17	4	5	55	.248	25	29	14	530	58	10	.983
1990	—Milwaukee (A.L.)	C-3B	135	474	55	131	21	4	6	59	.276	41	37	18	619	62	12	.983
1991	—Milwaukee (A.L.)	C-3-0-2	143	505	57	146	19	4	5	68	.289	26	33	5	665	†71	4	.995
1992	—Milwaukee (A.L.)	C-1-0-3	139	480	63	121	19	1	4	62	.252	46	41	14	699	74	6	.992
1993	—Milwaukee (A.L.)	3-0-1-C	148	552	66	151	38	3	7	79	.274	36	47	12	175	220	18	.956
Major league totals (7 years)			945	3335	380	896	157	19	39	429	.269	241	266	95	3886	635	69	.985

SUTCLIFFE, RICK
P, CARDINALS

PERSONAL: Born June 21, 1956, in Independence, Mo. . . . 6-7/239. . . . Throws right, bats left. . . . Full name: Richard Lee Sutcliffe. . . . Brother of Terry Sutcliffe, minor league pitcher (1979-81).

HIGH SCHOOL: Van Horn (Independence, Mo.).

TRANSACTIONS/CAREER NOTES: Selected by Los Angeles Dodgers organization in first round (21st pick overall) of free-agent draft (June 5, 1974). . . . On disabled list (May 3-24, 1977 and August 14-September 5, 1981). . . . Traded by Dodgers with 2B Jack Perconte to Cleveland Indians for OF Jorge Orta, C Jack Fimple and P Larry White (December 9, 1981). . . . Traded by Indians with C Ron Hassey and P George Frazier to Chicago Cubs for OF Mel Hall, OF Joe Carter, P Don Schulze and P Darryl Banks (June 13, 1984). . . . Granted free agency (November 8, 1984). . . . Re-signed by Cubs (December 14, 1984). . . . On disabled list (May 20-June 7, July 8-23 and July 29-September 27, 1985; June 30-August 3, 1986; and May 21-June 11, 1988). . . . On Chicago disabled list (March 31-August 29, 1990); included rehabilitation assignment to Iowa (April 26-May 1). . . . On Chicago disabled list (April 2-18, 1991). . . . On Chicago disabled list (June 9-August 6, 1991); included rehabilitation assignment to Peoria (July 10-11) and Iowa (July 15-20 and July 29-30). . . . Granted free agency (October 28, 1991). . . . Signed by Baltimore Orioles (December 19, 1991). . . . Granted free agency (October 26, 1992). . . . Re-signed by Orioles (November 23,

1992).... On suspended list (June 16-23, 1993).... On disabled list (August 23-September 11, 1993).... Granted free agency (November 1, 1993).... Signed by St. Louis Cardinals organization (January 31, 1994).
RECORDS: Shares major league single-season record for fewest games won by pitcher who led league in games won—18 (1987).
HONORS: Named N.L. Rookie Pitcher of the Year by THE SPORTING NEWS (1979).... Named N.L. Rookie of the Year by Baseball Writers' Association of America (1979).... Named N.L. Pitcher of the Year by THE SPORTING NEWS (1984).... Named righthanded pitcher on THE SPORTING NEWS N.L. All-Star team (1984).... Named N.L. Cy Young Award winner by Baseball Writers' Association of America (1984).... Named N.L. Comeback Player of the Year by THE SPORTING NEWS (1987).... Named A.L. Comeback Player of the Year by THE SPORTING NEWS (1992).
MISCELLANEOUS: Received base on balls in only appearance as pinch-hitter with Chicago (1991).

Year	Team (League)	W	L	Pct.	ERA	G	GS	CG	ShO	Sv.	IP	H	R	ER	BB	SO
1974	—Belling. (N'west)	10	3	.769	3.32	17	14	7	•2	1	95	79	42	35	48	69
1975	—Bakersfield (Calif.)	8	*16	.333	4.15	28	*28	10	0	0	193	*214	*115	*89	68	91
1976	—Waterbury (East.)	10	11	.476	3.18	30	26	8	0	0	187	*187	90	66	45	121
	—Los Angeles (N.L.)	0	0	...	0.00	1	1	0	0	0	5	2	0	0	1	3
1977	—Albuquerque (PCL)	3	10	.231	6.43	17	16	1	0	5	77	96	67	55	63	48
1978	—Albuquerque (PCL)	13	6	.684	4.45	30	27	6	0	0	184	179	101	91	92	99
	—Los Angeles (N.L.)	0	0	...	0.00	2	0	0	0	0	2	2	0	0	1	0
1979	—Los Angeles (N.L.)	17	10	.630	3.46	39	30	5	1	0	242	217	104	93	97	117
1980	—Los Angeles (N.L.)	3	9	.250	5.56	42	10	1	1	5	110	122	73	68	55	59
1981	—Los Angeles (N.L.)	2	2	.500	4.02	14	6	0	0	0	47	41	24	21	20	16
1982	—Cleveland (A.L.)■	14	8	.636	*2.96	34	27	6	1	1	216	174	81	71	98	142
1983	—Cleveland (A.L.)	17	11	.607	4.29	36	35	10	2	0	243⅓	251	131	116	102	160
1984	—Cleveland (A.L.)	4	5	.444	5.15	15	15	2	0	0	94⅓	111	60	54	46	58
	—Chicago (N.L.)■	16	1	.941	2.69	20	20	7	3	0	150⅓	123	53	45	39	155
1985	—Chicago (N.L.)	8	8	.500	3.18	20	20	6	3	0	130	119	51	46	44	102
1986	—Chicago (N.L.)	5	14	.263	4.64	28	27	4	1	0	176⅔	166	92	91	96	122
1987	—Chicago (N.L.)	*18	10	.643	3.68	34	34	6	1	0	237⅓	223	106	97	106	174
1988	—Chicago (N.L.)	13	14	.481	3.86	32	32	12	2	0	226	232	97	97	70	144
1989	—Chicago (N.L.)	16	11	.593	3.66	35	34	5	1	0	229	202	98	93	69	153
1990	—Iowa (Am. Assoc.)	0	2	.000	7.82	2	2	0	0	0	12⅔	18	13	11	7	12
	—Chicago (N.L.)	0	2	.000	5.82	5	5	0	0	0	21⅔	25	14	14	12	7
1991	—Chicago (N.L.)	6	5	.545	4.10	19	18	0	0	0	96⅔	96	52	44	45	52
	—Peoria (Midwest)	0	0	...	6.00	1	1	0	0	0	9	12	6	6	2	6
	—Iowa (Am. Assoc.)	1	2	.333	9.69	3	2	0	0	0	13	23	14	14	6	8
1992	—Baltimore (A.L.)■	16	15	.516	4.47	36	•36	5	2	0	237⅓	251	*123	*118	74	109
1993	—Baltimore (A.L.)	10	10	.500	5.75	29	28	3	0	0	166	212	112	106	74	80
A.L. totals (5 years)		61	49	.555	4.37	150	141	26	5	1	957	999	507	465	394	549
N.L. totals (13 years)		104	86	.547	3.81	291	237	46	13	5	1673⅔	1570	764	709	655	1104
Major league totals (17 years)		165	135	.550	4.02	441	378	72	18	6	2630⅔	2569	1271	1174	1049	1653

CHAMPIONSHIP SERIES RECORD

CHAMPIONSHIP SERIES NOTES: Hit home run in first at-bat (October 2, 1984).

Year	Team (League)	W	L	Pct.	ERA	G	GS	CG	ShO	Sv.	IP	H	R	ER	BB	SO
1984	—Chicago (N.L.)	1	1	.500	3.38	2	2	0	0	0	13⅓	9	6	5	8	10
1989	—Chicago (N.L.)	0	0	...	4.50	1	1	0	0	0	6	5	3	3	4	2
Champ. series totals (2 years)		1	1	.500	3.72	3	3	0	0	0	19⅓	14	9	8	12	12

ALL-STAR GAME RECORD

Year	League	W	L	Pct.	ERA	GS	CG	ShO	Sv.	IP	H	R	ER	BB	SO
1983	—American						Did not play.								
1987	—National	0	0	...	0.00	0	0	0	0	2	1	0	0	1	0
1989	—National	0	0	...	18.00	0	0	0	0	1	4	2	2	0	0
All-Star totals (2 years)		0	0	...	6.00	0	0	0	0	3	5	2	2	1	0

SUTKO, GLENN

C, PIRATES

PERSONAL: Born May 9, 1968, in Atlanta.... 6-3/225.... Throws right, bats right.... Full name: Glenn Edward Sutko.
HIGH SCHOOL: Forsyth (Cumming, Ga.).
COLLEGE: Spartanburg (S.C.) Methodist and Dekalb College (Ga.).
TRANSACTIONS/CAREER NOTES: Selected by Cincinnati Reds organization in 45th round of free-agent draft (June 2, 1987).... On Cedar Rapids disabled list (May 29-July 12, 1990).... On Nashville disabled list (July 27-August 5, 1991).... On Winston-Salem disabled list (April 8-May 7, 1993).... Released by Chattanooga, Reds organization (December 15, 1993).... Signed by Pittsburgh Pirates organization (January 10, 1994).
MISCELLANEOUS: Made one plate appearance after designated hitter moved to right field (1993).

			BATTING												FIELDING			
Year	Team (League)	Pos.	G	AB	R	H	2B	3B	HR	RBI	Avg.	BB	SO	SB	PO	A	E	Avg.
1988	—Billings (Pioneer)	C	30	84	3	13	2	1	1	8	.155	14	38	3	141	15	5	.969
1989	—Greensboro (S. Atl.)	C	109	333	44	78	21	0	7	41	.234	47	105	1	676	77	11	.986
1990	—Ced. Rap. (Midw.)	C	4	10	0	3	0	0	0	0	.300	0	2	0	21	2	0	1.000
	—Chatt. (South.)	C-1B	53	174	12	29	7	1	2	11	.167	8	66	1	351	33	4	.990
	—Cincinnati (N.L.)	C	1	1	0	0	0	0	0	0	.000	0	1	0	3	0	0	1.000
1991	—Chatt. (South.)	C	23	63	12	18	3	0	3	11	.286	9	20	0	168	21	1	.995
	—Cincinnati (N.L.)	C	10	10	0	1	0	0	0	1	.100	2	6	0	16	5	3	.875
	—Nashville (A.A.)	C	45	134	9	28	2	1	3	15	.209	22	67	1	228	39	4	.985
1992	—Chatt. (South.)	C-P	64	198	24	37	4	0	10	27	.187	17	90	3	337	53	8	.980
1993	—Winst.-Salem (Car.)	P-PR	31	1	1	0	0	0	0	0	.000	0	0	0	9	10	0	1.000
Major league totals (2 years)			11	11	0	1	0	0	0	1	.091	2	7	0	19	5	3	.889

RECORD AS PITCHER

Year	Team (League)	W	L	Pct.	ERA	G	GS	CG	ShO	Sv.	IP	H	R	ER	BB	SO
1992	—Chatt. (South.)	0	0	...	1.69	4	1	0	0	1	5⅓	5	1	1	3	4
1993	—Winst.-Salem (Car.)	5	7	.417	4.30	28	14	2	0	0	98⅓	112	54	47	33	68

SVEUM, DALE

IF, MARINERS

PERSONAL: Born November 23, 1963, in Richmond, Calif. . . . 6-3/185. . . . Throws right, bats both. . . . Full name: Dale Curtis Sveum. . . . Name pronounced SWAIM.

HIGH SCHOOL: Pinole Valley (Calif.).

TRANSACTIONS/CAREER NOTES: Selected by Milwaukee Brewers organization in first round (25th pick overall) of free-agent draft (June 7, 1982). . . . On Milwaukee disabled list (July 23-August 9, 1986). . . . On Milwaukee disabled list (March 19, 1989-entire season); included rehabilitation assignment to Beloit (June 30-July 5) and Stockton (July 6-18). . . . Traded by Brewers to Philadelphia Phillies for P Bruce Ruffin (December 11, 1991). . . . On disabled list (April 9-24, 1992). . . . Traded by Phillies to Chicago White Sox for P Keith Shepherd (August 10, 1992). . . . Granted free agency (October 26, 1992). . . . Signed by Oakland Athletics organization (January 21, 1993). . . . Released by A's (June 17, 1993). . . . Signed by Calgary, Seattle Mariners organization (June 27, 1993). . . . On Calgary disabled list (August 3-13 and August 18, 1993-remainder of season).

STATISTICAL NOTES: Led California League third basemen with 261 assists in 1983. . . . Led Texas League with 256 total bases in 1984. . . . Led Texas League third basemen with 111 putouts and 30 errors in 1984. . . . Led American League third basemen with 26 errors in 1986. . . . Hit three home runs in one game (July 17, 1987). . . . Switch-hit home runs in one game (July 17, 1987 and June 12, 1988). . . . Led American League shortstops with 27 errors in 1988.

							BATTING								FIELDING			
Year	Team (League)	Pos.	G	AB	R	H	2B	3B	HR	RBI	Avg.	BB	SO	SB	PO	A	E	Avg.
1982	—Pikeville (Appal.)	SS-3B	58	223	29	52	13	1	2	21	.233	20	50	6	84	158	36	.871
1983	—Stockton (Calif.)	3B-SS	135	533	70	139	26	5	5	70	.261	29	73	15	105	†281	40	.906
1984	—El Paso (Texas)	3B-SS	131	523	92	*172	*41	8	9	84	.329	43	72	6	†113	259	†30	.925
1985	—Vancouver (PCL)	3B-SS	122	415	42	98	17	3	6	48	.236	48	79	4	81	200	26	.915
1986	—Vancouver (PCL)	3B	28	105	16	31	3	2	1	23	.295	13	22	0	22	54	4	.950
	—Milwaukee (A.L.)	3B-SS-2B	91	317	35	78	13	2	7	35	.246	32	63	4	92	179	†30	.900
1987	—Milwaukee (A.L.)	SS-2B	153	535	86	135	27	3	25	95	.252	40	133	2	242	396	23	.965
1988	—Milwaukee (A.L.)	SS-2B	129	467	41	113	14	4	9	51	.242	21	122	1	209	375	†27	.956
1989	—Beloit (Midwest)	DH	6	15	0	2	1	0	0	2	.133	5	6	0	...	...	...	...
	—Stockton (Calif.)	DH	11	43	5	8	0	0	1	5	.186	6	14	0	...	...	...	...
1990	—Milwaukee (A.L.)	3-2-1-S	48	117	15	23	7	0	1	12	.197	12	30	0	59	63	6	.953
	—Denver (A.A.)	3-S-1-2	57	218	25	63	17	2	2	26	.289	20	49	1	134	102	12	.952
1991	—Milwaukee (A.L.)	SS-3B-2B	90	266	33	64	19	1	4	43	.241	32	78	2	85	189	10	.965
1992	—Philadelphia (N.L.)■.	SS-3B-1B	54	135	13	24	4	0	2	16	.178	16	39	0	78	100	8	.957
	—Chicago (A.L.)■........	SS-3B-1B	40	114	15	25	9	0	2	12	.219	12	29	1	43	98	8	.946
1993	—Tac.-Calg. (PCL)■ ...	2-3-1-S	45	163	41	51	12	1	8	32	.313	30	39	2	91	50	3	.979
	—Oakland (A.L.)	1-3-2-0-S	30	79	12	14	2	1	2	6	.177	16	21	0	128	17	3	.980
American League totals (7 years)			581	1895	237	452	91	11	50	254	.239	165	476	10	858	1317	107	.953
National League totals (1 year)			54	135	13	24	4	0	2	16	.178	16	39	0	78	100	8	.957
Major league totals (7 years)			635	2030	250	476	95	11	52	270	.234	181	515	10	936	1417	115	.953

SWAN, RUSS

P, INDIANS

PERSONAL: Born January 3, 1964, in Fremont, Calif. . . . 6-4/210. . . . Throws left, bats left. . . . Full name: Russell Howard Swan.

HIGH SCHOOL: Kennewick (Wash.).

COLLEGE: Spokane Falls Community College (Wash.) and Texas A&M.

TRANSACTIONS/CAREER NOTES: Selected by Houston Astros organization in second round of free-agent draft (January 17, 1984). . . . Selected by Seattle Mariners organization in secondary phase of free-agent draft (June 4, 1984). . . . Selected by San Francisco Giants organization in ninth round of free-agent draft (June 2, 1986). . . . Traded by Giants organization to Seattle Mariners for P Gary Eave (May 24, 1990). . . . On Seattle disabled list (July 8-September 1, 1990); included rehabilitation assignment to Calgary (August 16-31). . . . On disabled list (August 3-18, 1991). . . . On Calgary disabled list (July 15-August 3, 1993). . . . On Seattle disabled list (August 23, 1993-remainder of season). . . . Released by Mariners (November 12, 1993). . . . Signed by Cleveland Indians organization (January 21, 1994).

Year	Team (League)	W	L	Pct.	ERA	G	GS	CG	ShO	Sv.	IP	H	R	ER	BB	SO
1986	—Everett (N'west)	5	0	1.000	2.15	7	7	2	0	0	46	30	17	11	22	45
	—Clinton (Midwest)	3	3	.500	3.09	7	7	2	1	0	43⅔	36	18	15	8	37
1987	—Fresno (California)	6	3	.667	3.80	12	12	0	0	0	64	54	40	27	29	59
1988	—San Jose (Calif.)	7	0	1.000	2.23	11	11	2	1	0	76⅔	53	28	19	26	62
1989	—Shreveport (Texas)	2	3	.400	2.63	11	11	0	0	0	75⅓	62	25	22	22	56
	—San Francisco (N.L.)	0	2	.000	10.80	2	2	0	0	0	6⅔	11	10	8	4	2
	—Phoenix (PCL)	4	3	.571	3.36	14	13	1	0	0	83	75	37	31	29	49
1990	—San Francisco (N.L.)	0	1	.000	3.86	2	1	0	0	0	2⅓	6	4	1	4	1
	—Phoe.-Calg. (PCL)■......	3	6	.333	4.45	11	11	0	0	0	56⅔	69	35	28	27	35
	—Seattle (A.L.)	2	3	.400	3.64	11	8	0	0	0	47	42	22	19	18	15
1991	—Seattle (A.L.)	6	2	.750	3.43	63	0	0	0	2	78⅔	81	35	30	28	33
1992	—Seattle (A.L.)	3	10	.231	4.74	55	9	1	0	9	104⅓	104	60	55	45	45
1993	—Seattle (A.L.)	3	3	.500	9.15	23	0	0	0	0	19⅔	25	20	20	18	10
	—Calgary (PCL)	2	1	.667	8.44	9	0	0	0	0	10⅔	14	11	10	8	7
A.L. totals (4 years)		14	18	.438	4.47	152	17	1	0	11	249⅔	252	137	124	109	103
N.L. totals (2 years)		0	3	.000	9.00	4	3	0	0	0	9	17	14	9	8	3
Major league totals (5 years)		14	21	.400	4.63	156	20	1	0	11	258⅔	269	151	133	117	106

SWEENEY, MARK

OF, ANGELS

PERSONAL: Born October 26, 1969, in Framingham, Mass. . . . 6-1/195. . . . Throws left, bats left. . . . Full name: Mark Patrick Sweeney.

HIGH SCHOOL: Holliston (Mass.).

COLLEGE: Maine.

TRANSACTIONS/CAREER NOTES: Selected by Los Angeles Dodgers organization in 39th round of free-agent draft (June 4, 1990). . . . Selected by California Angels organization in ninth round of free-agent draft (June 3, 1991).

			BATTING											FIELDING			
Year	Team (League)	Pos.	G	AB	R	H	2B	3B	HR	RBI	Avg.	BB	SO	SB	PO	A	E	Avg.
1991	—Boise (Northwest)	OF	70	234	45	66	10	3	4	34	.282	*51	42	9	81	2	4	.954
1992	—Quad City (Midw.)	OF	120	424	65	115	20	5	14	76	.271	47	85	15	205	5	4	.981
1993	—Palm Springs (Cal.)	OF-1B	66	245	41	87	18	3	3	47	.355	42	29	9	145	2	7	.955
	—Midland (Texas)	OF	51	188	41	67	13	2	9	32	.356	27	22	1	85	3	1	.989

SWIFT, BILL

P, GIANTS

PERSONAL: Born October 27, 1961, in South Portland, Me. . . . 6-0/191. . . . Throws right, bats right. . . . Full name: William Charles Swift.
HIGH SCHOOL: South Portland (Portland, Me.).
COLLEGE: Maine.

TRANSACTIONS/CAREER NOTES: Selected by Minnesota Twins organization in second round of free-agent draft (June 6, 1983). . . . Selected by Seattle Mariners organization in first round (second pick overall) of free-agent draft (June 4, 1984). . . . On disabled list (May 6-21, 1985 and April 22, 1987-remainder of season). . . . On Seattle disabled list (March 28-April 27, 1989); included rehabilitation assignment to San Bernardino (April 18-27). . . . On disabled list (April 11-26, 1991). . . . Traded by Mariners with P Mike Jackson and P Dave Burba to San Francisco Giants for OF Kevin Mitchell and P Mike Remlinger (December 11, 1991). . . . On San Francisco disabled list (May 23-June 21 and August 25-September 9, 1992).
MISCELLANEOUS: Member of 1984 U.S. Olympic baseball team. . . . Appeared in five games as pinch-runner (1992).

Year	Team (League)	W	L	Pct.	ERA	G	GS	CG	ShO	Sv.	IP	H	R	ER	BB	SO
1985	—Chatt. (South.)	2	1	.667	3.69	7	7	0	0	0	39	34	16	16	21	21
	—Seattle (A.L.)	6	10	.375	4.77	23	21	0	0	0	120⅔	131	71	64	48	55
1986	—Seattle (A.L.)	2	9	.182	5.46	29	17	1	0	0	115⅓	148	85	70	55	55
	—Calgary (PCL)	4	4	.500	3.95	10	8	3	1	1	57	57	33	25	22	29
1987	—Calgary (PCL)	0	0	...	8.84	5	5	0	0	0	18⅓	32	22	18	13	5
1988	—Seattle (A.L.)	8	12	.400	4.59	38	24	6	1	0	174⅔	199	99	89	65	47
1989	—San Bern. (Calif.)	1	0	1.000	0.00	2	2	0	0	0	10	8	0	0	2	4
	—Seattle (A.L.)	7	3	.700	4.43	37	16	0	0	1	130	140	72	64	38	45
1990	—Seattle (A.L.)	6	4	.600	2.39	55	8	0	0	6	128	135	46	34	21	42
1991	—Seattle (A.L.)	1	2	.333	1.99	71	0	0	0	17	90⅓	74	22	20	26	48
1992	—San Francisco (N.L.)■	10	4	.714	*2.08	30	22	3	2	1	164⅔	144	41	38	43	77
1993	—San Francisco (N.L.)	21	8	.724	2.82	34	34	1	1	0	232⅔	195	82	73	55	157
	A.L. totals (6 years)	30	40	.429	4.04	253	86	7	1	24	759	827	395	341	253	292
	N.L. totals (2 years)	31	12	.721	2.51	64	56	4	3	1	397⅓	339	123	111	98	234
	Major league totals (8 years)	61	52	.540	3.52	317	142	11	4	25	1156⅓	1166	518	452	351	526

SWINDELL, GREG

P, ASTROS

PERSONAL: Born January 2, 1965, in Fort Worth, Tex. . . . 6-3/225. . . . Throws left, bats right. . . . Full name: Forest Gregory Swindell. . . . Name pronounced swin-DELL.
HIGH SCHOOL: Sharpstown (Tex.).
COLLEGE: Texas.

TRANSACTIONS/CAREER NOTES: Selected by Cleveland Indians organization in first round (second pick overall) of free-agent draft (June 2, 1986). . . . On disabled list (June 30, 1987-remainder of season and July 26-August 30, 1989). . . . Traded by Indians to Cincinnati Reds for P Jack Armstrong, P Scott Scudder and P Joe Turek (November 15, 1991). . . . On disabled list (August 23-September 7, 1992). . . . Granted free agency (October 26, 1992). . . . Signed by Houston Astros (December 4, 1992). . . . On disabled list (July 6-26, 1993).
HONORS: Named lefthanded pitcher on THE SPORTING NEWS college All-America team (1985-86).

Year	Team (League)	W	L	Pct.	ERA	G	GS	CG	ShO	Sv.	IP	H	R	ER	BB	SO
1986	—Waterloo (Midw.)	2	1	.667	1.00	3	3	0	0	0	18	12	2	2	3	25
	—Cleveland (A.L.)	5	2	.714	4.23	9	9	1	0	0	61⅔	57	35	29	15	46
1987	—Cleveland (A.L.)	3	8	.273	5.10	16	15	4	1	0	102⅓	112	62	58	37	97
1988	—Cleveland (A.L.)	18	14	.563	3.20	33	33	12	4	0	242	234	97	86	45	180
1989	—Cleveland (A.L.)	13	6	.684	3.37	28	28	5	2	0	184⅓	170	71	69	51	129
1990	—Cleveland (A.L.)	12	9	.571	4.40	34	34	3	0	0	214⅔	245	110	105	47	135
1991	—Cleveland (A.L.)	9	16	.360	3.48	33	33	7	0	0	238	241	112	92	31	169
1992	—Cincinnati (N.L.)■	12	8	.600	2.70	31	30	5	3	0	213⅔	210	72	64	41	138
1993	—Houston (N.L.)■	12	13	.480	4.16	31	30	1	1	0	190⅓	215	98	88	40	124
	A.L. totals (6 years)	60	55	.522	3.79	153	152	32	7	0	1043	1059	487	439	226	756
	N.L. totals (2 years)	24	21	.533	3.39	62	60	6	4	0	404	425	170	152	81	262
	Major league totals (8 years)	84	76	.525	3.68	215	212	38	11	0	1447	1484	657	591	307	1018

ALL-STAR GAME RECORD

Year	League	W	L	Pct.	ERA	GS	CG	ShO	Sv.	IP	H	R	ER	BB	SO
1989	—American	0	0	...	0.00	0	0	0	0	1⅔	2	0	0	0	3

SWINGLE, PAUL

P, ANGELS

PERSONAL: Born December 21, 1966, in Inglewood, Calif. . . . 6-0/185. . . . Throws right, bats right. . . . Full name: Paul Christopher Swingle. . . . Name pronounced SWING-gul.
HIGH SCHOOL: Dobson (Mesa, Ariz.).
COLLEGE: Grand Canyon (Ariz.).

TRANSACTIONS/CAREER NOTES: Selected by California Angels organization in 29th round of free-agent draft (June 3, 1989).

Year	Team (League)	W	L	Pct.	ERA	G	GS	CG	ShO	Sv.	IP	H	R	ER	BB	SO
1989	—Bend (Northwest)	1	0	1.000	2.95	9	0	0	0	0	18⅓	7	9	6	19	26
1990	—Boise (Northwest)	0	1	.000	0.66	14	0	0	0	6	13⅔	5	1	1	4	25
1991	—Palm Springs (Cal.)	5	4	.556	4.42	43	0	0	0	10	57	51	37	28	41	63

S

Year	Team (League)	W	L	Pct.	ERA	G	GS	CG	ShO	Sv.	IP	H	R	ER	BB	SO
1992	—Midland (Texas)	8	10	.444	4.69	25	25	2	0	0	149⅔	158	88	78	51	104
1993	—Vancouver (PCL)	2	9	.182	6.92	37	4	0	0	1	67⅔	85	61	52	32	61
	—California (A.L.)	0	1	.000	8.38	9	0	0	0	0	9⅔	15	9	9	6	6
Major league totals (1 year)		0	1	.000	8.38	9	0	0	0	0	9⅔	15	9	9	6	6

TABAKA, JEFF

P, BREWERS

PERSONAL: Born January 17, 1964, in Barberton, O.... 6-2/195.... Throws left, bats right.... Full name: Jeffrey Jon Tabaka.

HIGH SCHOOL: Copley (O.) Senior.

COLLEGE: Kent.

TRANSACTIONS/CAREER NOTES: Selected by Montreal Expos organization in free-agent draft (June 2, 1986).... On West Palm Beach disabled list (May 2-June 23, 1988).... Selected by Philadelphia Phillies from Expos organization in Rule 5 major league draft (December 5, 1988); Expos waived right to reclaim him as part of deal in which Expos traded P Floyd Youmans and P Jeff Parrett to Phillies for P Kevin Gross (December 6, 1988).... Released by Reading, Phillies organization (July 26, 1991).... Signed by Milwaukee Brewers organization (August 8, 1991).... On disabled list (June 18-July 4, 1992).... Granted free agency (October 15, 1992).... Signed by Brewers (October 30, 1992).... Selected by Florida Marlins in third round (71st pick overall) of expansion draft (November 17, 1992).... Granted free agency (March 21, 1993).... Signed by New Orleans, Brewers organization (March 26, 1993).... Granted free agency (October 15, 1993).... Re-signed by Brewers organization (January 6, 1994).

MISCELLANEOUS: Appeared in one game as designated hitter with New Orleans (1993).

Year	Team (League)	W	L	Pct.	ERA	G	GS	CG	ShO	Sv.	IP	H	R	ER	BB	SO
1986	—Jamestown (NYP)	2	4	.333	4.30	13	9	0	0	0	52⅓	51	31	25	34	57
1987	—W.P. Beach (FSL)	8	6	.571	4.17	28	15	0	0	5	95	90	46	44	58	71
1988	—W.P. Beach (FSL)	7	5	.583	1.71	16	16	2	2	0	95	71	38	18	34	52
	—Jacksonv. (South.)	1	0	1.000	6.55	2	2	0	0	0	11	14	8	8	5	7
1989	—Reading (Eastern)■	8	7	.533	4.65	21	17	6	1	0	100⅔	109	59	52	54	80
	—Scran./W.B. (Int'l)	0	4	.000	6.32	6	6	0	0	0	31⅓	32	26	22	23	15
1990	—Clearwater (FSL)	5	2	.714	3.03	8	5	0	0	0	35⅔	39	17	12	18	23
1991	—Reading (Eastern)	4	8	.333	5.07	21	20	1	1	0	108⅓	117	65	61	78	68
	—Stockton (Calif.)■	0	2	.000	5.19	4	4	0	0	0	17⅓	19	11	10	16	19
1992	—El Paso (Texas)	9	5	.643	2.52	50	0	0	0	10	82	67	23	23	38	75
1993	—New Orleans (A.A.)■	6	6	.500	3.24	53	0	0	0	1	58⅓	50	26	21	30	63

TACKETT, JEFF

C, ORIOLES

PERSONAL: Born December 1, 1965, in Fresno, Calif.... 6-2/205.... Throws right, bats right.... Full name: Jeffery Wilson Tackett.... Son of Terry Tackett, minor league pitcher (1961-65).

HIGH SCHOOL: Camarillo (Calif.).

TRANSACTIONS/CAREER NOTES: Selected by Baltimore Orioles organization in second round of free-agent draft (June 4, 1984).... On disabled list (May 22-31, 1987).

STATISTICAL NOTES: Led New York-Pennsylvania League catchers with 489 total chances in 1985.... Led International League catchers with 570 putouts, 62 assists, 644 total chances and 11 double plays in 1990.... Led International League catchers with 761 putouts, 85 assists, 852 total chances and 14 passed balls and tied for lead with 12 double plays in 1991.

			BATTING												FIELDING			
Year	Team (League)	Pos.	G	AB	R	H	2B	3B	HR	RBI	Avg.	BB	SO	SB	PO	A	E	Avg.
1984	—Bluefield (Appal.)	C	34	98	9	16	2	0	0	12	.163	23	28	1	215	22	5	.979
1985	—Day. Beach (FSL)	C-1B	40	103	8	20	5	2	0	10	.194	13	16	1	173	21	5	.975
	—Newark (NY-Penn)	C	62	187	21	39	6	0	0	22	.209	22	33	2	*412	*63	*14	.971
1986	—Hagerstown (Car.)	C-1B	83	246	53	70	15	1	0	21	.285	36	36	16	465	38	9	.982
1987	—Charlotte (South.)	C	61	205	18	46	6	1	0	13	.224	12	34	5	379	27	10	.976
1988	—Charlotte (South.)	C	81	272	24	56	9	0	0	18	.206	42	46	6	543	57	11	.982
1989	—Rochester (Int'l)	C-3B	67	199	13	36	3	1	2	17	.181	19	45	3	339	42	9	.977
1990	—Rochester (Int'l)	C-3B-1B	108	306	37	73	8	3	4	33	.239	47	50	4	†573	†63	12	.981
1991	—Rochester (Int'l)	C-3B-1B	126	433	64	102	18	2	6	50	.236	54	59	3	†779	†90	8	.991
	—Baltimore (A.L.)	C	6	8	1	1	0	0	0	0	.125	2	2	0	22	0	0	1.000
1992	—Baltimore (A.L.)	C-3B	65	179	21	43	8	1	5	24	.240	17	28	0	311	32	1	.997
1993	—Baltimore (A.L.)	C-P	39	87	8	15	3	0	0	9	.172	13	28	0	167	16	2	.989
	—Rochester (Int'l)	C	8	25	1	8	2	0	0	2	.320	3	8	0	56	3	2	.967
Major league totals (3 years)			110	274	30	59	11	1	5	33	.215	32	58	0	500	48	3	.995

RECORD AS PITCHER

Year	Team (League)	W	L	Pct.	ERA	G	GS	CG	ShO	Sv.	IP	H	R	ER	BB	SO
1993	—Baltimore (A.L.)	0	0	...	0.00	1	0	0	0	0	1	1	0	0	1	0

TANANA, FRANK

P

PERSONAL: Born July 3, 1953, in Detroit.... 6-3/205.... Throws left, bats left.... Full name: Frank Daryl Tanana.... Son of Frank Richard Tanana, minor league outfielder (1952-56).... Name pronounced tuh-NAN-uh.

HIGH SCHOOL: Detroit Catholic Central.

COLLEGE: Cal State Fullerton.

TRANSACTIONS/CAREER NOTES: Selected by California Angels organization in first round (13th pick overall) of free-agent draft (June 8, 1971).... On disabled list (July 9-September 4, 1979).... Traded by Angels with P Jim Dorsey and OF Joe Rudi to Boston Red Sox for OF Fred Lynn and P Steve Renko (January 23, 1981).... Granted free agency (November 13, 1981).... Signed by Texas Rangers (January 6, 1982).... Traded by Rangers to Detroit Tigers for P Duane James (June 20, 1985).... Granted free agency (November 9, 1987).... Re-signed by Tigers (February 17, 1988).... Granted free agency (November 13, 1989).... Re-signed by Tigers (November 20, 1989).... Granted free agency (November 3, 1992).... Signed by New York Mets (December 10, 1992).... Traded by Mets to New York Yankees for P Kenny Greer (September 17, 1993).... Grant-

ed free agency (October 29, 1993).
RECORDS: Holds A.L. career record for most home runs allowed—422. . . . Shares A.L. record for most consecutive hits allowed at start of game—5 (May 18, 1980).
HONORS: Named Texas League Pitcher of the Year (1973). . . . Named A.L. Rookie Pitcher of the Year by THE SPORTING NEWS (1974). . . . Named lefthanded pitcher on THE SPORTING NEWS A.L. All-Star team (1976-77).
STATISTICAL NOTES: Led A.L. with eight balks in 1978 and tied for lead with four in 1984.
MISCELLANEOUS: Appeared in one game as pinch-runner with Idaho Falls of Pioneer League (1971); did not pitch due to a sore arm. . . . Struck out in only at-bat (1991).

Year	Team (League)	W	L	Pct.	ERA	G	GS	CG	ShO	Sv.	IP	H	R	ER	BB	SO
1971	—							Did not pitch.								
1972	—Quad Cities (Mid.)	7	2	.778	2.79	19	19	3	2	0	129	111	48	40	57	134
1973	—El Paso (Texas)	16	6	.727	2.71	26	26	★15	4	0	★206	170	72	62	63	★197
	—Salt Lake City (PCL)	1	0	1.000	2.57	2	2	1	1	0	14	11	5	4	2	15
	—California (A.L.)	2	2	.500	3.12	4	4	2	1	0	26	20	11	9	8	22
1974	—California (A.L.)	14	19	.424	3.11	39	35	12	4	0	269	262	104	93	77	180
1975	—California (A.L.)	16	9	.640	2.63	34	33	16	5	0	257	211	80	75	73	★269
1976	—California (A.L.)	19	10	.655	2.44	34	34	23	2	0	288	212	88	78	73	261
1977	—California (A.L.)	15	9	.625	★2.54	31	31	20	★7	0	241	201	72	68	61	205
1978	—California (A.L.)	18	12	.600	3.65	33	33	10	4	0	239	239	108	97	60	137
1979	—California (A.L.)	7	5	.583	3.90	18	17	2	1	0	90	93	44	39	25	46
1980	—California (A.L.)	11	12	.478	4.15	32	31	7	0	0	204	223	107	94	45	113
1981	—Boston (A.L.)■	4	10	.286	4.02	24	23	5	2	0	141	142	70	63	43	78
1982	—Texas (A.L.)■	7	•18	.280	4.21	30	30	7	0	0	194⅓	199	102	91	55	87
1983	—Texas (A.L.)	7	9	.438	3.16	29	22	3	0	0	159⅓	144	70	56	49	108
1984	—Texas (A.L.)	15	15	.500	3.25	35	35	9	1	0	246⅓	234	117	89	81	141
1985	—Texas-Det. (A.L.)■	12	14	.462	4.27	33	33	4	0	0	215	220	112	102	57	159
1986	—Detroit (A.L.)	12	9	.571	4.16	32	31	3	1	0	188⅓	196	95	87	65	119
1987	—Detroit (A.L.)	15	10	.600	3.91	34	34	5	3	0	218⅔	216	106	95	56	146
1988	—Detroit (A.L.)	14	11	.560	4.21	32	32	2	0	0	203	213	105	95	64	127
1989	—Detroit (A.L.)	10	14	.417	3.58	33	33	6	1	0	223⅔	227	105	89	74	147
1990	—Detroit (A.L.)	9	8	.529	5.31	34	29	1	0	1	176⅓	190	104	104	66	114
1991	—Detroit (A.L.)	13	12	.520	3.77	33	33	3	2	0	217⅓	217	98	91	78	107
1992	—Detroit (A.L.)	13	11	.542	4.39	32	31	3	0	0	186⅔	188	102	91	90	91
1993	—New York (N.L.)■	7	15	.318	4.48	29	29	0	0	0	183	198	100	91	48	104
	—New York (A.L.)■	0	2	.000	3.20	3	3	0	0	0	19⅔	18	10	7	7	12
A.L. totals (21 years)		233	221	.513	3.63	609	587	143	34	1	4003⅔	3865	1810	1613	1207	2669
N.L. totals (1 year)		7	15	.318	4.48	29	29	0	0	0	183	198	100	91	48	104
Major league totals (21 years)		240	236	.504	3.66	638	616	143	34	1	4186⅔	4063	1910	1704	1255	2773

CHAMPIONSHIP SERIES RECORD

CHAMPIONSHIP SERIES NOTES: Holds career record for most hit batsmen—4. . . . Holds single-series record for most hit batsmen—3 (1987). . . . Holds single-game record for most hit batsmen—3 (October 11, 1987).

Year	Team (League)	W	L	Pct.	ERA	G	GS	CG	ShO	Sv.	IP	H	R	ER	BB	SO
1979	—California (A.L.)	0	0	...	3.60	1	1	0	0	0	5	6	2	2	2	3
1987	—Detroit (A.L.)	0	1	.000	5.06	1	1	0	0	0	5⅓	6	4	3	4	1
Champ. series totals (2 years)		0	1	.000	4.35	2	2	0	0	0	10⅓	12	6	5	6	4

ALL-STAR GAME RECORD

Year	League	W	L	Pct.	ERA	GS	CG	ShO	Sv.	IP	H	R	ER	BB	SO
1976	—American	0	0	...	13.50	0	0	0	0	2	3	3	3	1	0
1977	—American				Selected, did not play—injured.										
1978	—American							Did not play.							
All-Star totals (1 year)		0	0	...	13.50	0	0	0	0	2	3	3	3	1	0

TAPANI, KEVIN

P, TWINS

PERSONAL: Born February 18, 1964, in Des Moines, Ia. . . . 6-0/188. . . . Throws right, bats right. . . . Full name: Kevin Ray Tapani. . . . Name pronounced TAP-uh-nee.
HIGH SCHOOL: Escanaba (Mich.).
COLLEGE: Central Michigan (degree in finance, 1987).
TRANSACTIONS/CAREER NOTES: Selected by Chicago Cubs organization in ninth round of free-agent draft (June 3, 1985). . . . Selected by Oakland Athletics organization in second round of free-agent draft (June 2, 1986). . . . Traded by A's as part of an eight-player, three-team deal in which New York Mets traded P Jesse Orosco to A's (December 11, 1987). A's traded Orosco, SS Alfredo Griffin and P Jay Howell to Los Angeles Dodgers for P Bob Welch, P Matt Young and P Jack Savage. A's then traded Savage, P Wally Whitehurst and Tapani to Mets. . . . Traded by Mets with P Tim Drummond to Portland, Minnesota Twins organization (August 1, 1989), as partial completion of deal in which Twins traded P Frank Viola to Mets for P Rick Aguilera, P David West and three players to be named later (July 31, 1989); Twins acquired P Jack Savage to complete deal (October 16, 1989). . . . On disabled list (August 17-September 10, 1990).

Year	Team (League)	W	L	Pct.	ERA	G	GS	CG	ShO	Sv.	IP	H	R	ER	BB	SO
1986	—Medford (N'west)	1	0	1.000	0.00	2	2	0	0	0	8⅓	6	3	0	3	9
	—Modesto (Calif.)	6	1	.857	2.48	11	11	1	0	0	69	74	26	19	22	44
	—Huntsville (South.)	1	0	1.000	6.00	1	1	0	0	0	6	8	4	4	1	2
	—Tacoma (PCL)	0	1	.000	15.43	1	1	0	0	0	2⅓	5	6	4	1	1
1987	—Modesto (Calif.)	10	7	.588	3.76	24	24	6	1	0	148⅓	122	74	62	60	121
1988	—St. Lucie (Fla. St.)■	1	0	1.000	1.42	3	3	0	0	0	19	17	5	3	4	11
	—Jackson (Texas)	5	1	.833	2.74	24	5	0	0	3	62⅓	46	23	19	19	35
1989	—Tidewater (Int'l)	7	5	.583	3.47	17	17	2	1	0	109	113	49	42	25	63
	—New York (N.L.)	0	0	...	3.68	3	0	0	0	0	7⅓	5	3	3	4	2
	—Portland (PCL)■	4	2	.667	2.20	6	6	1	0	0	41	38	15	10	12	30
	—Minnesota (A.L.)	2	2	.500	3.86	5	5	0	0	0	32⅔	34	15	14	8	21

Year	Team (League)	W	L	Pct.	ERA	G	GS	CG	ShO	Sv.	IP	H	R	ER	BB	SO
1990	—Minnesota (A.L.)	12	8	.600	4.07	28	28	1	1	0	159⅓	164	75	72	29	101
1991	—Minnesota (A.L.)	16	9	.640	2.99	34	34	4	1	0	244	225	84	81	40	135
1992	—Minnesota (A.L.)	16	11	.593	3.97	34	34	4	1	0	220	226	103	97	48	138
1993	—Minnesota (A.L.)	12	15	.444	4.43	36	35	3	1	0	225⅔	243	123	111	57	150
A.L. totals (5 years)		58	45	.563	3.83	137	136	12	4	0	881⅔	892	400	375	182	545
N.L. totals (1 year)		0	0	...	3.68	3	0	0	0	0	7⅓	5	3	3	4	2
Major league totals (5 years)		58	45	.563	3.83	140	136	12	4	0	889	897	403	378	186	547

CHAMPIONSHIP SERIES RECORD

Year	Team (League)	W	L	Pct.	ERA	G	GS	CG	ShO	Sv.	IP	H	R	ER	BB	SO
1991	—Minnesota (A.L.)	0	1	.000	7.84	2	2	0	0	0	10⅓	16	9	9	3	9

WORLD SERIES RECORD

Year	Team (League)	W	L	Pct.	ERA	G	GS	CG	ShO	Sv.	IP	H	R	ER	BB	SO
1991	—Minnesota (A.L.)	1	1	.500	4.50	2	2	0	0	0	12	13	6	6	2	7

TARASCO, TONY

OF, BRAVES

PERSONAL: Born December 9, 1970, in New York. . . . 6-1/205. . . . Throws right, bats left. . . . Full name: Anthony Giacinto Tarasco.
HIGH SCHOOL: Santa Monica (Calif.).
TRANSACTIONS/CAREER NOTES: Selected by Atlanta Braves organization in 15th round of free-agent draft (June 1, 1988). . . . On disabled list (August 4-September 12, 1991).

			BATTING											FIELDING			
Year	Team (League)	Pos.	G	AB	R	H	2B	3B	HR	RBI	Avg.	BB	SO	SB	PO	A	E	Avg.
1988	—Idaho Falls (Pio.)	OF	7	10	1	0	0	0	0	1	.000	5	2	1	2	0	1	.667
	—GC Braves (GCL)	OF	21	64	10	15	6	1	0	4	.234	7	7	3	25	1	1	.963
1989	—Pulaski (Appal.)	OF	49	156	22	53	8	2	2	22	.340	21	20	7	45	4	3	.942
1990	—Sumter (S. Atl.)	OF	107	355	42	94	13	3	3	37	.265	37	57	9	173	14	9	.954
1991	—Durham (Carolina)	OF	78	248	31	62	8	2	12	38	.250	21	64	11	119	6	3	.977
1992	—Greenville (South.)	OF-2B	133	489	73	140	22	2	15	54	.286	27	84	33	209	17	5	.978
1993	—Richmond (Int'l)	OF	93	370	73	122	15	7	15	53	.330	36	54	19	143	8	2	.987
	—Atlanta (N.L.)	OF	24	35	6	8	2	0	0	2	.229	0	5	0	11	0	0	1.000
Major league totals (1 year)			24	35	6	8	2	0	0	2	.229	0	5	0	11	0	0	1.000

CHAMPIONSHIP SERIES RECORD

			BATTING											FIELDING			
Year	Team (League)	Pos.	G	AB	R	H	2B	3B	HR	RBI	Avg.	BB	SO	SB	PO	A	E	Avg.
1993	—Atlanta (N.L.)	OF-PR	2	1	0	0	0	0	0	0	.000	0	1	0	0	0	0	...

TARTABULL, DANNY

OF, YANKEES

PERSONAL: Born October 30, 1962, in Miami. . . . 6-1/204. . . . Throws right, bats right. . . . Full name: Danilo Mora Tartabull. . . . Son of Jose Tartabull, outfielder, Kansas City A's, Boston Red Sox and Oakland A's (1962-70); and brother of Jose Tartabull Jr., minor league outfielder (1986-88).
HIGH SCHOOL: Carol City (Miami).
TRANSACTIONS/CAREER NOTES: Selected by Cincinnati Reds organization in third round of free-agent draft (June 3, 1980). . . . Selected by Seattle Mariners organization in player compensation pool draft (January 20, 1983); pick received as compensation for Chicago White Sox signing free-agent P Floyd Bannister (December 13, 1982). . . . On disabled list (May 15-30, 1986). . . . Traded by Mariners with P Rick Luecken to Kansas City Royals for P Scott Bankhead, P Steve Shields and OF Mike Kingery (December 10, 1986). . . . On disabled list (June 15-30, 1989; April 11-May 18 and July 14-31, 1990). . . . Granted free agency (October 28, 1991). . . . Signed by New York Yankees (January 6, 1992). . . . On disabled list (April 21-May 8 and July 27-August 14, 1992 and May 25-June 15, 1993).
HONORS: Named Florida State League Most Valuable Player (1981). . . . Named Pacific Coast League Player of the Year (1985).
STATISTICAL NOTES: Led Florida State League third basemen with 29 errors in 1981. . . . Led Pacific Coast League shortstops with 68 double plays in 1984. . . . Led Pacific Coast League with .615 slugging percentage and 291 total bases in 1985. . . . Led Pacific Coast League shortstops with 35 errors in 1985. . . . Led A.L. with 21 game-winning RBIs in 1987. . . . Hit three home runs in one game (July 6, 1991). . . . Led A.L. with .593 slugging percentage in 1991.

			BATTING											FIELDING			
Year	Team (League)	Pos.	G	AB	R	H	2B	3B	HR	RBI	Avg.	BB	SO	SB	PO	A	E	Avg.
1980	—Billings (Pioneer)	3B-OF-2B	59	157	33	47	10	0	2	27	.299	37	24	7	34	54	14	.863
1981	—Tampa (Fla. St.)	3B-2B	127	422	86	131	★28	10	14	81	★.310	90	77	11	150	248	†39	.911
1982	—Waterbury (East.)	2B	126	409	64	93	17	3	17	63	.227	89	120	12	237	306	★32	.944
1983	—Chatt. (South.)■	2B	128	481	95	145	32	7	13	66	.301	47	63	25	252	405	23	.966
1984	—Salt Lake City (PCL)	SS	116	418	69	127	22	9	13	73	.304	57	69	11	181	333	24	.955
	—Seattle (A.L.)	SS-2B	10	20	3	6	1	0	2	7	.300	2	3	0	8	21	2	.935
1985	—Calgary (PCL)	SS-3B	125	473	102	142	14	3	★43	★109	.300	67	123	17	181	399	†36	.942
	—Seattle (A.L.)	SS-3B	19	61	8	20	7	1	1	7	.328	8	14	1	28	43	4	.947
1986	—Seattle (A.L.)	OF-2B-3B	137	511	76	138	25	6	25	96	.270	61	157	4	233	111	18	.950
1987	—Kansas City (A.L.)■	OF	158	582	95	180	27	3	34	101	.309	79	136	9	228	11	6	.976
1988	—Kansas City (A.L.)	OF	146	507	80	139	38	3	26	102	.274	76	119	8	227	8	9	.963
1989	—Kansas City (A.L.)	OF	133	441	54	118	22	0	18	62	.268	69	123	4	108	3	2	.982
1990	—Kansas City (A.L.)	OF	88	313	41	84	19	0	15	60	.268	36	93	1	81	1	3	.965
1991	—Kansas City (A.L.)	OF	132	484	78	153	35	3	31	100	.316	65	121	6	190	4	7	.965
1992	—New York (A.L.)■	OF	123	421	72	112	19	0	25	85	.266	103	115	2	143	3	3	.980
1993	—New York (A.L.)	OF	138	513	87	128	33	2	31	102	.250	92	156	0	88	3	2	.978
Major league totals (10 years)			1084	3853	594	1078	226	18	208	722	.280	591	1037	35	1334	208	56	.965

ALL-STAR GAME RECORD

Year	League	Pos.	AB	R	H	2B	3B	HR	RBI	Avg.	BB	SO	SB	PO	A	E	Avg.
			BATTING											FIELDING			
1991	—American	DH	2	0	0	0	0	0	0	.000	0	1	0	...	...	...	...

TATUM, JIM

3B/1B, ROCKIES

PERSONAL: Born October 9, 1967, in San Diego. . . . 6-2/200. . . . Throws right, bats right. . . . Full name: James Ray Tatum Jr.

HIGH SCHOOL: Santana (Santee, Calif.).

TRANSACTIONS/CAREER NOTES: Selected by San Diego Padres organization in third round of free-agent draft (June 3, 1985). . . . Released by Padres organization (June 8, 1988). . . . Signed as free agent by Cleveland Indians organization (September 14, 1989). . . . Released by Indians organization (May 24, 1990). . . . Signed by Milwaukee Brewers organization (June 21, 1990). . . . Selected by Colorado Rockies in second round (44th pick overall) of expansion draft (November 17, 1992). . . . Granted free agency (December 20, 1993). . . . Re-signed by Rockies organization (December 23, 1993).

HONORS: Named American Association Most Valuable Player (1992).

STATISTICAL NOTES: Led Northwest League third basemen with 149 assists, 27 errors, 214 total chances and 11 double plays in 1985. . . . Led South Atlantic League third basemen with 35 errors and 29 double plays in 1986. . . . Led South Atlantic League third basemen with 257 assists and tied for lead with 368 total chances in 1987. . . . Led Texas League in sacrifice flies with 20, in being hit by pitch with 15 and in grounding into double plays with 21 in 1991. . . . Led American Association with 261 total bases and 11 sacrifice flies in 1992.

Year	Team (League)	Pos.	G	AB	R	H	2B	3B	HR	RBI	Avg.	BB	SO	SB	PO	A	E	Avg.
			BATTING												FIELDING			
1985	—Spokane (N'west)	3B-SS	74	281	21	64	9	1	1	32	.228	20	60	0	51	†168	†30	.880
1986	—Char., S.C. (S. Atl.)	3B-2B-SS	120	431	55	112	19	2	10	62	.260	41	83	2	81	232	†41	.884
1987	—Char., S.C. (S. Atl.)	3B-SS-2B	128	468	52	131	22	2	9	72	.280	46	65	8	87	†259	24	.935
1988	—Wichita (Texas)	3B	118	402	38	105	26	1	8	54	.261	30	73	2	*97	195	27	.915
1989	—							Did not play.										
1990	—Cant./Akr. (East.)■	3B-1B	30	106	6	19	6	0	2	11	.179	6	19	1	57	51	12	.900
	—Stockton (Calif.)■	3B-1B	70	260	41	68	16	0	12	59	.262	13	49	4	160	108	7	.975
1991	—El Paso (Texas)	S-3-C-1-P	130	493	99	158	27	8	18	128	.320	63	79	5	190	263	31	.936
1992	—Denver (A.A.)	3B-OF	130	492	74	*162	*36	3	19	101	*.329	40	87	8	90	272	25	.935
	—Milwaukee (A.L.)	3B	5	8	0	1	0	0	0	0	.125	1	2	0	6	2	0	1.000
1993	—Colorado (N.L.)■	1B-3B-OF	92	98	7	20	5	0	1	12	.204	5	27	0	45	5	2	.962
	—Colo. Springs (PCL)	3B-1B	13	45	5	10	2	0	2	7	.222	2	9	0	8	21	3	.906
American League totals (1 year)			5	8	0	1	0	0	0	0	.125	1	2	0	6	2	0	1.000
National League totals (1 year)			92	98	7	20	5	0	1	12	.204	5	27	0	45	5	2	.962
Major league totals (2 years)			97	106	7	21	5	0	1	12	.198	6	29	0	51	7	2	.967

RECORD AS PITCHER

Year	Team (League)	W	L	Pct.	ERA	G	GS	CG	ShO	Sv.	IP	H	R	ER	BB	SO
1991	—El Paso (Texas)	0	0	...	0.00	1	0	0	0	0	1	1	0	0	0	0

TAUBENSEE, EDDIE

C, ASTROS

PERSONAL: Born October 31, 1968, in Beeville, Tex. . . . 6-4/205. . . . Throws right, bats left. . . . Full name: Edward Kenneth Taubensee. . . . Name pronounced TAW-ben-see.

HIGH SCHOOL: Lake Howell (Maitland, Fla.).

TRANSACTIONS/CAREER NOTES: Selected by Cincinnati Reds organization in sixth round of free-agent draft (June 2, 1986). . . . Selected by Oakland Athletics from Reds organization in Rule 5 major league draft (December 3, 1990). . . . Claimed on waivers by Cleveland Indians (April 4, 1991). . . . Traded by Indians with P Willie Blair to Houston Astros for OF Kenny Lofton and IF Dave Rohde (December 10, 1991).

STATISTICAL NOTES: Led Pioneer League with 19 passed balls in 1987. . . . Tied for South Atlantic League lead in double plays by catcher with seven in 1988.

Year	Team (League)	Pos.	G	AB	R	H	2B	3B	HR	RBI	Avg.	BB	SO	SB	PO	A	E	Avg.
			BATTING												FIELDING			
1986	—GC Reds (GCL)	C-1B	35	107	8	21	3	0	1	11	.196	11	33	0	208	27	8	.967
1987	—Billings (Pioneer)	C	55	162	24	43	7	0	5	28	.265	25	47	2	344	29	6	.984
1988	—Greensboro (S. Atl.)	C	103	330	36	85	16	1	10	41	.258	44	93	8	640	70	15	.979
	—Chatt. (South.)	C	5	12	2	2	0	0	1	1	.167	3	4	0	17	5	1	.957
1989	—Ced. Rap. (Midw.)	C	59	196	25	39	5	0	8	22	.199	25	55	4	400	9	1	.998
	—Chatt. (South.)	C	45	127	11	24	2	0	3	13	.189	11	28	0	213	31	6	.976
1990	—Ced. Rap. (Midw.)	C	122	417	57	108	21	1	16	62	.259	51	98	11	795	94	16	.982
1991	—Cleveland (A.L.)■	C	26	66	5	16	2	1	0	8	.242	5	16	0	89	6	2	.979
	—Colo. Springs (PCL)	C	91	287	53	89	23	3	13	39	.310	31	61	0	412	47	12	.975
1992	—Houston (N.L.)■	C	104	297	23	66	15	0	5	28	.222	31	78	2	557	66	5	.992
	—Tucson (PCL)	C	20	74	13	25	8	1	1	10	.338	8	17	0	127	10	4	.972
1993	—Houston (N.L.)	C	94	288	26	72	11	1	9	42	.250	21	44	1	551	41	5	.992
American League totals (1 year)			26	66	5	16	2	1	0	8	.242	5	16	0	89	6	2	.979
National League totals (2 years)			198	585	49	138	26	1	14	70	.236	52	122	3	1108	107	10	.992
Major league totals (3 years)			224	651	54	154	28	2	14	78	.237	57	138	3	1197	113	12	.991

TAVAREZ, JESUS

OF, MARLINS

PERSONAL: Born March 26, 1971, in Santo Domingo, Dominican Republic. . . . 6-0/170. . . . Throws right, bats both. . . . Full name: Jesus Rafael Tavarez. . . . Name pronounced tuh-VARE-ez.

TRANSACTIONS/CAREER NOTES: Signed as free agent by Seattle Mariners organization (June 8, 1989). . . . On disabled list (April 20-May 20, 1992). . . . Selected by Florida Marlins in first round (26th pick overall) of expansion draft (November 17, 1992). . . . On disabled list (May 18-June 4, 1993).

STATISTICAL NOTES: Tied for Carolina League lead in double plays by outfielder with four in 1990.
MISCELLANEOUS: Batted righthanded only (1990-92).

Year	Team (League)	Pos.	G	AB	R	H	2B	3B	HR	RBI	Avg.	BB	SO	SB	PO	A	E	Avg.
			BATTING												FIELDING			
1989 —	....		Dominican Summer League statistics unavailable.															
1990 —	Peninsula (Caro.)	OF	108	379	39	90	10	1	0	32	.237	20	79	40	228	•12	9	.964
1991 —	San Bern. (Calif.)	OF	124	466	80	132	11	3	5	41	.283	39	78	69	231	9	9	.964
1992 —	Jacksonv. (South.)	OF	105	392	38	101	9	2	3	25	.258	23	54	29	208	7	5	.977
1993 —	High Desert (Calif.)■	OF	109	444	104	130	21	8	7	71	.293	57	66	47	194	10	9	.958

TAVAREZ, JULIAN

P, INDIANS

PERSONAL: Born May 22, 1973, in Santiago, Dominican Republic. . . . 6-2/165. . . . Throws right, bats right.
HIGH SCHOOL: Santiago (Dominican Republic) Public School.
TRANSACTIONS/CAREER NOTES: Signed as free agent by Cleveland Indians organization (March 16, 1990).
STATISTICAL NOTES: Led Appalachian League with 10 hit batsmen in 1993.

Year	Team (League)	W	L	Pct.	ERA	G	GS	CG	ShO	Sv.	IP	H	R	ER	BB	SO
1990 —	Dom. Indians (DSL)	5	5	.500	3.29	14	12	3	0	0	82	85	53	30	48	33
1991 —	Dom. Indians (DSL)	8	2	.800	2.67	19	18	1	0	0	121⅓	95	41	36	28	75
1992 —	Burlington (Appal.)	6	3	.667	2.68	14	*14	2	•2	0	87⅓	86	41	26	12	69
1993 —	Kinston (Carolina)	11	5	.688	2.42	18	18	2	0	0	119	102	48	32	28	107
—	Cant./Akr. (East.)	2	1	.667	0.95	3	2	1	1	0	19	14	2	2	1	11
—	Cleveland (A.L.)	2	2	.500	6.57	8	7	0	0	0	37	53	29	27	13	19
Major league totals (1 year)		2	2	.500	6.57	8	7	0	0	0	37	53	29	27	13	19

TAYLOR, BILL

P, ATHLETICS

PERSONAL: Born October 16, 1961, in Monticello, Fla. . . . 6-8/200. . . . Throws right, bats right. . . . Full name: William Howell Taylor.
HIGH SCHOOL: Central (Thomasville, Ga.).
COLLEGE: Abraham Baldwin Agricultural College (Ga.).
TRANSACTIONS/CAREER NOTES: Selected by Texas Rangers organization in second round of free-agent draft (January 8, 1980). . . . Loaned by Rangers organization to Wausau, Seattle Mariners organization (April 5-June 23, 1982). . . . Granted free agency (October 22, 1988). . . . Signed by Las Vegas, San Diego Padres organization (March 30, 1989). . . . Granted free agency (October 22, 1989). . . . Signed by Atlanta Braves organization (August 16, 1990). . . . Selected by Toronto Blue Jays from Braves organization in Rule 5 major league draft (December 7, 1992). . . . Returned to Braves organization (April 3, 1993). . . . Granted free agency (October 15, 1993). . . . Signed by Oakland Athletics organization (December 13, 1993).

Year	Team (League)	W	L	Pct.	ERA	G	GS	CG	ShO	Sv.	IP	H	R	ER	BB	SO
1980 —	Asheville (S. Atl.)	0	2	.000	10.93	6	2	0	0	0	14	24	24	17	9	12
—	GC Rangers (GCL)	0	0	...	2.31	14	2	0	0	0	35	36	14	9	16	22
1981 —	Asheville (S. Atl.)	1	7	.125	4.64	14	12	1	0	0	64	76	43	33	35	44
—	GC Rangers (GCL)	4	2	.667	2.72	12	11	0	0	0	53	42	23	16	29	35
1982 —	Wau.-Bur. (Midw.)■	7	9	.438	4.18	37	9	2	0	3	112	100	64	52	63	95
1983 —	Salem (Carolina)	1	1	.500	6.26	7	7	1	0	0	41⅔	30	34	29	42	42
—	Tulsa (Texas)	5	8	.385	6.87	21	12	0	0	0	76	86	65	58	51	75
1984 —	Tulsa (Texas)	5	3	.625	3.83	42	2	0	0	7	80	65	38	34	51	80
1985 —	Tulsa (Texas)	3	9	.250	3.47	20	17	2	0	0	103⅔	84	55	40	48	87
1986 —	Tulsa (Texas)	3	7	.300	3.95	11	11	2	1	0	68⅓	65	40	30	37	64
—	Okla. City (A.A.)	5	5	.500	4.60	16	16	1	0	0	101⅔	94	56	52	57	68
1987 —	Okla. City (A.A.)	*12	9	.571	5.61	28	•28	0	0	0	168⅓	198	122	105	91	100
1988 —	Okla. City (A.A.)	4	8	.333	5.49	20	12	1	1	1	82	98	55	50	35	42
1989 —	Las Vegas (PCL)■	7	4	.636	5.13	47	0	0	0	1	79	93	48	45	27	71
1990 —	Durham (Carolina)■	0	0	...	3.24	5	0	0	0	0	8⅓	8	3	3	1	10
—	Richmond (Int'l)	0	0	...	0.00	2	0	0	0	0	2⅓	4	0	0	0	0
1991 —	Greenville (South.)	6	2	.750	1.51	•59	0	0	0	22	77⅓	49	16	13	15	65
1992 —	Richmond (Int'l)	2	3	.400	2.28	47	0	0	0	12	79	72	27	20	27	82
1993 —	Richmond (Int'l)	2	4	.333	1.98	59	0	0	0	*26	68⅓	56	19	15	26	81

TAYLOR, KERRY

P, PADRES

PERSONAL: Born January 25, 1971, in Bemidji, Minn. . . . 6-3/200. . . . Throws right, bats right. . . . Full name: Kerry Thomas Taylor.
HIGH SCHOOL: Roseau (Minn.).
COLLEGE: Bemidji (Minn.) State University.
TRANSACTIONS/CAREER NOTES: Signed as free agent by Minnesota Twins organization (June 26, 1989). . . . Selected by San Diego Padres from Twins organization in Rule 5 major league draft (December 7, 1992).

Year	Team (League)	W	L	Pct.	ERA	G	GS	CG	ShO	Sv.	IP	H	R	ER	BB	SO
1989 —	Elizabeth. (Appal.)	3	0	1.000	1.50	9	8	0	0	0	36	26	11	6	22	24
1990 —	GC Twins (GCL)	3	1	.750	3.57	14	•13	1	1	0	63	57	37	25	33	59
1991 —	Kenosha (Midwest)	7	11	.389	3.82	26	26	2	1	0	132	121	74	56	84	84
1992 —	Kenosha (Midwest)	10	9	.526	2.75	27	27	2	1	0	170⅓	150	71	52	68	158
1993 —	San Diego (N.L.)■	0	5	.000	6.45	36	7	0	0	0	68⅓	72	53	49	49	45
Major league totals (1 year)		0	5	.000	6.45	36	7	0	0	0	68⅓	72	53	49	49	45

TAYLOR, SCOTT

P, RED SOX

PERSONAL: Born August 2, 1967, in Defiance, O. . . . 6-1/190. . . . Throws left, bats left. . . . Full name: Rodney Scott Taylor.
HIGH SCHOOL: Defiance (O.).
COLLEGE: Bowling Green State.
TRANSACTIONS/CAREER NOTES: Selected by Boston Red Sox organization in 28th round of free-agent draft (June 1, 1988). . . .

On disabled list (June 15-July 4, 1989).... On New Britain disabled list (July 13, 1990-remainder of season).... On Pawtucket disabled list (June 10-17, 1991).

Year	Team (League)	W	L	Pct.	ERA	G	GS	CG	ShO	Sv.	IP	H	R	ER	BB	SO
1988	—Elmira (N.Y.-Penn)	1	0	1.000	0.00	2	1	0	0	0	3⅔	2	0	0	3	8
1989	—Lynchburg (Caro.)	5	3	.625	2.89	19	9	0	0	1	81	61	33	26	25	99
1990	—Lynchburg (Caro.)	5	6	.455	2.73	13	13	1	0	0	89	76	36	27	30	120
	—New Britain (East.)	0	2	.000	1.65	5	5	1	0	0	27⅓	23	8	5	13	27
1991	—Pawtucket (Int'l)	3	3	.500	3.46	7	7	1	0	0	39	32	19	15	17	35
	—New Britain (East.)	2	0	1.000	0.62	4	4	0	0	0	29	20	2	2	9	38
1992	—Pawtucket (Int'l)	9	11	.450	3.67	26	26	5	0	0	162	168	73	66	61	91
	—Boston (A.L.)	1	1	.500	4.91	4	1	0	0	0	14⅔	13	8	8	4	7
1993	—Pawtucket (Int'l)	7	7	.500	4.04	47	8	0	0	1	122⅔	132	61	55	48	88
	—Boston (A.L.)	0	1	.000	8.18	16	0	0	0	0	11	14	10	10	12	8
Major league totals (2 years)		1	2	.333	6.31	20	1	0	0	0	25⅔	27	18	18	16	15

TAYLOR, SCOTT M.

P, BREWERS

PERSONAL: Born October 3, 1966, in Topeka, Kan.... 6-3/200.... Throws right, bats right.... Full name: Scott Michael Taylor.
HIGH SCHOOL: Arkansas City (Kan.).
COLLEGE: Kansas.

TRANSACTIONS/CAREER NOTES: Selected by Seattle Mariners organization in 15th round of free-agent draft (June 1, 1988).... Traded by Mariners organization to Atlanta Braves organization for OF Dennis Hood (December 10, 1990).... Released by Greenville, Braves organization (June 18, 1992).... Signed by El Paso, Milwaukee Brewers organization (June 25, 1992).

Year	Team (League)	W	L	Pct.	ERA	G	GS	CG	ShO	Sv.	IP	H	R	ER	BB	SO
1989	—Wausau (Midwest)	9	7	.563	3.22	16	16	6	2	0	106⅓	92	49	38	37	65
	—Williamsport (East.)	1	4	.200	5.75	10	7	1	0	0	40⅔	49	26	26	20	22
1990	—San Bern. (Calif.)	8	8	.500	5.41	34	21	1	0	1	126⅓	148	100	76	69	86
1991	—Durham (Carolina)■	10	3	.769	2.18	24	16	2	0	3	111⅓	94	32	27	33	78
	—Greenville (South.)	3	4	.429	4.19	8	7	1	1	0	43	49	25	20	16	26
1992	—Greenville (South.)	1	1	.500	6.69	22	4	0	0	1	39	44	31	29	18	20
	—El Paso (Texas)■	4	2	.667	3.48	11	9	0	0	0	54⅓	45	21	21	19	37
1993	—El Paso (Texas)	6	6	.500	3.80	17	16	1	0	0	104⅓	105	53	44	31	76
	—New Orleans (A.A.)	5	1	.833	2.31	12	8	1	0	0	62⅓	48	17	16	21	47

TELFORD, ANTHONY

P

PERSONAL: Born March 6, 1966, in San Jose, Calif.... 6-0/189.... Throws right, bats right.... Full name: Anthony Charles Telford.
HIGH SCHOOL: Silver Creek (Calif.).
COLLEGE: San Jose State.

TRANSACTIONS/CAREER NOTES: Selected by Baltimore Orioles organization in third round of free-agent draft (June 2, 1987).... On disabled list (April 20, 1988-remainder of season).... On Frederick disabled list (April 7-18, 1989).... On Erie disabled list (June 16-30, 1989).... Granted free agency (October 15, 1993).

Year	Team (League)	W	L	Pct.	ERA	G	GS	CG	ShO	Sv.	IP	H	R	ER	BB	SO
1987	—Newark (NY-Penn)	1	0	1.000	1.02	6	2	0	0	0	17⅔	16	2	2	3	27
	—Hagerstown (Car.)	1	0	1.000	1.59	2	2	0	0	0	11⅓	9	2	2	5	10
	—Rochester (Int'l)	0	0	...	0.00	1	0	0	0	0	2	0	0	0	3	3
1988	—Hagerstown (Car.)	1	0	1.000	0.00	1	1	0	0	0	7	3	0	0	0	10
1989	—Frederick (Caro.)	2	1	.667	4.21	9	5	0	0	1	25⅔	25	15	12	12	19
1990	—Frederick (Caro.)	4	2	.667	1.68	8	8	1	0	0	53⅔	35	15	10	11	49
	—Hagerstown (East.)	10	2	.833	1.97	14	13	3	1	0	96	80	26	21	25	73
	—Baltimore (A.L.)	3	3	.500	4.95	8	8	0	0	0	36⅓	43	22	20	19	20
1991	—Rochester (Int'l)	•12	9	.571	3.95	27	25	3	0	0	157⅓	166	82	69	48	115
	—Baltimore (A.L.)	0	0	...	4.05	9	1	0	0	0	26⅔	27	12	12	6	24
1992	—Rochester (Int'l)	12	7	.632	4.18	27	26	3	0	0	*181	*183	89	84	64	129
1993	—Rochester (Int'l)	7	7	.500	4.27	38	6	0	0	2	90⅔	98	51	43	33	66
	—Baltimore (A.L.)	0	0	...	9.82	3	0	0	0	0	7⅓	11	8	8	1	6
Major league totals (3 years)		3	3	.500	5.12	20	9	0	0	0	70⅓	81	42	40	26	50

TELGHEDER, DAVID

P, METS

PERSONAL: Born November 11, 1966, in Middletown, N.Y.... 6-3/212.... Throws right, bats right.... Full name: David William Telgheder.... Name pronounced TELL-GATOR.
HIGH SCHOOL: Minisink Valley (Slate Hill, N.Y.).
COLLEGE: Massachusetts (received degree, 1989).

TRANSACTIONS/CAREER NOTES: Selected by New York Mets organization in 31st round of free-agent draft (June 5, 1989).
STATISTICAL NOTES: Pitched 1-0 no-hit victory against Pawtucket (May 15, 1992).

Year	Team (League)	W	L	Pct.	ERA	G	GS	CG	ShO	Sv.	IP	H	R	ER	BB	SO
1989	—Pittsfield (NYP)	5	3	.625	2.45	13	7	4	1	2	58⅔	43	18	16	9	65
1990	—Columbia (S. Atl.)	9	3	.750	1.54	14	13	5	1	0	99⅓	79	22	17	10	81
	—St. Lucie (Fla. St.)	9	4	.692	3.00	14	14	3	0	0	96	84	38	32	14	77
1991	—Williamsport (East.)	•13	11	.542	3.60	28	26	1	0	0	167⅔	185	81	67	33	90
1992	—Tidewater (Int'l)	6	*14	.300	4.21	28	27	3	2	0	169	173	87	79	36	118
1993	—Norfolk (Int'l)	7	3	.700	2.95	13	12	0	0	1	76⅓	81	29	25	19	52
	—New York (N.L.)	6	2	.750	4.76	24	7	0	0	0	75⅔	82	40	40	21	35
Major league totals (1 year)		6	2	.750	4.76	24	7	0	0	0	75⅔	82	40	40	21	35

TETTLETON, MICKEY

OF/DH/C, TIGERS

PERSONAL: Born September 16, 1960, in Oklahoma City.... 6-2/212.... Throws right, bats both.... Full name: Mickey Lee Tettleton.
HIGH SCHOOL: Southeast (Oklahoma City).
COLLEGE: Oklahoma State.

TRANSACTIONS/CAREER NOTES: Selected by Oakland Athletics organization in fifth round of free-agent draft (June 8, 1981).... On disabled list (July 16-August 13, 1982).... On Oakland disabled list (August 4-25, 1985); included rehabilitation assignment to Modesto (August 21-25).... On Oakland disabled list (May 9-June 16, 1986); included rehabilitation assignment to Modesto (May 23-June 13).... On Oakland disabled list (July 22-August 6, 1987); included rehabilitation assignment to Modesto (August 2-6).... Released by A's (March 28, 1988).... Signed by Rochester, Baltimore Orioles organization (April 5, 1988).... On disabled list (August 5-September 2, 1989).... Granted free agency (November 5, 1990).... Re-signed by Orioles (December 19, 1990).... Traded by Orioles to Detroit Tigers for P Jeff M. Robinson (January 11, 1991).
RECORDS: Holds major league single-season record for most strikeouts by switch-hitter—160 (1990).
HONORS: Named catcher on THE SPORTING NEWS A.L. All-Star team (1989 and 1991-92).... Named catcher on THE SPORTING NEWS A.L. Silver Slugger team (1989 and 1991-92).
STATISTICAL NOTES: Tied for Eastern League lead with eight intentional bases on balls received in 1984.... Led Eastern League catchers with .993 fielding percentage in 1984.... Switch-hit home runs in one game (June 13, 1988 and May 7, 1993, 12 innings).... Led A.L. catchers with .996 fielding percentage in 1992.

			BATTING												FIELDING			
Year	**Team (League)**	**Pos.**	**G**	**AB**	**R**	**H**	**2B**	**3B**	**HR**	**RBI**	**Avg.**	**BB**	**SO**	**SB**	**PO**	**A**	**E**	**Avg.**
1981	—Modesto (Calif.)	C-OF-1B	48	138	28	34	3	0	5	19	.246	46	33	2	235	31	14	.950
1982	—Modesto (Calif.)	C-OF	88	253	44	63	18	0	8	37	.249	63	46	4	424	36	8	.983
1983	—Modesto (Calif.)	C-OF	124	378	55	92	18	2	7	62	.243	82	71	1	582	46	11	.983
1984	—Alb./Colon. (East.)	C-0-1-3-S	86	281	32	65	18	0	5	47	.231	52	52	2	368	42	3	†.993
	—Oakland (A.L.)	C	33	76	10	20	2	1	1	5	.263	11	21	0	112	10	1	.992
1985	—Oakland (A.L.)	C	78	211	23	53	12	0	3	15	.251	28	59	2	344	24	4	.989
	—Modesto (Calif.)	C	4	14	1	3	3	0	0	2	.214	0	4	0	20	1	0	1.000
1986	—Oakland (A.L.)	C	90	211	26	43	9	0	10	35	.204	39	51	7	463	32	8	.984
	—Modesto (Calif.)	C	15	42	14	10	1	0	2	8	.238	19	9	2	40	3	2	.956
1987	—Oakland (A.L.)	C-1B	82	211	19	41	3	0	8	26	.194	30	65	1	435	29	6	.987
	—Modesto (Calif.)	C	3	11	4	4	1	0	2	2	.364	1	4	0	5	0	0	1.000
1988	—Rochester (Int'l)■	C-OF	19	41	9	10	3	1	1	4	.244	9	15	0	71	7	3	.963
	—Baltimore (A.L.)	C	86	283	31	74	11	1	11	37	.261	28	70	0	361	31	3	.992
1989	—Baltimore (A.L.)	C	117	411	72	106	21	2	26	65	.258	73	117	3	297	42	2	.994
1990	—Baltimore (A.L.)	C-1B-OF	135	444	68	99	21	2	15	51	.223	106	160	2	458	39	5	.990
1991	—Detroit (A.L.)■	C-OF-1B	154	501	85	132	17	2	31	89	.263	101	131	3	562	55	6	.990
1992	—Detroit (A.L.)	C-1B-OF	157	525	82	125	25	0	32	83	.238	•122	137	0	481	47	2	†.996
1993	—Detroit (A.L.)	1B-OF-C	152	522	79	128	25	4	32	110	.245	109	139	3	724	47	6	.992
	Major league totals (10 years)		1084	3395	495	821	146	12	169	516	.242	647	950	21	4237	356	43	.991

ALL-STAR GAME RECORD

			BATTING											FIELDING			
Year	**League**	**Pos.**	**AB**	**R**	**H**	**2B**	**3B**	**HR**	**RBI**	**Avg.**	**BB**	**SO**	**SB**	**PO**	**A**	**E**	**Avg.**
1989	—American	C	1	0	0	0	0	0	0	.000	0	0	0	2	0	0	1.000

TEUFEL, TIM

IF

PERSONAL: Born July 7, 1958, in Greenwich, Conn.... 6-0/175.... Throws right, bats right.... Full name: Timothy Shawn Teufel.... Name pronounced TUFF-el.
HIGH SCHOOL: St. Mary's (Greenwich, Conn.).
COLLEGE: St. Petersburg (Fla.) Junior College and Clemson.
TRANSACTIONS/CAREER NOTES: Selected by Milwaukee Brewers organization in 16th round of free-agent draft (June 6, 1978).... Selected by Chicago White Sox organization in secondary phase of free-agent draft (June 5, 1979).... Selected by Minnesota Twins organization in second round of free-agent draft (June 3, 1980).... Traded by Twins with OF Pat Crosby to New York Mets for OF Billy Beane, P Bill Latham and P Joe Klink (January 16, 1986).... On disabled list (June 16-July 1, 1987; May 17-June 11, 1988; and June 5-23, 1989).... Traded by Mets to San Diego Padres for SS Garry Templeton (May 31, 1991).... Granted free agency (October 30, 1991).... Re-signed by Padres (January 8, 1991).... Granted free agency (November 1, 1993).
HONORS: Named second baseman on THE SPORTING NEWS college All-America team (1980).... Named International League Player of the Year (1983).
STATISTICAL NOTES: Led International League second basemen with 304 putouts, 394 assists, 711 total chances and 109 double plays in 1983.

			BATTING												FIELDING			
Year	**Team (League)**	**Pos.**	**G**	**AB**	**R**	**H**	**2B**	**3B**	**HR**	**RBI**	**Avg.**	**BB**	**SO**	**SB**	**PO**	**A**	**E**	**Avg.**
1980	—Orlando (Southern)	2B	86	287	38	76	15	3	11	47	.265	49	61	3	196	246	17	.963
1981	—Orlando (Southern)	2B	128	416	69	103	21	5	17	60	.248	45	80	4	312	376	20	.972
1982	—Orlando (Southern)	2B	100	340	52	96	12	4	9	56	.282	67	51	16	231	185	15	.965
	—Toledo (Int'l)	2B	45	149	25	42	10	4	6	20	.282	15	23	1	99	139	3	.988
1983	—Toledo (Int'l)	2B-SS	136	471	103	152	27	6	27	100	.323	102	71	13	†306	†401	14	.981
	—Minnesota (A.L.)	2B-SS	21	78	11	24	7	1	3	6	.308	2	8	0	47	58	1	.991
1984	—Minnesota (A.L.)	2B	157	568	76	149	30	3	14	61	.262	76	73	1	315	*485	13	.984
1985	—Minnesota (A.L.)	2B	138	434	58	113	24	3	10	50	.260	48	70	4	237	352	12	.980
1986	—New York (N.L.)■	2B-1B-3B	93	279	35	69	20	1	4	31	.247	32	42	1	143	174	9	.972
1987	—New York (N.L.)	2B-1B	97	299	55	92	29	0	14	61	.308	44	53	3	139	214	11	.970
1988	—New York (N.L.)	2B-1B	90	273	35	64	20	0	4	31	.234	29	41	0	175	213	7	.982
1989	—New York (N.L.)	2B-1B	83	219	27	56	7	2	2	15	.256	32	50	1	261	112	10	.974
1990	—New York (N.L.)	1B-2B-3B	80	175	28	43	11	0	10	24	.246	15	33	0	141	58	4	.980
1991	—N.Y.-S.D. (N.L.)■	2B-3B-1B	117	341	41	74	16	0	12	44	.217	51	77	9	178	205	9	.977
1992	—San Diego (N.L.)	2B-3B-1B	101	246	23	55	10	0	6	25	.224	31	45	2	137	163	7	.977
1993	—San Diego (N.L.)	2B-3B-1B	96	200	26	50	11	2	7	31	.250	27	39	2	109	124	3	.987
	American League totals (3 years)		316	1080	145	286	61	7	27	117	.265	126	151	5	599	895	26	.983
	National League totals (8 years)		757	2032	270	503	124	5	59	262	.248	261	380	18	1283	1263	60	.977
	Major league totals (11 years)		1073	3112	415	789	185	12	86	379	.254	387	531	23	1882	2158	86	.979

CHAMPIONSHIP SERIES RECORD

Year	Team (League)	Pos.	G	AB	R	H	2B	3B	HR	RBI	Avg.	BB	SO	SB	PO	A	E	Avg.
				BATTING											FIELDING			
1986	—New York (N.L.)	2B	2	6	0	1	0	0	0	0	.167	0	0	0	2	8	0	1.000
1988	—New York (N.L.)	2B	1	3	0	0	0	0	0	0	.000	0	1	0	1	3	0	1.000
Championship series totals (2 years)			3	9	0	1	0	0	0	0	.111	0	1	0	3	11	0	1.000

WORLD SERIES RECORD

Year	Team (League)	Pos.	G	AB	R	H	2B	3B	HR	RBI	Avg.	BB	SO	SB	PO	A	E	Avg.
				BATTING											FIELDING			
1986	—New York (N.L.)	2B	3	9	1	4	1	0	1	1	.444	1	2	0	3	3	1	.857

TEWKSBURY, BOB

P, CARDINALS

PERSONAL: Born November 30, 1960, in Concord, N.H. . . . 6-4/208. . . . Throws right, bats right. . . . Full name: Robert Alan Tewksbury.
HIGH SCHOOL: Merrimack (Penacook, N.H.).
COLLEGE: Rutgers and St. Leo College (Fla.).

TRANSACTIONS/CAREER NOTES: Selected by New York Yankees organization in 19th round of free-agent draft (June 8, 1981). . . . On Fort Lauderdale disabled list (April 8-June 7, 1983). . . . On disabled list (April 9-27, 1984). . . . On Albany/Colonie disabled list (June 10-25, 1985). . . . Traded by Yankees with P Rich Scheid and P Dean Wilkins to Chicago Cubs for P Steve Trout (July 13, 1987). . . . On Chicago disabled list (August 13, 1987-remainder of season and May 22-June 12, 1988). . . . Granted free agency (October 15, 1988). . . . Signed by St. Louis Cardinals (December 16, 1988).

Year	Team (League)	W	L	Pct.	ERA	G	GS	CG	ShO	Sv.	IP	H	R	ER	BB	SO
1981	—Oneonta (NYP)	7	3	.700	3.60	14	14	6	1	0	85	85	43	34	37	62
1982	—Fort Lauder. (FSL)	*15	4	.789	*1.88	24	23	•13	*5	1	182⅓	146	46	38	47	92
1983	—Fort Lauder. (FSL)	2	0	1.000	0.00	2	2	1	0	0	16	6	1	0	1	5
	—Nashville (South.)	5	1	.833	2.82	7	7	3	0	0	51	49	20	16	10	15
1984	—Nashville (South.)	11	9	.550	2.83	26	26	6	0	0	172	185	69	54	42	78
1985	—Alb./Colon. (East.)	6	5	.545	3.54	17	17	4	2	0	106⅔	101	48	42	19	63
	—Columbus (Int'l)	3	0	1.000	1.02	6	6	1	1	0	44	27	5	5	5	21
1986	—New York (A.L.)	9	5	.643	3.31	23	20	2	0	0	130⅓	144	58	48	31	49
	—Columbus (Int'l)	1	0	1.000	2.70	2	2	0	0	0	10	6	3	3	2	4
1987	—New York (A.L.)	1	4	.200	6.75	8	6	0	0	0	33⅓	47	26	25	7	12
	—Columbus (Int'l)	6	1	.857	2.53	11	11	3	0	0	74⅔	68	23	21	11	32
	—Chicago (N.L.)■	0	4	.000	6.50	7	3	0	0	0	18	32	15	13	13	10
1988	—Iowa (Am. Assoc.)	4	2	.667	3.76	10	10	2	2	0	67	73	28	28	10	43
	—Chicago (N.L.)	0	0	...	8.10	1	1	0	0	0	3⅓	6	5	3	2	1
1989	—Louisville (A.A.)■	•13	5	.722	2.43	28	28	2	1	0	*189	170	63	51	34	72
	—St. Louis (N.L.)	1	0	1.000	3.30	7	4	1	1	0	30	25	12	11	10	17
1990	—St. Louis (N.L.)	10	9	.526	3.47	28	20	3	2	1	145⅓	151	67	56	15	50
	—Louisville (A.A.)	3	2	.600	2.43	6	6	0	0	0	40⅔	41	15	11	3	22
1991	—St. Louis (N.L.)	11	12	.478	3.25	30	30	3	0	0	191	206	86	69	38	75
1992	—St. Louis (N.L.)	16	5	*.762	2.16	33	32	5	0	0	233	217	63	56	20	91
1993	—St. Louis (N.L.)	17	10	.630	3.83	32	32	2	0	0	213⅔	*258	99	91	20	97
A.L. totals (2 years)		10	9	.526	4.01	31	26	2	0	0	163⅔	191	84	73	38	61
N.L. totals (7 years)		55	40	.579	3.23	138	122	14	3	1	834⅓	895	347	299	118	341
Major league totals (8 years)		65	49	.570	3.35	169	148	16	3	1	998	1086	431	372	156	402

ALL-STAR GAME RECORD

Year	League	W	L	Pct.	ERA	GS	CG	ShO	Sv.	IP	H	R	ER	BB	SO
1992	—National	0	0	...	21.60	0	0	0	0	1⅔	4	4	4	1	0

THIGPEN, BOBBY

P, MARINERS

PERSONAL: Born July 17, 1963, in Tallahassee, Fla. . . . 6-3/222. . . . Throws right, bats right. . . . Full name: Robert Thomas Thigpen.
HIGH SCHOOL: Aucilla Christian Academy (Monticello, Fla.).
COLLEGE: Seminole Community College (Fla.) and Mississippi State.

TRANSACTIONS/CAREER NOTES: Selected by Milwaukee Brewers organization in seventh round of free-agent draft (January 11, 1983). . . . Selected by Chicago White Sox organization in fourth round of free-agent draft (June 3, 1985). . . . Traded by White Sox to Philadelphia Phillies for P Jose DeLeon (August 10, 1993). . . . Granted free agency (November 1, 1993). . . . Signed by Seattle Mariners organization (January 31, 1994).
RECORDS: Holds major league single-season record for most saves—57 (1990).
HONORS: Named A.L. Fireman of the Year by THE SPORTING NEWS (1990).
STATISTICAL NOTES: Led Southern League with 11 hit batsmen in 1986.

Year	Team (League)	W	L	Pct.	ERA	G	GS	CG	ShO	Sv.	IP	H	R	ER	BB	SO
1985	—Niag. Falls (NYP)	2	3	.400	1.72	28	1	0	0	9	52⅓	30	12	10	19	74
	—Appleton (Midw.)	1	0	1.000	0.00	1	0	0	0	0	2⅔	1	0	0	1	4
1986	—Birm. (Southern)	8	11	.421	4.68	25	25	5	0	0	159⅔	182	97	83	54	90
	—Chicago (A.L.)	2	0	1.000	1.77	20	0	0	0	7	35⅔	26	7	7	12	20
1987	—Chicago (A.L.)	7	5	.583	2.73	51	0	0	0	16	89	86	30	27	24	52
	—Hawaii (PCL)	2	3	.400	6.15	9	9	2	1	0	52⅔	72	38	36	14	17
1988	—Chicago (A.L.)	5	8	.385	3.30	68	0	0	0	34	90	96	38	33	33	62
1989	—Chicago (A.L.)	2	6	.250	3.76	61	0	0	0	34	79	62	34	33	40	47
1990	—Chicago (A.L.)	4	6	.400	1.83	*77	0	0	0	*57	88⅔	60	20	18	32	70
1991	—Chicago (A.L.)	7	5	.583	3.49	67	0	0	0	30	69⅔	63	32	27	38	47
1992	—Chicago (A.L.)	1	3	.250	4.75	55	0	0	0	22	55	58	29	29	33	45

Year	Team (League)	W	L	Pct.	ERA	G	GS	CG	ShO	Sv.	IP	H	R	ER	BB	SO
1993	—Chicago (A.L.)	0	0	...	5.71	25	0	0	0	1	34⅔	51	25	22	12	19
	—Philadelphia (N.L.)■	3	1	.750	6.05	17	0	0	0	0	19⅓	23	13	13	9	10
A.L. totals (8 years)		28	33	.459	3.26	424	0	0	0	201	541⅔	502	215	196	224	362
N.L. totals (1 year)		3	1	.750	6.05	17	0	0	0	0	19⅓	23	13	13	9	10
Major league totals (8 years)		31	34	.477	3.35	441	0	0	0	201	561	525	228	209	233	372

CHAMPIONSHIP SERIES RECORD

Year	Team (League)	W	L	Pct.	ERA	G	GS	CG	ShO	Sv.	IP	H	R	ER	BB	SO
1993	—Philadelphia (N.L.)	0	0	...	5.40	2	0	0	0	0	1⅔	1	1	1	1	3

WORLD SERIES RECORD

Year	Team (League)	W	L	Pct.	ERA	G	GS	CG	ShO	Sv.	IP	H	R	ER	BB	SO
1993	—Philadelphia (N.L.)	0	0	...	0.00	2	0	0	0	0	2⅔	1	0	0	1	0

ALL-STAR GAME RECORD

Year	League	W	L	Pct.	ERA	GS	CG	ShO	Sv.	IP	H	R	ER	BB	SO
1990	—American	0	0	...	0.00	0	0	0	0	1	0	0	0	0	1

THOMAS, FRANK

1B, WHITE SOX

PERSONAL: Born May 27, 1968, in Columbus, Ga. . . . 6-5/257. . . . Throws right, bats right. . . . Full name: Frank Edward Thomas.
HIGH SCHOOL: Columbus (Ga.).
COLLEGE: Auburn.
TRANSACTIONS/CAREER NOTES: Selected by Chicago White Sox organization in first round (seventh pick overall) of free-agent draft (June 5, 1989).
HONORS: Named first baseman on THE SPORTING NEWS college All-America team (1989). . . . Named designated hitter on THE SPORTING NEWS A.L. All-Star team (1991). . . . Named designated hitter on THE SPORTING NEWS A.L. Silver Slugger team (1991). . . . Named Major League Player of the Year by THE SPORTING NEWS (1993). . . . Named first baseman on THE SPORTING NEWS A.L. All-Star team (1993). . . . Named first baseman on THE SPORTING NEWS A.L. Silver Slugger team (1993). . . . Named A.L. Most Valuable Player by Baseball Writers' Association of America (1993).
STATISTICAL NOTES: Led Southern League with .581 slugging percentage and .487 on-base percentage in 1990. . . . Led A.L. with .453 on-base percentage in 1991 and .439 in 1992. . . . Led A.L. first basemen with 1,533 total chances in 1992.

			BATTING												FIELDING			
Year	Team (League)	Pos.	G	AB	R	H	2B	3B	HR	RBI	Avg.	BB	SO	SB	PO	A	E	Avg.
1989	—GC Whi. Sox (GCL)	1B	17	52	8	19	5	0	1	11	.365	10	24	4	130	8	2	.986
	—Sarasota (Fla. St.)	1B	55	188	27	52	9	1	4	30	.277	31	33	0	420	31	7	.985
1990	—Birm. (Southern)	1B	109	353	85	114	27	5	18	71	.323	*112	74	7	954	77	14	.987
	—Chicago (A.L.)	1B	60	191	39	63	11	3	7	31	.330	44	54	0	428	26	5	.989
1991	—Chicago (A.L.)	1B	158	559	104	178	31	2	32	109	.318	*138	112	1	459	27	2	.996
1992	—Chicago (A.L.)	1B	160	573	108	185	•46	2	24	115	.323	•122	88	6	*1428	92	13	.992
1993	—Chicago (A.L.)	1B	153	549	106	174	36	0	41	128	.317	112	54	4	1222	83	15	.989
Major league totals (4 years)			531	1872	357	600	124	7	104	383	.321	416	308	11	3537	228	35	.991

CHAMPIONSHIP SERIES RECORD

CHAMPIONSHIP SERIES NOTES: Holds single-series record for most bases on balls received—10 (1993). . . . Shares single-game record for most bases on balls received—4 (October 5, 1993).

			BATTING												FIELDING			
Year	Team (League)	Pos.	G	AB	R	H	2B	3B	HR	RBI	Avg.	BB	SO	SB	PO	A	E	Avg.
1993	—Chicago (A.L.)	1B-DH	6	17	2	6	0	0	1	3	.353	10	5	0	24	3	0	1.000

ALL-STAR GAME RECORD

			BATTING											FIELDING			
Year	League	Pos.	AB	R	H	2B	3B	HR	RBI	Avg.	BB	SO	SB	PO	A	E	Avg.
1993	—American	PH-DH	1	0	1	0	0	0	0	1.000	0	0	0	...	...	...	...

THOMAS, LARRY

P, WHITE SOX

PERSONAL: Born October 25, 1969, in Miami. . . . 6-1/195. . . . Throws left, bats right. . . . Full name: Larry Wayne Thomas.
HIGH SCHOOL: Winthrop (Mass.).
COLLEGE: Maine.
TRANSACTIONS/CAREER NOTES: Selected by Chicago White Sox organization in second round of free-agent draft (June 3, 1991).

Year	Team (League)	W	L	Pct.	ERA	G	GS	CG	ShO	Sv.	IP	H	R	ER	BB	SO
1991	—Utica (N.Y.-Penn)	1	3	.250	1.47	11	10	0	0	0	73⅓	55	22	12	25	61
	—Birm. (Southern)	0	0	...	3.00	2	0	0	0	0	6	6	3	2	4	2
1992	—Sarasota (Fla. St.)	5	0	1.000	1.62	8	8	0	0	0	55⅔	44	14	10	7	50
	—Birm. (Southern)	8	6	.571	*1.94	17	17	3	0	0	120⅔	102	32	26	30	72
1993	—Nashville (A.A.)	4	6	.400	5.99	18	18	1	0	0	100⅔	114	73	67	32	67
	—Sarasota (Fla. St.)	4	2	.667	2.48	8	8	3	2	0	61⅔	52	19	17	15	27
	—Birm. (Southern)	0	1	.000	5.14	1	1	0	0	0	7	9	5	4	1	5

THOME, JIM

3B, INDIANS

PERSONAL: Born August 27, 1970, in Peoria, Ill. . . . 6-4/220. . . . Throws right, bats left. . . . Full name: James Howard Thome. . . . Name pronounced TOE-me.
HIGH SCHOOL: Limestone (Bartonville, Ill.).
COLLEGE: Illinois Central.
TRANSACTIONS/CAREER NOTES: Selected by Cleveland Indians organization in 13th round of free-agent draft (June 5, 1989). . . . On Cleveland disabled list (March 28-May 18, 1992); included rehabilitation assignment to Canton/Akron (May 9-18). . . . On

Cleveland disabled list (May 20-June 15, 1992); included rehabilitation assignment to Canton/Akron (June 1-15).
HONORS: Named International League Most Valuable Player (1993).
STATISTICAL NOTES: Led International League with .441 on-base percentage in 1993.

			BATTING												FIELDING			
Year	**Team (League)**	**Pos.**	**G**	**AB**	**R**	**H**	**2B**	**3B**	**HR**	**RBI**	**Avg.**	**BB**	**SO**	**SB**	**PO**	**A**	**E**	**Avg.**
1989	—GC Indians (GCL)	SS-3B	55	186	22	44	5	3	0	22	.237	21	33	6	65	144	21	.909
1990	—Burlington (Appal.)	3B	34	118	31	44	7	1	12	34	.373	27	18	6	28	79	11	.907
	—Kinston (Carolina)	3B	33	117	19	36	4	1	4	16	.308	24	26	4	10	66	8	.905
1991	—Cant./Akr. (East.)	3B	84	294	47	99	20	2	5	45	.337	44	58	8	41	167	17	.924
	—Colo. Springs (PCL)	3B	41	151	20	43	7	3	2	28	.285	12	29	0	28	84	6	.949
	—Cleveland (A.L.)	3B	27	98	7	25	4	2	1	9	.255	5	16	1	12	60	8	.900
1992	—Colo. Springs (PCL)	3B	12	48	11	15	4	1	2	14	.313	6	16	0	9	20	8	.784
	—Cleveland (A.L.)	3B	40	117	8	24	3	1	2	12	.205	10	34	2	21	61	11	.882
	—Cant./Akr. (East.)	3B	30	107	16	36	9	2	1	14	.336	24	30	0	11	35	4	.920
1993	—Charlotte (Int'l)	3B	115	410	85	136	21	4	25	*102	*.332	76	94	1	67	226	15	.951
	—Cleveland (A.L.)	3B	47	154	28	41	11	0	7	22	.266	29	36	2	29	86	6	.950
Major league totals (3 years)			114	369	43	90	18	3	10	43	.244	44	86	5	62	207	25	.915

THOMPSON, MILT

OF, PHILLIES

PERSONAL: Born January 5, 1959, in Washington, D.C.... 5-11/203.... Throws right, bats left.... Full name: Milton Bernard Thompson.
HIGH SCHOOL: Col. Zadok Magruder (Rockville, Md.).
COLLEGE: Howard (Washington, D.C.).
TRANSACTIONS/CAREER NOTES: Selected by Atlanta Braves organization in second round of free-agent draft (January 9, 1979). ... Traded by Braves with P Steve Bedrosian to Philadelphia Phillies for C Ozzie Virgil and P Pete Smith (December 10, 1985). ... Traded by Phillies to St. Louis Cardinals for C Steve Lake and OF Curt Ford (December 16, 1988).... Granted free agency (October 27, 1992).... Signed by Phillies (December 9, 1992).
STATISTICAL NOTES: Led Southern League outfielders with 336 total chances in 1982.... Led Southern League in caught stealing with 19 in 1982.... Led International League outfielders with 341 total chances in 1984.

			BATTING												FIELDING			
Year	**Team (League)**	**Pos.**	**G**	**AB**	**R**	**H**	**2B**	**3B**	**HR**	**RBI**	**Avg.**	**BB**	**SO**	**SB**	**PO**	**A**	**E**	**Avg.**
1979	—Greenw. (W. Car.)	OF	53	145	31	27	4	1	2	16	.186	32	39	16	85	8	3	.969
	—Kingsport (Appal.)	OF	26	94	22	31	8	4	1	11	.330	16	17	13	58	4	1	.984
1980	—Durham (Carolina)	OF	68	255	49	74	12	3	2	36	.290	42	62	38	159	8	5	.971
	—Savannah (South.)	OF	71	278	35	83	7	3	1	15	.299	19	67	22	133	11	6	.960
1981	—Savannah (South.)	OF	140	493	92	135	18	2	4	31	.274	87	105	46	226	17	8	.968
1982	—Savannah (South.)	OF	•144	526	83	132	20	7	6	45	.251	87	145	*68	*312	10	14	.958
	—Richmond (Int'l)	OF	3	6	2	1	0	0	0	0	.167	1	3	1	4	0	0	1.000
1983	—Richmond (Int'l)	OF	12	32	12	8	1	0	0	3	.250	10	5	6	30	0	1	.968
	—Savannah (South.)	OF-1B	115	386	84	117	21	4	5	36	.303	83	76	46	295	15	7	.978
1984	—Richmond (Int'l)	OF	134	503	•91	145	11	3	4	40	.288	83	86	47	*317	13	11	.968
	—Atlanta (N.L.)	OF	25	99	16	30	1	0	2	4	.303	11	11	14	37	6	2	.956
1985	—Richmond (Int'l)	OF	82	312	52	98	10	1	2	22	.314	32	30	34	209	3	4	.981
	—Atlanta (N.L.)	OF	73	182	17	55	7	2	0	6	.302	7	36	9	78	2	3	.964
1986	—Philadelphia (N.L.)■	OF	96	299	38	75	7	1	6	23	.251	26	62	19	212	1	2	.991
	—Portland (PCL)	OF	41	161	26	56	10	2	1	16	.348	15	20	21	101	1	1	.990
1987	—Philadelphia (N.L.)	OF	150	527	86	159	26	9	7	43	.302	42	87	46	354	4	4	.989
1988	—Philadelphia (N.L.)	OF	122	378	53	109	16	2	2	33	.288	39	59	17	278	5	5	.983
1989	—St. Louis (N.L.)■	OF	155	545	60	158	28	8	4	68	.290	39	91	27	348	5	8	.978
1990	—St. Louis (N.L.)	OF	135	418	42	91	14	7	6	30	.218	39	60	25	232	4	7	.971
1991	—St. Louis (N.L.)	OF	115	326	55	100	16	5	6	34	.307	32	53	16	207	8	2	.991
1992	—St. Louis (N.L.)	OF	109	208	31	61	9	1	4	17	.293	16	39	18	74	1	2	.974
1993	—Philadelphia (N.L.)■	OF	129	340	42	89	14	2	4	44	.262	40	57	9	162	6	1	.994
Major league totals (10 years)			1109	3322	440	927	138	37	41	302	.279	291	555	200	1982	42	36	.983

CHAMPIONSHIP SERIES RECORD

			BATTING												FIELDING			
Year	**Team (League)**	**Pos.**	**G**	**AB**	**R**	**H**	**2B**	**3B**	**HR**	**RBI**	**Avg.**	**BB**	**SO**	**SB**	**PO**	**A**	**E**	**Avg.**
1993	—Philadelphia (N.L.)	OF-PH-PR	6	13	2	3	1	0	0	0	.231	1	2	0	8	0	1	.889

WORLD SERIES RECORD

			BATTING												FIELDING			
Year	**Team (League)**	**Pos.**	**G**	**AB**	**R**	**H**	**2B**	**3B**	**HR**	**RBI**	**Avg.**	**BB**	**SO**	**SB**	**PO**	**A**	**E**	**Avg.**
1993	—Philadelphia (N.L.)	OF-PR	5	16	3	5	1	1	1	6	.313	1	2	0	10	0	1	.909

THOMPSON, ROBBY

2B, GIANTS

PERSONAL: Born May 10, 1962, in West Palm Beach, Fla.... 5-11/173.... Throws right, bats right.... Full name: Robert Randall Thompson.
HIGH SCHOOL: Forest Hill (West Palm Beach, Fla.).
COLLEGE: Palm Beach Junior College (Fla.) and Florida.
TRANSACTIONS/CAREER NOTES: Selected by Oakland Athletics organization in second round of free-agent draft (January 12, 1982).... Selected by Seattle Mariners organization in secondary phase of free-agent draft (June 7, 1982).... Selected by San Francisco Giants organization in secondary phase of free-agent draft (June 6, 1983).... On disabled list (April 28-May 13, 1987; April 29-May 22, 1992 and July 5-22, 1993).... Granted free agency (October 26, 1993).... Re-signed by Giants (November 13, 1993).
RECORDS: Holds major league single-game record for most times caught stealing—4 (June 27, 1986, 12 innings).
HONORS: Named N.L. Rookie Player of the Year by THE SPORTING NEWS (1986).... Named second baseman on THE SPORTING NEWS N.L. All-Star team (1993).... Won N.L. Gold Glove at second base (1993).... Named second baseman on THE SPORTING NEWS N.L. Silver Slugger team (1993).

T

STATISTICAL NOTES: Led Texas League second basemen with .982 fielding percentage, 291 putouts, 664 total chances and 91 double plays in 1985.... Led N.L. with 18 sacrifice hits in 1986.... Tied for N.L. lead in being hit by pitch with 13 in 1989.... Tied for N.L. lead in double plays by second baseman with 94 in 1990.... Hit for the cycle (April 22, 1991).... Led N.L. second basemen with 98 double plays in 1991 and 101 in 1992.

			BATTING												FIELDING			
Year	**Team (League)**	**Pos.**	**G**	**AB**	**R**	**H**	**2B**	**3B**	**HR**	**RBI**	**Avg.**	**BB**	**SO**	**SB**	**PO**	**A**	**E**	**Avg.**
1983	—Fresno (California) ..	2B	64	220	33	57	8	1	4	23	.259	18	62	4	118	185	11	.965
1984	—Fresno (California) ..	2B-SS-3B	102	325	53	81	11	0	8	43	.249	47	85	21	182	280	24	.951
1985	—Shreveport (Texas) ..	2B-SS	121	449	85	117	20	7	9	40	.261	65	101	28	†292	366	12	†.982
1986	—San Francisco (N.L.) ..	2B-SS	149	549	73	149	27	3	7	47	.271	42	112	12	255	451	17	.976
1987	—San Francisco (N.L.) ..	2B	132	420	62	110	26	5	10	44	.262	40	91	16	246	341	17	.972
1988	—San Francisco (N.L.) ..	2B	138	477	66	126	24	6	7	48	.264	40	111	14	255	365	14	.978
1989	—San Francisco (N.L.) ..	2B	148	547	91	132	26	*11	13	50	.241	51	133	12	307	425	8	.989
1990	—San Francisco (N.L.) ..	2B	144	498	67	122	22	3	15	56	.245	34	96	14	287	441	8	.989
1991	—San Francisco (N.L.) ..	2B	144	492	74	129	24	5	19	48	.262	63	95	14	320	402	11	.985
1992	—San Francisco (N.L.) ..	2B	128	443	54	115	25	1	14	49	.260	43	75	5	296	382	15	.978
1993	—San Francisco (N.L.) ..	2B	128	494	85	154	30	2	19	65	.312	45	97	10	273	384	8	.988
Major league totals (8 years)			1111	3920	572	1037	204	36	104	407	.265	358	810	97	2239	3191	98	.982

CHAMPIONSHIP SERIES RECORD

			BATTING												FIELDING			
Year	**Team (League)**	**Pos.**	**G**	**AB**	**R**	**H**	**2B**	**3B**	**HR**	**RBI**	**Avg.**	**BB**	**SO**	**SB**	**PO**	**A**	**E**	**Avg.**
1987	—San Francisco (N.L.) ..	2B-PH	7	20	4	2	0	1	1	2	.100	5	7	2	11	19	1	.968
1989	—San Francisco (N.L.) ..	2B	5	18	5	5	0	0	2	3	.278	3	2	0	10	13	0	1.000
Championship series totals (2 years)			12	38	9	7	0	1	3	5	.184	8	9	2	21	32	1	.981

WORLD SERIES RECORD

			BATTING												FIELDING			
Year	**Team (League)**	**Pos.**	**G**	**AB**	**R**	**H**	**2B**	**3B**	**HR**	**RBI**	**Avg.**	**BB**	**SO**	**SB**	**PO**	**A**	**E**	**Avg.**
1989	—San Francisco (N.L.) ..	2B-PH	4	11	0	1	0	0	0	2	.091	0	4	0	4	10	0	1.000

ALL-STAR GAME RECORD

ALL-STAR GAME NOTES: Named to N.L. All-Star team for 1988 game; replaced by Bob Walk due to injury.... Named to N.L. All-Star team for 1993 game; replaced by Gregg Jefferies due to injury.

			BATTING										FIELDING			
Year	**League**	**Pos.**	**AB**	**R**	**H**	**2B**	**3B**	**HR**	**RBI**	**Avg.**	**BB**	**SO**	**SB**	**PO**	**A**	**E**	**Avg.**
1988	—National....................		Selected, did not play—injured.														
1993	—National....................		Selected, did not play—injured.														

THOMPSON, RYAN

OF, METS

PERSONAL: Born November 4, 1967, in Chestertown, Md. ... 6-3/200. ... Throws right, bats right.... Full name: Ryan Orlando Thompson.

HIGH SCHOOL: Kent County (Rock Hall, Md.).

TRANSACTIONS/CAREER NOTES: Selected by Toronto Blue Jays organization in 13th round of free-agent draft (June 2, 1987).... On disabled list (May 29-June 7, 1991).... On Syracuse disabled list (May 4-11 and July 20-27, 1992).... Traded by Blue Jays to New York Mets (September 1, 1992), completing deal in which Mets traded P David Cone to Blue Jays for IF Jeff Kent and a player to be named later (August 27, 1992).

			BATTING												FIELDING			
Year	**Team (League)**	**Pos.**	**G**	**AB**	**R**	**H**	**2B**	**3B**	**HR**	**RBI**	**Avg.**	**BB**	**SO**	**SB**	**PO**	**A**	**E**	**Avg.**
1987	—Medicine Hat (Pio.) ..	OF	40	110	13	27	3	1	1	9	.245	6	34	1	56	2	4	.935
1988	—St. Cathar. (NYP)	OF	23	57	13	10	4	0	0	2	.175	24	21	2	29	1	4	.882
	—Dunedin (Fla. St.)	OF	17	29	2	4	0	0	1	2	.138	2	12	0	11	0	0	1.000
1989	—St. Cathar. (NYP)	OF	74	278	39	76	14	1	6	36	.273	16	60	9	111	•11	5	.961
1990	—Dunedin (Fla. St.)	OF	117	438	56	101	15	5	6	37	.231	20	100	18	237	7	7	.972
1991	—Knoxville (South.)	OF	114	403	48	97	14	3	8	40	.241	26	88	17	222	5	4	.983
1992	—Syracuse (Int'l)	OF	112	429	74	121	20	7	14	46	.282	43	114	10	270	8	4	.986
	—New York (N.L.)■......	OF	30	108	15	24	7	1	3	10	.222	8	24	2	77	2	1	.988
1993	—New York (N.L.)	OF	80	288	34	72	19	2	11	26	.250	19	81	2	228	4	3	.987
	—Norfolk (Int'l)	OF	60	224	39	58	11	2	12	34	.259	24	81	6	138	4	4	.973
Major league totals (2 years)			110	396	49	96	26	3	14	36	.242	27	105	4	305	6	4	.987

THON, DICKIE

IF

PERSONAL: Born June 20, 1958, in South Bend, Ind. ... 5-11/175.... Throws right, bats right. ... Full name: Richard William Thon.

HIGH SCHOOL: San Antonio (Rio Piedras, Puerto Rico).

TRANSACTIONS/CAREER NOTES: Signed as free agent by California Angels organization (November 23, 1975).... Traded by Angels to Houston Astros for P Ken Forsch (April 1, 1981).... On disabled list (April 9, 1984-remainder of season and May 19-June 8, 1985).... Granted free agency (November 12, 1985).... Re-signed by Astros (January 7, 1986).... On disabled list (June 6-23, 1986).... On Houston restricted list (April 3-18, 1987), then transferred to disabled list (April 19-May 10, 1987); included rehabilitation assignment to Tucson (April 19-May 8).... On disqualified list (July 4, 1987-remainder of season).... Granted free agency (November 9, 1987).... Signed by San Diego Padres (February 18, 1988).... Contract sold by Padres to Philadelphia Phillies (January 27, 1989).... On suspended list (June 29-July 1, 1990).... Granted free agency (November 4, 1991).... Signed by Texas Rangers (December 16, 1991).... On Texas disabled list (August 7-September 13, 1992).... Released by Rangers (October 5, 1992).... Signed by Denver, Milwaukee Brewers organization (February 2, 1993).... On Milwaukee disabled list (July 11-27, 1993).... Granted free agency (October 29, 1993).

RECORDS: Shares N.L. single-season record for fewest triples for league leader—10 (1982).

HONORS: Named shortstop on THE SPORTING NEWS N.L. All-Star team (1983).... Named shortstop on THE SPORTING NEWS N.L. Silver Slugger team (1983).

STATISTICAL NOTES: Led N.L. with 18 game-winning RBIs in 1983. . . . Tied for N.L. lead in double plays by shortstop with 86 in 1990.

Year	Team (League)	Pos.	G	AB	R	H	2B	3B	HR	RBI	Avg.	BB	SO	SB	PO	A	E	Avg.
			BATTING												FIELDING			
1976	—Quad Cities (Mid.)	SS	69	246	46	68	11	4	1	32	.276	33	19	19	96	193	32	.900
1977	—Salinas (Calif.)	SS	56	225	48	71	13	2	4	44	.316	28	27	10	95	162	13	.952
	—Salt Lake City (PCL)	SS	77	274	47	79	9	3	8	43	.288	29	35	14	129	242	26	.935
1978	—Salt Lake City (PCL)	2B-SS	130	439	67	113	17	3	1	47	.257	51	63	15	273	380	26	.962
1979	—Salt Lake City (PCL)	SS-2B	38	162	25	47	3	1	2	21	.290	15	16	14	70	120	11	.945
	—California (A.L.)	2B-SS-3B	35	56	6	19	3	0	0	8	.339	5	10	0	38	46	8	.913
1980	—Salt Lake City (PCL)	2B-SS	40	155	28	61	14	2	2	28	.394	12	14	9	81	107	12	.940
	—California (A.L.)	S-2-3-1	80	267	32	68	12	2	0	15	.255	10	28	7	70	124	10	.951
1981	—Houston (N.L.)■.......	2B-SS-3B	49	95	13	26	6	0	0	3	.274	9	13	6	53	63	6	.951
1982	—Houston (N.L.)	SS-3B-2B	136	496	73	137	31	*10	3	36	.276	37	48	37	183	412	17	.972
1983	—Houston (N.L.)	SS	154	619	81	177	28	9	20	79	.286	54	73	34	258	*533	28	.966
1984	—Houston (N.L.)	SS	5	17	3	6	0	1	0	1	.353	0	4	0	8	13	0	1.000
1985	—Houston (N.L.)	SS	84	251	26	63	6	1	6	29	.251	18	50	8	106	218	11	.967
1986	—Houston (N.L.)	SS	106	278	24	69	13	1	3	21	.248	29	49	6	142	210	10	.972
1987	—Tucson (PCL)	SS	14	48	10	13	4	0	0	6	.271	6	12	1	22	40	7	.899
	—Houston (N.L.)	SS	32	66	6	14	1	0	1	3	.212	16	13	3	21	53	6	.925
1988	—San Diego (N.L.)■.....	SS-2B-3B	95	258	36	68	12	2	1	18	.264	33	49	19	84	171	12	.955
1989	—Philadelphia (N.L.)■.	SS	136	435	45	118	18	4	15	60	.271	33	81	6	174	380	16	.972
1990	—Philadelphia (N.L.) ...	SS	149	552	54	141	20	4	8	48	.255	37	77	12	222	439	25	.964
1991	—Philadelphia (N.L.) ...	SS	146	539	44	136	18	4	9	44	.252	25	84	11	234	412	21	.969
1992	—Texas (A.L.)■	SS	95	275	30	68	15	3	4	37	.247	20	40	12	117	225	15	.958
1993	—Milwaukee (A.L.)■....	SS-3B-2B	85	245	23	66	10	1	1	33	.269	22	39	6	80	119	7	.966
American League totals (4 years)			295	843	91	221	40	6	5	93	.262	57	117	25	305	514	40	.953
National League totals (11 years)			1092	3606	405	955	153	36	66	342	.265	291	541	142	1485	2904	152	.967
Major league totals (15 years)			1387	4449	496	1176	193	42	71	435	.264	348	658	167	1790	3418	192	.964

DIVISION SERIES RECORD

Year	Team (League)	Pos.	G	AB	R	H	2B	3B	HR	RBI	Avg.	BB	SO	SB	PO	A	E	Avg.
			BATTING												FIELDING			
1981	—Houston (N.L.)	SS-PH	4	11	0	2	0	0	0	0	.182	0	0	0	5	10	1	.938

CHAMPIONSHIP SERIES RECORD

Year	Team (League)	Pos.	G	AB	R	H	2B	3B	HR	RBI	Avg.	BB	SO	SB	PO	A	E	Avg.
			BATTING												FIELDING			
1979	—California (A.L.)	PR-SS	1	0	1	0	0	0	0	0	...	0	0	0	0	0	0	...
1986	—Houston (N.L.)	SS-PH	6	12	1	3	0	0	1	1	.250	0	1	0	6	9	0	1.000
Championship series totals (2 years)			7	12	2	3	0	0	1	1	.250	0	1	0	6	9	0	1.000

ALL-STAR GAME RECORD

Year	League	Pos.	AB	R	H	2B	3B	HR	RBI	Avg.	BB	SO	SB	PO	A	E	Avg.
			BATTING											FIELDING			
1983	—National	PH-SS	3	0	1	0	0	0	0	.333	0	0	0	0	2	0	1.000

THURMAN, GARY

OF

PERSONAL: Born November 12, 1964, in Indianapolis. . . . 5-10/180. . . . Throws right, bats right. . . . Full name: Gary Montez Thurman Jr.

HIGH SCHOOL: Indianapolis North Central.

TRANSACTIONS/CAREER NOTES: Selected by Kansas City Royals organization in first round (21st pick overall) of free-agent draft (June 6, 1983). . . . On Kansas City disabled list (March 26-April 13, 1989). . . . On Kansas City disabled list (May 10-July 26, 1989); included rehabilitation assignment to Omaha (June 15-July 26). . . . On disabled list (August 6-September 9, 1991). . . . Claimed on waivers by Detroit Tigers (March 26, 1993). . . . Granted free agency (December 20, 1993).

RECORDS: Shares A.L. single-season record for most stolen bases without being caught stealing—16 (1989).

STATISTICAL NOTES: Led Gulf Coast League outfielders with 143 total chances in 1983. . . . Tied for South Atlantic League lead in caught stealing with 17 in 1984. . . . Led South Atlantic League outfielders with 329 total chances in 1984. . . . Led Florida State League outfielders with 396 total chances in 1985. . . . Tied for American Association lead in double plays by outfielder with six in 1987.

Year	Team (League)	Pos.	G	AB	R	H	2B	3B	HR	RBI	Avg.	BB	SO	SB	PO	A	E	Avg.
			BATTING												FIELDING			
1983	—GC Royals (GCL)	OF	59	203	32	52	8	2	0	19	.256	34	*58	31	*127	*13	3	.979
1984	—Char., S.C. (S. Atl.) ...	OF	129	478	71	109	6	8	6	51	.228	81	127	44	*311	5	13	.960
1985	—Fort Myers (FSL)	OF	134	453	68	137	9	9	0	45	.302	68	93	*70	*368	18	10	.975
1986	—Memphis (South.)	OF	131	525	88	164	24	12	7	62	.312	56	81	53	277	5	11	.962
	—Omaha (A.A.)	OF	3	2	1	1	0	0	0	0	.500	2	0	2	2	0	0	1.000
1987	—Omaha (A.A.)	OF	115	450	88	132	14	9	8	39	.293	48	84	*58	283	11	•8	.974
	—Kansas City (A.L.)	OF	27	81	12	24	2	0	0	5	.296	8	20	7	61	5	2	.971
1988	—Omaha (A.A.)	OF	106	422	77	106	12	6	3	40	.251	38	80	35	195	16	6	.972
	—Kansas City (A.L.)	OF	35	66	6	11	1	0	0	2	.167	4	20	5	36	1	2	.949
1989	—Kansas City (A.L.)	OF	72	87	24	17	2	1	0	5	.195	15	26	16	54	2	3	.949
	—Omaha (A.A.)	OF	17	64	5	14	3	2	0	3	.219	7	18	5	34	1	2	.946
1990	—Kansas City (A.L.)	OF	23	60	5	14	3	0	0	3	.233	2	12	1	32	0	0	1.000
	—Omaha (A.A.)	OF	98	381	65	126	14	8	0	26	.331	31	68	39	163	6	6	.966
1991	—Kansas City (A.L.)	OF	80	184	24	51	9	0	2	13	.277	11	42	15	129	2	4	.970
1992	—Kansas City (A.L.)	OF	88	200	25	49	6	3	0	20	.245	9	34	9	138	5	2	.986
1993	—Detroit (A.L.)■	OF	75	89	22	19	2	2	0	13	.213	11	30	7	54	3	3	.950
Major league totals (7 years)			400	767	118	185	25	6	2	61	.241	60	184	60	504	18	16	.970

TIMLIN, MIKE

P, BLUE JAYS

PERSONAL: Born March 10, 1966, in Midland, Tex.... 6-4/210.... Throws right, bats right.... Full name: Michael August Timlin.
HIGH SCHOOL: Midland (Tex.).
COLLEGE: Southwestern University (Tex.).
TRANSACTIONS/CAREER NOTES: Selected by Toronto Blue Jays organization in fifth round of free-agent draft (June 2, 1987).... On disabled list (April 4-May 2, 1989 and August 2-17, 1991).... On Toronto disabled list (March 27-June 12, 1992); included rehabilitation assignment to Dunedin (April 11-15 and May 24-June 5) and Syracuse (June 5-12).
STATISTICAL NOTES: Led South Atlantic League with 19 hit batsmen in 1988.

Year	Team (League)	W	L	Pct.	ERA	G	GS	CG	ShO	Sv.	IP	H	R	ER	BB	SO
1987	—Medicine Hat (Pio.)	4	8	.333	5.14	13	12	2	0	0	75⅓	79	50	43	26	66
1988	—Myrtle Beach (SAL)	10	6	.625	2.86	35	22	0	0	0	151	119	68	48	77	106
1989	—Dunedin (Fla. St.)	5	8	.385	3.25	33	7	1	0	7	88⅔	90	44	32	36	64
1990	—Dunedin (Fla. St.)	7	2	.778	1.43	42	0	0	0	22	50⅓	36	11	8	16	46
	—Knoxville (South.)	1	2	.333	1.73	17	0	0	0	8	26	20	6	5	7	21
1991	—Toronto (A.L.)	11	6	.647	3.16	63	3	0	0	3	108⅓	94	43	38	50	85
1992	—Dunedin (Fla. St.)	0	0	...	0.90	6	1	0	0	1	10	9	2	1	2	7
	—Syracuse (Int'l)	0	1	.000	8.74	7	1	0	0	3	11⅓	15	11	11	5	7
	—Toronto (A.L.)	0	2	.000	4.12	26	0	0	0	1	43⅔	45	23	20	20	35
1993	—Toronto (A.L.)	4	2	.667	4.69	54	0	0	0	1	55⅔	63	32	29	27	49
	—Dunedin (Fla. St.)	0	0	...	1.00	4	0	0	0	1	9	4	1	1	0	8
	Major league totals (3 years)	15	10	.600	3.77	143	3	0	0	5	207⅔	202	98	87	97	169

CHAMPIONSHIP SERIES RECORD

Year	Team (League)	W	L	Pct.	ERA	G	GS	CG	ShO	Sv.	IP	H	R	ER	BB	SO
1991	—Toronto (A.L.)	0	1	.000	3.18	4	0	0	0	0	5⅔	5	4	2	2	5
1992	—Toronto (A.L.)	0	0	...	6.75	2	0	0	0	0	1⅓	4	1	1	0	1
1993	—Toronto (A.L.)	0	0	...	3.86	1	0	0	0	0	2⅓	3	1	1	0	2
	Champ. series totals (3 years)	0	1	.000	3.86	7	0	0	0	0	9⅓	12	6	4	2	8

WORLD SERIES RECORD

Year	Team (League)	W	L	Pct.	ERA	G	GS	CG	ShO	Sv.	IP	H	R	ER	BB	SO
1992	—Toronto (A.L.)	0	0	...	0.00	2	0	0	0	1	1⅓	0	0	0	0	0
1993	—Toronto (A.L.)	0	0	...	0.00	2	0	0	0	0	2⅓	2	0	0	0	4
	World Series totals (2 years)	0	0	...	0.00	4	0	0	0	1	3⅔	2	0	0	0	4

TIMMONS, OZZIE

OF, CUBS

PERSONAL: Born September 18, 1970, in Tampa, Fla.... 6-2/205.... Throws right, bats right.... Full name: Osborne Llewellyn Timmons.
HIGH SCHOOL: Brandon (Fla.).
COLLEGE: University of Tampa (Fla.).
TRANSACTIONS/CAREER NOTES: Selected by Chicago White Sox organization in 44th round of free-agent draft (June 1, 1988).... Selected by Chicago Cubs organization in fifth round of free-agent draft (June 3, 1991).... On disabled list (August 9, 1993-remainder of season).

			BATTING												FIELDING			
Year	Team (League)	Pos.	G	AB	R	H	2B	3B	HR	RBI	Avg.	BB	SO	SB	PO	A	E	Avg.
1991	—Geneva (NY-Penn)	OF	73	294	35	65	10	1	•12	47	.221	18	39	4	118	3	4	.968
1992	—Winst.-Salem (Car.)	OF	86	305	64	86	18	0	18	56	.282	58	46	11	90	7	1	.990
	—Charlotte (South.)	OF	36	122	13	26	7	0	3	13	.213	12	26	2	41	3	1	.978
1993	—Orlando (Southern)	OF	107	359	65	102	22	2	18	58	.284	62	80	5	169	14	6	.968

TINGLEY, RON

C, MARLINS

PERSONAL: Born May 27, 1959, in Presque Isle, Me.... 6-2/194.... Throws right, bats right.... Full name: Ronald Irvin Tingley.
HIGH SCHOOL: Ramona (Riverside, Calif.).
TRANSACTIONS/CAREER NOTES: Selected by San Diego Padres organization in 10th round of free-agent draft (June 7, 1977).... On disabled list (April 10-29, 1980).... Traded by Padres organization to Seattle Mariners organization for SS Bill Wrona (April 1, 1984).... On disabled list (April 7-August 10, 1984).... Granted free agency (October 15, 1984).... Signed by Calgary, Mariners organization (January 15, 1985).... Granted free agency (October 15, 1985).... Signed by Richmond, Atlanta Braves organization (November 19, 1985).... Released by Braves organization (June 19, 1986).... Signed by Maine, Cleveland Indians organization (June 23, 1986).... Traded by Indians organization to California Angels for a player to be named later (September 6, 1989); Colorado Springs, Indians organization, acquired IF Mark McLemore to complete deal (August 17, 1990).... On California disabled list (August 4-September 1, 1990).... Granted free agency (October 15, 1990).... Signed by Edmonton, Angels organization (December 6, 1990).... Granted free agency (October 7, 1993).... Signed by Edmonton, Florida Marlins organization (November 3, 1993).

			BATTING												FIELDING			
Year	Team (League)	Pos.	G	AB	R	H	2B	3B	HR	RBI	Avg.	BB	SO	SB	PO	A	E	Avg.
1977	—Walla Walla (N'west)	OF	21	33	8	5	0	0	1	3	.152	2	9	0	5	2	0	1.000
1978	—Walla Walla (N'west)	OF-C	43	140	22	29	2	0	2	21	.207	21	38	2	149	16	8	.954
1979	—Santa Clara (Calif.)	C-OF-P	52	143	11	29	4	1	0	17	.203	18	37	0	258	42	8	.974
	—Amarillo (Texas)	C-OF	30	90	16	23	4	1	1	6	.256	14	17	2	133	17	4	.974
1980	—Reno (California)	C-OF	65	204	37	61	3	3	3	35	.299	33	35	46	333	46	10	.974
1981	—Amarillo (Texas)	C-1B-OF	116	379	72	109	9	★10	13	60	.288	52	98	8	607	47	11	.983
1982	—Hawaii (PCL)	C	115	362	45	95	13	8	6	42	.262	56	103	11	540	77	12	.981
	—San Diego (N.L.)	C	8	20	0	2	0	0	0	0	.100	0	7	0	40	4	2	.957
1983	—Las Vegas (PCL)	C	92	294	44	83	15	6	10	48	.282	39	85	9	449	55	12	.977
1984	—Salt L. City (PCL)■	C	3	2	1	1	0	0	1	1	.500	0	1	0	3	0	0	1.000
1985	—Calgary (PCL)	C-OF	83	277	36	70	11	3	11	47	.253	30	74	3	399	51	10	.978
1986	—Rich.-Maine (Int'l)■	C	58	174	13	35	2	1	3	13	.201	12	36	1	280	23	6	.981

Year	Team (League)	Pos.	G	AB	R	H	2B	3B	HR	RBI	Avg.	BB	SO	SB	PO	A	E	Avg.
			BATTING												FIELDING			
1987	—Buffalo (A.A.)	C-1B-3B	57	167	27	45	8	5	5	30	.269	25	42	1	306	37	6	.983
1988	—Colo. Springs (PCL)	C	44	130	11	37	5	1	3	20	.285	12	23	1	234	22	0	1.000
	—Cleveland (A.L.)	C	9	24	1	4	0	0	1	2	.167	2	8	0	48	6	0	1.000
1989	—Colo. Springs (PCL)	C-1B	66	207	28	54	8	2	6	39	.261	19	49	2	349	45	12	.970
	—California (A.L.)■	C	4	3	0	1	0	0	0	0	.333	1	0	0	7	1	1	.889
1990	—Edmonton (PCL)	C	54	172	27	46	9	2	5	23	.267	21	39	1	284	35	8	.976
	—California (A.L.)	C	5	3	0	0	0	0	0	0	.000	1	1	0	12	0	0	1.000
1991	—Edmonton (PCL)	C	17	55	11	16	5	0	3	15	.291	8	14	1	65	9	3	.961
	—California (A.L.)	C	45	115	11	23	7	0	1	13	.200	8	34	1	222	32	3	.988
1992	—California (A.L.)	C	71	127	15	25	2	1	3	8	.197	13	35	0	270	35	4	.987
1993	—California (A.L.)	C	58	90	7	18	7	0	0	12	.200	9	22	1	200	20	1	.995
American League totals (6 years)			192	362	34	71	16	1	5	35	.196	34	100	2	759	94	9	.990
National League totals (1 year)			8	20	0	2	0	0	0	0	.100	0	7	0	40	4	2	.957
Major league totals (7 years)			200	382	34	73	16	1	5	35	.191	34	107	2	799	98	11	.988

RECORD AS PITCHER

Year	Team (League)	W	L	Pct.	ERA	G	GS	CG	ShO	Sv.	IP	H	R	ER	BB	SO
1979	—Santa Clara (Calif.)	0	0	...	9.00	1	0	0	0	0	1	4	5	1	2	2

TINSLEY, LEE

OF, MARINERS

PERSONAL: Born March 4, 1969, in Shelbyville, Ky.... 5-10/185.... Throws right, bats both.... Full name: Lee Owen Tinsley.

HIGH SCHOOL: Shelby County (Ky.).

TRANSACTIONS/CAREER NOTES: Selected by Oakland Athletics organization in first round (11th pick overall) of free-agent draft (June 2, 1987).... Traded by A's with P Apolinar Garcia to Cleveland Indians for 3B Brook Jacoby (July 26, 1991).... Claimed on waivers by Seattle Mariners (September 21, 1992).

STATISTICAL NOTES: Tied for Northwest League lead in caught stealing with 10 in 1988.... Led Midwest League outfielders with 320 total chances in 1990.

Year	Team (League)	Pos.	G	AB	R	H	2B	3B	HR	RBI	Avg.	BB	SO	SB	PO	A	E	Avg.
			BATTING												FIELDING			
1987	—Medford (N'west)	OF	45	132	22	23	3	2	0	13	.174	35	57	9	77	2	4	.952
1988	—S. Oregon (N'west)	OF	72	256	56	64	8	2	3	28	.250	*66	*106	*42	127	6	6	.957
1989	—Madison (Midwest)	OF	123	397	51	72	10	2	6	31	.181	67	*177	19	274	7	8	.972
1990	—Madison (Midwest)	OF	132	482	88	121	14	12	12	59	.251	78	*175	44	*302	7	11	.966
1991	—Huntsville (South.)	OF	92	303	47	68	7	6	2	24	.224	52	97	36	175	3	7	.962
	—Cant./Akr. (East.)■	OF	38	139	26	41	7	2	3	8	.295	18	37	18	56	1	2	.966
1992	—Colo. Springs (PCL)	OF	27	81	19	19	2	1	0	4	.235	16	19	3	42	1	1	.977
	—Cant./Akr. (East.)	OF	96	349	65	100	9	8	5	38	.287	42	82	18	226	5	5	.979
1993	—Seattle (A.L.)■	OF	11	19	2	3	1	0	1	2	.158	2	9	0	9	0	1	.900
	—Calgary (PCL)	OF	111	450	95	136	25	*18	10	63	.302	50	98	34	241	4	3	.988
Major league totals (1 year)			11	19	2	3	1	0	1	2	.158	2	9	0	9	0	1	.900

TOLIVER, FRED

P

PERSONAL: Born February 3, 1961, in Natchez, Miss.... 6-1/170.... Throws right, bats right.... Full name: Freddie Lee Toliver.

HIGH SCHOOL: San Gorgonio (San Bernardino, Calif.).

TRANSACTIONS/CAREER NOTES: Selected by New York Yankees organization in third round of free-agent draft (June 5, 1979).... On Greensboro disabled list (May 23-June 6, 1980).... On disabled list (April 9-May 27, 1981).... Traded by Yankees organization to Cincinnati Reds organization (December 10, 1981), completing deal in which Reds traded OF Ken Griffey to Yankees for P Brian Ryder and a player to be named later (November 4, 1981).... On Denver disabled list (July 5-August 10, 1985).... Traded by Reds organization to Philadelphia Phillies organization (August 27, 1985), completing deal in which Phillies traded C Bo Diaz and P Greg Simpson to Reds for SS Tom Foley, C Alan Knicely and a player to be named later (August 8, 1985).... On Philadelphia disabled list (May 30-June 25 and July 8, 1986-remainder of season).... Traded by Phillies organization to Minnesota Twins organization for C Chris Calvert (February 5, 1988).... Traded by Twins organization to San Diego Padres for P Greg Booker (June 29, 1989).... Traded by Padres organization to Yankees organization (September 27, 1989), completing deal in which Yankees traded 3B Mike Pagliarulo and P Don Schulze to Padres for P Walt Terrell and a player to be named later (July 22, 1989).... Released by Yankees (April 2, 1990).... Signed by California Angels organization (May 25, 1990).... Granted free agency (October 15, 1990).... Re-signed by Angels organization (March 4, 1991).... Granted free agency (October 15, 1991).... Signed by Salinas, independent (April 7, 1992).... Contract sold by Salinas to Pittsburgh Pirates organization (July 23, 1992).... Granted free agency (October 15, 1993).

MISCELLANEOUS: Appeared in one game as pinch-runner with Minnesota (1989).

Year	Team (League)	W	L	Pct.	ERA	G	GS	CG	ShO	Sv.	IP	H	R	ER	BB	SO
1979	—Oneonta (NYP)	*10	2	.833	2.10	13	13	1	0	0	77	46	28	18	66	71
1980	—Fort Lauder. (FSL)	0	2	.000	14.63	3	3	0	0	0	8	14	15	13	10	4
	—Greensboro (S. Atl.)	6	8	.429	2.86	20	20	4	0	0	126	98	60	40	89	96
1981	—Greensboro (S. Atl.)	5	3	.625	3.49	17	14	2	1	0	80	67	38	31	56	62
1982	—Ced. Rap. (Midw.)■	6	7	.462	4.23	23	20	1	0	0	115	114	77	54	66	117
	—Indianapolis (A.A.)	2	2	.500	3.92	4	4	0	0	0	20⅔	20	10	9	13	19
1983	—Indianapolis (A.A.)	8	10	.444	4.54	26	26	6	1	0	166⅔	151	93	84	*110	112
1984	—Wichita (A.A.)	11	6	.647	4.83	32	23	6	0	0	164	142	90	88	*116	113
	—Cincinnati (N.L.)	0	0	...	0.90	3	1	0	0	0	10	7	2	1	7	4
1985	—Denver (A.A.)	11	3	.786	3.24	19	19	5	2	0	122⅓	113	50	44	56	84
	—Philadelphia (N.L.)■	0	4	.000	4.68	11	3	0	0	1	25	27	15	13	17	23
1986	—Portland (PCL)	1	3	.250	7.43	6	6	0	0	0	26⅔	31	23	22	14	15
	—Philadelphia (N.L.)	0	2	.000	3.51	5	5	0	0	0	25⅔	28	14	10	11	20
1987	—Maine (Int'l)	6	9	.400	4.62	22	21	•2	0	0	124⅔	114	70	64	67	80
	—Philadelphia (N.L.)	1	1	.500	5.64	10	4	0	0	0	30⅓	34	19	19	17	25

Year	Team (League)	W	L	Pct.	ERA	G	GS	CG	ShO	Sv.	IP	H	R	ER	BB	SO
1988	—Portland (PCL)■	7	2	.778	3.13	13	13	4	1	0	95	79	42	33	35	54
	—Minnesota (A.L.)	7	6	.538	4.24	21	19	0	0	0	114⅔	116	57	54	52	69
1989	—Minnesota (A.L.)	1	3	.250	7.76	7	5	0	0	0	29	39	26	25	15	11
	—Port.-L.V. (PCL)■	8	2	.800	2.57	13	13	4	2	0	84	72	32	24	31	72
	—San Diego (N.L.)	0	0	...	7.07	9	0	0	0	0	14	17	14	11	9	14
1990	—Palm Springs (Cal.)■	0	1	.000	2.87	7	1	0	0	0	15⅔	15	5	5	6	5
	—Edmonton (PCL)	8	2	.800	3.99	13	12	0	0	0	67⅔	71	34	30	28	45
1991	—Aguascal. (Mex.)	4	5	.444	5.97	12	11	2	0	0	69⅓	90	49	46	42	47
	—Edmonton (PCL)	7	4	.636	4.15	18	18	2	1	0	95⅓	89	48	44	49	68
1992	—Salinas (Calif.)■	5	8	.385	3.49	20	20	3	1	0	123⅔	125	63	48	47	104
	—Carolina (South.)■	1	2	.333	4.19	15	0	0	0	3	19⅓	22	11	9	10	24
1993	—Carolina (South.)	2	2	.500	3.15	33	0	0	0	12	40	32	16	14	24	48
	—Pittsburgh (N.L.)	1	0	1.000	3.74	12	0	0	0	0	21⅔	20	10	9	8	14
	—Buffalo (A.A.)	1	3	.250	3.65	13	0	0	0	1	12⅓	13	5	5	9	11
A.L. totals (2 years)		8	9	.471	4.95	28	24	0	0	0	143⅔	155	83	79	67	80
N.L. totals (6 years)		2	7	.222	4.48	50	13	0	0	1	126⅔	133	74	63	69	100
Major league totals (7 years)		10	16	.385	4.73	78	37	0	0	1	270⅓	288	157	142	136	180

TOMBERLIN, ANDY

OF

PERSONAL: Born November 7, 1966, in Monroe, N.C. . . . 5-11/160. . . . Throws left, bats left. . . . Full name: Andy Lee Tomberlin.

HIGH SCHOOL: Piedmont (Monroe, N.C.).

TRANSACTIONS/CAREER NOTES: Signed as free agent by Atlanta Braves organization (August 16, 1985). . . . On disabled list (April 10-May 28, 1991). . . . Granted free agency (October 15, 1992). . . . Signed by Buffalo, Pittsburgh Pirates organization (November 24, 1992). . . . On Buffalo disabled list (May 22-June 5 and June 30-July 27, 1993). . . . Granted free agency (October 13, 1993).

STATISTICAL NOTES: Tied for Carolina League lead with seven intentional base on balls received in 1989.

			BATTING											FIELDING			
Year	Team (League)	Pos.	G	AB	R	H	2B	3B	HR	RBI	Avg.	BB	SO	SB	PO	A	E	Avg.
1986	—Sumter (S. Atl.)	P	13	1	0	0	0	0	0	0	.000	1	1	0	2	2	2	.667
	—Pulaski (Appal.)	P	3	4	2	1	0	0	0	0	.250	2	1	0	0	5	0	1.000
1987	—Pulaski (Appal.)	P	14	7	1	2	0	0	0	1	.286	0	0	0	1	9	1	.909
1988	—Burlington (Midw.)	OF	43	134	24	46	7	3	3	18	.343	22	33	7	62	6	3	.958
	—Durham (Carolina)	OF-P	83	256	43	77	16	3	6	35	.301	49	42	16	152	2	3	.981
1989	—Durham (Carolina)	OF-1B-P	119	363	63	102	13	2	16	61	.281	54	82	35	442	16	1	.998
1990	—Greenville (South.)	OF-P	60	196	31	61	9	1	4	25	.311	20	35	9	95	4	3	.971
	—Richmond (Int'l)	OF-1B	80	283	36	86	19	3	4	31	.304	39	43	11	180	9	4	.979
1991	—Richmond (Int'l)	OF	93	329	47	77	13	2	2	24	.234	41	85	10	192	1	1	.995
1992	—Richmond (Int'l)	OF	118	406	69	110	16	5	9	47	.271	41	102	12	184	9	3	.985
1993	—Buffalo (A.A.)■	OF-P	68	221	41	63	11	6	12	45	.285	18	48	3	104	7	5	.957
	—Pittsburgh (N.L.)	OF	27	42	4	12	0	1	1	5	.286	2	14	0	9	1	0	1.000
Major league totals (1 year)			27	42	4	12	0	1	1	5	.286	2	14	0	9	1	0	1.000

RECORD AS PITCHER

Year	Team (League)	W	L	Pct.	ERA	G	GS	CG	ShO	Sv.	IP	H	R	ER	BB	SO
1986	—Sumter (S. Atl.)	1	0	1.000	4.62	13	0	0	0	0	25⅓	18	17	13	27	22
	—Pulaski (Appal.)	2	0	1.000	2.12	3	3	0	0	0	17	13	4	4	9	15
1987	—Pulaski (Appal.)	4	2	.667	4.43	12	6	0	0	0	44⅔	35	23	22	29	51
1988	—Durham (Carolina)	0	0	...	0.00	1	0	0	0	0	1	0	0	0	0	0
1989	—Durham (Carolina)	0	0	...	18.00	1	0	0	0	0	1	2	2	2	2	2
1990	—Greenville (South.)	0	0	...	0.00	1	0	0	0	0	1	1	0	0	1	1
1993	—Buffalo (A.A.)	0	0	...	0.00	2	0	0	0	0	2	0	0	0	3	1

TOMLIN, RANDY

P, PIRATES

PERSONAL: Born June 14, 1966, in Bainbridge, Md. . . . 5-10/182. . . . Throws left, bats left. . . . Full name: Randy Leon Tomlin.

COLLEGE: Liberty (Va.).

TRANSACTIONS/CAREER NOTES: Selected by Pittsburgh Pirates organization in 18th round of free-agent draft (June 1, 1988). . . . On Pittsburgh disabled list (May 29-July 10, 1993); included rehabilitation assignment to Carolina (June 29-July 6). . . . On Pittsburgh disabled list (August 27, 1993-remainder of season).

STATISTICAL NOTES: Pitched 1-0 no-hit victory for Salem against Kinston (May 28, 1989).

MISCELLANEOUS: Appeared in one game as pinch-runner (1991).

Year	Team (League)	W	L	Pct.	ERA	G	GS	CG	ShO	Sv.	IP	H	R	ER	BB	SO
1988	—Watertown (NYP)	7	5	.583	2.18	15	15	5	2	0	103⅓	75	31	25	25	87
1989	—Salem (Carolina)	12	6	.667	3.25	21	21	3	2	0	138⅔	131	60	50	43	99
	—Harrisburg (East.)	2	2	.500	0.84	5	5	1	1	0	32	18	6	3	6	31
1990	—Harrisburg (East.)	9	6	.600	2.28	19	18	4	•3	0	126⅓	101	43	32	34	92
	—Buffalo (A.A.)	0	0	...	3.38	3	1	0	0	0	8	12	3	3	1	3
	—Pittsburgh (N.L.)	4	4	.500	2.55	12	12	2	0	0	77⅔	62	24	22	12	42
1991	—Pittsburgh (N.L.)	8	7	.533	2.98	31	27	4	2	0	175	170	75	58	54	104
1992	—Pittsburgh (N.L.)	14	9	.609	3.41	35	33	1	1	0	208⅔	226	85	79	42	90
1993	—Pittsburgh (N.L.)	4	8	.333	4.85	18	18	1	0	0	98⅓	109	57	53	15	44
	—Carolina (South.)	1	0	1.000	0.75	2	2	0	0	0	12	7	1	1	1	9
Major league totals (4 years)		30	28	.517	3.41	96	90	8	3	0	559⅔	567	241	212	123	280

CHAMPIONSHIP SERIES RECORD

Year	Team (League)	W	L	Pct.	ERA	G	GS	CG	ShO	Sv.	IP	H	R	ER	BB	SO
1990	—Pittsburgh (N.L.)							Did not play.								

Year	Team (League)	W	L	Pct.	ERA	G	GS	CG	ShO	Sv.	IP	H	R	ER	BB	SO
1991	—Pittsburgh (N.L.)	0	0	...	3.00	1	1	0	0	0	6	6	2	2	2	1
1992	—Pittsburgh (N.L.)	0	0	...	6.75	2	0	0	0	0	2⅔	5	2	2	1	0
Champ. series totals (2 years)		0	0	...	4.15	3	1	0	0	0	8⅔	11	4	4	3	1

TORRES, SALOMON

P, GIANTS

PERSONAL: Born March 11, 1972, in San Pedro de Macoris, Dominican Republic. . . . 5-11/165. . . . Throws right, bats right. . . . Full name: Salomon Ramirez Torres.
HIGH SCHOOL: Centro Academico Rogus (San Pedro de Macoris, Dominican Republic).
TRANSACTIONS/CAREER NOTES: Signed as free agent by San Francisco Giants organization (September 15, 1989).
HONORS: Named Midwest League Most Valuable Player (1991).

Year	Team (League)	W	L	Pct.	ERA	G	GS	CG	ShO	Sv.	IP	H	R	ER	BB	SO
1990	—San Pedro (DSL)	11	1	.917	0.50	13	13	6	0	0	90	44	15	5	30	101
1991	—Clinton (Midwest)	•16	5	.762	*1.41	28	28	*8	3	0	*210⅓	148	48	33	47	*214
1992	—Shreveport (Texas)	6	10	.375	4.21	25	25	4	2	0	162⅓	167	93	76	34	151
1993	—Shreveport (Texas)	7	4	.636	2.70	12	12	2	1	0	83⅓	67	27	25	12	67
	—Phoenix (PCL)	7	4	.636	3.50	14	14	•4	1	0	105⅓	105	43	41	27	99
	—San Francisco (N.L.)	3	5	.375	4.03	8	8	0	0	0	44⅔	37	21	20	27	23
Major league totals (1 year)		3	5	.375	4.03	8	8	0	0	0	44⅔	37	21	20	27	23

TRACHSEL, STEVE

P, CUBS

PERSONAL: Born October 31, 1970, in Oxnard, Calif. . . . 6-4/205. . . . Throws right, bats right. . . . Full name: Stephen Christopher Trachsel. . . . Name pronounced TRACK-sul.
HIGH SCHOOL: Troy (Fullerton, Calif.).
COLLEGE: Fullerton (Calif.) College and Long Beach State.
TRANSACTIONS/CAREER NOTES: Selected by Chicago Cubs organization in eighth round of free-agent draft (June 3, 1991).
STATISTICAL NOTES: Pitched 4-2 no-hit victory for Winston-Salem against Peninsula (July 12, 1991, second game).

Year	Team (League)	W	L	Pct.	ERA	G	GS	CG	ShO	Sv.	IP	H	R	ER	BB	SO
1991	—Geneva (NY-Penn)	1	0	1.000	1.26	2	2	0	0	0	14⅓	10	2	2	6	7
	—Winst.-Salem (Car.)	4	4	.500	3.67	12	12	1	0	0	73⅔	70	38	30	19	69
1992	—Charlotte (South.)	•13	8	.619	3.06	29	•29	5	2	0	*191	180	76	65	35	135
1993	—Iowa (Am. Assoc.)	13	6	.684	3.96	27	26	1	1	0	170⅔	170	78	75	45	135
	—Chicago (N.L.)	0	2	.000	4.58	3	3	0	0	0	19⅔	16	10	10	3	14
Major league totals (1 year)		0	2	.000	4.58	3	3	0	0	0	19⅔	16	10	10	3	14

TRAMMELL, ALAN

SS, TIGERS

PERSONAL: Born February 21, 1958, in Garden Grove, Calif. . . . 6-0/185. . . . Throws right, bats right. . . . Full name: Alan Stuart Trammell. . . . Name pronounced TRAM-ull.
HIGH SCHOOL: Kearney (San Diego).
TRANSACTIONS/CAREER NOTES: Selected by Detroit Tigers organization in second round of free-agent draft (June 8, 1976). . . . On disabled list (July 9-31, 1984; June 29-July 17, 1988; June 4-23, 1989; July 18-August 13, 1991 and May 16, 1992-remainder of season). . . . Granted free agency (November 6, 1992). . . . Re-signed by Tigers (December 2, 1992). . . . On disabled list (April 2-17, 1993).
HONORS: Named Southern League Most Valuable Player (1977). . . . Won A.L. Gold Glove at shortstop (1980-81 and 1983-84). . . . Named A.L. Comeback Player of the Year by THE SPORTING NEWS (1983). . . . Named shortstop on THE SPORTING NEWS A.L. All-Star team (1987-88 and 1990). . . . Named shortstop on THE SPORTING NEWS A.L. Silver Slugger team (1987-88 and 1990).
STATISTICAL NOTES: Led A.L. with 16 sacrifice hits in 1981 and 15 in 1983. . . . Led A.L. shortstops with 102 double plays in 1990.

			BATTING												FIELDING			
Year	Team (League)	Pos.	G	AB	R	H	2B	3B	HR	RBI	Avg.	BB	SO	SB	PO	A	E	Avg.
1976	—Bristol (Appal.)	SS	41	140	27	38	2	2	0	7	.271	26	20	8	59	131	12	.941
	—Montgomery (Sou.)	SS	21	56	4	10	0	0	0	2	.179	7	12	3	40	64	2	.981
1977	—Montgomery (Sou.)	SS	134	454	78	132	9	*19	3	50	.291	56	92	4	188	397	27	.956
	—Detroit (A.L.)	SS	19	43	6	8	0	0	0	0	.186	4	12	0	15	34	2	.961
1978	—Detroit (A.L.)	SS	139	448	49	120	14	6	2	34	.268	45	56	3	239	421	14	.979
1979	—Detroit (A.L.)	SS	142	460	68	127	11	4	6	50	.276	43	55	17	245	388	26	.961
1980	—Detroit (A.L.)	SS	146	560	107	168	21	5	9	65	.300	69	63	12	225	412	13	.980
1981	—Detroit (A.L.)	SS	105	392	52	101	15	3	2	31	.258	49	31	10	181	347	9	.983
1982	—Detroit (A.L.)	SS	157	489	66	126	34	3	9	57	.258	52	47	19	259	459	16	.978
1983	—Detroit (A.L.)	SS	142	505	83	161	31	2	14	66	.319	57	64	30	236	367	13	.979
1984	—Detroit (A.L.)	SS	139	555	85	174	34	5	14	69	.314	60	63	19	180	314	10	.980
1985	—Detroit (A.L.)	SS	149	605	79	156	21	7	13	57	.258	50	71	14	225	400	15	.977
1986	—Detroit (A.L.)	SS	151	574	107	159	33	7	21	75	.277	59	57	25	238	445	22	.969
1987	—Detroit (A.L.)	SS	151	597	109	205	34	3	28	105	.343	60	47	21	222	421	19	.971
1988	—Detroit (A.L.)	SS	128	466	73	145	24	1	15	69	.311	46	46	7	195	355	11	.980
1989	—Detroit (A.L.)	SS	121	449	54	109	20	3	5	43	.243	45	45	10	188	396	9	.985
1990	—Detroit (A.L.)	SS	146	559	71	170	37	1	14	89	.304	68	55	12	232	409	14	.979
1991	—Detroit (A.L.)	SS-3B	101	375	57	93	20	0	9	55	.248	37	39	11	131	296	9	.979
1992	—Detroit (A.L.)	SS	29	102	11	28	7	1	1	11	.275	15	4	2	46	80	3	.977
1993	—Detroit (A.L.)	SS-3B-OF	112	401	72	132	25	3	12	60	.329	38	38	12	113	238	9	.975
Major league totals (17 years)			2077	7580	1149	2182	381	54	174	936	.288	797	793	224	3170	5782	214	.977

T

CHAMPIONSHIP SERIES RECORD

Year	Team (League)	Pos.	G	AB	R	H	2B	3B	HR	RBI	Avg.	BB	SO	SB	PO	A	E	Avg.
			BATTING												FIELDING			
1984	—Detroit (A.L.)	SS	3	11	2	4	0	1	1	3	.364	3	1	0	1	8	0	1.000
1987	—Detroit (A.L.)	SS	5	20	3	4	1	0	0	2	.200	1	2	0	6	9	1	.938
Championship series totals (2 years)			8	31	5	8	1	1	1	5	.258	4	3	0	7	17	1	.960

WORLD SERIES RECORD

WORLD SERIES NOTES: Named Most Valuable Player (1984).... Shares single-game record for batting in all club's runs—4 (October 13, 1984).

Year	Team (League)	Pos.	G	AB	R	H	2B	3B	HR	RBI	Avg.	BB	SO	SB	PO	A	E	Avg.
			BATTING												FIELDING			
1984	—Detroit (A.L.)	SS	5	20	5	9	1	0	2	6	.450	2	2	1	8	9	1	.944

ALL-STAR GAME RECORD

ALL-STAR GAME NOTES: Named to A.L. All-Star team for 1984 game; replaced by Alfredo Griffin due to injury.... Named to A.L. All-Star team for 1988 game; replaced by Cal Ripken Jr. due to injury.

Year	League	Pos.	AB	R	H	2B	3B	HR	RBI	Avg.	BB	SO	SB	PO	A	E	Avg.
			BATTING											FIELDING			
1980	—American	SS	0	0	0	0	0	0	0	...	0	0	0	0	0	0	...
1984	—American		Selected, did not play—injured.														
1985	—American	SS	1	0	0	0	0	0	0	.000	0	0	0	0	0	0	...
1987	—American	PH	1	0	0	0	0	0	0	.000	0	0	0	...	...	...	...
1988	—American		Selected, did not play—injured.														
1990	—American	PH	1	0	0	0	0	0	0	.000	0	0	0	...	...	...	...
All-Star Game totals (4 years)			3	0	0	0	0	0	0	.000	0	0	0	0	0	0	...

TREADWAY, JEFF

3B/2B, DODGERS

PERSONAL: Born January 22, 1963, in Columbus, Ga.... 5-11/170.... Throws right, bats left.... Full name: Hugh Jeffery Treadway.

HIGH SCHOOL: Griffin (Ga.).

COLLEGE: Middle Georgia College and Georgia.

TRANSACTIONS/CAREER NOTES: Selected by Montreal Expos organization in 18th round of free-agent draft (January 13, 1981).... Signed as free agent by Cincinnati Reds organization (January 29, 1984).... On disabled list (August 28-September 24, 1988).... Contract sold by Reds to Atlanta Braves (March 25, 1989).... On Atlanta disabled list (March 10-June 26, 1992); included rehabilitation assignment to Greenville (June 22-26).... Released by Braves (November 20, 1992).... Signed by Cleveland Indians organization (December 17, 1992).... Granted free agency (October 27, 1993).... Signed by Los Angeles Dodgers organization (December 14, 1993).

STATISTICAL NOTES: Hit three home runs in one game (May 26, 1990).

Year	Team (League)	Pos.	G	AB	R	H	2B	3B	HR	RBI	Avg.	BB	SO	SB	PO	A	E	Avg.
			BATTING												FIELDING			
1984	—Tampa (Fla. St.)	3B-2B	119	372	44	115	16	0	0	44	.309	54	40	13	128	184	25	.926
1985	—Vermont (Eastern)	2B	129	431	63	130	17	1	2	49	.302	71	40	6	271	332	15	.976
1986	—Vermont (Eastern)	2B	33	122	18	41	8	1	1	16	.336	23	12	3	68	102	5	.971
	—Denver (A.A.)	2B-3B	72	204	20	67	11	4	3	23	.328	19	12	3	75	153	6	.974
1987	—Nashville (A.A.)	2B	123	409	66	129	28	5	7	59	.315	52	41	2	236	362	12	*.980
	—Cincinnati (N.L.)	2B	23	84	9	28	4	0	2	4	.333	2	6	1	44	48	4	.958
1988	—Cincinnati (N.L.)	2B-3B	103	301	30	76	19	4	2	23	.252	27	30	2	189	253	8	.982
1989	—Atlanta (N.L.)■	2B-3B	134	473	58	131	18	3	8	40	.277	30	38	3	273	341	12	.981
1990	—Atlanta (N.L.)	2B	128	474	56	134	20	2	11	59	.283	25	42	3	241	360	15	.976
1991	—Atlanta (N.L.)	2B	106	306	41	98	17	2	3	32	.320	23	19	2	155	206	15	.960
1992	—Greenville (South.)	2B	4	11	1	5	2	0	0	1	.455	2	1	0	8	10	0	1.000
	—Atlanta (N.L.)	2B-3B	61	126	5	28	6	1	0	5	.222	9	16	1	53	85	1	.993
1993	—Cleveland (A.L.)■	3B-2B	97	221	25	67	14	1	2	27	.303	14	21	1	46	111	10	.940
American League totals (1 year)			97	221	25	67	14	1	2	27	.303	14	21	1	46	111	10	.940
National League totals (6 years)			555	1764	199	495	84	12	26	163	.281	116	151	12	955	1293	55	.976
Major league totals (7 years)			652	1985	224	562	98	13	28	190	.283	130	172	13	1001	1404	65	.974

CHAMPIONSHIP SERIES RECORD

Year	Team (League)	Pos.	G	AB	R	H	2B	3B	HR	RBI	Avg.	BB	SO	SB	PO	A	E	Avg.
			BATTING												FIELDING			
1991	—Atlanta (N.L.)	2B	1	3	0	1	0	0	0	0	.333	0	0	0	2	2	0	1.000
1992	—Atlanta (N.L.)	PH-2B	3	3	1	2	0	0	0	0	.667	0	1	0	0	1	0	1.000
Championship series totals (2 years)			4	6	1	3	0	0	0	0	.500	0	1	0	2	3	0	1.000

WORLD SERIES RECORD

Year	Team (League)	Pos.	G	AB	R	H	2B	3B	HR	RBI	Avg.	BB	SO	SB	PO	A	E	Avg.
			BATTING												FIELDING			
1991	—Atlanta (N.L.)	PH-2B	3	4	1	1	0	0	0	0	.250	1	2	0	1	3	1	.800
1992	—Atlanta (N.L.)	PH	1	1	0	0	0	0	0	0	.000	0	0	0	...	...	...	...
World Series totals (2 years)			4	5	1	1	0	0	0	0	.200	1	2	0	1	3	1	.800

TRLICEK, RICK

P, DODGERS

PERSONAL: Born April 26, 1969, in Houston.... 6-2/200.... Throws right, bats right.... Full name: Richard Alan Trlicek.... Name pronounced TRILL-a-CHECK.

HIGH SCHOOL: LaGrange (Tex.).

TRANSACTIONS/CAREER NOTES: Selected by Philadelphia Phillies organization in fourth round of free-agent draft (June 2, 1987).... Released by Phillies organization (March 23, 1989).... Signed by Atlanta Braves organization (April 2, 1989).... Traded by Braves organization to Toronto Blue Jays for C Ernie Whitt and OF Kevin Batiste (December 17, 1989).... On disabled list (August 4, 1991-remainder of season).... On Syracuse disabled list (July 31-September 8, 1992).... Claimed on waivers by Los Angeles Dodgers (March 16, 1993).... On suspended list (June 29-July 2, 1993).

Year	Team (League)	W	L	Pct.	ERA	G	GS	CG	ShO	Sv.	IP	H	R	ER	BB	SO
1987	—Utica (N.Y.-Penn)	2	5	.286	4.10	10	8	1	1	0	37⅓	43	28	17	31	22
1988	—Batavia (NY-Penn)	2	3	.400	7.39	8	8	0	0	0	31⅔	27	32	26	31	26
1989	—Sumter (S. Atl.)■	6	5	.545	2.59	15	15	0	0	0	93⅔	73	40	27	40	72
	—Durham (Carolina)	0	0	...	1.13	1	1	0	0	0	8	3	2	1	1	4
1990	—Dunedin (Fla. St.)■	5	8	.385	3.73	26	26	0	0	0	154⅓	128	74	64	72	125
1991	—Knoxville (South.)	2	5	.286	2.45	41	0	0	0	16	51⅓	36	26	14	22	55
1992	—Toronto (A.L.)	0	0	...	10.80	2	0	0	0	0	1⅔	2	2	2	2	1
	—Syracuse (Int'l)	1	1	.500	4.36	35	0	0	0	10	43⅓	37	22	21	31	35
1993	—Los Angeles (N.L.)■	1	2	.333	4.08	41	0	0	0	1	64	59	32	29	21	41
	A.L. totals (1 year)	0	0	...	10.80	2	0	0	0	0	1⅔	2	2	2	2	1
	N.L. totals (1 year)	1	2	.333	4.08	41	0	0	0	1	64	59	32	29	21	41
	Major league totals (2 years)	1	2	.333	4.25	43	0	0	0	1	65⅔	61	34	31	23	42

TROMBLEY, MIKE

P, TWINS

PERSONAL: Born April 14, 1967, in Springfield, Mass.... 6-2/208.... Throws right, bats right.... Full name: Michael Scott Trombley.
HIGH SCHOOL: Minnechaug Regional (Wilbraham, Mass.).
COLLEGE: Duke.
TRANSACTIONS/CAREER NOTES: Selected by Minnesota Twins organization in 14th round of free-agent draft (June 5, 1989).
STATISTICAL NOTES: Pitched 3-0 no-hit victory against Knoxville (August 8, 1991).... Led Pacific Coast League with 18 home runs allowed in 1992.

Year	Team (League)	W	L	Pct.	ERA	G	GS	CG	ShO	Sv.	IP	H	R	ER	BB	SO
1989	—Kenosha (Midwest)	5	1	.833	3.12	12	3	0	0	2	49	45	23	17	13	41
	—Visalia (California)	2	2	.500	2.14	6	6	2	1	0	42	31	12	10	11	36
1990	—Visalia (California)	14	6	.700	3.43	27	25	3	1	0	176	163	79	67	50	164
1991	—Orlando (Southern)	12	7	.632	2.54	27	27	7	2	0	*191	153	65	54	57	*175
1992	—Portland (PCL)	10	8	.556	3.65	25	25	2	0	0	165	149	70	67	58	*138
	—Minnesota (A.L.)	3	2	.600	3.30	10	7	0	0	0	46⅓	43	20	17	17	38
1993	—Minnesota (A.L.)	6	6	.500	4.88	44	10	0	0	2	114⅓	131	72	62	41	85
	Major league totals (2 years)	9	8	.529	4.43	54	17	0	0	2	160⅔	174	92	79	58	123

TSAMIS, GEORGE

P, TWINS

PERSONAL: Born June 14, 1967, in Campbell, Calif.... 6-2/175.... Throws left, bats right.... Full name: George Alex Tsamis.... Name pronounced SAY-miss.
HIGH SCHOOL: Countryside Senior (Clearwater, Fla.).
COLLEGE: Stetson.
TRANSACTIONS/CAREER NOTES: Selected by Toronto Blue Jays organization in 33rd round of free-agent draft (June 1, 1988).... Selected by Minnesota Twins organization in 15th round of free-agent draft (June 5, 1989).

Year	Team (League)	W	L	Pct.	ERA	G	GS	CG	ShO	Sv.	IP	H	R	ER	BB	SO
1989	—Visalia (California)	6	3	.667	3.05	15	13	3	0	0	94⅓	85	36	32	34	87
1990	—Visalia (California)	*17	4	.810	2.21	26	26	4	*3	0	183⅔	168	62	45	61	145
1991	—Orlando (Southern)	0	0	...	0.00	1	1	0	0	0	7	3	2	0	4	5
	—Portland (PCL)	10	8	.556	3.27	29	27	2	1	0	167⅔	183	75	61	66	71
1992	—Portland (PCL)	•13	4	.765	3.90	39	22	4	1	1	163⅔	*195	78	71	51	71
1993	—Portland (PCL)	1	2	.333	8.36	3	3	0	0	0	14	27	15	13	5	10
	—Minnesota (A.L.)	1	2	.333	6.19	41	0	0	0	1	68⅓	86	51	47	27	30
	Major league totals (1 year)	1	2	.333	6.19	41	0	0	0	1	68⅓	86	51	47	27	30

TUBBS, GREG

OF, WHITE SOX

PERSONAL: Born August 31, 1962, in Smithville, Tenn.... 5-9/185.... Throws right, bats right.... Full name: Gregory Alan Tubbs.
HIGH SCHOOL: Dekalb County (Smithville, Tenn.).
COLLEGE: Austin Peay State.
TRANSACTIONS/CAREER NOTES: Selected by Atlanta Braves organization in 22nd round of free-agent draft (June 4, 1984).... Traded by Braves organization to Pittsburgh Pirates organization for IF Rico Rossy (May 2, 1990).... Granted free agency (October 15, 1990).... Signed by Carolina, Pirates organization (January 28, 1991).... Granted free agency (October 15, 1991).... Signed by Buffalo, Pirates organization (November 13, 1991).... On disabled list (August 8-18, 1992).... Granted free agency (October 15, 1992).... Signed by Indianapolis, Cincinnati Reds organization (November 9, 1992).... Granted free agency (October 8, 1993).... Signed by Nashville, Chicago White Sox organization (November 22, 1993).
STATISTICAL NOTES: Led Southern League in caught stealing with 19 in 1987.... Led International League in caught stealing with 15 in 1989.... Led American Association in caught stealing with 19 in 1992.

						BATTING								FIELDING			
Year	Team (League)	Pos.	G	AB	R	H	2B	3B	HR	RBI	Avg.	BB	SO	SB	PO	A	E	Avg.
1984	—GC Braves (GCL)	OF	18	58	13	21	4	3	0	3	.362	15	5	5	24	2	0	1.000
	—Anderson (S. Atl.)	OF	50	174	25	53	5	2	2	11	.305	27	29	19	88	7	3	.969
1985	—Sumter (S. Atl.)	OF	61	239	53	85	11	7	6	36	.356	33	36	30	93	6	4	.961
	—Durham (Carolina)	OF	70	266	44	75	15	6	8	32	.282	36	52	29	188	3	2	.990
1986	—Greenville (South.)	OF	*144	536	95	144	21	7	5	56	.269	107	74	31	371	7	4	*.990
1987	—Greenville (South.)	OF	141	540	97	145	19	7	3	40	.269	*86	86	24	364	9	6	.984
1988	—Greenville (South.)	OF	29	101	13	24	1	1	0	12	.238	13	20	4	67	2	2	.972
	—Richmond (Int'l)	OF	78	228	43	56	14	2	2	11	.246	28	38	8	177	4	2	.989
1989	—Greenville (South.)	OF	11	27	4	5	0	0	0	1	.185	8	4	3	16	0	0	1.000
	—Richmond (Int'l)	OF	115	405	64	122	10	11	4	35	.301	47	49	19	199	3	1	.995

									BATTING							FIELDING			
Year	**Team (League)**	**Pos.**	**G**	**AB**	**R**	**H**	**2B**	**3B**	**HR**	**RBI**	**Avg.**	**BB**	**SO**	**SB**	**PO**	**A**	**E**	**Avg.**
1990	—Richmond (Int'l)	OF	11	23	3	5	0	0	0	1	.217	11	6	0	17	0	1	.944
	—M.C. Reds (Mex.)	OF	57	213	37	67	5	9	4	33	.315	36	45	11	103	8	5	.957
	—Harrisburg (East.)■	OF	54	213	35	60	6	5	3	21	.282	23	35	8	102	3	2	.981
1991	—Buffalo (A.A.)	OF	121	373	71	102	18	•11	3	34	.273	48	62	34	237	3	3	.988
1992	—Buffalo (A.A.)	OF	110	430	69	126	20	5	7	42	.293	57	64	20	264	6	3	.989
1993	—Indianapolis (A.A.)■	OF	97	334	59	102	21	4	10	45	.305	42	65	15	195	7	6	.971
	—Cincinnati (N.L.)	OF	35	59	10	11	0	0	1	2	.186	14	10	3	38	1	1	.975
Major league totals (1 year)			35	59	10	11	0	0	1	2	.186	14	10	3	38	1	1	.975

TUCKER, SCOOTER

C, ASTROS

PERSONAL: Born November 18, 1966, in Greenville, Miss. ... 6-2/205. ... Throws right, bats right. ... Full name: Eddie Jack Tucker.
HIGH SCHOOL: Washington (Greenville, Miss.).
COLLEGE: Delta State (Miss.).

TRANSACTIONS/CAREER NOTES: Selected by San Francisco Giants organization in fifth round of free-agent draft (June 1, 1988). ... Claimed on waivers by Houston Astros (September 25, 1991).
STATISTICAL NOTES: Led Texas League catchers with .995 fielding percentage, 673 putouts, 70 assists and 747 total chances in 1991.

									BATTING							FIELDING			
Year	**Team (League)**	**Pos.**	**G**	**AB**	**R**	**H**	**2B**	**3B**	**HR**	**RBI**	**Avg.**	**BB**	**SO**	**SB**	**PO**	**A**	**E**	**Avg.**
1988	—Everett (N'west)	C	45	153	24	40	5	0	3	23	.261	30	34	0	237	23	1	.996
1989	—Clinton (Midwest)	C-OF	126	426	44	105	20	2	3	43	.246	58	80	6	649	60	10	.986
1990	—San Jose (Calif.)	C-OF	123	439	59	123	28	2	5	71	.280	71	69	9	599	88	11	.984
1991	—Shreveport (Texas)	C-3B	110	352	49	100	29	1	4	49	.284	48	57	3	†673	†71	4	†.995
1992	—Tucson (PCL)■	C	83	288	36	87	15	1	1	29	.302	28	35	5	517	56	5	.991
	—Houston (N.L.)	C	20	50	5	6	1	0	0	3	.120	3	13	1	75	6	2	.976
1993	—Tucson (PCL)	C-1B-3B	98	318	54	87	20	2	1	37	.274	47	37	1	621	69	5	.993
	—Houston (N.L.)	C	9	26	1	5	1	0	0	3	.192	2	3	0	56	3	0	1.000
Major league totals (2 years)			29	76	6	11	2	0	0	6	.145	5	16	1	131	9	2	.986

TURANG, BRIAN

OF, MARINERS

PERSONAL: Born June 14, 1967, in Long Beach, Calif. ... 5-10/170. ... Throws right, bats right. ... Full name: Brian Craig Turang. ... Name pronounced tuh-RANG.
HIGH SCHOOL: Millikan (Long Beach, Calif.).
COLLEGE: Long Beach (Calif.) City College and Loyola Marymount.

TRANSACTIONS/CAREER NOTES: Selected by Milwaukee Brewers organization in 20th round of free-agent draft (June 2, 1987). ... Selected by Seattle Mariners organization in 51st round of free-agent draft (June 5, 1989). ... On Jacksonville disabled list (April 29-May 20, 1991). ... On San Bernardino disabled list (August 2, 1991-remainder of season). ... On disabled list (April 15-May 1, 1992).
STATISTICAL NOTES: Led Southern League second basemen with .976 fielding percentage, 283 putouts, 323 assists, 621 total chances and 75 double plays in 1992.

									BATTING							FIELDING			
Year	**Team (League)**	**Pos.**	**G**	**AB**	**R**	**H**	**2B**	**3B**	**HR**	**RBI**	**Avg.**	**BB**	**SO**	**SB**	**PO**	**A**	**E**	**Avg.**
1989	—Belling. (N'west)	2B-OF	60	207	42	59	10	3	4	11	.285	33	50	9	97	133	18	.927
1990	—San Bern. (Calif.)	2B-OF-SS	132	487	86	144	25	5	12	67	.296	69	98	25	239	304	14	.975
	—Calgary (PCL)	2B	3	9	1	2	0	0	0	1	.222	2	4	0	5	5	1	.909
1991	—Jacksonv. (South.)	2B-OF	41	130	14	28	6	2	0	7	.215	13	33	5	73	35	3	.973
	—San Bern. (Calif.)	2B-OF	34	100	9	18	2	1	0	4	.180	15	31	6	63	66	3	.977
1992	—Jacksonv. (South.)	2B-OF	129	483	67	121	21	3	14	63	.251	44	61	19	†286	†323	15	†.976
1993	—Calgary (PCL)	0-2-3-S	110	423	83	137	20	11	8	54	.324	40	48	24	221	75	13	.958
	—Seattle (A.L.)	OF-3B-2B	40	140	22	35	11	1	0	7	.250	17	20	6	72	2	1	.987
Major league totals (1 year)			40	140	22	35	11	1	0	7	.250	17	20	6	72	2	1	.987

TURNER, CHRIS

C, ANGELS

PERSONAL: Born March 23, 1969, in Bowling Green, Ky. ... 6-1/190. ... Throws right, bats right. ... Full name: Christopher Wan Turner.
HIGH SCHOOL: Warren Central (Bowling Green, Ky.).
COLLEGE: Western Kentucky (degree in psychology, 1991).

TRANSACTIONS/CAREER NOTES: Selected by California Angels organization in seventh round of free-agent draft (June 3, 1991).
STATISTICAL NOTES: Led Northwest League catchers with .997 fielding percentage in 1991. ... Led Pacific Coast League catchers with 17 passed balls in 1993.

									BATTING							FIELDING			
Year	**Team (League)**	**Pos.**	**G**	**AB**	**R**	**H**	**2B**	**3B**	**HR**	**RBI**	**Avg.**	**BB**	**SO**	**SB**	**PO**	**A**	**E**	**Avg.**
1991	—Boise (Northwest)	C-OF	52	163	26	37	5	0	2	29	.227	32	32	10	360	39	2	†.995
1992	—Quad City (Midw.)	C-1B	109	330	66	83	18	1	9	53	.252	85	65	8	727	98	9	.989
1993	—Vancouver (PCL)	C-1B	90	283	50	78	12	1	4	57	.276	49	44	6	524	56	6	.990
	—California (A.L.)	C	25	75	9	21	5	0	1	13	.280	9	16	1	116	14	1	.992
Major league totals (1 year)			25	75	9	21	5	0	1	13	.280	9	16	1	116	14	1	.992

TURNER, MATT

P, MARLINS

PERSONAL: Born February 18, 1967, in Lexington, Ky. ... 6-5/215. ... Throws right, bats right. ... Full name: William Matthew Turner.
HIGH SCHOOL: Lexington (Ky.) Catholic, then Lafayette (Lexington, Ky.).
COLLEGE: Middle Georgia College.

TRANSACTIONS/CAREER NOTES: Signed as free agent by Atlanta Braves organization (May 21, 1986). ... Traded by Braves with a player to be named later to Houston Astros for P Jim Clancy (July 31, 1991); Astros acquired P Earl Sanders to complete deal

(November 15, 1991).... Granted free agency (October 16, 1992).... Signed by Florida Marlins organization (October 21, 1992).

STATISTICAL NOTES: Tied for South Atlantic League lead with six balks in 1987.

Year	Team (League)	W	L	Pct.	ERA	G	GS	CG	ShO	Sv.	IP	H	R	ER	BB	SO
1986	—Pulaski (Appal.)	1	3	.250	4.62	18	5	0	0	2	48⅔	55	36	25	28	48
1987	—Sumter (S. Atl.)	2	3	.400	4.71	39	9	0	0	0	93⅔	91	61	49	48	102
1988	—Burlington (Midw.)	1	3	.250	6.55	7	6	0	0	0	34⅓	43	27	25	16	26
	—Sumter (S. Atl.)	1	0	1.000	4.60	7	0	0	0	0	15⅔	17	8	8	3	7
1989	—Durham (Carolina)	9	9	.500	2.44	53	3	0	0	1	118	95	38	32	47	114
1990	—Greenville (South.)	6	4	.600	2.66	40	0	0	0	4	67⅔	59	24	20	29	60
	—Richmond (Int'l)	2	3	.400	3.86	22	1	0	0	2	42	44	20	18	16	36
1991	—Richmond (Int'l)	1	3	.250	4.75	23	0	0	0	5	36	33	21	19	20	33
	—Tucson (PCL)■	1	1	.500	4.15	13	0	0	0	1	26	27	12	12	14	25
1992	—Tucson (PCL)	2	8	.200	3.51	63	0	0	0	14	100	93	52	39	40	84
1993	—Edmonton (PCL)■	0	0	...	0.66	12	0	0	0	10	13⅔	9	1	1	2	15
	—Florida (N.L.)	4	5	.444	2.91	55	0	0	0	0	68	55	23	22	26	59
Major league totals (1 year)		4	5	.444	2.91	55	0	0	0	0	68	55	23	22	26	59

URBANI, TOM

P, CARDINALS

PERSONAL: Born January 21, 1968, in Santa Cruz, Calif.... 6-1/190.... Throws left, bats left.... Full name: Thomas James Urbani.

HIGH SCHOOL: Harbor (Santa Cruz, Calif.).

COLLEGE: Cabrillo College (Calif.) and Long Beach State.

TRANSACTIONS/CAREER NOTES: Selected by Kansas City Royals organization in 33rd round of free-agent draft (June 2, 1986).... Selected by Texas Rangers organization in 34th round of free-agent draft (June 1, 1988).... Selected by Minnesota Twins organization in 29th round of free-agent draft (June 5, 1989).... Selected by St. Louis Cardinals organization in 13th round of free-agent draft (June 4, 1990).

Year	Team (League)	W	L	Pct.	ERA	G	GS	CG	ShO	Sv.	IP	H	R	ER	BB	SO
1990	—Johns. City (App.)	4	3	.571	3.35	9	9	0	0	0	48⅓	43	35	18	15	40
	—Hamilton (NYP)	0	4	.000	6.15	5	5	0	0	0	26⅓	33	26	18	15	17
1991	—Springfield (Midw.)	3	2	.600	2.08	8	8	0	0	0	47⅔	45	20	11	6	42
	—St. Peters. (FSL)	8	7	.533	2.35	19	19	2	1	0	118⅔	109	39	31	25	64
1992	—Arkansas (Texas)	4	6	.400	1.93	10	10	2	1	0	65⅓	49	23	14	15	41
	—Louisville (A.A.)	4	5	.444	4.67	16	16	0	0	0	88⅔	91	50	46	37	46
1993	—Louisville (A.A.)	9	5	.643	2.47	18	13	0	0	1	94⅔	86	29	26	23	65
	—St. Louis (N.L.)	1	3	.250	4.65	18	9	0	0	0	62	73	44	32	26	33
Major league totals (1 year)		1	3	.250	4.65	18	9	0	0	0	62	73	44	32	26	33

URIBE, JOSE

SS

PERSONAL: Born January 21, 1960, in San Cristobal, Dominican Republic.... 5-10/170.... Throws right, bats both.... Full name: Jose Alta Uribe.... Formerly known as Jose Alta Gonzalez.... Name pronounced yoo-REE-bay.

TRANSACTIONS/CAREER NOTES: Signed as free agent by New York Yankees organization (February 18, 1977).... Released by Yankees organization (July 5, 1977).... Signed by St. Louis Cardinals organization (August 18, 1980).... Traded by Cardinals with 1B David Green, 1B Gary Rajsich and P Dave LaPoint to San Francisco Giants for OF/1B Jack Clark (February 1, 1985).... On disabled list (April 11-30, May 5-20 and May 28-July 4, 1987; and May 31-June 16, 1988).... On San Francisco disabled list (April 4-19, 1991).... On San Francisco disabled list (June 18-July 23, 1991); included rehabilitation assignment to San Jose (July 4-10) and Phoenix (July 10-23).... On San Francisco disabled list (August 18-September 4, 1992).... Granted free agency (October 27, 1992).... Signed by Houston Astros (January 5, 1993).... Granted free agency (October 29, 1993).

STATISTICAL NOTES: Led Texas League shortstops with 88 double plays in 1982.... Led American Association shortstops with 664 total chances and 90 double plays in 1983.... Led American Association with 14 sacrifice hits in 1983.... Led American Association shortstops with 720 total chances and 96 double plays in 1984.... Led N.L. shortstops with 85 double plays in 1989.

				BATTING											FIELDING			
Year	Team (League)	Pos.	G	AB	R	H	2B	3B	HR	RBI	Avg.	BB	SO	SB	PO	A	E	Avg.
1981	—St. Peters. (FSL)	SS	128	463	54	124	15	2	0	40	.268	24	69	12	171	*387	32	.946
1982	—Arkansas (Texas)	SS	123	465	73	115	17	7	0	41	.247	40	65	16	185	385	36	.941
	—Louisville (A.A.)	SS	8	28	5	10	2	0	0	4	.357	1	4	0	15	18	1	.971
1983	—Louisville (A.A.)	SS	122	423	64	120	19	6	3	44	.284	35	45	26	206	425	*33	.950
1984	—Louisville (A.A.)	SS	145	484	68	135	20	2	3	46	.279	26	52	11	*233	*455	*32	*.956
	—St. Louis (N.L.)	SS-2B	8	19	4	4	0	0	0	3	.211	0	2	1	7	15	1	.957
1985	—San Francisco (N.L.)■	SS-2B	147	476	46	113	20	4	3	26	.237	30	57	8	209	438	26	.961
1986	—San Francisco (N.L.)	SS	157	453	46	101	15	1	3	43	.223	61	76	22	249	444	16	.977
1987	—San Francisco (N.L.)	SS	95	309	44	90	16	5	5	30	.291	24	35	12	145	286	13	.971
1988	—San Francisco (N.L.)	SS	141	493	47	124	10	7	3	35	.252	36	69	14	212	404	19	.970
1989	—San Francisco (N.L.)	SS	151	453	34	100	12	6	1	30	.221	34	74	6	225	436	18	.973
1990	—San Francisco (N.L.)	SS	138	415	35	103	8	6	1	24	.248	29	49	5	182	373	20	.965
1991	—San Francisco (N.L.)	SS	90	231	23	51	8	4	1	12	.221	20	33	3	98	218	11	.966
	—San Jose (Calif.)	SS	3	9	0	1	0	1	0	1	.111	1	2	0	5	6	0	1.000
	—Phoenix (PCL)	SS	11	41	7	14	1	1	0	4	.341	1	2	0	16	34	1	.980
1992	—San Francisco (N.L.)	SS	66	162	24	39	9	1	2	13	.241	14	25	2	75	157	7	.971
1993	—Houston (N.L.)■	SS	45	53	4	13	1	0	0	3	.245	8	5	1	34	51	5	.944
Major league totals (10 years)			1038	3064	307	738	99	34	19	219	.241	256	425	74	1436	2822	136	.969

CHAMPIONSHIP SERIES RECORD

				BATTING											FIELDING			
Year	Team (League)	Pos.	G	AB	R	H	2B	3B	HR	RBI	Avg.	BB	SO	SB	PO	A	E	Avg.
1987	—San Francisco (N.L.)	SS	7	26	1	7	1	0	0	2	.269	0	4	1	11	20	1	.969

Year	Team (League)	Pos.	G	AB	R	H	2B	3B	HR	RBI	Avg.	BB	SO	SB	PO	A	E	Avg.
			BATTING												FIELDING			
1989	—San Francisco (N.L.)..	SS	5	17	2	4	1	0	0	1	.235	1	5	1	6	9	2	.882
Championship series totals (2 years)			12	43	3	11	2	0	0	3	.256	1	9	2	17	29	3	.939

WORLD SERIES RECORD

Year	Team (League)	Pos.	G	AB	R	H	2B	3B	HR	RBI	Avg.	BB	SO	SB	PO	A	E	Avg.
			BATTING												FIELDING			
1989	—San Francisco (N.L.)..	SS	3	5	1	1	0	0	0	0	.200	0	0	0	1	3	0	1.000

VALDEZ, SERGIO

P

PERSONAL: Born September 7, 1965, in Elias Pina, Dominican Republic. . . . 6-1/190. . . . Throws right, bats right. . . . Full name: Sergio Sanchez Valdez.

TRANSACTIONS/CAREER NOTES: Signed as free agent by Montreal Expos organization (June 18, 1983). . . . On West Palm Beach disabled list (May 17-June 3, 1984). . . . Traded by Expos organization with P Nate Minchey and OF Kevin Dean to Atlanta Braves for P Zane Smith (July 2, 1989). . . . Claimed on waivers by Cleveland Indians (April 30, 1990). . . . Released by Indians (March 25, 1991). . . . Re-signed by Indians organization (April 3, 1991). . . . Granted free agency (October 16, 1991). . . . Signed by Montreal Expos organization (December 10, 1991). . . . On Ottawa disabled list (April 24-May 16, 1993). . . . Granted free agency (October 15, 1993).

Year	Team (League)	W	L	Pct.	ERA	G	GS	CG	ShO	Sv.	IP	H	R	ER	BB	SO
1983	—Calgary (Pioneer)	6	3	.667	5.57	13	13	1	0	0	72⅔	88	55	45	31	41
1984	—W.P. Beach (FSL)	0	0	...	8.74	5	0	0	0	0	11⅓	15	11	11	8	6
	—Jamestown (NYP)......	2	7	.222	4.03	13	12	5	1	0	76	78	47	34	33	46
1985	—Utica (N.Y.-Penn)......	6	5	.545	3.07	15	•15	5	0	0	105⅔	98	53	36	36	86
1986	—W.P. Beach (FSL)	*16	6	.727	2.47	24	24	6	•4	0	145⅔	119	48	40	46	108
	—Montreal (N.L.)	0	4	.000	6.84	5	5	0	0	0	25	39	20	19	11	20
1987	—Indianapolis (A.A.).....	10	7	.588	5.12	27	27	2	•2	0	158⅓	191	108	90	64	*128
1988	—Indianapolis (A.A.).....	5	4	.556	3.43	14	14	0	0	0	84	80	38	32	28	61
1989	—Indianapolis (A.A.).....	6	3	.667	3.28	19	12	0	0	1	90⅔	78	38	33	26	81
	—Atlanta (N.L.)■..........	1	2	.333	6.06	19	1	0	0	0	32⅔	31	24	22	17	26
1990	—Atlanta (N.L.)............	0	0	...	6.75	6	0	0	0	0	5⅓	6	4	4	3	3
	—Cleveland (A.L.)■.......	6	6	.500	4.75	24	13	0	0	0	102⅓	109	62	54	35	63
	—Colo. Springs (PCL)......	4	3	.571	5.19	7	7	2	1	0	43⅓	55	29	25	13	33
1991	—Colo. Springs (PCL).....	4	•12	.250	4.11	26	15	4	0	0	131⅓	139	67	60	27	71
	—Cleveland (A.L.)	1	0	1.000	5.51	6	0	0	0	0	16⅓	15	11	10	5	11
1992	—Indianapolis (A.A.)■....	4	2	.667	3.75	13	8	0	0	0	62⅓	59	29	26	13	41
	—Montreal (N.L.)...........	0	2	.000	2.41	27	0	0	0	0	37⅓	25	12	10	12	32
1993	—Ottawa (Int'l)	5	3	.625	3.12	30	4	0	0	1	83⅔	77	31	29	22	53
	—Montreal (N.L.)...........	0	0	...	9.00	4	0	0	0	0	3	4	4	3	1	2
A.L. totals (2 years)		7	6	.538	4.85	30	13	0	0	0	118⅔	124	73	64	40	74
N.L. totals (5 years)		1	8	.111	5.05	61	6	0	0	0	103⅓	105	64	58	44	83
Major league totals (6 years)		8	14	.364	4.95	91	19	0	0	0	222	229	137	122	84	157

VALENTIN, JOHN

SS, RED SOX

PERSONAL: Born February 18, 1967, in Mineola, N.Y. . . . 6-0/180. . . . Throws right, bats right. . . . Full name: John William Valentin. . . . Name pronounced VAL-en-tin.

HIGH SCHOOL: St. Anthony (Jersey City, N.J.).

COLLEGE: Seton Hall.

TRANSACTIONS/CAREER NOTES: Selected by Boston Red Sox organization in fifth round of free-agent draft (June 1, 1988). . . . On Boston disabled list (April 1-20, 1993); included rehabilitation assignment to Pawtucket (April 16-20).

STATISTICAL NOTES: Led New York-Pennsylvania League shortstops with .949 fielding percentage in 1988.

Year	Team (League)	Pos.	G	AB	R	H	2B	3B	HR	RBI	Avg.	BB	SO	SB	PO	A	E	Avg.
			BATTING												FIELDING			
1988	—Elmira (N.Y.-Penn)..	SS-3B	60	207	18	45	5	1	2	16	.217	36	35	5	96	175	14	†.951
1989	—Winter Haven (FSL)..	SS-3B	55	215	27	58	13	1	3	18	.270	13	29	4	99	177	12	.958
	—Lynchburg (Caro.)...	SS	75	264	47	65	7	2	8	34	.246	41	40	5	105	220	16	.953
1990	—New Britain (East.)..	SS	94	312	20	68	18	1	2	31	.218	25	46	1	139	266	21	.951
1991	—New Britain (East.)..	SS	23	81	8	16	3	0	0	5	.198	9	14	1	50	65	3	.975
	—Pawtucket (Int'l)......	SS	100	329	52	87	22	4	9	49	.264	60	42	0	184	300	25	.951
1992	—Pawtucket (Int'l)......	SS	97	331	47	86	18	1	9	29	.260	48	50	1	148	*358	20	.962
	—Boston (A.L.)...........	SS	58	185	21	51	13	0	5	25	.276	20	17	1	79	182	10	.963
1993	—Pawtucket (Int'l)......	SS	2	9	3	3	0	0	1	1	.333	0	1	0	8	9	0	1.000
	—Boston (A.L.)...........	SS	144	468	50	130	40	3	11	66	.278	49	77	3	238	432	20	.971
Major league totals (2 years)			202	653	71	181	53	3	16	91	.277	69	94	4	317	614	30	.969

VALENTIN, JOSE

SS, BREWERS

PERSONAL: Born October 12, 1969, in Manati, Puerto Rico. . . . 5-10/175. . . . Throws right, bats both. . . . Full name: Jose Antonio Valentin. . . . Brother of Jose Valentin, infielder, Minnesota Twins organization. . . . Name pronounced VAL-un-TEEN.

TRANSACTIONS/CAREER NOTES: Signed as free agent by San Diego Padres organization (October 12, 1986). . . . On disabled list (April 16-May 1 and May 18-July 11, 1990). . . . Traded by Padres with P Ricky Bones and OF Matt Mieske to Milwaukee Brewers for 3B Gary Sheffield and P Geoff Kellogg (March 27, 1992).

STATISTICAL NOTES: Led Texas League shortstops with 658 total chances in 1991. . . . Led American Association shortstops with 639 total chances and 70 double plays in 1992. . . . Led American Association shortstops with 211 putouts and 80 double plays in 1993.

Year	Team (League)	Pos.	G	AB	R	H	2B	3B	HR	RBI	Avg.	BB	SO	SB	PO	A	E	Avg.
			BATTING												FIELDING			
1987	—Spokane (N'west).....	SS	70	244	52	61	8	2	2	24	.250	35	38	8	101	175	26	.914
1988	—Char., S.C. (S. Atl.)...	SS	133	444	56	103	20	1	6	44	.232	45	83	11	204	412	60	.911

UV

Year	Team (League)	Pos.	G	AB	R	H	2B	3B	HR	RBI	Avg.	BB	SO	SB	PO	A	E	Avg.
			BATTING												FIELDING			
1989	—Riverside (Calif.)	SS	114	381	40	74	10	5	10	41	.194	37	93	8	*227	333	*46	.924
	—Wichita (Texas)	SS-3B	18	49	8	12	1	0	2	5	.245	5	12	1	26	45	8	.899
1990	—Wichita (Texas)	SS	11	36	4	10	2	0	0	2	.278	5	7	2	14	33	2	.959
1991	—Wichita (Texas)	SS	129	447	73	112	22	5	17	68	.251	55	115	8	176	*442	40	.939
1992	—Denver (A.A.)■	SS	*139	492	78	118	19	11	3	45	.240	53	99	9	*187	*414	*38	.941
	—Milwaukee (A.L.)	SS-2B	4	3	1	0	0	0	0	1	.000	0	0	0	1	1	1	.667
1993	—New Orleans (A.A.)	SS-1B	122	389	56	96	22	5	9	53	.247	47	87	9	†212	351	29	.951
	—Milwaukee (A.L.)	SS	19	53	10	13	1	2	1	7	.245	7	16	1	20	51	6	.922
Major league totals (2 years)			23	56	11	13	1	2	1	8	.232	7	16	1	21	52	7	.913

VALENZUELA, FERNANDO

P

PERSONAL: Born November 1, 1960, in Navajoa, Sonora, Mexico. . . . 5-11/202. . . . Throws left, bats left. . . . Full name: Fernando Anguamea Valenzuela. . . . Name pronounced VAL-en-ZWAY-luh.

TRANSACTIONS/CAREER NOTES: Contract sold by Puebla of Mexican League to Los Angeles Dodgers organization (July 6, 1979). . . . On disabled list (July 31-September 26, 1988). . . . Granted free agency (November 13, 1989). . . . Re-signed by Dodgers (December 15, 1989). . . . Granted free agency (November 5, 1990). . . . Re-signed by Dodgers (December 19, 1990). . . . Released by Dodgers (March 28, 1991). . . . Signed by California Angels organization (May 20, 1991). . . . On California disabled list (June 13-July 5, 1991). . . . Released by Angels (July 5, 1991). . . . Re-signed by Angels organization (July 10, 1991). . . . Released by Angels organization (September 10, 1991). . . . Signed by Toledo, Detroit Tigers organization (March 20, 1992). . . . Loaned by Toledo to Jalisco of Mexican League (March 20-June 3, 1992). . . . Contract acquired by Jalisco from Tigers organization (June 3, 1992). . . . Signed as free agent by Baltimore Orioles organization (February 27, 1993). . . . Granted free agency (October 29, 1993).

RECORDS: Shares modern major league rookie-season record for most shutout games won or tied—8 (1981). . . . Shares N.L. single-season record for fewest assists by pitcher who led league in assists—47 (1986).

HONORS: Named Major League Player of the Year by THE SPORTING NEWS (1981). . . . Named N.L. Pitcher of the Year by THE SPORTING NEWS (1981). . . . Named N.L. Rookie Pitcher of the Year by THE SPORTING NEWS (1981). . . . Named lefthanded pitcher on THE SPORTING NEWS N.L. All-Star team (1981 and 1986). . . . Named pitcher on THE SPORTING NEWS N.L. Silver Slugger team (1981 and 1983). . . . Named N.L. Cy Young Award winner by Baseball Writers' Association of America (1981). . . . Named N.L. Rookie of the Year by Baseball Writers' Association of America (1981). . . . Won N.L. Gold Glove at pitcher (1986).

STATISTICAL NOTES: Led Mexican Center League with 13 wild pitches in 1978. . . . Led N.L. with 14 wild pitches in 1987. . . . Pitched 6-0 no-hit victory against St. Louis (June 29, 1990).

MISCELLANEOUS: Appeared in one game as outfielder with no chances (1982). . . . Appeared in one game as first baseman with two putouts (1989).

Year	Team (League)	W	L	Pct.	ERA	G	GS	CG	ShO	Sv.	IP	H	R	ER	BB	SO
1978	—Guana. (Mex. Cen.)	5	6	.455	2.23	16	13	6	0	1	93	88	46	23	46	*91
1979	—Yucatan (Mexican)	10	12	.455	2.49	26	26	12	2	0	181	157	68	50	70	141
	—Lodi (California)■	1	2	.333	1.13	3	3	0	0	0	24	21	10	3	3	18
1980	—San Antonio (Tex.)	13	9	.591	3.10	27	25	11	4	0	174	156	70	60	70	*162
	—Los Angeles (N.L.)	2	0	1.000	0.00	10	0	0	0	1	18	8	2	0	5	16
1981	—Los Angeles (N.L.)	13	7	.650	2.48	25	•25	*11	*8	0	*192	140	55	53	61	*180
1982	—Los Angeles (N.L.)	19	13	.594	2.87	37	37	18	4	0	285	247	105	91	83	199
1983	—Los Angeles (N.L.)	15	10	.600	3.75	35	35	9	4	0	257	245	*122	107	99	189
1984	—Los Angeles (N.L.)	12	17	.414	3.03	34	34	12	2	0	261	218	109	88	*106	240
1985	—Los Angeles (N.L.)	17	10	.630	2.45	35	35	14	5	0	272⅓	211	92	74	101	208
1986	—Los Angeles (N.L.)	*21	11	.656	3.14	34	34	*20	3	0	269⅓	226	104	94	85	242
1987	—Los Angeles (N.L.)	14	14	.500	3.98	34	34	•12	1	0	251	*254	120	111	*124	190
1988	—Los Angeles (N.L.)	5	8	.385	4.24	23	22	3	0	1	142⅓	142	71	67	76	64
1989	—Los Angeles (N.L.)	10	13	.435	3.43	31	31	3	0	0	196⅔	185	89	75	98	116
1990	—Los Angeles (N.L.)	13	13	.500	4.59	33	33	5	2	0	204	223	112	*104	77	115
1991	—Palm Springs (Cal.)■	0	0	...	0.00	1	1	0	0	0	4	4	1	0	3	2
	—Midland (Texas)	3	1	.750	1.96	4	4	1	1	0	23	18	5	5	6	17
	—California (A.L.)	0	2	.000	12.15	2	2	0	0	0	6⅔	14	10	9	3	5
	—Edmonton (PCL)	3	3	.500	7.12	7	7	0	0	0	36⅔	48	34	29	17	36
1992	—Jalisco (Mexican)■	10	9	.526	3.86	22	22	•13	0	0	156⅓	154	81	67	51	98
1993	—Baltimore (A.L.)■	8	10	.444	4.94	32	31	5	2	0	178⅔	179	104	98	79	78
	—Rochester (Int'l)	0	1	.000	10.80	1	1	0	0	0	3⅓	6	4	4	3	1
	—Bowie (Eastern)	0	0	...	1.50	1	1	0	0	0	6	4	1	1	0	4
A.L. totals (2 years)		8	12	.400	5.20	34	33	5	2	0	185⅓	193	114	107	82	83
N.L. totals (11 years)		141	116	.549	3.31	331	320	107	29	2	2348⅔	2099	981	864	915	1759
Major league totals (13 years)		149	128	.538	3.45	365	353	112	31	2	2534	2292	1095	971	997	1842

DIVISION SERIES RECORD

Year	Team (League)	W	L	Pct.	ERA	G	GS	CG	ShO	Sv.	IP	H	R	ER	BB	SO
1981	—Los Angeles (N.L.)	1	0	1.000	1.06	2	2	1	0	0	17	10	2	2	3	10

CHAMPIONSHIP SERIES RECORD

CHAMPIONSHIP SERIES NOTES: Holds N.L. single-game record for most bases on balls allowed—8 (October 14, 1985). . . . Shares N.L. single-series record for most bases on balls allowed—10 (1985).

Year	Team (League)	W	L	Pct.	ERA	G	GS	CG	ShO	Sv.	IP	H	R	ER	BB	SO
1981	—Los Angeles (N.L.)	1	1	.500	2.45	2	2	0	0	0	14⅔	10	4	4	5	10
1983	—Los Angeles (N.L.)	1	0	1.000	1.13	1	1	0	0	0	8	7	1	1	4	5
1985	—Los Angeles (N.L.)	1	0	1.000	1.88	2	2	0	0	0	14⅓	11	3	3	10	13
Champ. series totals (3 years)		3	1	.750	1.95	5	5	0	0	0	37	28	8	8	19	28

WORLD SERIES RECORD

Year	Team (League)	W	L	Pct.	ERA	G	GS	CG	ShO	Sv.	IP	H	R	ER	BB	SO
1981	—Los Angeles (N.L.)	1	0	1.000	4.00	1	1	1	0	0	9	9	4	4	7	6

ALL-STAR GAME RECORD

ALL-STAR GAME NOTES: Shares single-game record for most consecutive strikeouts—5 (July 15, 1986).

Year	League	W	L	Pct.	ERA	GS	CG	ShO	Sv.	IP	H	R	ER	BB	SO
1981	—National	0	0	...	0.00	1	0	0	0	1	2	0	0	0	0
1982	—National	0	0	...	0.00	0	0	0	0	⅔	0	0	0	2	0
1983	—National						Did not play.								
1984	—National	0	0	...	0.00	0	0	0	0	2	2	0	0	0	3
1985	—National	0	0	...	0.00	0	0	0	0	1	0	0	0	1	1
1986	—National	0	0	...	0.00	0	0	0	0	3	1	0	0	0	5
All-Star totals (5 years)		0	0	...	0.00	1	0	0	0	7⅔	5	0	0	3	9

VALERA, JULIO

P, ANGELS

PERSONAL: Born October 13, 1968, in San Sebastian, Puerto Rico. . . . 6-2/215. . . . Throws right, bats right. . . . Full name: Julio Enrique Valera. . . . Name pronounced vuh-LAIR-uh.

HIGH SCHOOL: Manual Mendez Liciago (San Sebastian, Puerto Rico).

TRANSACTIONS/CAREER NOTES: Signed as free agent by New York Mets organization (February 6, 1986). . . . Traded by Mets with a player to be named later to California Angels for SS Dick Schofield (April 12, 1992); Angels acquired P Julian Vasquez from Mets to complete deal (October 6, 1992). . . . On disabled list (June 24, 1993-remainder of season).

Year	Team (League)	W	L	Pct.	ERA	G	GS	CG	ShO	Sv.	IP	H	R	ER	BB	SO
1986	—Kingsport (Appal.)	3	•10	.231	5.19	13	13	2	1	0	76⅓	91	58	44	29	64
1987	—Columbia (S. Atl.)	8	7	.533	2.80	22	22	2	2	0	125⅓	114	53	39	31	97
1988	—Columbia (S. Atl.)	15	11	.577	3.20	30	27	8	0	1	191	171	77	68	51	144
1989	—St. Lucie (Fla. St.)	4	2	.667	1.00	6	6	3	2	0	45	34	5	5	6	45
	—Jackson (Texas)	10	6	.625	*2.49	19	19	6	2	0	137⅓	123	47	38	36	107
	—Tidewater (Int'l)	1	1	.500	2.08	2	2	0	0	0	13	8	3	3	5	10
1990	—Tidewater (Int'l)	10	10	.500	3.02	24	24	9	2	1	158	146	66	53	39	133
	—New York (N.L.)	1	1	.500	6.92	3	3	0	0	0	13	20	11	10	7	4
1991	—Tidewater (Int'l)	10	10	.500	3.83	26	26	3	1	0	*176⅓	152	79	75	70	117
	—New York (N.L.)	0	0	...	0.00	2	0	0	0	0	2	1	0	0	4	3
1992	—Tidewater (Int'l)	1	0	1.000	0.00	1	1	0	0	0	6	5	0	0	2	7
	—California (A.L.)■	8	11	.421	3.73	30	28	4	2	0	188	188	82	78	64	113
1993	—California (A.L.)	3	6	.333	6.62	19	5	0	0	4	53	77	44	39	15	28
A.L. totals (2 years)		11	17	.393	4.37	49	33	4	2	4	241	265	126	117	79	141
N.L. totals (2 years)		1	1	.500	6.00	5	3	0	0	0	15	21	11	10	11	7
Major league totals (4 years)		12	18	.400	4.46	54	36	4	2	4	256	286	137	127	90	148

VALLE, DAVE

C, RED SOX

PERSONAL: Born October 30, 1960, in Bayside, N.Y. . . . 6-2/220. . . . Throws right, bats right. . . . Brother of John Valle, minor league outfielder (1972-84). . . . Name pronounced VALLEY.

HIGH SCHOOL: Holy Cross (Flushing, N.Y.).

TRANSACTIONS/CAREER NOTES: Selected by Seattle Mariners organization in second round of free-agent draft (June 6, 1978). . . . On disabled list (July 26-August 25, 1979; June 24-July 3, 1981; April 13-June 20 and June 27-July 7, 1983). . . . On Salt Lake City disabled list (May 4-17 and June 9-25, 1984). . . . On Seattle disabled list (April 26-July 19, 1985); included rehabilitation assignment to Calgary (June 26-July 12). . . . On disabled list (April 17-May 7, 1987 and July 23-September 2, 1988). . . . On Seattle disabled list (May 30-July 6, 1989); included rehabilitation assignment to Calgary (July 4-6). . . . On disabled list (May 18-June 17, 1990). . . . On suspended list (July 21-24, 1991). . . . On disabled list (May 9-26, 1992). . . . Granted free agency (October 26, 1993). . . . Signed by Boston Red Sox (December 30, 1993).

STATISTICAL NOTES: Led Northwest League catchers with six double plays and tied for lead with 23 passed balls in 1978. . . . Led California League catchers with 102 assists in 1980. . . . Led A.L. catchers with .997 fielding percentage in 1990. . . . Led A.L. in being hit by pitch with 17 in 1993. . . . Tied for A.L. lead in double plays by catcher with 13 in 1993.

			BATTING												FIELDING			
Year	Team (League)	Pos.	G	AB	R	H	2B	3B	HR	RBI	Avg.	BB	SO	SB	PO	A	E	Avg.
1978	—Belling. (N'west)	C	57	167	12	34	2	0	2	21	.204	16	34	3	*338	65	10	.976
1979	—Alexandria (Caro.)	C	58	169	17	36	5	0	6	25	.213	23	24	1	290	44	11	.968
1980	—San Jose (Calif.)	C-P	119	430	81	126	14	0	12	70	.293	50	54	6	570	†102	17	.975
1981	—Lynn (Eastern)	C	93	318	38	82	16	0	11	54	.258	36	48	3	445	56	6	.988
1982	—Salt Lake City (PCL)	C-1B	75	234	28	49	11	1	4	28	.209	26	26	0	347	49	11	.973
1983	—Chatt. (South.)	C-1B	53	176	20	42	11	0	3	22	.239	24	28	0	239	24	4	.985
1984	—Salt Lake City (PCL)	C	86	284	54	79	13	1	12	54	.278	45	36	0	433	34	6	.987
	—Seattle (A.L.)	C	13	27	4	8	1	0	1	4	.296	1	5	0	56	5	0	1.000
1985	—Seattle (A.L.)	C	31	70	2	11	1	0	0	4	.157	1	17	0	117	7	3	.976
	—Calgary (PCL)	C	42	131	17	45	8	0	6	26	.344	20	19	0	202	11	1	.995
1986	—Calgary (PCL)	C	105	353	71	110	21	2	21	72	.312	41	43	5	404	61	6	.987
	—Seattle (A.L.)	C-1B	22	53	10	18	3	0	5	15	.340	7	7	0	90	3	2	.979
1987	—Seattle (A.L.)	C-1B-OF	95	324	40	83	16	3	12	53	.256	15	46	2	422	34	5	.989
1988	—Seattle (A.L.)	C-1B	93	290	29	67	15	2	10	50	.231	18	38	0	490	47	6	.989
1989	—Seattle (A.L.)	C	94	316	32	75	10	3	7	34	.237	29	32	0	496	52	4	.993
	—Calgary (PCL)	C	2	6	0	0	0	0	0	0	.000	0	0	0	6	0	0	1.000
1990	—Seattle (A.L.)	C-1B	107	308	37	66	15	0	7	33	.214	45	48	1	633	44	2	†.997
1991	—Seattle (A.L.)	C	132	324	38	63	8	1	8	32	.194	34	49	0	676	52	6	.992
1992	—Seattle (A.L.)	C	124	367	39	88	16	1	9	30	.240	27	58	0	606	62	7	.990
1993	—Seattle (A.L.)	C	135	423	48	109	19	0	13	63	.258	48	56	1	*881	71	5	.995
Major league totals (10 years)			846	2502	279	588	104	10	72	318	.235	225	356	4	4467	377	40	.992

RECORD AS PITCHER

Year	Team (League)	W	L	Pct.	ERA	G	GS	CG	ShO	Sv.	IP	H	R	ER	BB	SO
1980	—San Jose (Calif.)	0	0	...	0.00	1	0	0	0	0	1	1	0	0	2	2

VAN BURKLEO, TY

1B/OF, ROCKIES

PERSONAL: Born October 7, 1963, in Oakland, Calif. . . . 6-5/225. . . . Throws left, bats left. . . . Full name: Tyler Lee Van Burkleo. . . . Son of Dutch Van Burkleo, minor league infielder (1952-59).
HIGH SCHOOL: Chatsworth (Calif.).

TRANSACTIONS/CAREER NOTES: Signed as free agent by Milwaukee Brewers organization (December 19, 1981). . . . Released by Brewers organization (June 27, 1984). . . . Signed by California Angels organization (August 4, 1984). . . . Released by Angels organization (June 2, 1987). . . . Played in Japan (1987-91). . . . Contract sold by Seibu Lions to Hiroshima Carp (November 16, 1990). . . . Released by Hiroshima following 1991 season. . . . Signed as free agent by Angels organization (January 15, 1992). . . . Granted free agency (October 15, 1993). . . . Signed by Colorado Springs, Colorado Rockies organization (December 2, 1993).
STATISTICAL NOTES: Led California League with 11 sacrifice flies in 1986.

			BATTING												FIELDING			
Year	Team (League)	Pos.	G	AB	R	H	2B	3B	HR	RBI	Avg.	BB	SO	SB	PO	A	E	Avg.
1982	—Beloit (Midwest)	1B	129	412	61	99	21	1	22	65	.240	77	135	5	1036	64	*23	.980
1983	—Stockton (Calif.)	1B	111	347	42	71	23	3	7	37	.205	40	117	8	759	57	16	.981
1984	—Stockton (Calif.)	1B	47	129	14	21	5	0	1	12	.163	22	48	2	301	16	4	.988
	—Peoria (Midwest)■	OF-1B	26	73	13	23	7	1	1	10	.315	15	27	4	83	1	4	.955
1985	—Redwood (Calif.)	1B-OF	118	366	53	101	20	5	10	52	.276	52	99	8	523	38	10	.982
1986	—Palm Springs (Cal.)	1B-OF	135	485	94	130	28	3	22	*108	.268	97	128	11	1124	73	15	.988
1987	—Midland (Texas)	OF-1B	48	183	38	60	12	4	12	33	.328	23	58	3	202	15	4	.982
	—Seibu (Jp. Pac.)■	1B-OF	34	122	19	34	...	...	6	20	.279	...	...	...	...	...	...	...
1988	—Seibu (Jp. Pac.)	1B-OF	118	366	67	98	10	2	38	90	.268	...	...	3	...	...	...	...
1989	—Seibu (Jp. Pac.)	DH	36	119	14	25	...	...	6	11	.210	16	34	0	...	...	...	...
1990	—Seibu (Jp. Pac.)	OF	41	112	22	22	...	...	9	22	.196	14	34	0	...	...	...	...
1991	—Hiroshima (Jp. Cn.)■	1B-OF	29	59	2	12	...	...	2	5	.203	14	22	0	...	...	...	...
1992	—Edmonton (PCL)■	1B-OF	135	458	83	125	28	7	19	88	.273	75	100	20	695	37	7	.991
1993	—Vancouver (PCL)	1B-OF	105	361	47	99	19	2	6	56	.274	51	89	7	781	51	13	.985
	—California (A.L.)	1B	12	33	2	5	3	0	1	1	.152	6	9	1	99	3	0	1.000
Major league totals (1 year)			12	33	2	5	3	0	1	1	.152	6	9	1	99	3	0	1.000

VANDER WAL, JOHN

OF/1B, EXPOS

PERSONAL: Born April 29, 1966, in Grand Rapids, Mich. . . . 6-2/190. . . . Throws left, bats left. . . . Full name: John Henry Vander Wal.
HIGH SCHOOL: Hudsonville (Mich.).
COLLEGE: Western Michigan.

TRANSACTIONS/CAREER NOTES: Selected by Houston Astros organization in eighth round of free-agent draft (June 4, 1984). . . . Selected by Montreal Expos organization in third round of free-agent draft (June 2, 1987).

			BATTING												FIELDING			
Year	Team (League)	Pos.	G	AB	R	H	2B	3B	HR	RBI	Avg.	BB	SO	SB	PO	A	E	Avg.
1987	—Jamestown (NYP)	OF	18	69	24	33	12	3	3	15	.478	3	14	3	20	0	0	1.000
	—W.P. Beach (FSL)	OF	50	189	29	54	11	2	2	22	.286	30	25	8	103	1	3	.972
1988	—W.P. Beach (FSL)	OF	62	231	50	64	15	2	10	33	.277	32	40	11	109	3	1	.991
	—Jacksonv. (South.)	OF	58	208	22	54	14	0	3	14	.260	17	49	3	99	0	0	1.000
1989	—Jacksonv. (South.)	OF	71	217	30	55	9	2	6	24	.253	22	51	2	72	3	1	.987
1990	—Indianapolis (A.A.)	OF	51	135	16	40	6	0	2	14	.296	13	28	0	48	4	2	.963
	—Jacksonv. (South.)	OF	77	277	45	84	25	3	8	40	.303	39	46	6	106	4	1	.991
1991	—Indianapolis (A.A.)	OF	133	478	84	140	36	8	15	71	.293	79	118	8	197	7	1	*.995
	—Montreal (N.L.)	OF	21	61	4	13	4	1	1	8	.213	1	18	0	29	0	0	1.000
1992	—Montreal (N.L.)	OF-1B	105	213	21	51	8	2	4	20	.239	24	36	3	122	6	2	.985
1993	—Montreal (N.L.)	1B-OF	106	215	34	50	7	4	5	30	.233	27	30	6	271	14	4	.986
Major league totals (3 years)			232	489	59	114	19	7	10	58	.233	52	84	9	422	20	6	.987

VANEGMOND, TIM

P, RED SOX

PERSONAL: Born May 31, 1969, in Shreveport, La. . . . 6-2/180. . . . Throws right, bats right. . . . Full name: Timothy Layne Vanegmond. . . . Name pronounced VAN-eg-mond.
HIGH SCHOOL: East Coweta (Senoia, Ga.).
COLLEGE: Southern Union State Junior College (Ala.) and Jacksonville (Ala.) State.
TRANSACTIONS/CAREER NOTES: Selected by Boston Red Sox organization in 17th round of free-agent draft (June 3, 1991).
STATISTICAL NOTES: Led Carolina League with 18 wild pitches in 1992. . . . Pitched 2-0 no-hit victory against Prince William (June 1, 1992). . . . Led Eastern League with 14 hit batsmen in 1993.

Year	Team (League)	W	L	Pct.	ERA	G	GS	CG	ShO	Sv.	IP	H	R	ER	BB	SO
1991	—GC Red Sox (GCL)	2	0	1.000	0.60	3	2	0	0	1	15	6	1	1	1	20
	—Winter Haven (FSL)	4	5	.444	3.03	13	10	4	2	2	68⅓	69	32	23	23	47
1992	—Lynchburg (Caro.)	12	4	.750	3.42	28	27	2	1	0	173⅔	161	73	66	52	140
1993	—New Britain (East.)	6	12	.333	3.97	29	*29	1	1	0	*190⅓	182	*99	84	44	*163

VanLANDINGHAM, BILL

P, GIANTS

PERSONAL: Born July 16, 1970, in Columbia, Tenn. . . . 6-2/210. . . . Throws right, bats right. . . . Full name: William Joseph VanLandingham.
HIGH SCHOOL: Battle Ground Academy (Franklin, Tenn.).
COLLEGE: Kentucky.

TRANSACTIONS/CAREER NOTES: Selected by San Francisco Giants organization in fifth round of free-agent draft (June 3, 1991).

. . . On San Jose disabled list (May 30-July 14, 1992).
STATISTICAL NOTES: Led Northwest League with 25 wild pitches in 1991.

Year	Team (League)	W	L	Pct.	ERA	G	GS	CG	ShO	Sv.	IP	H	R	ER	BB	SO
1991	—Everett (N'west)	•8	4	.667	4.09	15	15	0	0	0	77	58	43	35	*79	86
1992	—San Jose (Calif.)	1	3	.250	5.57	6	6	0	0	0	21	22	18	13	13	18
	—Clinton (Midwest)	0	4	.000	5.67	10	10	0	0	0	54	49	40	34	29	59
1993	—San Jose (Calif.)	•14	8	.636	5.12	27	•27	1	0	0	163⅓	167	103	*93	87	*171
	—Phoenix (PCL)	0	1	.000	6.43	1	1	0	0	0	7	8	6	5	0	2

VAN POPPEL, TODD

P, ATHLETICS

PERSONAL: Born December 9, 1971, in Hinsdale, Ill. . . . 6-5/210. . . . Throws right, bats right. . . . Full name: Todd Matthew Van Poppel.
HIGH SCHOOL: St. Martin (Arlington, Tex.).
TRANSACTIONS/CAREER NOTES: Selected by Oakland Athletics organization in first round (14th pick overall) of free-agent draft (June 4, 1990); pick received as part of compensation for Milwaukee Brewers signing Type A free agent Dave Parker. . . . On disabled list (May 28-September 11, 1992).

Year	Team (League)	W	L	Pct.	ERA	G	GS	CG	ShO	Sv.	IP	H	R	ER	BB	SO
1990	—S. Oregon (N'west)	1	1	.500	1.13	5	5	0	0	0	24	10	5	3	9	32
	—Madison (Midwest)	2	1	.667	3.95	3	3	0	0	0	13⅔	8	11	6	10	17
1991	—Huntsville (South.)	6	*13	.316	3.47	24	24	1	1	0	132⅓	118	69	51	90	115
	—Oakland (A.L.)	0	0	. . .	9.64	1	1	0	0	0	4⅔	7	5	5	2	6
1992	—Tacoma (PCL)	4	2	.667	3.97	9	9	0	0	0	45⅓	44	22	20	35	29
1993	—Tacoma (PCL)	4	8	.333	5.83	16	16	0	0	0	78⅔	67	53	51	54	71
	—Oakland (A.L.)	6	6	.500	5.04	16	16	0	0	0	84	76	50	47	62	47
Major league totals (2 years)		6	6	.500	5.28	17	17	0	0	0	88⅔	83	55	52	64	53

VanRYN, BEN

P, DODGERS

PERSONAL: Born August 19, 1971, in Fort Wayne, Ind. . . . 6-5/185. . . . Throws left, bats left. . . . Full name: Benjamin Ashley VanRyn. . . . Name pronounced VAN-RIN.
HIGH SCHOOL: East Noble (Kendallville, Ind.).
TRANSACTIONS/CAREER NOTES: Selected by Montreal Expos organization in supplemental round ("sandwich pick" between first and second round, 37th pick overall) of free-agent draft (June 4, 1990); pick received as part of compensation for New York Yankees signing Type A free agent Pascual Perez. . . . On Sumter disabled list (July 25-August 1, 1991). . . . Traded by Expos organization to Los Angeles Dodgers organization for OF Marc Griffin (December 10, 1991).
HONORS: Named Texas League Pitcher of the Year (1993).

Year	Team (League)	W	L	Pct.	ERA	G	GS	CG	ShO	Sv.	IP	H	R	ER	BB	SO
1990	—GC Expos (GCL)	5	3	.625	1.74	10	9	0	0	0	51⅔	44	13	10	15	56
1991	—Sumter (S. Atl.)	2	13	.133	6.50	20	20	0	0	0	109⅓	122	96	79	61	77
	—Jamestown (NYP)	3	3	.500	5.01	6	6	1	0	0	32⅓	37	19	18	12	23
1992	—Vero Beach (FSL)■	10	7	.588	3.20	26	25	1	1	0	137⅔	125	58	49	54	108
1993	—San Antonio (Tex.)	*14	4	.778	*2.21	21	21	1	0	0	134⅓	118	43	33	37	144
	—Albuquerque (PCL)	1	4	.200	10.73	6	6	0	0	0	24⅓	35	30	29	17	9

VAN SLYKE, ANDY

OF, PIRATES

PERSONAL: Born December 21, 1960, in Utica, N.Y. . . . 6-2/198. . . . Throws right, bats left. . . . Full name: Andrew James Van Slyke.
HIGH SCHOOL: New Hartford (N.Y.).
TRANSACTIONS/CAREER NOTES: Selected by St. Louis Cardinals organization in first round (sixth pick overall) of free-agent draft (June 5, 1979). . . . On disabled list (June 8, 1979-entire season and April 10-May 14, 1981). . . . Traded by Cardinals with C Mike LaValliere and P Mike Dunne to Pittsburgh Pirates for C Tony Pena (April 1, 1987). . . . On disabled list (April 17-May 12, 1989). . . . On Pittsburgh disabled list (June 15-August 27, 1993); included rehabilitation assignment to Carolina (August 16-19, 1993).
RECORDS: Shares major league single-game record for most unassisted double plays by outfielder—1 (July 7, 1992).
HONORS: Named N.L. Player of the Year by THE SPORTING NEWS (1988). . . . Named outfielder on THE SPORTING NEWS N.L. All-Star team (1988 and 1992). . . . Won N.L. Gold Glove as outfielder (1988-92). . . . Named outfielder on THE SPORTING NEWS N.L. Silver Slugger team (1988 and 1992).
STATISTICAL NOTES: Tied for N.L. lead in double plays by outfielder with four in 1985, six in 1987 and five in 1989. . . . Led N.L. with 13 sacrifice flies in 1988. . . . Led N.L. outfielders with 422 total chances in 1988.

			BATTING												FIELDING			
Year	Team (League)	Pos.	G	AB	R	H	2B	3B	HR	RBI	Avg.	BB	SO	SB	PO	A	E	Avg.
1979	—							Did not play.										
1980	—Gastonia (S. Atl.)	OF	126	426	62	115	15	4	8	59	.270	70	68	19	177	16	•16	.923
1981	—St. Peters. (FSL)	OF	94	282	42	62	11	3	1	25	.220	47	55	10	168	10	5	.973
1982	—Arkansas (Texas)	OF	123	416	83	116	13	*11	16	70	.279	61	85	37	266	17	7	.976
1983	—Louisville (A.A.)	3B-1B-OF	54	220	52	81	21	4	6	41	.368	31	30	13	201	78	16	.946
	—St. Louis (N.L.)	OF-3B-1B	101	309	51	81	15	5	8	38	.262	46	64	21	203	59	6	.978
1984	—St. Louis (N.L.)	OF-3B-1B	137	361	45	88	16	4	7	50	.244	63	71	28	357	82	8	.982
1985	—St. Louis (N.L.)	OF-1B	146	424	61	110	25	6	13	55	.259	47	54	34	237	13	1	.996
1986	—St. Louis (N.L.)	OF-1B	137	418	48	113	23	7	13	61	.270	47	85	21	415	34	8	.982
1987	—Pittsburgh (N.L.)■	OF-1B	157	564	93	165	36	11	21	82	.293	56	122	34	338	10	4	.989
1988	—Pittsburgh (N.L.)	OF	154	587	101	169	23	*15	25	100	.288	57	126	30	*406	12	4	.991
1989	—Pittsburgh (N.L.)	OF-1B	130	476	64	113	18	9	9	53	.237	47	100	16	344	9	4	.989
1990	—Pittsburgh (N.L.)	OF	136	493	67	140	26	6	17	77	.284	66	89	14	326	6	8	.976
1991	—Pittsburgh (N.L.)	OF	138	491	87	130	24	7	17	83	.265	71	85	10	273	8	1	.996
1992	—Pittsburgh (N.L.)	OF	154	614	103	•199	*45	12	14	89	.324	58	99	12	421	11	5	.989
1993	—Pittsburgh (N.L.)	OF	83	323	42	100	13	4	8	50	.310	24	40	11	205	2	1	.995
	—Carolina (South.)	OF	2	4	0	0	0	0	0	1	.000	1	3	0	0	0	0	. . .
Major league totals (11 years)			1473	5060	762	1408	264	86	152	738	.278	582	935	231	3525	246	50	.987

CHAMPIONSHIP SERIES RECORD

Year	Team (League)	Pos.	G	AB	R	H	2B	3B	HR	RBI	Avg.	BB	SO	SB	PO	A	E	Avg.
			BATTING												FIELDING			
1985	—St. Louis (N.L.)	OF-PR	5	11	1	1	0	0	0	1	.091	2	1	0	6	0	0	1.000
1990	—Pittsburgh (N.L.)	OF	6	24	3	5	1	1	0	3	.208	1	7	1	13	1	0	1.000
1991	—Pittsburgh (N.L.)	OF	7	25	3	4	2	0	1	2	.160	5	5	1	18	1	0	1.000
1992	—Pittsburgh (N.L.)	OF	7	29	1	8	3	1	0	4	.276	1	5	0	20	0	0	1.000
Championship series totals (4 years)			25	89	8	18	6	2	1	10	.202	9	18	2	57	2	0	1.000

WORLD SERIES RECORD

Year	Team (League)	Pos.	G	AB	R	H	2B	3B	HR	RBI	Avg.	BB	SO	SB	PO	A	E	Avg.
			BATTING												FIELDING			
1985	—St. Louis (N.L.)	OF-PH-PR	6	11	0	1	0	0	0	0	.091	0	5	0	8	0	0	1.000

ALL-STAR GAME RECORD

Year	League	Pos.	AB	R	H	2B	3B	HR	RBI	Avg.	BB	SO	SB	PO	A	E	Avg.
			BATTING											FIELDING			
1988	—National	OF	2	0	0	0	0	0	0	.000	0	0	0	2	0	0	1.000
1992	—National	OF	2	0	0	0	0	0	0	.000	0	0	0	0	0	0	...
1993	—National		Selected, did not play—injured.														
All-Star Game totals (2 years)			4	0	0	0	0	0	0	.000	0	0	0	2	0	0	1.000

VARSHO, GARY

OF, PIRATES

PERSONAL: Born June 20, 1961, in Marshfield, Wis. . . . 5-11/190. . . . Throws right, bats left. . . . Full name: Gary Andrew Varsho.

HIGH SCHOOL: Marshfield (Wis.).

COLLEGE: Wisconsin-Oshkosh.

TRANSACTIONS/CAREER NOTES: Selected by Chicago Cubs organization in fifth round of free-agent draft (June 7, 1982). . . . On disabled list (August 13, 1986-remainder of season). . . . Traded by Cubs to Pittsburgh Pirates for OF Steve Carter (March 29, 1991). . . . Claimed on waivers by Cincinnati Reds (November 25, 1992). . . . Granted free agency (October 7, 1993). . . . Signed by Pirates organization (January 5, 1994).

STATISTICAL NOTES: Led California League second basemen with 71 double plays in 1983. . . . Led Texas League second basemen with 650 total chances in 1984. . . . Led American Association in caught stealing with 17 in 1987.

Year	Team (League)	Pos.	G	AB	R	H	2B	3B	HR	RBI	Avg.	BB	SO	SB	PO	A	E	Avg.
			BATTING												FIELDING			
1982	—Quad Cities (Mid.)	2B	76	271	52	68	9	4	3	40	.251	49	50	30	190	180	14	.964
1983	—Salinas (Calif.)	2B	131	490	69	129	16	*13	3	57	.263	49	108	46	284	339	•33	.950
1984	—Midland (Texas)	2B	128	429	65	112	15	6	8	50	.261	49	86	27	*286	335	*29	.955
1985	—Pittsfield (Eastern)	1B-OF	115	418	62	101	14	6	3	37	.242	40	53	•40	670	51	6	.992
1986	—Pittsfield (Eastern)	OF-1B-2B	107	399	75	106	18	5	13	44	.266	38	52	*45	213	14	6	.974
1987	—Iowa (Am. Assoc.)	OF	132	504	87	152	23	9	9	48	.302	41	65	37	227	18	6	.976
1988	—Iowa (Am. Assoc.)	OF	66	234	46	65	16	5	4	26	.278	18	38	8	120	6	2	.984
	—Chicago (N.L.)	OF	46	73	6	20	3	0	0	5	.274	1	6	5	29	0	3	.906
1989	—Chicago (N.L.)	OF	61	87	10	16	4	2	0	6	.184	4	13	3	25	1	2	.929
	—Iowa (Am. Assoc.)	OF	31	112	13	26	3	1	2	13	.232	9	21	6	67	4	3	.959
1990	—Iowa (Am. Assoc.)	OF-1B-3B	63	229	35	69	9	0	7	33	.301	25	35	18	202	15	7	.969
	—Chicago (N.L.)	OF	46	48	10	12	4	0	0	1	.250	1	6	2	2	0	0	1.000
1991	—Pittsburgh (N.L.)■	OF-1B	99	187	23	51	11	2	4	23	.273	19	34	9	95	2	1	.990
1992	—Pittsburgh (N.L.)	OF	103	162	22	36	6	3	4	22	.222	10	32	5	62	1	1	.984
1993	—Cincinnati (N.L.)■	OF	77	95	8	22	6	0	2	11	.232	9	19	1	27	1	0	1.000
	—Indianapolis (A.A.)	OF-1B	32	121	19	35	8	1	3	18	.289	15	13	1	69	0	4	.945
Major league totals (6 years)			432	652	79	157	34	7	10	68	.241	44	110	25	240	5	7	.972

CHAMPIONSHIP SERIES RECORD

Year	Team (League)	Pos.	G	AB	R	H	2B	3B	HR	RBI	Avg.	BB	SO	SB	PO	A	E	Avg.
			BATTING												FIELDING			
1991	—Pittsburgh (N.L.)	PH	2	2	0	1	0	0	0	0	.500	0	1	0	...	...	...	...
1992	—Pittsburgh (N.L.)	PH-OF	2	2	0	1	0	0	0	0	.500	0	0	0	0	0	0	...
Championship series totals (2 years)			4	4	0	2	0	0	0	0	.500	0	1	0	0	0	0	...

VASQUEZ, JULIAN

P, ANGELS

PERSONAL: Born May 24, 1968, in Puerto Plata, Dominican Republic. . . . 6-3/185. . . . Throws right, bats right.

HIGH SCHOOL: Escuela Antera Mota (Puerto Plata, Dominican Republic).

TRANSACTIONS/CAREER NOTES: Signed as a free agent by New York Mets organization (July 22, 1986). . . . On Tidewater disabled list (July 22-September 18, 1992). . . . Traded by Mets to California Angels (October 6, 1992), completing deal in which Angels traded SS Dick Schofield to Mets for P Julio Valera and a player to be named later (April 12, 1992). . . . On California disabled list (April 5, 1993-entire season).

Year	Team (League)	W	L	Pct.	ERA	G	GS	CG	ShO	Sv.	IP	H	R	ER	BB	SO
1987	—Kingsport (Appal.)	2	3	.400	3.29	25	0	0	0	3	41	36	20	15	22	36
1988	—Kingsport (Appal.)	0	1	.000	3.19	19	2	0	0	10	31	19	13	11	13	30
1989	—Columbia (S. Atl.)	1	5	.167	3.88	37	0	0	0	7	58	47	30	25	32	61
1990	—Columbia (S. Atl.)	1	4	.200	2.17	25	0	0	0	9	29	28	15	7	17	37
1991	—St. Lucie (Fla. St.)	3	2	.600	0.28	56	0	0	0	•25	64	35	6	2	39	56
1992	—Binghamton (East.)	2	1	.667	1.35	24	0	0	0	17	26⅔	17	5	4	7	24
	—Tidewater (Int'l)	1	4	.200	5.56	20	0	0	0	6	22⅔	22	14	14	8	22
1993	—■							Did not play.								

VAUGHN, GREG

OF, BREWERS

PERSONAL: Born July 3, 1965, in Sacramento, Calif. . . . 6-0/205. . . . Throws right, bats right. . . . Full name: Gregory Lamont Vaughn.
HIGH SCHOOL: John F. Kennedy (Sacramento, Calif.).
COLLEGE: Sacramento (Calif.) City College and Miami (Fla.).

TRANSACTIONS/CAREER NOTES: Selected by St. Louis Cardinals organization in fifth round of free-agent draft (January 17, 1984). . . . Selected by Milwaukee Brewers organization in secondary phase of free-agent draft (June 4, 1984). . . . Selected by Pittsburgh Pirates organization in secondary phase of free-agent draft (January 9, 1985). . . . Selected by California Angels organization in secondary phase of free-agent draft (June 3, 1985). . . . Selected by Brewers organization in secondary phase of free-agent draft (June 2, 1986). . . . On disabled list (May 26-June 10, 1990).
HONORS: Named Midwest League co-Most Valuable Player (1987). . . . Named American Association Most Valuable Player (1989).
STATISTICAL NOTES: Led Midwest League with 292 total bases in 1987. . . . Led Texas League with 279 total bases in 1988. . . . Led American Association with .548 slugging percentage in 1989.

		BATTING												FIELDING			
Year Team (League)	Pos.	G	AB	R	H	2B	3B	HR	RBI	Avg.	BB	SO	SB	PO	A	E	Avg.
1986 —Helena (Pioneer)	OF	66	258	64	75	13	2	16	54	.291	30	69	23	99	5	3	.972
1987 —Beloit (Midwest)	OF	139	492	*120	150	31	6	*33	105	.305	102	115	36	247	11	10	.963
1988 —El Paso (Texas)	OF	131	505	*104	152	*39	2	*28	*105	.301	63	120	22	216	12	7	.970
1989 —Denver (A.A.)	OF	110	387	74	107	17	5	*26	*92	.276	62	94	20	140	4	3	.980
—Milwaukee (A.L.)	OF	38	113	18	30	3	0	5	23	.265	13	23	4	32	1	2	.943
1990 —Milwaukee (A.L.)	OF	120	382	51	84	26	2	17	61	.220	33	91	7	195	8	7	.967
1991 —Milwaukee (A.L.)	OF	145	542	81	132	24	5	27	98	.244	62	125	2	315	5	2	.994
1992 —Milwaukee (A.L.)	OF	141	501	77	114	18	2	23	78	.228	60	123	15	288	6	3	.990
1993 —Milwaukee (A.L.)	OF	154	569	97	152	28	2	30	97	.267	89	118	10	214	1	3	.986
Major league totals (5 years)		598	2107	324	512	99	11	102	357	.243	257	480	38	1044	21	17	.984

ALL-STAR GAME RECORD

		BATTING											FIELDING			
Year League	Pos.	AB	R	H	2B	3B	HR	RBI	Avg.	BB	SO	SB	PO	A	E	Avg.
1993 —American	OF	1	1	1	0	0	0	0	1.000	0	0	0	0	0	0	...

VAUGHN, MO

1B/DH, RED SOX

PERSONAL: Born December 15, 1967, in Norwalk, Conn. . . . 6-1/225. . . . Throws right, bats left. . . . Full name: Maurice Samuel Vaughn.
HIGH SCHOOL: Trinity Pawling Prep (Pawling, N.Y.).
COLLEGE: Seton Hall.

TRANSACTIONS/CAREER NOTES: Selected by Boston Red Sox organization in first round (23rd pick overall) of free-agent draft (June 9, 1989).

		BATTING												FIELDING			
Year Team (League)	Pos.	G	AB	R	H	2B	3B	HR	RBI	Avg.	BB	SO	SB	PO	A	E	Avg.
1989 —New Britain (East.)	1B	73	245	28	68	15	0	8	38	.278	25	47	1	541	45	•10	.983
1990 —Pawtucket (Int'l)	1B	108	386	62	114	26	1	22	72	.295	44	87	3	828	60	11	.988
1991 —Pawtucket (Int'l)	1B	69	234	35	64	10	0	14	50	.274	60	44	2	432	24	3	.993
—Boston (A.L.)	1B	74	219	21	57	12	0	4	32	.260	26	43	2	378	26	6	.985
1992 —Boston (A.L.)	1B	113	355	42	83	16	2	13	57	.234	47	67	3	741	57	*15	.982
—Pawtucket (Int'l)	1B	39	149	15	42	6	0	6	28	.282	18	35	1	368	15	8	.980
1993 —Boston (A.L.)	1B	152	539	86	160	34	1	29	101	.297	79	130	4	1110	70	*16	.987
Major league totals (3 years)		339	1113	149	300	62	3	46	190	.270	152	240	9	2229	153	37	.985

VELARDE, RANDY

SS/3B/OF, YANKEES

PERSONAL: Born November 24, 1962, in Midland, Tex. . . . 6-0/192. . . . Throws right, bats right. . . . Full name: Randy Lee Velarde. . . . Name pronounced vel-ARE-dee.
HIGH SCHOOL: Robert E. Lee (Midland, Tex.).
COLLEGE: Lubbock (Tex.) Christian College.

TRANSACTIONS/CAREER NOTES: Selected by Chicago White Sox organization in 19th round of free-agent draft (June 3, 1985). . . . Traded by White Sox organization with P Pete Filson to New York Yankees for P Scott Nielsen and IF Mike Soper (January 5, 1987). . . . On New York disabled list (August 9-29, 1989). . . . On New York disabled list (June 6-July 30, 1993); included rehabilitation assignment to Albany/Colonie (July 24-30).
STATISTICAL NOTES: Led Midwest League shortstops with 52 errors in 1986.

		BATTING												FIELDING			
Year Team (League)	Pos.	G	AB	R	H	2B	3B	HR	RBI	Avg.	BB	SO	SB	PO	A	E	Avg.
1985 —Niag. Falls (NYP)	0-S-2-3	67	218	28	48	7	3	1	16	.220	35	72	8	124	117	15	.941
1986 —Appleton (Midw.)	SS-3B-OF	124	417	55	105	31	4	11	50	.252	58	96	13	205	300	†54	.903
—Buffalo (A.A.)	SS	9	20	2	4	1	0	0	2	.200	2	4	1	9	28	3	.925
1987 —Alb./Colon. (East.)■	SS-OF	71	263	40	83	20	2	7	32	.316	25	47	8	128	254	17	.957
—Columbus (Int'l)	SS	49	185	21	59	10	6	5	33	.319	15	36	8	100	164	16	.943
—New York (A.L.)	SS	8	22	1	4	0	0	0	1	.182	0	6	0	8	20	2	.933
1988 —Columbus (Int'l)	SS-2B-3B	78	293	39	79	23	4	5	37	.270	25	71	7	123	271	25	.940
—New York (A.L.)	2B-SS-3B	48	115	18	20	6	0	5	12	.174	8	24	1	72	98	8	.955
1989 —Columbus (Int'l)	SS-3B	103	387	59	103	26	3	11	53	.266	38	105	3	150	295	22	.953
—New York (A.L.)	3B-SS	33	100	12	34	4	2	2	11	.340	7	14	0	26	61	4	.956
1990 —New York (A.L.)	3-S-0-2	95	229	21	48	6	2	5	19	.210	20	53	0	70	159	12	.950
1991 —New York (A.L.)	3B-SS-OF	80	184	19	45	11	1	1	15	.245	18	43	3	64	148	15	.934
1992 —New York (A.L.)	S-3-0-2	121	412	57	112	24	1	7	46	.272	38	78	7	179	257	15	.967
1993 —New York (A.L.)	OF-SS-3B	85	226	28	68	13	2	7	24	.301	18	39	2	102	92	9	.956
—Alb./Colon. (East.)	SS-OF	5	17	2	4	0	0	1	2	.235	2	2	0	6	12	2	.900
Major league totals (7 years)		470	1288	156	331	64	8	27	128	.257	109	257	13	521	835	65	.954

VELASQUEZ, GUILLERMO

1B, PADRES

PERSONAL: Born April 23, 1968, in Mexicali, Mexico. . . . 6-3/225. . . . Throws right, bats left. . . . Name pronounced veh-LAS-kez.
TRANSACTIONS/CAREER NOTES: Signed as free agent by Monterrey of Mexican League prior to 1986 season. . . . Contract sold by Monterrey to San Diego Padres organization (December 9, 1986).
STATISTICAL NOTES: Led Texas League first basemen with 1,173 total chances in 1991. . . . Led Pacific Coast League first basemen with .994 fielding percentage in 1992.

			BATTING												FIELDING			
Year	**Team (League)**	**Pos.**	**G**	**AB**	**R**	**H**	**2B**	**3B**	**HR**	**RBI**	**Avg.**	**BB**	**SO**	**SB**	**PO**	**A**	**E**	**Avg.**
1986	—Monterrey (Mex.)	1B	62	146	19	39	8	2	3	21	.267	8	24	1	353	11	4	.989
1987	—Char., S.C. (S. Atl.)■	1B	102	295	32	65	12	0	3	30	.220	16	65	2	695	58	12	.984
1988	—Char., S.C. (S. Atl.)	1B	135	520	55	149	28	3	11	90	.287	34	110	1	*1186	85	13	.990
1989	—Riverside (Calif.)	1B	139	544	73	152	30	2	9	69	.279	51	91	4	1073	95	*19	.984
1990	—Wichita (Texas)	1B	105	377	48	102	21	2	12	72	.271	35	66	0	631	50	14	.980
1991	—Wichita (Texas)	1B	130	501	72	148	26	3	21	100	.295	48	75	4	*1092	69	12	.990
1992	—Las Vegas (PCL)	1B-OF	136	512	68	158	*44	4	7	99	.309	44	94	3	1049	91	8	†.993
	—San Diego (N.L.)	1B-OF	15	23	1	7	0	0	1	5	.304	1	7	0	15	1	1	.941
1993	—San Diego (N.L.)	1B-OF	79	143	7	30	2	0	3	20	.210	13	35	0	225	21	4	.984
	—Las Vegas (PCL)	1B	30	129	23	43	6	1	5	24	.333	10	19	0	278	28	3	.990
	Major league totals (2 years)		94	166	8	37	2	0	4	25	.223	14	42	0	240	22	5	.981

VENTURA, ROBIN

3B, WHITE SOX

PERSONAL: Born July 14, 1967, in Santa Maria, Calif. . . . 6-1/198. . . . Throws right, bats left. . . . Full name: Robin Mark Ventura.
HIGH SCHOOL: Righetti (Santa Maria, Calif.).
COLLEGE: Oklahoma State.
TRANSACTIONS/CAREER NOTES: Selected by Chicago White Sox organization in first round (10th pick overall) of free-agent draft (June 1, 1988). . . . On suspended list (August 23-25, 1993).
HONORS: Named College Player of the Year by THE SPORTING NEWS (1987-88). . . . Named third baseman on THE SPORTING NEWS college All-America team (1987-88). . . . Named Golden Spikes Award winner by USA Baseball (1988). . . . Won A.L. Gold Glove at third base (1991-93).
STATISTICAL NOTES: Led Southern League with 12 intentional bases on balls received in 1989. . . . Led Southern League third basemen with .930 fielding percentage and tied for lead with 21 double plays in 1989. . . . Led A.L. third basemen with 134 putouts and 18 errors in 1991. . . . Led A.L. third basemen with 141 putouts, 372 assists, 536 total chances and tied for lead with 29 double plays in 1992. . . . Led A.L. third basemen with 404 total chances in 1993.
MISCELLANEOUS: Member of 1988 U.S. Olympic baseball team.

			BATTING												FIELDING			
Year	**Team (League)**	**Pos.**	**G**	**AB**	**R**	**H**	**2B**	**3B**	**HR**	**RBI**	**Avg.**	**BB**	**SO**	**SB**	**PO**	**A**	**E**	**Avg.**
1989	—Birm. (Southern)	3B-1B-2B	129	454	75	126	25	2	3	67	.278	93	51	9	108	249	27	†.930
	—Chicago (A.L.)	3B	16	45	5	8	3	0	0	7	.178	8	6	0	17	33	2	.962
1990	—Chicago (A.L.)	3B-1B	150	493	48	123	17	1	5	54	.249	55	53	1	116	268	25	.939
1991	—Chicago (A.L.)	3B-1B	157	606	92	172	25	1	23	100	.284	80	67	2	†225	291	†18	.966
1992	—Chicago (A.L.)	3B-1B	157	592	85	167	38	1	16	93	.282	93	71	2	†141	†375	23	.957
1993	—Chicago (A.L.)	3B-1B	157	554	85	145	27	1	22	94	.262	105	82	1	119	278	14	.966
	Major league totals (5 years)		637	2290	315	615	110	4	66	348	.269	341	279	6	618	1245	82	.958

CHAMPIONSHIP SERIES RECORD

			BATTING												FIELDING			
Year	**Team (League)**	**Pos.**	**G**	**AB**	**R**	**H**	**2B**	**3B**	**HR**	**RBI**	**Avg.**	**BB**	**SO**	**SB**	**PO**	**A**	**E**	**Avg.**
1993	—Chicago (A.L.)	3B-1B	6	20	2	4	0	0	1	5	.200	6	6	0	9	6	1	.938

ALL-STAR GAME RECORD

		BATTING											FIELDING			
Year	**League**	**Pos.**	**AB**	**R**	**H**	**2B**	**3B**	**HR**	**RBI**	**Avg.**	**BB**	**SO**	**SB**	**PO**	**A**	**E**	**Avg.**
1992	—American	3B	2	1	2	1	0	0	1	1.000	0	0	0	1	1	0	1.000

VERAS, QUILVIO

2B, METS

PERSONAL: Born April 3, 1971, in Santo Domingo, Dominican Republic. . . . 5-9/166. . . . Throws right, bats both. . . . Full name: Quilvio Alberto Perez Veras.
HIGH SCHOOL: Victor E. Liz (Santo Domingo, Dominican Republic).
TRANSACTIONS/CAREER NOTES: Signed as free agent by New York Mets organization (November 22, 1989).
STATISTICAL NOTES: Tied for Appalachian League lead in double plays by second baseman with 30 in 1991. . . . Led Appalachian League second basemen with 282 total chances in 1991. . . . Led South Atlantic League in on-base percentage with .441 and in caught stealing with 35 in 1992. . . . Led Eastern League in on-base percentage with .430 and in caught stealing with 19 in 1993. . . . Led Eastern League second basemen with 669 total chances in 1993.

			BATTING												FIELDING			
Year	**Team (League)**	**Pos.**	**G**	**AB**	**R**	**H**	**2B**	**3B**	**HR**	**RBI**	**Avg.**	**BB**	**SO**	**SB**	**PO**	**A**	**E**	**Avg.**
1990	—GC Mets (GCL)	2B	30	98	26	29	3	3	1	5	.296	19	16	16	45	76	3	.976
	—Kingsport (Appal.)	2B	24	94	21	36	6	0	1	14	.383	13	14	9	55	79	8	.944
1991	—Kingsport (Appal.)	2B	64	226	*54	76	11	4	1	16	.336	36	28	38	*113	*161	8	.972
	—Pittsfield (NYP)	2B-SS	5	15	3	4	0	1	0	2	.267	5	1	2	16	16	1	.970
1992	—Columbia (S. Atl.)	2B	117	414	97	132	24	10	2	40	*.319	84	52	*66	208	313	20	.963
1993	—Binghamton (East.)	2B	128	444	87	136	19	7	2	51	.306	*91	62	52	*274	*372	23	.966

VERES, RANDY

P, CUBS

PERSONAL: Born November 25, 1965, in San Francisco. . . . 6-3/210. . . . Throws right, bats right. . . . Full name: Randolph Ruhland Veres. . . . Name pronounced VER-es.
HIGH SCHOOL: Cordova (Rancho Cordova, Calif.).
COLLEGE: Sacramento (Calif.) City College.

TRANSACTIONS/CAREER NOTES: Selected by New York Mets organization in 32nd round of free-agent draft (June 4, 1984).... Selected by Milwaukee Brewers organization in secondary phase of free-agent draft (January 9, 1985).... On disabled list (August 17, 1986-remainder of season).... Signed as free agent by Richmond, Atlanta Braves organization (May 3, 1991).... Released by Richmond (June 12, 1991).... Signed by Phoenix, San Francisco Giants organization (June 19, 1991).... Granted free agency (September 15, 1991).... Re-signed by Giants organization (October 11, 1991).... On disabled list (May 16-September 8, 1992).... Granted free agency (October 15, 1992).... Signed by Canton/Akron, Cleveland Indians organization (June 15, 1993).... On disabled list (July 9-16, 1993).... Granted free agency (October 15, 1993).... Signed by Chicago Cubs (December 3, 1993).

Year	Team (League)	W	L	Pct.	ERA	G	GS	CG	ShO	Sv.	IP	H	R	ER	BB	SO
1985	—Helena (Pioneer)	7	4	.636	3.84	13	13	3	2	0	77⅓	66	43	33	36	67
1986	—Beloit (Midwest)	4	12	.250	3.89	23	22	3	1	0	113⅓	132	78	49	52	87
1987	—Beloit (Midwest)	10	6	.625	3.12	21	21	6	0	0	127	132	63	44	52	98
1988	—Stockton (Calif.)	8	4	.667	3.35	20	14	1	1	0	110	94	54	41	77	96
	—El Paso (Texas)	3	2	.600	3.66	6	6	0	0	0	39⅓	35	18	16	12	31
1989	—El Paso (Texas)	2	3	.400	4.78	8	8	0	0	0	43⅓	43	29	23	25	41
	—Denver (A.A.)	6	7	.462	3.95	17	17	2	1	0	107	108	57	47	38	80
	—Milwaukee (A.L.)	0	1	.000	4.32	3	1	0	0	0	8⅓	9	5	4	4	8
1990	—Denver (A.A.)	1	6	.143	5.19	16	7	0	0	2	50⅓	60	36	29	27	36
	—Milwaukee (A.L.)	0	3	.000	3.67	26	0	0	0	1	41⅔	38	17	17	16	16
1991	—Richmond (Int'l)■	0	2	.000	5.04	9	3	0	0	0	25	32	14	14	10	12
	—Phoenix (PCL)■	3	0	1.000	3.56	19	1	0	0	1	43	42	26	17	14	41
1992	—Phoenix (PCL)	0	2	.000	8.10	12	0	0	0	1	13⅓	14	12	12	13	13
1993	—Cant./Akr. (East.)■	1	5	.167	4.89	13	12	0	0	0	57	59	33	31	19	49
	Major league totals (2 years)	0	4	.000	3.78	29	1	0	0	1	50	47	22	21	20	24

VILLANUEVA, HECTOR

C/1B

PERSONAL: Born October 2, 1964, in San Juan, Puerto Rico.... 6-1/220.... Throws right, bats right.... Full name: Hector Balasquide Villanueva.

HIGH SCHOOL: Cupeyville (Rio Piedras, Puerto Rico).

COLLEGE: Alabama-Birmingham.

TRANSACTIONS/CAREER NOTES: Signed as free agent by Chicago Cubs organization (March 26, 1985).... On disabled list (June 7-22, 1987).... On Chicago disabled list (April 1-21, 1991).... Released by Cubs (November 6, 1992).... Signed by St. Louis Cardinals (December 8, 1992).... Released by Cardinals (August 8, 1993).

STATISTICAL NOTES: Led Carolina League with 12 sacrifice flies in 1986.

			BATTING												FIELDING			
Year	Team (League)	Pos.	G	AB	R	H	2B	3B	HR	RBI	Avg.	BB	SO	SB	PO	A	E	Avg.
1985	—Geneva (NY-Penn)	C	1	0	0	0	0	0	0	0	...	0	0	0	0	0	0	...
	—Peoria (Midwest)	C-P	65	193	22	45	7	0	1	19	.233	27	36	0	322	43	12	.968
1986	—Winst.-Salem (Car.)	C-1B	125	412	58	131	20	2	13	100	.318	81	42	6	653	72	6	.992
1987	—Pittsfield (Eastern)	C-1B	109	391	59	107	31	0	14	70	.274	43	38	3	489	58	4	.993
1988	—Pittsfield (Eastern)	1-C-3-P	127	436	50	137	24	3	10	75	.314	*71	58	5	840	98	11	.988
1989	—Iowa (Am. Assoc.)	C-1B-P	120	444	46	112	25	1	12	57	.252	32	95	1	618	67	6	.991
1990	—Iowa (Am. Assoc.)	C-1B	52	177	20	47	7	1	8	34	.266	19	36	0	263	27	0	1.000
	—Chicago (N.L.)	C-1B	52	114	14	31	4	1	7	18	.272	4	27	1	170	10	2	.989
1991	—Chicago (N.L.)	C-1B	71	192	23	53	10	1	13	32	.276	21	30	0	276	27	6	.981
	—Iowa (Am. Assoc.)	C	6	25	2	9	3	0	2	9	.360	1	6	0	15	0	0	1.000
1992	—Chicago (N.L.)	C-1B	51	112	9	17	6	0	2	13	.152	11	24	0	181	24	4	.981
	—Iowa (Am. Assoc.)	1B-C	49	159	21	38	8	0	9	35	.239	20	36	0	239	26	4	.985
1993	—St. Louis (N.L.)■	C	17	55	7	8	1	0	3	9	.145	4	17	0	86	3	0	1.000
	—Louisville (A.A.)	C-1B	40	124	13	30	9	0	5	20	.242	16	18	0	188	14	2	.990
	Major league totals (4 years)		191	473	53	109	21	2	25	72	.230	40	98	1	713	64	12	.985

RECORD AS PITCHER

Year	Team (League)	W	L	Pct.	ERA	G	GS	CG	ShO	Sv.	IP	H	R	ER	BB	SO
1985	—Peoria (Midwest)	0	0	...	0.00	1	0	0	0	0	1	0	0	0	1	1
1988	—Pittsfield (Eastern)	0	0	...	9.00	1	0	0	0	0	1	2	1	1	0	1
1989	—Iowa (Am. Assoc.)	0	0	...	18.00	1	0	0	0	0	1	3	2	2	1	0

VINA, FERNANDO

2B/SS, METS

PERSONAL: Born April 16, 1969, in Sacramento, Calif.... 5-9/170.... Throws right, bats left.... Name pronounced VEEN-ya.

HIGH SCHOOL: Valley (Sacramento, Calif.).

COLLEGE: Cosumnes River College (Calif.), Sacramento (Calif.) City College and Arizona State.

TRANSACTIONS/CAREER NOTES: Selected by New York Yankees organization in 51st round of free-agent draft (June 1, 1988).... Selected by New York Mets organization in ninth round of free-agent draft (June 4, 1990).... Selected by Seattle Mariners from Mets organization in Rule 5 major league draft (December 7, 1992).... Returned to Mets organization (June 15, 1993).

STATISTICAL NOTES: Tied for South Atlantic League lead in caught stealing with 22 in 1991.... Led South Atlantic League second basemen with 600 total chances and 61 double plays in 1991.... Led Florida State League second basemen with 85 double plays in 1992.

			BATTING												FIELDING			
Year	Team (League)	Pos.	G	AB	R	H	2B	3B	HR	RBI	Avg.	BB	SO	SB	PO	A	E	Avg.
1991	—Columbia (S. Atl.)	2B	129	498	77	135	23	6	6	50	.271	46	27	42	194	*385	21	*.965
1992	—St. Lucie (Fla. St.)	2B	111	421	61	124	15	5	1	42	.295	32	26	36	219	*360	17	.971
	—Tidewater (Int'l)	2B	11	30	3	6	0	0	0	2	.200	0	2	0	16	28	1	.978
1993	—Seattle (A.L.)■	2B-SS	24	45	5	10	2	0	0	2	.222	4	3	6	28	40	0	1.000
	—Norfolk (Int'l)■	SS-2B-OF	73	287	24	66	6	4	4	27	.230	7	17	16	146	232	14	.964
	Major league totals (1 year)		24	45	5	10	2	0	0	2	.222	4	3	6	28	40	0	1.000

VIOLA, FRANK

P, RED SOX

PERSONAL: Born April 19, 1960, in East Meadow, N.Y. . . . 6-4/210. . . . Throws left, bats left. . . . Full name: Frank John Viola Jr. . . . Name pronounced vy-OH-luh.
HIGH SCHOOL: East Meadow (New York).
COLLEGE: St. John's (N.Y.).
TRANSACTIONS/CAREER NOTES: Selected by Kansas City Royals organization in 16th round of free-agent draft (June 6, 1978). . . . Selected by Minnesota Twins organization in second round of free-agent draft (June 8, 1981). . . . Traded by Twins to New York Mets for P Rick Aguilera, P David West and three players to be named later (July 31, 1989); Portland, Twins organization, acquired P Kevin Tapani and P Tim Drummond (August 1, 1989), and Twins acquired P Jack Savage to complete deal (October 16, 1989). . . . Granted free agency (October 28, 1991). . . . Signed by Boston Red Sox (January 2, 1992).
RECORDS: Holds major league single-season record for fewest innings pitched for league leader—249⅔ (1990).
HONORS: Named A.L. Pitcher of the Year by THE SPORTING NEWS (1988). . . . Named lefthanded pitcher on THE SPORTING NEWS A.L. All-Star team (1988). . . . Named A.L. Cy Young Award winner by Baseball Writers' Association of America (1988). . . . Named lefthanded pitcher on THE SPORTING NEWS N.L. All-Star team (1990).

Year	Team (League)	W	L	Pct.	ERA	G	GS	CG	ShO	Sv.	IP	H	R	ER	BB	SO
1981	—Orlando (Southern)	5	4	.556	3.43	17	15	2	0	0	97	112	47	37	33	50
1982	—Toledo (Int'l)	2	3	.400	3.88	8	8	2	0	0	58	61	27	25	18	34
	—Minnesota (A.L.)	4	10	.286	5.21	22	22	3	1	0	126	152	77	73	38	84
1983	—Minnesota (A.L.)	7	15	.318	5.49	35	34	4	0	0	210	242	*141	*128	92	127
1984	—Minnesota (A.L.)	18	12	.600	3.21	35	35	10	4	0	257⅔	225	101	92	73	149
1985	—Minnesota (A.L.)	18	14	.563	4.09	36	36	9	0	0	250⅔	262	*136	114	68	135
1986	—Minnesota (A.L.)	16	13	.552	4.51	37	•37	7	1	0	245⅔	257	136	123	83	191
1987	—Minnesota (A.L.)	17	10	.630	2.90	36	36	7	1	0	251⅔	230	91	81	66	197
1988	—Minnesota (A.L.)	*24	7	*.774	2.64	35	35	7	2	0	255⅓	236	80	75	54	193
1989	—Minnesota (A.L.)	8	12	.400	3.79	24	24	7	1	0	175⅔	171	80	74	47	138
	—New York (N.L.)■	5	5	.500	3.38	12	12	2	1	0	85⅓	75	35	32	27	73
1990	—New York (N.L.)	20	12	.625	2.67	35	•35	7	3	0	*249⅔	227	83	74	60	182
1991	—New York (N.L.)	13	15	.464	3.97	35	35	3	0	0	231⅓	*259	112	102	54	132
1992	—Boston (A.L.)■	13	12	.520	3.44	35	35	6	1	0	238	214	99	91	89	121
1993	—Boston (A.L.)	11	8	.579	3.14	29	29	2	1	0	183⅔	180	76	64	72	91
	A.L. totals (10 years)	136	113	.546	3.75	324	323	62	12	0	2194⅓	2169	1017	915	682	1426
	N.L. totals (3 years)	38	32	.543	3.31	82	82	12	4	0	566⅓	561	230	208	141	387
	Major league totals (12 years)	174	145	.545	3.66	406	405	74	16	0	2760⅔	2730	1247	1123	823	1813

CHAMPIONSHIP SERIES RECORD

Year	Team (League)	W	L	Pct.	ERA	G	GS	CG	ShO	Sv.	IP	H	R	ER	BB	SO
1987	—Minnesota (A.L.)	1	0	1.000	5.25	2	2	0	0	0	12	14	8	7	5	9

WORLD SERIES RECORD

WORLD SERIES NOTES: Named Most Valuable Player (1987).

Year	Team (League)	W	L	Pct.	ERA	G	GS	CG	ShO	Sv.	IP	H	R	ER	BB	SO
1987	—Minnesota (A.L.)	2	1	.667	3.72	3	3	0	0	0	19⅓	17	8	8	3	16

ALL-STAR GAME RECORD

Year	League	W	L	Pct.	ERA	GS	CG	ShO	Sv.	IP	H	R	ER	BB	SO
1988	—American	1	0	1.000	0.00	1	0	0	0	2	0	0	0	0	1
1990	—National	0	0	. . .	0.00	0	0	0	0	1	1	0	0	0	0
1991	—National	0	0	. . .	0.00	0	0	0	0	1	0	0	0	1	0
	All-Star totals (3 years)	1	0	1.000	0.00	1	0	0	0	4	1	0	0	1	1

VITIELLO, JOE

1B, ROYALS

PERSONAL: Born April 11, 1970, in Cambridge, Mass. . . . 6-2/215. . . . Throws right, bats right. . . . Full name: Joseph David Vitiello.
HIGH SCHOOL: Stoneham (Mass.).
COLLEGE: Alabama.
TRANSACTIONS/CAREER NOTES: Selected by New York Yankees organization in 31st round of free-agent draft (June 1, 1988). . . . Selected by Kansas City Royals organization in first round (seventh pick overall) of free-agent draft (June 3, 1991). . . . On disabled list (April 12-23, 1992 and June 2-11, 1993).

			BATTING											FIELDING			
Year	Team (League)	Pos.	G	AB	R	H	2B	3B	HR	RBI	Avg.	BB	SO	SB	PO	A	E	Avg.
1991	—Eugene (N'west)	OF-1B	19	64	16	21	2	0	6	21	.328	11	18	1	49	4	1	.981
	—Memphis (South.)	OF-1B	36	128	15	28	4	1	0	18	.219	23	36	0	77	4	1	.988
1992	—Baseball City (FSL)	1B	115	400	52	113	16	1	8	65	.283	46	101	0	879	44	13	.986
1993	—Memphis (South.)	1B	117	413	62	119	25	2	15	66	.288	57	95	2	830	53	•17	.981

VITKO, JOE

P, METS

PERSONAL: Born February 1, 1970, in Somerville, N.J. . . . 6-8/210. . . . Throws right, bats right. . . . Full name: Joseph John Vitko III.
HIGH SCHOOL: Central Cambria (Ebensburg, Pa.).
COLLEGE: St. Francis (Pa.).
TRANSACTIONS/CAREER NOTES: Selected by New York Mets organization in 38th round of free-agent draft (June 1, 1988). . . . Selected by Mets organization in 24th round of free-agent draft (June 5, 1989). . . . On New York disabled list (March 30, 1993-entire season); included rehabilitation assignment to Gulf Coast Mets (August 24-28) and St. Lucie (August 28-September 6).
STATISTICAL NOTES: Tied for Eastern League lead with 12 hit batsmen in 1992.

Year	Team (League)	W	L	Pct.	ERA	G	GS	CG	ShO	Sv.	IP	H	R	ER	BB	SO
1989	—GC Mets (GCL)	4	1	.800	3.29	8	5	1	0	0	41	28	20	15	16	33
	—Pittsfield (NYP)	2	1	.667	0.91	5	5	1	1	0	29⅔	24	6	3	8	29
1990	—Columbia (S. Atl.)	8	1	.889	2.49	16	12	4	2	1	90⅓	70	29	25	30	72

Year	Team (League)	W	L	Pct.	ERA	G	GS	CG	ShO	Sv.	IP	H	R	ER	BB	SO
1991	—St. Lucie (Fla. St.)	11	8	.579	2.24	22	22	5	2	0	140⅓	102	40	35	39	105
1992	—Binghamton (East.)	12	8	.600	3.49	26	26	4	3	0	165	163	76	64	53	89
	—New York (N.L.)	0	1	.000	13.50	3	1	0	0	0	4⅔	12	11	7	1	6
1993	—GC Mets (GCL)	0	0	...	0.00	1	1	0	0	0	3	1	0	0	1	2
	—St. Lucie (Fla. St.)	0	0	...	1.29	2	2	0	0	0	7	4	1	1	1	5
Major league totals (1 year)		0	1	.000	13.50	3	1	0	0	0	4⅔	12	11	7	1	6

VIZCAINO, JOSE

IF, CUBS

PERSONAL: Born March 26, 1968, in San Cristobal, Dominican Republic. . . . 6-1/180. . . . Throws right, bats both. . . . Full name: Jose Luis Pimental Vizcaino. . . . Name pronounced VIS-ky-EE-no.
HIGH SCHOOL: Americo Tolentino (Palenque de San Cristobal, Dominican Republic).
TRANSACTIONS/CAREER NOTES: Signed as free agent by Los Angeles Dodgers organization (February 18, 1986). . . . Traded by Dodgers to Chicago Cubs for IF Greg Smith (December 14, 1990). . . . On disabled list (April 20-May 6 and August 26-September 16, 1992).
STATISTICAL NOTES: Led Gulf Coast League shortstops with 23 double plays in 1987. . . . Led Pacific Coast League shortstops with 611 total chances and 82 double plays in 1989.

			BATTING												FIELDING			
Year	Team (League)	Pos.	G	AB	R	H	2B	3B	HR	RBI	Avg.	BB	SO	SB	PO	A	E	Avg.
1987	—GC Dodgers (GCL)	SS-1B	49	150	26	38	5	1	0	12	.253	22	24	8	73	107	13	.933
1988	—Bakersfield (Calif.)	SS	122	433	77	126	11	4	0	38	.291	50	54	13	185	340	30	.946
1989	—Albuquerque (PCL)	SS	129	434	60	123	10	4	1	44	.283	33	41	16	*191	*390	*30	.951
	—Los Angeles (N.L.)	SS	7	10	2	2	0	0	0	0	.200	0	1	0	6	9	2	.882
1990	—Albuquerque (PCL)	2B-SS	81	276	46	77	10	2	2	38	.279	30	33	13	141	229	14	.964
	—Los Angeles (N.L.)	SS-2B	37	51	3	14	1	1	0	2	.275	4	8	1	23	27	2	.962
1991	—Chicago (N.L.)■	3B-SS-2B	93	145	7	38	5	0	0	10	.262	5	18	2	49	118	7	.960
1992	—Chicago (N.L.)	SS-3B-2B	86	285	25	64	10	4	1	17	.225	14	35	3	93	195	9	.970
1993	—Chicago (N.L.)	SS-3B-2B	151	551	74	158	19	4	4	54	.287	46	71	12	217	410	17	.974
Major league totals (5 years)			374	1042	111	276	35	9	5	83	.265	69	133	18	388	759	37	.969

VIZQUEL, OMAR

SS, INDIANS

PERSONAL: Born April 24, 1967, in Caracas, Venezuela. . . . 5-9/165. . . . Throws right, bats both. . . . Full name: Omar Enrique Vizquel. . . . Name pronounced vis-KEL.
HIGH SCHOOL: Francisco Espejo (Caracas, Venezuela).
TRANSACTIONS/CAREER NOTES: Signed as free agent by Seattle Mariners organization (April 1, 1984). . . . On Seattle disabled list (April 7-May 13, 1990); included rehabilitation assignment to Calgary (May 3-7) and San Bernardino (May 8-12). . . . On Seattle disabled list (April 13-May 11, 1992); included rehabilitation assignment to Calgary (May 5-11). . . . Traded by Mariners to Cleveland Indians for SS Felix Fermin, 1B Reggie Jefferson and cash (December 20, 1993).
HONORS: Won A.L. Gold Glove at shortstop (1993).
STATISTICAL NOTES: Led Midwest League shortstops with .969 fielding percentage in 1986. . . . Tied for A.L. lead in double plays by shortstop with 108 in 1993.
MISCELLANEOUS: Batted righthanded only (1984-88).

			BATTING												FIELDING			
Year	Team (League)	Pos.	G	AB	R	H	2B	3B	HR	RBI	Avg.	BB	SO	SB	PO	A	E	Avg.
1984	—Butte (Pioneer)	SS-2B	15	45	7	14	2	0	0	4	.311	3	8	2	13	29	5	.894
1985	—Belling. (N'west)	SS-2B	50	187	24	42	9	0	5	17	.225	12	27	4	85	175	19	.932
1986	—Wausau (Midwest)	SS-2B	105	352	60	75	13	2	4	28	.213	64	56	19	153	328	16	†.968
1987	—Salinas (Calif.)	SS-2B	114	407	61	107	12	8	0	38	.263	57	55	25	81	295	25	.938
1988	—Vermont (Eastern)	SS	103	374	54	95	18	2	2	35	.254	42	44	30	173	268	19	*.959
	—Calgary (PCL)	SS	33	107	10	24	2	3	1	12	.224	5	14	2	43	92	6	.957
1989	—Calgary (PCL)	SS	7	28	3	6	2	0	0	3	.214	3	4	0	15	14	0	1.000
	—Seattle (A.L.)	SS	143	387	45	85	7	3	1	20	.220	28	40	1	208	388	18	.971
1990	—Calgary (PCL)	SS	48	150	18	35	6	2	0	8	.233	13	10	4	70	142	6	.972
	—San Bern. (Calif.)	SS	6	28	5	7	0	0	0	3	.250	3	1	1	11	21	3	.914
	—Seattle (A.L.)	SS	81	255	19	63	3	2	2	18	.247	18	22	4	103	239	7	.980
1991	—Seattle (A.L.)	SS-2B	142	426	42	98	16	4	1	41	.230	45	37	7	224	422	13	.980
1992	—Seattle (A.L.)	SS	136	483	49	142	20	4	0	21	.294	32	38	15	223	403	7	*.989
	—Calgary (PCL)	SS	6	22	0	6	1	0	0	2	.273	1	3	0	14	21	1	.972
1993	—Seattle (A.L.)	SS	158	560	68	143	14	2	2	31	.255	50	71	12	245	475	15	.980
Major league totals (5 years)			660	2111	223	531	60	15	6	131	.252	173	208	39	1003	1927	60	.980

VOIGT, JACK

OF, ORIOLES

PERSONAL: Born May 17, 1966, in Sarasota, Fla. . . . 6-1/175. . . . Throws right, bats right. . . . Full name: John David Voigt.
HIGH SCHOOL: Venice (Fla.).
COLLEGE: Louisiana State.
TRANSACTIONS/CAREER NOTES: Selected by Baltimore Orioles organization in ninth round of free-agent draft (June 2, 1987).
STATISTICAL NOTES: Led New York-Pennsylvania League third basemen with .941 fielding percentage and 16 double plays in 1987. . . . Led Carolina League third basemen with .990 fielding percentage in 1989. . . . Led Carolina League with 11 sacrifice flies in 1990.

			BATTING												FIELDING			
Year	Team (League)	Pos.	G	AB	R	H	2B	3B	HR	RBI	Avg.	BB	SO	SB	PO	A	E	Avg.
1987	—Newark (NY-Penn)	3B-1B	63	219	41	70	10	1	11	52	*.320	33	45	1	63	141	11	†.949
	—Hagerstown (Car.)	1B	2	9	0	1	0	0	0	1	.111	1	4	0	9	0	2	.818
1988	—Hagerstown (Car.)	OF-1B	115	367	62	83	18	2	12	42	.226	66	92	5	213	11	6	.974
1989	—Frederick (Caro.)	OF-1B	127	406	61	107	26	5	10	77	.264	62	106	17	189	16	2	†.990

Year	Team (League)	Pos.	G	AB	R	H	2B	3B	HR	RBI	Avg.	BB	SO	SB	PO	A	E	Avg.
			BATTING												FIELDING			
1990	—Hagerstown (East.) ..	OF	126	418	55	107	26	2	12	70	.256	59	97	5	249	12	6	.978
1991	—Hagerstown (East.) ..	OF	29	90	15	22	3	0	0	6	.244	15	19	6	8	0	0	1.000
	—Rochester (Int'l)	OF-1B-3B	83	267	46	72	12	4	6	35	.270	40	53	9	198	32	3	.987
1992	—Rochester (Int'l)	OF-1B-3B	129	443	74	126	23	4	16	64	.284	58	102	9	330	36	10	.973
	—Baltimore (A.L.)	PR	1	0	0	0	0	0	0	0	...	0	0	0	...	...	...	...
1993	—Rochester (Int'l)	OF-3B-1B	18	61	16	22	6	1	3	11	.361	9	14	0	38	5	1	.977
	—Baltimore (A.L.)	OF-1B-3B	64	152	32	45	11	1	6	23	.296	25	33	1	101	6	1	.991
Major league totals (2 years)			65	152	32	45	11	1	6	23	.296	25	33	1	101	6	1	.991

WACHTER, DEREK

OF, BREWERS

PERSONAL: Born August 28, 1970, in Bethpage, N.Y. . . . 6-2/195. . . . Throws right, bats right. . . . Full name: Derek Jon Wachter. . . . Name pronounced WOCK-ter.
HIGH SCHOOL: Miller Place (N.Y.).
COLLEGE: Iona.
TRANSACTIONS/CAREER NOTES: Selected by Milwaukee Brewers organization in seventh round of free-agent draft (June 3, 1991).

Year	Team (League)	Pos.	G	AB	R	H	2B	3B	HR	RBI	Avg.	BB	SO	SB	PO	A	E	Avg.
			BATTING												FIELDING			
1991	—Ariz. Brewers (Ar.) ...	OF-1B	51	186	52	58	•16	5	6	42	.312	41	59	3	81	5	3	.966
1992	—Beloit (Midwest)	OF	111	363	53	98	17	*9	10	61	.270	43	113	6	139	1	8	.946
1993	—Stockton (Calif.)	OF	115	420	75	123	20	4	22	108	.293	64	93	3	130	6	3	.978

WAGNER, PAUL

P, PIRATES

PERSONAL: Born November 14, 1967, in Milwaukee. . . . 6-1/202. . . . Throws right, bats right. . . . Full name: Paul Alan Wagner.
HIGH SCHOOL: Washington (Germantown, Wis.).
COLLEGE: Illinois State.
TRANSACTIONS/CAREER NOTES: Selected by Pittsburgh Pirates organization in 12th round of free-agent draft (June 5, 1989). . . . On disabled list (August 3-19, 1993).

Year	Team (League)	W	L	Pct.	ERA	G	GS	CG	ShO	Sv.	IP	H	R	ER	BB	SO
1989	—Welland (NYP)	4	5	.444	4.47	13	10	0	0	0	50⅓	54	34	25	15	30
1990	—Augusta (S. Atl.)	7	7	.500	2.75	35	1	0	0	4	72	71	30	22	30	71
	—Salem (Carolina)	0	1	.000	5.00	11	4	0	0	2	36	39	22	20	17	28
1991	—Salem (Carolina)	11	6	.647	3.12	25	25	5	•2	0	158⅔	124	70	55	60	113
1992	—Carolina (South.)	6	6	.500	3.03	19	19	2	1	0	121⅔	104	52	41	47	101
	—Pittsburgh (N.L.)	2	0	1.000	0.69	6	1	0	0	0	13	9	1	1	5	5
	—Buffalo (A.A.)	3	3	.500	5.49	8	8	0	0	0	39⅓	51	27	24	14	19
1993	—Pittsburgh (N.L.)	8	8	.500	4.27	44	17	1	1	2	141⅓	143	72	67	42	114
Major league totals (2 years) ..		10	8	.556	3.97	50	18	1	1	2	154⅓	152	73	68	47	119

WAINHOUSE, DAVE

P, MARINERS

PERSONAL: Born November 7, 1967, in Toronto. . . . 6-2/185. . . . Throws right, bats left. . . . Full name: David Paul Wainhouse.
HIGH SCHOOL: Mercer Island (Wash.).
COLLEGE: Washington State.
TRANSACTIONS/CAREER NOTES: Selected by Montreal Expos organization in first round (19th pick overall) of free-agent draft (June 1, 1988). . . . On Harrisburg disabled list (April 25-May 3, 1991). . . . On disabled list (August 13-September 8, 1992). . . . Traded by Expos with P Kevin Foster to Seattle Mariners for IF Frank Bolick and a player to be named later (November 20, 1992); Expos organization acquired C Miah Bradbury to complete deal (December 8, 1992). . . . On Calgary disabled list (April 23-August 3, 1993).
MISCELLANEOUS: Member of 1988 Canadian Olympic baseball team.

Year	Team (League)	W	L	Pct.	ERA	G	GS	CG	ShO	Sv.	IP	H	R	ER	BB	SO
1989	—W.P. Beach (FSL)	1	5	.167	4.07	13	13	0	0	0	66⅓	75	35	30	19	26
1990	—W.P. Beach (FSL)	6	3	.667	2.11	12	12	2	1	0	76⅔	68	28	18	34	58
	—Jacksonv. (South.)	7	7	.500	4.33	17	16	2	0	0	95⅔	97	59	46	47	59
1991	—Harrisburg (East.)	2	2	.500	2.60	33	0	0	0	11	52	49	17	15	17	46
	—Indianapolis (A.A.)	2	0	1.000	4.08	14	0	0	0	1	28⅔	28	14	13	15	13
	—Montreal (N.L.)	0	1	.000	6.75	2	0	0	0	0	2⅔	2	2	2	4	1
1992	—Indianapolis (A.A.)	5	4	.556	4.11	44	0	0	0	21	46	48	22	21	24	37
1993	—Seattle (A.L.)■	0	0	...	27.00	3	0	0	0	0	2⅓	7	7	7	5	2
	—Calgary (PCL)	0	1	.000	4.02	13	0	0	0	5	15⅔	10	7	7	7	7
A.L. totals (1 year)		0	0	...	27.00	3	0	0	0	0	2⅓	7	7	7	5	2
N.L. totals (1 year)		0	1	.000	6.75	2	0	0	0	0	2⅔	2	2	2	4	1
Major league totals (2 years) ..		0	1	.000	16.20	5	0	0	0	0	5	9	9	9	9	3

WAKAMATSU, DON

C, RANGERS

PERSONAL: Born February 22, 1963, at Hood River, Ore. . . . 6-2/200. . . . Throws right, bats right. . . . Full name: Wilbur Donald Wakamatsu.
HIGH SCHOOL: Hayward (Calif.).
COLLEGE: Arizona State.
TRANSACTIONS/CAREER NOTES: Selected by Cincinnati Reds organization in 11th round of free-agent draft (June 7, 1985). . . . Released by Reds organization (March 29, 1989). . . . Signed by Birmingham, Chicago White Sox organization (April 4, 1989). . . . Granted free agency (October 7, 1991). . . . Signed by Los Angeles Dodgers (December 10, 1991). . . . On disabled list (May 22-June 4 and July 4, 1993-remainder of season). . . . Granted free agency (October 8, 1993). . . . Signed by Texas Rangers organization (October 29, 1993).
STATISTICAL NOTES: Led Pioneer League catchers with 416 total chances in 1985. . . . Led Southern League catchers with .990 fielding percentage in 1989.

Year	Team (League)	Pos.	G	AB	R	H	2B	3B	HR	RBI	Avg.	BB	SO	SB	PO	A	E	Avg.
			BATTING												FIELDING			
1985	—Billings (Pioneer)	C	58	196	20	49	7	0	0	24	.250	25	36	1	367	44	5	*.988
1986	—Tampa (Florida St.)	1B-C	112	361	41	100	18	2	1	66	.277	53	66	6	623	58	14	.980
1987	—Ced. Rap. (Midw.)	C-1B	103	365	33	79	13	1	7	41	.216	30	71	3	690	69	11	.986
1988	—Chatt. (South.)	C-1B-3B	79	235	22	56	9	1	1	26	.238	37	41	0	418	59	8	.984
1989	—Birm. (Southern)■	C-1B-3B	92	287	45	73	15	0	2	45	.254	32	55	7	503	57	8	†.986
1990	—Vancouver (PCL)	C	62	187	20	49	10	0	0	13	.262	13	35	2	285	33	2	.994
1991	—Vancouver (PCL)	C-1B	55	172	20	34	8	0	4	19	.198	12	39	0	267	31	3	.990
	—Chicago (A.L.)	C	18	31	2	7	0	0	0	0	.226	1	6	0	47	2	0	1.000
1992	—Albuquerque (PCL)■	C	60	167	22	54	10	0	2	15	.323	15	23	0	264	41	4	.987
1993	—Albuquerque (PCL)	C	54	181	30	61	11	1	7	31	.337	15	31	0	329	35	4	.989
	Major league totals (1 year)		18	31	2	7	0	0	0	0	.226	1	6	0	47	2	0	1.000

WAKEFIELD, TIM

P, PIRATES

PERSONAL: Born August 2, 1966, in Melbourne, Fla. . . . 6-2/204. . . . Throws right, bats right. . . . Full name: Timothy Stephen Wakefield.
HIGH SCHOOL: Eau Gallie (Melbourne, Fla.).
COLLEGE: Florida Tech.
TRANSACTIONS/CAREER NOTES: Selected by Pittsburgh Pirates organization in eighth round of free-agent draft (June 1, 1988).
HONORS: Named N.L. Rookie Pitcher of the Year by THE SPORTING NEWS (1992).
STATISTICAL NOTES: Led Carolina League with 24 home runs allowed in 1990.
MISCELLANEOUS: Appeared in one game as pinch-runner with Pittsburgh (1992).

Year	Team (League)	W	L	Pct.	ERA	G	GS	CG	ShO	Sv.	IP	H	R	ER	BB	SO
1989	—Welland (NYP)	1	1	.500	3.40	18	1	0	0	2	39⅔	30	17	15	21	42
1990	—Salem (Carolina)	10	•14	.417	4.73	28	•28	2	0	0	*190⅓	*187	109	*100	*85	127
1991	—Carolina (South.)	15	8	.652	2.90	26	25	•8	1	0	183	155	68	59	51	120
	—Buffalo (A.A.)	0	1	.000	11.57	1	1	0	0	0	4⅔	8	6	6	1	4
1992	—Buffalo (A.A.)	10	3	.769	3.06	20	20	*6	1	0	135⅓	122	52	46	51	71
	—Pittsburgh (N.L.)	8	1	.889	2.15	13	13	4	1	0	92	76	26	22	35	51
1993	—Pittsburgh (N.L.)	6	11	.353	5.61	24	20	3	2	0	128⅓	145	83	80	75	59
	—Carolina (South.)	3	5	.375	6.99	9	9	1	0	0	56⅔	68	48	44	22	36
	Major league totals (2 years)	14	12	.538	4.17	37	33	7	3	0	220⅓	221	109	102	110	110

CHAMPIONSHIP SERIES RECORD

CHAMPIONSHIP SERIES NOTES: Shares single-series record for most complete games—2 (1992). . . . Shares N.L. career record for most complete games—2.

Year	Team (League)	W	L	Pct.	ERA	G	GS	CG	ShO	Sv.	IP	H	R	ER	BB	SO
1992	—Pittsburgh (N.L.)	2	0	1.000	3.00	2	2	2	0	0	18	14	6	6	5	7

RECORD AS POSITION PLAYER

Year	Team (League)	Pos.	G	AB	R	H	2B	3B	HR	RBI	Avg.	BB	SO	SB	PO	A	E	Avg.
			BATTING												FIELDING			
1988	—Watertown (NYP)	1B	54	159	24	30	6	2	3	20	.189	25	57	3	377	25	8	.980
1989	—Augusta (S. Atl.)	3B-1B	11	34	5	8	2	1	0	5	.235	1	14	1	27	6	3	.917
	—Welland (NYP)	P-3-2-1	36	63	7	13	4	0	1	3	.206	3	21	1	26	31	8	.877

WALBECK, MATT

C, TWINS

PERSONAL: Born October 2, 1969, in Sacramento, Calif. . . . 5-11/190. . . . Throws right, bats both. . . . Full name: Matthew Lovick Walbeck.
HIGH SCHOOL: Sacramento (Calif.).
TRANSACTIONS/CAREER NOTES: Selected by Chicago Cubs organization in eighth round of free-agent draft (June 2, 1987). . . . On Winston-Salem disabled list (April 12-July 11, 1990). . . . On Charleston, W.Va. disabled list (September 5, 1992-remainder of season). . . . Traded by Cubs with P Dave Stevens to Minnesota Twins for P Willie Banks (November 24, 1993).
STATISTICAL NOTES: Tied for Carolina League lead with 10 sacrifice flies in 1991. . . . Led American Association catchers with 561 total chances and tied for lead with nine double plays in 1993.
MISCELLANEOUS: Batted righthanded only (1987-89).

Year	Team (League)	Pos.	G	AB	R	H	2B	3B	HR	RBI	Avg.	BB	SO	SB	PO	A	E	Avg.
			BATTING												FIELDING			
1987	—Wytheville (Appal.)	C	51	169	24	53	9	3	1	28	.314	22	39	0	293	22	1	*.997
1988	—Char., W.Va. (SAL)	C	104	312	28	68	9	0	2	24	.218	30	44	7	549	68	14	.978
1989	—Peoria (Midwest)	C	94	341	38	86	19	0	4	47	.252	20	47	5	605	72	11	.984
1990	—Peoria (Midwest)	C	25	66	2	15	1	0	0	5	.227	5	7	1	137	16	2	.987
1991	—Winst.-Salem (Car.)	C	91	260	25	70	11	0	3	41	.269	20	23	3	473	64	12	.978
1992	—Charlotte (South.)	C-1B	105	385	48	116	22	1	7	42	.301	33	56	0	552	80	10	.984
1993	—Chicago (N.L.)	C	11	30	2	6	2	0	1	6	.200	1	6	0	49	2	0	1.000
	—Iowa (Am. Assoc.)	C	87	331	31	93	18	2	6	43	.281	18	47	1	496	*64	1	*.998
	Major league totals (1 year)		11	30	2	6	2	0	1	6	.200	1	6	0	49	2	0	1.000

WALEWANDER, JIM

IF, MARLINS

PERSONAL: Born May 2, 1961, in Chicago. . . . 5-10/155. . . . Throws right, bats both. . . . Full name: James Lawrence Walewander. . . . Name pronounced WHALE-wonn-der.
COLLEGE: Iowa State.
TRANSACTIONS/CAREER NOTES: Selected by Detroit Tigers organization in ninth round of free-agent draft (June 6, 1983). . . . Granted free agency (October 15, 1989). . . . Signed by Columbus, New York Yankees organization (December 27, 1989). . . . Granted free agency (October 15, 1990). . . . Re-signed by Columbus (December 9, 1990). . . . Granted free agency (October

W

15, 1991).... Signed by Oklahoma City, Texas Rangers organization (July 15, 1992).... Granted free agency (October 15, 1992).... Signed by Vancouver, California Angels organization (January 20, 1993).... Granted free agency (October 8, 1993).... Signed by Edmonton, Florida Marlins organization (November 12, 1993).

STATISTICAL NOTES: Led Appalachian League second basemen with 188 assists, 325 total chances and 33 double plays in 1983. ... Led Florida State League second basemen with 329 putouts in 1984.... Led Florida State League second basemen with 698 total chances in 1985.... Led International League in on-base percentage with .408 and in being hit by pitch with 11 in 1990. ... Led International League in caught stealing with 19 in 1991.

			BATTING											FIELDING			
Year	Team (League)	Pos.	G	AB	R	H	2B	3B	HR	RBI	Avg.	BB	SO	SB	PO	A	E	Avg.
1983	—Bristol (Appal.)	2B-SS	•73	*285	56	91	14	2	4	28	.319	34	39	*35	140	222	16	.958
1984	—Lakeland (Fla. St.)	2B-SS-3B	137	502	70	136	16	2	0	36	.271	64	40	47	342	341	23	.967
1985	—Lakeland (Fla. St.)	2B	129	499	80	141	13	7	0	36	.283	48	28	30	267	*417	14	.980
	—Birm. (Southern)	2B	14	45	3	13	0	1	0	2	.289	2	3	0	22	33	1	.982
1986	—Glens Falls (East.)	2B-3B-SS	124	440	59	107	10	6	1	31	.243	43	54	25	207	291	18	.965
1987	—Toledo (Int'l)	2B	59	210	27	57	9	1	0	12	.271	28	31	18	129	139	12	.957
	—Detroit (A.L.)	2B-3B-SS	53	54	24	13	3	1	1	4	.241	7	6	2	26	58	1	.988
1988	—Detroit (A.L.)	2B-SS-3B	88	175	23	37	5	0	0	6	.211	12	26	11	125	154	6	.979
	—Toledo (Int'l)	2B	4	11	4	5	2	0	0	2	.455	3	3	2	12	10	1	.957
1989	—Toledo (Int'l)	2B-SS-3B	133	484	53	109	15	3	7	38	.225	57	72	32	182	282	24	.951
1990	—Columbus (Int'l)■	2-3-S-1	131	368	80	92	14	5	1	31	.250	*90	67	49	216	282	22	.958
	—New York (A.L.)	2B-3B-SS	9	5	1	1	1	0	0	1	.200	0	0	1	4	5	0	1.000
1991	—Columbus (Int'l)	S-3-2-1-0	126	408	81	92	11	3	3	38	.225	69	66	*54	181	298	20	.960
1992	—Okla. City (A.A.)■	2B	44	124	20	26	7	0	0	10	.210	17	18	5	69	108	5	.973
1993	—Vancouver (PCL)■	2-3-S-0	102	351	77	107	12	1	1	43	.305	60	57	36	165	224	8	.980
	—California (A.L.)	SS-2B	12	8	2	1	0	0	0	3	.125	5	1	1	9	13	0	1.000
Major league totals (4 years)			162	242	50	52	9	1	1	14	.215	24	33	15	164	230	7	.983

WALK, BOB

P

PERSONAL: Born November 26, 1956, in Van Nuys, Calif.... 6-3/217.... Throws right, bats right.... Full name: Robert Vernon Walk.

HIGH SCHOOL: Hart (Calif.).

COLLEGE: College of the Canyons (Calif.).

TRANSACTIONS/CAREER NOTES: Selected by California Angels organization in fifth round of free-agent draft (January 9, 1975). ... Selected by Philadelphia Phillies organization in fifth round of free-agent draft (January 7, 1976).... Selected by Phillies organization in secondary phase of free-agent draft (June 8, 1976).... Traded by Phillies to Atlanta Braves for OF Gary Mathews (March 25, 1981).... On Atlanta disabled list (May 26-August 9, 1981).... Released by Braves (March 26, 1984).... Signed by Pittsburgh Pirates organization (April 3, 1984).... On Pittsburgh disabled list (July 23, 1984-remainder of season). ... Granted free agency (November 4, 1988).... Re-signed by Pirates (November 27, 1988).... On disabled list (June 9-24, 1989; June 20-July 14 and August 6-25, 1990).... On Pittsburgh disabled list (April 15-May 14, 1991).... On Pittsburgh disabled list (July 27-September 1, 1991); included rehabilitation assignment to Carolina (August 28-30).... Granted free agency (November 4, 1991).... Re-signed by Pirates (December 31, 1991).... On disabled list (April 20-May 10 and June 2-20, 1992).... On suspended list (August 31-September 5, 1993).... Granted free agency (November 1, 1993).

STATISTICAL NOTES: Led Carolina League with 13 hit batsmen in 1978.... Tied for International League lead with 22 home runs allowed in 1983.... Led N.L. with 13 wild pitches in 1988.

Year	Team (League)	W	L	Pct.	ERA	G	GS	CG	ShO	Sv.	IP	H	R	ER	BB	SO
1977	—Sp'rt'brg (W. Caro.)	6	9	.400	3.64	15	15	7	1	0	99	90	55	40	46	66
	—Peninsula (Caro.)	0	2	.000	4.25	8	8	0	0	0	36	44	31	17	20	23
1978	—Peninsula (Caro.)	13	8	.619	2.12	26	26	9	0	0	187	147	58	44	64	150
1979	—Reading (Eastern)	12	7	.632	*2.24	24	24	11	1	0	185	156	62	46	77	*135
1980	—Okla. City (A.A.)	5	1	.833	2.94	8	8	0	0	0	49	39	21	16	17	36
	—Philadelphia (N.L.)	11	7	.611	4.56	27	27	2	0	0	152	163	82	77	71	94
1981	—Atlanta (N.L.)■	1	4	.200	4.60	12	8	0	0	0	43	41	25	22	23	16
	—Richmond (Int'l)	2	1	.667	2.45	4	3	0	0	0	22	18	7	6	11	13
1982	—Atlanta (N.L.)	11	9	.550	4.87	32	27	3	1	0	164⅓	179	101	89	59	84
1983	—Richmond (Int'l)	11	12	.478	5.21	28	•28	*11	2	0	*185	179	*119	*107	102	123
	—Atlanta (N.L.)	0	0	...	7.36	1	1	0	0	0	3⅔	7	3	3	2	4
1984	—Hawaii (PCL)■	9	5	.643	*2.26	18	18	5	3	0	127⅓	100	39	32	42	85
	—Pittsburgh (N.L.)	1	1	.500	2.61	2	2	0	0	0	10⅓	8	5	3	4	10
1985	—Hawaii (PCL)	*16	5	.762	*2.65	24	24	*12	1	0	173	143	57	51	61	124
	—Pittsburgh (N.L.)	2	3	.400	3.68	9	9	1	1	0	58⅔	60	27	24	18	40
1986	—Pittsburgh (N.L.)	7	8	.467	3.75	44	15	1	1	2	141⅔	129	66	59	64	78
1987	—Pittsburgh (N.L.)	8	2	.800	3.31	39	12	1	1	0	117	107	52	43	51	78
1988	—Pittsburgh (N.L.)	12	10	.545	2.71	32	32	1	1	0	212⅔	183	75	64	65	81
1989	—Pittsburgh (N.L.)	13	10	.565	4.41	33	31	2	0	0	196	208	106	96	65	83
1990	—Pittsburgh (N.L.)	7	5	.583	3.75	26	24	1	1	1	129⅔	136	59	54	36	73
1991	—Pittsburgh (N.L.)	9	2	.818	3.60	25	20	0	0	0	115	104	53	46	35	67
	—Carolina (South.)	0	1	.000	1.80	1	1	0	0	0	5	5	1	1	2	3
1992	—Pittsburgh (N.L.)	10	6	.625	3.20	36	19	1	0	2	135	132	54	48	43	60
1993	—Pittsburgh (N.L.)	13	14	.481	5.68	32	32	3	0	0	187	214	121	*118	70	80
Major league totals (14 years)		105	81	.565	4.03	350	259	16	6	5	1666	1671	829	746	606	848

CHAMPIONSHIP SERIES RECORD

Year	Team (League)	W	L	Pct.	ERA	G	GS	CG	ShO	Sv.	IP	H	R	ER	BB	SO
1980	—Philadelphia (N.L.)							Did not play.								
1982	—Atlanta (N.L.)	0	0	...	9.00	1	0	0	0	0	1	2	1	1	1	1
1990	—Pittsburgh (N.L.)	1	1	.500	4.85	2	2	0	0	0	13	11	7	7	2	8
1991	—Pittsburgh (N.L.)	0	0	...	1.93	3	0	0	0	1	9⅓	5	2	2	3	5
1992	—Pittsburgh (N.L.)	1	0	1.000	3.86	2	1	1	0	0	11⅔	6	5	5	7	6
Champ. series totals (4 years)		2	1	.667	3.86	8	3	1	0	1	35	24	15	15	13	20

W

WORLD SERIES RECORD

Year	Team (League)	W	L	Pct.	ERA	G	GS	CG	ShO	Sv.	IP	H	R	ER	BB	SO
1980	—Philadelphia (N.L.).....	1	0	1.000	7.71	1	1	0	0	0	7	8	6	6	3	3

ALL-STAR GAME RECORD

Year	League	W	L	Pct.	ERA	GS	CG	ShO	Sv.	IP	H	R	ER	BB	SO
1988	—National........................	0	0	...	0.00	0	0	0	0	⅓	0	0	0	0	0

WALKER, CHICO

2B/3B/OF

PERSONAL: Born November 26, 1958, in Jackson, Miss.... 5-9/185.... Throws right, bats both.... Full name: Cleotha Walker.

HIGH SCHOOL: Tilden (Chicago).

TRANSACTIONS/CAREER NOTES: Selected by Boston Red Sox organization in 22nd round of free-agent draft (June 8, 1976).... On disabled list (August 22-September 19, 1979).... Granted free agency (October 15, 1984).... Signed by Iowa, Chicago Cubs organization (November 9, 1984).... Traded by Cubs organization to California Angels for P Todd Fischer (October 16, 1987).... Granted free agency (October 15, 1988).... Signed by Toronto Blue Jays organization (January 28, 1989).... Granted free agency (October 22, 1989).... Signed by Chicago Cubs organization (April 25, 1990).... Granted free agency (December 20, 1991).... Re-signed by Cubs (December 23, 1991).... Claimed on waivers by New York Mets (May 7, 1992).... Released by Mets (October 4, 1993).

STATISTICAL NOTES: Led Eastern League in caught stealing with 16 in 1979.... Led International League second basemen with 667 total chances and tied for lead with 74 double plays in 1980.... Led International League with nine intentional bases on balls received in 1984.... Led American Association in total bases with 258 and in caught stealing with 22 in 1986.... Led American Association outfielders with 16 assists in 1986.

			BATTING											FIELDING			
Year	Team (League)	Pos.	G	AB	R	H	2B	3B	HR	RBI	Avg.	BB	SO	SB	PO	A	E	Avg.
1976	—Elmira (N.Y.-Penn)..	2B	22	28	9	5	1	2	0	1	.179	11	10	0	9	18	3	.900
1977	—Elmira (N.Y.-Penn)..	2B-SS	64	227	26	50	4	3	1	14	.220	29	39	10	122	196	15	.955
1978	—Winter Haven (FSL)..	SS-3B-2B	133	480	66	134	10	6	3	52	.279	43	71	17	172	380	42	.929
1979	—Bristol (Eastern)......	2B	123	498	75	132	19	★12	8	57	.265	44	77	29	252	357	23	.964
1980	—Pawtucket (Int'l)......	2B	139	536	59	146	18	7	8	52	.272	41	91	21	252	★394	★21	.969
	—Boston (A.L.)...........	2B	19	57	3	12	0	0	1	5	.211	6	10	3	15	31	2	.958
1981	—Pawtucket (Int'l)......	OF-2B-3B	138	535	50	148	21	5	17	68	.277	49	110	24	209	178	13	.968
	—Boston (A.L.)...........	2B	6	17	3	6	0	0	0	2	.353	1	2	0	4	10	0	1.000
1982	—Pawtucket (Int'l)......	0-2-3-S	133	494	71	124	22	2	15	66	.251	60	99	25	209	48	11	.959
1983	—Pawtucket (Int'l)......	3-0-S-2	125	442	78	119	18	1	18	56	.269	68	80	27	122	126	16	.939
	—Boston (A.L.)...........	OF	4	5	2	2	0	2	0	1	.400	0	0	0	4	1	0	1.000
1984	—Pawtucket (Int'l)......	2B-OF-3B	130	499	•91	131	26	5	18	51	.263	80	88	42	223	241	20	.959
	—Boston (A.L.)...........	2B	3	2	1	0	0	0	0	0	.000	0	1	0	0	1	0	1.000
1985	—Iowa (Am. Assoc.)■..	OF-3B	89	331	47	94	17	8	5	46	.284	50	60	42	177	6	5	.973
	—Chicago (N.L.).........	OF-2B	21	12	3	1	0	0	0	0	.083	0	5	1	4	0	0	1.000
1986	—Iowa (Am. Assoc.).......	OF-2B	138	530	97	•158	30	11	16	65	.298	62	68	•67	286	†38	8	.976
	—Chicago (N.L.).........	OF	28	101	21	28	3	2	1	7	.277	10	20	15	42	1	2	.956
1987	—Chicago (N.L.).........	OF-3B	47	105	15	21	4	0	0	7	.200	12	23	11	37	0	1	.974
	—Iowa (Am. Assoc.).....	0-2-3-S	90	315	64	77	13	3	8	31	.244	65	52	28	146	90	8	.967
1988	—Edmonton (PCL)■.....	OF-2B	79	304	58	88	17	4	7	39	.289	29	47	25	174	5	7	.962
	—California (A.L.).......	OF-2B-3B	33	78	8	12	1	0	0	2	.154	6	15	2	33	20	2	.964
1989	—Syracuse (Int'l)■......	OF-2B	123	431	61	103	11	5	12	63	.239	58	61	37	177	30	3	.986
1990	—Charlotte (South.)■..	OF-2B	88	310	49	82	15	1	12	45	.265	44	72	10	107	50	4	.975
	—Iowa (Am. Assoc.)....	OF	32	114	30	41	7	1	6	19	.360	25	17	9	37	6	2	.956
1991	—Chicago (N.L.)..........	3B-OF-2B	124	374	51	96	10	1	6	34	.257	33	57	13	106	89	8	.961
1992	—Chi.-N.Y. (N.L.)■......	3B-OF-2B	126	253	26	73	12	1	4	38	.289	27	50	15	54	85	8	.946
1993	—New York (N.L.)........	2B-3B-OF	115	213	18	48	7	1	5	19	.225	14	29	7	68	82	8	.949
American League totals (5 years)............			65	159	17	32	1	2	1	10	.201	13	28	5	56	63	4	.967
National League totals (6 years).............			461	1058	134	267	36	5	16	105	.252	96	184	62	311	257	27	.955
Major league totals (11 years)................			526	1217	151	299	37	7	17	115	.246	109	212	67	367	320	31	.957

WALKER, LARRY

OF, EXPOS

PERSONAL: Born December 1, 1966, in Maple Ridge, British Columbia, Canada.... 6-3/215.... Throws right, bats left.... Full name: Larry Kenneth Robert Walker.

HIGH SCHOOL: Maple Ridge (B.C.) Senior Secondary School.

TRANSACTIONS/CAREER NOTES: Signed as free agent by Montreal Expos organization (November 14, 1984).... On disabled list (April 4, 1988-entire season; June 28-July 13, 1991 and May 26-June 10, 1993).

HONORS: Named outfielder on THE SPORTING NEWS N.L. All-Star team (1992).... Won N.L. Gold Glove as outfielder (1992-93).... Named outfielder on THE SPORTING NEWS N.L. Silver Slugger team (1992).

			BATTING											FIELDING			
Year	Team (League)	Pos.	G	AB	R	H	2B	3B	HR	RBI	Avg.	BB	SO	SB	PO	A	E	Avg.
1985	—Utica (N.Y.-Penn)....	1B-3B	62	215	24	48	8	2	2	26	.223	18	57	12	354	62	8	.981
1986	—Burlington (Midw.)...	OF-3B	95	332	67	96	12	6	29	74	.289	46	112	16	106	51	10	.940
	—W.P. Beach (FSL).....	OF	38	113	20	32	7	5	4	16	.283	26	32	2	44	5	0	1.000
1987	—Jacksonv. (South.)..	OF	128	474	91	136	25	7	26	83	.287	67	120	24	263	9	9	.968
1988	—..................................		Did not play.															
1989	—Indianapolis (A.A.)...	OF	114	385	68	104	18	2	12	59	.270	50	87	36	241	★18	★11	.959
	—Montreal (N.L.).........	OF	20	47	4	8	0	0	0	4	.170	5	13	1	19	2	0	1.000
1990	—Montreal (N.L.).........	OF	133	419	59	101	18	3	19	51	.241	49	112	21	249	12	4	.985
1991	—Montreal (N.L.).........	OF-1B	137	487	59	141	30	2	16	64	.290	42	102	14	536	36	6	.990
1992	—Montreal (N.L.).........	OF	143	528	85	159	31	4	23	93	.301	41	97	18	269	16	2	.993
1993	—Montreal (N.L.).........	OF-1B	138	490	85	130	24	5	22	86	.265	80	76	29	316	16	6	.982
Major league totals (5 years)..................			571	1971	292	539	103	14	80	298	.273	217	400	83	1389	82	18	.988

ALL-STAR GAME RECORD

Year	League	Pos.	AB	R	H	2B	3B	HR	RBI	Avg.	BB	SO	SB	PO	A	E	Avg.
			BATTING											FIELDING			
1992	—National	PH	1	0	1	0	0	0	0	1.000	0	0	0	...	...	...	...

WALKER, PETE

P, METS

PERSONAL: Born April 8, 1969, in Beverly, Mass. . . . 6-2/195. . . . Throws right, bats right. . . . Full name: Peter Brian Walker.
HIGH SCHOOL: East Lyme (Conn.).
COLLEGE: Connecticut.
TRANSACTIONS/CAREER NOTES: Selected by New York Mets organization in seventh round of free-agent draft (June 4, 1990). . . . On disabled list (June 6-18, 1992 and April 25-May 9, 1993).

Year	Team (League)	W	L	Pct.	ERA	G	GS	CG	ShO	Sv.	IP	H	R	ER	BB	SO
1990	—Pittsfield (NYP)	5	7	.417	4.16	16	13	1	0	0	80	74	43	37	46	73
1991	—St. Lucie (Fla. St.)	10	12	.455	3.21	26	25	1	0	0	151⅓	145	77	54	52	95
1992	—Binghamton (East.)	7	12	.368	4.12	24	23	4	0	0	139⅔	159	77	64	46	72
1993	—Binghamton (East.)	4	9	.308	3.44	45	10	0	0	19	99⅓	89	45	38	46	89

WALLACH, TIM

3B, DODGERS

PERSONAL: Born September 14, 1957, in Huntington Park, Calif. . . . 6-3/202. . . . Throws right, bats right. . . . Full name: Timothy Charles Wallach.
HIGH SCHOOL: University (Irvine, Calif.).
COLLEGE: Saddleback Community College (Calif.) and Cal State Fullerton.
TRANSACTIONS/CAREER NOTES: Selected by California Angels organization in eighth round of free-agent draft (June 6, 1978). . . . Selected by Montreal Expos organization in first round (10th pick overall) of free-agent draft (June 5, 1979). . . . Traded by Expos to Los Angeles Dodgers for SS Tim Barker (December 24, 1992). . . . On disabled list (July 18-August 9, 1993).
HONORS: Named Golden Spikes Award winner by USA Baseball (1979). . . . Named College Player of the Year by THE SPORTING NEWS (1979). . . . Named first baseman on THE SPORTING NEWS college All-America team (1979). . . . Named third baseman on THE SPORTING NEWS N.L. All-Star team (1985 and 1987). . . . Won N.L. Gold Glove at third base (1985, 1988 and 1990). . . . Named third baseman on THE SPORTING NEWS N.L. Silver Slugger team (1985 and 1987).
STATISTICAL NOTES: Hit home run in first major league at-bat (September 6, 1980). . . . Led American Association with 295 total bases and tied for lead with nine sacrifice flies in 1980. . . . Led N.L. third basemen with 132 putouts in 1982, 162 in 1984, 128 in 1987 and 123 in 1988. . . . Led N.L. third basemen with 332 assists in 1984. . . . Led N.L. third basemen with 515 total chances in 1984 and 549 in 1985. . . . Led N.L. third basemen with 29 double plays in 1984, 34 in 1985 and tied for lead with 31 in 1988. . . . Led N.L. in being hit by pitch with 10 in 1986. . . . Tied for N.L. lead with 16 game-winning RBIs in 1987. . . . Hit three home runs in one game (May 4, 1987). . . . Led N.L. in grounding into double plays with 21 in 1989.

Year	Team (League)	Pos.	G	AB	R	H	2B	3B	HR	RBI	Avg.	BB	SO	SB	PO	A	E	Avg.
				BATTING											FIELDING			
1979	—Memphis (South.)	1B-3B	75	257	50	84	16	4	18	51	.327	37	53	0	290	35	4	.988
1980	—Denver (A.A.)	3B-OF-1B	134	512	103	144	29	7	36	124	.281	51	92	1	222	147	21	.946
	—Montreal (N.L.)	OF-1B	5	11	1	2	0	0	1	2	.182	1	5	0	12	0	0	1.000
1981	—Montreal (N.L.)	OF-1B-3B	71	212	19	50	9	1	4	13	.236	15	37	0	207	31	1	.996
1982	—Montreal (N.L.)	3B-OF-1B	158	596	89	160	31	3	28	97	.268	36	81	6	†132	287	23	.948
1983	—Montreal (N.L.)	3B	156	581	54	156	33	3	19	70	.269	55	97	0	*151	262	19	.956
1984	—Montreal (N.L.)	3B-SS	160	582	55	143	25	4	18	72	.246	50	101	3	†162	†332	21	.959
1985	—Montreal (N.L.)	3B	155	569	70	148	36	3	22	81	.260	38	79	9	*148	*383	18	.967
1986	—Montreal (N.L.)	3B	134	480	50	112	22	1	18	71	.233	44	72	8	94	270	16	.958
1987	—Montreal (N.L.)	3B-P	153	593	89	177	*42	4	26	123	.298	37	98	9	†128	292	21	.952
1988	—Montreal (N.L.)	3B-2B	159	592	52	152	32	5	12	69	.257	38	88	2	†124	329	18	.962
1989	—Montreal (N.L.)	3B-P	154	573	76	159	•42	0	13	77	.277	58	81	3	113	302	18	.958
1990	—Montreal (N.L.)	3B	161	626	69	185	37	5	21	98	.296	42	80	6	128	309	21	.954
1991	—Montreal (N.L.)	3B	151	577	60	130	22	1	13	73	.225	50	100	2	107	310	14	*.968
1992	—Montreal (N.L.)	3B-1B	150	537	53	120	29	1	9	59	.223	50	90	2	689	244	15	.984
1993	—Los Angeles (N.L.)■	3B-1B	133	477	42	106	19	1	12	62	.222	32	70	0	121	229	15	.959
Major league totals (14 years)			1900	7006	779	1800	379	32	216	967	.257	546	1079	50	2316	3580	220	.964

DIVISION SERIES RECORD

Year	Team (League)	Pos.	G	AB	R	H	2B	3B	HR	RBI	Avg.	BB	SO	SB	PO	A	E	Avg.
				BATTING											FIELDING			
1981	—Montreal (N.L.)	OF	4	4	1	1	1	0	0	0	.250	4	0	0	4	0	0	1.000

CHAMPIONSHIP SERIES RECORD

Year	Team (League)	Pos.	G	AB	R	H	2B	3B	HR	RBI	Avg.	BB	SO	SB	PO	A	E	Avg.
				BATTING											FIELDING			
1981	—Montreal (N.L.)	PH	1	1	0	0	0	0	0	0	.000	0	0	0	...	...	...	...

ALL-STAR GAME RECORD

Year	League	Pos.	AB	R	H	2B	3B	HR	RBI	Avg.	BB	SO	SB	PO	A	E	Avg.
			BATTING											FIELDING			
1984	—National	3B	1	0	0	0	0	0	0	.000	0	0	0	0	0	0	...
1985	—National	3B	2	1	1	1	0	0	0	.500	1	1	0	1	1	0	1.000
1987	—National	3B	3	0	0	0	0	0	0	.000	0	0	0	0	2	0	1.000
1989	—National	3B	1	0	0	0	0	0	0	.000	0	0	0	0	0	0	...
1990	—National	3B	2	0	0	0	0	0	0	.000	0	0	0	0	0	0	...
All-Star Game totals (5 years)			9	1	1	1	0	0	0	.111	1	1	0	1	3	0	1.000

RECORD AS PITCHER

Year	Team (League)	W	L	Pct.	ERA	G	GS	CG	ShO	Sv.	IP	H	R	ER	BB	SO
1987	—Montreal (N.L.)	0	0	...	0.00	1	0	0	0	0	1	1	0	0	0	0

Year	Team (League)	W	L	Pct.	ERA	G	GS	CG	ShO	Sv.	IP	H	R	ER	BB	SO
1989	—Montreal (N.L.)	0	0	...	9.00	1	0	0	0	0	1	2	1	1	0	0
Major league totals (2 years)		0	0	...	4.50	2	0	0	0	0	2	3	1	1	0	0

WALTERS, DAN

C

PERSONAL: Born August 15, 1966, in Brunswick, Me. ... 6-4/230. ... Throws right, bats right. ... Full name: Daniel Gene Walters.
HIGH SCHOOL: Santana (Santee, Calif.).
TRANSACTIONS/CAREER NOTES: Selected by Houston Astros organization in fifth round of free-agent draft (June 4, 1984). ... Traded by Astros organization to San Diego Padres organization for P Ed Vosberg (December 13, 1988). ... Granted free agency (November 22, 1993).
STATISTICAL NOTES: Led South Atlantic League catchers with 723 total chances in 1986. ... Led Florida State League catchers with 607 total chances in 1987. ... Tied for Southern League lead in double plays by catcher with six in 1988.

			BATTING												FIELDING			
Year	Team (League)	Pos.	G	AB	R	H	2B	3B	HR	RBI	Avg.	BB	SO	SB	PO	A	E	Avg.
1985	—Asheville (S. Atl.)	C	15	28	1	1	0	0	0	1	.036	1	11	0	54	8	2	.969
	—Auburn (NY-Penn)	C	44	144	15	30	6	0	0	10	.208	8	23	1	294	33	5	.985
1986	—Asheville (S. Atl.)	C	101	366	42	96	21	1	8	46	.262	14	59	1	655	62	6	*.992
1987	—Osceola (Fla. St.)	C	99	338	23	84	8	0	1	30	.249	33	42	2	*540	62	5	*.992
1988	—Columbus (South.)	C	98	305	31	71	10	1	7	28	.233	26	42	1	538	67	10	.984
1989	—Wichita (Texas)■	C	89	300	30	82	15	0	6	45	.273	25	31	0	424	35	6	.987
1990	—Wichita (Texas)	C	58	199	25	59	12	0	7	40	.296	21	21	0	276	41	3	.991
	—Las Vegas (PCL)	C-1B	53	184	19	47	9	0	3	26	.255	13	24	0	247	28	2	.993
1991	—Las Vegas (PCL)	C-1B	96	293	39	93	22	0	4	44	.317	22	35	0	449	46	10	.980
1992	—Las Vegas (PCL)	C	35	127	16	50	9	0	2	25	.394	10	12	0	200	23	6	.974
	—San Diego (N.L.)	C	57	179	14	45	11	1	4	22	.251	10	28	1	329	25	3	.992
1993	—San Diego (N.L.)	C	27	94	6	19	3	0	1	10	.202	7	13	0	138	21	5	.970
	—Las Vegas (PCL)	C	66	223	26	64	14	0	5	39	.287	14	26	1	245	14	2	.992
Major league totals (2 years)			84	273	20	64	14	1	5	32	.234	17	41	1	467	46	8	.985

WALTON, BRUCE

P, ROCKIES

PERSONAL: Born December 25, 1962, in Bakersfield, Calif. ... 6-2/195. ... Throws right, bats right. ... Full name: Bruce Kenneth Walton.
HIGH SCHOOL: North Bakersfield (Calif.).
COLLEGE: Hawaii.
TRANSACTIONS/CAREER NOTES: Selected by St. Louis Cardinals organization in 10th round of free-agent draft (June 8, 1981). ... Selected by Oakland Athletics organization in 16th round of free-agent draft (June 3, 1985). ... Granted free agency (October 15, 1992). ... Signed by Montreal Expos organization (December 7, 1992). ... Traded by Expos organization to Tucson, Houston Astros organization, for a player to be named later (August 9, 1993). ... Granted free agency (October 15, 1993). ... Signed by Colorado Rockies organization (December 3, 1993).
STATISTICAL NOTES: Pitched one inning, combining with starter Chris Nabholz (eight innings) in 4-0 no-hit victory for Ottawa against Richmond (May 24, 1993).

Year	Team (League)	W	L	Pct.	ERA	G	GS	CG	ShO	Sv.	IP	H	R	ER	BB	SO
1985	—Pocatello (Pioneer)	3	7	.300	4.11	18	9	2	0	3	76⅔	89	46	35	27	69
1986	—Madison (Midwest)	0	0	...	5.40	1	1	0	0	0	5	5	3	3	1	1
	—Modesto (Calif.)	13	7	.650	4.09	27	•27	4	0	0	176	*204	96	80	41	107
1987	—Modesto (Calif.)	8	6	.571	2.88	16	16	3	1	0	106⅓	97	44	34	27	84
	—Huntsville (South.)	2	2	.500	3.10	18	2	0	0	2	58	61	24	20	13	40
1988	—Huntsville (South.)	4	5	.444	4.56	42	3	0	0	3	116⅓	126	64	59	23	82
1989	—Tacoma (PCL)	8	6	.571	3.76	32	14	1	1	1	107⅔	118	59	45	27	76
1990	—Tacoma (PCL)	5	5	.500	3.11	46	5	0	0	7	98⅓	103	42	34	23	67
1991	—Tacoma (PCL)	1	1	.500	1.35	38	0	0	0	20	46⅔	39	11	7	5	49
	—Oakland (A.L.)	1	0	1.000	6.23	12	0	0	0	0	13	11	9	9	6	10
1992	—Oakland (A.L.)	0	0	...	9.90	7	0	0	0	0	10	17	11	11	3	7
	—Tacoma (PCL)	8	2	*.800	2.77	35	7	2	1	8	81⅓	76	29	25	21	60
1993	—Montreal (N.L.)■	0	0	...	9.53	4	0	0	0	0	5⅔	11	6	6	3	0
	—Ottawa (Int'l)	4	4	.500	1.05	40	0	0	0	16	42⅔	32	12	5	8	40
	—Tucson (PCL)■	2	0	1.000	1.80	13	0	0	0	7	15	12	4	3	3	14
A.L. totals (2 years)		1	0	1.000	7.83	19	0	0	0	0	23	28	20	20	9	17
N.L. totals (1 year)		0	0	...	9.53	4	0	0	0	0	5⅔	11	6	6	3	0
Major league totals (3 years)		1	0	1.000	8.16	23	0	0	0	0	28⅔	39	26	26	12	17

WALTON, JEROME

OF, REDS

PERSONAL: Born July 8, 1965, in Newnan, Ga. ... 6-1/175. ... Throws right, bats right. ... Full name: Jerome O'Terrell Walton.
HIGH SCHOOL: Enterprise (Ala.).
COLLEGE: Enterprise (Ala.) State Junior College.
TRANSACTIONS/CAREER NOTES: Selected by Chicago Cubs organization in second round of free-agent draft (January 14, 1986). ... On Chicago disabled list (May 11-June 11, 1989); included rehabilitation assignment to Iowa (June 6-11). ... On Chicago disabled list (June 18-August 2, 1990); included rehabilitation assignment to Iowa (July 29-August 1). ... On Chicago disabled list (March 28-April 24, 1992); included rehabilitation assignment to Iowa (April 17-24). ... On Iowa disabled list (July 1-September 14, 1992). ... Granted free agency (December 19, 1992). ... Signed by California Angels organization (January 29, 1993). ... Placed on Vancouver disabled list (July 19, 1993). ... Released by Angels organization (August 20, 1993). ... Signed by Cincinnati Reds organization (November 4, 1993).
HONORS: Named N.L. Rookie Player of the Year by THE SPORTING NEWS (1989). ... Named N.L. Rookie of the Year by Baseball Writers' Association of America (1989).
STATISTICAL NOTES: Led Appalachian League outfielders with 128 putouts and 131 total chances and tied for lead with two double plays in 1986. ... Led Midwest League in caught stealing with 25 in 1987.

Year	Team (League)	Pos.	G	AB	R	H	2B	3B	HR	RBI	Avg.	BB	SO	SB	PO	A	E	Avg.
			BATTING												FIELDING			
1986	—Wytheville (Appal.)..	OF-3B	62	229	48	66	7	4	5	34	.288	28	40	21	†130	7	3	.979
1987	—Peoria (Midwest)......	OF	128	472	102	158	24	11	6	38	.335	91	91	49	255	9	7	.974
1988	—Pittsfield (Eastern) ..	OF	120	414	64	137	26	2	3	49	*.331	41	69	42	270	11	2	*.993
1989	—Chicago (N.L.)	OF	116	475	64	139	23	3	5	46	.293	27	77	24	289	2	3	.990
	—Iowa (Am. Assoc.)....	OF	4	18	4	6	1	0	1	3	.333	1	5	2	8	0	0	1.000
1990	—Chicago (N.L.)	OF	101	392	63	103	16	2	2	21	.263	50	70	14	247	3	6	.977
	—Iowa (Am. Assoc.)....	OF	4	16	3	3	0	0	1	1	.188	2	4	0	6	1	0	1.000
1991	—Chicago (N.L.)	OF	123	270	42	59	13	1	5	17	.219	19	55	7	170	2	3	.983
1992	—Iowa (Am. Assoc.)....	OF	7	27	8	8	2	1	0	3	.296	4	6	1	10	0	0	1.000
	—Chicago (N.L.)	OF	30	55	7	7	0	1	0	1	.127	9	13	1	34	0	2	.944
1993	—California (A.L.)■.....	OF	5	2	2	0	0	0	0	0	.000	1	2	1	2	0	0	1.000
	—Vancouver (PCL)	OF	54	176	34	55	11	1	2	20	.313	16	24	5	82	3	0	1.000
American League totals (1 year)			5	2	2	0	0	0	0	0	.000	1	2	1	2	0	0	1.000
National League totals (4 years)			370	1192	176	308	52	7	12	85	.258	105	215	46	740	7	14	.982
Major league totals (5 years)			375	1194	178	308	52	7	12	85	.258	106	217	47	742	7	14	.982

CHAMPIONSHIP SERIES RECORD

CHAMPIONSHIP SERIES NOTES: Shares records for most at-bats—2; hits—2; and singles—2, in one inning (October 5, 1989, first inning).

Year	Team (League)	Pos.	G	AB	R	H	2B	3B	HR	RBI	Avg.	BB	SO	SB	PO	A	E	Avg.
			BATTING												FIELDING			
1989	—Chicago (N.L.)	OF	5	22	4	8	0	0	0	2	.364	2	2	0	11	0	0	1.000

WARD, DUANE

P, BLUE JAYS

PERSONAL: Born May 28, 1964, in Parkview, N.M. . . . 6-4/225. . . . Throws right, bats right. . . . Full name: Roy Duane Ward.

HIGH SCHOOL: Farmington (N.M.).

TRANSACTIONS/CAREER NOTES: Selected by Atlanta Braves organization in first round (ninth pick overall) of free-agent draft (June 7, 1982). . . . On disabled list (May 7-29 and July 14-August 7, 1984). . . . Traded by Braves organization to Toronto Blue Jays for P Doyle Alexander (July 6, 1986).

Year	Team (League)	W	L	Pct.	ERA	G	GS	CG	ShO	Sv.	IP	H	R	ER	BB	SO
1982	—GC Braves (GCL)	2	3	.400	4.53	8	8	1	0	0	45⅔	45	25	23	24	31
	—Anderson (S. Atl.)	1	2	.333	5.32	5	4	0	0	0	23⅔	24	16	14	15	18
1983	—Durham (Carolina).....	11	13	.458	4.29	28	28	6	2	0	178⅓	165	103	85	75	115
1984	—Greenville (South.).....	4	9	.308	4.99	21	20	4	0	0	104⅔	108	71	58	57	54
1985	—Greenville (South.).....	11	10	.524	4.20	28	24	3	0	0	150	141	83	70	*105	100
	—Richmond (Int'l)	0	1	.000	11.81	5	1	0	0	0	5⅓	8	9	7	8	3
1986	—Atlanta (N.L.)	0	1	.000	7.31	10	0	0	0	0	16	22	13	13	8	8
	—Rich.-Syrac. (Int'l)■..	7	5	.583	3.98	20	20	3	0	0	117⅔	125	56	52	52	67
	—Toronto (A.L.)	0	1	.000	13.50	2	1	0	0	0	2	3	4	3	4	1
1987	—Toronto (A.L.)	1	0	1.000	6.94	12	1	0	0	0	11⅔	14	9	9	12	10
	—Syracuse (Int'l)	2	2	.500	3.89	46	3	0	0	14	76⅓	59	35	33	42	67
1988	—Toronto (A.L.)	9	3	.750	3.30	64	0	0	0	15	111⅔	101	46	41	60	91
1989	—Toronto (A.L.)	4	10	.286	3.77	66	0	0	0	15	114⅔	94	55	48	58	122
1990	—Toronto (A.L.)	2	8	.200	3.45	73	0	0	0	11	127⅔	101	51	49	42	112
1991	—Toronto (A.L.)	7	6	.538	2.77	*81	0	0	0	23	107⅓	80	36	33	33	132
1992	—Toronto (A.L.)	7	4	.636	1.95	79	0	0	0	12	101⅓	76	27	22	39	103
1993	—Toronto (A.L.)	2	3	.400	2.13	71	0	0	0	•45	71⅔	49	17	17	25	97
A.L. totals (8 years)..............		32	35	.478	3.08	448	2	0	0	121	648	518	245	222	273	668
N.L. totals (1 year)		0	1	.000	7.31	10	0	0	0	0	16	22	13	13	8	8
Major league totals (8 years)..		32	36	.471	3.19	458	2	0	0	121	664	540	258	235	281	676

CHAMPIONSHIP SERIES RECORD

Year	Team (League)	W	L	Pct.	ERA	G	GS	CG	ShO	Sv.	IP	H	R	ER	BB	SO
1989	—Toronto (A.L.)	0	0	...	7.36	2	0	0	0	0	3⅔	6	3	3	3	5
1991	—Toronto (A.L.)	0	1	.000	6.23	2	0	0	0	1	4⅓	4	3	3	1	6
1992	—Toronto (A.L.)	1	0	1.000	6.75	3	0	0	0	0	4	5	3	3	1	2
1993	—Toronto (A.L.)	0	0	...	5.79	4	0	0	0	2	4⅔	4	3	3	3	8
Champ. series totals (4 years)		1	1	.500	6.48	11	0	0	0	3	16⅔	19	12	12	8	21

WORLD SERIES RECORD

WORLD SERIES NOTES: Shares single-series record for most games won as relief pitcher—2 (1992).

Year	Team (League)	W	L	Pct.	ERA	G	GS	CG	ShO	Sv.	IP	H	R	ER	BB	SO
1992	—Toronto (A.L.)	2	0	1.000	0.00	4	0	0	0	0	3⅓	1	0	0	1	6
1993	—Toronto (A.L.)	1	0	1.000	1.93	4	0	0	0	2	4⅔	3	2	1	0	7
World Series totals (2 years) .		3	0	1.000	1.13	8	0	0	0	2	8	4	2	1	1	13

ALL-STAR GAME RECORD

Year	League	W	L	Pct.	ERA	GS	CG	ShO	Sv.	IP	H	R	ER	BB	SO
1993	—American......................	0	0	...	0.00	0	0	0	0	1	0	0	0	0	2

WARD, TURNER

OF, BREWERS

PERSONAL: Born April 11, 1965, in Orlando, Fla. . . . 6-2/182. . . . Throws right, bats both. . . . Full name: Turner Max Ward.

HIGH SCHOOL: Satsuma (Ala.).

COLLEGE: South Alabama.

W

TRANSACTIONS/CAREER NOTES: Selected by New York Yankees organization in 18th round of free-agent draft (June 2, 1986).... Traded by Yankees organization with C Joel Skinner to Cleveland Indians organization for OF Mel Hall (March 19, 1989).... On Gulf Coast Indians disabled list (April 7-July 24, 1989).... Traded by Indians with P Tom Candiotti to Toronto Blue Jays for P Denis Boucher, OF Glenallen Hill, OF Mark Whiten and a player to be named later (June 27, 1991); Indians acquired cash instead of player to complete deal (October 15, 1991).... On Toronto disabled list (August 2-September 1, 1993); included rehabilitation assignment to Knoxville (August 21-September 1).... Claimed on waivers by Milwaukee Brewers (November 24, 1993).

STATISTICAL NOTES: Led Pacific Coast League outfielders with 292 putouts and 308 total chances in 1990.

			BATTING											FIELDING			
Year	Team (League)	Pos.	G	AB	R	H	2B	3B	HR	RBI	Avg.	BB	SO	SB	PO	A	E	Avg.
1986	—Oneonta (NYP)	OF-1B-3B	63	221	42	62	4	1	1	19	.281	31	39	6	97	6	5	.954
1987	—Fort Lauder. (FSL)	OF-3B	130	493	83	145	15	2	7	55	.294	64	83	25	332	11	8	.977
1988	—Columbus (Int'l)	OF	134	490	55	123	24	1	7	50	.251	48	100	28	223	5	1	*.996
1989	—GC Indians (GCL)■	DH	4	15	2	3	0	0	0	1	.200	2	2	1	...	...	...	...
	—Cant./Akr. (East.)	OF	30	93	19	28	5	1	0	3	.301	15	16	1	2	0	0	1.000
1990	—Colo. Springs (PCL)	OF-2B	133	495	89	148	24	9	6	65	.299	72	70	22	†292	7	9	.971
	—Cleveland (A.L.)	OF	14	46	10	16	2	1	1	10	.348	3	8	3	20	2	1	.957
1991	—Clev.-Tor. (A.L.)■	OF	48	113	12	27	7	0	0	7	.239	11	18	0	70	1	0	1.000
	—Colo. Springs (PCL)	OF	14	51	5	10	1	1	1	3	.196	6	9	2	30	0	1	.968
	—Syracuse (Int'l)	OF	59	218	40	72	11	3	7	32	.330	47	22	9	136	5	0	1.000
1992	—Toronto (A.L.)	OF	18	29	7	10	3	0	1	3	.345	4	4	0	18	1	0	1.000
	—Syracuse (Int'l)	OF	81	280	41	67	10	2	10	29	.239	44	43	7	143	3	5	.967
1993	—Toronto (A.L.)	OF-1B	72	167	20	32	4	2	4	28	.192	23	26	3	97	2	1	.990
	—Knoxville (South.)	OF	7	23	6	6	2	0	0	2	.261	7	3	3	20	0	0	1.000
Major league totals (4 years)			152	355	49	85	16	3	6	48	.239	41	56	6	205	6	2	.991

WATSON, ALLEN

P, CARDINALS

PERSONAL: Born November 18, 1970, in Jamaica, N.Y.... 6-3/190.... Throws left, bats left.... Full name: Allen Kenneth Watson.

HIGH SCHOOL: Christ the King (Queens, N.Y.).

COLLEGE: New York State Institute of Technology.

TRANSACTIONS/CAREER NOTES: Selected by St. Louis Cardinals organization in first round (21st pick overall) of free-agent draft (June 3, 1991); pick received as part of compensation for Toronto Blue Jays signing Type A free agent Ken Dayley.... On Savannah disabled list (August 19, 1991-remainder of season).

Year	Team (League)	W	L	Pct.	ERA	G	GS	CG	ShO	Sv.	IP	H	R	ER	BB	SO
1991	—Hamilton (NYP)	1	1	.500	2.52	8	8	0	0	0	39⅓	22	15	11	17	46
	—Savannah (S. Atl.)	1	1	.500	3.95	3	3	0	0	0	13⅔	16	7	6	8	12
1992	—St. Peters. (FSL)	5	4	.556	1.91	14	14	2	0	0	89⅔	81	31	19	18	80
	—Arkansas (Texas)	8	5	.615	2.15	14	14	3	1	0	96⅓	77	24	23	23	93
	—Louisville (A.A.)	1	0	1.000	1.46	2	2	0	0	0	12⅓	8	4	2	5	9
1993	—Louisville (A.A.)	5	4	.556	2.91	17	17	2	0	0	120⅔	101	46	39	31	86
	—St. Louis (N.L.)	6	7	.462	4.60	16	15	0	0	0	86	90	53	44	28	49
Major league totals (1 year)		6	7	.462	4.60	16	15	0	0	0	86	90	53	44	28	49

WATSON, RON

P, ANGELS

PERSONAL: Born September 12, 1968, in Newton, Mass.... 6-5/240.... Throws right, bats left.... Full name: Ronald Ralph Watson.

HIGH SCHOOL: Weston (Mass.).

COLLEGE: Eckerd (Fla.).

TRANSACTIONS/CAREER NOTES: Selected by California Angels organization in 39th round of free-agent draft (June 4, 1990).... On disabled list (April 9-May 15, 1993).

Year	Team (League)	W	L	Pct.	ERA	G	GS	CG	ShO	Sv.	IP	H	R	ER	BB	SO
1990	—Ariz. Angels (Ariz.)	2	3	.400	3.27	20	0	0	0	0	33	26	14	12	14	21
1991	—Boise (Northwest)	0	1	.000	6.23	18	3	0	0	0	26	35	28	18	15	27
1992	—Quad City (Midw.)	8	5	.615	1.29	40	0	0	0	10	70	43	20	10	42	69
1993	—Midland (Texas)	2	1	.667	3.88	36	0	0	0	3	46⅓	39	22	20	43	41

WAWRUCK, JAMES

OF, ORIOLES

PERSONAL: Born April 23, 1970, in Hartford, Conn.... 5-11/185.... Throws left, bats left.... Full name: James William Wawruck.

HIGH SCHOOL: Loomis Chaffee (Windsor, Conn.).

COLLEGE: Vermont.

TRANSACTIONS/CAREER NOTES: Selected by Baltimore Orioles organization in fifth round of free-agent draft (June 3, 1991).... On disabled list (April 9-16, 1992).

			BATTING											FIELDING			
Year	Team (League)	Pos.	G	AB	R	H	2B	3B	HR	RBI	Avg.	BB	SO	SB	PO	A	E	Avg.
1991	—GC Orioles (GCL)	OF	14	45	6	17	1	1	0	6	.378	6	4	2	10	0	0	1.000
	—Frederick (Caro.)	OF	22	83	15	23	3	0	0	7	.277	7	14	10	16	0	1	.941
1992	—Frederick (Caro.)	OF	102	350	61	108	18	4	8	46	.309	47	69	11	118	7	6	.954
1993	—Bowie (Eastern)	OF	128	475	59	141	21	5	4	44	.297	43	66	28	210	4	2	*.991

WAYNE, GARY

P, DODGERS

PERSONAL: Born November 30, 1962, in Dearborn, Mich.... 6-3/193.... Throws left, bats left.... Full name: Gary Anthony Wayne.

HIGH SCHOOL: Crestwood (Dearborn Heights, Mich.).

COLLEGE: Michigan.

TRANSACTIONS/CAREER NOTES: Selected by Oakland Athletics organization in 23rd round of free-agent draft (June 6, 1983).... Selected by Montreal Expos organization in fourth round of free-agent draft (June 4, 1984).... On disabled list (April 7-

August 24, 1988).... Selected by Minnesota Twins from Expos organization in Rule 5 major league draft (December 5, 1988). ... Traded by Twins with P Rob Wassenaar to Colorado Rockies for P Brett Merriman (March 26, 1993).... Granted free agency (December 20, 1993).... Signed by Los Angeles Dodgers organization (January 6, 1994).

Year	Team (League)	W	L	Pct.	ERA	G	GS	CG	ShO	Sv.	IP	H	R	ER	BB	SO
1984	—W.P. Beach (FSL)	3	5	.375	3.87	13	12	2	0	0	74⅓	70	38	32	49	46
1985	—Jacksonv. (South.)	3	12	.200	5.29	21	20	2	0	0	102	108	67	60	70	62
	—W.P. Beach (FSL)	2	2	.500	5.58	8	4	0	0	0	30⅔	37	23	19	22	18
1986	—W.P. Beach (FSL)	2	5	.286	1.61	47	0	0	0	*25	61⅓	48	16	11	25	55
1987	—Jacksonv. (South.)	5	1	.833	2.35	56	0	0	0	10	80⅓	56	23	21	35	78
1988	—Indianapolis (A.A.)	0	0	...	6.14	8	0	0	0	1	7⅓	9	5	5	3	6
1989	—Minnesota (A.L.)■	3	4	.429	3.30	60	0	0	0	1	71	55	28	26	36	41
1990	—Minnesota (A.L.)	1	1	.500	4.19	38	0	0	0	1	38⅔	38	19	18	13	28
	—Portland (PCL)	2	4	.333	3.41	22	0	0	0	5	31⅔	29	14	12	13	30
1991	—Portland (PCL)	4	5	.444	2.79	51	0	0	0	8	67⅔	63	27	21	31	66
	—Minnesota (A.L.)	1	0	1.000	5.11	8	0	0	0	1	12⅓	11	7	7	4	7
1992	—Minnesota (A.L.)	3	3	.500	2.63	41	0	0	0	0	48	46	18	14	19	29
	—Portland (PCL)	0	1	.000	2.35	14	0	0	0	5	23	23	11	6	1	20
1993	—Colorado (N.L.)■	5	3	.625	5.05	65	0	0	0	1	62⅓	68	40	35	26	49
	A.L. totals (4 years)	8	8	.500	3.44	147	0	0	0	3	170	150	72	65	72	105
	N.L. totals (1 year)	5	3	.625	5.05	65	0	0	0	1	62⅓	68	40	35	26	49
	Major league totals (5 years)	13	11	.542	3.87	212	0	0	0	4	232⅓	218	112	100	98	154

WEATHERS, DAVE

P, MARLINS

PERSONAL: Born September 25, 1969, in Lawrenceburg, Tenn.... 6-3/205.... Throws right, bats right.... Full name: John David Weathers.
HIGH SCHOOL: Loretto (Tenn.).
COLLEGE: Motlow State Community College (Tenn.).
TRANSACTIONS/CAREER NOTES: Selected by Toronto Blue Jays organization in third round of free-agent draft (June 1, 1988).... On Syracuse disabled list (May 11-July 31, 1992).... Selected by Florida Marlins in second round (29th pick overall) of expansion draft (November 17, 1992).

Year	Team (League)	W	L	Pct.	ERA	G	GS	CG	ShO	Sv.	IP	H	R	ER	BB	SO
1988	—St. Cathar. (NYP)	4	4	.500	3.02	15	12	0	0	0	62⅔	58	30	21	26	36
1989	—Myrtle Beach (SAL)	11	•13	.458	3.86	31	*31	2	0	0	172⅔	163	99	74	86	111
1990	—Dunedin (Fla. St.)	10	7	.588	3.70	27	•27	2	0	0	158	158	82	65	59	96
1991	—Knoxville (South.)	10	7	.588	2.45	24	22	5	2	0	139⅓	121	51	38	49	114
	—Toronto (A.L.)	1	0	1.000	4.91	15	0	0	0	0	14⅔	15	9	8	17	13
1992	—Syracuse (Int'l)	1	4	.200	4.66	12	10	0	0	0	48⅓	48	29	25	21	30
	—Toronto (A.L.)	0	0	...	8.10	2	0	0	0	0	3⅓	5	3	3	2	3
1993	—Edmonton (PCL)■	11	4	•.733	3.83	22	22	3	1	0	141	150	77	60	47	117
	—Florida (N.L.)	2	3	.400	5.12	14	6	0	0	0	45⅔	57	26	26	13	34
	A.L. totals (2 years)	1	0	1.000	5.50	17	0	0	0	0	18	20	12	11	19	16
	N.L. totals (1 year)	2	3	.400	5.12	14	6	0	0	0	45⅔	57	26	26	13	34
	Major league totals (3 years)	3	3	.500	5.23	31	6	0	0	0	63⅔	77	38	37	32	50

WEBSTER, LENNY

C, TWINS

PERSONAL: Born February 10, 1965, in New Orleans.... 5-9/195.... Throws right, bats right.... Full name: Leonard Irell Webster.
HIGH SCHOOL: Lutcher (La.).
COLLEGE: Grambling State.
TRANSACTIONS/CAREER NOTES: Selected by Minnesota Twins organization in 16th round of free-agent draft (June 7, 1982).... Selected by Twins organization in 21st round of free-agent draft (June 3, 1985).
HONORS: Named Midwest League Most Valuable Player (1988).

			BATTING												FIELDING			
Year	Team (League)	Pos.	G	AB	R	H	2B	3B	HR	RBI	Avg.	BB	SO	SB	PO	A	E	Avg.
1986	—Kenosha (Midwest)	C	22	65	2	10	2	0	0	8	.154	10	12	0	87	9	0	1.000
	—Elizabeth. (Appal.)	C	48	152	29	35	4	0	3	14	.230	22	21	1	88	11	3	.971
1987	—Kenosha (Midwest)	C	52	140	17	35	7	0	3	17	.250	17	20	2	228	29	5	.981
1988	—Kenosha (Midwest)	C	129	465	82	134	23	2	11	87	.288	71	47	3	606	96	14	.980
1989	—Visalia (California)	C	63	231	36	62	7	0	5	39	.268	27	27	2	352	57	4	.990
	—Orlando (Southern)	C	59	191	29	45	7	0	2	17	.236	44	20	2	293	46	4	.988
	—Minnesota (A.L.)	C	14	20	3	6	2	0	0	1	.300	3	2	0	32	0	0	1.000
1990	—Orlando (Southern)	C	126	455	69	119	31	0	8	71	.262	68	57	0	629	70	9	.987
	—Minnesota (A.L.)	C	2	6	1	2	1	0	0	0	.333	1	1	0	9	0	0	1.000
1991	—Portland (PCL)	C	87	325	43	82	18	0	7	34	.252	24	32	1	477	65	6	*.989
	—Minnesota (A.L.)	C	18	34	7	10	1	0	3	8	.294	6	10	0	61	10	1	.986
1992	—Minnesota (A.L.)	C	53	118	10	33	10	1	1	13	.280	9	11	0	190	11	1	.995
1993	—Minnesota (A.L.)	C	49	106	14	21	2	0	1	8	.198	11	8	1	177	13	0	1.000
	Major league totals (5 years)		136	284	35	72	16	1	5	30	.254	30	32	1	469	34	2	.996

WEBSTER, MITCH

OF, DODGERS

PERSONAL: Born May 16, 1959, in Larned, Kan.... 6-1/191.... Throws left, bats both.... Full name: Mitchell Dean Webster.
HIGH SCHOOL: Larned (Kan.).
TRANSACTIONS/CAREER NOTES: Selected by Los Angeles Dodgers organization in 23rd round of free-agent draft (June 7, 1977).... Selected by Syracuse, Toronto Blue Jays organization from Dodgers organization in Rule 5 minor league draft (December 4, 1979).... Traded by Blue Jays organization to Montreal Expos for a player to be named later (June 22, 1985); Blue Jays organization acquired P Cliff Young to complete deal (September 10, 1985).... Traded by Expos to Chicago Cubs for OF Dave Martinez (July 14, 1988).... On disabled list (May 14-29, 1989).... Traded by Cubs to

W

Cleveland Indians for OF Dave Clark (November 20, 1989).... Traded by Indians to Pittsburgh Pirates for P Mike York (May 16, 1991).... Traded by Pirates to Dodgers for OF Jose Gonzales (July 3, 1991).... Granted free agency (October 30, 1991).... Re-signed by Dodgers (December 6, 1991).... Granted free agency (October 27, 1992).... Re-signed by Dodgers (December 4, 1992).

RECORDS: Shares major league single-season record for fewest double plays by outfielder (150 or more games)—0 (1987).

STATISTICAL NOTES: Led International League outfielders with 385 total chances and five double plays in 1982.

				BATTING											FIELDING			
Year	Team (League)	Pos.	G	AB	R	H	2B	3B	HR	RBI	Avg.	BB	SO	SB	PO	A	E	Avg.
1977	—Lethbridge (Pio.)	OF	55	168	45	59	4	0	0	31	.351	36	21	13	81	3	8	.913
1978	—Clinton (Midwest)	OF	45	157	18	38	3	1	0	9	.242	19	26	8	92	6	7	.933
	—Lethbridge (Pio.)	OF	55	182	58	58	5	1	0	18	.319	45	22	18	77	3	0	*1.000
1979	—Clinton (Midwest)	OF	123	473	95	*154	17	7	2	40	*.326	58	54	10	*272	10	10	.966
1980	—Syracuse (Int'l)■	OF	49	161	23	35	4	2	1	12	.217	8	18	4	112	3	5	.958
	—Kinston (Carolina)	OF	65	258	43	76	7	3	0	28	.295	21	21	16	129	8	5	.965
1981	—Knoxville (South.)	OF	140	554	89	163	26	6	1	42	.294	45	56	52	317	7	10	.970
1982	—Syracuse (Int'l)	OF	137	513	95	144	21	7	13	68	.281	67	55	12	*367	16	2	*.995
1983	—Syracuse (Int'l)	OF-1B	135	462	77	120	26	8	9	45	.260	68	60	21	266	16	10	.966
	—Toronto (A.L.)	OF	11	11	2	2	0	0	0	0	.182	1	1	0	5	0	0	1.000
1984	—Toronto (A.L.)	OF-1B	26	22	9	5	2	1	0	4	.227	1	7	0	16	0	2	.889
	—Syracuse (Int'l)	OF	95	360	60	108	22	5	3	25	.300	51	36	16	239	7	7	.972
1985	—Toronto (A.L.)	OF	4	1	0	0	0	0	0	0	.000	0	0	0	0	0	0	...
	—Syracuse (Int'l)	OF	47	189	32	52	5	3	3	23	.275	20	24	5	83	10	1	.989
	—Montreal (N.L.)■	OF	74	212	32	58	8	2	11	30	.274	20	33	15	133	3	1	.993
1986	—Montreal (N.L.)	OF	151	576	89	167	31	*13	8	49	.290	57	78	36	325	12	8	.977
1987	—Montreal (N.L.)	OF	156	588	101	165	30	8	15	63	.281	70	95	33	266	8	5	.982
1988	—Mont.-Chi. (N.L.)■	OF	151	523	69	136	16	8	6	39	.260	55	87	22	322	3	6	.982
1989	—Chicago (N.L.)	OF	98	272	40	70	12	4	3	19	.257	30	55	14	161	3	6	.965
1990	—Cleveland (A.L.)■	OF-1B	128	437	58	110	20	6	12	55	.252	20	61	22	345	3	5	.986
1991	—Cleveland (A.L.)	OF	13	32	2	4	0	0	0	0	.125	3	9	2	24	0	0	1.000
	—Pitts.-L.A. (N.L.)■	OF-1B	94	171	21	38	8	5	2	19	.222	18	52	0	87	2	2	.978
1992	—Los Angeles (N.L.)	OF	135	262	33	70	12	5	6	35	.267	27	49	11	130	0	3	.977
1993	—Los Angeles (N.L.)	OF	88	172	26	42	6	2	2	14	.244	11	24	4	75	1	4	.950
American League totals (5 years)			182	503	71	121	22	7	12	59	.241	25	78	24	390	3	7	.983
National League totals (8 years)			947	2776	411	746	123	47	53	268	.269	288	473	135	1499	32	35	.978
Major league totals (11 years)			1129	3279	482	867	145	54	65	327	.264	313	551	159	1889	35	42	.979

CHAMPIONSHIP SERIES RECORD

				BATTING											FIELDING			
Year	Team (League)	Pos.	G	AB	R	H	2B	3B	HR	RBI	Avg.	BB	SO	SB	PO	A	E	Avg.
1989	—Chicago (N.L.)	OF-PH	3	3	0	1	0	0	0	0	.333	0	0	0	0	0	0	...

WEDGE, ERIC

C/1B, ROCKIES

PERSONAL: Born January 27, 1968, in Fort Wayne, Ind.... 6-3/220.... Throws right, bats right.... Full name: Eric Michael Wedge.

HIGH SCHOOL: Northrop (Fort Wayne, Ind.).

COLLEGE: Wichita State.

TRANSACTIONS/CAREER NOTES: Selected by Boston Red Sox organization in third round of free-agent draft (June 5, 1989).... On Pawtucket disabled list (May 15-22 and May 24-July 10, 1991; and June 3-10 and June 25-July 28, 1992).... Selected by Colorado Rockies in second round (48th pick overall) of expansion draft (November 17, 1992).... On Colorado disabled list (March 27-June 17, 1993); included rehabilitation assignment to Central Valley (May 28-June 3) and Colorado Springs (June 3-16).... On Colorado disabled list (June 17-July 26, 1993).

STATISTICAL NOTES: Led Eastern League catchers with eight double plays in 1990.

				BATTING											FIELDING			
Year	Team (League)	Pos.	G	AB	R	H	2B	3B	HR	RBI	Avg.	BB	SO	SB	PO	A	E	Avg.
1989	—Elmira (N.Y.-Penn)	C	41	145	20	34	6	2	7	22	.234	15	21	1	283	30	2	.994
	—New Britain (East.)	C	14	40	3	8	2	0	0	2	.200	5	10	0	83	9	0	1.000
1990	—New Britain (East.)	C	103	339	36	77	13	1	5	47	.227	50	54	1	583	62	9	.986
1991	—Pawtucket (Int'l)	C	53	163	24	38	14	1	5	18	.233	25	26	0	282	36	6	.981
	—New Britain (East.)	C	2	8	0	2	0	0	0	2	.250	0	2	0	6	1	0	1.000
	—Winter Haven (FSL)	C	8	21	2	5	0	0	1	1	.238	3	7	1	17	2	0	1.000
	—Boston (A.L.)	PH	1	1	0	1	0	0	0	0	1.000	0	0	0	...	...	...	...
1992	—Pawtucket (Int'l)	C	65	211	28	63	9	0	11	40	.299	32	40	0	209	20	3	.987
	—Boston (A.L.)	C	27	68	11	17	2	0	5	11	.250	13	18	0	19	2	0	1.000
1993	—Central Vall. (Cal.)■	C	6	23	6	7	0	0	3	11	.304	2	6	0	30	0	0	1.000
	—Colo. Springs (PCL)	C-1B	38	90	17	24	6	0	3	13	.267	16	22	0	134	22	3	.981
	—Colorado (N.L.)	C	9	11	2	2	0	0	0	1	.182	0	4	0	6	1	0	1.000
American League totals (2 years)			28	69	11	18	2	0	5	11	.261	13	18	0	19	2	0	1.000
National League totals (1 year)			9	11	2	2	0	0	0	1	.182	0	4	0	6	1	0	1.000
Major league totals (3 years)			37	80	13	20	2	0	5	12	.250	13	22	0	25	3	0	1.000

WEGMAN, BILL

P, BREWERS

PERSONAL: Born December 19, 1962, in Cincinnati.... 6-5/235.... Throws right, bats right.... Full name: William Edward Wegman.

HIGH SCHOOL: Oak Hill (Cincinnati).

TRANSACTIONS/CAREER NOTES: Selected by Milwaukee Brewers organization in fifth round of free-agent draft (June 8, 1981).... On Vancouver disabled list (June 18-August 11, 1984).... On disabled list (August 7-22, 1987; May 21-June 7, 1988; and June 1, 1989-remainder of season).... On Milwaukee disabled list (June 3, 1990-remainder of season); included rehabilitation assignment to Beloit (June 27).... On Milwaukee disabled list (April 5-May 3, 1991); included rehabilitation assignment to Beloit (April 13-30) and Denver (April 30-May 3).... On Milwaukee disabled list (July 7-

September 14, 1993).
STATISTICAL NOTES: Led California League with five balks in 1983.... Led Pacific Coast League with 21 home runs allowed in 1985.
MISCELLANEOUS: Appeared in two games as pinch-runner (1986).... Appeared in one game as pinch-runner (1988).

Year	Team (League)	W	L	Pct.	ERA	G	GS	CG	ShO	Sv.	IP	H	R	ER	BB	SO
1981	—Butte (Pioneer)	6	5	.545	4.17	14	13	4	0	0	82	94	51	38	44	47
1982	—Beloit (Midwest)	12	6	.667	2.81	25	25	10	1	0	179⅔	176	77	56	38	129
1983	—Stockton (Calif.)	*16	5	.762	*1.30	24	23	•15	•4	0	186⅔	149	33	27	45	135
1984	—El Paso (Texas)	4	5	.444	2.67	10	10	4	0	0	64	62	25	19	15	42
	—Vancouver (PCL)	0	3	.000	1.95	6	3	0	0	1	27⅔	30	11	6	8	16
1985	—Vancouver (PCL)	10	11	.476	4.02	28	28	8	2	0	188	187	93	84	52	113
	—Milwaukee (A.L.)	2	0	1.000	3.57	3	3	0	0	0	17⅔	17	8	7	3	6
1986	—Milwaukee (A.L.)	5	12	.294	5.13	35	32	2	0	0	198⅓	217	120	113	43	82
1987	—Milwaukee (A.L.)	12	11	.522	4.24	34	33	7	0	0	225	229	113	106	53	102
1988	—Milwaukee (A.L.)	13	13	.500	4.12	32	31	4	1	0	199	207	104	91	50	84
1989	—Milwaukee (A.L.)	2	6	.250	6.71	11	8	0	0	0	51	69	44	38	21	27
1990	—Denver (A.A.)	1	0	1.000	3.29	3	3	0	0	0	13⅔	10	5	5	7	14
	—Milwaukee (A.L.)	2	2	.500	4.85	8	5	1	1	0	29⅔	37	21	16	6	20
	—Beloit (Midwest)	0	0	...	0.00	1	1	0	0	0	2	1	0	0	1	2
1991	—Beloit (Midwest)	0	2	.000	1.64	3	3	0	0	0	11	11	5	2	1	12
	—Denver (A.A.)	0	0	...	2.57	1	1	0	0	0	7	6	2	2	1	1
	—Milwaukee (A.L.)	15	7	.682	2.84	28	28	7	2	0	193⅓	176	76	61	40	89
1992	—Milwaukee (A.L.)	13	14	.481	3.20	35	35	7	0	0	261⅔	251	104	93	55	127
1993	—Milwaukee (A.L.)	4	14	.222	4.48	20	18	5	0	0	120⅔	135	70	60	34	50
Major league totals (9 years)		68	79	.463	4.06	206	193	33	4	0	1296⅓	1338	660	585	305	587

WEGMANN, TOM

P, METS

PERSONAL: Born August 29, 1968, in Dyersville, Ia.... 6-0/185.... Throws right, bats right.... Full name: Thomas Joseph Wegmann.
HIGH SCHOOL: Beckman (Dyersville, Ia.).
COLLEGE: Muscatine (Ia.) Community College and Middle Tennessee State.
TRANSACTIONS/CAREER NOTES: Signed as free agent by New York Mets organization (June 15, 1990).... On St. Lucie disabled list (June 17-July 6 and August 13, 1991-remainder of season).
STATISTICAL NOTES: Pitched 7-0 perfect game for Kingsport against Pulaski (July 31, 1990, first game).

Year	Team (League)	W	L	Pct.	ERA	G	GS	CG	ShO	Sv.	IP	H	R	ER	BB	SO
1990	—GC Mets (GCL)	0	0	...	0.00	2	0	0	0	0	2	0	0	0	0	4
	—Kingsport (Appal.)	5	4	.556	2.67	14	12	4	•2	0	84⅓	53	34	25	30	103
1991	—Columbia (S. Atl.)	5	0	1.000	0.56	7	6	1	1	0	48	21	7	3	9	69
	—St. Lucie (Fla. St.)	4	3	.571	2.51	13	11	0	0	1	61	46	19	17	14	69
1992	—Binghamton (East.)	9	2	*.818	2.58	27	11	2	0	1	97⅔	73	29	28	27	93
	—Tidewater (Int'l)	2	3	.400	4.42	7	6	0	0	0	36⅔	38	19	18	17	38
1993	—Norfolk (Int'l)	5	3	.625	3.23	44	2	0	0	2	86⅓	68	33	31	34	99

WEHNER, JOHN

IF/OF, PIRATES

PERSONAL: Born June 29, 1967, in Pittsburgh.... 6-3/205.... Throws right, bats right.... Full name: John Paul Wehner.... Name pronounced WAY-ner.
HIGH SCHOOL: Carrick (Pittsburgh).
COLLEGE: Indiana.
TRANSACTIONS/CAREER NOTES: Selected by Pittsburgh Pirates organization in seventh round of free-agent draft (June 1, 1988).... On Pittsburgh disabled list (August 29-October 7, 1991).
STATISTICAL NOTES: Led New York-Pennsylvania League third basemen with 219 total chances and 14 double plays in 1988.... Led Carolina League third basemen with 403 total chances and tied for lead with 24 double plays in 1989.... Led Eastern League third basemen with 476 total chances and 40 double plays in 1990.

			BATTING												FIELDING			
Year	Team (League)	Pos.	G	AB	R	H	2B	3B	HR	RBI	Avg.	BB	SO	SB	PO	A	E	Avg.
1988	—Watertown (NYP)	3B	70	265	41	73	6	0	3	31	.275	21	39	18	*65	137	17	.922
1989	—Salem (Carolina)	3B	*137	*515	69	*155	32	6	14	73	.301	42	81	21	*89	*278	36	.911
1990	—Harrisburg (East.)	3B	•138	*511	71	147	27	1	4	62	.288	40	51	24	*109	*317	*50	.895
1991	—Carolina (South.)	3B-1B	61	234	30	62	5	1	3	21	.265	24	32	17	182	134	10	.969
	—Buffalo (A.A.)	3B	31	112	18	34	9	2	1	15	.304	14	12	6	30	69	8	.925
	—Pittsburgh (N.L.)	3B	37	106	15	36	7	0	0	7	.340	7	17	3	23	65	6	.936
1992	—Buffalo (A.A.)	2B-1B-3B	60	223	37	60	13	2	7	27	.269	29	30	10	226	122	7	.980
	—Pittsburgh (N.L.)	3B-1B-2B	55	123	11	22	6	0	0	4	.179	12	22	3	96	64	4	.976
1993	—Pittsburgh (N.L.)	OF-3B-2B	29	35	3	5	0	0	0	0	.143	6	10	0	17	8	0	1.000
	—Buffalo (A.A.)	3B-2B-OF	89	330	61	83	22	2	7	34	.252	40	53	17	133	256	17	.958
Major league totals (3 years)			121	264	29	63	13	0	0	11	.239	25	49	6	136	137	10	.965

CHAMPIONSHIP SERIES RECORD

			BATTING												FIELDING			
Year	Team (League)	Pos.	G	AB	R	H	2B	3B	HR	RBI	Avg.	BB	SO	SB	PO	A	E	Avg.
1992	—Pittsburgh (N.L.)	PH	2	2	0	0	0	0	0	0	.000	0	2	0	...	...	...	...

WEISS, WALT

SS, ROCKIES

PERSONAL: Born November 28, 1963, in Tuxedo, N.Y.... 6-0/175.... Throws right, bats both.... Full name: Walter William Weiss Jr.
HIGH SCHOOL: Suffern (N.Y.).
COLLEGE: North Carolina.
TRANSACTIONS/CAREER NOTES: Selected by Baltimore Orioles organization in 10th round of free-agent draft (June 7, 1982).... Selected by Oakland Athletics organization in first round (11th pick overall) of free-agent draft (June 3, 1985).... On Oakland

disabled list (May 18-July 31, 1989); included rehabilitation assignment to Tacoma (July 18-25) and Modesto (July 26-31). ... On disabled list (August 23-September 7, 1990; April 15-30 and June 7, 1991-remainder of season).... On Oakland disabled list (March 30-June 3, 1992); included rehabilitation assignment to Tacoma (May 26-June 3).... Traded by A's to Florida Marlins for C Eric Helfand and a player to be named later (November 17, 1992); A's acquired P Scott Baker from Marlins to complete deal (November 20, 1992).... Granted free agency (October 25, 1993).... Signed by Colorado Rockies (January 7, 1994).

HONORS: Named A.L. Rookie Player of the Year by THE SPORTING NEWS (1988).... Named A.L. Rookie of the Year by Baseball Writers' Association of America (1988).

			BATTING												FIELDING			
Year	Team (League)	Pos.	G	AB	R	H	2B	3B	HR	RBI	Avg.	BB	SO	SB	PO	A	E	Avg.
1985	—Pocatello (Pioneer)	SS	40	158	19	49	9	3	0	21	.310	12	18	6	51	126	11	.941
	—Modesto (Calif.)	SS	30	122	17	24	4	1	0	7	.197	12	20	3	36	97	7	.950
1986	—Madison (Midwest)	SS	84	322	50	97	15	5	2	54	.301	33	66	12	143	251	20	.952
	—Huntsville (South.)	SS	46	160	19	40	2	1	0	13	.250	11	39	5	72	142	11	.951
1987	—Huntsville (South.)	SS	91	337	43	96	16	2	1	32	.285	47	67	23	152	259	17	.960
	—Oakland (A.L.)	SS	16	26	3	12	4	0	0	1	.462	2	2	1	8	30	1	.974
	—Tacoma (PCL)	SS	46	179	35	47	4	3	0	17	.263	28	31	8	76	140	11	.952
1988	—Oakland (A.L.)	SS	147	452	44	113	17	3	3	39	.250	35	56	4	254	431	15	.979
1989	—Oakland (A.L.)	SS	84	236	30	55	11	0	3	21	.233	21	39	6	106	195	15	.953
	—Tacoma (PCL)	SS	2	9	1	1	1	0	0	1	.111	0	0	0	0	3	1	.750
	—Modesto (Calif.)	SS	5	8	1	3	0	0	0	1	.375	4	1	0	6	9	0	1.000
1990	—Oakland (A.L.)	SS	138	445	50	118	17	1	2	35	.265	46	53	9	194	373	12	.979
1991	—Oakland (A.L.)	SS	40	133	15	30	6	1	0	13	.226	12	14	6	64	99	5	.970
1992	—Tacoma (PCL)	SS	4	13	2	3	1	0	0	3	.231	2	1	0	8	14	1	.957
	—Oakland (A.L.)	SS	103	316	36	67	5	2	0	21	.212	43	39	6	144	270	19	.956
1993	—Florida (N.L.)■	SS	158	500	50	133	14	2	1	39	.266	79	73	7	229	406	15	.977
	American League totals (6 years)		528	1608	178	395	60	7	8	130	.246	159	203	32	770	1398	67	.970
	National League totals (1 year)		158	500	50	133	14	2	1	39	.266	79	73	7	229	406	15	.977
	Major league totals (7 years)		686	2108	228	528	74	9	9	169	.250	238	276	39	999	1804	82	.972

CHAMPIONSHIP SERIES RECORD

			BATTING												FIELDING			
Year	Team (League)	Pos.	G	AB	R	H	2B	3B	HR	RBI	Avg.	BB	SO	SB	PO	A	E	Avg.
1988	—Oakland (A.L.)	SS	4	15	2	5	2	0	0	2	.333	0	4	0	7	10	0	1.000
1989	—Oakland (A.L.)	SS-PR	4	9	2	1	1	0	0	0	.111	1	1	1	5	9	0	1.000
1990	—Oakland (A.L.)	SS	2	7	2	0	0	0	0	0	.000	2	2	0	2	7	1	.900
1992	—Oakland (A.L.)	SS	3	6	1	1	0	0	0	0	.167	2	1	2	5	6	0	1.000
	Championship series totals (4 years)		13	37	7	7	3	0	0	2	.189	5	8	3	19	32	1	.981

WORLD SERIES RECORD

			BATTING												FIELDING			
Year	Team (League)	Pos.	G	AB	R	H	2B	3B	HR	RBI	Avg.	BB	SO	SB	PO	A	E	Avg.
1988	—Oakland (A.L.)	SS	5	16	1	1	0	0	0	0	.063	0	1	0	5	11	1	.941
1989	—Oakland (A.L.)	SS	4	15	3	2	0	0	1	1	.133	2	2	0	7	8	0	1.000
	World Series totals (2 years)		9	31	4	3	0	0	1	1	.097	2	3	0	12	19	1	.969

WELCH, BOB

P, ATHLETICS

PERSONAL: Born November 3, 1956, in Detroit.... 6-3/198.... Throws right, bats right.... Full name: Robert Lynn Welch.

HIGH SCHOOL: Hazel Park (Ferndale, Mich.).

COLLEGE: Eastern Michigan.

TRANSACTIONS/CAREER NOTES: Selected by Chicago Cubs organization in 14th round of free-agent draft (June 5, 1974).... Selected by Los Angeles Dodgers organization in first round (20th pick overall) of free-agent draft (June 7, 1977).... On Los Angeles disabled list (April 29-June 5, 1985); included rehabilitation assignment to Vero Beach (May 21-June 5).... Traded by Dodgers as part of an eight-player, three-team deal in which New York Mets sent P Jesse Orosco to Oakland Athletics. A's traded Orosco, SS Alfredo Griffin and P Jay Howell to Dodgers for Welch, P Matt Young and P Jack Savage. A's then traded Savage, P Wally Whitehurst and P Kevin Tapani to Mets (December 11, 1987).... On disabled list (June 13-30, 1989).... Granted free agency (November 5, 1990).... Re-signed by A's (December 15, 1990).... On disabled list (March 28-May 2, May 27-June 14 and August 8-September 11, 1992 and August 8-24, 1993).

HONORS: Named A.L. Pitcher of the Year by THE SPORTING NEWS (1990).... Named righthanded pitcher on THE SPORTING NEWS A.L. All-Star team (1990).... Named A.L. Cy Young Award winner by Baseball Writers' Association of America (1990).

MISCELLANEOUS: Appeared in one game as outfielder with no chances (1982).... Appeared in one game as pinch-runner (1991).

Year	Team (League)	W	L	Pct.	ERA	G	GS	CG	ShO	Sv.	IP	H	R	ER	BB	SO
1977	—San Antonio (Tex.)	4	5	.444	4.44	14	14	1	1	0	71	94	44	35	17	56
1978	—Albuquerque (PCL)	5	1	.833	3.78	11	11	2	0	0	69	72	33	29	19	53
	—Los Angeles (N.L.)	7	4	.636	2.03	23	13	4	3	3	111	92	28	25	26	66
1979	—Los Angeles (N.L.)	5	6	.455	4.00	25	12	1	0	5	81	82	42	36	32	64
1980	—Los Angeles (N.L.)	14	9	.609	3.28	32	32	3	2	0	214	190	85	78	79	141
1981	—Los Angeles (N.L.)	9	5	.643	3.45	23	23	2	1	0	141	141	56	54	41	88
1982	—Los Angeles (N.L.)	16	11	.593	3.36	36	36	9	3	0	235⅔	199	94	88	81	176
1983	—Los Angeles (N.L.)	15	12	.556	2.65	31	31	4	3	0	204	164	73	60	72	156
1984	—Los Angeles (N.L.)	13	13	.500	3.78	31	29	3	1	0	178⅔	191	86	75	58	126
1985	—Los Angeles (N.L.)	14	4	.778	2.31	23	23	8	3	0	167⅓	141	49	43	35	96
	—Vero Beach (FSL)	0	0	...	2.12	3	3	0	0	0	17	15	4	4	1	9
1986	—Los Angeles (N.L.)	7	13	.350	3.28	33	33	7	3	0	235⅔	227	95	86	55	183
1987	—Los Angeles (N.L.)	15	9	.625	3.22	35	35	6	•4	0	251⅔	204	94	90	86	196
1988	—Oakland (A.L.)■	17	9	.654	3.64	36	36	4	2	0	244⅔	237	107	99	81	158
1989	—Oakland (A.L.)	17	8	.680	3.00	33	33	1	0	0	209⅔	191	82	70	78	137

Year	Team (League)	W	L	Pct.	ERA	G	GS	CG	ShO	Sv.	IP	H	R	ER	BB	SO
1990	—Oakland (A.L.)	*27	6	*.818	2.95	35	35	2	2	0	238	214	90	78	77	127
1991	—Oakland (A.L.)	12	13	.480	4.58	35	•35	7	1	0	220	220	124	112	91	101
1992	—Oakland (A.L.)	11	7	.611	3.27	20	20	0	0	0	123⅔	114	47	45	43	47
1993	—Oakland (A.L.)	9	11	.450	5.29	30	28	0	0	0	166⅔	208	102	98	56	[illegible]
A.L. totals (6 years)		93	54	.633	3.76	189	187	14	5	0	1202⅔	1184	552	502	426	633
N.L. totals (10 years)		115	86	.572	3.14	292	267	47	23	8	1820	1631	702	635	565	1292
Major league totals (16 years)		208	140	.598	3.39	481	454	61	28	8	3022⅔	2815	1254	1137	991	1925

DIVISION SERIES RECORD

Year	Team (League)	W	L	Pct.	ERA	G	GS	CG	ShO	Sv.	IP	H	R	ER	BB	SO
1981	—Los Angeles (N.L.)	0	0	...	0.00	1	0	0	0	0	1	0	0	0	1	1

CHAMPIONSHIP SERIES RECORD

Year	Team (League)	W	L	Pct.	ERA	G	GS	CG	ShO	Sv.	IP	H	R	ER	BB	SO
1978	—Los Angeles (N.L.)	1	0	1.000	2.08	1	0	0	0	0	4⅓	2	1	1	0	5
1981	—Los Angeles (N.L.)	0	0	...	5.40	3	0	0	0	1	1⅔	2	1	1	0	2
1983	—Los Angeles (N.L.)	0	1	.000	6.75	1	1	0	0	0	1⅓	0	2	1	2	0
1985	—Los Angeles (N.L.)	0	1	.000	6.75	1	1	0	0	0	2⅔	5	4	2	6	2
1988	—Oakland (A.L.)	0	0	...	27.00	1	1	0	0	0	1⅔	6	5	5	2	0
1989	—Oakland (A.L.)	1	0	1.000	3.18	1	1	0	0	0	5⅔	8	2	2	1	4
1990	—Oakland (A.L.)	1	0	1.000	1.23	1	1	0	0	0	7⅓	6	1	1	3	4
1992	—Oakland (A.L.)	0	0	...	2.57	1	1	0	0	0	7	7	2	2	1	7
Champ. series totals (8 years)		3	2	.600	4.26	10	6	0	0	1	31⅔	36	18	15	15	24

WORLD SERIES RECORD

Year	Team (League)	W	L	Pct.	ERA	G	GS	CG	ShO	Sv.	IP	H	R	ER	BB	SO
1978	—Los Angeles (N.L.)	0	1	.000	6.23	3	0	0	0	1	4⅓	4	3	3	2	6
1981	—Los Angeles (N.L.)	0	0	...	...	1	1	0	0	0	0	3	2	2	1	0
1988	—Oakland (A.L.)	0	0	...	1.80	1	1	0	0	0	5	6	1	1	3	8
1989	—Oakland (A.L.)							Did not play.								
1990	—Oakland (A.L.)	0	0	...	4.91	1	1	0	0	0	7⅓	9	4	4	2	2
World Series totals (4 years)		0	1	.000	5.40	6	3	0	0	1	16⅔	22	10	10	8	16

ALL-STAR GAME RECORD

Year	League	W	L	Pct.	ERA	GS	CG	ShO	Sv.	IP	H	R	ER	BB	SO
1980	—National	0	0	...	6.00	0	0	0	0	3	5	2	2	1	4
1990	—American	0	0	...	0.00	1	0	0	0	2	1	0	0	0	1
All-Star totals (2 years)		0	0	...	3.60	1	0	0	0	5	6	2	2	1	5

WELLS, BOB

P, PHILLIES

PERSONAL: Born November 1, 1966, in Yakima, Wash.... 6-0/180.... Throws right, bats right.... Full name: Robert Lee Wells.

HIGH SCHOOL: Eisenhower (Yakima, Wash.).

COLLEGE: Spokane Falls Community College (Wash.).

TRANSACTIONS/CAREER NOTES: Signed as free agent by Philadelphia Phillies organization (August 18, 1988).... On Reading disabled list (July 21, 1991-remainder of season).... On Scranton/Wilkes-Barre disabled list (April 9-28, 1992).... On Reading disabled list (June 9, 1992-remainder of season and April 8-June 13, 1993).

Year	Team (League)	W	L	Pct.	ERA	G	GS	CG	ShO	Sv.	IP	H	R	ER	BB	SO
1989	—Martinsville (App.)	0	0	...	4.50	4	0	0	0	0	6	8	5	3	2	3
1990	—Spartanburg (SAL)	5	8	.385	2.87	20	19	2	0	0	113	94	47	36	40	73
	—Clearwater (FSL)	0	2	.000	4.91	6	1	0	0	1	14⅔	17	9	8	6	11
1991	—Clearwater (FSL)	7	2	.778	3.11	24	9	1	0	0	75⅓	63	27	26	19	66
	—Reading (Eastern)	1	0	1.000	3.60	1	1	0	0	0	5	4	2	2	1	3
1992	—Clearwater (FSL)	1	0	1.000	3.86	9	0	0	0	5	9⅓	10	4	4	3	9
	—Reading (Eastern)	0	1	.000	1.17	3	3	0	0	0	15⅓	12	2	2	5	11
1993	—Clearwater (FSL)	1	0	1.000	0.98	12	1	0	0	2	27⅔	23	5	3	6	24
	—Scran./W.B. (Int'l)	1	1	.500	2.79	11	0	0	0	0	19⅓	19	7	6	5	8

WELLS, DAVID

P, TIGERS

PERSONAL: Born May 20, 1963, in Torrance, Calif.... 6-4/225.... Throws left, bats left.... Full name: David Lee Wells.

HIGH SCHOOL: Point Loma (San Diego).

TRANSACTIONS/CAREER NOTES: Selected by Toronto Blue Jays organization in second round of free-agent draft (June 7, 1982).... On Knoxville disabled list (June 28, 1984-remainder of season).... On disabled list (April 10, 1985-entire season).... On Knoxville disabled list (July 7-August 20, 1986).... Released by Blue Jays (March 30, 1993).... Signed by Detroit Tigers (April 3, 1993).... On disabled list (August 1-20, 1993).... Granted free agency (October 28, 1993).... Re-signed by Tigers (December 13, 1993).

Year	Team (League)	W	L	Pct.	ERA	G	GS	CG	ShO	Sv.	IP	H	R	ER	BB	SO
1982	—Medicine Hat (Pio.)	4	3	.571	5.18	12	12	1	0	0	64⅓	71	42	37	32	53
1983	—Kinston (Carolina)	6	5	.545	3.73	25	25	5	0	0	157	141	81	65	71	115
1984	—Kinston (Carolina)	1	6	.143	4.71	7	7	0	0	0	42	51	29	22	19	44
	—Knoxville (South.)	3	2	.600	2.59	8	8	3	1	0	59	58	22	17	17	34
1985	—							Did not play.								
1986	—Florence (S. Atl.)	0	0	...	3.55	4	1	0	0	0	12⅔	7	6	5	9	14
	—Ventura (Calif.)	2	1	.667	1.89	5	2	0	0	0	19	13	5	4	4	26
	—Knoxville (South.)	1	3	.250	4.05	10	7	1	0	0	40	42	24	18	18	32
	—Syracuse (Int'l)	0	1	.000	9.82	3	0	0	0	0	3⅔	6	4	4	1	2

Year	Team (League)	W	L	Pct.	ERA	G	GS	CG	ShO	Sv.	IP	H	R	ER	BB	SO
1987	—Syracuse (Int'l)	4	6	.400	3.87	43	12	0	0	6	109⅓	102	49	47	32	106
	—Toronto (A.L.)	4	3	.571	3.99	18	2	0	0	1	29⅓	37	14	13	12	32
1988	—Toronto (A.L.)	3	5	.375	4.62	41	0	0	0	4	64⅓	65	36	33	31	56
	—Syracuse (Int'l)	0	0	...	0.00	6	0	0	0	3	5⅔	7	1	0	2	8
1989	—Toronto (A.L.)	7	4	.636	2.40	54	0	0	0	2	86⅓	66	25	23	28	78
1990	—Toronto (A.L.)	11	6	.647	3.14	43	25	0	0	3	189	165	72	66	45	115
1991	—Toronto (A.L.)	15	10	.600	3.72	40	28	2	0	1	198⅓	188	88	82	49	106
1992	—Toronto (A.L.)	7	9	.438	5.40	41	14	0	0	2	120	138	84	72	36	62
1993	—Detroit (A.L.)■............	11	9	.550	4.19	32	30	0	0	0	187	183	93	87	42	139
Major league totals (7 years)..		58	46	.558	3.87	269	99	2	0	13	874⅓	842	412	376	243	588

CHAMPIONSHIP SERIES RECORD

Year	Team (League)	W	L	Pct.	ERA	G	GS	CG	ShO	Sv.	IP	H	R	ER	BB	SO
1989	—Toronto (A.L.)	0	0	...	0.00	1	0	0	0	0	1	0	1	0	2	1
1991	—Toronto (A.L.)	0	0	...	2.35	4	0	0	0	0	7⅔	6	2	2	2	9
1992	—Toronto (A.L.)							Did not play.								
Champ. series totals (2 years)		0	0	...	2.08	5	0	0	0	0	8⅔	6	3	2	4	10

WORLD SERIES RECORD

Year	Team (League)	W	L	Pct.	ERA	G	GS	CG	ShO	Sv.	IP	H	R	ER	BB	SO
1992	—Toronto (A.L.)	0	0	...	0.00	4	0	0	0	0	4⅓	1	0	0	2	3

WENDELL, TURK

P, CUBS

PERSONAL: Born May 19, 1967, in Pittsfield, Mass. . . . 6-2/190. . . . Throws right, bats both. . . . Full name: Steven John Wendell.

HIGH SCHOOL: Wahconah Regional (Dalton, Mass.).

COLLEGE: Quinnipiac College (Conn.).

TRANSACTIONS/CAREER NOTES: Selected by Atlanta Braves organization in fifth round of free-agent draft (June 1, 1988). . . . Traded by Braves with P Yorkis Perez to Chicago Cubs for P Mike Bielecki and C Damon Berryhill (September 29, 1991). . . . On disabled list (May 4, 1992-remainder of season).

Year	Team (League)	W	L	Pct.	ERA	G	GS	CG	ShO	Sv.	IP	H	R	ER	BB	SO
1988	—Pulaski (Appal.)	3	•8	.273	3.83	14	14	★6	1	0	★101	85	50	43	30	87
1989	—Burlington (Midw.)	9	11	.450	2.21	22	22	•9	★5	0	159	127	63	39	41	153
	—Greenville (South.).....	0	0	...	9.82	1	1	0	0	0	3⅔	7	5	4	1	3
	—Durham (Carolina).....	2	0	1.000	1.13	3	3	1	0	0	24	13	4	3	6	27
1990	—Durham (Carolina).....	1	3	.250	1.86	6	5	1	0	0	38⅔	24	10	8	15	26
	—Greenville (South.).....	4	9	.308	5.74	36	13	1	1	2	91	105	70	58	48	85
1991	—Greenville (South.).....	11	3	★.786	2.56	25	20	1	1	0	147⅔	130	47	42	51	122
	—Richmond (Int'l)	0	2	.000	3.43	3	3	1	0	0	21	20	9	8	16	18
1992	—Iowa (Am. Assoc.)■ ...	2	0	1.000	1.44	4	4	0	0	0	25	17	7	4	15	12
1993	—Iowa (Am. Assoc.)	10	8	.556	4.60	25	25	3	0	0	148⅔	148	88	76	47	110
	—Chicago (N.L.)............	1	2	.333	4.37	7	4	0	0	0	22⅔	24	13	11	8	15
Major league totals (1 year) ...		1	2	.333	4.37	7	4	0	0	0	22⅔	24	13	11	8	15

WERTZ, BILL

P, INDIANS

PERSONAL: Born January 15, 1967, in Cleveland. . . . 6-6/220. . . . Throws right, bats right. . . . Full name: William Charles Wertz.

HIGH SCHOOL: Central Catholic (Cleveland).

COLLEGE: Ohio State.

TRANSACTIONS/CAREER NOTES: Selected by Cleveland Indians organization in 31st round of free-agent draft (June 5, 1989). . . . Loaned by Indians organization to Reno, independent (April 4-June 18, 1990).

Year	Team (League)	W	L	Pct.	ERA	G	GS	CG	ShO	Sv.	IP	H	R	ER	BB	SO
1989	—GC Indians (GCL)	4	3	.571	3.14	12	11	1	•1	0	66	57	23	23	36	56
1990	—Reno (California)■	1	3	.250	6.60	17	9	0	0	0	61⅓	61	58	45	52	52
	—Watertown (NYP)■....	•10	2	.833	2.86	14	14	2	0	0	•100⅔	81	39	32	48	92
1991	—Columbus (S. Atl.)......	6	8	.429	2.97	49	0	0	0	9	91	81	41	30	32	95
1992	—Cant./Akr. (East.)	8	4	.667	1.20	57	0	0	0	8	97⅓	75	16	13	30	69
1993	—Charlotte (Int'l)	7	2	.778	1.95	28	1	0	0	0	50⅔	42	18	11	14	47
	—Cleveland (A.L.)	2	3	.400	3.62	34	0	0	0	0	59⅔	54	28	24	32	53
Major league totals (1 year) ...		2	3	.400	3.62	34	0	0	0	0	59⅔	54	28	24	32	53

WEST, DAVID

P, PHILLIES

PERSONAL: Born September 1, 1964, in Memphis, Tenn. . . . 6-6/255. . . . Throws left, bats left. . . . Full name: David Lee West.

HIGH SCHOOL: Craigmont (Memphis, Tenn.).

TRANSACTIONS/CAREER NOTES: Selected by New York Mets organization in fourth round of free-agent draft (June 6, 1983). . . . Traded by Mets with P Rick Aguilera and three players to be named later to Minnesota Twins for P Frank Viola (July 31, 1989); Portland, Twins organization, acquired P Kevin Tapani and P Tim Drummond (August 1, 1989), and Twins acquired P Jack Savage to complete deal (October 16, 1989). . . . On disabled list (September 7, 1990-remainder of season). . . . On Minnesota disabled list (April 7-July 2, 1991); included rehabilitation assignment to Orlando (May 12-15) and Portland (June 14-July 2). . . . Traded by Twins to Philadelphia Phillies for P Mike Hartley (December 5, 1992).

STATISTICAL NOTES: Led New York-Pennsylvania League with 16 wild pitches in 1984. . . . Pitched 3-0 no-hit victory against Spartanburg (August 14, 1985). . . . Pitched six innings, combining with Larry Casian (two innings) and Greg Johnson (one inning) in 5-0 no-hit victory for Portland against Vancouver (June 7, 1992).

Year	Team (League)	W	L	Pct.	ERA	G	GS	CG	ShO	Sv.	IP	H	R	ER	BB	SO
1983	—GC Mets (GCL)	2	4	.333	2.85	12	10	0	0	0	53⅔	41	28	17	52	56
1984	—Columbia (S. Atl.).......	3	5	.375	6.23	12	12	0	0	0	60⅔	41	47	42	68	60
	—Little Falls (NYP)	6	4	.600	3.34	13	11	0	0	0	62	43	35	23	62	79

Year	Team (League)	W	L	Pct.	ERA	G	GS	CG	ShO	Sv.	IP	H	R	ER	BB	SO
1985	—Columbia (S. Atl.)	10	9	.526	4.56	26	25	5	2	0	150	105	97	76	*111	194
1986	—Lynchburg (Caro.)	1	6	.143	5.16	13	13	1	0	0	75	76	50	43	53	70
	—Columbia (S. Atl.)	10	3	.769	2.91	13	13	3	1	0	92⅔	74	41	30	56	101
1987	—Jackson (Texas)	10	7	.588	2.81	25	25	4	•2	0	166⅔	152	67	52	*81	*186
1988	—Tidewater (Int'l)	12	4	*.750	*1.80	23	23	7	1	0	160⅓	106	42	32	*97	143
	—New York (N.L.)	1	0	1.000	3.00	2	1	0	0	0	6	6	2	2	3	3
1989	—Tidewater (Int'l)	7	4	.636	2.37	12	12	5	1	0	87⅓	60	31	23	29	69
	—New York (N.L.)	0	2	.000	7.40	11	2	0	0	0	24⅓	25	20	20	14	19
	—Minnesota (A.L.)■	3	2	.600	6.41	10	5	0	0	0	39⅓	48	29	28	19	31
1990	—Minnesota (A.L.)	7	9	.438	5.10	29	27	2	0	0	146⅓	142	88	83	78	92
1991	—Minnesota (A.L.)	4	4	.500	4.54	15	12	0	0	0	71⅓	66	37	36	28	52
	—Orlando (Southern)	0	0	...	0.00	1	1	0	0	0	⅓	0	0	0	0	0
	—Portland (PCL)	1	1	.500	6.32	4	4	0	0	0	15⅔	12	11	11	12	15
1992	—Portland (PCL)	7	6	.538	4.43	19	18	1	0	0	101⅔	88	51	50	65	87
	—Minnesota (A.L.)	1	3	.250	6.99	9	3	0	0	0	28⅓	32	24	22	20	19
1993	—Philadelphia (N.L.)■	6	4	.600	2.92	76	0	0	0	3	86⅓	60	37	28	51	87
A.L. totals (4 years)		15	18	.455	5.33	63	47	2	0	0	285⅓	288	178	169	145	194
N.L. totals (3 years)		7	6	.538	3.86	89	3	0	0	3	116⅔	91	59	50	68	109
Major league totals (6 years)		22	24	.478	4.90	152	50	2	0	3	402	379	237	219	213	303

CHAMPIONSHIP SERIES RECORD

Year	Team (League)	W	L	Pct.	ERA	G	GS	CG	ShO	Sv.	IP	H	R	ER	BB	SO
1991	—Minnesota (A.L.)	1	0	1.000	0.00	2	0	0	0	0	5⅔	1	0	0	4	4
1993	—Philadelphia (N.L.)	0	0	...	13.50	3	0	0	0	0	2⅔	5	5	4	2	5
Champ. series totals (2 years)		1	0	1.000	4.32	5	0	0	0	0	8⅓	6	5	4	6	9

WORLD SERIES RECORD

Year	Team (League)	W	L	Pct.	ERA	G	GS	CG	ShO	Sv.	IP	H	R	ER	BB	SO
1991	—Minnesota (A.L.)	0	0	...	...	2	0	0	0	0	0	2	4	4	4	0
1993	—Philadelphia (N.L.)	0	0	...	27.00	3	0	0	0	0	1	5	3	3	1	0
World Series totals (2 years)		0	0	...	63.00	5	0	0	0	0	1	7	7	7	5	0

WESTON, MICKEY

P

PERSONAL: Born March 26, 1961, in Flint, Mich. . . . 6-1/187. . . . Throws right, bats right. . . . Full name: Michael Lee Weston.

HIGH SCHOOL: Lake Fenton (Fenton, Mich.).

COLLEGE: Eastern Michigan.

TRANSACTIONS/CAREER NOTES: Selected by New York Mets organization in 12th round of free-agent draft (June 7, 1982). . . . On disabled list (April 8-18 and May 23-June 25, 1986). . . . Granted free agency (October 15, 1988). . . . Signed by Rochester, Baltimore Orioles organization (November 28, 1988). . . . On Baltimore disabled list (June 23-August 22, 1989); included rehabilitation assignment to Rochester (August 2-21). . . . Traded by Orioles to Toronto Blue Jays for P Paul Kilgus (December 14, 1990). . . . Granted free agency (October 16, 1991). . . . Signed by Scranton/Wilkes-Barre, Philadelphia Phillies organization (December 18, 1991). . . . Granted free agency (October 16, 1992). . . . Signed by Tidewater, Mets organization (January 4, 1993). . . . Granted free agency (October 15, 1993).

Year	Team (League)	W	L	Pct.	ERA	G	GS	CG	ShO	Sv.	IP	H	R	ER	BB	SO
1982	—Little Falls (NYP)	7	6	.538	5.07	17	13	2	0	0	92⅓	105	63	52	22	67
1983	—Columbia (S. Atl.)	2	2	.500	4.34	37	1	0	0	6	74⅔	87	48	36	22	46
1984	—Columbia (S. Atl.)	6	5	.545	1.84	32	2	0	0	2	63⅔	58	27	13	27	40
1985	—Lynchburg (Caro.)	6	5	.545	2.15	49	3	1	1	10	100⅓	81	29	24	22	62
1986	—Jackson (Texas)	4	4	.500	4.33	34	4	0	0	2	70⅔	73	40	34	27	36
1987	—Jackson (Texas)	8	4	.667	3.40	58	1	0	0	3	82	96	39	31	18	50
1988	—Jackson (Texas)	8	5	.615	*2.23	30	14	1	0	0	125⅓	127	50	31	20	61
	—Tidewater (Int'l)	2	1	.667	1.52	4	4	2	1	0	29⅔	21	6	5	5	16
1989	—Rochester (Int'l)■	8	3	.727	2.09	23	14	2	1	4	112	103	30	26	19	51
	—Baltimore (A.L.)	1	0	1.000	5.54	7	0	0	0	1	13	18	8	8	2	7
1990	—Rochester (Int'l)	11	1	.917	1.98	29	12	2	0	6	109⅓	93	36	24	22	58
	—Baltimore (A.L.)	0	1	.000	7.71	9	2	0	0	0	21	28	20	18	6	9
1991	—Syracuse (Int'l)■	•12	6	.667	3.74	27	25	3	0	0	166	193	85	69	36	60
	—Toronto (A.L.)	0	0	...	0.00	2	0	0	0	0	2	1	0	0	1	1
1992	—Scran./W.B. (Int'l)■	10	6	.625	3.11	26	24	2	1	1	170⅔	165	65	59	29	79
	—Philadelphia (N.L.)	0	1	.000	12.27	1	1	0	0	0	3⅔	7	5	5	1	0
1993	—Norfolk (Int'l)■	10	9	.526	4.24	21	20	3	0	0	127⅓	149	77	60	18	41
	—New York (N.L.)	0	0	...	7.94	4	0	0	0	0	5⅔	11	5	5	1	2
A.L. totals (3 years)		1	1	.500	6.50	18	2	0	0	1	36	47	28	26	9	17
N.L. totals (2 years)		0	1	.000	9.64	5	1	0	0	0	9⅓	18	10	10	2	2
Major league totals (5 years)		1	2	.333	7.15	23	3	0	0	1	45⅓	65	38	36	11	19

W

WETTELAND, JOHN

P, EXPOS

PERSONAL: Born August 21, 1966, in San Mateo, Calif. . . . 6-2/215. . . . Throws right, bats right. . . . Full name: John Karl Wetteland.

HIGH SCHOOL: Cardinal Newman (Santa Rosa, Calif.).

COLLEGE: College of San Mateo (Calif.).

TRANSACTIONS/CAREER NOTES: Selected by New York Mets organization in 12th round of free-agent draft (June 4, 1984). . . . Selected by Los Angeles Dodgers organization in secondary phase of free-agent draft (January 9, 1985). . . . Selected by Detroit Tigers from Dodgers organization in Rule 5 major league draft (December 7, 1987). . . . Returned to Dodgers organization (March 29, 1988). . . . On Albuquerque disabled list (May 1-8 and June 3-29, 1991). . . . Traded by Dodgers with P Tim Belcher to Cincinnati Reds for OF Eric Davis and P Kip Gross (November 25, 1991). . . . Traded by Reds with P Bill Risley to Montreal Expos for OF Dave Martinez, P Scott Ruskin and SS Willie Greene (December 11, 1991). . . . On Montreal disabled list (March

23-April 23, 1993); included rehabilitation assignment to West Palm Beach (April 18-23).
STATISTICAL NOTES: Tied for Florida State League lead with 11 home runs allowed and 17 wild pitches in 1987. . . . Led Texas League with 22 wild pitches in 1988.

Year	Team (League)	W	L	Pct.	ERA	G	GS	CG	ShO	Sv.	IP	H	R	ER	BB	SO
1985	—Great Falls (Pio.)	1	1	.500	3.92	11	2	0	0	0	20⅔	17	10	9	15	23
1986	—Bakersfield (Calif.)	0	7	.000	5.78	15	12	4	0	0	67	71	50	43	46	38
	—Great Falls (Pio.)	4	3	.571	5.45	12	12	1	0	0	69⅓	70	51	42	40	59
1987	—Vero Beach (FSL)	12	7	.632	3.13	27	27	7	2	0	175⅔	150	81	61	92	144
1988	—San Antonio (Tex.)■	10	8	.556	3.88	25	25	3	1	0	162⅓	141	74	70	•77	140
1989	—Albuquerque (PCL)	5	3	.625	3.65	10	10	1	0	0	69	61	28	28	20	73
	—Los Angeles (N.L.)	5	8	.385	3.77	31	12	0	0	1	102⅔	81	46	43	34	96
1990	—Los Angeles (N.L.)	2	4	.333	4.81	22	5	0	0	0	43	44	28	23	17	36
	—Albuquerque (PCL)	2	2	.500	5.59	8	5	1	0	0	29	27	19	18	13	26
1991	—Albuquerque (PCL)	4	3	.571	2.79	41	4	0	0	20	61⅓	48	22	19	26	55
	—Los Angeles (N.L.)	1	0	1.000	0.00	6	0	0	0	0	9	5	2	0	3	9
1992	—Montreal (N.L.)■	4	4	.500	2.92	67	0	0	0	37	83⅓	64	27	27	36	99
1993	—W.P. Beach (FSL)	0	0	...	0.00	2	2	0	0	0	3	0	0	0	0	6
	—Montreal (N.L.)	9	3	.750	1.37	70	0	0	0	43	85⅓	58	17	13	28	113
	Major league totals (5 years)	21	19	.525	2.95	196	17	0	0	81	323⅓	252	120	106	118	353

WHISENANT, MATT

P, MARLINS

PERSONAL: Born June 8, 1971, in Los Angeles. . . . 6-3/200. . . . Throws left, bats both. . . . Full name: Matthew Michael Whisenant.
HIGH SCHOOL: La Canada (Calif.).
COLLEGE: Glendale (Ariz.) Community College.
TRANSACTIONS/CAREER NOTES: Selected by Philadelphia Phillies organization in 18th round of free-agent draft (June 5, 1989). . . . Traded by Phillies organization with P Joel Adamson to Florida Marlins organization for P Danny Jackson (November 17, 1992). . . . On disabled list (July 13, 1993-remainder of season).

Year	Team (League)	W	L	Pct.	ERA	G	GS	CG	ShO	Sv.	IP	H	R	ER	BB	SO
1990	—Princeton (Appal.)	0	0	...	11.40	9	2	0	0	0	15	16	27	19	20	25
1991	—Batavia (NY-Penn)	2	1	.667	2.45	11	10	0	0	0	47⅔	31	19	13	42	55
1992	—Spartanburg (SAL)	11	7	.611	3.23	27	27	2	0	0	150⅔	117	69	54	85	151
1993	—Kane Co. (Midw.)■	2	6	.250	4.69	15	15	0	0	0	71	68	45	37	56	74

WHITAKER, LOU

2B, TIGERS

PERSONAL: Born May 12, 1957, in Brooklyn, N.Y. . . . 5-11/180. . . . Throws right, bats left. . . . Full name: Louis Rodman Whitaker.
HIGH SCHOOL: Martinsville (Va.).
TRANSACTIONS/CAREER NOTES: Selected by Detroit Tigers organization in fifth round of free-agent draft (June 4, 1975). . . . On disabled list (May 3-14, 1977 and June 13-28, 1979). . . . Granted free agency (November 2, 1992). . . . Re-signed by Tigers (December 7, 1992).
HONORS: Named Florida State League Most Valuable Player (1976). . . . Named A.L. Rookie of the Year by Baseball Writers' Association of America (1978). . . . Named second baseman on THE SPORTING NEWS A.L. All-Star team (1983-84). . . . Named second baseman on THE SPORTING NEWS A.L. Silver Slugger team (1983-85 and 1987). . . . Won A.L. Gold Glove at second base (1983-85).
STATISTICAL NOTES: Led Florida State League second basemen with 30 double plays in 1976. . . . Led A.L. second basemen with 811 total chances and 120 double plays in 1982.

				BATTING											FIELDING			
Year	Team (League)	Pos.	G	AB	R	H	2B	3B	HR	RBI	Avg.	BB	SO	SB	PO	A	E	Avg.
1975	—Bristol (Appal.)	3B-SS	42	114	17	27	6	1	1	17	.237	25	13	1	38	82	16	.882
1976	—Lakeland (Fla. St.)	3B	124	343	*70	129	12	5	1	62	.376	55	51	48	*99	*267	*30	*.924
1977	—Montgomery (Sou.)	2B	107	396	*81	111	13	4	3	48	.280	58	52	38	208	285	15	.970
	—Detroit (A.L.)	2B	11	32	5	8	1	0	0	2	.250	4	6	2	17	18	0	1.000
1978	—Detroit (A.L.)	2B	139	484	71	138	12	7	3	58	.285	61	65	7	301	458	17	.978
1979	—Detroit (A.L.)	2B	127	423	75	121	14	8	3	42	.286	78	66	20	280	369	9	.986
1980	—Detroit (A.L.)	2B	145	477	68	111	19	1	1	45	.233	73	79	8	340	428	12	.985
1981	—Detroit (A.L.)	2B	•109	335	48	88	14	4	5	36	.263	40	42	5	227	*354	9	.985
1982	—Detroit (A.L.)	2B	152	560	76	160	22	8	15	65	.286	48	58	11	331	*470	10	*.988
1983	—Detroit (A.L.)	2B	161	643	94	206	40	6	12	72	.320	67	70	17	299	447	13	.983
1984	—Detroit (A.L.)	2B	143	558	90	161	25	1	13	56	.289	62	63	6	290	405	15	.979
1985	—Detroit (A.L.)	2B	152	609	102	170	29	8	21	73	.279	80	56	6	314	414	11	.985
1986	—Detroit (A.L.)	2B	144	584	95	157	26	6	20	73	.269	63	70	13	276	421	11	.984
1987	—Detroit (A.L.)	2B	149	604	110	160	38	6	16	59	.265	71	108	13	275	416	17	.976
1988	—Detroit (A.L.)	2B	115	403	54	111	18	2	12	55	.275	66	61	2	218	284	8	.984
1989	—Detroit (A.L.)	2B	148	509	77	128	21	1	28	85	.251	89	59	6	*327	393	11	.985
1990	—Detroit (A.L.)	2B	132	472	75	112	22	2	18	60	.237	74	71	8	286	372	6	.991
1991	—Detroit (A.L.)	2B	138	470	94	131	26	2	23	78	.279	90	45	4	255	361	4	*.994
1992	—Detroit (A.L.)	2B	130	453	77	126	26	0	19	71	.278	81	46	6	256	312	9	.984
1993	—Detroit (A.L.)	2B	119	383	72	111	32	1	9	67	.290	78	46	3	236	322	11	.981
	Major league totals (17 years)		2214	7999	1283	2199	385	63	218	997	.275	1125	1011	137	4528	6244	173	.984

CHAMPIONSHIP SERIES RECORD

				BATTING											FIELDING			
Year	Team (League)	Pos.	G	AB	R	H	2B	3B	HR	RBI	Avg.	BB	SO	SB	PO	A	E	Avg.
1984	—Detroit (A.L.)	2B	3	14	3	2	0	0	0	0	.143	0	3	0	5	6	0	1.000
1987	—Detroit (A.L.)	2B	5	17	4	3	0	0	1	1	.176	7	3	1	11	14	0	1.000
	Championship series totals (2 years)		8	31	7	5	0	0	1	1	.161	7	6	1	16	20	0	1.000

WORLD SERIES RECORD

Year	Team (League)	Pos.	G	AB	R	H	2B	3B	HR	RBI	Avg.	BB	SO	SB	PO	A	E	Avg.
			BATTING												FIELDING			
1984	—Detroit (A.L.)	2B	5	18	6	5	2	0	0	0	.278	4	4	0	15	18	0	1.000

ALL-STAR GAME RECORD

ALL-STAR GAME NOTES: Named to A.L. All-Star team for 1987 game; replaced by Harold Reynolds due to injury.

Year	League	Pos.	AB	R	H	2B	3B	HR	RBI	Avg.	BB	SO	SB	PO	A	E	Avg.
			BATTING											FIELDING			
1983	—American	PH-2B	1	1	1	0	1	0	2	1.000	0	0	0	1	0	0	1.000
1984	—American	2B	3	0	2	1	0	0	0	.667	0	0	0	0	5	0	1.000
1985	—American	2B	2	0	0	0	0	0	0	.000	0	0	0	1	1	0	1.000
1986	—American	2B	2	1	1	0	0	1	2	.500	0	1	0	0	3	0	1.000
1987	—American		Selected, did not play—injured.														
All-Star Game totals (4 years)			8	2	4	1	1	1	4	.500	0	1	0	2	9	0	1.000

WHITE, DERRICK

1B, EXPOS

PERSONAL: Born October 12, 1969, in San Rafael, Calif. . . . 6-1/220. . . . Throws right, bats right. . . . Full name: Derrick Ramon White.
HIGH SCHOOL: Terra Linda (San Rafael, Calif.).
COLLEGE: Santa Rosa (Calif.) Junior College and Oklahoma.
TRANSACTIONS/CAREER NOTES: Selected by Minnesota Twins organization in 23rd round of free-agent draft (June 5, 1989). . . . Selected by Philadelphia Phillies organization in ninth round of free-agent draft (June 4, 1990). . . . Selected by Montreal Expos organization in sixth round of free-agent draft (June 3, 1991). . . . On Ottawa disabled list (April 8-May 4, 1993).
STATISTICAL NOTES: Led Eastern League first basemen with 1,294 total chances and 110 double plays in 1992.

Year	Team (League)	Pos.	G	AB	R	H	2B	3B	HR	RBI	Avg.	BB	SO	SB	PO	A	E	Avg.
			BATTING												FIELDING			
1991	—Jamestown (NYP)	OF-1B	72	271	46	89	10	4	6	50	.328	40	46	8	402	18	8	.981
1992	—Harrisburg (East.)	1B	134	495	63	137	19	2	13	81	.277	40	73	17	*1178	*106	10	*.992
1993	—W.P. Beach (FSL)	1B	6	25	1	5	0	0	0	1	.200	1	2	2	38	4	0	1.000
	—Ottawa (Int'l)	1B	67	249	32	70	15	1	4	29	.281	20	52	10	632	49	8	.988
	—Montreal (N.L.)	1B	17	49	6	11	3	0	2	4	.224	2	12	2	129	8	1	.993
	—Harrisburg (East.)	1B	21	79	14	18	1	0	2	12	.228	5	17	2	171	11	2	.989
Major league totals (1 year)			17	49	6	11	3	0	2	4	.224	2	12	2	129	8	1	.993

WHITE, DEVON

OF, BLUE JAYS

PERSONAL: Born December 29, 1962, in Kingston, Jamaica. . . . 6-2/190. . . . Throws right, bats both. . . . Full name: Devon Markes White. . . . Name pronounced de-VON.
HIGH SCHOOL: Park West (New York).
TRANSACTIONS/CAREER NOTES: Selected by California Angels organization in sixth round of free-agent draft (June 8, 1981). . . . On suspended list (June 11-12 and July 19, 1982-remainder of season). . . . On Edmonton disabled list (May 12-22, 1986). . . . On disabled list (May 7-June 10, 1988). . . . Traded by Angels organization with P Willie Fraser and a player to be named later to Toronto Blue Jays for OF Junior Felix, IF Luis Sojo and a player to be named later (December 2, 1990); Blue Jays acquired P Marcus Moore and Angels acquired C Ken Rivers to complete deal (December 4, 1990).
RECORDS: Shares major league record for most stolen bases in one inning—3 (September 9, 1989, sixth inning).
HONORS: Won A.L. Gold Glove as outfielder (1988-89 and 1991-93).
STATISTICAL NOTES: Led Midwest League outfielders with 286 total chances in 1983. . . . Led California League outfielders with 351 total chances in 1984. . . . Led Pacific Coast League outfielders with 339 total chances in 1986. . . . Switch-hit home runs in one game (June 23, 1987; June 29, 1990 and June 1, 1992). . . . Led A.L. outfielders with 449 total chances in 1987, 448 in 1991 and 458 in 1992.

Year	Team (League)	Pos.	G	AB	R	H	2B	3B	HR	RBI	Avg.	BB	SO	SB	PO	A	E	Avg.
			BATTING												FIELDING			
1981	—Idaho Falls (Pio.)	OF-3B-1B	30	106	10	19	2	0	0	10	.179	12	34	4	33	10	3	.935
1982	—Danville (Midwest)	OF	57	186	21	40	6	1	1	11	.215	11	41	11	89	3	8	.920
1983	—Peoria (Midwest)	OF	117	430	69	109	17	6	13	66	.253	36	124	32	267	8	11	.962
	—Nashua (Eastern)	OF	17	70	11	18	7	2	0	2	.257	7	22	5	37	0	3	.925
1984	—Redwood (Calif.)	OF	138	520	101	147	25	5	7	55	.283	56	118	36	*322	16	13	.963
1985	—Midland (Texas)	OF	70	260	52	77	10	4	4	35	.296	35	46	38	176	10	4	.979
	—Edmonton (PCL)	OF	66	277	53	70	16	5	4	39	.253	24	77	21	205	6	2	.991
	—California (A.L.)	OF	21	7	7	1	0	0	0	0	.143	1	3	3	10	1	0	1.000
1986	—Edmonton (PCL)	OF	112	461	84	134	25	10	14	60	.291	31	90	*42	317	•16	6	.982
	—California (A.L.)	OF	29	51	8	12	1	1	1	3	.235	6	8	13	49	0	2	.961
1987	—California (A.L.)	OF	159	639	103	168	33	5	24	87	.263	39	135	32	*424	16	9	.980
1988	—California (A.L.)	OF	122	455	76	118	22	2	11	51	.259	23	84	17	364	7	9	.976
1989	—California (A.L.)	OF	156	636	86	156	18	13	12	56	.245	31	129	44	430	10	5	.989
1990	—California (A.L.)	OF	125	443	57	96	17	3	11	44	.217	44	116	21	302	11	9	.972
	—Edmonton (PCL)	OF	14	55	9	20	4	4	0	6	.364	7	12	4	31	1	3	.914
1991	—Toronto (A.L.)■	OF	156	642	110	181	40	10	17	60	.282	55	135	33	*439	8	1	*.998
1992	—Toronto (A.L.)	OF	153	641	98	159	26	7	17	60	.248	47	133	37	*443	8	7	.985
1993	—Toronto (A.L.)	OF	146	598	116	163	42	6	15	52	.273	57	127	34	399	6	3	.993
Major league totals (9 years)			1067	4112	661	1054	199	47	108	413	.256	303	870	234	2860	67	45	.985

CHAMPIONSHIP SERIES RECORD

CHAMPIONSHIP SERIES NOTES: Holds career record for highest batting average (50 or more at-bats)—.392. . . . Holds single-series record for most times caught stealing—4 (1992). . . . Shares A.L. single-series record for most hits—12 (1993). . . . Shares A.L. single-game record for most at-bats—6 (October 11, 1992, 11 innings).

Year	Team (League)	Pos.	G	AB	R	H	2B	3B	HR	RBI	Avg.	BB	SO	SB	PO	A	E	Avg.
			BATTING												FIELDING			
1986	—California (A.L.)	OF-PR	4	2	2	1	0	0	0	0	.500	0	1	0	3	0	0	1.000
1991	—Toronto (A.L.)	OF	5	22	5	8	1	0	0	0	.364	2	3	3	16	0	0	1.000
1992	—Toronto (A.L.)	OF	6	23	2	8	2	0	0	2	.348	5	6	0	16	0	1	.941
1993	—Toronto (A.L.)	OF	6	27	3	12	1	1	1	2	.444	1	5	0	15	0	0	1.000
Championship series totals (4 years)			21	74	12	29	4	1	1	4	.392	8	15	3	50	0	1	.980

WORLD SERIES RECORD

Year	Team (League)	Pos.	G	AB	R	H	2B	3B	HR	RBI	Avg.	BB	SO	SB	PO	A	E	Avg.
			BATTING												FIELDING			
1992	—Toronto (A.L.)	OF	6	26	2	6	1	0	0	2	.231	0	6	1	22	0	0	1.000
1993	—Toronto (A.L.)	OF	6	24	8	7	3	2	1	7	.292	4	7	1	16	0	0	1.000
World Series totals (2 years)			12	50	10	13	4	2	1	9	.260	4	13	2	38	0	0	1.000

ALL-STAR GAME RECORD

Year	League	Pos.	AB	R	H	2B	3B	HR	RBI	Avg.	BB	SO	SB	PO	A	E	Avg.
			BATTING											FIELDING			
1989	—American	OF	1	0	0	0	0	0	0	.000	0	0	0	0	0	0	...
1993	—American	OF	2	1	1	1	0	0	1	.500	0	0	1	1	0	0	1.000
All-Star Game totals (2 years)			3	1	1	1	0	0	1	.333	0	0	1	1	0	0	1.000

WHITE, GABE

P, EXPOS

PERSONAL: Born November 20, 1971, in Sebring, Fla. . . . 6-2/200. . . . Throws left, bats left. . . . Full name: Gabriel Allen White.

HIGH SCHOOL: Sebring (Fla.).

TRANSACTIONS/CAREER NOTES: Selected by Montreal Expos organization in supplemental round ("sandwich pick" between first and second round, 28th pick overall) of free-agent draft (June 4, 1990); pick received as part of compensation for California Angels signing Type A free agent Mark Langston. . . . On Harrisburg disabled list (July 2-27, 1993).

Year	Team (League)	W	L	Pct.	ERA	G	GS	CG	ShO	Sv.	IP	H	R	ER	BB	SO
1990	—GC Expos (GCL)	4	2	.667	3.14	11	11	1	0	0	57⅓	50	21	20	12	41
1991	—Sumter (S. Atl.)	6	9	.400	3.26	24	24	5	0	0	149	127	73	54	53	140
1992	—Rockford (Midw.)	14	8	.636	2.84	27	27	7	0	0	187	148	73	59	61	*176
1993	—Harrisburg (East.)	7	2	.778	2.16	16	16	2	1	0	100	80	30	24	28	80
	—Ottawa (Int'l)	2	1	.667	3.12	6	6	1	1	0	40⅓	38	15	14	6	28

WHITE, JIMMY

OF, ASTROS

PERSONAL: Born December 1, 1972, in Tampa, Fla. . . . 6-1/170. . . . Throws right, bats left. . . . Full name: Jimmy Lee White Jr.

HIGH SCHOOL: Brandon (Fla.).

TRANSACTIONS/CAREER NOTES: Selected by Houston Astros organization in sixth round of free-agent draft (June 4, 1990).

Year	Team (League)	Pos.	G	AB	R	H	2B	3B	HR	RBI	Avg.	BB	SO	SB	PO	A	E	Avg.
			BATTING												FIELDING			
1990	—GC Astros (GCL)	OF	52	180	32	44	6	4	0	18	.244	29	50	11	71	9	2	.976
1991	—Asheville (S. Atl.)	OF	128	437	66	112	22	2	8	43	.256	43	133	12	214	12	5	.978
1992	—Burlington (Midw.)	OF	102	370	39	106	20	7	1	47	.286	38	84	17	170	•17	7	.964
	—Asheville (S. Atl.)	OF	24	83	12	28	6	1	2	14	.337	7	15	5	54	4	2	.967
1993	—Osceola (Fla. St.)	OF	125	447	80	123	9	12	7	37	.275	54	120	24	270	16	•12	.960

WHITE, RICK

P, PIRATES

PERSONAL: Born December 23, 1968, in Springfield, O. . . . 6-4/215. . . . Throws right, bats right. . . . Full name: Richard Allen White.

HIGH SCHOOL: Kenton Ridge (Springfield, O.).

COLLEGE: Paducah (Ky.) Community College.

TRANSACTIONS/CAREER NOTES: Selected by Pittsburgh Pirates organization in 15th round of free-agent draft (June 4, 1990). . . . On Carolina disabled list (May 15-July 6, 1993). . . . On Buffalo disabled list (August 28-September 4, 1993).

Year	Team (League)	W	L	Pct.	ERA	G	GS	CG	ShO	Sv.	IP	H	R	ER	BB	SO
1990	—GC Pirates (GCL)	3	1	.750	0.76	7	6	0	0	0	35⅔	26	11	3	4	27
	—Welland (NYP)	1	4	.200	3.26	9	5	1	0	0	38⅔	39	19	14	14	43
1991	—Augusta (S. Atl.)	4	4	.500	3.00	34	0	0	0	6	63	68	26	21	18	52
	—Salem (Carolina)	2	3	.400	4.66	13	5	1	0	1	46⅓	41	27	24	9	36
1992	—Salem (Carolina)	7	9	.438	3.80	18	18	•5	0	0	120⅔	116	58	51	24	70
	—Carolina (South.)	1	7	.125	4.21	10	10	1	0	0	57⅔	59	32	27	18	45
1993	—Carolina (South.)	4	3	.571	3.50	12	12	1	0	0	69⅓	59	29	27	12	52
	—Buffalo (A.A.)	0	3	.000	3.54	7	3	0	0	0	28	25	13	11	8	16

W

WHITE, RONDELL

OF, EXPOS

PERSONAL: Born February 23, 1972, in Milledgeville, Ga. . . . 6-1/205. . . . Throws right, bats right. . . . Full name: Rondell Bernard White.

HIGH SCHOOL: Jones County (Gray, Ga.).

TRANSACTIONS/CAREER NOTES: Selected by Montreal Expos organization in first round (24th pick overall) of free-agent draft (June 4, 1990); pick received as part of compensation for California Angels signing Type A free agent Mark Langston.

STATISTICAL NOTES: Led Gulf Coast League with 96 total bases in 1990.

Year	Team (League)	Pos.	G	AB	R	H	2B	3B	HR	RBI	Avg.	BB	SO	SB	PO	A	E	Avg.
			BATTING												FIELDING			
1990	—GC Expos (GCL)	OF	57	221	33	66	7	4	5	34	.299	17	33	10	71	1	2	.973
1991	—Sumter (S. Atl.)	OF	123	465	80	122	23	6	13	68	.262	57	109	50	215	6	3	*.987
1992	—W.P. Beach (FSL)	OF	111	450	80	142	10	*12	4	41	.316	46	78	42	187	2	3	.984
	—Harrisburg (East.)	OF	21	89	22	27	7	1	2	7	.303	6	14	6	29	1	2	.938
1993	—Harrisburg (East.)	OF	90	372	72	122	16	10	12	52	.328	22	72	21	179	4	1	.995
	—Ottawa (Int'l)	OF	37	150	28	57	8	2	7	32	.380	12	20	10	79	0	1	.988
	—Montreal (N.L.)	OF	23	73	9	19	3	1	2	15	.260	7	16	1	33	0	0	1.000
Major league totals (1 year)			23	73	9	19	3	1	2	15	.260	7	16	1	33	0	0	1.000

WHITEHURST, WALLY

P, PADRES

PERSONAL: Born April 11, 1964, in Shreveport, La.... 6-3/200.... Throws right, bats right.... Full name: Walter Richard Whitehurst.
HIGH SCHOOL: Terrebonne (Houma, La.).
COLLEGE: New Orleans.

TRANSACTIONS/CAREER NOTES: Selected by Oakland Athletics organization in third round of free-agent draft (June 3, 1985).... Traded by A's as part of an eight-player, three-team deal in which New York Mets sent P Jesse Orosco to A's. A's traded Orosco, SS Alfredo Griffin and P Jay Howell to Los Angeles Dodgers for P Bob Welch, P Matt Young and P Jack Savage. A's then traded Savage, Whitehurst and P Kevin Tapani to Mets (December 11, 1987).... On disabled list (July 26-August 10, 1991).... Traded by Mets with OF D.J. Dozier and a player to be named later to San Diego Padres for SS Tony Fernandez (October 26, 1992); Padres acquired C Raul Casanova from Mets to complete deal (December 7, 1992).... On San Diego disabled list (March 29-May 11, 1993); included rehabilitation assignment to Wichita (April 18-May 10).... On San Diego disabled list (July 27-August 13 and August 20-September 24, 1993).
STATISTICAL NOTES: Tied for Northwest League lead with seven hit batsmen and two balks in 1985.

Year	Team (League)	W	L	Pct.	ERA	G	GS	CG	ShO	Sv.	IP	H	R	ER	BB	SO
1985	—Medford (N'west)	7	5	.583	3.58	14	14	2	0	0	88	92	51	35	29	•91
	—Modesto (Calif.)	1	0	1.000	1.80	2	2	0	0	0	10	10	3	2	5	5
1986	—Madison (Midwest)	6	1	.857	0.59	8	8	5	•4	0	61	42	8	4	16	57
	—Huntsville (South.)	9	5	.643	4.64	19	19	2	0	0	104⅔	114	66	54	46	54
1987	—Huntsville (South.)	11	10	.524	3.98	28	28	5	•3	0	183⅓	192	104	81	42	106
1988	—Tidewater (Int'l)■	10	11	.476	3.05	26	26	3	1	0	165	145	65	56	32	113
1989	—Tidewater (Int'l)	8	7	.533	3.25	21	20	3	1	0	133	123	54	48	32	95
	—New York (N.L.)	0	1	.000	4.50	9	1	0	0	0	14	17	7	7	5	9
1990	—New York (N.L.)	1	0	1.000	3.29	38	0	0	0	2	65⅔	63	27	24	9	46
	—Tidewater (Int'l)	1	0	1.000	2.00	2	2	0	0	0	9	7	2	2	1	10
1991	—New York (N.L.)	7	12	.368	4.19	36	20	0	0	1	133⅓	142	67	62	25	87
1992	—New York (N.L.)	3	9	.250	3.62	44	11	0	0	0	97	99	45	39	33	70
1993	—Wichita (Texas)■	1	0	1.000	1.27	4	4	0	0	0	21⅓	11	4	3	5	14
	—San Diego (N.L.)	4	7	.364	3.83	21	19	0	0	0	105⅔	109	47	45	30	57
Major league totals (5 years)		15	29	.341	3.83	148	51	0	0	3	415⅔	430	193	177	102	269

WHITEN, MARK

OF, CARDINALS

PERSONAL: Born November 25, 1966, in Pensacola, Fla.... 6-3/215.... Throws right, bats both.... Full name: Mark Anthony Whiten.... Name pronounced WHITT-en.
HIGH SCHOOL: Pensacola (Fla.).
COLLEGE: Pensacola (Fla.) Junior College.

TRANSACTIONS/CAREER NOTES: Selected by Toronto Blue Jays organization in fifth round of free-agent draft (January 14, 1986).... On suspended list (May 23-25, 1991).... Traded by Blue Jays with P Denis Boucher, OF Glenallen Hill and a player to be named later to Cleveland Indians for P Tom Candiotti and OF Turner Ward (June 27, 1991); Indians acquired cash instead of player to complete deal (October 15, 1991).... Traded by Indians to St. Louis Cardinals for P Mark Clark and SS Juan Andujar (March 31, 1993).
RECORDS: Shares major league single-game records for most home runs—4 (September 7, 1993, second game); and most runs batted in—12 (September 7, 1993, second game).... Shares major league record for most runs batted in during doubleheader—13 (September 7, 1993).... Shares N.L. record for most runs batted in during two consecutive games—13 (September 7, 1993, first and second games).
STATISTICAL NOTES: Tied for Pioneer League lead in being hit by pitch with six in 1986.... Led South Atlantic League outfielders with 322 total chances and tied for lead with four double plays in 1987.... Led South Atlantic League in being hit by pitch with 16 and tied for lead in intentional bases on balls received with 10 in 1987.... Led Southern League in being hit by pitch with 11 in 1989.... Switch-hit home runs in one game (September 14, 1993).
MISCELLANEOUS: Batted righthanded only (1988-89).

Year	Team (League)	Pos.	G	AB	R	H	2B	3B	HR	RBI	Avg.	BB	SO	SB	PO	A	E	Avg.
			BATTING												FIELDING			
1986	—Medicine Hat (Pio.)	OF	•70	270	53	81	16	3	10	44	.300	29	56	22	111	9	*10	.923
1987	—Myrtle Beach (SAL)	OF	*139	494	90	125	22	5	15	64	.253	76	149	49	*292	*18	12	.963
1988	—Dunedin (Fla. St.)	OF	99	385	61	97	8	5	7	37	.252	41	69	17	200	*21	9	.961
	—Knoxville (South.)	OF	28	108	20	28	3	1	2	9	.259	12	20	6	62	3	4	.942
1989	—Knoxville (South.)	OF	129	423	75	109	13	6	12	47	.258	60	114	11	223	17	8	.968
1990	—Syracuse (Int'l)	OF	104	390	65	113	19	4	14	48	.290	37	72	14	158	14	6	.966
	—Toronto (A.L.)	OF	33	88	12	24	1	1	2	7	.273	7	14	2	60	3	0	1.000
1991	—Tor.-Clev. (A.L.)■	OF	116	407	46	99	18	7	9	45	.243	30	85	4	256	13	7	.975
1992	—Cleveland (A.L.)	OF	148	508	73	129	19	4	9	43	.254	72	102	16	321	14	7	.980
1993	—St. Louis (N.L.)■	OF	152	562	81	142	13	4	25	99	.253	58	110	15	329	9	10	.971
American League totals (3 years)			297	1003	131	252	38	12	20	95	.251	109	201	22	637	30	14	.979
National League totals (1 year)			152	562	81	142	13	4	25	99	.253	58	110	15	329	9	10	.971
Major league totals (4 years)			449	1565	212	394	51	16	45	194	.252	167	311	37	966	39	24	.977

WHITESIDE, MATT

P, RANGERS

PERSONAL: Born August 8, 1967, in Charleston, Mo. . . . 6-0/195. . . . Throws right, bats right. . . . Full name: Matthew Christopher Whiteside.
HIGH SCHOOL: Charleston (Mo.).
COLLEGE: Arkansas State (degree in physical education).
TRANSACTIONS/CAREER NOTES: Selected by Texas Rangers organization in 25th round of free-agent draft (June 4, 1990).

Year	Team (League)	W	L	Pct.	ERA	G	GS	CG	ShO	Sv.	IP	H	R	ER	BB	SO
1990	—Butte (Pioneer)	4	4	.500	3.45	18	5	0	0	2	57⅓	57	33	22	25	45
1991	—Gastonia (S. Atl.)	3	1	.750	2.15	48	0	0	0	29	62⅔	44	19	15	21	71
1992	—Tulsa (Texas)	0	1	.000	2.41	33	0	0	0	21	33⅔	31	9	9	3	30
	—Okla. City (A.A.)	1	0	1.000	0.79	12	0	0	0	8	11⅓	7	1	1	3	13
	—Texas (A.L.)	1	1	.500	1.93	20	0	0	0	4	28	26	8	6	11	13
1993	—Texas (A.L.)	2	1	.667	4.32	60	0	0	0	1	73	78	37	35	23	39
	—Okla. City (A.A.)	2	1	.667	5.56	8	0	0	0	1	11⅓	17	7	7	8	10
	Major league totals (2 years)	3	2	.600	3.65	80	0	0	0	5	101	104	45	41	34	52

WHITMORE, DARRELL

OF, MARLINS

PERSONAL: Born November 18, 1968, in Front Royal, Va. . . . 6-1/210. . . . Throws right, bats left. . . . Full name: Darrell Lamont Whitmore.
HIGH SCHOOL: Warren County (Front Royal, Va.).
COLLEGE: West Virginia.
TRANSACTIONS/CAREER NOTES: Selected by Toronto Blue Jays organization in 10th round of free-agent draft (June 2, 1987). . . . Selected by Blue Jays organization in 58th round of free-agent draft (June 1, 1988). . . . Selected by Cleveland Indians organization in second round of free-agent draft (June 4, 1990); pick received as compensation for Seattle Mariners signing Type B free agent Pete O'Brien. . . . On temporary inactive list (July 2, 1991-remainder of season). . . . Selected by Florida Marlins in first round (16th pick overall) of expansion draft (November 17, 1992).

			BATTING												FIELDING			
Year	Team (League)	Pos.	G	AB	R	H	2B	3B	HR	RBI	Avg.	BB	SO	SB	PO	A	E	Avg.
1990	—Burlington (Appal.)	OF	30	112	18	27	3	2	0	13	.241	9	30	9	28	1	4	.879
1991	—Watertown (NYP)	OF	6	19	2	7	2	1	0	9	.368	3	2	0	0	0	0	...
1992	—Kinston (Carolina)	OF	121	443	71	124	22	2	10	52	.280	56	92	17	184	6	8	.960
1993	—Edmonton (PCL)■	OF	73	273	52	97	24	2	9	62	.355	22	53	11	171	7	4	.978
	—Florida (N.L.)	OF	76	250	24	51	8	2	4	19	.204	10	72	4	140	3	3	.979
	Major league totals (1 year)		76	250	24	51	8	2	4	19	.204	10	72	4	140	3	3	.979

WICKANDER, KEVIN

P, REDS

PERSONAL: Born January 4, 1965, in Fort Dodge, Ia. . . . 6-3/205. . . . Throws left, bats left. . . . Full name: Kevin Dean Wickander. . . . Name pronounced WICK-and-er.
HIGH SCHOOL: Cortez (Phoenix).
COLLEGE: Grand Canyon (Ariz.).
TRANSACTIONS/CAREER NOTES: Selected by Cleveland Indians organization in second round of free-agent draft (June 2, 1986). . . . On disabled list (May 31, 1990-remainder of season). . . . On Colorado Springs temporary inactive list (May 25-June 29, 1991). . . . Traded by Indians to Cincinnati Reds for a player to be named later (May 7, 1993); Indians acquired P Todd Ruyak to complete deal (June 4, 1993). . . . On Cincinnati disabled list (June 2-21, 1993); included rehabilitation assignment to Indianapolis (June 16-21). . . . On Cincinnati disabled list (July 2-19, 1993).

Year	Team (League)	W	L	Pct.	ERA	G	GS	CG	ShO	Sv.	IP	H	R	ER	BB	SO
1986	—Batavia (NY-Penn)	3	4	.429	2.72	11	9	0	0	0	46⅓	30	19	14	27	63
1987	—Kinston (Carolina)	9	6	.600	3.42	25	25	2	1	0	147⅓	128	69	56	75	118
1988	—Williamsport (East.)	1	0	1.000	0.63	24	0	0	0	16	28⅔	14	3	2	9	33
	—Colo. Springs (PCL)	0	2	.000	7.16	19	0	0	0	0	32⅔	44	30	26	27	22
1989	—Colo. Springs (PCL)	1	3	.250	2.95	45	0	0	0	11	42⅔	40	14	14	27	41
	—Cleveland (A.L.)	0	0	...	3.38	2	0	0	0	0	2⅔	6	1	1	2	0
1990	—Cleveland (A.L.)	0	1	.000	3.65	10	0	0	0	0	12⅓	14	6	5	4	10
1991	—Cant./Akr. (East.)	1	2	.333	3.96	20	0	0	0	0	25	24	14	11	13	21
	—Colo. Springs (PCL)	1	0	1.000	2.45	11	0	0	0	2	11	8	3	3	5	9
1992	—Colo. Springs (PCL)	0	0	...	1.64	8	0	0	0	2	11	4	2	2	6	18
	—Cleveland (A.L.)	2	0	1.000	3.07	44	0	0	0	1	41	39	14	14	28	38
1993	—Cleveland (A.L.)	0	0	...	4.15	11	0	0	0	0	8⅔	15	7	4	3	3
	—Cincinnati (N.L.)■	1	0	1.000	6.75	33	0	0	0	0	25⅓	32	20	19	19	20
	—Indianapolis (A.A.)	0	0	...	0.00	1	1	0	0	0	3	2	0	0	1	2
	A.L. totals (4 years)	2	1	.667	3.34	67	0	0	0	1	64⅔	74	28	24	37	51
	N.L. totals (1 year)	1	0	1.000	6.75	33	0	0	0	0	25⅓	32	20	19	19	20
	Major league totals (4 years)	3	1	.750	4.30	100	0	0	0	1	90	106	48	43	56	71

WICKMAN, BOB

P, YANKEES

PERSONAL: Born February 6, 1969, in Green Bay, Wis. . . . 6-1/212. . . . Throws right, bats right. . . . Full name: Robert Joe Wickman.
HIGH SCHOOL: Oconto Falls (Wis.).
COLLEGE: Wisconsin-Whitewater.
TRANSACTIONS/CAREER NOTES: Selected by Chicago White Sox organization in second round of free-agent draft (June 4, 1990). . . . Traded by White Sox organization with P Melido Perez and P Domingo Jean to New York Yankees organization for 2B Steve Sax and cash (January 10, 1992).

Year	Team (League)	W	L	Pct.	ERA	G	GS	CG	ShO	Sv.	IP	H	R	ER	BB	SO
1990	—GC Whi. Sox (GCL)	2	0	1.000	2.45	2	2	0	0	0	11	7	4	3	1	15
	—Sarasota (Fla. St.)	0	1	.000	1.98	2	2	0	0	0	13⅔	17	7	3	4	8
	—South Bend (Mid.)	7	2	.778	1.38	9	9	3	0	0	65⅓	50	16	10	16	50
1991	—Sarasota (Fla. St.)	5	1	.833	2.05	7	7	1	1	0	44	43	16	10	11	32
	—Birm. (Southern)	6	10	.375	3.56	20	20	4	1	0	131⅓	127	68	52	50	81

Year	Team (League)	W	L	Pct.	ERA	G	GS	CG	ShO	Sv.	IP	H	R	ER	BB	SO
1992	—Columbus (Int'l)■	12	5	.706	2.92	23	23	2	1	0	157	131	61	51	55	108
	—New York (A.L.)	6	1	.857	4.11	8	8	0	0	0	50⅓	51	25	23	20	21
1993	—New York (A.L.)	14	4	.778	4.63	41	19	1	1	4	140	156	82	72	69	70
Major league totals (2 years)		20	5	.800	4.49	49	27	1	1	4	190⅓	207	107	95	89	91

WILKERSON, CURTIS

2B

PERSONAL: Born April 26, 1961, in Petersburg, Va.... 5-9/173.... Throws right, bats both.... Full name: Curtis Vernon Wilkerson.

HIGH SCHOOL: Dinwiddie (Va.).

TRANSACTIONS/CAREER NOTES: Selected by Texas Rangers organization in fourth round of free-agent draft (June 3, 1980).... On disabled list (May 19-June 21, 1983).... Traded by Rangers with P Mitch Williams, P Paul Kilgus, P Steve Wilson, IF Luis Benitez and OF Pablo Delgado to Chicago Cubs for OF Rafael Palmeiro, P Jamie Moyer and P Drew Hall (December 5, 1988).... Granted free agency (November 5, 1990).... Signed by Pittsburgh Pirates (January 9, 1991).... Granted free agency (November 5, 1991).... Signed by Kansas City Royals organization (January 28, 1992).... Granted free agency (November 3, 1992).... Re-signed by Royals (December 8, 1992).... On disabled list (May 17, 1993-remainder of season).... Granted free agency (October 15, 1993).

STATISTICAL NOTES: Tied for Texas League lead with 11 sacrifice hits in 1982.

			BATTING												FIELDING			
Year	Team (League)	Pos.	G	AB	R	H	2B	3B	HR	RBI	Avg.	BB	SO	SB	PO	A	E	Avg.
1980	—GC Rangers (GCL)	SS-2B	37	105	15	20	2	0	0	8	.190	8	26	1	38	86	17	.879
1981	—Asheville (S. Atl.)	SS-2B	106	333	45	68	7	3	0	19	.204	26	53	12	188	372	28	.952
1982	—Burlington (Midw.)	SS-2B	56	198	18	50	6	0	0	13	.253	15	33	21	78	159	16	.937
	—Tulsa (Texas)	SS	72	266	32	71	6	3	2	14	.267	15	31	12	102	225	18	.948
1983	—Okla. City (A.A.)	SS	89	343	51	107	19	4	3	31	.312	38	55	14	135	272	19	.955
	—Texas (A.L.)	SS-2B-3B	16	35	7	6	0	1	0	1	.171	2	5	3	18	31	1	.980
1984	—Texas (A.L.)	SS-2B	153	484	47	120	12	0	1	26	.248	22	72	12	227	391	30	.954
1985	—Texas (A.L.)	SS-2B	129	360	35	88	11	6	0	22	.244	22	63	14	165	328	21	.959
1986	—Texas (A.L.)	2B-SS	110	236	27	56	10	3	0	15	.237	11	42	9	125	199	13	.961
1987	—Texas (A.L.)	SS-2B-3B	85	138	28	37	5	3	2	14	.268	6	16	6	79	98	6	.967
1988	—Texas (A.L.)	2B-SS-3B	117	338	41	99	12	5	0	28	.293	26	43	9	186	299	15	.970
1989	—Chicago (N.L.)■	3-2-S-0	77	160	18	39	4	2	1	10	.244	8	33	4	42	91	8	.943
1990	—Chicago (N.L.)	3-2-S-0	77	186	21	41	5	1	0	16	.220	7	36	2	49	93	14	.910
1991	—Pittsburgh (N.L.)■	2B-SS-3B	85	191	20	36	9	1	2	18	.188	15	40	2	73	124	2	.990
1992	—Kansas City (A.L.)■	SS-2B-3B	111	296	27	74	10	1	2	29	.250	18	47	18	148	257	10	.976
1993	—Kansas City (A.L.)	2B-SS	12	28	1	4	0	0	0	0	.143	1	6	2	8	25	0	1.000
American League totals (8 years)			733	1915	213	484	60	19	5	135	.253	108	294	73	956	1628	96	.964
National League totals (3 years)			239	537	59	116	18	4	3	44	.216	30	109	8	164	308	24	.952
Major league totals (11 years)			972	2452	272	600	78	23	8	179	.245	138	403	81	1120	1936	120	.962

CHAMPIONSHIP SERIES RECORD

			BATTING												FIELDING			
Year	Team (League)	Pos.	G	AB	R	H	2B	3B	HR	RBI	Avg.	BB	SO	SB	PO	A	E	Avg.
1989	—Chicago (N.L.)	PH-PR-3B	3	2	1	1	0	0	0	0	.500	0	0	0	0	0	0	...
1991	—Pittsburgh (N.L.)	PH	4	4	0	0	0	0	0	0	.000	0	3	0	...	...	...	...
Championship series totals (2 years)			7	6	1	1	0	0	0	0	.167	0	3	0	0	0	0	...

WILKINS, RICK

C, CUBS

PERSONAL: Born June 4, 1967, in Jacksonville, Fla.... 6-2/210.... Throws right, bats left.... Full name: Richard David Wilkins.

HIGH SCHOOL: The Bolles School (Jacksonville, Fla.).

COLLEGE: Florida Community College and Furman.

TRANSACTIONS/CAREER NOTES: Selected by Chicago Cubs organization in 23rd round of free-agent draft (June 2, 1986).

STATISTICAL NOTES: Led Appalachian League with eight intentional bases on balls received in 1987.... Led Appalachian League catchers with .989 fielding percentage, 483 putouts and 540 total chances and tied for lead with six double plays in 1987.... Led Midwest League catchers with 984 total chances in 1988.... Led Carolina League catchers with 860 total chances and tied for lead with eight double plays in 1989.... Led Southern League catchers with 857 total chances, 11 double plays and 15 passed balls in 1990.

			BATTING												FIELDING			
Year	Team (League)	Pos.	G	AB	R	H	2B	3B	HR	RBI	Avg.	BB	SO	SB	PO	A	E	Avg.
1987	—Geneva (NY-Penn)	C-1B	75	243	35	61	8	2	8	43	.251	58	40	7	†503	51	7	†.988
1988	—Peoria (Midwest)	C	137	490	54	119	30	1	8	63	.243	67	110	4	*864	*101	*19	.981
1989	—Winst.-Salem (Car.)	C	132	445	61	111	24	1	12	54	.249	50	87	6	*764	*78	*18	.979
1990	—Charlotte (South.)	C	127	449	48	102	18	1	17	71	.227	43	95	4	*740	*103	14	.984
1991	—Iowa (Am. Assoc.)	C-OF	38	107	12	29	3	1	5	14	.271	11	17	1	204	24	3	.987
	—Chicago (N.L.)	C	86	203	21	45	9	0	6	22	.222	19	56	3	373	42	3	.993
1992	—Chicago (N.L.)	C	83	244	20	66	9	1	8	22	.270	28	53	0	408	47	3	.993
	—Iowa (Am. Assoc.)	C	47	155	20	43	11	2	5	28	.277	19	42	0	177	18	2	.990
1993	—Chicago (N.L.)	C	136	446	78	135	23	1	30	73	.303	50	99	2	717	89	3	.996
Major league totals (3 years)			305	893	119	246	41	2	44	117	.275	97	208	5	1498	178	9	.995

WILLIAMS, BERNIE

OF, YANKEES

PERSONAL: Born September 13, 1968, in San Juan, Puerto Rico.... 6-2/200.... Throws right, bats both.... Full name: Bernabe Figueroa Williams.

TRANSACTIONS/CAREER NOTES: Signed as free agent by New York Yankees organization (September 13, 1985).... On disabled list (July 15, 1988-remainder of season and May 13-June 7, 1993).

RECORDS: Shares major league single-game record (nine innings) for most strikeouts—5 (August 21, 1991).

STATISTICAL NOTES: Led Gulf Coast League outfielders with 123 total chances in 1986.... Tied for Gulf Coast League lead in caught stealing with 12 in 1986.... Led Eastern League in caught stealing with 18 in 1990.... Led Eastern League outfielders with 307 total chances and tied for lead with four double plays in 1990.
MISCELLANEOUS: Batted righthanded only (1986-88).

			BATTING												FIELDING			
Year	Team (League)	Pos.	G	AB	R	H	2B	3B	HR	RBI	Avg.	BB	SO	SB	PO	A	E	Avg.
1986	—GC Yankees (GCL)....	OF	61	230	*45	62	5	3	2	25	.270	39	40	33	*117	3	3	.976
1987	—Fort Lauder. (FSL)...	OF	25	71	11	11	3	0	0	4	.155	18	22	9	49	1	0	1.000
	—Oneonta (NYP).........	OF	25	93	13	32	4	0	0	15	.344	10	14	9	40	0	2	.952
1988	—Prin. William (Car.)..	OF	92	337	72	113	16	7	7	45	*.335	65	65	29	186	8	5	.975
1989	—Columbus (Int'l).......	OF	50	162	21	35	8	1	2	16	.216	25	38	11	112	2	1	.991
	—Alb./Colon. (East.)...	OF	91	314	63	79	11	8	11	42	.252	60	72	26	180	5	5	.974
1990	—Alb./Colon. (East.)...	OF	134	466	*91	131	28	5	8	54	.281	*98	97	*39	*288	15	4	.987
1991	—Columbus (Int'l).......	OF	78	306	52	90	14	6	8	37	.294	38	43	9	164	2	1	.994
	—New York (A.L.)........	OF	85	320	43	76	19	4	3	34	.238	48	57	10	230	3	5	.979
1992	—New York (A.L.)........	OF	62	261	39	73	14	2	5	26	.280	29	36	7	187	5	1	.995
	—Columbus (Int'l).......	OF	95	363	68	111	23	*9	8	50	.306	52	61	20	205	2	2	.990
1993	—New York (A.L.)........	OF	139	567	67	152	31	4	12	68	.268	53	106	9	366	5	4	.989
Major league totals (3 years)			286	1148	149	301	64	10	20	128	.262	130	199	26	783	13	10	.988

WILLIAMS, BRIAN

P, ASTROS

PERSONAL: Born February 15, 1969, in Lancaster, S.C.... 6-2/195.... Throws right, bats right.... Full name: Brian O'Neal Williams.
HIGH SCHOOL: Lewisville (Fort Lawn, S.C.).
COLLEGE: South Carolina.
TRANSACTIONS/CAREER NOTES: Selected by Pittsburgh Pirates organization in third round of free-agent draft (June 2, 1987).... Selected by Houston Astros organization in supplemental round ("sandwich pick" between first and second round, 31st pick overall) of free-agent draft (June 4, 1990); pick received as part of compensation for San Francisco Giants signing Type A free agent Kevin Bass.... On Tucson disabled list (May 25-June 1, 1992).... On Houston disabled list (August 5-20, 1993); included rehabilitation assignment to Tucson (August 15-20).
MISCELLANEOUS: Appeared in four games as pinch-runner with Houston (1992).

Year	Team (League)	W	L	Pct.	ERA	G	GS	CG	ShO	Sv.	IP	H	R	ER	BB	SO
1990	—Auburn (NY-Penn)....	0	0	...	4.05	3	3	0	0	0	6⅔	6	5	3	6	7
1991	—Osceola (Fla. St.)......	6	4	.600	2.91	15	15	0	0	0	89⅔	72	41	29	40	67
	—Jackson (Texas).......	2	1	.667	4.20	3	3	0	0	0	15	17	8	7	7	15
	—Tucson (PCL)............	0	1	.000	4.93	7	7	0	0	0	38⅓	39	25	21	22	29
	—Houston (N.L.)..........	0	1	.000	3.75	2	2	0	0	0	12	11	5	5	4	4
1992	—Tucson (PCL)............	6	1	.857	4.50	12	12	0	0	0	70	78	37	35	26	58
	—Houston (N.L.)..........	7	6	.538	3.92	16	16	0	0	0	96⅓	92	44	42	42	54
1993	—Houston (N.L.)..........	4	4	.500	4.83	42	5	0	0	3	82	76	48	44	38	56
	—Tucson (PCL)............	1	0	1.000	0.00	2	0	0	0	0	3	1	0	0	0	3
Major league totals (3 years)..		11	11	.500	4.30	60	23	0	0	3	190⅓	179	97	91	84	114

WILLIAMS, GEORGE

C/OF, ATHLETICS

PERSONAL: Born April 22, 1969, in La Crosse, Wis.... 5-10/190.... Throws right, bats both.... Full name: George Erik Williams.
HIGH SCHOOL: La Crosse (Wis.) Central.
COLLEGE: Texas-Pan American.
TRANSACTIONS/CAREER NOTES: Selected by Oakland Athletics organization in 24th round of free-agent draft (June 3, 1991).
STATISTICAL NOTES: Tied for Midwest League lead with six intentional bases on balls received in 1992.

			BATTING												FIELDING			
Year	Team (League)	Pos.	G	AB	R	H	2B	3B	HR	RBI	Avg.	BB	SO	SB	PO	A	E	Avg.
1991	—S. Oregon (N'west)...	C-3B	55	174	24	41	10	0	2	24	.236	38	36	9	126	44	6	.966
1992	—Madison (Midwest)..	C-OF	115	349	56	106	18	2	5	42	.304	76	53	9	455	57	18	.966
1993	—Huntsville (South.)...	C-OF-3B	124	434	80	128	26	2	14	77	.295	67	66	6	430	63	11	.978

WILLIAMS, GERALD

OF, YANKEES

PERSONAL: Born August 10, 1966, in New Orleans.... 6-2/190.... Throws right, bats right.... Full name: Gerald Floyd Williams.
COLLEGE: Grambling State.
TRANSACTIONS/CAREER NOTES: Selected by New York Yankees organization in 14th round of free-agent draft (June 2, 1987).
STATISTICAL NOTES: Led Carolina League outfielders with 307 total chances in 1989.... Led International League outfielders with 354 total chances in 1992.... Tied for International League lead in double plays by outfielder with five in 1992.

			BATTING												FIELDING			
Year	Team (League)	Pos.	G	AB	R	H	2B	3B	HR	RBI	Avg.	BB	SO	SB	PO	A	E	Avg.
1987	—Oneonta (NYP).........	OF	29	115	26	42	6	2	2	29	.365	16	18	6	68	3	3	.959
1988	—Prin. William (Car.)..	OF	54	159	20	29	3	0	2	18	.182	15	47	6	71	2	3	.961
	—Fort Lauder. (FSL)...	OF	63	212	21	40	7	2	2	17	.189	16	56	4	163	2	6	.965
1989	—Prin. William (Car.)..	OF	134	454	63	104	19	6	13	69	.229	51	120	15	*292	7	8	.974
1990	—Fort Lauder. (FSL)...	OF	50	204	25	59	4	5	7	43	.289	16	52	19	115	1	3	.975
	—Alb./Colon. (East.)...	OF	96	324	54	81	17	2	13	58	.250	35	74	18	210	6	7	.969
1991	—Alb./Colon. (East.)...	OF	45	175	28	50	15	0	5	32	.286	18	26	18	109	4	3	.974
	—Columbus (Int'l).......	OF	61	198	20	51	8	3	2	27	.258	16	39	9	124	1	3	.977
1992	—Columbus (Int'l).......	OF	*142	547	92	*156	31	6	16	86	.285	38	98	36	*332	*14	8	.977
	—New York (A.L.)........	OF	15	27	7	8	2	0	3	6	.296	0	3	2	20	1	2	.913
1993	—Columbus (Int'l).......	OF	87	336	53	95	19	6	8	38	.283	20	66	29	191	6	3	.985
	—New York (A.L.)........	OF	42	67	11	10	2	3	0	6	.149	1	14	2	41	2	2	.956
Major league totals (2 years)			57	94	18	18	4	3	3	12	.191	1	17	4	61	3	4	.941

W

WILLIAMS, JEFF

P, MARINERS

PERSONAL: Born April 16, 1969, in Salina, Kan. . . . 6-4/230. . . . Throws right, bats right. . . . Full name: Jeffrey Jay Williams.
HIGH SCHOOL: North (Wichita, Kan.).
COLLEGE: Wichita State.
TRANSACTIONS/CAREER NOTES: Selected by Philadelphia Phillies organization in 17th round of free-agent draft (June 2, 1987). . . . Selected by Baltimore Orioles organization in supplemental round ("sandwich pick" between second and third round) of free-agent draft (June 4, 1990); pick received as compensation for Montreal Expos signing Type C free agent Dave Schmidt. . . . On disabled list (April 8-22 and September 11-18, 1993). . . . Claimed on waivers by Seattle Mariners (December 22, 1993).
STATISTICAL NOTES: Tied for Eastern League lead with 15 wild pitches in 1992.

Year	Team (League)	W	L	Pct.	ERA	G	GS	CG	ShO	Sv.	IP	H	R	ER	BB	SO
1990	—Bluefield (Appal.)	2	0	1.000	1.59	9	0	0	0	0	11⅓	7	3	2	5	14
	—Frederick (Caro.)	2	1	.667	4.68	16	0	0	0	1	25	23	17	13	17	31
1991	—Frederick (Caro.)	1	2	.333	2.70	12	0	0	0	6	16⅔	17	6	5	6	20
	—Hagerstown (East.)	3	5	.375	2.60	39	0	0	0	17	55⅓	52	23	16	32	42
1992	—Hagerstown (East.)	8	10	.444	4.83	36	15	3	0	6	123	148	91	66	70	82
1993	—Rochester (Int'l)	2	5	.286	5.76	33	5	0	0	1	86	95	59	55	47	59

WILLIAMS, MATT

3B, GIANTS

PERSONAL: Born November 28, 1965, in Bishop, Calif. . . . 6-2/216. . . . Throws right, bats right. . . . Full name: Matthew Derrick Williams. . . . Grandson of Bert Griffith, outfielder/first baseman, Brooklyn Dodgers and Washington Senators (1922-24).
HIGH SCHOOL: Carson (Nev.).
COLLEGE: UNLV.
TRANSACTIONS/CAREER NOTES: Selected by New York Mets organization in 27th round of free-agent draft (June 6, 1983). . . . Selected by San Francisco Giants organization in first round (third pick overall) of free-agent draft (June 2, 1986). . . . On disabled list (June 28-July 14, 1993).
HONORS: Named shortstop on THE SPORTING NEWS college All-America team (1986). . . . Named third baseman on THE SPORTING NEWS N.L. All-Star team (1990 and 1993). . . . Named third baseman on THE SPORTING NEWS N.L. Silver Slugger team (1990 and 1993). . . . Won N.L. Gold Glove at third base (1991 and 1993).
STATISTICAL NOTES: Led N.L. third basemen with 33 double plays in both 1990 and 1992 and 34 in 1993. . . . Tied for N.L. lead in total chances by third baseman with 465 in 1990. . . . Led N.L. third basemen with 131 putouts in 1991.

			BATTING												FIELDING			
Year	Team (League)	Pos.	G	AB	R	H	2B	3B	HR	RBI	Avg.	BB	SO	SB	PO	A	E	Avg.
1986	—Everett (N'west)	SS	4	17	3	4	0	1	1	10	.235	1	4	0	5	10	2	.882
	—Clinton (Midwest)	SS	68	250	32	60	14	3	7	29	.240	23	62	3	89	150	10	.960
1987	—Phoenix (PCL)	3B-2B-SS	56	211	36	61	15	2	6	37	.289	19	53	6	53	136	14	.931
	—San Francisco (N.L.)	SS-3B	84	245	28	46	9	2	8	21	.188	16	68	4	110	234	9	.975
1988	—Phoenix (PCL)	3-S-2-0	82	306	45	83	19	1	12	51	.271	13	56	6	56	173	13	.946
	—San Francisco (N.L.)	3B-SS	52	156	17	32	6	1	8	19	.205	8	41	0	48	108	7	.957
1989	—San Francisco (N.L.)	3B-SS	84	292	31	59	18	1	18	50	.202	14	72	1	90	168	10	.963
	—Phoenix (PCL)	3B-SS-OF	76	284	61	91	20	2	26	61	.320	32	51	9	57	197	11	.958
1990	—San Francisco (N.L.)	3B	159	617	87	171	27	2	33	*122	.277	33	138	7	*140	306	19	.959
1991	—San Francisco (N.L.)	3B-SS	157	589	72	158	24	5	34	98	.268	33	128	5	†134	295	16	.964
1992	—San Francisco (N.L.)	3B	146	529	58	120	13	5	20	66	.227	39	109	7	105	289	*23	.945
1993	—San Francisco (N.L.)	3B	145	579	105	170	33	4	38	110	.294	27	80	1	117	266	12	.970
	Major league totals (7 years)		827	3007	398	756	130	20	159	486	.251	170	636	25	744	1666	96	.962

CHAMPIONSHIP SERIES RECORD

CHAMPIONSHIP SERIES NOTES: Holds N.L. single-series record for most runs batted in—9 (1989).

			BATTING												FIELDING			
Year	Team (League)	Pos.	G	AB	R	H	2B	3B	HR	RBI	Avg.	BB	SO	SB	PO	A	E	Avg.
1987	—San Francisco (N.L.)								Did not play.									
1989	—San Francisco (N.L.)	3B-SS	5	20	2	6	1	0	2	9	.300	0	2	0	5	12	0	1.000
	Championship series totals (1 year)		5	20	2	6	1	0	2	9	.300	0	2	0	5	12	0	1.000

WORLD SERIES RECORD

			BATTING												FIELDING			
Year	Team (League)	Pos.	G	AB	R	H	2B	3B	HR	RBI	Avg.	BB	SO	SB	PO	A	E	Avg.
1989	—San Francisco (N.L.)	SS-3B	4	16	1	2	0	0	1	1	.125	0	6	0	4	12	0	1.000

ALL-STAR GAME RECORD

			BATTING											FIELDING			
Year	League	Pos.	AB	R	H	2B	3B	HR	RBI	Avg.	BB	SO	SB	PO	A	E	Avg.
1990	—National	PH	1	0	0	0	0	0	0	.000	0	1	0	...	...	...	...

W

WILLIAMS, MIKE

P, PHILLIES

PERSONAL: Born July 29, 1968, in Radford, Va. . . . 6-2/199. . . . Throws right, bats right. . . . Full name: Michael Darren Williams.
HIGH SCHOOL: Giles (Pearisburg, Va.).
COLLEGE: Virginia Tech.
TRANSACTIONS/CAREER NOTES: Selected by Philadelphia Phillies organization in 14th round of free-agent draft (June 4, 1990).

Year	Team (League)	W	L	Pct.	ERA	G	GS	CG	ShO	Sv.	IP	H	R	ER	BB	SO
1990	—Batavia (NY-Penn)	2	3	.400	2.30	27	0	0	0	11	47	39	17	12	13	42
1991	—Clearwater (FSL)	7	3	.700	1.74	14	14	2	1	0	93⅓	65	23	18	14	76
	—Reading (Eastern)	7	5	.583	3.69	16	15	2	1	0	102⅓	93	44	42	36	51
1992	—Reading (Eastern)	1	2	.333	5.17	3	3	0	0	0	15⅔	17	10	9	7	12
	—Scran./W.B. (Int'l)	9	1	*.900	2.43	16	16	3	1	0	92⅔	84	26	25	30	59
	—Philadelphia (N.L.)	1	1	.500	5.34	5	5	1	0	0	28⅔	29	20	17	7	5

Year	Team (League)	W	L	Pct.	ERA	G	GS	CG	ShO	Sv.	IP	H	R	ER	BB	SO
1993	—Scran./W.B. (Int'l)	9	2	*.818	2.87	14	13	1	1	0	97⅓	93	34	31	16	53
	—Philadelphia (N.L.)	1	3	.250	5.29	17	4	0	0	0	51	50	32	30	22	33
Major league totals (2 years)		2	4	.333	5.31	22	9	1	0	0	79⅔	79	52	47	29	38

WILLIAMS, MITCH

P, ASTROS

PERSONAL: Born November 17, 1964, in Santa Ana, Calif. . . . 6-4/205. . . . Throws left, bats left. . . . Full name: Mitchell Steven Williams. . . . Brother of Bruce Williams, minor league pitcher (1981-85).
HIGH SCHOOL: West Linn (Ore.).

TRANSACTIONS/CAREER NOTES: Selected by San Diego Padres organization in eighth round of free-agent draft (June 7, 1982). . . . Selected by Texas Rangers from Padres organization in Rule 5 major league draft (December 3, 1984). . . . Returned to Padres organization (April 6, 1985). . . . Traded by Padres organization to Rangers for 3B Randy Asadoor (April 6, 1985). . . . On suspended list (May 2-4, 1988). . . . Traded by Rangers with P Paul Kilgus, P Steve Wilson, IF Curtis Wilkerson, IF Luis Benitez and OF Pablo Delgado to Chicago Cubs for OF Rafael Palmeiro, P Jamie Moyer and P Drew Hall (December 5, 1988). . . . On disabled list (June 12-July 12, 1990). . . . Traded by Cubs to Philadelphia Phillies for P Chuck McElroy and P Bob Scanlan (April 7, 1991). . . . Granted free agency (October 31, 1991). . . . Re-signed by Phillies (December 18, 1991). . . . Traded by Phillies to Houston Astros for P Doug Jones and P Jeff Juden (December 2, 1993).
RECORDS: Holds major league rookie-season record for most games pitched—80 (1986).
STATISTICAL NOTES: Led Northwest League pitchers with 14 wild pitches and tied for lead with two balks in 1983.

Year	Team (League)	W	L	Pct.	ERA	G	GS	CG	ShO	Sv.	IP	H	R	ER	BB	SO
1982	—Walla Walla (N'west)	3	4	.429	4.78	12	12	0	0	0	58⅓	37	37	31	*72	66
1983	—Reno (California)	1	7	.125	7.14	11	11	0	0	0	58	58	56	46	60	44
	—Spokane (N'west)	7	6	.538	4.48	14	•14	3	1	0	92⅓	84	51	•46	55	87
1984	—Reno (California)	9	8	.529	4.99	26	26	3	1	0	164	163	113	91	127	165
1985	—Salem (Carolina)■	6	9	.400	5.45	22	21	1	0	0	99	57	64	60	*117	138
	—Tulsa (Texas)	2	2	.500	4.64	6	6	0	0	0	33	17	24	17	48	37
1986	—Texas (A.L.)	8	6	.571	3.58	*80	0	0	0	8	98	69	39	39	79	90
1987	—Texas (A.L.)	8	6	.571	3.23	85	1	0	0	6	108⅔	63	47	39	94	129
1988	—Texas (A.L.)	2	7	.222	4.63	67	0	0	0	18	68	48	38	35	47	61
1989	—Chicago (N.L.)■	4	4	.500	2.64	*76	0	0	0	36	81⅔	71	27	24	52	67
1990	—Chicago (N.L.)	1	8	.111	3.93	59	2	0	0	16	66⅓	60	38	29	50	55
1991	—Philadelphia (N.L.)■	12	5	.706	2.34	69	0	0	0	30	88⅓	56	24	23	62	84
1992	—Philadelphia (N.L.)	5	8	.385	3.78	66	0	0	0	29	81	69	39	34	64	74
1993	—Philadelphia (N.L.)	3	7	.300	3.34	65	0	0	0	43	62	56	30	23	44	60
A.L. totals (3 years)		18	19	.486	3.70	232	1	0	0	32	274⅔	180	124	113	220	280
N.L. totals (5 years)		25	32	.439	3.16	335	2	0	0	154	379⅓	312	158	133	272	340
Major league totals (8 years)		43	51	.457	3.39	567	3	0	0	186	654	492	282	246	492	620

CHAMPIONSHIP SERIES RECORD

Year	Team (League)	W	L	Pct.	ERA	G	GS	CG	ShO	Sv.	IP	H	R	ER	BB	SO
1989	—Chicago (N.L.)	0	0	...	0.00	2	0	0	0	0	1	1	0	0	0	2
1993	—Philadelphia (N.L.)	2	0	1.000	1.69	4	0	0	0	2	5⅓	6	2	1	2	5
Champ. series totals (2 years)		2	0	1.000	1.42	6	0	0	0	2	6⅓	7	2	1	2	7

WORLD SERIES RECORD

Year	Team (League)	W	L	Pct.	ERA	G	GS	CG	ShO	Sv.	IP	H	R	ER	BB	SO
1993	—Philadelphia (N.L.)	0	2	.000	20.25	3	0	0	0	1	2⅔	5	6	6	4	1

ALL-STAR GAME RECORD

Year	League	W	L	Pct.	ERA	GS	CG	ShO	Sv.	IP	H	R	ER	BB	SO
1989	—National	0	0	...	0.00	0	0	0	0	1	0	0	0	1	1

WILLIAMS, TODD

P, DODGERS

PERSONAL: Born February 13, 1971, in Syracuse, N.Y. . . . 6-3/185. . . . Throws right, bats right. . . . Full name: Todd Michael Williams.
HIGH SCHOOL: East Syracuse (N.Y.) Minoa.
COLLEGE: Onondaga Community College (N.Y.).

TRANSACTIONS/CAREER NOTES: Selected by Los Angeles Dodgers organization in 54th round of free-agent draft (June 4, 1990).

Year	Team (League)	W	L	Pct.	ERA	G	GS	CG	ShO	Sv.	IP	H	R	ER	BB	SO
1991	—Great Falls (Pio.)	5	2	.714	2.72	28	0	0	0	8	53	50	26	16	24	59
1992	—Bakersfield (Calif.)	0	0	...	2.30	13	0	0	0	9	15⅔	11	4	4	7	11
	—San Antonio (Tex.)	7	4	.636	3.27	39	0	0	0	13	44	47	17	16	23	35
1993	—Albuquerque (PCL)	5	5	.500	4.99	*65	0	0	0	*21	70⅓	87	44	39	31	56

WILLIAMS, WOODY

P, BLUE JAYS

PERSONAL: Born August 19, 1966, in Houston. . . . 6-0/190. . . . Throws right, bats right. . . . Full name: Gregory Scott Williams.
HIGH SCHOOL: Cy-Fair (Houston).
COLLEGE: Houston.

TRANSACTIONS/CAREER NOTES: Selected by Toronto Blue Jays organization in 28th round of free-agent draft (June 1, 1988). . . . On disabled list (April 9-May 17, 1992).

Year	Team (League)	W	L	Pct.	ERA	G	GS	CG	ShO	Sv.	IP	H	R	ER	BB	SO
1988	—St. Cathar. (NYP)	8	2	.800	1.54	12	12	2	0	0	76	48	22	13	21	58
	—Knoxville (South.)	2	2	.500	3.81	6	4	0	0	0	28⅓	27	13	12	12	25
1989	—Dunedin (Fla. St.)	3	5	.375	2.32	20	9	0	0	3	81⅓	63	26	21	27	60
	—Knoxville (South.)	3	5	.375	3.55	14	12	2	•2	1	71	61	32	28	33	51

Year	Team (League)	W	L	Pct.	ERA	G	GS	CG	ShO	Sv.	IP	H	R	ER	BB	SO
1990	—Knoxville (South.)	7	9	.438	3.14	42	12	0	0	5	126	111	55	44	39	74
	—Syracuse (Int'l)	0	1	.000	10.00	3	0	0	0	0	9	15	10	10	4	8
1991	—Knoxville (South.)	3	2	.600	3.59	18	1	0	0	3	42⅔	42	18	17	14	37
	—Syracuse (Int'l)	3	4	.429	4.12	31	0	0	0	6	54⅔	52	27	25	27	37
1992	—Syracuse (Int'l)	6	8	.429	3.13	25	16	1	0	1	120⅔	115	46	42	41	81
1993	—Syracuse (Int'l)	1	1	.500	2.20	12	0	0	0	3	16⅓	15	5	4	5	16
	—Toronto (A.L.)	3	1	.750	4.38	30	0	0	0	0	37	40	18	18	22	24
	—Dunedin (Fla. St.)	0	0	...	0.00	2	0	0	0	0	4	0	0	0	2	2
Major league totals (1 year)		3	1	.750	4.38	30	0	0	0	0	37	40	18	18	22	24

WILLIAMSON, MARK

P, ORIOLES

PERSONAL: Born July 21, 1959, in Corpus Christi, Tex. . . . 6-0/185. . . . Throws right, bats right. . . . Full name: Mark Alan Williamson.
HIGH SCHOOL: Mt. Miguel (Calif.).
COLLEGE: Grossmont College (Calif.) and San Diego State (degree in mechanical engineering).
TRANSACTIONS/CAREER NOTES: Selected by Kansas City Royals organization in 12th round of free-agent draft (June 8, 1981). . . . Selected by San Diego Padres organization in fourth round of free-agent draft (June 7, 1982). . . . Traded by Padres organization with C Terry Kennedy to Baltimore Orioles for P Storm Davis (October 30, 1986). . . . On disabled list (March 31-April 22 and August 19, 1990-remainder of season; and August 14-September 1, 1991). . . . On Baltimore disabled list (April 16-September 4, 1992); included rehabilitation assignment to Hagerstown (July 22-August 6) and Rochester (August 6-20). . . . Granted free agency (December 19, 1992). . . . Re-signed by Orioles (January 12, 1993). . . . Granted free agency (October 13, 1993). . . . Re-signed by Orioles organization (February 3, 1994).
STATISTICAL NOTES: Pitched one inning, combining with starter Bob Milacki (six innings), Mike Flanagan (one inning) and Gregg Olson (one inning) in 2-0 no-hit victory against Oakland (July 13, 1991).

Year	Team (League)	W	L	Pct.	ERA	G	GS	CG	ShO	Sv.	IP	H	R	ER	BB	SO
1982	—Reno (California)	7	5	.583	4.39	26	0	0	0	9	41	34	24	20	18	30
1983	—Beaumont (Texas)	6	3	.667	4.03	47	1	0	0	3	82⅔	90	45	37	30	39
1984	—Reno (California)	10	12	.455	2.90	56	1	0	0	15	93	105	41	30	23	69
1985	—Beaumont (Texas)	10	9	.526	2.86	42	0	0	0	8	78⅔	72	27	25	23	64
1986	—Las Vegas (PCL)	10	3	*.769	3.36	*65	0	0	0	•16	104⅓	103	47	39	36	81
1987	—Baltimore (A.L.)■	8	9	.471	4.03	61	2	0	0	3	125	122	59	56	41	73
	—Rochester (Int'l)	0	1	.000	6.75	1	0	0	0	0	4	6	3	3	1	1
1988	—Baltimore (A.L.)	5	8	.385	4.90	37	10	2	0	2	117⅔	125	70	64	40	69
	—Rochester (Int'l)	2	3	.400	3.34	12	3	1	0	2	29⅔	38	11	11	5	25
1989	—Baltimore (A.L.)	10	5	.667	2.93	65	0	0	0	9	107⅓	105	35	35	30	55
1990	—Baltimore (A.L.)	8	2	.800	2.21	49	0	0	0	1	85⅓	65	25	21	28	60
1991	—Baltimore (A.L.)	5	5	.500	4.48	65	0	0	0	4	80⅓	87	42	40	35	53
1992	—Baltimore (A.L.)	0	0	...	0.96	12	0	0	0	1	18⅔	16	3	2	10	14
	—Hagerstown (East.)	0	1	.000	4.91	6	5	0	0	0	14⅔	13	9	8	2	8
	—Rochester (Int'l)	0	0	...	0.00	4	0	0	0	2	3⅔	2	0	0	0	1
1993	—Baltimore (A.L.)	7	5	.583	4.91	48	1	0	0	0	88	106	54	48	25	45
Major league totals (7 years)		43	34	.558	3.85	337	13	2	0	20	622⅓	626	288	266	209	369

WILLIS, CARL

P, TWINS

PERSONAL: Born December 28, 1960, in Danville, Va. . . . 6-4/213. . . . Throws right, bats left. . . . Full name: Carl Blake Willis.
HIGH SCHOOL: Piedmont Academy (Providence, N.C.).
COLLEGE: UNC Wilmington.
TRANSACTIONS/CAREER NOTES: Selected by San Francisco Giants organization in 31st round of free-agent draft (June 7, 1982). . . . Selected by Detroit Tigers organization in 23rd round of free-agent draft (June 6, 1983). . . . Traded by Tigers to Cincinnati Reds (September 1, 1984), completing deal in which Reds traded P Bill Scherrer to Tigers for cash and a player to be named later (August 27, 1984). . . . Selected by California Angels from Reds organization in Rule 5 major league draft (December 10, 1985). . . . Returned to Reds organization (April 6, 1986). . . . Traded by Reds organization to Chicago White Sox for OF Darrell Pruitt (January 19, 1988). . . . Selected by Edmonton, Angels organization, from White Sox organization in Rule 5 minor league draft (December 6, 1988). . . . Granted free agency (October 22, 1989). . . . Signed by Colorado Springs, Cleveland Indians organization (December 20, 1989). . . . Granted free agency (October 15, 1990). . . . Signed by Portland, Minnesota Twins organization (December 12, 1990). . . . On Minnesota disabled list (March 30-May 14, 1993); included rehabilitation assignment to Portland (May 6-14).

Year	Team (League)	W	L	Pct.	ERA	G	GS	CG	ShO	Sv.	IP	H	R	ER	BB	SO
1983	—Bristol (Appal.)	0	1	.000	3.38	2	0	0	0	0	2⅔	0	1	1	4	3
	—Lakeland (Fla. St.)	3	0	1.000	0.00	4	0	0	0	0	9⅔	6	0	0	5	7
	—Birm. (Southern)	3	1	.750	3.98	14	0	0	0	2	20⅓	16	9	9	7	13
1984	—Evansville (A.A.)	5	3	.625	3.73	40	1	0	0	16	60⅓	59	26	25	20	27
	—Detroit (A.L.)	0	2	.000	7.31	10	2	0	0	0	16	25	13	13	5	4
	—Cincinnati (N.L.)■	0	1	.000	3.72	7	0	0	0	1	9⅔	8	4	4	2	3
1985	—Cincinnati (N.L.)	1	0	1.000	9.22	11	0	0	0	1	13⅔	21	18	14	5	6
	—Denver (A.A.)	4	4	.500	4.15	37	1	0	0	8	78	82	39	36	30	27
1986	—Denver (A.A.)	1	3	.250	4.68	20	1	0	0	8	32⅔	29	22	17	16	16
	—Cincinnati (N.L.)	1	3	.250	4.47	29	0	0	0	0	52⅓	54	29	26	32	24
1987	—Nashville (A.A.)	6	4	.600	3.33	53	0	0	0	5	83⅔	97	39	31	30	54
1988	—Vancouver (PCL)■	4	4	.500	4.22	40	1	0	0	4	64	77	36	30	16	44
	—Chicago (A.L.)	0	0	...	8.25	6	0	0	0	0	12	17	12	11	7	6
1989	—Edmonton (PCL)■	5	7	.417	3.69	36	10	0	0	5	112⅓	137	54	46	36	47
1990	—Colo. Springs (PCL)■	5	3	.625	6.39	41	6	0	0	2	98⅔	136	80	70	32	42
1991	—Portland (PCL)■	1	1	.500	1.64	3	1	0	0	0	11	5	4	2	0	0
	—Minnesota (A.L.)	8	3	.727	2.63	40	0	0	0	2	89	76	31	26	19	53
1992	—Minnesota (A.L.)	7	3	.700	2.72	59	0	0	0	1	79⅓	73	25	24	11	45

Year	Team (League)	W	L	Pct.	ERA	G	GS	CG	ShO	Sv.	IP	H	R	ER	BB	SO
1993	—Portland (PCL)	0	0	...	2.25	2	0	0	0	0	4	6	2	1	1	2
	—Minnesota (A.L.)	3	0	1.000	3.10	53	0	0	0	5	58	56	23	20	17	44
A.L. totals (5 years)		18	8	.692	3.33	168	2	0	0	8	254 ⅓	247	104	94	59	152
N.L. totals (3 years)		2	4	.333	5.23	47	0	0	0	2	75⅔	83	51	44	39	33
Major league totals (7 years)		20	12	.625	3.76	215	2	0	0	10	330	330	155	138	98	185

CHAMPIONSHIP SERIES RECORD

Year	Team (League)	W	L	Pct.	ERA	G	GS	CG	ShO	Sv.	IP	H	R	ER	BB	SO
1991	—Minnesota (A.L.)	0	0	...	0.00	3	0	0	0	0	5⅓	2	0	0	0	3

WORLD SERIES RECORD

Year	Team (League)	W	L	Pct.	ERA	G	GS	CG	ShO	Sv.	IP	H	R	ER	BB	SO
1991	—Minnesota (A.L.)	0	0	...	5.14	4	0	0	0	0	7	6	4	4	2	2

WILSON, BRANDON

SS, WHITE SOX

PERSONAL: Born February 26, 1969, in Owensboro, Ky. ... 6-1/170. ... Throws right, bats right. ... Full name: Brandon Lee Wilson.
HIGH SCHOOL: Owensboro (Ky.).
COLLEGE: Kentucky.
TRANSACTIONS/CAREER NOTES: Selected by Chicago White Sox organization in 18th round of free-agent draft (June 4, 1990).
STATISTICAL NOTES: Led Midwest League shortstops with 585 total chances and 75 double plays in 1991. ... Tied for Southern League lead in errors by shortstop with 35 in 1993.

			BATTING												FIELDING			
Year	Team (League)	Pos.	G	AB	R	H	2B	3B	HR	RBI	Avg.	BB	SO	SB	PO	A	E	Avg.
1990	—GC Whi. Sox (GCL)	SS-2B	11	41	4	11	1	0	0	5	.268	4	5	3	15	33	6	.889
	—Utica (N.Y.-Penn)	SS-2B	53	165	31	41	2	0	0	14	.248	28	45	14	19	36	6	.902
1991	—South Bend (Mid.)	SS	125	463	75	145	18	6	2	49	.313	61	70	41	*203	*353	29	*.950
	—Birm. (Southern)	SS	2	10	3	4	1	0	0	2	.400	0	2	0	4	7	0	1.000
1992	—Sarasota (Fla. St.)	SS	103	399	68	118	22	6	4	54	.296	45	64	30	151	278	33	.929
	—Birm. (Southern)	SS	27	107	10	29	4	0	0	4	.271	4	16	5	33	76	4	.965
1993	—Birm. (Southern)	SS-2B	137	500	76	135	19	5	2	48	.270	52	77	*43	217	315	‡35	.938

WILSON, CRAIG

3B

PERSONAL: Born November 28, 1964, in Anne Arundel County, Md. ... 5-11/210. ... Throws right, bats right.
HIGH SCHOOL: Annapolis (Md.).
COLLEGE: Anne Arundel Community College (Md.).
TRANSACTIONS/CAREER NOTES: Selected by St. Louis Cardinals organization in 20th round of free-agent draft (June 4, 1984). ... Traded by Cardinals with OF Felix Jose to Kansas City Royals for 3B Gregg Jefferies and OF Ed Gerald (February 12, 1993). ... On Omaha temporary inactive list (April 8-May 18, 1993). ... Granted free agency (December 20, 1993).
STATISTICAL NOTES: Led Midwest League third basemen with .932 fielding percentage in 1985. ... Led Midwest League second basemen with 653 total chances and 86 double plays in 1986. ... Led American Association third basemen with 264 assists, 26 errors, 386 total chances and 28 double plays in 1988.

			BATTING												FIELDING			
Year	Team (League)	Pos.	G	AB	R	H	2B	3B	HR	RBI	Avg.	BB	SO	SB	PO	A	E	Avg.
1984	—Erie (N.Y.-Penn)	2B-3B-SS	72	282	53	83	18	4	7	46	.294	29	27	10	169	206	14	.964
1985	—Springfield (Midw.)	3B-2B	133	504	64	132	16	4	8	52	.262	47	67	33	156	293	27	†.943
1986	—Springfield (Midw.)	2B	127	496	106	136	17	6	1	49	.274	65	49	44	*292	*343	18	*.972
1987	—St. Peters. (FSL)	3B-2B	38	162	35	58	6	4	0	28	.358	14	5	12	35	91	6	.955
	—Louisville (A.A.)	2B-3B	21	70	10	15	2	0	1	8	.214	3	5	0	22	51	2	.973
	—Arkansas (Texas)	2-3-S-0	66	238	37	69	13	1	1	26	.290	30	19	9	117	164	8	.972
1988	—Louisville (A.A.)	3B-2B	133	497	59	127	27	2	1	46	.256	54	46	6	98	†271	†26	.934
1989	—Arkansas (Texas)	2B-3B	55	224	41	71	12	1	1	40	.317	21	14	8	127	150	12	.958
	—Louisville (A.A.)	2B-3B	75	278	37	81	18	3	1	30	.291	14	25	1	130	151	18	.940
	—St. Louis (N.L.)	3B	6	4	1	1	0	0	0	1	.250	1	2	0	1	0	1	.500
1990	—Louisville (A.A.)	2B-3B	57	204	30	57	9	2	2	23	.279	28	15	5	78	139	12	.948
	—St. Louis (N.L.)	3-0-2-1	55	121	13	30	2	0	0	7	.248	8	14	0	45	30	1	.987
1991	—St. Louis (N.L.)	3-0-1-2	60	82	5	14	2	0	0	13	.171	6	10	0	30	14	2	.957
1992	—St. Louis (N.L.)	3B-2B-OF	61	106	6	33	6	0	0	13	.311	10	18	1	24	47	3	.959
	—Louisville (A.A.)	2B-OF-3B	20	81	13	24	5	1	0	5	.296	5	8	3	41	38	6	.929
1993	—Omaha (A.A.)■	3B-1B	65	234	26	65	13	1	3	28	.278	20	24	7	50	115	9	.948
	—Kansas City (A.L.)	3B-OF-2B	21	49	6	13	1	0	1	3	.265	7	6	1	8	22	1	.968
American League totals (1 year)			21	49	6	13	1	0	1	3	.265	7	6	1	8	22	1	.968
National League totals (4 years)			182	313	25	78	10	0	0	34	.249	25	44	1	100	91	7	.965
Major league totals (5 years)			203	362	31	91	11	0	1	37	.251	32	50	2	108	113	8	.965

WILSON, DAN

C, MARINERS

PERSONAL: Born March 25, 1969, in Arlington Heights, Ill. ... 6-3/190. ... Throws right, bats right. ... Full name: Daniel Allen Wilson.
HIGH SCHOOL: Barrington (Ill.).
COLLEGE: Minnesota.
TRANSACTIONS/CAREER NOTES: Selected by New York Mets organization in 26th round of free-agent draft (June 2, 1987). ... Selected by Cincinnati Reds organization in first round (seventh pick overall) of free-agent draft (June 4, 1990). ... Traded by Reds with P Bobby Ayala to Seattle Mariners for P Erik Hanson and 2B Bret Boone (November 2, 1993).
STATISTICAL NOTES: Led American Association catchers with 810 total chances in 1992.

			BATTING											FIELDING			
Year	Team (League)	Pos.	G	AB	R	H	2B	3B	HR	RBI	Avg.	BB	SO	SB	PO	A	E	Avg.
1990	—Char., W.Va. (SAL) ..	C	32	113	16	28	9	1	2	17	.248	13	17	0	190	24	1	.995
1991	—Char., W.Va. (SAL) ..	C	52	197	25	62	11	1	3	29	.315	25	21	1	355	41	3	.992
	—Chatt. (South.)	C	81	292	32	75	19	2	2	38	.257	21	39	2	486	49	4	.993
1992	—Nashville (A.A.)........	C	106	366	27	92	16	1	4	34	.251	31	58	1	*733	*69	*8	.990
	—Cincinnati (N.L.).......	C	12	25	2	9	1	0	0	3	.360	3	8	0	42	4	0	1.000
1993	—Cincinnati (N.L.).......	C	36	76	6	17	3	0	0	8	.224	9	16	0	146	9	1	.994
	—Indianapolis (A.A.)...	C	51	191	18	50	11	1	1	17	.262	19	31	1	314	24	2	.994
Major league totals (2 years)	....		48	101	8	26	4	0	0	11	.257	12	24	0	188	13	1	.995

WILSON, DESI

1B/OF, RANGERS

PERSONAL: Born May 9, 1969, in Glen Cove, N.Y. . . . 6-7/230. . . . Throws left, bats left. . . . Full name: Desi Bernard Wilson.

HIGH SCHOOL: Glen Cove (N.Y.).

COLLEGE: Fairleigh Dickinson.

TRANSACTIONS/CAREER NOTES: Selected by Boston Red Sox organization in 15th round of free-agent draft (June 2, 1987). . . . Selected by Houston Astros organization in 87th round of free-agent draft (June 5, 1989). . . . Selected by Texas Rangers organization in 30th round of free-agent draft (June 3, 1991).

			BATTING											FIELDING			
Year	Team (League)	Pos.	G	AB	R	H	2B	3B	HR	RBI	Avg.	BB	SO	SB	PO	A	E	Avg.
1991	—GC Rangers (GCL)....	OF	8	25	1	4	2	0	0	7	.160	3	2	0	2	0	0	1.000
1992	—Butte (Pioneer).........	OF	72	253	45	81	9	4	5	42	.320	31	45	13	90	8	9	.916
1993	—Charlotte (Fla. St.) ...	1B-OF	131	511	83	•156	21	7	3	70	.305	50	90	29	859	57	15	.984

WILSON, GLENN

OF

PERSONAL: Born December 22, 1958, in Baytown, Tex. . . . 6-1/190. . . . Throws right, bats right. . . . Full name: Glenn Dwight Wilson.

HIGH SCHOOL: Channelview (Tex.).

COLLEGE: Sam Houston State.

TRANSACTIONS/CAREER NOTES: Selected by Detroit Tigers organization in first round (18th pick overall) of free-agent draft (June 3, 1980). . . . On Evansville disabled list (May 27-June 9 and June 17-27, 1982). . . . Traded by Tigers with C/1B John Wockenfuss to Philadelphia Phillies for 1B Dave Bergman and P Willie Hernandez (March 24, 1984). . . . Traded by Phillies with OF Dave Brundage and P Mike Jackson to Seattle Mariners for OF Phil Bradley and P Tim Fortugno (December 9, 1987). . . . Traded by Mariners to Pittsburgh Pirates for OF Darnell Coles (July 22, 1988). . . . On disabled list (August 5-20, 1988). . . . Traded by Pirates to Houston Astros for OF Billy Hatcher (August 18, 1989). . . . Granted free agency (November 5, 1990). . . . Signed by Atlanta Braves (February 13, 1991). . . . On Richmond restricted list (May 14-June 7, 1991). . . . Released by Braves organization (June 7, 1991). . . . Signed by Pirates organization (January 14, 1993). . . . Released by Pirates (June 17, 1993). . . . Signed by Buffalo, Pirates organization (June 17, 1993). . . . On Buffalo disabled list (August 3-11 and September 3-10, 1993). . . . Granted free agency (October 15, 1993).

RECORDS: Shares major league single-season record for fewest double plays by outfielder who led league in double plays—4 (1985).

HONORS: Named third baseman on THE SPORTING NEWS college All-America team (1980).

STATISTICAL NOTES: Led N.L. outfielders with five double plays in 1986, six in 1990 and tied for lead with four in 1985. . . . Led N.L. outfielders with 18 assists and 11 errors in 1987.

			BATTING											FIELDING			
Year	Team (League)	Pos.	G	AB	R	H	2B	3B	HR	RBI	Avg.	BB	SO	SB	PO	A	E	Avg.
1980	—Montgomery (Sou.) ..	3B	77	284	36	75	16	2	7	31	.264	14	52	3	56	189	*33	.881
1981	—Birm. (Southern)	OF	124	496	77	152	24	6	18	82	.306	23	56	7	292	18	5	.984
	—Evansville (A.A.)	OF-1B	10	37	5	9	2	0	2	7	.243	3	7	0	16	2	0	1.000
1982	—Detroit (A.L.)	OF	84	322	39	94	15	1	12	34	.292	15	51	2	215	8	3	.987
	—Evansville (A.A.)	OF	42	165	24	46	7	2	10	33	.279	9	37	4	96	6	3	.971
1983	—Detroit (A.L.)	OF	144	503	55	135	25	6	11	65	.268	25	79	1	225	12	3	.988
1984	—Philadelphia (N.L.)■.	OF-3B	132	341	28	82	21	3	6	31	.240	17	56	7	153	7	7	.958
1985	—Philadelphia (N.L.) ...	OF	161	608	73	167	39	5	14	102	.275	35	117	7	343	*18	*12	.968
1986	—Philadelphia (N.L.) ...	OF	155	584	70	158	30	4	15	84	.271	42	91	5	331	*20	4	.989
1987	—Philadelphia (N.L.) ...	OF-P	154	569	55	150	21	2	14	54	.264	38	82	3	315	†19	†11	.968
1988	—Seattle (A.L.)■..........	OF	78	284	28	71	10	1	3	17	.250	15	52	1	140	4	3	.980
	—Pittsburgh (N.L.)■....	OF	37	126	11	34	8	0	2	15	.270	3	18	0	66	1	1	.985
1989	—Pitts.-Hou. (N.L.)■...	OF-1B	128	432	50	115	26	4	11	64	.266	37	53	1	249	13	6	.978
1990	—Houston (N.L.)..........	OF-1B	118	368	42	90	14	0	10	55	.245	26	64	0	227	12	6	.976
1991	—Richmond (Int'l)■.....	OF	29	100	13	27	4	0	2	15	.270	13	21	1	40	0	3	.930
1992	—..............................		Out of organized baseball.															
1993	—Buffalo (A.A.)	OF	61	201	32	56	14	1	12	43	.279	16	38	0	59	4	1	.984
	—Pittsburgh (N.L.)	OF	10	14	0	2	0	0	0	0	.143	0	9	0	5	2	1	.875
American League totals (3 years)	....		306	1109	122	300	50	8	26	116	.271	55	182	4	580	24	9	.985
National League totals (8 years)	....		895	3042	329	798	159	18	72	405	.262	198	490	23	1689	92	48	.974
Major league totals (10 years)	....		1201	4151	451	1098	209	26	98	521	.265	253	672	27	2269	116	57	.977

ALL-STAR GAME RECORD

			BATTING										FIELDING			
Year	League	Pos.	AB	R	H	2B	3B	HR	RBI	Avg.	BB	SO	SB	PO	A	E	Avg.
1985	—National.....................	PH	1	0	0	0	0	0	0	.000	0	1	0	...	...	...	...

RECORD AS PITCHER

Year	Team (League)	W	L	Pct.	ERA	G	GS	CG	ShO	Sv.	IP	H	R	ER	BB	SO
1987	—Philadelphia (N.L.).....	0	0	...	0.00	1	0	0	0	0	1	0	0	0	0	1

WILSON, NIGEL

OF, MARLINS

PERSONAL: Born January 12, 1970, in Oshawa, Ont. . . . 6-1/185. . . . Throws left, bats left. . . . Full name: Nigel Edward Wilson.
HIGH SCHOOL: Ajax (Ont.).
TRANSACTIONS/CAREER NOTES: Signed as free agent by Toronto Blue Jays organization (July 30, 1987). . . . Selected by Florida Marlins in first round (second pick overall) of expansion draft (November 17, 1992). . . . On Edmonton disabled list (June 18-July 24, 1993).
STATISTICAL NOTES: Led Florida State League with 217 total bases and .477 slugging percentage in 1991. . . . Led Southern League with 269 total bases in 1992. . . . Tied for Pacific Coast League lead in being hit by pitch with 10 in 1993.

			BATTING											FIELDING			
Year	**Team (League)**	**Pos.**	**G**	**AB**	**R**	**H**	**2B**	**3B**	**HR**	**RBI**	**Avg.**	**BB**	**SO**	**SB**	**PO**	**A**	**E**	**Avg.**
1988	—St. Cathar. (NYP)	OF	40	103	12	21	1	2	2	11	.204	12	32	8	50	3	5	.914
1989	—St. Cathar. (NYP)	OF	42	161	17	35	5	2	4	18	.217	11	50	8	37	2	3	.929
1990	—Myrtle Beach (SAL)	OF	110	440	77	120	23	9	16	62	.273	30	71	22	127	7	10	.931
1991	—Dunedin (Fla. St.)	OF	119	455	64	137	18	★13	12	55	.301	29	99	27	196	7	8	.962
1992	—Knoxville (South.)	OF	137	521	85	143	•34	7	26	69	.274	33	137	13	192	6	9	.957
1993	—Edmonton (PCL)■	OF	96	370	66	108	26	7	17	68	.292	25	108	8	121	13	2	.985
	—Florida (N.L.)	OF	7	16	0	0	0	0	0	0	.000	0	11	0	4	0	0	1.000
Major league totals (1 year)			7	16	0	0	0	0	0	0	.000	0	11	0	4	0	0	1.000

WILSON, STEVE

P, DODGERS

PERSONAL: Born December 13, 1964, in Victoria, B.C. . . . 6-4/224. . . . Throws left, bats left. . . . Full name: Stephen Douglas Wilson.
HIGH SCHOOL: Eric Hamber (Vancouver, B.C.).
COLLEGE: Portland.
TRANSACTIONS/CAREER NOTES: Selected by Texas Rangers organization in fourth round of free-agent draft (June 3, 1985). . . . Traded by Rangers with P Mitch Williams, P Paul Kilgus, IF Curtis Wilkerson, IF Luis Benitez and OF Pablo Delgado to Chicago Cubs for OF Rafael Palmeiro, P Jamie Moyer and P Drew Hall (December 5, 1988). . . . Traded by Cubs to Los Angeles Dodgers for P Jeff Hartsock (September 6, 1991). . . . On Albuquerque disabled list (June 22-August 1, 1993).
MISCELLANEOUS: Appeared in one game as pinch-runner with Chicago (1991).

Year	**Team (League)**	**W**	**L**	**Pct.**	**ERA**	**G**	**GS**	**CG**	**ShO**	**Sv.**	**IP**	**H**	**R**	**ER**	**BB**	**SO**
1985	—Burlington (Midw.)	3	5	.375	4.58	21	10	0	0	0	72⅔	71	44	37	27	76
1986	—Tulsa (Texas)	7	13	.350	4.87	24	24	2	0	0	136⅔	117	83	74	★103	95
1987	—Charlotte (Fla. St.)	9	5	.643	2.44	20	17	1	1	0	107	81	41	29	44	80
1988	—Tulsa (Texas)	15	7	.682	3.16	25	25	5	3	0	165⅓	147	72	58	53	132
	—Texas (A.L.)	0	0	...	5.87	3	0	0	0	0	7⅔	7	5	5	4	1
1989	—Chicago (N.L.)■	6	4	.600	4.20	53	8	0	0	2	85⅔	83	43	40	31	65
1990	—Chicago (N.L.)	4	9	.308	4.79	45	15	1	0	1	139	140	77	74	43	95
1991	—Iowa (Am. Assoc.)	3	8	.273	3.87	25	16	1	0	0	114	102	55	49	45	84
	—Chi.-L.A. (N.L.)■	0	0	...	2.61	19	0	0	0	2	20⅔	14	7	6	9	14
1992	—Los Angeles (N.L.)	2	5	.286	4.19	60	0	0	0	0	66⅔	74	37	31	29	54
1993	—Los Angeles (N.L.)	1	0	1.000	4.56	25	0	0	0	1	25⅔	30	13	13	14	23
	—Albuquerque (PCL)	0	3	.000	4.38	13	12	0	0	0	51⅓	57	29	25	14	44
A.L. totals (1 year)		0	0	...	5.87	3	0	0	0	0	7⅔	7	5	5	4	1
N.L. totals (5 years)		13	18	.419	4.37	202	23	1	0	6	337⅔	341	177	164	126	251
Major league totals (6 years)		13	18	.419	4.40	205	23	1	0	6	345⅓	348	182	169	130	252

CHAMPIONSHIP SERIES RECORD

Year	**Team (League)**	**W**	**L**	**Pct.**	**ERA**	**G**	**GS**	**CG**	**ShO**	**Sv.**	**IP**	**H**	**R**	**ER**	**BB**	**SO**
1989	—Chicago (N.L.)	0	1	.000	4.91	2	0	0	0	0	3⅔	3	5	2	1	4

WILSON, TREVOR

P, GIANTS

PERSONAL: Born June 7, 1966, in Torrance, Calif. . . . 6-0/204. . . . Throws left, bats left. . . . Full name: Trevor Kirk Wilson.
HIGH SCHOOL: Oregon City (Ore.).
COLLEGE: Oregon State.
TRANSACTIONS/CAREER NOTES: Selected by San Francisco Giants organization in eighth round of free-agent draft (June 3, 1985). . . . On San Francisco disabled list (August 22-September 6, 1990 and March 27-April 18, 1992). . . . On suspended list (June 26-29, 1992). . . . On San Francisco disabled list (May 21-June 5, 1993). . . . On San Francisco disabled list (July 3-August 10, 1993); included rehabilitation assignment to San Jose (August 3-10). . . . On San Francisco disabled list (August 24-September 15, 1993).
STATISTICAL NOTES: Tied for Northwest League lead with two balks in 1985. . . . Tied for N.L. lead with seven balks in 1992.
MISCELLANEOUS: Appeared in one game as pinch-runner (1992).

Year	**Team (League)**	**W**	**L**	**Pct.**	**ERA**	**G**	**GS**	**CG**	**ShO**	**Sv.**	**IP**	**H**	**R**	**ER**	**BB**	**SO**
1985	—Everett (N'west)	2	4	.333	4.23	17	7	0	0	3	55⅓	67	36	26	26	50
1986	—Clinton (Midwest)	6	11	.353	4.27	34	21	0	0	2	130⅔	126	70	62	64	84
1987	—Clinton (Midwest)	10	6	.625	2.01	26	26	3	2	0	161⅓	130	60	36	77	146
1988	—Shreveport (Texas)	5	4	.556	1.86	12	11	0	0	0	72⅔	55	19	15	23	53
	—Phoenix (PCL)	2	3	.400	5.05	11	9	0	0	0	51⅔	49	35	29	33	49
	—San Francisco (N.L.)	0	2	.000	4.09	4	4	0	0	0	22	25	14	10	8	15
1989	—Phoenix (PCL)	7	7	.500	3.12	23	20	2	0	0	115⅓	109	49	40	76	77
	—San Francisco (N.L.)	2	3	.400	4.35	14	4	0	0	0	39⅓	28	20	19	24	22
1990	—Phoenix (PCL)	5	5	.500	3.82	11	10	2	1	0	66	63	31	28	44	45
	—San Francisco (N.L.)	8	7	.533	4.00	27	17	3	2	0	110⅓	87	52	49	49	66
1991	—San Francisco (N.L.)	13	11	.542	3.56	44	29	2	1	0	202	173	87	80	77	139
1992	—San Francisco (N.L.)	8	14	.364	4.21	26	26	1	1	0	154	152	82	72	64	88
1993	—San Francisco (N.L.)	7	5	.583	3.60	22	18	1	0	0	110	110	45	44	40	57
	—San Jose (Calif.)	1	0	1.000	0.00	2	2	0	0	0	10	4	0	0	3	8
Major league totals (6 years)		38	42	.475	3.87	137	98	7	4	0	637⅔	575	300	274	262	387

WILSON, WILLIE

OF, CUBS

PERSONAL: Born July 9, 1955, in Montgomery, Ala. . . . 6-3/200. . . . Throws right, bats both. . . . Full name: Willie James Wilson.
HIGH SCHOOL: Summit (N.J.).
TRANSACTIONS/CAREER NOTES: Selected by Kansas City Royals organization in first round (18th pick overall) of free-agent draft (June 5, 1974). . . . On disabled list (August 21-September 6, 1983). . . . On suspended list (December 15, 1983-May 15, 1984). . . . On disabled list (May 27-June 17, 1989). . . . Granted free agency (November 13, 1989). . . . Re-signed by Royals (December 7, 1989). . . . Granted free agency (November 5, 1990). . . . Signed by Oakland Athletics (December 3, 1990). . . . On disabled list (August 15-September 1, 1991 and August 17-September 1, 1992). . . . Granted free agency (October 27, 1992). . . . Signed by Chicago Cubs (December 18, 1992).
RECORDS: Holds major league single-season records for most at-bats—705 (1980); and most at-bats by switch-hitter—705 (1980). . . . Shares major league single-season records for collecting 100 or more hits righthanded and lefthanded (1980); and most hits by switch-hitter—230 (1980). . . . Holds A.L. career record for highest stolen-base percentage (300 or more attempts)—.833. . . . Holds A.L. single-season record for most triples by switch-hitter—21 (1985). . . . Shares A.L. records for most years leading league in triples—5; and most consecutive stolen bases without being caught stealing—32 (July 23 through September 23, 1980). . . . Shares A.L. single-season record for fewest times caught stealing (50 or more stolen bases)—8 (1983).
HONORS: Named Midwest League Most Valuable Player (1975). . . . Named outfielder on THE SPORTING NEWS A.L. Silver Slugger team (1980 and 1982). . . . Won A.L. Gold Glove as outfielder (1980).
STATISTICAL NOTES: Led Midwest League in being hit by pitch with 13 in 1975. . . . Switch-hit home runs in one game (June 15, 1979).

			BATTING											FIELDING			
Year	Team (League)	Pos.	G	AB	R	H	2B	3B	HR	RBI	Avg.	BB	SO	SB	PO	A	E	Avg.
1974	—GC Royals (GCL)	OF	47	155	30	39	3	5	1	14	.252	10	51	*24	92	8	4	.962
1975	—Waterloo (Midw.)	OF	127	486	92	*132	18	4	8	73	.272	26	99	*76	249	•17	*17	.940
1976	—Jacksonv. (South.)	OF	107	388	54	98	13	6	1	35	.253	26	72	37	273	5	8	.972
	—Kansas City (A.L.)	OF	12	6	0	1	0	0	0	0	.167	0	2	2	6	1	1	.875
1977	—Omaha (A.A.)	OF	132	495	67	139	10	6	4	47	.281	24	106	*74	*278	7	11	.963
	—Kansas City (A.L.)	OF	13	34	10	11	2	0	0	1	.324	1	8	6	24	0	1	.960
1978	—Kansas City (A.L.)	OF	127	198	43	43	8	2	0	16	.217	16	33	46	171	6	4	.978
1979	—Kansas City (A.L.)	OF	154	588	113	185	18	13	6	49	.315	28	92	*83	384	12	6	.985
1980	—Kansas City (A.L.)	OF	161	*705	*133	*230	28	•15	3	49	.326	28	81	79	482	9	6	.988
1981	—Kansas City (A.L.)	OF	102	439	54	133	10	7	1	32	.303	18	42	34	299	*14	4	.987
1982	—Kansas City (A.L.)	OF	136	585	87	194	19	*15	3	46	*.332	26	81	37	376	4	5	.987
1983	—Kansas City (A.L.)	OF	137	576	90	159	22	8	2	33	.276	33	75	59	354	3	9	.975
1984	—Kansas City (A.L.)	OF	128	541	81	163	24	9	2	44	.301	39	56	47	383	6	4	.990
1985	—Kansas City (A.L.)	OF	141	605	87	168	25	*21	4	43	.278	29	94	43	378	4	2	.995
1986	—Kansas City (A.L.)	OF	156	631	77	170	20	7	9	44	.269	31	97	34	408	4	3	.993
1987	—Kansas City (A.L.)	OF	146	610	97	170	18	*15	4	30	.279	32	88	59	342	3	1	*.997
1988	—Kansas City (A.L.)	OF	147	591	81	155	17	•11	1	37	.262	22	106	35	365	1	4	.989
1989	—Kansas City (A.L.)	OF	112	383	58	97	17	7	3	43	.253	27	78	24	252	2	6	.977
1990	—Kansas City (A.L.)	OF	115	307	49	89	13	3	2	42	.290	30	57	24	187	2	0	1.000
1991	—Oakland (A.L.)■	OF	113	294	38	70	14	4	0	28	.238	18	43	20	176	2	3	.983
1992	—Oakland (A.L.)	OF	132	396	38	107	15	5	0	37	.270	35	65	28	355	2	7	.981
1993	—Chicago (N.L.)■	OF	105	221	29	57	11	3	1	11	.258	11	40	7	109	1	1	.991
American League totals (17 years)			2032	7489	1136	2145	270	142	40	574	.286	413	1098	660	4942	75	66	.987
National League totals (1 year)			105	221	29	57	11	3	1	11	.258	11	40	7	109	1	1	.991
Major league totals (18 years)			2137	7710	1165	2202	281	145	41	585	.286	424	1138	667	5051	76	67	.987

DIVISION SERIES RECORD

			BATTING											FIELDING			
Year	Team (League)	Pos.	G	AB	R	H	2B	3B	HR	RBI	Avg.	BB	SO	SB	PO	A	E	Avg.
1981	—Kansas City (A.L.)	OF	3	13	0	4	0	0	0	1	.308	0	0	0	6	0	0	1.000

CHAMPIONSHIP SERIES RECORD

			BATTING											FIELDING			
Year	Team (League)	Pos.	G	AB	R	H	2B	3B	HR	RBI	Avg.	BB	SO	SB	PO	A	E	Avg.
1978	—Kansas City (A.L.)	OF-PR	3	4	0	1	0	0	0	0	.250	0	2	0	2	0	0	1.000
1980	—Kansas City (A.L.)	OF	3	13	2	4	2	1	0	4	.308	1	2	0	6	1	0	1.000
1984	—Kansas City (A.L.)	OF	3	13	0	2	0	0	0	0	.154	1	2	0	10	0	0	1.000
1985	—Kansas City (A.L.)	OF	7	29	5	9	0	0	1	2	.310	1	5	1	12	0	0	1.000
1992	—Oakland (A.L.)	OF	6	22	0	5	1	0	0	0	.227	1	5	7	16	0	0	1.000
Championship series totals (5 years)			22	81	7	21	3	1	1	6	.259	4	16	8	46	1	0	1.000

WORLD SERIES RECORD

WORLD SERIES NOTES: Holds single-series record for most strikeouts—12 (1980). . . . Shares record for most at-bats in one inning—2 (October 18, 1980, first inning).

			BATTING											FIELDING			
Year	Team (League)	Pos.	G	AB	R	H	2B	3B	HR	RBI	Avg.	BB	SO	SB	PO	A	E	Avg.
1980	—Kansas City (A.L.)	OF	6	26	3	4	1	0	0	0	.154	4	12	2	15	1	0	1.000
1985	—Kansas City (A.L.)	OF	7	30	2	11	0	1	0	3	.367	1	4	3	19	1	0	1.000
World Series totals (2 years)			13	56	5	15	1	1	0	3	.268	5	16	5	34	2	0	1.000

ALL-STAR GAME RECORD

			BATTING										FIELDING			
Year	League	Pos.	AB	R	H	2B	3B	HR	RBI	Avg.	BB	SO	SB	PO	A	E	Avg.
1982	—American	OF	2	0	0	0	0	0	0	.000	0	1	0	1	0	0	1.000
1983	—American	OF	1	0	1	1	0	0	1	1.000	0	0	0	2	0	0	1.000
All-Star Game totals (2 years)			3	0	1	1	0	0	1	.333	0	1	0	3	0	0	1.000

WINFIELD, DAVE

DH/OF, TWINS

PERSONAL: Born October 3, 1951, in St. Paul, Minn. ... 6-6/245. ... Throws right, bats right. ... Full name: David Mark Winfield.
HIGH SCHOOL: St. Paul (Minn.) Central.
COLLEGE: Minnesota (received degree).
TRANSACTIONS/CAREER NOTES: Selected by Baltimore Orioles organization in 40th round of free-agent draft (June 5, 1969). ... Selected by San Diego Padres organization in first round (fourth pick overall) of free-agent draft (June 5, 1973). ... Granted free agency (October 22, 1980). ... Signed by New York Yankees (December 15, 1980). ... On disabled list (May 20-June 4, 1982; April 16-May 1, 1984; and March 19, 1989-entire season). ... Traded by Yankees to California Angels for P Mike Witt (May 11, 1990). ... Granted free agency (October 30, 1991). ... Signed by Toronto Blue Jays (December 19, 1991). ... Granted free agency (November 2, 1992). ... Signed by Minnesota Twins (December 17, 1992).
HONORS: Named outfielder on THE SPORTING NEWS college All-America team (1973). ... Named outfielder on THE SPORTING NEWS N.L. All-Star team (1979). ... Won N.L. Gold Glove as outfielder (1979-80). ... Named outfielder on THE SPORTING NEWS A.L. Silver Slugger team (1981-85). ... Named outfielder on THE SPORTING NEWS A.L. All-Star team (1982-84). ... Won A.L. Gold Glove as outfielder (1982-85 and 1987). ... Named A.L. Comeback Player of the Year by THE SPORTING NEWS (1990). ... Named designated hitter on THE SPORTING NEWS A.L. All-Star team (1992). ... Named designated hitter on THE SPORTING NEWS A.L. Silver Slugger team (1992).
STATISTICAL NOTES: Led N.L. with 333 total bases and 24 intentional bases on balls received in 1979. ... Hit three home runs in one game (April 13, 1991). ... Hit for the cycle (June 24, 1991).
MISCELLANEOUS: Selected by Atlanta Hawks in fifth round (79th pick overall) of 1973 NBA draft. ... Selected by Utah Stars in sixth round (58th pick overall) of 1973 ABA draft. ... Selected by Minnesota Vikings in 17th round (429th pick overall) of 1973 NFL draft.

			BATTING												FIELDING			
Year	**Team (League)**	**Pos.**	**G**	**AB**	**R**	**H**	**2B**	**3B**	**HR**	**RBI**	**Avg.**	**BB**	**SO**	**SB**	**PO**	**A**	**E**	**Avg.**
1973	—San Diego (N.L.)	OF-1B	56	141	9	39	4	1	3	12	.277	12	19	0	65	1	3	.957
1974	—San Diego (N.L.)	OF	145	498	57	132	18	4	20	75	.265	40	96	9	276	11	•12	.960
1975	—San Diego (N.L.)	OF	143	509	74	136	20	2	15	76	.267	69	82	23	302	9	9	.972
1976	—San Diego (N.L.)	OF	137	492	81	139	26	4	13	69	.283	65	78	26	304	*15	6	.982
1977	—San Diego (N.L.)	OF	157	615	104	169	29	7	25	92	.275	58	75	16	368	15	11	.972
1978	—San Diego (N.L.)	OF-1B	158	587	88	181	30	5	24	97	.308	55	81	21	328	8	7	.980
1979	—San Diego (N.L.)	OF	159	597	97	184	27	10	34	*118	.308	85	71	15	344	14	5	.986
1980	—San Diego (N.L.)	OF	162	558	89	154	25	6	20	87	.276	79	83	23	273	20	4	.987
1981	—New York (A.L.)■	OF	105	388	52	114	25	1	13	68	.294	43	41	11	196	1	3	.985
1982	—New York (A.L.)	OF	140	539	84	151	24	8	37	106	.280	45	64	5	279	*17	8	.974
1983	—New York (A.L.)	OF	152	598	99	169	26	8	32	116	.283	58	77	15	313	5	7	.978
1984	—New York (A.L.)	OF	141	567	106	193	34	4	19	100	.340	53	71	6	306	3	2	.994
1985	—New York (A.L.)	OF	155	633	105	174	34	6	26	114	.275	52	96	19	316	13	3	.991
1986	—New York (A.L.)	OF-3B	154	565	90	148	31	5	24	104	.262	77	106	6	292	9	5	.984
1987	—New York (A.L.)	OF	156	575	83	158	22	1	27	97	.275	76	96	5	253	6	3	.989
1988	—New York (A.L.)	OF	149	559	96	180	37	2	25	107	.322	69	88	9	276	3	3	.989
1989	—								Did not play.									
1990	—N.Y.-Calif. (A.L.)■	OF	132	475	70	127	21	2	21	78	.267	52	81	0	177	7	2	.989
1991	—California (A.L.)	OF	150	568	75	149	27	4	28	86	.262	56	109	7	198	7	2	.990
1992	—Toronto (A.L.)■	OF	156	583	92	169	33	3	26	108	.290	82	89	2	52	1	0	1.000
1993	—Minnesota (A.L.)■	OF-1B	143	547	72	148	27	2	21	76	.271	45	106	2	91	3	0	1.000
American League totals (12 years)			1733	6597	1024	1880	341	46	299	1160	.285	708	1024	87	2749	75	38	.987
National League totals (8 years)			1117	3997	599	1134	179	39	154	626	.284	463	585	133	2260	93	57	.976
Major league totals (20 years)			2850	10594	1623	3014	520	85	453	1786	.285	1171	1609	220	5009	168	95	.982

DIVISION SERIES RECORD

			BATTING												FIELDING			
Year	**Team (League)**	**Pos.**	**G**	**AB**	**R**	**H**	**2B**	**3B**	**HR**	**RBI**	**Avg.**	**BB**	**SO**	**SB**	**PO**	**A**	**E**	**Avg.**
1981	—New York (A.L.)	OF	5	20	2	7	3	0	0	0	.350	1	5	0	10	1	0	1.000

CHAMPIONSHIP SERIES RECORD

CHAMPIONSHIP SERIES NOTES: Shares A.L. single-game record for most at-bats—6 (October 11, 1992, 11 innings).

			BATTING												FIELDING			
Year	**Team (League)**	**Pos.**	**G**	**AB**	**R**	**H**	**2B**	**3B**	**HR**	**RBI**	**Avg.**	**BB**	**SO**	**SB**	**PO**	**A**	**E**	**Avg.**
1981	—New York (A.L.)	OF	3	13	2	2	1	0	0	2	.154	2	2	1	6	0	0	1.000
1992	—Toronto (A.L.)	DH	6	24	7	6	1	0	2	3	.250	4	2	0	...	...	...	...
Championship series totals (2 years)			9	37	9	8	2	0	2	5	.216	6	4	1	6	0	0	1.000

WORLD SERIES RECORD

			BATTING												FIELDING			
Year	**Team (League)**	**Pos.**	**G**	**AB**	**R**	**H**	**2B**	**3B**	**HR**	**RBI**	**Avg.**	**BB**	**SO**	**SB**	**PO**	**A**	**E**	**Avg.**
1981	—New York (A.L.)	OF	6	22	0	1	0	0	0	1	.045	5	4	1	13	1	0	1.000
1992	—Toronto (A.L.)	OF-DH	6	22	0	5	1	0	0	3	.227	2	3	0	7	0	0	1.000
World Series totals (2 years)			12	44	0	6	1	0	0	4	.136	7	7	1	20	1	0	1.000

ALL-STAR GAME RECORD

ALL-STAR GAME NOTES: Holds career record for most doubles—7. ... Shares record for most consecutive games with one or more hits—7. ... Shares single-game record for most at-bats in nine-inning game—5 (July 17, 1979).

			BATTING											FIELDING			
Year	**League**	**Pos.**	**AB**	**R**	**H**	**2B**	**3B**	**HR**	**RBI**	**Avg.**	**BB**	**SO**	**SB**	**PO**	**A**	**E**	**Avg.**
1977	—National	OF	2	0	2	1	0	0	2	1.000	0	0	0	1	0	0	1.000
1978	—National	OF	2	1	1	0	0	0	0	.500	0	0	0	1	0	0	1.000
1979	—National	OF	5	1	1	1	0	0	1	.200	0	1	0	3	0	0	1.000
1980	—National	OF	2	0	0	0	0	0	1	.000	0	0	0	2	0	0	1.000
1981	—American	OF	4	0	0	0	0	0	0	.000	1	0	0	0	1	0	1.000
1982	—American	OF	2	0	1	0	0	0	0	.500	0	0	0	0	0	0	...

Year	League	Pos.	AB	R	H	2B	3B	HR	RBI	Avg.	BB	SO	SB	PO	A	E	Avg.
			BATTING											FIELDING			
1983	—American	OF	3	2	3	1	0	0	1	1.000	0	0	0	3	0	0	1.000
1984	—American	OF	4	0	1	1	0	0	0	.250	0	0	0	2	1	0	1.000
1985	—American	OF	3	0	1	0	0	0	0	.333	0	0	1	0	0	0	...
1986	—American	OF	1	1	1	1	0	0	0	1.000	0	0	0	0	0	0	...
1987	—American	OF	5	0	1	1	0	0	0	.200	1	0	0	2	0	0	1.000
1988	—American	OF	3	1	1	1	0	0	0	.333	0	0	0	1	0	0	1.000
All-Star Game totals (12 years)			36	6	13	7	0	0	5	.361	2	1	1	15	2	0	1.000

WINNINGHAM, HERM

OF, ROCKIES

PERSONAL: Born December 1, 1961, in Orangeburg, S.C. ... 5-11/185. ... Throws right, bats left.

HIGH SCHOOL: Orangeburg (S.C.).

COLLEGE: DeKalb Community College South (Ga.).

TRANSACTIONS/CAREER NOTES: Selected by Pittsburgh Pirates organization in 38th round of free-agent draft (June 5, 1979).... Selected by Milwaukee Brewers organization in secondary phase of free-agent draft (January 8, 1980).... Selected by Montreal Expos organization in secondary phase of free-agent draft (June 3, 1980).... Selected by New York Mets organization in secondary phase of free-agent draft (January 13, 1981).... On Tidewater disabled list (August 9-September 20, 1983).... Traded by Mets with IF Hubie Brooks, C Mike Fitzgerald and P Floyd Youmans to Expos for C Gary Carter (December 10, 1984).... On Montreal disabled list (June 24-July 13, 1985); included rehabilitation assignment to Indianapolis (July 4-13).... Traded by Expos with C Jeff Reed and P Randy St. Claire to Cincinnati Reds for OF Tracy Jones and P Pat Pacillo (July 13, 1988).... On disabled list (June 6-21, 1989).... Granted free agency (November 5, 1991).... Signed by Boston Red Sox (January 29, 1992).... Granted free agency (November 6, 1992).... Signed by Buffalo, Pittsburgh Pirates organization (March 11, 1993).... Released by Buffalo (April 3, 1993).... Signed by Pawtucket, Red Sox organization (April 8, 1993).... Released by Pawtucket (June 18, 1993).... Signed by Norfolk, New York Mets organization (July 28, 1993).... Granted free agency (October 15, 1993).... Signed by Colorado Rockies organization (December 9, 1993).

RECORDS: Shares modern major league single-game record for most triples—3 (August 15, 1990, 12 innings).

Year	Team (League)	Pos.	G	AB	R	H	2B	3B	HR	RBI	Avg.	BB	SO	SB	PO	A	E	Avg.
				BATTING											FIELDING			
1981	—Kingsport (Appal.)	OF	58	204	44	52	7	4	2	14	.255	33	31	20	128	3	2	*.985
1982	—Lynchburg (Caro.)	OF	120	430	65	127	20	5	6	61	.295	64	106	50	235	6	5	.980
1983	—Jackson (Texas)	OF	78	288	54	102	13	6	4	41	.354	43	44	17	157	5	6	.964
	—Tidewater (Int'l)	OF	29	113	18	30	5	2	1	11	.265	10	29	6	70	1	3	.959
1984	—Tidewater (Int'l)	OF	115	406	50	114	20	3	3	47	.281	48	81	23	228	8	4	.983
	—New York (N.L.)	OF	14	27	5	11	1	1	0	5	.407	1	7	2	7	0	0	1.000
1985	—Montreal (N.L.)■	OF	125	312	30	74	6	5	3	21	.237	28	72	20	229	6	4	.983
	—Indianapolis (A.A.)	OF	11	35	3	6	0	0	0	2	.171	3	7	2	22	0	1	.957
1986	—Montreal (N.L.)	OF-SS	90	185	23	40	6	3	4	11	.216	18	51	12	97	2	2	.980
	—Indianapolis (A.A.)	OF	51	201	35	54	5	7	4	24	.269	14	47	23	106	3	1	.991
1987	—Montreal (N.L.)	OF	137	347	34	83	20	3	4	41	.239	34	68	29	225	5	6	.975
1988	—Mont.-Cin. (N.L.)■	OF	100	203	16	47	3	4	0	21	.232	17	45	12	128	1	1	.992
	—Indianapolis (A.A.)	OF	3	10	2	2	0	1	0	1	.200	0	3	1	6	0	0	1.000
1989	—Cincinnati (N.L.)	OF	115	251	40	63	11	3	3	13	.251	24	50	14	146	3	3	.980
1990	—Cincinnati (N.L.)	OF	84	160	20	41	8	5	3	17	.256	14	31	6	89	3	0	1.000
1991	—Cincinnati (N.L.)	OF	98	169	17	38	6	1	1	4	.225	11	40	4	99	2	5	.953
1992	—Boston (A.L.)■	OF	105	234	27	55	8	1	1	14	.235	10	53	6	112	7	3	.975
1993	—Paw.-Nor. (Int'l)■	OF	95	338	46	86	10	4	7	33	.254	37	73	15	187	5	5	.975
American League totals (1 year)			105	234	27	55	8	1	1	14	.235	10	53	6	112	7	3	.975
National League totals (8 years)			763	1654	185	397	61	25	18	133	.240	147	364	99	1020	22	21	.980
Major league totals (9 years)			868	1888	212	452	69	26	19	147	.239	157	417	105	1132	29	24	.980

CHAMPIONSHIP SERIES RECORD

Year	Team (League)	Pos.	G	AB	R	H	2B	3B	HR	RBI	Avg.	BB	SO	SB	PO	A	E	Avg.
				BATTING											FIELDING			
1990	—Cincinnati (N.L.)	OF-PH	3	7	1	2	1	0	0	1	.286	1	1	1	7	0	0	1.000

WORLD SERIES RECORD

Year	Team (League)	Pos.	G	AB	R	H	2B	3B	HR	RBI	Avg.	BB	SO	SB	PO	A	E	Avg.
				BATTING											FIELDING			
1990	—Cincinnati (N.L.)	PH-OF	2	4	1	2	0	0	0	0	.500	0	0	0	3	0	0	1.000

WITHEM, SHANNON

P, TIGERS

PERSONAL: Born September 21, 1972, in Ann Arbor, Mich.... 6-3/185.... Throws right, bats right. ... Full name: Shannon Bolt Withem. ... Name pronounced WITH-em.

HIGH SCHOOL: Willow Run (Ypsilanti, Mich.).

TRANSACTIONS/CAREER NOTES: Selected by Detroit Tigers organization in fifth round of free-agent draft (June 4, 1990).

STATISTICAL NOTES: Tied for Appalachian League lead with 12 wild pitches in 1990.

Year	Team (League)	W	L	Pct.	ERA	G	GS	CG	ShO	Sv.	IP	H	R	ER	BB	SO
1990	—Bristol (Eastern)	3	*9	.250	5.23	14	13	0	0	0	62	70	43	36	35	48
1991	—Fayetteville (SAL)	2	6	.250	8.50	11	11	0	0	0	47⅔	71	53	45	28	19
	—Niag. Falls (NYP)	1	2	.333	3.33	8	3	0	0	0	27	26	12	10	11	17
1992	—Fayetteville (SAL)	1	3	.250	4.74	22	2	0	0	2	38	40	23	20	20	34
1993	—Lakeland (Fla. St.)	10	2	.833	3.42	16	16	2	1	0	113	108	47	43	24	62

WITT, BOBBY

P, ATHLETICS

PERSONAL: Born May 11, 1964, in Arlington, Va.... 6-2/205.... Throws right, bats right.... Full name: Robert Andrew Witt.

HIGH SCHOOL: Canton (Mass.).

COLLEGE: Oklahoma.

W

TRANSACTIONS/CAREER NOTES: Selected by Cincinnati Reds organization in seventh round of free-agent draft (June 7, 1982). . . . Selected by Texas Rangers organization in first round (third pick overall) of free-agent draft (June 3, 1985). . . . On Texas disabled list (May 21-June 20, 1987); included rehabilitation assignment to Oklahoma City (June 7-12) and Tulsa (June 13). . . . On Texas disabled list (May 27-July 31, 1991); included rehabilitation assignment to Oklahoma City (July 22-29). . . . Traded by Rangers with OF Ruben Sierra, P Jeff Russell and cash to Oakland Athletics for OF Jose Canseco (August 31, 1992).
RECORDS: Shares major league record for most strikeouts in one inning—4 (August 2, 1987, second inning).
HONORS: Named righthanded pitcher on THE SPORTING NEWS college All-America team (1985).
STATISTICAL NOTES: Led A.L. with 22 wild pitches in 1986 and tied for lead with 16 in 1988.
MISCELLANEOUS: Member of 1984 U.S. Olympic baseball team. . . . Struck out in only appearance as pinch-hitter with Texas (1987). . . . Appeared in two games as pinch-runner (1990).

Year	Team (League)	W	L	Pct.	ERA	G	GS	CG	ShO	Sv.	IP	H	R	ER	BB	SO
1985	—Tulsa (Texas)	0	6	.000	6.43	11	8	0	0	0	35	26	26	25	44	39
1986	—Texas (A.L.)	11	9	.550	5.48	31	31	0	0	0	157⅔	130	104	96	*143	174
1987	—Texas (A.L.)	8	10	.444	4.91	26	25	1	0	0	143	114	82	78	*140	160
	—Okla. City (A.A.)	1	0	1.000	9.00	1	1	0	0	0	5	5	5	5	3	2
	—Tulsa (Texas)	0	1	.000	5.40	1	1	0	0	0	5	5	9	3	6	2
1988	—Texas (A.L.)	8	10	.444	3.92	22	22	13	2	0	174⅓	134	83	76	101	148
	—Okla. City (A.A.)	4	6	.400	4.34	11	11	3	0	0	76⅔	69	42	37	47	70
1989	—Texas (A.L.)	12	13	.480	5.14	31	31	5	1	0	194⅓	182	123	•111	*114	166
1990	—Texas (A.L.)	17	10	.630	3.36	33	32	7	1	0	222	197	98	83	110	221
1991	—Texas (A.L.)	3	7	.300	6.09	17	16	1	1	0	88⅔	84	66	60	74	82
	—Okla. City (A.A.)	1	1	.500	1.13	2	2	0	0	0	8	3	1	1	8	12
1992	—Texas-Oak. (A.L.)■	10	14	.417	4.29	31	31	0	0	0	193	183	99	92	114	125
1993	—Oakland (A.L.)	14	13	.519	4.21	35	33	5	1	0	220	226	112	103	91	131
Major league totals (8 years)		83	86	.491	4.52	226	221	32	6	0	1393	1250	767	699	887	1207

CHAMPIONSHIP SERIES RECORD

Year	Team (League)	W	L	Pct.	ERA	G	GS	CG	ShO	Sv.	IP	H	R	ER	BB	SO
1992	—Oakland (A.L.)	0	0	...	18.00	1	0	0	0	0	1	2	2	2	1	1

WITT, MIKE

P

PERSONAL: Born July 20, 1960, in Fullerton, Calif. . . . 6-7/208. . . . Throws right, bats right. . . . Full name: Michael Atwater Witt.
HIGH SCHOOL: Servite (Calif.).
COLLEGE: Cypress (Calif.) College.
TRANSACTIONS/CAREER NOTES: Selected by California Angels organization in fourth round of free-agent draft (June 6, 1978). . . . Granted free agency (November 9, 1987). . . . Re-signed by Angels (December 22, 1987). . . . Traded by Angels to New York Yankees for OF Dave Winfield (May 11, 1990). . . . On New York disabled list (June 9-August 7, 1990). . . . Granted free agency (December 7, 1990). . . . Re-signed by Yankees (January 2, 1991). . . . On New York disabled list (March 29-June 7, 1991); included rehabilitation assignment to Columbus (June 1-2). . . . On New York disabled list (June 14, 1991-remainder of season); included rehabilitation assignment to Albany/Colonie (July 17-19). . . . On New York disabled list (April 3, 1992-entire season); included rehabilitation assignment to Gulf Coast Yankees (June 25-July 3). . . . On New York disabled list (March 28-April 25, 1993); included rehabilitation assignment to Columbus (April 13-18). . . . On New York disabled list (June 2-17, 1993). . . . On New York disabled list (June 18, 1993-remainder of season); included rehabilitation assignment to Albany/Colonie (August 15-20) and Columbus (August 20-September 7). . . . Granted free agency (October 27, 1993).
STATISTICAL NOTES: Tied for A.L. lead with 11 hit batsmen in 1981. . . . Pitched 1-0 perfect game against Texas (September 30, 1984). . . . Pitched two innings, combining with starter Mark Langston (seven innings) in 1-0 no-hit victory for California against Seattle (April 11, 1990).

Year	Team (League)	W	L	Pct.	ERA	G	GS	CG	ShO	Sv.	IP	H	R	ER	BB	SO
1978	—Idaho Falls (Pio.)	7	1	.875	3.56	13	13	3	0	0	86	88	45	34	26	79
1979	—Salinas (Calif.)	8	10	.444	5.11	30	26	2	0	0	141	156	96	80	70	94
1980	—Salinas (Calif.)	7	3	.700	2.10	13	13	3	0	0	90	85	30	21	35	76
	—El Paso (Texas)	5	5	.500	5.79	12	12	2	0	0	70	72	53	45	39	64
1981	—California (A.L.)	8	9	.471	3.28	22	21	7	1	0	129	123	60	47	47	75
1982	—California (A.L.)	8	6	.571	3.51	33	26	5	1	0	179⅔	177	77	70	47	85
1983	—California (A.L.)	7	14	.333	4.91	43	19	2	0	5	154	173	90	84	75	77
1984	—California (A.L.)	15	11	.577	3.47	34	34	9	2	0	246⅔	227	103	95	84	196
1985	—California (A.L.)	15	9	.625	3.56	35	35	6	1	0	250	228	115	99	98	180
1986	—California (A.L.)	18	10	.643	2.84	34	34	14	3	0	269	218	95	85	73	208
1987	—California (A.L.)	16	14	.533	4.01	36	36	10	0	0	247	252	128	110	84	192
1988	—California (A.L.)	13	16	.448	4.15	34	34	12	2	0	249⅔	263	*130	115	87	133
1989	—California (A.L.)	9	15	.375	4.54	33	33	5	0	0	220	252	119	•111	48	123
1990	—Calif.-N.Y. (A.L.)■	5	9	.357	4.00	26	16	2	1	1	117	106	62	52	47	74
1991	—Columbus (Int'l)	0	0	...	9.00	1	1	0	0	0	4	7	4	4	3	5
	—New York (A.L.)	0	1	.000	10.13	2	2	0	0	0	5⅓	8	7	6	1	0
	—Alb./Colon. (East.)	0	0	...	9.00	1	1	0	0	0	2	2	2	2	2	2
1992	—GC Yankees (GCL)	1	0	1.000	0.00	3	3	0	0	0	12	7	1	0	2	13
1993	—Columbus (Int'l)	1	0	1.000	1.98	3	3	0	0	0	13⅔	11	3	3	5	11
	—New York (A.L.)	3	2	.600	5.27	9	9	0	0	0	41	39	26	24	22	30
	—Alb./Colon. (East.)	0	0	...	0.00	1	0	0	0	0	2	2	0	0	0	2
Major league totals (12 years)		117	116	.502	3.83	341	299	72	11	6	2108⅓	2066	1012	898	713	1373

CHAMPIONSHIP SERIES RECORD

Year	Team (League)	W	L	Pct.	ERA	G	GS	CG	ShO	Sv.	IP	H	R	ER	BB	SO
1982	—California (A.L.)	0	0	...	6.00	1	0	0	0	0	3	2	2	2	2	3
1986	—California (A.L.)	1	0	1.000	2.55	2	2	1	0	0	17⅔	13	5	5	2	8
Champ. series totals (2 years)		1	0	1.000	3.05	3	2	1	0	0	20⅔	15	7	7	4	11

ALL-STAR GAME RECORD

Year	League	W	L	Pct.	ERA	GS	CG	ShO	Sv.	IP	H	R	ER	BB	SO
1986	—American	Did not play.													
1987	—American	Did not play.													

WOHLERS, MARK
P, BRAVES

PERSONAL: Born January 23, 1970, in Holyoke, Mass. . . . 6-4/207. . . . Throws right, bats right. . . . Full name: Mark Edward Wohlers.
HIGH SCHOOL: Holyoke (Mass.).
TRANSACTIONS/CAREER NOTES: Selected by Atlanta Braves organization in eighth round of free-agent draft (June 1, 1988).
HONORS: Named Southern League Outstanding Pitcher (1991).
STATISTICAL NOTES: Pitched two innings, combining with starter Kent Mercker (six innings) and Alejandro Pena (one inning) in 1-0 no-hit victory for Atlanta against San Diego (September 11, 1991).

Year	Team (League)	W	L	Pct.	ERA	G	GS	CG	ShO	Sv.	IP	H	R	ER	BB	SO
1988	—Pulaski (Appal.)	5	3	.625	3.32	13	9	1	0	0	59⅔	47	37	22	50	49
1989	—Sumter (S. Atl.)	2	7	.222	6.49	14	14	0	0	0	68	74	55	49	59	51
	—Pulaski (Appal.)	1	1	.500	5.48	14	8	0	0	0	46	48	36	28	28	50
1990	—Greenville (South.)	0	1	.000	4.02	14	0	0	0	6	15⅔	14	7	7	14	20
	—Sumter (S. Atl.)	5	4	.556	1.88	37	2	0	0	5	52⅔	27	13	11	20	85
1991	—Greenville (South.)	0	0	...	0.57	28	0	0	0	21	31⅓	9	4	2	13	44
	—Richmond (Int'l)	1	0	1.000	1.03	23	0	0	0	11	26⅓	23	4	3	12	22
	—Atlanta (N.L.)	3	1	.750	3.20	17	0	0	0	2	19⅔	17	7	7	13	13
1992	—Richmond (Int'l)	0	2	.000	3.93	27	2	0	0	9	34⅓	32	16	15	17	33
	—Atlanta (N.L.)	1	2	.333	2.55	32	0	0	0	4	35⅓	28	11	10	14	17
1993	—Richmond (Int'l)	1	3	.250	1.84	25	0	0	0	4	29⅓	21	7	6	11	39
	—Atlanta (N.L.)	6	2	.750	4.50	46	0	0	0	0	48	37	25	24	22	45
Major league totals (3 years)		10	5	.667	3.58	95	0	0	0	6	103	82	43	41	49	75

CHAMPIONSHIP SERIES RECORD

Year	Team (League)	W	L	Pct.	ERA	G	GS	CG	ShO	Sv.	IP	H	R	ER	BB	SO
1991	—Atlanta (N.L.)	0	0	...	0.00	3	0	0	0	0	1⅔	3	0	0	1	1
1992	—Atlanta (N.L.)	0	0	...	0.00	3	0	0	0	0	3	2	0	0	1	2
1993	—Atlanta (N.L.)	0	1	.000	3.38	4	0	0	0	0	5⅓	2	2	2	3	10
Champ. series totals (3 years)		0	1	.000	1.80	10	0	0	0	0	10	7	2	2	5	13

WORLD SERIES RECORD

Year	Team (League)	W	L	Pct.	ERA	G	GS	CG	ShO	Sv.	IP	H	R	ER	BB	SO
1991	—Atlanta (N.L.)	0	0	...	0.00	3	0	0	0	0	1⅔	2	0	0	2	1
1992	—Atlanta (N.L.)	0	0	...	0.00	2	0	0	0	0	⅔	0	0	0	1	0
World Series totals (2 years)		0	0	...	0.00	5	0	0	0	0	2⅓	2	0	0	3	1

WOMACK, TONY
SS, PIRATES

PERSONAL: Born September 25, 1969, in Danville, Va. . . . 5-9/153. . . . Throws right, bats left. . . . Full name: Anthony Darrell Womack.
HIGH SCHOOL: Gretna (Va.).
COLLEGE: Guilford (N.C.).
TRANSACTIONS/CAREER NOTES: Selected by Pittsburgh Pirates organization in seventh round of free-agent draft (June 3, 1991). . . . On disabled list (April 17-26 and August 28, 1992-remainder of season).

			BATTING												FIELDING			
Year	Team (League)	Pos.	G	AB	R	H	2B	3B	HR	RBI	Avg.	BB	SO	SB	PO	A	E	Avg.
1991	—Welland (NYP)	SS-2B	45	166	30	46	3	0	1	8	.277	17	39	26	78	109	16	.921
1992	—Augusta (S. Atl.)	SS-2B	102	380	62	93	8	3	0	18	.245	41	59	50	186	291	40	.923
1993	—Salem (Carolina)	SS	72	304	41	91	11	3	2	18	.299	13	34	28	130	223	28	.927
	—Carolina (South.)	SS	60	247	41	75	7	2	0	23	.304	17	34	21	102	169	11	.961
	—Pittsburgh (N.L.)	SS	15	24	5	2	0	0	0	0	.083	3	3	2	11	22	1	.971
Major league totals (1 year)			15	24	5	2	0	0	0	0	.083	3	3	2	11	22	1	.971

WOOD, TED
OF, EXPOS

PERSONAL: Born January 4, 1967, in Mansfield, O. . . . 6-2/187. . . . Throws left, bats left. . . . Full name: Edward Robert Wood Jr.
HIGH SCHOOL: Orange (Pepper Pike, O.).
COLLEGE: New Orleans.
TRANSACTIONS/CAREER NOTES: Selected by San Francisco Giants in supplemental round ("sandwich pick" between first and second round, 29th pick overall) of free-agent draft (June 1, 1988); pick received as part of compensation for California Angels signing Type A free agent Chili Davis. . . . On San Francisco disabled list (August 27-September 19, 1992). . . . Claimed on waivers by Montreal Expos (March 23, 1993). . . . On Ottawa disabled list (July 26-August 5, 1993).
HONORS: Named outfielder on THE SPORTING NEWS college All-America team (1988).
MISCELLANEOUS: Member of 1988 U.S. Olympic baseball team.

			BATTING												FIELDING			
Year	Team (League)	Pos.	G	AB	R	H	2B	3B	HR	RBI	Avg.	BB	SO	SB	PO	A	E	Avg.
1989	—Shreveport (Texas)	OF	114	349	44	90	13	1	0	43	.258	51	72	9	200	4	3	.986
1990	—Shreveport (Texas)	OF	•131	456	81	121	22	*11	17	72	.265	74	76	17	247	8	6	.977
1991	—Phoenix (PCL)	OF	*137	512	90	159	38	6	11	*109	.311	*86	96	12	275	8	10	.966
	—San Francisco (N.L.)	OF	10	25	0	3	0	0	0	1	.120	2	11	0	10	0	1	.909
1992	—Phoenix (PCL)	OF-1B	110	418	70	127	24	7	7	63	.304	48	74	9	275	13	6	.980
	—San Francisco (N.L.)	OF	24	58	5	12	2	0	1	3	.207	6	15	0	35	0	1	.972

W

Year	Team (League)	Pos.	G	AB	R	H	2B	3B	HR	RBI	Avg.	BB	SO	SB	PO	A	E	Avg.
			BATTING												FIELDING			
1993	—Montreal (N.L.)■	OF	13	26	4	5	1	0	0	3	.192	3	3	0	16	0	0	1.000
	—Ottawa (Int'l)	OF	83	231	39	59	11	4	1	21	.255	38	54	12	108	6	0	1.000
Major league totals (3 years)			47	109	9	20	3	0	1	7	.183	11	29	0	61	0	2	.968

WOODS, TYRONE

OF, EXPOS

PERSONAL: Born August 19, 1969, in Dade City, Fla.... 6-1/220.... Throws right, bats right.... Full name: William Tyrone Woods.

HIGH SCHOOL: Hernando (Brooksville, Fla.).

TRANSACTIONS/CAREER NOTES: Selected by Montreal Expos organization in fifth round of free-agent draft (June 1, 1988).... On disabled list (April 11-24, 1991).

Year	Team (League)	Pos.	G	AB	R	H	2B	3B	HR	RBI	Avg.	BB	SO	SB	PO	A	E	Avg.
			BATTING												FIELDING			
1988	—GC Expos (GCL)	3B	43	149	12	18	2	0	2	12	.121	7	47	2	31	44	10	.882
1989	—Jamestown (NYP)	3B	63	209	23	55	6	4	9	29	.263	20	59	8	37	98	18	.882
1990	—Rockford (Midw.)	OF	123	455	50	110	27	5	8	46	.242	45	121	5	166	13	7	.962
1991	—W.P. Beach (FSL)	OF	96	295	34	65	15	3	5	31	.220	28	85	4	85	5	4	.957
1992	—Rockford (Midw.)	OF	101	374	54	109	22	3	12	47	.291	34	83	15	166	9	10	.946
	—W.P. Beach (FSL)	OF	15	56	7	16	1	2	1	7	.286	6	15	2	28	2	2	.938
	—Harrisburg (East.)	OF	4	4	0	0	0	0	0	0	.000	0	3	0	0	0	0	...
1993	—Harrisburg (East.)	OF-1B-3B	106	318	51	80	15	1	16	59	.252	35	77	4	188	13	4	.980

WOODSON, KERRY

P, MARINERS

PERSONAL: Born May 18, 1969, in Jacksonville, Fla.... 6-2/190.... Throws right, bats right.... Full name: Walter Browne Woodson IV.

HIGH SCHOOL: Carmel (Calif.).

COLLEGE: San Jose (Calif.) City College.

TRANSACTIONS/CAREER NOTES: Selected by Seattle Mariners organization in 29th round of free-agent draft (June 1, 1988).... On disabled list (August 13, 1990-remainder of season).... On Jacksonville disabled list (April 11-May 29, 1991).... On Seattle disabled list (August 12-September 7 and September 17, 1992-remainder of season).... On Seattle disabled list (March 26, 1993-entire season).

STATISTICAL NOTES: Led California League with 12 hit batsmen in 1990.

Year	Team (League)	W	L	Pct.	ERA	G	GS	CG	ShO	Sv.	IP	H	R	ER	BB	SO
1989	—Belling. (N'west)	3	4	.429	4.75	12	12	0	0	0	60⅔	63	42	32	27	53
1990	—San Bern. (Calif.)	8	6	.571	3.10	27	23	1	1	0	136⅔	111	62	47	83	131
1991	—San Bern. (Calif.)	2	0	1.000	1.95	5	5	0	0	0	27⅔	33	13	6	16	14
	—Jacksonv. (South.)	4	6	.400	3.06	13	13	2	0	0	79⅓	73	35	27	39	50
1992	—Jacksonv. (South.)	5	4	.556	3.57	11	11	0	0	0	68	74	31	27	36	55
	—Calgary (PCL)	1	4	.200	3.43	10	0	0	0	2	21	20	15	8	12	9
	—Seattle (A.L.)	0	1	.000	3.29	8	1	0	0	0	13⅔	12	7	5	11	6
1993	—							Did not play.								
Major league totals (1 year)		0	1	.000	3.29	8	1	0	0	0	13⅔	12	7	5	11	6

WOODSON, TRACY

3B/1B, PIRATES

PERSONAL: Born October 5, 1962, in Richmond, Va.... 6-3/216.... Throws right, bats right.... Full name: Tracy Michael Woodson.

HIGH SCHOOL: Benedictine (Richmond, Va.).

COLLEGE: North Carolina State.

TRANSACTIONS/CAREER NOTES: Selected by Los Angeles Dodgers organization in third round of free-agent draft (June 4, 1984).... On Los Angeles disabled list (June 19-July 4, 1989).... Traded by Dodgers to Chicago White Sox for P Jeff Bittiger (November 9, 1989).... Released by White Sox organization (November 30, 1990).... Signed by Atlanta Braves organization (February 8, 1991).... Granted free agency (October 15, 1991).... Signed by Louisville, St. Louis Cardinals organization (December 26, 1991).... Granted free agency (October 15, 1993).... Signed by Buffalo, Pittsburgh Pirates organization (November 22, 1993).

STATISTICAL NOTES: Led Florida State League third basemen with .926 fielding percentage, 111 putouts and 408 total chances in 1985.... Led Texas League third basemen with .947 fielding percentage, 135 putouts and 413 total chances in 1986.... Tied for Pacific Coast League lead in grounding into double plays with 18 in 1990.... Led American Association third basemen with 108 putouts in 1992.

Year	Team (League)	Pos.	G	AB	R	H	2B	3B	HR	RBI	Avg.	BB	SO	SB	PO	A	E	Avg.
			BATTING												FIELDING			
1984	—Vero Beach (FSL)	1B	76	256	29	56	9	0	4	36	.219	27	41	7	630	38	9	.987
1985	—Vero Beach (FSL)	3B-1B	138	504	55	126	30	4	9	62	.250	50	78	10	†131	270	30	†.930
1986	—San Antonio (Tex.)	3B-SS	131	495	65	133	27	3	18	90	.269	33	59	4	†135	259	22	†.947
1987	—Los Angeles (N.L.)	3B-1B	53	136	14	31	8	1	1	11	.228	9	21	1	58	58	4	.967
	—Albuquerque (PCL)	3B-1B	67	259	37	75	13	2	5	44	.290	17	22	1	285	90	15	.962
1988	—Albuquerque (PCL)	1-3-2-S	85	313	46	100	27	1	17	73	.319	39	48	1	493	131	14	.978
	—Los Angeles (N.L.)	3B-1B	65	173	15	43	4	1	3	15	.249	7	32	1	160	60	6	.973
1989	—Albuquerque (PCL)	3B-1B	89	325	49	95	21	0	14	59	.292	32	40	2	296	132	13	.971
	—Los Angeles (N.L.)	3B	4	6	0	0	0	0	0	0	.000	0	1	0	1	1	0	1.000
1990	—Vancouver (PCL)■	3B-1B	131	480	70	128	22	5	17	81	.267	50	70	6	470	163	16	.975
1991	—Richmond (Int'l)■	3B-1B-OF	120	441	43	122	20	3	6	56	.277	28	43	1	277	166	20	.957
1992	—Louisville (A.A.)■	3-0-1-S	109	412	62	122	23	2	12	59	.296	24	46	4	†127	271	26	.939
	—St. Louis (N.L.)	3B-1B	31	114	9	35	8	0	1	22	.307	3	10	0	43	38	3	.964
1993	—St. Louis (N.L.)	3B-1B	62	77	4	16	2	0	0	2	.208	1	14	0	56	25	4	.953
Major league totals (5 years)			215	506	42	125	22	2	5	50	.247	20	78	2	318	182	17	.967

CHAMPIONSHIP SERIES RECORD

Year	Team (League)	Pos.	BATTING G	AB	R	H	2B	3B	HR	RBI	Avg.	BB	SO	SB	FIELDING PO	A	E	Avg.
1988	—Los Angeles (N.L.) ...	1B-PH	3	4	0	1	0	0	0	0	.250	0	1	0	3	0	0	1.000

WORLD SERIES RECORD

Year	Team (League)	Pos.	BATTING G	AB	R	H	2B	3B	HR	RBI	Avg.	BB	SO	SB	FIELDING PO	A	E	Avg.
1988	—Los Angeles (N.L.) ...	PH-1B	4	4	0	0	0	0	0	1	.000	0	0	0	6	1	0	1.000

WORRELL, TIM

P, PADRES

PERSONAL: Born July 5, 1967, in Pasadena, Calif. . . . 6-4/220. . . . Throws right, bats right. . . . Full name: Timothy Howard Worrell. . . . Brother of Todd Worrell, pitcher, Los Angeles Dodgers. . . . Name pronounced wor-RELL.
HIGH SCHOOL: Maranatha (Sierra Madre, Calif.).
COLLEGE: Biola University (Calif.).
TRANSACTIONS/CAREER NOTES: Selected by San Diego Padres organization in 20th round of free-agent draft (June 5, 1989).
STATISTICAL NOTES: Pitched 2-0 no-hit victory for Las Vegas against Phoenix (September 5, 1992).

Year	Team (League)	W	L	Pct.	ERA	G	GS	CG	ShO	Sv.	IP	H	R	ER	BB	SO
1989	—							Did not play.								
1990	—Char., S.C. (S. Atl.)	5	8	.385	4.64	20	19	3	0	0	110⅔	120	65	57	28	68
1991	—Waterloo (Midw.)	8	4	.667	3.34	14	14	3	2	0	86⅓	70	36	32	33	83
	—High Desert (Calif.)	5	2	.714	4.24	11	11	2	0	0	63⅔	65	32	30	33	70
1992	—Wichita (Texas)	8	6	.571	2.86	19	19	1	1	0	125⅔	115	46	40	32	109
	—Las Vegas (PCL)	4	2	.667	4.26	10	10	1	1	0	63⅓	61	32	30	19	32
1993	—Las Vegas (PCL)	5	6	.455	5.48	15	14	2	0	0	87	102	61	53	26	89
	—San Diego (N.L.)	2	7	.222	4.92	21	16	0	0	0	100⅔	104	63	55	43	52
Major league totals (1 year)		2	7	.222	4.92	21	16	0	0	0	100⅔	104	63	55	43	52

WORRELL, TODD

P, DODGERS

PERSONAL: Born September 28, 1959, in Arcadia, Calif. . . . 6-5/222. . . . Throws right, bats right. . . . Full name: Todd Roland Worrell. . . . Brother of Tim Worrell, pitcher, San Diego Padres. . . . Name pronounced wor-RELL.
HIGH SCHOOL: Maranatha (Sierra Madre, Calif.).
COLLEGE: Biola College, Calif. (bachelor of science degree in Christian education).
TRANSACTIONS/CAREER NOTES: Selected by St. Louis Cardinals organization in first round (21st pick overall) of free-agent draft (June 7, 1982). . . . On St. Louis disabled list (May 14-June 7, 1989); included rehabilitation assignment to Louisville (June 6-7). . . . On disabled list (March 31, 1990-entire season). . . . On St. Louis disabled list (April 4, 1991-entire season); included rehabilitation assignment to Louisville (May 4-10). . . . Granted free agency (October 26, 1992). . . . Signed by Los Angeles Dodgers (December 9, 1992). . . . On Los Angeles disabled list (April 8-May 27, 1993); included rehabilitation assignment to Bakersfield (May 23-27). . . . On Los Angeles disabled list (June 11-July 15, 1993); included rehabilitation assignment to Albuquerque (June 30-July 15).
RECORDS: Holds major league rookie-season record for most saves—36 (1986).
HONORS: Named righthanded pitcher on THE SPORTING NEWS college All-America team (1982). . . . Named N.L. Rookie Pitcher of the Year by THE SPORTING NEWS (1986). . . . Named N.L. Fireman of the Year by THE SPORTING NEWS (1986). . . . Named N.L. Rookie of the Year by Baseball Writers' Association of America (1986).
MISCELLANEOUS: Appeared in two games as outfielder with no chances (1986). . . . Appeared in one game as outfielder with no chances (1987 and St. Louis, 1989).

Year	Team (League)	W	L	Pct.	ERA	G	GS	CG	ShO	Sv.	IP	H	R	ER	BB	SO
1982	—Erie (N.Y.-Penn)	4	1	.800	3.31	9	8	0	0	0	51⅔	52	23	19	15	57
1983	—Louisville (A.A.)	4	2	.667	4.74	15	14	1	0	0	79⅔	76	49	42	42	46
	—Arkansas (Texas)	5	2	.714	3.07	10	10	4	0	0	70⅓	57	33	24	37	74
1984	—Arkansas (Texas)	3	10	.231	4.49	18	18	5	0	0	100⅓	109	72	50	67	88
	—St. Peters. (FSL)	3	2	.600	2.09	8	7	2	0	0	47⅓	41	22	11	24	33
1985	—Louisville (A.A.)	8	6	.571	3.60	34	17	2	1	11	127⅔	114	59	51	47	*126
	—St. Louis (N.L.)	3	0	1.000	2.91	17	0	0	0	5	21⅔	17	7	7	7	17
1986	—St. Louis (N.L.)	9	10	.474	2.08	74	0	0	0	*36	103⅔	86	29	24	41	73
1987	—St. Louis (N.L.)	8	6	.571	2.66	75	0	0	0	33	94⅔	86	29	28	34	92
1988	—St. Louis (N.L.)	5	9	.357	3.00	68	0	0	0	32	90	69	32	30	34	78
1989	—St. Louis (N.L.)	3	5	.375	2.96	47	0	0	0	20	51⅔	42	21	17	26	41
	—Louisville (A.A.)	0	0	...	0.00	1	1	0	0	0	1	0	0	0	0	1
1990	—							Did not play.								
1991	—Louisville (A.A.)	0	0	...	18.00	3	3	0	0	0	3	4	6	6	3	4
1992	—St. Louis (N.L.)	5	3	.625	2.11	67	0	0	0	3	64	45	15	15	25	64
1993	—Los Angeles (N.L.)■	1	1	.500	6.05	35	0	0	0	5	38⅔	46	28	26	11	31
	—Bakersfield (Calif.)	0	0	...	0.00	2	2	0	0	0	2	1	0	0	0	5
	—Albuquerque (PCL)	1	0	1.000	1.04	7	2	0	0	0	8⅔	7	2	1	2	13
Major league totals (7 years)		34	34	.500	2.85	383	0	0	0	134	464⅓	391	161	147	178	396

CHAMPIONSHIP SERIES RECORD

CHAMPIONSHIP SERIES NOTES: Appeared in one game as outfielder (1987).

Year	Team (League)	W	L	Pct.	ERA	G	GS	CG	ShO	Sv.	IP	H	R	ER	BB	SO
1985	—St. Louis (N.L.)	1	0	1.000	1.42	4	0	0	0	0	6⅓	4	1	1	2	3
1987	—St. Louis (N.L.)	0	0	...	2.08	3	0	0	0	1	4⅓	4	1	1	1	6
Champ. series totals (2 years)		1	0	1.000	1.69	7	0	0	0	1	10⅔	8	2	2	3	9

WORLD SERIES RECORD

WORLD SERIES NOTES: Shares single-game record for most consecutive strikeouts—6 (October 24, 1985).

Year	Team (League)	W	L	Pct.	ERA	G	GS	CG	ShO	Sv.	IP	H	R	ER	BB	SO
1985	—St. Louis (N.L.)	0	1	.000	3.86	3	0	0	0	1	4⅔	4	2	2	2	6
1987	—St. Louis (N.L.)	0	0	...	1.29	4	0	0	0	2	7	6	1	1	4	3
World Series totals (2 years)		0	1	.000	2.31	7	0	0	0	3	11⅔	10	3	3	6	9

ALL-STAR GAME RECORD

Year	League	W	L	Pct.	ERA	GS	CG	ShO	Sv.	IP	H	R	ER	BB	SO
1988	—National	0	0	...	0.00	0	0	0	0	1	0	0	0	0	0

WRONA, RICK

C

PERSONAL: Born December 10, 1963, in Tulsa, Okla.... 6-1/185.... Throws right, bats right.... Full name: Richard James Wrona.... Brother of Bill Wrona, minor league infielder (1983-89).... Name pronounced RO-nah.
HIGH SCHOOL: Bishop Kelly (Tulsa, Okla.).
COLLEGE: Wichita State.
TRANSACTIONS/CAREER NOTES: Selected by Chicago Cubs organization in fifth round of free-agent draft (June 3, 1985).... Granted free agency (October 12, 1990).... Signed by Milwaukee Brewers (November 2, 1990).... Released by Brewers (April 1, 1991).... Signed by Tulsa, Texas Rangers organization (May 13, 1991).... Released by Tulsa (June 18, 1991).... Signed by Cincinnati Reds organization (November 12, 1991).... On Nashville disabled list (May 20-June 1, 1992).... Granted free agency (October 15, 1992).... Signed by Nashville, Chicago White Sox organization (December 29, 1992).... Granted free agency (October 15, 1993).
MISCELLANEOUS: Batted as switch-hitter (1985).

			BATTING												FIELDING			
Year	Team (League)	Pos.	G	AB	R	H	2B	3B	HR	RBI	Avg.	BB	SO	SB	PO	A	E	Avg.
1985	—Peoria (Midwest)	C	6	16	2	4	1	0	0	2	.250	2	5	0	31	1	2	.941
	—Winst.-Salem (Car.)	C	20	49	4	11	4	0	0	2	.224	3	15	0	90	10	3	.971
1986	—Winst.-Salem (Car.)	C-0-3-1	91	267	43	68	15	0	4	32	.255	25	37	5	464	74	11	.980
1987	—Pittsfield (Eastern)	C-1B	70	218	22	48	10	3	1	25	.220	7	32	5	299	49	9	.975
1988	—Pittsfield (Eastern)	C	5	6	0	0	0	0	0	1	.000	1	2	0	11	1	0	1.000
	—Iowa (Am. Assoc.)	C	83	193	28	51	9	0	2	23	.264	17	34	0	347	36	7	.982
	—Chicago (N.L.)	C	4	6	0	0	0	0	0	0	.000	0	1	0	11	0	1	.917
1989	—Chicago (N.L.)	C	38	92	11	26	2	1	2	14	.283	2	21	0	158	15	3	.983
	—Iowa (Am. Assoc.)	C-1B-OF	60	189	15	41	8	3	2	13	.217	7	40	1	340	41	6	.984
1990	—Chicago (N.L.)	C	16	29	3	5	0	0	0	0	.172	2	11	1	55	9	2	.970
	—Iowa (Am. Assoc.)	C-1B	58	146	16	33	4	0	2	15	.226	10	35	0	311	37	6	.983
1991	—Tulsa (Texas)■	C-OF	27	82	4	13	0	1	3	7	.159	5	18	0	109	14	2	.984
1992	—Cincinnati (N.L.)■	C-1B	11	23	0	4	0	0	0	0	.174	0	3	0	52	5	2	.966
	—Nashville (A.A.)	C-OF-3B	40	118	16	29	8	2	2	10	.246	5	21	1	180	12	5	.975
1993	—Nashville (A.A.)■	C	73	184	24	39	13	0	3	22	.212	11	35	0	400	52	5	.989
	—Chicago (A.L.)	C	4	8	0	1	0	0	0	1	.125	0	4	0	12	0	0	1.000
American League totals (1 year)			4	8	0	1	0	0	0	1	.125	0	4	0	12	0	0	1.000
National League totals (4 years)			69	150	14	35	2	1	2	14	.233	4	36	1	276	29	8	.974
Major league totals (5 years)			73	158	14	36	2	1	2	15	.228	4	40	1	288	29	8	.975

CHAMPIONSHIP SERIES RECORD

			BATTING												FIELDING			
Year	Team (League)	Pos.	G	AB	R	H	2B	3B	HR	RBI	Avg.	BB	SO	SB	PO	A	E	Avg.
1989	—Chicago (N.L.)	C	2	5	0	0	0	0	0	0	.000	0	3	0	9	1	0	1.000

YAUGHN, KIP

P, MARLINS

PERSONAL: Born July 20, 1969, in Walnut Creek, Calif.... 6-0/180.... Throws right, bats right.... Full name: Kip Edwin Yaughn.
HIGH SCHOOL: Antioch (Calif.) then Clayton Valley (Concord, Calif.).
COLLEGE: Arizona State.
TRANSACTIONS/CAREER NOTES: Selected by Baltimore Orioles organization in 13th round of free-agent draft (June 4, 1990).... On disabled list (July 6-August 28, 1992).... Selected by Florida Marlins in first round (24th pick overall) of expansion draft (November 17, 1992).... On Florida disabled list (March 27-August 9, 1993); included rehabilitation assignment to High Desert (August 1-9).

Year	Team (League)	W	L	Pct.	ERA	G	GS	CG	ShO	Sv.	IP	H	R	ER	BB	SO
1990	—Wausau (Midwest)	2	4	.333	5.29	10	10	0	0	0	51	46	32	30	29	47
1991	—Frederick (Caro.)	11	8	.579	3.94	27	27	1	0	0	162	168	88	71	76	155
1992	—Hagerstown (East.)	7	8	.467	3.48	18	18	5	0	0	116⅓	88	52	45	33	106
1993	—High Desert (Calif.)■	0	0	...	6.86	6	6	0	0	0	21	25	17	16	13	13
	—Edmonton (PCL)	1	0	1.000	0.00	1	1	0	0	0	5	6	0	0	1	2

YELDING, ERIC

2B, CUBS

PERSONAL: Born February 22, 1965, in Montrose, Ala.... 5-11/165.... Throws right, bats right.... Full name: Eric Girard Yelding.
HIGH SCHOOL: Fairhope (Montrose, Ala.).
COLLEGE: Chipola Junior College (Fla.).
TRANSACTIONS/CAREER NOTES: Selected by Toronto Blue Jays organization in first round (19th pick overall) of free-agent draft (January 17, 1984).... Selected by Chicago Cubs from Blue Jays organization in Rule 5 major league draft (December 5, 1988).... Claimed on waivers by Houston Astros (April 3, 1989).... On suspended list for one game (April 19, 1991).... On Tucson disabled list (August 12-September 13, 1991).... Traded by Astros to Chicago White Sox (July 10, 1992), completing deal in which White Sox traded P Rich Scheid to Astros for a player to be named later (July 4, 1992).... Released by White Sox organization (August 24, 1992).... Signed by Cincinnati Reds organization (November 16, 1992).... Released by Reds organization (March 23, 1993).... Signed by Iowa, Cubs organization (March 30, 1993).... Granted free agency (October 3, 1993).... Re-signed by Cubs organization (January 11, 1994).

STATISTICAL NOTES: Led Pioneer League in caught stealing with 11 in 1984. . . . Led Carolina League in caught stealing with 26 in 1985. . . . Led California League shortstops with 573 total chances in 1986. . . . Led International League in caught stealing with 23 in 1988. . . . Led International League second basemen with 21 errors in 1988. . . . Led N.L. in caught stealing with 25 in 1990.

			BATTING												FIELDING			
Year	Team (League)	Pos.	G	AB	R	H	2B	3B	HR	RBI	Avg.	BB	SO	SB	PO	A	E	Avg.
1984	—Medicine Hat (Pio.) ..	OF	67	*304	61	94	14	6	4	29	.309	26	46	31	99	9	13	.893
1985	—Kinston (Carolina) ...	OF	135	526	59	137	14	4	2	31	.260	33	70	*62	310	10	9	.973
1986	—Vent. Co. (Calif.)	SS	131	*560	83	157	14	7	4	40	.280	33	84	41	*231	284	*58	.899
1987	—Myrtle Beach (SAL) ..	SS	88	357	53	109	12	2	1	31	.305	18	30	73	126	226	45	.887
	—Knoxville (South.)	SS	39	150	23	30	6	1	0	7	.200	12	25	10	64	92	14	.918
1988	—Syracuse (Int'l)	2B-SS	•138	*556	•69	139	15	2	1	38	.250	36	102	*59	222	310	†35	.938
1989	—Houston (N.L.)■........	SS-2B-OF	70	90	19	21	2	0	0	9	.233	7	19	11	37	57	3	.969
1990	—Houston (N.L.)..........	0-S-2-3	142	511	69	130	9	5	1	28	.254	39	87	64	315	124	17	.963
1991	—Houston (N.L.)..........	SS-OF	78	276	19	67	11	1	1	20	.243	13	46	11	114	166	20	.933
	—Tucson (PCL)	SS	11	43	6	17	3	0	0	3	.395	4	4	4	22	24	2	.958
1992	—Tucs.-Vanc. (PCL)■	OF-SS	93	338	47	89	11	5	0	29	.263	26	67	32	154	113	13	.954
	—Houston (N.L.)..........	OF-SS	9	8	1	2	0	0	0	0	.250	0	3	0	1	0	0	1.000
1993	—Chicago (N.L.)■........	2-3-0-S	69	108	14	22	5	1	1	10	.204	11	22	3	52	86	4	.972
	Major league totals (5 years)		368	993	122	242	27	7	3	67	.244	70	177	89	519	433	44	.956

YOUNG, ANTHONY

P, METS

PERSONAL: Born January 19, 1966, in Houston. . . . 6-2/200. . . . Throws right, bats right. . . . Full name: Anthony Wayne Young.

HIGH SCHOOL: Furr (Houston).

COLLEGE: Houston.

TRANSACTIONS/CAREER NOTES: Selected by Montreal Expos organization in 10th round of free-agent draft (June 4, 1984). . . . Selected by New York Mets organization in 38th round of free-agent draft (June 2, 1987). . . . On disabled list (July 19, 1989-remainder of season and June 11-18, 1990).

RECORDS: Holds major league record for most consecutive games lost—27 (May 6, 1992 through July 24, 1993). . . . Holds modern N.L. rookie-season record for most consecutive games lost—14 (1992).

HONORS: Named Texas League Pitcher of the Year (1990).

Year	Team (League)	W	L	Pct.	ERA	G	GS	CG	ShO	Sv.	IP	H	R	ER	BB	SO
1987	—Little Falls (NYP)	3	4	.429	4.53	14	9	0	0	0	53⅔	58	37	27	25	48
1988	—Little Falls (NYP)	3	5	.375	2.20	15	10	4	0	0	73⅔	51	33	18	34	75
1989	—Columbia (S. Atl.).......	9	6	.600	3.49	21	17	8	1	0	129	115	60	50	55	127
1990	—Jackson (Texas)........	*15	3	.833	*1.65	23	23	3	1	0	158	116	38	29	52	95
1991	—Tidewater (Int'l).........	7	9	.438	3.73	25	25	3	1	0	164	172	74	68	67	93
	—New York (N.L.)	2	5	.286	3.10	10	8	0	0	0	49⅓	48	20	17	12	20
1992	—New York (N.L.)	2	14	.125	4.17	52	13	1	0	15	121	134	66	56	31	64
1993	—New York (N.L.)	1	16	.059	3.77	39	10	1	0	3	100⅓	103	62	42	42	62
	—Norfolk (Int'l)	1	1	.500	1.13	3	3	0	0	0	16	14	2	2	5	8
	Major league totals (3 years) ..	5	35	.125	3.82	101	31	2	0	18	270⅔	285	148	115	85	146

IN MEMORIAM

YOUNG, CLIFF

P

PERSONAL: Born August 2, 1964, in Willis, Tex. . . . Died November 4, 1993. . . . 6-4/210. . . . Threw left, batted left. . . . Full name: Clifford Raphael Young.

HIGH SCHOOL: Willis (Tex.).

TRANSACTIONS/CAREER NOTES: Selected by Montreal Expos organization in fifth round of free-agent draft (June 6, 1983). . . . On suspended list (May 23-30, 1984). . . . Traded by Expos organization to Toronto Blue Jays organization (September 10, 1985), completing deal in which Blue Jays traded OF Mitch Webster to Expos for a player to be named later (June 22, 1985). . . . On disabled list (August 20-30, 1986). . . . Selected by Oakland Athletics from Blue Jays organization in Rule 5 major league draft (December 8, 1986). . . . Returned to Blue Jays organization (April 6, 1987). . . . Traded by Blue Jays organization to California Angels for P DeWayne Buice (March 9, 1989). . . . On disabled list (August 4-23, 1992). . . . Granted free agency (October 15, 1992). . . . Signed by Charlotte, Cleveland Indians organization (January 5, 1993). . . . On Cleveland disabled list (July 26, 1993-remainder of season). . . . Granted free agency (October 15, 1993).

STATISTICAL NOTES: Led Florida State League with 13 home runs allowed in 1986.

Year	Team (League)	W	L	Pct.	ERA	G	GS	CG	ShO	Sv.	IP	H	R	ER	BB	SO
1983	—Calgary (Pioneer)	7	1	.875	5.11	13	13	4	0	0	79⅓	98	55	45	32	72
1984	—Gastonia (S. Atl.)	8	10	.444	4.18	24	24	7	2	0	144⅓	117	77	67	68	121
1985	—W.P. Beach (FSL)	15	5	.750	3.98	25	25	7	0	0	153⅔	149	77	68	57	112
1986	—Knoxville (South.)■....	12	*14	.462	3.89	31	*31	1	0	0	*203⅔	*232	111	88	71	121
1987	—Knoxville (South.)■....	8	9	.471	4.45	42	12	0	0	1	119⅓	148	76	59	43	81
1988	—Syracuse (Int'l)...........	9	6	.600	3.42	33	18	4	1	1	147⅓	133	68	56	32	75
1989	—Edmonton (PCL)■......	8	9	.471	4.79	31	21	2	1	0	139	158	80	74	32	89
1990	—Edmonton (PCL)	7	4	.636	2.42	30	0	0	0	4	52	45	15	14	10	30
	—California (A.L.)	1	1	.500	3.52	17	0	0	0	0	30⅔	40	14	12	7	19
1991	—California (A.L.)	1	0	1.000	4.26	11	0	0	0	0	12⅔	12	6	6	3	6
	—Edmonton (PCL)	4	8	.333	4.90	34	8	0	0	5	71⅔	88	53	39	25	39
1992	—Edmonton (PCL)	10	8	.556	5.59	28	20	5	1	0	143⅓	174	94	89	42	104
1993	—Charlotte (Int'l)■........	3	1	.750	2.15	5	5	1	1	0	37⅔	30	10	9	2	21
	—Cleveland (A.L.)	3	3	.500	4.62	21	7	0	0	1	60⅓	74	35	31	18	31
	Major league totals (3 years) ..	5	4	.556	4.25	49	7	0	0	1	103⅔	126	55	49	28	56

YOUNG, CURT

P

PERSONAL: Born April 16, 1960, in Saginaw, Mich. . . . 6-1/175. . . . Throws left, bats right. . . . Full name: Curtis Allen Young.

HIGH SCHOOL: Arthur Hill (Saginaw, Mich.).

COLLEGE: Central Michigan.

TRANSACTIONS/CAREER NOTES: Selected by Oakland Athletics organization in fourth round of free-agent draft (June 8, 1981). . . . On Oakland disabled list (May 3-July 5, 1985); included rehabilitation assignment to Modesto (June 29-July 5). . . . On disabled list (June 30-July 20, 1987 and June 2-17, 1991). . . . Granted free agency (October 28, 1991). . . . Signed by Omaha, Kansas City Royals organization (February 12, 1992). . . . Released by Royals (June 10, 1992). . . . Signed by Columbus, New York Yankees organization (June 16, 1992). . . . On New York disabled list (August 5-September 1, 1992). . . . Granted free agency (November 6, 1992). . . . Signed by A's organization (December 7, 1992). . . . On Oakland disabled list (June 15-July 5 and July 6, 1993-remainder of season). . . . Released by A's (October 8, 1993).

MISCELLANEOUS: Appeared in one game as pinch-runner (1990). . . . Made an out in only at-bat (1991).

Year	Team (League)	W	L	Pct.	ERA	G	GS	CG	ShO	Sv.	IP	H	R	ER	BB	SO
1981	—Medford (N'west)	2	2	.500	4.25	8	8	3	1	0	53	45	27	25	32	49
	—Modesto (Calif.)	2	1	.667	3.48	5	4	1	0	0	31	28	15	12	16	22
1982	—Modesto (Calif.)	15	8	.652	3.47	28	*28	12	1	0	205	189	90	79	81	162
1983	—Tacoma (PCL)	12	9	.571	5.05	27	25	2	0	0	158⅔	175	94	89	52	109
	—Oakland (A.L.)	0	1	.000	16.00	8	2	0	0	0	9	17	17	16	5	5
1984	—Tacoma (PCL)	6	4	.600	3.78	14	14	5	1	0	95⅓	88	45	40	28	61
	—Oakland (A.L.)	9	4	.692	4.06	20	17	2	1	0	108⅔	118	53	49	31	41
1985	—Oakland (A.L.)	0	4	.000	7.24	19	7	0	0	0	46	57	38	37	22	19
	—Modesto (Calif.)	0	0	...	4.76	2	2	0	0	0	5⅔	7	4	3	6	3
	—Tacoma (PCL)	2	0	1.000	3.60	3	3	0	0	0	15	10	7	6	7	8
1986	—Tacoma (PCL)	4	0	1.000	2.00	4	4	1	0	0	27	16	7	6	6	28
	—Oakland (A.L.)	13	9	.591	3.45	29	27	5	2	0	198	176	88	76	57	116
1987	—Oakland (A.L.)	13	7	.650	4.08	31	31	6	0	0	203	194	102	92	44	124
1988	—Oakland (A.L.)	11	8	.579	4.14	26	26	1	0	0	156⅓	162	77	72	50	69
1989	—Oakland (A.L.)	5	9	.357	3.73	25	20	1	0	0	111	117	56	46	47	55
1990	—Oakland (A.L.)	9	6	.600	4.85	26	21	0	0	0	124⅓	124	70	67	53	56
1991	—Oakland (A.L.)	4	2	.667	5.00	41	1	0	0	0	68⅓	74	38	38	34	27
1992	—Omaha (A.A.)■	0	1	.000	5.40	2	2	0	0	0	10	15	6	6	2	6
	—K.C.-N.Y. (A.L.)■	4	2	.667	3.99	23	7	0	0	0	67⅔	80	35	30	17	20
	—Columbus (Int'l)	3	0	1.000	3.38	3	3	0	0	0	16	16	6	6	6	2
1993	—Tacoma (PCL)■	6	1	.857	1.93	10	10	1	0	0	65⅓	53	23	14	16	31
	—Oakland (A.L.)	1	1	.500	4.30	3	3	0	0	0	14⅔	14	7	7	6	4
	Major league totals (11 years)	69	53	.566	4.31	251	162	15	3	0	1107	1133	581	530	366	536

CHAMPIONSHIP SERIES RECORD

Year	Team (League)	W	L	Pct.	ERA	G	GS	CG	ShO	Sv.	IP	H	R	ER	BB	SO
1988	—Oakland (A.L.)	0	0	...	0.00	1	0	0	0	0	1⅓	1	1	0	0	2
1989	—Oakland (A.L.)							Did not play.								
1990	—Oakland (A.L.)							Did not play.								
	Champ. series totals (1 year)	0	0	...	0.00	1	0	0	0	0	1⅓	1	1	0	0	2

WORLD SERIES RECORD

Year	Team (League)	W	L	Pct.	ERA	G	GS	CG	ShO	Sv.	IP	H	R	ER	BB	SO
1988	—Oakland (A.L.)	0	0	...	0.00	1	0	0	0	0	1	1	0	0	0	0
1989	—Oakland (A.L.)							Did not play.								
1990	—Oakland (A.L.)	0	0	...	0.00	1	0	0	0	0	1	1	0	0	0	0
	World Series totals (2 years)	0	0	...	0.00	2	0	0	0	0	2	2	0	0	0	0

YOUNG, ERIC

OF/2B, ROCKIES

PERSONAL: Born May 18, 1967, in New Brunswick, N.J. . . . 5-9/180. . . . Throws right, bats right. . . . Full name: Eric Orlando Young.

HIGH SCHOOL: New Brunswick (N.J.).

COLLEGE: Rutgers.

TRANSACTIONS/CAREER NOTES: Selected by Los Angeles Dodgers organization in 43rd round of free-agent draft (June 5, 1989). . . . Selected by Colorado Rockies in first round (11th pick overall) of expansion draft (November 17, 1992).

STATISTICAL NOTES: Led Florida State League second basemen with 24 errors in 1990. . . . Led Texas League in caught stealing with 26 in 1991. . . . Led Texas League second basemen with .974 fielding percentage in 1991.

			BATTING												FIELDING			
Year	Team (League)	Pos.	G	AB	R	H	2B	3B	HR	RBI	Avg.	BB	SO	SB	PO	A	E	Avg.
1989	—GC Dodgers (GCL)	2B	56	197	53	65	11	5	2	22	.330	33	16	*41	104	128	*15	.939
1990	—Vero Beach (FSL)	2B-OF	127	460	*101	132	23	7	2	50	.287	69	35	*76	156	218	†25	.937
1991	—San Antonio (Tex.)	2B-OF	127	461	82	129	17	4	3	35	.280	67	36	*70	206	282	13	†.974
	—Albuquerque (PCL)	2B	1	5	0	2	0	0	0	0	.400	0	0	0	1	2	0	1.000
1992	—Albuquerque (PCL)	2B	94	350	61	118	16	5	3	49	.337	33	18	28	210	287	•20	.961
	—Los Angeles (N.L.)	2B	49	132	9	34	1	0	1	11	.258	8	9	6	85	114	9	.957
1993	—Colorado (N.L.)■	2B-OF	144	490	82	132	16	8	3	42	.269	63	41	42	254	230	18	.964
	Major league totals (2 years)		193	622	91	166	17	8	4	53	.267	71	50	48	339	344	27	.962

YOUNG, ERNIE

OF, ATHLETICS

PERSONAL: Born July 8, 1969, in Chicago. . . . 6-1/190. . . . Throws right, bats right. . . . Full name: Ernest Wesley Young.

HIGH SCHOOL: Mendel Catholic (Chicago).

COLLEGE: Lewis (Ill.).

TRANSACTIONS/CAREER NOTES: Selected by Oakland Athletics organization in 10th round of free-agent draft (June 4, 1990). . . . On disabled list (July 11, 1992-remainder of season).

STATISTICAL NOTES: Led California League with .635 slugging percentage in 1993.

			BATTING												FIELDING			
Year	Team (League)	Pos.	G	AB	R	H	2B	3B	HR	RBI	Avg.	BB	SO	SB	PO	A	E	Avg.
1990	—S. Oregon (N'west)...	OF	50	168	34	47	6	2	6	23	.280	29	53	4	62	5	2	.971
1991	—Madison (Midwest)..	OF	114	362	75	92	19	2	15	71	.254	58	115	20	204	9	7	.968
1992	—Modesto (Calif.)........	OF	74	253	55	63	12	4	11	33	.249	47	74	11	126	11	6	.958
1993	—Modesto (Calif.)........	OF	85	301	83	92	18	6	23	71	.306	72	92	23	178	8	3	.984
	—Huntsville (South.)...	OF	45	120	26	25	5	0	5	15	.208	24	36	8	97	8	4	.963

YOUNG, GERALD

OF

PERSONAL: Born October 22, 1964, in Tele, Honduras. . . . 6-2/185. . . . Throws right, bats both. . . . Full name: Gerald Anthony Young.

HIGH SCHOOL: Valley (Santa Ana, Calif.).

TRANSACTIONS/CAREER NOTES: Selected by New York Mets organization in fifth round of free-agent draft (June 7, 1982). . . . Traded by Mets organization with IF Manny Lee to Houston Astros (August 31, 1984), as partial completion of deal in which Mets acquired IF Ray Knight for three players to be named later (August 28, 1984); Astros acquired P Mitch Cook to complete deal (September 10, 1984). . . . On Houston disabled list (April 1-June 25, 1992); included rehabilitation assignment to Tucson (May 6-14, May 30-June 4 and June 18-25). . . . Granted free agency (October 5, 1992). . . . Signed by Colorado Rockies (October 29, 1992). . . . Released by Rockies (May 19, 1993). . . . Signed by Indianapolis, Cincinnati Reds organization (June 4, 1993). . . . Released by Indianapolis (July 20, 1993). . . . Signed by Calgary, Seattle Mariners organization (August 7, 1993). . . . Granted free agency (October 15, 1993).

STATISTICAL NOTES: Tied for Appalachian League lead in being hit by pitch with six in 1982. . . . Led Appalachian League shortstops with 38 errors in 1982. . . . Tied for Florida State League lead in double plays by outfielder with five in 1985. . . . Led Southern League in caught stealing with 27 in 1986. . . . Led N.L. in caught stealing with 25 in 1989 and tied for lead with 27 in 1988. . . . Led N.L. outfielders with 428 total chances and tied for lead with five double plays in 1989.

			BATTING												FIELDING			
Year	Team (League)	Pos.	G	AB	R	H	2B	3B	HR	RBI	Avg.	BB	SO	SB	PO	A	E	Avg.
1982	—Kingsport (Appal.)...	SS-2B-3B	59	197	27	35	6	1	0	15	.178	33	52	7	79	170	†39	.865
1983	—GC Mets (GCL)..........	OF-SS	56	177	34	42	7	2	1	14	.237	35	29	11	88	9	7	.933
1984	—Columbia (S. Atl.).....	OF	124	396	69	84	14	3	1	52	.212	84	69	43	254	7	4	.985
1985	—Osceola (Fla. St.)■...	OF	133	474	88	121	20	9	3	48	.255	86	48	31	251	11	5	.981
1986	—Columbus (South.)...	OF	136	539	101	151	30	4	9	62	.280	67	57	*54	317	22	13	.963
1987	—Tucson (PCL)...........	OF	86	340	59	99	15	5	2	31	.291	47	32	43	232	7	7	.972
	—Houston (N.L.)..........	OF	71	274	44	88	9	2	1	15	.321	26	27	26	143	5	3	.980
1988	—Houston (N.L.)..........	OF	149	576	79	148	21	9	0	37	.257	66	66	65	357	10	3	.992
1989	—Houston (N.L.)..........	OF	146	533	71	124	17	3	0	38	.233	74	60	34	*412	*15	1	*.998
1990	—Houston (N.L.)..........	OF	57	154	15	27	4	1	1	4	.175	20	23	6	99	4	1	.990
	—Tucson (PCL)...........	OF	49	183	37	61	7	4	0	24	.333	40	18	14	112	8	6	.952
1991	—Tucson (PCL)...........	OF	24	79	14	24	2	3	0	17	.304	14	8	3	45	4	0	1.000
	—Houston (N.L.)..........	OF	108	142	26	31	3	1	1	11	.218	24	17	16	96	4	0	1.000
1992	—Tucson (PCL)...........	OF	20	74	15	23	2	1	0	2	.311	14	4	13	43	5	1	.980
	—Houston (N.L.)..........	OF	74	76	14	14	1	1	0	4	.184	10	11	6	53	0	2	.964
1993	—Colorado (N.L.)■.......	OF	19	19	5	1	0	0	0	1	.053	4	1	0	15	0	2	.882
	—Indianapolis (A.A.)■.	OF	32	103	15	31	10	0	1	6	.301	18	7	7	53	0	0	1.000
	—Calgary (PCL)■........	OF	26	104	19	31	8	2	1	10	.298	20	16	7	58	1	4	.937
Major league totals (7 years)			624	1774	254	433	55	17	3	110	.244	224	205	153	1175	38	12	.990

YOUNG, KEVIN

1B, PIRATES

PERSONAL: Born June 16, 1969, in Alpena, Mich. . . . 6-2/219. . . . Throws right, bats right. . . . Full name: Kevin Stacey Young.

HIGH SCHOOL: Washington (Kansas City, Kan.).

COLLEGE: Kansas City Kansas Community College, then Southern Mississippi.

TRANSACTIONS/CAREER NOTES: Selected by Pittsburgh Pirates organization in seventh round of free-agent draft (June 4, 1990).

STATISTICAL NOTES: Tied for Southern League lead in errors by third baseman with 26 in 1991. . . . Tied for American Association lead in being hit by pitch with 11 in 1992. . . . Led American Association third basemen with 300 assists, 32 errors, 436 total chances and 41 double plays in 1992. . . . Led N.L. first basemen with .998 fielding percentage in 1993.

			BATTING												FIELDING			
Year	Team (League)	Pos.	G	AB	R	H	2B	3B	HR	RBI	Avg.	BB	SO	SB	PO	A	E	Avg.
1990	—Welland (NYP)..........	SS	72	238	46	58	16	2	5	30	.244	31	36	10	*79	118	26	.883
1991	—Salem (Carolina)......	3B	56	201	38	63	12	4	6	28	.313	20	34	3	54	93	12	.925
	—Carolina (South.).....	3B-1B	75	263	36	90	19	6	3	33	.342	15	38	9	157	116	‡28	.907
	—Buffalo (A.A.)...........	3B-1B	4	9	1	2	1	0	0	2	.222	0	0	1	6	6	2	.857
1992	—Buffalo (A.A.)...........	3B-1B	137	490	*91	154	29	6	8	65	.314	67	67	18	129	†313	†32	.932
	—Pittsburgh (N.L.)......	3B-1B	10	7	2	4	0	0	0	4	.571	2	0	1	3	1	1	.800
1993	—Pittsburgh (N.L.)......	1B-3B	141	449	38	106	24	3	6	47	.236	36	82	2	1122	112	3	†.998
Major league totals (2 years)			151	456	40	110	24	3	6	51	.241	38	82	3	1125	113	4	.997

YOUNG, MATT

P

PERSONAL: Born August 9, 1958, in Pasadena, Calif. . . . 6-3/210. . . . Throws left, bats left. . . . Full name: Matthew John Young.

HIGH SCHOOL: St. Francis (La Canada, Calif.).

COLLEGE: Pasadena (Calif.) City College and UCLA.

TRANSACTIONS/CAREER NOTES: Selected by Boston Red Sox organization in second round of free-agent draft (January 10, 1978). . . . Selected by Seattle Mariners organization in second round of free-agent draft (June 3, 1980). . . . On Seattle disabled list (July 4-29, 1984). . . . Traded by Mariners to Los Angeles Dodgers for P Dennis Powell and IF Mike Watters (December 10, 1986). . . . Traded by Dodgers as part of an eight-player, three-team deal in which New York Mets traded P Jesse Orosco to Oakland Athletics (December 11, 1987). A's traded Orosco with SS Alfredo Griffin and P Jay Howell to Dodgers for Young, P Bob Welch and P Jack Savage. A's then traded Savage with P Wally Whitehurst and P Kevin Tapani to Mets. . . . On disabled list (April 3, 1988-entire season). . . . Released by A's (December 21, 1988). . . . Re-signed by A's (January 19, 1989). . . . On Oakland disabled list (March 19-June 13, 1989); included rehabilitation assignment to Modesto (May 16 and

May 25-June 2) and Tacoma (June 3-9).... Granted free agency (November 13, 1989).... Signed by Mariners (December 15, 1989).... Granted free agency (November 5, 1990).... Signed by Red Sox (December 4, 1990).... On Boston disabled list (June 5-August 1, 1991); included rehabilitation assignment to Pawtucket (July 22-August 1).... On disabled list (June 29-July 15, 1992).... Released by Red Sox (March 30, 1993).... Signed by Cleveland Indians organization (April 6, 1993).... Released by Indians (August 9, 1993).... Signed by Syracuse, Toronto Blue Jays organization (August 12, 1993).... Released by Syracuse (September 8, 1993).

RECORDS: Shares major league record for most strikeouts in one inning—4 (September 9, 1990, first inning).

STATISTICAL NOTES: Pitched no-hit game against Cleveland in which he completed eight innings but lost, 2-1 (April 12, 1992, first game).

Year	Team (League)	W	L	Pct.	ERA	G	GS	CG	ShO	Sv.	IP	H	R	ER	BB	SO
1980	—Belling. (N'west)	4	5	.444	4.93	12	12	3	1	3	73	73	46	40	62	53
1981	—Lynn (Eastern)	3	9	.250	4.00	14	14	3	0	3	81	80	47	36	38	57
1982	—Salt Lake City (PCL)	12	10	.545	4.65	29	26	8	4	8	176	192	113	91	75	118
1983	—Seattle (A.L.)	11	15	.423	3.27	33	32	5	2	5	203⅔	178	86	74	79	130
1984	—Seattle (A.L.)	6	8	.429	5.72	22	22	1	0	1	113⅓	141	81	72	57	73
	—Salt Lake City (PCL)	6	0	1.000	1.51	6	6	0	0	0	41⅔	32	9	7	20	37
1985	—Seattle (A.L.)	12	*19	.387	4.91	37	35	5	2	5	218⅓	242	135	119	76	136
1986	—Seattle (A.L.)	8	6	.571	3.82	65	5	1	0	1	103⅔	108	50	44	46	82
1987	—Los Angeles (N.L.)■	5	8	.385	4.47	47	0	0	0	0	54⅓	62	30	27	17	42
1988	—■							Did not play.								
1989	—Modesto (Calif.)	0	0	...	0.75	3	3	0	0	0	12	9	1	1	6	13
	—Tacoma (PCL)	1	1	.500	2.45	2	2	0	0	0	11	8	4	3	5	6
	—Oakland (A.L.)	1	4	.200	6.75	26	4	0	0	0	37⅓	42	31	28	31	27
1990	—Seattle (A.L.)■	8	18	.308	3.51	34	33	7	1	7	225⅓	198	106	88	107	176
1991	—Boston (A.L.)■	3	7	.300	5.18	19	16	0	0	40	88⅔	92	55	51	53	69
	—Pawtucket (Int'l)	1	0	1.000	4.50	2	2	0	0	00	8	8	4	4	6	7
1992	—Boston (A.L.)	0	4	.000	4.58	28	8	1	0	0	70⅔	69	42	36	42	57
1993	—Charl.-Syrac. (Int.)■	5	1	.833	2.37	10	8	1	0	0	49⅓	33	15	13	19	55
	—Cleveland (A.L.)	1	6	.143	5.21	22	8	0	0	0	74⅓	75	45	43	57	65
	A.L. totals (9 years)	50	87	.365	4.40	286	163	20	5	19	1135⅓	1145	631	555	548	815
	N.L. totals (1 year)	5	8	.385	4.47	47	0	0	0	0	54⅓	62	30	27	17	42
	Major league totals (10 years)	55	95	.367	4.40	333	163	20	5	19	1189⅔	1207	661	582	565	857

CHAMPIONSHIP SERIES RECORD

Year	Team (League)	W	L	Pct.	ERA	G	GS	CG	ShO	Sv.	IP	H	R	ER	BB	SO
1989	—Oakland (A.L.)	0	0	...	0.00	1	0	0	0	0	⅓	0	0	0	2	0

WORLD SERIES RECORD

Year	Team (League)	W	L	Pct.	ERA	G	GS	CG	ShO	Sv.	IP	H	R	ER	BB	SO
1989	—Oakland (A.L.)							Did not play.								

ALL-STAR GAME RECORD

Year	League	W	L	Pct.	ERA	GS	CG	ShO	Sv.	IP	H	R	ER	BB	SO
1983	—American	0	0	...	0.00	0	0	0	0	1	0	0	0	0	1

YOUNG, PETE

P, EXPOS

PERSONAL: Born March 19, 1968, in Meadville, Miss.... 6-0/225.... Throws right, bats right.... Full name: Bryan Owen Young.

HIGH SCHOOL: McComb (Miss.).

COLLEGE: Mississippi State.

TRANSACTIONS/CAREER NOTES: Selected by Cincinnati Reds organization in 22nd round of free-agent draft (June 2, 1986).... Selected by Montreal Expos organization in sixth round of free-agent draft (June 5, 1989).

Year	Team (League)	W	L	Pct.	ERA	G	GS	CG	ShO	Sv.	IP	H	R	ER	BB	SO
1989	—Jamestown (NYP)	5	2	.714	1.94	18	10	0	0	4	65	63	18	14	14	62
1990	—W.P. Beach (FSL)	8	3	.727	2.47	39	12	0	0	19	109⅓	106	36	30	27	62
1991	—Sumter (S. Atl.)	0	0	...	9.00	1	0	0	0	0	1	1	1	1	1	2
	—Harrisburg (East.)	7	5	.583	2.60	54	0	0	0	13	90	82	28	26	24	74
1992	—Indianapolis (A.A.)	6	2	.750	3.51	36	0	0	0	7	48⅔	53	19	19	21	34
	—Montreal (N.L.)	0	0	...	3.98	13	0	0	0	0	20⅓	18	9	9	9	11
1993	—Ottawa (Int'l)	4	5	.444	3.72	48	0	0	0	1	72⅔	63	32	30	33	46
	—Montreal (N.L.)	1	0	1.000	3.38	4	0	0	0	0	5⅓	4	2	2	0	3
	Major league totals (2 years)	1	0	1.000	3.86	17	0	0	0	0	25⅔	22	11	11	9	14

YOUNT, ROBIN

OF

PERSONAL: Born September 16, 1955, in Danville, Ill.... 6-0/180.... Throws right, bats right.... Brother of Larry Yount, pitcher, Houston Astros (1971).

HIGH SCHOOL: Taft (Woodland Hills, Calif.).

TRANSACTIONS/CAREER NOTES: Selected by Milwaukee Brewers organization in first round (third pick overall) of free-agent draft (June 5, 1973).... On disabled list (March 28-May 3, 1978).... Granted free agency (November 13, 1989).... Re-signed by Brewers (December 19, 1989).... On disabled list (July 6-30, 1991).... Granted free agency (November 8, 1992).... Re-signed by Brewers (January 7, 1993).... On disabled list (April 27-May 14, 1993).... Granted free agency (November 4, 1993).

RECORDS: Holds major league career record for most sacrifice flies—123.

HONORS: Named shortstop on THE SPORTING NEWS A.L. All-Star team (1978, 1980 and 1982).... Named shortstop on THE SPORTING NEWS A.L. Silver Slugger team (1980 and 1982).... Named Major League Player of the Year by THE SPORTING NEWS (1982).... Named A.L. Player of the Year by THE SPORTING NEWS (1982).... Won A.L. Gold Glove at shortstop (1982).... Named A.L. Most Valuable Player by Baseball Writers' Association of America (1982 and 1989).... Named outfielder on THE SPORTING NEWS A.L. All-Star team (1989).... Named outfielder on THE SPORTING NEWS A.L. Silver Slugger

team (1989).
STATISTICAL NOTES: Led A.L. shortstops with 831 total chances and 104 double plays and tied for lead with 290 putouts in 1976. . . . Led A.L. with 367 total bases and .578 slugging percentage in 1982. . . . Led A.L. outfielders with .997 fielding percentage in 1986. . . . Hit for the cycle (June 12, 1988).

			BATTING												FIELDING			
Year	**Team (League)**	**Pos.**	**G**	**AB**	**R**	**H**	**2B**	**3B**	**HR**	**RBI**	**Avg.**	**BB**	**SO**	**SB**	**PO**	**A**	**E**	**Avg.**
1973	—Newark (NY-Penn)..	SS	64	242	29	69	15	3	3	25	.285	31	26	8	43	85	18	.877
1974	—Milwaukee (A.L.)......	SS	107	344	48	86	14	5	3	26	.250	12	46	7	148	327	19	.962
1975	—Milwaukee (A.L.)......	SS	147	558	67	149	28	2	8	52	.267	33	69	12	273	402	*44	.939
1976	—Milwaukee (A.L.)......	SS-OF	•161	638	59	161	19	3	2	54	.252	38	69	16	‡290	510	31	.963
1977	—Milwaukee (A.L.)......	SS	154	605	66	174	34	4	4	49	.288	41	80	16	256	449	29	.960
1978	—Milwaukee (A.L.)......	SS	127	502	66	147	23	9	9	71	.293	24	43	16	246	453	30	.959
1979	—Milwaukee (A.L.)......	SS	149	577	72	154	26	5	8	51	.267	35	52	11	267	517	25	.969
1980	—Milwaukee (A.L.)......	SS	143	611	121	179	*49	10	23	87	.293	26	67	20	239	455	28	.961
1981	—Milwaukee (A.L.)......	SS	96	377	50	103	15	5	10	49	.273	22	37	4	161	370	8	*.985
1982	—Milwaukee (A.L.)......	SS	156	635	129	*210	•46	12	29	114	.331	54	63	14	253	*489	24	.969
1983	—Milwaukee (A.L.)......	SS	149	578	102	178	42	*10	17	80	.308	72	58	12	256	420	19	.973
1984	—Milwaukee (A.L.)......	SS	160	624	105	186	27	7	16	80	.298	67	67	14	199	402	18	.971
1985	—Milwaukee (A.L.)......	OF-1B	122	466	76	129	26	3	15	68	.277	49	56	10	267	5	8	.971
1986	—Milwaukee (A.L.)......	OF-1B	140	522	82	163	31	7	9	46	.312	62	73	14	365	9	2	†.995
1987	—Milwaukee (A.L.)......	OF	158	635	99	198	25	9	21	103	.312	76	94	19	380	5	5	.987
1988	—Milwaukee (A.L.)......	OF	*162	621	92	190	38	•11	13	91	.306	63	63	22	444	12	2	.996
1989	—Milwaukee (A.L.)......	OF	160	614	101	195	38	9	21	103	.318	63	71	19	361	8	7	.981
1990	—Milwaukee (A.L.)......	OF	158	587	98	145	17	5	17	77	.247	78	89	15	*422	3	4	.991
1991	—Milwaukee (A.L.)......	OF	130	503	66	131	20	4	10	77	.260	54	79	6	315	1	2	.994
1992	—Milwaukee (A.L.)......	OF	150	557	71	147	40	3	8	77	.264	53	81	15	371	6	2	.995
1993	—Milwaukee (A.L.)......	OF-1B	127	454	62	117	25	3	8	51	.258	44	93	9	342	7	1	.997
Major league totals (20 years).................			2856	11008	1632	3142	583	126	251	1406	.285	966	1350	271	5855	4850	308	.972

DIVISION SERIES RECORD

			BATTING												FIELDING			
Year	**Team (League)**	**Pos.**	**G**	**AB**	**R**	**H**	**2B**	**3B**	**HR**	**RBI**	**Avg.**	**BB**	**SO**	**SB**	**PO**	**A**	**E**	**Avg.**
1981	—Milwaukee (A.L.)......	SS	5	19	4	6	0	1	0	1	.316	2	2	1	6	16	1	.957

CHAMPIONSHIP SERIES RECORD

			BATTING												FIELDING			
Year	**Team (League)**	**Pos.**	**G**	**AB**	**R**	**H**	**2B**	**3B**	**HR**	**RBI**	**Avg.**	**BB**	**SO**	**SB**	**PO**	**A**	**E**	**Avg.**
1982	—Milwaukee (A.L.)......	SS	5	16	1	4	0	0	0	0	.250	5	0	0	11	12	1	.958

WORLD SERIES RECORD

WORLD SERIES NOTES: Shares single-game record for most at-bats in nine-inning game—6 (October 12, 1982).

			BATTING												FIELDING			
Year	**Team (League)**	**Pos.**	**G**	**AB**	**R**	**H**	**2B**	**3B**	**HR**	**RBI**	**Avg.**	**BB**	**SO**	**SB**	**PO**	**A**	**E**	**Avg.**
1982	—Milwaukee (A.L.)......	SS	7	29	6	12	3	0	1	6	.414	2	2	0	20	19	3	.929

ALL-STAR GAME RECORD

			BATTING											FIELDING			
Year	**League**	**Pos.**	**AB**	**R**	**H**	**2B**	**3B**	**HR**	**RBI**	**Avg.**	**BB**	**SO**	**SB**	**PO**	**A**	**E**	**Avg.**
1980	—American..................	SS	2	0	0	0	0	0	0	.000	0	0	0	3	2	0	1.000
1982	—American..................	SS	3	0	0	0	0	0	0	.000	0	1	0	0	2	0	1.000
1983	—American..................	SS	2	1	0	0	0	0	1	.000	1	1	0	0	1	0	1.000
All-Star Game totals (3 years)......................			7	1	0	0	0	0	1	.000	1	2	0	3	5	0	1.000

ZAMBRANO, EDDIE

OF/1B, CUBS

PERSONAL: Born February 1, 1966, in Maracaibo, Venezuela. . . . 6-3/200. . . . Throws right, bats right. . . . Full name: Eduardo Jose Zambrano. . . . Brother of Bob Zambrano, third baseman, Cubs organization; and brother of Jose Zambrano, outfielder, Boston Red Sox organization.
HIGH SCHOOL: San Martin (Maracaibo, Venezuela).
TRANSACTIONS/CAREER NOTES: Signed as free agent by Boston Red Sox organization (November 1, 1984). . . . Selected by Cleveland Indians organization from Red Sox organization in Rule 5 minor league draft (December 5, 1989). . . . Released by Indians organization (July 7, 1990). . . . Signed by Pittsburgh Pirates organization (January 10, 1991). . . . Granted free agency (October 15, 1991). . . . Signed by Buffalo, Pirates organization (November 13, 1991). . . . Granted free agency (October 15, 1992). . . . Signed by Iowa, Chicago Cubs organization (November 24, 1992).
HONORS: Named American Association Most Valuable Player (1993).
STATISTICAL NOTES: Led American Association with 11 intentional bases on balls received in 1993.

			BATTING												FIELDING			
Year	**Team (League)**	**Pos.**	**G**	**AB**	**R**	**H**	**2B**	**3B**	**HR**	**RBI**	**Avg.**	**BB**	**SO**	**SB**	**PO**	**A**	**E**	**Avg.**
1985	—Greensboro (S. Atl.)..	OF	115	443	63	120	17	3	1	51	.271	31	61	1	221	10	5	.979
1986	—Greensboro (S. Atl.)..	OF	112	395	68	94	16	5	12	65	.238	42	80	4	180	11	7	.965
1987	—Winter Haven (FSL)..	OF	69	225	33	60	16	1	11	32	.267	27	47	1	167	7	4	.978
	—New Britain (East.)..	OF	33	118	16	29	11	1	2	11	.246	10	21	1	62	3	3	.956
1988	—New Britain (East.)..	OF	121	381	36	85	13	1	8	30	.223	30	70	10	252	13	7	.974
1989	—New Britain (East.)..	OF	54	169	15	37	8	1	3	11	.219	14	27	3	120	4	2	.984
1990	—Kinston (Carolina)■.	OF	63	204	26	50	7	2	3	30	.245	29	36	1	108	8	4	.967
1991	—Carolina (South.)■...	OF	83	269	28	68	17	3	3	39	.253	22	56	4	141	8	2	.987
	—Buffalo (A.A.)..........	OF	48	144	19	49	8	5	3	35	.340	17	25	1	86	2	0	1.000
1992	—Buffalo (A.A.)..........	OF	126	394	47	112	22	4	16	79	.284	51	75	3	235	15	1	.996

Year	Team (League)	Pos.	G	AB	R	H	2B	3B	HR	RBI	Avg.	BB	SO	SB	PO	A	E	Avg.
			BATTING												FIELDING			
1993	—Iowa (Am. Assoc.)■..	OF-1B	133	469	95	142	29	2	32	*115	.303	54	93	10	503	40	7	.987
	—Chicago (N.L.)	OF-1B	8	17	1	5	0	0	0	2	.294	1	3	0	14	0	1	.933
Major league totals (1 year)			8	17	1	5	0	0	0	2	.294	1	3	0	14	0	1	.933

ZAUN, GREG

C, ORIOLES

PERSONAL: Born April 14, 1971, in Glendale, Calif. . . . 5-10/170. . . . Throws right, bats both. . . . Full name: Gregory Owen Zaun. . . . Nephew of Rick Dempsey, current manager, Albuquerque, Los Angeles Dodgers organization, and major league catcher with six teams (1969-92).
HIGH SCHOOL: St. Francis (La Canada, Calif.).
TRANSACTIONS/CAREER NOTES: Selected by Baltimore Orioles organization in 17th round of free-agent draft (June 5, 1989). . . . On Bowie disabled list (June 17-July 15, 1993).
STATISTICAL NOTES: Led Appalachian League catchers with 460 putouts and 501 total chances in 1990. . . . Led Midwest League catchers with 796 total chances in 1991. . . . Led Carolina League catchers with 746 putouts, 91 assists, 18 errors, 855 total chances and 10 double plays in 1992.

Year	Team (League)	Pos.	G	AB	R	H	2B	3B	HR	RBI	Avg.	BB	SO	SB	PO	A	E	Avg.
			BATTING												FIELDING			
1990	—Wausau (Midwest) ..	C	37	100	3	13	0	1	1	7	.130	7	17	0	270	26	3	.990
	—Bluefield (Appal.)	C-3-S-P	61	184	29	55	5	2	2	21	.299	23	15	5	†462	34	10	.980
1991	—Kane Co. (Midw.)	C	113	409	67	112	17	5	4	51	.274	50	41	4	*697	83	16	.980
1992	—Frederick (Caro.)	C-2B	108	383	54	96	18	6	6	52	.251	42	45	3	†746	†91	†18	.979
1993	—Bowie (Eastern)	C-2-3-P	79	258	25	79	10	0	3	38	.306	27	26	4	423	51	10	.979
	—Rochester (Int'l)	C	21	78	10	20	4	2	1	11	.256	6	11	0	141	18	4	.975

RECORD AS PITCHER

Year	Team (League)	W	L	Pct.	ERA	G	GS	CG	ShO	Sv.	IP	H	R	ER	BB	SO
1990	—Bluefield (Appal.)	0	0	...	0.00	1	0	0	0	0	1	1	0	0	1	1
1993	—Bowie (Eastern)	0	0	...	0.00	1	0	0	0	0	2⅓	1	0	0	0	0

ZEILE, TODD

3B, CARDINALS

PERSONAL: Born September 9, 1965, in Van Nuys, Calif. . . . 6-1/190. . . . Throws right, bats right. . . . Full name: Todd Edward Zeile. . . . Husband of Julianne McNamara, Olympic gold-medal gymnast (1984). . . . Name pronounced ZEEL.
HIGH SCHOOL: Hart (Newhall, Calif.).
COLLEGE: UCLA.
TRANSACTIONS/CAREER NOTES: Selected by Kansas City Royals organization in 30th round of free-agent draft (June 6, 1983). . . . Selected by St. Louis Cardinals organization in supplemental round ("sandwich pick" between second and third round) of free-agent draft (June 2, 1986); pick received as compensation for New York Yankees signing Type C free agent Ivan DeJesus.
RECORDS: Holds N.L. single-season record for fewest putouts by third baseman (150 or more games)—83 (1993).
HONORS: Named Midwest League co-Most Valuable Player (1987).
STATISTICAL NOTES: Led New York-Pennsylvania League with six sacrifice flies in 1986. . . . Tied for New York-Pennsylvania League lead in double plays by catcher with seven in 1986. . . . Led Texas League catchers with 687 putouts and 761 total chances in 1988. . . . Led American Association catchers with .992 fielding percentage and 17 passed balls in 1989.

Year	Team (League)	Pos.	G	AB	R	H	2B	3B	HR	RBI	Avg.	BB	SO	SB	PO	A	E	Avg.
			BATTING												FIELDING			
1986	—Erie (N.Y.-Penn)	C	70	248	40	64	14	1	14	*63	.258	37	52	5	407	*66	8	.983
1987	—Springfield (Midw.) ..	C-3B	130	487	94	142	24	4	25	*106	.292	70	85	1	867	79	14	.985
1988	—Arkansas (Texas)	C-OF-1B	129	430	95	117	33	2	19	75	.272	83	64	6	†697	66	10	.987
1989	—Louisville (A.A.)	C-3B-1B	118	453	71	131	26	3	19	85	.289	45	78	0	583	71	6	†.991
	—St. Louis (N.L.)	C	28	82	7	21	3	1	1	8	.256	9	14	0	125	10	4	.971
1990	—St. Louis (N.L.)	C-3-1-0	144	495	62	121	25	3	15	57	.244	67	77	2	648	106	15	.980
1991	—St. Louis (N.L.)	3B	155	565	76	158	36	3	11	81	.280	62	94	17	124	290	*25	.943
1992	—St. Louis (N.L.)	3B	126	439	51	113	18	4	7	48	.257	68	70	7	81	235	13	.960
	—Louisville (A.A.)	3B	21	74	11	23	4	1	5	13	.311	9	13	0	15	41	5	.918
1993	—St. Louis (N.L.)	3B	157	571	82	158	36	1	17	103	.277	70	76	5	83	310	33	.923
Major league totals (5 years)			610	2152	278	571	118	12	51	297	.265	276	331	31	1061	951	90	.957

ZIMMERMAN, MIKE

P, PIRATES

PERSONAL: Born February 6, 1969, in Brooklyn, N.Y. . . . 6-0/180. . . . Throws right, bats right. . . . Full name: Michael Alan Zimmerman.
HIGH SCHOOL: Lincoln (Brooklyn, N.Y.).
COLLEGE: South Alabama.
TRANSACTIONS/CAREER NOTES: Selected by Pittsburgh Pirates organization in supplemental round ("sandwich pick" between first and second round, 27th pick overall) of free-agent draft (June 4, 1990); pick received as part of compensation for Los Angeles Dodgers signing Type A free agent Jim Gott.
STATISTICAL NOTES: Led Carolina League with 14 hit batsmen and 20 wild pitches in 1991. . . . Pitched seven innings, combining with Dennis Tafoya (one inning) in 1-0 no-hit victory against Chattanooga (May 8, 1992).

Year	Team (League)	W	L	Pct.	ERA	G	GS	CG	ShO	Sv.	IP	H	R	ER	BB	SO
1990	—Welland (NYP)	2	0	1.000	0.68	9	0	0	0	2	13⅓	7	4	1	9	22
	—Salem (Carolina)	1	1	.500	5.96	19	0	0	0	8	25⅔	28	19	17	16	24
1991	—Salem (Carolina)	4	2	.667	4.37	49	1	0	0	9	70	51	47	34	72	63
1992	—Carolina (South.)	4	•15	.211	3.82	27	27	1	0	0	153	141	82	65	75	107
1993	—Buffalo (A.A.)	3	1	.750	4.08	33	0	0	0	1	46⅓	45	23	21	28	32
	—Carolina (South.)	2	3	.400	3.60	33	0	0	0	9	45	40	26	18	21	30

ZINTER, ALAN

1B/OF, METS

PERSONAL: Born May 19, 1968, in El Paso, Tex.... 6-2/185.... Throws right, bats both.... Full name: Alan Michael Zinter.
HIGH SCHOOL: J.M. Hanks (El Paso, Tex.).
COLLEGE: Arizona.
TRANSACTIONS/CAREER NOTES: Selected by San Diego Padres organization in 23rd round of free-agent draft (June 2, 1986).... Selected by New York Mets organization in first round (24th pick overall) of free-agent draft (June 5, 1989).
HONORS: Named catcher on THE SPORTING NEWS college All-America team (1989).
STATISTICAL NOTES: Tied for Eastern League lead with 11 passed balls in 1991.

			BATTING											FIELDING			
Year	Team (League)	Pos.	G	AB	R	H	2B	3B	HR	RBI	Avg.	BB	SO	SB	PO	A	E	Avg.
1989	—Pittsfield (NYP)	C	12	41	11	15	2	1	2	12	.366	12	4	0	33	3	0	1.000
	—St. Lucie (Fla. St.)	C-1B-OF	48	159	17	38	10	0	3	32	.239	18	31	0	196	21	8	.964
1990	—St. Lucie (Fla. St.)	C	98	333	63	97	19	6	7	63	.291	54	70	8	500	54	11	.981
	—Jackson (Texas)	C	6	20	2	4	1	0	0	1	.200	3	11	1	31	2	0	1.000
1991	—Williamsport (East.)	C	124	422	44	93	13	6	9	54	.220	59	106	3	523	45	10	.983
1992	—Binghamton (East.)	1B	128	431	63	96	13	5	16	50	.223	70	117	0	963	51	12	.988
1993	—Binghamton (East.)	1-0-C-3	134	432	68	113	24	4	24	87	.262	90	105	1	709	49	11	.986

ZOSKY, EDDIE

SS, BLUE JAYS

PERSONAL: Born February 10, 1968, in Whittier, Calif.... 6-0/180.... Throws right, bats right.... Full name: Edward James Zosky.... Name pronounced ZAH-skee.
HIGH SCHOOL: St. Paul's (Sante Fe Springs, Calif.).
COLLEGE: Fresno State.
TRANSACTIONS/CAREER NOTES: Selected by New York Mets organization in fifth round of free-agent draft (June 2, 1986).... Selected by Toronto Blue Jays organization in first round (19th pick overall) of free-agent draft (June 5, 1989).... On Toronto disabled list (March 26-August 11, 1993); included rehabilitation assignment to Hagerstown (July 26-August 2) and Syracuse (August 2-11).
HONORS: Named shortstop on THE SPORTING NEWS college All-America team (1989).
STATISTICAL NOTES: Led Southern League shortstops with 80 double plays in 1990.... Led International League shortstops with 616 total chances and 88 double plays in 1991.

			BATTING											FIELDING			
Year	Team (League)	Pos.	G	AB	R	H	2B	3B	HR	RBI	Avg.	BB	SO	SB	PO	A	E	Avg.
1989	—Knoxville (South.)	SS	56	208	21	46	5	3	2	14	.221	10	32	1	94	135	8	.966
1990	—Knoxville (South.)	SS	115	450	53	122	20	7	3	45	.271	26	72	3	*196	295	31	*.941
1991	—Syracuse (Int'l)	SS	119	511	69	135	18	4	6	39	.264	35	82	9	*221	*371	24	*.961
	—Toronto (A.L.)	SS	18	27	2	4	1	1	0	2	.148	0	8	0	12	26	0	1.000
1992	—Syracuse (Int'l)	SS	96	342	31	79	11	6	4	38	.231	19	53	3	123	249	27	.932
	—Toronto (A.L.)	SS	8	7	1	2	0	1	0	1	.286	0	2	0	2	10	1	.923
1993	—Hagerstown (SAL)	SS	5	20	2	2	0	0	0	1	.100	2	1	0	10	15	0	1.000
	—Syracuse (Int'l)	SS	28	93	9	20	5	0	0	8	.215	1	20	0	48	71	5	.960
Major league totals (2 years)			26	34	3	6	1	2	0	3	.176	0	10	0	14	36	1	.980

ZUPCIC, BOB

OF, RED SOX

PERSONAL: Born August 18, 1966, in Pittsburgh.... 6-4/225.... Throws right, bats right.... Name pronounced ZUP-sik.
HIGH SCHOOL: Bishop Egan (Fairless Hills, Pa.).
COLLEGE: Oral Roberts.
TRANSACTIONS/CAREER NOTES: Selected by Boston Red Sox in supplemental round ("sandwich pick" between first and second round, 32nd pick overall) of free-agent draft (June 2, 1987); pick received as compensation for Red Sox failing to sign 1986 No. 1 pick Greg McMurtry.
HONORS: Named outfielder on THE SPORTING NEWS college All-America team (1987).

			BATTING											FIELDING			
Year	Team (League)	Pos.	G	AB	R	H	2B	3B	HR	RBI	Avg.	BB	SO	SB	PO	A	E	Avg.
1987	—Elmira (N.Y.-Penn)	OF	66	238	39	72	12	2	7	37	.303	17	35	5	131	1	4	.971
1988	—Lynchburg (Caro.)	OF	135	482	69	143	33	5	13	97	.297	60	64	10	250	9	3	.989
1989	—New Britain (East.)	OF	94	346	37	75	12	2	2	28	.217	19	55	15	186	12	6	.971
	—Pawtucket (Int'l)	OF	27	94	8	24	7	1	1	11	.255	3	15	1	61	4	0	1.000
1990	—New Britain (East.)	OF	132	461	45	98	26	1	2	41	.213	36	65	10	286	10	4	.987
1991	—Pawtucket (Int'l)	OF	129	429	70	103	27	1	18	70	.240	55	58	11	255	13	2	.993
	—Boston (A.L.)	OF	18	25	3	4	0	0	1	3	.160	1	6	0	14	0	2	.875
1992	—Pawtucket (Int'l)	OF	9	25	3	8	1	0	2	5	.320	8	6	0	19	0	0	1.000
	—Boston (A.L.)	OF	124	392	46	108	19	1	3	43	.276	25	60	2	241	11	6	.977
1993	—Boston (A.L.)	OF	141	286	40	69	24	2	2	26	.241	27	54	5	179	7	4	.979
Major league totals (3 years)			283	703	89	181	43	3	6	72	.257	53	120	7	434	18	12	.974

MAJOR LEAGUE MANAGERS

ALOU, FELIPE

EXPOS

PERSONAL: Born May 12, 1935, in Haina, Dominican Republic. . . . 6-1/195. . . . Threw right, batted right. . . . Full name: Felipe Rojas Alou. . . . Father of Moises Alou, outfielder, Expos; brother of Jesus Alou, major league outfielder with four teams (1965-75 and 1978-79); and brother of Matty Alou, major league outfielder with six teams (1960-74).

COLLEGE: University of Santo Domingo (Dominican Republic).

TRANSACTIONS/CAREER NOTES: Signed as free agent by New York Giants organization (November 14, 1955). . . . Giants franchise moved from New York to San Francisco (1958). . . . Traded by Giants with P Billy Hoeft, C Ed Bailey and a player to be named later to Milwaukee Braves for P Bob Hendley, P Bob Shaw and C Del Crandall (December 3, 1963); Giants sent IF Ernie Bowman to Braves to complete deal (January 8, 1964). . . . On disabled list (June 24-July 25, 1964). . . . Braves franchise moved from Milwaukee to Atlanta (1966). . . . Traded by Braves to Oakland Athletics for P Jim Nash (December 3, 1969). . . . Traded by A's to New York Yankees for P Rob Gardner and P Ron Klimkowski (April 9, 1971). . . . Contract sold by Yankees on waivers to Montreal Expos (September 5, 1973). . . . Contract sold by Expos to Milwaukee Brewers (December 7, 1973). . . . Released by Brewers (April 29, 1974).

HONORS: Named first baseman on THE SPORTING NEWS N.L. All-Star team (1966).

STATISTICAL NOTES: Led N.L. with 355 total bases in 1966.

			BATTING												FIELDING			
Year	**Team (League)**	**Pos.**	**G**	**AB**	**R**	**H**	**2B**	**3B**	**HR**	**RBI**	**Avg.**	**BB**	**SO**	**SB**	**PO**	**A**	**E**	**Avg.**
1956	—Lake Charl. (Evan.)	OF	5	9	1	2	0	0	0	1	.222	...	...	0	6	1	0	1.000
	—Cocoa (Florida St.)	OF-3B	119	445	111	169	15	6	21	99	*.380	68	40	*48	199	60	23	.918
1957	—Minneapolis (A.A.)	OF	24	57	7	12	2	0	0	3	.211	5	8	1	32	1	1	.971
	—Springfield (East.)	OF-3B	106	359	45	110	14	3	12	71	.306	27	29	18	215	26	9	.964
1958	—Phoenix (PCL)	OF	55	216	61	69	16	2	13	42	.319	17	24	10	150	3	3	.981
	—San Francisco (N.L.)	OF	75	182	21	46	9	2	4	16	.253	19	34	4	126	2	2	.985
1959	—San Francisco (N.L.)	OF	95	247	38	68	13	2	10	33	.275	17	38	5	111	2	3	.974
1960	—San Francisco (N.L.)	OF	106	322	48	85	17	3	8	44	.264	16	42	10	156	5	7	.958
1961	—San Francisco (N.L.)	OF	132	415	59	120	19	0	18	52	.289	26	41	11	196	10	2	.990
1962	—San Francisco (N.L.)	OF	154	561	96	177	30	3	25	98	.316	33	66	10	262	7	8	.971
1963	—San Francisco (N.L.)	OF	157	565	75	159	31	9	20	82	.281	27	87	11	279	9	4	.986
1964	—Milwaukee (N.L.)■	OF-1B	121	415	60	105	26	3	9	51	.253	30	41	5	329	12	5	.986
1965	—Milwaukee (N.L.)	0-1-3-S	143	555	80	165	29	2	23	78	.297	31	63	8	626	43	6	.991
1966	—Atlanta (N.L.)	1-0-3-S	154	*666	*122	*218	32	6	31	74	.327	24	51	5	935	64	13	.987
1967	—Atlanta (N.L.)	1B-OF	140	574	76	157	26	3	15	43	.274	32	50	6	864	34	9	.990
1968	—Atlanta (N.L.)	OF	160	*662	72	•210	37	5	11	57	.317	48	56	12	379	8	8	.980
1969	—Atlanta (N.L.)	OF	123	476	54	134	13	1	5	32	.282	23	23	4	260	4	3	.989
1970	—Oakland (A.L.)■	OF-1B	154	575	70	156	25	3	8	55	.271	32	31	10	290	11	7	.977
1971	—Oak.-N.Y. (A.L.)■	OF-1B	133	469	52	135	21	6	8	69	.288	32	25	5	513	23	4	.993
1972	—New York (A.L.)	1B-OF	120	324	33	90	18	1	6	37	.278	22	27	1	669	54	7	.990
1973	—New York (A.L.)	1B-OF	93	280	25	66	12	0	4	27	.236	9	25	0	512	31	7	.987
	—Montreal (N.L.)■	OF-1B	19	48	4	10	1	0	1	4	.208	2	4	0	30	3	0	1.000
1974	—Milwaukee (A.L.)■	OF	3	3	0	0	0	0	0	0	.000	0	2	0	0	0	1	.000
American League totals (5 years)			503	1651	180	447	76	10	26	188	.271	95	110	16	1984	119	26	.988
National League totals (13 years)			1579	5688	805	1654	283	39	180	664	.291	328	596	91	4553	203	70	.985
Major league totals (17 years)			2082	7339	985	2101	359	49	206	852	.286	423	706	107	6537	322	96	.986

CHAMPIONSHIP SERIES RECORD

			BATTING												FIELDING			
Year	**Team (League)**	**Pos.**	**G**	**AB**	**R**	**H**	**2B**	**3B**	**HR**	**RBI**	**Avg.**	**BB**	**SO**	**SB**	**PO**	**A**	**E**	**Avg.**
1969	—Atlanta (N.L.)	PH	1	1	0	0	0	0	0	0	.000	0	0	0	...	...	...	...

WORLD SERIES RECORD

			BATTING												FIELDING			
Year	**Team (League)**	**Pos.**	**G**	**AB**	**R**	**H**	**2B**	**3B**	**HR**	**RBI**	**Avg.**	**BB**	**SO**	**SB**	**PO**	**A**	**E**	**Avg.**
1962	—San Francisco (N.L.)	OF	7	26	2	7	1	1	0	1	.269	1	4	0	8	0	1	.889

ALL-STAR GAME RECORD

			BATTING											FIELDING			
Year	**League**	**Pos.**	**AB**	**R**	**H**	**2B**	**3B**	**HR**	**RBI**	**Avg.**	**BB**	**SO**	**SB**	**PO**	**A**	**E**	**Avg.**
1962	—National	OF	0	0	0	0	0	0	1	...	0	0	0	0	0	0	...
1966	—National		Did not play.														
1968	—National	OF	0	0	0	0	0	0	0	...	0	0	0	0	0	0	...
All-Star Game totals (2 years)			0	0	0	0	0	0	1	...	0	0	0	0	0	0	...

RECORD AS MANAGER

BACKGROUND: Spring training instructor, Montreal Expos (1976). . . . Coach, Expos (1979-80, 1984 and October 8, 1991-May 22, 1992).

HONORS: Named Florida State League Manager of the Year (1990).

		REGULAR SEASON				POSTSEASON							
						Playoff		Champ. Series		World Series		All-Star Game	
Year	**Team (League)**	**W**	**L**	**Pct.**	**Pos.**	**W**	**L**	**W**	**L**	**W**	**L**	**W**	**L**
1977	—West Palm Beach (Florida State)	77	55	.583	1st (S)	1	2	—	—	—	—	—	—
1978	—Memphis (Southern)	71	73	.493	2nd (W)	—	—	—	—	—	—	—	—
1981	—Denver (American Association)	76	60	.559	2nd (W)	4	0	—	—	—	—	—	—
1982	—Wichita (American Association)	70	67	.511	2nd (W)	—	—	—	—	—	—	—	—

Year Team (League)	W	L	Pct.	Pos.	Playoff W	Playoff L	Champ. Series W	Champ. Series L	World Series W	World Series L	All-Star Game W	All-Star Game L
	REGULAR SEASON				POSTSEASON							
1983 —Wichita (American Association)	65	71	.478	3rd (W)	—	—	—	—	—	—	—	—
1985 —Indianapolis (American Association)	61	81	.430	4th (E)	—	—	—	—	—	—	—	—
1986 —West Palm Beach (Florida State)	80	55	.593	1st (S)	3	3	—	—	—	—	—	—
1987 —West Palm Beach (Florida State)	75	63	.543	2nd (S)	—	—	—	—	—	—	—	—
1988 —West Palm Beach (Florida State)	41	27	.603	2nd (E)	—	—	—	—	—	—	—	—
—(Second half)	30	36	.455	3rd (E)	2	2	—	—	—	—	—	—
1989 —West Palm Beach (Florida State)	39	31	.557	T2nd (E)	—	—	—	—	—	—	—	—
—(Second half)	35	33	.515	2nd (E)	—	—	—	—	—	—	—	—
1990 —West Palm Beach (Florida State)	49	19	.721	1st (E)	—	—	—	—	—	—	—	—
—(Second half)	43	21	.672	1st (E)	3	3	—	—	—	—	—	—
1991 —West Palm Beach (Florida State)	33	31	.516	4th (E)	—	—	—	—	—	—	—	—
—(Second half)	39	28	.582	2nd (E)	6	1	—	—	—	—	—	—
1992 —Montreal (N.L.)	70	55	.560	2nd (E)	—	—	—	—	—	—	—	—
1993 —Montreal (N.L.)	94	68	.580	2nd (E)	—	—	—	—	—	—	—	—
Major league totals (2 years)	164	123	.571									

NOTES:

1977— Lost to St. Petersburg in semifinals.
1978— Memphis tied one game.
1981— Defeated Omaha for league championship.
1986— Defeated Winter Haven, two games to none, in semifinals; lost to St. Petersburg, three games to one, in league championship.
1988— Defeated Vero Beach, two games to none, in first round; lost to Osceola, two games to none, in semifinals.
1990— Defeated Lakeland, two games to one, in semifinals; lost to Vero Beach, two games to one, in league championship.
1991— Defeated Vero Beach, two games to one, in first round; defeated Lakeland, two games to none, in semifinals; defeated Clearwater, two games to none, in league championship.
1992— Replaced Montreal manager Tom Runnells with club in fourth place, record of 17-20 (May 22).

ANDERSON, SPARKY

TIGERS

PERSONAL: Born February 22, 1934, in Bridgewater, S.D. . . . 5-9/168. . . . Threw right, batted right. . . . Full name: George Lee Anderson.
HIGH SCHOOL: Dorsey (Los Angeles).
TRANSACTIONS/CAREER NOTES: Signed by Santa Barbara, Brooklyn Dodgers organization (January 30, 1953). . . . Dodgers franchise moved from Brooklyn to Los Angeles (1958). . . . Recalled by Los Angeles Dodgers and traded to Philadelphia Phillies for P Jim Golden, P Gene Snyder and OF Eldon (Rip) Repulski (December 23, 1958). . . . On Toronto disabled list (August 13-September 13, 1961 and August 12-23, 1962).
STATISTICAL NOTES: Led California League shortstops with 83 double plays in 1953. . . . Led Western League with 20 sacrifice hits in 1954. . . . Tied for Texas League lead with 22 sacrifice hits in 1955. . . . Led Texas League second basemen with 117 double plays in 1955. . . . Led Pacific Coast League second basemen with .985 fielding percentage, 523 putouts, 486 assists, 1,024 total chances and 135 double plays and tied for lead with 15 errors in 1957. . . . Led International League second basemen with 104 double plays in 1958 and 89 in 1960. . . . Led International League with 15 sacrifice hits in 1960.

Year Team (League)	Pos.	G	AB	R	H	2B	3B	HR	RBI	Avg.	BB	SO	SB	PO	A	E	Avg.
			BATTING											FIELDING			
1953 —Santa Barb. (Calif.)	SS	•141	*598	98	157	21	4	5	55	.263	57	47	13	*277	395	32	.955
1954 —Pueblo (Western)	2B	147	497	72	147	13	5	0	62	.296	80	35	14	*397	432	20	•.976
1955 —Fort Worth (Texas)	2B	158	594	86	158	24	1	0	42	.266	69	35	6	*456	*469	18	*.981
1956 —Montreal (Int'l)	2B	140	453	65	135	17	5	0	47	.298	53	28	4	372	391	15	.981
1957 —Los Angeles (PCL)	2B-SS	•168	619	74	161	15	0	2	35	.260	72	48	8	†524	†488	‡15	†.985
1958 —Montreal (Int'l)	2B	•155	580	78	156	35	5	2	56	.269	47	50	21	*387	*464	10	*.988
1959 —Philadelphia (N.L.)■	2B	152	477	42	104	9	3	0	34	.218	42	53	6	343	403	12	.984
1960 —Toronto (Int'l)■	2B	148	543	67	123	11	5	5	21	.227	41	36	12	319	*416	12	.984
1961 —Toronto (Int'l)	2B	97	275	30	66	17	0	0	22	.240	34	33	5	189	203	6	.985
1962 —Toronto (Int'l)	2B	124	432	56	111	18	2	2	38	.257	49	32	2	282	327	8	*.987
1963 —Toronto (Int'l)	2B	116	358	56	89	12	5	3	25	.249	37	45	3	226	256	6	*.988
Major league totals (1 year)		152	477	42	104	9	3	0	34	.218	42	53	6	343	403	12	.984

RECORD AS MANAGER

BACKGROUND: Coach, San Diego Padres (1969).
HONORS: Coach, N.L. All-Star team (1974). . . . Coach, A.L. All-Star team (1982, 1984 and 1993). . . . Named A.L. Manager of the Year by Baseball Writers' Association of America (1984 and 1987). . . . Named A.L. Manager of the Year by THE SPORTING NEWS (1987).

Year Team (League)	W	L	Pct.	Pos.	Playoff W	Playoff L	Champ. Series W	Champ. Series L	World Series W	World Series L	All-Star Game W	All-Star Game L
	REGULAR SEASON				POSTSEASON							
1964 —Toronto (International)	80	72	.526	5th	—	—	—	—	—	—	—	—
1965 —Rock Hill (Western Carolinas)	24	40	.375	8th	—	—	—	—	—	—	—	—
—(Second half)	35	23	.603	1st	2	0	—	—	—	—	—	—
1966 —St. Petersburg (Florida State)	42	24	.636	2nd	—	—	—	—	—	—	—	—
—(Second half)	49	21	.700	1st	2	3	—	—	—	—	—	—
1967 —Modesto (California)	38	32	.543	T2nd	—	—	—	—	—	—	—	—
—(Second half)	41	29	.586	1st	0	2	—	—	—	—	—	—
1968 —Asheville (Southern)	86	54	.614	1st	—	—	—	—	—	—	—	—
1970 —Cincinnati (N.L.)	102	60	.630	1st (W)	—	—	3	0	1	4	—	—
1971 —Cincinnati (N.L.)	79	83	.488	T4th (W)	—	—	—	—	—	—	0	1
1972 —Cincinnati (N.L.)	95	59	.619	1st (W)	—	—	3	2	3	4	—	—
1973 —Cincinnati (N.L.)	99	63	.611	1st (W)	—	—	2	3	—	—	1	0

Year	Team (League)	Regular Season W	L	Pct.	Pos.	Postseason: Playoff W	L	Champ. Series W	L	World Series W	L	All-Star Game W	L
1974	—Cincinnati (N.L.)	98	64	.605	2nd (W)	—	—	—	—	—	—	—	—
1975	—Cincinnati (N.L.)	108	54	.667	1st (W)	—	—	3	0	4	3	—	—
1976	—Cincinnati (N.L.)	102	60	.630	1st (W)	—	—	3	0	4	0	1	0
1977	—Cincinnati (N.L.)	88	74	.543	2nd (W)	—	—	—	—	—	—	1	0
1978	—Cincinnati (N.L.)	92	69	.571	2nd (W)	—	—	—	—	—	—	—	—
1979	—Detroit (A.L.)	56	50	.528	5th (E)	—	—	—	—	—	—	—	—
1980	—Detroit (A.L.)	84	78	.519	5th (E)	—	—	—	—	—	—	—	—
1981	—Detroit (A.L.)	31	26	.544	4th (E)	—	—	—	—	—	—	—	—
	—(Second half)	29	23	.558	3rd (E)	—	—	—	—	—	—	—	—
1982	—Detroit (A.L.)	83	79	.512	4th (E)	—	—	—	—	—	—	—	—
1983	—Detroit (A.L.)	92	70	.568	2nd (E)	—	—	—	—	—	—	—	—
1984	—Detroit (A.L.)	104	58	.642	1st (E)	—	—	3	0	4	1	—	—
1985	—Detroit (A.L.)	84	77	.522	3rd (E)	—	—	—	—	—	—	0	1
1986	—Detroit (A.L.)	87	75	.537	3rd (E)	—	—	—	—	—	—	—	—
1987	—Detroit (A.L.)	98	64	.605	1st (E)	—	—	1	4	—	—	—	—
1988	—Detroit (A.L.)	88	74	.543	2nd (E)	—	—	—	—	—	—	—	—
1989	—Detroit (A.L.)	59	103	.364	7th (E)	—	—	—	—	—	—	—	—
1990	—Detroit (A.L.)	79	83	.488	3rd (E)	—	—	—	—	—	—	—	—
1991	—Detroit (A.L.)	84	78	.519	T2nd (E)	—	—	—	—	—	—	—	—
1992	—Detroit (A.L.)	75	87	.463	6th (E)	—	—	—	—	—	—	—	—
1993	—Detroit (A.L.)	85	77	.525	T3rd (E)	—	—	—	—	—	—	—	—
	American League totals (15 years)	1218	1102	.525		—	—	4	4	4	1	0	1
	National League totals (9 years)	863	586	.596		—	—	14	5	12	11	3	1
	Major league totals (24 years)	2081	1688	.552		—	—	18	9	16	12	3	2

NOTES:

1965—Defeated Salisbury (first-half winner) in playoff.
1966—Lost to Leesburg (first-half winner) in playoff.
1967—Lost to San Jose (first-half winner) in playoff.
1970—Defeated Pittsburgh in N.L. Championship Series; lost to Baltimore in World Series.
1972—Defeated Pittsburgh in N.L. Championship Series; lost to Oakland in World Series.
1973—Lost to New York Mets in N.L. Championship Series.
1975—Defeated Pittsburgh in N.L. Championship Series; defeated Boston in World Series.
1976—Defeated Philadelphia in N.L. Championship Series; defeated New York Yankees in World Series.
1979—Replaced Detroit manager Les Moss (and interim manager Dick Tracewski) with club in fifth place, record of 29-26 (June 14).
1984—Defeated Kansas City in A.L. Championship Series; defeated San Diego in World Series.
1987—Lost to Minnesota in A.L. Championship Series.
1989—Record includes period in which Anderson took time off (May 19-June 4); club was 9-8 under temporary manager Dick Tracewski.

BAKER, DUSTY

GIANTS

PERSONAL: Born June 15, 1949, in Riverside, Calif. . . . 6-2/200. . . . Threw right, batted right. . . . Full name: Johnnie B. Baker Jr.
HIGH SCHOOL: Del Campo (Fair Oaks, Calif.).
COLLEGE: American River College (Calif.).

TRANSACTIONS/CAREER NOTES: Selected by Atlanta Braves organization in 26th round of free-agent draft (June 6, 1967). . . . On West Palm Beach restricted list (April 5-June 13, 1968). . . . On Atlanta military list (January 24-April 3, 1969 and June 17-July 3, 1972). . . . Traded by Braves with 1B/3B Ed Goodson to Los Angeles Dodgers for OF Jimmy Wynn, 2B Lee Lacy, 1B/OF Tom Paciorek and IF Jerry Royster (November 17, 1975). . . . Released on waivers by Dodgers (February 10, 1984); San Francisco Giants claim rejected (February 16, 1984). . . . Granted free agency (February 21, 1984). . . . Signed by Giants (April 1, 1984). . . . On restricted list (April 2-11, 1984). . . . Traded by Giants to Oakland Athletics for P Ed Puikunas and C Dan Winters (March 24, 1985). . . . Granted free agency (November 10, 1986).
RECORDS: Shares major league records for most plate appearances, most at-bats and most times faced pitcher as batsman in one inning—3 (September 20, 1972, second inning); most stolen bases in one inning—3 (June 27, 1984, third inning). . . . Holds N.L. single-season record for fewest chances accepted by an outfielder (150 or more games)—235 (1977).
HONORS: Named outfielder on THE SPORTING NEWS N.L. All-Star team (1980). . . . Named outfielder on THE SPORTING NEWS N.L. Silver Slugger team (1980-81). . . . Won N.L. Gold Glove as outfielder (1981).
STATISTICAL NOTES: Led N.L. outfielders with 407 total chances in 1973.

Year	Team (League)	Pos.	G	Batting: AB	R	H	2B	3B	HR	RBI	Avg.	BB	SO	SB	Fielding: PO	A	E	Avg.
1967	—Austin (Texas)	OF	9	39	6	9	1	0	0	1	.231	2	7	0	17	0	1	.944
1968	—W.P. Beach (FSL)	OF	6	21	2	4	0	0	0	2	.190	1	4	0	6	2	0	1.000
	—Greenw. (W. Car.)	OF	52	199	45	68	11	3	6	39	.342	23	39	6	82	1	3	.965
	—Atlanta (N.L.)	OF	6	5	0	2	0	0	0	0	.400	0	1	0	0	0	0	...
1969	—Shreveport (Texas)	OF	73	265	40	68	5	1	9	31	.257	36	41	2	135	10	3	.980
	—Richmond (Int'l)	OF-3B	25	89	7	22	4	0	0	8	.247	11	22	3	40	9	4	.925
	—Atlanta (N.L.)	OF	3	7	0	0	0	0	0	0	.000	0	3	0	2	0	0	1.000
1970	—Richmond (Int'l)	OF	118	461	97	150	29	3	11	51	.325	53	45	10	236	10	7	.972
	—Atlanta (N.L.)	OF	13	24	3	7	0	0	0	4	.292	2	4	0	11	1	3	.800
1971	—Richmond (Int'l)	OF-3B	80	341	62	106	23	2	11	41	.311	25	37	10	136	13	4	.974
	—Atlanta (N.L.)	OF	29	62	2	14	2	0	0	4	.226	1	14	0	29	1	0	1.000
1972	—Atlanta (N.L.)	OF	127	446	62	143	27	2	17	76	.321	45	68	4	344	8	4	.989
1973	—Atlanta (N.L.)	OF	159	604	101	174	29	4	21	99	.288	67	72	24	*390	10	7	.983
1974	—Atlanta (N.L.)	OF	149	574	80	147	35	0	20	69	.256	71	87	18	359	10	7	.981
1975	—Atlanta (N.L.)	OF	142	494	63	129	18	2	19	72	.261	67	57	12	287	10	3	.990
1976	—Los Angeles (N.L.)■	OF	112	384	36	93	13	0	4	39	.242	31	54	2	254	3	1	.996
1977	—Los Angeles (N.L.)	OF	153	533	86	155	26	1	30	86	.291	58	89	2	227	8	3	.987

Year	Team (League)	Pos.	G	AB	R	H	2B	3B	HR	RBI	Avg.	BB	SO	SB	PO	A	E	Avg.
			BATTING												FIELDING			
1978	—Los Angeles (N.L.) ...	OF	149	522	62	137	24	1	11	66	.262	47	66	12	250	13	4	.985
1979	—Los Angeles (N.L.) ...	OF	151	554	86	152	29	1	23	88	.274	56	70	11	289	14	3	.990
1980	—Los Angeles (N.L.) ...	OF	153	579	80	170	26	4	29	97	.294	43	66	12	308	5	3	.991
1981	—Los Angeles (N.L.) ...	OF	103	400	48	128	17	3	9	49	.320	29	43	10	181	8	2	.990
1982	—Los Angeles (N.L.) ...	OF	147	570	80	171	19	1	23	88	.300	56	62	17	226	7	6	.975
1983	—Los Angeles (N.L.) ...	OF	149	531	71	138	25	1	15	73	.260	72	59	7	249	4	5	.981
1984	—San Francisco (N.L.)■	OF	100	243	31	71	7	2	3	32	.292	40	27	4	112	1	3	.974
1985	—Oakland (A.L.)■........	1B-OF	111	343	48	92	15	1	14	52	.268	50	47	2	465	29	5	.990
1986	—Oakland (A.L.)	OF-1B	83	242	25	58	8	0	4	19	.240	27	37	0	90	4	0	1.000
American League totals (2 years)			194	585	73	150	23	1	18	71	.256	77	84	2	555	33	5	.992
National League totals (17 years)			1845	6532	891	1831	297	22	224	942	.280	685	842	135	3518	103	54	.985
Major league totals (19 years)			2039	7117	964	1981	320	23	242	1013	.278	762	926	137	4073	136	59	.986

DIVISION SERIES RECORD

Year	Team (League)	Pos.	G	AB	R	H	2B	3B	HR	RBI	Avg.	BB	SO	SB	PO	A	E	Avg.
			BATTING												FIELDING			
1981	—Los Angeles (N.L.) ...	OF	5	18	2	3	1	0	0	1	.167	2	0	0	12	0	0	1.000

CHAMPIONSHIP SERIES RECORD

CHAMPIONSHIP SERIES NOTES: Named N.L. Championship Series Most Valuable Player (1977).... Shares single-game record for most grand slams—1 (October 5, 1977).... Shares record for most runs batted in in one inning—4 (October 5, 1977, fourth inning).... Shares N.L. single-game record for most hits—4 (October 7, 1978).

Year	Team (League)	Pos.	G	AB	R	H	2B	3B	HR	RBI	Avg.	BB	SO	SB	PO	A	E	Avg.
			BATTING												FIELDING			
1977	—Los Angeles (N.L.) ...	OF	4	14	4	5	1	0	2	8	.357	2	3	0	3	0	0	1.000
1978	—Los Angeles (N.L.) ...	OF	4	15	1	7	2	0	0	1	.467	3	0	0	5	0	0	1.000
1981	—Los Angeles (N.L.) ...	OF	5	19	3	6	1	0	0	3	.316	1	0	0	10	0	1	.909
1983	—Los Angeles (N.L.) ...	OF	4	14	4	5	1	0	1	1	.357	2	0	0	9	0	0	1.000
Championship series totals (4 years)			17	62	12	23	5	0	3	13	.371	8	3	0	27	0	1	.964

WORLD SERIES RECORD

Year	Team (League)	Pos.	G	AB	R	H	2B	3B	HR	RBI	Avg.	BB	SO	SB	PO	A	E	Avg.
			BATTING												FIELDING			
1977	—Los Angeles (N.L.) ...	OF	6	24	4	7	0	0	1	5	.292	0	2	0	11	0	1	.917
1978	—Los Angeles (N.L.) ...	OF	6	21	2	5	0	0	1	1	.238	1	3	0	12	0	0	1.000
1981	—Los Angeles (N.L.) ...	OF	6	24	3	4	0	0	0	1	.167	1	6	0	13	0	0	1.000
World Series totals (3 years)			18	69	9	16	0	0	2	7	.232	2	11	0	36	0	1	.973

ALL-STAR GAME RECORD

Year	League	Pos.	AB	R	H	2B	3B	HR	RBI	Avg.	BB	SO	SB	PO	A	E	Avg.
			BATTING											FIELDING			
1981	—National....................	OF	2	0	1	0	0	0	0	.500	0	0	0	2	0	0	1.000
1982	—National....................	OF	2	0	0	0	0	0	0	.000	0	0	0	0	0	0	...
All-Star Game totals (2 years)			4	0	1	0	0	0	0	.250	0	0	0	2	0	0	1.000

RECORD AS MANAGER

BACKGROUND: Coach, San Francisco Giants (1988-92).... Manager, Scottsdale Scorpions, Giants organization, Arizona Fall League (1992, record: 20-22, second place/Northern Division).

HONORS: Named N.L. Manager of the Year by Baseball Writers' Association of America (1993).

Year	Team (League)	W	L	Pct.	Pos.	Playoff W	Playoff L	Champ. Series W	Champ. Series L	World Series W	World Series L	All-Star Game W	All-Star Game L
		REGULAR SEASON				POSTSEASON							
1993	—San Francisco (N.L.)	103	59	.636	2nd (W)	—	—	—	—	—	—	—	—

BAYLOR, DON

ROCKIES

PERSONAL: Born June 28, 1949, in Austin, Tex.... 6-1/220.... Threw right, batted right.... Full name: Donald Edward Baylor.... Cousin of Pat Ballage, safety, Indianapolis Colts of National Football League (1986 and 1987).

HIGH SCHOOL: Stephen F. Austin (Austin, Tex.).

COLLEGE: Miami-Dade Junior College and Blinn Junior College (Tex.).

TRANSACTIONS/CAREER NOTES: Selected by Baltimore Orioles organization in second round of free-agent draft (June 6, 1967).... Traded by Orioles with P Mike Torrez and P Paul Mitchell to Oakland Athletics for OF Reggie Jackson, P Ken Holtzman and P Bill Van Bommel (April 2, 1976).... Granted free agency (November 1, 1976).... Signed by California Angels (November 16, 1976).... On disabled list (May 11-June 26, 1980).... Granted free agency (November 10, 1982).... Signed by New York Yankees (December 1, 1982).... Traded by Yankees to Boston Red Sox for DH Mike Easler (March 28, 1986).... Traded by Red Sox to Minnesota Twins for a player to be named later (August 31, 1987); Red Sox acquired P Enrique Rios to complete deal (December 18, 1987).... Released by Twins (December 21, 1987).... Signed by A's (February 9, 1988).... Granted free agency (November 4, 1988).

RECORDS: Holds major league career record for most times hit by pitch—267.... Shares major league records for most consecutive home runs in two consecutive games—4 (July 1 [1] and 2 [3], 1975, bases on balls included); and most long hits in opening game of season—4 (2 doubles, 1 triple, 1 home run, April 6, 1973).... Shares major league record for most times caught stealing in one inning—2 (June 15, 1974, ninth inning).... Shares modern major league single-game record for most at-bats—7 (August 25, 1979).... Holds A.L. single-season record for most times hit by pitch—35 (1986).

HONORS: Named Appalachian League Player of the Year (1967).... Named Minor League Player of the Year by THE SPORTING NEWS (1970).... Named A.L. Player of the Year by THE SPORTING NEWS (1979).... Named A.L. Most Valuable Player by Baseball Writers' Association of America (1979).... Named designated hitter on THE SPORTING NEWS A.L. All-Star team

(1979, 1985-86).... Named designated hitter on THE SPORTING NEWS A.L. Silver Slugger team (1983, 1985-86).
STATISTICAL NOTES: Led Appalachian League with 135 total bases and tied for lead in caught stealing with 6 in 1967.... Led Texas League in being hit by pitch with 13 in 1969.... Led International League with 296 total bases in 1970.... Led International League in being hit by pitch with 19 in 1970 and 16 in 1971.... Led A.L. in being hit by pitch with 13 in 1973, 20 in 1976, 18 in 1978, 23 in 1984, 24 in 1985, 35 in 1986, 28 in 1987 and tied for lead with 13 in 1975.... Hit three home runs in one game (July 2, 1975).... Led A.L. with 12 sacrifice flies in 1978.... Led A.L. with 21 game-winning RBIs in 1982.

			BATTING												FIELDING			
Year	**Team (League)**	**Pos.**	**G**	**AB**	**R**	**H**	**2B**	**3B**	**HR**	**RBI**	**Avg.**	**BB**	**SO**	**SB**	**PO**	**A**	**E**	**Avg.**
1967	—Bluefield (Appal.)	OF	•67	246	50	*85	10	*8	8	47	*.346	35	52	*26	106	5	5	.957
1968	—Stockton (Calif.)	OF	68	244	52	90	6	3	7	40	.369	35	65	14	135	3	7	.952
	—Elmira (Eastern)	OF	6	24	4	8	1	1	1	3	.333	3	4	1	10	1	0	1.000
	—Rochester (Int'l)	OF	15	46	4	10	2	0	0	4	.217	3	17	1	29	1	4	.882
1969	—Miami (Florida St.)	OF	17	56	13	21	5	4	3	24	.375	7	8	3	30	2	3	.914
	—Dall./Fort W. (Tex.)	OF	109	406	71	122	17	•10	11	57	.300	48	77	19	241	7	*13	.950
1970	—Rochester (Int'l)	OF	•140	508	*127	166	*34	*15	22	107	.327	76	99	26	286	5	7	.977
	—Baltimore (A.L.)	OF	8	17	4	4	0	0	0	4	.235	2	3	1	15	0	0	1.000
1971	—Rochester (Int'l)	OF	136	492	104	154	•31	10	20	95	.313	79	73	25	210	4	9	.960
	—Baltimore (A.L.)	OF	1	2	0	0	0	0	0	1	.000	2	1	0	4	0	0	1.000
1972	—Baltimore (A.L.)	OF-1B	102	320	33	81	13	3	11	38	.253	29	50	24	206	4	5	.977
1973	—Baltimore (A.L.)	OF-1B	118	405	64	116	20	4	11	51	.286	35	48	32	228	10	6	.975
1974	—Baltimore (A.L.)	OF-1B	137	489	66	133	22	1	10	59	.272	43	56	29	260	2	5	.981
1975	—Baltimore (A.L.)	OF-1B	145	524	79	148	21	6	25	76	.282	53	64	32	286	8	5	.983
1976	—Oakland (A.L.)■	OF-1B	157	595	85	147	25	1	15	68	.247	58	72	52	781	45	12	.986
1977	—California (A.L.)■	OF-1B	154	561	87	141	27	0	25	75	.251	62	76	26	280	16	7	.977
1978	—California (A.L.)	OF-1B	158	591	103	151	26	0	34	99	.255	56	71	22	194	9	6	.971
1979	—California (A.L.)	OF-1B	•162	628	*120	186	33	3	36	*139	.296	71	51	22	203	3	5	.976
1980	—California (A.L.)	OF	90	340	39	85	12	2	5	51	.250	24	32	6	119	4	4	.969
1981	—California (A.L.)	1B-OF	103	377	52	90	18	1	17	66	.239	42	51	3	38	3	0	1.000
1982	—California (A.L.)	DH	157	608	80	160	24	1	24	93	.263	57	69	10	...	...	...	...
1983	—New York (A.L.)■	OF-1B	144	534	82	162	33	3	21	85	.303	40	53	17	23	2	1	.962
1984	—New York (A.L.)	OF	134	493	84	129	29	1	27	89	.262	38	68	1	8	0	1	.889
1985	—New York (A.L.)	DH	142	477	70	110	24	1	23	91	.231	52	90	0	...	...	...	...
1986	—Boston (A.L.)■	1B-OF	160	585	93	139	23	1	31	94	.238	62	111	3	71	4	1	.987
1987	—Bos.-Minn. (A.L.)■	DH	128	388	67	95	9	0	16	63	.245	45	59	5	...	...	...	...
1988	—Oakland (A.L.)■	DH	92	264	28	58	7	0	7	34	.220	34	44	0	...	...	...	...
	Major league totals (19 years)		2292	8198	1236	2135	366	28	338	1276	.260	805	1069	285	2716	110	58	.980

CHAMPIONSHIP SERIES RECORD

CHAMPIONSHIP SERIES NOTES: Holds career record for most clubs played with—5.... Holds single-series record for most runs batted in—10 (1982).... Shares single-game records for most times reached base safely—5 (October 8, 1986); and most grand slams—1 (October 9, 1982).... Shares record for most runs batted in in one inning—4 (October 9, 1982, eighth inning).... Holds A.L. record for most consecutive games with one or more hits—12 (1982 [last three games], 1986-87).... Shares A.L. single-game record for most runs batted in—5 (October 5, 1982).

			BATTING												FIELDING			
Year	**Team (League)**	**Pos.**	**G**	**AB**	**R**	**H**	**2B**	**3B**	**HR**	**RBI**	**Avg.**	**BB**	**SO**	**SB**	**PO**	**A**	**E**	**Avg.**
1973	—Baltimore (A.L.)	OF-PH	4	11	3	3	0	0	0	1	.273	3	5	0	7	0	0	1.000
1974	—Baltimore (A.L.)	OF	4	15	0	4	0	0	0	0	.267	0	2	0	9	0	0	1.000
1979	—California (A.L.)	DH-OF	4	16	2	3	0	0	1	2	.188	1	2	0	4	0	0	1.000
1982	—California (A.L.)	DH	5	17	2	5	1	1	1	10	.294	2	0	0	...	...	...	...
1986	—Boston (A.L.)	DH	7	26	6	9	3	0	1	2	.346	4	5	0	...	...	...	...
1987	—Minnesota (A.L.)	PH-DH	2	5	0	2	0	0	0	1	.400	0	0	0	...	...	...	...
1988	—Oakland (A.L.)	DH	2	6	0	0	0	0	0	1	.000	1	2	0	...	...	...	...
	Championship series totals (7 years)		28	96	13	26	4	1	3	17	.271	11	16	0	20	0	0	1.000

WORLD SERIES RECORD

WORLD SERIES NOTES: Shares record for most at-bats in one inning—2 (October 17, 1987, fourth inning).

			BATTING												FIELDING			
Year	**Team (League)**	**Pos.**	**G**	**AB**	**R**	**H**	**2B**	**3B**	**HR**	**RBI**	**Avg.**	**BB**	**SO**	**SB**	**PO**	**A**	**E**	**Avg.**
1986	—Boston (A.L.)	DH-PH	4	11	1	2	1	0	0	1	.182	1	3	0	...	...	...	...
1987	—Minnesota (A.L.)	DH-PH	5	13	3	5	0	0	1	3	.385	1	1	0	...	...	...	...
1988	—Oakland (A.L.)	PH	1	1	0	0	0	0	0	0	.000	0	1	0	...	...	...	...
	World Series totals (3 years)		10	25	4	7	1	0	1	4	.280	2	5	0	...	...	...	...

ALL-STAR GAME RECORD

			BATTING											FIELDING			
Year	**League**	**Pos.**	**AB**	**R**	**H**	**2B**	**3B**	**HR**	**RBI**	**Avg.**	**BB**	**SO**	**SB**	**PO**	**A**	**E**	**Avg.**
1979	—American	OF	4	2	2	1	0	0	1	.500	0	0	0	1	0	0	1.000

RECORD AS MANAGER

BACKGROUND: Special assistant to general manager, Milwaukee Brewers (September 5-December 4, 1989).... Coach, Brewers (December 4, 1989-91).... Coach, St. Louis Cardinals (1992).

		REGULAR SEASON				POSTSEASON							
						Playoff		Champ. Series		World Series		All-Star Game	
Year	**Team (League)**	**W**	**L**	**Pct.**	**Pos.**	**W**	**L**	**W**	**L**	**W**	**L**	**W**	**L**
1993	—Colorado (N.L.)	67	95	.414	6th (W)	—	—	—	—	—	—	—	—

COLLINS, TERRY

ASTROS

PERSONAL: Born May 27, 1949, in Midland, Mich. . . . 5-8/160. . . . Threw right, batted left. . . . Full name: Terry Lee Collins.
HIGH SCHOOL: Midland (Mich.).
COLLEGE: Eastern Michigan (bachelor of science degree).
TRANSACTIONS/CAREER NOTES: Selected by Pittsburgh Pirates organization in 19th round of free-agent draft (June 8, 1971). . . . Released by Pirates organization (January 7, 1974). . . . Signed by Los Angeles Dodgers organization (January 14, 1974). . . . On disabled list (July 2-August 6, 1976). . . . Served as player/coach for Waterbury (1975) and Albuquerque (1977). . . . Released by Dodgers organization (February 28, 1978). . . . Signed by Dodgers organization as coach (March 13, 1978). . . . Released by Dodgers organization (May 14, 1978). . . . Signed by Dodgers organization as player (May 14, 1978). . . . On disabled list (June 26-July 6, 1978). . . . Signed as player/coach for Albuquerque for 1979. . . . On temporary inactive list (entire 1979 season). . . . Released by Dodgers organization (December 7, 1979). . . . Signed by Dodgers organization as coach (January 30, 1980). . . . Signed by Dodgers organization as player/coach (May 18, 1980). . . . On disabled list (May 29-July 1 and July 12-August 17, 1980). . . . Released by Dodgers organization (September 18, 1980). . . . Signed by Dodgers organization as player/manager (August 17, 1984). . . . Released by Dodgers organization as player (September 28, 1984).
STATISTICAL NOTES: Led New York-Pennsylvania League shortstops with 310 total chances and 37 double plays in 1971.

			BATTING												FIELDING			
Year	**Team (League)**	**Pos.**	**G**	**AB**	**R**	**H**	**2B**	**3B**	**HR**	**RBI**	**Avg.**	**BB**	**SO**	**SB**	**PO**	**A**	**E**	**Avg.**
1971	—Niag. Falls (NYP)	SS	70	265	51	81	12	3	1	26	.306	36	35	12	*112	*179	19	*.939
1972	—Salem (Carolina)	2B	126	459	77	116	17	7	1	41	.253	70	75	8	*254	333	*25	.959
1973	—Sherbrooke (East.)	2-0-3-P-S	114	324	52	76	9	0	0	20	.235	59	54	7	177	206	12	.970
1974	—Waterbury (East.)■	2B-SS	86	230	28	46	3	2	1	23	.200	46	42	2	144	243	11	.972
1975	—Waterbury (East.)	SS	4	9	2	1	0	0	0	1	.111	3	2	0	3	9	2	.857
	—Albuquerque (PCL)	2B-SS-3B	64	153	24	48	5	4	0	10	.314	18	19	2	87	53	11	.927
1976	—Albuquerque (PCL)	3B-OF-SS	67	174	23	42	4	5	2	24	.241	19	21	6	46	64	3	.973
1977	—Albuquerque (PCL)	2-3-S-P	54	158	27	39	6	3	0	15	.247	32	21	2	64	113	9	.952
1978	—Albuquerque (PCL)	2-3-S-P-0-1	72	217	29	60	9	4	1	22	.276	21	20	4	115	162	12	.958
1979	—								Did not play.									
1980	—Albuquerque (PCL)	DH	11	14	1	2	0	0	0	1	.143	3	4	1	...	...	...	...
1981	—								Did not play.									
1982	—								Did not play.									
1983	—								Did not play.									
1984	—Albuquerque (PCL)	SS-2B	3	6	1	1	0	0	0	0	.167	0	0	0	5	3	0	1.000

RECORD AS PITCHER

Year	Team (League)	W	L	Pct.	ERA	G	GS	CG	ShO	Sv.	IP	H	R	ER	BB	SO
1973	—Sherbrooke (East.)	0	0	...	2.25	3	0	0	0	2	4	3	1	1	3	0
1977	—Albuquerque (PCL)	0	0	...	0.00	1	0	0	0	0	2	2	0	0	0	1
1978	—Albuquerque (PCL)	0	0	...	0.00	2	0	0	0	1	3	1	0	0	1	1

RECORD AS MANAGER

BACKGROUND: Player/coach, Waterbury, Dodgers organization (1975). . . . Player/coach, Albuquerque, Dodgers organization (1977-80). . . . Coach, Pittsburgh Pirates (November 26, 1991-November 17, 1993).
HONORS: Named Minor League Manager of the Year by THE SPORTING NEWS (1987). . . . Named Pacific Coast League Manager of the Year (1988).

		REGULAR SEASON				POSTSEASON							
						Playoff		Champ. Series		World Series		All-Star Game	
Year	**Team (League)**	**W**	**L**	**Pct.**	**Pos.**	**W**	**L**	**W**	**L**	**W**	**L**	**W**	**L**
1981	—Lodi (California)	30	40	.429	7th	—	—	—	—	—	—	—	—
	—(Second half)	43	27	.614	T2nd	5	2	—	—	—	—	—	—
1982	—Vero Beach (Florida State)	38	31	.551	2nd (S)	—	—	—	—	—	—	—	—
	—(Second half)	42	22	.656	1st (S)	1	2	—	—	—	—	—	—
1983	—San Antonio (Texas)	33	34	.493	3rd (W)	—	—	—	—	—	—	—	—
	—(Second half)	3	4	.429		—	—	—	—	—	—	—	—
	—Albuquerque, second half (Pacific Coast)	42	26	.618	1st (S)	3	5	—	—	—	—	—	—
1984	—Albuquerque (Pacific Coast)	36	36	.500	5th (S)	—	—	—	—	—	—	—	—
	—(Second half)	26	45	.366	5th (S)	—	—	—	—	—	—	—	—
1985	—Albuquerque (Pacific Coast)	36	35	.507	4th (S)	—	—	—	—	—	—	—	—
	—(Second half)	31	41	.431	4th (S)	—	—	—	—	—	—	—	—
1986	—Albuquerque (Pacific Coast)	28	43	.394	5th (S)	—	—	—	—	—	—	—	—
	—(Second half)	26	45	.366	5th (S)	—	—	—	—	—	—	—	—
1987	—Albuquerque (Pacific Coast)	43	27	.614	1st (S)	—	—	—	—	—	—	—	—
	—(Second half)	34	38	.472	4th (S)	6	1	—	—	—	—	—	—
1988	—Albuquerque (Pacific Coast)	38	33	.535	2nd (S)	—	—	—	—	—	—	—	—
	—(Second half)	48	23	.676	1st (S)	0	3	—	—	—	—	—	—
1989	—Buffalo (American Association)	80	62	.563	2nd (E)	—	—	—	—	—	—	—	—
1990	—Buffalo (American Association)	85	62	.578	2nd (E)	—	—	—	—	—	—	—	—
1991	—Buffalo (American Association)	81	62	.566	1st (E)	2	3	—	—	—	—	—	—

NOTES:
1981—Defeated Reno, two games to one, in semifinals; defeated Visalia, three games to two, in league championship.
1982—Lost to Fort Lauderdale in playoffs.
1983—Replaced Albuquerque manager Del Crandall (June 29). Defeated Las Vegas, three games to two, in playoffs; lost to Portland, three games to none, in league championship.
1987—Defeated Las Vegas, three games to none, in playoffs; defeated Calgary, three games to one, in league championship.
1988—Lost to Las Vegas in playoffs.
1991—Lost to Denver in league championship.

COX, BOBBY

BRAVES

PERSONAL: Born May 21, 1941, in Tulsa, Okla. . . . 6-0/185. . . . Threw right, batted right. . . . Full name: Robert Joe Cox.
HIGH SCHOOL: Selma (Calif.).
COLLEGE: Reedley Junior College (Calif.).
TRANSACTIONS/CAREER NOTES: Signed by Los Angeles Dodgers organization (1959). . . . Selected by Chicago Cubs organization from Dodgers organization in Rule 5 minor league draft (November 30, 1964). . . . Acquired by Atlanta Braves organization (1966). . . . On Austin disabled list (May 8-18 and May 30-June 9, 1966). . . . On disabled list (May 1-June 12, 1967). . . . Traded by Braves to New York Yankees for C Bob Tillman and P Dale Roberts (December 7, 1967); Roberts later was transferred to Richmond. . . . On disabled list (May 28-June 18, 1970). . . . Released by Yankees organization (September 22, 1970). . . . Signed by Fort Lauderdale, Yankees organization (July 17, 1971). . . . Released as player by Fort Lauderdale (August 28, 1971).
STATISTICAL NOTES: Led Alabama-Florida League shortstops with 71 double plays in 1961. . . . Led Pacific Coast League third basemen with .954 fielding percentage in 1965.

			BATTING												FIELDING			
Year	**Team (League)**	**Pos.**	**G**	**AB**	**R**	**H**	**2B**	**3B**	**HR**	**RBI**	**Avg.**	**BB**	**SO**	**SB**	**PO**	**A**	**E**	**Avg.**
1960	—Reno (California)	2B	125	440	99	112	20	5	13	75	.255	95	129	28	282	*385	*39	.945
1961	—Salem (Northwest)	2B	14	44	3	9	2	0	0	2	.205	0	14	0	25	25	2	.962
	—Pan. City (Ala.-Fla.)	2B	92	335	66	102	27	4	17	73	.304	48	72	17	220	247	8	*.983
1962	—Salem (Northwest)	3B-2B	*141	514	83	143	26	7	16	82	.278	63	119	7	174	296	28	.944
1963	—Albuquerque (Tex.)	3B	17	53	5	15	2	0	2	5	.283	3	12	1	8	27	1	.972
	—Great Falls (Pio.)	3B	109	407	103	137	*31	4	19	85	.337	73	84	7	82	211	21	*.933
1964	—Albuquerque (Tex.)	2B	138	523	98	152	29	13	16	91	.291	52	84	8	*322	*415	*28	.963
1965	—Salt L. City (PCL)■	3B-2B	136	473	58	125	32	1	12	55	.264	35	96	1	133	337	22	†.955
1966	—Tacoma (PCL)	3B-2B	10	34	2	4	1	0	0	4	.118	6	9	0	23	15	0	1.000
	—Austin (Texas)■	2B-3B	92	339	35	77	11	1	7	30	.227	25	55	7	140	216	12	.967
1967	—Richmond (Int'l)	3B-1B	99	350	52	104	17	4	14	51	.297	34	73	3	84	136	8	.965
1968	—New York (A.L.)■	3B	135	437	33	100	15	1	7	41	.229	41	85	3	98	279	17	.957
1969	—New York (A.L.)	3B-2B	85	191	17	41	7	1	2	17	.215	34	41	0	50	147	11	.947
1970	—Syracuse (Int'l)	3B-SS-2B	90	251	34	55	15	0	9	30	.219	49	40	0	86	163	13	.950
1971	—Fort Lauder. (FSL)	2B-P	4	9	1	1	0	0	0	0	.111	1	0	0	4	5	0	1.000
	Major league totals (2 years)		220	628	50	141	22	2	9	58	.225	75	126	3	148	426	28	.953

RECORD AS PITCHER

Year	**Team (League)**	**W**	**L**	**Pct.**	**ERA**	**G**	**GS**	**CG**	**ShO**	**Sv.**	**IP**	**H**	**R**	**ER**	**BB**	**SO**
1971	—Fort Lauder. (FSL)	0	1	.000	5.40	3	0	0	0	0	10	15	9	6	5	4

RECORD AS MANAGER

BACKGROUND: Minor league instructor, New York Yankees (October 28, 1970-March 24, 1971). . . . Player/manager, Fort Lauderdale, Yankees organization (1971). . . . Coach, Yankees (1977).
HONORS: Coach, A.L. All-Star team (1985). . . . Named Major League Manager of the Year by THE SPORTING NEWS (1985). . . . Named A.L. Manager of the Year by Baseball Writers' Association of America (1985). . . . Named N.L. Manager of the Year by THE SPORTING NEWS (1991 and 1993). . . . Named N.L. Manager of the Year by Baseball Writers' Association of America (1991).

		REGULAR SEASON				POSTSEASON							
						Playoff		Champ. Series		World Series		All-Star Game	
Year	**Team (League)**	**W**	**L**	**Pct.**	**Pos.**	**W**	**L**	**W**	**L**	**W**	**L**	**W**	**L**
1971	—Fort Lauderdale (Florida State)	71	70	.504	4th (E)	—	—	—	—	—	—	—	—
1972	—West Haven (Eastern)	84	56	.600	1st (A)	3	0	—	—	—	—	—	—
1973	—Syracuse (International)	76	70	.521	3rd (A)	—	—	—	—	—	—	—	—
1974	—Syracuse (International)	74	70	.514	2nd (N)	—	—	—	—	—	—	—	—
1975	—Syracuse (International)	72	64	.529	3rd	—	—	—	—	—	—	—	—
1976	—Syracuse (International)	82	57	.590	2nd	6	1	—	—	—	—	—	—
1978	—Atlanta (N.L.)	69	93	.426	6th (W)	—	—	—	—	—	—	—	—
1979	—Atlanta (N.L.)	66	94	.413	6th (W)	—	—	—	—	—	—	—	—
1980	—Atlanta (N.L.)	81	80	.503	4th (W)	—	—	—	—	—	—	—	—
1981	—Atlanta (N.L.)	25	29	.463	4th (W)	—	—	—	—	—	—	—	—
	—(Second half)	25	27	.481	5th (W)	—	—	—	—	—	—	—	—
1982	—Toronto (A.L.)	78	84	.481	T6th (E)	—	—	—	—	—	—	—	—
1983	—Toronto (A.L.)	89	73	.549	4th (E)	—	—	—	—	—	—	—	—
1984	—Toronto (A.L.)	89	73	.549	2nd (E)	—	—	—	—	—	—	—	—
1985	—Toronto (A.L.)	99	62	.615	1st (E)	—	—	3	4	—	—	—	—
1990	—Atlanta (N.L.)	40	57	.412	6th (W)	—	—	—	—	—	—	—	—
1991	—Atlanta (N.L.)	94	68	.580	1st (W)	—	—	4	3	3	4	—	—
1992	—Atlanta (N.L.)	98	64	.605	1st (W)	—	—	4	3	2	4	0	1
1993	—Atlanta (N.L.)	104	58	.642	1st (W)	—	—	2	4	—	—	0	1
	American League totals (4 years)	355	292	.549		—	—	3	4	—	—	—	—
	National League totals (8 years)	602	570	.514		—	—	10	10	5	8	0	2
	Major league totals (12 years)	957	862	.526		—	—	13	14	5	8	0	2

NOTES:
1972—Defeated Three Rivers in playoff.
1976—Defeated Memphis, three games to none, in playoffs; defeated Richmond, three games to one, in league championship.
1985—Lost to Kansas City in A.L. Championship Series.
1990—Replaced Atlanta manager Russ Nixon with club in sixth place, record of 25-40 (June 22).
1991—Defeated Pittsburgh in N.L. Championship Series; lost to Minnesota in World Series.
1992—Defeated Pittsburgh in N.L. Championship Series; lost to Toronto in World Series.
1993—Lost to Philadelphia in N.L. Championship Series.

FREGOSI, JIM

PHILLIES

PERSONAL: Born April 4, 1942, in San Francisco. . . . 6-2/197. . . . Threw right, batted right. . . . Full name: James Louis Fregosi. . . . Father of Jim Fregosi Jr., minor league shortstop (1985-87).
HIGH SCHOOL: Serra (San Mateo, Calif.).
COLLEGE: Menlo College (Calif.).
TRANSACTIONS/CAREER NOTES: Signed by Boston Red Sox organization (September 6, 1959). . . . Selected by Los Angeles Angels in A.L. expansion draft (December 14, 1960). . . . On disabled list (July 12-August 5, 1961). . . . Traded by Angels to New York Mets for P Nolan Ryan, P Don Rose, OF Leroy Stanton and C Francisco Estrada (December 10, 1971). . . . Traded by Mets to Texas Rangers for a player to be named later (July 11, 1973); deal settled with cash. . . . On disabled list (April 22-May 12, 1977). . . . Traded by Rangers to Pittsburgh Pirates for 1B/C Ed Kirkpatrick (June 15, 1977). . . . Released by Pirates in order to accept managerial position with California Angels (June 1, 1978).
RECORDS: Shares major league single-game record for most double plays started by shortstop (nine-inning game)—5 (May 1, 1966, first game).
HONORS: Named shortstop on THE SPORTING NEWS A.L. All-Star team (1964 and 1967). . . . Won A.L. Gold Glove at shortstop (1967).
STATISTICAL NOTES: Tied for American Association lead in double plays by shortstop with 100 in 1961. . . . Led American League with 15 sacrifice hits in 1965. . . . Led American League shortstops with 125 double plays in 1966 and tied for lead with 92 in 1968. . . . Led American League shortstops with 531 assists and tied for lead with 35 errors in 1966.

			BATTING											FIELDING			
Year	Team (League)	Pos.	G	AB	R	H	2B	3B	HR	RBI	Avg.	BB	SO	SB	PO	A	E	Avg.
1960	—Alpine (Soph.)	IF-OF	112	404	96	108	17	7	6	58	.267	74	99	4	198	261	39	.922
1961	—Dall./Fort W. (A.A.)	SS	150	516	54	131	18	4	6	50	.254	50	70	6	247	*495	*53	.933
	—Los Angeles (A.L.)	SS	11	27	7	6	0	0	0	3	.222	1	4	0	12	22	2	.944
1962	—Dall./Fort W. (A.A.)	SS-OF	64	219	25	62	9	3	1	14	.283	32	37	1	94	164	22	.921
	—Los Angeles (A.L.)	SS	58	175	15	51	3	4	3	23	.291	18	27	2	96	150	15	.943
1963	—Los Angeles (A.L.)	SS	154	592	83	170	29	12	9	50	.287	36	104	2	271	446	27	.964
1964	—Los Angeles (A.L.)	SS	147	505	86	140	22	9	18	72	.277	72	87	8	225	421	23	.966
1965	—California (A.L.)	SS	161	602	66	167	19	7	15	64	.277	54	107	13	*312	481	26	.968
1966	—California (A.L.)	SS-1B	162	611	78	154	32	7	13	67	.252	67	89	17	299	†531	‡35	.960
1967	—California (A.L.)	SS	151	590	75	171	23	6	9	56	.290	49	77	9	258	435	25	.965
1968	—California (A.L.)	SS	159	614	77	150	21	*13	9	49	.244	60	101	9	273	454	29	.962
1969	—California (A.L.)	SS	161	580	78	151	22	6	12	47	.260	93	86	9	255	465	21	.972
1970	—California (A.L.)	SS-1B	158	601	95	167	33	5	22	82	.278	69	92	0	313	475	20	.975
1971	—California (A.L.)	SS-1B-OF	107	347	31	81	15	1	5	33	.233	39	61	2	241	251	22	.957
1972	—New York (N.L.)■	3B-SS-1B	101	340	31	79	15	4	5	32	.232	38	71	0	91	162	15	.944
1973	—New York (N.L.)	S-3-1-0	45	124	7	29	4	1	0	11	.234	20	25	1	47	70	9	.929
	—Texas (A.L.)■	3B-1B-SS	45	157	25	42	6	2	6	16	.268	12	31	0	98	53	5	.968
1974	—Texas (A.L.)	1B-3B	78	230	31	60	5	0	12	34	.261	22	41	0	331	73	5	.988
1975	—Texas (A.L.)	1B-3B	77	191	25	50	5	0	7	33	.262	20	39	0	356	35	6	.985
1976	—Texas (A.L.)	1B-2B	58	133	17	31	7	0	2	12	.233	23	33	2	183	18	2	.990
1977	—Texas (A.L.)	1B	13	28	4	7	1	0	1	5	.250	3	4	0	31	4	0	1.000
	—Pittsburgh (N.L.)■	1B-3B	36	56	10	16	1	1	3	16	.286	13	10	2	99	5	2	.981
1978	—Pittsburgh (N.L.)	3B-1B-2B	20	20	3	4	1	0	0	1	.200	6	8	0	14	4	2	.900
American League totals (16 years)			1700	5983	793	1598	243	72	143	646	.267	638	983	73	3554	4314	263	.968
National League totals (4 years)			202	540	51	128	21	6	8	60	.237	77	114	3	251	241	28	.946
Major league totals (18 years)			1902	6523	844	1726	264	78	151	706	.265	715	1097	76	3805	4555	291	.966

ALL-STAR GAME RECORD

			BATTING										FIELDING			
Year	League	Pos.	AB	R	H	2B	3B	HR	RBI	Avg.	BB	SO	SB	PO	A	E	Avg.
1964	—American	SS	4	1	1	0	0	0	1	.250	0	1	0	4	1	0	1.000
1966	—American	SS	2	0	0	0	0	0	0	.000	0	1	0	0	1	0	1.000
1967	—American	SS	4	0	1	0	0	0	0	.250	0	2	0	2	3	0	1.000
1968	—American	SS	3	0	1	1	0	0	0	.333	0	1	0	1	6	0	1.000
1969	—American	SS	1	0	0	0	0	0	0	.000	0	0	0	0	0	0	...
1970	—American	PH	1	0	0	0	0	0	0	.000	0	0	0	...	...	...	...
All-Star Game totals (6 years)			15	1	3	1	0	0	1	.200	0	5	0	7	11	0	1.000

RECORD AS MANAGER

BACKGROUND: Special assignment scout and coach, Philadelphia Phillies (1989-90). . . . Minor league pitching instructor and special assignment scout, Phillies (beginning of 1991 season-April 23, 1991).
HONORS: Named American Association Manager of the Year (1983). . . . Named American Association co-Manager of the Year (1985). . . . Named Minor League Manager of the Year by THE SPORTING NEWS (1985). . . . Coach, A.L. All-Star team (1987). . . . Coach, N.L. All-Star team (1993).

		REGULAR SEASON				POSTSEASON							
						Playoff		Champ. Series		World Series		All-Star Game	
Year	Team (League)	W	L	Pct.	Pos.	W	L	W	L	W	L	W	L
1978	—California (A.L.)	62	54	.534	T2nd (W)	—	—	—	—	—	—	—	—
1979	—California (A.L.)	88	74	.543	1st (W)	—	—	1	3	—	—	—	—
1980	—California (A.L.)	65	95	.406	6th (W)	—	—	—	—	—	—	—	—
1981	—California (A.L.)	22	25	.468									
1983	—Louisville (American Association)	78	57	.578	1st (E)	3	6	—	—	—	—	—	—
1984	—Louisville (American Association)	79	76	.510	4th	8	3	—	—	—	—	—	—
1985	—Louisville (American Association)	74	68	.521	1st (E)	4	1	—	—	—	—	—	—
1986	—Louisville (American Association)	32	34	.485	3rd (E)	—	—	—	—	—	—	—	—
	—Chicago (A.L.)	45	51	.469	5th (W)	—	—	—	—	—	—	—	—
1987	—Chicago (A.L.)	77	85	.475	5th (W)	—	—	—	—	—	—	—	—
1988	—Chicago (A.L.)	71	90	.441	5th (W)	—	—	—	—	—	—	—	—

Year	Team (League)	W	L	Pct.	Pos.	Playoff W	Playoff L	Champ. Series W	Champ. Series L	World Series W	World Series L	All-Star Game W	All-Star Game L
		REGULAR SEASON				POSTSEASON							
1991	—Philadelphia (N.L.)	74	75	.497	3rd (E)	—	—	—	—	—	—	—	—
1992	—Philadelphia (N.L.)	70	92	.432	6th (E)	—	—	—	—	—	—	—	—
1993	—Philadelphia (N.L.)	97	65	.599	1st (E)	—	—	4	2	2	4	—	—
	American League totals (7 years)	430	474	.476		—	—	1	3	—	—	—	—
	National League totals (3 years)	241	232	.510		—	—	4	2	2	4	—	—
	Major league totals (10 years)	671	706	.487		—	—	5	5	2	4	—	—

NOTES:

1978—Replaced California manager Dave Garcia with club in third place, record of 25-21 (June 1).
1979—Lost to Baltimore in A.L. Championship Series.
1981—Replaced as California manager by Gene Mauch with club in fourth place (May 28).
1983—Defeated Oklahoma City, three games to two, in playoff; lost to Denver, four games to none, in championship playoff.
1984—Defeated Indianapolis, four games to two, in playoff; defeated Denver, four games to one, in championship playoff.
1985—Defeated Oklahoma City, four games to one, in championship playoff.
1986—Replaced manager Tony La Russa (record of 26-38) and interim manager Doug Rader (1-1) with club in fifth place, record of 27-39 (June 22).
1991—Replaced Philadelphia manager Nick Leyva with club in sixth place, record of 4-9 (April 23).
1993—Defeated Atlanta in N.L. Championship Series; lost to Toronto in World Series.

GARNER, PHIL

BREWERS

PERSONAL: Born April 30, 1949, in Jefferson City, Tenn. . . . 5-10/177. . . . Threw right, batted right. . . . Full name: Philip Mason Garner.
HIGH SCHOOL: Beardon (Knoxville, Tenn.).
COLLEGE: Tennessee (received bachelor of science degree in general business, 1973).
TRANSACTIONS/CAREER NOTES: Selected by Montreal Expos organization in eighth round of free-agent draft (June 4, 1970). . . . Selected by Oakland Athletics organization in secondary phase of free-agent draft (January 13, 1971). . . . Traded by A's with IF Tommy Helms and P Chris Batton to Pittsburgh Pirates for P Doc Medich, P Dave Giusti, P Rick Langford, P Doug Bair, OF Mitchell Page and OF Tony Armas (March 15, 1977). . . . On Pittsburgh disabled list (April 2-23, 1981). . . . Traded by Pirates to Houston Astros for 2B Johnny Ray and two players to be named later (August 31, 1981); Pirates organization acquired OF Kevin Houston and P Randy Niemann to complete deal (September 9, 1981). . . . Granted free agency (November 12, 1986). . . . Re-signed by Astros (January 6, 1987). . . . Traded by Astros to Los Angeles Dodgers for a player to be named later (June 19, 1987); Astros organization acquired P Jeff Edwards to complete deal (June 26, 1987). . . . Granted free agency (November 9, 1987). . . . Signed by San Francisco Giants (January 28, 1988). . . . On San Francisco disabled list (April 13-September 2, 1988); included rehabilitation assignment to Phoenix (August 5-24). . . . Granted free agency (November 3, 1988).
RECORDS: Shares major league record for most grand slams in two consecutive games—2 (September 14 and 15, 1978). . . . Shares N.L. single-month record for most grand slams—2 (September 1978).
STATISTICAL NOTES: Led Pacific Coast League third basemen with 104 putouts, 261 assists, 35 errors, 400 total chances and 23 double plays in 1973. . . . Led A.L. second basemen with 26 errors in 1975. . . . Led A.L. second basemen with 865 total chances in 1976. . . . Led N.L. second basemen with 499 assists, 21 errors, 869 total chances and 116 double plays in 1980.

Year	Team (League)	Pos.	G	AB	R	H	2B	3B	HR	RBI	Avg.	BB	SO	SB	PO	A	E	Avg.
			BATTING												FIELDING			
1971	—Burlington (Midw.)	3B	116	439	73	122	22	4	11	70	.278	49	73	8	★122	203	29	.918
1972	—Birm. (Southern)	3B	71	264	45	74	10	6	12	40	.280	27	43	3	74	116	13	.936
	—Iowa (Am. Assoc.)	3B	70	247	33	60	18	4	9	22	.243	30	73	7	50	140	10	.950
1973	—Tucson (PCL)	3B-2B	138	516	87	149	23	12	14	73	.289	72	90	3	†107	†270	†35	.915
	—Oakland (A.L.)	3B	9	5	0	0	0	0	0	0	.000	0	3	0	2	3	0	1.000
1974	—Tucson (PCL)	3B-SS	96	388	78	128	29	10	11	51	.330	53	58	8	92	182	15	.948
	—Oakland (A.L.)	3B-SS-2B	30	28	4	5	1	0	0	1	.179	1	5	1	11	24	1	.972
1975	—Oakland (A.L.)	2B-SS	•160	488	46	120	21	5	6	54	.246	30	65	4	355	427	†26	.968
1976	—Oakland (A.L.)	2B	159	555	54	145	29	12	8	74	.261	36	71	35	378	★465	22	.975
1977	—Pittsburgh (N.L.)■	3B-2B-SS	153	585	99	152	35	10	17	77	.260	55	65	32	223	351	17	.971
1978	—Pittsburgh (N.L.)	3B-2B-SS	154	528	66	138	25	9	10	66	.261	66	71	27	258	389	28	.959
1979	—Pittsburgh (N.L.)	3B-2B-SS	150	549	76	161	32	8	11	59	.293	55	74	17	234	396	22	.966
1980	—Pittsburgh (N.L.)	2B-SS	151	548	62	142	27	6	5	58	.259	46	53	32	349	†500	†21	.976
1981	—Pitts.-Hou. (N.L.)■	2B	87	294	35	73	9	3	1	26	.248	36	32	10	183	250	12	.973
1982	—Houston (N.L.)	2B-3B	155	588	65	161	33	8	13	83	.274	40	92	24	285	464	17	.978
1983	—Houston (N.L.)	3B	154	567	76	135	24	2	14	79	.238	63	84	18	100	311	24	.945
1984	—Houston (N.L.)	3B-2B	128	374	60	104	17	6	4	45	.278	43	63	3	136	251	12	.970
1985	—Houston (N.L.)	3B-2B	135	463	65	124	23	10	6	51	.268	34	72	4	101	229	21	.940
1986	—Houston (N.L.)	3B-2B	107	313	43	83	14	3	9	41	.265	30	45	12	66	152	23	.905
1987	—Hou.-L.A. (N.L.)■	3B-2B-SS	113	238	29	49	9	0	5	23	.206	28	44	6	65	144	13	.941
1988	—San Francisco (N.L.)■	3B	15	13	0	2	0	0	0	1	.154	1	3	0	0	0	0	...
	—Phoenix (PCL)	2B-3B	17	45	5	12	2	1	1	5	.267	4	4	0	12	22	0	1.000
	American League totals (4 years)		358	1076	104	270	51	17	14	129	.251	67	144	40	746	919	49	.971
	National League totals (12 years)		1502	5060	676	1324	248	65	95	609	.262	497	698	185	2000	3437	210	.963
	Major league totals (16 years)		1860	6136	780	1594	299	82	109	738	.260	564	842	225	2746	4356	259	.965

DIVISION SERIES RECORD

Year	Team (League)	Pos.	G	AB	R	H	2B	3B	HR	RBI	Avg.	BB	SO	SB	PO	A	E	Avg.
			BATTING												FIELDING			
1981	—Houston (N.L.)	2B	5	18	1	2	0	0	0	0	.111	3	3	0	6	8	1	.933

CHAMPIONSHIP SERIES RECORD

Year	Team (League)	Pos.	G	AB	R	H	2B	3B	HR	RBI	Avg.	BB	SO	SB	PO	A	E	Avg.
			BATTING												FIELDING			
1975	—Oakland (A.L.)	2B	3	5	0	0	0	0	0	0	.000	0	1	0	7	4	1	.917

Year	Team (League)	Pos.	G	AB	R	H	2B	3B	HR	RBI	Avg.	BB	SO	SB	PO	A	E	Avg.
			BATTING												FIELDING			
1979	—Pittsburgh (N.L.)	2B-SS	3	12	4	5	0	1	1	1	.417	1	0	0	8	9	0	1.000
1986	—Houston (N.L.)	3B	3	9	1	2	1	0	0	2	.222	1	2	0	1	9	0	1.000
Championship series totals (3 years)			9	26	5	7	1	1	1	3	.269	2	3	0	16	22	1	.974

WORLD SERIES RECORD

WORLD SERIES NOTES: Shares single-series record for collecting one or more hits in each game (1979).

Year	Team (League)	Pos.	G	AB	R	H	2B	3B	HR	RBI	Avg.	BB	SO	SB	PO	A	E	Avg.
			BATTING												FIELDING			
1979	—Pittsburgh (N.L.)	2B	7	24	4	12	4	0	0	5	.500	3	1	0	21	23	2	.957

ALL-STAR GAME RECORD

Year	League	Pos.	AB	R	H	2B	3B	HR	RBI	Avg.	BB	SO	SB	PO	A	E	Avg.
			BATTING											FIELDING			
1976	—American	2B	1	0	0	0	0	0	0	.000	0	1	0	1	1	0	1.000
1980	—National	2B	2	1	1	0	0	0	0	.500	1	1	1	1	3	0	1.000
1981	—National	2B	0	0	0	0	0	0	0	...	0	0	0	0	0	0	...
All-Star Game totals (3 years)			3	1	1	0	0	0	0	.333	1	2	1	2	4	0	1.000

RECORD AS MANAGER

BACKGROUND: Coach, Houston Astros (1989-91).

Year	Team (League)	W	L	Pct.	Pos.	Playoff W	Playoff L	Champ. Series W	Champ. Series L	World Series W	World Series L	All-Star Game W	All-Star Game L
		REGULAR SEASON				POSTSEASON							
1992	—Milwaukee (A.L.)	92	70	.568	2nd (E)	—	—	—	—	—	—	—	—
1993	—Milwaukee (A.L.)	69	93	.426	7th (E)	—	—	—	—	—	—	—	—
Major league totals (2 years)		161	163	.497									

NOTES:

1993— On suspended list (September 24-27); club went 1-2 under third base coach Duffy Dyer.

GASTON, CITO

BLUE JAYS

PERSONAL: Born March 17, 1944, in San Antonio. . . . 6-4/210. . . . Threw right, batted right. . . . Full name: Clarence Edwin Gaston.

HIGH SCHOOL: Holy Cross (Corpus Christi, Tex.).

TRANSACTIONS/CAREER NOTES: Signed by Milwaukee Braves organization (March 22, 1964). . . . On Binghamton disabled list (May 26-July 6, 1964). . . . On disabled list (August 2-29, 1965). . . . Braves franchise moved from Milwaukee to Atlanta (1966). . . . Selected by San Diego Padres in expansion draft (October 14, 1968). . . . On disabled list (May 17-June 2, 1972). . . . Traded by Padres to Braves for P Danny Frisella (November 7, 1974). . . . Contract sold by Braves to Pittsburgh Pirates (September 22, 1978). . . . Granted free agency (November 2, 1978). . . . Signed by Santo Domingo of Inter-American League (April 10, 1979). . . . On suspended list (June 21-30, 1979). . . . Granted free agency when Inter-American League folded (June 30, 1979). . . . Signed by Leon of Mexican League (July 22, 1979).

STATISTICAL NOTES: Led New York-Pennsylvania League with 255 total bases in 1966.

Year	Team (League)	Pos.	G	AB	R	H	2B	3B	HR	RBI	Avg.	BB	SO	SB	PO	A	E	Avg.
			BATTING												FIELDING			
1964	—Binghamton (NYP)	OF	11	21	1	5	2	0	1	4	.238	1	9	0	8	0	1	.889
	—Greenville (W. Car.)	OF	49	165	15	38	6	3	0	16	.230	8	47	1	62	5	5	.931
1965	—W.P. Beach (FSL)	OF	70	202	14	38	5	3	0	9	.188	33	50	0	111	4	5	.958
1966	—Batavia (NY-Penn)	OF	114	433	84	143	18	5	*28	*104	.330	59	84	8	214	12	13	.946
	—Austin (Texas)	OF	4	10	2	3	1	1	0	4	.300	2	2	0	10	0	0	1.000
1967	—Austin (Texas)	OF	136	505	72	154	24	6	10	70	.305	45	104	6	274	8	12	.959
	—Atlanta (N.L.)	OF	9	25	1	3	0	1	0	1	.120	0	5	1	7	1	2	.800
1968	—Richmond (Int'l)	OF	21	71	9	17	4	0	2	8	.239	8	21	0	43	0	0	1.000
	—Shreveport (Texas)	OF	96	340	49	95	15	4	6	57	.279	28	55	12	203	3	9	.958
1969	—San Diego (N.L.)■	OF	129	391	20	90	11	7	2	28	.230	24	117	4	243	12	11	.959
1970	—San Diego (N.L.)	OF	146	584	92	186	26	9	29	93	.318	41	142	4	310	7	8	.975
1971	—San Diego (N.L.)	OF	141	518	57	118	13	9	17	61	.228	24	121	1	271	8	5	.982
1972	—San Diego (N.L.)	OF	111	379	30	102	14	0	7	44	.269	22	76	0	158	10	4	.977
1973	—San Diego (N.L.)	OF	133	476	51	119	18	4	16	57	.250	20	88	0	198	16	•12	.947
1974	—San Diego (N.L.)	OF	106	267	19	57	11	0	6	33	.213	16	51	0	119	7	1	.992
1975	—Atlanta (N.L.)■	OF-1B	64	141	17	34	4	0	6	15	.241	17	33	1	80	2	3	.965
1976	—Atlanta (N.L.)	OF-1B	69	134	15	39	4	0	4	25	.291	13	21	1	58	2	1	.984
1977	—Atlanta (N.L.)	OF-1B	56	85	6	23	4	0	3	21	.271	5	19	1	44	4	1	.980
1978	—Atl.-Pitts. (N.L.)■	OF-1B	62	120	6	28	1	0	1	9	.233	3	20	0	66	2	3	.958
1979	—San Dom. (In.-Am.)■	...	40	148	22	48	5	0	1	14	.324	...	...	1	...	...	...	...
	—Leon (Mexican)■	OF	24	83	5	28	2	0	1	8	.337	10	16	0	24	0	0	1.000
1980	—Leon (Mexican)	1B	48	185	16	44	5	0	4	27	.238	11	26	0	126	3	3	.977
Major league totals (11 years)			1026	3120	314	799	106	30	91	387	.256	185	693	13	1554	71	51	.970

ALL-STAR GAME RECORD

Year	League	Pos.	AB	R	H	2B	3B	HR	RBI	Avg.	BB	SO	SB	PO	A	E	Avg.
			BATTING											FIELDING			
1970	—National	OF	2	0	0	0	0	0	0	.000	1	0	0	2	0	0	1.000

RECORD AS MANAGER

BACKGROUND: Minor league instructor, Atlanta Braves organization (1981). . . . Coach, Toronto Blue Jays (1982-May 15, 1989).

HONORS: Coach, A.L. All-Star team (1991). . . . Named co-Sportsman of the Year by THE SPORTING NEWS (1993).

Year	Team (League)	W	L	Pct.	Pos.	Playoff W	Playoff L	Champ. Series W	Champ. Series L	World Series W	World Series L	All-Star Game W	All-Star Game L
		REGULAR SEASON				POSTSEASON							
1989	—Toronto (A.L.)	77	49	.611	1st (E)	—	—	1	4	—	—	—	—
1990	—Toronto (A.L.)	86	76	.531	2nd (E)	—	—	—	—	—	—	—	—
1991	—Toronto (A.L.)	91	71	.562	1st (E)	—	—	1	4	—	—	—	—
1992	—Toronto (A.L.)	96	66	.593	1st (E)	—	—	4	2	4	2	—	—
1993	—Toronto (A.L.)	95	67	.586	1st (E)	—	—	4	2	4	2	1	0
	Major league totals (5 years)	445	329	.575				10	12	8	4	1	0

NOTES:

1989—Replaced Toronto manager Jimy Williams with club in seventh place, record of 12-24 (May 15); lost to Oakland in A.L. Championship Series.

1991—Record includes time taken off because of back injury (August 21-September 27); Blue Jays were 19-14 under temporary manager Gene Tenace during that time; lost to Minnesota in A.L. Championship Series.

1992—Defeated Oakland in A.L. Championship Series; defeated Atlanta in World Series.

1993—Defeated Chicago in A.L. Championship Series; defeated Philadelphia in World Series.

GREEN, DALLAS

METS

PERSONAL: Born August 4, 1934, in Newport, Del. . . . 6-5/210. . . . Threw right, batted left. . . . Full name: George Dallas Green Jr. . . . Father of John Green, minor league pitcher (1985-90).

HIGH SCHOOL: Conrad (Wilmington, Del.).

COLLEGE: Delaware (bachelor of science degree, 1981).

TRANSACTIONS/CAREER NOTES: Signed as free agent by Philadelphia Phillies organization (June 9, 1955). . . . On disabled list (May 25-June 12, 1959). . . . Contract sold by Phillies organization to Washington Senators (April 11, 1965). . . . Returned to Phillies organization (May 11, 1965). . . . Contract sold by Phillies organization to New York Mets organization (July 22, 1966). . . . Returned to Phillies organization (August 10, 1966). . . . Served as player/coach for Reading (1967). . . . Released by Phillies (September 22, 1967).

Year	Team (League)	W	L	Pct.	ERA	G	GS	CG	ShO	Sv.	IP	H	R	ER	BB	SO
1955	—Reidsville (Caro.)	1	1	.500	10.06	7	2	1	0	...	17	25	22	19	16	8
	—Mattoon (Miss.-O.V.)	4	3	.571	3.44	11	8	5	3	...	55	43	29	21	42	85
1956	—Salt L. City (Pio.)	17	12	.586	3.58	33	31	17	1	...	239	182	126	95	*187	*226
1957	—Miami (Int'l)	0	1	.000	10.50	2	2	0	0	...	6	6	8	7	4	5
	—H.P.-Thomas.(Caro.)	12	9	.571	4.02	25	20	8	2	...	159	143	84	71	92	147
1958	—Miami (Int'l)	7	10	.412	3.74	31	22	5	0	...	159	135	73	66	70	103
1959	—Buffalo (Int'l)	9	5	.643	2.94	17	15	6	2	...	101	94	39	33	28	72
1960	—Buffalo (Int'l)	3	4	.429	3.36	11	11	4	0	...	75	72	35	28	26	44
	—Philadelphia (N.L.)	3	6	.333	4.05	23	10	5	1	...	109	100	54	49	44	51
1961	—Philadelphia (N.L.)	2	4	.333	4.85	42	10	1	1	...	128	160	77	69	47	51
1962	—Philadelphia (N.L.)	6	6	.500	3.84	37	10	2	0	...	129	145	58	55	43	58
1963	—Philadelphia (N.L.)	7	5	.583	3.23	40	14	4	0	...	120	134	53	43	38	68
1964	—Arkansas (PCL)	4	1	.800	2.63	7	6	2	0	...	48	46	15	14	9	34
	—Philadelphia (N.L.)	2	1	.667	5.79	25	0	0	0	...	42	63	31	27	14	21
1965	—Washington (A.L.)■	0	0	...	3.21	6	2	0	0	...	14	14	6	5	3	6
	—Arkansas (PCL)■	12	7	.632	3.66	23	23	12	1	...	172	180	81	70	36	119
1966	—San Diego (PCL)	14	9	.609	3.82	26	26	11	3	...	184	200	91	78	28	90
	—New York (N.L.)■	0	0	...	5.40	4	0	0	0	...	5	6	3	3	2	1
1967	—Reading (Eastern)■	6	2	.750	1.77	8	8	7	3	...	66	59	20	13	12	42
	—Philadelphia (N.L.)	0	0	...	9.00	8	0	0	0	...	15	25	16	15	6	12
	A.L. totals (1 year)	0	0	...	3.21	6	2	0	0	...	14	14	6	5	3	6
	N.L. totals (7 years)	20	22	.476	4.29	179	44	12	2	...	548	633	292	261	194	262
	Major league totals (8 years)	20	22	.476	4.26	185	46	12	2	...	562	647	298	266	197	268

RECORD AS MANAGER

BACKGROUND: Player/coach, Reading, Phillies organization (1967). . . . Assistant farm director, Phillies (November 19, 1969-June 2, 1972). . . . Director of minor leagues, Phillies (June 2, 1972-August 31, 1979). . . . General manager, Chicago Cubs (1982-87). . . . Scout, New York Mets (1991-May 19, 1993).

HONORS: Named Appalachian League Manager of the Year (1969). . . . Named Major League Executive of the Year by THE SPORTING NEWS (1984).

Year	Team (League)	W	L	Pct.	Pos.	Playoff W	Playoff L	Champ. Series W	Champ. Series L	World Series W	World Series L	All-Star Game W	All-Star Game L
		REGULAR SEASON				POSTSEASON							
1968	—Huron (Northern)	26	43	.377	5th	—	—	—	—	—	—	—	—
1969	—Pulaski (Appalachian)	38	28	.576	1st (N)	—	—	—	—	—	—	—	—
1979	—Philadelphia (N.L.)	19	11	.633	4th (E)	—	—	—	—	—	—	—	—
1980	—Philadelphia (N.L.)	91	71	.562	1st (E)	—	—	3	2	4	2	—	—
1981	—Philadelphia (N.L.)	34	21	.618	1st (E)	—	—	—	—	—	—	1	0
	—(Second half)	25	27	.481	3rd (E)	2	3	—	—	—	—	—	—
1989	—New York (A.L.)	56	65	.463		—	—	—	—	—	—	—	—
1993	—New York (N.L.)	46	78	.371	7th (E)	—	—	—	—	—	—	—	—
	National League totals (4 years)	215	208	.508		2	3	3	2	4	2	1	0
	American League totals (1 year)	56	65	.463		—	—	—	—	—	—	—	—
	Major league totals (5 years)	271	273	.498		2	3	3	2	4	2	1	0

NOTES:

1979—Replaced Philadelphia manager Danny Ozark with club in fifth place, record of 65-67 (August 31).

1980—Defeated Houston in N.L. Championship Series; defeated Kansas City in World Series.

1981—Lost to Montreal in divisional playoffs.
1989—Replaced by Bucky Dent as New York manager with club in sixth place (August 18).
1993—Replaced New York manager Jeff Torborg with club in seventh place, record of 13-25 (May 19).

HARGROVE, MIKE

INDIANS

PERSONAL: Born October 26, 1949, in Perryton, Tex. . . . 6-0/195. . . . Threw left, batted left. . . . Full name: Dudley Michael Hargrove.
HIGH SCHOOL: Perryton (Tex.).
COLLEGE: Northwestern State, Okla. (received bachelor of science degree in physical education and social sciences).
TRANSACTIONS/CAREER NOTES: Selected by Texas Rangers organization in 25th round of free-agent draft (June 6, 1972). . . . Traded by Rangers with 3B Kurt Bevacqua and C Bill Fahey to San Diego Padres for OF Oscar Gamble, C Dave Roberts and cash (October 25, 1978). . . . Traded by Padres to Cleveland Indians for OF Paul Dade (June 14, 1979). . . . Granted free agency (November 12, 1985).
HONORS: Named Western Carolinas League Player of the Year (1973). . . . Named A.L. Rookie Player of the Year by THE SPORTING NEWS (1974). . . . Named A.L. Rookie of the Year by Baseball Writers' Association of America (1974).
STATISTICAL NOTES: Led New York-Pennsylvania League first basemen with 58 double plays in 1972. . . . Led Western Carolinas League with 247 total bases in 1973. . . . Led Western Carolinas League first basemen with 118 double plays in 1973. . . . Led A.L. first basemen with 1,489 total chances in 1980. . . . Led A.L. with .432 on-base percentage in 1981.

			BATTING												FIELDING			
Year	**Team (League)**	**Pos.**	**G**	**AB**	**R**	**H**	**2B**	**3B**	**HR**	**RBI**	**Avg.**	**BB**	**SO**	**SB**	**PO**	**A**	**E**	**Avg.**
1972	—Geneva (NY-Penn)...	1B	•70	243	38	65	8	0	4	37	.267	52	44	3	★537	•40	10	★.983
1973	—Gastonia (W. Car.)...	1B	•130	456	88	★160	★35	8	12	82	★.351	68	47	10	★1121	•77	14	★.988
1974	—Texas (A.L.)............	1B-OF	131	415	57	134	18	6	4	66	.323	49	42	0	638	72	9	.987
1975	—Texas (A.L.)............	OF-1B	145	519	82	157	22	2	11	62	.303	79	66	4	513	45	13	.977
1976	—Texas (A.L.)............	1B	151	541	80	155	30	1	7	58	.287	★97	64	2	1222	110	★21	.984
1977	—Texas (A.L.)............	1B	153	525	98	160	28	4	18	69	.305	103	59	2	1393	100	11	.993
1978	—Texas (A.L.)............	1B	146	494	63	124	24	1	7	40	.251	★107	47	2	1221	★116	★17	.987
1979	—San Diego (N.L.)■.....	1B	52	125	15	24	5	0	0	8	.192	25	15	0	323	17	5	.986
	—Cleveland (A.L.)■.....	OF-1B	100	338	60	110	21	4	10	56	.325	63	40	2	356	16	2	.995
1980	—Cleveland (A.L.)	1B	160	589	86	179	22	2	11	85	.304	111	36	4	★1391	88	10	.993
1981	—Cleveland (A.L.)	1B	94	322	43	102	21	0	2	49	.317	60	16	5	766	76	•9	.989
1982	—Cleveland (A.L.)	1B	160	591	67	160	26	1	4	65	.271	101	58	2	1293	★123	5	.996
1983	—Cleveland (A.L.)	1B	134	469	57	134	21	4	3	57	.286	78	40	0	1098	115	7	.994
1984	—Cleveland (A.L.)	1B	133	352	44	94	14	2	2	44	.267	53	38	0	790	83	8	.991
1985	—Cleveland (A.L.)	1B-OF	107	284	31	81	14	1	1	27	.285	39	29	1	599	66	6	.991
American League totals (12 years)..........			1614	5439	768	1590	261	28	80	678	.292	940	535	24	11280	1010	118	.990
National League totals (1 year)..............			52	125	15	24	5	0	0	8	.192	25	15	0	323	17	5	.986
Major league totals (12 years)................			1666	5564	783	1614	266	28	80	686	.290	965	550	24	11603	1027	123	.990

ALL-STAR GAME RECORD

			BATTING										FIELDING			
Year	**League**	**Pos.**	**AB**	**R**	**H**	**2B**	**3B**	**HR**	**RBI**	**Avg.**	**BB**	**SO**	**SB**	**PO**	**A**	**E**	**Avg.**
1975	—American..................	PH	1	0	0	0	0	0	0	.000	0	0	0	...	...	...	...

RECORD AS MANAGER

BACKGROUND: Minor league coach, Cleveland Indians organization (1986). . . . Coach, Indians (1990-July 6, 1991).
HONORS: Named Carolina League Manager of the Year (1987). . . . Named Pacific Coast League Manager of the Year (1989).

		REGULAR SEASON				POSTSEASON							
						Playoff		Champ. Series		World Series		All-Star Game	
Year	**Team (League)**	**W**	**L**	**Pct.**	**Pos.**	**W**	**L**	**W**	**L**	**W**	**L**	**W**	**L**
1987	—Kinston (Carolina)	33	37	.471	T3rd (S)	—	—	—	—	—	—	—	—
	—(Second half)	42	28	.600	1st (S)	3	3	—	—	—	—	—	—
1988	—Williamsport (Eastern).........................	66	73	.475	6th	—	—	—	—	—	—	—	—
1989	—Colorado Springs (Pacific Coast)............	44	26	.629	1st (S)	—	—	—	—	—	—	—	—
	—(Second half)	34	38	.472	3rd (S)	2	3	—	—	—	—	—	—
1991	—Cleveland (A.L.)	32	53	.376	7th (E)	—	—	—	—	—	—	—	—
1992	—Cleveland (A.L.)	76	86	.469	T4th (E)	—	—	—	—	—	—	—	—
1993	—Cleveland (A.L.)	76	86	.469	6th (E)	—	—	—	—	—	—	—	—
Major league totals (3 years)..............................		184	225	.450									

NOTES:
1987—Defeated Winston-Salem, two games to none, in playoffs; lost to Salem, three games to one, in league championship.
1989—Lost to Albuquerque in playoffs.
1991—Replaced Cleveland manager John McNamara with club in seventh place, record of 25-52 (July 6).

HOBSON, BUTCH

RED SOX

PERSONAL: Born August 17, 1951, in Tuscaloosa, Ala. . . . 6-1/190. . . . Threw right, batted right. . . . Full name: Clell Lavern Hobson Jr. . . . Son of Clell Hobson, minor league infielder (1953-57).
HIGH SCHOOL: Bessemer (Ala.).
COLLEGE: Alabama.
TRANSACTIONS/CAREER NOTES: Selected by Boston Red Sox organization in eighth round of free-agent draft (June 5, 1973). . . . On disabled list (July 27-August 11 and August 23-September 7, 1980). . . . Traded by Red Sox with SS Rick Burleson to California Angels for 3B Carney Lansford, P Mark Clear and OF Rick Miller (December 10, 1980). . . . Traded by Angels to New York Yankees for P Bill Castro (March 24, 1982). . . . On disabled list (April 1-24, 1982 and August 1-14, 1985). . . . Released by Yankees organization (September 17, 1985).
STATISTICAL NOTES: Led Eastern League with 201 total bases in 1975. . . . Led International League third basemen with 89 putouts and 204 assists in 1976.

			BATTING												FIELDING			
Year	Team (League)	Pos.	G	AB	R	H	2B	3B	HR	RBI	Avg.	BB	SO	SB	PO	A	E	Avg.
1973	—Winst.-Salem (Car.) ..	3B-OF	17	39	8	7	2	1	0	5	.179	14	8	0	10	10	1	.952
1974	—Winst.-Salem (Car.) ..	OF-3B-1B	119	423	66	120	18	8	14	74	.284	39	75	2	211	79	12	.960
1975	—Bristol (Eastern)	3B	•138	471	68	125	25	3	15	73	.265	48	90	6	102	309	28	.936
	—Boston (A.L.)	3B	2	4	0	1	0	0	0	0	.250	0	2	0	1	3	0	1.000
1976	—Rhode Island (Int'l) ..	3B-SS	90	360	56	103	21	1	25	72	.286	33	81	1	†91	†204	15	.952
	—Boston (A.L.)	3B	76	269	34	63	7	5	8	34	.234	15	62	0	60	146	14	.936
1977	—Boston (A.L.)	3B	159	593	77	157	33	5	30	112	.265	27	*162	5	128	272	23	.946
1978	—Boston (A.L.)	3B	147	512	65	128	26	2	17	80	.250	50	122	1	122	261	*43	.899
1979	—Boston (A.L.)	3B-2B	146	528	74	138	26	7	28	93	.261	30	78	3	110	251	25	.935
1980	—Boston (A.L.)	3B	93	324	35	74	6	0	11	39	.228	25	69	1	52	109	16	.910
1981	—California (A.L.)■	3B	85	268	27	63	7	4	4	36	.235	35	60	1	85	139	•17	.929
1982	—New York (A.L.)■	1B	30	58	2	10	2	0	0	3	.172	1	14	0	37	2	2	.951
	—Columbus (Int'l)	1B-3B	27	83	17	27	5	1	4	20	.325	18	13	0	44	14	4	.935
1983	—Columbus (Int'l)	3B-1B	112	379	68	93	17	4	19	63	.245	56	76	2	91	149	11	.956
1984	—Columbus (Int'l)	3B-1B	116	382	49	96	18	1	13	56	.251	48	63	0	207	121	12	.965
1985	—Columbus (Int'l)	3B-1B	107	347	44	82	9	1	12	56	.236	47	64	0	123	138	16	.942
	Major league totals (8 years)		738	2556	314	634	107	23	98	397	.248	183	569	11	595	1183	140	.927

RECORD AS MANAGER

HONORS: Named International League Manager of the Year (1991).

		REGULAR SEASON				POSTSEASON							
						Playoff		Champ. Series		World Series		All-Star Game	
Year	Team (League)	W	L	Pct.	Pos.	W	L	W	L	W	L	W	L
1987	—Columbia (South Atlantic)	35	35	.500	5th (S)	—	—	—	—	—	—	—	—
	—(Second half)	29	40	.420	6th (S)	—	—	—	—	—	—	—	—
1988	—Columbia (South Atlantic)	38	32	.543	4th (S)	—	—	—	—	—	—	—	—
	—(Second half)	36	31	.537	2nd (S)	—	—	—	—	—	—	—	—
1989	—New Britain (Eastern)	60	76	.441	8th	—	—	—	—	—	—	—	—
1990	—New Britain (Eastern)	72	67	.518	4th	3	5	—	—	—	—	—	—
1991	—Pawtucket (International)	79	64	.552	1st (E)	0	3	—	—	—	—	—	—
1992	—Boston (A.L.)	73	89	.451	7th (E)	—	—	—	—	—	—	—	—
1993	—Boston (A.L.)	80	82	.494	5th (E)	—	—	—	—	—	—	—	—
	Major league totals (2 years)	153	171	.472									

NOTES:

1990—Defeated Albany/Colonie, three games to two, in playoffs; lost to London, three games to none, in league championship.
1991—Lost to Columbus in playoffs.

JOHNSON, DAVEY

REDS

PERSONAL: Born January 30, 1943, in Orlando, Fla. . . . 6-1/182. . . . Threw right, batted right. . . . Full name: David Allen Johnson.
HIGH SCHOOL: Alamo Heights (San Antonio, Tex.).
COLLEGE: Texas A&M, Trinity University, Tex. (bachelor of science degree in mathematics), and Johns Hopkins.
TRANSACTIONS/CAREER NOTES: Signed as free agent by Baltimore Orioles organization (June 2, 1962). . . . On Rochester disabled list (August 7-September 1, 1965). . . . Traded by Orioles with P Pat Dobson, P Roric Harrison and C Johnny Oates to Atlanta Braves for C Earl Williams and IF Taylor Duncan (November 30, 1972). . . . Released by Braves (April 11, 1975). . . . Signed by Yomiuri Giants of Japan Central League (1975). . . . Released by Yomiuri (January 21, 1977). . . . Signed by Philadelphia Phillies (February 3, 1977). . . . On disabled list (June 15-July 1, 1977). . . . Traded by Phillies to Chicago Cubs for P Larry Anderson (August 6, 1978). . . . Released by Cubs (October 17, 1978). . . . Served as player/manager with Miami of Inter-American League (1979). . . . Granted free agency when league folded (June 30, 1979).
RECORDS: Shares major league single-season records for most home runs by second baseman—42 (1973, also had one home run as pinch-hitter); fewest triples (150 or more games)—0 (1973); and most grand slams by pinch-hitter—2 (1978).
HONORS: Won A.L. Gold Glove at second base (1969-71). . . . Named second baseman on THE SPORTING NEWS A.L. All-Star team (1970). . . . Named N.L. Comeback Player of the Year by THE SPORTING NEWS (1973). . . . Named second baseman on THE SPORTING NEWS N.L. All-Star team (1973).
STATISTICAL NOTES: Led California League shortstops with 63 double plays in 1962. . . . Led A.L. second basemen with 19 errors in 1966. . . . Tied for A.L. lead in putouts by second baseman with 379 in 1970. . . . Tied for A.L. lead with eight sacrifice flies in 1967. . . . Led A.L. second basemen with 103 double plays in 1971. . . . Led N.L. second basemen with 877 total chances and tied for lead with 106 double plays in 1973.

			BATTING												FIELDING			
Year	Team (League)	Pos.	G	AB	R	H	2B	3B	HR	RBI	Avg.	BB	SO	SB	PO	A	E	Avg.
1962	—Stockton (Calif.)	SS	97	343	58	106	18	•12	10	63	.309	43	61	8	135	307	40	*.917
1963	—Elmira (Eastern)	SS-2B	63	233	47	76	11	6	13	42	.326	29	42	12	115	155	12	.957
	—Rochester (Int'l)	2B-OF	63	211	31	52	9	3	6	22	.246	25	39	4	141	138	11	.962
1964	—Rochester (Int'l)	2B-SS	•155	590	87	156	29	14	19	73	.264	71	95	7	326	445	39	.952
1965	—Baltimore (A.L.)	3B-2B-SS	20	47	5	8	3	0	0	1	.170	5	6	3	11	37	3	.941
	—Rochester (Int'l)	SS	52	193	29	58	9	3	4	22	.301	16	34	4	96	161	10	.963
1966	—Baltimore (A.L.)	2B-SS	131	501	47	129	20	3	7	56	.257	31	64	3	294	357	†20	.970
1967	—Baltimore (A.L.)	2B-3B	148	510	62	126	30	3	10	64	.247	59	82	4	344	351	14	.980
1968	—Baltimore (A.L.)	2B-SS	145	504	50	122	24	4	9	56	.242	44	80	7	294	370	15	.978
1969	—Baltimore (A.L.)	2B-SS	142	511	52	143	34	1	7	57	.280	57	52	3	358	370	12	.984
1970	—Baltimore (A.L.)	2B-SS	149	530	68	149	27	1	10	53	.281	66	68	2	‡382	391	8	.990
1971	—Baltimore (A.L.)	2B	142	510	67	144	26	1	18	72	.282	51	55	3	361	367	12	.984
1972	—Baltimore (A.L.)	2B	118	376	31	83	22	3	5	32	.221	52	68	1	286	307	6	*.990
1973	—Atlanta (N.L.)■	2B	157	559	84	151	25	0	43	99	.270	81	93	5	383	464	*30	.966
1974	—Atlanta (N.L.)	1B-2B	136	454	56	114	18	0	15	62	.251	75	59	1	789	231	11	.989

Year	Team (League)	Pos.	BATTING G	AB	R	H	2B	3B	HR	RBI	Avg.	BB	SO	SB	FIELDING PO	A	E	Avg.
1975	—Atlanta (N.L.)	PH	1	1	0	1	1	0	0	1	1.000	0	0	0	...	...	...	...
	—Yomiuri (Jp. Cen.)■	3B-SS	91	289	29	57	7	0	13	38	.197	32	71	1	85	157	11	.957
1976	—Yomiuri (Jp. Cen.)	2B-3B-1B	108	371	48	102	16	2	26	74	.275	55	62	1	226	28	11	.958
1977	—Philadelphia (N.L.)■	1B-2B-3B	78	156	23	50	9	1	8	36	.321	23	20	1	299	31	0	1.000
1978	—Phil.-Chi. (N.L.)■	3B-2B-1B	68	138	19	32	3	1	4	20	.232	15	28	0	61	63	11	.919
1979	—Miami (In.-Am.)■	1B	10	25	7	6	2	0	1	2	.240	...	...	0	...	...	...	...
American League totals (8 years)			995	3489	382	904	186	16	66	391	.259	365	475	26	2330	2550	90	.982
National League totals (5 years)			440	1308	182	348	56	2	70	218	.266	194	200	7	1532	789	52	.978
Major league totals (13 years)			1435	4797	564	1252	242	18	136	609	.261	559	675	33	3862	3339	142	.981

CHAMPIONSHIP SERIES RECORD

Year	Team (League)	Pos.	BATTING G	AB	R	H	2B	3B	HR	RBI	Avg.	BB	SO	SB	FIELDING PO	A	E	Avg.
1969	—Baltimore (A.L.)	2B	3	13	2	3	0	0	0	0	.231	2	1	0	5	11	0	1.000
1970	—Baltimore (A.L.)	2B	3	11	4	4	0	0	2	4	.364	1	1	0	11	4	0	1.000
1971	—Baltimore (A.L.)	2B	3	10	2	3	2	0	0	0	.300	3	1	0	5	6	1	.917
1977	—Philadelphia (N.L.)	1B	1	4	0	1	0	0	0	2	.250	0	1	0	8	0	0	1.000
Championship series totals (4 years)			10	38	8	11	2	0	2	6	.289	6	4	0	29	21	1	.980

WORLD SERIES RECORD

Year	Team (League)	Pos.	BATTING G	AB	R	H	2B	3B	HR	RBI	Avg.	BB	SO	SB	FIELDING PO	A	E	Avg.
1966	—Baltimore (A.L.)	2B	4	14	1	4	1	0	0	1	.286	0	1	0	12	12	0	1.000
1969	—Baltimore (A.L.)	2B	5	16	1	1	0	0	0	0	.063	2	1	0	8	15	0	1.000
1970	—Baltimore (A.L.)	2B	5	16	2	5	2	0	0	2	.313	5	2	0	15	9	0	1.000
1971	—Baltimore (A.L.)	2B	7	27	1	4	0	0	0	3	.148	0	1	0	18	12	0	1.000
World Series totals (4 years)			21	73	5	14	3	0	0	6	.192	7	5	0	53	48	0	1.000

ALL-STAR GAME RECORD

Year	League	Pos.	BATTING AB	R	H	2B	3B	HR	RBI	Avg.	BB	SO	SB	FIELDING PO	A	E	Avg.
1968	—American	2B	1	0	0	0	0	0	0	.000	0	1	0	1	1	0	1.000
1969	—American		Selected, did not play—injured.														
1970	—American	2B	5	0	1	0	0	0	0	.200	0	1	0	5	1	0	1.000
1973	—National	2B	1	0	0	0	0	0	0	.000	0	0	0	1	1	0	1.000
All-Star Game totals (3 years)			7	0	1	0	0	0	0	.143	0	2	0	7	3	0	1.000

RECORD AS MANAGER

BACKGROUND: Player/manager, Miami, Inter-American League (1979).... Instructor, New York Mets organization (1982).... Consultant, Cincinnati Reds (December 31, 1992-May 24, 1993).

HONORS: Coach, N.L. All-Star team (1986).

Year	Team (League)	REGULAR SEASON W	L	Pct.	Pos.	POSTSEASON Playoff W	Playoff L	Champ. Series W	Champ. Series L	World Series W	World Series L	All-Star Game W	All-Star Game L
1979	—Miami (Inter-American)	43	17	.717	1st	—	—	—	—	—	—	—	—
	—(Second half)	8	4	.667	1st	—	—	—	—	—	—	—	—
1981	—Jackson (Texas)	39	27	.591	1st (E)	—	—	—	—	—	—	—	—
	—(Second half)	29	39	.426	3rd (E)	5	1	—	—	—	—	—	—
1983	—Tidewater (International)	71	68	.511	4th	6	3	—	—	—	—	—	—
1984	—New York (N.L.)	90	72	.556	2nd (E)	—	—	—	—	—	—	—	—
1985	—New York (N.L.)	98	64	.605	2nd (E)	—	—	—	—	—	—	—	—
1986	—New York (N.L.)	108	54	.667	1st (E)	—	—	4	2	4	3	—	—
1987	—New York (N.L.)	92	70	.568	2nd (E)	—	—	—	—	—	—	1	0
1988	—New York (N.L.)	100	60	.625	1st (E)	—	—	3	4	—	—	—	—
1989	—New York (N.L.)	87	75	.537	2nd (E)	—	—	—	—	—	—	—	—
1990	—New York (N.L.)	20	22	.476		—	—	—	—	—	—	—	—
1993	—Cincinnati (N.L.)	53	65	.449	5th (W)	—	—	—	—	—	—	—	—
Major league totals (8 years)		648	482	.573				7	6	4	3	1	0

NOTES:

1979— Inter-American League folded June 30. Miami finished first in both halves of season and was declared league champion.
1981— Defeated Tulsa, two games to one, in playoffs; defeated San Antonio, three games to none, in league championship.
1983— Defeated Columbus, three games to two, in playoffs; defeated Richmond, three games to one, in league championship.
1986— Defeated Houston in N.L. Championship Series; defeated Boston in World Series.
1988— Lost to Los Angeles in N.L. Championship Series.
1990— Replaced as New York manager by Bud Harrelson with club in fourth place (May 29).
1993— Replaced Cincinnati manager Tony Perez with club in fifth place, record of 20-24 (May 24).

KELLY, TOM

TWINS

PERSONAL: Born August 15, 1950, in Graceville, Minn.... 5-11/185.... Threw left, batted left.... Full name: Jay Thomas Kelly.

HIGH SCHOOL: St. Mary's (South Amboy, N.J.).

COLLEGE: Mesa (Ariz.) Community College and Monmouth College (N.J.).

TRANSACTIONS/CAREER NOTES: Selected by Seattle Pilots organization in eighth round of free-agent draft (June 7, 1968).... Seattle franchise moved to Milwaukee and renamed Brewers (1970).... On temporary inactive list (April 16-20, April 25-30 and August 21, 1970-remainder of season).... On military list (August 27, 1970-February 3, 1971).... Released by Jacksonville (April 6, 1971).... Signed by Charlotte, Minnesota Twins organization (April 28, 1971).... Loaned by Twins organization

to Rochester, Baltimore Orioles organization (April 5-September 22, 1976).... On temporary inactive list (April 15-19, 1977). ... On disabled list (July 25-August 4, 1977).... Released by Toledo (December 18, 1978).... Signed by Visalia, Twins organization (January 2, 1979).... Released by Visalia (December 2, 1980).
STATISTICAL NOTES: Led Pacific Coast League outfielders with six double plays in 1972.

			BATTING											FIELDING			
Year	**Team (League)**	**Pos.**	**G**	**AB**	**R**	**H**	**2B**	**3B**	**HR**	**RBI**	**Avg.**	**BB**	**SO**	**SB**	**PO**	**A**	**E**	**Avg.**
1968	—Newark (NY-Penn)	OF	65	218	50	69	11	4	2	10	.317	43	31	★16	★144	★9	3	.981
1969	—Clinton (Midwest)	OF	100	269	47	60	10	2	6	35	.223	82	31	10	158	15	4	.977
1970	—Jacksonv. (South.)	OF-1B	93	266	33	64	10	1	8	38	.241	41	37	2	204	19	4	.982
1971	—Charlotte (South.)■	1B-OF	100	303	50	89	17	0	6	41	.294	59	52	2	508	38	9	.984
1972	—Tacoma (PCL)	OF-1B	132	407	76	114	19	2	10	52	.280	70	95	4	282	19	10	.968
1973	—Tacoma (PCL)	OF-1B	114	337	67	87	10	2	17	49	.258	89	64	4	200	20	6	.973
1974	—Tacoma (PCL)	OF-1B	115	357	68	110	16	0	18	69	.308	78	41	4	514	41	3	.995
1975	—Tacoma (PCL)	OF-1B	62	202	38	51	5	0	9	29	.252	47	36	6	185	12	6	.970
	—Minnesota (A.L.)	1B-OF	49	127	11	23	5	0	1	11	.181	15	22	0	360	28	6	.985
1976	—Rochester (Int'l)■	OF-1B	127	405	71	117	19	3	18	70	.289	85	71	2	323	28	4	.989
1977	—Tacoma (PCL)■	1B-OF-P	113	363	80	99	12	1	12	64	.273	78	61	11	251	15	6	.978
1978	—Toledo (Int'l)	1B-OF	119	325	47	74	13	0	10	49	.228	★91	61	2	556	46	5	.992
1979	—Visalia (California)	1B-P	2	0	0	0	0	0	0	0	...	1	0	0	3	4	0	1.000
Major league totals (1 year)			49	127	11	23	5	0	1	11	.181	15	22	0	360	28	6	.985

RECORD AS PITCHER

Year	**Team (League)**	**W**	**L**	**Pct.**	**ERA**	**G**	**GS**	**CG**	**ShO**	**Sv.**	**IP**	**H**	**R**	**ER**	**BB**	**SO**
1977	—Tacoma (PCL)	0	0	...	6.00	1	0	0	0	0	3	2	2	2	3	0
1979	—Visalia (California)	1	0	1.000	2.25	1	1	0	0	0	8	5	3	2	7	2
1980	—Visalia (California)	0	0	...	0.69	2	1	0	0	0	13	12	1	1	6	2

RECORD AS MANAGER

BACKGROUND: Player/manager, Tacoma, Minnesota Twins organization (June 1977-remainder of season).... Player/coach, Toledo, Twins organization (1978).... Coach, Twins (1983-September 11, 1986).
HONORS: Named California League Manager of the Year (1979).... Named California League co-Manager of the Year (1980). ... Named Southern League Manager of the Year (1981).... Coach, A.L. All-Star team (1991).... Named A.L. Manager of the Year by THE SPORTING NEWS (1991).... Named A.L. Manager of the Year by Baseball Writers' Association of America (1991).

		REGULAR SEASON				POSTSEASON							
						Playoff		Champ. Series		World Series		All-Star Game	
Year	**Team (League)**	**W**	**L**	**Pct.**	**Pos.**	**W**	**L**	**W**	**L**	**W**	**L**	**W**	**L**
1977	—Tacoma (Pacific Coast)	28	26	.519	3rd (W)	—	—	—	—	—	—	—	—
1979	—Visalia (California)	44	26	.629	1st (S)	1	2	—	—	—	—	—	—
	—(Second half)	42	28	.600	2nd (S)	—	—	—	—	—	—	—	—
1980	—Visalia (California)	27	43	.386	4th (S)	—	—	—	—	—	—	—	—
	—(Second half)	44	26	.629	1st (S)	2	3	—	—	—	—	—	—
1981	—Orlando (Southern)	42	27	.609	1st (E)	6	2	—	—	—	—	—	—
	—(Second half)	37	36	.507	3rd (E)	—	—	—	—	—	—	—	—
1982	—Orlando (Southern)	31	38	.449	5th (E)	—	—	—	—	—	—	—	—
	—(Second half)	43	32	.573	2nd (E)	—	—	—	—	—	—	—	—
1986	—Minnesota (A.L.)	12	11	.522	6th (W)	—	—	—	—	—	—	—	—
1987	—Minnesota (A.L.)	85	77	.525	1st (W)	—	—	4	1	4	3	—	—
1988	—Minnesota (A.L.)	91	71	.562	2nd (W)	—	—	—	—	—	—	1	0
1989	—Minnesota (A.L.)	80	82	.494	5th (W)	—	—	—	—	—	—	—	—
1990	—Minnesota (A.L.)	74	88	.457	7th (W)	—	—	—	—	—	—	—	—
1991	—Minnesota (A.L.)	95	67	.586	1st (W)	—	—	4	1	4	3	—	—
1992	—Minnesota (A.L.)	90	72	.556	2nd (W)	—	—	—	—	—	—	1	0
1993	—Minnesota (A.L.)	71	91	.438	T5th (W)	—	—	—	—	—	—	—	—
Major league totals (8 years)		598	559	.517		—	—	8	2	8	6	2	0

NOTES:
1977—Replaced Tacoma manager Del Wilber with record of 40-49 and became player/manager (June).
1979—Lost to San Jose in semifinals.
1980—Defeated Fresno, two games to one, in semifinals; lost to Stockton, three games to none, in league championship.
1981—Defeated Savannah, three games to one, in semifinals; defeated Nashville, three games to one, in league championship.
1986—Replaced Minnesota manager Ray Miller with club in seventh place, record of 59-80 (September 12).
1987—Defeated Detroit in A.L. Championship Series; defeated St. Louis in World Series.
1991—Defeated Toronto in A.L. Championship Series; defeated Atlanta in World Series.

KENNEDY, KEVIN

RANGERS

PERSONAL: Born September 26, 1954, in Los Angeles.... 6-3/220.... Threw right, batted right.... Full name: Kevin Curtis Kennedy.
HIGH SCHOOL: Taft (Woodland Hills, Calif.).
COLLEGE: San Diego State and Cal State Northridge (bachelor of arts degree in accounting).
TRANSACTIONS/CAREER NOTES: Selected by Baltimore Orioles organization in eighth round of free-agent draft (June 8, 1976). ... On Rochester disabled list (June 10-July 6, 1981).... Released by Orioles organization (July 6, 1981).... Signed by St. Louis Cardinals organization (July 12, 1981).... Released by Cardinals organization (April 25, 1982).... Signed by Los Angeles Dodgers organization (April 29, 1982).... Granted free agency (October 22, 1982).... Served as coach of Lodi, Dodgers organization (February 9-May 16, 1983).... Signed as player by Albuquerque, Dodgers organization (May 16, 1983).... Released by Albuquerque (June 2, 1983).... Re-signed as coach of Lodi (June 2, 1983).
STATISTICAL NOTES: Led International League catchers with 10 double plays in 1979.

Year	Team (League)	Pos.	G	AB	R	H	2B	3B	HR	RBI	Avg.	BB	SO	SB	PO	A	E	Avg.
			BATTING												FIELDING			
1976	—Bluefield (Appal.)	C	21	81	9	22	4	0	1	10	.272	10	9	1	160	25	3	.984
	—Charlotte (South.)	C	40	123	21	27	4	0	0	5	.220	18	19	2	210	24	2	.992
1977	—Charlotte (South.)	C	36	115	12	29	7	0	0	14	.252	11	18	0	194	22	7	.969
	—Rochester (Int'l)	C	14	43	2	12	2	0	0	3	.279	0	4	0	67	3	1	.986
1978	—Rochester (Int'l)	C	123	410	46	104	17	2	4	58	.254	41	67	3	548	53	8	.987
1979	—Rochester (Int'l)	C	109	360	28	71	8	4	3	32	.197	26	40	0	586	56	7	.989
1980	—Rochester (Int'l)	C	77	232	21	61	8	0	1	28	.263	21	33	0	318	37	4	.989
1981	—Rochester (Int'l)	C	24	71	5	13	2	0	0	5	.183	4	12	0	91	11	4	.962
	—Springfield (A.A.)■	C	9	23	2	3	1	0	0	0	.130	3	3	0	37	2	0	1.000
1982	—Louisville (A.A.)	C	4	9	0	1	0	0	0	1	.111	2	2	0	18	1	1	.950
	—Albuquerque (PCL)■	C-P	51	137	17	39	5	0	3	20	.285	10	22	3	217	22	7	.972
1983	—Albuquerque (PCL)	C-P	2	3	1	0	0	0	0	2	.000	1	0	0	9	0	0	1.000

RECORD AS PITCHER

Year	Team (League)	W	L	Pct.	ERA	G	GS	CG	ShO	Sv.	IP	H	R	ER	BB	SO
1982	—Albuquerque (PCL)	0	0	...	9.00	1	0	0	0	0	1	2	1	1	0	0
1983	—Albuquerque (PCL)	0	0	...	0.00	1	0	0	0	0	1⅓	1	0	0	0	0

RECORD AS MANAGER

BACKGROUND: Coach, Lodi, Los Angeles Dodgers organization (February 9-May 16 and June 2, 1983-remainder of season).... Director, minor league field operations, Montreal Expos (October 31, 1991-May 22, 1992).... Coach, Expos (May 22, 1992-remainder of season).

HONORS: Named Pioneer League Manager of the Year (1985).... Named Pacific Coast League Manager of the Year (1990).

Year	Team (League)	W	L	Pct.	Pos.	Playoff W	Playoff L	Champ. Series W	Champ. Series L	World Series W	World Series L	All-Star Game W	All-Star Game L
		REGULAR SEASON				POSTSEASON							
1984	—Great Falls (Pioneer)	37	31	.544	2nd (N)	—	—	—	—	—	—	—	—
1985	—Great Falls (Pioneer)	54	16	.771	1st (N)	2	3	—	—	—	—	—	—
1986	—Great Falls (Pioneer)	40	30	.571	2nd	1	3	—	—	—	—	—	—
1987	—Bakersfield (California)	41	31	.569	2nd (S)	0	1	—	—	—	—	—	—
	—(Second half)	37	34	.521	2nd (S)	—	—	—	—	—	—	—	—
1988	—San Antonio (Texas)	42	26	.618	1st (W)	—	—	—	—	—	—	—	—
	—(Second half)	31	34	.477	3rd (W)	0	2	—	—	—	—	—	—
1989	—Albuquerque (Pacific Coast)	36	35	.507	3rd (S)	—	—	—	—	—	—	—	—
	—(Second half)	44	27	.620	1st (S)	4	5	—	—	—	—	—	—
1990	—Albuquerque (Pacific Coast)	46	25	.648	1st (S)	—	—	—	—	—	—	—	—
	—(Second half)	45	26	.634	1st (S)	6	2	—	—	—	—	—	—
1991	—Albuquerque (Pacific Coast)	38	30	.559	3rd (S)	—	—	—	—	—	—	—	—
	—(Second half)	42	28	.600	2nd (S)	—	—	—	—	—	—	—	—
1993	—Texas (A.L.)	86	76	.531	2nd (W)	—	—	—	—	—	—	—	—
	Major league totals (1 year)	86	76	.531									

NOTES:

1985— Lost to Salt Lake City in league championship.
1987— Lost to El Paso in one-game playoff for first-half title.
1986— Lost to Salt Lake City in league championship.
1988— Lost to El Paso in playoffs.
1989— Defeated Colorado Springs, three games to two, in playoffs; lost to Vancouver, three games to one, in league championship.
1990— Defeated Colorado Springs, three games to two, in playoffs; defeated Edmonton, three games to none, in league championship.

LACHEMANN, RENE

MARLINS

PERSONAL: Born May 4, 1945, in Los Angeles.... 6-0/200.... Threw right, batted right.... Full name: Rene George Lachemann.... Brother of Marcel Lachemann, current coach, Marlins, and pitcher, Oakland Athletics (1969-71); and brother of Bill Lachemann, current manager, Arizona League Angels, California Angels organization, and minor league catcher (1955-63).... Name pronounced LATCH-man.

HIGH SCHOOL: Dorsey (Los Angeles).

COLLEGE: Southern California.

TRANSACTIONS/CAREER NOTES: Signed as free agent by Kansas City Athletics organization (September 18, 1963).... On Mobile disabled list (July 19-29, 1966).... A's franchise moved from Kansas City to Oakland (October 1967).... Released by A's organization (October 26, 1972).

STATISTICAL NOTES: Led Midwest League catchers with 14 double plays in 1964.... Led Pacific Coast League catchers with 889 total chances and 13 double plays in 1967.

Year	Team (League)	Pos.	G	AB	R	H	2B	3B	HR	RBI	Avg.	BB	SO	SB	PO	A	E	Avg.
			BATTING												FIELDING			
1964	—Burlington (Midw.)	C	99	335	52	94	14	1	*24	82	.281	33	74	0	743	55	10	.988
	—Birm. (Southern)	C	3	6	1	4	1	0	0	1	.667	0	0	0	7	1	0	1.000
1965	—Kansas City (A.L.)	C	92	216	20	49	7	1	9	29	.227	12	57	0	361	27	8	.980
1966	—Mobile (Southern)	C	119	434	48	111	17	1	15	65	.256	32	104	0	819	48	13	.985
	—Kansas City (A.L.)	C	7	5	0	1	1	0	0	0	.200	0	1	0	10	1	0	1.000
1967	—Vancouver (PCL)	C	123	410	26	91	16	0	6	53	.222	31	100	0	*811	68	10	.989
1968	—Oakland (A.L.)	C	19	60	3	9	1	0	0	4	.150	1	11	0	82	5	3	.967
	—Vancouver (PCL)	C-1B	63	193	14	48	7	0	4	14	.249	18	48	0	351	22	7	.982
1969	—Iowa (Am. Assoc.)	1B-C	107	415	47	106	18	1	20	66	.255	35	91	1	782	62	10	.988
1970	—Iowa (Am. Assoc.)	1-3-2-C	61	171	25	44	10	0	5	20	.257	22	36	0	365	29	7	.983
1971	—Iowa (Am. Assoc.)	1-3-C-2	92	314	42	76	16	1	17	48	.242	23	76	1	542	65	10	.984
1972	—Iowa (Am. Assoc.)	1-C-0-3	95	236	25	51	6	0	11	37	.216	44	61	1	347	18	6	.984
	Major league totals (3 years)		118	281	23	59	9	1	9	33	.210	13	69	0	453	33	11	.978

RECORD AS MANAGER

BACKGROUND: Coach, Boston Red Sox (October 29, 1984-86).... Coach, Oakland Athletics (November 18, 1986-92).
HONORS: Named Southern League Manager of the Year (1976).

		REGULAR SEASON				POSTSEASON							
						Playoff		Champ. Series		World Series		All-Star Game	
Year	Team (League)	W	L	Pct.	Pos.	W	L	W	L	W	L	W	L
1973	—Burlington (Midwest)	24	23	.511	5th (S)	—	—	—	—	—	—	—	—
	—(Second half)	30	32	.484	3rd (S)	—	—	—	—	—	—	—	—
1974	—Burlington (Midwest)	29	28	.509	2nd (S)	—	—	—	—	—	—	—	—
	—(Second half)	32	31	.508	2nd (S)	—	—	—	—	—	—	—	—
1975	—Modesto (California)	33	37	.471	6th	—	—	—	—	—	—	—	—
	—(Second half)	35	35	.500	5th	—	—	—	—	—	—	—	—
1976	—Chattanooga (Southern)	34	30	.532	1st (W)	—	—	—	—	—	—	—	—
	—(Second half)	36	38	.486	2nd (W)	0	1	—	—	—	—	—	—
1977	—San Jose (Pacific Coast)	64	80	.444	4th	—	—	—	—	—	—	—	—
1978	—San Jose (Pacific Coast)	53	87	.379	5th	—	—	—	—	—	—	—	—
1979	—Spokane (Pacific Coast)	39	32	.549	2nd (N)	—	—	—	—	—	—	—	—
	—(Second half)	29	47	.382	5th (N)	—	—	—	—	—	—	—	—
1980	—Spokane (Pacific Coast)	24	41	.369	5th (N)	—	—	—	—	—	—	—	—
	—(Second half)	36	39	.480	2nd (N)	—	—	—	—	—	—	—	—
1981	—Spokane (Pacific Coast)	11	9	.550		—	—	—	—	—	—	—	—
	—Seattle (A.L.)	15	18	.455	6th (W)	—	—	—	—	—	—	—	—
	—Seattle (second half)	23	29	.442	5th (W)	—	—	—	—	—	—	—	—
1982	—Seattle (A.L.)	76	86	.469	4th (W)	—	—	—	—	—	—	—	—
1983	—Seattle (A.L.)	26	47	.356		—	—	—	—	—	—	—	—
1984	—Milwaukee (A.L.)	67	94	.416	7th (E)	—	—	—	—	—	—	—	—
1993	—Florida (N.L.)	64	98	.395	6th (E)	—	—	—	—	—	—	—	—
	A.L. totals (4 years)	207	274	.430									
	N.L. totals (1 year)	64	98	.395									
	Major league totals (5 years)	271	372	.421		—	—	—	—	—	—	—	—

NOTES:
1976—Lost to Montgomery in one-game playoff in West Division championship.
1981—Left Spokane (second place) to replace Seattle manager Maury Wills with club in seventh place, record of 6-18 (May 6).
1983—Replaced as Seattle manager by Del Crandall with club in seventh place (June 25).

LAMONT, GENE

WHITE SOX

PERSONAL: Born December 25, 1946, in Rockford, Ill. ... 6-1/190. ... Threw right, batted both.... Full name: Gene William Lamont.
HIGH SCHOOL: Hiawatha (Kirkland, Ill).
COLLEGE: Northern Illinois and Western Illinois.
TRANSACTIONS/CAREER NOTES: Selected by Detroit Tigers organization in first round (13th pick overall) of free-agent draft (June 29, 1965).... On disabled list (May 18-28, 1966).... On temporary inactive list (May 20-25, 1967).... On military list (May 25, 1967-remainder of season).... On temporary inactive list (July 15-31, 1972). ... Traded by Tigers to Atlanta Braves organization for C Bob Didier (May 14, 1973).... Selected by Tigers from Braves organization in Rule 5 major league draft (December 3, 1973).... Released by Evansville, Tigers organization (December 20, 1977).
STATISTICAL NOTES: Led Southern League catchers with nine errors in 1969. ... Led Southern League catchers with 730 putouts, 72 assists, 814 total chances, 9 double plays and 15 passed balls in 1972. ... Led American Association catchers with eight double plays in 1976.

			BATTING												FIELDING			
Year	Team (League)	Pos.	G	AB	R	H	2B	3B	HR	RBI	Avg.	BB	SO	SB	PO	A	E	Avg.
1965	—Syracuse (Int'l)	C	5	9	1	1	0	0	1	1	.111	0	6	0	...	...	...	...
	—Day. Beach (FSL)	C	38	104	9	24	5	1	1	16	.231	13	33	1	222	19	3	.988
1966	—States. (W. Caro.)	C	45	137	14	27	4	2	3	19	.197	21	49	1	283	28	8	.975
	—Rocky Mount (Car.)	C	36	102	9	26	4	1	2	9	.255	16	23	0	213	19	5	.979
1967	—Rocky Mount (Car.)	C	19	56	4	8	2	0	1	5	.143	8	8	0	107	16	1	.992
1968	—Rocky Mount (Car.)	C-OF-3B	101	304	36	76	10	0	4	39	.250	24	60	1	498	72	7	.988
1969	—Montgomery (Sou.)	C-3B	86	268	24	63	15	1	3	29	.235	32	37	0	410	92	†16	.969
1970	—Toledo (Int'l)	C-3B-OF	74	230	27	61	9	1	4	32	.265	19	46	1	313	59	5	.987
	—Detroit (A.L.)	C	15	44	3	13	3	1	1	4	.295	2	9	0	87	8	0	1.000
1971	—Toledo (Int'l)	C	63	180	17	41	8	1	5	19	.228	19	29	0	321	43	9	.976
	—Detroit (A.L.)	C	7	15	2	1	0	0	0	1	.067	0	5	0	38	2	2	.952
1972	—Montgomery (Sou.)	C-OF	119	385	47	105	19	1	6	51	.273	64	72	1	†731	†72	12	.985
	—Detroit (A.L.)	C	1	0	0	0	0	0	0	0	...	0	0	0	1	0	0	1.000
1973	—Richmond (Int'l)■	C-1B	101	275	29	69	11	1	2	25	.251	41	64	0	411	34	3	.993
1974	—Detroit (A.L.)■	C	60	92	9	20	4	0	3	8	.217	7	19	0	204	21	6	.974
1975	—Detroit (A.L.)	C	4	8	1	3	1	0	0	1	.375	0	2	1	14	3	1	.944
	—Evansville (A.A.)	C	49	130	15	40	9	0	3	20	.308	20	20	1	211	23	4	.983
1976	—Evansville (A.A.)	C	96	269	23	63	13	0	5	25	.234	36	47	2	467	47	7	.987
1977	—Evansville (A.A.)	C	3	5	0	2	1	0	0	0	.400	1	1	0	4	1	0	1.000
	Major league totals (5 years)		87	159	15	37	8	1	4	14	.233	9	35	1	344	34	9	.977

RECORD AS MANAGER

BACKGROUND: Coach, Pittsburgh Pirates (1986-91).
HONORS: Named Southern League Manager of the Year (1982).... Named A.L. Manager of the Year by Baseball Writers' Association of America (1993).

		REGULAR SEASON				POSTSEASON							
						Playoff		Champ. Series		World Series		All-Star Game	
Year	Team (League)	W	L	Pct.	Pos.	W	L	W	L	W	L	W	L
1978	—Fort Myers (Florida State)	38	30	.559	1st (S)	0	1	—	—	—	—	—	—
	—(Second half)	33	36	.478	5th (S)	—	—	—	—	—	—	—	—
1979	—Fort Myers (Florida State)	38	32	.543	3rd (S)	—	—	—	—	—	—	—	—
	—(Second half)	31	37	.456	4th (S)	—	—	—	—	—	—	—	—
1980	—Jacksonville (Southern)	31	40	.437	4th (E)	—	—	—	—	—	—	—	—
	—(Second half)	32	41	.438	5th (E)	—	—	—	—	—	—	—	—
1981	—Jacksonville (Southern)	34	36	.486	4th (E)	—	—	—	—	—	—	—	—
	—(Second half)	31	41	.431	4th (E)	—	—	—	—	—	—	—	—
1982	—Jacksonville (Southern)	41	31	.569	1st (E)	—	—	—	—	—	—	—	—
	—(Second half)	42	30	.583	1st (E)	4	4	—	—	—	—	—	—
1983	—Jacksonville (Southern)	36	36	.500	2nd (E)	—	—	—	—	—	—	—	—
	—(Second half)	41	32	.562	1st (E)	4	4	—	—	—	—	—	—
1984	—Omaha (American Association)	68	86	.442	8th	—	—	—	—	—	—	—	—
1985	—Omaha (American Association)	73	69	.514	3rd (W)	—	—	—	—	—	—	—	—
1992	—Chicago (A.L.)	86	76	.531	3rd (W)	—	—	—	—	—	—	—	—
1993	—Chicago (A.L.)	94	68	.580	1st (W)	—	—	2	4	—	—	—	—
	Major league totals (2 years)	180	144	.556		—	—	2	4	—	—	—	—

NOTES:

1978—Lost to Miami in Southern Division championship.

1981—Jacksonville tied one game.

1982—Defeated Columbus, three games to one, in Eastern Division championship; lost to Nashville, three games to one, in league championship.

1983—Defeated Savannah, three games to one, in Eastern Division championship; lost to Birmingham, three games to one, in league championship.

1993—Lost to Toronto in A.L. Championship Series.

LA RUSSA, TONY

ATHLETICS

PERSONAL: Born October 4, 1944, in Tampa, Fla. . . . 6-0/185. . . . Threw right, batted right. . . . Full name: Anthony La Russa Jr.

HIGH SCHOOL: Jefferson (Tampa, Fla.).

COLLEGE: University of Tampa (Fla.), South Florida (degree in industrial management) and Florida State (law degree, 1980).

TRANSACTIONS/CAREER NOTES: Signed by Kansas City Athletics organization (June 6, 1962). . . . On disabled list (May 9-September 8, 1964; June 3-July 15, 1965; and April 12-May 6 and July 3-September 5, 1967). . . . A's franchise moved from Kansas City to Oakland (October 1967). . . . Contract sold by A's to Atlanta Braves (August 14, 1971). . . . Traded by Braves to Chicago Cubs for P Tom Phoebus (October 20, 1972). . . . Contract sold by Cubs to Pittsburgh Pirates organization (March 23, 1974). . . . Released by Pirates organization (April 4, 1975). . . . Signed by Chicago White Sox organization (April 7, 1975). . . . On disabled list (August 8-18, 1976). . . . Contract sold by White Sox to St. Louis Cardinals organization (December 13, 1976). . . . Named Cardinals coach (June 20, 1977). . . . Released by Cardinals organization (September 29, 1977).

STATISTICAL NOTES: Led International League in being hit by pitch with 11 in 1972.

			BATTING												FIELDING			
Year	Team (League)	Pos.	G	AB	R	H	2B	3B	HR	RBI	Avg.	BB	SO	SB	PO	A	E	Avg.
1962	—Day. Beach (FSL)	SS	64	225	37	58	7	0	1	32	.258	42	47	11	135	173	38	.890
	—Binghamton (East.)	SS-2B	12	43	3	8	0	0	0	4	.186	5	9	2	20	27	8	.855
1963	—Kansas City (A.L.)	SS-2B	34	44	4	11	1	1	0	1	.250	7	12	0	29	25	2	.964
1964	—Lewiston (N'west)	2B-SS	90	329	50	77	22	1	1	25	.234	53	56	10	188	218	18	.958
1965	—Birm. (Southern)	2B	75	259	24	50	11	2	1	18	.193	26	37	5	202	161	21	.945
1966	—Modesto (Calif.)	2B	81	316	67	92	20	1	7	54	.291	44	37	18	201	212	20	.954
	—Mobile (Southern)	2B	51	170	20	50	9	4	4	26	.294	23	24	4	117	133	10	.962
1967	—Birm. (Southern)	2B	41	139	12	32	6	1	5	22	.230	10	11	3	88	120	5	.977
1968	—Oakland (A.L.)	PH	5	3	0	1	0	0	0	0	.333	0	0	0	...	...	...	...
	—Vancouver (PCL)	2B	122	455	55	109	16	8	5	29	.240	52	58	4	249	321	14	*.976
1969	—Iowa (Am. Assoc.)	2B	67	235	37	72	11	1	4	27	.306	0	1	5	177	222	15	.964
	—Oakland (A.L.)	PH	8	8	0	0	0	0	0	0	.000	42	30	0	...	...	...	...
1970	—Iowa (Am. Assoc.)	2B	22	88	13	22	5	0	2	5	.250	9	14	0	52	59	3	.974
	—Oakland (A.L.)	2B	52	106	6	21	4	1	0	6	.198	15	19	0	67	89	5	.969
1971	—Iowa (Am. Assoc.)	2-3-S-0	28	107	21	31	5	1	2	11	.290	10	11	0	70	85	2	.987
	—Oakland (A.L.)	2B-SS-3B	23	8	3	0	0	0	0	0	.000	0	4	0	8	7	2	.882
	—Atlanta (N.L.)■	2B	9	7	1	2	0	0	0	0	.286	1	1	0	8	6	1	.933
1972	—Richmond (Int'l)	2B	122	389	68	120	13	2	10	42	.308	72	41	0	305	289	20	.967
1973	—Wichita (A.A.)■	2B-1B-3B	106	392	82	123	16	0	5	75	.314	60	46	10	423	213	26	.961
	—Chicago (N.L.)	PR	1	0	1	0	0	0	0	0	...	0	0	0	...	...	...	...
1974	—Char., W.Va. (Int'l)■	2B	139	457	50	119	17	1	8	35	.260	51	50	4	262	*378	17	.974
1975	—Denver (A.A.)■	3-0-S-2	118	354	87	99	23	2	7	46	.280	70	46	13	95	91	10	.949
1976	—Iowa (Am. Assoc.)	3-2-S-1-0-P	107	332	53	86	11	0	4	34	.259	40	43	10	132	160	22	.930
1977	—New Orleans (A.A.)■	2B-3B	50	128	17	24	2	2	3	6	.188	20	21	0	66	87	7	.956
	American League totals (5 years)		122	169	13	33	5	2	0	7	.195	64	65	0	104	121	9	.962
	National League totals (2 years)		10	7	2	2	0	0	0	0	.286	1	1	0	8	6	1	.933
	Major league totals (6 years)		132	176	15	35	5	2	0	7	.199	65	66	0	112	127	10	.960

RECORD AS PITCHER

Year	Team (League)	W	L	Pct.	ERA	G	GS	CG	ShO	Sv.	IP	H	R	ER	BB	SO
1976	—Iowa (Am. Assoc.)	0	0	...	3.00	3	0	0	0	0	3	3	1	1	0	0

RECORD AS MANAGER

BACKGROUND: Coach, St. Louis Cardinals organization (June 20-September 29, 1977). . . . Coach, Chicago White Sox (July 3,

1978-remainder of season).
RECORDS: Shares major league single-season record for most clubs managed—2 (1986).
HONORS: Named Major League Manager of the Year by THE SPORTING NEWS (1983).... Named A.L. Manager of the Year by Baseball Writers' Association of America (1983, 1988 and 1992).... Coach, A.L. All-Star team (1984 and 1987).... Named A.L. Manager of the Year by THE SPORTING NEWS (1988 and 1992).

		REGULAR SEASON				POSTSEASON							
						Playoff		Champ. Series		World Series		All-Star Game	
Year	Team (League)	W	L	Pct.	Pos.	W	L	W	L	W	L	W	L
1978	—Knoxville (Southern)	49	21	.700	1st (W)	—	—	—	—	—	—	—	—
	—(Second half)	4	4	.500		—	—	—	—	—	—	—	—
1979	—Iowa (American Association)	54	52	.509		—	—	—	—	—	—	—	—
	—Chicago (A.L.)	27	27	.500	5th (W)	—	—	—	—	—	—	—	—
1980	—Chicago (A.L.)	70	90	.438	5th (W)	—	—	—	—	—	—	—	—
1981	—Chicago (A.L.)	31	22	.585	3rd (W)	—	—	—	—	—	—	—	—
	—(Second half)	23	30	.434	6th (W)	—	—	—	—	—	—	—	—
1982	—Chicago (A.L.)	87	75	.537	3rd (W)	—	—	—	—	—	—	—	—
1983	—Chicago (A.L.)	99	63	.611	1st (W)	—	—	1	3	—	—	—	—
1984	—Chicago (A.L.)	74	88	.457	T5th (W)	—	—	—	—	—	—	—	—
1985	—Chicago (A.L.)	85	77	.525	3rd (W)	—	—	—	—	—	—	—	—
1986	—Chicago (A.L.)	26	38	.406		—	—	—	—	—	—	—	—
	—Oakland (A.L.)	45	34	.570	T3rd (W)	—	—	—	—	—	—	—	—
1987	—Oakland (A.L.)	81	81	.500	3rd (W)	—	—	—	—	—	—	—	—
1988	—Oakland (A.L.)	104	58	.642	1st (W)	—	—	4	0	1	4	—	—
1989	—Oakland (A.L.)	99	63	.611	1st (W)	—	—	4	1	4	0	1	0
1990	—Oakland (A.L.)	103	59	.636	1st (W)	—	—	4	0	0	4	1	0
1991	—Oakland (A.L.)	84	78	.519	4th (W)	—	—	—	—	—	—	1	0
1992	—Oakland (A.L.)	96	66	.593	1st (W)	—	—	2	4	—	—	—	—
1993	—Oakland (A.L.)	68	94	.420	7th (W)	—	—	—	—	—	—	—	—
	Major league totals (15 years)	1202	1043	.535				15	8	5	8	3	0

NOTES:
1978—Became Chicago White Sox coach and replaced as Knoxville manager by Joe Jones with club in third place (July 3).
1979—Replaced as Iowa manager by Joe Sparks with club in second place (August 3); replaced Chicago manager Don Kessinger with club in fifth place, record of 46-60 (August 3).
1983—Lost to Baltimore in A.L. Championship Series.
1986—Replaced as White Sox manager by interim manager Doug Rader with club in sixth place (June 20); replaced Oakland manager Jackie Moore (record of 29-44) and interim manager Jeff Newman (2-8) with club in seventh place, record of 31-52 (July 7).
1988—Defeated Boston in A.L. Championship Series; lost to Los Angeles in World Series.
1989—Defeated Toronto in A.L. Championship Series; defeated San Francisco in World Series.
1990—Defeated Boston in A.L. Championship Series; lost to Cincinnati in World Series.
1992—Lost to Toronto in A.L. Championship Series.
1993—On suspended list (October 1-remainder of season); club was managed by the coaching staff.

LASORDA, TOM

DODGERS

PERSONAL: Born September 22, 1927, in Norristown, Pa.... 5-9/195.... Threw left, batted left.... Full name: Thomas Charles Lasorda.... Name pronounced luh-SORR-duh.
HIGH SCHOOL: Norristown (Pa.).
TRANSACTIONS/CAREER NOTES: On National Defense list (May 14, 1946-February 2, 1948).... On disabled list (July 9-19, 1948).... Selected by Nashua, Brooklyn Dodgers organization, from Philadelphia Phillies organization in Rule 5 minor league draft (November 24, 1948).... Contract sold by Brooklyn Dodgers organization to Kansas City Athletics (March 2, 1956).... Traded by A's to New York Yankees for P Wally Burnette and cash (July 11, 1956).... Contract sold by Yankees organization to Dodgers organization (May 26, 1957).... Released by Dodgers organization (July 9, 1960).
RECORDS: Shares N.L. record for most wild pitches in one inning—3 (May 5, 1955, first inning).
HONORS: Named International League Pitcher of the Year (1958).
STATISTICAL NOTES: Led Canadian-American League with 20 wild pitches in 1948.... Led International League with 14 wild pitches in 1953.

Year	Team (League)	W	L	Pct.	ERA	G	GS	CG	ShO	Sv.	IP	H	R	ER	BB	SO
1945	—Concord (N.C. St.)	3	12	.200	4.09	27	13	6	0	...	121	115	84	55	100	91
1946	—							In military service.								
1947	—							In military service.								
1948	—Schen. (Can.-Am.)	9	12	.429	4.64	32	18	11	0	...	192	180	122	99	153	195
1949	—Greenville (S. Atl.)	7	7	.500	2.93	45	15	6	0	...	178	141	81	58	138	151
1950	—Montreal (Int'l)	9	4	.692	3.70	31	17	7	0	...	146	136	73	60	82	85
1951	—Montreal (Int'l)	12	8	.600	3.49	31	21	11	1	...	165	145	75	64	87	80
1952	—Montreal (Int'l)	14	5	.737	3.66	33	27	12	5	...	182	156	90	74	93	77
1953	—Montreal (Int'l)	17	8	.680	2.81	36	29	12	3	...	208	171	77	65	94	122
1954	—Montreal (Int'l)	14	5	.737	3.51	23	21	13	1	...	154	142	66	60	79	75
	—Brooklyn (N.L.)	0	0	...	5.00	4	0	0	0	...	9	8	5	5	5	5
1955	—Brooklyn (N.L.)	0	0	...	13.50	4	1	0	0	...	4	5	6	6	6	4
	—Montreal (Int'l)	9	8	.529	3.27	22	21	11	3	...	143	125	58	52	62	92
1956	—Kansas City (A.L.)■	0	4	.000	6.20	18	5	0	0	...	45	40	38	31	45	28
	—Denver (A.A.)■	3	4	.429	4.99	16	13	2	0	...	83	94	54	46	34	54
1957	—Denver (A.A.)	0	2	.000	12.18	6	4	0	0	...	17	29	25	23	6	8
	—Los Angeles (PCL)■	7	10	.412	3.89	29	20	5	1	...	132	134	73	57	59	72
1958	—Montreal (Int'l)	★18	6	.750	2.50	34	31	★16	•5	...	★230	191	77	64	76	126
1959	—Montreal (Int'l)	12	8	.600	3.83	29	28	10	2	...	188	192	93	80	•77	64
1960	—Montreal (Int'l)	2	5	.286	8.20	12	10	1	0	...	45	79	48	41	24	17
	A.L. totals (1 year)	0	4	.000	6.20	18	5	0	0	...	45	40	38	31	45	28
	N.L. totals (2 years)	0	0	...	7.62	8	1	0	0	...	13	13	11	11	11	9
	Major league totals (3 years)	0	4	.000	6.52	26	6	0	0	...	58	53	49	42	56	37

RECORD AS MANAGER

BACKGROUND: Scout, Los Angeles Dodgers (1961-65). . . . Manager, Los Angeles farm team in Arizona Instructional League (1969). . . . Coach, Dodgers (1973-76).

HONORS: Named Pioneer League Manager of the Year (1967). . . . Named Pacific Coast League co-Manager of the Year (1970). . . . Named Minor League Manager of the Year by THE SPORTING NEWS (1970). . . . Coach, N.L. All-Star team (1977, 1983-84, 1986 and 1993). . . . Named N.L. Manager of the Year by Baseball Writers' Association of America (1983 and 1988). . . . Named N.L. co-Manager of the Year by THE SPORTING NEWS (1988).

	REGULAR SEASON				POSTSEASON							
					Playoff		Champ. Series		World Series		All-Star Game	
Year Team (League)	W	L	Pct.	Pos.	W	L	W	L	W	L	W	L
1965 —Pocatello (Pioneer)	33	33	.500	T2nd	—	—	—	—	—	—	—	—
1966 —Ogden (Pioneer)	39	27	.591	1st	—	—	—	—	—	—	—	—
1967 —Ogden (Pioneer)	41	25	.621	1st	—	—	—	—	—	—	—	—
1968 —Ogden (Pioneer)	39	25	.609	1st	—	—	—	—	—	—	—	—
1969 —Spokane (Pacific Coast)	71	73	.493	2nd (N)	—	—	—	—	—	—	—	—
1970 —Spokane (Pacific Coast)	94	52	.630	1st (N)	4	0	—	—	—	—	—	—
1971 —Spokane (Pacific Coast)	69	76	.476	3rd (N)	—	—	—	—	—	—	—	—
1972 —Albuquerque (Pacific Coast)	92	56	.622	1st (E)	3	1	—	—	—	—	—	—
1976 —Los Angeles (N.L.)	2	2	.500	2nd (W)	—	—	—	—	—	—	—	—
1977 —Los Angeles (N.L.)	98	64	.605	1st (W)	—	—	3	1	2	4	—	—
1978 —Los Angeles (N.L.)	95	67	.586	1st (W)	—	—	3	1	2	4	1	0
1979 —Los Angeles (N.L.)	79	83	.488	3rd (W)	—	—	—	—	—	—	1	0
1980 —Los Angeles (N.L.)	92	71	.564	2nd (W)	—	—	—	—	—	—	—	—
1981 —Los Angeles (N.L.)	36	21	.632	1st (W)	—	—	—	—	—	—	—	—
—(Second half)	27	26	.509	4th (W)	3	2	3	2	4	2	—	—
1982 —Los Angeles (N.L.)	88	74	.543	2nd (W)	—	—	—	—	—	—	1	0
1983 —Los Angeles (N.L.)	91	71	.562	1st (W)	—	—	1	3	—	—	—	—
1984 —Los Angeles (N.L.)	79	83	.488	4th (W)	—	—	—	—	—	—	—	—
1985 —Los Angeles (N.L.)	95	67	.586	1st (W)	—	—	2	4	—	—	—	—
1986 —Los Angeles (N.L.)	73	89	.451	5th (W)	—	—	—	—	—	—	—	—
1987 —Los Angeles (N.L.)	73	89	.451	4th (W)	—	—	—	—	—	—	—	—
1988 —Los Angeles (N.L.)	94	67	.584	1st (W)	—	—	4	3	4	1	—	—
1989 —Los Angeles (N.L.)	77	83	.481	4th (W)	—	—	—	—	—	—	0	1
1990 —Los Angeles (N.L.)	86	76	.531	2nd (W)	—	—	—	—	—	—	—	—
1991 —Los Angeles (N.L.)	93	69	.574	2nd (W)	—	—	—	—	—	—	—	—
1992 —Los Angeles (N.L.)	63	99	.389	6th (W)	—	—	—	—	—	—	—	—
1993 —Los Angeles (N.L.)	81	81	.500	4th (W)	—	—	—	—	—	—	—	—
Major league totals (18 years)	1422	1282	.526		3	2	16	14	12	11	3	1

NOTES:

1970— Defeated Hawaii in championship playoff.
1972— Defeated Eugene in championship playoff.
1976— Replaced retiring Los Angeles manager Walter Alston with club in second place, record of 90-68 (September 29).
1977— Defeated Philadelphia in N.L. Championship Series; lost to New York Yankees in World Series.
1978— Defeated Philadelphia in N.L. Championship Series; lost to New York Yankees in World Series.
1981— Defeated Houston in divisional playoffs; defeated Montreal in N.L. Championship Series; defeated New York Yankees in World Series.
1983— Lost to Philadelphia in N.L. Championship Series.
1985— Lost to St. Louis in N.L. Championship Series.
1988— Defeated New York Mets in N.L. Championship Series; defeated Oakland in World Series.

LEYLAND, JIM

PIRATES

PERSONAL: Born December 15, 1944, in Toledo, O. . . . 5-11/170. . . . Threw right, batted right. . . . Full name: James Richard Leyland. . . . Name pronounced LEE-lund.

HIGH SCHOOL: Perrysburg (O.).

TRANSACTIONS/CAREER NOTES: Signed as free agent by Detroit Tigers organization (September 21, 1963). . . . On disabled list (June 15-27, 1964). . . . Released by Rocky Mount, Tigers organization (March 27, 1971).

		BATTING											FIELDING			
Year Team (League)	Pos.	G	AB	R	H	2B	3B	HR	RBI	Avg.	BB	SO	SB	PO	A	E	Avg.
1964 —Lakeland (Fla. St.)	C	52	129	8	25	0	1	0	8	.194	18	33	1	268	17	6	.979
—Cocoa Tigers (CRL)	C	24	52	2	12	1	1	0	4	.231	13	7	1	122	15	3	.979
1965 —Jamestown (NYP)	C-3B-P	82	211	18	50	7	2	1	21	.237	37	44	2	318	36	6	.983
1966 —Rocky Mount (Car.)	C	67	173	24	42	6	0	0	16	.243	32	35	0	369	23	1	.997
1967 —Montgomery (Sou.)	C	62	171	11	40	3	0	1	16	.234	16	27	0	350	25	6	.984
1968 —Montgomery (Sou.)	C-3B-SS	81	264	19	51	3	0	1	20	.193	14	54	2	511	43	7	.988
1969 —Montgomery (Sou.)	C	16	39	1	8	0	0	0	1	.205	4	7	0	64	6	3	.959
—Lakeland (Fla. St.)	C-P	60	179	20	43	8	0	1	16	.240	31	17	0	321	28	4	.989
1970 —Montgomery (Sou.)	C	2	3	0	0	0	0	0	0	.000	0	0	0	6	0	1	.857

RECORD AS PITCHER

Year Team (League)	W	L	Pct.	ERA	G	GS	CG	ShO	Sv.	IP	H	R	ER	BB	SO
1965 —Jamestown (NYP)	0	0	...	0.00	1	0	0	0	...	2	2	0	0	0	1
1969 —Lakeland (Fla. St.)	0	0	...	9.00	1	0	0	0	0	2	4	2	2	0	1

RECORD AS MANAGER

BACKGROUND: Coach, Detroit Tigers organization (1970-June 5, 1971); served as player/coach (1970). . . . Coach, Chicago White Sox (1982-85).

HONORS: Named Florida State League Manager of the Year (1977-78). . . . Named American Association Manager of the Year (1979). . . . Named N.L. co-Manager of the Year by THE SPORTING NEWS (1988). . . . Coach, N.L. All-Star team (1990-91).

. . . Named N.L. Manager of the Year by THE SPORTING NEWS (1990 and 1992). . . . Named N.L. Manager of the Year by Baseball Writers' Association of America (1990 and 1992).

		REGULAR SEASON				POSTSEASON							
						Playoff		Champ. Series		World Series		All-Star Game	
Year	Team (League)	W	L	Pct.	Pos.	W	L	W	L	W	L	W	L
1971	—Bristol (Appalachian)	31	35	.470	3rd (S)	—	—	—	—	—	—	—	—
1972	—Clinton (Midwest)	22	41	.349	5th (N)	—	—	—	—	—	—	—	—
	—(Second half)	27	36	.429	4th (N)	—	—	—	—	—	—	—	—
1973	—Clinton (Midwest)	36	26	.581	2nd (N)	—	—	—	—	—	—	—	—
	—(Second half)	37	25	.597	1st (N)	0	2	—	—	—	—	—	—
1974	—Montgomery (Southern)	61	76	.445	3rd (W)	—	—	—	—	—	—	—	—
1975	—Clinton (Midwest)	29	31	.483	4th (S)	—	—	—	—	—	—	—	—
	—(Second half)	38	30	.559	2nd (S)	—	—	—	—	—	—	—	—
1976	—Lakeland (Florida State)	74	64	.536	2nd (N)	4	0	—	—	—	—	—	—
1977	—Lakeland (Florida State)	85	53	.616	1st (N)	5	1	—	—	—	—	—	—
1978	—Lakeland (Florida State)	31	38	.449	4th (N)	—	—	—	—	—	—	—	—
	—(Second half)	47	22	.681	1st (N)	2	2	—	—	—	—	—	—
1979	—Evansville (American Association)	78	58	.574	1st (E)	4	2	—	—	—	—	—	—
1980	—Evansville (American Association)	61	74	.452	2nd (E)	—	—	—	—	—	—	—	—
1981	—Evansville (American Association)	73	63	.537	1st (E)	1	3	—	—	—	—	—	—
1986	—Pittsburgh (N.L.)	64	98	.395	6th (E)	—	—	—	—	—	—	—	—
1987	—Pittsburgh (N.L.)	80	82	.494	T4th (E)	—	—	—	—	—	—	—	—
1988	—Pittsburgh (N.L.)	85	75	.525	2nd (E)	—	—	—	—	—	—	—	—
1989	—Pittsburgh (N.L.)	74	88	.457	5th (E)	—	—	—	—	—	—	—	—
1990	—Pittsburgh (N.L.)	95	67	.586	1st (E)	—	—	2	4	—	—	—	—
1991	—Pittsburgh (N.L.)	98	64	.605	1st (E)	—	—	3	4	—	—	—	—
1992	—Pittsburgh (N.L.)	96	66	.593	1st (E)	—	—	3	4	—	—	—	—
1993	—Pittsburgh (N.L.)	75	87	.463	5th (E)	—	—	—	—	—	—	—	—
	Major league totals (8 years)	667	627	.515		—	—	8	12	—	—	—	—

NOTES:

1973—Lost to Wisconsin Rapids in playoff.
1976—Defeated Miami, two games to none, in semifinals; defeated Tampa, two games to none, in league championship.
1977—Defeated Miami, two games to none, in semifinals; defeated St. Petersburg, three games to one, in league championship.
1978—Defeated St. Petersburg, one game to none, in Northern Division championship; lost to Miami, two games to one, in league championship.
1979—Defeated Oklahoma City in league championship.
1981—Lost to Denver in semifinals.
1985—Served as acting manager of Chicago White Sox (record of 1-1), with club in fourth place, while manager Tony La Russa served a suspension (August 10 and 11).
1990—Lost to Cincinnati in N.L. Championship Series.
1991—Lost to Atlanta in N.L. Championship Series.
1992—Lost to Atlanta in N.L. Championship Series.
1993—On suspended list (August 27-September 1).

McRAE, HAL

ROYALS

PERSONAL: Born July 10, 1945, in Avon Park, Fla. . . . 5-11/185. . . . Threw right, batted right. . . . Full name: Harold Abraham McRae. . . . Father of Brian McRae, outfielder, Royals.
HIGH SCHOOL: Douglas (Sebring, Fla.).
COLLEGE: Florida A&M.

TRANSACTIONS/CAREER NOTES: Selected by Cincinnati Reds organization in sixth round of free-agent draft (June, 1965). . . . On disabled list (June 23-July 6, 1966; April 26-May 7, 1967; April 18-May 28 and July 4-August 5, 1969). . . . Traded with P Wayne Simpson to Kansas City Royals for P Roger Nelson and OF Richie Scheinblum (November 30, 1972). . . . On disabled list (June 11-August 2, 1979 and May 13-June 2, 1980). . . . Granted free agency (November 10, 1982). . . . Re-signed by Royals (November 15, 1982). . . . Granted free agency (November 12, 1985). . . . Re-signed by Royals (December 8, 1985). . . . Released by Royals (December 19,1986). . . . Re-signed by Royals as player/coach (January 12, 1987). . . . Released as player (July 21, 1987).
RECORDS: Shares major league doubleheader record for most long hits—6 (August 27, 1974, five doubles, one home run).
HONORS: Named designated hitter on THE SPORTING NEWS A.L. All-Star Team (1976-77 and 1982). . . . Named designated hitter on THE SPORTING NEWS A.L. Silver Slugger Team (1982).
STATISTICAL NOTES: Led A.L. with .406 on-base percentage in 1976. . . . Led A.L. in being hit by pitch with 13 in 1977.

			BATTING												FIELDING			
Year	Team (League)	Pos.	G	AB	R	H	2B	3B	HR	RBI	Avg.	BB	SO	SB	PO	A	E	Avg.
1965	—Tampa (Fla. St.)	OF	22	65	3	10	3	0	0	4	.154	4	15	1	19	0	0	1.000
1966	—Peninsula (Caro.)	2B	109	394	65	113	19	4	11	56	.287	29	59	10	252	226	*28	.945
1967	—Buffalo (Int'l)	2B	73	259	30	65	14	3	10	34	.251	7	43	7	133	208	23	.937
	—Knoxville (South.)	2B	51	186	26	54	10	3	6	25	.290	11	20	2	140	136	12	.958
1968	—Indianapolis (PCL)	2B-OF	119	444	64	131	31	11	16	65	.295	23	65	15	222	307	14	.974
	—Cincinnati (N.L.)	2B	17	51	1	10	1	0	0	2	.196	4	14	1	33	30	5	.926
1969	—Indianapolis (A.A.)	OF	17	41	2	9	1	0	0	4	.220	4	7	0	0	0	0	...
1970	—Cincinnati (N.L.)	OF-3B-2B	70	165	18	41	6	1	8	23	.248	15	23	0	53	7	1	.984
1971	—Cincinnati (N.L.)	OF	99	337	39	89	24	2	9	34	.264	11	35	3	167	6	6	.966
1972	—Cincinnati (N.L.)	OF-3B	61	97	9	27	4	0	5	26	.278	2	10	0	16	14	6	.833
1973	—Kansas City (A.L.)■	OF-3B	106	338	36	79	18	3	9	50	.234	34	38	2	101	6	5	.955
1974	—Kansas City (A.L.)	OF-3B	148	539	71	167	36	4	15	88	.310	54	68	11	132	3	7	.951
1975	—Kansas City (A.L.)	OF-3B	126	480	57	147	38	6	5	71	.306	47	47	11	207	7	3	.986
1976	—Kansas City (A.L.)	OF	149	527	75	175	34	5	8	73	.332	64	43	22	63	2	2	.970
1977	—Kansas City (A.L.)	OF	•162	641	104	191	*54	11	21	92	.298	59	43	18	81	8	4	.957
1978	—Kansas City (A.L.)	OF	156	623	90	170	39	5	16	72	.273	51	62	17	3	1	0	1.000

Year	Team (League)	Pos.	G	AB	R	H	2B	3B	HR	RBI	Avg.	BB	SO	SB	PO	A	E	Avg.
			BATTING												FIELDING			
1979	—Kansas City (A.L.)....	DH	101	393	55	113	32	4	10	74	.288	38	46	5	...	...	...	...
1980	—Kansas City (A.L.)....	OF	124	489	73	145	39	5	14	83	.297	29	56	10	17	0	0	1.000
1981	—Kansas City (A.L.)....	OF	101	389	38	106	23	2	7	36	.272	34	33	3	10	0	1	.909
1982	—Kansas City (A.L.)....	OF	159	613	91	189	•46	8	27	*133	.308	55	61	4	1	0	1	.500
1983	—Kansas City (A.L.)....	DH	157	589	84	183	41	6	12	82	.311	50	68	2	...	...	...	...
1984	—Kansas City (A.L.)....	DH	106	317	30	96	13	4	3	42	.303	34	47	0	...	...	...	...
1985	—Kansas City (A.L.)....	DH	112	320	41	83	19	0	14	70	.259	44	45	0	...	...	...	...
1986	—Kansas City (A.L.)....	DH	112	278	22	70	14	0	7	37	.252	18	39	0	...	...	...	...
1987	—Kansas City (A.L.)....	DH	18	32	5	10	3	0	1	9	.313	5	1	0	...	...	...	...
American League totals (15 years)			1837	6568	872	1924	449	63	169	1012	.293	616	697	105	615	27	23	.965
National League totals (4 years)			247	650	67	167	35	3	22	85	.257	32	82	4	269	57	18	.948
Major league totals (19 years)			2084	7218	939	2091	484	66	191	1097	.290	648	779	109	884	84	41	.959

DIVISION SERIES RECORD

Year	Team (League)	Pos.	G	AB	R	H	2B	3B	HR	RBI	Avg.	BB	SO	SB	PO	A	E	Avg.
			BATTING												FIELDING			
1981	—Kansas City (A.L.)....	DH	3	11	0	1	1	0	0	0	.091	1	1	0	...	...	...	...

CHAMPIONSHIP SERIES RECORD

CHAMPIONSHIP SERIES NOTES: Holds career record for most times caught stealing—6. . . . Shares career record for most doubles—7.

Year	Team (League)	Pos.	G	AB	R	H	2B	3B	HR	RBI	Avg.	BB	SO	SB	PO	A	E	Avg.
			BATTING												FIELDING			
1970	—Cincinnati (N.L.).......	OF	2	4	0	0	0	0	0	0	.000	0	2	0	2	0	0	1.000
1972	—Cincinnati (N.L.).......	PH	1	0	0	0	0	0	0	0	...	0	0	0	...	...	...	...
1976	—Kansas City (A.L.)....	OF	5	17	2	2	1	1	0	1	.118	1	4	0	5	1	0	1.000
1977	—Kansas City (A.L.)....	OF	5	18	6	8	3	0	1	2	.444	3	1	0	2	1	0	1.000
1978	—Kansas City (A.L.)....	DH	4	14	0	3	0	0	0	2	.214	2	2	1	...	...	...	...
1980	—Kansas City (A.L.)....	DH	3	10	0	2	0	0	0	0	.200	1	3	0	...	...	...	...
1984	—Kansas City (A.L.)....	PH	2	2	0	2	1	0	0	1	1.000	0	0	0	...	...	...	...
1985	—Kansas City (A.L.)....	DH	6	23	1	6	2	0	0	3	.261	1	6	0	...	...	...	...
Championship series totals (8 years)			28	88	9	23	7	1	1	9	.261	8	18	1	9	2	0	1.000

WORLD SERIES RECORD

Year	Team (League)	Pos.	G	AB	R	H	2B	3B	HR	RBI	Avg.	BB	SO	SB	PO	A	E	Avg.
			BATTING												FIELDING			
1970	—Cincinnati (N.L.).......	OF	3	11	1	5	2	0	0	3	.455	0	1	0	2	1	0	1.000
1972	—Cincinnati (N.L.).......	OF	5	9	1	4	1	0	0	2	.444	0	1	0	4	0	0	1.000
1980	—Kansas City (A.L.)....	DH	6	24	3	9	3	0	0	1	.375	2	2	0	...	...	...	...
1985	—Kansas City (A.L.)....	PH	3	1	0	0	0	0	0	0	.000	1	0	0	...	...	...	...
World Series totals (4 years)			17	45	5	18	6	0	0	6	.400	3	4	0	6	1	0	1.000

ALL-STAR GAME RECORD

Year	League	Pos.	AB	R	H	2B	3B	HR	RBI	Avg.	BB	SO	SB	PO	A	E	Avg.
			BATTING											FIELDING			
1975	—American..................	PH	1	0	0	0	0	0	0	.000	0	0	0	...	...	...	...
1976	—American..................	PH	1	0	0	0	0	0	0	.000	0	0	0	...	...	...	...
1982	—American..................	PH	0	0	0	0	0	0	0	...	1	0	0	...	...	...	...
All-Star Game totals (3 years)			2	0	0	0	0	0	0	.000	1	0	0	...	...	...	...

RECORD AS MANAGER

BACKGROUND: Player/hitting coach, Kansas City Royals (beginning of 1987 season-July 21, 1987). . . . Hitting coach, Royals (July 21, 1987-remainder of season). . . . Minor league hitting instructor, Pittsburgh Pirates (1988-89). . . . Hitting instructor, Montreal Expos (1990-May 24, 1991).
HONORS: Coach, A.L. All-Star team (1992).

Year	Team (League)	W	L	Pct.	Pos.	Playoff W	Playoff L	Champ. Series W	Champ. Series L	World Series W	World Series L	All-Star Game W	All-Star Game L
		REGULAR SEASON				POSTSEASON							
1991	—Kansas City (A.L.)	66	58	.532	6th (W)	—	—	—	—	—	—	—	—
1992	—Kansas City (A.L.)	72	90	.444	T5th (W)	—	—	—	—	—	—	—	—
1993	—Kansas City (A.L.)	84	78	.519	3rd (W)	—	—	—	—	—	—	—	—
Major league totals (3 years)		222	226	.496									

NOTES:
1991—Replaced Kansas City manager John Wathan (record of 15-22) and interim manager Bob Schaefer (1-0) with club in seventh place, record of 16-22 (May 24). . . . Placed on suspended list (August 13); reinstated (August 14).

OATES, JOHNNY

ORIOLES

PERSONAL: Born January 21, 1946, in Sylva, N.C. . . . 5-11/185. . . . Threw right, batted left. . . . Full name: Johnny Lane Oates.
HIGH SCHOOL: Prince George (Va.).
COLLEGE: Virginia Tech (received bachelor of science degree in health and physical education).
TRANSACTIONS/CAREER NOTES: Selected by Chicago White Sox organization in second round of free-agent draft (June 1966). . . . Selected by Baltimore Orioles organization in secondary phase of free-agent draft (January 28, 1967). . . . On military list (April 21-August 22, 1970). . . . Traded by Orioles with P Pat Dobson, P Roric Harrison and 2B Dave Johnson to Atlanta Braves for C Earl Williams and IF Taylor Duncan (November 30, 1972). . . . On disabled list (July 17-September 2, 1973). . . . Traded

by Braves with 1B Dick Allen to Philadelphia Phillies for C Jim Essian, OF Barry Bonnell and cash (May 7, 1975).... On disabled list (April 14-June 1, 1976).... Traded by Phillies with P Quency Hill to Los Angeles Dodgers for IF Ted Sizemore (December 20, 1976).... Released by Dodgers (March 27, 1980).... Signed by New York Yankees (April 4, 1980).... Granted free agency (November 13, 1980).... Re-signed by Yankees organization (January 23, 1981).... On Columbus disabled list (August 3-25, 1981).... Released by Yankees organization (October 27, 1981).

STATISTICAL NOTES: Led International League catchers with 727 total chances in 1971.... Led N.L. with 15 passed balls in 1974.... Tied for N.L. lead in double plays by catcher with 10 in 1975.

			BATTING											FIELDING			
Year	**Team (League)**	**Pos.**	**G**	**AB**	**R**	**H**	**2B**	**3B**	**HR**	**RBI**	**Avg.**	**BB**	**SO**	**SB**	**PO**	**A**	**E**	**Avg.**
1967	—Bluefield (Appal.)	C	5	12	5	5	1	0	1	4	.417	2	0	0	23	5	0	1.000
	—Miami (Florida St.)	C-OF	48	156	22	45	5	2	3	19	.288	24	13	2	271	37	8	.975
1968	—Miami (Florida St.)	C-OF	70	194	24	51	9	3	0	23	.263	33	14	2	384	42	3	.993
1969	—Dall./Fort W. (Tex.)	C	66	191	24	55	12	2	1	18	.288	20	9	0	253	42	4	.987
1970	—Rochester (Int'l)	C	9	16	1	6	1	0	0	4	.375	4	2	0	24	2	0	1.000
	—Baltimore (A.L.)	C	5	18	2	5	0	1	0	2	.278	2	0	0	30	1	2	.939
1971	—Rochester (Int'l)	C	114	346	49	96	16	3	7	44	.277	49	31	10	*648	*73	6	.992
1972	—Baltimore (A.L.)	C	85	253	20	66	12	1	4	21	.261	28	31	5	391	31	2	*.995
1973	—Atlanta (N.L.)■	C	93	322	27	80	6	0	4	27	.248	22	31	1	409	57	9	.981
1974	—Atlanta (N.L.)	C	100	291	22	65	10	0	1	21	.223	23	24	2	434	55	4	.992
1975	—Atl.-Phil. (N.L.)■	C	98	287	28	81	15	0	1	25	.282	34	33	1	450	45	5	.990
1976	—Philadelphia (N.L.)	C	37	99	10	25	2	0	0	8	.253	8	12	0	155	15	1	.994
1977	—Los Angeles (N.L.)■	C	60	156	18	42	4	0	3	11	.269	11	11	1	258	37	4	.987
1978	—Los Angeles (N.L.)	C	40	75	5	23	1	0	0	6	.307	5	3	0	77	10	4	.956
1979	—Los Angeles (N.L.)	C	26	46	4	6	2	0	0	2	.130	4	1	0	64	13	2	.975
1980	—New York (A.L.)■	C	39	64	6	12	3	0	1	3	.188	2	3	1	99	10	1	.991
1981	—New York (A.L.)	C	10	26	4	5	1	0	0	0	.192	2	0	0	49	3	2	.963
	American League totals (4 years)		139	361	32	88	16	2	5	26	.244	34	34	6	569	45	7	.989
	National League totals (7 years)		454	1276	114	322	40	0	9	100	.252	107	115	5	1847	232	29	.986
	Major league totals (11 years)		593	1637	146	410	56	2	14	126	.250	141	149	11	2416	277	36	.987

CHAMPIONSHIP SERIES RECORD

			BATTING											FIELDING			
Year	**Team (League)**	**Pos.**	**G**	**AB**	**R**	**H**	**2B**	**3B**	**HR**	**RBI**	**Avg.**	**BB**	**SO**	**SB**	**PO**	**A**	**E**	**Avg.**
1976	—Philadelphia (N.L.)	C	1	1	0	0	0	0	0	0	.000	0	0	0	1	0	0	1.000

WORLD SERIES RECORD

			BATTING											FIELDING			
Year	**Team (League)**	**Pos.**	**G**	**AB**	**R**	**H**	**2B**	**3B**	**HR**	**RBI**	**Avg.**	**BB**	**SO**	**SB**	**PO**	**A**	**E**	**Avg.**
1977	—Los Angeles (N.L.)	C	1	1	0	0	0	0	0	0	.000	0	0	0	1	0	0	1.000
1978	—Los Angeles (N.L.)	C	1	1	0	1	0	0	0	0	1.000	1	0	0	3	1	0	1.000
	World Series totals (2 years)		2	2	0	1	0	0	0	0	.500	1	0	0	4	1	0	1.000

RECORD AS MANAGER

BACKGROUND: Player/coach, Columbus, New York Yankees organization (July 30, 1981-remainder of season).... Coach, Chicago Cubs (1984-87).... Coach, Baltimore Orioles (1989-May 23, 1991).

HONORS: Named International League Manager of the Year (1988).... Coach, A.L. All-Star team (1993).... Named A.L. Manager of the Year by THE SPORTING NEWS (1993).

		REGULAR SEASON				POSTSEASON							
						Playoff		Champ. Series		World Series		All-Star Game	
Year	**Team (League)**	**W**	**L**	**Pct.**	**Pos.**	**W**	**L**	**W**	**L**	**W**	**L**	**W**	**L**
1982	—Nashville (Southern)	32	38	.457	4th (W)	—	—	—	—	—	—	—	—
	—(Second half)	45	29	.608	1st (W)	6	2	—	—	—	—	—	—
1983	—Columbus (International)	83	57	.593	1st	2	3	—	—	—	—	—	—
1988	—Rochester (International)	77	64	.546	1st (W)	5	5	—	—	—	—	—	—
1991	—Baltimore (A.L.)	54	71	.432	6th (E)	—	—	—	—	—	—	—	—
1992	—Baltimore (A.L.)	89	73	.549	3rd (E)	—	—	—	—	—	—	—	—
1993	—Baltimore (A.L.)	85	77	.525	T3rd (E)	—	—	—	—	—	—	—	—
	Major league totals (3 years)	228	221	.508									

NOTES:

1982—Defeated Knoxville, three games to one, in playoffs; defeated Jacksonville, three games to one, in league championship.

1983—Lost to Tidewater in playoffs.

1988—Defeated Tidewater, three games to one, in league championship; lost to Indianapolis (American Association), four games to two, in AAA-Alliance championship.

1991—Replaced Baltimore manager Frank Robinson with club in seventh place, record of 13-24 (May 23).

PINIELLA, LOU

MARINERS

PERSONAL: Born August 28, 1943, in Tampa, Fla.... 6-2/199.... Threw right, batted right.... Full name: Louis Victor Piniella.... Cousin of Dave Magadan, third baseman, Florida Marlins.... Name pronounced pin-ELL-uh.

HIGH SCHOOL: Jesuit (Tampa, Fla.).

COLLEGE: Tampa.

TRANSACTIONS/CAREER NOTES: Signed as free agent by Cleveland Indians organization (June 9, 1962).... Selected by Washington Senators organization from Jacksonville, Indians organization, in Rule 5 major league draft (November 26, 1962).... On military list (March 9-July 20, 1964).... Traded by Senators organization to Baltimore Orioles organization (August 4, 1964), completing deal in which Orioles traded P Lester (Buster) Narum to Senators for cash and a player to be named later (March 31, 1964).... On suspended list (June 27-29, 1965).... Traded by Orioles organization to Indians organization for C Camilo Carreon (March 10, 1966).... On temporary inactive list (May 19-22, 1967).... On disabled list (May 22-June 6, 1968)....

On temporary inactive list (June 6-25, 1968).... Selected by Seattle Pilots in expansion draft (October 15, 1968).... Traded by Pilots to Kansas City Royals for OF Steve Whitaker and P John Gelnar (April 1, 1969).... On military list (August 7-22, 1969).... On disabled list (May 5-June 8, 1971).... Traded by Royals with P Ken Wright to New York Yankees for P Lindy McDaniel (December 7, 1973).... On disabled list (June 17-July 6, 1975; August 23-September 7, 1981; and March 30-April 22, 1983).... Placed on voluntarily retired list (June 17, 1984).
RECORDS: Shares major league record for most assists by outfielder in one inning—2 (May 27, 1974, third inning).
HONORS: Named A.L. Rookie of the Year by Baseball Writers' Association of America (1969).
STATISTICAL NOTES: Led A.L. in grounding into double plays with 25 in 1972.

			BATTING												FIELDING			
Year	**Team (League)**	**Pos.**	**G**	**AB**	**R**	**H**	**2B**	**3B**	**HR**	**RBI**	**Avg.**	**BB**	**SO**	**SB**	**PO**	**A**	**E**	**Avg.**
1962	—Selma (Ala.-Fla.)	OF	70	278	40	75	10	5	8	44	.270	10	57	4	94	6	9	.917
1963	—Peninsula (Caro.)■	OF	143	548	71	170	29	4	16	77	.310	34	70	8	271	*23	8	.974
1964	—Aberdeen (North.)	OF	20	74	8	20	8	3	0	12	.270	6	9	1	37	1	1	.974
	—Baltimore (A.L.)■	PH	4	1	0	0	0	0	0	0	.000	0	0	0	...	...	...	...
1965	—Elmira (Eastern)	OF	126	490	64	122	29	6	11	64	.249	22	57	5	176	5	7	.963
1966	—Portland (PCL)■	OF	133	457	47	132	22	3	7	52	.289	20	52	6	177	11	11	.945
1967	—Portland (PCL)	OF	113	396	46	122	20	1	8	56	.308	23	47	2	199	7	6	.972
1968	—Portland (PCL)	OF	88	331	49	105	15	3	13	62	.317	19	31	0	167	6	7	.961
	—Cleveland (A.L.)	OF	6	5	1	0	0	0	0	1	.000	0	0	1	1	0	0	1.000
1969	—Kansas City (A.L.)■	OF	135	493	43	139	21	6	11	68	.282	33	56	2	278	13	7	.977
1970	—Kansas City (A.L.)	OF-1B	144	542	54	163	24	5	11	88	.301	35	42	3	250	6	4	.985
1971	—Kansas City (A.L.)	OF	126	448	43	125	21	5	3	51	.279	21	43	5	201	6	3	.986
1972	—Kansas City (A.L.)	OF	151	574	65	179	*33	4	11	72	.312	34	59	7	275	8	7	.976
1973	—Kansas City (A.L.)	OF	144	513	53	128	28	1	9	69	.250	30	65	5	196	9	3	.986
1974	—New York (A.L.)■	OF-1B	140	518	71	158	26	0	9	70	.305	32	58	1	270	16	3	.990
1975	—New York (A.L.)	OF	74	199	7	39	4	1	0	22	.196	16	22	0	65	5	1	.986
1976	—New York (A.L.)	OF	100	327	36	92	16	6	3	38	.281	18	34	0	199	10	4	.981
1977	—New York (A.L.)	OF-1B	103	339	47	112	19	3	12	45	.330	20	31	2	86	3	2	.978
1978	—New York (A.L.)	OF	130	472	67	148	34	5	6	69	.314	34	36	3	213	4	7	.969
1979	—New York (A.L.)	OF	130	461	49	137	22	2	11	69	.297	17	31	3	204	13	4	.982
1980	—New York (A.L.)	OF	116	321	39	92	18	0	2	27	.287	29	20	0	157	8	5	.971
1981	—New York (A.L.)	OF	60	159	16	44	9	0	5	18	.277	13	9	0	69	2	1	.986
1982	—New York (A.L.)	OF	102	261	33	80	17	1	6	37	.307	18	18	0	68	2	0	1.000
1983	—New York (A.L.)	OF	53	148	19	43	9	1	2	16	.291	11	12	1	67	4	3	.959
1984	—New York (A.L.)	OF	29	86	8	26	4	1	1	6	.302	7	5	0	40	3	0	1.000
Major league totals (18 years)			1747	5867	651	1705	305	41	102	766	.291	368	541	33	2639	112	54	.981

DIVISION SERIES RECORD

			BATTING												FIELDING			
Year	**Team (League)**	**Pos.**	**G**	**AB**	**R**	**H**	**2B**	**3B**	**HR**	**RBI**	**Avg.**	**BB**	**SO**	**SB**	**PO**	**A**	**E**	**Avg.**
1981	—New York (A.L.)	DH-PH	4	10	1	2	1	0	1	3	.200	0	0	0	...	...	...	...

CHAMPIONSHIP SERIES RECORD

			BATTING												FIELDING			
Year	**Team (League)**	**Pos.**	**G**	**AB**	**R**	**H**	**2B**	**3B**	**HR**	**RBI**	**Avg.**	**BB**	**SO**	**SB**	**PO**	**A**	**E**	**Avg.**
1976	—New York (A.L.)	DH-PH	4	11	1	3	1	0	0	0	.273	0	1	0	...	...	...	...
1977	—New York (A.L.)	OF-DH	5	21	1	7	3	0	0	2	.333	0	1	0	9	1	0	1.000
1978	—New York (A.L.)	OF	4	17	2	4	0	0	0	0	.235	0	3	0	13	0	0	1.000
1980	—New York (A.L.)	OF	2	5	1	1	0	0	1	1	.200	2	1	0	5	0	0	1.000
1981	—New York (A.L.)	PH-DH-OF	3	5	2	3	0	0	1	3	.600	0	0	0	0	0	0	...
Championship series totals (5 years)			18	59	7	18	4	0	2	6	.305	2	6	0	27	1	0	1.000

WORLD SERIES RECORD

WORLD SERIES NOTES: Shares single-series record for collecting one or more hits in each game (1978).

			BATTING												FIELDING			
Year	**Team (League)**	**Pos.**	**G**	**AB**	**R**	**H**	**2B**	**3B**	**HR**	**RBI**	**Avg.**	**BB**	**SO**	**SB**	**PO**	**A**	**E**	**Avg.**
1976	—New York (A.L.)	DH-OF-PH	4	9	1	3	1	0	0	0	.333	0	0	0	1	0	0	1.000
1977	—New York (A.L.)	OF	6	22	1	6	0	0	0	3	.273	0	3	0	16	1	1	.944
1978	—New York (A.L.)	OF	6	25	3	7	0	0	0	4	.280	0	0	1	14	1	0	1.000
1981	—New York (A.L.)	OF-PH	6	16	2	7	1	0	0	3	.438	0	1	1	7	0	0	1.000
World Series totals (4 years)			22	72	7	23	2	0	0	10	.319	0	4	2	38	2	1	.976

ALL-STAR GAME RECORD

			BATTING										FIELDING			
Year	**League**	**Pos.**	**AB**	**R**	**H**	**2B**	**3B**	**HR**	**RBI**	**Avg.**	**BB**	**SO**	**SB**	**PO**	**A**	**E**	**Avg.**
1972	—American	PH	1	0	0	0	0	0	0	.000	0	0	0	...	...	...	...

RECORD AS MANAGER

BACKGROUND: Coach, New York Yankees (June 25, 1984-85).... Vice-president/general manager, Yankees (beginning of 1988 season-June 22, 1988).... Special adviser, Yankees (1989).

		REGULAR SEASON				POSTSEASON							
						Playoff		Champ. Series		World Series		All-Star Game	
Year	**Team (League)**	**W**	**L**	**Pct.**	**Pos.**	**W**	**L**	**W**	**L**	**W**	**L**	**W**	**L**
1986	—New York (A.L.)	90	72	.556	2nd (E)	—	—	—	—	—	—	—	—
1987	—New York (A.L.)	89	73	.549	4th (E)	—	—	—	—	—	—	—	—
1988	—New York (A.L.)	45	48	.484	5th (E)	—	—	—	—	—	—	—	—
1990	—Cincinnati (N.L.)	91	71	.562	1st (W)	—	—	4	2	4	0	—	—
1991	—Cincinnati (N.L.)	74	88	.457	5th (W)	—	—	—	—	—	—	0	1

Year	Team (League)	W	L	Pct.	Pos.	Playoff W	Playoff L	Champ. Series W	Champ. Series L	World Series W	World Series L	All-Star Game W	All-Star Game L
1992	—Cincinnati (N.L.)	90	72	.556	2nd (W)	—	—	—	—	—	—	—	—
1993	—Seattle (A.L.)	82	80	.506	4th (W)	—	—	—	—	—	—	—	—
	American League totals (4 years)	306	273	.528		—	—	—	—	—	—	—	—
	National League totals (3 years)	255	231	.525		—	—	4	2	4	0	0	1
	Major league totals (7 years)	561	504	.527		—	—	4	2	4	0	0	1

NOTES:

1988—Replaced New York manager Billy Martin with club in second place, record of 40-28 (June 23).

1990—Defeated Pittsburgh in N.L. Championship Series; defeated Oakland in World Series.

RIGGLEMAN, JIM

PADRES

PERSONAL: Born December 9, 1952, in Fort Dix, N.J. . . . 5-11/175. . . . Threw right, batted right. . . . Full name: James David Riggleman.

HIGH SCHOOL: Richard Montgomery (Rockville, Md.).

COLLEGE: Frostburg (Md.) State (degree in physical education).

TRANSACTIONS/CAREER NOTES: Selected by Los Angeles Dodgers organization in fourth round of free-agent draft (June 5, 1974). . . . Traded by Dodgers organization to St. Louis Cardinals organization for C Sergio Robles (July 19, 1976). . . . On Springfield disabled list (April 14-July 3, 1978). . . . Released by Arkansas to become coach (May 25, 1981).

STATISTICAL NOTES: Led Eastern League third basemen with 30 double plays in 1975.

Year	Team (League)	Pos.	G	AB	R	H	2B	3B	HR	RBI	Avg.	BB	SO	SB	PO	A	E	Avg.
			BATTING												FIELDING			
1974	—Waterbury (East.)	2B-3B	80	252	29	67	13	1	8	41	.266	25	56	1	159	175	20	.944
1975	—Waterbury (East.)	3B	129	439	61	113	14	7	11	57	.257	54	86	14	109	267	53	.876
1976	—Waterbury (East.)	OF-3B	84	287	38	75	14	2	6	39	.261	31	47	4	99	29	18	.877
	—Arkansas (Texas)■	3B-OF-1B	47	154	29	46	9	1	5	25	.299	19	13	1	38	73	10	.917
1977	—Arkansas (Texas)	3B	27	93	10	26	7	2	0	11	.280	16	9	6	25	48	5	.936
	—New Orleans (A.A.)	3B-OF-SS	103	346	52	83	16	0	17	52	.240	34	65	10	88	149	24	.908
1978	—Arkansas (Texas)	3B-OF	59	174	34	51	8	1	4	34	.293	43	39	2	29	60	14	.864
1979	—Arkansas (Texas)	3B-OF-1B	46	110	17	30	9	0	1	23	.273	13	23	5	34	22	4	.933
	—Springfield (A.A.)	3B-OF-1B	35	93	9	22	4	0	2	9	.237	5	26	3	47	4	6	.895
1980	—Arkansas (Texas)	3B-OF	127	431	84	127	29	7	21	90	.295	60	67	28	123	243	26	.934
1981	—Arkansas (Texas)	OF-3B	37	133	17	32	7	1	1	15	.241	16	29	3	56	22	5	.940

RECORD AS MANAGER

BACKGROUND: Coach, Arkansas, St. Louis Cardinals organization, (May 25, 1981-remainder of season). . . . Coach, Louisville, Cardinals organization (April 13-May 31, 1982). . . . Director of player development, Cardinals (June 21, 1988-remainder of season). . . . Coach, Cardinals (1989-90).

Year	Team (League)	W	L	Pct.	Pos.	Playoff W	Playoff L	Champ. Series W	Champ. Series L	World Series W	World Series L	All-Star Game W	All-Star Game L
1982	—St. Petersburg (Florida State)	8	4	.667	2nd	—	—	—	—	—	—	—	—
	—(Second half)	35	30	.538	2nd	—	—	—	—	—	—	—	—
1983	—St. Petersburg (Florida State)	33	35	.485	T3rd	—	—	—	—	—	—	—	—
	—(Second half)	37	29	.561	2nd	—	—	—	—	—	—	—	—
1984	—St. Petersburg (Florida State)	39	38	.506	3rd	—	—	—	—	—	—	—	—
	—(Second half)	32	35	.478	3rd	—	—	—	—	—	—	—	—
1985	—Arkansas (Texas)	33	30	.524	1st (E)	—	—	—	—	—	—	—	—
	—(Second half)	31	40	.437	4th (E)	0	2	—	—	—	—	—	—
1986	—Arkansas (Texas)	35	28	.556	3rd (E)	—	—	—	—	—	—	—	—
	—(Second half)	32	39	.451	3rd (E)	—	—	—	—	—	—	—	—
1987	—Arkansas (Texas)	36	29	.554	2nd (E)	—	—	—	—	—	—	—	—
	—(Second half)	36	34	.514	3rd (E)	—	—	—	—	—	—	—	—
1988	—Arkansas (Texas)	30	37	.448	3rd (E)	—	—	—	—	—	—	—	—
	—(Second half)	2	1	.667		—	—	—	—	—	—	—	—
1991	—Las Vegas (Pacific Coast)	36	34	.514	4th (S)	—	—	—	—	—	—	—	—
	—(Second half)	29	41	.414	5th (S)	—	—	—	—	—	—	—	—
1992	—Las Vegas (Pacific Coast)	41	31	.569	1st (S)	—	—	—	—	—	—	—	—
	—(Second half)	33	39	.458	3rd (S)	2	3	—	—	—	—	—	—
	—San Diego (N.L.)	4	8	.333	3rd (W)	—	—	—	—	—	—	—	—
1993	—San Diego (N.L.)	61	101	.377		—	—	—	—	—	—	—	—
	Major league totals (2 years)	65	109	.374									

NOTES:

1982—Replaced St. Petersburg manager Nick Leyva with club in fourth place, record of 26-30 (June 4).

1985—Lost to Jackson in semifinals.

1988—Replaced as Arkansas manager by Darold Knowles (June 21).

1992—Lost to Colorado Springs in semifinals. Replaced San Diego manager Greg Riddoch with club in third place, record of 78-72 (September 23).

RODGERS, BUCK

ANGELS

PERSONAL: Born August 16, 1938, in Delaware, O. . . . 6-1/190. . . . Threw right, batted both. . . . Full name: Robert Leroy Rodgers.

HIGH SCHOOL: Prospect (O.).

COLLEGE: Ohio Wesleyan and Ohio Northern.

TRANSACTIONS/CAREER NOTES: Signed by Detroit Tigers organization (July 14, 1956). . . . On Knoxville disabled list (May 24-June 3, 1959). . . . Selected by Los Angeles Angels from Tigers in A.L. expansion draft (December 14, 1960). . . . On Hawaii dis-

abled list (May 4-June 11, 1969).... Released by Angels (October 22, 1969).... Signed by Salinas, Angels organization (August 24, 1975).... Released as player by Salinas (September 15, 1975).... Signed by El Paso, Angels organization (July 15, 1977).... Released as player by El Paso (August 14, 1977).
RECORDS: Holds A.L. rookie-season record for most games by catcher—150 (1962).
STATISTICAL NOTES: Led New York-Pennsylvania League catchers with 77 assists and 24 errors in 1957.... Led Pioneer League catchers with 16 errors in 1958.... Led South Atlantic League catchers with 11 errors in 1959.... Led A.L. catchers with 14 double plays in 1962 and 14 in 1964.... Led A.L. catchers with 73 assists in 1967.

							BATTING								FIELDING			
Year	**Team (League)**	**Pos.**	**G**	**AB**	**R**	**H**	**2B**	**3B**	**HR**	**RBI**	**Avg.**	**BB**	**SO**	**SB**	**PO**	**A**	**E**	**Avg.**
1956	—Jamestown (Pony)	OF	48	153	28	36	8	1	6	26	.235	27	55	3	43	6	3	.942
1957	—Erie (N.Y.-Penn)	C-OF	114	430	79	127	26	4	12	80	.295	47	55	6	568	†77	†25	.963
1958	—Lancaster (East.)	C	19	63	8	16	3	0	3	8	.254	7	11	1	111	11	2	.984
	—Idaho Falls (Pio.)	C-OF	99	378	73	115	15	6	12	74	.304	467	39	3	524	45	†20	.966
1959	—Birm. (Southern)	C	3	13	1	1	0	1	0	2	.077	0	0	0	28	0	1	.966
	—Knoxville (S. Atl.)	OF-C	105	355	53	102	18	6	7	55	.287	47	38	3	565	60	†13	.980
1960	—Denver (A.A.)	C	23	84	12	20	7	1	3	12	.238	7	6	0	127	15	4	.973
	—Birm. (Southern)	C	93	313	36	77	14	1	5	38	.246	33	29	0	456	*68	7	.987
1961	—Dall./Fort W. (A.A.)■	C	124	427	55	122	22	3	3	62	.286	47	37	2	*595	*70	11	.984
	—Los Angeles (A.L.)	C	16	56	8	18	2	0	2	13	.321	1	6	0	71	11	3	.965
1962	—Los Angeles (A.L.)	C	155	565	65	146	34	6	6	61	.258	45	68	1	826	73	•10	.989
1963	—Los Angeles (A.L.)	C	100	300	24	70	6	0	4	23	.233	29	35	2	416	48	*10	.979
1964	—Los Angeles (A.L.)	C	148	514	38	125	18	3	4	54	.243	40	71	4	884	*87	*13	.987
1965	—California (A.L.)	C	132	411	33	86	14	3	1	32	.209	35	61	4	682	52	7	.991
1966	—California (A.L.)	C	133	454	45	107	20	3	7	48	.236	29	57	3	662	*69	6	.992
1967	—California (A.L.)	C-OF	139	429	29	94	13	3	6	41	.219	34	55	1	728	†73	7	.991
1968	—California (A.L.)	C	91	258	13	49	6	0	1	14	.190	16	48	2	407	50	7	.985
1969	—Hawaii (PCL)	C-3B	44	145	15	37	5	0	0	12	.255	17	16	2	215	26	4	.984
	—California (A.L.)	C	18	46	4	9	1	0	0	2	.196	5	8	0	74	9	0	1.000
1970	—								Did not play.									
1971	—								Did not play.									
1972	—								Did not play.									
1973	—								Did not play.									
1974	—								Did not play.									
1975	—Salinas (Calif.)	DH	4	3	1	1	0	0	0	0	.333	3	1	0	...	...	...	...
1976	—								Did not play.									
1977	—El Paso (Texas)	PH	1	0	0	0	0	0	0	0	...	0	0	0	...	...	...	...
	Major league totals (9 years)		932	3033	259	704	114	18	31	288	.232	234	409	17	4750	472	63	.988

RECORD AS MANAGER

BACKGROUND: Coach, Minnesota Twins (1970-74).... Player/manager, Salinas, California Angels organization (August 24-September 15, 1975).... Coach, San Francisco Giants (1976).... Player/manager, El Paso, Angels organization (July 15-August 14, 1977).... Coach, Milwaukee Brewers (1978-80).
RECORDS: Shares major league single-season record for most clubs managed—2 (1991).
HONORS: Named Texas League Manager of the Year (1977).... Named American Association Manager of the Year (1984).... Named Minor League Manager of the Year by THE SPORTING NEWS (1984).... Named N.L. Manager of the Year by THE SPORTING NEWS (1987).... Named N.L. Manager of the Year by Baseball Writers' Association of America (1987).... Coach, N.L. All-Star team (1988-89).

		REGULAR SEASON				POSTSEASON							
						Playoff		Champ. Series		World Series		All-Star Game	
Year	**Team (League)**	**W**	**L**	**Pct.**	**Pos.**	**W**	**L**	**W**	**L**	**W**	**L**	**W**	**L**
1975	—Salinas (California)	35	35	.500	5th	—	—	—	—	—	—	—	—
	—(Second half)	32	38	.457	6th	—	—	—	—	—	—	—	—
1977	—El Paso (Texas)	38	24	.613	1st (W)	—	—	—	—	—	—	—	—
	—(Second half)	40	28	.588	1st (W)	0	2	—	—	—	—	—	—
1980	—Milwaukee (A.L.)	13	10	.565	3rd (E)	—	—	—	—	—	—	—	—
1981	—Milwaukee (A.L.)	31	25	.554	3rd (E)	—	—	—	—	—	—	—	—
	—(Second half)	31	22	.585	1st (E)	2	3	—	—	—	—	—	—
1982	—Milwaukee (A.L.)	23	24	.489		—	—	—	—	—	—	—	—
1984	—Indianapolis (American Association)	91	63	.591	1st	2	4	—	—	—	—	—	—
1985	—Montreal (N.L.)	84	77	.522	3rd (E)	—	—	—	—	—	—	—	—
1986	—Montreal (N.L.)	78	83	.484	4th (E)	—	—	—	—	—	—	—	—
1987	—Montreal (N.L.)	91	71	.562	3rd (E)	—	—	—	—	—	—	—	—
1988	—Montreal (N.L.)	81	81	.500	3rd (E)	—	—	—	—	—	—	—	—
1989	—Montreal (N.L.)	81	81	.500	4th (E)	—	—	—	—	—	—	—	—
1990	—Montreal (N.L.)	85	77	.525	3rd (E)	—	—	—	—	—	—	—	—
1991	—Montreal (N.L.)	20	29	.408		—	—	—	—	—	—	—	—
	—California (A.L.)	20	18	.526	7th (E)	—	—	—	—	—	—	—	—
1992	—California (A.L.)	72	90	.444	T5th (W)	—	—	—	—	—	—	—	—
1993	—California (A.L.)	71	91	.438	T5th (W)	—	—	—	—	—	—	—	—
	American League totals (6 years)	261	280	.482		2	3	—	—	—	—	—	—
	National League totals (7 years)	520	499	.510		—	—	—	—	—	—	—	—
	Major league totals (12 years)	781	779	.501		2	3	—	—	—	—	—	—

NOTES:
1977—Lost to Arkansas in league championship.
1980—Began season as temporary Milwaukee manager for George Bamberger, who was ill. Bamberger returned with club in second place, record of 26-21 (June 6). Rodgers named manager after Bamberger retired with club in fourth place, record of 73-66 (September 7).

1981—Lost to New York Yankees in divisional playoff.
1982—Replaced as Milwaukee manager by Harvey Kuenn with club tied for fifth place (June 2).
1984—Lost to Louisville in semifinal playoff series.
1991—Replaced as Montreal manager by Tom Runnells with club in sixth place (June 3); replaced Doug Rader as California manager with club in seventh place, record of 61-63 (August 26).
1992—Record includes time missed due to bus-crash injuries (May 21-August 28); club was 39-50 under interim manager John Wathan.

SHOWALTER, BUCK

YANKEES

PERSONAL: Born May 23, 1956, in DeFuniak Springs, Fla. . . . 5-9/195. . . . Threw left, batted left. . . . Full name: William Nathaniel Showalter III.
COLLEGE: Chipola Junior College (Fla.) and Mississippi State.
TRANSACTIONS/CAREER NOTES: Selected by New York Yankees organization in fifth round of free-agent draft (June 7, 1977). . . . On disabled list (July 1-11 and July 19-August 4, 1981).
STATISTICAL NOTES: Led Southern League first basemen with 1,281 putouts in 1982.

				BATTING											FIELDING			
Year	**Team (League)**	**Pos.**	**G**	**AB**	**R**	**H**	**2B**	**3B**	**HR**	**RBI**	**Avg.**	**BB**	**SO**	**SB**	**PO**	**A**	**E**	**Avg.**
1977	—Fort Lauder. (FSL) ...	OF	56	196	32	71	8	1	1	25	.362	36	13	4	96	2	2	.980
1978	—West Haven (East.)..	OF	123	429	52	124	13	2	3	46	.289	55	34	19	192	•15	7	.967
1979	—West Haven (East.)..	1B-OF	129	469	71	131	7	3	6	51	.279	36	30	8	575	52	7	.989
1980	—Nashville (South.)	OF-1B	142	550	84	*178	19	3	1	82	.324	53	23	6	71	2	1	.986
1981	—Columbus (Int'l)	OF	14	37	6	7	1	0	1	3	.189	3	0	0	11	0	1	.917
	—Nashville (South.)	OF-1B	90	307	46	81	17	6	0	38	.264	46	16	3	201	14	7	.968
1982	—Nashville (South.)	1B-OF	132	517	66	*152	29	3	3	46	.294	61	42	2	†1282	51	13	.990
1983	—Nashville (South.)	1B-OF-P	89	297	35	82	13	4	1	37	.276	39	22	1	127	6	2	.985
	—Columbus (Int'l)	1B-P	18	63	9	15	3	0	1	8	.238	7	3	1	139	14	1	.994

RECORD AS PITCHER

Year	**Team (League)**	**W**	**L**	**Pct.**	**ERA**	**G**	**GS**	**CG**	**ShO**	**Sv.**	**IP**	**H**	**R**	**ER**	**BB**	**SO**
1983	—Nashville (South.)......	0	0	...	9.00	1	0	0	0	0	1	2	1	1	0	1
	—Columbus (Int'l).........	0	0	...	0.00	1	0	0	0	0	2	0	0	0	0	2

RECORD AS MANAGER

BACKGROUND: Minor league coach, New York Yankees organization (1984). . . . Coach, Yankees (1990-91).
HONORS: Named New York-Pennsylvania League Manager of the Year (1985). . . . Named Eastern League Manager of the Year (1989). . . . Coach, A.L. All-Star team (1992).

		REGULAR SEASON				POSTSEASON							
						Playoff		Champ. Series		World Series		All-Star Game	
Year	**Team (League)**	**W**	**L**	**Pct.**	**Pos.**	**W**	**L**	**W**	**L**	**W**	**L**	**W**	**L**
1985	—Oneonta (New York-Pennsylvania).............	55	23	.705	1st (N)	3	0	—	—	—	—	—	—
1986	—Oneonta (New York-Pennsylvania).............	59	18	.766	1st (Y)	0	1	—	—	—	—	—	—
1987	—Fort Lauderdale (Florida State)	85	53	.616	1st (S)	5	1	—	—	—	—	—	—
1988	—Fort Lauderdale (Florida State)	39	29	.574	3rd (E)	—	—	—	—	—	—	—	—
	—(Second half)	30	36	.455	T3rd (E)	—	—	—	—	—	—	—	—
1989	—Albany/Colonie (Eastern)	92	48	.657	1st	6	2	—	—	—	—	—	—
1992	—New York (A.L.)	76	86	.469	T4th (E)	—	—	—	—	—	—	—	—
1993	—New York (A.L.)	88	74	.543	2nd (E)	—	—	—	—	—	—	—	—
	Major league totals (2 years)................................	164	160	.506									

NOTES:
1985—Defeated Geneva in one-game semifinal playoff; defeated Auburn, two games to none, in league championship.
1986—Lost to Newark in playoffs.
1987—Defeated Lakeland, two games to none, in playoffs; defeated Osceola, three games to one, in league championship.
1989—Defeated Reading, three games to one, in playoffs; defeated Harrisburg, three games to one, in league championship.

TORRE, JOE

CARDINALS

PERSONAL: Born July 18, 1940, in Brooklyn, N.Y. . . . 6-1/210. . . . Threw right, batted right. . . . Full name: Joseph Paul Torre. . . . Brother of Frank Torre, first baseman, Milwaukee Braves, Philadelphia Phillies (1956-60, 1962-63). . . . Name pronounced TORE-ee.
HIGH SCHOOL: St. Francis Prep (Brooklyn, N.Y.).
TRANSACTIONS/CAREER NOTES: Signed by Jacksonville, Milwaukee Braves organization (August 24, 1959). . . . On military list (September 30, 1962-March 26, 1963). . . . Braves franchise moved from Milwaukee to Atlanta (1966). . . . On disabled list (April 18-May 9, 1968). . . . Traded by Braves to St. Louis Cardinals for 1B Orlando Cepeda (March 17, 1969). . . . Traded by Cardinals to New York Mets for P Tommy Moore and P Ray Sadecki (October 13, 1974). . . . Released as player by Mets (June 18, 1977).
RECORDS: Shares major league single-game record for most times grounded into double play—4 (July 21, 1975).
HONORS: Named catcher on THE SPORTING NEWS N.L. All-Star team (1964-66). . . . Won N.L. Gold Glove at catcher (1965). . . . Named Major League Player of the Year by THE SPORTING NEWS (1971). . . . Named N.L. Player of the Year by THE SPORTING NEWS (1971). . . . Named third baseman on THE SPORTING NEWS N.L. All-Star team (1971). . . . Named N.L. Most Valuable Player by Baseball Writers' Association of America (1971).
STATISTICAL NOTES: Led N.L. catchers with .995 fielding percentage in 1964 and .996 in 1968. . . . Led N.L. in grounding into double plays with 26 in 1964, 22 in 1965, 22 in 1967 and 21 in 1968. . . . Led N.L. catchers with 12 double plays in 1967. . . . Led N.L. with 352 total bases in 1971. . . . Hit for the cycle (June 27, 1973). . . . Led N.L. first basemen with 102 assists and 144 double plays in 1974.

				BATTING											FIELDING			
Year	**Team (League)**	**Pos.**	**G**	**AB**	**R**	**H**	**2B**	**3B**	**HR**	**RBI**	**Avg.**	**BB**	**SO**	**SB**	**PO**	**A**	**E**	**Avg.**
1960	—Eau Claire (North.)...	C	117	369	63	127	23	3	16	74	*.344	70	45	7	636	64	9	.987
	—Milwaukee (N.L.)......	PH	2	2	0	1	0	0	0	0	.500	0	1	0	...	...	...	...

Year	Team (League)	Pos.	G	AB	R	H	2B	3B	HR	RBI	Avg.	BB	SO	SB	PO	A	E	Avg.
			BATTING												FIELDING			
1961	—Louisville (A.A.)	C	27	111	18	38	8	2	3	24	.342	6	9	0	185	14	2	.990
	—Milwaukee (N.L.)	C	113	406	40	113	21	4	10	42	.278	28	60	3	494	50	10	.982
1962	—Milwaukee (N.L.)	C	80	220	23	62	8	1	5	26	.282	24	24	1	325	39	5	.986
1963	—Milwaukee (N.L.)	C-1B-OF	142	501	57	147	19	4	14	71	.293	42	79	1	919	76	6	.994
1964	—Milwaukee (N.L.)	C-1B	154	601	87	193	36	5	20	109	.321	36	67	4	1081	94	7	†.994
1965	—Milwaukee (N.L.)	C-1B	148	523	68	152	21	1	27	80	.291	61	79	0	1022	73	8	.993
1966	—Atlanta (N.L.)	C-1B	148	546	83	172	20	3	36	101	.315	60	61	0	874	87	12	.988
1967	—Atlanta (N.L.)	C-1B	135	477	67	132	18	1	20	68	.277	75	49	2	785	81	8	.991
1968	—Atlanta (N.L.)	C-1B	115	424	45	115	11	2	10	55	.271	34	72	1	733	48	2	†.997
1969	—St. Louis (N.L.)■	1B-C	159	602	72	174	29	6	18	101	.289	66	85	0	1360	91	7	.995
1970	—St. Louis (N.L.)	C-3B-1B	•161	624	89	203	27	9	21	100	.325	70	91	2	651	162	13	.984
1971	—St. Louis (N.L.)	3B	161	634	97	★230	34	8	24	★137	★.363	63	70	4	★136	271	•21	.951
1972	—St. Louis (N.L.)	3B-1B	149	544	71	157	26	6	11	81	.289	54	74	3	336	198	15	.973
1973	—St. Louis (N.L.)	1B-3B	141	519	67	149	17	2	13	69	.287	65	78	2	881	128	12	.988
1974	—St. Louis (N.L.)	1B-3B	147	529	59	149	28	1	11	70	.282	69	68	1	1173	†121	14	.989
1975	—New York (N.L.)■	3B-1B	114	361	33	89	16	3	6	35	.247	35	55	0	172	157	15	.956
1976	—New York (N.L.)	1B-3B	114	310	36	95	10	3	5	31	.306	21	35	1	593	52	7	.989
1977	—New York (N.L.)	1B-3B	26	51	2	9	3	0	1	9	.176	2	10	0	83	3	1	.989
Major league totals (18 years)			2209	7874	996	2342	344	59	252	1185	.297	805	1058	25	11618	1731	163	.988

ALL-STAR GAME RECORD

Year	League	Pos.	AB	R	H	2B	3B	HR	RBI	Avg.	BB	SO	SB	PO	A	E	Avg.
			BATTING											FIELDING			
1963	—National								Did not play.								
1964	—National	C	2	0	0	0	0	0	0	.000	0	0	0	5	0	0	1.000
1965	—National	C	4	1	1	0	0	1	2	.250	0	0	0	5	1	0	1.000
1966	—National	C	3	0	0	0	0	0	0	.000	0	1	0	5	0	0	1.000
1967	—National	C	2	0	0	0	0	0	0	.000	0	0	0	4	1	0	1.000
1970	—National	PH	1	0	0	0	0	0	0	.000	0	0	0	...	...	...	...
1971	—National	3B	3	0	0	0	0	0	0	.000	0	1	0	1	0	0	1.000
1972	—National	3B	3	0	0	0	0	0	0	.000	0	1	0	1	2	0	1.000
1973	—National	1B-3B	3	0	0	0	0	0	0	.000	0	0	0	5	0	0	1.000
All-Star Game totals (8 years)			21	1	1	0	0	1	2	.048	0	3	0	26	4	0	1.000

RECORD AS MANAGER

BACKGROUND: Player/manager, New York Mets (May 31-June 18, 1977).
HONORS: Coach, N.L. All-Star team (1983 and 1992).

Year	Team (League)	W	L	Pct.	Pos.	Playoff W	Playoff L	Champ. Series W	Champ. Series L	World Series W	World Series L	All-Star Game W	All-Star Game L
		REGULAR SEASON				POSTSEASON							
1977	—New York (N.L.)	49	68	.419	6th (E)	—	—	—	—	—	—	—	—
1978	—New York (N.L.)	66	96	.407	6th (E)	—	—	—	—	—	—	—	—
1979	—New York (N.L.)	63	99	.389	6th (E)	—	—	—	—	—	—	—	—
1980	—New York (N.L.)	67	95	.414	5th (E)	—	—	—	—	—	—	—	—
1981	—New York (N.L.)	17	34	.333	5th (E)	—	—	—	—	—	—	—	—
	—(Second half)	24	28	.462	4th (E)	—	—	—	—	—	—	—	—
1982	—Atlanta (N.L.)	89	73	.549	1st (W)	—	—	0	3	—	—	—	—
1983	—Atlanta (N.L.)	88	74	.543	2nd (W)	—	—	—	—	—	—	—	—
1984	—Atlanta (N.L.)	80	82	.494	T2nd (W)	—	—	—	—	—	—	—	—
1990	—St. Louis (N.L.)	24	34	.414	6th (E)	—	—	—	—	—	—	—	—
1991	—St. Louis (N.L.)	84	78	.519	2nd (E)	—	—	—	—	—	—	—	—
1992	—St. Louis (N.L.)	83	79	.512	3rd (E)	—	—	—	—	—	—	—	—
1993	—St. Louis (N.L.)	87	75	.537	3rd (E)	—	—	—	—	—	—	—	—
Major league totals (12 years)		821	915	.473		—	—	0	3	—	—	—	—

NOTES:
1977—Replaced New York manager Joe Frazier with club in sixth place, record of 15-30 (May 31); served as player/manager (May 31-June 18, when released as player).
1982—Lost to St. Louis in N.L. Championship Series.
1990—Replaced St. Louis manager Whitey Herzog (record of 33-47) and interim manager Red Schoendienst (13-11) with club in sixth place, record of 46-58 (August 1).

TREBELHORN, TOM

CUBS

PERSONAL: Born January 27, 1948, in Portland, Ore. . . . 5-11/178. . . . Threw right, batted left. . . . Full name: Thomas Lynn Trebelhorn.
HIGH SCHOOL: Cleveland (Portland, Ore.).
COLLEGE: Portland State (bachelor of science degree in history and teaching, 1970).
TRANSACTIONS/CAREER NOTES: Selected by Bend (affiliate of Hawaii, Pacific Coast League) of Northwest League in sixth round of free-agent draft (June 4, 1970). . . . Contract sold to Oakland Athletics organization (September 2, 1972). . . . Released by A's organization (June 17, 1975).
STATISTICAL NOTES: Led N.L. catchers with five double plays in 1970. . . . Led Northwest League catchers with .997 fielding percentage in 1971. . . . Tied for Northwest League lead in double plays by catcher with three in 1972.
MISCELLANEOUS: Player/coach (1974).

Year	Team (League)	Pos.	G	AB	R	H	2B	3B	HR	RBI	Avg.	BB	SO	SB	PO	A	E	Avg.
			BATTING												FIELDING			
1970	—Bend (Northwest)	C-3-2-0	68	198	33	48	4	1	4	32	.242	42	49	3	296	48	12	.966
1971	—Bend (Northwest)	C-OF	51	149	28	47	13	3	3	38	.315	17	22	3	282	33	2	†.994

Year	Team (League)	Pos.	G	AB	R	H	2B	3B	HR	RBI	Avg.	BB	SO	SB	PO	A	E	Avg.
			BATTING												FIELDING			
1972	—Walla Walla (N'west)..	C	42	124	17	25	5	1	2	20	.202	20	13	1	272	19	4	.986
1973	—Birm. (Southern)■....	3B-C-1B	33	89	9	18	5	0	2	13	.202	15	9	0	87	31	8	.937
	—Burlington (Midw.)...	C-1B	43	146	23	33	6	0	2	20	.226	23	19	0	298	25	5	.985
1974	—Birm. (Southern)	C-3B	8	9	1	2	1	0	0	0	.222	1	3	0	13	1	1	.933
	—Lewiston (N'west)....	P-PH	7	2	0	0	0	0	0	0	.000	0	2	0	1	2	0	1.000

RECORD AS PITCHER

Year	Team (League)	W	L	Pct.	ERA	G	GS	CG	ShO	Sv.	IP	H	R	ER	BB	SO
1974	—Lewiston (N'west)	1	0	1.000	0.75	5	0	0	0	0	12	7	1	1	2	2

RECORD AS MANAGER

BACKGROUND: Player/coach, Lewiston, Oakland A's organization (1974).... Coach, Portland, Cleveland Indians organization (1978).... Coach, Portland, Pittsburgh Pirates organization (1980-81).... Coach, Milwaukee Brewers (1984 and beginning of 1986 season-September 25, 1986).... Coach, Chicago Cubs (November 25, 1991-October 13, 1993).
HONORS: Coach, A.L. All-Star team (1988).

Year	Team (League)	W	L	Pct.	Pos.	Playoff W	Playoff L	Champ. Series W	Champ. Series L	World Series W	World Series L	All-Star Game W	All-Star Game L
		REGULAR SEASON				POSTSEASON							
1975	—Boise (Northwest)	39	39	.500	3rd (S)	—	—	—	—	—	—	—	—
1976	—Boise (Northwest)	33	38	.465	3rd (S)	—	—	—	—	—	—	—	—
1977	—Modesto (California)	31	39	.443	4th	—	—	—	—	—	—	—	—
	—(Second half)	22	48	.314	6th	—	—	—	—	—	—	—	—
1979	—Batavia (New York-Pennsylvania)	37	34	.521	3rd (W)	—	—	—	—	—	—	—	—
1982	—Portland (Pacific Coast)	32	39	.451	5th (N)	—	—	—	—	—	—	—	—
	—(Second half)	33	40	.452	5th (N)	—	—	—	—	—	—	—	—
1983	—Hawaii (Pacific Coast)	32	40	.444	T4th (S)	—	—	—	—	—	—	—	—
	—(Second half)	40	31	.563	2nd (S)	—	—	—	—	—	—	—	—
1985	—Vancouver (Pacific Coast)	38	34	.528	2nd (N)	—	—	—	—	—	—	—	—
	—(Second half)	41	30	.577	1st (N)	6	0	—	—	—	—	—	—
1986	—Milwaukee (A.L.)	6	3	.667	6th (E)	—	—	—	—	—	—	—	—
1987	—Milwaukee (A.L.)	91	71	.562	3rd (E)	—	—	—	—	—	—	—	—
1988	—Milwaukee (A.L.)	87	75	.537	T3rd (E)	—	—	—	—	—	—	—	—
1989	—Milwaukee (A.L.)	81	81	.500	4th (E)	—	—	—	—	—	—	—	—
1990	—Milwaukee (A.L.)	74	88	.457	6th (E)	—	—	—	—	—	—	—	—
1991	—Milwaukee (A.L.)	83	79	.512	4th (E)	—	—	—	—	—	—	—	—
	Major league totals (6 years)	422	397	.515									

NOTES:
1985—Defeated Calgary, three games to none, for division championship; defeated Phoenix, three games to none, in league championship.
1986—Replaced retiring Milwaukee manager George Bamberger with club in sixth place, record of 71-81 (September 26).

1994 BASEBALL HALL OF FAME ENSHRINEE

CARLTON, STEVE

P

PERSONAL: Born December 22, 1944, in Miami. . . . 6-5/210. . . . Threw left, batted left. . . . Full name: Steven Norman Carlton.
HIGH SCHOOL: North Miami.
COLLEGE: Miami-Dade (South) Community College.

TRANSACTIONS/CAREER NOTES: Signed as free agent by St. Louis Cardinals organization (October 8, 1963). . . . Traded by Cardinals to Philadelphia Phillies for P Rick Wise (February 25, 1972). . . . On disabled list (June 21-September 2, 1985). . . . Released by Phillies (June 24, 1986). . . . Signed by San Francisco Giants (July 4, 1986). . . . Released by Giants (August 7, 1986). . . . Signed by Chicago White Sox (August 12, 1986). . . . Granted free agency (November 12, 1986). . . . Signed by Cleveland Indians (April 4, 1987). . . . Traded by Indians to Minnesota Twins for a player to be named later (July 31, 1987); Indians organization acquired P Jeff Perry to complete deal (August 18, 1987). . . . Released by Twins (December 21, 1987). . . . Re-signed by Twins (January 29, 1988). . . . Released by Twins (April 28, 1988).
RECORDS: Holds major league single-game records for most strikeouts by lefthanded pitcher—19 (September 15, 1969); most strikeouts by losing pitcher—19 (September 15, 1969). . . . Holds N.L. career records for most years pitched—22; most consecutive years pitched—22; most games started—677; most consecutive starting assignments—534; most bases on balls issued—1,717; most strikeouts—4,000; most years with 100 or more strikeouts—18; and most consecutive years with 100 or more strikeouts—18. . . . Holds N.L. single-season record for most balks—11 (1979). . . . Shares N.L. single-game record for most strikeouts—19 (September 15, 1969). . . . Shares modern N.L. single-season record for most games won by lefthanded pitcher—27 (1972).
HONORS: Named lefthanded pitcher on THE SPORTING NEWS N.L. All-Star team (1969, 1971-72, 1977, 1979-80 and 1982). . . . Named N.L. Pitcher of the Year by THE SPORTING NEWS (1972, 1977, 1980 and 1982). . . . Named N.L. Cy Young Award winner by Baseball Writers' Association of America (1972, 1977, 1980 and 1982). . . . Won N.L. Gold Glove at pitcher (1981).
STATISTICAL NOTES: Led N.L. with seven balks in 1977, 11 in 1979, seven in 1980, nine each in 1982 and 1983 and tied for lead with seven each in 1975, 1978 and 1984. . . . Led N.L. with 30 home runs allowed in 1978. . . . Led N.L. with 17 wild pitches in 1980.

Year	Team (League)	W	L	Pct.	ERA	G	GS	CG	ShO	Sv.	IP	H	R	ER	BB	SO
1964	—Rock Hill (W. Car.)	10	1	.909	1.03	11	11	5	2	...	79	39	17	9	36	91
	—Winnipeg (North.)	4	4	.500	3.36	12	12	4	2	...	75	63	40	28	48	79
	—Tulsa (Texas)	1	1	.500	2.63	4	3	0	0	...	24	16	13	7	18	21
1965	—St. Louis (N.L.)	0	0	...	2.52	15	2	0	0	...	25	27	7	7	8	21
1966	—Tulsa (Pac. Coast)	9	5	.643	3.59	19	19	10	1	...	128	110	65	51	54	108
	—St. Louis (N.L.)	3	3	.500	3.12	9	9	2	1	...	52	56	22	18	18	25
1967	—St. Louis (N.L.)	14	9	.609	2.98	30	28	11	2	...	193	173	71	64	62	168
1968	—St. Louis (N.L.)	13	11	.542	2.99	34	33	10	5	...	232	214	87	77	61	162
1969	—St. Louis (N.L.)	17	11	.607	2.17	31	31	12	2	0	236	185	66	57	93	210
1970	—St. Louis (N.L.)	10	*19	.345	3.72	34	33	13	2	0	254	239	123	105	109	193
1971	—St. Louis (N.L.)	20	9	.690	3.56	37	36	18	4	0	273	275	120	108	98	172
1972	—Philadelphia (N.L.)■	*27	10	.730	*1.98	41	*41	*30	8	0	*346	*257	84	76	87	*310
1973	—Philadelphia (N.L.)	13	*20	.394	3.90	40	•40	•18	3	0	•293	*293	*146	*127	113	223
1974	—Philadelphia (N.L.)	16	13	.552	3.22	39	39	17	1	0	291	249	118	104	*136	*240
1975	—Philadelphia (N.L.)	15	14	.517	3.56	37	37	14	3	0	255	217	116	101	104	192
1976	—Philadelphia (N.L.)	20	7	*.741	3.13	35	35	13	2	0	253	224	94	88	72	195
1977	—Philadelphia (N.L.)	*23	10	.697	2.64	36	36	17	2	0	283	229	99	83	89	198
1978	—Philadelphia (N.L.)	16	13	.552	2.84	34	34	12	3	0	247	228	91	78	63	161
1979	—Philadelphia (N.L.)	18	11	.621	3.62	35	35	13	4	0	251	202	112	101	89	213
1980	—Philadelphia (N.L.)	*24	9	.727	2.34	38	•38	13	3	0	*304	243	87	79	90	*286
1981	—Philadelphia (N.L.)	13	4	.765	2.42	24	24	10	1	0	190	152	59	51	62	179
1982	—Philadelphia (N.L.)	*23	11	.676	3.10	38	*38	*19	*6	0	*295 2/3	*253	114	102	86	*286
1983	—Philadelphia (N.L.)	15	16	.484	3.11	37	37	8	3	0	*283 2/3	*277	117	98	84	*275
1984	—Philadelphia (N.L.)	13	7	.650	3.58	33	33	1	0	0	229	214	104	91	79	163
1985	—Philadelphia (N.L.)	1	8	.111	3.33	16	16	0	0	0	92	84	43	34	53	48
1986	—Phil.-S.F. (N.L.)■	5	11	.313	5.89	22	22	0	0	0	113	138	90	74	61	80
	—Chicago (A.L.)■	4	3	.571	3.69	10	10	0	0	0	63 1/3	58	30	26	25	40
1987	—Clev.-Minn. (A.L.)■	6	14	.300	5.74	32	21	3	0	1	152	165	111	97	86	91
1988	—Minnesota (A.L.)	0	1	.000	16.76	4	1	0	0	0	9 2/3	20	19	18	5	5
A.L. totals (3 years)		10	18	.357	5.64	46	32	3	0	1	225	243	160	141	116	136
N.L. totals (22 years)		319	226	.585	3.11	695	677	251	55	0	4991 1/3	4429	1970	1723	1717	4000
Major league totals (24 years)		329	244	.574	3.22	741	709	254	55	1	5216 1/3	4672	2130	1864	1833	4136

DIVISION SERIES RECORD

Year	Team (League)	W	L	Pct.	ERA	G	GS	CG	ShO	Sv.	IP	H	R	ER	BB	SO
1981	—Philadelphia (N.L.)	0	2	.000	3.86	2	2	0	0	0	14	14	6	6	8	13

CHAMPIONSHIP SERIES RECORD

CHAMPIONSHIP SERIES NOTES: Holds career record for most bases on balls issued—28. . . . Shares career record for most home runs hit by pitcher—1. . . . Holds N.L. career records for most games started—8; most innings pitched—53 2/3; most hits allowed—53; most earned runs allowed—21. . . . Shares N.L. career record for most games won—4.

Year	Team (League)	W	L	Pct.	ERA	G	GS	CG	ShO	Sv.	IP	H	R	ER	BB	SO
1976	—Philadelphia (N.L.)	0	1	.000	5.14	1	1	0	0	0	7	8	5	4	5	6
1977	—Philadelphia (N.L.)	0	1	.000	6.94	2	2	0	0	0	11 2/3	13	9	9	8	6
1978	—Philadelphia (N.L.)	1	0	1.000	4.00	1	1	1	0	0	9	8	4	4	2	8

Year	Team (League)	W	L	Pct.	ERA	G	GS	CG	ShO	Sv.	IP	H	R	ER	BB	SO
1980	—Philadelphia (N.L.).....	1	0	1.000	2.19	2	2	0	0	0	12⅓	11	3	3	8	6
1983	—Philadelphia (N.L.).....	2	0	1.000	0.66	2	2	0	0	0	13⅔	13	1	1	5	13
Champ. series totals (5 years)		4	2	.667	3.52	8	8	1	0	0	53⅔	53	22	21	28	39

WORLD SERIES RECORD

Year	Team (League)	W	L	Pct.	ERA	G	GS	CG	ShO	Sv.	IP	H	R	ER	BB	SO
1967	—St. Louis (N.L.)..........	0	1	.000	0.00	1	1	0	0	...	6	3	1	0	2	5
1968	—St. Louis (N.L.)..........	0	0	...	6.75	2	0	0	0	...	4	7	3	3	1	3
1980	—Philadelphia (N.L.).....	2	0	1.000	2.40	2	2	0	0	0	15	14	5	4	9	17
1983	—Philadelphia (N.L.).....	0	1	.000	2.70	1	1	0	0	0	6⅔	5	3	2	3	7
World Series totals (4 years) .		2	2	.500	2.56	6	4	0	0	0	31⅔	29	12	9	15	32

ALL-STAR GAME RECORD

Year	League	W	L	Pct.	ERA	GS	CG	ShO	Sv.	IP	H	R	ER	BB	SO
1968	—National........................	0	0	...	0.00	0	0	0	...	1	0	0	0	0	1
1969	—National........................	1	0	1.000	6.00	1	0	0	0	3	2	2	2	1	2
1971	—National........................							Did not play.							
1972	—National........................	0	0	...	0.00	0	0	0	0	1	0	0	0	1	0
1974	—National........................							Did not play.							
1977	—National........................							Did not play.							
1979	—National........................	0	0	...	27.00	1	0	0	0	1	2	3	3	1	0
1980	—National........................							Did not play.							
1981	—National........................							Did not play.							
1982	—National........................	0	0	...	0.00	0	0	0	0	2	1	0	0	2	4
All-Star totals (5 years)		1	0	1.000	5.63	2	0	0	0	8	5	5	5	5	7

1993 AMERICAN LEAGUE STATISTICAL LEADERS

BATTING

BATTING AVERAGE
.363 John Olerud, Tor.
.332 Paul Molitor, Tor.
.326 Roberto Alomar, Tor.
.325 Kenny Lofton, Clev.
.321 Carlos Baerga, Clev.
.317 Frank Thomas, Chi.
.315 Mike Greenwell, Bos.

RUNS
124 Rafael Palmeiro, Tex.
121 Paul Molitor, Tor.
116 Kenny Lofton, Clev.
116 Devon White, Tor.
114 R. Henderson, Oak.-Tor.
113 Ken Griffey Jr., Sea.
113 Tony Phillips, Det.

HITS
211 Paul Molitor, Tor.
200 Carlos Baerga, Clev.
200 John Olerud, Tor.
192 Roberto Alomar, Tor.
185 Kenny Lofton, Clev.
184 Kirby Puckett, Minn.
182 Travis Fryman, Det.

TOTAL BASES
359 Ken Griffey Jr., Sea.
339 Juan Gonzalez, Tex.
333 Frank Thomas, Chi.
331 Rafael Palmeiro, Tex.
330 John Olerud, Tor.
328 Albert Belle, Clev.
324 Paul Molitor, Tor.

DOUBLES
54 John Olerud, Tor.
42 Devon White, Tor.
40 Rafael Palmeiro, Tex.
40 John Valentin, Bos.
39 Kirby Puckett, Minn.
38 Three players tied

TRIPLES
14 Lance Johnson, Chi.
13 Joey Cora, Chi.
10 David Hulse, Tex.
9 Tony Fernandez, Tor.
9 Brian McRae, K.C.
8 Brady Anderson, Balt.
8 Kenny Lofton, Clev.

HOME RUNS
46 Juan Gonzalez, Tex.
45 Ken Griffey Jr., Sea.
41 Frank Thomas, Chi.
38 Albert Belle, Clev.
37 Rafael Palmeiro, Tex.
33 Joe Carter, Tor.
33 Dean Palmer, Tex.

RUNS BATTED IN
129 Albert Belle, Clev.
128 Frank Thomas, Chi.
121 Joe Carter, Tor.
118 Juan Gonzalez, Tex.
117 Cecil Fielder, Det.
114 Carlos Baerga, Clev.
112 Chili Davis, Calif.

WALKS
132 Tony Phillips, Det.
120 R. Henderson, Oak.-Tor.
114 John Olerud, Tor.
112 Frank Thomas, Chi.
109 Mickey Tettleton, Det.
105 Robin Ventura, Chi.
100 Jay Buhner, Sea.

STRIKEOUTS
169 Rob Deer, Det.-Bos.
156 Danny Tartabull, N.Y.
154 Dean Palmer, Tex.
144 Jay Buhner, Sea.
139 Mickey Tettleton, Det.
135 Two players tied

ON-BASE PERCENTAGE
.473 John Olerud, Tor.
.443 Tony Phillips, Det.
.432 R. Henderson, Oak.-Tor.
.426 Frank Thomas, Chi.
.416 Chris Hoiles, Balt.
.408 Three players tied

SLUGGING PERCENTAGE
.632 Juan Gonzalez, Tex.
.617 Ken Griffey Jr., Sea.
.607 Frank Thomas, Chi.
.599 John Olerud, Tor.
.585 Chris Hoiles, Balt.
.554 Rafael Palmeiro, Tex.
.552 Albert Belle, Clev.

STOLEN BASES
70 Kenny Lofton, Clev.
55 Roberto Alomar, Tor.
55 Luis Polonia, Calif.
53 R. Henderson, Oak.-Tor.
48 Chad Curtis, Calif.
35 Lance Johnson, Chi.
34 Devon White, Tor.

HARDEST TO FAN (PLATE APP. PER SO)
36.7 Felix Fermin, Clev.
19.8 Brian Harper, Minn.
17.5 Lance Johnson, Chi.
15.6 C. Knoblauch, Minn.
15.2 Scott Fletcher, Bos.
14.2 Don Mattingly, N.Y.

HOME RUN RATIO (AT-BATS PER HOME RUN)
11.7 Juan Gonzalez, Tex.
12.9 Ken Griffey Jr., Sea.
13.4 Frank Thomas, Chi.
14.4 Chris Hoiles, Balt.
15.6 Albert Belle, Clev.
15.7 Dean Palmer, Tex.

HARDEST TO DOUBLE UP (AT-BATS PER GIDP)
199.3 Devon White, Tor.
140.0 Brady Anderson, Balt.
121.3 Harold Reynolds, Balt.
104.4 Mickey Tettleton, Det.
103.8 Dean Palmer, Tex.
99.8 Felix Jose, K.C.

PITCHING

EARNED-RUN AVERAGE
2.56 Kevin Appier, K.C.
2.95 Wilson Alvarez, Chi.
3.00 Jimmy Key, N.Y.
3.13 Alex Fernandez, Chi.
3.14 Frank Viola, Bos.
3.15 Chuck Finley, Calif.
3.20 Mark Langston, Calif.

WINS
22 Jack McDowell, Chi.
19 Pat Hentgen, Tor.
19 Randy Johnson, Sea.
18 Kevin Appier, K.C.
18 Alex Fernandez, Chi.
18 Jimmy Key, N.Y.
16 Four pitchers tied

WINNING PERCENTAGE (MINIMUM 15 DECISIONS)
.824 Juan Guzman, Tor.
.778 Bob Wickman, N.Y.
.750 Jimmy Key, N.Y.
.706 Jason Bere, Chi.
.706 Dave Fleming, Sea.
.704 Randy Johnson, Sea.

SAVES
45 Jeff Montgomery, K.C.
45 Duane Ward, Tor.
40 Tom Henke, Tex.
38 Roberto Hernandez, Chi.
36 Dennis Eckersley, Oak.
34 Rick Aguilera, Minn.
33 Jeff Russell, Bos.

GAMES
80 Greg Harris, Bos.
73 Scott Radinsky, Chi.
71 Tony Fossas, Bos.
71 Jeff Nelson, Sea.
71 Duane Ward, Tor.
70 Three pitchers tied

GAMES STARTED
36 Cal Eldred, Mil.
36 Mike Moore, Det.
35 Chuck Finley, Calif.
35 Mark Langston, Calif.
35 Kevin Tapani, Minn.
34 11 pitchers tied

COMPLETE GAMES
13 Chuck Finley, Calif.
12 Kevin Brown, Tex.
10 Randy Johnson, Sea.
10 Jack McDowell, Chi.
8 Cal Eldred, Mil.
7 Three pitchers tied

SHUTOUTS
4 Jack McDowell, Chi.
3 Kevin Brown, Tex.
3 Randy Johnson, Sea.
3 Mike Moore, Det.
2 Five pitchers tied

INNINGS PITCHED
258.0 Cal Eldred, Mil.
256.2 Jack McDowell, Chi.
256.1 Mark Langston, Calif.
255.1 Randy Johnson, Sea.
254.0 David Cone, K.C.
251.1 Chuck Finley, Calif.
247.1 Alex Fernandez, Chi.

HITS ALLOWED
266 Scott Erickson, Minn.
261 Jack McDowell, Chi.
254 Jaime Navarro, Mil.
243 Chuck Finley, Calif.
243 Kevin Tapani, Minn.
232 Cal Eldred, Mil.
232 Jose Mesa, Clev.

WALKS
122 Wilson Alvarez, Chi.
114 David Cone, K.C.
110 Juan Guzman, Tor.
99 Randy Johnson, Sea.
91 Cal Eldred, Mil.
91 Bobby Witt, Oak.
89 Mike Moore, Det.

STRIKEOUTS
308 Randy Johnson, Sea.
196 Mark Langston, Calif.
194 Juan Guzman, Tor.
191 David Cone, K.C.
187 Chuck Finley, Calif.
186 Kevin Appier, K.C.
180 Cal Eldred, Mil.

HOME RUNS ALLOWED
35 Mike Moore, Det.
32 Cal Eldred, Mil.
31 Danny Darwin, Bos.
28 Ricky Bones, Mil.
28 Bill Gullickson, Det.
27 Alex Fernandez, Chi.
27 Pat Hentgen, Tor.

FEWEST WALKS PER 9 INN.
1.6 Jimmy Key, N.Y.
1.9 Danny Darwin, Bos.
2.0 David Wells, Det.
2.3 Kevin Tapani, Minn.
2.3 John Doherty, Det.
2.4 Three pitchers tied

STRIKEOUTS PER 9 INN.
10.9 Randy Johnson, Sea.
8.2 Melido Perez, N.Y.
7.9 Juan Guzman, Tor.
7.5 Roger Clemens, Bos.
7.2 Willie Banks, Minn.
7.1 Roger Pavlik, Tex.
7.0 Two pitchers tied

OPP. BATTING AVG. AGAINST
.203 Randy Johnson, Sea.
.212 Kevin Appier, K.C.
.223 David Cone, K.C.
.228 Ben McDonald, Balt.
.229 Chris Bosio, Sea.
.230 Danny Darwin, Bos.
.230 Wilson Alvarez, Chi.

1993 NATIONAL LEAGUE STATISTICAL LEADERS

BATTING

BATTING AVERAGE

.370	Andres Galarraga, Colo.
.358	Tony Gwynn, S.D.
.342	Gregg Jefferies, St.L.
.336	Barry Bonds, S.F.
.325	Mark Grace, Chi.
.320	Jeff Bagwell, Hou.
.318	Mike Piazza, L.A.

RUNS

143	Lenny Dykstra, Phil.
129	Barry Bonds, S.F.
113	Ron Gant, Atl.
111	Fred McGriff, S.D.-Atl.
110	Jeff Blauser, Atl.
105	Matt Williams, S.F.
104	Two players tied

HITS

194	Lenny Dykstra, Phil.
193	Mark Grace, Chi.
188	Marquis Grissom, Mont.
187	Jay Bell, Pitts.
186	Gregg Jefferies, St.L.
182	Jeff Blauser, Atl.
181	Two players tied

TOTAL BASES

365	Barry Bonds, S.F.
325	Matt Williams, S.F.
309	Ron Gant, Atl.
307	Lenny Dykstra, Phil.
307	Mike Piazza, L.A.
306	Fred McGriff, S.D.-Atl.
301	David Justice, Atl.

DOUBLES

45	Charlie Hayes, Colo.
44	Lenny Dykstra, Phil.
43	Dante Bichette, Colo.
41	Craig Biggio, Hou.
41	Tony Gwynn, S.D.
40	Bernard Gilkey, St.L.
39	Mark Grace, Chi.

TRIPLES

13	Steve Finley, Hou.
10	Brett Butler, L.A.
9	Jay Bell, Pitts.
9	Mickey Morandini, Phil.
8	Vince Coleman, N.Y.
8	Al Martin, Pitts.
8	Eric Young, Colo.

HOME RUNS

46	Barry Bonds, S.F.
40	David Justice, Atl.
38	Matt Williams, S.F.
37	Fred McGriff, S.D.-Atl.
36	Ron Gant, Atl.
35	Mike Piazza, L.A.
34	Two players tied

RUNS BATTED IN

123	Barry Bonds, S.F.
120	David Justice, Atl.
117	Ron Gant, Atl.
112	Mike Piazza, L.A.
110	Matt Williams, S.F.
105	Darren Daulton, Phil.
103	Todd Zeile, St.L.

WALKS

129	Lenny Dykstra, Phil.
126	Barry Bonds, S.F.
117	Darren Daulton, Phil.
111	John Kruk, Phil.
86	Brett Butler, L.A.
85	Jeff Blauser, Atl.
85	Dave Hollins, Phil.

STRIKEOUTS

147	Cory Snyder, L.A.
135	Jeff Conine, Fla.
135	Sammy Sosa, Chi.
130	Orestes Destrade, Fla.
124	Phil Plantier, S.D.
122	Three players tied

ON-BASE PERCENTAGE

.458	Barry Bonds, S.F.
.430	John Kruk, Phil.
.420	Lenny Dykstra, Phil.
.414	Orlando Merced, Pitts.
.408	Gregg Jefferies, St.L.
.403	Andres Galarraga, Colo.
.401	Jeff Blauser, Atl.

SLUGGING PERCENTAGE

.677	Barry Bonds, S.F.
.602	Andres Galarraga, Colo.
.561	Matt Williams, S.F.
.561	Mike Piazza, L.A.
.549	Fred McGriff, S.D.-Atl.
.526	Dante Bichette, Colo.
.522	Two players tied

STOLEN BASES

58	Chuck Carr, Fla.
53	Marquis Grissom, Mont.
47	Otis Nixon, Atl.
46	Gregg Jefferies, St.L.
46	Darren Lewis, S.F.
43	Delino DeShields, Mont.
42	Eric Young, Colo.

HARDEST TO FAN (PLATE APP. PER SO)

33.5	Ozzie Smith, St.L.
28.1	Tony Gwynn, S.D.
21.1	Mark Grace, Chi.
19.1	Gregg Jefferies, St.L.
14.3	Darren Lewis, S.F.
13.8	Eric Young, Colo.

HOME RUN RATIO (AT-BATS PER HOME RUN)

11.7	Barry Bonds, S.F.
13.6	Phil Plantier, S.D.
14.6	David Justice, Atl.
14.8	Bobby Bonilla, N.Y.
15.1	Fred McGriff, S.D.-Atl.
15.2	Matt Williams, S.F.

HARDEST TO DOUBLE UP (AT-BATS PER GIDP)

255.0	Darren Daulton, Phil.
130.5	Darren Lewis, S.F.
115.5	Phil Plantier, S.D.
101.2	Brett Butler, L.A.
100.0	Walt Weiss, Fla.
96.0	Al Martin, Pitts.

PITCHING

EARNED-RUN AVERAGE

2.36	Greg Maddux, Atl.
2.48	Jose Rijo, Cin.
2.77	Mark Portugal, Hou.
2.82	Bill Swift, S.F.
2.92	Steve Avery, Atl.
2.98	Pete Harnisch, Hou.
3.12	Tom Candiotti, L.A.

WINS

22	John Burkett, S.F.
22	Tom Glavine, Atl.
21	Bill Swift, S.F.
20	Greg Maddux, Atl.
18	Steve Avery, Atl.
18	Mark Portugal, Hou.
17	Bob Tewksbury, St.L.

WINNING PERCENTAGE (MINIMUM 15 DECISIONS)

.818	Mark Portugal, Hou.
.800	Tommy Greene, Phil.
.786	Tom Glavine, Atl.
.759	John Burkett, S.F.
.750	Steve Avery, Atl.
.724	Bill Swift, S.F.

SAVES

53	Randy Myers, Chi.
48	Rod Beck, S.F.
45	Bryan Harvey, Fla.
43	John Wetteland, Mont.
43	Mitch Williams, Phil.
43	Lee Smith, St.L.
27	Mike Stanton, Atl.

GAMES

81	Mike Jackson, S.F.
76	Rod Beck, S.F.
76	David West, Phil.
74	Greg McMichael, Atl.
73	Rob Murphy, St.L.
73	Randy Myers, Chi.
72	Xavier Hernandez, Hou.

GAMES STARTED

36	Tom Glavine, Atl.
36	Greg Maddux, Atl.
36	Jose Rijo, Cin.
35	Steve Avery, Atl.
35	John Smoltz, Atl.
35	Greg Harris, S.D.-Colo.
34	Seven pitchers tied

COMPLETE GAMES

8	Greg Maddux, Atl.
7	Curt Schilling, Phil.
7	Tommy Greene, Phil.
7	Terry Mulholland, Phil.
7	Doug Drabek, Hou.
7	Dwight Gooden, N.Y.
5	Two pitchers tied

SHUTOUTS

4	Pete Harnisch, Hou.
3	Ramon Martinez, L.A.
2	11 pitchers tied

INNINGS PITCHED

267.0	Greg Maddux, Atl.
257.1	Jose Rijo, Cin.
243.2	John Smoltz, Atl.
239.1	Tom Glavine, Atl.
237.2	Doug Drabek, Hou.
235.1	Curt Schilling, Phil.
232.2	Bill Swift, S.F.

HITS ALLOWED

258	Bob Tewksbury, St.L.
242	Doug Drabek, Hou.
239	Greg Harris, Colo.
236	Tom Glavine, Atl.
234	Curt Schilling, Phil.
228	Greg Maddux, Atl.
224	Two pitchers tied

WALKS

104	Ramon Martinez, L.A.
100	John Smoltz, Atl.
90	Tom Glavine, Atl.
87	Ryan Bowen, Fla.
86	Andy Benes, S.D.
85	Ben Rivera, Phil.
80	Danny Jackson, Phil.

STRIKEOUTS

227	Jose Rijo, Cin.
208	John Smoltz, Atl.
197	Greg Maddux, Atl.
186	Curt Schilling, Phil.
185	Pete Harnisch, Hou.
179	Andy Benes, S.D.
167	Tommy Greene, Phil.

HOME RUNS ALLOWED

33	Greg Harris, S.D.-Colo.
29	Jack Armstrong, Fla.
27	Dennis Martinez, Mont.
26	Frank Tanana, N.Y.
25	Jose Guzman, Chi.
24	K. Bottenfield, Mont.-Colo.
24	Greg Swindell, Hou.

FEWEST WALKS PER 9 INN.

0.8	Bob Tewksbury, St.L.
1.5	Rene Arocha, St.L.
1.6	John Burkett, S.F.
1.7	Steve Avery, Atl.
1.8	Greg Maddux, Atl.
1.9	Terry Mulholland, Phil.
1.9	Greg Swindell, Hou.

STRIKEOUTS PER 9 INN.

7.9	Jose Rijo, Cin.
7.7	John Smoltz, Atl.
7.7	Jose Guzman, Chi.
7.6	Pete Harnisch, Hou.
7.5	Tommy Greene, Phil.
7.4	Darryl Kile, Hou.
7.1	Curt Schilling, Phil.

OPP. BATTING AVG. AGAINST

.214	Pete Harnisch, Hou.
.226	Bill Swift, S.F.
.230	Jose Rijo, Cin.
.230	John Smoltz, Atl.
.232	Greg Maddux, Atl.
.232	Andy Benes, S.D.
.233	Tommy Greene, Phil.